Account Title	Classification	Financial Statement	Normal Balance
L			
Land	Plant Asset	Balance Sheet	Debit
Loss on Disposal of Plant Assets	Other Expense	Income Statement	Debit
M			
Maintenance and Repairs Expense	Operating Expense	Income Statement	Debit
Mortgage Payable	Long-Term Liability	Balance Sheet	Credit
N			
Notes Payable	Current Liability/ Long-Term Liability	Balance Sheet	Credit
P			
Patents	Intangible Asset	Balance Sheet	Debit
Paid-in Capital in Excess of Par— Common Stock	Stockholders' Equity	Balance Sheet	Credit
Paid-in Capital in Excess of Par— Preferred Stock	Stockholders' Equity	Balance Sheet	Credit
Preferred Stock	Stockholders' Equity	Balance Sheet	Credit
Premium on Bonds Payable	Long-Term Liability—Adjunct	Balance Sheet	Credit
Prepaid Insurance	Current Asset	Balance Sheet	Debit
R			
Rent Expense	Operating Expense	Income Statement	Debit
Retained Earnings	Stockholders' Equity	Balance Sheet and Retained Earnings Statement	Credit
S			
Salaries and Wages Expense	Operating Expense	Income Statement	Debit
Salaries and Wages Payable	Current Liability	Balance Sheet	Credit
Sales Discounts	Revenue—Contra	Income Statement	Debit
Sales Returns and Allowances	Revenue—Contra	Income Statement	Debit
Sales Revenue	Revenue	Income Statement	Credit
Selling Expenses	Operating Expense	Income Statement	Debit
Service Revenue	Revenue	Income Statement	Credit
Short-Term Investments	Current Asset	Balance Sheet	Debit
Stock Investments	Current Asset/Long-Term Investment	Balance Sheet	Debit
Supplies	Current Asset	Balance Sheet	Debit
Supplies Expense	Operating Expense	Income Statement	Debit
T			
Treasury Stock	Stockholders' Equity	Balance Sheet	Debit
U			
Unearned Service Revenue	Current Liability	Balance Sheet	Credit
Utilities Expense	Operating Expense	Income Statement	Debit

(1) The normal balance for Income Summary will be credit when there is a net income, debit when there is a net loss. The Income Summary account does not appear on any financial statement.

(2) If a periodic system is used, Inventory also appears on the income statement in the calculation of cost of goods sold.

The following is a sample chart of accounts. It does not represent a comprehensive chart of all the accounts used in this textbook but rather those accounts that are commonly used. This sample chart of accounts is for a company that generates both service revenue as well as sales revenue. It uses the perpetual approach to inventory. If a periodic system was used, the following temporary accounts would be needed to record inventory purchases: Purchases; Freight-In; Purchase Returns and Allowances; and Purchase Discounts.

CHART OF ACCOUNTS

Assets	Liabilities	Stockholders' Equity	Revenues	Expenses
Cash	Notes Payable	Common Stock	Service Revenue	Administrative Expenses
Accounts Receivable	Accounts Payable	Paid-in Capital in Excess of Par— Common Stock	Sales Revenue	Amortization Expense
Allowance for Doubtful Accounts	Unearned Service Revenue	Preferred Stock	Sales Discounts	Bad Debt Expense
Interest Receivable	Salaries and Wages Payable	Paid-in Capital in Excess of Par— Preferred Stock	Sales Returns and Allowances	Cost of Goods Sold
Inventory	Interest Payable	Treasury Stock	Interest Revenue	Depreciation Expense
Supplies	Dividends Payable	Retained Earnings	Gain on Disposal of Plant Assets	Freight-Out
Prepaid Insurance	Income Taxes Payable	Dividends		Income Tax Expense
Land	Bonds Payable	Income Summary		Insurance Expense
Equipment	Discount on Bonds Payable			Interest Expense
Accumulated Depreciation— Equipment	Premium on Bonds Payable			Loss on Disposal of Plant Assets
Buildings	Mortgage Payable			Maintenance and Repairs Expense
Accumulated Depreciation— Buildings				Rent Expense
Copyrights				Salaries and Wages Expense
Goodwill				Selling Expenses
Patents				Supplies Expense
				Utilities Expense

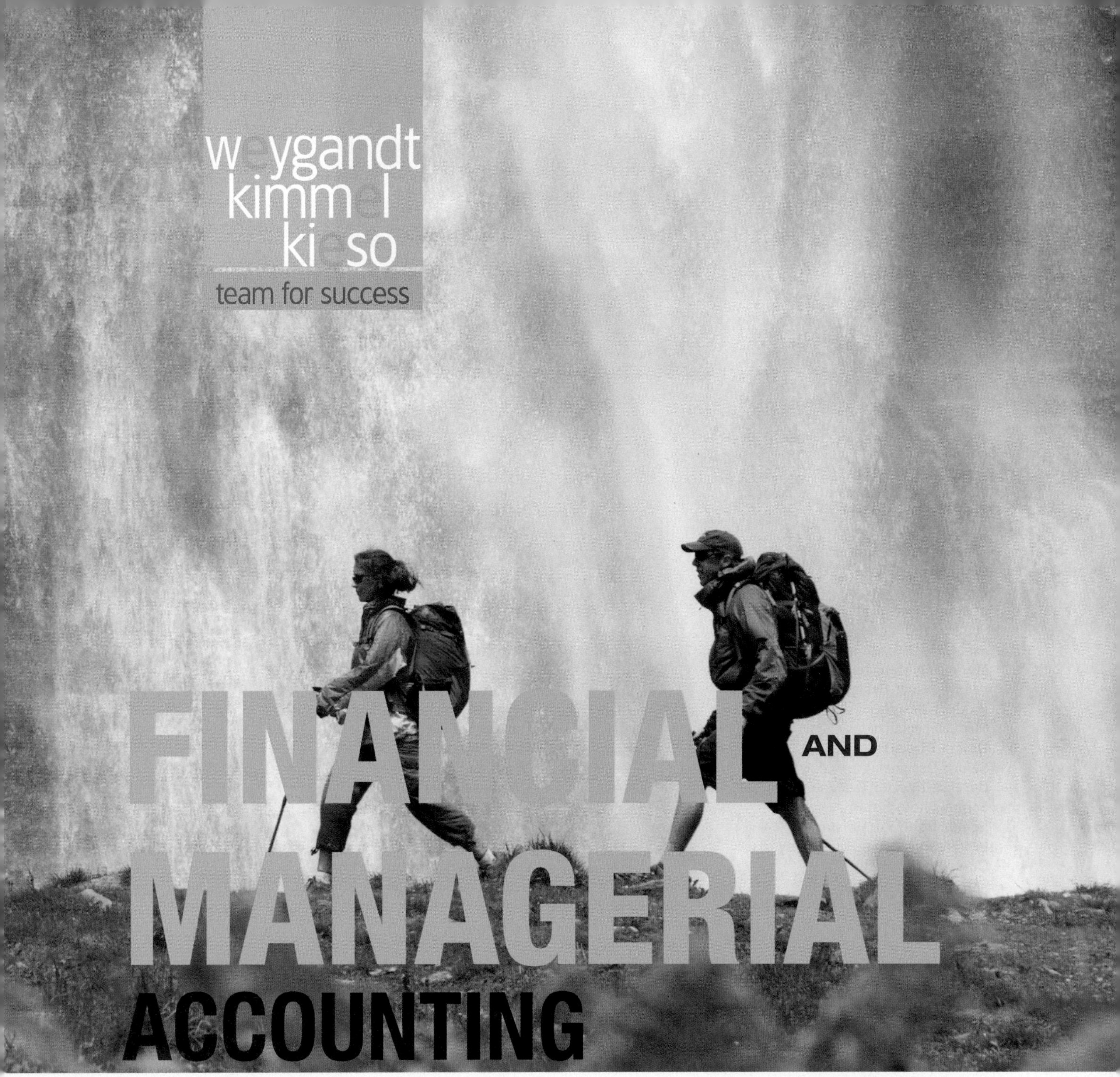

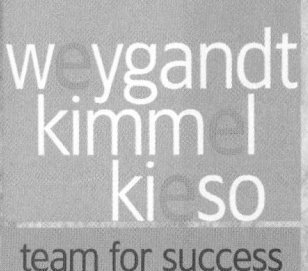

weygandt
kimmel
kieso
team for success

FINANCIAL AND MANAGERIAL ACCOUNTING

WILEY

John Wiley & Sons, Inc.

Jerry J. Weygandt PhD, CPA
University of Wisconsin—Madison
Madison, Wisconsin

Paul D. Kimmel PhD, CPA
University of Wisconsin—Milwaukee
Milwaukee, Wisconsin

Donald E. Kieso PhD, CPA
Northern Illinois University
DeKalb, Illinois

Dedicated to
the **Wiley sales representatives**
who sell our books and service
our adopters in a professional
and ethical manner, and to
Enid, Merlynn, and Donna

Vice President & Executive Publisher	George Hoffman
Associate Publisher	Christopher DeJohn
Operations Manager	Yana Mermel
Senior Content Editor	Ed Brislin
Development Editor	Terry Ann Tatro
Development Editor	Margaret Thompson
Content Manager	Dorothy Sinclair
Senior Production Editor	Valerie A. Vargas
Associate Director of Marketing	Amy Scholz
Marketing Manager	Karolina Zarychta Honsa
Lead Product Designer	Allison Morris
Product Designer	Greg Chaput
Media Specialist	Daniela DiMaggio
Design Director	Harry Nolan
Senior Designer	Maureen Eide
Cover & Interior Designer	Kristine Carney
Senior Photo Editor	Mary Ann Price
Senior Editorial Assistant	Jacqueline Kepping
Production Management Services	Ingrao Associates
Cover Photo Credit	© Bill Stevenson/Aurora Photos

This book was set in New Aster by Aptara®, Inc. and printed and bound by Courier-Kendallville. The cover was printed by Courier-Kendallville.

Founded in 1807, John Wiley & Sons, Inc. has been a valued source of knowledge and understanding for more than 200 years, helping people around the world meet their needs and fulfill their aspirations. Our company is built on a foundation of principles that include responsibility to the communities we serve and where we live and work. In 2008, we launched a Corporate Citizenship Initiative, a global effort to address the environmental, social, economic, and ethical challenges we face in our business. Among the issues we are addressing are carbon impact, paper specifications and procurement, ethical conduct within our business and among our vendors, and community and charitable support. For more information, please visit our website: www.wiley.com/go/citizenship.

ISBN-13 978-1-118-00423-4

Printed in the United States of America

10 9 8 7 6

From the Authors

Dear Student,

Why This Course? *Remember your biology course in high school? Did you have one of those "invisible man" models (or maybe something more high-tech than that) that gave you the opportunity to look "inside" the human body? This accounting course offers something similar: To understand a business, you have to understand the financial insides of a business organization. An introductory accounting course will help you understand the essential financial components of businesses. Whether you are looking at a large multinational company like Microsoft or Starbucks or a single-owner software consulting business or coffee shop, knowing the fundamentals of accounting will help you understand what is happening. As an employee, a manager, an investor, a business owner, or a director of your own personal finances—any of which roles you will have at some point in your life—you will make better decisions for having taken this course.*

> "Whether you are looking at a large multinational company like Microsoft or Starbucks or a single-owner software consulting business or coffee shop, knowing the fundamentals of accounting will help you understand what is happening."

Why This Book? *This textbook contains features to help you learn best, whatever your learning style. To understand what your learning style is, spend about 10 minutes to take the learning style quiz at the book's companion website. Then, look at page xiii for how you can apply an understanding of your learning style to this course. When you know more about your own learning style, browse through pages xiv–xvii. These pages describe the main features you will find in this textbook and explain their purpose.*

How To Succeed? *We've asked many students and many instructors whether there is a secret for success in this course. The nearly unanimous answer turns out to be not much of a secret: "Do the homework." This is one course where doing is learning. The more time you spend on the homework assignments—using the various tools that this textbook provides—the more likely you are to learn the essential concepts, techniques, and methods of accounting. Besides the textbook itself, the book's companion website also offers various support resources.*

Good luck in this course. We hope you enjoy the experience and that you put to good use throughout a lifetime of success the knowledge you obtain in this course. We are sure you will not be disappointed.

Jerry J. Weygandt
Paul D. Kimmel
Donald E. Kieso

Your Team for Success in Accounting

Wiley Accounting is your partner in accounting education. We want to be the first publisher you think of when it comes to quality content, reliable technology, innovative resources, professional training, and unparalleled support for your accounting classroom.

Your Wiley Accounting Team for Success is comprised of three distinctive advantages that you won't find with any other publisher:

- Author Commitment
- Wiley Faculty Network
- WileyPLUS

kieso
weygandt
kimmel
warfield

team for success

Author Commitment:

A Proven Author Team of Inspired Teachers

The Team for Success authors bring years of industry and academic experience to the development of each textbook that relates accounting concepts to real-world experiences. This cohesive team brings continuity of writing style, pedagogy, and problem material to each course from Principles to Intermediate so you and your students can seamlessly progress from introductory through advanced courses in accounting.

The authors understand the mindset and time limitations of today's students. They demonstrate an intangible ability to effectively deliver complex information so it is clear and understandable while staying one step ahead of emerging global trends in business.

Wiley Faculty Network:
A Team of Educators Dedicated to Your Professional Development

The Wiley Faculty Network (WFN) is a global group of seasoned accounting professionals who share best practices in teaching with their peers. Our Virtual Guest Lecture Series provides the opportunity you need for professional development in an online environment that is relevant, convenient, and collaborative. The quality of these seminars and workshops meets the strictest standards, so we are proud to be able to offer valuable CPE credits to attendees.

With 24 faculty mentors in accounting, it's easy to find help with your most challenging curriculum questions—just ask our experts!

www.wileyplus.com

WileyPLUS:
An Experienced Team of Support Professionals

The *WileyPLUS* Account Managers understand the time constraints of busy instructors who want to provide the best resources available to their students with minimal headaches and planning time. They know how intimidating new software can be, so they are sure to make the transition easy and painless.

Account Managers act as your personal contact and expert resource for training, course set-up, and shortcuts throughout the *WileyPLUS* experience.

Your success as an educator directly correlates to student success, and that's our goal. The Wiley Accounting Team for Success truly strives for YOUR success! Partner with us today!

www.wileyteamforsuccess.com

Author Commitment
Collaboration. Innovation. Experience.

After decades of success as authors of textbooks like this one, Jerry Weygandt, Paul Kimmel, and Don Kieso understand that teaching accounting goes beyond simply presenting data. The authors are truly effective because they know that teaching is about telling compelling stories in ways that make each concept come to life.

Teacher / Author / Professional

Through their textbooks, supplements, online learning tools, and classrooms, these authors have developed a comprehensive pedagogy that engages students in learning and faculty with teaching.

These authors collaborate throughout the entire process. The end result is a true collaboration where each author brings his individual experience and talent to the development of every paragraph, page, and chapter, thus creating a truly well-rounded, thorough view on any given accounting topic.

Many Ways in One Direction

Our **Team for Success** has developed a teaching system that addresses every learning style. Each year brings new insights, feedback, ideas, and improvements on how to deliver the material to every student with a passion for the subject in a format that gives them the best chance to succeed.

The key to the team's approach is in understanding that, just as there are many different ways to learn, there are also many different ways to teach.

In Their Own Words

Visit the Wiley **Team for Success** website to hear from the authors first-hand as they discuss their teaching styles, collaboration, and the future of accounting.

www.wileyteamforsuccess.com

Author Commitment

Jerry Weygandt

Jerry J. Weygandt, PhD, CPA, is Arthur Andersen Alumni Emeritus Professor of Accounting at the University of Wisconsin—Madison. He holds a Ph.D. in accounting from the University of Illinois. Articles by Professor Weygandt have appeared in the *Accounting Review, Journal of Accounting Research, Accounting Horizons, Journal of Accountancy,* and other academic and professional journals. These articles have examined such financial reporting issues as accounting for price-level adjustments, pensions, convertible securities, stock option contracts, and interim reports. Professor Weygandt is author of other accounting and financial reporting books and is a member of the American Accounting Association, the American Institute of Certified Public Accountants, and the Wisconsin Society of Certified Public Accountants. He has served on numerous committees of the American Accounting Association and as a member of the editorial board of the Accounting Review; he also has served as President and Secretary-Treasurer of the American Accounting Association. In addition, he has been actively involved with the American Institute of Certified Public Accountants and has been a member of the Accounting Standards Executive Committee (AcSEC) of that organization. He has served on the FASB task force that examined the reporting issues related to accounting for income taxes and served as a trustee of the Financial Accounting Foundation. Professor Weygandt has received the Chancellor's Award for Excellence in Teaching and the Beta Gamma Sigma Dean's Teaching Award. He is on the board of directors of M & I Bank of Southern Wisconsin. He is the recipient of the Wisconsin Institute of CPA's Outstanding Educator's Award and the Lifetime Achievement Award. In 2001 he received the American Accounting Association's Outstanding Educator Award.

Paul Kimmel

Paul D. Kimmel, PhD, CPA, received his bachelor's degree from the University of Minnesota and his doctorate in accounting from the University of Wisconsin. He is an Associate Professor at the University of Wisconsin—Milwaukee, and has public accounting experience with Deloitte & Touche (Minneapolis). He was the recipient of the UWM School of Business Advisory Council Teaching Award, the Reggie Taite Excellence in Teaching Award and a three-time winner of the Outstanding Teaching Assistant Award at the University of Wisconsin. He is also a recipient of the Elijah Watts Sells Award for Honorary Distinction for his results on the CPA exam. He is a member of the American Accounting Association and the Institute of Management Accountants and has published articles in *Accounting Review, Accounting Horizons, Advances in Management Accounting, Managerial Finance, Issues in Accounting Education, Journal of Accounting Education,* as well as other journals. His research interests include accounting for financial instruments and innovation in accounting education. He has published papers and given numerous talks on incorporating critical thinking into accounting education, and helped prepare a catalog of critical thinking resources for the Federated Schools of Accountancy.

Don Kieso

Donald E. Kieso, PhD, CPA, received his bachelor's degree from Aurora University and his doctorate in accounting from the University of Illinois. He has served as chairman of the Department of Accountancy and is currently the KPMG Emeritus Professor of Accountancy at Northern Illinois University. He has public accounting experience with Price Waterhouse & Co. (San Francisco and Chicago) and Arthur Andersen & Co. (Chicago) and research experience with the Research Division of the American Institute of Certified Public Accountants (New York). He has done post doctorate work as a Visiting Scholar at the University of California at Berkeley and is a recipient of NIU's Teaching Excellence Award and four Golden Apple Teaching Awards. Professor Kieso is the author of other accounting and business books and is a member of the American Accounting Association, the American Institute of Certified Public Accountants, and the Illinois CPA Society. He has served as a member of the Board of Directors of the Illinois CPA Society, then AACSB's Accounting Accreditation Committees, the State of Illinois Comptroller's Commission, as Secretary-Treasurer of the Federation of Schools of Accountancy, and as Secretary-Treasurer of the American Accounting Association. Professor Kieso is currently serving on the Board of Trustees and Executive Committee of Aurora University, as a member of the Board of Directors of Kishwaukee Community Hospital, and as Treasurer and Director of Valley West Community Hospital. From 1989 to 1993 he served as a charter member of the national Accounting Education Change Commission. He is the recipient of the Outstanding Accounting Educator Award from the Illinois CPA Society, the FSA's Joseph A. Silvoso Award of Merit, the NIU Foundation's Humanitarian Award for Service to Higher Education, a Distinguished Service Award from the Illinois CPA Society, and in 2003 an honorary doctorate from Aurora University.

IFRS

Ready When You Are

The emerging importance of

International Financial Reporting Standards presents challenges in how you teach and how your students learn accounting.

The **Wiley Accounting Team for Success** is ready when you are to help prepare you and your students for the integration of IFRS into your courses.

No matter where you are in this transition, Wiley Accounting is here to provide the tools you need to fully incorporate IFRS into your accounting courses. We offer the most extensive **Products**, **Content**, **Services**, **Support**, and **Training** available today—leading the way to prepare you and your students for success!

Innovative Products New IFRS Editions of **Kieso, Intermediate Accounting** and **Weygandt, Financial Accounting** are the most current and only textbooks available based fully on International Financial Reporting Standards. Wiley Accounting also offers numerous IFRS resources that can serve to supplement your course.

Exclusive Content Our accounting publications feature more quality and current coverage of IFRS topics than any other textbook available today! The Wiley Accounting Team for Success authors integrate IFRS content within each chapter through features like **A Look at IFRS**, which demonstrates how international standards apply to each U.S. GAAP topic, as well as provides an opportunity for practical application. **International Insights** also provide an international perspective of the accounting topic discussed in the text.

Support & Services Wiley Accounting features a dedicated **IFRS website** (at *www.wileyifrs.com*) and an **Accounting Weekly Updates website** (at *www. wileyaccountingupdates.com*) to make sure you have the most current resources available.

Timely Training Wiley Accounting and the **Wiley Faculty Network** provides free IFRS virtual training workshops, IFRS Guest Lectures, and IFRS "Boot Camps" featuring authors Paul Kimmel and Terry Warfield. You can also earn **CPE credit** for attending these sessions.

To learn more about how the Wiley Accounting Team for Success can help your students succeed, visit **www.wileyteamforsuccess.com** or contact your Wiley sales representative today.

Wiley Managerial Accounting Video Series

Watch managerial accounting in action!

New Managerial Accounting Videos use a variety of real-life, successful companies you already know to demonstrate and reinforce concepts taught in your managerial accounting course.

Companies you will learn about include:

Pizza Hut • Southwest Airlines • Starbucks • Method • Holland America Line • Jones Soda Co. • Zappos • Babycakes • Tribeca Grand • Precor • Whole Foods Market

Check out these videos in your *WileyPLUS* course. Simply go to "Course Materials" in *WileyPLUS* and type the keyword "video" in the search box.

WILEY PLUS
www.wileyplus.com

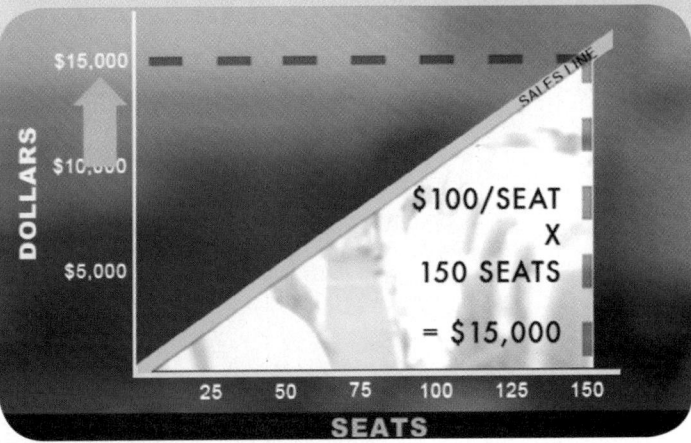

WILEY

WileyPLUS

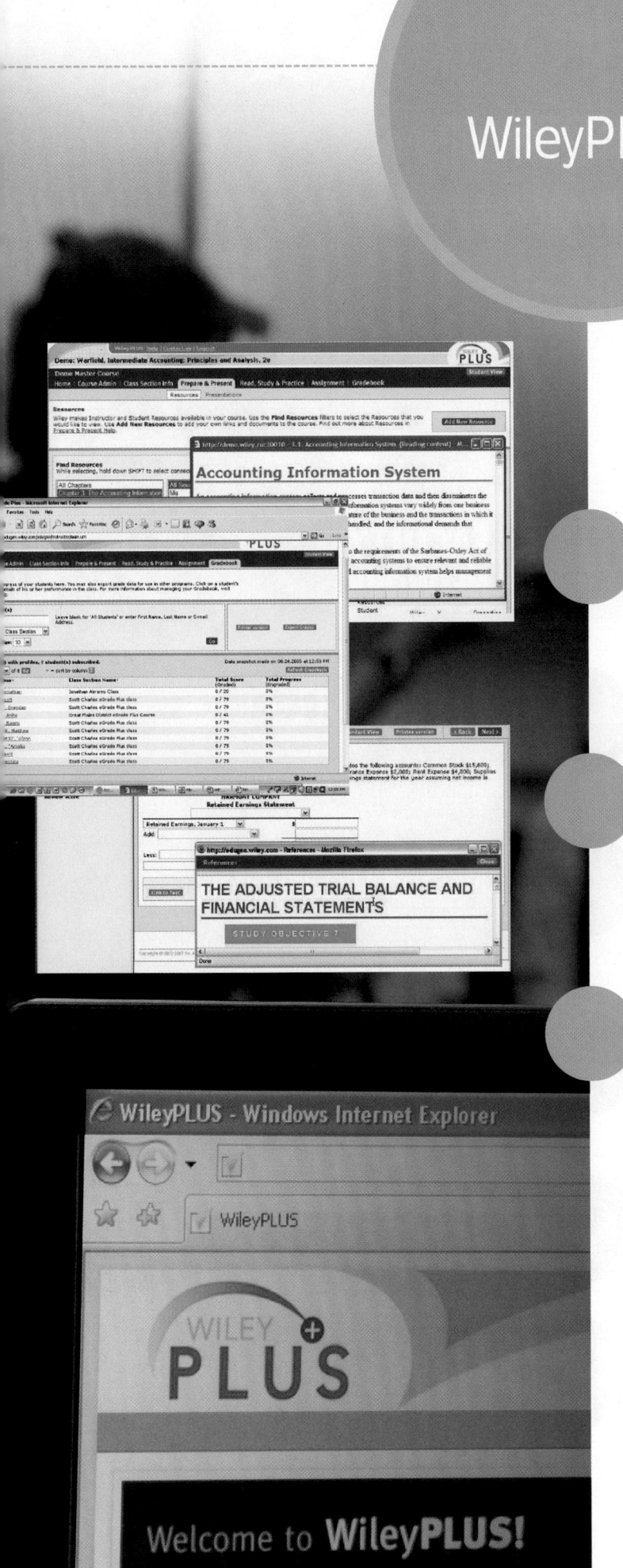

Prepare and Present

Create outstanding class presentations using a wealth of resources, such as PowerPoint™ slides, interactive simulations, and more. Plus you can easily upload any materials you have created into your course and combine them with the resources contained in *WileyPLUS*.

Track Your Progress

Keep track of your students' progress via an instructor's gradebook, which allows you to analyze individual and overall class results. This gives you an accurate and realistic assessment of your students' progress and level of understanding.

Create Assignments

Automate the assigning and grading of homework or quizzes by using the provided question banks or by writing your own. Student results will be automatically graded and recorded in your gradebook. *WileyPLUS* also links homework problems to relevant sections of the online text, hints, or solutions—context-sensitive help where students need it most!

The Wiley Faculty Network

The Place Where Faculty Connect ...

The Wiley Faculty Network is a global community of faculty connected by a passion for teaching and a drive to learn and share. Connect with the Wiley Faculty Network to collaborate with your colleagues, find a mentor, attend virtual and live events, and view a wealth of resources all designed to help you grow as an educator. Embrace the art of teaching—great things happen where faculty connect!

Discover innovative ideas and gain knowledge you can use.

- Training
- Virtual Guest Lectures
- Live Events

Explore your resources and development opportunities.

- Teaching Resources
- Archived Guest Lectures
- Recorded Presentations
- Professional Development Modules

Connect with colleagues— your greatest resource.

- Find a Mentor
- Interest Groups
- Blog

Find out more at
www.WHEREFACULTYCONNECT.com

Virtual Guest Lectures

Connect with recognized leaders across disciplines and collaborate with your peers on timely topics and discipline-specific issues, many of which offer CPE credit.

Live and Virtual Events

These invitation-only, discipline-specific events are organized through a close partnership between the WFN, Wiley, and the academic community near the event location.

Technology Training

Discover a wealth of topic- and technology-specific training presented by subject matter experts, authors, and faculty where and when you need it.

Teaching Resources

Propel your teaching and student learning to the next level with quality peer-reviewed case studies, testimonials, classroom tools, and checklists.

Connect with Colleagues

Achieve goals and tackle challenges more easily by enlisting the help of your peers. Connecting with colleagues through the WFN can help you improve your teaching experience.

What TYPE of learner are you?

Understanding each of these basic learning styles enables the authors to engage students' minds and motivate them to do their best work, ultimately improving the experience for both students and faculty.

	Intake: To take in the information	To make a study package	Text features that may help you the most	Output: To do well on exams
VISUAL	• Pay close attention to charts, drawings, and handouts your instructors use. • Underline. • Use different colors. • Use symbols, flow charts, graphs, different arrangements on the page, white spaces.	Convert your lecture notes into "page pictures." To do this: • Use the "Intake" strategies. • Reconstruct images in different ways. • Redraw pages from memory. • Replace words with symbols and initials. • Look at your pages.	The Navigator/Feature Story/Preview Infographics/Illustrations Accounting equation analyses Highlighted words Comprehensive DO IT! Problem/Action Plan Questions/Exercises/Problems Financial Reporting Problem Comparative Analysis Problem Real-World Focus	• Recall your "page pictures." • Draw diagrams where appropriate. • Practice turning your visuals back into words.
AURAL	• Attend lectures and tutorials. • Discuss topics with students and instructors. • Explain new ideas to other people. • Use a tape recorder. • Leave spaces in your lecture notes for later recall. • Describe overheads, pictures, and visuals to somebody who was not in class.	You may take poor notes because you prefer to listen. Therefore: • Expand your notes by talking with others and with information from your textbook. • Tape-record summarized notes and listen. • Read summarized notes out loud. • Explain your notes to another "aural" person.	Preview Insight Boxes DO IT! Action Plan Summary of Learning Objectives Glossary Comprehensive DO IT! Problem/Action Plan Self-Test Questions Questions/Exercises/Problems Financial Reporting Problem Comparative Analysis Problem Real-World Focus Decision-Making Across the Organization Communication Activity Ethics Case	• Talk with the instructor. • Spend time in quiet places recalling the ideas. • Practice writing answers to old exam questions. • Say your answers out loud.
READING/WRITING	• Use lists and headings. • Use dictionaries, glossaries, and definitions. • Read handouts, textbooks, and supplementary library readings. • Use lecture notes.	• Write out words again and again. • Reread notes silently. • Rewrite ideas and principles into other words. • Turn charts, diagrams, and other illustrations into statements.	The Navigator/Feature Story/Study Objectives/Preview DO IT! Action Plan Summary of Learning Objectives Glossary/Self-Test Questions Questions/Exercises/Problems Writing Problems Financial Reporting Problem Comparative Analysis Problem Real-World Focus Decision-Making Across the Organization Communication Activity All About You	• Write exam answers. • Practice with multiple-choice questions. • Write paragraphs, beginnings and endings. • Write your lists in outline form. • Arrange your words into hierarchies and points.
KINESTHETIC	• Use all your senses. • Go to labs, take field trips. • Listen to real-life examples. • Pay attention to applications. • Use hands-on approaches. • Use trial-and-error methods.	You may take poor notes because topics do not seem concrete or relevant. Therefore: • Put examples in your summaries. • Use case studies and applications to help with principles and abstract concepts. • Talk about your notes with another "kinesthetic" person. • Use pictures and photographs that illustrate an idea.	The Navigator/Feature Story/Preview Infographics/Illustrations DO IT! Action Plan Summary of Learning Objectives Comprehensive DO IT! Problem/Action Plan Self-Test Questions Questions/Exercises/Problems Financial Reporting Problem Comparative Analysis Problem Real-World Focus Decision-Making Across the Organization Communication Activity All About You	• Write practice answers. • Role-play the exam situation.

Textbook Features

In this First Edition, we include numerous pedagogical tools that expand our emphasis on student learning. Our goal is to provide a teaching and learning package that instructors and students will rate as the highest in customer satisfaction.

The Accounting Cycle

For many students, success in an introductory accounting course hinges on developing a sound conceptual understanding of the accounting cycle. As a result, we have developed a framework to help students visualize how to analyze, journalize, and post transaction data.

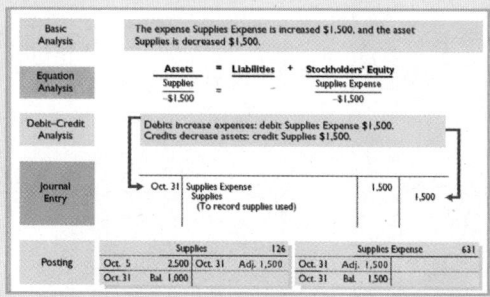

Accounting Principles

For many students, learning about the conceptual framework can be somewhat tedious. Yet, at the same time, we believe that students need a good understanding of the accounting assumptions, principles, and constraints that accountants use as a basis for recording and reporting financial information. As a result, we decided to integrate our discussion of accounting principles throughout the textbook as they relate to the topic at hand. However, we also realize that students might find it helpful to have a summary of all the concepts, which we provide in the **Chapter 3 Appendix**, *Concepts in Action*.

Chart of Accounts

It is important to always try to eliminate unnecessary barriers to student understanding. Sometimes, the accounting course can seem unnecessarily complicated to students because so many account titles are used. In order to reduce possible confusion and to keep students focused on those concepts that really matter, we streamlined the number of accounts used in the textbook, supplements, and *WileyPLUS*. See inside the front cover of the textbook for a sample chart of accounts, which represent the majority of the account titles used.

Accounting Equation Analyses

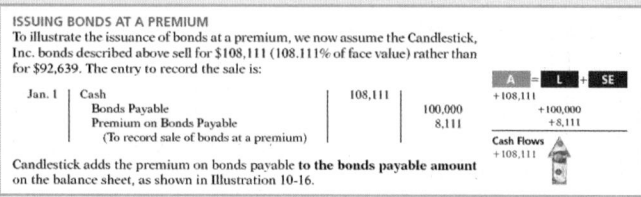

We include **accounting equation analyses** in the margin next to key journal entries. They will help students understand the impact of an accounting transaction on the components of the accounting equation, on the stockholders' equity accounts, and on the company's cash flows.

Real-World Emphasis

One of the goals of the introductory accounting course is to orient students to the application of accounting principles and techniques in practice. Accordingly, we use numerous examples from real companies throughout the textbook. The names of these real companies are highlighted in red.

Also, throughout the chapters, **Insight** and **Accounting Across the Organization** boxes show how people, often in non-accounting functions, in actual companies make decisions using accounting information. These high-interest boxes focus on various themes—ethics, international, investor, and corporate social responsibility concerns. *Guideline Answers* to the critical thinking questions are provided at the end of each chapter.

ACCOUNTING ACROSS THE ORGANIZATION

Wall Street No Friend of Facebook

In the 1990s, it was the dream of every young technology entrepreneur to start a company and do an initial public offering (IPO), that is, list company shares on a stock exchange. It seemed like there was a never-ending supply of 20-something-year-old technology entrepreneurs that made millions doing IPOs of companies that never made a profit and eventually failed. In sharp contrast to this is Mark Zuckerberg, the 27-year-old founder and CEO of Facebook. If Facebook did an IPO, he would make billions of dollars. But, he is in no hurry to go public. Because his company doesn't need to invest in factories, distribution systems, or even marketing, it doesn't need to raise a lot of cash. Also, by not going public, Zuckerberg has more control over the direction of the company. Right now, he and the other founders don't have to answer to outside shareholders, who might be more concerned about short-term investment horizons rather than long-term goals. In addition, publicly traded companies face many more financial reporting disclosure requirements.

Source: Jessica E. Vascellaro, "Facebook CEO in No Rush to 'Friend' Wall Street," Wall Street Journal Online (March 4, 2010).

? Why has Mark Zuckerberg, the CEO and founder of Facebook, delayed taking his company's shares public through an initial public offering (IPO)? (See page 596.)

PEOPLE, PLANET, AND PROFIT INSIGHT

Selling Green

Here is a question an executive of PepsiCo was asked: Should PepsiCo market green? The executive indicated that the company should, as he believes it's the No. 1 thing consumers all over the world care about. Here are some thoughts on this issue:

If you are going to market green, what are some things we've learned? I'll share with you one thing we've learned at PepsiCo.

Sun Chips are part of the food business I run. It's a "healthy snack." We decided that Sun Chips, if it's a healthy snack, should be made in facilities that have a net-zero footprint. In other words, I want off the electric grid everywhere we make Sun Chips. We did that. Sun Chips should be made in a facility that puts back more water than it uses. It does that. And we partnered with our suppliers and came out with the world's first compostable chip package.

Now, there was an issue with this package: It was louder than the New York subway, louder than jet engines taking off. What would a company that's committed to green do: walk away or stay committed? If your people are passionate, they're going to fix it for you as long as you stay committed. Six months later, the compostable bag has half the noise of our current package.

So the view today is: we should market green, we should be proud to do it . . . it has to be a 360 process, both internal and external. And if you do that, you can monetize environmental sustainability for the shareholders.

Source: "Four Problems—and Solutions," Wall Street Journal (March 7, 2011), p. R2.

? What is meant by "monetize environmental sustainability" for shareholders? (See page 267.)

People, Planet, and Profit

Today's companies are evaluating not just their profitability but also their corporate social responsibility. To that end, we have profiled some of these companies, such as PepsiCo, to highlight their sustainable business practices.

Anatomy of a Fraud

Our *Anatomy of a Fraud* stories highlight some real-world frauds. We describe the situation, note the extent of the fraud, and then discuss the missing internal control activity that would likely have prevented or uncovered the fraud.

ANATOMY OF A FRAUD

Bobbi Jean Donnelly, the office manager for Mod Fashions Corporations design center, was responsible for preparing the design center budget and reviewing expense reports submitted by design center employees. Her desire to upgrade her wardrobe got the better of her, and she enacted a fraud that involved filing expense-reimbursement requests for her own personal clothing purchases. She was able to conceal the fraud because she was responsible for reviewing all expense reports, including her own. In addition, she sometimes was given ultimate responsibility for signing off on the expense reports when her boss was "too busy." Also, because she controlled the budget, when she submitted her expenses, she coded them to budget items that she knew were running under budget, so that they would not catch anyone's attention.

Total take: $275,000

The Missing Control

Independent internal verification. Bobbi Jean's boss should have verified her expense reports. When asked what he thought her expenses for a year were, the boss said about $10,000. At $115,000 per year, her actual expenses were more than 10 times what would have been expected. However, because he was "too busy" to verify her expense reports or to review the budget, he never noticed.

Source: Adapted from Wells, Fraud Casebook (2007), pp. 79–90.

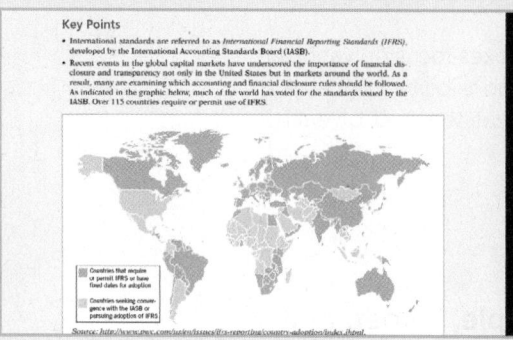

Kellogg Company		
Balance Sheet (partial)		
($ in millions)		
Stockholders' equity		
Common stock, $0.25 par value, 1,000,000,000 shares authorized		
Issued: 418,669,193 shares		$ 105
Capital in excess of par value		388
Retained earnings		4,217
Treasury stock, at cost 28,618,052 shares		(1,357)
Accumulated other comprehensive income (loss)		(827)
Total stockholders' equity		$ 2,526

Financial Statements

Students will be more willing to commit time and energy to a topic when they believe it is relevant to their future careers. There is no better way to demonstrate relevance than to ground discussions in the real world. To that end, we include financial statements from actual companies regularly throughout the textbook.

International Financial Reporting Standards

To reflect the constant changes in the accounting environment, we have included a comprehensive section at the end of each chapter on International Financial Reporting Standards (IFRS). *A Look at IFRS* includes an overview section, addresses differences between GAAP and IFRS (*Key Points*), describes convergence efforts (*Looking to the Future*), and provides students with the opportunity to test their understanding through self-test questions and exercises (*IFRS Practice*). An international financial reporting problem is also included, based on Zetar plc's (a U.K. candy company) financial statements, provided in Appendix C of the textbook.

International Insights (and *International Notes* in the margin) also provide a global perspective of the accounting topics discussed in the textbook.

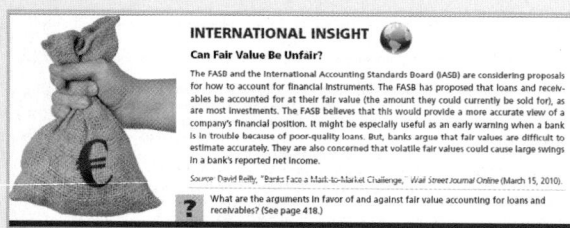

INTERNATIONAL INSIGHT

Can Fair Value Be Unfair?

The FASB and the International Accounting Standards Board (IASB) are considering proposals for how to account for financial instruments. The FASB has proposed that loans and receivables be accounted for at their fair value (the amount they could currently be sold for), as are most investments. The FASB believes that this would provide a more accurate view of a company's financial position. It might be especially useful as an early warning when a bank is in trouble because of poor-quality loans. But, banks argue that fair values are difficult to estimate accurately. They are also concerned that volatile fair values could cause large swings in a bank's reported net income.

Source: David Reilly, "Banks Face a Mark-to-Market Challenge," Wall Street Journal Online (March 15, 2010).

? What are the arguments in favor of and against fair value accounting for loans and receivables? (See page 418.)

DO IT! Exercises

Brief **DO IT!** exercises ask students to apply their newly acquired knowledge. The **DO IT!** exercises include an *Action Plan*, which reviews the necessary steps to complete the exercise, as well as a *Solution* so students can have immediate feedback. A Comprehensive **DO IT!** problem at the end of each chapter allows students a final check of their understanding before they do their homework. **DO IT!** Review problems are part of the end-of-chapter homework material.

Marginal Notes

Helpful Hints in the margin further clarify concepts being discussed. **Ethics Notes** point out ethical points related to the nearby text discussion. **Alternative Terminology** lets students know about interchangeable words and phrases. **International Notes** provide a global perspective of the accounting topics being discussed.

Managerial Decision-Making

Beginning in Chapter 15, we introduce Current Designs, a kayak-making company based in Winona, Minnesota. We then follow-up with a decision-making problem in every subsequent chapter based on this real-world company. Each problem presents realistic managerial accounting situations that students must analyze to determine the best course of action. In addition, many of these end-of-chapter activities also have an accompanying video.

Managerial Accounting Video Series

Through the use of real-world, cutting-edge companies, these videos engage students with a dynamic overview of managerial accounting topics and motivate them through the detailed tools, examples, and discussions presented in their textbook, *WileyPLUS* course, and classroom lectures.

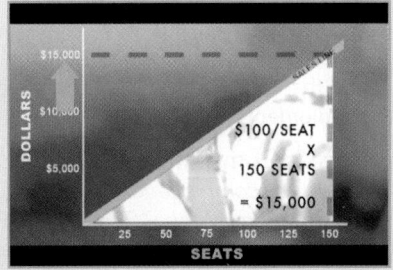

Comprehensive Homework Material

Each chapter concludes with Self-Test Questions, Questions, Brief Exercises, **DO IT!** Review, Exercises, and Problems. Many chapters also include a Comprehensive Problem. An icon identifies Exercises and Problems that can be solved using **Excel templates** at the book's companion website. The **Continuing Cookie Chronicle** and the **Waterways Continuing Problem** use the business activities of two fictional companies to help students apply financial and managerial accounting topics to realistic entrepreneurial situations.

Broadening Your Perspective Section

The **Broadening Your Perspective** section at the end of each chapter presents short cases that require analytical, decision-making, and critical thinking skills. Elements in this section include the following:

- Financial Reporting Problem: PepsiCo, Inc.
- Comparative Analysis Problem: PepsiCo, Inc. vs. The Coca-Cola Company
- Real-World Focus
- Decision-Making Across the Organization
- Decision-Making at Current Designs
- Managerial Analysis

- Communication Activity
- Ethics Case
- All About You
- Considering People, Planet, and Profit
- Considering Your Costs and Benefits
- FASB Codification Activity

These assignments are designed to help develop students' decision-making and critical-thinking skills.

Teaching and Learning Supplementary Material

For Instructors

In addition to the support instructors receive from *WileyPLUS* and the Wiley Faculty Network, we offer the following useful supplements.

Book's Companion Website. On this website, *www.wiley.com/college/weygandt*, instructors will find the Solutions Manual, Test Bank, Instructor's Manual, Computerized Test Bank, and other resources.

Solutions Manual. The Solutions Manual contains detailed solutions to all questions, brief exercises, exercises, and problems in the textbook, as well as suggested answers to the questions and cases. The estimated time to complete exercises, problems, and cases is provided.

Instructor's Manual. Included in each chapter are lecture outlines with teaching tips, chapter reviews, illustrations, and review quizzes.

Test Bank and Computerized Test Bank. The test bank and computerized test bank allow instructors to tailor examinations according to study objectives and learning outcomes, including AACSB, AICPA, and IMA professional standards. Achievement tests, comprehensive examinations, and a final exam are included.

PowerPoint™. The PowerPoint™ presentations contain a combination of key concepts, images, and problems from the textbook.

Blackboard. Blackboard offers an integrated set of course management tools that enable instructors to easily design, develop, and manage Web-based and Web-enhanced courses.

For Students

Book's Companion Website. On this website, students will find:

- *Exercises: Set B* and *Challenge Exercises*
- *Problems: Set C*
- *Self-Tests and Additional Self-Tests*
- *Appendices E–H*
- *Cases for Managerial Decision-Making*

Study Guide. Each chapter of the Study Guide contains a chapter review, chapter outline, and a glossary of key terms. Demonstration problems, multiple-choice, true/false, matching, and other exercises are also included.

Working Papers and Excel Working Papers. The working papers are printed templates that can help students correctly format their textbook accounting solutions.

Excel Primer: Using Excel in Accounting. The online Excel primer and accompanying Excel templates allow students to complete select end-of-chapter exercises and problems identified by a spreadsheet icon in the margin of the textbook.

Managerial Accounting Video Series. Through the examples of real-world, cutting-edge companies, these videos engage students with a dynamic overview of managerial accounting topics and motivate them through the detailed tools, examples, and discussions presented in their textbook, *WileyPLUS* course, and classroom lectures.

Mobile Applications. Quizzing and reviewing content is available for download on iTunes.

Acknowledgments

Financial & Managerial Accounting has benefited greatly from the input of focus group participants, manuscript reviewers, ancillary authors, and proofers. We greatly appreciate the constructive suggestions and innovative ideas of reviewers and the creativity and accuracy of the ancillary authors and checkers.

Dawn Addington
Central New Mexico Community College

Audrey Agnello
Niagara County Community College

Matt Anderson
Michigan State University

Joe Anthony
Michigan State University

Art Baja
Ohlone College

Felicia Baldwin
City College of Chicago— Richard J. Daley

Richard Barnhart
Grand Rapids Community College

John Blahnik
Lorain County Community College

David Bland
Cape Fear Community College

Bruce Bradford
Fairfield University

Brian Bratten
University of Kentucky—Lexington

Jerry Braun
Daytona State College

Leroy Bugger
Edison State College

Erin Burrell
University of Central Florida

Lisa Capozzoli
College of DuPage

Bruce Cassel
SUNY Dutchess Community College

Renee Castrigano
Cleveland State University

Gayle Chaky
Dutchess Community College

Linda Chambers
Miles College

Milton Chavez-Arias
Ohlone College

Kung Chen
University of Nebraska—Lincoln

Toni Clegg
Delta College

Cheryl Copeland
California State University, Fresno

Suzanne Counte
St. Louis Community College— Meramec

Paul Croitoru
Wilbur Wright College

Robin D'Agati
Palm Beach State College

Karl Dahlberg
Rutgers University—Newark

Dori Danko
Grand Valley State University

Alan Davis
Community College of Philadelphia

Larry DeGaetano
Montclair State University

Andrew DeJoseph
College of Mount Saint Vincent

Naman Desai
University of Central Florida

Ron Dustin
Fresno City College

Barbara Eide
University of Wisconsin—La Crosse

Martin Epstein
Central New Mexico Community College

Ann Esarco
McHenry County College

Caroline Falconetti
Nassau Community College

Janet Farler
Pima Community College

Roger Gee
San Diego Mesa College

Severin Grabski
Michigan State University

Hassan Hefzi
California State Polytechnic University—Pomona

Merrilly Hoffman
San Jacinto College

Janice Holmes
Louisiana State University—Baton Rouge

Bambi Hora
University of Central Oklahoma

John Hoskins
University of Alabama—Huntsville

Leslie Hubbard
Solano Community College

Daniel Hunt
Ivy Technical Community College

John Illig
State College of Florida

Jeff Jones
College of Southern Nevada— Henderson

Nancy Kelly
Middlesex Community College

Ridgway Knight
Santa Monica College

Don Kovacic
California State University, San Marcos

Richard Larkin

Jason Lee
SUNY Plattsburgh

Harold Little
Western Kentucky University

Lois Mahoney
Eastern Michigan University

Maria Mari
Miami Dade College

Linda Marquis
Northern Kentucky University

Maureen McBeth
College of DuPage

Florence McGovern
Bergen Community College

Mary Michel
Manhattan College

Jeanette Milius
Iowa Western Community College

Earl Mitchell
Santa Ana College

April Mohr
Kentucky Community College

Mary Beth Nelson
North Shore Community College

Michael Newman
University of Houston

Oluwakemi Onwuchekwa
University of Central Florida

James Onyeocha
South Carolina State University

Hong Pak
California State Polytechnic University— Pomona

Judy Peterson
Monmouth College

Richard Pettit
Mountain View College

James Racic
Lakeland Community College

Robert Rambo
Roger Williams University

Raymond Reisig
Pace University—Pleasantville

Luther Ross
Central Piedmont Community College

Susan Sadowski
Shippensburg University/UMUC

Richard Sarkisian
Camden County College

Karl Schindl
University of Wisconsin—Manitowoc

Debbie Seifert
Illinois State University

Valerie Simmons
University of Southern Mississippi

Mike Skaff
College of the Sequoias

Chuck Smith
Iowa Western Community College

Ashley Soliz
Delta State University

Jalal Soroosh
Loyola University Maryland

Patrick Stegman
College of Lake County

Grace Stuart-Tuggle
Palm Beach State College

Karen Tabak
Maryville University

Diane Tanner
University of North Florida

Geoffrey Tickell
Indiana University of Pennsylvania

Joan Van Hise
Fairfield University

Richard Van Ness
Schenectady County Community College

Cynthia Vanoosterum
Ivy Community College

Sheila Viel
University of Wisconsin—Milwaukee

Robert Walsh
University of Dallas

Barbara Warschawski
Schenectady County Community College

Bob Willis
Rogers State University

Jeffrey Wong
Bellevue College

Marj Yuschak
Rutgers University—New Brunswick

Judith Zander
Grossmont College

WileyPLUS Developers and Reviewers

Carole Brandt-Fink
Laura McNally
Melanie Yon

Ancillary Authors, Contributors, Proofers, and Accuracy Checkers

LuAnn Bean
Florida Institute of Technology

Jack Borke
University of Wisconsin—Platteville

Sandra Cohen
Columbia College Chicago

Jim Emig
Villanova University

Larry Falcetto
Emporia State University

Mark Gleason
Metropolitan State University

Coby Harmon
University of California—Santa Barbara

Benjamin Huegel
St. Mary's University

Douglas Kieso
Aurora University

Kirk Lynch
Sandhills Community College

Kevin McNelis
New Mexico State University

Jill Misuraca
University of Tampa

Barbara Muller
Arizona State University

Yvonne Phang
Borough of Manhattan Community College

John Plouffe
California State University—Los Angeles

Rex Schildhouse
San Diego Community College—Miramar

Teresa Speck
St. Mary's University

Lynn Stallworth
Appalachian State University

Ellen Sweatt
Georgia Perimeter College

Diane Tanner
University of North Florida

Joan Van Hise
Fairfield University

Doris Warmflash
SUNY, Westchester Community College

Dick Wasson
San Diego State University

Andrea Weickgenannt
Xavier University

Bernie Weinrich
Lindenwood University

We appreciate the exemplary support and commitment given to us by associate publisher Chris DeJohn, senior acquisitions editor Michael McDonald, marketing manager Karolina Zarychta Honsa, operations manager Yana Mermel, senior content editor Ed Brislin, development editors Terry Ann Tatro and Margaret Thompson, lead product designer Allie Morris, product designer Greg Chaput, vice president of higher education production and manufacturing Ann Berlin, designers Maureen Eide and Kristine Carney, illustration editor Anna Melhorn, photo editor Mary Ann Price, project editor Suzanne Ingrao of Ingrao Associates, indexer Steve Ingle, Denise Showers at Aptara, Cyndy Taylor, and project manager Angel Chavez at Integra. All of these professionals provided innumerable services that helped the textbook take shape.

We also thank Benjamin Huegel and Teresa Speck of St. Mary's University for their extensive efforts in the preparation of the homework materials related to Current Designs. We also appreciate the considerable support provided to us by the following people at Current Designs: Mike Cichanowski, Jim Brown, Diane Buswell, and Jake Greseth. We also benefited from the assistance and suggestions provided to us by Joan Van Hise in the preparation of materials related to sustainability.

Finally, our thanks to Amy Scholz, Susan Elbe, George Hoffman, Tim Stookesberry, Joe Heider, and Steve Smith for their support and leadership in Wiley's College Division. We will appreciate suggestions and comments from users—instructors and students alike. You can send your thoughts and ideas about the textbook to us via email at: *wileyauthorfeedback@gmail.com*.

Jerry J. Weygandt
Madison, Wisconsin

Paul D. Kimmel
Milwaukee, Wisconsin

Donald E. Kieso
DeKalb, Illinois

Brief Contents

APPENDICES

*Available online at www.wiley.com/college/weygandt

Contents

Feature Story

Knowing the Numbers

Many students who take this course do not plan to be accountants. If you are in that group, you might be thinking, "If I'm not going to be an accountant, why do I need to know accounting?" In response, consider the quote from Harold Geneen, the former chairman of IT&T: "To be good at your business, you have to know the numbers—cold."

Success in any business comes back to the numbers. You will rely on them to make decisions, and managers will use them to evaluate your performance. That is true whether your job involves marketing, production, management, or information systems.

In business, accounting and financial statements are the means for communicating the numbers. If you don't know how to read financial statements, you can't really know your business.

Many companies spend significant resources teaching their employees basic accounting so that they can read financial statements and understand how their actions affect the company's financial results. One such company is Springfield ReManufacturing Corporation (SRC). When Jack Stack and 11 other managers purchased SRC for 10 cents a share, it was a failing division of International Harvester. Jack's 119 employees, however, were counting on him for their livelihood. He decided that for the company to

The Navigator is a learning system designed to prompt you to use the learning aids in the chapter and set priorities as you study.

Learning Objectives give you a framework for learning the specific concepts covered in the chapter.

Learning Objectives

After studying this chapter, you should be able to:

1 Explain what accounting is.
2 Identify the users and uses of accounting.
3 Understand why ethics is a fundamental business concept.
4 Explain generally accepted accounting principles.
5 Explain the monetary unit assumption and the economic entity assumption.
6 State the accounting equation, and define its components.
7 Analyze the effects of business transactions on the accounting equation.
8 Understand the four financial statements and how they are prepared.

 ✔ The Navigator

survive, every employee needed to think like a businessperson and to act like an owner. To accomplish this, all employees at SRC took basic accounting courses and participated in weekly reviews of the company's financial statements. SRC survived, and eventually thrived. To this day, every employee (now numbering more than 1,000) undergoes this same training.

Many other companies have adopted this approach, which is called "open-book management." Even in companies that do not practice open-book management, employers generally assume that managers in all areas of the company are "financially literate."

Taking this course will go a long way to making you financially literate. In this book, you will learn how to read and prepare financial statements, and how to use basic tools to evaluate financial results. Appendices A and B provide real financial statements of two well-known U.S. companies, PepsiCo, Inc. and The Coca-Cola Company. Appendix C includes the financial statements of Zetar plc, a U.K. candy company. Throughout this textbook, we attempt to increase your familiarity with financial reporting by providing numerous references, questions, and exercises that encourage you to explore these financial statements.

 **The Navigator**

*The **Feature Story** helps you picture how the chapter topic relates to the real world of accounting and business. You will find references to the story throughout the chapter.*

Preview of Chapter 1

The opening story about Springfield ReManufacturing Corporation highlights the importance of having good financial information and knowing how to use it to make effective business decisions. Whatever your pursuits or occupation, the need for financial information is inescapable. You cannot earn a living, spend money, buy on credit, make an investment, or pay taxes without receiving, using, or dispensing financial information. Good decision-making depends on good information.

The purpose of this chapter is to show you that accounting is the system used to provide useful financial information. The content and organization of Chapter 1 are as follows.

*The **Preview** describes and outlines the major topics and subtopics you will see in the chapter.*

ACCOUNTING IN ACTION

What Is Accounting?	The Building Blocks of Accounting	The Basic Accounting Equation	Using the Accounting Equation	Financial Statements
• Three activities • Who uses accounting data	• Ethics in financial reporting • Generally accepted accounting principles • Measurement principles • Assumptions	• Assets • Liabilities • Stockholders' equity	• Transaction analysis • Summary of transactions	• Income statement • Retained earnings statement • Balance sheet • Statement of cash flows

✔ **The Navigator**

What Is Accounting?

Essential terms are printed in blue when they first appear, and are defined in the end-of-chapter glossary.

What consistently ranks as one of the top career opportunities in business? What frequently rates among the most popular majors on campus? What was the undergraduate degree chosen by Nike founder Phil Knight, Home Depot co-founder Arthur Blank, former acting director of the Federal Bureau of Investigation (FBI) Thomas Pickard, and numerous members of Congress? Accounting.[1] Why did these people choose accounting? They wanted to understand what was happening financially to their organizations. Accounting is the financial information system that provides these insights. In short, to understand your organization, you have to know the numbers.

Accounting consists of three basic activities—it **identifies**, **records**, and **communicates** the economic events of an organization to interested users. Let's take a closer look at these three activities.

Three Activities

As a starting point to the accounting process, a company identifies the **economic events relevant to its business**. Examples of economic events are the sale of snack chips by PepsiCo, the providing of telephone services by AT&T, and the payment of wages by Ford Motor Company.

Once a company like PepsiCo identifies economic events, it **records** those events in order to provide a history of its financial activities. Recording consists of keeping a **systematic**, **chronological diary of events**, measured in dollars and cents. In recording, PepsiCo also classifies and summarizes economic events.

Finally, PepsiCo **communicates** the collected information to interested users by means of **accounting reports**. The most common of these reports are called **financial statements**. To make the reported financial information meaningful, PepsiCo reports the recorded data in a standardized way. It accumulates information resulting from similar transactions. For example, PepsiCo accumulates all sales transactions over a certain period of time and reports the data as one amount in the company's financial statements. Such data are said to be reported **in the aggregate**. By presenting the recorded data in the aggregate, the accounting process simplifies a multitude of transactions and makes a series of activities understandable and meaningful.

A vital element in communicating economic events is the accountant's ability to **analyze and interpret** the reported information. Analysis involves use of ratios, percentages, graphs, and charts to highlight significant financial trends and relationships. Interpretation involves **explaining the uses**, **meaning**, **and limitations of reported data**. Appendix A of this textbook shows the financial statements of PepsiCo, Inc. Appendix B illustrates the financial statements of The Coca-Cola Company. We refer to these statements at various places throughout the textbook. (In addition, in the *A Look at IFRS* section at the end of each chapter, the U.K. company Zetar plc is analyzed.) At this point, these financial statements probably strike you as complex and confusing. By the end of this course, you'll be surprised at your ability to understand, analyze, and interpret them.

Illustration 1-1 summarizes the activities of the accounting process.

---

[1]The appendix to this chapter describes job opportunities for accounting majors and explains why accounting is such a popular major.

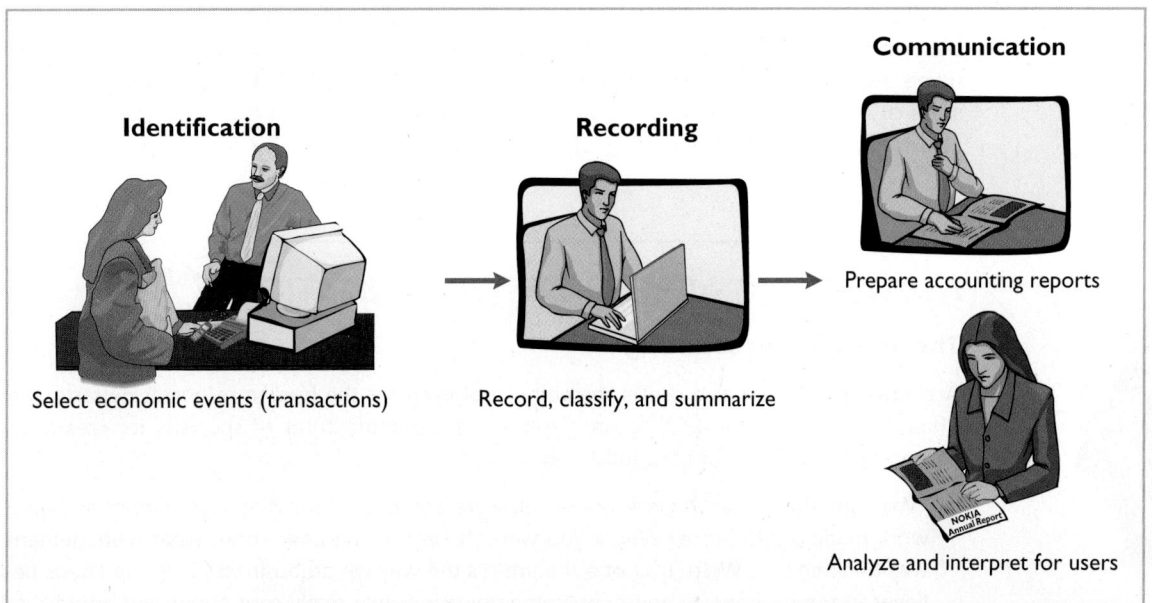

Identification

Select economic events (transactions)

Recording

Record, classify, and summarize

Communication

Prepare accounting reports

Analyze and interpret for users

Illustration 1-1
The activities of the accounting process

You should understand that the accounting process **includes** the bookkeeping function. **Bookkeeping** usually involves **only** the recording of economic events. It is therefore just one part of the accounting process. In total, accounting involves **the entire process of identifying, recording, and communicating economic events.**[2]

Who Uses Accounting Data

The specific financial information that a user needs depends upon the kinds of decisions the user makes. There are two broad groups of users of financial information: internal users and external users.

INTERNAL USERS

Internal users of accounting information are managers who plan, organize, and run the business. These include marketing managers, production supervisors, finance directors, and company officers. In running a business, internal users must answer many important questions, as shown in Illustration 1-2.

LEARNING OBJECTIVE   2

Identify the users and uses of accounting.

Illustration 1-2
Questions that internal users ask

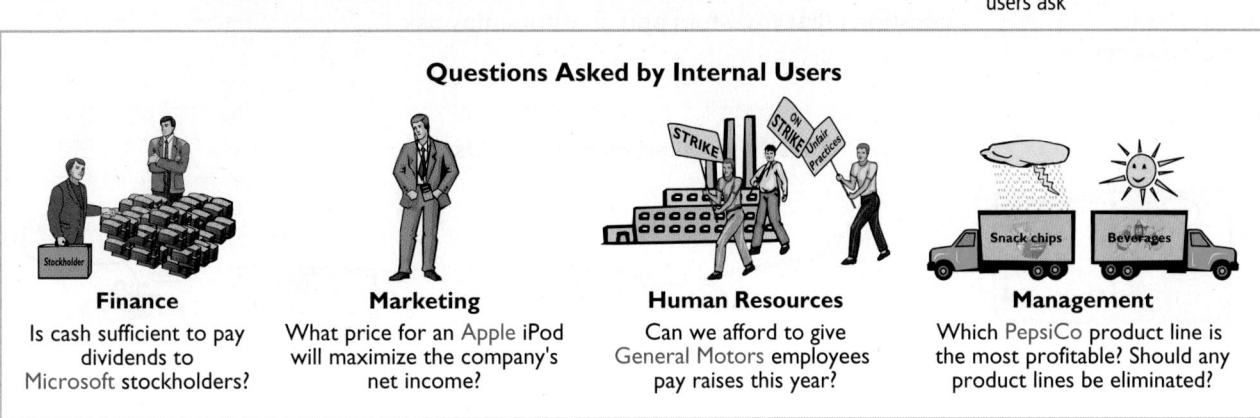

Questions Asked by Internal Users

Finance
Is cash sufficient to pay dividends to Microsoft stockholders?

Marketing
What price for an Apple iPod will maximize the company's net income?

Human Resources
Can we afford to give General Motors employees pay raises this year?

Management
Which PepsiCo product line is the most profitable? Should any product lines be eliminated?

---

[2]The origins of accounting are generally attributed to the work of Luca Pacioli, an Italian Renaissance mathematician. Pacioli was a close friend and tutor to Leonardo da Vinci and a contemporary of Christopher Columbus. In his 1494 text *Summa de Arithmetica, Geometria, Proportione et Proportionalite*, Pacioli described a system to ensure that financial information was recorded efficiently and accurately.

To answer these and other questions, internal users need detailed information on a timely basis. **Managerial accounting** provides internal reports to help users make decisions about their companies. Examples are financial comparisons of operating alternatives, projections of income from new sales campaigns, and forecasts of cash needs for the next year.

ACCOUNTING ACROSS THE ORGANIZATION

The Scoop on Accounting

Accounting can serve as a useful recruiting tool even for the human resources department. Rhino Foods, located in Burlington, Vermont, is a manufacturer of specialty ice cream. Its corporate website includes the following:

"Wouldn't it be great to work where you were part of a team? Where your input and hard work made a difference? Where you weren't kept in the dark about what management was thinking? . . . Well—it's not a dream! It's the way we do business . . . Rhino Foods believes in family, honesty and open communication—we really care about and appreciate our employees—and it shows. Operating results are posted and monthly group meetings inform all employees about what's happening in the Company. Employees also share in the Company's profits, in addition to having an excellent comprehensive benefits package."

Source: www.rhinofoods.com/workforus/workforus.html.

Accounting Across the Organization boxes demonstrate applications of accounting information in various business functions.

 What are the benefits to the company and to the employees of making the financial statements available to all employees? (See page 48.)

EXTERNAL USERS

External users are individuals and organizations outside a company who want financial information about the company. The two most common types of external users are investors and creditors. **Investors** (owners) use accounting information to make decisions to buy, hold, or sell ownership shares of a company. **Creditors** (such as suppliers and bankers) use accounting information to evaluate the risks of granting credit or lending money. Illustration 1-3 shows some questions that investors and creditors may ask.

Illustration 1-3
Questions that external users ask

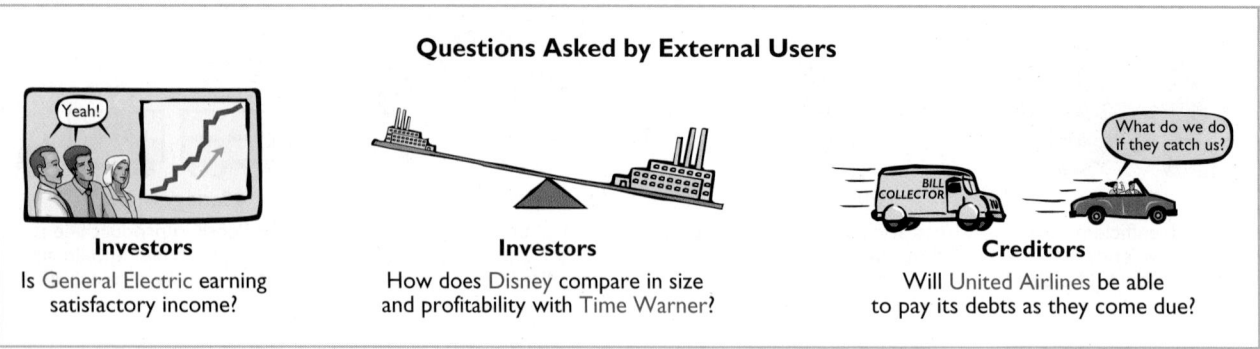

Questions Asked by External Users

Investors
Is General Electric earning satisfactory income?

Investors
How does Disney compare in size and profitability with Time Warner?

Creditors
Will United Airlines be able to pay its debts as they come due?

Financial accounting answers these questions. It provides economic and financial information for investors, creditors, and other external users. The information needs of external users vary considerably. **Taxing authorities**, such as the Internal Revenue Service, want to know whether the company complies with tax laws. **Regulatory agencies**, such as the Securities and Exchange Commission or the Federal Trade Commission, want to know whether the company is operating within prescribed rules. **Customers** are interested in whether a company like General Motors will continue to honor product warranties and support its product lines. **Labor unions**, such as the Major League Baseball Players Association, want to know whether the owners have the ability to pay increased wages and benefits.

The Building Blocks of Accounting

A doctor follows certain standards in treating a patient's illness. An architect follows certain standards in designing a building. An accountant follows certain standards in reporting financial information. For these standards to work, a fundamental business concept must be at work—ethical behavior.

Ethics in Financial Reporting

People won't gamble in a casino if they think it is "rigged." Similarly, people won't play the stock market if they think stock prices are rigged. In recent years, the financial press has been full of articles about financial scandals at Enron, WorldCom, HealthSouth, AIG, and others. As the scandals came to light, mistrust of financial reporting in general grew. One article in the *Wall Street Journal* noted that "repeated disclosures about questionable accounting practices have bruised investors' faith in the reliability of earnings reports, which in turn has sent stock prices tumbling." Imagine trying to carry on a business or invest money if you could not depend on the financial statements to be honestly prepared. Information would have no credibility. There is no doubt that a sound, well-functioning economy depends on accurate and dependable financial reporting.

> **LEARNING OBJECTIVE   3**
>
> **Understand why ethics is a fundamental business concept.**

United States regulators and lawmakers were very concerned that the economy would suffer if investors lost confidence in corporate accounting because of unethical financial reporting. In response, Congress passed the **Sarbanes-Oxley Act** (SOX, or Sarbox). Its intent is to reduce unethical corporate behavior and decrease the likelihood of future corporate scandals. As a result of SOX, top management must now certify the accuracy of financial information. In addition, penalties for fraudulent financial activity are much more severe. Also, SOX increased the independence of the outside auditors who review the accuracy of corporate financial statements and increased the oversight role of boards of directors.

> ### Ethics Note
>
> Circus-founder P.T. Barnum is alleged to have said, "Trust everyone, but cut the deck." What Sarbanes-Oxley does is to provide measures that (like cutting the deck of playing cards) help ensure that fraud will not occur.

The standards of conduct by which one's actions are judged as right or wrong, honest or dishonest, fair or not fair, are **ethics**. Effective financial reporting depends on sound ethical behavior. To sensitize you to ethical situations in business and to give you practice at solving ethical dilemmas, we address ethics in a number of ways in this book:

Ethics Notes help sensitize you to some of the ethical issues in accounting.

1. A number of the *Feature Stories* and other parts of the textbook discuss the central importance of ethical behavior to financial reporting.

2. *Ethics Insight* boxes and marginal *Ethics Notes* highlight ethics situations and issues in actual business settings.

3. Many of the *People, Planet, and Profit Insight* boxes focus on ethical issues that companies face in measuring and reporting social and environmental issues.

4. At the end of the chapter, an *Ethics Case* simulates a business situation and asks you to put yourself in the position of a decision-maker in that case.

When analyzing these various ethics cases, as well as experiences in your own life, it is useful to apply the three steps outlined in Illustration 1-4.

Illustration 1-4
Steps in analyzing ethics cases and situations

1. Recognize an ethical situation and the ethical issues involved.

Use your personal ethics to identify ethical situations and issues. Some businesses and professional organizations provide written codes of ethics for guidance in some business situations.

2. Identify and analyze the principal elements in the situation.

Identify the *stakeholders*—persons or groups who may be harmed or benefited. Ask the question: What are the responsibilities and obligations of the parties involved?

3. Identify the alternatives, and weigh the impact of each alternative on various stakeholders.

Select the most ethical alternative, considering all the consequences. Sometimes there will be one right answer. Other situations involve more than one right solution; these situations require an evaluation of each and a selection of the best alternative.

Insights provide examples of business situations from various perspectives—ethics, investor, international, and corporate social responsibility.

ETHICS INSIGHT

The Numbers Behind Not-for-Profit Organizations

Accounting plays an important role for a wide range of business organizations worldwide. Just as the integrity of the numbers matters for business, it matters at least as much for not-for-profit organizations. Proper control and reporting help ensure that money is used the way donors intended. Donors are less inclined to give to an organization if they think the organization is subject to waste or theft. The accounting challenges of some large international not-for-profits rival those of the world's largest businesses. For example, after the Haitian earthquake, the Haitian-born musician Wyclef Jean was criticized for the poor accounting controls in a relief fund that he founded. Since then, he has hired a new accountant and improved the transparency regarding funds raised and spent.

 What benefits does a sound accounting system provide to a not-for-profit organization? (See page 48.)

LEARNING OBJECTIVE   **4**

Explain generally accepted accounting principles.

Generally Accepted Accounting Principles

The accounting profession has developed standards that are generally accepted and universally practiced. This common set of standards is called **generally accepted accounting principles (GAAP)**. These standards indicate how to report economic events.

The primary accounting standard-setting body in the United States is the **Financial Accounting Standards Board (FASB)**. The **Securities and Exchange Commission (SEC)** is the agency of the U.S. government that oversees U.S. financial markets and accounting standard-setting bodies. The SEC relies on the FASB to develop accounting standards, which public companies must follow. Many countries outside of the United States have adopted the accounting standards issued by the **International Accounting Standards Board (IASB)**. These standards are called **International Financial Reporting Standards (IFRS)**.

As markets become more global, it is often desirable to compare the result of companies from different countries that report using different accounting standards. In order to increase comparability, in recent years the two standard-setting bodies have made efforts to reduce the differences between U.S. GAAP and IFRS. This process is referred to as **convergence**. As a result of these convergence efforts, it is likely that someday there will be a single set of high-quality accounting standards that are used by companies around the world. Because convergence is such an important issue, we highlight any major differences between GAAP and IFRS in *International Notes* (as shown in the margin here) and provide a more in-depth discussion in the *A Look at IRFS* section at the end of each chapter.

> ### International Note
> Over 100 countries use International Financial Reporting Standards (called IFRS). For example, all companies in the European Union follow international standards. The differences between U.S. and international standards are not generally significant.

International Notes *high-light differences between U.S. and international accounting standards.*

Measurement Principles

GAAP generally uses one of two measurement principles, the cost principle or the fair value principle. Selection of which principle to follow generally relates to trade-offs between relevance and faithful representation. **Relevance** means that financial information is capable of making a difference in a decision. **Faithful representation** means that the numbers and descriptions match what really existed or happened—it is factual.

Helpful Hint
Relevance and *faithful representation* are two primary qualities that make accounting information useful for decision-making.

Helpful Hints *further clarify concepts being discussed.*

COST PRINCIPLE

The **cost principle** (or historical cost principle) dictates that companies record assets at their cost. This is true not only at the time the asset is purchased, but also over the time the asset is held. For example, if Best Buy purchases land for $300,000, the company initially reports it in its accounting records at $300,000. But what does Best Buy do if, by the end of the next year, the fair value of the land has increased to $400,000? Under the cost principle, it continues to report the land at $300,000.

FAIR VALUE PRINCIPLE

The **fair value principle** states that assets and liabilities should be reported at fair value (the price received to sell an asset or settle a liability). Fair value information may be more useful than historical cost for certain types of assets and liabilities. For example, certain investment securities are reported at fair value because market value information is usually readily available for these types of assets. In determining which measurement principle to use, companies weigh the factual nature of cost figures versus the relevance of fair value. In general, most companies choose to use cost. Only in situations where assets are actively traded, such as investment securities, do companies apply the fair value principle extensively.

INTERNATIONAL INSIGHT

The Korean Discount

If you think that accounting standards don't matter, consider recent events in South Korea. For many years, international investors complained that the financial reports of South Korean companies were inadequate and inaccurate. Accounting practices there often resulted in huge differences between stated revenues and actual revenues. Because investors did not have faith in the accuracy of the numbers, they were unwilling to pay as much for the shares of these companies relative to shares of comparable companies in different countries. This difference in stock price was often referred to as the "Korean discount."

In response, Korean regulators decided that, beginning in 2011, companies will have to comply with international accounting standards. This change was motivated by a desire to "make the country's businesses more transparent" in order to build investor confidence and spur economic growth. Many other Asian countries, including China, India, Japan, and Hong Kong, have also decided either to adopt international standards or to create standards that are based on the international standards.

Source: Evan Ramstad, "End to 'Korea Discount'?" *Wall Street Journal* (March 16, 2007).

 What is meant by the phrase "make the country's businesses more transparent"? Why would increasing transparency spur economic growth? (See page 48.)

Assumptions

LEARNING OBJECTIVE **5**

Explain the monetary unit assumption and the economic entity assumption.

Assumptions provide a foundation for the accounting process. Two main assumptions are the **monetary unit assumption** and the **economic entity assumption**.

MONETARY UNIT ASSUMPTION

The **monetary unit assumption** requires that companies include in the accounting records only transaction data that can be expressed in money terms. This assumption enables accounting to quantify (measure) economic events. The monetary unit assumption is vital to applying the cost principle.

This assumption prevents the inclusion of some relevant information in the accounting records. For example, the health of a company's owner, the quality of service, and the morale of employees are not included. The reason: Companies cannot quantify this information in money terms. Though this information is important, companies record only events that can be measured in money.

ECONOMIC ENTITY ASSUMPTION

An economic entity can be any organization or unit in society. It may be a company (such as Crocs, Inc.), a governmental unit (the state of Ohio), a municipality (Seattle), a school district (St. Louis District 48), or a church (Southern Baptist). The **economic entity assumption** requires that the activities of the entity be kept separate and distinct from the activities of its owner and all other economic entities. To illustrate, Sally Rider, owner of Sally's Boutique, must keep her personal living costs separate from the expenses of the boutique. Similarly, McDonald's, Coca-Cola, and Cadbury-Schweppes are segregated into separate economic entities for accounting purposes.

Ethics Note

The importance of the economic entity assumption is illustrated by scandals involving Adelphia. In this case, senior company employees entered into transactions that blurred the line between the employees' financial interests and those of the company. For example, Aldephia guaranteed over $2 billion of loans to the founding family.

PROPRIETORSHIP A business owned by one person is generally a **proprietorship**. The owner is often the manager/operator of the business. Small service-type businesses (plumbing companies, beauty salons, and auto repair shops), farms, and small retail stores (antique shops, clothing stores, and used-book stores) are often proprietorships. **Usually only a relatively small amount of money (capital) is necessary to start in business as a proprietorship. The owner (proprietor) receives any profits, suffers any losses, and is personally liable for all debts of the business.** There is no legal distinction between the business as an economic unit and the owner, but the accounting records of the business activities are kept separate from the personal records and activities of the owner.

PARTNERSHIP A business owned by two or more persons associated as partners is a **partnership**. In most respects a partnership is like a proprietorship except that more than one owner is involved. Typically a partnership agreement (written or oral) sets forth such terms as initial investment, duties of each partner, division of net income (or net loss), and settlement to be made upon death or withdrawal of a partner. Each partner generally has unlimited personal liability for the debts of the partnership. **Like a proprietorship, for accounting purposes the partnership transactions must be kept separate from the personal activities of the partners.** Partnerships are often used to organize retail and service-type businesses, including professional practices (lawyers, doctors, architects, and certified public accountants).

CORPORATION A business organized as a separate legal entity under state corporation law and having ownership divided into transferable shares of stock is a **corporation**. The holders of the shares (stockholders) **enjoy limited liability**; that is, they are not personally liable for the debts of the corporate entity. Stockholders **may transfer all or part of their ownership shares to other investors at any time** (i.e., sell their shares). The ease with which ownership can change adds to the attractiveness of investing in a corporation. Because ownership can be transferred without dissolving the corporation, the corporation **enjoys an unlimited life**.

Although the combined number of proprietorships and partnerships in the United States is more than five times the number of corporations, the revenue produced by corporations is eight times greater. Most of the largest companies in the United States—for example, ExxonMobil, Ford, Wal-Mart Stores Inc., Citigroup, and Apple—are corporations.

> ## DO IT!

Basic Concepts

The DO IT! exercises ask you to put newly acquired knowledge to work. They outline the Action Plan necessary to complete the exercise, and they show a Solution.

Action Plan
✔ Review the basic concepts learned to date.
✔ Develop an understanding of the key terms used.

Indicate whether each of the five statements presented below is true or false.

1. The three steps in the accounting process are identification, recording, and communication.
2. The two most common types of external users are investors and company officers.
3. Congress passed the Sarbanes-Oxley Act to reduce unethical behavior and decrease the likelihood of future corporate scandals.
4. The primary accounting standard-setting body in the United States is the Financial Accounting Standards Board (FASB).
5. The cost principle dictates that companies record assets at their cost. In later periods, however, the fair value of the asset must be used if fair value is higher than its cost.

Solution

> 1. True 2. False. The two most common types of external users are investors and creditors. 3. True. 4. True. 5. False. The cost principle dictates that companies record assets at their cost. Under the cost principle, the company must also use cost in later periods.

Related exercise material: **E1-1, E1-2, E1-3, E1-4,** and **DO IT!** 1-1.

 The Navigator

The Basic Accounting Equation

LEARNING OBJECTIVE 6

State the accounting equation, and define its components.

The two basic elements of a business are what it owns and what it owes. **Assets** are the resources a business owns. For example, Google has total assets of approximately $40.5 billion. Liabilities and owner's equity are the rights or claims against these resources. Thus, Google has $40.5 billion of claims against its $40.5 billion of assets. Claims of those to whom the company owes money (creditors) are called **liabilities**. Claims of owners are called **stockholders' equity**. Google has liabilities of $4.5 billion and stockholders' equity of $36 billion.

We can express the relationship of assets, liabilities, and stockholders' equity as an equation, as shown in Illustration 1-5.

Illustration 1-5
The basic accounting equation

| Assets | = | Liabilities | + | Stockholders' Equity |

This relationship is the **basic accounting equation**. Assets must equal the sum of liabilities and stockholders' equity. Liabilities appear before stockholders' equity in the basic accounting equation because they are paid first if a business is liquidated.

The accounting equation applies to all **economic entities** regardless of size, nature of business, or form of business organization. It applies to a small proprietorship such as a corner grocery store as well as to a giant corporation such as PepsiCo. The equation provides the **underlying framework** for recording and summarizing economic events.

Let's look in more detail at the categories in the basic accounting equation.

Assets

As noted above, **assets** are resources a business owns. The business uses its assets in carrying out such activities as production and sales. The common characteristic possessed by all assets is **the capacity to provide future services or benefits**. In a business, that service potential or future economic benefit eventually results in cash inflows (receipts). For example, consider Campus Pizza, a local restaurant. It owns a delivery truck that provides economic benefits from delivering pizzas. Other assets of Campus Pizza are tables, chairs, jukebox, cash register, oven, tableware, and, of course, cash.

Liabilities

Liabilities are claims against assets—that is, existing debts and obligations. Businesses of all sizes usually borrow money and purchase merchandise on credit. These economic activities result in payables of various sorts:

- Campus Pizza, for instance, purchases cheese, sausage, flour, and beverages on credit from suppliers. These obligations are called **accounts payable**.
- Campus Pizza also has a **note payable** to First National Bank for the money borrowed to purchase the delivery truck.
- Campus Pizza may also have **salaries and wages payable** to employees and **sales and real estate taxes payable** to the local government.

All of these persons or entities to whom Campus Pizza owes money are its **creditors**.

Creditors may legally force the liquidation of a business that does not pay its debts. In that case, the law requires that creditor claims be paid **before** ownership claims.

Stockholders' Equity

The ownership claim on total assets is **stockholders' equity**. It is equal to total assets minus total liabilities. Here is why: The assets of a business are claimed by either creditors or stockholders. To find out what belongs to stockholders, we subtract creditors' claims (the liabilities) from the assets. The remainder is the stockholders' claim on the assets—stockholders' equity. It is often referred to as **residual equity**—that is, the equity "left over" after creditors' claims are satisfied.

The stockholders' equity section of a corporation's balance sheet generally consists of (1) common stock and (2) retained earnings.

COMMON STOCK

A corporation may obtain funds by selling shares of stock to investors. **Common stock** is the term used to describe the total amount paid in by stockholders for the shares they purchase.

RETAINED EARNINGS

The **retained earnings** section of the balance sheet is determined by three items: revenues, expenses, and dividends.

REVENUES Revenues are the gross increases in stockholders' equity resulting from business activities entered into for the purpose of earning income. Generally, revenues result from selling merchandise, performing services, renting property, and lending money.

Revenues usually result in an increase in an asset. They may arise from different sources and are called various names depending on the nature of the business. Campus Pizza, for instance, has two categories of sales revenues—pizza sales and beverage sales. Other titles for and sources of revenue common to many businesses are sales, fees, services, commissions, interest, dividends, royalties, and rent.

Helpful Hint
In some situations, accountants use the term *owner's equity* and in others *owners' equity*. *Owner's* refers to one *owner* (the case with a sole proprietorship), and *owners'* refers to multiple owners (the case with partnerships). The term *stockholders' equity* refers to ownership in corporations.

Helpful Hint
The effect of revenues is positive—an increase in stockholders' equity coupled with an increase in assets or a decrease in liabilities.

Helpful Hint
The effect of expenses is negative—a decrease in stockholders' equity coupled with a decrease in assets or an increase in liabilities.

EXPENSES Expenses are the cost of assets consumed or services used in the process of earning revenue. **They are decreases in stockholders' equity that result from operating the business.** Like revenues, expenses take many forms and are called various names depending on the type of asset consumed or service used. For example, Campus Pizza recognizes the following types of expenses: cost of ingredients (flour, cheese, tomato paste, meat, mushrooms, etc.); cost of beverages; wages expense; utilities expense (electric, gas, and water expense); telephone expense; delivery expense (gasoline, repairs, licenses, etc.); supplies expense (napkins, detergents, aprons, etc.); rent expense; interest expense; and property tax expense.

DIVIDENDS Net income represents an increase in net assets which are then available to distribute to stockholders. The distribution of cash or other assets to stockholders is called a **dividend**. Dividends reduce retained earnings. However, dividends are **not an expense**. A corporation first determines its revenues and expenses and then computes net income or net loss. If it has net income, and decides it has no better use for that income, a corporation may decide to distribute a dividend to its owners (the stockholders).

In summary, the principal sources (increases) of stockholders' equity are investments by stockholders and revenues from business operations. In contrast, reductions (decreases) in stockholders' equity result from expenses and dividends. These relationships are shown in Illustration 1-6.

Illustration 1-6
Increases and decreases in stockholders' equity

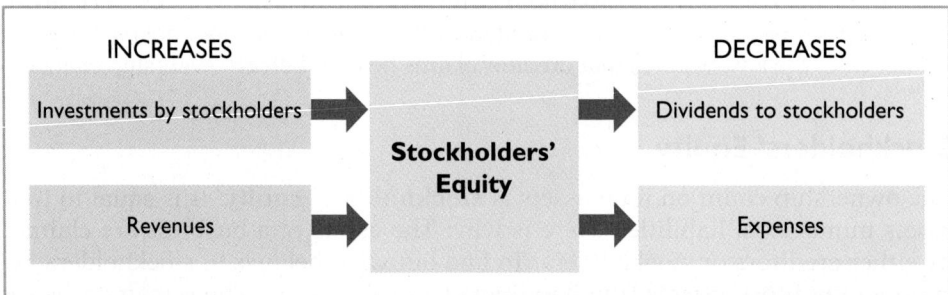

> **DO IT!**

Stockholders' Equity Effects

Action Plan

✔ Understand the sources of revenue.

✔ Understand what causes expenses.

✔ Review the rules for changes in stockholders' equity: Investments and revenues increase stockholders' equity. Expenses and dividends decrease stockholders' equity.

✔ Recognize that dividends are distributions of cash or other assets to stockholders.

Classify the following items as issuance of stock (I), dividends (D), revenues (R), or expenses (E). Then indicate whether each item increases or decreases stockholders' equity.

(1) Rent Expense   (3) Dividends
(2) Service Revenue   (4) Salaries and Wages Expense

Solution

1. Rent Expense is an expense (E); it decreases stockholders' equity.   2. Service Revenue is a revenue (R); it increases stockholders' equity.   3. Dividends is a distribution to stockholders (D); it decreases stockholders' equity.   4. Salaries and Wages Expense is an expense (E); it decreases stockholders' equity.

Related exercise material: **BE1-1, BE1-2, BE1-3, BE1-4, BE1-5, E1-5, E1-6, E1-7, and DO IT! 1-2.**

Using the Accounting Equation

Transactions (**business transactions**) are a business's economic events recorded by accountants. Transactions may be external or internal. **External transactions** involve economic events between the company and some outside enterprise. For example, Campus Pizza's purchase of cooking equipment from a supplier, payment of monthly rent to the landlord, and sale of pizzas to customers are external transactions. **Internal transactions** are economic events that occur entirely within one company. The use of cooking and cleaning supplies are internal transactions for Campus Pizza.

Companies carry on many activities that do not represent business transactions. Examples are hiring employees, answering the telephone, talking with customers, and placing merchandise orders. Some of these activities may lead to business transactions: Employees will earn wages, and suppliers will deliver ordered merchandise. The company must analyze each event to find out if it affects the components of the accounting equation. If it does, the company will record the transaction. Illustration 1-7 demonstrates the transaction-identification process.

LEARNING OBJECTIVE   **7**

Analyze the effects of business transactions on the accounting equation.

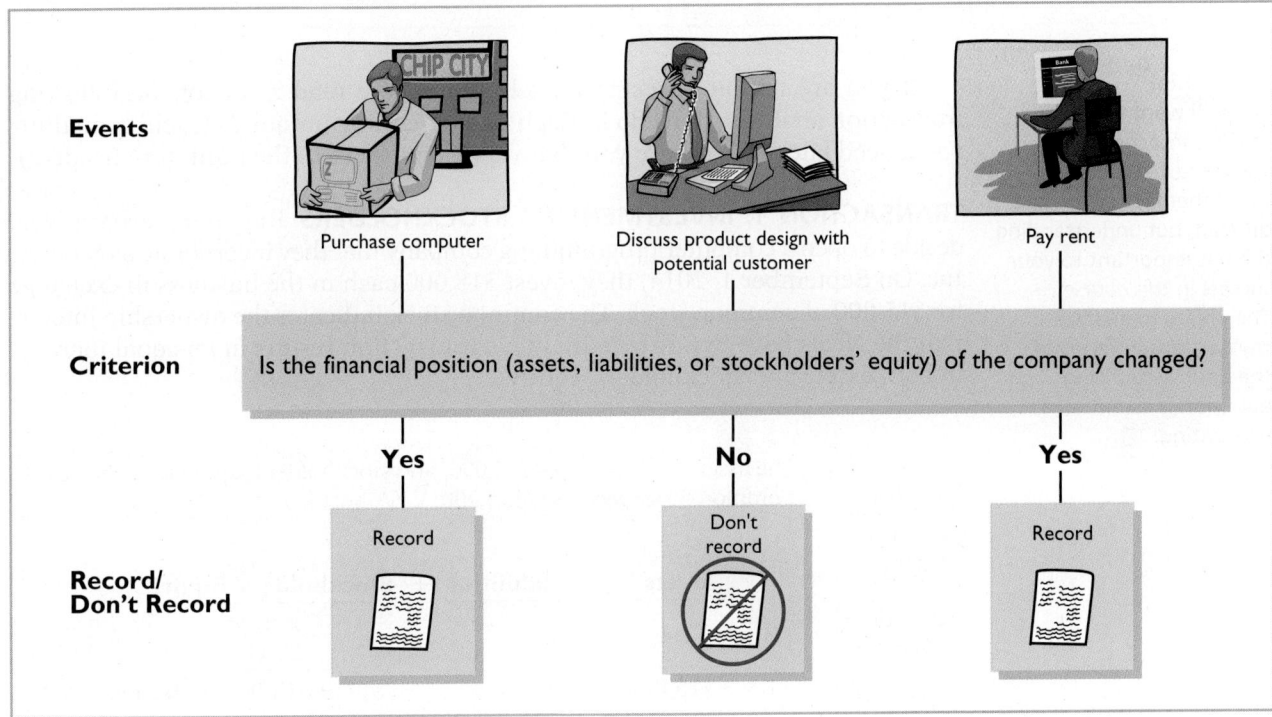

Illustration 1-7
Transaction-identification process

Each transaction must have a dual effect on the accounting equation. For example, if an asset is increased, there must be a corresponding (1) decrease in another asset, (2) increase in a specific liability, or (3) increase in stockholders' equity.

Two or more items could be affected. For example, as one asset is increased $10,000, another asset could decrease $6,000 and a liability could increase $4,000. Any change in a liability or ownership claim is subject to similar analysis.

Transaction Analysis

In order to analyze transactions, we will examine a computer programming business (Softbyte Inc.) during its first month of operations. As part of this analysis, we will expand the basic accounting equation. This will allow us to better illustrate the impact of transactions on stockholders' equity. Recall that stockholders' equity is comprised of two parts: common stock and retained earnings. Common stock is affected when the company issues new shares of stock in exchange for cash. Retained earnings is affected when the company earns revenue, incurs expenses, or pays dividends. Illustration 1-8 shows the **expanded accounting equation**.

Illustration 1-8
Expanded accounting equation

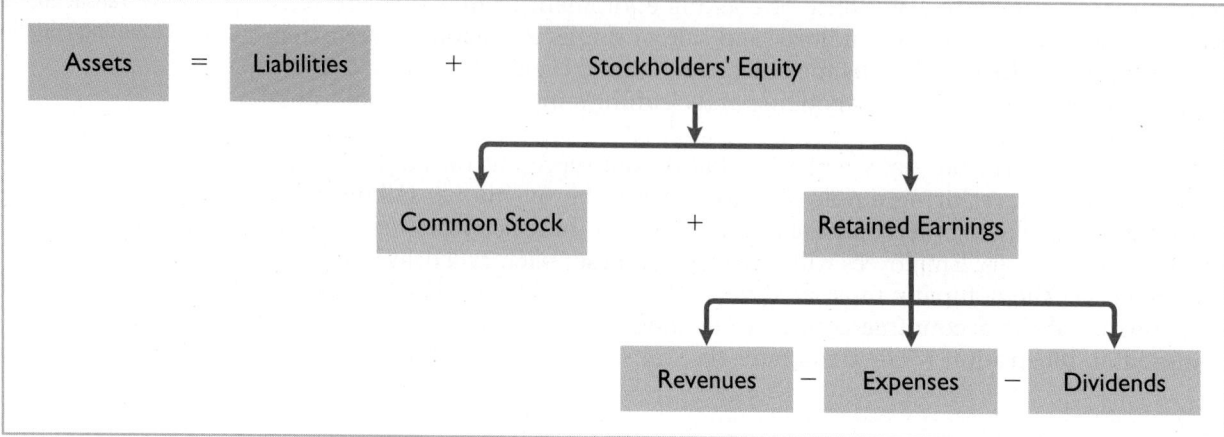

If you are tempted to skip ahead after you've read a few of the following transaction analyses, don't do it. Each has something unique to teach, something you'll need later. (We assure you that we've kept them to the minimum needed!)

TRANSACTION 1. INVESTMENT BY STOCKHOLDERS Ray and Barbara Neal decide to open a computer programming company that they incorporate as Softbyte Inc. On September 1, 2014, they invest $15,000 cash in the business in exchange for $15,000 of common stock. The common stock indicates the ownership interest that the Neals have in Softbyte Inc. This transaction results in an equal increase in both assets and stockholders' equity.

Basic Analysis	The asset Cash increases $15,000, and stockholders' equity identified as Common Stock increases $15,000.

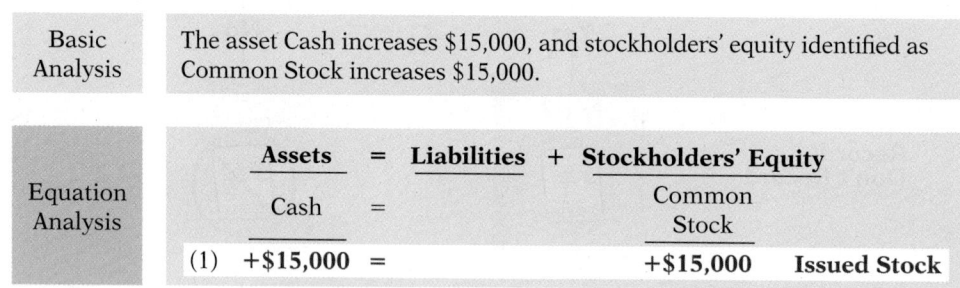

Observe that the equality of the basic equation has been maintained. Note also that the source of the increase in stockholders' equity (in this case, issued stock) is indicated. Why does this matter? Because investments by stockholders do not represent revenues, and they are excluded in determining net income. Therefore, it is necessary to make clear that the increase is an investment rather than revenue from operations. Additional investments (i.e., investments made by stockholders after the corporation has been initially formed) have the same effect on stockholders' equity as the initial investment.

TRANSACTION 2. PURCHASE OF EQUIPMENT FOR CASH Softbyte Inc. purchases computer equipment for $7,000 cash. This transaction results in an equal increase and decrease in total assets, though the composition of assets changes.

Basic Analysis	Cash decreases $7,000, and the asset Equipment increases $7,000.

		Assets		= Liabilities +	Stockholders' Equity
		Cash	+ Equipment =		Common Stock
		$15,000			$15,000
Equation Analysis	(2)	−7,000	+$7,000		
		$ 8,000 +	$ 7,000 =		$15,000
			$15,000		

Observe that total assets are still $15,000. Common stock also remains at $15,000, the amount of the original investment.

TRANSACTION 3. PURCHASE OF SUPPLIES ON CREDIT Softbyte Inc. purchases for $1,600 from Acme Supply Company computer paper and other supplies expected to last several months. Acme agrees to allow Softbyte to pay this bill in October. This transaction is a purchase on account (a credit purchase). Assets increase because of the expected future benefits of using the paper and supplies, and liabilities increase by the amount due Acme Company.

Basic Analysis	The asset Supplies increases $1,600, and the liability Accounts Payable increases by $1,600.

		Assets			=	Liabilities	+	Stockholders' Equity
		Cash	+ Supplies +	Equipment =		Accounts Payable	+	Common Stock
		$8,000		$7,000				$15,000
Equation Analysis	(3)		+$1,600			+$1,600		
		$8,000 +	$ 1,600 +	$7,000 =		$ 1,600	+	$15,000
			$16,600			$16,600		

Total assets are now $16,600. This total is matched by a $1,600 creditor's claim and a $15,000 ownership claim.

TRANSACTION 4. SERVICES PROVIDED FOR CASH Softbyte Inc. receives $1,200 cash from customers for programming services it has provided. This transaction represents Softbyte's principal revenue-producing activity. Recall that **revenue increases stockholders' equity**.

Basic Analysis	Cash increases $1,200, and revenues (specifically, Service Revenue) increase $1,200.

		Assets			= Liabilities +		Stockholders' Equity			
					Accounts	Common		Retained Earnings		
		Cash	+ Supplies +	Equipment =	Payable +	Stock	+	Rev.	− Exp. −	Div.
		$8,000	$1,600	$7,000	$1,600	$15,000				
Equation Analysis	(4)	+1,200						+$1,200		Service Revenue
		$9,200 +	$1,600 +	$7,000 =	$1,600 +	$15,000	+	$ 1,200		
			$17,800			$17,800				

The two sides of the equation balance at $17,800. Service Revenue is included in determining Softbyte's net income.

Note that we do not have room to give details for each individual revenue and expense account in this illustration. Thus, revenues (and expenses when we get to them) are summarized under one column heading for Revenues and one for Expenses. However, it is important to keep track of the category (account) titles affected (e.g., Service Revenue) as they will be needed when we prepare financial statements later in the chapter.

TRANSACTION 5. PURCHASE OF ADVERTISING ON CREDIT Softbyte receives a bill for $250 from the *Daily News* for advertising but postpones payment until a later date. This transaction results in an increase in liabilities and a decrease in stockholders' equity.

Basic Analysis	Accounts Payable increases $250, and stockholders' equity decreases $250 due to Advertising Expense.

Equation Analysis

		Assets			= Liabilities +		Stockholders' Equity			
	Cash	+ Supplies +	Equipment	=	Accounts Payable	+ Common Stock	+	Retained Earnings		
								Rev.	− Exp. −	Div.
	$9,200	$1,600	$7,000		$1,600	$15,000		$1,200		
(5)					+250				−$250	Advertising Expense
	$9,200 +	$1,600 +	$7,000	=	$1,850 +	$15,000 +		$1,200	− $ 250	
		$17,800					$17,800			

The two sides of the equation still balance at $17,800. Retained Earnings decreases when Softbyte incurs the expense. Expenses do not have to be paid in cash at the time they are incurred. When Softbyte pays at a later date, the liability Accounts Payable will decrease and the asset Cash will decrease (see Transaction 8). The cost of advertising is an expense (rather than an asset) because Softbyte has used the benefits. Advertising Expense is included in determining net income.

TRANSACTION 6. SERVICES RENDERED FOR CASH AND CREDIT Softbyte Inc. provides $3,500 of programming services for customers. The company receives cash of $1,500 from customers, and it bills the balance of $2,000 on account. This transaction results in an equal increase in assets and stockholders' equity.

Basic Analysis	Three specific items are affected: Cash increases $1,500, Accounts Receivable increases $2,000, and Service Revenue increases $3,500.

Equation Analysis

		Assets				= Liabilities +		Stockholders' Equity			
	Cash +	Accounts Receivable	+ Supplies +	Equipment	=	Accounts Payable	+ Common Stock	+	Retained Earnings		
									Rev.	− Exp. −	Div.
	$ 9,200		$1,600	$7,000		$1,850	$15,000		$1,200	$250	
(6)	+1,500	+$2,000							+3,500		Service Revenue
	$10,700 +	$ 2,000 +	$1,600 +	$7,000	=	$1,850 +	$15,000 +		$4,700	− $250	
			$21,300					$21,300			

Softbyte earns revenues when it provides the service, and therefore it recognizes $3,500 in revenue. In exchange for this service, it received $1,500 in Cash and Accounts Receivable of $2,000. This Accounts Receivable represents customers' promise to pay $2,000 to Softbyte in the future. When it later receives collections on account, Softbyte will increase Cash and will decrease Accounts Receivable (see Transaction 9).

TRANSACTION 7. PAYMENT OF EXPENSES Softbyte pays the following expenses in cash for September: store rent $600, salaries and wages of employees $900, and utilities $200. These payments result in an equal decrease in assets and expenses.

Basic Analysis	Cash decreases $1,700, and the specific expense categories (Rent Expense, Salaries and Wages Expense, and Utilities Expense) decrease stockholders' equity by the same amount.

		Assets			=	Liabilities +		Stockholders' Equity			
	Cash +	Accounts Receivable	+ Supplies +	Equipment =		Accounts Payable	+ Common Stock	+	Retained Earnings		
								Rev.	− Exp.	− Div.	
	$10,700	$2,000	$1,600	$7,000		$1,850	$15,000	$4,700	$ 250		
(7)	−1,700								−600		Rent Exp.
									−900		Sal./Wages Exp.
									−200		Utilities Exp.
	$ 9,000 +	$2,000	+ $1,600 +	$7,000	=	$1,850	+ $15,000	+ $4,700	− $1,950		
		$19,600						$19,600			

The two sides of the equation now balance at $19,600. Three lines are required in the analysis to indicate the different types of expenses that have been incurred.

TRANSACTION 8. PAYMENT OF ACCOUNTS PAYABLE Softbyte pays its $250 *Daily News* bill in cash. The company previously (in Transaction 5) recorded the bill as an increase in Accounts Payable and a decrease in stockholders' equity.

Basic Analysis	This cash payment "on account" decreases the asset Cash by $250 and also decreases the liability Accounts Payable by $250.

		Assets			=	Liabilities +		Stockholders' Equity			
	Cash +	Accounts Receivable	+ Supplies +	Equipment =		Accounts Payable	+ Common Stock	+	Retained Earnings		
								Rev.	− Exp.	− Div.	
	$9,000	$2,000	$1,600	$7,000		$1,850	$15,000	$4,700	$1,950		
(8)	−250					−250					
	$8,750 +	$2,000	+ $1,600 +	$7,000	=	$1,600	+ $15,000	+ $4,700	− $1,950		
		$19,350						$19,350			

Observe that the payment of a liability related to an expense that has previously been recorded does not affect stockholders' equity. Softbyte recorded the expense (in Transaction 5) and should not record it again.

TRANSACTION 9. RECEIPT OF CASH ON ACCOUNT Softbyte receives $600 in cash from customers who had been billed for services (in Transaction 6). This transaction does not change total assets, but it changes the composition of those assets.

Basic Analysis	Cash increases $600, and Accounts Receivable decreases $600.

Equation Analysis

	Assets				=	Liabilities +		Stockholders' Equity			
	Cash +	Accounts Receivable	+ Supplies +	Equipment =		Accounts Payable	+ Common Stock +	Retained Earnings			
								Rev. −	Exp.	− Div.	
	$8,750	$2,000	$1,600	$7,000		$1,600	$15,000	$4,700	$1,950		
(9)	+600	−600									
	$9,350 +	$1,400 +	$1,600 +	$7,000 =		$1,600 +	$15,000 +	$4,700 −	$1,950		
		$19,350						$19,350			

Note that the collection of an account receivable for services previously billed and recorded does not affect stockholders' equity. Softbyte already recorded this revenue (in Transaction 6) and should not record it again.

TRANSACTION 10. DIVIDENDS The corporation pays a dividend of $1,300 in cash to Ray and Barbara Neal, the stockholders of Softbyte Inc. This transaction results in an equal decrease in assets and stockholders' equity.

Basic Analysis	Cash decreases $1,300, and stockholders' equity decreases $1,300 due to dividends.

Equation Analysis

	Assets				=	Liabilities +		Stockholders' Equity			
	Cash +	Accounts Receivable	+ Supplies +	Equipment =		Accounts Payable	+ Common Stock +	Retained Earnings			
								Rev. −	Exp.	− Div.	
	$9,350	$1,400	$1,600	$7,000		$1,600	$15,000	$4,700	$1,950		
(10)	−1,300									−$1,300	Dividends
	$8,050 +	$1,400 +	$1,600 +	$7,000 =		$1,600 +	$15,000 +	$4,700 −	$1,950 −	$1,300	
		$18,050						$18,050			

Note that the dividend reduces retained earnings, which is part of stockholders' equity. **Dividends are not expenses.** Like stockholders' investments, dividends are excluded in determining net income.

Summary of Transactions

Illustration 1-9 summarizes the September transactions of Softbyte Inc. to show their cumulative effect on the basic accounting equation. It also indicates the transaction number and the specific effects of each transaction. Finally, Illustration 1-9 demonstrates a number of significant facts:

1. Each transaction must be analyzed in terms of its effect on:
   (a) The three components of the basic accounting equation.
   (b) Specific types (kinds) of items within each component.
2. The two sides of the equation must always be equal.
3. The Common Stock and Retained Earnings columns indicate the causes of each change in the stockholders' claim on assets.

Trans-action	Cash	+	Accounts Receivable	+ Supplies	+ Equipment =	Accounts Payable	+	Common Stock	+	Rev.	− Exp.	− Div.	
			Assets			**= Liabilities +**		**Stockholders' Equity**					
										Retained Earnings			
(1)	+$15,000						+	$15,000					Issued Stock
(2)	−7,000				+$7,000								
(3)				+$1,600		+$1,600							
(4)	+1,200									+$1,200			Service Revenue
(5)						+250					−$250		Advert. Expense
(6)	+1,500		+$2,000							+3,500			Service Revenue
(7)	−1,700										−600		Rent Expense
											−900		Sal./Wages Exp.
											−200		Utilities Expense
(8)	−250					−250							
(9)	+600		−600										
(10)	−1,300											−$1,300	Dividends
	$ 8,050 +		$1,400 +	$1,600 +	$7,000 =	$1,600 +		$15,000 +		$4,700 −	$1,950 −	$1,300	
			$18,050					**$18,050**					

Illustration 1-9
Tabular summary of Softbyte Inc. transactions

There! You made it through transaction analysis. If you feel a bit shaky on any of the transactions, it might be a good idea at this point to get up, take a short break, and come back again for a brief (10- to 15-minute) review of the transactions, to make sure you understand them before you go on to the next section.

> DO IT!

Tabular Analysis

Action Plan

✔ Analyze the effects of each transaction on the accounting equation.

✔ Use appropriate category names (not descriptions).

✔ Keep the accounting equation in balance.

Transactions made by Virmari & Co., a public accounting firm, for the month of August are shown below. Prepare a tabular analysis which shows the effects of these transactions on the expanded accounting equation, similar to that shown in Illustration 1-9.

1. Stockholders purchased shares of stock for $25,000 cash.
2. The company purchased $7,000 of office equipment on credit.
3. The company received $8,000 cash in exchange for services performed.
4. The company paid $850 for this month's rent.
5. The company paid a dividend of $1,000 in cash to stockholders.

Solution

Transaction	Cash	+ Equipment =	Accounts Payable	+	Common Stock	+	Rev.	− Exp.	− Div.	
	Assets		**= Liabilities +**		**Stockholders' Equity**					
							Retained Earnings			
(1)	+$25,000				+$25,000					
(2)		+$7,000	+$7,000							
(3)	+8,000						+$8,000			Service Revenue
(4)	−850							−$850		Rent Expense
(5)	−1,000								− $1,000	Dividends
	$31,150 +	$7,000 =	$7,000 +		$25,000 +		$8,000 −	$850 −	$1,000	
	$38,150				**$38,150**					

Related exercise material: **BE1-6, BE1-7, BE1-8, BE1-9, E1-6, E1-7, E1-8, E1-9, E1-10, and** DO IT! **1-3.**

 The Navigator

Financial Statements

Companies prepare four financial statements from the summarized accounting data:

1. An **income statement** presents the revenues and expenses and resulting net income or net loss for a specific period of time.
2. A **retained earnings statement** summarizes the changes in retained earnings for a specific period of time.
3. A **balance sheet** reports the assets, liabilities, and stockholders' equity of a company at a specific date.
4. A **statement of cash flows** summarizes information about the cash inflows (receipts) and outflows (payments) for a specific period of time.

These statements provide relevant financial data for internal and external users. Illustration 1-10 shows the financial statements of Softbyte Inc. Note that the statements shown in Illustration 1-10 are interrelated:

1. Net income of $2,750 on the **income statement** is added to the beginning balance of retained earnings in the **retained earnings statement**.
2. Retained earnings of $1,450 at the end of the reporting period shown in the **retained earnings statement** is reported on the **balance sheet**.
3. Cash of $8,050 on the **balance sheet** is reported on the **statement of cash flows**.

Also, explanatory notes and supporting schedules are an integral part of every set of financial statements. We illustrate these notes and schedules in later chapters of this textbook.

Be sure to carefully examine the format and content of each statement in Illustration 1-10. We describe the essential features of each in the following sections.

Income Statement

The income statement reports the success or profitability of the company's operations over a specific period of time. For example, Softbyte Inc.'s income statement is dated "For the Month Ended September 30, 2014." It is prepared from the data appearing in the revenue and expense columns of Illustration 1-9 (page 21). The heading of the statement identifies the company, the type of statement, and the time period covered by the statement.

The income statement lists revenues first, followed by expenses. Finally, the statement shows net income (or net loss). When revenues exceed expenses, **net income** results. When expenses exceed revenues, a **net loss** results.

Although practice varies, we have chosen in our illustrations and homework solutions to list expenses in order of magnitude. (We will consider alternative formats for the income statement in later chapters.)

Note that the income statement does not include investment and dividend transactions between the stockholders and the business in measuring net income. For example, as explained earlier, the cash dividend from Softbyte Inc. was not regarded as a business expense. This type of transaction is considered a reduction of retained earnings, which causes a decrease in stockholders' equity.

Retained Earnings Statement

Softbyte Inc.'s retained earnings statement reports the changes in retained earnings for a specific period of time. The time period is the same as that covered by

Illustration 1-10
Financial statements and their interrelationships

Softbyte Inc. **Income Statement** **For the Month Ended September 30, 2014**		
Revenues		
Service revenue		$ 4,700
Expenses		
Salaries and wages expense	$900	
Rent expense	600	
Advertising expense	250	
Utilities expense	200	
Total expenses		1,950
Net income		$2,750

Helpful Hint
The heading of each statement identifies the company, the type of statement, and the specific date or time period covered by the statement.

Softbyte Inc. **Retained Earnings Statement** **For the Month Ended September 30, 2014**	
Retained earnings, September 1	$ 0
Add: Net income	2,750
	2,750
Less: Dividends	1,300
Retained earnings, September 30	$1,450

①

Helpful Hint
Note that final sums are double-underlined, and negative amounts (in the statement of cash flows) are presented in parentheses.

Softbyte Inc. **Balance Sheet** **September 30, 2014**		
Assets		
Cash		$ 8,050
Accounts receivable		1,400
Supplies		1,600
Equipment		7,000
Total assets		$18,050
Liabilities and Stockholders' Equity		
Liabilities		
Accounts payable		$ 1,600
Stockholders' equity		
Common stock	$15,000	
Retained earnings	1,450	16,450
Total liabilities and stockholder's equity		$18,050

②

Softbyte Inc. **Statement of Cash Flows** **For the Month Ended September 30, 2014**		
Cash flows from operating activities		
Cash receipts from revenues	$ 3,300	
Cash payments for expenses	(1,950)	
Net cash provided by operating activities		1,350
Cash flows from investing activities		
Purchase of equipment		(7,000)
Cash flows from financing activities		
Sale of common stock	$15,000)	
Payment of cash dividends	(1,300)	13,700
Net increase in cash		8,050
Cash at the beginning of the period		0
Cash at the end of the period		$8,050

③

Helpful Hint
The arrows in this illustration show the interrelationships of the four financial statements.
1. Net income is computed first and is needed to determine the ending balance in retained earnings.
2. The ending balance in retained earnings is needed in preparing the balance sheet.
3. The cash shown on the balance sheet is needed in preparing the statement of cash flows.

the income statement ("For the Month Ended September 30, 2014"). Data for the preparation of the retained earnings statement come from the retained earnings columns of the tabular summary (Illustration 1-9) and from the income statement (Illustration 1-10, page 23).

The first line of the statement shows the beginning retained earnings amount. Then come net income and dividends. The retained earnings ending balance is the final amount on the statement. The information provided by this statement indicates the reasons why retained earnings increased or decreased during the period. If there is a net loss, it is deducted with dividends in the retained earnings statement.

Balance Sheet

Softbyte Inc.'s balance sheet reports the assets, liabilities, and stockholders' equity at a specific date (September 30, 2014). The company prepares the balance sheet from the column headings and the month-end data shown in the last line of the tabular summary (Illustration 1-9).

Observe that the balance sheet lists assets at the top, followed by liabilities and stockholders' equity. Total assets must equal total liabilities and stockholders' equity. Softbyte Inc. reports only one liability, Accounts Payable, on its balance sheet. In most cases, there will be more than one liability. When two or more liabilities are involved, a customary way of listing is as shown in Illustration 1-11.

Illustration 1-11
Presentation of liabilities

Liabilities	
Notes payable	$ 10,000
Accounts payable	63,000
Salaries and wages payable	18,000
Total liabilities	**$91,000**

The balance sheet is like a snapshot of the company's financial condition at a specific moment in time (usually the month-end or year-end).

Statement of Cash Flows

Helpful Hint
Investing activities pertain to investments made by the company, not investments made by the owners.

The statement of cash flows provides information on the cash receipts and payments for a specific period of time. The statement of cash flows reports (1) the cash effects of a company's operations during a period, (2) its investing transactions, (3) its financing transactions, (4) the net increase or decrease in cash during the period, and (5) the cash amount at the end of the period.

Reporting the sources, uses, and change in cash is useful because investors, creditors, and others want to know what is happening to a company's most liquid resource. The statement of cash flows provides answers to the following simple but important questions.

1. Where did cash come from during the period?
2. What was cash used for during the period?
3. What was the change in the cash balance during the period?

As shown in Softbyte Inc.'s statement of cash flows in Illustration 1-10, cash increased $8,050 during the period. Net cash flow provided from operating activities increased cash $1,350. Cash flow from investing transactions decreased cash $7,000. And cash flow from financing transactions increased cash $13,700. At this time, you need not be concerned with how these amounts are determined. Chapter 13 will examine in detail how the statement is prepared.

PEOPLE, PLANET, AND PROFIT INSIGHT

Beyond Financial Statements

Should we expand our financial statements beyond the income statement, retained earnings statement, balance sheet, and statement of cash flows? Some believe we should take into account ecological and social performance, in addition to financial results, in evaluating a company. The argument is that a company's responsibility lies with anyone who is influenced by its actions. In other words, a company should be interested in benefiting many different parties, instead of only maximizing stockholder's interests.

A socially responsible business does not exploit or endanger any group of individuals. It follows fair trade practices, provides safe environments for workers, and bears responsibility for environmental damage. Granted, measurement of these factors is difficult. How to report this information is also controversial. But, many interesting and useful efforts are underway. Throughout this textbook, we provide additional insights into how companies are attempting to meet the challenge of measuring and reporting their contributions to society, as well as their financial results, to stockholders.

? Why might a company's stockholders be interested in its environmental and social performance? (See page 48.)

> DO IT!

Financial Statement Items

Presented below is selected information related to Flanagan Corporation at December 31, 2014. Flanagan reports financial information monthly.

Equipment	$10,000	Utilities Expense	$ 4,000
Cash	8,000	Accounts Receivable	9,000
Service Revenue	36,000	Salaries and Wages Expense	7,000
Rent Expense	11,000	Notes Payable	16,500
Accounts Payable	2,000	Dividends	5,000

(a) Determine the total assets of Flanagan at December 31, 2014.

(b) Determine the net income that Flanagan reported for December 2014.

(c) Determine the stockholders' equity of Flanagan at December 31, 2014.

Solution

Action Plan

✔ Remember the basic accounting equation: assets must equal liabilities plus stockholders' equity.

✔ Review previous financial statements to determine how total assets, net income, and stockholders' equity are computed.

(a) The total assets are $27,000, comprised of Cash $8,000, Accounts Receivable $9,000, and Equipment $10,000.

(b) Net income is $14,000, computed as follows.

Revenues		
Service revenue		$36,000
Expenses		
Rent expense	$11,000	
Salaries and wages expense	7,000	
Utilities expense	4,000	
Total expenses		22,000
Net income		$14,000

(c) The ending stockholders' equity of Flanagan Corporation is $8,500. By rewriting the accounting equation, we can compute stockholders' equity as assets minus liabilities, as follows.

Total assets [as computed in (a)]		$27,000
Less: Liabilities		
Notes payable	$16,500	
Accounts payable	2,000	18,500
Stockholders' equity		$ 8,500

Note that it is not possible to determine the corporation's stockholders' equity in any other way, because the beginning total for stockholders' equity is not provided.

Related exercise material: **BE1-10, BE1-11, E1-9, E1-12, E1-13, E1-14, E1-15, E1-16, and** DO IT! **1-4.**

✔ **The Navigator**

> **Comprehensive DO IT!**

*The **Comprehensive DO IT!** is a final review of the chapter. The **Action Plan** gives tips about how to approach the problem, and the **Solution** demonstrates both the form and content of complete answers.*

Legal Services Inc. was incorporated on July 1, 2014. During the first month of operations, the following transactions occurred.

1. Stockholders invested $10,000 in cash in exchange for common stock of Legal Services Inc.
2. Paid $800 for July rent on office space.
3. Purchased office equipment on account $3,000.
4. Provided legal services to clients for cash $1,500.
5. Borrowed $700 cash from a bank on a note payable.
6. Performed legal services for client on account $2,000.
7. Paid monthly expenses: salaries $500, utilities $300, and advertising $100.

Instructions

(a) Prepare a tabular summary of the transactions.

(b) Prepare the income statement, retained earnings statement, and balance sheet at July 31 for Legal Services Inc.

Solution to Comprehensive DO IT!

(a)

Trans-action	Cash	+	Accounts Receivable	+	Equipment	=	Notes Payable	+	Accounts Payable	+	Common Stock	+	Rev.	−	Exp.	−	Div.	
(1)	+$10,000					=					+$10,000							Issued Stock
(2)	−800														−$800			Rent Expense
(3)					+$3,000	=			+$3,000									
(4)	+1,500												+$1,500					Service Revenue
(5)	+700						+$700											
(6)			+$2,000										+2,000					Service Revenue
(7)	−500														−500			Sal./Wages Exp.
	−300														−300			Utilities Expense
	−100														−100			Advertising Expense
	$10,500	+	$2,000	+	$3,000	=	$700	+	$3,000	+	$10,000	+	$3,500	−	$1,700			

$15,500 $15,500

Assets = **Liabilities** + **Stockholder's Equity** (Retained Earnings)

Action Plan

✔ Make sure that assets equal liabilities plus stockholders' equity after each transaction.

✔ Investments and revenues increase stockholders' equity. Dividends and expenses decrease stockholders' equity.

✔ Prepare the financial statements in the order listed.

✔ The income statement shows revenues and expenses for a period of time.

✔ The retained earnings statement shows the changes in retained earnings for the same period of time as the income statement.

✔ The balance sheet reports assets, liabilities, and stockholders' equity at a specific date.

(b)

Legal Services Inc. Income Statement For the Month Ended July 31, 2014		
Revenues		
Service revenue		$3,500
Expenses		
Rent expense	$800	
Salaries and wages expense	500	
Utilities expense	300	
Advertising expense	100	
Total expenses		1,700
Net income		$1,800

Legal Services Inc. Retained Earnings Statement For the Month Ended July 31, 2014	
Retained earnings, July 1	$ –0–
Add: Net income	1,800
Retained earnings, July 31	$1,800

Legal Services Inc. Balance Sheet July 31, 2014		
Assets		
Cash		$10,500
Accounts receivable		2,000
Equipment		3,000
Total assets		$15,500
Liabilities and Stockholder's Equity		
Liabilities		
Notes payable	$ 700	
Accounts payable	3,000	
Total liabilities		$ 3,700
Stockholder's equity		
Common stock	10,000	
Retained earnings	1,800	11,800
Total liabilities and stockholder's equity		$15,500

 The Navigator

SUMMARY OF LEARNING OBJECTIVES

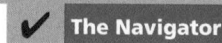
The Navigator

1 Explain what accounting is. Accounting is an information system that identifies, records, and communicates the economic events of an organization to interested users.

2 Identify the users and uses of accounting. The major users and uses of accounting are as follows. (a) Management uses accounting information to plan, organize, and run the business. (b) Investors (owners) decide whether to buy, hold, or sell their financial interests on the basis of accounting data. (c) Creditors (suppliers and bankers) evaluate the risks of granting credit or lending money on the basis of accounting information. Other groups that use accounting information are taxing authorities, regulatory agencies, customers, and labor unions.

3 Understand why ethics is a fundamental business concept. Ethics are the standards of conduct by which actions are judged as right or wrong. Effective financial reporting depends on sound ethical behavior.

4 Explain generally accepted accounting principles. Generally accepted accounting principles are a common set of standards used by accountants.

5 Explain the monetary unit assumption and the economic entity assumption. The monetary unit assumption requires that companies include in the accounting records only transaction data that can be expressed in terms of money. The economic entity assumption requires that the activities of each economic entity be kept separate from the activities of its owner(s) and other economic entities.

6 State the accounting equation, and define its components. The basic accounting equation is:

$$\text{Assets} = \text{Liabilities} + \text{Stockholders' Equity}$$

Assets are resources a business owns. Liabilities are creditorship claims on total assets. Stockholders' equity is the ownership claim on total assets.

The expanded accounting equation is:

$$\text{Assets} = \text{Liabilities} + \text{Common Stock}$$
$$+ \text{Revenues} - \text{Expenses} - \text{Dividends}$$

Common stock is affected when the company issues new shares of stock in exchange for cash. Revenues are increases in assets resulting from income-earning activities. Expenses are the costs of assets consumed or services used in the process of earning revenue. Dividends are payments the company makes to its stockholders.

7 Analyze the effects of business transactions on the accounting equation. Each business transaction must have a dual effect on the accounting equation. For example, if an individual asset increases, there must be a corresponding (1) decrease in another asset, or (2) increase in a specific liability, or (3) increase in stockholders' equity.

8 Understand the four financial statements and how they are prepared. An income statement presents the revenues and expenses, and resulting net income or net loss, for a specific period of time. A retained earnings statement summarizes the changes in retained earnings for a specific period of time. A balance sheet reports the assets, liabilities, and stockholders' equity at a specific date. A statement of cash flows summarizes information about the cash inflows (receipts) and outflows (payments) for a specific period of time.

GLOSSARY

Accounting The information system that identifies, records, and communicates the economic events of an organization to interested users. (p. 4).

Assets Resources a business owns. (p. 13).

Balance sheet A financial statement that reports the assets, liabilities, and stockholders' equity of a company at a specific date. (p. 22).

Basic accounting equation Assets = Liabilities + Stockholders' Equity. (p. 12).

Bookkeeping A part of accounting that involves only the recording of economic events. (p. 5).

Common stock Term used to describe the total amount paid in by stockholders for the shares they purchase. (p. 13).

Convergence Effort to reduce differences between U.S. GAAP and IFRS to enhance comparability. (p. 9).

Corporation A business organized as a separate legal entity under state corporation law, having ownership divided into transferable shares of stock. (p. 11).

Cost principle An accounting principle that states that companies should record assets at their cost. (p. 9).

Dividend A distribution by a corporation to its stockholders. (p. 14).

Economic entity assumption An assumption that requires that the activities of the entity be kept separate and distinct from the activities of its owner and all other economic entities. (p. 10).

Ethics The standards of conduct by which one's actions are judged as right or wrong, honest or dishonest, fair or not fair. (p. 7).

Expanded accounting equation Assets = Liabilities + Common Stock + Revenues − Expenses − Dividends. (p. 16).

Expenses The cost of assets consumed or services used in the process of earning revenue. (p. 14).

Fair value principle An accounting principle stating that assets and liabilities should be reported at fair value (the price received to sell an asset or settle a liability). (p. 9).

Faithful representation Numbers and descriptions match what really existed or happened—it is factual. (p. 9).

Financial accounting The field of accounting that provides economic and financial information for investors, creditors, and other external users. (p. 6).

Financial Accounting Standards Board (FASB) A private organization that establishes generally accepted accounting principles in the United States (GAAP). (p. 9).

Generally accepted accounting principles (GAAP) Common standards that indicate how to report economic events. (p. 8).

Income statement A financial statement that presents the revenues and expenses and resulting net income or net loss of a company for a specific period of time. (p. 22).

International Accounting Standards Board (IASB) An accounting standard-setting body that issues standards adopted by many countries outside of the United States. (p. 9).

International Financial Reporting Standards (IFRS) International accounting standards set by the International Accounting Standards Board (IASB). (p. 9).

Liabilities Creditor claims on total assets. (p. 13).

Managerial accounting The field of accounting that provides internal reports to help users make decisions about their companies. (p. 6).

Monetary unit assumption An assumption stating that companies include in the accounting records only transaction data that can be expressed in terms of money. (p. 10).

Net income The amount by which revenues exceed expenses. (p. 22).

Net loss The amount by which expenses exceed revenues. (p. 22).

Partnership A business owned by two or more persons associated as partners. (p. 11).

Proprietorship A business owned by one person. (p. 10).

Relevance Financial information that is capable of making a difference in a decision. (p. 9).

Retained earnings statement A financial statement that summarizes the changes in retained earnings for a specific period of time. (p. 22).

Revenues The gross increase in stockholders' equity resulting from business activities entered into for the purpose of earning income. (p. 13).

Sarbanes-Oxley Act (SOX) Law passed by Congress in 2002 intended to reduce unethical corporate behavior. (p. 7).

Securities and Exchange Commission (SEC) A governmental agency that oversees U.S. financial markets and accounting standard-setting bodies. (p. 9).

Statement of cash flows A financial statement that summarizes information about the cash inflows (receipts) and cash outflows (payments) for a specific period of time. (p. 22).

Stockholders' equity The ownership claim on a corporation's total assets. (p. 13).

Transactions The economic events of a business that are recorded by accountants. (p. 15).

APPENDIX 1A ACCOUNTING CAREER OPPORTUNITIES

Why is accounting such a popular major and career choice? First, there are a lot of jobs. In many cities in recent years, the demand for accountants exceeded the supply. Not only are there a lot of jobs, but there are a wide array of opportunities. As one accounting organization observed, "accounting is one degree with 360 degrees of opportunity."

LEARNING OBJECTIVE 9

Explain the career opportunities in accounting.

Accounting is also hot because it is obvious that accounting matters. Interest in accounting has increased, ironically, because of the attention caused by the accounting failures of companies such as Enron and WorldCom. These widely publicized scandals revealed the important role that accounting plays in society. Most people want to make a difference, and an accounting career provides many opportunities to contribute to society. Finally, the Sarbanes-Oxley Act (SOX) (see page 7) significantly increased the accounting and internal control requirements for corporations. This dramatically increased demand for professionals with accounting training.

Accountants are in such demand that it is not uncommon for accounting students to have accepted a job offer a year before graduation. As the following discussion reveals, the job options of people with accounting degrees are virtually unlimited.

Public Accounting

Individuals in **public accounting** offer expert service to the general public, in much the same way that doctors serve patients and lawyers serve clients. A major portion of public accounting involves **auditing**. In auditing, a certified public accountant (CPA) examines company financial statements and provides an opinion as to how accurately the financial statements present the company's results and financial position. Analysts, investors, and creditors rely heavily on these "audit opinions," which CPAs have the exclusive authority to issue.

Taxation is another major area of public accounting. The work that tax specialists perform includes tax advice and planning, preparing tax returns, and representing clients before governmental agencies such as the Internal Revenue Service.

A third area in public accounting is **management consulting**. It ranges from installing basic accounting software or highly complex enterprise resource planning systems, to providing support services for major marketing projects and merger and acquisition activities.

Many CPAs are entrepreneurs. They form small- or medium-sized practices that frequently specialize in tax or consulting services.

Private Accounting

Instead of working in public accounting, you might choose to be an employee of a for-profit company such as Starbucks, Google, or PepsiCo. In **private (or managerial) accounting**, you would be involved in activities such as cost accounting (finding the cost of producing specific products), budgeting, accounting information system design and support, and tax planning and preparation. You might also be a member of your company's internal audit team. In response to SOX, the internal auditors' job of reviewing the company's operations to ensure compliance with company policies and to increase efficiency has taken on increased importance.

Alternatively, many accountants work for not-for-profit organizations such as the Red Cross or the Bill and Melinda Gates Foundation, or for museums, libraries, or performing arts organizations.

Governmental Accounting

Another option is to pursue one of the many accounting opportunities in governmental agencies. For example, the Internal Revenue Service (IRS), Federal Bureau of Investigation (FBI), and the Securities and Exchange Commission (SEC) all employ accountants. The FBI has a stated goal that at least 15 percent of its new agents should be CPAs. There is also a very high demand for accounting educators at public colleges and universities and in state and local governments.

Forensic Accounting

Forensic accounting uses accounting, auditing, and investigative skills to conduct investigations into theft and fraud. It is listed among the top 20 career paths of the future. The job of forensic accountants is to catch the perpetrators of the estimated $600 billion per year of theft and fraud occurring at U.S. companies. This includes tracing money-laundering and identity-theft activities as well as tax evasion. Insurance companies hire forensic accountants to detect insurance frauds such as arson, and law offices employ forensic accountants to identify marital assets in divorces. Forensic accountants often have FBI, IRS, or similar government experience.

"Show Me the Money"

How much can a new accountant make? Take a look at the average salaries for college graduates in public and private accounting.[3] Keep in mind if you also have a CPA license, you'll make 10–15% more when you start out.

Employer	Jr. Level (0–3 yrs.)	Sr. Level (4–6 yrs.)
Public accounting (large firm)	$48,750–$69,250	$66,750–$86,000
Public accounting (small firm)	$41,000–$56,000	$54,000–$69,750
Corporate accounting (large company)	$38,000–$57,250	$55,750–$73,500
Corporate accounting (small company)	$33,500–$49,000	$46,500–$58,750

Illustration 1A-1
Salary estimates for jobs in public and corporate accounting

Serious earning potential over time gives CPAs great job security. Here are some examples of upper-level salaries for managers in corporate accounting. Note that geographic region, experience, education, CPA certification, and company size each play a role in determining salary.

Position	Large Company	Small to Medium Company
Chief financial officer	$183,250–$384,000	$94,250–$175,750
Corporate controller	$122,000–$180,000	$80,500–$134,750
Tax manager	$ 92,250–$130,250	$74,250–$100,250

Illustration 1A-2
Upper-level management salaries in corporate accounting

For up-to-date salary estimates, as well as a wealth of additional information regarding accounting as a career, check out *www.startheregoplaces.com*.

SUMMARY OF LEARNING OBJECTIVE FOR APPENDIX 1A   ✔ The Navigator

9 Explain the career opportunities in accounting. Accounting offers many different jobs in fields such as public and private accounting, government, and forensic accounting. Accounting is a popular major because there are many different types of jobs, with unlimited potential for career advancement.

GLOSSARY FOR APPENDIX 1A

Auditing The examination of financial statements by a certified public accountant in order to express an opinion as to the fairness of presentation. (p. 30).

Forensic accounting An area of accounting that uses accounting, auditing, and investigative skills to conduct investigations into theft and fraud. (p. 30).

Management consulting An area of public accounting ranging from development of accounting and computer systems to support services for marketing projects and merger and acquisition activities. (p. 30).

Private (or managerial) accounting An area of accounting within a company that involves such activities as cost accounting, budgeting, design and support of accounting information systems, and tax planning and preparation. (p. 30).

Public accounting An area of accounting in which the accountant offers expert service to the general public. (p. 30).

Taxation An area of public accounting involving tax advice, tax planning, preparing tax returns, and representing clients before governmental agencies. (p. 30).

---

[3]*"http://www.startheregoplaces.com/why-accounting/salary-and-demand/* (accessed April 24, 2011).

 Self-Test, Brief Exercises, Exercises, Problem Set A, and many more components are available for practice in WileyPLUS.

Note: All asterisked Questions, Exercises, and Problems relate to material in the appendix to the chapter.

SELF-TEST QUESTIONS

Answers are on page 48.

(LO 1) **1.** Which of the following is *not* a step in the accounting process?
  (a) Identification.   (c) Recording.
  (b) Verification.   (d) Communication.

(LO 2) **2.** Which of the following statements about users of accounting information is *incorrect*?
  (a) Management is an internal user.
  (b) Taxing authorities are external users.
  (c) Present creditors are external users.
  (d) Regulatory authorities are internal users.

(LO 4) **3.** The cost principle states that:
  (a) assets should be initially recorded at cost and adjusted when the fair value changes.
  (b) activities of an entity are to be kept separate and distinct from its owner.
  (c) assets should be recorded at their cost.
  (d) only transaction data capable of being expressed in terms of money be included in the accounting records.

(LO 5) **4.** Which of the following statements about basic assumptions is *correct*?
  (a) Basic assumptions are the same as accounting principles.
  (b) The economic entity assumption states that there should be a particular unit of accountability.
  (c) The monetary unit assumption enables accounting to measure employee morale.
  (d) Partnerships are not economic entities.

(LO 5) **5.** The three types of business entities are:
  (a) proprietorships, small businesses, and partnerships.
  (b) proprietorships, partnerships, and corporations.
  (c) proprietorships, partnerships, and large businesses.
  (d) financial, manufacturing, and service companies.

(LO 6) **6.** Net income will result during a time period when:
  (a) assets exceed liabilities.
  (b) assets exceed revenues.
  (c) expenses exceed revenues.
  (d) revenues exceed expenses.

(LO 7) **7.** Performing services on account will have the following effects on the components of the basic accounting equation:
  (a) increase assets and decrease stockholders' equity.
  (b) increase assets and increase stockholders' equity.
  (c) increase assets and increase liabilities.
  (d) increase liabilities and increase stockholders' equity.

(LO 7) **8.** As of December 31, 2014, Stoneland Company has assets of $3,500 and stockholders' equity of $2,000. What are the liabilities for Stoneland Company as of December 31, 2014?
  (a) $1,500. (b) $1,000. (c) $2,500. (d) $2,000.

(LO 7) **9.** Which of the following events is *not* recorded in the accounting records?
  (a) Equipment is purchased on account.
  (b) An employee is terminated.
  (c) A cash investment is made into the business.
  (d) The company pays a cash dividend.

(LO 7) **10.** During 2014, Gibson Company's assets decreased $50,000 and its liabilities decreased $90,000. Its stockholders' equity therefore:
  (a) increased $40,000.   (c) decreased $40,000.
  (b) decreased $140,000.   (d) increased $140,000.

(LO 7) **11.** Payment of an account payable affects the components of the accounting equation in the following way:
  (a) decreases stockholders' equity and decreases liabilities.
  (b) increases assets and decreases liabilities.
  (c) decreases assets and increases stockholders' equity.
  (d) decreases assets and decreases liabilities.

(LO 8) **12.** Which of the following statements is *false*?
  (a) A statement of cash flows summarizes information about the cash inflows (receipts) and outflows (payments) for a specific period of time.
  (b) A balance sheet reports the assets, liabilities, and stockholders' equity at a specific date.
  (c) An income statement presents the revenues, expenses, changes in stockholders' equity, and resulting net income or net loss for a specific period of time.
  (d) A retained earnings statement summarizes the changes in retained earnings for a specific period of time.

(LO 8) **13.** On the last day of the period, Jim Otto Company buys a $900 machine on credit. This transaction will affect the:
  (a) income statement only.
  (b) balance sheet only.
  (c) income statement and retained earnings statement only.
  (d) income statement, retained earnings statement, and balance sheet.

(LO 8) **14.** The financial statement that reports assets, liabilities, and stockholders' equity is the:
  (a) income statement.
  (b) retained earnings statement.
  (c) balance sheet.
  (d) statement of cash flows.

(LO 9) *15. Services provided by a public accountant include:
  (a) auditing, taxation, and management consulting.
  (b) auditing, budgeting, and management consulting.
  (c) auditing, budgeting, and cost accounting.
  (d) internal auditing, budgeting, and management consulting.

Go to the book's companion website, www.wiley.com/college/weygandt, for additional Self-Test Questions.

✔ The Navigator

QUESTIONS

1. "Accounting is ingrained in our society and it is vital to our economic system." Do you agree? Explain.
2. Identify and describe the steps in the accounting process.
3. (a) Who are internal users of accounting data? (b) How does accounting provide relevant data to these users?
4. What uses of financial accounting information are made by (a) investors and (b) creditors?
5. "Bookkeeping and accounting are the same." Do you agree? Explain.
6. Jackie Remmers Travel Agency purchased land for $85,000 cash on December 10, 2014. At December 31, 2014, the land's value has increased to $93,000. What amount should be reported for land on Jackie Remmers' balance sheet at December 31, 2014? Explain.
7. What is the monetary unit assumption?
8. What is the economic entity assumption?
9. What are the three basic forms of profit-oriented business organizations?
10. Teresa Alvarez is the owner of a successful printing shop. Recently, her business has been increasing, and Teresa has been thinking about changing the organization of her business from a proprietorship to a corporation. Discuss some of the advantages Teresa would enjoy if she were to incorporate her business.
11. What is the basic accounting equation?
12. (a) Define the terms assets, liabilities, and stockholders' equity.
    (b) What items affect stockholders' equity?
13. Which of the following items are liabilities of Designer Jewelry Stores?
    (a) Cash.   (f) Equipment.
    (b) Accounts payable.   (h) Service revenue.
    (c) Dividends.   (g) Salaries and wages
    (d) Accounts receivable.   payable.
    (e) Supplies.   (i) Rent expense.
14. Can a business enter into a transaction in which only the left side of the basic accounting equation is affected? If so, give an example.
15. Are the following events recorded in the accounting records? Explain your answer in each case.
    (a) The president of the company dies.
    (b) Supplies are purchased on account.
    (c) An employee is fired.
16. Indicate how the following business transactions affect the basic accounting equation.
    (a) Paid cash for janitorial services.
    (b) Purchased equipment for cash.
    (c) Invested cash in the business for stock.
    (d) Paid accounts payable in full.
17. Listed below are some items found in the financial statements of Alex Greenway Co. Indicate in which financial statement(s) the following items would appear.
    (a) Service revenue.   (e) Retained earnings.
    (b) Equipment.   (f) Salaries and wages
    (c) Advertising expense.   payable.
    (d) Accounts receivable.
18. In February 2014, Paula Klink invested an additional $10,000 in Midtown Company. Midtown's accountant, Jon Shin, recorded this receipt as an increase in cash and revenues. Is this treatment appropriate? Why or why not?
19. "A company's net income appears directly on the income statement and the retained earnings statement, and it is included indirectly in the company's balance sheet." Do you agree? Explain.
20. Jardine Enterprises had a stockholders' equity balance of $158,000 at the beginning of the period. At the end of the accounting period, the stockholders' equity balance was $198,000.
    (a) Assuming no additional investment or distributions during the period, what is the net income for the period?
    (b) Assuming an additional investment of $13,000 but no distributions during the period, what is the net income for the period?
21. Summarized operations for H. J. Oslo Co. for the month of July are as follows.
    Revenues earned: for cash $30,000; on account $70,000.
    Expenses incurred: for cash $26,000; on account $40,000.
    Indicate for H. J. Oslo Co. (a) the total revenues, (b) the total expenses, and (c) net income for the month of July.
22. The basic accounting equation is: Assets = Liabilities + Stockholders' Equity. Replacing the words in that equation with dollar amounts, what is The Coca-Cola Company's accounting equation at December 31, 2010?

BRIEF EXERCISES

BE1-1 Presented below is the basic accounting equation. Determine the missing amounts.

Use basic accounting equation.

(LO 6)

	Assets	=	Liabilities	+	Stockholders' Equity
(a)	$90,000		$50,000		?
(b)	?		$45,000		$70,000
(c)	$94,000		?		$60,000

*Use basic accounting
equation.*

(LO 6)

BE1-2 Given the accounting equation, answer each of the following questions.
(a) The liabilities of Shumway Company are $120,000 and the stockholders' equity is $232,000. What is the amount of Shumway Company's total assets?
(b) The total assets of Shumway Company are $190,000 and its stockholders' equity is $80,000. What is the amount of its total liabilities?
(c) The total assets of Shumway Company are $600,000 and its liabilities are equal to one half of its total assets. What is the amount of Shumway Company's stockholders' equity?

*Use basic accounting
equation.*

(LO 6)

BE1-3 At the beginning of the year, Gonzales Company had total assets of $870,000 and total liabilities of $500,000. Answer the following questions.
(a) If total assets increased $150,000 during the year and total liabilities decreased $80,000, what is the amount of stockholders' equity at the end of the year?
(b) During the year, total liabilities increased $100,000 and stockholders' equity decreased $70,000. What is the amount of total assets at the end of the year?
(c) If total assets decreased $80,000 and stockholders' equity increased $120,000 during the year, what is the amount of total liabilities at the end of the year?

*Solve accounting
equation.*

(LO 6)

BE1-4 Use the accounting equation to answer each of the following questions.
(a) The liabilities of Alli Company are $90,000. Common stock account is $150,000; dividends are $40,000; revenues, $450,000; and expenses, $320,000. What is the amount of Alli Company's total assets?
(b) The total assets of Planke Company are $57,000. Common stock account is $23,000; dividends are $7,000; revenues, $50,000; and expenses, $35,000. What is the amount of the company's total liabilities?
(c) The total assets of Thao Co. are $600,000 and its liabilities are equal to two-thirds of its total assets. What is the amount of Thao Co.'s stockholders' equity?

*Identify assets, liabilities,
and stockholders' equity.*

(LO 6)

BE1-5 Indicate whether each of the following items is an asset (A), liability (L), or part of stockholders' equity (SE).
_____ (a) Accounts receivable   _____ (d) Supplies
_____ (b) Salaries and wages payable   _____ (e) Owner's investment
_____ (c) Equipment   _____ (f) Notes payable

*Determine effect of
transactions on basic
accounting equation.*

(LO 7)

BE1-6 Presented below are three business transactions. On a sheet of paper, list the letters (a), (b), and (c) with columns for assets, liabilities, and stockholders' equity. For each column, indicate whether the transactions increased (+), decreased (−), or had no effect (NE) on assets, liabilities, and stockholders' equity.
(a) Purchased supplies on account.
(b) Received cash for providing a service.
(c) Paid expenses in cash.

*Determine effect of
transactions on
accounting equation.*

(LO 7)

BE1-7 Follow the same format as BE1-6 above. Determine the effect on assets, liabilities, and stockholders' equity of the following three transactions.
(a) Stockholders invested cash in the business for common stock.
(b) Paid a cash dividend.
(c) Received cash from a customer who had previously been billed for services provided.

*Classify items affecting
stockholders' equity.*

(LO 6)

BE1-8 Classify each of the following items as dividends (D), revenue (R), or expense (E).
_____ (a) Advertising expense   _____ (e) Dividends
_____ (b) Service revenue   _____ (f) Rent revenue
_____ (c) Insurance expense   _____ (g) Utilities expense
_____ (d) Salaries and wages expense

*Determine effect of
transactions on
stockholders' equity.*

(LO 6)

BE1-9 Presented below are three transactions. Mark each transaction as affecting common stock (C), dividends (D), revenue (R), expense (E), or not affecting stockholders' equity (NSE).
_____ (a) Received cash for services performed
_____ (b) Paid cash to purchase equipment
_____ (c) Paid employee salaries.

Prepare a balance sheet.

(LO 8)

BE1-10 In alphabetical order below are balance sheet items for Grande Company at December 31, 2014. Kit Grande is the owner of Grande Company. Prepare a balance sheet, following the format of Illustration 1-10.

Accounts payable	$85,000
Accounts receivable	$72,500
Cash	$44,000
Common stock	$31,500

BE1-11 Indicate whether the following items would appear on the income statement (IS), balance sheet (BS), or retained earnings statement (RE).

_____ (a) Notes payable   _____ (d) Cash
_____ (b) Advertising expense _____ (e) Service revenue
_____ (c) Common stock   _____ (f) Dividends

Determine where items appear on financial statements.

(LO 8)

> DO IT! REVIEW

DO IT! 1-1 Indicate whether each of the five statements presented below is true or false.

1. The three steps in the accounting process are identification, recording, and examination.
2. The two most common types of external users are investors and creditors.
3. Congress passed the Sarbanes-Oxley Act to ensure that investors invest only in companies that will be profitable.
4. The primary accounting standard-setting body in the United States is the Securities and Exchange Commission (SEC).
5. The cost principle dictates that companies record assets at their cost and continue to report them at their cost over the time the asset is held.

Review basic concepts.

(LO 1, 2, 4)

DO IT! 1-2 Classify the following items as issuance of stock (I), dividends (D), revenues (R), or expenses (E). Then indicate whether each item increases or decreases stockholders' equity.

1. Dividends   3. Advertising expense
2. Rent revenue   4. Stockholders invest cash in the business

Evaluate effects of transactions on stockholders' equity.

(LO 6)

DO IT! 1-3 Transactions made by Callahan and Co., a law firm, for the month of March are shown below. Prepare a tabular analysis which shows the effects of these transactions on the accounting equation, similar to that shown in Illustration 1-9.

1. The company provided $23,000 of services for customers, on credit.
2. The company received $23,000 in cash from customers who had been billed for services (in transaction 1).
3. The company received a bill for $2,000 of advertising, but will not pay it until a later date.
4. The company paid a dividend of $5,000 in cash to stockholders.

Prepare tabular analysis.

(LO 7)

DO IT! 1-4 Presented below is selected information related to Narrow Gage Company at December 31, 2014. Narrow Gage reports financial information monthly.

Calculate effects of transactions on financial statement items.

(LO 8)

Accounts Payable	$ 3,000	Salaries and Wages Expense	$16,500
Cash	9,000	Notes Payable	25,000
Advertising Expense	6,000	Rent Expense	9,800
Service Revenue	54,000	Accounts Receivable	13,500
Equipment	29,000	Dividends	7,500

(a) Determine the total assets of Narrow Gage Company at December 31, 2014.
(b) Determine the net income that Narrow Gage Company reported for December 2014.
(c) Determine the stockholders' equity of Narrow Gage Company at December 31, 2014.

✔ **The Navigator**

EXERCISES

E1-1 Sondgeroth Company performs the following accounting tasks during the year.

_____Analyzing and interpreting information.
_____Classifying economic events.
_____Explaining uses, meaning, and limitations of data.
_____Keeping a systematic chronological diary of events.

Classify the three activities of accounting.

(LO 1)

_____Measuring events in dollars and cents.
_____Preparing accounting reports.
_____Reporting information in a standard format.
_____Selecting economic activities relevant to the company.
_____Summarizing economic events.

Accounting is "an information system that **identifies**, **records**, and **communicates** the economic events of an organization to interested users."

Instructions

Categorize the accounting tasks performed by Sondgeroth as relating to either the identification (I), recording (R), or communication (C) aspects of accounting.

Identify users of accounting information.

(LO 2)

E1-2 (a) The following are users of financial statements.

_____Customers _____Securities and Exchange Commission
_____Internal Revenue Service _____Store manager
_____Labor unions _____Suppliers
_____Marketing manager _____Vice president of finance
_____Production supervisor

Instructions

Identify the users as being either **external users** or **internal users**.

(b) The following questions could be asked by an internal user or an external user.

_____ Can we afford to give our employees a pay raise?
_____ Did the company earn a satisfactory income?
_____ Do we need to borrow in the near future?
_____ How does the company's profitability compare to other companies?
_____ What does it cost us to manufacture each unit produced?
_____ Which product should we emphasize?
_____ Will the company be able to pay its short-term debts?

Instructions

Identify each of the questions as being more likely asked by an **internal user** or an **external user**.

Discuss ethics and the cost principle.

(LO 3)

E1-3 Leon Manternach, president of Manternach Company, has instructed Carla Ruden, the head of the accounting department for Manternach Company, to report the company's land in the company's accounting reports at its fair value of $170,000 instead of its cost of $100,000. Manternach says, "Showing the land at $170,000 will make our company look like a better investment when we try to attract new investors next month."

Instructions

Explain the ethical situation involved for Carla Ruden, identifying the stakeholders and the alternatives.

Use accounting concepts.

(LO 4, 5)

E1-4 The following situations involve accounting principles and assumptions.

1. Julia Company owns buildings that are worth substantially more than they originally cost. In an effort to provide more relevant information, Julia reports the buildings at fair value in its accounting reports.
2. Dekalb Company includes in its accounting records only transaction data that can be expressed in terms of money.
3. Omar Shariff, president of Omar's Oasis, records his personal living costs as expenses of the Oasis.

Instructions

For each of the three situations, state if the accounting method used is correct or incorrect. If correct, identify which principle or assumption supports the method used. If incorrect, identify which principle or assumption has been violated.

Classify accounts as assets, liabilities, and stockholders' equity.

(LO 6)

E1-5 Robinson Cleaners has the following balance sheet items.

Accounts payable   Accounts receivable
Cash   Notes payable
Equipment   Salaries and wages payable
Supplies   Common stock

Instructions
Classify each item as an asset, liability, or stockholders' equity.

E1-6 Selected transactions for Spring Green Lawn Care Company are listed below.

1. Sold common stock for cash to start business.
2. Paid monthly rent.
3. Purchased equipment on account.
4. Billed customers for services performed.
5. Paid dividends.
6. Received cash from customers billed in (4).
7. Incurred advertising expense on account.
8. Purchased additional equipment for cash.
9. Received cash from customers when service was performed.

Analyze the effect of transactions.

(LO 6, 7)

Instructions
List the numbers of the above transactions and describe the effect of each transaction on assets, liabilities, and stockholders' equity. For example, the first answer is (1) Increase in assets and increase in stockholders' equity.

E1-7 Collins Computer Timeshare Company entered into the following transactions during May 2014.

1. Purchased computer terminals for $20,000 from Digital Equipment on account.
2. Paid $3,000 cash for May rent on storage space.
3. Received $15,000 cash from customers for contracts billed in April.
4. Provided computer services to Schmidt Construction Company for $2,400 cash.
5. Paid Central States Power Co. $11,000 cash for energy usage in May.
6. Stockholders invested an additional $32,000 in the business.
7. Paid Digital Equipment for the terminals purchased in (1) above.
8. Incurred advertising expense for May of $900 on account.

Analyze the effect of transactions on assets, liabilities, and stockholders' equity.

(LO 6, 7)

Instructions
Indicate with the appropriate letter whether each of the transactions above results in:
(a) An increase in assets and a decrease in assets.
(b) An increase in assets and an increase in stockholders' equity.
(c) An increase in assets and an increase in liabilities.
(d) A decrease in assets and a decrease in stockholders' equity.
(e) A decrease in assets and a decrease in liabilities.
(f) An increase in liabilities and a decrease in stockholders' equity.
(g) An increase in stockholders' equity and a decrease in liabilities.

E1-8 An analysis of the transactions made by J. L. Kang & Co., a certified public accounting firm, for the month of August is shown below. Each increase and decrease in stockholders' equity is explained.

Analyze transactions and compute net income.

(LO 7, 8)

	Assets				= Liabilities +	Stockholders' Equity				
Cash	+ Accounts Receivable	+ Supplies	+ Equipment =		Accounts Payable	+ Common Stock	+ Retained Earnings			
							Rev. −	Exp. −	Div.	
1. +$15,000						+$15,000				
2. −2,000			+$5,000		+$3,000					
3. −750		+$750								
4. +4,600	+$4,500						+$9,100			Service Revenue
5. −1,500					−1,500					
6. −2,000									−$2,000	
7. −650								−$650		Rent Expense
8. +450	−450									
9. −3,900								−3,900		Sal./Wages Expense
10.					+500			−500		Utilities Expense

Instructions
(a) ⬛▦▦▷ Describe each transaction that occurred for the month.
(b) Determine how much stockholders' equity increased for the month.
(c) Compute the amount of net income for the month.

*Prepare financial
statements.*

(LO 8)

E1-9 An analysis of transactions for J. L. Kang & Co. was presented in E1–8.

Instructions

Prepare an income statement and a retained earnings statement for August and a balance sheet at August 31, 2014.

*Determine net income
(or loss).*

(LO 7)

E1-10 Kimmy Company had the following assets and liabilities on the dates indicated.

December 31	Total Assets	Total Liabilities
2013	$400,000	$260,000
2014	$480,000	$300,000
2015	$590,000	$400,000

Kimmy began business on January 1, 2013, with an investment of $100,000 from stockholders.

Instructions

From an analysis of the change in stockholders' equity during the year, compute the net income (or loss) for:

(a) 2013, assuming Kimmy paid $15,000 in dividends for the year.
(b) 2014, assuming stockholders made an additional investment of $50,000 and Kimmy paid no dividends in 2014.
(c) 2015, assuming stockholders made an additional investment of $15,000 and Kimmy paid dividends of $30,000 in 2015.

*Analyze financial
statements items.*

(LO 6, 7)

E1-11 Two items are omitted from each of the following summaries of balance sheet and income statement data for two corporations for the year 2014, Steven Craig and Georgia Enterprises.

	Steven Craig	Georgia Enterprises
Beginning of year:		
Total assets	$ 97,000	$129,000
Total liabilities	85,000	(c)
Total stockholders' equity	(a)	75,000
End of year:		
Total assets	160,000	180,000
Total liabilities	120,000	50,000
Total stockholders' equity	40,000	130,000
Changes during year in stockholders' equity:		
Additional investment	(b)	25,000
Dividends	24,000	(d)
Total revenues	215,000	100,000
Total expenses	175,000	55,000

Instructions

Determine the missing amounts.

*Prepare income statement
and retained earnings
statement.*

(LO 8)

E1-12 The following information relates to Karen Weigel Co. for the year 2014.

Retained earnings, January 1, 2014	$48,000	Advertising expense	$ 1,800
Dividends during 2014	5,000	Rent expense	10,400
Service revenue	62,500	Utilities expense	3,100
Salaries and wages expense	28,000		

Instructions

After analyzing the data, prepare an income statement and a retained earnings statement for the year ending December 31, 2014.

*Correct an incorrectly
prepared balance sheet.*

(LO 8)

E1-13 Lynn Dreise is the bookkeeper for Sanculi Company. Lynn has been trying to get the balance sheet of Sanculi Company to balance. Sanculi's balance sheet is shown on the next page.

Sanculi Company
Balance Sheet
December 31, 2014

Assets		Liabilities	
Cash	$14,000	Accounts payable	$20,000
Supplies	8,000	Accounts receivable	(8,500)
Equipment	48,000	Common stock	50,000
Dividends	9,000	Retained earnings	17,500
Total assets	$79,000	Total liabilities and stockholders' equity	$79,000

Instructions

Prepare a correct balance sheet.

E1-14 Bear Park, a public camping ground near the Lake Mead National Recreation Area, has compiled the following financial information as of December 31, 2014.

Compute net income and prepare a balance sheet.

(LO 8)

Revenues during 2014—camping fees	$140,000	Notes payable	$ 60,000
Revenues during 2014—general store	47,000	Expenses during 2014	150,000
Accounts payable	11,000	Supplies on hand	2,500
Cash on hand	20,000	Common stock	20,000
Original cost of equipment	105,500	Retained earnings	?
Fair value of equipment	140,000		

Instructions

(a) Determine Bear Park's net income for 2014.

(b) Prepare a balance sheet for Bear Park as of December 31, 2014.

E1-15 Presented below is financial information related to the 2014 operations of Donna Marie Cruise Company.

Prepare an income statement.

(LO 8)

Maintenance and repairs expense	$ 97,000
Utilities expense	10,000
Salaries and wages expense	142,000
Advertising expense	3,500
Ticket revenue	335,000

Instructions

Prepare the 2014 income statement for Donna Marie Cruise Company.

E1-16 Presented below is information related to Williams and Douglas, Attorneys at Law.

Prepare a retained earnings statement.

(LO 8)

Retained earnings, January 1, 2014	$ 23,000
Legal service revenue—2014	340,000
Total expenses—2014	211,000
Assets, January 1, 2014	85,000
Liabilities, January 1, 2014	62,000
Assets, December 31, 2014	168,000
Liabilities, December 31, 2014	80,000
Dividends—2014	64,000

Instructions

Prepare the 2014 retained earnings statement for Williams and Douglas, Attorneys at Law.

E1-17 This information is for Belleview Company for the year ended December 31, 2014.

Prepare a cash flow statement.

(LO 8)

Cash received from revenues from customers	$600,000
Cash received for issuance of common stock	280,000
Cash paid for new equipment	100,000
Cash dividends paid	20,000
Cash paid for expenses	430,000
Cash balance 1/1/14	30,000

Instructions

Prepare the 2014 statement of cash flows for Belleview Company.

EXERCISES: SET B AND CHALLENGE EXERCISES

Visit the book's companion website, at **www.wiley.com/college/weygandt,** and choose the Student Companion site to access Exercise Set B and Challenge Exercises.

PROBLEMS: SET A

Analyze transactions and compute net income.

(LO 6, 7)

Check figures next to some Problems give you a key number, to let you know if you are on the right track with your solution.

(a) Total assets $13,140

(b) Net income $3,890

P1-1A Kinney's Repair Inc. was started on May 1. A summary of May transactions is presented below.

1. Stockholders invested $10,000 cash in the business in exchange for common stock.
2. Purchased equipment for $5,000 cash.
3. Paid $400 cash for May office rent.
4. Paid $500 cash for supplies.
5. Incurred $250 of advertising costs in the *Beacon News* on account.
6. Received $4,700 in cash from customers for repair service.
7. Declared and paid a $1,000 cash dividend.
8. Paid part-time employee salaries $1,000.
9. Paid utility bills $140.
10. Provided repair service on account to customers $980.
11. Collected cash of $120 for services billed in transaction (10).

Instructions

(a) Prepare a tabular analysis of the transactions, using the following column headings: Cash, Accounts Receivable, Supplies, Equipment, Accounts Payable, Common Stock, and Retained Earnings (with separate columns for Revenues, Expenses, and Dividends). Include margin explanations for any changes in Retained Earnings. Revenue is called Service Revenue.

(b) From an analysis of the Retained Earnings columns, compute the net income or net loss for May.

Analyze transactions and prepare income statement, retained earnings statement, and balance sheet.

(LO 6, 7, 8)

P1-2A On August 31, the balance sheet of Donahue Veterinary Clinic showed Cash $9,000, Accounts Receivable $1,700, Supplies $600, Equipment $6,000, Accounts Payable $3,600, Common Stock $13,000, and Retained Earnings $700. During September, the following transactions occurred.

1. Paid $2,900 cash for accounts payable due.
2. Collected $1,300 of accounts receivable.
3. Purchased additional office equipment for $2,100, paying $800 in cash and the balance on account.
4. Earned revenue of $7,300, of which $2,500 is collected in cash and the balance is due in October.
5. Declared and paid a $400 cash dividend.
6. Paid salaries $1,700, rent for September $900, and advertising expense $200.
7. Incurred utilities expense for month on account $170.
8. Received $10,000 from Capital Bank on a 6-month note payable.

Instructions

(a) Ending cash $15,900

(b) Net income $4,330
Total assets $29,800

(a) Prepare a tabular analysis of the September transactions beginning with August 31 balances. The column headings should be as follows: Cash + Accounts Receivable + Supplies + Equipment = Notes Payable + Accounts Payable + Common Stock + Retained Earnings + Revenues − Expenses − Dividends.

(b) Prepare an income statement for September, a retained earnings statement for September, and a balance sheet at September 30.

Prepare income statement, retained earnings statement, and balance sheet.

(LO 8)

P1-3A On May 1, Blue Sky Flying School, a company that provides flying lessons, was started with an investment of $45,000 cash in the business. Following are the assets and liabilities of the company on May 31, 2014, and the revenues and expenses for the month of May.

Cash	$ 4,500	Notes Payable	$28,000
Accounts Receivable	7,200	Rent Expense	1,200
Equipment	64,000	Maintenance and	
Service Revenue	6,800	Repairs Expense	400
Advertising Expense	500	Gasoline Expense	2,500
Accounts Payable	1,400	Utilities Expense	400

No additional investments were made in May, but the company paid dividends of $500 during the month.

Instructions

(a) Prepare an income statement and a retained earnings statement for the month of May and a balance sheet at May 31.

(b) Prepare an income statement and a retained earnings statement for May assuming the following data are not included above: (1) $900 of revenue was earned and billed but not collected at May 31, and (2) $1,500 of gasoline expense was incurred but not paid.

(a) Net income $1,800
Total assets $75,700
(b) Net income $1,200

P1-4A Matt Stiner started a delivery service, Stiner Deliveries, on June 1, 2014. The following transactions occurred during the month of June.

Analyze transactions and prepare financial statements.

(LO 6, 7, 8)

June	1	Stockholders invested $10,000 cash in the business in exchange for common stock.
	2	Purchased a used van for deliveries for $14,000. Matt paid $2,000 cash and signed a note payable for the remaining balance.
	3	Paid $500 for office rent for the month.
	5	Performed $4,800 of services on account.
	9	Declared and paid $300 in cash dividends.
	12	Purchased supplies for $150 on account.
	15	Received a cash payment of $1,250 for services provided on June 5.
	17	Purchased gasoline for $100 on account.
	20	Received a cash payment of $1,500 for services provided.
	23	Made a cash payment of $500 on the note payable.
	26	Paid $250 for utilities.
	29	Paid for the gasoline purchased on account on June 17.
	30	Paid $1,000 for employee salaries.

Instructions

(a) Show the effects of the previous transactions on the accounting equation using the following format.

(a) Total assets $25,800

		Assets			=	**Liabilities**	+		**Stockholders' Equity**			
Date	Cash +	Accounts Receivable	+ Supplies +	Equipment =		Notes Payable	+ Accounts Payable	+ Common Stock	+	Rev. −	Retained Earnings Exp. −	Div.

Include margin explanations for any changes in the Retained Earnings account in your analysis.

(b) Prepare an income statement for the month of June.
(c) Prepare a balance sheet at June 30, 2014.

(b) Net income $4,450
(c) Cash $8,100

P1-5A Financial statement information about four different companies is as follows.

Determine financial statement amounts and prepare retained earnings statement.

(LO 7, 8)

	Crosby Company	Stills Company	Nash Company	Young Company
January 1, 2014				
Assets	$ 75,000	$110,000	(g)	$150,000
Liabilities	50,000	(d)	$ 75,000	(j)
Stockholders' equity	(a)	60,000	45,000	100,000
December 31, 2014				
Assets	(b)	137,000	200,000	(k)
Liabilities	55,000	75,000	(h)	80,000
Stockholders' equity	40,000	(e)	130,000	140,000
Stockholders' equity changes in year				
Additional investment	(c)	15,000	10,000	15,000
Dividends	10,000	(f)	14,000	10,000
Total revenues	350,000	420,000	(i)	500,000
Total expenses	330,000	385,000	342,000	(l)

Instructions

(a) Determine the missing amounts. (*Hint:* For example, to solve for (a), Assets − Liabilities = Stockholders' Equity = $25,000.)

(b) Prepare the retained earnings statement for Stills Company. Assume beginning retained earnings was $20,000.

(c) ▭▭▭▶ Write a memorandum explaining the sequence for preparing financial statements and the interrelationship of the retained earnings statement to the income statement and balance sheet.

PROBLEMS: SET B

Analyze transactions and compute net income.

(LO 6, 7)

P1-1B On April 1, Holly Dahl established Holiday Travel Agency. The following transactions were completed during the month.

1. Stockholders invested $10,000 cash in the business in exchange for common stock.
2. Paid $400 cash for April office rent.
3. Purchased office equipment for $2,500 cash.
4. Incurred $300 of advertising costs in the *Chicago Tribune*, on account.
5. Paid $600 cash for office supplies.
6. Earned $8,500 for services provided: $2,000 cash is received from customers, and the balance of $6,500 is billed to customers on account.
7. Declared and paid a $200 cash dividend.
8. Paid *Chicago Tribune* amount due in transaction (4).
9. Paid employees' salaries $2,200.
10. Received $5,700 in cash from customers billed previously in transaction (6).

Instructions

(a) Ending cash $11,500

(a) Prepare a tabular analysis of the transactions using the following column headings: Cash, Accounts Receivable, Supplies, Equipment, Accounts Payable, Common Stock, and Retained Earnings (with separate columns for Revenues, Expenses, and Dividends). Include margin explanation for any changes in Retained Earnings.

(b) Net income $5,600

(b) From an analysis of the Retained Earnings columns, compute the net income or net loss for April.

Analyze transactions and prepare income statement, retained earnings statement, and balance sheet.

(LO 6, 7, 8)

P1-2B Mandy Arnold opened a law office, Mandy Arnold, Attorney at Law, on July 1, 2014. On July 31, the balance sheet showed Cash $4,000, Accounts Receivable $1,500, Supplies $500, Equipment $5,000, Accounts Payable $4,200, and Common Stock $6,000, and Retained Earnings $800. During August, the following transactions occurred.

1. Collected $1,400 of accounts receivable due from clients.
2. Paid $2,700 cash for accounts payable due.
3. Earned revenue of $7,900 of which $3,000 is collected in cash and the balance is due in September.
4. Purchased additional office equipment for $1,000, paying $400 in cash and the balance on account.
5. Paid salaries $3,000, rent for August $900, and advertising expenses $350.
6. Declared and paid a $450 cash dividend.
7. Received $2,000 from Standard Federal Bank; the money was borrowed on a 4-month note payable.
8. Incurred utility expenses for month on account $210.

Instructions

(a) Ending expenses $4,460

(a) Prepare a tabular analysis of the August transactions beginning with July 31 balances. The column headings should be as follows: Cash + Accounts Receivable + Supplies + Equipment = Notes Payable + Accounts Payable + Common Stock + Retained Earnings + Revenues − Expenses − Dividends.

(b) Net income $3,440
    Total assets $14,100

(b) Prepare an income statement for August, a retained earnings statement for August, and a balance sheet at August 31.

P1-3B Angelic Cosmetics Co., a company that provides individual skin care treatment, was started on June 1 with an investment of $25,000 cash. Following are the assets and liabilities of the company at June 30 and the revenues and expenses for the month of June.

Prepare income statement, retained earnings statement, and balance sheet.

(LO 8)

Cash	$10,000	Notes Payable	$13,000
Accounts Receivable	4,000	Accounts Payable	1,400
Service Revenue	5,500	Rent Expense	1,600
Supplies	2,000	Gasoline Expense	600
Advertising Expense	500	Utilities Expense	300
Equipment	25,000		

Stockholders made no additional investments in June. The company paid a cash dividend of $900 during the month.

Instructions
(a) Prepare an income statement and a retained earnings statement for the month of June and a balance sheet at June 30, 2014.
(b) Prepare an income statement and a retained earnings statement for June assuming the following data are not included above: (1) $800 of revenue was earned and billed but not collected at June 30, and (2) $100 of gasoline expense was incurred but not paid.

*(a) Net income $2,500
Total assets $41,000
(b) Net income $3,200*

P1-4B Jessi Paulis started a consulting firm, Paulis Consulting, on May 1, 2014. The following transactions occurred during the month of May.

Analyze transactions and prepare financial statements.

(LO 6, 7, 8)

May	1	Paulis invested $8,000 cash in the business in exchange for stock.
	2	Paid $800 for office rent for the month.
	3	Purchased $500 of supplies on account.
	5	Paid $50 to advertise in the *County News*.
	9	Received $3,000 cash for services provided.
	12	Declared and paid a $700 cash dividend.
	15	Performed $3,300 of services on account.
	17	Paid $2,100 for employee salaries.
	20	Paid for the supplies purchased on account on May 3.
	23	Received a cash payment of $2,000 for services provided on account on May 15.
	26	Borrowed $5,000 from the bank on a note payable.
	29	Purchased office equipment for $2,300 on account.
	30	Paid $150 for utilities.

Instructions
(a) Show the effects of the previous transactions on the accounting equation using the following format.

(a) Total assets $17,800

		Assets			=	Liabilities	+		Stockholders' Equity		
Date	Cash +	Accounts Receivable	+ Supplies + Equipment =			Notes Payable +	Accounts Payable +	Common Stock +	Retained Earnings		
									Rev. −	Exp. −	Div.

Include margin explanations for any changes in the Retained Earnings account in your analysis.

(b) Prepare an income statement for the month of May.
(c) Prepare a balance sheet at May 31, 2014.

*(b) Net income $3,200
(c) Cash $13,700*

P1-5B Financial statement information about four different companies is shown on the next page.

Determine financial state-ment amounts and prepare retained earnings statement.

(LO 7, 8)

Instructions
(a) Determine the missing amounts. (*Hint:* For example, to solve for (a), Assets − Liabilities = Stockholders' Equity = $28,000.)
(b) Prepare the retained earnings statement for John Company. Assume beginning retained earnings was $0.
(c) ▭▭▭▭▶ Write a memorandum explaining the sequence for preparing financial statements and the interrelationship of the retained earnings statement to the income statement and balance sheet.

	John Company	Paul Company	George Company	Ringo Company
January 1, 2014				
Assets	$ 78,000	$ 90,000	(g)	$150,000
Liabilities	50,000	(d)	$ 75,000	(j)
Stockholders' equity	(a)	50,000	54,000	100,000
December 31, 2014				
Assets	(b)	117,000	180,000	(k)
Liabilities	55,000	79,000	(h)	80,000
Stockholders' equity	40,000	(e)	100,000	145,000
Stockholders' equity changes in year				
Additional investment	(c)	8,000	10,000	15,000
Dividends	10,000	(f)	12,000	10,000
Total revenues	350,000	390,000	(i)	500,000
Total expenses	335,000	400,000	360,000	(l)

PROBLEMS: SET C

Visit the book's website, at **www.wiley.com/college/weygandt**, and choose the Student Companion site to access Problem Set C.

CONTINUING COOKIE CHRONICLE

*The **Continuing Cookie Chronicle** starts in this chapter and continues in every chapter. You also can find this problem at the book's companion website.*

CCC1 Natalie Koebel spent much of her childhood learning the art of cookie-making from her grandmother. They passed many happy hours mastering every type of cookie imaginable and later creating new recipes that were both healthy and delicious. Now at the start of her second year in college, Natalie is investigating various possibilities for starting her own business as part of the requirements of the entrepreneurship program in which she is enrolled.

A long-time friend insists that Natalie has to somehow include cookies in her business plan. After a series of brainstorming sessions, Natalie settles on the idea of operating a cookie-making school. She will start on a part-time basis and offer her services in people's homes. Now that she has started thinking about it, the possibilities seem endless. During the fall, she will concentrate on holiday cookies. She will offer individual lessons and group sessions (which will probably be more entertainment than education for the participants). Natalie also decides to include children in her target market.

The first difficult decision is coming up with the perfect name for her business. In the end, she settles on "Cookie Creations" and then moves on to more important issues.

Instructions

(a) What form of business organization—proprietorship, partnership, or corporation—do you recommend that Natalie use for her business? Discuss the benefits and weaknesses of each form and give the reasons for your choice.

(b) Will Natalie need accounting information? If yes, what information will she need and why? How often will she need this information?

(c) Identify specific asset, liability, and owner's/stockholders' equity accounts that Cookie Creations will likely use to record its business transactions.

(d) Should Natalie open a separate bank account for the business? Why or why not?

Broadening Your PERSPECTIVE

Financial Reporting and Analysis

Financial Reporting Problem: PepsiCo, Inc.

BYP1-1 The actual financial statements of PepsiCo, Inc., as presented in the company's 2010 Annual Report, are contained in Appendix A (at the back of the textbook).

Instructions
Refer to PepsiCo's financial statements and answer the following questions.

(a) What were PepsiCo's total assets at December 25, 2010? At December 26, 2009?
(b) How much cash (and cash equivalents) did PepsiCo have on December 25, 2010?
(c) What amount of accounts payable did PepsiCo report on December 25, 2010? On December 26, 2009?
(d) What were PepsiCo's net sales in 2008? In 2009? In 2010?
(e) What is the amount of the change in PepsiCo's net income from 2009 to 2010?

Comparative Analysis Problem: PepsiCo, Inc. vs. The Coca-Cola Company

BYP1-2 PepsiCo's financial statements are presented in Appendix A. The Coca-Cola Company's financial statements are presented in Appendix B.

Instructions
Refer to the financial statements and answer the following questions.
(a) Based on the information contained in these financial statements, determine the following for each company.

   (1) Total assets at December 25, 2010, for PepsiCo, and for Coca-Cola at December 31, 2010.
   (2) Accounts (notes) receivable, net at December 25, 2010, for PepsiCo and at December 31, 2010, for Coca-Cola.
   (3) Net sales for year ended in 2010.
   (4) Net income for year ended in 2010.
(b) What conclusions concerning the two companies can be drawn from these data?

Real-World Focus

BYP1-3 This exercise will familiarize you with skill requirements, job descriptions, and salaries for accounting careers.

Address: **www.careers-in-accounting.com**, or go to **www.wiley.com/college/weygandt**

Instructions
Go to the site shown above. Answer the following questions.

(a) What are the three broad areas of accounting (from "Skills and Talents Required")?
(b) List eight skills required in accounting.
(c) How do the three accounting areas differ in terms of these eight required skills?
(d) Explain one of the key job functions in accounting.
(e) What is the salary range for a junior staff accountant to a Big 4 firm?

Critical Thinking

Decision-Making Across the Organization

BYP1-4 Lucy and Nick Lars, local golf stars, opened the Chip-Shot Driving Range Company on March 1, 2014. They invested $20,000 cash and received common stock in exchange for their investment. A caddy shack was constructed for cash at a cost of $6,000, and $800 was spent on golf balls and golf clubs. The Lars leased five acres of land at a cost of $1,000 per month and paid the first month's rent. During the first month, advertising costs totaled $750, of which $150 was unpaid at March 31, and $400 was paid to members of the high school golf team for retrieving golf balls. All revenues from customers were deposited in the company's bank account. On March 15, Lucy and Nick received a dividend of $800. A $100 utility bill was received on March 31 but was not paid. On March 31, the balance in the company's bank account was $15,100.

Lucy and Nick thought they had a pretty good first month of operations. But, their estimates of profitability ranged from a loss of $4,900 to net income of $1,650.

Instructions
With the class divided into groups, answer the following.

(a) How could the Lars have concluded that the business operated at a loss of $4,900? Was this a valid basis on which to determine net income?

(b) How could the Lars have concluded that the business operated at a net income of $1,650? (*Hint:* Prepare a balance sheet at March 31.) Was this a valid basis on which to determine net income?

(c) Without preparing an income statement, determine the actual net income for March.

(d) What was the revenue earned in March?

Communication Activity

BYP1-5 Erin Danielle, the bookkeeper for New York Company, has been trying to get the balance sheet to balance. The company's balance sheet is shown below.

New York Company			
Balance Sheet			
For the Month Ended December 31, 2014			
Assets		**Liabilities**	
Equipment	$22,500	Common stock	$23,000
Cash	9,000	Accounts receivable	(6,000)
Supplies	2,000	Retained earnings	(2,000)
Accounts payable	(8,000)	Notes payable	10,500
	$25,500		$25,500

Instructions
Explain to Erin Danielle in a memo why the original balance sheet is incorrect, and what should be done to correct it.

Ethics Case

BYP1-6 After numerous campus interviews, Jeff Hunter, a senior at Great Northern College, received two office interview invitations from the Baltimore offices of two large firms. Both firms offered to cover his out-of-pocket expenses (travel, hotel, and meals). He scheduled the interviews for both firms on the same day, one in the morning and one in the afternoon. At the conclusion of each interview, he submitted to both firms his total out-of-pocket expenses for the trip to Baltimore: mileage $112 (280 miles at $0.40), hotel $130, meals $36, parking and tolls $18, for a total of $296. He believes this approach is appropriate. If he had made two trips, his cost would have been two times $296. He is also certain that neither firm knew he had visited the other on that same trip. Within 10 days, Jeff received two checks in the mail, each in the amount of $296.

Instructions
(a) Who are the stakeholders (affected parties) in this situation?
(b) What are the ethical issues in this case?
(c) What would you do in this situation?

All About You

BYP1-7 Some people are tempted to make their finances look worse to get financial aid. Companies sometimes also manage their financial numbers in order to accomplish certain goals. Earnings management is the planned timing of revenues, expenses, gains, and losses to smooth out bumps in net income. In managing earnings, companies' actions vary from being within the range of ethical activity, to being both unethical and illegal attempts to mislead investors and creditors.

Instructions

Provide responses for each of the following questions.

(a) Discuss whether you think each of the following actions (adapted from *www.finaid.org/fafsa/*) to increase the chances of receiving financial aid is ethical.
   (1) Spend down the student's assets and income first, before spending parents' assets and income.
   (2) Accelerate necessary expenses to reduce available cash. For example, if you need a new car, buy it before applying for financial aid.
   (3) State that a truly financially dependent child is independent.
   (4) Have a parent take an unpaid leave of absence for long enough to get below the "threshold" level of income.
(b) What are some reasons why a *company* might want to overstate its earnings?
(c) What are some reasons why a *company* might want to understate its earnings?
(d) Under what circumstances might an otherwise ethical person decide to illegally overstate or understate earnings?

BYP1-8 When companies need money, they go to investors or creditors. Before investors or creditors will give a company cash, they want to know the company's financial position and performance. They want to see the company's financial statements—the balance sheet and the income statement. When students need money for school, they often apply for financial aid. When you apply for financial aid, you must submit your own version of a financial statement—the Free Application for Federal Student Aid (FAFSA) form.

Suppose you have $4,000 in cash and $4,000 in credit card bills. The more cash and other assets that you have, the less likely you are to get financial aid. Also, if you have a lot of consumer debt (credit card bills), schools are not more likely to loan you money. To increase your chances of receiving aid, should you use the cash to pay off your credit card bills, and therefore make yourself look "worse off" to the financial aid decision-makers?

YES: You are playing within the rules. You are not hiding assets. You are simply restructuring your assets and liabilities to best conform with the preferences that are built into the federal aid formulas.

NO: You are engaging in a transaction solely to take advantage of a loophole in the federal aid rules. In doing so, you are potentially depriving someone who is actually worse off than you from receiving aid.

Instructions

Write a response indicating your position regarding this situation. Provide support for your view.

FASB Codification Activity

BYP1-9 The FASB has developed the Financial Accounting Standards Board Accounting Standards Codification (or more simply "the Codification"). The FASB's primary goal in developing the Codification is to provide in one place all the authoritative literature related to a particular topic. To provide easy access to the Codification, the FASB also developed the Financial Accounting Standards Board Codification Research System (CRS). CRS is an online, real-time database that provides easy access to the Codification. The Codification and the related CRS provide a topically organized structure, subdivided into topic, subtopics, sections, and paragraphs, using a numerical index system.

You may find this system useful in your present and future studies, and so we have provided an opportunity to use this online system as part of the *Broadening Your Perspective* section.

Instructions

Academic access to the FASB Codification is available through university subscriptions, obtained from the American Accounting Association (at *http://aaahq.org/FASB/Access.cfm*), for an annual fee of $150. This subscription covers an unlimited number of students within a single institution. Once this access has been obtained by your school, you should log in (at *http://aaahq.org/ascLogin. cfm*) and familiarize yourself with the resources that are accessible at the FASB Codification site.

Answers to Chapter Questions

Answers to Insight and Accounting Across the Organization Questions

p. 6 The Scoop on Accounting Q: What are the benefits to the company and to the employees of making the financial statements available to all employees? **A:** If employees can read and use financial reports, a company will benefit in the following ways. The *marketing department* will make better decisions about products to offer and prices to charge. The *finance department* will make better decisions about debt and equity financing and how much to distribute in dividends. The *production department* will make better decisions about when to buy new equipment and how much inventory to produce. The *human resources department* will be better able to determine whether employees can be given raises. Finally, *all employees* will be better informed about the basis on which they are evaluated, which will increase employee morale.

p. 8 The Numbers Behind Not-for-Profit Organizations Q: What benefits does a sound accounting system provide to a not-for-profit organization? **A:** Accounting provides at least two benefits to not-for-profit organizations. First, it helps to ensure that money is used in the way that donors intended. Second, it assures donors that their money is not going to waste and thus increases the likelihood of future donations.

p. 10 The Korean Discount Q: What is meant by the phrase "make the country's businesses more transparent"? Why would increasing transparency spur economic growth? **A:** Transparency refers to the extent to which outsiders have knowledge regarding a company's financial performance and financial position. If a company lacks transparency, its financial reports do not adequately inform investors of critical information that is needed to make investment decisions. If corporate transparency is increased, investors will be more willing to supply the financial capital that businesses need in order to grow, which would spur the country's economic growth.

p. 12 Spinning the Career Wheel Q: How might accounting help you? **A:** You will need to understand financial reports in any enterprise with which you are associated. Whether you become a manager, a doctor, a lawyer, a social worker, a teacher, an engineer, an architect, or an entrepreneur, a working knowledge of accounting is relevant.

p. 25 Beyond Financial Statements Q: Why might a company's stockholders be interested in its environmental and social performance? **A:** Many companies now recognize that being a socially responsible organization is not only the right thing to do, but it also is good for business. Many investment professionals understand, for example, that environmental, social, and proper corporate governance of companies affects the performance of their investment portfolios. For example, British Petroleum's oil leak disaster is a classic example of the problems that can occur for a company and its stockholders. BP's stock price was slashed, its dividend reduced, its executives replaced, and its reputation badly damaged. It is interesting that socially responsible investment funds are now gaining momentum in the marketplace such that companies now recognize this segment as an important investment group.

Answers to Self-Test Questions

1. b **2.** d **3.** c **4.** b **5.** b **6.** d **7.** b **8.** a ($3,500 − $2,000) **9.** b **10.** a ($90,000 − $50,000)
11. d **12.** c **13.** b **14.** c *15. a

A Look at IFRS

Most agree that there is a need for one set of international accounting standards. Here is why:

Multinational corporations. Today's companies view the entire world as their market. For example, Coca-Cola, Intel, and McDonald's generate more than 50% of their sales outside the United States, and many foreign companies, such as Toyota, Nestlé, and Sony, find their largest market to be the United States.

Mergers and acquisitions. The mergers between Fiat/Chrysler and Vodafone/Mannesmann suggest that we will see even more such business combinations in the future.

Information technology. As communication barriers continue to topple through advances in technology, companies and individuals in different countries and markets are becoming more comfortable buying and selling goods and services from one another.

Financial markets. Financial markets are of international significance today. Whether it is currency, equity securities (stocks), bonds, or derivatives, there are active markets throughout the world trading these types of instruments.

Key Points

- International standards are referred to as *International Financial Reporting Standards (IFRS)*, developed by the International Accounting Standards Board (IASB).

- Recent events in the global capital markets have underscored the importance of financial disclosure and transparency not only in the United States but in markets around the world. As a result, many are examining which accounting and financial disclosure rules should be followed. As indicated in the graphic below, much of the world has voted for the standards issued by the IASB. Over 115 countries require or permit use of IFRS.

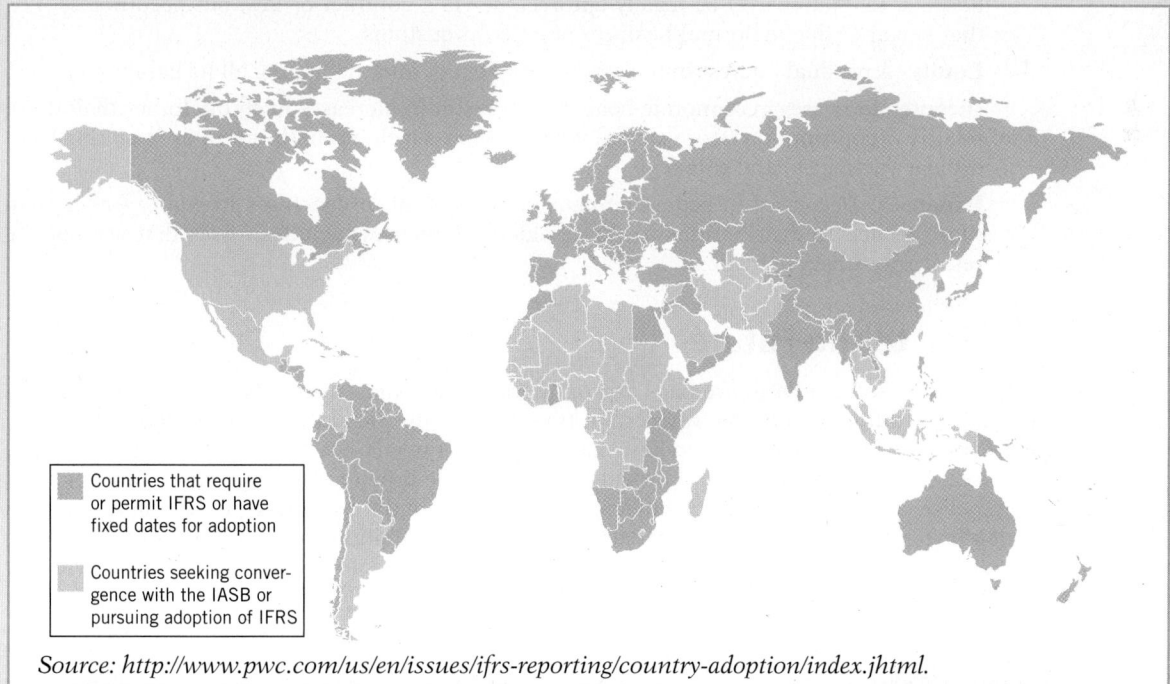

Countries that require or permit IFRS or have fixed dates for adoption

Countries seeking convergence with the IASB or pursuing adoption of IFRS

Source: http://www.pwc.com/us/en/issues/ifrs-reporting/country-adoption/index.jhtml.

- U.S standards, referred to as generally accepted accounting principles (GAAP), are developed by the Financial Accounting Standards Board (FASB). The fact that there are differences between what is in this textbook (which is based on U.S. standards) and IFRS should not be surprising because the FASB and IASB have responded to different user needs. In some countries, the primary users of financial statements are private investors. In others, the primary users are tax authorities or central government planners. It appears that the United States and the international standard-setting environment are primarily driven by meeting the needs of investors and creditors.

- The internal control standards applicable to Sarbanes-Oxley (SOX) apply only to large public companies listed on U.S. exchanges. There is a continuing debate as to whether non-U.S. companies should have to comply with this extra layer of regulation. Debate about international companies (non-U.S.) adopting SOX-type standards centers on whether the benefits exceed the costs. The concern is that the higher costs of SOX compliance are making the U.S. securities markets less competitive.

- The textbook mentions a number of ethics violations, such as Enron, WorldCom, and AIG. These problems have also occurred internationally, for example, at Satyam Computer Services (India), Parmalat (Italy), and Royal Ahold (the Netherlands).

- IFRS tends to be simpler in its accounting and disclosure requirements; some people say more "principles-based." GAAP is more detailed; some people say it is more "rules-based." This difference in approach has resulted in a debate about the merits of "principles-based" versus "rules-based" standards.

- U.S. regulators have recently eliminated the need for foreign companies that trade shares in U.S. markets to reconcile their accounting with GAAP.

- The three most common forms of business organization, proprietorships, partnerships, and corporations, are also found in countries that use IFRS. Because the choice of business organization is influenced by factors such as legal environment, tax rates and regulations, and degree of entrepreneurism, the relative use of each form will vary across countries.

- The conceptual framework that underlies IFRS is very similar to that used to develop GAAP. The basic definitions provided in this textbook for the key elements of financial statements, that is, assets, liabilities, equity, revenues (**referred to as income**), and expenses, are simplified versions of the official definitions provided by the FASB. The more substantive definitions, using the IASB definitional structure, are as follows.

  Assets. A resource controlled by the entity as a result of past events and from which future economic benefits are expected to flow to the entity.

  Liabilities. A present obligation of the entity arising from past events, the settlement of which is expected to result in an outflow from the entity of resources embodying economic benefits. Liabilities may be legally enforceable via a contract or law, but need not be, i.e., they can arise due to normal business practice or customs.

  Equity. A residual interest in the assets of the entity after deducting all its liabilities.

  Income. Increases in economic benefits that result in increases in equity (other than those related to contributions from shareholders). Income includes both revenues (resulting from ordinary activities) and gains.

  Expenses. Decreases in economic benefits that result in decreases in equity (other than those related to distributions to shareholders). Expenses includes losses that are not the result of ordinary activities.

Looking to the Future

Both the IASB and the FASB are hard at work developing standards that will lead to the elimination of major differences in the way certain transactions are accounted for and reported. In fact, at one time the IASB stated that no new major standards would become effective until 2011. The major reason for this policy was to provide companies the time to translate and implement IFRS into practice, as much has happened in a very short period of time. Consider, for example, that as a result of a joint project on the conceptual framework, the definitions of the most fundamental elements (assets, liabilities, equity, revenues, and expenses) may actually change. However, whether the IASB adopts internal control provisions similar to those in SOX remains to be seen.

IFRS Practice

IFRS Self-Test Questions

1. Which of the following is *not* a reason why a single set of high-quality international accounting standards would be beneficial?
    (a) Mergers and acquisition activity.
    (b) Financial markets.

(c) Multinational corporations.

(d) GAAP is widely considered to be a superior reporting system.

2. The Sarbanes-Oxley Act determines:
   (a) international tax regulations.
   (b) internal control standards as enforced by the IASB.
   (c) internal control standards of U.S. publicly traded companies.
   (d) U.S. tax regulations.

3. IFRS is considered to be more:
   (a) principles-based and less rules-based than GAAP.
   (b) rules-based and less principles-based than GAAP.
   (c) detailed than GAAP.
   (d) None of the above.

4. Which of the following statements is *false*?
   (a) IFRS is based on a conceptual framework that is similar to that used to develop GAAP.
   (b) Assets are defined by the IASB as resources controlled by the entity as a result of past events and from which future economic benefits are expected to flow to the entity.
   (c) Non-U.S. companies that trade shares in U.S. markets must reconcile their accounting with GAAP.
   (d) Proprietorships, partnerships, and corporations are also found in countries that use IFRS.

5. Which of the following statements is *true*?
   (a) Under IFRS, the term income refers to what would be called revenues and gains under GAAP.
   (b) The term income is not used under IFRS.
   (c) The term income refers only to gains on investments.
   (d) Under IFRS, expenses include distributions to owners.

IFRS Exercises

IFRS1-1 Who are the two key international players in the development of international accounting standards? Explain their role.

IFRS1-2 What might explain the fact that different accounting standard-setters have developed accounting standards that are sometimes quite different in nature?

IFRS1-3 What is the benefit of a single set of high-quality accounting standards?

IFRS1-4 Discuss the potential advantages and disadvantages that countries outside the United States should consider before adopting regulations, such as those in the Sarbanes-Oxley Act, that increase corporate internal control requirements.

International Financial Reporting Problem: Zetar plc

IFRS1-5 The financial statements of Zetar plc are presented in Appendix C. The company's complete annual report, including the notes to its financial statements, is available at *www.zetarplc.com*.

Instructions

Visit Zetar's corporate website and answer the following questions from Zetar's 2010 annual report.

(a) What accounting firm performed the audit of Zetar's financial statements?

(b) What is the address of the company's corporate headquarters?

(c) What is the company's reporting currency?

(d) What two segments does the company operate in, and what were the sales for each segment in the year ended April 30, 2010?

Answers to IFRS Self-Test Questions

1. d 2. c 3. a 4. c 5. a

 Remember to go back to The Navigator box on the chapter opening page and check off your completed work.

Chapter 2

The Recording Process

Accidents Happen

How organized are you financially? Take a short quiz. Answer *yes* or *no* to each question:

- Does your wallet contain so many debit card receipts that you've been declared a walking fire hazard?
- Was Dwight Howard playing high school basketball the last time you balanced your checkbook?
- Have you ever been tempted to burn down your house so you don't have to try to find all of the receipts and records that you need to fill out your tax return?

If you think it is hard to keep track of the many transactions that make up *your* life, imagine what it is like for a major corporation like Fidelity Investments. Fidelity is one of the largest mutual fund management firms in the world. If you had your life savings invested at Fidelity Investments, you might be just slightly displeased if, when you checked your balance online, a message appeared on the screen indicating that your account information was lost.

To ensure the accuracy of your balance and the security of your funds, Fidelity Investments, like all other companies large and small, relies on a sophisticated accounting information system. That's not to say that Fidelity or any other

Learning Objectives

After studying this chapter, you should be able to:

1 Explain what an account is and how it helps in the recording process.

2 Define debits and credits and explain their use in recording business transactions.

3 Identify the basic steps in the recording process.

4 Explain what a journal is and how it helps in the recording process.

5 Explain what a ledger is and how it helps in the recording process.

6 Explain what posting is and how it helps in the recording process.

7 Prepare a trial balance and explain its purposes.

 ✔ **The Navigator**

company is error-free. In fact, if you've ever overdrawn your bank account because you failed to track your debit card purchases properly, you may take some comfort from one accountant's mistake at Fidelity Investments. The accountant failed to include a minus sign while doing a calculation, making what was actually a $1.3 billion loss look like a $1.3 billion— yes, *billion*—gain! Fortunately, like most accounting errors, it was detected before any real harm was done.

No one expects that kind of mistake at a company like Fidelity, which has

sophisticated computer systems and top investment managers. In explaining the mistake to shareholders, a spokesperson wrote, "Some people have asked how, in this age of technology, such a mistake could be made. While many of our processes are computerized, accounting systems are complex and dictate that some steps must be handled manually by our managers and accountants, and people can make mistakes."

Preview of Chapter 2

In Chapter 1, we analyzed business transactions in terms of the accounting equation. We then presented the cumulative effects of these transactions in tabular form. Imagine a company like Fidelity Investments (as in the Feature Story) using the same tabular format as Softbyte Inc. to keep track of its transactions. In a single day, Fidelity engages in thousands of business transactions. To record each transaction this way would be impractical, expensive, and unnecessary. Instead, companies use a set of procedures and records to keep track of transaction data more easily. This chapter introduces and illustrates these basic procedures and records.

The content and organization of Chapter 2 are as follows.

THE RECORDING PROCESS

The Account	Steps in the Recording Process	The Recording Process Illustrated	The Trial Balance
• Debits and credits • Stockholders' equity relationships • Summary of debit/credit rules	• Journal • Ledger • Posting	• Summary illustration of journalizing and posting	• Limitations of a trial balance • Locating errors • Use of dollar signs

✔ **The Navigator**

The Account

An **account** is an individual accounting record of increases and decreases in a specific asset, liability, or owner's equity item. For example, Softbyte Inc. (the company discussed in Chapter 1) would have separate accounts for Cash, Accounts Receivable, Accounts Payable, Service Revenue, Salaries and Wages Expense, and so on. (Note that whenever we are referring to a specific account, we capitalize the name.)

In its simplest form, an account consists of three parts: (1) a title, (2) a left or debit side, and (3) a right or credit side. Because the format of an account resembles the letter T, we refer to it as a **T-account**. Illustration 2-1 shows the basic form of an account.

Illustration 2-1
Basic form of account

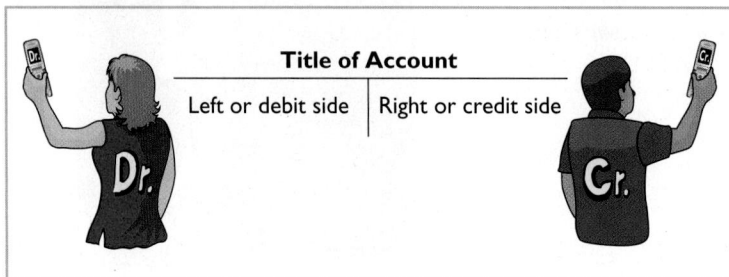

	Title of Account	
Left or debit side		Right or credit side

We use this form often throughout this book to explain basic accounting relationships.

Debits and Credits

The term **debit** indicates the left side of an account, and **credit** indicates the right side. They are commonly abbreviated as **Dr.** for debit and **Cr.** for credit. They **do not** mean increase or decrease, as is commonly thought. We use the terms *debit* and *credit* repeatedly in the recording process to describe **where** entries are made in accounts. For example, the act of entering an amount on the left side of an account is called **debiting** the account. Making an entry on the right side is **crediting** the account.

When comparing the totals of the two sides, an account shows a **debit balance** if the total of the debit amounts exceeds the credits. An account shows a **credit balance** if the credit amounts exceed the debits. Note the position of the debit side and credit side in Illustration 2-1.

The procedure of recording debits and credits in an account is shown in Illustration 2-2 for the transactions affecting the Cash account of Softbyte Inc. The data are taken from the Cash column of the tabular summary in Illustration 1-9 (page 21).

Illustration 2-2
Tabular summary and account form for Softbyte's Cash account

Tabular Summary		Account Form			
Cash			**Cash**		
$15,000		(Debits)	15,000	(Credits)	7,000
−7,000			1,200		1,700
1,200			1,500		250
1,500			600		1,300
−1,700					
−250		Balance	8,050		
600		(Debit)			
−1,300					
$ 8,050					

Every positive item in the tabular summary represents a receipt of cash; every negative amount represents a payment of cash. **Notice that in the account form we record the increases in cash as debits, and the decreases in cash as credits.** For example, the $15,000 receipt of cash (in red) is debited to Cash, and the −$7,000 payment of cash (in blue) is credited to Cash.

Having increases on one side and decreases on the other reduces recording errors and helps in determining the totals of each side of the account as well as the account balance. The balance is determined by netting the two sides (subtracting one amount from the other). The account balance, a debit of $8,050, indicates that Softbyte had $8,050 more increases than decreases in cash. That is, since it started with a balance of zero, it has $8,050 in its Cash account.

DEBIT AND CREDIT PROCEDURE

In Chapter 1, you learned the effect of a transaction on the basic accounting equation. Remember that each transaction must affect two or more accounts to keep the basic accounting equation in balance. In other words, for each transaction, debits must equal credits. The equality of debits and credits provides the basis for the **double-entry system** of recording transactions.

Under the double-entry system, the dual (two-sided) effect of each transaction is recorded in appropriate accounts. This system provides a logical method for recording transactions. The double-entry system also helps ensure the accuracy of the recorded amounts and helps to detect errors such as those at Fidelity Investments as discussed in the Feature Story. If every transaction is recorded with equal debits and credits, the sum of all the debits to the accounts must equal the sum of all the credits.

The double-entry system for determining the equality of the accounting equation is much more efficient than the plus/minus procedure used in Chapter 1. On the following pages, we will illustrate debit and credit procedures in the double-entry system.

> **International Note**
>
> Rules for accounting for specific events sometimes differ across countries. For example, European companies rely less on historical cost and more on fair value than U.S. companies. Despite the differences, the double-entry accounting system is the basis of accounting systems worldwide.

DR./CR. PROCEDURES FOR ASSETS AND LIABILITIES

In Illustration 2-2 for Softbyte Inc. increases in Cash—an asset—were entered on the left side, and decreases in Cash were entered on the right side. We know that both sides of the basic equation (Assets = Liabilities + Stockholders' Equity) must be equal. It therefore follows that increases and decreases in liabilities will have to be recorded *opposite from* increases and decreases in assets. Thus, increases in liabilities must be entered on the right or credit side, and decreases in liabilities must be entered on the left or debit side. The effects that debits and credits have on assets and liabilities are summarized in Illustration 2-3.

Debits	Credits
Increase assets	Decrease assets
Decrease liabilities	Increase liabilities

Illustration 2-3
Debit and credit effects—assets and liabilities

Asset accounts normally show debit balances. That is, debits to a specific asset account should exceed credits to that account. Likewise, **liability accounts normally show credit balances**. That is, credits to a liability account should exceed debits to that account. The **normal balance** of an account is on the side where an increase in the account is recorded. Illustration 2-4 (page 56) shows the normal balances for assets and liabilities.

Illustration 2-4
Normal balances—assets and liabilities

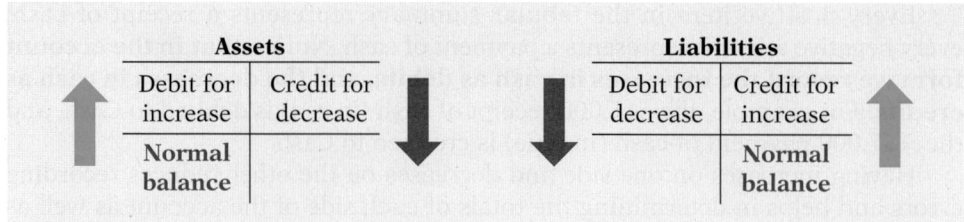

Knowing the normal balance in an account may help you trace errors. For example, a credit balance in an asset account such as Land or a debit balance in a liability account such as Salaries and Wages Payable usually indicates an error. Occasionally, though, an abnormal balance may be correct. The Cash account, for example, will have a credit balance when a company has overdrawn its bank balance (i.e., written a check that "bounced").

STOCKHOLDERS' EQUITY

As Chapter 1 indicated, there are five subdivisions of stockholders' equity: common stock, retained earnings, dividends, revenues, and expenses. In a double-entry system, companies keep accounts for each of these subdivisions, as explained below.

COMMON STOCK Companies issue **common stock** in exchange for the owners' investment paid in to the corporation. Credits increase the Common Stock account, and debits decrease it. For example, when an owner invests cash in the business in exchange for shares of the corporation's stock, the company debits (increases) Cash and credits (increases) Common Stock.

Illustration 2-5 shows the rules of debit and credit for the Common Stock account.

Illustration 2-5
Debit and credit effects—common stock

Debits	**Credits**
Decrease Common Stock	Increase Common Stock

We can diagram the normal balance in Common Stock as follows.

Illustration 2-6
Normal balance—common stock

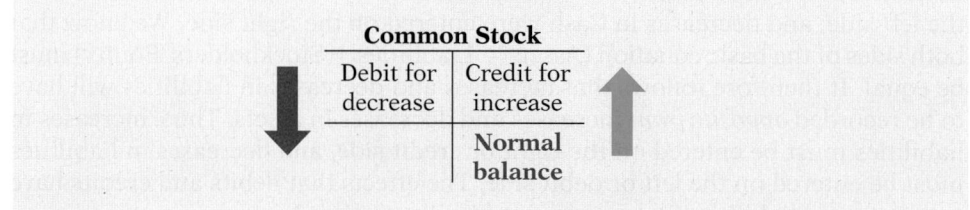

Helpful Hint
The rules for debit and credit and the normal balances of common stock and retained earnings are the same as for liabilities.

RETAINED EARNINGS **Retained earnings** is net income that is kept (retained) in the business. It represents the portion of stockholders' equity that the company has accumulated through the profitable operation of the business. Credits (net income) increase the Retained Earnings account, and debits (dividends or net losses) decrease it, as Illustration 2-7 shows.

Illustration 2-7
Debit and credit effects and normal balance—retained earnings

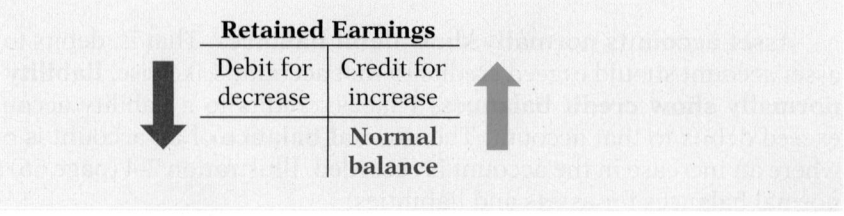

DIVIDENDS A dividend is a company's distribution to its stockholders on a pro rata (equal) basis. The most common form of a distribution is a **cash dividend**. Dividends reduce the stockholders' claims on retained earnings. Debits increase the Dividends account, and credits decrease it. Illustration 2-8 shows that this account normally has a debit balance.

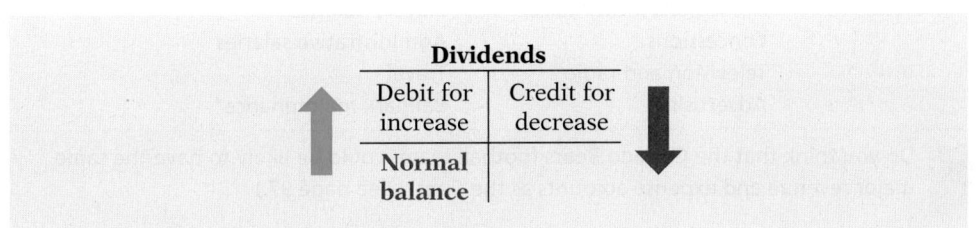

Illustration 2-8
Debit and credit effect and normal balance—dividends

REVENUES AND EXPENSES

The purpose of earning revenues is to benefit the stockholders of the business. When a company earns revenues, stockholders' equity increases. Revenues are a subdivision of stockholders' equity that provides information as to **why** stockholders' equity increased. Credits increase revenue accounts and debits decrease them. Therefore, **the effect of debits and credits on revenue accounts is the same as their effect on stockholders' equity**.

Expenses have the opposite effect: expenses decrease stockholders' equity. Since expenses decrease net income, and revenues increase it, it is logical that the increase and decrease sides of expense accounts should be the reverse of revenue accounts. Thus, debits increase expense accounts, and credits decrease them.

Illustration 2-9 shows the effect of debits and credits on revenues and expenses.

Helpful Hint
Because revenues increase stockholders' equity, a revenue account has the same debit/credit rules as the Common Stock account. Expenses have the opposite effect.

Debits	Credits
Decrease revenues	Increase revenues
Increase expenses	Decrease expenses

Illustration 2-9
Debit and credit effects—revenues and expenses

Credits to revenue accounts should exceed debits. Debits to expense accounts should exceed credits. Thus, revenue accounts normally show credit balances, and expense accounts normally show debit balances. We can diagram the normal balance as follows.

Illustration 2-10
Normal balances—revenues and expenses

	Revenues			Expenses	
	Debit for decrease	Credit for increase		Debit for increase	Credit for decrease
		Normal balance		Normal balance	

Stockholders' Equity Relationships

As Chapter 1 indicated, companies report common stock and retained earnings in the stockholders' equity section of the balance sheet. They report dividends on the retained earnings statement. And they report revenues and expenses on the income statement. Dividends, revenues, and expenses are eventually transferred to retained earnings at the end of the period. As a result, a change in any one of these three items affects stockholders' equity. Illustration 2-11 shows the relationships related to stockholders' equity.

Illustration 2-11
Stockholders' equity relationships

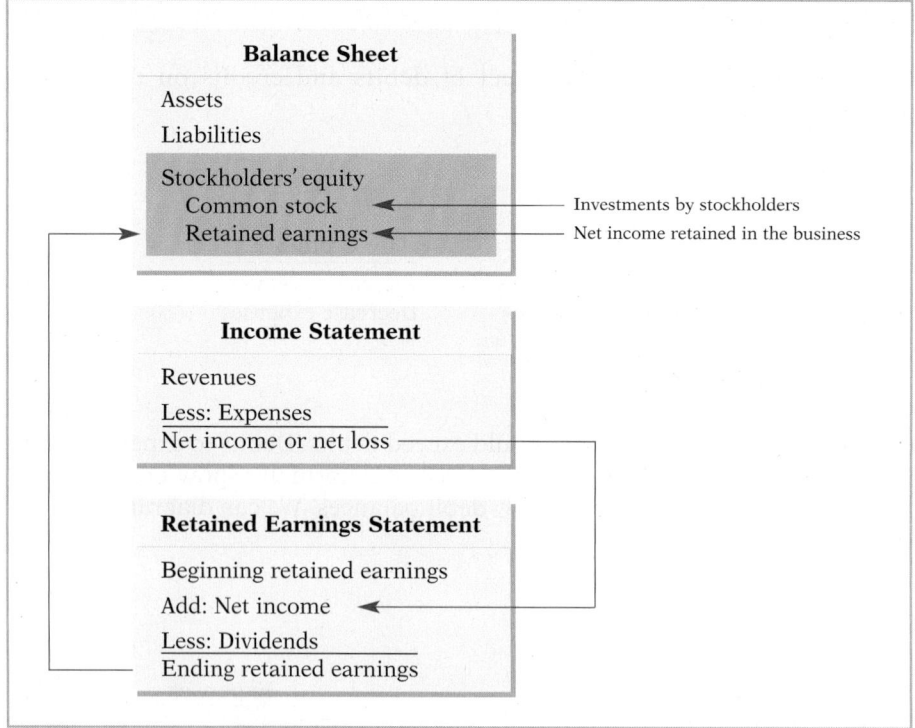

Summary of Debit/Credit Rules

Illustration 2-12 shows a summary of the debit/credit rules and effects on each type of account. Study this diagram carefully. It will help you understand the fundamentals of the double-entry system.

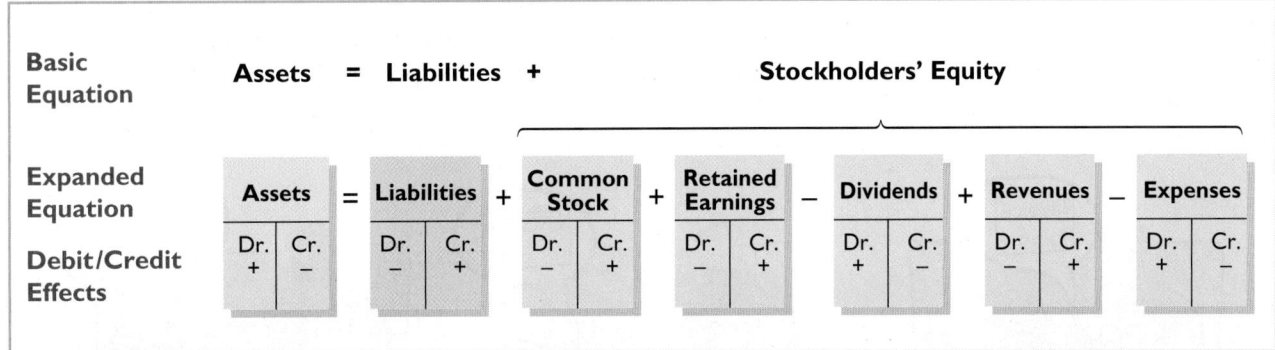

Illustration 2-12
Summary of debit/credit rules

> **DO IT!**

Normal Balances

Action Plan

✔ Determine the types of accounts needed. Kate will need asset accounts for each different type of asset she invests in the business, and liability accounts for any debts she incurs.

✔ Understand the types of stockholders' equity accounts. When Kate begins the business, she will need only Common Stock. Later, she will need other stockholders' equity accounts.

Kate Browne, president of Hair It Is, Inc., has just rented space in a shopping mall in which she will open and operate a beauty salon. A friend has advised Kate to set up a double-entry set of accounting records in which to record all of her business transactions.

Identify the balance sheet accounts that Hair It Is, Inc., will likely need to record the transactions needed to establish and open the business. Also, indicate whether the normal balance of each account is a debit or a credit.

Solution

Hair It Is, Inc., would likely need the following accounts to record the transactions needed to ready the beauty salon for opening day:

Cash (debit balance)	Equipment (debit balance)
Supplies (debit balance)	Accounts Payable (credit balance)
Notes Payable (credit balance), if the business borrows money	Common Stock (credit balance)

Related exercise material: **BE2-1, BE2-2, BE2-5, E2-1, E2-2, E2-4, and DO IT! 2-1.**

✔ **The Navigator**

Steps in the Recording Process

Although it is possible to enter transaction information directly into the accounts without using a journal, few businesses do so. Practically every business uses three basic steps in the recording process:

1. Analyze each transaction for its effects on the accounts.

2. Enter the transaction information in a *journal*.

3. Transfer the journal information to the appropriate accounts in the *ledger*.

The recording process begins with the transaction. **Business documents**, such as a sales slip, a check, a bill, or a cash register tape, provide evidence of the transaction. The company analyzes this evidence to determine the transaction's

LEARNING OBJECTIVE 3

Identify the basic steps in the recording process.

effects on specific accounts. The company then enters the transaction in the journal. Finally, it transfers the journal entry to the designated accounts in the ledger. Illustration 2-13 shows the recording process.

Illustration 2-13
The recording process

The steps in the recording process occur repeatedly. In Chapter 1, we illustrated the first step, the analysis of transactions, and will give further examples in this and later chapters. The other two steps in the recording process are explained in the next sections.

The Journal

Companies initially record transactions in chronological order (the order in which they occur). Thus, the **journal** is referred to as the book of original entry. For each transaction, the journal shows the debit and credit effects on specific accounts.

Companies may use various kinds of journals, but every company has the most basic form of journal, a **general journal**. Typically, a general journal has spaces for dates, account titles and explanations, references, and two amount columns. (See the format of the journal in Illustration 2-14, page 61.) *Whenever we use the term "journal" in this textbook, we mean the general journal, unless we specify otherwise.*

The journal makes several significant contributions to the recording process:

1. It discloses in one place the **complete effects of a transaction**.

2. It provides a **chronological record** of transactions.

3. It helps **to prevent or locate errors** because the debit and credit amounts for each entry can be easily compared.

JOURNALIZING

Entering transaction data in the journal is known as **journalizing**. Companies make separate journal entries for each transaction. A complete entry consists of: (1) the date of the transaction, (2) the accounts and amounts to be debited and credited, and (3) a brief explanation of the transaction.

Illustration 2-14 shows the technique of journalizing, using the first two transactions of Softbyte Inc. On September 1, stockholders invested $15,000 cash in the corporation in exchange for shares of stock, and Softbyte purchased computer equipment for $7,000 cash. The number J1 indicates that the company records these two entries on the first page of the general journal. (The boxed numbers correspond to explanations in the list below the illustration.)

Illustration 2-14
Technique of journalizing

General Journal				J1
Date	**Account Titles and Explanation**	**Ref.**	**Debit**	**Credit**
2014		5		
Sept. 1	2 Cash		15,000	
1	3 Common Stock			15,000
	4 (Issued shares of stock for cash)			
1	Equipment		7,000	
	Cash			7,000
	(Purchase equipment for cash)			

1 The date of the transaction is entered in the Date column.

2 The debit account title (that is, the account to be debited) is entered first at the extreme left margin of the column headed "Account Titles and Explanation," and the amount of the debit is recorded in the Debit column.

3 The credit account title (that is, the account to be credited) is indented and entered on the next line in the column headed "Account Titles and Explanation," and the amount of the credit is recorded in the Credit column.

4 A brief explanation of the transaction appears on the line below the credit account title. A space is left between journal entries. The blank space separates individual journal entries and makes the entire journal easier to read.

5 The column titled Ref. (which stands for Reference) is left blank when the journal entry is made. This column is used later when the journal entries are transferred to the ledger accounts.

It is important to use correct and specific account titles in journalizing. Erroneous account titles lead to incorrect financial statements. However, some flexibility exists initially in selecting account titles. The main criterion is that each title must appropriately describe the content of the account. Once a company chooses the specific title to use, it should record under that account title all later transactions involving the account.[1]

SIMPLE AND COMPOUND ENTRIES

Some entries involve only two accounts, one debit and one credit. (See, for example, the entries in Illustration 2-14.) An entry like these is considered a **simple entry**. Some transactions, however, require more than two accounts in journalizing. An entry that requires three or more accounts is a **compound entry**. To illustrate, assume that on July 1, Butler Company purchases a delivery truck costing $14,000. It pays $8,000 cash now and agrees to pay the remaining $6,000 on account (to be paid later). The compound entry is as follows.

Illustration 2-15
Compound journal entry

General Journal				J1
Date	**Account Titles and Explanation**	**Ref.**	**Debit**	**Credit**
2014				
July 1	Equipment		14,000	
	Cash			8,000
	Accounts Payable			6,000
	(Purchased truck for cash with balance on account)			

---

[1]*In homework problems, you should use specific account titles when they are given.* When account titles are not given, you may select account titles that identify the nature and content of each account. The account titles used in journalizing should not contain explanations such as Cash Paid or Cash Received.

In a compound entry, the standard format requires that all debits be listed before the credits.

> ## DO IT!

Recording Business Activities

As president and sole stockholder, Kate Browne engaged in the following activities in establishing her beauty salon, Hair It Is, Inc.

1. Opened a bank account in the name of Hair It Is, Inc. and deposited $20,000 of her own money in this account in exchange for shares of common stock.

2. Purchased equipment on account (to be paid in 30 days) for a total cost of $4,800.

3. Interviewed three applicants for the position of beautician.

In what form (type of record) should Hair It Is, Inc., record these three activities? Prepare the entries to record the transactions.

Solution

Action Plan

✔ Understand which activities need to be recorded and which do not. Any that have economic effects should be recorded in a journal.

✔ Analyze the effects of transactions on asset, liability, and stockholders' equity accounts.

Each transaction that is recorded is entered in the general journal. The three activities would be recorded as follows.

1. Cash	20,000	
Common Stock		20,000
(Issued shares of stock for cash)		
2. Equipment	4,800	
Accounts Payable		4,800
(Purchase of equipment on account)		
3. No entry because no transaction has occurred.		

Related exercise material: **BE2-3, BE2-6, E2-3, E2-5, E2-6, E2-7, and DO IT! 2-2.**

✔ **The Navigator**

The Ledger

LEARNING OBJECTIVE   5

Explain what a ledger is and how it helps in the recording process.

The entire group of accounts maintained by a company is the **ledger**. The ledger keeps in one place all the information about changes in specific account balances.

Companies may use various kinds of ledgers, but every company has a general ledger. A **general ledger** contains all the asset, liability, and stockholders' equity accounts, as shown in Illustration 2-16. *Whenever we use the term "ledger" in this textbook, we mean the general ledger, unless we specify otherwise.*

Illustration 2-16
The general ledger

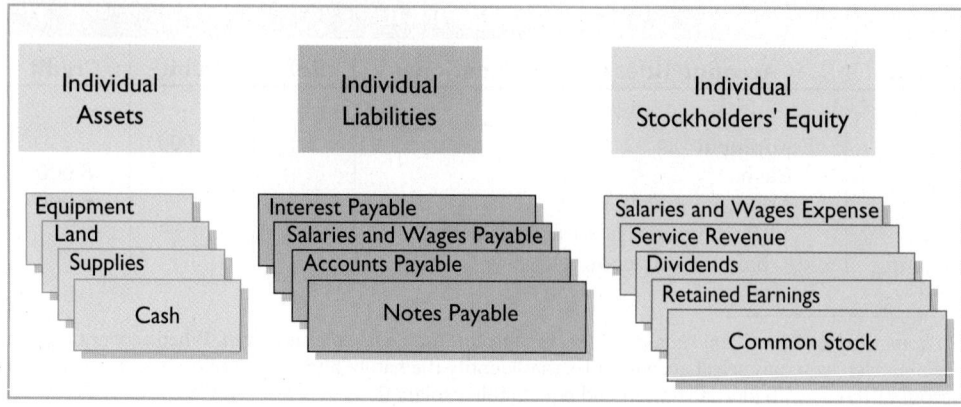

Companies arrange the ledger in the sequence in which they present the accounts in the financial statements, beginning with the balance sheet accounts. First in order are the asset accounts, followed by liability accounts, stockholders' equity accounts, revenues, and expenses. Each account is numbered for easier identification.

The ledger provides the balance in each of the accounts and keeps track of changes in these balances. For example, the Cash account shows the amount of cash available to meet current obligations. The Accounts Receivable account shows amounts due from customers. The Accounts Payable account shows amounts owned to creditors.

ACCOUNTING ACROSS THE ORGANIZATION

What Would Sam Do?

In his autobiography Sam Walton described the double-entry accounting system he used when Wal-Mart was just getting started: "We kept a little pigeonhole on the wall for the cash receipts and paperwork of each [Wal-Mart] store. I had a blue binder ledger book for each store. When we added a store, we added a pigeonhole. We did this at least up to twenty stores. Then once a month, the bookkeeper and I would enter the merchandise, enter the sales, enter the cash, and balance it."

Source: Sam Walton, *Made in America* (New York: Doubleday, 1992), p. 53.

 Why did Sam Walton keep separate pigeonholes and blue binders? Why bother to keep separate records for each store? (See page 97.)

STANDARD FORM OF ACCOUNT

The simple T-account form used in accounting textbooks is often very useful for illustration purposes. However, in practice, the account forms used in ledgers are much more structured. Illustration 2-17 shows a typical form, using assumed data from a cash account.

Cash					No. 101
Date	**Explanation**	**Ref.**	**Debit**	**Credit**	**Balance**
2014					
June 1			25,000		25,000
2				8,000	17,000
3			4,200		21,200
9			7,500		28,700
17				11,700	17,000
20				250	16,750
30				7,300	9,450

Illustration 2-17
Three-column form of account

This is called the **three-column form of account.** It has three money columns—debit, credit, and balance. The balance in the account is determined after each transaction. Companies use the explanation space and reference columns to provide special information about the transaction.

Posting

LEARNING OBJECTIVE 6

Explain what posting is and how it helps in the recording process.

Transferring journal entries to the ledger accounts is called **posting**. This phase of the recording process accumulates the effects of journalized transactions into the individual accounts. Posting involves the following steps.

1. In the **ledger**, enter, in the appropriate columns of the account(s) debited, the date, journal page, and debit amount shown in the journal.

2. In the reference column of the **journal**, write the account number to which the debit amount was posted.

3. In the **ledger**, enter, in the appropriate columns of the account(s) credited, the date, journal page, and credit amount shown in the journal.

4. In the reference column of the **journal**, write the account number to which the credit amount was posted.

Illustration 2-18 shows these four steps using Softbyte Inc.'s first journal entry, the issuance of common stock for $15,000 cash. The boxed numbers indicate the sequence of the steps.

Illustration 2-18
Posting a journal entry

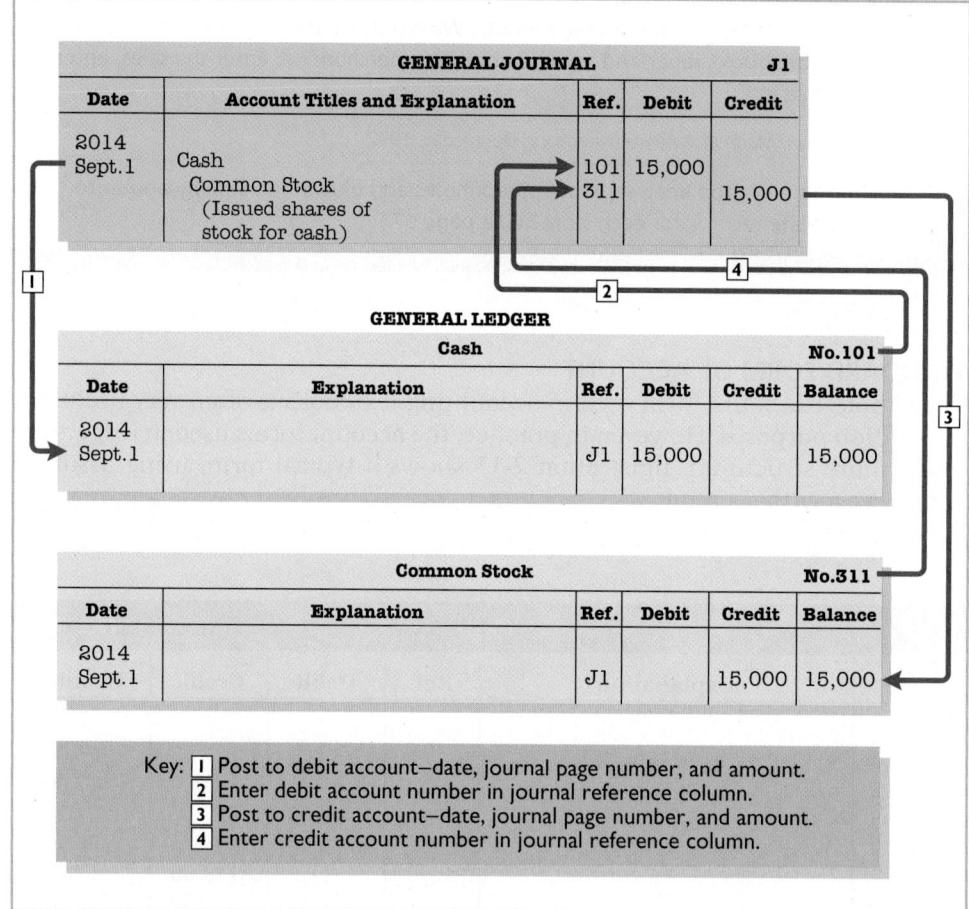

Posting should be performed in chronological order. That is, the company should post all the debits and credits of one journal entry before proceeding to the next journal entry. Postings should be made on a timely basis to ensure that the ledger is up to date.[2]

---

[2]*In homework problems, you can journalize all transactions before posting any of the journal entries.*

The reference column **of a ledger** account indicates the journal page from which the transaction was posted.[3] The explanation space of the ledger account is used infrequently because an explanation already appears in the journal.

CHART OF ACCOUNTS

The number and type of accounts differ for each company. The number of accounts depends on the amount of detail management desires. For example, the management of one company may want a single account for all types of utility expense. Another may keep separate expense accounts for each type of utility, such as gas, electricity, and water. Similarly, a small company like Softbyte Inc. will have fewer accounts than a corporate giant like Dell. Softbyte may be able to manage and report its activities in 20 to 30 accounts, while Dell may require thousands of accounts to keep track of its worldwide activities.

Most companies have a **chart of accounts**. This chart lists the accounts and the account numbers that identify their location in the ledger. The numbering system that identifies the accounts usually starts with the balance sheet accounts and follows with the income statement accounts.

Helpful Hint
On the textbook's endpapers, you will also find an expanded chart of accounts.

In this and the next two chapters, we will be explaining the accounting for Pioneer Advertising Agency Inc. (a service company). The ranges of the account numbers are as follows.

- Accounts 101–199 indicate asset accounts
- 200–299 indicate liabilities
- 300–399 indicate stockholders' equity accounts
- 400–499, revenues
- 500–799, expenses
- 800–899, other revenues
- 900–999, other expenses.

Illustration 2-19 shows the chart of accounts for Pioneer Advertising Agency Inc. Accounts shown in red are used in this chapter. Accounts shown in black are explained in later chapters.

Pioneer Advertising Agency Inc. Chart of Accounts	
Assets	**Stockholders' Equity**
101 Cash	**311 Common Stock**
112 Accounts Receivable	320 Retained Earnings
126 Supplies	**332 Dividends**
130 Prepaid Insurance	350 Income Summary
157 Equipment	
158 Accumulated Depreciation— Equipment	**Revenues**
	400 Service Revenue
Liabilities	**Expenses**
200 Notes Payable	631 Supplies Expense
201 Accounts Payable	711 Depreciation Expense
209 Unearned Service Revenue	722 Insurance Expense
212 Salaries and Wages Payable	**726 Salaries and Wages Expense**
230 Interest Payable	**729 Rent Expense**
	905 Interest Expense

Illustration 2-19
Chart of accounts for Pioneer Advertising Agency Inc.

---

[3]After the last entry has been posted, the accountant should scan the reference column **in the journal**, to confirm that all postings have been made.

You will notice that there are gaps in the numbering system of the chart of accounts for Pioneer Advertising. Gaps are left to permit the insertion of new accounts as needed during the life of the business.

The Recording Process Illustrated

Illustrations 2-20 through 2-29 show the basic steps in the recording process, using the October transactions of Pioneer Advertising Agency Inc. Pioneer's accounting period is a month. A basic analysis and a debit-credit analysis precede the journalizing and posting of each transaction. For simplicity, we use the T-account form in the illustrations instead of the standard account form.

Study these transaction analyses carefully. **The purpose of transaction analysis is first to identify the type of account involved, and then to determine whether to make a debit or a credit to the account.** You should always perform this type of analysis before preparing a journal entry. Doing so will help you understand the journal entries discussed in this chapter as well as more complex journal entries in later chapters.

In addition, an Accounting Cycle Tutorial is available in *WileyPLUS*. It provides an interactive presentation of the steps in the accounting cycle, using the examples in the illustrations on the following pages.

Illustration 2-20
Investment of cash by stockholders

Helpful Hint
Follow these steps:
1. Determine what type of account is involved.
2. Determine what items increased or decreased and by how much.
3. Translate the increases and decreases into debits and credits.

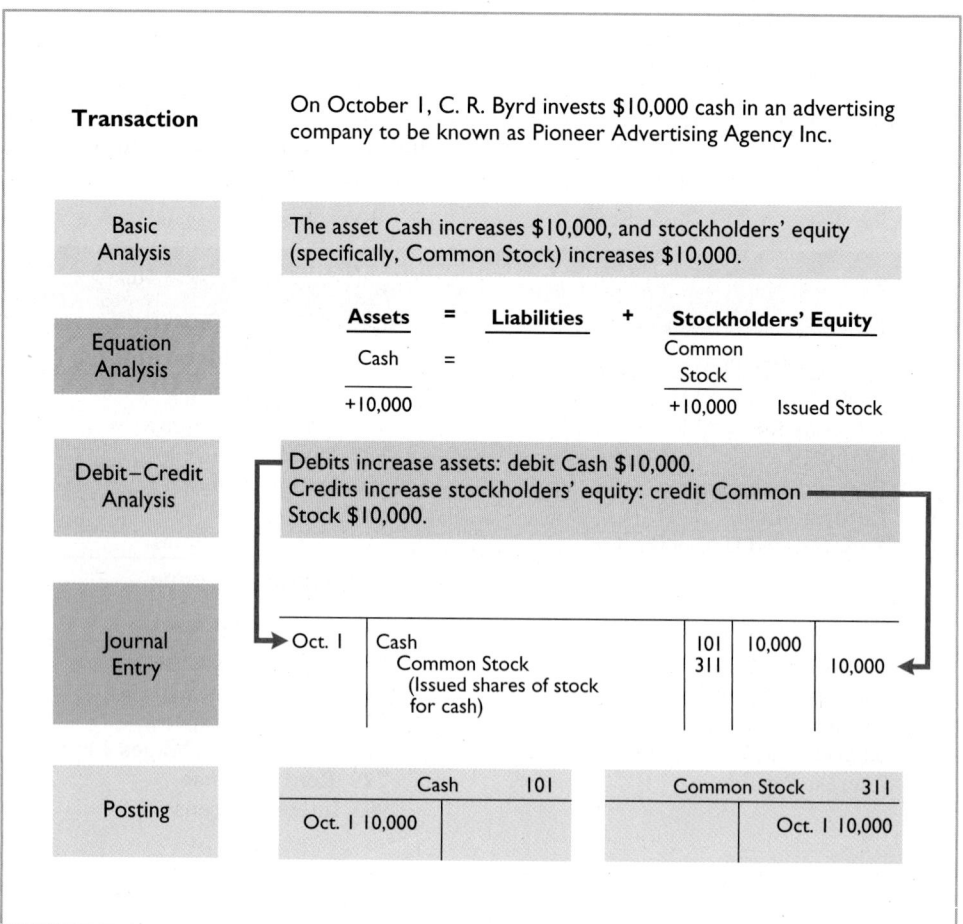

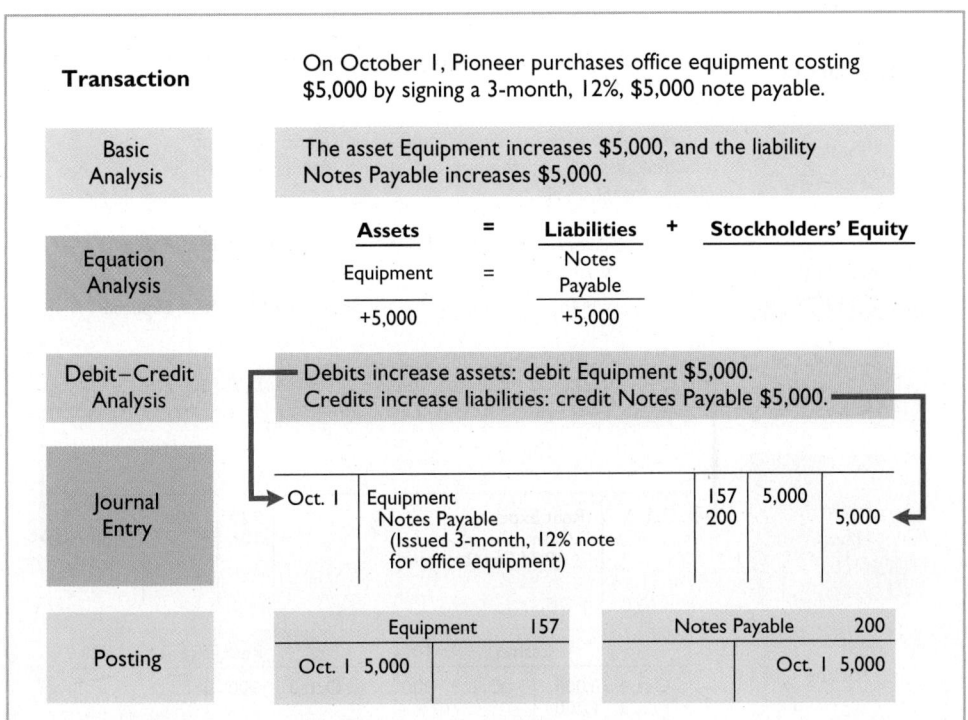

Transaction

On October 1, Pioneer purchases office equipment costing $5,000 by signing a 3-month, 12%, $5,000 note payable.

Basic Analysis

The asset Equipment increases $5,000, and the liability Notes Payable increases $5,000.

Equation Analysis

Assets	=	**Liabilities**	+	**Stockholders' Equity**
Equipment	=	Notes Payable		
+5,000		+5,000		

Debit–Credit Analysis

Debits increase assets: debit Equipment $5,000.
Credits increase liabilities: credit Notes Payable $5,000.

Journal Entry

Oct. 1	Equipment	157	5,000	
	Notes Payable	200		5,000
	(Issued 3-month, 12% note for office equipment)			

Posting

Equipment	157		Notes Payable	200
Oct. 1 5,000				Oct. 1 5,000

Illustration 2-21
Purchase of office equipment

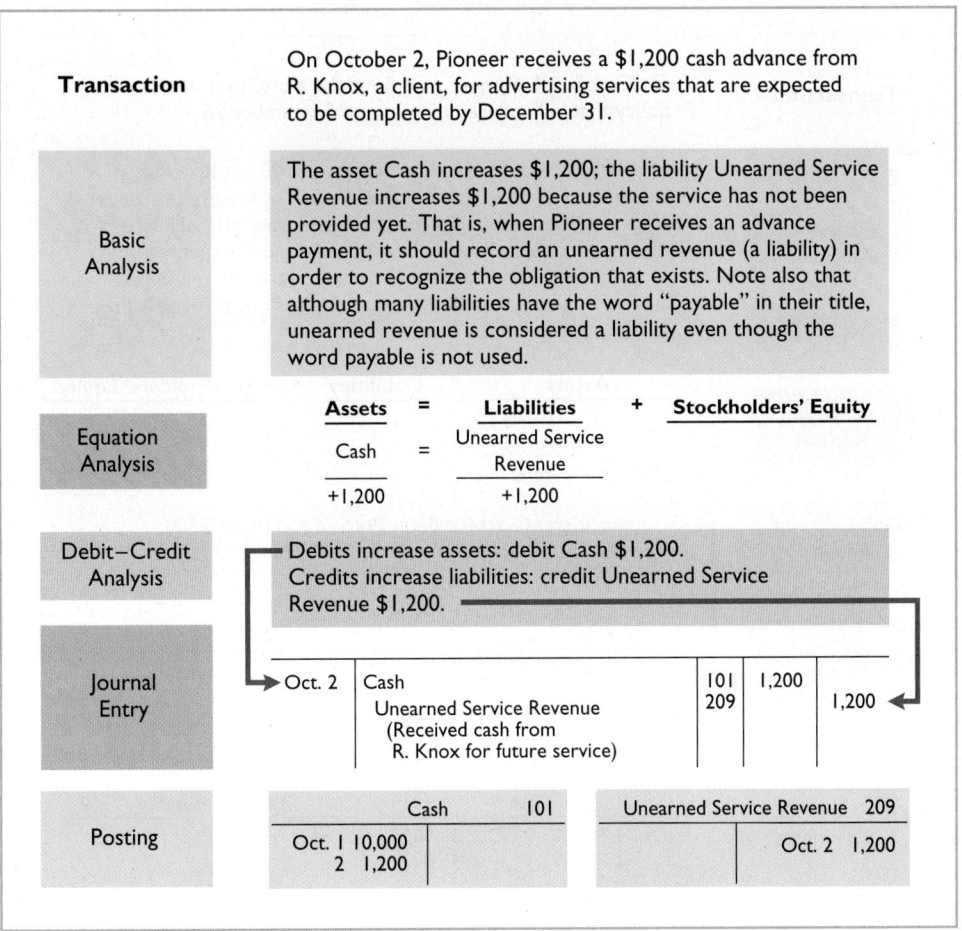

Transaction

On October 2, Pioneer receives a $1,200 cash advance from R. Knox, a client, for advertising services that are expected to be completed by December 31.

Basic Analysis

The asset Cash increases $1,200; the liability Unearned Service Revenue increases $1,200 because the service has not been provided yet. That is, when Pioneer receives an advance payment, it should record an unearned revenue (a liability) in order to recognize the obligation that exists. Note also that although many liabilities have the word "payable" in their title, unearned revenue is considered a liability even though the word payable is not used.

Equation Analysis

Assets	=	**Liabilities**	+	**Stockholders' Equity**
Cash	=	Unearned Service Revenue		
+1,200		+1,200		

Debit–Credit Analysis

Debits increase assets: debit Cash $1,200.
Credits increase liabilities: credit Unearned Service Revenue $1,200.

Journal Entry

Oct. 2	Cash	101	1,200	
	Unearned Service Revenue	209		1,200
	(Received cash from R. Knox for future service)			

Posting

Cash	101		Unearned Service Revenue	209
Oct. 1 10,000				Oct. 2 1,200
2 1,200				

Illustration 2-22
Receipt of cash for future service

Illustration 2-23
Payment of monthly rent

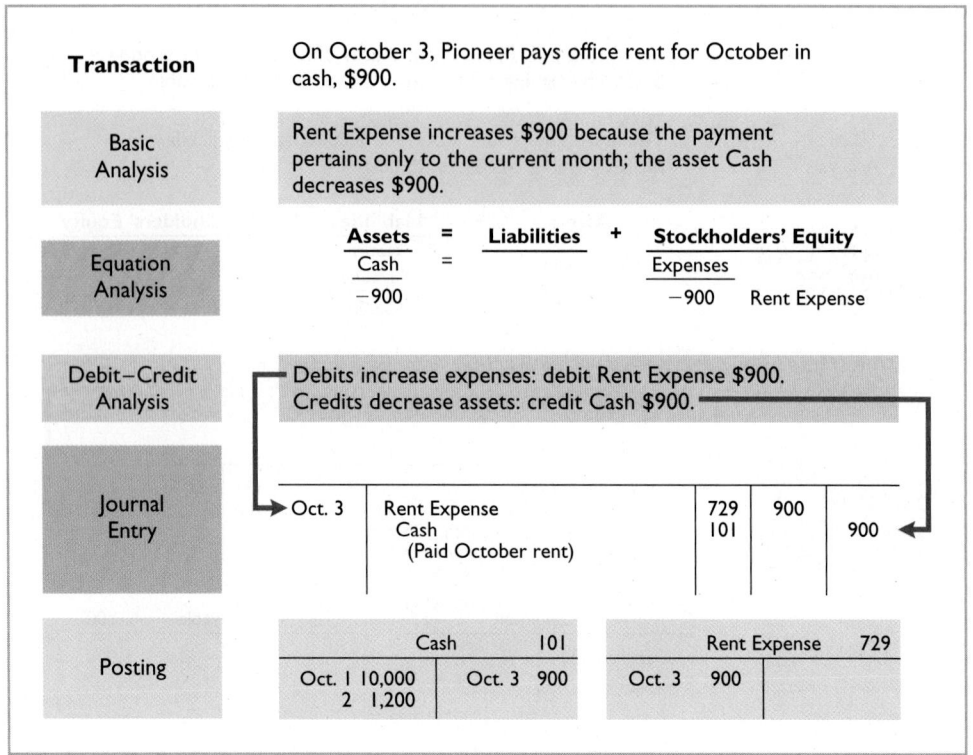

Transaction	On October 3, Pioneer pays office rent for October in cash, $900.
Basic Analysis	Rent Expense increases $900 because the payment pertains only to the current month; the asset Cash decreases $900.
Equation Analysis	**Assets = Liabilities + Stockholders' Equity** Cash = Expenses −900 −900 Rent Expense
Debit–Credit Analysis	Debits increase expenses: debit Rent Expense $900. Credits decrease assets: credit Cash $900.
Journal Entry	Oct. 3 Rent Expense ..... 729 900 Cash ..... 101 900 (Paid October rent)
Posting	Cash 101 Oct. 1 10,000 Oct. 3 900 2 1,200 Rent Expense 729 Oct. 3 900

Illustration 2-24
Payment for insurance

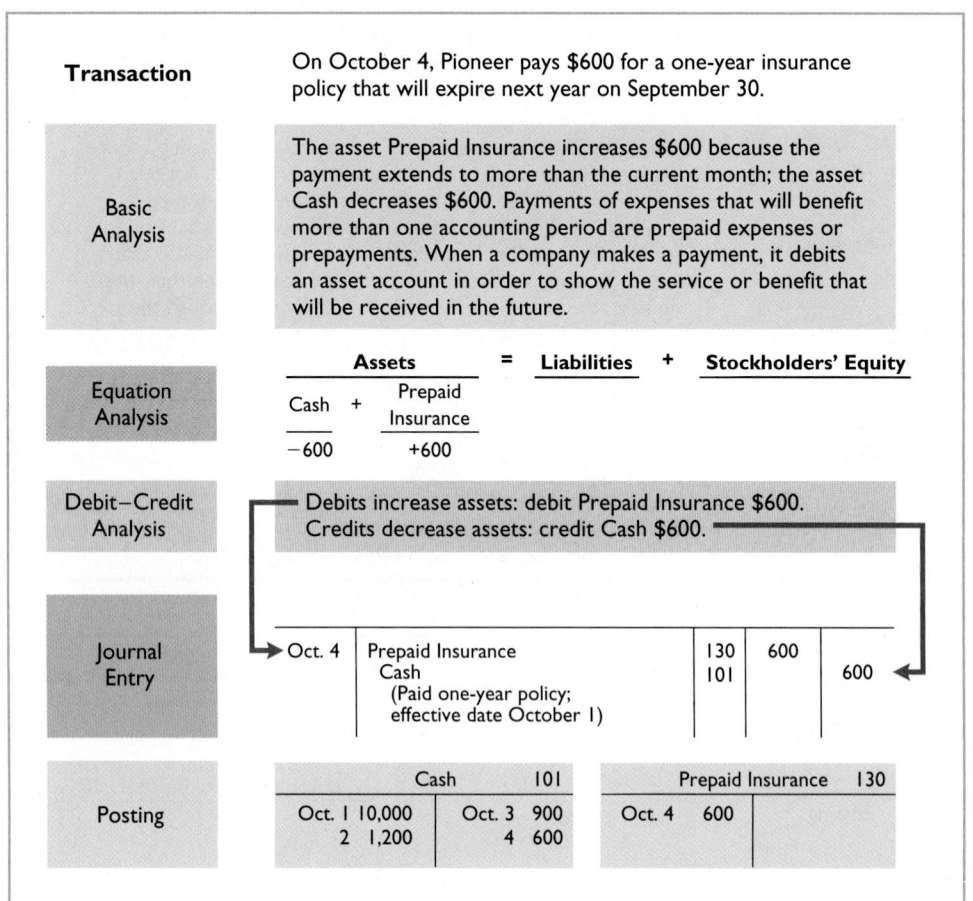

Transaction	On October 4, Pioneer pays $600 for a one-year insurance policy that will expire next year on September 30.
Basic Analysis	The asset Prepaid Insurance increases $600 because the payment extends to more than the current month; the asset Cash decreases $600. Payments of expenses that will benefit more than one accounting period are prepaid expenses or prepayments. When a company makes a payment, it debits an asset account in order to show the service or benefit that will be received in the future.
Equation Analysis	**Assets = Liabilities + Stockholders' Equity** Cash + Prepaid Insurance −600 +600
Debit–Credit Analysis	Debits increase assets: debit Prepaid Insurance $600. Credits decrease assets: credit Cash $600.
Journal Entry	Oct. 4 Prepaid Insurance ..... 130 600 Cash ..... 101 600 (Paid one-year policy; effective date October 1)
Posting	Cash 101 Oct. 1 10,000 Oct. 3 900 2 1,200 4 600 Prepaid Insurance 130 Oct. 4 600

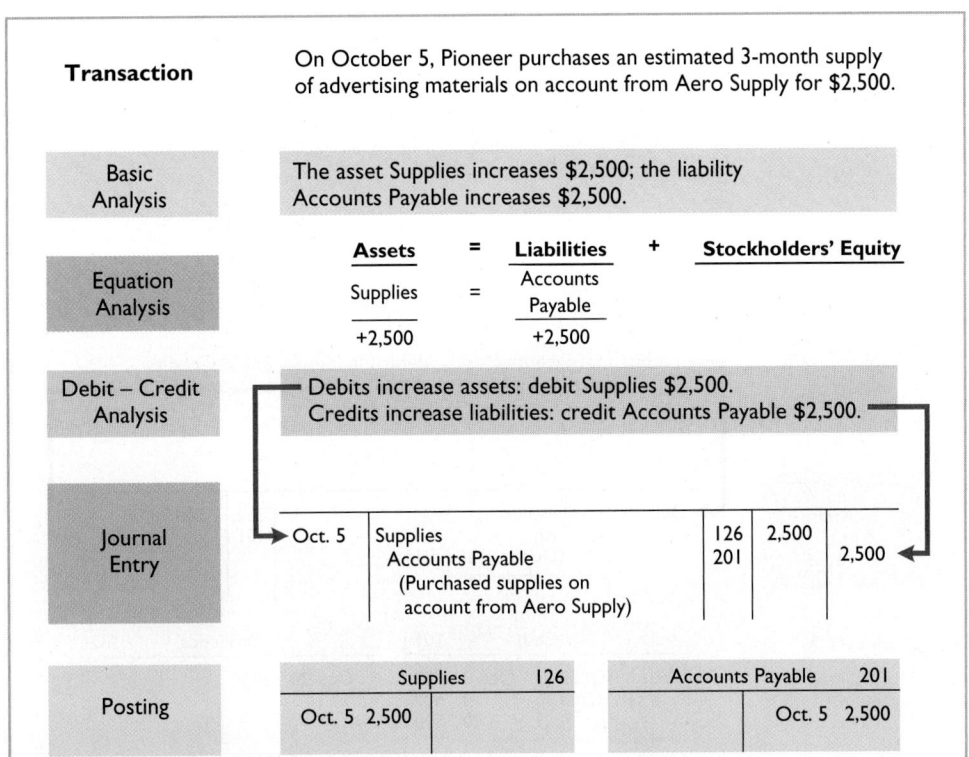

Illustration 2-25
Purchase of supplies on credit

Transaction	On October 5, Pioneer purchases an estimated 3-month supply of advertising materials on account from Aero Supply for $2,500.		
Basic Analysis	The asset Supplies increases $2,500; the liability Accounts Payable increases $2,500.		

	Assets	=	Liabilities	+	Stockholders' Equity
Equation Analysis	Supplies	=	Accounts Payable		
	+2,500		+2,500		

Debit – Credit Analysis: Debits increase assets: debit Supplies $2,500. Credits increase liabilities: credit Accounts Payable $2,500.

Journal Entry

Oct. 5	Supplies	126	2,500	
	Accounts Payable	201		2,500
	(Purchased supplies on account from Aero Supply)			

Posting

Supplies	126
Oct. 5 2,500	

Accounts Payable	201
	Oct. 5 2,500

Illustration 2-26
Hiring of employees

Event	On October 9, Pioneer hires four employees to begin work on October 15. Each employee is to receive a weekly salary of $500 for a 5-day work week, payable every 2 weeks—first payment made on October 26.
Basic Analysis	A business transaction has not occurred. There is only an agreement between the employer and the employees to enter into a business transaction beginning on October 15. Thus, a debit–credit analysis is not needed because there is no accounting entry. (See transaction of October 26 for first entry.)

Illustration 2-27
Declaration and payment of dividend

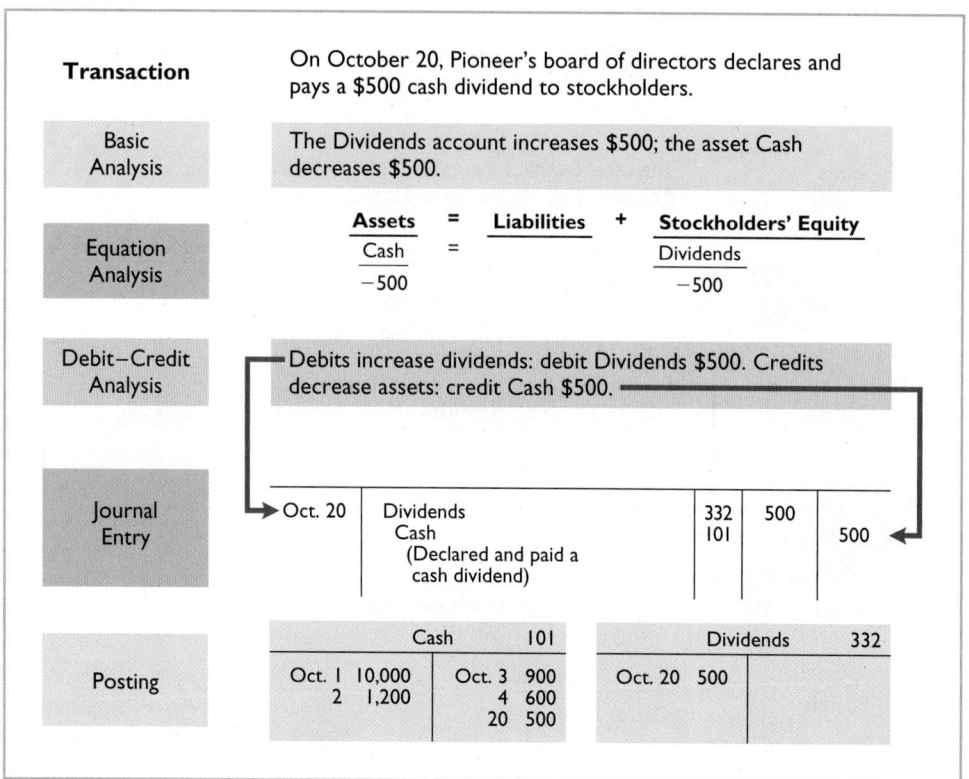

Illustration 2-28
Payment of salaries

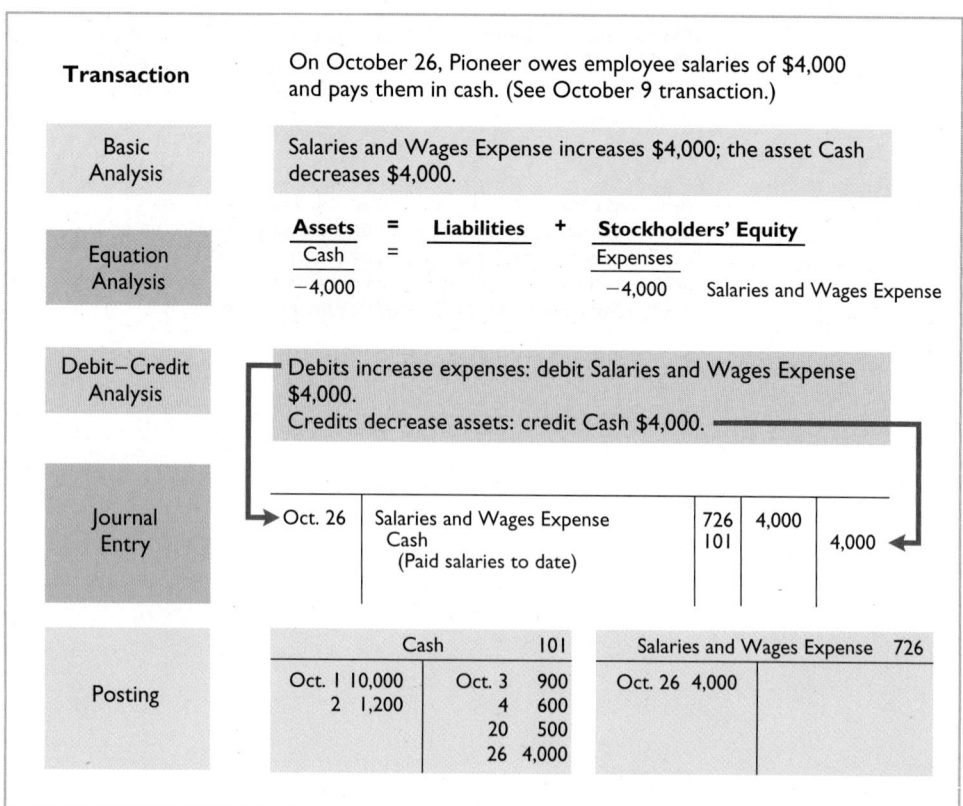

Illustration 2-29
Receipt of cash for services
provided

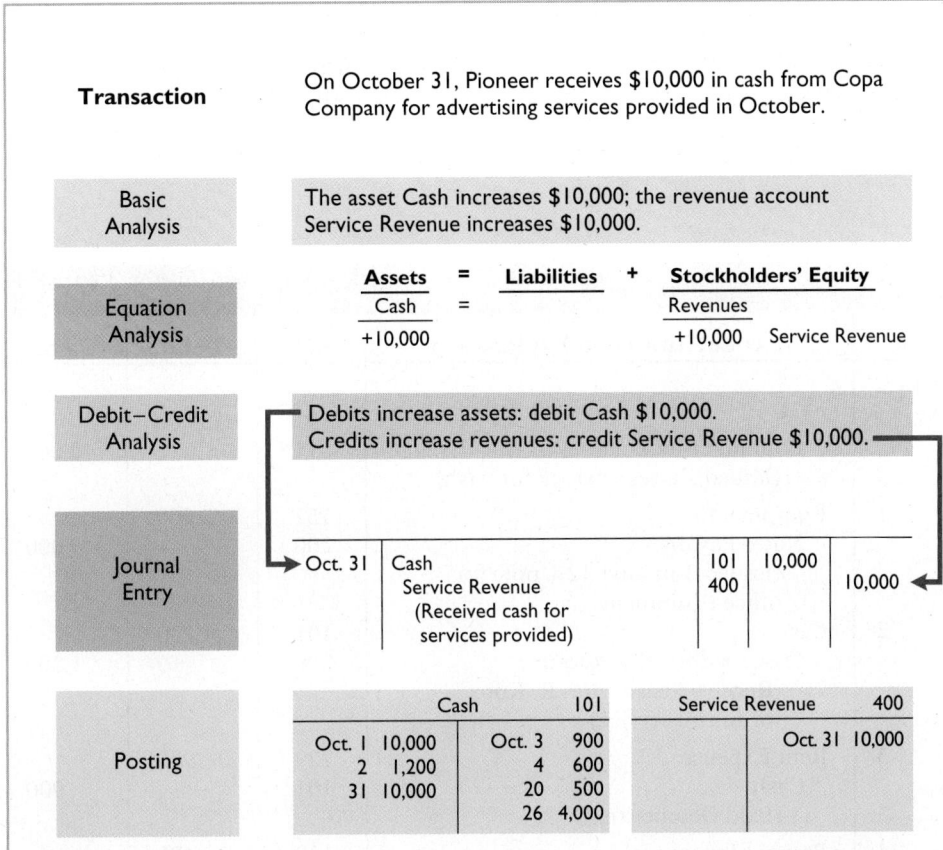

Transaction	On October 31, Pioneer receives $10,000 in cash from Copa Company for advertising services provided in October.
Basic Analysis	The asset Cash increases $10,000; the revenue account Service Revenue increases $10,000.

Equation Analysis

Assets	=	Liabilities	+	Stockholders' Equity
Cash	=			Revenues
+10,000				+10,000 Service Revenue

Debit–Credit Analysis

Debits increase assets: debit Cash $10,000.
Credits increase revenues: credit Service Revenue $10,000.

Journal Entry

Oct. 31	Cash	101	10,000	
	Service Revenue	400		10,000
	(Received cash for services provided)			

Posting

Cash			101
Oct. 1 10,000	Oct. 3 900		
2 1,200	4 600		
31 10,000	20 500		
	26 4,000		

Service Revenue	400
	Oct. 31 10,000

> DO IT!

Posting

Kate Browne recorded the following transactions in a general journal during the month of March.

Mar. 4	Cash	2,280	
	Service Revenue		2,280
Mar. 15	Salaries and Wages Expense	400	
	Cash		400
Mar. 19	Utilities Expense	92	
	Cash		92

Post these entries to the Cash account of the general ledger to determine the ending balance in cash. The beginning balance in Cash on March 1 was $600.

Action Plan

✔ Recall that posting involves transferring the journalized debits and credits to specific accounts in the ledger.

✔ Determine the ending balance by netting the total debits and credits.

Solution

Cash			
3/1	600	3/15	400
3/4	2,280	3/19	92
3/31 Bal.	2,388		

Related exercise material: **BE2-7, BE2-8, E2-8, E2-12, and DO IT! 2-3.**

 The Navigator

Summary Illustration of Journalizing and Posting

Illustration 2-30 shows the journal for Pioneer Advertising Agency Inc. for October. Illustration 2-31 shows the ledger, with all balances in red.

Illustration 2-30
General journal entries

	General Journal				Page J1
Date	**Account Titles and Explanation**	**Ref.**	**Debit**		**Credit**
2014					
Oct. 1	Cash	101	10,000		
	Common Stock	311			10,000
	(Issued shares of stock for cash)				
1	Equipment	157	5,000		
	Notes Payable	200			5,000
	(Issued 3-month, 12% note for office equipment)				
2	Cash	101	1,200		
	Unearned Service Revenue	209			1,200
	(Received cash from R. Knox for future service)				
3	Rent Expense	729	900		
	Cash	101			900
	(Paid October rent)				
4	Prepaid Insurance	130	600		
	Cash	101			600
	(Paid one-year policy; effective date October 1)				
5	Supplies	126	2,500		
	Accounts Payable	201			2,500
	(Purchased supplies on account from Aero Supply)				
20	Dividends	332	500		
	Cash	101			500
	(Declared and paid a cash dividend)				
26	Salaries and Wages Expense	726	4,000		
	Cash	101			4,000
	(Paid salaries to date)				
31	Cash	101	10,000		
	Service Revenue	400			10,000
	(Received cash for services provided)				

General Ledger

Cash No. 101

Date	Explanation	Ref.	Debit	Credit	Balance
2014					
Oct. 1		J1	10,000		10,000
2		J1	1,200		11,200
3		J1		900	10,300
4		J1		600	9,700
20		J1		500	9,200
26		J1		4,000	5,200
31		J1	10,000		**15,200**

Supplies No. 126

Date	Explanation	Ref.	Debit	Credit	Balance
2014					
Oct. 5		J1	2,500		**2,500**

Prepaid Insurance No. 130

Date	Explanation	Ref.	Debit	Credit	Balance
2014					
Oct. 4		J1	600		**600**

Equipment No. 157

Date	Explanation	Ref.	Debit	Credit	Balance
2014					
Oct. 1		J1	5,000		**5,000**

Notes Payable No. 200

Date	Explanation	Ref.	Debit	Credit	Balance
2014					
Oct. 1		J1		5,000	**5,000**

Accounts Payable No. 201

Date	Explanation	Ref.	Debit	Credit	Balance
2014					
Oct. 5		J1		2,500	**2,500**

Unearned Service Revenue No. 209

Date	Explanation	Ref.	Debit	Credit	Balance
2014					
Oct. 2		J1		1,200	**1,200**

Common Stock No. 311

Date	Explanation	Ref.	Debit	Credit	Balance
2014					
Oct. 1		J1		10,000	**10,000**

Dividends No. 332

Date	Explanation	Ref.	Debit	Credit	Balance
2014					
Oct. 20		J1	500		**500**

Service Revenue No. 400

Date	Explanation	Ref.	Debit	Credit	Balance
2014					
Oct. 31		J1		10,000	**10,000**

Salaries and Wages Expense No. 726

Date	Explanation	Ref.	Debit	Credit	Balance
2014					
Oct. 26		J1	4,000		**4,000**

Rent Expense No. 729

Date	Explanation	Ref.	Debit	Credit	Balance
2014					
Oct. 3		J1	900		**900**

Illustration 2-31
General ledger

The Trial Balance

A **trial balance** is a list of accounts and their balances at a given time. Customarily, companies prepare a trial balance at the end of an accounting period. They list accounts in the order in which they appear in the ledger. Debit balances appear in the left column and credit balances in the right column.

  The trial balance proves the mathematical equality of debits and credits after posting. Under the double-entry system, this equality occurs when the sum of the debit account balances equals the sum of the credit account balances. **A trial balance may also uncover errors in journalizing and posting.** For example, a trial balance may well have detected the error at Fidelity Investments discussed in the Feature Story. **In addition, a trial balance is useful in the preparation of financial statements**, as we will explain in the next two chapters.

LEARNING OBJECTIVE **7**

Prepare a trial balance and explain its purposes.

The steps for preparing a trial balance are:

1. List the account titles and their balances.
2. Total the debit and credit columns.
3. Prove the equality of the two columns.

Illustration 2-32 shows the trial balance prepared from Pioneer Advertising's ledger. Note that the total debits ($28,700) equal the total credits ($28,700).

Illustration 2-32
A trial balance

Helpful Hint
To sum a column of figures is sometimes referred to as to *foot* the column. The column is then said to be *footed.*

Pioneer Advertising Agency Inc. Trial Balance October 31, 2014		
	Debit	**Credit**
Cash	$ 15,200	
Supplies	2,500	
Prepaid Insurance	600	
Equipment	5,000	
Notes Payable		$ 5,000
Accounts Payable		2,500
Unearned Service Revenue		1,200
Common Stock		10,000
Dividends	500	
Service Revenue		10,000
Salaries and Wages Expense	4,000	
Rent Expense	900	
	$28,700	$28,700

Helpful Hint
A trial balance is so named because it is a test to see if the sum of the debit balances equals the sum of the credit balances.

A trial balance is a necessary checkpoint for uncovering certain types of errors. For example, if only the debit portion of a journal entry has been posted, the trial balance would bring this error to light.

Limitations of a Trial Balance

A trial balance does not guarantee freedom from recording errors, however. Numerous errors may exist even though the totals of the trial balance columns agree. For example, the trial balance may balance even when (1) a transaction is not journalized, (2) a correct journal entry is not posted, (3) a journal entry is posted twice, (4) incorrect accounts are used in journalizing or posting, or (5) offsetting errors are made in recording the amount of a transaction. As long as equal debits and credits are posted, even to the wrong account or in the wrong amount, the total debits will equal the total credits. **The trial balance does not prove that the company has recorded all transactions or that the ledger is correct.**

Ethics Note

An *error* is the result of an unintentional mistake; it is neither ethical nor unethical. An *irregularity* is an intentional misstatement, which is viewed as unethical.

Locating Errors

Errors in a trial balance generally result from mathematical mistakes, incorrect postings, or simply transcribing data incorrectly. What do you do if you are faced with a trial balance that does not balance? First, determine the amount of the difference between the two columns of the trial balance. After this amount is known, the following steps are often helpful:

1. If the error is $1, $10, $100, or $1,000, re-add the trial balance columns and recompute the account balances.

2. If the error is divisible by 2, scan the trial balance to see whether a balance equal to half the error has been entered in the wrong column.

3. If the error is divisible by 9, retrace the account balances on the trial balance to see whether they are incorrectly copied from the ledger. For example, if a balance was $12 and it was listed as $21, a $9 error has been made. Reversing the order of numbers is called a **transposition error**.

4. If the error is not divisible by 2 or 9, scan the ledger to see whether an account balance in the amount of the error has been omitted from the trial balance, and scan the journal to see whether a posting of that amount has been omitted.

Use of Dollar Signs

Note that dollar signs do not appear in journals or ledgers. Dollar signs are typically used only in the trial balance and the financial statements. Generally, a dollar sign is shown only for the first item in the column and for the total of that column. A single line (a totaling rule) is placed under the column of figures to be added or subtracted. Total amounts are double-underlined to indicate they are final sums. Negative signs or parentheses do not appear in journals or ledgers.

INVESTOR INSIGHT

Why Accuracy Matters

While most companies record transactions very carefully, the reality is that mistakes still happen. For example, bank regulators fined Bank One Corporation (now Chase) $1.8 million because they felt that the unreliability of the bank's accounting system caused it to violate regulatory requirements.

Also, in recent years Fannie Mae, the government-chartered mortgage association, announced a series of large accounting errors. These announcements caused alarm among investors, regulators, and politicians because they fear that the errors may suggest larger, undetected problems. This is important because the home-mortgage market depends on Fannie Mae to buy hundreds of billions of dollars of mortgages each year from banks, thus enabling the banks to issue new mortgages.

Finally, before a major overhaul of its accounting system, the financial records of Waste Management, Inc. were in such disarray that 10,000 of the company's 57,000 employees were receiving pay slips that were in error.

The Sarbanes-Oxley Act was created to minimize the occurrence of errors like these by increasing every employee's responsibility for accurate financial reporting.

? In order for these companies to prepare and issue financial statements, their accounting equations (debits and credits) must have been in balance at year-end. How could these errors or misstatements have occurred? (See page 97.)

> ## DO IT!

Trial Balance

The following accounts come from the ledger of SnowGo Corporation at December 31, 2014.

157	Equipment	$88,000		311	Common Stock	$20,000
332	Dividends	8,000		212	Salaries and	
201	Accounts Payable	22,000			Wages Payable	2,000
726	Salaries and			200	Notes Payable	19,000
	Wages Expense	42,000		722	Utilities Expense	3,000
112	Accounts Receivable	4,000		130	Prepaid Insurance	6,000
400	Service Revenue	95,000		101	Cash	7,000

Prepare a trial balance in good form.

Solution

Action Plan

✔ Determine normal balances and list accounts in the order they appear in the ledger.

✔ Accounts with debit balances appear in the left column, and those with credit balances in the right column.

✔ Total the debit and credit columns to prove equality.

SnowGo Corporation
Trial Balance
December 31, 2014

	Debit	Credit
Cash	$ 7,000	
Accounts Receivable	4,000	
Prepaid Insurance	6,000	
Equipment	88,000	
Notes Payable		$ 19,000
Accounts Payable		22,000
Salaries and Wages Payable		2,000
Common Stock		20,000
Dividends	8,000	
Service Revenue		95,000
Utilities Expense	3,000	
Salaries and Wages Expense	42,000	
	$158,000	$158,000

Related exercise material: **BE2-9, BE2-10, E2-9, E2-10, E2-11, E2-13, E2-14, and** DO IT! **2-4.**

✔ **The Navigator**

> ## Comprehensive DO IT!

Transactions

Bob Sample and other student investors opened Campus Laundromat Inc. on September 1, 2014. During the first month of operations, the following transactions occurred.

Sept. 1 Stockholders invested $20,000 cash in the business.
2 Paid $1,000 cash for store rent for the month of September.
3 Purchased washers and dryers for $25,000, paying $10,000 in cash and signing a $15,000, 6-month, 12% note payable.
4 Paid $1,200 for a one-year accident insurance policy.
10 Received a bill from the *Daily News* for advertising the opening of the laundromat $200.
20 Declared and paid a cash dividend to stockholders $700.
30 Determined that cash receipts for laundry fees for the month were $6,200.

The chart of accounts for the company is the same as for Pioneer Advertising Agency Inc. except for the following: No. 610 Advertising Expense.

Instructions

(a) Journalize the September transactions. (Use J1 for the journal page number.)

(b) Open ledger accounts and post the September transactions.

(c) Prepare a trial balance at September 30, 2014.

Solution to Comprehensive DO IT!

(a)	GENERAL JOURNAL			J1
Date	**Account Titles and Explanation**	**Ref.**	**Debit**	**Credit**
2014				
Sept. 1	Cash	101	20,000	
	Common Stock	311		20,000
	(Stockholders' investment of cash in business)			
2	Rent Expense	729	1,000	
	Cash	101		1,000
	(Paid September rent)			
3	Equipment	157	25,000	
	Cash	101		10,000
	Notes Payable	200		15,000
	(Purchased laundry equipment for cash and 6-month, 12% note payable)			
4	Prepaid Insurance	130	1,200	
	Cash	101		1,200
	(Paid one-year insurance policy)			
10	Advertising Expense	610	200	
	Accounts Payable	201		200
	(Received bill from *Daily News* for advertising)			
20	Dividends	332	700	
	Cash	101		700
	(Declared and paid a cash dividend)			
30	Cash	101	6,200	
	Service Revenue	400		6,200
	(Received cash for services provided)			

Action Plan

✔ Make separate journal entries for each transaction.

✔ In journalizing, make sure debits equal credits.

✔ In journalizing, use specific account titles taken from the chart of accounts.

✔ Provide appropriate description of each journal entry.

✔ Arrange ledger in statement order, beginning with the balance sheet accounts.

✔ Post in chronological order.

✔ Use numbers in the reference column to indicate the amount has been posted.

✔ In the trial balance, list accounts in the order in which they appear in the ledger.

✔ List debit balances in the left column, and credit balances in the right column.

(b)   **GENERAL LEDGER**

	Cash				No. 101
Date	**Explanation**	**Ref.**	**Debit**	**Credit**	**Balance**
2014					
Oct. 1		J1	20,000		20,000
2		J1		1,000	19,000
3		J1		10,000	9,000
4		J1		1,200	7,800
20		J1		700	7,100
30		J1	6,200		13,300

	Prepaid Insurance				No. 130
Date	**Explanation**	**Ref.**	**Debit**	**Credit**	**Balance**
2014					
Sept. 4		J1	1,200		1,200

	Notes Payable				No. 200
Date	**Explanation**	**Ref.**	**Debit**	**Credit**	**Balance**
2014					
Sept. 3		J1		15,000	15,000

	Accounts Payable				No. 201
Date	**Explanation**	**Ref.**	**Debit**	**Credit**	**Balance**
2014					
Sept. 10		J1		200	200

	Common Stock				No. 311
Date	**Explanation**	**Ref.**	**Debit**	**Credit**	**Balance**
2014					
Sept. 1		J1		20,000	20,000

Equipment					No. 157
Date	Explanation	Ref.	Debit	Credit	Balance
2014					
Sept. 3		J1	25,000		25,000

Dividends					No. 332
Date	Explanation	Ref.	Debit	Credit	Balance
2014					
Sept. 20		J1	700		700

Service Revenue					No. 400
Date	Explanation	Ref.	Debit	Credit	Balance
2014					
Sept. 30		J1		6,200	6,200

Advertising Expense					No. 610
Date	Explanation	Ref.	Debit	Credit	Balance
2014					
Sept. 10		J1	200		200

Rent Expense					No. 729
Date	Explanation	Ref.	Debit	Credit	Balance
2014					
Sept. 2		J1	1,000		1,000

(c)

Campus Laundromat Inc.
Trial Balance
September 30, 2014

	Debit	Credit
Cash	$13,300	
Prepaid Insurance	1,200	
Equipment	25,000	
Notes Payable		$15,000
Accounts Payable		200
Common Stock		20,000
Dividends	700	
Service Revenue		6,200
Advertising Expense	200	
Rent Expense	1,000	
	$41,400	$41,400

SUMMARY OF LEARNING OBJECTIVES

1 Explain what an account is and how it helps in the recording process. An account is a record of increases and decreases in specific asset, liability, or stockholders' equity items.

2 Define debits and credits and explain their use in recording business transactions. The terms debit and credit are synonymous with left and right. Assets, dividends, and expenses are increased by debits and decreased by credits. Liabilities, common stock, retained earnings, and revenues are increased by credits and decreased by debits.

3 Identify the basic steps in the recording process. The basic steps in the recording process are (a) analyze each transaction for its effects on the accounts, (b) enter the transaction information in a journal, and (c) transfer the journal information to the appropriate accounts in the ledger.

4 Explain what a journal is and how it helps in the recording process. The initial accounting record of a transaction is entered in a journal before the data are entered in the accounts. A journal (a) discloses in one place the complete effects of a transaction, (b) provides a chronological record of transactions, and (c) prevents or locates errors because the debit and credit amounts for each entry can be easily compared.

5 Explain what a ledger is and how it helps in the recording process. The ledger is the entire group of accounts maintained by a company. The ledger keeps in one place all the information about changes in specific account balances.

6 Explain what posting is and how it helps in the recording process. Posting is the transfer of journal entries to the ledger accounts. This phase of the recording process accumulates the effects of journalized transactions in the individual accounts.

7 Prepare a trial balance and explain its purposes. A trial balance is a list of accounts and their balances at a given time. Its primary purpose is to prove the equality of debits and credits after posting. A trial balance also uncovers errors in journalizing and posting and is useful in preparing financial statements.

GLOSSARY

Account A record of increases and decreases in specific asset, liability, or stockholders' equity items. (p. 54).

Chart of accounts A list of accounts and the account numbers that identify their location in the ledger. (p. 65).

Common stock Issued in exchange for the owners' investment paid in to the corporation. (p. 56).

Compound entry A journal entry that involves three or more accounts. (p. 61).

Credit The right side of an account. (p. 54).

Debit The left side of an account. (p. 54).

Dividend A distribution by a corporation to its stockholders on a pro rata (equal) basis. (p. 57).

Double-entry system A system that records in appropriate accounts the dual effect of each transaction. (p. 55).

General journal The most basic form of journal. (p. 60).

General ledger A ledger that contains all asset, liability, and stockholders' equity accounts. (p. 62).

Journal An accounting record in which transactions are initially recorded in chronological order. (p. 60).

Journalizing The entering of transaction data in the journal. (p. 60).

Ledger The entire group of accounts maintained by a company. (p. 62).

Normal balance An account balance on the side where an increase in the account is recorded. (p. 55).

Posting The procedure of transferring journal entries to the ledger accounts. (p. 64).

Retained earnings Net income that is kept (retained) in the business. (p. 56).

Simple entry A journal entry that involves only two accounts. (p. 61).

T-account The basic form of an account. (p. 54).

Three-column form of account A form with columns for debit, credit, and balance amounts in an account. (p. 63).

Trial balance A list of accounts and their balances at a given time. (p. 73).

 Self-Test, Brief Exercises, Exercises, Problem Set A, and many more resources are available for practice in WileyPLUS.

SELF-TEST QUESTIONS

Answers are on page 97.

(LO 1) **1.** Which of the following statements about an account is *true*?
 (a) In its simplest form, an account consists of two parts.
 (b) An account is an individual accounting record of increases and decreases in specific asset, liability, and stockholders' equity items.
 (c) There are separate accounts for specific assets and liabilities but only one account for stockholders' equity items.
 (d) The left side of an account is the credit or decrease side.

(LO 2) **2.** Debits:
 (a) increase both assets and liabilities.
 (b) decrease both assets and liabilities.
 (c) increase assets and decrease liabilities.
 (d) decrease assets and increase liabilities.

(LO 2) **3.** A revenue account:
 (a) is increased by debits.
 (b) is decreased by credits.
 (c) has a normal balance of a debit.
 (d) is increased by credits.

(LO 2) **4.** Accounts that normally have debit balances are:
 (a) assets, expenses, and revenues.
 (b) assets, expenses, and common stock.
 (c) assets, liabilities, and dividends.
 (d) assets, dividends, and expenses.

5. The expanded accounting equation is: (LO 3)
 (a) Assets + Liabilities = Common Stock + Retained Earnings + Dividends + Revenues + Expenses
 (b) Assets = Liabilities + Common Stock + Retained Earnings + Dividends + Revenues − Expenses
 (c) Assets = Liabilities − Common Stock − Retained Earnings − Dividends − Revenues − Expenses
 (d) Assets = Liabilities + Common Stock + Retained Earnings − Dividends + Revenues − Expenses

6. Which of the following is *not* part of the recording (LO 2) process?
 (a) Analyzing transactions.
 (b) Preparing a trial balance.
 (c) Entering transactions in a journal.
 (d) Posting transactions.

7. Which of the following statements about a journal is (LO 4) *false*?
 (a) It is not a book of original entry.
 (b) It provides a chronological record of transactions.
 (c) It helps to locate errors because the debit and credit amounts for each entry can be readily compared.
 (d) It discloses in one place the complete effect of a transaction.

8. The purchase of supplies on account should result in: (LO 4)
 (a) a debit to Supplies Expense and a credit to Cash.
 (b) a debit to Supplies Expense and a credit to Supplies.

(c) a debit to Supplies and a credit to Accounts Payable.

(d) a debit to Supplies and a credit to Accounts Receivable.

(LO 5) **9.** The order of the accounts in the ledger is:

(a) assets, revenues, expenses, liabilities, common stock, dividends.

(b) assets, liabilities, common stock, dividends, revenues, expenses.

(c) common stock, assets, revenues, expenses, liabilities, dividends.

(d) revenues, assets, expenses, liabilities, common stock, dividends.

(LO 5) **10.** A ledger:

(a) contains only asset and liability accounts.

(b) should show accounts in alphabetical order.

(c) is a collection of the entire group of accounts maintained by a company.

(d) is a book of original entry.

(LO 6) **11.** Posting:

(a) normally occurs before journalizing.

(b) transfers ledger transaction data to the journal.

(c) is an optional step in the recording process.

(d) transfers journal entries to ledger accounts.

(LO 6) **12.** Before posting a payment of $5,000, the Accounts Payable of Senator Corporation had a normal balance of $16,000. The balance after posting this transaction was:

(a) $21,000.   (b) $5,000.

(c) $11,000.   (d) Cannot be determined.

13. A trial balance: (LO 7)

(a) is a list of accounts with their balances at a given time.

(b) proves the mathematical accuracy of journalized transactions.

(c) will not balance if a correct journal entry is posted twice.

(d) proves that all transactions have been recorded.

14. A trial balance will not balance if: (LO 7)

(a) a correct journal entry is posted twice.

(b) the purchase of supplies on account is debited to Supplies and credited to Cash.

(c) a $100 cash dividend is debited to Dividends for $1,000 and credited to Cash for $100.

(d) a $450 payment on account is debited to Accounts Payable for $45 and credited to Cash for $45.

15. The trial balance of Clooney Corporation had ac- (LO 7) counts with the following normal balances: Cash $5,000, Service Revenue $85,000, Salaries and Wages Payable $4,000, Salaries and Wages Expense $40,000, Rent Expense $10,000, Common Stock $42,000, Dividends $15,000, and Equipment $61,000. In preparing a trial balance, the total in the debit column is:

(a) $131,000.

(b) $216,000.

(c) $91,000.

(d) $116,000.

Go to the book's companion website, www.wiley.com/college/weygandt, for additional Self-Test Questions.

 The Navigator

QUESTIONS

1. Describe the parts of a T-account.

2. "The terms *debit* and *credit* mean increase and decrease, respectively." Do you agree? Explain.

3. Jason Hilbert, a fellow student, contends that the double-entry system means each transaction must be recorded twice. Is Jason correct? Explain.

4. Sandra Browne, a beginning accounting student, believes debit balances are favorable and credit balances are unfavorable. Is Sandra correct? Discuss.

5. State the rules of debit and credit as applied to (a) asset accounts, (b) liability accounts, and (c) the stockholders' equity accounts (revenue, expenses, dividends, common stock, and retained earnings).

6. What is the normal balance for each of the following accounts? (a) Accounts Receivable. (b) Cash. (c) Dividends. (d) Accounts Payable. (e) Service Revenue. (f) Salaries and Wages Expense. (g) Common Stock.

7. Indicate whether each of the following accounts is an asset, a liability, or a stockholders' equity account and whether it has a normal debit or credit balance: (a) Accounts Receivable, (b) Accounts Payable, (c) Equipment, (d) Dividends, (e) Supplies.

8. For the following transactions, indicate the account debited and the account credited.

(a) Supplies are purchased on account.

(b) Cash is received on signing a note payable.

(c) Employees are paid salaries in cash.

9. Indicate whether the following accounts generally will have (a) debit entries only, (b) credit entries only, or (c) both debit and credit entries.

(1) Cash.

(2) Accounts Receivable.

(3) Dividends.

(4) Accounts Payable.

(5) Salaries and Wages Expense.

(6) Service Revenue.

10. What are the basic steps in the recording process?

11. What are the advantages of using a journal in the recording process?

12. (a) When entering a transaction in the journal, should the debit or credit be written first?

(b) Which should be indented, the debit or credit?

13. Describe a compound entry, and provide an example.

14. (a) Should business transaction debits and credits be recorded directly in the ledger accounts?

(b) What are the advantages of first recording transactions in the journal and then posting to the ledger?

15. The account number is entered as the last step in posting the amounts from the journal to the ledger. What is the advantage of this step?

16. Journalize the following business transactions.

(a) Alberto Rivera invests $9,000 cash in the business in exchange for shares of common stock.

(b) Insurance of $800 is paid for the year.

(c) Supplies of $2,000 are purchased on account.

(d) Cash of $7,500 is received for services rendered.

17. (a) What is a ledger?

(b) What is a chart of accounts and why is it important?

18. What is a trial balance and what are its purposes?

19. Joe Kirby is confused about how accounting information flows through the accounting system. He believes the flow of information is as follows.

(a) Debits and credits posted to the ledger.

(b) Business transaction occurs.

(c) Information entered in the journal.

(d) Financial statements are prepared.

(e) Trial balance is prepared.

Is Joe correct? If not, indicate to Joe the proper flow of the information.

20. Two students are discussing the use of a trial balance. They wonder whether the following errors, each considered separately, would prevent the trial balance from balancing. What would you tell them?

(a) The bookkeeper debited Cash for $600 and credited Salaries and Wages Expense for $600 for payment of wages.

(b) Cash collected on account was debited to Cash for $900 and Service Revenue was credited for $90.

21. **PEPSICO** What are the normal balances for PepsiCo's Cash, Accounts Payable, and Interest Expense accounts?

BRIEF EXERCISES

BE2-1 For each of the following accounts indicate the effects of (a) a debit and (b) a credit on the accounts and (c) the normal balance of the account.

1. Accounts Payable.
2. Advertising Expense.
3. Service Revenue.
4. Accounts Receivable.
5. Common Stock.
6. Dividends.

Indicate debit and credit effects and normal balance.

(LO 2)

BE2-2 Transactions for the Kaustav Sen Company, which provides welding services, for the month of June are presented below. Identify the accounts to be debited and credited for each transaction.

June 1 Kaustav Sen invests $4,000 cash in exchange for shares of common stock in a small welding business.

2 Purchases equipment on account for $900.

3 $800 cash is paid to landlord for June rent.

12 Bills L. Nigh $300 for welding work done on account.

Identify accounts to be debited and credited.

(LO 2)

BE2-3 Using the data in BE2-2, journalize the transactions. (You may omit explanations.)

Journalize transactions.

(LO 4)

BE2-4 ▭▭▭▷ Tim Weber, a fellow student, is unclear about the basic steps in the recording process. Identify and briefly explain the steps in the order in which they occur.

Identify and explain steps in recording process.

(LO 3)

BE2-5 J.A. Motzek Inc. has the following transactions during August of the current year. Indicate (a) the effect on the accounting equation and (b) the debit-credit analysis illustrated on pages 66–71 of the text.

Aug. 1 Opens an office as a financial advisor, investing $5,000 in cash in exchange for common stock.

4 Pays insurance in advance for 6 months, $1,800 cash.

16 Receives $1,100 from clients for services provided.

27 Pays secretary $1,000 salary.

Indicate basic and debit-credit analysis.

(LO 2)

BE2-6 Using the data in BE2-5, journalize the transactions. (You may omit explanations.)

Journalize transactions.

(LO 4)

Post journal entries to T-accounts.

(LO 6)

BE2-7 Selected transactions for the Gilles Company are presented in journal form below. Post the transactions to T-accounts. Make one T-account for each item and determine each account's ending balance.

				J1
Date	**Account Titles and Explanation**	**Ref.**	**Debit**	**Credit**
May 5	Accounts Receivable		5,000	
	Service Revenue			5,000
	(Billed for services provided)			
12	Cash		2,100	
	Accounts Receivable			2,100
	(Received cash in payment of account)			
15	Cash		3,000	
	Service Revenue			3,000
	(Received cash for services provided)			

Post journal entries to standard form of account.

(LO 6)

BE2-8 Selected journal entries for the Gilles Company are presented in BE2-7. Post the transactions using the standard form of account.

Prepare a trial balance.

(LO 7)

BE2-9 From the ledger balances given below, prepare a trial balance for the Starr Company at June 30, 2014. List the accounts in the order shown on page 74 of the text. All account balances are normal.

Accounts Payable $9,000, Cash $6,800, Common Stock $20,000, Dividends $1,200, Equipment $17,000, Service Revenue $6,000, Accounts Receivable $3,000, Salaries and Wages Expense $6,000, and Rent Expense $1,000.

Prepare a correct trial balance.

(LO 7)

BE2-10 An inexperienced bookkeeper prepared the following trial balance. Prepare a correct trial balance, assuming all account balances are normal.

Cheng Company
Trial Balance
December 31, 2014

	Debit	**Credit**
Cash	$16,800	
Prepaid Insurance		$ 3,500
Accounts Payable		3,000
Unearned Service Revenue	4,200	
Common Stock		13,000
Dividends		4,500
Service Revenue		25,600
Salaries and Wages Expense	18,600	
Rent Expense		2,400
	$39,600	$52,000

> **DO IT! REVIEW**

Identify normal balances.

(LO 2)

DO IT! 2-1 Graham Kahl has just rented space in a strip mall. In this space, he will open a photography studio, to be called "Picture This!" A friend has advised Graham to set up a double-entry set of accounting records in which to record all of his business transactions.

Identify the balance sheet accounts that Graham will likely need to record the transactions needed to open his business (a corporation). Indicate whether the normal balance of each account is a debit or credit.

DO IT! **2-2** Graham Kahl engaged in the following activities in establishing his photography studio, Picture This!:

Record business activities.

(LO 4)

1. Opened a bank account in the name of Picture This! and deposited $8,000 of his own money into this account in exchange for common stock.
2. Purchased photography supplies at a total cost of $1,600. The business paid $400 in cash and the balance is on account.
3. Obtained estimates on the cost of photography equipment from three different manufacturers.

In what form (type of record) should Graham record these three activities? Prepare the entries to record the transactions.

DO IT! **2-3** Graham Kahl recorded the following transactions during the month of April.

Post transactions.

(LO 6)

April 3	Cash	3,700	
	Service Revenue		3,700
April 16	Rent Expense	600	
	Cash		600
April 20	Salaries and Wages Expense	500	
	Cash		500

Post these entries to the Cash T-account of the general ledger to determine the ending balance in cash. The beginning balance in cash on April 1 was $1,600.

DO IT! **2-4** The following accounts are taken from the ledger of Chillin' Company at December 31, 2014.

Prepare a trial balance.

(LO 7)

200	Notes Payable	$20,000	101	Cash	$6,000
311	Common Stock	25,000	120	Supplies	5,000
157	Equipment	76,000	522	Rent Expense	2,000
332	Dividends	8,000	220	Salaries and	
726	Salaries and			Wages Payable	3,000
	Wages Expense	38,000	201	Accounts Payable	9,000
400	Service Revenue	86,000	112	Accounts Receivable	8,000

Prepare a trial balance in good form.

✔ **The Navigator**

EXERCISES

E2-1 Larry Burns has prepared the following list of statements about accounts.

Analyze statements about accounting and the recording process.

(LO 1)

1. An account is an accounting record of either a specific asset or a specific liability.
2. An account shows only increases, not decreases, in the item it relates to.
3. Some items, such as cash and accounts receivable, are combined into one account.
4. An account has a left, or credit side, and a right, or debit side.
5. A simple form of an account consisting of just the account title, the left side, and the right side, is called a T-account.

Instructions
Identify each statement as true or false. If false, indicate how to correct the statement.

E2-2 Selected transactions for B. Madar, an interior decorating firm, in its first month of business, are shown below and on page 84.

Identify debits, credits, and normal balances.

(LO 2)

Jan. 2 Invested $15,000 cash in the business in exchange for common stock.
    3 Purchased used car for $7,000 cash for use in the business.
    9 Purchased supplies on account for $500.
    11 Billed customers $1,800 for services performed.

16 Paid $200 cash for advertising.
20 Received $700 cash from customers billed on January 11.
23 Paid creditor $300 cash on balance owed.
28 Declared and paid a $1,000 cash dividend.

Instructions
For each transaction indicate the following.

(a) The basic type of account debited and credited (asset, liability, stockholders' equity).
(b) The specific account debited and credited (cash, rent expense, service revenue, etc.).
(c) Whether the specific account is increased or decreased.
(d) The normal balance of the specific account.

Use the following format, in which the January 2 transaction is given as an example.

	Account Debited				Account Credited			
	(a)	**(b)**	**(c)**	**(d)**	**(a)**	**(b)**	**(c)**	**(d)**
	Basic	**Specific**		**Normal**	**Basic**	**Specific**		**Normal**
Date	**Type**	**Account**	**Effect**	**Balance**	**Type**	**Account**	**Effect**	**Balance**
Jan. 2	Asset	Cash	Increase	Debit	Stockholders' Equity	Common Stock	Increase	Credit

Journalize transactions.
(LO 4)

E2-3 Data for B. Madar, interior decorating, are presented in E2-2.

Instructions
Journalize the transactions using journal page J1. (You may omit explanations.)

Analyze transactions and determine their effect on accounts.
(LO 2)

E2-4 Presented below is information related to Robbins Real Estate Agency.

Oct. 1 Lynn Robbins begins business as a real estate agent with a cash investment of $20,000 in exchange for common stock.
2 Hires an administrative assistant.
3 Purchases office furniture for $1,900, on account.
6 Sells a house and lot for N. Fennig; bills N. Fennig $3,200 for realty services provided.
27 Pays $850 on the balance related to the transaction of October 3.
30 Pays the administrative assistant $2,500 in salary for October.

Instructions
Prepare the debit-credit analysis for each transaction as illustrated on pages 66–71.

Journalize transactions.
(LO 4)

E2-5 Transaction data for Robbins Real Estate Agency are presented in E2-4.

Instructions
Journalize the transactions. (You may omit explanations.)

Analyze transactions and journalize.
(LO 2, 3, 4)

E2-6 Elvira Industries had the following transactions.

1. Borrowed $5,000 from the bank by signing a note.
2. Paid $2,500 cash for a computer.
3. Purchased $450 of supplies on account.

Instructions
(a) Indicate what accounts are increased and decreased by each transaction.
(b) Journalize each transaction. (Omit explanations.)

Analyze transactions and journalize.
(LO 2, 3, 4)

E2-7 Rockford Enterprises had the following selected transactions.

1. Kris Rockford invested $5,000 cash in the business in exchange for common stock.
2. Paid office rent of $1,100.
3. Performed consulting services and billed a client $4,700.
4. Declared and paid a $700 cash dividend.

Instructions
(a) Indicate the effect each transaction has on the accounting equation (Assets = Liabilities + Stockholders' Equity), using plus and minus signs.
(b) Journalize each transaction. (Omit explanations.)

E2-8 Rachel Manny has prepared the following list of statements about the general ledger.

1. The general ledger contains all the asset and liability accounts, but no stockholders' equity accounts.
2. The general ledger is sometimes referred to as simply the ledger.
3. The accounts in the general ledger are arranged in alphabetical order.
4. Each account in the general ledger is numbered for easier identification.
5. The general ledger is a book of original entry.

Analyze statements about the ledger.

(LO 5)

Instructions
Identify each statement as true or false. If false, indicate how to correct the statement.

E2-9 Selected transactions from the journal of Roberta Mendez, investment broker, are presented below.

Post journal entries and prepare a trial balance.

(LO 6, 7)

Date	Account Titles and Explanation	Ref.	Debit	Credit
Aug. 1	Cash		5,000	
	Common Stock			5,000
	(Investment of cash for stock)			
10	Cash		2,700	
	Service Revenue			2,700
	(Received cash for services provided)			
12	Equipment		5,000	
	Cash			1,000
	Notes Payable			4,000
	(Purchased office equipment for cash and notes payable)			
25	Account Receivable		1,600	
	Service Revenue			1,600
	(Billed clients for services provided)			
31	Cash		850	
	Accounts Receivable			850
	(Receipt of cash on account)			

Instructions
(a) Post the transactions to T-accounts.
(b) Prepare a trial balance at August 31, 2014.

E2-10 The T-accounts below summarize the ledger of Padre Landscaping Company at the end of the first month of operations.

Journalize transactions from account data and prepare a trial balance.

(LO 4, 7)

	Cash		No. 101
4/1	10,000	4/15	720
4/12	900	4/25	1,500
4/29	400		
4/30	1,000		

	Accounts Receivable		No. 112
4/7	3,200	4/29	400

	Supplies		No. 126
4/4	1,800		

	Accounts Payable		No. 201
4/25	1,500	4/4	1,800

Unearned Service Revenue		No. 209
	4/30	1,000

Common Stock		No. 311
	4/1	10,000

Service Revenue		No. 400
	4/7	3,200
	4/12	900

Salaries and Wages Expense		No. 726
415	720	

Instructions

(a) Prepare the complete general journal (including explanations) from which the postings to Cash were made.

(b) Prepare a trial balance at April 30, 2014.

Journalize transactions from account data and prepare a trial balance.

(LO 4, 7)

E2-11 Presented below is the ledger for Sparks Co.

	Cash		No. 101
10/1	5,000	10/4	400
10/10	650	10/12	1,500
10/10	3,000	10/15	280
10/20	500	10/30	300
10/25	2,000	10/31	500

	Accounts Receivable		No. 112
10/6	800	10/20	500
10/20	940		

	Supplies		No. 126
10/4	400		

	Equipment		No. 157
10/3	2,000		

	Notes Payable		No. 200
		10/10	3,000

	Accounts Payable		No. 201
10/12	1,500	10/3	2,000

	Common Stock		No. 311
		10/1	5,000
		10/25	2,000

	Dividends		No. 332
10/30	300		

	Service Revenue		No. 400
		10/6	800
		10/10	650
		10/20	940

	Salaries and Wages Expense		No. 726
10/31	500		

	Rent Expense		No. 729
10/15	280		

Instructions

(a) Reproduce the journal entries for the transactions that occurred on October 1, 10, and 20, and provide explanations for each.

(b) Determine the October 31 balance for each of the accounts above, and prepare a trial balance at October 31, 2014.

Prepare journal entries and post using standard account form.

(LO 4, 6)

E2-12 Selected transactions for Neve Campbell Company during its first month in business are presented below.

Sept. 1 Invested $10,000 cash in the business in exchange for common stock.
  5 Purchased equipment for $12,000 paying $4,000 in cash and the balance on account.
  25 Paid $2,400 cash on balance owed for equipment.
  30 Declared and paid a $500 cash dividend.

Campbell's chart of accounts shows No. 101 Cash, No. 157 Equipment, No. 201 Accounts Payable, No. 311 Common Stock; No. 332 Dividends.

Instructions

(a) Journalize the transactions on page J1 of the journal. (Omit explanations.)

(b) Post the transactions using the standard account form.

Analyze errors and their effects on trial balance.

(LO 7)

E2-13 The bookkeeper for Stan Tucci Equipment Repair made a number of errors in journalizing and posting, as described below.

1. A credit posting of $400 to Accounts Receivable was omitted.
2. A debit posting of $750 for Prepaid Insurance was debited to Insurance Expense.
3. A collection from a customer of $100 in payment of its account owed was journalized and posted as a debit to Cash $100 and a credit to Service Revenue $100.
4. A credit posting of $300 to Property Taxes Payable was made twice.
5. A cash purchase of supplies for $250 was journalized and posted as a debit to Supplies $25 and a credit to Cash $25.
6. A debit of $495 to Advertising Expense was posted as $459.

Instructions

For each error:

(a) Indicate whether the trial balance will balance.
(b) If the trial balance will not balance, indicate the amount of the difference.
(c) Indicate the trial balance column that will have the larger total.

Consider each error separately. Use the following form, in which error (1) is given as an example.

	(a)	(b)	(c)
Error	**In Balance**	**Difference**	**Larger Column**
(1)	No	$400	debit

E2-14 The accounts in the ledger of Tempus Fugit Delivery Service contain the following balances on July 31, 2014.

Prepare a trial balance.
(LO 2, 7)

Accounts Receivable	$10,642	Prepaid Insurance	$ 1,968
Accounts Payable	8,396	Maintenance and Repairs Expense	961
Cash	?	Service Revenue	10,610
Equipment	49,360	Dividends	700
Gasoline Expense	758	Common Stock	40,000
Utilities Expense	523	Salaries and Wages Expense	4,428
Notes Payable	26,450	Salaries and Wages Payable	815
		Retained Earnings	4,636

Instructions

Prepare a trial balance with the accounts arranged as illustrated in the chapter and fill in the missing amount for Cash.

E2-15 The statement of cash flows classifies each transaction as an operating activity, an investing activity, or a financing activity. Operating activities are the types of activities the company performs to generate profits. Investing activities include the purchase of long-lived assets such as equipment or the purchase of investment securities. Financing activities are borrowing money, issuing shares of stock, and paying dividends.

Identify cash flow activities.
(LO 7)

Presented below are the following transactions.

1. Issued stock for $20,000 cash.
2. Issued note payable for $10,000 cash.
3. Purchased office equipment for $11,000 cash.
4. Received $15,000 cash for services provided.
5. Paid $1,000 cash for rent.
6. Paid $600 cash dividend to stockholders.
7. Paid $6,500 cash for salaries.

Instructions

Classify each of these transactions as operating, investing, or financing activities.

EXERCISES: SET B AND CHALLENGE EXERCISES

Visit the book's companion website, at **www.wiley.com/college/weygandt**, and choose the Student Companion site to access Exercise Set B and Challenge Exercises.

PROBLEMS: SET A

P2-1A Prairie Park was started on April 1 by C. J. Amaro and associates. The following selected events and transactions occurred during April.

Journalize a series of transactions.
(LO 2, 4)

Apr.	1	Stockholders invested $50,000 cash in the business in exchange for common stock.
	4	Purchased land costing $30,000 for cash.
	8	Incurred advertising expense of $1,800 on account.
	11	Paid salaries to employees $1,500.

12   Hired park manager at a salary of $4,000 per month, effective May 1.
13   Paid $1,500 cash for a one-year insurance policy.
17   Declared and paid a $1,400 cash dividend.
20   Received $5,700 in cash for admission fees.
25   Sold 100 coupon books for $30 each. Each book contains 10 coupons that entitle the holder to one admission to the park.
30   Received $8,900 in cash admission fees.
30   Paid $900 on balance owed for advertising incurred on April 8.

Amaro uses the following accounts: Cash, Prepaid Insurance, Land, Accounts Payable, Unearned Service Revenue, Common Stock; Dividends; Service Revenue, Advertising Expense, and Salaries and Wages Expense.

Instructions
Journalize the April transactions.

Journalize transactions, post, and prepare a trial balance.

(LO 2, 4, 6, 7)

P2-2A Kara Shin is a licensed CPA. During the first month of operations of her business, Kara Shin, Inc., the following events and transactions occurred.

May 1   Stockholders invested $20,000 cash in exchange for common stock.
2   Hired a secretary-receptionist at a salary of $2,000 per month.
3   Purchased $1,500 of supplies on account from Hartig Supply Company.
7   Paid office rent of $900 cash for the month.
11   Completed a tax assignment and billed client $2,800 for services provided.
12   Received $3,500 advance on a management consulting engagement.
17   Received cash of $1,200 for services completed for Lucille Co.
31   Paid secretary-receptionist $2,000 salary for the month.
31   Paid 40% of balance due Hartig Supply Company.

Kara uses the following chart of accounts: No. 101 Cash, No. 112 Accounts Receivable, No. 126 Supplies, No. 201 Accounts Payable, No. 209 Unearned Service Revenue, No. 311 Common Stock, No. 400 Service Revenue, No. 726 Salaries and Wages Expense, and No. 729 Rent Expense.

Instructions

Trial balance totals $28,400

(a) Journalize the transactions.
(b) Post to the ledger accounts.
(c) Prepare a trial balance on May 31, 2014.

Journalize and post transactions and prepare a trial balance.

(LO 2, 4, 6, 7)

P2-3A Mark Hockenberry owns and manages a computer repair service, which had the following trial balance on December 31, 2013 (the end of its fiscal year).

Byte Repair Service, Inc.
Trial Balance
December 31, 2013

Cash	$ 8,000	
Accounts Receivable	15,000	
Supplies	13,000	
Prepaid Rent	3,000	
Equipment	21,000	
Accounts Payable		$19,000
Common Stock		30,000
Retained Earnings		11,000
	$60,000	$60,000

Summarized transactions for January 2014 were as follows.

1. Advertising costs, paid in cash, $1,000.
2. Additional supplies acquired on account $4,000.
3. Miscellaneous expenses, paid in cash, $1,700.
4. Cash collected from customers in payment of accounts receivable $13,000.
5. Cash paid to creditors for accounts payable due $15,000.
6. Repair services performed during January: for cash $5,000; on account $9,000.
7. Wages for January, paid in cash, $3,000.
8. Dividends during January were $2,000.

Instructions

(a) Open T-accounts for each of the accounts listed in the trial balance, and enter the opening balances for 2014.

(b) Prepare journal entries to record each of the January transactions. (Omit explanations.)

(c) Post the journal entries to the accounts in the ledger. (Add accounts as needed.)

(d) Prepare a trial balance as of January 31, 2014.

Trial balance totals $63,000

P2-4A The trial balance of the Garland Company shown below does not balance.

Prepare a correct trial balance.

(LO 7)

Garland Company
Trial Balance
May 31, 2014

	Debit	Credit
Cash	$ 3,850	
Accounts Receivable		$ 2,750
Prepaid Insurance	700	
Equipment	12,000	
Accounts Payable		4,500
Unearned Service Revenue	560	
Common Stock		11,700
Service Revenue	8,690	
Salaries and Wages Expense	4,200	
Advertising Expense		1,100
Utilities Expense	800	
	$30,800	$20,050

Your review of the ledger reveals that each account has a normal balance. You also discover the following errors.

1. The totals of the debit sides of Prepaid Insurance, Accounts Payable, and Utilities Expense were each understated $100.

2. Transposition errors were made in Accounts Receivable and Service Revenue. Based on postings made, the correct balances were $2,570 and $8,960, respectively.

3. A debit posting to Salaries and Wages Expense of $200 was omitted.

4. A $1,000 cash dividend was debited to Common Stock for $1,000 and credited to Cash for $1,000.

5. A $520 purchase of supplies on account was debited to Equipment for $520 and credited to Cash for $520.

6. A cash payment of $450 for advertising was debited to Advertising Expense for $45 and credited to Cash for $45.

7. A collection from a customer for $420 was debited to Cash for $420 and credited to Accounts Payable for $420.

Instructions

Prepare a correct trial balance. Note that the chart of accounts includes the following: Dividends and Supplies. (*Hint:* It helps to prepare the correct journal entry for the transaction described and compare it to the mistake made.)

Trial balance totals $26,720

P2-5A The Classic Theater opened on April 1. All facilities were completed on March 31. At this time, the ledger showed No. 101 Cash $6,000, No. 140 Land $10,000, No. 145 Buildings (concession stand, projection room, ticket booth, and screen) $8,000, No. 157 Equipment $6,000, No. 201 Accounts Payable $2,000, No. 275 Mortgage Payable $8,000, and No. 311 Common Stock $20,000. During April, the following events and transactions occurred.

Journalize transactions, post, and prepare a trial balance.

(LO 2, 4, 6, 7)

Apr. 2 Paid film rental of $800 on first movie.

  3 Ordered two additional films at $1,000 each.

  9 Received $1,800 cash from admissions.

  10 Made $2,000 payment on mortgage and $1,000 for accounts payable due.

  11 Classic Theater contracted with D. Zarle Company to operate the concession stand. Zarle is to pay 18% of gross concession receipts (payable monthly) for the rental of the concession stand.

  12 Paid advertising expenses $300.

20   Received one of the films ordered on April 3 and was billed $1,000. The film will be shown in April.

25   Received $5,200 cash from admissions.

29   Paid salaries $1,600.

30   Received statement from D. Zarle showing gross concession receipts of $1,000 and the balance due to The Classic Theater of $180 ($1,000 × 18%) for April. Zarle paid one-half of the balance due and will remit the remainder on May 5.

30   Prepaid $900 rental on special film to be run in May.

In addition to the accounts identified above, the chart of accounts shows No. 112 Accounts Receivable, No. 136 Prepaid Rent, No. 400 Service Revenue, No. 429 Rent Revenue, No. 610 Advertising Expense, No. 726 Salaries and Wages Expense, and No. 729 Rent Expense.

Trial balance totals $35,180

Instructions

(a) Enter the beginning balances in the ledger as of April 1. Insert a check mark (✓) in the reference column of the ledger for the beginning balance.

(b) Journalize the April transactions.

(c) Post the April journal entries to the ledger. Assume that all entries are posted from page 1 of the journal.

(d) Prepare a trial balance on April 30, 2014.

PROBLEMS: SET B

Journalize a series of transactions.

(LO 2, 4)

P2-1B Surepar Disc Golf Course was opened on March 1 by Bill Arnsdorf. The following selected events and transactions occurred during March:

Mar. 1   Invested $60,000 cash in the business in exchange for common stock.

3   Purchased Lee's Golf Land for $38,000 cash. The price consists of land $23,000, shed $9,000, and equipment $6,000. (Make one compound entry.)

5   Advertised the opening of the driving range and miniature golf course, paying advertising expenses of $1,600.

6   Paid cash $2,400 for a one-year insurance policy.

10   Purchased golf discs and other equipment for $1,050 from Parton Company payable in 30 days.

18   Received $340 in cash for golf fees earned.

19   Sold 100 coupon books for $18 each. Each book contains 4 coupons that enable the holder to play one round of disc golf.

25   Declared and paid an $800 cash dividend.

30   Paid salaries of $250.

30   Paid Parton Company in full.

31   Received $200 cash for fees earned.

Bill Arnsdorf uses the following accounts: Cash, Prepaid Insurance, Land, Buildings, Equipment, Accounts Payable, Unearned Service Revenue, Common Stock, Dividends, Service Revenue, Advertising Expense, and Salaries and Wages Expense.

Instructions

Journalize the March transactions.

Journalize transactions, post, and prepare a trial balance.

(LO 2, 4, 6, 7)

P2-2B Judi Dench is a licensed dentist. During the first month of the operation of her business, the following events and transactions occurred.

April 1   Stockholders invested $40,000 cash in exchange for common stock.

1   Hired a secretary-receptionist at a salary of $600 per week payable monthly.

2   Paid office rent for the month $1,400.

3   Purchased dental supplies on account from Halo Company $5,200.

10   Provided dental services and billed insurance companies $6,600.

11   Received $1,000 cash advance from Rich Welk for an implant.

20   Received $2,100 cash for services completed and delivered to Phil Stueben.

30   Paid secretary-receptionist for the month $2,400.

30   Paid $1,900 to Halo Company for accounts payable due.

Judi uses the following chart of accounts: No. 101 Cash, No. 112 Accounts Receivable, No. 126 Supplies, No. 201 Accounts Payable, No. 209 Unearned Service Revenue, No. 311 Common Stock, No. 400 Service Revenue, No. 726 Salaries and Wages Expense, and No. 729 Rent Expense.

Instructions

(a) Journalize the transactions.

(b) Post to the ledger accounts.

(c) Prepare a trial balance on April 30, 2014.

Trial balance totals $53,000

P2-3B Chamberlain Services was formed on May 1, 2014. The following transactions took place during the first month.

Journalize transactions, post, and prepare a trial balance.

(LO 2, 4, 6, 7)

Transactions on May 1:

1. Stockholders invested $50,000 cash in exchange for common stock.
2. Hired two employees to work in the warehouse. They will each be paid a salary of $2,800 per month.
3. Signed a 2-year rental agreement on a warehouse; paid $24,000 cash in advance for the first year.
4. Purchased furniture and equipment costing $30,000. A cash payment of $8,000 was made immediately; the remainder will be paid in 6 months.
5. Paid $1,800 cash for a one-year insurance policy on the furniture and equipment.

Transactions during the remainder of the month:

6. Purchased basic office supplies for $750 cash.
7. Purchased more office supplies for $1,300 on account.
8. Total revenues earned were $20,000—$8,000 cash and $12,000 on account.
9. Paid $400 to suppliers for accounts payable due.
10. Received $3,000 from customers in payment of accounts receivable.
11. Received utility bills in the amount of $260, to be paid next month.
12. Paid the monthly salaries of the two employees, totalling $5,600.

Instructions

(a) Prepare journal entries to record each of the events listed. (Omit explanations.)

(b) Post the journal entries to T-accounts.

(c) Prepare a trial balance as of May 31, 2014.

Trial balance totals $93,160

P2-4B The trial balance of Ron Salem Co. shown below does not balance.

Prepare a correct trial balance.

(LO 7)

Ron Salem Co.
Trial Balance
June 30, 2014

	Debit	Credit
Cash		$ 3,840
Accounts Receivable	$ 2,898	
Supplies	800	
Equipment	3,000	
Accounts Payable		2,666
Unearned Service Revenue	2,200	
Common Stock		9,000
Dividends	800	
Service Revenue		2,380
Salaries and Wages Expense	3,400	
Utilities Expense	910	
	$14,008	$17,886

Each of the listed accounts has a normal balance per the general ledger. An examination of the ledger and journal reveals the following errors.

1. Cash received from a customer in payment of its account was debited for $570, and Accounts Receivable was credited for the same amount. The actual collection was for $750.
2. The purchase of a computer on account for $620 was recorded as a debit to Supplies for $620 and a credit to Accounts Payable for $620.
3. Services were performed on account for a client for $890. Accounts Receivable was debited for $890, and Service Revenue was credited for $89.
4. A debit posting to Salaries and Wages Expense of $700 was omitted.
5. A payment of a balance due for $309 was credited to Cash for $309 and credited to Accounts Payable for $390.
6. The payment of a $600 cash dividend was debited to Salaries and Wages Expense for $600 and credited to Cash for $600.

Trial balance totals $16,348

Journalize transactions, post, and prepare a trial balance.

(LO 2, 4, 6, 7)

Instructions

Prepare a correct trial balance. (*Hint:* It helps to prepare the correct journal entry for the transaction described and compare it to the mistake made.)

P2-5B The Russo Theater, owned by Alan Russo, will begin operations in March. The Russo will be unique in that it will show only triple features of sequential theme movies. As of March 1, the ledger of Russo showed No. 101 Cash $8,000, No. 140 Land $21,000, No. 145 Buildings (concession stand, projection room, ticket booth, and screen) $10,000, No. 157 Equipment $8,000, No. 201 Accounts Payable $7,000, and No. 311 Common Stock $40,000. During the month of March, the following events and transactions occurred.

Mar.   2   Rented the three *Indiana Jones* movies to be shown for the first 3 weeks of March. The film rental was $3,500; $1,000 was paid in cash and $2,500 will be paid on March 10.

     3   Ordered the *Lord of the Rings* movies to be shown the last 10 days of March. It will cost $240 per night.

     9   Received $4,000 cash from admissions.

    10   Paid balance due on *Indiana Jones* movies rental and $1,600 on March 1 accounts payable.

    11   Russo Theater contracted with M. Brewer to operate the concession stand. Brewer is to pay 15% of gross concession receipts (payable monthly) for the right to operate the concession stand.

    12   Paid advertising expenses $450.

    20   Received $5,000 cash from customers for admissions.

    20   Received the *Lord of Rings* movies and paid the rental fee of $2,400.

    31   Paid salaries of $2,500.

    31   Received statement from M. Brewer showing gross receipts from concessions of $5,000 and the balance due to Russo Theater of $750 ($5,000 × 15%) for March. Brewer paid one-half the balance due and will remit the remainder on April 5.

    31   Received $9,000 cash from customers for admissions.

In addition to the accounts identified above, the chart of accounts includes No. 112 Accounts Receivable, No. 400 Service Revenue, No. 429 Rent Revenue, No. 610 Advertising Expense, No. 729 Rent Expense, and No. 726 Salaries and Wages Expense.

Instructions

(a) Enter the beginning balances in the ledger. Insert a check mark (✓) in the reference column of the ledger for the beginning balance.

(b) Journalize the March transactions.

(c) Post the March journal entries to the ledger. Assume that all entries are posted from page 1 of the journal.

Trial balance totals $64,150   (d) Prepare a trial balance on March 31, 2014.

PROBLEMS: SET C

Visit the book's companion website, at **www.wiley.com/college/weygandt**, and choose the Student Companion site to access Problem Set C.

CONTINUING COOKIE CHRONICLE

(*Note:* This is a continuation of the Cookie Chronicle from Chapter 1.)

CCC2 After researching the different forms of business organization, Natalie Koebel decides to operate "Cookie Creations" as a corporation. She then starts the process of getting the business running. In November 2014, the following activities take place.

Nov.   8   Natalie cashes her U.S. Savings Bonds and receives $520, which she deposits in her personal bank account.

     8   She opens a bank account under the name "Cookie Creations" and transfers $500 from her personal account to the new account in exchange for common stock.

11   Natalie pays $65 to have advertising brochures and posters printed. She plans to distribute these as opportunities arise. (*Hint:* Use Advertising Expense.)

13   She buys baking supplies, such as flour, sugar, butter, and chocolate chips, for $125 cash.

14   Natalie starts to gather some baking equipment to take with her when teaching the cookie classes. She has an excellent top-of-the-line food processor and mixer that originally cost her $750. Natalie decides to start using it only in her new business. She estimates that the equipment is currently worth $300. She invests the equipment in the business in exchange for common stock.

16   Natalie realizes that her initial cash investment is not enough. Her grandmother lends her $2,000 cash, for which Natalie signs a note payable in the name of the business. Natalie deposits the money in the business bank account. (*Hint:* The note does not have to be repaid for 24 months. As a result, the notes payable should be reported in the accounts as the last liability and also on the balance sheet as the last liability.)

17   She buys more baking equipment for $900 cash.

20   She teaches her first class and collects $125 cash.

25   Natalie books a second class for December 4 for $150. She receives $30 cash in advance as a down payment.

30   Natalie pays $1,320 for a one-year insurance policy that will expire on December 1, 2015.

Instructions

(a) Prepare journal entries to record the November transactions.
(b) Post the journal entries to general ledger accounts.
(c) Prepare a trial balance at November 30.

Broadening Your PERSPECTIVE

Financial Reporting and Analysis

Financial Reporting Problem: PepsiCo, Inc.

BYP2-1 The financial statements of PepsiCo, Inc. are presented in Appendix A. The notes accompanying the statements contain the following selected accounts, stated in millions of dollars.

Accounts Payable	Income Taxes Payable
Accounts Receivable	Interest Expense
Property, Plant, and Equipment	Inventory

Instructions

(a) Answer the following questions.
   (1) What is the increase and decrease side for each account?
   (2) What is the normal balance for each account?
(b) Identify the probable other account in the transaction and the effect on that account when:
   (1) Accounts Receivable is decreased.
   (2) Accounts Payable is decreased.
   (3) Inventory is increased.
(c) Identify the other account(s) that ordinarily would be involved when:
   (1) Interest Expense is increased.
   (2) Property, Plant, and Equipment is increased.

Comparative Analysis Problem: PepsiCo, Inc. vs. The Coca-Cola Company

BYP2-2 PepsiCo's financial statements are presented in Appendix A. Financial statements of The Coca-Cola Company are presented in Appendix B.

Instructions

(a) Based on the information contained in the financial statements, determine the normal balance of the listed accounts for each company.

Pepsi	Coca-Cola
1. Inventory	1. Accounts Receivable
2. Property, Plant, and Equipment	2. Cash and Cash Equivalents
3. Accounts Payable	3. Cost of Goods Sold (expense)
4. Interest Expense	4. Sales (revenue)

(b) Identify the other account ordinarily involved when:
   (1) Accounts Receivable is increased.
   (2) Salaries and Wages Payable is decreased.
   (3) Property, Plant, and Equipment is increased.
   (4) Interest Expense is increased.

Real-World Focus

BYP2-3 Much information about specific companies is available on the Internet. Such information includes basic descriptions of the company's location, activities, industry, financial health, and financial performance.

Address: **biz.yahoo.com/i,** or go to **www.wiley.com/college/weygandt**

Steps

1. Type in a company name, or use index to find company name.
2. Choose **Profile**. Perform instructions (a)–(c) below.
3. Click on the company's specific industry to identify competitors. Perform instructions (d)–(g) below.

Instructions

Answer the following questions.

(a) What is the company's industry?
(b) What was the company's total sales?
(c) What was the company's net income?
(d) What are the names of four of the company's competitors?
(e) Choose one of these competitors.
(f) What is this competitor's name? What were its sales? What was its net income?
(g) Which of these two companies is larger by size of sales? Which one reported higher net income?

Critical Thinking

Decision-Making Across the Organization

BYP2-4 Amy Torbert operates Hollins Riding Academy. The academy's primary sources of revenue are riding fees and lesson fees, which are paid on a cash basis. Amy also boards horses for owners, who are billed monthly for boarding fees. In a few cases, boarders pay in advance of expected use. For its revenue transactions, the academy maintains the following accounts: No. 1 Cash, No. 5 Boarding Accounts Receivable, No. 27 Unearned Boarding Revenue, No. 51 Riding Revenue, No. 52 Lesson Revenue, and No. 53 Boarding Revenue.

The academy owns 10 horses, a stable, a riding corral, riding equipment, and office equipment. These assets are accounted for in accounts No. 11 Horses, No. 12 Building, No. 13 Riding Corral, No. 14 Riding Equipment, and No. 15 Office Equipment.

For its expenses, the academy maintains the following accounts: No. 6 Hay and Feed Supplies, No. 7 Prepaid Insurance, No. 21 Accounts Payable, No. 60 Salaries Expense, No. 61 Advertising Expense, No. 62 Utilities Expense, No. 63 Veterinary Expense, No. 64 Hay and Feed Expense, and No. 65 Insurance Expense.

Amy makes periodic payments of cash dividends to stockholders. To record stockholders' equity in the business and dividends, Torbert maintains three accounts: No. 50 Common Stock, No. 51 Retained Earnings, and No. 52 Dividends.

During the first month of operations, an inexperienced bookkeeper was employed. Amy Torbert asks you to review the following eight entries of the 50 entries made during the month. In each case, the explanation for the entry is correct.

May 1	Cash	18,000	
	Common Stock		18,000
	(Invested $18,000 cash in exchange for stock)		
5	Cash	250	
	Riding Revenue		250
	(Received $250 cash for lessons provided)		
7	Cash	500	
	Boarding Revenue		500
	(Received $500 for boarding of horses beginning June 1)		
14	Riding Equipment	80	
	Cash		800
	(Purchased desk and other office equipment for $800 cash)		
15	Salaries Expense	440	
	Cash		440
	(Issued dividend checks to stockholders)		
20	Cash	148	
	Riding Revenue		184
	(Received $184 cash for riding fees)		
30	Veterinary Expense	75	
	Accounts Payable		75
	(Received bill of $75 from veterinarian for services rendered)		
31	Hay and Feed Expense	1,500	
	Cash		1,500
	(Purchased an estimated 2 months' supply of feed and hay for $1,700 on account)		

Instructions

With the class divided into groups, answer the following.

(a) Identify each journal entry that is correct. For each journal entry that is incorrect, prepare the entry that should have been made by the bookkeeper.

(b) Which of the incorrect entries would prevent the trial balance from balancing?

(c) What was the correct net income for May, assuming the bookkeeper reported net income of $4,600 after posting all 50 entries?

(d) What was the correct cash balance at May 31, assuming the bookkeeper reported a balance of $12,475 after posting all 50 entries (and the only errors occurred in the items listed above)?

Communication Activity

BYP2-5 Shandler's Maid Company offers home cleaning service. Two recurring transactions for the company are billing customers for services rendered and paying employee salaries. For example, on March 15, bills totaling $6,000 were sent to customers and $2,000 was paid in salaries to employees.

Instructions

Write a memo to your instructor that explains and illustrates the steps in the recording process for each of the March 15 transactions. Use the format illustrated in the text under the heading, "The Recording Process Illustrated" (page 66).

Ethics Case

BYP2-6 Sara Rankin is the assistant chief accountant at Hokey Company, a manufacturer of computer chips and cellular phones. The company presently has total sales of $20 million. It is the end of the first quarter. Sara is hurriedly trying to prepare a general ledger trial balance so that quarterly financial statements can be prepared and released to management and the regulatory agencies. The total credits on the trial balance exceed the debits by $1,000. In order to meet the 4 p.m. deadline, Sara decides to force the debits and credits into balance by adding the amount of the difference to the Equipment account. She chose Equipment because it is one of the larger account balances; percentage-wise, it will be the least misstated. Sara "plugs" the difference! She believes that the difference will not affect anyone's decisions. She wishes that she had another few days to find the error but realizes that the financial statements are already late.

Instructions
(a) Who are the stakeholders in this situation?
(b) What are the ethical issues involved in this case?
(c) What are Sara's alternatives?

All About You

BYP2-7 Every company needs to plan in order to move forward. Its top management must consider where it wants the company to be in three to five years. Like a company, you need to think about where you want to be three to five years from now, and you need to start taking steps now in order to get there.

Instructions
Provide responses to each of the following items.
(a) Where would you like to be working in three to five years? Describe your plan for getting there by identifying between five and 10 specific steps that you need to take in order to get there.
(b) In order to get the job you want, you will need a résumé. Your résumé is the equivalent of a company's annual report. It needs to provide relevant and reliable information about your past accomplishments so that employers can decide whether to "invest" in you. Do a search on the Internet to find a good résumé format. What are the basic elements of a résumé?
(c) A company's annual report provides information about a company's accomplishments. In order for investors to use the annual report, the information must be reliable; that is, users must have faith that the information is accurate and believable. How can you provide assurance that the information on your résumé is reliable?
(d) Prepare a résumé assuming that you have accomplished the five to 10 specific steps you identified in part (a). Also, provide evidence that would give assurance that the information is reliable.

BYP2-8 If you haven't already done so, in the not-too-distant future you will prepare a résumé. In some ways, your résumé is like a company's annual report. Its purpose is to enable others to evaluate your past, in an effort to predict your future.

A résumé is your opportunity to create a positive first impression. It is important that it be impressive—but it should also be accurate. In order to increase their job prospects, some people are tempted to "inflate" their résumés by overstating the importance of some past accomplishments or positions. In fact, you might even think that "everybody does it" and that if you don't do it, you will be at a disadvantage.

David Edmondson, the president and CEO of well-known electronics retailer Radio Shack, overstated his accomplishments by claiming that he had earned a bachelor's of science degree, when in fact he had not. Apparently, his employer had not done a background check to ensure the accuracy of his résumé. Should Radio Shack have fired him?

YES: Radio Shack is a publicly traded company. Investors, creditors, employees, and others doing business with the company will not trust it if its leader is known to have poor integrity. The "tone at the top" is vital to creating an ethical organization.

NO: Mr. Edmondson had been a Radio Shack employee for 11 years. He had served the company in a wide variety of positions, and had earned the position of CEO through exceptional performance. While the fact that he lied 11 years earlier on his résumé was unfortunate, his service since then made this past transgression irrelevant. In addition, the company was in the midst of a massive restructuring, which included closing 700 of its 7,000 stores. It could not afford additional upheaval at this time.

Instructions
Write a response indicating your position regarding this situation. Provide support for your view.

Answers to Chapter Questions

Answers to Insight and Accounting Across the Organization Questions

p. 58 Keeping Score Q: Do you think that the Chicago Bears football team would be likely to have the same major revenue and expense accounts as the Cubs? **A:** Because their businesses are similar—professional sports—many of the revenue and expense accounts for the baseball and football teams might be similar.

p. 63 What Would Sam Do? Q: Why did Sam Walton keep separate pigeonholes and blue binders? **A:** Using separate pigeonholes and blue binders for each store enabled Walton to accumulate and track the performance of each individual store easily. **Q:** Why bother to keep separate records for each store? **A:** Keeping separate records for each store provided Walton with more information about performance of individual stores and managers, and greater control. Walton would want and need the same advantages if he were starting his business today. The difference is that he might now use a computerized system for small businesses.

p. 75 Why Accuracy Matters Q: In order for these companies to prepare and issue financial statements, their accounting equations (debits and credits) must have been in balance at year-end. How could these errors or misstatements have occurred? **A:** A company's accounting equation (its books) can be in balance yet its financial statements have errors or misstatements because of the following: entire transactions were not recorded; transactions were recorded at wrong amounts; transactions were recorded in the wrong accounts; transactions were recorded in the wrong accounting period. Audits of financial statements uncover some, but obviously not all, errors or misstatements.

Answers to Self-Test Questions

1. b **2.** c **3.** d **4.** d **5.** d **6.** b **7.** a **8.** c **9.** b **10.** c **11.** d **12.** c ($16,000 − $5,000)
13. a **14.** c **15.** a ($5,000 + $40,000 + $10,000 + $15,000 + $61,000)

A Look at IFRS

International companies use the same set of procedures and records to keep track of transaction data. Thus, the material in Chapter 2 dealing with the account, general rules of debit and credit, and steps in the recording process—the journal, ledger, chart of accounts, and trial balance—is the same under both GAAP and IFRS.

Key Points

- Transaction analysis is the same under IFRS and GAAP but, as you will see in later chapters, different standards sometimes impact how transactions are recorded.

- Rules for accounting for specific events sometimes differ across countries. For example, European companies rely less on historical cost and more on fair value than U.S. companies. Despite the differences, the double-entry accounting system is the basis of accounting systems worldwide.

- Both the IASB and FASB go beyond the basic definitions provided in this textbook for the key elements of financial statements, that is, assets, liabilities, equity, revenues, and expenses. The more substantive definitions, using the IASB definitional structure, are provided in the Chapter 1 *A Look at IFRS* discussion.

- A trial balance under IFRS follows the same format as shown in the textbook.

- As shown in the textbook, dollars signs are typically used only in the trial balance and the financial statements. The same practice is followed under IFRS, using the currency sign of the country that the reporting company is headquartered.

- In February 2010, the SEC expressed a desire to continue working toward a single set of high-quality standards. In deciding whether the United States should adopt IFRS, some of the issues the SEC said should be considered are:

  ♦ Whether IFRS is sufficiently developed and consistent in application.

  ♦ Whether the IASB is sufficiently independent.

  ♦ Whether IFRS is established for the benefit of investors.

  ♦ The issues involved in educating investors about IFRS.

  ♦ The impact of a switch to IFRS on U.S. laws and regulations.

  ♦ The impact on companies including changes to their accounting systems, contractual arrangements, corporate governance, and litigation.

  ♦ The issues involved in educating accountants, so they can prepare statements under IFRS.

Looking to the Future

The basic recording process shown in this textbook is followed by companies across the globe. It is unlikely to change in the future. The definitional structure of assets, liabilities, equity, revenues, and expenses may change over time as the IASB and FASB evaluate their overall conceptual framework for establishing accounting standards.

IFRS Practice

IFRS Self-Test Questions

1. Which statement is *correct* regarding IFRS?
   (a) IFRS reverses the rules of debits and credits, that is, debits are on the right and credits are on the left.
   (b) IFRS uses the same process for recording transactions as GAAP.
   (c) The chart of accounts under IFRS is different because revenues follow assets.
   (d) None of the above statements are correct.

2. The expanded accounting equation under IFRS is as follows:
   (a) Assets = Liabilities + Common Stock + Retained Earnings + Dividends + Revenues − Expenses.
   (b) Assets + Liabilities = Common Stock + Retained Earnings − Dividends + Revenues − Expenses.
   (c) Assets = Liabilities + Common Stock + Retained Earnings − Dividends + Revenues − Expenses.
   (d) Assets = Liabilities + Common Stock + Retained Earnings − Dividends − Revenues − Expenses.

3. A trial balance:
   (a) is the same under IFRS and GAAP.
   (b) proves that transactions are recorded correctly.
   (c) proves that all transactions have been recorded.
   (d) will not balance if a correct journal entry is posted twice.

4. One difference between IFRS and GAAP is that:
   (a) GAAP uses accrual-accounting concepts and IFRS uses primarily the cash basis of accounting.
   (b) IFRS uses a different posting process than GAAP.
   (c) IFRS uses more fair value measurements than GAAP.
   (d) the limitations of a trial balance are different between IFRS and GAAP.

5. The general policy for using proper currency signs (dollar, yen, pound, etc.) is the same for both IFRS and this textbook. This policy is as follows:
   (a) Currency signs only appear in ledgers and journal entries.
   (b) Currency signs are only shown in the trial balance.
   (c) Currency signs are shown for all compound journal entries.
   (d) Currency signs are shown in trial balances and financial statements.

IFRS Exercise

IFRS2-1 Describe some of the issues the SEC must consider in deciding whether the United States should adopt IFRS.

International Financial Reporting Problem: Zetar plc

IFRS2-2 The financial statements of Zetar plc are presented in Appendix C. The company's complete annual report, including the notes to its financial statements, is available at *www.zetarplc.com*.

Instructions

Describe in which statement each of the following items is reported, and the position in the statement (e.g., current asset).

(a) Other administrative expenses.

(b) Cash at bank.

(c) Borrowings and overdrafts.

(d) Finance costs.

Answers to IFRS Self-Test Questions

1. b **2.** c **3.** a **4.** c **5.** d

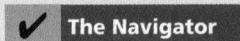
✔ **The Navigator**

Chapter 3

Adjusting the Accounts

Feature Story

What Was Your Profit?

The accuracy of the financial reporting system depends on answers to a few fundamental questions: At what point has revenue been recognized? At what point is the earnings process complete? When have expenses really been incurred?

During the 1990s, the stock prices of dot-com companies boomed. Most dot-coms earned most of their revenue from selling advertising space on their websites. To boost reported revenue, some dot-coms began swapping website ad space. Company A would put an ad for its website on company B's website, and company B would put an ad for its website on company A's website. No money changed hands, but each company recorded revenue (for the value of the space that it gave the other company on its site). This practice did little to boost net income, and it resulted in no additional cash flow—but it did boost *reported revenue*. Regulators eventually put an end to this misleading practice.

Another type of transgression results from companies recording revenues or expenses in the wrong year. In fact, shifting revenues and expenses is one of the most common abuses of financial accounting. Xerox admitted reporting billions of dollars of lease revenue in periods earlier than it should have been reported. And

---

Learning Objectives

After studying this chapter, you should be able to:

1 Explain the time period assumption.

2 Explain the accrual basis of accounting.

3 Explain the reasons for adjusting entries.

4 Identify the major types of adjusting entries.

5 Prepare adjusting entries for deferrals.

6 Prepare adjusting entries for accruals.

7 Describe the nature and purpose of an adjusted trial balance.

 ✔ **The Navigator**

WorldCom stunned the financial markets with its admission that it had boosted net income by billions of dollars by delaying the recognition of expenses until later years.

Unfortunately, revelations such as these have become all too common in the corporate world. It is no wonder that a U.S. Trust survey of affluent Americans reported that 85% of respondents believed that there should be tighter regulation of financial disclosures; 66% said they did not trust the management of publicly traded companies.

Why did so many companies violate basic financial reporting rules and sound ethics? Many speculate that as stock prices climbed, executives were under increasing pressure to meet higher and higher earnings expectations. If actual results weren't as good as hoped for, some gave in to temptation and "adjusted" their numbers to meet market expectations.

✔ **The Navigator**

Preview of **Chapter 3**

In Chapter 1, you learned a neat little formula: Net income = Revenues − Expenses. In Chapter 2, you learned some rules for recording revenue and expense transactions. Guess what? Things are not really that nice and neat. In fact, it is often difficult for companies to determine in what time period they should report some revenues and expenses. In other words, in measuring net income, timing is everything.

The content and organization of Chapter 3 are as follows.

ADJUSTING THE ACCOUNTS		
Timing Issues	**The Basics of Adjusting Entries**	**The Adjusted Trial Balance and Financial Statements**
• Fiscal and calendar years • Accrual- vs. cash-basis accounting • Recognizing revenues and expenses	• Types of adjusting entries • Adjusting entries for deferrals • Adjusting entries for accruals • Summary of basic relationships	• Preparing the adjusted trial balance • Preparing financial statements

✔ **The Navigator**

Timing Issues

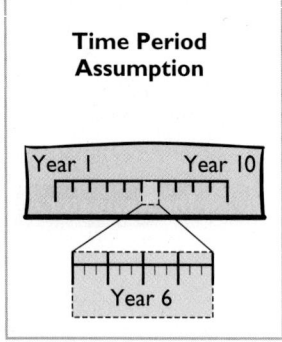

Time Period Assumption

Year I   Year 10

Year 6

Alternative Terminology
The time period assumption is also called the *periodicity assumption.*

We would need no adjustments if we could wait to prepare financial statements until a company ended its operations. At that point, we could easily determine its final balance sheet and the amount of lifetime income it earned.

However, most companies need immediate feedback about how well they are doing. For example, management usually wants monthly financial statements, and the Internal Revenue Service requires all businesses to file annual tax returns. Therefore, **accountants divide the economic life of a business into artificial time periods**. This convenient assumption is referred to as the **time period assumption.**

Many business transactions affect more than one of these arbitrary time periods. For example, the airplanes purchased by Southwest Airlines five years ago are still in use today. We must determine the relevance of each business transaction to specific accounting periods. (How much of the cost of an airplane contributed to operations this year?)

Fiscal and Calendar Years

Both small and large companies prepare financial statements periodically in order to assess their financial condition and results of operations. **Accounting time periods are generally a month, a quarter, or a year.** Monthly and quarterly time periods are called **interim periods.** Most large companies must prepare both quarterly and annual financial statements.

An accounting time period that is one year in length is a **fiscal year**. A fiscal year usually begins with the first day of a month and ends twelve months later on the last day of a month. Most businesses use the **calendar year** (January 1 to December 31) as their accounting period. Some do not. Companies whose fiscal year differs from the calendar year include Delta Air Lines, June 30, and Walt Disney Productions, September 30. Sometimes a company's year-end will vary from year to year. For example, PepsiCo's fiscal year ends on the Friday closest to December 31, which was December 29 in 2009 and December 31 in 2010.

Accrual- versus Cash-Basis Accounting

What you will learn in this chapter is **accrual-basis accounting.** Under the accrual basis, companies record transactions that change a company's financial statements **in the periods in which the events occur.** For example, using the accrual basis to determine net income means companies recognize revenues when they actually perform the services (rather than when they receive cash). It also means recognizing expenses when incurred (rather than when paid).

An alternative to the accrual basis is the cash basis. Under **cash-basis accounting**, companies record revenue when they receive cash. They record an expense when they pay out cash. The cash basis seems appealing due to its simplicity, but it often produces misleading financial statements. It fails to record revenue for a company that has provided services but for which it has not received the cash. As a result, it does not match expenses with earned revenues. **Cash-basis accounting is not in accordance with generally accepted accounting principles (GAAP).**

Individuals and some small companies do use cash-basis accounting. The cash basis is justified for small businesses because they often have few receivables and payables. Medium and large companies use accrual-basis accounting.

Recognizing Revenues and Expenses

It can be difficult to determine the amount of revenues and expenses to report in a given accounting period. Two principles help in this task: the revenue recognition principle and the expense recognition principle.

REVENUE RECOGNITION PRINCIPLE

When a company agrees to perform a service or sell a product to a customer, it has a performance obligation. When the company meets this performance obligation, it recognizes revenue. The **revenue recognition principle** therefore requires that companies recognize revenue in the accounting period in which the performance obligation is satisfied.[1] To illustrate, assume that Dave's Dry Cleaning cleans clothing on June 30, but customers do not claim and pay for their clothes until the first week of July. Under the revenue recognition principle, Dave's recognizes revenue in June when it performed the service, rather than in July when it received the cash. At June 30, Dave's would report a receivable on its balance sheet and revenue in its income statement for the service performed.

EXPENSE RECOGNITION PRINCIPLE

Accountants follow a simple rule in recognizing expenses: "Let the expenses follow the revenues." Thus, expense recognition is tied to revenue recognition. In the dry cleaning example, this means that Dave's should report the salary expense incurred in performing the June 30 cleaning service in the same period in which it recognizes the service revenue. The critical issue in expense recognition is when the expense makes its contribution to revenue. This may or may not be the same period in which the expense is paid. If Dave's does not pay the salary incurred on June 30 until July, it would report salaries payable on its June 30 balance sheet.

This practice of expense recognition is referred to as the **expense recognition principle** (often referred to as the **matching principle**). It dictates that efforts (expenses) be matched with results (revenues). Illustration 3-1 summarizes the revenue and expense recognition principles.

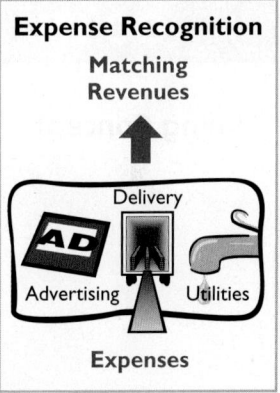

Revenue Recognition

Revenue should be recognized in the accounting period in which services are performed.

Expense Recognition

Illustration 3-1
GAAP relationships in revenue and expense recognition

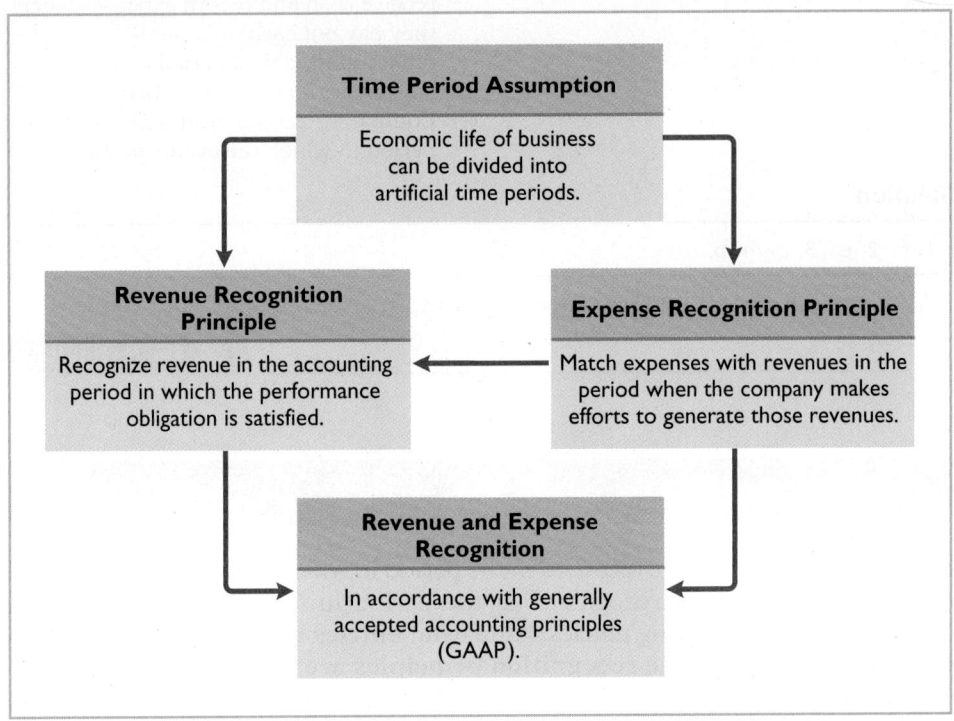

Time Period Assumption

Economic life of business can be divided into artificial time periods.

Revenue Recognition Principle

Recognize revenue in the accounting period in which the performance obligation is satisfied.

Expense Recognition Principle

Match expenses with revenues in the period when the company makes efforts to generate those revenues.

Revenue and Expense Recognition

In accordance with generally accepted accounting principles (GAAP).

---

[1]The defination for the revenue recognitions principle is based on the revised exposure draft issued by the FASB.

ETHICS INSIGHT

Cooking the Books?

Allegations of abuse of the revenue recognition principle have become all too common in recent years. For example, it was alleged that Krispy Kreme sometimes doubled the number of doughnuts shipped to wholesale customers at the end of a quarter to boost quarterly results. The customers shipped the unsold doughnuts back after the beginning of the next quarter for a refund. Conversely, Computer Associates International was accused of backdating sales—that is, saying that a sale that occurred at the beginning of one quarter occurred at the end of the previous quarter in order to achieve the previous quarter's sales targets.

? What motivates sales executives and finance and accounting executives to participate in activities that result in inaccurate reporting of revenues? (See page 158.)

> DO IT!

Timing Concepts

Numerous timing concepts are discussed on pages 102–103. A list of concepts is provided in the left column below, with a description of the concept in the right column below. There are more descriptions provided than concepts. Match the description of the concept to the concept.

1. ____Accrual-basis accounting.
2. ____Calendar year.
3. ____Time period assumption.
4. ____Expense recognition principle.

(a) Monthly and quarterly time periods.
(b) Efforts (expenses) should be matched with results (revenues).
(c) Accountants divide the economic life of a business into artificial time periods.
(d) Companies record revenues when they receive cash and record expenses when they pay out cash.
(e) An accounting time period that starts on January 1 and ends on December 31.
(f) Companies record transactions in the period in which the events occur.

Action Plan

✔ Review the glossary terms identified on pages 102–103 and 126.

✔ Study carefully the revenue recognition principle, the expense recognition principle, and the time period assumption.

Solution

1. f   2. e   3. c   4. b

Related exercise material: **E3-1, E3-2, E3-3, and** `DO IT!` **3-1.**

 ✔ **The Navigator**

The Basics of Adjusting Entries

LEARNING OBJECTIVE   3

Explain the reasons for adjusting entries.

In order for revenues to be recorded in the period in which services are performed, and for expenses to be recognized in the period in which they are incurred, companies make adjusting entries. **Adjusting entries ensure that the revenue recognition and expense recognition principles are followed.**

Adjusting entries are necessary because the **trial balance**—the first pulling together of the transaction data—may not contain up-to-date and complete data. This is true for several reasons:

1. Some events are not recorded daily because it is not efficient to do so. Examples are the use of supplies and the earning of wages by employees.

2. Some costs are not recorded during the accounting period because these costs expire with the passage of time rather than as a result of recurring daily transactions. Examples are charges related to the use of buildings and equipment, rent, and insurance.

3. Some items may be unrecorded. An example is a utility service bill that will not be received until the next accounting period.

Adjusting entries are required every time a company prepares financial statements. The company analyzes each account in the trial balance to determine whether it is complete and up to date for financial statement purposes. **Every adjusting entry will include one income statement account and one balance sheet account.**

International Note

Internal controls are a system of checks and balances designed to detect and prevent fraud and errors. The Sarbanes-Oxley Act requires U.S. companies to enhance their systems of internal control. However, many foreign companies do not have to meet strict internal control requirements. Some U.S. companies believe that this gives foreign firms an unfair advantage because developing and maintaining internal controls can be very expensive.

Types of Adjusting Entries

Adjusting entries are classified as either **deferrals** or **accruals**. As Illustration 3-2 shows, each of these classes has two subcategories.

LEARNING OBJECTIVE 4

Identify the major types of adjusting entries.

Illustration 3-2
Categories of adjusting entries

Deferrals:
1. Prepaid expenses: Expenses paid in cash before they are used or consumed.
2. Unearned revenues: Cash received before services are performed.

Accruals:
1. Accrued revenues: Revenues for services performed but not yet received in cash or recorded.
2. Accrued expenses: Expenses incurred but not yet paid in cash or recorded.

Subsequent sections give examples of each type of adjustment. Each example is based on the October 31 trial balance of Pioneer Advertising Agency Inc. from Chapter 2, reproduced in Illustration 3-3.

Illustration 3-3
Trial balance

Pioneer Advertising Agency Inc. Trial Balance October 31, 2014		
	Debit	**Credit**
Cash	$15,200	
Supplies	2,500	
Prepaid Insurance	600	
Equipment	5,000	
Notes Payable		$ 5,000
Accounts Payable		2,500
Unearned Service Revenue		1,200
Common Stock		10,000
Retained Earnings		–0–
Dividends	500	
Service Revenue		10,000
Salaries and Wages Expense	4,000	
Rent Expense	900	
	$28,700	$28,700

We assume that Pioneer Advertising uses an accounting period of one month. Thus, monthly adjusting entries are made. The entries are dated October 31.

Adjusting Entries for Deferrals

LEARNING OBJECTIVE   **5**

Prepare adjusting entries for deferrals.

To defer means to postpone or delay. **Deferrals** are costs or revenues that are recognized at a date later than the point when cash was originally exchanged. Companies make adjusting entries for deferrals to record the portion of the deferred item that was incurred as an expense or recognized as revenue during the current accounting period. The two types of deferrals are prepaid expenses and unearned revenues.

PREPAID EXPENSES

When companies record payments of expenses that will benefit more than one accounting period, they record an asset called **prepaid expenses** or **prepayments**. When expenses are prepaid, an asset account is increased (debited) to show the service or benefit that the company will receive in the future. Examples of common prepayments are insurance, supplies, advertising, and rent. In addition, companies make prepayments when they purchase buildings and equipment.

Prepaid expenses are costs that expire either with the passage of time (e.g., rent and insurance) **or through use** (e.g., supplies). The expiration of these costs does not require daily entries, which would be impractical and unnecessary. Accordingly, companies postpone the recognition of such cost expirations until they prepare financial statements. At each statement date, they make adjusting entries to record the expenses applicable to the current accounting period and to show the remaining amounts in the asset accounts.

Prior to adjustment, assets are overstated and expenses are understated. Therefore, as shown in Illustration 3-4, **an adjusting entry for prepaid expenses results in an increase (a debit) to an expense account and a decrease (a credit) to an asset account.**

Illustration 3-4
Adjusting entries for prepaid expenses

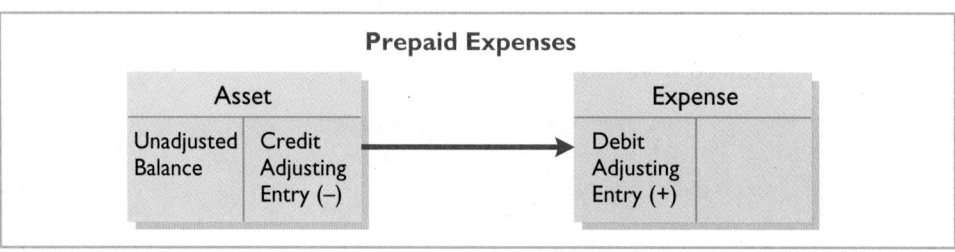

Prepaid Expenses

Asset		Expense	
Unadjusted Balance	Credit Adjusting Entry (−)	Debit Adjusting Entry (+)	

Supplies

Oct. 5

Supplies purchased; record asset

Pioneer Advertising Agency

Oct. 31
Supplies used; record supplies expense

Let's look in more detail at some specific types of prepaid expenses, beginning with supplies.

SUPPLIES The purchase of supplies, such as paper and envelopes, results in an increase (a debit) to an asset account. During the accounting period, the company uses supplies. Rather than record supplies expense as the supplies are used, companies recognize supplies expense at the **end** of the accounting period. At the end of the accounting period, the company counts the remaining supplies. The difference between the unadjusted balance in the Supplies (asset) account and the actual cost of supplies on hand represents the supplies used (an expense) for that period (page 107).

Recall from Chapter 2 that Pioneer Advertising Agency Inc. purchased supplies costing $2,500 on October 5. Pioneer recorded the purchase by increasing (debiting) the asset Supplies. This account shows a balance of $2,500 in the October 31 trial balance. An inventory count at the close of business on October 31 reveals that $1,000 of supplies are still on hand. Thus, the cost of supplies used is $1,500 ($2,500 − $1,000). This use of supplies decreases an asset, Supplies. It also decreases stockholders' equity by increasing an expense account, Supplies Expense. This is shown in Illustration 3-5.

Illustration 3-5
Adjustment for supplies

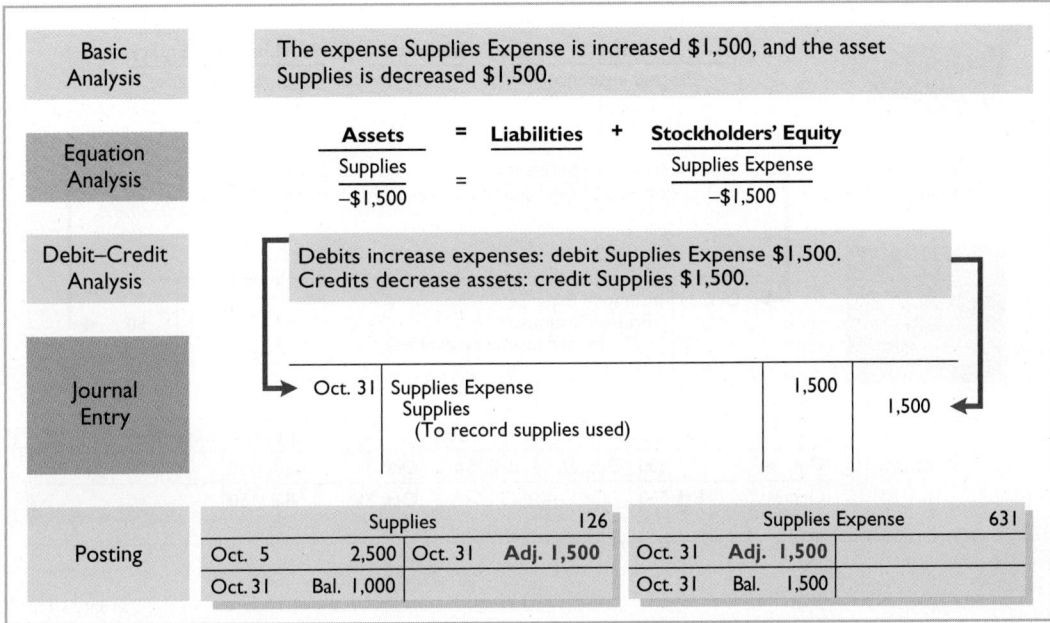

After adjustment, the asset account Supplies shows a balance of $1,000, which is equal to the cost of supplies on hand at the statement date. In addition, Supplies Expense shows a balance of $1,500, which equals the cost of supplies used in October. **If Pioneer does not make the adjusting entry, October expenses will be understated and net income overstated by $1,500. Moreover, both assets and stockholders' equity will be overstated by $1,500 on the October 31 balance sheet.**

INSURANCE Companies purchase insurance to protect themselves from losses due to fire, theft, and unforeseen events. Insurance must be paid in advance, often for more than one year. The cost of insurance (premiums) paid in advance is recorded as an increase (debit) in the asset account Prepaid Insurance. At the financial statement date, companies increase (debit) Insurance Expense and decrease (credit) Prepaid Insurance for the cost of insurance that has expired during the period.

On October 4, Pioneer Advertising paid $600 for a one-year fire insurance policy. Coverage began on October 1. Pioneer recorded the payment by increasing (debiting) Prepaid Insurance. This account shows a balance of $600 in the October 31 trial balance. Insurance of $50 ($600 ÷ 12) expires each month. The expiration of prepaid insurance decreases an asset, Prepaid Insurance. It also decreases stockholders' equity by increasing an expense account, Insurance Expense.

As shown in Illustration 3-6 (page 108), the asset Prepaid Insurance shows a balance of $550, which represents the unexpired cost for the remaining 11 months of coverage. At the same time, the balance in Insurance Expense equals the insurance cost that expired in October. If Pioneer does not make this adjustment, October

expenses are understated by $50 and net income is overstated by $50. Moreover, as the accounting equation shows, both assets and stockholders' equity will be overstated by $50 on the October 31 balance sheet.

Illustration 3-6
Adjustment for insurance

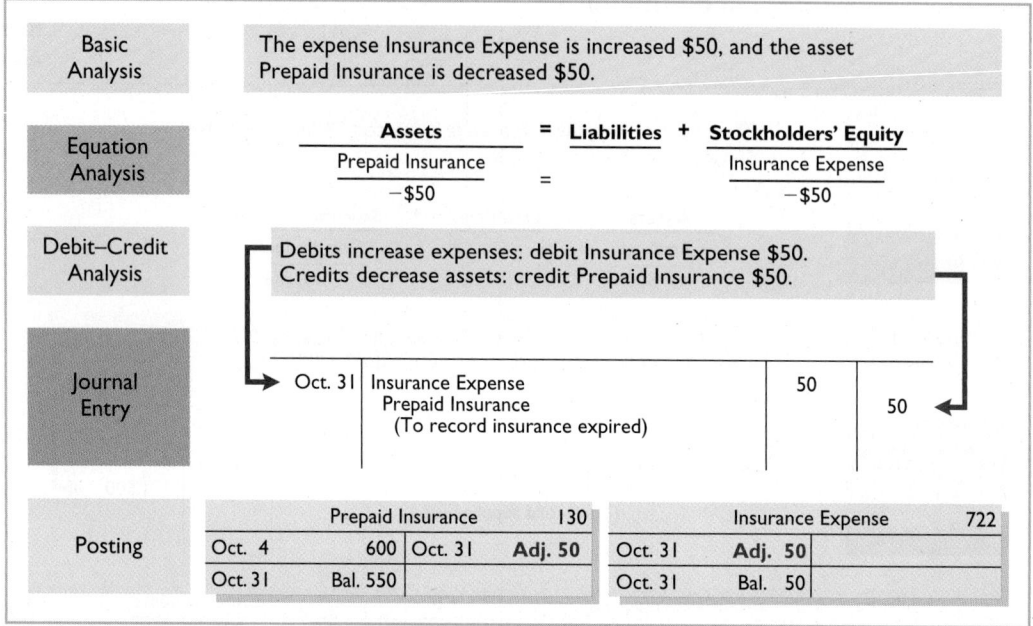

DEPRECIATION A company typically owns a variety of assets that have long lives, such as buildings, equipment, and motor vehicles. The period of service is referred to as the **useful life** of the asset. Because a building is expected to provide service for many years, it is recorded as an asset, rather than an expense, on the date it is acquired. As explained in Chapter 1, companies record such assets **at cost**, as required by the cost principle. To follow the expense recognition principle, companies allocate a portion of this cost as an expense during each period of the asset's useful life. **Depreciation** is the process of allocating the cost of an asset to expense over its useful life.

Need for Adjustment. The acquisition of long-lived assets is essentially a long-term prepayment for the use of an asset. An adjusting entry for depreciation is needed to recognize the cost that has been used (an expense) during the period and to report the unused cost (an asset) at the end of the period. One very important point to understand: **Depreciation is an allocation concept, not a valuation concept.** That is, depreciation **allocates an asset's cost to the periods in which it is used. Depreciation does not attempt to report the actual change in the value of the asset**.

For Pioneer Advertising, assume that depreciation on the equipment is $480 a year, or $40 per month. As shown in Illustration 3-7 on the next page, rather than decrease (credit) the asset account directly, Pioneer instead credits Accumulated Depreciation—Equipment. Accumulated Depreciation is called a **contra asset account.** Such an account is offset against an asset account on the balance sheet. Thus, the Accumulated Depreciation—Equipment account offsets the asset Equipment. This account keeps track of the total amount of depreciation expense taken over the life of the asset. To keep the accounting equation in balance, Pioneer decreases stockholders' equity by increasing an expense account, Depreciation Expense.

Depreciation

Oct. 2

Equipment purchased; record asset

Equipment			
Oct	Nov	Dec	Jan
$40	$40	$40	$40
Feb	March	April	May
$40	$40	$40	$40
June	July	Aug	Sept
$40	$40	$40	$40
Depreciation = $480/year			

Oct. 31

Depreciation recognized; record depreciation expense

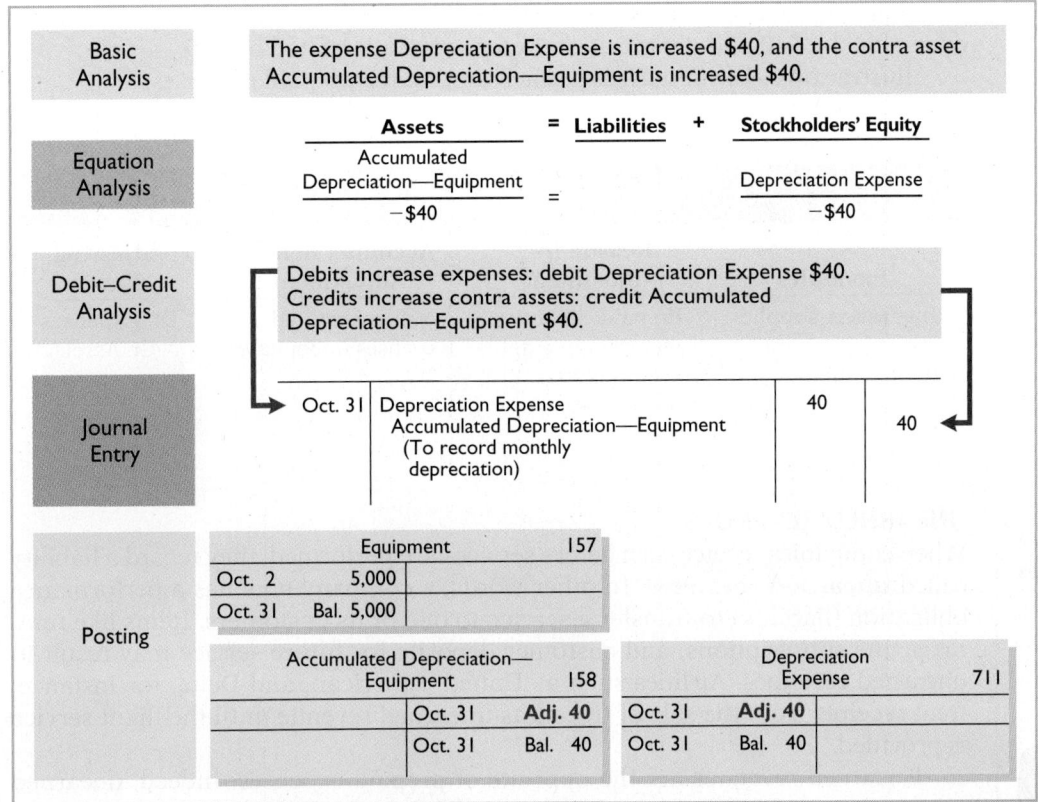

| Basic Analysis | The expense Depreciation Expense is increased $40, and the contra asset Accumulated Depreciation—Equipment is increased $40. |

Illustration 3-7
Adjustment for depreciation

The balance in the Accumulated Depreciation—Equipment account will increase $40 each month, and the balance in Equipment remains $5,000.

Helpful Hint
All contra accounts have increases, decreases, and normal balances opposite to the account to which they relate.

Statement Presentation. As indicated, Accumulated Depreciation—Equipment is a contra asset account. It is offset against Equipment on the balance sheet. The normal balance of a contra asset account is a credit. A theoretical alternative to using a contra asset account would be to decrease (credit) the asset account by the amount of depreciation each period. But using the contra account is preferable for a simple reason: It discloses *both* the original cost of the equipment *and* the total cost that has expired to date. Thus, in the balance sheet, Pioneer deducts Accumulated Depreciation—Equipment from the related asset account, as shown in Illustration 3-8.

Equipment	$ 5,000
Less: Accumulated depreciation—equipment	40
	$4,960

Illustration 3-8
Balance sheet presentation of accumulated depreciation

Book value is the difference between the cost of any depreciable asset and its related accumulated depreciation. In Illustration 3-8, the book value of the equipment at the balance sheet date is $4,960. The book value and the fair value of the asset are generally two different values. As noted earlier, **the purpose of depreciation is not valuation but a means of cost allocation**.

Depreciation expense identifies the portion of an asset's cost that expired during the period (in this case, in October). The accounting equation shows that without

Alternative Terminology
Book value is also referred to as *carrying value*.

this adjusting entry, total assets, total stockholders' equity, and net income are overstated by $40 and depreciation expense is understated by $40.

Illustration 3-9 summarizes the accounting for prepaid expenses.

Illustration 3-9
Accounting for prepaid expenses

Accounting for Prepaid Expenses

Examples	Reason for Adjustment	Accounts Before Adjustment	Adjusting Entry
Insurance, supplies, advertising, rent, depreciation	Prepaid expenses recorded in asset accounts have been used.	Assets overstated. Expenses understated.	Dr. Expenses Cr. Assets

UNEARNED REVENUES

Unearned Revenues

Oct. 2

Thank you in advance for your work.

I will finish by Dec. 31

~ $1,200

Cash is received in advance; liability is recorded

Oct. 31
Some service has been performed; some revenue is recorded

When companies receive cash before services are performed, they record a liability called **unearned revenues**. In other words, a company now has a performance obligation (liability) to transfer a service to one of its customers. Items like rent, magazine subscriptions, and customer deposits for future service may result in unearned revenues. Airlines such as United, American, and Delta, for instance, treat receipts from the sale of tickets as unearned revenue until the flight service is provided.

Unearned revenues are the opposite of prepaid expenses. Indeed, unearned revenue on the books of one company is likely to be a prepaid expense on the books of the company that has made the advance payment. For example, if identical accounting periods are assumed, a landlord will have unearned rent revenue when a tenant has prepaid rent.

When a company receives payment for services to be performed in a future accounting period, it increases (credits) an unearned revenue (a liability) account to recognize the liability that exists. The company subsequently recognizes revenues when it performs the service. During the accounting period, it is not practical to make daily entries as the company provides services. Instead, the company delays recognition of revenue until the adjustment process. Then, the company makes an adjusting entry to record the revenue for services performed during the period and to show the liability that remains at the end of the accounting period. Typically, prior to adjustment, liabilities are overstated and revenues are understated. Therefore, as shown in Illustration 3-10, **the adjusting entry for unearned revenues results in a decrease (a debit) to a liability account and an increase (a credit) to a revenue account**.

Illustration 3-10
Adjusting entries for unearned revenues

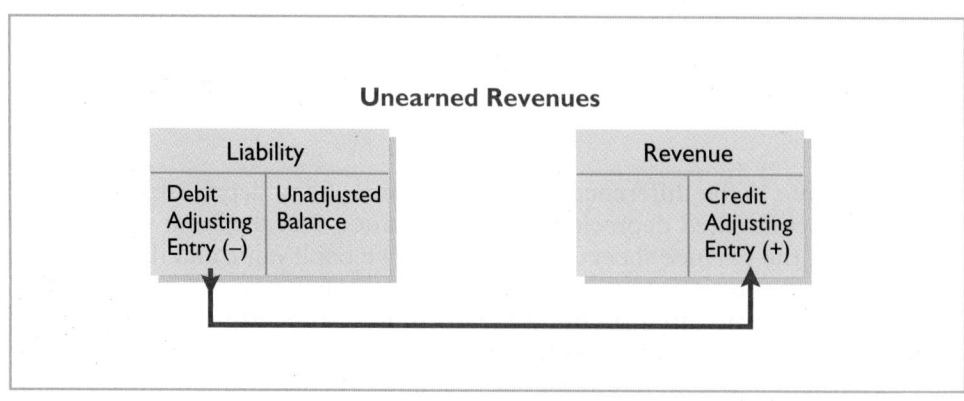

Pioneer Advertising received $1,200 on October 2 from R. Knox for advertising services expected to be completed by December 31. Pioneer credited the payment to Unearned Service Revenue, and this liability account shows a balance of $1,200 in the October 31 trial balance. From an evaluation of the service Pioneer performed for Knox during October, the company determines that it should recognize $400 of revenue in October. The liability (Unearned Service Revenue) is therefore decreased, and stockholder's equity (Service Revenue) is increased.

As shown in Illustration 3-11, the liability Unearned Service Revenue now shows a balance of $800. That amount represents the remaining advertising services expected to be performed in the future. At the same time, Service Revenue shows total revenue recognized in October of $10,400. **Without this adjustment, revenues and net income are understated by $400 in the income statement. Moreover, liabilities are overstated and stockholders' equity is understated by $400 on the October 31 balance sheet.**

Alternative Terminology
Unearned revenue is sometimes referred to as *deferred revenue*.

Illustration 3-11
Service revenue accounts after adjustment

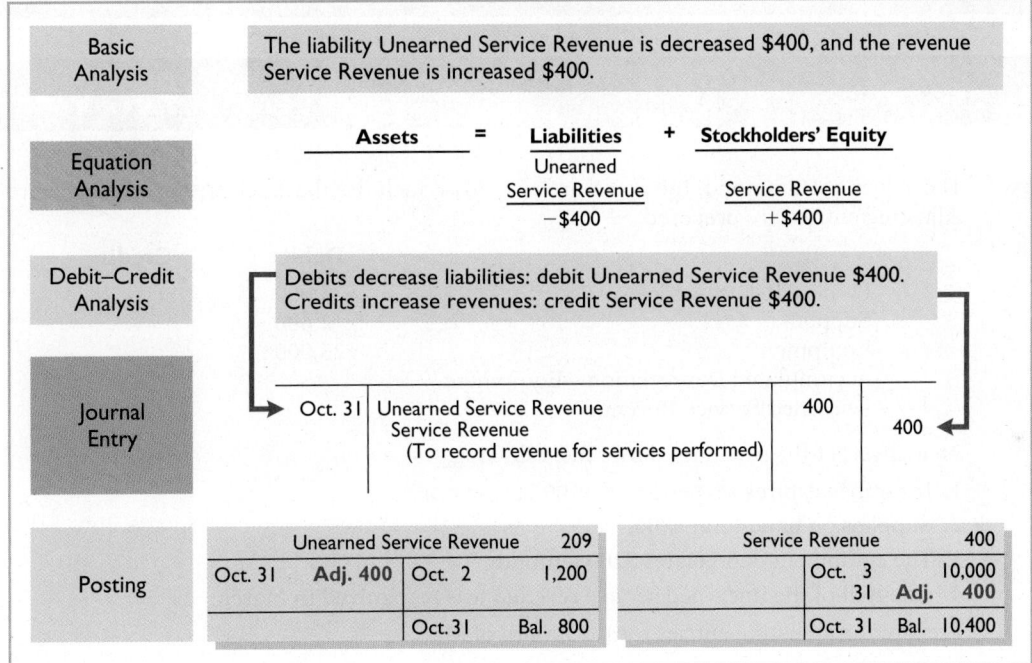

Illustration 3-12 summarizes the accounting for unearned revenues.

Illustration 3-12
Accounting for unearned revenues

	Accounting for Unearned Revenues		
Examples	**Reason for Adjustment**	**Accounts Before Adjustment**	**Adjusting Entry**
Rent, magazine subscriptions, customer deposits for future service	Unearned revenues recorded in liability accounts are now recognized as revenue for services performed.	Liabilities overstated. Revenues understated.	Dr. Liabilities Cr. Revenues

ACCOUNTING ACROSS THE ORGANIZATION

Turning Gift Cards into Revenue

Those of you who are marketing majors (and even most of you who are not) know that gift cards are among the hottest marketing tools in merchandising today. Customers purchase gift cards and give them to someone for later use. In a recent year, gift-card sales topped $95 billion.

Although these programs are popular with marketing executives, they create accounting questions. Should revenue be recorded at the time the gift card is sold, or when it is exercised? How should expired gift cards be accounted for? In its 2009 balance sheet, Best Buy reported unearned revenue related to gift cards of $479 million.

Source: Robert Berner, "Gift Cards: No Gift to Investors," *BusinessWeek* (March 14, 2005), p. 86.

 Suppose that Robert Jones purchases a $100 gift card at Best Buy on December 24, 2013, and gives it to his wife, Mary Jones, on December 25, 2013. On January 3, 2014, Mary uses the card to purchase $100 worth of CDs. When do you think Best Buy should recognize revenue and why? (See page 158.)

> ## DO IT!

Adjusting Entries for Deferrals

The ledger of Hammond, Inc., on March 31, 2014, includes these selected accounts before adjusting entries are prepared.

	Debit	Credit
Prepaid Insurance	$ 3,600	
Supplies	2,800	
Equipment	25,000	
Accumulated Depreciation—Equipment		$5,000
Unearned Service Revenue		9,200

An analysis of the accounts shows the following.

1. Insurance expires at the rate of $100 per month.
2. Supplies on hand total $800.
3. The equipment depreciates $200 a month.
4. One-half of the unearned service revenue was recognized in March.

Prepare the adjusting entries for the month of March.

Solution

Action Plan

✔ Make adjusting entries at the end of the period for revenues recognized and expenses incurred in the period.

✔ Don't forget to make adjusting entries for deferrals. Failure to adjust for deferrals leads to overstatement of the asset or liability and understatement of the related expense or revenue.

1. Insurance Expense	100	
Prepaid Insurance		100
(To record insurance expired)		
2. Supplies Expense	2,000	
Supplies		2,000
(To record supplies used)		
3. Depreciation Expense	200	
Accumulated Depreciation—Equipment		200
(To record monthly depreciation)		
4. Unearned Service Revenue	4,600	
Service Revenue		4,600
(To record revenue for services performed)		

Related exercise material: **BE3-3, BE3-4, BE3-5, BE3-6, and DO IT! 3-2.**

 The Navigator

Adjusting Entries for Accruals

The second category of adjusting entries is **accruals**. Prior to an accrual adjustment, the revenue account (and the related asset account) or the expense account (and the related liability account) are understated. Thus, the adjusting entry for accruals will **increase both a balance sheet and an income statement account**.

ACCRUED REVENUES

Revenues for services performed but not yet recorded at the statement date are **accrued revenues**. Accrued revenues may accumulate (accrue) with the passing of time, as in the case of interest revenue. These are unrecorded because the earning of interest does not involve daily transactions. Companies do not record interest revenue on a daily basis because it is often impractical to do so. Accrued revenues also may result from services that have been performed but not yet billed or collected, as in the case of commissions and fees. These may be unrecorded because only a portion of the total service has been provided and the clients won't be billed until the service has been completed.

An adjusting entry records the receivable that exists at the balance sheet date and the revenue for the services performed during the period. Prior to adjustment, both assets and revenues are understated. As shown in Illustration 3-13, **an adjusting entry for accrued revenues results in an increase (a debit) to an asset account and an increase (a credit) to a revenue account**.

Accrued Revenues

Oct. 31

Revenue and receivable are recorded for unbilled services

Nov. 10

Cash is received; receivable is reduced

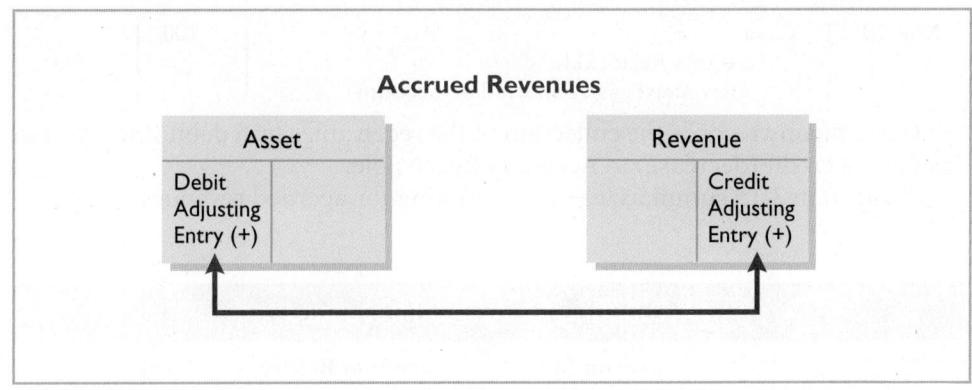

Accrued Revenues

Asset		Revenue	
Debit Adjusting Entry (+)			Credit Adjusting Entry (+)

Illustration 3-13
Adjusting entries for accrued revenues

Helpful Hint
For accruals, there may have been no prior entry, and the accounts requiring adjustment may both have zero balances prior to adjustment.

In October, Pioneer Advertising Agency Inc. recognized $200 for advertising services performed that were not billed to clients on or before October 31. Because these services are not billed, they are not recorded. The accrual of unrecorded service revenue increases an asset account, Accounts Receivable. It also increases stockholders' equity by increasing a revenue account, Service Revenue, as shown in Illustration 3-14 (page 114).

The asset Accounts Receivable shows that clients owe Pioneer $200 at the balance sheet date. The balance of $10,600 in Service Revenue represents the total revenue for services performed by Pioneer during the month ($10,000 + $400 + $200). **Without the adjusting entry, assets and stockholders' equity on the balance sheet and revenues and net income on the income statement are understated.**

Illustration 3-14
Adjustment for accrued revenue

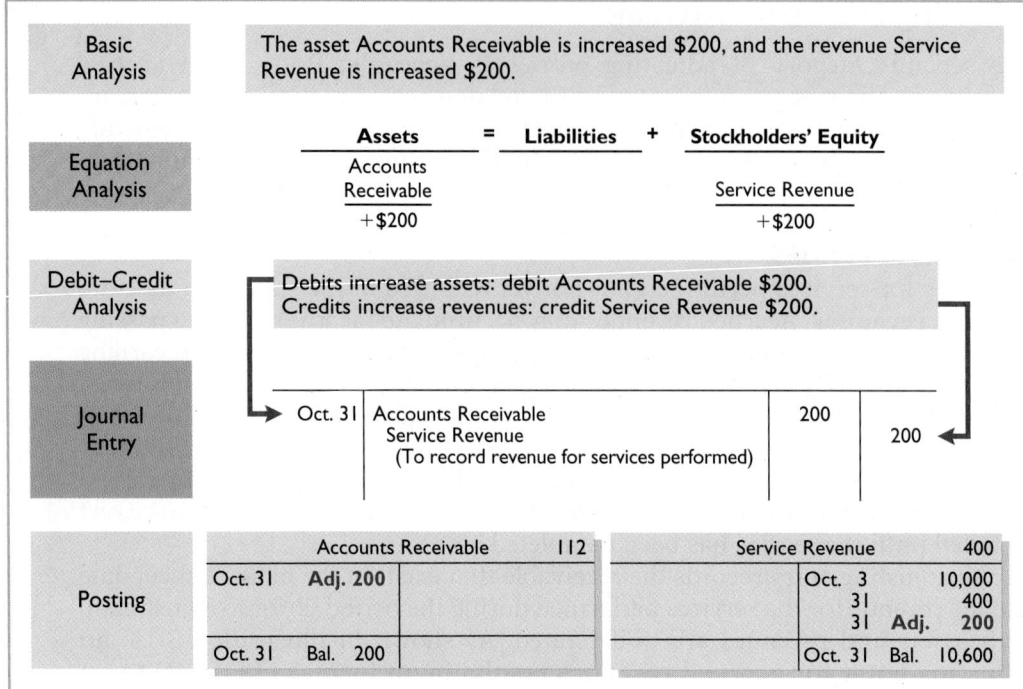

Equation analyses summarize the effects of transactions on the three elements of the accounting equation, as well as the effect on cash flows.

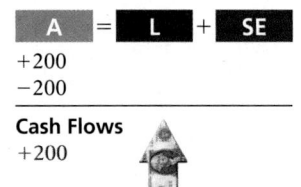

A	=	L	+	SE
+200				
−200				

Cash Flows
+200

On November 10, Pioneer receives cash of $200 for the services performed in October and makes the following entry.

Nov. 10	Cash	200	
	Accounts Receivable		200
	(To record cash collected on account)		

The company records the collection of the receivables by a debit (increase) to Cash and a credit (decrease) to Accounts Receivable.

Illustration 3-15 summarizes the accounting for accrued revenues.

Illustration 3-15
Accounting for accrued revenues

	Accounting for Accrued Revenues			
Examples	**Reason for Adjustment**	**Accounts Before Adjustment**	**Adjusting Entry**	
Interest, rent, services performed but not collected	Services performed but not yet recorded.	Assets understated. Revenues understated.	Dr. Assets Cr. Revenues	

ACCRUED EXPENSES

Expenses incurred but not yet paid or recorded at the statement date are called **accrued expenses**. Interest, taxes, and salaries are common examples of accrued expenses.

Companies make adjustments for accrued expenses to record the obligations that exist at the balance sheet date and to recognize the expenses that apply to the current accounting period. Prior to adjustment, both liabilities and expenses are understated. Therefore, as Illustration 3-16 shows, **an adjusting entry for accrued expenses results in an increase (a debit) to an expense account and an increase (a credit) to a liability account**.

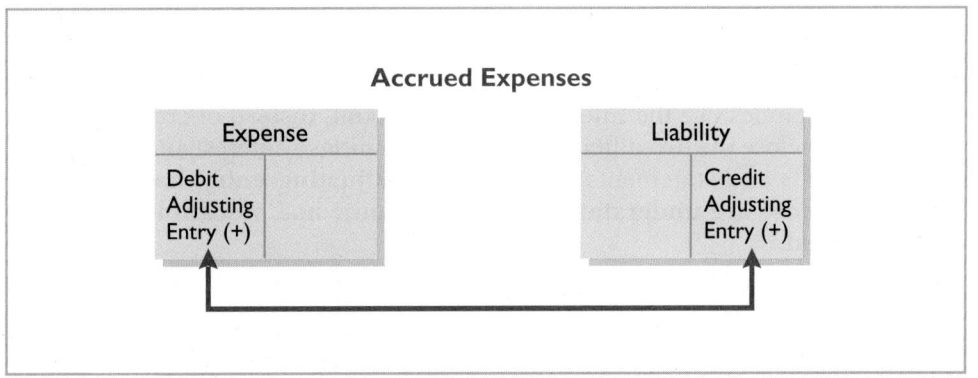

Illustration 3-16
Adjusting entries for accrued expenses

Let's look in more detail at some specific types of accrued expenses, beginning with accrued interest.

ACCRUED INTEREST Pioneer Advertising signed a three-month note payable in the amount of $5,000 on October 1. The note requires Pioneer to pay interest at an annual rate of 12%.

The amount of the interest recorded is determined by three factors: (1) the face value of the note; (2) the interest rate, which is always expressed as an annual rate; and (3) the length of time the note is outstanding. For Pioneer, the total interest due on the $5,000 note at its maturity date three months in the future is $150 ($5,000 × 12% × $\frac{3}{12}$), or $50 for one month. Illustration 3-17 shows the formula for computing interest and its application to Pioneer for the month of October.

Face Value of Note	×	Annual Interest Rate	×	Time in Terms of One Year	=	Interest
$5,000	×	12%	×	$\frac{1}{12}$	=	$50

Illustration 3-17
Formula for computing interest

Helpful Hint
In computing interest, we express the time period as a fraction of a year.

Illustration 3-18
Adjustment for accrued interest

As Illustration 3-18 shows, the accrual of interest at October 31 increases a liability account, Interest Payable. It also decreases stockholders' equity by increasing an expense account, Interest Expense.

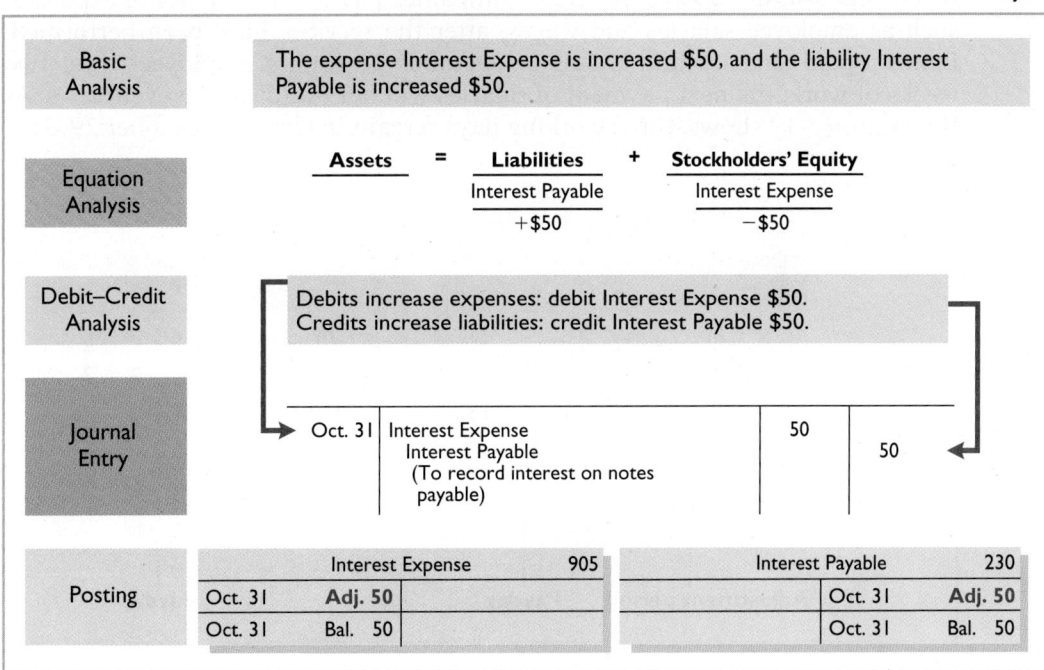

Interest Expense shows the interest charges for the month of October. Interest Payable shows the amount of interest the company owes at the statement date. Pioneer will not pay the interest until the note comes due at the end of three months. Companies use the Interest Payable account, instead of crediting Notes Payable, to disclose the two different types of obligations—interest and principal—in the accounts and statements. **Without this adjusting entry, liabilities and interest expense are understated, and net income and stockholders' equity are overstated.**

INTERNATIONAL INSIGHT

Cashing In on Accrual Accounting

The Chinese government, like most governments, uses cash accounting. A recent report, however, noted that it decided to use accrual accounting versus cash accounting for about $38 billion of expenditures in a recent budget projection. The Chinese government decided to expense the amount in the year in which the expenditures were originally allocated rather than when the payments would be made. Why did it do this? It enabled the government to keep its projected budget deficit below a 3% threshold. While the Chinese government was able to keep its projected shortfall below 3%, it did suffer some criticism for its inconsistent accounting. Critics charge that this inconsistent treatment reduces the transparency of China's accounting information. That is, it is not easy for outsiders to accurately evaluate what is really going on.

Source: Andrew Batson, "China Altered Budget Accounting to Reduce Deficit Figure," *Wall Street Journal Online* (March 15, 2010).

? Accrual accounting is often considered superior to cash accounting. Why, then, were some people critical of China's use of accrual accounting in this instance? (See page 159.)

ACCRUED SALARIES AND WAGES Companies pay for some types of expenses, such as employee salaries and wages, after the services have been performed. Pioneer paid salaries and wages on October 26 for its employees' first two weeks of work; the next payment of salaries will not occur until November 9. As Illustration 3-19 shows, three working days remain in October (October 29–31).

Illustration 3-19
Calendar showing Pioneer's pay periods

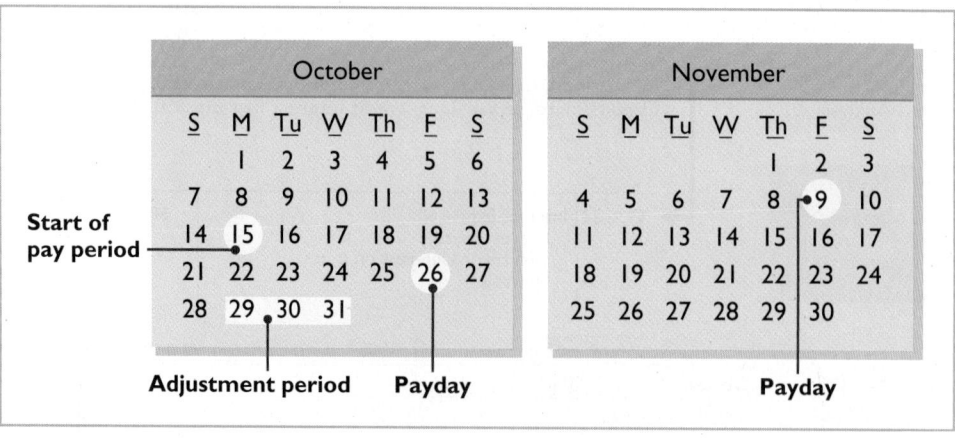

At October 31, the salaries and wages for these three days represent an accrued expense and a related liability to Pioneer. The employees receive total salaries and wages of $2,000 for a five-day work week, or $400 per day. Thus, accrued salaries and wages at October 31 are $1,200 ($400 × 3). This accrual increases a liability, Salaries and Wages Payable. It also decreases stockholders' equity by increasing an expense account, Salaries and Wages Expense, as shown in Illustration 3-20.

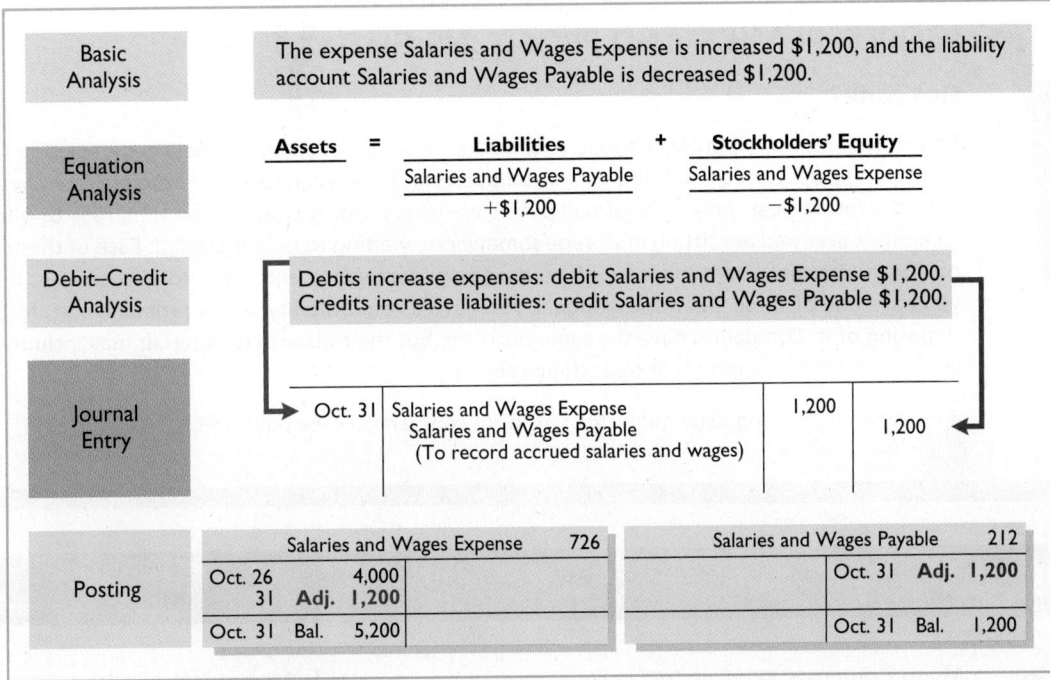

Illustration 3-20
Adjustment for accrued salaries and wages

After this adjustment, the balance in Salaries and Wages Expense of $5,200 (13 days × $400) is the actual salary and wages expense for October. The balance in Salaries and Wages Payable of $1,200 is the amount of the liability for salaries and wages Pioneer owes as of October 31. **Without the $1,200 adjustment for salaries and wages, Pioneer's expenses are understated $1,200 and its liabilities are understated $1,200.**

Pioneer Advertising pays salaries and wages every two weeks. Consequently, the next payday is November 9, when the company will again pay total salaries and wages of $4,000. The payment consists of $1,200 of salaries and wages payable at October 31 plus $2,800 of salaries and wages expense for November (7 working days, as shown in the November calendar × $400). Therefore, Pioneer makes the following entry on November 9.

Nov. 9	Salaries and Wages Payable	1,200	
	Salaries and Wages Expense	2,800	
	Cash		4,000
	(To record November 9 payroll)		

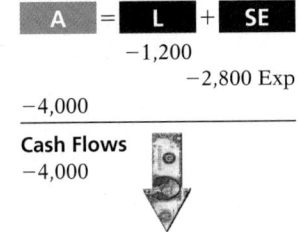

A = L + SE
−1,200
−2,800 Exp
−4,000
Cash Flows
−4,000

This entry eliminates the liability for Salaries and Wages Payable that Pioneer recorded in the October 31 adjusting entry, and it records the proper amount of Salaries and Wages Expense for the period between November 1 and November 9.

Illustration 3-21 (page 118) summarizes the accounting for accrued expenses.

Illustration 3-21
Accounting for accrued
expenses

	Accounting for Accrued Expenses			
Examples	**Reason for Adjustment**	**Accounts Before Adjustment**	**Adjusting Entry**
Interest, rent, salaries	Expenses have been incurred but not yet paid in cash or recorded.	Expenses understated. Liabilities understated.	Dr. Expenses Cr. Liabilities

PEOPLE, PLANET, AND PROFIT INSIGHT

Got Junk?

Do you have an old computer or two in your garage? How about an old TV that needs replacing? Many people do. Approximately 163,000 computers and televisions become obsolete *each day.* Yet, in a recent year, only 11% of computers were recycled. It is estimated that 75% of all computers ever sold are sitting in storage somewhere, waiting to be disposed of. Each of these old TVs and computers is loaded with lead, cadmium, mercury, and other toxic chemicals. If you have one of these electronic gadgets, you have a responsibility, and a probable cost, for disposing of it. Companies have the same problem, but their discarded materials may include lead paint, asbestos, and other toxic chemicals.

? What accounting issue might this cause for companies? (See page 159.)

> DO IT!

Adjusting Entries for Accruals

Micro Computer Services Inc. began operations on August 1, 2014. At the end of August 2014, management attempted to prepare monthly financial statements. The following information relates to August.

1. At August 31, the company owed its employees $800 in salaries and wages that will be paid on September 1.

2. On August 1, the company borrowed $30,000 from a local bank on a 15-year mortgage. The annual interest rate is 10%.

3. Revenue for services performed but unrecorded for August totaled $1,100.

Prepare the adjusting entries needed at August 31, 2014.

Solution

Action Plan

✔ Make adjusting entries at the end of the period for revenues recognized and expenses incurred in the period.

✔ Don't forget to make adjusting entries for accruals. Adjusting entries for accruals will increase both a balance sheet and an income statement account.

1. Salaries and Wages Expense	800	
Salaries and Wages Payable		800
(To record accrued salaries)		
2. Interest Expense	250	
Interest Payable		250
(To record accrued interest: $30,000 \times 10\% \times \frac{1}{12} = \$250$)		
3. Accounts Receivable	1,100	
Service Revenue		1,100
(To record revenue for services performed)		

Related exercise material: **BE3-7, E3-5, E3-6, E3-7, E3-8, E3-9, E3-10, E3-11, E3-12,** and **DO IT! 3-3.**

 The Navigator

Summary of Basic Relationships

Illustration 3-22 summarizes the four basic types of adjusting entries. Take some time to study and analyze the adjusting entries. Be sure to note that **each adjusting entry affects one balance sheet account and one income statement account.**

Illustration 3-22
Summary of adjusting entries

Type of Adjustment	Accounts Before Adjustment	Adjusting Entry
Prepaid expenses	Assets overstated. Expenses understated.	Dr. Expenses Cr. Assets
Unearned revenues	Liabilities overstated. Revenues understated.	Dr. Liabilities Cr. Revenues
Accrued revenues	Assets understated. Revenues understated.	Dr. Assets Cr. Revenues
Accrued expenses	Expenses understated. Liabilities understated.	Dr. Expenses Cr. Liabilities

Illustrations 3-23 (below) and 3-24 (on page 120) show the journalizing and posting of adjusting entries for Pioneer Advertising Agency Inc. on October 31. The ledger identifies all adjustments by the reference J2 because they have been recorded on page 2 of the general journal. The company may insert a center caption "Adjusting Entries" between the last transaction entry and the first adjusting entry in the journal. When you review the general ledger in Illustration 3-24, note that the entries highlighted in color are the adjustments.

Illustration 3-23
General journal showing adjusting entries

	General Journal			J2
Date	**Account Titles and Explanation**	**Ref.**	**Debit**	**Credit**
2014	*Adjusting Entries*			
Oct. 31	Supplies Expense	631	1,500	
	Supplies	126		1,500
	(To record supplies used)			
31	Insurance Expense	722	50	
	Prepaid Insurance	130		50
	(To record insurance expired)			
31	Depreciation Expense	711	40	
	Accumulated Depreciation—Equipment	158		40
	(To record monthly depreciation)			
31	Unearned Service Revenue	209	400	
	Service Revenue	400		400
	(To record revenue for services performed)			
31	Accounts Receivable	112	200	
	Service Revenue	400		200
	(To record revenue for services performed)			
31	Interest Expense	905	50	
	Interest Payable	230		50
	(To record interest on notes payable)			
31	Salaries and Wages Expense	726	1,200	
	Salaries and Wages Payable	212		1,200
	(To record accrued salaries and wages)			

Helpful Hint
1. Adjusting entries should not involve debits or credits to cash.
2. Evaluate whether the adjustment makes sense. For example, an adjustment to recognize supplies used should increase supplies expense.
3. Double-check all computations.
4. Each adjusting entry affects one balance sheet account and one income statement account.

Illustration 3-24
General ledger after adjustment

General Ledger

Cash   No. 101

Date	Explanation	Ref.	Debit	Credit	Balance
2014					
Oct. 1		J1	10,000		10,000
2		J1	1,200		11,200
3		J1		900	10,300
4		J1		600	9,700
20		J1		500	9,200
26		J1		4,000	5,200
31		J1	10,000		15,200

Accounts Receivable   No. 112

Date	Explanation	Ref.	Debit	Credit	Balance
2014					
Oct. 31	Adj. entry	J2	200		200

Supplies   No. 126

Date	Explanation	Ref.	Debit	Credit	Balance
2014					
Oct. 5		J1	2,500		2,500
31	Adj. entry	J2		1,500	1,000

Prepaid Insurance   No. 130

Date	Explanation	Ref.	Debit	Credit	Balance
2014					
Oct. 4		J1	600		600
31	Adj. entry	J2		50	550

Equipment   No. 157

Date	Explanation	Ref.	Debit	Credit	Balance
2014					
Oct. 1		J1	5,000		5,000

Accumulated Depreciation—Equipment   No. 158

Date	Explanation	Ref.	Debit	Credit	Balance
2014					
Oct. 31	Adj. entry	J2		40	40

Notes Payable   No. 200

Date	Explanation	Ref.	Debit	Credit	Balance
2014					
Oct. 1		J1		5,000	5,000

Accounts Payable   No. 201

Date	Explanation	Ref.	Debit	Credit	Balance
2014					
Oct. 5		J1		2,500	2,500

Unearned Service Revenue   No. 209

Date	Explanation	Ref.	Debit	Credit	Balance
2014					
Oct. 2		J1		1,200	1,200
31	Adj. entry	J2	400		800

Salaries and Wages Payable   No. 212

Date	Explanation	Ref.	Debit	Credit	Balance
2014					
Oct. 31	Adj. entry	J2		1,200	1,200

Interest Payable   No. 230

Date	Explanation	Ref.	Debit	Credit	Balance
2014					
Oct. 31	Adj. entry	J2		50	50

Common Stock   No. 311

Date	Explanation	Ref.	Debit	Credit	Balance
2014					
Oct. 1		J1		10,000	10,000

Retained Earnings   No. 320

Date	Explanation	Ref.	Debit	Credit	Balance
2014					

Dividends   No. 332

Date	Explanation	Ref.	Debit	Credit	Balance
2014					
Oct. 20		J1	500		500

Service Revenue   No. 400

Date	Explanation	Ref.	Debit	Credit	Balance
2014					
Oct. 31		J1		10,000	10,000
31	Adj. entry	J2		400	10,400
31	Adj. entry	J2		200	10,600

Supplies Expense   No. 631

Date	Explanation	Ref.	Debit	Credit	Balance
2014					
Oct. 31	Adj. entry	J2	1,500		1,500

Depreciation Expense   No. 711

Date	Explanation	Ref.	Debit	Credit	Balance
2014					
Oct. 31	Adj. entry	J2	40		40

Insurance Expense   No. 722

Date	Explanation	Ref.	Debit	Credit	Balance
2014					
Oct. 31	Adj. entry	J2	50		50

Salaries and Wages Expense   No. 726

Date	Explanation	Ref.	Debit	Credit	Balance
2014					
Oct. 26		J1	4,000		4,000
31	Adj. entry	J2	1,200		5,200

Rent Expense   No. 729

Date	Explanation	Ref.	Debit	Credit	Balance
2014					
Oct. 3		J1	900		900

Interest Expense   No. 905

Date	Explanation	Ref.	Debit	Credit	Balance
2014					
Oct. 31	Adj. entry	J2	50		50

The Adjusted Trial Balance and Financial Statements

After a company has journalized and posted all adjusting entries, it prepares another trial balance from the ledger accounts. This trial balance is called an **adjusted trial balance**. It shows the balances of all accounts, including those adjusted, at the end of the accounting period. The purpose of an adjusted trial balance is to **prove the equality** of the total debit balances and the total credit balances in the ledger after all adjustments. Because the accounts contain all data needed for financial statements, the adjusted trial balance is the **primary basis for the preparation of financial statements**.

LEARNING OBJECTIVE   7

Describe the nature and purpose of an adjusted trial balance.

Preparing the Adjusted Trial Balance

Illustration 3-25 presents the adjusted trial balance for Pioneer Advertising Agency Inc. prepared from the ledger accounts in Illustration 3-24. The amounts affected by the adjusting entries are highlighted in color. Compare these amounts to those in the unadjusted trial balance in Illustration 3-3 on page 105. In this comparison, you will see that there are more accounts in the adjusted trial balance as a result of the adjusting entries made at the end of the month.

Illustration 3-25
Adjusted trial balance

Pioneer Advertising Agency Inc.
Adjusted Trial Balance
October 31, 2014

	Dr.	Cr.
Cash	$15,200	
Accounts Receivable	200	
Supplies	1,000	
Prepaid Insurance	550	
Equipment	5,000	
Accumulated Depreciation—Equipment		$ 40
Notes Payable		5,000
Accounts Payable		2,500
Interest Payable		50
Unearned Service Revenue		800
Salaries and Wages Payable		1,200
Common Stock		10,000
Retained Earnings		–0–
Dividends	500	
Service Revenue		10,600
Salaries and Wages Expense	5,200	
Supplies Expense	1,500	
Rent Expense	900	
Insurance Expense	50	
Interest Expense	50	
Depreciation Expense	40	
	$30,190	$30,190

Preparing Financial Statements

Companies can prepare financial statements directly from the adjusted trial balance. Illustrations 3-26 and 3-27 present the interrelationships of data in the adjusted trial balance and the financial statements.

As Illustration 3-26 shows, companies prepare the income statement from the revenue and expense accounts. Next, they use the Retained Earnings and Dividends accounts and the net income (or net loss) from the income statement to prepare the retained earnings statement. As Illustration 3-27 shows, companies then prepare the balance sheet from the asset and liability accounts and the ending retained earnings balance as reported in the retained earnings statement.

Illustration 3-26

Preparation of the income statement and retained earnings statement from the adjusted trial balance

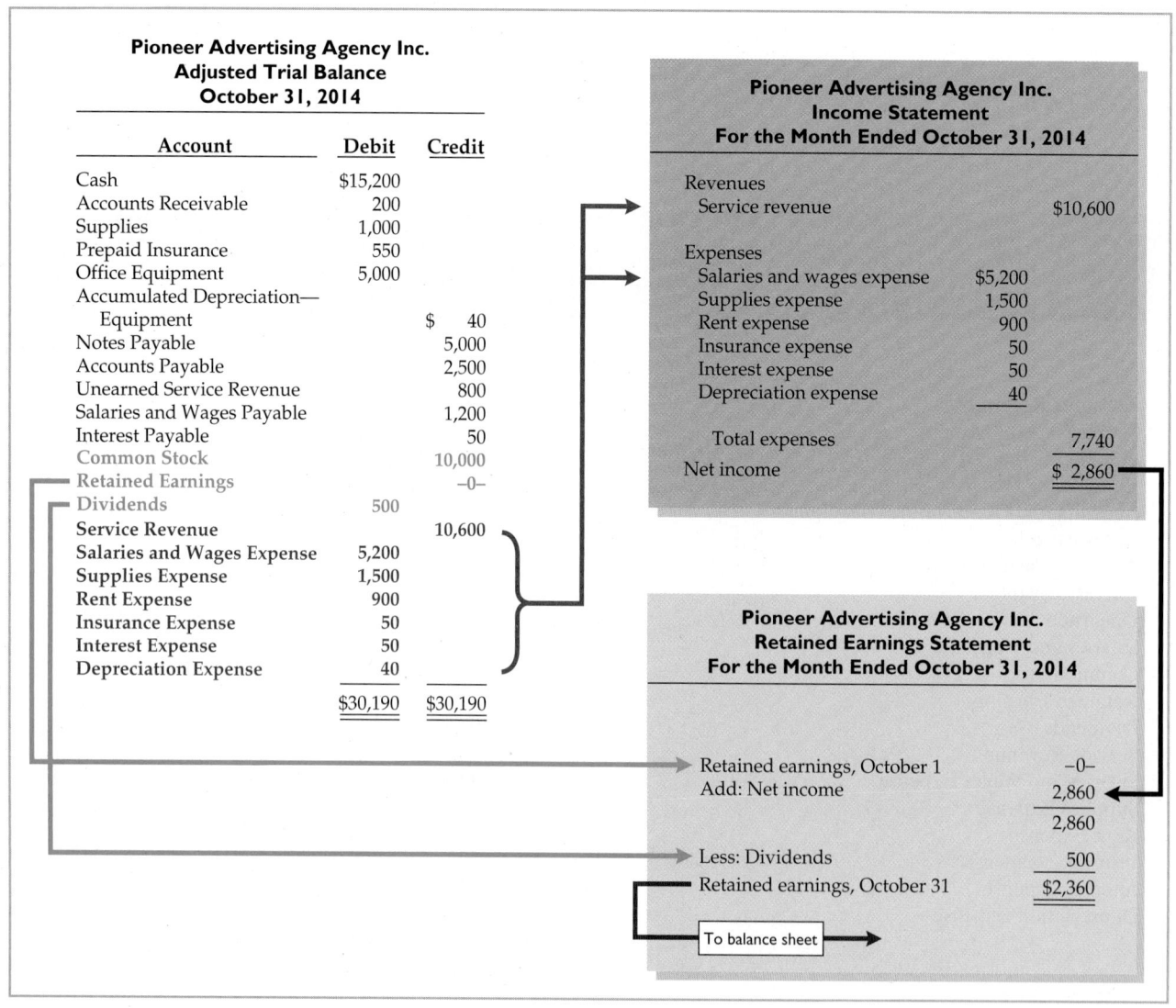

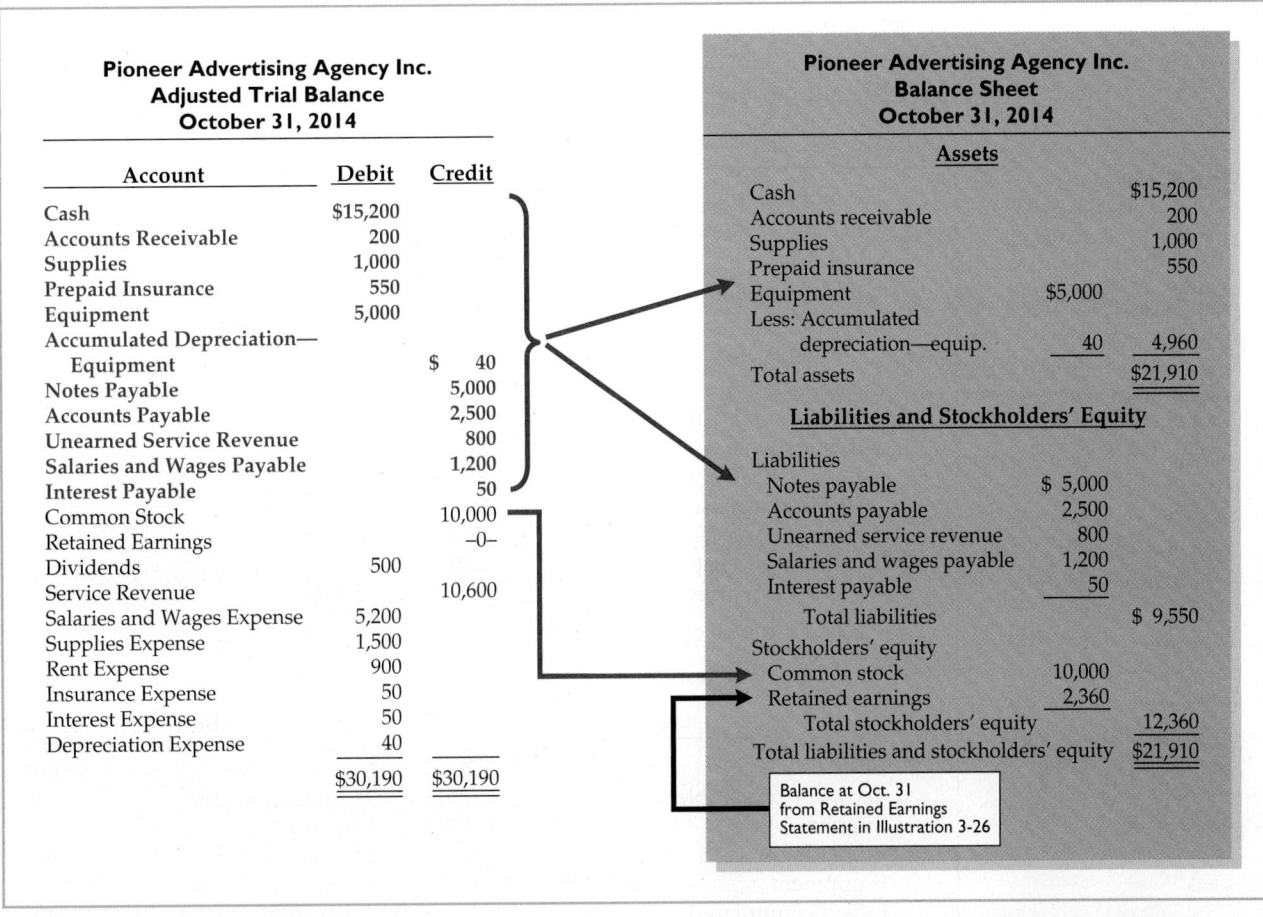

Pioneer Advertising Agency Inc.
Adjusted Trial Balance
October 31, 2014

Account	Debit	Credit
Cash	$15,200	
Accounts Receivable	200	
Supplies	1,000	
Prepaid Insurance	550	
Equipment	5,000	
Accumulated Depreciation—		
Equipment		$ 40
Notes Payable		5,000
Accounts Payable		2,500
Unearned Service Revenue		800
Salaries and Wages Payable		1,200
Interest Payable		50
Common Stock		10,000
Retained Earnings		–0–
Dividends	500	
Service Revenue		10,600
Salaries and Wages Expense	5,200	
Supplies Expense	1,500	
Rent Expense	900	
Insurance Expense	50	
Interest Expense	50	
Depreciation Expense	40	
	$30,190	$30,190

Pioneer Advertising Agency Inc.
Balance Sheet
October 31, 2014

Assets

Cash		$15,200
Accounts receivable		200
Supplies		1,000
Prepaid insurance		550
Equipment	$5,000	
Less: Accumulated		
depreciation—equip.	40	4,960
Total assets		$21,910

Liabilities and Stockholders' Equity

Liabilities		
Notes payable	$ 5,000	
Accounts payable	2,500	
Unearned service revenue	800	
Salaries and wages payable	1,200	
Interest payable	50	
Total liabilities		$ 9,550
Stockholders' equity		
Common stock	10,000	
Retained earnings	2,360	
Total stockholders' equity		12,360
Total liabilities and stockholders' equity		$21,910

Balance at Oct. 31
from Retained Earnings
Statement in Illustration 3-26

Illustration 3-27
Preparation of the balance sheet
from the adjusted trial balance

> **DO IT!**

Trial balance

Skolnick Co. was organized on April 1, 2014. The company prepares quarterly financial statements. The adjusted trial balance amounts at June 30 are shown below.

	Debits		Credits
Cash	$ 6,700	Accumulated Depreciation—Equipment	$ 850
Accounts Receivable	600	Notes Payable	5,000
Prepaid Rent	900	Accounts Payable	1,510
Supplies	1,000	Salaries and Wages Payable	400
Equipment	15,000	Interest Payable	50
Dividends	600	Unearned Rent Revenue	500
Salaries and Wages Expense	9,400	Common Stock	14,000
Rent Expense	1,500	Service Revenue	14,200
Depreciation Expense	850	Rent Revenue	800
Supplies Expense	200		
Utilities Expense	510		
Interest Expense	50		
Total debits	$37,310	Total credits	$37,310

(a) Determine the net income for the quarter April 1 to June 30.

(b) Determine the total assets and total liabilities at June 30, 2014, for Skolnick Co.

(c) Determine the amount that appears for Retained Earnings at June 30, 2014.

Solution

Action Plan

✔ In an adjusted trial balance, all assets, liability, revenue, and expense accounts are properly stated.

✔ To determine the ending balance in Retained Earnings, add net income and subtract dividends.

(a) The net income is determined by adding revenues and subtracting expenses. The net income is computed as follows.

Revenues		
Service revenue	$14,200	
Rent revenue	800	
Total revenues		$15,000
Expenses		
Salaries and wages expense	$ 9,400	
Rent expense	1,500	
Depreciation expense	850	
Utilities expense	510	
Supplies expense	200	
Interest expense	50	
Total expenses		12,510
Net income		$ 2,490

(b) Total assets and liabilities are computed as follows.

Assets			Liabilities	
Cash		$ 6,700	Notes payable	$5,000
Accounts receivable		600	Accounts payable	1,510
Supplies		1,000	Unearned rent	
Prepaid rent		900	revenue	500
Equipment	$15,000		Salaries and wages	
Less: Accumulated			payable	400
depreciation—			Interest payable	50
equipment	850	14,150		
Total assets		$23,350	Total liabilities	$7,460

(c)

Retained earnings, April 1	$ 0
Add: Net income	2,490
Less: Dividends	600
Retained earnings, June 30	$ 1,890

Related exercise material: **BE3-9, BE3-10, E3-11, E3-13, and** DO IT! **3-4.**

✔ **The Navigator**

> Comprehensive DO IT!

The Green Thumb Lawn Care Inc. began on April 1. At April 30, the trial balance shows the following balances for selected accounts.

Prepaid Insurance	$ 3,600
Equipment	28,000
Notes Payable	20,000
Unearned Service Revenue	4,200
Service Revenue	1,800

Analysis reveals the following additional data.

1. Prepaid insurance is the cost of a 2-year insurance policy, effective April 1.
2. Depreciation on the equipment is $500 per month.
3. The note payable is dated April 1. It is a 6-month, 12% note.
4. Seven customers paid for the company's 6 months' lawn service package of $600 beginning in April. The company performed services for these customers in April.
5. Lawn services provided other customers but not recorded at April 30 totaled $1,500.

Instructions

Prepare the adjusting entries for the month of April. Show computations.

Solution to Comprehensive

Action Plan

✔ Note that adjustments are being made for one month.

✔ Make computations carefully.

✔ Select account titles carefully.

✔ Make sure debits are made first and credits are indented.

✔ Check that debits equal credits for each entry.

GENERAL JOURNAL					J1
Date	**Account Titles and Explanation**	**Ref.**	**Debit**		**Credit**
	Adjusting Entries				
Apr. 30	Insurance Expense		150		
	Prepaid Insurance				150
	(To record insurance expired: $3,600 ÷ 24 = $150 per month)				
30	Depreciation Expense		500		
	Accumulated Depreciation—Equipment				500
	(To record monthly depreciation)				
30	Interest Expense		200		
	Interest Payable				200
	(To record interest on notes payable: $20,000 × 12% × 1/12 = $200)				
30	Unearned Service Revenue		700		
	Service Revenue				700
	(To record revenue for services performed: $600 ÷ 6 = $100; $100 per month × 7 = $700)				
30	Accounts Receivable		1,500		
	Service Revenue				1,500
	(To record revenue for services performed)				

 The Navigator

SUMMARY OF LEARNING OBJECTIVES

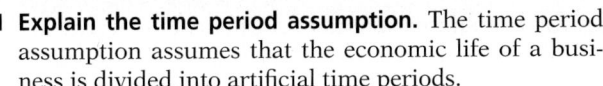 **The Navigator**

1 **Explain the time period assumption.** The time period assumption assumes that the economic life of a business is divided into artificial time periods.

2 **Explain the accrual basis of accounting.** Accrual-basis accounting means that companies record events that change a company's financial statements in the periods in which those events occur, rather than in the periods in which the company receives or pays cash.

3 **Explain the reasons for adjusting entries.** Companies make adjusting entries at the end of an accounting period.

Such entries ensure that companies recognize revenues in the period in which the performance obligation is satisfied and recognize expenses in the period in which they are incurred.

4 **Identify the major types of adjusting entries.** The major types of adjusting entries are deferrals (prepaid expenses and unearned revenues) and accruals (accrued revenues and accrued expenses).

5 **Prepare adjusting entries for deferrals.** Deferrals are either prepaid expenses or unearned revenues.

Companies make adjusting entries for deferrals to record the portion of the prepayment that represents the expense incurred or the revenue for services performed in the current accounting period.

6 Prepare adjusting entries for accruals. Accruals are either accrued revenues or accrued expenses. Companies make adjusting entries for accruals to record revenues for services performed and expenses incurred in the current accounting period that have not been recognized through daily entries.

7 Describe the nature and purpose of an adjusted trial balance. An adjusted trial balance shows the balances of all accounts, including those that have been adjusted, at the end of an accounting period. Its purpose is to prove the equality of the total debit balances and total credit balances in the ledger after all adjustments.

GLOSSARY

Accrual-basis accounting Accounting basis in which companies record transactions that change a company's financial statements in the periods in which the events occur. (p. 102).

Accruals Adjusting entries for either accrued revenues or accrued expenses. (p. 105).

Accrued expenses Expenses incurred but not yet paid in cash or recorded. (p. 114).

Accrued revenues Revenues for services performed but not yet received in cash or recorded. (p. 113).

Adjusted trial balance A list of accounts and their balances after the company has made all adjustments. (p. 121).

Adjusting entries Entries made at the end of an accounting period to ensure that companies follow the revenue and expense recognition principles. (p. 104).

Book value The difference between the cost of a depreciable asset and its related accumulated depreciation. (p. 109).

Calendar year An accounting period that extends from January 1 to December 31. (p. 102).

Cash-basis accounting Accounting basis in which companies record revenue when they receive cash and an expense when they pay cash. (p. 102).

Contra asset account An account offset against an asset account on the balance sheet. (p. 108).

Deferrals Adjusting entries for either prepaid expenses or unearned revenues. (p. 105).

Depreciation The allocation of the cost of an asset to expense over its useful life in a rational and systematic manner. (p. 108).

Expense recognition (matching) principle The principle that companies match efforts (expenses) with accomplishments (revenues). (p. 103).

Fiscal year An accounting period that is one year in length. (p. 102).

Interim periods Monthly or quarterly accounting time periods. (p. 102).

Prepaid expenses (prepayments) Expenses paid in cash before they are used or consumed. (p. 106).

Revenue recognition principle The principle that companies recognize revenue in the accounting period in which the performance obligation is satisfied. (p. 103).

Time period assumption An assumption that accountants can divide the economic life of a business into artificial time periods. (p. 102).

Unearned revenues Cash received before services are performed. (p. 110).

Useful life The length of service of a long-lived asset. (p. 108).

APPENDIX **3A** ALTERNATIVE TREATMENT OF PREPAID EXPENSES AND UNEARNED REVENUES

LEARNING OBJECTIVE   8

Prepare adjusting entries for the alternative treatment of deferrals.

In discussing adjusting entries for prepaid expenses and unearned revenues, we illustrated transactions for which companies made the initial entries to balance sheet accounts. In the case of prepaid expenses, the company debited the prepayment to an asset account. In the case of unearned revenue, the company credited a liability account to record the cash received.

Some companies use an alternative treatment: (1) When a company prepays an expense, it debits that amount to an expense account. (2) When it receives payment for future services, it credits the amount to a revenue account. In this appendix, we describe the circumstances that justify such entries and the different adjusting entries that may be required. This alternative treatment of prepaid expenses and unearned revenues has the same effect on the financial statements as the procedures described in the chapter.

Prepaid Expenses

Prepaid expenses become expired costs either through the passage of time (e.g., insurance) or through consumption (e.g., advertising supplies). If, at the time of purchase, the company expects to consume the supplies before the next financial statement date, **it may choose to debit (increase) an expense account rather than an asset account. This alternative treatment is simply more convenient**.

Assume that Pioneer Advertising Agency Inc. expects that it will use before the end of the month all of the supplies purchased on October 5. A debit of $2,500 to Supplies Expense (rather than to the asset account Supplies) on October 5 will eliminate the need for an adjusting entry on October 31. At October 31, the Supplies Expense account will show a balance of $2,500, which is the cost of supplies used between October 5 and October 31.

But what if the company does not use all the supplies? For example, what if an inventory of $1,000 of advertising supplies remains on October 31? Obviously, the company would need to make an adjusting entry. Prior to adjustment, the expense account Supplies Expense is overstated $1,000, and the asset account Supplies is understated $1,000. Thus, Pioneer makes the following adjusting entry.

Oct. 31	Supplies	1,000	
	Supplies Expense		1,000
	(To record supplies inventory)		

After the company posts the adjusting entry, the accounts show:

Supplies				Supplies Expense			
10/31 **Adj.**	**1,000**			10/5	2,500	10/31 **Adj.**	**1,000**
				10/31 **Bal.**	**1,500**		

A = L + SE
+1,000
+1,000 Exp

Cash Flows
no effect

Illustration 3A-1
Prepaid expenses accounts after adjustment

After adjustment, the asset account Supplies shows a balance of $1,000, which is equal to the cost of supplies on hand at October 31. In addition, Supplies Expense shows a balance of $1,500. This is equal to the cost of supplies used between October 5 and October 31. Without the adjusting entry expenses are overstated and net income is understated by $1,000 in the October income statement. Also, both assets and stockholders' equity are understated by $1,000 on the October 31 balance sheet.

Illustration 3A-2 compares the entries and accounts for advertising supplies in the two adjustment approaches.

Prepayment Initially Debited to Asset Account (per chapter)				Prepayment Initially Debited to Expense Account (per appendix)			
Oct. 5	Supplies	2,500		Oct. 5	Supplies Expense	2,500	
	Accounts Payable		2,500		Accounts Payable		2,500
Oct. 31	Supplies Expense	1,500		Oct. 31	Supplies	1,000	
	Supplies		1,500		Supplies Expense		1,000

Illustration 3A-2
Adjustment approaches— a comparison

After Pioneer posts the entries, the accounts appear as follows.

Illustration 3A-3
Comparison of accounts

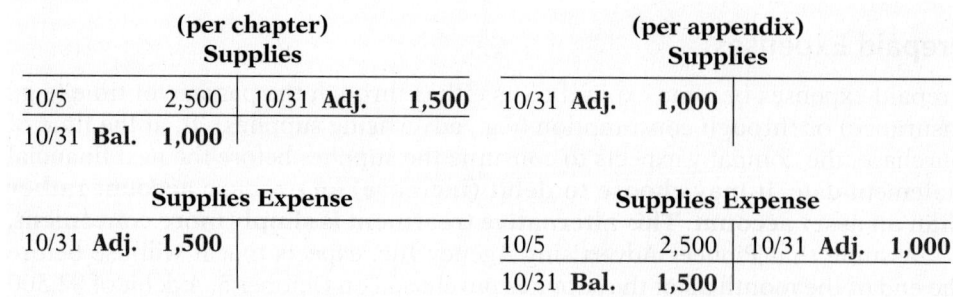

	(per chapter) Supplies				**(per appendix)** Supplies		
10/5	2,500	10/31 **Adj.**	1,500	10/31 **Adj.**	1,000		
10/31 **Bal.**	1,000						

	Supplies Expense				**Supplies Expense**		
10/31 **Adj.**	1,500			10/5	2,500	10/31 **Adj.**	1,000
				10/31 **Bal.**	1,500		

Note that the account balances under each alternative are the same at October 31: Supplies $1,000, and Supplies Expense $1,500.

Unearned Revenues

Unearned revenues are recognized as revenue at the time services are performed. Similar to the case for prepaid expenses, companies may credit (increase) a revenue account when they receive cash for future services.

To illustrate, assume that Pioneer Advertising Agency Inc. received $1,200 for future services on October 2. Pioneer expects to perform the services before October 31.[2] In such a case, the company credits Service Revenue. If Pioneer in fact performs the service before October 31, no adjustment is needed.

However, if at the statement date Pioneer has not performed $800 of the services, it would make an adjusting entry. Without the entry, the revenue account Service Revenue is overstated $800, and the liability account Unearned Service Revenue is understated $800. Thus, Pioneer makes the following adjusting entry.

Helpful Hint
The required adjusted balances here are Service Revenue $400 and Unearned Service Revenue $800.

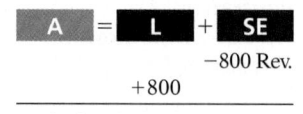
−800 Rev.
+800

Cash Flows
no effect

Oct. 31	Service Revenue		800	
	Unearned Service Revenue			800
	(To record unearned service revenue)			

After Pioneer posts the adjusting entry, the accounts show:

Illustration 3A-4
Unearned service revenue accounts after adjustment

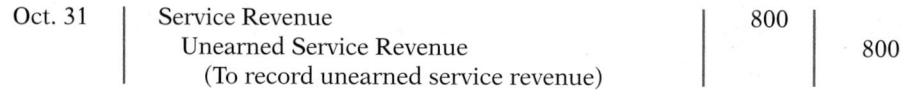

	Unearned Service Revenue				**Service Revenue**			
	10/31 **Adj.**	800	10/31 **Adj.**	800	10/2	1,200		
					10/31 **Bal.**	400		

The liability account Unearned Service Revenue shows a balance of $800. This equals the services that will be performed in the future. In addition, the balance in Service Revenue equals the services performed in October. Without the adjusting entry, both revenues and net income are overstated by $800 in the October income statement. Also, liabilities are understated by $800, and stockholders' equity is overstated by $800 on the October 31 balance sheet.

Illustration 3A-5 compares the entries and accounts for initially recording unearned service revenue in (1) a liability account or (2) a revenue account.

---

[2]This example focuses only on the alternative treatment of unearned revenues. For simplicity, we have ignored the entries to Service Revenue pertaining to the immediate recognition of revenue ($10,000) and the adjusting entry for accrued revenue ($200).

Illustration 3A-5
Adjustment approaches—a comparison

Unearned Service Revenue Initially Credited to Liability Account (per chapter)			Unearned Service Revenue Initially Credited to Revenue Account (per appendix)		
Oct. 2 Cash	1,200		Oct. 2 Cash	1,200	
Unearned Service			Service Revenue		1,200
Revenue		1,200			
Oct. 31 Unearned Service			Oct. 31 Service Revenue	800	
Revenue	400		Unearned Service		
Service Revenue		400	Revenue		800

After Pioneer posts the entries, the accounts appear as follows.

Illustration 3A-6
Comparison of accounts

(per chapter)
Unearned Service Revenue

10/31 **Adj.**	400	10/2	1,200
		10/31 **Bal.**	800

(per appendix)
Unearned Service Revenue

		10/31 **Adj.**	800

Service Revenue

		10/31 **Adj.**	400

Service Revenue

10/31 **Adj.**	800	10/2	1,200
		10/31 **Bal.**	400

Note that the balances in the accounts are the same under the two alternatives: Unearned Service Revenue $800, and Service Revenue $400.

Summary of Additional Adjustment Relationships

Illustration 3A-7
Summary of basic relationships for deferrals.

Illustration 3A-7 provides a summary of basic relationships for deferrals.

Type of Adjustment	Reason for Adjustment	Account Balances before Adjustment	Adjusting Entry
Prepaid expenses	(a) Prepaid expenses initially recorded in asset accounts have been used.	Assets overstated. Expenses understated.	Dr. Expenses Cr. Assets
	(b) Prepaid expenses initially recorded in expense accounts have not been used.	**Assets understated.** **Expenses overstated.**	**Dr. Assets** **Cr. Expenses**
Unearned revenues	(a) Unearned revenues initially recorded in liability accounts are now recognized as revenue.	Liabilities overstated. Revenues understated.	Dr. Liabilities Cr. Revenues
	(b) Unearned revenues initially recorded in revenue accounts are still unearned.	**Liabilities understated.** **Revenues overstated.**	**Dr. Revenues** **Cr. Liabilities**

Alternative adjusting entries **do not apply** to accrued revenues and accrued expenses because **no entries occur before companies make these types of adjusting entries**.

SUMMARY OF LEARNING OBJECTIVE FOR APPENDIX 3A

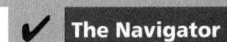 ✔ **The Navigator**

8 Prepare adjusting entries for the alternative treatment of deferrals. Companies may initially debit prepayments to an expense account. Likewise, they may credit unearned revenues to a revenue account. At the end of the period, these accounts may be overstated. The adjusting entries for prepaid expenses are a debit to an asset account and a credit to an expense account. Adjusting entries for unearned revenues are a debit to a revenue account and a credit to a liability account.

LEARNING OBJECTIVE **9**

Discuss financial reporting concepts.

This appendix provides a summary of the concepts in action used in this textbook. In addition, it provides other useful concepts which accountants use as a basis for recording and reporting financial information.

Qualities of Useful Information

Recently, the FASB and IASB completed the first phase of a joint project in which they developed a conceptual framework to serve as the basis for future accounting standards. The framework begins by stating that the primary objective of financial reporting is to provide financial information that is **useful** to investors and creditors for making decisions about providing capital. According to the FASB, useful information should possess two fundamental qualities, relevance and faithful representation, as shown in Illustration 3B-1.

Illustration 3B-1
Fundamental qualities of useful information

Relevance Accounting information is considered **relevant** if it would make a difference in a business decision. Information is considered relevant if it provides information that has **predictive value**, that is, helps provide accurate expectations about the future, and has **confirmatory value**, that is, confirms or corrects prior expectations.

Faithful Representation Faithful representation means that information accurately depicts what really happened. To provide a faithful representation, information must be **complete** (nothing important has been omitted) and **neutral** (is not biased toward one position or another).

ENHANCING QUALITIES

In addition to the two fundamental qualities, the FASB and IASB also describe a number of enhancing qualities of useful information. These include **comparability**, **consistency**, **verifiability**, **timeliness**, and **understandability**. In accounting, **comparability** results when different companies use the same accounting principles. Another characteristic that enhances comparability is consistency. **Consistency** means that a company uses the same accounting principles and methods from year to year. Information is **verifiable** if we are able to prove that it is free from error. For accounting information to be relevant, it must be **timely**. That is, it must be available to decision-makers before it loses its capacity to influence decisions. For example, public companies like Google or Best Buy must provide their annual reports to investors within 60 days of their year-end. Information has the quality of **understandability** if it is presented in a clear and concise fashion, so that reasonably informed users of that information can interpret it and comprehend its meaning.

Assumptions in Financial Reporting

To develop accounting standards, the FASB relies on some key assumptions, as shown in Illustration 3B-2. These include assumptions about the monetary unit, economic entity, time period, going concern, and accrual basis.

Illustration 3B-2
Key assumptions in financial reporting

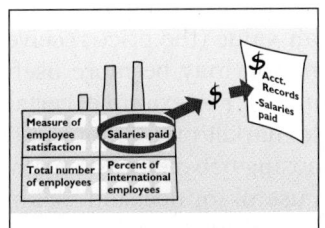

Monetary Unit Assumption The monetary unit assumption (discussed in Chapter 1) requires that only those things that can be expressed in money are included in the accounting records. This means that certain important information needed by investors, creditors, and managers, such as customer satisfaction, is not reported in the financial statements.

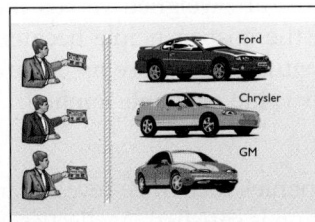

Economic Entity Assumption The economic entity assumption (discussed in Chapter 1) states that the activities of the entity must be kept separate and distinct from the activities of the owner. In order to assess a company's performance and financial position accurately, it is important that we not blur company transactions with personal transactions (especially those of its managers) or transactions of other companies.

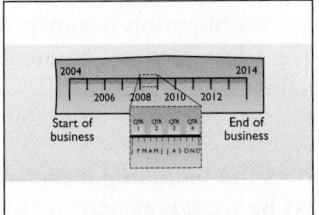

Time Period (Periodicity) Assumption Notice that the income statement, retained earnings statement, and statement of cash flows all cover periods of one year, and the balance sheet is prepared at the end of each year. The time period assumption (discussed in Chapter 3) states that the life of a business can be divided into artificial time periods and that useful reports covering those periods can be prepared for the business.

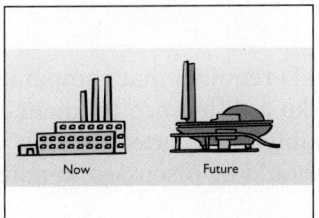

Going Concern Assumption The going concern assumption (discussed in Chapter 9) states that the business will remain in operation for the foreseeable future. Of course, many businesses do fail, but in general, it is reasonable to assume that the business will continue operating.

Accrual-Basis Assumption The accrual-basis accounting assumption (discussed in Chapter 3) means that transactions that change a company's financial statements are recorded in the periods in which the events occur. Accrual-basis accounting is addressed in more detail in Chapter 4.

Ethics Note

The importance of the economic entity assumption is illustrated by scandals involving Adelphia. In this case, senior company employees entered into transactions that blurred the line between the employees' financial interests and those of the company. For example, Adelphia guaranteed over $2 billion of loans to the founding family.

Principles in Financial Reporting

MEASUREMENT PRINCIPLES

GAAP generally uses one of two measurement principles, the cost principle or the fair value principle. Selection of which principle to follow generally relates to trade-offs between relevance and faithful representation.

COST PRINCIPLE The **cost principle** (or *historical cost principle,* discussed in Chapter 1) dictates that companies record assets at their cost. This is true not only at the time the asset is purchased but also over the time the asset is held. For example, if land that was purchased for $30,000 increases in value to $40,000, it continues to be reported at $30,000.

FAIR VALUE PRINCIPLE The **fair value principle** (discussed in Chapter 1) indicates that assets and liabilities should be reported at fair value (the price received to sell an asset or settle a liability). Fair value information may be more useful than historical cost for certain types of assets and liabilities. For example, certain investment securities are reported at fair value because market price information is often readily available for these types of assets. In choosing between cost and fair value, two qualities that make accounting information useful for decision-making are used—relevance and faithful representation. In determining which measurement principle to use, the factual nature of cost figures are weighed versus the relevance of fair value. In general, most assets follow the cost principle because market values are representationally faithful. Only in situations where assets are actively traded, such as investment securities, is the fair value principle applied.

REVENUE RECOGNITION PRINCIPLE

The **revenue recognition principle** requires that companies recognize revenue in the accounting period in which the performance obligation is satisfied. As discussed in Chapter 3, in a service company, revenue is recognized at the time the service is performed. In a merchandising company, the performance obligation is generally satisfied when the goods transfer from the seller to the buyer (discussed in Chapter 4). At this point, the sales transaction is complete and the sales price established.

EXPENSE RECOGNITION PRINCIPLE

The **expense recognition principle** (often referred to as the *matching principle*, discussed in Chapter 3) dictates that efforts (expenses) be matched with results (revenues). Thus, expenses follow revenues.

FULL DISCLOSURE PRINCIPLE

The **full disclosure principle** (discussed in Chapter 11) requires that companies disclose all circumstances and events that would make a difference to financial statement users. If an important item cannot reasonably be reported directly in one of the four types of financial statements, then it should be discussed in notes that accompany the statements.

Constraints In Financial Reporting

Efforts to provide useful financial information can be costly to a company. Therefore, the profession has agreed upon **constraints** to ensure that companies apply accounting rules in a reasonable fashion, from the perspectives of both the company and the user. The constraints are the materiality and cost constraints, as shown in Illustration 3B-3.

Illustration 3B-3
Constraints in financial reporting

Materiality Constraint The materiality constraint (discussed in Chapter 9) relates to a financial statement item's impact on a company's overall financial condition and operations. An item is **material** when its **size** makes it likely to influence the decision of an investor or creditor. It is **immaterial** if it is too small to impact a decision-maker. If the item does not make a difference, the company does not have to follow GAAP in reporting it.

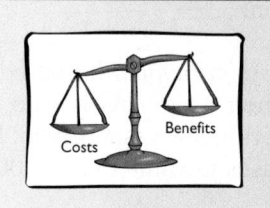

Cost Constraint The cost constraint (discussed in Chapter 1) relates to the fact that providing information is costly. In deciding whether companies should be required to provide a certain type of information, accounting standard-setters weigh the cost that companies will incur to provide the information against the benefit that financial statement users will gain from having the information available.

SUMMARY OF LEARNING OBJECTIVE FOR APPENDIX 3B

✔ **The Navigator**

9 Discuss financial reporting concepts. To be judged useful, information should have the primary characteristics of relevance and faithful representation. In addition, it should be comparable, consistent, verifiable, timely, and understandable.

The *monetary unit assumption* requires that companies include in the accounting records only transaction data that can be expressed in terms of money. The *economic entity assumption* states that economic events can be identified with a particular unit of accountability. The *time period assumption* states that the economic life of a business can be divided into artificial time periods and that meaningful accounting reports can be prepared for each period. The *going concern assumption* states that the company will continue in

operation long enough to carry out its existing objectives and commitments. The *accrual-basis accounting assumption* means that transactions are recorded in the periods in which the events occur.

The *cost principle* states that companies should record assets at their cost. The *fair value principle* indicates that assets and liabilities should be reported at fair value. The *revenue recognition principle* requires that companies recognize revenue in the accounting period in which the performance obligation is satisfied. The *expense recognition principle* dictates that efforts (expenses) be matched with results (revenues). The *full disclosure principle* requires that companies disclose circumstances and events that matter to financial statement users.

The major constraints are materiality and cost.

GLOSSARY FOR APPENDIX 3B

Accrual-basis accounting assumption Transactions that change a company's financial statements are recorded in the periods in which the events occur. (p. 131).

Comparability Ability to compare the accounting information of different companies because they use the same accounting principles. (p. 130).

Consistency Use of the same accounting principles and methods from year to year within a company. (p. 130).

Cost constraint Constraint of determining whether the cost that companies will incur to provide the information will outweigh the benefit that financial statement users will gain from having the information available. (p. 132).

Cost principle An accounting principle that states that companies should record assets at their cost. (p. 131).

Economic entity assumption An assumption that every economic entity can be separately identified and accounted for. (p. 131).

Expense recognition principle Efforts (expenses) should be matched with results (revenues). (p. 132)

Fair value principle Assets and liabilities should be reported at fair value (the price received to sell an asset or settle a liability). (p. 132).

Faithful representation Information that is complete, neutral, and free from error. (p. 130).

Full disclosure principle Accounting principle that dictates that companies disclose circumstances and

events that make a difference to financial statement users. (p. 132).

Going concern assumption The assumption that the company will continue in operation for the foreseeable future. (p. 131).

Materiality constraint The constraint of determining whether an item is large enough to likely influence the decision of an investor or creditor. (p. 132).

Monetary unit assumption An assumption that requires that only those things that can be expressed in money are included in the accounting records. (p. 131).

Relevance The quality of information that indicates the information makes a difference in a decision. (p. 130).

Revenue recognition principle Companies recognize revenue in the accounting period in which the performance obligation is satisfied. (p. 132).

Timely Information that is available to decision-makers before it loses its capacity to influence decisions. (p. 130).

Time period assumption An assumption that the life of a business can be divided into artificial time periods and that useful reports covering those periods can be prepared for the business. (p. 131).

Understandability Information presented in a clear and concise fashion so that users can interpret it and comprehend its meaning. (p. 130).

Verifiable Information that is proven to be free from error. (p. 130).

Note: All Questions, Exercises, and Problems marked with an asterisk relate to material in the appendices to the chapter.

SELF-TEST QUESTIONS

Answers are on page 159.

(LO 1) **1.** The time period assumption states that:
   (a) revenue should be recognized in the accounting period in which a performance obligation is satisfied.
   (b) expenses should be matched with revenues.
   (c) the economic life of a business can be divided into artificial time periods.
   (d) the fiscal year should correspond with the calendar year.

(LO 1) **2.** The time period assumption states that:
   (a) companies must wait until the calendar year is completed to prepare financial statements.
   (b) companies use the fiscal year to report financial information.
   (c) the economic life of a business can be divided into artificial time periods.
   (d) companies record information in the time period in which the events occur.

(LO 2) **3.** Which of the following statements about the accrual basis of accounting is *false*?
   (a) Events that change a company's financial statements are recorded in the periods in which the events occur.
   (b) Revenue is recognized in the period in which services are performed.
   (c) This basis is in accord with generally accepted accounting principles.
   (d) Revenue is recorded only when cash is received, and expense is recorded only when cash is paid.

(LO 2) **4.** The principle or assumption dictating that efforts (expenses) be matched with accomplishments (revenues) is the:
   (a) expense recognition principle.
   (b) cost assumption.
   (c) time period principle.
   (d) revenue recognition principle.

(LO 3) **5.** Adjusting entries are made to ensure that:
   (a) expenses are recognized in the period in which they are incurred.
   (b) revenues are recorded in the period in which services are provided.
   (c) balance sheet and income statement accounts have correct balances at the end of an accounting period.
   (d) All of the above.

(LO 4) **6.** Each of the following is a major type (or category) of adjusting entries *except:*
   (a) prepaid expenses.   (c) accrued expenses.
   (b) accrued revenues.   (d) recognized revenues.

(LO 5) **7.** The trial balance shows Supplies $1,350 and Supplies Expense $0. If $600 of supplies are on hand at the end of the period, the adjusting entry is:
   (a) Supplies   600
        Supplies Expense   600
   (b) Supplies   750
        Supplies Expense   750
   (c) Supplies Expense   750
        Supplies   750
   (d) Supplies Expense   600
        Supplies   600

(LO 5) **8.** Adjustments for prepaid expenses:
   (a) decrease assets and increase revenues.
   (b) decrease expenses and increase assets.
   (c) decrease assets and increase expenses.
   (d) decrease revenues and increase assets.

(LO 5) **9.** Accumulated Depreciation is:
   (a) a contra asset account.
   (b) an expense account.
   (c) a stockholders' equity account.
   (d) a liability account.

(LO 5) **10.** Queenan Company computes depreciation on delivery equipment at $1,000 for the month of June. The adjusting entry to record this depreciation is as follows.
   (a) Depreciation Expense   1,000
        Accumulated Depreciation—
        Queenan Company   1,000
   (b) Depreciation Expense   1,000
        Equipment   1,000
   (c) Depreciation Expense   1,000
        Accumulated Depreciation—
        Equipment   1,000
   (d) Equipment Expense   1,000
        Accumulated Depreciation—
        Equipment   1,000

(LO 5) **11.** Adjustments for unearned revenues:
   (a) decrease liabilities and increase revenues.
   (b) have an assets and revenues account relationship.
   (c) increase assets and increase revenues.
   (d) decrease revenues and decrease assets.

(LO 6) **12.** Adjustments for accrued revenues:
   (a) have a liabilities and revenues account relationship.
   (b) have an assets and revenues account relationship.
   (c) decrease assets and revenues.
   (d) decrease liabilities and increase revenues.

(LO 6) **13.** Kathy Siska earned a salary of $400 for the last week of September. She will be paid on October 1. The adjusting entry for Kathy's employer at September 30 is:

(a) No entry is required.

(b)	Salaries and Wages Expense	400	
	Salaries and Wages Payable		400
(c)	Salaries and Wages Expense	400	
	Cash		400
(d)	Salaries and Wages Payable	400	
	Cash		400

(LO 7) **14.** Which of the following statements is *incorrect* concerning the adjusted trial balance?

(a) An adjusted trial balance proves the equality of the total debit balances and the total credit balances in the ledger after all adjustments are made.

(b) The adjusted trial balance provides the primary basis for the preparation of financial statements.

(c) The adjusted trial balance lists the account balances segregated by assets and liabilities.

(d) The adjusted trial balance is prepared after the adjusting entries have been journalized and posted.

(LO 8) *15. The trial balance shows Supplies $0 and Supplies Expense $1,500. If $800 of supplies are on hand at the end of the period, the adjusting entry is:

(a) Debit Supplies $800 and credit Supplies Expense $800.

(b) Debit Supplies Expense $800 and credit Supplies $800.

(c) Debit Supplies $700 and credit Supplies Expense $700.

(d) Debit Supplies Expense $700 and credit Supplies $700.

*16. Neutrality is an ingredient of: (LO 9)

	Faithful Representation	Relevance
(a)	Yes	Yes
(b)	No	No
(c)	Yes	No
(d)	No	Yes

*17. What accounting constraint allows a company to ig-   (LO 9) nore GAAP if an item is too small to impact a decision?

(a) Comparability.   (c) Cost.

(b) Materiality.   (d) Consistency.

Go to the book's companion website, www.wiley.com/college/weygandt, for additional Self-Test Questions.

 The Navigator

QUESTIONS

1. (a) How does the time period assumption affect an accountant's analysis of business transactions?

(b) Explain the terms *fiscal year, calendar year,* and *interim periods*.

2. State two generally accepted accounting principles that relate to adjusting the accounts.

3. Gabe Corts, a lawyer, accepts a legal engagement in March, performs the work in April, and is paid in May. If Corts' law firm prepares monthly financial statements, when should it recognize revenue from this engagement? Why?

4. Why do accrual-basis financial statements provide more useful information than cash-basis statements?

5. In completing the engagement in Question 3, Corts pays no costs in March, $2,200 in April, and $2,500 in May (incurred in April). How much expense should the firm deduct from revenues in the month when it recognizes the revenue? Why?

6. "Adjusting entries are required by the cost principle of accounting." Do you agree? Explain.

7. Why may a trial balance not contain up-to-date and complete financial information?

8. Distinguish between the two categories of adjusting entries, and identify the types of adjustments applicable to each category.

9. What is the debit/credit effect of a prepaid expense adjusting entry?

10. "Depreciation is a valuation process that results in the reporting of the fair value of the asset." Do you agree? Explain.

11. Explain the differences between depreciation expense and accumulated depreciation.

12. M. Gibbs Company purchased equipment for $18,000. By the current balance sheet date, $7,000 had been depreciated. Indicate the balance sheet presentation of the data.

13. What is the debit/credit effect of an unearned revenue adjusting entry?

14. A company fails to recognize revenue for services performed but not yet received in cash or recorded. Which of the following accounts are involved in the adjusting entry: (a) asset, (b) liability, (c) revenue, or (d) expense? For the accounts selected, indicate whether they would be debited or credited in the entry.

15. A company fails to recognize an expense incurred but not paid. Indicate which of the following accounts is debited and which is credited in the adjusting entry: (a) asset, (b) liability, (c) revenue, or (d) expense.

16. A company makes an accrued revenue adjusting entry for $900 and an accrued expense adjusting entry for $700. How much was net income understated prior to these entries? Explain.

17. On January 9, a company pays $6,000 for salaries and wages, of which $2,000 was reported as Salaries and Wages Payable on December 31. Give the entry to record the payment.

18. For each of the following items before adjustment, indicate the type of adjusting entry (prepaid expense, unearned revenue, accrued revenue, or accrued expense) that is needed to correct the misstatement. If an item could result in more than one type of adjusting entry, indicate each of the types.

(a) Assets are understated.

(b) Liabilities are overstated.

(c) Liabilities are understated.
(d) Expenses are understated.
(e) Assets are overstated.
(f) Revenue is understated.

19. One-half of the adjusting entry is given below. Indicate the account title for the other half of the entry.
    (a) Salaries and Wages Expense is debited.
    (b) Depreciation Expense is debited.
    (c) Interest Payable is credited.
    (d) Supplies is credited.
    (e) Accounts Receivable is debited.
    (f) Unearned Service Revenue is debited.

20. "An adjusting entry may affect more than one balance sheet or income statement account." Do you agree? Why or why not?

21. Why is it possible to prepare financial statements directly from an adjusted trial balance?

22. **PEPSICO** What was PepsiCo's depreciation and amortization expense for 2010 and 2009?

*23. L. Thomas Company debits Supplies Expense for all purchases of supplies and credits Rent Revenue for all advanced rentals. For each type of adjustment, give the adjusting entry.

*24. (a) What is the primary objective of financial reporting?
     (b) Identify the characteristics of useful accounting information.

*25. Dan Fineman, the president of King Company, is pleased. King substantially increased its net income in 2014 while keeping its unit inventory relatively the same. Howard Gross, chief accountant, cautions Dan, however. Gross says that since King changed its method of inventory valuation, there is a consistency problem and it is difficult to determine whether King is better off. Is Gross correct? Why or why not?

*26. What is the distinction between comparability and consistency?

*27. Describe the two constraints inherent in the presentation of accounting information.

*28. Laurie Belk is president of Better Books. She has no accounting background. Belk cannot understand why fair value is not used as the basis for all accounting measurement and reporting. Discuss.

*29. What is the economic entity assumption? Give an example of its violation.

BRIEF EXERCISES

Indicate why adjusting entries are needed.

(LO 3)

BE3-1 The ledger of Basler Company includes the following accounts. Explain why each account may require adjustment.
(a) Prepaid Insurance
(b) Depreciation Expense
(c) Unearned Service Revenue
(d) Interest Payable

Identify the major types of adjusting entries.

(LO 4, 5, 6)

BE3-2 Lucci Company accumulates the following adjustment data at December 31. Indicate (a) the type of adjustment (prepaid expense, accrued revenues and so on), and (b) the status of accounts before adjustment (overstated or understated).

1. Supplies of $100 are on hand.
2. Services provided but not recorded total $870.
3. Interest of $200 has accumulated on a note payable.
4. Rent collected in advance totaling $560 has been recognized.

Prepare adjusting entry for supplies.

(LO 5)

BE3-3 Wow Advertising Company's trial balance at December 31 shows Supplies $6,700 and Supplies Expense $0. On December 31, there are $1,900 of supplies on hand. Prepare the adjusting entry at December 31, and using T-accounts, enter the balances in the accounts, post the adjusting entry, and indicate the adjusted balance in each account.

Prepare adjusting entry for depreciation.

(LO 5)

BE3-4 At the end of its first year, the trial balance of Wooster Company shows Equipment $32,000 and zero balances in Accumulated Depreciation—Equipment and Depreciation Expense. Depreciation for the year is estimated to be $6,000. Prepare the adjusting entry for depreciation at December 31, post the adjustments to T-accounts, and indicate the balance sheet presentation of the equipment at December 31.

Prepare adjusting entry for prepaid expense.

(LO 5)

BE3-5 On July 1, 2014, Pizner Co. pays $13,200 to Orlow Insurance Co. for a 3-year insurance contract. Both companies have fiscal years ending December 31. For Pizner Co., journalize and post the entry on July 1 and the adjusting entry on December 31.

Prepare adjusting entry for unearned revenue.

(LO 5)

BE3-6 Using the data in BE3-5, journalize and post the entry on July 1 and the adjusting entry on December 31 for Orlow Insurance Co. Orlow uses the accounts Unearned Service Revenue and Service Revenue.

BE3-7 The bookkeeper for Easton Company asks you to prepare the following accrued adjusting entries at December 31.

1. Interest on notes payable of $360 is accrued.
2. Services provided but not recorded total $1,750.
3. Salaries earned by employees of $900 have not been recorded.

Use the following account titles: Service Revenue, Accounts Receivable, Interest Expense, Interest Payable, Salaries and Wages Expense, and Salaries and Wages Payable.

Prepare adjusting entries for accruals.

(LO 6)

BE3-8 The trial balance of Gleason Company includes the following balance sheet accounts, which may require adjustment. For each account that requires adjustment, indicate (a) the type of adjusting entry (prepaid expenses, unearned revenues, accrued revenues, and accrued expenses) and (b) the related account in the adjusting entry.

Analyze accounts in an unadjusted trial balance.

(LO 4, 5, 6)

Accounts Receivable   Interest Payable
Prepaid Insurance   Unearned Service Revenue
Accumulated Depreciation—Equipment

BE3-9 The adjusted trial balance of Lopez Company at December 31, 2014, includes the following accounts: Common Stock $15,600; Dividends $6,000; Service Revenue $38,400; Salaries and Wages Expense $16,000; Insurance Expense $2,000; Rent Expense $4,400; Supplies Expense $1,500; and Depreciation Expense $1,300. Prepare an income statement for the year.

Prepare an income statement from an adjusted trial balance.

(LO 7)

BE3-10 Partial adjusted trial balance data for Lopez Company is presented in BE3-9. Prepare a retained earnings statement for the year assuming net income is $13,200 for the year and Retained Earnings is $7,240 on January 1.

Prepare a retained earnings statement from an adjusted trial balance.

(LO 7)

*BE3-11 Lim Company records all prepayments in income statement accounts. At April 30, the trial balance shows Supplies Expense $2,800, Service Revenue $9,200, and zero balances in related balance sheet accounts. Prepare the adjusting entries at April 30 assuming (a) $1,000 of supplies on hand and (b) $2,000 of service revenue should be reported as unearned.

Prepare adjusting entries under alternative treatment of deferrals.

(LO 8)

*BE3-12 The accompanying chart shows the qualitative characteristics of useful accounting information. Fill in the blanks.

Identify characteristics of useful information.

(LO 9)

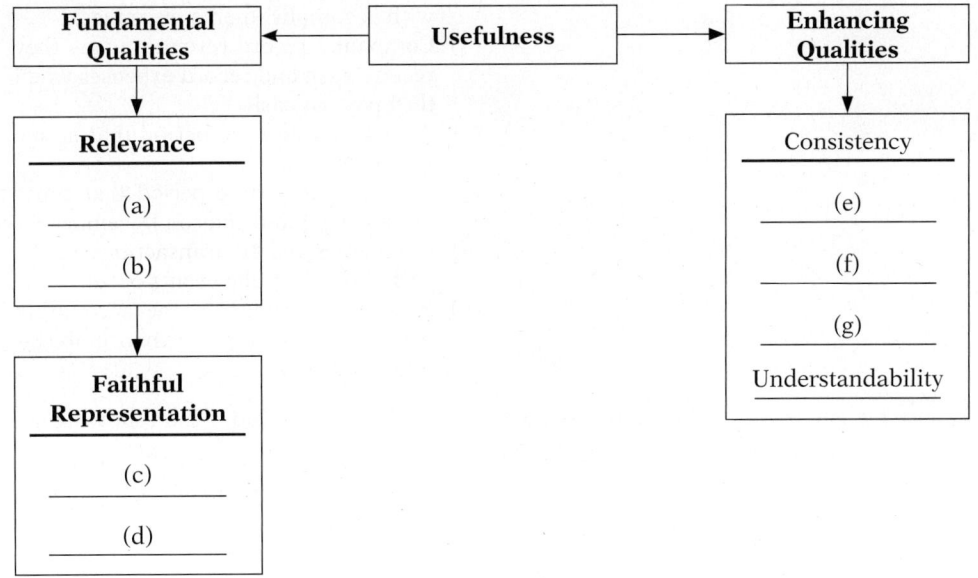

*BE3-13 Given the *characteristics* of useful accounting information, complete each of the following statements.

Identify characteristics of useful information.

(LO 9)

(a) For information to be _____, it should have predictive and confirmatory value.
(b) _____ is the quality of information that gives assurance that it is free from error and bias.
(c) _____ means using the same accounting principles and methods from year to year within a company.

Identify characteristics of useful information.

(LO 9)

*BE3-14 Here are some qualitative characteristics of useful accounting information:

1. Predictive value   3. Verifiable
2. Neutral   4. Timely

Match each qualitative characteristic to one of the following statements.

———— (a) Accounting information should help provide accurate expectations about future events.

———— (b) Accounting information cannot be selected, prepared, or presented to favor one set of interested users over another.

———— (c) Accounting information must be proved to be free of error.

———— (d) Accounting information must be available to decision-makers before it loses its capacity to influence their decisions.

Define full disclosure principle.

(LO 9)

*BE3-15 The full disclosure principle dictates that:

(a) financial statements should disclose all assets at their cost.

(b) financial statements should disclose only those events that can be measured in dollars.

(c) financial statements should disclose all events and circumstances that would matter to users of financial statements.

(d) financial statements should not be relied on unless an auditor has expressed an unqualified opinion on them.

> DO IT! REVIEW

Identify timing concepts.

(LO 1, 2)

DO IT! 3-1 Numerous timing concepts are discussed on pages 102–103. A list of concepts is provided below in the left column, with a description of the concept in the right column. There are more descriptions provided than concepts. Match the description of the concept to the concept.

1. _____ Cash-basis accounting.
2. _____ Fiscal year.
3. _____ Revenue recognition principle.
4. _____ Expense recognition principle.

(a) Monthly and quarterly time periods.

(b) Accountants divide the economic life of a business into artificial time periods.

(c) Efforts (expenses) should be matched with accomplishments (revenues).

(d) Companies record revenues when they receive cash and record expenses when they pay out cash.

(e) An accounting time period that is one year in length.

(f) An accounting time period that starts on January 1 and ends on December 31.

(g) Companies record transactions in the period in which the events occur.

(h) Recognize revenue in the accounting period in which a performance obligation is satisfied.

Prepare adjusting entries for deferrals.

(LO 5)

DO IT! 3-2 The ledger of Lafayette, Inc. on March 31, 2014, includes the following selected accounts before adjusting entries.

	Debit	Credit
Prepaid Insurance	2,400	
Supplies	2,500	
Equipment	30,000	
Unearned Service Revenue		9,000

An analysis of the accounts shows the following.

1. Insurance expires at the rate of $300 per month.
2. Supplies on hand total $1,400.
3. The equipment depreciates $200 per month.
4. 2/5 of the unearned service revenue was recognized in March.

Prepare the adjusting entries for the month of March.

DO IT! 3-3 Pegasus Computer Services began operations in July 2014. At the end of the month, the company is trying to prepare monthly financial statements. Pegasus has the following information for the month.

Prepare adjusting entries for accruals.

(LO 6)

1. At July 31, Pegasus owed employees $1,300 in salaries that the company will pay in August.
2. On July 1, Pegasus borrowed $20,000 from a local bank on a 10-year note. The annual interest rate is 9%.
3. Service revenue unrecorded in July totaled $2,400.

Prepare the adjusting entries needed at July 31, 2014.

DO IT! 3-4 Phelps Co. was organized on April 1, 2014. The company prepares quarterly financial statements. The adjusted trial balance amounts at June 30 are shown below.

Calculate amounts from trial balance.

(LO 7)

Debits		Credits	
Cash	$ 5,190	Accumulated Depreciation—	$ 700
Accounts Receivable	480	Equipment	
Prepaid Rent	720	Notes Payable	4,000
Supplies	920	Accounts Payable	790
Equipment	12,000	Salaries and Wages Payable	300
Dividends	500	Interest Payable	40
Salaries and Wages Expense	7,400	Unearned Rent Revenue	400
Rent Expense	1,200	Common Stock	11,200
Depreciation Expense	700	Service Revenue	11,360
Supplies Expense	160	Rent Revenue	900
Utilities Expense	380	Total credits	$29,690
Interest Expense	40		
Total debits	$29,690		

(a) Determine the net income for the quarter April 1 to June 30.
(b) Determine the total assets and total liabilities at June 30, 2014, for Phelps Company.
(c) Determine the amount that appears for Retained Earnings at June 30, 2014.

 The Navigator

EXERCISES

E3-1 Fred Mosure has prepared the following list of statements about the time period assumption.

Explain the time period assumption.

(LO 1)

1. Adjusting entries would not be necessary if a company's life were not divided into artificial time periods.
2. The IRS requires companies to file annual tax returns.
3. Accountants divide the economic life of a business into artificial time periods, but each transaction affects only one of these periods.
4. Accounting time periods are generally a month, a quarter, or a year.
5. A time period lasting one year is called an interim period.
6. All fiscal years are calendar years, but not all calendar years are fiscal years.

Instructions
Identify each statement as true or false. If false, indicate how to correct the statement.

E3-2 On numerous occasions, proposals have surfaced to put the federal government on the accrual basis of accounting. This is no small issue. If this basis were used, it would mean that billions in unrecorded liabilities would have to be booked, and the federal deficit would increase substantially.

Distinguish between cash and accrual basis of accounting.

(LO 2)

Instructions ▭▭▭▭▷

(a) What is the difference between accrual-basis accounting and cash-basis accounting?

(b) Why would politicians prefer the cash basis over the accrual basis?

(c) Write a letter to your senator explaining why the federal government should adopt the accrual basis of accounting.

Compute cash and accrual accounting income.

(LO 2)

E3-3 Concordia Industries collected $105,000 from customers in 2014. Of the amount collected, $28,000 was from revenue accrued from services performed in 2013. In addition, Concordia recognized $44,000 of revenue in 2014, which will not be collected until 2015.

Concordia Industries also paid $72,000 for expenses in 2014. Of the amount paid, $30,000 was for expenses incurred on account in 2013. In addition, Concordia incurred $37,000 of expenses in 2014, which will not be paid until 2015.

Instructions

(a) Compute 2014 cash-basis net income.

(b) Compute 2014 accrual-basis net income.

Identify the type of adjusting entry needed.

(LO 4)

E3-4 Waverly Corporation encounters the following situations:

1. Waverly collects $1,750 from a customer in 2014 for services to be performed in 2015.
2. Waverly incurs utility expense which is not yet paid in cash or recorded.
3. Waverly employees worked 3 days in 2014 but will not be paid until 2015.
4. Waverly performs services for a customer but has not yet received cash or recorded the transaction.
5. Waverly paid $2,400 rent on December 1 for the 4 months starting December 1.
6. Waverly received cash for future services and recorded a liability until the service was performed.
7. Waverly performed consulting services for a client in December 2014. On December 31, it had not billed the client for services provided of $1,200.
8. Waverly paid cash for an expense and recorded an asset until the item was used up.
9. Waverly purchased $750 of supplies in 2014; at year-end, $400 of supplies remain unused.
10. Waverly purchased equipment on January 1, 2014; the equipment will be used for 5 years.
11. Waverly borrowed $10,000 on October 1, 2014, signing an 8% one-year note payable.

Instructions

Identify what type of adjusting entry (prepaid expense, unearned revenue, accrued expense, or accrued revenue) is needed in each situation, at December 31, 2014.

Prepare adjusting entries from selected data.

(LO 5, 6)

E3-5 Dan Luther Company has the following balances in selected accounts on December 31, 2014.

Accounts Receivable	$ –0–
Accumulated Depreciation—Equipment	–0–
Equipment	7,000
Interest Payable	–0–
Notes Payable	8,000
Prepaid Insurance	2,100
Salaries and Wages Payable	–0–
Supplies	2,450
Unearned Service Revenue	30,000

All the accounts have normal balances. The information below has been gathered at December 31, 2014.

1. Dan Luther Company borrowed $8,000 by signing a 10%, one-year note on October 1, 2014.
2. A count of supplies on December 31, 2014, indicates that supplies of $780 are on hand.
3. Depreciation on the equipment for 2014 is $1,000.
4. Dan Luther Company paid $2,100 for 12 months of insurance coverage on June 1, 2014.
5. On December 1, 2014, Dan Luther collected $30,000 for consulting services to be performed from December 1, 2014, through March 31, 2015.
6. Dan Luther performed consulting services for a client in December 2014. The client will be billed $3,900.

7. Dan Luther Company pays its employees total salaries of $9,000 every Monday for the preceding 5-day week (Monday through Friday). On Monday, December 29, employees were paid for the week ending December 26. All employees worked the last 3 days of 2014.

Instructions

Prepare adjusting entries for the seven items described on page 140 and above.

E3-6 Orwell Company accumulates the following adjustment data at December 31.

1. Services provided but not recorded total $1,420.
2. Supplies of $300 have been used.
3. Utility expenses of $225 are unpaid.
4. Unearned service revenue of $260 is recognized for services performed.
5. Salaries of $800 are unpaid.
6. Prepaid insurance totaling $380 has expired.

Identify types of adjustments and account relationships.

(LO 4, 5, 6)

Instructions

For each of the above items indicate the following.

(a) The type of adjustment (prepaid expense, unearned revenue, accrued revenue, or accrued expense).
(b) The status of accounts before adjustment (overstatement or understatement).

E3-7 The ledger of Villa Rental Agency on March 31 of the current year includes the selected accounts, shown below, before adjusting entries have been prepared.

Prepare adjusting entries from selected account data.

(LO 5, 6)

	Debit	Credit
Prepaid Insurance	$ 3,600	
Supplies	2,800	
Equipment	25,000	
Accumulated		
Depreciation—Equipment		$ 8,400
Notes Payable		20,000
Unearned Rent Revenue		9,900
Rent Revenue		60,000
Interest Expense	–0–	
Salaries and Wages Expense	14,000	

An analysis of the accounts shows the following.

1. The equipment depreciates $300 per month.
2. One-third of the unearned rent revenue was recognized during the quarter.
3. Interest of $500 is accrued on the notes payable.
4. Supplies on hand total $650.
5. Insurance expires at the rate of $200 per month.

Instructions

Prepare the adjusting entries at March 31, assuming that adjusting entries are made **quarterly**. Additional accounts are: Depreciation Expense, Insurance Expense, Interest Payable, and Supplies Expense.

E3-8 Kari Engle, D.D.S., opened a dental practice on January 1, 2014. During the first month of operations, the following transactions occurred.

Prepare adjusting entries.

(LO 5, 6)

1. Performed services for patients who had dental plan insurance. At January 31, $875 of such services were performed but not yet recorded.
2. Utility expenses incurred but not paid prior to January 31 totaled $520.
3. Purchased dental equipment on January 1 for $80,000, paying $20,000 in cash and signing a $60,000, 3-year note payable. The equipment depreciates $400 per month. Interest is $500 per month.
4. Purchased a six-month malpractice insurance policy on January 1 for $18,000.
5. Purchased $1,600 of dental supplies. On January 31, determined that $700 of supplies were on hand.

Instructions

Prepare the adjusting entries on January 31. Account titles are: Accumulated Depreciation—Equipment, Depreciation Expense, Service Revenue, Accounts Receivable, Insurance Expense, Interest Expense, Interest Payable, Prepaid Insurance, Supplies, Supplies Expense, Utilities Expense, and Accounts Payable.

Prepare adjusting entries.

(LO 5, 6)

E3-9 The trial balance for Pioneer Advertising Agency Inc. is shown in Illustration 3-3, page 105. In lieu of the adjusting entries shown in the text at October 31, assume the following adjustment data.

1. Supplies on hand at October 31 total $800.
2. Expired insurance for the month is $100.
3. Depreciation for the month is $50.
4. Unearned service revenue recognized in October totals $600.
5. Services provided but not recorded at October 31 are $300.
6. Interest accrued at October 31 is $70.
7. Accrued salaries at October 31 are $1,200.

Instructions

Prepare the adjusting entries for the items above.

Prepare correct income statement.

(LO 2, 5, 6, 7)

E3-10 The income statement of Midland Co. for the month of July shows net income of $1,500 based on Service Revenue $5,500, Salaries and Wages Expense $2,300, Supplies Expense $1,200, and Utilities Expense $500. In reviewing the statement, you discover the following.

1. Insurance expired during July of $400 was omitted.
2. Supplies expense includes $300 of supplies that are still on hand at July 31.
3. Depreciation on equipment of $150 was omitted.
4. Accrued but unpaid salaries and wages at July 31 of $280 were not included.
5. Services performed but unrecorded totaled $920.

Instructions

Prepare a correct income statement for July 2014.

Analyze adjusted data.

(LO 4, 5, 6, 7)

E3-11 A partial adjusted trial balance of Ruiz Company at January 31, 2014, shows the following.

Ruiz Company
Adjusted Trial Balance
January 31, 2014

	Debit	Credit
Supplies	$ 850	
Prepaid Insurance	2,400	
Salaries and Wages Payable		$ 800
Unearned Service Revenue		750
Supplies Expense	950	
Insurance Expense	400	
Salaries and Wages Expense	2,500	
Service Revenue		2,000

Instructions

Answer the following questions, assuming the year begins January 1.

(a) If the amount in Supplies Expense is the January 31 adjusting entry, and $670 of supplies was purchased in January, what was the balance in Supplies on January 1?

(b) If the amount in Insurance Expense is the January 31 adjusting entry, and the original insurance premium was for one year, what was the total premium and when was the policy purchased?

Journalize basic transactions and adjusting entries.

(LO 5, 6, 7)

(c) If $3,300 of salaries was paid in January, what was the balance in Salaries and Wages Payable at December 31, 2013?

E3-12 Selected accounts of Welch Company are shown on the next page.

Supplies Expense

7/31	800	

Supplies				**Salaries and Wages Payable**		
7/1 Bal.	1,100	7/31	800		7/31	1,200
7/10	200					

Accounts Receivable		**Unearned Service Revenue**			
7/31	620	7/31	900	7/1 Bal.	1,500
				7/20	750

Salaries and Wages Expense		**Service Revenue**		
7/15	1,200		7/14	2,000
7/31	1,200		7/31	900
			7/31	620

Instructions

After analyzing the accounts, journalize (a) the July transactions and (b) the adjusting entries that were made on July 31. (*Hint:* July transactions were for cash.)

E3-13 The trial balances before and after adjustment for Matusiak Company at the end of its fiscal year are presented below.

Prepare adjusting entries from analysis of trial balances.

(LO 5, 6, 7)

Matusiak Company
Trial Balance
August 31, 2014

	Before Adjustment		After Adjustment	
	Dr.	Cr.	Dr.	Cr.
Cash	$10,400		$10,400	
Accounts Receivable	8,800		10,000	
Supplies	2,300		700	
Prepaid Insurance	4,000		2,500	
Equipment	14,000		14,000	
Accumulated Depreciation—Equipment		$ 3,600		$ 4,900
Accounts Payable		5,800		5,800
Salaries and Wages Payable		–0–		1,100
Unearned Rent Revenue		1,500		800
Common Stock		12,000		12,000
Retained Earnings		3,600		3,600
Service Revenue		34,000		35,200
Rent Revenue		11,000		11,700
Salaries and Wages Expense	17,000		18,100	
Supplies Expense	–0–		1,600	
Rent Expense	15,000		15,000	
Insurance Expense	–0–		1,500	
Depreciation Expense	–0–		1,300	
	$71,500	$71,500	$75,100	$75,100

Instructions

Prepare the adjusting entries that were made.

*Prepare financial statements
from adjusted trial balance.*

(LO 7)

E3-14 The adjusted trial balance for Matusiak Company is given in E3-13.

Instructions
Prepare the income and retained earnings statements for the year and the balance sheet at August 31.

*Record transactions on
accrual basis; convert
revenue to cash receipts.*

(LO 5, 6)

E3-15 The following data are taken from the comparative balance sheets of Newman Billiards Club, which prepares its financial statements using the accrual basis of accounting.

December 31	2014	2013
Accounts receivable from members	$12,000	$ 9,000
Unearned service revenue	17,000	20,000

Members are billed based upon their use of the club's facilities. Unearned service revenues arise from the sale of gift certificates, which members can apply to their future use of club facilities. The 2014 income statement for the club showed that service revenue of $153,000 was recognized during the year.

Instructions
(*Hint:* You will probably find it helpful to use T-accounts to analyze these data.)

(a) Prepare journal entries for each of the following events that took place during 2014.
   (1) Accounts receivable from 2013 were all collected.
   (2) Gift certificates outstanding at the end of 2013 were all redeemed.
   (3) An additional $35,000 worth of gift certificates were sold during 2014. A portion of these was used by the recipients during the year; the remainder was still outstanding at the end of 2014.
   (4) Services provided to members for 2014 were billed to members.
   (5) Accounts receivable for 2014 (i.e., those billed in item [4] above) were partially collected.
(b) Determine the amount of cash received by the club, with respect to member services, during 2014.

*Compute cash flow from
operations and net income.*

(LO 2)

E3-16 In its first year of operations, Anya Company recognized $30,000 in service revenue, $4,800 of which was on account and still outstanding at year-end. The remaining $25,200 was received in cash from customers.

The company incurred operating expenses of $17,000. Of these expenses $12,000 was paid in cash; $5,000 was still owed on account at year-end. In addition, Anya prepaid $2,600 for insurance coverage that would not be used until the second year of operations.

Instructions
(a) Compute Anya's first-year cash flow from operations.
(b) Compute Anya's first-year net income under accrual-basis accounting.
(c) Which basis of accounting (cash or accrual) provides more useful information for decision-makers?

Journalize adjusting entries.

(LO 8)

*E3-17 Rogert Company has the following balances in selected accounts on December 31, 2014.

Service Revenue	$40,000
Insurance Expense	2,880
Supplies Expense	2,450

All the accounts have normal balances. Rogert Company debits prepayments to expense accounts when paid, and credits unearned revenues to revenue accounts when received. The following information below has been gathered at December 31, 2014.

1. Rogert Company paid $2,880 for 12 months of insurance coverage on April 1, 2014.
2. On December 1, 2014, Rogert Company collected $40,000 for consulting services to be performed from December 1, 2014, through March 31, 2015.
3. A count of supplies on December 31, 2014, indicates that supplies of $420 are on hand.

Instructions
Prepare the adjusting entries needed at December 31, 2014.

*E3-18 At Beloit Company, prepayments are debited to expense when paid, and unearned revenues are credited to revenue when cash is received. During January of the current year, the following transactions occurred.

Journalize transactions and adjusting entries.

(LO 8)

Jan. 2   Paid $2,640 for fire insurance protection for the year.
     10   Paid $1,700 for supplies.
     15   Received $6,400 for services to be performed in the future.

On January 31, it is determined that $2,500 of the services were performed and that there are $650 of supplies on hand.

Instructions
(a) Journalize and post the January transactions. (Use T-accounts.)
(b) Journalize and post the adjusting entries at January 31.
(c) Determine the ending balance in each of the accounts.

*E3-19 Presented below are the assumptions and principles discussed in this chapter.

Identify accounting assumptions and principles.

(LO 9)

1. Full disclosure principle.
2. Going concern assumption.
3. Monetary unit assumption.
4. Time period assumption.
5. Cost principle.
6. Economic entity assumption.

Instructions
Identify by number the accounting assumption or principle that is described below. Do not use a number more than once.

_____ (a) Is the rationale for why plant assets are not reported at liquidation value. (*Note:* Do not use the cost principle.)
_____ (b) Indicates that personal and business record-keeping should be separately maintained.
_____ (c) Assumes that the dollar is the "measuring stick" used to report on financial performance.
_____ (d) Separates financial information into time periods for reporting purposes.
_____ (e) Measurement basis used when a reliable estimate of fair value is not available.
_____ (f) Dictates that companies should disclose all circumstances and events that make a difference to financial statement users.

*E3-20 Rosman Co. had three major business transactions during 2014.

Identify the assumption or principle that has been violated.

(LO 9)

(a) Reported at its fair value of $260,000 merchandise inventory with a cost of $208,000.
(b) The president of Rosman Co., Jay Rosman, purchased a truck for personal use and charged it to his expense account.
(c) Rosman Co. wanted to make its 2014 income look better, so it added 2 more weeks to the year (a 54-week year). Previous years were 52 weeks.

Instructions
In each situation, identify the assumption or principle that has been violated, if any, and discuss what the company should have done.

*E3-21 The following are characteristics, assumptions, principles, or constraints that guide the FASB when it creates accounting standards.

Identity financial accounting concepts and principles.

(LO 9)

Relevance	Expense recognition principle
Faithful representation	Time period assumption
Comparability	Going concern assumption
Consistency	Cost principle
Monetary unit assumption	Full disclosure principle
Economic entity assumption	Materiality constraint

Match each item above with a description below.

1. _____ Ability to easily evaluate one company's results relative to another's.
2. _____ Belief that a company will continue to operate for the foreseeable future.
3. _____ The judgment concerning whether an item is large enough to matter to decision-makers.

4. _____ The reporting of all information that would make a difference to financial statement users.
5. _____ The practice of preparing financial statements at regular intervals.
6. _____ The quality of information that indicates the information makes a difference in a decision.
7. _____ A belief that items should be reported on the balance sheet at the price that was paid to acquire the item.
8. _____ A company's use of the same accounting principles and methods from year to year.
9. _____ Tracing accounting events to particular companies.
10. _____ The desire to minimize errors and bias in financial statements.
11. _____ Reporting only those things that can be measured in dollars.
12. _____ Dictates that efforts (expenses) be matched with results (revenues).

Comment on the objectives and qualitative characteristics of accounting information

(LO 9)

*E3-22 Net Nanny Software International Inc., headquartered in Vancouver, specializes in Internet safety and computer security products for both the home and commercial markets. In a recent balance sheet, it reported a deficit (negative retained earnings) of US $5,678,288. It has reported only net losses since its inception. In spite of these losses, Net Nanny's common shares have traded anywhere from a high of $3.70 to a low of $0.32 on the Canadian Venture Exchange.

Net Nanny's financial statements have historically been prepared in Canadian dollars. Recently, the company adopted the U.S. dollar as its reporting currency.

Instructions ▭▭▭▷
(a) What is the objective of financial reporting? How does this objective meet or not meet Net Nanny's investors' needs?
(b) Why would investors want to buy Net Nanny's shares if the company has consistently reported losses over the last few years? Include in your answer an assessment of the relevance of the information reported on Net Nanny's financial statements.
(c) Comment on how the change in reporting information from Canadian dollars to U.S. dollars likely affected the readers of Net Nanny's financial statements. Include in your answer an assessment of the comparability of the information.

Comment on the objectives and qualitative characteristics of financial reporting.

(LO 9)

*E3-23 A friend of yours, Ana Gehrig, recently completed an undergraduate degree in science and has just started working with a biotechnology company. Ana tells you that the owners of the business are trying to secure new sources of financing which are needed in order for the company to proceed with development of a new health care product. Ana said that her boss told her that the company must put together a report to present to potential investors.

Ana thought that the company should include in this package the detailed scientific findings related to the Phase I clinical trials for this product. She said, "I know that the biotech industry sometimes has only a 10% success rate with new products, but if we report all the scientific findings, everyone will see what a sure success this is going to be! The president was talking about the importance of following some set of accounting principles. Why do we need to look at some accounting rules? What they need to realize is that we have scientific results that are quite encouraging, some of the most talented employees around, and the start of some really great customer relationships. We haven't made any sales yet, but we will. We just need the funds to get through all the clinical testing and get government approval for our product. Then these investors will be quite happy that they bought in to our company early!"

Instructions ▭▭▭▷
(a) What is accounting information?
(b) Comment on how Ana's suggestions for what should be reported to prospective investors conforms to the qualitative characteristics of accounting information. Do you think that the things that Ana wants to include in the information for investors will conform to financial reporting guidelines?

EXERCISES: SET B AND CHALLENGE EXERCISES

Visit the book's companion website, at **www.wiley.com/college/weygandt**, and choose the Student Companion site to access Exercise Set B and Challenge Exercises.

PROBLEMS: SET A

P3-1A Joey Cuono started his own consulting firm, Cuono Company, on June 1, 2014. The trial balance at June 30 is shown below.

Prepare adjusting entries, post to ledger accounts, and prepare adjusted trial balance.

(LO 5, 6, 7)

Cuono Company
Trial Balance
June 30, 2014

Account Number		Debit	Credit
101	Cash	$ 6,200	
112	Accounts Receivable	6,000	
126	Supplies	2,000	
130	Prepaid Insurance	3,000	
157	Equipment	14,400	
201	Accounts Payable		$ 4,700
209	Unearned Service Revenue		4,000
311	Common Stock		20,000
400	Service Revenue		7,900
726	Salaries and Wages Expense	4,000	
729	Rent Expense	1,000	
		$36,600	$36,600

In addition to those accounts listed on the trial balance, the chart of accounts for Cuono Company also contains the following accounts and account numbers: No. 158 Accumulated Depreciation—Equipment, No. 212 Salaries and Wages Payable, No. 631 Supplies Expense, No. 711 Depreciation Expense, No. 722 Insurance Expense, and No. 732 Utilities Expense.

Other data:

1. Supplies on hand at June 30 are $1,100.
2. A utility bill for $150 has not been recorded and will not be paid until next month.
3. The insurance policy is for a year.
4. $2,500 of unearned service revenue is recognized for services performed at the end of the month.
5. Salaries of $1,600 are accrued at June 30.
6. The equipment has a 4-year life with no salvage value. It is being depreciated at $300 per month for 48 months.
7. Invoices representing $2,100 of services performed during the month have not been recorded as of June 30.

Instructions
(a) Prepare the adjusting entries for the month of June. Use J3 as the page number for your journal.
(b) Post the adjusting entries to the ledger accounts. Enter the totals from the trial balance as beginning account balances and place a check mark in the posting reference column.
(c) Prepare an adjusted trial balance at June 30, 2014.

(c) Adj. trial balance $40,750

Prepare adjusting entries, post, and prepare adjusted trial balance, and financial statements.

(LO 5, 6, 7)

P3-2A Lazy River Resort opened for business on June 1 with eight air-conditioned units. Its trial balance before adjustment on August 31 is as follows.

Lazy River Resort, Inc.
Trial Balance
August 31, 2014

Account Number		Debit	Credit
101	Cash	$ 19,600	
126	Supplies	3,300	
130	Prepaid Insurance	6,000	
140	Land	25,000	
143	Buildings	125,000	
157	Equipment	26,000	
201	Accounts Payable		$ 6,500
208	Unearned Rent Revenue		7,400
275	Mortgage Payable		80,000
311	Common Stock		100,000
332	Dividends	5,000	
429	Rent Revenue		80,000
622	Maintenance and Repairs Expense	3,600	
726	Salaries and Wages Expense	51,000	
732	Utilities Expense	9,400	
		$273,900	$273,900

In addition to those accounts listed on the trial balance, the chart of accounts for Lazy River Resort also contains the following accounts and account numbers: No. 112 Accounts Receivable, No. 144 Accumulated Depreciation—Buildings, No. 158 Accumulated Depreciation—Equipment, No. 212 Salaries and Wages Payable, No. 230 Interest Payable, No. 631 Supplies Expense, No. 711 Depreciation Expense, No. 718 Interest Expense, and No. 722 Insurance Expense.

Other data:

1. Insurance expires at the rate of $400 per month.
2. A count on August 31 shows $900 of supplies on hand.
3. Annual depreciation is $4,500 on buildings and $2,400 on equipment.
4. Unearned rent revenue of $4,100 was recognized for services performed prior to August 31.
5. Salaries of $400 were unpaid at August 31.
6. Rentals of $3,700 were due from tenants at August 31. (Use Accounts Receivable.)
7. The mortgage interest rate is 9% per year. (The mortgage was taken out on August 1.)

(c) Adj. trial balance $280,325

(d) Net income $17,475
Ending retained earnings
$12,475

Total assets $203,275

Instructions
(a) Journalize the adjusting entries on August 31 for the 3-month period June 1–August 31.
(b) Prepare a ledger using the three-column form of account. Enter the trial balance amounts and post the adjusting entries. (Use J1 as the posting reference.)
(c) Prepare an adjusted trial balance on August 31.
(d) Prepare an income statement and a retained earnings statement for the 3 months ending August 31 and a balance sheet as of August 31.

Prepare adjusting entries and financial statements.

(LO 5, 6, 7)

P3-3A Costello Advertising Agency Inc. was founded by Pat Costello in January of 2013. Presented on the next page are both the adjusted and unadjusted trial balances as of December 31, 2014.

(b) Net income $38,450
Ending retained earnings
$31,950

Total assets $69,000

(c) (1) 6%
(2) $4,500

Instructions
(a) Journalize the annual adjusting entries that were made.
(b) Prepare an income statement and a retained earnings statement for the year ending December 31, 2014, and a balance sheet at December 31.
(c) Answer the following questions.
   (1) If the note has been outstanding 6 months, what is the annual interest rate on that note?
   (2) If the company paid $14,500 in salaries in 2014, what was the balance in Salaries and Wages Payable on December 31, 2013?

Costello Advertising Agency, Inc.
Trial Balance
December 31, 2014

	Unadjusted Dr.	Unadjusted Cr.	Adjusted Dr.	Adjusted Cr.
Cash	$11,000		$11,000	
Accounts Receivable	20,000		23,500	
Supplies	8,600		5,000	
Prepaid Insurance	3,350		2,500	
Equipment	60,000		60,000	
Accumulated Depreciation—Equipment		$ 28,000		$ 33,000
Accounts Payable		5,000		5,000
Interest Payable		–0–		150
Notes Payable		5,000		5,000
Unearned Service Revenue		7,200		5,600
Salaries and Wages Payable		–0–		1,300
Common Stock		20,000		20,000
Retained Earnings		5,500		5,500
Dividends	12,000		12,000	
Service Revenue		58,600		63,700
Salaries and Wages Expense	10,000		11,300	
Insurance Expense			850	
Interest Expense	350		500	
Depreciation Expense			5,000	
Supplies Expense			3,600	
Rent Expense	4,000		4,000	
	$129,300	$129,300	$139,250	$139,250

P3-4A A review of the ledger of Bellingham Company at December 31, 2014, produces the following data pertaining to the preparation of annual adjusting entries.

Preparing adjusting entries.
(LO 5, 6)
1. Salaries and wages expense $2,200

1. Salaries and Wages Payable $0. There are eight salaried employees. Salaries are paid every Friday for the current week. Five employees receive a salary of $800 each per week, and three employees earn $500 each per week. Assume December 31 is a Tuesday. Employees do not work weekends. All employees worked the last 2 days of December.

2. Unearned Rent Revenue $324,000. The company began subleasing office space in its new building on November 1. At December 31, the company had the following rental contracts that are paid in full for the entire term of the lease.

2. Rent revenue $74,000

Date	Term (in months)	Monthly Rent	Number of Leases
Nov. 1	6	$4,000	5
Dec. 1	6	$8,500	4

3. Prepaid Advertising $15,600. This balance consists of payments on two advertising contracts. The contracts provide for monthly advertising in two trade magazines. The terms of the contracts are as follows.

3. Advertising expense $5,200

Contract	Date	Amount	Number of Magazine Issues
A650	May 1	$6,000	12
B974	Oct. 1	9,600	24

The first advertisement runs in the month in which the contract is signed.

4. Notes Payable $100,000. This balance consists of a note for one year at an annual interest rate of 9%, dated June 1.

4. Interest expense $5,250

Instructions
Prepare the adjusting entries at December 31, 2014. (Show all computations.)

Journalize transactions and follow through accounting cycle to preparation of financial statements.

(LO 5, 6, 7)

P3-5A On September 1, 2014, the account balances of Beck Equipment Repair, Inc. were as follows.

No.	Debits		No.	Credits	
101	Cash	$ 4,880	158	Accumulated Depreciation—Equipment	$ 2,100
112	Accounts Receivable	3,520	201	Accounts Payable	3,400
126	Supplies	2,000	209	Unearned Service Revenue	1,400
157	Equipment	18,000	212	Salaries and Wages Payable	500
			311	Common Stock	10,000
			320	Retained Earnings	11,000
		$28,400			$28,400

During September, the following summary transactions were completed.

Sept. 8 Paid $1,700 for salaries due employees, of which $1,200 is for September.
10 Received $1,200 cash from customers on account.
12 Received $3,400 cash for services performed in September.
15 Purchased store equipment on account $3,000.
17 Purchased supplies on account $1,200.
20 Paid creditors $4,500 on account.
22 Paid September rent $500.
25 Paid salaries $1,050.
27 Performed services on account and billed customers for services provided $1,600.
29 Received $750 from customers for future service.

Adjustment data consist of:

1. Supplies on hand $1,700.
2. Accrued salaries payable $400.
3. Depreciation is $140 per month.
4. Unearned service revenue of $1,450 is recognized for services performed.

Instructions
(a) Enter the September 1 balances in the ledger accounts.
(b) Journalize the September transactions.
(c) Post to the ledger accounts. Use J1 for the posting reference. Use the following additional accounts: No. 400 Service Revenue, No. 631 Supplies Expense, No. 711 Depreciation Expense, No. 726 Salaries and Wages Expense, and No. 729 Rent Expense.

(d) Trial balance $33,350
(f) Adj. trial balance $33,890
(g) Net income $1,660
    Ending retained earnings $12,660
    Total assets $26,860

(d) Prepare a trial balance at September 30.
(e) Journalize and post adjusting entries.
(f) Prepare an adjusted trial balance.
(g) Prepare an income statement and a retained earnings statement for September and a balance sheet at September 30.

Prepare adjusting entries, adjusted trial balance, and financial statements using appendix.

(LO 5, 6, 7, 8)

*P3-6A Alpha Graphics Company, Inc. was organized on January 1, 2014. At the end of the first 6 months of operations, the trial balance contained the accounts shown below.

Debits		Credits	
Cash	$ 8,400	Notes Payable	$ 20,000
Accounts Receivable	14,000	Accounts Payable	9,000
Equipment	45,000	Common Stock	22,000
Insurance Expense	2,880	Service Revenue	58,280
Salaries and Wages Expense	30,000		
Supplies Expense	3,900		
Advertising Expense	1,900		
Rent Expense	1,500		
Utilities Expense	1,700		
	$109,280		$109,280

Analysis reveals the following additional data.

1. The $3,900 balance in Supplies Expense represents supplies purchased in January. At June 30, $680 of supplies are on hand.
2. The note payable was issued on February 1. It is a 9%, 6-month note.
3. The balance in Insurance Expense is the premium on a one-year policy, dated March 1, 2014.
4. Service revenues are credited to revenue when received. At June 30, service revenue of $1,100 is still not performed for the customer.
5. Depreciation is $2,250 per year.

Instructions
(a) Journalize the adjusting entries at June 30. (Assume adjustments are recorded every 6 months.)
(b) Prepare an adjusted trial balance.
(c) Prepare an income statement and a retained earnings statement for the 6 months ended June 30 and a balance sheet at June 30.

(b) Adj. trial balance $111,155
(c) Net income $16,025
Ending retained earnings $16,025
Total assets $68,875

PROBLEMS: SET B

P3-1B Lynda Rigg started her own consulting firm, Vektek Consulting, Inc. on May 1, 2014. The trial balance at May 31 is as follows.

Prepare adjusting entries, post to ledger accounts, and prepare an adjusted trial balance.

(LO 5, 6, 7)

Vektek Consulting, Inc.
Trial Balance
May 31, 2014

Account Number		Debit	Credit
101	Cash	$ 7,700	
112	Accounts Receivable	4,000	
126	Supplies	1,500	
130	Prepaid Insurance	2,400	
157	Equipment	12,000	
201	Accounts Payable		$ 4,500
209	Unearned Service Revenue		2,600
311	Common Stock		16,000
400	Service Revenue		8,500
726	Salaries and Wages Expense	3,000	
729	Rent Expense	1,000	
		$31,600	$31,600

In addition to those accounts listed on the trial balance, the chart of accounts for Vektek Consulting also contains the following accounts and account numbers: No. 158 Accumulated Depreciation—Equipment, No. 212 Salaries and Wages Payable, No. 631 Supplies Expense, No. 711 Depreciation Expense, No. 722 Insurance Expense, and No. 736 Utilities Expense.

Other data:

1. $500 of supplies have been used during the month.
2. Utilities expense incurred but not paid on May 31, 2014, $200.
3. The insurance policy is for 2 years.
4. $1,000 of the balance in the Unearned Service Revenue account remains unearned at the end of the month.
5. May 31 is a Wednesday, and employees are paid on Fridays. Vektek Consulting has two employees, who are paid $500 each for a 5-day work week.
6. The office equipment has a 5-year life with no salvage value. It is being depreciated at $200 per month for 60 months.
7. Invoices representing $1,400 of services performed during the month have not been recorded as of May 31.

Instructions

(a) Prepare the adjusting entries for the month of May. Use J4 as the page number for your journal.

(b) Post the adjusting entries to the ledger accounts. Enter the totals from the trial balance as beginning account balances and place a check mark in the posting reference column.

(c) Prepare an adjusted trial balance at May 31, 2014.

(c) Adj. trial balance $34,000

Prepare adjusting entries, post, and prepare adjusted trial balance, and financial statements.

(LO 5, 6, 7)

P3-2B The Badger Motel, Inc. opened for business on May 1, 2014. Its trial balance before adjustment on May 31 is as follows.

Badger Motel, Inc.
Trial Balance
May 31, 2014

Account Number		Debit	Credit
101	Cash	$ 2,500	
126	Supplies	1,520	
130	Prepaid Insurance	2,400	
140	Land	14,000	
141	Buildings	58,000	
157	Equipment	15,000	
201	Accounts Payable		$ 4,800
208	Unearned Rent Revenue		3,300
275	Mortgage Payable		38,000
311	Common Stock		40,000
429	Rent Revenue		12,300
610	Advertising Expense	780	
726	Salaries and Wages Expense	3,300	
732	Utilities Expense	900	
		$98,400	$98,400

In addition to those accounts listed on the trial balance, the chart of accounts for Badger Motel, Inc. also contains the following accounts and account numbers: No. 142 Accumulated Depreciation—Buildings, No. 158 Accumulated Depreciation—Equipment, No. 212 Salaries and Wages Payable, No. 230 Interest Payable, No. 631 Supplies Expense, No. 711 Depreciation Expense, No. 718 Interest Expense, and No. 722 Insurance Expense.

Other data:

1. Prepaid insurance is a 1-year policy starting May 1, 2014.
2. A count of supplies shows $350 of unused supplies on May 31.
3. Annual depreciation is $2,640 on the buildings and $1,500 on equipment.
4. The mortgage interest rate is 12%. (The mortgage was taken out on May 1.)
5. Two-thirds of the unearned rent revenue has been recognized for services performed.
6. Salaries of $750 are accrued and unpaid at May 31.

Instructions

(c) Adj. trial balance $99,875

(d) Net income $6,675

Ending retained earnings $6,675

Total assets $91,705

(a) Journalize the adjusting entries on May 31.

(b) Prepare a ledger using the three-column form of account. Enter the trial balance amounts and post the adjusting entries. (Use J1 as the posting reference.)

(c) Prepare an adjusted trial balance on May 31.

(d) Prepare an income statement and a retained earnings statement for the month of May and a balance sheet at May 31.

Prepare adjusting entries and financial statements.

(LO 5, 6, 7)

P3-3B Medina Co., Inc. was organized on July 1, 2014. Quarterly financial statements are prepared. The unadjusted and adjusted trial balances as of September 30 are shown on the next page.

Medina Co., Inc.
Trial Balance
September 30, 2014

	Unadjusted Dr.	Unadjusted Cr.	Adjusted Dr.	Adjusted Cr.
Cash	$ 8,700		$ 8,700	
Accounts Receivable	10,400		11,500	
Supplies	1,900		650	
Prepaid Rent	2,200		1,200	
Equipment	20,000		20,000	
Accumulated Depreciation—Equipment		$ –0–		$ 1,125
Notes Payable		10,000		10,000
Accounts Payable		3,200		3,200
Salaries and Wages Payable		–0–		725
Interest Payable		–0–		100
Unearned Rent Revenue		1,900		1,050
Common Stock		22,000		22,000
Dividends	1,000		1,000	
Service Revenue		16,800		17,900
Rent Revenue		1,710		2,560
Salaries and Wages Expense	8,000		8,725	
Rent Expense	1,900		2,900	
Depreciation Expense			1,125	
Supplies Expense			1,250	
Utilities Expense	1,510		1,510	
Interest Expense			100	
	$55,610	$55,610	$58,660	$58,660

Instructions
(a) Journalize the adjusting entries that were made.
(b) Prepare an income statement and a retained earnings statement for the 3 months ending September 30 and a balance sheet at September 30.
(c) If the note bears interest at 12%, how many months has it been outstanding?

(b) Net income $4,850
Ending retained earnings $3,850
Total assets $40,925

P3-4B A review of the ledger of Khan Company at December 31, 2014, produces the following data pertaining to the preparation of annual adjusting entries.

Prepare adjusting entries
(LO 5, 6)

1. Prepaid Insurance $9,300. The company has separate insurance policies on its buildings and its motor vehicles. Policy B4564 on the building was purchased on April 1, 2013, for $6,000. The policy has a term of 3 years. Policy A2958 on the vehicles was purchased on January 1, 2014, for $4,800. This policy has a term of 2 years.

1. Insurance expense $4,400

2. Unearned Rent Revenue $429,000. The company began subleasing office space in its new building on November 1. At December 31, the company had the following rental contracts that are paid in full for the entire term of the lease.

2. Rent revenue $84,000

Date	Term (in months)	Monthly Rent	Number of Leases
Nov. 1	9	$5,000	5
Dec. 1	6	$8,500	4

3. Notes Payable $120,000. This balance consists of a note for 9 months at an annual interest rate of 9%, dated November 1.

3. Interest expense $1,800

4. Salaries and Wages Payable $0. There are eight salaried employees. Salaries are paid every Friday for the current week. Five employees receive a salary of $640 each per week, and three employees earn $500 each per week. Assume December 31 is a Wednesday. Employees do not work weekends. All employees worked the last 3 days of December.

4. Salaries and wages expense $2,820

Instructions
Prepare the adjusting entries at December 31, 2014.

Journalize transactions and follow through accounting cycle to preparation of financial statements.

(LO 5, 6, 7)

P3-5B On November 1, 2014, the account balances of Samone Equipment Repair, Inc. were as follows.

No.	Debits		No.	Credits	
101	Cash	$ 2,400	158	Accumulated Depreciation—Equipment	$ 2,000
112	Accounts Receivable	4,450	201	Accounts Payable	2,600
126	Supplies	1,800	209	Unearned Service Revenue	1,360
157	Equipment	16,000	212	Salaries and Wages Payable	700
			311	Common Stock	10,000
			320	Retained Earnings	7,990
		$24,650			$24,650

During November, the following summary transactions were completed.

Nov. 8 Paid $1,500 for salaries due employees, of which $700 is for October salaries.
  10 Received $3,420 cash from customers on account.
  12 Received $3,100 cash for services performed in November.
  15 Purchased equipment on account $2,000.
  17 Purchased supplies on account $700.
  20 Paid creditors on account $2,700.
  22 Paid November rent $500.
  25 Paid salaries $1,500.
  27 Performed services on account and billed customers for services provided $1,900.
  29 Received $350 from customers for future service.

Adjustment data consist of:

1. Supplies on hand $1,400.
2. Accrued salaries payable $350.
3. Depreciation for the month is $200.
4. Unearned service revenue of $1,380 is recognized for services performed.

Instructions

(a) Enter the November 1 balances in the ledger accounts.
(b) Journalize the November transactions.
(c) Post to the ledger accounts. Use J1 for the posting reference. Use the following additional accounts: No. 400 Service Revenue, No. 631 Supplies Expense, No. 711 Depreciation Expense, No. 726 Salaries and Wages Expense, and No. 729 Rent Expense.

(d) Trial balance $29,300
(f) Adj. trial balance $29,850
(g) Net income $1,930
    Ending retained earnings
    $9,920
    Total assets $23,200

(d) Prepare a trial balance at November 30.
(e) Journalize and post adjusting entries.
(f) Prepare an adjusted trial balance.
(g) Prepare an income statement and a retained earnings statement for November and a balance sheet at November 30.

PROBLEMS: SET C

Visit the book's companion website, at **www.wiley.com/college/weygandt**, and choose the Student Companion site to access Problem Set C.

CONTINUING COOKIE CHRONICLE

(*Note:* This is a continuation of the Cookie Chronicle from Chapters 1–2. Use the information from the previous chapters and follow the instructions on the next page using the general ledger accounts you have already prepared.)

CCC3 It is the end of November and Natalie has been in touch with her grandmother. Her grandmother asked Natalie how well things went in her first month of business. Natalie, too, would like to know if the company has been profitable or not during November.

Natalie realizes that in order to determine Cookie Creations' income, she must first make adjustments.

Natalie puts together the following additional information.

1. A count reveals that $35 of baking supplies were used during November.
2. Natalie estimates that all of her baking equipment will have a useful life of 5 years or 60 months. (Assume Natalie decides to record a full month's worth of depreciation, regardless of when the equipment was obtained by the business.)
3. Natalie's grandmother has decided to charge interest of 6% on the note payable extended on November 16. The loan plus interest is to be repaid in 24 months. (Assume that half a month of interest accrued during November.)
4. On November 30, a friend of Natalie's asks her to teach a class at the neighborhood school. Natalie agrees and teaches a group of 35 first-grade students how to make Santa Claus cookies. The next day, Natalie prepares an invoice for $300 and leaves it with the school principal. The principal says that he will pass the invoice along to the head office, and it will be paid sometime in December.
5. Natalie receives a utilities bill for $45. The bill is for utilities consumed by Natalie's business during November and is due December 15.

Instructions
Using the information that you have gathered through Chapter 2, and based on the new information above, do the following.

(a) Prepare and post the adjusting journal entries.
(b) Prepare an adjusted trial balance.
(c) Using the adjusted trial balance, calculate Cookie Creations' net income or net loss for the month of November. Do not prepare an income statement.

Broadening Your PERSPECTIVE

Financial Reporting and Analysis

Financial Reporting Problem: PepsiCo, Inc.

BYP3-1 The financial statements of PepsiCo, Inc. are presented in Appendix A at the end of this textbook.

Instructions
(a) Using the consolidated financial statements and related information, identify items that may result in adjusting entries for prepayments.
(b) Using the consolidated financial statements and related information, identify items that may result in adjusting entries for accruals.
(c) Using the Selected Financial Data and 5-Year Summary, what has been the trend since 2006 for net income?

Comparative Analysis Problem: PepsiCo, Inc. vs. The Coca-Cola Company

BYP3-2 PepsiCo's financial statements are presented in Appendix A. Financial statements for The Coca-Cola Company are presented in Appendix B.

Instructions
Based on information contained in these financial statements, determine the following for each company.

(a) Net increase (decrease) in property, plant, and equipment (net) from 2009 to 2010.
(b) Increase (decrease) in selling, general, and administrative expenses from 2009 to 2010.
(c) Increase (decrease) in long-term debt (obligations) from 2009 to 2010.

(d) Increase (decrease) in net income from 2009 to 2010.

(e) Increase (decrease) in cash and cash equivalents from 2009 to 2010.

Real-World Focus

BYP3-3 No financial decision-maker should ever rely solely on the financial information reported in the annual report to make decisions. It is important to keep abreast of financial news. This activity demonstrates how to search for financial news on the Web.

Address: http://biz.yahoo.com/i, or go to **www.wiley.com/college/weygandt**

Steps

1. Type in either Wal-Mart, Target Corp., or Kmart.
2. Choose **News**.
3. Select an article that sounds interesting to you and that would be relevant to an investor in these companies.

Instructions

(a) What was the source of the article (e.g., Reuters, Businesswire, Prnewswire)?

(b) Assume that you are a personal financial planner and that one of your clients owns stock in the company. Write a brief memo to your client summarizing the article and explaining the implications of the article for their investment.

Critical Thinking

Decision-Making Across the Organization

BYP3-4 Happy Trails Park, Inc. was organized on April 1, 2013, by Alicia Henry. Alicia is a good manager but a poor accountant. From the trial balance prepared by a part-time bookkeeper, Alicia prepared the following income statement for the quarter that ended March 31, 2014.

Happy Trails Park, Inc.
Income Statement
For the Quarter Ended March 31, 2014

Revenues		
Rent revenue		$88,000
Operating expenses		
Advertising	$ 5,200	
Salaries and wages	28,800	
Utilities	750	
Depreciation	800	
Maintenance and repairs	4,000	
Total operating expenses		39,550
Net income		$48,450

Alicia thought that something was wrong with the statement because net income had never exceeded $20,000 in any one quarter. Knowing that you are an experienced accountant, she asks you to review the income statement and other data.

You first look at the trial balance. In addition to the account balances reported above in the income statement, the ledger contains the following additional selected balances at March 31, 2014.

Supplies	$ 6,200
Prepaid Insurance	7,500
Notes Payable	12,000

You then make inquiries and discover the following.

1. Rent revenue includes advanced rentals for summer occupancy $14,000.
2. There were $1,450 of supplies on hand at March 31.
3. Prepaid insurance resulted from the payment of a one-year policy on January 1, 2014.
4. The mail on April 1, 2014, brought the following bills: advertising for week of March 24, $130; repairs made March 10, $260; and utilities, $120.
5. There are four employees, who receive wages totaling $300 per day. At March 31, 2 days' salaries and wages have been incurred but not paid.
6. The note payable is a 3-month, 10% note dated January 1, 2014.

Instructions
With the class divided into groups, answer the following.

(a) Prepare a correct income statement for the quarter ended March 31, 2014.
(b) Explain to Alicia the generally accepted accounting principles that she did not recognize in preparing her income statement and their effect on her results.

(a) Net income
    $26,415
(b) Effect on result is
    $22,035

Communication Activity

BYP3-5 In reviewing the accounts of Maribeth Co. at the end of the year, you discover that adjusting entries have not been made.

Instructions
Write a memo to Maribeth Danon, the owner of Maribeth Co., that explains the following: the nature and purpose of adjusting entries, why adjusting entries are needed, and the types of adjusting entries that may be made.

Ethics Case

BYP3-6 Watkin Company is a pesticide manufacturer. Its sales declined greatly this year due to the passage of legislation outlawing the sale of several of Watkin's chemical pesticides. In the coming year, Watkin will have environmentally safe and competitive chemicals to replace these discontinued products. Sales in the next year are expected to greatly exceed any prior year's. The decline in sales and profits appears to be a one-year aberration. But even so, the company president fears a large dip in the current year's profits. He believes that such a dip could cause a significant drop in the market price of Watkin's stock and make the company a takeover target.

To avoid this possibility, the company president calls in Diane Leno, controller, to discuss this period's year-end adjusting entries. He urges her to accrue every possible revenue and to defer as many expenses as possible. He says to Diane, "We need the revenues this year, and next year can easily absorb expenses deferred from this year. We can't let our stock price be hammered down!" Diane didn't get around to recording the adjusting entries until January 17, but she dated the entries December 31 as if they were recorded then. Diane also made every effort to comply with the president's request.

Instructions
(a) Who are the stakeholders in this situation?
(b) What are the ethical considerations of (1) the president's request and (2) Diane's dating the adjusting entries December 31?
(c) Can Diane accrue revenues and defer expenses and still be ethical?

All About You

BYP3-7 Companies must report or disclose in their financial statements information about all liabilities, including potential liabilities related to environmental clean-up. There are many situations in which you will be asked to provide personal financial information about your assets, liabilities, revenue, and expenses. Sometimes you will face difficult decisions regarding what to disclose and how to disclose it.

Instructions
Suppose that you are putting together a loan application to purchase a home. Based on your income and assets, you qualify for the mortgage loan, but just barely. How would you address each

of the following situations in reporting your financial position for the loan application? Provide responses for each of the following situations.

(a) You signed a guarantee for a bank loan that a friend took out for $20,000. If your friend doesn't pay, you will have to pay. Your friend has made all of the payments so far, and it appears he will be able to pay in the future.

(b) You were involved in an auto accident in which you were at fault. There is the possibility that you may have to pay as much as $50,000 as part of a settlement. The issue will not be resolved before the bank processes your mortgage request.

(c) The company at which you work isn't doing very well, and it has recently laid off employees. You are still employed, but it is quite possible that you will lose your job in the next few months.

BYP3-8 Many companies have potential pollution or environmental-disposal problems—not only for electronic gadgets, but also for the lead paint or asbestos they sold. How do we fit these issues into the accounting equation? Are these costs and related liabilities that companies should report?

YES: As more states impose laws holding companies responsible, and as more courts levy pollution-related fines, it becomes increasingly likely that companies will have to pay large amounts in the future.

NO: The amounts still are too difficult to estimate. Putting inaccurate estimates on the financial statements reduces their usefulness. Instead, why not charge the costs later, when the actual environmental cleanup or disposal occurs, at which time the company knows the actual cost?

Instructions
Write a response indicating your position regarding this situation. Provide support for your view.

FASB Codification Activity

BYP3-9 If your school has a subscription to the FASB Codification, go to *http://aaahq.org/asclogin. cfm* to log in and prepare responses to the following.

Instructions
Access the glossary ("Master Glossary") to answer the following.

(a) What is the definition of revenue?
(b) What is the definition of compensation?

Answers to Chapter Questions

Answers to Insight and Accounting Across the Organization Questions

p. 104 Cooking the Books? Q: What motivates sales executives and finance and accounting executives to participate in activities that result in inaccurate reporting of revenues? **A:** Sales executives typically receive bonuses based on their ability to meet quarterly sales targets. In addition, they often face the possibility of losing their jobs if they miss those targets. Executives in accounting and finance are very aware of the earnings targets of Wall Street analysts and investors. If they fail to meet these targets, the company's stock price will fall. As a result of these pressures, executives sometimes knowingly engage in unethical efforts to misstate revenues. As a result of the Sarbanes-Oxley Act, the penalties for such behavior are now much more severe.

p. 112 Turning Gift Cards into Revenue Q: Suppose that Robert Jones purchases a $100 gift card at Best Buy on December 24, 2013, and gives it to his wife, Mary Jones, on December 25, 2013. On January 3, 2014, Mary uses the card to purchase $100 worth of CDs. When do you think Best Buy should recognize revenue and why? **A:** According to the revenue recognition principle, companies should recognize revenue when the performance obligation is satisfied. In this case, revenue is not recognized until Best Buy provides the goods. Thus, when Best Buy receives cash in exchange for the gift card on December 24, 2013, it should recognize a liability, Unearned Revenue, for $100. On January 3, 2014, when Mary Jones exchanges the card for merchandise, Best Buy should recognize revenue and eliminate $100 from the balance in the Unearned Revenue account.

p. 116 Cashing In on Accrual Accounting Q: Accrual accounting is often considered superior to cash accounting. Why, then, were some people critical of China's use of accrual accounting in this instance? **A:** In this case, some people were critical because, in general, China uses cash accounting. By switching to accrual accounting for this transaction, China was not being consistent in its accounting practices. Lack of consistency reduces the transparency and usefulness of accounting information.

p. 118 Got Junk? Q: What accounting issue might this cause for companies? **A:** The balance sheet should provide a fair representation of what a company owns and what it owes. If significant obligations of the company are not reported on the balance sheet, the company's net worth (its equity) will be overstated. While it is true that it is not possible to estimate the *exact* amount of future environmental cleanup costs, it is becoming clear that companies will be held accountable. Therefore, it doesn't seem reasonable to not accrue for environmental costs. Recognition of these liabilities provides a more accurate picture of the company's financial position. It also has the potential to improve the environment. As companies are forced to report these amounts on their financial statements, they will start to look for more effective and efficient means to reduce toxic waste and therefore reduce their costs.

Answers to Self-Test Questions

1. c **2.** c **3.** d **4.** a **5.** d **6.** d **7.** c ($1,350 − $600) **8.** c **9.** a **10.** c **11.** a **12.** b **13.** b
14. c *15. a *16. c *17. b

A Look at IFRS

It is often difficult for companies to determine in what time period they should report particular revenues and expenses. Both the IASB and FASB are working on a joint project to develop a common conceptual framework, as well as a revenue recognition project, that will enable companies to better use the same principles to record transactions consistently over time.

Key Points

- In this chapter, you learned accrual-basis accounting applied under GAAP. Companies applying IFRS also use accrual-basis accounting to ensure that they record transactions that change a company's financial statements in the period in which events occur.

- Similar to GAAP, cash-basis accounting is not in accordance with IFRS.

- IFRS also divides the economic life of companies into artificial time periods. Under both GAAP and IFRS, this is referred to as the *time period assumption*.

- IFRS requires that companies present a complete set of financial statements, including comparative information annually.

- The **general** revenue recognition principles required by GAAP that are used in this textbook are similar to those under IFRS.

- As the Feature Story illustrates, revenue recognition fraud is a major issue in U.S. financial reporting. The same situation occurs in other countries, as evidenced by revenue recognition breakdowns at Dutch software company Baan NV, Japanese electronics giant NEC, and Dutch grocer Ahold NV.

- Under IFRS, revaluation of items such as land and buildings is permitted. IFRS allows depreciation based on revaluation of assets, which is not permitted under GAAP.

- The terminology used for revenues and gains, and expenses and losses, differs somewhat between IFRS and GAAP. For example, income under IFRS is defined as:

    Increases in economic benefits during the accounting period in the form of inflows or enhancements of assets or decreases of liabilities that result in increases in equity, other than those relating to contributions from shareholders.

Income includes *both* revenues, which arise during the normal course of operating activities, and gains, which arise from activities outside of the normal sales of goods and services. The term income is not used this way under GAAP. Instead, under GAAP income refers to the net difference between revenues and expenses. Expenses under IFRS are defined as:

> Decreases in economic benefits during the accounting period in the form of outflows or depletions of assets or incurrences of liabilities that result in decreases in equity other than those relating to distributions to shareholders.

Note that under IFRS, expenses include both those costs incurred in the normal course of operations, as well as losses that are not part of normal operations. This is in contrast to GAAP, which defines each separately.

Looking to the Future

The IASB and FASB have recently completed a joint project on revenue recognition. The purpose of this project was to develop comprehensive guidance on when to recognize revenue. This approach focuses on changes in assets and liabilities as the basis for revenue recognition. It is hoped that this approach will lead to more consistent accounting in this area. For more on this topic, see *www.fasb.org/project/revenue_recognition.shtml*.

IFRS Practice

IFRS Self-Test Questions

1. GAAP:
   (a) provides the same type of guidance as IFRS for revenue recognition.
   (b) provides only general guidance on revenue recognition, compared to the detailed guidance provided by IFRS.
   (c) allows revenue to be recognized when a customer makes an order.
   (d) requires that revenue not be recognized until cash is received.

2. Which of the following statements is *false*?
   (a) IFRS employs the time period assumption.
   (b) IFRS employs accrual accounting.
   (c) IFRS requires that revenues and costs must be capable of being measured reliably.
   (d) IFRS uses the cash basis of accounting.

3. As a result of the revenue recognition project by the FASB and IASB:
   (a) revenue recognition places more emphasis on when the service obligation is satisfied.
   (b) revenue recognition places more emphasis on when revenue is realized.
   (c) revenue recognition places more emphasis on when changes occur in assets and liabilities.
   (d) revenue is no longer recorded unless cash has been received.

4. Which of the following is *false*?
   (a) Under IFRS, the term *income* describes both revenues and gains.
   (b) Under IFRS, the term *expenses* includes losses.
   (c) Under IFRS, firms do not engage in the closing process.
   (d) IFRS has fewer standards than GAAP that address revenue recognition.

5. Accrual-basis accounting:
   (a) is optional under IFRS.
   (b) results in companies recording transactions that change a company's financial statements in the period in which events occur.
   (c) has been eliminated as a result of the IASB/FASB joint project on revenue recognition.
   (d) is not consistent with the IASB conceptual framework.

IFRS Exercises

IFRS3-1 Compare and contrast the rules regarding revenue recognition under IFRS versus GAAP.

IFRS3-2 Under IFRS, do the definitions of revenues and expenses include gains and losses? Explain.

International Financial Reporting Problem: Zetar plc

IFRS3-3 The financial statements of Zetar plc are presented in Appendix C. The company's complete annual report, including the notes to its financial statements, is available at *www.zetarplc. com*.

Instructions

Visit Zetar's corporate website and answer the following questions from Zetar's 2010 annual report.

(a) From the notes to the financial statements, how does the company determine the amount of revenue to record at the time of a sale?

(b) From the notes to the financial statements, how does the company determine whether a sale has occurred?

(c) Using the consolidated income statement and consolidated statement of financial position, identify items that may result in adjusting entries for deferrals.

(d) Using the consolidated income statement, identify two items that may result in adjusting entries for accruals.

Answers to IFRS Self-Test Questions

1. a   **2.** d   **3.** c   **4.** c   **5.** b

✔ **The Navigator**

Chapter 4

Completing the Accounting Cycle

Feature Story

Everyone Likes to Win

When Ted Castle was a hockey coach at the University of Vermont, his players were self-motivated by their desire to win. Hockey was a game you either won or lost. But at Rhino Foods, Inc., a bakery-foods company he founded in Burlington, Vermont, he discovered that manufacturing-line workers were not so self-motivated. Ted thought, what if he turned the food-making business into a game, with rules, strategies, and trophies?

Ted knew that in a game, knowing the score is all-important. He felt only if the employees know the score—know exactly how the business is doing daily, weekly, monthly—could he turn food-making into a game. But Rhino is a closely held, family-owned business, and its financial statements and profits were confidential. Ted wondered, should he open Rhino's books to the employees?

A consultant put Ted's concerns in perspective when he said, "Imagine you're playing touch football. You play for an hour or two, and the whole time I'm sitting there with a book, keeping score. All of a sudden I blow the whistle, and I say, 'OK, that's it. Everybody go home.' I close my book and walk away. How would you feel?" Ted opened his books and revealed the financial statements to his employees.

Learning Objectives

After studying this chapter, you should be able to:

1. Prepare a worksheet.
2. Explain the process of closing the books.
3. Describe the content and purpose of a post-closing trial balance.
4. State the required steps in the accounting cycle.
5. Explain the approaches to preparing correcting entries.
6. Identify the sections of a classified balance sheet.

 The Navigator

The next step was to teach employees the rules and strategies of how to "win" at making food. The first lesson: "Your opponent at Rhino is expenses. You must cut and control expenses." Ted and his staff distilled those lessons into daily scorecards—production reports and income statements—that keep Rhino's employees up-to-date on the game. At noon each day, Ted posts the previous day's results at the entrance to the production room. Everyone checks whether they made or lost money on what they produced the day before. And it's not just an academic exercise: There's a bonus check for each employee at the end of every four-week "game" that meets profitability guidelines.

Rhino has flourished since the first game. Employment has increased from 20 to 130 people, while both revenues and profits have grown dramatically.

 The Navigator

Preview of **Chapter 4**

At Rhino Foods, Inc., financial statements help employees understand what is happening in the business. In Chapter 3, we prepared financial statements directly from the adjusted trial balance. However, with so many details involved in the end-of-period accounting procedures, it is easy to make errors. One way to minimize errors in the records and to simplify the end-of-period procedures is to use a worksheet.

In this chapter, we will explain the role of the worksheet in accounting. We also will study the remaining steps in the accounting cycle, especially the closing process, again using Pioneer Advertising Agency Inc. as an example. Then we will consider correcting entries and classified balance sheets. The content and organization of Chapter 4 are as follows.

COMPLETING THE ACCOUNTING CYCLE

Using a Worksheet	Closing the Books	Summary of Accounting Cycle	Classified Balance Sheet
• Steps in preparation • Preparing financial statements • Preparing adjusting entries	• Preparing closing entries • Posting closing entries • Preparing a post-closing trial balance	• Reversing entries—An optional step • Correcting entries—An avoidable step	• Current assets • Long-term investments • Property, plant, and equipment • Intangible assets • Current liabilities • Long-term liabilities • Stockholders' equity

✔ **The Navigator**

Using a Worksheet

A **worksheet** is a multiple-column form used in the adjustment process and in preparing financial statements. As its name suggests, the worksheet is a working tool. **It is not a permanent accounting record**; it is neither a journal nor a part of the general ledger. The worksheet is merely a device used in preparing adjusting entries and the financial statements. Companies generally computerize worksheets using an electronic spreadsheet program such as Excel.

Illustration 4-1 shows the basic form of a worksheet and the five steps for preparing it. Each step is performed in sequence. **The use of a worksheet is optional.** When a company chooses to use one, it prepares financial statements from the worksheet. It enters the adjustments in the worksheet columns and then journalizes and posts the adjustments after it has prepared the financial statements. Thus, worksheets make it possible to provide the financial statements to management and other interested parties at an earlier date.

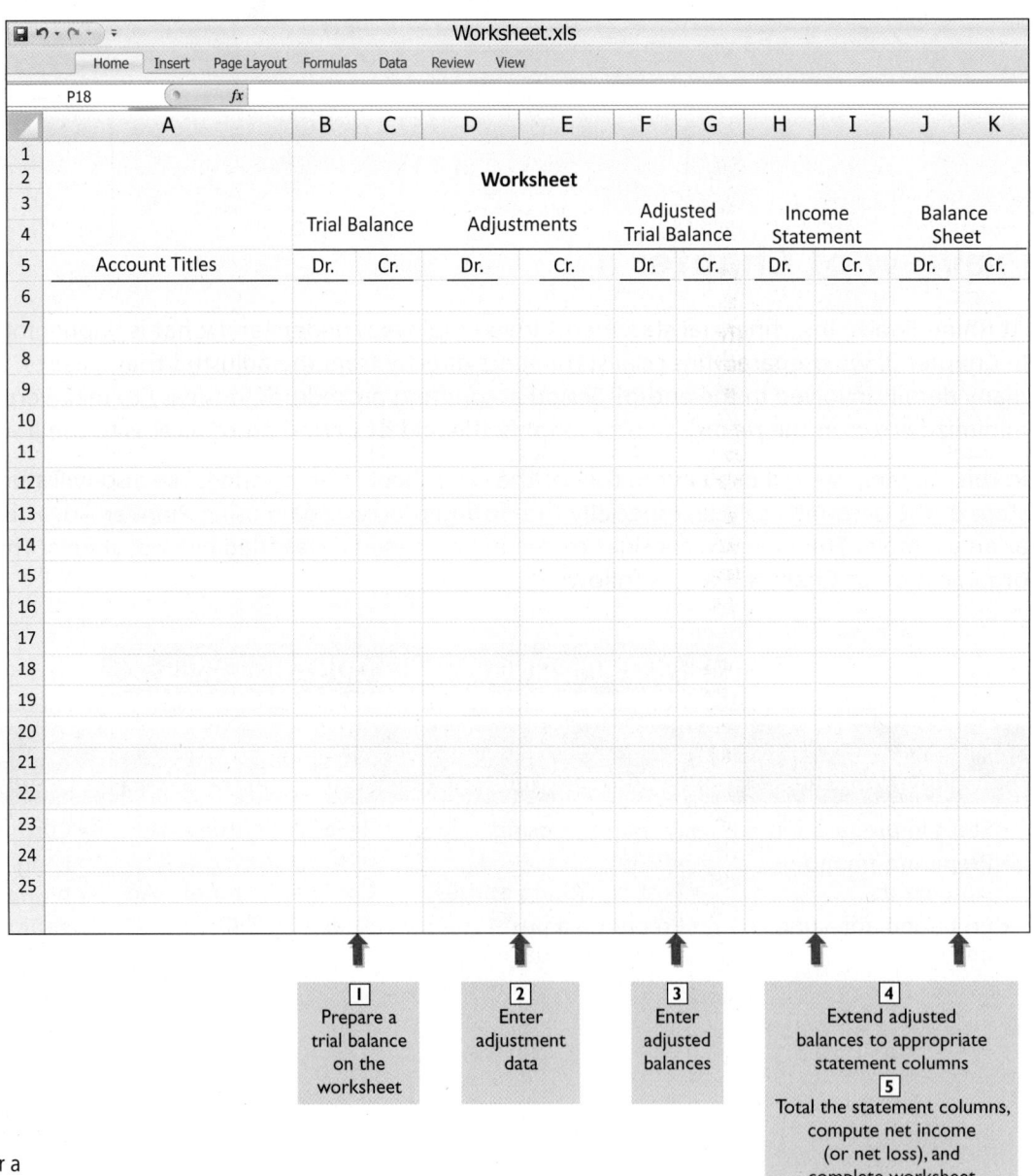

Illustration 4-1
Form and procedure for a worksheet

Steps in Preparing a Worksheet

We will use the October 31 trial balance and adjustment data of Pioneer Advertising Agency Inc., from Chapter 3, to illustrate how to prepare a worksheet. We describe each step of the process and demonstrate these steps in Illustration 4-2 (page 166) and transparencies 4-3A, B, C, and D.

STEP 1. PREPARE A TRIAL BALANCE ON THE WORKSHEET

Enter all ledger accounts with balances in the account titles space. Enter debit and credit amounts from the ledger in the trial balance columns. Illustration 4-2 shows the worksheet trial balance for Pioneer Advertising Agency Inc. This trial balance is the same one that appears in Illustration 2-32 (page 74) and Illustration 3-3 (page 105).

STEP 2. ENTER THE ADJUSTMENTS IN THE ADJUSTMENTS COLUMNS

Turn over the first transparency, Illustration 4-3A. When using a worksheet, enter all adjustments in the adjustments columns. In entering the adjustments, use applicable trial balance accounts. If additional accounts are needed, insert them on the lines immediately below the trial balance totals. A different letter identifies the debit and credit for each adjusting entry. The term used to describe this process is **keying. Companies do not journalize the adjustments until after they complete the worksheet and prepare the financial statements.**

The adjustments for Pioneer Advertising Agency Inc. are the same as the adjustments in Illustration 3-23 (page 119). They are keyed in the adjustments columns of the worksheet as follows.

(a) Pioneer debits an additional account, Supplies Expense, $1,500 for the cost of supplies used, and credits Supplies $1,500.

(b) Pioneer debits an additional account, Insurance Expense, $50 for the insurance that has expired, and credits Prepaid Insurance $50.

(c) The company needs two additional depreciation accounts. It debits Depreciation Expense $40 for the month's depreciation, and credits Accumulated Depreciation—Equipment $40.

(d) Pioneer debits Unearned Service Revenue $400 for services provided, and credits Service Revenue $400.

(e) Pioneer debits an additional account, Accounts Receivable, $200 for services provided but not billed, and credits Service Revenue $200.

(f) The company needs two additional accounts relating to interest. It debits Interest Expense $50 for accrued interest, and credits Interest Payable $50.

(g) Pioneer debits Salaries and Wages Expense $1,200 for accrued salaries, and credits an additional account, Salaries and Wages Payable, $1,200.

After Pioneer has entered all the adjustments, the adjustments columns are totaled to prove their equality.

STEP 3. ENTER ADJUSTED BALANCES IN THE ADJUSTED TRIAL BALANCE COLUMNS

Turn over the second transparency, Illustration 4-3B. Pioneer determines the adjusted balance of an account by combining the amounts entered in the first four columns of the worksheet for each account. For example, the Prepaid Insurance account in the trial balance columns has a $600 debit balance and a $50 credit in the adjustments columns. The result is a $550 debit balance recorded in the adjusted trial balance columns. **For each account, the amount**

(**Note:** Text continues on page 167, following acetate overlays.)

Illustration 4-2

Preparing a trial balance

	Pioneer Advertising.xls

Home Insert Page Layout Formulas Data Review View

P18   fx

Pioneer Advertising Agency Inc.
Worksheet
For the Month Ended October 31, 2014

Account Titles	Trial Balance Dr.	Trial Balance Cr.	Adjustments Dr.	Adjustments Cr.	Adjusted Trial Balance Dr.	Adjusted Trial Balance Cr.	Income Statement Dr.	Income Statement Cr.	Balance Sheet Dr.	Balance Sheet Cr.
Cash	15,200									
Supplies	2,500									
Prepaid Insurance	600									
Equipment	5,000									
Notes Payable		5,000								
Accounts Payable		2,500								
Unearned Service Revenue		1,200								
Common Stock		10,000								
Dividends	500									
Service Revenue		10,000								
				(e)						
Salaries and Wages Expense	4,000									
Rent Expense	900									
Totals	28,700	28,700								

Include all accounts with balances from ledger.

Trial balance amounts come directly from ledger accounts.

in the adjusted trial balance columns is the balance that will appear in the ledger after journalizing and posting the adjusting entries. The balances in these columns are the same as those in the adjusted trial balance in Illustration 3-25 (page 121).

After Pioneer has entered all account balances in the adjusted trial balance columns, the columns are totaled to prove their equality. If the column totals do not agree, the financial statement columns will not balance and the financial statements will be incorrect.

STEP 4. EXTEND ADJUSTED TRIAL BALANCE AMOUNTS TO APPROPRIATE FINANCIAL STATEMENT COLUMNS

Turn over the third transparency, Illustration 4-3C. The fourth step is to extend adjusted trial balance amounts to the income statement and balance sheet columns of the worksheet. Pioneer enters balance sheet accounts in the appropriate balance sheet debit and credit columns. For instance, it enters Cash in the balance sheet debit column, and Notes Payable in the credit column. Pioneer extends Accumulated Depreciation—Equipment to the balance sheet credit column; the reason is that accumulated depreciation is a contra-asset account with a credit balance.

Helpful Hint
Every adjusted trial balance amount must be extended to one of the four statement columns.

Because the worksheet does not have columns for the retained earnings statement, Pioneer extends the balance in Common Stock and Retained Earnings, if any, to the balance sheet credit column. In addition, it extends the balance in Dividends to the balance sheet debit column because it is a stockholders' equity account with a debit balance.

The company enters the expense and revenue accounts such as Salaries and Wages Expense and Service Revenue in the appropriate income statement columns. Illustration 4-3C shows all of these extensions.

STEP 5. TOTAL THE STATEMENT COLUMNS, COMPUTE THE NET INCOME (OR NET LOSS), AND COMPLETE THE WORKSHEET

Turn over the fourth transparency, Illustration 4-3D. The company now must total each of the financial statement columns. The net income or loss for the period is the difference between the totals of the two income statement columns. If total credits exceed total debits, the result is net income. In such a case, as shown in Illustration 4-3D, the company inserts the words "Net Income" in the account titles space. It then enters the amount in the income statement debit column and the balance sheet credit column. **The debit amount balances the income statement columns; the credit amount balances the balance sheet columns.** In addition, the credit in the balance sheet column indicates the increase in stockholders' equity resulting from net income.

What if total debits in the income statement columns exceed total credits? In that case, the company has a net loss. It enters the amount of the net loss in the income statement credit column and the balance sheet debit column.

After entering the net income or net loss, the company determines new column totals. The totals shown in the debit and credit income statement columns will match. So will the totals shown in the debit and credit balance sheet columns. If either the income statement columns or the balance sheet columns are not equal after the net income or net loss has been entered, there is an error in the worksheet. Illustration 4-3D shows the completed worksheet for Pioneer Advertising Agency Inc.

Preparing Financial Statements from a Worksheet

After a company has completed a worksheet, it has at hand all the data required for preparation of financial statements. The income statement is prepared from the income statement columns. The balance sheet and retained earnings statement are prepared from the balance sheet columns. Illustration 4-4 (page 168)

Illustration 4-4
Financial statements from a
worksheet

Pioneer Advertising Agency Inc.
Income Statement
For the Month Ended October 31, 2014

Revenues		
Service revenue		$10,600
Expenses		
Salaries and wages expense	$5,200	
Supplies expense	1,500	
Rent expense	900	
Insurance expense	50	
Interest expense	50	
Depreciation expense	40	
Total expenses		7,740
Net income		$ 2,860

Pioneer Advertising Agency Inc.
Retained Earnings Statement
For the Month Ended October 31, 2014

Retained earnings, October 1	$ –0–
Add: Net income	2,860
	2,860
Less: Dividends	500
Retained earnings, October 31	$2,360

Pioneer Advertising Agency Inc.
Balance Sheet
October 31, 2014

Assets

Cash		$15,200
Accounts receivable		200
Supplies		1,000
Prepaid insurance		550
Equipment	$5,000	
Less: Accumulated depreciation—equipment	40	4,960
Total assets		$21,910

Liabilities and Stockholders' Equity

Liabilities		
Notes payable	$5,000	
Accounts payable	2,500	
Interest payable	50	
Unearned service revenue	800	
Salaries and wages payable	1,200	
Total liabilities		$ 9,550
Stockholders' equity		
Common stock	10,000	
Retained earnings	2,360	
Total stockholders' equity		12,360
Total liabilities and stockholders' equity		$21,910

shows the financial statements prepared from Pioneer's worksheet. At this point, the company has not journalized or posted adjusting entries. Therefore, ledger balances for some accounts are not the same as the financial statement amounts.

The amount shown for common stock on the worksheet does not change from the beginning to the end of the period unless the company issues additional stock during the period. Because there was no balance in Pioneer's retained earnings, the account is not listed on the worksheet. Only after dividends and net income (or loss) are posted to retained earnings does this account have a balance at the end of the first year of the business.

Using a worksheet, companies can prepare financial statements before they journalize and post adjusting entries. **However, the completed worksheet is not a substitute for formal financial statements.** The format of the data in the financial statement columns of the worksheet is not the same as the format of the financial statements. **A worksheet is essentially a working tool of the accountant**; companies do not distribute it to management and other parties.

Accounting Cycle Tutorial—Preparing Financial Statements and Closing the Books

Preparing Adjusting Entries from a Worksheet

A worksheet is not a journal, and it cannot be used as a basis for posting to ledger accounts. To adjust the accounts, the company must journalize the adjustments and post them to the ledger. **The adjusting entries are prepared from the adjustments columns of the worksheet.** The reference letters in the adjustments columns and the explanations of the adjustments at the bottom of the worksheet help identify the adjusting entries. The journalizing and posting of adjusting entries **follows** the preparation of financial statements when a worksheet is used. The adjusting entries on October 31 for Pioneer Advertising Agency Inc. are the same as those shown in Illustration 3-23 (page 119).

Helpful Hint
Note that writing the explanation to the adjustment at the bottom of the worksheet is not required.

> **DO IT!**

Worksheet

Action Plan

✔ Balance sheet: Extend assets to debit column. Extend liabilities to credit column. Extend contra assets to credit column. Extend dividends account to debit column.

✔ Income statement: Extend expenses to debit column. Extend revenues to credit column.

Susan Elbe is preparing a worksheet. Explain to Susan how she should extend the following adjusted trial balance accounts to the financial statement columns of the worksheet.

Cash
Accumulated Depreciation
Accounts Payable
Dividends
Service Revenue
Salaries and Wages Expense

Solution

Income statement debit column—Salaries and Wages Expense
Income statement credit column—Service Revenue
Balance sheet debit column—Cash; Dividends
Balance sheet credit column—Accumulated Depreciation; Accounts Payable

Related exercise material: **BE4-1, BE4-2, BE4-3, E4-1, E4-2, E4-5, E4-6, and DO IT! 4-1.**

 The Navigator

Closing the Books

LEARNING OBJECTIVE **2**

Explain the process of closing the books.

Alternative Terminology
Temporary accounts are sometimes called *nominal accounts*, and permanent accounts are sometimes called *real accounts*.

Illustration 4-5
Temporary versus permanent accounts

Helpful Hint
A contra-asset account, such as accumulated depreciation, is a permanent account also.

At the end of the accounting period, the company makes the accounts ready for the next period. This is called **closing the books**. In closing the books, the company distinguishes between temporary and permanent accounts.

Temporary accounts relate only to a given accounting period. They include all income statement accounts and the Dividends account. **The company closes all temporary accounts at the end of the period.**

In contrast, **permanent accounts** relate to one or more future accounting periods. They consist of all balance sheet accounts, including stockholders' equity accounts. **Permanent accounts are not closed from period to period.** Instead, the company carries forward the balances of permanent accounts into the next accounting period. Illustration 4-5 identifies the accounts in each category.

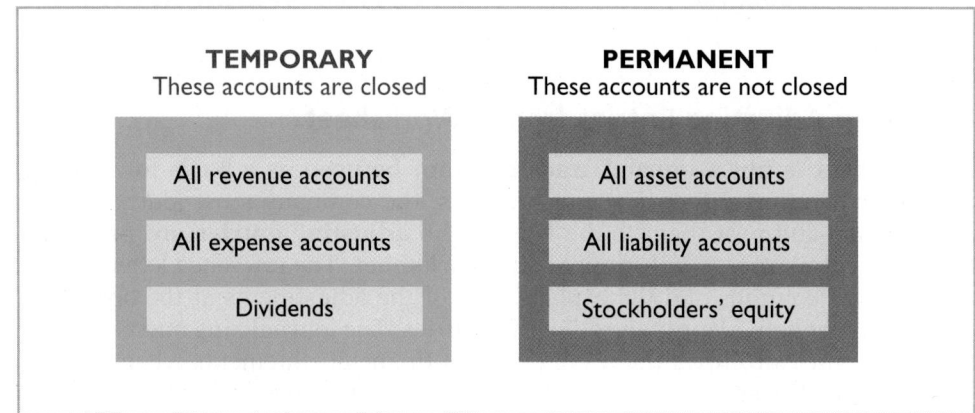

TEMPORARY	PERMANENT
These accounts are closed	These accounts are not closed
All revenue accounts	All asset accounts
All expense accounts	All liability accounts
Dividends	Stockholders' equity

Preparing Closing Entries

At the end of the accounting period, the company transfers temporary account balances to the permanent stockholders' equity account, Retained Earnings, by means of closing entries.

Closing entries formally recognize in the ledger the transfer of net income (or net loss) and Dividends to Retained Earnings. The retained earnings statement shows the results of these entries. **Closing entries also produce a zero balance in each temporary account.** The temporary accounts are then ready to accumulate data in the next accounting period separate from the data of prior periods. Permanent accounts are not closed.

Journalizing and posting closing entries is a required step in the accounting cycle. (See Illustration 4-12 on page 177.) The company performs this step after it has prepared financial statements. In contrast to the steps in the cycle that you have already studied, companies generally journalize and post closing entries **only at the end of the annual accounting period**. Thus, all temporary accounts will contain data for the entire year.

In preparing closing entries, companies could close each income statement account directly to Retained Earnings. However, to do so would result in excessive detail in the permanent Retained Earnings account. Instead, companies close the revenue and expense accounts to another temporary account, **Income Summary**, and they transfer the resulting net income or net loss from this account to Retained Earnings.

Companies **record closing entries in the general journal**. A center caption, Closing Entries, inserted in the journal between the last adjusting entry and the first closing entry, identifies these entries. Then the company posts the closing entries to the ledger accounts.

Companies generally prepare closing entries directly from the adjusted balances in the ledger. They could prepare separate closing entries for each nominal account, but the following four entries accomplish the desired result more efficiently:

1. Debit each revenue account for its balance, and credit Income Summary for total revenues.
2. Debit Income Summary for total expenses, and credit each expense account for its balance.
3. Debit Income Summary and credit Retained Earnings for the amount of net income.
4. Debit Retained Earnings for the balance in the Dividends account, and credit Dividends for the same amount.

Illustration 4-6 presents a diagram of the closing process. In it, the boxed numbers refer to the four entries required in the closing process.

Helpful Hint
Dividends is closed directly to Retained Earnings and *not* to Income Summary because Dividends is not an expense.

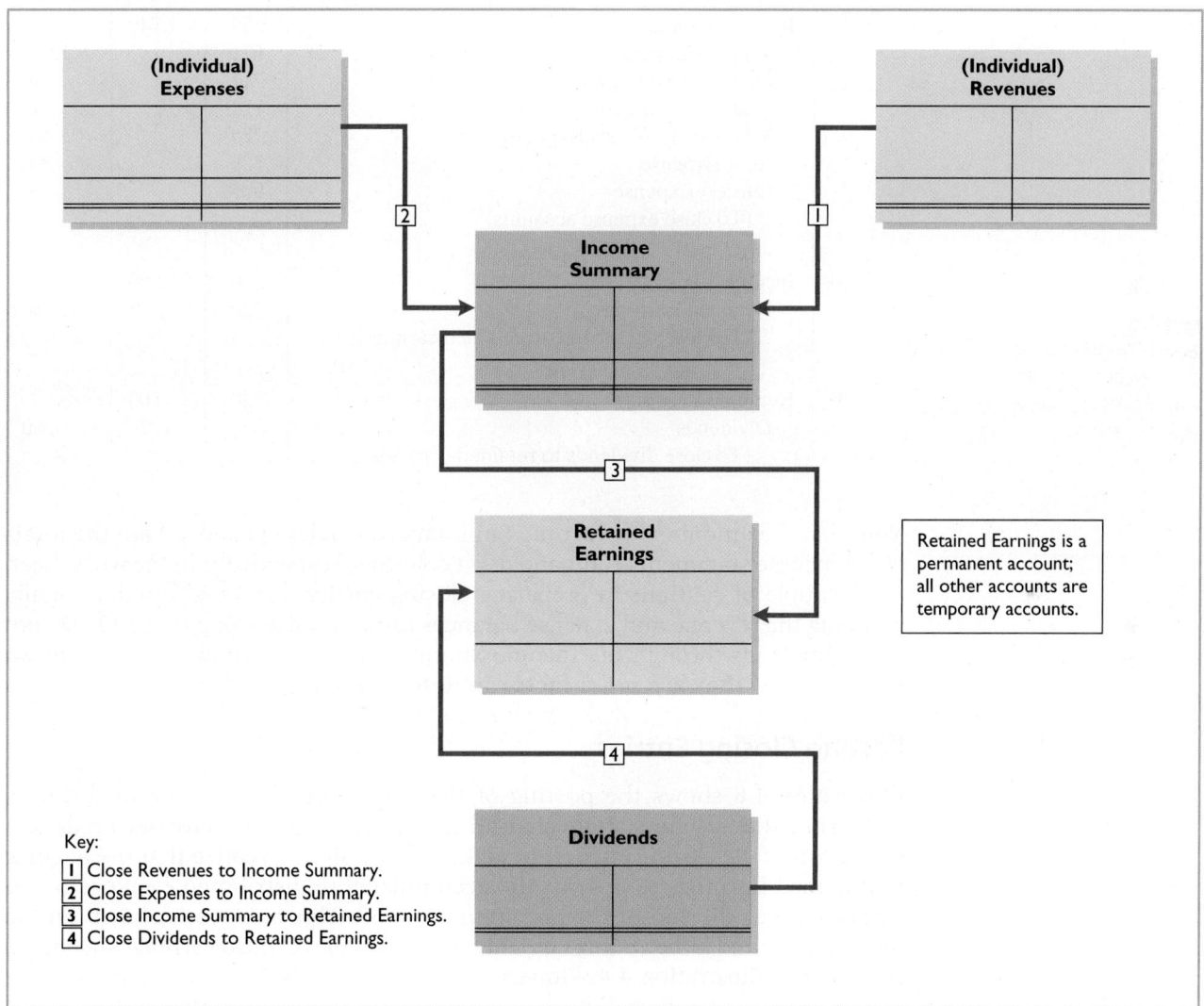

Key:
[1] Close Revenues to Income Summary.
[2] Close Expenses to Income Summary.
[3] Close Income Summary to Retained Earnings.
[4] Close Dividends to Retained Earnings.

Retained Earnings is a permanent account; all other accounts are temporary accounts.

Illustration 4-6
Diagram of closing process—proprietorship

If there were a net loss (because expenses exceeded revenues), entry 3 in Illustration 4-6 would be reversed: there would be a credit to Income Summary and a debit to Retained Earnings.

CLOSING ENTRIES ILLUSTRATED

In practice, companies generally prepare closing entries only at the end of the annual accounting period. However, to illustrate the journalizing and posting of closing entries, we will assume that Pioneer Advertising Agency Inc. closes its books monthly. Illustration 4-7 shows the closing entries at October 31. (The numbers in parentheses before each entry correspond to the four entries diagrammed in Illustration 4-6.)

Illustration 4-7
Closing entries journalized

	General Journal			J3
Date	**Account Titles and Explanation**	**Ref.**	**Debit**	**Credit**
	Closing Entries			
2014	(1)			
Oct. 31	Service Revenue	400	10,600	
	Income Summary	350		10,600
	(To close revenue account)			
	(2)			
31	Income Summary	350	7,740	
	Supplies Expense	631		1,500
	Depreciation Expense	711		40
	Insurance Expense	722		50
	Salaries and Wages Expense	726		5,200
	Rent Expense	729		900
	Interest Expense	905		50
	(To close expense accounts)			
	(3)			
31	Income Summary	350	2,860	
	Retained Earnings	320		2,860
	(To close net income to retained earnings)			
	(4)			
31	Retained Earnings	320	500	
	Dividends	332		500
	(To close dividends to retained earnings)			

Note that the amounts for Income Summary in entries (1) and (2) are the totals of the income statement credit and debit columns, respectively, in the worksheet.

A couple of cautions in preparing closing entries: (1) Avoid unintentionally doubling the revenue and expense balances rather than zeroing them. (2) Do not close Dividends through the Income Summary account. **Dividends are not an expense, and they are not a factor in determining net income.**

Posting Closing Entries

Illustration 4-8 shows the posting of the closing entries and the underlining (ruling) of the accounts. Note that all temporary accounts have zero balances after posting the closing entries. In addition, you should realize that the balance in Retained Earnings represents the accumulated undistributed earnings of the corporation at the end of the accounting period. This balance is shown on the balance sheet and is the ending amount reported on the retained earnings statement, as shown in Illustration 4-4. Pioneer uses the Income Summary account only in closing. It does not journalize and post entries to this account during the year.

As part of the closing process, Pioneer totals, balances, and double-underlines its temporary accounts—revenues, expenses, and Dividends, as shown in T-account form in Illustration 4-8. It does not close its permanent accounts—assets, liabilities, and stockholders' equity (Common Stock and Retained Earnings). Instead, Pioneer draws a single underline beneath the current-period entries for the permanent accounts. The account balance is then entered below the single rule and is carried forward to the next period. (For example, see Retained Earnings.)

Helpful Hint
The balance in Income Summary before it is closed must equal the net income or net loss for the period.

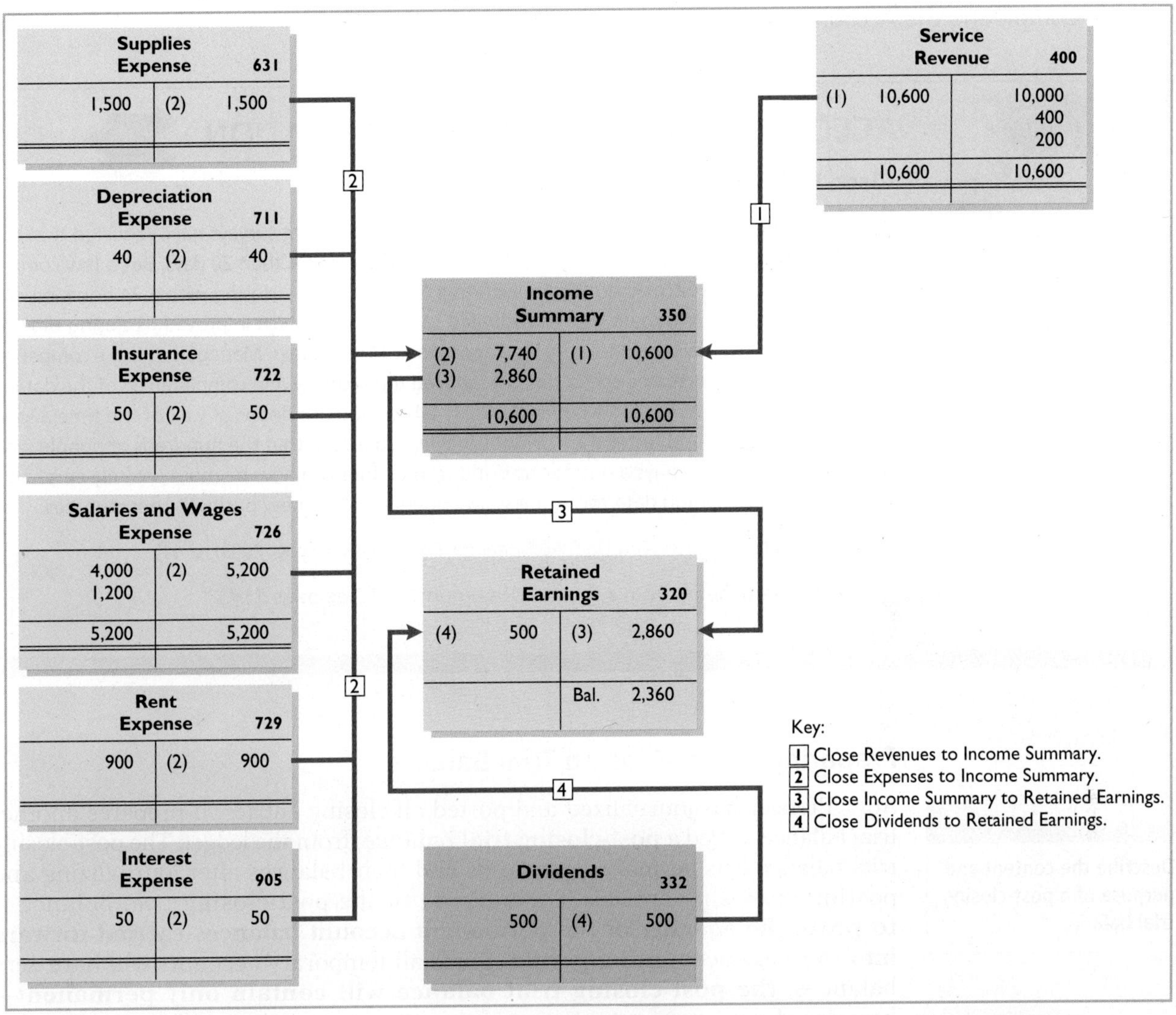

Supplies Expense 631

1,500		(2)	1,500

Depreciation Expense 711

40		(2)	40

Insurance Expense 722

50		(2)	50

Salaries and Wages Expense 726

4,000		(2)	5,200
1,200			
5,200			5,200

Rent Expense 729

900		(2)	900

Interest Expense 905

50		(2)	50

Service Revenue 400

(1)	10,600		10,000
			400
			200
	10,600		10,600

Income Summary 350

(2)	7,740	(1)	10,600
(3)	2,860		
	10,600		10,600

Retained Earnings 320

(4)	500	(3)	2,860
		Bal.	2,360

Dividends 332

	500	(4)	500

Key:
1. Close Revenues to Income Summary.
2. Close Expenses to Income Summary.
3. Close Income Summary to Retained Earnings.
4. Close Dividends to Retained Earnings.

Illustration 4-8
Posting of closing entries

> DO IT!

Closing Entries

Action Plan
✔ Close Income Summary to Retained Earnings.
✔ Close Dividends to Retained Earnings.

The worksheet for Hancock Company shows the following in the financial statement columns:

Dividends $15,000
Common stock $42,000
Net income $18,000

Prepare the closing entries at December 31 that affect stockholders' equity.

Solution

Dec. 31	Income Summary	18,000	
	Retained Earnings		18,000
	(To close net income to retained earnings)		
31	Retained Earnings	15,000	
	Dividends		15,000
	(To close dividends to retained earnings)		

Related exercise material: **BE4-4, BE4-5, BE4-6, E4-4, E4-7, E4-8, E4-10, E4-11, and DO IT! 4-2.**

ACCOUNTING ACROSS THE ORGANIZATION

Cisco Performs the Virtual Close

Technology has dramatically shortened the closing process. Recent surveys have reported that the average company now takes only six to seven days to close, rather than 20 days. But a few companies do much better. Cisco Systems can perform a "virtual close"—closing within 24 hours on any day in the quarter. The same is true at Lockheed Martin Corp., which improved its closing time by 85% in just the last few years. Not very long ago it took 14 to 16 days. Managers at these companies emphasize that this increased speed has not reduced the accuracy and completeness of the data.

This is not just showing off. Knowing exactly where you are financially all of the time allows the company to respond faster than competitors. It also means that the hundreds of people who used to spend 10 to 20 days a quarter tracking transactions can now be more usefully employed on things such as mining data for business intelligence to find new business opportunities.

Source: "Reporting Practices: Few Do It All," *Financial Executive* (November 2003), p. 11.

? Who else benefits from a shorter closing process? (See page 214.)

Preparing a Post-Closing Trial Balance

> **LEARNING OBJECTIVE 3**
>
> Describe the content and purpose of a post-closing trial balance.

After Pioneer has journalized and posted all closing entries, it prepares another trial balance, called a **post-closing trial balance**, from the ledger. The post-closing trial balance lists permanent accounts and their balances after journalizing and posting of closing entries. The purpose of the post-closing trial balance is **to prove the equality of the permanent account balances carried forward into the next accounting period**. Since all temporary accounts will have zero balances, **the post-closing trial balance will contain only permanent— balance sheet—accounts**.

Illustration 4-9 shows the post-closing trial balance for Pioneer Advertising Agency Inc.

Illustration 4-9
Post-closing trial balance

Pioneer Advertising Agency Inc.
Post-Closing Trial Balance
October 31, 2014

	Debit	Credit
Cash	$15,200	
Accounts Receivable	200	
Supplies	1,000	
Prepaid Insurance	550	
Equipment	5,000	
Accumulated Depreciation—Equipment		$ 40
Notes Payable		5,000
Accounts Payable		2,500
Unearned Service Revenue		800
Salaries and Wages Payable		1,200
Interest Payable		50
Common Stock		10,000
Retained Earnings		2,360
	$21,950	$21,950

Pioneer prepares the post-closing trial balance from the permanent accounts in the ledger. Illustration 4-10 shows the permanent accounts in Pioneer's general ledger.

Illustration 4-10
General ledger, permanent accounts

(Permanent Accounts Only)

General Ledger

Cash — No. 101

Date	Explanation	Ref.	Debit	Credit	Balance
2014					
Oct. 1		J1	10,000		10,000
2		J1	1,200		11,200
3		J1		900	10,300
4		J1		600	9,700
20		J1		500	9,200
26		J1		4,000	5,200
31		J1	10,000		**15,200**

Accounts Receivable — No. 112

Date	Explanation	Ref.	Debit	Credit	Balance
2014					
Oct. 31	Adj. entry	J2	**200**		**200**

Supplies — No. 126

Date	Explanation	Ref.	Debit	Credit	Balance
2014					
Oct. 5		J1	2,500		2,500
31	Adj. entry	J2		**1,500**	**1,000**

Prepaid Insurance — No. 130

Date	Explanation	Ref.	Debit	Credit	Balance
2014					
Oct. 4		J1	600		600
31	Adj. entry	J2		**50**	**550**

Equipment — No. 157

Date	Explanation	Ref.	Debit	Credit	Balance
2014					
Oct. 1		J1	5,000		**5,000**

Accumulated Depreciation—Equipment — No. 158

Date	Explanation	Ref.	Debit	Credit	Balance
2014					
Oct. 31	Adj. entry	J2		**40**	**40**

Notes Payable — No. 200

Date	Explanation	Ref.	Debit	Credit	Balance
2014					
Oct. 1		J1		5,000	**5,000**

Accounts Payable — No. 201

Date	Explanation	Ref.	Debit	Credit	Balance
2014					
Oct. 5		J1		2,500	**2,500**

Unearned Service Revenue — No. 209

Date	Explanation	Ref.	Debit	Credit	Balance
2014					
Oct. 2		J1		1,200	1,200
31	Adj. entry	J2	400		**800**

Salaries and Wages Payable — No. 212

Date	Explanation	Ref.	Debit	Credit	Balance
2014					
Oct. 31	Adj. entry	J2		**1,200**	**1,200**

Interest Payable — No. 230

Date	Explanation	Ref.	Debit	Credit	Balance
2014					
Oct. 31	Adj. entry	J2		**50**	**50**

Common Stock — No. 311

Date	Explanation	Ref.	Debit	Credit	Balance
2014					
Oct. 1		J1		10,000	10,000

Retained Earnings — No. 320

Date	Explanation	Ref.	Debit	Credit	Balance
2014					
Oct. 1					–0–
31	Closing entry	J3		2,860	2,860
31	Closing entry	J3	500		2,360

Note: The permanent accounts for Pioneer Advertising Agency Inc. are shown here; the temporary accounts are shown in Illustration 4-11. Both permanent and temporary accounts are part of the general ledger; we segregated them here to aid in learning.

A post-closing trial balance provides evidence that the company has properly journalized and posted the closing entries. It also shows that the accounting equation is in balance at the end of the accounting period. However, like the trial balance, it does not prove that Pioneer has recorded all transactions or that the ledger is correct.

For example, the post-closing trial balance still will balance even if a transaction is not journalized and posted or if a transaction is journalized and posted twice.

The remaining accounts in the general ledger are temporary accounts, shown in Illustration 4-11. After Pioneer correctly posts the closing entries, each temporary account has a zero balance. These accounts are double-underlined to finalize the closing process.

Illustration 4-11

General ledger, temporary accounts

(Temporary Accounts Only)

General Ledger

Dividends   No. 332

Date	Explanation	Ref.	Debit	Credit	Balance
2014					
Oct. 20		J1	500		500
31	Closing entry	J3		500	–0–

Income Summary   No. 350

Date	Explanation	Ref.	Debit	Credit	Balance
2014					
Oct. 31	Closing entry	J3		10,600	10,600
31	Closing entry	J3	7,740		2,860
31	Closing entry	J3	2,860		–0–

Service Revenue   No. 400

Date	Explanation	Ref.	Debit	Credit	Balance
2014					
Oct. 31		J1		10,000	10,000
31	Adj. entry	J2		400	10,400
31	Adj. entry	J2		200	10,600
31	Closing entry	J3	10,600		–0–

Supplies Expense   No. 631

Date	Explanation	Ref.	Debit	Credit	Balance
2014					
Oct. 31	Adj. entry	J2	1,500		1,500
31	Closing entry	J3		1,500	–0–

Depreciation Expense   No. 711

Date	Explanation	Ref.	Debit	Credit	Balance
2014					
Oct. 31	Adj. entry	J2	40		40
31	Closing entry	J3		40	–0–

Insurance Expense   No. 722

Date	Explanation	Ref.	Debit	Credit	Balance
2014					
Oct. 31	Adj. entry	J2	50		50
31	Closing entry	J3		50	–0–

Salaries and Wages Expense   No. 726

Date	Explanation	Ref.	Debit	Credit	Balance
2014					
Oct. 26		J1	4,000		4,000
31	Adj. entry	J2	1,200		5,200
31	Closing entry	J3		5,200	–0–

Rent Expense   No. 729

Date	Explanation	Ref.	Debit	Credit	Balance
2014					
Oct. 3		J1	900		900
31	Closing entry	J3		900	–0–

Interest Expense   No. 905

Date	Explanation	Ref.	Debit	Credit	Balance
2014					
Oct. 31	Adj. entry	J2	50		50
31	Closing entry	J3		50	–0–

> *Note:* The temporary accounts for Pioneer Advertising Agency Inc. are shown here; Illustration 4-10 shows the permanent accounts. Both permanent and temporary accounts are part of the general ledger; they are segregated here to aid in learning.

Summary of the Accounting Cycle

LEARNING OBJECTIVE   **4**

State the required steps in the accounting cycle.

Illustration 4-12 summarizes the steps in the accounting cycle. You can see that the cycle begins with the analysis of business transactions and ends with the preparation of a post-closing trial balance.

Steps 1–3 may occur daily during the accounting period, as explained in Chapter 2. Companies perform Steps 4–7 on a periodic basis, such as monthly, quarterly, or annually. Steps 8 and 9—closing entries, and a post-closing trial balance—usually take place only at the end of a company's **annual** accounting period.

Illustration 4-12
Steps in the accounting cycle

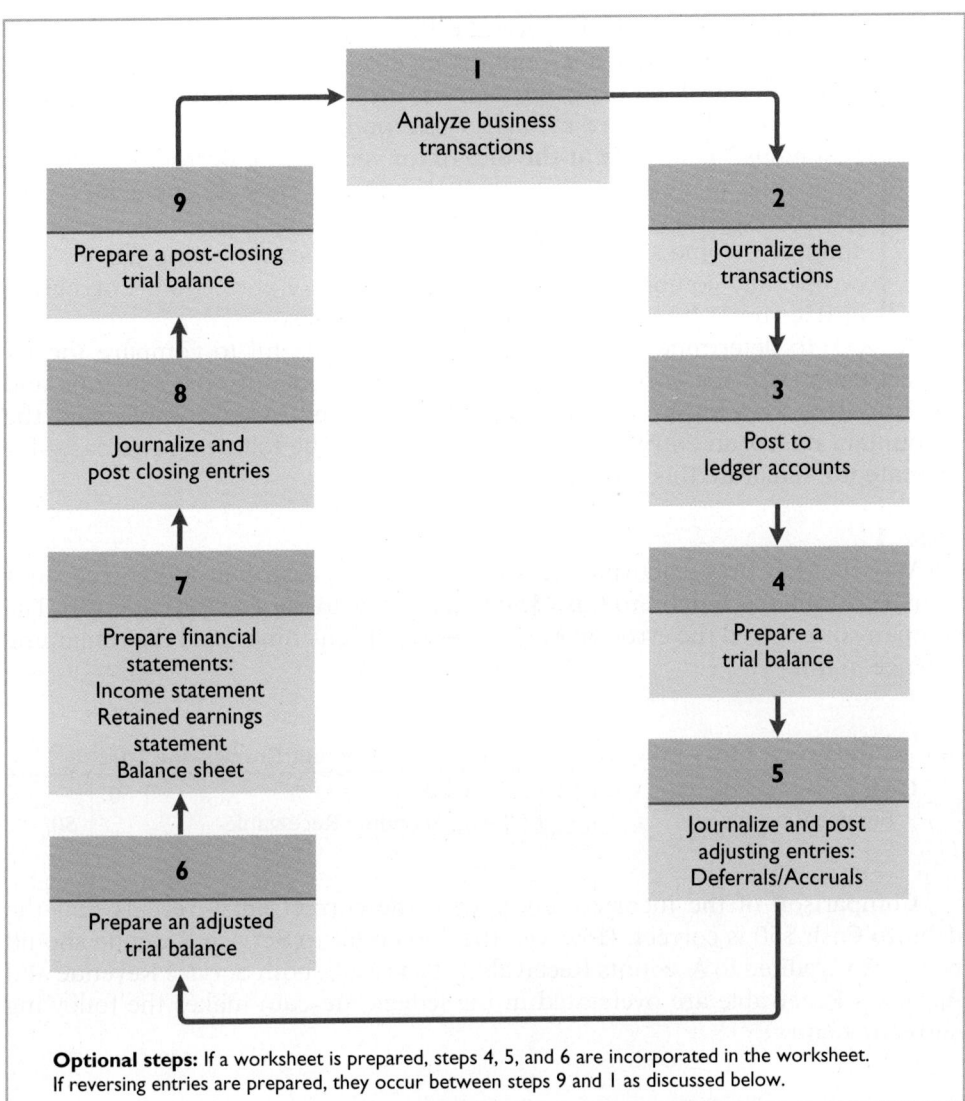

Optional steps: If a worksheet is prepared, steps 4, 5, and 6 are incorporated in the worksheet. If reversing entries are prepared, they occur between steps 9 and 1 as discussed below.

There are also two **optional steps** in the accounting cycle. As you have seen, companies may use a worksheet in preparing adjusting entries and financial statements. In addition, they may use reversing entries, as explained below.

Reversing Entries—An Optional Step

Some accountants prefer to reverse certain adjusting entries by making a **reversing entry** at the beginning of the next accounting period. A reversing entry is the exact opposite of the adjusting entry made in the previous period. **Use of reversing entries is an optional bookkeeping procedure; it is not a required step in the accounting cycle.** Accordingly, we have chosen to cover this topic in Appendix 4A at the end of the chapter.

Correcting Entries—An Avoidable Step

Unfortunately, errors may occur in the recording process. Companies should correct errors, **as soon as they discover them**, by journalizing and posting **correcting entries**. If the accounting records are free of errors, no correcting entries are needed.

LEARNING OBJECTIVE   **5**

Explain the approaches to preparing correcting entries.

Ethics Note

When companies find errors in previously released income statements, they restate those numbers. Perhaps because of the increased scrutiny caused by Sarbanes-Oxley, in a recent year companies filed a record 1,195 restatements.

You should recognize several differences between correcting entries and adjusting entries. First, adjusting entries are an integral part of the accounting cycle. Correcting entries, on the other hand, are unnecessary if the records are error-free. Second, companies journalize and post adjustments **only at the end of an accounting period**. In contrast, companies make correcting entries **whenever they discover an error**. Finally, adjusting entries always affect at least one balance sheet account and one income statement account. In contrast, correcting entries may involve any combination of accounts in need of correction. **Correcting entries must be posted before closing entries.**

To determine the correcting entry, it is useful to compare the incorrect entry with the correct entry. Doing so helps identify the accounts and amounts that should—and should not—be corrected. After comparison, the accountant makes an entry to correct the accounts. The following two cases for Mercato Co. illustrate this approach.

CASE 1

On May 10, Mercato Co. journalized and posted a $50 cash collection on account from a customer as a debit to Cash $50 and a credit to Service Revenue $50. The company discovered the error on May 20, when the customer paid the remaining balance in full.

Illustration 4-13
Comparison of entries

Incorrect Entry (May 10)			Correct Entry (May 10)		
Cash	50		Cash	50	
Service Revenue		50	Accounts Receivable		50

Comparison of the incorrect entry with the correct entry reveals that the debit to Cash $50 is correct. However, the $50 credit to Service Revenue should have been credited to Accounts Receivable. As a result, both Service Revenue and Accounts Receivable are overstated in the ledger. Mercato makes the following correcting entry.

Illustration 4-14
Correcting entry

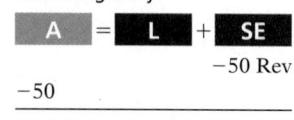

−50

Cash Flows
no effect

	Correcting Entry				
May 20	Service Revenue			50	
	Accounts Receivable				50
	(To correct entry of May 10)				

CASE 2

On May 18, Mercato purchased on account equipment costing $450. The transaction was journalized and posted as a debit to Equipment $45 and a credit to Accounts Payable $45. The error was discovered on June 3, when Mercato received the monthly statement for May from the creditor.

Illustration 4-15
Comparison of entries

Incorrect Entry (May 18)			Correct Entry (May 18)		
Equipment	45		Equipment	450	
Accounts Payable		45	Accounts Payable		450

Comparison of the two entries shows that two accounts are incorrect. Equipment is understated $405, and Accounts Payable is understated $405. Mercato makes the following correcting entry.

Correcting Entry

June 3	Equipment	405	
	Accounts Payable		405
	(To correct entry of May 18)		

A = L + SE
+405
+405

Cash Flows
no effect

Illustration 4-16
Correcting entry

Instead of preparing a correcting entry, **it is possible to reverse the incorrect entry and then prepare the correct entry**. This approach will result in more entries and postings than a correcting entry, but it will accomplish the desired result.

ACCOUNTING ACROSS THE ORGANIZATION

Yale Express Loses Some Transportation Bills

Yale Express, a short-haul trucking firm, turned over much of its cargo to local truckers to complete deliveries. Yale collected the entire delivery charge; when billed by the local trucker, Yale sent payment for the final phase to the local trucker. Yale used a cutoff period of 20 days into the next accounting period in making its adjusting entries for accrued liabilities. That is, it waited 20 days to receive the local truckers' bills to determine the amount of the unpaid but incurred delivery charges as of the balance sheet date.

On the other hand, Republic Carloading, a nationwide, long-distance freight forwarder, frequently did not receive transportation bills from truckers to whom it passed on cargo until months after the year-end. In making its year-end adjusting entries, Republic waited for months in order to include all of these outstanding transportation bills.

When Yale Express merged with Republic Carloading, Yale's vice president employed the 20-day cutoff procedure for both firms. As a result, millions of dollars of Republic's accrued transportation bills went unrecorded. When the company detected the error and made correcting entries, these and other errors changed a reported profit of $1.14 million into a loss of $1.88 million!

What might Yale Express's vice president have done to produce more accurate financial statements without waiting months for Republic's outstanding transportation bills? (See page 214.)

The Classified Balance Sheet

The balance sheet presents a snapshot of a company's financial position at a point in time. To improve users' understanding of a company's financial position, companies often use a classified balance sheet. A **classified balance sheet** groups together similar assets and similar liabilities, using a number of standard classifications and sections. This is useful because items within a group have similar economic characteristics. A classified balance sheet generally contains the standard classifications listed in Illustration 4-17.

LEARNING OBJECTIVE 6

Identify the sections of a classified balance sheet.

Assets	Liabilities and Stockholders' Equity
Current assets	Current liabilities
Long-term investments	Long-term liabilities
Property, plant, and equipment	Stockholders' equity
Intangible assets	

Illustration 4-17
Standard balance sheet classifications

These groupings help financial statement readers determine such things as (1) whether the company has enough assets to pay its debts as they come due, and (2) the claims of short- and long-term creditors on the company's total assets. Many of these groupings can be seen in the balance sheet of Franklin Corporation shown in Illustration 4-18 below. In the sections that follow, we explain each of these groupings.

Illustration 4-18
Classified balance sheet

Franklin Corporation Balance Sheet October 31, 2014			
Assets			
Current assets			
Cash		$ 6,600	
Short-term investments		2,000	
Accounts receivable		7,000	
Notes receivable		1,000	
Inventory		3,000	
Supplies		2,100	
Prepaid insurance		400	
Total current assets			$22,100
Long-term investments			
Investment in stock of Walters Corp.		5,200	
Investment in real estate		2,000	7,200
Property, plant, and equipment			
Land		10,000	
Equipment	$24,000		
Less: Accumulated depreciation— equipment	5,000	19,000	29,000
Intangible assets			
Patents			3,100
Total assets			$61,400
Liabilities and Stockholders' Equity			
Current liabilities			
Notes payable		$11,000	
Accounts payable		2,100	
Salaries and wages payable		1,600	
Unearned service revenue		900	
Interest payable		450	
Total current liabilities			$16,050
Long-term liabilities			
Mortgage payable		10,000	
Notes payable		1,300	
Total long-term liabilities			11,300
Total liabilities			27,350
Stockholders' equity			
Common stock		20,000	
Retained earnings		14,050	
Total stockholders' equity			34,050
Total liabilities and stockholders' equity			$61,400

Helpful Hint
Recall that the basic accounting equation is Assets = Liabilities + Stockholders' Equity.

Current Assets

Current assets are assets that a company expects to convert to cash or use up within one year or its operating cycle, whichever is longer. In Illustration 4-18, Franklin Corporation had current assets of $22,100. For most businesses, the cutoff for classification as current assets is one year from the balance sheet date. For example, accounts receivable are current assets because the company will collect them and convert them to cash within one year. Supplies is a current asset because the company expects to use it up in operations within one year.

Some companies use a period longer than one year to classify assets and liabilities as current because they have an operating cycle longer than one year. The **operating cycle** of a company is the average time that it takes to purchase inventory, sell it on account, and then collect cash from customers. For most businesses this cycle takes less than a year, so they use a one-year cutoff. But, for some businesses, such as vineyards or airplane manufacturers, this period may be longer than a year. **Except where noted, we will assume that companies use one year to determine whether an asset or liability is current or long-term.**

Common types of current assets are (1) cash, (2) short-term investments (such as short-term U.S. government securities), (3) receivables (notes receivable, accounts receivable, and interest receivable), (4) inventories, and (5) prepaid expenses (supplies and insurance). **On the balance sheet, companies usually list these items in the order in which they expect to convert them into cash.**

Illustration 4-19 presents the current assets of Southwest Airlines Co.

Illustration 4-19
Current assets section

Southwest Airlines Co.
Balance Sheet (partial)
(in millions)

Current assets	
Cash and cash equivalents	$1,390
Short-term investments	369
Accounts receivable	241
Inventories	181
Prepaid expenses and other current assets	420
Total current assets	$2,601

As explained later in the chapter, a company's current assets are important in assessing its short-term debt-paying ability.

Long-Term Investments

Long-term investments are generally, (1) investments in stocks and bonds of other companies that are normally held for many years, and (2) long-term assets such as land or buildings that a company is not currently using in its operating activities. In Illustration 4-18, Franklin Corporation reported total long-term investments of $7,200 on its balance sheet.

Yahoo! Inc. reported long-term investments in its balance sheet as shown in Illustration 4-20 (page 182).

Alternative Terminology
Long-term investments are often referred to simply as *investments*.

Illustration 4-20
Long-term investments section

Yahoo! Inc.
Balance Sheet (partial)
(in thousands)

Long-term investments
Long-term investments in marketable securities $90,266

Property, Plant, and Equipment

Property, plant, and equipment are assets with relatively long useful lives that a company is currently using in operating the business. This category (sometimes called *fixed assets*) includes land, buildings, machinery and equipment, delivery equipment, and furniture. In Illustration 4-18, Franklin Corporation reported property, plant, and equipment of $29,000.

> ### International Note
>
> Recently, China adopted International Financial Reporting Standards (IFRS). This was done in an effort to reduce fraud and increase investor confidence in financial reports. Under these standards, many items, such as property, plant, and equipment, may be reported at current fair values, rather than historical cost.

Depreciation is the practice of allocating the cost of assets to a number of years. Companies do this by systematically assigning a portion of an asset's cost as an expense each year (rather than expensing the full purchase price in the year of purchase). The assets that the company depreciates are reported on the balance sheet at cost less accumulated depreciation. The **accumulated depreciation** account shows the total amount of depreciation that the company has expensed thus far in the asset's life. In Illustration 4-18, Franklin Corporation reported accumulated depreciation of $5,000.

Illustration 4-21 presents the property, plant, and equipment of Cooper Tire & Rubber Company.

Illustration 4-21
Property, plant, and equipment section

Cooper Tire & Rubber Company
Balance Sheet (partial)
(in thousands)

Property, plant, and equipment		
Land and land improvements	$ 41,553	
Buildings	298,706	
Machinery and equipment	1,636,091	
Molds, cores, and rings	268,158	$2,244,508
Less: Accumulated depreciation		1,252,692
		$ 991,816

Intangible Assets

Helpful Hint
Sometimes intangible assets are reported under a broader heading called *"Other assets."*

Many companies have long-lived assets that do not have physical substance yet often are very valuable. We call these assets **intangible assets**. One common intangible asset is goodwill. Others include patents, copyrights, and trademarks or trade names that give the company **exclusive right** of use for a specified period of time. In Illustration 4-18, Franklin Corporation reported intangible assets of $3,100.

Illustration 4-22 shows the intangible assets of media giant Time Warner, Inc.

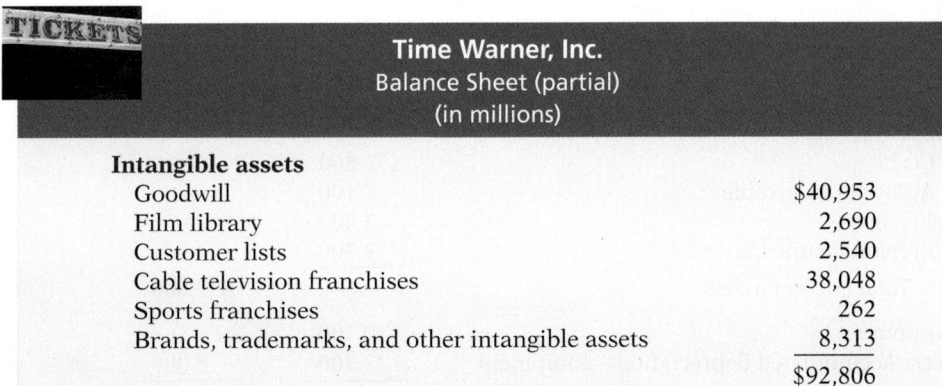

Time Warner, Inc.
Balance Sheet (partial)
(in millions)

Intangible assets	
Goodwill	$40,953
Film library	2,690
Customer lists	2,540
Cable television franchises	38,048
Sports franchises	262
Brands, trademarks, and other intangible assets	8,313
	$92,806

Illustration 4-22
Intangible assets section

PEOPLE, PLANET, AND PROFIT INSIGHT

Regaining Goodwill

After falling to unforeseen lows amidst scandals, recalls, and economic crises, the American public's positive perception of the reputation of corporate America is on the rise. Overall corporate reputation is experiencing rehabilitation as the American public gives high marks overall to corporate America, specific industries, and the largest number of individual companies in a dozen years. This is according to the findings of the 2011 Harris Interactive RQ Study, which measures the reputations of the 60 most visible companies in the U.S.

The survey focuses on six reputational dimensions that influence reputation and consumer behavior. The six dimensions, along with the five corporations that ranked highest within each, are as follows.

- **Social Responsibility:** (1) Whole Foods Market, (2) Johnson & Johnson, (3) Google, (4) The Walt Disney Company, (5) Procter & Gamble Co.
- **Emotional Appeal:** (1) Johnson & Johnson, (2) amazon.com, (3) UPS, (4) General Mills, (5) Kraft Foods
- **Financial Performance:** (1) Google, (2) Berkshire Hathaway, (3) Apple, (4) Intel, (5) The Walt Disney Company
- **Products and Services:** (1) Intel Corporation, (2) 3M Company, (3) Johnson & Johnson, (4) Google, (5) Procter & Gamble Co.

Source: www.harrisinteractive.com.

 Name two industries today which are probably rated low on the reputational characteristics of "being trusted" and "having high ethical standards." (See page 214.)

> DO IT!

Asset Section of Classified Balance Sheet

Baxter Hoffman recently received the following information related to Hoffman Company's December 31, 2014, balance sheet.

Prepaid insurance	$ 2,300	Inventory	$3,400
Cash	800	Accumulated depreciation—	
Equipment	10,700	equipment	2,700
		Accounts receivable	1,100

Prepare the asset section of Hoffman Company's classified balance sheet.

Action Plan

✔ Present current assets first. Current assets are cash and other resources that the company expects to convert to cash or use up within one year.

✔ Present current assets in the order in which the company expects to convert them into cash.

✔ Subtract accumulated depreciation—equipment from equipment to determine net equipment.

Solution

Assets

Current assets		
Cash	$ 800	
Accounts receivable	1,100	
Inventory	3,400	
Prepaid insurance	2,300	
Total current assets		$ 7,600
Equipment	10,700	
Less: Accumulated depreciation—equipment	2,700	8,000
Total assets		$15,600

Related exercise material: **BE4-10** and **DO IT! 4-3**.

The Navigator ✔

Ethics Note

A company that has more current assets than current liabilities can increase the ratio of current assets to current liabilities by using cash to pay off some current liabilities. This gives the appearance of being more liquid. Do you think this move is ethical?

Current Liabilities

In the liabilities and stockholders' equity section of the balance sheet, the first grouping is current liabilities. **Current liabilities** are obligations that the company is to pay within the coming year or its operating cycle, whichever is longer. Common examples are accounts payable, wages payable, bank loans payable, interest payable, and taxes payable. Also included as current liabilities are current maturities of long-term obligations—payments to be made within the next year on long-term obligations. In Illustration 4-18, Franklin Corporation reported five different types of current liabilities, for a total of $16,050.

Within the current liabilities section, companies usually list notes payable first, followed by accounts payable. Other items then follow in the order of their magnitude. *In your homework, you should present notes payable first, followed by accounts payable, and then other liabilities in order of magnitude.*

Illustration 4-23 shows the current liabilities section adapted from the balance sheet of Marcus Corporation.

Illustration 4-23
Current liabilities section

Marcus Corporation
Balance Sheet (partial)
(in thousands)

Current liabilities	
Notes payable	$ 239
Accounts payable	24,242
Current maturities of long-term debt	57,250
Other current liabilities	27,477
Income taxes payable	11,215
Salary and wages payable	6,720
Total current liabilities	$127,143

Users of financial statements look closely at the relationship between current assets and current liabilities. This relationship is important in evaluating a company's **liquidity**—its ability to pay obligations expected to be due within the next year. When current assets exceed current liabilities at the balance sheet date, the likelihood for paying the liabilities is favorable. When the reverse is true, short-term creditors may not be paid, and the company may ultimately be forced into bankruptcy.

ACCOUNTING ACROSS THE ORGANIZATION

Can a Company Be Too Liquid?

There actually is a point where a company can be too liquid—that is, it can have too much working capital (current assets less current liabilities). While it is important to be liquid enough to be able to pay short-term bills as they come due, a company does not want to tie up its cash in extra inventory or receivables that are not earning the company money.

By one estimate from the REL Consultancy Group, the thousand largest U.S. companies have on their books cumulative excess working capital of $764 billion. Based on this figure, companies could have reduced debt by 36% or increased net income by 9%. Given that managers throughout a company are interested in improving profitability, it is clear that they should have an eye toward managing working capital. They need to aim for a "Goldilocks solution"—not too much, not too little, but just right.

Source: K. Richardson, "Companies Fall Behind in Cash Management," *Wall Street Journal* (June 19, 2007).

? What can various company managers do to ensure that working capital is managed efficiently to maximize net income? (See page 214.)

Long-Term Liabilities

Long-term liabilities are obligations that a company expects to pay **after** one year. Liabilities in this category include bonds payable, mortgages payable, long-term notes payable, lease liabilities, and pension liabilities. Many companies report long-term debt maturing after one year as a single amount in the balance sheet and show the details of the debt in notes that accompany the financial statements. Others list the various types of long-term liabilities. In Illustration 4-18, Franklin Corporation reported long-term liabilities of $11,300. *In your home-work, list long-term liabilities in the order of their magnitude.*

Illustration 4-24 shows the long-term liabilities that The Procter & Gamble Company reported in its balance sheet.

Illustration 4-24
Long-term liabilities section

The Procter & Gamble Company Balance Sheet (partial) (in millions)	
Long-term liabilities	
Long-term debt	$23,375
Deferred income taxes	12,015
Other noncurrent liabilities	5,147
Total long-term liabilities	$40,537

Stockholders' (Owners') Equity

The content of the owners' equity section varies with the form of business orga-nization. In a proprietorship, there is one capital account. In a partnership, there is a capital account for each partner. Corporations divide owners' equity into two accounts—Common Stock (sometimes referred to as Capital Stock) and Retained Earnings. Corporations record stockholders' investments in the company by debiting an asset account and crediting the Common Stock account. They record in the Retained Earnings account income retained for use in the business. Corporations combine the Common Stock and Retained Earnings accounts and report them on the balance sheet as **stockholders' equity**. (We'll learn more about these corporation accounts in later chapters.) Nordstrom, Inc. recently reported its stockholders' equity section as follows.

Illustration 4-25
Stockholders' equity section

Nordstrom, Inc.
Balance Sheet (partial)
($ in thousands)

Stockholders' equity	
Common stock, 271,331 shares	$ 685,934
Retained earnings	1,406,747
Total stockholders' equity	$2,092,681

> DO IT!

Balance Sheet Classifications

The following accounts were taken from the financial statements of Callahan Company.

_____ Salaries and wages payable
_____ Service revenue
_____ Interest payable
_____ Goodwill
_____ Short-term investments
_____ Mortgage payable (due in 3 years)

_____ Investment in real estate
_____ Equipment
_____ Accumulated depreciation— equipment
_____ Depreciation expense
_____ Common stock
_____ Unearned service revenue

Match each of the following accounts to its proper balance sheet classification, shown below. If the item would not appear on a balance sheet, use "NA."

Current assets (CA)
Long-term investments (LTI)
Property, plant, and equipment (PPE)
Intangible assets (IA)

Current liabilities (CL)
Long-term liabilities (LTL)
Stockholders' equity (SE)

Solution

Action Plan

✔ Analyze whether each financial statement item is an asset, liability, or stockholders' equity.

✔ Determine if asset and liability items are short-term or long-term.

__CL__	Salaries and wages payable		__LTI__	Investment in real estate
__NA__	Service revenue		__PPE__	Equipment
__CL__	Interest payable		__PPE__	Accumulated depreciation— equipment
__IA__	Goodwill			
__CA__	Short-term investments		__NA__	Depreciation expense
__LTL__	Mortgage payable (due in 3 years)		__SE__	Common stock
			__CL__	Unearned service revenue

Related exercise material: **BE4-11, E4-14, E4-15, E4-16, E4-17,** and **DO IT!** **4-4.**

 The Navigator

> **Comprehensive DO IT!**

At the end of its first month of operations, Watson Answering Service Inc. has the following unadjusted trial balance.

Action Plan

✔ In completing the worksheet, be sure to (a) key the adjustments; (b) start at the top of the adjusted trial balance columns and extend adjusted balances to the correct statement columns; and (c) enter net income (or net loss) in the proper columns.

✔ In preparing a classified balance sheet, know the contents of each of the sections.

✔ In journalizing closing entries, remember that there are only four entries and that Dividends are closed to Retained Earnings.

Watson Answering Service Inc.
August 31, 2014
Trial Balance

	Debit	Credit
Cash	$ 5,400	
Accounts Receivable	2,800	
Supplies	1,300	
Prepaid Insurance	2,400	
Equipment	60,000	
Notes Payable		$40,000
Accounts Payable		2,400
Common Stock		30,000
Dividends	1,000	
Service Revenue		4,900
Salaries and Wages Expense	3,200	
Utilities Expense	800	
Advertising Expense	400	
	$77,300	$77,300

Other data:

1. Insurance expires at the rate of $200 per month.
2. $1,000 of supplies are on hand at August 31.
3. Monthly depreciation on the equipment is $900.
4. Interest of $500 on the notes payable has accrued during August.

Instructions
(a) Prepare a worksheet.
(b) Prepare a classified balance sheet assuming $35,000 of the notes payable are long-term.
(c) Journalize the closing entries.

Solution to Comprehensive DO IT!

(a)
Watson Answering Service Inc.
Worksheet for the Month Ended August 31, 2014

Account Titles	Trial Balance Dr.	Cr.	Adjustments Dr.	Cr.	Adjusted Trial Balance Dr.	Cr.	Income Statement Dr.	Cr.	Balance Sheet Dr.	Cr.
Cash	5,400				5,400				5,400	
Accounts Receivable	2,800				2,800				2,800	
Supplies	1,300			(b) 300	1,000				1,000	
Prepaid Insurance	2,400			(a) 200	2,200				2,200	
Equipment	60,000				60,000				60,000	
Notes Payable		40,000				40,000				40,000
Accounts Payable		2,400				2,400				2,400
Common Stock		30,000				30,000				30,000
Dividends	1,000				1,000				1,000	
Service Revenue		4,900				4,900		4,900		
Salaries and Wages Expense	3,200				3,200		3,200			
Utilities Expense	800				800		800			
Advertising Expense	400				400		400			
Totals	77,300	77,300								

	Adjustments Dr.	Adjustments Cr.	Adjusted Trial Balance Dr.	Adjusted Trial Balance Cr.	Income Statement Dr.	Income Statement Cr.	Balance Sheet Dr.	Balance Sheet Cr.
Insurance Expense	(a) 200		200		200			
Supplies Expense	(b) 300		300		300			
Depreciation Expense	(c) 900		900		900			
Accumulated Depreciation—Equipment		(c) 900		900				900
Interest Expense	(d) 500		500		500			
Interest Payable		(d) 500		500				500
Totals	1,900	1,900	78,700	78,700	6,300	4,900	72,400	73,800
Net Loss						1,400	1,400	
Totals					6,300	6,300	73,800	73,800

Explanation: (a) Insurance expired, (b) Supplies used, (c) Depreciation expensed, (d) Interest accrued.

(b)

Watson Answering Service Inc.
Balance Sheet
August 31, 2014

Assets

Current assets		
Cash	$ 5,400	
Accounts receivable	2,800	
Supplies	1,000	
Prepaid insurance	2,200	
Total current assets		$11,400
Property, plant, and equipment		
Equipment	60,000	
Less: Accumulated depreciation—equipment	900	59,100
Total assets		$70,500

Liabilities and Stockholders' Equity

Current liabilities		
Notes payable	$ 5,000	
Accounts payable	2,400	
Interest payable	500	
Total current liabilities		$ 7,900
Long-term liabilities		
Notes payable		35,000
Total liabilities		42,900
Stockholders' equity		
Common stock	30,000	
Retained earnings	(2,400)*	
Total stockholders' equity		27,600
Total liabilities and stockholders' equity		$70,500

*Net loss $1,400, plus dividends of $1,000.

(c)

Aug. 31	Service Revenue	4,900	
	Income Summary		4,900
	(To close revenue account)		
31	Income Summary	6,300	
	Salaries and Wages Expense		3,200
	Depreciation Expense		900
	Utilities Expense		800
	Interest Expense		500

		Advertising Expense			400
		Supplies Expense			300
		Insurance Expense			200
		(To close expense accounts)			
	31	Retained Earnings		1,400	
		Income Summary			1,400
		(To close net loss to retained earnings)			
	31	Retained Earnings		1,000	
		Dividends			1,000
		(To close dividends to retained earnings)			

✔ **The Navigator**

SUMMARY OF LEARNING OBJECTIVES

✔ **The Navigator**

1 Prepare a worksheet. The steps in preparing a worksheet are as follows. (a) Prepare a trial balance on the worksheet. (b) Enter the adjustments in the adjustments columns. (c) Enter adjusted balances in the adjusted trial balance columns. (d) Extend adjusted trial balance amounts to appropriate financial statement columns. (e) Total the statement columns, compute net income (or net loss), and complete the worksheet.

2 Explain the process of closing the books. Closing the books occurs at the end of an accounting period. The process is to journalize and post closing entries and then underline and balance all accounts. In closing the books, companies make separate entries to close revenues and expenses to Income Summary, Income Summary to Retained Earnings, and Dividends to Retained Earnings. Only temporary accounts are closed.

3 Describe the content and purpose of a post-closing trial balance. A post-closing trial balance contains the balances in permanent accounts that are carried forward to the next accounting period. The purpose of this trial balance is to prove the equality of these balances.

4 State the required steps in the accounting cycle. The required steps in the accounting cycle are: (1) analyze business transactions, (2) journalize the transactions, (3) post to ledger accounts, (4) prepare a trial balance, (5) journalize and post adjusting entries, (6) prepare an adjusted trial balance, (7) prepare financial statements, (8) journalize and post closing entries, and (9) prepare a post-closing trial balance.

5 Explain the approaches to preparing correcting entries. One way to determine the correcting entry is to compare the incorrect entry with the correct entry. After comparison, the company makes a correcting entry to correct the accounts. An alternative to a correcting entry is to reverse the incorrect entry and then prepare the correct entry.

6 Identify the sections of a classified balance sheet. A classified balance sheet categorizes assets as current assets; long-term investments; property, plant, and equipment; and intangibles. Liabilities are classified as either current or long-term. There is also a stockholders' (owners') equity section, which varies with the form of business organization.

GLOSSARY

Classified balance sheet A balance sheet that contains standard classifications or sections. (p. 179).

Closing entries Entries made at the end of an accounting period to transfer the balances of temporary accounts to a permanent stockholders' equity account, Retained Earnings. (p. 170).

Correcting entries Entries to correct errors made in recording transactions. (p. 177).

Current assets Assets that a company expects to convert to cash or use up within one year. (p. 181).

Current liabilities Obligations that a company expects to pay within the coming year. (p. 184).

Income Summary A temporary account used in closing revenue and expense accounts. (p. 170).

Intangible assets Noncurrent assets that do not have physical substance. (p. 182).

Liquidity The ability of a company to pay obligations expected to be due within the next year. (p. 184).

Long-term investments Generally, (1) investments in stocks and bonds of other companies that companies normally hold for many years, and (2) long-term assets, such as land and buildings, not currently being used in operations. (p. 181).

Long-term liabilities Obligations that a company expects to pay after one year. (p. 185).

Operating cycle The average time that it takes to purchase inventory, sell it on account, and then collect cash from customers. (p. 181).

Permanent (real) accounts Accounts that relate to one or more accounting periods. Consist of all balance sheet accounts. Balances are carried forward to next accounting period. (p. 170).

Post-closing trial balance A list of permanent accounts and their balances after a company has journalized and posted closing entries. (p. 174).

Property, plant, and equipment Assets with relatively long useful lives and currently being used in operations. (p. 182).

Reversing entry An entry, made at the beginning of the next accounting period, that is the exact opposite of the adjusting entry made in the previous period. (p. 177).

Stockholders' equity The combination of common stock and retained earnings accounts. Often referred to as the ownership claim of shareholders on total assets. It is to a corporation what owner's equity is to a proprietorship. (p. 186).

Temporary (nominal) accounts Accounts that relate only to a given accounting period. Consist of all income statement accounts and the dividends account. All temporary accounts are closed at end of the accounting period. (p. 170).

Worksheet A multiple-column form that may be used in making adjusting entries and in preparing financial statements. (p. 164).

APPENDIX 4A REVERSING ENTRIES

LEARNING OBJECTIVE **7**

Prepare reversing entries.

After preparing the financial statements and closing the books, it is often helpful to reverse some of the adjusting entries before recording the regular transactions of the next period. Such entries are **reversing entries**. Companies make **a reversing entry at the beginning of the next accounting period**. Each reversing entry **is the exact opposite of the adjusting entry made in the previous period**. The recording of reversing entries is an **optional step** in the accounting cycle.

The purpose of reversing entries is to simplify the recording of a subsequent transaction related to an adjusting entry. For example, in Chapter 3 (page 117), the payment of salaries after an adjusting entry resulted in two debits: one to Salaries and Wages Payable and the other to Salaries and Wages Expense. With reversing entries, the company can debit the entire subsequent payment to Salaries and Wages Expense. **The use of reversing entries does not change the amounts reported in the financial statements.** What it does is simplify the recording of subsequent transactions.

Reversing Entries Example

Companies most often use reversing entries to reverse two types of adjusting entries: accrued revenues and accrued expenses. To illustrate the optional use of reversing entries for accrued expenses, we will use the salaries expense transactions for Pioneer Advertising Agency Inc. as illustrated in Chapters 2, 3, and 4. The transaction and adjustment data are as follows.

1. October 26 (initial salary entry): Pioneer pays $4,000 of salaries and wages earned between October 15 and October 26.

2. October 31 (adjusting entry): Salaries and wages earned between October 29 and October 31 are $1,200. The company will pay these in the November 9 payroll.

3. November 9 (subsequent salary entry): Salaries and wages paid are $4,000. Of this amount, $1,200 applied to accrued salaries and wages payable and $2,800 was earned between November 1 and November 9.

Illustration 4A-1 shows the entries with and without reversing entries.

Without Reversing Entries (per chapter)				With Reversing Entries (per appendix)		
Initial Salary Entry				**Initial Salary Entry**		
Oct. 26	Salaries and Wages Expense	4,000		Oct. 26	(Same entry)	
	Cash		4,000			
Adjusting Entry				**Adjusting Entry**		
Oct. 31	Salaries and Wages Expense	1,200		Oct. 31	(Same entry)	
	Salaries and Wages Payable		1,200			
Closing Entry				**Closing Entry**		
Oct. 31	Income Summary	5,200		Oct. 31	(Same entry)	
	Salaries and Wages Expense		5,200			
Reversing Entry				**Reversing Entry**		
Nov. 1	No reversing entry is made.			Nov. 1	**Salaries and Wages Payable**	**1,200**
					Salaries and Wages Expense	**1,200**
Subsequent Salary Entry				**Subsequent Salary Entry**		
Nov. 9	Salaries and Wages Payable	1,200		Nov. 9	**Salaries and Wages Expense**	**4,000**
	Salaries and Wages Expense	2,800			**Cash**	**4,000**
	Cash		4,000			

Illustration 4A-1
Comparative entries—not reversing vs. reversing

The first three entries are the same whether or not Pioneer uses reversing entries. The last two entries are different. The November 1 **reversing entry** eliminates the $1,200 balance in Salaries and Wages Payable created by the October 31 adjusting entry. The reversing entry also creates a $1,200 credit balance in the Salaries and Wages Expense account. As you know, it is unusual for an expense account to have a credit balance. The balance is correct in this instance, though, because it anticipates that the entire amount of the first salaries and wages payment in the new accounting period will be debited to Salaries and Wages Expense. This debit will eliminate the credit balance. The resulting debit balance in the expense account will equal the salaries and wages expense incurred in the new accounting period ($2,800 in this example).

If Pioneer makes reversing entries, it can debit all cash payments of expenses to the expense account. This means that on November 9 (and every payday) Pioneer can debit Salaries and Wages Expense for the amount paid, without regard to any accrued salaries and wages payable. Being able to make the **same entry each time** simplifies the recording process: The company can record subsequent transactions as if the related adjusting entry had never been made.

Illustration 4A-2 shows the posting of the entries with reversing entries.

Salaries and Wages Expense				Salaries and Wages Payable			
10/26 Paid	4,000	10/31 Closing	5,200	**11/1 Reversing**	**1,200**	10/31 Adjusting	1,200
31 Adjusting	1,200						
	5,200		5,200				
11/9 Paid	4,000	**11/1 Reversing**	**1,200**				

Illustration 4A-2
Postings with reversing entries

A company can also use reversing entries for accrued revenue adjusting entries. For Pioneer Advertising Inc., the adjusting entry was Accounts Receivable (Dr.) $200 and Service Revenue (Cr.) $200. Thus, the reversing entry on November 1 is:

−200 Rev

−200

Cash Flows
no effect

Nov. 1	Service Revenue	200	
	Accounts Receivable		200
	(To reverse October 31 adjusting entry)		

When Pioneer collects the accrued service revenue, it debits Cash and credits Service Revenue.

SUMMARY OF LEARNING OBJECTIVE FOR APPENDIX 4A ✔ The Navigator

7 Prepare reversing entries. Reversing entries are the opposite of the adjusting entries made in the preceding period. Some companies choose to make reversing entries at the beginning of a new accounting period to simplify the recording of later transactions related to the adjusting entries. In most cases, only accrued adjusting entries are reversed.

WILEY PLUS Self-Test, Brief Exercises, Exercises, Problem Set A, and many more components are available for practice in WileyPLUS

Note: All Questions, Exercises, and Problems marked with an asterisk relate to material in the appendix to the chapter.

SELF-TEST QUESTIONS

Answers are on page 214.

(LO 1) **1.** Which of the following statements is *incorrect* concerning the worksheet?
   (a) The worksheet is essentially a working tool of the accountant.
   (b) The worksheet is distributed to management and other interested parties.
   (c) The worksheet cannot be used as a basis for posting to ledger accounts.
   (d) Financial statements can be prepared directly from the worksheet before journalizing and posting the adjusting entries.

(LO 1) **2.** In a worksheet, net income is entered in the following columns:
   (a) income statement (Dr) and balance sheet (Dr).
   (b) income statement (Cr) and balance sheet (Dr).
   (c) income statement (Dr) and balance sheet (Cr).
   (d) income statement (Cr) and balance sheet (Cr).

(LO 1) **3.** In the unadjusted trial balance of its worksheet for the year ended December 31, 2014, Taitum Company reported Equipment of $120,000. The year-end adjusting entries require an adjustment of $15,000 for depreciation expense for the equipment. After adjustment, the following adjusted amount should be reported:

   (a) A debit of $105,000 for Equipment in the balance sheet column.
   (b) A credit of $15,000 for Depreciation Expense—Equipment in the income statement column.
   (c) A debit of $120,000 for Equipment in the balance sheet column.
   (d) A debit of $15,000 for Accumulated Depreciation—Equipment in the balance sheet column.

(LO 2) **4.** An account that will have a zero balance after closing entries have been journalized and posted is:
   (a) Service Revenue.
   (b) Supplies.
   (c) Prepaid Insurance.
   (d) Accumulated Depreciation—Equipment.

(LO 2) **5.** When a net loss has occurred, Income Summary is:
   (a) debited and Retained Earnings is credited.
   (b) credited and Retained Earnings is debited.
   (c) debited and Dividends is credited.
   (d) credited and Dividends is debited.

(LO 2) **6.** The closing process involves separate entries to close (1) expenses, (2) dividends, (3) revenues, and (4) income summary. The correct sequencing of the entries is:
   (a) (4), (3), (2), (1)   (c) (3), (1), (4), (2)
   (b) (1), (2), (3), (4)   (d) (3), (2), (1), (4)

(LO 3) **7.** Which types of accounts will appear in the post-closing trial balance?
   (a) Permanent (real) accounts.
   (b) Temporary (nominal) accounts.
   (c) Accounts shown in the income statement columns of a worksheet.
   (d) None of the above.

(LO 4) **8.** All of the following are required steps in the accounting cycle *except:*
   (a) journalizing and posting closing entries.
   (b) preparing financial statements.
   (c) journalizing the transactions.
   (d) preparing a worksheet.

(LO 4) **9.** The proper order of the following steps in the accounting cycle is:
   (a) prepare unadjusted trial balance, journalize transactions, post to ledger accounts, journalize and post adjusting entries.
   (b) journalize transactions, prepare unadjusted trial balance, post to ledger accounts, journalize and post adjusting entries.
   (c) journalize transactions, post to ledger accounts, prepare unadjusted trial balance, journalize and post adjusting entries.
   (d) prepare unadjusted trial balance, journalize and post adjusting entries, journalize transactions, post to ledger accounts.

(LO 5) **10.** When Alexander Company purchased supplies worth $500, it incorrectly recorded a credit to Supplies for $5,000 and a debit to Cash for $5,000. Before correcting this error:
   (a) Cash is overstated and Supplies is overstated.
   (b) Cash is understated and Supplies is understated.
   (c) Cash is understated and Supplies is overstated.
   (d) Cash is overstated and Supplies is understated.

(LO 5) **11.** Cash of $100 received at the time the service was provided was journalized and posted as a debit to Cash $100 and a credit to Accounts Receivable $100. Assuming the incorrect entry is not reversed, the correcting entry is:
   (a) debit Service Revenue $100 and credit Accounts Receivable $100.
   (b) debit Accounts Receivable $100 and credit Service Revenue $100.
   (c) debit Cash $100 and credit Service Revenue $100.
   (d) debit Accounts Receivable $100 and credit Cash $100.

(LO 6) **12.** The correct order of presentation in a classified balance sheet for the following current assets is:
   (a) accounts receivable, cash, prepaid insurance, inventory.
   (b) cash, inventory, accounts receivable, prepaid insurance.
   (c) cash, accounts receivable, inventory, prepaid insurance.
   (d) inventory, cash, accounts receivable, prepaid insurance.

(LO 6) **13.** A company has purchased a tract of land. It expects to build a production plant on the land in approximately 5 years. During the 5 years before construction, the land will be idle. The land should be reported as:
   (a) property, plant, and equipment.
   (b) land expense.
   (c) a long-term investment.
   (d) an intangible asset.

(LO 6) **14.** In a classified balance sheet, assets are usually classified using the following categories:
   (a) current assets; long-term assets; property, plant, and equipment; and intangible assets.
   (b) current assets; long-term investments; property, plant, and equipment; and tangible assets.
   (c) current assets; long-term investments; tangible assets; and intangible assets.
   (d) current assets; long-term investments; property, plant, and equipment; and intangible assets.

(LO 6) **15.** Current assets are listed:
   (a) by expected conversion to cash.
   (b) by importance.
   (c) by longevity.
   (d) alphabetically.

(LO 7) ***16.** On December 31, Frank Voris Company correctly made an adjusting entry to recognize $2,000 of accrued salaries payable. On January 8 of the next year, total salaries of $3,400 were paid. Assuming the correct reversing entry was made on January 1, the entry on January 8 will result in a credit to Cash $3,400 and the following debit(s):
   (a) Salaries and Wages Payable $1,400, and Salaries and Wages Expense $2,000.
   (b) Salaries and Wages Payable $2,000 and Salaries and Wages Expense $1,400.
   (c) Salaries and Wages Expense $3,400.
   (d) Salaries and Wages Payable $3,400.

Go to the book's companion website, www.wiley.com/college/weygandt, for additional Self-Test Questions.

✔ **The Navigator**

QUESTIONS

1. "A worksheet is a permanent accounting record and its use is required in the accounting cycle." Do you agree? Explain.

2. Explain the purpose of the worksheet.

3. What is the relationship, if any, between the amount shown in the adjusted trial balance column for an account and that account's ledger balance?

4. If a company's revenues are $125,000 and its expenses are $113,000, in which financial statement columns of the worksheet will the net income of $12,000 appear? When expenses exceed revenues, in which columns will the difference appear?

5. Why is it necessary to prepare formal financial statements if all of the data are in the statement columns of the worksheet?

6. Identify the account(s) debited and credited in each of the four closing entries, assuming the company has net income for the year.

7. Describe the nature of the Income Summary account and identify the types of summary data that may be posted to this account.

8. What are the content and purpose of a post-closing trial balance?

9. Which of the following accounts would not appear in the post-closing trial balance? Interest Payable; Equipment; Depreciation Expense; Dividends; Unearned Service Revenue; Accumulated Depreciation—Equipment; and Service Revenue.

10. Distinguish between a reversing entry and an adjusting entry. Are reversing entries required?

11. Indicate, in the sequence in which they are made, the three required steps in the accounting cycle that involve journalizing.

12. Identify, in the sequence in which they are prepared, the three trial balances that are often used to report financial information about a company.

13. How do correcting entries differ from adjusting entries?

14. What standard classifications are used in preparing a classified balance sheet?

15. What is meant by the term "operating cycle?"

16. Define current assets. What basis is used for arranging individual items within the current assets section?

17. Distinguish between long-term investments and property, plant, and equipment.

18. (a) What is the term used to describe the owners' equity section of a corporation? (b) Identify the two owners' equity accounts in a corporation and indicate the purpose of each.

19. ⬤ **PEPSICO** Using PepsiCo's annual report, determine its current liabilities at December 31, 2010, and December 26, 2009. Were current liabilities higher or lower than current assets in these two years?

*20. Triumph Company prepares reversing entries. If the adjusting entry for interest payable is reversed, what type of an account balance, if any, will there be in Interest Payable and Interest Expense after the reversing entry is posted?

*21. At December 31, accrued salaries payable totaled $3,500. On January 10, total salaries of $9,200 are paid. (a) Assume that reversing entries are made at January 1. Give the January 10 entry, and indicate the Salaries and Wages Expense account balance after the entry is posted. (b) Repeat part (a) assuming reversing entries are not made.

BRIEF EXERCISES

List the steps in preparing a worksheet.

(LO 1)

BE4-1 The steps in using a worksheet are presented in random order below. List the steps in the proper order by placing numbers 1–5 in the blank spaces.

(a) _____ Prepare a trial balance on the worksheet.
(b) _____ Enter adjusted balances.
(c) _____ Extend adjusted balances to appropriate statement columns.
(d) _____ Total the statement columns, compute net income (loss), and complete the worksheet.
(e) _____ Enter adjustment data.

Prepare partial worksheet.

(LO 1)

BE4-2 The ledger of Keo Company includes the following unadjusted balances: Prepaid Insurance $3,000, Service Revenue $61,000, and Salaries and Wages Expense $25,000. Adjusting entries are required for (a) expired insurance $1,300; (b) services provided $1,100, but unbilled and uncollected; and (c) accrued salaries payable $800. Enter the unadjusted balances and adjustments into a worksheet and complete the worksheet for all accounts. *Note:* You will need to add the following accounts: Accounts Receivable, Salaries and Wages Payable, and Insurance Expense.

Identify worksheet columns for selected accounts.

(LO 1)

BE4-3 The following selected accounts appear in the adjusted trial balance columns of the worksheet for Cesar Company: Accumulated Depreciation; Depreciation Expense; Common Stock; Dividends; Service Revenue; Supplies; and Accounts Payable. Indicate the financial statement column (income statement Dr., balance sheet Cr., etc.) to which each balance should be extended.

Prepare closing entries from ledger balances.

(LO 2)

BE4-4 The ledger of Rowen Company contains the following balances: Retained Earnings $30,000; Dividends $2,000; Service Revenue $47,000; Salaries and Wages Expense $27,000; and Supplies Expense $5,000. Prepare the closing entries at December 31.

Post closing entries; underline and balance T-accounts.

(LO 2)

BE4-5 Using the data in BE4-4, enter the balances in T-accounts, post the closing entries, and underline and balance the accounts.

BE4-6 The income statement for Mosquera Golf Club for the month ending July 31 shows Service Revenue $19,200, Salaries and Wages Expense $8,800, Maintenance and Repairs Expense $2,500, and Net Income $7,900. Prepare the entries to close the revenue and expense accounts. Post the entries to the revenue and expense accounts, and complete the closing process for these accounts using the three-column form of account.

Journalize and post closing entries using the three-column form of account.

(LO 2)

BE4-7 Using the data in BE4-3, identify the accounts that would be included in a post-closing trial balance.

Identify post-closing trial balance accounts.

(LO 3)

BE4-8 The steps in the accounting cycle are listed in random order below. List the steps in proper sequence, assuming no worksheet is prepared, by placing numbers 1–9 in the blank spaces.

List the required steps in the accounting cycle in sequence.

(LO 4)

(a) _____ Prepare a trial balance.
(b) _____ Journalize the transactions.
(c) _____ Journalize and post closing entries.
(d) _____ Prepare financial statements.
(e) _____ Journalize and post adjusting entries.
(f) _____ Post to ledger accounts.
(g) _____ Prepare a post-closing trial balance.
(h) _____ Prepare an adjusted trial balance.
(i) _____ Analyze business transactions.

BE4-9 At Rafeul Company, the following errors were discovered after the transactions had been journalized and posted. Prepare the correcting entries.

Prepare correcting entries.

(LO 5)

1. A collection on account from a customer for $690 was recorded as a debit to Cash $690 and a credit to Service Revenue $690.
2. The purchase of store supplies on account for $1,580 was recorded as a debit to Supplies $1,850 and a credit to Accounts Payable $1,850.

BE4-10 The balance sheet debit column of the worksheet for Kren Company includes the following accounts: Accounts Receivable $12,500; Prepaid Insurance $3,600; Cash $6,700; Supplies $5,200; and Short-Term Investments $4,900. Prepare the current assets section of the balance sheet, listing the accounts in proper sequence.

Prepare the current assets section of a balance sheet.

(LO 6)

BE4-11 The following are the major balance sheet classifications:

Classify accounts on balance sheet.

(LO 6)

Current assets (CA)
Long-term investments (LTI)
Property, plant, and equipment (PPE)
Intangible assets (IA)

Current liabilities (CL)
Long-term liabilities (LTL)
Stockholders' equity (SE)

Match each of the following accounts to its proper balance sheet classification.

_____ Accounts payable
_____ Accounts receivable
_____ Accumulated depreciation—buildings
_____ Buildings
_____ Cash
_____ Copyrights

_____ Income taxes payable
_____ Debt investment (long-term)
_____ Land
_____ Inventory
_____ Patents
_____ Supplies

*BE4-12 At October 31, Prasad Company made an accrued expense adjusting entry of $1,680 for salaries. Prepare the reversing entry on November 1, and indicate the balances in Salaries and Wages Payable and Salaries and Wages Expense after posting the reversing entry.

Prepare reversing entries.

(LO 7)

> DO IT! REVIEW

DO IT! **4-1** Janet Adams is preparing a worksheet. Explain to Janet how she should extend the following adjusted trial balance accounts to the financial statement columns of the worksheet.

Prepare a worksheet.

(LO 1)

Service Revenue
Notes Payable
Common Stock

Accounts Receivable
Accumulated Depreciation
Utilities Expense

Prepare closing entries.

(LO 2)

DO IT! 4-2 The worksheet for Olympic Company shows the following in the financial statement columns.

Dividends	$15,000
Common Stock	70,000
Net income	47,000

Prepare the closing entries at December 31 that affect stockholders' equity.

Prepare assets section of the balance sheet.

(LO 6)

DO IT! 4-3 Tyler Pahl recently received the following information related to Pahl Company's December 31, 2014, balance sheet.

Inventory	$ 4,100	Short-term investments	$1,200
Cash	3,900	Accumulated depreciation	5,200
Equipment	21,700	Accounts receivable	4,300
Investments in stock (long-term)	6,500		

Prepare the assets section of Pahl Company's classified balance sheet.

Match accounts to balance sheet classifications.

(LO 6)

DO IT! 4-4 The following accounts were taken from the financial statements of Orville Company.

_____ Interest revenue
_____ Utilities payable
_____ Accounts payable
_____ Supplies
_____ Bonds payable
_____ Trademarks

_____ Common stock
_____ Accumulated depreciation—equipment
_____ Equipment
_____ Salaries and wages expense
_____ Investment in real estate
_____ Unearned rent revenue

Match each of the accounts to its proper balance sheet classification, as shown below. If the item would not appear on a balance sheet, use "NA."

Current assets (CA)
Long-term investments (LTI)
Property, plant, and equipment (PPE)
Intangible assets (IA)

Current liabilities (CL)
Long-term liabilities (LTL)
Stockholders' equity (SE)

✔ **The Navigator**

EXERCISES

Complete the worksheet.

(LO 1)

E4-1 The trial balance columns of the worksheet for Cajon Company at June 30, 2014, are as follows.

Cajon Company
Worksheet
For the Month Ended June 30, 2014

	Trial Balance	
Account Titles	**Dr.**	**Cr.**
Cash	$4,020	
Accounts Receivable	2,440	
Supplies	1,900	
Accounts Payable		$1,120
Unearned Service Revenue		240
Common Stock		5,000
Service Revenue		3,100
Salaries and Wages Expense	860	
Miscellaneous Expense	240	
	$9,460	$9,460

Other data:

1. A physical count reveals $500 of supplies on hand.
2. $100 of the unearned revenue is still unearned at month-end.
3. Accrued salaries are $250.

Instructions
Enter the trial balance on a worksheet and complete the worksheet.

E4-2 The adjusted trial balance columns of the worksheet for Albanese Company are as follows.

Complete the worksheet.
(LO 1)

Albanese Company
Worksheet (partial)
For the Month Ended April 30, 2014

Account Titles	Adjusted Trial Balance Dr.	Cr.	Income Statement Dr.	Cr.	Balance Sheet Dr.	Cr.
Cash	7,442					
Accounts Receivable	7,840					
Prepaid Rent	2,280					
Equipment	23,000					
Accumulated Depreciation—Equip.		4,800				
Notes Payable		5,700				
Accounts Payable		5,672				
Common Stock		22,000				
Retained Earnings		4,000				
Dividends	3,000					
Service Revenue		12,590				
Salaries and Wages Expense	9,840					
Rent Expense	760					
Depreciation Expense	600					
Interest Expense	57					
Interest Payable		57				
Totals	54,819	54,819				

Instructions
Complete the worksheet.

Prepare financial statements from worksheet.

E4-3 Worksheet data for Albanese Company are presented in E4-2. No common stock was issued during April.

(LO 1, 6)

Instructions
Prepare an income statement, a retained earnings statement, and a classified balance sheet.

E4-4 Worksheet data for Albanese Company are presented in E4-2.

Journalize and post closing entries and prepare a post-closing trial balance.

Instructions
(a) Journalize the closing entries at April 30.
(b) Post the closing entries to Income Summary and Retained Earnings. Use T-accounts.
(c) Prepare a post-closing trial balance at April 30.

(LO 2, 3)

E4-5 The adjustments columns of the worksheet for Munoz Company are shown below.

Prepare adjusting entries from a worksheet, and extend balances to worksheet columns.

Account Titles	Adjustments Debit	Credit
Accounts Receivable	600	
Prepaid Insurance		400
Accumulated Depreciation—Equipment		900
Salaries and Wages Payable		500
Service Revenue		600
Salaries and Wages Expense	500	
Insurance Expense	400	
Depreciation Expense	900	
	2,400	2,400

(LO 1)

Instructions
(a) Prepare the adjusting entries.
(b) Assuming the adjusted trial balance amount for each account is normal, indicate the financial statement column to which each balance should be extended.

Derive adjusting entries from worksheet data.

(LO 1)

E4-6 Selected worksheet data for Freeman Company are presented below.

Account Titles	Trial Balance		Adjusted Trial Balance	
	Dr.	Cr.	Dr.	Cr.
Accounts Receivable	?		34,000	
Prepaid Insurance	26,000		18,000	
Supplies	7,000		?	
Accumulated Depreciation—Equipment		12,000		?
Salaries and Wages Payable		?		5,000
Service Revenue		88,000		95,000
Insurance Expense			?	
Depreciation Expense			10,000	
Supplies Expense			4,700	
Salaries and Wages Expense	?		49,000	

Instructions
(a) Fill in the missing amounts.
(b) Prepare the adjusting entries that were made.

Prepare closing entries, and prepare a post-closing trial balance.

(LO 2, 3)

E4-7 Lanza Company had the following adjusted trial balance.

Lanza Company
Adjusted Trial Balance
For the Month Ended June 30, 2014

Account Titles	Adjusted Trial Balance	
	Debits	Credits
Cash	$ 3,712	
Accounts Receivable	3,904	
Supplies	480	
Accounts Payable		$ 1,556
Unearned Service Revenue		160
Common Stock		4,000
Retained Earnings		1,760
Dividends	600	
Service Revenue		4,300
Salaries and Wages Expense	1,344	
Miscellaneous Expense	180	
Supplies Expense	1,900	
Salaries and Wages Payable		344
	$12,120	$12,120

Instructions
(a) Prepare closing entries at June 30, 2014.
(b) Prepare a post-closing trial balance.

Journalize and post closing entries, and prepare a post-closing trial balance.

(LO 2, 3)

E4-8 Roth Company ended its fiscal year on July 31, 2014. The company's adjusted trial balance as of the end of its fiscal year is as shown on the next page.

Roth Company
Adjusted Trial Balance
July 31, 2014

No.	Account Titles	Debits	Credits
101	Cash	$ 9,840	
112	Accounts Receivable	8,140	
157	Equipment	15,900	
167	Accumulated Depreciation—Equip.		$ 5,400
201	Accounts Payable		2,220
208	Unearned Rent Revenue		3,800
311	Common Stock		18,000
320	Retained Earnings		20,260
332	Dividends	12,000	
404	Service Revenue		64,000
429	Rent Revenue		6,500
711	Depreciation Expense	3,700	
720	Salaries and Wages Expense	55,700	
732	Utilities Expense	14,900	
		$120,180	$120,180

Instructions
(a) Prepare the closing entries using page J15.
(b) Post to Retained Earnings and No. 350 Income Summary accounts. (Use the three-column form.)
(c) Prepare a post-closing trial balance at July 31.

E4-9 The adjusted trial balance for Roth Company is presented in E4-8.

Prepare financial statements.

(LO 6)

Instructions
(a) Prepare an income statement and a retained earnings statement for the year.
(b) Prepare a classified balance sheet at July 31.

E4-10 Patrick Kellogg has prepared the following list of statements about the accounting cycle.

Answer questions related to the accounting cycle.

(LO 4)

1. "Journalize the transactions" is the first step in the accounting cycle.
2. Reversing entries are a required step in the accounting cycle.
3. Correcting entries do not have to be part of the accounting cycle.
4. If a worksheet is prepared, some steps of the accounting cycle are incorporated into the worksheet.
5. The accounting cycle begins with the analysis of business transactions and ends with the preparation of a post-closing trial balance.
6. All steps of the accounting cycle occur daily during the accounting period.
7. The step of "post to the ledger accounts" occurs before the step of "journalize the transactions."
8. Closing entries must be prepared before financial statements can be prepared.

Instructions
Identify each statement as true or false. If false, indicate how to correct the statement.

E4-11 Selected accounts for Michelle's Salon are presented below. All June 30 postings are from closing entries.

Prepare closing entries.

(LO 2)

Salaries and Wages Expense									
6/10	3,200	6/30	8,800						
6/28	5,600								

Service Revenue			
6/30	18,100	6/15	9,700
		6/24	8,400

Retained Earnings			
6/30	2,200	6/1	12,000
		6/30	5,400
		Bal.	15,200

Supplies Expense			
6/12	600	6/30	900
6/24	300		

Rent Expense			
6/1	3,000	6/30	3,000

Dividends			
6/13	1,000	6/30	2,200
6/25	1,200		

Instructions
(a) Prepare the closing entries that were made.
(b) Post the closing entries to Income Summary.

Prepare correcting entries.

(LO 5)

E4-12 Joshua Company discovered the following errors made in January 2014.

1. A payment of Salaries and Wages Expense of $700 was debited to Equipment and credited to Cash, both for $700.
2. A collection of $800 from a client on account was debited to Cash $300 and credited to Service Revenue $300.
3. The purchase of equipment on account for $760 was debited to Equipment $670 and credited to Accounts Payable $670.

Instructions
(a) Correct the errors by reversing the incorrect entry and preparing the correct entry.
(b) Correct the errors without reversing the incorrect entry.

Prepare correcting entries.

(LO 5)

E4-13 Kogan Company has an inexperienced accountant. During the first 2 weeks on the job, the accountant made the following errors in journalizing transactions. All entries were posted as made.

1. A payment on account of $840 to a creditor was debited to Accounts Payable $480 and credited to Cash $480.
2. The purchase of supplies on account for $380 was debited to Equipment $38 and credited to Accounts Payable $38.
3. A $500 cash dividend was debited to Salaries and Wages Expense $500 and credited to Cash $500.

Instructions
Prepare the correcting entries.

Prepare a classified balance sheet.

(LO 6)

E4-14 The adjusted trial balance for Rego Bowling Alley at December 31, 2014, contains the following accounts.

Debits		**Credits**	
Buildings	$128,000	Common Stock	$ 80,000
Accounts Receivable	7,540	Retained Earnings	28,000
Prepaid Insurance	4,680	Accumulated Depreciation—Buildings	42,600
Cash	18,040	Accounts Payable	12,300
Equipment	62,400	Notes Payable	95,000
Land	67,000	Accumulated Depreciation—Equipment	18,720
Insurance Expense	780	Interest Payable	2,600
Depreciation Expense	7,360	Service Revenue	19,180
Interest Expense	2,600		$298,400
	$298,400		

Instructions
(a) Prepare a classified balance sheet; assume that $15,000 of the note payable will be paid in 2015.
(b) ⬛▭▭▷ Comment on the liquidity of the company.

Classify accounts on balance sheet.

(LO 6)

E4-15 The following are the major balance sheet classifications.

Current assets (CA)	Current liabilities (CL)
Long-term investments (LTI)	Long-term liabilities (LTL)
Property, plant, and equipment (PPE)	Stockholders' equity (SE)
Intangible assets (IA)	

Instructions
Classify each of the following accounts taken from Geraldo Company's balance sheet.

_____ Accounts payable	_____ Accumulated depreciation
_____ Accounts receivable	_____ Buildings
_____ Cash	_____ Land
_____ Common stock	_____ Long-term debt
_____ Patents	_____ Supplies
_____ Salaries and wages payable	_____ Equipment
_____ Inventory	_____ Prepaid expenses
_____ Investments	

E4-16 The following items were taken from the financial statements of Sexton Company. (All dollars are in thousands.)

Prepare a classified balance sheet.

(LO 6)

Long-term debt	$ 1,000	Accumulated depreciation	$ 4,125
Prepaid insurance	680	Accounts payable	1,444
Equipment	11,500	Notes payable (due after 2015)	800
Long-term investments	1,200	Common stock	10,000
Short-term investments	3,619	Retained earnings	4,750
Notes payable (due in 2015)	500	Accounts receivable	1,696
Cash	2,668	Inventory	1,256

Instructions

Prepare a classified balance sheet in good form as of December 31, 2014.

E4-17 These financial statement items are for Emjay Company at year-end, July 31, 2014.

Prepare financial statements.

(LO 1, 6)

Salaries and wages payable	$ 2,080	Notes payable (long-term)	$ 1,800
Salaries and wages expense	50,700	Cash	14,200
Utilities expense	22,600	Accounts receivable	9,180
Equipment	30,000	Accumulated depreciation—equip.	6,000
Accounts payable	4,100	Dividends	3,000
Service revenue	62,000	Depreciation expense	2,500
Rent revenue	8,500	Retained earnings (beginning	
Common stock	25,000	of the year)	22,700

Instructions

(a) Prepare an income statement and a retained earnings statement for the year.
(b) Prepare a classified balance sheet at July 31.

*E4-18 Grogan Company pays salaries of $9,000 every Monday for the preceding 5-day week (Monday through Friday). Assume December 31 falls on a Thursday, so Grogan's employees have worked 4 days without being paid.

Use reversing entries.

(LO 7)

Instructions

(a) Assume the company does not use reversing entries. Prepare the December 31 adjusting entry and the entry on Monday, January 4, when Grogan pays the payroll.
(b) Assume the company does use reversing entries. Prepare the December 31 adjusting entry, the January 1 reversing entry, and the entry on Monday, January 4, when Grogan pays the payroll.

*E4-19 On December 31, the adjusted trial balance of Select Employment Agency shows the following selected data.

Prepare closing and reversing entries.

(LO 2, 4, 7)

| Accounts Receivable | $24,500 | Service Revenue | $93,800 |
| Interest Expense | 8,300 | Interest Payable | 1,300 |

Analysis shows that adjusting entries were made to (1) accrue $5,000 of service revenue and (2) accrue $1,300 interest expense.

Instructions

(a) Prepare the closing entries for the temporary accounts shown above at December 31.
(b) Prepare the reversing entries on January 1.
(c) Post the entries in (a) and (b). Underline and balance the accounts. (Use T-accounts.)
(d) Prepare the entries to record (1) the collection of the accrued revenue on January 10 and (2) the payment of all interest due ($3,000) on January 15.
(e) Post the entries in (d) to the temporary accounts.

EXERCISES: SET B AND CHALLENGE EXERCISES

Visit the book's companion website, at **www.wiley.com/college/weygandt**, and choose the Student Companion site to access Exercise Set B and Challenge Exercises.

PROBLEMS: SET A

Prepare worksheet, financial statements, and adjusting and closing entries.

(LO 1, 2, 6)

P4-1A Sherlock Holmes began operations as a private investigator on January 1, 2014. The trial balance columns of the worksheet for Sherlock Holmes, P.I., Inc. at March 31 are as follows.

Sherlock Holmes P.I., Inc.
Worksheet
For the Quarter Ended March 31, 2014

Account Titles	Trial Balance	
	Dr.	Cr.
Cash	11,410	
Accounts Receivable	5,920	
Supplies	1,250	
Prepaid Insurance	2,400	
Equipment	30,000	
Notes Payable		10,000
Accounts Payable		12,350
Common Stock		20,000
Dividends	600	
Service Revenue		14,200
Salaries and Wages Expense	2,240	
Travel Expense	1,300	
Rent Expense	1,200	
Miscellaneous Expense	230	
	56,550	56,550

Other data:

1. Supplies on hand total $480.
2. Depreciation is $720 per quarter.
3. Interest accrued on 6-month note payable, issued January 1, $300.
4. Insurance expires at the rate of $200 per month.
5. Services provided but unbilled at March 31 total $1,080.

(a) Adjusted trial balance
   $58,650
(b) Net income $7,920
   Total assets $49,970

Complete worksheet; prepare financial statements, closing entries, and post-closing trial balance.

(LO 1, 2, 3, 6) **GLS**

Instructions
(a) Enter the trial balance on a worksheet and complete the worksheet.
(b) Prepare an income statement and a retained earnings statement for the quarter and a classified balance sheet at March 31.
(c) Journalize the adjusting entries from the adjustments columns of the worksheet.
(d) Journalize the closing entries from the financial statement columns of the worksheet.

P4-2A The adjusted trial balance columns of the worksheet for Watson Company are as follows.

Watson Company
Worksheet
For the Year Ended December 31, 2014

Account No.	Account Titles	Adjusted Trial Balance Dr.	Adjusted Trial Balance Cr.
101	Cash	17,800	
112	Accounts Receivable	14,400	
126	Supplies	2,300	
130	Prepaid Insurance	4,400	
151	Equipment	46,000	
152	Accumulated Depreciation—Equipment		18,000
200	Notes Payable		20,000
201	Accounts Payable		8,000
212	Salaries and Wages Payable		2,600
230	Interest Payable		1,000
311	Common Stock		15,000
320	Retained Earnings		9,800
332	Dividends	12,000	
400	Service Revenue		86,200
610	Advertising Expense	10,000	
631	Supplies Expense	3,700	
711	Depreciation Expense	6,000	
722	Insurance Expense	4,000	
726	Salaries and Wages Expense	39,000	
905	Interest Expense	1,000	
	Totals	160,600	160,600

Instructions
(a) Complete the worksheet by extending the balances to the financial statement columns.
(b) Prepare an income statement, a retained earnings statement, and a classified balance sheet. (*Note:* $5,000 of the notes payable become due in 2015.)
(c) Prepare the closing entries. Use J14 for the journal page.
(d) Post the closing entries. Use the three-column form of account. Income Summary is account No. 350.
(e) Prepare a post-closing trial balance.

(a) Net income $22,500
(b) Current assets $38,900
   Current liabilities $16,600

(e) Post-closing trial balance $84,900

P4-3A The completed financial statement columns of the worksheet for Hubbs Company are shown below and on the next page.

Prepare financial statements, closing entries, and post-closing trial balance.

(LO 1, 2, 3, 6)

Hubbs Company
Worksheet
For the Year Ended December 31, 2014

Account No.	Account Titles	Income Statement Dr.	Income Statement Cr.	Balance Sheet Dr.	Balance Sheet Cr.
101	Cash			6,200	
112	Accounts Receivable			7,500	
130	Prepaid Insurance			1,800	
157	Equipment			33,000	
167	Accumulated Depreciation—Equip.				9,900
201	Accounts Payable				11,700
212	Salaries and Wages Payable				3,000
311	Common Stock				20,000
320	Retained Earnings				9,700
332	Dividends			4,000	
400	Service Revenue		47,000		
622	Maintenance and Repairs Expense	4,100			
711	Depreciation Expense	3,300			

Account No.	Account Titles	Income Statement Dr.	Cr.	Balance Sheet Dr.	Cr.
722	Insurance Expense	2,200			
726	Salaries and Wages Expense	35,200			
732	Utilities Expense	4,000			
	Totals	48,800	47,000	52,500	54,300
	Net Loss		1,800	1,800	
		48,800	48,800	54,300	54,300

Instructions

(a) Prepare an income statement, a retained earnings statement, and a classified balance sheet.

(b) Prepare the closing entries.

(c) Post the closing entries, and underline and balance the accounts. (Use T-accounts.) Income Summary is account No. 350.

(d) Prepare a post-closing trial balance.

P4-4A Excelsior Amusement Park has a fiscal year ending on September 30. Selected data from the September 30 worksheet are presented below.

Excelsior Amusement Park
Worksheet
For the Year Ended September 30, 2014

	Trial Balance Dr.	Cr.	Adjusted Trial Balance Dr.	Cr.
Cash	34,400		34,400	
Supplies	18,600		2,200	
Prepaid Insurance	29,900		10,900	
Land	80,000		80,000	
Equipment	120,000		120,000	
Accumulated Depreciation—Equip.		36,200		42,200
Accounts Payable		14,600		14,600
Unearned Ticket Revenue		3,900		1,000
Mortgage Payable		50,000		50,000
Common Stock		60,000		60,000
Retained Earnings		36,100		36,100
Dividends	14,000		14,000	
Ticket Revenue		277,900		280,800
Salaries and Wages Expense	98,000		98,000	
Maintenance and Repairs Expense	30,500		30,500	
Advertising Expense	9,400		9,400	
Utilities Expense	16,900		16,900	
Property Tax Expense	21,000		24,000	
Interest Expense	6,000		8,000	
Totals	478,700	478,700		
Insurance Expense			19,000	
Supplies Expense			16,400	
Interest Payable				2,000
Depreciation Expense			6,000	
Property Taxes Payable				3,000
Totals			489,700	489,700

Instructions

(a) Prepare a complete worksheet.

(b) Prepare a classified balance sheet. (*Note:* $15,000 of the mortgage note payable is due for payment in the next fiscal year.)

(c) Journalize the adjusting entries using the worksheet as a basis.

(d) Journalize the closing entries using the worksheet as a basis.

(e) Prepare a post-closing trial balance.

(a) Net loss $1,800
  Ending retained earnings $3,900
  Total assets $38,600

(d) Post-closing trial balance $48,500

Complete worksheet; prepare classified balance sheet, entries, and post-closing trial balance.

(LO 1, 2, 3, 6)

(a) Net income $52,600
(b) Total current assets $47,500

(e) Post-closing trial balance $247,500

P4-5A Lynda Hines opened Fresh Step Carpet Cleaners on March 1. During March, the following transactions were completed.

Complete all steps in accounting cycle.

(LO 1, 2, 3, 4, 6)

Mar.	1	Stockholders invested $14,000 cash in the business in exchange for common stock.
	1	Purchased used truck for $8,000, paying $3,000 cash and the balance on account.
	3	Purchased cleaning supplies for $1,200 on account.
	5	Paid $1,800 cash on one-year insurance policy effective March 1.
	14	Billed customers $4,800 for cleaning services.
	18	Paid $1,500 cash on amount owed on truck and $500 on amount owed on cleaning supplies.
	20	Paid $1,800 cash for employee salaries.
	21	Collected $1,600 cash from customers billed on March 14.
	28	Billed customers $2,500 for cleaning services.
	31	Paid gasoline for month on truck $320.
	31	Declared and paid $800 cash dividends.

The chart of accounts for Fresh Step Carpet Cleaners contains the following accounts: No. 101 Cash, No. 112 Accounts Receivable, No. 128 Supplies, No. 130 Prepaid Insurance, No. 157 Equipment, No. 158 Accumulated Depreciation—Equipment, No. 201 Accounts Payable, No. 212 Salaries and Wages Payable, No. 311 Common Stock, No. 320 Retained Earnings, No. 332 Dividends, No. 350 Income Summary, No. 400 Service Revenue, No. 633 Gasoline Expense, No. 634 Supplies Expense, No. 711 Depreciation Expense, No. 722 Insurance Expense, and No. 726 Salaries and Wages Expense.

Instructions

(a) Journalize and post the March transactions. Use page J1 for the journal and the three-column form of account.

(b) Prepare a trial balance at March 31 on a worksheet.

(c) Enter the following adjustments on the worksheet and complete the worksheet.

(b) Trial balance $25,500
(c) Adjusted trial balance
  $27,270

(1) Unbilled revenue for services performed at March 31 was $750.

(2) Depreciation on equipment for the month was $300.

(3) One-twelfth of the insurance expired.

(4) An inventory count shows $250 of cleaning supplies on hand at March 31.

(5) Accrued but unpaid employee salaries were $720.

(d) Prepare the income statement and a retained earnings statement for March and a classified balance sheet at March 31.

(d) Net income $3,810
  Total assets $21,930

(e) Journalize and post adjusting entries. Use page J2 for the journal.

(f) Journalize and post closing entries and complete the closing process. Use page J3 for the journal.

(g) Post-closing trial balance
  $22,230

(g) Prepare a post-closing trial balance at March 31.

P4-6A Sara Yu, CPA, was retained by Info Cable to prepare financial statements for April 2014. Yu accumulated all the ledger balances per Info's records and found the following.

Analyze errors and prepare correcting entries and trial balance.

(LO 5)

Info Cable
Trial Balance
April 30, 2014

	Debit	Credit
Cash	$ 4,100	
Accounts Receivable	3,200	
Supplies	800	
Equipment	10,600	
Accumulated Depreciation—Equip.		$ 1,250
Accounts Payable		2,100
Salaries and Wages Payable		700
Unearned Service Revenue		890
Common Stock		10,000
Retained Earnings		2,880
Service Revenue		5,450
Salaries and Wages Expense	3,300	
Advertising Expense	480	
Miscellaneous Expense	290	
Depreciation Expense	500	
	$23,270	$23,270

Sara Yu reviewed the records and found the following errors.

1. Cash received from a customer on account was recorded as $950 instead of $590.
2. A payment of $75 for advertising expense was entered as a debit to Miscellaneous Expense $75 and a credit to Cash $75.
3. The first salary payment this month was for $1,850, which included $700 of salaries payable on March 31. The payment was recorded as a debit to Salaries and Wages Expense $1,850 and a credit to Cash $1,850. (No reversing entries were made on April 1.)
4. The purchase on account of a printer costing $310 was recorded as a debit to Supplies and a credit to Accounts Payable for $310.
5. A cash payment of repair expense on equipment for $125 was recorded as a debit to Equipment $152 and a credit to Cash $152.

Instructions

(a) Prepare an analysis of each error showing (1) the incorrect entry, (2) the correct entry, and (3) the correcting entry. Items 4 and 5 occurred on April 30, 2014.

Trial balance $22,570

(b) Prepare a correct trial balance.

PROBLEMS: SET B

Prepare worksheet, financial statements, and adjusting and closing entries.

(LO 1, 2, 6)

P4-1B The trial balance columns of the worksheet for Firmament Roofing at March 31, 2014, are as follows.

Firmament Roofing
Worksheet
For the Month Ended March 31, 2014

Account Titles	Trial Balance	
	Dr.	Cr.
Cash	2,720	
Accounts Receivable	2,700	
Supplies	1,500	
Equipment	11,000	
Accumulated Depreciation—Equipment		1,250
Accounts Payable		2,500
Unearned Service Revenue		550
Common Stock		10,000
Dividends	1,100	
Service Revenue		6,300
Salaries and Wages Expense	1,300	
Miscellaneous Expense	280	
	20,600	20,600

Other data:

1. A physical count reveals only $550 of roofing supplies on hand.
2. Depreciation for March is $250.
3. Unearned revenue amounted to $290 at March 31.
4. Accrued salaries are $480.

(a) Adjusted trial balance
$21,330

(b) Net income $3,300
Total assets $15,470

Complete worksheet; prepare financial statements, closing entries, and post-closing trial balance.

(LO 1, 2, 3, 6)

Instructions

(a) Enter the trial balance on a worksheet and complete the worksheet.
(b) Prepare an income statement and a retained earnings statement for the month of March and a classified balance sheet at March 31. Common stock of $10,000 was issued for cash at the beginning of March.
(c) Journalize the adjusting entries from the adjustments columns of the worksheet.
(d) Journalize the closing entries from the financial statement columns of the worksheet.

P4-2B The adjusted trial balance columns of the worksheet for Eagle Company, owned by Jeff Spiegel, are as follows.

Eagle Company
Worksheet
For the Year Ended December 31, 2014

Account No.	Account Titles	Adjusted Trial Balance Dr.	Cr.
101	Cash	5,300	
112	Accounts Receivable	10,800	
126	Supplies	1,500	
130	Prepaid Insurance	2,000	
151	Equipment	27,000	
152	Accumulated Depreciation—Equipment		5,600
200	Notes Payable		15,000
201	Accounts Payable		4,600
212	Salaries and Wages Payable		2,400
230	Interest Payable		600
311	Common Stock		10,000
320	Retained Earnings		4,200
332	Dividends	5,000	
400	Service Revenue		59,000
610	Advertising Expense	8,400	
631	Supplies Expense	4,000	
711	Depreciation Expense	5,600	
722	Insurance Expense	3,200	
726	Salaries and Wages Expense	28,000	
905	Interest Expense	600	
	Totals	101,400	101,400

Instructions
(a) Complete the worksheet by extending the balances to the financial statement columns.
(b) Prepare an income statement, a retained earnings statement, and a classified balance sheet. (*Note:* $3,000 of the notes payable become due in 2015.)
(c) Prepare the closing entries. Use J14 for the journal page.
(d) Post the closing entries. Use the three-column form of account. Income Summary is No. 350.
(e) Prepare a post-closing trial balance.

(a) Net income $9,200

(b) Current assets $19,600; Current liabilities $10,600

(e) Post-closing trial balance $46,600

P4-3B The completed financial statement columns of the worksheet for Lathrop Company are shown below and on the next page.

Prepare financial statements, closing entries, and post-closing trial balance.

(LO 1, 2, 3, 6)

Lathrop Company
Worksheet
For the Year Ended December 31, 2014

Account No.	Account Titles	Income Statement Dr.	Cr.	Balance Sheet Dr.	Cr.
101	Cash			8,900	
112	Accounts Receivable			10,800	
130	Prepaid Insurance			2,800	
157	Equipment			28,000	
167	Accumulated Depreciation—Equip.				4,500
201	Accounts Payable				2,000
212	Salaries and Wages Payable				2,400
311	Common Stock				12,000
320	Retained Earnings				16,400
332	Dividends			8,000	
400	Service Revenue		56,000		
622	Maintenance and Repairs Expense	1,600			

Account No.	Account Titles	Income Statement Dr.	Income Statement Cr.	Balance Sheet Dr.	Balance Sheet Cr.
711	Depreciation Expense	3,000			
722	Insurance Expense	1,800			
726	Salaries and Wages Expense	27,000			
732	Utilities Expense	1,400			
	Totals	34,800	56,000	58,500	37,300
	Net Income	21,200			21,200
		56,000	56,000	58,500	58,500

Instructions

(a) Ending retained earnings $29,600;

Total current assets $22,500

(d) Post-closing trial balance $50,500

(a) Prepare an income statement, a retained earnings statement, and a classified balance sheet.

(b) Prepare the closing entries.

(c) Post the closing entries, and underline and balance the accounts. (Use T-accounts.) Income Summary is account No. 350.

(d) Prepare a post-closing trial balance.

Complete worksheet; prepare classified balance sheet, entries, and post-closing trial balance.

(LO 1, 2, 3, 6)

P4-4B Kumar Management Services Inc. began business on January 1, 2014, with a capital investment of $120,000. The company manages condominiums for owners (Service Revenue) and rents space in its own office building (Rent Revenue). The trial balance and adjusted trial balance columns of the worksheet at the end of the first year are as follows.

Kumar Management Services Inc.
Worksheet
For the Year Ended December 31, 2014

Account Titles	Trial Balance Dr.	Trial Balance Cr.	Adjusted Trial Balance Dr.	Adjusted Trial Balance Cr.
Cash	13,800		13,800	
Accounts Receivable	26,300		26,300	
Prepaid Insurance	3,600		1,800	
Land	67,000		67,000	
Buildings	127,000		127,000	
Equipment	59,000		59,000	
Accounts Payable		12,500		12,500
Unearned Rent Revenue		8,000		3,500
Mortgage Payable		120,000		120,000
Common Stock		80,000		80,000
Retained Earnings		54,000		54,000
Dividends	16,000		16,000	
Service Revenue		90,700		90,700
Rent Revenue		26,000		30,500
Salaries and Wages Expense	42,000		42,000	
Advertising Expense	17,500		17,500	
Utilities Expense	19,000		19,000	
Totals	391,200	391,200		
Insurance Expense			1,800	
Depreciation Expense			6,600	
Accumulated Depreciation—Buildings				3,000
Accumulated Depreciation—Equipment				3,600
Interest Expense			9,600	
Interest Payable				9,600
Totals			407,400	407,400

Instructions

(a) Net income $24,700

(b) Total current assets $41,900

(a) Prepare a complete worksheet.

(b) Prepare a classified balance sheet. (*Note:* $25,000 of the mortgage note payable is due for payment next year.)

(c) Journalize the adjusting entries.
(d) Journalize the closing entries.
(e) Prepare a post-closing trial balance.

(e) Post-closing trial balance
$294,900

P4-5B Tom Brennan opened Brennan's Cleaning Service on July 1, 2014. During July the following transactions were completed.

*Complete all steps in
accounting cycle.*

| July | 1 | Stockholders invested $20,000 cash in the business in exchange for common stock. |

(LO 1, 2, 3, 4, 6)

	1	Purchased used truck for $12,000, paying $4,000 cash and the balance on account.
	3	Purchased cleaning supplies for $2,100 on account.
	5	Paid $1,800 cash on one-year insurance policy effective July 1.
	12	Billed customers $5,900 for cleaning services.
	18	Paid $1,500 cash on amount owed on truck and $1,400 on amount owed on cleaning supplies.
	20	Paid $4,500 cash for employee salaries.
	21	Collected $4,400 cash from customers billed on July 12.
	25	Billed customers $8,000 for cleaning services.
	31	Paid gasoline for month on truck $350.
	31	Declared and paid a $1,200 cash dividend.

The chart of accounts for Brennan's Cleaning Service contains the following accounts: No. 101 Cash, No. 112 Accounts Receivable, No. 128 Supplies, No. 130 Prepaid Insurance, No. 157 Equipment, No. 158 Accumulated Depreciation—Equipment, No. 201 Accounts Payable, No. 212 Salaries and Wages Payable, No. 311 Common Stock, No. 320 Retained Earnings, No. 332 Dividends, No. 350 Income Summary, No. 400 Service Revenue, No. 633 Gasoline Expense, No. 634 Supplies Expense, No. 711 Depreciation Expense, No. 722 Insurance Expense, and No. 726 Salaries and Wages Expense.

Instructions
(a) Journalize and post the July transactions. Use page J1 for the journal and the three-column form of account.
(b) Prepare a trial balance at July 31 on a worksheet.
(c) Enter the following adjustments on the worksheet and complete the worksheet.
    (1) Services provided but unbilled and uncollected at July 31 were $3,300.
    (2) Depreciation on equipment for the month was $500.
    (3) One-twelfth of the insurance expired.
    (4) An inventory count shows $600 of cleaning supplies on hand at July 31.
    (5) Accrued but unpaid employee salaries were $2,200.
(d) Prepare the income statement and retained earnings statement for July and a classified balance sheet at July 31.
(e) Journalize and post adjusting entries. Use page J2 for the journal.
(f) Journalize and post closing entries and complete the closing process. Use page J3 for the journal.
(g) Prepare a post-closing trial balance at July 31.

(b) Trial balance $41,100
(c) Adjusted trial balance
    $47,100

(d) Net income $8,000;
    Total assets $36,200

(g) Post-closing trial balance
    $36,700

PROBLEMS: SET C

Visit the book's companion website, at **www.wiley.com/college/weygandt**, and choose the Student Companion site to access Problem Set C.

COMPREHENSIVE PROBLEM: CHAPTERS 2 TO 4

CP4 Mary Coleman opened Mary's Maids Cleaning Service on July 1, 2014. During July, the company completed the following transactions.

| July | 1 | Stockholders invested $15,000 cash in the business in exchange for common stock. |
| | 1 | Purchased a used truck for $10,000, paying $3,000 cash and the balance on account. |

July   3   Purchased cleaning supplies for $1,700 on account.
       5   Paid $1,800 on a one-year insurance policy, effective July 1.
      12   Billed customers $4,200 for cleaning services.
      18   Paid $1,000 of amount owed on truck, and $400 of amount owed on cleaning supplies.
      20   Paid $1,900 for employee salaries.
      21   Collected $2,400 from customers billed on July 12.
      25   Billed customers $2,100 for cleaning services.
      31   Paid gasoline for the month on the truck, $400.
      31   Declared and paid a $500 cash dividend.

The chart of accounts for Mary's Maids Cleaning Service contains the following accounts: No. 101 Cash, No. 112 Accounts Receivable, No. 128 Supplies, No. 130 Prepaid Insurance, No. 157 Equipment, No. 158 Accumulated Depreciation—Equipment, No. 201 Accounts Payable, No. 212 Salaries and Wages Payable, No. 311 Common Stock, No. 320 Retained Earnings, No. 332 Dividends, No. 350 Income Summary, No. 400 Service Revenue, No. 633 Gasoline Expense, No. 634 Supplies Expense, No. 711 Depreciation Expense, No. 722 Insurance Expense, and No. 726 Salaries and Wages Expense.

Instructions
(a) Journalize and post the July transactions. Use page J1 for the journal.

(b) Trial balance totals $28,600

(b) Prepare a trial balance at July 31 on a worksheet.
(c) Enter the following adjustments on the worksheet, and complete the worksheet.
    (1) Unbilled fees for services performed at July 31 were $1,300.
    (2) Depreciation on equipment for the month was $200.
    (3) One-twelfth of the insurance expired.
    (4) An inventory count shows $280 of cleaning supplies on hand at July 31.
    (5) Accrued but unpaid employee salaries were $630.

(d) Net income $2,900
    Total assets $25,330

(d) Prepare the income statement and retained earnings statement for July, and a classified balance sheet at July 31, 2014.
(e) Journalize and post the adjusting entries. Use page J2 for the journal.
(f) Journalize and post the closing entries, and complete the closing process. Use page J3 for the journal.

(g) Trial balance totals $25,530

(g) Prepare a post-closing trial balance at July 31.

CONTINUING COOKIE CHRONICLE

(*Note:* This is a continuation of the Cookie Chronicle from Chapters 1–3.)

CCC4 Natalie had a very busy December. At the end of the month, after journalizing and posting the December transactions and adjusting entries, Natalie prepared the following adjusted trial balance.

Cookie Creations
Adjusted Trial Balance
December 31, 2014

	Debit	Credit
Cash	$1,180	
Accounts Receivable	875	
Supplies	350	
Prepaid Insurance	1,210	
Equipment	1,200	
Accumulated Depreciation—Equipment		$ 40
Accounts Payable		75
Salaries and Wages Payable		56
Unearned Service Revenue		300
Notes Payable		2,000
Interest Payable		15

Common Stock		800
Dividends	500	
Service Revenue		4,515
Salaries and Wages Expense	1,006	
Utilities Expense	125	
Advertising Expense	165	
Supplies Expense	1,025	
Depreciation Expense	40	
Insurance Expense	110	
Interest Expense	15	
	$7,801	$7,801

Instructions

Using the information in the adjusted trial balance, do the following.

(a) Prepare an income statement and a retained earnings statement for the 2 months ended December 31, 2014, and a classified balance sheet at December 31, 2014. The note payable has a stated interest rate of 6%, and the principal and interest are due on November 16, 2016.

(b) Natalie has decided that her year-end will be December 31, 2014. Prepare closing entries as of December 31, 2014.

(c) Prepare a post-closing trial balance.

Broadening Your PERSPECTIVE

Financial Reporting and Analysis

Financial Reporting Problem: PepsiCo, Inc.

BYP4-1 The financial statements of PepsiCo, Inc. are presented in Appendix A at the end of this textbook.

Instructions

Answer the questions below using the Consolidated Balance Sheet and the Notes to Consolidated Financial Statements section.

(a) What were PepsiCo's total current assets at December 25, 2010, and December 26, 2009?
(b) Are assets that PepsiCo included under current assets listed in proper order? Explain.
(c) How are PepsiCo's assets classified?
(d) What are "cash equivalents"?
(e) What were PepsiCo's total current liabilities at December 25, 2010, and December 26, 2009?

Comparative Analysis Problem: PepsiCo, Inc. vs. The Coca-Cola Company

BYP4-2 PepsiCo's financial statements are presented in Appendix A. Financial statements for The Coca-Cola Company are presented in Appendix B.

Instructions

(a) Based on the information contained in these financial statements, determine each of the following for PepsiCo at December 25, 2010, and for Coca-Cola at December 31, 2010.
    (1) Total current assets.
    (2) Net amount of property, plant, and equipment (land, buildings, and equipment).
    (3) Total current liabilities.
    (4) Total equity.
(b) What conclusions concerning the companies' respective financial positions can be drawn?

Real-World Focus

BYP4-3 Numerous companies have established home pages on the Internet, e.g., Capt'n Eli Root Beer Company *(www.captneli.com/rootbeer.php)* and Kodak *(www.kodak.com)*.

Instructions
Examine the home pages of any two companies and answer the following questions.

(a) What type of information is available?
(b) Is any accounting-related information presented?
(c) Would you describe the home page as informative, promotional, or both? Why?

Critical Thinking

Decision-Making Across the Organization

BYP4-4 Everclean Janitorial Service was started 2 years ago by Lauren Baird. Because business has been exceptionally good, Lauren decided on July 1, 2014, to expand operations by acquiring an additional truck and hiring two more assistants. To finance the expansion, Lauren obtained on July 1, 2014, a $25,000, 10% bank loan, payable $10,000 on July 1, 2015, and the balance on July 1, 2016. The terms of the loan require the borrower to have $10,000 more current assets than current liabilities at December 31, 2014. If these terms are not met, the bank loan will be refinanced at 15% interest. At December 31, 2014, the accountant for Everclean Janitorial Service prepared the balance sheet shown below.

Lauren presented the balance sheet to the bank's loan officer on January 2, 2015, confident that the company had met the terms of the loan. The loan officer was not impressed. She said, "We need financial statements audited by a CPA." A CPA was hired and immediately realized that the balance sheet had been prepared from a trial balance and not from an adjusted trial balance. The adjustment data at the balance sheet date consisted of the following.

(1) Unbilled janitorial services performed were $3,900.
(2) Janitorial supplies on hand were $2,100.
(3) Prepaid insurance was a 3-year policy dated January 1, 2014.
(4) December expenses incurred but unpaid at December 31, $620.
(5) Interest on the bank loan was not recorded.
(6) The amounts for property, plant, and equipment presented in the balance sheet were reported net of accumulated depreciation (cost less accumulated depreciation). These amounts were $4,000 for cleaning equipment and $5,000 for delivery trucks as of January 1, 2014. Depreciation for 2014 was $2,000 for cleaning equipment and $5,000 for delivery trucks.

Everclean Janitorial Service
Balance Sheet
December 31, 2014

Assets		Liabilities and Stockholders' Equity	
Current assets		Current liabilities	
Cash	$ 5,500	Notes payable	$10,000
Accounts receivable	9,000	Accounts payable	1,500
Janitorial supplies	5,200	Total current liabilities	11,500
Prepaid insurance	4,800	Long-term liability	
Total current assets	24,500	Notes payable	15,000
Property, plant, and equipment		Total liabilities	26,500
Cleaning equipment (net)	22,000	Stockholders' equity	
Delivery trucks (net)	34,000	Common stock	30,000
Total property, plant, and equipment	56,000	Retained earnings	24,000
Total assets	$80,500	Total liabilities and stockholders' equity	$80,500

Instructions
With the class divided into groups, answer the following.

(a) Prepare a correct balance sheet.
(b) Were the terms of the bank loan met? Explain.

Communication Activity

BYP4-5 The accounting cycle is important in understanding the accounting process.

Instructions
Write a memo to your instructor that lists the steps of the accounting cycle in the order they should be completed. End with a paragraph that explains the optional steps in the cycle.

Ethics Case

BYP4-6 As the controller of Take No Prisoners Perfume Company, you discover a misstatement that overstated net income in the prior year's financial statements. The misleading financial statements appear in the company's annual report which was issued to banks and other creditors less than a month ago. After much thought about the consequences of telling the president, Phil McNally, about this misstatement, you gather your courage to inform him. Phil says, "Hey! What they don't know won't hurt them. But, just so we set the record straight, we'll adjust this year's financial statements for last year's misstatement. We can absorb that misstatement better in this year than in last year anyway! Just don't make such a mistake again."

Instructions
(a) Who are the stakeholders in this situation?
(b) What are the ethical issues in this situation?
(c) What would you do as a controller in this situation?

All About You

BYP4-7 Companies prepare balance sheets in order to know their financial position at a specific point in time. This enables them to make a comparison to their position at previous points in time, and gives them a basis for planning for the future. In order to evaluate your financial position, you need to prepare a personal balance sheet. Assume that you have compiled the following information regarding your finances. (*Hint:* Some of the items might not be used in your personal balance sheet.)

Amount owed on student loan balance (long-term)	$ 5,000
Balance in checking account	1,200
Certificate of deposit (6-month)	3,000
Annual earnings from part-time job	12,800
Automobile	7,000
Balance on automobile loan (current portion)	1,500
Balance on automobile loan (long-term portion)	4,000
Home computer	1,100
Amount owed to you by younger brother	300
Balance in money market account	1,800
Annual tuition	6,400
Video and stereo equipment	1,250
Balance owed on credit card (current portion)	190
Balance owed on credit card (long-term portion)	1,850

Instructions
Prepare a personal balance sheet using the format you have learned for a classified balance sheet for a company. For the equity account, use Owner's Equity.

FASB Codification Activity

BYP4-8 If your school has a subscription to the FASB Codification, go to *http://aaahq.org/ascLogin.cfm* to log in and prepare responses to the following.

Instructions
(a) Access the glossary ("Master Glossary") at the FASB Codification website to answer the following.
  (1) What is the definition of current assets?
  (2) What is the definition of current liabilities?
(b) A company wants to offset its accounts payable against its cash account and show a cash amount net of accounts payable on its balance sheet. Identify the criteria (found in the FASB Codification) under which a company has the right of set off. Does the company have the right to offset accounts payable against the cash account?

Answers to Chapter Questions

Answers to Insight and Accounting Across the Organization Questions

p. 174 Cisco Performs the Virtual Close Q: Who else benefits from a shorter closing process? **A:** Investors benefit from a shorter closing process. The shorter the closing, the sooner the company can report its financial results. This means that the financial information is more timely and therefore more relevant to investors.

p. 179 Yale Express Loses Some Transportation Bills Q: What might Yale Express's vice president have done to produce more accurate financial statements without waiting months for Republic's outstanding transportation bills? **A:** Yale's vice president could have engaged his accountants and auditors to prepare an adjusting entry based on an estimate of the outstanding transportation bills. (The estimate could have been made using past experience and the current volume of business.)

p. 183 Regaining Goodwill Q: Name two industries today which are probably rated low on the reputational characteristics of "being trusted" and "having high ethical standards." **A:** Two possible industries are financial companies (Goldman Sachs or AIG) or oil companies (BP).

p. 185 Can a Company Be Too Liquid? Q: What can various company managers do to ensure that working capital is managed efficiently to maximize net income? **A:** Marketing and sales managers must understand that by extending generous repayment terms, they are expanding the company's receivables balance and slowing the company's cash flow. Production managers must strive to minimize the amount of excess inventory on hand. Managers must coordinate efforts to speed up the collection of receivables, while also ensuring that the company pays its payables on time but never too early.

Answers to Self-Test Questions

1. b **2.** c **3.** c **4.** a **5.** b **6.** c **7.** a **8.** d **9.** c **10.** d **11.** b **12.** c **13.** c **14.** d **15.** a ***16.** c

A Look at IFRS

The classified balance sheet, although generally required internationally, contains certain variations in format when reporting under IFRS.

Key Points

- The procedures of the closing process are applicable to all companies, whether they are using IFRS or GAAP.

- IFRS recommends but does not require the use of the title "statement of financial position" rather than balance sheet.

- The format of statement of financial position information is often presented differently under IFRS. Although no specific format is required, most companies that follow IFRS present statement of financial position information in this order:

  ♦ Noncurrent assets
  ♦ Current assets
  ♦ Equity
  ♦ Noncurrent liabilities
  ♦ Current liabilities

- IFRS requires a classified statement of financial position except in very limited situations. IFRS follows the same guidelines as this textbook for distinguishing between current and noncurrent assets and liabilities.

- Under IFRS, current assets are usually listed in the reverse order of liquidity. For example, under GAAP cash is listed first, but under IFRS it is listed last.

- Some companies report the subtotal *net assets*, which equals total assets minus total liabilities. See, for example, the statement of financial position of Zetar plc in Appendix C.

- IFRS has many differences in terminology that you will notice in this textbook. For example, in the sample statement of financial position illustrated below, notice in the investment category that stock is called shares.

Franklin Corporation
Statement of Financial Position
October 31, 2014

Assets

Intangible assets			
Patents			$ 3,100
Property, plant, and equipment			
Land		$10,000	
Equipment	$24,000		
Less: Accumulated depreciation	5,000	19,000	29,000
Long-term investments			
Investment in shares of Walters Corp.		5,200	
Investment in real estate		2,000	7,200
Current assets			
Prepaid insurance		400	
Supplies		2,100	
Inventories		3,000	
Notes receivable		1,000	
Accounts receivable		7,000	
Short-term investments		2,000	
Cash		6,600	22,100
Total assets			$61,400

Equity and Liabilities

Equity			
Share capital		$20,000	
Retained earnings		14,050	$34,050
Non-current liabilities			
Mortgage payable		10,000	
Notes payable		1,300	11,300
Current liabilities			
Notes payable		11,000	
Accounts payable		2,100	
Salaries payable		1,600	
Unearned service revenue		900	
Interest payable		450	16,050
Total equity and liabilities			$61,400

- Both IFRS and GAAP require disclosures about (1) accounting policies followed, (2) judgments that management has made in the process of applying the entity's accounting policies, and (3) the key assumptions and estimation uncertainty that could result in a material adjustment to the carrying amounts of assets and liabilities within the next financial year.

- Comparative prior-period information must be presented and financial statements must be prepared annually.

- Both GAAP and IFRS are increasing the use of fair value to report assets. However, at this point IFRS has adopted it more broadly. As examples, under IFRS companies can apply fair value to property, plant, and equipment; natural resources; and in some cases intangible assets.

Looking to the Future

The IASB and the FASB are working on a project to converge their standards related to financial statement presentation. A key feature of the proposed framework is that each of the statements will be organized in the same format, to separate an entity's financing activities from its operating and investing activities and, further, to separate financing activities into transactions with owners and creditors. Thus, the same classifications used in the statement of financial position would also be used in the income statement and the statement of cash flows. The project has three phases. You can follow the joint financial presentation project at the following link: *http://www.fasb.org/project/financial_statement_presentation.shtml*.

The IASB and the FASB face a difficult task in attempting to update, modify, and complete a converged conceptual framework. For example, how do companies choose between information that is highly relevant but difficult to verify versus information that is less relevant but easy to verify? How do companies define control when developing a definition of an asset? Is a liability the future sacrifice itself or the obligation to make the sacrifice? Should a single measurement method, such as historical cost or fair value, be used, or does it depend on whether it is an asset or liability that is being measured? It appears that the new document will be a significant improvement over its predecessors and will lead to principles-based standards, which will help financial statement users make better decisions.

IFRS Practice

IFRS Self-Test Questions

1. Which of the following statements is *false?*
   (a) Assets equals liabilities plus equity.
   (b) Under IFRS, companies sometimes net liabilities against assets to report "net assets."
   (c) The FASB and IASB are working on a joint conceptual framework project.
   (d) Under IFRS, the statement of financial position is usually referred to as the statement of assets and equity.

2. A company has purchased a tract of land and expects to build a production plant on the land in approximately 5 years. During the 5 years before construction, the land will be idle. Under IFRS, the land should be reported as:
   (a) land expense.
   (b) property, plant, and equipment.
   (c) an intangible asset.
   (d) a long-term investment.

3. Current assets under IFRS are listed generally:
   (a) by importance.
   (b) in the reverse order of their expected conversion to cash.
   (c) by longevity.
   (d) alphabetically.

4. Companies that use IFRS:
   (a) may report all their assets on the statement of financial position at fair value.
   (b) may offset assets against liabilities and show net assets and net liabilities on their statement of financial positions, rather than the underlying detailed line items.
   (c) may report noncurrent assets before current assets on the statement of financial position.
   (s) do not have any guidelines as to what should be reported on the statement of financial position.

5. Companies that follow IFRS to prepare a statement of financial position generally use the following order of classification:
   (a) current assets, current liabilities, noncurrent assets, noncurrent liabilities, equity.
   (b) noncurrent assets, noncurrent liabilities, current assets, current liabilities, equity.
   (c) noncurrent assets, current assets, equity, noncurrent liabilities, current liabilities.
   (d) equity, noncurrent assets, current assets, noncurrent liabilities, current liabilities.

IFRS Exercises

IFRS4-1 In what ways does the format of a statement of financial of position under IFRS often differ from a balance sheet presented under GAAP?

IFRS4-2 What term is commonly used under IFRS in reference to the balance sheet?

IFRS4-3 The statement of financial position for Diaz Company includes the following accounts (in pounds): Accounts Receivable £12,500; Prepaid Insurance £3,600; Cash £15,400; Supplies £5,200; and Short-Term Investments £6,700. Prepare the current assets section of the statement of financial position, listing the accounts in proper sequence.

IFRS4-4 Zurich Company recently received the following information (in Swiss francs) related to the company's December 31, 2014, statement of financial position.

Inventories	CHF 2,700	Short-term investments	CHF 120
Cash	13,100	Accumulated depreciation—	
Equipment	21,700	equipment	5,700
Investments in shares		Accounts receivable	4,300
(long-term)	6,500		

Prepare the assets section of the company's classified statement of financial position.

IFRS4-5 The following information is available for Rego Bowling Alley at December 31, 2014.

Buildings	$128,000	Share Capital	$90,000
Accounts Receivable	7,540	Retained Earnings	22,000
Prepaid Insurance	4,680	Accumulated Depreciation—Buildings	42,600
Cash	18,040	Accounts Payable	12,300
Equipment	62,400	Notes Payable	95,000
Land	67,000	Accumulated Depreciation—Equipment	18,720
Insurance Expense	780	Interest Payable	2,600
Depreciation Expense	7,360	Service Revenues	15,180
Interest Expense	2,600		

Prepare a classified statement of financial position; assume that $13,900 of the notes payable will be paid in 2015.

IFRS4-6 Brian Hopkins is interested in comparing the liquidity and solvency of a U.S. software company with a Chinese competitor. Is this possible if the two companies report using different currencies?

International Comparative Analysis Problem: PepsiCo vs. Zetar plc

IFRS4-7 The financial statements of Zetar plc are presented in Appendix C. The company's complete annual report, including the notes to its financial statements, is available at *www.zetarplc.com*.

Instructions

Identify five differences in the format of the statement of financial position used by Zetar plc compared to a company, such as PepsiCo, that follows GAAP. (PepsiCo's financial statements are available in Appendix A.)

Answers to IFRS Self-Test Questions
1. d   **2.** d   **3.** b   **4.** c   **5.** c

 **The Navigator**

 Remember to go back to The Navigator box on the chapter opening page and check off your completed work.

Chapter 5

Accounting for Merchandising Operations

Feature Story

Who Doesn't Shop at Wal-Mart?

In his book *The End of Work,* Jeremy Rifkin notes that until the 20th century the word *consumption* evoked negative images. To be labeled a "consumer" was an insult. (In fact, one of the deadliest diseases in history, tuberculosis, was often referred to as "consumption.") Twentieth-century merchants realized, however, that in order to prosper, they had to convince people of the need for things not previously needed. For example, General Motors made annual changes in its cars so that people would be discontented with the cars they already owned. Thus began consumerism.

Today, consumption describes the U.S. lifestyle in a nutshell. We consume twice as much today per person as we did at the end of World War II. The amount of U.S. retail space per person is vastly greater than that of any other country. It appears that we live to shop.

The first great retail giant was Sears Roebuck. It started as a catalog company enabling people in rural areas to buy things by mail. For decades, it was the uncontested merchandising leader.

Today, Wal-Mart Stores, Inc. is the undisputed champion provider of basic (and perhaps not-so-basic) human needs. Wal-Mart opened its first store in 1962, and it now has

Learning Objectives

After studying this chapter, you should be able to:

1 Identify the differences between service and merchandising companies.

2 Explain the recording of purchases under a perpetual inventory system.

3 Explain the recording of sales revenues under a perpetual inventory system.

4 Explain the steps in the accounting cycle for a merchandising company.

5 Distinguish between a multiple-step and a single-step income statement.

 The Navigator

more than 8,000 stores, serving more than 100 million customers every week. A key cause of Wal-Mart's incredible growth is its amazing system of inventory control and distribution. Wal-Mart has a management information system that employs six satellite channels, from which company computers receive 8.4 million updates every minute on what items customers buy and the relationship among items sold to each person.

Measured by sales revenues, Wal-Mart is the largest company in the world. In six years, it went from selling almost no groceries to being America's largest grocery retailer.

It would appear that things have never looked better at Wal-Mart. On the other hand, a *Wall Street Journal* article entitled "How to Sell More to Those Who Think It's Cool to Be Frugal" suggests that consumerism as a way of life might be dying. Don't bet your high-definition 3D TV on it though.

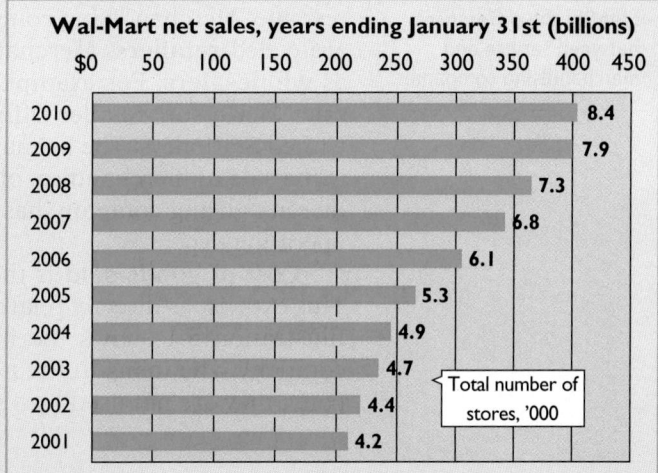

Wal-Mart net sales, years ending January 31st (billions)

Year	Net sales	Total number of stores, '000
2010		8.4
2009		7.9
2008		7.3
2007		6.8
2006		6.1
2005		5.3
2004		4.9
2003		4.7
2002		4.4
2001		4.2

Source: "How Big Can It Grow?" *The Economist* (April 17, 2004), pp. 67–69, and *www.walmart.com* (accessed November 23, 2010).

✔ **The Navigator**

Preview of **Chapter 5**

Merchandising is one of the largest and most influential industries in the United States. It is likely that a number of you will work for a merchandiser. Therefore, understanding the financial statements of merchandising companies is important. In this chapter, you will learn the basics about reporting merchandising transactions. In addition, you will learn how to prepare and analyze a commonly used form of the income statement—the multiple-step income statement. The content and organization of the chapter are as follows.

ACCOUNTING FOR MERCHANDISING OPERATIONS

Merchandising Operations	Recording Purchases of Merchandise	Recording Sales of Merchandise	Completing the Accounting Cycle	Forms of Financial Statements
• Operating cycles • Flow of costs—perpetual and periodic inventory systems	• Freight costs • Purchase returns and allowances • Purchase discounts • Summary of purchasing transactions	• Sales returns and allowances • Sales discounts	• Adjusting entries • Closing entries • Summary of merchandising entries	• Multiple-step income statement • Single-step income statement • Classified balance sheet

✔ **The Navigator**

Merchandising Operations

Wal-Mart, Kmart, and Target are called merchandising companies because they buy and sell merchandise rather than perform services as their primary source of revenue. Merchandising companies that purchase and sell directly to consumers are called **retailers**. Merchandising companies that sell to retailers are known as **wholesalers**. For example, retailer Walgreens might buy goods from wholesaler McKesson; retailer Office Depot might buy office supplies from wholesaler United Stationers. The primary source of revenues for merchandising companies is the sale of merchandise, often referred to simply as **sales revenue** or **sales**. A merchandising company has two categories of expenses: cost of goods sold and operating expenses.

Cost of goods sold is the total cost of merchandise sold during the period. This expense is directly related to the revenue recognized from the sale of goods. Illustration 5-1 shows the income measurement process for a merchandising company. The items in the two blue boxes are unique to a merchandising company; they are not used by a service company.

Illustration 5-1
Income measurement process for a merchandising company

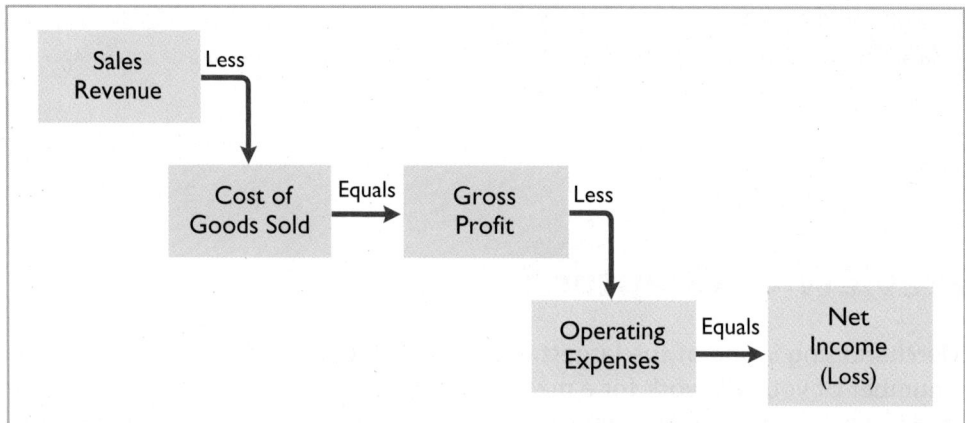

Operating Cycles

The operating cycle of a merchandising company ordinarily is longer than that of a service company. The purchase of merchandise inventory and its eventual sale lengthen the cycle. Illustration 5-2 contrasts the operating cycles of service and merchandising companies. Note that the added asset account for a merchandising company is the Inventory account. Companies report inventory as a current asset on the balance sheet.

Flow of Costs

The flow of costs for a merchandising company is as follows: Beginning inventory plus the cost of goods purchased is the cost of goods available for sale. As goods are sold, they are assigned to cost of goods sold. Those goods that are not sold by the end of the accounting period represent ending inventory. Illustration 5-3 describes these relationships. Companies use one of two systems to account for inventory: a **perpetual inventory system** or a **periodic inventory system**.

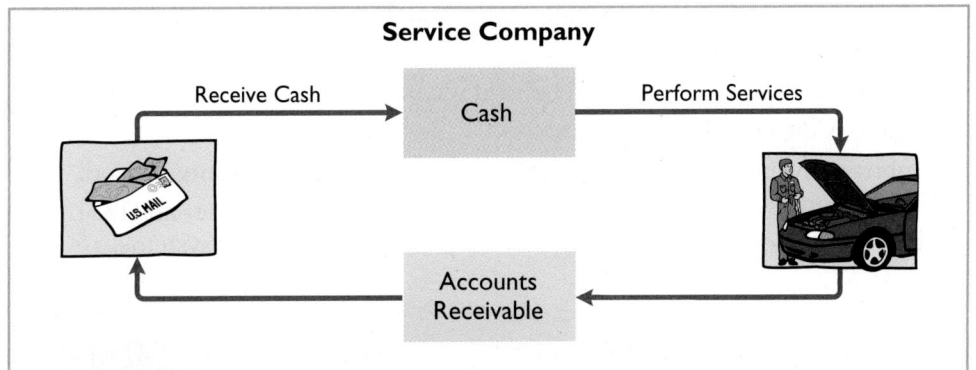

Illustration 5-2
Operating cycles for a service company and a merchandising company

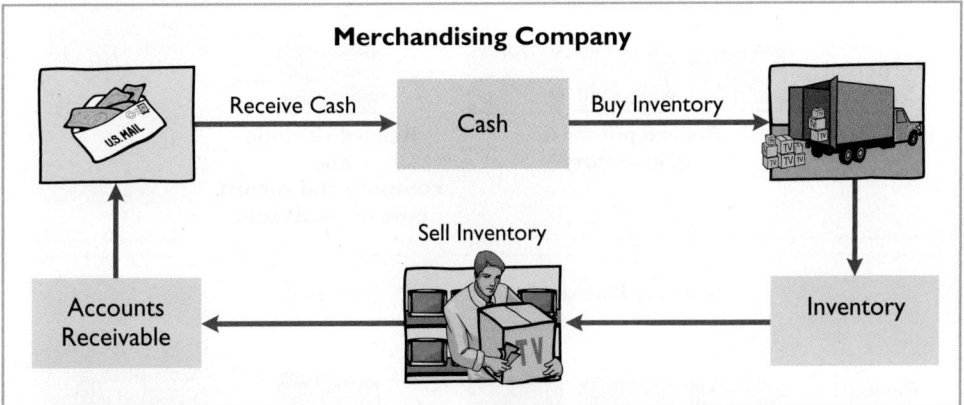

PERPETUAL SYSTEM

In a **perpetual inventory system**, companies keep detailed records of the cost of each inventory purchase and sale. These records continuously—perpetually—show the inventory that should be on hand for every item. For example, a Ford dealership has separate inventory records for each automobile, truck, and van on its lot and showroom floor. Similarly, a Kroger grocery store uses bar codes and optical scanners to keep a daily running record of every box of cereal and every jar of jelly that it buys and sells. Under a perpetual inventory system, a company determines the cost of goods sold **each time a sale occurs**.

Helpful Hint
For control purposes, companies take a physical inventory count under the perpetual system, even though it is not needed to determine cost of goods sold.

PERIODIC SYSTEM

In a **periodic inventory system**, companies do not keep detailed inventory records of the goods on hand throughout the period. Instead, they determine the cost of goods sold **only at the end of the accounting period**—that is, periodically. At that point, the company takes a physical inventory count to determine the cost of goods on hand.

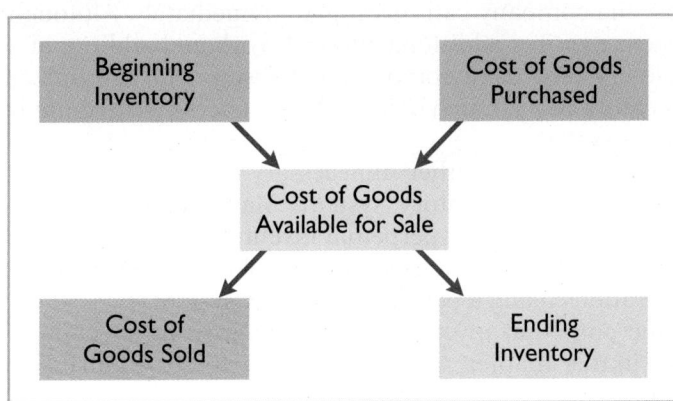

Illustration 5-3
Flow of costs

To determine the cost of goods sold under a periodic inventory system, the following steps are necessary:

1. Determine the cost of goods on hand at the beginning of the accounting period.
2. Add to it the cost of goods purchased.
3. Subtract the cost of goods on hand at the end of the accounting period.

Illustration 5-4 graphically compares the sequence of activities and the timing of the cost of goods sold computation under the two inventory systems.

Illustration 5-4
Comparing perpetual and periodic inventory systems

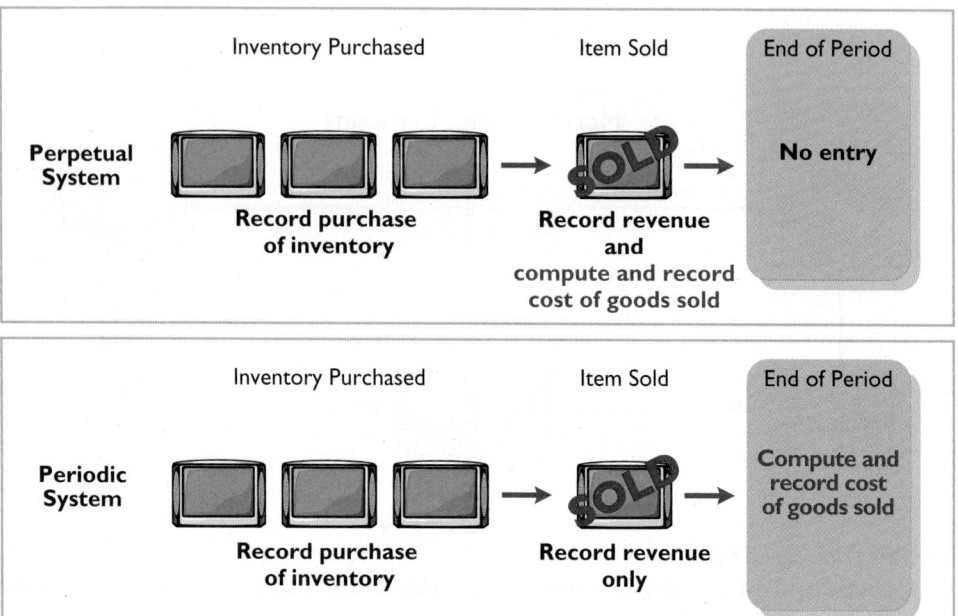

ADDITIONAL CONSIDERATIONS

Companies that sell merchandise with high unit values, such as automobiles, furniture, and major home appliances, have traditionally used perpetual systems. The growing use of computers and electronic scanners has enabled many more companies to install perpetual inventory systems. The perpetual inventory system is so named because the accounting records continuously—perpetually—show the quantity and cost of the inventory that should be on hand at any time.

A perpetual inventory system provides better control over inventories than a periodic system. Since the inventory records show the quantities that should be on hand, the company can count the goods at any time to see whether the amount of goods actually on hand agrees with the inventory records. If shortages are uncovered, the company can investigate immediately. Although a perpetual inventory system requires additional clerical work and additional cost to maintain the subsidiary records, a computerized system can minimize this cost. As noted in the Feature Story, much of Wal-Mart's success is attributed to its sophisticated inventory system.

Some businesses find it either unnecessary or uneconomical to invest in a computerized perpetual inventory system. Many small merchandising businesses, in particular, find that a perpetual inventory system costs more than it is worth. Managers of these businesses can control their merchandise and manage day-to-day operations using a periodic inventory system.

Because the perpetual inventory system is growing in popularity and use, we illustrate it in this chapter. Appendix 5A describes the journal entries for the periodic system.

INVESTOR INSIGHT

Morrow Snowboards Improves Its Stock Appeal

Investors are often eager to invest in a company that has a hot new product. However, when snowboard-maker Morrow Snowboards, Inc., issued shares of stock to the public for the first time, some investors expressed reluctance to invest in Morrow because of a number of accounting control problems. To reduce investor concerns, Morrow implemented a perpetual inventory system to improve its control over inventory. In addition, it stated that it would perform a physical inventory count every quarter until it felt that the perpetual inventory system was reliable.

 If a perpetual system keeps track of inventory on a daily basis, why do companies ever need to do a physical count? (See page 267.)

Recording Purchases of Merchandise

Companies purchase inventory using cash or credit (on account). They normally record purchases when they receive the goods from the seller. Business documents provide written evidence of the transaction. A canceled check or a cash register receipt, for example, indicates the items purchased and amounts paid for each cash purchase. Companies record cash purchases by an increase in Inventory and a decrease in Cash.

A **purchase invoice** should support each credit purchase. This invoice indicates the total purchase price and other relevant information. However, the purchaser does not prepare a separate purchase invoice. Instead, the purchaser uses as a purchase invoice a copy of the sales invoice sent by the seller. In Illustration 5-5 (page 224), for example, Sauk Stereo (the buyer) uses as a purchase invoice the sales invoice prepared by PW Audio Supply, Inc. (the seller).

Sauk Stereo makes the following journal entry to record its purchase from PW Audio Supply. The entry increases (debits) Inventory and increases (credits) Accounts Payable.

> **LEARNING OBJECTIVE 2**
>
> Explain the recording of purchases under a perpetual inventory system.

May 4	Inventory	3,800	
	Accounts Payable		3,800
	(To record goods purchased on account from PW Audio Supply)		

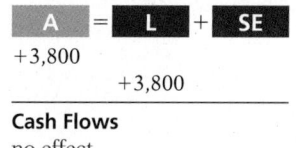

A = L + SE
+3,800
+3,800

Cash Flows
no effect

Under the perpetual inventory system, companies record purchases of merchandise for sale in the Inventory account. Thus, Wal-Mart would increase (debit) Inventory for clothing, sporting goods, and anything else purchased for resale to customers.

Not all purchases are debited to Inventory, however. Companies record purchases of assets acquired for use and not for resale, such as supplies, equipment, and similar items, as increases to specific asset accounts rather than to Inventory. For example, to record the purchase of materials used to make shelf signs or for cash register receipt paper, Wal-Mart would increase Supplies.

Freight Costs

The sales agreement should indicate who—the seller or the buyer—is to pay for transporting the goods to the buyer's place of business. When a common carrier

Illustration 5-5
Sales invoice used as purchase invoice by Sauk Stereo

INVOICE NO. 731

PW AUDIO SUPPLY, INC.

27 CIRCLE DRIVE
HARDING, MICHIGAN 48281

▼

S	Firm Name	Sauk Stereo
O		
L	Attention of	James Hoover, Purchasing Agent
D		
	Address	125 Main Street
T		
O	Chelsea Illinois 60915	
	City State Zip	

Date 5/4/14	Salesperson Malone	Terms 2/10, n/30	FOB Shipping Point		
Catalog No.	Description		Quantity	Price	Amount
X572Y9820	Printed Circuit Board-prototype		1	2,300	$2,300
A2547Z45	Production Model Circuits		5	300	1,500

IMPORTANT: ALL RETURNS MUST BE MADE WITHIN 10 DAYS	**TOTAL**	**$3,800**

Helpful Hint
To better understand the contents of this invoice, identify these items:
1. Seller
2. Invoice date
3. Purchaser
4. Salesperson
5. Credit terms
6. Freight terms
7. Goods sold: catalog number, description, quantity, price per unit
8. Total invoice amount

such as a railroad, trucking company, or airline transports the goods, the carrier prepares a freight bill in accord with the sales agreement.

Freight terms are expressed as either FOB shipping point or FOB destination. The letters FOB mean **free on board**. Thus, **FOB shipping point** means that the seller places the goods free on board the carrier, and the buyer pays the freight costs. Conversely, **FOB destination** means that the seller places the goods free on board to the buyer's place of business, and the seller pays the freight. For example, the sales invoice in Illustration 5-5 indicates FOB shipping point. Thus, the buyer (Sauk Stereo) pays the freight charges. Illustration 5-6 illustrates these shipping terms.

Illustration 5-6
Shipping terms

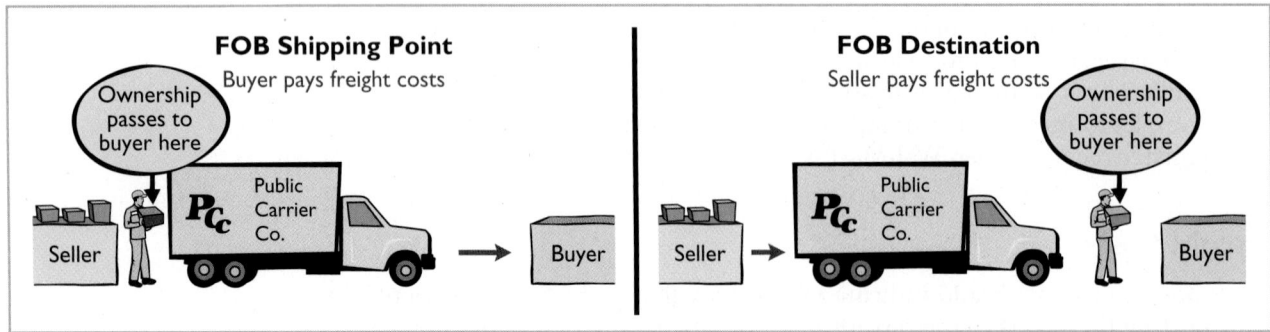

FREIGHT COSTS INCURRED BY THE BUYER

When the buyer incurs the transportation costs, these costs are considered part of the cost of purchasing inventory. Therefore, the buyer debits (increases) the account Inventory. For example, if upon delivery of the goods on May 6, Sauk Stereo (the buyer) pays Acme Freight Company $150 for freight charges, the entry on Sauk Stereo's books is:

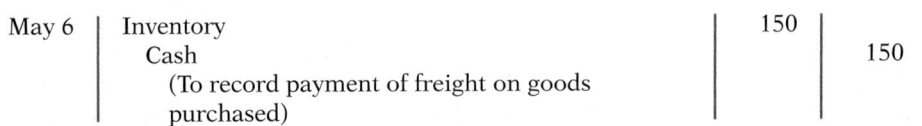

May 6	Inventory	150	
	Cash		150
	(To record payment of freight on goods purchased)		

A	=	L	+	SE
+150				
−150				

Cash Flows
−150

Thus, any freight costs incurred by the buyer are part of the cost of merchandise purchased. The reason: Inventory cost should include all costs to acquire the inventory, including freight necessary to deliver the goods to the buyer. Companies recognize these costs as cost of goods sold when the inventory is sold.

FREIGHT COSTS INCURRED BY THE SELLER

In contrast, **freight costs incurred by the seller on outgoing merchandise are an operating expense to the seller**. These costs increase an expense account titled Freight-Out or Delivery Expense. If the freight terms on the invoice had required PW Audio Supply (the seller) to pay the freight charges, the entry by PW Audio Supply would be:

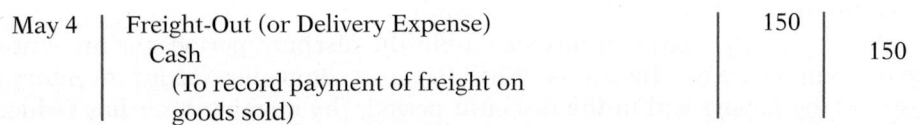

May 4	Freight-Out (or Delivery Expense)	150	
	Cash		150
	(To record payment of freight on goods sold)		

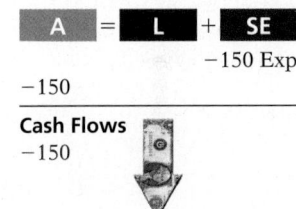

A	=	L	+	SE
				−150 Exp
−150				

Cash Flows
−150

When the seller pays the freight charges, it will usually establish a higher invoice price for the goods to cover the shipping expense.

Purchase Returns and Allowances

A purchaser may be dissatisfied with the merchandise received because the goods are damaged or defective, of inferior quality, or do not meet the purchaser's specifications. In such cases, the purchaser may return the goods to the seller for credit if the sale was made on credit, or for a cash refund if the purchase was for cash. This transaction is known as a **purchase return**. Alternatively, the purchaser may choose to keep the merchandise if the seller is willing to grant an allowance (deduction) from the purchase price. This transaction is known as a **purchase allowance**.

    Assume that on May 8 Sauk Stereo returned goods costing $300 to PW Audio Supply. The following entry by Sauk Stereo for the returned merchandise decreases (debits) Accounts Payable and decreases (credits) Inventory.

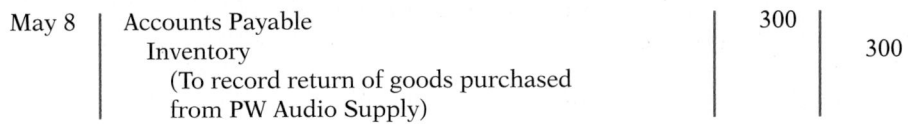

May 8	Accounts Payable	300	
	Inventory		300
	(To record return of goods purchased from PW Audio Supply)		

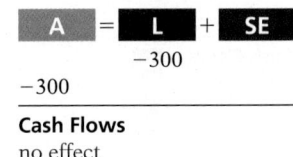

A	=	L	+	SE
		−300		
−300				

Cash Flows
no effect

Because Sauk Stereo increased Inventory when the goods were received, Inventory is decreased when Sauk Stereo returns the goods (or when it is granted an allowance).

    Suppose instead that Sauk Stereo chose to keep the goods after being granted a $50 allowance (reduction in price). It would reduce (debit) Accounts Payable and reduce (credit) Inventory for $50.

Purchase Discounts

The credit terms of a purchase on account may permit the buyer to claim a cash discount for prompt payment. The buyer calls this cash discount a **purchase discount**. This incentive offers advantages to both parties: The purchaser saves money, and the seller shortens the operating cycle by more quickly converting the accounts receivable into cash.

Credit terms specify the amount of the cash discount and time period in which it is offered. They also indicate the time period in which the purchaser is expected to pay the full invoice price. In the sales invoice in Illustration 5-5 (page 224), credit terms are 2/10, n/30, which is read "two-ten, net thirty." This means that the buyer may take a 2% cash discount on the invoice price less ("net of") any returns or allowances, if payment is made within 10 days of the invoice date (the **discount period**). Otherwise, the invoice price, less any returns or allowances, is due 30 days from the invoice date.

Alternatively, the discount period may extend to a specified number of days following the month in which the sale occurs. For example, 1/10 EOM (end of month) means that a 1% discount is available if the invoice is paid within the first 10 days of the next month.

When the seller elects not to offer a cash discount for prompt payment, credit terms will specify only the maximum time period for paying the balance due. For example, the invoice may state the time period as n/30, n/60, or n/10 EOM. This means, respectively, that the buyer must pay the net amount in 30 days, 60 days, or within the first 10 days of the next month.

When the buyer pays an invoice within the discount period, the amount of the discount decreases Inventory. Why? Because companies record inventory at cost and, by paying within the discount period, the merchandiser has reduced that cost. To illustrate, assume Sauk Stereo pays the balance due of $3,500 (gross invoice price of $3,800 less purchase returns and allowances of $300) on May 14, the last day of the discount period. The cash discount is $70 ($3,500 × 2%), and Sauk Stereo pays $3,430 ($3,500 − $70). The entry Sauk Stereo makes to record its May 14 payment decreases (debits) Accounts Payable by the amount of the gross invoice price, reduces (credits) Inventory by the $70 discount, and reduces (credits) Cash by the net amount owed.

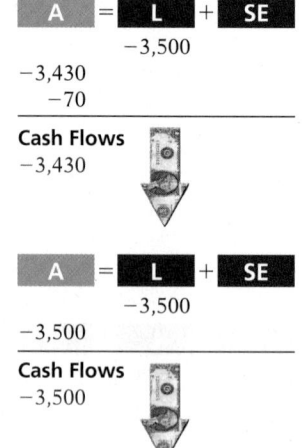

A	=	L	+	SE
		−3,500		
−3,430				
−70				

Cash Flows
−3,430

May 14	Accounts Payable	3,500	
	Cash		3,430
	Inventory		70
	(To record payment within discount period)		

If Sauk Stereo failed to take the discount, and instead made full payment of $3,500 on June 3, it would debit Accounts Payable and credit Cash for $3,500 each.

A	=	L	+	SE
		−3,500		
−3,500				

Cash Flows
−3,500

June 3	Accounts Payable	3,500	
	Cash		3,500
	(To record payment with no discount taken)		

A merchandising company usually should take all available discounts. Passing up the discount may be viewed as **paying interest** for use of the money. For example, passing up the discount offered by PW Audio Supply would be comparable to Sauk Stereo paying an interest rate of 2% for the use of $3,500 for 20 days. This is the equivalent of an annual interest rate of approximately 36.5% (2% × 365/20). Obviously, it would be better for Sauk Stereo to borrow at prevailing bank interest rates of 6% to 10% than to lose the discount.

Summary of Purchasing Transactions

The following T-account (with transaction descriptions in blue) provides a summary of the effect of the previous transactions on Inventory. Sauk Stereo originally purchased $3,800 worth of inventory for resale. It then returned $300 of goods. It paid $150 in freight charges, and finally, it received a $70 discount off the balance owed because it paid within the discount period. This results in a balance in Inventory of $3,580.

		Inventory			
Purchase	May 4	3,800	May 8	300	Purchase return
Freight-in	6	150	14	70	Purchase discount
Balance		3,580			

> DO IT!

Purchase Transactions

On September 5, De La Hoya Company buys merchandise on account from Junot Diaz Company. The selling price of the goods is $1,500, and the cost to Diaz Company was $800. On September 8, De La Hoya returns defective goods with a selling price of $200. Record the transactions on the books of De La Hoya Company.

Solution

Action Plan

✔ Purchaser records goods at cost.

✔ When goods are returned, purchaser reduces Inventory.

Sept. 5	Inventory	1,500	
	Accounts Payable		1,500
	(To record goods purchased on account)		
8	Accounts Payable	200	
	Inventory		200
	(To record return of defective goods)		

Related exercise material: **BE5-2, BE5-4, E5-2, E5-3, E5-4, and** DO IT! **5-1.**

 The Navigator

Recording Sales of Merchandise

LEARNING OBJECTIVE   3

Explain the recording of sales revenues under a perpetual inventory system.

In accordance with the revenue recognition principle, companies record sales revenue when the performance obligation is satisfied. Typically, the performance obligation is satisfied when the goods transfer from the seller to the buyer. At this point, the sales transaction is complete and the sales price established.

Sales may be made on credit or for cash. A **business document** should support every sales transaction, to provide written evidence of the sale. **Cash register tapes** provide evidence of cash sales. A **sales invoice**, like the one shown in Illustration 5-5 (page 224), provides support for a credit sale. The original copy of the invoice goes to the customer, and the seller keeps a copy for use in recording the sale. The invoice shows the date of sale, customer name, total sales price, and other relevant information.

The seller makes two entries for each sale. **The first entry records the sale**: The seller increases (debits) Cash (or Accounts Receivable, if a credit sale), and also increases (credits) Sales Revenue. **The second entry records the cost of**

the merchandise sold: The seller increases (debits) Cost of Goods Sold, and also decreases (credits) Inventory for the cost of those goods. As a result, the Inventory account will show at all times the amount of inventory that should be on hand.

To illustrate a credit sales transaction, PW Audio Supply records its May 4 sale of $3,800 to Sauk Stereo (see Illustration 5-5) as follows (assume the merchandise cost PW Audio Supply $2,400).

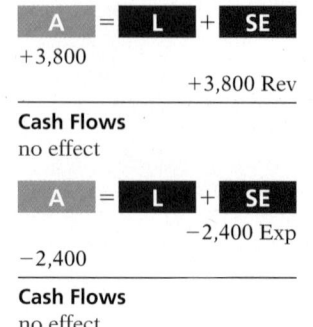

May 4	Accounts Receivable	3,800	
	Sales Revenue		3,800
	(To record credit sale to Sauk Stereo per invoice #731)		
4	Cost of Goods Sold	2,400	
	Inventory		2,400
	(To record cost of merchandise sold on invoice #731 to Sauk Stereo)		

For internal decision-making purposes, merchandising companies may use more than one sales account. For example, PW Audio Supply may decide to keep separate sales accounts for its sales of TV sets, DVD recorders, and microwave ovens. Wal-Mart might use separate accounts for sporting goods, children's clothing, and hardware—or it might have even more narrowly defined accounts. By using separate sales accounts for major product lines, rather than a single combined sales account, company management can more closely monitor sales trends and respond more strategically to changes in sales patterns. For example, if TV sales are increasing while microwave oven sales are decreasing, PW Audio Supply might reevaluate both its advertising and pricing policies on these items to ensure they are optimal.

On its income statement presented to outside investors, a merchandising company normally would provide only a single sales figure—the sum of all of its individual sales accounts. This is done for two reasons. First, providing detail on all of its individual sales accounts would add considerable length to its income statement. Second, companies do not want their competitors to know the details of their operating results. However, Microsoft recently expanded its disclosure of revenue from three to five types. The reason: The additional categories will better enable financial statement users to evaluate the growth of the company's consumer and Internet businesses.

Ethics Note

Many companies are trying to improve the quality of their financial reporting. For example, General Electric now provides more detail on its revenues and operating profits.

At the end of "Anatomy of a Fraud" stories, which describe some recent real-world frauds, we discuss the missing internal control activity that would likely have prevented or uncovered the fraud.

ANATOMY OF A FRAUD[1]

Holly Harmon was a cashier at a national superstore for only a short while when she began stealing merchandise using three methods. First, her husband or friends took UPC labels from cheaper items and put them on more expensive items. Holly then scanned the goods at the register. Second, Holly rang an item up but then voided the sale and left the merchandise in the shopping cart. A third approach was to put goods into large plastic containers. She rang up the plastic containers but not the goods within them. One day, Holly did not call in sick or show up for work. In such instances, the company reviews past surveillance tapes to look for suspicious activity by employees. This enabled the store to observe the thefts and to identify the participants.

---

[1]The "Anatomy of a Fraud" stories in this textbook are adapted from *Fraud Casebook: Lessons from the Bad Side of Business,* edited by Joseph T. Wells (Hoboken, NJ: John Wiley & Sons, Inc., 2007). Used by permission. The names of some of the people and organizations in the stories are fictitious, but the facts in the stories are true.

Total take: $12,000

The Missing Controls
Human resource controls. A background check would have revealed Holly's previous criminal record. She would not have been hired as a cashier.
Physical controls. Software can flag high numbers of voided transactions or a high number of sales of low-priced goods. Random comparisons of video records with cash register records can ensure that the goods reported as sold on the register are the same goods that are shown being purchased on the video recording. Finally, employees should be aware that they are being monitored.

Source: Adapted from Wells, *Fraud Casebook* (2007), pp. 251–259.

Sales Returns and Allowances

We now look at the "flipside" of purchase returns and allowances, which the seller records as **sales returns and allowances**. These are transactions where the seller either accepts goods back from the buyer (a return) or grants a reduction in the purchase price (an allowance) so the buyer will keep the goods. PW Audio Supply's entries to record credit for returned goods involve (1) an increase (debit) in Sales Returns and Allowances (a contra account to Sales Revenue) and a decrease (credit) in Accounts Receivable at the $300 selling price, and (2) an increase (debit) in Inventory (assume a $140 cost) and a decrease (credit) in Cost of Goods Sold, as shown below (assuming that the goods were not defective).

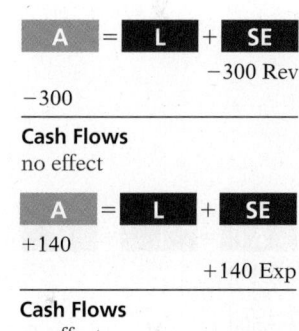

May 8	Sales Returns and Allowances	300	
	Accounts Receivable		300
	(To record credit granted to Sauk Stereo for returned goods)		
8	Inventory	140	
	Cost of Goods Sold		140
	(To record cost of goods returned)		

A = L + SE
−300 Rev
−300
Cash Flows
no effect

A = L + SE
+140
+140 Exp
Cash Flows
no effect

If Sauk Stereo returns goods because they are damaged or defective, then PW Audio Supply's entry to Inventory and Cost of Goods Sold should be for the fair value of the returned goods, rather than their cost. For example, if the returned goods were defective and had a fair value of $50, PW Audio Supply would debit Inventory for $50, and would credit Cost of Goods Sold for $50.

What happens if the goods are not returned but the seller grants the buyer an allowance by reducing the purchase price? In this case, the seller debits Sales Returns and Allowances and credits Accounts Receivable for the amount of the allowance.

As mentioned above, Sales Returns and Allowances is a **contra-revenue account** to Sales Revenue. The normal balance of Sales Returns and Allowances is a debit. Companies use a contra account, instead of debiting Sales Revenue, to disclose in the accounts and in the income statement the amount of sales returns and allowances. Disclosure of this information is important to management: Excessive returns and allowances may suggest problems—inferior merchandise, inefficiencies in filling orders, errors in billing customers, or delivery or shipment mistakes. Moreover, a decrease (debit) recorded directly to Sales Revenue would obscure the relative importance of sales returns and allowances as a percentage of sales. It also could distort comparisons between total sales in different accounting periods.

ACCOUNTING ACROSS THE ORGANIZATION

Should Costco Change Its Return Policy?

In most industries, sales returns are relatively minor. But returns of consumer electronics can really take a bite out of profits. Recently, the marketing executives at Costco Wholesale Corp. faced a difficult decision. Costco has always prided itself on its generous return policy. Most goods have had an unlimited grace period for returns. A new policy will require that certain electronics must be returned within 90 days of their purchase. The reason? The cost of returned products such as high-definition TVs, computers, and iPods cut an estimated 8¢ per share off Costco's earnings per share, which was $2.30.

Source: Kris Hudson, "Costco Tightens Policy on Returning Electronics," *Wall Street Journal* (February 27, 2007), p. B4.

 If a company expects significant returns, what are the implications for revenue recognition? (See page 267.)

Sales Discounts

As mentioned in our discussion of purchase transactions, the seller may offer the customer a cash discount—called by the seller a **sales discount**—for the prompt payment of the balance due. Like a purchase discount, a sales discount is based on the invoice price less returns and allowances, if any. The seller increases (debits) the Sales Discounts account for discounts that are taken. For example, PW Audio Supply makes the following entry to record the cash receipt on May 14 from Sauk Stereo within the discount period.

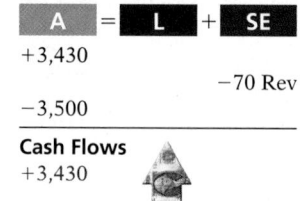

	A	=	L	+	SE
	+3,430				
					−70 Rev
	−3,500				

Cash Flows
+3,430

Date	Account	Debit	Credit
May 14	Cash	3,430	
	Sales Discounts	70	
	Accounts Receivable		3,500
	(To record collection within 2/10, n/30 discount period from Sauk Stereo)		

Like Sales Returns and Allowances, Sales Discounts is a **contra-revenue account** to Sales Revenue. Its normal balance is a debit. PW Audio Supply uses this account, instead of debiting Sales Revenue, to disclose the amount of cash discounts taken by customers. If Sauk Stereo does not take the discount, PW Audio Supply increases (debits) Cash for $3,500 and decreases (credits) Accounts Receivable for the same amount at the date of collection.

The following T-accounts summarize the three sales-related transactions and show their combined effect on net sales.

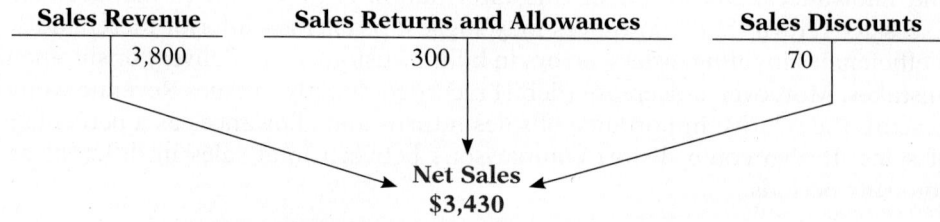

> DO IT!

Sales Transactions

On September 5, De La Hoya Company buys merchandise on account from Junot Diaz Company. The selling price of the goods is $1,500, and the cost to Diaz Company was $800. On September 8, De La Hoya returns defective goods with a selling price of $200 and a fair value of $30. Record the transactions on the books of Junot Diaz Company.

Action Plan

✔ Seller records both the sale and the cost of goods sold at the time of the sale.

✔ When goods are returned, the seller records the return in a contra account, Sales Returns and Allowances, and reduces Accounts Receivable. Any goods returned increase Inventory and reduce Cost of Goods Sold.

✔ Defective or damaged inventory is recorded at fair value (scrap value).

Solution

Sept. 5	Accounts Receivable		1,500	
	Sales Revenue			1,500
	(To record credit sale)			
5	Cost of Goods Sold		800	
	Inventory			800
	(To record cost of goods sold on account)			
8	Sales Returns and Allowances		200	
	Accounts Receivable			200
	(To record credit granted for receipt of returned goods)			
8	Inventory		30	
	Cost of Goods Sold			30
	(To record fair value of goods returned)			

Related exercise material: **BE5-2, BE5-3, E5-3, E5-4, E5-5, and** DO IT! **5-2.**

✔ **The Navigator**

PEOPLE, PLANET, AND PROFIT INSIGHT

Selling Green

Here is a question an executive of PepsiCo was asked: Should PepsiCo market green? The executive indicated that the company should, as he believes it's the No. 1 thing consumers all over the world care about. Here are some thoughts on this issue:

If you are going to market green, what are some things we've learned? I'll share with you one thing we've learned at PepsiCo.

Sun Chips are part of the food business I run. It's a "healthy snack." We decided that Sun Chips, if it's a healthy snack, should be made in facilities that have a net-zero footprint. In other words, I want off the electric grid everywhere we make Sun Chips. We did that. Sun Chips should be made in a facility that puts back more water than it uses. It does that. And we partnered with our suppliers and came out with the world's first compostable chip package.

Now, there was an issue with this package: It was louder than the New York subway, louder than jet engines taking off. What would a company that's committed to green do: walk away or stay committed? If your people are passionate, they're going to fix it for you as long as you stay committed. Six months later, the compostable bag has half the noise of our current package.

So the view today is: we should market green, we should be proud to do it . . . it has to be a 360 process, both internal and external. And if you do that, you can monetize environmental sustainability for the shareholders.

Source: "Four Problems—and Solutions," *Wall Street Journal* (March 7, 2011), p. R2.

? What is meant by "monetize environmental sustainability" for shareholders? (See page 267.)

Completing the Accounting Cycle

Up to this point, we have illustrated the basic entries for transactions relating to purchases and sales in a perpetual inventory system. Now we consider the remaining steps in the accounting cycle for a merchandising company. Each of the required steps described in Chapter 4 for service companies apply to merchandising companies. Appendix 5B to this chapter shows use of a worksheet by a merchandiser (an optional step).

Adjusting Entries

A merchandising company generally has the same types of adjusting entries as a service company. However, a merchandiser using a perpetual system will require one additional adjustment to make the records agree with the actual inventory on hand. Here's why: At the end of each period, for control purposes, a merchandising company that uses a perpetual system will take a physical count of its goods on hand. The company's unadjusted balance in Inventory usually does not agree with the actual amount of inventory on hand. The perpetual inventory records may be incorrect due to recording errors, theft, or waste. Thus, the company needs to adjust the perpetual records to make the recorded inventory amount agree with the inventory on hand. **This involves adjusting Inventory and Cost of Goods Sold.**

For example, suppose that PW Audio Supply has an unadjusted balance of $40,500 in Inventory. Through a physical count, PW Audio Supply determines that its actual merchandise inventory at year-end is $40,000. The company would make an adjusting entry as follows.

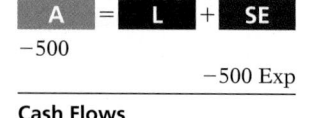

−500

−500 Exp

Cash Flows
no effect

Cost of Goods Sold	500	
Inventory		500
(To adjust inventory to physical count)		

Closing Entries

A merchandising company, like a service company, closes to Income Summary all accounts that affect net income. In journalizing, the company credits all temporary accounts with debit balances, and debits all temporary accounts with credit balances, as shown below for PW Audio Supply. Note that PW Audio Supply closes Cost of Goods Sold to Income Summary.

Helpful Hint
The easiest way to prepare the first two closing entries is to identify the temporary accounts by their balances and then prepare one entry for the credits and one for the debits.

Dec. 31	Sales Revenue	480,000	
	Income Summary		480,000
	(To close income statement accounts with		
	credit balances)		
31	Income Summary	450,000	
	Sales Returns and Allowances		12,000
	Sales Discounts		8,000
	Cost of Goods Sold		316,000
	Salaries and Wages Expense		64,000
	Freight-Out		7,000
	Advertising Expense		16,000
	Utilities Expense		17,000
	Depreciation Expense		8,000
	Insurance Expense		2,000
	(To close income statement accounts with		
	debit balances)		

31	Income Summary	30,000	
	Retained Earnings		30,000
	(To close net income to retained earnings)		

31	Retained Earnings	15,000	
	Dividends		15,000
	(To close dividends to retained earnings)		

After PW Audio Supply has posted the closing entries, all temporary accounts have zero balances. Also, Retained Earnings has a balance that is carried over to the next period.

Summary of Merchandising Entries

Illustration 5-7 summarizes the entries for the merchandising accounts using a perpetual inventory system.

Illustration 5-7
Daily recurring and adjusting and closing entries

	Transactions	Daily Recurring Entries	Dr.	Cr.
Sales Transactions	Selling merchandise to customers.	Cash or Accounts Receivable	XX	
		Sales Revenue		XX
		Cost of Goods Sold	XX	
		Inventory		XX
	Granting sales returns or allowances to customers.	Sales Returns and Allowances	XX	
		Cash or Accounts Receivable		XX
		Inventory	XX	
		Cost of Goods Sold		XX
	Paying freight costs on sales; FOB destination.	Freight-Out	XX	
		Cash		XX
	Receiving payment from customers within discount period	Cash	XX	
		Sales Discounts	XX	
		Accounts Receivable		XX
Purchase Transactions	Purchasing merchandise for resale.	Inventory	XX	
		Cash or Accounts Payable		XX
	Paying freight costs on merchandise purchased; FOB shipping point.	Inventory	XX	
		Cash		XX
	Receiving purchase returns or allowances from suppliers.	Cash or Accounts Payable	XX	
		Inventory		XX
	Paying suppliers within discount period.	Accounts Payable	XX	
		Inventory		XX
		Cash		XX

	Events	Adjusting and Closing Entries		
	Adjust because book amount is higher than the inventory amount determined to be on hand.	Cost of Goods Sold	XX	
		Inventory		XX
	Closing temporary accounts with credit balances.	Sales Revenue	XX	
		Income Summary		XX
	Closing temporary accounts with debit balances.	Income Summary	XX	
		Sales Returns and Allowances		XX
		Sales Discounts		XX
		Cost of Goods Sold		XX
		Freight-Out		XX
		Expenses		XX

> DO IT!

Closing Entries

The trial balance of Celine's Sports Wear Shop at December 31 shows Inventory $25,000, Sales Revenue $162,400, Sales Returns and Allowances $4,800, Sales Discounts $3,600, Cost of Goods Sold $110,000, Rent Revenue $6,000, Freight-Out $1,800, Rent Expense $8,800, and Salaries and Wages Expense $22,000. Prepare the closing entries for the above accounts.

Solution

Action Plan

✔ Close all temporary accounts with credit balances to Income Summary by debiting these accounts.

✔ Close all temporary accounts with debit balances, except dividends, to Income Summary by crediting these accounts.

The two closing entries are:

Dec. 31	Sales Revenue	162,400	
	Rent Revenue	6,000	
	Income Summary		168,400
	(To close accounts with credit balances)		
31	Income Summary	151,000	
	Cost of Goods Sold		110,000
	Sales Returns and Allowances		4,800
	Sales Discounts		3,600
	Freight-Out		1,800
	Rent Expense		8,800
	Salaries and Wages Expense		22,000
	(To close accounts with debit balances)		

Related exercise material: **BE5-5, BE5-6, E5-6, E5-7, E5-8, and** DO IT! **5-3.**

✔ **The Navigator**

Forms of Financial Statements

Merchandising companies widely use the classified balance sheet introduced in Chapter 4 and one of two forms for the income statement. This section explains the use of these financial statements by merchandisers.

Multiple-Step Income Statement

The **multiple-step income statement** is so named because it shows several steps in determining net income. Two of these steps relate to the company's principal operating activities. A multiple-step statement also distinguishes between **operating** and **nonoperating activities**. Finally, the statement also highlights intermediate components of income and shows subgroupings of expenses.

Income Statement Presentation of Sales

The multiple-step income statement begins by presenting **sales revenue**. It then deducts contra-revenue accounts—sales returns and allowances, and sales discounts—to arrive at **net sales**. Illustration 5-8 presents the sales revenues section for PW Audio Supply, using assumed data.

Illustration 5-8
Computation of net sales

PW Audio Supply, Inc. Income Statement (partial)		
Sales revenues		
Sales revenue		$ 480,000
Less: Sales returns and allowances	$12,000	
Sales discounts	8,000	20,000
Net sales		**$460,000**

This presentation discloses the key data about the company's principal revenue-producing activities.

GROSS PROFIT

From Illustration 5-1, you learned that companies deduct cost of goods sold from sales revenue in order to determine **gross profit.** For this computation, companies use **net sales** (which takes into consideration Sales Returns and Allowances and Sales Discounts) as the amount of sales revenue. On the basis of the sales data in Illustration 5-8 (net sales of $460,000) and cost of goods sold under the perpetual inventory system (assume $316,000), PW Audio Supply's gross profit is $144,000, computed as follows.

Illustration 5-9
Computation of gross profit

Net sales	$ 460,000
Cost of goods sold	316,000
Gross profit	**$144,000**

We also can express a company's gross profit as a percentage, called the **gross profit rate.** To do so, we divide the amount of gross profit by net sales. For PW Audio Supply, the **gross profit rate** is 31.3%, computed as follows.

Illustration 5-10
Gross profit rate formula
and computation

Gross Profit	÷	Net Sales	=	Gross Profit Rate
$144,000	÷	$460,000	=	31.3%

Analysts generally consider the gross profit **rate** to be more useful than the gross profit **amount.** The rate expresses a more meaningful (qualitative) relationship between net sales and gross profit. For example, a gross profit of $1,000,000 may sound impressive. But if it is the result of a gross profit rate of only 7%, it is not so impressive. The gross profit rate tells how many cents of each sales dollar go to gross profit.

Gross profit represents the **merchandising profit** of a company. It is not a measure of the overall profitability, because operating expenses are not yet deducted. But managers and other interested parties closely watch the amount and trend of gross profit. They compare current gross profit with amounts reported in past periods. They also compare the company's gross profit rate with rates of competitors and with industry averages. Such comparisons provide information about the effectiveness of a company's purchasing function and the soundness of its pricing policies.

OPERATING EXPENSES AND NET INCOME

Operating expenses are the next component in measuring net income for a merchandising company. They are the expenses incurred in the process of earning sales revenue. These expenses are similar in merchandising and service companies. At PW Audio Supply, operating expenses were $114,000. The company determines its net income by subtracting operating expenses from gross profit. Thus, net income is $30,000, as shown below.

Illustration 5-11
Operating expenses in computing net income

Gross profit	$144,000
Operating expenses	**114,000**
Net income	$ 30,000

The net income amount is the so-called "bottom line" of a company's income statement.

Ethics Note

Companies manage earnings in various ways. ConAgra Foods recorded a nonrecurring gain for $186 million from the sale of Pilgrim's Pride stock to help meet an earnings projection for the quarter.

NONOPERATING ACTIVITIES

Nonoperating activities consist of various revenues and expenses and gains and losses that are unrelated to the company's main line of operations. When nonoperating items are included, the label "**Income from operations**" (or "Operating income") precedes them. This label clearly identifies the results of the company's normal operations, an amount determined by subtracting cost of goods sold and operating expenses from net sales. The results of nonoperating activities are shown in the categories "**Other revenues and gains**" and "**Other expenses and losses.**" Illustration 5-12 lists examples of each.

Illustration 5-12
Other items of nonoperating activities

Other Revenues and Gains

Interest revenue from notes receivable and marketable securities.

Dividend revenue from investments in common stock.

Rent revenue from subleasing a portion of the store.

Gain from the sale of property, plant, and equipment.

Other Expenses and Losses

Interest expense on notes and loans payable.

Casualty losses from recurring causes, such as vandalism and accidents.

Loss from the sale or abandonment of property, plant, and equipment.

Loss from strikes by employees and suppliers.

Merchandising companies report the nonoperating activities in the income statement immediately after the company's operating activities. Illustration 5-13 shows these sections for PW Audio Supply, Inc., using assumed data.

The distinction between operating and nonoperating activities is crucial to many external users of financial data. These users view operating income as sustainable and many nonoperating activities as nonrecurring. Therefore, when forecasting next year's income, analysts put the most weight on this year's operating income, and less weight on this year's nonoperating activities.

ETHICS INSIGHT

Disclosing More Details

After Enron, increased investor criticism and regulator scrutiny forced many companies to improve the clarity of their financial disclosures. For example, IBM announced that it would begin providing more detail regarding its "Other gains and losses." It had previously included these items in its selling, general, and administrative expenses, with little disclosure.

Disclosing other gains and losses in a separate line item on the income statement will not have any effect on bottom-line income. However, analysts complained that burying these details in the selling, general, and administrative expense line reduced their ability to fully understand how well IBM was performing. For example previously if IBM sold off one of its buildings at a gain, it would include this gain in the selling, general and administrative expense line item, thus reducing that expense. This made it appear that the company had done a better job of controlling operating expenses than it actually had.

Other companies that also recently announced changes to increase the informativeness of their income statements include PepsiCo and General Electric.

? Why have investors and analysts demanded more accuracy in isolating "Other gains and losses" from operating items? (See page 267.)

PW Audio Supply, Inc.
Income Statement
For the Year Ended December 31, 2014

Illustration 5-13
Multiple-step income statement

Calculation of gross profit

Sales revenues		
Sales revenue		$480,000
Less: Sales returns and allowances	$12,000	
Sales discounts	8,000	20,000
Net sales		460,000
Cost of goods sold		316,000
Gross profit		144,000

Calculation of income from operations

Operating expenses		
Salaries and wages expense	64,000	
Utilities expense	17,000	
Advertising expense	16,000	
Depreciation expense	8,000	
Freight-out	7,000	
Insurance expense	2,000	
Total operating expenses		114,000
Income from operations		30,000
Other revenues and gains		
Interest revenue	3,000	
Gain on disposal of plant assets	600	3,600

Results of nonoperating activities

Other expenses and losses		
Interest expense	1,800	
Casualty loss from vandalism	200	2,000
Net income		$ 31,600

Single-Step Income Statement

Another income statement format is the **single-step income statement**. The statement is so named because only one step—subtracting total expenses from total revenues—is required in determining net income.

In a single-step statement, all data are classified into two categories: (1) **revenues**, which include both operating revenues and other revenues and gains; and (2) **expenses**, which include cost of goods sold, operating expenses, and other expenses and losses. Illustration 5-14 shows a single-step statement for PW Audio Supply.

Illustration 5-14
Single-step income statement

PW Audio Supply, Inc. Income Statement For the Year Ended December 31, 2014		
Revenues		
Net sales		$460,000
Interest revenue		3,000
Gain on disposal of plant assets		600
Total revenues		463,600
Expenses		
Cost of goods sold	$316,000	
Operating expenses	114,000	
Interest expense	1,800	
Casualty loss from vandalism	200	
Total expenses		432,000
Net income		$ 31,600

There are two primary reasons for using the single-step format: (1) A company does not realize any type of profit or income until total revenues exceed total expenses, so it makes sense to divide the statement into these two categories. (2) The format is simpler and easier to read. *For homework problems, however, you should use the single-step format only when specifically instructed to do so.*

Classified Balance Sheet

In the balance sheet, merchandising companies report inventory as a current asset immediately below accounts receivable. Recall from Chapter 4 that companies generally list current asset items in the order of their closeness to cash (liquidity). Inventory is less close to cash than accounts receivable because the goods must first be sold and then collection made from the customer. Illustration 5-15 presents the assets section of a classified balance sheet for PW Audio Supply.

Illustration 5-15
Assets section of a classified balance sheet

Helpful Hint
The $40,000 is the cost of the inventory on hand, not its expected selling price.

PW Audio Supply, Inc. Balance Sheet (Partial) December 31, 2014		
Assets		
Current assets		
Cash		$ 9,500
Accounts receivable		16,100
Inventory		40,000
Prepaid insurance		1,800
Total current assets		67,400
Property, plant, and equipment		
Equipment	$80,000	
Less: Accumulated depreciation—equipment	24,000	56,000
Total assets		$123,400

> DO IT!

Financial Statement Classifications

You are presented with the following list of accounts from the adjusted trial balance for merchandiser Gorman Company. Indicate in which financial statement and under what classification each of the following would be reported.

Accounts Payable
Accounts Receivable
Accumulated Depreciation—Buildings
Accumulated Depreciation—Equipment
Advertising Expense
Buildings
Cash
Common Stock
Depreciation Expense
Dividends
Equipment
Freight-Out
Gain on Disposal of Plant Assets

Insurance Expense
Interest Expense
Interest Payable
Inventory
Land
Notes Payable (due in 3 years)
Property Taxes Payable
Salaries and Wages Expense
Salaries and Wages Payable
Sales Returns and Allowances
Sales Revenue
Utilities Expense

Solution

Action Plan

✔ Review the major sections of the income statement, sales revenues, cost of goods sold, operating expenses, other revenues and gains, and other expenses and losses.

✔ Add net income to beginning retained earnings and deduct dividends to arrive at ending retained earnings in the retained earnings statement.

✔ Review the major sections of the balance sheet, income statement, and retained earnings statement.

Account	Financial Statement	Classification
Accounts Payable	Balance sheet	Current liabilities
Accounts Receivable	Balance sheet	Current assets
Accumulated Depreciation— Buildings	Balance sheet	Property, plant, and equipment
Accumulated Depreciation— Equipment	Balance sheet	Property, plant, and equipment
Advertising Expense	Income statement	Operating expenses
Buildings	Balance sheet	Property, plant, and equipment
Cash	Balance sheet	Current assets
Common Stock	Balance sheet	Stockholders' equity
Depreciation Expense	Income statement	Operating expenses
Dividends	Retained earnings statement	Deduction section
Equipment	Balance sheet	Property, plant, and equipment
Freight-Out	Income statement	Operating expenses
Gain on Disposal of Plant Assets	Income statement	Other revenues and gains
Insurance Expense	Income statement	Operating expenses
Interest Expense	Income statement	Other expenses and losses
Interest Payable	Balance sheet	Current liabilities
Inventory	Balance sheet	Current assets
Land	Balance sheet	Property, plant, and equipment
Notes Payable	Balance sheet	Long-term liabilities
Property Taxes Payable	Balance sheet	Current liabilities
Salaries and Wages Expense	Income statement	Operating expenses
Salaries and Wages Payable	Balance sheet	Current liabilities
Sales Returns and Allowances	Income statement	Sales revenues
Sales Revenue	Income statement	Sales revenues
Utilities Expense	Income statement	Operating expenses

Related exercise material: **BE5-7, BE5-8, BE5-9, E5-9, E5-10, E5-12, E5-13, E5-14, and** DO IT! **5-4.**

 ✔ **The Navigator**

The adjusted trial balance columns of Falcetto Company's worksheet for the year ended December 31, 2014, are as follows.

Debit		**Credit**	
Cash	14,500	Accumulated Depreciation—	18,000
Accounts Receivable	11,100	Equipment	
Inventory	29,000	Notes Payable	25,000
Prepaid Insurance	2,500	Accounts Payable	10,600
Equipment	95,000	Common Stock	50,000
Dividends	12,000	Retained Earnings	31,000
Sales Returns and Allowances	6,700	Sales Revenue	536,800
Sales Discounts	5,000	Interest Revenue	2,500
Cost of Goods Sold	363,400		673,900
Freight-Out	7,600		
Advertising Expense	12,000		
Salaries and Wages Expense	56,000		
Utilities Expense	18,000		
Rent Expense	24,000		
Depreciation Expense	9,000		
Insurance Expense	4,500		
Interest Expense	3,600		
	673,900		

Instructions
Prepare a multiple-step income statement for Falcetto Company.

Solution to Comprehensive **DO IT!**

Action Plan

✔ Remember that the key components of the income statement are net sales, cost of goods sold, gross profit, total operating expenses, and net income (loss). Report these components in the right-hand column of the income statement.

✔ Put nonoperating items after income from operations.

Falcetto Company
Income Statement
For the Year Ended December 31, 2014

Sales revenues		
Sales revenue		$536,800
Less: Sales returns and allowances	$ 6,700	
Sales discounts	5,000	11,700
Net sales		525,100
Cost of goods sold		363,400
Gross profit		161,700
Operating expenses		
Salaries and wages expense	56,000	
Rent expense	24,000	
Utilities expense	18,000	
Advertising expense	12,000	
Depreciation expense	9,000	
Freight-out	7,600	
Insurance expense	4,500	
Total operating expenses		131,100
Income from operations		30,600
Other revenues and gains		
Interest revenue	2,500	
Other expenses and losses		
Interest expense	3,600	1,100
Net income		$ 29,500

SUMMARY OF LEARNING OBJECTIVES

✔ The Navigator

1 **Identify the differences between service and merchandising companies.** Because of inventory, a merchandising company has sales revenue, cost of goods sold, and gross profit. To account for inventory, a merchandising company must choose between a perpetual and a periodic inventory system.

2 **Explain the recording of purchases under a perpetual inventory system.** The company debits the Inventory account for all purchases of merchandise and freight-in, and credits it for purchase discounts and purchase returns and allowances.

3 **Explain the recording of sales revenues under a perpetual inventory system.** When a merchandising company sells inventory, it debits Accounts Receivable (or Cash), and credits Sales Revenue for the **selling price** of the merchandise. At the same time, it debits Cost of

Goods Sold, and credits Inventory for the cost of the inventory items sold. Sales returns and allowances and sales discounts are debited.

4 **Explain the steps in the accounting cycle for a merchandising company.** Each of the required steps in the accounting cycle for a service company applies to a merchandising company. A worksheet is again an optional step. Under a perpetual inventory system, the company must adjust the Inventory account to agree with the physical count.

5 **Distinguish between a multiple-step and a single-step income statement.** A multiple-step income statement shows numerous steps in determining net income, including nonoperating activities sections. A single-step income statement classifies all data under two categories, revenues or expenses, and determines net income in one step.

GLOSSARY

Contra-revenue account An account that is offset against a revenue account on the income statement. (p. 229).

Cost of goods sold The total cost of merchandise sold during the period. (p. 220).

FOB destination Freight terms indicating that the seller places the goods free on board to the buyer's place of business, and the seller pays the freight. (p. 224).

FOB shipping point Freight terms indicating that the seller places goods free on board the carrier, and the buyer pays the freight costs. (p. 224).

Gross profit The excess of net sales over the cost of goods sold. (p. 235).

Gross profit rate Gross profit expressed as a percentage, by dividing the amount of gross profit by net sales. (p. 235).

Income from operations Income from a company's principal operating activity; determined by subtracting cost of goods sold and operating expenses from net sales. (p. 236).

Multiple-step income statement An income statement that shows several steps in determining net income. (p. 234).

Net sales Sales less sales returns and allowances and less sales discounts. (p. 234).

Nonoperating activities Various revenues, expenses, gains, and losses that are unrelated to a company's main line of operations. (p. 236).

Operating expenses Expenses incurred in the process of earning sales revenues. (p. 235).

Other expenses and losses A nonoperating-activities section of the income statement that shows expenses and losses unrelated to the company's main line of operations. (p. 236).

Other revenues and gains A nonoperating-activities section of the income statement that shows revenues and gains unrelated to the company's main line of operations. (p. 236).

Periodic inventory system An inventory system under which the company does not keep detailed inventory records throughout the accounting period but determines the cost of goods sold only at the end of an accounting period. (p. 221).

Perpetual inventory system An inventory system under which the company keeps detailed records of the cost of each inventory purchase and sale, and the records continuously show the inventory that should be on hand. (p. 221).

Purchase allowance A deduction made to the selling price of merchandise, granted by the seller so that the buyer will keep the merchandise. (p. 225).

Purchase discount A cash discount claimed by a buyer for prompt payment of a balance due. (p. 226).

Purchase invoice A document that supports each credit purchase. (p. 223).

Purchase return A return of goods from the buyer to the seller for a cash or credit refund. (p. 225).

Sales discount A reduction given by a seller for prompt payment of a credit sale. (p. 230).

Sales invoice A document that supports each credit sale. (p. 227).

Sales returns and allowances Purchase returns and allowances from the seller's perspective. See *Purchase return* and *Purchase allowance*, above. (p. 229).

Sales revenue (Sales) The primary source of revenue in a merchandising company. (p. 220).

Single-step income statement An income statement that shows only one step in determining net income. (p. 237).

APPENDIX 5A PERIODIC INVENTORY SYSTEM

As described in this chapter, companies may use one of two basic systems of accounting for inventories: (1) the perpetual inventory system or (2) the periodic inventory system. In the chapter, we focused on the characteristics of the perpetual inventory system. In this appendix, we discuss and illustrate the **periodic inventory system**. One key difference between the two systems is the point at which the company computes cost of goods sold. For a visual reminder of this difference, refer back to Illustration 5-4 (page 222).

Determining Cost of Goods Sold Under a Periodic System

Determining cost of goods sold is different when a periodic inventory system is used rather than a perpetual system. As you have seen, a company using a **perpetual system** makes an entry to record cost of goods sold and to reduce inventory *each time a sale is made*. A company using a **periodic system** does not determine cost of goods sold *until the end of the period*. At the end of the period the company performs a count to determine the ending balance of inventory. It then **calculates cost of goods sold by subtracting ending inventory from the goods available for sale**. Goods available for sale is the sum of beginning inventory plus purchases, as shown in Illustration 5A-1.

Illustration 5A-1
Basic formula for cost of goods sold using the periodic system

$$
\begin{array}{l}
 \text{Beginning Inventory} \\
+\ \underline{\text{Cost of Goods Purchased}} \\
 \text{Cost of Goods Available for Sale} \\
-\ \underline{\text{Ending Inventory}} \\
 \text{Cost of Goods Sold}
\end{array}
$$

Another difference between the two approaches is that the perpetual system directly adjusts the Inventory account for any transaction that affects inventory (such as freight costs, returns, and discounts). The periodic system does not do this. Instead, it creates different accounts for purchases, freight costs, returns, and discounts. These various accounts are shown in Illustration 5A-2, which presents the calculation of cost of goods sold for PW Audio Supply using the periodic approach.

Illustration 5A-2
Cost of goods sold for a merchandiser using a periodic inventory system

PW Audio Supply, Inc. Cost of Goods Sold For the Year Ended December 31, 2014			
Cost of goods sold			
Inventory, January 1			$ 36,000
Purchases		$325,000	
Less: Purchase returns and allowances	$10,400		
Purchase discounts	6,800	17,200	
Net purchases		307,800	
Add: Freight-in		12,200	
Cost of goods purchased			320,000
Cost of goods available for sale			356,000
Inventory, December 31			40,000
Cost of goods sold			**$316,000**

Helpful Hint
The far right column identifies the primary items that make up cost of goods sold of $316,000. The middle column explains cost of goods purchased of $320,000. The left column reports contra purchase items of $17,200.

Note that the basic elements from Illustration 5A-1 are highlighted in Illustration 5A-2. You will learn more in Chapter 6 about how to determine cost of goods sold using the periodic system.

The use of the periodic inventory system does not affect the form of presentation in the balance sheet. As under the perpetual system, a company reports inventory in the current assets section.

Recording Merchandise Transactions

In a **periodic inventory system**, companies record revenues from the sale of merchandise when sales are made, just as in a perpetual system. Unlike the perpetual system, however, companies **do not attempt on the date of sale to record the cost of the merchandise sold**. Instead, they take a physical inventory count at the **end of the period** to determine (1) the cost of the merchandise then on hand and (2) the cost of the goods sold during the period. And, **under a periodic system, companies record purchases of merchandise in the Purchases account rather than the Inventory account**. Also, in a periodic system, purchase returns and allowances, purchase discounts, and freight costs on purchases are recorded in separate accounts.

To illustrate the recording of merchandise transactions under a periodic inventory system, we will use purchase/sale transactions between PW Audio Supply, Inc. and Sauk Stereo, as illustrated for the perpetual inventory system in this chapter.

Recording Purchases of Merchandise

On the basis of the sales invoice (Illustration 5-5, shown on page 224) and receipt of the merchandise ordered from PW Audio Supply, Sauk Stereo records the $3,800 purchase as follows.

May 4	Purchases	3,800	
	Accounts Payable		3,800
	(To record goods purchased on account from PW Audio Supply)		

Helpful Hint
Be careful not to debit purchases of equipment or supplies to a Purchases account.

Purchases is a temporary account whose normal balance is a debit.

FREIGHT COSTS

When the purchaser directly incurs the freight costs, it debits the account Freight-In (or Transportation-In). For example, if Sauk Stereo pays Acme Freight Company $150 for freight charges on its purchase from PW Audio Supply on May 6, the entry on Sauk Stereo's books is:

May 6	Freight-In (Transportation-In)	150	
	Cash		150
	(To record payment of freight on goods purchased)		

Like Purchases, Freight-In is a temporary account whose normal balance is a debit. **Freight-In is part of cost of goods purchased.** The reason is that cost of goods purchased should include any freight charges necessary to bring the goods to the purchaser. Freight costs are not subject to a purchase discount. Purchase discounts apply only to the invoice cost of the merchandise.

Alternative Terminology
Freight-in is also called *transportation-in*.

PURCHASE RETURNS AND ALLOWANCES

Sauk Stereo returns $300 of goods to PW Audio Supply and prepares the following entry to recognize the return.

May 8	Accounts Payable	300	
	Purchase Returns and Allowances		300
	(To record return of goods purchased		
	from PW Audio Supply)		

Purchase Returns and Allowances is a temporary account whose normal balance is a credit.

PURCHASE DISCOUNTS

On May 14, Sauk Stereo pays the balance due on account to PW Audio Supply, taking the 2% cash discount allowed by PW Audio Supply for payment within 10 days. Sauk Stereo records the payment and discount as follows.

May 14	Accounts Payable ($3,800 − $300)	3,500	
	Purchase Discounts ($3,500 × .02)		70
	Cash		3,430
	(To record payment within		
	the discount period)		

Purchase Discounts is a temporary account whose normal balance is a credit.

Recording Sales of Merchandise

The seller, PW Audio Supply, records the sale of $3,800 of merchandise to Sauk Stereo on May 4 (sales invoice No. 731, Illustration 5-5, page 224) as follows.

May 4	Accounts Receivable	3,800	
	Sales Revenue		3,800
	(To record credit sales per invoice #731		
	to Sauk Stereo)		

SALES RETURNS AND ALLOWANCES

To record the returned goods received from Sauk Stereo on May 8, PW Audio Supply records the $300 sales return as follows.

May 8	Sales Returns and Allowances	300	
	Accounts Receivable		300
	(To record credit granted to Sauk		
	Stereo for returned goods)		

SALES DISCOUNTS

On May 14, PW Audio Supply receives payment of $3,430 on account from Sauk Stereo. PW Audio Supply honors the 2% cash discount and records the payment of Sauk Stereo's account receivable in full as follows.

May 14	Cash	3,430	
	Sales Discounts ($3,500 × .02)	70	
	Accounts Receivable ($3,800 − $300)		3,500
	(To record collection within 2/10, n/30		
	discount period from Sauk Stereo)		

COMPARISON OF ENTRIES—PERPETUAL VS. PERIODIC

Illustration 5A-3 summarizes the periodic inventory entries shown in this appendix and compares them to the perpetual-system entries from the chapter. Entries that differ in the two systems are shown in color.

	Entries on Sauk Stereo's Books				
Transaction	**Perpetual Inventory System**			**Periodic Inventory System**	

May 4 Purchase of merchandise on credit.	Inventory
	    Accounts Payable
		3,800	3,800	Purchases
				    Accounts Payable
					3,800
					    3,800

6 Freight costs on purchases.	Inventory
	    Cash
		150	150	Freight-In
				    Cash
					150
					    150

8 Purchase returns and allowances.	Accounts Payable
	    Inventory
		300	300	Accounts Payable
				    Purchase Returns
				    and Allowances
					300
					
					    300

14 Payment on account with a discount.	Accounts Payable
	    Cash
	    Inventory
		3,500	3,430
			70
				Accounts Payable
				    Cash
				    Purchase Discounts
					3,500
					    3,430
					    70

	Entries on PW Audio Supply's Books				
Transaction	**Perpetual Inventory System**			**Periodic Inventory System**	

May 4 Sale of merchandise on credit.	Accounts Receivable
	    Sales Revenue
		3,800	3,800	Accounts Receivable
				    Sales Revenue
					3,800
					    3,800

	Cost of Goods Sold
	    Inventory
		2,400	2,400	No entry for cost of
				    goods sold	

8 Return of merchandise sold.	Sales Returns and
	Allowances
	    Accounts Receivable
		300	300	Sales Returns and
				Allowances
				    Accounts Receivable
					300
					    300

	Inventory Cost of Goods Sold	140	140	No entry	

14 Cash received on account with a discount.	Cash
	Sales Discounts
	    Accounts Receivable
		3,430
		70
			3,500	Cash
				Sales Discounts
				    Accounts Receivable
					3,430
					70
					    3,500

Illustration 5A-3
Comparison of entries for perpetual and periodic inventory systems

SUMMARY OF LEARNING OBJECTIVE FOR APPENDIX 5A

6 **Explain the recording of purchases and sales of inventory under a periodic inventory system.** In recording purchases under a periodic system, companies must make entries for (a) cash and credit purchases, (b) purchase returns and allowances, (c) purchase discounts, and (d) freight costs. In recording sales, companies must make entries for (a) cash and credit sales, (b) sales returns and allowances, and (c) sales discounts.

APPENDIX 5B WORKSHEET FOR A MERCHANDISING COMPANY

Using a Worksheet

As indicated in Chapter 4, a worksheet enables companies to prepare financial statements before they journalize and post adjusting entries. The steps in preparing a worksheet for a merchandising company are the same as for a service company (see pages 164–167). Illustration 5B-1 (page 246) shows the worksheet for PW Audio Supply (excluding nonoperating items). The unique accounts for a merchandiser using a perpetual inventory system are in boldface letters and in red.

LEARNING OBJECTIVE 7

Prepare a worksheet for a merchandising company.

| | | | | | PW Audio Supply.xls | | | | | | |

	A	B	C	D	E	F	G	H	I	J	K
1											
2					**PW Audio Supply, Inc.**						
3					**Worksheet**						
4					**For the Year Ended December 31, 2014**						
5		Trial Balance		Adjustments		Adjusted Trial Balance		Income Statement		Balance Sheet	
6											
7	Accounts	Dr.	Cr.	Dr.	Cr.	Dr.	Cr.	Dr.	Cr.	Dr.	Cr.
8	Cash	9,500				9,500				9,500	
9	Accounts Receivable	16,100				16,100				16,100	
10	**Inventory**	**40,500**			(a) 500	40,000				40,000	
11	Prepaid Insurance	3,800			(b) 2,000	1,800				1,800	
12	Equipment	80,000				80,000				80,000	
13	Accumulated Depreciation—Equipment		16,000		(c) 8,000		24,000				24,000
14	Accounts Payable		20,400				20,400				20,400
15	Common Stock		50,000				50,000				50,000
16	Retained Earnings		33,000				33,000				33,000
17	Dividends	15,000				15,000				15,000	
18	**Sales Revenue**		480,000				480,000		480,000		
19	**Sales Returns and** Allowances	**12,000**				12,000		12,000			
20	**Sales Discounts**	**8,000**				8,000		8,000			
21	**Cost of Goods Sold**	**315,500**		(a) 500		316,000		316,000			
22	Freight-Out	7,000				7,000		7,000			
23	Advertising Expense	16,000				16,000		16,000			
24	Salaries and Wages Expense	59,000		(d) 5,000		64,000		64,000			
25	Utilities Expense	17,000				17,000		17,000			
26	Totals	599,400	599,400								
27	Insurance Expense			(b) 2,000		2,000		2,000			
28	Depreciation Expense			(c) 8,000		8,000		8,000			
29	Salaries and Wages Payable				(d) 5,000		5,000				5,000
30	Totals			15,500	15,500	612,400	612,400	450,000	480,000	162,400	132,400
31	Net Income							30,000			30,000
32	Totals							480,000	480,000	162,400	162,400
33											

Key: (a) Adjustment to inventory on hand. (b) Insurance expired. (c) Depreciation expense. (d) Salaries accrued.

Illustration 5B-1
Worksheet for merchandising company

TRIAL BALANCE COLUMNS
Data for the trial balance come from the ledger balances of PW Audio Supply at December 31. The amount shown for Inventory, $40,500, is the year-end inventory amount from the perpetual inventory system.

ADJUSTMENTS COLUMNS
A merchandising company generally has the same types of adjustments as a service company. As you see in the worksheet, adjustments (b), (c), and (d) are for insurance, depreciation, and salaries. Pioneer Advertising Agency Inc. as illustrated in Chapters 3 and 4, also had these adjustments. Adjustment (a) was required to adjust the perpetual inventory carrying amount to the actual count.

After PW Audio Supply enters all adjustments data on the worksheet, it establishes the equality of the adjustments column totals. It then extends the balances in all accounts to the adjusted trial balance columns.

ADJUSTED TRIAL BALANCE

The adjusted trial balance shows the balance of all accounts after adjustment at the end of the accounting period.

INCOME STATEMENT COLUMNS

Next, the merchandising company transfers the accounts and balances that affect the income statement from the adjusted trial balance columns to the income statement columns. PW Audio Supply shows sales of $480,000 in the credit column. It shows the contra-revenue accounts Sales Returns and Allowances $12,000 and Sales Discounts $8,000 in the debit column. The difference of $460,000 is the net sales shown on the income statement (Illustration 5-13, page 237).

Finally, the company totals all the credits in the income statement column and compares those totals to the total of the debits in the income statement column. If the credits exceed the debits, the company has net income. PW Audio Supply has net income of $30,000. If the debits exceed the credits, the company would report a net loss.

BALANCE SHEET COLUMNS

The major difference between the balance sheets of a service company and a merchandiser is inventory. PW Audio Supply shows the ending inventory amount of $40,000 in the balance sheet debit column. The information to prepare the retained earnings statement is also found in these columns. That is, the retained earnings beginning balance is $33,000. The dividends are $15,000. Net income results when the total of the debit column exceeds the total of the credit column in the balance sheet columns. A net loss results when the total of the credits exceeds the total of the debit balances.

SUMMARY OF LEARNING OBJECTIVE FOR APPENDIX 5B

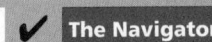 ✔ The Navigator

7 Prepare a worksheet for a merchandising company. The steps in preparing a worksheet for a merchandising company are the same as for a service company.

The unique accounts for a merchandiser are Inventory, Sales Revenue, Sales Returns and Allowances, Sales Discounts, and Cost of Goods Sold.

 WILEY PLUS

Self-Test, Brief Exercises, Exercises, Problem Set A, and many more components are available for practice in WileyPLUS.

Note: All asterisked Questions, Exercises, and Problems relate to material in the appendix to the chapter.

SELF-TEST QUESTIONS

Answers are on page 267.

(LO 1) **1.** Gross profit will result if:
   (a) operating expenses are less than net income.
   (b) sales revenues are greater than operating expenses.
   (c) sales revenues are greater than cost of goods sold.
   (d) operating expenses are greater than cost of goods sold.

2. Under a perpetual inventory system, when goods are (LO 2) purchased for resale by a company:
   (a) purchases on account are debited to Inventory.
   (b) purchases on account are debited to Purchases.
   (c) purchase returns are debited to Purchase Returns and Allowances.
   (d) freight costs are debited to Freight-Out.

(LO 3) **3.** The sales accounts that normally have a debit balance are:
  (a) Sales Discounts.
  (b) Sales Returns and Allowances.
  (c) Both (a) and (b).
  (d) Neither (a) nor (b).

(LO 3) **4.** A credit sale of $750 is made on June 13, terms 2/10, net/30. A return of $50 is granted on June 16. The amount received as payment in full on June 23 is:
  (a) $700.   (c) $685.
  (b) $686.   (d) $650.

(LO 2) **5.** Which of the following accounts will normally appear in the ledger of a merchandising company that uses a perpetual inventory system?
  (a) Purchases.   (c) Cost of Goods Sold.
  (b) Freight-In.   (d) Purchase Discounts.

(LO 3) **6.** To record the sale of goods for cash in a perpetual inventory system:
  (a) only one journal entry is necessary to record cost of goods sold and reduction of inventory.
  (b) only one journal entry is necessary to record the receipt of cash and the sales revenue.
  (c) two journal entries are necessary: one to record the receipt of cash and sales revenue, and one to record the cost of goods sold and reduction of inventory.
  (d) two journal entries are necessary: one to record the receipt of cash and reduction of inventory, and one to record the cost of goods sold and sales revenue.

(LO 4) **7.** The steps in the accounting cycle for a merchandising company are the same as those in a service company *except*:
  (a) an additional adjusting journal entry for inventory may be needed in a merchandising company.
  (b) closing journal entries are not required for a merchandising company.
  (c) a post-closing trial balance is not required for a merchandising company.
  (d) a multiple-step income statement is required for a merchandising company.

(LO 5) **8.** The multiple-step income statement for a merchandising company shows each of the following features *except*:
  (a) gross profit.
  (b) cost of goods sold.
  (c) a sales revenue section.
  (d) investing activities section.

9. If sales revenues are $400,000, cost of goods sold is (LO 5) $310,000, and operating expenses are $60,000, the gross profit is:
  (a) $30,000.   (c) $340,000.
  (b) $90,000.   (d) $400,000.

10. A single-step income statement: (LO 5)
  (a) reports gross profit.
  (b) does not report cost of goods sold.
  (c) reports sales revenues and "Other revenues and gains" in the revenues section of the income statement.
  (d) reports operating income separately.

11. Which of the following appears on both a single-step (LO 5) and a multiple-step income statement?
  (a) inventory.
  (b) gross profit.
  (c) income from operations.
  (d) cost of goods sold.

*12. In determining cost of goods sold: (LO 6)
  (a) purchase discounts are deducted from net purchases.
  (b) freight-out is added to net purchases.
  (c) purchase returns and allowances are deducted from net purchases.
  (d) freight-in is added to net purchases.

*13. If beginning inventory is $60,000, cost of goods (LO 6) purchased is $380,000, and ending inventory is $50,000, cost of goods sold is:
  (a) $390,000.   (c) $330,000.
  (b) $370,000.   (d) $420,000.

*14. When goods are purchased for resale by a company (LO 6) using a periodic inventory system:
  (a) purchases on account are debited to Inventory.
  (b) purchases on account are debited to Purchases.
  (c) purchase returns are debited to Purchase Returns and Allowances.
  (d) freight costs are debited to Purchases.

*15. In a worksheet, Inventory is shown in the following (LO 7) columns:
  (a) Adjusted trial balance debit and balance sheet debit.
  (b) Income statement debit and balance sheet debit.
  (c) Income statement credit and balance sheet debit.
  (d) Income statement credit and adjusted trial balance debit.

Go to the book's companion website, www.wiley.com/college/weygandt, for additional Self-Test Questions.

 **The Navigator**

QUESTIONS

1. (a) "The steps in the accounting cycle for a merchandising company are different from the accounting cycle for a service company." Do you agree or disagree? (b) Is the measurement of net income for a merchandising company conceptually the same as for a service company? Explain.

2. Why is the normal operating cycle for a merchandising company likely to be longer than for a service company?

3. (a) How do the components of revenues and expenses differ between merchandising and service companies? (b) Explain the income measurement process in a merchandising company.

4. How does income measurement differ between a merchandising and a service company?

5. When is cost of goods sold determined in a perpetual inventory system?

6. Distinguish between FOB shipping point and FOB destination. Identify the freight terms that will result in a debit to Inventory by the buyer and a debit to Freight-Out by the seller.

7. Explain the meaning of the credit terms 2/10, n/30.

8. Goods costing $2,500 are purchased on account on July 15 with credit terms of 2/10, n/30. On July 18, a $200 credit memo is received from the supplier for damaged goods. Give the journal entry on July 24 to record payment of the balance due within the discount period using a perpetual inventory system.

9. Karen Lloyd believes revenues from credit sales may be earned before they are collected in cash. Do you agree? Explain.

10. (a) What is the primary source document for recording (1) cash sales, (2) credit sales. (b) Using XXs for amounts, give the journal entry for each of the transactions in part (a).

11. A credit sale is made on July 10 for $700, terms 2/10, n/30. On July 12, $100 of goods are returned for credit. Give the journal entry on July 19 to record the receipt of the balance due within the discount period.

12. Explain why the Inventory account will usually require adjustment at year-end.

13. Prepare the closing entries for the Sales Revenue account, assuming a balance of $180,000 and the Cost of Goods Sold account with a $125,000 balance.

14. What merchandising account(s) will appear in the post-closing trial balance?

15. Regis Co. has sales revenue of $109,000, cost of goods sold of $70,000, and operating expenses of $23,000. What is its gross profit and its gross profit rate?

16. Kathy Ho Company reports net sales of $800,000, gross profit of $570,000, and net income of $240,000. What are its operating expenses?

17. Identify the distinguishing features of an income statement for a merchandising company.

18. Identify the sections of a multiple-step income statement that relate to (a) operating activities, and (b) nonoperating activities.

19. How does the single-step form of income statement differ from the multiple-step form?

20. ⊛ **PEPSICO** Determine PepsiCo's gross profit rate for 2010 and 2009. Indicate whether it increased or decreased from 2009 to 2010.

*21. Identify the accounts that are added to or deducted from Purchases to determine the cost of goods purchased. For each account, indicate whether it is added or deducted.

*22. Goods costing $2,000 are purchased on account on July 15 with credit terms of 2/10, n/30. On July 18, a $200 credit was received from the supplier for damaged goods. Give the journal entry on July 24 to record payment of the balance due within the discount period, assuming a periodic inventory system.

*23. Indicate the columns of the worksheet in which (a) inventory and (b) cost of goods sold will be shown.

BRIEF EXERCISES

BE5-1 Presented below are the components in Clearwater Company's income statement. Determine the missing amounts.

Compute missing amounts in determining net income.

(LO 1)

	Sales Revenue	Cost of Goods Sold	Gross Profit	Operating Expenses	Net Income
(a)	$75,000	?	$30,000	?	$10,800
(b)	$108,000	$55,000	?	?	$29,500
(c)	?	$83,900	$79,600	$39,500	?

BE5-2 Giovanni Company buys merchandise on account from Gordon Company. The selling price of the goods is $780, and the cost of the goods is $560. Both companies use perpetual inventory systems. Journalize the transaction on the books of both companies.

Journalize perpetual inventory entries.

(LO 2, 3)

BE5-3 Prepare the journal entries to record the following transactions on Benson Company's books using a perpetual inventory system.
(a) On March 2, Benson Company sold $800,000 of merchandise to Edgebrook Company, terms 2/10, n/30. The cost of the merchandise sold was $620,000.
(b) On March 6, Edgebrook Company returned $120,000 of the merchandise purchased on March 2. The cost of the returned merchandise was $90,000.
(c) On March 12, Benson Company received the balance due from Edgebrook Company.

Journalize sales transactions.

(LO 3)

BE5-4 From the information in BE5-3, prepare the journal entries to record these transactions on Edgebrook Company's books under a perpetual inventory system.

Journalize purchase transactions.

(LO 2)

BE5-5 At year-end, the perpetual inventory records of Salsa Company showed merchandise inventory of $98,000. The company determined, however, that its actual inventory on hand was $94,600. Record the necessary adjusting entry.

Prepare adjusting entry for merchandise inventory.

(LO 4)

BE5-6 Orlaida Company has the following merchandise account balances: Sales Revenue $192,000, Sales Discounts $2,000, Cost of Goods Sold $105,000, and Inventory $40,000. Prepare the entries to record the closing of these items to Income Summary.

Prepare closing entries for merchandise accounts.

(LO 4)

Prepare sales revenues section of income statement.

(LO 5)

BE5-7 Piccola Company provides the following information for the month ended October 31, 2014: sales on credit $280,000, cash sales $100,000, sales discounts $5,000, sales returns and allowances $18,000. Prepare the sales revenues section of the income statement based on this information.

Contrast presentation in multiple-step and single-step income statements.

(LO 5)

BE5-8 ▭▭▭▻ Explain where each of the following items would appear on (1) a multiple-step income statement, and on (2) a single-step income statement: (a) gain on sale of equipment, (b) interest expense, (c) casualty loss from vandalism, and (d) cost of goods sold.

Compute net sales, gross profit, income from operations, and gross profit rate.

(LO 5)

BE5-9 Assume Jose Company has the following reported amounts: Sales revenue $506,000, Sales returns and allowances $13,000, Cost of goods sold $330,000, Operating expenses $110,000. Compute the following: (a) net sales, (b) gross profit, (c) income from operations, and (d) gross profit rate. (Round to one decimal place.)

Compute net purchases and cost of goods purchased.

(LO 6)

*BE5-10** Assume that Guardian Company uses a periodic inventory system and has these account balances: Purchases $430,000; Purchase Returns and Allowances $13,000; Purchase Discounts $8,000; and Freight-In $16,000. Determine net purchases and cost of goods purchased.

Compute cost of goods sold and gross profit.

(LO 6)

*BE5-11** Assume the same information as in BE5-10 and also that Guardian Company has beginning inventory of $60,000, ending inventory of $90,000, and net sales of $680,000. Determine the amounts to be reported for cost of goods sold and gross profit.

Journalize purchase transactions.

(LO 6)

*BE5-12** Prepare the journal entries to record these transactions on Huntington Company's books using a periodic inventory system.
(a) On March 2, Huntington Company purchased $900,000 of merchandise from Saunder Company, terms 2/10, n/30.
(b) On March 6, Huntington Company returned $184,000 of the merchandise purchased on March 2.
(c) On March 12, Huntington Company paid the balance due to Saunder Company.

Identify worksheet columns for selected accounts.

(LO 7)

*BE5-13** Presented below is the format of the worksheet presented in the chapter.

Trial Balance		Adjustments		Adjusted Trial Balance		Income Statement		Balance Sheet	
Dr.	Cr.	Dr.	Cr.	Dr.	Cr.	Dr.	Cr.	Dr.	Cr.

Indicate where the following items will appear on the worksheet: (a) Cash, (b) Inventory, (c) Sales revenue, and (d) Cost of goods sold.

Example:
Cash: Trial balance debit column; Adjusted trial balance debit column; and Balance sheet debit column.

> DO IT! REVIEW

Record transactions of purchasing company.

(LO 2)

DO IT! **5-1** On October 5, Gibson Company buys merchandise on account from Quincy Company. The selling price of the goods is $4,700, and the cost to Quincy Company is $3,100. On October 8, Gibson returns defective goods with a selling price of $650 and a fair value of $160. Record the transactions on the books of Gibson Company.

Record transactions of selling company.

(LO 3)

DO IT! **5-2** Assume information similar to that in **DO IT!** **5-1**. That is: On October 5, Gibson Company buys merchandise on account from Quincy Company. The selling price of the goods is $4,700, and the cost to Quincy Company is $3,100. On October 8, Gibson returns defective goods with a selling price of $650 and a fair value of $160. Record the transactions on the books of Quincy Company.

Prepare closing entries for a merchandising company.

(LO 4)

DO IT! **5-3** The trial balance of Optique's Boutique at December 31 shows Inventory $21,000, Sales Revenue $156,000, Sales Returns and Allowances $4,000, Sales Discounts $3,000, Cost of Goods Sold $92,400, Interest Revenue $3,000, Freight-Out $1,900, Utilities Expense $7,400, and Salaries and Wages Expense $19,500. Prepare the closing entries for Optique.

DO IT! 5-4 Dorothea Company is preparing its multiple-step income statement, retained earnings statement, and classified balance sheet. Using the column heads *Account, Financial Statement*, and *Classification*, indicate in which financial statement and under what classification each of the following would be reported.

Classify financial statement accounts.

(LO 5)

Account	**Financial Statement**	**Classification**
Accounts Payable		
Accounts Receivable		
Accumulated Depreciation— Buildings		
Cash		
Casualty Loss from Vandalism		
Common Stock		
Cost of Goods Sold		
Depreciation Expense		
Dividends		
Equipment		
Freight-Out		
Insurance Expense		
Interest Payable		
Inventory		
Land		
Notes Payable (due in 5 years)		
Property Taxes Payable		
Salaries and Wages Expense		
Salaries and Wages Payable		
Sales Returns and Allowances		
Sales Revenue		
Unearned Rent Revenue		
Utilities Expense		

 The Navigator

EXERCISES

E5-1 Mr. Soukup has prepared the following list of statements about service companies and merchandisers.

Answer general questions about merchandisers.

(LO 1)

1. Measuring net income for a merchandiser is conceptually the same as for a service company.
2. For a merchandiser, sales less operating expenses is called gross profit.
3. For a merchandiser, the primary source of revenues is the sale of inventory.
4. Sales salaries and wages is an example of an operating expense.
5. The operating cycle of a merchandiser is the same as that of a service company.
6. In a perpetual inventory system, no detailed inventory records of goods on hand are maintained.
7. In a periodic inventory system, the cost of goods sold is determined only at the end of the accounting period.
8. A periodic inventory system provides better control over inventories than a perpetual system.

Instructions

Identify each statement as true or false. If false, indicate how to correct the statement.

E5-2 Information related to Duffy Co. is presented below.

Journalize purchases transactions.

(LO 2)

1. On April 5, purchased merchandise from Thomas Company for $25,000, terms 2/10, net/30, FOB shipping point.
2. On April 6, paid freight costs of $900 on merchandise purchased from Thomas.
3. On April 7, purchased equipment on account for $26,000.

4. On April 8, returned damaged merchandise to Thomas Company and was granted a $2,600 credit for returned merchandise.
5. On April 15, paid the amount due to Thomas Company in full.

Instructions
(a) Prepare the journal entries to record these transactions on the books of Duffy Co. under a perpetual inventory system.
(b) Assume that Duffy Co. paid the balance due to Thomas Company on May 4 instead of April 15. Prepare the journal entry to record this payment.

Journalize perpetual inventory entries.

(LO 2, 3)

E5-3 On September 1, Roshek Office Supply had an inventory of 30 calculators at a cost of $22 each. The company uses a perpetual inventory system. During September, the following transactions occurred.

Sept. 6   Purchased 90 calculators at $20 each from Harlow Co., terms 2/10, n/30.
     9   Paid freight of $180 on calculators purchased from Harlow Co.
   10   Returned 3 calculators to Harlow Co. for $66 credit (including freight) because they did not meet specifications.
   12   Sold 26 calculators costing $22 (including freight) for $33 each to Village Book Store, terms n/30.
   14   Granted credit of $33 to Village Book Store for the return of one calculator that was not ordered.
   20   Sold 40 calculators costing $22 for $32 each to Dixie Card Shop, terms n/30.

Instructions
Journalize the September transactions.

Prepare purchase and sale entries.

(LO 2, 3)

E5-4 On June 10, Rebecca Company purchased $7,600 of merchandise from Clinton Company, FOB shipping point, terms 2/10, n/30. Rebecca pays the freight costs of $400 on June 11. Damaged goods totaling $300 are returned to Clinton for credit on June 12. The fair value of these goods is $70. On June 19, Rebecca pays Clinton Company in full, less the purchase discount. Both companies use a perpetual inventory system.

Instructions
(a) Prepare separate entries for each transaction on the books of Rebecca Company.
(b) Prepare separate entries for each transaction for Clinton Company. The merchandise purchased by Rebecca on June 10 had cost Clinton $4,300.

Journalize sales transactions.

(LO 3)

E5-5 Presented below are transactions related to Yarrow Company.

1. On December 3, Yarrow Company sold $570,000 of merchandise to Lampkins Co., terms 1/10, n/30, FOB shipping point. The cost of the merchandise sold was $364,800.
2. On December 8, Lampkins Co. was granted an allowance of $20,000 for merchandise purchased on December 3.
3. On December 13, Yarrow Company received the balance due from Lampkins Co.

Instructions
(a) Prepare the journal entries to record these transactions on the books of Yarrow Company using a perpetual inventory system.
(b) Assume that Yarrow Company received the balance due from Lampkins Co. on January 2 of the following year instead of December 13. Prepare the journal entry to record the receipt of payment on January 2.

Prepare sales revenues section and closing entries.

(LO 4, 5)

E5-6 The adjusted trial balance of Mendoza Company shows the following data pertaining to sales at the end of its fiscal year October 31, 2014: Sales Revenue $820,000, Freight-Out $16,000, Sales Returns and Allowances $28,000, and Sales Discounts $13,000.

Instructions
(a) Prepare the sales revenues section of the income statement.
(b) Prepare separate closing entries for (1) sales, and (2) the contra accounts to sales.

Prepare adjusting and closing entries.

(LO 4)

E5-7 Twix Company had the following account balances at year-end: Cost of Goods Sold $60,000; Inventory $15,000; Operating Expenses $29,000; Sales Revenue $115,000; Sales Discounts $1,300; and Sales Returns and Allowances $1,700. A physical count of inventory determines that merchandise inventory on hand is $13,600.

Instructions
(a) Prepare the adjusting entry necessary as a result of the physical count.
(b) Prepare closing entries.

E5-8 Presented below is information related to Taylor Co. for the month of January 2014.

Prepare adjusting and closing entries.

(LO 4)

Ending inventory per		Insurance expense	$ 12,000
perpetual records	$ 21,600	Rent expense	20,000
Ending inventory actually		Salaries and wages expense	59,000
on hand	21,000	Sales discounts	8,000
Cost of goods sold	208,000	Sales returns and allowances	13,000
Freight-out	7,000	Sales revenue	378,000

Instructions
(a) Prepare the necessary adjusting entry for inventory.
(b) Prepare the necessary closing entries.

E5-9 Presented below is information for Bach Company for the month of March 2014.

Prepare multiple-step income statement.

(LO 5)

Cost of goods sold	$212,000	Rent expense	$ 32,000
Freight-out	9,000	Sales discounts	6,600
Insurance expense	6,000	Sales returns and allowances	13,000
Salaries and wages expense	58,000	Sales revenue	380,000

Instructions
(a) Prepare a multiple-step income statement.
(b) Compute the gross profit rate.

E5-10 In its income statement for the year ended December 31, 2014, Michael Company reported the following condensed data.

Prepare multiple-step and single-step income statements.

(LO 5)

Operating expenses	$ 725,000	Interest revenue	$ 33,000
Cost of goods sold	1,256,000	Loss on disposal of plant assets	17,000
Interest expense	70,000	Net sales	2,200,000

Instructions
(a) Prepare a multiple-step income statement.
(b) Prepare a single-step income statement.

E5-11 An inexperienced accountant for Gulliver Company made the following errors in recording merchandising transactions.

Prepare correcting entries for sales and purchases.

(LO 2, 3)

1. A $175 refund to a customer for faulty merchandise was debited to Sales Revenue $175 and credited to Cash $175.
2. A $150 credit purchase of supplies was debited to Inventory $150 and credited to Cash $150.
3. A $215 sales discount was debited to Sales Revenue.
4. A cash payment of $20 for freight on merchandise purchases was debited to Freight-Out $200 and credited to Cash $200.

Instructions
Prepare separate correcting entries for each error, assuming that the incorrect entry is not reversed. (Omit explanations.)

E5-12 In 2014, Endeaver Company had net sales of $860,000 and cost of goods sold of $533,200. Operating expenses were $221,000, and interest expense was $7,000. Endeaver prepares a multiple-step income statement.

Compute various income measures.

(LO 5)

Instructions
(a) Compute Endeaver's gross profit.
(b) Compute the gross profit rate. Why is this rate computed by financial statement users?
(c) What is Endeaver's income from operations and net income?
(d) If Endeaver prepared a single-step income statement, what amount would it report for net income?
(e) In what section of its classified balance sheet should Endeaver report merchandise inventory?

E5-13 Presented below is financial information for two different companies.

Compute missing amounts and compute gross profit rate.

(LO 5)

	Lee Company	Chan Company
Sales revenue	$90,000	(d)
Sales returns	(a)	$ 5,000
Net sales	81,000	98,000
Cost of goods sold	56,000	(e)
Gross profit	(b)	37,500
Operating expenses	12,000	(f)
Net income	(c)	15,000

Instructions

(a) Determine the missing amounts.

(b) Determine the gross profit rates. (Round to one decimal place.)

Compute missing amounts.

(LO 5)

E5-14 Financial information is presented below for three different companies.

	Athena Cosmetics	Harry Grocery	Panama Wholesalers
Sales revenue	$90,000	$ (e)	$122,000
Sales returns and allowances	(a)	5,000	12,000
Net sales	86,000	95,000	(i)
Cost of goods sold	56,000	(f)	(j)
Gross profit	(b)	22,000	24,000
Operating expenses	15,000	(g)	18,000
Income from operations	(c)	(h)	(k)
Other expenses and losses	4,000	3,000	(l)
Net income	(d)	11,000	5,000

Instructions

Determine the missing amounts.

Prepare cost of goods sold section.

(LO 6)

*E5-15 The trial balance of Roman Company at the end of its fiscal year, August 31, 2014, includes these accounts: Inventory $17,200; Purchases $149,000; Sales Revenue $190,000; Freight-In $5,000; Sales Returns and Allowances $3,000; Freight-Out $1,000; and Purchase Returns and Allowances $6,000. The ending inventory is $14,000.

Instructions

Prepare a cost of goods sold section for the year ending August 31 (periodic inventory).

Compute various income statement items.

(LO 6)

*E5-16 On January 1, 2014, Clover Corporation had inventory of $50,000. At December 31, 2014, Clover had the following account balances.

Freight-in	$ 4,000
Purchases	509,000
Purchase discounts	6,000
Purchase returns and allowances	8,000
Sales revenue	840,000
Sales discounts	7,000
Sales returns and allowances	11,000

At December 31, 2014, Clover determines that its ending inventory is $60,000.

Instructions

(a) Compute Clover's 2014 gross profit.

(b) Compute Clover's 2014 operating expenses if net income is $130,000 and there are no nonoperating activities.

Prepare cost of goods sold section.

(LO 6)

*E5-17 Below is a series of cost of goods sold sections for companies Alpha, Beta, Chi, and Decca.

	Alpha	Beta	Chi	Decca
Beginning inventory	$ 150	$ 70	$1,000	$ (j)
Purchases	1,620	1,060	(g)	43,590
Purchase returns and allowances	40	(d)	290	(k)
Net purchases	(a)	1,030	6,210	41,090
Freight-in	95	(e)	(h)	2,240
Cost of goods purchased	(b)	1,280	7,940	(l)
Cost of goods available for sale	1,825	1,350	(i)	49,530
Ending inventory	310	(f)	1,450	6,230
Cost of goods sold	(c)	1,260	7,490	43,300

Instructions

Fill in the lettered blanks to complete the cost of goods sold sections.

Journalize purchase transactions.

(LO 6)

*E5-18 This information relates to Olaf Co.

1. On April 5, purchased merchandise from DeVito Company for $18,000, terms 2/10, net/30, FOB shipping point.

2. On April 6, paid freight costs of $820 on merchandise purchased from DeVito Company.

3. On April 7, purchased equipment on account for $30,000.

4. On April 8, returned some of April 5 merchandise, which cost $2,800, to DeVito Company.
5. On April 15, paid the amount due to DeVito Company in full.

Instructions

(a) Prepare the journal entries to record these transactions on the books of Olaf Co. using a periodic inventory system.
(b) Assume that Olaf Co. paid the balance due to DeVito Company on May 4 instead of April 15. Prepare the journal entry to record this payment.

E5-19 Presented below is information related to Chile Co.

Journalize purchase transactions.

(LO 6)

1. On April 5, purchased merchandise from Graham Company for $16,000, terms 2/10, net/30, FOB shipping point.
2. On April 6, paid freight costs of $800 on merchandise purchased from Graham.
3. On April 7, purchased equipment on account from Reed Mfg. Co. for $27,000.
4. On April 8, returned merchandise, which cost $4,000, to Graham Company.
5. On April 15, paid the amount due to Graham Company in full.

Instructions

(a) Prepare the journal entries to record these transactions on the books of Chile Co. using a periodic inventory system.
(b) Assume that Chile Co. paid the balance due to Graham Company on May 4 instead of April 15. Prepare the journal entry to record this payment.

E5-20 Presented below are selected accounts for Higley Company as reported in the worksheet at the end of May 2014.

Complete worksheet.

(LO 7)

Accounts	Adjusted Trial Balance		Income Statement		Balance Sheet	
	Dr.	Cr.	Dr.	Cr.	Dr.	Cr.
Cash	9,000					
Inventory	76,000					
Sales Revenue		460,000				
Sales Returns and Allowances	10,000					
Sales Discounts	9,000					
Cost of Goods Sold	288,000					

Instructions

Complete the worksheet by extending amounts reported in the adjusted trial balance to the appropriate columns in the worksheet. Do not total individual columns.

E5-21 The trial balance columns of the worksheet for Adelle Company at June 30, 2014, are as follows.

Prepare a worksheet.

(LO 7)

Adelle Company
Worksheet
For the Month Ended June 30, 2014

Account Titles	Trial Balance	
	Debit	Credit
Cash	$ 2,120	
Accounts Receivable	2,440	
Inventory	11,640	
Accounts Payable		$ 1,120
Common Stock		4,000
Sales Revenue		42,500
Cost of Goods Sold	20,560	
Operating Expenses	10,860	
	$47,620	$47,620

Other data:
Operating expenses incurred on account, but not yet recorded, total $1,500.

Instructions

Enter the trial balance on a worksheet and complete the worksheet.

EXERCISES: SET B AND CHALLENGE EXERCISES

Visit the book's companion website, at **www.wiley.com/college/weygandt**, and choose the Student Companion site to access Exercise Set B and Challenge Exercises.

PROBLEMS: SET A

Journalize purchase and sales transactions under a perpetual inventory system.

(LO 2, 3)

P5-1A Ready-Set-Go Co. distributes suitcases to retail stores and extends credit terms of 1/10, n/30 to all of its customers. At the end of June, Ready-Set-Go's inventory consisted of suitcases costing $1,200. During the month of July, the following merchandising transactions occurred.

July 1 Purchased suitcases on account for $1,500 from Trunk Manufacturers, FOB destination, terms 2/10, n/30. The appropriate party also made a cash payment of $100 for freight on this date.

3 Sold suitcases on account to Satchel World for $2,200. The cost of suitcases sold is $1,400.

9 Paid Trunk Manufacturers in full.

12 Received payment in full from Satchel World.

17 Sold suitcases on account to Lady GoGo for $1,400. The cost of the suitcases sold was $1,010.

18 Purchased suitcases on account for $1,900 from Holiday Manufacturers, FOB shipping point, terms 1/10, n/30. The appropriate party also made a cash payment of $125 for freight on this date.

20 Received $300 credit (including freight) for suitcases returned to Holiday Manufacturers.

21 Received payment in full from Lady GoGo.

22 Sold suitcases on account to Vagabond for $2,250. The cost of suitcases sold was $1,350.

30 Paid Holiday Manufacturers in full.

31 Granted Vagabond $200 credit for suitcases returned costing $120.

Ready-Set-Go's chart of accounts includes the following: No. 101 Cash, No. 112 Accounts Receivable, No. 120 Inventory, No. 201 Accounts Payable, No. 401 Sales Revenue, No. 412 Sales Returns and Allowances, No. 414 Sales Discounts, and No. 505 Cost of Goods Sold.

Instructions

Journalize the transactions for the month of July for Ready-Set-Go using a perpetual inventory system.

Journalize, post, and prepare a partial income statement.

(LO 2, 3, 5)

P5-2A Shmi Distributing Company completed the following merchandising transactions in the month of April. At the beginning of April, the ledger of Shmi showed Cash of $8,000 and Common Stock of $8,000.

Apr. 2 Purchased merchandise on account from Walker Supply Co. $6,200, terms 1/10, n/30.

4 Sold merchandise on account $5,500, FOB destination, terms 1/10, n/30. The cost of the merchandise sold was $3,400.

5 Paid $240 freight on April 4 sale.

6 Received credit from Walker Supply Co. for merchandise returned $500.

11 Paid Walker Supply Co. in full, less discount.

13 Received collections in full, less discounts, from customers billed on April 4.

14 Purchased merchandise for cash $3,800.

16 Received refund from supplier for returned goods on cash purchase of April 14, $500.

18 Purchased merchandise from Benjamin Distributors $4,500, FOB shipping point, terms 2/10, n/30.

20 Paid freight on April 18 purchase $160.

23 Sold merchandise for cash $7,400. The merchandise sold had a cost of $4,120.

Apr. 26 Purchased merchandise for cash $2,300.
    27 Paid Benjamin Distributors in full, less discount.
    29 Made refunds to cash customers for defective merchandise $90. The returned merchandise had a fair value of $30.
    30 Sold merchandise on account $3,400, terms n/30. The cost of the merchandise sold was $1,900.

Shmi Distributing Company's chart of accounts includes the following: No. 101 Cash, No. 112 Accounts Receivable, No. 120 Inventory, No. 201 Accounts Payable, No. 311 Common Stock, No. 401 Sales Revenue, No. 412 Sales Returns and Allowances, No. 414 Sales Discounts, No. 505 Cost of Goods Sold, and No. 644 Freight-Out.

Instructions
(a) Journalize the transactions using a perpetual inventory system.
(b) Enter the beginning cash and capital balances, and post the transactions. (Use J1 for the journal reference.)
(c) Prepare the income statement through gross profit for the month of April 2014.

(c) Gross profit $6,765

Prepare financial statements and adjusting and closing entries.

(LO 4, 5)

P5-3A Starz Department Store is located near the Towne Shopping Mall. At the end of the company's calendar year on December 31, 2014, the following accounts appeared in two of its trial balances.

	Unadjusted	Adjusted		Unadjusted	Adjusted
Accounts Payable	$ 79,300	$ 80,300	Interest Revenue	$ 4,000	$ 4,000
Accounts Receivable	50,300	50,300	Inventory	75,000	75,000
Accumulated Depr.—Buildings	42,100	52,500	Mortgage Payable	80,000	80,000
Accumulated Depr.—Equipment	29,600	42,900	Prepaid Insurance	9,600	2,400
Buildings	290,000	290,000	Property Tax Expense		4,800
Cash	23,800	23,800	Property Taxes Payable		4,800
Common Stock	112,000	112,000	Retained Earnings	64,600	64,600
Cost of Goods Sold	412,700	412,700	Salaries and Wages Expense	108,000	108,000
Depreciation Expense		23,700	Sales Commissions Expense	10,200	14,500
Dividends	24,000	24,000	Sales Commissions Payable		4,300
Equipment	110,000	110,000	Sales Returns and Allowances	8,000	8,000
Insurance Expense		7,200	Sales Revenue	724,000	724,000
Interest Expense	3,000	8,600	Utilities Expense	11,000	12,000
Interest Payable		5,600			

Instructions
(a) Prepare a multiple-step income statement, a retained earnings statement, and a classified balance sheet. $16,000 of the mortgage payable is due for payment next year.
(b) Journalize the adjusting entries that were made.
(c) Journalize the closing entries that are necessary.

(a) Net income $128,500
Retained earnings $169,100
Total assets $456,100

Journalize, post, and prepare a trial balance.

(LO 2, 3, 4)

P5-4A J. Ackbar, a former professional tennis star, operates Ackbar's Tennis Shop at the Miller Lake Resort. At the beginning of the current season, the ledger of Ackbar's Tennis Shop showed Cash $2,200, Inventory $1,800, and Common Stock $4,000. The following transactions were completed during April.

Apr. 4 Purchased racquets and balls from Jay-Mac Co. $760, FOB shipping point, terms 2/10, n/30.
    6 Paid freight on purchase from Jay-Mac Co. $40.
    8 Sold merchandise to members $1,150, terms n/30. The merchandise sold had a cost of $790.
    10 Received credit of $60 from Jay-Mac Co. for a racquet that was returned.
    11 Purchased tennis shoes from Venus Sports for cash, $420.
    13 Paid Jay-Mac Co. in full.
    14 Purchased tennis shirts and shorts from Everett Sportswear $800, FOB shipping point, terms 3/10, n/60.
    15 Received cash refund of $50 from Venus Sports for damaged merchandise that was returned.
    17 Paid freight on Everett Sportswear purchase $30.
    18 Sold merchandise to members $980, terms n/30. The cost of the merchandise sold was $520.

Apr. 20 Received $600 in cash from members in settlement of their accounts.
　　　 21 Paid Everett Sportswear in full.
　　　 27 Granted an allowance of $40 to members for tennis clothing that did not fit properly.
　　　 30 Received cash payments on account from members, $820.

The chart of accounts for the tennis shop includes the following: No. 101 Cash, No. 112 Accounts Receivable, No. 120 Inventory, No. 201 Accounts Payable, No. 311 Common Stock, No. 401 Sales Revenue, No. 412 Sales Returns and Allowances, and No. 505 Cost of Goods Sold.

Instructions
(a) Journalize the April transactions using a perpetual inventory system.
(b) Enter the beginning balances in the ledger accounts and post the April transactions. (Use J1 for the journal reference.)
(c) Prepare a trial balance on April 30, 2014.

(c) Total debits $6,130

Determine cost of goods sold and gross profit under periodic approach.

(LO 6)

*P5-5A At the end of Apex Department Store's fiscal year on December 31, 2014, these accounts appeared in its adjusted trial balance.

Freight-In	$ 5,600
Inventory	40,500
Purchases	442,000
Purchase Discounts	12,000
Purchase Returns and Allowances	6,400
Sales Revenue	718,000
Sales Returns and Allowances	18,000

Additional facts:

1. Merchandise inventory on December 31, 2014, is $65,000.
2. Apex Department Store uses a periodic system.

Instructions

Gross profit $295,300

Prepare an income statement through gross profit for the year ended December 31, 2014.

Calculate missing amounts and assess profitability.

(LO 6)

*P5-6A Valerie Fons operates a retail clothing operation. She purchases all merchandise inventory on credit and uses a periodic inventory system. The Accounts Payable account is used for recording inventory purchases only; all other current liabilities are accrued in separate accounts. You are provided with the following selected information for the fiscal years 2011–2014.

	2011	**2012**	**2013**	**2014**
Inventory (ending)	$13,000	$ 11,300	$ 14,700	$ 12,200
Accounts payable (ending)	20,000			
Sales revenue		225,700	240,300	235,000
Purchases of merchandise				
inventory on account		141,000	150,000	132,000
Cash payments to suppliers		135,000	161,000	127,000

Instructions

(a) 2013 $146,600

(a) Calculate cost of goods sold for each of the 2012, 2013, and 2014 fiscal years.
(b) Calculate the gross profit for each of the 2012, 2013, and 2014 fiscal years.

(c) 2013 Ending accts payable $16,000

(c) Calculate the ending balance of accounts payable for each of the 2012, 2013, and 2014 fiscal years.
(d) Sales declined in fiscal 2014. Does that mean that profitability, as measured by the gross profit rate, necessarily also declined? Explain, calculating the gross profit rate for each fiscal year to help support your answer. (Round to one decimal place.)

Journalize, post, and prepare trial balance and partial income statement using periodic approach.

(LO 6)

GLS

*P5-7A At the beginning of the current season, the ledger of Village Tennis Shop showed Cash $2,500; Inventory $1,700; and Common Stock $4,200. The following transactions were completed during April.

Apr. 4 Purchased racquets and balls from Lowell Co. $860, terms 3/10, n/30.
　　　 6 Paid freight on Lowell Co. purchase $74.
　　　 8 Sold merchandise to members $900, terms n/30.
　　　 10 Received credit of $60 from Lowell Co. for a racquet that was returned.

Apr. 11 Purchased tennis shoes from Volker Sports for cash $300.
     13 Paid Lowell Co. in full.
     14 Purchased tennis shirts and shorts from Linzey Sportswear $700, terms 2/10, n/60.
     15 Received cash refund of $50 from Volker Sports for damaged merchandise that was returned.
     17 Paid freight on Linzey Sportswear purchase $30.
     18 Sold merchandise to members $1,200, terms n/30.
     20 Received $500 in cash from members in settlement of their accounts.
     21 Paid Linzey Sportswear in full.
     27 Granted an allowance of $25 to members for tennis clothing that did not fit properly.
     30 Received cash payments on account from members $620.

The chart of accounts for the tennis shop includes Cash, Accounts Receivable, Inventory, Accounts Payable, Common Stock, Sales Revenue, Sales Returns and Allowances, Purchases, Purchase Returns and Allowances, Purchase Discounts, and Freight-In.

Instructions
(a) Journalize the April transactions using a periodic inventory system.
(b) Using T-accounts, enter the beginning balances in the ledger accounts and post the April transactions.
(c) Prepare a trial balance on April 30, 2014.
(d) Prepare an income statement through gross profit, assuming inventory on hand at April 30 is $2,296.

(c) Tot. trial balance $6,448
(d) Gross profit $855

*P5-8A The trial balance of Mr. Rosiak Fashion Center contained the following accounts at November 30, the end of the company's fiscal year.

Complete accounting cycle beginning with a worksheet.

(LO 4, 5, 7)

Mr. Rosiak Fashion Center
Trial Balance
November 30, 2014

	Debit	Credit
Cash	$ 8,700	
Accounts Receivable	27,700	
Inventory	44,700	
Supplies	6,200	
Equipment	133,000	
Accumulated Depreciation—Equipment		$ 23,000
Notes Payable		51,000
Accounts Payable		48,500
Common Stock		50,000
Retained Earnings		38,000
Dividends	8,000	
Sales Revenue		755,200
Sales Returns and Allowances	12,800	
Cost of Goods Sold	497,400	
Salaries and Wages Expense	136,000	
Advertising Expense	24,400	
Utilities Expense	14,000	
Maintenance and Repairs Expense	12,100	
Freight-Out	16,700	
Rent Expense	24,000	
Totals	$965,700	$965,700

Adjustment data:

1. Supplies on hand totaled $2,100.
2. Depreciation is $11,500 on the equipment.
3. Interest of $4,000 is accrued on notes payable at November 30.
4. Inventory actually on hand is $44,520.

(a) Adj. trial balance
$981,200
Net loss $1,980
(b) Gross profit $244,820
Total assets $181,520

Instructions

(a) Enter the trial balance on a worksheet, and complete the worksheet.
(b) Prepare a multiple-step income statement and a retained earnings statement for the year, and a classified balance sheet as of November 30, 2014. Notes payable of $6,000 are due in January 2015.
(c) Journalize the adjusting entries.
(d) Journalize the closing entries.
(e) Prepare a post-closing trial balance.

PROBLEMS: SET B

Journalize purchase and sales transactions under a perpetual inventory system.

(LO 2, 3)

P5-1B Book Nook Warehouse distributes hardcover books to retail stores and extends credit terms of 2/10, n/30 to all of its customers. At the end of May, Book Nook's inventory consisted of books purchased for $1,800. During June, the following merchandising transactions occurred.

June 1 Purchased books on account for $1,850 from Phantom Publishers, FOB destination, terms 2/10, n/30. The appropriate party also made a cash payment of $50 for the freight on this date.

3 Sold books on account to Ex Libris for $2,500. The cost of the books sold was $1,440.

6 Received $150 credit for books returned to Phantom Publishers.

9 Paid Phantom Publishers in full, less discount.

15 Received payment in full from Ex Libris.

17 Sold books on account to Bargain Books for $1,800. The cost of the books sold was $1,020.

20 Purchased books on account for $1,500 from Bookem Publishers, FOB destination, terms 2/15, n/30. The appropriate party also made a cash payment of $50 for the freight on this date.

24 Received payment in full from Bargain Books.

26 Paid Bookem Publishers in full, less discount.

28 Sold books on account to Corner Bookstore for $1,300. The cost of the books sold was $850.

30 Granted Corner Bookstore $120 credit for books returned costing $72.

Book Nook Warehouse's chart of accounts includes the following: No. 101 Cash, No. 112 Accounts Receivable, No. 120 Inventory, No. 201 Accounts Payable, No. 401 Sales Revenue, No. 412 Sales Returns and Allowances, No. 414 Sales Discounts, and No. 505 Cost of Goods Sold.

Instructions

Journalize the transactions for the month of June for Book Nook Warehouse using a perpetual inventory system.

Journalize, post, and prepare a partial income statement.

(LO 2, 3, 5)

P5-2B Copple Hardware Store completed the following merchandising transactions in the month of May. At the beginning of May, the ledger of Copple showed Cash of $5,000 and Common Stock of $5,000.

May 1 Purchased merchandise on account from Nute's Wholesale Supply $4,200, terms 2/10, n/30.

2 Sold merchandise on account $2,300, terms 1/10, n/30. The cost of the merchandise sold was $1,300.

5 Received credit from Nute's Wholesale Supply for merchandise returned $500.

9 Received collections in full, less discounts, from customers billed on sales of $2,300 on May 2.

10 Paid Nute's Wholesale Supply in full, less discount.

11 Purchased supplies for cash $400.

12 Purchased merchandise for cash $1,400.

15 Received refund for poor quality merchandise from supplier on cash purchase $150.

17 Purchased merchandise from Sherrick Distributors $1,300, FOB shipping point, terms 2/10, n/30.

May 19 Paid freight on May 17 purchase $130.

24 Sold merchandise for cash $3,200. The merchandise sold had a cost of $2,000.

25 Purchased merchandise from Herbert, Inc. $620, FOB destination, terms 2/10, n/30.

27 Paid Sherrick Distributors in full, less discount.

29 Made refunds to cash customers for defective merchandise $90. The returned merchandise had a fair value of $40.

31 Sold merchandise on account $1,000 terms n/30. The cost of the merchandise sold was $560.

Copple Hardware's chart of accounts includes the following: No. 101 Cash, No. 112 Accounts Receivable, No. 120 Inventory, No. 126 Supplies, No. 201 Accounts Payable, No. 311 Common Stock, No. 401 Sales Revenue, No. 412 Sales Returns and Allowances, No. 414 Sales Discounts, and No. 505 Cost of Goods Sold.

Instructions

(a) Journalize the transactions using a perpetual inventory system.

(b) Enter the beginning cash and common stock balances and post the transactions. (Use J1 for the journal reference.)

(c) Prepare an income statement through gross profit for the month of May 2014.

(c) Gross profit $2,567

P5-3B The Moulton Store is located in midtown Metropolis. During the past several years, net income has been declining because of suburban shopping centers. At the end of the company's fiscal year on November 30, 2014, the following accounts appeared in two of its trial balances.

Prepare financial statements and adjusting and closing entries.

(LO 4, 5)

	Unadjusted	Adjusted		Unadjusted	Adjusted
Accounts Payable	$ 25,200	$ 25,200	Notes Payable	$ 37,000	$ 37,000
Accounts Receivable	30,500	30,500	Prepaid Insurance	10,500	3,500
Accumulated Depr.—Equip.	22,000	33,000	Property Tax Expense		3,500
Cash	26,000	26,000	Property Taxes Payable		3,500
Common Stock	50,000	50,000	Rent Expense	15,000	15,000
Cost of Goods Sold	507,000	507,000	Retained Earnings	61,700	61,700
Depreciation Expense		11,000	Salaries and Wages Expense	96,000	96,000
Dividends	8,000	8,000	Sales Commissions Expense	6,500	13,500
Equipment	154,300	154,300	Sales Commissions Payable		7,000
Freight-Out	6,500	6,500	Sales Returns and Allowances	9,000	9,000
Insurance Expense		7,000	Sales Revenue	706,000	706,000
Interest Expense	6,100	6,100	Utilities Expense	8,500	8,500
Interest Revenue	8,000	8,000			
Inventory	26,000	26,000			

Instructions

(a) Prepare a multiple-step income statement, a retained earnings statement, and a classified balance sheet. Notes payable are due in 2017.

(b) Journalize the adjusting entries that were made.

(c) Journalize the closing entries that are necessary.

(a) Net income $30,900
  Retained earnings $84,600
  Total assets $207,300

P5-4B Bill Kokott, a former disc golf star, operates Bill's Discorama. At the beginning of the current season on April 1, the ledger of Bill's Discorama showed Cash $1,850, Inventory $2,150, and Common Stock $4,000. The following transactions were completed during April.

Journalize, post, and prepare a trial balance.

(LO 2, 3, 4)

Apr. 5 Purchased golf discs, bags, and other inventory on account from Ellis Co. $1,200, FOB shipping point, terms 2/10, n/60.

7 Paid freight on the Ellis purchase $75.

9 Received credit from Ellis Co. for merchandise returned $100.

10 Sold merchandise on account for $930, terms n/30. The merchandise sold had a cost of $540.

12 Purchased disc golf shirts and other accessories on account from Penguin Sportswear $720, terms 1/10, n/30.

14 Paid Ellis Co. in full, less discount.

17 Received credit from Penguin Sportswear for merchandise returned $120.

20 Made sales on account for $610, terms n/30. The cost of the merchandise sold was $370.

Apr. 21   Paid Penguin Sportswear in full, less discount.
    27   Granted an allowance to members for clothing that was flawed $20.
    30   Received payments on account from customers $960.

The chart of accounts for the store includes the following: No. 101 Cash, No. 112 Accounts Receivable, No. 120 Inventory, No. 201 Accounts Payable, No. 311 Common Stock, No. 401 Sales Revenue, No. 412 Sales Returns and Allowances, and No. 505 Cost of Goods Sold.

Instructions

(a) Journalize the April transactions using a perpetual inventory system.
(b) Enter the beginning balances in the ledger accounts and post the April transactions. (Use J1 for the journal reference.)

(c) Total debits $5,540

(c) Prepare a trial balance on April 30, 2014.

Determine cost of goods sold and gross profit under periodic approach.

(LO 6)

*P5-5B At the end of Stampfer Department Store's fiscal year on November 30, 2014, these accounts appeared in its adjusted trial balance.

Freight-In	$ 7,500
Inventory	40,000
Purchases	585,000
Purchase Discounts	5,300
Purchase Returns and Allowances	2,900
Sales Revenue	1,000,000
Sales Returns and Allowances	28,000

Additional facts:

1. Merchandise inventory on November 30, 2014, is $54,600.
2. Stampfer Department Store uses a periodic system.

Instructions

Gross profit $402,300

Prepare an income statement through gross profit for the year ended November 30, 2014.

Calculate missing amounts and assess profitability.

(LO 6)

*P5-6B Psang Inc. operates a retail operation that purchases and sells home entertainment products. The company purchases all merchandise inventory on credit and uses a periodic inventory system. The Accounts Payable account is used for recording inventory purchases only; all other current liabilities are accrued in separate accounts. You are provided with the following selected information for the fiscal years 2011 through 2014, inclusive.

	2011	2012	2013	2014
Income Statement Data				
Sales revenue		$53,000	$ (e)	$46,000
Cost of goods sold		(a)	13,800	14,300
Gross profit		38,300	35,200	(i)
Operating expenses		35,900	(f)	28,600
Net income		$ (b)	$ 2,500	$ (j)
Balance Sheet Data				
Inventory	$7,200	$ (c)	$ 8,100	$ (k)
Accounts payable	3,200	3,400	2,500	(l)
Additional Information				
Purchases of merchandise inventory on account		$14,200	$ (g)	$13,200
Cash payments to suppliers		(d)	(h)	13,600

(c) $6,700
(g) $15,200
(i) $31,700

Instructions

(a) Calculate the missing amounts.
(b) Sales declined over the 3-year fiscal period, 2012–2014. Does that mean that profitability necessarily also declined? Explain, computing the gross profit rate and the profit margin ratio for each fiscal year to help support your answer. (Round to one decimal place.)

Journalize, post, and prepare trial balance and partial income statement using periodic approach.

(LO 6)

GLS

*P5-7B At the beginning of the current season on April 1, the ledger of Tri-State Pro Shop showed Cash $3,000; Inventory $4,000; and Common Stock $7,000. These transactions occurred during April 2014.

Apr. 5 Purchased golf bags, clubs, and balls on account from Balata Co. $1,300, FOB ship-
          ping point, terms 2/10, n/60.
      7 Paid freight on Balata Co. purchases $70.
      9 Received credit from Balata Co. for merchandise returned $100.
     10 Sold merchandise on account to members $670, terms n/30.
     12 Purchased golf shoes, sweaters, and other accessories on account from Arrow Sports-
          wear $450, terms 1/10, n/30.
     14 Paid Balata Co. in full.
     17 Received credit from Arrow Sportswear for merchandise returned $50.
     20 Made sales on account to members $600, terms n/30.
     21 Paid Arrow Sportswear in full.
     27 Granted credit to members for clothing that had flaws $55.
     30 Received payments on account from members $630.

The chart of accounts for the pro shop includes Cash, Accounts Receivable, Inventory,
Accounts Payable, Common Stock, Sales Revenue, Sales Returns and Allowances, Purchases, Purchase Returns and Allowances, Purchase Discounts, and Freight-In.

Instructions
(a) Journalize the April transactions using a periodic inventory system.
(b) Using T-accounts, enter the beginning balances in the ledger accounts and post the
     April transactions.
(c) Prepare a trial balance on April 30, 2014.
(d) Prepare an income statement through gross profit, assuming merchandise inventory
     on hand at April 30 is $4,824.

(c) Tot. trial balance $8,448
Gross profit $397

PROBLEMS: SET C

Visit the book's companion website, at **www.wiley.com/college/weygandt**, and choose
the Student Companion site to access Problem Set C.

COMPREHENSIVE PROBLEM

CP5 On December 1, 2014, Jurczyk Distributing Company had the following account
balances.

	Debits		**Credits**
Cash	$ 7,200	Accumulated Depreciation—	
Accounts Receivable	4,600	Equipment	$ 2,200
Inventory	12,000	Accounts Payable	4,500
Supplies	1,200	Salaries and Wages Payable	1,000
Equipment	22,000	Common Stock	30,000
	$47,000	Retained Earnings	9,300
			$47,000

During December, the company completed the following summary transactions.

Dec. 6 Paid $1,600 for salaries and wages due employees, of which $600 is for December
          and $1,000 is for November salaries and wages payable.
      8 Received $2,100 cash from customers in payment of account (no discount allowed).
     10 Sold merchandise for cash $6,600. The cost of the merchandise sold was $4,100.
     13 Purchased merchandise on account from Gong Co. $9,000, terms 2/10, n/30.
     15 Purchased supplies for cash $2,000.
     18 Sold merchandise on account $12,000, terms 3/10, n/30. The cost of the merchandise
          sold was $8,400.
     20 Paid salaries and wages $1,800.
     23 Paid Gong Co. in full, less discount.
     27 Received collections in full, less discounts, from customers billed on December 18.

Adjustment data:
1. Accrued salaries and wages payable $800.
2. Depreciation $200 per month.
3. Supplies on hand $1,700.

Instructions
(a) Journalize the December transactions using a perpetual inventory system.
(b) Enter the December 1 balances in the ledger T-accounts and post the December transactions. Use Cost of Goods Sold, Depreciation Expense, Salaries and Wages Expense, Sales Revenue, Sales Discounts, and Supplies Expense.
(c) Journalize and post adjusting entries.

(d) Totals $65,600
(e) Net income $840

(d) Prepare an adjusted trial balance.
(e) Prepare an income statement and a retained earnings statement for December and a classified balance sheet at December 31.

CONTINUING COOKIE CHRONICLE

(*Note:* This is a continuation of the Cookie Chronicle from Chapters 1–4.)

CCC5 Because Natalie has had such a successful first few months, she is considering other opportunities to develop her business. One opportunity is the sale of fine European mixers. The owner of Kzinski Supply Company has approached Natalie to become the exclusive U.S. distributor of these fine mixers in her state. The current cost of a mixer is approximately $575 (U.S.), and Natalie would sell each one for $1,150. Natalie comes to you for advice on how to account for these mixers.

Go to the book's companion website, www.wiley.com/college/weygandt, to see the completion of this problem.

Broadening Your PERSPECTIVE

Financial Reporting and Analysis

Financial Reporting Problem: PepsiCo, Inc.

BYP5-1 The financial statements of PepsiCo, Inc. are presented in Appendix A at the end of this textbook.

Instructions
Answer the following questions using PepsiCo's Consolidated Statement of Income.

(a) What was the percentage change in (1) sales and in (2) net income from 2008 to 2009 and from 2009 to 2010?
(b) What was the company's gross profit rate in 2008, 2009, and 2010?
(c) What was the company's percentage of net income to net sales in 2008, 2009, and 2010? Comment on any trend in this percentage.

Comparative Analysis Problem: PepsiCo, Inc. vs. The Coca-Cola Company

BYP5-2 PepsiCo's financial statements are presented in Appendix A. Financial statements of The Coca-Cola Company are presented in Appendix B.

Instructions

(a) Based on the information contained in these financial statements, determine each of the following for each company.
  (1) Gross profit for 2010.
  (2) Gross profit rate for 2010.
  (3) Operating income for 2010.
  (4) Percentage change in operating income from 2009 to 2010.
(b) What conclusions concerning the relative profitability of the two companies can you draw from these data?

Real-World Focus

BYP5-3 No financial decision-maker should ever rely solely on the financial information reported in the annual report to make decisions. It is important to keep abreast of financial news. This activity demonstrates how to search for financial news on the Web.

Address: **biz.yahoo.com/i,** or go to **www.wiley.com/college/weygandt**

Steps
1. Type in either PepsiCo or Coca-Cola.
2. Choose **News**.
3. Select an article that sounds interesting to you.

Instructions
(a) What was the source of the article (e.g., Reuters, Businesswire, PR Newswire)?
(b) Assume that you are a personal financial planner and that one of your clients owns stock in the company. Write a brief memo to your client, summarizing the article and explaining the implications of the article for their investment.

Critical Thinking

Decision-Making Across the Organization

BYP5-4 Three years ago, Debbie Sells and her brother-in-law Mike Mooney opened Family Department Store. For the first two years, business was good, but the following condensed income results for 2013 were disappointing.

Family Department Store
Income Statement
For the Year Ended December 31, 2013

Net sales		$700,000
Cost of goods sold		553,000
Gross profit		147,000
Operating expenses		
Selling expenses	$100,000	
Administrative expenses	20,000	120,000
Net income		$ 27,000

Debbie believes the problem lies in the relatively low gross profit rate (gross profit divided by net sales) of 21%. Mike believes the problem is that operating expenses are too high.

Debbie thinks the gross profit rate can be improved by making both of the following changes. She does not anticipate that these changes will have any effect on operating expenses.

1. Increase average selling prices by 20%. This increase is expected to lower sales volume so that total sales will increase only 5%.
2. Buy merchandise in larger quantities and take all purchase discounts. These changes are expected to increase the gross profit rate by 3 percentage points.

Mike thinks expenses can be cut by making both of the following changes. He feels that these changes will not have any effect on net sales.

1. Cut 2013 sales salaries of $60,000 in half and give sales personnel a commission of 2% of net sales.
2. Reduce store deliveries to one day per week rather than twice a week; this change will reduce 2013 delivery expenses of $30,000 by 40%.

Debbie and Mike come to you for help in deciding the best way to improve net income.

Instructions

With the class divided into groups, answer the following.

(a) Prepare a condensed income statement for 2014, assuming (1) Debbie's changes are implemented and (2) Mike's ideas are adopted.
(b) What is your recommendation to Debbie and Mike?
(c) Prepare a condensed income statement for 2014, assuming both sets of proposed changes are made.

Communication Activity

BYP5-5 The following situation is in chronological order.

1. Dexter decides to buy a surfboard.
2. He calls Boardin USA Co. to inquire about their surfboards.
3. Two days later, he requests Boardin USA Co. to make him a surfboard.
4. Three days later, Boardin USA Co. sends Dexter a purchase order to fill out.
5. He sends back the purchase order.
6. Boardin USA Co. receives the completed purchase order.
7. Boardin USA Co. completes the surfboard.
8. Dexter picks up the surfboard.
9. Boardin USA Co. bills Dexter.
10. Boardin USA Co. receives payment from Dexter.

Instructions

In a memo to the president of Boardin USA Co., answer the following.

(a) When should Boardin USA Co. record the sale?
(b) Suppose that with his purchase order, Dexter is required to make a down payment. Would that change your answer?

Ethics Case

BYP5-6 Anita Zurbrugg was just hired as the assistant treasurer of Yorktown Stores. The company is a specialty chain store with nine retail stores concentrated in one metropolitan area. Among other things, the payment of all invoices is centralized in one of the departments Anita will manage. Her primary responsibility is to maintain the company's high credit rating by paying all bills when due and to take advantage of all cash discounts.

Chris Dadian, the former assistant treasurer who has been promoted to treasurer, is training Anita in her new duties. He instructs Anita that she is to continue the practice of preparing all checks "net of discount" and dating the checks the last day of the discount period. "But," Chris continues, "we always hold the checks at least 4 days beyond the discount period before mailing them. That way, we get another 4 days of interest on our money. Most of our creditors need our business and don't complain. And, if they scream about our missing the discount period, we blame it on the mail room or the post office. We've only lost one discount out of every hundred we take that way. I think everybody does it. By the way, welcome to our team!"

Instructions

(a) What are the ethical considerations in this case?
(b) Who are the stakeholders that are harmed or benefitted in this situation?
(c) Should Anita continue the practice started by Chris? Does she have any choice?

All About You

BYP5-7 There are many situations in business where it is difficult to determine the proper period in which to record revenue. Suppose that after graduation with a degree in finance, you take a job as a manager at a consumer electronics store called Pacifica Electronics. The company has expanded rapidly in order to compete with Best Buy. Pacifica has also begun selling gift cards for its electronic products. The cards are available in any dollar amount and allow the holder of the card to purchase an item for up to 2 years from the time the card is purchased. If the card is not used during that 2 years, it expires.

Instructions
Answer the following questions.

At what point should the revenue from the gift cards be recognized? Should the revenue be recognized at the time the card is sold, or should it be recorded when the card is redeemed? Explain the reasoning to support your answers.

FASB Codification Activity

BYP5-8 If your school has a subscription to the FASB Codification, go to *http://aaahq.org/ascLogin.cfm* to log in and prepare responses to the following

(a) Access the glossary ("Master Glossary") to answer the following.
 (1) What is the definition provided for inventory?
 (2) What is a customer?
(b) What guidance does the Codification provide concerning reporting inventories above cost?

Answers to Chapter Questions

Answers to Insight and Accounting Across the Organization Questions

p. 223 Morrow Snowboards Improves Its Stock Appeal Q: If a perpetual system keeps track of inventory on a daily basis, why do companies ever need to do a physical count? **A:** A perpetual system keeps track of all sales and purchases on a continuous basis. This provides a constant record of the number of units in the inventory. However, if employees make errors in recording sales or purchases, or if there is theft, the inventory value will not be correct. As a consequence, all companies do a physical count of inventory at least once a year.

p. 230 Should Costco Change Its Return Policy? Q: If a company expects significant returns, what are the implications for revenue recognition? **A:** If a company expects significant returns, it should make an adjusting entry at the end of the year reducing sales by the estimated amount of sales returns. This is necessary so as not to overstate the amount of revenue recognized in the period.

p. 231 Selling Green Q: What is meant by "monetize environmental sustainability" for shareholders? **A:** By marketing green, not only does PepsiCo help the environment in the long run, but it also leads to long-term profitability as well. In other words, sound sustainability practices are good business and lead to sound financial results.

p. 237 Disclosing More Details Q: Why have investors and analysts demanded more accuracy in isolating "Other gains and losses" from operating items? **A:** Greater accuracy in the classification of operating versus nonoperating ("Other gains and losses") items permits investors and analysts to judge the real operating margin, the results of continuing operations, and management's ability to control operating expenses.

Answers to Self-Test Questions

1. c **2.** a **3.** c **4.** b (($750 − $50) × .98) **5.** c **6.** c **7.** a **8.** d **9.** b ($400,000 − $310,000)
10. c **11.** d ***12.** d ***13.** a ($60,000 + $380,000 − $50,000) ***14.** b ***15.** a

A Look at IFRS

The basic accounting entries for merchandising are the same under both GAAP and IFRS. The income statement is a required statement under both sets of standards. The basic format is similar although some differences do exist.

Key Points

- Under both GAAP and IFRS, a company can choose to use either a perpetual or a periodic system.
- Inventories are defined by IFRS as held-for-sale in the ordinary course of business, in the process of production for such sale, or in the form of materials or supplies to be consumed in the production process or in the providing of services.
- Under GAAP, companies generally classify income statement items by function. Classification by function leads to descriptions like administration, distribution, and manufacturing. Under IFRS, companies must classify expenses by either nature or function. Classification by nature leads to descriptions such as the following: salaries, depreciation expense, and utilities expense. If a company uses the functional-expense method on the income statement, disclosure by nature is required in the notes to the financial statements.
- Presentation of the income statement under GAAP follows either a single-step or multiple-step format. IFRS does not mention a single-step or multiple-step approach.
- Under IFRS, revaluation of land, buildings, and intangible assets is permitted. The initial gains and losses resulting from this revaluation are reported as adjustments to equity, often referred to as *other comprehensive income*. The effect of this difference is that the use of IFRS results in more transactions affecting equity (other comprehensive income) but not net income.
- *IAS 1*, "Presentation of Financial Statements," provides general guidelines for the reporting of income statement information. Subsequently, a number of international standards have been issued that provide additional guidance to issues related to income statement presentation.
- Similar to GAAP, comprehensive income under IFRS includes unrealized gains and losses (such as those on so-called "non-trading" securities) that are not included in the calculation of net income.
- IFRS requires that two years of income statement information be presented, whereas GAAP requires three years.

Looking to the Future

The IASB and FASB are working on a project that would rework the structure of financial statements. Specifically, this project will address the issue of how to classify various items in the income statement. A main goal of this new approach is to provide information that better represents how businesses are run. In addition, this approach draws attention away from just one number—net income. It will adopt major groupings similar to those currently used by the statement of cash flows (operating, investing, and financing), so that numbers can be more readily traced across statements. For example, the amount of income that is generated by operations would be traceable to the assets and liabilities used to generate the income. Finally, this approach would also provide detail, beyond that currently seen in most statements (either GAAP or IFRS), by requiring that line items be presented both by function and by nature. The new financial statement format was heavily influenced by suggestions from financial statement analysts.

IFRS Practice

IFRS Self-Test Questions

1. Which of the following would *not* be included in the definition of inventory under IFRS?
   (a) Photocopy paper held for sale by an office-supply store.
   (b) Stereo equipment held for sale by an electronics store.
   (c) Used office equipment held for sale by the human relations department of a plastics company.
   (d) All of the above would meet the definition.

2. Which of the following would *not* be a line item of a company reporting costs by nature?
(a) Depreciation expense.
(b) Salaries expense.
(c) Interest expense.
(d) Manufacturing expense

3. Which of the following would *not* be a line item of a company reporting costs by function?
(a) Administration.
(b) Manufacturing.
(c) Utilities expense.
(d) Distribution.

4. Which of the following statements is *false*?
(a) IFRS specifically requires use of a multiple-step income statement.
(b) Under IFRS, companies can use either a perpetual or periodic system.
(c) The proposed new format for financial statements was heavily influenced by the suggestions of financial statement analysts.
(d) The new income statement format will try to de-emphasize the focus on the "net income" line item.

5. Under the new format for financial statements being proposed under a joint IASB/FASB project:
(a) all financial statements would adopt headings similar to the current format of the balance sheet.
(b) financial statements would be presented consistent with the way management usually run companies.
(c) companies would be required to report income statement line items by function only.
(d) the amount of detail shown in the income statement would decrease compared to current presentations.

IFRS Exercises

IFRS5-1 Explain the difference between the "nature-of-expense" and "function-of-expense" classifications.

IFRS5-2 For each of the following income statement line items, state whether the item is a "by nature" expense item or a "by function" expense item.

_____ Cost of goods sold
_____ Depreciation expense
_____ Salaries and wages expense
_____ Selling expenses
_____ Utilities expense
_____ Delivery expense
_____ General and administrative expenses

IFRS5-3 Atlantis Company reported the following amounts (in euros) in 2014: net income, €150,000; unrealized gain related to revaluation of buildings, €10,000; and unrealized loss on non-trading securities, €(35,000). Determine Atlantis's total comprehensive income for 2014.

International Financial Reporting Problem: Zetar plc

IFRS5-4 The financial statements of Zetar plc are presented in Appendix C. The company's complete annual report, including the notes to its financial statements, is available at *www.zetarplc.com*.

Instructions

(a) Is Zetar using a multiple-step or a single-step income statement format? Explain how you made your determination.

(b) Instead of "interest expense," what label does Zetar use for interest costs that it incurs?

(c) Using the notes to the company's financial statements, explain what each of the following are:
(1) Adjusted results.
(2) One-off items.

Answers to IFRS Self-Test Questions

1. c **2.** d **3.** c **4.** a **5.** b

✔ **The Navigator**

✔ Remember to go back to The Navigator box on the chapter opening page and check off your completed work.

Chapter 6

Inventories

Feature Story

"Where Is That Spare Bulldozer Blade?"

Let's talk inventory—big, bulldozer-size inventory. Caterpillar Inc. is the world's largest manufacturer of construction and mining equipment, diesel and natural gas engines, and industrial gas turbines. It sells its products in over 200 countries, making it one of the most successful U.S. exporters. More than 70% of its productive assets are located domestically, and nearly 50% of its sales are foreign.

During the 1980s, Caterpillar's profitability suffered, but today it is very successful. A big part of this turnaround can be attributed to

effective management of its inventory. Imagine what it costs Caterpillar to have too many bulldozers sitting around in inventory—a situation the company definitely wants to avoid. Conversely, Caterpillar must make sure it has enough inventory to meet demand.

At one time during a 7-year period, Caterpillar's sales increased by 100%, while its inventory increased by only 50%. To achieve this dramatic reduction in the amount of resources tied up in inventory, while continuing to meet customers' needs, Caterpillar used a two-pronged approach. First, it completed a factory modernization program, which dramatically increased its production efficiency. The program

---

Learning Objectives

After studying this chapter, you should be able to:

1 Describe the steps in determining inventory quantities.

2 Explain the accounting for inventories and apply the inventory cost flow methods.

3 Explain the financial effects of the inventory cost flow assumptions.

4 Explain the lower-of-cost-or-market basis of accounting for inventories.

5 Indicate the effects of inventory errors on the financial statements.

6 Compute and interpret the inventory turnover ratio.

 ✔ **The Navigator**

reduced by 60% the amount of inventory the company processed at any one time. It also reduced by an incredible 75% the time it takes to manufacture a part.

Second, Caterpillar dramatically improved its parts distribution system. It ships more than 100,000 items daily from its 23 distribution centers strategically located around the world (10 *million* square feet of warehouse space—remember, we're talking bulldozers). The company can virtually guarantee that it can get any part to anywhere in the world within 24 hours.

After these changes, Caterpillar had record exports, profits, and revenues. It would seem that things couldn't be

better. But industry analysts, as well as the company's managers, thought otherwise. In order to maintain Caterpillar's position as the industry leader, management began another major overhaul of inventory production and inventory management processes. The goal: to cut the number of repairs in half, increase productivity by 20%, and increase inventory turnover by 40%.

In short, Caterpillar's ability to manage its inventory has been a key reason for its past success, and inventory management will very likely play a huge part in its ability to succeed in the future.

✔ **The Navigator**

Preview of **Chapter 6**

In the previous chapter, we discussed the accounting for merchandise inventory using a perpetual inventory system. In this chapter, we explain the methods used to calculate the cost of inventory on hand at the balance sheet date and the cost of goods sold.

The content and organization of this chapter are as follows.

INVENTORIES				
Classifying Inventory	**Determining Inventory Quantities**	**Inventory Costing**	**Inventory Errors**	**Statement Presentation and Analysis**
• Finished goods • Work in process • Raw materials	• Taking a physical inventory • Determining ownership of goods	• Specific identification • Cost flow assumptions • Financial statement and tax effects • Consistent use • Lower-of-cost-or-market	• Income statement effects • Balance sheet effects	• Presentation • Analysis

✔ **The Navigator**

Classifying Inventory

How a company classifies its inventory depends on whether the firm is a merchandiser or a manufacturer. In a *merchandising* company, such as those described in Chapter 5, inventory consists of many different items. For example, in a grocery store, canned goods, dairy products, meats, and produce are just a few of the inventory items on hand. These items have two common characteristics: (1) They are owned by the company, and (2) they are in a form ready for sale to customers in the ordinary course of business. Thus, merchandisers need only one inventory classification, **merchandise inventory**, to describe the many different items that make up the total inventory.

In a *manufacturing* company, some inventory may not yet be ready for sale. As a result, manufacturers usually classify inventory into three categories: finished goods, work in process, and raw materials. **Finished goods inventory** is manufactured items that are completed and ready for sale. **Work in process** is that portion of manufactured inventory that has been placed into the production process but is not yet complete. **Raw materials** are the basic goods that will be used in production but have not yet been placed into production.

For example, Caterpillar classifies earth-moving tractors completed and ready for sale as **finished goods**. It classifies the tractors on the assembly line in various stages of production as **work in process**. The steel, glass, tires, and other components that are on hand waiting to be used in the production of tractors are identified as **raw materials**.

By observing the levels and changes in the levels of these three inventory types, financial statement users can gain insight into management's production plans. For example, low levels of raw materials and high levels of finished goods suggest that management believes it has enough inventory on hand, and production will be slowing down—perhaps in anticipation of a recession. On the other hand, high levels of raw materials and low levels of finished goods probably signal that management is planning to step up production.

Many companies have significantly lowered inventory levels and costs using **just-in-time (JIT) inventory** methods. Under a just-in-time method, companies manufacture or purchase goods just in time for use. Dell is famous for having developed a system for making computers in response to individual customer requests. Even though it makes each computer to meet each customer's particular specifications, Dell is able to assemble the computer and put it on a truck in less than 48 hours. The success of the JIT system depends on reliable suppliers. By integrating its information systems with those of its suppliers, Dell reduced its inventories to nearly zero. This is a huge advantage in an industry where products become obsolete nearly overnight.

The accounting concepts discussed in this chapter apply to the inventory classifications of both merchandising and manufacturing companies. Our focus here is on merchandise inventory.

Helpful Hint
Regardless of the classification, companies report all inventories under Current Assets on the balance sheet.

ACCOUNTING ACROSS THE ORGANIZATION

A Big Hiccup

JIT can save a company a lot of money, but it isn't without risk. An unexpected disruption in the supply chain can cost a company a lot of money. Japanese automakers experienced just such a disruption when a 6.8-magnitude earthquake caused major damage to the company that produces 50% of their piston rings. The rings themselves cost only $1.50, but without them you cannot make a car. No other supplier could quickly begin producing sufficient quantities of the rings to match the desired specifications. As a result, the auto-makers were forced to shut down production for a few days—a loss of tens of thousands of cars.

Source: Amy Chozick, "A Key Strategy of Japan's Car Makers Backfires," *Wall Street Journal* (July 20, 2007).

? What steps might the companies take to avoid such a serious disruption in the future? (See page 320.)

Determining Inventory Quantities

No matter whether they are using a periodic or perpetual inventory system, all companies need to determine inventory quantities at the end of the accounting period. If using a perpetual system, companies take a physical inventory for two reasons:

LEARNING OBJECTIVE   **1**

Describe the steps in determining inventory quantities.

1. To check the accuracy of their perpetual inventory records.
2. To determine the amount of inventory lost due to wasted raw materials, shoplifting, or employee theft.

Companies using a periodic inventory system take a physical inventory to determine the inventory on hand at the balance sheet date, and to determine the cost of goods sold for the period.

Determining inventory quantities involves two steps: (1) taking a physical inventory of goods on hand and (2) determining the ownership of goods.

Taking a Physical Inventory

Companies take a physical inventory at the end of the accounting period. Taking a physical inventory involves actually counting, weighing, or measuring each kind of inventory on hand. In many companies, taking an inventory is a formidable task. Retailers such as Target, True Value Hardware, or Home Depot have thousands of different inventory items. An inventory count is generally more accurate when goods are not being sold or received during the counting. Consequently, companies often "take inventory" when the business is closed or when business is slow. Many retailers close early on a chosen day in January—after the holiday sales and returns, when inventories are at their lowest level—to count inventory. Recall from Chapter 5 that Wal-Mart Stores, Inc. has a year-end of January 31.

Ethics Note

In a famous fraud, a salad oil company filled its storage tanks mostly with water. The oil rose to the top, so auditors thought the tanks were full of oil. The company also said it had more tanks than it really did: It repainted numbers on the tanks to confuse auditors.

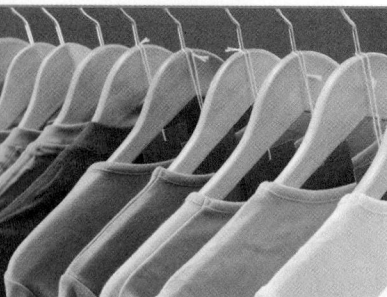

ETHICS INSIGHT

Falsifying Inventory to Boost Income

Managers at women's apparel maker Leslie Fay were convicted of falsifying inventory records to boost net income—and consequently to boost management bonuses. In another case, executives at Craig Consumer Electronics were accused of defrauding lenders by manipulating inventory records. The indictment said the company classified "defective goods as new or refurbished" and claimed that it owned certain shipments "from overseas suppliers" when, in fact, Craig either did not own the shipments or the shipments did not exist.

 What effect does an overstatement of inventory have on a company's financial statements? (See page 320.)

Determining Ownership of Goods

One challenge in computing inventory quantities is determining what inventory a company owns. To determine ownership of goods, two questions must be answered: Do all of the goods included in the count belong to the company? Does the company own any goods that were not included in the count?

GOODS IN TRANSIT

A complication in determining ownership is **goods in transit** (on board a truck, train, ship, or plane) at the end of the period. The company may have purchased goods that have not yet been received, or it may have sold goods that have not yet been delivered. To arrive at an accurate count, the company must determine ownership of these goods.

Goods in transit should be included in the inventory of the company that has legal title to the goods. Legal title is determined by the terms of the sale, as shown in Illustration 6-1 and described below.

Illustration 6-1
Terms of sale

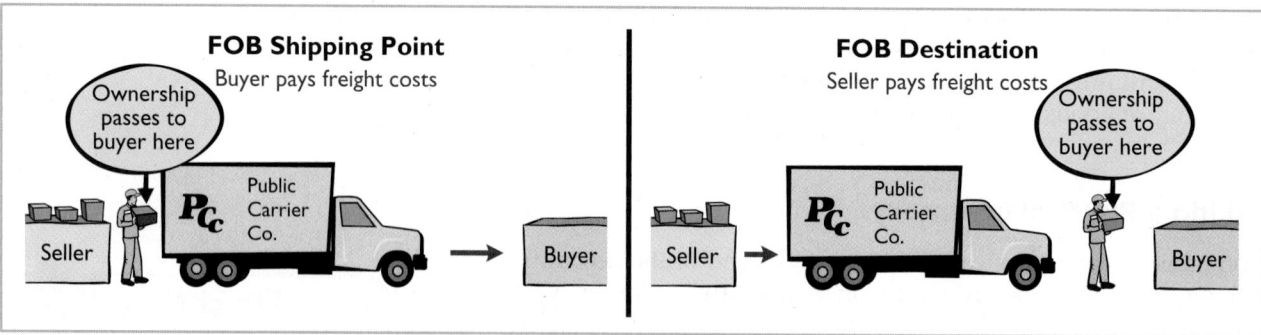

1. When the terms are **FOB (free on board) shipping point**, ownership of the goods passes to the buyer when the public carrier accepts the goods from the seller.
2. When the terms are **FOB destination**, ownership of the goods remains with the seller until the goods reach the buyer.

If goods in transit at the statement date are ignored, inventory quantities may be seriously miscounted. Assume, for example, that Hargrove Company has

20,000 units of inventory on hand on December 31. It also has the following goods in transit:

1. Sales of 1,500 units shipped December 31 FOB destination.

2. Purchases of 2,500 units shipped FOB shipping point by the seller on December 31.

Hargrove has legal title to both the 1,500 units sold and the 2,500 units purchased. If the company ignores the units in transit, it would understate inventory quantities by 4,000 units (1,500 + 2,500).

As we will see later in the chapter, inaccurate inventory counts affect not only the inventory amount shown on the balance sheet but also the cost of goods sold calculation on the income statement.

CONSIGNED GOODS

In some lines of business, it is common to hold the goods of other parties and try to sell the goods for them for a fee, but without taking ownership of the goods. These are called **consigned goods**.

For example, you might have a used car that you would like to sell. If you take the item to a dealer, the dealer might be willing to put the car on its lot and charge you a commission if it is sold. Under this agreement, the dealer **would not take ownership** of the car, which would still belong to you. Therefore, if an inventory count were taken, the car would not be included in the dealer's inventory.

Many car, boat, and antique dealers sell goods on consignment to keep their inventory costs down and to avoid the risk of purchasing an item that they will not be able to sell. Today, even some manufacturers are making consignment agreements with their suppliers in order to keep their inventory levels low.

> DO IT!

Rules of Ownership

Hasbeen Company completed its inventory count. It arrived at a total inventory value of $200,000. As a new member of Hasbeen's accounting department, you have been given the information listed below. Discuss how this information affects the reported cost of inventory.

1. Hasbeen included in the inventory goods held on consignment for Falls Co., costing $15,000.

2. The company did not include in the count purchased goods of $10,000 which were in transit (terms: FOB shipping point).

3. The company did not include in the count sold inventory with a cost of $12,000 which was in transit (terms: FOB shipping point).

Solution

Action Plan

✔ Apply the rules of ownership to goods held on consignment.

✔ Apply the rules of ownership to goods in transit.

The goods of $15,000 held on consignment should be deducted from the inventory count. The goods of $10,000 purchased FOB shipping point should be added to the inventory count. Sold goods of $12,000 which were in transit FOB shipping point should not be included in the ending inventory. Thus, inventory should be carried at $195,000 ($200,000 − $15,000 + $10,000).

Related exercise material: **BE6-1, E6-1, E6-2, and** DO IT! **6-1.**

 The Navigator

ANATOMY OF A FRAUD

Ted Nickerson, CEO of clock manufacturer Dally Industries, was feared by all of his employees. Ted also had expensive tastes. To support his expensive tastes, Ted took out large loans, which he collateralized with his shares of Dally Industries stock. If the price of Dally's stock fell, he was required to provide the bank with more shares of stock. To achieve target net income figures and thus maintain the stock price, Ted coerced employees in the company to alter inventory figures. Inventory quantities were manipulated by changing the amounts on inventory control tags after the year-end physical inventory count. For example, if a tag said there were 20 units of a particular item, the tag was changed to 220. Similarly, the unit costs that were used to determine the value of ending inventory were increased from, for example, $125 per unit to $1,250. Both of these fraudulent changes had the effect of increasing the amount of reported ending inventory. This reduced cost of goods sold and increased net income.

Total take: $245,000

The Missing Control
Independent internal verification. The company should have spot-checked its inventory records periodically, verifying that the number of units in the records agreed with the amount on hand and that the unit costs agreed with vendor price sheets.

Source: Adapted from Wells, *Fraud Casebook* (2007), pp. 502–509.

Inventory Costing

LEARNING OBJECTIVE 2

Explain the accounting for inventories and apply the inventory cost flow methods.

Inventory is accounted for at cost. Cost includes all expenditures necessary to acquire goods and place them in a condition ready for sale. For example, freight costs incurred to acquire inventory are added to the cost of inventory, but the cost of shipping goods to a customer are a selling expense.

After a company has determined the quantity of units of inventory, it applies unit costs to the quantities to compute the total cost of the inventory and the cost of goods sold. This process can be complicated if a company has purchased inventory items at different times and at different prices.

For example, assume that Crivitz TV Company purchases three identical 50-inch TVs on different dates at costs of $700, $750, and $800. During the year, Crivitz sold two sets at $1,200 each. These facts are summarized in Illustration 6-2.

Illustration 6-2
Data for inventory costing example

Purchases			
February 3	1 TV	at	$700
March 5	1 TV	at	$750
May 22	1 TV	at	$800
Sales			
June 1	2 TVs	for	$2,400 ($1,200 × 2)

Cost of goods sold will differ depending on which two TVs the company sold. For example, it might be $1,450 ($700 + $750), or $1,500 ($700 + $800), or $1,550 ($750 + $800). In this section, we discuss alternative costing methods available to Crivitz.

Specific Identification

If Crivitz can positively identify which particular units it sold and which are still in ending inventory, it can use the **specific identification method** of inventory costing. For example, if Crivitz sold the TVs it purchased on February 3 and May 22, then its cost of goods sold is $1,500 ($700 + $800), and its ending inventory is $750 (see Illustration 6-3). Using this method, companies can accurately determine ending inventory and cost of goods sold.

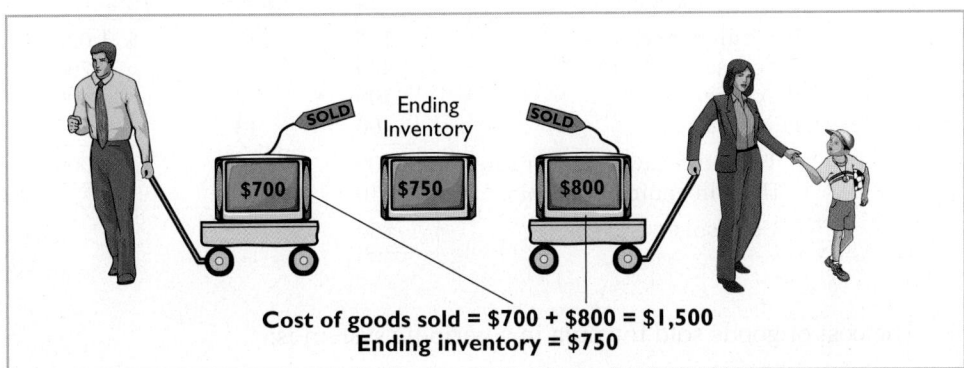

Illustration 6-3
Specific identification method

Specific identification requires that companies keep records of the original cost of each individual inventory item. Historically, specific identification was possible only when a company sold a limited variety of high-unit-cost items that could be identified clearly from the time of purchase through the time of sale. Examples of such products are cars, pianos, or expensive antiques.

Today, bar coding, electronic product codes, and radio frequency identification make it theoretically possible to do specific identification with nearly any type of product. The reality is, however, that this practice is still relatively rare. Instead, rather than keep track of the cost of each particular item sold, most companies make assumptions, called **cost flow assumptions**, about which units were sold.

Ethics Note

A major disadvantage of the specific identification method is that management may be able to manipulate net income. For example, it can boost net income by selling units purchased at a low cost, or reduce net income by selling units purchased at a high cost.

Cost Flow Assumptions

Because specific identification is often impractical, other cost flow methods are permitted. These differ from specific identification in that they **assume** flows of costs that may be unrelated to the physical flow of goods. There are three assumed cost flow methods:

1. First-in, first-out (FIFO)
2. Last-in, first-out (LIFO)
3. Average-cost

There is no accounting requirement that the cost flow assumption be consistent with the physical movement of the goods. Company management selects the appropriate cost flow method.

To demonstrate the three cost flow methods, we will use a *periodic* inventory system. We assume a periodic system for two main reasons. First, many small companies use periodic rather than perpetual systems. Second, **very few companies use *perpetual* LIFO, FIFO, or average-cost** to cost their inventory and related cost of goods sold. Instead, companies that use perpetual systems often use an assumed cost (called a standard cost) to record cost of goods sold at the time of sale. Then, at the end of the period when they count their inventory, they recalculate cost of goods sold using *periodic* FIFO, LIFO, or average-cost and adjust cost of goods sold to this recalculated number.[1]

To illustrate the three inventory cost flow methods, we will use the data for Houston Electronics' Astro condensers, shown in Illustration 6-4.

Illustration 6-4
Data for Houston Electronics

Houston Electronics Astro Condensers				
Date	**Explanation**	**Units**	**Unit Cost**	**Total Cost**
Jan. 1	Beginning inventory	100	$10	$ 1,000
Apr. 15	Purchase	200	11	2,200
Aug. 24	Purchase	300	12	3,600
Nov. 27	Purchase	400	13	5,200
	Total units available for sale	1,000		$12,000
	Units in ending inventory	450		
	Units sold	550		

The cost of goods sold formula in a periodic system is:

(Beginning Inventory + Purchases) − Ending Inventory = Cost of Goods Sold

Houston Electronics had a total of 1,000 units available to sell during the period (beginning inventory plus purchases). The total cost of these 1,000 units is $12,000, referred to as *cost of goods available for sale*. A physical inventory taken at December 31 determined that there were 450 units in ending inventory. Therefore, Houston sold 550 units (1,000 − 450) during the period. To determine the cost of the 550 units that were sold (the cost of goods sold), we assign a cost to the ending inventory and subtract that value from the cost of goods available for sale. The value assigned to the ending inventory **will depend on which cost flow method we use**. No matter which cost flow assumption we use, though, the sum of cost of goods sold plus the cost of the ending inventory must equal the cost of goods available for sale—in this case, $12,000.

FIRST-IN, FIRST-OUT (FIFO)

The **first-in, first-out (FIFO) method** assumes that the **earliest goods** purchased are the first to be sold. FIFO often parallels the actual physical flow of merchandise. That is, it generally is good business practice to sell the oldest units first. Under the FIFO method, therefore, the **costs** of the earliest goods purchased are the first to be recognized in determining cost of goods sold. (This does not necessarily mean that the oldest units *are* sold first, but that the costs of the oldest units are *recognized* first. In a bin of picture hangers at the hardware store, for example, no one really knows, nor would it matter, which hangers are sold first.) Illustration 6-5 shows the allocation of the cost of goods available for sale at Houston Electronics under FIFO.

---

[1]Also, some companies use a perpetual system to keep track of units, but they do not make an entry for perpetual cost of goods sold. In addition, firms that employ LIFO tend to use *dollar-value LIFO*, a method discussed in upper-level courses. FIFO periodic and FIFO perpetual give the same result. Therefore, firms should not incur the additional cost to use FIFO perpetual. Few firms use perpetual average-cost because of the added cost of record-keeping. Finally, for instructional purposes, we believe it is easier to demonstrate the cost flow assumptions under the periodic system, which makes it more pedagogically appropriate.

Cost of Goods Available for Sale

Date	Explanation	Units	Unit Cost	Total Cost
Jan. 1	Beginning inventory	100	$10	$ 1,000
Apr. 15	Purchase	200	11	2,200
Aug. 24	Purchase	300	12	3,600
Nov. 27	Purchase	400	13	5,200
	Total	1,000		$12,000

Illustration 6-5
Allocation of costs—FIFO method

Helpful Hint
Note the sequencing of the allocation:
(1) Compute ending inventory, and
(2) determine cost of goods sold.

Helpful Hint
Another way of thinking about the calculation of FIFO ending inventory is the *LISH assumption*—last in still here.

Step 1: Ending Inventory

Date	Units	Unit Cost	Total Cost
Nov. 27	400	$13	$5,200
Aug. 24	50	12	600
Total	450		$5,800

Step 2: Cost of Goods Sold

Cost of goods available for sale	$12,000
Less: Ending inventory	5,800
Cost of goods sold	$ 6,200

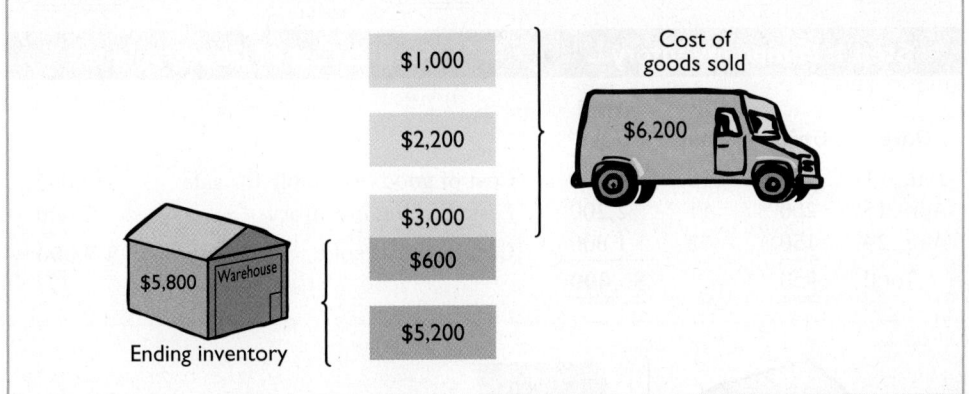

Under FIFO, since it is assumed that the first goods purchased were the first goods sold, ending inventory is based on the prices of the most recent units purchased. That is, **under FIFO, companies obtain the cost of the ending inventory by taking the unit cost of the most recent purchase and working backward until all units of inventory have been costed**. In this example, Houston Electronics prices the 450 units of ending inventory using the *most recent* prices. The last purchase was 400 units at $13 on November 27. The remaining 50 units are priced using the unit cost of the second most recent purchase, $12, on August 24. Next, Houston Electronics calculates cost of goods sold by subtracting the cost of the units **not sold** (ending inventory) from the cost of all goods available for sale.

Illustration 6-6 demonstrates that companies also can calculate cost of goods sold by pricing the 550 units sold using the prices of the first 550 units acquired. Note that of the 300 units purchased on August 24, only 250 units are assumed sold. This agrees with our calculation of the cost of ending inventory, where 50 of these units were assumed unsold and thus included in ending inventory.

Date	Units	Unit Cost	Total Cost
Jan. 1	100	$10	$ 1,000
Apr. 15	200	11	2,200
Aug. 24	250	12	3,000
Total	550		$6,200

Illustration 6-6
Proof of cost of goods sold

LAST-IN, FIRST-OUT (LIFO)

The **last-in, first-out (LIFO) method** assumes that the **latest goods** purchased are the first to be sold. LIFO seldom coincides with the actual physical flow of inventory. (Exceptions include goods stored in piles, such as coal or hay, where goods are removed from the top of the pile as they are sold.) Under the LIFO method, the **costs** of the latest goods purchased are the first to be recognized in determining cost of goods sold. Illustration 6-7 shows the allocation of the cost of goods available for sale at Houston Electronics under LIFO.

Illustration 6-7
Allocation of costs—LIFO method

Cost of Goods Available for Sale				
Date	**Explanation**	**Units**	**Unit Cost**	**Total Cost**
Jan. 1	Beginning inventory	100	$10	$ 1,000
Apr. 15	Purchase	200	11	2,200
Aug. 24	Purchase	300	12	3,600
Nov. 27	Purchase	400	13	5,200
	Total	1,000		$12,000

Step 1: Ending Inventory				Step 2: Cost of Goods Sold	
Date	**Units**	**Unit Cost**	**Total Cost**		
Jan. 1	100	$10	$ 1,000	Cost of goods available for sale	$12,000
Apr. 15	200	11	2,200	Less: Ending inventory	5,000
Aug. 24	150	12	1,800	Cost of goods sold	$ 7,000
Total	450		$5,000		

Helpful Hint
Another way of thinking about the calculation of LIFO ending inventory is the *FISH assumption*—first in still here.

Under LIFO, since it is assumed that the first goods sold were those that were most recently purchased, ending inventory is based on the prices of the oldest units purchased. That is, **under LIFO, companies obtain the cost of the ending inventory by taking the unit cost of the earliest goods available for sale and working forward until all units of inventory have been costed**. In this example, Houston Electronics prices the 450 units of ending inventory using the *earliest* prices. The first purchase was 100 units at $10 in the January 1 beginning inventory. Then, 200 units were purchased at $11. The remaining 150 units needed are priced at $12 per unit (August 24 purchase). Next, Houston Electronics calculates cost of goods sold by subtracting the cost of the units **not sold** (ending inventory) from the cost of all goods available for sale.

Illustration 6-8 demonstrates that companies also can calculate cost of goods sold by pricing the 550 units sold using the prices of the last 550 units acquired. Note that of the 300 units purchased on August 24, only 150 units are assumed sold. This agrees with our calculation of the cost of ending inventory, where 150 of these units were assumed unsold and thus included in ending inventory.

Date	Units	Unit Cost	Total Cost
Nov. 27	400	$13	$ 5,200
Aug. 24	150	12	1,800
Total	550		$7,000

Illustration 6-8
Proof of cost of goods sold

Under a periodic inventory system, which we are using here, **all goods purchased during the period are assumed to be available for the first sale, regardless of the date of purchase.**

AVERAGE-COST

The **average-cost method** allocates the cost of goods available for sale on the basis of the **weighted-average unit cost** incurred. The average-cost method assumes that goods are similar in nature. Illustration 6-9 presents the formula and a sample computation of the weighted-average unit cost.

Cost of Goods Available for Sale	÷	Total Units Available for Sale	=	Weighted-Average Unit Cost
$12,000	÷	1,000	=	$12.00

Illustration 6-9
Formula for weighted-average unit cost

The company then applies the weighted-average unit cost to the units on hand to determine the cost of the ending inventory. Illustration 6-10 (page 282) shows the allocation of the cost of goods available for sale at Houston Electronics using average-cost.

We can verify the cost of goods sold under this method by multiplying the units sold times the weighted-average unit cost ($550 \times \$12 = \$6,600$). Note that this method does not use the average of the unit costs. That average is $11.50 ($10 + $11 + $12 + $13 = $46; $46 \div 4$). The average-cost method instead uses the average **weighted by** the quantities purchased at each unit cost.

> DO IT!

Cost Flow Methods

The accounting records of Shumway Ag Implement show the following data.

Beginning inventory	4,000 units at $ 3
Purchases	6,000 units at $ 4
Sales	7,000 units at $12

Determine the cost of goods sold during the period under a periodic inventory system using (a) the FIFO method, (b) the LIFO method, and (c) the average-cost method.

Solution

Action Plan

✔ Understand the periodic inventory system.

✔ Allocate costs between goods sold and goods on hand (ending inventory) for each cost flow method.

✔ Compute cost of goods sold for each method.

Cost of goods available for sale = (4,000 × $3) + (6,000 × $4) = $36,000
Ending inventory = 10,000 − 7,000 = 3,000 units

(a) FIFO: $36,000 − (3,000 × $4) = $24,000

(b) LIFO: $36,000 − (3,000 × $3) = $27,000

(c) Average cost per unit: [(4,000 @ $3) + (6,000 @ $4)] ÷ 10,000 = $3.60
Average-cost: $36,000 − (3,000 × $3.60) = $25,200

Related exercise material: **BE6-3, BE6-4, BE6-5, E6-3, E6-4, E6-5, E6-6, E6-7, E6-8, and DO IT! 6-2.**

 ✔ The Navigator

Illustration 6-10
Allocation of costs—
average-cost method

Cost of Goods Available for Sale

Date	Explanation	Units	Unit Cost	Total Cost
Jan. 1	Beginning inventory	100	$10	$ 1,000
Apr. 15	Purchase	200	11	2,200
Aug. 24	Purchase	300	12	3,600
Nov. 27	Purchase	400	13	5,200
	Total	1,000		**$12,000**

Step 1: Ending Inventory			Step 2: Cost of Goods Sold	
$12,000 ÷ 1,000 = $12.00			Cost of goods available for sale	$12,000
			Less: Ending inventory	5,400
Units	**Unit Cost**	**Total Cost**	Cost of goods sold	**$ 6,600**
450	$12.00	**$5,400**		

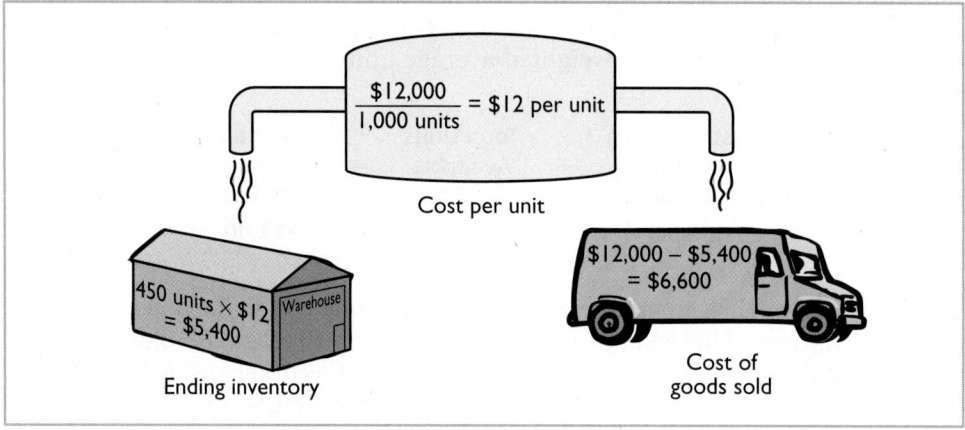

$$\frac{\$12,000}{1,000 \text{ units}} = \$12 \text{ per unit}$$

Cost per unit

450 units × $12 = $5,400   Warehouse

Ending inventory

$12,000 − $5,400 = $6,600

Cost of goods sold

Financial Statement and Tax Effects of Cost Flow Methods

Each of the three assumed cost flow methods is acceptable for use. For example, Reebok International Ltd. and Wendy's International currently use the FIFO method of inventory costing. Campbell Soup Company, Krogers, and Walgreen Drugs use LIFO for part or all of their inventory. Bristol-Myers Squibb, Starbucks, and Motorola use the average-cost method. In fact, a company may also use more than one cost flow method at the same time. Stanley Black & Decker Manufacturing Company, for example, uses LIFO for domestic inventories and FIFO for foreign inventories. Illustration 6-11 (in the margin) shows the use of the three cost flow methods in the 500 largest U.S. companies.

The reasons companies adopt different inventory cost flow methods are varied, but they usually involve one of three factors: (1) income statement effects, (2) balance sheet effects, or (3) tax effects.

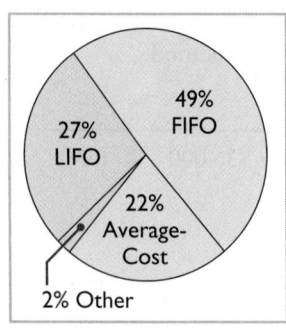

Illustration 6-11
Use of cost flow methods in major U.S. companies

INCOME STATEMENT EFFECTS

To understand why companies might choose a particular cost flow method, let's examine the effects of the different cost flow assumptions on the financial statements of Houston Electronics. The condensed income statements in Illustration 6-12 assume that Houston sold its 550 units for $11,500, had operating expenses of $2,000, and is subject to an income tax rate of 30%.

Illustration 6-12
Comparative effects of cost flow methods

Houston Electronics Condensed Income Statements			
	FIFO	**LIFO**	**Average-Cost**
Sales revenue	$11,500	$11,500	$11,500
Beginning inventory	1,000	1,000	1,000
Purchases	11,000	11,000	11,000
Cost of goods available for sale	12,000	12,000	12,000
Ending inventory	**5,800**	**5,000**	**5,400**
Cost of goods sold	6,200	7,000	6,600
Gross profit	5,300	4,500	4,900
Operating expenses	2,000	2,000	2,000
Income before income taxes*	3,300	2,500	2,900
Income tax expense (30%)	990	750	870
Net income	**$ 2,310**	**$ 1,750**	**$ 2,030**

*We are assuming that Houston Electronics is a corporation, and corporations are required to pay income taxes.

Note the cost of goods available for sale ($12,000) is the same under each of the three inventory cost flow methods. However, the ending inventories and the costs of goods sold are different. This difference is due to the unit costs that the company allocated to cost of goods sold and to ending inventory. Each dollar of difference in ending inventory results in a corresponding dollar difference in income before income taxes. For Houston, an $800 difference exists between FIFO and LIFO cost of goods sold.

In periods of changing prices, the cost flow assumption can have a significant impact on income and on evaluations based on income. In most instances, prices are rising (inflation). In a period of inflation, FIFO produces a higher net income because the lower unit costs of the first units purchased are matched against revenues. In a period of rising prices (as is the case in the Houston example), FIFO reports the highest net income ($2,310) and LIFO the lowest ($1,750); average-cost falls in the middle ($2,030). If prices are falling, the results from the use of FIFO and LIFO are reversed. FIFO will report the lowest net income and LIFO the highest.

To management, higher net income is an advantage. It causes external users to view the company more favorably. In addition, management bonuses, if based on net income, will be higher. Therefore, when prices are rising (which is usually the case), companies tend to prefer FIFO because it results in higher net income.

Some argue that the use of LIFO in a period of inflation enables the company to avoid reporting **paper** (or **phantom**) **profit** as economic gain. To illustrate, assume that Kralik Company buys 200 units of a product at $20 per unit on January 10 and 200 more on December 31 at $24 each. During the year, Kralik sells 200 units at $30 each. Illustration 6-13 shows the results under FIFO and LIFO.

Illustration 6-13
Income statement effects compared

	FIFO	**LIFO**
Sales (200 × $30)	$6,000	$6,000
Cost of goods sold	4,000 (200 × $20)	4,800 (200 × $24)
Gross profit	$2,000	$1,200

Under LIFO, Kralik Company has recovered the current replacement cost ($4,800) of the units sold. Thus, the gross profit in economic terms is real. However, under FIFO, the company has recovered only the January 10 cost ($4,000). To replace the units sold, it must reinvest $800 (200 × $4) of the gross profit. Thus, $800 of the gross profit is said to be phantom or illusory. As a result, reported net income is also overstated in real terms.

BALANCE SHEET EFFECTS

A major advantage of the FIFO method is that in a period of inflation, the costs allocated to ending inventory will approximate their current cost. For example, for Houston Electronics, 400 of the 450 units in the ending inventory are costed under FIFO at the higher November 27 unit cost of $13.

Conversely, a major shortcoming of the LIFO method is that in a period of inflation, the costs allocated to ending inventory may be significantly understated in terms of current cost. The understatement becomes greater over prolonged periods of inflation if the inventory includes goods purchased in one or more prior accounting periods. For example, Caterpillar has used LIFO for 50 years. Its balance sheet shows ending inventory of $6,360 million. But, the inventory's actual current cost if FIFO had been used is $9,363 million.

TAX EFFECTS

We have seen that both inventory on the balance sheet and net income on the income statement are higher when companies use FIFO in a period of inflation. Yet, many companies have selected LIFO. Why? The reason is that LIFO results in the lowest income taxes (because of lower net income) during times of rising prices. For example, at Houston Electronics, income taxes are $750 under LIFO, compared to $990 under FIFO. The tax savings of $240 makes more cash available for use in the business.

Using Inventory Cost Flow Methods Consistently

Whatever cost flow method a company chooses, it should use that method consistently from one accounting period to another. This approach is often referred to as the concept of **consistency**, which means that a company uses the same accounting principles and methods from year to year. Consistent application enhances the comparability of financial statements over successive time periods. In contrast, using the FIFO method one year and the LIFO method the next year would make it difficult to compare the net incomes of the two years.

Although consistent application is preferred, it does not mean that a company may *never* change its inventory costing method. When a company adopts a different method, it should disclose in the financial statements the change and its effects on net income. Illustration 6-14 shows a typical disclosure, using information from the financial statements of Quaker Oats (now a unit of PepsiCo).

Helpful Hint
A tax rule, often referred to as the *LIFO conformity rule*, requires that if companies use LIFO for tax purposes they must also use it for financial reporting purposes. This means that if a company chooses the LIFO method to reduce its tax bills, it will also have to report lower net income in its financial statements.

Illustration 6-14
Disclosure of change in cost flow method

Quaker Oats
Notes to the Financial Statements

Note 1: Effective July 1, the Company adopted the LIFO cost flow assumption for valuing the majority of U.S. Grocery Products inventories. The Company believes that the use of the LIFO method better matches current costs with current revenues. The effect of this change on the current year was to decrease net income by $16.0 million.

INTERNATIONAL INSIGHT

Is LIFO Fair?

ExxonMobil Corporation, like many U.S. companies, uses LIFO to value its inventory for financial reporting and tax purposes. In one recent year, this resulted in a cost of goods sold figure that was $5.6 billion higher than under FIFO. By increasing cost of goods sold, ExxonMobil reduces net income, which reduces taxes. Critics say that LIFO provides an unfair "tax dodge." As Congress looks for more sources of tax revenue, some lawmakers favor the elimination of LIFO. Supporters of LIFO argue that the method is conceptually sound because it matches current costs with current revenues. In addition, they point out that this matching provides protection against inflation.

International accounting standards do not allow the use of LIFO. Because of this, the net income of foreign oil companies such as BP and Royal Dutch Shell are not directly comparable to U.S. companies, which makes analysis difficult.

Source: David Reilly, "Big Oil's Accounting Methods Fuel Criticism," *Wall Street Journal* (August 8, 2006), p. C1.

? What are the arguments for and against the use of LIFO? (See page 320.)

Lower-of-Cost-or-Market

The value of inventory for companies selling high-technology or fashion goods can drop very quickly due to changes in technology or fashion. These circumstances sometimes call for inventory valuation methods other than those presented so far. For example, at one time purchasing managers at Ford decided to make a large purchase of palladium, a precious metal used in vehicle emission devices. They made this purchase because they feared a future shortage. The shortage did not materialize, and by the end of the year the price of palladium had plummeted. Ford's inventory was then worth $1 billion less than its original cost. Do you think Ford's inventory should have been stated at cost, in accordance with the cost principle, or at its lower replacement cost?

> **LEARNING OBJECTIVE 4**
>
> Explain the lower-of-cost-or-market basis of accounting for inventories.

As you probably reasoned, this situation requires a departure from the cost basis of accounting. When the value of inventory is lower than its cost, companies can "write down" the inventory to its market value. This is done by valuing the inventory at the **lower-of-cost-or-market (LCM)** in the period in which the price decline occurs. LCM is an example of the accounting concept of conservatism, which means that the best choice among accounting alternatives is the method that is least likely to overstate assets and net income.

> **International Note**
>
> Under U.S. GAAP, companies cannot reverse inventory write-downs if inventory increases in value in subsequent periods. IFRS permits companies to reverse write-downs in some circumstances.

Companies apply LCM to the items in inventory after they have used one of the cost flow methods (specific identification, FIFO, LIFO, or average-cost) to determine cost. Under the LCM basis, market is defined as **current replacement cost**, not selling price. For a merchandising company, market is the cost of purchasing the same goods at the present time from the usual suppliers in the usual quantities. Current replacement cost is used because a decline in the replacement cost of an item usually leads to a decline in the selling price of the item.

To illustrate the application of LCM, assume that Ken Tuckie TV has the following lines of merchandise with costs and market values as indicated. LCM produces the results shown in Illustration 6-15 (page 286). Note that the amounts shown in the final column are the lower-of-cost-or-market amounts for each item.

Illustration 6-15
Computation of lower-of-cost-or-market

	Cost	Market	Lower-of-Cost-or-Market
Flat-screen TVs	$60,000	$55,000	$ 55,000
Satellite radios	45,000	52,000	45,000
DVD recorders	48,000	45,000	45,000
DVDs	15,000	14,000	14,000
Total inventory			$159,000

Inventory Errors

LEARNING OBJECTIVE   **5**

Indicate the effects of inventory errors on the financial statements.

Unfortunately, errors occasionally occur in accounting for inventory. In some cases, errors are caused by failure to count or price the inventory correctly. In other cases, errors occur because companies do not properly recognize the transfer of legal title to goods that are in transit. When errors occur, they affect both the income statement and the balance sheet.

Income Statement Effects

Under a periodic inventory system, both the beginning and ending inventories appear in the income statement. The ending inventory of one period automatically becomes the beginning inventory of the next period. Thus, inventory errors affect the computation of cost of goods sold and net income in two periods.

The effects on cost of goods sold can be computed by entering incorrect data in the formula in Illustration 6-16 and then substituting the correct data.

Illustration 6-16
Formula for cost of goods sold

Beginning Inventory	+	Cost of Goods Purchased	−	Ending Inventory	=	Cost of Goods Sold

If the error understates *beginning* inventory, cost of goods sold will be understated. If the error understates *ending* inventory, cost of goods sold will be overstated. Illustration 6-17 shows the effects of inventory errors on the current year's income statement.

Illustration 6-17
Effects of inventory errors on current year's income statement

When Inventory Error:	Cost of Goods Sold Is:	Net Income Is:
Understates beginning inventory	Understated	Overstated
Overstates beginning inventory	Overstated	Understated
Understates ending inventory	Overstated	Understated
Overstates ending inventory	Understated	Overstated

 Ethics Note

Inventory fraud increases during recessions. Such fraud includes pricing inventory at amounts in excess of its actual value, or claiming to have inventory when no inventory exists. Inventory fraud usually overstates ending inventory, thereby understating cost of goods sold and creating higher income.

So far, the effects of inventory errors are fairly straightforward. Now, though, comes the (at first) surprising part: An error in the ending inventory of the current period will have a **reverse effect on net income of the next accounting period**. Illustration 6-18 shows this effect. As you study the illustration, you will see that the reverse effect comes from the fact that understating ending inventory in 2013 results in understating beginning inventory in 2014 and overstating net income in 2014.

Over the two years, though, total net income is correct because the errors **offset each other**. Notice that total income using incorrect data is $35,000 ($22,000 + $13,000), which is the same as the total income of $35,000 ($25,000 + $10,000) using correct data. Also note in this example

Sample Company							
Condensed Income Statements							
	2013				**2014**		
	Incorrect		Correct		Incorrect		Correct
Sales revenue		$80,000		$80,000		$90,000	$90,000
Beginning inventory	$20,000		$20,000		**$12,000**	**$15,000**	
Cost of goods purchased	40,000		40,000		68,000	68,000	
Cost of goods available for sale	60,000		60,000		80,000	83,000	
Ending inventory	**12,000**		**15,000**		23,000	23,000	
Cost of goods sold		48,000		45,000	57,000		60,000
Gross profit		32,000		35,000	33,000		30,000
Operating expenses		10,000		10,000	20,000		20,000
Net income		$22,000		$25,000	$13,000		$10,000

$(3,000)
Net income
understated

$3,000
Net income
overstated

**The errors cancel. Thus the combined total
income for the 2-year period is correct.**

Illustration 6-18
Effects of inventory errors on two years' income statements

that an error in the beginning inventory does not result in a corresponding error in the ending inventory for that period. The correctness of the ending inventory depends entirely on the accuracy of taking and costing the inventory at the balance sheet date under the periodic inventory system.

Balance Sheet Effects

Companies can determine the effect of ending inventory errors on the balance sheet by using the basic accounting equation: Assets = Liabilities + Stockholders' Equity. Errors in the ending inventory have the effects shown in Illustration 6-19.

Illustration 6-19
Effects of ending inventory errors on balance sheet

Ending Inventory Error	Assets	Liabilities	Stockholders' Equity
Overstated	Overstated	No effect	Overstated
Understated	Understated	No effect	Understated

The effect of an error in ending inventory on the subsequent period was shown in Illustration 6-18. Recall that if the error is not corrected, the combined total net income for the two periods would be correct. Thus, total stockholders' equity reported on the balance sheet at the end of 2014 will also be correct.

> DO IT!

**LCM Basis;
Inventory Errors**

(a) Tracy Company sells three different types of home heating stoves (gas, wood, and pellet). The cost and market value of its inventory of stoves are as follows.

	Cost	Market
Gas	$ 84,000	$ 79,000
Wood	250,000	280,000
Pellet	112,000	101,000

Action Plan

✔ Determine whether cost or market value is lower for each inventory type.

✔ Sum the lowest value of each inventory type to determine the total value of inventory.

Action Plan

✔ An ending inventory error in one period will have an equal and opposite effect on cost of goods sold and net income in the next period.

✔ After two years, the errors have offset each other.

Determine the value of the company's inventory under the lower-of-cost-or-market approach.

Solution

The lowest value for each inventory type is gas $79,000, wood $250,000, and pellet $101,000. The total inventory value is the sum of these amounts, $430,000.

(b) Visual Company overstated its 2013 ending inventory by $22,000. Determine the impact this error has on ending inventory, cost of goods sold, and stockholders' equity in 2013 and 2014.

Solution

	2013	2014
Ending inventory	$22,000 overstated	No effect
Cost of goods sold	$22,000 understated	$22,000 overstated
Stockholders' equity	$22,000 overstated	No effect

Related exercise material: **BE6-7, BE6-8, E6-9, E6-10, E6-11, E6-12,** and **6-3.**

✔ **The Navigator**

Statement Presentation and Analysis

Presentation

As indicated in Chapter 5, inventory is classified in the balance sheet as a current asset immediately below receivables. In a multiple-step income statement, cost of goods sold is subtracted from sales. There also should be disclosure of (1) the major inventory classifications, (2) the basis of accounting (cost, or lower-of-cost-or-market), and (3) the cost method (FIFO, LIFO, or average).

Wal-Mart Stores, Inc., for example, in its January 31, 2011, balance sheet reported inventories of $36,318 million under current assets. The accompanying notes to the financial statements, as shown in Illustration 6-20, disclosed the following information.

Illustration 6-20
Inventory disclosures by Wal-Mart

Wal-Mart Stores, Inc.
Notes to the Financial Statements

Note 1: Summary of Significant Accounting Policies

Inventories

The Company values inventories at the lower of cost or market as determined primarily by the retail method of accounting, using the last-in, first-out ("LIFO") method for substantially all of the Walmart U.S. segment's merchandise inventories. The retail method of accounting results in inventory being valued at the lower of cost or market since permanent markdowns are currently taken as a reduction of the retail value of inventory. The Sam's Club segment's merchandise is valued based on the weighted-average cost using the LIFO method. Inventories for the Walmart International operations are primarily valued by the retail method of accounting and are stated using the first-in, first-out ("FIFO") method. At January 31, 2011 and 2010, our inventories valued at LIFO approximate those inventories as if they were valued at FIFO.

As indicated in this note, Wal-Mart values its inventories at the lower-of-cost-or-market using LIFO and FIFO.

Analysis

The amount of inventory carried by a company has significant economic consequences. And inventory management is a double-edged sword that requires constant attention. On the one hand, management wants to have a great variety and quantity on hand so that customers have a wide selection and items are always in stock. But, such a policy may incur high carrying costs (e.g., investment, storage, insurance, obsolescence, and damage). On the other hand, low inventory levels lead to stock-outs and lost sales. Common ratios used to manage and evaluate inventory levels are inventory turnover and a related measure, days in inventory.

Inventory turnover measures the number of times on average the inventory is sold during the period. Its purpose is to measure the liquidity of the inventory. The inventory turnover is computed by dividing cost of goods sold by the average inventory during the period. Unless seasonal factors are significant, average inventory can be computed from the beginning and ending inventory balances. For example, Wal-Mart reported in its 2011 annual report a beginning inventory of $32,713 million, an ending inventory of $36,318 million, and cost of goods sold for the year ended January 31, 2011, of $315,287 million. The inventory turnover formula and computation for Wal-Mart are shown below.

Cost of Goods Sold	÷	Average Inventory	=	Inventory Turnover
$315,287	÷	$\dfrac{\$36,318 + \$32,713}{2}$	=	9.13 times

Illustration 6-21
Inventory turnover formula and computation for Wal-Mart

A variant of the inventory turnover ratio is **days in inventory**. This measures the average number of days inventory is held. It is calculated as 365 divided by the inventory turnover ratio. For example, Wal-Mart's inventory turnover of 9.13 times divided into 365 is approximately 40 days. This is the approximate time that it takes a company to sell the inventory once it arrives at the store.

There are typical levels of inventory in every industry. Companies that are able to keep their inventory at lower levels and higher turnovers and still satisfy customer needs are the most successful.

ACCOUNTING ACROSS THE ORGANIZATION

Improving Inventory Control with RFID

Wal-Mart improved its inventory control with the introduction of radio frequency identification (RFID). Much like bar codes, which tell a retailer the number of boxes of a specific product it has, RFID goes a step farther, helping to distinguish one box of a specific product from another. RFID uses technology similar to that used by keyless remotes that unlock car doors.

Companies currently use RFID to track shipments from supplier to distribution center to store. Other potential uses include monitoring product expiration dates and acting quickly on product recalls. Wal-Mart also anticipates faster returns and warranty processing using RFID. This technology will further assist Wal-Mart managers in their efforts to ensure that their store has just the right type of inventory, in just the right amount, in just the right place. Other companies are also interested in RFID. Best Buy has spent millions researching possible applications in its stores.

? Why is inventory control important to managers such as those at Wal-Mart and Best Buy? (See page 320.)

> **DO IT!**

Inventory Turnover

Early in 2014, Westmoreland Company switched to a just-in-time inventory system. Its sales, cost of goods sold, and inventory amounts for 2013 and 2014 are shown below.

	2013	2014
Sales revenue	$2,000,000	$1,800,000
Cost of goods sold	1,000,000	910,000
Beginning inventory	290,000	210,000
Ending inventory	210,000	50,000

Determine the inventory turnover and days in inventory for 2013 and 2014. Discuss the changes in the amount of inventory, the inventory turnover and days in inventory, and the amount of sales across the two years.

Solution

	2013	2014
Inventory turnover ratio	$\dfrac{\$1,000,000}{(\$290,000 + \$210,000)/2} = 4$	$\dfrac{\$910,000}{(\$210,000 + \$50,000)/2} = 7$
Days in inventory	$365 \div 4 = 91.3$ days	$365 \div 7 = 52.1$ days

The company experienced a very significant decline in its ending inventory as a result of the just-in-time inventory. This decline improved its inventory turnover ratio and its days in inventory. However, its sales declined by 10%. It is possible that this decline was caused by the dramatic reduction in the amount of inventory that was on hand, which increased the likelihood of "stock-outs." To determine the optimal inventory level, management must weigh the benefits of reduced inventory against the potential lost sales caused by stock-outs.

Related exercise material: **BE6-9, E6-13, E6-14, and**  **6-4.**

Action Plan

✔ To find the inventory turnover ratio, divide cost of goods sold by average inventory.

✔ To determine days in inventory, divide 365 days by the inventory turnover ratio.

✔ Just-in-time inventory reduces the amount of inventory on hand, which reduces carrying costs. Reducing inventory levels by too much has potential negative implications for sales.

✔ **The Navigator**

> Comprehensive **DO IT! 1**

Gerald D. Englehart Company has the following inventory, purchases, and sales data for the month of March.

Inventory:	March 1	200 units @ $4.00	$ 800
Purchases:			
	March 10	500 units @ $4.50	2,250
	March 20	400 units @ $4.75	1,900
	March 30	300 units @ $5.00	1,500
Sales:			
	March 15	500 units	
	March 25	400 units	

The physical inventory count on March 31 shows 500 units on hand.

Instructions

Under a **periodic inventory system**, determine the cost of inventory on hand at March 31 and the cost of goods sold for March under (a) (FIFO), (b) (LIFO), and (c) average-cost.

Solution to Comprehensive DO IT! 1

Action Plan

✔ Compute the total goods available for sale, in both units and dollars.

✔ Compute the cost of ending inventory under the periodic FIFO method by allocating to the units on hand the **latest costs**.

✔ Compute the cost of ending inventory under the periodic LIFO method by allocating to the units on hand the **earliest costs**.

✔ Compute the cost of ending inventory under the periodic average-cost method by allocating to the units on hand a **weighted-average cost**.

The cost of goods available for sale is $6,450, as follows.

Inventory:		200 units @ $4.00	$ 800
Purchases:			
	March 10	500 units @ $4.50	2,250
	March 20	400 units @ $4.75	1,900
	March 30	300 units @ $5.00	1,500
Total:		1,400	$6,450

Under a **periodic inventory system**, the cost of goods sold under each cost flow method is as follows.

FIFO Method

Ending inventory:

Date	Units	Unit Cost	Total Cost	
March 30	300	$5.00	$1,500	
March 20	200	4.75	950	$2,450

Cost of goods sold: $6,450 − $2,450 = $4,000

LIFO Method

Ending inventory:

Date	Units	Unit Cost	Total Cost	
March 1	200	$4.00	$ 800	
March 10	300	4.50	1,350	$2,150

Cost of goods sold: $6,450 − $2,150 = $4,300

Average-Cost Method

Average unit cost: $6,450 ÷ 1,400 = $4.607
Ending inventory: 500 × $4.607 = $2,303.50

Cost of goods sold: $6,450 − $2,303.50 = $4,146.50

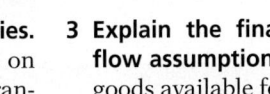
✔ **The Navigator**

SUMMARY OF LEARNING OBJECTIVES

✔ **The Navigator**

1 Describe the steps in determining inventory quantities. The steps are (1) take a physical inventory of goods on hand and (2) determine the ownership of goods in transit or on consignment.

2 Explain the accounting for inventories and apply the inventory cost flow methods. The primary basis of accounting for inventories is cost. Cost of goods available for sale includes (a) cost of beginning inventory and (b) cost of goods purchased. The inventory cost flow methods are specific identification and three assumed cost flow methods—FIFO, LIFO, and average-cost.

3 Explain the financial effects of the inventory cost flow assumptions. Companies may allocate the cost of goods available for sale to cost of goods sold and ending inventory by specific identification or by a method based on an assumed cost flow. When prices are rising, the first-in, first-out (FIFO) method results in lower cost of goods sold and higher net income than the other methods. The reverse is true when prices are falling. In the balance sheet, FIFO results in an ending inventory that is closest to current value; inventory under LIFO is the farthest from current value. LIFO results in the lowest income taxes.

4 Explain the lower-of-cost-or-market basis of accounting for inventories. Companies may use the lower-of-cost-or-market (LCM) basis when the current replacement cost (market) is less than cost. Under LCM, companies recognize the loss in the period in which the price decline occurs.

5 Indicate the effects of inventory errors on the financial statements. *In the income statement of the current year:* (a) An error in beginning inventory will have a reverse effect on net income. (b) An error in ending inventory will have a similar effect on net income. In the following period, its effect on net income for that period is reversed, and total net income for the two years will be correct.

In the balance sheet: Ending inventory errors will have the same effect on total assets and total stockholders' equity and no effect on liabilities.

6 Compute and interpret the inventory turnover ratio. The inventory turnover ratio is cost of goods sold divided by average inventory. To convert it to average days in inventory, divide 365 days by the inventory turnover ratio.

GLOSSARY

Average-cost method Inventory costing method that uses the weighted-average unit cost to allocate to ending inventory and cost of goods sold the cost of goods available for sale. (p. 281).

Consigned goods Goods held for sale by one party although ownership of the goods is retained by another party. (p. 275).

Consistency concept Dictates that a company use the same accounting principles and methods from year to year. (p. 284).

Current replacement cost The current cost to replace an inventory item. (p. 285).

Days in inventory Measure of the average number of days inventory is held; calculated as 365 divided by inventory turnover ratio. (p. 289).

Finished goods inventory Manufactured items that are completed and ready for sale. (p. 272).

First-in, first-out (FIFO) method Inventory costing method that assumes that the costs of the earliest goods purchased are the first to be recognized as cost of goods sold. (p. 278).

FOB (free on board) destination Freight terms indicating that ownership of the goods remains with the seller until the goods reach the buyer. (p. 274).

FOB (free on board) shipping point Freight terms indicating that ownership of the goods passes to the buyer when the public carrier accepts the goods from the seller. (p. 274).

Inventory turnover A ratio that measures the number of times on average the inventory sold during the period; computed by dividing cost of goods sold by the average inventory during the period. (p. 289).

Just-in-time (JIT) inventory method Inventory system in which companies manufacture or purchase goods just in time for use. (p. 272).

Last-in, first-out (LIFO) method Inventory costing method that assumes the costs of the latest units purchased are the first to be allocated to cost of goods sold. (p. 280).

Lower-of-cost-or-market (LCM) basis A basis whereby inventory is stated at the lower of either its cost or its market value as determined by current replacement cost. (p. 285).

Raw materials Basic goods that will be used in production but have not yet been placed into production. (p. 272).

Specific identification method An actual physical flow costing method in which items still in inventory are specifically costed to arrive at the total cost of the ending inventory. (p. 277).

Weighted-average unit cost Average cost that is weighted by the number of units purchased at each unit cost. (p. 281).

Work in process That portion of manufactured inventory that has been placed into the production process but is not yet complete. (p. 272).

APPENDIX 6A   INVENTORY COST FLOW METHODS IN PERPETUAL INVENTORY SYSTEMS

LEARNING OBJECTIVE **7**

Apply the inventory cost flow methods to perpetual inventory records.

What inventory cost flow methods do companies employ if they use a perpetual inventory system? Simple—they can use any of the inventory cost flow methods described in the chapter. To illustrate the application of the three assumed cost flow methods (FIFO, LIFO, and average-cost), we will use the data shown in Illustration 6A-1 and in this chapter for Houston Electronics' Astro Condenser.

Illustration 6A-1
Inventoriable units and costs

	Houston Electronics				
	Astro Condensers				
Date	Explanation	Units	Units Cost	Total Cost	Balance in Units
1/1	Beginning inventory	100	$10	$ 1,000	100
4/15	Purchases	200	11	2,200	300
8/24	Purchases	300	12	3,600	600
9/10	Sale	550			50
11/27	Purchases	400	13	5,200	450
				$12,000	

First-In, First-Out (FIFO)

Under FIFO, the company charges to cost of goods sold the cost of the earliest goods on hand **prior to each sale**. Therefore, the cost of goods sold on September 10 consists of the units on hand January 1 and the units purchased April 15 and August 24. Illustration 6A-2 shows the inventory under a FIFO method perpetual system.

Illustration 6A-2
Perpetual system—FIFO

Date	Purchases	Cost of Goods Sold	Balance (in units and cost)
January 1			(100 @ $10) $1,000
April 15	(200 @ $11) $2,200		(100 @ $10) (200 @ $11) } $3,200
August 24	(300 @ $12) $3,600		(100 @ $10) (200 @ $11) (300 @ $12) } $6,800
September 10		(100 @ $10) (200 @ $11) (250 @ $12)	(50 @ $12) $ 600
		$6,200	— Cost of goods sold
November 27	(400 @ $13) $5,200		(50 @ $12) (400 @ $13) } $5,800 — Ending inventory

The ending inventory in this situation is $5,800, and the cost of goods sold is $6,200 [(100 @ $10) + (200 @ $11) + (250 @ $12)].

Compare Illustrations 6-5 (page 279) and 6A-2. You can see that the results under FIFO in a perpetual system are the **same as in a periodic system**. In both cases, the ending inventory is $5,800 and cost of goods sold is $6,200. Regardless of the system, the first costs in are the costs assigned to cost of goods sold.

Last-In, First-Out (LIFO)

Under the LIFO method using a perpetual system, the company charges to cost of goods sold the cost of the most recent purchase prior to sale. Therefore, the cost of the goods sold on September 10 consists of all the units from the August 24 and April 15 purchases plus 50 of the units in beginning inventory. Illustration 6A-3 (page 294) shows the computation of the ending inventory under the LIFO method.

Illustration 6A-3
Perpetual system—LIFO

Date	Purchases		Cost of Goods Sold	Balance (in units and cost)	
January 1				(100 @ $10)	$1,000
April 15	(200 @ $11)	$2,200		(100 @ $10) (200 @ $11)	$3,200
August 24	(300 @ $12)	$3,600		(100 @ $10) (200 @ $11) (300 @ $12)	$6,800
September 10			(300 @ $12) (200 @ $11) (50 @ $10)	(50 @ $10)	$ 500
			$6,300		
November 27	(400 @ $13)	$5,200		(50 @ $10) (400 @ $13)	$5,700

Cost of goods sold

Ending inventory

The use of LIFO in a perpetual system will usually produce cost allocations that differ from those using LIFO in a periodic system. In a perpetual system, the company allocates the latest units purchased *prior to each sale* to cost of goods sold. In contrast, in a periodic system, the latest units purchased *during the period* are allocated to cost of goods sold. Thus, when a purchase is made after the last sale, the LIFO periodic system will apply this purchase to the previous sale. Compare Illustrations 6-7 (page 280) and 6A-3. Illustration 6-7 shows that the 400 units at $13 purchased on November 27 applied to the sale of 550 units (on September 10). Under the LIFO perpetual system in Illustration 6A-3, the 400 units at $13 purchased on November 27 are all applied to the ending inventory.

The ending inventory in this LIFO perpetual illustration is $5,700, and cost of goods sold is $6,300, as compared to the LIFO periodic Illustration 6-7 (on page 280) where the ending inventory is $5,000 and cost of goods sold is $7,000.

Average-Cost

The average-cost method in a perpetual inventory system is called the **moving-average method**. Under this method, the company computes a new average **after each purchase**, by dividing the cost of goods available for sale by the units on hand. The average cost is then applied to (1) the units sold, to determine the cost of goods sold, and (2) the remaining units on hand, to determine the ending inventory amount. Illustration 6A-4 shows the application of the moving-average cost method by Houston Electronics.

Illustration 6A-4
Perpetual system—average-cost method

Date	Purchases		Cost of Goods Sold	Balance (in units and cost)	
January 1				(100 @ $10)	$ 1,000
April 15	(200 @ $11)	$2,200		(300 @ $10.667)	$ 3,200
August 24	(300 @ $12)	$3,600		(600 @ $11.333)	$ 6,800
September 10			(550 @ $11.333)	(50 @ $11.333)	$ 567
			$6,233		
November 27	(400 @ $13)	$5,200		(450 @ $12.816)	**$5,767**

Cost of goods sold

Ending inventory

As indicated, Houston Electronics computes **a new average each time it makes a purchase**. On April 15, after it buys 200 units for $2,200, a total of 300 units costing $3,200 ($1,000 + $2,200) are on hand. The average unit cost is $10.667 ($3,200 ÷ 300). On August 24, after Houston Electronics buys 300 units for $3,600, a total of 600 units costing $6,800 ($1,000 + $2,200 + $3,600) are on hand, at an average cost per unit of $11.333 ($6,800 ÷ 600). Houston Electronics uses this unit cost of $11.333 in costing sales until it makes another purchase, when the company computes a new unit cost. Accordingly, the unit cost of the 550 units sold (on September 10) is $11.333, and the total cost of goods sold is $6,233. On November 27, following the purchase of 400 units for $5,200, there are 450 units on hand costing $5,767 ($567 + $5,200) with a new average cost of $12.816 ($5,767 ÷ 450).

Compare this moving-average cost under the perpetual inventory system to Illustration 6-10 (on page 282) showing the average-cost method under a periodic inventory system.

> Comprehensive **DO IT! 2**

Comprehensive DO IT! 1 on page 290 showed cost of goods sold computations under a periodic inventory system. Now let's assume that Gerald D. Englehart Company uses a perpetual inventory system. The company has the same inventory, purchases, and sales data for the month of March as shown earlier:

Inventory:	March 1	200 units @ $4.00	$ 800	
Purchases:	March 10	500 units @ $4.50	2,250	
	March 20	400 units @ $4.75	1,900	
	March 30	300 units @ $5.00	1,500	
Sales:	March 15	500 units		
	March 25	400 units		

The physical inventory count on March 31 shows 500 units on hand.

Instructions
Under a **perpetual inventory system**, determine the cost of inventory on hand at March 31 and the cost of goods sold for March under (a) FIFO, (b) LIFO, and (c) average-cost.

Solution to Comprehensive DO IT! 2

Action Plan

✔ Compute the cost of goods sold under the perpetual FIFO method by allocating to the goods sold the **earliest** cost of goods purchased.

✔ Compute the cost of goods sold under the perpetual LIFO method by allocating to the goods sold the **latest** cost of goods purchased.

✔ Compute the cost of goods sold under the perpetual average-cost method by allocating to the goods sold a **moving-average** cost.

The cost of goods available for sale is $6,450, as follows.

Inventory:		200 units @ $4.00	$ 800
Purchases:	March 10	500 units @ $4.50	2,250
	March 20	400 units @ $4.75	1,900
	March 30	300 units @ $5.00	1,500
Total:		1,400	$6,450

Under a **perpetual inventory system**, the cost of goods sold under each cost flow method is as follows.

FIFO Method

Date	Purchases	Cost of Goods Sold	Balance
March 1			(200 @ $4.00) $ 800
March 10	(500 @ $4.50) $2,250		(200 @ $4.00)
			(500 @ $4.50) $3,050
March 15		(200 @ $4.00)	
		(300 @ $4.50)	(200 @ $4.50) $ 900
		$2,150	

Date	Purchases	Cost of Goods Sold	Balance
March 20	(400 @ $4.75) $1,900		(200 @ $4.50) (400 @ $4.75) } $2,800
March 25		(200 @ $4.50) (200 @ $4.75) ——————— $1,850	(200 @ $4.75) $ 950
March 30	(300 @ $5.00) $1,500		(200 @ $4.75) (300 @ $5.00) } $2,450
	Ending inventory $2,450	Cost of goods sold: $2,150 + $1,850 = $4,000	

LIFO Method

Date	Purchases	Cost of Goods Sold	Balance
March 1			(200 @ $4.00) $ 800
March 10	(500 @ $4.50) $2,250		(200 @ $4.00) (500 @ $4.50) } $3,050
March 15		(500 @ $4.50) $2,250	(200 @ $4.00) $ 800
March 20	(400 @ $4.75) $1,900		(200 @ $4.00) (400 @ $4.75) } $2,700
March 25		(400 @ $4.75) $1,900	(200 @ $4.00) $ 800
March 30	(300 @ $5.00) $1,500		(200 @ $4.00) (300 @ $5.00) } $2,300
	Ending inventory $2,300	Cost of goods sold: $2,250 + $1,900 = $4,150	

Moving-Average Cost Method

Date	Purchases	Cost of Goods Sold	Balance
March 1			(200 @ $4.00) $ 800
March 10	(500 @ $4.50) $2,250		(700 @ $4.357) $3,050
March 15		(500 @ $4.357) $ 2,179	(200 @ $4.357) $ 871
March 20	(400 @ $4.75) $1,900		(600 @ $4.618) $2,771
March 25		(400 @ $4.618) $ 1,847	(200 @ $4.618) $ 924
March 30	(300 @ $5.00) $1,500		(500 @ $4.848) $2,424
	Ending inventory $2,424	Cost of goods sold: $2,179 + $1,847 = $4,026	

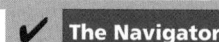

✔ The Navigator

SUMMARY OF LEARNING OBJECTIVE FOR APPENDIX 6A   ✔ The Navigator

7 Apply the inventory cost flow methods to perpetual inventory records. Under FIFO and a perpetual inventory system, companies charge to cost of goods sold the cost of the earliest goods on hand prior to each sale. Under LIFO and a perpetual system, companies charge to cost of goods sold the cost of the most recent purchase prior to sale. Under the moving-average (average cost) method and a perpetual system, companies compute a new average cost after each purchase.

APPENDIX **6B**   ESTIMATING INVENTORIES

LEARNING OBJECTIVE 8

Describe the two methods of estimating inventories.

In the chapter, we assumed that a company would be able to physically count its inventory. What if it cannot? What if the inventory were destroyed by fire or flood, for example? In that case, the company would use an estimate.

Two circumstances explain why companies sometimes estimate inventories. First, a casualty such as fire, flood, or earthquake may make it impossible to take a physical inventory. Second, managers may want monthly or quarterly financial statements, but a physical inventory is taken only annually. The need for estimating inventories occurs primarily with a periodic inventory system because of the absence of perpetual inventory records.

There are two widely used methods of estimating inventories: (1) the gross profit method, and (2) the retail inventory method.

Gross Profit Method

The **gross profit method** estimates the cost of ending inventory by applying a gross profit rate to net sales. This method is relatively simple but effective. Accountants, auditors, and managers frequently use the gross profit method to test the reasonableness of the ending inventory amount. It will detect large errors.

To use this method, a company needs to know its net sales, cost of goods available for sale, and gross profit rate. The company then can estimate its gross profit for the period. Illustration 6B-1 shows the formulas for using the gross profit method.

Step 1:	Net Sales	−	Estimated Gross Profit	=	Estimated Cost of Goods Sold	
Step 2:	Cost of Goods Available for Sale	−	Estimated Cost of Goods Sold	=	Estimated Cost of Ending Inventory	

Illustration 6B-1
Gross profit method formulas

To illustrate, assume that Kishwaukee Company wishes to prepare an income statement for the month of January. Its records show net sales of $200,000, beginning inventory $40,000, and cost of goods purchased $120,000. In the preceding year, the company realized a 30% gross profit rate. It expects to earn the same rate this year. Given these facts and assumptions, Kishwaukee can compute the estimated cost of the ending inventory at January 31 under the gross profit method as follows.

Illustration 6B-2
Example of gross profit method

Step 1:

Net sales	$ 200,000
Less: Estimated gross profit (30% × $200,000)	60,000
Estimated cost of goods sold	**$140,000**

Step 2:

Beginning inventory	$ 40,000
Cost of goods purchased	120,000
Cost of goods available for sale	160,000
Less: Estimated cost of goods sold	140,000
Estimated cost of ending inventory	**$ 20,000**

The gross profit method is based on the assumption that the gross profit rate will remain constant. But, it may not remain constant, due to a change in merchandising policies or in market conditions. In such cases, the company should adjust the rate to reflect current operating conditions. In some cases, companies can obtain a more accurate estimate by applying this method on a department or product-line basis.

Note that companies should not use the gross profit method to prepare financial statements at the end of the year. These statements should be based on a physical inventory count.

Retail Inventory Method

A retail store such as Home Depot, Ace Hardware, or Wal-Mart has thousands of different types of merchandise at low unit costs. In such cases, it is difficult and time-consuming to apply unit costs to inventory quantities. An alternative is to use the **retail inventory method** to estimate the cost of inventory. Most retail companies can establish a relationship between cost and sales price. The company then applies the cost-to-retail percentage to the ending inventory at retail prices to determine inventory at cost.

Under the retail inventory method, a company's records must show both the cost and retail value of the goods available for sale. Illustration 6B-3 presents the formulas for using the retail inventory method.

Illustration 6B-3
Retail inventory method formulas

Step 1:	Goods Available for Sale at Retail	−	Net Sales	=	Ending Inventory at Retail
Step 2:	Goods Available for Sale at Cost	÷	Goods Available for Sale at Retail	=	Cost-to-Retail Ratio
Step 3:	Ending Inventory at Retail	×	Cost-to-Retail Ratio	=	Estimated Cost of Ending Inventory

We can demonstrate the logic of the retail method by using unit-cost data. Assume that Ortiz Inc. has marked 10 units purchased at $7 to sell for $10 per unit. Thus, the cost-to-retail ratio is 70% ($70 ÷ $100). If four units remain unsold, their retail value is $40 (4 × $10), and their cost is $28 ($40 × 70%). This amount agrees with the total cost of goods on hand on a per unit basis (4 × $7).

Illustration 6B-4 shows application of the retail method for Valley West Co. Note that it is not necessary to take a physical inventory to determine the estimated cost of goods on hand at any given time.

Illustration 6B-4
Application of retail inventory method

	At Cost	At Retail
Beginning inventory	$14,000	$ 21,500
Goods purchased	61,000	78,500
Goods available for sale	$75,000	100,000
Net sales		70,000
Step (1) Ending inventory at retail =		$ 30,000

Step (1) Ending inventory at retail =
Step (2) Cost-to-retail ratio = $75,000 ÷ $100,000 = 75%
Step (3) Estimated cost of ending inventory = $30,000 × 75% = $22,500

The retail inventory method also facilitates taking a physical inventory at the end of the year. Valley West can value the goods on hand at the prices marked on the merchandise and then apply the cost-to-retail ratio to the goods on hand at retail to determine the ending inventory at cost.

> **Helpful Hint**
> In determining inventory at retail, companies use selling prices of the units.

The major disadvantage of the retail method is that it is an averaging technique. Thus, it may produce an incorrect inventory valuation if the mix of the ending inventory is not representative of the mix in the goods available for sale. Assume, for example, that the cost-to-retail ratio of 75% for Valley West consists of equal proportions of inventory items that have cost-to-retail ratios of 70%, 75%, and 80%. If the ending inventory contains only items with a 70% ratio, an incorrect inventory cost will result. Companies can minimize this problem by applying the retail method on a department or product-line basis.

SUMMARY OF LEARNING OBJECTIVE FOR APPENDIX 6B

 ✔ **The Navigator**

8 Describe the two methods of estimating inventories. The two methods of estimating inventories are the gross profit method and the retail inventory method. Under the gross profit method, companies apply a gross profit rate to net sales to determine estimated cost of goods sold. They then subtract estimated cost of goods sold from cost of goods available for sale to determine the estimated cost of the ending inventory.

Under the retail inventory method, companies compute a cost-to-retail ratio by dividing the cost of goods available for sale by the retail value of the goods available for sale. They then apply this ratio to the ending inventory at retail to determine the estimated cost of the ending inventory.

GLOSSARY FOR APPENDIX 6B

Gross profit method A method for estimating the cost of the ending inventory by applying a gross profit rate to net sales and subtracting estimated cost of goods sold from cost of goods available for sale. (p. 297).

Retail inventory method A method for estimating the cost of the ending inventory by applying a cost-to-retail ratio to the ending inventory at retail. (p. 298).

 **Self-Test, Brief Exercises, Exercises, Problem Set A, and many more components are available for practice in WileyPLUS.**

Note: All asterisked Questions, Exercises, and Problems relate to material in the appendices to the chapter.

SELF-TEST QUESTIONS

Answers are on page 320.

(LO 1) **1.** Which of the following should *not* be included in the physical inventory of a company?
   (a) Goods held on consignment from another company.
   (b) Goods shipped on consignment to another company.
   (c) Goods in transit from another company shipped FOB shipping point.
   (d) None of the above.

(LO 1) **2.** As a result of a thorough physical inventory, Railway Company determined that it had inventory worth $180,000 at December 31, 2014. This count did not take into consideration the following facts. Rogers Consignment store currently has goods worth $35,000 on its sales floor that belong to Railway but are being sold on consignment by Rogers. The selling price of these goods is $50,000. Railway purchased $13,000 of goods that were shipped on December 27, FOB destination, that will be received by Railway on January 3. Determine the correct amount of inventory that Railway should report.
   (a) $230,000.
   (b) $215,000.
   (c) $228,000.
   (d) $193,000.

(LO 2)   **3.** Cost of goods available for sale consists of two elements: beginning inventory and:
  (a) ending inventory.
  (b) cost of goods purchased.
  (c) cost of goods sold.
  (d) All of the above.

(LO 2)   **4.** Tinker Bell Company has the following:

	Units	Unit Cost
Inventory, Jan. 1	8,000	$11
Purchase, June 19	13,000	12
Purchase, Nov. 8	5,000	13

If Tinker Bell has 9,000 units on hand at December 31, the cost of the ending inventory under FIFO is:
  (a) $99,000.   (c) $113,000.
  (b) $108,000.   (d) $117,000.

(LO 2)   **5.** Using the data in Question 4 above, the cost of the ending inventory under LIFO is:
  (a) $113,000.   (c) $99,000.
  (b) $108,000.   (d) $100,000.

(LO 2)   **6.** Davidson Electronics has the following:

	Units	Unit Cost
Inventory, Jan. 1	5,000	$ 8
Purchase, April 2	15,000	$10
Purchase, Aug. 28	20,000	$12

If Davidson has 7,000 units on hand at December 31, the cost of ending inventory under the average-cost method is:
  (a) $84,000.   (c) $56,000.
  (b) $70,000.   (d) $75,250.

(LO 3)   **7.** In periods of rising prices, LIFO will produce:
  (a) higher net income than FIFO.
  (b) the same net income as FIFO.
  (c) lower net income than FIFO.
  (d) higher net income than average-cost.

(LO 3)   **8.** Factors that affect the selection of an inventory costing method do *not* include:
  (a) tax effects.
  (b) balance sheet effects.
  (c) income statement effects.
  (d) perpetual vs. periodic inventory system.

(LO 4)   **9.** Rickety Company purchased 1,000 widgets and has 200 widgets in its ending inventory at a cost of $91 each and a current replacement cost of $80 each. The ending inventory under lower-of-cost-or-market is:
  (a) $91,000.   (c) $18,200.
  (b) $80,000.   (d) $16,000.

10. Atlantis Company's ending inventory is understated (LO 5) $4,000. The effects of this error on the current year's cost of goods sold and net income, respectively, are:
  (a) understated, overstated.
  (b) overstated, understated.
  (c) overstated, overstated.
  (d) understated, understated.

11. Harold Company overstated its inventory by $15,000 at (LO 4) December 31, 2013. It did not correct the error in 2013 or 2014. As a result, Harold's stockholders' equity was:
  (a) overstated at December 31, 2013, and understated at December 31, 2014.
  (b) overstated at December 31, 2013, and properly stated at December 31, 2014.
  (c) understated at December 31, 2013, and understated at December 31, 2014.
  (d) overstated at December 31, 2013, and overstated at December 31, 2014.

12. Which of these would cause the inventory turnover (LO 6) ratio to increase the most?
  (a) Increasing the amount of inventory on hand.
  (b) Keeping the amount of inventory on hand constant but increasing sales.
  (c) Keeping the amount of inventory on hand constant but decreasing sales.
  (d) Decreasing the amount of inventory on hand and increasing sales.

13. Carlos Company had beginning inventory of $80,000, (LO 5) ending inventory of $110,000, cost of goods sold of $285,000, and sales of $475,000. Carlos's days in inventory is:
  (a) 73 days.   (c) 102.5 days.
  (b) 121.7 days.   (d) 84.5 days.

*14. Songbird Company has sales of $150,000 and cost of (LO 8) goods available for sale of $135,000. If the gross profit rate is 30%, the estimated cost of the ending inventory under the gross profit method is:
  (a) $15,000.   (c) $45,000.
  (b) $30,000.   (d) $75,000.

*15. In a perpetual inventory system: (LO 7)
  (a) LIFO cost of goods sold will be the same as in a periodic inventory system.
  (b) average costs are based entirely on unit cost averages.
  (c) a new average is computed under the average-cost method after each sale.
  (d) FIFO cost of goods sold will be the same as in a periodic inventory system.

Go to the book's companion website, www.wiley.com/college/weygandt, for additional Self-Test Questions.

 **The Navigator**

QUESTIONS

1. "The key to successful business operations is effective inventory management." Do you agree? Explain.

2. An item must possess two characteristics to be classified as inventory by a merchandiser. What are these two characteristics?

3. Your friend Art Mega has been hired to help take the physical inventory in Jaegar Hardware Store. Explain to Art Mega what this job will entail.

4. (a) Hanson Company ships merchandise to Fox Company on December 30. The merchandise reaches the buyer on January 6. Indicate the terms of sale that will result in the goods being included in (1) Hanson's December 31 inventory, and (2) Fox's December 31 inventory.

(b) Under what circumstances should Hanson Company include consigned goods in its inventory?

5. Topp Hat Shop received a shipment of hats for which it paid the wholesaler $2,970. The price of the hats was $3,000 but Topp was given a $30 cash discount and required to pay freight charges of $80. In addition, Topp paid $130 to cover the travel expenses of an employee who negotiated the purchase of the hats. What amount will Topp record for inventory? Why?

6. Explain the difference between the terms FOB shipping point and FOB destination.

7. Jason Bradley believes that the allocation of inventoriable costs should be based on the actual physical flow of the goods. Explain to Jason why this may be both impractical and inappropriate.

8. What is a major advantage and a major disadvantage of the specific identification method of inventory costing?

9. "The selection of an inventory cost flow method is a decision made by accountants." Do you agree? Explain. Once a method has been selected, what accounting requirement applies?

10. Which assumed inventory cost flow method:
    (a) usually parallels the actual physical flow of merchandise?
    (b) assumes that goods available for sale during an accounting period are identical?
    (c) assumes that the latest units purchased are the first to be sold?

11. In a period of rising prices, the inventory reported in Barto Company's balance sheet is close to the current cost of the inventory. Phelan Company's inventory is considerably below its current cost. Identify the inventory cost flow method being used by each company. Which company has probably been reporting the higher gross profit?

12. Olsen Company has been using the FIFO cost flow method during a prolonged period of rising prices. During the same time period, Olsen has been paying out all of its net income as dividends. What adverse effects may result from this policy?

13. Steve Kerns is studying for the next accounting midterm examination. What should Steve know about (a) departing from the cost basis of accounting for inventories and (b) the meaning of "market" in the lower-of-cost-or-market method?

14. Steering Music Center has 5 CD players on hand at the balance sheet date. Each cost $100. The current replacement cost is $90 per unit. Under the lower-of-cost-or-market basis of accounting for inventories, what value should be reported for the CD players on the balance sheet? Why?

15. Maggie Stores has 20 toasters on hand at the balance sheet date. Each cost $28. The current replacement cost is $30 per unit. Under the lower-of-cost-or-market basis of accounting for inventories, what value should Maggie report for the toasters on the balance sheet? Why?

16. Cohen Company discovers in 2014 that its ending inventory at December 31, 2013, was $7,600 understated. What effect will this error have on (a) 2013 net income, (b) 2014 net income, and (c) the combined net income for the 2 years?

17. Raglan Company's balance sheet shows Inventory $162,800. What additional disclosures should be made?

18. Under what circumstances might inventory turnover be too high? That is, what possible negative consequences might occur?

19. **PEPSICO** What inventory cost flow does PepsiCo use for its inventories? (*Hint:* you will need to examine the notes for PepsiCo's financial statements.)

*20. "When perpetual inventory records are kept, the results under the FIFO and LIFO methods are the same as they would be in a periodic inventory system." Do you agree? Explain.

*21. How does the average-cost method of inventory costing differ between a perpetual inventory system and a periodic inventory system?

*22. When is it necessary to estimate inventories?

*23. Both the gross profit method and the retail inventory method are based on averages. For each method, indicate the average used, how it is determined, and how it is applied.

*24. Edmonds Company has net sales of $400,000 and cost of goods available for sale of $300,000. If the gross profit rate is 40%, what is the estimated cost of the ending inventory? Show computations.

*25. Park Shoe Shop had goods available for sale in 2014 with a retail price of $120,000. The cost of these goods was $84,000. If sales during the period were $90,000, what is the ending inventory at cost using the retail inventory method?

BRIEF EXERCISES

BE6-1 Dayne Company identifies the following items for possible inclusion in the taking of a physical inventory. Indicate whether each item should be included or excluded from the inventory taking.

Identify items to be included in taking a physical inventory.

(LO 1)

(a) Goods shipped on consignment by Dayne to another company.
(b) Goods in transit from a supplier shipped FOB destination.

(c) Goods sold but being held for customer pickup.

(d) Goods held on consignment from another company.

BE6-2 The ledger of Perez Company includes the following items: (a) Freight-In, (b) Purchase Returns and Allowances, (c) Purchases, (d) Sales Discounts, and (e) Purchase Discounts. Identify which items are included in goods available for sale.

BE6-3 In its first month of operations, Rusch Company made three purchases of merchandise in the following sequence: (1) 300 units at $6, (2) 400 units at $7, and (3) 200 units at $8. Assuming there are 450 units on hand, compute the cost of the ending inventory under the (a) FIFO method and (b) LIFO method. Rusch uses a periodic inventory system.

BE6-4 Data for Rusch Company are presented in BE6-3. Compute the cost of the ending inventory under the average-cost method, assuming there are 450 units on hand.

BE6-5 The management of Muni Corp. is considering the effects of various inventory-costing methods on its financial statements and its income tax expense. Assuming that the price the company pays for inventory is increasing, which method will:

(a) Provide the highest net income?

(b) Provide the highest ending inventory?

(c) Result in the lowest income tax expense?

(d) Result in the most stable earnings over a number of years?

BE6-6 In its first month of operation, Marquis Company purchased 100 units of inventory for $6, then 200 units for $7, and finally 150 units for $8. At the end of the month, 200 units remained. Compute the amount of phantom profit that would result if the company used FIFO rather than LIFO. Explain why this amount is referred to as *phantom profit*. The company uses the periodic method.

BE6-7 Pena Appliance Center accumulates the following cost and market data at December 31.

Inventory Categories	Cost Data	Market Data
Cameras	$12,000	$12,100
Camcorders	9,500	9,200
DVD players	14,000	12,800

Compute the lower-of-cost-or-market valuation for the company's total inventory.

BE6-8　Farr Company reports net income of $90,000 in 2014. However, ending inventory was understated $5,000. What is the correct net income for 2014? What effect, if any, will this error have on total assets as reported in the balance sheet at December 31, 2014?

BE6-9 At December 31, 2014, the following information was available for J. Simon Company: ending inventory $40,000, beginning inventory $60,000, cost of goods sold $300,000, and sales revenue $380,000. Calculate inventory turnover and days in inventory for J. Simon Company.

*****BE6-10** Abbott's Department Store uses a perpetual inventory system. Data for product E2-D2 include the following purchases.

Date	Number of Units	Unit Price
May 7	50	$11
July 28	30	13

On June 1, Abbott's sold 30 units, and on August 27, 35 more units. Prepare the perpetual inventory schedule for the above transactions using (a) FIFO, (b) LIFO, and (c) moving-average cost.

*****BE6-11** At May 31, Stuart Company has net sales of $330,000 and cost of goods available for sale of $230,000. Compute the estimated cost of the ending inventory, assuming the gross profit rate is 40%.

*****BE6-12** On June 30, Dusto Fabrics has the following data pertaining to the retail inventory method: Goods available for sale: at cost $35,000, at retail $50,000; net sales $42,000; and ending inventory at retail $8,000. Compute the estimated cost of the ending inventory using the retail inventory method.

> DO IT! REVIEW

DO IT! 6-1 Brazille Company just took its physical inventory. The count of inventory items on hand at the company's business locations resulted in a total inventory cost of $300,000. In reviewing the details of the count and related inventory transactions, you have discovered the following.

Apply rules of ownership to determine inventory cost.

(LO 1)

1. Brazille has sent inventory costing $21,000 on consignment to Nikki Company. All of this inventory was at Nikki's showrooms on December 31.

2. The company did not include in the count inventory (cost, $20,000) that was purchased on December 28, terms FOB shipping point. The goods were in transit on December 31.

3. The company did not include in the count inventory (cost, $17,000) that was sold with terms of FOB shipping point. The goods were in transit on December 31.

Compute the correct December 31 inventory.

DO IT! 6-2 The accounting records of Connor Electronics show the following data.

Compute cost of goods sold under different cost flow methods.

(LO 2)

Beginning inventory	3,000 units at $5
Purchases	8,000 units at $7
Sales	9,400 units at $10

Determine cost of goods sold during the period under a periodic inventory system using (a) the FIFO method, (b) the LIFO method, and (c) the average-cost method. (Round unit cost to nearest tenth of a cent.)

DO IT! 6-3 (a) Wahl Company sells three different categories of tools (small, medium, and large). The cost and market value of its inventory of tools are as follows.

Compute inventory value under LCM.

(LO 4)

	Cost	Market Value
Small	$ 64,000	$ 73,000
Medium	290,000	260,000
Large	152,000	149,000

Determine the value of the company's inventory under the lower-of-cost-or-market approach.

(b) Rhodee Company understated its 2013 ending inventory by $28,000. Determine the impact this error has on ending inventory, cost of goods sold, and stockholders' equity in 2013 and 2014.

DO IT! 6-4 Early in 2014, Racine Company switched to a just-in-time inventory system. Its sales, cost of goods sold, and inventory amounts for 2013 and 2014 are shown below.

Compute inventory turnover ratio and assess inventory level.

(LO 6)

	2013	2014
Sales	$3,120,000	$3,713,000
Cost of goods sold	1,200,000	1,425,000
Beginning inventory	180,000	220,000
Ending inventory	220,000	100,000

Determine the inventory turnover and days in inventory for 2013 and 2014. Discuss the changes in the amount of inventory, the inventory turnover and days in inventory, and the amount of sales across the two years.

EXERCISES

E6-1 Premier Bank and Trust is considering giving Alou Company a loan. Before doing so, management decides that further discussions with Alou's accountant may be desirable. One area of particular concern is the inventory account, which has a year-end balance of $297,000. Discussions with the accountant reveal the following.

Determine the correct inventory amount.

(LO 1)

1. Alou sold goods costing $38,000 to Comerico Company, FOB shipping point, on December 28. The goods are not expected to arrive at Comerico until January 12. The goods were not included in the physical inventory because they were not in the warehouse.
2. The physical count of the inventory did not include goods costing $95,000 that were shipped to Alou FOB destination on December 27 and were still in transit at year-end.
3. Alou received goods costing $19,000 on January 2. The goods were shipped FOB shipping point on December 26 by Grant Co. The goods were not included in the physical count.
4. Alou sold goods costing $35,000 to Emerick Co., FOB destination, on December 30. The goods were received at Emerick on January 8. They were not included in Alou's physical inventory.
5. Alou received goods costing $44,000 on January 2 that were shipped FOB shipping point on December 29. The shipment was a rush order that was supposed to arrive December 31. This purchase was included in the ending inventory of $297,000.

Instructions
Determine the correct inventory amount on December 31.

Determine the correct inventory amount.

(LO 1)

E6-2 Kale Wilson, an auditor with Sneed CPAs, is performing a review of Platinum Company's inventory account. Platinum did not have a good year, and top management is under pressure to boost reported income. According to its records, the inventory balance at year-end was $740,000. However, the following information was not considered when determining that amount.

1. Included in the company's count were goods with a cost of $250,000 that the company is holding on consignment. The goods belong to Superior Corporation.
2. The physical count did not include goods purchased by Platinum with a cost of $40,000 that were shipped FOB destination on December 28 and did not arrive at Platinum's warehouse until January 3.
3. Included in the inventory account was $17,000 of office supplies that were stored in the warehouse and were to be used by the company's supervisors and managers during the coming year.
4. The company received an order on December 29 that was boxed and sitting on the loading dock awaiting pick-up on December 31. The shipper picked up the goods on January 1 and delivered them on January 6. The shipping terms were FOB shipping point. The goods had a selling price of $49,000 and a cost of $33,000. The goods were not included in the count because they were sitting on the dock.
5. On December 29, Platinum shipped goods with a selling price of $80,000 and a cost of $60,000 to District Sales Corporation FOB shipping point. The goods arrived on January 3. District Sales had only ordered goods with a selling price of $10,000 and a cost of $8,000. However, a sales manager at Platinum had authorized the shipment and said that if District wanted to ship the goods back next week, it could.
6. Included in the count was $48,000 of goods that were parts for a machine that the company no longer made. Given the high-tech nature of Platinum's products, it was unlikely that these obsolete parts had any other use. However, management would prefer to keep them on the books at cost, "since that is what we paid for them, after all."

Instructions
Prepare a schedule to determine the correct inventory amount. Provide explanations for each item above, saying why you did or did not make an adjustment for each item.

Calculate cost of goods sold using specific identification and FIFO.

(LO 2, 3)

E6-3 On December 1, Discount Electronics Ltd. has three DVD players left in stock. All are identical, all are priced to sell at $150. One of the three DVD players left in stock, with serial #1012, was purchased on June 1 at a cost of $100. Another, with serial #1045, was purchased on November 1 for $90. The last player, serial #1056, was purchased on November 30 for $84.

Instructions
(a) Calculate the cost of goods sold using the FIFO periodic inventory method assuming that two of the three players were sold by the end of December, Discount Electronics' year-end.
(b) If Discount Electronics used the specific identification method instead of the FIFO method, how might it alter its earnings by "selectively choosing" which particular players to sell to the two customers? What would Discount's cost of goods sold be if the company wished to minimize earnings? Maximize earnings?
(c) Which of the two inventory methods do you recommend that Discount use? Explain why.

E6-4 Sherper's Boards sells a snowboard, Xpert, that is popular with snowboard enthusiasts. Information relating to Sherper's purchases of Xpert snowboards during September is shown below. During the same month, 121 Xpert snowboards were sold. Sherper's uses a periodic inventory system.

Compute inventory and cost of goods sold using FIFO and LIFO.

(LO 2)

Date	Explanation	Units	Unit Cost	Total Cost
Sept. 1	Inventory	23	$ 97	$ 2,231
Sept. 12	Purchases	45	102	4,590
Sept. 19	Purchases	20	104	2,080
Sept. 26	Purchases	44	105	4,620
	Totals	132		$13,521

Instructions

(a) Compute the ending inventory at September 30 and cost of goods sold using the FIFO and LIFO methods. Prove the amount allocated to cost of goods sold under each method.

(b) For both FIFO and LIFO, calculate the sum of ending inventory and cost of goods sold. What do you notice about the answers you found for each method?

E6-5 Zambian Co. uses a periodic inventory system. Its records show the following for the month of May, in which 68 units were sold.

Compute inventory and cost of goods sold using FIFO and LIFO.

(LO 2)

		Units	Unit Cost	Total Cost
May 1	Inventory	30	$ 9	$270
15	Purchases	25	11	275
24	Purchases	35	12	420
	Totals	90		$965

Instructions

Compute the ending inventory at May 31 and cost of goods sold using the FIFO and LIFO methods. Prove the amount allocated to cost of goods sold under each method.

E6-6 Eastland Company reports the following for the month of June.

Compute inventory and cost of goods sold using FIFO and LIFO.

(LO 2, 3)

		Units	Unit Cost	Total Cost
June 1	Inventory	200	$5	$1,000
12	Purchase	300	6	1,800
23	Purchase	500	7	3,500
30	Inventory	160		

Instructions

(a) Compute the cost of the ending inventory and the cost of goods sold under (1) FIFO and (2) LIFO.

(b) Which costing method gives the higher ending inventory? Why?

(c) Which method results in the higher cost of goods sold? Why?

E6-7 Givens Company had 100 units in beginning inventory at a total cost of $10,000. The company purchased 200 units at a total cost of $26,000. At the end of the year, Givens had 75 units in ending inventory.

Compute inventory under FIFO, LIFO, and average-cost.

(LO 2, 3)

Instructions

(a) Compute the cost of the ending inventory and the cost of goods sold under (1) FIFO, (2) LIFO, and (3) average-cost.

(b) Which cost flow method would result in the highest net income?

(c) Which cost flow method would result in inventories approximating current cost in the balance sheet?

(d) Which cost flow method would result in Givens paying the least taxes in the first year?

E6-8 Inventory data for Eastland Company are presented in E6-6.

Compute inventory and cost of goods sold using average-cost.

(LO 2, 3)

Instructions

(a) Compute the cost of the ending inventory and the cost of goods sold using the average-cost method.

(b) Will the results in (a) be higher or lower than the results under (1) FIFO and (2) LIFO?

(c) Why is the average unit cost not $6?

Determine ending inventory under LCM.

(LO 4)

E6-9 Kinshasa Camera Shop uses the lower-of-cost-or-market basis for its inventory. The following data are available at December 31.

Item	Units	Unit Cost	Market
Cameras:			
Minolta	8	$170	$156
Canon	6	150	152
Light meters:			
Vivitar	12	125	115
Kodak	14	115	135

Instructions

Determine the amount of the ending inventory by applying the lower-of-cost-or-market basis.

Compute lower-of-cost-or-market.

(LO 4)

E6-10 Fenton Company applied FIFO to its inventory and got the following results for its ending inventory.

Cameras	100 units at a cost per unit of $68
DVD players	150 units at a cost per unit of $75
iPods	125 units at a cost per unit of $80

The cost of purchasing units at year-end was cameras $70, DVD players $69, and iPods $78.

Instructions

Determine the amount of ending inventory at lower-of-cost-or-market.

Determine effects of inventory errors.

(LO 5)

E6-11 Delhi Hardware reported cost of goods sold as follows.

	2013	2014
Beginning inventory	$ 20,000	$ 30,000
Cost of goods purchased	150,000	175,000
Cost of goods available for sale	170,000	205,000
Ending inventory	30,000	35,000
Cost of goods sold	$140,000	$170,000

Delhi made two errors: (1) 2013 ending inventory was overstated $2,000, and (2) 2014 ending inventory was understated $6,000.

Instructions

Compute the correct cost of goods sold for each year.

Prepare correct income statements.

(LO 5)

E6-12 Horner Watch Company reported the following income statement data for a 2-year period.

	2013	2014
Sales revenue	$210,000	$250,000
Cost of goods sold		
Beginning inventory	32,000	44,000
Cost of goods purchased	173,000	202,000
Cost of goods available for sale	205,000	246,000
Ending inventory	44,000	52,000
Cost of goods sold	161,000	194,000
Gross profit	$ 49,000	$ 56,000

Horner uses a periodic inventory system. The inventories at January 1, 2013, and December 31, 2014, are correct. However, the ending inventory at December 31, 2013, was understated $6,000.

Instructions

(a) Prepare correct income statement data for the 2 years.

(b) What is the cumulative effect of the inventory error on total gross profit for the 2 years?

(c) ▭▭▭▭▭▶ Explain in a letter to the president of Horner Watch Company what has happened, i.e., the nature of the error and its effect on the financial statements.

E6-13 This information is available for Sepia Photo Corporation for 2012, 2013, and 2014.

Compute inventory turnover, days in inventory, and gross profit rate.

(LO 6)

	2012	**2013**	**2014**
Beginning inventory	$ 100,000	$ 330,000	$ 400,000
Ending inventory	330,000	400,000	480,000
Cost of goods sold	900,000	1,120,000	1,300,000
Sales revenue	1,200,000	1,600,000	1,900,000

Instructions

Calculate inventory turnover, days in inventory, and gross profit rate (from Chapter 5) for Sepia's Photo Corporation for 2012, 2013, and 2014. Comment on any trends.

Compute inventory turnover and days in inventory.

(LO 6)

E6-14 The cost of goods sold computations for Silver Company and Gold Company are shown below.

	Silver Company	**Gold Company**
Beginning inventory	$ 47,000	$ 71,000
Cost of goods purchased	200,000	290,000
Cost of goods available for sale	247,000	361,000
Ending inventory	55,000	69,000
Cost of goods sold	$192,000	$292,000

Instructions

(a) Compute inventory turnover and days in inventory for each company.

(b) Which company moves its inventory more quickly?

*E6-15 Roselle Appliance uses a perpetual inventory system. For its flat-screen television sets, the January 1 inventory was 3 sets at $600 each. On January 10, Roselle purchased 6 units at $648 each. The company sold 2 units on January 8 and 4 units on January 15.

Apply cost flow methods to perpetual records.

(LO 7)

Instructions

Compute the ending inventory under (1) FIFO, (2) LIFO, and (3) moving-average cost.

*E6-16 Eastland Company reports the following for the month of June.

Calculate inventory and cost of goods sold using three cost flow methods in a perpetual inventory system.

(LO 7)

Date	Explanation	Units	Unit Cost	Total Cost
June 1	Inventory	200	$5	$1,000
12	Purchase	300	6	1,800
23	Purchase	500	7	3,500
30	Inventory	160		

Instructions

(a) Calculate the cost of the ending inventory and the cost of goods sold for each cost flow assumption, using a perpetual inventory system. Assume a sale of 400 units occurred on June15 for a selling price of $8 and a sale of 440 units on June 27 for $9.

(b) How do the results differ from E6-6 and E6-8?

(c) Why is the average unit cost not $6 [($5 + $6 + $7) ÷ 3 = $6]?

*E6-17 Information about Sherper's Boards is presented in E6-4. Additional data regarding Sherper's sales of Xpert snowboards are provided below. Assume that Sherper's uses a perpetual inventory system.

Apply cost flow methods to perpetual records.

(LO 7)

Date		Units	Unit Price	Total Revenue
Sept. 5	Sale	12	$199	$ 2,388
Sept. 16	Sale	50	203	10,150
Sept. 29	Sale	59	209	12,331
	Totals	121		$24,869

Instructions

(a) Compute ending inventory at September 30 using FIFO, LIFO, and moving-average cost.

(b) Compare ending inventory using a perpetual inventory system to ending inventory using a periodic inventory system (from E6-4).

(c) Which inventory cost flow method (FIFO, LIFO) gives the same ending inventory value under both periodic and perpetual? Which method gives different ending inventory values?

Use the gross profit method to estimate inventory.

(LO 8)

*E6-18 Adler Company reported the following information for November and December 2014.

	November	December
Cost of goods purchased	$500,000	$ 610,000
Inventory, beginning-of-month	100,000	120,000
Inventory, end-of-month	120,000	????
Sales revenue	750,000	1,000,000

Adler's ending inventory at December 31 was destroyed in a fire.

Instructions
(a) Compute the gross profit rate for November.
(b) Using the gross profit rate for November, determine the estimated cost of inventory lost in the fire.

Determine merchandise lost using the gross profit method of estimating inventory.

(LO 8)

*E6-19 The inventory of Florence Company was destroyed by fire on March 1. From an examination of the accounting records, the following data for the first 2 months of the year are obtained: Sales Revenue $51,000, Sales Returns and Allowances $1,000, Purchases $31,200, Freight-In $1,200, and Purchase Returns and Allowances $1,800.

Instructions
Determine the merchandise lost by fire, assuming:

(a) A beginning inventory of $20,000 and a gross profit rate of 40% on net sales.
(b) A beginning inventory of $30,000 and a gross profit rate of 32% on net sales.

Determine ending inventory at cost using retail method.

(LO 8)

*E6-20 Peacock Shoe Store uses the retail inventory method for its two departments, Women's Shoes and Men's Shoes. The following information for each department is obtained.

Item	Women's Shoes	Men's Shoes
Beginning inventory at cost	$ 36,500	$ 45,000
Cost of goods purchased at cost	148,000	136,300
Net sales	178,000	185,000
Beginning inventory at retail	46,000	60,000
Cost of goods purchased at retail	179,000	185,000

Instructions
Compute the estimated cost of the ending inventory for each department under the retail inventory method.

EXERCISES: SET B AND CHALLENGE EXERCISES

Visit the book's companion website, at **www.wiley.com/college/weygandt**, and choose the Student Companion site to access Exercise Set B and Challenge Exercises.

PROBLEMS: SET A

Determine items and amounts to be recorded in inventory.

(LO 1)

P6-1A Columbus Limited is trying to determine the value of its ending inventory at February 28, 2014, the company's year-end. The accountant counted everything that was in the warehouse as of February 28, which resulted in an ending inventory valuation of $48,000. However, she didn't know how to treat the following transactions so she didn't record them.

(a) On February 26, Columbus shipped to a customer goods costing $800. The goods were shipped FOB shipping point, and the receiving report indicates that the customer received the goods on March 2.
(b) On February 26, Shira Inc. shipped goods to Columbus FOB destination. The invoice price was $350. The receiving report indicates that the goods were received by Columbus on March 2.
(c) Columbus had $620 of inventory at a customer's warehouse "on approval." The customer was going to let Columbus know whether it wanted the merchandise by the end of the week, March 4.
(d) Columbus also had $400 of inventory on consignment at a Palletine craft shop.

(e) On February 26, Columbus ordered goods costing $750. The goods were shipped FOB shipping point on February 27. Columbus received the goods on March 1.

(f) On February 28, Columbus packaged goods and had them ready for shipping to a customer FOB destination. The invoice price was $350; the cost of the items was $220. The receiving report indicates that the goods were received by the customer on March 2.

(g) Columbus had damaged goods set aside in the warehouse because they are no longer saleable. These goods cost $400 and Columbus originally expected to sell these items for $600.

Instructions

For each of the above transactions, specify whether the item in question should be included in ending inventory and, if so, at what amount. For each item that is not included in ending inventory, indicate who owns it and what account, if any, it should have been recorded in.

P6-2A Dyna Distribution markets CDs of the performing artist King James. At the beginning of March, Dyna had in beginning inventory 1,500 King James CDs with a unit cost of $7. During March, Dyna made the following purchases of King James CDs.

| March 5 | 3,500 @ $8 | March 21 | 2,000 @ $10 |
| March 13 | 4,000 @ $9 | March 26 | 2,000 @ $11 |

During March, 10,000 units were sold. Dyna uses a periodic inventory system.

Determine cost of goods sold and ending inventory using FIFO, LIFO, and average-cost with analysis.

(LO 2, 3)

Instructions

(a) Determine the cost of goods available for sale.

(b) Determine (1) the ending inventory and (2) the cost of goods sold under each of the assumed cost flow methods (FIFO, LIFO, and average-cost). Prove the accuracy of the cost of goods sold under the FIFO and LIFO methods.

(c) Which cost flow method results in (1) the highest inventory amount for the balance sheet and (2) the highest cost of goods sold for the income statement?

(b) (2) Cost of goods sold:
FIFO $84,500
LIFO $94,000
Average $89,615

P6-3A Milo Company had a beginning inventory of 400 units of Product Kimbo at a cost of $8 per unit. During the year, purchases were:

| Feb. 20 | 300 units at $9 | Aug. 12 | 600 units at $11 |
| May 5 | 500 units at $10 | Dec. 8 | 200 units at $12 |

Milo Company uses a periodic inventory system. Sales totaled 1,500 units.

Determine cost of goods sold and ending inventory using FIFO, LIFO, and average-cost with analysis.

(LO 2, 3)

Instructions

(a) Determine the cost of goods available for sale.

(b) Determine (1) the ending inventory and (2) the cost of goods sold under each of the assumed cost flow methods (FIFO, LIFO, and average-cost). Prove the accuracy of the cost of goods sold under the FIFO and LIFO methods.

(c) Which cost flow method results in (1) the lowest inventory amount for the balance sheet, and (2) the lowest cost of goods sold for the income statement?

(b) Cost of goods sold:
FIFO $14,200
LIFO $15,800
Average $14,925

P6-4A The management of Red Robin Co. is reevaluating the appropriateness of using its present inventory cost flow method, which is average-cost. They request your help in determining the results of operations for 2014 if either the FIFO method or the LIFO method had been used. For 2014, the accounting records show the following data.

Compute ending inventory, prepare income statements, and answer questions using FIFO and LIFO.

(LO 2, 3)

Inventories		Purchases and Sales	
Beginning (10,000 units)	$22,800	Total net sales (225,000 units)	$865,000
Ending (15,000 units)		Total cost of goods purchased (230,000 units)	578,500

Purchases were made quarterly as follows.

Quarter	Units	Unit Cost	Total Cost
1	60,000	$2.30	$138,000
2	50,000	2.50	125,000
3	50,000	2.60	130,000
4	70,000	2.65	185,500
	230,000		$578,500

Operating expenses were $147,000, and the company's income tax rate is 32%.

Instructions

(a) Prepare comparative condensed income statements for 2014 under FIFO and LIFO. (Show computations of ending inventory.)

(b) ▯▭▭▭▷ Answer the following questions for management.

  (1) Which cost flow method (FIFO or LIFO) produces the more meaningful inventory amount for the balance sheet? Why?

  (2) Which cost flow method (FIFO or LIFO) produces the more meaningful net income? Why?

  (3) Which cost flow method (FIFO or LIFO) is more likely to approximate actual physical flow of the goods? Why?

  (4) How much additional cash will be available for management under LIFO than under FIFO? Why?

  (5) Will gross profit under the average-cost method be higher or lower than (i) FIFO and (ii) LIFO? (*Note:* It is not necessary to quantify your answer.)

Calculate ending inventory, cost of goods sold, gross profit, and gross profit rate under periodic method; compare results.

(LO 2, 3)

P6-5A You are provided with the following information for Matthew Inc. for the month ended October 31, 2014. Matthew uses a periodic method for inventory.

Date	Description	Units	Unit Cost or Selling Price
October 1	Beginning inventory	60	$24
October 9	Purchase	120	26
October 11	Sale	100	35
October 17	Purchase	70	27
October 22	Sale	65	40
October 25	Purchase	80	28
October 29	Sale	120	40

Instructions

(a) Calculate (i) ending inventory, (ii) cost of goods sold, (iii) gross profit, and (iv) gross profit rate under each of the following methods.

  (1) LIFO.

  (2) FIFO.

  (3) Average-cost.

(b) Compare results for the three cost flow assumptions.

Compare specific identification, FIFO and LIFO under periodic method; use cost flow assumption to influence earnings.

(LO 2, 3)

P6-6A You have the following information for Greco Diamonds. Greco Diamonds uses the periodic method of accounting for its inventory transactions. Greco only carries one brand and size of diamonds—all are identical. Each batch of diamonds purchased is carefully coded and marked with its purchase cost.

March 1	Beginning inventory 150 diamonds at a cost of $310 per diamond.
March 3	Purchased 200 diamonds at a cost of $350 each.
March 5	Sold 180 diamonds for $600 each.
March 10	Purchased 350 diamonds at a cost of $380 each.
March 25	Sold 400 diamonds for $650 each.

Instructions

(a) Assume that Greco Diamonds uses the specific identification cost flow method.

  (1) Demonstrate how Greco Diamonds could maximize its gross profit for the month by specifically selecting which diamonds to sell on March 5 and March 25.

  (2) Demonstrate how Greco Diamonds could minimize its gross profit for the month by selecting which diamonds to sell on March 5 and March 25.

(b) Assume that Greco Diamonds uses the FIFO cost flow assumption. Calculate cost of goods sold. How much gross profit would Greco Diamonds report under this cost flow assumption?

(c) Assume that Greco Diamonds uses the LIFO cost flow assumption. Calculate cost of goods sold. How much gross profit would the company report under this cost flow assumption?

Compute ending inventory, prepare income statements, and answer questions using FIFO and LIFO.

(LO 2, 3)

(d) Which cost flow method should Greco Diamonds select? Explain.

P6-7A The management of Mumba Inc. asks your help in determining the comparative effects of the FIFO and LIFO inventory cost flow methods. For 2014, the accounting records provide the data shown at the top of the next page.

Inventory, January 1 (10,000 units)	$ 35,000
Cost of 120,000 units purchased	501,000
Selling price of 100,000 units sold	665,000
Operating expenses	130,000

Units purchased consisted of 40,000 units at $4.00 on May 10; 60,000 units at $4.20 on August 15; and 20,000 units at $4.45 on November 20. Income taxes are 28%.

Instructions
(a) Prepare comparative condensed income statements for 2014 under FIFO and LIFO. (Show computations of ending inventory.)
(b) ▭▭▭▶ Answer the following questions for management in the form of a business letter.
　(1) Which inventory cost flow method produces the most meaningful inventory amount for the balance sheet? Why?
　(2) Which inventory cost flow method produces the most meaningful net income? Why?
　(3) Which inventory cost flow method is most likely to approximate the actual physical flow of the goods? Why?
　(4) How much more cash will be available for management under LIFO than under FIFO? Why?
　(5) How much of the gross profit under FIFO is illusionary in comparison with the gross profit under LIFO?

Gross profit:
FIFO　$260,000
LIFO　$244,000

*P6-8A Tempo Ltd. is a retailer operating in Dartmouth, Nova Scotia. Tempo uses the perpetual inventory method. All sales returns from customers result in the goods being returned to inventory; the inventory is not damaged. Assume that there are no credit transactions; all amounts are settled in cash. You are provided with the following information for Tempo Ltd. for the month of January 2014.

Calculate cost of goods sold and ending inventory for FIFO, moving-average cost, and LIFO under the perpetual system; compare gross profit under each assumption.

(LO 7)

Date	Description	Quantity	Unit Cost or Selling Price
December 31	Ending inventory	150	$19
January 2	Purchase	100	21
January 6	Sale	150	40
January 9	Sale return	10	40
January 9	Purchase	75	24
January 10	Purchase return	15	24
January 10	Sale	50	45
January 23	Purchase	100	26
January 30	Sale	160	50

Instructions
(a) For each of the following cost flow assumptions, calculate (i) cost of goods sold, (ii) ending inventory, and (iii) gross profit.
　(1) LIFO.　(2) FIFO.　(3) Moving-average cost.
(b) Compare results for the three cost flow assumptions.

Gross profit:
LIFO　$8,000
FIFO　$8,420
Average　$8,266

*P6-9A Dominican Appliance Mart began operations on May 1. It uses a perpetual inventory system. During May, the company had the following purchases and sales for its Model 25 Sureshot camera.

Determine ending inventory under a perpetual inventory system.

(LO 7)

Date	Purchases Units	Purchases Unit Cost	Sales Units
May 1	7	$155	
4			4
8	8	$170	
12			5
15	6	$185	
20			3
25			5

Instructions
(a) Determine the ending inventory under a perpetual inventory system using (1) FIFO, (2) moving-average cost, and (3) LIFO.

(a) FIFO　$740
Average　$702
LIFO　$635

(b) Which costing method produces (1) the highest ending inventory valuation and (2) the lowest ending inventory valuation?

Estimate inventory loss using gross profit method.

(LO 8)

*P6-10A Fram Company lost 70% of its inventory in a fire on March 25, 2014. The accounting records showed the following gross profit data for February and March.

	February	March (to 3/25)
Net sales	$300,000	$260,000
Net purchases	197,800	191,000
Freight-in	2,900	4,000
Beginning inventory	4,500	25,200
Ending inventory	25,200	?

Fram Company is fully insured for fire losses but must prepare a report for the insurance company.

Instructions
(a) Compute the gross profit rate for the month of February.
(b) Using the gross profit rate for February, determine both the estimated total inventory and inventory lost in the fire in March.

Compute ending inventory using retail method.

(LO 8)

*P6-11A Thai Department Store uses the retail inventory method to estimate its monthly ending inventories. The following information is available for two of its departments at August 31, 2014.

	Sporting Goods		Jewelry and Cosmetics	
	Cost	Retail	Cost	Retail
Net sales		$1,010,000		$1,150,000
Purchases	$675,000	1,066,000	$741,000	1,158,000
Purchase returns	(26,000)	(40,000)	(12,000)	(20,000)
Purchase discounts	(12,360)	—	(2,440)	—
Freight-in	9,000	—	14,000	—
Beginning inventory	47,360	74,000	39,440	62,000

At December 31, Thai Department Store takes a physical inventory at retail. The actual retail values of the inventories in each department are Sporting Goods $85,000, and Jewelry and Cosmetics $54,000.

Instructions
(a) Determine the estimated cost of the ending inventory for each department on August 31, 2014, using the retail inventory method.
(b) Compute the ending inventory at cost for each department at **December 31**, assuming the cost-to-retail ratios are 60% for Sporting Goods and 64% for Jewelry and Cosmetics.

PROBLEMS: SET B

Determine items and amounts to be recorded in inventory.

(LO 1)

P6-1B Banff Limited is trying to determine the value of its ending inventory as of February 28, 2014, the company's year-end. The following transactions occurred, and the accountant asked your help in determining whether they should be recorded or not.

(a) On February 26, Banff shipped goods costing $800 to a customer and charged the customer $1,000. The goods were shipped with terms FOB shipping point and the receiving report indicates that the customer received the goods on March 2.
(b) On February 26, Vendor Inc. shipped goods to Banff under terms FOB shipping point. The invoice price was $450 plus $30 for freight. The receiving report indicates that the goods were received by Banff on March 2.
(c) Banff had $720 of inventory isolated in the warehouse. The inventory is designated for a customer who has requested that the goods be shipped on March 10.
(d) Also included in Banff's warehouse is $700 of inventory that Jasper Producers shipped to Banff on consignment.

(e) On February 26, Banff issued a purchase order to acquire goods costing $900. The goods were shipped with terms FOB destination on February 27. Banff received the goods on March 2.

(f) On February 26, Banff shipped goods to a customer under terms FOB destination. The invoice price was $350; the cost of the items was $200. The receiving report indicates that the goods were received by the customer on February 28.

Instructions

For each of the above transactions, specify whether the item in question should be included in ending inventory, and if so, at what amount.

P6-2B Doom's Day Distribution markets CDs of the performing artist Marilynn. At the beginning of October, Doom's Day had in beginning inventory 2,000 of Marilynn's CDs with a unit cost of $7. During October, Doom's Day made the following purchases of Marilynn's CDs.

Determine cost of goods sold and ending inventory using FIFO, LIFO, and average-cost with analysis.

(LO 2, 3)

Oct. 3	3,000 @ $8	Oct. 19	4,000 @ $10
Oct. 9	5,500 @ $9	Oct. 25	2,000 @ $11

During October, 13,500 units were sold. Doom's Day uses a periodic inventory system.

Instructions

(a) Determine the cost of goods available for sale.

(b) Determine (1) the ending inventory and (2) the cost of goods sold under each of the assumed cost flow methods (FIFO, LIFO, and average-cost). Prove the accuracy of the cost of goods sold under the FIFO and LIFO methods.

(c) Which cost flow method results in (1) the highest inventory amount for the balance sheet and (2) the highest cost of goods sold for the income statement?

(b)(2) Cost of goods sold:
FIFO $117,500
LIFO $127,500
Average $122,317

P6-3B Collins Company had a beginning inventory on January 1 of 100 units of Product 4-18-15 at a cost of $21 per unit. During the year, the following purchases were made.

Determine cost of goods sold and ending inventory, using FIFO, LIFO, and average-cost with analysis.

(LO 2, 3)

Mar. 15	300 units at $24	Sept. 4	300 units at $28
July 20	200 units at $25	Dec. 2	100 units at $30

700 units were sold. Collins Company uses a periodic inventory system.

Instructions

(a) Determine the cost of goods available for sale.

(b) Determine (1) the ending inventory, and (2) the cost of goods sold under each of the assumed cost flow methods (FIFO, LIFO, and average-cost). Prove the accuracy of the cost of goods sold under the FIFO and LIFO methods.

(c) Which cost flow method results in (1) the highest inventory amount for the balance sheet, and (2) the highest cost of goods sold for the income statement?

(b)(2) Cost of goods sold:
FIFO $17,100
LIFO $18,800
Average $17,990

P6-4B The management of Gilbert Inc. is reevaluating the appropriateness of using its present inventory cost flow method, which is average-cost. The company requests your help in determining the results of operations for 2014 if either the FIFO or the LIFO method had been used. For 2014, the accounting records show these data:

Compute ending inventory, prepare income statements, and answer questions using FIFO and LIFO.

(LO 2, 3)

Inventories		Purchases and Sales	
Beginning (8,000 units)	$16,000	Total net sales (188,000 units)	$780,000
Ending (15,000 units)		Total cost of goods purchased	
		(195,000 units)	480,500

Purchases were made quarterly as follows.

Quarter	Units	Unit Cost	Total Cost
1	50,000	$2.20	$110,000
2	40,000	2.40	96,000
3	45,000	2.50	112,500
4	60,000	2.70	162,000
	195,000		$480,500

Operating expenses were $130,000, and the company's income tax rate is 36%.

Instructions

(a) Prepare comparative condensed income statements for 2014 under FIFO and LIFO. (Show computations of ending inventory.)

(b) ▣▤▤▤▷ Answer the following questions for management.

(1) Which cost flow method (FIFO or LIFO) produces the more meaningful inventory amount for the balance sheet? Why?

(2) Which cost flow method (FIFO or LIFO) produces the more meaningful net income? Why?

(3) Which cost flow method (FIFO or LIFO) is more likely to approximate the actual physical flow of goods? Why?

(4) How much more cash will be available for management under LIFO than under FIFO? Why?

(5) Will gross profit under the average-cost method be higher or lower than FIFO? Than LIFO? (*Note:* It is not necessary to quantify your answer.)

P6-5B You are provided with the following information for Lahti Inc. for the month ended June 30, 2014. Lahti uses the periodic method for inventory.

Date	Description	Quantity	Unit Cost or Selling Price
June 1	Beginning inventory	40	$40
June 4	Purchase	135	43
June 10	Sale	110	70
June 11	Sale return	15	70
June 18	Purchase	55	46
June 18	Purchase return	10	46
June 25	Sale	60	75
June 28	Purchase	30	50

Instructions

(a) Calculate (i) ending inventory, (ii) cost of goods sold, (iii) gross profit, and (iv) gross profit rate under each of the following methods.

(1) LIFO.   (2) FIFO.   (3) Average-cost.

(b) Compare results for the three cost flow assumptions.

P6-6B You are provided with the following information for Gas Guzzlers. Gas Guzzlers uses the periodic method of accounting for its inventory transactions.

March 1	Beginning inventory 2,200 liters at a cost of 60¢ per liter.
March 3	Purchased 2,500 liters at a cost of 65¢ per liter.
March 5	Sold 2,200 liters for $1.05 per liter.
March 10	Purchased 4,000 liters at a cost of 72¢ per liter.
March 20	Purchased 2,500 liters at a cost of 80¢ per liter.
March 30	Sold 5,500 liters for $1.25 per liter.

Instructions

(a) Prepare partial income statements through gross profit, and calculate the value of ending inventory that would be reported on the balance sheet, under each of the following cost flow assumptions. (Round ending inventory and cost of goods sold to the nearest dollar.)

(1) Specific identification method assuming:

(i) The March 5 sale consisted of 1,100 liters from the March 1 beginning inventory and 1,100 liters from the March 3 purchase; and

(ii) The March 30 sale consisted of the following number of units sold from beginning inventory and each purchase: 450 liters from March 1; 850 liters from March 3; 2,900 liters from March 10; 1,300 liters from March 20.

(2) FIFO.

(3) LIFO.

(b) How can companies use a cost flow method to justify price increases? Which cost flow method would best support an argument to increase prices?

P6-7B The management of Creek Co. asks your help in determining the comparative effects of the FIFO and LIFO inventory cost flow methods. For 2014, the accounting records provide the data shown at the top of the next page.

Inventory, January 1 (10,000 units)	$ 47,000
Cost of 100,000 units purchased	532,000
Selling price of 85,000 units sold	740,000
Operating expenses	140,000

Units purchased consisted of 35,000 units at $5.10 on May 10; 35,000 units at $5.30 on August 15; and 30,000 units at $5.60 on November 20. Income taxes are 32%.

Instructions
(a) Prepare comparative condensed income statements for 2014 under FIFO and LIFO. (Show computations of ending inventory.)
(b) ▭▭▭▶ Answer the following questions for management.
    (1) Which inventory cost flow method produces the most meaningful inventory amount for the balance sheet? Why?
    (2) Which inventory cost flow method produces the most meaningful net income? Why?
    (3) Which inventory cost flow method is most likely to approximate actual physical flow of the goods? Why?
    (4) How much additional cash will be available for management under LIFO than under FIFO? Why?
    (5) How much of the gross profit under FIFO is illusory in comparison with the gross profit under LIFO?

(a) Net income
FIFO $109,480
LIFO $98,260

*P6-8B Yuan Li Inc. is a retailer operating in Edmonton, Alberta. Yuan Li uses the perpetual inventory method. All sales returns from customers result in the goods being returned to inventory; the inventory is not damaged. Assume that there are no credit transactions; all amounts are settled in cash. You are provided with the following information for Yuan Li Inc. for the month of January 2014.

Calculate cost of goods sold and ending inventory under LIFO, FIFO, and moving-average cost under the perpetual system; compare gross profit under each assumption.

(LO 7)

Date	Description	Quantity	Unit Cost or Selling Price
January 1	Beginning inventory	100	$14
January 5	Purchase	150	17
January 8	Sale	110	28
January 10	Sale return	10	28
January 15	Purchase	55	19
January 16	Purchase return	5	19
January 20	Sale	80	32
January 25	Purchase	30	22

Instructions
(a) For each of the following cost flow assumptions, calculate (i) cost of goods sold, (ii) ending inventory, and (iii) gross profit.
    (1) LIFO.   (2) FIFO.   (3) Moving-average cost.
(b) Compare results for the three cost flow assumptions.

Gross profit:
LIFO $2,200
FIFO $2,600
Average $2,452

*P6-9B Lemansky Co. began operations on July 1. It uses a perpetual inventory system. During July, the company had the following purchases and sales.

Determine ending inventory under a perpetual inventory system.

(LO 7)

Date	Purchases Units	Purchases Unit Cost	Sales Units
July 1	5	$120	
July 6			3
July 11	6	$136	
July 14			4
July 21	8	$147	
July 27			6

Instructions
(a) Determine the ending inventory under a perpetual inventory system using (1) FIFO, (2) moving-average cost, and (3) LIFO.
(b) Which costing method produces the highest ending inventory valuation?

(a) Ending inventory
FIFO $882
Avg $852
LIFO $806

Compute gross profit rate and inventory loss using gross profit method.

(LO 8)

*P6-10B Bristol Company lost all of its inventory in a fire on December 26, 2014. The accounting records showed the following gross profit data for November and December.

	November	December (to 12/26)
Net sales	$600,000	$700,000
Beginning inventory	30,000	33,000
Purchases	368,000	420,000
Purchase returns and allowances	13,300	14,900
Purchase discounts	8,500	9,500
Freight-in	4,800	5,900
Ending inventory	33,000	?

Bristol is fully insured for fire losses but must prepare a report for the insurance company.

Instructions

(a) Compute the gross profit rate for November.

(b) Using the gross profit rate for November, determine the estimated cost of the inventory lost in the fire.

Compute ending inventory using retail method.

(LO 8)

*P6-11B Hooked on Books uses the retail inventory method to estimate its monthly ending inventories. The following information is available for two of its departments at October 31, 2014.

	Hardcovers		Paperbacks	
	Cost	Retail	Cost	Retail
Beginning inventory	$ 420,000	$ 700,000	$ 280,000	$ 360,000
Purchases	2,094,000	3,200,000	1,155,000	1,540,000
Freight-in	26,000		12,000	
Purchase discounts	44,000		22,000	
Net sales		3,100,000		1,570,000

At December 31, Hooked on Books takes a physical inventory at retail. The actual retail values of the inventories in each department are Hardcovers $790,000 and Paperbacks $335,000.

Instructions

(a) Determine the estimated cost of the ending inventory for each department at October 31, 2014, using the retail inventory method.

(b) Compute the ending inventory at cost for each department at December 31, assuming the cost-to-retail ratios for the year are 65% for Hardcovers and 77% for Paperbacks.

PROBLEMS: SET C

Visit the book's companion website, at **www.wiley.com/college/weygandt**, and choose the Student Companion site to access Problem Set C.

COMPREHENSIVE PROBLEM

CP6 On December 1, 2014, Seattle Company had the account balances shown below.

Debits			Credits	
Cash	$ 4,650	Accumulated Depreciation—Equipment	$ 1,500
Accounts Receivable	3,900	Accounts Payable	3,000
Inventory	1,950*	Common Stock	20,000
Equipment	21,000	Retained Earnings	7,000
	$31,500		$31,500

*(3,000 × $0.65)

The following transactions occurred during December.

Dec. 3 Purchased 4,000 units of inventory on account at a cost of $0.72 per unit.
     5 Sold 4,400 units of inventory on account for $0.92 per unit. (It sold 3,000 of the $0.65 units and 1,400 of the $0.72.)
     7 Granted the December 5 customer $180 credit for 200 units of inventory returned costing $150. These units were returned to inventory.
   17 Purchased 2,200 units of inventory for cash at $0.78 each.
   22 Sold 2,000 units of inventory on account for $0.95 per unit. (It sold 2,000 of the $0.72 units.)

Adjustment data:
1. Accrued salaries payable $400.
2. Depreciation $200 per month.

Instructions
(a) Journalize the December transactions and adjusting entries, assuming Seattle uses the perpetual inventory method.
(b) Enter the December 1 balances in the ledger T-accounts and post the December transactions. In addition to the accounts mentioned above, use the following additional accounts: Cost of Goods Sold, Depreciation Expense, Salaries and Wages Expense, Salaries and Wages Payable, Sales Revenue, and Sales Returns and Allowances.
(c) Prepare an adjusted trial balance as of December 31, 2014.
(d) Prepare an income statement for December 2014 and a classified balance sheet at December 31, 2014.
(e) Compute ending inventory and cost of goods sold under FIFO, assuming Seattle Company uses the periodic inventory system.
(f) Compute ending inventory and cost of goods sold under LIFO, assuming Seattle Company uses the periodic inventory system.

CONTINUING COOKIE CHRONICLE

(*Note:* This is a continuation of the Cookie Chronicle from Chapters 1–5.)

CCC6 Natalie is busy establishing both divisions of her business (cookie classes and mixer sales) and completing her business degree. Her goals for the next 11 months are to sell one mixer per month and to give two to three classes per week.

    The cost of the fine European mixers is expected to increase. Natalie has just negotiated new terms with Kzinski that include shipping costs in the negotiated purchase price (mixers will be shipped FOB destination). Natalie must choose a cost flow assumption for her mixer inventory.

Go to the book's companion website, www.wiley.com/college/weygandt, to see the completion of this problem.

Broadening Your **PERSPECTIVE**

Financial Reporting and Analysis

Financial Reporting Problem: PepsiCo, Inc.

BYP6-1 The notes that accompany a company's financial statements provide informative details that would clutter the amounts and descriptions presented in the statements. Refer to the financial statements of PepsiCo, Inc. and the Notes to Consolidated Financial Statements in Appendix A.

PEPSICO

Instructions

Answer the following questions. Complete the requirements in millions of dollars, as shown in PepsiCo's annual report.

(a) What did PepsiCo report for the amount of inventories in its consolidated balance sheet at December 25, 2010? At December 26, 2009?

(b) Compute the dollar amount of change and the percentage change in inventories between 2009 and 2010. Compute inventory as a percentage of current assets at December 25, 2010.

(c) How does PepsiCo value its inventories? Which inventory cost flow method does PepsiCo use? (See Notes to the Financial Statements.)

(d) What is the cost of sales (cost of goods sold) reported by PepsiCo for 2010, 2009, and 2008? Compute the percentage of cost of sales to net sales in 2010.

Comparative Analysis Problem: PepsiCo, Inc. vs. The Coca-Cola Company

 **BYP6-2** PepsiCo's financial statements are presented in Appendix A. Financial statements of The Coca-Cola Company are presented in Appendix B.

Instructions

(a) Based on the information contained in these financial statements, compute the following 2010 ratios for each company.
   (1) Inventory turnover ratio.
   (2) Days in inventory.

(b) What conclusions concerning the management of the inventory can you draw from these data?

Real-World Focus

BYP6-3 A company's annual report usually will identify the inventory method used. Knowing that, you can analyze the effects of the inventory method on the income statement and balance sheet.

Address: **www.cisco.com,** or go to **www.wiley.com/college/weygandt**

Instructions

Answer the following questions based on the current year's annual report on Cisco's website.

(a) At Cisco's fiscal year-end, what was the inventory on the balance sheet?
(b) How has this changed from the previous fiscal year-end?
(c) How much of the inventory was finished goods?
(d) What inventory method does Cisco use?

Critical Thinking

Decision-Making Across the Organization

 **BYP6-4** On April 10, 2014, fire damaged the office and warehouse of Ehlert Company. Most of the accounting records were destroyed, but the following account balances were determined as of March 31, 2014: Inventory (January 1, 2014), $80,000; Sales Revenue (January 1–March 31, 2014), $180,000; Purchases (January 1–March 31, 2014), $94,000.

The company's fiscal year ends on December 31. It uses a periodic inventory system.

From an analysis of the April bank statement, you discover cancelled checks of $4,200 for cash purchases during the period April 1–10. Deposits during the same period totaled $20,500. Of that amount, 60% were collections on accounts receivable, and the balance was cash sales.

Correspondence with the company's principal suppliers revealed $12,400 of purchases on account from April 1 to April 10. Of that amount, $1,900 was for merchandise in transit on April 10 that was shipped FOB destination.

Correspondence with the company's principal customers produced acknowledgments of credit sales totaling $37,000 from April 1 to April 10. It was estimated that $5,600 of credit sales will never be acknowledged or recovered from customers.

Ehlert Company reached an agreement with the insurance company that its fire-loss claim should be based on the average of the gross profit rates for the preceding 2 years. The financial statements for 2012 and 2013 showed the following data.

	2013	2012
Net sales	$600,000	$480,000
Cost of goods purchased	404,000	346,400
Beginning inventory	60,000	40,000
Ending inventory	80,000	60,000

Inventory with a cost of $17,000 was salvaged from the fire.

Instructions

With the class divided into groups, answer the following.

(a) Determine the balances in (1) Sales Revenue and (2) Purchases at April 10.

*(b) Determine the average gross profit rate for the years 2012 and 2013. (*Hint:* Find the gross profit rate for each year and divide the sum by 2.)

*(c) Determine the inventory loss as a result of the fire, using the gross profit method.

Communication Activity

BYP6-5 You are the controller of Classic Toys Inc. Kathy McDonnell, the president, recently mentioned to you that she found an error in the 2013 financial statements which she believes has corrected itself. She determined, in discussions with the Purchasing Department, that 2013 ending inventory was overstated by $1 million. Kathy says that the 2014 ending inventory is correct. Thus, she assumes that 2014 income is correct. Kathy says to you, "What happened has happened— there's no point in worrying about it anymore."

Instructions

You conclude that Kathy is incorrect. Write a brief, tactful memo to Kathy, clarifying the situation.

Ethics Case

BYP6-6 Paeth Wholesale Corp. uses the LIFO method of inventory costing. In the current year, profit at Paeth is running unusually high. The corporate tax rate is also high this year, but it is scheduled to decline significantly next year. In an effort to lower the current year's net income and to take advantage of the changing income tax rate, the president of Paeth Wholesale instructs the plant accountant to recommend to the purchasing department a large purchase of inventory for delivery 3 days before the end of the year. The price of the inventory to be purchased has doubled during the year, and the purchase will represent a major portion of the ending inventory value.

Instructions

(a) What is the effect of this transaction on this year's and next year's income statement and income tax expense? Why?

(b) If Paeth Wholesale had been using the FIFO method of inventory costing, would the president give the same directive?

(c) Should the plant accountant order the inventory purchase to lower income? What are the ethical implications of this order?

All About You

BYP6-7 Some of the largest business frauds ever perpetrated have involved the misstatement of inventory. Two classics were at Leslie Fay and McKesson Corporation.

Instructions

There is considerable information regarding inventory frauds available on the Internet. Search for information about one of the two cases mentioned above, or inventory fraud at any other company, and prepare a short explanation of the nature of the inventory fraud.

BYP6-8 Suppose you own a number of wine shops selling mid-level as well as expensive bottled wine. You have been experiencing significant losses from theft at your stores. You suspect that it is a combination of both employee and customer theft. Assuming that it would be cost-effective, would you install video cameras to reduce both employee theft and customer theft?

YES: Most employees and customers are honest. However, some will steal if given the opportunity. Management has a responsibility to employ reasonable, cost-effective approaches to safeguard company assets.

NO: The use of video technology to monitor employees and customers sends a message of distrust. You run the risk of alienating your employees (who may well figure out a way around the cameras anyway). Cameras might also reduce the welcoming atmosphere for your customers, who might find the cameras offensive.

Instructions
Write a response indicating your position regarding the situation, provide support for your view.

FASB Codification Activity

BYP6-9 If your school has a subscription to the FASB Codification, go to *http://aaahq.org/ascLogin. cfm* to log in and prepare responses to the following.

(a) The primary basis for accounting for inventories is cost. How is cost defined in the Codification?
(b) What does the Codification state regarding the use of consistency in the selection or employment of a basis for inventory?
(c) What does the Codification indicate is a justification for the use of the lower-of-cost-or-market for inventory valuation?

Answers to Chapter Questions

Answers to Insight and Accounting Across the Organization Questions

p. 273 A Big Hiccup Q: What steps might the companies take to avoid such a serious disruption in the future? **A:** The manufacturer of the piston rings should spread its manufacturing facilities across a few locations that are far enough apart that they would not all be at risk at once. In addition, the automakers might consider becoming less dependent on a single supplier.

p. 274 Falsifying Inventory to Boost Income Q: What effect does an overstatement of inventory have on a company's financial statements? **A:** The balance sheet looks stronger because inventory and retained earnings are overstated. The income statement looks better because cost of goods sold is understated and income is overstated.

p. 285 Is LIFO Fair? Q: What are the arguments for and against the use of LIFO? **A:** Proponents of LIFO argue that it is conceptually superior because it matches the most recent cost with the most recent selling price. Critics contend that it artificially understates the company's net income and consequently reduces tax payments. Also, because most foreign companies are not allowed to use LIFO, its use by U.S. companies reduces the ability of investors to compare U.S. companies with foreign companies.

p. 289 Improving Inventory Control with RFID Q: Why is inventory control important to managers such as those at Wal-Mart and Best Buy? **A:** In the very competitive environment of discount retailing, where Wal-Mart and Best Buy are major players, small differences in price matter to the customer. Wal-Mart sells a high volume of inventory at a low gross profit rate. When operating in a high-volume, low-margin environment, small cost savings can mean the difference between being profitable or going out of business.

Answers to Self-Test Questions

1. a   **2.** b ($180,000 + $35,000)   **3.** b   **4.** c [(5,000 × $13) + (4,000 × $12)]   **5.** d [(8,000 × $11) + (1,000 × $12)]   **6.** d ((5,000 × $8) + (15,000 × $10) + (20,000 × $12)) ÷ 40,000 = $10.75; $10.75 × 7,000   **7.** c   **8.** d   **9.** d (200 × $80)   **10.** b   **11.** b   **12.** d   **13.** b $285,000 ÷ [($80,000 + $110,000) ÷ 2] = 3; 365 ÷ 3   ***14.** b [$150,000 − (30% × $150,000)] = $105,000; $135,000 − $105,000   ***15.** d

A Look at IFRS

The major IFRS requirements related to accounting and reporting for inventories are the same as GAAP. The major differences are that IFRS prohibits the use of the LIFO cost flow assumption and determines market in the lower-of-cost-or-market inventory valuation differently.

Key Points

- The requirements for accounting for and reporting inventories are more principles-based under IFRS. That is, GAAP provides more detailed guidelines in inventory accounting.

- The definitions for inventory are essentially similar under IFRS and GAAP. Both define inventory as assets held-for-sale in the ordinary course of business, in the process of production for sale (work in process), or to be consumed in the production of goods or services (e.g., raw materials).

- Who owns the goods—goods in transit or consigned goods—as well as the costs to include in inventory, are accounted for the same under IFRS and GAAP.

- Both GAAP and IFRS permit specific identification where appropriate. IFRS actually requires that the specific identification method be used where the inventory items are not interchangeable (i.e., can be specifically identified). If the inventory items are not specifically identifiable, a cost flow assumption is used. GAAP does not specify situations in which specific identification must be used.

- A major difference between IFRS and GAAP relates to the LIFO cost flow assumption. GAAP permits the use of LIFO for inventory valuation. IFRS prohibits its use. FIFO and average-cost are the only two acceptable cost flow assumptions permitted under IFRS.

- IFRS requires companies to use the same cost flow assumption for all goods of a similar nature. GAAP has no specific requirement in this area.

- In the lower-of-cost-or-market test for inventory valuation, IFRS defines market as net realizable value. Net realizable value is the estimated selling price in the ordinary course of business, less the estimated costs of completion and estimated selling expenses. In other words, net realizable value is the best estimate of the net amounts that inventories are expected to realize. GAAP, on the other hand, defines market as essentially replacement cost.

- Under GAAP, if inventory is written down under the lower-of-cost-or-market valuation, the new basis is now considered its cost. As a result, the inventory may not be written back up to its original cost in a subsequent period. Under IFRS, the write-down may be reversed in a subsequent period up to the amount of the previous write-down. Both the write-down and any subsequent reversal should be reported on the income statement as an expense. An item-by-item approach is generally followed under IFRS.

- An example of the use of lower-of-cost-or-net realizable value under IFRS follows.

Mendel Company has the following four items in its ending inventory as of December 31, 2014. The company uses the lower-of-cost-or-net realizable value approach for inventory valuation following IFRS.

Item No.	Cost	Net Realizable Value
1320	$3,600	$3,400
1333	4,000	4,100
1428	2,800	2,100
1510	5,000	4,700

The computation of the ending inventory value to be reported in the financial statements at December 31, 2014, is as follows.

Item No.	Cost	Net Realizable Value	LCNRV
1320	$ 3,600	$ 3,400	$ 3,400
1333	4,000	4,100	4,000
1428	2,800	2,100	2,100
1510	5,000	4,700	4,700
Total	$15,400	$14,300	$14,200

- Unlike property, plant, and equipment, IFRS does not permit the option of valuing inventories at fair value. As indicated above, IFRS requires inventory to be written down, but inventory cannot be written up above its original cost.
- Similar to GAAP, certain agricultural products and mineral products can be reported at net realizable value using IFRS.

Looking to the Future

One convergence issue that will be difficult to resolve relates to the use of the LIFO cost flow assumption. As indicated, IFRS specifically prohibits its use. Conversely, the LIFO cost flow assumption is widely used in the United States because of its favorable tax advantages. In addition, many argue that LIFO from a financial reporting point of view provides a better matching of current costs against revenue and, therefore, enables companies to compute a more realistic income.

IFRS Practice

IFRS Self-Test Questions

1. Which of the following should *not* be included in the inventory of a company using IFRS?
   (a) Goods held on consignment from another company.
   (b) Goods shipped on consignment to another company.
   (c) Goods in transit from another company shipped FOB shipping point.
   (d) None of the above.

2. Which method of inventory costing is prohibited under IFRS?
   (a) Specific identification.
   (c) FIFO.
   (b) LIFO.
   (d) Average-cost.

3. Yang Company purchased 2,000 widgets and has 400 widgets in its ending inventory at a cost of $90 each and a current replacement cost of $80 each. The net realizable value of each unit in the ending inventory is $70. The ending inventory under lower-of-cost-or-net realizable value is:
   (a) $36,000.
   (c) $28,000.
   (b) $32,000.
   (d) None of the above.

4. Specific identification:
   (a) must be used under IFRS if the inventory items are not interchangeable.
   (b) cannot be used under IFRS.
   (c) cannot be used under GAAP.
   (d) must be used under IFRS if it would result in the most conservative net income.

5. IFRS requires the following:
   (a) Ending inventory is written up and down to net realizable value each reporting period.
   (b) Ending inventory is written down to net realizable value but cannot be written up.
   (c) Ending inventory is written down to net realizable value and may be written up in future periods to its net realizable value but not above its original cost.
   (d) Ending inventory is written down to net realizable value and may be written up in future periods to its net realizable value.

IFRS Exercises

IFRS6-1 Briefly describe some of the similarities and differences between GAAP and IFRS with respect to the accounting for inventories.

IFRS6-2 LaTour Inc. is based in France and prepares its financial statements in accordance with IFRS. In 2014, it reported (in euros) cost of goods sold of €578 million and average inventory of €154 million. Briefly discuss how analysis of LaTour's inventory turnover ratio (and comparisons to a company using GAAP) might be affected by differences in inventory accounting between IFRS and GAAP.

IFRS6-3 Franklin Company has the following four items in its ending inventory as of December 31, 2014. The company uses the lower-of-cost-or-net realizable value approach for inventory valuation following IFRS.

Item No.	Cost	Net Realizable Value
AB	$1,700	$1,400
TRX	2,200	2,300
NWA	7,800	7,100
SGH	3,000	3,700

Compute the lower-of-cost-or-net realizable value.

International Financial Reporting Problem: Zetar plc

IFRS6-4 The financial statements of Zetar plc are presented in Appendix C. The company's complete annual report, including the notes to its financial statements, is available at *www.zetarplc.com*.

Instructions

Using the notes to the company's financial statements, answer the following questions.

(a) What cost flow assumption does the company use to value inventory?

(b) What was the amount of expense that the company reported for inventory write-downs during 2010?

(c) What amount of raw materials, work in process, and finished goods inventory did the company report at April 30, 2010?

Answers to IFRS Self-Test Questions

1. a **2.** b **3.** c **4.** a **5.** c

 ✔ **The Navigator**

Chapter 7

Fraud, Internal Control, and Cash

Feature Story

Minding the Money in Moose Jaw

If you're ever looking for a cappuccino in Moose Jaw, Saskatchewan, stop by Stephanie's Gourmet Coffee and More, located on Main Street. Staff there serve, on average, 650 cups of coffee a day, including both regular and specialty coffees, not to mention soups, Italian sandwiches, and a wide assortment of gourmet cheesecakes.

"We've got high school students who come here, and students from the community college," says owner/manager Stephanie Mintenko, who has run the place since opening it in 1995. "We have customers who are

retired, and others who are working people and have only 30 minutes for lunch. We have to be pretty quick."

That means that the cashiers have to be efficient. Like most businesses where purchases are low-cost and high-volume, cash control has to be simple.

"We have an electronic cash register, but it's not the fancy new kind where you just punch in the item," explains Ms. Mintenko. "You have to punch in the prices." The machine does keep track of sales in several categories, however. Cashiers punch a button to indicate whether each item is a beverage, a meal, or a Wi-Fi charge for the cafe's Internet service. An internal tape in the machine keeps a record of

Learning Objectives

After studying this chapter, you should be able to:

1 Define fraud and internal control.

2 Identify the principles of internal control activities.

3 Explain the applications of internal control principles to cash receipts.

4 Explain the applications of internal control principles to cash disbursements.

5 Describe the operation of a petty cash fund.

6 Indicate the control features of a bank account.

7 Prepare a bank reconciliation.

8 Explain the reporting of cash.

 The Navigator

all transactions; the customer receives a receipt only upon request.

There is only one cash register. "Up to three of us might operate it on any given shift, including myself," says Ms. Mintenko.

She and her staff do two "cashouts" each day—one with the shift change at 5:00 p.m. and one when the shop closes at 10:00 p.m. At each cashout, they count the cash in the register drawer. That amount, minus the cash change carried forward (the float), should match the shift total on the

register tape. If there's a discrepancy, they do another count. Then, if necessary, "we go through the whole tape to find the mistake," she explains. "It usually turns out to be someone who punched in $18 instead of $1.80, or something like that."

Ms. Mintenko sends all the cash tapes and float totals to a bookkeeper, who double-checks everything and provides regular reports. "We try to keep the accounting simple, so we can concentrate on making great coffee and food."

✔ **The Navigator**

Preview of Chapter 7

As the story about recording cash sales at Stephanie's Gourmet Coffee and More indicates, control of cash is important to ensure that fraud does not occur. Companies also need controls to safeguard other types of assets. For example, Stephanie's undoubtedly has controls to prevent the theft of food and supplies, and controls to prevent the theft of tableware and dishes from its kitchen.

In this chapter, we explain the essential features of an internal control system and how it prevents fraud. We also describe how those controls apply to a specific asset—cash. The applications include some controls with which you may be already familiar, such as the use of a bank.

The content and organization of Chapter 7 are as follows.

FRAUD, INTERNAL CONTROL, AND CASH

Fraud and Internal Control	Cash Controls	Control Features: Use of a Bank	Reporting Cash
• Fraud • The Sarbanes-Oxley Act • Internal control • Principles of internal control activities • Limitations	• Cash receipts controls • Cash disbursements controls	• Making deposits • Writing checks • Bank statements • Reconciling the bank account • Electronic funds transfer (EFT) system	• Cash equivalents • Restricted cash

✔ **The Navigator**

Fraud and Internal Control

The Feature Story describes many of the internal control procedures used by Stephanie's Gourmet Coffee and More. These procedures are necessary to discourage employees from fraudulent activities.

Fraud

A **fraud** is a dishonest act by an employee that results in personal benefit to the employee at a cost to the employer. Examples of fraud reported in the financial press include:

- A bookkeeper in a small company diverted $750,000 of bill payments to a personal bank account over a three-year period.
- A shipping clerk with 28 years of service shipped $125,000 of merchandise to himself.
- A computer operator embezzled $21 million from Wells Fargo Bank over a two-year period.
- A church treasurer "borrowed" $150,000 of church funds to finance a friend's business dealings.

Illustration 7-1
Fraud triangle

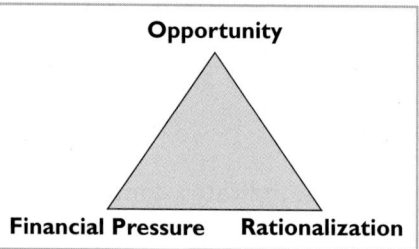

Why does fraud occur? The three main factors that contribute to fraudulent activity are depicted by the **fraud triangle** in Illustration 7-1 (in the margin).

The most important element of the fraud triangle is **opportunity**. For an employee to commit fraud, the workplace environment must provide opportunities that an employee can take advantage of. Opportunities occur when the workplace lacks sufficient controls to deter and detect fraud. For example, inadequate monitoring of employee actions can create opportunities for theft and can embolden employees because they believe they will not be caught.

A second factor that contributes to fraud is **financial pressure**. Employees sometimes commit fraud because of personal financial problems caused by too much debt. Or, they might commit fraud because they want to lead a lifestyle that they cannot afford on their current salary.

The third factor that contributes to fraud is **rationalization**. In order to justify their fraud, employees rationalize their dishonest actions. For example, employees sometimes justify fraud because they believe they are underpaid while the employer is making lots of money. Employees feel justified in stealing because they believe they deserve to be paid more.

The Sarbanes-Oxley Act

What can be done to prevent or to detect fraud? After numerous corporate scandals came to light in the early 2000s, Congress addressed this issue by passing the **Sarbanes-Oxley Act (SOX)**. Under SOX, all publicly traded U.S. corporations are required to maintain an adequate system of internal control. Corporate executives and boards of directors must ensure that these controls are reliable and effective. In addition, independent outside auditors must attest to the adequacy of the internal control system. Companies that fail to comply are subject to fines, and company officers can be imprisoned. SOX also created the Public Company Accounting Oversight Board (PCAOB), to establish auditing standards and regulate auditor activity.

One poll found that 60% of investors believe that SOX helps safeguard their stock investments. Many say they would be unlikely to invest in a company that fails to follow SOX requirements. Although some corporate executives have criticized the time and expense involved in following the SOX requirements, SOX appears to be working well. For example, the chief accounting officer of Eli Lily noted that SOX triggered a comprehensive review of how the company documents controls. This review uncovered redundancies and pointed out controls that needed to be added. In short, it added up to time and money well spent. And the finance chief at General Electric noted, "We have seen value in SOX. It helps build investors' trust and gives them more confidence."[1]

Internal Control

Internal control consists of all the related methods and measures adopted within an organization to safeguard its assets, enhance the reliability of its accounting records, increase efficiency of operations, and ensure compliance with laws and regulations. Internal control systems have five primary components as listed below.[2]

- **A control environment.** It is the responsibility of top management to make it clear that the organization values integrity and that unethical activity will not be tolerated. This component is often referred to as the "tone at the top."
- **Risk assessment.** Companies must identify and analyze the various factors that create risk for the business and must determine how to manage these risks.
- **Control activities.** To reduce the occurrence of fraud, management must design policies and procedures to address the specific risks faced by the company.
- **Information and communication.** The internal control system must capture and communicate all pertinent information both down and up the organization, as well as communicate information to appropriate external parties.
- **Monitoring.** Internal control systems must be monitored periodically for their adequacy. Significant deficiencies need to be reported to top management and/or the board of directors.

PEOPLE, PLANET, AND PROFIT INSIGHT

And the Controls Are . . .

Internal controls are important for an effective financial reporting system. The same is true for sustainability reporting. An effective system of internal controls for sustainability reporting will help in the following ways: (1) prevent the unauthorized use of data; (2) provide reasonable assurance that the information is accurate, valid, and complete; and (3) report information that is consistent with the overall sustainability accounting policies. With these types of controls, users will have the confidence that they can use the sustainability information effectively.

Some regulators are calling for even more assurance through audits of this information. Companies that potentially can cause environmental damage through greenhouse gases are subject to reporting requirements as well as companies in the mining and extractive industries. And, as demand for more information in the sustainability area expands, the need for audits of this information will grow.

? Why is sustainability information important to investors? (See page 374.)

---

[1]"Corporate Regulation Must Be Working—There's a Backlash," *Wall Street Journal*, (June 16, 2004), p. C1; and Judith Burns, "Is Sarbanes-Oxley Working?" *Wall Street Journal*, (June 21, 2004), pp. R8–R9.

[2]The Committee of Sponsoring Organizations of the Treadway Commission, "Internal Control—Integrated Framework," *www.coso.org/publications/executive_summary_integrated_framework.htm* (accessed March 2008).

LEARNING OBJECTIVE   2

Identify the principles of internal control activities.

Principles of Internal Control Activities

Each of the five components of an internal control system is important. Here, we will focus on one component, the control activities. The reason? These activities are the backbone of the company's efforts to address the risks it faces, such as fraud. The specific control activities used by a company will vary, depending on management's assessment of the risks faced. This assessment is heavily influenced by the size and nature of the company.

The six principles of control activities are as follows.

- Establishment of responsibility
- Segregation of duties
- Documentation procedures
- Physical controls
- Independent internal verification
- Human resource controls

We explain these principles in the following sections. You should recognize that they apply to most companies and are relevant to both manual and computerized accounting systems.

Transfer of Cash Drawers

ESTABLISHMENT OF RESPONSIBILITY

An essential principle of internal control is to assign responsibility to specific employees. **Control is most effective when only one person is responsible for a given task.**

To illustrate, assume that the cash on hand at the end of the day in a Safeway supermarket is $10 short of the cash rung up on the cash register. If only one person has operated the register, the shift manager can quickly determine responsibility for the shortage. If two or more individuals have worked the register, it may be impossible to determine who is responsible for the error. In the Feature Story, the principle of establishing responsibility does not appear to be strictly applied by Stephanie's Gourmet Coffee and More, since three people operate the cash register on any given shift.

Establishing responsibility often requires limiting access only to authorized personnel, and then identifying those personnel. For example, the automated systems used by many companies have mechanisms such as identifying passcodes that keep track of who made a journal entry, who rang up a sale, or who entered an inventory storeroom at a particular time. Use of identifying passcodes enables the company to establish responsibility by identifying the particular employee who carried out the activity.

ANATOMY OF A FRAUD

Maureen Frugali was a training supervisor for claims processing at Colossal Healthcare. As a standard part of the claims processing training program, Maureen created fictitious claims for use by trainees. These fictitious claims were then sent to the accounts payable department. After the training claims had been processed, she was to notify Accounts Payable of all fictitious claims, so that they would not be paid. However, she did not inform Accounts Payable about every fictitious claim. She created some fictitious claims for entities that she controlled (that is, she would receive the payment), and she let Accounts Payable pay her.

Total take: $11 million

The Missing Control
Establishment of responsibility. The health-care company did not adequately restrict the responsibility for authoring and approving claims transactions. The training supervisor should not have been authorized to create claims in the company's "live" system.

Source: Adapted from Wells, *Fraud Casebook* (2007), pp. 61–70.

SEGREGATION OF DUTIES
Segregation of duties is indispensable in an internal control system. There are two common applications of this principle:

1. Different individuals should be responsible for related activities.
2. The responsibility for record-keeping for an asset should be separate from the physical custody of that asset.

The rationale for segregation of duties is this: **The work of one employee should, without a duplication of effort, provide a reliable basis for evaluating the work of another employee.** For example, the personnel that design and program computerized systems should not be assigned duties related to day-to-day use of the system. Otherwise, they could design the system to benefit them personally and conceal the fraud through day-to-day use.

SEGREGATION OF RELATED ACTIVITIES Making one individual responsible for related activities increases the potential for errors and irregularities. For example, companies should assign related *purchasing activities* to different individuals. Related purchasing activities include ordering merchandise, order approval, receiving goods, authorizing payment, and paying for goods or services. Various frauds are possible when one person handles related purchasing activities. For example:

- If a purchasing agent is allowed to order goods without obtaining supervisory approval, the likelihood of the purchasing agent receiving kickbacks from suppliers increases.
- If an employee who orders goods also handles receipt of the goods and invoice, as well as payment authorization, he or she might authorize payment for a fictitious invoice.

These abuses are less likely to occur when companies divide the purchasing tasks.

Similarly, companies should assign related *sales activities* to different individuals. Related selling activities include making a sale, shipping (or delivering) the goods to the customer, billing the customer, and receiving payment. Various frauds are possible when one person handles related sales transactions. For example:

- If a salesperson can make a sale without obtaining supervisory approval, he or she might make sales at unauthorized prices to increase sales commissions.
- A shipping clerk who also has access to accounting records could ship goods to himself.
- A billing clerk who handles billing and receipt could understate the amount billed for sales made to friends and relatives.

These abuses are less likely to occur when companies divide the sales tasks: The salespeople make the sale; the shipping department ships the goods on the basis of the sales order; and the billing department prepares the sales invoice after comparing the sales order with the report of goods shipped.

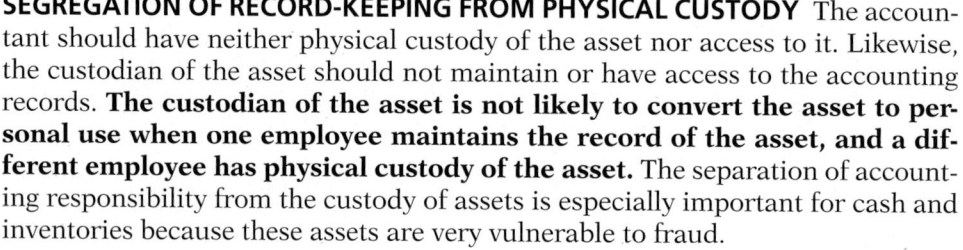

ANATOMY OF A FRAUD

Lawrence Fairbanks, the assistant vice-chancellor of communications at Aesop University, was allowed to make purchases of under $2,500 for his department without external approval. Unfortunately, he also sometimes bought items for himself, such as expensive antiques and other collectibles. How did he do it? He replaced the vendor invoices he received with fake vendor invoices that he created. The fake invoices had descriptions that were more consistent with the communications department's purchases. He submitted these fake invoices to the accounting department as the basis for their journal entries and to the accounts payable department as the basis for payment.

Total take: $475,000

The Missing Control
Segregation of duties. The university had not properly segregated related purchasing activities. Lawrence was ordering items, receiving the items, and receiving the invoice. By receiving the invoice, he had control over the documents that were used to account for the purchase and thus was able to substitute a fake invoice.

Source: Adapted from Wells, *Fraud Casebook* (2007), pp. 3–15.

Accounting Employee A
Maintains cash
balances per books

Segregation of Duties
(Accountability for assets)

Assistant Cashier B
Maintains custody
of cash on hand

SEGREGATION OF RECORD-KEEPING FROM PHYSICAL CUSTODY The accountant should have neither physical custody of the asset nor access to it. Likewise, the custodian of the asset should not maintain or have access to the accounting records. **The custodian of the asset is not likely to convert the asset to personal use when one employee maintains the record of the asset, and a different employee has physical custody of the asset.** The separation of accounting responsibility from the custody of assets is especially important for cash and inventories because these assets are very vulnerable to fraud.

ANATOMY OF A FRAUD

Angela Bauer was an accounts payable clerk for Aggasiz Construction Company. She prepared and issued checks to vendors and reconciled bank statements. Angela perpetrated a fraud in this way: She wrote checks for costs that the company had not actually incurred (e.g., fake taxes). A supervisor then approved and signed the checks. Before issuing the check, though, Angela would "white-out" the payee line on the check and change it to personal accounts that she controlled. She was able to conceal the theft because she also reconciled the bank account. That is, nobody else ever saw that the checks had been altered.

Total take: $570,000

The Missing Control
Segregation of duties. Aggasiz Construction Company did not properly segregate record-keeping from physical custody. Angela had physical custody of the checks, which essentially was control of the cash. She also had record-keeping responsibility because she prepared the bank reconciliation.

Source: Adapted from Wells, *Fraud Casebook* (2007), pp. 100–107.

DOCUMENTATION PROCEDURES

Documents provide evidence that transactions and events have occurred. At Stephanie's Gourmet Coffee and More, the cash register tape is the restaurant's documentation for the sale and the amount of cash received. Similarly, a shipping document indicates that the goods have been shipped, and a sales invoice indicates that the company has billed the customer for the goods. By requiring signatures (or initials) on the documents, the company can identify the individual(s) responsible for the transaction or event. Companies should document transactions when the transaction occurs.

Companies should establish procedures for documents. First, whenever possible, companies should use **prenumbered documents, and all documents should be accounted for**. Prenumbering helps to prevent a transaction from being recorded more than once, or conversely, from not being recorded at all. Second, the control system should require that employees **promptly forward source documents for accounting entries to the accounting department**. **This control measure helps to ensure timely recording of the transaction** and contributes directly to the accuracy and reliability of the accounting records.

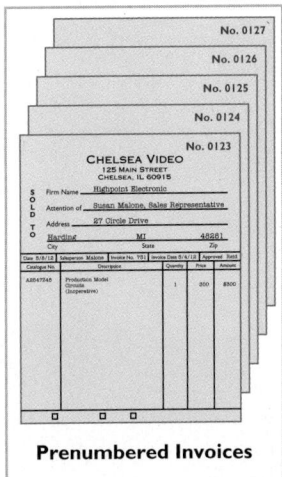

Prenumbered Invoices

ANATOMY OF A FRAUD

To support their reimbursement requests for travel costs incurred, employees at Mod Fashions Corporation's design center were required to submit receipts. The receipts could include the detailed bill provided for a meal, or the credit card receipt provided when the credit card payment is made, or a copy of the employee's monthly credit card bill that listed the item. A number of the designers who frequently traveled together came up with a fraud scheme: They submitted claims for the same expenses. For example, if they had a meal together that cost $200, one person submitted the detailed meal bill, another submitted the credit card receipt, and a third submitted a monthly credit card bill showing the meal as a line item. Thus, all three received a $200 reimbursement.

Total take: $75,000

The Missing Control
Documentation procedures. Mod Fashions should require the original, detailed receipt. It should not accept photocopies, and it should not accept credit card statements. In addition, documentation procedures could be further improved by requiring the use of a corporate credit card (rather than a personal credit card) for all business expenses.

Source: Adapted from Wells, *Fraud Casebook* (2007), pp. 79–90.

PHYSICAL CONTROLS

Use of physical controls is essential. *Physical controls* relate to the safeguarding of assets and enhance the accuracy and reliability of the accounting records. Illustration 7-2 shows examples of these controls.

Illustration 7-2
Physical controls

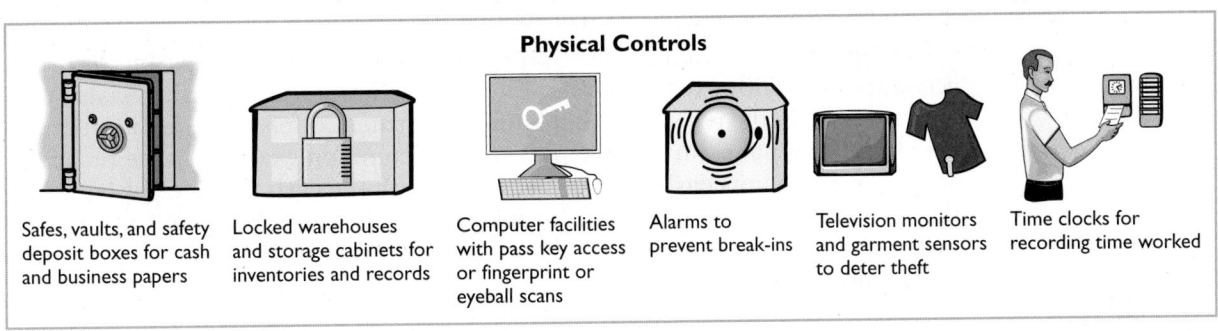

Physical Controls

| Safes, vaults, and safety deposit boxes for cash and business papers | Locked warehouses and storage cabinets for inventories and records | Computer facilities with pass key access or fingerprint or eyeball scans | Alarms to prevent break-ins | Television monitors and garment sensors to deter theft | Time clocks for recording time worked |

ANATOMY OF A FRAUD

At Centerstone Health, a large insurance company, the mailroom each day received insurance applications from prospective customers. Mailroom employees scanned the applications into electronic documents before the applications were processed. Once the applications are scanned they can be accessed online by authorized employees.

Insurance agents at Centerstone Health earn commissions based upon successful applications. The sales agent's name is listed on the application. However, roughly 15% of the applications are from customers who did not work with a sales agent. Two friends—Alex, an employee in record-keeping, and Parviz, a sales agent—thought up a way to perpetrate a fraud. Alex identified scanned applications that did not list a sales agent. After business hours, he entered the mailroom and found the hard-copy applications that did not show a sales agent. He wrote in Parviz's name as the sales agent and then rescanned the application for processing. Parviz received the commission, which the friends then split.

Total take: $240,000

The Missing Control

Physical controls. Centerstone Health lacked two basic physical controls that could have prevented this fraud. First, the mailroom should have been locked during nonbusiness hours, and access during business hours should have been tightly controlled. Second, the scanned applications supposedly could be accessed only by authorized employees using their passwords. However, the password for each employee was the same as the employee's user ID. Since employee user-ID numbers were available to all other employees, all employees knew all other employees' passwords. Unauthorized employees could access the scanned applications. Thus, Alex could enter the system using another employee's password and access the scanned applications.

Source: Adapted from Wells, *Fraud Casebook* (2007), pp. 316–326.

INDEPENDENT INTERNAL VERIFICATION

Most internal control systems provide for **independent internal verification**. This principle involves the review of data prepared by employees. To obtain maximum benefit from independent internal verification:

1. Companies should verify records periodically or on a surprise basis.

2. An employee who is independent of the personnel responsible for the information should make the verification.

3. Discrepancies and exceptions should be reported to a management level that can take appropriate corrective action.

Independent internal verification is especially useful in comparing recorded accountability with existing assets. The reconciliation of the cash register tape with the cash in the register at Stephanie's Gourmet Coffee and More is an example of this internal control principle. Another common example is the reconciliation of a company's cash balance per books with the cash balance per bank and the verification of the perpetual inventory records through a count of physical inventory. Illustration 7-3 shows the relationship between this principle and the segregation of duties principle.

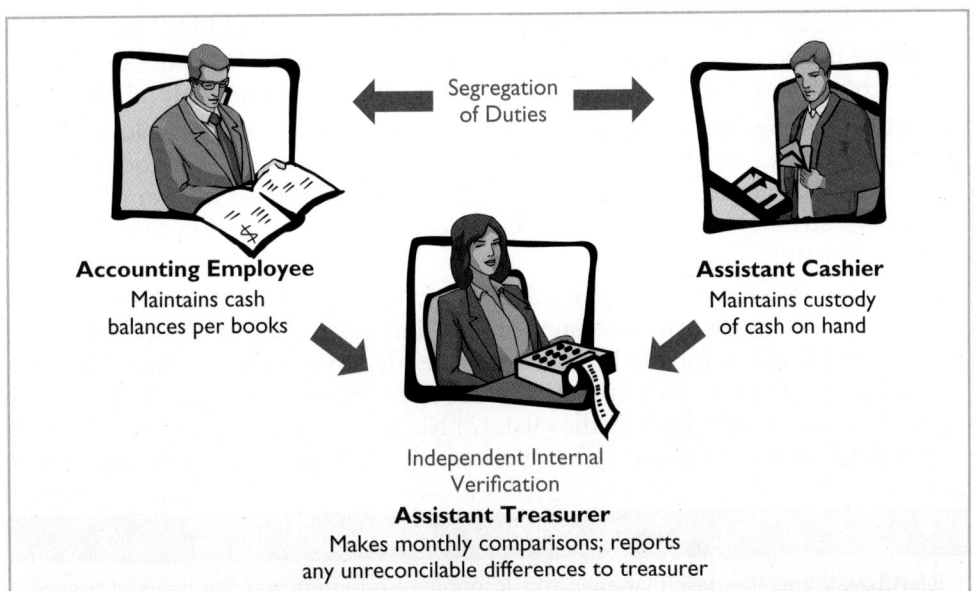

Illustration 7-3
Comparison of segregation of duties principle with independent internal verification principle

ANATOMY OF A FRAUD

Bobbi Jean Donnelly, the office manager for Mod Fashions Corporations design center, was responsible for preparing the design center budget and reviewing expense reports submitted by design center employees. Her desire to upgrade her wardrobe got the better of her, and she enacted a fraud that involved filing expense-reimbursement requests for her own personal clothing purchases. She was able to conceal the fraud because she was responsible for reviewing all expense reports, including her own. In addition, she sometimes was given ultimate responsibility for signing off on the expense reports when her boss was "too busy." Also, because she controlled the budget, when she submitted her expenses, she coded them to budget items that she knew were running under budget, so that they would not catch anyone's attention.

Total take: $275,000

The Missing Control

Independent internal verification. Bobbi Jean's boss should have verified her expense reports. When asked what he thought her expenses for a year were, the boss said about $10,000. At $115,000 per year, her actual expenses were more than 10 times what would have been expected. However, because he was "too busy" to verify her expense reports or to review the budget, he never noticed.

Source: Adapted from Wells, *Fraud Casebook* (2007), pp. 79–90.

Large companies often assign independent internal verification to internal auditors. **Internal auditors** are company employees who continuously evaluate the effectiveness of the company's internal control systems. They review the activities of departments and individuals to determine whether prescribed internal controls are being followed. They also recommend improvements when needed. In fact, most fraud is discovered by the company through internal mechanisms such as existing internal controls and internal audits. For example, the alleged fraud at WorldCom, involving billions of dollars, was uncovered by an internal auditor.

HUMAN RESOURCE CONTROLS

Human resource control activities include the following.

1. **Bond employees who handle cash. Bonding** involves obtaining insurance protection against theft by employees. It contributes to the safeguarding of cash in

two ways: First, the insurance company carefully screens all individuals before adding them to the policy and may reject risky applicants. Second, bonded employees know that the insurance company will vigorously prosecute all offenders.

2. **Rotate employees' duties and require employees to take vacations.** These measures deter employees from attempting thefts since they will not be able to permanently conceal their improper actions. Many banks, for example, have discovered employee thefts when the employee was on vacation or assigned to a new position.

3. **Conduct thorough background checks.** Many believe that the most important and inexpensive measure any business can take to reduce employee theft and fraud is for the human resources department to conduct thorough background checks. Two tips: (1) Check to see whether job applicants actually graduated from the schools they list. (2) Never use the telephone numbers for previous employers given on the reference sheet; always look them up yourself.

ANATOMY OF A FRAUD

Ellen Lowry was the desk manager and Josephine Rodriquez was the head of housekeeping at the Excelsior Inn, a luxury hotel. The two best friends were so dedicated to their jobs that they never took vacations, and they frequently filled in for other employees. In fact, Ms. Rodriquez, whose job as head of housekeeping did not include cleaning rooms, often cleaned rooms herself, "just to help the staff keep up." These two "dedicated" employees, working as a team, found a way to earn a little more cash. Ellen, the desk manager, provided significant discounts to guests who paid with cash. She kept the cash and did not register the guest in the hotel's computerized system. Instead, she took the room out of circulation "due to routine maintenance." Because the room did not show up as being used, it did not receive a normal housekeeping assignment. Instead, Josephine, the head of housekeeping, cleaned the rooms during the guests' stay.

Total take: $95,000

The Missing Control
Human resource controls. Ellen, the desk manager, had been fired by a previous employer after being accused of fraud. If the Excelsior Inn had conducted a thorough background check, it would not have hired her. The hotel fraud was detected when Ellen missed work for a few days due to illness. A system of mandatory vacations and rotating days off would have increased the chances of detecting the fraud before it became so large.

Source: Adapted from Wells, *Fraud Casebook* (2007), pp. 145–155.

ACCOUNTING ACROSS THE ORGANIZATION

SOX Boosts the Role of Human Resources

Under SOX, a company needs to keep track of employees' degrees and certifications to ensure that employees continue to meet the specified requirements of a job. Also, to ensure proper employee supervision and proper separation of duties, companies must develop and monitor an organizational chart. When one corporation went through this exercise, it found that out of 17,000 employees, there were 400 people who did not report to anyone. The corporation also had 35 people who reported to each other. In addition, if an employee complains of an unfair firing and mentions financial issues at the company, HR must refer the case to the company audit committee and possibly to its legal counsel.

 Why would unsupervised employees or employees who report to each other represent potential internal control threats? (See page 374.)

Limitations of Internal Control

Companies generally design their systems of internal control to provide **reasonable assurance** of proper safeguarding of assets and reliability of the accounting records. The concept of reasonable assurance rests on the premise that the costs of establishing control procedures should not exceed their expected benefit.

To illustrate, consider shoplifting losses in retail stores. Stores could eliminate such losses by having a security guard stop and search customers as they leave the store. But, store managers have concluded that the negative effects of such a procedure cannot be justified. Instead, they have attempted to control shoplifting losses by less costly procedures. They post signs saying, "We reserve the right to inspect all packages" and "All shoplifters will be prosecuted." They use hidden TV cameras and store detectives to monitor customer activity, and they install sensor equipment at exits.

The **human element** is an important factor in every system of internal control. A good system can become ineffective as a result of employee fatigue, carelessness, or indifference. For example, a receiving clerk may not bother to count goods received and may just "fudge" the counts. Occasionally, two or more individuals may work together to get around prescribed controls. Such **collusion** can significantly reduce the effectiveness of a system, eliminating the protection offered by segregation of duties. No system of internal control is perfect.

The size of the business also may impose limitations on internal control. A small company, for example, may find it difficult to segregate duties or to provide for independent internal verification.

> **Helpful Hint**
> Controls may vary with the risk level of the activity. For example, management may consider cash to be high risk and maintaining inventories in the stockroom as low risk. Thus, management would have stricter controls for cash.

ETHICS INSIGHT

Big Theft at Small Companies

A study by the Association of Certified Fraud Examiners indicates that businesses with fewer than 100 employees are most at risk for employee theft. In fact, 38% of frauds occurred at companies with fewer than 100 employees. The median loss at small companies was $200,000, which was higher than the median fraud at companies with more than 10,000 employees ($147,000). A $200,000 loss can threaten the very existence of a small company.

Source: 2008 Report to the Nation on Occupational Fraud and Abuse, Association of Certified Fraud Examiners, *www.acfe.com/documents/2008-rttn.pdf*, p. 26.

? Why are small companies more susceptible to employee theft? (See page 374.)

> DO IT!

Control Activities

Identify which control activity is violated in each of the following situations, and explain how the situation creates an opportunity for a fraud.

1. The person with primary responsibility for reconciling the bank account is also the company's accountant and makes all bank deposits.
2. Wellstone Company's treasurer received an award for distinguished service because he had not taken a vacation in 30 years.
3. In order to save money spent on order slips and to reduce time spent keeping track of order slips, a local bar/restaurant does not buy prenumbered order slips.

Action Plan

✔ Familiarize yourself with each of the control activities summarized on page 328.

✔ Understand the nature of the frauds that each control activity is intended to address.

Solution

1. Violates the control activity of segregation of duties. Record-keeping should be separate from physical custody. As a consequence, the employee could embezzle cash and make journal entries to hide the theft.

2. Violates the control activity of human resource controls. Key employees must take vacations. Otherwise, the treasurer, who manages the company's cash, might embezzle cash and use his position to conceal the theft.

3. Violates the control activity of documentation procedures. If prenumbered documents are not used, then it is virtually impossible to account for the documents. As a consequence, an employee could write up a dinner sale, receive the cash from the customer, and then throw away the order slip and keep the cash.

Related exercise material: **BE7-1, BE7-2, BE7-3, BE7-4, E7-1, and DO IT! 7-1.**

✔ **The Navigator**

Cash Controls

LEARNING OBJECTIVE 3

Explain the applications of internal control principles to cash receipts.

Cash is the one asset that is readily convertible into any other type of asset. It also is easily concealed and transported, and is highly desired. Because of these characteristics, **cash is the asset most susceptible to fraudulent activities**. In addition, because of the large volume of cash transactions, numerous errors may occur in executing and recording them. To safeguard cash and to ensure the accuracy of the accounting records for cash, effective internal control over cash is critical.

Cash Receipts Controls

Illustration 7-4
Application of internal control principles to cash receipts

Illustration 7-4 shows how the internal control principles explained earlier apply to cash receipts transactions. As you might expect, companies vary considerably

Cash Receipts Controls

Establishment of Responsibility

Only designated personnel are authorized to handle cash receipts (cashiers)

Segregation of Duties

Different individuals receive cash, record cash receipts, and hold the cash

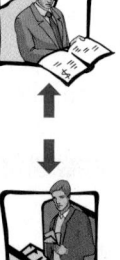

Documentation Procedures

Use remittance advice (mail receipts), cash register tapes, and deposit slips

Physical Controls

Store cash in safes and bank vaults; limit access to storage areas; use cash registers

Independent Internal Verification

Supervisors count cash receipts daily; treasurer compares total receipts to bank deposits daily

Human Resource Controls

Bond personnel who handle cash; require employees to take vacations; conduct background checks

in how they apply these principles. To illustrate internal control over cash receipts, we will examine control activities for a retail store with both over-the-counter and mail receipts.

OVER-THE-COUNTER RECEIPTS

In retail businesses, control of over-the-counter receipts centers on cash registers that are visible to customers. A cash sale is rung up on a cash register, with the amount clearly visible to the customer. This activity prevents the cashier from ringing up a lower amount and pocketing the difference. The customer receives an itemized cash register receipt slip and is expected to count the change received. The cash register's tape is locked in the register until a supervisor removes it. This tape accumulates the daily transactions and totals.

At the end of the clerk's shift, the clerk counts the cash and sends the cash and the count to the cashier. The cashier counts the cash, prepares a deposit slip, and deposits the cash at the bank. The cashier also sends a duplicate of the deposit slip to the accounting department to indicate cash received. The supervisor removes the cash register tape and sends it to the accounting department as the basis for a journal entry to record the cash received. Illustration 7-5 summarizes this process.

Illustration 7-5
Control of over-the-counter receipts

Helpful Hint
Flowcharts such as this one enhance the understanding of the flow of documents, the processing steps, and the internal control procedures.

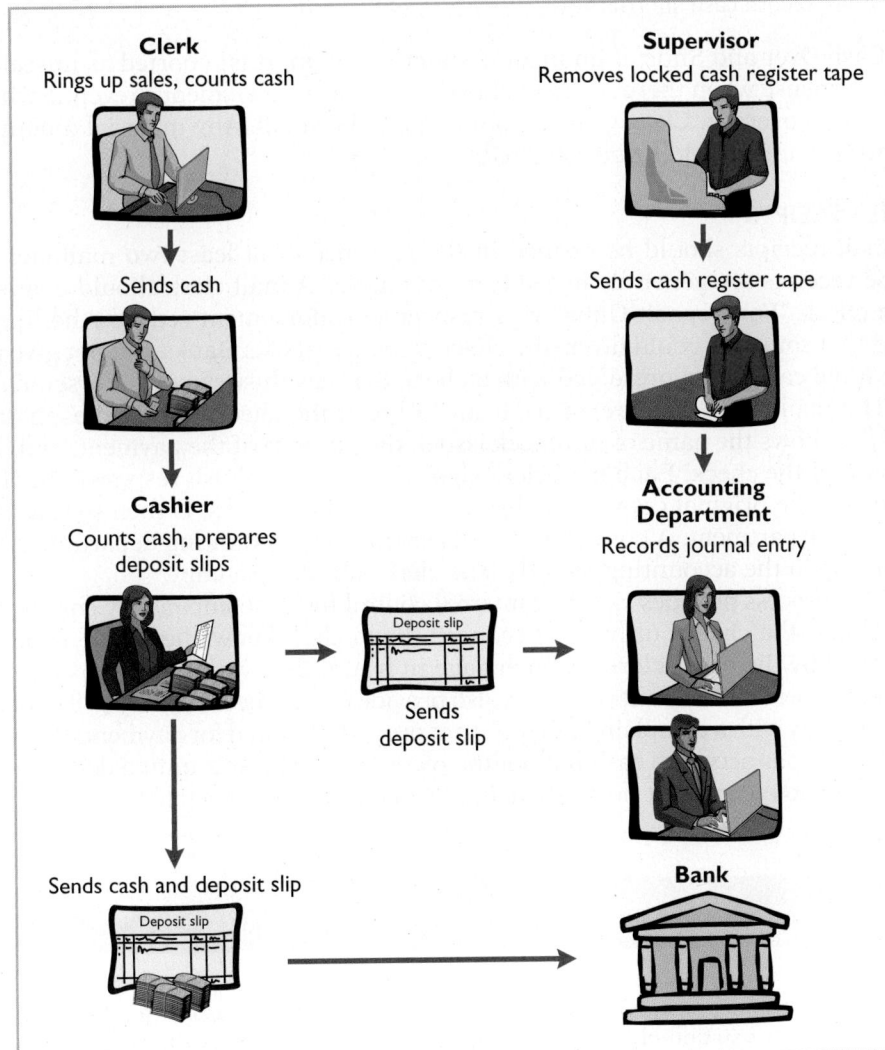

This system for handling cash receipts uses an important internal control principle—segregation of record-keeping from physical custody. The supervisor has access to the cash register tape but **not** to the cash. The clerk and the cashier have access to the cash but **not** to the register tape. In addition, the cash register tape provides documentation and enables independent internal verification. Use of these three principles of internal control (segregation of record-keeping from physical custody, documentation, and independent internal verification) provides an effective system of internal control. Any attempt at fraudulent activity should be detected unless there is collusion among the employees.

In some instances, the amount deposited at the bank will not agree with the cash recorded in the accounting records based on the cash register tape. These differences often result because the clerk hands incorrect change back to the retail customer. In this case, the difference between the actual cash and the amount reported on the cash register tape is reported in a Cash Over and Short account. For example, suppose that the cash register tape indicated sales of $6,956.20 but the amount of cash was only $6,946.10. A cash shortfall of $10.10 exists. To account for this cash shortfall and related cash, the company makes the following entry.

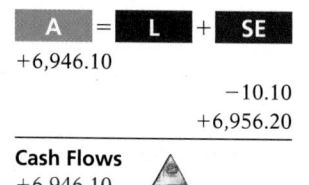

A = L + SE
+6,946.10
              −10.10
              +6,956.20

Cash Flows
+6,946.10

Cash	6,946.10	
Cash Over and Short	10.10	
Sales Revenue		6,956.20
(To record cash shortfall)		

Cash Over and Short is an income statement item. It is reported as miscellaneous expense when there is a cash shortfall, and as miscellaneous revenue when there is an overage. Clearly, the amount should be small. Any material amounts in this account should be investigated.

MAIL RECEIPTS

All mail receipts should be opened in the presence of at least two mail clerks. These receipts are generally in the form of checks. A mail clerk should endorse each check "For Deposit Only." This restrictive endorsement reduces the likelihood that someone could divert the check to personal use. Banks will not give an individual cash when presented with a check that has this type of endorsement.

The mail clerks prepare, in triplicate, a list of the checks received each day. This list shows the name of the check issuer, the purpose of the payment, and the amount of the check. Each mail clerk signs the list to establish responsibility for the data. The original copy of the list, along with the checks, is then sent to the cashier's department. A copy of the list is sent to the accounting department for recording in the accounting records. The clerks also keep a copy.

This process provides excellent internal control for the company. By employing two clerks, the chance of fraud is reduced. Each clerk knows he or she is being observed by the other clerk(s). To engage in fraud, they would have to collude. The customers who submit payments also provide control because they will contact the company with a complaint if they are not properly credited for payment. Because the cashier has access to cash but not the records, and the accounting department has access to records but not cash, neither can engage in undetected fraud.

> **DO IT!**

Control over Cash Receipts

L. R. Cortez is concerned about the control over cash receipts in his fast-food restaurant, Big Cheese. The restaurant has two cash registers. At no time do more than two employees take customer orders and ring up sales. Work shifts for employees range from 4 to 8 hours. Cortez asks your help in installing a good system of internal control over cash receipts.

Action Plan

✔ Differentiate among the internal control principles of (1) establishing responsibility, (2) using physical controls, and (3) independent internal verification.

✔ Design an effective system of internal control over cash receipts.

Solution

Cortez should assign a cash register to each employee at the start of each work shift, with register totals set at zero. Each employee should be instructed to use only the assigned register and to ring up all sales. Each customer should be given a receipt. At the end of the shift, the employee should do a cash count. A separate employee should compare the cash count with the register tape, to be sure they agree. In addition, Cortez should install an automated system that would enable the company to compare orders rung up on the register to orders processed by the kitchen.

Related exercise material: **BE7-5, E7-2, and** **7-2.**

✔ The Navigator

Cash Disbursements Controls

Companies disburse cash for a variety of reasons, such as to pay expenses and liabilities or to purchase assets. **Generally, internal control over cash disbursements is more effective when companies pay by check rather than by cash.** One exception is **for incidental amounts that are paid out of petty cash.**[3]

Companies generally issue checks only after following specified control procedures. Illustration 7-6 (page 340) shows how principles of internal control apply to cash disbursements.

LEARNING OBJECTIVE 4

Explain the applications of internal control principles to cash disbursements.

VOUCHER SYSTEM CONTROLS

Most medium and large companies use vouchers as part of their internal control over cash disbursements. A **voucher system** is a network of approvals by authorized individuals, acting independently, to ensure that all disbursements by check are proper.

The system begins with the authorization to incur a cost or expense. It ends with the issuance of a check for the liability incurred. A **voucher** is an authorization form prepared for each expenditure. Companies require vouchers for all types of cash disbursements except those from petty cash.

The starting point in preparing a voucher is to fill in the appropriate information about the liability on the face of the voucher. The vendor's invoice provides most of the needed information. Then, an employee in accounts payable records the voucher (in a journal called a **voucher register**) and files it according to the date on which it is to be paid. The company issues and sends a check on that date, and stamps the voucher "paid." The paid voucher is sent to the accounting department for recording (in a journal called the **check register**). A voucher system involves two journal entries, one to record the liability when the voucher is issued and a second to pay the liability that relates to the voucher.

The use of a voucher system improves internal control over cash disbursements. First, the authorization process inherent in a voucher system establishes responsibility. Each individual has responsibility to review the underlying documentation to ensure that it is correct. In addition, the voucher system keeps track of the documents that back up each transaction. By keeping these documents in one place, a supervisor can independently verify the authenticity of each transaction. Consider, for example, the case of Aesop University presented on page 330. Aesop did not use a voucher system for transactions under $2,500. As a consequence,

---

[3]We explain the operation of a petty cash fund on pages 340–342.

Cash Disbursements Controls

Establishment of Responsibility

Only designated personnel are authorized to sign checks (treasurer) and approve vendors

Physical Controls

Store blank checks in safes, with limited access; print check amounts by machine in indelible ink

Segregation of Duties

Different individuals approve and make payments; check signers do not record disbursements

Independent Internal Verification

Compare checks to invoices; reconcile bank statement monthly

Documentation Procedures

Use prenumbered checks and account for them in sequence; each check must have an approved invoice; require employees to use corporate credit cards for reimbursable expenses; stamp invoices "paid"

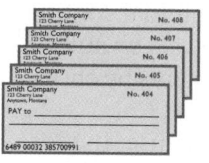

Human Resource Controls

Bond personnel who handle cash; require employees to take vacations; conduct background checks

Illustration 7-6
Application of internal control principles to cash disbursements

there was no independent verification of the documents, which enabled the employee to submit fake invoices to hide his unauthorized purchases.

PETTY CASH FUND CONTROLS

LEARNING OBJECTIVE 5

Describe the operation of a petty cash fund.

As you learned earlier in the chapter, better internal control over cash disbursements is possible when companies make payments by check. However, using checks to pay small amounts is both impractical and a nuisance. For instance, a company would not want to write checks to pay for postage due, working lunches, or taxi fares. A common way of handling such payments, while maintaining satisfactory control, is to use a **petty cash fund** to pay relatively small amounts. The operation of a petty cash fund, often called an **imprest system**, involves (1) establishing the fund, (2) making payments from the fund, and (3) replenishing the fund.[4]

---

[4]The term "imprest" means an advance of money for a designated purpose.

ESTABLISHING THE PETTY CASH FUND Two essential steps in establishing a petty cash fund are: (1) appointing a petty cash custodian who will be responsible for the fund, and (2) determining the size of the fund. Ordinarily, a company expects the amount in the fund to cover anticipated disbursements for a three- to four-week period.

To establish the fund, a company issues a check payable to the petty cash custodian for the stipulated amount. For example, if Laird Company decides to establish a $100 fund on March 1, the general journal entry is:

Mar. 1	Petty Cash	100	
	Cash		100
	(To establish a petty cash fund)		

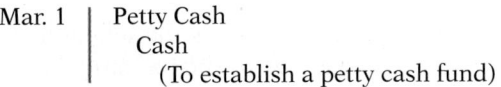

A	=	L	+	SE

+100
−100

Cash Flows
no effect

The fund custodian cashes the check and places the proceeds in a locked petty cash box or drawer. Most petty cash funds are established on a fixed-amount basis. The company will make no additional entries to the Petty Cash account unless management changes the stipulated amount of the fund. For example, if Laird Company decides on July 1 to increase the size of the fund to $250, it would debit Petty Cash $150 and credit Cash $150.

Ethics Note

Petty cash funds are authorized and legitimate. In contrast, "slush" funds are unauthorized and hidden (under the table).

MAKING PAYMENTS FROM THE PETTY CASH FUND The petty cash custodian has the authority to make payments from the fund that conform to prescribed management policies. Usually, management limits the size of expenditures that come from petty cash. Likewise, it may not permit use of the fund for certain types of transactions (such as making short-term loans to employees).

Each payment from the fund must be documented on a prenumbered petty cash receipt (or petty cash voucher), as shown in Illustration 7-7. The signatures of both the fund custodian and the person receiving payment are required on the receipt. If other supporting documents such as a freight bill or invoice are available, they should be attached to the petty cash receipt.

Helpful Hint
The petty cash receipt satisfies two internal control procedures: (1) establishing responsibility (signature of custodian), and (2) documentation procedures.

Illustration 7-7
Petty cash receipt

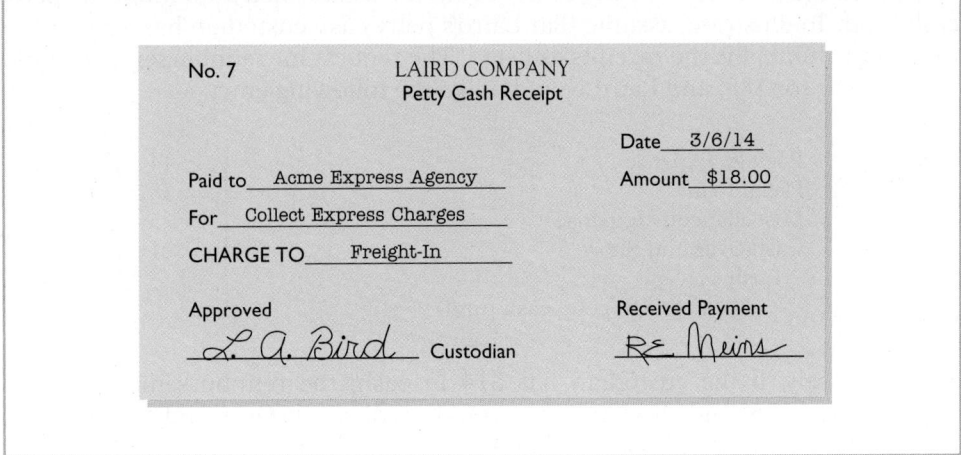

| No. 7 | LAIRD COMPANY |
| | Petty Cash Receipt |

Date __3/6/14__

Paid to __Acme Express Agency__   Amount __$18.00__

For __Collect Express Charges__

CHARGE TO __Freight-In__

Approved   Received Payment

__L. A. Bird__ Custodian   __R. E. Meins__

The fund custodian keeps the receipts in the petty cash box until the fund is replenished. The sum of the petty cash receipts and the money in the fund should equal the established total at all times. Management can (and should) make surprise counts at any time to determine whether the fund is being maintained correctly.

Ethics Note

Internal control over a petty cash fund is strengthened by: (1) having a supervisor make surprise counts of the fund to confirm whether the paid petty cash receipts and fund cash equal the imprest amount, and (2) canceling or mutilating the paid petty cash receipts so they cannot be resubmitted for reimbursement.

The company does not make an accounting entry to record a payment when it is made from petty cash. It is considered both inexpedient and unnecessary to do so. Instead, the company recognizes the accounting effects of each payment when it replenishes the fund.

REPLENISHING THE PETTY CASH FUND   When the money in the petty cash fund reaches a minimum level, the company replenishes the fund. The petty cash custodian initiates a request for reimbursement. The individual prepares a schedule (or summary) of the payments that have been made and sends the schedule, supported by petty cash receipts and other documentation, to the treasurer's office. The treasurer's office examines the receipts and supporting documents to verify that proper payments from the fund were made. The treasurer then approves the request and issues a check to restore the fund to its established amount. At the same time, all supporting documentation is stamped "paid" so that it cannot be submitted again for payment.

To illustrate, assume that on March 15 Laird's petty cash custodian requests a check for $87. The fund contains $13 cash and petty cash receipts for postage $44, freight-out $38, and miscellaneous expenses $5. The general journal entry to record the check is:

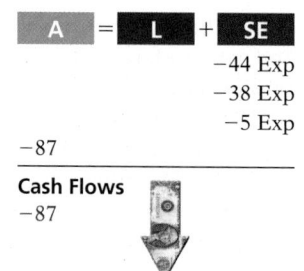

−44 Exp
−38 Exp
−5 Exp
−87

Cash Flows
−87

Mar. 15	Postage Expense	44	
	Freight-Out	38	
	Miscellaneous Expense	5	
	Cash		87
	(To replenish petty cash fund)		

Note that the reimbursement entry does not affect the Petty Cash account. Replenishment changes the composition of the fund by replacing the petty cash receipts with cash. It does not change the balance in the fund.

Occasionally, in replenishing a petty cash fund, the company may need to recognize a cash shortage or overage. This results when the total of the cash plus receipts in the petty cash box does not equal the established amount of the petty cash fund. To illustrate, assume that Laird's petty cash custodian has only $12 in cash in the fund plus the receipts as listed. The request for reimbursement would therefore be for $88, and Laird would make the following entry.

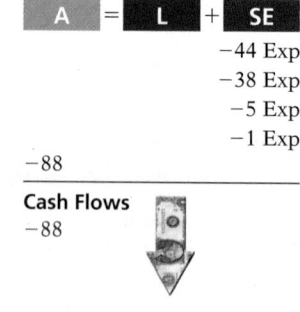

−44 Exp
−38 Exp
−5 Exp
−1 Exp
−88

Cash Flows
−88

Mar. 15	Postage Expense	44	
	Freight-Out	38	
	Miscellaneous Expense	5	
	Cash Over and Short	1	
	Cash		88
	(To replenish petty cash fund)		

Conversely, if the custodian has $14 in cash, the reimbursement request would be for $86, and the company would credit Cash Over and Short for $1 (overage). A company reports a debit balance in Cash Over and Short in the income statement as miscellaneous expense. It reports a credit balance in the account as miscellaneous revenue. The company closes Cash Over and Short to Income Summary at the end of the year.

Companies should replenish a petty cash fund at the end of the accounting period, regardless of the cash in the fund. Replenishment at this time is necessary in order to recognize the effects of the petty cash payments on the financial statements.

Helpful Hint
Cash over and short situations result from mathematical errors or from failure to keep accurate records.

ETHICS INSIGHT

How Employees Steal

A recent study by the Association of Certified Fraud Examiners found that two-thirds of all employee thefts involved a fraudulent disbursement by an employee. The most common form (28.3% of cases) was fraudulent billing schemes. In these, the employee causes the company to issue a payment to the employee by submitting a bill for nonexistent goods or services, purchases of personal goods by the employee, or inflated invoices. The following graph shows various types of fraudulent disbursements and the median loss from each.

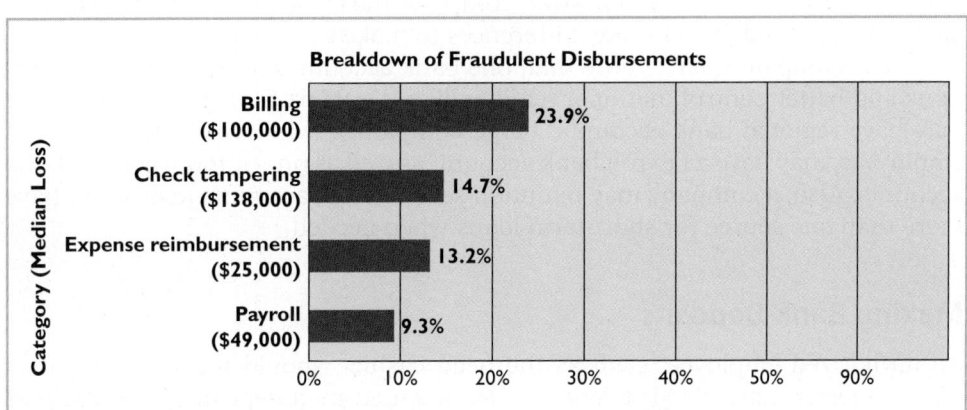

Breakdown of Fraudulent Disbursements

Category (Median Loss):
- Billing ($100,000): 23.9%
- Check tampering ($138,000): 14.7%
- Expense reimbursement ($25,000): 13.2%
- Payroll ($49,000): 9.3%

Source: 2008 Report to the Nation on Occupational Fraud and Abuse, Association of Certified Fraud Examiners, www.acfe.com/documents/2008_rttn.pdf, p. 13.

? How can companies reduce the likelihood of fraudulent disbursements? (See page 375.)

> DO IT!

Petty Cash Fund

Action Plan

✔ To establish the fund, set up a separate general ledger account.

✔ Determine how much cash is needed to replenish the fund: subtract the cash remaining from the petty cash fund balance.

✔ Total the petty cash receipts. Determine any cash over or short—the difference between the cash needed to replenish the fund and the total of the petty cash receipts.

✔ Record the expenses incurred according to the petty cash receipts when replenishing the fund.

Bateer Company established a $50 petty cash fund on July 1. On July 30, the fund had $12 cash remaining and petty cash receipts for postage $14, office supplies $10, and delivery expense $15. Prepare journal entries to establish the fund on July 1 and to replenish the fund on July 30.

Solution

July 1	Petty Cash	50	
	Cash		50
	(To establish petty cash fund)		
30	Postage Expense	14	
	Supplies	10	
	Delivery Expense	15	
	Cash Over and Short		1
	Cash ($50 – $12)		38
	(To replenish petty cash)		

Related exercise material: **BE7-9, E7-7, E7-8, and DO IT! 7-3.**

 The Navigator

Control Features: Use of a Bank

The use of a bank contributes significantly to good internal control over cash. A company can safeguard its cash by using a bank as a depository and as a clearing house for checks received and written. Use of a bank minimizes the amount of currency that a company must keep on hand. Also, use of a bank facilitates the control of cash because it creates a double record of all bank transactions—one by the company and the other by the bank. The asset account Cash maintained by the company should have the same balance as the bank's liability account for that company. A **bank reconciliation** compares the bank's balance with the company's balance and explains any differences to make them agree.

Many companies have more than one bank account. For efficiency of operations and better control, national retailers like Wal-Mart Stores, Inc. and Target may have regional bank accounts. Large companies, with tens of thousands of employees, may have a payroll bank account, as well as one or more general bank accounts. Also, a company may maintain several bank accounts in order to have more than one source for short-term loans when needed.

Making Bank Deposits

An authorized employee, such as the head cashier, should make a company's bank deposits. Each deposit must be documented by a deposit slip (ticket), as shown in Illustration 7-8.

Illustration 7-8
Deposit slip

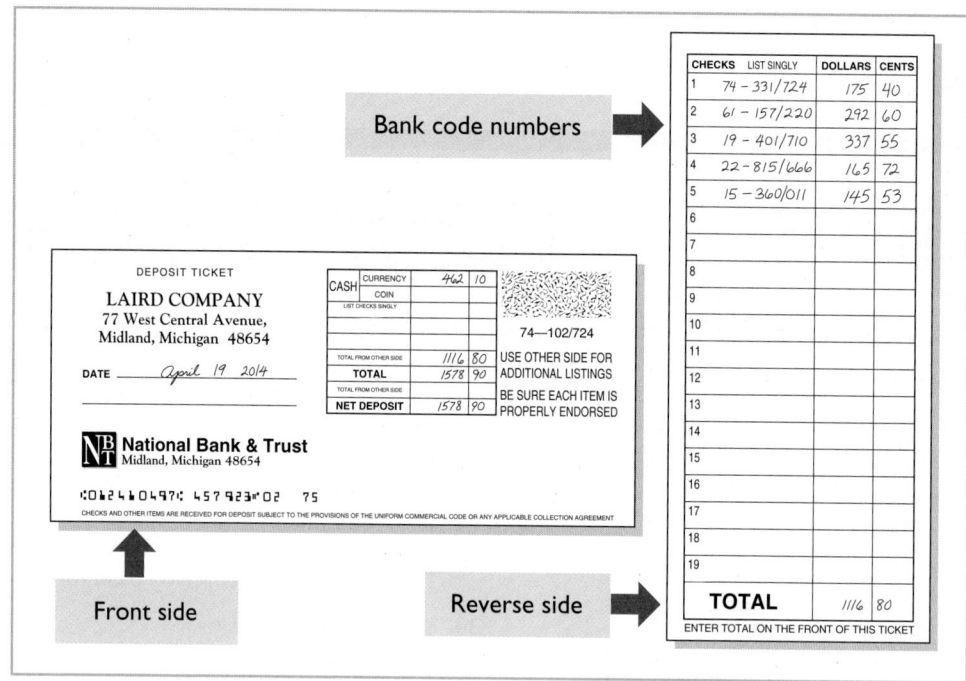

Deposit slips are prepared in duplicate. The bank retains the original; the depositor keeps the duplicate, machine-stamped by the bank to establish its authenticity.

Writing Checks

Most of us write checks without thinking very much about them. A **check** is a written order signed by the depositor directing the bank to pay a specified sum of money to a designated recipient. There are three parties to a check: (1) the **maker** (or drawer) who issues the check, (2) the **bank** (or payer) on which the check is drawn, and (3) the **payee** to whom the check is payable. A check is a **negotiable instrument** that one party can transfer to another party by endorsement. Each check should be accompanied by an explanation of its purpose. In many companies, a remittance advice attached to the check, as shown in Illustration 7-9, explains the check's purpose.

Illustration 7-9
Check with remittance advice

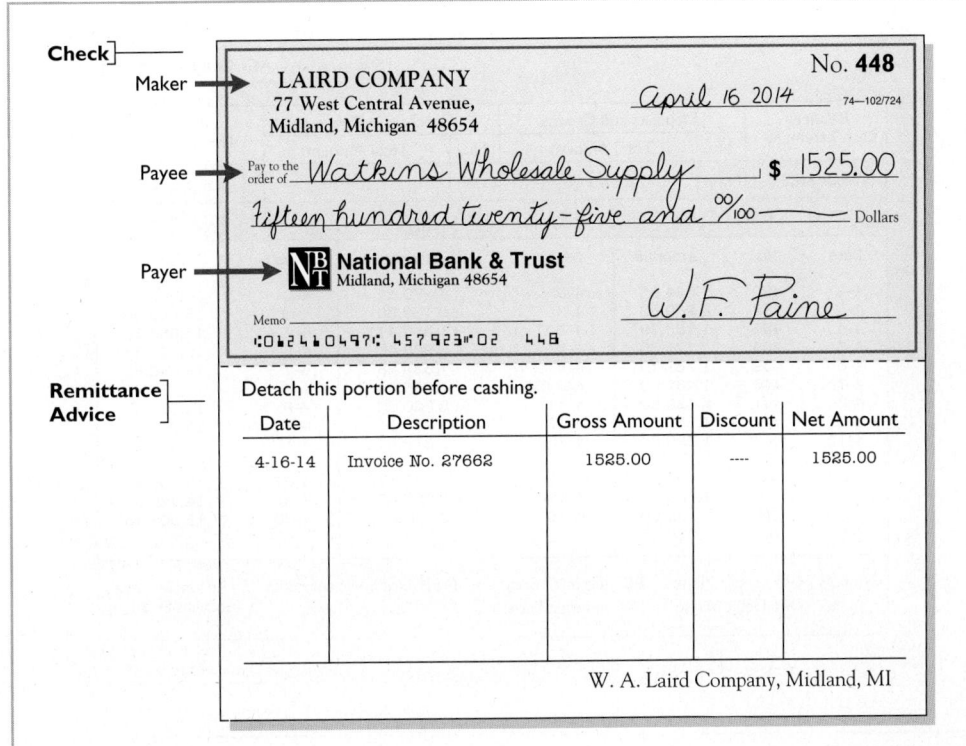

It is important to know the balance in the checking account at all times. To keep the balance current, the depositor should enter each deposit and check on running-balance memo forms (or online statements) provided by the bank or on the check stubs in the checkbook.

Bank Statements

If you have a personal checking account, you are probably familiar with bank statements. A **bank statement** shows the depositor's bank transactions and balances.[5] Each month, a depositor receives a statement from the bank. Illustration 7-10 (page 346) presents a typical bank statement. It shows (1) checks paid and other debits that reduce the balance in the depositor's account, (2) deposits and other credits that increase the balance in the account, and (3) the account balance after each day's transactions.

The bank statement lists in numerical sequence all "paid" checks, along with the date the check was paid and its amount. Upon paying a check, the bank

Helpful Hint
Essentially, the bank statement is a copy of the bank's records sent to the customer (or available online) for review.

---

[5]Our presentation assumes that the depositor makes all adjustments at the end of the month. In practice, a company may also make journal entries during the month as it reviews information from the bank regarding its account.

Illustration 7-10
Bank statement

Helpful Hint
The bank *credits* to the customer's account every deposit it receives. The reverse occurs when the bank "pays" a check issued by a company on its checking account balance. Payment reduces the bank's liability. Thus, the bank *debits* check payments to the customer's account with the bank.

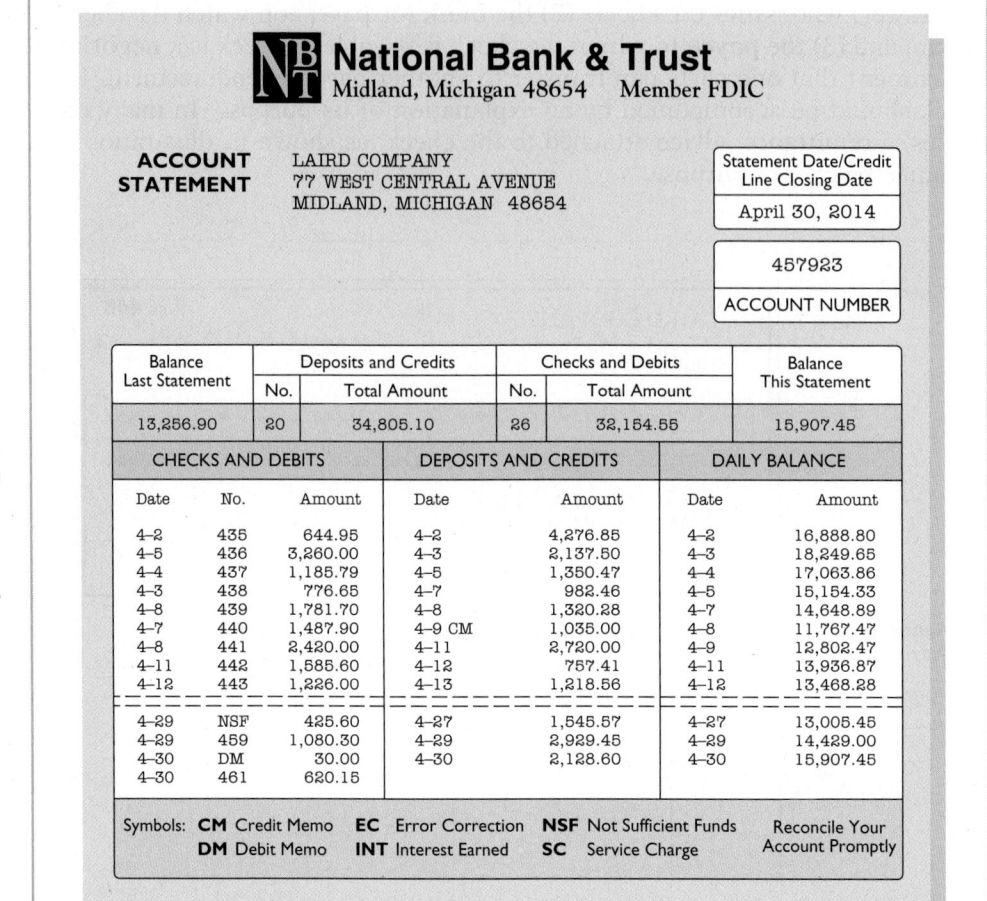

stamps the check "paid"; a paid check is sometimes referred to as a **canceled** check. On the statement, the bank also includes memoranda explaining other debits and credits it made to the depositor's account.

DEBIT MEMORANDUM

Some banks charge a monthly fee for their services. Often, they charge this fee only when the average monthly balance in a checking account falls below a specified amount. They identify the fee, called a **bank service charge**, on the bank statement by a symbol such as **SC**. The bank also sends with the statement a debit memorandum explaining the charge noted on the statement. Other debit memoranda may also be issued for other bank services such as the cost of printing checks, issuing traveler's checks, and wiring funds to other locations. The symbol **DM** is often used for such charges.

Banks also use a debit memorandum when a deposited check from a customer "bounces" because of insufficient funds. For example, assume that Scott Company, a customer of Laird Company, sends a check for $800 to Laird Company for services provided. Unfortunately, Scott does not have sufficient funds at its bank to pay for these services. In such a case, Scott's bank marks the check **NSF** (not sufficient funds) and returns it to Laird's (the depositor's) bank. Laird's bank then debits Laird's account, as shown by the symbol NSF on the bank statement in Illustration 7-10. The bank sends the NSF check and debit memorandum to Laird as notification of the charge. Laird then records an Account Receivable from Scott Company (the writer of the bad check) and reduces cash for the NSF check.

CREDIT MEMORANDUM
Sometimes a depositor asks the bank to collect its notes receivable. In such a case, the bank will credit the depositor's account for the cash proceeds of the note. This is illustrated by the symbol **CM** on the Laird Company bank statement. The bank issues and sends with the statement a credit memorandum to explain the entry. Many banks also offer interest on checking accounts. The interest earned may be indicated on the bank statement by the symbol **CM** or **INT**.

Reconciling the Bank Account

The bank and the depositor maintain independent records of the depositor's checking account. People tend to assume that the respective balances will always agree. In fact, the two balances are seldom the same at any given time, and both balances differ from the "correct" or "true" balance. Therefore, it is necessary to make the balance per books and the balance per bank agree with the correct or true amount—a process called **reconciling the bank account**. The need for agreement has two causes:

1. **Time lags** that prevent one of the parties from recording the transaction in the same period as the other party.
2. **Errors** by either party in recording transactions.

Time lags occur frequently. For example, several days may elapse between the time a company mails a check to a payee and the date the bank pays the check. Similarly, when the depositor uses the bank's night depository to make its deposits, there will be a difference of at least one day between the time the depositor records the deposit and the time the bank does so. A time lag also occurs whenever the bank mails a debit or credit memorandum to the depositor.

The incidence of errors depends on the effectiveness of the internal controls of the depositor and the bank. Bank errors are infrequent. However, either party could accidentally record a $450 check as $45 or $540. In addition, the bank might mistakenly charge a check to a wrong account by keying in an incorrect account name or number.

> **LEARNING OBJECTIVE 7**
>
> Prepare a bank reconciliation.

RECONCILIATION PROCEDURE
The bank reconciliation should be prepared by an employee who has no other responsibilities pertaining to cash. If a company fails to follow this internal control principle of independent internal verification, cash embezzlements may go unnoticed. For example, a cashier who prepares the reconciliation can embezzle cash and conceal the embezzlement by misstating the reconciliation. Thus, the bank accounts would reconcile, and the embezzlement would not be detected.

In reconciling the bank account, it is customary to reconcile the balance per books and balance per bank to their adjusted (correct or true) cash balances. The starting point in preparing the reconciliation is to enter the balance per bank statement and balance per books on the reconciliation schedule. The company then makes various adjustments, as shown in Illustration 7-11 (page 348).

The following steps should reveal all the reconciling items that cause the difference between the two balances.

Step 1. Deposits in transit. Compare the individual deposits listed on the bank statement with deposits in transit from the preceding bank reconciliation and with the deposits per company records or duplicate deposit slips. Deposits recorded by the depositor that have not been recorded by the bank are the **deposits in transit**. Add these deposits to the balance per bank.

> **Helpful Hint**
> Deposits in transit and outstanding checks are reconciling items because of time lags.

Illustration 7-11
Bank reconciliation
adjustments

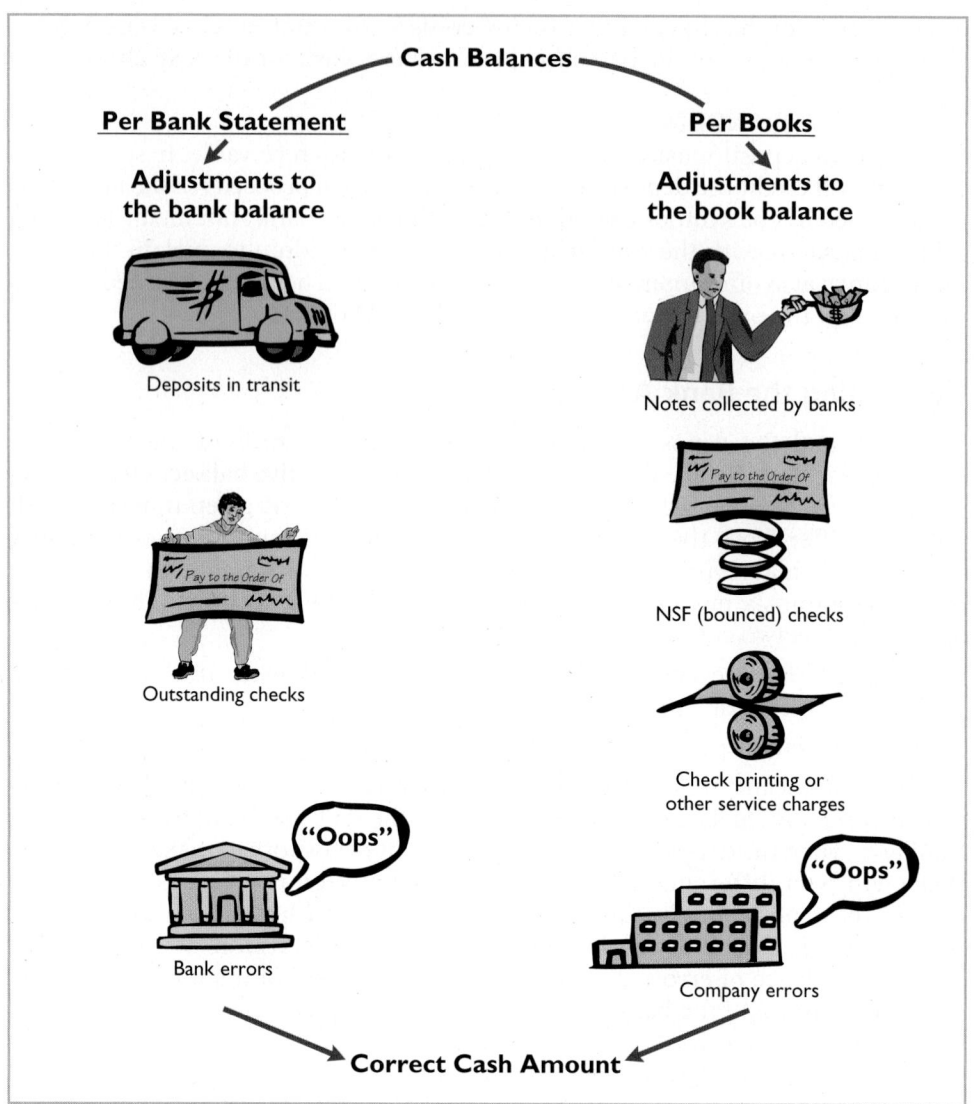

Step 2. Outstanding checks. Compare the paid checks shown on the bank statement with (a) checks outstanding from the previous bank reconciliation, and (b) checks issued by the company as recorded in the cash payments journal (or in the check register in your personal checkbook). Issued checks recorded by the company but that have not yet been paid by the bank are **outstanding checks**. Deduct outstanding checks from the balance per the bank.

Step 3. Errors. Note any errors discovered in the foregoing steps and list them in the appropriate section of the reconciliation schedule. For example, if the company mistakenly recorded as $169 a paid check correctly written for $196, it would deduct the error of $27 from the balance per books. All errors made by the depositor are reconciling items in determining the adjusted cash balance per books. In contrast, all errors made by the bank are reconciling items in determining the adjusted cash balance per the bank.

Step 4. Bank memoranda. Trace bank memoranda to the depositor's records. List in the appropriate section of the reconciliation schedule any unrecorded memoranda. For example, the company would deduct from the balance per books a $5 debit memorandum for bank service charges. Similarly, it would add to the balance per books $32 of interest earned.

BANK RECONCILIATION ILLUSTRATED

The bank statement for Laird Company, in Illustration 7-10, shows a balance per bank of $15,907.45 on April 30, 2014. On this date the balance of cash per books is $11,589.45. Using the four reconciliation steps, Laird determines the following reconciling items.

Step 1. Deposits in transit: April 30 deposit (received by bank on May 1). $2,201.40

Step 2. Outstanding checks: No. 453, $3,000.00; no. 457, $1,401.30; no. 460, $1,502.70.   5,904.00

Step 3. Errors: Laird wrote check no. 443 for $1,226.00 and the bank correctly paid that amount. However, Laird recorded the check as $1,262.00.   36.00

Step 4. Bank memoranda:
    a. Debit—NSF check from J. R. Baron for $425.60   425.60
    b. Debit—Charge for printing company checks $30.00   30.00
    c. Credit—Collection of note receivable for $1,000 plus interest earned $50, less bank collection fee $15.00   1,035.00

Illustration 7-12 shows Laird's bank reconciliation.

> **Helpful Hint**
> Note in the bank statement on page 346 that checks no. 459 and 461 have been paid but check no. 460 is not listed. Thus, this check is outstanding. If a complete bank statement were provided, checks no. 453 and 457 would also not be listed. The amounts for these three checks are obtained from the company's cash payments records.

Laird Company
Bank Reconciliation
April 30, 2014

Cash balance per bank statement		$ 15,907.45
Add: Deposits in transit		2,201.40
		18,108.85
Less: Outstanding checks		
No. 453	$3,000.00	
No. 457	1,401.30	
No. 460	1,502.70	5,904.00
Adjusted cash balance per bank		**$12,204.85**
Cash balance per books		$ 11,589.45
Add: Collection of note receivable $1,000, plus interest earned $50, less collection fee $15	$1,035.00	
Error in recording check no. 443	36.00	1,071.00
		12,660.45
Less: NSF check	425.60	
Bank service charge	30.00	455.60
Adjusted cash balance per books		**$12,204.85**

Illustration 7-12
Bank reconciliation

> **Alternative Terminology**
> The terms *adjusted cash balance*, *true cash balance*, and *correct cash balance* are used interchangeably.

> **Helpful Hint**
> The entries that follow are adjusting entries. In prior chapters, Cash was an account that did not require adjustment. That was a simplifying assumption for learning purposes because we had not yet explained a bank reconciliation.

ENTRIES FROM BANK RECONCILIATION

The company records each reconciling item used to determine the **adjusted cash balance per books. If the company does not journalize and post these items, the Cash account will not show the correct balance.** Laird Company would make the following entries on April 30.

COLLECTION OF NOTE RECEIVABLE This entry involves four accounts. Assuming that the interest of $50 has not been accrued and the collection fee is charged to Miscellaneous Expense, the entry is:

Apr. 30	Cash	1,035.00	
	Miscellaneous Expense	15.00	
	Notes Receivable		1,000.00
	Interest Revenue		50.00
	(To record collection of note receivable by bank)		

BOOK ERROR The cash disbursements journal shows that check no. 443 was a payment on account to Andrea Company, a supplier. The correcting entry is:

Apr. 30	Cash	36.00	
	Accounts Payable—Andrea Company		36.00
	(To correct error in recording check no. 443)		

NSF CHECK As indicated earlier, an NSF check becomes an account receivable to the depositor. The entry is:

Apr. 30	Accounts Receivable—J. R. Baron	425.60	
	Cash		425.60
	(To record NSF check)		

BANK SERVICE CHARGES Depositors debit check printing charges (DM) and other bank service charges (SC) to Miscellaneous Expense because they are usually nominal in amount. The entry is:

Apr. 30	Miscellaneous Expense	30.00	
	Cash		30.00
	(To record charge for printing company checks)		

Instead of making four separate entries, Laird could combine them into one compound entry.

After Laird has posted the entries, the Cash account will show the following.

Cash

Apr. 30 Bal.		11,589.45	Apr. 30		425.60
30		1,035.00	30		30.00
30		36.00			
Apr. 30 Bal.		**12,204.85**			

Illustration 7-13
Adjusted balance in cash account

The adjusted cash balance in the ledger should agree with the adjusted cash balance per books in the bank reconciliation in Illustration 7-12 (page 349).

What entries does the bank make? If the company discovers any bank errors in preparing the reconciliation, it should notify the bank. The bank then can make the necessary corrections in its records. The bank does not make any entries for deposits in transit or outstanding checks. Only when these items reach the bank will the bank record these items.

Electronic Funds Transfer (EFT) System

It is not surprising that companies and banks have developed approaches to transfer funds among parties without the use of paper (deposit tickets, checks, etc.). Such procedures, called **electronic funds transfers (EFT)**, are disbursement systems that use wire, telephone, or computers to transfer cash balances from one

(margin annotations)

A = L + SE
+1,035
−15 Exp
−1,000
+50 Rev
Cash Flows
+1,035

A = L + SE
+36
+36
Cash Flows
+36

A = L + SE
+425.60
−425.60
Cash Flows
−425.60

A = L + SE
−30 Exp
−30
Cash Flows
−30

location to another. Use of EFT is quite common. For example, many employees receive no formal payroll checks from their employers. Instead, employers send electronic payroll data to the appropriate banks. Also, individuals now frequently make regular payments such as those for house, car, and utilities by EFT.

EFT transfers normally result in better internal control since no cash or checks are handled by company employees. This does not mean that opportunities for fraud are eliminated. In fact, the same basic principles related to internal control apply to EFT transfers. For example, without proper segregation of duties and authorizations, an employee might be able to redirect electronic payments into a personal bank account and conceal the theft with fraudulent accounting entries.

INVESTOR INSIGHT

Madoff's Ponzi Scheme

No recent fraud has generated more interest and rage than the one perpetrated by Bernard Madoff. Madoff was an elite New York investment fund manager who was highly regarded by securities regulators. Investors flocked to him because he delivered very steady returns of between 10% and 15%, no matter whether the market was going up or going down. However, for many years, Madoff did not actually invest the cash that people gave to him. Instead, he was running a Ponzi scheme: He paid returns to existing investors using cash received from new investors. As long as the size of his investment fund continued to grow from new investments at a rate that exceeded the amounts that he needed to pay out in returns, Madoff was able to operate his fraud smoothly. To conceal his misdeeds, he fabricated false investment statements that were provided to investors. In addition, Madoff hired an auditor that never verified the accuracy of the investment records but automatically issued unqualified opinions each year. Although a competing fund manager warned the SEC a number of times over a nearly 10-year period that he thought Madoff was engaged in fraud, the SEC never aggressively investigated the allegations. Investors, many of which were charitable organizations, lost more than $18 billion. Madoff was sentenced to a jail term of 150 years.

? How was Madoff able to conceal such a giant fraud? (See page 375.)

> DO IT!

Bank Reconciliation

Sally Kist owns Linen Kist Fabrics. Sally asks you to explain how she should treat the following reconciling items when reconciling the company's bank account: (1) a debit memorandum for an NSF check, (2) a credit memorandum for a note collected by the bank, (3) outstanding checks, and (4) a deposit in transit.

Solution

Sally should treat the reconciling items as follows.

(1) NSF check: Deduct from balance per books.

(2) Collection of note: Add to balance per books.

(3) Outstanding checks: Deduct from balance per bank.

(4) Deposit in transit: Add to balance per bank.

Action Plan

✔ Understand the purpose of a bank reconciliation.

✔ Identify time lags and explain how they cause reconciling items.

Related exercise material: **BE7-11, BE7-12, BE7-13, BE7-14, E7-9, E7-10, E7-11, E7-12, E7-13, and DO IT! 7-4.**

 ✔ The Navigator

Reporting Cash

Cash consists of coins, currency (paper money), checks, money orders, and money on hand or on deposit in a bank or similar depository. Companies report cash in two different statements: the balance sheet and the statement of cash flows. The balance sheet reports the amount of cash available at a given point in time. The statement of cash flows shows the sources and uses of cash during a period of time. The statement of cash flows was introduced in Chapter 1 and will be discussed in much detail in Chapter 13. In this section, we discuss some important points regarding the presentation of cash in the balance sheet.

When presented in a balance sheet, cash on hand, cash in banks, and petty cash are often combined and reported simply as **Cash**. Because it is the most liquid asset owned by the company, cash is listed first in the current assets section of the balance sheet.

Cash Equivalents

Many companies use the designation "Cash and cash equivalents" in reporting cash. (See Illustration 7-14 for an example.) **Cash equivalents** are short-term, highly liquid investments that are both:

1. Readily convertible to known amounts of cash, and

2. So near their maturity that their market value is relatively insensitive to changes in interest rates.

Illustration 7-14
Balance sheet presentation of cash

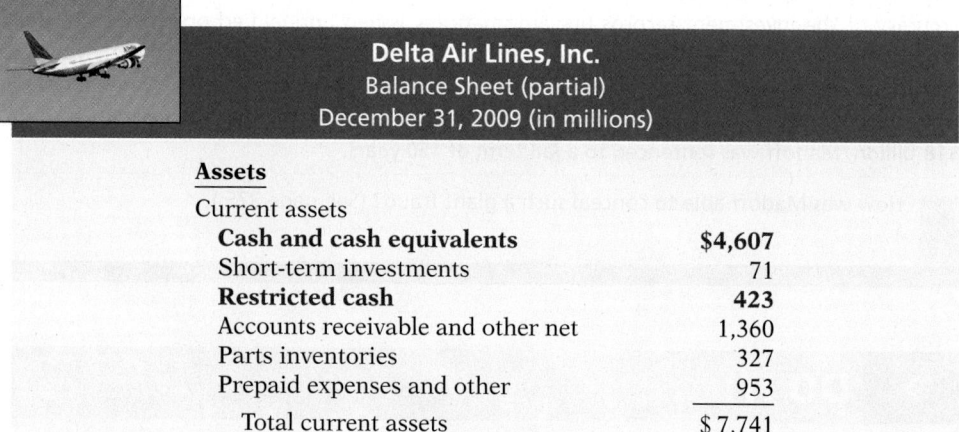

Delta Air Lines, Inc.
Balance Sheet (partial)
December 31, 2009 (in millions)

Assets

Current assets	
Cash and cash equivalents	$4,607
Short-term investments	71
Restricted cash	423
Accounts receivable and other net	1,360
Parts inventories	327
Prepaid expenses and other	953
Total current assets	$ 7,741

Examples of cash equivalents are Treasury bills, commercial paper (short-term corporate notes), and money market funds. All typically are purchased with cash that is in excess of immediate needs.

Occasionally, a company will have a net negative balance in its bank account. In this case, the company should report the negative balance among current liabilities. For example, farm equipment manufacturer Ag-Chem recently reported "Checks outstanding in excess of cash balances" of $2,145,000 among its current liabilities.

Restricted Cash

A company may have **restricted cash**, cash that is not available for general use but rather is restricted for a special purpose. For example, landfill companies are often required to maintain a fund of restricted cash to

Ethics Note

Recently, some companies were forced to restate their financial statements because they had too broadly interpreted which types of investments could be treated as cash equivalents. By reporting these items as cash equivalents, the companies made themselves look more liquid.

ensure they will have adequate resources to cover closing and clean-up costs at the end of a landfill site's useful life. McKessor Corp. recently reported restricted cash of $962 million to be paid out as the result of investor lawsuits.

Cash restricted in use should be reported separately on the balance sheet as restricted cash. If the company expects to use the restricted cash within the next year, it reports the amount as a current asset. When this is not the case, it reports the restricted funds as a noncurrent asset.

Illustration 7-14 shows restricted cash reported in the financial statements of Delta Air Lines. The company is required to maintain restricted cash as collateral to support insurance obligations related to workers' compensation claims. Delta does not have access to these funds for general use, and so it must report them separately, rather than as part of cash and cash equivalents.

> Comprehensive DO IT!

Poorten Company's bank statement for May 2014 shows the following data.

Balance 5/1	$12,650	Balance 5/31	$14,280
Debit memorandum:		Credit memorandum:	
NSF check	$175	Collection of note receivable	$505

The cash balance per books at May 31 is $13,319. Your review of the data reveals the following.

1. The NSF check was from Copple Co., a customer.
2. The note collected by the bank was a $500, 3-month, 12% note. The bank charged a $10 collection fee. No interest has been accrued.
3. Outstanding checks at May 31 total $2,410.
4. Deposits in transit at May 31 total $1,752.
5. A Poorten Company check for $352, dated May 10, cleared the bank on May 25. The company recorded this check, which was a payment on account, for $325.

Instructions
(a) Prepare a bank reconciliation at May 31.
(b) Journalize the entries required by the reconciliation.

Solution to Comprehensive DO IT!

Action Plan

✔ Follow the four steps in the reconciliation procedure (pp. 347–349).

✔ Work carefully to minimize mathematical errors in the reconciliation.

✔ Prepare entries from reconciling items per books.

✔ Make sure the cash ledger balance after posting the reconciling entries agrees with the adjusted cash balance per books.

(a)
Poorten Company
Bank Reconciliation
May 31, 2014

Cash balance per bank statement		$14,280
Add: Deposits in transit		1,752
		16,032
Less: Outstanding checks		2,410
Adjusted cash balance per bank		$13,622
Cash balance per books		$13,319
Add: Collection of note receivable $500, plus $15		
interest, less collection fee $10		505
		13,824
Less: NSF check	$175	
Error in recording check	27	202
Adjusted cash balance per books		$13,622

(b)

May 31	Cash		505	
	Miscellaneous Expense		10	
	Notes Receivable			500
	Interest Revenue			15
	(To record collection of note by bank)			
31	Accounts Receivable—Copple Co.		175	
	Cash			175
	(To record NSF check from Copple Co.)			
31	Accounts Payable		27	
	Cash			27
	(To correct error in recording check)			

✔ The Navigator

SUMMARY OF LEARNING OBJECTIVES

✔ The Navigator

1 Define fraud and internal control. A fraud is a dishonest act by an employee that results in personal benefit to the employee at a cost to the employer. The fraud triangle refers to the three factors that contribute to fraudulent activity by employees: opportunity, financial pressure, and rationalization. Internal control consists of all the related methods and measures adopted within an organization to safeguard its assets, enhance the reliability of its accounting records, increase efficiency of operations, and ensure compliance with laws and regulations.

2 Identify the principles of internal control activities. The principles of internal control are establishment of responsibility; segregation of duties; documentation procedures; physical controls; independent internal verification; and human resource controls such as bonding and requiring employees to take vacations.

3 Explain the applications of internal control principles to cash receipts. Internal controls over cash receipts include: (a) designating specific personnel to handle cash; (b) assigning different individuals to receive cash, record cash, and maintain custody of cash; (c) using remittance advices for mail receipts, cash register tapes for over-the-counter receipts, and deposit slips for bank deposits; (d) using company safes and bank vaults to store cash with access limited to authorized personnel, and using cash registers in executing over-the-counter receipts; (e) making independent daily counts of register receipts and daily comparison of total receipts with total deposits; and (f) bonding personnel that handle cash and requiring them to take vacations.

4 Explain the applications of internal control principles to cash disbursements. Internal controls over cash disbursements include: (a) having specific individuals such as the treasurer authorized to sign checks and approve invoices; (b) assigning different individuals to approve

items for payment, pay the items, and record the payment; (c) using prenumbered checks and accounting for all checks, with each check supported by an approved invoice (d) storing blank checks in a safe or vault with access restricted to authorized personnel, and using a checkwriting machine to imprint amounts on checks; (e) comparing each check with the approved invoice before issuing the check, and making monthly reconciliations of bank and book balances; and (f) bonding personnel who handle cash, requiring employees to take vacations, and conducting background checks.

5 Describe the operation of a petty cash fund. Companies operate a petty cash fund to pay relatively small amounts of cash. They must establish the fund, make payments from the fund, and replenish the fund when the cash in the fund reaches a minimum level.

6 Indicate the control features of a bank account. A bank account contributes to good internal control by providing physical controls for the storage of cash. It minimizes the amount of currency that a company must keep on hand, and it creates a double record of a depositor's bank transactions.

7 Prepare a bank reconciliation. It is customary to reconcile the balance per books and balance per bank to their adjusted balances. The steps in the reconciling process are to determine deposits in transit, outstanding checks, errors by the depositor or the bank, and unrecorded bank memoranda.

8 Explain the reporting of cash. Companies list cash first in the current assets section of the balance sheet. In some cases, they report cash together with cash equivalents. Cash restricted for a special purpose is reported separately as a current asset or as a noncurrent asset, depending on when the cash is expected to be used.

GLOSSARY

Bank reconciliation The process of comparing the bank's balance of an account with the company's balance and explaining any differences to make them agree. (p. 344).

Bank service charge A fee charged by a bank for the use of its services. (p. 346).

Bank statement A monthly statement from the bank that shows the depositor's bank transactions and balances. (p. 345).

Bonding Obtaining insurance protection against misappropriation of assets by employees. (p. 333).

Cash Resources that consist of coins, currency, checks, money orders, and money on hand or on deposit in a bank or similar depository. (p. 352).

Cash equivalents Short-term, highly liquid investments that can be converted to a specific amount of cash. (p. 352).

Check A written order signed by a bank depositor, directing the bank to pay a specified sum of money to a designated recipient. (p. 344).

Deposits in transit Deposits recorded by the depositor but not yet been recorded by the bank. (p. 347).

Electronic funds transfer (EFT) A disbursement system that uses wire, telephone, or computers to transfer funds from one location to another. (p. 350).

Fraud A dishonest act by an employee that results in personal benefit to the employee at a cost to the employer. (p. 326).

Fraud triangle The three factors that contribute to fraudulent activity by employees: opportunity, financial pressure, and rationalization. (p. 326).

Internal auditors Company employees who continuously evaluate the effectiveness of the company's internal control system. (p. 333).

Internal control All of the related methods and activities adopted within an organization to safeguard its assets and enhance the accuracy and reliability of its accounting records. (p. 327).

NSF check A check that is not paid by a bank because of insufficient funds in a customer's bank account. (p. 346).

Outstanding checks Checks issued and recorded by a company but not yet paid by the bank. (p. 348).

Petty cash fund A cash fund used to pay relatively small amounts. (p. 340).

Restricted cash Cash that must be used for a special purpose. (p. 352).

Sarbanes-Oxley Act (SOX) Regulations passed by Congress to try to reduce unethical corporate behavior. (p. 326).

Voucher An authorization form prepared for each payment in a voucher system. (p. 339).

Voucher system A network of approvals by authorized individuals acting independently to ensure that all disbursements by check are proper. (p. 339).

 Self-Test, Brief Exercises, Exercises, Problem Set A, and many more components are available for practice in WileyPLUS.

SELF-TEST QUESTIONS

Answers are on page 375.

(LO 1) 1. Which of the following is *not* an element of the fraud triangle?
(a) Rationalization.
(b) Financial pressure.
(c) Segregation of duties.
(d) Opportunity.

(LO 1) 2. An organization uses internal control to enhance the accuracy and reliability of its accounting records and to:
(a) safeguard its assets.
(b) prevent fraud.
(c) produce correct financial statements.
(d) deter employee dishonesty.

(LO 1) 3. Which of the following was *not* a result of the Sarbanes-Oxley Act?
(a) Companies must file financial statements with the Internal Revenue Service.

(b) All publicly traded companies must maintain adequate internal controls.
(c) The Public Company Accounting Oversight Board was created to establish auditing standards and regulate auditor activity.
(d) Corporate executives and board of directors must ensure that controls are reliable and effective, and they can be fined or imprisoned for failure to do so.

4. The principles of internal control do *not* include: **(LO 2)**
(a) establishment of responsibility.
(b) documentation procedures.
(c) management responsibility.
(d) independent internal verification.

5. Physical controls do *not* include: **(LO 2)**
(a) safes and vaults to store cash.
(b) independent bank reconciliations.

(c) locked warehouses for inventories.

(d) bank safety deposit boxes for important papers.

(LO 3)   **6.** Permitting only designated personnel to handle cash receipts is an application of the principle of:

(a) segregation of duties.

(b) establishment of responsibility.

(c) independent check.

(d) human resource controls.

(LO 3)   **7.** Which of the following control activities is *not* relevant to when a company uses a computerized (rather than manual) accounting system?

(a) Establishment of responsibility.

(b) Segregation of duties.

(c) Independent internal verification.

(d) All of these control activities are relevant to a computerized system.

(LO 4)   **8.** The use of prenumbered checks in disbursing cash is an application of the principle of:

(a) establishment of responsibility.

(b) segregation of duties.

(c) physical controls.

(d) documentation procedures.

(LO 5)   **9.** A company writes a check to replenish a $100 petty cash fund when the fund contains receipts of $94 and $4 in cash. In recording the check, the company should:

(a) debit Cash Over and Short for $2.

(b) debit Petty Cash for $94.

(c) credit Cash for $94.

(d) credit Petty Cash for $2.

10. The control features of a bank account do *not* include: (LO 6)

(a) having bank auditors verify the correctness of the bank balance per books.

(b) minimizing the amount of cash that must be kept on hand.

(c) providing a double record of all bank transactions.

(d) safeguarding cash by using a bank as a depository.

11. In a bank reconciliation, deposits in transit are: (LO 7)

(a) deducted from the book balance.

(b) added to the book balance.

(c) added to the bank balance.

(d) deducted from the bank balance.

12. The reconciling item in a bank reconciliation that   (LO 7) will result in an adjusting entry by the depositor is:

(a) outstanding checks.

(b) deposit in transit.

(c) a bank error.

(d) bank service charges.

13. Which of the following items in a cash drawer at   (LO 8) November 30 is *not* cash?

(a) Money orders.

(b) Coins and currency.

(c) A customer check dated December 1.

(d) A customer check dated November 28.

14. Which of the following statements correctly describes   (LO 8) the reporting of cash?

(a) Cash cannot be combined with cash equivalents.

(b) Restricted cash funds may be combined with cash.

(c) Cash is listed first in the current assets section.

(d) Restricted cash funds cannot be reported as a current asset.

Go to the book's companion website, www.wiley.com/college/weygandt, for additional Self-Test Questions.

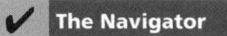 **The Navigator**

QUESTIONS

1. A local bank reported that it lost $150,000 as the result of an employee fraud. Travis Witt is not clear on what is meant by an "employee fraud." Explain the meaning of fraud to Travis and give an example of frauds that might occur at a bank.

2. Fraud experts often say that there are three primary factors that contribute to employee fraud. Identify the three factors and explain what is meant by each.

3. Identify and describe the five components of a good internal control system.

4. "Internal control is concerned only with enhancing the accuracy of the accounting records." Do you agree? Explain.

5. What principles of internal control apply to most organizations?

6. At the corner grocery store, all sales clerks make change out of one cash register drawer. Is this a violation of internal control? Why?

7. Pam Duffy is reviewing the principle of segregation of duties. What are the two common applications of this principle?

8. How do documentation procedures contribute to good internal control?

9. What internal control objectives are met by physical controls?

10. (a) Explain the control principle of independent internal verification. (b) What practices are important in applying this principle?

11. The management of Yaeger Company asks you, as the company accountant, to explain (a) the concept of reasonable assurance in internal control and (b) the importance of the human factor in internal control.

12. Yorkville Fertilizer Co. owns the following assets at the balance sheet date.

Cash in bank savings account	$ 6,000
Cash on hand	850
Cash refund due from the IRS	1,000
Checking account balance	12,000
Postdated checks	500

What amount should Yorkville report as cash in the balance sheet?

13. What principle(s) of internal control is (are) involved in making daily cash counts of over-the-counter receipts?

14. Aurora Department Stores has just installed new electronic cash registers in its stores. How do cash registers improve internal control over cash receipts?

15. At Oswego Wholesale Company, two mail clerks open all mail receipts. How does this strengthen internal control?

16. "To have maximum effective internal control over cash disbursements, all payments should be made by check." Is this true? Explain.

17. Ted Rampolla Company's internal controls over cash disbursements provide for the treasurer to sign checks imprinted by a check-writing machine in indelible ink after comparing the check with the approved invoice. Identify the internal control principles that are present in these controls.

18. How do the principles of (a) physical controls and (b) documentation controls apply to cash disbursements?

19. (a) What is a voucher system? (b) What principles of internal control apply to a voucher system?

20. What is the essential feature of an electronic funds transfer (EFT) procedure?

21. (a) Identify the three activities that pertain to a petty cash fund, and indicate an internal control principle that is applicable to each activity. (b) When are journal entries required in the operation of a petty cash fund?

22. "The use of a bank contributes significantly to good internal control over cash." Is this true? Why or why not?

23. Faye Uhlik is confused about the lack of agreement between the cash balance per books and the balance per bank. Explain the causes for the lack of agreement to Faye, and give an example of each cause.

24. What are the four steps involved in finding differences between the balance per books and balance per bank?

25. Pauline Duche asks your help concerning an NSF check. Explain to Pauline (a) what an NSF check is, (b) how it is treated in a bank reconciliation, and (c) whether it will require an adjusting entry.

26. (a) "Cash equivalents are the same as cash." Do you agree? Explain. (b) How should restricted cash funds be reported on the balance sheet?

27. ◈ PEPSICO At what amount does PepsiCo report cash and cash equivalents in its 2010 consolidated balance sheet?

BRIEF EXERCISES

BE7-1 Match each situation with the fraud triangle factor"—opportunity, financial pressure, or rationalization"—that best describes it.

1. An employee's monthly credit card payments are nearly 75% of his or her monthly earnings.
2. An employee earns minimum wage at a firm that has reported record earnings for each of the last five years.
3. An employee has an expensive gambling habit.
4. An employee has check-writing and signing responsibilities for a small company, as well as reconciling the bank account.

Identify fraud triangle concepts.

(LO 1)

BE7-2 Bridget Harrard has prepared the following list of statements about internal control.

1. One of the objectives of internal control is to safeguard assets from employee theft, robbery, and unauthorized use.
2. One of the objectives of internal control is to enhance the accuracy and reliability of the accounting records.
3. No laws require U.S. corporations to maintain an adequate system of internal control.

Identify each statement as true or false. If false, indicate how to correct the statement.

Indicate internal control concepts.

(LO 1)

BE7-3 Emily Cooper is the new owner of Preferred Parking. She has heard about internal control but is not clear about its importance for her business. Explain to Emily the four purposes of internal control and give her one application of each purpose for Preferred Parking.

Explain the importance of internal control.

(LO 1)

BE7-4 The internal control procedures in Naperville Company provide that:

1. Employees who have physical custody of assets do not have access to the accounting records.
2. Each month, the assets on hand are compared to the accounting records by an internal auditor.
3. A prenumbered shipping document is prepared for each shipment of goods to customers.

Identify the principles of internal control that are being followed.

Identify internal control principles.

(LO 2)

BE7-5 Syracuse Company has the following internal control procedures over cash receipts. Identify the internal control principle that is applicable to each procedure.

1. All over-the-counter receipts are entered on cash registers.
2. All cashiers are bonded.
3. Daily cash counts are made by cashier department supervisors.

Identify the internal control principles applicable to cash receipts.

(LO 3)

4. The duties of receiving cash, recording cash, and custody of cash are assigned to different individuals.
5. Only cashiers may operate cash registers.

Make journal entries for cash overage and shortfall.

(LO 3)

BE7-6 The cash register tape for Goodmood Industries reported sales of $6,891.50. Record the journal entry that would be necessary for each of the following situations. (a) Cash to be accounted for exceeds cash on hand by $46.25. (b) Cash on hand exceeds cash to be accounted for by $28.32.

Make journal entry using cash count sheet.

(LO 3)

BE7-7 While examining cash receipts information, the accounting department determined the following information: opening cash balance $180, cash on hand $1,125.74, and cash sales per register tape $950.83. Prepare the required journal entry based upon the cash count sheet.

Identify the internal control principles applicable to cash disbursements.

(LO 4)

BE7-8 Helena Company has the following internal control procedures over cash disbursements. Identify the internal control principle that is applicable to each procedure.

1. Company checks are prenumbered.
2. The bank statement is reconciled monthly by an internal auditor.
3. Blank checks are stored in a safe in the treasurer's office.
4. Only the treasurer or assistant treasurer may sign checks.
5. Check signers are not allowed to record cash disbursement transactions.

Prepare entry to replenish a petty cash fund.

(LO 5)

BE7-9 On March 20, Batavia's petty cash fund of $100 is replenished when the fund contains $9 in cash and receipts for postage $52, freight-out $26, and travel expense $10. Prepare the journal entry to record the replenishment of the petty cash fund.

Identify the control features of a bank account.

(LO 6)

BE7-10 Louis Whited is uncertain about the control features of a bank account. Explain the control benefits of (a) a check and (b) a bank statement.

Indicate location of reconciling items in a bank reconciliation.

(LO 7)

BE7-11 The following reconciling items are applicable to the bank reconciliation for Hinckley Company: (1) outstanding checks, (2) bank debit memorandum for service charge, (3) bank credit memorandum for collecting a note for the depositor, and (4) deposits in transit. Indicate how each item should be shown on a bank reconciliation.

Identify reconciling items that require adjusting entries.

(LO 7)

BE7-12 Using the data in BE7-11, indicate (a) the items that will result in an adjustment to the depositor's records and (b) why the other items do not require adjustment.

Prepare partial bank reconciliation.

(LO 7)

BE7-13 At July 31, Shabbona Company has the following bank information: cash balance per bank $7,420, outstanding checks $762, deposits in transit $1,620, and a bank service charge $20. Determine the adjusted cash balance per bank at July 31.

Prepare partial bank reconciliation.

(LO 7)

BE7-14 At August 31, DeKalb Company has a cash balance per books of $8,900 and the following additional data from the bank statement: charge for printing DeKalb Company checks $35, interest earned on checking account balance $40, and outstanding checks $800. Determine the adjusted cash balance per books at August 31.

Explain the statement presentation of cash balances.

(LO 8)

BE7-15 Plano Company has the following cash balances: Cash in Bank $15,742, Payroll Bank Account $5,000, and Plant Expansion Fund Cash $45,000. Explain how each balance should be reported on the balance sheet.

> DO IT! REVIEW

Identify violations of control activities.

(LO 2)

DO IT! **7-1** Identify which control activity is violated in each of the following situations, and explain how the situation creates an opportunity for fraud or inappropriate accounting practices.

1. Once a month, the sales department sends sales invoices to the accounting department to be recorded.
2. Sam Hustad orders merchandise for Green Lake Company; he also receives merchandise and authorizes payment for merchandise.
3. Several clerks at Ralph's Foods use the same cash register drawer.

DO IT! 7-2 Jerry Holman is concerned with control over mail receipts at Midtown Sporting Goods. All mail receipts are opened by Don Judd. Don sends the checks to the accounting department, where they are stamped "For Deposit Only." The accounting department records and deposits the mail receipts weekly. Jerry asks for your help in installing a good system of internal control over mail receipts.

Design system of internal control over cash receipts.

(LO 3)

DO IT! 7-3 Markee Company established a $100 petty cash fund on August 1. On August 31, the fund had $6 cash remaining and petty cash receipts for postage $31, office supplies $42, and miscellaneous expense $16. Prepare journal entries to establish the fund on August 1 and replenish the fund on August 31.

Make journal entries for petty cash fund.

(LO 5)

DO IT! 7-4 Jon Rapp owns Rapp Blankets. Jon asks you to explain how he should treat the following reconciling items when reconciling the company's bank account.

1. Outstanding checks.
2. A deposit in transit.
3. The bank charged to our account a check written by another company.
4. A debit memorandum for a bank service charge.

Explain treatment of items in bank reconciliation.

(LO 7)

✔ **The Navigator**

EXERCISES

E7-1 Sue Ernesto is the owner of Ernesto's Pizza. Ernesto's is operated strictly on a carryout basis. Customers pick up their orders at a counter where a clerk exchanges the pizza for cash. While at the counter, the customer can see other employees making the pizzas and the large ovens in which the pizzas are baked.

Identify the principles of internal control.

(LO 2)

Instructions
Identify the six principles of internal control and give an example of each principle that you might observe when picking up your pizza. (*Note:* It may not be possible to observe all the principles.)

E7-2 The following control procedures are used at Aldean Company for over-the-counter cash receipts.

1. To minimize the risk of robbery, cash in excess of $100 is stored in an unlocked attaché case in the stock room until it is deposited in the bank.
2. All over-the-counter receipts are registered by three clerks who use a cash register with a single cash drawer.
3. The company accountant makes the bank deposit and then records the day's receipts.
4. At the end of each day, the total receipts are counted by the cashier on duty and reconciled to the cash register total.
5. Cashiers are experienced; they are not bonded.

Identify internal control weaknesses over cash receipts and suggest improvements.

(LO 2, 3)

Instructions
(a) For each procedure, explain the weakness in internal control, and identify the control principle that is violated.
(b) For each weakness, suggest a change in procedure that will result in good internal control.

E7-3 The following control procedures are used in Morgan's Boutique Shoppe for cash disbursements.

1. The company accountant prepares the bank reconciliation and reports any discrepancies to the owner.
2. The store manager personally approves all payments before signing and issuing checks.
3. Each week, 100 company checks are left in an unmarked envelope on a shelf behind the cash register.
4. After payment, bills are filed in a paid invoice folder.
5. The company checks are unnumbered.

Identify internal control weaknesses over cash disbursements and suggest improvements.

(LO 2, 4)

Instructions

(a) For each procedure, explain the weakness in internal control, and identify the internal control principle that is violated.

(b) For each weakness, suggest a change in the procedure that will result in good internal control.

Identify internal control weaknesses for cash disbursements and suggest improvements.

(LO 4)

E7-4 At Teresa Company, checks are not prenumbered because both the purchasing agent and the treasurer are authorized to issue checks. Each signer has access to unissued checks kept in an unlocked file cabinet. The purchasing agent pays all bills pertaining to goods purchased for resale. Prior to payment, the purchasing agent determines that the goods have been received and verifies the mathematical accuracy of the vendor's invoice. After payment, the invoice is filed by vendor name, and the purchasing agent records the payment in the cash disbursements journal. The treasurer pays all other bills following approval by authorized employees. After payment, the treasurer stamps all bills PAID, files them by payment date, and records the checks in the cash disbursements journal. Teresa Company maintains one checking account that is reconciled by the treasurer.

Instructions

(a) List the weaknesses in internal control over cash disbursements.

(b) ▭▭▭▷ Write a memo to the company treasurer indicating your recommendations for improvement.

Indicate whether procedure is good or weak internal control.

(LO 2, 3, 4)

E7-5 Listed below are five procedures followed by Parson Company.

1. Several individuals operate the cash register using the same register drawer.
2. A monthly bank reconciliation is prepared by someone who has no other cash responsibilities.
3. Fran Vorbeck writes checks and also records cash payment journal entries.
4. One individual orders inventory, while a different individual authorizes payments.
5. Unnumbered sales invoices from credit sales are forwarded to the accounting department every four weeks for recording.

Instructions

Indicate whether each procedure is an example of good internal control or of weak internal control. If it is an example of good internal control, indicate which internal control principle is being followed. If it is an example of weak internal control, indicate which internal control principle is violated. Use the table below.

Procedure	IC Good or Weak?	Related Internal Control Principle
1.		
2.		
3.		
4.		
5.		

Indicate whether procedure is good or weak internal control.

(LO 2, 3, 4)

E7-6 Listed below are five procedures followed by Bingham Company.

1. Employees are required to take vacations.
2. Any member of the sales department can approve credit sales.
3. Blake Nayak ships goods to customers, bills customers, and receives payment from customers.
4. Total cash receipts are compared to bank deposits daily by someone who has no other cash responsibilities.
5. Time clocks are used for recording time worked by employees.

Instructions

Indicate whether each procedure is an example of good internal control or of weak internal control. If it is an example of good internal control, indicate which internal control principle is being followed. If it is an example of weak internal control, indicate which internal control principle is violated. Use the table below.

Procedure	IC Good or Weak?	Related Internal Control Principle
1.		
2.		
3.		
4.		
5.		

E7-7 LaSalle Company established a petty cash fund on May 1, cashing a check for $100. The company reimbursed the fund on June 1 and July 1 with the following results.

Prepare journal entries for a petty cash fund.

(LO 5)

June 1: Cash in fund $1.75. Receipts: delivery expense $31.25; postage expense $41.00; and miscellaneous expense $25.00.

July 1: Cash in fund $3.25. Receipts: delivery expense $21.00; entertainment expense $51.00; and miscellaneous expense $24.75.

On July 10, LaSalle increased the fund from $100 to $150.

Instructions
Prepare journal entries for LaSalle Company for May 1, June 1, July 1, and July 10.

E7-8 Kickapoo Company uses an imprest petty cash system. The fund was established on March 1 with a balance of $100. During March, the following petty cash receipts were found in the petty cash box.

Prepare journal entries for a petty cash fund.

(LO 5)

Date	Receipt No.	For	Amount
3/5	1	Stamp Inventory	$39
7	2	Freight-Out	17
9	3	Miscellaneous Expense	6
11	4	Travel Expense	24
14	5	Miscellaneous Expense	7

The fund was replenished on March 15 when the fund contained $4 in cash. On March 20, the amount in the fund was increased to $150.

Instructions
Journalize the entries in March that pertain to the operation of the petty cash fund.

E7-9 Lisa Ceja is unable to reconcile the bank balance at January 31. Lisa's reconciliation is as follows.

Prepare bank reconciliation and adjusting entries.

(LO 7)

Cash balance per bank	$3,660.20
Add: NSF check	590.00
Less: Bank service charge	25.00
Adjusted balance per bank	$4,225.20
Cash balance per books	$3,825.20
Less: Deposits in transit	480.00
Add: Outstanding checks	930.00
Adjusted balance per books	$4,275.20

Instructions
(a) Prepare a correct bank reconciliation.
(b) Journalize the entries required by the reconciliation.

E7-10 On April 30, the bank reconciliation of Perrin Company shows three outstanding checks: no. 254, $650; no. 255, $720; and no. 257, $410. The May bank statement and the May cash payments journal show the following.

Determine outstanding checks.

(LO 7)

Bank Statement			Cash Payments Journal		
Checks Paid			Checks Issued		
Date	Check No.	Amount	Date	Check No.	Amount
5/4	254	650	5/2	258	159
5/2	257	410	5/5	259	275
5/17	258	159	5/10	260	820
5/12	259	275	5/15	261	500
5/20	261	500	5/22	262	750
5/29	263	480	5/24	263	480
5/30	264	560	5/29	264	560

Prepare bank reconciliation and adjusting entries.

(LO 7)

Instructions
Using step 2 in the reconciliation procedure, list the outstanding checks at May 31.

E7-11 The following information pertains to Worthy Video Company.

1. Cash balance per bank, July 31, $7,293.
2. July bank service charge not recorded by the depositor $28.
3. Cash balance per books, July 31, $7,384.
4. Deposits in transit, July 31, $1,500.
5. Bank collected $800 note for Worthy in July, plus interest $36, less fee $20. The collection has not been recorded by Worthy, and no interest has been accrued.
6. Outstanding checks, July 31, $621.

Instructions
(a) Prepare a bank reconciliation at July 31.
(b) Journalize the adjusting entries at July 31 on the books of Worthy Video Company.

Prepare bank reconciliation and adjusting entries.

(LO 7)

E7-12 The information below relates to the Cash account in the ledger of Wasson Company.

Balance September 1—$17,150; Cash deposited—$64,000.
Balance September 30—$17,404; Checks written—$63,746.

The September bank statement shows a balance of $16,122 on September 30 and the following memoranda.

Credits		Debits	
Collection of $1,500 note plus interest $30	$1,530	NSF check: Violet Jones	$725
Interest earned on checking account	$45	Safety deposit box rent	$65

At September 30, deposits in transit were $4,450, and outstanding checks totaled $2,383.

Instructions
(a) Prepare the bank reconciliation at September 30.
(b) Prepare the adjusting entries at September 30, assuming (1) the NSF check was from a customer on account, and (2) no interest had been accrued on the note.

Compute deposits in transit and outstanding checks for two bank reconciliations.

(LO 7)

E7-13 The cash records of Satter Company show the following four situations.

1. The June 30 bank reconciliation indicated that deposits in transit total $920. During July, the general ledger account Cash shows deposits of $15,750, but the bank statement indicates that only $15,600 in deposits were received during the month.
2. The June 30 bank reconciliation also reported outstanding checks of $880. During the month of July, Satter Company books show that $17,200 of checks were issued. The bank statement showed that $16,400 of checks cleared the bank in July.
3. In September, deposits per the bank statement totaled $26,700, deposits per books were $25,400, and deposits in transit at September 30 were $2,600.
4. In September, cash disbursements per books were $23,700, checks clearing the bank were $24,000, and outstanding checks at September 30 were $2,100.

There were no bank debit or credit memoranda. No errors were made by either the bank or Satter Company.

Instructions
Answer the following questions.

(a) In situation (1), what were the deposits in transit at July 31?
(b) In situation (2), what were the outstanding checks at July 31?
(c) In situation (3), what were the deposits in transit at August 31?
(d) In situation (4), what were the outstanding checks at August 31?

Show presentation of cash in financial statements.

(LO 8)

E7-14 Nayak Company has recorded the following items in its financial records.

Cash in bank	$ 41,000
Cash in plant expansion fund	100,000
Cash on hand	8,000
Highly liquid investments	34,000
Petty cash	500
Receivables from customers	89,000
Stock investments	61,000

The cash in bank is subject to a compensating balance of $5,000. The highly liquid investments had maturities of 3 months or less when they were purchased. The stock investments will be sold in the next 6 to 12 months. The plant expansion project will begin in 3 years.

Instructions

(a) What amount should Nayak report as "Cash and cash equivalents" on its balance sheet?

(b) Where should the items not included in part (a) be reported on the balance sheet?

(c) What disclosures should Nayak make in its financial statements concerning "cash and cash equivalents"?

EXERCISES: SET B AND CHALLENGE EXERCISES

Visit the book's companion website, at **www.wiley.com/college/weygandt**, and choose the Student Companion site to access Exercise Set B and Challenge Exercises.

PROBLEMS: SET A

P7-1A Mainland Supply Company recently changed its system of internal control over cash disbursements. The system includes the following features.

Instead of being unnumbered and manually prepared, all checks must now be prenumbered and written by using the new checkwriting machine purchased by the company. Before a check can be issued, each invoice must have the approval of Erin McGarry, the purchasing agent, and Barb Speas, the receiving department supervisor. Checks must be signed by either Amaika Blake, the treasurer, or Ken Yost, the assistant treasurer. Before signing a check, the signer is expected to compare the amount of the check with the amount on the invoice.

After signing a check, the signer stamps the invoice PAID and inserts within the stamp, the date, check number, and amount of the check. The "paid" invoice is then sent to the accounting department for recording.

Blank checks are stored in a safe in the treasurer's office. The combination to the safe is known only by the treasurer and assistant treasurer. Each month, the bank statement is reconciled with the bank balance per books by the assistant chief accountant. All employees who handle or account for cash are bonded.

Identify internal control principles over cash disbursements.

(LO 2, 4)

Instructions

Identify the internal control principles and their application to cash disbursements of Mainland Supply Company.

P7-2A Arial Company maintains a petty cash fund for small expenditures. The following transactions occurred over a 2-month period.

Journalize and post petty cash fund transactions.

(LO 5)

July 1 Established petty cash fund by writing a check on Coulter Bank for $200.

15 Replenished the petty cash fund by writing a check for $198.00. On this date the fund consisted of $2.00 in cash and the following petty cash receipts: freight-out $87.00, postage expense $51.40, entertainment expense $46.60, and miscellaneous expense $11.20.

31 Replenished the petty cash fund by writing a check for $192.00. At this date, the fund consisted of $8.00 in cash and the following petty cash receipts: freight-out $82.10, charitable contributions expense $45.00, postage expense $25.50, and miscellaneous expense $39.40.

Aug. 15   Replenished the petty cash fund by writing a check for $187.00. On this date, the fund consisted of $13.00 in cash and the following petty cash receipts: freight-out $75.60, entertainment expense $43.00, postage expense $33.00, and miscellaneous expense $37.00.

16   Increased the amount of the petty cash fund to $300 by writing a check for $100.

31   Replenished petty cash fund by writing a check for $277.00. On this date, the fund consisted of $23 in cash and the following petty cash receipts: postage expense $133.00, travel expense $95.60, and freight-out $47.10.

Instructions

(a) July 15, Cash short $1.80

(b) Aug. 31 balance $300

(a) Journalize the petty cash transactions.
(b) Post to the Petty Cash account.
(c) What internal control features exist in a petty cash fund?

Prepare a bank reconciliation and adjusting entries.

(LO 7)

P7-3A On May 31, 2014, Terrell Company had a cash balance per books of $6,781.50. The bank statement from Home Town State Bank on that date showed a balance of $6,804.60. A comparison of the statement with the cash account revealed the following facts.

1. The statement included a debit memo of $40 for the printing of additional company checks.
2. Cash sales of $836.15 on May 12 were deposited in the bank. The cash receipts journal entry and the deposit slip were incorrectly made for $886.15. The bank credited Terrell Company for the correct amount.
3. Outstanding checks at May 31 totaled $276.25. Deposits in transit were $1,916.15.
4. On May 18, the company issued check No. 1181 for $685 to Barry Dietz on account. The check, which cleared the bank in May, was incorrectly journalized and posted by Terrell Company for $658.
5. A $3,000 note receivable was collected by the bank for Terrell Company on May 31 plus $80 interest. The bank charged a collection fee of $20. No interest has been accrued on the note.
6. Included with the cancelled checks was a check issued by Bridges Company to Jon Newton for $600 that was incorrectly charged to Terrell Company by the bank.
7. On May 31, the bank statement showed an NSF charge of $680 for a check issued by Sandy Grifton, a customer, to Terrell Company on account.

Instructions

(a) Adjusted cash balance per bank $9,044.50

(a) Prepare the bank reconciliation at May 31, 2014.
(b) Prepare the necessary adjusting entries for Terrell Company at May 31, 2014.

Prepare a bank reconciliation and adjusting entries from detailed data.

(LO 7)

P7-4A The bank portion of the bank reconciliation for Rintala Company at November 30, 2014, was as follows.

Rintala Company
Bank Reconciliation
November 30, 2014

Cash balance per bank		$14,367.90
Add: Deposits in transit		2,530.20
		16,898.10

Less: Outstanding checks		
Check Number	Check Amount	
3451	$2,260.40	
3470	720.10	
3471	844.50	
3472	1,426.80	
3474	1,050.00	6,301.80
Adjusted cash balance per bank		$10,596.30

The adjusted cash balance per bank agreed with the cash balance per books at November 30.

The December bank statement showed the following checks and deposits.

Bank Statement

	Checks			Deposits	
Date	**Number**	**Amount**	**Date**	**Amount**	
12-1	3451	$ 2,260.40	12-1	$ 2,530.20	
12-2	3471	844.50	12-4	1,211.60	
12-7	3472	1,426.80	12-8	2,365.10	
12-4	3475	1,640.70	12-16	2,672.70	
12-8	3476	1,300.00	12-21	2,945.00	
12-10	3477	2,130.00	12-26	2,567.30	
12-15	3479	3,080.00	12-29	2,836.00	
12-27	3480	600.00	12-30	1,025.00	
12-30	3482	475.50	Total	$18,152.90	
12-29	3483	1,140.00			
12-31	3485	540.80			
	Total	$15,438.70			

The cash records per books for December showed the following.

Cash Payments Journal

Date	Number	Amount	Date	Number	Amount
12-1	3475	$1,640.70	12-20	3482	$ 475.50
12-2	3476	1,300.00	12-22	3483	1,140.00
12-2	3477	2,130.00	12-23	3484	798.00
12-4	3478	621.30	12-24	3485	450.80
12-8	3479	3,080.00	12-30	3486	1,889.50
12-10	3480	600.00	Total		$14,933.20
12-17	3481	807.40			

Cash Receipts Journal

Date	Amount
12-3	$ 1,211.60
12-7	2,365.10
12-15	2,672.70
12-20	2,954.00
12-25	2,567.30
12-28	2,836.00
12-30	1,025.00
12-31	1,190.40
Total	$16,822.10

The bank statement contained two memoranda:

1. A credit of $3,645 for the collection of a $3,500 note for Rintala Company plus interest of $160 and less a collection fee of $15. Rintala Company has not accrued any interest on the note.
2. A debit of $572.80 for an NSF check written by D. Chagnon, a customer. At December 31, the check had not been redeposited in the bank.

At December 31, the cash balance per books was $12,485.20, and the cash balance per the bank statement was $20,154.30. The bank did not make any errors, but two errors were made by Rintala Company.

Instructions

(a) Using the four steps in the reconciliation procedure, prepare a bank reconciliation at December 31.
(b) Prepare the adjusting entries based on the reconciliation. (*Hint:* The correction of any errors pertaining to recording checks should be made to Accounts Payable. The correction of any errors relating to recording cash receipts should be made to Accounts Receivable.)

(a) Adjusted balance per books $15,458.40

Prepare a bank reconciliation and adjusting entries.

(LO 7)

P7-5A Cayemberg Company maintains a checking account at the Commerce Bank. At July 31, selected data from the ledger balance and the bank statement are shown below.

	Cash in Bank	
	Per Books	**Per Bank**
Balance, July 1	$17,600	$16,800
July receipts	81,400	
July credits		82,470
July disbursements	77,150	
July debits		74,756
Balance, July 31	$21,850	$24,514

Analysis of the bank data reveals that the credits consist of $81,000 of July deposits and a credit memorandum of $1,470 for the collection of a $1,400 note plus interest revenue of $70. The July debits per bank consist of checks cleared $74,700 and a debit memorandum of $56 for printing additional company checks.

You also discover the following errors involving July checks: (1) A check for $230 to a creditor on account that cleared the bank in July was journalized and posted as $320. (2) A salary check to an employee for $255 was recorded by the bank for $155.

The June 30 bank reconciliation contained only two reconciling items: deposits in transit $7,000 and outstanding checks of $6,200.

Instructions

(a) Adjusted balance per books
  $23,354

(a) Prepare a bank reconciliation at July 31, 2014.
(b) Journalize the adjusting entries to be made by Cayemberg Company. Assume that interest on the note has not been accrued.

Identify internal control weaknesses in cash receipts and cash disbursements.

(LO 2, 3, 4)

P7-6A Nature Hill Middle School wants to raise money for a new sound system for its auditorium. The primary fund-raising event is a dance at which the famous disc jockey Obnoxious Al will play classic and not-so-classic dance tunes. Rob Drexler, the music and theater instructor, has been given the responsibility for coordinating the fund-raising efforts. This is Rob's first experience with fund-raising. He decides to put the eighth-grade choir in charge of the event; he will be a relatively passive observer.

Rob had 500 unnumbered tickets printed for the dance. He left the tickets in a box on his desk and told the choir students to take as many tickets as they thought they could sell for $5 each. In order to ensure that no extra tickets would be floating around, he told them to dispose of any unsold tickets. When the students received payment for the tickets, they were to bring the cash back to Rob and he would put it in a locked box in his desk drawer.

Some of the students were responsible for decorating the gymnasium for the dance. Rob gave each of them a key to the money box and told them that if they took money out to purchase materials, they should put a note in the box saying how much they took and what it was used for. After 2 weeks the money box appeared to be getting full, so Rob asked Erik Radley to count the money, prepare a deposit slip, and deposit the money in a bank account Rob had opened.

The day of the dance, Rob wrote a check from the account to pay the DJ. Obnoxious Al, however, said that he accepted only cash and did not give receipts. So Rob took $200 out of the cash box and gave it to Al. At the dance, Rob had Sobia Hamm working at the entrance to the gymnasium, collecting tickets from students, and selling tickets to those who had not prepurchased them. Rob estimated that 400 students attended the dance.

The following day, Rob closed out the bank account, which had $250 in it, and gave that amount plus the $180 in the cash box to Principal Coleman. Principal Coleman seemed surprised that, after generating roughly $2,000 in sales, the dance netted only $430 in cash. Rob did not know how to respond.

Instructions

Identify as many internal control weaknesses as you can in this scenario, and suggest how each could be addressed.

PROBLEMS: SET B

P7-1B Orpheum Theater is located in the Brooklyn Mall. A cashier's booth is located near the entrance to the theater. Three cashiers are employed. One works from 1–5 P.M., another from 5–9 P.M. The shifts are rotated among the three cashiers. The cashiers receive cash from customers and operate a machine that ejects serially numbered tickets. The rolls of tickets are inserted and locked into the machine by the theater manager at the beginning of each cashier's shift.

Identify internal control weaknesses over cash receipts.

(LO 2, 3)

After purchasing a ticket, the customer takes the ticket to an usher stationed at the entrance of the theater lobby some 60 feet from the cashier's booth. The usher tears the ticket in half, admits the customer, and returns the ticket stub to the customer. The other half of the ticket is dropped into a locked box by the usher.

At the end of each cashier's shift, the theater manager removes the ticket rolls from the machine and makes a cash count. The cash count sheet is initialed by the cashier. At the end of the day, the manager deposits the receipts in total in a bank night deposit vault located in the mall. The manager also sends copies of the deposit slip and the initialed cash count sheets to the theater company treasurer for verification and to the company's accounting department. Receipts from the first shift are stored in a safe located in the manager's office.

Instructions

(a) Identify the internal control principles and their application to the cash receipts transactions of the Orpheum Theater.

(b) If the usher and cashier decide to collaborate to misappropriate cash, what actions might they take?

P7-2B McArtor Company maintains a petty cash fund for small expenditures. The following transactions occurred over a 2-month period.

Journalize and post petty cash fund transactions.

(LO 5)

July 1 Established petty cash fund by writing a check on Star Bank for $100.
     15 Replenished the petty cash fund by writing a check for $94.90. On this date, the fund consisted of $5.10 in cash and the following petty cash receipts: freight-out $51.00, postage expense $20.50, entertainment expense $23.10, and miscellaneous expense $4.10.
     31 Replenished the petty cash fund by writing a check for $92.90. At this date, the fund consisted of $7.10 in cash and the following petty cash receipts: freight-out $43.50, charitable contributions expense $20.00, postage expense $20.10, and miscellaneous expense $9.30.
Aug. 15 Replenished the petty cash fund by writing a check for $98.00. On this date, the fund consisted of $2.00 in cash and the following petty cash receipts: freight-out $40.20, entertainment expense $21.00, postage expense $14.00, and miscellaneous expense $19.80.
     16 Increased the amount of the petty cash fund to $150 by writing a check for $50.
     31 Replenished the petty cash fund by writing a check for $137.00. On this date, the fund consisted of $13 in cash and the following petty cash receipts: freight-out $74.00, entertainment expense $43.20, and postage expense $17.70.

Instructions

(a) Journalize the petty cash transactions.
(b) Post to the Petty Cash account.
(c) What internal control features exist in a petty cash fund?

(a) July 15 Cash over $3.80
(b) Aug. 31 balance $150

P7-3B Aglife Genetics Company of Lancaster, Wisconsin, spreads herbicides and applies liquid fertilizer for local farmers. On May 31, 2014, the company's Cash account per its general ledger showed the following balance.

Prepare a bank reconciliation and adjusting entries.

(LO 7)

	CASH				NO. 101
Date	Explanation	Ref.	Debit	Credit	Balance
May 31	Balance				13,287

The bank statement from Lancaster State Bank on that date showed the following balance.

<table>
<tr><th></th><th>Lancaster State Bank</th><th></th></tr>
<tr><th>Checks and Debits</th><th>Deposits and Credits</th><th>Daily Balance</th></tr>
<tr><td>XXX</td><td>XXX</td><td>5/31   12,732</td></tr>
</table>

A comparison of the details on the bank statement with the details in the cash account revealed the following facts.

1. The statement included a debit memo of $35 for the printing of additional company checks.
2. Cash sales of $1,720 on May 12 were deposited in the bank. The cash receipts journal entry and the deposit slip were incorrectly made for $1,820. The bank credited Aglife Genetics Company for the correct amount.
3. Outstanding checks at May 31 totaled $1,425, and deposits in transit were $2,100.
4. On May 18, the company issued check no. 1181 for $1,102 to M. Datz on account. The check, which cleared the bank in May, was incorrectly journalized and posted by Aglife Genetics Company for $110.
5. A $4,000 note receivable was collected by the bank for Aglife Genetics Company on May 31 plus $80 interest. The bank charged a collection fee of $25. No interest has been accrued on the note.
6. Included with the cancelled checks was a check issued by Bohr Company to Carol Mertz for $900 that was incorrectly charged to Aglife Genetics Company by the bank.
7. On May 31, the bank statement showed an NSF charge of $1,908 for a check issued by Tyler Gricius, a customer, to Aglife Genetics Company on account.

Instructions

(a) Adj. cash bal. $14,307

(a) Prepare the bank reconciliation at May 31, 2014.
(b) Prepare the necessary adjusting entries for Aglife Genetics Company at May 31, 2014.

Prepare a bank reconciliation and adjusting entries from detailed data.

(LO 7)

P7-4B The bank portion of the bank reconciliation for Goulet Company at October 31, 2014, was as follows.

Goulet Company
Bank Reconciliation
October 31, 2014

Cash balance per bank		$6,000
Add: Deposits in transit		842
		6,842
Less: Outstanding checks		
Check Number	Check Amount	
2451	$700	
2470	396	
2471	464	
2472	170	
2474	578	2,308
Adjusted cash balance per bank		$4,534

The adjusted cash balance per bank agreed with the cash balance per books at October 31.

The November bank statement showed the following checks and deposits:

Bank Statement

	Checks			Deposits	
Date	Number	Amount	Date		Amount
11-1	2470	$ 396	11-1		$ 842
11-2	2471	464	11-4		666
11-5	2474	578	11-8		545
11-4	2475	903	11-13		1,416
11-8	2476	1,556	11-18		810
11-10	2477	330	11-21		1,624
11-15	2479	980	11-25		1,412
11-18	2480	714	11-28		908
11-27	2481	382	11-30		652
11-30	2483	317	Total		$8,875
11-29	2486	495			
	Total	$7,115			

The cash records per books for November showed the following.

Cash Payments Journal

Date	Number	Amount	Date	Number	Amount
11-1	2475	$ 903	11-20	2483	$ 317
11-2	2476	1,556	11-22	2484	460
11-2	2477	330	11-23	2485	525
11-4	2478	300	11-24	2486	495
11-8	2479	890	11-29	2487	340
11-10	2480	714	11-30	2488	635
11-15	2481	382	Total		$8,197
11-18	2482	350			

Cash Receipts Journal

Date	Amount
11-3	$ 666
11-7	545
11-12	1,416
11-17	810
11-20	1,642
11-24	1,412
11-27	908
11-29	652
11-30	1,581
Total	$9,632

The bank statement contained two bank memoranda:

1. A credit of $1,375 for the collection of a $1,300 note for Goulet Company plus interest of $91 and less a collection fee of $16. Goulet Company has not accrued any interest on the note.
2. A debit for the printing of additional company checks $35.

At November 30, the cash balance per books was $5,969, and the cash balance per the bank statement was $9,100. The bank did not make any errors, but two errors were made by Goulet Company.

Instructions
(a) Using the four steps in the reconciliation procedure described on pages 347–349, prepare a bank reconciliation at November 30.
(b) Prepare the adjusting entries based on the reconciliation. (*Hint:* The correction of any errors pertaining to recording checks should be made to Accounts Payable. The correction of any errors relating to recording cash receipts should be made to Accounts Receivable).

(a) Adjusted cash balance per bank $7,201

P7-5B Tizani Company's bank statement from Eastern National Bank at August 31, 2014, shows the information below.

Prepare a bank reconciliation and adjusting entries.

(LO 7)

Balance, August 1	$11,284	Bank credit memoranda:		
August deposits	47,521	Collection of note		
Checks cleared in August	46,175	receivable plus $105		
Balance, August 31	17,146	interest	$4,505	
		Interest earned	41	
		Bank debit memorandum:		
		Safety deposit box rent	30	

A summary of the Cash account in the ledger for August shows: Balance, August 1, $10,559; receipts $50,050; disbursements $47,794; and balance, August 31, $12,815. Analysis reveals that the only reconciling items on the July 31 bank reconciliation were a deposit in transit for $2,200 and outstanding checks of $2,925. The deposit in transit was the first deposit recorded by the bank in August. In addition, you determine that there were two errors involving company checks drawn in August: (1) A check for $340 to a creditor on account that cleared the bank in August was journalized and posted for $430. (2) A salary check to an employee for $275 was recorded by the bank for $277.

Instructions

(a) Adjusted balance per books
$17,421

(a) Prepare a bank reconciliation at August 31.

(b) Journalize the adjusting entries to be made by Tizani Company at August 31. Assume that interest on the note has not been accrued by the company.

Prepare a comprehensive bank reconciliation with theft and internal control deficiencies.

(LO 2, 3, 4, 7)

P7-6B Stupendous Company is a very profitable small business. It has not, however, given much consideration to internal control. For example, in an attempt to keep clerical and office expenses to a minimum, the company has combined the jobs of cashier and bookkeeper. As a result, Jake Burnett handles all cash receipts, keeps the accounting records, and prepares the monthly bank reconciliations.

The balance per the bank statement on October 31, 2014, was $15,313. Outstanding checks were: no. 62 for $107.74, no. 183 for $127.50, no. 284 for $215.26, no. 862 for $132.10, no. 863 for $192.78, and no. 864 for $140.49. Included with the statement was a credit memorandum of $460 indicating the collection of a note receivable for Stupendous Company by the bank on October 25. This memorandum has not been recorded by Stupendous Company.

The company's ledger showed one cash account with a balance of $18,608.81. The balance included undeposited cash on hand. Because of the lack of internal controls, Burnett took for personal use all of the undeposited receipts in excess of $3,226.18. He then prepared the following bank reconciliation in an effort to conceal his theft of cash.

Bank Reconciliation

Cash balance per books, October 31		$18,608.81
Add: Outstanding checks		
No. 862	$132.10	
No. 863	192.78	
No. 864	140.49	390.37
		18,999.18
Less: Undeposited receipts		3,226.18
Unadjusted balance per bank, October 31		15,773.00
Less: Bank credit memorandum		460.00
Cash balance per bank statement, October 31		$15,313.00

Instructions

(a) Adjusted balance per books
$17,623.31

(a) Prepare a correct bank reconciliation. (*Hint:* Deduct the amount of the theft from the adjusted balance per books.)

(b) Indicate the three ways that Burnett attempted to conceal the theft and the dollar amount pertaining to each method.

(c) What principles of internal control were violated in this case?

PROBLEMS: SET C

Visit the book's companion website, at **www.wiley.com/college/weygandt**, and choose the Student Companion site to access Problem Set C.

COMPREHENSIVE PROBLEM

CP7 On December 1, 2014, Westmoreland Company had the following account balances.

	Debits		Credits
Cash	$18,200	Accumulated Depreciation—	
Notes Receivable	2,000	Equipment	$ 3,000
Accounts Receivable	7,500	Accounts Payable	6,100
Inventory	16,000	Common Stock	50,000
Prepaid Insurance	1,600	Retained Earnings	14,200
Equipment	28,000		$73,300
	$73,300		

During December, the company completed the following transactions.

Dec. 7 Received $3,600 cash from customers in payment of account (no discount allowed).
12 Purchased merchandise on account from Alice Co. $12,000, terms 1/10, n/30.
17 Sold merchandise on account $16,000, terms 2/10, n/30. The cost of the merchandise sold was $10,000.
19 Paid salaries $2,200.
22 Paid Alice Co. in full, less discount.
26 Received collections in full, less discounts, from customers billed on December 17.
31 Received $2,700 cash from customers in payment of account (no discount allowed).

Adjustment data:

1. Depreciation $200 per month.
2. Insurance expired $400.

Instructions
(a) Journalize the December transactions. (Assume a perpetual inventory system.)
(b) Enter the December 1 balances in the ledger T-accounts and post the December transactions. Use Cost of Goods Sold, Depreciation Expense, Insurance Expense, Salaries and Wages Expense, Sales Revenue, and Sales Discounts.
(c) The statement from Dodge County Bank on December 31 showed a balance of $25,930. A comparison of the bank statement with the Cash account revealed the following facts.
1. The bank collected a note receivable of $2,000 for Westmoreland Company on December 15.
2. The December 31 receipts were deposited in a night deposit vault on December 31. These deposits were recorded by the bank in January.
3. Checks outstanding on December 31 totaled $1,210.
4. On December 31, the bank statement showed a NSF charge of $680 for a check received by the company from K. Quinn, a customer, on account.

Prepare a bank reconciliation as of December 31 based on the available information. (*Hint:* The cash balance per books is $26,100. This can be proven by finding the balance in the Cash account from parts (a) and (b).)
(d) Journalize the adjusting entries resulting from the bank reconciliation and adjustment data.
(e) Post the adjusting entries to the ledger T-accounts.
(f) Prepare an adjusted trial balance.
(g) Prepare an income statement for December and a classified balance sheet at December 31.

CONTINUING COOKIE CHRONICLE

(*Note:* This is a continuation of the Cookie Chronicle from Chapters 1–6.)

CCC7 Part 1 Natalie is struggling to keep up with the recording of her accounting transactions. She is spending a lot of time marketing and selling mixers and giving her cookie classes. Her friend John is an accounting student who runs his own accounting service. He has asked Natalie if she would like to have him do her accounting. John and Natalie meet and discuss her business.

Part 2　Natalie decides that she cannot afford to hire John to do her accounting. One way that she can ensure that her cash account does not have any errors and is accurate and up-to-date is to prepare a bank reconciliation at the end of each month. Natalie would like you to help her.

Go to the book's companion website, www.wiley.com/college/weygandt, to see the completion of this problem.

Broadening Your **PERSPECTIVE**

Financial Reporting and Analysis

Financial Reporting Problem: PepsiCo, Inc.

BYP7-1　The financial statements of PepsiCo, Inc. are presented in Appendix A at the end of this textbook.

Instructions
(a) What comments, if any, are made about cash in the report of the independent registered public accounting firm?
(b) What data about cash and cash equivalents are shown in the consolidated balance sheet?
(c) In its notes to Consolidated Financial Statements, how does PepsiCo define cash equivalents?
(d) In the section "Management's Report on Internal Control Over Financial Reporting," what does PepsiCo's management say about internal control? (See page A-35 in Appendix A of the back of the book.)

Comparative Analysis Problem: PepsiCo, Inc. vs. The Coca-Cola Company

BYP7-2　PepsiCo's financial statements are presented in Appendix A. Financial statements of The Coca-Cola Company are presented in Appendix B.

Instructions
(a) Based on the information contained in these financial statements, determine each of the following for each company:
　(1) Cash and cash equivalents balance at December 25, 2010, for PepsiCo and at December 31, 2010, for Coca-Cola.
　(2) Increase (decrease) in cash and cash equivalents from 2009 to 2010.
　(3) Cash provided by operating activities during the year ended December 2010 (from statement of cash flows).
(b) What conclusions concerning the management of cash can be drawn from these data?

Real-World Focus

BYP7-3　All organizations should have systems of internal control. Universities are no exception. This site discusses the basics of internal control in a university setting.

Address: **www.bc.edu/offices/audit/controls,** or go to **www.wiley.com/college/weygandt**

Steps: Go to the site shown above.

Instructions
The front page of this site provides links to pages that answer six critical questions. Use these links to answer the following questions.

(a) In a university setting, who has responsibility for evaluating the adequacy of the system of internal control?
(b) What do reconciliations ensure in the university setting? Who should review the reconciliation?
(c) What are some examples of physical controls?
(d) What are two ways to accomplish inventory counts?

Critical Thinking

Decision-Making Across the Organization

BYP7-4 The board of trustees of a local church is concerned about the internal accounting controls for the offering collections made at weekly services. The trustees ask you to serve on a three-person audit team with the internal auditor of a local college and a CPA who has just joined the church.

At a meeting of the audit team and the board of trustees, you learn the following.

1. The church's board of trustees has delegated responsibility for the financial management and audit of the financial records to the finance committee. This group prepares the annual budget and approves major disbursements. It is not involved in collections or record-keeping. No audit has been made in recent years because the same trusted employee has kept church records and served as financial secretary for 15 years. The church does not carry any fidelity insurance.
2. The collection at the weekly service is taken by a team of ushers who volunteer to serve one month. The ushers take the collection plates to a basement office at the rear of the church. They hand their plates to the head usher and return to the church service. After all plates have been turned in, the head usher counts the cash received. The head usher then places the cash in the church safe along with a notation of the amount counted. The head usher volunteers to serve for 3 months.
3. The next morning, the financial secretary opens the safe and recounts the collection. The secretary withholds $150–$200 in cash, depending on the cash expenditures expected for the week, and deposits the remainder of the collections in the bank. To facilitate the deposit, church members who contribute by check are asked to make their checks payable to "Cash."
4. Each month, the financial secretary reconciles the bank statement and submits a copy of the reconciliation to the board of trustees. The reconciliations have rarely contained any bank errors and have never shown any errors per books.

Instructions

With the class divided into groups, answer the following.

(a) Indicate the weaknesses in internal accounting control over the handling of collections.
(b) List the improvements in internal control procedures that you plan to make at the next meeting of the audit team for (1) the ushers, (2) the head usher, (3) the financial secretary, and (4) the finance committee.
(c) What church policies should be changed to improve internal control?

Communication Activity

BYP7-5 As a new auditor for the CPA firm of Murphy, Mooney, and Feeney, you have been assigned to review the internal controls over mail cash receipts of Stillwater Company. Your review reveals the following: Checks are promptly endorsed "For Deposit Only," but no list of the checks is prepared by the person opening the mail. The mail is opened either by the cashier or by the employee who maintains the accounts receivable records. Mail receipts are deposited in the bank weekly by the cashier.

Instructions

Write a letter to Jack Meyer, owner of Stillwater Company, explaining the weaknesses in internal control and your recommendations for improving the system.

Ethics Case

BYP7-6 You are the assistant controller in charge of general ledger accounting at Springtime Bottling Company. Your company has a large loan from an insurance company. The loan agreement requires that the company's cash account balance be maintained at $200,000 or more, as reported monthly.

At June 30, the cash balance is $80,000, which you report to Anne Shirley, the financial vice president. Anne excitedly instructs you to keep the cash receipts book open for one additional day for purposes of the June 30 report to the insurance company. Anne says, "If we don't get that cash balance over $200,000, we'll default on our loan agreement. They could close us down, put us all out of our jobs!" Anne continues, "I talked to Oconto Distributors (one of Springtime's largest customers) this morning. They said they sent us a check for $150,000 yesterday. We should receive it tomorrow. If we include just that one check in our cash balance, we'll be in the clear. It's in the mail!"

Instructions

(a) Who will suffer negative effects if you do not comply with Anne Shirley's instructions? Who will suffer if you do comply?
(b) What are the ethical considerations in this case?
(c) What alternatives do you have?

All About You

BYP7-7 As you may already know, potential security risks may arise from your personal computer. It is important to keep in mind, however, that there are also many other ways that your identity can be stolen other than from your computer. The federal government provides many resources to help protect you from identity thieves.

Instructions

Go to **http://onguardonline.gov/idtheft.html**, and click on **ID Theft Faceoff**. Complete the quiz provided there.

BYP7-8 Identity thieves determine your identity by going through your mail or trash, stealing your credit cards, redirecting mail through change of address forms, or acquiring personal information you share on unsecured sites. In a recent year, more than 7 million people were victims of identity theft.

Do you feel it is safe to store personal financial data (such as Social Security numbers and bank and credit account numbers) on your computer?

YES: I have anti-virus software that will detect and stop any intruder.

NO: Even the best anti-virus software does not detect every kind of intruder.

Instructions

Write a response indicating your position regarding the situation. Provide support for your view.

FASB Codification Activity

BYP7-9 If your school has a subscription to the FASB Codification, go to *http://aaahq.org/ascLogin. cfm* to log in and prepare responses to the following.

(a) How is cash defined in the Codification?
(b) How are cash equivalents defined in the Codification?
(c) What are the disclosure requirements related to cash and cash equivalents?

Answers to Chapter Questions

Answers to Insight and Accounting Across the Organization Questions

p. 327 And the Controls Are... Q: Why is sustainability information important to investors? **A:** Investors, customers, suppliers, and employees want more information about companies' long-term impact on society. There is a growing awareness that sustainability issues can affect a company's financial performance. Proper reporting on sustainability issues develops a solid reputation for transparency and provides confidence to shareholders.

p. 334 SOX Boosts the Role of Human Resources Q: Why would unsupervised employees or employees who report to each other represent potential internal control threats? **A:** An unsupervised employee may have a fraudulent job (or may even be a fictitious person), e.g., a person drawing a paycheck without working. Or, if two employees supervise each other, there is no real separation of duties, and they can conspire to defraud the company.

p. 335 Big Theft at Small Companies Q: Why are small companies more susceptible to employee theft? **A:** The high degree of trust often found in small companies makes them more vulnerable. Also, small companies tend to have less sophisticated systems of internal control, and they usually lack internal auditors. In addition, it is very hard to achieve some internal control features, such as segregation of duties, when you have very few employees.

p. 343 How Employees Steal Q: How can companies reduce the likelihood of fraudulent disbursements? **A:** To reduce the occurrence of fraudulent disbursements, a company should follow the procedures discussed in this chapter. These include having only designated personnel sign checks; having different personnel approve payments and make payments; ensuring that check signers do not record disbursements; using prenumbered checks and matching each check to an approved invoice; storing blank checks securely; reconciling the bank statement; and stamping invoices PAID.

p. 351 Madoff's Ponzi Scheme Q: How was Madoff able to conceal such a giant fraud? **A:** Madoff fabricated false investment statements that were provided to investors. In addition, his auditor never verified these investment statements even though the auditor gave him an unqualified opinion each year.

Answers to Self-Test Questions

1. c **2.** a **3.** a **4.** c **5.** b **6.** b **7.** d **8.** d **9.** a ($100 − ($94 + $4)) **10.** a **11.** c **12.** d **13.** c **14.** c

A Look at IFRS

Fraud can occur anywhere. And because the three main factors that contribute to fraud are universal in nature, the principles of internal control activities are used globally by companies. While Sarbanes-Oxley (SOX) does not apply to international companies, most large international companies have internal controls similar to those indicated in the chapter. IFRS and GAAP are very similar in accounting for cash. *IAS No. 1 (revised)*, "Presentation of Financial Statements," is the only standard that discusses issues specifically related to cash.

Key Points

- The fraud triangle discussed in this chapter is applicable to all international companies. Some of the major frauds on an international basis are Parmalat (Italy), Royal Ahold (the Netherlands), and Satyam Computer Services (India).

- Rising economic crime poses a growing threat to companies, with nearly half of all organizations worldwide being victims of fraud in a recent two-year period (*PricewaterhouseCoopers' Global Economic Crime Survey*, 2005). Specifically, 44% of Romanian companies surveyed experienced fraud in the past two years.

- Globally, the number of companies reporting fraud increased from 37% to 45% since 2003, a 22% increase. The cost to companies was an average US$1.7 million in losses from "tangible frauds," that is, those that result in an immediate and direct financial loss. These include asset misappropriation, false pretenses, and counterfeiting (*PricewaterhouseCoopers' Global Economic Crime Survey*, 2005).

- Accounting scandals both in the United States and internationally have re-ignited the debate over the relative merits of GAAP, which takes a "rules-based" approach to accounting, versus IFRS, which takes a "principles-based" approach. The FASB announced that it intends to introduce more principles-based standards.

- On a lighter note, at one time Ig Nobel Prize in Economics went to the CEOs of those companies involved in the corporate accounting scandals of that year for "adapting the mathematical concept of imaginary numbers for use in the business world." A parody of the Nobel Prizes, the Ig Nobel Prizes (read Ignoble, as not noble) are given each year in early October for 10 achievements that "first make people laugh, and then make them think." Organized by the scientific humor magazine *Annals of Improbable Research (AIR)*, they are presented by a group that includes genuine Nobel laureates at a ceremony at Harvard University's Sanders Theater. (See *en.wikipedia.org/wiki/Ig_Nobel_Prize*.)

- Internal controls are a system of checks and balances designed to prevent and detect fraud and errors. While most companies have these systems in place, many have never completely documented them, nor had an independent auditor attest to their effectiveness. Both of these actions are required under SOX.

- Companies find that internal control review is a costly process but badly needed. One study estimates the cost of SOX compliance for U.S. companies at over $35 billion, with audit fees doubling in the first year of compliance. At the same time, examination of internal controls indicates lingering problems in the way companies operate. One study of first compliance with the internal-control testing provisions documented material weaknesses for about 13% of companies reporting in a two-year period (*PricewaterhouseCoopers' Global Economic Crime Survey*, 2005).

- The SOX internal control standards apply only to companies listed on U.S. exchanges. There is continuing debate over whether foreign issuers should have to comply with this extra layer of regulation.

- The accounting and internal control procedures related to cash are essentially the same under both IFRS and this textbook. In addition, the definition used for cash equivalents is the same.

- Most companies report cash and cash equivalents together under IFRS, as shown in this textbook. In addition, IFRS follows the same accounting policies related to the reporting of restricted cash.

- IFRS defines cash and cash equivalents as follows.
  - **Cash** is comprised of cash on hand and demand deposits.
  - **Cash equivalents** are short-term, highly liquid investments that are readily convertible to known amounts of cash and which are subject to an insignificant risk of changes in value.

- Under IFRS, cash and cash equivalents are often shown last in the statement of financial position.

Looking to the Future

Ethics has become a very important aspect of reporting. Different cultures have different perspectives on bribery and other questionable activities, and consequently penalties for engaging in such activities vary considerably across countries.

High-quality international accounting requires both high-quality accounting standards and high-quality auditing. Similar to the convergence of GAAP and IFRS, there is movement to improve international auditing standards. The International Auditing and Assurance Standards Board (IAASB) functions as an independent standard-setting body. It works to establish high-quality auditing and assurance and quality-control standards throughout the world. Whether the IAASB adopts internal control provisions similar to those in SOX remains to be seen. You can follow developments in the international audit arena at *http://www.ifac.org/iaasb/*.

Under proposed new standards for financial statements, companies would not be allowed to combine cash equivalents with cash.

IFRS Practice

IFRS Self-Test Questions

1. Non-U.S companies that follow IFRS:
   (a) do not normally use the principles of internal control activities described in this textbook.
   (b) often offset cash with accounts payable on the balance sheet.
   (c) are not required to follow SOX.
   (d) None of the above.

2. Which of the following is the correct accounting under IFRS for cash?
   (a) Cash cannot be combined with cash equivalents.
   (b) Restricted cash funds may be reported as a current or non-current asset depending on the circumstances.
   (c) Restricted cash funds cannot be reported as a current asset.
   (d) Cash on hand is not reported on the balance sheet as Cash.

3. The Sarbanes-Oxley Act applies to:
   (a) all U.S. companies listed on U.S. exchanges.
   (b) all companies that list stock on any stock exchange in any country.
   (c) all European companies listed on European exchanges.
   (d) Both (a) and (c).

4. High-quality international accounting requires both high-quality accounting standards and:
   (a) a reconsideration of SOX to make it less onerous.
   (b) high-quality auditing standards.
   (c) government intervention to ensure that the public interest is protected.
   (d) the development of new principles of internal control activities.

5. Cash equivalents under IFRS:
   (a) are significantly different than the cash equivalents discussed in the textbook.
   (b) are generally disclosed separately from cash.
   (c) may be required to be reported separately from cash in the future.
   (d) None of the above.

IFRS Exercises

IFRS7-1 Some people argue that the internal control requirements of the Sarbanes-Oxley Act (SOX) put U.S. companies at a competitive disadvantage to companies outside the United States. Discuss the competitive implications (both pros and cons) of SOX.

IFRS7-2 State whether each of the following is true or false. For those that are false, explain why.

(a) A proposed new financial accounting standard would not allow cash equivalents to be reported in combination with cash.

(b) Perspectives on bribery and penalties for engaging in bribery are the same across all countries.

(c) Cash equivalents are comprised of cash on hand and demand deposits.

(d) SOX was created by the International Accounting Standards Board.

International Financial Reporting Problem: Zetar plc

IFRS7-3 The financial statements of Zetar plc are presented in Appendix C. The company's complete annual report, including the notes to its financial statements, is available at *www.zetarplc.com*.

Instructions

Using the notes to the company's financial statements, answer the following questions.

(a) Which committee of the board of directors is responsible for considering management's reports on internal control?

(b) What are the company's key control procedures?

(c) Does the company have an internal audit department?

(d) In what section or sections does Zetar report its bank overdrafts?

Answers to IFRS Self-Test Questions

1. c   2. b   3. a   4. b   5. c

 **The Navigator**

Chapter 8

Accounting for Receivables

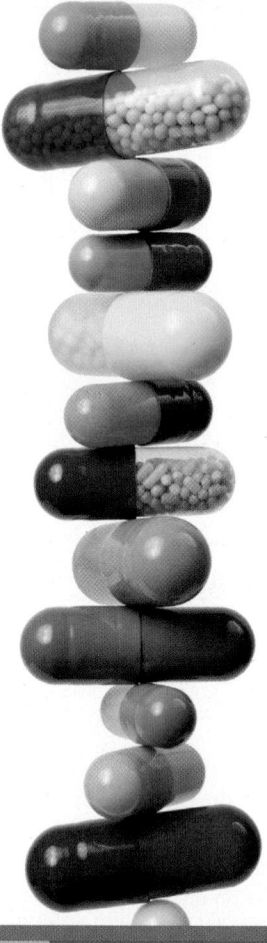

A Dose of Careful Management Keeps Receivables Healthy

"Sometimes you have to know when to be very tough, and sometimes you can give them a bit of a break," says Vivi Su. She's not talking about her children, but about the customers of a subsidiary of pharmaceutical company Whitehall-Robins, where she works as supervisor of credit and collections.

For example, while the company's regular terms are 1/15, n/30 (1% discount if paid within 15 days), a customer might ask for and receive a few days of grace and still get the discount. Or a customer might place

orders above its credit limit, in which case, depending on its payment history and the circumstances, Ms. Su might authorize shipment of the goods anyway.

"It's not about drawing a line in the sand, and that's all," she explains. "You want a good relationship with your customers—but you also need to bring in the money."

"The money," in Whitehall-Robins's case, amounts to some $170 million in sales a year. Nearly all of it comes in through the credit accounts Ms. Su manages. The process starts with the decision to grant a customer an account in the first place, Ms. Su explains. The sales rep gives the customer a credit application. "My

Learning Objectives

After studying this chapter, you should be able to:

1 Identify the different types of receivables.

2 Explain how companies recognize accounts receivable.

3 Distinguish between the methods and bases companies use to value accounts receivable.

4 Describe the entries to record the disposition of accounts receivable.

5 Compute the maturity date of and interest on notes receivable.

6 Explain how companies recognize notes receivable.

7 Describe how companies value notes receivable.

8 Describe the entries to record the disposition of notes receivable.

9 Explain the statement presentation and analysis of receivables.

 The Navigator

department reviews this application very carefully; a customer needs to supply three good references, and we also run a check with a credit firm like Equifax. If we accept them, then based on their size and history, we assign a credit limit."

Once accounts are established, the company supervises them very carefully. "I get an aging report every single day," says Ms. Su.

"The rule of thumb is that we should always have at least 85% of receivables current—meaning they were billed less than 30 days ago," she continues. "But we try to do even better than that—I like to see 90%." Similarly, her guideline is never to have more than 5% of receivables at over 90 days. But long before that figure is reached, "we jump on it," she says firmly.

At 15 days overdue, Whitehall-Robins phones the client. Often there's a reasonable explanation for the delay—an invoice may have gone astray, or the payables clerk is away. "But if a customer keeps on delaying, and tells us several times that it'll

only be a few more days, we know there's a problem," says Ms. Su. After 45 days, "I send a letter. Then a second notice is sent in writing. After the third and final notice, the client has 10 days to pay, and then I hand it over to a collection agency, and it's out of my hands."

Ms. Su's boss, Terry Norton, records an estimate for bad debts every year, based on a percentage of receivables. The percentage depends on the current aging history. He also calculates and monitors the company's receivables turnover ratio, which the company reports in its financial statements. "I think of it in terms of collection period of DSO—days of sales outstanding," he explains.

Ms. Su knows that she and Mr. Norton are crucial to the profitability of Whitehall-Robins. "Receivables are generally the second-largest asset of any company (after its capital assets)," she points out. "So it's no wonder we keep a very close eye on them."

✔ **The Navigator**

Preview of **Chapter 8**

As indicated in the Feature Story, receivables are a significant asset for many pharmaceutical companies. Because a large portion of sales in the United States are done on credit, receivables are important to companies in other industries as well. As a consequence, companies must pay close attention to their receivables and manage them carefully. In this chapter, you will learn what journal entries companies make when they sell products, when they collect cash from those sales, and when they write off accounts they cannot collect.

The content and organization of the chapter are as follows.

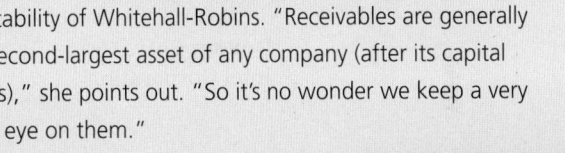

ACCOUNTING FOR RECEIVABLES			
Types of Receivables	**Accounts Receivable**	**Notes Receivable**	**Statement Presentation and Analysis**
• Accounts receivable • Notes receivable • Other receivables	• Recognizing accounts receivable • Valuing accounts receivable • Disposing of accounts receivable	• Determining maturity date • Computing interest • Recognizing notes receivable • Valuing notes receivable • Disposing of notes receivable	• Presentation • Analysis

✔ **The Navigator**

Types of Receivables

LEARNING OBJECTIVE   **1**

Identify the different types of receivables.

The term **receivables** refers to amounts due from individuals and companies. Receivables are claims that are expected to be collected in cash. The management of receivables is a very important activity for any company that sells goods or services on credit.

Receivables are important because they represent one of a company's most liquid assets. For many companies, receivables are also one of the largest assets. For example, receivables represented 21.9% of the current assets of pharmaceutical giant Rite Aid in 2011. Illustration 8-1 lists receivables as a percentage of total assets for five other well-known companies in a recent year.

Illustration 8-1
Receivables as a percentage of assets

Company	Receivables as a Percentage of Total Assets
General Electric	52%
Ford Motor Company	42%
Minnesota Mining and Manufacturing Company (3M)	14%
DuPont Co.	17%
Intel Corporation	5%

The relative significance of a company's receivables as a percentage of its assets depends on various factors: its industry, the time of year, whether it extends long-term financing, and its credit policies. To reflect important differences among receivables, they are frequently classified as (1) accounts receivable, (2) notes receivable, and (3) other receivables.

Accounts receivable are amounts customers owe on account. They result from the sale of goods and services. Companies generally expect to collect accounts receivable within 30 to 60 days. They are usually the most significant type of claim held by a company.

Notes receivable are a written promise (as evidenced by a formal instrument) for amounts to be received. The note normally requires the collection of interest and extends for time periods of 60–90 days or longer. Notes and accounts receivable that result from sales transactions are often called **trade receivables**.

Ethics Note

Companies report receivables from employees separately in the financial statements. The reason: Sometimes those assets are not the result of an "arm's-length" transaction.

Other receivables include nontrade receivables such as interest receivable, loans to company officers, advances to employees, and income taxes refundable. These do not generally result from the operations of the business. Therefore, they are generally classified and reported as separate items in the balance sheet.

Accounts Receivable

Three accounting issues associated with accounts receivable are:

1. **Recognizing** accounts receivable.
2. **Valuing** accounts receivable.
3. **Disposing** of accounts receivable.

Recognizing Accounts Receivable

Recognizing accounts receivable is relatively straightforward. A service organization records a receivable when it provides service on account. A merchandiser records accounts receivable at the point of sale of merchandise on account. When a merchandiser sells goods, it increases (debits) Accounts Receivable and increases (credits) Sales Revenue.

LEARNING OBJECTIVE 2

Explain how companies recognize accounts receivable.

The seller may offer terms that encourage early payment by providing a discount. Sales returns also reduce receivables. The buyer might find some of the goods unacceptable and choose to return the unwanted goods.

To review, assume that Jordache Co. on July 1, 2014, sells merchandise on account to Polo Company for $1,000, terms 2/10, n/30. On July 5, Polo returns merchandise worth $100 to Jordache Co. On July 11, Jordache receives payment from Polo Company for the balance due. The journal entries to record these transactions on the books of Jordache Co. are as follows. **(Cost of goods sold entries are omitted.)**

> **Ethics Note**
>
> In exchange for lower interest rates, some companies have eliminated the 25-day grace period before finance charges kick in. Be sure you read the fine print in any credit agreement you sign.

July 1	Accounts Receivable—Polo Company	1,000	
	Sales Revenue		1,000
	(To record sales on account)		
July 5	Sales Returns and Allowances	100	
	Accounts Receivable—Polo Company		100
	(To record merchandise returned)		
July 11	Cash ($900 − $18)	882	
	Sales Discounts ($900 × .02)	18	
	Accounts Receivable—Polo Company		900
	(To record collection of accounts receivable)		

> **Helpful Hint**
> These entries are the same as those described in Chapter 5. For simplicity, we have omitted inventory and cost of goods sold from this set of journal entries and from end-of-chapter material.

Some retailers issue their own credit cards. When you use a retailer's credit card (JCPenney, for example), the retailer charges interest on the balance due if not paid within a specified period (usually 25–30 days).

To illustrate, assume that you use your JCPenney credit card to purchase clothing with a sales price of $300 on June 1, 2014. JCPenney will increase (debit) Accounts Receivable for $300 and increase (credit) Sales Revenue for $300 (cost of goods sold entry omitted) as follows.

June 1	Accounts Receivable	300	
	Sales Revenue		300
	(To record sales on account)		

A	=	L	+	SE
+300				
				+300 Rev

Cash Flows
no effect

Assuming that you owe $300 at the end of the month, and JCPenney charges 1.5% per month on the balance due, the adjusting entry that JCPenney makes to record interest revenue of $4.50 ($300 × 1.5%) on June 30 is as follows.

June 30	Accounts Receivable	4.50	
	Interest Revenue		4.50
	(To record interest on amount due)		

A	=	L	+	SE
+4.50				
				+4.50 Rev

Cash Flows
no effect

Interest revenue is often substantial for many retailers.

ANATOMY OF A FRAUD

Tasanee was the accounts receivable clerk for a large non-profit foundation that provided performance and exhibition space for the performing and visual arts. Her responsibilities included activities normally assigned to an accounts receivable clerk, such as recording revenues from various sources that included donations, facility rental fees, ticket revenue, and bar receipts. However, she was also responsible for handling all cash and checks from the time they were received until the time she deposited them, as well as preparing the bank reconciliation. Tasanee took advantage of her situation by falsifying bank deposits and bank reconciliations so that she could steal cash from the bar receipts. Since nobody else logged the donations or matched the donation receipts to pledges prior to Tasanee receiving them, she was able to offset the cash that was stolen against donations that she received but didn't record. Her crime was made easier by the fact that her boss, the company's controller, only did a very superficial review of the bank reconciliation and thus didn't notice that some numbers had been cut out from other documents and taped onto the bank reconciliation.

Total take: $1.5 million

The Missing Controls

Segregation of duties. The foundation should not have allowed an accounts receivable clerk, whose job was to record receivables, to also handle cash, record cash, make deposits, and especially prepare the bank reconciliation.

Independent internal verification. The controller was supposed to perform a thorough review of the bank reconciliation. Because he did not, he was terminated from his position.

Source: Adapted from Wells, *Fraud Casebook* (2007), pp. 183–194.

Valuing Accounts Receivable

Alternative Terminology
You will sometimes see *Bad Debt Expense* called *Uncollectible Accounts Expense.*

Once companies record receivables in the accounts, the next question is: How should they report receivables in the financial statements? Companies report accounts receivable on the balance sheet as an asset. But determining the **amount** to report is sometimes difficult because some receivables will become uncollectible.

Each customer must satisfy the credit requirements of the seller before the credit sale is approved. Inevitably, though, some accounts receivable become uncollectible. For example, a customer may not be able to pay because of a decline in its sales revenue due to a downturn in the economy. Similarly, individuals may be laid off from their jobs or faced with unexpected hospital bills. Companies record credit losses as debits to **Bad Debt Expense** (or Uncollectible Accounts Expense). Such losses are a normal and necessary risk of doing business on a credit basis.

Recently, when U.S. home prices fell, home foreclosures rose, and the economy in general slowed, lenders experienced huge increases in their bad debt expense. For example, during a recent quarter Wachovia (a large U.S. bank now owned be Wells Fargo) increased bad debt expense from $108 million to $408 million. Similarly, American Express increased its bad debt expense by 70%.

Two methods are used in accounting for uncollectible accounts: (1) the direct write-off method and (2) the allowance method. The following sections explain these methods.

DIRECT WRITE-OFF METHOD FOR UNCOLLECTIBLE ACCOUNTS

Under the **direct write-off method**, when a company determines a particular account to be uncollectible, it charges the loss to Bad Debt Expense. Assume, for example, that Warden Co. writes off as uncollectible M. E. Doran's $200 balance on December 12. Warden's entry is:

Dec. 12	Bad Debt Expense	200	
	Accounts Receivable—M. E. Doran		200
	(To record write-off of M. E. Doran account)		

A	=	L	+	SE
				−200 Exp
−200				

Cash Flows
no effect

Under this method, Bad Debt Expense will show only **actual losses** from uncollectibles. The company will report accounts receivable at its gross amount.

Although this method is simple, its use can reduce the usefulness of both the income statement and balance sheet. Consider the following example. Assume that in 2014, Quick Buck Computer Company decided it could increase its revenues by offering computers to college students without requiring any money down and with no credit-approval process. On campuses across the country, it distributed one million computers with a selling price of $800 each. This increased Quick Buck's revenues and receivables by $800 million. The promotion was a huge success! The 2014 balance sheet and income statement looked great. Unfortunately, during 2015, nearly 40% of the customers defaulted on their loans. This made the 2015 income statement and balance sheet look terrible. Illustration 8-2 shows the effect of these events on the financial statements if the direct write-off method is used.

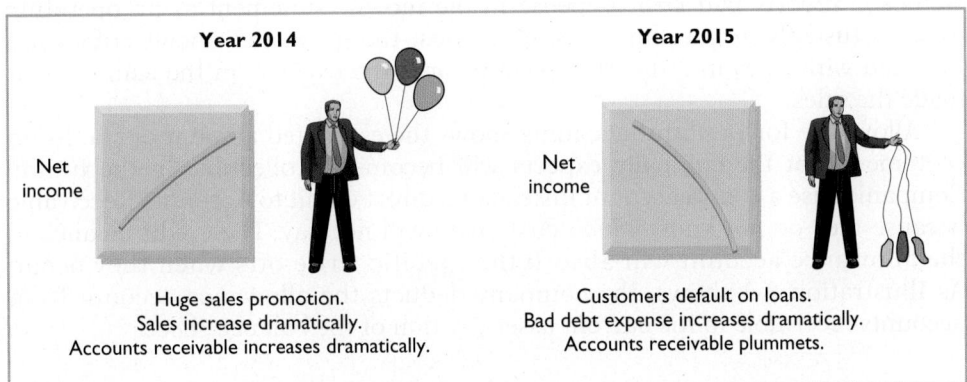

Illustration 8-2
Effects of direct write-off method

Year 2014

Net income

Huge sales promotion.
Sales increase dramatically.
Accounts receivable increases dramatically.

Year 2015

Net income

Customers default on loans.
Bad debt expense increases dramatically.
Accounts receivable plummets.

Under the direct write-off method, companies often record bad debt expense in a period different from the period in which they record the revenue. The method does not attempt to match bad debt expense to sales revenues in the income statement. Nor does the direct write-off method show accounts receivable in the balance sheet at the amount the company actually expects to receive. **Consequently, unless bad debt losses are insignificant, the direct write-off method is not acceptable for financial reporting purposes.**

ALLOWANCE METHOD FOR UNCOLLECTIBLE ACCOUNTS

The **allowance method** of accounting for bad debts involves estimating uncollectible accounts at the end of each period. This provides better matching on the income statement. It also ensures that companies state receivables on the balance sheet at their cash (net) realizable value. **Cash (net) realizable value** is the net amount the company expects to receive in cash. It excludes amounts that the company estimates it will not collect. Thus, this method reduces receivables in the balance sheet by the amount of estimated uncollectible receivables.

GAAP requires the allowance method for financial reporting purposes when bad debts are material in amount. This method has three essential features:

1. Companies **estimate** uncollectible accounts receivable. They match this estimated expense **against revenues** in the same accounting period in which they record the revenues.

Helpful Hint
In this context, *material* means significant or important to financial statement users.

2. Companies debit estimated uncollectibles to Bad Debt Expense and credit them to Allowance for Doubtful Accounts through an adjusting entry at the end of each period. Allowance for Doubtful Accounts is a contra account to Accounts Receivable.

3. When companies write off a specific account, they debit actual uncollectibles to Allowance for Doubtful Accounts and credit that amount to Accounts Receivable.

RECORDING ESTIMATED UNCOLLECTIBLES To illustrate the allowance method, assume that Hampson Furniture has credit sales of $1,200,000 in 2014. Of this amount, $200,000 remains uncollected at December 31. The credit manager estimates that $12,000 of these sales will be uncollectible. The adjusting entry to record the estimated uncollectibles increases (debits) Bad Debt Expense and increases (credits) Allowance for Doubtful Accounts, as follows.

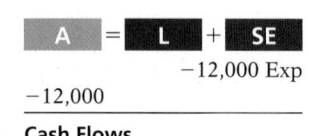

−12,000

Cash Flows
no effect

Dec. 31	Bad Debt Expense	12,000	
	Allowance for Doubtful Accounts		12,000
	(To record estimate of uncollectible accounts)		

Hampson reports Bad Debt Expense in the income statement as an operating expense (usually as a selling expense). Thus, the estimated uncollectibles are matched with sales in 2014. Hampson records the expense in the same year it made the sales.

Allowance for Doubtful Accounts shows the estimated amount of claims on customers that the company expects will become uncollectible in the future. Companies use a contra account instead of a direct credit to Accounts Receivable because they do not know *which* customers will not pay. The credit balance in the allowance account will absorb the specific write-offs when they occur. As Illustration 8-3 shows, the company deducts the allowance account from accounts receivable in the current assets section of the balance sheet.

Illustration 8-3
Presentation of allowance for doubtful accounts

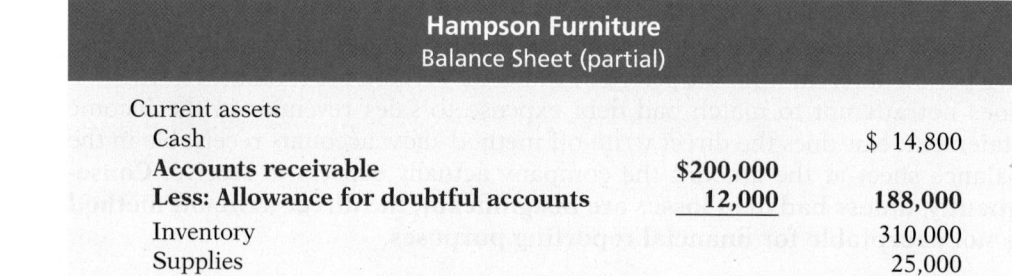

Hampson Furniture		
Balance Sheet (partial)		
Current assets		
Cash		$ 14,800
Accounts receivable	$200,000	
Less: Allowance for doubtful accounts	12,000	188,000
Inventory		310,000
Supplies		25,000
Total current assets		$537,800

Helpful Hint
Cash realizable value is sometimes referred to as *accounts receivable (net)*.

The amount of $188,000 in Illustration 8-3 represents the expected **cash realizable value** of the accounts receivable at the statement date. **Companies do not close Allowance for Doubtful Accounts at the end of the fiscal year.**

RECORDING THE WRITE-OFF OF AN UNCOLLECTIBLE ACCOUNT As described in the Feature Story, companies use various methods of collecting past-due accounts, such as letters, calls, and legal action. When they have exhausted all means of collecting a past-due account and collection appears impossible, the company should write off the account. In the credit card industry, for example, it is standard practice to write off accounts that are 210 days past due. To prevent premature or unauthorized write-offs, authorized management personnel should formally approve each write-off. To maintain good internal control, companies should not authorize someone to write off accounts who also has daily responsibilities related to cash or receivables.

To illustrate a receivables write-off, assume that the financial vice president of Hampson Furniture authorizes a write-off of the $500 balance owed by R. A. Ware on March 1, 2015. The entry to record the write-off is:

Mar. 1	Allowance for Doubtful Accounts	500	
	Accounts Receivable—R. A. Ware		500
	(Write-off of R. A. Ware account)		

A = L + SE
+500
−500

Cash Flows
no effect

Bad Debt Expense does not increase when the write-off occurs. **Under the allowance method, companies debit every bad debt write-off to the allowance account rather than to Bad Debt Expense.** A debit to Bad Debt Expense would be incorrect because the company has already recognized the expense when it made the adjusting entry for estimated bad debts. Instead, the entry to record the write-off of an uncollectible account reduces both Accounts Receivable and Allowance for Doubtful Accounts. After posting, the general ledger accounts will appear as in Illustration 8-4.

Accounts Receivable				Allowance for Doubtful Accounts			
Jan. 1 Bal. 200,000	Mar. 1	500		Mar. 1	500	Jan. 1 Bal.	12,000
Mar. 1 Bal. 199,500						Mar. 1 Bal.	11,500

Illustration 8-4
General ledger balances after write-off

A write-off affects **only balance sheet accounts**—not income statement accounts. The write-off of the account reduces both Accounts Receivable and Allowance for Doubtful Accounts. Cash realizable value in the balance sheet, therefore, remains the same, as Illustration 8-5 shows.

	Before Write-Off	After Write-Off
Accounts receivable	$ 200,000	$ 199,500
Allowance for doubtful accounts	12,000	11,500
Cash realizable value	**$188,000**	**$188,000**

Illustration 8-5
Cash realizable value comparison

RECOVERY OF AN UNCOLLECTIBLE ACCOUNT Occasionally, a company collects from a customer after it has written off the account as uncollectible. The company makes two entries to record the recovery of a bad debt: (1) It reverses the entry made in writing off the account. This reinstates the customer's account. (2) It journalizes the collection in the usual manner.

To illustrate, assume that on July 1, R. A. Ware pays the $500 amount that Hampson had written off on March 1. Hampson makes these entries:

(1)

July 1	Accounts Receivable—R. A. Ware	500	
	Allowance for Doubtful Accounts		500
	(To reverse write-off of R. A. Ware account)		

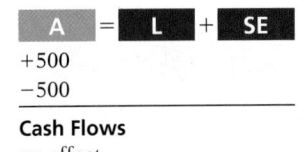

A = L + SE
+500
−500

Cash Flows
no effect

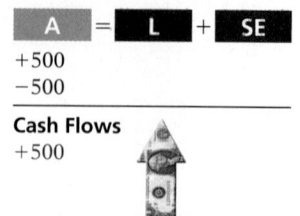

Cash Flows
+500

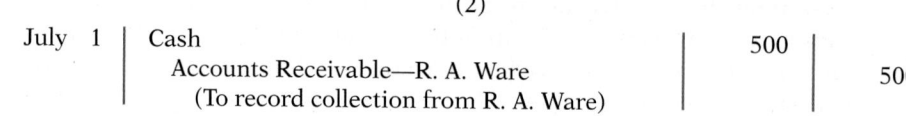

(2)

July 1	Cash	500	
	Accounts Receivable—R. A. Ware		500
	(To record collection from R. A. Ware)		

Note that the recovery of a bad debt, like the write-off of a bad debt, affects **only balance sheet accounts**. The net effect of the two entries above is a debit to Cash and a credit to Allowance for Doubtful Accounts for $500. Accounts Receivable and the Allowance for Doubtful Accounts both increase in entry (1) for two reasons. First, the company made an error in judgment when it wrote off the account receivable. Second, after R. A. Ware did pay, Accounts Receivable in the general ledger and Ware's account in the subsidiary ledger should show the collection for possible future credit purposes.

ESTIMATING THE ALLOWANCE For Hampson Furniture in Illustration 8-3, the amount of the expected uncollectibles was given. However, in "real life," companies must estimate that amount when they use the allowance method. Two bases are used to determine this amount: **(1) percentage of sales**, and **(2) percentage of receivables**. Both bases are generally accepted. The choice is a management decision. It depends on the relative emphasis that management wishes to give to expenses and revenues on the one hand or to cash realizable value of the accounts receivable on the other. The choice is whether to emphasize income statement or balance sheet relationships. Illustration 8-6 compares the two bases.

Illustration 8-6
Comparison of bases for estimating uncollectibles

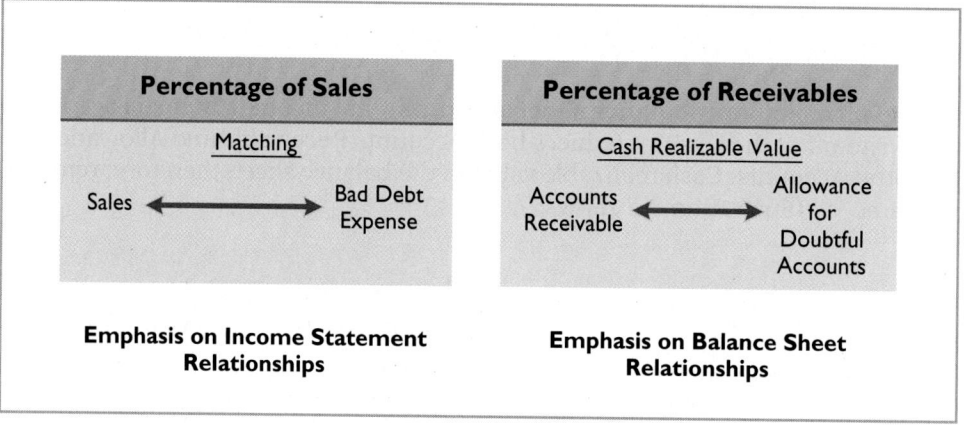

The percentage-of-sales basis results in a better matching of expenses with revenues—an income statement viewpoint. The percentage-of-receivables basis produces the better estimate of cash realizable value—a balance sheet viewpoint. Under both bases, the company must determine its past experience with bad debt losses.

Percentage-of-Sales. In the **percentage-of-sales basis**, management estimates what percentage of credit sales will be uncollectible. This percentage is based on past experience and anticipated credit policy.

The company applies this percentage to either total credit sales or net credit sales of the current year. To illustrate, assume that Gonzalez Company elects to use the percentage-of-sales basis. It concludes that 1% of net credit sales will become uncollectible. If net credit sales for 2014 are $800,000, the estimated bad debt expense is $8,000 (1% × $800,000). The adjusting entry is:

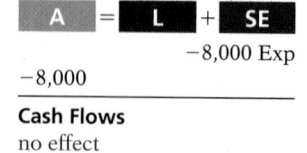

Cash Flows
no effect

Dec. 31	Bad Debt Expense	8,000	
	Allowance for Doubtful Accounts		8,000
	(To record estimated bad debts for year)		

After the adjusting entry is posted, assuming the allowance account already has a credit balance of $1,723, the accounts of Gonzalez Company will show the following:

Illustration 8-7
Bad debt accounts after posting

Bad Debt Expense		Allowance for Doubtful Accounts	
Dec. 31 Adj. **8,000**		Jan. 1 Bal. 1,723	
		Dec. 31 Adj. **8,000**	
		Dec. 31 Bal. 9,723	

This basis of estimating uncollectibles emphasizes the matching of expenses with revenues. As a result, Bad Debt Expense will show a direct percentage relationship to the sales base on which it is computed. **When the company makes the adjusting entry, it disregards the existing balance in Allowance for Doubtful Accounts.** The adjusted balance in this account should be a reasonable approximation of the realizable value of the receivables. If actual write-offs differ significantly from the amount estimated, the company should modify the percentage for future years.

Percentage-of-Receivables.

Under the **percentage-of-receivables basis**, management estimates what percentage of receivables will result in losses from uncollectible accounts. The company prepares an **aging schedule**, in which it classifies customer balances by the length of time they have been unpaid. Because of its emphasis on time, the analysis is often called **aging the accounts receivable**. In the Feature Story, Whitehall-Robins prepared an aging report daily.

After the company arranges the accounts by age, it determines the expected bad debt losses. It applies percentages based on past experience to the totals in each category. The longer a receivable is past due, the less likely it is to be collected. Thus, the estimated percentage of uncollectible debts increases as the number of days past due increases. Illustration 8-8 shows an aging schedule for Dart Company. Note that the estimated percentage uncollectible increases from 2% to 40% as the number of days past due increases.

Illustration 8-8
Aging schedule

	A	B	C	D	E	F	G
1				**Number of Days Past Due**			
2			**Not**				
3	**Customer**	**Total**	**Yet Due**	**1–30**	**31–60**	**61–90**	**Over 90**
4	T. E. Adert	$ 600		$ 300		$ 200	$ 100
5	R. C. Bortz	300	$ 300				
6	B. A. Carl	450		200	$ 250		
7	O. L. Diker	700	500			200	
8	T. O. Ebbet	600			300		300
9	Others	36,950	26,200	5,200	2,450	1,600	1,500
10		$39,600	$27,000	$5,700	$3,000	$2,000	$1,900
11	Estimated Percentage Uncollectible		2%	4%	10%	20%	40%
12	Total Estimated Bad Debts	$ 2,228	$ 540	$ 228	$ 300	$ 400	$ 760
13							

Total estimated bad debts for Dart Company ($2,228) represent the amount of existing customer claims the company expects will become uncollectible in the future. This amount represents the **required balance** in Allowance for Doubtful

Accounts at the balance sheet date. **The amount of the bad debt adjusting entry is the difference between the required balance and the existing balance in the allowance account.** If the trial balance shows Allowance for Doubtful Accounts with a credit balance of $528, the company will make an adjusting entry for $1,700 ($2,228 − $528), as shown here.

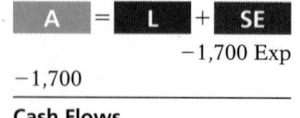

A = L + SE
−1,700 Exp
−1,700

Cash Flows
no effect

Dec. 31	Bad Debt Expense	1,700	
	Allowance for Doubtful Accounts		1,700
	(To adjust allowance account to total estimated uncollectibles)		

After Dart posts its adjusting entry, its accounts will appear as follows.

Illustration 8-9
Bad debt accounts after posting

Bad Debt Expense		Allowance for Doubtful Accounts	
Dec. 31 Adj. **1,700**		Bal. 528	
		Dec. 31 Adj. **1,700**	
		Bal. 2,228	

Occasionally, the allowance account will have a **debit balance** prior to adjustment. This occurs when write-offs during the year have exceeded previous provisions for bad debts. In such a case, the company **adds the debit balance to the required balance** when it makes the adjusting entry. Thus, if there had been a $500 debit balance in the allowance account before adjustment, the adjusting entry would have been for $2,728 ($2,228 + $500) to arrive at a credit balance of $2,228. The percentage-of-receivables basis will normally result in the better approximation of cash realizable value.

> DO IT!

Uncollectible Accounts Receivable

Brule Co. has been in business five years. The ledger at the end of the current year shows:

Accounts Receivable	$30,000 Dr.
Sales Revenue	$180,000 Cr.
Allowance for Doubtful Accounts	$2,000 Dr.

Bad debts are estimated to be 10% of receivables. Prepare the entry to adjust Allowance for Doubtful Accounts.

Action Plan

✔ Report receivables at their cash (net) realizable value.

✔ Estimate the amount the company does not expect to collect.

✔ Consider the existing balance in the allowance account when using the percentage-of-receivables basis.

Solution

The following entry should be made to bring the balance in Allowance for Doubtful Accounts up to a balance of $3,000 (10% × $30,000):

Bad Debt Expense [(10% × $30,000) + $2,000]	5,000	
Allowance for Doubtful Accounts		5,000
(To record estimate of uncollectible accounts)		

Related exercise material: **BE8-3, BE8-6, BE8-7, E8-3, E8-4, E8-5,** and **DO IT! 8-1.**

✔ **The Navigator**

LEARNING OBJECTIVE 4

Describe the entries to record the disposition of accounts receivable.

Disposing of Accounts Receivable

In the normal course of events, companies collect accounts receivable in cash and remove the receivables from the books. However, as credit sales and receivables have grown in significance, the "normal course of events" has changed.

Companies now frequently sell their receivables to another company for cash, thereby shortening the cash-to-cash operating cycle.

Companies sell receivables for two major reasons. First, **they may be the only reasonable source of cash**. When money is tight, companies may not be able to borrow money in the usual credit markets. Or, if money is available, the cost of borrowing may be prohibitive.

A second reason for selling receivables is that **billing and collection are often time-consuming and costly**. It is often easier for a retailer to sell the receivables to another party with expertise in billing and collection matters. Credit card companies such as MasterCard, Visa, and Discover specialize in billing and collecting accounts receivable.

SALE OF RECEIVABLES

A common sale of receivables is a sale to a factor. A **factor** is a finance company or bank that buys receivables from businesses and then collects the payments directly from the customers. Factoring is a multibillion dollar business.

Factoring arrangements vary widely. Typically, the factor charges a commission to the company that is selling the receivables. This fee ranges from 1–3% of the amount of receivables purchased. To illustrate, assume that Hendredon Furniture factors $600,000 of receivables to Federal Factors. Federal Factors assesses a service charge of 2% of the amount of receivables sold. The journal entry to record the sale by Hendredon Furniture is as follows.

Cash	588,000	
Service Charge Expense (2% × $600,000)	12,000	
Accounts Receivable		600,000
(To record the sale of accounts receivable)		

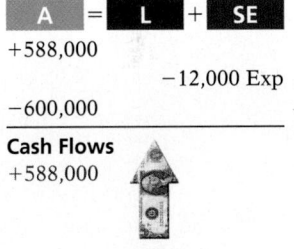

A = L + SE
+588,000
−12,000 Exp
−600,000

Cash Flows
+588,000

If the company often sells its receivables, it records the service charge expense (such as that incurred by Hendredon) as selling expense. If the company infrequently sells receivables, it may report this amount in the "Other expenses and losses" section of the income statement.

CREDIT CARD SALES

Over one billion credit cards are in use in the United States—more than three credit cards for every man, woman, and child in this country. Visa, MasterCard, and American Express are the national credit cards that most individuals use. Three parties are involved when national credit cards are used in retail sales: (1) the credit card issuer, who is independent of the retailer; (2) the retailer; and (3) the customer. A retailer's acceptance of a national credit card is another form of selling (factoring) the receivable.

Illustration 8-10 (page 390) shows the major advantages of national credit cards to the retailer. In exchange for these advantages, the retailer pays the credit card issuer a fee of 2–6% of the invoice price for its services.

ACCOUNTING FOR CREDIT CARD SALES The retailer generally considers sales from the use of national credit card sales as *cash sales*. The retailer must pay to the bank that issues the card a fee for processing the transactions. The retailer records the credit card slips in a similar manner as checks deposited from a cash sale.

To illustrate, Anita Ferreri purchases $1,000 of compact discs for her restaurant from Karen Kerr Music Co., using her Visa First Bank Card. First Bank charges a service fee of 3%. The entry to record this transaction by Karen Kerr Music is as follows.

Cash	970	
Service Charge Expense	30	
Sales Revenue		1,000
(To record Visa credit card sales)		

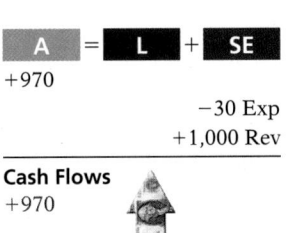

A = L + SE
+970
−30 Exp
+1,000 Rev

Cash Flows
+970

Illustration 8-10
Advantages of credit cards
to the retailer

Issuer does credit investigation
of customer

Credit card issuer   Customer   Retailer

Issuer maintains customer
accounts

Issuer undertakes collection
process and absorbs any losses

Retailer receives cash more
quickly from credit card issuer

ACCOUNTING ACROSS THE ORGANIZATION

How Does a Credit Card Work?

Most of you know how to *use* a credit card, but do you know what happens in the transaction and how the transaction is processed? Suppose that you use a Visa card to purchase some new ties at Nordstrom. The salesperson swipes your card, which allows the information on the magnetic strip on the back of the card to be read. The salesperson then enters the amount of the purchase. The machine contacts the Visa computer, which routes the call back to the bank that issued your Visa card. The issuing bank verifies that the account exists, that the card is not stolen, and that you have not exceeded your credit limit. At this point, the slip is printed, which you sign.

Visa acts as the clearing agent for the transaction. It transfers funds from the issuing bank to Nordstrom's bank account. Generally this transfer of funds, from sale to the receipt of funds in the merchant's account, takes two to three days.

In the meantime, Visa puts a pending charge on your account for the amount of the tie purchase; that amount counts immediately against your available credit limit. At the end of the billing period, Visa sends you an invoice (your credit card bill) which shows the various charges you made, and the amounts that Visa expended on your behalf, for the month. You then must "pay the piper" for your stylish new ties.

 Assume that Nordstrom prepares a bank reconciliation at the end of each month. If some credit card sales have not been processed by the bank, how should Nordstrom treat these transactions on its bank reconciliation? (See page 418.)

> ## DO IT!

Disposition of Accounts Receivable

Mehl Wholesalers Co. has been expanding faster than it can raise capital. According to its local banker, the company has reached its debt ceiling. Mehl's suppliers (creditors) are demanding payment within 30 days of the invoice date for goods acquired, but Mehl's customers are slow in paying (60–90 days). As a result, Mehl has a cash flow problem.

Mehl needs $120,000 in cash to safely cover next Friday's payroll. Its balance of outstanding accounts receivables totals $750,000. What might Mehl do to alleviate this cash crunch? Record the entry that Mehl would make when it raises the needed cash.

Solution

Action Plan

✔ To speed up the collection of cash, sell receivables to a factor.

✔ Calculate service charge expense as a percentage of the factored receivables.

Assuming that Mehl Wholesalers factors $125,000 of its accounts receivable at a 1% service charge, it would make the following entry.

Cash	123,750	
Service Charge Expense (1% × $125,000)	1,250	
Accounts Receivable		125,000
(To record sale of receivables to factor)		

Related exercise material: **BE8-8, E8-7, E8-8, E8-9, and 8-2.**

✔ **The Navigator**

Notes Receivable

Companies may also grant credit in exchange for a formal credit instrument known as a promissory note. A **promissory note** is a written promise to pay a specified amount of money on demand or at a definite time. Promissory notes may be used (1) when individuals and companies lend or borrow money, (2) when the amount of the transaction and the credit period exceed normal limits, or (3) in settlement of accounts receivable.

In a promissory note, the party making the promise to pay is called the **maker**. The party to whom payment is to be made is called the **payee**. The note may specifically identify the payee by name or may designate the payee simply as the bearer of the note.

In the note shown in Illustration 8-11 (page 392), Calhoun Company is the maker, and Wilma Company is the payee. To Wilma Company, the promissory note is a note receivable. To Calhoun Company, it is a note payable.

Notes receivable give the holder a stronger legal claim to assets than do accounts receivable. Like accounts receivable, notes receivable can be readily sold to another party. Promissory notes are negotiable instruments (as are checks), which means that they can be transferred to another party by endorsement.

Companies frequently accept notes receivable from customers who need to extend the payment of an outstanding account receivable. They often require such notes from high-risk customers. In some industries (such as the pleasure and sport boat industry), all credit sales are supported by notes. The majority of notes, however, originate from loans.

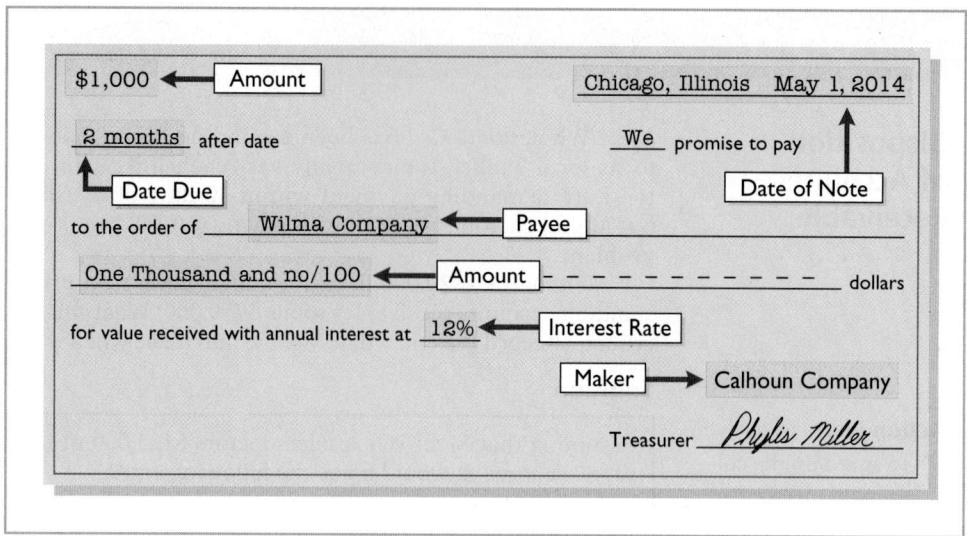

The basic issues in accounting for notes receivable are the same as those for accounts receivable:

1. **Recognizing** notes receivable.
2. **Valuing** notes receivable.
3. **Disposing** of notes receivable.

On the following pages, we will look at these issues. Before we do, we need to consider two issues that do not apply to accounts receivable: maturity date and computing interest.

Determining the Maturity Date

When the life of a note is expressed in terms of months, you find the date when it matures by counting the months from the date of issue. For example, the maturity date of a three-month note dated May 1 is August 1. A note drawn on the last day of a month matures on the last day of a subsequent month. That is, a July 31 note due in two months matures on September 30.

When the due date is stated in terms of days, you need to count the exact number of days to determine the maturity date. In counting, **omit the date the note is issued but include the due date.** For example, the maturity date of a 60-day note dated July 17 is September 15, computed as follows.

Term of note		60 days
July (31 − 17)	14	
August	31	45
Maturity date: September		**15**

Illustration 8-13 shows three ways of stating the maturity date of a promissory note.

Illustration 8-13
Maturity date of different notes

Computing Interest

Illustration 8-14 gives the basic formula for computing interest on an interest-bearing note.

Face Value of Note	×	Annual Interest Rate	×	Time in Terms of One Year	=	Interest

Illustration 8-14
Formula for computing interest

Helpful Hint
The interest rate specified is the *annual* rate.

The interest rate specified in a note is an **annual** rate of interest. The time factor in the computation in Illustration 8-14 expresses the fraction of a year that the note is outstanding. When the maturity date is stated in days, the time factor is often the number of days divided by 360. When counting days, omit the date that the note is issued but include the due date. When the due date is stated in months, the time factor is the number of months divided by 12. Illustration 8-15 shows computation of interest for various time periods.

Illustration 8-15
Computation of interest

Terms of Note	Interest Computation
	Face × Rate × Time = Interest
$ 730, 18%, 120 days	$ 730 × 18% × 120/360 = $ 43.80
$1,000, 15%, 6 months	$1,000 × 15% × 6/12 = $ 75.00
$2,000, 12%, 1 year	$2,000 × 12% × 1/1 = $240.00

There are different ways to calculate interest. For example, the computation in Illustration 8-15 assumes 360 days for the length of the year. Most financial instruments use 365 days to compute interest. *For homework problems, assume 360 days to simplify computations.*

Recognizing Notes Receivable

To illustrate the basic entry for notes receivable, we will use Calhoun Company's $1,000, two-month, 12% promissory note dated May 1. Assuming that Calhoun Company wrote the note to settle an open account, Wilma Company makes the following entry for the receipt of the note.

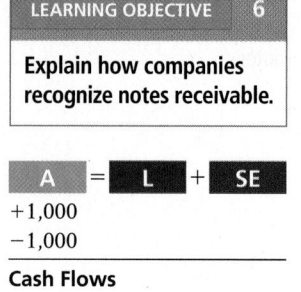

A	**=**	**L**	**+**	**SE**

+1,000
−1,000

Cash Flows
no effect

May 1	Notes Receivable	1,000	
	Accounts Receivable—Calhoun Company		1,000
	(To record acceptance of Calhoun Company note)		

The company records the note receivable at its **face value**, the amount shown on the face of the note. No interest revenue is reported when the note is accepted because the revenue recognition principle does not recognize revenue until the performance obligation is satisfied. Interest is earned (accrued) as time passes.

If a company lends money using a note, the entry is a debit to Notes Receivable and a credit to Cash in the amount of the loan.

Valuing Notes Receivable

Valuing short-term notes receivable is the same as valuing accounts receivable. Like accounts receivable, companies report short-term notes receivable at their **cash (net) realizable value**. The notes receivable allowance account is Allowance for Doubtful Accounts. The estimations involved in determining cash realizable value and in recording bad debt expense and the related allowance are done similarly to accounts receivable.

INTERNATIONAL INSIGHT

Can Fair Value Be Unfair?

The FASB and the International Accounting Standards Board (IASB) are considering proposals for how to account for financial instruments. The FASB has proposed that loans and receivables be accounted for at their fair value (the amount they could currently be sold for), as are most investments. The FASB believes that this would provide a more accurate view of a company's financial position. It might be especially useful as an early warning when a bank is in trouble because of poor-quality loans. But, banks argue that fair values are difficult to estimate accurately. They are also concerned that volatile fair values could cause large swings in a bank's reported net income.

Source: David Reilly, "Banks Face a Mark-to-Market Challenge," *Wall Street Journal Online* (March 15, 2010).

? What are the arguments in favor of and against fair value accounting for loans and receivables? (See page 418.)

Disposing of Notes Receivable

Notes may be held to their maturity date, at which time the face value plus accrued interest is due. In some situations, the maker of the note defaults, and the payee must make an appropriate adjustment. In other situations, similar to accounts receivable, the holder of the note speeds up the conversion to cash by selling the receivables (described later in this chapter).

HONOR OF NOTES RECEIVABLE

A note is **honored** when its maker pays in full at its maturity date. For each interest-bearing note, the **amount due at maturity** is the face value of the note plus interest for the length of time specified on the note.

To illustrate, assume that Wolder Co. lends Higley Co. $10,000 on June 1, accepting a five-month, 9% interest note. In this situation, interest is $375 ($10,000 × 9% × $\frac{5}{12}$). The amount due, the maturity value, is $10,375 ($10,000 + $375). To obtain payment, Wolder (the payee) must present the note either to Higley Co. (the maker) or to the maker's agent, such as a bank. If Wolder presents the note to Higley Co. on November 1, the maturity date, Wolder's entry to record the collection is:

Nov. 1	Cash	10,375	
	Notes Receivable		10,000
	Interest Revenue ($10,000 × 9% × $\frac{5}{12}$)		375
	(To record collection of Higley note and interest)		

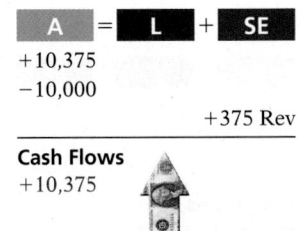

A = L + SE
+10,375
−10,000
           +375 Rev

Cash Flows
+10,375

ACCRUAL OF INTEREST RECEIVABLE

Suppose instead that Wolder Co. prepares financial statements as of September 30. The timeline in Illustration 8-16 presents this situation.

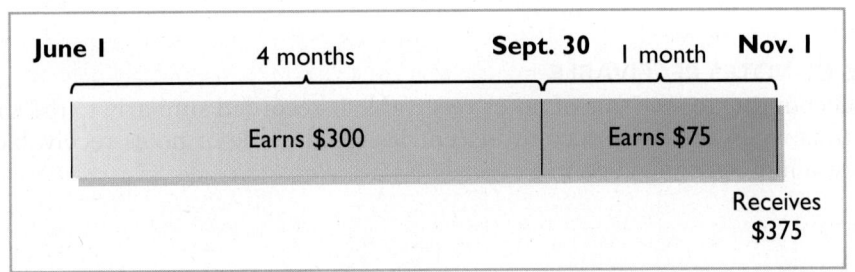

Illustration 8-16
Timeline of interest earned

To reflect interest earned but not yet received, Wolder must accrue interest on September 30. In this case, the adjusting entry by Wolder is for four months of interest, or $300, as shown below.

Sept. 30	Interest Receivable ($10,000 × 9% × $\frac{4}{12}$)	300	
	Interest Revenue		300
	(To accrue 4 months' interest on Higley note)		

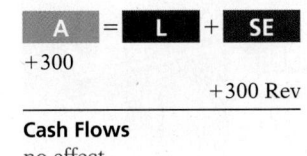

A = L + SE
+300
           +300 Rev

Cash Flows
no effect

At the note's maturity on November 1, Wolder receives $10,375. This amount represents repayment of the $10,000 note as well as five months of interest, or $375, as shown below. The $375 is comprised of the $300 Interest Receivable accrued on September 30 plus $75 earned during October. Wolder's entry to record the honoring of the Higley note on November 1 is:

Nov. 1	Cash [$10,000 + ($10,000 × 9% × $\frac{5}{12}$)]	10,375	
	Notes Receivable		10,000
	Interest Receivable		300
	Interest Revenue ($10,000 × 9% × $\frac{1}{12}$)		75
	(To record collection of Higley note and interest)		

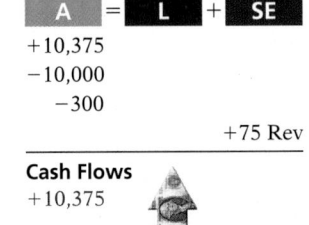

A = L + SE
+10,375
−10,000
−300
           +75 Rev

Cash Flows
+10,375

In this case, Wolder credits Interest Receivable because the receivable was established in the adjusting entry on September 30.

DISHONOR OF NOTES RECEIVABLE

A **dishonored (defaulted) note** is a note that is not paid in full at maturity. A dishonored note receivable is no longer negotiable. However, the payee still has a claim against the maker of the note for both the note and the interest. Therefore, the note holder usually transfers the Notes Receivable account to an account receivable.

To illustrate, assume that Higley Co. on November 1 indicates that it cannot pay at the present time. The entry to record the dishonor of the note depends on whether Wolder Co. expects eventual collection. If it does expect eventual collection, Wolder Co. debits the amount due (face value and interest) on the note to Accounts Receivable. It would make the following entry at the time the note is dishonored (assuming no previous accrual of interest).

A	=	L	+	SE
+10,375				
−10,000				
				+375 Rev

Cash Flows
no effect

Nov. 1	Accounts Receivable—Higley	10,375		
	Notes Receivable		10,000	
	Interest Revenue		375	
	(To record the dishonor of Higley note)			

If instead, on November 1, there is no hope of collection, the note holder would write off the face value of the note by debiting Allowance for Doubtful Accounts. No interest revenue would be recorded because collection will not occur.

SALE OF NOTES RECEIVABLE

The accounting for the sale of notes receivable is recorded similarly to the sale of accounts receivable. The accounting entries for the sale of notes receivable are left for a more advanced course.

ACCOUNTING ACROSS THE ORGANIZATION

Bad Information Can Lead to Bad Loans

Many factors have contributed to the recent credit crisis. One significant factor that resulted in many bad loans was a failure by lenders to investigate loan customers sufficiently. For example, Countrywide Financial Corporation wrote many loans under its "Fast and Easy" loan program. That program allowed borrowers to provide little or no documentation for their income or their assets. Other lenders had similar programs, which earned the nickname "liars' loans." One study found that in these situations, 60% of applicants overstated their incomes by more than 50% in order to qualify for a loan. Critics of the banking industry say that because loan officers were compensated for loan volume, and because banks were selling the loans to investors rather than holding them, the lenders had little incentive to investigate the borrowers' creditworthiness.

Source: Glenn R. Simpson and James R. Hagerty, "Countrywide Loss Focuses Attention on Underwriting," *Wall Street Journal* (April 30, 2008), p. B1; and Michael Corkery, "Fraud Seen as Driver in Wave of Foreclosures," *Wall Street Journal* (December 21, 2007), p. A1.

? What steps should the banks have taken to ensure the accuracy of financial information provided on loan applications? (See page 418.)

> DO IT!

Notes Receivable

Gambit Stores accepts from Leonard Co. a $3,400, 90-day, 6% note dated May 10 in settlement of Leonard's overdue account. (a) What is the maturity date of the note? (b) What entry does Gambit make at the maturity date, assuming Leonard pays the note and interest in full at that time?

Solution

Action Plan

✔ Count the exact number of days to determine the maturity date. Omit the date the note is issued, but include the due date.

✔ Determine whether interest was accrued.

✔ Compute the accrued interest.

✔ Prepare the entry for payment of the note and interest.

✔ The entry to record interest at maturity in this solution assumes no interest has been previously accrued on this note.

(a) The maturity date is August 8, computed as follows.

Term of note:		90 days
May (31−10)	21	
June	30	
July	31	82
Maturity date: August		8

(b) The interest payable at the maturity date is $51, computed as follows.

Face	×	Rate	×	Time	=	Interest
$3,400	×	6%	×	90/360	=	$51

The entry recorded by Gambit Stores at the maturity date is:

Cash	3,451	
Notes Receivable		3,400
Interest Revenue		51
(To record collection of Leonard note)		

Related exercise material: **BE8-9, BE8-10, BE8-11, E8-10, E8-11, E8-12, E8-13, and DO IT! 8-3.**

 ✔ **The Navigator**

Statement Presentation and Analysis

Presentation

Companies should identify in the balance sheet or in the notes to the financial statements each of the major types of receivables. Short-term receivables appear in the current assets section of the balance sheet. Short-term investments appear before short-term receivables because these investments are more liquid (nearer to cash). Companies report both the gross amount of receivables and the allowance for doubtful accounts.

> **LEARNING OBJECTIVE   9**
>
> **Explain the statement presentation and analysis of receivables.**

In a multiple-step income statement, companies report bad debt expense and service charge expense as selling expenses in the operating expenses section. Interest revenue appears under "Other revenues and gains" in the nonoperating activities section of the income statement.

Analysis

Investors and corporate managers compute financial ratios to evaluate the liquidity of a company's accounts receivable. They use the **accounts receivable turnover ratio** to assess the liquidity of the receivables. This ratio measures the number of times, on average, the company collects accounts receivable during the period. It is computed by dividing net credit sales (net sales less cash sales) by the average net accounts receivable during the year. Unless seasonal factors are significant, average net accounts receivable outstanding can be computed from the beginning and ending balances of net accounts receivable.

For example, in 2009 Cisco Systems had net sales of $32,420 million for the year. It had a beginning accounts receivable (net) balance of $3,177 million and an ending accounts receivable (net) balance of $4,929 million. Assuming that Cisco's sales were all on credit, its accounts receivable turnover ratio is computed as follows.

Illustration 8-17
Accounts receivable turnover ratio and computation

Net Credit Sales	÷	Average Net Accounts Receivable	=	Accounts Receivable Turnover
$32,420	÷	$\dfrac{\$3,177 + \$4,929}{2}$	=	8 times

The result indicates an accounts receivable turnover ratio of 8 times per year. The higher the turnover ratio, the more liquid the company's receivables.

A variant of the accounts receivable turnover ratio that makes the liquidity even more evident is its conversion into an **average collection period** in terms of days. This is done by dividing the turnover ratio into 365 days. For example, Cisco's turnover of 8 times is divided into 365 days, as shown in Illustration 8-18, to obtain approximately 46 days. This means that it takes Cisco 46 days to collect its accounts receivable.

Illustration 8-18
Average collection period for receivables formula and computation

Days in Year	÷	Accounts Receivable Turnover	=	Average Collection Period in Days
365 days	÷	8 times	=	46 days

Companies frequently use the average collection period to assess the effectiveness of a company's credit and collection policies. The general rule is that the collection period should not greatly exceed the credit term period (that is, the time allowed for payment).

> DO IT!

Analysis of Receivables

In 2014, Phil Mickelson Company has net credit sales of $923,795 for the year. It had a beginning accounts receivable (net) balance of $38,275 and an ending accounts receivable (net) balance of $35,988. Compute Phil Mickelson Company's (a) accounts receivable turnover and (b) average collection period in days.

Solution

Action Plan

✔ Review the formula to compute the accounts receivable turnover.

✔ Make sure that both the beginning and ending accounts receivable balances are considered in the computation.

✔ Review the formula to compute the average collection period in days.

(a)

Net credit sales	÷	Average net accounts receivable	=	Accounts receivable turnover
$923,795	÷	$\dfrac{38,275 + 35,988}{2}$	=	24.9 times

(b)

Days in year	÷	Accounts receivable turnover	=	Average collection period in days
365	÷	24.9 times	=	14.7 days

Related exercise material: **BE8-12, E8-14, and** **DO IT!** **8-4.**

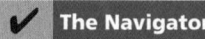
✔ The Navigator

> ### Comprehensive DO IT!

The following selected transactions relate to Dylan Company.

Mar. 1 Sold $20,000 of merchandise to Potter Company, terms 2/10, n/30.
11 Received payment in full from Potter Company for balance due.
12 Accepted Juno Company's $20,000, 6-month, 12% note for balance due on existing accounts receivable.
13 Made Dylan Company credit card sales for $13,200.
15 Made Visa credit card sales totaling $6,700. A 3% service fee is charged by Visa.
Apr. 11 Sold accounts receivable of $8,000 to Harcot Factor. Harcot Factor assesses a service charge of 2% of the amount of receivables sold.
13 Received collections of $8,200 on Dylan Company credit card sales and added finance charges of 1.5% to the remaining balances.
May 10 Wrote off as uncollectible $16,000 of accounts receivable. Dylan uses the percentage-of-sales basis to estimate bad debts.
June 30 Credit sales recorded during the first 6 months total $2,000,000. The bad debt percentage is 1% of credit sales. At June 30, the balance in the allowance account is $3,500.
July 16 One of the accounts receivable written off in May was from J. Simon, who pays the amount due, $4,000, in full.

Instructions

Prepare the journal entries for the transactions.

Solution to Comprehensive DO IT!

Action Plan

✔ Generally, record accounts receivable at invoice price.

✔ Recognize that sales returns and allowances and cash discounts reduce the amount received on accounts receivable.

✔ Record service charge expense on the seller's books when accounts receivable are sold.

✔ Prepare an adjusting entry for bad debt expense.

✔ Ignore any balance in the allowance account under the percentage-of-sales basis. Recognize the balance in the allowance account under the percentage-of-receivables basis.

✔ Record write-offs of accounts receivable only in balance sheet accounts.

Mar.	1	Accounts Receivable—Potter	20,000	
		Sales Revenue		20,000
		(To record sales on account)		
	11	Cash	19,600	
		Sales Discounts (2% × $20,000)	400	
		Accounts Receivable—Potter		20,000
		(To record collection of accounts receivable)		
	12	Notes Receivable	20,000	
		Accounts Receivable—Juno		20,000
		(To record acceptance of Juno Company note)		
	13	Accounts Receivable	13,200	
		Sales Revenue		13,200
		(To record company credit card sales)		
	15	Cash	6,499	
		Service Charge Expense (3% × $6,700)	201	
		Sales Revenue		6,700
		(To record credit card sales)		
Apr.	11	Cash	7,840	
		Service Charge Expense (2% × $8,000)	160	
		Accounts Receivable		8,000
		(To record sale of receivables to factor)		
	13	Cash	8,200	
		Accounts Receivable		8,200
		(To record collection of accounts receivable)		
		Accounts Receivable [($13,200 − $8,200) × 1.5%]	75	
		Interest Revenue		75
		(To record interest on amount due)		
May	10	Allowance for Doubtful Accounts	16,000	
		Accounts Receivable		16,000
		(To record write-off of accounts receivable)		

June 30	Bad Debt Expense ($2,000,000 × 1%)	20,000	
	Allowance for Doubtful Accounts		20,000
	(To record estimate of uncollectible accounts)		
July 16	Accounts Receivable—J. Simon	4,000	
	Allowance for Doubtful Accounts		4,000
	(To reverse write-off of accounts receivable)		
	Cash	4,000	
	Accounts Receivable—J. Simon		4,000
	(To record collection of accounts receivable)		

✔ **The Navigator**

SUMMARY OF LEARNING OBJECTIVES

 The Navigator

1 Identify the different types of receivables. Receivables are frequently classified as (1) accounts, (2) notes, and (3) other. Accounts receivable are amounts customers owe on account. Notes receivable are claims for which lenders issue formal instruments of credit as proof of the debt. Other receivables include nontrade receivables such as interest receivable, loans to company officers, advances to employees, and income taxes refundable.

2 Explain how companies recognize accounts receivable. Companies record accounts receivable when they provide a service on account or at the point-of-sale of merchandise on account. Sales revenues are reduced by sales returns and allowances. Cash discounts reduce the amount received on accounts receivable. When interest is charged on a past due receivable, the company adds this interest to the accounts receivable balance and recognizes it as interest revenue.

3 Distinguish between the methods and bases companies use to value accounts receivable. There are two methods of accounting for uncollectible accounts: the allowance method and the direct write-off method. Companies may use either the percentage-of-sales or the percentage-of-receivables basis to estimate uncollectible accounts using the allowance method. The percentage-of-sales basis emphasizes the expense recognition (matching) principle. The percentage-of-receivables basis emphasizes the cash realizable value of the accounts receivable. An aging schedule is often used with this basis.

4 Describe the entries to record the disposition of accounts receivable. When a company collects an account receivable, it credits Accounts Receivable. When a company sells (factors) an account receivable, a service charge expense reduces the amount received.

5 Compute the maturity date of and interest on notes receivable. For a note stated in months, the maturity date is found by counting the months from the date of issue. For a note stated in days, the number of days is counted, omitting the issue date and counting the due date. The formula for computing interest is: Face value × Interest rate × Time.

6 Explain how companies recognize notes receivable. Companies record notes receivable at face value. In some cases, it is necessary to accrue interest prior to maturity. In this case, companies debit Interest Receivable and credit Interest Revenue.

7 Describe how companies value notes receivable. As with accounts receivable, companies report notes receivable at their cash (net) realizable value. The notes receivable allowance account is Allowance for Doubtful Accounts. The computation and estimations involved in valuing notes receivable at cash realizable value, and in recording the proper amount of bad debt expense and related allowance, are similar to those for accounts receivable.

8 Describe the entries to record the disposition of notes receivable. Notes can be held to maturity. At that time the face value plus accrued interest is due, and the note is removed from the accounts. In many cases, the holder of the note speeds up the conversion by selling the receivable to another party (a factor). In some situations, the maker of the note dishonors the note (defaults), in which case the company transfers the note and accrued interest to an account receivable or writes off the note.

9 Explain the statement presentation and analysis of receivables. Companies should identify in the balance sheet or in the notes to the financial statements each major type of receivable. Short-term receivables are considered current assets. Companies report the gross amount of receivables and the allowance for doubtful accounts. They report bad debt and service charge expenses in the multiple-step income statement as operating (selling) expenses; interest revenue appears under other revenues and gains in the nonoperating activities section of the statement. Managers and investors evaluate accounts receivable for liquidity by computing a turnover ratio and an average collection period.

GLOSSARY

Accounts receivable Amounts owed by customers on account. (p. 380).

Accounts receivable turnover ratio A measure of the liquidity of accounts receivable; computed by dividing net credit sales by average net accounts receivable. (p. 397).

Aging the accounts receivable The analysis of customer balances by the length of time they have been unpaid. (p. 387).

Allowance method A method of accounting for bad debts that involves estimating uncollectible accounts at the end of each period. (p. 383).

Average collection period The average amount of time that a receivable is outstanding; calculated by dividing 365 days by the accounts receivable turnover ratio. (p. 398).

Bad Debt Expense An expense account to record uncollectible receivables. (p. 382).

Cash (net) realizable value The net amount a company expects to receive in cash. (p. 383).

Direct write-off method A method of accounting for bad debts that involves expensing accounts at the time they are determined to be uncollectible. (p. 382).

Dishonored (defaulted) note A note that is not paid in full at maturity. (p. 396).

Factor A finance company or bank that buys receivables from businesses and then collects the payments directly from the customers. (p. 389).

Maker The party in a promissory note who is making the promise to pay. (p. 391).

Notes receivable Written promise (as evidenced by a formal instrument) for amounts to be received. (p. 380).

Other receivables Various forms of nontrade receivables, such as interest receivable and income taxes refundable. (p. 380).

Payee The party to whom payment of a promissory note is to be made. (p. 391).

Percentage-of-receivables basis Management estimates what percentage of receivables will result in losses from uncollectible accounts. (p. 387).

Percentage-of-sales basis Management estimates what percentage of credit sales will be uncollectible. (p. 386).

Promissory note A written promise to pay a specified amount of money on demand or at a definite time. (p. 391).

Receivables Amounts due from individuals and other companies. (p. 380).

Trade receivables Notes and accounts receivable that result from sales transactions. (p. 380).

 **Self-Test, Brief Exercises, Exercises, Problem Set A, and many more components are available for practice in WileyPLUS.**

SELF-TEST QUESTIONS

Answers are on page 419.

(LO 1) **1.** Receivables are frequently classified as:
(a) accounts receivable, company receivables, and other receivables.
(b) accounts receivable, notes receivable, and employee receivables.
(c) accounts receivable and general receivables.
(d) accounts receivable, notes receivable, and other receivables.

(LO 2) **2.** Buehler Company on June 15 sells merchandise on account to Chaz Co. for $1,000, terms 2/10, n/30. On June 20, Chaz Co. returns merchandise worth $300 to Buehler Company. On June 24, payment is received from Chaz Co. for the balance due. What is the amount of cash received?
(a) $700. (c) $686.
(b) $680. (d) None of the above.

(LO 3) **3.** Which of the following approaches for bad debts is best described as a balance sheet method?
(a) Percentage-of-receivables basis.
(b) Direct write-off method.
(c) Percentage-of-sales basis.
(d) Both a and b.

4. Hughes Company has a credit balance of $5,000 (LO 3) in its Allowance for Doubtful Accounts before any adjustments are made at the end of the year. Based on review and aging of its accounts receivable at the end of the year, Hughes estimates that $60,000 of its receivables are uncollectible. The amount of bad debt expense which should be reported for the year is:
(a) $5,000. (c) $60,000.
(b) $55,000. (d) $65,000.

5. Use the same information as in question 4, except that (LO 3) Hughes has a debit balance of $5,000 in its Allowance for Doubtful Accounts before any adjustments are made at the end of the year. In this situation, the amount of bad debt expense that should be reported for the year is:
(a) $5,000. (c) $60,000.
(b) $55,000. (d) $65,000.

6. Net sales for the month are $800,000, and bad debts (LO 3) are expected to be 1.5% of net sales. The company uses the percentage-of-sales basis. If Allowance for Doubtful Accounts has a credit balance of $15,000 before adjustment, what is the balance after adjustment?
(a) $15,000. (c) $23,000.
(b) $27,000. (d) $31,000.

(LO 3) **7.** In 2014, Roso Carlson Company had net credit sales of $750,000. On January 1, 2014, Allowance for Doubtful Accounts had a credit balance of $18,000. During 2014, $30,000 of uncollectible accounts receivable were written off. Past experience indicates that 3% of net credit sales become uncollectible. What should be the adjusted balance of Allowance for Doubtful Accounts at December 31, 2014?

(a) $10,050.   (c) $22,500.
(b) $10,500.   (d) $40,500.

(LO 3) **8.** An analysis and aging of the accounts receivable of Prince Company at December 31 reveals the following data.

Accounts receivable	$800,000
Allowance for doubtful accounts per books before adjustment	50,000
Amounts expected to become uncollectible	65,000

The cash realizable value of the accounts receivable at December 31, after adjustment, is:

(a) $685,000.   (c) $800,000.
(b) $750,000.   (d) $735,000.

(LO 6) **9.** One of the following statements about promissory notes is incorrect. The *incorrect* statement is:

(a) The party making the promise to pay is called the maker.
(b) The party to whom payment is to be made is called the payee.
(c) A promissory note is not a negotiable instrument.
(d) A promissory note is often required from high-risk customers.

(LO 4) **10.** Which of the following statements about Visa credit card sales is *incorrect*?

(a) The credit card issuer makes the credit investigation of the customer.
(b) The retailer is not involved in the collection process.
(c) Two parties are involved.
(d) The retailer receives cash more quickly than it would from individual customers on account.

(LO 4) **11.** Blinka Retailers accepted $50,000 of Citibank Visa credit card charges for merchandise sold on July 1. Citibank charges 4% for its credit card use. The entry to record this transaction by Blinka Retailers will include a credit to Sales Revenue of $50,000 and a debit(s) to:

(a) Cash $48,000
    and Service Charge Expense $2,000
(b) Accounts Receivable $48,000
    and Service Charge Expense $2,000
(c) Cash $50,000
(d) Accounts Receivable $50,000

(LO 6) **12.** Foti Co. accepts a $1,000, 3-month, 6% promissory note in settlement of an account with Bartelt Co. The entry to record this transaction is as follows.

(a) Notes Receivable   1,015
      Accounts Receivable   1,015
(b) Notes Receivable   1,000
      Accounts Receivable   1,000
(c) Notes Receivable   1,000
      Sales Revenue   1,000
(d) Notes Receivable   1,030
      Accounts Receivable   1,030

(LO 8) **13.** Ginter Co. holds Kolar Inc.'s $10,000, 120-day, 9% note. The entry made by Ginter Co. when the note is collected, assuming no interest has been previously accrued, is:

(a) Cash   10,300
      Notes Receivable   10,300
(b) Cash   10,000
      Notes Receivable   10,000
(c) Accounts Receivable   10,300
      Notes Receivable   10,000
      Interest Revenue   300
(d) Cash   10,300
      Notes Receivable   10,000
      Interest Revenue   300

(LO 9) **14.** Accounts and notes receivable are reported in the current assets section of the balance sheet at:

(a) cash (net) realizable value
(b) net book value.
(c) lower-of-cost-or-market value.
(d) invoice cost.

(LO 9) **15.** Oliveras Company had net credit sales during the year of $800,000 and cost of goods sold of $500,000. The balance in accounts receivable at the beginning of the year was $100,000, and the end of the year it was $150,000. What were the accounts receivable turnover ratio and the average collection period in days?

(a) 4.0 and 91.3 days.   (c) 6.4 and 57 days.
(b) 5.3 and 68.9 days.   (d) 8.0 and 45.6 days.

Go to the book's companion website, **www.wiley.com/college/weygandt**, for additional Self-Test Questions.

 ✔ **The Navigator**

QUESTIONS

1. What is the difference between an account receivable and a note receivable?

2. What are some common types of receivables other than accounts receivable and notes receivable?

3. Texaco Oil Company issues its own credit cards. Assume that Texaco charges you $40 interest on an

unpaid balance. Prepare the journal entry that Texaco makes to record this revenue.

4. What are the essential features of the allowance method of accounting for bad debts?

5. Roger Holloway cannot understand why cash realizable value does not decrease when an uncollectible account is written off under the allowance method. Clarify this point for Roger Holloway.

6. Distinguish between the two bases that may be used in estimating uncollectible accounts.

7. Borke Company has a credit balance of $3,200 in Allowance for Doubtful Accounts. The estimated bad debt expense under the percentage-of-sales basis is $3,700. The total estimated uncollectibles under the percentage-of-receivables basis is $5,800. Prepare the adjusting entry under each basis.

8. How are bad debts accounted for under the direct write-off method? What are the disadvantages of this method?

9. Freida Company accepts both its own credit cards and national credit cards. What are the advantages of accepting both types of cards?

10. An article recently appeared in the *Wall Street Journal* indicating that companies are selling their receivables at a record rate. Why are companies selling their receivables?

11. WestSide Textiles decides to sell $800,000 of its accounts receivable to First Factors Inc. First Factors assesses a service charge of 3% of the amount of receivables sold. Prepare the journal entry that WestSide Textiles makes to record this sale.

12. Your roommate is uncertain about the advantages of a promissory note. Compare the advantages of a note receivable with those of an account receivable.

13. How may the maturity date of a promissory note be stated?

14. Indicate the maturity date of each of the following promissory notes:

Date of Note	Terms
(a) March 13	one year after date of note
(b) May 4	3 months after date
(c) June 20	30 days after date
(d) July 1	60 days after date

15. Compute the missing amounts for each of the following notes.

	Principal	Annual Interest Rate	Time	Total Interest
(a)	?	9%	120 days	$ 450
(b)	$30,000	10%	3 years	?
(c)	$60,000	?	5 months	$3,000
(d)	$45,000	8%	?	$1,200

16. In determining interest revenue, some financial institutions use 365 days per year and others use 360 days. Why might a financial institution use 360 days?

17. Jana Company dishonors a note at maturity. What are the options available to the lender?

18. General Motors Corporation has accounts receivable and notes receivable. How should the receivables be reported on the balance sheet?

19. The accounts receivable turnover ratio is 8.14, and average net receivables during the period are $400,000. What is the amount of net credit sales for the period?

20. **PEPSICO** What percentage does PepsiCo's allowance for doubtful accounts represent as a percentage of its gross receivables?

BRIEF EXERCISES

BE8-1 Presented below are three receivables transactions. Indicate whether these receivables are reported as accounts receivable, notes receivable, or other receivables on a balance sheet.
(a) Sold merchandise on account for $64,000 to a customer.
(b) Received a promissory note of $57,000 for services performed.
(c) Advanced $8,000 to an employee.

Identify different types of receivables.

(LO 1)

BE8-2 Record the following transactions on the books of Galaxy Co.
(a) On July 1, Galaxy Co. sold merchandise on account to Kingston Inc. for $17,200, terms 2/10, n/30.
(b) On July 8, Kingston Inc. returned merchandise worth $3,800 to Galaxy Co.
(c) On July 11, Kingston Inc. paid for the merchandise.

Record basic accounts receivable transactions.

(LO 2)

BE8-3 During its first year of operations, Energy Company had credit sales of $3,000,000; $600,000 remained uncollected at year-end. The credit manager estimates that $31,000 of these receivables will become uncollectible.
(a) Prepare the journal entry to record the estimated uncollectibles.
(b) Prepare the current assets section of the balance sheet for Energy Company. Assume that in addition to the receivables it has cash of $90,000, inventory of $118,000, and prepaid insurance of $7,500.

Prepare entry for allowance method and partial balance sheet.

(LO 3, 9)

BE8-4 At the end of 2014, Endrun Co. has accounts receivable of $700,000 and an allowance for doubtful accounts of $54,000. On January 24, 2015, the company learns that its receivable from Marcello is not collectible, and management authorizes a write-off of $6,200.
(a) Prepare the journal entry to record the write-off.
(b) What is the cash realizable value of the accounts receivable (1) before the write-off and (2) after the write-off?

Prepare entry for write-off; determine cash realizable value.

(LO 3)

Prepare entries for collection of bad debt write-off.
(LO 3)

BE8-5 Assume the same information as BE8-4. On March 4, 2015, Endrun Co. receives payment of $6,200 in full from Marcello. Prepare the journal entries to record this transaction.

Prepare entry using percentage-of-sales method.
(LO 3)

BE8-6 Hamblin Co. elects to use the percentage-of-sales basis in 2014 to record bad debt expense. It estimates that 2% of net credit sales will become uncollectible. Sales revenues are $800,000 for 2014, sales returns and allowances are $38,000, and the allowance for doubtful accounts has a credit balance of $9,000. Prepare the adjusting entry to record bad debt expense in 2014.

Prepare entry using percentage-of-receivables method.
(LO 3)

BE8-7 Gleason Co. uses the percentage-of-receivables basis to record bad debt expense. It estimates that 1% of accounts receivable will become uncollectible. Accounts receivable are $420,000 at the end of the year, and the allowance for doubtful accounts has a credit balance of $1,500.
(a) Prepare the adjusting journal entry to record bad debt expense for the year.
(b) If the allowance for doubtful accounts had a debit balance of $740 instead of a credit balance of $1,500, determine the amount to be reported for bad debt expense.

Prepare entries to dispose of accounts receivable.
(LO 4)

BE8-8 Presented below are two independent transactions.
(a) Fiesta Restaurant accepted a Visa card in payment of a $175 lunch bill. The bank charges a 4% fee. What entry should Fiesta make?
(b) St. Charles Company sold its accounts receivable of $70,000. What entry should St. Charles make, given a service charge of 3% on the amount of receivables sold?

Compute interest and determine maturity dates on notes.
(LO 5)

BE8-9 Compute interest and find the maturity date for the following notes.

	Date of Note	Principal	Interest Rate (%)	Terms
(a)	June 10	$80,000	6%	60 days
(b)	July 14	$64,000	7%	90 days
(c)	April 27	$12,000	8%	75 days

Determine maturity dates and compute interest and rates on notes.
(LO 5)

BE8-10 Presented below are data on three promissory notes. Determine the missing amounts.

	Date of Note	Terms	Maturity Date	Principal	Annual Interest Rate	Total Interest
(a)	April 1	60 days	?	$600,000	5%	?
(b)	July 2	30 days	?	90,000	?	$600
(c)	March 7	6 months	?	120,000	10%	?

Prepare entry for notes receivable exchanged for account receivable.
(LO 6)

BE8-11 On January 10, 2014, Wilfer Co. sold merchandise on account to Elgin Co. for $11,600, n/30. On February 9, Elgin Co. gave Wilfer Co. a 9% promissory note in settlement of this account. Prepare the journal entry to record the sale and the settlement of the account receivable.

Compute ratios to analyze receivables.
(LO 9)

BE8-12 The financial statements of Minnesota Mining and Manufacturing Company (3M) report net sales of $20.0 billion. Accounts receivable (net) are $2.7 billion at the beginning of the year and $2.8 billion at the end of the year. Compute 3M's accounts receivable turnover ratio. Compute 3M's average collection period for accounts receivable in days.

> DO IT! REVIEW

Prepare entry for uncollectible accounts.
(LO 3)

DO IT! **8-1** Todd Company has been in business several years. At the end of the current year, the ledger shows:

Accounts Receivable	$ 310,000 Dr.
Sales Revenue	2,200,000 Cr.
Allowance for Doubtful Accounts	4,700 Cr.

Bad debts are estimated to be 5% of receivables. Prepare the entry to adjust Allowance for Doubtful Accounts.

DO IT! **8-2** Paltrow Distributors is a growing company whose ability to raise capital has not been growing as quickly as its expanding assets and sales. Paltrow's local banker has indicated that the company cannot increase its borrowing for the foreseeable future. Paltrow's suppliers are demanding payment for goods acquired within 30 days of the invoice date, but Paltrow's customers are slow in paying for their purchases (60–90 days). As a result, Paltrow has a cash flow problem.

Prepare entry for factored accounts.

(LO 4)

Paltrow needs $160,000 to cover next Friday's payroll. Its balance of outstanding accounts receivable totals $1,000,000. What might Paltrow do to alleviate this cash crunch? Record the entry that Paltrow would make when it raises the needed cash. (Assume a 3% service charge.)

DO IT! **8-3** Karbon Wholesalers accepts from Bazaar Stores a $6,200, 4-month, 9% note dated May 31 in settlement of Bazaar's overdue account. (a) What is the maturity date of the note? (b) What is the entry made by Karbon at the maturity date, assuming Bazaar pays the note and interest in full at that time?

Prepare entries for notes receivable.

(LO 5, 8)

DO IT! **8-4** In 2014, Lauren Company has net credit sales of $1,480,000 for the year. It had a beginning accounts receivable (net) balance of $112,000 and an ending accounts receivable (net) balance of $108,000. Compute Lauren Company's (a) accounts receivable turnover and (b) average collection period in days.

Compute ratios for receivables.

(LO 9)

 ✔ **The Navigator**

EXERCISES

E8-1 Presented below are selected transactions of Menge Company. Menge sells in large quantities to other companies and also sells its product in a small retail outlet.

Journalize entries related to accounts receivable.

(LO 2)

March	1	Sold merchandise on account to Lynda Company for $3,800, terms 2/10, n/30.
	3	Lynda Company returned merchandise worth $500 to Menge.
	9	Menge collected the amount due from Lynda Company from the March 1 sale.
	15	Menge sold merchandise for $200 in its retail outlet. The customer used his Menge credit card.
	31	Menge added 1.5% monthly interest to the customer's credit card balance.

Instructions
Prepare journal entries for the transactions above.

E8-2 Presented below are two independent situations.

Journalize entries for recognizing accounts receivable.

(LO 2)

(a) On January 6, Bennett Co. sells merchandise on account to Jackie Inc. for $7,000, terms 2/10, n/30. On January 16, Jackie Inc. pays the amount due. Prepare the entries on Bennett's books to record the sale and related collection.

(b) On January 10, Connor Bybee uses his Sheridan Co. credit card to purchase merchandise from Sheridan Co. for $9,000. On February 10, Bybee is billed for the amount due of $9,000. On February 12, Bybee pays $6,000 on the balance due. On March 10, Bybee is billed for the amount due, including interest at 2% per month on the unpaid balance as of February 12. Prepare the entries on Sheridan Co.'s books related to the transactions that occurred on January 10, February 12, and March 10.

E8-3 The ledger of Elburn Company at the end of the current year shows Accounts Receivable $110,000, Sales Revenue $840,000, and Sales Returns and Allowances $28,000.

Journalize entries to record allowance for doubtful accounts using two different bases.

(LO 3)

Instructions
(a) If Elburn uses the direct write-off method to account for uncollectible accounts, journalize the adjusting entry at December 31, assuming Elburn determines that T. Thum's $1,400 balance is uncollectible.

(b) If Allowance for Doubtful Accounts has a credit balance of $2,100 in the trial balance, journalize the adjusting entry at December 31, assuming bad debts are expected to be (1) 1% of net sales, and (2) 10% of accounts receivable.

(c) If Allowance for Doubtful Accounts has a debit balance of $200 in the trial balance, journalize the adjusting entry at December 31, assuming bad debts are expected to be (1) 0.75% of net sales and (2) 6% of accounts receivable.

Determine bad debt expense; prepare the adjusting entry for bad debt expense.

(LO 3)

E8-4 Leland Company has accounts receivable of $98,100 at March 31. An analysis of the accounts shows the following information.

Month of Sale	Balance, March 31
March	$65,000
February	17,600
January	8,500
Prior to January	7,000
	$98,100

Credit terms are 2/10, n/30. At March 31, Allowance for Doubtful Accounts has a credit balance of $900 prior to adjustment. The company uses the percentage-of-receivables basis for estimating uncollectible accounts. The company's estimate of bad debts is shown below.

Age of Accounts	Estimated Percentage Uncollectible
1–30 days	2.0%
31–60 days	5.0%
61–90 days	30.0%
Over 90 days	50.0%

Instructions
(a) Determine the total estimated uncollectibles.
(b) Prepare the adjusting entry at March 31 to record bad debt expense.

Journalize write-off and recovery.

(LO 3)

E8-5 At December 31, 2013, Crawford Company had a balance of $15,000 in Allowance for Doubtful Accounts. During 2014, Crawford wrote off accounts totaling $14,100. One of those accounts ($1,800) was later collected. At December 31, 2014, an aging schedule indicated that the balance in Allowance for Doubtful Accounts should be $19,000.

Instructions
Prepare journal entries to record the 2014 transactions of Crawford Company.

Journalize percentage-of-sales basis, write-off, recovery.

(LO 3)

E8-6 On December 31, 2013, Russell Co. estimated that 2% of its net sales of $360,000 will become uncollectible. The company recorded this amount as an addition to Allowance for Doubtful Accounts. On May 11, 2014, Russell Co. determined that the B. Vetter account was uncollectible and wrote off $1,100. On June 12, 2014, Vetter paid the amount previously written off.

Instructions
Prepare the journal entries on December 31, 2013, May 11, 2014, and June 12, 2014.

Journalize entries for the sale of accounts receivable.

(LO 4)

E8-7 Presented below are two independent situations.

(a) On March 3, Hinckley Appliances sells $620,000 of its receivables to Universal Factors Inc. Universal Factors assesses a finance charge of 3% of the amount of receivables sold. Prepare the entry on Hinckley Appliances' books to record the sale of the receivables.
(b) On May 10, Cody Company sold merchandise for $3,500 and accepted the customer's America Bank MasterCard. America Bank charges a 5% service charge for credit card sales. Prepare the entry on Cody Company's books to record the sale of merchandise.

Journalize entries for credit card sales.

(LO 4)

E8-8 Presented below are two independent situations.

(a) On April 2, Julie Keiser uses her JCPenney Company credit card to purchase merchandise from a JCPenney store for $1,500. On May 1, Keiser is billed for the $1,500 amount due. Keiser pays $900 on the balance due on May 3. On June 1, Keiser receives a bill for the amount due, including interest at 1.0% per month on the unpaid balance as of May 3. Prepare the entries on JCPenney Co.'s books related to the transactions that occurred on April 2, May 3, and June 1.
(b) On July 4, Avalon Restaurant accepts a Visa card for a $200 dinner bill. Visa charges a 3% service fee. Prepare the entry on Avalon's books related to this transaction.

E8-9 Burtonville Stores accepts both its own and national credit cards. During the year, the following selected summary transactions occurred.

Jan. 15 Made Burtonville credit card sales totaling $18,000. (There were no balances prior to January 15.)
20 Made Visa credit card sales (service charge fee 2%) totaling $4,800.
Feb. 10 Collected $10,000 on Burtonville credit card sales.
15 Added finance charges of 1.5% to Burtonville credit card account balances.

Journalize credit card sales, and indicate the statement presentation of financing charges and service charge expense.

(LO 4)

Instructions
(a) Journalize the transactions for Burtonville Stores.
(b) Indicate the statement presentation of the financing charges and the credit card service charge expense for Burtonville Stores.

E8-10 Reeves Supply Co. has the following transactions related to notes receivable during the last 2 months of 2014.

Nov. 1 Loaned $15,000 cash to Norma Jeanne on a 1-year, 9% note.
Dec. 11 Sold goods to Bob Sharbo, Inc., receiving a $6,750, 90-day, 8% note.
16 Received a $4,400, 6-month, 12% note in exchange for Richard Russo's outstanding accounts receivable.
31 Accrued interest revenue on all notes receivable.

Journalize entries for notes receivable transactions.

(LO 5, 6)

Instructions
(a) Journalize the transactions for Reeves Supply Co.
(b) Record the collection of the Jeanne note at its maturity in 2015.

E8-11 Record the following transactions for Taylor Co. in the general journal.

2014

May 1 Received a $7,500, 1-year, 9% note in exchange for Len Monroe's outstanding accounts receivable.
Dec. 31 Accrued interest on the Monroe note.
Dec. 31 Closed the interest revenue account.

Journalize entries for notes receivable.

(LO 5, 6)

2015

May 1 Received principal plus interest on the Monroe note. (No interest has been accrued in 2015.)

E8-12 Bieber Company had the following select transactions.

May 1, 2014 Accepted Crane Company's 1-year, 12% note in settlement of a $16,000 account receivable.
July 1, 2014 Loaned $25,000 cash to Sam Howard on a 9-month, 10% note.
Dec. 31, 2014 Accrued interest on all notes receivable.
Apr. 1, 2015 Sam Howard dishonored its note; Bieber expects it will eventually collect.
May 1, 2015 Received principal plus interest on the Crane note.

Prepare entries for note receivable transactions.

(LO 5, 6, 8)

Instructions
Prepare journal entries to record the transactions. Bieber prepares adjusting entries once a year on December 31.

E8-13 On May 2, Ottawa Company lends $7,600 to Cortland, Inc., issuing a 6-month, 8% note. At the maturity date, November 2, Cortland indicates that it cannot pay.

Journalize entries for dishonor of notes receivable.

(LO 5, 8)

Instructions
(a) Prepare the entry to record the issuance of the note.
(b) Prepare the entry to record the dishonor of the note, assuming that Ottawa Company expects collection will occur.
(c) Prepare the entry to record the dishonor of the note, assuming that Ottawa Company does not expect collection in the future.

E8-14 Lashkova Company had accounts receivable of $100,000 on January 1, 2014. The only transactions that affected accounts receivable during 2014 were net credit sales of $1,000,000, cash collections of $920,000, and accounts written off of $30,000.

Compute accounts receivable turnover and average collection period.

(LO 9)

Instructions
(a) Compute the ending balance of accounts receivable.
(b) Compute the accounts receivable turnover ratio for 2014.
(c) Compute the average collection period in days.

EXERCISES: SET B AND CHALLENGE EXERCISES

Visit the book's companion website, at **www.wiley.com/college/weygandt**, and choose the Student Companion site to access Exercise Set B and Challenge Exercises.

PROBLEMS: SET A

Prepare journal entries related to bad debt expense.

(LO 2, 3, 9)

P8-1A At December 31, 2013, Dean Co. reported the following information on its balance sheet.

Accounts receivable	$960,000
Less: Allowance for doubtful accounts	70,000

During 2014, the company had the following transactions related to receivables.

1. Sales on account	$3,315,000
2. Sales returns and allowances	50,000
3. Collections of accounts receivable	2,810,000
4. Write-offs of accounts receivable deemed uncollectible	90,000
5. Recovery of bad debts previously written off as uncollectible	29,000

Instructions

(a) Prepare the journal entries to record each of these five transactions. Assume that no cash discounts were taken on the collections of accounts receivable.

(b) Accounts receivable $1,325,000
ADA $9,000

(b) Enter the January 1, 2014, balances in Accounts Receivable and Allowance for Doubtful Accounts, post the entries to the two accounts (use T-accounts), and determine the balances.

(c) Bad debt expense $116,000

(c) Prepare the journal entry to record bad debt expense for 2014, assuming that an aging of accounts receivable indicates that expected bad debts are $125,000.

(d) Compute the accounts receivable turnover ratio for 2014.

Compute bad debt amounts.

(LO 3)

P8-2A Information related to Hamilton Company for 2014 is summarized below.

Total credit sales	$2,500,000
Accounts receivable at December 31	970,000
Bad debts written off	66,000

Instructions

(a) What amount of bad debt expense will Hamilton Company report if it uses the direct write-off method of accounting for bad debts?

(b) Assume that Hamilton Company estimates its bad debt expense to be 3% of credit sales. What amount of bad debt expense will Hamilton record if it has an Allowance for Doubtful Accounts credit balance of $4,000?

(c) Assume that Hamilton Company estimates its bad debt expense based on 7% of accounts receivable. What amount of bad debt expense will Hamilton record if it has an Allowance for Doubtful Accounts credit balance of $3,000?

(d) Assume the same facts as in (c), except that there is a $3,000 debit balance in Allowance for Doubtful Accounts. What amount of bad debt expense will Hamilton record?

(e) ◻▭▭▶ What is the weakness of the direct write-off method of reporting bad debt expense?

P8-3A Presented below is an aging schedule for Sycamore Company.

Journalize entries to record transactions related to bad debts.

(LO 2, 3)

			Worksheet.xls				
Home	Insert	Page Layout	Formulas	Data	Review	View	

| | P18 | | fx | | | | |

	A	B	C	D	E	F	G
1				**Number of Days Past Due**			
2	**Customer**	**Total**	**Not Yet Due**	**1–30**	**31–60**	**61–90**	**Over 90**
3							
4	Anders	$ 28,000		$12,000	$16,000		
5	Blake	40,000	$ 40,000				
6	Cyrs	57,000	16,000	6,000		$35,000	
7	De Jong	34,000					$34,000
8	Others	132,000	96,000	16,000	14,000		6,000
9		$291,000	$152,000	$34,000	$30,000	$35,000	$40,000
10	Estimated percentage uncollectible		2%	6%	13%	25%	60%
11	Total estimated bad debts	$ 41,730	$ 3,040	$ 2,040	$ 3,900	$ 8,750	$24,000
12							

At December 31, 2014, the unadjusted balance in Allowance for Doubtful Accounts is a credit of $9,000.

Instructions

(a) Journalize and post the adjusting entry for bad debts at December 31, 2014.

(b) Journalize and post to the allowance account the following events and transactions in the year 2015.

   (1) On March 31, a $1,000 customer balance originating in 2014 is judged uncollectible.

   (2) On May 31, a check for $1,000 is received from the customer whose account was written off as uncollectible on March 31.

(c) Journalize the adjusting entry for bad debts on December 31, 2015, assuming that the unadjusted balance in Allowance for Doubtful Accounts is a debit of $800 and the aging schedule indicates that total estimated bad debts will be $31,600.

(a) Bad debt expense $32,730

(c) Bad debt expense $32,400

P8-4A Mineo Inc. uses the allowance method to estimate uncollectible accounts receivable. The company produced the following aging of the accounts receivable at year-end.

Journalize transactions related to bad debts.

(LO 2, 3)

			Worksheet.xls				
Home	Insert	Page Layout	Formulas	Data	Review	View	

| | P18 | | fx | | | | |

	A	B	C	D	E	F	G
1			**Number of Days Outstanding**				
2		**Total**	**0–30**	**31–60**	**61–90**	**91–120**	**Over 120**
3							
4	Accounts receivable	193,000	70,000	46,000	39,000	23,000	$15,000
5	% uncollectible		1%	3%	5%	8%	10%
6	Estimated bad debts						
7							

Instructions

(a) Calculate the total estimated bad debts based on the above information.

(b) Prepare the year-end adjusting journal entry to record the bad debts using the aged uncollectible accounts receivable determined in (a). Assume the current balance in Allowance for Doubtful Accounts is a $3,000 debit.

(c) Of the above accounts, $5,000 is determined to be specifically uncollectible. Prepare the journal entry to write off the uncollectible account.

(a) Tot. est. bad debts $7,370

(d) The company collects $5,000 subsequently on a specific account that had previously been determined to be uncollectible in (c). Prepare the journal entry(ies) necessary to restore the account and record the cash collection.

(e) Comment on how your answers to (a)–(d) would change if Mineo Inc. used 3% of *total* accounts receivable, rather than aging the accounts receivable. What are the advantages to the company of aging the accounts receivable rather than applying a percentage to total accounts receivable?

Journalize entries to record transactions related to bad debts.

(LO 3)

P8-5A At December 31, 2014, the trial balance of Roberto Company contained the following amounts before adjustment.

	Debits	**Credits**
Accounts Receivable	$385,000	
Allowance for Doubtful Accounts		$ 800
Sales Revenue		918,000

Instructions

(a) Based on the information given, which method of accounting for bad debts is Roberto Company using—the direct write-off method or the allowance method? How can you tell?

(b) Prepare the adjusting entry at December 31, 2014, for bad debt expense under each of the following independent assumptions.

(1) An aging schedule indicates that $11,750 of accounts receivable will be uncollectible.

(2) The company estimates that 1% of sales will be uncollectible.

(b) (2) $9,180

(c) Repeat part (b) assuming that instead of a credit balance there is an $800 debit balance in Allowance for Doubtful Accounts.

(d) During the next month, January 2015, a $3,000 account receivable is written off as uncollectible. Prepare the journal entry to record the write-off.

(e) Repeat part (d) assuming that Roberto uses the direct write-off method instead of the allowance method in accounting for uncollectible accounts receivable.

(f) What type of account is Allowance for Doubtful Accounts? How does it affect how accounts receivable is reported on the balance sheet at the end of the accounting period?

Prepare entries for various notes receivable transactions.

(LO 2, 4, 5, 8, 9)

GLS

P8-6A Hilo Company closes its books monthly. On September 30, selected ledger account balances are:

Notes Receivable	$31,000
Interest Receivable	170

Notes Receivable include the following.

Date	Maker	Face	Term	Interest
Aug. 16	Demaster Inc.	$ 8,000	60 days	8%
Aug. 25	Skinner Co.	9,000	60 days	10%
Sept. 30	Almer Corp.	14,000	6 months	9%

Interest is computed using a 360-day year. During October, the following transactions were completed.

Oct.	7	Made sales of $6,300 on Hilo credit cards.
	12	Made sales of $1,200 on MasterCard credit cards. The credit card service charge is 3%.
	15	Added $460 to Hilo customer balance for finance charges on unpaid balances.
	15	Received payment in full from Demaster Inc. on the amount due.
	24	Received notice that the Skinner note has been dishonored. (Assume that Skinner is expected to pay in the future.)

Instructions

(a) Journalize the October transactions and the October 31 adjusting entry for accrued interest receivable.

(b) Accounts receivable
$15,910

(b) Enter the balances at October 1 in the receivable accounts. Post the entries to all of the receivable accounts.

(c) Total receivables $30,015

(c) Show the balance sheet presentation of the receivable accounts at October 31.

P8-7A On January 1, 2014, Derek Company had Accounts Receivable $139,000, Notes Receivable $30,000, and Allowance for Doubtful Accounts $13,200. The note receivable is from Kaye Noonan Company. It is a 4-month, 12% note dated December 31, 2013. Derek Company prepares financial statements annually. During the year, the following selected transactions occurred.

Prepare entries for various receivable transactions.

(LO 2, 4, 5, 6, 7, 8)

Jan. 5 Sold $24,000 of merchandise to Zwingle Company, terms n/15.
  20 Accepted Zwingle Company's $24,000, 3-month, 9% note for balance due.
Feb. 18 Sold $8,000 of merchandise to Gerard Company and accepted Gerard's $8,000, 6-month, 8% note for the amount due.
Apr. 20 Collected Zwingle Company note in full.
  30 Received payment in full from Kaye Noonan Company on the amount due.
May 25 Accepted Isabella Inc.'s $4,000, 3-month, 7% note in settlement of a past-due balance on account.
Aug. 18 Received payment in full from Gerard Company on note due.
  25 The Isabella Inc. note was dishonored. Isabella Inc. is not bankrupt; future payment is anticipated.
Sept. 1 Sold $12,000 of merchandise to Fernando Company and accepted a $12,000, 6-month, 10% note for the amount due.

Instructions
Journalize the transactions.

PROBLEMS: SET B

P8-1B At December 31, 2013, Globe Trotter Imports reported the following information on its balance sheet.

Prepare journal entries related to bad debt expense.

(LO 2, 3, 9)

Accounts receivable	$220,000
Less: Allowance for doubtful accounts	15,000

During 2014, the company had the following transactions related to receivables.

1. Sales on account	$2,400,000
2. Sales returns and allowances	45,000
3. Collections of accounts receivable	2,250,000
4. Write-offs of accounts receivable deemed uncollectible	13,000
5. Recovery of bad debts previously written off as uncollectible	2,000

Instructions
(a) Prepare the journal entries to record each of these five transactions. Assume that no cash discounts were taken on the collections of accounts receivable.
(b) Enter the January 1, 2014, balances in Accounts Receivable and Allowance for Doubtful Accounts. Post the entries to the two accounts (use T-accounts), and determine the balances.
(c) Prepare the journal entry to record bad debt expense for 2014, assuming that an aging of accounts receivable indicates that estimated bad debts are $22,000.
(d) Compute the accounts receivable turnover ratio for the year 2014.

(b) Accounts receivable
$312,000
ADA $4,000
(c) Bad debt expense
$18,000

P8-2B Information related to Shin Company for 2014 is summarized below.

Compute bad debt amounts.

(LO 3)

Total credit sales	$920,000
Accounts receivable at December 31	369,000
Bad debts written off	23,400

Instructions
(a) What amount of bad debt expense will Shin Company report if it uses the direct write-off method of accounting for bad debts?
(b) Assume that Shin Company decides to estimate its bad debt expense to be 3% of credit sales. What amount of bad debt expense will Shin record if Allowance for Doubtful Accounts has a credit balance of $3,000?

(c) Assume that Shin Company decides to estimate its bad debt expense based on 7% of accounts receivable. What amount of bad debt expense will Shin Company record if Allowance for Doubtful Accounts has a credit balance of $4,000?

(d) Assume the same facts as in (c), except that there is a $2,000 debit balance in Allowance for Doubtful Accounts. What amount of bad debt expense will Shin record?

(e) ▱▱▱▱▶ What is the weakness of the direct write-off method of reporting bad debt expense?

Journalize entries to record transactions related to bad debts.

(LO 2, 3)

P8-3B Presented below is an aging schedule for Garry Owen Company.

				Number of Days Past Due			
Customer	Total	Not Yet Due	1–30	31–60	61–90	Over 90
Alma	$ 26,000		$11,500	$14,500		
Browne	45,000	$ 45,000				
Conlon	75,000	22,500	7,500		$45,000	
Dalton	57,000					$57,000
Others	189,000	138,000	22,500	19,500		9,000
	$392,000	$205,500	$41,500	$34,000	$45,000	$66,000
Estimated percentage uncollectible		2%	6%	10%	25%	50%
Total estimated bad debts	$ 54,250	$ 4,110	$ 2,490	$ 3,400	$11,250	$33,000

At December 31, 2014, the unadjusted balance in Allowance for Doubtful Accounts is a credit of $14,000.

Instructions

(a) Bad debt expense $40,250

(a) Journalize and post the adjusting entry for bad debts at December 31, 2014.

(b) Journalize and post to the allowance account the following events and transactions in the year 2015.

    (1) March 1, a $1,900 customer balance originating in 2014 is judged uncollectible.

    (2) May 1, a check for $1,900 is received from the customer whose account was written off as uncollectible on March 1.

(c) Bad debt expense $45,700

(c) Journalize the adjusting entry for bad debts on December 31, 2015. Assume that the unadjusted balance in Allowance for Doubtful Accounts is a debit of $3,400, and the aging schedule indicates that total estimated bad debts will be $42,300.

Journalize transactions related to bad debts.

(LO 2, 3)

P8-4B The following represents selected information taken from a company's aging schedule to estimate uncollectible accounts receivable at year-end.

		Number of Days Outstanding				
	Total	0–30	31–60	61–90	91–120	Over 120
Accounts receivable	$383,000	$220,000	$90,000	$40,000	$18,000	$15,000
% uncollectible		1%	3%	5%	8%	10%
Estimated bad debts						

Instructions

(a) Calculate the total estimated bad debts based on the above information.

(b) Prepare the year-end adjusting journal entry to record the bad debts using the allowance method and the aged uncollectible accounts receivable determined in (a). Assume the current balance in Allowance for Doubtful Accounts is a $1,600 credit.

(c) Of the above accounts, $1,100 is determined to be specifically uncollectible. Prepare the journal entry to write off the uncollectible accounts.

(d) The company subsequently collects $700 on a specific account that had previously been determined to be uncollectible in (c). Prepare the journal entry(ies) necessary to restore the account and record the cash collection.

(e) Explain how establishing an allowance account satisfies the expense recognition principle.

(a) Tot. est. bad debts $9,840

P8-5B At December 31, 2014, the trial balance of Mariette Company contained the following amounts before adjustment.

Journalize entries to record transactions related to bad debts.

(LO 3)

	Debits	**Credits**
Accounts Receivable	$250,000	
Allowance for Doubtful Accounts		$ 1,400
Sales Revenue		600,000

Instructions

(a) Prepare the adjusting entry at December 31, 2014, to record bad debt expense under each of the following independent assumptions.

   (1) An aging schedule indicates that $13,800 of accounts receivable will be uncollectible.

   (2) The company estimates that 2% of sales will be uncollectible.

(a) (2) $12,000

(b) Repeat part (a) assuming that instead of a credit balance, there is a $1,400 debit balance in Allowance for Doubtful Accounts.

(c) During the next month, January 2015, a $3,200 account receivable is written off as uncollectible. Prepare the journal entry to record the write-off.

(d) Repeat part (c) assuming that Mariette Company uses the direct write-off method instead of the allowance method in accounting for uncollectible accounts receivable.

(e) ▭▭▭▭▶ What are the advantages of using the allowance method in accounting for uncollectible accounts as compared to the direct write-off method?

P8-6B Gehrig Co. closes its books monthly. On June 30, selected ledger account balances are:

Prepare entries for various notes receivable transactions.

(LO 2, 4, 5, 8, 9)

Notes Receivable	$60,000
Interest Receivable	435

Notes Receivable include the following.

Date	Maker	Face	Term	Interest
May 16	Fulton Inc.	$12,000	60 days	9%
May 25	Ascot Co.	30,000	60 days	10%
June 30	Trayer Corp.	18,000	6 months	12%

During July, the following transactions were completed.

July 5	Made sales of $7,200 on Gehrig Co. credit cards.
14	Made sales of $1,300 on Visa credit cards. The credit card service charge is 3%.
14	Added $510 to Gehrig Co. credit card customer balances for finance charges on unpaid balances.
15	Received payment in full from Fulton Inc. on the amount due.
24	Received notice that the Ascot Co. note has been dishonored. (Assume that Ascot Co. is expected to pay in the future.)

Instructions

(a) Journalize the July transactions and the July 31 adjusting entry for accrued interest receivable. (Interest is computed using 360 days.)

(b) Enter the balances at July 1 in the receivable accounts. Post the entries to all of the receivable accounts.

(c) Show the balance sheet presentation of the receivable accounts at July 31.

(b) Accounts receivable $38,210

(c) Total receivables $56,390

Prepare entries for various
receivable transactions.

(LO 2, 4, 5, 6, 7, 8)

P8-7B On January 1, 2014, Valdez Company had Accounts Receivable $91,000 and Allowance for Doubtful Accounts $8,100. Valdez Company prepares financial statements annually. During the year, the following selected transactions occurred.

Jan. 5 Sold $8,400 of merchandise to Patrick Company, terms n/30.
Feb. 2 Accepted a $8,400, 4-month, 10% promissory note from Patrick Company for the balance due.
      12 Sold $13,500 of merchandise to Marguerite Company and accepted Marguerite's $13,500, 2-month, 10% note for the balance due.
      26 Sold $7,000 of merchandise to Felton Co., terms n/10.
Apr. 5 Accepted a $7,000, 3-month, 8% note from Felton Co. for the balance due.
      12 Collected Marguerite Company note in full.
June 2 Collected Patrick Company note in full.
July 5 Felton Co. dishonors its note of April 5. It is expected that Felton will eventually pay the amount owed.
      15 Sold $14,000 of merchandise to Planke Co. and accepted Planke's $14,000, 3-month, 12% note for the amount due.
Oct. 15 Planke Co.'s note was dishonored. Planke Co. is bankrupt, and there is no hope of future settlement.

Instructions
Journalize the transactions.

PROBLEMS: SET C

Visit the book's companion website, at **www.wiley.com/college/weygandt**, and choose the Student Companion site to access Problem Set C.

COMPREHENSIVE PROBLEM

CP8 Victoria Company's balance sheet at December 31, 2013, is presented below.

Victoria Company
Balance Sheet
December 31, 2013

Cash	$13,100	Accounts payable	$ 8,750
Accounts receivable	19,780	Common stock	20,000
Allowance for doubtful accounts	(800)	Retained earnings	12,730
Inventory	9,400		$41,480
	$41,480		

During January 2014, the following transactions occurred. Victoria uses the perpetual inventory method.

Jan. 1 Victoria accepted a 4-month, 8% note from Leon Company in payment of Leon's $1,500 account.
      3 Victoria wrote off as uncollectible the accounts of Barker Corporation ($450) and Elmo Company ($330).
      8 Victoria purchased $17,200 of inventory on account.
      11 Victoria sold for $25,000 on account inventory that cost $17,500.
      15 Victoria sold inventory that cost $780 to Joe Haribo for $1,200. Haribo charged this amount on his Visa First Bank card. The service fee charged Victoria by First Bank is 3%.
      17 Victoria collected $22,900 from customers on account.
      21 Victoria paid $16,300 on accounts payable.

24   Victoria received payment in full ($330) from Elmo Company on the account written off on January 3.
27   Victoria purchased advertising supplies for $1,400 cash.
31   Victoria paid other operating expenses, $3,218.

Adjustment data:

1. Interest is recorded for the month on the note from January 1.
2. Bad debts are expected to be 5% of the January 31, 2014, accounts receivable.
3. A count of advertising supplies on January 31, 2014, reveals that $470 remains unused.

Instructions
(You may want to set up T-accounts to determine ending balances.)

(a) Prepare journal entries for the transactions listed above and adjusting entries. (Include entries for cost of goods sold using the perpetual system.)
(b) Prepare an adjusted trial balance at January 31, 2014.
(c) Prepare an income statement and a retained earnings statement for the month ending January 31, 2014, and a classified balance sheet as of January 31, 2014.

CONTINUING COOKIE CHRONICLE

(*Note:* This is a continuation of the Cookie Chronicle from Chapters 1–7.)

CCC8 One of Natalie's friends, Curtis Lesperance, runs a coffee shop where he sells specialty coffees and prepares and sells muffins and cookies. He is eager to buy one of Natalie's fine European mixers, which would enable him to make larger batches of muffins and cookies. However, Curtis cannot afford to pay for the mixer for at least 30 days. He asks Natalie if she would be willing to sell him the mixer on credit. Natalie comes to you for advice.

Go to the book's companion website, www.wiley.com/college/weygandt, to see the completion of this problem.

Broadening Your PERSPECTIVE

Financial Reporting and Analysis

Financial Reporting Problem: CAF Company

BYP8-1 CAF Company sells office equipment and supplies to many organizations in the city and surrounding area on contract terms of 2/10, n/30. In the past, over 75% of the credit customers have taken advantage of the discount by paying within 10 days of the invoice date.

The number of customers taking the full 30 days to pay has increased within the last year. Current indications are that less than 60% of the customers are now taking the discount. Bad debts as a percentage of gross credit sales have risen from the 2.5% provided in past years to about 4.5% in the current year.

The company's Finance Committee has requested more information on the collections of accounts receivable. The controller responded to this request with the report reproduced below.

CAF Company
Accounts Receivable Collections
May 31, 2014

The fact that some credit accounts will prove uncollectible is normal. Annual bad debt write-offs have been 2.5% of gross credit sales over the past 5 years. During the last fiscal year, this percentage increased to slightly less than 4.5%. The current Accounts Receivable balance is $1,400,000. The condition of this balance in terms of age and probability of collection is as follows.

Proportion of Total	Age Categories	Probability of Collection
60%	not yet due	98%
22%	less than 30 days past due	96%
9%	30 to 60 days past due	94%
5%	61 to 120 days past due	91%
$2\frac{1}{2}\%$	121 to 180 days past due	75%
$1\frac{1}{2}\%$	over 180 days past due	30%

Allowance for Doubtful Accounts had a credit balance of $29,500 on June 1, 2013. CAF has provided for a monthly bad debt expense accrual during the current fiscal year based on the assumption that 4.5% of gross credit sales will be uncollectible. Total gross credit sales for the 2013–2014 fiscal year amounted to $2,800,000. Write-offs of bad accounts during the year totaled $102,000.

Instructions

(a) Prepare an accounts receivable aging schedule for CAF Company using the age categories identified in the controller's report to the Finance Committee showing the following.

   (1) The amount of accounts receivable outstanding for each age category and in total.

   (2) The estimated amount that is uncollectible for each category and in total.

(b) Compute the amount of the year-end adjustment necessary to bring Allowance for Doubtful Accounts to the balance indicated by the age analysis. Then prepare the necessary journal entry to adjust the accounting records.

(c) In a recessionary environment with tight credit and high interest rates:

   (1) Identify steps CAF Company might consider to improve the accounts receivable situation.

   (2) Then evaluate each step identified in terms of the risks and costs involved.

Comparative Analysis Problem: PepsiCo, Inc. vs. The Coca-Cola Company

BYP8-2 PepsiCo, Inc.'s financial statements are presented in Appendix A. Financial statements of The Coca-Cola Company are presented in Appendix B.

Instructions

(a) Based on the information in these financial statements, compute the following 2010 ratios for each company. (Assume all sales are credit sales and that PepsiCo's receivables on its balance sheet are all trade receivables.)

   (1) Accounts receivable turnover ratio.

   (2) Average collection period for receivables.

(b) What conclusions about managing accounts receivable can you draw from these data?

Real-World Focus

BYP8-3 *Purpose:* To learn more about factoring from websites that provide factoring services.

Address: www.ccapital.net, or go to www.wiley.com/college/weygandt

Steps: Go to the website, click on **invoice Factoring**, and answer the following questions.

(a) What are some of the benefits of factoring?

(b) What is the range of the percentages of the typical discount rate?

(c) If a company factors its receivables, what percentage of the value of the receivables can it expect to receive from the factor in the form of cash, and how quickly will it receive the cash?

Critical Thinking

Decision-Making Across the Organization

BYP8-4 Hilda and Tim Piwek own Campus Fashions. From its inception, Campus Fashions has sold merchandise on either a cash or credit basis, but no credit cards have been accepted. During the past several months, the Piweks have begun to question their sales policies. First, they have lost

some sales because of refusing to accept credit cards. Second, representatives of two metropolitan banks have been persuasive in almost convincing them to accept their national credit cards. One bank, City National Bank, has stated that its credit card fee is 4%.

The Piweks decide that they should determine the cost of carrying their own credit sales. From the accounting records of the past 3 years, they accumulate the following data.

	2014	2013	2012
Net credit sales	$500,000	$650,000	$400,000
Collection agency fees for slow-paying customers	2,450	2,500	2,300
Salary of part-time accounts receivable clerk	4,100	4,100	4,100

Credit and collection expenses as a percentage of net credit sales are uncollectible accounts 1.6%, billing and mailing costs 0.5%, and credit investigation fee on new customers 0.15%.

Hilda and Tim also determine that the average accounts receivable balance outstanding during the year is 5% of net credit sales. The Piweks estimate that they could earn an average of 8% annually on cash invested in other business opportunities.

Instructions
With the class divided into groups, answer the following.
(a) Prepare a table showing, for each year, total credit and collection expenses in dollars and as a percentage of net credit sales.
(b) Determine the net credit and collection expense in dollars and as a percentage of sales after considering the revenue not earned from other investment opportunities.
(c) Discuss both the financial and nonfinancial factors that are relevant to the decision.

Communication Activity

BYP8-5 Lily Pao, a friend of yours, overheard a discussion at work about changes her employer wants to make in accounting for uncollectible accounts. Lily knows little about accounting, and she asks you to help make sense of what she heard. Specifically, she asks you to explain the differences between the percentage-of-sales, percentage-of-receivables, and the direct write-off methods for uncollectible accounts.

Instructions
In a letter of one page (or less), explain to Lily the three methods of accounting for uncollectibles. Be sure to discuss differences among these methods.

Ethics Case

BYP8-6 The controller of Vestin Co. believes that the yearly allowance for doubtful accounts for Vestin Co. should be 2% of net credit sales. The president of Vestin Co., nervous that the stockholders might expect the company to sustain its 10% growth rate, suggests that the controller increase the allowance for doubtful accounts to 4%. The president thinks that the lower net income, which reflects a 6% growth rate, will be a more sustainable rate for Vestin Co.

Instructions
(a) Who are the stakeholders in this case?
(b) Does the president's request pose an ethical dilemma for the controller?
(c) Should the controller be concerned with Vestin Co.'s growth rate? Explain your answer.

All About You

BYP8-7 Credit card usage in the United States is substantial. Many startup companies use credit cards as a way to help meet short-term financial needs. The most common forms of debt for startups are use of credit cards and loans from relatives.

Suppose that you start up Brothers Sandwich Shop. You invested your savings of $20,000 and borrowed $70,000 from your relatives. Although sales in the first few months are good, you see that you may not have sufficient cash to pay expenses and maintain your inventory at acceptable levels, at least in the short term. You decide you may need to use one or more credit cards to fund the possible cash shortfall.

Instructions

(a) Go to the Internet and find two sources that provide insight into how to compare credit card terms.

(b) Develop a list, in descending order of importance, as to what features are most important to you in selecting a credit card for your business.

(c) Examine the features of your present credit card. (If you do not have a credit card, select a likely one online for this exercise.) Given your analysis above, what are the three major disadvantages of your present credit card?

BYP8-8 Individuals need to evaluate their personal credit positions using the same thought processes used by business people. Some of you might consider the idea of not having a credit card a ridiculous proposition. But the reality is that the misuse of credit cards brings financial hardship to millions of Americans each year. Credit card companies aggressively market their cards with images of glamour and happiness. But, there isn't much glamour in paying an 18% to 21% interest rate, and there is very little happiness to be found in filing for personal bankruptcy.

Should you cut up your credit card(s)?

YES: Americans are carrying huge personal debt burdens. Credit cards encourage unnecessary, spontaneous expenditures. The interest rates on credit cards are extremely high, which causes debt problems to escalate exponentially.

NO: Credit cards are a necessity for transactions in today's economy. In fact, many transactions are difficult or impossible to carry out without a credit card. People should learn to use credit cards responsibly.

Instructions

Write a response indicating your position regarding the situation. Provide support for your view.

FASB Codification Activity

BYP8-9 If your school has a subscription to the FASB Codification, go to *http://aaahq.org/ascLogin.cfm* to log in and prepare responses to the following.

(a) How are receivables defined in the Codification?

(b) What are the conditions under which losses from uncollectible receivables (Bad Debt Expense) should be reported?

Answers to Chapter Questions

Answers to Insight and Accounting Across the Organization Questions

p. 390 How Does a Credit Card Work? Q: Assume that Nordstrom prepares a bank reconciliation at the end of each month. If some credit card sales have not been processed by the bank, how should Nordstrom treat these transactions on its bank reconciliation? **A:** Nordstrom would treat the credit card receipts as deposits in transit. It has already recorded the receipts as cash. Its bank will increase Nordstrom's cash account when it receives the receipts.

p. 394 Can Fair Value Be Unfair? Q: What are the arguments in favor of and against fair value accounting for loans and receivables? **A:** Arguments in favor of fair value accounting for loans and receivables are that fair value would provide a more accurate view of a company's financial position. This might provide a useful early warning of when a bank or other financial institution was in trouble because its loans were of poor quality. But, banks argue that estimating fair values is very difficult to do accurately. They are also concerned that volatile fair values could cause large swings in a bank's reported net income.

p. 396 Bad Information Can Lead to Bad Loans Q: What steps should the banks have taken to ensure the accuracy of financial information provided on loan applications? **A:** At a minimum, the bank should have requested copies of recent income tax forms and contacted the supposed employer to verify income. To verify ownership and value of assets, it should have examined bank statements, investment statements, and title documents and should have employed appraisers.

Answers to Self-Test Questions

1. d **2.** c ($1,000 − $300) × (100% − 2%) **3.** a **4.** b ($60,000 − $5,000) **5.** d ($60,000 + $5,000) **6.** b ($800,000 × 1.5%) + $15,000 **7.** b ($750,000 × 3%) + ($18,000 − $30,000) **8.** d ($800,000 − $65,000) **9.** c **10.** c **11.** a **12.** b **13.** d $10,000 + ($10,000 × 120/360 × 9%) **14.** a **15.** c $800,000 ÷ [($100,000 + $150,000) ÷ 2]

A Look at IFRS

The basic accounting and reporting issues related to recognition and measurement of receivables, such as the use of allowance accounts, how to record discounts, use of the allowance method to account for bad debts, and factoring, are essentially the same between IFRS and GAAP.

Key Points

- IFRS requires that loans and receivables be accounted for at amortized cost, adjusted for allowances for doubtful accounts. IFRS sometimes refers to these allowances as *provisions*. The entry to record the allowance would be:

Bad Debt Expense	xxxxxx	
Allowance for Doubtful Accounts		xxxxxx

- Although IFRS implies that receivables with different characteristics should be reported separately, there is no standard that mandates this segregation.

- The FASB and IASB have worked to implement fair value measurement (the amount they currently could be sold for) for financial instruments. Both Boards have faced bitter opposition from various factions. As a consequence, the Boards have adopted a piecemeal approach; the first step is disclosure of fair value information in the notes. The second step is the fair value option, which permits, but does not require, companies to record some types of financial instruments at fair values in the financial statements.

- IFRS requires a two-tiered approach to test whether the value of loans and receivables are impaired. First, a company should look at specific loans and receivables to determine whether they are impaired. Then, the loans and receivables as a group should be evaluated for impairment. GAAP does not prescribe a similar two-tiered approach.

- IFRS and GAAP differ in the criteria used to determine how to record a factoring transaction. IFRS is a combination of an approach focused on risks and rewards and loss of control. GAAP uses loss of control as the primary criterion. In addition, IFRS permits partial derecognition of receivables; GAAP does not.

Looking to the Future

It appears likely that the question of recording fair values for financial instruments will continue to be an important issue to resolve as the Boards work toward convergence. Both the IASB and the FASB have indicated that they believe that financial statements would be more transparent and understandable if companies recorded and reported all financial instruments at fair value.

That said, in *IFRS 9*, which was issued in 2009, the IASB created a split model, where some financial instruments are recorded at fair value, but other financial assets, such as loans and receivables, can be accounted for at amortized cost if certain criteria are met. Critics say that this can result in two companies with identical securities accounting for those securities in different ways. A proposal by the FASB would require that nearly all financial instruments, including loans and receivables, be accounted for at fair value. It has been suggested that *IFRS 9* will likely be changed or replaced as the FASB and IASB continue to deliberate the best treatment for financial instruments. In fact, one past member of the IASB said that companies should ignore *IFRS 9* and continue to report under the old standard, because in his opinion, it was extremely likely that it would be changed before the mandatory adoption date of the standard arrived in 2013.

IFRS Practice

IFRS Self-Test Questions

1. Under IFRS, loans and receivables are to be reported on the balance sheet at:
   (a) amortized cost.
   (b) amortized cost adjusted for estimated loss provisions.
   (c) historical cost.
   (d) replacement cost.

2. Which of the following statements is *false*?
   (a) Loans and receivables include equity securities purchased by the company.
   (b) Loans and receivables include credit card receivables.
   (c) Loans and receivables include amounts owed by employees as a result of company loans to employees.
   (d) Loans and receivables include amounts resulting from transactions with customers.

3. In recording a factoring transaction:
   (a) IFRS focuses on loss of control.
   (b) GAAP focuses on loss of control and risks and rewards.
   (c) IFRS and GAAP allow partial derecognition.
   (d) IFRS allows partial derecognition

4. Under IFRS:
   (a) the entry to record estimated uncollected accounts is the same as GAAP.
   (b) loans and receivables should only be tested for impairment as a group.
   (c) it is always acceptable to use the direct write-off method.
   (d) all financial instruments are recorded at fair value.

5. Which of the following statements is *true*?
   (a) The fair value option requires that some types of financial instruments be recorded at fair value.
   (b) The fair value option allows, but does not require, that some types of financial instruments be recorded at amortized cost.
   (c) The fair value option allows, but does not require, that some types of financial instruments be recorded at fair value.
   (d) The FASB and IASB would like to reduce the reliance on fair value accounting for financial instruments in the future.

IFRS Exercise

IFRS8-1 What are some steps taken by both the FASB and IASB to move to fair value measurement for financial instruments? In what ways have some of the approaches differed?

International Financial Reporting Problem: Zetar plc

IFRS8-2 The financial statements of **Zetar plc** are presented in Appendix C. The company's complete annual report, including the notes to its financial statements, is available at *www.zetarplc.com*.

Instructions

Use the company's annual report to answer the following questions.

(a) According to the Operational Review of Financial Performance, what was one reason why the balance in receivables increased relative to the previous year?

(b) According to the notes to the financial statements, how are loans and receivables defined?

(c) In the notes to the financial statements, the company reports a "one off item" related to receivables. Explain what this item was.

(d) Using information in the notes to the financial statements, determine what percentage the provision for impairment of receivables was as a percentage of total trade receivables for 2010 and 2009. How did the ratio change from 2009 to 2010, and what does this suggest about the company's receivables?

Answers to IFRS Self-Test Questions

1. b   **2.** a   **3.** d   **4.** a   **5.** c

 **The Navigator**

✔ **Remember to go back to The Navigator box on the chapter opening page and check off your completed work.**

Chapter 9

Plant Assets, Natural Resources, and Intangible Assets

Feature Story

How Much for a Ride to the Beach?

It's spring break. Your plane has landed, you've finally found your bags, and you're dying to hit the beach—but first you need a "vehicular unit" to get you there. As you turn away from baggage claim, you see a long row of rental agency booths. Many are names you are familiar with—Hertz, Avis, and Budget. But a booth at the far end catches your eye—Rent-A-Wreck. Now there's a company making a clear statement!

Any company that relies on equipment to generate revenues must make decisions about what kind of equipment to buy, how long to keep it, and how vigorously to maintain it. Rent-A-Wreck has decided to rent used rather than new cars and trucks. It rents these vehicles across the United States, Europe, and Asia. While the big-name agencies push vehicles with that "new car smell," Rent-A-Wreck competes on price.

Rent-A-Wreck's message is simple: Rent a used car and save some cash. It's not a message that appeals to everyone. If you're a marketing

Learning Objectives

After studying this chapter, you should be able to:

1 Describe how the cost principle applies to plant assets.

2 Explain the concept of depreciation and how to compute it.

3 Distinguish between revenue and capital expenditures, and explain the entries for each.

4 Explain how to account for the disposal of a plant asset.

5 Compute periodic depletion of natural resources.

6 Explain the basic issues related to accounting for intangible assets.

7 Indicate how plant assets, natural resources, and intangible assets are reported.

 The Navigator

executive wanting to impress a big client, you probably don't want to pull up in a Rent-A-Wreck car. But if you want to get from point A to point B for the minimum cash per mile, then Rent-A-Wreck is playing your tune. The company's message seems to be getting across to the right clientele. Revenues have increased significantly.

When you rent a car from Rent-A-Wreck, you are renting from an independent business person. This owner has paid a "franchise fee" for the right to use the Rent-A-Wreck

name. In order to gain a franchise, he or she must meet financial and other criteria, and must agree to run the rental agency according to rules prescribed by Rent-A-Wreck. Some of these rules require that each franchise maintain its cars in a reasonable fashion. This ensures that, though you won't be cruising down Daytona Beach's Atlantic Avenue in a Mercedes convertible, you can be reasonably assured that you won't be calling a towtruck.

✔ **The Navigator**

Preview of **Chapter 9**

The accounting for long-term assets has important implications for a company's reported results. In this chapter, we explain the application of the cost principle of accounting to property, plant, and equipment, such as Rent-A-Wreck vehicles, as well as to natural resources and intangible assets, such as the "Rent-A-Wreck" trademark. We also describe the methods that companies may use to allocate an asset's cost over its useful life. In addition, we discuss the accounting for expenditures incurred during the useful life of assets, such as the cost of replacing tires and brake pads on rental cars.

The content and organization of Chapter 9 are as follows.

PLANT ASSETS, NATURAL RESOURCES, AND INTANGIBLE ASSETS			
Plant Assets	**Natural Resources**	**Intangible Assets**	**Statement Presentation and Analysis**
• Determining the cost of plant assets • Depreciation • Expenditures during useful life • Plant asset disposals	• Depletion	• Accounting for intangibles • Research and development costs	• Presentation • Analysis

✔ **The Navigator**

Plant Assets

Plant assets are resources that have three characteristics. They have a physical substance (a definite size and shape), are used in the operations of a business, and are not intended for sale to customers. They are also called **property, plant, and equipment; plant and equipment**; and **fixed assets**. These assets are expected to provide services to the company for a number of years. Except for land, plant assets decline in service potential over their useful lives.

Because plant assets play a key role in ongoing operations, companies keep plant assets in good operating condition. They also replace worn-out or outdated plant assets, and expand productive resources as needed. Many companies have substantial investments in plant assets. Illustration 9-1 shows the percentages of plant assets in relation to total assets of companies in a number of industries.

Illustration 9-1
Percentages of plant assets in relation to total assets

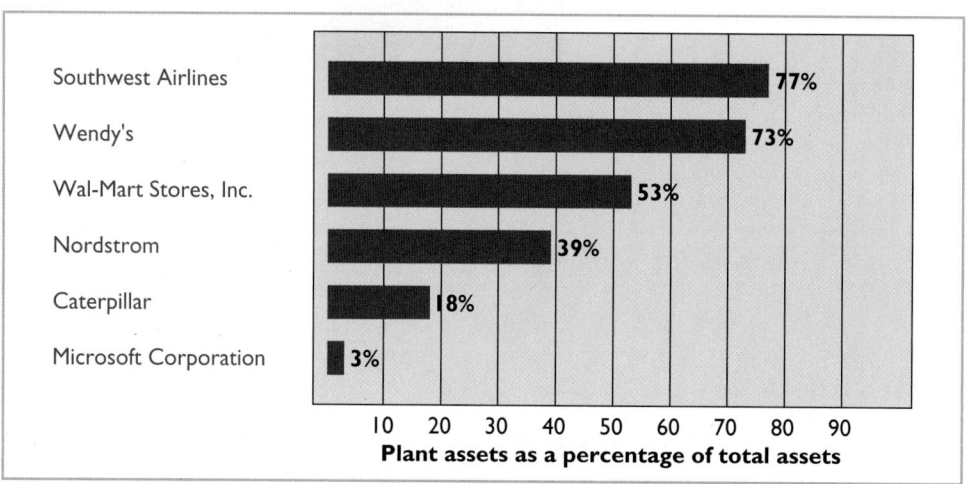

Determining the Cost of Plant Assets

The cost principle requires that companies record plant assets at cost. Thus, Rent-A-Wreck records its vehicles at cost. **Cost consists of all expenditures necessary to acquire the asset and make it ready for its intended use.** For example, the cost of factory machinery includes the purchase price, freight costs paid by the purchaser, and installation costs. Once cost is established, the company uses that amount as the basis of accounting for the plant asset over its useful life.

In the following sections, we explain the application of the cost principle to each of the major classes of plant assets.

LAND

Companies often use **land** as a building site for a manufacturing plant or office site. The cost of land includes (1) the cash purchase price, (2) closing costs such as title and attorney's fees, (3) real estate brokers' commissions, and (4) accrued property taxes and other liens assumed by the purchaser. For example, if the cash price is $50,000 and the purchaser agrees to pay accrued taxes of $5,000, the cost of the land is $55,000.

Companies record as debits (increases) to the Land account all necessary costs incurred to make land **ready for its intended use**. When a company acquires vacant land, these costs include expenditures for clearing, draining, filling, and grading. Sometimes, the land has a building on it that must be removed before construction of a new building. In this case, the company debits to the

Helpful Hint
Management's intended use is important in applying the cost principle.

Land account all demolition and removal costs, less any proceeds from salvaged materials.

To illustrate, assume that Hayes Company acquires real estate at a cash cost of $100,000. The property contains an old warehouse that is razed at a net cost of $6,000 ($7,500 in costs less $1,500 proceeds from salvaged materials). Additional expenditures are the attorney's fee, $1,000, and the real estate broker's commission, $8,000. The cost of the land is $115,000, computed as shown in Illustration 9-2.

Illustration 9-2
Computation of cost of land

Land	
Cash price of property	$ 100,000
Net removal cost of warehouse	6,000
Attorney's fee	1,000
Real estate broker's commission	8,000
Cost of land	**$115,000**

When Hayes records the acquisition, it debits Land for $115,000 and credits Cash for $115,000.

LAND IMPROVEMENTS

Land improvements are structural additions made to land. Examples are driveways, parking lots, fences, landscaping, and underground sprinklers. The cost of land improvements includes all expenditures necessary to make the improvements ready for their intended use. For example, the cost of a new parking lot for Home Depot includes the amount paid for paving, fencing, and lighting. Thus, Home Depot debits to Land Improvements the total of all of these costs.

Land improvements have limited useful lives, and their maintenance and replacement are the responsibility of the company. As a result, companies expense (depreciate) the cost of land improvements over their useful lives.

BUILDINGS

Buildings are facilities used in operations, such as stores, offices, factories, warehouses, and airplane hangars. Companies debit to the Buildings account all necessary expenditures related to the purchase or construction of a building. When a building is **purchased**, such costs include the purchase price, closing costs (attorney's fees, title insurance, etc.) and real estate broker's commission. Costs to make the building ready for its intended use include expenditures for remodeling and replacing or repairing the roof, floors, electrical wiring, and plumbing. When a new building is **constructed**, cost consists of the contract price plus payments for architects' fees, building permits, and excavation costs.

In addition, companies charge certain interest costs to the Buildings account. Interest costs incurred to finance the project are included in the cost of the building when a significant period of time is required to get the building ready for use. In these circumstances, interest costs are considered as necessary as materials and labor. However, the inclusion of interest costs in the cost of a constructed building is **limited to the construction period**. When construction has been completed, the company records subsequent interest payments on funds borrowed to finance the construction as debits (increases) to Interest Expense.

EQUIPMENT

Equipment includes assets used in operations, such as store check-out counters, office furniture, factory machinery, delivery trucks, and airplanes. The cost of equipment, such as Rent-A-Wreck vehicles, consists of the cash purchase price, sales taxes, freight charges, and insurance during transit paid by the purchaser. It also includes expenditures required in assembling, installing, and testing the unit. However, Rent-A-Wreck does not include motor vehicle licenses and accident insurance on company vehicles in the cost of equipment. These costs represent annual recurring expenditures and do not benefit future periods. Thus, they are treated as expenses as they are incurred.

To illustrate, assume Merten Company purchases factory machinery at a cash price of $50,000. Related expenditures are for sales taxes $3,000, insurance during shipping $500, and installation and testing $1,000. The cost of the factory machinery is $54,500, computed in Illustration 9-3.

Illustration 9-3
Computation of cost of factory machinery

Factory Machinery	
Cash price	$ 50,000
Sales taxes	3,000
Insurance during shipping	500
Installation and testing	1,000
Cost of factory machinery	**$54,500**

Merten makes the following summary entry to record the purchase and related expenditures.

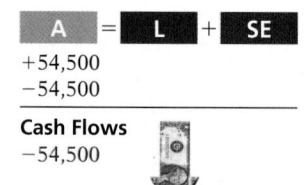

A = L + SE
+54,500
−54,500

Cash Flows
−54,500

Equipment	54,500	
Cash		54,500
(To record purchase of factory machine)		

For another example, assume that Lenard Company purchases a delivery truck at a cash price of $22,000. Related expenditures consist of sales taxes $1,320, painting and lettering $500, motor vehicle license $80, and a three-year accident insurance policy $1,600. The cost of the delivery truck is $23,820, computed as follows.

Illustration 9-4
Computation of cost of delivery truck

Delivery Truck	
Cash price	$ 22,000
Sales taxes	1,320
Painting and lettering	500
Cost of delivery truck	**$23,820**

Lenard treats the cost of the motor vehicle license as an expense, and the cost of the insurance policy as a prepaid asset. Thus, Lenard makes the following entry to record the purchase of the truck and related expenditures:

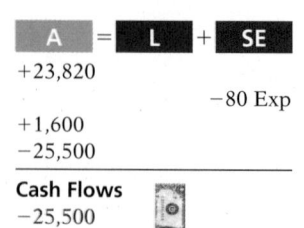

A = L + SE
+23,820
          −80 Exp
+1,600
−25,500

Cash Flows
−25,500

Equipment	23,820	
License Expense	80	
Prepaid Insurance	1,600	
Cash		25,500
(To record purchase of delivery truck and related expenditures)		

ACCOUNTING ACROSS THE ORGANIZATION

Many U.S. Firms Use Leases

Leasing is big business for U.S. companies. For example, business investment in equipment in a recent year totaled $709 billion. Leasing accounted for about 31% of all business investment ($218 billion).

Who does the most leasing? Interestingly, major banks such as Continental Bank, J.P. Morgan Leasing, and US Bancorp Equipment Finance are the major lessors. Also, many companies have established separate leasing companies, such as Boeing Capital Corporation, Dell Financial Services, and John Deere Capital Corporation. And, as an excellent example of the magnitude of leasing, leased planes account for nearly 40% of the U.S. fleet of commercial airlines. In addition, leasing is becoming increasingly common in the hotel industry. Marriott, Hilton, and InterContinental are increasingly choosing to lease hotels that are owned by someone else.

? Why might airline managers choose to lease rather than purchase their planes?
(See page 469.)

> DO IT!

Cost of Plant Assets

Action Plan

✔ Identify expenditures made in order to get delivery equipment ready for its intended use.

✔ Treat operating costs as expenses.

Assume that Drummond Heating and Cooling Co. purchases a delivery truck for $15,000 cash, plus sales taxes of $900 and delivery costs of $500. The buyer also pays $200 for painting and lettering, $600 for an annual insurance policy, and $80 for a motor vehicle license. Explain how each of these costs would be accounted for.

Solution

> The first four payments ($15,000, $900, $500, and $200) are expenditures necessary to make the truck ready for its intended use. Thus, the cost of the truck is $16,600. The payments for insurance and the license are operating costs and therefore are expensed.

Related exercise material: **BE9-1, BE9-2, E9-1, E9-2, E9-3,** and **DO IT!** 9-1.

✔ **The Navigator**

Depreciation

As explained in Chapter 3, **depreciation** **is the process of allocating to expense the cost of a plant asset over its useful (service) life in a rational and systematic manner**. Cost allocation enables companies to properly match expenses with revenues in accordance with the expense recognition principle (see Illustration 9-5).

LEARNING OBJECTIVE   **2**

Explain the concept of depreciation and how to compute it.

Illustration 9-5
Depreciation as a cost allocation concept

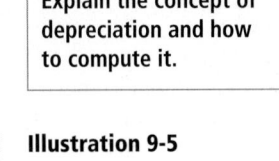

It is important to understand that **depreciation is a process of cost allocation**. **It is not a process of asset valuation.** No attempt is made to measure the change in an asset's fair value during ownership. So, the **book value** (cost less accumulated depreciation) of a plant asset may be quite different from its fair value. In fact, if an asset is fully depreciated, it can have a zero book value but still have a significant fair value.

Depreciation applies to three classes of plant assets: land improvements, buildings, and equipment. Each asset in these classes is considered to be a **depreciable asset**. Why? Because the usefulness to the company and revenue-producing ability of each asset will decline over the asset's useful life. Depreciation **does not apply to land** because its usefulness and revenue-producing ability generally remain intact over time. In fact, in many cases, the usefulness of land is greater over time because of the scarcity of good land sites. Thus, **land is not a depreciable asset**.

During a depreciable asset's useful life, its revenue-producing ability declines because of **wear and tear**. A delivery truck that has been driven 100,000 miles will be less useful to a company than one driven only 800 miles.

Revenue-producing ability may also decline because of obsolescence. **Obsolescence** is the process of becoming out of date before the asset physically wears out. For example, major airlines moved from Chicago's Midway Airport to Chicago-O'Hare International Airport because Midway's runways were too short for jumbo jets. Similarly, many companies replace their computers long before they originally planned to do so because improvements in new computing technology make the old computers obsolete.

Recognizing depreciation on an asset does not result in an accumulation of cash for replacement of the asset. The balance in Accumulated Depreciation represents the total amount of the asset's cost that the company has charged to expense. It is not a cash fund.

Note that the concept of depreciation is consistent with the going-concern assumption. The **going-concern assumption** states that the company will continue in operation for the foreseeable future. If a company does not use a going-concern assumption, then plant assets should be stated at their fair value. In that case, depreciation of these assets is not needed.

FACTORS IN COMPUTING DEPRECIATION

Three factors affect the computation of depreciation, as shown in Illustration 9-6.

Illustration 9-6
Three factors in computing depreciation

Helpful Hint
Depreciation expense is reported on the income statement. Accumulated depreciation is reported on the balance sheet as a deduction from plant assets.

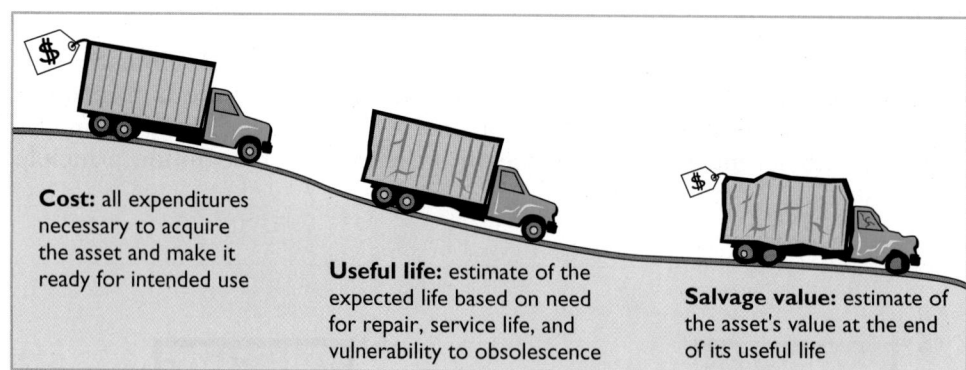

Cost: all expenditures necessary to acquire the asset and make it ready for intended use

Useful life: estimate of the expected life based on need for repair, service life, and vulnerability to obsolescence

Salvage value: estimate of the asset's value at the end of its useful life

1. **Cost.** Earlier, we explained the issues affecting the cost of a depreciable asset. Recall that companies record plant assets at cost, in accordance with the cost principle.

2. **Useful life.** **Useful life** is an estimate of the expected *productive life*, also called *service life*, of the asset for its owner. Useful life may be expressed in terms of time, units of activity (such as machine hours), or units of output. Useful life is an estimate. In making the estimate, management considers such factors as the intended use of the asset, its expected repair and maintenance, and its vulnerability to obsolescence. Past experience with similar assets is often helpful in deciding on expected useful life. We might reasonably expect Rent-A-Wreck and Avis to use different estimated useful lives for their vehicles.

3. **Salvage value.** **Salvage value** is an estimate of the asset's value at the end of its useful life. This value may be based on the asset's worth as scrap or on its expected trade-in value. Like useful life, salvage value is an estimate. In making the estimate, management considers how it plans to dispose of the asset and its experience with similar assets.

Alternative Terminology
Another term sometimes used for salvage value is *residual value*.

DEPRECIATION METHODS

Depreciation is generally computed using one of the following methods:

1. Straight-line
2. Units-of-activity
3. Declining-balance

Each method is acceptable under generally accepted accounting principles. Management selects the method(s) it believes to be appropriate. The objective is to select the method that best measures an asset's contribution to revenue over its useful life. Once a company chooses a method, it should apply it consistently over the useful life of the asset. Consistency enhances the comparability of financial statements. Depreciation affects the balance sheet through accumulated depreciation and the income statement through depreciation expense.

We will compare the three depreciation methods using the following data for a small delivery truck purchased by Barb's Florists on January 1, 2014.

Cost	$ 13,000
Expected salvage value	$ 1,000
Estimated useful life in years	5
Estimated useful life in miles	100,000

Illustration 9-7
Delivery truck data

Illustration 9-8 (in the margin) shows the use of the primary depreciation methods in 600 of the largest companies in the United States.

STRAIGHT-LINE Under the **straight-line method**, companies expense the same amount of depreciation for each year of the asset's useful life. It is measured solely by the passage of time.

To compute depreciation expense under the straight-line method, companies need to determine depreciable cost. **Depreciable cost** is the cost of the asset less its salvage value. It represents the total amount subject to depreciation. Under the straight-line method, to determine annual depreciation expense, we divide depreciable cost by the asset's useful life. Illustration 9-9 (page 430) shows the computation of the first year's depreciation expense for Barb's Florists.

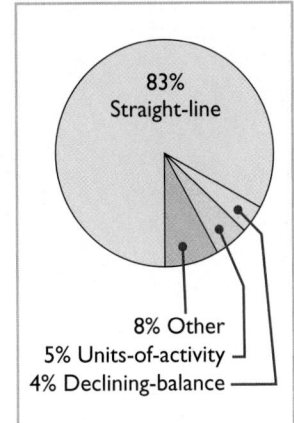

83% Straight-line

8% Other
5% Units-of-activity
4% Declining-balance

Illustration 9-8
Use of depreciation methods in 600 large U.S. companies

Illustration 9-9
Formula for straight-line method

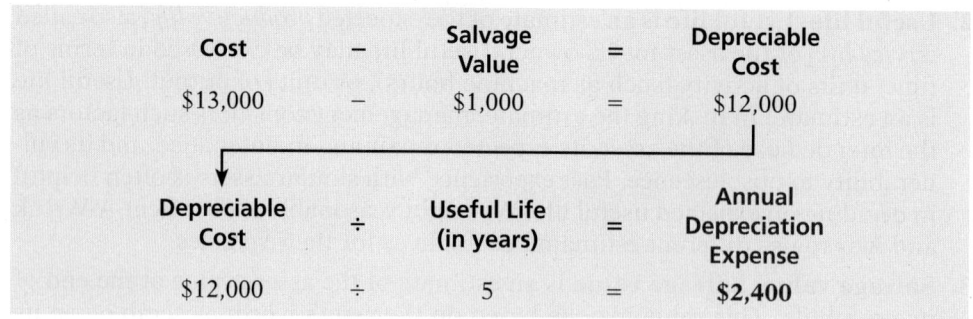

Cost	−	Salvage Value	=	Depreciable Cost
$13,000	−	$1,000	=	$12,000

Depreciable Cost	÷	Useful Life (in years)	=	Annual Depreciation Expense
$12,000	÷	5	=	$2,400

Alternatively, we also can compute an annual **rate** of depreciation. In this case, the rate is 20% (100% ÷ 5 years). When a company uses an annual straight-line rate, it applies the percentage rate to the depreciable cost of the asset. Illustration 9-10 shows a **depreciation schedule** using an annual rate.

Illustration 9-10
Straight-line depreciation schedule

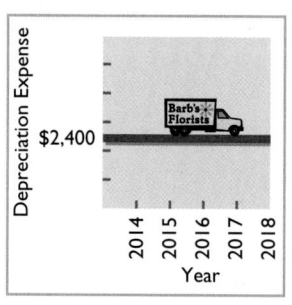

	Barb's Florists					
	Computation			Annual	End of Year	
Year	Depreciable Cost	× Depreciation Rate	=	Depreciation Expense	Accumulated Depreciation	Book Value
2014	$12,000	20%		$2,400	$ 2,400	$10,600*
2015	12,000	20		2,400	4,800	8,200
2016	12,000	20		2,400	7,200	5,800
2017	12,000	20		2,400	9,600	3,400
2018	12,000	20		2,400	12,000	1,000

*Book value = Cost − Accumulated depreciation = ($13,000 − $2,400).

Note that the depreciation expense of $2,400 is the same each year. The book value (computed as cost minus accumulated depreciation) at the end of the useful life is equal to the expected $1,000 salvage value.

What happens to these computations for an asset purchased **during** the year, rather than on January 1? In that case, it is necessary to **prorate the annual depreciation** on a time basis. If Barb's Florists had purchased the delivery truck on April 1, 2014, the company would own the truck for nine months of the first year (April–December). Thus, depreciation for 2014 would be $1,800 ($12,000 × 20% × 9/12 of a year).

The straight-line method predominates in practice. Such large companies as Campbell Soup, Marriott, and General Mills use the straight-line method. It is simple to apply, and it matches expenses with revenues when the use of the asset is reasonably uniform throughout the service life.

Alternative Terminology
Another term often used is the *units-of-production method.*

UNITS-OF-ACTIVITY Under the **units-of-activity method**, useful life is expressed in terms of the total units of production or use expected from the asset, rather than as a time period. The units-of-activity method is ideally suited to factory machinery. Manufacturing companies can measure production in units of output or in machine hours. This method can also be used for such assets as delivery equipment (miles driven) and airplanes (hours in use). The units-of-activity method is generally not suitable for buildings or furniture because depreciation for these assets is more a function of time than of use.

To use this method, companies estimate the total units of activity for the entire useful life, and then divide these units into depreciable cost. The resulting number represents the depreciable cost per unit. The depreciable cost per unit is then applied to the units of activity during the year to determine the annual depreciation expense.

To illustrate, assume that Barb's Florists drives its delivery truck 15,000 miles in the first year. Illustration 9-11 shows the units-of-activity formula and the computation of the first year's depreciation expense.

Helpful Hint
Under any method, depreciation stops when the asset's book value equals expected salvage value.

Depreciable Cost	÷	Total Units of Activity	=	Depreciable Cost per Unit
$12,000	÷	100,000 miles	=	$0.12

Depreciable Cost per Unit	×	Units of Activity during the Year	=	Annual Depreciation Expense
$0.12	×	15,000 miles	=	**$1,800**

Illustration 9-11
Formula for units-of-activity method

The units-of-activity depreciation schedule, using assumed mileage, is as follows.

		Barb's Florists			
	Computation		**Annual**	**End of Year**	
Year	**Units of Activity** ×	**Depreciation Cost/Unit** =	**Depreciation Expense**	**Accumulated Depreciation**	**Book Value**
2014	15,000	$0.12	**$1,800**	$ 1,800	$11,200*
2015	30,000	0.12	**3,600**	5,400	7,600
2016	20,000	0.12	**2,400**	7,800	5,200
2017	25,000	0.12	**3,000**	10,800	2,200
2018	10,000	0.12	**1,200**	12,000	**1,000**

*($13,000 − $1,800).

Illustration 9-12
Units-of-activity depreciation schedule

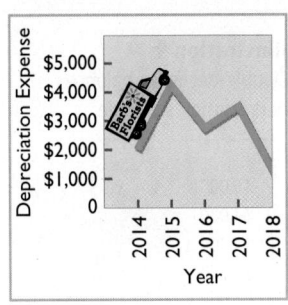

This method is easy to apply for assets purchased mid-year. In such a case, the company computes the depreciation using the productivity of the asset for the partial year.

The units-of-activity method is not nearly as popular as the straight-line method (see Illustration 9-8, page 429), primarily because it is often difficult for companies to reasonably estimate total activity. However, some very large companies, such as Chevron and Boise Cascade (a forestry company), do use this method. When the productivity of an asset varies significantly from one period to another, the units-of-activity method results in the best matching of expenses with revenues.

DECLINING-BALANCE The **declining-balance method** produces a decreasing annual depreciation expense over the asset's useful life. The method is so named because the periodic depreciation is based on a **declining book value** (cost less accumulated depreciation) of the asset. With this method, companies compute annual depreciation expense by multiplying the book value at the beginning of the year by the declining-balance depreciation rate. **The depreciation rate remains constant from year to year, but the book value to which the rate is applied declines each year.**

At the beginning of the first year, book value is the cost of the asset. This is because the balance in accumulated depreciation at the beginning of the asset's useful life is zero. In subsequent years, book value is the difference between cost and accumulated depreciation to date. Unlike the other depreciation methods, the declining-balance method does not use depreciable cost in computing annual depreciation expense. That is, **it ignores salvage value in determining the amount to which the declining-balance rate is applied**. Salvage value, however, does limit the total depreciation that can be taken. Depreciation stops when the asset's book value equals expected salvage value.

A common declining-balance rate is double the straight-line rate. The method is often called the **double-declining-balance method**. If Barb's Florists uses the double-declining-balance method, it uses a depreciation rate of 40% (2 × the straight-line rate of 20%). Illustration 9-13 shows the declining-balance formula and the computation of the first year's depreciation on the delivery truck.

Illustration 9-13
Formula for declining-balance method

Book Value at Beginning of Year	×	Declining-Balance Rate	=	Annual Depreciation Expense
$13,000	×	40%	=	$5,200

The depreciation schedule under this method is as follows.

Illustration 9-14
Double-declining-balance depreciation schedule

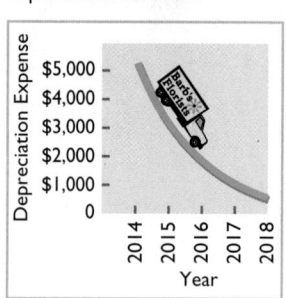

	Barb's Florists					

| | Computation | | | Annual | End of Year | |
Year	Book Value Beginning of Year	×	Depreciation Rate	= Depreciation Expense	Accumulated Depreciation	Book Value
2014	$13,000		40%	$5,200	$ 5,200	$7,800
2015	7,800		40	3,120	8,320	4,680
2016	4,680		40	1,872	10,192	2,808
2017	2,808		40	1,123	11,315	1,685
2018	1,685		40	685*	12,000	1,000

*Computation of $674 ($1,685 × 40%) is adjusted to $685 in order for book value to equal salvage value.

Helpful Hint
The method recommended for an asset that is expected to be significantly more productive in the first half of its useful life is the declining-balance method.

The delivery equipment is 69% depreciated ($8,320 ÷ $12,000) at the end of the second year. Under the straight-line method, the truck would be depreciated 40% ($4,800 ÷ $12,000) at that time. Because the declining-balance method produces higher depreciation expense in the early years than in the later years, it is considered an **accelerated-depreciation method**. The declining-balance method is compatible with the expense recognition principle. It matches the higher depreciation expense in early years with the higher benefits received in these years. It also recognizes lower depreciation expense in later years, when the asset's contribution to revenue is less. Some assets lose usefulness rapidly because of obsolescence. In these cases, the declining-balance method provides the most appropriate depreciation amount.

When a company purchases an asset during the year, it must prorate the first year's declining-balance depreciation on a time basis. For example, if Barb's Florists had purchased the truck on April 1, 2014, depreciation for 2014 would become $3,900 ($13,000 × 40% × 9/12). The book value at the beginning of 2015 is then $9,100 ($13,000 − $3,900), and the 2015 depreciation is $3,640 ($9,100 × 40%). Subsequent computations would follow from those amounts.

> DO IT!

Straight-Line Depreciation

On January 1, 2014, Iron Mountain Ski Corporation purchased a new snow-grooming machine for $50,000. The machine is estimated to have a 10-year life with a $2,000 salvage value. What journal entry would Iron Mountain Ski Corporation make at December 31, 2014, if it uses the straight-line method of depreciation?

Solution

Action Plan

✔ Calculate depreciable cost (Cost − Salvage value).

✔ Divide the depreciable cost by the asset's estimated useful life.

$$\text{Depreciation expense} = \frac{\text{Cost} - \text{Salvage value}}{\text{Useful life}} = \frac{\$50,000 - \$2,000}{10} = \$4,800$$

The entry to record the first year's depreciation would be:

Dec. 31	Depreciation Expense	4,800	
	Accumulated Depreciation—Equipment		4,800
	(To record annual depreciation on snow-grooming machine)		

Related exercise material: **BE9-3, BE9-4,** and **DO IT! 9-2.**

✔ **The Navigator**

COMPARISON OF METHODS Illustration 9-15 compares annual and total depreciation expense under each of the three methods for Barb's Florists.

Year	Straight-Line	Units-of-Activity	Declining-Balance
2014	$ 2,400	$ 1,800	$ 5,200
2015	2,400	3,600	3,120
2016	2,400	2,400	1,872
2017	2,400	3,000	1,123
2018	2,400	1,200	685
	$12,000	$12,000	$12,000

Illustration 9-15
Comparison of depreciation methods

Annual depreciation varies considerably among the methods, but **total depreciation is the same for the five-year period** under all three methods. Each method is acceptable in accounting because each recognizes in a rational and systematic manner the decline in service potential of the asset. Illustration 9-16 (page 434) graphs the depreciation expense pattern under each method.

Illustration 9-16
Patterns of depreciation

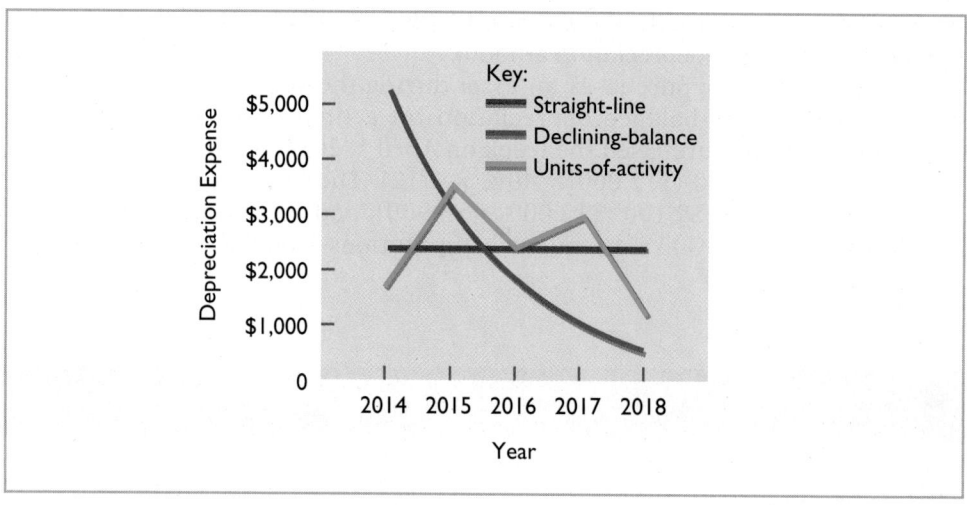

DEPRECIATION AND INCOME TAXES

The Internal Revenue Service (IRS) allows taxpayers to deduct depreciation expense when they compute taxable income. However, the IRS does not require taxpayers to use the same depreciation method on the tax return that is used in preparing financial statements.

Many corporations use straight-line in their financial statements to maximize net income. At the same time, they use a special accelerated-depreciation method on their tax returns to minimize their income taxes. Taxpayers must use on their tax returns either the straight-line method or a special accelerated-depreciation method called the **Modified Accelerated Cost Recovery System** (MACRS).

REVISING PERIODIC DEPRECIATION

Depreciation is one example of the use of estimation in the accounting process. Management should periodically review annual depreciation expense. If wear and tear or obsolescence indicate that annual depreciation estimates are inadequate or excessive, the company should change the amount of depreciation expense.

When a change in an estimate is required, the company makes the change in **current and future years**. **It does not change depreciation in prior periods.** The rationale is that continual restatement of prior periods would adversely affect confidence in financial statements.

To determine the new annual depreciation expense, the company first computes the asset's depreciable cost at the time of the revision. It then allocates the revised depreciable cost to the remaining useful life.

To illustrate, assume that Barb's Florists decides on January 1, 2017, to extend the useful life of the truck one year (a total life of six years) and increase its salvage value to $2,200. The company has used the straight-line method to depreciate the asset to date. Depreciation per year was $2,400 [($13,000 − $1,000) ÷ 5]. Accumulated depreciation after three years (2014–2016) is $7,200 ($2,400 × 3), and book value is $5,800 ($13,000 − $7,200). The new annual depreciation is $1,200, computed as follows.

Helpful Hint
Use a step-by-step approach: (1) determine new depreciable cost; (2) divide by remaining useful life.

Illustration 9-17
Revised depreciation computation

Book value, 1/1/17	$ 5,800	
Less: Salvage value	2,200	
Depreciable cost	$ 3,600	
Remaining useful life	3 years	(2017–2019)
Revised annual depreciation ($3,600 ÷ 3)	**$ 1,200**	

Barb's Florists makes no entry for the change in estimate. On December 31, 2017, during the preparation of adjusting entries, it records depreciation expense of $1,200. Companies must describe in the financial statements significant changes in estimates.

> DO IT!

Revised Depreciation

Action Plan

✔ Calculate remaining depreciable cost.

✔ Divide remaining depreciable cost by new remaining life.

Chambers Corporation purchased a piece of equipment for $36,000. It estimated a 6-year life and $6,000 salvage value. Thus, straight-line depreciation was $5,000 per year [($36,000 − $6,000) ÷ 6]. At the end of year three (before the depreciation adjustment), it estimated the new total life to be 10 years and the new salvage value to be $2,000. Compute the revised depreciation.

Solution

Original depreciation expense = [($36,000 − $6,000) ÷ 6] = $5,000
Accumulated depreciation after 2 years = 2 × $5,000 = $10,000
Book value = $36,000 − $10,000 = $26,000

Book value after 2 years of depreciation	$26,000
Less: New salvage value	2,000
Depreciable cost	24,000
Remaining useful life	8 years
Revised annual depreciation ($24,000 ÷ 8)	$ 3,000

Related exercise material: **BE9-7, E9-8, and** **9-3.**

✔ **The Navigator**

Expenditures During Useful Life

LEARNING OBJECTIVE 3

Distinguish between revenue and capital expenditures, and explain the entries for each.

During the useful life of a plant asset, a company may incur costs for ordinary repairs, additions, or improvements. **Ordinary repairs** are expenditures to **maintain** the operating efficiency and productive life of the unit. They usually are fairly small amounts that occur frequently. Examples are motor tune-ups and oil changes, the painting of buildings, and the replacing of worn-out gears on machinery. Companies record such repairs as debits to Maintenance and Repairs Expense as they are incurred. Because they are immediately charged as an expense against revenues, these costs are often referred to as **revenue expenditures**.

In contrast, **additions and improvements** are costs incurred to **increase** the operating efficiency, productive capacity, or useful life of a plant asset. They are usually material in amount and occur infrequently. Additions and improvements increase the company's investment in productive facilities. Companies generally debit these amounts to the plant asset affected. They are often referred to as **capital expenditures**.

Companies must use good judgment in deciding between a revenue expenditure and capital expenditure. For example, assume that Rodriguez Co. purchases a number of wastepaper baskets. Although the proper accounting would appear to be to capitalize and then depreciate these wastepaper baskets over their useful life, it would be more usual for Rodriguez to expense them immediately. This practice is justified on the basis of **materiality**. Materiality refers to the impact of an item's size on a company's financial operations. The **materiality concept** states that if an item would not make a difference in decision-making, the company does not have to follow GAAP in reporting that item.

ANATOMY OF A FRAUD

Bernie Ebbers was the founder and CEO of the phone company WorldCom. The company engaged in a series of increasingly large, debt-financed acquisitions of other companies. These acquisitions made the company grow quickly, which made the stock price increase dramatically. However, because the acquired companies all had different accounting systems, WorldCom's financial records were a mess. When WorldCom's performance started to flatten out, Bernie coerced WorldCom's accountants to engage in a number of fraudulent activities to make net income look better than it really was and thus prop up the stock price. One of these frauds involved treating $7 billion of line costs as capital expenditures. The line costs, which were rental fees paid to other phone companies to use their phone lines, had always been properly expensed in previous years. Capitalization delayed expense recognition to future periods and thus boosted current-period profits.

Total take: $7 billion

The Missing Controls

Documentation procedures. The company's accounting system was a disorganized collection of non-integrated systems, which resulted from a series of corporate acquisitions. Top management took advantage of this disorganization to conceal its fraudulent activities.

Independent internal verification. A fraud of this size should have been detected by a routine comparison of the actual physical assets with the list of physical assets shown in the accounting records.

Plant Asset Disposals

> **LEARNING OBJECTIVE 4**
>
> **Explain how to account for the disposal of a plant asset.**

Companies dispose of plant assets that are no longer useful to them. Illustration 9-18 below shows the three ways in which companies make plant asset disposals.

Whatever the disposal method, the company must determine the book value of the plant asset at the disposal date to determine the gain or loss. Recall that the book value is the difference between the cost of the plant asset and the accumulated depreciation to date. If the disposal occurs at any time during the year, the company must record depreciation for the fraction of the year to the date of disposal. The company then eliminates the book value by reducing (debiting) Accumulated Depreciation for the total depreciation associated with that asset to the date of disposal and reducing (crediting) the asset account for the cost of the asset.

Illustration 9-18
Methods of plant asset disposal

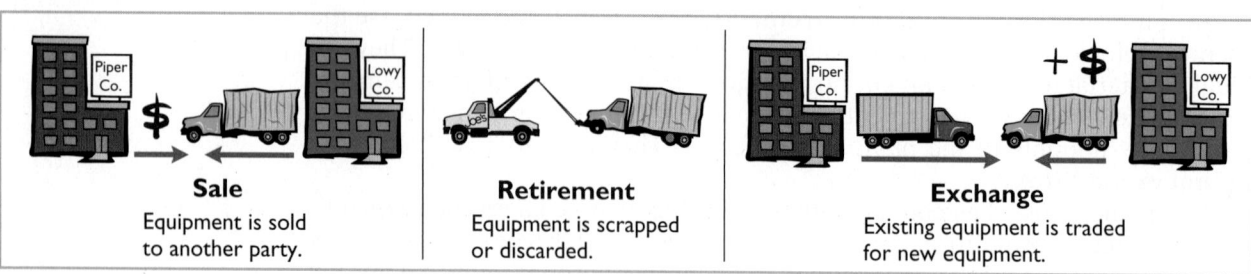

Sale	Retirement	Exchange
Equipment is sold to another party.	Equipment is scrapped or discarded.	Existing equipment is traded for new equipment.

In this chapter, we examine the accounting for the retirement and sale of plant assets. In the appendix to the chapter, we discuss and illustrate the accounting for exchanges of plant assets.

RETIREMENT OF PLANT ASSETS

To illustrate the retirement of plant assets, assume that Hobart Enterprises retires its computer printers, which cost $32,000. The accumulated depreciation on these printers is $32,000. The equipment, therefore, is fully depreciated (zero book value). The entry to record this retirement is as follows.

Accumulated Depreciation—Equipment		32,000	
Equipment			32,000
(To record retirement of fully depreciated			
equipment)			

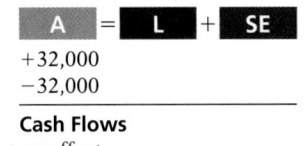

Cash Flows
no effect

Helpful Hint
When a company disposes of a plant asset, the company must remove from the accounts all amounts related to the asset. This includes the original cost in the asset account and the total depreciation to date in the accumulated depreciation account.

What happens if a fully depreciated plant asset is still useful to the company? In this case, the asset and its accumulated depreciation continue to be reported on the balance sheet, without further depreciation adjustment, until the company retires the asset. Reporting the asset and related accumulated depreciation on the balance sheet informs the financial statement reader that the asset is still in use. Once fully depreciated, no additional depreciation should be taken, even if an asset is still being used. In no situation can the accumulated depreciation on a plant asset exceed its cost.

If a company retires a plant asset before it is fully depreciated, and no cash is received for scrap or salvage value, a loss on disposal occurs. For example, assume that Sunset Company discards delivery equipment that cost $18,000 and has accumulated depreciation of $14,000. The entry is as follows.

Accumulated Depreciation—Equipment		14,000	
Loss on Disposal of Plant Assets		4,000	
Equipment			18,000
(To record retirement of delivery equipment			
at a loss)			

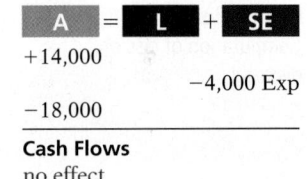

Cash Flows
no effect

Companies report a loss on disposal of plant assets in the "Other expenses and losses" section of the income statement.

SALE OF PLANT ASSETS

In a disposal by sale, the company compares the book value of the asset with the proceeds received from the sale. If the proceeds of the sale **exceed** the book value of the plant asset, **a gain on disposal occurs**. If the proceeds of the sale **are less than** the book value of the plant asset sold, **a loss on disposal occurs**.

Only by coincidence will the book value and the fair value of the asset be the same when the asset is sold. Gains and losses on sales of plant assets are therefore quite common. For example, Delta Airlines reported a $94,343,000 gain on the sale of five Boeing B727-200 aircraft and five Lockheed L-1011-1 aircraft.

GAIN ON SALE To illustrate a gain on sale of plant assets, assume that on July 1, 2014, Wright Company sells office furniture for $16,000 cash. The office furniture originally cost $60,000. As of January 1, 2014, it had accumulated depreciation of $41,000. Depreciation for the first six months of 2014 is $8,000. Wright records depreciation expense and updates accumulated depreciation to July 1 with the following entry.

July 1	Depreciation Expense	8,000	
	Accumulated Depreciation—Equipment		8,000
	(To record depreciation expense for		
	the first 6 months of 2014)		

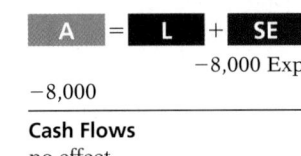

Cash Flows
no effect

After the accumulated depreciation balance is updated, the company computes the gain or loss. The gain or loss is the difference between the proceeds from the sale and the book value at the date of disposal. Illustration 9-19 (page 438) shows this computation for Wright Company, which has a gain on disposal of $5,000.

Illustration 9-19
Computation of gain on disposal

Cost of office furniture	$60,000
Less: Accumulated depreciation ($41,000 + $8,000)	49,000
Book value at date of disposal	11,000
Proceeds from sale	16,000
Gain on disposal of plant asset	**$ 5,000**

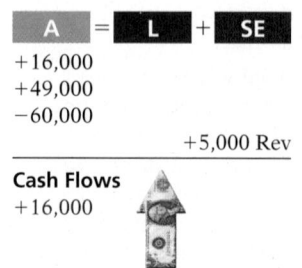

A = L + SE
+16,000
+49,000
−60,000
　　　　+5,000 Rev

Cash Flows
+16,000

Wright records the sale and the gain on disposal of the plant asset as follows.

July 1	Cash	16,000	
	Accumulated Depreciation—Equipment	49,000	
	Equipment		60,000
	Gain on Disposal of Plant Assets		5,000
	(To record sale of office furniture		
	at a gain)		

Companies report a gain on disposal of plant assets in the "Other revenues and gains" section of the income statement.

LOSS ON SALE Assume that instead of selling the office furniture for $16,000, Wright sells it for $9,000. In this case, Wright computes a loss of $2,000 as follows.

Illustration 9-20
Computation of loss on disposal

Cost of office furniture	$60,000
Less: Accumulated depreciation	49,000
Book value at date of disposal	11,000
Proceeds from sale	9,000
Loss on disposal of plant asset	**$ 2,000**

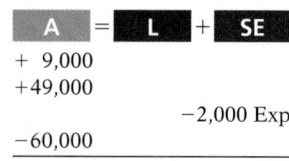

A = L + SE
+ 9,000
+49,000
　　　　−2,000 Exp
−60,000

Cash Flows
+9,000

Wright records the sale and the loss on disposal of the plant asset as follows.

July 1	Cash	9,000	
	Accumulated Depreciation—Equipment	49,000	
	Loss on Disposal of Plant Assets	2,000	
	Equipment		60,000
	(To record sale of office furniture at a loss)		

Companies report a loss on disposal of plant assets in the "Other expenses and losses" section of the income statement.

> **DO IT!**

Plant Asset Disposal

Overland Trucking has an old truck that cost $30,000, and it has accumulated depreciation of $16,000 on this truck. Overland has decided to sell the truck. (a) What entry would Overland Trucking make to record the sale of the truck for $17,000 cash? (b) What entry would Overland Trucking make to record the sale of the truck for $10,000 cash?

Action Plan

✔ At the time of disposal, determine the book value of the asset.

✔ Compare the asset's book value with the proceeds received to determine whether a gain or loss has occurred.

Solution

(a) Sale of truck for cash at a gain:

Cash	17,000	
Accumulated Depreciation—Equipment	16,000	
Equipment		30,000
Gain on Disposal of Plant Assets [$17,000 − ($30,000 − $16,000)]		3,000
(To record sale of truck at a gain)		

(b) Sale of truck for cash at a loss:

Cash	10,000	
Accumulated Depreciation—Equipment	16,000	
Loss on Disposal of Plant Assets [$10,000 − ($30,000 − $16,000)]	4,000	
Equipment		30,000
(To record sale of truck at a loss)		

Related exercise material: **BE9-9, BE9-10, E9-9, E9-10, and DO IT! 9-4.**

✔ **The Navigator**

Natural Resources

Natural resources consist of standing timber and underground deposits of oil, gas, and minerals. These long-lived productive assets have two distinguishing characteristics: (1) They are physically extracted in operations (such as mining, cutting, or pumping). (2) They are replaceable only by an act of nature.

The acquisition cost of a natural resource is the price needed to acquire the resource **and** prepare it for its intended use. For an already-discovered resource, such as an existing coal mine, cost is the price paid for the property.

The allocation of the cost of natural resources to expense in a rational and systematic manner over the resource's useful life is called **depletion**. (That is, *depletion* is to natural resources as *depreciation* is to plant assets.) **Companies generally use the units-of-activity method** (learned earlier in the chapter) **to compute depletion.** The reason is that **depletion generally is a function of the units extracted during the year.**

Under the units-of-activity method, companies divide the total cost of the natural resource minus salvage value by the number of units estimated to be in the resource. The result is a **depletion cost per unit of product.** They then multiply the depletion cost per unit by the number of units extracted and sold. The result is the **annual depletion expense**. Illustration 9-21 shows the formula to compute depletion expense.

LEARNING OBJECTIVE 5

Compute periodic depletion of natural resources.

Helpful Hint
On a balance sheet, natural resources may be described more specifically as *timberlands, mineral deposits, oil reserves*, and so on.

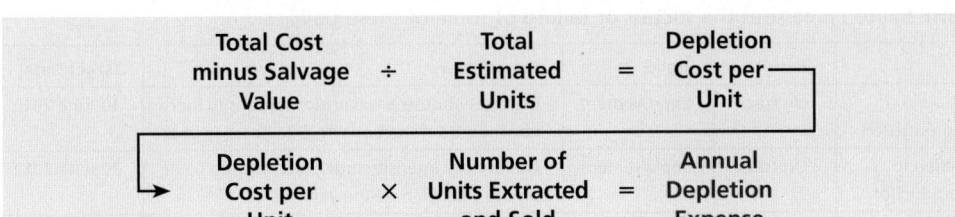

Illustration 9-21
Formula to compute depletion expense

To illustrate, assume that Lane Coal Company invests $5 million in a mine estimated to have 10 million tons of coal and no salvage value. In the first year, Lane extracts and sells 800,000 tons of coal. Using the formulas above, Lane computes the depletion expense as follows.

$5,000,000 ÷ 10,000,000 = $0.50 depletion cost per ton

$0.50 × 800,000 = $400,000 annual depletion expense

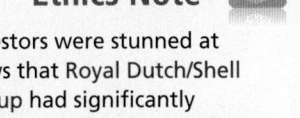

Ethics Note

Investors were stunned at news that Royal Dutch/Shell Group had significantly overstated its reported oil reserves—and perhaps had done so intentionally.

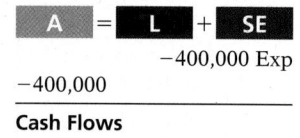

−400,000

Cash Flows
no effect

Lane records depletion expense for the first year of operation as follows.

Dec. 31	Depletion Expense	400,000	
	Accumulated Depletion		400,000
	(To record depletion expense on coal deposits)		

The company reports the account Depletion Expense as a part of the cost of producing the product. Accumulated Depletion is a contra-asset account, similar to accumulated depreciation. It is deducted from the cost of the natural resource in the balance sheet, as Illustration 9-22 shows.

Illustration 9-22
Statement presentation of accumulated depletion

Lane Coal Company		
Balance Sheet (partial)		
Coal mine	$5,000,000	
Less: Accumulated depletion	**400,000**	$4,600,000

Many companies do not use an Accumulated Depletion account. In such cases, the company credits the amount of depletion directly to the natural resources account.

Sometimes, a company will extract natural resources in one accounting period but not sell them until a later period. In this case, the company does not expense the depletion until it sells the resource. It reports the amount not sold as inventory in the current assets section.

PEOPLE, PLANET, AND PROFIT INSIGHT

Sustainability Report Please

Sustainability reports identify how the company is meeting its corporate social responsibilities. Many companies, both large and small, are now issuing these reports. For example, companies such as Disney, Best Buy, Microsoft, Ford, and ConocoPhilips issue these reports. Presented below is an adapted section of BHP Billiton's (a global mining, oil, and gas company) sustainability report on its environmental policies. These policies are to (1) take action to address the challenges of climate change, (2) set and achieve targets that reduce pollution, and (3) enhance biodiversity by assessing and considering ecological values and land-use aspects. Here is how BHP Billiton measures the success or failure of some of these policies:

Environment	Result	Trend	Commentary	Target Date
Aggregate Group target of 6% reduction in greenhouse gas emissions per unit of production	On track	Improvement	Our greenhouse gas emissions intensity index has reduced 7% on our FY2006 baseline year	30 June 2012
Aggregate Group target of 13% reduction in carbon-based energy use per unit of production	On track	Improvement	Our energy intensity index has reduced 6% on our FY2006 baseline year	30 June 2012
Aggregate Group target of a 10% improvement in the ratio of water recycled/reused to high-quality water consumed	On track	Deterioration	Our water use index has improved 7% on our FY2007 baseline year	30 June 2012

In addition to the environment, BHP Billiton has sections in its sustainability report which discuss people, safety, health, and community.

Source: BHP Billiton, *2010 Sustainability Report.*

 Why do you believe companies issue sustainability reports? (See page 469.)

Intangible Assets

Intangible assets are rights, privileges, and competitive advantages that result from the ownership of long-lived assets that do not possess physical substance. Evidence of intangibles may exist in the form of contracts or licenses. Intangibles may arise from the following sources:

1. Government grants, such as patents, copyrights, licenses, trademarks, and trade names.
2. Acquisition of another business, in which the purchase price includes a payment for *goodwill*.
3. Private monopolistic arrangements arising from contractual agreements, such as franchises and leases.

Some widely known intangibles are Microsoft's patents, McDonald's franchises, Apple's trade name iPod, J.K. Rowlings' copyrights on the *Harry Potter* books, and the trademark Rent-A-Wreck in the Feature Story.

LEARNING OBJECTIVE   6

Explain the basic issues related to accounting for intangible assets.

Accounting for Intangible Assets

Companies record intangible assets at cost. Intangibles are categorized as having either a limited life or an indefinite life. If an intangible has a **limited life**, the company allocates its cost over the asset's useful life using a process similar to depreciation. The process of allocating the cost of intangibles is referred to as **amortization**. The cost of intangible assets with **indefinite lives should not be amortized**.

To record amortization of an intangible asset, a company increases (debits) Amortization Expense and decreases (credits) the specific intangible asset. (Unlike depreciation, no contra account, such as Accumulated Amortization, is usually used.)

Intangible assets are typically amortized on a straight-line basis. For example, the legal life of a patent is 20 years. Companies **amortize the cost of a patent over its 20-year life or its useful life, whichever is shorter**. To illustrate the computation of patent amortization, assume that National Labs purchases a patent at a cost of $60,000. If National estimates the useful life of the patent to be eight years, the annual amortization expense is $7,500 ($60,000 ÷ 8). National records the annual amortization as follows.

Helpful Hint
Amortization is to intangibles what *depreciation* is to plant assets and *depletion* is to natural resources.

Dec. 31	Amortization Expense	7,500	
	Patents		7,500
	(To record patent amortization)		

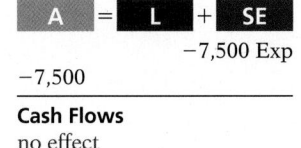

A = L + SE
−7,500   −7,500 Exp

Cash Flows
no effect

Companies classify Amortization Expense as an operating expense in the income statement.

There is a difference between intangible assets and plant assets in determining cost. For plant assets, cost includes both the purchase price of the asset and the costs incurred in designing and constructing the asset. In contrast, cost for an intangible asset includes **only the purchase price**. Companies expense any costs incurred in developing an intangible asset.

PATENTS

A **patent** is an exclusive right issued by the U.S. Patent Office that enables the recipient to manufacture, sell, or otherwise control an invention for a period of 20 years from the date of the grant. A patent is nonrenewable. But, companies can extend the legal life of a patent by obtaining new patents for improvements or other changes in the basic design. **The initial cost of a patent is the cash or cash equivalent price paid to acquire the patent.**

The saying, "A patent is only as good as the money you're prepared to spend defending it," is very true. Most patents are subject to litigation by competitors. Any legal costs an owner incurs in successfully defending a patent in an infringement suit are considered necessary to establish the patent's validity. **The owner adds those costs to the Patents account and amortizes them over the remaining life of the patent.**

The patent holder amortizes the cost of a patent over its 20-year legal life or its useful life, whichever is shorter. Companies consider obsolescence and inadequacy in determining useful life. These factors may cause a patent to become economically ineffective before the end of its legal life.

COPYRIGHTS

The federal government grants **copyrights**, which give the owner the exclusive right to reproduce and sell an artistic or published work. Copyrights extend for the life of the creator plus 70 years. The cost of a copyright is the **cost of acquiring and defending it**. The cost may be only the small fee paid to the U.S. Copyright Office. Or, it may amount to much more if an infringement suit is involved.

The useful life of a copyright generally is significantly shorter than its legal life. Therefore, copyrights usually are amortized over a relatively short period of time.

TRADEMARKS AND TRADE NAMES

A **trademark** or **trade name** is a word, phrase, jingle, or symbol that identifies a particular enterprise or product. Trade names like Wheaties, Monopoly, Big Mac, Kleenex, Coca-Cola, and Jeep create immediate product identification. They also generally enhance the sale of the product. The creator or original user may obtain exclusive legal right to the trademark or trade name by registering it with the U.S. Patent Office. Such registration provides 20 years of protection. The registration may be renewed indefinitely as long as the trademark or trade name is in use.

If a company purchases the trademark or trade name, its cost is the purchase price. If a company develops and maintains the trademark or trade name, any costs related to these activities are expensed as incurred. Because trademarks and trade names have indefinite lives, they are not amortized.

FRANCHISES AND LICENSES

When you fill up your tank at the corner Shell station, eat lunch at Subway, or rent a car from Rent-A-Wreck, you are dealing with franchises. A **franchise** is a contractual arrangement between a franchisor and a franchisee. The franchisor grants the franchisee the right to sell certain products, provide specific services, or use certain trademarks or trade names, usually within a designated geographic area.

Another type of franchise is that entered into between a governmental body (commonly municipalities) and a company. This franchise permits the company to use public property in performing its services. Examples are the use of city streets for a bus line or taxi service, use of public land for telephone and electric lines, and the use of airwaves for radio or TV broadcasting. Such operating rights are referred to as **licenses**. Franchises and licenses may by granted for a definite period of time, an indefinite period, or perpetually.

When a company can identify costs with the purchase of a franchise or license, it should recognize an intangible asset. Companies should amortize the cost of a limited-life franchise (or license) over its useful life. If the life is indefinite, the cost is not amortized. Annual payments made under a franchise agreement are recorded as **operating expenses** in the period in which they are incurred.

GOODWILL

Usually, the largest intangible asset that appears on a company's balance sheet is goodwill. **Goodwill** represents the value of all favorable attributes that relate to a company that are not attributable to any other specific asset. These include exceptional management, desirable location, good customer relations, skilled employees, high-quality products, and harmonious relations with labor unions. Goodwill is unique: Unlike assets such as investments and plant assets, which can be sold *individually* in the marketplace, goodwill can be identified only with the business as a whole.

If goodwill can be identified only with the business as a whole, how can its amount be determined? One could try to put a dollar value on the factors listed above (exceptional management, desirable location, and so on). But, the results would be very subjective, and such subjective valuations would not contribute to the reliability of financial statements. **Therefore, companies record goodwill only when an entire business is purchased. In that case, goodwill is the excess of cost over the fair value of the net assets (assets less liabilities) acquired.**

In recording the purchase of a business, the company debits (increases) the identifiable acquired assets, credits liabilities at their fair values, credits cash for the purchase price, and records the difference as goodwill. **Goodwill is not amortized** because it is considered to have an indefinite life. Companies report goodwill in the balance sheet under intangible assets.

INTERNATIONAL INSIGHT

Should Companies Write Up Goodwill?

Softbank Corp. is Japan's biggest Internet company. At one time, it boosted the profit margin of its mobile-phone unit from 3.2% to 11.2% through what appeared to some as accounting tricks. What did it do? It wrote down the value of its mobile-phone-unit assets by half. This would normally result in a huge loss. But rather than take a loss, the company wrote up goodwill by the same amount. How did this move increase earnings? The assets were being depreciated over 10 years, but the company amortizes goodwill over 20 years. (Amortization of goodwill was allowed under the accounting standards it followed at that time.) While the new treatment did not break any rules, the company was criticized by investors for not providing sufficient justification or a detailed explanation for the sudden shift in policy.

Source: Andrew Morse and Yukari Iwatani Kane, "Softbank's Accounting Shift Raises Eyebrows," *Wall Street Journal* (August 28, 2007), p. C1.

 Do you think that this treatment would be allowed under U.S. GAAP? (See page 469.)

Research and Development Costs

Research and development costs are expenditures that may lead to patents, copyrights, new processes, and new products. Many companies spend considerable sums of money on research and development (R&D). For example, in a recent year, IBM spent over $5.1 billion on R&D.

Research and development costs present accounting problems. For one thing, it is sometimes difficult to assign the costs to specific projects. Also, there are uncertainties in identifying the extent and timing of future benefits. As a result,

Helpful Hint
Research and development (R&D) costs are not intangible assets. But because they may lead to patents and copyrights, we discuss them in this section.

companies usually record R&D costs **as an expense when incurred**, whether the research and development is successful or not.

To illustrate, assume that Laser Scanner Company spent $3 million on R&D that resulted in two highly successful patents. It spent $20,000 on legal fees for the patents. The company would add the lawyers' fees to the patent account. The R&D costs, however, cannot be included in the cost of the patent. Instead, the company would record the R&D costs as an expense when incurred.

Many disagree with this accounting approach. They argue that expensing R&D costs leads to understated assets and net income. Others, however, argue that capitalizing these costs will lead to highly speculative assets on the balance sheet. Who is right is difficult to determine.

> ## DO IT!

Classification Concepts

Match the statement with the term most directly associated with it.

Copyrights   Depletion
Intangible assets   Franchises
Research and development costs

1. _____ The allocation of the cost of a natural resource to expense in a rational and systematic manner.

2. _____ Rights, privileges, and competitive advantages that result from the ownership of long-lived assets that do not possess physical substance.

3. _____ An exclusive right granted by the federal government to reproduce and sell an artistic or published work.

4. _____ A right to sell certain products or services or to use certain trademarks or trade names within a designated geographic area.

5. _____ Costs incurred by a company that often lead to patents or new products. These costs must be expensed as incurred.

Action Plan

✔ Know that the accounting for intangibles often depends on whether the item has a finite or indefinite life.

✔ Recognize the many similarities and differences between the accounting for natural resources, plant assets, and intangible assets.

Solution

1. Depletion
2. Intangible assets
3. Copyrights
4. Franchises
5. Research and development costs

Related exercise material: **BE9-11, BE9-12, E9-11, E9-12, E9-13, and** DO IT! **9-5.**

✔ **The Navigator**

Statement Presentation and Analysis

LEARNING OBJECTIVE   7

Indicate how plant assets, natural resources, and intangible assets are reported.

Presentation

Usually, companies combine plant assets and natural resources under "Property, plant, and equipment" in the balance sheet. They show intangibles separately. Companies disclose either in the balance sheet or the notes the balances of the major classes of assets, such as land, buildings, and equipment, and accumulated depreciation by major classes or in total. In addition, they should describe the depreciation and amortization methods that were used, as well as disclose the amount of depreciation and amortization expense for the period.

Illustration 9-23 shows a typical financial statement presentation of property, plant, and equipment and intangibles for The Procter & Gamble Company (P&G) in its 2010 balance sheet. The notes to P&G's financial statements present greater details about the accounting for its long-term tangible and intangible assets.

The Procter & Gamble Company
Balance Sheet (partial)
(in millions)

	June 30	
	2010	2009
Property, plant, and equipment		
Buildings	$ 6,868	$ 6,724
Machinery and equipment	29,294	29,042
Land	850	885
	37,012	36,651
Accumulated depreciation	(17,768)	(17,189)
Net property, plant, and equipment	19,244	19,462
Goodwill and other intangible assets		
Goodwill	54,012	56,512
Trademarks and other intangible assets, net	31,636	32,606
Net goodwill and other intangible assets	$85,648	$89,118

Illustration 9-23
P&G's presentation of property, plant, and equipment, and intangible assets

Illustration 9-24 shows another comprehensive presentation of property, plant, and equipment from the balance sheet of Owens-Illinois, Inc. The notes to the financial statements of Owens-Illinois identify the major classes of property, plant, and equipment. They also indicate that depreciation and amortization are by the straight-line method, and depletion is by the units-of-activity method.

Owens-Illinois, Inc.
Balance Sheet (partial)
(in millions)

Property, plant, and equipment			
Timberlands, at cost, less accumulated depletion		$ 95.4	
Buildings and equipment, at cost	$2,207.1		
Less: Accumulated depreciation	1,229.0	978.1	
Total property, plant, and equipment			$1,073.5
Intangibles			
Patents			410.0
Total			$1,483.5

Illustration 9-24
Owens-Illinois' presentation of property, plant, and equipment, and intangible assets

Analysis

Using ratios, we can analyze how efficiently a company uses its assets to generate sales. The **asset turnover ratio** analyzes the productivity of a company's assets. It tells us how many dollars of sales a company generates for each dollar invested in assets. This ratio is computed by dividing net sales by average total assets for the period. The formula in Illustration 9-25 shows the computation of the asset turnover ratio for The Procter & Gamble Company. P&G's net sales for 2010 were $78,938 million. Its total ending assets were $128,172 million, and beginning assets were $134,833 million.

Illustration 9-25
Asset turnover formula and computation

Net Sales	÷	Average Total Assets	=	Asset Turnover Ratio
$78,938	÷	$\dfrac{\$128,172 + \$134,833}{2}$	=	.60 times

Thus, each dollar invested in assets produced $0.60 in sales for P&G. If a company is using its assets efficiently, each dollar of assets will create a high amount of sales. This ratio varies greatly among different industries—from those that are asset-intensive (utilities) to those that are not (services).

> **Comprehensive DO IT! 1**

DuPage Company purchases a factory machine at a cost of $18,000 on January 1, 2014. DuPage expects the machine to have a salvage value of $2,000 at the end of its 4-year useful life.

During its useful life, the machine is expected to be used 160,000 hours. Actual annual hourly use was 2014, 40,000; 2015, 60,000; 2016, 35,000; and 2017, 25,000.

Instructions
Prepare depreciation schedules for the following methods: (a) straight-line, (b) units-of-activity, and (c) declining-balance using double the straight-line rate.

Solution to Comprehensive DO IT! 1

Action Plan

✔ Under the straight-line method, apply the depreciation rate to depreciable cost.

✔ Under the units-of-activity method, compute the depreciable cost per unit by dividing depreciable cost by total units of activity.

✔ Under the declining-balance method, apply the depreciation rate to **book value** at the beginning of the year.

(a)

Straight-Line Method

Year	Depreciable Cost* ×	Depreciation Rate =	Annual Depreciation Expense	Accumulated Depreciation	Book Value
2014	$16,000	25%	$4,000	$ 4,000	$14,000**
2015	16,000	25%	4,000	8,000	10,000
2016	16,000	25%	4,000	12,000	6,000
2017	16,000	25%	4,000	16,000	2,000

*$18,000 − $2,000.
**$18,000 − $4,000.

(b)

Units-of-Activity Method

Year	Units of Activity ×	Depreciable Cost/Unit =	Annual Depreciation Expense	Accumulated Depreciation	Book Value
2014	40,000	$0.10*	$4,000	$ 4,000	$14,000
2015	60,000	0.10	6,000	10,000	8,000
2016	35,000	0.10	3,500	13,500	4,500
2017	25,000	0.10	2,500	16,000	2,000

*($18,000 − $2,000) ÷ 160,000.

(c)

Declining-Balance Method

	Computation				End of Year	
Year	Book Value Beginning of Year	×	Depreciation Rate*	=	Annual Depreciation Expense	Accumulated Depreciation	Book Value
2014	$18,000		50%		$9,000	$ 9,000	$9,000
2015	9,000		50%		4,500	13,500	4,500
2016	4,500		50%		2,250	15,750	2,250
2017	2,250		50%		250**	16,000	2,000

*¼ × 2.
**Adjusted to $250 because ending book value should not be less than expected salvage value.

 The Navigator

> Comprehensive **DO IT! 2**

On January 1, 2014, Skyline Limousine Co. purchased a limo at an acquisition cost of $28,000. The vehicle has been depreciated by the straight-line method using a 4-year service life and a $4,000 salvage value. The company's fiscal year ends on December 31.

Instructions
Prepare the journal entry or entries to record the disposal of the limousine assuming that it was:

(a) Retired and scrapped with no salvage value on January 1, 2018.

(b) Sold for $5,000 on July 1, 2017.

Solution to Comprehensive **DO IT!** 2

Action Plan

✔ At the time of disposal, determine the book value of the asset.

✔ Recognize any gain or loss from disposal of the asset.

✔ Remove the book value of the asset from the records by debiting Accumulated Depreciation for the total depreciation to date of disposal and crediting the asset account for the cost of the asset.

(a) 1/1/18	Accumulated Depreciation—Equipment	24,000	
	Loss on Disposal of Plant Assets	4,000	
	Equipment		28,000
	(To record retirement of limousine)		
(b) 7/1/17	Depreciation Expense	3,000	
	Accumulated Depreciation—Equipment		3,000
	(To record depreciation to date of disposal)		
	Cash	5,000	
	Accumulated Depreciation—Equipment	21,000	
	Loss on Disposal of Plant Assets	2,000	
	Equipment		28,000
	(To record sale of limousine)		

 The Navigator

SUMMARY OF LEARNING OBJECTIVES

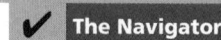
1 Describe how the cost principle applies to plant assets. The cost of plant assets includes all expenditures necessary to acquire the asset and make it ready for its intended use. Once cost is established, a company uses that amount as the basis of accounting for the plant asset over its useful life.

2 Explain the concept of depreciation and how to compute it. Depreciation is the allocation of the cost of a plant asset to expense over its useful (service) life in a rational and systematic manner. Depreciation is not a process of valuation, nor is it a process that results in an accumulation of cash.

Three depreciation methods are:

Method	Effect on Annual Depreciation	Formula
Straight-line	Constant amount	Depreciable cost ÷ Useful life (in years)
Units-of-activity	Varying amount	Depreciable cost per unit × Units of activity during the year
Declining-balance	Decreasing amount	Book value at beginning of year × Declining-balance rate

Companies make revisions of periodic depreciation in present and future periods, not retroactively. They determine the new annual depreciation by dividing the depreciable cost at the time of the revision by the remaining useful life.

3 Distinguish between revenue and capital expenditures, and explain the entries for each. Companies incur revenue expenditures to maintain the operating efficiency and productive life of an asset. They debit these expenditures to Maintenance and Repairs Expense as incurred. Capital expenditures increase the operating efficiency, productive capacity, or expected useful life of the asset. Companies generally debit these expenditures to the plant asset affected.

4 Explain how to account for the disposal of a plant asset. The accounting for disposal of a plant asset through retirement or sale is as follows.
(a) Eliminate the book value of the plant asset at the date of disposal.
(b) Record cash proceeds, if any.
(c) Account for the difference between the book value and the cash proceeds as a gain or loss on disposal.

5 Compute periodic depletion of natural resources. Companies compute depletion cost per unit by dividing the total cost of the natural resource minus salvage value by the number of units estimated to be in the resource. They then multiply the depletion cost per unit by the number of units extracted and sold.

6 Explain the basic issues related to accounting for intangible assets. The process of allocating the cost of an intangible asset is referred to as amortization. The cost of intangible assets with indefinite lives are not amortized. Companies normally use the straight-line method for amortizing intangible assets.

7 Indicate how plant assets, natural resources, and intangible assets are reported. Companies usually combine plant assets and natural resources under property, plant, and equipment; they show intangibles separately under intangible assets. Either within the balance sheet or in the notes, companies should disclose the balances of the major classes of assets, such as land, buildings, and equipment, and accumulated depreciation by major classes or in total. They also should describe the depreciation and amortization methods used, and should disclose the amount of depreciation and amortization expense for the period. The asset turnover ratio measures the productivity of a company's assets in generating sales.

GLOSSARY

Accelerated-depreciation method Depreciation method that produces higher depreciation expense in the early years than in the later years. (p. 432).

Additions and improvements Costs incurred to increase the operating efficiency, productive capacity, or useful life of a plant asset. (p. 435).

Amortization The allocation of the cost of an intangible asset to expense over its useful life in a systematic and rational manner. (p. 441).

Asset turnover ratio A measure of how efficiently a company uses its assets to generate sales; calculated as net sales divided by average total assets. (p. 445).

Capital expenditures Expenditures that increase the company's investment in productive facilities. (p. 435).

Copyrights Exclusive grant from the federal government that allows the owner to reproduce and sell an artistic or published work. (p. 442).

Declining-balance method Depreciation method that applies a constant rate to the declining book value of the asset and produces a decreasing annual depreciation expense over the useful life of the asset. (p. 431).

Depletion The allocation of the cost of a natural resource to expense in a rational and systematic manner over the resource's useful life. (p. 439).

Depreciation The process of allocating to expense the cost of a plant asset over its useful (service) life in a rational and systematic manner. (p. 427).

Depreciable cost The cost of a plant asset less its salvage value. (p. 429).

Franchise (license) A contractual arrangement under which the franchisor grants the franchisee the right to sell certain products, provide specific services, or use certain trademarks or trade names, usually within a designated geographic area. (p. 442).

Going-concern assumption States that the company will continue in operation for the foreseeable future. (p. 428).

Goodwill The value of all favorable attributes that relate to a company that is not attributable to any other specific asset. (p. 443).

Intangible assets Rights, privileges, and competitive advantages that result from the ownership of long-lived assets that do not possess physical substance. (p. 441).

Licenses Operating rights to use public property, granted to a business by a governmental agency. (p. 442).

Materiality concept If an item would not make a difference in decision-making, a company does not have to follow GAAP in reporting it. (p. 435).

Natural resources Assets that consist of standing timber and underground deposits of oil, gas, or minerals. (p. 439).

Ordinary repairs Expenditures to maintain the operating efficiency and productive life of the plant asset. (p. 435).

Patent An exclusive right issued by the U.S. Patent Office that enables the recipient to manufacture, sell, or otherwise control an invention for a period of 20 years from the date of the grant. (p. 441).

Plant assets Tangible resources that are used in the operations of the business and are not intended for sale to customers. (p. 424).

Research and development (R&D) costs Expenditures that may lead to patents, copyrights, new processes, or new products. (p. 443).

Revenue expenditures Expenditures that are immediately charged against revenues as an expense. (p. 435).

Salvage value An estimate of an asset's value at the end of its useful life. (p. 429).

Straight-line method Depreciation method in which periodic depreciation is the same for each year of the asset's useful life. (p. 429).

Trademark (trade name) A word, phrase, jingle, or symbol that identifies a particular enterprise or product. (p. 442).

Units-of-activity method Depreciation method in which useful life is expressed in terms of the total units of production or use expected from an asset. (p. 430).

Useful life An estimate of the expected productive life, also called service life, of an asset. (p. 429).

APPENDIX 9A EXCHANGE OF PLANT ASSETS

Ordinarily, companies record a gain or loss on the exchange of plant assets. The rationale for recognizing a gain or loss is that most exchanges have **commercial substance**. An exchange has commercial substance if the future cash flows change as a result of the exchange.

> **LEARNING OBJECTIVE   8**
>
> Explain how to account for the exchange of plant assets.

To illustrate, Ramos Co. exchanges some of its equipment for land held by Brodhead Inc. It is likely that the timing and amount of the cash flows arising from the land will differ significantly from the cash flows arising from the equipment. As a result, both Ramos and Brodhead are in different economic positions. Therefore, **the exchange has commercial substance**, and the companies recognize a gain or loss in the exchange. Because most exchanges have commercial substance (even when similar assets are exchanged), we illustrate only this type of situation, for both a loss and a gain.

Loss Treatment

To illustrate an exchange that results in a loss, assume that Roland Company exchanged a set of used trucks plus cash for a new semi-truck. The used trucks have a combined book value of $42,000 (cost $64,000 less $22,000 accumulated depreciation). Roland's purchasing agent, experienced in the second-hand market, indicates that the used trucks have a fair value of $26,000. In addition to the trucks, Roland must pay $17,000 for the semi-truck. Roland computes the cost of the semi-truck as follows.

Illustration 9A-1
Cost of semi-truck

Fair value of used trucks	$26,000
Cash paid	17,000
Cost of semi-truck	$43,000

Roland incurs a loss on disposal of plant assets of $16,000 on this exchange. The reason is that the book value of the used trucks is greater than the fair value of these trucks. The computation is as follows.

Illustration 9A-2
Computation of loss on disposal

Book value of used trucks ($64,000 − $22,000)	$ 42,000
Fair value of used trucks	26,000
Loss on disposal of plant assets	**$16,000**

In recording an exchange at a loss, three steps are required: (1) eliminate the book value of the asset given up, (2) record the cost of the asset acquired, and (3) recognize the loss on disposal of plant assets. Roland Company thus records the exchange on the loss as follows.

A	=	L	+	SE

+43,000
+22,000

        −16,000 Exp

−64,000
−17,000

Cash Flows
−17,000

Equipment (new)	43,000	
Accumulated Depreciation—Equipment	22,000	
Loss on Disposal of Plant Assets	16,000	
Equipment (old)		64,000
Cash		17,000
(To record exchange of used trucks for semi-truck)		

Gain Treatment

To illustrate a gain situation, assume that Mark Express Delivery decides to exchange its old delivery equipment plus cash of $3,000 for new delivery equipment. The book value of the old delivery equipment is $12,000 (cost $40,000 less accumulated depreciation $28,000). The fair value of the old delivery equipment is $19,000.

The cost of the new asset is the fair value of the old asset exchanged plus any cash paid (or other consideration given up). The cost of the new delivery equipment is $22,000, computed as follows.

Illustration 9A-3
Cost of new delivery equipment

Fair value of old delivery equipment	$ 19,000
Cash paid	3,000
Cost of new delivery equipment	**$22,000**

A gain results when the fair value of the old delivery equipment is greater than its book value. For Mark Express, there is a gain of $7,000 on disposal of plant assets, computed as follows.

Illustration 9A-4
Computation of gain on disposal

Fair value of old delivery equipment	$19,000
Book value of old delivery equipment ($40,000 − $28,000)	12,000
Gain on disposal of plant assets	**$ 7,000**

Mark Express Delivery records the exchange as follows.

Equipment (new)	22,000			+22,000
Accumulated Depreciation—Equipment (old)	28,000			+28,000
Equipment (old)		40,000		−40,000
Gain on Disposal of Plant Assets		7,000		+7,000 Rev
Cash		3,000		−3,000
(To record exchange of old delivery equipment for new delivery equipment)				

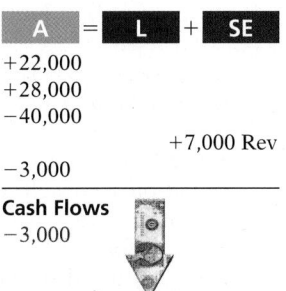

A = L + SE

+22,000
+28,000
−40,000
+7,000 Rev
−3,000

Cash Flows
−3,000

In recording an exchange at a gain, the following three steps are involved: (1) eliminate the book value of the asset given up, (2) record the cost of the asset acquired, and (3) recognize the gain on disposal of plant assets. Accounting for exchanges of plant assets becomes more complex if the transaction does not have commercial substance. This issue is discussed in more advanced accounting classes.

SUMMARY OF LEARNING OBJECTIVE FOR APPENDIX 9A   ✔ The Navigator

8 Explain how to account for the exchange of plant assets. Ordinarily, companies record a gain or loss on the exchange of plant assets. The rationale for recognizing a gain or loss is that most exchanges have commercial substance. An exchange has commercial substance if the future cash flows change as a result of the exchange.

 **WILEY PLUS**   Self-Test, Brief Exercises, Exercises, Problem Set A, and many more components are available for practice in WileyPLUS.

Note: All asterisked Questions, Exercises, and Problems relate to material in the appendix to the chapter.

SELF-TEST QUESTIONS

Answers are on page 469.

(LO 1) **1.** Erin Danielle Company purchased equipment and incurred the following costs.

Cash price	$24,000
Sales taxes	1,200
Insurance during transit	200
Installation and testing	400
Total costs	$25,800

What amount should be recorded as the cost of the equipment?
(a) $24,000.   (c) $25,400.
(b) $25,200.   (d) $25,800.

(LO 2) **2.** Depreciation is a process of:
(a) valuation.   (c) cash accumulation.
(b) cost allocation.   (d) appraisal.

(LO 2) **3.** Micah Bartlett Company purchased equipment on January 1, 2013, at a total invoice cost of $400,000. The equipment has an estimated salvage value of $10,000 and an estimated useful life of 5 years. The amount of accumulated depreciation at December 31, 2014, if the straight-line method of depreciation is used, is:
(a) $80,000.   (c) $78,000.
(b) $160,000.   (d) $156,000.

(LO 2) **4.** Ann Torbert purchased a truck for $11,000 on January 1, 2013. The truck will have an estimated salvage value of $1,000 at the end of 5 years. Using the units-of-activity method, the balance in accumulated depreciation at December 31, 2014, can be computed by the following formula:
(a) ($11,000 ÷ Total estimated activity) × Units of activity for 2014.
(b) ($10,000 ÷ Total estimated activity) × Units of activity for 2014.
(c) ($11,000 ÷ Total estimated activity) × Units of activity for 2013 and 2014.
(d) ($10,000 ÷ Total estimated activity) × Units of activity for 2013 and 2014.

(LO 2) **5.** Jefferson Company purchased a piece of equipment on January 1, 2014. The equipment cost $60,000 and has an estimated life of 8 years and a salvage value of $8,000. What was the depreciation expense for the asset for 2015 under the double-declining-balance method?
(a) $6,500.   (c) $15,000.
(b) $11,250.   (d) $6,562.

(LO 2) **6.** When there is a change in estimated depreciation:
(a) previous depreciation should be corrected.

(b) current and future years' depreciation should be revised.

(c) only future years' depreciation should be revised.

(d) None of the above.

(LO 2) **7.** Able Towing Company purchased a tow truck for $60,000 on January 1, 2012. It was originally depreciated on a straight-line basis over 10 years with an assumed salvage value of $12,000. On December 31, 2014, before adjusting entries had been made, the company decided to change the remaining estimated life to 4 years (including 2014) and the salvage value to $2,000. What was the depreciation expense for 2014?

(a) $6,000.   (c) $15,000.

(b) $4,800.   (d) $12,100.

(LO 3) **8.** Additions to plant assets are:

(a) revenue expenditures.

(b) debited to the Maintenance and Repairs Expense account.

(c) debited to the Purchases account.

(d) capital expenditures.

(LO 4) **9.** Bennie Razor Company has decided to sell one of its old manufacturing machines on June 30, 2014. The machine was purchased for $80,000 on January 1, 2010, and was depreciated on a straight-line basis for 10 years assuming no salvage value. If the machine was sold for $26,000, what was the amount of the gain or loss recorded at the time of the sale?

(a) $18,000.   (c) $22,000.

(b) $54,000.   (d) $46,000.

(LO 5) **10.** Maggie Sharrer Company expects to extract 20 million tons of coal from a mine that cost $12 million. If no salvage value is expected and 2 million tons are mined and sold in the first year, the entry to record depletion will include a:

(a) debit to Accumulated Depletion of $2,000,000.

(b) credit to Depletion Expense of $1,200,000.

(c) debit to Depletion Expense of $1,200,000.

(d) credit to Accumulated Depletion of $2,000,000.

(LO 6) **11.** Which of the following statements is *false*?

(a) If an intangible asset has a finite life, it should be amortized.

(b) The amortization period of an intangible asset can exceed 20 years.

(c) Goodwill is recorded only when a business is purchased.

(d) Research and development costs are expensed when incurred, except when the research and development expenditures result in a successful patent.

(LO 6) **12.** Martha Beyerlein Company incurred $150,000 of research and development costs in its laboratory to develop a patent granted on January 2, 2014. On July 31, 2014, Beyerlein paid $35,000 for legal fees in a successful defense of the patent. The total amount debited to Patents through July 31, 2014, should be:

(a) $150,000.   (c) $185,000.

(b) $35,000.   (d) $170,000.

(LO 7) **13.** Indicate which of the following statements is true.

(a) Since intangible assets lack physical substance, they need be disclosed only in the notes to the financial statements.

(b) Goodwill should be reported as a contra-account in the stockholders' equity section.

(c) Totals of major classes of assets can be shown in the balance sheet, with asset details disclosed in the notes to the financial statements.

(d) Intangible assets are typically combined with plant assets and natural resources and shown in the property, plant, and equipment section.

(LO 7) **14.** Lake Coffee Company reported net sales of $180,000, net income of $54,000, beginning total assets of $200,000, and ending total assets of $300,000. What was the company's asset turnover ratio?

(a) 0.90   (c) 0.72

(b) 0.20   (d) 1.39

(LO 8) ***15.** Schopenhauer Company exchanged an old machine, with a book value of $39,000 and a fair value of $35,000, and paid $10,000 cash for a similar new machine. The transaction has commercial substance. At what amount should the machine acquired in the exchange be recorded on Schopenhauer's books?

(a) $45,000.   (c) $49,000.

(b) $46,000.   (d) $50,000.

(LO 8) ***16.** In exchanges of assets in which the exchange has commercial substance:

(a) neither gains nor losses are recognized immediately.

(b) gains, but not losses, are recognized immediately.

(c) losses, but not gains, are recognized immediately.

(d) both gains and losses are recognized immediately.

Go to the book's companion website, www.wiley.com/college/weygandt, for additional Self-Test Questions.

QUESTIONS

1. Rick Baden is uncertain about the applicability of the cost principle to plant assets. Explain the principle to Rick.

2. What are some examples of land improvements?

3. Lexa Company acquires the land and building owned by Malta Company. What types of costs may be in-

curred to make the asset ready for its intended use if Lexa Company wants to use (a) only the land, and (b) both the land and the building?

4. In a recent newspaper release, the president of Wanzo Company asserted that something has to be done about depreciation. The president said, "Depreciation does not come close to accumulating the cash needed to replace the asset at the end of its useful life." What is your response to the president?

5. Jeremy is studying for the next accounting examination. He asks your help on two questions: (a) What is salvage value? (b) Is salvage value used in determining periodic depreciation under each depreciation method? Answer Jeremy's questions.

6. Contrast the straight-line method and the units-of-activity method as to (a) useful life, and (b) the pattern of periodic depreciation over useful life.

7. Contrast the effects of the three depreciation methods on annual depreciation expense.

8. In the fourth year of an asset's 5-year useful life, the company decides that the asset will have a 6-year service life. How should the revision of depreciation be recorded? Why?

9. Distinguish between revenue expenditures and capital expenditures during useful life.

10. How is a gain or loss on the sale of a plant asset computed?

11. Luis Corporation owns a machine that is fully depreciated but is still being used. How should Luis account for this asset and report it in the financial statements?

12. What are natural resources, and what are their distinguishing characteristics?

13. Explain what depletion is and how it is computed.

14. What are the similarities and differences between the terms depreciation, depletion, and amortization?

15. Spectrum Company hires an accounting intern who says that intangible assets should always be amortized over their legal lives. Is the intern correct? Explain.

16. Goodwill has been defined as the value of all favorable attributes that relate to a business. What types of attributes could result in goodwill?

17. Mark Gannon, a business major, is working on a case problem for one of his classes. In the case problem, the company needs to raise cash to market a new product it developed. Sara Bates, an engineering major, takes one look at the company's balance sheet and says, "This company has an awful lot of goodwill. Why don't you recommend that they sell some of it to raise cash?" How should Mark respond to Sara?

18. Under what conditions is goodwill recorded?

19. Often, research and development costs provide companies with benefits that last a number of years. (For example, these costs can lead to the development of a patent that will increase the company's income for many years.) However, generally accepted accounting principles require that such costs be recorded as an expense when incurred. Why?

20. McDonald's Corporation reports total average assets of $28.9 billion and net sales of $20.5 billion. What is the company's asset turnover ratio?

21. Alpha Corporation and Zito Corporation operate in the same industry. Alpha uses the straight-line method to account for depreciation; Zito uses an accelerated method. Explain what complications might arise in trying to compare the results of these two companies.

22. Wanzo Corporation uses straight-line depreciation for financial reporting purposes but an accelerated method for tax purposes. Is it acceptable to use different methods for the two purposes? What is Wanzo's motivation for doing this?

23. You are comparing two companies in the same industry. You have determined that Lam Corp. depreciates its plant assets over a 40-year life, whereas Shuey Corp. depreciates its plant assets over a 20-year life. Discuss the implications this has for comparing the results of the two companies.

24. Zelm Company is doing significant work to revitalize its warehouses. It is not sure whether it should capitalize these costs or expense them. What are the implications for current-year net income and future net income of expensing versus capitalizing these costs?

25. PEPSICO What classifications and amounts are shown in PepsiCo's Note 4 to explain its total property, plant, and equipment (net) of $19,058 million?

26. When assets are exchanged in a transaction involving commercial substance, how is the gain or loss on disposal of plant assets computed?

*27. Morris Refrigeration Company trades in an old machine on a new model when the fair value of the old machine is greater than its book value. The transaction has commercial substance. Should Morris recognize a gain on disposal of plant assets? If the fair value of the old machine is less than its book value, should Morris recognize a loss on disposal of plant assets?

BRIEF EXERCISES

BE9-1 The following expenditures were incurred by Rosenberg Company in purchasing land: cash price $64,000, accrued taxes $3,000, attorneys' fees $2,500, real estate broker's commission $2,000, and clearing and grading $3,800. What is the cost of the land?

Determine the cost of land.
(LO 1)

BE9-2 Jawson Company incurs the following expenditures in purchasing a truck: cash price $30,000, accident insurance $2,000, sales taxes $1,800, motor vehicle license $160, and painting and lettering $400. What is the cost of the truck?

Determine the cost of a truck.
(LO 1)

Compute straight-line depreciation.

(LO 2)

BE9-3 Weller Company acquires a delivery truck at a cost of $42,000. The truck is expected to have a salvage value of $9,000 at the end of its 4-year useful life. Compute annual depreciation for the first and second years using the straight-line method.

Compute depreciation and evaluate treatment.

(LO 2)

BE9-4 Pioneer Company purchased land and a building on January 1, 2014. Management's best estimate of the value of the land was $100,000 and of the building $200,000. But management told the accounting department to record the land at $225,000 and the building at $75,000. The building is being depreciated on a straight-line basis over 20 years with no salvage value. Why do you suppose management requested this accounting treatment? Is it ethical?

Compute declining-balance depreciation.

(LO 2)

BE9-5 Depreciation information for Weller Company is given in BE9-3. Assuming the declining-balance depreciation rate is double the straight-line rate, compute annual depreciation for the first and second years under the declining-balance method.

Compute depreciation using the units-of-activity method.

(LO 2)

BE9-6 Freemont Taxi Service uses the units-of-activity method in computing depreciation on its taxicabs. Each cab is expected to be driven 150,000 miles. Taxi no. 10 cost $33,500 and is expected to have a salvage value of $500. Taxi no. 10 is driven 36,000 miles in year 1 and 22,000 miles in year 2. Compute the depreciation for each year.

Compute revised depreciation.

(LO 2)

BE9-7 On January 1, 2014, the Vasquez Company ledger shows Equipment $32,000 and Accumulated Depreciation—Equipment $9,000. The depreciation resulted from using the straight-line method with a useful life of 10 years and salvage value of $2,000. On this date, the company concludes that the equipment has a remaining useful life of only 4 years with the same salvage value. Compute the revised annual depreciation.

Prepare entries for delivery truck costs.

(LO 3)

BE9-8 Tong Company had the following two transactions related to its delivery truck.

1. Paid $45 for an oil change.
2. Paid $580 to install special gear unit, which increases the operating efficiency of the truck.

Prepare Tong's journal entries to record these two transactions.

Prepare entries for disposal by retirement.

(LO 4)

BE9-9 Prepare journal entries to record the following.
(a) Perez Company retires its delivery equipment, which cost $44,000. Accumulated depreciation is also $44,000 on this delivery equipment. No salvage value is received.
(b) Assume the same information as (a), except that accumulated depreciation is $39,000, instead of $44,000, on the delivery equipment.

Prepare entries for disposal by sale.

(LO 4)

BE9-10 Arma Company sells equipment on September 30, 2014, for $20,000 cash. The equipment originally cost $72,000 and as of January 1, 2014, had accumulated depreciation of $42,000. Depreciation for the first 9 months of 2014 is $4,800. Prepare the journal entries to (a) update depreciation to September 30, 2014, and (b) record the sale of the equipment.

Prepare depletion expense entry and balance sheet presentation for natural resources.

(LO 5)

BE9-11 Midwest Mining Co. purchased for $7 million a mine that is estimated to have 28 million tons of ore and no salvage value. In the first year, 5 million tons of ore are extracted and sold.
(a) Prepare the journal entry to record depletion expense for the first year.
(b) Show how this mine is reported on the balance sheet at the end of the first year.

Prepare amortization expense entry and balance sheet presentation for intangibles.

(LO 6)

BE9-12 Felipe Company purchases a patent for $120,000 on January 2, 2014. Its estimated useful life is 8 years.
(a) Prepare the journal entry to record amortization expense for the first year.
(b) Show how this patent is reported on the balance sheet at the end of the first year.

Classify long-lived assets on balance sheet.

(LO 7)

BE9-13 Information related to plant assets, natural resources, and intangibles at the end of 2014 for Loomis Company is as follows: buildings $1,300,000; accumulated depreciation—buildings $650,000; goodwill $410,000; coal mine $500,000; accumulated depletion—coal mine $122,000. Prepare a partial balance sheet of Loomis Company for these items.

Analyze long-lived assets.

(LO 7)

BE9-14 In its 2010 annual report, Target reported beginning total assets of $44.5 billion; ending total assets of $43.7 billion; and net sales of $65.8 billion. Compute Target's asset turnover ratio.

Prepare entry for disposal by exchange.

(LO 8)

*BE9-15 Cordero Company exchanges old delivery equipment for new delivery equipment. The book value of the old delivery equipment is $33,000 (cost $61,000 less accumulated depreciation $28,000). Its fair value is $19,000, and cash of $5,000 is paid. Prepare the entry to record the exchange, assuming the transaction has commercial substance.

Prepare entry for disposal by exchange.

(LO 8)

*BE9-16 Assume the same information as BE9-15, except that the fair value of the old delivery equipment is $36,000. Prepare the entry to record the exchange.

> DO IT! REVIEW

DO IT! 9-1 Yockey Company purchased a delivery truck. The total cash payment was $27,820 including the following items.

Negotiated purchase price	$24,000
Installation of special shelving	1,100
Painting and lettering	780
Motor vehicle license	140
Annual insurance policy	500
Sales tax	1,300
Total paid	$27,820

Explain accounting for cost of plant assets.

(LO 1)

Explain how each of these costs would be accounted for.

DO IT! 9-2 On January 1, 2014, Rolling Hills Country Club purchased a new riding mower for $18,000. The mower is expected to have an 8-year life with a $2,000 salvage value. What journal entry would Rolling Hills make at December 31, 2014, if it uses straight-line depreciation?

Calculate depreciation expense and make journal entry.

(LO 2)

DO IT! 9-3 Savin Corporation purchased a piece of equipment for $50,000. It estimated a 6-year life and $2,000 salvage value. At the end of year four (before the depreciation adjustment), it estimated the new total life to be 8 years and the new salvage value to be $4,000. Compute the revised depreciation.

Calculated revised depreciation.

(LO 2)

DO IT! 9-4 Forgetta Manufacturing has old equipment that cost $48,000. The equipment has accumulated depreciation of $28,000 and a fair value of $26,000. Forgetta has decided to sell the equipment.

(a) What entry would Forgetta make to record the sale of the equipment for $26,000 cash?
(b) What entry would Forgetta make to record the sale of the equipment for $15,000 cash?

Make journal entries to record plant asset disposal.

(LO 4)

DO IT! 9-5 Match the statement with the term most directly associated with it.

Goodwill	Amortization
Intangible assets	Franchises
Research and development costs	

Match intangibles classifications concepts.

(LO 5, 6)

1. _____ Rights, privileges, and competitive advantages that result from the ownership of long-lived assets that do not possess physical substance.
2. _____ The allocation of the cost of an intangible asset to expense in a rational and systematic manner.
3. _____ A right to sell certain products or services, or use certain trademarks or trade names within a designated geographic area.
4. _____ Costs incurred by a company that often lead to patents or new products. These costs must be expensed as incurred.
5. _____ The excess of the cost of a company over the fair value of the net assets acquired.

✔ **The Navigator**

EXERCISES

E9-1 The following expenditures relating to plant assets were made by Devereaux Company during the first 2 months of 2014.

1. Paid $5,000 of accrued taxes at time plant site was acquired.
2. Paid $400 insurance to cover possible accident loss on new factory machinery while the machinery was in transit.
3. Paid $850 sales taxes on new delivery truck.

Determine cost of plant acquisitions.

(LO 1)

4. Paid $17,500 for parking lots and driveways on new plant site.
5. Paid $310 to have company name and advertising slogan painted on new delivery truck.
6. Paid $8,000 for installation of new factory machinery.
7. Paid $900 for one-year accident insurance policy on new delivery truck.
8. Paid $90 motor vehicle license fee on the new truck.

Instructions
(a) ▭▭▭▭▷ Explain the application of the cost principle in determining the acquisition cost of plant assets.
(b) List the numbers of the foregoing transactions, and opposite each indicate the account title to which each expenditure should be debited.

Determine property, plant, and equipment costs.

(LO 1)

E9-2 Bliesmer Company incurred the following costs.

1. Sales tax on factory machinery purchased	$ 5,000
2. Painting of and lettering on truck immediately upon purchase	700
3. Installation and testing of factory machinery	2,000
4. Real estate broker's commission on land purchased	3,500
5. Insurance premium paid for first year's insurance on new truck	1,100
6. Cost of landscaping on property purchased	7,200
7. Cost of paving parking lot for new building constructed	17,900
8. Cost of clearing, draining, and filling land	12,600
9. Architect's fees on self-constructed building	10,000

Instructions
Indicate to which account Bliesmer would debit each of the costs.

Determine acquisition costs of land.

(LO 1)

E9-3 On March 1, 2014, Rollinger Company acquired real estate on which it planned to construct a small office building. The company paid $80,000 in cash. An old warehouse on the property was razed at a cost of $9,400; the salvaged materials were sold for $1,700. Additional expenditures before construction began included $1,100 attorney's fee for work concerning the land purchase, $5,000 real estate broker's fee, $7,800 architect's fee, and $12,700 to put in driveways and a parking lot.

Instructions
(a) Determine the amount to be reported as the cost of the land.
(b) For each cost not used in part (a), indicate the account to be debited.

Understand depreciation concepts.

(LO 2)

E9-4 Ann Tremel has prepared the following list of statements about depreciation.

1. Depreciation is a process of asset valuation, not cost allocation.
2. Depreciation provides for the proper matching of expenses with revenues.
3. The book value of a plant asset should approximate its fair value.
4. Depreciation applies to three classes of plant assets: land, buildings, and equipment.
5. Depreciation does not apply to a building because its usefulness and revenue-producing ability generally remain intact over time.
6. The revenue-producing ability of a depreciable asset will decline due to wear and tear and to obsolescence.
7. Recognizing depreciation on an asset results in an accumulation of cash for replacement of the asset.
8. The balance in accumulated depreciation represents the total cost that has been charged to expense.
9. Depreciation expense and accumulated depreciation are reported on the income statement.
10. Four factors affect the computation of depreciation: cost, useful life, salvage value, and residual value.

Instructions
Identify each statement as true or false. If false, indicate how to correct the statement.

Compute depreciation under units-of-activity method.

(LO 2)

E9-5 Wheeler Bus Lines uses the units-of-activity method in depreciating its buses. One bus was purchased on January 1, 2014, at a cost of $145,000. Over its 4-year useful life, the bus is expected to be driven 100,000 miles. Salvage value is expected to be $15,000.

Instructions
(a) Compute the depreciable cost per unit.
(b) Prepare a depreciation schedule assuming actual mileage was: 2014, 26,000; 2015, 32,000; 2016, 25,000; and 2017, 17,000.

E9-6 Xanadu Company purchased a new machine on October 1, 2014, at a cost of $96,000. The company estimated that the machine will have a salvage value of $12,000. The machine is expected to be used for 10,000 working hours during its 5-year life.

Determine depreciation for partial periods.

(LO 2)

Instructions

Compute the depreciation expense under the following methods for the year indicated.

(a) Straight-line for 2014.
(b) Units-of-activity for 2014, assuming machine usage was 1,700 hours.
(c) Declining-balance using double the straight-line rate for 2014 and 2015.

E9-7 Tanger Company purchased a delivery truck for $36,000 on January 1, 2014. The truck has an expected salvage value of $6,000, and is expected to be driven 100,000 miles over its estimated useful life of 8 years. Actual miles driven were 15,000 in 2014 and 12,000 in 2015.

Compute depreciation using different methods.

(LO 2)

Instructions

(a) Compute depreciation expense for 2014 and 2015 using (1) the straight-line method, (2) the units-of-activity method, and (3) the double-declining-balance method.
(b) Assume that Tanger uses the straight-line method.
   (1) Prepare the journal entry to record 2014 depreciation.
   (2) Show how the truck would be reported in the December 31, 2014, balance sheet.

E9-8 Steve Grant, the new controller of Greenbriar Company, has reviewed the expected useful lives and salvage values of selected depreciable assets at the beginning of 2014. His findings are as follows.

Compute revised annual depreciation.

(LO 2)

Type of Asset	Date Acquired	Cost	Accumulated Depreciation 1/1/14	Useful Life in Years Old	Useful Life in Years Proposed	Salvage Value Old	Salvage Value Proposed
Building	1/1/06	$800,000	$152,000	40	50	$40,000	$18,000
Warehouse	1/1/09	100,000	18,000	25	20	10,000	3,700

All assets are depreciated by the straight-line method. Greenbriar Company uses a calendar year in preparing annual financial statements. After discussion, management has agreed to accept Grant's proposed changes.

Instructions

(a) Compute the revised annual depreciation on each asset in 2014. (Show computations.)
(b) Prepare the entry (or entries) to record depreciation on the building in 2014.

E9-9 Presented below are selected transactions at Tomas Company for 2014.

Journalize entries for disposal of plant assets.

(LO 4)

Jan.   1   Retired a piece of machinery that was purchased on January 1, 2004. The machine cost $58,000 on that date. It had a useful life of 10 years with no salvage value.

June 30   Sold a computer that was purchased on January 1, 2011. The computer cost $40,000. It had a useful life of 5 years with no salvage value. The computer was sold for $14,000.

Dec. 31   Discarded a delivery truck that was purchased on January 1, 2010. The truck cost $33,000. It was depreciated based on a 6-year useful life with a $3,000 salvage value.

Instructions

Journalize all entries required on the above dates, including entries to update depreciation, where applicable, on assets disposed of. Tomas Company uses straight-line depreciation. (Assume depreciation is up to date as of December 31, 2013.)

E9-10 Francis Company owns equipment that cost $50,000 when purchased on January 1, 2011. It has been depreciated using the straight-line method based on estimated salvage value of $8,000 and an estimated useful life of 5 years.

Journalize entries for disposal of equipment.

(LO 4)

Instructions

Prepare Francis Company's journal entries to record the sale of the equipment in these four independent situations.

(a) Sold for $28,000 on January 1, 2014.
(b) Sold for $28,000 on May 1, 2014.
(c) Sold for $11,000 on January 1, 2014.
(d) Sold for $11,000 on October 1, 2014.

Journalize entries for natural resources depletion.

(LO 5)

E9-11 On July 1, 2014, Sutton Inc. invested $720,000 in a mine estimated to have 800,000 tons of ore of uniform grade. During the last 6 months of 2014, 120,000 tons of ore were mined and sold.

Instructions
(a) Prepare the journal entry to record depletion expense.
(b) Assume that the 120,000 tons of ore were mined, but only 90,000 units were sold. How are the costs applicable to the 30,000 unsold units reported?

Prepare adjusting entries for amortization.

(LO 6)

E9-12 The following are selected 2014 transactions of Yosuke Corporation.

Jan. 1   Purchased a small company and recorded goodwill of $150,000. Its useful life is indefinite.

May 1   Purchased for $84,000 a patent with an estimated useful life of 5 years and a legal life of 20 years.

Instructions
Prepare necessary adjusting entries at December 31 to record amortization required by the events above.

Prepare entries to set up appropriate accounts for different intangibles; amortize intangible assets.

(LO 6)

E9-13 Nelson Company, organized in 2014, has the following transactions related to intangible assets.

1/2/14	Purchased patent (8-year life)	$560,000
4/1/14	Goodwill purchased (indefinite life)	360,000
7/1/14	10-year franchise; expiration date 7/1/2024	440,000
9/1/14	Research and development costs	223,000

Instructions
Prepare the necessary entries to record these intangibles. All costs incurred were for cash. Make the adjusting entries as of December 31, 2014, recording any necessary amortization and reflecting all balances accurately as of that date.

Calculate asset turnover ratio.

(LO 7)

E9-14 During 2014, Otaki Corporation reported net sales of $5,200,000 and net income of $1,500,000. Its balance sheet reported average total assets of $1,600,000.

Instructions
Calculate the asset turnover ratio.

Journalize entries for exchanges.

(LO 8)

*E9-15 Presented below are two independent transactions. Both transactions have commercial substance.

1. Global Co. exchanged old trucks (cost $64,000 less $22,000 accumulated depreciation) plus cash of $17,000 for new trucks. The old trucks had a fair value of $38,000.
2. Rijo Inc. trades its used machine (cost $12,000 less $4,000 accumulated depreciation) for a new machine. In addition to exchanging the old machine (which had a fair value of $9,000), Rijo also paid cash of $2,700.

Instructions
(a) Prepare the entry to record the exchange of assets by Global Co.
(b) Prepare the entry to record the exchange of assets by Rijo Inc.

Journalize entries for the exchange of plant assets.

(LO 8)

*E9-16 Jay's Delivery Company and Astro's Express Delivery exchanged delivery trucks on January 1, 2014. Jay's truck cost $22,000. It has accumulated depreciation of $16,000 and a fair value of $4,000. Astro's truck cost $10,000. It has accumulated depreciation of $7,000 and a fair value of $4,000. The transaction has commercial substance.

Instructions
(a) Journalize the exchange for Jay's Delivery Company.
(b) Journalize the exchange for Astro's Express Delivery.

EXERCISES: SET B AND CHALLENGE EXERCISES

Visit the book's companion website, at **www.wiley.com/college/weygandt**, and choose the Student Companion site to access Exercise Set B and Challenge Exercises.

PROBLEMS: SET A

P9-1A Ripley Company was organized on January 1. During the first year of operations, the following plant asset expenditures and receipts were recorded in random order.

Determine acquisition costs of land and building.

(LO 1)

Debits

1.	Cost of filling and grading the land	$ 6,000
2.	Full payment to building contractor	780,000
3.	Real estate taxes on land paid for the current year	5,000
4.	Cost of real estate purchased as a plant site (land $100,000 and building $45,000)	145,000
5.	Excavation costs for new building	35,000
6.	Architect's fees on building plans	10,000
7.	Accrued real estate taxes paid at time of purchase of real estate	2,000
8.	Cost of parking lots and driveways	14,000
9.	Cost of demolishing building to make land suitable for construction of new building	15,000
		$1,012,000

Credit

10.	Proceeds from salvage of demolished building	$ 3,600

Instructions
Analyze the foregoing transactions using the following column headings. Insert the number of each transaction in the Item column, and insert the amounts in the appropriate columns. For amounts entered in the Other Accounts column, also indicate the account titles.

Totals

Land $164,400
Buildings $825,000

Item	Land	Buildings	Other Accounts

P9-2A In recent years, Freeman Transportation purchased three used buses. Because of frequent turnover in the accounting department, a different accountant selected the depreciation method for each bus, and various methods were selected. Information concerning the buses is summarized below.

Compute depreciation under different methods.

(LO 2)

Bus	Acquired	Cost	Salvage Value	Useful Life in Years	Depreciation Method
1	1/1/12	$ 96,000	$ 6,000	5	Straight-line
2	1/1/12	140,000	10,000	4	Declining-balance
3	1/1/13	92,000	8,000	5	Units-of-activity

For the declining-balance method, the company uses the double-declining rate. For the units-of-activity method, total miles are expected to be 120,000. Actual miles of use in the first 3 years were 2013, 24,000; 2014, 36,000; and 2015, 31,000.

Instructions
(a) Compute the amount of accumulated depreciation on each bus at December 31, 2014.
(b) If Bus 2 was purchased on April 1 instead of January 1, what is the depreciation expense for this bus in (1) 2012 and (2) 2013?

(a) Bus 2, 2013, $105,000

P9-3A On January 1, 2014, Thao Company purchased the following two machines for use in its production process.

Compute depreciation under different methods.

(LO 2)

Machine A: The cash price of this machine was $35,000. Related expenditures included: sales tax $1,700, shipping costs $150, insurance during shipping $80, installation and testing costs $70, and $100 of oil and lubricants to be used with the machinery during its first year of operations. Thao estimates that the useful life of the machine is 5 years with a $5,000 salvage value remaining at the end of that time period. Assume that the straight-line method of depreciation is used.

Machine B: The recorded cost of this machine was $80,000. Thao estimates that the useful life of the machine is 4 years with a $5,000 salvage value remaining at the end of that time period.

Instructions

(a) Prepare the following for Machine A.
  (1) The journal entry to record its purchase on January 1, 2014.
  (2) The journal entry to record annual depreciation at December 31, 2014.
(b) Calculate the amount of depreciation expense that Thao should record for Machine B each year of its useful life under the following assumptions.
  (1) Thao uses the straight-line method of depreciation.
  (2) Thao uses the declining-balance method. The rate used is twice the straight-line rate.
  (3) Thao uses the units-of-activity method and estimates that the useful life of the machine is 125,000 units. Actual usage is as follows: 2014, 42,000 units; 2015, 35,000 units; 2016, 28,000 units; 2017, 20,000 units.
(c) Which method used to calculate depreciation on Machine B reports the highest amount of depreciation expense in year 1 (2014)? The highest amount in year 4 (2017)? The highest total amount over the 4-year period?

(b) (2) 2014 DDB
depreciation $40,000

Calculate revisions to depreciation expense.

(LO 2)

P9-4A At the beginning of 2012, Mansen Company acquired equipment costing $80,000. It was estimated that this equipment would have a useful life of 6 years and a residual value of $8,000 at that time. The straight-line method of depreciation was considered the most appropriate to use with this type of equipment. Depreciation is to be recorded at the end of each year.

During 2014 (the third year of the equipment's life), the company's engineers reconsidered their expectations, and estimated that the equipment's useful life would probably be 7 years (in total) instead of 6 years. The estimated residual value was not changed at that time. However, during 2017 the estimated residual value was reduced to $4,400.

Instructions

Indicate how much depreciation expense should be recorded each year for this equipment, by completing the following table.

Year	Depreciation Expense	Accumulated Depreciation
2012		
2013		
2014		
2015		
2016		
2017		
2018		

2018 depreciation expense,
$11,400

Journalize a series of equipment transactions related to purchase, sale, retirement, and depreciation.

(LO 2, 4, 7)

P9-5A At December 31, 2013, Walton Company reported the following as plant assets.

Land		$ 3,000,000
Buildings	$26,500,000	
Less: Accumulated depreciation—buildings	12,100,000	14,400,000
Equipment	40,000,000	
Less: Accumulated depreciation—equipment	5,000,000	35,000,000
Total plant assets		$52,400,000

During 2014, the following selected cash transactions occurred.

April 1 Purchased land for $2,200,000.
May 1   Sold equipment that cost $750,000 when purchased on January 1, 2010. The equipment was sold for $460,000.
June 1 Sold land purchased on June 1, 2004 for $1,800,000. The land cost $300,000.
July 1 Purchased equipment for $2,400,000.
Dec. 31 Retired equipment that cost $500,000 when purchased on December 31, 2004. No salvage value was received.

Instructions

(a) Journalize the above transactions. The company uses straight-line depreciation for buildings and equipment. The buildings are estimated to have a 50-year life and no salvage value. The equipment is estimated to have a 10-year useful life and no salvage value. Update depreciation on assets disposed of at the time of sale or retirement.
(b) Record adjusting entries for depreciation for 2014.
(c) Prepare the plant assets section of Walton's balance sheet at December 31, 2014.

(b) Depreciation Expense—
Buildings $530,000;
Equipment $3,995,000
(c) Total plant assets
$51,675,000

P9-6A Yount Co. has equipment that cost $50,000 and that has been depreciated $22,000. Record the disposal under the following assumptions.

(a) It was scrapped as having no value.
(b) It was sold for $25,000.
(c) It was sold for $31,000.

Record disposals

(LO 4)

P9-7A The intangible assets section of Glover Company at December 31, 2013, is presented below.

Patents ($60,000 cost less $6,000 amortization)	$54,000
Franchises ($48,000 cost less $19,200 amortization)	28,800
Total	$82,800

The patent was acquired in January 2013 and has a useful life of 10 years. The franchise was acquired in January 2010 and also has a useful life of 10 years. The following cash transactions may have affected intangible assets during 2014.

Jan. 2	Paid $36,000 legal costs to successfully defend the patent against infringement by another company.
Jan.–June	Developed a new product, incurring $140,000 in research and development costs. A patent was granted for the product on July 1. Its useful life is equal to its legal life.
Sept. 1	Paid $58,000 to an extremely large defensive lineman to appear in commercials advertising the company's products. The commercials will air in September and October.
Oct. 1	Acquired a franchise for $100,000. The franchise has a useful life of 50 years.

Instructions
(a) Prepare journal entries to record the transactions above.
(b) Prepare journal entries to record the 2014 amortization expense.
(c) Prepare the intangible assets section of the balance sheet at December 31, 2014.

Prepare entries to record transactions related to acquisition and amortization of intangibles; prepare the intangible assets section.

(LO 6, 7)

(b) Amortization Expense (patents) $10,000
Amortization Expense (franchises) $5,300
(c) Total intangible assets $203,500

P9-8A Due to rapid turnover in the accounting department, a number of transactions involving intangible assets were improperly recorded by the Buek Company in 2014.

1. Buek developed a new manufacturing process, incurring research and development costs of $147,000. The company also purchased a patent for $60,000. In early January, Buek capitalized $207,000 as the cost of the patents. Patent amortization expense of $10,350 was recorded based on a 20-year useful life.
2. On July 1, 2014, Buek purchased a small company and as a result acquired goodwill of $80,000. Buek recorded a half-year's amortization in 2014, based on a 50-year life ($800 amortization). The goodwill has an indefinite life.

Instructions
Prepare all journal entries necessary to correct any errors made during 2014. Assume the books have not yet been closed for 2014.

Prepare entries to correct errors made in recording and amortizing intangible assets.

(LO 6)

R&D Exp. $147,000

P9-9A Dirkson Company and Hawkins Corporation, two corporations of roughly the same size, are both involved in the manufacture of in-line skates. Each company depreciates its plant assets using the straight-line approach. An investigation of their financial statements reveals the following information.

Calculate and comment on asset turnover ratio.

(LO 7)

	Dirkson Co.	Hawkins Corp.
Net income	$ 400,000	$ 450,000
Sales revenue	1,200,000	1,140,000
Average total assets	2,000,000	1,500,000
Average plant assets	1,500,000	800,000

Instructions
(a) For each company, calculate the asset turnover ratio.
(b) Based on your calculations in part (a), comment on the relative effectiveness of the two companies in using their assets to generate sales and produce net income.

Determine acquisition costs of land and building.

(LO 1)

P9-1B Foxx Company was organized on January 1. During the first year of operations, the following plant asset expenditures and receipts were recorded in random order.

Debits

1.	Accrued real estate taxes paid at time of purchase of real estate	$ 9,000
2.	Real estate taxes on land paid for the current year	6,500
3.	Full payment to building contractor	500,000
4.	Excavation costs for new building	19,000
5.	Cost of real estate purchased as a plant site (land $75,000 and building $25,000)	100,000
6.	Cost of parking lots and driveways	18,000
7.	Architect's fees on building plans	9,000
8.	Installation cost of fences around property	6,000
9.	Cost of demolishing building to make land suitable for construction of new building	19,000
		$686,500

Credit

10.	Proceeds from salvage of demolished building	$ 3,800

Instructions

Analyze the foregoing transactions using the following column headings. Insert the number of each transaction in the Item column, and insert the amounts in the appropriate columns. For amounts entered in the Other Accounts column, also indicate the account title.

Totals

Land $124,200
Buildings $528,000

Item	Land	Buildings	Other Accounts

Compute depreciation under different methods.

(LO 2)

P9-2B In recent years, Hrubeck Company purchased three machines. Because of heavy turnover in the accounting department, a different accountant was in charge of selecting the depreciation method for each machine, and each selected a different method. Information concerning the machines is summarized below.

Machine	Acquired	Cost	Salvage Value	Useful Life in Years	Depreciation Method
1	1/1/11	$105,000	$ 5,000	8	Straight-line
2	1/1/12	150,000	10,000	10	Declining-balance
3	11/1/14	100,000	15,000	6	Units-of-activity

For the declining-balance method, the company uses the double-declining rate. For the units-of-activity method, total machine hours are expected to be 25,000. Actual hours of use in the first 3 years were 2014, 1,300; 2015, 4,100; and 2016, 5,500.

Instructions

(a) Machine 2, 2013, $24,000

(a) Compute the amount of accumulated depreciation on each machine at December 31, 2014.
(b) If Machine 2 had been purchased on May 1 instead of January 1, what would be the depreciation expense for this machine in (1) 2012 and (2) 2013?

Compute depreciation under different methods.

(LO 2)

P9-3B On January 1, 2014, Abraham Company purchased the following two machines for use in its production process.

Machine A: The cash price of this machine was $55,000. Related expenditures included: sales tax $2,750, shipping costs $100, insurance during shipping $75, installation and testing costs $75, and $90 of oil and lubricants to be used with the machinery during its first year of operation. Abraham estimates that the useful life of the machine is 4 years with a $6,000 salvage value remaining at the end of that time period.

Machine B: The recorded cost of this machine was $130,000. Abraham estimates that the useful life of the machine is 5 years with a $10,000 salvage value remaining at the end of that time period.

Instructions

(a) Prepare the following for Machine A.
   (1) The journal entry to record its purchase on January 1, 2014.
   (2) The journal entry to record annual depreciation at December 31, 2014, assuming the straight-line method of depreciation is used.

(b) Calculate the amount of depreciation expense that Abraham should record for Machine B each year of its useful life under the following assumption.
   (1) Abraham uses the straight-line method of depreciation.
   (2) Abraham uses the declining-balance method. The rate used is twice the straight-line rate.
   (3) Abraham uses the units-of-activity method and estimates the useful life of the machine is 24,000 units. Actual usage is as follows: 2014, 4,700 units; 2015, 7,000 units; 2016, 8,000 units; 2017, 2,500 units; 2018, 1,800 units.

(c) Which method used to calculate depreciation on Machine B reports the lowest amount of depreciation expense in year 1 (2014)? The lowest amount in year 5 (2018)? The lowest total amount over the 5-year period?

(a) (2) $13,000

P9-4B At the beginning of 2012, Bellamy Company acquired equipment costing $60,000. It was estimated that this equipment would have a useful life of 6 years and a residual value of $6,000 at that time. The straight-line method of depreciation was considered the most appropriate to use with this type of equipment. Depreciation is to be recorded at the end of each year.

Calculate revisions to depreciation expense.

(LO 2)

During 2014 (the third year of the equipment's life), the company's engineers reconsidered their expectations, and estimated that the equipment's useful life would probably be 7 years (in total) instead of 6 years. The estimated residual value was not changed at that time. However, during 2017 the estimated residual value was reduced to $3,000.

Instructions

Indicate how much depreciation expense should be recorded for this equipment each year by completing the following table.

Year	Depreciation Expense	Accumulated Depreciation
2012		
2013		
2014		
2015		
2016		
2017		
2018		

2018 depreciation expense, $8,700

P9-5B At December 31, 2013, Durango Company reported the following as plant assets.

Journalize a series of equipment transactions related to purchase, sale, retirement, and depreciation.

(LO 2, 4, 7)

Land		$ 2,000,000
Buildings	$28,500,000	
Less: Accumulated depreciation—buildings	12,100,000	16,400,000
Equipment	30,000,000	
Less: Accumulated depreciation—equipment	4,000,000	26,000,000
Total plant assets		$44,400,000

During 2014, the following selected cash transactions occurred.

April 1 Purchased land for $1,200,000.
May 1 Sold equipment that cost $420,000 when purchased on January 1, 2010. The equipment was sold for $246,000.
June 1 Sold land purchased on June 1, 2004, for $1,000,000. The land cost $310,000.
Oct. 1 Purchased equipment for $1,280,000.
Dec. 31 Retired equipment that cost $300,000 when purchased on December 31, 2004. No salvage value was received.

Instructions

(a) Journalize the above transactions. Durango uses straight-line depreciation for buildings and equipment. The buildings are estimated to have a 50-year useful life and no salvage value. The equipment is estimated to have a 10-year useful life and no salvage value. Update depreciation on assets disposed of at the time of sale or retirement.

(b) Depreciation Expense— Buildings $570,000; Equipment $2,960,000

(b) Record adjusting entries for depreciation for 2014.

(c) Prepare the plant assets section of Durango's balance sheet at December 31, 2014.

P9-6B Kellogg's has equipment that cost $40,000 and that has been depreciated $29,000. Record the disposal under the following assumptions.

(a) It was scrapped as having no value.

(b) It was sold for $24,000.

(c) It was sold for $10,000.

P9-7B The intangible assets section of Whitley Company at December 31, 2013, is presented below.

Patents ($100,000 cost less $10,000 amortization)	$ 90,000
Copyrights ($80,000 cost less $32,000 amortization)	48,000
Total	$138,000

The patent was acquired in January 2013 and has a useful life of 10 years. The copyright was acquired in January 2010 and also has a useful life of 10 years. The following cash transactions may have affected intangible assets during 2014.

Jan. 2	Paid $54,000 legal costs to successfully defend the patent against infringement by another company.
Jan.–June	Developed a new product, incurring $230,000 in research and development costs. A patent was granted for the product on July 1. Its useful life is equal to its legal life.
Sept. 1	Paid $125,000 to an Xgames star to appear in commercials advertising the company's products. The commercials will air in September and October.
Nov. 1	Acquired a copyright for $180,000. The copyright has a useful life of 40 years.

Instructions

(a) Prepare journal entries to record the transactions above.

(b) Prepare journal entries to record the 2014 amortization expense for intangible assets.

(c) Prepare the intangible assets section of the balance sheet at December 31, 2014.

(d) ▭▭▭▶ Prepare the note to the financials on Whitley's intangibles as of December 31, 2014.

P9-8B Due to rapid turnover in the accounting department, a number of transactions involving intangible assets were improperly recorded by Goslin Company in 2014.

1. Goslin developed a new manufacturing process, incurring research and development costs of $110,000. The company also purchased a patent for $70,000. In early January, Goslin capitalized $180,000 as the cost of the patents. Patent amortization expense of $9,000 was recorded based on a 20-year useful life.

2. On July 1, 2014, Goslin purchased a small company and as a result acquired goodwill of $200,000. Goslin recorded a half-year's amortization in 2014, based on a 40-year life ($2,500 amortization). The goodwill has an indefinite life.

Instructions

Prepare all journal entries necessary to correct any errors made during 2014. Assume the books have not yet been closed for 2014.

P9-9B Nina Corporation and Vernon Corporation, two corporations of roughly the same size, are both involved in the manufacture of canoes and sea kayaks. Each company depreciates its plant assets using the straight-line approach. An investigation of their financial statements reveals the following information.

	Nina Corp.	Vernon Corp.
Net income	$ 300,000	$ 325,000
Sales revenue	1,100,000	930,000
Average total assets	1,000,000	1,020,000
Average plant assets	750,000	770,000

Instructions

(a) For each company, calculate the asset turnover ratio.

(b) ▭▭▭▶ Based on your calculations in part (a), comment on the relative effectiveness of the two companies in using their assets to generate sales and produce net income.

PROBLEMS: SET C

Visit the book's companion website, at **www.wiley.com/college/weygandt**, and choose the Student Companion site to access Problem Set C.

COMPREHENSIVE PROBLEM: CHAPTERS 3 TO 9

CP9 Raymond Company's trial balance at December 31, 2014, is presented below. All 2014 transactions have been recorded except for the items described below and on page 466.

	Debit	Credit
Cash	$ 28,000	
Accounts Receivable	36,800	
Notes Receivable	10,000	
Interest Receivable	–0–	
Inventory	36,200	
Prepaid Insurance	4,400	
Land	20,000	
Buildings	160,000	
Equipment	60,000	
Patents	8,000	
Allowance for Doubtful Accounts		$ 300
Accumulated Depreciation—Buildings		49,000
Accumulated Depreciation—Equipment		24,000
Accounts Payable		28,300
Income Taxes Payable		–0–
Salaries and Wages Payable		–0–
Unearned Rent Revenue		6,000
Notes Payable (due in 2015)		11,000
Interest Payable		–0–
Notes Payable (due after 2015)		35,000
Common Stock		50,000
Retained Earnings		63,600
Dividends	12,000	
Sales Revenue		910,000
Interest Revenue		–0–
Rent Revenue		–0–
Gain on Disposal of Plant Assets		–0–
Bad Debt Expense	–0–	
Cost of Goods Sold	630,000	
Depreciation Expense	–0–	
Income Tax Expense	–0–	
Insurance Expense	–0–	
Interest Expense	–0–	
Other Operating Expenses	61,800	
Amortization Expense	–0–	
Salaries and Wages Expense	110,000	
Total	$1,177,200	$1,177,200

Unrecorded transactions:

1. On May 1, 2014, Raymond purchased equipment for $13,000 plus sales taxes of $780 (all paid in cash).
2. On July 1, 2014, Raymond sold for $3,500 equipment which originally cost $5,000. Accumulated depreciation on this equipment at January 1, 2014, was $1,800; 2014 depreciation prior to the sale of the equipment was $450.

3. On December 31, 2014, Raymond sold for $9,400 on account inventory that cost $6,600.
4. Raymond estimates that uncollectible accounts receivable at year-end is $4,000.
5. The note receivable is a one-year, 8% note dated April 1, 2014. No interest has been recorded.
6. The balance in prepaid insurance represents payment of a $4,400 6-month premium on October 1, 2014.
7. The building is being depreciated using the straight-line method over 40 years. The salvage value is $20,000.
8. The equipment owned prior to this year is being depreciated using the straight-line method over 5 years. The salvage value is 10% of cost.
9. The equipment purchased on May 1, 2014, is being depreciated using the straight-line method over 5 years, with a salvage value of $1,000.
10. The patent was acquired on January 1, 2014, and has a useful life of 10 years from that date.
11. Unpaid salaries and wages at December 31, 2014, total $2,200.
12. The unearned rent revenue of $6,000 was received on December 1, 2014, for 4 months rent.
13. Both the short-term and long-term notes payable are dated January 1, 2014, and carry a 9% interest rate. All interest is payable in the next 12 months.
14. Income tax expense was $17,000. It was unpaid at December 31.

Instructions
(a) Prepare journal entries for the transactions listed above.
(b) Prepare an updated December 31, 2014, trial balance.
(c) Prepare a 2014 income statement and a 2014 retained earnings statement.
(d) Prepare a December 31, 2014, classified balance sheet.

(b) Totals $1,228,294
(c) Net income $68,256
(d) Total assets $271,996

CONTINUING COOKIE CHRONICLE

(*Note:* This is a continuation of the Cookie Chronicle from Chapters 1–8.)

CCC9 Natalie is also thinking of buying a van that will be used only for business. Natalie is concerned about the impact of the van's cost on her income statement and balance sheet. She has come to you for advice on calculating the van's depreciation.

Go to the book's companion website, www.wiley.com/college/weygandt, to see the completion of this problem.

Broadening Your PERSPECTIVE

Financial Reporting and Analysis

Financial Reporting Problem: PepsiCo, Inc.

BYP9-1 The financial statements and the Notes to Consolidated Financial Statements of PepsiCo, Inc. are presented in Appendix A.

Instructions
Refer to PepsiCo's financial statements and answer the following questions.

(a) What was the total cost and book value of property, plant, and equipment at December 25, 2010?
(b) What method or methods of depreciation are used by the company for financial reporting purposes?

(c) What was the amount of depreciation and amortization expense for each of the three years 2008–2010?

(d) Using the statement of cash flows, what is the amount of capital spending in 2010 and 2009?

(e) Where does the company disclose its intangible assets, and what types of intangibles did it have at December 25, 2010?

Comparative Analysis Problem: PepsiCo, Inc. vs. The Coca-Cola Company

BYP9-2 PepsiCo's financial statements are presented in Appendix A. Financial statements of The Coca-Cola Company are presented in Appendix B.   **PEPSICO**

Instructions

(a) Compute the asset turnover ratio for each company for 2010.

(b) What conclusions concerning the efficiency of assets can be drawn from these data?

Real-World Focus

BYP9-3 *Purpose:* Use an annual report to identify a company's plant assets and the depreciation method used.

Address: **www.annualreports.com**, or go to **www.wiley.com/college/weygandt**

Steps

1. Select a particular company.
2. Search by company name.
3. Follow instructions below.

Instructions

Answer the following questions.

(a) What is the name of the company?

(b) What is the Internet address of the annual report?

(c) At fiscal year-end, what is the net amount of its plant assets?

(d) What is the accumulated depreciation?

(e) Which method of depreciation does the company use?

Critical Thinking

Decision-Making Across the Organization

BYP9-4 Givens Company and Runge Company are two companies that are similar in many respects. One difference is that Givens Company uses the straight-line method and Runge Company uses the declining-balance method at double the straight-line rate. On January 2, 2012, both companies acquired the depreciable assets shown below.

Asset	Cost	Salvage Value	Useful Life
Buildings	$320,000	$20,000	40 years
Equipment	125,000	10,000	10 years

Including the appropriate depreciation charges, annual net income for the companies in the years 2012, 2013, and 2014 and total income for the 3 years were as follows.

	2012	2013	2014	Total
Givens Company	$84,000	$88,400	$90,000	$262,400
Runge Company	68,000	76,000	85,000	229,000

At December 31, 2014, the balance sheets of the two companies are similar except that Runge Company has more cash than Givens Company.

Linda Yanik is interested in buying one of the companies. She comes to you for advice.

Instructions

With the class divided into groups, answer the following.

(a) Determine the annual and total depreciation recorded by each company during the 3 years.

(b) Assuming that Runge Company also uses the straight-line method of depreciation instead of the declining-balance method as in (a), prepare comparative income data for the 3 years.

(c) Which company should Linda Yanik buy? Why?

Communication Activity

BYP9-5 The following was published with the financial statements to American Exploration Company.

American Exploration Company
Notes to the Financial Statements

Property, Plant, and Equipment—The Company accounts for its oil and gas exploration and production activities using the successful efforts method of accounting. Under this method, acquisition costs for proved and unproved properties are capitalized when incurred. . . . The costs of drilling exploratory wells are capitalized pending determination of whether each well has discovered proved reserves. If proved reserves are not discovered, such drilling costs are charged to expense. . . . Depletion of the cost of producing oil and gas properties is computed on the units- of-activity method.

Instructions

Write a brief memo to your instructor discussing American Exploration Company's note regarding property, plant, and equipment. Your memo should address what is meant by the "successful efforts method" and "units-of-activity method."

Ethics Case

BYP9-6 Dieker Container Company is suffering declining sales of its principal product, nonbiodegradeable plastic cartons. The president, Edward Mohling, instructs his controller, Betty Fetters, to lengthen asset lives to reduce depreciation expense. A processing line of automated plastic extruding equipment, purchased for $3.1 million in January 2014, was originally estimated to have a useful life of 8 years and a salvage value of $300,000. Depreciation has been recorded for 2 years on that basis. Edward wants the estimated life changed to 12 years total, and the straight-line method continued. Betty is hesitant to make the change, believing it is unethical to increase net income in this manner. Edward says, "Hey, the life is only an estimate, and I've heard that our competition uses a 12-year life on their production equipment."

Instructions

(a) Who are the stakeholders in this situation?

(b) Is the change in asset life unethical, or is it simply a good business practice by an astute president?

(c) What is the effect of Edward Mohling's proposed change on income before taxes in the year of change?

All About You

BYP9-7 The Feature Story at the beginning of the chapter discussed the company Rent-A-Wreck. Note that the trade name Rent-A-Wreck is a very important asset to the company, as it creates immediate product identification. As indicated in the chapter, companies invest substantial sums to ensure that their product is well-known to the consumer. Test your knowledge of who owns some famous brands and their impact on the financial statements.

Instructions

(a) Provide an answer to the five multiple-choice questions below.

(1) Which company owns both Taco Bell and Pizza Hut?

(a) McDonald's.   (c) Yum Brands.

(b) CKE.   (d) Wendy's.

(2) Dairy Queen belongs to:

(a) Breyer.   (c) GE.

(b) Berkshire Hathaway.   (d) The Coca-Cola Company.

(3) Phillip Morris, the cigarette maker, is owned by:

(a) Altria.   (c) Boeing.

(b) GE.   (d) ExxonMobil.

(4) AOL, a major Internet provider, belongs to:

(a) Microsoft.   (c) NBC.

(b) Cisco.   (d) Time Warner.

(5) ESPN, the sports broadcasting network, is owned by:

(a) Procter & Gamble.   (c) Walt Disney.

(b) Altria.   (d) The Coca-Cola Company.

(b) How do you think the value of these brands is reported on the appropriate company's balance sheet?

FASB Codification Activity

BYP9-8 If your school has a subscription to the FASB Codification, go to *http://aaahq.org/ascLogin. cfm* to log in and prepare responses to the following.

(a) What does it mean to capitalize an item?

(b) What is the definition provided for an intangible asset?

(c) Your great-uncle, who is a CPA, is impressed that you are taking an accounting class. Based on his experience, he believes that depreciation is something that companies do based on past practice, not on the basis of authoritative guidance. Provide the authoritative literature to support the practice of fixed-asset depreciation.

Answers to Chapter Questions

Answers to Insight and Accounting Across the Organization Questions

p. 427 Many U.S. Firms Use Leases Q: Why might airline managers choose to lease rather than purchase their planes? **A:** The reasons for leasing include favorable tax treatment, better financing options, increased flexibility, reduced risk of obsolescence, and often less debt shown on the balance sheet.

p. 440 Sustainability Report Please Q: Why do you believe companies issue sustainability reports? **A:** It is important that companies clearly describe the things they value in addition to overall profitability. Most companies recognize that the health, safety, and environmental protections of their workforce and community are important components in developing strategies for continued growth and longevity. Without a strong commitment to the principles of corporate social responsibility, it is unlikely that a company will be able to maintain long-term stability and profitability. The development of a sustainability report helps companies to consider these issues and develop measures to assess whether they are meeting their goals in this area.

p. 443 Should Companies Write Up Goodwill? Q: Do you think that this treatment would be allowed under U.S. GAAP? **A:** The write-down of assets would have been allowed if it could be shown that the assets had declined in value (an impairment). However, the creation of goodwill to offset the write-down would not have been allowed. Goodwill can be recorded only when it results from the acquisition of a business. It cannot be recorded as the result of being created internally.

Answers to Self-Test Questions

1. d ($24,000 + $1,200 + $200 + $400)   **2.** b   **3.** d [($400,000 − $10,000) ÷ 5] × 2   **4.** d   **5.** b $60,000 × 25% = $15,000; ($60,000 − $15,000) × 25% = $11,250   **6.** b   **7.** d [($60,000 − $12,000) ÷ 10] × 2 = $9,600; ($60,000 − $9,600 − $2,000) ÷ 4   **8.** d   **9.** a [($80,000 ÷ 10) × 4.5] = $36,000; ($80,000 − $36,000) − $26,000   **10.** c ($12 million ÷ 20 million) × 2 million   **11.** d   **12.** b **13.** c   **14.** c $180,000 ÷ [($200,000 + $300,000) ÷ 2]   ***15.** a ($35,000 + $10,000)   ***16.** d

A Look at IFRS

IFRS follows most of the same principles as GAAP in the accounting for property, plant, and equipment. There are, however, some significant differences in the implementation: IFRS allows the use of revaluation of property, plant, and equipment, and it also requires the use of component depreciation. In addition, there are some significant differences in the accounting for both intangible assets and impairments.

Key Points

- The definition for plant assets for both IFRS and GAAP is essentially the same.

- Both international standards and GAAP follow the cost principle when accounting for property, plant, and equipment at date of acquisition. Cost consists of all expenditures necessary to acquire the asset and make it ready for its intended use.

- Under both IFRS and GAAP, interest costs incurred during construction are capitalized. Recently, IFRS converged to GAAP requirements in this area.

- IFRS, like GAAP, capitalizes all direct costs in self-constructed assets such as raw materials and labor. IFRS does not address the capitalization of fixed overhead, although in practice these costs are generally capitalized.

- IFRS also views depreciation as an allocation of cost over an asset's useful life. IFRS permits the same depreciation methods (e.g., straight-line, accelerated, and units-of-activity) as GAAP. However, a major difference is that IFRS requires component depreciation. *Component depreciation* specifies that any significant parts of a depreciable asset that have different estimated useful lives should be separately depreciated. Component depreciation is allowed under GAAP but is seldom used.

    To illustrate, assume that Lexure Construction builds an office building for $4,000,000, not including the cost of the land. If the $4,000,000 is allocated over the 40-year useful life of the building, Lexure reports $100,000 of depreciation per year, assuming straight-line depreciation and no disposal value. However, assume that $320,000 of the cost of the building relates to personal property and $600,000 relates to land improvements. The personal property has a depreciable life of 5 years, and the land improvements have a depreciable life of 10 years. In accordance with IFRS, Lexure must use component depreciation. It must reclassify $320,000 of the cost of the building to personal property and $600,000 to the cost of land improvements. Assuming that Lexure uses straight-line depreciation, component depreciation for the first year of the office building is computed as follows.

Building cost adjusted ($4,000,000 − $320,000 − $600,000)	$3,080,000
Building cost depreciation per year ($3,080,000/40)	$ 77,000
Personal property depreciation ($320,000/5)	64,000
Land improvements depreciation ($600,000/10)	60,000
Total component depreciation in first year	$ 201,000

- IFRS uses the term *residual value*, rather than salvage value, to refer to an owner's estimate of an asset's value at the end of its useful life for that owner.

- IFRS allows companies to revalue plant assets to fair value at the reporting date. Companies that choose to use the revaluation framework must follow revaluation procedures. If revaluation is used, it must be applied to all assets in a class of assets. Assets that are experiencing rapid price changes must be revalued on an annual basis, otherwise less frequent revaluation is acceptable.

    To illustrate asset revaluation accounting, assume that Pernice Company applies revaluation to plant assets with a carrying value of $1,000,000, a useful life of 5 years, and no residual value. Pernice makes the following journal entries in year 1, assuming straight-line depreciation.

Depreciation Expense	200,000	
Accumulated Depreciation—Plant Assets		200,000
(To record depreciation expense in year 1)		

After this entry, Pernice's plant assets have a carrying amount of $800,000 ($1,000,000 − $200,000). At the end of year 1, independent appraisers determine that the asset has a fair value of $850,000. To report the plant assets at fair value, or $850,000, Pernice eliminates the Accumulated Depreciation—Plant Assets account, reduces Plant Assets to its fair value of $850,000, and records Revaluation Surplus of $50,000. The entry to record the revaluation is as follows.

Accumulated Depreciation—Plant Assets	200,000	
Plant Assets		150,000
Revaluation Surplus		50,000
(To record adjusting the plant assets to fair value)		

Thus, Pernice follows a two-step process. First, Pernice records depreciation based on the cost basis of $1,000,000. As a result, it reports depreciation expense of $200,000 on the income statement. Second, it records the revaluation. It does this by eliminating any accumulated depreciation, adjusting the recorded value of the plant assets to fair value, and debiting or crediting the Revaluation Surplus account. In this example, the revaluation surplus is $50,000, which is the difference between the fair value of $850,000 and the book value of $800,000. Revaluation surplus is an example of an item reported as other comprehensive income, as discussed in the A Look at IFRS section of Chapter 5. Pernice now reports the following information in its statement of financial position at the end of year 1.

Plant assets ($1,000,000 − $150,000)	$850,000
Accumulated depreciation—plant assets	0
	$850,000
Revaluation surplus (equity)	$ 50,000

As indicated, $850,000 is the new basis of the asset. Pernice reports depreciation expense of $200,000 in the income statement and $50,000 in other comprehensive income. Assuming no change in the total useful life, depreciation in year 2 will be $212,500 ($850,000 ÷ 4).

- Under both GAAP and IFRS, changes in the depreciation method used and changes in useful life are handled in current and future periods. Prior periods are not affected. GAAP recently conformed to international standards in the accounting for changes in depreciation methods.

- The accounting for subsequent expenditures, such as ordinary repairs and additions, are essentially the same under IFRS and GAAP.

- The accounting for plant asset disposals is essentially the same under IFRS and GAAP.

- Initial costs to acquire natural resources are essentially the same under IFRS and GAAP.

- The definition of intangible assets is essentially the same under IFRS and GAAP.

- As in GAAP, under IFRS the costs associated with research and development are segregated into the two components. Costs in the research phase are always expensed under both IFRS and GAAP. Under IFRS, however, costs in the development phase are capitalized as Development Costs once technological feasibility is achieved.

  To illustrate, assume that Laser Scanner Company spent $1 million on research and $2 million on development of new products. Of the $2 million in development costs, $500,000 was incurred prior to technological feasibility and $1,500,000 was incurred after technological feasibility had been demonstrated. The company would record these costs as follows.

Research Expense	1,000,000	
Development Expense	500,000	
Development Costs	1,500,000	
Cash		3,000,000
(To record research and development costs)		

- IFRS permits revaluation of intangible assets (except for goodwill). GAAP prohibits revaluation of intangible assets.

- IFRS requires an impairment test at each reporting date for plant assets and intangibles and records an impairment if the asset's carrying amount exceeds its recoverable amount. The recoverable amount is the higher of the asset's fair value less costs to sell or its value-in-use. Value-in-use is the future cash flows to be derived from the particular asset, discounted to present value. Under GAAP, impairment loss is measured as the excess of the carrying amount over the asset's fair value.

- IFRS allows reversal of impairment losses when there has been a change in economic conditions or in the expected use of the asset. Under GAAP, impairment losses cannot be reversed for assets to be held and used; the impairment loss results in a new cost basis for the asset. IFRS and GAAP are similar in the accounting for impairments of assets held for disposal.

- The accounting for exchanges of nonmonetary assets has recently converged between IFRS and GAAP. GAAP now requires that gains on exchanges of nonmonetary assets be recognized if the exchange has commercial substance. This is the same framework used in IFRS.

Looking to the Future

With respect to revaluations, as part of the conceptual framework project, the Boards will examine the measurement bases used in accounting. It is too early to say whether a converged conceptual framework will recommend fair value measurement (and revaluation accounting) for plant assets and intangibles. However, this is likely to be one of the more contentious issues, given the long-standing use of historical cost as a measurement basis in GAAP.

The IASB and FASB have identified a project that would consider expanded recognition of internally generated intangible assets. IFRS permits more recognition of intangibles compared to GAAP. Thus, it will be challenging to develop converged standards for intangible assets, given the long-standing prohibition on capitalizing internally generated intangible assets and research and development costs in GAAP.

IFRS Practice

IFRS Self-Test Questions

1. Which of the following statements is *correct*?
   (a) Both IFRS and GAAP permit revaluation of property, plant, and equipment and intangible assets (except for goodwill).
   (b) IFRS permits revaluation of property, plant, and equipment and intangible assets (except for goodwill).
   (c) Both IFRS and GAAP permit revaluation of property, plant, and equipment but not intangible assets.
   (d) GAAP permits revaluation of property, plant, and equipment but not intangible assets.

2. International Company has land that cost $450,000 but now has a fair value of $600,000. International Company decides to use the revaluation method specified in IFRS to account for the land. Which of the following statements is *correct*?
   (a) International Company must continue to report the land at $450,000.
   (b) International Company would report a net income increase of $150,000 due to an increase in the value of the land.
   (c) International Company would debit Revaluation Surplus for $150,000.
   (d) International Company would credit Revaluation Surplus by $150,000.

3. Francisco Corporation is constructing a new building at a total initial cost of $10,000,000. The building is expected to have a useful live of 50 years with no residual value. The building's finished surfaces (e.g., roof cover and floor cover) are 5% of this cost and have a useful life of 20 years. Building services systems (e.g., electric, heating, and plumbing) are 20% of the cost and have a useful life of 25 years. The depreciation in the first year using component depreciation, assuming straight-line depreciation with no residual value, is:
   (a) $200,000.   (c) $255,000.
   (b) $215,000.   (d) None of the above.

4. Research and development costs are:
   (a) expensed under GAAP.   (c) expensed under both GAAP and IFRS.
   (b) expensed under IFRS.   (d) None of the above.

5. Under IFRS, value-in-use is defined as:
   (a) net realizable value.   (c) future cash flows discounted to present value.
   (b) fair value.   (d) total future undiscounted cash flows.

IFRS Exercises

IFRS9-1 What is component depreciation, and when must it be used?

IFRS9-2 What is revaluation of plant assets? When should revaluation be applied?

IFRS9-3 Some product development expenditures are recorded as development expenses and others as development costs. Explain the difference between these accounts and how a company decides which classification is appropriate.

IFRS9-4 Mandall Company constructed a warehouse for $280,000. Mandall estimates that the warehouse has a useful life of 20 years and no residual value. Construction records indicate that $40,000 of the cost of the warehouse relates to its heating, ventilation, and air conditioning (HVAC) system, which has an estimated useful life of only 10 years. Compute the first year of depreciation expense using straight-line component depreciation.

IFRS9-5 At the end of its first year of operations, Brianna Company chose to use the revaluation framework allowed under IFRS. Brianna's ledger shows Plant Assets $480,000 and Accumulated Depreciation—Plant Assets $60,000. Prepare journal entries to record the following.

(a) Independent appraisers determine that the plant assets have a fair value of $460,000.

(b) Independent appraisers determine that the plant assets have a fair value of $400,000.

IFRS9-6 Newell Industries spent $300,000 on research and $600,000 on development of a new product. Of the $600,000 in development costs, $400,000 was incurred prior to technological feasibility and $200,000 after technological feasibility had been demonstrated. Prepare the journal entry to record research and development costs.

International Financial Statement Analysis: Zetar plc

IFRS9-7 The financial statements of Zetar plc are presented in Appendix C.

Instructions

Use the company's annual report, available at *www.zetarplc.com*, to answer the following questions.

(a) According to the notes to the financial statements, what method or methods does the company use to depreciate "plant and equipment?" What rate does it use to depreciate plant and equipment?

(b) According to the notes to the financial statements, how often is goodwill tested for impairment?

(c) Using the notes to the financial statements, as well as information from the statement of cash flows, prepare the journal entry to record the disposal of property, plant, and equipment during 2010. (Round your amounts to the nearest thousand.)

Answers to IFRS Self-Test Questions

1. b **2.** d **3.** c ($10,000,000 × .05/20) + ($10,000,000 × .20/25) + ($10,000,000 × .75/50) **4.** a **5.** c

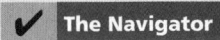 **The Navigator**

✔ Remember to go back to The Navigator box on the chapter opening page and check off your completed work.

Chapter 10

Liabilities

Feature Story

Financing His Dreams

What would you do if you had a great idea for a new product but couldn't come up with the cash to get the business off the ground? Small businesses often cannot attract investors. Nor can they obtain traditional debt financing through bank loans or bond issuances. Instead, they often resort to unusual, and costly, forms of nontraditional financing.

Such was the case for Wilbert Murdock. Murdock grew up in a New York housing project, and always had great ambitions. This ambitious spirit led him into some business ventures

that failed: a medical diagnostic tool, a device to eliminate carpal tunnel syndrome, custom-designed sneakers, and a device to keep people from falling asleep while driving.

Another idea was computerized golf clubs that analyze a golfer's swing and provide immediate feedback. Murdock saw great potential in the idea: Many golfers are willing to shell out considerable sums of money for devices that might improve their game. But Murdock had no cash to develop his product, and banks and other lenders had shied away. Rather than give up, Murdock resorted to credit cards—in a big way. He quickly owed $25,000 to credit card companies.

Learning Objectives

After studying this chapter, you should be able to:

1 Explain a current liability, and identify the major types of current liabilities.

2 Describe the accounting for notes payable.

3 Explain the accounting for other current liabilities.

4 Explain why bonds are issued, and identify the types of bonds.

5 Prepare the entries for the issuance of bonds and interest expense.

6 Describe the entries when bonds are redeemed or converted.

7 Describe the accounting for long-term notes payable.

8 Identify the methods for the presentation and analysis of long-term liabilities.

 ✔ The Navigator

While funding a business with credit cards might sound unusual, it isn't. A recent study found that one-third of businesses with fewer than 20 employees financed at least part of their operations with credit cards. As Murdock explained, credit cards are an appealing way to finance a start-up because "credit-card companies don't care how the money is spent." However, they do care how they are paid. And so Murdock faced high interest charges and a barrage of credit card collection letters.

Murdock's debt forced him to sacrifice nearly everything in order to keep his business afloat. His car stopped running, he barely had enough money to buy food, and he lived and worked out of a dimly lit apartment in his mother's basement. Through it all he tried to maintain a positive spirit, joking that, if he becomes successful, he might some day get to appear in an American Express commercial.

Source: Rodney Ho, "Banking on Plastic: To Finance a Dream, Many Entrepreneurs Binge on Credit Cards," *Wall Street Journal* (March 9, 1998), p. A1.

✔ **The Navigator**

Preview of **Chapter 10**

Inventor-entrepreneur Wilbert Murdock, as you can tell from the Feature Story, had to use multiple credit cards to finance his business ventures. Murdock's credit card debts would be classified as *current liabilities* because they are due every month. Yet, by making minimal payments and paying high interest each month, Murdock used this credit source long-term. Some credit card balances remain outstanding for years as they accumulate interest.

Earlier, we defined liabilities as creditors' claims on total assets and as existing debts and obligations. These claims, debts, and obligations must be settled or paid at some time **in the future** by the transfer of assets or services. The future date on which they are due or payable (maturity date) is a significant feature of liabilities. This "future date" feature gives rise to two basic classifications of liabilities: (1) current liabilities and (2) long-term liabilities. Our discussion in this chapter is divided into these two classifications.

The content and organization of Chapter 10 are as follows.

LIABILITIES	
Current Liabilities	**Long-Term Liabilities**
• Notes payable • Sales taxes payable • Payroll and payroll taxes • Unearned revenues • Current maturities of long-term debt • Statement presentation and analysis	• Bond basics • Accounting for bond issues • Accounting for bond retirements • Accounting for long-term notes payable • Statement presentation and analysis

✔ **The Navigator**

Current Liabilities

As explained in Chapter 4, a **current liability** is a debt with two key features: (1) The company reasonably expects to pay the debt from existing current assets or through the creation of other current liabilities. (2) The company will pay the debt within one year or the operating cycle, whichever is longer. Debts that do not meet **both criteria** are classified as long-term liabilities.

Companies must carefully monitor the relationship of current liabilities to current assets. This relationship is critical in evaluating a company's short-term debt-paying ability. A company that has more current liabilities than current assets may not be able to meet its current obligations when they become due.

Current liabilities include notes payable, accounts payable, and unearned revenues. They also include accrued liabilities such as taxes, salaries and wages, and interest payable. In the sections that follow, we discuss a few of the common types of current liabilities.

Notes Payable

Companies record obligations in the form of written notes as **notes payable**. Notes payable are often used instead of accounts payable because they give the lender formal proof of the obligation in case legal remedies are needed to collect the debt. Companies frequently issue notes payable to meet short-term financing needs. Notes payable usually require the borrower to pay interest.

Notes are issued for varying periods of time. **Those due for payment within one year of the balance sheet date are usually classified as current liabilities.**

To illustrate the accounting for notes payable, assume that First National Bank agrees to lend $100,000 on September 1, 2014, if Cole Williams Co. signs a $100,000, 12%, four-month note maturing on January 1. When a company issues an interest-bearing note, the amount of assets it receives upon issuance of the note generally equals the note's face value. Cole Williams Co. therefore will receive $100,000 cash and will make the following journal entry.

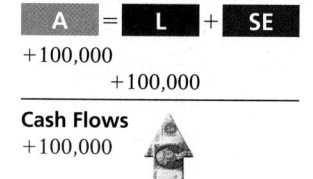

A = L + SE
+100,000
+100,000

Cash Flows
+100,000

Sept. 1	Cash	100,000	
	Notes Payable		100,000
	(To record issuance of 12%, 4-month note to First National Bank)		

Interest accrues over the life of the note, and the company must periodically record that accrual. If Cole Williams Co. prepares financial statements annually, it makes an adjusting entry at December 31 to recognize interest expense and interest payable of $4,000 ($100,000 × 12% × 4/12). Illustration 10-1 shows the formula for computing interest and its application to Cole Williams Co.'s note.

Illustration 10-1
Formula for computing interest

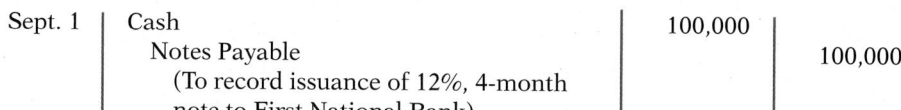

Face Value of Note	×	Annual Interest Rate	×	Time in Terms of One Year	=	Interest
$100,000	×	12%	×	4/12	=	**$4,000**

A = L + SE
−4,000 Exp
+4,000

Cash Flows
no effect

Cole Williams makes an adjusting entry as follows.

Dec. 31	Interest Expense	4,000	
	Interest Payable		4,000
	(To accrue interest for 4 months on First National Bank note)		

In the December 31 financial statements, the current liabilities section of the balance sheet will show notes payable $100,000 and interest payable $4,000. In addition, the company will report interest expense of $4,000 under "Other expenses and losses" in the income statement. If Cole Williams Co. prepared financial statements monthly, the adjusting entry at the end of each month would have been $1,000 ($100,000 × 12% × 1/12).

At maturity (January 1, 2015), Cole Williams Co. must pay the face value of the note ($100,000) plus $4,000 interest ($100,000 × 12% × 4/12). It records payment of the note and accrued interest as follows.

Jan. 1	Notes Payable	100,000	
	Interest Payable	4,000	
	Cash		104,000
	(To record payment of First National Bank interest-bearing note and accrued interest at maturity)		

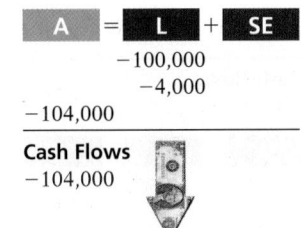

A = L + SE
−100,000
−4,000
−104,000

Cash Flows
−104,000

Sales Taxes Payable

As a consumer, you know that many of the products you purchase at retail stores are subject to sales taxes. Many states also are now collecting sales taxes on purchases made on the Internet as well. Sales taxes are expressed as a percentage of the sales price. The selling company collects the tax from the customer when the sale occurs. Periodically (usually monthly), the retailer remits the collections to the state's department of revenue.

Under most state sales tax laws, the selling company must enter separately on the cash register the amount of the sale and the amount of the sales tax collected. (Gasoline sales are a major exception.) The company then uses the cash register readings to credit Sales Revenue and Sales Taxes Payable. For example, if the March 25 cash register reading for Cooley Grocery shows sales of $10,000 and sales taxes of $600 (sales tax rate of 6%), the journal entry is:

> **LEARNING OBJECTIVE 3**
>
> **Explain the accounting for other current liabilities.**

Mar. 25	Cash	10,600	
	Sales Revenue		10,000
	Sales Taxes Payable		600
	(To record daily sales and sales taxes)		

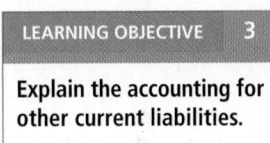

A = L + SE
+10,600
+10,000 Rev
+600

Cash Flows
+10,600

When the company remits the taxes to the taxing agency, it debits Sales Taxes Payable and credits Cash. The company does not report sales taxes as an expense. It simply forwards to the government the amount paid by the customers. Thus, Cooley Grocery serves only as a **collection agent** for the taxing authority.

Sometimes, companies do not enter sales taxes separately on the cash register. To determine the amount of sales in such cases, divide total receipts by 100% plus the sales tax percentage. To illustrate, assume that in the above example Cooley Grocery enters total receipts of $10,600. The receipts from the sales are equal to the sales price (100%) plus the tax percentage (6% of sales), or 1.06 times the sales total. We can compute the sales amount as follows.

$$\$10,600 \div 1.06 = \$10,000$$

Thus, Cooley Grocery could find the sales tax amount it must remit to the state ($600) by subtracting sales from total receipts ($10,600 − $10,000).

Helpful Hint
Alternatively, Cooley could find the tax by multiplying sales by the sales tax rate ($10,000 × .06).

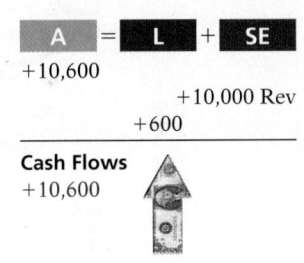

Payroll and Payroll Taxes Payable

Every employer incurs liabilities relating to employees' salaries and wages. One is the amount of salaries and wages owed to employees—**salaries and wages payable**. Another is the amount required by law to be withheld from employees' gross pay. Until a company remits these **withholding taxes** (federal and state income taxes, and Social Security taxes) to the governmental taxing authorities, they are credited to appropriate liability accounts. For example, if a corporation withholds taxes from its employees' wages and salaries, it would record accrual and payment of a $100,000 payroll, as shown below.

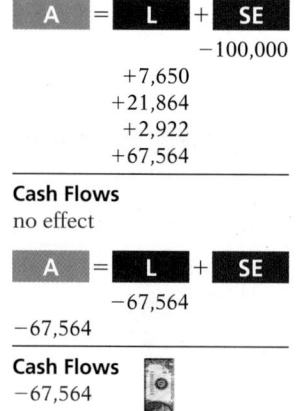

A	=	L	+	SE
				−100,000
		+7,650		
		+21,864		
		+2,922		
		+67,564		

Cash Flows
no effect

A	=	L	+	SE
		−67,564		
−67,564				

Cash Flows
−67,564

Mar. 7	Salaries and Wages Expense	100,000	
	FICA Taxes Payable[1]		7,650
	Federal Income Taxes Payable		21,864
	State Income Taxes Payable		2,922
	Salaries and Wages Payable		67,564
	(To record payroll and withholding taxes for the week ending March 7)		
Mar. 11	Salaries and Wages Payable	67,564	
	Cash		67,564
	(To record payment of the March 7 payroll)		

Illustration 10-2 summarizes the types of payroll deductions.

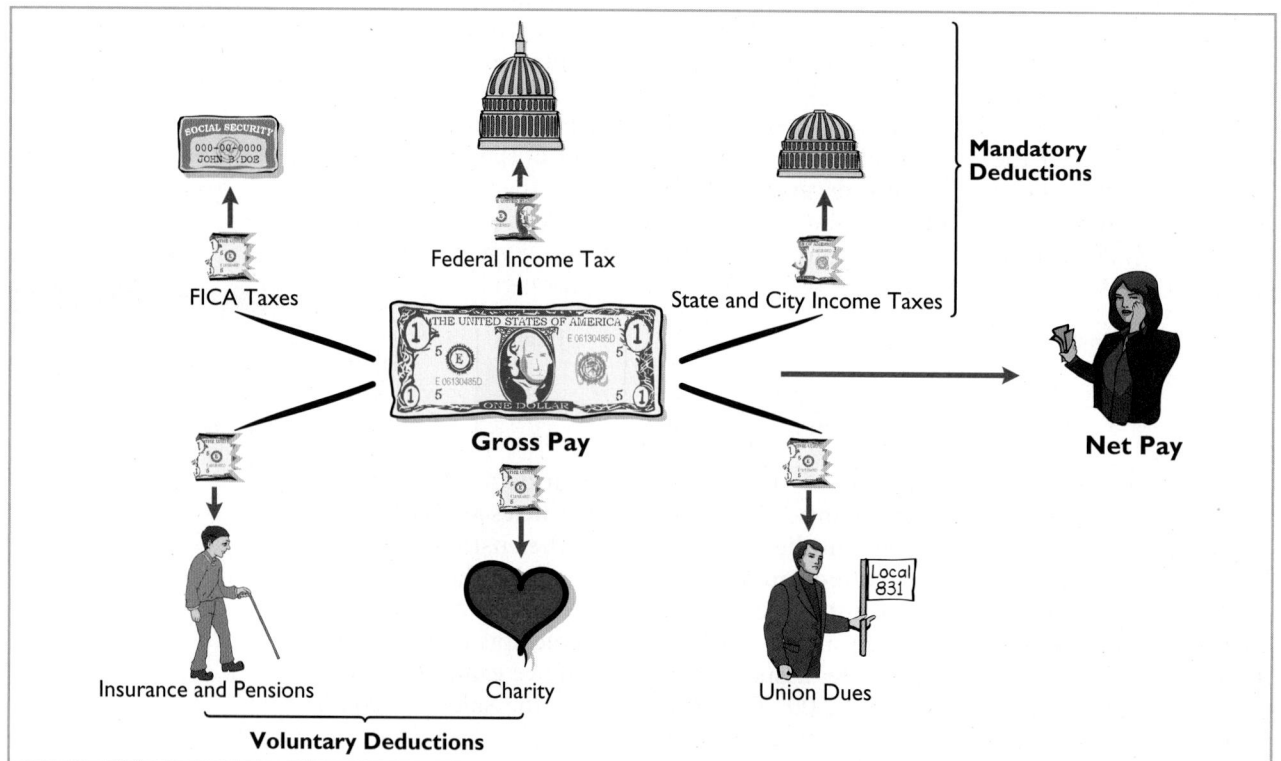

Illustration 10-2
Payroll deductions

Also, with every payroll, the employer incurs liabilities to pay various **payroll taxes** levied upon the employer. These payroll taxes include the employer's share of Social Security taxes and the state and federal unemployment taxes. Based on the $100,000 payroll in the previous example, the company would make the following entry to record the employer's expense and liability for these payroll taxes.

---

[1]Recently, FICA taxes include 6.2% of the first $106,800 for Old-Age, Survivors, and Disability Insurance (OASDI) and 1.45% of all wages for Medicare (HI).

Mar. 7	Payroll Tax Expense	13,850	
	FICA Taxes Payable		7,650
	Federal Unemployment Taxes Payable		800
	State Unemployment Taxes Payable		5,400
	(To record employer's payroll taxes on March 7 payroll)		

A = L + SE

−13,850

+7,650
+800
+5,400

Cash Flows
no effect

Illustration 10-3 shows the types of taxes levied on employers.

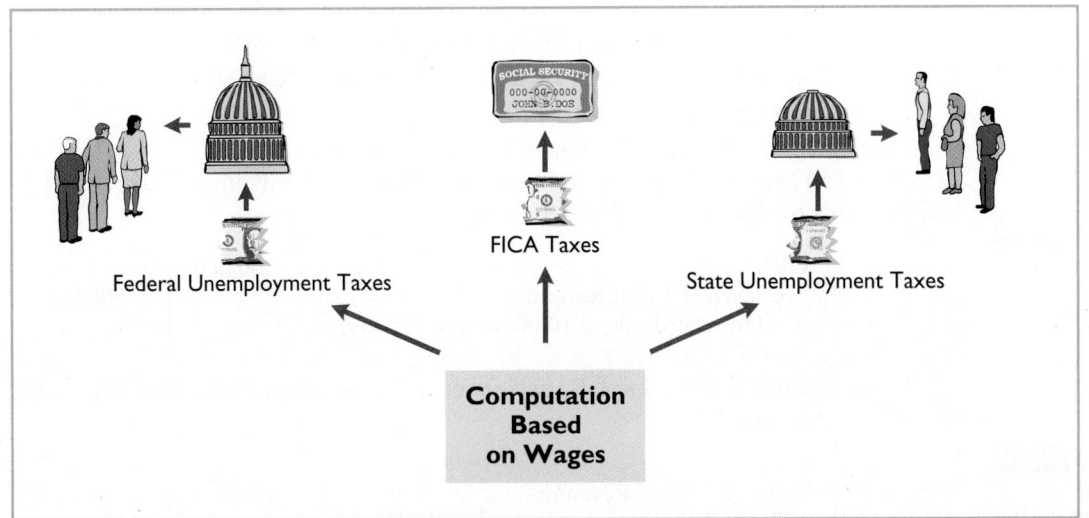

Illustration 10-3
Employer payroll taxes

Companies classify the payroll and payroll tax liability accounts as current liabilities because these amounts must be paid to employees or remitted to taxing authorities in the near term. Taxing authorities impose substantial fines and penalties on employers if the withholding and payroll taxes are not computed correctly and paid on time.

ACCOUNTING ACROSS THE ORGANIZATION

It Costs $74,000 to Put $44,000 in Sally's Pocket

Sally works for Bogan Communications, a small company in New Jersey that provides audio systems. She makes $59,000 a year but only nets $44,000. What happened to the other $15,000? Well, $2,376 goes for Sally's share of the medical and dental insurance that Bogan provides, $126 for state unemployment insurance, $149 for disability insurance, and $856 for Medicare. New Jersey takes $1,893 in income taxes, and the federal government gets $3,658 for Social Security and another $6,250 for income tax withholding. All of this adds up to some 22% of Sally's gross pay going to Washington or Trenton.

Employing Sally costs Bogan plenty too. Bogan has to write checks for $74,000 so Sally can receive her $59,000 in base pay. Health insurance is the biggest cost: While Sally pays nearly $2,400 for coverage, Bogan pays the rest—$9,561. Then, the federal and state governments take $56 for federal unemployment coverage, $149 for disability insurance, $300 for workers' comp, and $505 for state unemployment insurance. Finally, the government requires Bogan to pay $856 for Sally's Medicare and $3,658 for her Social Security.

When you add it all up, it costs $74,000 to put $44,000 in Sally's pocket and to give her $12,000 in benefits.

Source: Michael P. Fleischer, "Why I'm Not Hiring," *Wall Street Journal* (August 9, 2010), p. A17.

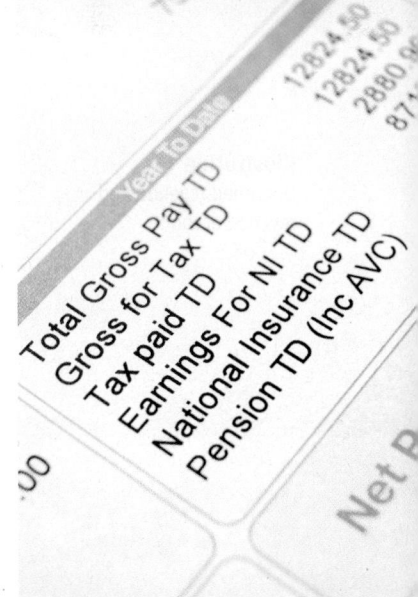

? How are the Social Security and Medicare taxes computed for Sally's salary?
(See page 533.)

Unearned Revenues

A magazine publisher, such as Sports Illustrated, receives customers' checks when they order magazines. An airline company, such as American Airlines, often receives cash when it sells tickets for future flights. Season tickets for concerts, sporting events, and theater programs are also paid for in advance. How do companies account for unearned revenues that are received before goods are delivered or services are provided?

1. When a company receives the advance payment, it debits Cash and credits a current liability account identifying the source of the unearned revenue.

2. When the company recognizes revenue, it debits an unearned revenue account and credits a revenue account.

To illustrate, assume that Superior University sells 10,000 season football tickets at $50 each for its five-game home schedule. The university makes the following entry for the sale of season tickets.

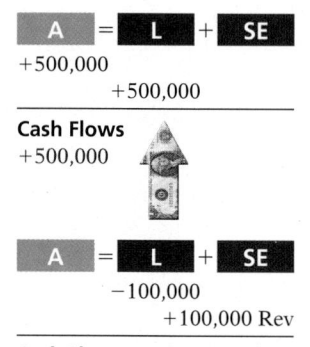

+500,000
        +500,000

Cash Flows
+500,000

Aug. 6	Cash	500,000	
	Unearned Ticket Revenue		500,000
	(To record sale of 10,000 season tickets)		

As each game is completed, Superior records the recognition of revenue with the following entry.

−100,000
        +100,000 Rev

Cash Flows
no effect

Sept. 7	Unearned Ticket Revenue	100,000	
	Ticket Revenue		100,000
	(To record football ticket revenue)		

The account Unearned Ticket Revenue represents unearned revenue, and Superior reports it as a current liability. As the school recognizes revenue, it reclassifies the amount from unearned revenue to Ticket Revenue. Unearned revenue is material for some companies. In the airline industry, for example, tickets sold for future flights represent almost 50% of total current liabilities. At United Air Lines, unearned ticket revenue was its largest current liability, recently amounting to over $1 billion.

Illustration 10-4 shows specific unearned revenue and revenue accounts used in selected types of businesses.

Illustration 10-4
Unearned revenue and revenue accounts

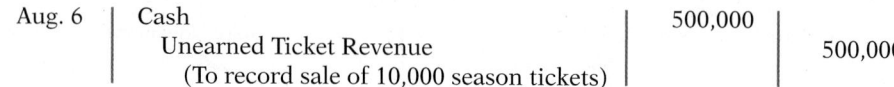

| Type of Business | Account Title | |
	Unearned Revenue	Revenue Recognized
Airline	Unearned Ticket Revenue	Ticket Revenue
Magazine publisher	Unearned Subscription Revenue	Subscription Revenue
Hotel	Unearned Rent Revenue	Rent Revenue

Current Maturities of Long-Term Debt

Companies often have a portion of long-term debt that comes due in the current year. That amount is considered a current liability. As an example, assume that Wendy Construction issues a five-year interest-bearing $25,000 note on January 1, 2013. This note specifies that each January 1, starting January 1, 2014, Wendy should pay $5,000 of the note. When the company prepares financial statements on December 31, 2013, it should report $5,000 as a current liability and $20,000 as a long-term liability. (The $5,000 amount is the portion of the note that is due to be paid within the next 12 months.) Companies often identify current maturities of long-term debt on the balance sheet as **long-term debt due within one year**.

It is not necessary to prepare an adjusting entry to recognize the current maturity of long-term debt. At the balance sheet date, all obligations due within one year are classified as current, and all other obligations as long-term.

> DO IT!

Current Liabilities

You and several classmates are studying for the next accounting examination. They ask you to answer the following questions.

1. If cash is borrowed on a $50,000, 6-month, 12% note on September 1, how much interest expense would be incurred by December 31?

Action Plan

✔ Use the interest formula: Face value of note × Annual interest rate × Time in terms of one year.

✔ Divide total receipts by 100% plus the tax rate to determine sales; then subtract sales from the total receipts.

✔ Determine what fraction of the total unearned rent was recognized this year.

2. How is the sales tax amount determined when the cash register total includes sales taxes?

3. If $15,000 is collected in advance on November 1 for 3 months' rent, what amount of rent revenue is recognized by December 31?

Solution

1. $50,000 × 12% × 4/12 = $2,000

2. First, divide the total cash register receipts by 100% plus the sales tax percentage to find the sales amount. Second, subtract the sales amount from the total cash register receipts to determine the sales taxes.

3. $15,000 × 2/3 = $10,000

Related exercise material: **BE10-2, BE10-3, BE10-4, E10-1, E10-2, E10-3, E10-4, and** DO IT! **10-1.**

✔ **The Navigator**

Statement Presentation and Analysis

PRESENTATION

As indicated in Chapter 4, current liabilities are the first category under liabilities on the balance sheet. Each of the principal types of current liabilities is listed separately. In addition, companies disclose the terms of notes payable and other key information about the individual items in the notes to the financial statements.

Companies seldom list current liabilities in the order of liquidity. The reason is that varying maturity dates may exist for specific obligations such as notes payable. A more common method of presenting current liabilities is to list them by **order of magnitude**, with the largest ones first. Or, as a matter of custom, many companies show notes payable first and then accounts payable, regardless of amount. Then, the remaining current liabilities are listed by magnitude. (*Use this approach in your homework.*) Illustration 10-5 (page 482) provides an adapted excerpt from Caterpillar Inc.'s balance sheet, which indicates its order of presentation.

ANALYSIS

Use of current and noncurrent classifications makes it possible to analyze a company's liquidity. **Liquidity** refers to the ability to pay maturing obligations and meet unexpected needs for cash. The relationship of current assets to current liabilities is critical in analyzing liquidity. We can express this relationship as a dollar amount (working capital) and as a ratio (the current ratio).

Illustration 10-5
Balance sheet presentation
of current liabilities

Caterpillar Inc. Balance Sheet December 31, 2010 (in millions)	
Assets	
Current assets	$31,810
Property, plant and equipment (net)	12,539
Other long-term assets	19,671
Total assets	$64,020
Liabilities and Stockholders' Equity	
Current liabilities	
Short-term borrowings (notes payable)	$ 4,056
Accounts payable	5,856
Accrued expenses	2,880
Accrued wages, salaries, and employee benefits	1,670
Customer advances	1,831
Dividends payable	281
Other current liabilities	1,521
Long-term debt due within one year	3,925
Total current liabilities	22,020
Noncurrent liabilities	30,675
Total liabilities	52,695
Stockholders' equity	11,325
Total liabilities and stockholders' equity	$64,020

Helpful Hint
For other examples of
current liabilities sections,
refer to the PepsiCo and
Coca-Cola balance sheets
in Appendices A and B.

The excess of current assets over current liabilities is **working capital**. Illustration 10-6 shows the formula for the computation of Caterpillar's working capital (dollar amounts in millions).

Illustration 10-6
Working capital formula and
computation

Current Assets	−	Current Liabilities	=	Working Capital
$31,810	−	$22,020	=	$9,790

As an absolute dollar amount, working capital offers limited informational value. For example, $1 million of working capital may be far more than needed for a small company but inadequate for a large corporation. Also, $1 million of working capital may be adequate for a company at one time but inadequate at another time.

The **current ratio** permits us to compare the liquidity of different-sized companies and of a single company at different times. The current ratio is calculated as current assets divided by current liabilities. The formula for this ratio is illustrated below, along with its computation using Caterpillar's current asset and current liability data (dollar amounts in millions).

Illustration 10-7
Current ratio formula and
computation

Current Assets	÷	Current Liabilities	=	Current Ratio
$31,810	÷	$22,020	=	1.44:1

Historically, companies and analysts considered a current ratio of 2:1 to be the standard for a good credit rating. In recent years, however, many healthy companies have maintained ratios well below 2:1 by improving management of their current assets and liabilities. Caterpillar's ratio of 1.44:1 is adequate but certainly below the standard of 2:1.

ANATOMY OF A FRAUD

Art was a custodial supervisor for a large school district. The district was supposed to employ between 35 and 40 regular custodians, as well as 3 or 4 substitute custodians to fill in when regular custodians were missing. Instead, in addition to the regular custodians, Art "hired" 77 substitutes. In fact, almost none of these people worked for the district. Instead, Art submitted time cards for these people, collected their checks at the district office, and personally distributed the checks to the "employees." If a substitute's check was for $1,200, that person would cash the check, keep $200, and pay Art $1,000.

Total take: $150,000

The Missing Controls

Human resource controls. Thorough background checks should be performed. No employees should begin work until they have been approved by the Board of Education and entered into the payroll system. No employees should be entered into the payroll system until they have been approved by a supervisor. All paychecks should be distributed directly to employees at the official school locations by designated employees.

Independent internal verification. Budgets should be reviewed monthly to identify situations where actual costs significantly exceed budgeted amounts.

Source: Adapted from Wells, *Fraud Casebook* (2007), pp. 164–171.

Long-Term Liabilities

Long-term liabilities are obligations that are expected to be paid after one year. In this section, we will explain the accounting for the principal types of obligations reported in the long-term liability section of the balance sheet. These obligations often are in the form of bonds or long-term notes.

Bond Basics

Bonds are a form of interest-bearing notes payable. To obtain **large amounts of long-term capital**, corporate management usually must decide whether to issue common stock (equity financing) or bonds. Bonds offer three advantages over common stock, as shown in Illustration 10-8 (page 484).

> **LEARNING OBJECTIVE 4**
>
> Explain why bonds are issued, and identify the types of bonds.

As the illustration shows, one reason to issue bonds is that they do not affect stockholder control. Because bondholders do not have voting rights, owners can raise capital with bonds and still maintain corporate control. In addition, bonds are attractive to corporations because the cost of bond interest is tax-deductible. As a result of this tax treatment, which stock dividends do not offer, bonds may result in lower cost of capital than equity financing.

To illustrate the third advantage, on earnings per share, assume that Microsystems, Inc. is considering two plans for financing the construction of a new

Illustration 10-8
Advantages of bond financing over common stock

Bond Financing	Advantages
	1. **Stockholder control is not affected.** Bondholders do not have voting rights, so current owners (stockholders) retain full control of the company.
	2. **Tax savings result.** Bond interest is deductible for tax purposes; dividends on stock are not.
	3. **Earnings per share may be higher.** Although bond interest expense reduces net income, earnings per share on common stock often is higher under bond financing because no additional shares of common stock are issued.

$5 million plant. Plan A involves issuance of 200,000 shares of common stock at the current market price of $25 per share. Plan B involves issuance of $5 million, 8% bonds at face value. Income before interest and taxes on the new plant will be $1.5 million. Income taxes are expected to be 30%. Microsystems currently has 100,000 shares of common stock outstanding. Illustration 10-9 shows the alternative effects on earnings per share.

Illustration 10-9
Effects on earnings per share—stocks vs. bonds

	Plan A Issue Stock	Plan B Issue Bonds
Income before interest and taxes	$1,500,000	$1,500,000
Interest (8% × $5,000,000)	—	400,000
Income before income taxes	1,500,000	1,100,000
Income tax expense (30%)	450,000	330,000
Net income	$1,050,000	$ 770,000
Outstanding shares	300,000	100,000
Earnings per share	**$3.50**	**$7.70**

Note that net income is $280,000 less ($1,050,000 − $770,000) with long-term debt financing (bonds). However, earnings per share is higher because there are 200,000 fewer shares of common stock outstanding.

One disadvantage in using bonds is that the company must **pay interest** on a periodic basis. In addition, the company must also **repay the principal** at the due date. A company with fluctuating earnings and a relatively weak cash position may have great difficulty making interest payments when earnings are low.

A corporation may also obtain long-term financing from notes payable and leasing. However, notes payable and leasing are seldom sufficient to furnish the amount of funds needed for plant expansion and major projects like new buildings.

Bonds are sold in relatively small denominations (usually $1,000 multiples). As a result of their size and the variety of their features, bonds attract many investors.

Helpful Hint
Besides corporations, governmental agencies and universities also issue bonds to raise capital.

TYPES OF BONDS

Bonds may have many different features. In the following sections, we describe the types of bonds commonly issued.

SECURED AND UNSECURED BONDS **Secured bonds** have specific assets of the issuer pledged as collateral for the bonds. A bond secured by real estate, for example, is called a **mortgage bond**. A bond secured by specific assets set aside to retire the bonds is called a **sinking fund bond**.

Unsecured bonds, also called **debenture bonds**, are issued against the general credit of the borrower. Companies with good credit ratings use these bonds extensively. For example, at one time, DuPont reported over $2 billion of debenture bonds outstanding.

TERM AND SERIAL BONDS Bonds that mature—are due for payment—at a single specified future date are **term bonds**. In contrast, bonds that mature in installments are **serial bonds**.

REGISTERED AND BEARER BONDS Bonds issued in the name of the owner are **registered bonds**. Interest payments on registered bonds are made by check to bondholders of record. Bonds not registered are **bearer** (or **coupon**) **bonds**. Holders of bearer bonds must send in coupons to receive interest payments. Most bonds issued today are registered bonds.

CONVERTIBLE AND CALLABLE BONDS Bonds that can be converted into common stock at the bondholder's option are **convertible bonds**. The conversion feature generally is attractive to bond buyers. Bonds that the issuing company can retire at a stated dollar amount prior to maturity are **callable bonds**. A call feature is included in nearly all corporate bond issues.

ISSUING PROCEDURES

State laws grant corporations the power to issue bonds. Both the board of directors and stockholders usually must approve bond issues. **In authorizing the bond issue, the board of directors must stipulate the number of bonds to be authorized, total face value, and contractual interest rate.** The total bond authorization often exceeds the number of bonds the company originally issues. This gives the corporation the flexibility to issue more bonds, if needed, to meet future cash requirements.

The **face value** is the amount of principal the issuing company must pay at the maturity date. The **maturity date** is the date that the final payment is due to the investor from the issuing company. The **contractual interest rate**, often referred to as the **stated rate**, is the rate used to determine the amount of cash interest the borrower pays and the investor receives. Usually the contractual rate is stated as an annual rate. Interest is generally paid semiannually.

The terms of the bond issue are set forth in a legal document called a **bond indenture**. The indenture shows the terms and summarizes the rights of the bondholders and their trustees, and the obligations of the issuing company. The **trustee** (usually a financial institution) keeps records of each bondholder, maintains custody of unissued bonds, and holds conditional title to pledged property.

In addition, the issuing company arranges for the printing of **bond certificates**. The indenture and the certificate are separate documents. As shown in Illustration 10-10 (page 486), a bond certificate provides the following information: name of the issuer, face value, contractual interest rate, and maturity date. An investment company that specializes in selling securities generally sells the bonds for the issuing company.

> ### Ethics Note
>
> Some companies try to minimize the amount of debt reported on their balance sheet by not reporting certain types of commitments as liabilities. This subject is of intense interest in the financial community.

BOND TRADING

Bondholders have the opportunity to convert their holdings into cash at any time by selling the bonds at the current market price on national securities exchanges.

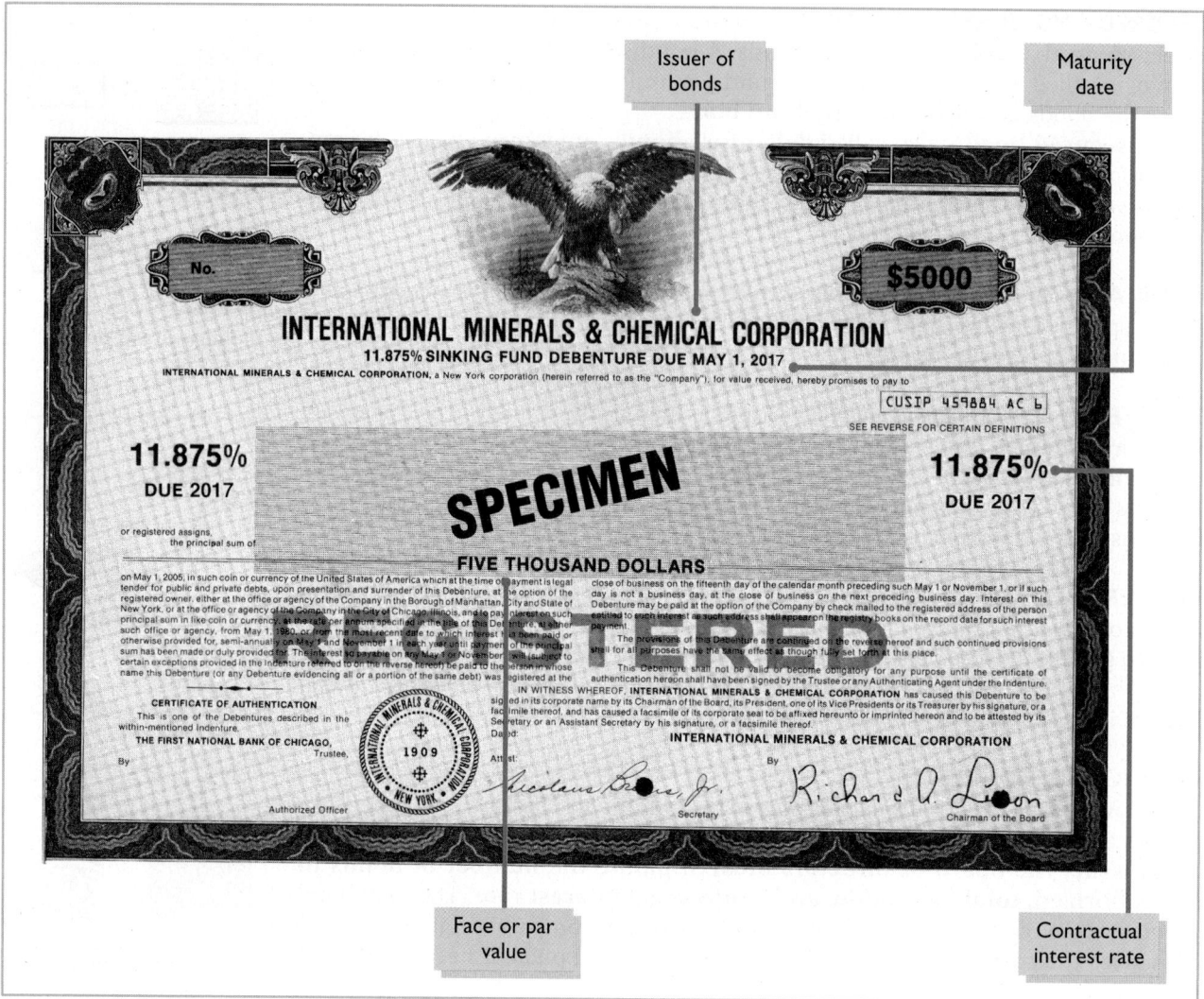

Illustration 10-10
Bond certificate

Bond prices are quoted as a percentage of the face value of the bond, which is usually $1,000. A $1,000 bond with a quoted price of 97 means that the selling price of the bond is 97% of face value, or $970. Newspapers and the financial press publish bond prices and trading activity daily as shown in Illustration 10-11.

Illustration 10-11
Market information for bonds

Bonds	Maturity	Close	Yield	Est. Volume (000)
Boeing Co. 5.125	Feb. 15, 2014	96.595	5.747	33,965

Helpful Hint
(1) What is the price of a $1,000 bond trading at 95¼?
(2) What is the price of a $1,000 bond trading at 101⅞?
Answers: (1) $952.50.
(2) $1,018.75.

This bond listing indicates that Boeing Co. has outstanding 5.125%, $1,000 bonds that mature in 2014. They currently yield a 5.747% return. On this day, $33,965,000 of these bonds were traded. At the close of trading, the price was 96.595% of face value, or $965.95.

A corporation makes journal entries **only when it issues or buys back bonds,** or when bondholders convert bonds into common stock. For example, DuPont **does not journalize** transactions between its bondholders and other investors. If Tom Smith sells his DuPont bonds to Faith Jones, DuPont does not journalize the transaction. (DuPont or its trustee does, however, keep records of the names of bondholders in the case of registered bonds.)

DETERMINING THE MARKET PRICE OF BONDS

If you were an investor wanting to purchase a bond, how would you determine how much to pay? To be more specific, assume that Coronet, Inc. issues a **zero-interest bond** (pays no interest) with a face value of $1,000,000 due in 20 years. For this bond, the only cash you receive is a million dollars at the end of 20 years. Would you pay a million dollars for this bond? We hope not! A million dollars received 20 years from now is not the same as a million dollars received today.

Same dollars at different times are not equal.

The term **time value of money** is used to indicate the relationship between time and money—that a dollar received today is worth more than a dollar promised at some time in the future. If you had a million dollars today, you would invest it. From that investment, you would earn interest such that at the end of 20 years, you would have much more than a million dollars. If someone is going to pay you a million dollars 20 years from now, you would want to find its equivalent today. In other words, you would want to determine how much you must invest today at current interest rates to have a million dollars in 20 years. The amount that must be invested today at a given rate of interest over a specified time is called **present value**.

The present value of a bond is the value at which it should sell in the marketplace. Market price therefore is a function of the three factors that determine present value: (1) the dollar amounts to be received, (2) the length of time until the amounts are received, and (3) the market rate of interest. The **market interest rate** is the rate investors demand for loaning funds. Appendix 10A discusses the process of finding the present value for bonds. Appendix D also provides additional material for time value of money computations.

ACCOUNTING ACROSS THE ORGANIZATION

When to Go Long-Term

A decision that all companies must make is to what extent to rely on short-term versus long-term financing. The critical nature of this decision was highlighted in the fall of 2001, after the World Trade Center disaster. Prior to September 11, short-term interest rates had been extremely low relative to long-term rates. In order to minimize interest costs, many companies were relying very heavily on short-term financing to purchase things they normally would have used long-term debt for. The problem with short-term financing is that it requires companies to continually find new financing as each loan comes due. This makes them vulnerable to sudden changes in the economy.

After September 11, lenders and short-term investors became very reluctant to loan money. This put the squeeze on many companies: As short-term loans came due, they were unable to refinance. Some were able to get other financing but at extremely high rates (for example, 12% as compared to 3%). Others were unable to get loans and instead had to sell assets to generate cash for their immediate needs.

Source: Henny Sender, "Firms Feel Consequences of Short-Term Borrowing," *Wall Street Journal Online* (October 12, 2001).

? Based on this story, what is a good general rule to use in choosing between short-term and long-term financing? (See page 533.)

> **DO IT!**

Bond Terminology

State whether each of the following statements is true or false.

_____ 1. Mortgage bonds and sinking fund bonds are both examples of secured bonds.

_____ 2. Unsecured bonds are also known as debenture bonds.

_____ 3. The stated rate is the rate investors demand for loaning funds.

_____ 4. The face value is the amount of principal the issuing company must pay at the maturity date.

_____ 5. The bond issuer must make journal entries to record transfers of its bonds among investors.

Action Plan

✔ Review the types of bonds and the basic terms associated with bonds.

Solution

1. True.

2. True.

3. False.   The stated rate is the contractual interest rate used to determine the amount of cash interest the borrower pays.

4. True.

5. False.   The bond issuer makes journal entries only when it issues or buys back bonds, when it records interest, and when bonds are converted.

Related exercise material: **BE10-7, E10-8, E10-9, and DO IT! 10-2.**

✔ **The Navigator**

Accounting for Bond Issues

LEARNING OBJECTIVE   5

Prepare the entries for the issuance of bonds and interest expense.

As indicated earlier, a corporation records bond transactions when it issues (sells) or retires (buys back) bonds and when bondholders convert bonds into common stock. If bondholders sell their bond investments to other investors, the issuing firm receives no further money on the transaction, **nor does the issuing corporation journalize the transaction** (although it does keep records of the names of bondholders in some cases).

Bonds may be issued at face value, below face value (discount), or above face value (premium). Bond prices for both new issues and existing bonds are quoted as **a percentage of the face value of the bond. Face value is usually $1,000.** Thus, a $1,000 bond with a quoted price of 97 means that the selling price of the bond is 97% of face value, or $970.

ISSUING BONDS AT FACE VALUE

To illustrate the accounting for bonds issued at face value, assume that on January 1, 2014, Candlestick, Inc. issues $100,000, five-year, 10% bonds at 100 (100% of face value). The entry to record the sale is:

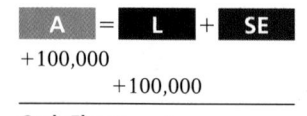

+100,000
        +100,000

Cash Flows
+100,000

Jan. 1	Cash	100,000	
	Bonds Payable		100,000
	(To record sale of bonds at face value)		

Candlestick reports bonds payable in the long-term liabilities section of the balance sheet because the maturity date is January 1, 2019 (more than one year away).

Over the term (life) of the bonds, companies make entries to record bond interest. Interest on bonds payable is computed in the same manner as interest on notes payable, as explained on page 476. Assume that interest is payable semi-annually on January 1 and July 1 on the Candlestick bonds. In that case, Candlestick must pay interest of $5,000 ($100,000 × 10% × 6/12) on July 1, 2014. The entry for the payment, assuming no previous accrual of interest, is:

July 1	Interest Expense	5,000	
	Cash		5,000
	(To record payment of bond interest)		

A = L + SE
−5,000 Exp
−5,000

Cash Flows
−5,000

At December 31, Candlestick recognizes the $5,000 of interest expense incurred since July 1 with the following adjusting entry:

Dec. 31	Interest Expense	5,000	
	Interest Payable		5,000
	(To accrue bond interest)		

A = L + SE
−5,000 Exp
+5,000

Cash Flows
no effect

Companies classify interest payable as a current liability because it is scheduled for payment within the next year. When Candlestick pays the interest on January 1, 2015, it debits (decreases) Interest Payable and credits (decreases) Cash for $5,000.

Candlestick records the payment on January 1 as follows.

Jan. 1	Interest Payable	5,000	
	Cash		5,000
	(To record payment of bond interest)		

DISCOUNT OR PREMIUM ON BONDS

In the Candlestick illustrations above, we assumed that the contractual (stated) interest rate and the market (effective) interest rate paid on the bonds were the same. Recall that the **contractual interest rate** is the rate applied to the face (par) value to arrive at the interest paid in a year. The **market interest rate** is the rate investors demand for loaning funds to the corporation. When the contractual interest rate and the market interest rate are the same, bonds sell **at face value (par value)**.

However, market interest rates change daily. The type of bond issued, the state of the economy, current industry conditions, and the company's performance all affect market interest rates. As a result, contractual and market interest rates often differ. To make bonds salable when the two rates differ, bonds sell below or above face value.

To illustrate, suppose that a company issues 10% bonds at a time when other bonds of similar risk are paying 12%. Investors will not be interested in buying the 10% bonds, so their value will fall below their face value. When a bond is sold for less than its face value, the difference between the face value of a bond and its selling price is called a **discount**. As a result of the decline in the bonds' selling price, the actual interest rate incurred by the company increases to the level of the current market interest rate.

Conversely, if the market rate of interest is **lower than** the contractual interest rate, investors will have to pay more than face value for the bonds. That is, if the market rate of interest is 8% but the contractual interest rate on the bonds is 10%, the price of the bonds will be bid up. When a bond is sold for more than its face value, the difference between the face value and its selling price is called a **premium**. Illustration 10-12 (page 490) shows these relationships graphically.

Illustration 10-12
Interest rates and bond prices

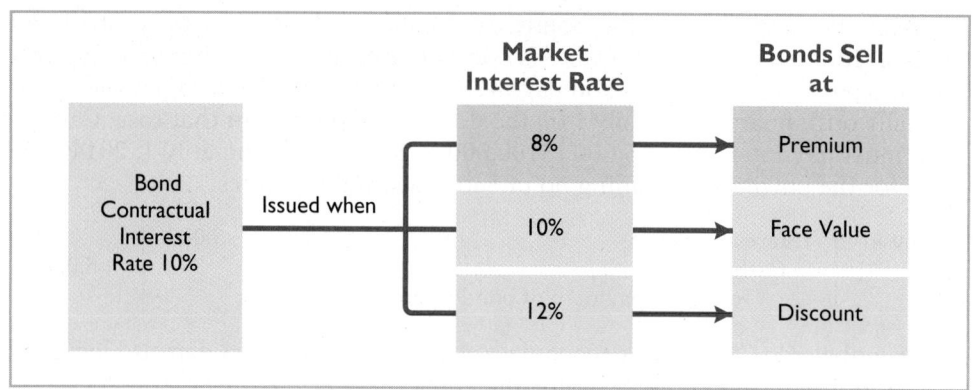

Helpful Hint

**Discount on
Bonds Payable**

Increase	Decrease
Debit	Credit
↓	
Normal	
Balance	

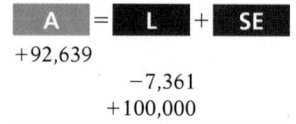

+92,639

−7,361
+100,000

Cash Flows

+92,639

Issuance of bonds at an amount different from face value is quite common. By the time a company prints the bond certificates and markets the bonds, it will be a coincidence if the market rate and the contractual rate are the same. Thus, the issuance of bonds at a discount does not mean that the issuer's financial strength is suspect. Conversely, the sale of bonds at a premium does not indicate that the financial strength of the issuer is exceptional.

ISSUING BONDS AT A DISCOUNT

To illustrate issuance of bonds at a discount, assume that on January 1, 2014, Candlestick, Inc. sells $100,000, five-year, 10% bonds for $92,639 (92.639% of face value). Interest is payable on July 1 and January 1. The entry to record the issuance is:

Jan. 1	Cash	92,639	
	Discount on Bonds Payable	7,361	
	Bonds Payable		100,000
	(To record sale of bonds at a discount)		

Although Discount on Bonds Payable has a debit balance, **it is not an asset**. Rather, it is a **contra account**. This account is **deducted from bonds payable** on the balance sheet, as shown in Illustration 10-13.

Illustration 10-13
Statement presentation of discount on bonds payable

Candlestick, Inc.		
Balance Sheet (partial)		
Long-term liabilities		
Bonds payable	$100,000	
Less: Discount on bonds payable	**7,361**	$92,639

Helpful Hint
Carrying value (book value) of bonds issued at a discount is determined by subtracting the balance of the discount account from the balance of the Bonds Payable account.

The $92,639 represents the **carrying (or book) value** of the bonds. On the date of issue, this amount equals the market price of the bonds.

The issuance of bonds below face value—at a discount—causes the total cost of borrowing to differ from the bond interest paid. That is, the issuing corporation must pay not only the contractual interest rate over the term of the bonds, but also the face value (rather than the issuance price) at maturity. Therefore, the difference between the issuance price and face value of the bonds—the discount—is an **additional cost of borrowing**. The company records this additional cost as **interest expense** over the life of the bonds. Appendices 10B and 10C show the procedures for recording this additional cost.

The total cost of borrowing $92,639 for Candlestick, Inc. is $57,361, computed as follows.

Illustration 10-14
Total cost of borrowing—bonds issued at a discount

Bonds Issued at a Discount

Semiannual interest payments	
($100,000 × 10% × ½ = $5,000; $5,000 × 10)	$ 50,000
Add: Bond discount ($100,000 − $92,639)	7,361
Total cost of borrowing	**$57,361**

Alternatively, we can compute the total cost of borrowing as follows.

Illustration 10-15
Alternative computation of total cost of borrowing—bonds issued at a discount

Bonds Issued at a Discount

Principal at maturity	$100,000
Semiannual interest payments ($5,000 × 10)	50,000
Cash to be paid to bondholders	150,000
Cash received from bondholders	92,639
Total cost of borrowing	**$ 57,361**

ISSUING BONDS AT A PREMIUM

To illustrate the issuance of bonds at a premium, we now assume the Candlestick, Inc. bonds described above sell for $108,111 (108.111% of face value) rather than for $92,639. The entry to record the sale is:

Jan. 1	Cash	108,111	
	Bonds Payable		100,000
	Premium on Bonds Payable		8,111
	(To record sale of bonds at a premium)		

A = L + SE
+108,111
　　　+100,000
　　　+8,111

Cash Flows
+108,111

Candlestick adds the premium on bonds payable **to the bonds payable amount** on the balance sheet, as shown in Illustration 10-16.

Illustration 10-16
Statement presentation of bond premium

Candlestick, Inc.
Balance Sheet (partial)

Long-term liabilities		
Bonds payable	$100,000	
Add: Premium on bonds payable	**8,111**	$108,111

The sale of bonds above face value causes the total cost of borrowing to be **less than the bond interest paid**. The reason: The borrower is not required to pay the bond premium at the maturity date of the bonds. Thus, the bond premium is considered to be **a reduction in the cost of borrowing**. The company credits the bond premium to Interest Expense over the life of the bonds. Appendices 10B and 10C show the procedures for recording this reduction in the cost of borrowing. The total cost of borrowing $108,111 for Candlestick, Inc. is computed as follows.

Helpful Hint
Premium on Bonds Payable

Decrease	Increase
Debit	Credit
	↓
	Normal
	Balance

Illustration 10-17
Total cost of borrowing—
bonds issued at a premium

Bonds Issued at a Premium	
Semiannual interest payments	
($100,000 × 10% × ½ = $5,000; $5,000 × 10)	$ 50,000
Less: Bond premium ($108,111 − $100,000)	8,111
Total cost of borrowing	**$41,889**

Alternatively, we can compute the cost of borrowing as follows.

Illustration 10-18
Alternative computation of
total cost of borrowing—bonds
issued at a premium

Bonds Issued at a Premium	
Principal at maturity	$100,000
Semiannual interest payments ($5,000 × 10)	50,000
Cash to be paid to bondholders	150,000
Cash received from bondholders	108,111
Total cost of borrowing	**$ 41,889**

> DO IT!

Bond Issuance

Giant Corporation issues $200,000 of bonds for $189,000. (a) Prepare the journal entry to record the issuance of the bonds, and (b) show how the bonds would be reported on the balance sheet at the date of issuance.

Solution

Action Plan

✔ Record cash received, bonds payable at face value, and the difference as a discount or premium.

✔ Report discount as a deduction from bonds payable and premium as an addition to bonds payable.

(a)

Cash	189,000	
Discount on Bonds Payable	11,000	
Bonds Payable		200,000
(To record sale of bonds at a discount)		

(b)

Long-term liabilities		
Bonds payable	$200,000	
Less: Discount on bonds payable	11,000	$189,000

Related exercise material: **BE10-8, BE10-9, BE10-10, E10-12, and** DO IT! **10-3.**

✔ **The Navigator**

Accounting for Bond Retirements

LEARNING OBJECTIVE 6

Describe the entries when bonds are redeemed or converted.

An issuing corporation retires bonds either when it buys back (redeems) the bonds or when bondholders convert them into common stock. We explain the entries for these transactions in the following sections.

REDEEMING BONDS AT MATURITY

Regardless of the issue price of bonds, the book value of the bonds at maturity will equal their face value. Assuming that the company pays and records separately the interest for the last interest period, Candlestick records the redemption of its bonds at maturity as follows.

Jan.1	Bonds Payable		100,000	
	Cash			100,000
	(To record redemption of bonds at maturity)			

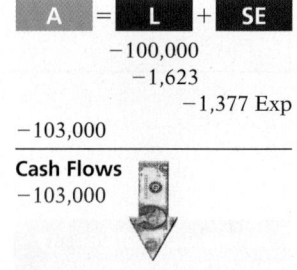

A = L + SE
−100,000
−100,000

Cash Flows
−100,000

REDEEMING BONDS BEFORE MATURITY

Bonds also may be redeemed before maturity. A company may decide to retire bonds before maturity to reduce interest cost and to remove debt from its balance sheet. A company should retire debt early only if it has sufficient cash resources.

When a company retires bonds before maturity, it is necessary to (1) eliminate the carrying value of the bonds at the redemption date; (2) record the cash paid; and (3) recognize the gain or loss on redemption. The **carrying value** of the bonds is the face value of the bonds less any remaining bond discount or plus any remaining bond premium at the redemption date.

To illustrate, assume that Candlestick, Inc. has sold its bonds at a premium. At the end of the eighth period, Candlestick retires these bonds at 103 after paying the semiannual interest. Assume also that the carrying value of the bonds at the redemption date is $101,623. Candlestick makes the following entry to record the redemption at the end of the eighth interest period (January 1, 2018):

Helpful Hint
Question: A bond is redeemed prior to its maturity date. Its carrying value exceeds its redemption price. Will the retirement result in a gain or a loss on redemption?
Answer: Gain.

Jan.1	Bonds Payable		100,000	
	Premium on Bonds Payable		1,623	
	Loss on Bond Redemption		1,377	
	Cash			103,000
	(To record redemption of bonds at 103)			

A = L + SE
−100,000
−1,623
−1,377 Exp
−103,000

Cash Flows
−103,000

Note that the loss of $1,377 is the difference between the cash paid of $103,000 and the carrying value of the bonds of $101,623.

CONVERTING BONDS INTO COMMON STOCK

Convertible bonds have features that are attractive both to bondholders and to the issuer. The conversion often gives bondholders an opportunity to benefit if the market price of the common stock increases substantially. Until conversion, though, the bondholder receives interest on the bond. For the issuer of convertible bonds, the bonds sell at a higher price and pay a lower rate of interest than comparable debt securities without the conversion option. Many corporations, such as Intel, Ford, and Wells Fargo, have convertible bonds outstanding.

When the issuing company records a conversion, the company ignores the current market prices of the bonds and stock. Instead, the company transfers the **carrying value** of the bonds to paid-in capital accounts. **No gain or loss is recognized.**

To illustrate, assume that on July 1 Saunders Associates converts $100,000 bonds sold at face value into 2,000 shares of $10 par value common stock. Both the bonds and the common stock have a market value of $130,000. Saunders makes the following entry to record the conversion:

July 1	Bonds Payable		100,000	
	Common Stock			20,000
	Paid-in Capital in Excess of Par—			
	Common Stock			80,000
	(To record bond conversion)			

A = L + SE
−100,000
+20,000 CS
+80,000 CS

Cash Flows
no effect

Note that the company does not consider the current market value of the bonds and stock ($130,000) in making the entry. This method of recording the bond conversion is often referred to as the **carrying (or book) value method**.

> DO IT!

Bond Redemption

Action Plan

✔ Determine and eliminate the carrying value of the bonds.
✔ Record the cash paid.
✔ Compute and record the gain or loss (the difference between the first two items).

R & B Inc. issued $500,000, 10-year bonds at a premium. Prior to maturity, when the carrying value of the bonds is $508,000, the company retires the bonds at 102. Prepare the entry to record the redemption of the bonds.

Solution

There is a loss on redemption: The cash paid, $510,000 ($500,000 × 102%), is greater than the carrying value of $508,000. The entry is:

Bonds Payable	500,000	
Premium on Bonds Payable	8,000	
Loss on Bond Redemption	2,000	
Cash		510,000
(To record redemption of bonds at 102)		

Related exercise material: **BE10-11, E10-13, E10-14, and** **DO IT!** **10-4.**

✔ **The Navigator**

Accounting for Long-Term Notes Payable

LEARNING OBJECTIVE **7**

Describe the accounting for long-term notes payable.

The use of notes payable in long-term debt financing is quite common. **Long-term notes payable** are similar to short-term interest-bearing notes payable except that the term of the notes exceeds one year. In periods of unstable interest rates, lenders may tie the interest rate on long-term notes to changes in the market rate for comparable loans. Examples are the 8.03% adjustable rate notes issued by General Motors and the floating-rate notes issued by American Express Company.

A long-term note may be secured by a **mortgage** that pledges title to specific assets as security for a loan. Individuals widely use **mortgage notes payable** to purchase homes, and many small and some large companies use them to acquire plant assets. At one time, approximately 18% of McDonald's long-term debt related to mortgage notes on land, buildings, and improvements.

Like other long-term notes payable, the mortgage loan terms may stipulate either a **fixed** or an **adjustable** interest rate. The interest rate on a fixed-rate mortgage remains the same over the life of the mortgage. The interest rate on an adjustable-rate mortgage is adjusted periodically to reflect changes in the market rate of interest. Typically, the terms require the borrower to make equal installment payments over the term of the loan. Each payment consists of (1) interest on the unpaid balance of the loan and (2) a reduction of loan principal. While the total amount of the payment remains constant, the interest decreases each period, while the portion applied to the loan principal increases.

Companies initially record mortgage notes payable at face value. They subsequently make entries for each installment payment. To illustrate, assume that Porter Technology Inc. issues a $500,000, 12%, 20-year mortgage note on December 31, 2014, to obtain needed financing for a new research laboratory. The terms provide for semiannual installment payments of $33,231 (not including real estate taxes and insurance). The installment payment schedule for the first two years is as follows.

Semiannual Interest Period	(A) Cash Payment	(B) Interest Expense (D) × 6%	(C) Reduction of Principal (A) − (B)	(D) Principal Balance (D) − (C)
12/31/14				$500,000
06/30/15	$33,231	$30,000	$3,231	496,769
12/31/15	33,231	29,806	3,425	493,344
06/30/16	33,231	29,601	3,630	489,714
12/31/16	33,231	29,383	3,848	485,866

Illustration 10-19
Mortgage installment payment schedule

Porter records the mortgage loan on December 31, 2014, as follows.

Dec. 31	Cash	500,000	
	Mortgage Payable		500,000
	(To record mortgage loan)		

A = L + SE
+500,000
      +500,000

Cash Flows
+500,000

On June 30, 2015, Porter records the first installment payment as follows.

June 30	Interest Expense	30,000	
	Mortgage Payable	3,231	
	Cash		33,231
	(To record semiannual payment on		
	mortgage)		

A = L + SE
             −30,000 Exp
    −3,231
−33,231

Cash Flows
−33,231

In the balance sheet, the company reports the reduction in principal for the next year as a current liability, and it classifies the remaining unpaid principal balance as a long-term liability. At December 31, 2015, the total liability is $493,344. Of that amount, $7,478 ($3,630 + $3,848) is current, and $485,866 ($493,344 − $7,478) is long-term.

> DO IT!

Long-Term Note

Cole Research issues a $250,000, 8%, 20-year mortgage note to obtain needed financing for a new lab. The terms call for semiannual payments of $12,631 each. Prepare the entries to record the mortgage loan and the first installment payment.

Action Plan

✔ Record the issuance of the note as a cash receipt and a liability.

✔ Each installment payment consists of interest and payment of principal.

Solution

Cash		250,000	
Mortgage Payable			250,000
(To record mortgage loan)			
Interest Expense		10,000*	
Mortgage Payable		2,361	
Cash			12,361
(To record semiannual payment on mortgage)			

*Interest expense = $250,000 × 8% × 6/12.

Related exercise material: **BE10-12, E10-15,** and **DO IT! 10-5.**

 The Navigator

ACCOUNTING ACROSS THE ORGANIZATION

Bonds versus Notes?

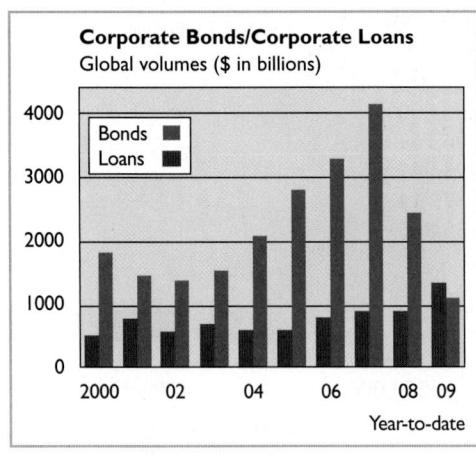

Corporate Bonds/Corporate Loans
Global volumes ($ in billions)

Companies have a choice in the form of long-term borrowing they undertake—issue bonds or issue notes. Notes are generally issued to a single lender (usually through a loan from a bank). Bonds, on the other hand, allow the company to divide the borrowing into many small investing units, thereby enabling more than one investor to participate in the borrowing. As indicated in the graph to the left, companies are recently borrowing more from bond investors than from banks and other loan providers in a bid to lock in cheap, long-term funding.

Why this trend? For one thing, low interest rates and rising inflows into fixed-income funds have triggered record bond issuances as banks cut back lending. In addition, for some high-rated companies, it can be riskier to borrow from a bank than the bond markets. The reason: High-rated companies tended to rely on short-term financing to fund working capital but were left stranded when these markets froze up. Some are now financing themselves with longer-term bonds instead.

Source: A. Sakoui and N. Bullock, "Companies Choose Bonds for Cheap Funds," *Financial Times* (October 12, 2009).

 Why might companies prefer bond financing instead of short-term financing?
(See page 533.)

Statement Presentation and Analysis

LEARNING OBJECTIVE **8**

Identify the methods for the presentation and analysis of long-term liabilities.

PRESENTATION

Companies report long-term liabilities in a separate section of the balance sheet immediately following current liabilities, as shown in Illustration 10-20. Alternatively, companies may present summary data in the balance sheet, with detailed data (interest rates, maturity dates, conversion privileges, and assets pledged as collateral) shown in a supporting schedule.

Illustration 10-20
Balance sheet presentation of long-term liabilities

Lax Corporation Balance Sheet (partial)		
Long-term liabilities		
Bonds payable 10% due in 2017	$1,000,000	
Less: Discount on bonds payable	80,000	$ 920,000
Mortgage payable, 11%, due in 2023 and secured by plant assets		500,000
Lease liability		440,000
Total long-term liabilities		$1,860,000

Companies report the current maturities of long-term debt under current liabilities if they are to be paid from current assets.

ANALYSIS

Long-term creditors and stockholders are interested in a company's long-run solvency. Of particular interest is the company's ability to pay interest as it comes due and to repay the face value of the debt at maturity. Here we look at two ratios that provide information about debt-paying ability and long-run solvency.

The **debt to total assets ratio** measures the percentage of the total assets provided by creditors. As shown in the formula in Illustration 10-21, it is computed by dividing total debt (both current and long-term liabilities) by total assets. The higher the percentage of debt to total assets, the greater the risk that the company may be unable to meet its maturing obligations.

The **times interest earned ratio** indicates the company's ability to meet interest payments as they come due. It is computed by dividing income before income taxes and interest expense by interest expense.

To illustrate these ratios, we will use data from Kellogg Company's recent annual report. The company had total liabilities of $8,925 million, total assets of $11,200 million, interest expense of $295 million, income taxes of $476 million, and net income of $1,208 million. Kellogg's debt to total assets ratio and times interest earned ratio are shown below.

Total Debt	÷	Total Assets	=	Debt to Total Assets
$8,925	÷	$11,200	=	79.7%

Income before Income Taxes and Interest Expense	÷	Interest Expense	=	Times Interest Earned
$1,208 + $476 + $295	÷	$295	=	6.71 times

Illustration 10-21
Debt to total assets and times interest earned ratios, with computations

Kellogg has a relatively high debt to total assets percentage of 79.7%. Its interest coverage of 6.71 times is considered safe.

INVESTOR INSIGHT

"Covenant-Lite" Debt

In many corporate loans and bond issuances, the lending agreement specifies debt covenants. These covenants typically are specific financial measures, such as minimum levels of retained earnings, cash flows, times interest earned ratios, or other measures that a company must maintain during the life of the loan. If the company violates a covenant, it is considered to have violated the loan agreement. The creditors can then demand immediate repayment, or they can renegotiate the loan's terms. Covenants protect lenders because they enable lenders to step in and try to get their money back before the borrower gets too deep into trouble.

During the 1990s, most traditional loans specified between three to six covenants or "triggers." In more recent years, when lots of cash was available, lenders began reducing or completely eliminating covenants from loan agreements in order to be more competitive with other lenders. When the economy declined, lenders lost big money when companies defaulted.

Source: Cynthia Koons, "Risky Business: Growth of 'Covenant-Lite' Debt," *Wall Street Journal* (June 18, 2007), p. C2.

 How can financial ratios such as those covered in this chapter provide protection for creditors? (See page 533.)

> ## Comprehensive DO IT!

Snyder Software Inc. has successfully developed a new spreadsheet program. To produce and market the program, the company needed $2 million of additional financing. On January 1, 2014, Snyder borrowed money as follows.

1. Snyder issued $500,000, 11%, 10-year convertible bonds. The bonds sold at face value and pay semiannual interest on January 1 and July 1. Each $1,000 bond is convertible into 30 shares of Snyder's $20 par value common stock.

2. Snyder issued $1 million, 10%, 10-year bonds at face value. Interest is payable semiannually on January 1 and July 1.

3. Snyder also issued a $500,000, 12%, 15-year mortgage payable. The terms provide for semiannual installment payments of $36,324 on June 30 and December 31.

Instructions

1. For the convertible bonds, prepare journal entries for:
   (a) The issuance of the bonds on January 1, 2014.
   (b) Interest expense on July 1 and December 31, 2014.
   (c) The payment of interest on January 1, 2015.
   (d) The conversion of all bonds into common stock on January 1, 2015, when the market price of the common stock was $67 per share.

2. For the 10-year, 10% bonds:
   (a) Journalize the issuance of the bonds on January 1, 2014.
   (b) Prepare the journal entries for interest expense in 2014. Assume no accrual of interest on July 1.
   (c) Prepare the entry for the redemption of the bonds at 101 on January 1, 2017, after paying the interest due on this date.

3. For the mortgage payable:
   (a) Prepare the entry for the issuance of the note on January 1, 2014.
   (b) Prepare a payment schedule for the first four installment payments.
   (c) Indicate the current and noncurrent amounts for the mortgage payable at December 31, 2014.

Solution to Comprehensive DO IT!

Action Plan

✔ Compute interest semi-annually (six months).

✔ Record the accrual and payment of interest on appropriate dates.

✔ Record the conversion of the bonds into common stock by removing the book (carrying) value of the bonds from the liability account.

1. (a) 2014				
Jan. 1	Cash		500,000	
	Bonds Payable			500,000
	(To record issue of 11%, 10-year convertible bonds at face value)			
(b) 2014				
July 1	Interest Expense		27,500	
	Cash ($500,000 × 0.055)			27,500
	(To record payment of semiannual interest)			
Dec. 31	Interest Expense		27,500	
	Interest Payable			27,500
	(To record accrual of semiannual bond interest)			
(c) 2015				
Jan. 1	Interest Payable		27,500	
	Cash			27,500
	(To record payment of accrued interest)			

(d) 2015

Jan. 1	Bonds Payable	500,000	
	Common Stock		300,000*
	Paid-in Capital in Excess of Par—Common Stock		200,000
	(To record conversion of bonds into common stock)		

*($500,000 ÷ $1,000 = 500 bonds; 500 × 30 = 15,000 shares; 15,000 × $20 = $300,000)

Action Plan

✔ Record the issuance of the bonds.

✔ Compute interest expense for each period.

✔ Compute the loss on bond redemption as the excess of the cash paid over the carrying value of the redeemed bonds.

2. (a) 2014

Jan. 1	Cash	1,000,000	
	Bonds Payable		1,000,000
	(To record issuance of bonds)		

(b) 2014

July 1	Interest Expense	50,000	
	Cash		50,000
	(To record payment of semiannual interest)		
Dec. 31	Interest Expense	50,000	
	Interest Payable		50,000
	(To record accrual of semiannual interest)		

(c) 2017

Jan. 1	Bonds Payable	1,000,000	
	Loss on Bond Redemption	10,000*	
	Cash		1,010,000
	(To record redemption of bonds at 101)		

*($1,010,000 − $1,000,000)

Action Plan

✔ Compute periodic interest expense on a mortgage payable, recognizing that as the principal amount decreases, so does the interest expense.

✔ Record mortgage payments, recognizing that each payment consists of (1) interest on the unpaid loan balance and (2) a reduction of the loan principal.

3. (a) 2014

Jan. 1	Cash	500,000	
	Mortgage Payable		500,000
	(To record issuance of mortgage payable)		

(b)

Semiannual Interest Period	Cash Payment	Interest Expense	Reduction of Principal	Principal Balance
Issue date				$500,000
1	$36,324	$30,000	$6,324	493,676
2	36,324	29,621	6,703	486,973
3	36,324	29,218	7,106	479,867
4	36,324	28,792	7,532	472,335

(c) Current liability $14,638 ($7,106 + $7,532)
    Long-term liability $472,335

 **The Navigator**

SUMMARY OF LEARNING OBJECTIVES

✔ **The Navigator**

1 **Explain a current liability, and identify the major types of current liabilities.** A current liability is a debt that a company can reasonably expect to pay (1) from existing current assets or through the creation of other current liabilities, and (2) within one year or the operating cycle, whichever is longer. The major types of current liabilities are notes payable, accounts payable, sales taxes payable, unearned revenues, and accrued liabilities such as taxes, salaries and wages, and interest payable.

2 Describe the accounting for notes payable. When a promissory note is interest-bearing, the amount of assets received upon the issuance of the note is generally equal to the face value of the note. Interest expense accrues over the life of the note. At maturity, the amount paid equals the face value of the note plus accrued interest.

3 Explain the accounting for other current liabilities. Companies record sales taxes payable at the time the related sales occur. The company serves as a collection agent for the taxing authority. Sales taxes are not an expense to the company. Companies initially record unearned revenues in an Unearned Revenue account. As a company recognizes revenue, a transfer from unearned revenue to revenue occurs. Companies report the current maturities of long-term debt as a current liability in the balance sheet.

4 Explain why bonds are issued, and identify the types of bonds. Companies may sell bonds to investors to raise long-term capital. Bonds offer the following advantages over common stock: (a) stockholder control is not affected, (b) tax savings result, and (c) earnings per share of common stock may be higher. The following types of bonds may be issued: secured and unsecured, term and serial bonds, registered and bearer bonds, and convertible and callable bonds.

5 Prepare the entries for the issuance of bonds and interest expense. When companies issue bonds, they debit Cash for the cash proceeds and credit Bonds Payable for the face value of the bonds. The account

Premium on Bonds Payable shows a bond premium; Discount on Bonds Payable shows a bond discount.

6 Describe the entries when bonds are redeemed or converted. When bondholders redeem bonds at maturity, the issuing company credits Cash and debits Bonds Payable for the face value of the bonds. When bonds are redeemed before maturity, the issuing company (a) eliminates the carrying value of the bonds at the redemption date, (b) records the cash paid, and (c) recognizes the gain or loss on redemption. When bonds are converted to common stock, the issuing company transfers the carrying (or book) value of the bonds to appropriate paid-in capital accounts; no gain or loss is recognized.

7 Describe the accounting for long-term notes payable. Each payment consists of (1) interest on the unpaid balance of the loan and (2) a reduction of loan principal. The interest decreases each period, while the portion applied to the loan principal increases.

8 Identify the methods for the presentation and analysis of long-term liabilities. Companies should report the nature and amount of each long-term debt in the balance sheet or in the notes accompanying the financial statements. Stockholders and long-term creditors are interested in a company's long-run solvency. Debt to total assets and times interest earned are two ratios that provide information about debt-paying ability and long-run solvency.

GLOSSARY

Bearer (coupon) bonds Bonds not registered in the name of the owner. (p. 485).

Bond certificate A legal document that indicates the name of the issuer, the face value of the bonds, the contractual interest rate and maturity date of the bonds. (p. 485).

Bond indenture A legal document that sets forth the terms of the bond issue. (p. 485).

Bonds A form of interest-bearing notes payable issued by corporations, universities, and governmental entities. (p. 483).

Callable bonds Bonds that are subject to retirement at a stated dollar amount prior to maturity at the option of the issuer. (p. 485).

Contractual interest rate Rate used to determine the amount of cash interest the borrower pays and the investor receives. (p. 485).

Convertible bonds Bonds that permit bondholders to convert them into common stock at the bondholders' option. (p. 485).

Current ratio A measure of a company's liquidity; computed as current assets divided by current liabilities. (p. 482).

Debenture bonds Bonds issued against the general credit of the borrower. Also called unsecured bonds. (p. 485).

Debt to total assets ratio A solvency measure that indicates the percentage of total assets provided by creditors; computed as total debt divided by total assets. (p. 497).

Discount (on a bond) The difference between the face value of a bond and its selling price, when the bond is sold for less than its face value. (p. 489).

Face value Amount of principal the issuer must pay at the maturity date of the bond. (p. 485).

Long-term liabilities Obligations expected to be paid after one year. (p. 483).

Market interest rate The rate investors demand for loaning funds to the corporation. (p. 487).

Maturity date The date on which the final payment on the bond is due from the bond issuer to the investor. (p. 485).

Mortgage bond A bond secured by real estate. (p. 485).

Mortgage notes payable A long-term note secured by a mortgage that pledges title to specific assets as security for a loan. (p. 494).

Notes payable Obligations in the form of written notes. (p. 476).

Premium (on a bond) The difference between the selling price and the face value of a bond, when the bond is sold for more than its face value. (p. 489).

Registered bonds Bonds issued in the name of the owner. (p. 485).

Secured bonds Bonds that have specific assets of the issuer pledged as collateral. (p. 485).

Serial bonds Bonds that mature in installments. (p. 485).

Sinking fund bonds Bonds secured by specific assets set aside to retire them. (p. 485).

Term bonds Bonds that mature at a single specified future date. (p. 485).

Times interest earned ratio A solvency measure that indicates a company's ability to meet interest payments;

computed by dividing income before income taxes and interest expense by interest expense. (p. 497).

Time value of money The relationship between time and money. A dollar received today is worth more than a dollar promised at some time in the future. (p. 487).

Unsecured bonds Bonds issued against the general credit of the borrower. Also called debenture bonds. (p. 485).

Working capital A measure of a company's liquidity; computed as current assets minus current liabilities. (p. 482).

APPENDIX 10A   PRESENT VALUE CONCEPTS RELATED TO BOND PRICING

Congratulations! You have a winning lottery ticket, and the state has provided you with three possible options for payment. They are:

1. Receive $10,000,000 in three years.

2. Receive $7,000,000 immediately.

3. Receive $3,500,000 at the end of each year for three years.

Which of these options would you select? The answer is not easy to determine at a glance. To make a dollar-maximizing choice, you must perform present value computations. A present value computation is based on the concept of time value of money. Time value of money concepts are useful for the lottery situation and for pricing other amounts to be received in the future. This appendix discusses how to use present value concepts to price bonds. It also will tell you how to determine what option you should take as a lottery winner.

> **LEARNING OBJECTIVE   9**
>
> **Compute the market price of a bond.**

Present Value of Face Value

To illustrate present value concepts, assume that you are willing to invest a sum of money that will yield $1,000 at the end of one year. In other words, what amount would you need to invest today to have $1,000 one year from now? If you want to earn 10%, the investment (or present value) is $909.09 ($1,000 ÷ 1.10). Illustration 10A-1 shows the computation.

Present value	×	(1 + Interest rate)	=	Future amount
Present value	×	(1 + 10%)	=	$1,000
Present value			=	$1,000 ÷ 1.10
Present value			=	**$909.09**

Illustration 10A-1
Present value computation—$1,000 discounted at 10% for one year

The future amount ($1,000), the interest rate (10%), and the number of periods (1) are known. We can depict the variables in this situation as shown in the time diagram in Illustration 10A-2.

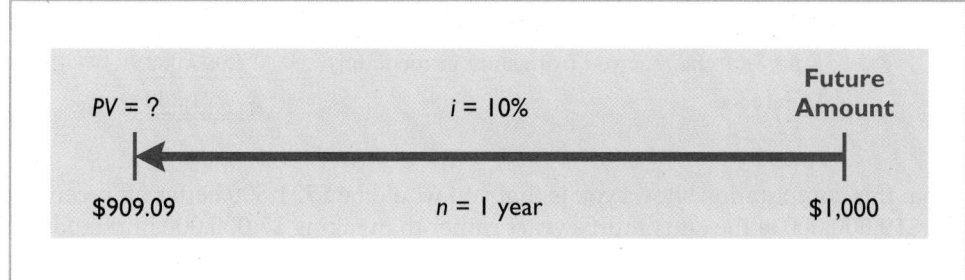

Illustration 10A-2
Finding present value if discounted for one period

If you are to receive the single future amount of $1,000 **in two years**, discounted at 10%, its present value is $826.45 [($1,000 ÷ 1.10) ÷ 1.10], depicted as follows.

Illustration 10A-3
Finding present value if discounted for two periods

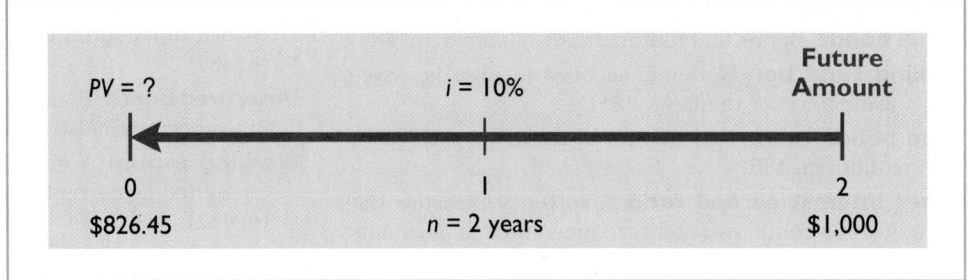

We also can determine the present value of 1 through tables that show the present value of 1 for *n* periods. In Table 10A-1, *n* is the number of discounting periods involved. The percentages are the periodic interest rates, and the 5-digit decimal numbers in the respective columns are the factors for the present value of 1.

When using Table 10A-1, we multiply the future amount by the present value factor specified at the intersection of the number of periods and the interest rate. For example, the present value factor for 1 period at an interest rate of 10% is .90909, which equals the $909.09 ($1,000 × .90909) computed in Illustration 10A-1.

Table 10A-1
Present Value of 1

(*n*) Periods	4%	5%	6%	7%	8%	9%	10%	11%	12%	15%
1	.96154	.95238	.94340	.93458	.92593	.91743	.90909	.90090	.89286	.86957
2	.92456	.90703	.89000	.87344	.85734	.84168	.82645	.81162	.79719	.75614
3	.88900	.86384	.83962	.81630	.79383	.77218	.75132	.73119	.71178	.65752
4	.85480	.82270	.79209	.76290	.73503	.70843	.68301	.65873	.63552	.57175
5	.82193	.78353	.74726	.71299	.68058	.64993	.62092	.59345	.56743	.49718
6	.79031	.74622	.70496	.66634	.63017	.59627	.56447	.53464	.50663	.43233
7	.75992	.71068	.66506	.62275	.58349	.54703	.51316	.48166	.45235	.37594
8	.73069	.67684	.62741	.58201	.54027	.50187	.46651	.43393	.40388	.32690
9	.70259	.64461	.59190	.54393	.50025	.46043	.42410	.39092	.36061	.28426
10	.67556	.61391	.55839	.50835	.46319	.42241	.38554	.35218	.32197	.24719

For two periods at an interest rate of 10%, the present value factor is .82645, which equals the $826.45 ($1,000 × .82645) computed previously.

Let's now go back to our lottery example. Given the present value concepts just learned, we can determine whether receiving $10,000,000 in three years is better than receiving $7,000,000 today, assuming the appropriate discount rate is 9%. The computation is as follows.

Illustration 10A-4
Present value of $10,000,000 to be received in three years

$10,000,000 × PV of 1 due in 3 years at 9% =	
$10,000,000 × .77218 (Table 10A-1)	$7,721,800
Amount to be received from state immediately	7,000,000
Difference	$ 721,800

What this computation shows you is that you would be $721,800 better off receiving the $10,000,000 at the end of three years rather than taking $7,000,000 immediately.

Present Value of Interest Payments (Annuities)

In addition to receiving the face value of a bond at maturity, an investor also receives periodic interest payments over the life of the bonds. These periodic payments are called **annuities**.

In order to compute the present value of an annuity, we need to know (1) the interest rate, (2) the number of interest payments, and (3) the amount of the periodic receipts or payments. To illustrate the computation of the present value of an annuity, assume that you will receive $1,000 cash annually for three years and the interest rate is 10%. The time diagram in Illustration 10A-5 depicts this situation.

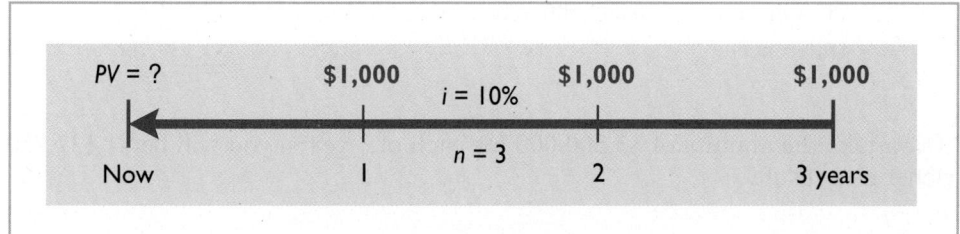

Illustration 10A-5
Time diagram for a three-year annuity

The present value in this situation may be computed as follows.

Future Amount	×	Present Value of 1 Factor at 10%	=	Present Value
$1,000 (1 year away)		.90909		$ 909.09
1,000 (2 years away)		.82645		826.45
1,000 (3 years away)		.75132		751.32
		2.48686		**$2,486.86**

Illustration 10A-6
Present value of a series of future amounts computation

We also can use annuity tables to value annuities. As illustrated in Table 10A-2 below, these tables show the present value of 1 to be received periodically for a given number of payments.

Table 10A-2									
Present Value of an Annuity of 1									
(n) Payments	**4%**	**5%**	**6%**	**7%**	**8%**	**9%**	**10%**	**11%**	**12%**	**15%**
1	.96154	.95238	.94340	.93458	.92593	.91743	.90909	.90090	.89286	.86957
2	1.88609	1.85941	1.83339	1.80802	1.78326	1.75911	1.73554	1.71252	1.69005	1.62571
3	2.77509	2.72325	2.67301	2.62432	2.57710	2.53130	2.48685	2.44371	2.40183	2.28323
4	3.62990	3.54595	3.46511	3.38721	3.31213	3.23972	3.16986	3.10245	3.03735	2.85498
5	4.45182	4.32948	4.21236	4.10020	3.99271	3.88965	3.79079	3.69590	3.60478	3.35216
6	5.24214	5.07569	4.91732	4.76654	4.62288	4.48592	4.35526	4.23054	4.11141	3.78448
7	6.00205	5.78637	5.58238	5.38929	5.20637	5.03295	4.86842	4.71220	4.56376	4.16042
8	6.73274	6.46321	6.20979	5.97130	5.74664	5.53482	5.33493	5.14612	4.96764	4.48732
9	7.43533	7.10782	6.80169	6.51523	6.24689	5.99525	5.75902	5.53705	5.32825	4.77158
10	8.11090	7.72173	7.36009	7.02358	6.71008	6.41766	6.14457	5.88923	5.65022	5.01877

From Table 10A-2, you can see that the present value factor of an annuity of 1 for three payments at 10% is 2.48685.[2] This present value factor is the total of the three individual present value factors as shown in Illustration 10A-6. Applying this amount to the annual cash flow of $1,000 produces a present value of $2,486.85.

Let's now go back to our lottery example. We determined that you would get more money if you wait and take the $10,000,000 in three years rather than take $7,000,000 immediately. But, there is still another option—to receive $3,500,000 at the end of **each year** for three years (an annuity). The computation to evaluate this option (again assuming a 9% discount rate) is as follows.

Illustration 10A-7
Present value of lottery payments to be received over three years

$3,500,000 × PV of 1 due yearly for 3 years at 9% =	
$3,500,000 × 2.53130 (Table 10A-2)	$8,859,550
Present value of $10,000,000 to be received in 3 years	7,721,800
Difference	$1,137,750

If you take the annuity of $3,500,000 for each of 3 years, you will be $1,137,750 richer as a result.

Time Periods and Discounting

We have used an **annual** interest rate to determine present value. Present value computations may also be done over shorter periods of time, such as monthly, quarterly, or semiannually. When the time frame is less than one year, it is necessary to convert the annual interest rate to the shorter time frame.

Assume, for example, that the investor in Illustration 10A-6 received $500 **semiannually** for three years instead of $1,000 annually. In this case, the number of payments becomes 6 (3 × 2), the interest rate is 5% (10% ÷ 2), the present value factor from Table 10A-2 is 5.07569, and the present value of the future cash flows is $2,537.85 (5.07569 × $500). This amount is slightly higher than the $2,486.86 computed in Illustration 10A-6 because interest is computed twice during the same year. That is, interest is earned on the first half year's interest.

Computing the Market Price of a Bond

The present value (or market price) of a bond is a function of three variables: (1) the payment amounts, (2) the length of time until the amounts are paid, and (3) the interest (discount) rate.

The first variable (dollars to be paid) is made up of two elements: (1) a series of interest payments (an annuity), and (2) the principal amount (a single sum). To compute the present value of the bond, we must discount both the interest payments and the principal amount.

When the investor's interest (discount) rate is equal to the bond's contractual interest rate, the present value of the bonds will equal the face value of the bonds. To illustrate, assume a bond issue of 10%, five-year bonds with a face value of $100,000 with interest payable **semiannually** on January 1 and July 1. If the discount rate is the same as the contractual rate, the bonds will sell **at face value**. In this case, the investor will receive: (1) $100,000 at maturity and (2) a series of ten $5,000 interest payments [$100,000 × (10% ÷ 2)] over the term of the bonds. The length of time is expressed in terms of interest periods (in this case, 10) and the discount rate per interest period (5%). The time diagram in Illustration 10A-8 depicts the variables involved in this discounting situation.

---

[2]The difference of .00001 between 2.48686 and 2.48685 is due to rounding.

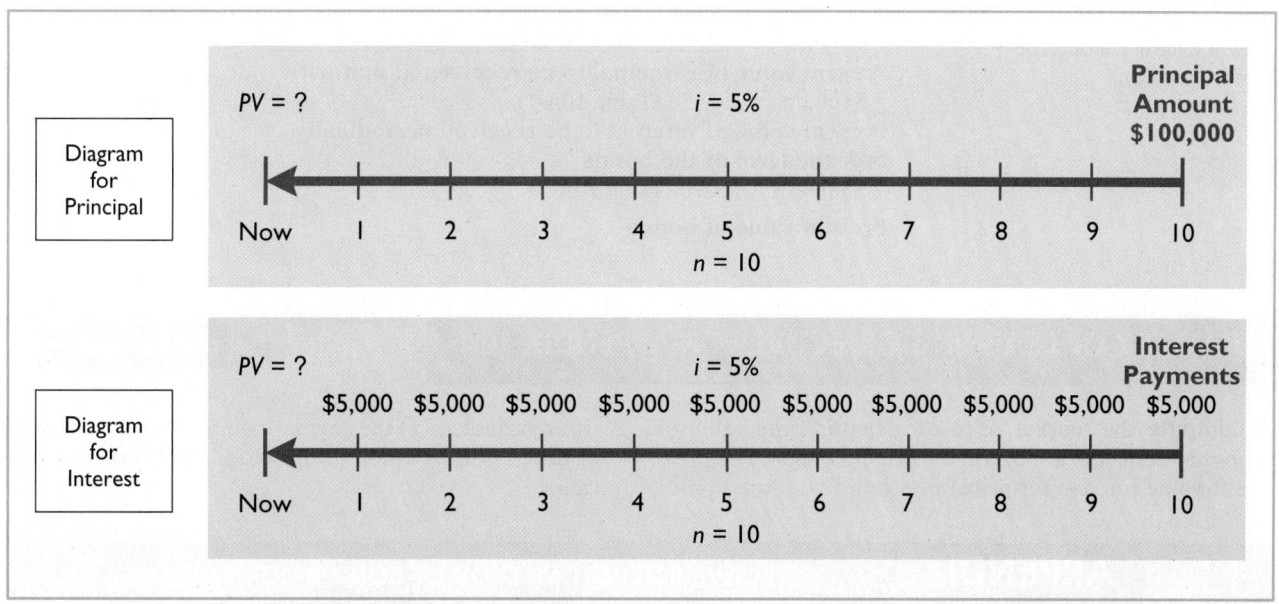

Illustration 10A-8
Time diagram for the present value of a 10%, five-year bond paying interest semiannually

The computation of the present value of Candlestick's bonds, assuming they were issued at face value (page 488), is shown below.

Illustration 10A-9
Present value of principal and interest (face value)

10% Contractual Rate—10% Discount Rate

Present value of principal to be received at maturity	
$100,000 × PV of 1 due in 10 periods at 5%	
$100,000 × .61391 (Table 10A-1)	$ 61,391
Present value of interest to be received periodically	
over the term of the bonds	
$5,000 × PV of 1 due periodically for 10 periods at 5%	
$5,000 × 7.72173 (Table 10A-2)	38,609*
Present value of bonds	**$100,000**

*Rounded.

Now assume that the investor's required rate of return is 12%, not 10%. The future amounts are again $100,000 and $5,000, respectively. But now we must use a discount rate of 6% (12% ÷ 2). The present value of Candlestick's bonds issued at a discount (page 490) is $92,639 as computed below.

Illustration 10A-10
Present value of principal and interest (discount)

10% Contractual Rate—12% Discount Rate

Present value of principal to be received at maturity	
$100,000 × .55839 (Table 10A-1)	$ 55,839
Present value of interest to be received periodically	
over the term of the bonds	
$5,000 × 7.36009 (Table 10A-2)	36,800
Present value of bonds	**$92,639**

If the discount rate is 8% and the contractual rate is 10%, the present value of Candlestick's bonds issued at a premium (page 491) is $108,111, computed as shown in Illustration 10A-11 (page 506).

Illustration 10A-11
Present value of principal and interest (premium)

10% Contractual Rate—8% Discount Rate	
Present value of principal to be received at maturity	
$100,000 × .67556 (Table 10A-1)	$ 67,556
Present value of interest to be received periodically over the term of the bonds	
$5,000 × 8.11090 (Table 10A-2)	40,555
Present value of bonds	**$108,111**

SUMMARY OF LEARNING OBJECTIVE FOR APPENDIX 10A   ✔ The Navigator

9 Compute the market price of a bond. Time value of money concepts are useful for pricing bonds. The present value (or market price) of a bond is a function of three variables: (1) the payment amounts, (2) the length of time until the amounts are paid, and (3) the interest rate.

APPENDIX **10B** EFFECTIVE-INTEREST METHOD OF BOND AMORTIZATION

LEARNING OBJECTIVE 10

Apply the effective-interest method of amortizing bond discount and bond premium.

Under the **effective-interest method**, the amortization of bond discount or bond premium results in periodic interest expense equal to a **constant percentage** of the carrying value of the bonds. The effective-interest method results in varying amounts of amortization and interest expense per period but **a constant percentage rate**.

The following steps are required under the effective-interest method.

1. Compute the **bond interest expense**. To do so, multiply the carrying value of the bonds at the beginning of the interest period by the effective-interest rate.
2. Compute the **bond interest paid** (or accrued). To do so, multiply the face value of the bonds by the contractual interest rate.
3. Compute the **amortization amount**. To do so, determine the difference between the amounts computed in steps (1) and (2).

Illustration 10B-1 depicts these steps.

Illustration 10B-1
Computation of amortization—effective-interest method

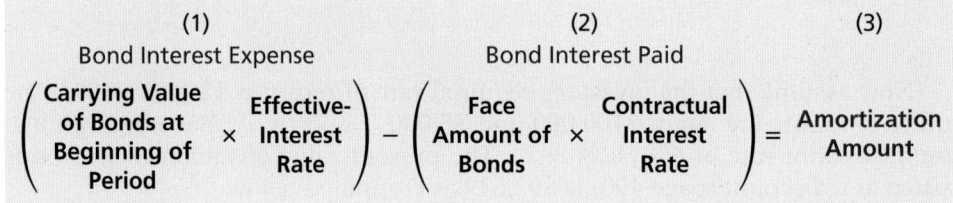

When the difference between the straight-line method of amortization (Appendix 10C) and the effective-interest method is material, GAAP requires the use of the effective-interest method.

Amortizing Bond Discount

To illustrate the effective-interest method of bond discount amortization, assume that Candlestick, Inc. issues $100,000 of 10%, five-year bonds on January 1, 2014, with interest payable each July 1 and January 1 (pages 490–491). The bonds sell for $92,639 (92.639% of face value). This sales price results in a bond discount of $7,361 ($100,000 − $92,639) and an effective-interest rate of 12%. A bond discount amortization schedule, as shown in Illustration 10B-2, facilitates the recording of interest expense and the discount amortization. Note that interest expense as a percentage of carrying value remains constant at 6%.

		Candlestick Inc.xls			

Home   Insert   Page Layout   Formulas   Data   Review   View

P18   fx

	A	B	C	D	E	F
1			**Candlestick, Inc.**			
2			Bond Discount Amortization			
3			Effective-Interest Method—Semiannual Interest Payments			
4			10% Bonds Issued at 12%			
5			**(B)**		**(D)**	**(E)**
6			Interest Expense	**(C)**	Unamortized	Bond
7	Semiannual	**(A)**	to Be Recorded	Discount	Discount	Carrying Value
8	Interest Periods	Interest to Be Paid (5% × $100,000)	(6% × Preceding Bond Carrying Value)	Amortization (B) – (A)	(D) – (C)	($100,000 – D)
9	Issue date				$7,361	$92,639
10	1	$ 5,000	$ 5,558 (6% × $92,639)	$ 558	6,803	93,197
11	2	5,000	5,592 (6% × $93,197)	592	6,211	93,789
12	3	5,000	5,627 (6% × $93,789)	627	5,584	94,416
13	4	5,000	5,665 (6% × $94,416)	665	4,919	95,081
14	5	5,000	5,705 (6% × $95,081)	705	4,214	95,786
15	6	5,000	5,747 (6% × $95,786)	747	3,467	96,533
16	7	5,000	5,792 (6% × $96,533)	792	2,675	97,325
17	8	5,000	5,840 (6% × $97,325)	840	1,835	98,165
18	9	5,000	5,890 (6% × $98,165)	890	945	99,055
19	10	5,000	5,945* (6% × $99,055)	945	–0–	100,000
20		$50,000	$57,361	$7,361		
21						
22	Column **(A)** remains constant because the face value of the bonds ($100,000) is multiplied by the semiannual contractual interest rate (5%) each period.					
23	Column **(B)** is computed as the preceding bond carrying value times the semiannual effective-interest rate (6%).					
24	Column **(C)** indicates the discount amortization each period.					
25	Column **(D)** decreases each period until it reaches zero at maturity.					
26	Column **(E)** increases each period until it equals face value at maturity.					
27						
28	*$2 difference due to rounding.					

Illustration 10B-2
Bond discount amortization
schedule

We have highlighted columns (A), (B), and (C) in the amortization schedule to emphasize their importance. These three columns provide the numbers for each period's journal entries. They are the primary reason for preparing the schedule.

For the first interest period, the computations of interest expense and the bond discount amortization are:

Interest expense ($92,639 × 6%)	$5,558
Contractual interest ($100,000 × 5%)	5,000
Bond discount amortization	**$ 558**

Illustration 10B-3
Computation of bond discount
amortization

Candlestick records the payment of interest and amortization of bond discount on July 1, 2014, as follows.

July 1	Interest Expense	5,558	
	Discount on Bonds Payable		558
	Cash		5,000
	(To record payment of bond interest and amortization of bond discount)		

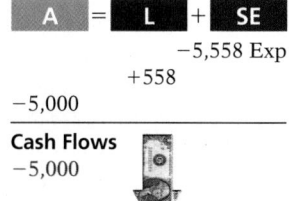

A = L + SE

−5,558 Exp
+558
−5,000

Cash Flows
−5,000

For the second interest period, bond interest expense will be $5,592 ($93,197 × 6%), and the discount amortization will be $592. At December 31, Candlestick makes the following adjusting entry.

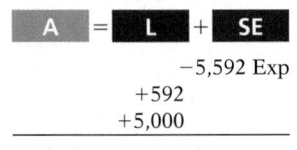

−5,592 Exp
+592
+5,000

Cash Flows
no effect

Dec. 31	Interest Expense	5,592	
	Discount on Bonds Payable		592
	Interest Payable		5,000
	(To record accrued interest and		
	amortization of bond discount)		

Total interest expense for 2014 is $11,150 ($5,558 + $5,592). On January 1, Candlestick records payment of the interest by a debit to Interest Payable and a credit to Cash.

Helpful Hint
When a bond sells for $108,111, it is quoted as 108.111% of face value. Note that $108,111 can be proven as shown in Appendix 10A.

Amortizing Bond Premium

The amortization of bond premium by the effective-interest method is similar to the procedures described for bond discount. For example, assume that Candlestick, Inc. issues $100,000, 10%, five-year bonds on January 1, 2014, with interest payable on July 1 and January 1 (pages 491–492). In this case, the bonds sell for $108,111. This sales price results in bond premium of $8,111 and an effective-interest rate of 8%. Illustration 10B-4 shows the bond premium amortization schedule.

Illustration 10B-4
Bond premium amortization schedule

			Candlestick Inc.xls			
	Home Insert Page Layout Formulas Data Review View					
	P18	*fx*				
	A	B	C	D	E	F
1			**Candlestick, Inc.**			
2			**Bond Premium Amortization**			
3			**Effective-Interest Method—Semiannual Interest Payments**			
4			**10% Bonds Issued at 8%**			
5						
6			**(B)**		**(D)**	**(E)**
7	**Semiannual**	**(A)**	**Interest Expense to Be Recorded**	**(C)**	**Unamortized**	**Bond**
8	**Interest**	**Interest to Be Paid**	**(4% × Preceding Bond**	**Premium**	**Premium**	**Carrying Value**
9	**Periods**	**(5% × $100,000)**	**Carrying Value)**	**Amortization (A) – (B)**	**(D) – (C)**	**($100,000 + D)**
10	Issue date				$8,111	$108,111
11	1	$ 5,000	$ 4,324 (4% × $108,111)	$ 676	7,435	107,435
12	2	5,000	4,297 (4% × $107,435)	703	6,732	106,732
13	3	5,000	4,269 (4% × $106,732)	731	6,001	106,001
14	4	5,000	4,240 (4% × $106,001)	760	5,241	105,241
15	5	5,000	4,210 (4% × $105,241)	790	4,451	104,451
16	6	5,000	4,178 (4% × $104,451)	822	3,629	103,629
17	7	5,000	4,145 (4% × $103,629)	855	2,774	102,774
18	8	5,000	4,111 (4% × $102,774)	889	1,885	101,885
19	9	5,000	4,075 (4% × $101,885)	925	960	100,960
20	10	5,000	4,040* (4% × $100,960)	960	−0−	100,000
21		$50,000	$41,889	$8,111		
22						
23	Column **(A)** remains constant because the face value of the bonds ($100,000) is multiplied by the semiannual contractual interest rate (5%) each period.					
24	Column **(B)** is computed as the carrying value of the bonds times the semiannual effective-interest rate (4%).					
25	Column **(C)** indicates the premium amortization each period.					
26	Column **(D)** decreases each period until it reaches zero at maturity.					
27	Column **(E)** decreases each period until it equals face value at maturity.					
28						
29	*$2 difference due to rounding.					

For the first interest period, the computations of interest expense and the bond premium amortization are:

Interest expense ($108,111 × 4%)	$4,324	
Contractual interest ($100,000 × 5%)	5,000	
Bond premium amortization	**$ 676**	

Illustration 10B-5
Computation of bond premium amortization

Candlestick records payments on the first interest date as follows.

July 1	Interest Expense	4,324	
	Premium on Bonds Payable	676	
	Cash		5,000
	(To record payment of bond interest and amortization of bond premium)		

A = L + SE

−4,324 Exp
−676
−5,000

Cash Flows
−5,000

For the second interest period, interest expense will be $4,297, and the premium amortization will be $703. Total bond interest expense for 2014 is $8,621 ($4,324 + $4,297).

> DO IT!

Action Plan

✔ Compute interest expense by multiplying bond carrying value at the beginning of the period by the effective-interest rate.

✔ Compute credit to cash (or interest payable) by multiplying the face value of the bonds by the contractual interest rate.

✔ Compute bond premium or discount amortization, which is the difference between interest expense and cash paid.

✔ Interest expense decreases when the effective-interest method is used for bonds issued at a premium. The reason is that a constant percentage is applied to a decreasing book value to compute interest expense.

Gardner Corporation issues $1,750,000, 10-year, 12% bonds on January 1, 2014, at $1,968,090, to yield 10%. The bonds pay semiannual interest July 1 and January 1. Gardner uses the effective-interest method of amortization.

Instructions

(a) Prepare the journal entry to record the issuance of the bonds.

(b) Prepare the journal entry to record the payment of interest on July 1, 2014.

Solution to Comprehensive DO IT! for Appendix 10B

(a) 2014				
Jan. 1	Cash		1,968,090	
	Bonds Payable			1,750,000
	Premium on Bonds Payable			218,090
	(To record issuance of bonds at a premium)			
(b) 2014				
July 1	Interest Expense		98,405*	
	Premium on Bonds Payable		6,595**	
	Cash			105,000
	(To record payment of semiannual interest and amortization of bond premium)			

*($1,968,090 × 5%)
**($105,000 − $98,405)

✔ **The Navigator**

✔ The Navigator

SUMMARY OF LEARNING OBJECTIVE FOR APPENDIX 10B

10 Apply the effective-interest method of amortizing bond discount and bond premium. The effective-interest method results in varying amounts of amortization and interest expense per period but a *constant* *percentage rate* of interest. When the difference between the straight-line and effective-interest method is material, GAAP requires the use of the effective-interest method.

GLOSSARY FOR APPENDIX 10B

Effective-interest method of amortization A method of amortizing bond discount or bond premium that results in periodic interest expense equal to a constant percentage of the carrying value of the bonds. (p. 506).

APPENDIX 10C STRAIGHT-LINE AMORTIZATION

> **LEARNING OBJECTIVE 11**
>
> Apply the straight-line method of amortizing bond discount and bond premium.

Amortizing Bond Discount

Under the **straight-line method of amortization**, the amortization of bond discount or bond premium results in periodic interest expense of the same amount in each interest period. In other words, the straight-line method results in a constant amount of amortization and interest expense per period. The amount is determined using the formula in Illustration 10C-1.

Illustration 10C-1
Formula for straight-line method of bond discount amortization

Bond Discount	÷	Number of Interest Periods	=	Bond Discount Amortization

In the Candlestick, Inc. example (pages 490–491), the company sold $100,000, five-year, 10% bonds on January 1, 2014, for $92,639. This price resulted in a $7,361 bond discount ($100,000 − $92,639). Interest is payable on July 1 and January 1. The bond discount amortization for each interest period is $736 ($7,361 ÷ 10). Candlestick records the payment of bond interest and the amortization of bond discount on the first interest date (July 1, 2014) as follows.

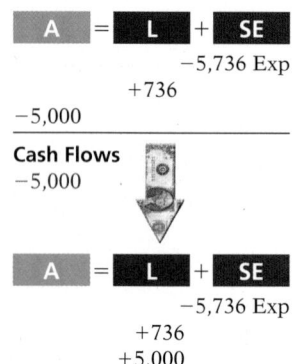

A = L + SE
            −5,736 Exp
       +736
−5,000
Cash Flows
−5,000

July 1	Interest Expense	5,736	
	Discount on Bonds Payable		736
	Cash		5,000
	(To record payment of bond interest and amortization of bond discount)		

At December 31, Candlestick makes the following adjusting entry.

A = L + SE
            −5,736 Exp
       +736
       +5,000
Cash Flows
no effect

Dec. 31	Interest Expense	5,736	
	Discount on Bonds Payable		736
	Interest Payable		5,000
	(To record accrued bond interest and amortization of bond discount)		

Over the term of the bonds, the balance in Discount on Bonds Payable will decrease annually by the **same amount** until it has a zero balance at the maturity date of the bonds. Thus, the carrying value of the bonds at maturity will be equal to the face value.

It is useful to prepare a bond discount amortization schedule as shown in Illustration 10C-2. The schedule shows interest expense, discount amortization, and the carrying value of the bond for each interest period. As indicated, the interest expense recorded **each period** for the Candlestick bond is $5,736. Also note that the carrying value of the bond increases $736 each period until it reaches its face value $100,000 at the end of period 10.

Illustration 10C-2
Bond discount amortization schedule

	Candlestick Inc.xls				
Home Insert Page Layout Formulas Data Review View					
P18		fx			
	A	B	C	D	E	F

	A	B	C	D	E	F
1	**Candlestick, Inc.**				
2	**Bond Discount Amortization**				
3	**Straight-Line Method—Semiannual Interest Payments**				
4					
5 6 7	**Semiannual Interest Periods**	**(A) Interest to Be Paid (5% × $100,000)**	**(B) Interest Expense to Be Recorded (A) + (C)**	**(C) Discount Amortization ($7,361 ÷ 10)**	**(D) Unamortized Discount (D) – (C)**	**(E) Bond Carrying Value ($100,000 – D)**
8	Issue date				$7,361	$92,639
9	1	$ 5,000	$ 5,736	$ 736	6,625	93,375
10	2	5,000	5,736	736	5,889	94,111
11	3	5,000	5,736	736	5,153	94,847
12	4	5,000	5,736	736	4,417	95,583
13	5	5,000	5,736	736	3,681	96,319
14	6	5,000	5,736	736	2,945	97,055
15	7	5,000	5,736	736	2,209	97,791
16	8	5,000	5,736	736	1,473	98,527
17	9	5,000	5,736	736	737	99,263
18	10	5,000	5,737*	737*	–0–	100,000
19		$50,000	$57,361	$7,361		
20						
21	Column **(A)** remains constant because the face value of the bonds ($100,000) is multiplied by the semiannual contractual interest rate (5%) each period.					
22	Column **(B)** is computed as the interest paid (Column A) plus the discount amortization (Column C).					
23	Column **(C)** indicates the discount amortization each period.					
24	Column **(D)** decreases each period by the same amount until it reaches zero at maturity.					
25	Column **(E)** increases each period by the same amount of discount amortization until it equals the face value at maturity.					
26						
27	*One dollar difference due to rounding.					

We have highlighted columns (A), (B), and (C) in the amortization schedule to emphasize their importance. These three columns provide the numbers for each period's journal entries. They are the primary reason for preparing the schedule.

Amortizing Bond Premium

The amortization of bond premium parallels that of bond discount. Illustration 10C-3 presents the formula for determining bond premium amortization under the straight-line method.

Bond Premium	÷	Number of Interest Periods	=	Bond Premium Amortization

Illustration 10C-3
Formula for straight-line method of bond premium amortization

Continuing our example, assume that Candlestick sells the bonds for $108,111 rather than $92,639 (pages 491–492). This sale price results in a bond premium of $8,111 ($108,111 − $100,000). The bond premium amortization for each interest period is $811 ($8,111 ÷ 10). Candlestick records the first payment of interest on July 1 as follows.

A = L + SE

−4,189 Exp
−811
−5,000

Cash Flows
−5,000

July 1	Interest Expense	4,189	
	Premium on Bonds Payable	811	
	Cash		5,000
	(To record payment of bond interest and		
	amortization of bond premium)		

At December 31, the company makes the following adjusting entry.

A = L + SE

−4,189 Exp
−811
+5,000

Cash Flows
no effect

Dec. 31	Interest Expense	4,189	
	Premium on Bonds Payable	811	
	Interest Payable		5,000
	(To record accrued bond interest and		
	amortization of bond premium)		

Over the term of the bonds, the balance in Premium on Bonds Payable will decrease annually **by the same amount** until it has a zero balance at maturity.

It is useful to prepare a bond premium amortization schedule as shown in Illustration 10C-4. It shows interest expense, premium amortization, and the carrying

Illustration 10C-4
Bond premium amortization schedule

Candlestick Inc.xls

Home   Insert   Page Layout   Formulas   Data   Review   View

P18   fx

Candlestick, Inc.
Bond Premium Amortization
Straight-Line Method—Semiannual Interest Payments

Semiannual Interest Periods	(A) Interest to Be Paid (5% × $100,000)	(B) Interest Expense to Be Recorded (A) – (C)	(C) Premium Amortization ($8,111 ÷ 10)	(D) Unamortized Premium (D) – (C)	(E) Bond Carrying Value ($100,000 + D)
Issue date				$8,111	$108,111
1	$ 5,000	$ 4,189	$ 811	7,300	107,300
2	5,000	4,189	811	6,489	106,489
3	5,000	4,189	811	5,678	105,678
4	5,000	4,189	811	4,867	104,867
5	5,000	4,189	811	4,056	104,056
6	5,000	4,189	811	3,245	103,245
7	5,000	4,189	811	2,434	102,434
8	5,000	4,189	811	1,623	101,623
9	5,000	4,189	811	812	100,812
10	5,000	4,188*	812*	–0–	100,000
	$50,000	$41,889	$8,111		

Column (A) remains constant because the face value of the bonds ($100,000) is multiplied by the semiannual contractual interest rate (5%) each period.

Column (B) is computed as the interest paid (Column A) less the premium amortization (Column C).

Column (C) indicates the premium amortization each period.

Column (D) decreases each period by the same amount until it reaches zero at maturity.

Column (E) decreases each period by the amount of premium amortization until it equals the face value at maturity.

*One dollar difference due to rounding.

value of the bond. The interest expense recorded each period for the Candlestick bond is $4,189. Also note that the carrying value of the bond decreases $811 each period until it reaches its face value of $100,000 at the end of period 10.

> DO IT!

Action Plan

✔ Compute credit to cash (or interest payable) by multiplying the face value of the bonds by the contractual interest rate.

✔ Compute bond premium or discount amortization by dividing bond premium or discount by the total number of periods.

✔ Understand that interest expense decreases when bonds are issued at a premium. The reason is that the amortization of premium reduces the total cost of borrowing.

Glenda Corporation issues $1,750,000, 10-year, 12% bonds on January 1, 2014, for $1,968,090 to yield 10%. The bonds pay semiannual interest July 1 and January 1. Glenda uses the straight-line method of amortization.

Instructions

(a) Prepare the journal entry to record the issuance of the bonds.

(b) Prepare the journal entry to record the payment of interest on July 1, 2014.

Solution to Comprehensive DO IT! **for Appendix 10C**

(a) 2014			
Jan. 1	Cash	1,968,090	
	Bonds Payable		1,750,000
	Premium on Bonds Payable		218,090
(b) 2014			
July 1	Interest Expense	94,095.50**	
	Premium on Bonds Payable	10,904.50*	
	Cash		105,000

*$218,090 ÷ 20
**$105,000 − $10,904.50

 The Navigator

SUMMARY OF LEARNING OBJECTIVE FOR APPENDIX 10C

✔ **The Navigator**

11 Apply the straight-line method of amortizing bond discount and bond premium. The straight-line method of amortization results in a *constant amount* of amortization and interest expense per period.

GLOSSARY FOR APPENDIX 10C

Straight-line method of amortization A method of amortizing bond discount or bond premium that results in allocating the same amount to interest expense in each interest period. (p. 510).

Self-Test, Brief Exercises, Exercises, Problem Set A, and many more components are available for practice in WileyPLUS.

Note: All asterisked Questions, Exercises, and Problems relate to material in the appendices to the chapter.

SELF-TEST QUESTIONS

Answers are on page 533.

(LO 1) **1.** The time period for classifying a liability as current is one year or the operating cycle, whichever is:
(a) longer.   (c) probable.
(b) shorter.   (d) possible.

(LO 1) **2.** To be classified as a current liability, a debt must be expected to be paid:
(a) out of existing current assets.
(b) by creating other current liabilities.
(c) within 2 years.
(d) Both (a) and (b).

(LO 2) **3.** Maggie Sharrer Company borrows $88,500 on September 1, 2014, from Sandwich State Bank by signing an $88,500, 12%, one-year note. What is the accrued interest at December 31, 2014?
(a) $2,655.   (c) $4,425.
(b) $3,540.   (d) $10,620.

(LO 3) **4.** Becky Sherrick Company has total proceeds from sales of $4,515. If the proceeds include sales taxes of 5%, the amount to be credited to Sales Revenue is:
(a) $4,000.   (c) $4,289.25.
(b) $4,300.   (d) No correct answer given.

(LO 3) **5.** Employer payroll taxes do *not* include:
(a) federal unemployment taxes.
(b) state unemployment taxes.
(c) federal income taxes.
(d) FICA taxes.

(LO 3) **6.** Sensible Insurance Company collected a premium of $18,000 for a 1-year insurance policy on April 1. What amount should Sensible report as a current liability for Unearned Insurance Premiums at December 31?
(a) $0.   (c) $13,500.
(b) $4,500.   (d) $18,000.

(LO 4) **7.** The term used for bonds that are unsecured is:
(a) callable bonds.   (c) debenture bonds.
(b) indenture bonds.   (d) bearer bonds.

(LO 5) **8.** Karson Inc. issues 10-year bonds with a maturity value of $200,000. If the bonds are issued at a premium, this indicates that:
(a) the contractual interest rate exceeds the market interest rate.
(b) the market interest rate exceeds the contractual interest rate.
(c) the contractual interest rate and the market interest rate are the same.
(d) no relationship exists between the two rates.

(LO 6) **9.** Gester Corporation retires its $100,000 face value bonds at 105 on January 1, following the payment of semiannual interest. The carrying value of the bonds at the redemption date is $103,745. The entry to record the redemption will include a:

(a) credit of $3,745 to Loss on Bond Redemption.
(b) debit of $3,745 to Premium on Bonds Payable.
(c) credit of $1,255 to Gain on Bond Redemption.
(d) debit of $5,000 to Premium on Bonds Payable.

10. Colson Inc. converts $600,000 of bonds sold at face (LO 6) value into 10,000 shares of common stock, par value $1. Both the bonds and the stock have a market value of $760,000. What amount should be credited to Paid-in Capital in Excess of Par—Common Stock as a result of the conversion?
(a) $10,000.   (c) $600,000.
(b) $160,000.   (d) $590,000.

11. Andrews Inc. issues a $497,000, 10%, 3-year mortgage (LO 7) note on January 1. The note will be paid in three annual installments of $200,000, each payable at the end of the year. What is the amount of interest expense that should be recognized by Andrews Inc. in the second year?
(a) $16,567.   (c) $34,670.
(b) $49,700.   (d) $346,700.

12. Howard Corporation issued a 20-year mortgage note (LO 7) payable on January 1, 2014. At December 31, 2014, the unpaid principal balance will be reported as:
(a) a current liability.
(b) a long-term liability.
(c) part current and part long-term liability.
(d) interest payable.

13. For 2014, Corn Flake Corporation reported net income (LO 8) of $300,000. Interest expense was $40,000 and income taxes were $100,000. The times interest earned ratio was:
(a) 3 times.   (c) 7.5 times.
(b) 4.4 times.   (d) 11 times.

*__14.__ The market price of a bond is dependent on: (LO 9)
(a) the payment amounts.
(b) the length of time until the amounts are paid.
(c) the interest rate.
(d) All of the above.

*__15.__ On January 1, Besalius Inc. issued $1,000,000, 9% (LO 10) bonds for $938,554. The market rate of interest for these bonds is 10%. Interest is payable annually on December 31. Besalius uses the effective-interest method of amortizing bond discount. At the end of the first year, Besalius should report unamortized bond discount of:
(a) $54,900.   (c) $51,610.
(b) $57,591.   (d) $51,000.

*__16.__ On January 1, Dias Corporation issued $1,000,000, (LO 10) 10%, 5-year bonds with interest payable on July 1 and January 1. The bonds sold for $1,081,105. The market rate of interest for these bonds was 8%. On the first interest date, using the effective-interest method, the debit entry to Interest Expense is for:
(a) $50,000.   (c) $43,244.
(b) $54,055.   (d) $100,811.

(LO 11) *17. On January 1, Hurley Corporation issues $500,000, 5-year, 12% bonds at 96 with interest payable on July 1 and January 1. The entry on July 1 to record payment of bond interest and the amortization of bond discount using the straight-line method will include a:
(a) debit to Interest Expense $30,000.
(b) debit to Interest Expense $60,000.

(c) credit to Discount on Bonds Payable $4,000.
(d) credit to Discount on Bonds Payable $2,000.

*18. For the bonds issued in Question 17 above, what is (LO 11) the carrying value of the bonds at the end of the third interest period?
(a) $486,000.   (c) $472,000.
(b) $488,000.   (d) $464,000.

Go to the book's companion website, www.wiley.com/college/weygandt, for additional Self-Test Questions.

QUESTIONS

1. Brenda Gable believes a current liability is a debt that can be expected to be paid in one year. Is Brenda correct? Explain.

2. McGuire Company obtains $30,000 in cash by signing a 9%, 6-month, $30,000 note payable to First Bank on July 1. McGuire's fiscal year ends on September 30. What information should be reported for the note payable in the annual financial statements?

3. (a) Your roommate says, "Sales taxes are reported as an expense in the income statement." Do you agree? Explain.
   (b) Planet Hollywood has cash proceeds from sales of $7,400. This amount includes $400 of sales taxes. Give the entry to record the proceeds.

4. Ottawa University sold 10,000 season football tickets at $90 each for its five-game home schedule. What entries should be made (a) when the tickets were sold, and (b) after each game?

5. What is liquidity? What are two measures of liquidity?

6. Identify three taxes commonly withheld by the employer from an employee's gross pay.

7. (a) What are long-term liabilities? Give three examples.
   (b) What is a bond?

8. (a) As a source of long-term financing, what are the major advantages of bonds over common stock?
   (b) What are the major disadvantages in using bonds for long-term financing?

9. Contrast the following types of bonds: (a) secured and unsecured, (b) term and serial, (c) registered and bearer, and (d) convertible and callable.

10. The following terms are important in issuing bonds: (a) face value, (b) contractual interest rate, (c) bond indenture, and (d) bond certificate. Explain each of these terms.

11. Describe the two major obligations incurred by a company when bonds are issued.

12. Assume that Bedazzled Inc. sold bonds with a face value of $100,000 for $104,000. Was the market interest rate equal to, less than, or greater than the bonds' contractual interest rate? Explain.

13. If a 6%, 10-year, $800,000 bond is issued at face value and interest is paid semiannually, what is the amount of the interest payment at the end of the first semiannual period?

14. If the Bonds Payable account has a balance of $900,000 and the Discount on Bonds Payable account has a balance of $60,000, what is the carrying value of the bonds?

15. Which accounts are debited and which are credited if a bond issue originally sold at a premium is redeemed before maturity at 97 immediately following the payment of interest?

16. Karistad Corporation is considering issuing a convertible bond. What is a convertible bond? Discuss the advantages of a convertible bond from the standpoint of (a) the bondholders and (b) the issuing corporation.

17. Roy Toth, a friend of yours, has recently purchased a home for $125,000, paying $25,000 down and the remainder financed by a 6.5%, 20-year mortgage, payable at $745.57 per month. At the end of the first month, Roy receives a statement from the bank indicating that only $203.90 of principal was paid during the month. At this rate, he calculates that it will take over 40 years to pay off the mortgage. Is he right? Discuss.

18. In general, what are the requirements for the financial statement presentation of long-term liabilities?

*19. Ginny Bellis is discussing the advantages of the effective-interest method of bond amortization with her accounting staff. What do you think Ginny is saying?

*20. Redbone Corporation issues $500,000 of 8%, 5-year bonds on January 1, 2014, at 104. If Redbone uses the effective-interest method in amortizing the premium, will the annual interest expense increase or decrease over the life of the bonds? Explain.

*21. Vera Cruz and Sven Varberg are discussing how the market price of a bond is determined. Vera believes that the market price of a bond is solely a function of the amount of the principal payment at the end of the term of a bond. Is she right? Discuss.

*22. Explain the straight-line method of amortizing discount and premium on bonds payable.

*23. Fleming Corporation issues $400,000 of 7%, 5-year bonds on January 1, 2014, at 105. Assuming that the straight-line method is used to amortize the premium, what is the total amount of interest expense for 2014?

Identify whether obligations are current liabilities.

(LO 1)

BE10-1 Cardinal Company has the following obligations at December 31: (a) a note payable for $100,000 due in 2 years, (b) a 10-year mortgage payable of $300,000 payable in ten $30,000 annual payments, (c) interest payable of $12,000 on the mortgage, and (d) accounts payable of $60,000. For each obligation, indicate whether it should be classified as a current liability. (Assume an operating cycle of less than one year.)

Prepare entries for an interest-bearing note payable.

(LO 2)

BE10-2 Becky Company borrows $60,000 on July 1 from the bank by signing a $60,000, 10%, one-year note payable.

(a) Prepare the journal entry to record the proceeds of the note.
(b) Prepare the journal entry to record accrued interest at December 31, assuming adjusting entries are made only at the end of the year.

Compute and record sales taxes payable.

(LO 3)

BE10-3 Goodwin Auto Supply does not segregate sales and sales taxes at the time of sale. The register total for March 16 is $13,440. All sales are subject to a 5% sales tax. Compute sales taxes payable, and make the entry to record sales taxes payable and sales.

Prepare entries for unearned revenues.

(LO 3)

BE10-4 Wichita University sells 4,000 season basketball tickets at $180 each for its 10-game home schedule. Give the entry to record (a) the sale of the season tickets and (b) the revenue recognized for playing the first home game.

Compute gross earnings and net pay.

(LO 3)

BE10-5 Sandi Teter's regular hourly wage rate is $14, and she receives an hourly rate of $21 for work in excess of 40 hours. During a January pay period, Sandi works 47 hours. Sandi's federal income tax withholding is $95, and she has no voluntary deductions. Compute Sandi Teter's gross earnings and net pay for the pay period.

Record a payroll and the payment of wages.

(LO 3)

BE10-6 Data for Sandi Teter are presented in BE10-5. Prepare the journal entries to record (a) Sandi's pay for the period and (b) the payment of Sandi's wages. Use January 15 for the end of the pay period and the payment date.

Compare bond versus stock financing.

(LO 4)

BE10-7 Shaffer Inc. is considering two alternatives to finance its construction of a new $2 million plant.

(a) Issuance of 200,000 shares of common stock at the market price of $10 per share.
(b) Issuance of $2 million, 7% bonds at face value.

Complete the following table, and indicate which alternative is preferable.

	Issue Stock	Issue Bond
Income before interest and taxes	$700,000	$700,000
Interest expense from bonds	_____	_____
Income before income taxes		
Income tax expense (30%)	_____	_____
Net income	$_____	$_____
Outstanding shares	_____	500,000
Earnings per share	_____	_____

Prepare entries for bonds issued at face value.

(LO 5)

BE10-8 Quincey Corporation issued 4,000, 6%, 5-year, $1,000 bonds dated January 1, 2014, at 100.

(a) Prepare the journal entry to record the sale of these bonds on January 1, 2014.
(b) Prepare the journal entry to record the first interest payment on July 1, 2014 (interest payable semiannually), assuming no previous accrual of interest.
(c) Prepare the adjusting journal entry on December 31, 2014, to record interest expense.

Prepare entries for bonds sold at a discount and a premium.

(LO 5)

BE10-9 Sandstone Company issues $1 million, 10-year, 5% bonds at 97, with interest payable on July 1 and January 1.

(a) Prepare the journal entry to record the sale of these bonds on January 1, 2014.
(b) Assuming instead that the above bonds sold for 104, prepare the journal entry to record the sale of these bonds on January 1, 2014.

BE10-10 Carrolla Company has issued three different bonds during 2014. Interest is payable semiannually on each of these bonds.

1. On January 1, 2014, 1,000, 8%, 5-year, $1,000 bonds dated January 1, 2014, were issued at face value.
2. On July 1, $800,000, 9%, 5-year bonds dated July 1, 2014, were issued at 102.
3. On September 1, $200,000, 7%, 5-year bonds dated September 1, 2014, were issued at 97.

Prepare the journal entry to record each bond transaction at the date of issuance.

Prepare entries for bonds issued.

(LO 5)

BE10-11 The balance sheet for Prism Consulting reports the following information on July 1, 2014.

Prepare entry for redemption of bonds.

(LO 6)

> Long-term liabilities
>   Bonds payable $1,000,000
>   Less: Discount on bonds payable   40,000 $960,000

Prism decides to redeem these bonds at 101 after paying semiannual interest. Prepare the journal entry to record the redemption on July 1, 2014.

BE10-12 McEntire Inc. issues a $400,000, 10%, 10-year mortgage note on December 31, 2014, to obtain financing for a new building. The terms provide for semiannual installment payments of $32,097. Prepare the entry to record the mortgage loan on December 31, 2014, and the first installment payment.

Prepare entries for long-term notes payable.

(LO 7)

BE10-13 Presented below are long-term liability items for Suarez Company at December 31, 2014. Prepare the long-term liabilities section of the balance sheet for Suarez Company.

Prepare statement presentation of long-term liabilities.

(LO 8)

> Bonds payable, due 2016 $500,000
> Lease liability   60,000
> Notes payable, due 2019   80,000
> Discount on bonds payable   42,000

*BE10-14 (a) What is the present value of $10,000 due 8 periods from now, discounted at 8%?
        (b) What is the present value of $20,000 to be received at the end of each of 6 periods, discounted at 10%?

Determine present value.

(LO 9)

*BE10-15 Presented below is the partial bond discount amortization schedule for Cardosa Corp. Cardosa uses the effective-interest method of amortization.

Use effective-interest method of bond amortization.

(LO 10)

Semiannual Interest Periods	Interest to Be Paid	Interest Expense to Be Recorded	Discount Amortization	Unamortized Discount	Bond Carrying Value
Issue date				$71,062	$928,938
1	$30,000	$32,513	$2,513	68,549	931,451
2	30,000	32,601	2,601	65,948	934,052

(a) Prepare the journal entry to record the payment of interest and the discount amortization at the end of period 1.
(b) ▭▭▭▷ Explain why interest expense is greater than interest paid.
(c) Explain why interest expense will increase each period.

*BE10-16 Stella Company issues $3 million, 10-year, 9% bonds at 96, with interest payable on July 1 and January 1. The straight-line method is used to amortize bond discount.

Prepare entries for bonds issued at a discount.

(LO 11)

(a) Prepare the journal entry to record the sale of these bonds on January 1, 2014.
(b) Prepare the journal entry to record interest expense and bond discount amortization on July 1, 2014, assuming no previous accrual of interest.

*BE10-17 Allman Inc. issues $2 million, 5-year, 10% bonds at 102, with interest payable on July 1 and January 1. The straight-line method is used to amortize bond premium.

Prepare entries for bonds issued at a premium.

(LO 11)

(a) Prepare the journal entry to record the sale of these bonds on January 1, 2014.
(b) Prepare the journal entry to record interest expense and bond premium amortization on July 1, 2014, assuming no previous accrual of interest.

> DO IT! REVIEW

Answer questions about current liabilities.

(LO 2, 3)

DO IT! **10-1** You and several classmates are studying for the next accounting examination. They ask you to answer the following questions:

1. If cash is borrowed on a $70,000, 9-month, 9% note on August 1, how much interest expense would be incurred by December 31?
2. The cash register total including sales taxes is $42,000, and the sales tax rate is 5%. What is the sales taxes payable?
3. If $42,000 is collected in advance on December 1 for 6-month magazine subscriptions, what amount of subscription revenue is recognized by December 31?

Evaluate statements about bonds.

(LO 4)

DO IT! **10-2** State whether each of the following statements is true or false.

_____ 1. Mortgage bonds and sinking fund bonds are both examples of debenture bonds.
_____ 2. Convertible bonds are also known as callable bonds.
_____ 3. The market rate is the rate investors demand for loaning funds.
_____ 4. Semiannual interest on bonds is equal to the face value times the stated rate times 6/12.
_____ 5. The present value of a bond is the value at which it should sell in the market.

Prepare journal entry for bond issuance and show balance sheet presentation.

(LO 5)

DO IT! **10-3** Ellis Corporation issues $300,000 of bonds for $308,000. (a) Prepare the journal entry to record the issuance of the bonds, and (b) show how the bonds would be reported on the balance sheet at the date of issuance.

Prepare entry for bond redemption.

(LO 6)

DO IT! **10-4** Jeske Corporation issued $400,000 of 10-year bonds at a discount. Prior to maturity, when the carrying value of the bonds was $390,000, the company retired the bonds at 98. Prepare the entry to record the redemption of the bonds.

Prepare entries for mortgage note and installment payment on note.

(LO 7)

DO IT! **10-5** Mattsen Orchard issues a $390,000, 5%, 15-year mortgage note to obtain needed financing for a new lab. The terms call for semiannual payments of $18,633 each. Prepare the entries to record the mortgage loan and the first installment payment.

 The Navigator

EXERCISES

Prepare entries for interest-bearing notes.

(LO 2)

E10-1 Padillio Company had the following transactions involving notes payable.

July 1, 2014	Borrows $60,000 from Fourth National Bank by signing a 9-month, 8% note.
Nov. 1, 2014	Borrows $50,000 from Livingston State Bank by signing a 3-month, 9% note.
Dec. 31, 2014	Prepares adjusting entries.
Feb. 1, 2015	Pays principal and interest to Livingston State Bank.
Apr. 1, 2015	Pays principal and interest to Fourth National Bank.

Instructions
Prepare journal entries for each of the transactions.

Prepare entries for interest-bearing notes.

(LO 2)

E10-2 On June 1, Yoon Company borrows $70,000 from First Bank on a 6-month, $70,000, 9% note.

Instructions
(a) Prepare the entry on June 1.
(b) Prepare the adjusting entry on June 30.
(c) Prepare the entry at maturity (December 1), assuming monthly adjusting entries have been made through November 30.
(d) What was the total financing cost (interest expense)?

E10-3 In providing accounting services to small businesses, you encounter the following situations pertaining to cash sales.

1. Jackson Company enters sales and sales taxes separately on its cash register. On April 10, the register totals are sales $30,000 and sales taxes $1,650.
2. Pearson Company does not segregate sales and sales taxes. Its register total for April 15 is $20,330, which includes a 7% sales tax.

Journalize sales and related taxes.

(LO 3)

Instructions
Prepare the entry to record the sales transactions and related taxes for each client.

E10-4 Nevin Company publishes a monthly sports magazine, *Fishing Preview*. Subscriptions to the magazine cost $18 per year. During November 2014, Nevin sells 12,000 subscriptions beginning with the December issue. Nevin prepares financial statements quarterly and recognizes subscription revenue at the end of the quarter. The company uses the accounts Unearned Subscription Revenue and Subscription Revenue.

Journalize unearned subscription revenue.

(LO 3)

Instructions
(a) Prepare the entry in November for the receipt of the subscriptions.
(b) Prepare the adjusting entry at December 31, 2014, to record sales revenue recognized in December 2014.
(c) Prepare the adjusting entry at March 31, 2015, to record sales revenue recognized in the first quarter of 2015.

E10-5 Dan Noll's gross earnings for the week were $1,780, his federal income tax withholding was $303, and his FICA total was $136.

Calculate and record net pay.

(LO 3)

Instructions
(a) What was Noll's net pay for the week?
(b) Journalize the entry for the recording of his pay in the general journal. (*Note:* Use Salaries and Wages Payable; not Cash.)
(c) Record the issuing of the check for Noll's pay in the general journal.

E10-6 According to the accountant of Ulster Inc., its payroll taxes for the week were as follows: $137.68 for FICA taxes, $13.77 for federal unemployment taxes, and $92.93 for state unemployment taxes.

Record accrual of payroll taxes.

(LO 3)

Instructions
Journalize the entry to record the accrual of the payroll taxes.

E10-7 The following financial data were reported by 3M Company for 2009 and 2010 (dollars in millions).

Calculate current ratio and working capital before and after paying accounts payable.

(LO 3)

3M Company Balance Sheets (partial)		
	2010	**2009**
Current assets		
Cash and cash equivalents	$ 3,377	$ 3,040
Accounts receivable, net	3,615	3,250
Inventories	3,155	2,639
Other current assets	2,068	1,866
Total current assets	$12,215	$10,795
Current liabilities	$ 6,089	$ 4,897

Instructions
(a) Calculate the current ratio and working capital for 3M for 2009 and 2010.
(b) Suppose that at the end of 2010, 3M management used $200 million cash to pay off $200 million of accounts payable. How would its current ratio and working capital have changed?

E10-8 Liane Hansen has prepared the following list of statements about bonds.

Evaluate statements about bonds.

(LO 4)

1. Bonds are a form of interest-bearing notes payable.
2. When seeking long-term financing, an advantage of issuing bonds over issuing common stock is that stockholder control is not affected.
3. When seeking long-term financing, an advantage of issuing common stock over issuing bonds is that tax savings result.

4. Secured bonds have specific assets of the issuer pledged as collateral for the bonds.
5. Secured bonds are also known as debenture bonds.
6. Bonds that mature in installments are called term bonds.
7. A conversion feature may be added to bonds to make them more attractive to bond buyers.
8. The rate used to determine the amount of cash interest the borrower pays is called the stated rate.
9. Bond prices are usually quoted as a percentage of the face value of the bond.
10. The present value of a bond is the value at which it should sell in the marketplace.

Instructions
Identify each statement as true or false. If false, indicate how to correct the statement.

Compare two alternatives of financing—issuance of common stock vs. issuance of bonds.

(LO 4)

E10-9 Global Airlines is considering two alternatives for the financing of a purchase of a fleet of airplanes. These two alternatives are:

1. Issue 60,000 shares of common stock at $40 per share. (Cash dividends have not been paid nor is the payment of any contemplated.)
2. Issue 10%, 10-year bonds at face value for $2,400,000.

It is estimated that the company will earn $800,000 before interest and taxes as a result of this purchase. The company has an estimated tax rate of 30% and has 90,000 shares of common stock outstanding prior to the new financing.

Instructions
Determine the effect on net income and earnings per share for these two methods of financing.

Prepare entries for issuance of bonds, and payment and accrual of bond interest.

(LO 5)

E10-10 On January 1, Payne Company issued $200,000, 8%, 10-year bonds at face value. Interest is payable semiannually on July 1 and January 1.

Instructions
Prepare journal entries to record the following.

(a) The issuance of the bonds.
(b) The payment of interest on July 1, assuming that interest was not accrued on June 30.
(c) The accrual of interest on December 31.

Prepare entries for bonds issued at face value.

(LO 5)

E10-11 On January 1, Disch Company issued $400,000, 7%, 5-year bonds at face value. Interest is payable semiannually on July 1 and January 1.

Instructions
Prepare journal entries to record the following events.

(a) The issuance of the bonds.
(b) The payment of interest on July 1, assuming no previous accrual of interest.
(c) The accrual of interest on December 31.

Prepare entries to record issuance of bonds at discount and premium.

(LO 5)

E10-12 Pueblo Company issued $300,000 of 5-year, 8% bonds at 98 on January 1, 2014. The bonds pay interest twice a year.

Instructions
(a) (1) Prepare the journal entry to record the issuance of the bonds.
   (2) Compute the total cost of borrowing for these bonds.
(b) Repeat the requirements from part (a), assuming the bonds were issued at 104.

Prepare entries for bond interest and redemption.

(LO 5, 6)

E10-13 The following section is taken from Barton Corp.'s balance sheet at December 31, 2013.

Current liabilities	
Interest payable	$ 56,000
Long-term liabilities	
Bonds payable, 7%, due January 1, 2018	1,600,000

Bond interest is payable semiannually on January 1 and July 1. The bonds are callable on any interest date.

Instructions
(a) Journalize the payment of the bond interest on January 1, 2014.
(b) Assume that on January 1, 2014, after paying interest, Barton calls bonds having a face value of $600,000. The call price is 104. Record the redemption of the bonds.
(c) Prepare the entry to record the payment of interest on July 1, 2014, assuming no previous accrual of interest on the remaining bonds.

E10-14 Presented below are three independent situations.

1. Voris Corporation retired $130,000 face value, 12% bonds on June 30, 2014, at 102. The carrying value of the bonds at the redemption date was $117,500. The bonds pay semiannual interest, and the interest payment due on June 30, 2014, has been made and recorded.
2. Lampe Inc. retired $150,000 face value, 12.5% bonds on June 30, 2014, at 97. The carrying value of the bonds at the redemption date was $151,000. The bonds pay semiannual interest, and the interest payment due on June 30, 2014, has been made and recorded.
3. Keho Company has $80,000, 8%, 12-year convertible bonds outstanding. These bonds were sold at face value and pay semiannual interest on June 30 and December 31 of each year. The bonds are convertible into 30 shares of Keho $5 par value common stock for each $1,000 worth of bonds. On December 31, 2014, after the bond interest has been paid, $40,000 face value bonds were converted. The market price of Keho common stock was $44 per share on December 31, 2014.

Prepare entries for redemption of bonds and conversion of bonds into common stock.

(LO 6)

Instructions

For each independent situation above, prepare the appropriate journal entry for the redemption or conversion of the bonds.

E10-15 Tucki Co. receives $240,000 when it issues a $240,000, 8%, mortgage note payable to finance the construction of a building at December 31, 2014. The terms provide for semiannual installment payments of $17,660 on June 30 and December 31.

Prepare entries to record mortgage note and installment payments.

(LO 7)

Instructions

Prepare the journal entries to record the mortgage loan and the first two installment payments.

E10-16 The adjusted trial balance for Matthews Corporation at the end of the current year contained the following accounts.

Prepare long-term liabilities section.

(LO 8)

Interest Payable	$ 9,000
Lease Liability	59,500
Bonds Payable, due 2019	180,000
Premium on Bonds Payable	24,000

Instructions

Prepare the long-term liabilities section of the balance sheet.

*E10-17 Styx Corporation is issuing $250,000 of 8%, 5-year bonds when potential bond investors want a return of 10%. Interest is payable semiannually.

Compute market price of bonds.

(LO 9)

Instructions

Compute the market price (present value) of the bonds.

*E10-18 Grande Corporation issued $500,000, 9%, 10-year bonds on January 1, 2014, for $468,844. This price resulted in an effective-interest rate of 10% on the bonds. Interest is payable semiannually on July 1 and January 1. Grande uses the effective-interest method to amortize bond premium or discount.

Prepare entries for issuance of bonds, payment of interest, and amortization of discount using effective-interest method.

(LO 5, 10)

Instructions

Prepare the journal entries to record the following. (Round to the nearest dollar.)

(a) The issuance of the bonds.
(b) The payment of interest and the discount amortization on July 1, 2014, assuming that interest was not accrued on June 30.
(c) The accrual of interest and the discount amortization on December 31, 2014.

*E10-19 Evelynn Company issued $300,000, 8%, 10-year bonds on January 1, 2014, for $321,319. This price resulted in an effective-interest rate of 7% on the bonds. Interest is payable semiannually on July 1 and January 1. Evelynn uses the effective-interest method to amortize bond premium or discount.

Prepare entries for issuance of bonds, payment of interest, and amortization of premium using effective-interest method.

(LO 5, 10)

Instructions

Prepare the journal entries to record the following. (Round to the nearest dollar.)

(a) The issuance of the bonds.
(b) The payment of interest and the premium amortization on July 1, 2014, assuming that interest was not accrued on June 30.
(c) The accrual of interest and the premium amortization on December 31, 2014.

Prepare entries to record issuance of bonds, payment of interest, amortization of premium, and redemption at maturity.

(LO 5, 11)

*E10-20 Manilow Company issued $700,000, 9%, 20-year bonds on January 1, 2014, at 103. Interest is payable semiannually on July 1 and January 1. Manilow uses straight-line amortization for bond premium or discount.

Instructions

Prepare the journal entries to record the following.

(a) The issuance of the bonds.
(b) The payment of interest and the premium amortization on July 1, 2014, assuming that interest was not accrued on June 30.
(c) The accrual of interest and the premium amortization on December 31, 2014.
(d) The redemption of the bonds at maturity, assuming interest for the last interest period has been paid and recorded.

Prepare entries to record issuance of bonds, payment of interest, amortization of discount, and redemption at maturity.

(LO 5, 11)

*E10-21 Newton Company issued $600,000, 7%, 10-year bonds on December 31, 2013, for $575,000. Interest is payable semiannually on June 30 and December 31. Newton Company uses the straight-line method to amortize bond premium or discount.

Instructions

Prepare the journal entries to record the following.

(a) The issuance of the bonds.
(b) The payment of interest and the discount amortization on June 30, 2014.
(c) The payment of interest and the discount amortization on December 31, 2014.
(d) The redemption of the bonds at maturity, assuming interest for the last interest period has been paid and recorded.

EXERCISES: SET B AND CHALLENGE EXERCISES

Visit the book's companion website, at **www.wiley.com/college/weygandt**, and choose the Student Companion site to access Exercise Set B and Challenge Exercises.

PROBLEMS: SET A

Prepare current liability entries, adjusting entries, and current liabilities section.

(LO 1, 2, 3)

P10-1A On January 1, 2014, the ledger of Shumway Company contains the following liability accounts.

Accounts Payable	$52,000
Sales Taxes Payable	5,800
Unearned Service Revenue	14,000

During January, the following selected transactions occurred.

Jan. 5 Sold merchandise for cash totaling $22,470, which includes 7% sales taxes.
 12 Provided services for customers who had made advance payments of $10,000. (Credit Service Revenue.)
 14 Paid state revenue department for sales taxes collected in December 2013 ($5,800).
 20 Sold 600 units of a new product on credit at $50 per unit, plus 7% sales tax.
 21 Borrowed $14,000 from DeKalb Bank on a 3-month, 8%, $14,000 note.
 25 Sold merchandise for cash totaling $12,947, which includes 7% sales taxes.

Instructions

(a) Journalize the January transactions.
(b) Journalize the adjusting entries at January 31 for the outstanding notes payable. (*Hint:* Use one-third of a month for the DeKalb Bank note.)
(c) Current liability total
  $74,448
(c) Prepare the current liabilities section of the balance sheet at January 31, 2014. Assume no change in accounts payable.

P10-2A The following are selected transactions of Graves Company. Graves prepares financial statements quarterly.

Journalize and post note transactions; show balance sheet presentation.

(LO 2)

Jan. 2 Purchased merchandise on account from Ally Company, $30,000, terms 2/10, n/30. (Graves uses the perpetual inventory system.)

Feb. 1 Issued a 6%, 2-month, $30,000 note to Ally in payment of account.

Mar. 31 Accrued interest for 2 months on Ally note.

Apr. 1 Paid face value and interest on Ally note.

July 1 Purchased equipment from Clark Equipment paying $8,000 in cash and signing a 7%, 3-month, $40,000 note.

Sept. 30 Accrued interest for 3 months on Clark note.

Oct. 1 Paid face value and interest on Clark note.

Dec. 1 Borrowed $15,000 from the Jonas Bank by issuing a 3-month, 6% note with a face value of $15,000.

Dec. 31 Recognized interest expense for 1 month on Jonas Bank note.

Instructions

(a) Prepare journal entries for the listed transactions and events.

(b) Post to the accounts Notes Payable, Interest Payable, and Interest Expense.

(c) Show the balance sheet presentation of notes and interest payable at December 31.

(d) What is total interest expense for the year?

(d) $1,075

P10-3A On May 1, 2014, Hopkins Corp. issued $720,000, 7%, 5-year bonds at face value. The bonds were dated May 1, 2014, and pay interest semiannually on May 1 and November 1. Financial statements are prepared annually on December 31.

Prepare entries to record issuance of bonds, interest accrual, and bond redemption.

(LO 5, 6, 8)

Instructions

(a) Prepare the journal entry to record the issuance of the bonds.

(b) Prepare the adjusting entry to record the accrual of interest on December 31, 2014.

(c) Show the balance sheet presentation on December 31, 2014.

(d) Prepare the journal entry to record payment of interest on May 1, 2015, assuming no accrual of interest from January 1, 2015, to May 1, 2015.

(d) Int. exp. $16,800

(e) Prepare the journal entry to record payment of interest on November 1, 2015.

(f) Assume that on November 1, 2015, Hopkins calls the bonds at 102. Record the redemption of the bonds.

(f) Loss $14,400

P10-4A Formosa Electric sold $400,000, 9%, 10-year bonds on January 1, 2014. The bonds were dated January 1 and paid interest on January 1 and July 1. The bonds were sold at 105.

Prepare entries to record issuance of bonds, interest accrual, and bond redemption.

(LO 5, 6, 8)

Instructions

(a) Prepare the journal entry to record the issuance of the bonds on January 1, 2014.

(b) At December 31, 2014, the balance in the Premium on Bonds Payable account is $18,000. Show the balance sheet presentation of accrued interest and the bond liability at December 31, 2014.

(c) On January 1, 2016, when the carrying value of the bonds was $416,000, the company redeemed the bonds at 105. Record the redemption of the bonds assuming that interest for the period has already been paid.

(c) Loss $4,000

P10-5A Otto Electronics issues a $800,000, 8%, 10-year mortgage note on December 31, 2013. The proceeds from the note are to be used in financing a new research laboratory. The terms of the note provide for semiannual installment payments, exclusive of real estate taxes and insurance, of $58,865. Payments are due June 30 and December 31.

Prepare installment payments schedule and journal entries for a mortgage note payable.

(LO 7)

(b) June 30 Mortgage
       Payable debit $26,865

(c) Current liability—2014
       $59,276

Instructions

(a) Prepare an installment payments schedule for the first 2 years.

(b) Prepare the entries for (1) the loan and (2) the first two installment payments.

(c) Show how the total mortgage liability should be reported on the balance sheet at December 31, 2014.

Prepare entries to record issuance of bonds, payment of interest, and amortization of bond premium using effective-interest method.

(LO 5, 10)

P10-6A On July 1, 2014, Strigel Corporation issued $5,000,000, 10%, 10-year bonds at $5,679,533. This price resulted in an effective-interest rate of 8% on the bonds. Strigel uses the effective-interest method to amortize bond premium or discount. The bonds pay semiannual interest July 1 and January 1.

(c) Amortization $22,819

(d) Amortization $23,731

(e) Amortization $24,681

Prepare entries to record issuance of bonds, payment of interest, and amortization of discount using effective-interest method. In addition, answer questions.

(LO 5, 10)

(a) (3) Amortization $7,123

(a) (4) Amortization $7,479

(b) Bond carrying value $3,397,066

Prepare entries to record issuance of bonds, interest accrual, and straight-line amortization for 2 years.

(LO 5, 11)

(b) Amortization $4,000
(d) Premium on bonds payable $64,000

Prepare entries to record issuance of bonds, interest, and straight-line amortization of bond premium and discount.

(LO 5, 11)

(a) Amortization $4,500
(b) Amortization $6,000
(c) Premium on bonds payable $85,500
Discount on bonds payable $114,000

Instructions

(Round all computations to the nearest dollar.)

(a) Prepare the journal entry to record the issuance of the bonds on July 1, 2014.
(b) Prepare an amortization table through December 31, 2015 (3 interest periods) for this bond issue.
(c) Prepare the journal entry to record the accrual of interest and the amortization of the premium on December 31, 2014.
(d) Prepare the journal entry to record the payment of interest and the amortization of the premium on July 1, 2015, assuming no accrual of interest on June 30.
(e) Prepare the journal entry to record the accrual of interest and the amortization of the premium on December 31, 2015.

*P10-7A On July 1, 2014, Kingston Company issued $3,600,000, 9%, 10-year bonds at $3,375,680. This price resulted in an effective-interest rate of 10% on the bonds. Kingston uses the effective-interest method to amortize bond premium or discount. The bonds pay semiannual interest July 1 and January 1.

Instructions

(Round all computations to the nearest dollar.)

(a) Prepare the journal entries to record the following transactions.
  (1) The issuance of the bonds on July 1, 2014.
  (2) The accrual of interest and the amortization of the discount on December 31, 2014.
  (3) The payment of interest and the amortization of the discount on July 1, 2015, assuming no accrual of interest on June 30.
  (4) The accrual of interest and the amortization of the discount on December 31, 2015.
(b) Show the proper balance sheet presentation for the liability for bonds payable on the December 31, 2015, balance sheet.
(c) Provide the answers to the following questions in letter form.
  (1) What amount of interest expense is reported for 2015?
  (2) Would the bond interest expense reported in 2015 be the same as, greater than, or less than the amount that would be reported if the straight-line method of amortization were used?
  (3) Determine the total cost of borrowing over the life of the bond.
  (4) Would the total bond interest expense be greater than, the same as, or less than the total interest expense that would be reported if the straight-line method of amortization were used?

*P10-8A Guehler Electric sold $2,000,000, 9%, 10-year bonds on January 1, 2014. The bonds were dated January 1 and pay interest July 1 and January 1. Guehler Electric uses the straight-line method to amortize bond premium or discount. The bonds were sold at 104. Assume no interest is accrued on June 30.

Instructions

(a) Prepare the journal entry to record the issuance of the bonds on January 1, 2014.
(b) Prepare a bond premium amortization schedule for the first 4 interest periods.
(c) Prepare the journal entries for interest and the amortization of the premium in 2014 and 2015.
(d) Show the balance sheet presentation of the bond liability at December 31, 2015.

*P10-9A Jaggar Company sold $3,000,000, 8%, 10-year bonds on July 1, 2014. The bonds were dated July 1, 2014, and pay interest July 1 and January 1. Jaggar Company uses the straight-line method to amortize bond premium or discount. Assume no interest is accrued on June 30.

Instructions

(a) Prepare all the necessary journal entries to record the issuance of the bonds and bond interest expense for 2014, assuming that the bonds sold at 103.
(b) Prepare journal entries as in part (a) assuming that the bonds sold at 96.
(c) Show balance sheet presentation for each bond issue at December 31, 2014.

*P10-10A The following is taken from the Millette Company balance sheet.

Prepare entries to record interest payments, straight-line premium amortization, and redemption of bonds.

(LO 6, 11)

Millette Company
Balance Sheet (partial)
December 31, 2013

Current liabilities
  Interest payable (for 6 months
    from July 1 to December 31) $ 90,000
Long-term liabilities
  Bonds payable, 6% due January 1, 2024 $3,000,000
  Add: Premium on bonds payable   180,000   3,180,000

Interest is payable semiannually on January 1 and July 1. The bonds are callable on any semiannual interest date. Millette uses straight-line amortization for any bond premium or discount. From December 31, 2013, the bonds will be outstanding for an additional 10 years (120 months).

Instructions
(a) Journalize the payment of bond interest on January 1, 2014.
(b) Prepare the entry to amortize bond premium and to pay the interest due on July 1, 2014, assuming no accrual of interest on June 30.
(c) Assume that on July 1, 2014, after paying interest, Millette Company calls bonds having a face value of $1,200,000. The call price is 101. Record the redemption of the bonds.
(d) Prepare the adjusting entry at December 31, 2014, to amortize bond premium and to accrue interest on the remaining bonds.

(b) Amortization $9,000

(c) Gain $56,400

(d) Amortization $5,400

PROBLEMS: SET B

P10-1B On January 1, 2014, the ledger of Zaur Company contains the following liability accounts.

Prepare current liability entries, adjusting entries, and current liabilities section.

(LO 1, 2, 3)

Accounts Payable	$42,500
Sales Taxes Payable	5,800
Unearned Service Revenue	15,000

During January, the following selected transactions occurred.

Jan. 1 Borrowed $15,000 in cash from Platteville Bank on a 4-month, 6%, $15,000 note.
     5 Sold merchandise for cash totaling $9,434, which includes 6% sales taxes.
   12 Provided services for customers who had made advance payments of $9,000. (Credit Service Revenue.)
   14 Paid state treasurer's department for sales taxes collected in December 2013, $5,800.
   20 Sold 700 units of a new product on credit at $44 per unit, plus 6% sales tax.
   25 Sold merchandise for cash totaling $16,536, which includes 6% sales taxes.

Instructions
(a) Journalize the January transactions.
(b) Journalize the adjusting entries at January 31 for the outstanding notes payable.
(c) Prepare the current liabilities section of the balance sheet at January 31, 2014. Assume no change in accounts payable.

(c) Current liability total
$66,893

P10-2B On June 1, 2014, Sator Corp. issued $1,200,000, 8%, 5-year bonds at face value. The bonds were dated June 1, 2014, and pay interest semiannually on June 1 and December 1. Financial statements are prepared annually on December 31.

Prepare entries to record issuance of bonds, interest accrual, and bond redemption.

(LO 5, 6, 8)

Instructions
(a) Prepare the journal entry to record the issuance of the bonds.
(b) Prepare the adjusting entry to record the accrual of interest on December 31, 2014.
(c) Show the balance sheet presentation on December 31, 2014.
(d) Prepare the journal entry to record payment of interest on June 1, 2015, assuming no accrual of interest from January 1, 2015, to June 1, 2015.

(d) Int. exp. $40,000

(f) Loss $12,000

(e) Prepare the journal entry to record payment of interest on December 1, 2015.
(f) Assume that on December 1, 2015, Sator calls the bonds at 101. Record the redemption of the bonds.

P10-3B Booker Co. sold $300,000, 10%, 10-year bonds on January 1, 2014. The bonds were dated January 1, and interest is paid on January 1 and July 1. The bonds were sold at 104.

Prepare entries to record issuance of bonds, interest accrual, and bond redemption.

(LO 5, 6, 8)

Instructions
(a) Prepare the journal entry to record the issuance of the bonds on January 1, 2014.
(b) At December 31, 2014, the balance in the Premium on Bonds Payable account is $10,800. Show the balance sheet presentation of accrued interest and the bond liability at December 31, 2014.

(c) Loss $5,400

(c) On January 1, 2016, when the carrying value of the bonds was $309,600, the company redeemed the bonds at 105. Record the redemption of the bonds assuming that interest for the period has already been paid.

Prepare installment payments schedule and journal entries for a mortgage note payable.

(LO 7, 8)

P10-4B Hamilton's Electronics issues a $380,000, 8%, 10-year mortgage note on December 31, 2013, to help finance a plant expansion program. The terms provide for semiannual installment payments, not including real estate taxes and insurance, of $27,961. Payments are due June 30 and December 31.

Instructions
(a) Prepare an installment payments schedule for the first 2 years.
(b) Prepare the entries for (1) the mortgage loan and (2) the first two installment payments.
(c) Show how the total mortgage liability should be reported on the balance sheet at December 31, 2014.

(b) June 30 Mortgage Payable debit $12,761

(c) Current liability—2014: $28,156

Prepare entries to record issuance of bonds, payment of interest, and amortization of bond discount using effective-interest method.

(LO 5, 10)

*P10-5B On July 1, 2014, Visnak Satellites issued $4,500,000, 7%, 10-year bonds at $4,194,218. This price resulted in an effective-interest rate of 8% on the bonds. Visnak uses the effective-interest method to amortize bond premium or discount. The bonds pay semiannual interest July 1 and January 1.

Instructions
(Round all computations to the nearest dollar.)
(a) Prepare the journal entry to record the issuance of the bonds on July 1, 2014.
(b) Prepare an amortization table through December 31, 2015 (3 interest periods) for this bond issue.

(c) Amortization $10,269

(c) Prepare the journal entry to record the accrual of interest and the amortization of the discount on December 31, 2014.

(d) Amortization $10,679

(d) Prepare the journal entry to record the payment of interest and the amortization of the discount on July 1, 2015, assuming that interest was not accrued on June 30.

(e) Amortization $11,107

(e) Prepare the journal entry to record the accrual of interest and the amortization of the discount on December 31, 2015.

Prepare entries to record issuance of bonds, payment of interest, and amortization of premium using effective-interest method. In addition, answer questions.

(LO 5, 10)

*P10-6B On July 1, 2014, Keokuk Chemical Company issued $4,000,000, 6%, 10-year bonds at $4,311,783. This price resulted in a 5% effective-interest rate on the bonds. Keokuk uses the effective-interest method to amortize bond premium or discount. The bonds pay semiannual interest on each July 1 and January 1.

Instructions
(Round all computations to the nearest dollar.)
(a) Prepare the journal entries to record the following transactions.
   (1) The issuance of the bonds on July 1, 2014.
   (2) The accrual of interest and the amortization of the premium on December 31, 2014.
   (3) The payment of interest and the amortization of the premium on July 1, 2015, assuming no accrual of interest on June 30.
   (4) The accrual of interest and the amortization of the premium on December 31, 2015.

(a) (2) Amortization $12,205
(a) (3) Amortization $12,511

(a) (4) Amortization $12,823
(b) Bond carrying value $4,274,244

(b) Show the proper balance sheet presentation for the liability for bonds payable on the December 31, 2015, balance sheet.
(c) ✏️➤ Provide the answers to the following questions in letter form.
   (1) What amount of interest expense is reported for 2015?
   (2) Would the bond interest expense reported in 2015 be the same as, greater than, or less than the amount that would be reported if the straight-line method of amortization were used?

	Eastland Company	Westside Company
Current liabilities	$440,200	$431,500
Long-term liabilities	78,000	82,000
Total liabilities	518,200	513,500
Stockholders' equity	442,750	420,050
Total liabilities and stockholders' equity	$960,950	$933,550

You have been engaged as a consultant to conduct a review of the two companies. Your goal is to determine which of them is in the stronger financial position.

Your review of their financial statements quickly reveals that the two companies have not followed the same accounting practices. The differences and your conclusions regarding them are summarized below.

1. Eastland Company has used the allowance method of accounting for bad debts. A review shows that the amount of its write-offs each year has been quite close to the allowances that have been provided. It therefore seems reasonable to have confidence in its current estimate of bad debts.

   Westside Company has used the direct write-off method for bad debts, and it has been somewhat slow to write off its uncollectible accounts. Based upon an aging analysis and review of its accounts receivable, it is estimated that $18,000 of its existing accounts will probably prove to be uncollectible.

2. Eastland Company has determined the cost of its merchandise inventory on a LIFO basis. The result is that its inventory appears on the balance sheet at an amount that is below its current replacement cost. Based upon a detailed physical examination of its merchandise on hand, the current replacement cost of its inventory is estimated at $513,000.

   Westside Company has used the FIFO method of valuing its merchandise inventory. Its ending inventory appears on the balance sheet at an amount that quite closely approximates its current replacement cost.

3. Eastland Company estimated a useful life of 12 years and a salvage value of $30,000 for its plant and equipment. It has been depreciating them on a straight-line basis.

   Westside Company has the same type of plant and equipment. However, it estimated a useful life of 10 years and a salvage value of $10,000. It has been depreciating its plant and equipment using the double-declining-balance method.

   Based upon engineering studies of these types of plant and equipment, you conclude that Westside's estimates and method for calculating depreciation are the more appropriate.

4. Among its current liabilities, Eastland has included the portions of long-term liabilities that become due within the next year. Westside has not done so.

   You find that $16,000 of Westside's $82,000 of long-term liabilities are due to be repaid in the current year.

Instructions

(a) Revise the balance sheets presented above so that the data are comparable and reflect the current financial position for each of the two companies.

(b) ▭▭▭▷ Prepare a brief report to your client stating your conclusions.

(a) Total assets:
Eastland $934,325
Westside $915,550

CONTINUING COOKIE CHRONICLE

(*Note:* This is a continuation of the Cookie Chronicle from Chapters 1–9.)

CCC10 Recall that Cookie Creations sells fine European mixers that it purchases from Kzinski Supply Co. Kzinski warrants the mixers to be free of defects in material and workmanship for a period of one year from the date of original purchase. If the mixer has such a defect, Kzinski will repair or replace the mixer free of charge for parts and labor.

Go to the book's companion website, www.wiley.com/college/weygandt, to see the completion of this problem.

Financial Reporting and Analysis

Financial Reporting Problem: PepsiCo, Inc.

BYP10-1 The financial statements of PepsiCo, Inc. and the notes to consolidated financial statements appear in Appendix A.

Instructions

Refer to PepsiCo's financial statements and answer the following questions about current and contingent liabilities and payroll costs.

(a) What were PepsiCo's total current liabilities at December 25, 2010? What was the increase/decrease in PepsiCo's total current liabilities from the prior year?

(b) In PepsiCo's Note 2 ("Our Significant Accounting Policies"), the company explains the nature of its contingencies. Under what conditions does PepsiCo recognize (record and report) liabilities for contingencies?

(c) What were the components of total current liabilities on December 25, 2010?

(d) What was PepsiCo's total long-term debt at December 25, 2010? What was the increase/decrease in total long-term debt from the prior year? What does Note 9 to the financial statements indicate about the composition of PepsiCo's long-term debt obligation?

(e) What are the total long-term contractual commitments that PepsiCo reports as of December 25, 2010? (See Note 9.)

Comparative Analysis Problem: PepsiCo, Inc. vs. The Coca-Cola Company

BYP10-2 PepsiCo, Inc.'s financial statements are presented in Appendix A. Financial statements of The Coca-Cola Company are presented in Appendix B.

Instructions

(a) At December 25, 2010, what was PepsiCo's largest current liability account? What were its total current liabilities? At December 31, 2010, what was Coca-Cola's largest current liability account? What were its total current liabilities?

(b) Based on information contained in those financial statements, compute the following 2010 values for each company.
   (1) Working capital.
   (2) Current ratio.

(c) What conclusions concerning the relative liquidity of these companies can be drawn from these data?

(d) Based on the information contained in these financial statements, compute the following 2010 ratios for each company.
   (1) Debt to total assets.
   (2) Times interest earned.

(e) What conclusions concerning the companies' long-run solvency can be drawn from these ratios?

Real-World Focus

BYP10-3 *Purpose:* Bond or debt securities pay a stated rate of interest. This rate of interest is dependent on the risk associated with the investment. Fitch Ratings provides ratings for companies that issue debt securities.

Address: **www.fitchratings.com**, or go to **www.wiley.com/college/weygandt**

Instructions

Answer the following questions.

(a) In what year did Fitch introduce its bond rating scale? (See **History** in **About Us**.)

(b) What letter values are assigned to debt investments that are considered "investment grade" and "speculative grade"? (See **Ratings Definitions**.)

(c) Search the Internet to identify two other major credit rating agencies.

Critical Thinking

Decision-Making Across the Organization

*BYP10-4 On January 1, 2012, Fleming Corporation issued $2,400,000 of 5-year, 7% bonds at 96; the bonds pay interest semiannually on July 1 and January 1. By January 1, 2014, the market rate of interest for bonds of risk similar to those of Fleming Corporation had risen. As a result, the market value of these bonds was $2,000,000 on January 1, 2014—below their carrying value. Debra Fleming, president of the company, suggests repurchasing all of these bonds in the open market at the $2,000,000 price. To do so the company will have to issue $2,000,000 (face value) of new 10-year, 10% bonds at par. The president asks you, as controller, "What is the feasibility of my proposed repurchase plan?"

Instructions

With the class divided into groups, answer the following.

(a) What is the carrying value of the outstanding Fleming Corporation 5-year bonds on January 1, 2014? (Assume straight-line amortization.)

(b) Prepare the journal entry to retire the 5-year bonds on January 1, 2014. Prepare the journal entry to issue the new 10-year bonds.

(c) Prepare a short memo to the president in response to her request for advice. List the economic factors that you believe should be considered for her repurchase proposal.

Communication Activity

BYP10-5 Ron Seiser, president of Seiser Corporation, is considering the issuance of bonds to finance an expansion of his business. He has asked you to (1) discuss the advantages of bonds over common stock financing, (2) indicate the types of bonds he might issue, and (3) explain the issuing procedures used in bond transactions.

Instructions

Write a memo to the president, answering his request.

Ethics Case

BYP10-6 Dylan Horn is the president, founder, and majority owner of Wesley Medical Corporation, an emerging medical technology products company. Wesley is in dire need of additional capital to keep operating and to bring several promising products to final development, testing, and production. Dylan, as owner of 51% of the outstanding stock, manages the company's operations. He places heavy emphasis on research and development and on long-term growth. The other principal stockholder is Mary Sommers who, as a nonemployee investor, owns 40% of the stock. Mary would like to deemphasize the R&D functions and emphasize the marketing function, to maximize short-run sales and profits from existing products. She believes this strategy would raise the market price of Wesley's stock.

All of Dylan's personal capital and borrowing power is tied up in his 51% stock ownership. He knows that any offering of additional shares of stock will dilute his controlling interest because he won't be able to participate in such an issuance. But, Mary has money and would likely buy enough shares to gain control of Wesley. She then would dictate the company's future direction, even if it meant replacing Dylan as president and CEO.

The company already has considerable debt. Raising additional debt will be costly, will adversely affect Wesley's credit rating, and will increase the company's reported losses due to the growth in interest expense. Mary and the other minority stockholders express opposition to the assumption of additional debt, fearing the company will be pushed to the brink of bankruptcy. Wanting to maintain his control and to preserve the direction of "his" company, Dylan is doing everything to avoid a stock issuance. He is contemplating a large issuance of bonds, even if it means the bonds are issued with a high effective-interest rate.

Instructions
(a) Who are the stakeholders in this situation?
(b) What are the ethical issues in this case?
(c) What would you do if you were Dylan?

All About You

BYP10-7 Medical costs are substantial and rising. But, will they be the most substantial expense over your lifetime? Not likely. Will it be housing or food? Again, not likely. The answer is taxes. On average, Americans work 99 days to afford their taxes. Companies, too, have large tax burdens. They look very hard at tax issues in deciding where to build their plants and where to locate their administrative headquarters.

Instructions
(a) Determine what your state income taxes are if your taxable income is $60,000 and you file as a single taxpayer in the state in which you live.
(b) Assume that you own a home worth $200,000 in your community and the tax rate is 2.1%. Compute the property taxes you would pay.
(c) Assume that the total gasoline bill for your automobile is $1,200 a year (300 gallons at $4 per gallon). What are the amounts of state and federal taxes that you pay on the $1,200?
(d) Assume that your purchases for the year total $9,000. Of this amount, $5,000 was for food and prescription drugs. What is the amount of sales tax you would pay on these purchases? (Many states do not levy a sales tax on food or prescription drugs. Does yours?)
(e) Determine what your Social Security taxes are if your income is $60,000.
(f) Determine what your federal income taxes are if your taxable income is $60,000 and you file as a single taxpayer.
(g) Determine your total taxes paid based on the above calculations, and determine the percentage of income that you would pay in taxes based on the following formula: Total taxes paid ÷ Total income.

BYP10-8 Some employees are encouraging and setting up preventive health-care programs. Here are the percentages for five unhealthy behaviors for individuals with some college education: current cigarette smoker (22.9%), five or more alcoholic drinks at one sitting during at least once in the past year (30%), physically inactive (30%), obese (25.2%), or sleep less than 6 hours per day (30.3%).

Suppose you own a business. About a quarter of your employees smoke, and an even higher percentage are overweight. You decide to implement a mandatory health program that requires employees to quit smoking and to exercise regularly, with regular monitoring. If employees do not participate in the program, they will have to pay their own insurance premiums. Is this fair?

YES: It is the responsibility of management to try to maximize a company's profit. Employees with unhealthy habits drive up the cost of health insurance because they require more frequent and more costly medical attention.

NO: What people do on their own time is their own business. This represents an invasion of privacy, and is a form of discrimination.

Instructions
Write a response indicating your position regarding the situation. Provide support for your view.

FASB Codification Activity

BYP10-9 If your school has a subscription to the FASB Codification, go to *http://aaahq.org/ascLogin. cfm* to log in and prepare responses to the following.
(a) What is the definition of current liabilities?
(b) What is the long-term obligation?
(c) What guidance does the Codification provide for the disclosure of long-term obligations?

Answers to Chapter Questions

Answers to Insight and Accounting Across the Organization Questions

p. 479 It Costs $74,000 to Put $44,000 in Sally's Pocket Q: How are the Social Security and Medicare taxes computed for Sally's salary? **A:** As indicated in the story, Sally's gross earnings were $59,000. The Social Security tax is 6.2% for both employee and employer up to gross earnings of $106,800 (2010 guidelines). As shown, both Sally and Bogan pay $3,661, which is 6.2% × $59,000. In addition, the Medicare tax is 1.45% on all gross earnings for both employee and employer. As shown, both Sally and Bogan pay $856, which is 1.45% × $59,000.

p. 487 When to Go Long-Term Q: Based on this story, what is a good general rule to use in choosing between short-term and long-term financing? **A:** In general, it is best to finance short-term assets with short-term liabilities and long-term assets with long-term liabilities, in order to reduce the likelihood of a liquidity crunch such as this.

p. 496 Bonds versus Notes? Q: Why might companies prefer bond financing instead of short-term financing? **A:** In some cases, it is difficult to get loans from banks. In addition, low interest rates have encouraged companies to go more long-term and fix their rate. Recently, short-term loans suddenly froze, leading to liquidity problems for certain companies.

p. 497 "Covenant-Lite" Debt Q: How can financial ratios such as those covered in this chapter provide protection for creditors? **A:** Financial ratios such as the current ratio, debt to total assets ratio, and the times interest earned ratio provide indications of a company's liquidity and solvency. By specifying minimum levels of liquidity and solvency, as measured by these ratios, a creditor creates triggers that enable it to step in before a company's financial situation becomes too dire.

Answers to Self-Test Questions

1. a **2.** d **3.** b ($88,500 × 12% × 4/12) **4.** b ($4,515 ÷ 1.05) **5.** c **6.** b ($18,000 × 3/12) **7.** c
8. a **9.** b **10.** d $600,000 − (10,000 × $1) **11.** c $200,000 − (10% × $497,000) = $150,300; ($497,000 − $150,300) × 10% **12.** c **13.** d ($300,000 + $40,000 + $100,000) ÷ $40,000 ***14.** d
*15. b [($938,554 × 10%) − ($1,000,000 × 9%)] = $3,855; ($1,000,000 − $938,554) − $3,855
*16. c ($1,081,105 × 8%) ÷ 2 ***17.** d [$500,000 − (96% × $500,000)] = $20,000; ($20,000 ÷ 10)
*18. a (500,000 × .96) = 480,000; ($480,000 + $2,000 + $2,000 + $2,000)

A Look at IFRS

IFRS and GAAP have similar definitions of liabilities. IFRS related to reporting and recognition of liabilities are found in *IAS 1 (revised)* ("Presentation of Financial Statements") and *IAS 37* ("Provisions, Contingent Liabilities, and Contingent Assets"). The general recording procedures for payroll are similar although differences occur depending on the types of benefits that are provided in different countries. For example, companies in other countries often have different forms of pensions, unemployment benefits, welfare payments, and so on. The accounting for various forms of compensation plans under IFRS is found in *IAS 19* ("Employee Benefits") and *IFRS 2* ("Share-based Payments"). *IAS 19* addresses the accounting for a wide range of compensation elements, including wages, bonuses, post-employment benefits, and compensated absences. Both of these standards were recently amended, resulting in significant convergence between IFRS and GAAP.

Key Points

- The basic definition of a liability under GAAP and IFRS is very similar. In a more technical way, liabilities are defined by the IASB as a present obligation of the entity arising from past events, the settlement of which is expected to result in an outflow from the entity of resources embodying economic benefits. Liabilities may be legally enforceable via a contract or law but need not be; that is, they can arise due to normal business practice or customs.

- IFRS requires that companies classify liabilities as current or noncurrent on the face of the statement of financial position (balance sheet), except in industries where a *presentation* based on liquidity would be considered to provide more useful information (such as financial institutions).When current liabilities (also called short-term liabilities) are presented, they are generally presented in order of liquidity.

- Under IFRS, liabilities are classified as current if they are expected to be paid within 12 months.

- Similar to GAAP, items are normally reported in order of liquidity. Companies sometimes show liabilities before assets. Also, they will sometimes show long-term liabilities before current liabilities.

- Under IFRS, companies sometimes will net current liabilities against current assets to show working capital on the face of the statement of financial position. (This is evident in the Zetar financial statements in Appendix C.)

- The basic calculation for bond valuation is the same under GAAP and IFRS. In addition, the accounting for bond liability transactions is essentially the same between GAAP and IFRS.

- IFRS requires use of the effective-interest method for amortization of bond discounts and premiums. GAAP also requires the effective-interest method, except that it allows use of the straight-line method where the difference is not material. Under IFRS, companies do not use a premium or discount account but instead show the bond at its net amount. For example, if a $100,000 bond was issued at 97, under IFRS a company would record:

| Cash | 97,000 | |
| Bonds Payable | | 97,000 |

- The accounting for convertible bonds differs between IFRS and GAAP. GAAP requires that the proceeds from the issuance of convertible debt be shown solely as debt. Unlike GAAP, IFRS splits the proceeds from the convertible bond between an equity component and a debt component. The equity conversion rights are reported in equity.

  To illustrate, assume that Harris Corp. issues convertible 7% bonds with a face value of $1,000,000 and receives $1,000,000. Comparable bonds without a conversion feature would have required a 9% rate of interest. To determine how much of the proceeds would be allocated to debt and how much to equity, the promised payments of the bond obligation would be discounted at the market rate of 9%. Suppose that this results in a present value of $850,000. The entry to record the issuance would be:

Cash	1,000,000	
Bonds Payable		850,000
Share Premium—Conversion Equity		150,000

Looking to the Future

The FASB and IASB are currently involved in two projects, each of which has implications for the accounting for liabilities. One project is investigating approaches to differentiate between debt and equity instruments. The other project, the elements phase of the conceptual framework project, will evaluate the definitions of the fundamental building blocks of accounting. The results of these projects could change the classification of many debt and equity securities.

IFRS Practice

IFRS Self-Test Questions

1. Which of the following is *false*?
   (a) Under IFRS, current liabilities must always be presented before noncurrent liabilities.
   (b) Under IFRS, an item is a current liability if it will be paid within the next 12 months.
   (c) Under IFRS, current liabilities are shown in order of liquidity.
   (d) Under IFRS, a liability is only recognized if it is a present obligation.

2. The accounting for bonds payable is:
   (a) essentially the same under IFRS and GAAP.
   (b) differs in that GAAP requires use of the straight-line method for amortization of bond premium and discount.

(c) the same except that market prices may be different because the present value calculations are different between IFRS and GAAP.

(d) not covered by IFRS.

3. Stevens Corporation issued 5% convertible bonds with a total face value of $3,000,000 for $3,000,000. If the bonds had not had a conversion feature, they would have sold for $2,600,000. Under IFRS, the entry to record the transaction would require a credit to:

(a) Bonds Payable for $3,000,000.

(b) Bonds Payable for $400,000.

(c) Share Premium—Conversion Equity for $400,000.

(d) Discount on Bonds Payable for $400,000.

4. Which of the following is *true* regarding accounting for amortization of bond discount and premium?

(a) Both IFRS and GAAP must use the effective-interest method.

(b) GAAP must use the effective-interest method, but IFRS may use either the effective-interest method or the straight-line method.

(c) IFRS is required to use the effective-interest method.

(d) GAAP is required to use the straight-line method.

5. The joint projects of the FASB and IASB could potentially:

(a) change the definition of liabilities.

(b) change the definition of equity.

(c) change the definition of assets.

(d) All of the above.

IFRS Exercises

IFRS10-1 Briefly describe some of the similarities and differences between GAAP and IFRS with respect to the accounting for liabilities.

IFRS10-2 Ratzlaff Company issues (in euros) €2 million, 10-year, 8% bonds at 97, with interest payable on July 1 and January 1.

Instructions

(a) Prepare the journal entry to record the sale of these bonds on January 1, 2014.

(b) Assuming instead that the above bonds sold for 104, prepare the journal entry to record the sale of these bonds on January 1, 2014.

IFRS10-3 Archer Company issued (in pounds) £4,000,000 par value, 7% convertible bonds at 99 for cash. The net present value of the debt without the conversion feature is £3,800,000. Prepare the journal entry to record the issuance of the convertible bonds.

International Financial Statement Analysis: Zetar plc

IFRS10-4 The financial statements of Zetar plc are presented on Appendix C. The company's complete annual report, including the notes to its financial statements, is available at *www.zetarplc.com*.

Instructions

Use the company's annual report to answer the following questions.

(a) According to the notes to the financial statements, what types of transactions do trade payables relate to? What was the average amount of time it took the company to pay its payables?

(b) Note 2 (B) discusses provisions that the company records for certain types of activities. What do the provisions relate to, what are the estimates based on, and what could cause those estimates to change in subsequent periods?

(c) What was the average interest rate paid on bank loans and overdrafts?

Answers to IFRS Self-Test Questions

1. a   2. a   3. c   4. c   5. d

 **The Navigator**

 Remember to go back to The Navigator box on the chapter opening page and check off your completed work.

Chapter 11

Corporations: Organization, Stock Transactions, Dividends, and Retained Earnings

Feature **Story**

What's Cooking?

What major U.S. corporation got its start 41 years ago with a waffle iron? *Hint:* It doesn't sell food. *Another hint:* Swoosh. *Another hint:* "Just do it." That's right, Nike. In 1971, Nike co-founder Bill Bowerman put a piece of rubber into a kitchen waffle iron, and the trademark waffle sole was born. It seems fair to say that at Nike, "They don't make 'em like they used to."

Nike was co-founded by Bowerman and Phil Knight, a member of Bowerman's University of Oregon track team. Each began in the shoe business independently during the early 1960s. Bowerman got his start by making hand-crafted running shoes for his University of Oregon track team. Knight, after completing graduate school, started a small business importing low-cost, high-quality shoes from Japan. In 1964, the two joined

✔ **The Navigator**

☐ Scan Learning Objectives

☐ Read Feature Story

☐ Read Preview

☐ Read text and answer **DO IT!** p. 545
    ☐ p. 547 ☐ p. 550 ☐ p. 554 ☐ p. 560
    ☐ p. 563 ☐ p. 567 ☐ p. 570

☐ Work Comprehensive **DO IT!** p. 571

☐ Review Summary of Learning Objectives

☐ Answer Self-Test Questions

☐ Complete Assignments

☐ Go to **WileyPLUS** for practice and tutorials

 Read A Look at IFRS p. 597

Learning Objectives

After studying this chapter, you should be able to:

1 Identify the major characteristics of a corporation.

2 Record the issuance of common stock.

3 Explain the accounting for treasury stock.

4 Differentiate preferred stock from common stock.

5 Prepare the entries for cash dividends and stock dividends.

6 Identify the items reported in a retained earnings statement.

7 Prepare and analyze a comprehensive stockholders' equity section.

✔ **The Navigator**

forces, each contributing $500, and formed Blue Ribbon Sports, a partnership that marketed Japanese shoes.

It wasn't until 1971 that the company began manufacturing its own line of shoes. With the new shoes came a new corporate name—Nike—the Greek goddess of victory. It is hard to imagine that the company that now boasts a stable full of world-class athletes as promoters at one time had part-time employees selling shoes out of car trunks at track meets. Nike has achieved its success through relentless innovation combined with unbridled promotion.

By 1980, Nike was sufficiently established and issued its first stock to the public. That same year, it created a stock ownership program for its employees, allowing them to share in the company's success. Since then,

Nike has enjoyed phenomenal growth, with 2011 sales reaching $20.7 billion and total dividends paid of $569 million.

Nike is not alone in its quest for the top of the sport shoe world. Reebok used to be Nike's arch rival (get it? "arch"), but then Reebok was acquired by the German company adidas. Now adidas pushes Nike every step of the way.

The shoe market is fickle, with new styles becoming popular almost daily and vast international markets still lying untapped. Whether one of these two giants does eventually take control of the pedi-planet remains to be seen. Meanwhile, the shareholders sit anxiously in the stands as this Olympic-size drama unfolds.

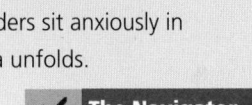

✔ The Navigator

Preview of **Chapter 11**

Corporations like Nike and adidas have substantial resources at their disposal. In fact, the corporation is the dominant form of business organization in the United States in terms of sales, earnings, and number of employees. All of the 500 largest companies in the United States are corporations. In this chapter, we will explain the essential features of a corporation and the accounting for a corporation's capital stock transactions.

The content and organization of Chapter 11 are as follows.

CORPORATIONS: ORGANIZATION, STOCK TRANSACTIONS, DIVIDENDS, AND RETAINED EARNINGS				
The Corporate Form of Organization	**Accounting for Stock Transactions**	**Dividends**	**Retained Earnings**	**Statement Presentation and Analysis**
• Characteristics • Formation • Stockholder rights • Stock issue considerations • Corporate capital	• Common Stock • Treasury Stock • Preferred stock	• Cash dividends • Stock dividends • Stock splits	• Retained earnings restrictions • Prior period adjustments • Retained earnings statement	• Presentation • Analysis

✔ The Navigator

The Corporate Form of Organization

LEARNING OBJECTIVE 1

Identify the major characteristics of a corporation.

In 1819, Chief Justice John Marshall defined a corporation as "an artificial being, invisible, intangible, and existing only in contemplation of law." This definition is the foundation for the prevailing legal interpretation that a **corporation** is an **entity separate and distinct from its owners**.

A corporation is created by law, and its continued existence depends upon the statutes of the state in which it is incorporated. As a legal entity, a corporation has most of the rights and privileges of a person. The major exceptions relate to privileges that only a living person can exercise, such as the right to vote or to hold public office. A corporation is subject to the same duties and responsibilities as a person. For example, it must abide by the laws, and it must pay taxes.

Two common ways to classify corporations are by **purpose** and by **ownership**. A corporation may be organized for the purpose of making a profit, or it may be not-for-profit. For-profit corporations include such well-known companies as McDonald's, Nike, PepsiCo, and Google. Not-for-profit corporations are organized for charitable, medical, or educational purposes. Examples are the Salvation Army and the American Cancer Society.

Classification by ownership differentiates publicly held and privately held corporations. A **publicly held corporation** may have thousands of stockholders. Its stock is regularly traded on a national securities exchange such as the New York Stock Exchange. Examples are IBM, Caterpillar, and General Electric.

Alternative Terminology
Privately held corporations are also referred to as *closely held corporations.*

In contrast, a **privately held corporation** usually has only a few stockholders, and does not offer its stock for sale to the general public. Privately held companies are generally much smaller than publicly held companies, although some notable exceptions exist. Cargill Inc., a private corporation that trades in grain and other commodities, is one of the largest companies in the United States.

Characteristics of a Corporation

In 1964, when Nike's founders, Knight and Bowerman, were just getting started in the running shoe business, they formed their original organization as a partnership. In 1968, they reorganized the company as a corporation. A number of characteristics distinguish corporations from proprietorships and partnerships. We explain the most important of these characteristics below.

Legal existence separate from owners

SEPARATE LEGAL EXISTENCE

As an entity separate and distinct from its owners, the corporation acts under its own name rather than in the name of its stockholders. Nike may buy, own, and sell property. It may borrow money, and may enter into legally binding contracts in its own name. It may also sue or be sued, and it pays its own taxes.

In a partnership, the acts of the owners (partners) bind the partnership. In contrast, the acts of its owners (stockholders) do not bind the corporation unless such owners are **agents** of the corporation. For example, if you owned shares of Nike stock, you would not have the right to purchase inventory for the company unless you were designated as an agent of the corporation.

Limited liability of stockholders

LIMITED LIABILITY OF STOCKHOLDERS

Since a corporation is a separate legal entity, creditors have recourse only to corporate assets to satisfy their claims. The liability of stockholders is normally limited to their investment in the corporation. Creditors have no legal claim on the personal assets of the owners unless fraud has occurred. Even in the event of bankruptcy, stockholders' losses are generally limited to their capital investment in the corporation.

TRANSFERABLE OWNERSHIP RIGHTS

Shares of capital stock give ownership in a corporation. These shares are transferable units. Stockholders may dispose of part or all of their interest in a corporation simply by selling their stock. The transfer of an ownership interest in a partnership requires the consent of each owner. In contrast, the transfer of stock is entirely at the discretion of the stockholder. It does not require the approval of either the corporation or other stockholders.

**Transferable
ownership rights**

The transfer of ownership rights between stockholders normally has no effect on the daily operating activities of the corporation. Nor does it affect the corporation's assets, liabilities, and total ownership equity. The transfer of these ownership rights is a transaction between individual owners. After it first issues the capital stock, the company does not participate in such transfers.

ABILITY TO ACQUIRE CAPITAL

It is relatively easy for a corporation to obtain capital through the issuance of stock. Investors buy stock in a corporation to earn money over time as the share price grows, and because a stockholder has limited liability and shares of stock are readily transferable. Also, individuals can become stockholders by investing relatively small amounts of money. In sum, the ability of a successful corporation to obtain capital is virtually unlimited.

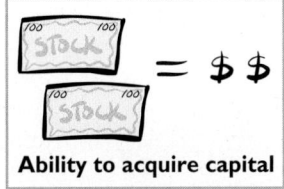

Ability to acquire capital

CONTINUOUS LIFE

The life of a corporation is stated in its charter. The life may be perpetual, or it may be limited to a specific number of years. If it is limited, the company can extend the life through renewal of the charter. Since a corporation is a separate legal entity, its continuance as a going concern is not affected by the withdrawal, death, or incapacity of a stockholder, employee, or officer. As a result, a successful company can have a continuous and perpetual life.

Continuous life

CORPORATION MANAGEMENT

Stockholders legally own the corporation. However, they manage the corporation indirectly through a board of directors they elect. Philip Knight is the chairman of Nike. The board, in turn, formulates the operating policies for the company. The board also selects officers, such as a president and one or more vice presidents, to execute policy and to perform daily management functions. As a result of the Sarbanes-Oxley Act, the board is now required to monitor management's actions more closely. Many feel that the failures of Enron and WorldCom could have been avoided by more diligent boards.

Illustration 11-1 (page 540) presents a typical organization chart showing the delegation of responsibility. The chief executive officer (CEO) has overall responsibility for managing the business. As the organization chart shows, the CEO delegates responsibility to other officers. The chief accounting officer is the **controller**. The controller's responsibilities include (1) maintaining the accounting records, (2) maintaining an adequate system of internal control, and (3) preparing financial statements, tax returns, and internal reports. The **treasurer** has custody of the corporation's funds and is responsible for maintaining the company's cash position.

> ### Ethics Note
> Managers who are not owners are often compensated based on the performance of the firm. They thus may be tempted to exaggerate firm performance by inflating income figures.

The organizational structure of a corporation enables a company to hire professional managers to run the business. On the other hand, the separation of ownership and management often reduces an owner's ability to actively manage the company.

GOVERNMENT REGULATIONS

A corporation is subject to numerous state and federal regulations. For example, state laws usually prescribe the requirements for issuing stock, the distributions of

Illustration 11-1
Corporation organization chart

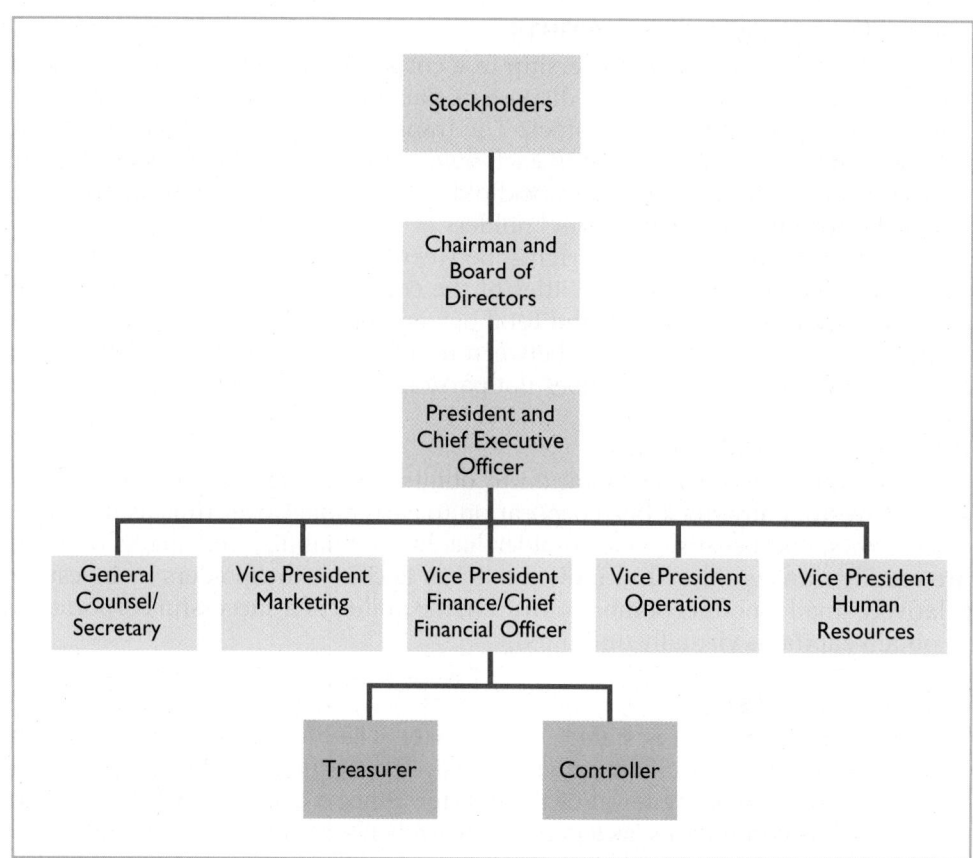

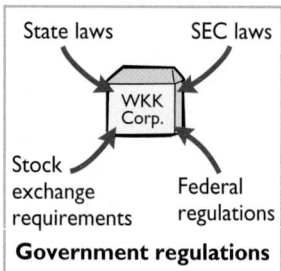

Government regulations

earnings permitted to stockholders, and the effects of retiring stock. Federal securities laws govern the sale of capital stock to the general public. Also, most publicly held corporations are required to make extensive disclosure of their financial affairs to the Securities and Exchange Commission (SEC) through quarterly and annual reports. In addition, when a corporation lists its stock on organized securities exchanges, it must comply with the reporting requirements of these exchanges. Government regulations are designed to protect the owners of the corporation.

ADDITIONAL TAXES

Owners of proprietorships and partnerships report their share of earnings on their personal income tax returns. The individual owner then pays taxes on this amount. Corporations, on the other hand, must pay federal and state income taxes **as a separate legal entity**. These taxes are substantial.

Additional taxes

In addition, stockholders must pay taxes on cash dividends (pro rata distributions of net income). Thus, many argue that the government taxes corporate income **twice (double taxation)**—once at the corporate level, and again at the individual level.

In summary, Illustration 11-2 shows the advantages and disadvantages of a corporation compared to a proprietorship and a partnership.

Illustration 11-2
Advantages and disadvantages of a corporation

Advantages	Disadvantages
Separate legal existence	Corporation management—separation of ownership and management
Limited liability of stockholders	
Transferable ownership rights	Government regulations
Ability to acquire capital	Additional taxes
Continuous life	
Corporation management—professional managers	

Forming a Corporation

A corporation is formed by grant of a state **charter**. The charter is a document that describes the name and purpose of the corporation, the types and number of shares of stock that are authorized to be issued, the names of the individuals that formed the company, and the number of shares that these individuals agreed to purchase. Regardless of the number of states in which a corporation has operating divisions, it is incorporated in only one state.

Alternative Terminology
The charter is often referred to as the *articles of incorporation*.

It is to the company's advantage to incorporate in a state whose laws are favorable to the corporate form of business organization. For example, although General Motors has its headquarters in Michigan, it is incorporated in New Jersey. In fact, more and more corporations have been incorporating in states with rules that favor existing management. For example, Gulf Oil changed its state of incorporation to Delaware to thwart possible unfriendly takeovers. There, certain defensive tactics against takeovers can be approved by the board of directors alone, without a vote by shareholders.

Upon receipt of its charter from the state of incorporation, the corporation establishes **by-laws**. The by-laws establish the internal rules and procedures for conducting the affairs of the corporation. Corporations engaged in interstate commerce must also obtain a **license** from each state in which they do business. The license subjects the corporation's operating activities to the general corporation laws of the state.

Costs incurred in the formation of a corporation are called **organization costs**. These costs include legal and state fees, and promotional expenditures involved in the organization of the business. **Corporations expense organization costs as incurred**. To determine the amount and timing of future benefits is so difficult that it is standard procedure to take a conservative approach of expensing these costs immediately.

ACCOUNTING ACROSS THE ORGANIZATION

Wall Street No Friend of Facebook

In the 1990s, it was the dream of every young technology entrepreneur to start a company and do an initial public offering (IPO), that is, list company shares on a stock exchange. It seemed like there was a never-ending supply of 20-something-year-old technology entrepreneurs that made millions doing IPOs of companies that never made a profit and eventually failed. In sharp contrast to this is Mark Zuckerberg, the 27-year-old founder and CEO of Facebook. If Facebook did an IPO, he would make billions of dollars. But, he is in no hurry to go public. Because his company doesn't need to invest in factories, distribution systems, or even marketing, it doesn't need to raise a lot of cash. Also, by not going public, Zuckerberg has more control over the direction of the company. Right now, he and the other founders don't have to answer to outside shareholders, who might be more concerned about short-term investment horizons rather than long-term goals. In addition, publicly traded companies face many more financial reporting disclosure requirements.

Source: Jessica E. Vascellaro, "Facebook CEO in No Rush to 'Friend' Wall Street," *Wall Street Journal Online* (March 4, 2010).

? Why has Mark Zuckerberg, the CEO and founder of Facebook, delayed taking his company's shares public through an initial public offering (IPO)? (See page 596.)

Ownership Rights of Stockholders

When chartered, the corporation may begin selling ownership rights in the form of shares of stock. When a corporation has only one class of stock, it is **common stock**. Each share of common stock gives the stockholder the ownership rights pictured in Illustration 11-3. The articles of incorporation or the by-laws state the ownership rights of a share of stock.

Illustration 11-3
Ownership rights of stockholders

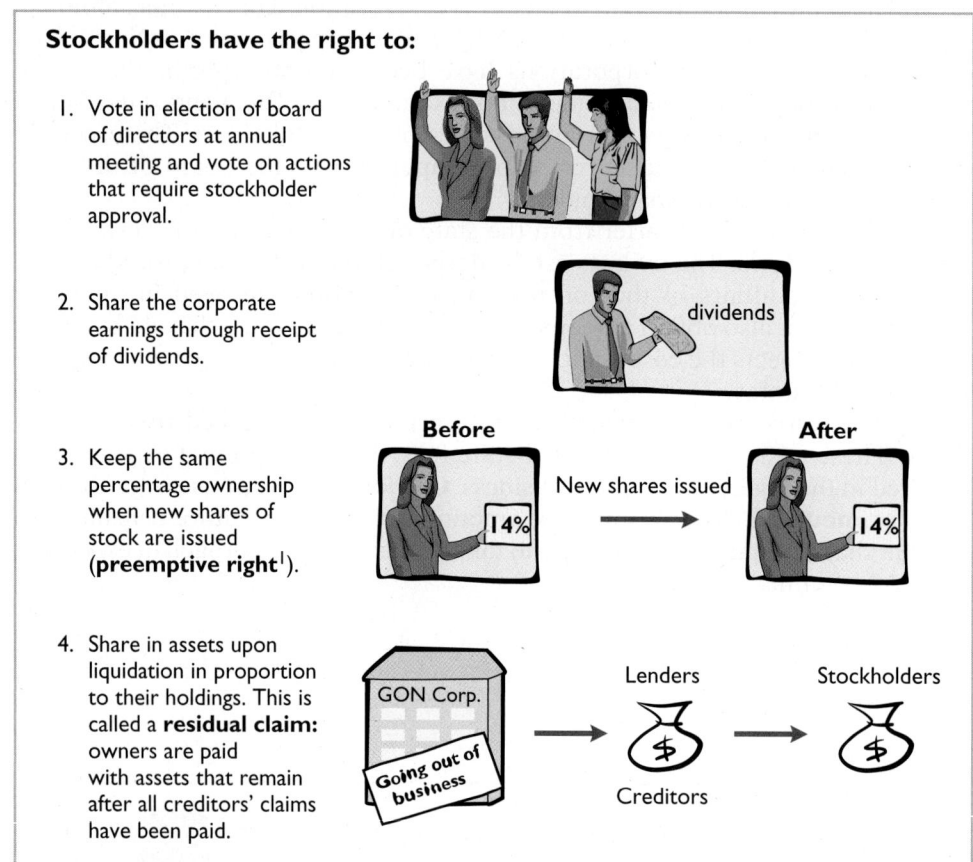

Stockholders have the right to:

1. Vote in election of board of directors at annual meeting and vote on actions that require stockholder approval.

2. Share the corporate earnings through receipt of dividends.

3. Keep the same percentage ownership when new shares of stock are issued (**preemptive right**[1]).

4. Share in assets upon liquidation in proportion to their holdings. This is called a **residual claim:** owners are paid with assets that remain after all creditors' claims have been paid.

Proof of stock ownership is evidenced by a form known as a **stock certificate**. As Illustration 11-4 shows, the face of the certificate shows the name of the corporation, the stockholder's name, the class and special features of the stock, the number of shares owned, and the signatures of authorized corporate officials. Prenumbered certificates facilitate accountability. They may be issued for any quantity of shares.

Stock Issue Considerations

In considering the issuance of stock, a corporation must resolve a number of basic questions: How many shares should it authorize for sale? How should it

---

[1]A number of companies have eliminated the preemptive right because they believe it makes an unnecessary and cumbersome demand on management. For example, by stockholder approval, IBM has dropped its preemptive right for stockholders.

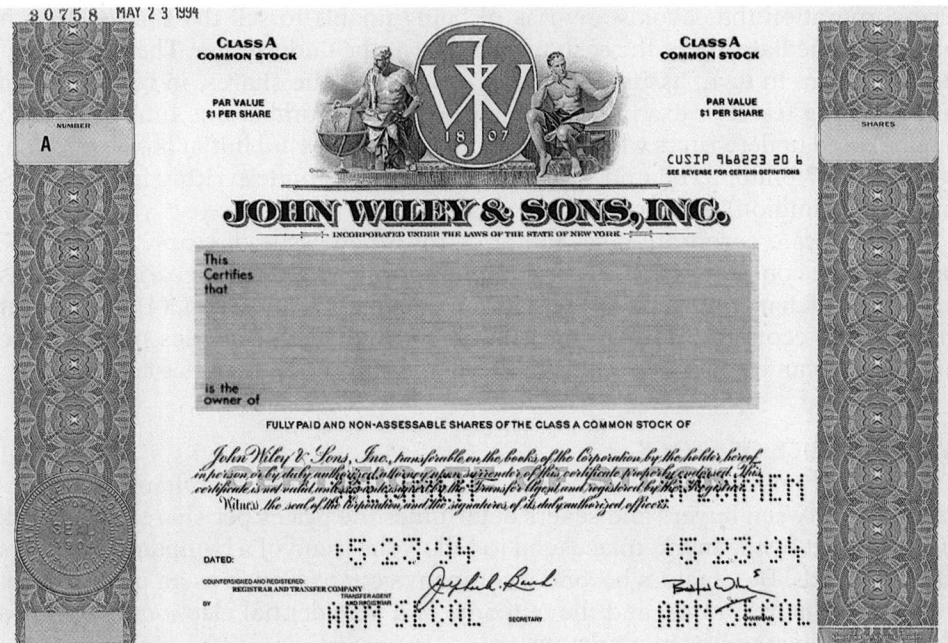

Illustration 11-4
A stock certificate

issue the stock? At what price should it issue the shares? What value should the corporation assign to the stock? These questions are addressed in the following sections.

AUTHORIZED STOCK

The charter indicates the amount of stock that a corporation is **authorized** to sell. The total amount of **authorized stock** at the time of incorporation normally anticipates both initial and subsequent capital needs. As a result, the number of shares authorized generally exceeds the number initially sold. If it sells all authorized stock, a corporation must obtain consent of the state to amend its charter before it can issue additional shares.

The authorization of capital stock does not result in a formal accounting entry. This event has no immediate effect on either corporate assets or stockholders' equity. However, the number of authorized shares is often reported in the stockholders' equity section. It is then simple to determine the number of unissued shares that the corporation can issue without amending the charter: subtract the total shares issued from the total authorized. For example, if Advanced Micro was authorized to sell 100,000 shares of common stock and issued 80,000 shares, 20,000 shares would remain unissued.

ISSUANCE OF STOCK

A corporation can issue common stock **directly** to investors. Or, it can issue the stock **indirectly** through an investment banking firm that specializes in bringing securities to the attention of prospective investors. Direct issue is typical in closely held companies. Indirect issue is customary for a publicly held corporation.

In an indirect issue, the investment banking firm may agree to **underwrite** the entire stock issue. In this arrangement, the investment banker buys the stock from the corporation at a stipulated price and resells the shares to investors.

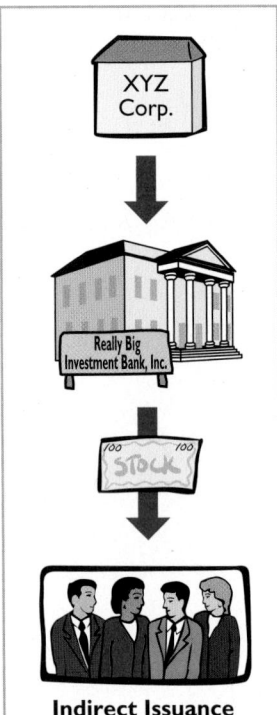

Indirect Issuance

The corporation thus avoids any risk of being unable to sell the shares. Also, it obtains immediate use of the cash received from the underwriter. The investment banking firm, in turn, assumes the risk of reselling the shares, in return for an underwriting fee.[2] For example, Google (the world's number-one Internet search engine) used underwriters when it issued a highly successful initial public offering, raising $1.67 billion. The underwriters charged a 3% underwriting fee (approximately $50 million) on Google's stock offering.

How does a corporation set the price for a new issue of stock? Among the factors to be considered are (1) the company's anticipated future earnings, (2) its expected dividend rate per share, (3) its current financial position, (4) the current state of the economy, and (5) the current state of the securities market. The calculation can be complex and is properly the subject of a finance course.

MARKET PRICE OF STOCK

The stock of publicly held companies is traded on organized exchanges. The interaction between buyers and sellers determines the prices per share. In general, the prices set by the marketplace tend to follow the trend of a company's earnings and dividends. But, factors beyond a company's control, such as an oil embargo, changes in interest rates, and the outcome of a presidential election, may cause day-to-day fluctuations in market prices.

The trading of capital stock on securities exchanges involves the transfer of **already issued shares** from an existing stockholder to another investor. These transactions have **no impact** on a corporation's stockholders' equity.

INVESTOR INSIGHT

How to Read Stock Quotes

Organized exchanges trade the stock of publicly held companies at dollar prices per share established by the interaction between buyers and sellers. For each listed security, the financial press reports the high and low prices of the stock during the year, the total volume of stock traded on a given day, the high and low prices for the day, and the closing market price, with the net change for the day. Nike is listed on the New York Stock Exchange. Here is a listing for Nike:

| Stock | 52 Weeks | | Volume | High | Low | Close | Net Change |
	High	Low					
Nike	78.55	48.76	5,375,651	72.44	69.78	70.61	−1.69

These numbers indicate the following. The high and low market prices for the last 52 weeks have been $78.55 and $48.76. The trading volume for the day was 5,375,651 shares. The high, low, and closing prices for that date were $72.44, $69.78, and $70.61, respectively. The net change for the day was a decrease of $1.69 per share.

? For stocks traded on organized exchanges, how are the dollar prices per share established? What factors might influence the price of shares in the marketplace? (See page 596.)

---

[2]Alternatively, the investment banking firm may agree only to enter into a **best-efforts** contract with the corporation. In such cases, the banker agrees to sell as many shares as possible at a specified price. The corporation bears the risk of unsold stock. Under a best-efforts arrangement, the banking firm is paid a fee or commission for its services.

PAR AND NO-PAR VALUE STOCKS

Par value stock is capital stock to which the charter has assigned a value per share. Years ago, par value determined the **legal capital** per share that a company must retain in the business for the protection of corporate creditors; that amount was not available for withdrawal by stockholders. Thus, in the past, most states required the corporation to sell its shares at par or above.

However, par value was often immaterial relative to the value of the company's stock—even at the time of issue. Thus, its usefulness as a protective device to creditors was questionable. For example, Loews Corporation's par value is $0.01 per share, yet a new issue in 2010 would have sold at a **market price** in the $35 per share range. Thus, par has no relationship with market price; in the vast majority of cases, it is an immaterial amount. As a consequence, today many states do not require a par value. Instead, they use other means to protect creditors.

No-par value stock is capital stock to which the charter has not assigned a value. No-par value stock is fairly common today. For example, Nike and Procter & Gamble both have no-par stock. In many states, the board of directors assigns a **stated value** to no-par shares.

> DO IT!

Corporate Organization

Indicate whether each of the following statements is true or false.

_____ 1. Similar to partners in a partnership, stockholders of a corporation have unlimited liability.

_____ 2. It is relatively easy for a corporation to obtain capital through the issuance of stock.

_____ 3. The separation of ownership and management is an advantage of the corporate form of business.

_____ 4. The journal entry to record the authorization of capital stock includes a credit to the appropriate capital stock account.

_____ 5. All states require a par value per share for capital stock.

Solution

1. False. The liability of stockholders is normally limited to their investment in the corporation.

2. True.

3. False. The separation of ownership and management is a disadvantage of the corporate form of business.

4. False. The authorization of capital stock does not result in a formal accounting entry.

5. False. Many states do not require a par value.

Action Plan

✔ Review the characteristics of a corporation and understand which are advantages and which are disadvantages.

✔ Understand that corporations raise capital through the issuance of stock, which can be par or no-par.

Related exercise material: **BE11-1, E11-1, E11-2, and DO IT! 11-1.**

✔ **The Navigator**

Corporate Capital

Owners' equity is identified by various names: **stockholders' equity, shareholders' equity**, or **corporate capital**. The stockholders' equity section of a corporation's balance sheet consists of two parts: (1) paid-in (contributed) capital and (2) retained earnings (earned capital).

The distinction between **paid-in capital** and **retained earnings** is important from both a legal and a financial point of view. Legally, corporations can make distributions of earnings (declare dividends) out of retained earnings in all states. However, in many states they cannot declare dividends out of paid-in capital. Management, stockholders, and others often look to retained earnings for the continued existence and growth of the corporation.

PAID-IN CAPITAL

Paid-in capital is the total amount of cash and other assets paid in to the corporation by stockholders in exchange for capital stock. As noted earlier, when a corporation has only one class of stock, it is **common stock**.

RETAINED EARNINGS

Retained earnings is net income that a corporation retains for future use. Net income is recorded in Retained Earnings by a closing entry that debits Income Summary and credits Retained Earnings. For example, assuming that net income for Delta Robotics in its first year of operations is $130,000, the closing entry is:

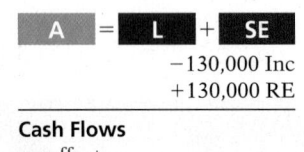

A = L + SE
−130,000 Inc
+130,000 RE

Cash Flows
no effect

Income Summary	130,000	
Retained Earnings		130,000
(To close Income Summary and transfer net income		
to retained earnings)		

If Delta Robotics has a balance of $800,000 in common stock at the end of its first year, its stockholders' equity section is as follows.

Illustration 11-5
Stockholders' equity section

Delta Robotics
Balance Sheet (partial)

Stockholders' equity		
Paid-in capital		
Common stock	$800,000	
Retained earnings	130,000	
Total stockholders' equity		**$930,000**

Illustration 11-6 compares the owners' equity (stockholders' equity) accounts reported on a balance sheet for a proprietorship and a corporation.

Illustration 11-6
Comparison of owners' equity accounts

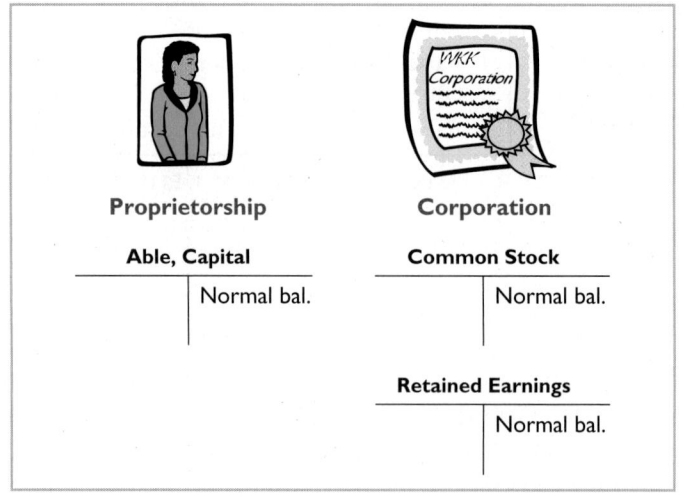

> ## DO IT!

Corporate Capital

At the end of its first year of operation, Doral Corporation has $750,000 of common stock and net income of $122,000. Prepare (a) the closing entry for net income and (b) the stockholders' equity section at year-end.

Solution

Action Plan

✔ Record net income in Retained Earnings by a closing entry in which Income Summary is debited and Retained Earnings is credited.

✔ In the stockholders' equity section, show (1) paid-in capital and (2) retained earnings.

(a)	Income Summary	122,000	
	Retained Earnings		122,000
	(To close Income Summary and transfer		
	net income to retained earnings)		
(b)	Stockholders' equity		
	Paid-in capital		
	Common stock	$750,000	
	Retained earnings	122,000	
	Total stockholders' equity		$872,000

Related exercise material: **DO IT! 11-2.**

✔ **The Navigator**

PEOPLE, PLANET, AND PROFIT INSIGHT

The Impact of Corporate Social Responsibility

A 2010 survey conducted by Institutional Shareholder Services, a proxy advisory firm, shows that 83% of investors now believe environmental and social factors can have a significant impact on shareholder value over the long term. This belief is clearly visible in the rising level of support for shareholder proposals requesting action related to social and environmental issues.

    The following table shows that the number of corporate social responsibility (CSR) related shareholder proposals rose from 150 in 2000 to 191 in 2010. Moreover, those proposals garnered average voting support of 18.4% of votes cast versus just 7.5% a decade earlier.

Trends in Shareholder Proposals on Corporate Responsibility

	2000	2005	2010
Number of proposals voted	150	155	191
Average voting support	7.5%	9.9%	18.4%
Percent proposals receiving > 10% support	16.7%	31.2%	52.1%

Source: Investor Responsibility Research Center, Ernst & Young, *Seven Questions CEOs and Boards Should Ask About: "Triple Bottom Line" Reporting.*

? Why are CSR-related shareholder proposals increasing? (See page 596.)

Accounting for Stock Transactions

Accounting for Common Stock Issues

Let's now look at how to account for issues of common stock. The primary objectives in accounting for the issuance of common stock are (1) to identify the specific sources of paid-in capital, and (2) to maintain the distinction between paid-in capital and retained earnings. **The issuance of common stock affects only paid-in capital accounts.**

ISSUING PAR VALUE COMMON STOCK FOR CASH

As discussed earlier, par value does not indicate a stock's market price. Therefore, the cash proceeds from issuing par value stock may be equal to, greater than, or less than par value. When the company records issuance of common stock for cash, it credits to Common Stock the par value of the shares. It records in a separate paid-in capital account the portion of the proceeds that is above or below par value.

To illustrate, assume that Hydro-Slide, Inc. issues 1,000 shares of $1 par value common stock at par for cash. The entry to record this transaction is:

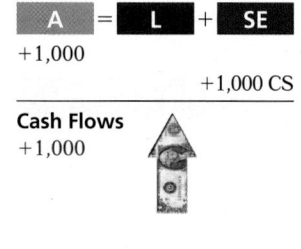

Cash Flows
+1,000

Cash	1,000	
Common Stock		1,000
(To record issuance of 1,000 shares of $1 par common stock at par)		

Now assume that Hydro-Slide issues an additional 1,000 shares of the $1 par value common stock for cash at $5 per share. The amount received above the par value, in this case $4 ($5 − $1), is credited to Paid-in Capital in Excess of Par—Common Stock. The entry is:

Cash Flows
+5,000

Cash	5,000	
Common Stock		1,000
Paid-in Capital in Excess of Par—Common Stock		4,000
(To record issuance of 1,000 shares of $1 par common stock)		

The total paid-in capital from these two transactions is $6,000, and the legal capital is $2,000. Assuming Hydro-Slide, Inc. has retained earnings of $27,000, Illustration 11-7 shows the company's stockholders' equity section.

Illustration 11-7
Stockholders' equity—paid-in capital in excess of par

Alternative Terminology
Paid-in Capital in Excess of Par is also called *Premium on Stock.*

Hydro-Slide, Inc.	
Balance Sheet (partial)	
Stockholders' equity	
Paid-in capital	
Common stock	$ 2,000
Paid-in capital in excess of par— common stock	**4,000**
Total paid-in capital	6,000
Retained earnings	27,000
Total stockholders' equity	$33,000

When a corporation issues stock for less than par value, it debits the account Paid-in Capital in Excess of Par—Common Stock if a credit balance exists in this account. If a credit balance does not exist, then the corporation debits to Retained Earnings the amount less than par. This situation occurs only rarely:

Most states do not permit the sale of common stock below par value because stockholders may be held personally liable for the difference between the price paid upon original sale and par value.

ISSUING NO-PAR COMMON STOCK FOR CASH

When no-par common stock has a stated value, the entries are similar to those illustrated for par value stock. The corporation credits the stated value to Common Stock. Also, when the selling price of no-par stock exceeds stated value, the corporation credits the excess to Paid-in Capital in Excess of Stated Value—Common Stock.

For example, assume that instead of $1 par value stock, Hydro-Slide, Inc. has $5 stated value no-par stock and the company issues 5,000 shares at $8 per share for cash. The entry is:

Cash	40,000	
Common Stock		25,000
Paid-in Capital in Excess of Stated Value—Common Stock		15,000
(To record issue of 5,000 shares of $5 stated value no-par stock)		

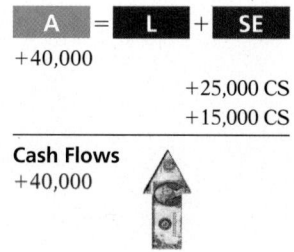

Hydro-Slide, Inc. reports Paid-in Capital in Excess of Stated Value—Common Stock as part of paid-in capital in the stockholders' equity section.

What happens when no-par stock does not have a stated value? In that case, the corporation credits the entire proceeds to Common Stock. Thus, if Hydro-Slide does not assign a stated value to its no-par stock, it records the issuance of the 5,000 shares at $8 per share for cash as follows.

Cash	40,000	
Common Stock		40,000
(To record issue of 5,000 shares of no-par stock)		

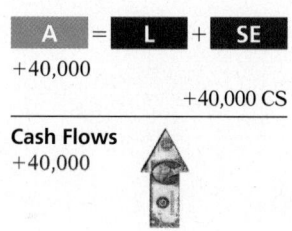

ISSUING COMMON STOCK FOR SERVICES OR NONCASH ASSETS

Corporations also may issue stock for services (compensation to attorneys or consultants) or for noncash assets (land, buildings, and equipment). In such cases, what cost should be recognized in the exchange transaction? To comply with the **cost principle,** in a noncash transaction **cost is the cash equivalent price.** Thus, **cost is either the fair value of the consideration given up, or the fair value of the consideration received**, whichever is more clearly determinable.

To illustrate, assume that attorneys have helped Jordan Company incorporate. They have billed the company $5,000 for their services. They agree to accept 4,000 shares of $1 par value common stock in payment of their bill. At the time of the exchange, there is no established market price for the stock. In this case, the fair value of the consideration received, $5,000, is more clearly evident. Accordingly, Jordan Company makes the following entry.

Organization Expense	5,000	
Common Stock		4,000
Paid-in Capital in Excess of Par—Common Stock		1,000
(To record issuance of 4,000 shares of $1 par value stock to attorneys)		

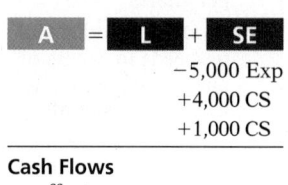

As explained on page 541, organization costs are expensed as incurred.

In contrast, assume that Athletic Research Inc. is an existing publicly held corporation. Its $5 par value stock is actively traded at $8 per share. The company issues 10,000 shares of stock to acquire land recently advertised for sale at $90,000. The most clearly evident value in this noncash transaction is the market price of the consideration given, $80,000. The company records the transaction as follows.

A = L + SE
+80,000
+50,000 CS
+30,000 CS

Cash Flows
no effect

Land	80,000	
Common Stock		50,000
Paid-in Capital in Excess of Par—Common Stock		30,000
(To record issuance of 10,000 shares of $5 par value stock for land)		

As illustrated in these examples, **the par value of the stock is never a factor in determining the cost of the assets received**. This is also true of the stated value of no-par stock.

ANATOMY OF A FRAUD

The president, chief operating officer, and chief financial officer of SafeNet, a software encryption company, were each awarded employee stock options by the company's board of directors as part of their compensation package. Stock options enable an employee to buy a company's stock sometime in the future at the price that existed when the stock option was awarded. For example, suppose that you received stock options today, when the stock price of your company was $30. Three years later, if the stock price rose to $100, you could "exercise" your options and buy the stock for $30 per share, thereby making $70 per share. After being awarded their stock options, the three employees changed the award dates in the company's records to dates in the past, when the company's stock was trading at historical lows. For example, using the previous example, they would choose a past date when the stock was selling for $10 per share, rather than the $30 price on the actual award date. In our example, this would increase the profit from exercising the options to $90 per share.

Total take: $1.7 million

The Missing Control
Independent internal verification. The company's board of directors should have ensured that the awards were properly administered. For example, the date on the minutes from the board meeting could be compared to the dates that were recorded for the awards. In addition, the dates should again be confirmed upon exercise.

> DO IT!

Issuance of Stock

Action Plan

✔ In issuing shares for cash, credit Common Stock for par value per share.

✔ Credit any additional proceeds in excess of par to a separate paid-in capital account.

✔ When stock is issued for services, use the cash equivalent price.

✔ For the cash equivalent price, use either the fair value of what is given up or the fair value of what is received, whichever is more clearly determinable.

Cayman Corporation begins operations on March 1 by issuing 100,000 shares of $10 par value common stock for cash at $12 per share. On March 15, it issues 5,000 shares of common stock to attorneys in settlement of their bill of $50,000 for organization costs. Journalize the issuance of the shares, assuming the stock is not publicly traded.

Solution

Mar. 1	Cash	1,200,000	
	Common Stock		1,000,000
	Paid-in Capital in Excess of Par— Common Stock		200,000
	(To record issuance of 100,000 shares at $12 per share)		
Mar. 15	Organization Expense	50,000	
	Common Stock		50,000
	(To record issuance of 5,000 shares for attorneys' fees)		

Related exercise material: **BE11-2, BE11-3, BE11-4, E11-3, E11-4, and DO IT! 11-3.**

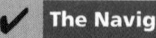 ✔ **The Navigator**

Accounting for Treasury Stock

Treasury stock is a corporation's own stock that it has issued and subsequently reacquired from shareholders, but not retired. A corporation may acquire treasury stock for various reasons:

1. To reissue the shares to officers and employees under bonus and stock compensation plans.
2. To signal to the stock market that management believes the stock is underpriced, in the hope of enhancing its market price.
3. To have additional shares available for use in the acquisition of other companies.
4. To reduce the number of shares outstanding and thereby increase earnings per share.

Another infrequent reason for purchasing shares is that management may want to eliminate hostile shareholders by buying them out.

Many corporations have treasury stock. For example, approximately 70% of U.S. companies have treasury stock.[3] In a recent year, Nike purchased more than 6 million treasury shares.

Helpful Hint
Treasury shares do not have dividend rights or voting rights.

PURCHASE OF TREASURY STOCK

Companies generally account for treasury stock by **the cost method**. This method uses the cost of the shares purchased to value the treasury stock. Under the cost method, the company debits **Treasury Stock** for the **price paid to reacquire the shares**. When the company disposes of the shares, it credits to Treasury Stock **the same amount** it paid to reacquire the shares.

To illustrate, assume that on January 1, 2014, the stockholders' equity section of Mead, Inc. has 100,000 shares of $5 par value common stock outstanding (all issued at par value) and Retained Earnings of $200,000. The stockholders' equity section before purchase of treasury stock is as follows.

Mead, Inc.	
Balance Sheet (partial)	
Stockholders' equity	
Paid-in capital	
Common stock, $5 par value, 100,000 shares	
issued and outstanding	$500,000
Retained earnings	200,000
Total stockholders' equity	$700,000

Illustration 11-8
Stockholders' equity with no treasury stock

On February 1, 2014, Mead acquires 4,000 shares of its stock at $8 per share. The entry is:

Feb. 1	Treasury Stock	32,000	
	Cash		32,000
	(To record purchase of 4,000 shares of treasury stock at $8 per share)		

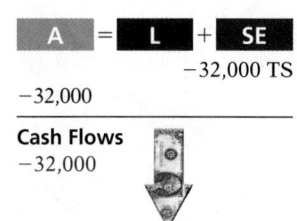

A = L + SE
−32,000 TS
−32,000
Cash Flows
−32,000

Note that Mead debits Treasury Stock for the cost of the shares purchased. Is the original paid-in capital account, Common Stock, affected? No, because the number of issued shares does not change. In the stockholders' equity section of

---

[3]*Accounting Trends & Techniques 2010* (New York: American Institute of Certified Public Accountants).

the balance sheet, Mead deducts treasury stock from total paid-in capital and retained earnings. Treasury Stock is a **contra stockholders' equity account**. Thus, the acquisition of treasury stock reduces stockholders' equity.

The stockholders' equity section of Mead, Inc. after purchase of treasury stock is as follows.

Illustration 11-9
Stockholders' equity
with treasury stock

Mead, Inc.	
Balance Sheet (partial)	
Stockholders' equity	
Paid-in capital	
Common stock, $5 par value, 100,000 shares issued	
and 96,000 shares outstanding	$500,000
Retained earnings	200,000
Total paid-in capital and retained earnings	700,000
Less: Treasury stock (4,000 shares)	**32,000**
Total stockholders' equity	$668,000

Ethics Note

The purchase of treasury stock reduces the cushion for creditors and preferred stockholders. A restriction for the cost of treasury stock purchased is often required. The restriction is usually applied to retained earnings.

Mead discloses in the balance sheet both the number of shares issued (100,000) and the number in the treasury (4,000). The difference is the number of shares of stock outstanding (96,000). The term **outstanding stock** means the number of shares of issued stock that are being held by stockholders.

Some maintain that companies should report treasury stock as an asset because it can be sold for cash. Under this reasoning, companies should also show unissued stock as an asset, clearly an erroneous conclusion. Rather than being an asset, treasury stock reduces stockholder claims on corporate assets. This effect is correctly shown by reporting treasury stock as a deduction from total paid-in capital and retained earnings.

ACCOUNTING ACROSS THE ORGANIZATION

Why Did Reebok Buy Its Own Stock?

In a bold (and some would say risky) move, Reebok at one time bought back nearly a *third* of its shares. This repurchase of shares dramatically reduced Reebok's available cash. In fact, the company borrowed significant funds to accomplish the repurchase. In a press release, management stated that it was repurchasing the shares because it believed its stock was severely underpriced. The repurchase of so many shares was meant to signal management's belief in good future earnings.

Skeptics, however, suggested that Reebok's management was repurchasing shares to make it less likely that another company would acquire Reebok (in which case Reebok's top managers would likely lose their jobs). By depleting its cash, Reebok became a less likely acquisition target. Acquiring companies like to purchase companies with large cash balances so they can pay off debt used in the acquisition.

 What signal might a large stock repurchase send to investors regarding management's belief about the company's growth opportunities? (See page 596.)

DISPOSAL OF TREASURY STOCK

Treasury stock is usually sold or retired. The accounting for its sale differs when treasury stock is sold above cost than when it is sold below cost.

SALE OF TREASURY STOCK ABOVE COST If the selling price of the treasury shares is equal to their cost, the company records the sale of the shares by a debit to Cash and a credit to Treasury Stock. When the selling price of the shares is greater than their cost, the company credits the difference to Paid-in Capital from Treasury Stock.

To illustrate, assume that on July 1, Mead, Inc. sells for $10 per share the 1,000 shares of its treasury stock, previously acquired at $8 per share. The entry is as follows.

July 1	Cash	10,000	
	Treasury Stock		8,000
	Paid-in Capital from Treasury Stock		2,000
	(To record sale of 1,000 shares of treasury stock above cost)		

Mead does not record a $2,000 gain on sale of treasury stock for two reasons: (1) Gains on sales occur when **assets** are sold, and treasury stock is not an asset. (2) A corporation does not realize a gain or suffer a loss from stock transactions with its own stockholders. Thus, companies should not include in net income any paid-in capital arising from the sale of treasury stock. Instead, they report Paid-in Capital from Treasury Stock separately on the balance sheet, as a part of paid-in capital.

SALE OF TREASURY STOCK BELOW COST When a company sells treasury stock below its cost, it usually debits to Paid-in Capital from Treasury Stock the excess of cost over selling price. Thus, if Mead, Inc. sells an additional 800 shares of treasury stock on October 1 at $7 per share, it makes the following entry.

Oct. 1	Cash	5,600	
	Paid-in Capital from Treasury Stock	800	
	Treasury Stock		6,400
	(To record sale of 800 shares of treasury stock below cost)		

Observe the following from the two sales entries: (1) Mead credits Treasury Stock at cost in each entry. (2) Mead uses Paid-in Capital from Treasury Stock for the difference between cost and the resale price of the shares. (3) The original paid-in capital account, Common Stock, is not affected. **The sale of treasury stock increases both total assets and total stockholders' equity.**

After posting the foregoing entries, the treasury stock accounts will show the following balances on October 1.

	Treasury Stock				Paid-in Capital from Treasury Stock		
Feb. 1	32,000	July 1	8,000	Oct. 1	800	July 1	2,000
		Oct. 1	6,400			Oct. 1 Bal.	1,200
Oct. 1 Bal.	17,600						

When a company fully depletes the credit balance in Paid-in Capital from Treasury Stock, it debits to Retained Earnings any additional excess of cost over selling price. To illustrate, assume that Mead, Inc. sells its remaining 2,200 shares at $7 per share on December 1. The excess of cost over selling price is $2,200

Helpful Hint
Treasury stock transactions are classified as capital stock transactions. As in the case when stock is issued, the income statement is not involved.

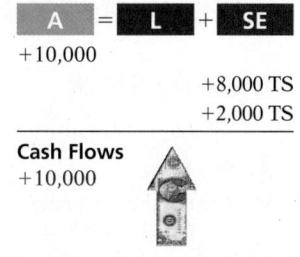

A = L + SE
+10,000
          +8,000 TS
          +2,000 TS

Cash Flows
+10,000

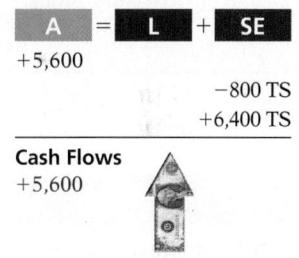

A = L + SE
+5,600
          −800 TS
          +6,400 TS

Cash Flows
+5,600

Illustration 11-10
Treasury stock accounts

[2,200 × ($8 − $7)]. In this case, Mead debits $1,200 of the excess to Paid-in Capital from Treasury Stock. It debits the remainder to Retained Earnings. The entry is:

A = L + SE			
+15,400			

Dec. 1	Cash	15,400	
	Paid-in Capital from Treasury Stock	1,200	
	Retained Earnings	1,000	
	Treasury Stock		17,600
	(To record sale of 2,200 shares of treasury		
	stock at $7 per share)		

−1,200 TS
−1,000 RE
+17,600 TS

Cash Flows
+15,400

> DO IT!

Treasury Stock

Action Plan

✔ Record the purchase of treasury stock at cost.

✔ When treasury stock is sold above its cost, credit the excess of the selling price over cost to Paid-in Capital from Treasury Stock.

✔ When treasury stock is sold below its cost, debit the excess of cost over selling price to Paid-in Capital from Treasury Stock.

Santa Anita Inc. purchases 3,000 shares of its $50 par value common stock for $180,000 cash on July 1. It will hold the shares in the treasury until resold. On November 1, the corporation sells 1,000 shares of treasury stock for cash at $70 per share. Journalize the treasury stock transactions.

Solution

July 1	Treasury Stock	180,000	
	Cash		180,000
	(To record the purchase of 3,000		
	shares at $60 per share)		
Nov. 1	Cash	70,000	
	Treasury Stock		60,000
	Paid-in Capital from Treasury Stock		10,000
	(To record the sale of 1,000 shares		
	at $70 per share)		

Related exercise material: **BE11-5, E11-5, and DO IT! 11-4.**

✔ **The Navigator**

Accounting for Preferred Stock

LEARNING OBJECTIVE   **4**

Differentiate preferred stock from common stock.

To appeal to more investors, a corporation may issue an additional class of stock, called preferred stock. **Preferred stock** has contractual provisions that give it some preference or priority over common stock. Typically, preferred stockholders have a priority as to (1) distributions of earnings (dividends) and (2) assets in the event of liquidation. However, they generally do not have voting rights.

Like common stock, corporations may issue preferred stock for cash or for noncash assets. The entries for these transactions are similar to the entries for common stock. When a corporation has more than one class of stock, each paid-in capital account title should identify the stock to which it relates. A company might have the following accounts: Preferred Stock, Common Stock, Paid-in Capital in Excess of Par—Preferred Stock, and Paid-in Capital in Excess of Par—Common Stock. For example, if Stine Corporation issues 10,000 shares of $10 par value preferred stock for $12 cash per share, the entry to record the issuance is:

A = L + SE			
+120,000			

	Cash	120,000	
	Preferred Stock		100,000
	Paid-in Capital in Excess of Par—Preferred Stock		20,000
	(To record the issuance of 10,000 shares of		
	$10 par value preferred stock)		

+100,000 PS
+20,000 PS

Cash Flows
+120,000

Preferred stock may have either a par value or no-par value. In the stockholders' equity section of the balance sheet, companies list preferred stock first because of its dividend and liquidation preferences over common stock.

We discuss various features associated with the issuance of preferred stock on the following pages.

DIVIDEND PREFERENCES

As indicated above, **preferred stockholders have the right to receive dividends before common stockholders**. For example, if the dividend rate on preferred stock is $5 per share, common shareholders will not receive any dividends in the current year until preferred stockholders have received $5 per share. The first claim to dividends does not, however, guarantee the payment of dividends. Dividends depend on many factors, such as adequate retained earnings and availability of cash. If a company does not pay dividends to preferred stockholders, it cannot of course pay dividends to common stockholders.

For preferred stock, companies state the per share dividend amount as a percentage of the par value or as a specified amount. For example, Earthlink specifies a 3% dividend on its $100 par value preferred, whereas PepsiCo pays $4.56 per share on its no-par value stock.

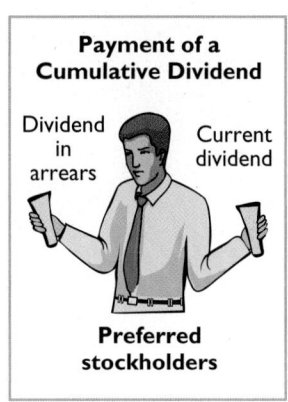

Dividend Preference

CUMULATIVE DIVIDEND Preferred stock often contains a **cumulative dividend** feature. This means that preferred stockholders must be paid both current-year dividends and any unpaid prior-year dividends before common stockholders receive dividends. When preferred stock is cumulative, preferred dividends not declared in a given period are called **dividends in arrears**.

To illustrate, assume that Scientific Leasing has 5,000 shares of 7%, $100 par value, cumulative preferred stock outstanding. Each $100 share pays a $7 dividend (.07 × $100). The annual dividend is $35,000 (5,000 × $7 per share). If dividends are two years in arrears, preferred stockholders are entitled to receive the following dividends in the current year.

Dividends in arrears ($35,000 × 2)	$ 70,000
Current-year dividends	35,000
Total preferred dividends	**$105,000**

Illustration 11-11
Computation of total dividends to preferred stock

The company cannot pay dividends to common stockholders until it pays the entire preferred dividend. In other words, companies cannot pay dividends to common stockholders while any preferred dividends are in arrears.

Are dividends in arrears considered a liability? **No—no payment obligation exists until the board of directors declares a dividend.** However, companies should disclose in the notes to the financial statements the amount of dividends in arrears. Doing so enables investors to assess the potential impact of this commitment on the corporation's financial position.

Companies that are unable to meet their dividend obligations are not looked upon favorably by the investment community. As a financial officer noted in discussing one company's failure to pay its cumulative preferred dividend for a period of time, "Not meeting your obligations on something like that is a major black mark on your record." The accounting entries for preferred stock dividends are explained later in this chapter.

Payment of a Cumulative Dividend

Dividend in arrears

Current dividend

Preferred stockholders

LIQUIDATION PREFERENCE

Most preferred stocks also have a preference on corporate assets if the corporation fails. This feature provides security for the preferred stockholder. The preference to assets may be for the par value of the shares or for a specified liquidating value. For example, Commonwealth Edison's preferred stock entitles its holders to receive $31.80 per share, plus accrued and unpaid dividends, in the event of liquidation. The liquidation preference establishes the respective claims of creditors and preferred stockholders in litigation involving bankruptcy lawsuits.

Dividends

LEARNING OBJECTIVE　**5**

Prepare the entries for cash dividends and stock dividends.

A dividend is a corporation's distribution of cash or stock to its stockholders on a pro rata (proportional to ownership) basis. Pro rata means that if you own 10% of the common shares, you will receive 10% of the dividend. Dividends can take four forms: cash, property, scrip (a promissory note to pay cash), or stock. Cash dividends predominate in practice. Also, companies declare stock dividends with some frequency. These two forms of dividends will be the focus of discussion in this chapter.

Investors are very interested in a company's dividend practices. In the financial press, **dividends are generally reported quarterly as a dollar amount per share**. (Sometimes they are reported on an annual basis.) For example, Nike's **quarterly** dividend rate in the fourth quarter of 2010 was 27 cents per share. The dividend rate for the fourth quarter of 2010 for GE was 12 cents, and for ConAgra Foods it was 28 cents.

Cash Dividends

A **cash dividend** is a pro rata distribution of cash to stockholders. For a corporation to pay a cash dividend, it must have:

1. **Retained earnings.** The legality of a cash dividend depends on the laws of the state in which the company is incorporated. Payment of cash dividends from retained earnings is legal in all states. In general, cash dividend distributions from only the balance in common stock (legal capital) are illegal.

   A dividend declared out of paid-in capital is termed a **liquidating dividend**. Such a dividend reduces or "liquidates" the amount originally paid in by stockholders. Statutes vary considerably with respect to cash dividends based on paid-in capital in excess of par or stated value. Many states permit such dividends.

2. **Adequate cash.** The legality of a dividend and the ability to pay a dividend are two different things. For example, Nike, with retained earnings of over $4.8 billion, could legally declare a dividend of at least $4.8 billion. But Nike's cash balance is only $1.8 billion.

   Before declaring a cash dividend, a company's board of directors must carefully consider both current and future demands on the company's cash resources. In some cases, current liabilities may make a cash dividend inappropriate. In other cases, a major plant expansion program may warrant only a relatively small dividend.

3. **A declaration of dividends.** A company does not pay dividends unless its board of directors decides to do so, at which point the board "declares" the dividend. The board of directors has full authority to determine the amount of income to distribute in the form of a dividend and the amount to retain in the business. Dividends do not accrue like interest on a note payable, and they are not a liability until declared.

   The amount and timing of a dividend are important issues for management to consider. The payment of a large cash dividend could lead to liquidity problems for the company. On the other hand, a small dividend or a missed dividend may cause unhappiness among stockholders. Many stockholders expect to receive a reasonable cash payment from the company on a periodic basis. Many companies declare and pay cash dividends quarterly. On the other hand, a number of high-growth companies pay no dividends, preferring to conserve cash to finance future capital expenditures.

ENTRIES FOR CASH DIVIDENDS

Three dates are important in connection with dividends: (1) the declaration date, (2) the record date, and (3) the payment date. Normally, there are two to four weeks between each date. Companies make accounting entries on the declaration date and the payment date.

On the **declaration date**, the board of directors formally declares (authorizes) the cash dividend and announces it to stockholders. Declaration of a cash dividend **commits the corporation to a legal obligation**. The obligation is binding and cannot be rescinded. The company makes an entry to recognize the increase in Cash Dividends and the increase in the liability Dividends Payable.

To illustrate, assume that on December 1, 2014, the directors of Media General declare a 50¢ per share cash dividend on 100,000 shares of $10 par value common stock. The dividend is $50,000 (100,000 × 50¢). The entry to record the declaration is:

Declaration Date

Dec. 1	Cash Dividends	50,000	
	Dividends Payable		50,000
	(To record declaration of cash dividend)		

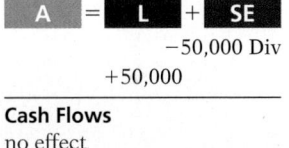

A = L + SE
$-50,000$ Div
$+50,000$

Cash Flows
no effect

Media General debits the account Cash Dividends. Cash dividends decrease retained earnings. We use the specific title Cash Dividends to differentiate it from other types of dividends, such as stock dividends. Dividends Payable is a current liability: It will normally be paid within the next several months.

When using a dividend account, the company transfers the balance of that account to Retained Earnings at the end of the year by a closing entry. Whichever account is used for the dividend declaration, the effect is the same: Retained earnings decreases, and a current liability increases. *For homework problems, you should use the Cash Dividends account for recording dividend declarations.*

At the **record date**, the company determines ownership of the outstanding shares for dividend purposes. The stockholders' records maintained by the corporation supply this information. In the interval between the declaration date and the record date, the corporation updates its stock ownership records. For Media General, the record date is December 22. No entry is required on this date because the corporation's liability recognized on the declaration date is unchanged.

Helpful Hint
The purpose of the record date is to identify the persons or entities that will receive the dividend, not to determine the amount of the dividend liability.

Record Date

| Dec. 22 | No entry necessary | | |

On the **payment date**, the company makes cash dividend payments to the stockholders of record (as of December 22) and records the payment of the dividend. If January 20 is the payment date for Media General, the entry on that date is:

Payment Date

Jan. 20	Dividends Payable	50,000	
	Cash		50,000
	(To record payment of cash dividend)		

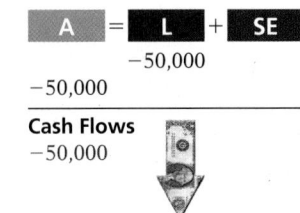

A = L + SE
$-50,000$
$-50,000$

Cash Flows
$-50,000$

Note that payment of the dividend reduces both current assets and current liabilities. It has no effect on stockholders' equity. The **cumulative effect** of the **declaration and payment** of a cash dividend is to **decrease both stockholders'**

equity and total assets. Illustration 11-12 summarizes the three important dates associated with dividends for Media General.

Illustration 11-12
Key dividend dates

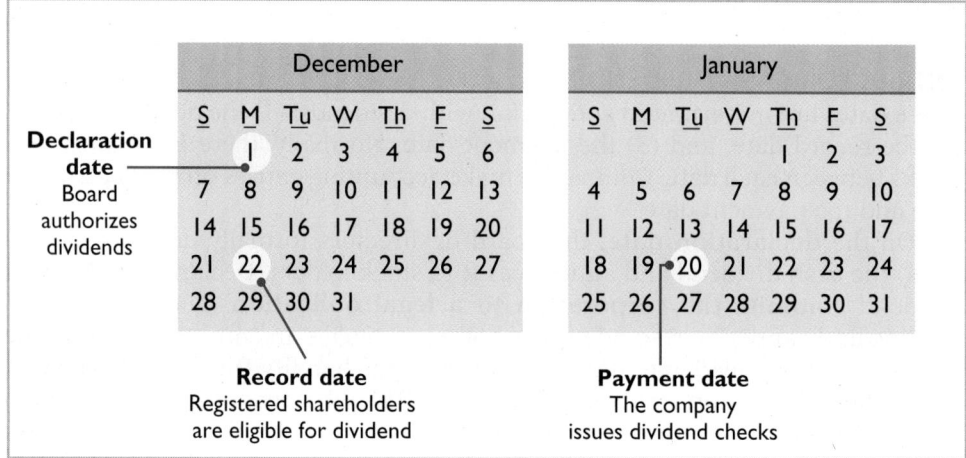

ALLOCATING CASH DIVIDENDS BETWEEN PREFERRED AND COMMON STOCK

As explained earlier in the chapter, preferred stock has priority over common stock in regard to dividends. Holders of cumulative preferred stock must be paid any unpaid prior-year dividends and its current year's dividend before common stockholders receive dividends.

To illustrate, assume that at December 31, 2014, IBR Inc. has 1,000 shares of 8%, $100 par value cumulative preferred stock. It also has 50,000 shares of $10 par value common stock outstanding. The dividend per share for preferred stock is $8 ($100 par value × 8%). The required annual dividend for preferred stock is therefore $8,000 (1,000 × $8). At December 31, 2014, the directors declare a $6,000 cash dividend. In this case, the entire dividend amount goes to preferred stockholders because of their dividend preference. The entry to record the declaration of the dividend is:

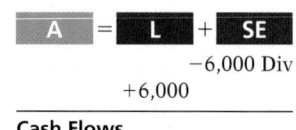

−6,000 Div
+6,000

Cash Flows
no effect

Dec. 31	Cash Dividends	6,000	
	Dividends Payable		6,000
	(To record $6 per share cash dividend		
	to preferred stockholders)		

Because of the cumulative feature, dividends of $2 ($8 − $6) per share are in arrears on preferred stock for 2014. IBR must pay these dividends to preferred stockholders before it can pay any future dividends to common stockholders. IBR should disclose dividends in arrears in the financial statements.

At December 31, 2015, IBR declares a $50,000 cash dividend. The allocation of the dividend to the two classes of stock is as follows.

Illustration 11-13
Allocating dividends to preferred and common stock

Total dividend		$50,000
Allocated to preferred stock		
Dividends in arrears, 2014 (1,000 × $2)	$2,000	
2015 dividend (1,000 × $8)	8,000	10,000
Remainder allocated to common stock		$40,000

The entry to record the declaration of the dividend is:

Dec. 31	Cash Dividends	50,000	
	Dividends Payable		50,000
	(To record declaration of cash dividends of $10,000 to preferred stock and $40,000 to common stock)		

A = L + SE
−50,000 Div
+50,000

Cash Flows
no effect

If IBR's preferred stock is not cumulative, preferred stockholders receive only $8,000 in dividends in 2015. Common stockholders receive $42,000.

ACCOUNTING ACROSS THE ORGANIZATION

Up, Down, and ??

The decision whether to pay a dividend, and how much to pay, is a very important management decision. As the chart below shows, from 2002 to 2007, many companies substantially increased their dividends, and total dividends paid by U.S. companies hit record levels. One reason for the increase is that Congress lowered, from 39% to 15%, the tax rate paid by investors on dividends received, making dividends more attractive to investors.

Then the financial crisis of 2008 occurred. As result, in 2009, 804 companies cut their dividends (see chart), the highest level since the S&P started collecting data in 1995. In 2010, more companies started to increase their dividends. However, potential higher taxes on dividends coming in the future and the possibility of a low-growth economy may stall any significant increase.

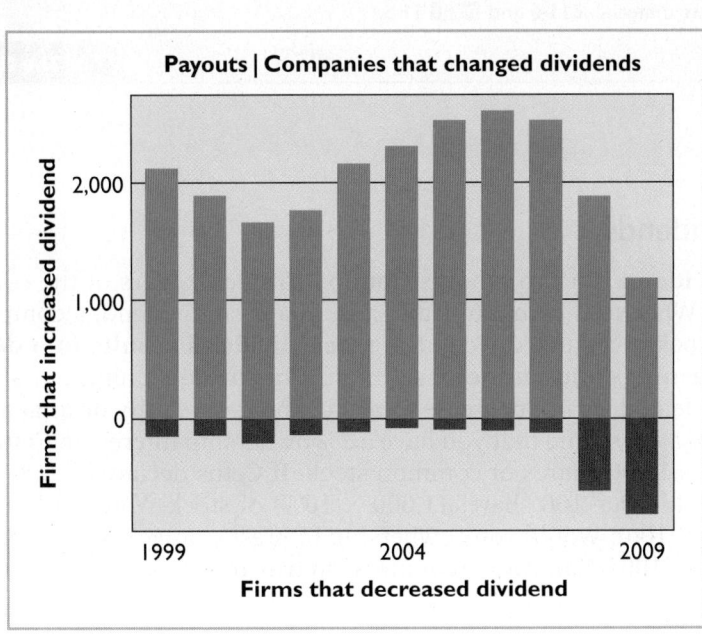

Payouts | Companies that changed dividends

Source: Matt Phillips and Jay Miller, "Last Year's Dividend Slash Was $58 Billion," *Wall Street Journal* (January 8, 2010), p. C5.

? What factors must management consider in deciding how large a dividend to pay? (See page 596.)

> DO IT!

Dividends on Preferred and Common Stock

MasterMind Corporation has 2,000 shares of 6%, $100 par value preferred stock outstanding at December 31, 2014. At December 31, 2014, the company declared a $60,000 cash dividend. Determine the dividend paid to preferred stockholders and common stockholders under each of the following scenarios.

1. The preferred stock is noncumulative, and the company has not missed any dividends in previous years.

2. The preferred stock is noncumulative, and the company did not pay a dividend in each of the two previous years.

3. The preferred stock is cumulative, and the company did not pay a dividend in each of the two previous years.

Solution

Action Plan

✔ Determine dividends on preferred shares by multiplying the dividend rate times the par value of the stock times the number of preferred shares.

✔ Understand the cumulative feature: If preferred stock is cumulative, then any missed dividends (dividends in arrears) and the current year's dividend must be paid to preferred stockholders before dividends are paid to common stockholders.

1. The company has not missed past dividends and the preferred stock is noncumulative. Thus, the preferred stockholders are paid only this year's dividend. The dividend paid to preferred stockholders would be $12,000 (2,000 × .06 × $100). The dividend paid to common stockholders would be $48,000 ($60,000 − $12,000).

2. The preferred stock is noncumulative; thus, past unpaid dividends do not have to be paid. The dividend paid to preferred stockholders would be $12,000 (2,000 × .06 × $100). The dividend paid to common stockholders would be $48,000 ($60,000 − $12,000).

3. The preferred stock is cumulative; thus, dividends that have been missed (dividends in arrears) must be paid. The dividend paid to preferred stockholders would be $36,000 (3 × 2,000 × .06 × $100). The dividend paid to common stockholders would be $24,000 ($60,000 − $36,000).

Related exercise material: **E11-6 and** DO IT! **11-5.**

 The Navigator

Stock Dividends

A **stock dividend** is a pro rata distribution to stockholders of the corporation's own stock. Whereas a company pays cash in a cash dividend, a company issues shares of stock in a stock dividend. **A stock dividend results in a decrease in retained earnings and an increase in paid-in capital.** Unlike a cash dividend, a stock dividend does not decrease total stockholders' equity or total assets.

To illustrate, assume that you have a 2% ownership interest in Cetus Inc.; you own 20 of its 1,000 shares of common stock. If Cetus declares a 10% stock dividend, it would issue 100 shares (1,000 × 10%) of stock. You would receive two shares (2% × 100). Would your ownership interest change? No, it would remain at 2% (22 ÷ 1,100). **You now own more shares of stock, but your ownership interest has not changed.** Illustration 11-14 shows the effect of a stock dividend for stockholders.

Cetus has disbursed no cash, and has assumed no liabilities. What, then, are the purposes and benefits of a stock dividend? Corporations issue stock dividends generally for one or more of the following reasons.

1. To satisfy stockholders' dividend expectations without spending cash.

2. To increase the marketability of the corporation's stock. When the number of shares outstanding increases, the market price per share decreases. Decreasing

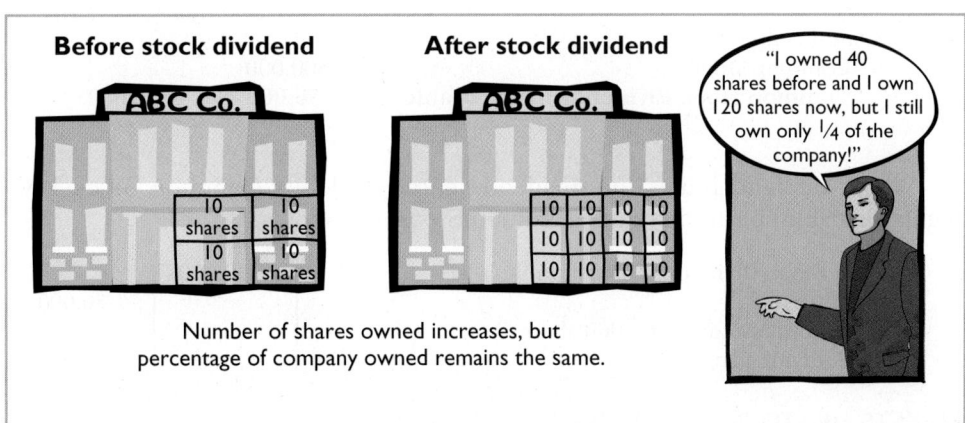

Illustration 11-14
Effect of stock dividend for
stockholders

the market price of the stock makes it easier for smaller investors to purchase the shares.

3. To emphasize that a portion of stockholders' equity has been permanently reinvested in the business (and is unavailable for cash dividends).

When the dividend is declared, the board of directors determines the size of the stock dividend and the value assigned to each dividend.

Generally, if the company issues a **small stock dividend** (less than 20–25% of the corporation's issued stock), the value assigned to the dividend is the fair value per share. This treatment is based on the assumption that a small stock dividend will have little effect on the market price of the shares previously outstanding. Thus, many stockholders consider small stock dividends to be distributions of earnings equal to the fair market value of the shares distributed. If a company issues a **large stock dividend** (greater than 20–25%), the value assigned to the dividend is the par or stated value. Small stock dividends predominate in practice. Thus, we will illustrate only entries for small stock dividends.

ENTRIES FOR STOCK DIVIDENDS

To illustrate the accounting for small stock dividends, assume that Medland Corporation has a balance of $300,000 in retained earnings. It declares a 10% stock dividend on its 50,000 shares of $10 par value common stock. The current fair market value of its stock is $15 per share. The number of shares to be issued is 5,000 (10% × 50,000). Therefore the total amount to be debited to Stock Dividends is $75,000 (5,000 × $15). The entry to record the declaration of the stock dividend is as follows.

Stock Dividends	75,000	
Common Stock Dividends Distributable		50,000
Paid-in Capital in Excess of Par—Common Stock		25,000
(To record declaration of 10% stock dividend)		

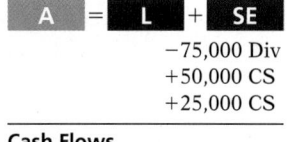

A = L + SE
−75,000 Div
+50,000 CS
+25,000 CS

Cash Flows
no effect

Medland debits Stock Dividends for the fair market value of the stock issued ($15 × 5,000). (Similar to Cash Dividends, Stock Dividends decrease retained earnings.) Medland also credits Common Stock Dividends Distributable for the par value of the dividend shares ($10 × 5,000), and credits Paid-in Capital in Excess of Par—Common Stock for the excess over par ($5 × 5,000).

Common Stock Dividends Distributable is a **stockholders' equity account**. It is not a liability because assets will not be used to pay the dividend. If the company prepares a balance sheet before it issues the dividend shares, it reports the distributable account under paid-in capital as shown in Illustration 11-15 (page 562).

Illustration 11-15
Statement presentation of common stock dividends distributable

Paid-in capital		
Common stock	$500,000	
Common stock dividends distributable	**50,000**	$550,000

When Medland issues the dividend shares, it debits Common Stock Dividends Distributable and credits Common Stock, as follows.

Common Stock Dividends Distributable	50,000	
Common Stock		50,000
(To record issuance of 5,000 shares in a		
stock dividend)		

A = L + SE

      −50,000 CS
      +50,000 CS

Cash Flows
no effect

EFFECTS OF STOCK DIVIDENDS

How do stock dividends affect stockholders' equity? They **change the composition of stockholders' equity** because they transfer to paid-in capital a portion of retained earnings. However, **total stockholders' equity remains the same.** Stock dividends also have no effect on the par or stated value per share. But, the number of shares outstanding increases. Illustration 11-16 shows these effects for Medland Corporation.

Illustration 11-16
Stock dividend effects

	Before Dividend	After Dividend
Stockholders' equity		
Paid-in capital		
Common stock, $10 par	$ 500,000	$ 550,000
Paid-in capital in excess of par—common stock	—	25,000
Total paid-in capital	500,000	575,000
Retained earnings	300,000	225,000
Total stockholders' equity	**$800,000**	**$800,000**
Outstanding shares	**50,000**	**55,000**
Par value per share	**$10.00**	**$10.00**

In this example, total paid-in capital increases by $75,000 (50,000 shares × 10% × $15) and retained earnings decreases by the same amount. Note also that total stockholders' equity remains unchanged at $800,000. The number of shares increases by 5,000 (50,000 × 10%).

Stock Splits

A stock split, like a stock dividend, involves issuance of additional shares to stockholders according to their percentage ownership. **However, a stock split results in a reduction in the par or stated value per share.** The purpose of a stock split is to increase the marketability of the stock by lowering its market price per share. This, in turn, makes it easier for the corporation to issue additional stock.

The effect of a split on market price is generally *inversely proportional* to the size of the split. For example, after a recent 2-for-1 stock split, the market price of Nike's stock fell from $111 to approximately $55. The lower market price stimulated market activity, and within one year the stock was trading above $100 again.

In a stock split, the number of shares increases in the same proportion that par or stated value per share decreases. For example, in a 2-for-1 split, one share of $10 par value stock is exchanged for two shares of $5 par value stock. **A stock split does not have any effect on total paid-in capital, retained earnings, or total stockholders' equity.** But, the number of shares outstanding increases, and par value per

Helpful Hint
A stock split changes the par value per share but does not affect any balances in stockholders' equity.

share decreases. Illustration 11-17 shows these effects for Medland Corporation, assuming that it splits its 50,000 shares of common stock on a 2-for-1 basis.

Illustration 11-17
Stock split effects

	Before Stock Split	After Stock Split
Stockholders' equity		
Paid-in capital		
Common stock	$ 500,000	$ 500,000
Paid-in capital in excess of par— common stock	–0–	–0–
Total paid-in capital	500,000	500,000
Retained earnings	300,000	300,000
Total stockholders' equity	**$800,000**	**$800,000**
Outstanding shares	50,000	100,000
Par value per share	$10.00	$5.00

A stock split does not affect the balances in any stockholders' equity accounts. Therefore **it is not necessary to journalize a stock split**.

Illustration 11-18 summarizes the differences between stock splits and stock dividends.

Illustration 11-18
Differences between the effects of stock splits and stock dividends

Item	Stock Split	Stock Dividend
Total paid-in capital	No change	Increase
Total retained earnings	No change	Decrease
Total par value (common stock)	No change	Increase
Par value per share	Decrease	No change
Total stockholders' equity	No change	No change

INVESTOR INSIGHT

A No-Split Philosophy

Warren Buffett's company, Berkshire Hathaway, has two classes of shares. Until recently, the company had never split either class of stock. As a result, the class A stock had a market price of $97,000 and the class B sold for about $3,200 per share. Because the price per share is so high, the stock does not trade as frequently as the stock of other companies. Mr. Buffett has always opposed stock splits because he feels that a lower stock price attracts short-term investors. He appears to be correct. For example, while more than 6 million shares of IBM are exchanged on the average day, only about 1,000 class A shares of Berkshire are traded. Despite Mr. Buffett's aversion to splits, in order to accomplish a recent acquisition, Berkshire decided to split its class B shares 50 to 1.

Source: Scott Patterson, "Berkshire Nears Smaller Baby B's," *Wall Street Journal Online* (January 19, 2010).

? Why does Warren Buffett usually oppose stock splits? (See page 596.)

> DO IT!

Stock Dividends and Stock Splits

Sing CD Company has had five years of record earnings. Due to this success, the market price of its 500,000 shares of $2 par value common stock has tripled from $15 per share to $45. During this period, paid-in capital remained the same at $2,000,000. Retained earnings increased from $1,500,000 to $10,000,000. President Joan Elbert is considering either

Action Plan

✔ Calculate the stock dividend's effect on retained earnings by multiplying the number of new shares times the market price of the stock (or par value for a large stock dividend).

✔ Recall that a stock dividend increases the number of shares without affecting total stockholders' equity.

✔ Recall that a stock split only increases the number of shares outstanding and decreases the par value per share.

a 10% stock dividend or a 2-for-1 stock split. She asks you to show the before-and-after effects of each option on retained earnings and total stockholders' equity.

Solution

The stock dividend amount is $2,250,000 [(500,000 × 10%) × $45]. The new balance in retained earnings is $7,750,000 ($10,000,000 − $2,250,000). The retained earnings balance after the stock split is the same as it was before the split: $10,000,000. Total stockholders' equity does not change. The effects on the stockholders' equity accounts are as follows.

	Original Balances	After Dividend	After Split
Paid-in capital	$ 2,000,000	$ 4,250,000	$ 2,000,000
Retained earnings	10,000,000	7,750,000	10,000,000
Total stockholders' equity	$12,000,000	$12,000,000	$12,000,000
Shares outstanding	500,000	550,000	1,000,000

Related exercise material: **BE11-8, BE11-9, E11-14, E11-15, and** **11-6.**

✔ **The Navigator**

Retained Earnings

Recall that **retained earnings** is net income that a company retains in the business. The balance in retained earnings is part of the stockholders' claim on the total assets of the corporation. It does not, though, represent a claim on any specific asset. Nor can the amount of retained earnings be associated with the balance of any asset account. For example, a $100,000 balance in retained earnings does not mean that there should be $100,000 in cash. The reason is that the company may have used the cash resulting from the excess of revenues over expenses to purchase buildings, equipment, and other assets.

To demonstrate that retained earnings and cash may be quite different, Illustration 11-19 shows recent amounts of retained earnings and cash in selected companies.

Illustration 11-19
Retained earnings and cash balances

	(in millions)	
Company	Retained Earnings	Cash
Disney Co.	$24,207	$3,670
Intel Corp.	28,984	6,598
Kellogg Co.	4,217	1,026
Amazon.com	(1,837)	1,022

Helpful Hint
Remember that Retained Earnings is a stockholders' equity account, whose normal balance is a credit.

Remember that when a company has net income, it closes net income to retained earnings. The closing entry is a debit to Income Summary and a credit to Retained Earnings.

When a company has a **net loss** (expenses exceed revenues), it also closes this amount to retained earnings. The closing entry in this case is a debit to Retained Earnings and a credit to Income Summary. This is done even if it results in a debit balance in Retained Earnings. **Companies do not debit net losses to paid-in capital accounts.** To do so would destroy the distinction between paid-in and earned capital. If cumulative losses exceed cumulative income over a company's life, a debit balance in Retained Earnings results. A debit balance in Retained Earnings is identified as a **deficit**. A company reports a deficit as a deduction in the stockholders' equity section, as shown below.

Balance Sheet (partial)

Stockholders' equity	
Paid-in capital	
Common stock	$800,000
Retained earnings (deficit)	**(50,000)**
Total stockholders' equity	$750,000

Illustration 11-20
Stockholders' equity with deficit

Retained Earnings Restrictions

The balance in retained earnings is generally available for dividend declarations. Some companies state this fact. For example, Lockheed Martin Corporation states the following in the notes to its financial statements.

Lockheed Martin Corporation
Notes to the Financial Statements

At December 31, retained earnings were unrestricted and available for dividend payments.

Illustration 11-21
Disclosure of unrestricted retained earnings

In some cases, there may be **retained earnings restrictions**. These make a portion of the retained earnings balance currently unavailable for dividends. Restrictions result from one or more of the following causes.

1. **Legal restrictions.** Many states require a corporation to restrict retained earnings for the cost of treasury stock purchased. The restriction keeps intact the corporation's legal capital that is being temporarily held as treasury stock. When the company sells the treasury stock, the restriction is lifted.

2. **Contractual restrictions.** Long-term debt contracts may restrict retained earnings as a condition for the loan. The restriction limits the use of corporate assets for payment of dividends. Thus, it increases the likelihood that the corporation will be able to meet required loan payments.

3. **Voluntary restrictions.** The board of directors may voluntarily create retained earnings restrictions for specific purposes. For example, the board may authorize a restriction for future plant expansion. By reducing the amount of retained earnings available for dividends, the company makes more cash available for the planned expansion.

Companies generally disclose **retained earnings restrictions** in the notes to the financial statements. For example, as shown in Illustration 11-22 (page 566), Tektronix Inc., a manufacturer of electronic measurement devices, had total retained earnings of $774 million, but the unrestricted portion was only $223.8 million.

Illustration 11-22
Disclosure of restriction

Tektronix Inc.
Notes to the Financial Statements

Certain of the Company's debt agreements require compliance with debt covenants. Management believes that the Company is in compliance with such requirements. The Company had unrestricted retained earnings of $223.8 million after meeting those requirements.

Prior Period Adjustments

Suppose that a corporation has closed its books and issued financial statements. The corporation then discovers that it made a material error in reporting net income of a prior year. How should the company record this situation in the accounts and report it in the financial statements?

The correction of an error in previously issued financial statements is known as a **prior period adjustment**. The company makes the correction directly to Retained Earnings, because the effect of the error is now in this account. The net income for the prior period has been recorded in retained earnings through the journalizing and posting of closing entries.

To illustrate, assume that General Microwave discovers in 2014 that it understated depreciation expense on equipment in 2013 by $300,000 due to computational errors. These errors overstated both net income for 2013 and the current balance in retained earnings. The entry for the prior period adjustment, ignoring all tax effects, is as follows.

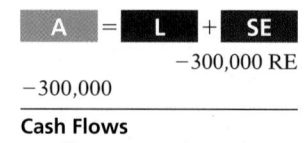

A = L + SE
−300,000 RE
−300,000

Cash Flows
no effect

Retained Earnings	300,000	
Accumulated Depreciation—Equipment		300,000
(To adjust for understatement of depreciation		
in a prior period)		

A debit to an income statement account in 2014 is incorrect because the error pertains to a prior year.

Companies report prior period adjustments in the retained earnings statement.[4] They add (or deduct, as the case may be) these adjustments from the beginning retained earnings balance. This results in an adjusted beginning balance. For example, assuming a beginning balance of $800,000 in retained earnings, General Microwave reports the prior period adjustment as follows.

Illustration 11-23
Statement presentation of prior period adjustments

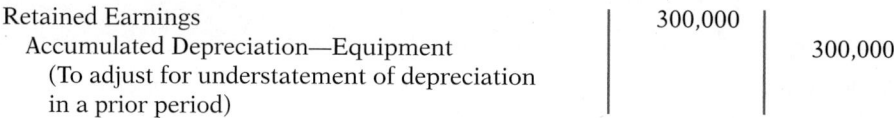

General Microwave
Retained Earnings Statement (partial)

Balance, January 1, as reported	$ 800,000
Correction for overstatement of net income	
in prior period (depreciation error)	**(300,000)**
Balance, January 1, as adjusted	$ 500,000

Again, reporting the correction in the current year's income statement would be incorrect because it applies to a prior year's income statement.

---

[4] A complete retained earnings statement is shown in Illustration 11-25 on the next page.

Retained Earnings Statement

The **retained earnings statement** shows the changes in retained earnings during the year. The company prepares the statement from the Retained Earnings account. Illustration 11-24 shows (in account form) transactions that affect retained earnings.

Retained Earnings

1. Net loss	1. Net income
2. Prior period adjustments for overstatement of net income	2. Prior period adjustments for understatement of net income
3. Cash dividends and stock dividends	
4. Some disposals of treasury stock	

Illustration 11-24
Debits and credits to retained earnings

As indicated, net income increases retained earnings, and a net loss decreases retained earnings. Prior period adjustments may either increase or decrease retained earnings. Both cash dividends and stock dividends decrease retained earnings. The circumstances under which treasury stock transactions decrease retained earnings are explained on page 565.

A complete retained earnings statement for Graber Inc., based on assumed data, is as follows.

Illustration 11-25
Retained earnings statement

Graber Inc.
Retained Earnings Statement
For the Year Ended December 31, 2014

Balance, January 1, as reported		$1,050,000
Correction for understatement of net income in prior period (inventory error)		50,000
Balance, January 1, as adjusted		1,100,000
Add: Net income		360,000
		1,460,000
Less: Cash dividends	$100,000	
Stock dividends	200,000	300,000
Balance, December 31		$1,160,000

> ## DO IT!

Retained Earnings Statement

Vega Corporation has retained earnings of $5,130,000 on January 1, 2014. During the year, Vega earned $2,000,000 of net income. It declared and paid a $250,000 cash dividend. In 2014, Vega recorded an adjustment of $180,000 due to the understatement (from a mathematical error) of 2013 depreciation expense. Prepare a retained earnings statement for 2014.

Action Plan

✔ Recall that a retained earnings statement begins with retained earnings, as reported at the end of the previous year.

✔ Add or subtract any prior period adjustments to arrive at the adjusted beginning figure.

✔ Add net income and subtract dividends declared to arrive at the ending balance in retained earnings.

Solution

Vega Corporation Retained Earnings Statement For the Year Ended December 31, 2014	
Balance, January 1, as reported	$5,130,000
Correction for overstatement of net income in prior period (depreciation error)	(180,000)
Balance, January 1, as adjusted	4,950,000
Add: Net income	2,000,000
	6,950,000
Less: Cash dividends	250,000
Balance, December 31	$6,700,000

Related exercise material: **BE11-10, BE11-11, E11-17, E11-18, and DO IT! 11-7.**

✔ **The Navigator**

Statement Presentation and Analysis

LEARNING OBJECTIVE   7

Prepare and analyze a comprehensive stockholders' equity section.

In the stockholders' equity section of the balance sheet, paid-in capital and retained earnings are reported. The specific sources of paid-in capital are identified. Within paid-in capital, two classifications are recognized:

1. **Capital stock.** This category consists of preferred and common stock. Preferred stock is shown before common stock because of its preferential rights. Par value, shares authorized, shares issued, and shares outstanding are reported for each class of stock.

2. **Additional paid-in capital.** This includes the excess of amounts paid over par or stated value and paid-in capital from treasury stock.

Presentation

Illustration 11-26 presents the stockholders' equity section of Graber Inc.'s balance sheet. Note the following: (1) "Common stock dividends distributable" is shown under "Capital stock," in "Paid-in capital." (2) A note (Note R) discloses a retained earnings restriction.

Illustration 11-26
Comprehensive stockholders' equity section

Graber Inc. Balance Sheet (partial)		
Stockholders' equity		
Paid-in capital		
Capital stock		
9% Preferred stock, $100 par value, cumulative, callable at $120, 10,000 shares authorized, 6,000 shares issued and outstanding		$ 600,000
Common stock, no par, $5 stated value, 500,000 shares authorized, 400,000 shares issued and 390,000 outstanding	$2,000,000	
Common stock dividends distributable	**50,000**	2,050,000
Total capital stock		2,650,000

Illustration 11-26
(cont'd.)

Additional paid-in capital		
In excess of par—preferred stock	30,000	
In excess of stated value—common stock	1,050,000	
Total additional paid-in capital		1,080,000
Total paid-in capital		3,730,000
Retained earnings (see Note R)		1,160,000
Total paid-in capital and retained earnings		4,890,000
Less: Treasury stock (10,000 common shares)		80,000
Total stockholders' equity		$4,810,000

Note R: Retained earnings is restricted for the cost of treasury stock, $80,000.

The stockholders' equity section of Graber Inc. in Illustration 11-26 includes most of the accounts discussed in this chapter. The disclosures pertaining to Graber's common stock indicate that the company issued 400,000 shares; 100,000 shares are unissued (500,000 authorized less 400,000 issued); and 390,000 shares are outstanding (400,000 issued less 10,000 shares in treasury).

Published annual reports often combine and report as a single amount the individual sources of additional paid-in capital, as shown in Illustration 11-27. In addition, authorized shares are sometimes not reported.

Illustration 11-27
Published stockholders'
equity section

Kellogg Company
Balance Sheet (partial)
($ in millions)

Stockholders' equity	
Common stock, $0.25 par value, 1,000,000,000 shares authorized	
Issued: 418,669,193 shares	$ 105
Capital in excess of par value	388
Retained earnings	4,217
Treasury stock, at cost 28,618,052 shares	(1,357)
Accumulated other comprehensive income (loss)	(827)
Total stockholders' equity	$ 2,526

In practice, companies sometimes use the term "Capital surplus" in place of "Additional paid-in capital," and "Earned surplus" in place of "Retained earnings." The use of the term "surplus" suggests that the company has available an excess amount of funds. Such is not necessarily the case. Therefore, **the term "surplus" should not be employed in accounting**. Unfortunately, a number of companies still do use it.

Instead of presenting a detailed stockholders' equity section in the balance sheet and a retained earnings statement, many companies prepare a **stockholders' equity statement**. This statement shows the changes (1) in each stockholders' equity account and (2) in total that occurred during the year. An example of a stockholders' equity statement appears in PepsiCo's financial statements in Appendix A (page A-7) and in an appendix to this chapter (Illustration 11A-1).

Analysis

Investors and analysts can measure profitability from the viewpoint of the common stockholder by the **return on common stockholders' equity**. This ratio shows how many dollars of net income the company earned for each dollar invested by the common stockholders. It is computed by dividing **net income available to**

common stockholders (which is net income minus preferred stock dividends) by average common stockholders' equity.

To illustrate, Walt Disney Company's beginning-of-the-year and end-of-the-year common stockholders' equity were $31,820 and $30,753 million, respectively. Its net income was $4,687 million, and no preferred stock was outstanding. The return on common stockholders' equity ratio is computed as follows.

Illustration 11-28
Return on common stockholders' equity ratio and computation

Net Income Available to Common Stockholders	÷	Average Common Stockholders' Equity	=	Return on Common Stockholders' Equity
($4,687 − $0)	÷	$\dfrac{(\$31{,}820 + \$30{,}753)}{2}$	=	15.0%

As shown above, if a company has preferred stock, we would deduct the amount of **preferred dividends** from the company's net income to compute income available to common stockholders. Also, the par value of preferred stock is deducted from total average stockholders' equity to arrive at the amount of common stockholders' equity.

> DO IT!

Stockholders' Equity and EPS

On January 1, 2014, Siena Corporation purchased 2,000 shares of treasury stock. Other information regarding Siena Corporation is provided below.

	2013	2014
Net income	$110,000	$110,000
Dividends on preferred stock	$10,000	$10,000
Dividends on common stock	$2,000	$1,600
Weighted-average number of shares outstanding	10,000	8,000*
Common stockholders' equity, beginning of year	$500,000	$400,000*
Common stockholders' equity, end of year	$500,000	$400,000

*Adjusted for purchase of treasury stock.

Compute (a) return on common stockholders' equity for each year and (b) earnings per share for each year, and (c) discuss the changes in each.

Solution

Action Plan

✔ Determine return on common stockholders' equity by dividing net income available to common stockholders by the average common stockholders' equity.

✔ Determine earnings per share by dividing net income available to common stockholders by the weighted-average number of common shares outstanding.

(a)

	2013	**2014**
Return on common stockholders' equity	$\dfrac{(\$110{,}000 - \$10{,}000)}{(\$500{,}000 + \$500{,}000)/2} = 20\%$	$\dfrac{(\$110{,}000 - \$10{,}000)}{(\$400{,}000 + \$400{,}000)/2} = 25\%$

(b)

Earnings per share	$\dfrac{(\$110{,}000 - \$10{,}000)}{10{,}000} = \$10$	$\dfrac{(\$110{,}000 - \$10{,}000)}{8{,}000} = \$12.50$

(c) Between 2013 and 2014, return on common stockholders' equity improved from 20% to 25%. Earnings per share increased from $10 to $12.50. While this would appear to be good news for the company's common stockholders, these increases should be carefully evaluated. It is important to note that net income did not change during this period. The increase in both ratios was due to the purchase of treasury shares, which reduced the denominator of each ratio. As the company repurchases its own shares, it becomes more reliant on debt and thus increases its risk.

Related exercise material: **E11-22 and** DO IT! **11-8.**

✔ The Navigator

> Comprehensive **DO IT!**

Rolman Corporation is authorized to issue 1,000,000 shares of $5 par value common stock. In its first year, the company has the following stock transactions.

Jan. 10   Issued 400,000 shares of stock at $8 per share.
July 1   Issued 100,000 shares of stock for land. The land had an asking price of $900,000. The stock is currently selling on a national exchange at $8.25 per share.
Sept. 1   Purchased 10,000 shares of common stock for the treasury at $9 per share.
Dec. 1   Sold 4,000 shares of the treasury stock at $10 per share.

Instructions
(a) Journalize the transactions.
(b) Prepare the stockholders' equity section assuming the company had retained earnings of $200,000 at December 31.

Solution to Comprehensive DO IT!

Action Plan

✔ When common stock has a par value, credit Common Stock for par value.
✔ Use fair value in a noncash transaction.
✔ Debit and credit the Treasury Stock account at cost.
✔ Record differences between the cost and selling price of treasury stock in stockholders' equity accounts, not as gains or losses.

(a)				
Jan. 10	Cash		3,200,000	
	Common Stock			2,000,000
	Paid-in Capital in Excess of Par— Common Stock			1,200,000
	(To record issuance of 400,000 shares of $5 par value stock)			
July 1	Land		825,000	
	Common Stock			500,000
	Paid-in Capital in Excess of Par— Common Stock			325,000
	(To record issuance of 100,000 shares of $5 par value stock for land)			
Sept. 1	Treasury Stock		90,000	
	Cash			90,000
	(To record purchase of 10,000 shares of treasury stock at cost)			
Dec. 1	Cash		40,000	
	Treasury Stock			36,000
	Paid-in Capital from Treasury Stock			4,000
	(To record sale of 4,000 shares of treasury stock above cost)			

(b)
Rolman Corporation
Balance Sheet (partial)

Stockholders' equity		
Paid-in capital		
Capital stock		
Common stock, $5 par value, 1,000,000 shares authorized, 500,000 shares issued, 494,000 shares outstanding		$2,500,000
Additional paid-in capital		
In excess of par—common stock	$1,525,000	
From treasury stock	4,000	
Total additional paid-in capital		1,529,000
Total paid-in capital		4,029,000
Retained earnings		200,000
Total paid-in capital and retained earnings		4,229,000
Less: Treasury stock (6,000 shares)		(54,000)
Total stockholders' equity		$4,175,000

✔ The Navigator

SUMMARY OF LEARNING OBJECTIVES

1 Identify the major characteristics of a corporation. The major characteristics of a corporation are separate legal existence, limited liability of stockholders, transferable ownership rights, ability to acquire capital, continuous life, corporation management, government regulations, and additional taxes.

2 Record the issuance of common stock. When the issuance of common stock for cash is recorded, the par value of the shares is credited to Common Stock. The portion of the proceeds that is above or below par value is recorded in a separate paid-in capital account. When no-par common stock has a stated value, the entries are similar to those for par value stock. When no-par stock does not have a stated value, the entire proceeds are credited to Common Stock.

3 Explain the accounting for treasury stock. The cost method is generally used in accounting for treasury stock. Under this approach, Treasury Stock is debited at the price paid to reacquire the shares. The same amount is credited to Treasury Stock when the shares are sold. The difference between the sales price and cost is recorded in stockholders' equity accounts, not in income statement accounts.

4 Differentiate preferred stock from common stock. Preferred stock has contractual provisions that give it priority over common stock in certain areas. Typically, preferred stockholders have a preference to (1) dividends and (2) assets in liquidation. They usually do not have voting rights.

5 Prepare the entries for cash dividends and stock dividends. Entries for both cash and stock dividends are required on the declaration date and the payment date. At the *declaration date* the entries are cash dividend—debit Cash Dividends and credit Dividends Payable; small stock dividend—debit Stock Dividends, credit Paid-in Capital in Excess of Par (or Stated Value) and credit Common Stock Dividends Distributable. On the *payment date*, the entries for cash and stock dividends are cash dividend—debit Dividends Payable and credit Cash; small stock dividend—debit Common Stock Dividends Distributable and credit Common Stock.

6 Identify the items that are reported in a retained earnings statement. Each of the individual debits and credits to retained earnings should be reported in the retained earnings statement. Additions consist of net income and prior period adjustments to correct understatements of prior years' net income. Deductions consist of net loss, adjustments to correct overstatements of prior years' net income, cash and stock dividends, and some disposals of treasury stock.

7 Prepare and analyze a comprehensive stockholders' equity section. In the stockholders' equity section, paid-in capital and retained earnings are reported and specific sources of paid-in capital are identified. Within paid-in capital, two classifications are shown: capital stock and additional paid-in capital. If a corporation has treasury stock, the cost of treasury stock is deducted from total paid-in capital and retained earnings to obtain total stockholders' equity. One measure of profitability is the return on common stockholders' equity. It is calculated by dividing net income minus preferred stock dividends by average common stockholders' equity.

GLOSSARY

Authorized stock The amount of stock that a corporation is authorized to sell as indicated in its charter. (p. 543).

Cash dividend A pro rata distribution of cash to stockholders. (p. 556).

Charter A document that is issued by a state to set forth important terms and features regarding the creation of a corporation. (p. 541).

Corporation A business organized as a legal entity separate and distinct from its owners under state corporation law. (p. 538).

Cumulative dividend A feature of preferred stock entitling the stockholder to receive current and unpaid prior-year dividends before common stockholders receive any dividends. (p. 555).

Declaration date The date the board of directors formally declares the dividend and announces it to stockholders. (p. 557).

Deficit A debit balance in retained earnings. (p. 565).

Dividend A corporation's distribution of cash or stock to its stockholders on a pro rata (proportional) basis. (p. 556).

Liquidating dividend A dividend declared out of paid-in capital. (p. 556).

No-par value stock Capital stock that has not been assigned a value in the corporate charter. (p. 545).

Organization costs Costs incurred in the formation of a corporation. (p. 541).

Outstanding stock Capital stock that has been issued and is being held by stockholders. (p. 552).

Paid-in capital Total amount of cash and other assets paid in to the corporation by stockholders in exchange for capital stock. (p. 546).

Par value stock Capital stock that has been assigned a value per share in the corporate charter. (p. 545).

Payment date The date dividend checks are mailed to stockholders. (p. 557).

Preferred stock Capital stock that has some contractual preferences over common stock. (p. 554).

Prior period adjustment The correction of an error in previously issued financial statements. (p. 566).

Privately held corporation A corporation that has only a few stockholders and whose stock is not available for sale to the general public. (p. 538).

Publicly held corporation A corporation that may have thousands of stockholders and whose stock is regularly traded on a national securities exchange. (p. 538).

Record date The date when ownership of outstanding shares is determined for dividend purposes. (p. 557).

Retained earnings Net income that a corporation retains for future use. (p. 546).

Retained earnings restrictions Circumstances that make a portion of retained earnings currently unavailable for dividends. (p. 565).

Retained earnings statement A financial statement that shows the changes in retained earnings during the year. (p. 567).

Return on common stockholders' equity ratio A ratio that measures profitability from the stockholders' point of view. It is computed by dividing net income available to common stockholders by average common stockholders' equity. (p. 569).

Stated value The amount per share assigned by the board of directors to no-par stock that becomes legal capital per share. (p. 545).

Stock dividend A pro rata distribution of the corporation's own stock to stockholders. (p. 560).

Stockholders' equity statement A statement that shows the changes in each stockholders' equity account and in total stockholders' equity during the year. (p. 569).

Stock split The issuance of additional shares of stock to stockholders accompanied by a reduction in the par or stated value per share. (p. 562).

Treasury stock A corporation's own stock that the corporation has issued and reacquired but not retired. (p. 551).

APPENDIX 11A   STOCKHOLDERS' EQUITY STATEMENT

When balance sheets and income statements are presented by a corporation, changes in the separate accounts comprising stockholders' equity should also be disclosed. Disclosure of such changes is necessary to make the financial statements sufficiently informative for users. The disclosures may be made in an additional statement or in the notes to the financial statements.

Many corporations make the disclosures in a **stockholders' equity statement**. The statement shows the changes in **each** stockholders' equity account and in **total** stockholders' equity during the year. As shown in Illustration 11A-1, the stockholders' equity statement is prepared in columnar form. It contains columns for each account and for total stockholders' equity. The transactions are then identified and their effects are shown in the appropriate columns.

LEARNING OBJECTIVE 8

Describe the use and content of the stockholders' equity statement.

Illustration 11A-1
Stockholders' equity statement

Hampton Corporation
Stockholders' Equity Statement
For the Year Ended December 31, 2014

	Common Stock ($5 Par)	Paid-in Capital in Excess of Par—Common Stock	Retained Earnings	Treasury Stock	Total
Balance January 1	$300,000	$200,000	$650,000	$(34,000)	$1,116,000
Issued 5,000 shares of common stock at $15	25,000	50,000			75,000
Declared a $40,000 cash dividend			(40,000)		(40,000)
Purchased 2,000 shares for treasury at $16				(32,000)	(32,000)
Net income for year			240,000		240,000
Balance December 31	$325,000	$250,000	$850,000	$(66,000)	$1,359,000

In practice, additional columns are usually provided to show the number of shares of issued stock and treasury stock. The stockholders' equity statement for PepsiCo, for a three-year period, is shown in Appendix A. **When a stockholders' equity statement is presented, a retained earnings statement is not necessary** because the retained earnings column explains the changes in this account.

SUMMARY OF LEARNING OBJECTIVE FOR APPENDIX 11A

 The Navigator

8 Describe the use and content of the stockholders' equity statement. Corporations must disclose changes in stockholders' equity accounts and may choose to do so by issuing a separate stockholders' equity statement. This statement, prepared in columnar form, shows changes in each stockholders' equity account and in total stockholders' equity during the accounting period. When this statement is presented, a retained earnings statement is not necessary.

APPENDIX **11B** BOOK VALUE—ANOTHER PER SHARE AMOUNT

Book Value per Share

LEARNING OBJECTIVE   9

Compute book value per share.

You have learned about a number of per share amounts in this chapter. Another per share amount of some importance is **book value per share**. It represents **the equity a common stockholder has in the net assets of the corporation** from owning one share of stock. Remember that the net assets (total assets minus total liabilities) of a corporation must be equal to total stockholders' equity. Therefore, the formula for computing book value per share when a company has only one class of stock outstanding is:

Illustration 11B-1
Book value per share formula

Total Stockholders' Equity	÷	Number of Common Shares Outstanding	=	Book Value per Share

Thus, if Marlo Corporation has total stockholders' equity of $1,500,000 (common stock $1,000,000 and retained earnings $500,000) and 50,000 shares of common stock outstanding, book value per share is $30 ($1,500,000 ÷ 50,000).

When a company has both preferred and common stock, the computation of book value is more complex. Since preferred stockholders have a prior claim on net assets over common stockholders, their equity must be deducted from total stockholders' equity. Then we can determine the stockholders' equity that applies to the common stock. The computation of book value per share involves the following steps.

1. **Compute the preferred stock equity.** This equity is equal to the sum of the call price of preferred stock plus any cumulative dividends in arrears. If the preferred stock does not have a call price, the par value of the stock is used.

2. **Determine the common stock equity.** Subtract the preferred stock equity from total stockholders' equity.

3. **Determine book value per share.** Divide common stock equity by shares of common stock outstanding.

EXAMPLE

We will use the stockholders' equity section of Graber Inc. shown in Illustration 11-26. Graber's preferred stock is callable at $120 per share and is cumulative. Assume that dividends on Graber's preferred stock were in arrears for one year, $54,000 (6,000 × $9). The computation of preferred stock equity (Step 1 in the preceding list) is:

Call price (6,000 shares × $120)	$720,000	**Illustration 11B-2**
Dividends in arrears (6,000 shares × $9)	54,000	Computation of preferred stock equity—Step 1
Preferred stock equity	**$774,000**	

The computation of book value (Steps 2 and 3) is as follows.

Total stockholders' equity	$4,810,000	**Illustration 11B-3**
Less: **Preferred stock equity**	774,000	Computation of book value per share with preferred
Common stock equity	**$4,036,000**	stock—Steps 2 and 3
Shares of common stock outstanding	390,000	
Book value per share ($4,036,000 ÷ 390,000)	**$10.35**	

Note that we used the call price of $120 instead of the par value of $100. Note also that the paid-in capital in excess of par value of preferred stock, $30,000, **is not assigned to the preferred stock equity**. Preferred stockholders ordinarily do not have a right to amounts paid-in in excess of par value. Therefore, such amounts are assigned to the common stock equity in computing book value.

Book Value versus Market Value

Be sure you understand that **book value per share may not equal market value per share**. Book value generally is based on recorded costs. Market value reflects the subjective judgments of thousands of stockholders and prospective investors about a company's potential for future earnings and dividends. Market value per share may exceed book value per share, but that fact does not necessarily mean that the stock is overpriced. The correlation between book value and the annual range of a company's market value per share is often remote, as indicated by the following recent data.

Company	Book Value (year-end)	Market Range (for the year)	
The Limited, Inc.	$13.38	$31.03–$22.89	**Illustration 11B-4**
H. J. Heinz Company	$ 7.48	$40.61–$34.53	Book and market values compared
Cisco Systems	$ 3.66	$21.24–$17.01	
Wal-Mart Stores	$12.79	$50.87–$42.31	

Book value per share **is useful** in determining the trend of a stockholder's per share equity in a corporation. It is also significant in many contracts and in court cases where the rights of individual parties are based on cost information.

SUMMARY OF LEARNING OBJECTIVE FOR APPENDIX 11B

✔ **The Navigator**

9 Compute book value per share. Book value per share represents the equity a common stockholder has in the net assets of a corporation from owning one share of stock. When there is only common stock outstanding, the formula for computing book value is: Total stockholders' equity ÷ Number of common shares outstanding = Book value per share.

GLOSSARY FOR APPENDIX 11B

Book value per share The equity a common stockholder has in the net assets of the corporation from owning one share of stock. (p. 574).

 **Self-Test, Brief Exercises, Exercises, Problem Set A, and many more components are available for practice in WileyPLUS.**

Note: All asterisked Questions, Exercises, and Problems relate to material in the appendices to the chapter.

SELF-TEST QUESTIONS

Answers are on page 596.

(LO 1) **1.** Which of the following is *not* a major advantage of a corporation?
    (a) Separate legal existence.
    (b) Continuous life.
    (c) Government regulations.
    (d) Transferable ownership rights.

(LO 1) **2.** A major disadvantage of a corporation is:
    (a) limited liability of stockholders.
    (b) additional taxes.
    (c) transferable ownership rights.
    (d) None of the above.

(LO 2) **3.** Which of the following statements is *false*?
    (a) Ownership of common stock gives the owner a voting right.
    (b) The stockholders' equity section begins with paid-in capital.
    (c) The authorization of capital stock does not result in a formal accounting entry.
    (d) Legal capital per share applies to par value stock but not to no-par value stock.

(LO 2) **4.** ABC Corporation issues 1,000 shares of $10 par value common stock at $12 per share. In recording the transaction, credits are made to:
    (a) Common Stock $10,000 and Paid-in Capital in Excess of Stated Value $2,000.
    (b) Common Stock $12,000.
    (c) Common Stock $10,000 and Paid-in Capital in Excess of Par $2,000.
    (d) Common Stock $10,000 and Retained Earnings $2,000.

(LO 3) **5.** XYZ, Inc. sells 100 shares of $5 par value treasury stock at $13 per share. If the cost of acquiring the shares was $10 per share, the entry for the sale should include credits to:
    (a) Treasury Stock $1,000 and Paid-in Capital from Treasury Stock $300.
    (b) Treasury Stock $500 and Paid-in Capital from Treasury Stock $800.
    (c) Treasury Stock $1,000 and Retained Earnings $300.
    (d) Treasury Stock $500 and Paid-in Capital in Excess of Par $800.

(LO 3) **6.** In the stockholders' equity section, the cost of treasury stock is deducted from:
    (a) total paid-in capital and retained earnings.
    (b) retained earnings.
    (c) total stockholders' equity.
    (d) common stock in paid-in capital.

(LO 4) **7.** Preferred stock may have priority over common stock *except* in:
    (a) dividends.
    (b) assets in the event of liquidation.
    (c) cumulative dividend features.
    (d) voting.

(LO 4, 5) **8.** M-Bot Corporation has 10,000 shares of 8%, $100 par value, cumulative preferred stock outstanding at December 31, 2014. No dividends were declared in 2012 or 2013. If M-Bot wants to pay $375,000 of dividends in 2014, common stockholders will receive:
    (a) $0.   (c) $215,000.
    (b) $295,000.   (d) $135,000.

(LO 5) **9.** Entries for cash dividends are required on the:
  (a) declaration date and the payment date.
  (b) record date and the payment date.
  (c) declaration date, record date, and payment date.
  (d) declaration date and the record date.

(LO 5) **10.** Which of the following statements about small stock dividends is *true*?
  (a) A debit to Retained Earnings for the par value of the shares issued should be made.
  (b) A small stock dividend decreases total stockholders' equity.
  (c) Market price per share should be assigned to the dividend shares.
  (d) A small stock dividend ordinarily will have an effect on par value per share of stock.

(LO 6) **11.** All *but one* of the following is reported in a retained earnings statement. The exception is:
  (a) cash and stock dividends.
  (b) net income and net loss.
  (c) sales revenue.
  (d) prior period adjustments.

(LO 6) **12.** A prior period adjustment is:
  (a) reported in the income statement as a nontypical item.
  (b) a correction of an error that is recorded directly to retained earnings.
  (c) reported directly in the stockholders' equity section.
  (d) reported in the retained earnings statement as an adjustment of the ending balance of retained earnings.

(LO 7) **13.** In the stockholders' equity section of the balance sheet, common stock:
  (a) is listed before preferred stock.
  (b) is added to total capital stock.
  (c) is part of paid-in capital.
  (d) is part of additional paid-in capital.

14. Which of the following is *not* reported under additional paid-in capital? (LO 7)
  (a) Paid-in capital in excess of par value.
  (b) Common stock.
  (c) Paid-in capital in excess of stated value.
  (d) Paid-in capital from treasury stock.

15. Katie Inc. reported net income of $186,000 during (LO 7) 2014 and paid dividends of $26,000 on common stock. It also has 10,000 shares of 6%, $100 par value, noncumulative preferred stock outstanding. Common stockholders' equity was $1,200,000 on January 1, 2014, and $1,600,000 on December 31, 2014. The company's return on common stockholders' equity for 2014 is:
  (a) 10.0%.   (c) 7.1%.
  (b) 9.0%.   (d) 13.3%.

***16.** When a stockholders' equity statement is presented, (LO 8) it is not necessary to prepare a (an):
  (a) retained earnings statement.
  (b) balance sheet.
  (c) income statement.
  (d) None of the above.

***17.** The ledger of JFK, Inc. shows common stock, common treasury stock, and no preferred stock. For this (LO 9) company, the formula for computing book value per share is:
  (a) total paid-in capital and retained earnings divided by the number of shares of common stock issued.
  (b) common stock divided by the number of shares of common stock issued.
  (c) total stockholders' equity divided by the number of shares of common stock outstanding.
  (d) total stockholders' equity divided by the number of shares of common stock issued.

Go to the book's companion website, www.wiley.com/college/weygandt, for additional Self-Test Questions.

✔ **The Navigator**

QUESTIONS

1. Mark Adler, a student, asks your help in understanding the following characteristics of a corporation: (a) separate legal existence, (b) limited liability of stockholders, and (c) transferable ownership rights. Explain these characteristics to Mark.

2. (a) Your friend Paula Leuck cannot understand how the characteristic of corporation management is both an advantage and a disadvantage. Clarify this problem for Paula.
  (b) Identify and explain two other disadvantages of a corporation.

3. (a) The following terms pertain to the forming of a corporation: (1) charter, (2) by-laws, and (3) organization costs. Explain the terms.

  (b) Lisa Bast believes a corporation must be incorporated in the state in which its headquarters' office is located. Is Lisa correct? Explain.

4. What are the basic ownership rights of common stockholders in the absence of restrictive provisions?

5. A corporation has been defined as an entity separate and distinct from its owners. In what ways is a corporation a separate legal entity?

6. (a) What are the two principal components of stockholders' equity?
  (b) What is paid-in capital? Give three examples.

7. The corporate charter of Keller Corporation allows the issuance of a maximum of 100,000 shares of common stock. During its first two years of operations, Keller sold 70,000 shares to shareholders and reacquired 7,000 of these shares. After these transactions, how many shares are authorized, issued, and outstanding?

8. Which is the better investment—common stock with a par value of $5 per share, or common stock with a par value of $20 per share? Why?

9. What factors help determine the market value of stock?

10. Why is common stock usually not issued at a price that is less than par value?

11. Land appraised at $84,000 is purchased by issuing 1,000 shares of $10 par value common stock. The market price of the shares at the time of the exchange, based on active trading in the securities market, is $95 per share. Should the land be recorded at $10,000, $84,000, or $95,000? Explain.

12. For what reasons might a company like IBM repurchase some of its stock (treasury stock)?

13. Luz, Inc. purchases 1,000 shares of its own previously issued $5 par common stock for $9,000. Assuming the shares are held in the treasury, what effect does this transaction have on (a) net income, (b) total assets, (c) total paid-in capital, and (d) total stockholders' equity?

14. The treasury stock purchased in Question 13 is resold by Luz, Inc. for $13,000. What effect does this transaction have on (a) net income, (b) total assets, (c) total paid-in capital, and (d) total stockholders' equity?

15. (a) What are the principal differences between common stock and preferred stock?
    (b) Preferred stock may be cumulative. Discuss this feature.
    (c) How are dividends in arrears presented in the financial statements?

16. Identify the events that result in credits and debits to retained earnings.

17. Indicate how each of the following accounts should be classified in the stockholders' equity section.
    (a) Common stock
    (b) Paid-in capital in excess of par—common stock
    (c) Retained earnings
    (d) Treasury stock

(e) Paid-in capital from treasury stock
(f) Paid-in capital in excess of stated value—common stock
(g) Preferred stock

18. Tim Miotke maintains that adequate cash is the only requirement for the declaration of a cash dividend. Is Tim correct? Explain.

19. (a) Three dates are important in connection with cash dividends. Identify these dates, and explain their significance to the corporation and its stockholders.
    (b) Identify the accounting entries that are made for a cash dividend and the date of each entry.

20. Contrast the effects of a cash dividend and a stock dividend on a corporation's balance sheet.

21. Travis Plum asks, "Since stock dividends don't change anything, why declare them?" What is your answer to Travis?

22. Meloy Corporation has 30,000 shares of $9 par value common stock outstanding when it announces a 3-for-1 stock split. Before the split, the stock had a market price of $120 per share. After the split, how many shares of stock will be outstanding? What will be the approximate market price per share?

23. The board of directors is considering either a stock split or a stock dividend. They understand that total stockholders' equity will remain the same under either action. However, they are not sure of the different effects of the two types of actions on other aspects of stockholders' equity. Explain the differences to the directors.

24. What is a prior period adjustment, and how is it reported in the financial statements?

25. What is the purpose of a retained earnings restriction? Identify the possible causes of retained earnings restrictions.

*26. What is the formula for computing book value per share when a corporation has only common stock?

*27. Emko Inc's common stock has a per value of $1, a book value of $24, and a current market price of $18. Explain why these amounts are all different.

BRIEF EXERCISES

List the advantages and disadvantages of a corporation.
(LO 1)

BE11-1 Kari Home is studying for her accounting midterm examination. Identify for Kari the advantages and disadvantages of the corporate form of business organization.

Prepare entries for issuance of par value common stock.
(LO 2)

BE11-2 On May 10, Chen Corporation issues 2,000 shares of $6 par value common stock for cash at $13 per share. Journalize the issuance of the stock.

Prepare entries for issuance of no-par value common stock.
(LO 2)

BE11-3 On June 1, Federia Inc. issues 4,000 shares of no-par common stock at a cash price of $6 per share. Journalize the issuance of the shares assuming the stock has a stated value of $2 per share.

Prepare entries for issuance of stock in a noncash transaction.
(LO 2)

BE11-4 Alou Inc.'s $10 par value common stock is actively traded at a market price of $15 per share. Alou issues 5,000 shares to purchase land advertised for sale at $81,000. Journalize the issuance of the stock in acquiring the land.

BE11-5 On July 1, Naperville Corporation purchases 500 shares of its $2 par value common stock for the treasury at a cash price of $8 per share. On September 1, it sells 300 shares of the treasury stock for cash at $9 per share. Journalize the two treasury stock transactions.

Prepare entries for treasury stock transactions.
(LO 3)

BE11-6 Chard Inc. issues 5,000 shares of $100 par value preferred stock for cash at $118 per share. Journalize the issuance of the preferred stock.

Prepare entries for issuance of preferred stock.
(LO 4)

BE11-7 Fields Corporation has 80,000 shares of common stock outstanding. It declares a $2 per share cash dividend on November 1 to stockholders of record on December 1. The dividend is paid on December 31. Prepare the entries on the appropriate dates to record the declaration and payment of the cash dividend.

Prepare entries for a cash dividend.
(LO 5)

BE11-8 Valiant Corporation has 56,000 shares of $10 par value common stock outstanding. It declares a 10% stock dividend on December 1 when the market price per share is $16. The dividend shares are issued on December 31. Prepare the entries for the declaration and payment of the stock dividend.

Prepare entries for a stock dividend.
(LO 5)

BE11-9 The stockholders' equity section of Neely Corporation consists of common stock ($10 par) $2,000,000 and retained earnings $500,000. A 15% stock dividend (30,000 shares) is declared when the market price per share is $14. Show the before-and-after effects of the dividend on the following.
(a) The components of stockholders' equity.
(b) Shares outstanding.
(c) Par value per share.

Show before-and-after effects of a stock dividend.
(LO 5)

BE11-10 For the year ending December 31, 2014, Abbott Inc. reports net income $140,000 and dividends $55,000. Prepare the retained earnings statement for the year assuming the balance in retained earnings on January 1, 2014, was $220,000.

Prepare a retained earnings statement.
(LO 6)

BE11-11 The balance in retained earnings on January 1, 2014, for Sandra Inc. was $800,000. During the year, the corporation paid cash dividends of $60,000 and distributed a stock dividend of $8,000. In addition, the company determined that it had understated its depreciation expense in prior years by $44,000. Net income for 2014 was $120,000. Prepare the retained earnings statement for 2014.

Prepare a retained earnings statement.
(LO 6)

BE11-12 Garcia Corporation has the following accounts at December 31: Common Stock, $10 par, 5,000 shares issued, $50,000; Paid-in Capital in Excess of Par—Common Stock $32,000; Retained Earnings $45,000; and Treasury Stock, 500 shares, $9,000. Prepare the stockholders' equity section of the balance sheet.

Prepare stockholders' equity section.
(LO 7)

*BE11-13 The balance sheet for Lauren Inc. shows the following: total paid-in capital and retained earnings $877,000, total stockholders' equity $817,000, common stock issued 44,000 shares, and common stock outstanding 38,000 shares. Compute the book value per share. (No preferred stock is outstanding.)

Compute book value per share.
(LO 9)

> DO IT! REVIEW

DO IT! 11-1 Indicate whether each of the following statements is true or false.
_____1. The corporation is an entity separate and distinct from its owners.
_____2. The liability of stockholders is normally limited to their investment in the corporation.
_____3. The relative lack of government regulation is an advantage of the corporate form of business.
_____4. There is no journal entry to record the authorization of capital stock.
_____5. No-par value stock is quite rare today.

Analyze statements about corporate organization.
(LO 1)

DO IT! 11-2 At the end of its first year of operation, Jaeger Corporation has $1,000,000 of common stock and net income of $228,000. Prepare (a) the closing entry for net income and (b) the stockholders' equity section at year-end.

Close net income and prepare stockholders' equity section.
(LO 1)

DO IT! 11-3 Walton Corporation began operations on April 1 by issuing 50,000 shares of $2 par value common stock for cash at $13 per share. On April 19, it issued 2,000 shares of common stock to attorneys in settlement of their bill of $27,500 for organization costs. Journalize both issuances, assuming the stock is not publicly traded.

Journalize issuance of stock.
(LO 2)

Journalize treasury stock transactions.

(LO 3)

DO IT! **11-4** Delsman Corporation purchased 2,000 shares of its $5 par value common stock for $128,000 on August 1. It will hold these shares in the treasury until resold. On December 1, the corporation sold 1,200 shares of treasury stock for cash at $72 per share. Journalize the treasury stock transactions.

Determine dividends paid to preferred and common stockholders.

(LO 5)

DO IT! **11-5** Inmann Corporation has 4,000 shares of 7%, $100 par value preferred stock outstanding at December 31, 2014. At December 31, 2014, the company declared a $110,000 cash dividend. Determine the dividend paid to preferred stockholders and common stockholders under each of the following scenarios.

1. The preferred stock is noncumulative, and the company has not missed any dividends in previous years.
2. The preferred stock is noncumulative, and the company did not pay a dividend in each of the two previous years.
3. The preferred stock is cumulative, and the company did not pay a dividend in each of the two previous years.

Determine effects of stock dividend and stock split.

(LO 5)

DO IT! **11-6** Sentry Company has had 4 years of net income. Due to this success, the market price of its 400,000 shares of $2 par value common stock has increased from $12 per share to $49. During this period, paid-in capital remained the same at $2,400,000. Retained earnings increased from $1,800,000 to $12,000,000. President T. Boldt is considering either a 15% stock dividend or a 2-for-1 stock split. He asks you to show the before-and-after effects of each option on (a) retained earnings and (b) total stockholders' equity.

Prepare a retained earnings statement.

(LO 6)

DO IT! **11-7** Raymond Corporation has retained earnings of $3,100,000 on January 1, 2014. During the year, Raymond earned $1,200,000 of net income. It declared and paid a $150,000 cash dividend. In 2014, Raymond recorded an adjustment of $86,000 due to the overstatement (from mathematical error) of 2013 depreciation expense. Prepare a retained earnings statement for 2014.

Compute return on stockholders' equity and discuss changes.

(LO 7)

DO IT! **11-8** On January 1, 2014, Leonard Corporation purchased 1,000 shares of treasury stock. Other information regarding Leonard Corporation is provided below.

	2013	2014
Net income	$200,000	$210,000
Dividends on preferred stock	$30,000	$30,000
Dividends on common stock	$20,000	$25,000
Weighted-average number of common shares outstanding	10,000	9,000
Common stockholders' equity beginning of year	$600,000	$760,000
Common stockholders' equity end of year	$760,000	$830,000

Compute (a) return on common stockholders' equity for each year and (b) discuss the changes in each.

 The Navigator

EXERCISES

Identify characteristics of a corporation.

(LO 1)

E11-1 Victoria has prepared the following list of statements about corporations.

1. A corporation is an entity separate and distinct from its owners.
2. As a legal entity, a corporation has most of the rights and privileges of a person.
3. Most of the largest U.S. corporations are privately held corporations.
4. Corporations may buy, own, and sell property; borrow money; enter into legally binding contracts; and sue and be sued.
5. The net income of a corporation is not taxed as a separate entity.
6. Creditors have a legal claim on the personal assets of the owners of a corporation if the corporation does not pay its debts.
7. The transfer of stock from one owner to another requires the approval of either the corporation or other stockholders.

8. The board of directors of a corporation legally owns the corporation.
9. The chief accounting officer of a corporation is the controller.
10. Corporations are subject to fewer state and federal regulations than partnerships or proprietorships.

Instructions

Identify each statement as true or false. If false, indicate how to correct the statement.

E11-2 Victoria (see E11-1) has studied the information you gave her in that exercise and has come to you with more statements about corporations.

Identify characteristics of a corporation.

(LO 1, 2)

1. Corporation management is both an advantage and a disadvantage of a corporation compared to a proprietorship or a partnership.
2. Limited liability of stockholders, government regulations, and additional taxes are the major disadvantages of a corporation.
3. When a corporation is formed, organization costs are recorded as an asset.
4. Each share of common stock gives the stockholder the ownership rights to vote at stockholder meetings, share in corporate earnings, keep the same percentage ownership when new shares of stock are issued, and share in assets upon liquidation.
5. The number of issued shares is always greater than or equal to the number of authorized shares.
6. A journal entry is required for the authorization of capital stock.
7. Publicly held corporations usually issue stock directly to investors.
8. The trading of capital stock on a securities exchange involves the transfer of already issued shares from an existing stockholder to another investor.
9. The market price of common stock is usually the same as its par value.
10. Retained earnings is the total amount of cash and other assets paid in to the corporation by stockholders in exchange for capital stock.

Instructions

Identify each statement as true or false. If false, indicate how to correct the statement.

E11-3 During its first year of operations, Branden Corporation had the following transactions pertaining to its common stock.

Journalize issuance of common stock.

(LO 2)

Jan. 10   Issued 70,000 shares for cash at $4 per share.
July 1   Issued 30,000 shares for cash at $7 per share.

Instructions

(a) Journalize the transactions, assuming that the common stock has a par value of $4 per share.
(b) Journalize the transactions, assuming that the common stock is no-par with a stated value of $1 per share.

E11-4 Luis Corporation issued 1,000 shares of stock.

Journalize issuance of common stock.

(LO 2)

Instructions

Prepare the entry for the issuance under the following assumptions.

(a) The stock had a par value of $5 per share and was issued for a total of $48,000.
(b) The stock had a stated value of $5 per share and was issued for a total of $48,000.
(c) The stock had no par or stated value and was issued for a total of $48,000.
(d) The stock had a par value of $5 per share and was issued to attorneys for services during incorporation valued at $48,000.
(e) The stock had a par value of $5 per share and was issued for land worth $48,000.

E11-5 Kathleen Corporation purchased from its stockholders 5,000 shares of its own previously issued stock for $250,000. It later resold 1,500 shares for $54 per share, then 2,000 more shares for $49 per share, and finally 1,500 shares for $40 per share.

Journalize treasury stock transactions.

(LO 3)

Instructions

Prepare journal entries for the purchase of the treasury stock and the three sales of treasury stock.

E11-6 Robydek Corporation issued 100,000 shares of $20 par value, cumulative, 9% preferred stock on January 1, 2012, for $2,080,000. In December 2014, Robydek declared its first dividend of $550,000.

Differentiate between preferred and common stock.

(LO 4)

Instructions

(a) Prepare Robydek's journal entry to record the issuance of the preferred stock.

(b) If the preferred stock is *not* cumulative, how much of the $550,000 would be paid to **common** stockholders?

(c) If the preferred stock is cumulative, how much of the $550,000 would be paid to **common** stockholders?

Journalize issuance of common and preferred stock and purchase of treasury stock.

(LO 2, 3, 4)

E11-7 Fallow Co. had the following transactions during the current period.

Mar. 2   Issued 5,000 shares of $1 par value common stock to attorneys in payment of a bill for $38,000 for services provided in helping the company to incorporate.

June 12   Issued 60,000 shares of $1 par value common stock for cash of $475,000.

July 11   Issued 1,000 shares of $100 par value preferred stock for cash at $110 per share.

Nov. 28   Purchased 2,000 shares of treasury stock for $18,000.

Instructions

Journalize the transactions.

Journalize noncash common stock transactions.

(LO 2)

E11-8 As an auditor for the CPA firm of Gratis and Goode, you encounter the following situations in auditing different clients.

1. JR Corporation is a closely held corporation whose stock is not publicly traded. On December 5, the corporation acquired land by issuing 5,000 shares of its $10 par value common stock. The owners' asking price for the land was $138,000, and the fair value of the land was $124,000.

2. Novak Corporation is a publicly held corporation whose common stock is traded on the securities markets. On June 1, it acquired land by issuing 20,000 shares of its $10 par value stock. At the time of the exchange, the land was advertised for sale at $250,000. The stock was selling at $11 per share.

Instructions

Prepare the journal entries for each of the situations above.

Journalize treasury stock transactions.

(LO 3)

E11-9 On January 1, 2014, the stockholders' equity section of Bergin Corporation shows common stock ($5 par value) $1,500,000; paid-in capital in excess of par $1,000,000; and retained earnings $1,200,000. During the year, the following treasury stock transactions occurred.

Mar. 1   Purchased 50,000 shares for cash at $12 per share.

July 1   Sold 10,000 treasury shares for cash at $14 per share.

Sept. 1   Sold 8,000 treasury shares for cash at $11 per share.

Instructions

(a) Journalize the treasury stock transactions.

(b) Restate the entry for September 1, assuming the treasury shares were sold at $9 per share.

Journalize preferred stock transactions and indicate statement presentation.

(LO 4, 7)

E11-10 Suliman Corporation is authorized to issue both preferred and common stock. The par value of the preferred is $50. During the first year of operations, the company had the following events and transactions pertaining to its preferred stock.

Feb. 1   Issued 12,000 shares for cash at $53 per share.

July 1   Issued 23,000 shares for cash at $57 per share.

Instructions

(a) Journalize the transactions.

(b) Post to the stockholders' equity accounts.

(c) Indicate the financial statement presentation of the related accounts.

Answer questions about stockholders' equity section.

(LO 2, 3, 4, 7)

E11-11 The stockholders' equity section of Ahab Corporation at December 31 is as follows.

Ahab Corporation
Balance Sheet (partial)

Paid-in capital	
Preferred stock, cumulative, 10,000 shares authorized, 5,000 shares issued and outstanding	$ 300,000
Common stock, no par, 750,000 shares authorized, 600,000 shares issued	1,200,000
Total paid-in capital	1,500,000
Retained earnings	1,858,000
Total paid-in capital and retained earnings	3,358,000
Less: Treasury stock (75,000 common shares)	75,000
Total stockholders' equity	$3,283,000

Instructions

⬛️▶ From a review of the stockholders' equity section, as chief accountant, write a memo to the president of the company answering the following questions.

(a) How many shares of common stock are outstanding?
(b) Assuming there is a stated value, what is the stated value of the common stock?
(c) What is the par value of the preferred stock?
(d) If the annual dividend on preferred stock is $30,000, what is the dividend rate on preferred stock?
(e) If dividends of $60,000 were in arrears on preferred stock, what would be the balance in Retained Earnings?

E11-12 Anya Corporation recently hired a new accountant with extensive experience in accounting for partnerships. Because of the pressure of the new job, the accountant was unable to review his textbooks on the topic of corporation accounting. During the first month, the accountant made the following entries for the corporation's capital stock.

Prepare correct entries for capital stock transactions.

(LO 2, 3, 4)

May 2	Cash	130,000	
	Capital Stock		130,000
	(Issued 10,000 shares of $10 par value common stock at $13 per share)		
10	Cash	580,000	
	Capital Stock		580,000
	(Issued 10,000 shares of $50 par value preferred stock at $58 per share)		
15	Capital Stock	18,000	
	Cash		18,000
	(Purchased 1,200 shares of common stock for the treasury at $15 per share)		
31	Cash	8,000	
	Capital Stock		5,000
	Gain on Sale of Stock		3,000
	(Sold 500 shares of treasury stock at $16 per share)		

Instructions

On the basis of the explanation for each entry, prepare the entry that should have been made for the capital stock transactions.

E11-13 On January 1, Chevon Corporation had 98,000 shares of no-par common stock issued and outstanding. The stock has a stated value of $4 per share. During the year, the following occurred.

Journalize cash dividends; indicate statement presentation.

(LO 5)

Apr. 1   Issued 25,000 additional shares of common stock for $17 per share.
June 15   Declared a cash dividend of $1 per share to stockholders of record on June 30.
July 10   Paid the $1 cash dividend.
Dec. 1   Issued 2,000 additional shares of common stock for $19 per share.
      15   Declared a cash dividend on outstanding shares of $1.20 per share to stockholders of record on December 31.

Instructions

(a) Prepare the entries, if any, on each of the three dividend dates.
(b) How are dividends and dividends payable reported in the financial statements prepared at December 31?

E11-14 On January 1, 2014, Lanie Corporation had $1,000,000 of common stock outstanding that was issued at par. It also had retained earnings of $750,000. The company issued 40,000 shares of common stock at par on July 1 and earned net income of $400,000 for the year.

Journalize stock dividends.

(LO 5)

Instructions

Journalize the declaration of a 15% stock dividend on December 10, 2014, for the following independent assumptions.

(a) Par value is $8, and market price is $18.
(b) Par value is $5, and market price is $20.

Compare effects of a stock dividend and a stock split.

(LO 5)

E11-15 On October 31, the stockholders' equity section of Hillman Company consists of common stock $300,000 and retained earnings $900,000. Hillman is considering the following two courses of action: (1) declaring a 5% stock dividend on the 50,000, $6 par value shares outstanding, or (2) effecting a 2-for-1 stock split that will reduce par value to $3 per share. The current market price is $13 per share.

Instructions

Prepare a tabular summary of the effects of the alternative actions on the components of stockholders' equity, outstanding shares, and par value per share. Use the following column headings: Before Action, After Stock Dividend, and After Stock Split.

Prepare correcting entries for dividends and a stock split.

(LO 5)

E11-16 Before preparing financial statements for the current year, the chief accountant for Paul Company discovered the following errors in the accounts.

1. The declaration and payment of $50,000 cash dividend was recorded as a debit to Interest Expense $50,000 and a credit to Cash $50,000.
2. A 10% stock dividend (1,200 shares) was declared on the $10 par value stock when the market price per share was $17. The only entry made was Stock Dividends (Dr.) $12,000 and Dividend Payable (Cr.) $12,000. The shares have not been issued.
3. A 4-for-1 stock split involving the issue of 400,000 shares of $5 par value common stock for 100,000 shares of $20 par value common stock was recorded as a debit to Retained Earnings $2,000,000 and a credit to Common Stock $2,000,000.

Instructions

Prepare the correcting entries at December 31.

Prepare a retained earnings statement.

(LO 6)

E11-17 On January 1, 2014, Richard Corporation had retained earnings of $550,000. During the year, Richard had the following selected transactions.

1. Declared cash dividends $96,000.
2. Corrected overstatement of 2013 net income because of depreciation error $40,000.
3. Earned net income $350,000.
4. Declared stock dividends $80,000.

Instructions

Prepare a retained earnings statement for the year.

Prepare a retained earnings statement.

(LO 6)

E11-18 Bindra Company reported retained earnings at December 31, 2013, of $340,000. Bindra had 200,000 shares of common stock outstanding throughout 2014.

The following transactions occurred during 2014.

1. An error was discovered: in 2012, depreciation expense was recorded at $66,000, but the correct amount was $50,000.
2. A cash dividend of $0.50 per share was declared and paid.
3. A 5% stock dividend was declared and distributed when the market price per share was $14 per share.
4. Net income was $285,000.

Instructions

Prepare a retained earnings statement for 2014.

Classify stockholders' equity accounts.

(LO 7)

E11-19 The ledger of Summit Corporation contains the following accounts: Common Stock, Preferred Stock, Treasury Stock, Paid-in Capital in Excess of Par—Preferred Stock, Paid-in Capital in Excess of Stated Value—Common Stock, Paid-in Capital from Treasury Stock, and Retained Earnings.

Instructions

Classify each account using the following table headings.

	Paid-in Capital			
Account	**Capital Stock**	**Additional**	**Retained Earnings**	**Other**

Prepare a stockholders' equity section.

(LO 7)

E11-20 The following accounts appear in the ledger of Alexis Inc. after the books are closed at December 31.

Common Stock, no par, $1 stated value, 400,000 shares authorized;	
300,000 shares issued	$ 300,000
Common Stock Dividends Distributable	30,000
Paid-in Capital in Excess of Stated Value—Common Stock	1,200,000
Preferred Stock, $5 par value, 8%, 40,000 shares authorized;	
30,000 shares issued	150,000
Retained Earnings	800,000
Treasury Stock (10,000 common shares)	65,000
Paid-in Capital in Excess of Par—Preferred Stock	50,000

Instructions

Prepare the stockholders' equity section at December 31, assuming retained earnings is restricted for plant expansion in the amount of $150,000.

E11-21 Perrin Company reported the following balances at December 31, 2013: common stock $400,000; paid-in capital in excess of par—common stock $220,000; and retained earnings $250,000. During 2014, the following transactions affected stockholder's equity.

Prepare stockholders' equity section.

(LO 7)

1. Issued preferred stock with a par value of $125,000 for $165,000.
2. Purchased treasury stock (common) for $40,000.
3. Earned net income of $140,000.
4. Declared and paid cash dividends of $48,000.

Instructions

Prepare the stockholders' equity section of Perrin Company's December 31, 2014, balance sheet.

E11-22 In 2014, Reliant Corporation had net sales of $600,000 and cost of goods sold of $360,000. Operating expenses were $153,000, and interest expense was $7,500. The corporation's tax rate is 25%. The corporation declared preferred dividends of $12,000 in 2014, and its average common stockholders' equity during the year was $180,000.

Prepare an income statement and compute return on equity.

(LO 7)

Instructions

(a) Prepare an income statement for Reliant Corporation.
(b) Compute Reliant Corporation's return on common stockholders' equity for 2014.

*E11-23 In a recent year, the stockholders' equity section of Aluminum Company of America (Alcoa) showed the following (in alphabetical order): additional paid-in capital $6,101, common stock $925, preferred stock $56, retained earnings $7,428, and treasury stock 2,828. All dollar data are in millions.

Prepare a stockholders' equity section.

(LO 7, 9)

The preferred stock has 557,740 shares authorized, with a par value of $100 and an annual $3.75 per share cumulative dividend preference. At December 31, 557,649 shares of preferred are issued and 546,024 shares are outstanding. There are 1.8 billion shares of $1 par value common stock authorized, of which 924.6 million are issued and 844.8 million are outstanding at December 31.

Instructions

(a) Prepare the stockholders' equity section, including disclosure of all relevant data.
(b) Compute the book value per share of common stock, assuming there are no preferred dividends in arrears. (Round to two decimals.)

*E11-24 At December 31, Gorden Corporation has total stockholders' equity of $3,200,000. Included in this total are preferred stock $500,000 and paid-in capital in excess of par—preferred stock $50,000. There are 10,000 shares of $50 par value, 8% cumulative preferred stock outstanding. At year-end, 200,000 shares of common stock are outstanding.

Compute book value per share with preferred stock.

(LO 4, 9)

Instructions

Compute the book value per share of common stock, under each of the following assumptions.

(a) There are no preferred dividends in arrears, and the preferred stock does not have a call price.
(b) Preferred dividends are one year in arrears, and the preferred stock has a call price of $60 per share.

Compute book value per share; indicate account balances after a stock dividend.

(LO 5, 7, 9)

*E11-25 On October 1, Venden Corporation's stockholders' equity is as follows.

Common stock, $5 par value	$400,000
Paid-in capital in excess of par—common stock	25,000
Retained earnings	225,000
Total stockholders' equity	$650,000

On October 1, Venden declares and distributes a 15% stock dividend when the market price of the stock is $15 per share.

Instructions

(a) Compute the book value per share (1) before the stock dividend and (2) after the stock dividend. (Round to two decimals)

(b) Indicate the balances in the three stockholders' equity accounts after the stock dividend shares have been distributed.

EXERCISES: SET B AND CHALLENGE EXERCISES

Visit the book's companion website, at **www.wiley.com/college/weygandt**, and choose the Student Companion site to access Exercise Set B and Challenge Exercises.

PROBLEMS: SET A

Journalize stock transactions, post, and prepare paid-in capital section.

(LO 2, 4, 7)

P11-1A Burke Corporation was organized on January 1, 2014. It is authorized to issue 10,000 shares of 8%, $100 par value preferred stock, and 500,000 shares of no-par common stock with a stated value of $2 per share. The following stock transactions were completed during the first year.

Jan. 10	Issued 100,000 shares of common stock for cash at $5 per share.
Mar. 1	Issued 5,000 shares of preferred stock for cash at $105 per share.
Apr. 1	Issued 18,000 shares of common stock for land. The asking price of the land was $98,000. The fair value of the land was $92,000.
May 1	Issued 80,000 shares of common stock for cash at $4.50 per share.
Aug. 1	Issued 10,000 shares of common stock to attorneys in payment of their bill of $30,000 for services provided in helping the company organize.
Sept. 1	Issued 10,000 shares of common stock for cash at $5 per share.
Nov. 1	Issued 1,000 shares of preferred stock for cash at $108 per share.

Instructions

(a) Journalize the transactions.

(b) Post to the stockholders' equity accounts. (Use J5 as the posting reference.)

(c) Total paid-in capital $1,665,000

(c) Prepare the paid-in capital section of stockholders' equity at December 31, 2014.

Journalize and post treasury stock transactions, and prepare stockholders' equity section.

(LO 3, 7)

P11-2A Elston Corporation had the following stockholders' equity accounts on January 1, 2014: Common Stock ($5 par) $400,000, Paid-in Capital in Excess of Par—Common Stock $200,000, and Retained Earnings $100,000. In 2014, the company had the following treasury stock transactions.

Mar. 1	Purchased 5,000 shares at $9 per share.
June 1	Sold 500 shares at $12 per share.
Sept. 1	Sold 2,500 shares at $10 per share.
Dec. 1	Sold 1,000 shares at $6 per share.

Elston Corporation uses the cost method of accounting for treasury stock. In 2014, the company reported net income of $34,000.

Instructions

(a) Journalize the treasury stock transactions, and prepare the closing entry at December 31, 2014, for net income.

(b) Open accounts for (1) Paid-in Capital from Treasury Stock, (2) Treasury Stock, and (3) Retained Earnings. Post to these accounts using J10 as the posting reference.

(c) Prepare the stockholders' equity section for Elston Corporation at December 31, 2014.

(b) Treasury Stock $9,000
(c) Total stockholders' equity
   $726,000

P11-3A The stockholders' equity accounts of Terrell Corporation on January 1, 2014, were as follows.

Preferred Stock (9%, $50 par, cumulative, 10,000 shares authorized)	$ 400,000
Common Stock ($1 stated value, 2,000,000 shares authorized)	1,000,000
Paid-in Capital in Excess of Par—Preferred Stock	100,000
Paid-in Capital in Excess of Stated Value—Common Stock	1,450,000
Retained Earnings	1,816,000
Treasury Stock (20,000 common shares)	50,000

Journalize and post transactions, prepare stockholders' equity section.

(LO 2, 3, 4, 7)

During 2014, the corporation had the following transactions and events pertaining to its stockholders' equity.

Feb. 1   Issued 25,000 shares of common stock for $120,000.
Apr. 14   Sold 9,000 shares of treasury stock—common for $46,000.
Sept. 3   Issued 7,000 shares of common stock for a patent valued at $42,000.
Nov. 10   Purchased 1,000 shares of common stock for the treasury at a cost of $6,000.
Dec. 31   Determined that net income for the year was $452,000.

No dividends were declared during the year.

Instructions

(a) Journalize the transactions and the closing entry for net income.

(b) Enter the beginning balances in the accounts, and post the journal entries to the stockholders' equity accounts. (Use J5 for the posting reference.)

(c) Prepare a stockholders' equity section at December 31, 2014, including the disclosure of the preferred dividends in arrears.

(c) Total stockholders' equity
   $5,370,000

P11-4A On January 1, 2014, Prasad Corporation had the following stockholders' equity accounts.

Common Stock ($25 par value, 48,000 shares issued and outstanding)	$1,200,000
Paid-in Capital in Excess of Par—Common Stock	200,000
Retained Earnings	600,000

Prepare dividend entries and stockholders' equity section.

(LO, 5, 7)

During the year, the following transactions occurred.

Feb. 1   Declared a $1 cash dividend per share to stockholders of record on February 15, payable March 1.
Mar. 1   Paid the dividend declared in February.
Apr. 1   Announced a 5-for-1 stock split. Prior to the split, the market price per share was $36.
July 1   Declared a 10% stock dividend to stockholders of record on July 15, distributable July 31. On July 1, the market price of the stock was $7 per share.
     31   Issued the shares for the stock dividend.
Dec. 1   Declared a $0.40 per share dividend to stockholders of record on December 15, payable January 5, 2015.
     31   Determined that net income for the year was $350,000.

Instructions

(a) Journalize the transactions and the closing entries for net income and dividends.

(b) Enter the beginning balances, and post the entries to the stockholders' equity accounts. (*Note:* Open additional stockholders' equity accounts as needed.)

(c) Prepare a stockholders' equity section at December 31.

(c) Total stockholders' equity
   $2,196,400

P11-5A The post-closing trial balance of Russo Corporation at December 31, 2014, contains the following stockholders' equity accounts.

Preferred Stock (15,000 shares issued)	$ 750,000
Common Stock (250,000 shares issued)	2,500,000
Paid-in Capital in Excess of Par—Preferred Stock	250,000
Paid-in Capital in Excess of Par—Common Stock	425,000
Common Stock Dividends Distributable	250,000
Retained Earnings	1,054,000

Prepare retained earnings statement and stockholders' equity section, and compute earnings per share.

(LO 5, 6, 7)

A review of the accounting records reveals the following.

1. No errors have been made in recording 2014 transactions or in preparing the closing entry for net income.
2. Preferred stock is $50 par, 7%, and cumulative; 15,000 shares have been outstanding since January 1, 2013.
3. Authorized stock is 20,000 shares of preferred, 500,000 shares of common with a $10 par value.
4. The January 1 balance in Retained Earnings was $1,200,000.
5. On July 1, 20,000 shares of common stock were issued for cash at $16 per share.
6. On September 1, the company discovered an understatement error of $80,000 in computing depreciation in 2013. The net of tax effect of $56,000 was properly debited directly to Retained Earnings.
7. A cash dividend of $250,000 was declared and properly allocated to preferred and common stock on October 1. No dividends were paid to preferred stockholders in 2013.
8. On December 31, a 10% common stock dividend was declared out of retained earnings on common stock when the market price per share was $17.
9. Net income for the year was $585,000.
10. On December 31, 2014, the directors authorized disclosure of a $200,000 restriction of retained earnings for plant expansion. (Use Note X.)

Instructions
(a) Reproduce the Retained Earnings account for 2014.
(b) Prepare a retained earnings statement for 2014.

(c) Total stockholders' equity, $5,229,000

(c) Prepare a stockholders' equity section at December 31, 2014.
(d) Compute the allocation of the cash dividend to preferred and common stock.

Prepare entries for stock transactions and prepare stockholders' equity section.

(LO 2, 3, 4, 7)

P11-6A Jude Corporation has been authorized to issue 20,000 shares of $100 par value, 10%, noncumulative preferred stock and 1,000,000 shares of no-par common stock. The corporation assigned a $2.50 stated value to the common stock. At December 31, 2014, the ledger contained the following balances pertaining to stockholders' equity.

Preferred Stock	$ 120,000
Paid-in Capital in Excess of Par—Preferred Stock	12,000
Common Stock	1,000,000
Paid-in Capital in Excess of Stated Value—Common Stock	1,600,000
Treasury Stock (1,000 common shares)	9,000
Paid-in Capital from Treasury Stock	1,000
Retained Earnings	82,000

The preferred stock was issued for land having a fair value of $132,000. All common stock issued was for cash. In November, 1,500 shares of common stock were purchased for the treasury at a per share cost of $9. In December, 500 shares of treasury stock were sold for $11 per share. No dividends were declared in 2014.

Instructions
(a) Prepare the journal entries for the:
(1) Issuance of preferred stock for land.
(2) Issuance of common stock for cash.
(3) Purchase of common treasury stock for cash.

(b) Total stockholders' equity $2,806,000

(4) Sale of treasury stock for cash.
(b) Prepare the stockholders' equity section at December 31, 2014.

Prepare dividend entries and stockholders' equity section.

(LO 5, 7)

P11-7A On January 1, 2014, Primo Corporation had the following stockholders' equity accounts.

Common Stock ($10 par value, 75,000 shares issued and outstanding)	$750,000
Paid-in Capital in Excess of Par—Common Stock	200,000
Retained Earnings	540,000

During the year, the following transactions occurred.

Jan. 15 Declared a $1 cash dividend per share to stockholders of record on January 31, payable February 15.
Feb. 15 Paid the dividend declared in January.

Apr. 15   Declared a 10% stock dividend to stockholders of record on April 30, distribut-
          able May 15. On April 15, the market price of the stock was $14 per share.
May 15   Issued the shares for the stock dividend.
July 1   Announced a 2-for-1 stock split. The market price per share prior to the an-
          nouncement was $15. (The new par value is $5.)
Dec. 1   Declared a $0.60 per share cash dividend to stockholders of record on December 15,
          payable January 10, 2015.
      31 Determined that net income for the year was $250,000.

Instructions
(a) Journalize the transactions and the closing entries for net income and dividends.
(b) Enter the beginning balances, and post the entries to the stockholders' equity accounts.
    (*Note:* Open additional stockholders' equity accounts as needed.)
(c) Prepare a stockholders' equity section at December 31.

*(c) Total stockholders' equity
$1,566,000*

*P11-8A The following stockholders' equity accounts arranged alphabetically are in the
ledger of Westin Corporation at December 31, 2014.

*Prepare stockholders' equity
section; compute book value
per share.*

(LO 7, 9)

Common Stock ($10 stated value)	$1,500,000
Paid-in Capital from Treasury Stock	6,000
Paid-in Capital in Excess of Stated Value—Common Stock	690,000
Paid-in Capital in Excess of Par—Preferred Stock	42,400
Preferred Stock (8%, $100 par, noncumulative)	360,000
Retained Earnings	776,000
Treasury Stock—Common (7,000 shares)	92,000

Instructions
(a) Prepare a stockholders' equity section at December 31, 2014.
(b) Compute the book value per share of the common stock, assuming the preferred stock
    has a call price of $110 per share.

*Total stockholders' equity
$3,282,400*

*P11-9A On January 1, 2014, Goodhue Inc. had the following stockholders' equity balances.

*Prepare stockholders' equity
statement.*

(LO 7, 8)

Common Stock (400,000 shares issued)	$800,000
Paid-in Capital in Excess of Par—Common Stock	500,000
Common Stock Dividends Distributable	120,000
Retained Earnings	600,000

During 2014, the following transactions and events occurred.

1. Issued 60,000 shares of $2 par value common stock as a result of 15% stock dividend
   declared on December 15, 2013.
2. Issued 30,000 shares of common stock for cash at $4 per share.
3. Purchased 25,000 shares of common stock for the treasury at $5 per share.
4. Declared and paid a cash dividend of $111,000.
5. Sold 8,000 shares of treasury stock for cash at $5 per share.
6. Earned net income of $360,000.

Instructions
Prepare a stockholders' equity statement for the year.

*Total stockholders' equity
$2,304,000*

PROBLEMS: SET B

P11-1B Welles Corporation was organized on January 1, 2014. It is authorized to issue
20,000 shares of 6%, $40 par value preferred stock, and 500,000 shares of no-par common
stock with a stated value of $1 per share. The following stock transactions were completed
during the first year.

*Journalize stock transactions,
post, and prepare paid-in
capital section.*

(LO 2, 4, 7)

Jan. 10   Issued 80,000 shares of common stock for cash at $3 per share.
Mar. 1   Issued 10,000 shares of preferred stock for cash at $45 per share.
Apr. 1   Issued 25,000 shares of common stock for land. The asking price of the land was
          $90,000. The company's estimate of fair value of the land was $75,000.
May 1   Issued 75,000 shares of common stock for cash at $4 per share.
Aug. 1   Issued 10,000 shares of common stock to attorneys in payment of their bill for
          $44,000 for services provided in helping the company organize.

Sept. 1 Issued 5,000 shares of common stock for cash at $6 per share.
Nov. 1 Issued 2,000 shares of preferred stock for cash at $48 per share.

Instructions

(c) Total paid-in capital
$1,235,000

(a) Journalize the transactions.
(b) Post to the stockholders' equity accounts. (Use J1 as the posting reference.)
(c) Prepare the paid-in capital section of stockholders' equity at December 31, 2014.

Journalize and post treasury stock transactions, and prepare stockholders' equity section.

(LO 3, 7)

P11-2B Plover Corporation had the following stockholders' equity accounts on January 1, 2014: Common Stock ($1 par) $400,000, Paid-in Capital in Excess of Par—Common Stock $500,000, and Retained Earnings $100,000. In 2014, the company had the following treasury stock transactions.

Mar. 1 Purchased 5,000 shares at $7 per share.
June 1 Sold 800 shares at $10 per share.
Sept. 1 Sold 1,700 shares at $9 per share.
Dec. 1 Sold 1,000 shares at $5 per share.

Plover Corporation uses the cost method of accounting for treasury stock. In 2014, the company reported net income of $80,000.

Instructions

(a) Journalize the treasury stock transactions, and prepare the closing entry at December 31, 2014, for net income.
(b) Treasury Stock $10,500
(c) Total stockholders' equity
$1,073,300
(b) Open accounts for (1) Paid-in Capital from Treasury Stock, (2) Treasury Stock, and (3) Retained Earnings. Post to these accounts using J12 as the posting reference.
(c) Prepare the stockholders' equity section for Plover Corporation at December 31, 2014.

Journalize and post transactions, prepare stockholders' equity section.

(LO 2, 3, 4, 7)

P11-3B The stockholders' equity accounts of Marya Corporation on January 1, 2014, were as follows.

Preferred Stock (9%, $100 par, cumulative, 5,000 shares authorized)	$300,000
Common Stock ($3 stated value, 300,000 shares authorized)	660,000
Paid-in Capital in Excess of Par—Preferred Stock	20,000
Paid-in Capital in Excess of Stated Value—Common Stock	396,000
Retained Earnings	488,000
Treasury Stock (5,000 common shares)	30,000

During 2014, the corporation had the following transactions and events pertaining to its stockholders' equity.

Feb. 1 Issued 3,000 shares of common stock for $19,500.
Mar. 20 Purchased 1,500 additional shares of common treasury stock at $6 per share.
June 14 Sold 4,000 shares of treasury stock—common for $26,000.
Sept. 3 Issued 2,000 shares of common stock for a patent valued at $14,000.
Dec. 31 Determined that net income for the year was $350,000.

No dividends were declared during the year.

Instructions

(a) Journalize the transactions and the closing entry for net income.
(b) Enter the beginning balances in the accounts and post the journal entries to the stockholders' equity accounts. (Use J1 as the posting reference.)
(c) Total stockholders' equity
$2,234,500
(c) Prepare a stockholders' equity section at December 31, 2014, including the disclosure of the preferred dividends in arrears.

Prepare dividend entries and stockholders' equity section.

(LO 5, 7)

P11-4B On January 1, 2014, Dixon Corporation had the following stockholders' equity accounts.

Common Stock ($4 par value, 250,000 shares issued and outstanding)	$1,000,000
Paid-in Capital in Excess of Par—Common Stock	200,000
Retained Earnings	840,000

During the year, the following transactions occurred.

Jan. 15 Declared a $1 cash dividend per share to stockholders of record on January 31, payable February 15.
Feb. 15 Paid the dividend declared in January.
Apr. 15 Declared a 10% stock dividend to stockholders of record on April 30, distributable May 15. On April 15, the market price of the stock was $11 per share.

May 15 Issued the shares for the stock dividend.

July 1 Announced a 2-for-1 stock split. The market price per share prior to the announcement was $12. (The new par value is $2.00.)

Dec. 1 Declared a $0.50 per share cash dividend to stockholders of record on December 15, payable January 10, 2015.

      31 Determined that net income for the year was $264,000.

Instructions

(a) Journalize the transactions and the closing entries for net income and dividends.

(b) Enter the beginning balances, and post the entries to the stockholders' equity accounts. (*Note:* Open additional stockholders' equity accounts as needed.)

(c) Prepare a stockholders' equity section at December 31.

(c) Total stockholders' equity
$1,779,000

P11-5B On December 31, 2013, Andes Company had 1,500,000 shares of $10 par common stock issued and outstanding. The stockholders' equity accounts at December 31, 2013, had the following balances.

Common Stock	$15,000,000
Additional Paid-in Capital	1,500,000
Retained Earnings	900,000

Prepare retained earnings statement and stockholders' equity section.

(LO 6, 7)

Transactions during 2014 and other information related to stockholders' equity accounts were as follows.

1. On January 10, 2014, Andes issued at $105 per share 100,000 shares of $100 par value, 8% cumulative preferred stock.

2. On February 8, 2014, Andes reacquired 20,000 shares of its common stock for $14 per share.

3. On June 8, 2014, Andes declared a cash dividend of $1 per share on the common stock outstanding, payable on July 10, 2014, to stockholders of record on July 1, 2014.

4. On December 15, 2014, Andes declared the yearly cash dividend on preferred stock, payable January 10, 2015, to stockholders of record on December 15, 2014.

5. Net income for the year is $3,600,000.

6. It was discovered that depreciation expense had been understated in 2013 by $65,000.

Instructions

(a) Prepare a retained earnings statement for the year ended December 31, 2014.

(b) Prepare the stockholders' equity section of Andes's balance sheet at December 31, 2014.

(b) Total stockholders' equity
$28,875,000

P11-6B The ledger of Paisley Corporation at December 31, 2014, after the books have been closed, contains the following stockholders' equity accounts.

Preferred Stock (8,000 shares issued)	$ 800,000
Common Stock (400,000 shares issued)	2,000,000
Paid-in Capital in Excess of Par—Preferred Stock	100,000
Paid-in Capital in Excess of Stated—Common Stock	1,220,000
Common Stock Dividends Distributable	200,000
Retained Earnings	2,520,000

Prepare retained earnings statement and stockholders' equity section, and compute earnings per share.

(LO 5, 6, 7)

A review of the accounting records reveals the following.

1. No errors have been made in recording 2014 transactions or in preparing the closing entry for net income.

2. Preferred stock is 8%, $100 par value, noncumulative, and callable at $125. Since January 1, 2013, 8,000 shares have been outstanding; 20,000 shares are authorized.

3. Common stock is no-par with a stated value of $5 per share; 600,000 shares are authorized.

4. The January 1 balance in Retained Earnings was $2,450,000.

5. On October 1, 100,000 shares of common stock were sold for cash at $8 per share.

6. A cash dividend of $500,000 was declared and properly allocated to preferred and common stock on November 1. No dividends were paid to preferred stockholders in 2013.

7. On December 31, a 10% common stock dividend was declared out of retained earnings on common stock when the market price per share was $10.

8. Net income for the year was $970,000.

9. On December 31, 2014, the directors authorized disclosure of a $100,000 restriction of retained earnings for plant expansion. (Use Note A.)

Instructions

(a) Reproduce the Retained Earnings account (T-account) for 2014.

(c) Total stockholders' equity
$6,840,000

(b) Prepare a retained earnings statement for 2014.

(c) Prepare a stockholders' equity section at December 31, 2014.

(d) Compute the allocation of the cash dividend to preferred and common stock.

Prepare stockholders' equity section; compute book value per share.

(LO 7, 9)

*****P11-7B** The following stockholders' equity accounts arranged alphabetically are in the ledger of Crivello Corporation at December 31, 2014.

Common Stock ($3 stated value)	$2,400,000
Paid-in Capital from Treasury Stock	10,000
Paid-in Capital in Excess of Stated Value—Common Stock	1,600,000
Paid-in Capital in Excess of Par—Preferred Stock	220,000
Preferred Stock (8%, $50 par, noncumulative)	800,000
Retained Earnings	1,448,000
Treasury Stock—Common (10,000 shares)	75,000

Instructions

Total stockholders' equity
$6,403,000

(a) Prepare a stockholders' equity section at December 31, 2014.

(b) Compute the book value per share of the common stock, assuming the preferred stock has a call price of $60 per share.

PROBLEMS: SET C

Visit the book's companion website, at **www.wiley.com/college/weygandt**, and choose the Student Companion site to access Problem Set C.

COMPREHENSIVE PROBLEM

CP11-1 Voltaire Corporation's balance sheet at December 31, 2013, is presented below.

Voltaire Corporation
Balance Sheet
December 31, 2013

Cash	$ 24,600	Accounts payable	$ 25,600
Accounts receivable	45,500	Common stock ($1 par)	50,000
Allowance for doubtful		Retained earnings	147,400
accounts	(1,500)		$223,000
Supplies	4,400		
Land	40,000		
Buildings	130,000		
Accumulated depreciation—buildings	(20,000)		
	$223,000		

During 2014, the following transactions occurred.

1. On January 1, 2014, Voltaire issued 1,500 shares of $20 par, 6% preferred stock for $33,000.
2. On January 1, 2014, Voltaire also issued 900 shares of the $1 par value common stock for $6,300.
3. Voltaire performed services for $276,000 on account.
4. On April 1, 2014, Voltaire collected fees of $36,000 in advance for services to be performed from April 1, 2014, to March 31, 2015.
5. Voltaire collected $267,000 from customers on account.
6. Voltaire bought $26,100 of supplies on account.
7. Voltaire paid $32,200 on accounts payable.

8. Voltaire reacquired 400 shares of its common stock on June 1, 2014, for $8 per share.
9. Paid other operating expenses of $188,200.
10. On December 31, 2014, Voltaire declared the annual preferred stock dividend and a $.50 per share dividend on the outstanding common stock, all payable on January 15, 2015.
11. An account receivable of $1,300 which originated in 2013 is written off as uncollectible.

Adjustment data:

1. A count of supplies indicates that $5,900 of supplies remain unused at year-end.
2. Recorded revenue recognized from item 4 above.
3. The allowance for doubtful accounts should have a balance of $3,500 at year end.
4. Depreciation is recorded on the building on a straight-line basis based on a 30-year life and a salvage value of $10,000.
5. The income tax rate is 30%. (*Hint:* Prepare the income statement up to income before taxes and multiply by 30% to compute the amount.)

Instructions
(You may want to set up T-accounts to determine ending balances.)

(a) Prepare journal entries for the transactions listed above and adjusting entries.
(b) Prepare an adjusted trial balance at December 31, 2014.
(c) Prepare an income statement and a retained earnings statement for the year ending December 31, 2014, and a classified balance sheet as of December 31, 2014.

(b) Totals $647,620
(c) Net income $58,030
    Tot. assets $344,900

CONTINUING COOKIE CHRONICLE

(*Note:* This is a continuation of the Cookie Chronicle from Chapters 1–10.)

CCC11 Natalie and her friend Curtis Lesperance decide that they can benefit from joining Cookie Creations and Curtis's coffee shop. In the first part of this problem, they come to you with questions about setting up a corporation for their new business. In the second part of the problem, they want your help in preparing financial information following the first year of operations of their new business, Cookie & Coffee Creations.

Go to the book's companion website, www.wiley.com/college/weygandt, to see the completion of this problem.

Broadening Your PERSPECTIVE

Financial Reporting and Analysis

Financial Reporting Problem: PepsiCo, Inc.

BYP11-1 The stockholders' equity section for PepsiCo, Inc. is shown in Appendix A. You will also find data relative to this problem on other pages of the appendix.

PEPSICO

Instructions
(a) What is the par or stated value per share of PepsiCo's common stock?
(b) What percentage of PepsiCo's authorized common stock was issued at December 25, 2010?
(c) How many shares of common stock were outstanding at December 25, 2010, and at December 26, 2009?
*(d) What was the book value per share at December 25, 2010, and at December 26, 2009?
(e) What were the high and low market prices per share in the fourth quarter of fiscal 2010, as reported under Selected Financial Data?

Comparative Analysis Problem: PepsiCo, Inc. vs. The Coca-Cola Company

BYP11-2 PepsiCo's financial statements are presented in Appendix A. Financial statements of The Coca-Cola Company are presented in Appendix B.

Instructions
(a) Based on the information contained in these financial statements, compute the 2010 book value per share for each company. (*Hint:* Use the value reported for "common shareholders' equity" as the numerator for PepsiCo.)
(b) Compare the market value per share for each company to the book value per share at year-end 2010. Assume that the market value of Coca-Cola's stock was $65.77 at year-end 2010.
(c) Why are book value and market value per share different?
(d) Compute earnings per share and return on common stockholders' equity for both companies for 2010. Assume PepsiCo's weighted-average shares were 1,590 million and Coca-Cola's weighted-average shares were 2,308 million. Can these measures be used to compare the profitability of the two companies? Why or why not?
(e) What was the total amount of dividends paid by each company in 2010?

Real-World Focus

BYP11-3 Use the stockholders' equity section of an annual report and identify the major components.

Address: **www.annualreports.com,** or go to **www.wiley.com/college/weygandt**

Steps
1. From Annual Reports Homepage, choose **Search by Alphabet**, and choose a letter.
2. Select a particular company.
3. Choose Annual Report.
4. Follow instructions below.

Instructions
Answer the following questions.

(a) What is the company's name?
(b) What classes of capital stock has the company issued?
(c) For each class of stock:
    (1) How many shares are authorized, issued, and/or outstanding?
    (2) What is the par value?
(d) What are the company's retained earnings?
(e) Has the company acquired treasury stock? How many shares?

Critical Thinking

Decision-Making Across the Organization

BYP11-4 The stockholders' meeting for Kissinger Corporation has been in progress for some time. The chief financial officer for Kissinger is presently reviewing the company's financial statements and is explaining the items that comprise the stockholders' equity section of the balance sheet for the current year. The stockholders' equity section of Kissinger Corporation at December 31, 2014, is as follows.

Kissinger Corporation
Balance Sheet (partial)
December 31, 2014

Paid-in capital	
Capital stock	
Preferred stock, authorized 1,000,000 shares cumulative, $100 par value, $8 per share, 6,000 shares issued and outstanding	$ 600,000
Common stock, authorized 5,000,000 shares, $1 par value, 3,000,000 shares issued, and 2,700,000 outstanding	3,000,000
Total capital stock	3,600,000

Additional paid-in capital		
In excess of par—preferred stock	$ 50,000	
In excess of par—common stock	25,000,000	
Total additional paid-in capital		25,050,000
Total paid-in capital		28,650,000
Retained earnings		900,000
Total paid-in capital and retained earnings		29,550,000
Less: Treasury stock (300,000 common shares)		9,300,000
Total stockholders' equity		$20,250,000

At the meeting, stockholders have raised a number of questions regarding the stockholders' equity section.

Instructions

With the class divided into groups, answer the following questions as if you were the chief financial officer for Kissinger Corporation.

(a) "What does the cumulative provision related to the preferred stock mean?"

(b) "I thought the common stock was presently selling at $29.75, but the company has the stock stated at $1 per share. How can that be?"

(c) "Why is the company buying back its common stock? Furthermore, the treasury stock has a debit balance because it is subtracted from stockholders' equity. Why is treasury stock not reported as an asset if it has a debit balance?"

Communication Activity

BYP11-5 Jerrod Platt, your uncle, is an inventor who has decided to incorporate. Uncle Jerrod knows that you are an accounting major at U.N.O. In a recent letter to you, he ends with the question, "I'm filling out a state incorporation application. Can you tell me the difference in the following terms: (1) authorized stock, (2) issued stock, (3) outstanding stock, and (4) preferred stock?"

Instructions

In a brief note, differentiate for Uncle Jerrod among the four different stock terms. Write the letter to be friendly, yet professional.

Ethics Case

BYP11-6 The R&D division of Hancock Chemical Corp. has just developed a chemical for sterilizing the vicious Brazilian "killer bees" which are invading Mexico and the southern states of the United States. The president of Hancock is anxious to get the chemical on the market to boost the company's profits. He believes his job is in jeopardy because of decreasing sales and profits. Hancock has an opportunity to sell this chemical in Central American countries, where the laws are much more relaxed than in the United States.

The director of Hancock's R&D division strongly recommends further testing in the laboratory for side-effects of this chemical on other insects, birds, animals, plants, and even humans. He cautions the president, "We could be sued from all sides if the chemical has tragic side-effects that we didn't even test for in the labs." The president answers, "We can't wait an additional year for your lab tests. We can avoid losses from such lawsuits by establishing a separate wholly owned corporation to shield Hancock Corp. from such lawsuits. We can't lose any more than our investment in the new corporation, and we'll invest in just the patent covering this chemical. We'll reap the benefits if the chemical works and is safe, and avoid the losses from lawsuits if it's a disaster." The following week, Hancock creates a new wholly owned corporation called Badell Inc., sells the chemical patent to it for $10, and watches the spraying begin.

Instructions

(a) Who are the stakeholders in this situation?

(b) Are the president's motives and actions ethical?

(c) Can Hancock shield itself against losses of Badell Inc.?

All About You

BYP11-7 A high percentage of Americans own stock in corporations. As a shareholder in a corporation, you will receive an annual report. One of the goals of this course is for you to learn how to navigate your way around an annual report.

Instructions

Use PepsiCo Inc.'s annual report provided in Appendix A to answer the following questions.

(a) What CPA firm performed the audit of PepsiCo's financial statements?
(b) What was the amount of PepsiCo's earnings per share in 2010?
(c) What was net revenue in 2010?
(d) How many shares of treasury stock did the company have at the end of 2010?
(e) How much cash did PepsiCo spend on capital expenditures in 2010?
(f) Over what life does the company depreciate its buildings?
(g) What was the total amount of dividends paid in 2010?

FASB Codification Activity

BYP11-8 If your school has a subscription to the FASB Codification, go to *http://aaahq.org/ascLogin.cfm* to log in and prepare responses to the following.

(a) What is the stock dividend?
(b) What is a stock split?
(c) At what percentage point does the issuance of additional shares qualify as a stock dividend, as opposed to a stock split?

Answers to Chapter Questions

Answers to Insight and Accounting Across the Organization Questions

p. 541 Wall Street No Friend of Facebook Q: Why has Mark Zuckerberg, the CEO and founder of Facebook, delayed taking his company's shares public through an initial public offering (IPO)? **A:** Facebook doesn't need to invest in factories, distribution systems, or even marketing, so it doesn't need to raise a lot of cash. Also, by not going public, Zuckerberg has more control over the direction of the company. In addition, publicly traded companies face many more financial reporting disclosure requirements.

p. 544 How to Read Stock Quotes Q: For stocks traded on organized stock exchanges, how are the dollar prices per share established? **A:** The dollar prices per share are established by the interaction between buyers and sellers of the shares. **Q:** What factors might influence the price of shares in the marketplace? **A:** The price of shares is influenced by a company's earnings and dividends as well as by factors beyond a company's control, such as changes in interest rates, labor strikes, scarcity of supplies or resources, and politics. The number of willing buyers and sellers (demand and supply) also plays a part in the price of shares.

p. 547 The Impact of Corporate Social Responsibility Q: Why are CSR-related shareholder proposals increasing? **A:** The increase in shareholder proposals reflect a growing belief that a company's social and environmental policies correlate strongly with its risk-management strategy and ultimately its financial performance.

p. 552 Why Did Reebok Buy Its Own Stock? Q: What signal might a large stock repurchase send to investors regarding management's belief about the company's growth opportunities? **A:** When a company has many growth opportunities it will normally conserve its cash in order to be better able to fund expansion. A large use of cash to buy back stock (and essentially shrink the company) would suggest that management was not optimistic about its growth opportunities.

p. 559 Up, Down, and ?? Q: What factors must management consider in deciding how large a dividend to pay? **A:** Management must consider the size of the company's retained earnings balance, the amount of available cash, the company's expected near-term cash needs, the company's growth opportunities, and what level of dividend the company will be able to sustain based upon its expected future earnings.

p. 563 A No-Split Philosophy Q: Why does Warren Buffett usually oppose stock splits? **A:** Mr. Buffett prefers to attract shareholders that make a long-term commitment to his company, as opposed to traders that only hold their investment for a short period of time. He believes that a high stock price discourages short-term investment.

Answers to Self-Test Questions

1. c **2.** b **3.** d **4.** c **5.** a **6.** a **7.** d **8.** d **9.** a **10.** c **11.** c **12.** b **13.** c **14.** b **15.** b
$186,000 - (6\% \times \$100 \times 10,000) = \$126,000$ ***16.** a   ***17.** c

A Look at IFRS

The accounting for transactions related to stockholders' equity, such as issuance of shares and purchase of treasury stock, are similar under both IFRS and GAAP. Major differences relate to terminology used, introduction of items such as revaluation surplus, and presentation of stockholders' equity information. The basic accounting for cash and stock dividends is essentially the same under both GAAP and IFRS although IFRS terminology may differ.

Key Points

- Under IFRS, the term *reserves* is used to describe all equity accounts other than those arising from contributed (paid-in) capital. This would include, for example, reserves related to retained earnings, asset revaluations, and fair value differences.

- Many countries have a different mix of investor groups than in the United States. For example, in Germany, financial institutions like banks are not only major creditors of corporations but often are the largest corporate stockholders as well. In the United States, Asia, and the United Kingdom, many companies rely on substantial investment from private investors.

- There are often terminology differences for equity accounts. The following summarizes some of the common differences in terminology.

GAAP	IFRS
Common stock	Share capital—ordinary
Stockholders	Shareholders
Par value	Nominal or face value
Authorized stock	Authorized share capital
Preferred stock	Share capital—preference
Paid-in capital	Issued/allocated share capital
Paid-in capital in excess of par—common stock	Share premium—ordinary
Paid-in capital in excess of par—preferred stock	Share premium—preference
Retained earnings	Retained earnings or Retained profits
Retained earnings deficit	Accumulated losses
Accumulated other comprehensive income	General reserve and other reserve accounts

As an example of how similar transactions use different terminology under IFRS, consider the accounting for the issuance of 1,000 shares of $1 par value common stock for $5 per share. Under IFRS, the entry is as follows.

Cash	5,000	
Share Capital—Ordinary		1,000
Share Premium—Ordinary		4,000

- The accounting for treasury stock differs somewhat between IFRS and GAAP. (However, many of the differences are beyond the scope of this course.) Like GAAP, IFRS does not allow a company to record gains or losses on purchases of its own shares. One difference worth noting is that, when a company purchases its own shares, IFRS treats it as a reduction of stockholders' equity, but it does not specify which particular stockholders' equity accounts are to be affected. Therefore, it could be shown as an increase to a contra-equity account (Treasury Stock) or a decrease to retained earnings or share capital.

- A major difference between IFRS and GAAP relates to the account Revaluation Surplus. Revaluation surplus arises under IFRS because companies are permitted to revalue their property, plant, and equipment to fair value under certain circumstances. This account is part of general reserves under IFRS and is not considered contributed capital.

- IFRS often uses terms such as *retained profits* or *accumulated profit or loss* to describe retained earnings. The term *retained earnings* is also often used.

- The accounting related to prior period adjustment is essentially the same under IFRS and GAAP. IFRS addresses the accounting for errors in *IAS 8* ("Accounting Policies, Changes in Accounting Estimates, and Errors"). One area where IFRS and GAAP differ in reporting relates to error corrections in previously issued financial statements. While IFRS requires restatement with some exceptions, GAAP does not permit any exceptions.

- Equity is given various descriptions under IFRS, such as shareholder's equity, owners' equity, capital and reserves, and shareholders' funds.
- The income statement using IFRS is called the *statement of comprehensive income*. A statement of comprehensive income is presented in a one- or two-statement format. The single-statement approach includes all items of income and expense, as well as each component of other comprehensive income or loss by its individual characteristic. In the two-statement approach, a traditional income statement is prepared. It is then followed by a statement of comprehensive income, which starts with net income or loss and then adds other comprehensive income or loss items. Regardless of which approach is reported, income tax expense is required to be reported.
- The computations related to earnings per share are essentially the same under IFRS and GAAP.

Looking to the Future

The IASB and the FASB are currently working on a project related to financial statement presentation. An important part of this study is to determine whether certain line items, subtotals, and totals should be clearly defined and required to be displayed in the financial statements. For example, it is likely that the statement of stockholders' equity and its presentation will be examined closely.

Both the IASB and FASB are working toward convergence of any remaining differences related to earnings per share computations. This convergence will deal with highly technical changes beyond the scope of this textbook.

IFRS Practice

IFRS Self-Test Questions

1. Under IFRS, a purchase by a company of its own shares is recorded by:
   (a) an increase in Treasury Stock.
   (b) a decrease in contributed capital.
   (c) a decrease in share capital.
   (d) All of these are acceptable treatments.

2. Which of the following is *true*?
   (a) In the United States, the primary corporate stockholders are financial institutions.
   (b) Share capital means total assets under IFRS.
   (c) The IASB and FASB are presently studying how financial statement information should be presented.
   (d) The accounting for treasury stock differs extensively between GAAP and IFRS.

3. Under IFRS, the amount of capital received in excess of par value would be credited to:
   (a) Retained Earnings.   (c) Share Premium.
   (b) Contributed Capital.   (d) Par value is not used under IFRS.

4. Which of the following is *false*?
   (a) Under GAAP, companies cannot record gains on transactions involving their own shares.
   (b) Under IFRS, companies cannot record gains on transactions involving their own shares.
   (c) Under IFRS, the statement of stockholders' equity is a required statement.
   (d) Under IFRS, a company records a revaluation surplus when it experiences an increase in the price of its common stock.

5. Which of the following does *not* represent a pair of GAAP/IFRS-comparable terms?
   (a) Additional paid-in capital/Share premium.
   (b) Treasury stock/Repurchase reserve.
   (c) Common stock/Share capital.
   (d) Preferred stock/Preference shares.

6. The basic accounting for cash dividends and stock dividends:
   (a) is different under IFRS versus GAAP.
   (b) is the same under IFRS and GAAP.
   (c) differs only for the accounting for cash dividends between GAAP and IFRS.
   (d) differs only for the accounting for stock dividends between GAAP and IFRS.

7. Which item in *not* considered part of reserves?
   (a) Accumulated other comprehensive income.   (c) Retained earnings.
   (b) Revaluation surplus.   (d) Issued shares.

8. Under IFRS, a statement of comprehensive income must include:
   (a) accounts payable.
   (b) retained earnings.
   (c) income tax expense.
   (d) preference stock.

9. Which set of terms can be used to describe total stockholders' equity under IFRS?
   (a) Shareholders' equity, capital and reserves, other comprehensive income.
   (b) Capital and reserves, shareholders' equity, shareholders' funds.
   (c) Capital and reserves, retained earnings, shareholders' equity.
   (d) All of the above.

10. Earnings per share computations related to IFRS and GAAP:
    (a) are essentially similar.
    (b) result in an amount referred to as earnings per share.
    (c) must deduct preferred (preference) dividends when computing earnings per share.
    (d) All of the above.

IFRS Exercises

IFRS11-1 On May 10, Romano Corporation issues 1,000 shares of $10 par value ordinary shares for cash at $18 per share. Journalize the issuance of the shares.

IFRS11-2 Ingram Corporation has the following accounts (in euros) at December 31: Share Capital—Ordinary, €10 par, 5,000 shares issued, €50,000; Share Premium—Ordinary €10,000; Retained Earnings €45,000; and Treasury Shares—Ordinary, 500 shares, €11,000. Prepare the equity section of the statement of financial position.

IFRS11-3 Sorocaba Co. had the following transactions during the current period.

Mar. 2   Issued 5,000 shares of $1 par value ordinary shares to attorneys in payment of a bill for $30,000 for services provided in helping the company to incorporate.
June 12   Issued 60,000 shares of $1 par value ordinary shares for cash of $375,000.
July 11   Issued 1,000 shares of $100 par value preference shares for cash at $110 per share.
Nov. 28   Purchased 2,000 treasury shares for $80,000.

Instructions

Journalize the above transactions.

International Financial Reporting Problem: Zetar plc

IFRS11-4 The financial statements of Zetar plc are presented in Appendix C. The company's complete annual report, including the notes to its financial statements, is available at *www.zetarplc.com*.

Instructions

Use the company's annual report to answer the following questions.

(a) Using the information in the statement of changes in equity, prepare the journal entry to record the issuance of ordinary shares during the year ended April 30, 2010.

(b) Examine the equity section of the company's balance sheet. For each item in the equity section, provide the comparable label that would be used under GAAP.

(c) Did the company declare and pay any dividends for the year ended April 30, 2010?

(d) Compute the company's return on ordinary shareholders' equity for the year ended April 30, 2010.

(e) What was Zetar's earnings per share for the year ended April 30, 2010?

Answers to IFRS Self-Test Questions

1. d   **2.** c   **3.** c   **4.** d   **5.** b   **6.** b   **7.** d   **8.** c   **9.** b   **10.** d

✔ The Navigator

✔ Remember to go back to The Navigator box on the chapter opening page and check off your completed work.

Chapter 12

Investments

Feature Story

"Is There Anything Else We Can Buy?"

In a rapidly changing world, you must change rapidly or suffer the consequences. In business, change requires investment.

A case in point is found in the entertainment industry. Technology is bringing about innovations so quickly that it is nearly impossible to guess which technologies will last and which will soon fade away. For example, will both satellite TV and cable TV survive, or will just one succeed? Or, will both be replaced by something else?

Consider the publishing industry as well. Will paper newspapers and magazines be replaced completely by online news? If you are a publisher, you have to make your best guess about what the future holds and invest accordingly.

Time Warner, Inc. lives at the center of this arena. It is not an environment for the timid, and Time Warner's philosophy is anything but that. Instead, it might be characterized as, "If we can't beat you, we will buy you." Its mantra is "invest, invest, invest." A list of Time Warner's holdings gives an idea of its reach:

Magazines: *People, Time, Life, Sports Illustrated, Fortune.*

Book publishers: Time-Life Books, Book-of-the-Month Club, Little, Brown & Co, Sunset Books.

Learning Objectives

After studying this chapter, you should be able to:

1 Discuss why corporations invest in debt and stock securities.

2 Explain the accounting for debt investments.

3 Explain the accounting for stock investments.

4 Describe the use of consolidated financial statements.

5 Indicate how debt and stock investments are reported in financial statements.

6 Distinguish between short-term and long-term investments.

 ✔ **The Navigator**

Television and movies: Warner Bros. ("ER," "Without a Trace," the WB Network), HBO, and movies like *Harry Potter and the Deathly Hollows: Part 2* and *Batman Begins.*

Broadcasting: TNT, CNN news, and Turner's library of thousands of classic movies.

Internet: America Online and AOL Anywhere.

Time Warner owns more information and entertainment copyrights and brands than any other company in the world.

The merger of America Online (AOL) with Time Warner, one of the biggest mergers ever, was originally perceived by many as the gateway to the future. In actuality, it was a financial disaster. It is largely responsible for much of the decline in Time Warner's stock price, from a high of $95.80 to a recent level of $32. Ted Turner, who was at one time Time Warner's largest shareholder, lost billions of dollars on the deal and eventually sold most of his shares. In 2009, Time Warner completed a spin-off of AOL after years of trying to integrate the two companies. One analyst called the failed deal "a nine-year adventure akin to a marathon through mud."

 **The Navigator**

Preview of **Chapter 12**

Time Warner's management believes in aggressive growth through investing in the stock of existing companies. Besides purchasing stock, companies also purchase other securities such as bonds issued by corporations or by governments. Companies can make investments for a short or long period of time, as a passive investment, or with the intent to control another company. As you will see in this chapter, the way in which a company accounts for its investments is determined by a number of factors.

The content and organization of Chapter 12 are as follows.

INVESTMENTS			
Why Corporations Invest	**Accounting for Debt Investments**	**Accounting for Stock Investments**	**Valuing and Reporting Investments**
• Cash management • Investment income • Strategic reasons	• Recording acquisition of bonds • Recording bond interest • Recording sale of bonds	• Holdings of less than 20% • Holdings between 20% and 50% • Holdings of more than 50%	• Categories of securities • Balance sheet presentation • Realized and unrealized gain or loss • Classified balance sheet

✔ **The Navigator**

Why Corporations Invest

LEARNING OBJECTIVE   1

Discuss why corporations invest in debt and stock securities.

Corporations purchase investments in debt or stock securities generally for one of three reasons. First, a corporation may **have excess cash** that it does not need for the immediate purchase of operating assets. For example, many companies experience seasonal fluctuations in sales. A Cape Cod marina has more sales in the spring and summer than in the fall and winter. (The reverse is true for an Aspen ski shop.) At the end of an operating cycle, the marina may have cash on hand that is temporarily idle until the start of another operating cycle. It may invest the excess funds to earn a greater return—interest and dividends—than it would get by just holding the funds in the bank. Illustration 12-1 depicts the role that such temporary investments play in the operating cycle.

Illustration 12-1
Temporary investments and the operating cycle

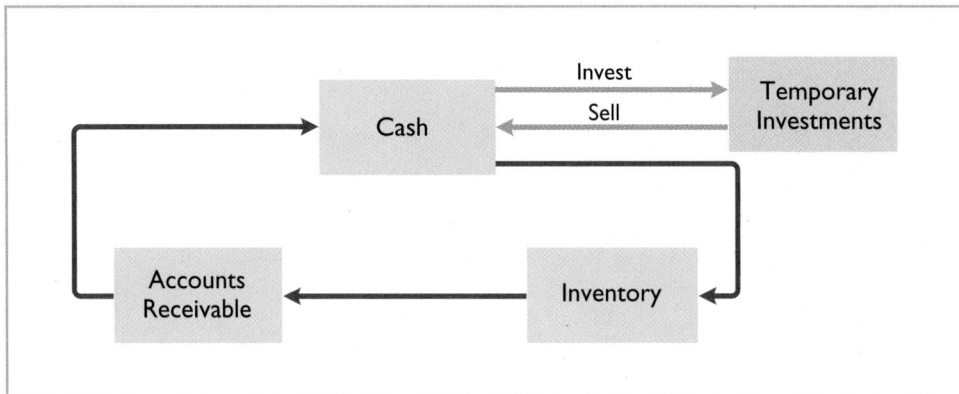

Excess cash may also result from economic cycles. For example, when the economy is booming, General Electric generates considerable excess cash. It uses some of this cash to purchase new plant and equipment, and pays out some of the cash in dividends. But, it may also invest excess cash in liquid assets in anticipation of a future downturn in the economy. It can then liquidate these investments during a recession, when sales slow and cash is scarce.

When investing excess cash for short periods of time, corporations invest in low-risk, highly liquid securities—most often short-term government securities. It is generally not wise to invest short-term excess cash in shares of common stock because stock investments can experience rapid price changes. If you did invest your short-term excess cash in stock and the price of the stock declined significantly just before you needed cash again, you would be forced to sell your stock investment at a loss.

A second reason some companies purchase investments is to generate **earnings from investment income**. For example, banks make most of their earnings by lending money, but they also generate earnings by investing in debt. Conversely, mutual stock funds invest primarily in equity securities in order to benefit from stock-price appreciation and dividend revenue.

Third, companies also invest for **strategic reasons**. A company can exercise some influence over a customer or supplier by purchasing a significant, but not controlling, interest in that company. Or, a company may purchase a noncontrolling interest in another company in a related industry in which it wishes to establish a presence. For example, Time Warner initially purchased an interest of less than 20% in Turner Broadcasting to have a stake in Turner's expanding business opportunities. At a later date, Time Warner acquired the remaining 80%. Subsequently, Time Warner merged with AOL and became AOL Time Warner, Inc. Now, it is again just Time Warner, Inc., as indicated in the Feature Story.

A corporation may also choose to purchase a controlling interest in another company. For example, as the *Accounting Across the Organization* box on page 608 shows, Procter & Gamble purchased Gillette. Such purchases might be done to enter a new industry without incurring the tremendous costs and risks associated with starting from scratch. Or, a company might purchase another company in its same industry.

In summary, businesses invest in other companies for the reasons shown in Illustration 12-2.

Illustration 12-2
Why corporations invest

Reason	Typical Investment
To house excess cash until needed	Low-risk, high-liquidity, short-term securities such as government-issued securities
To generate earnings *I need 1,000 Treasury bills by tonight.*	Debt securities (banks and other financial institutions) and stock securities (mutual funds and pension funds)
To meet strategic goals	Stocks of companies in a related industry or in an unrelated industry that the company wishes to enter

Accounting for Debt Investments

Debt investments are investments in government and corporation bonds. In accounting for debt investments, companies make entries to record (1) the acquisition, (2) the interest revenue, and (3) the sale.

LEARNING OBJECTIVE   **2**

Explain the accounting for debt investments.

Recording Acquisition of Bonds

At acquisition, the cost principle applies. Cost includes all expenditures necessary to acquire these investments, such as the price paid plus brokerage fees (commissions), if any.

Assume, for example, that Kuhl Corporation acquires 50 Doan Inc. 8%, 10-year, $1,000 bonds on January 1, 2014, for $54,000, including brokerage fees of $1,000. The entry to record the investment is:

Jan. 1	Debt Investments	54,000	
	Cash		54,000
	(To record purchase of 50 Doan Inc. bonds)		

A = **L** + **SE**
+54,000
−54,000

Cash Flows
−54,000

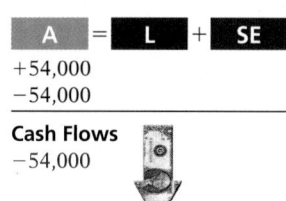

Recording Bond Interest

The Doan, Inc. bonds pay interest of $2,000 semiannually on July 1 and January 1 ($50,000 × 8% × ½). The entry for the receipt of interest on July 1 is:

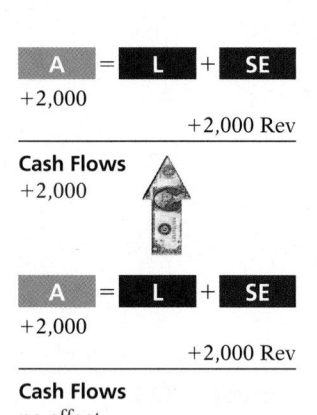

July 1	Cash	2,000	
	Interest Revenue		2,000
	(To record receipt of interest on Doan Inc. bonds)		

If Kuhl Corporation's fiscal year ends on December 31, it accrues the interest of $2,000 earned since July 1. The adjusting entry is:

Dec. 31	Interest Receivable	2,000	
	Interest Revenue		2,000
	(To accrue interest on Doan Inc. bonds)		

Kuhl reports Interest Receivable as a current asset in the balance sheet. It reports Interest Revenue under "Other revenues and gains" in the income statement.

Kuhl reports receipt of the interest on January 1 as follows.

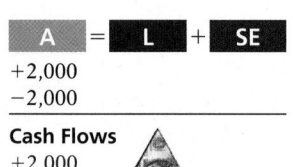

Jan. 1	Cash	2,000	
	Interest Receivable		2,000
	(To record receipt of accrued interest)		

A credit to Interest Revenue at this time is incorrect because the company earned and accrued interest revenue in the *preceding* accounting period.

Recording Sale of Bonds

When Kuhl sells the bonds, it credits the investment account for the cost of the bonds. Kuhl records as a gain or loss any difference between the net proceeds from the sale (sales price less brokerage fees) and the cost of the bonds.

Assume, for example, that Kuhl Corporation receives net proceeds of $58,000 on the sale of the Doan Inc. bonds on January 1, 2015, after receiving the interest due. Since the securities cost $54,000, the company realizes a gain of $4,000. It records the sale as:

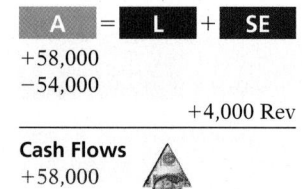

Jan. 1	Cash	58,000	
	Debt Investments		54,000
	Gain on Sale of Debt Investments		4,000
	(To record sale of Doan Inc. bonds)		

Kuhl reports the gain on sale of debt investments under "Other revenues and gains" in the income statement and reports losses under "Other expenses and losses."

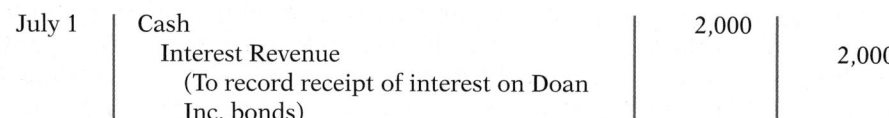

> **DO IT!**

Debt Investments

Waldo Corporation had the following transactions pertaining to debt investments.

Jan. 1   Purchased 30, $1,000 Hillary Co. 10% bonds for $30,000, plus brokerage fees of $900. Interest is payable semiannually on July 1 and January 1.

July 1   Received semiannual interest on Hillary Co. bonds.

July 1   Sold 15 Hillary Co. bonds for $15,000, less $400 brokerage fees.

(a) Journalize the transactions, and (b) prepare the adjusting entry for the accrual of interest on December 31.

Action Plan

✔ Record bond investments at cost.

✔ Record interest when received and/or accrued.

✔ When bonds are sold, credit the investment account for the cost of the bonds.

✔ Record any difference between the cost and the net proceeds as a gain or loss.

Solution

(a)	Jan. 1	Debt Investments	30,900	
		Cash		30,900
		(To record purchase of 30 Hillary Co. bonds)		
	July 1	Cash	1,500	
		Interest Revenue ($30,000 × .10 × 6/12)		1,500
		(To record receipt of interest on Hillary Co. bonds)		
	July 1	Cash	14,600	
		Loss on Sale of Debt Investments	850	
		Debt Investments ($30,900 × 15/30)		15,450
		(To record sale of 15 Hillary Co. bonds)		
(b)	Dec. 31	Interest Receivable	750	
		Interest Revenue ($15,000 × .10 × 6/12)		750
		(To accrue interest on Hillary Co. bonds)		

Related exercise material: **BE12-1, E12-2, E12-3, and DO IT! 12-1.**

✔ **The Navigator**

Accounting for Stock Investments

Stock investments are investments in the capital stock of other corporations. When a company holds stock (and/or debt) of several different corporations, the group of securities is identified as an **investment portfolio**.

The accounting for investments in common stock depends on the extent of the investor's influence over the operating and financial affairs of the issuing corporation (the **investee**). Illustration 12-3 shows the general guidelines.

LEARNING OBJECTIVE 3

Explain the accounting for stock investments.

Illustration 12-3
Accounting guidelines for stock investments

Investor's Ownership Interest in Investee's Common Stock	Presumed Influence on Investee	Accounting Guidelines
Less than 20%	Insignificant	Cost method
Between 20% and 50%	Significant	Equity method
More than 50%	Controlling	Consolidated financial statements

Companies are required to use judgment instead of blindly following the guidelines.[1] On the following pages, we will explain the application of each guideline.

---

[1] Among the questions that are considered in determining an investor's influence are these: (1) Does the investor have representation on the investee's board? (2) Does the investor participate in the investee's policy-making process? (3) Are there material transactions between the investor and investee? (4) Is the common stock held by other stockholders concentrated or dispersed?

Holdings of Less than 20%

In accounting for stock investments of less than 20%, companies use the cost method. Under the **cost method**, companies record the investment at cost, and recognize revenue only when cash dividends are received.

RECORDING ACQUISITION OF STOCK INVESTMENTS

At acquisition, the cost principle applies. Cost includes all expenditures necessary to acquire these investments, such as the price paid plus any brokerage fees (commissions).

Assume, for example, that on July 1, 2014, Sanchez Corporation acquires 1,000 shares (10% ownership) of Beal Corporation common stock. Sanchez pays $40 per share plus brokerage fees of $500. The entry for the purchase is:

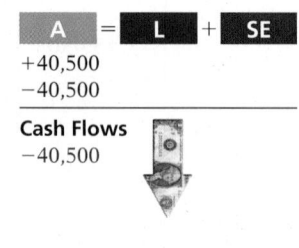

July 1	Stock Investments	40,500	
	Cash		40,500
	(To record purchase of 1,000 shares of Beal Corporation common stock)		

RECORDING DIVIDENDS

During the time Sanchez owns the stock, it makes entries for any cash dividends received. If Sanchez receives a $2 per share dividend on December 31, the entry is:

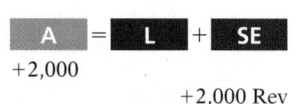

Dec. 31	Cash (1,000 × $2)	2,000	
	Dividend Revenue		2,000
	(To record receipt of a cash dividend)		

Sanchez reports Dividend Revenue under "Other revenues and gains" in the income statement. Unlike interest on notes and bonds, dividends do not accrue. Therefore, companies do not make adjusting entries to accrue dividends.

RECORDING SALE OF STOCK

When a company sells a stock investment, it recognizes as a gain or a loss the difference between the net proceeds from the sale (sales price less brokerage fees) and the cost of the stock.

Assume that Sanchez Corporation receives net proceeds of $39,500 on the sale of its Beal stock on February 10, 2015. Because the stock cost $40,500, Sanchez incurred a loss of $1,000. The entry to record the sale is:

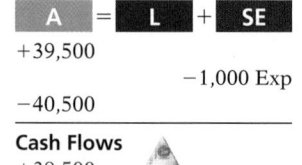

Feb. 10	Cash	39,500	
	Loss on Sale of Stock Investments	1,000	
	Stock Investments		40,500
	(To record sale of Beal common stock)		

Sanchez reports the loss under "Other expenses and losses" in the income statement. It would show a gain on sale under "Other revenues and gains."

Holdings Between 20% and 50%

When an investor company owns only a small portion of the shares of stock of another company, the investor cannot exercise control over the investee. But, when an investor owns between 20% and 50% of the common stock of a corporation, it is presumed that the investor has significant influence over the financial and operating activities of the investee. The investor probably has a representative on the investee's board of directors and, through that representative, may exercise some control over the investee. The investee company in some sense becomes part of the investor company.

For example, even prior to purchasing all of Turner Broadcasting, Time Warner owned 20% of Turner. Because it exercised significant control over major decisions made by Turner, Time Warner used an approach called the equity method. Under the **equity method**, **the investor records its share of the net income of the investee in the year when it is earned**. An alternative might be to delay recognizing the investor's share of net income until the investee declares a cash dividend. But, that approach would ignore the fact that the investor and investee are, in some sense, one company, making the investor better off by the investee's earned income.

Under the equity method, the investor company initially records the investment in common stock at cost. After that, it **adjusts** the investment account annually to show the investor's equity in the investee. Each year, the investor does the following. (1) It increases (debits) the investment account and increases (credits) revenue for its share of the investee's net income.[2] (2) The investor also decreases (credits) the investment account for the amount of dividends received. The investment account is reduced for dividends received because payment of a dividend decreases the net assets of the investee.

> **Helpful Hint**
> Under the equity method, the investor recognizes revenue on the accrual basis—i.e., when it is earned by the investee.

RECORDING ACQUISITION OF STOCK INVESTMENTS

Assume that Milar Corporation acquires 30% of the common stock of Beck Company for $120,000 on January 1, 2014. The entry to record this transaction is:

Jan. 1	Stock Investments	120,000	
	Cash		120,000
	(To record purchase of Beck common stock)		

A = L + SE
+120,000
−120,000

Cash Flows
−120,000

RECORDING REVENUE AND DIVIDENDS

For 2014, Beck reports net income of $100,000. It declares and pays a $40,000 cash dividend. Milar records (1) its share of Beck's income, $30,000 (30% × $100,000) and (2) the reduction in the investment account for the dividends received, $12,000 ($40,000 × 30%). The entries are:

(1)

Dec. 31	Stock Investments	30,000	
	Revenue from Stock Investments		30,000
	(To record 30% equity in Beck's 2014 net income)		

A = L + SE
+30,000
                    +30,000 Rev

Cash Flows
no effect

(2)

Dec. 31	Cash	12,000	
	Stock Investments		12,000
	(To record dividends received)		

A = L + SE
+12,000
−12,000

Cash Flows
+12,000

After Milar posts the transactions for the year, its investment and revenue accounts will show the following.

Stock Investments			
Jan. 1	120,000	Dec. 31	12,000
Dec. 31	30,000		
Dec. 31 Bal.	138,000		

Revenue from Stock Investments		
	Dec. 31	30,000

Illustration 12-4
Investment and revenue accounts after posting

During the year, the net increase in the investment account was $18,000. As indicated above, the investment account increased by $30,000 due to Milar's share of

---

[2]Or, the investor increases (debits) a loss account and decreases (credits) the investment account for its share of the investee's net loss.

Beck's income, and it decreased by $12,000 due to dividends received from Beck. In addition, Milar reports $30,000 of revenue from its investment, which is 30% of Beck's net income of $100,000.

Note that the difference between reported revenue under the cost method and reported revenue under the equity method can be significant. For example, Milar would report only $12,000 (30% × $40,000) of dividend revenue if it used the cost method.

Holdings of More than 50%

A company that owns more than 50% of the common stock of another entity is known as the **parent company**. The entity whose stock the parent company owns is called the **subsidiary (affiliated) company**. Because of its stock ownership, the parent company has a **controlling interest** in the subsidiary.

When a company owns more than 50% of the common stock of another company, it usually prepares **consolidated financial statements**. These statements present the total assets and liabilities controlled by the parent company. They also present the total revenues and expenses of the subsidiary companies. Companies prepare consolidated statements **in addition to** the financial statements for the parent and individual subsidiary companies.

As noted earlier, when Time Warner had a 20% investment in Turner, it reported this investment in a single line item—Other Investments. After the merger, Time Warner instead consolidated Turner's results with its own. Under this approach, Time Warner included Turner's individual assets and liabilities with its own: its plant and equipment were added to Time Warner's plant and equipment, its receivables were added to Time Warner's receivables, and so on.

Helpful Hint
If parent (A) has three wholly owned subsidiaries (B, C, & D), there are four separate legal entities. From the viewpoint of the shareholders of the parent company, there is only one economic entity.

ACCOUNTING ACROSS THE ORGANIZATION

How Procter & Gamble Accounts for Gillette

Recently, Procter & Gamble Company acquired Gillette Company for $53.4 billion. The common stockholders of Procter & Gamble elect the board of directors of the company, who, in turn, select the officers and managers of the company. Procter & Gamble's board of directors controls the property owned by the corporation, which includes the common stock of Gillette. Thus, they are in a position to elect the board of directors of Gillette and, in effect, control its operations. These relationships are graphically illustrated here.

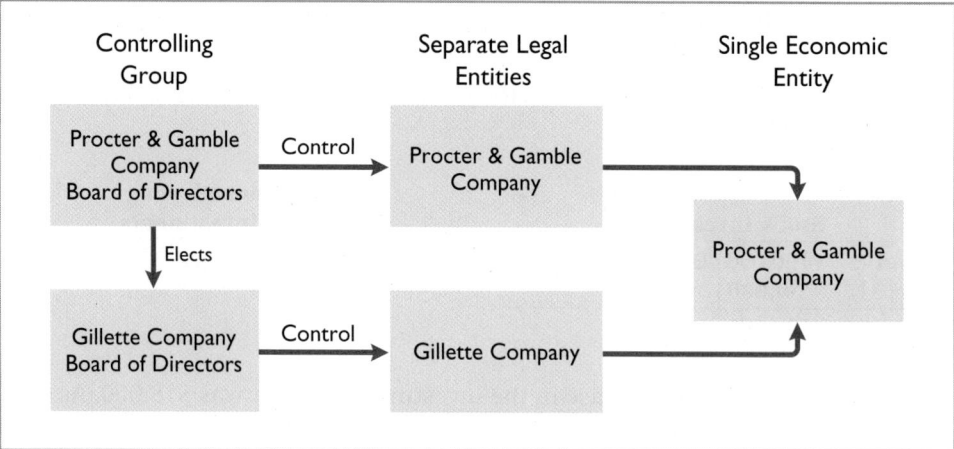

? Where on Procter & Gamble's balance sheet will you find its investment in Gillette Company? (See page 641.)

Consolidated statements are useful to the stockholders, board of directors, and managers of the parent company. These statements indicate the magnitude and scope of operations of the companies under common control. For example, regulators and the courts undoubtedly used the consolidated statements of AT&T to determine whether a breakup of the company was in the public interest. Listed below are three companies that prepare consolidated statements and some of the companies they have owned. One, Disney, is Time Warner's arch rival.

PepsiCo	Cendant	The Disney Company
Frito-Lay	Howard Johnson	Capital Cities/ABC, Inc.
Tropicana	Ramada Inn	Disneyland, Disney World
Quaker Oats	Century 21	Mighty Ducks
Pepsi-Cola	Coldwell Banker	Anaheim Angels
Gatorade	Avis	ESPN

Illustration 12-5
Examples of consolidated companies and their subsidiaries

> DO IT!

Stock Investments

Presented below are two independent situations.

1. Rho Jean Inc. acquired 5% of the 400,000 shares of common stock of Stillwater Corp. at a total cost of $6 per share on May 18, 2014. On August 30, Stillwater declared and paid a $75,000 dividend. On December 31, Stillwater reported net income of $244,000 for the year.

2. Debbie, Inc. obtained significant influence over North Sails by buying 40% of North Sails' 60,000 outstanding shares of common stock at a cost of $12 per share on January 1, 2014. On April 15, North Sails declared and paid a cash dividend of $45,000. On December 31, North Sails reported net income of $120,000 for the year.

Prepare all necessary journal entries for 2014 for (1) Rho Jean Inc. and (2) Debbie, Inc.

Solution

Action Plan

✔ Presume that the investor has relatively little influence over the investee when an investor owns less than 20% of the common stock of another corporation. In this case, net income earned by the investee is not considered a proper basis for recognizing income from the investment by the investor.

✔ Presume significant influence for investments of 20%–50%. Therefore, record the investor's share of the net income of the investee.

(1)	May 18	Stock Investments (20,000 × $6)	120,000	
		Cash		120,000
		(To record purchase of 20,000 shares of Stillwater Co. stock)		
	Aug. 30	Cash	3,750	
		Dividend Revenue ($75,000 × 5%)		3,750
		(To record receipt of cash dividend)		
(2)	Jan. 1	Stock Investments (60,000 × 40% × $12)	288,000	
		Cash		288,000
		(To record purchase of 24,000 shares of North Sails' stock)		
	Apr. 15	Cash	18,000	
		Stock Investments ($45,000 × 40%)		18,000
		(To record receipt of cash dividend)		
	Dec. 31	Stock Investments ($120,000 × 40%)	48,000	
		Revenue from Stock Investments		48,000
		(To record 40% equity in North Sails' net income)		

Related exercise material: **BE12-2, BE12-3, E12-4, E12-5, E12-6, E12-7, E12-8, and** DO IT! **12-2.**

 The Navigator

Valuing and Reporting Investments

LEARNING OBJECTIVE **5**

Indicate how debt and stock investments are reported in financial statements.

The value of debt and stock investments may fluctuate greatly during the time they are held. For example, in one 12-month period, the stock price of Time Warner hit a high of $58.50 and a low of $9. In light of such price fluctuations, how should companies value investments at the balance sheet date? Valuation could be at cost, at fair value, or at the lower-of-cost-or-market value.

Many people argue that fair value offers the best approach because it represents the expected cash realizable value of securities. **Fair value** is the amount for which a security could be sold in a normal market. Others counter that, unless a security is going to be sold soon, the fair value is not relevant because the price of the security will likely change again.

Categories of Securities

For purposes of valuation and reporting at a financial statement date, companies classify debt investments into two categories:

1. **Trading securities** are bought and held primarily for sale in the near term to generate income on short-term price differences.

2. **Held-for-collection securities** are debt securities that the investor has the intent and ability to hold to maturity.[3]

Stock investments are also classified into two categories:

1. **Trading securities** (as defined above).

2. **Non-trading securities** are held for purposes other than trading. For example, a company may hold a stock investment to sell a product in a particular area.

Stock investments have no maturity date and therefore are never classified as held-for-collection securities.

Illustration 12-6 shows the valuation guidelines for these securities. **These guidelines apply to all debt securities and to those stock investments in which the holdings are less than 20%.**

Illustration 12-6
Valuation guidelines

Trading (Both Debt and Stock)	Non-Trading (Stock Only)	Held-for-Collection (Debt Only)
"We'll sell within ten days."	"We'll hold the stock for a while to see how it performs."	"We intend to hold until maturity."
At fair value with changes reported in net income	At fair value with changes reported in the stockholders' equity section	At amortized cost

---

[3]This category is provided for completeness. The accounting and valuation issues related to held-for-collection securities are discussed in more advanced accounting courses. The discussion in valuing and reporting investments is based on the revised exposure draft issued by the FASB.

TRADING SECURITIES

Companies hold trading securities with the intention of selling them in a short period (generally less than a month). *Trading* means frequent buying and selling. As indicated in Illustration 12-7, companies adjust trading securities to fair value at the end of each period, and report changes from cost as part of net income. The changes are reported as **unrealized gains or losses** because the securities have not been sold. The unrealized gain or loss is the difference between the **total cost** of trading securities and their **total fair value**. Companies classify trading securities as current assets.

Illustration 12-7 shows the cost and fair values for investments Pace Corporation classified as trading securities on December 31, 2014. Pace has an unrealized gain of $7,000 because total fair value of $147,000 is $7,000 greater than total cost of $140,000.

Helpful Hint
The fact that trading securities are short-term investments increases the likelihood that they will be sold at fair value (the company may not be able to time their sale) and the likelihood that there will be realized gains or losses.

Trading Securities, December 31, 2014			
Investments	Cost	Fair Value	Unrealized Gain (Loss)
Yorkville Company bonds	$ 50,000	$ 48,000	$(2,000)
Kodak Company stock	90,000	99,000	9,000
Total	$140,000	$147,000	$ 7,000

Illustration 12-7
Valuation of trading securities

Pace records fair value and unrealized gain or loss through an adjusting entry at the time it prepares financial statements. In this entry, the company uses a valuation allowance account, Fair Value Adjustment—Trading, to record the difference between the total cost and the total fair value of the securities. The adjusting entry for Pace Corporation is:

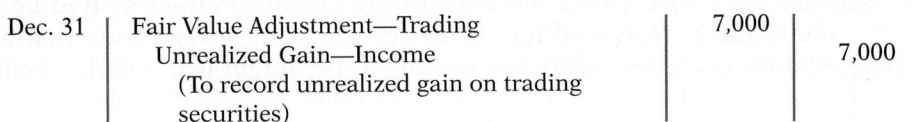

Dec. 31	Fair Value Adjustment—Trading	7,000	
	Unrealized Gain—Income		7,000
	(To record unrealized gain on trading securities)		

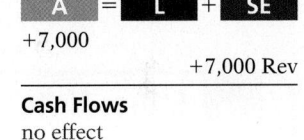

A	=	L	+	SE
+7,000				
				+7,000 Rev

Cash Flows
no effect

The use of a Fair Value Adjustment—Trading account enables Pace to maintain a record of the investment cost. It needs actual cost to determine the gain or loss realized when it sells the securities. Pace adds the debit balance (or subtracts a credit balance) of the Fair Value Adjustment—Trading account to the cost of the investments to arrive at a fair value for the trading securities.

The fair value of the securities is the amount Pace reports on its balance sheet. It reports the unrealized gain in the income statement in the "Other revenues and gains" section. The term "Income" in the account title indicates that the gain affects net income.

If the total cost of the trading securities is greater than total fair value, an unrealized loss has occurred. In such a case, the adjusting entry is a debit to Unrealized Loss—Income and a credit to Fair Value Adjustment—Trading. Companies report the unrealized loss under "Other expenses and losses" in the income statement.

The Fair Value Adjustment—Trading account is carried forward into future accounting periods. The company does not make any entry to the account until the end of each reporting period. At that time, the company adjusts the balance in the account to the difference between cost and fair value. For trading securities, it closes the Unrealized Gain (Loss)—Income account at the end of the reporting period.

ACCOUNTING ACROSS THE ORGANIZATION

And the Correct Way to Report Investments Is...?

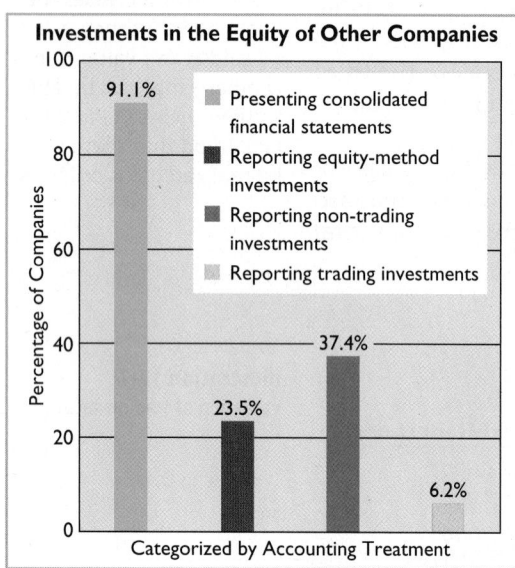

Investments in the Equity of Other Companies

The accompanying graph presents an estimate of the percentage of companies on the major exchanges that have investments in the equity of other entities.

As the graph indicates, many companies have equity investments of some type. These investments can be substantial. For example, the total amount of equity-method investments appearing on company balance sheets is approximately $403 billion, and the amount shown in the income statements in any one year for all companies is approximately $38 billion.

Source: "Report and Recommendations Pursuant to Section 401(c) of the Sarbanes-Oxley Act of 2002 on Arrangements with Off-Balance Sheet Implications, Special Purpose Entities, and Transparency of Filings by Issuers," United States Securities and Exchange Commission—Office of Chief Accountant, Office of Economic Analyses, Division of Corporation Finance (June 2005), pp. 36–39.

 Why might the use of the equity method not lead to full disclosure in the financial statements? (See page 641.)

NON-TRADING SECURITIES

As indicated earlier, debt investments are classified either as trading or held-for-collection securities. Stock investments are classified either as trading or non-trading. **Non-trading securities** are stock investments that are held for purposes other than trading. If the intent is to sell the securities within the next year or operating cycle, the investor classifies the securities as current assets in the balance sheet. Otherwise, it classifies them as long-term assets in the investments section of the balance sheet.

> **Ethics Note**
>
> Some managers seem to hold their non-trading securities that have experienced losses, while selling those that have gains, thus increasing income. Do you think this is ethical?

Companies report non-trading securities at fair value. The procedure for determining fair value and the unrealized gain or loss for these securities is the same as for trading securities. To illustrate, assume that Ingrao Corporation has two securities that it classifies as non-trading. Illustration 12-8 provides information on the cost, fair value, and amount of the unrealized gain or loss on December 31, 2014. There is an unrealized loss of $9,537 because total cost of $293,537 is $9,537 more than total fair value of $284,000.

Illustration 12-8
Valuation of non-trading securities

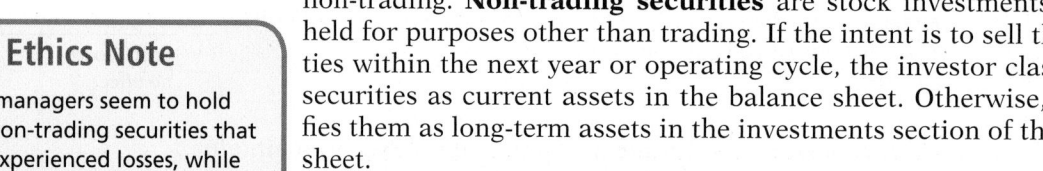

Non-Trading Securities, December 31, 2014

Investments	Cost	Fair Value	Unrealized Gain (Loss)
Campbell Soup Corporation stock	$ 93,537	$103,600	$10,063
Hershey Company stock	200,000	180,400	(19,600)
Total	$293,537	$284,000	$ (9,537)

Both the adjusting entry and the reporting of the unrealized gain or loss for Ingrao's non-trading securities differ from those illustrated for trading securities. The differences result because Ingrao does not expect to sell these securities in the near term. Thus, prior to actual sale, it is more likely that changes in fair value may change either unrealized gains or losses. Therefore, Ingrao does not report an unrealized gain or loss in the income statement. Instead, it reports it as a **separate component of stockholders' equity**.

In the adjusting entry, Ingrao identifies the fair value adjustment account with non-trading securities, and it identifies the unrealized gain or loss account with stockholders' equity. Ingrao records the unrealized loss of $9,537 as follows.

> ### Ethics Note
> At one time, the SEC accused investment bank Morgan Stanley of overstating the value of certain bond investments by $75 million. The SEC stated that, in applying market value accounting, Morgan Stanley used its own more-optimistic assumptions rather than relying on external pricing sources.

Dec. 31	Unrealized Gain or Loss—Equity	9,537	
	Fair Value Adjustment—Non-Trading		9,537
	(To record unrealized loss on non-trading		
	securities)		

A = L + SE

−9,537   −9,537 Exp

Cash Flows
no effect

If total fair value exceeds total cost, Ingrao debits Fair Value Adjustment—Non-Trading and credits Unrealized Gain or Loss—Equity.

For non-trading securities, the company carries forward the Unrealized Gain or Loss—Equity account to future periods. At each future balance sheet date, Ingrao adjusts the Fair Value Adjustment—Non-Trading and the Unrealized Gain or Loss—Equity accounts to show the difference between cost and fair value at that time.

> DO IT!

Trading and Non-Trading Securities

Action Plan

✔ Mark trading securities to fair value and report the adjustment in current-period income.

✔ Mark non-trading securities to fair value and report the adjustment as a separate component of stockholders' equity.

Some of Powderhorn Corporation's investment securities are classified as trading securities and some are classified as non-trading. The cost and fair value of each category at December 31, 2014, are shown below.

	Cost	Fair Value	Unrealized Gain (Loss)
Trading securities	$93,600	$94,900	$1,300
Non-trading securities	$48,800	$51,400	$2,600

At December 31, 2013, the Fair Value Adjustment—Trading account had a debit balance of $9,200, and the Fair Value Adjustment—Non-Trading account had a credit balance of $5,750. Prepare the required journal entries for each group of securities for December 31, 2014.

Solution

Trading securities:

Unrealized Loss—Income	7,900*	
Fair Value Adjustment—Trading		7,900
(To record unrealized loss on trading securities)		

*$9,200 − $1,300

Non-trading securities:

Fair Value Adjustment—Non-Trading	8,350**	
Unrealized Gain or Loss—Equity		8,350
(To record unrealized gain on non-trading securities)		

**$5,750 + $2,600

Related exercise material: **BE12-4, BE12-5, BE12-6, BE12-7, E12-10, E12-11, E12-12, and** DO IT! **12-3.**

 ✔ **The Navigator**

Balance Sheet Presentation

In the balance sheet, companies classify investments as either short-term or long-term.

SHORT-TERM INVESTMENTS

Short-term investments (also called **marketable securities**) are securities held by a company that are (1) **readily marketable** and (2) **intended to be converted into cash** within the next year or operating cycle, whichever is longer. Investments that do not meet **both criteria** are classified as **long-term investments**.

Helpful Hint
Trading securities are always classified as short-term. Non-trading securities can be either short-term or long-term.

READILY MARKETABLE An investment is readily marketable when it can be sold easily whenever the need for cash arises. Short-term paper[4] meets this criterion. It can be readily sold to other investors. Stocks and bonds traded on organized securities exchanges, such as the New York Stock Exchange, are readily marketable. They can be bought and sold daily. In contrast, there may be only a limited market for the securities issued by small corporations, and no market for the securities of a privately held company.

INTENT TO CONVERT Intent to convert means that management intends to sell the investment within the next year or operating cycle, whichever is longer. Generally, this criterion is satisfied when the investment is considered a resource that the investor will use whenever the need for cash arises. For example, a ski resort may invest idle cash during the summer months with the intent to sell the securities to buy supplies and equipment shortly before the winter season. This investment is considered short-term even if lack of snow cancels the next ski season and eliminates the need to convert the securities into cash as intended.

Because of their high liquidity, short-term investments appear immediately below Cash in the "Current assets" section of the balance sheet. They are reported at fair value. For example, Pace Corporation would report its trading securities as shown in Illustration 12-9.

Illustration 12-9
Presentation of short-term investments

Pace Corporation Balance Sheet (partial)	
Current assets	
Cash	$ 21,000
Short-term investments, at fair value	147,000

LONG-TERM INVESTMENTS

Companies generally report long-term investments in a separate section of the balance sheet immediately below "Current assets," as shown later in Illustration 12-12 (page 616). Long-term investments in non-trading securities are reported at fair value. Investments in common stock accounted for under the equity method are reported at equity.

Presentation of Realized and Unrealized Gain or Loss

Companies must present in the financial statements gains and losses on investments, whether realized or unrealized. In the income statement, companies

---

[4]**Short-term paper** includes (1) certificates of deposit (CDs) issued by banks, (2) money market certificates issued by banks and savings and loan associations, (3) Treasury bills issued by the U.S. government, and (4) commercial paper (notes) issued by corporations with good credit ratings.

report gains and losses in the nonoperating activities section under the categories listed in Illustration 12-10. Interest and dividend revenue are also reported in that section.

Other Revenue and Gains	Other Expenses and Losses
Interest Revenue	Loss on Sale of Investments
Dividend Revenue	Unrealized Loss—Income
Gain on Sale of Investments	
Unrealized Gain—Income	

Illustration 12-10
Nonoperating items related to investments

As indicated earlier, companies report an unrealized gain or loss on non-trading securities as a separate component of stockholders' equity. To illustrate, assume that Dawson Inc. has common stock of $3,000,000, retained earnings of $1,500,000, and an unrealized loss on non-trading securities of $100,000. Illustration 12-11 shows the balance sheet presentation of the unrealized loss.

Illustration 12-11
Unrealized loss in stockholders' equity section

Dawson Inc. Balance Sheet (partial)	
Stockholders' equity	
Common stock	$3,000,000
Retained earnings	1,500,000
Total paid-in capital and retained earnings	4,500,000
Less: Unrealized loss on non-trading securities	**100,000**
Total stockholders' equity	$4,400,000

Note that the loss decreases stockholders' equity. An unrealized gain is added to stockholders' equity. Reporting the unrealized gain or loss in the stockholders' equity section serves two purposes: (1) It reduces the volatility of net income due to fluctuations in fair value. (2) It informs the financial statement user of the gain or loss that would occur if the securities were sold at fair value.

Companies must report items such as this, which affect stockholders' equity but are not included in the calculation of net income, as part of a more inclusive measure called *comprehensive income*. We discuss comprehensive income more fully in Chapter 14.

Classified Balance Sheet

We have presented many sections of classified balance sheets in this and preceding chapters. The classified balance sheet in Illustration 12-12 (page 616) includes, in one place, key topics from previous chapters: the issuance of par value common stock, restrictions of retained earnings, and issuance of long-term bonds. From this chapter, the statement includes (highlighted in red) short-term and long-term investments. The investments in short-term securities are considered trading securities. The long-term investments in stock of less than 20% owned companies are considered non-trading securities. Illustration 12-12 also includes a long-term investment reported at equity and descriptive notations within the statement, such as the basis for valuing inventory and one note to the statement.

Illustration 12-12
Classified balance sheet

Pace Corporation
Balance Sheet
December 31, 2014

Assets

Current assets
  Cash .... $ 21,000
  Short-term investments, at fair value **147,000**
  Accounts receivable .... $ 84,000
  Less: Allowance for doubtful accounts 4,000   80,000
  Inventory, at FIFO cost 43,000
  Prepaid insurance 23,000
    Total current assets 314,000
Investments
  Investments in stock of less than 20%
  owned companies, at fair value **50,000**
  Investment in stock of 20–50% owned
  company, at equity **150,000**
    Total investments 200,000
Property, plant, and equipment
  Land 200,000
  Buildings $800,000
  Less: Accumulated depreciation—buildings 200,000   600,000
  Equipment 180,000
  Less: Accumulated depreciation—equipment 54,000   126,000
    Total property, plant, and equipment 926,000
Intangible assets
  Goodwill 270,000
    Total assets $1,710,000

Liabilities and Stockholders' Equity

Current liabilities
  Accounts payable .... $ 185,000
  Income taxes payable 60,000
  Interest payable 10,000
    Total current liabilities 255,000
Long-term liabilities
  Bonds payable, 10%, due 2021 .... $ 300,000
  Less: Discount on bonds payable 10,000
    Total long-term liabilities 290,000
    Total liabilities 545,000
Stockholders' equity
  Paid-in capital
    Common stock, $10 par value, 200,000 shares
      authorized, 80,000 shares issued and
      outstanding 800,000
  Paid-in capital in excess of par—
    common stock 100,000
    Total paid-in capital 900,000
  Retained earnings (Note 1) 255,000
    Total paid-in capital and retained earnings 1,155,000
  Add: Unrealized gain on non-trading
    securities **10,000**
    Total stockholders' equity 1,165,000
    Total liabilities and stockholders' equity $1,710,000

Note 1. Retained earnings of $100,000 is restricted for plant expansion.

> DO IT!

Financial Statement Presentation of Investments

Identify where each of the following items would be reported in the financial statements.

1. Interest earned on investments in bonds.
2. Fair value adjustment—non-trading.
3. Unrealized loss on non-trading securities.
4. Gain on sale of investments in stock.
5. Unrealized gain on trading securities.

Use the following possible categories:

Balance sheet:

Current assets	Current liabilities
Investments	Long-term liabilities
Property, plant, and equipment	Stockholders' equity
Intangible assets	

Income statement:

Other revenues and gains   Other expenses and losses

Action Plan

✔ Classify investments as current assets if they will be held for less than one year.

✔ Report unrealized gains or losses on trading securities in income.

✔ Report unrealized gains or losses on non-trading securities in equity.

✔ Report realized earnings on investments in the income statement as "Other revenues and gains" or as "Other expenses and losses."

Solution

Item	Financial Statement	Category
1. Interest earned on investments in bonds.	Income statement	Other revenues and gains
2. Fair value adjustment—non-trading	Balance sheet	Investments
3. Unrealized loss on non-trading securities	Balance sheet	Stockholders' equity
4. Gain on sale of investments in stock	Income statement	Other revenues and gains
5. Unrealized gain on trading securities	Income statement	Other revenues and gains

Related exercise material: **BE12-6, BE12-7, BE12-8, E12-10, E12-11, E12-12, and DO IT! 12-4.**

✔ **The Navigator**

> Comprehensive DO IT!

In its first year of operations, DeMarco Company had the following selected transactions in stock investments that are considered trading securities.

June 1   Purchased for cash 600 shares of Sanburg common stock at $24 per share, plus $300 brokerage fees.

July 1   Purchased for cash 800 shares of Cey Corporation common stock at $33 per share, plus $600 brokerage fees.

Sept. 1   Received a $1 per share cash dividend from Cey Corporation.

Nov. 1   Sold 200 shares of Sanburg common stock for cash at $27 per share, less $150 brokerage fees.

Dec. 15   Received a $0.50 per share cash dividend on Sanburg common stock.

At December 31, the fair values per share were Sanburg $25 and Cey $30.

Instructions

(a) Journalize the transactions.

(b) Prepare the adjusting entry at December 31 to report the securities at fair value.

Action Plan

✔ Include the price paid plus brokerage fees in the cost of the investment.

✔ Compute the gain or loss on sales as the difference between net selling price and the cost of the securities.

✔ Base the adjustment to fair value on the total difference between the cost and the fair value of the securities.

Solution to Comprehensive DO IT!

(a) June 1	Stock Investments		14,700	
	Cash [(600 × $24) + $300]			14,700
	(To record purchase of 600 shares of Sanburg common stock)			
July 1	Stock Investments		27,000	
	Cash [(800 × $33) + $600]			27,000
	(To record purchase of 800 shares of Cey common stock)			
Sept. 1	Cash (800 × $1.00)		800	
	Dividend Revenue			800
	(To record receipt of $1 per share cash dividend from Cey Corporation)			
Nov. 1	Cash [(200 × $27) − $150]		5,250	
	Stock Investments ($14,700 × 200/600)			4,900
	Gain on Sale of Stock Investments			350
	(To record sale of 200 shares of Sanburg common stock)			
Dec. 15	Cash [(600 − 200) × $0.50]		200	
	Dividend Revenue			200
	(To record receipt of $0.50 per share dividend from Sanburg)			
(b) Dec. 31	Unrealized Loss—Income		2,800	
	Fair Value Adjustment—Trading			2,800
	(To record unrealized loss on trading securities)			

Investment	Cost	Fair Value	Unrealized Gain (Loss)
Sanburg common stock	$ 9,800	$10,000	$ 200
Cey common stock	27,000	24,000	(3,000)
Totals	$36,800	$34,000	$(2,800)

✔ **The Navigator**

SUMMARY OF LEARNING OBJECTIVES

✔ **The Navigator**

1 Discuss why corporations invest in debt and stock securities. Corporations invest for three primary reasons: (a) They have excess cash. (b) They view investments as a significant revenue source. (c) They have strategic goals such as gaining control of a competitor or moving into a new line of business.

2 Explain the accounting for debt investments. Companies record investments in debt securities when they purchase bonds, receive or accrue interest, and sell the bonds. They report gains or losses on the sale of bonds in the "Other revenues and gains" or "Other expenses and losses" sections of the income statement.

3 Explain the accounting for stock investments. Companies record investments in common stock when they purchase the stock, receive dividends, and sell the stock. When ownership is less than 20%, the cost method is used. When ownership is between 20% and 50%, the equity method should be used. When ownership is more than 50%, companies prepare consolidated financial statements.

4 Describe the use of consolidated financial statements. When a company owns more than 50% of the common stock of another company, it usually prepares consolidated financial statements. These statements indicate the magnitude and scope of operations of the companies under common control.

5 Indicate how debt and stock investments are reported in financial statements. Investments in debt securities are classified as trading or held-for-collection securities for valuation and reporting purposes. Stock investments are classified either as trading or non-trading. Stock investments have no maturity date and therefore are never classified as held-for-collection. Trading securities are reported as current assets at fair value, with changes from cost reported in net income. Non-trading securities are also reported at fair value, with the changes from cost reported in stockholders' equity. Non-trading securities

are classified as short-term or long-term, depending on their expected future sale date.

6 Distinguish between short-term and long-term investments. Short-term investments are securities that are (a) readily marketable and (b) intended to be converted to cash within the next year or operating cycle, whichever is longer. Investments that do not meet both criteria are classified as long-term investments.

GLOSSARY

Consolidated financial statements Financial statements that present the assets and liabilities controlled by the parent company and the total revenues and expenses of the subsidiary companies. (p. 608).

Controlling interest Ownership of more than 50% of the common stock of another entity. (p. 608).

Cost method An accounting method in which the investment in common stock is recorded at cost, and revenue is recognized only when cash dividends are received. (p. 606).

Debt investments Investments in government and corporation bonds. (p. 603).

Equity method An accounting method in which the investment in common stock is initially recorded at cost, and the investment account is then adjusted annually to show the investor's equity in the investee. (p. 607).

Fair value Amount for which a security could be sold in a normal market. (p. 610).

Held-for-collection securities Debt securities that the investor has the intent and ability to hold to maturity (p. 610).

Investment portfolio A group of stocks and/or debt securities in different corporations held for investment purposes. (p. 605).

Long-term investments Investments that are not readily marketable or that management does not intend to convert into cash within the next year or operating cycle, whichever is longer. (p. 614).

Non-trading securities Stock investments that are held for purposes other than trading. (p. 610).

Parent company A company that owns more than 50% of the common stock of another entity. (p. 608).

Short-term investments Investments that are readily marketable and intended to be converted into cash within the next year or operating cycle, whichever is longer. (p. 614).

Stock investments Investments in the capital stock of other corporations. (p. 605).

Subsidiary (affiliated) company A company in which more than 50% of its stock is owned by another company. (p. 608).

Trading securities Securities bought and held primarily for sale in the near term to generate income on short-term price differences. (p. 610).

APPENDIX 12A   PREPARING CONSOLIDATED FINANCIAL STATEMENTS

Most of the large U.S. corporations are holding companies that own other corporations. They therefore prepare **consolidated** financial statements that combine the separate companies.

> **LEARNING OBJECTIVE 7**
>
> Describe the form and content of consolidated financial statements as well as how to prepare them.

Consolidated Balance Sheet

Companies prepare consolidated balance sheets from the individual balance sheets of their affiliated companies. They do not prepare consolidated statements from ledger accounts kept by the consolidated entity because only the separate legal entities maintain accounting records.

All items in the individual balance sheets are included in the consolidated balance sheet except amounts that pertain to transactions between the affiliated companies. Transactions between the affiliated companies are identified as intercompany transactions. The process of excluding these transactions in preparing consolidated statements is referred to as **intercompany eliminations**. These eliminations are necessary to avoid overstating assets, liabilities, and stockholders' equity in the consolidated balance sheet. For example, amounts owed by a subsidiary to a parent company and the related receivable reported by the parent company would be eliminated. The objective in a consolidated balance sheet is to show only obligations to and receivables from parties who are not part of the affiliated group of companies.

To illustrate, assume that on January 1, 2014, Powers Construction Company pays $150,000 in cash for 100% of Serto Brick Company's common stock. Powers Company records the investment at cost, as required by the cost principle. Illustration 12A-1 presents the separate balance sheets of the two companies immediately after the purchase, together with combined and consolidated data.[5] Powers obtains the balances in the "combined" column by adding the items in the separate balance sheets of the affiliated companies. The combined totals do not represent a consolidated balance sheet because there has been a double-counting of assets and stockholders' equity in the amount of $150,000.

Helpful Hint
Eliminations are aptly named because they eliminate duplicate data. They are not adjustments.

Illustration 12A-1
Combined and consolidated data

	Powers Company and Serto Company Balance Sheet January 1, 2014			
Assets	**Powers Company**	**Serto Company**	**Combined Data**	**Consolidated Data**
Current assets	$ 50,000	$ 80,000	$130,000	**$130,000**
Investment in Serto Company common stock	150,000		150,000	**–0–**
Plant and equipment (net)	325,000	145,000	470,000	**470,000**
Total assets	$525,000	$225,000	$750,000	**$600,000**
Liabilities and Stockholders' Equity				
Current liabilities	$ 50,000	$ 75,000	$125,000	**$125,000**
Common stock	300,000	100,000	400,000	**300,000**
Retained earnings	175,000	50,000	225,000	**175,000**
Total liabilities and stockholders' equity	$525,000	$225,000	$750,000	**$600,000**

The Investment in Serto Company common stock that appears on the balance sheet of Powers Company represents an interest in the net assets of Serto. As a result, there has been a double-counting of assets. Similarly, there has been a double-counting in stockholders' equity because the common stock of Serto Company is completely owned by the stockholders of Powers Company.

The balances in the consolidated data column are the amounts that should appear in the consolidated balance sheet. The double-counting has been eliminated by showing Investment in Serto Company at zero and by reporting only the common stock and retained earnings of Powers Company as stockholders' equity.

USE OF A WORKSHEET—COST EQUAL TO BOOK VALUE
The preparation of consolidated balance sheets is usually facilitated by the use of a worksheet. As shown in Illustration 12A-2, the worksheet for a consolidated balance sheet contains columns for (1) the balance sheet data for the separate

---

[5]We use condensed data throughout this material to keep details at a minimum.

legal entities, (2) intercompany eliminations, and (3) consolidated data. All data in the worksheet relate to the preceding example in which Powers Company acquires 100% ownership of Serto Company for $150,000. In this case, the cost of the investment, $150,000, is equal to the book value [$150,000 ($225,000 − $75,000)] of the subsidiary's net assets. The intercompany elimination results in a credit to the investment account maintained by Powers Company for its balance, $150,000, and debits to the Common Stock and Retained Earnings accounts of Serto Company for their respective balances, $100,000 and $50,000.

Illustration 12A-2
Worksheet—Cost equal to book value

Powers Company.xls

Powers Company and Subsidiary
Worksheet—Consolidated Balance Sheet
January 1, 2014 (Acquisition Date)

	Powers Company	Serto Company	Eliminations Dr.	Eliminations Cr.	Consolidated Data
Assets					
Current assets	50,000	80,000			130,000
Investment in Serto Company common stock	150,000			150,000	–0–
Plant and equipment (net)	325,000	145,000			470,000
Totals	525,000	225,000			600,000
Liabilities and Stockholders' Equity					
Current liabilities	50,000	75,000			125,000
Common stock—Powers Company	300,000				300,000
Common stock—Serto Company		100,000	100,000		–0–
Retained earnings—Powers Company	175,000				175,000
Retained earnings—Serto Company		50,000	50,000		–0–
Totals	525,000	225,000	150,000	150,000	600,000

It is important to recognize that companies make intercompany eliminations solely on the worksheet to present correct consolidated data. Neither of the affiliated companies journalizes or posts the eliminations. Therefore, eliminations do not affect the ledger accounts. Powers Company's investment account and Serto Company's common stock and retained earnings accounts are reported by the separate entities in preparing their own financial statements.

Helpful Hint
As in the case of the worksheets explained earlier in this textbook, consolidated worksheets are also optional.

USE OF A WORKSHEET—COST ABOVE BOOK VALUE

The cost of acquiring the common stock of another company may be above or below its book value. The management of the parent company may pay more than book value for the stock. Why? Because it believes the fair values of identifiable assets such as land, buildings, and equipment are higher than their recorded book values. Or, it may believe the subsidiary's future earnings prospects warrant a payment for goodwill.

To illustrate, assume the same data used above, except that Powers Company pays $165,000 in cash for 100% of Serto's common stock. The excess of cost over book value is $15,000 ($165,000 − $150,000). Powers recognizes this amount separately in eliminating the parent company's investment account, as shown in

Helpful Hint
The consolidated worksheet is another useful spreadsheet application. This is an easier worksheet to attempt since the required instructions are very straightforward.

Illustration 12A-3. Total assets and total liabilities and stockholders' equity are the same as in the preceding example ($600,000). However, in this case, total assets include $15,000 of Excess of Cost Over Book Value of Subsidiary. The disposition of the excess is explained in the next section.

Illustration 12A-3
Worksheet—Cost above book value

	Powers Company	Serto Company	Eliminations Dr.	Eliminations Cr.	Consolidated Data
Powers Company and Subsidiary					
Worksheet—Consolidated Balance Sheet					
January 1, 2014 (Acquisition Date)					
Assets					
Current assets	35,000	80,000			115,000
Investment in Serto Company common stock	165,000			165,000	–0–
Plant and equipment (net)	325,000	145,000			470,000
Excess of cost over book value of subsidiary			15,000		15,000
Totals	525,000	225,000			600,000
Liabilities and Stockholders' Equity					
Current liabilities	50,000	75,000			125,000
Common stock—Powers Company	300,000				300,000
Common stock—Serto Company		100,000	100,000		–0–
Retained earnings—Powers Company	175,000				175,000
Retained earnings—Serto Company		50,000	50,000		–0–
Totals	525,000	225,000	165,000	165,000	600,000

Note that a separate line is added to the worksheet for the excess of cost over book value of subsidiary.

CONTENT OF A CONSOLIDATED BALANCE SHEET

To illustrate a consolidated balance sheet, we will use the worksheet shown in Illustration 12A-3. This worksheet shows an excess of cost over book value of $15,000. In the consolidated balance sheet, Powers first allocates this amount to specific assets, such as plant and equipment and inventory, if their fair values on the acquisition date exceed their book values. Any remainder is considered to be goodwill. For Serto Company, assume that the fair value of the plant and equipment is $155,000. Thus, Powers allocates $10,000 of the excess of cost over book value to property and equipment, and the remainder, $5,000, to goodwill. Illustration 12A-4 shows the condensed consolidated balance sheet of Powers Company.

Through innovative financial restructuring, The Coca-Cola Company at one time eliminated a substantial amount of non-intercompany debt. It sold to the public 51% of two bottling companies. The "49% solution," as insiders call the strategy, enabled Coca-Cola to keep effective control over the businesses, and it swept $3 billion of debt from its consolidated balance sheet. (It no longer consolidated the two bottling companies.) At the same time the new companies obtained independent access to equity markets to satisfy their own large appetites for capital.

Illustration 12A-4
Consolidated balance sheet

Powers Company
Consolidated Balance Sheet
January 1, 2014

Assets

Current assets		$115,000
Plant and equipment (net)		480,000
Goodwill		5,000
Total assets		$600,000

Liabilities and Stockholders' Equity

Current liabilities		$125,000
Stockholders' equity		
Common stock	$300,000	
Retained earnings	175,000	475,000
Total liabilities and stockholders' equity		$600,000

Consolidated Income Statement

Affiliated companies also prepare a consolidated income statement. This statement shows the results of operations of affiliated companies as though they are one economic unit. This means that the statement shows only revenue and expense transactions between the consolidated entity and companies and individuals who are outside the affiliated group.

Consequently, all intercompany revenue and expense transactions must be eliminated. Intercompany transactions such as sales between affiliates and interest on loans charged by one affiliate to another must be eliminated. A worksheet facilitates the preparation of consolidated income statements in the same manner as it does for the balance sheet.

SUMMARY OF LEARNING OBJECTIVE FOR APPENDIX 12A

✔ **The Navigator**

7 Describe the form and content of consolidated financial statements as well as how to prepare them. Consolidated financial statements are similar in form and content to the financial statements of an individual corporation. A consolidated balance sheet shows the assets and liabilities controlled by the parent company. A consolidated income statement shows the results of operations of affiliated companies as though they are one economic unit. The worksheet for a consolidated balance sheet contains columns for (a) the balance sheet data for the separate entities, (b) intercompany eliminations, and (c) consolidated data.

GLOSSARY FOR APPENDIX 12A

Intercompany eliminations Eliminations made to exclude the effects of intercompany transactions in preparing consolidated statements. (p. 620).

Intercompany transactions Transactions between affiliated companies. (p. 620).

Note: All Questions, Exercises, and Problems marked with an asterisk relate to material in the appendix to the chapter.

SELF-TEST QUESTIONS

Answers are on page 641.

(LO 1) **1.** Which of the following is *not* a primary reason why corporations invest in debt and equity securities?
  (a) They wish to gain control of a competitor.
  (b) They have excess cash.
  (c) They wish to move into a new line of business.
  (d) They are required to by law.

(LO 2) **2.** Debt investments are initially recorded at:
  (a) cost.
  (b) cost plus accrued interest.
  (c) fair value.
  (d) None of the above.

(LO 2) **3.** Hanes Company sells debt investments costing $26,000 for $28,000, plus accrued interest that has been recorded. In journalizing the sale, credits are to:
  (a) Debt Investments and Loss on Sale of Debt Investments.
  (b) Debt Investments, Gain on Sale of Debt Investments, and Interest Receivable.
  (c) Stock Investments and Interest Receivable.
  (d) No correct answer is given.

(LO 3) **4.** Pryor Company receives net proceeds of $42,000 on the sale of stock investments that cost $39,500. This transaction will result in reporting in the income statement a:
  (a) loss of $2,500 under "Other expenses and losses."
  (b) loss of $2,500 under "Operating expenses."
  (c) gain of $2,500 under "Other revenues and gains."
  (d) gain of $2,500 under "Operating revenues."

(LO 3) **5.** The equity method of accounting for long-term investments in stock should be used when the investor has significant influence over an investee and owns:
  (a) between 20% and 50% of the investee's common stock.
  (b) 20% or more of the investee's common stock.
  (c) more than 50% of the investee's common stock.
  (d) less than 20% of the investee's common stock.

(LO 3) **6.** Assume that Horicon Corp acquired 25% of the common stock of Sheboygan Corp. on January 1, 2014, for $300,000. During 2014 Sheboygan Corp. reported net income of $160,000 and paid total dividends of $60,000. If Horicon uses the equity method to account for its investment, the balance in the investment account on December 31, 2014, will be:
  (a) $300,000.   (c) $400,000.
  (b) $325,000.   (d) $340,000.

(LO 3) **7.** Using the information in Self-Test Question 6, what entry would Horicon make to record the receipt of the dividend from Sheboygan?
  (a) Debit Cash and credit Revenue from Stock Investments.
  (b) Debit Cash Dividends and credit Revenue from Stock Investments.
  (c) Debit Cash and credit Stock Investments.
  (d) Debit Cash and credit Dividend Revenue.

(LO 3) **8.** You have a controlling interest if:
  (a) you own more than 20% of a company's stock.
  (b) you are the president of the company.
  (c) you use the equity method.
  (d) you own more than 50% of a company's stock.

(LO 4) **9.** Which of the following statements is *not true*? Consolidated financial statements are useful to:
  (a) determine the profitability of specific subsidiaries.
  (b) determine the total profitability of companies under common control.
  (c) determine the breadth of a parent company's operations.
  (d) determine the full extent of total obligations of companies under common control.

(LO 5) **10.** At the end of the first year of operations, the total cost of the trading securities portfolio is $120,000. Total fair value is $115,000. The financial statements should show:
  (a) a reduction of an asset of $5,000 and a realized loss of $5,000.
  (b) a reduction of an asset of $5,000 and an unrealized loss of $5,000 in the stockholders' equity section.
  (c) a reduction of an asset of $5,000 in the current assets section and an unrealized loss of $5,000 in "Other expenses and losses."
  (d) a reduction of an asset of $5,000 in the current assets section and a realized loss of $5,000 in "Other expenses and losses."

(LO 5) **11.** At December 31, 2014, the fair value of non-trading securities is $41,300 and the cost is $39,800. At January 1, 2014, there was a credit balance of $900 in the Fair Value Adjustment—Non-Trading account. The required adjusting entry would be:
  (a) Debit Fair Value Adjustment—Non-Trading for $1,500 and credit Unrealized Gain or Loss—Equity for $1,500.
  (b) Debit Fair Value Adjustment—Non-Trading for $600 and credit Unrealized Gain or Loss—Equity for $600.
  (c) Debit Fair Value Adjustment—Non-Trading for $2,400 and credit Unrealized Gain or Loss—Equity for $2,400.
  (d) Debit Unrealized Gain or Loss—Equity for $2,400 and credit Fair Value Adjustment—Non-Trading for $2,400.

(LO 5) **12.** In the balance sheet, a debit balance in Unrealized Gain or Loss—Equity is reported as a(n):
  (a) increase to stockholders' equity.
  (b) decrease to stockholders' equity.
  (c) loss in the income statement.
  (d) loss in the retained earnings statement.

(LO 6) **13.** Short-term debt investments must be readily marketable and expected to be sold within:
  (a) 3 months from the date of purchase.
  (b) the next year or operating cycle, whichever is shorter.

(c) the next year or operating cycle, whichever is longer.

(d) the operating cycle.

(LO 7) *14. Pate Company pays $175,000 for 100% of Sinko's common stock when Sinko's stockholders' equity consists of Common Stock $100,000 and Retained Earnings $60,000. In the worksheet for the consolidated balance sheet, the eliminations will include a:

(a) credit to Investment in Sinko Common Stock $160,000.

(b) credit to Excess of Book Value over Cost of Subsidiary $15,000.

(c) debit to Retained Earnings $75,000.

(d) debit to Excess of Cost over Book Value of Subsidiary $15,000.

(LO 7) *15. Which of the following statements about intercompany eliminations is *true*?

(a) They are not journalized or posted by any of the subsidiaries.

(b) They do not affect the ledger accounts of any of the subsidiaries.

(c) They are made solely on the worksheet to arrive at correct consolidated data.

(d) All of these statements are true.

*16. Which one of the following statements about consolidated income statements is *false*? (LO 7)

(a) A worksheet facilitates the preparation of the statement.

(b) The consolidated income statement shows the results of operations of affiliated companies as a single economic unit.

(c) All revenue and expense transactions between parent and subsidiary companies are eliminated.

(d) When a subsidiary is wholly owned, the form and content of the statement will differ from the income statement of an individual corporation.

Go to the book's companion website, www.wiley.com/college/weygandt, for additional Self-Test Questions.

✔ **The Navigator**

QUESTIONS

1. What are the reasons that corporations invest in securities?

2. (a) What is the cost of an investment in bonds?
   (b) When is interest on bonds recorded?

3. Tino Martinez is confused about losses and gains on the sale of debt investments. Explain to Tino (a) how the gain or loss is computed, and (b) the statement presentation of the gains and losses.

4. Olindo Company sells Gish's bonds costing $40,000 for $45,000, including $500 of accrued interest. In recording the sale, Olindo books a $5,000 gain. Is this correct? Explain.

5. What is the cost of an investment in stock?

6. To acquire Kinston Corporation stock, R. Neal pays $62,000 in cash, plus $1,200 broker's fees. What entry should be made for this investment?

7. (a) When should a long-term investment in common stock be accounted for by the equity method?
   (b) When is revenue recognized under this method?

8. Rijo Corporation uses the equity method to account for its ownership of 30% of the common stock of Pippen Packing. During 2014, Pippen reported a net income of $80,000 and declares and pays cash dividends of $10,000. What recognition should Rijo Corporation give to these events?

9. What constitutes "significant influence" when an investor's financial interest is below the 50% level?

10. Distinguish between the cost and equity methods of accounting for investments in stocks.

11. What are consolidated financial statements?

12. What are the classification guidelines for investments at a balance sheet date?

13. Tina Eddings is the controller of Mendez Inc. At December 31, the company's investments in trading securities cost $74,000. They have a fair value of $70,000. Indicate how Tina would report these data in the financial statements prepared on December 31.

14. Using the data in Question 13, how would Tina report the data if the investment were long-term and the securities were classified as non-trading?

15. Hashmi Company's investments in non-trading securities at December 31 show total cost of $195,000 and total fair value of $205,000. Prepare the adjusting entry.

16. Using the data in Question 15, prepare the adjusting entry assuming the securities are classified as trading securities.

17. What is the proper statement presentation of the account Unrealized Loss—Equity?

18. What purposes are served by reporting Unrealized Gain or Loss—Equity in the stockholders' equity section?

19. Altoona Wholesale Supply owns stock in Key Corporation. Altoona intends to hold the stock indefinitely because of some negative tax consequences if sold. Should the investment in Key be classified as a short-term investment? Why or why not?

20.  What does PepsiCo state regarding its accounting policy involving consolidated financial statements?

*21. (a) What asset and stockholders' equity balances are eliminated in preparing a consolidated balance sheet for a parent and a wholly owned subsidiary? (b) Why are they eliminated?

*22. Roscoe Company pays $318,000 to purchase all the outstanding common stock of Lia Corporation. At the date of purchase, the net assets of Lia have a book value of $290,000. Roscoe's management allocates $20,000 of the excess cost to undervalued land on the books of Lia. What should be done with the rest of the excess?

BRIEF EXERCISES

Journalize entries for debt investments.
(LO 2)

BE12-1 Kimmel Corporation purchased debt investments for $52,000 on January 1, 2014. On July 1, 2014, Kimmel received cash interest of $2,340. Journalize the purchase and the receipt of interest. Assume that no interest has been accrued.

Journalize entries for stock investments.
(LO 3)

BE12-2 On August 1, Paul Company buys 1,000 shares of Merlynn common stock for $35,000 cash, plus brokerage fees of $700. On December 1, Paul sells the stock investments for $40,000 in cash. Journalize the purchase and sale of the common stock.

Record transactions under the equity method of accounting.
(LO 3)

BE12-3 Texas Company owns 25% of Plano Company. For the current year, Plano reports net income of $180,000 and declares and pays a $50,000 cash dividend. Record Texas's equity in Plano's net income and the receipt of dividends from Plano.

Prepare adjusting entry using fair value.
(LO 5)

BE12-4 The cost of the trading securities of Hardy Company at December 31, 2014, is $62,000. At December 31, 2014, the fair value of the securities is $59,000. Prepare the adjusting entry to record the securities at fair value.

Indicate statement presentation using fair value.
(LO 5, 6)

BE12-5 For the data presented in BE12-4, show the financial statement presentation of the trading securities and related accounts.

Prepare adjusting entry using fair value.
(LO 5)

BE12-6 Latrobe Corporation holds as a long-term investment non-trading stock securities costing $72,000. At December 31, 2014, the fair value of the securities is $66,000. Prepare the adjusting entry to record the securities at fair value.

Indicate statements presentation using fair value.
(LO 5, 6)

BE12-7 For the data presented in BE12-6, show the financial statement presentation of the non-trading securities and related accounts. Assume the non-trading securities are noncurrent.

Prepare investments section of balance sheet.
(LO 5, 6)

BE12-8 Gurnee Corporation has the following long-term investments: (1) Common stock of Kornas Co. (10% ownership) held as non-trading securities, cost $108,000, fair value $115,000. (2) Common stock of Kozanecki Inc. (30% ownership), cost $210,000, equity $270,000. Prepare the investments section of the balance sheet.

Prepare partial consolidated worksheet when cost equals book value.
(LO 7)

*BE12-9 Paula Company acquires 100% of the common stock of Shannon Company for $190,000 cash. On the acquisition date, Shannon's ledger shows Common Stock $120,000 and Retained Earnings $70,000. Complete the worksheet for the following accounts: Paula—Investment in Shannon Common Stock, Shannon—Common Stock, and Shannon—Retained Earnings.

Prepare partial consolidated worksheet when cost exceeds book value.
(LO 7)

*BE12-10 Data for the Paula and Shannon companies are given in BE12-9. Instead of paying $190,000, assume that Paula pays $200,000 to acquire the 100% interest in Shannon Company. Complete the worksheet for the accounts identified in BE12-9 and for the excess of cost over book value.

> DO IT! REVIEW

Make journal entry for bond purchase and adjusting entry for interest accrual.
(LO 2)

DO IT! **12-1** Kurtyka Corporation had the following transactions relating to debt investments:

Jan. 1   Purchased 50, $1,000, 12% Nordica Company bonds for $50,000 plus broker's fees of $1,500. Interest is payable semiannually on January 1 and July 1.
July 1   Received semiannual interest from Nordica Company bonds.
July 1   Sold 30 Nordica Company bonds for $30,000, less $800 broker's fees.

(a) Journalize the transactions, and (b) prepare the adjusting entry for the accrual of interest on December 31.

Make journal entries for stock investments.
(LO 3)

DO IT! **12-2** Presented below are two independent situations:

1. Lorfeld Inc. acquired 10% of the 500,000 shares of common stock of Northbrook Corporation at a total cost of $11 per share on June 17, 2014. On September 3, Northbrook declared and paid a $160,000 dividend. On December 31, Northbrook reported net income of $550,000 for the year.

2. Saa Corporation obtained significant influence over McCarthy Company by buying 30% of McCarthy's 100,000 outstanding shares of common stock at a cost of $18 per share on January 1, 2014. On May 15, McCarthy declared and paid a cash dividend of $150,000. On December 31, McCarthy reported net income of $270,000 for the year.

Prepare all necessary journal entries for 2014 for (a) McCarthy and (b) Saa.

DO IT! 12-3 Some of McEleeven Corporation's investment securities are classified as trading securities and some are classified as non-trading. The cost and fair value of each category at December 31, 2014, were as follows.

Make journal entries for trading and non-trading securities.

(LO 5)

	Cost	Fair Value	Unrealized Gain (Loss)
Trading securities	$96,300	$84,900	$(11,400)
Non-trading securities	$59,000	$63,200	$ 4,200

At December 31, 2013, the Fair Value Adjustment—Trading account had a debit balance of $2,200, and the Fair Value Adjustment—Non-Trading account had a credit balance of $7,750. Prepare the required journal entries for each group of securities for December 31, 2014.

DO IT! 12-4 Identify where each of the following items would be reported in the financial statements.

Indicate financial statement presentation of investments.

(LO 6)

1. Loss on sale of investments in stock.
2. Unrealized gain on non-trading securities.
3. Fair value adjustment—trading.
4. Interest earned on investments in bonds.
5. Unrealized loss on trading securities.

Use the following possible categories:

Balance sheet:

Current assets	Current liabilities
Investments	Long-term liabilities
Property, plant, and equipment	Stockholders' equity
Intangible assets	

Income statement:

Other revenues and gains	Other expenses and losses

 The Navigator

EXERCISES

E12-1 Mr. Wellington is studying for an accounting test and has developed the following questions about investments.

Understand debt and stock investments.

(LO 1)

1. What are three reasons why companies purchase investments in debt or stock securities?
2. Why would a corporation have excess cash that it does not need for operations?
3. What is the typical investment when investing cash for short periods of time?
4. What are the typical investments when investing cash to generate earnings?
5. Why would a company invest in securities that provide no current cash flows?
6. What is the typical stock investment when investing cash for strategic reasons?

Instructions

Provide answers for Mr. Wellington.

E12-2 Floyd Corporation had the following transactions pertaining to debt investments.

Journalize debt investment transactions and accrue interest.

(LO 2)

Jan. 1	Purchased 50 8%, $1,000 Petal Co. bonds for $50,000 cash plus brokerage fees of $900. Interest is payable semiannually on July 1 and January 1.
July 1	Received semiannual interest on Petal Co. bonds.
July 1	Sold 30 Petal Co. bonds for $34,000 less $500 brokerage fees.

Instructions

(a) Journalize the transactions.

(b) Prepare the adjusting entry for the accrual of interest at December 31.

Journalize debt investment transactions, accrue interest, and record sale.

(LO 2)

E12-3 Brook Company purchased 70 Meissner Company 12%, 10-year, $1,000 bonds on January 1, 2014, for $73,000. Brook Company also had to pay $500 of broker's fees. The bonds pay interest semiannually on July 1 and January 1. On January 1, 2015, after receipt of interest, Brook Company sold 40 of the bonds for $40,100.

Instructions

Prepare the journal entries to record the transactions described above.

Journalize stock investment transactions.

(LO 3)

E12-4 Diann Company had the following transactions pertaining to stock investments.

Feb. 1   Purchased 600 shares of Ronn common stock (2%) for $6,000 cash, plus brokerage fees of $200.

July 1   Received cash dividends of $1 per share on Ronn common stock.

Sept. 1   Sold 300 shares of Ronn common stock for $4,400, less brokerage fees of $100.

Dec. 1   Received cash dividends of $1 per share on Ronn common stock.

Instructions

(a) Journalize the transactions.

(b) Explain how dividend revenue and the gain (loss) on sale should be reported in the income statement.

Journalize transactions for investments in stocks.

(LO 3)

E12-5 Spring Inc. had the following transactions pertaining to investments in common stock.

Jan. 1   Purchased 2,500 shares of Angeltide Corporation common stock (5%) for $140,000 cash plus $2,100 broker's commission.

July 1   Received a cash dividend of $3 per share.

Dec. 1   Sold 500 shares of Angeltide Corporation common stock for $32,000 cash, less $800 broker's commission.

Dec. 31   Received a cash dividend of $3 per share.

Instructions

Journalize the transactions.

Journalize transactions for investments in stocks.

(LO 3)

E12-6 On February 1, Minitori Company purchased 500 shares (2% ownership) of Becker Company common stock for $30 per share plus brokerage fees of $400. On March 20, Minitori Company sold 100 shares of Becker stock for $2,900, less a $50 brokerage fee. Minitori received a dividend of $1.00 per share on April 25. On June 15, Minitori sold 200 shares of Becker stock for $7,400, less a $90 brokerage fee. On July 28, Minitori received a dividend of $1.25 per share.

Instructions

Prepare the journal entries to record the transactions described above.

Journalize and post transactions under the equity method.

(LO 3)

E12-7 On January 1, Vince Corporation purchased a 25% equity in Morelli Corporation for $180,000. At December 31, Morelli declared and paid a $60,000 cash dividend and reported net income of $200,000.

Instructions

(a) Journalize the transactions.

(b) Determine the amount to be reported as an investment in Morelli stock at December 31.

Journalize entries under cost and equity methods.

(LO 3, 5)

E12-8 Presented below are two independent situations.

1. Chicory Cosmetics acquired 15% of the 200,000 shares of common stock of Racine Fashion at a total cost of $13 per share on March 18, 2014. On June 30, Racine declared and paid a $60,000 dividend. On December 31, Racine reported net income of $122,000 for the year. At December 31, the market price of Racine Fashion was $15 per share. The stock is classified as non-trading.

2. Frank, Inc., obtained significant influence over Nowak Corporation by buying 30% of Nowak's 30,000 outstanding shares of common stock at a total cost of $9 per share on January 1, 2014. On June 15, Nowak declared and paid a cash dividend of $30,000. On December 31, Nowak reported a net income of $80,000 for the year.

Instructions

Prepare all the necessary journal entries for 2014 for (a) Chicory Cosmetics and (b) Frank, Inc.

Understand the usefulness of consolidated statements.

(LO 4)

E12-9 Edna Company purchased 70% of the outstanding common stock of Damen Corporation.

Instructions

(a) Explain the relationship between Edna Company and Damen Corporation.

(b) How should Edna account for its investment in Damen?

(c) Why is the accounting treatment described in (b) useful?

E12-10 At December 31, 2014, the trading securities for Oglesbee, Inc. are as follows.

Prepare adjusting entry to record fair value, and indicate statement presentation.

(LO 5, 6)

Security	Cost	Fair Value
A	$17,500	$16,000
B	12,500	14,000
C	23,000	19,000
	$53,000	$49,000

Instructions

(a) Prepare the adjusting entry at December 31, 2014, to report the securities at fair value.

(b) Show the balance sheet and income statement presentation at December 31, 2014, after adjustment to fair value.

E12-11 Data for investments in stock classified as trading securities are presented in E12-10. Assume instead that the investments are classified as non-trading securities. They have the same cost and fair value. The securities are considered to be a long-term investment.

Prepare adjusting entry to record fair value, and indicate statement presentation.

(LO 5, 6)

Instructions

(a) Prepare the adjusting entry at December 31, 2014, to report the securities at fair value.

(b) Show the statement presentation at December 31, 2014, after adjustment to fair value.

(c) ▭▭▭▶ E. Devonshire, a member of the board of directors, does not understand the reporting of the unrealized gains or losses. Write a letter to Ms. Devonshire explaining the reporting and the purposes that it serves.

E12-12 Zippydah Company has the following data at December 31, 2014.

Prepare adjusting entries for fair value, and indicate statement presentation for two classes of securities.

(LO 5, 6)

Securities	Cost	Fair Value
Trading	$120,000	$124,000
Non-trading	100,000	94,000

The non-trading securities are held as a long-term investment.

Instructions

(a) Prepare the adjusting entries to report each class of securities at fair value.

(b) Indicate the statement presentation of each class of securities and the related unrealized gain (loss) accounts.

*E12-13 On January 1, 2014, Lennon Corporation acquires 100% of Ono Inc. for $220,000 in cash. The condensed balance sheets of the two corporations immediately following the acquisition are as follows.

Prepare consolidated worksheet when cost equals book value.

(LO 7)

	Lennon Corporation	Ono Inc.
Current assets	$ 60,000	$ 50,000
Investment in Ono Inc. common stock	220,000	
Plant and equipment (net)	300,000	220,000
	$580,000	$270,000
Current liabilities	$180,000	$ 50,000
Common stock	230,000	80,000
Retained earnings	170,000	140,000
	$580,000	$270,000

Instructions

Prepare a worksheet for a consolidated balance sheet.

*E12-14 Data for the Lennon and Ono corporations are presented in E12-13. Assume that instead of paying $220,000 in cash for Ono Inc., Lennon Corporation pays $225,000 in cash. Thus, at the acquisition date, the assets of Lennon Corporation are current assets $55,000, investment in Ono Inc. common stock $225,000, and plant and equipment (net) $300,000.

Prepare consolidated worksheet when cost exceeds book value.

(LO 7)

Instructions

Prepare a worksheet for a consolidated balance sheet.

EXERCISES: SET B AND CHALLENGE EXERCISES

Visit the book's companion website, at **www.wiley.com/college/weygandt**, and choose the Student Companion site to access Exercise Set B and Challenge Exercises.

PROBLEMS: SET A

Journalize debt investment transactions and show financial statement presentation.

(LO 2, 5, 6)

P12-1A Pagnucci Carecenters Inc. provides financing and capital to the health-care industry, with a particular focus on nursing homes for the elderly. The following selected transactions relate to bonds acquired as an investment by Pagnucci, whose fiscal year ends on December 31.

2014

Jan. 1   Purchased at face value $2,000,000 of Franco Nursing Centers, Inc., 10-year, 8% bonds dated January 1, 2014, directly from Franco.
July 1   Received the semiannual interest on the Franco bonds.
Dec. 31   Accrual of interest at year-end on the Franco bonds.

(Assume that all intervening transactions and adjustments have been properly recorded and that the number of bonds owned has not changed from December 31, 2014, to December 31, 2016.)

2017

Jan. 1   Received the semiannual interest on the Franco bonds.
Jan. 1   Sold $1,000,000 Franco bonds at 106. The broker deducted $6,000 for commissions and fees on the sale.
July 1   Received the semiannual interest on the Franco bonds.
Dec. 31   Accrual of interest at year-end on the Franco bonds.

Instructions

(a) Journalize the listed transactions for the years 2014 and 2017.
(b) Show the balance sheet presentation of the bonds and interest receivable at December 31, 2014. Assume the investments are considered long-term.

(a) Gain on sale of debt investments $54,000

Journalize investment transactions, prepare adjusting entry, and show statement presentation.

(LO 2, 3, 5, 6)

P12-2A In January 2014, the management of Stefan Company concludes that it has sufficient cash to permit some short-term investments in debt and stock securities. During the year, the following transactions occurred.

Feb. 1   Purchased 600 shares of Superior common stock for $31,800, plus brokerage fees of $600.
Mar. 1   Purchased 800 shares of Pawlik common stock for $20,000, plus brokerage fees of $400.
Apr. 1   Purchased 50 $1,000, 7% Venice bonds for $50,000, plus $1,000 brokerage fees. Interest is payable semiannually on April 1 and October 1.
July 1   Received a cash dividend of $0.60 per share on the Superior common stock.
Aug. 1   Sold 200 shares of Superior common stock at $58 per share less brokerage fees of $200.
Sept. 1   Received a $1 per share cash dividend on the Pawlik common stock.
Oct. 1   Received the semiannual interest on the Venice bonds.
Oct. 1   Sold the Venice bonds for $50,000 less $1,000 brokerage fees.

At December 31, the fair value of the Superior common stock was $55 per share. The fair value of the Pawlik common stock was $24 per share.

Instructions

(a) Journalize the transactions and post to the accounts Debt Investments and Stock Investments. (Use the T-account form.)
(b) Prepare the adjusting entry at December 31, 2014, to report the investment securities at fair value. All securities are considered to be trading securities.

(a) Gain on sale of stock investments $600

(c) Show the balance sheet presentation of investment securities at December 31, 2014.
(d) Identify the income statement accounts and give the statement classification of each account.

P12-3A On December 31, 2013, Ogallala Associates owned the following securities, held as a long-term investment. The securities are not held for influence or control of the investee.

Journalize transactions and adjusting entry for stock investments.

(LO 3, 5, 6)

Common Stock	Shares	Cost
Carlene Co.	2,000	$60,000
Riverdale Co.	5,000	45,000
Raczynski Co.	1,500	30,000

On December 31, 2013, the total fair value of the securities was equal to its cost. In 2014, the following transactions occurred.

July 1   Received $1 per share semiannual cash dividend on Riverdale Co. common stock.
Aug. 1   Received $0.50 per share cash dividend on Carlene Co. common stock.
Sept. 1   Sold 1,500 shares of Riverdale Co. common stock for cash at $8 per share, less brokerage fees of $300.
Oct. 1   Sold 800 shares of Carlene Co. common stock for cash at $33 per share, less brokerage fees of $500.
Nov. 1   Received $1 per share cash dividend on Raczynski Co. common stock.
Dec. 15   Received $0.50 per share cash dividend on Carlene Co. common stock.
    31   Received $1 per share semiannual cash dividend on Riverdale Co. common stock.

At December 31, the fair values per share of the common stocks were Carlene Co. $32, Riverdale Co. $8, and Raczynski Co. $18.

Instructions
(a) Journalize the 2014 transactions and post to the account Stock Investments. (Use the T-account form.)
(b) Prepare the adjusting entry at December 31, 2014, to show the securities at fair value. The stock should be classified as non-trading securities.
(c) Show the balance sheet presentation of the investments at December 31, 2014. At this date, Ogallala Associates has common stock $1,500,000 and retained earnings $1,000,000.

(b) Unrealized loss $4,100

P12-4A Control Alt Design acquired 30% of the outstanding common stock of Walter Company on January 1, 2014, by paying $800,000 for the 45,000 shares. Walter declared and paid $0.30 per share cash dividends on March 15, June 15, September 15, and December 15, 2014. Walter reported net income of $320,000 for the year. At December 31, 2014, the market price of Walter common stock was $24 per share.

Prepare entries under the cost and equity methods, and tabulate differences.

(LO 3)

Instructions
(a) Prepare the journal entries for Control Alt Design for 2014 assuming Control Alt Design cannot exercise significant influence over Walter. Use the cost method and assume that Walter common stock should be classified as a trading security.
(b) Prepare the journal entries for Control Alt Design for 2014, assuming Control Alt Design can exercise significant influence over Walter. Use the equity method.
(c) Indicate the balance sheet and income statement account balances at December 31, 2014, under each method of accounting.

(a) Total dividend revenue $54,000

(b) Revenue from investments $96,000

P12-5A The following securities are in Amberwood Company's portfolio of long-term non-trading securities at December 31, 2013.

Journalize stock investment transactions and show statement presentation.

(LO 3, 5, 6)

	Cost
1,000 shares of Reginald Corporation common stock	$52,000
1,400 shares of Elderberry Corporation common stock	84,000
1,200 shares of Mattoon Corporation preferred stock	33,600

On December 31, 2013, the total cost of the portfolio equaled total fair value. Amberwood had the following transactions related to the securities during 2014.

Jan. 20   Sold all 1,000 shares of Reginald Corporation common stock at $55 per share less brokerage fees of $600.

28   Purchased 400 shares of $70 par value common stock of Hachito Corporation at $78 per share, plus brokerage fees of $480.

30   Received a cash dividend of $1.15 per share on Elderberry Corp. common stock.

Feb. 8   Received cash dividends of $0.40 per share on Mattoon Corp. preferred stock.

18   Sold all 1,200 shares of Mattoon Corp. preferred stock at $27 per share less brokerage fees of $360.

July 30   Received a cash dividend of $1.00 per share on Elderberry Corp. common stock.

Sept. 6   Purchased an additional 900 shares of $10 par value common stock of Hachito Corporation at $82 per share, plus brokerage fees of $1,200.

Dec. 1   Received a cash dividend of $1.50 per share on Hachito Corporation common stock.

At December 31, 2014, the fair values of the securities were:

Elderberry Corporation common stock	$64 per share
Hachito Corporation common stock	$72 per share

Instructions

(a) Prepare journal entries to record the transactions.
(b) Post to the investment accounts. (Use T-accounts.)
(c) Prepare the adjusting entry at December 31, 2014 to report the portfolio at fair value.
(d) Show the balance sheet presentation at December 31, 2014, for the investment-related accounts.

(a) Gain on sale of stock investments $2,400

(c) Unrealized loss $7,480

Prepare a balance sheet.

(LO 5, 6)

P12-6A The following data, presented in alphabetical order, are taken from the records of Radar Corporation.

Accounts payable	$ 240,000
Accounts receivable	140,000
Accumulated depreciation—buildings	180,000
Accumulated depreciation—equipment	52,000
Allowance for doubtful accounts	6,000
Bonds payable (10%, due 2020)	500,000
Buildings	950,000
Cash	42,000
Common stock ($10 par value; 500,000 shares authorized, 150,000 shares issued)	1,500,000
Dividends payable	80,000
Equipment	275,000
Fair value adjustment—non-trading securities (Dr)	8,000
Goodwill	200,000
Income taxes payable	120,000
Inventory	170,000
Investment in Mara common stock (30% ownership), at equity	380,000
Investment in Sasse common stock (10% ownership), at cost	278,000
Land	390,000
Notes payable (due 2015)	70,000
Paid-in capital in excess of par—common stock	130,000
Premium on bonds payable	40,000
Prepaid insurance	16,000
Retained earnings	103,000
Short-term investments, at fair value (and cost)	180,000
Unrealized gain—non-trading securities	8,000

The investment in Sasse common stock is considered to be a long-term non-trading security.

Instructions

Total assets $2,791,000

Prepare a classified balance sheet at December 31, 2014.

P12-7A Robinson Corporation purchased all the outstanding common stock of Hoffman Plastics, Inc. on December 31, 2014. Just before the purchase, the condensed balance sheets of the two companies appeared as follows.

*P12-7A Robinson Corporation purchased all the outstanding common stock of Hoffman Plastics, Inc. on December 31, 2014. Just before the purchase, the condensed balance sheets of the two companies appeared as follows.

Prepare consolidated worksheet and balance sheet when cost exceeds book value.

(LO 7)

	Robinson Corporation	Hoffman Plastics, Inc.
Current assets	$1,480,000	$ 435,500
Plant and equipment (net)	2,100,000	676,000
	$3,580,000	$1,111,500
Current liabilities	$ 578,000	$ 92,500
Common stock	1,950,000	525,000
Retained earnings	1,052,000	494,000
	$3,580,000	$1,111,500

Robinson used current assets of $1,225,000 to acquire the stock of Hoffman Plastics. The excess of this purchase price over the book value of Hoffman Plastics' net assets is determined to be attributable $86,000 to Hoffman Plastics' plant and equipment and the remainder to goodwill.

Instructions
(a) Prepare the entry for Robinson's acquisition of Hoffman Plastics, Inc. stock.
(b) Prepare a consolidated worksheet at December 31, 2014.
(c) Prepare a consolidated balance sheet at December 31, 2014.

Excess of cost over book value $120,000

PROBLEMS: SET B

P12-1B Cheese Farms is a grower of hybrid seed corn for Steenbergen Genetics Corporation. It has had two exceptionally good years and has elected to invest its excess funds in bonds. The selected transactions, shown below, relate to bonds acquired as an investment by Cheese Farms, whose fiscal year ends on December 31.

Journalize debt investment transactions and show financial statement presentation.

(LO 2, 5, 6)

2014

Jan. 1 Purchased at face value $400,000 of Stombaugh Corporation 10-year, 9% bonds dated January 1, 2014, directly from the issuing corporation.
July 1 Received the semiannual interest on the Stombaugh bonds.
Dec. 31 Accrual of interest at year-end on the Stombaugh bonds.

(Assume that all intervening transactions and adjustments have been properly recorded and the number of bonds owned has not changed from December 31, 2014, to December 31, 2016.)

2017

Jan. 1 Received the semiannual interest on the Stombaugh bonds.
Jan. 1 Sold $200,000 of Stombaugh bonds at 114. The broker deducted $7,000 for commissions and fees on the sale.
July 1 Received the semiannual interest on the Stombaugh bonds.
Dec. 31 Accrual of interest at year-end on the Stombaugh bonds.

Instructions
(a) Journalize the listed transactions for the years 2014 and 2017.
(b) Show the balance sheet presentation of the bonds and interest receivable at December 31, 2014. Assume the investments are considered long-term.

(a) Gain on sale of debt investments $21,000

P12-2B In January 2014, the management of Gina Company concludes that it has sufficient cash to purchase some short-term investments in debt and stock securities. During the year, the following transactions occurred.

Feb. 1 Purchased 500 shares of Joy common stock for $30,000, plus brokerage fees of $800.
Mar. 1 Purchased 600 shares of Aurelius common stock for $20,000, plus brokerage fees of $300.

Journalize investment transactions, prepare adjusting entry, and show statement presentation.

(LO 2, 3, 5, 6)

Apr. 1 Purchased 40 $1,000, 9% Sikich bonds for $40,000, plus $1,200 brokerage fees. Interest is payable semiannually on April 1 and October 1.

July 1 Received a cash dividend of $0.60 per share on the Joy common stock.

Aug. 1 Sold 300 shares of Joy common stock at $69 per share, less brokerage fees of $350.

Sept. 1 Received a $1 per share cash dividend on the Aurelius common stock.

Oct. 1 Received the semiannual interest on the Sikich bonds.

Oct. 1 Sold the Sikich bonds for $45,000, less $1,000 brokerage fees.

At December 31, the fair value of the Joy common stock was $66 per share. The fair value of the Aurelius common stock was $29 per share.

Instructions

(a) Journalize the transactions and post to the accounts Debt Investments and Stock Investments. (Use the T-account form.)

(b) Unrealized loss $2,020

(b) Prepare the adjusting entry at December 31, 2014, to report the investments at fair value. All securities are considered to be trading securities.

(c) Show the balance sheet presentation of investment securities at December 31, 2014.

(d) Identify the income statement accounts and give the statement classification of each account.

Journalize transactions and adjusting entry for stock investments.

(LO 3, 5, 6)

P12-3B On December 31, 2013, Eli Associates owned the following securities, held as long-term investments.

Common Stock	Shares	Cost
Trowbridge Co.	4,000	$100,000
Holly Co.	5,000	30,000
Oriental Motors Co.	3,000	60,000

On this date, the total fair value of the securities was equal to its cost. The securities are not held for influence or control over the investees. In 2014, the following transactions occurred.

July 1 Received $1 per share semiannual cash dividend on Holly Co. common stock.

Aug. 1 Received $0.50 per share cash dividend on Trowbridge Co. common stock.

Sept. 1 Sold 1,500 shares of Holly Co. common stock for cash at $8 per share, less brokerage fees of $300.

Oct. 1 Sold 600 shares of Trowbridge Co. common stock for cash at $30 per share, less brokerage fees of $600.

Nov. 1 Received $1 per share cash dividend on Oriental Motor Co. common stock.

Dec. 15 Received $0.50 per share cash dividend on Trowbridge Co. common stock.

31 Received $1 per share semiannual cash dividend on Holly Co. common stock.

At December 31, the fair values per share of the common stocks were Trowbridge Co. $23, Holly Co. $7, and Oriental Motors Co. $19.

Instructions

(a) Gain on sale, $2,700 and $2,400

(a) Journalize the 2014 transactions and post to the account Stock Investments. (Use the T-account form.)

(b) Prepare the adjusting entry at December 31, 2014, to show the securities at fair value. The stock should be classified as non-trading securities.

(c) Show the balance sheet presentation of the investment-related accounts at December 31, 2014. At this date, Eli Associates has common stock $2,000,000 and retained earnings $1,200,000.

Prepare entries under the cost and equity methods, and tabulate differences.

(LO 3)

P12-4B Tuecke's Concrete acquired 20% of the outstanding common stock of Drew, Inc. on January 1, 2014, by paying $1,100,000 for 40,000 shares. Drew declared and paid a $0.50 per share cash dividend on June 30 and again on December 31, 2014. Drew reported net income of $600,000 for the year. At December 31, 2014, the market price of Drew's common stock was $30 per share.

Instructions

(a) Total dividend revenue $40,000

(a) Prepare the journal entries for Tuecke's Concrete for 2014, assuming Tuecke's cannot exercise significant influence over Drew. Use the cost method and assume Drew common stock should be classified as non-trading.

(b) Prepare the journal entries for Tuecke's Concrete for 2014, assuming Tuecke's can exercise significant influence over Drew. Use the equity method.

(c) Indicate the balance sheet and income statement account balances at December 31, 2014, under each method of accounting.

(b) Revenue from investment $120,000

P12-5B The following are in Verbitsky's Company's portfolio of long-term non-trading securities at December 31, 2013.

Journalize stock investment transactions and show statement presentation.

(LO 3, 5, 6)

	Cost
700 shares of Sasha Corporation common stock	$35,000
900 shares of Ukraine Corporation common stock	42,000
800 shares of Zaba Corporation preferred stock	22,400

On December 31, the total cost of the portfolio equaled total fair value. Verbitsky's Company had the following transactions related to the securities during 2014.

Jan. 7   Sold 700 shares of Sasha Corporation common stock at $56 per share, less brokerage fees of $700.

10   Purchased 300 shares, $70 par value common stock of Vanucci Corporation at $78 per share, plus brokerage fees of $240.

26   Received a cash dividend of $1.15 per share on Ukraine Corporation common stock.

Feb. 2   Received cash dividends of $0.40 per share on Zaba Corporation preferred stock.

10   Sold all 800 shares of Zaba Corporation preferred stock at $26 per share less brokerage fees of $180.

July 1   Received a cash dividend of $1.00 per share on Ukraine Corporation common stock.

Sept. 1   Purchased an additional 800 shares of the $70 par value common stock of Vanucci Corporation at $75 per share, plus brokerage fees of $900.

Dec. 15   Received a cash dividend of $1.50 per share on Vanucci Corporation common stock.

At December 31, 2014, the fair values of the securities were:

Ukraine Corporation common stock	$48 per share
Vanucci Corporation common stock	$72 per share

Instructions

(a) Prepare journal entries to record the transactions.

(b) Post to the investment accounts. (Use T-accounts.)

(c) Prepare the adjusting entry at December 31, 2014, to report the portfolio at fair value.

(d) Show the balance sheet presentation at December 31, 2014, for the investment-related accounts.

(a) Loss on sale $1,780

(c) Unrealized loss $4,140

P12-6B The following data, presented in alphabetical order, are taken from the records of Redlands Corporation.

Prepare a balance sheet.

(LO 5, 6)

Accounts payable	$ 375,000
Accounts receivable	135,000
Accumulated depreciation—buildings	270,000
Accumulated depreciation—equipment	80,000
Allowance for doubtful accounts	10,000
Bonds payable (10%, due 2024)	600,000
Buildings	1,350,000
Cash	210,000
Common stock ($5 par value; 500,000 shares authorized, 440,000 shares issued)	2,200,000
Discount on bonds payable	30,000
Dividends payable	75,000
Equipment	415,000
Goodwill	300,000
Income taxes payable	180,000
Inventory	255,000
Investment in Bonita Inc. stock (30% ownership), at equity	900,000

Land	780,000
Notes payable (due 2015)	110,000
Paid-in capital in excess of par—common stock	300,000
Prepaid insurance	25,000
Retained earnings	480,000
Short-term investments, at fair value (and cost)	280,000

Total assets $4,290,000

Instructions
Prepare a classified balance sheet at December 31, 2014.

Prepare consolidated worksheet and balance sheet when cost exceeds book value.

(LO 7)

*P12-7B Patel Company purchased all the outstanding common stock of Singh Company on December 31, 2014. Just before the purchase, the condensed balance sheets of the two companies were as follows.

	Patel Company	Singh Company
Current assets	$1,478,000	$379,000
Plant and equipment (net)	1,882,000	351,000
	$3,360,000	$730,000
Current liabilities	$ 870,000	$ 90,000
Common stock	1,947,000	360,000
Retained earnings	543,000	280,000
	$3,360,000	$730,000

Patel used current assets of $710,000 to acquire the stock of Singh. The excess of this purchase price over the book value of Patel's net assets is determined to be attributable $20,000 to Singh's plant and equipment and the remainder to goodwill.

Instructions

Excess of cost over book value $50,000

(a) Prepare the entry for Patel Company's acquisition of Singh Company stock.
(b) Prepare a consolidated worksheet at December 31, 2014.
(c) Prepare a consolidated balance sheet at December 31, 2014.

PROBLEMS: SET C

Visit the book's companion website, at **www.wiley.com/college/weygandt**, and choose the Student Companion site to access Problem Set C.

COMPREHENSIVE PROBLEM: CHAPTERS 11 TO 12

CP12 Part I   Mindy Feldkamp and her two colleagues, Oscar Lopez and Lori Melton, are personal trainers at an upscale health spa/resort in Tampa, Florida. They want to start a health club that specializes in health plans for people in the 50+ age range. The growing population in this age range and strong consumer interest in the health benefits of physical activity have convinced them they can profitably operate their own club. In addition to many other decisions, they need to determine what type of business organization they want. Oscar believes there are more advantages to the corporate form than a partnership, but he hasn't yet convinced Mindy and Lori. They have come to you, a small-business consulting specialist, seeking information and advice regarding the choice of starting a partnership versus a corporation.

Instructions

(a) ▭▭▭▭▷ Prepare a memo (dated May 26, 2013) that describes the advantages and disadvantages of both partnerships and corporations. Advise Mindy, Oscar, and Lori regarding which organizational form you believe would better serve their purposes. Make sure to include reasons supporting your advice.

Part II   After deciding to incorporate, each of the three investors receives 20,000 shares of $2 par common stock on June 12, 2013, in exchange for their co-owned building ($200,000 fair value) and $100,000 total cash they contributed to the business. The next decision that Mindy, Oscar, and Lori need to make is how to obtain financing for renovation and equipment. They understand the difference between equity securities and debt securities, but do not understand the tax, net income, and earnings per share consequences of equity versus debt financing on the future of their business.

Instructions
(b) Prepare notes for a discussion with the three entrepreneurs in which you will compare the consequences of using equity versus debt financing. As part of your notes, show the differences in interest and tax expense assuming $1,400,000 is financed with common stock, and then alternatively with debt. Assume that when common stock is used, 140,000 shares will be issued. When debt is used, assume the interest rate on debt is 9%, the tax rate is 32%, and income before interest and taxes is $300,000. (You may want to use an electronic spreadsheet.)

Part III   During the discussion about financing, Lori mentions that one of her clients, Roberto Marino, has approached her about buying a significant interest in the new club. Having an interested investor sways the three to issue equity securities to provide the financing they need. On July 21, 2013, Mr. Marino buys 90,000 shares at a price of $10 per share.

 The club, LifePath Fitness, opens on January 12, 2014, and after a slow start begins to produce the revenue desired by the owners. The owners decide to pay themselves a stock dividend since cash has been less than abundant since they opened their doors. The 10% stock dividend is declared by the owners on July 27, 2014. The market price of the stock is $3 on the declaration date. The date of record is July 31, 2014 (there have been no changes in stock ownership since the initial issuance), and the issue date is August 15, 2014. By the middle of the fourth quarter of 2014, the cash flow of LifePath Fitness has improved to the point that the owners feel ready to pay themselves a cash dividend. They declare a $0.05 cash dividend per share on December 4, 2014. The record date is December 14, 2014, and the payment date is December 24, 2014.

Instructions
(c) (1) Record all of the transactions related to the common stock of LifePath Fitness during the years 2013 and 2014. (2) Indicate how many shares are issued and outstanding after the stock dividend is issued.

Part IV   Since the club opened, a major concern has been the pool facilities. Although the existing pool is adequate, Mindy, Oscar, and Lori all desire to make LifePath a cutting-edge facility. Until the end of 2014, financing concerns prevented this improvement. However, because there has been steady growth in clientele, revenue, and income since the fourth quarter of 2014, the owners have explored possible financing options. They are hesitant to issue stock and change the ownership mix because they have been able to work together as a team with great effectiveness. They have formulated a plan to issue secured term bonds to raise the needed $600,000 for the pool facilities. By the end of April 2015, everything was in place for the bond issue to go ahead. On June 1, 2015, the bonds were issued for $548,000. The bonds pay semiannual interest of 3% (6% annual) on December 1 and June 1 of each year. The bonds mature in 10 years, and amortization is computed using the straight-line method.

Instructions
(d) Record (1) the issuance of the secured bonds, (2) the interest payment made on December 1, 2015, (3) the adjusting entry required at December 31, 2015, and (4) the interest payment made on June 1, 2016.

Part V   Mr. Marino's purchase of the stock of LifePath Fitness was done through his business. The stock investment has always been accounted for using the cost method on his firm's books. However, early in 2016 he decided to take his company public. He is preparing an IPO (initial public offering), and he needs to have the firm's financial statements audited. One of the issues to be resolved is to restate the stock investment in LifePath Fitness using the equity method, since Mr. Marino's ownership percentage is greater than 20%.

Instructions

(e) (1) Give the entries that would have been made on Marino's books if the equity method of accounting for investments had been used from the initial investment through 2015. Assume the following data for LifePath.

	2013	**2014**	**2015**
Net income	$30,000	$70,000	$105,000
Total cash dividends	$ 2,100	$20,000	$ 50,000

(2) Compute the balance in the Stock Investments account (as it relates to LifePath Fitness) at the end of 2015.

CONTINUING COOKIE CHRONICLE

(*Note:* This is a continuation of the Cookie Chronicle from Chapters 1–11.)

CCC12 Natalie has been approached by Ken Thornton, a shareholder of The Beanery Coffee Inc. Ken wants to retire and would like to sell his 1,000 shares in The Beanery Coffee, which represents 30% of all shares issued. The Beanery is currently operated by Ken's twin daughters, who each own 35% of the common shares. The Beanery not only operates a coffee shop but also roasts and sells beans to retailers, under the name "Rocky Mountain Beanery."

Ken has met with Curtis and Natalie to discuss the business operation. All have concluded that there would be many advantages for Cookie & Coffee Creations Inc. to acquire an interest in The Beanery Coffee. Despite the apparent advantages, however, Natalie and Curtis are still not convinced that they should participate in this business venture.

Go to the book's companion website, www.wiley.com/college/weygandt, to see the completion of this problem.

Broadening Your PERSPECTIVE

Financial Reporting and Analysis

Financial Reporting Problem: Pepsico, Inc.

BYP12-1 The annual report of PepsiCo, Inc. is presented in Appendix A.

Instructions

(a) See Note 1 to the financial statements and indicate what the consolidated financial statements include.

(b) Using PepsiCo's consolidated statement of cash flows, determine how much was spent for capital acquisitions during the current year.

Comparative Analysis Problem: PepsiCo, Inc. vs. The Coca-Cola Company

BYP12-2 PepsiCo's financial statements are presented in Appendix A. Financial statements of The Coca-Cola Company are presented in Appendix B.

Instructions

(a) Based on the information contained in these financial statements, determine the following for each company.

(1) Net cash used for investing (investment) activities for the current year (from the statement of cash flows).

(2) Cash used for capital expenditures during the current year.

(b) Each of PepsiCo's financial statements is labeled "consolidated." What has been consolidated? That is, from the contents of PepsiCo's annual report, identify by name the six divisions that have been consolidated. (*Hint:* PepsiCo uses abbreviations to describe each division. You will need to look up the meaning of each of these abbreviations.)

Real-World Focus

BYP12-3 Most publicly traded companies are examined by numerous analysts. These analysts often don't agree about a company's future prospects. In this exercise, you will find analysts' ratings about companies and make comparisons over time and across companies in the same industry. You will also see to what extent the analysts experienced "earnings surprises." Earnings surprises can cause changes in stock prices.

Address: **biz.yahoo.com/i/** or go to **www.wiley.com/college/weygandt**

Steps
1. Choose a company.
2. Use the index to find the company's name.
3. Choose **Research**.

Instructions
(a) How many analysts rated the company?
(b) What percentage rated it a strong buy?
(c) What was the average rating for the week?
(d) Did the average rating improve or decline relative to the previous week?
(e) What was the amount of the earnings surprise percentage during the last quarter?

Critical Thinking

Decision-Making Across the Organization

BYP12-4 At the beginning of the question-and-answer portion of the annual stockholders' meeting of Kemper Corporation, stockholder Mike Kerwin asks, "Why did management sell the holdings in UMW Company at a loss when this company has been very profitable during the period Kemper held its stock?"

Since president Tony Chavez has just concluded his speech on the recent success and bright future of Kemper, he is taken aback by this question and responds, "I remember we paid $1,300,000 for that stock some years ago. I am sure we sold that stock at a much higher price. You must be mistaken."

Kerwin retorts, "Well, right here in footnote number 7 to the annual report it shows that 240,000 shares, a 30% interest in UMW, were sold on the last day of the year. Also, it states that UMW earned $520,000 this year and paid out $160,000 in cash dividends. Further, a summary statement indicates that in past years, while Kemper held UMW stock, UMW earned $1,240,000 and paid out $440,000 in dividends. Finally, the income statement for this year shows a loss on the sale of UMW stock of $180,000. So, I doubt that I am mistaken."

Red-faced, president Chavez turns to you.

Instructions
With the class divided into groups, answer the following.

(a) What dollar amount did Kemper receive upon the sale of the UMW stock?
(b) Explain why both stockholder Kerwin and president Chavez are correct.

Communication Activity

BYP12-5 Bunge Corporation has purchased two securities for its portfolio. The first is a stock investment in Longley Corporation, one of its suppliers. Bunge purchased 10% of Longley with the intention of holding it for a number of years, but has no intention of purchasing more shares. The second investment was a purchase of debt securities. Bunge purchased the debt securities because its analysts believe that changes in market interest rates will cause these securities to increase in value in a short period of time. Bunge intends to sell the securities as soon as they have increased in value.

Instructions

Write a memo to Max Scholes, the chief financial officer, explaining how to account for each of these investments. Explain what the implications for reported income are from this accounting treatment.

Ethics Case

BYP12-6 Bartlet Financial Services Company holds a large portfolio of debt and stock securities as an investment. The total fair value of the portfolio at December 31, 2014, is greater than total cost. Some securities have increased in value and others have decreased. Deb Faust, the financial vice president, and Jan McCabe, the controller, are in the process of classifying for the first time the securities in the portfolio.

Faust suggests classifying the securities that have increased in value as trading securities in order to increase net income for the year. She wants to classify the securities that have decreased in value as long-term non-trading securities, so that the decreases in value will not affect 2014 net income.

McCabe disagrees. She recommends classifying the securities that have decreased in value as trading securities and those that have increased in value as long-term non-trading securities. McCabe argues that the company is having a good earnings year and that recognizing the losses now will help to smooth income for this year. Moreover, for future years, when the company may not be as profitable, the company will have built-in gains.

Instructions

(a) Will classifying the securities as Faust and McCabe suggest actually affect earnings as each says it will?

(b) Is there anything unethical in what Faust and McCabe propose? Who are the stakeholders affected by their proposals?

(c) Assume that Faust and McCabe properly classify the portfolio. At year-end, Faust proposes to sell the securities that will increase 2014 net income, and McCabe proposes to sell the securities that will decrease 2014 net income. Is this unethical?

All About You

BYP12-7 The Securities and Exchange Commission (SEC) is the primary regulatory agency of U.S. financial markets. Its job is to ensure that the markets remain fair for all investors. The following SEC sites provide useful information for investors.

Address: **www.sec.gov/answers.shtml** and **http://www.sec.gov/investor/tools/quiz.htm**.

Instructions

(a) Go to the first SEC site and find the definition of the following terms.
   (i)   Ask price.
   (ii) Margin.
   (iii) Prospectus.
   (iv) Index fund.
(b) Go to the second SEC site and take the short quiz.

BYP12-8 You've got $3,000 in credit card bills at an 18% interest rate. Your employer has a 401(k) plan in which it will match your contributions, up to 10% of your annual salary. Should you pay off your credit card bills before you start putting money into the 401(k)?

YES: Paying off an 18% debt, and thus avoiding 18% interest payments, is essentially equivalent to earning 18% on investments. Reducing your debts reduces your financial vulnerability.

NO: You need to get in the savings habit as soon as possible. You should take part of the money you would have used to pay off your debt each month and instead put it into the 401(k).

Instructions

Write a response indicating your position regarding the situation. Provide support for your view.

FASB Codification Activity

BYP12-9 If your school has a subscription to the FASB Codification, go to *http://aaahq.org/ascLogin.cfm* to log in and prepare responses to the following.

(a) What is the definition of a trading security?
(b) What is the definition of non-trading security?
(c) What is definition of a holding gain or loss?

Answers to Chapter Questions

Answers to Insight and Accounting Across the Organization Questions

p. 608 How Procter & Gamble Accounts for Gillette Q: Where on Procter & Gamble's balance sheet will you find its investment in Gillette Company? **A:** Because Procter & Gamble owns Gillette, Procter & Gamble does not report Gillette in the investment section of its balance sheet. Instead, Gillette's assets and liabilities are included and commingled with the assets and liabilities of Procter & Gamble.

p. 612 And the Correct Way to Report Investments Is... ? Q: Why might the use of the equity method not lead to full disclosure in the financial statements? **A:** Under the equity method, the investment in common stock of another company is initially recorded at cost. After that, the investment account is adjusted at each reporting date to show the investor's equity in the investee. However, on the investor's balance sheet, only the investment account is shown. The pro-rata share of the investee's assets and liabilities are not reported. Because the pro-rata share of the investee's assets and liabilities are not shown, some argue that the full disclosure principle is violated.

Answers to Self-Test Questions

1. d **2.** a **3.** b **4.** c **5.** a **6.** b $300,000 + [25\% \times (\$160,000 - \$60,000)]$ **7.** c **8.** d **9.** a
10. c **11.** c ($41,300 - \$39,800) + \$900$) **12.** b **13.** c ***14.** d $175,000 - \$160,000$ ***15.** d ***16.** d

A Look at IFRS

The accounting and reporting for investments under IFRS and GAAP are very similar. Recently, the FASB issued a reporting standard that essentially converges to a previously issued IASB standard.

Key Points

- The basic accounting entries to record the acquisition of debt securities, the receipt of interest, and the sale of debt securities are the same under IFRS and GAAP.

- The basic accounting entries to record the acquisition of stock investments, the receipt of dividends, and the sale of stock securities are the same under IFRS and GAAP.

- Both IFRS and GAAP use the same criteria to determine whether the equity method of accounting should be used—that is, significant influence with a general guide of over 20% ownership, IFRS uses the term *associate investment* rather than equity investment to describe its investment under the equity method.

- Under IFRS, both the investor and an associate company should follow the same accounting policies. As a result, in order to prepare financial information, adjustments are made to the associate's policies to conform to the investor's books. GAAP does not have that requirement.

- The basis for consolidation under IFRS is control. Under GAAP, a bipolar approach is used, which is a risk-and-reward model (often referred to as a variable-entity approach) and a voting-interest approach. However, under both systems, for consolidation to occur, the investor company must generally own 50% of another company.

- Both IFRS and GAAP require that companies determine how to measure their financial assets based on two criteria:

  - The company's business model for managing their financial assets; and
  - The contractual cash flow characteristics of the financial asset.

  If a company has (1) a business model whose objective is to hold assets in order to collect contractual cash flows and (2) the contractual terms of the financial asset gives specified dates to cash flows that are solely payments of principal and interest on the principal amount outstanding, then the company should use cost (often referred to as amortized cost).

  For example, assume that Mitsubishi purchases a bond investment that it intends to hold-for-collection. Its business model for this type of investment is to collect interest and then principal at maturity. The payment dates for the interest rate and principal are stated on the bond. In this case, Mitsubishi accounts for the investment at cost. If, on the other hand, Mitsubishi purchased the bonds as part of a trading strategy to speculate on interest rate changes (a trading investment), then the debt investment is reported at fair value. As a result, only debt investments such as receivables, loans, and bond investments that meet the two criteria above are recorded at amortized cost. All other debt investments are recorded and reported at fair value.

- Both IFRS and GAAP use held-for-collection (debt investments), trading (both debt and equity investments), and non-trading equity investment classifications. These classifications are based on the business model used to manage the investments and the type of security.

- The accounting for trading investments is the same between GAAP and IFRS. Also, held-for-collection investments are accounted for at amortized cost. Gains and losses on non-trading equity investments (IFRS) are reported in other comprehensive income.

- Unrealized gains and losses related to non-trading securities are reported in other comprehensive income under GAAP and IFRS. These gains and losses that accumulate are then reported in the balance sheet.

- IFRS does not use Other Revenues and Gains or Other Expenses and Losses in its income statement presentation. It will generally classify these items as unusual items or financial items.

Looking to the Future

As indicated earlier, both the FASB and IASB have indicated (conceptually) that they believe that all financial instruments should be reported at fair value and that changes in fair value should be reported as part of net income. However, both the FASB and IASB have decided to permit amortized cost for debt investments held-for-collection. Hopefully, they will eventually arrive at fair value measurement for all financial instruments.

IFRS Practice

IFRS Self-Test Questions

1. The following asset is *not* considered a financial asset under IFRS:
   - (a) trading securities.
   - (b) equity securities.
   - (c) held-for-collection securities.
   - (d) inventories.

2. Under IFRS, the equity method of accounting for long-term investments in common stock should be used when the investor has significant influence over an investee and owns:
   - (a) between 20% and 50% of the investee's common stock.
   - (b) 30% or more of the investee's common stock.
   - (c) more than 50% of the investee's common stock.
   - (d) less than 20% of the investee's common stock.

3. Under IFRS, at the end of the first year of operations, the total cost of the trading investments portfolio is $120,000. Total fair value is $115,000. The financial statement should show:

(a) a reduction in the carrying value of the asset of $5,000 and an unrealized loss of $5,000 in the income statement.

(b) a reduction in the carrying value of the asset of $5,000 and an unrealized loss of $5,000 in the stockholders' equity section.

(c) a reduction in the carrying value of the asset of $5,000 in the current assets section and an unrealized loss of $5,000 in other comprehensive income.

(d) a reduction in the carrying value of the asset of $5,000 in the current assets section and a realized loss of $5,000 in other expenses and losses.

4. Under IFRS, unrealized gains on non-trading stock investments should:

(a) be reported as other revenues and gains in the income statement as part of net income.

(b) be reported as other gains on the income statement as part of net income.

(c) not be reported on the income statement or balance sheet.

(d) be reported as other comprehensive income.

5. Under IFRS, the unrealized loss on trading investments should be reported:

(a) as part of other comprehensive loss reducing net income.

(b) on the income statement reducing net income.

(c) as part of other comprehensive loss not affecting net income.

(d) directly to stockholders' equity bypassing the income statement.

Answers to IFRS Self-Test Questions

1. d   **2.** a   **3.** a   **4.** d   **5.** b

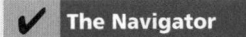

✔ **The Navigator**

Chapter 13

Statement of Cash Flows

Feature Story

Got Cash?

In today's environment, companies must be ready to respond to changes quickly in order to survive and thrive. This requires that they manage their cash very carefully. One company that managed cash successfully in its early years was Microsoft. During those years, the company paid much of its payroll with stock options (rights to purchase company stock in the future at a given price) instead of cash. This strategy conserved cash and turned more than a thousand of its employees into millionaires during the company's first 20 years of business.

In recent years, Microsoft has had a different kind of cash problem. Now that it has reached a more "mature" stage in life, it generates so much cash—roughly $1 billion per month—that it cannot always figure out what to do with it. At one time, Microsoft had accumulated $60 billion.

The company said it was accumulating cash to invest in new opportunities, buy other companies, and pay off pending lawsuits. But for many years, the federal government blocked attempts by Microsoft to buy anything other than small firms because it feared that purchase of a large firm would only increase Microsoft's monopolistic position.

Microsoft's stockholders have complained for years that holding all this cash was putting a drag on the company's profitability. Why? Because Microsoft had the cash invested in very low-yielding government securities.

Learning Objectives

After studying this chapter, you should be able to:

1 Indicate the usefulness of the statement of cash flows.

2 Distinguish among operating, investing, and financing activities.

3 Prepare a statement of cash flows using the indirect method.

4 Analyze the statement of cash flows.

 The Navigator

Stockholders felt that the company either should find new investment projects that would bring higher returns, or return some of the cash to stockholders.

Finally, Microsoft announced a plan to return cash to stockholders, by paying a special one-time $32 billion dividend. This special dividend was so large that, according to the U.S. Commerce Department, it caused total personal income in the United States to rise by 3.7% in one month—the largest increase ever recorded by the agency. (It also made the holiday season brighter, especially for retailers in the Seattle area.) Microsoft also doubled its regular annual dividend to $3.50 per share. Further, it announced that it would spend another $30 billion buying treasury stock. In addition, Microsoft more recently offered to buy Yahoo! for

$44.6 billion (Yahoo! declined the offer). Dividends, stock buybacks, and acquisitions will help to deplete some of its massive cash horde. But as you will see in this chapter, for a cash-generating machine like Microsoft, the company will be anything but cash-starved.

Interestingly, in 2010 Google found itself in a position similar to Microsoft's. Its cash pile of $26.5 billion was nearly 20% of the company's value. That's enough to pay a dividend of $80 per share. Unless it can find large, worthwhile projects to invest in, Google will also need to return a big chunk of its cash to shareholders.

Source: "Business: An End to Growth? Microsoft's Cash Bonanza," *The Economist* (July 23, 2005), p. 61.

 **The Navigator**

Preview of **Chapter 13**

The balance sheet, income statement, and retained earnings statement do not always show the whole picture of the financial condition of a company or institution. In fact, looking at the financial statements of some well-known companies, a thoughtful investor might ask questions like these: How did Eastman Kodak finance cash dividends of $649 million in a year in which it earned only $17 million? How could United Airlines purchase new planes that cost $1.9 billion in a year in which it reported a net loss of over $2 billion? How did the companies that spent a combined fantastic $3.4 trillion on mergers and acquisitions in a recent year finance those deals? Answers to these and similar questions can be found in this chapter, which presents the statement of cash flows.

The content and organization of this chapter are as follows.

STATEMENT OF CASH FLOWS		
Statement of Cash Flows: Usefulness and Format	**Preparing the Statement of Cash Flows—Indirect Method**	**Using Cash Flows to Evaluate a Company**
• Usefulness • Classifications • Significant noncash activities • Format • Preparation • Indirect and direct methods	• Step 1: Operating activities • Step 2: Investing and financing activities • Step 3: Net change in cash	• Free cash flow

✔ **The Navigator**

Statement of Cash Flows: Usefulness and Format

The balance sheet, income statement, and retained earnings statement provide only limited information about a company's cash flows (cash receipts and cash payments). For example, comparative balance sheets show the increase in property, plant, and equipment during the year. But, they do not show how the additions were financed or paid for. The income statement shows net income. But, it does not indicate the amount of cash generated by operating activities. The retained earnings statement shows cash dividends declared but not the cash dividends paid during the year. None of these statements presents a detailed summary of where cash came from and how it was used.

Usefulness of the Statement of Cash Flows

LEARNING OBJECTIVE 1

Indicate the usefulness of the statement of cash flows.

The **statement of cash flows** reports the cash receipts, cash payments, and net change in cash resulting from operating, investing, and financing activities during a period. The information in a statement of cash flows should help investors, creditors, and others assess:

1. **The entity's ability to generate future cash flows.** By examining relationships between items in the statement of cash flows, investors can make predictions of the amounts, timing, and uncertainty of future cash flows better than they can from accrual-basis data.

2. **The entity's ability to pay dividends and meet obligations.** If a company does not have adequate cash, it cannot pay employees, settle debts, or pay dividends. Employees, creditors, and stockholders should be particularly interested in this statement because it alone shows the flows of cash in a business.

 Ethics Note

Though we would discourage reliance on cash flows to the exclusion of accrual accounting, comparing cash from operations to net income can reveal important information about the "quality" of reported net income. Such a comparison can reveal the extent to which net income provides a good measure of actual performance.

3. **The reasons for the difference between net income and net cash provided (used) by operating activities.** Net income provides information on the success or failure of a business. However, some financial statement users are critical of accrual-basis net income because it requires many estimates. As a result, users often challenge the reliability of the number. Such is not the case with cash. Many readers of the statement of cash flows want to know the reasons for the difference between net income and net cash provided by operating activities. Then, they can assess for themselves the reliability of the income number.

4. **The cash investing and financing transactions during the period.** By examining a company's investing and financing transactions, a financial statement reader can better understand why assets and liabilities changed during the period.

Classification of Cash Flows

LEARNING OBJECTIVE 2

Distinguish among operating, investing, and financing activities.

The statement of cash flows classifies cash receipts and cash payments as operating, investing, and financing activities. Transactions and other events characteristic of each kind of activity are as follows.

1. **Operating activities** include the cash effects of transactions that create revenues and expenses. They thus enter into the determination of net income.

2. **Investing activities** include (a) acquiring and disposing of investments and property, plant, and equipment, and (b) lending money and collecting the loans.

3. **Financing activities** include (a) obtaining cash from issuing debt and repaying the amounts borrowed, and (b) obtaining cash from stockholders, repurchasing shares, and paying dividends.

The operating activities category is the most important. It shows the cash provided by company operations. This source of cash is generally considered to be the best measure of a company's ability to generate sufficient cash to continue as a going concern.

Illustration 13-1 lists typical cash receipts and cash payments within each of the three classifications. **Study the list carefully.** It will prove very useful in solving homework exercises and problems.

Illustration 13-1
Typical receipt and payment classifications

TYPES OF CASH INFLOWS AND OUTFLOWS

Operating activities—Income statement items
Cash inflows:
From sale of goods or services.
From interest received and dividends received.
Cash outflows:
To suppliers for inventory.
To employees for services.
To government for taxes.
To lenders for interest.
To others for expenses.

Operating activities

Investing activities—Changes in investments and long-term assets
Cash inflows:
From sale of property, plant, and equipment.
From sale of investments in debt or equity securities of other entities.
From collection of principal on loans to other entities.
Cash outflows:
To purchase property, plant, and equipment.
To purchase investments in debt or equity securities of other entities.
To make loans to other entities.

Investing activities

Financing activities—Changes in long-term liabilities and stockholders' equity
Cash inflows:
From sale of common stock.
From issuance of long-term debt (bonds and notes).
Cash outflows:
To stockholders as dividends.
To redeem long-term debt or reacquire capital stock (treasury stock).

Financing activities

Note the following general guidelines:

1. Operating activities involve income statement items.

2. Investing activities involve cash flows resulting from changes in investments and long-term asset items.

3. Financing activities involve cash flows resulting from changes in long-term liability and stockholders' equity items.

Companies classify as operating activities some cash flows related to investing or financing activities. For example, receipts of investment revenue (interest and dividends) are classified as operating activities. So are payments of interest to lenders. Why are these considered operating activities? **Because companies report these items in the income statement, where results of operations are shown.**

Significant Noncash Activities

Not all of a company's significant activities involve cash. Examples of significant noncash activities are:

1. Direct issuance of common stock to purchase assets.

2. Conversion of bonds into common stock.

3. Direct issuance of debt to purchase assets.

4. Exchanges of plant assets.

Helpful Hint
Do not include noncash investing and financing activities in the body of the statement of cash flows. Report this information in a separate schedule.

Companies do not report in the body of the statement of cash flows significant financing and investing activities that do not affect cash. Instead, they report these activities in either a **separate schedule** at the bottom of the statement of cash flows or in a **separate note or supplementary schedule** to the financial statements. The reporting of these noncash activities in a separate schedule satisfies the **full disclosure principle**.

In solving homework assignments, you should present significant noncash investing and financing activities in a separate schedule at the bottom of the statement of cash flows. (See the last entry in Illustration 13-2, on page 649, for an example.)

ACCOUNTING ACROSS THE ORGANIZATION

Net *What?*

Net income is not the same as net cash provided by operating activities. Below are some results from recent annual reports (dollars in millions). Note the wide disparity among these companies, all of which engaged in retail merchandising.

Company	Net Income	Net Cash Provided by Operating Activities
Kohl's Corporation	$ 1,083	$ 1,234
Wal-Mart Stores, Inc.	11,284	20,169
J.C. Penney Company, Inc.	1,153	1,255
Costco Wholesale Corp.	1,082	2,076
Target Corporation	2,849	4,125

 In general, why do differences exist between net income and net cash provided by operating activities? (See page 706.)

Format of the Statement of Cash Flows

The general format of the statement of cash flows presents the results of the three activities discussed previously—operating, investing, and financing—plus the significant noncash investing and financing activities. Illustration 13-2 shows a widely used form of the statement of cash flows.

Illustration 13-2
Format of statement of cash flows

Company Name
Statement of Cash Flows
Period Covered

Cash flows from operating activities		
(List of individual items)	XX	
Net cash provided (used) by operating activities		XXX
Cash flows from investing activities		
(List of individual inflows and outflows)	XX	
Net cash provided (used) by investing activities		XXX
Cash flows from financing activities		
(List of individual inflows and outflows)	XX	
Net cash provided (used) by financing activities		XXX
Net increase (decrease) in cash		XXX
Cash at beginning of period		XXX
Cash at end of period		XXX
Noncash investing and financing activities		
(List of individual noncash transactions)		XXX

The cash flows from operating activities section always appears first, followed by the investing activities section and then the financing activities section. The sum of the operating, investing, and financing sections equals the net increase or decrease in cash for the period. This amount is combined with the beginning cash balance to arrive at the ending cash balance—the same amount reported on the balance sheet.

> **DO IT!**

Classification of Cash Flows

Action Plan
✔ Identify the three types of activities used to report all cash inflows and outflows.

✔ Report as operating activities the cash effects of transactions that create revenues and expenses and enter into the determination of net income.

✔ Report as investing activities transactions that (a) acquire and dispose of investments and long-term assets and (b) lend money and collect loans.

During its first week, Duffy & Stevenson Company had these transactions.

1. Issued 100,000 shares of $5 par value common stock for $800,000 cash.
2. Borrowed $200,000 from Castle Bank, signing a 5-year note bearing 8% interest.
3. Purchased two semi-trailer trucks for $170,000 cash.
4. Paid employees $12,000 for salaries and wages.
5. Collected $20,000 cash for services provided.

Classify each of these transactions by type of cash flow activity.

Action Plan (cont'd)

✔ Report as financing activities transactions that (a) obtain cash from issuing debt and repay the amounts borrowed and (b) obtain cash from stockholders and pay them dividends.

Solution

1. Financing activity	4. Operating activity
2. Financing activity	5. Operating activity
3. Investing activity	

Related exercise material: **BE13-1, BE13-2, BE13-3, E13-1, E13-2, E13-3, and** **DO IT!** **13-1.**

Preparing the Statement of Cash Flows

Companies prepare the statement of cash flows differently from the three other basic financial statements. First, it is not prepared from an adjusted trial balance. It requires detailed information concerning the changes in account balances that occurred between two points in time. An adjusted trial balance will not provide the necessary data. Second, the statement of cash flows deals with cash receipts and payments. As a result, the company **must adjust** the effects of the use of accrual accounting **to determine cash flows**.

The information to prepare this statement usually comes from three sources:

- **Comparative balance sheets.** Information in the comparative balance sheets indicates the amount of the changes in assets, liabilities, and stockholders' equities from the beginning to the end of the period.

- **Current income statement.** Information in this statement helps determine the amount of cash provided or used by operations during the period.

- **Additional information.** Such information includes transaction data that are needed to determine how cash was provided or used during the period.

Preparing the statement of cash flows from these data sources involves three major steps, explained in Illustration 13-3 on the next page.

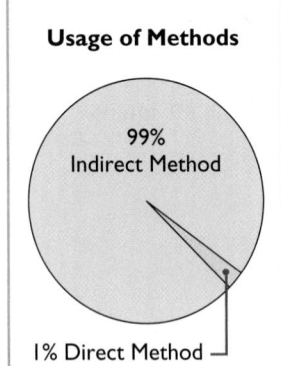

Usage of Methods

99% Indirect Method

1% Direct Method

Indirect and Direct Methods

In order to perform Step 1, a company **must convert net income from an accrual basis to a cash basis**. This conversion may be done by either of two methods: (1) the indirect method or (2) the direct method. **Both methods arrive at the same total amount** for "Net cash provided by operating activities." They differ in **how** they arrive at the amount.

The **indirect method** adjusts net income for items that do not affect cash. A great majority of companies (99%) use this method, as shown in the chart on the left.[1] Companies favor the indirect method for two reasons: (1) It is easier and less costly to prepare, and (2) it focuses on the differences between net income and net cash flow from operating activities.

The **direct method** shows operating cash receipts and payments, making it more consistent with the objective of a statement of cash flows. The FASB has expressed a preference for the direct method but allows the use of either method.

The next section illustrates the more popular indirect method. Appendix 13B illustrates the direct method.

---

[1]*Accounting Trends and Techniques—2010* (New York: American Institute of Certified Public Accountants, 2010).

Step 1: Determine net cash provided/used by operating activities by converting net income from an accrual basis to a cash basis.

Buying & selling goods

This step involves analyzing not only the current year's income statement but also comparative balance sheets and selected additional data.

Step 2: Analyze changes in noncurrent asset and liability accounts and record as investing and financing activities, or disclose as noncash transactions.

Investing   Financing

This step involves analyzing comparative balance sheet data and selected additional information for their effects on cash.

Step 3: Compare the net change in cash on the statement of cash flows with the change in the Cash account reported on the balance sheet to make sure the amounts agree.

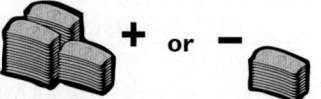

+ or −

The difference between the beginning and ending cash balances can be easily computed from comparative balance sheets.

Illustration 13-3
Three major steps in preparing the statement of cash flows

Preparing the Statement of Cash Flows—Indirect Method

To explain how to prepare a statement of cash flows using the indirect method, we use financial information from Computer Services Company. Illustration 13-4 presents Computer Services' current- and previous-year balance sheets, its current-year income statement, and related financial information for the current year.

LEARNING OBJECTIVE   3

Prepare a statement of cash flows using the indirect method.

Illustration 13-4
Comparative balance sheets, income statement, and additional information for Computer Services Company

Computer Services Company Comparative Balance Sheets December 31			
Assets	**2014**	**2013**	**Change in Account Balance Increase/Decrease**
Current assets			
Cash	$ 55,000	$ 33,000	$ 22,000 Increase
Accounts receivable	20,000	30,000	10,000 Decrease
Inventory	15,000	10,000	5,000 Increase
Prepaid expenses	5,000	1,000	4,000 Increase
Property, plant, and equipment			
Land	130,000	20,000	110,000 Increase
Buildings	160,000	40,000	120,000 Increase
Accumulated depreciation—buildings	(11,000)	(5,000)	6,000 Increase
Equipment	27,000	10,000	17,000 Increase
Accumulated depreciation—equipment	(3,000)	(1,000)	2,000 Increase
Total assets	$398,000	$138,000	

Illustration 13-4
(cont'd.)

Liabilities and Stockholders' Equity			
Current liabilities			
Accounts payable	$ 28,000	$ 12,000	$ 16,000 Increase
Income taxes payable	6,000	8,000	2,000 Decrease
Long-term liabilities			
Bonds payable	130,000	20,000	110,000 Increase
Stockholders' equity			
Common stock	70,000	50,000	20,000 Increase
Retained earnings	164,000	48,000	116,000 Increase
Total liabilities and stockholders' equity	$398,000	$138,000	

Computer Services Company
Income Statement
For the Year Ended December 31, 2014

Sales revenue		$507,000
Cost of goods sold	$150,000	
Operating expenses (excluding depreciation)	111,000	
Depreciation expense	9,000	
Loss on disposal of plant assets	3,000	
Interest expense	42,000	315,000
Income before income tax		192,000
Income tax expense		47,000
Net income		$145,000

Additional information for 2014:
1. Depreciation expense was comprised of $6,000 for building and $3,000 for equipment.
2. The company sold equipment with a book value of $7,000 (cost $8,000, less accumulated depreciation $1,000) for $4,000 cash.
3. Issued $110,000 of long-term bonds in direct exchange for land.
4. A building costing $120,000 was purchased for cash. Equipment costing $25,000 was also purchased for cash.
5. Issued common stock for $20,000 cash.
6. The company declared and paid a $29,000 cash dividend.

We will now apply the three steps to the information provided for Computer Services Company. *(Appendix 13C demonstrates an approach that employs T-accounts to prepare the statement of cash flows. Many students find this approach helpful. We encourage you to give it a try as you walk through the Computer Services example.)*

Step 1: Operating Activities

DETERMINE NET CASH PROVIDED/USED BY OPERATING ACTIVITIES BY CONVERTING NET INCOME FROM AN ACCRUAL BASIS TO A CASH BASIS
To determine net cash provided by operating activities under the indirect method, companies **adjust net income in numerous ways**. A useful starting point is to understand **why** net income must be converted to net cash provided by operating activities.

Under generally accepted accounting principles, most companies use the accrual basis of accounting. This basis requires that companies record revenue when earned and record expenses when incurred. Earned revenues may include credit sales for which the company has not yet collected cash. Expenses incurred may include some items that the company has not yet paid in cash. Thus, net income under the accrual basis is not the same as net cash provided by operating activities.

Therefore, under the indirect method, companies must adjust net income to convert certain items to the cash basis. The indirect method (or reconciliation method) starts with net income and converts it to net cash provided by operating activities. Illustration 13-5 lists the three types of adjustments.

Net Income	+/−	Adjustments	=	Net Cash Provided/ Used by Operating Activities
		• **Add back noncash expenses**, such as depreciation expense, amortization, or depletion.		
		• **Deduct gains and add losses** that resulted from investing and financing activities.		
		• **Analyze changes** to noncash current asset and current liability accounts.		

Illustration 13-5
Three types of adjustments to convert net income to net cash provided by operating activities

We explain the three types of adjustments in the next three sections.

DEPRECIATION EXPENSE

Computer Services' income statement reports depreciation expense of $9,000. Although depreciation expense reduces net income, it does not reduce cash. In other words, depreciation expense is a noncash charge. The company must add it back to net income to arrive at net cash provided by operating activities. Computer Services reports depreciation expense in the statement of cash flows as shown below.

Helpful Hint
Depreciation is similar to any other expense in that it reduces net income. It differs in that it does not involve a current cash outflow. That is why it must be *added back* to net income to arrive at cash provided by operating activities.

Illustration 13-6
Adjustment for depreciation

Cash flows from operating activities	
Net income	$145,000
Adjustments to reconcile net income to net cash provided by operating activities:	
Depreciation expense	**9,000**
Net cash provided by operating activities	$154,000

As the first adjustment to net income in the statement of cash flows, companies frequently list depreciation and similar noncash charges such as amortization of intangible assets, depletion expense, and bad debt expense.

LOSS ON DISPOSAL OF PLANT ASSETS

Illustration 13-1 (page 647) states that cash received from the sale (disposal) of plant assets should be reported in the investing activities section. Because of this, **companies must eliminate from net income all gains and losses related to the disposal of plant assets, to arrive at cash provided by operating activities**.

In our example, Computer Services' income statement reports a $3,000 loss on disposal of plant assets (book value $7,000, less $4,000 cash received from disposal of plant assets). The company's loss of $3,000 should not be included in the operating activities section of the statement of cash flows. Illustration 13-7 shows that the $3,000 loss is eliminated by adding $3,000 back to net income to arrive at net cash provided by operating activities.

Illustration 13-7
Adjustment for loss on disposal of plant assets

Cash flows from operating activities		
Net income		$145,000
Adjustments to reconcile net income to net cash provided by operating activities:		
Depreciation expense	$9,000	
Loss on disposal of plant assets	**3,000**	12,000
Net cash provided by operating activities		$157,000

If a gain on disposal occurs, the company deducts the gain from its net income in order to determine net cash provided by operating activities. **In the case of either a gain or a loss, companies report the actual amount of cash received from the sale as a source of cash in the investing activities section of the statement of cash flows.**

CHANGES TO NONCASH CURRENT ASSET AND CURRENT LIABILITY ACCOUNTS

A final adjustment in reconciling net income to net cash provided by operating activities involves examining all changes in current asset and current liability accounts. The accrual accounting process records revenues in the period earned and expenses in the period incurred. For example, companies use Accounts Receivable to record amounts owed to the company for sales that have been made but for which cash collections have not yet been received. They use the Prepaid Insurance account to reflect insurance that has been paid for, but which has not yet expired, and therefore has not been expensed. Similarly, the Salaries and Wages Payable account reflects salaries and wages expense that has been incurred by the company but has not been paid.

As a result, we need to adjust net income for these accruals and prepayments to determine net cash provided by operating activities. Thus, we must analyze the change in each current asset and current liability account to determine its impact on net income and cash.

CHANGES IN NONCASH CURRENT ASSETS. The adjustments required for changes in noncash current asset accounts are as follows. **Deduct from net income increases in current asset accounts, and add to net income decreases in current asset accounts, to arrive at net cash provided by operating activities.** We can observe these relationships by analyzing the accounts of Computer Services Company.

DECREASE IN ACCOUNTS RECEIVABLE Computer Services Company's accounts receivable decreased by $10,000 (from $30,000 to $20,000) during the period. For Computer Services, this means that cash receipts were $10,000 higher than sales revenue. The Accounts Receivable account in Illustration 13-8 shows that Computer Services Company had $507,000 in sales revenue (as reported on the income statement), but it collected $517,000 in cash.

Illustration 13-8
Analysis of accounts receivable

Accounts Receivable				
1/1/14	Balance	30,000	**Receipts from customers**	517,000
	Sales revenue	**507,000**		
12/31/14	Balance	20,000		

To adjust net income to net cash provided by operating activities, the company adds to net income the decrease of $10,000 in accounts receivable (see Illustration 13-9). When the Accounts Receivable balance increases, cash receipts are lower than sales revenue earned under the accrual basis. Therefore, the company deducts from net income the amount of the increase in accounts receivable, to arrive at net cash provided by operating activities.

INCREASE IN INVENTORY Computer Services Company's Inventory balance increased $5,000 (from $10,000 to $15,000) during the period. The change in the Inventory account reflects the difference between the amount of inventory purchased and the amount sold. For Computer Services, this means that the cost of merchandise purchased exceeded the cost of goods sold by $5,000. As a result, cost of goods sold does not reflect $5,000 of cash payments made for merchandise. The company deducts from net income this inventory increase of $5,000 during the period, to arrive at net cash provided by operating activities (see Illustration 13-9). If inventory decreases, the company adds to net income the amount of the change, to arrive at net cash provided by operating activities.

INCREASE IN PREPAID EXPENSES Computer Services' prepaid expenses increased during the period by $4,000. This means that cash paid for expenses is higher than expenses reported on an accrual basis. In other words, the company has made cash payments in the current period, but will not charge expenses to income until future periods (as charges to the income statement). To adjust net income to net cash provided by operating activities, the company deducts from net income the $4,000 increase in prepaid expenses (see Illustration 13-9).

Illustration 13-9
Adjustments for changes in current asset accounts

Cash flows from operating activities		
Net income		$145,000
Adjustments to reconcile net income to net cash provided by operating activities:		
Depreciation expense	$ 9,000	
Loss on disposal of plant assets	3,000	
Decrease in accounts receivable	**10,000**	
Increase in inventory	**(5,000)**	
Increase in prepaid expenses	**(4,000)**	13,000
Net cash provided by operating activities		$158,000

If prepaid expenses decrease, reported expenses are higher than the expenses paid. Therefore, the company adds to net income the decrease in prepaid expenses, to arrive at net cash provided by operating activities.

CHANGES IN CURRENT LIABILITIES. The adjustments required for changes in current liability accounts are as follows. **Add to net income increases in current liability accounts, and deduct from net income decreases in current liability accounts, to arrive at net cash provided by operating activities.**

INCREASE IN ACCOUNTS PAYABLE For Computer Services Company, Accounts Payable increased by $16,000 (from $12,000 to $28,000) during the period. That means the company received $16,000 more in goods than it actually paid for. As shown in Illustration 13-10 (page 656), to adjust net income to determine net cash provided by operating activities, the company adds to net income the $16,000 increase in Accounts Payable.

DECREASE IN INCOME TAXES PAYABLE When a company incurs income tax expense but has not yet paid its taxes, it records income taxes payable. A change in the Income Taxes Payable account reflects the difference between income tax expense incurred and income tax actually paid. Computer Services' Income Taxes Payable account decreased by $2,000. That means the $47,000 of income tax expense reported on the income statement was $2,000 less than the amount of taxes paid during the period of $49,000. As shown in Illustration 13-10, to adjust net income to a cash basis, the company must reduce net income by $2,000.

Illustration 13-10
Adjustments for changes in current liability accounts

Cash flows from operating activities		
Net income		$145,000
Adjustments to reconcile net income to net cash provided by operating activities:		
Depreciation expense	$ 9,000	
Loss on disposal of plant assets	3,000	
Decrease in accounts receivable	10,000	
Increase in inventory	(5,000)	
Increase in prepaid expenses	(4,000)	
Increase in accounts payable	**16,000**	
Decrease in income taxes payable	**(2,000)**	27,000
Net cash provided by operating activities		$172,000

Illustration 13-10 shows that, after starting with net income of $145,000, the sum of all of the adjustments to net income was $27,000. This resulted in net cash provided by operating activities of $172,000.

Summary of Conversion to Net Cash Provided by Operating Activities—Indirect Method

As shown in the previous illustrations, the statement of cash flows prepared by the indirect method starts with net income. It then adds or deducts items to arrive at net cash provided by operating activities. The required adjustments are of three types:

1. Noncash charges such as depreciation, amortization, and depletion.

2. Gains and losses on the disposal of plant assets.

3. Changes in noncash current asset and current liability accounts.

Illustration 13-11 provides a summary of these changes.

Illustration 13-11
Adjustments required to convert net income to net cash provided by operating activities

		Adjustments Required to Convert Net Income to Net Cash Provided by Operating Activities
Noncash Charges	Depreciation expense	Add
	Patent amortization expense	Add
	Depletion expense	Add
Gains and Losses	Loss on disposal of plant assets	Add
	Gain on disposal of plant assets	Deduct
Changes in Current Assets and Current Liabilities	Increase in current asset account	Deduct
	Decrease in current asset account	Add
	Increase in current liability account	Add
	Decrease in current liability account	Deduct

ETHICS INSIGHT

Cash Flow Isn't Always What It Seems

Some managers have taken actions that artificially increase cash flow from operating activities. They do this by moving negative amounts out of the operating section and into the investing or financing section.

For example, WorldCom, Inc. disclosed that it had improperly capitalized expenses: It had moved $3.8 billion of cash outflows from the "Cash from operating activities" section of the statement of cash flows to the "Investing activities" section, thereby greatly enhancing cash provided by operating activities. Similarly, Dynegy, Inc. restated its statement of cash flows because it had improperly included in operating activities, instead of in financing activities, $300 million from natural gas trading. The restatement resulted in a drop of 37% in cash flow from operating activities.

Source: Henny Sender, "Sadly, These Days Even Cash Flow Isn't Always What It Seems to Be," *Wall Street Journal* (May 8, 2002).

? For what reasons might managers at WorldCom and at Dynegy take the actions noted above? (See page 706.)

> DO IT!

Cash from Operating Activities

Action Plan

✔ Add noncash charges such as depreciation back to net income to compute net cash provided by operating activities.

✔ Deduct from net income gains on the disposal of plant assets, or add losses back to net income, to compute net cash provided by operating activities.

✔ Use changes in non-cash current asset and current liability accounts to compute net cash provided by operating activities.

Josh's PhotoPlus reported net income of $73,000 for 2014. Included in the income statement were depreciation expense of $7,000 and a gain on disposal of plant assets of $2,500. Josh's comparative balance sheets show the following balances.

	12/31/13	12/31/14
Accounts receivable	$17,000	$21,000
Accounts payable	6,000	2,200

Calculate net cash provided by operating activities for Josh's PhotoPlus.

Solution

Cash flows from operating activities		
Net income		$73,000
Adjustments to reconcile net income to net cash provided by operating activities:		
Depreciation expense	$ 7,000	
Gain on disposal of plant assets	(2,500)	
Increase in accounts receivable	(4,000)	
Decrease in accounts payable	(3,800)	(3,300)
Net cash provided by operating activities		$69,700

Related exercise material: **BE13-4, BE13-5, BE13-6, E13-4, E13-5, E13-6, E13-7, E13-8,** and **DO IT!** **13-2.**

 The Navigator

Step 2: Investing and Financing Activities

ANALYZE CHANGES IN NONCURRENT ASSET AND LIABILITY ACCOUNTS AND RECORD AS INVESTING AND FINANCING ACTIVITIES, OR DISCLOSE AS NONCASH TRANSACTIONS

INCREASE IN LAND As indicated from the change in the Land account and the additional information, the company purchased land of $110,000 through the issuance of long-term bonds. The issuance of bonds payable for land has no effect on cash. But, it is a significant noncash investing and financing activity that merits disclosure in a separate schedule. (See Illustration 13-13 on pages 659–660.)

INCREASE IN BUILDINGS As the additional data indicate, Computer Services Company acquired an office building for $120,000 cash. This is a cash outflow reported in the investing section. (See Illustration 13-13 on pages 659–660.)

INCREASE IN EQUIPMENT The Equipment account increased $17,000. The additional information explains that this was a net increase that resulted from two transactions: (1) a purchase of equipment of $25,000, and (2) the sale for $4,000 of equipment costing $8,000. These transactions are investing activities. The company should report each transaction separately. Thus, it reports the purchase of equipment as an outflow of cash for $25,000. It reports the sale as an inflow of cash for $4,000. The T-account below shows the reasons for the change in this account during the year.

Illustration 13-12
Analysis of equipment

	Equipment			
1/1/14	Balance	10,000	Cost of equipment sold	8,000
	Purchase of equipment	**25,000**		
12/31/14	Balance	27,000		

The following entry shows the details of the equipment sale transaction.

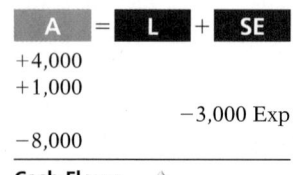

+4,000
+1,000
−3,000 Exp
−8,000

Cash Flows
+4,000

Cash	4,000	
Accumulated Depreciation—Equipment	1,000	
Loss on Disposal of Plant Assets	3,000	
Equipment		8,000

INCREASE IN BONDS PAYABLE The Bonds Payable account increased $110,000. As indicated in the additional information, the company acquired land from the issuance of these bonds. It reports this noncash transaction in a separate schedule at the bottom of the statement.

INCREASE IN COMMON STOCK The balance sheet reports an increase in Common Stock of $20,000. The additional information section notes that this increase resulted from the issuance of new shares of stock. This is a cash inflow reported in the financing section.

INCREASE IN RETAINED EARNINGS Retained earnings increased $116,000 during the year. This increase can be explained by two factors: (1) Net income of $145,000 increased retained earnings. (2) Dividends of $29,000 decreased retained earnings. The company adjusts net income to net cash provided by operating activities in the operating activities section. Payment of the dividends (not the declaration) is a **cash outflow that the company reports as a financing activity**.

Helpful Hint
When companies issue stocks or bonds for cash, the actual proceeds will appear in the statement of cash flows as a financing inflow (rather than the par value of the stocks or face value of bonds).

ANATOMY OF A FRAUD

For more than a decade, the top executives at the Italian dairy products company Parmalat engaged in multiple frauds which overstated cash and other assets by more than $1 billion while understating liabilities by between $8 and $12 billion. Much of the fraud involved creating fictitious sources and uses of cash. Some of these activities incorporated sophisticated financial transactions with subsidiaries created with the help of large international financial institutions. However, much of the fraud employed very basic, even sloppy, forgery of documents. For example, when outside auditors requested confirmation of bank accounts (such as a fake $4.8 billion account in the Cayman Islands), documents were created on scanners, with signatures that were cut and pasted from other documents. These were then passed through a fax machine numerous times to make them look real (if difficult to read). Similarly, fictitious bills were created in order to divert funds to other businesses owned by the Tanzi family (who controlled Parmalat).

Total take: Billions of dollars

THE MISSING CONTROL
Independent internal verification. Internal auditors at the company should have independently verified bank accounts and major transfers of cash to outside companies that were controlled by the Tanzi family.

STATEMENT OF CASH FLOWS—2014

Using the previous information, we can now prepare a statement of cash flows for 2014 for Computer Services Company as shown in Illustration 13-13.

Step 3: Net Change in Cash

COMPARE THE NET CHANGE IN CASH ON THE STATEMENT OF CASH FLOWS WITH THE CHANGE IN THE CASH ACCOUNT REPORTED ON THE BALANCE SHEET TO MAKE SURE THE AMOUNTS AGREE

Illustration 13-13 indicates that the net change in cash during the period was an increase of $22,000. This agrees with the change in Cash account reported on the balance sheet in Illustration 13-4 (page 651).

Illustration 13-13
Statement of cash flows, 2014—indirect method

Computer Services Company		
Statement of Cash Flows—Indirect Method		
For the Year Ended December 31, 2014		
Cash flows from operating activities		
Net income		$ 145,000
Adjustments to reconcile net income to net cash		
provided by operating activities:		
Depreciation expense	$ 9,000	
Loss on disposal of plant assets	3,000	
Decrease in accounts receivable	10,000	
Increase in inventory	(5,000)	
Increase in prepaid expenses	(4,000)	
Increase in accounts payable	16,000	
Decrease in income taxes payable	(2,000)	27,000
Net cash provided by operating activities		172,000
Cash flows from investing activities		
Purchase of building	(120,000)	
Purchase of equipment	(25,000)	
Disposal of plant assets	4,000	
Net cash used by investing activities		(141,000)

Helpful Hint
Note that in the investing and financing activities sections, positive numbers indicate cash inflows (receipts), and negative numbers indicate cash outflows (payments).

Illustration 13-13
(cont'd.)

Cash flows from financing activities			
Issuance of common stock		20,000	
Payment of cash dividends		(29,000)	
Net cash used by financing activities			(9,000)
Net increase in cash			22,000
Cash at beginning of period			33,000
Cash at end of period			$ 55,000
Noncash investing and financing activities			
Issuance of bonds payable to purchase land			$ 110,000

> **DO IT!**

Indirect Method

Use the information below and on the next page to prepare a statement of cash flows using the indirect method.

Reynolds Company
Comparative Balance Sheets
December 31

Assets	2014	2013	Change Increase/Decrease
Cash	$ 54,000	$ 37,000	$ 17,000 Increase
Accounts receivable	68,000	26,000	42,000 Increase
Inventory	54,000	–0–	54,000 Increase
Prepaid expenses	4,000	6,000	2,000 Decrease
Land	75,000	70,000	5,000 Increase
Buildings	200,000	200,000	–0–
Accumulated depreciation—buildings	(21,000)	(11,000)	10,000 Increase
Equipment	193,000	68,000	125,000 Increase
Accumulated depreciation—equipment	(28,000)	(10,000)	18,000 Increase
Totals	$599,000	$386,000	
Liabilities and Stockholders' Equity			
Accounts payable	$ 23,000	$ 40,000	$ 17,000 Decrease
Accrued expenses payable	10,000	–0–	10,000 Increase
Bonds payable	140,000	150,000	10,000 Decrease
Common stock ($1 par)	220,000	60,000	160,000 Increase
Retained earnings	206,000	136,000	70,000 Increase
Totals	$599,000	$386,000	

Helpful Hint

1. Determine net cash provided/used by operating activities, recognizing that operating activities generally relate to changes in current assets and current liabilities.
2. Determine net cash provided/used by investing activities, recognizing that investing activities generally relate to changes in noncurrent assets.
3. Determine net cash provided/used by financing activities, recognizing that financing activities generally relate to changes in long-term liabilities and stockholders' equity accounts.

Reynolds Company
Income Statement
For the Year Ended December 31, 2014

Sales revenue		$890,000
Cost of goods sold	$465,000	
Operating expenses	221,000	
Interest expense	12,000	
Loss on disposal of plant assets	2,000	700,000
Income before income taxes		190,000
Income tax expense		65,000
Net income		$125,000

Additional information:

1. Operating expenses include depreciation expense of $33,000.
2. Equipment with a cost of $41,000 and a book value of $36,000 was sold for $34,000 cash.
3. Land was sold at its book value for cash.
4. Interest expense of $12,000 was paid in cash.
5. Equipment with a cost of $166,000 was purchased for cash.
6. Bonds of $10,000 were redeemed at their face value for cash.
7. Common stock ($1 par) of $130,000 was issued for cash.
8. Cash dividends of $55,000 were declared and paid in 2014.
9. Common stock of $30,000 was issued in exchange for land.

Solution

Action Plan

✔ Determine net cash provided/used by operating activities by adjusting net income for items that did not affect cash.

✔ Determine net cash provided/used by investing activities and financing activities.

✔ Determine the net increase/decrease in cash.

Reynolds Company
Statement of Cash Flows—Indirect Method
For the Year Ended December 31, 2014

Cash flows from operating activities		
Net income		$ 125,000
Adjustments to reconcile net income to net cash provided by operating activities:		
Depreciation expense	$ 33,000	
Loss on disposal of plant assets	2,000	
Increase in accounts receivable	(42,000)	
Increase in inventory	(54,000)	
Decrease in prepaid expenses	2,000	
Decrease in accounts payable	(17,000)	
Increase in accrued expenses payable	10,000	(66,000)
Net cash provided by operating activities		59,000
Cash flows from investing activities		
Sale of land	25,000	
Disposal of plant assets	34,000	
Purchase of equipment	(166,000)	
Net cash used by investing activities		(107,000)
Cash flows from financing activities		
Redemption of bonds	(10,000)	
Sale of common stock	130,000	
Payment of dividends	(55,000)	
Net cash provided by financing activities		65,000
Net increase in cash		17,000
Cash at beginning of period		37,000
Cash at end of period		$ 54,000
Noncash investing and financing activities		
Issued common stock in exchange for land		$ 30,000

Related exercise material: **BE13-4, BE13-5, BE13-6, BE13-7, E13-4, E13-5, E13-6, E13-7, E13-8, and E13-9.**

 The Navigator

Using Cash Flows to Evaluate a Company

LEARNING OBJECTIVE   **4**

Analyze the statement of cash flows.

Traditionally, investors and creditors have most commonly used ratios based on numbers derived from accrual accounting. These days, cash-based ratios are gaining increased acceptance among analysts.

Free Cash Flow

In the statement of cash flows, cash provided by operating activities is intended to indicate the cash-generating capability of the company. Analysts have noted, however, that **cash provided by operating activities fails to take into account that a company must invest in new fixed assets** just to maintain its current level of operations. Companies also must at least **maintain dividends at current levels** to satisfy investors. The measurement of free cash flow provides additional insight regarding a company's cash-generating ability. **Free cash flow** describes the cash remaining from operations after adjustment for capital expenditures and dividends.

Consider the following example: Suppose that MPC produced and sold 10,000 personal computers this year. It reported $100,000 cash provided by operating activities. In order to maintain production at 10,000 computers, MPC invested $15,000 in equipment. It chose to pay $5,000 in dividends. Its free cash flow was $80,000 ($100,000 − $15,000 − $5,000). The company could use this $80,000 either to purchase new assets to expand the business or to pay an $80,000 dividend and continue to produce 10,000 computers. In practice, free cash flow is often calculated with the formula in Illustration 13-14. (Alternative definitions also exist.)

Illustration 13-14
Free cash flow

Free Cash Flow	=	Cash Provided by Operating Activities	−	Capital Expenditures	−	Cash Dividends

Illustration 13-15 provides basic information (in billions) excerpted from the 2009 statement of cash flows of Microsoft Corporation.

Illustration 13-15
Microsoft cash flow information ($ in millions)

Microsoft Corporation
Statement of Cash Flows (partial)
2009

Cash provided by operating activities		$ 19,037
Cash flows from investing activities		
Additions to property and equipment	$ (3,119)	
Purchases of investments	(36,850)	
Sales of investments	19,806	
Acquisitions of companies	(868)	
Maturities of investments	6,191	
Other	(930)	
Cash used by investing activities		(15,770)
Cash paid for dividends		(4,468)

Microsoft's free cash flow is calculated as shown in Illustration 13-16.

Cash provided by operating activities	$ 19,037
Less: Expenditures on property, plant, and equipment	3,119
Dividends paid	4,468
Free cash flow	**$11,450**

Illustration 13-16
Calculation of Microsoft's free cash flow ($ in millions)

Microsoft generated approximately $11.4 billion of free cash flow. This is a tremendous amount of cash generated in a single year. It is available for the acquisition of new assets, the retirement of stock or debt, or the payment of dividends.

Also note that Microsoft's cash from operations of $19 billion exceeds its 2009 net income of $14.6 billion. This lends additional credibility to Microsoft's income number as an indicator of potential future performance. If anything, Microsoft's net income might understate its actual performance.

As another example, consider Oracle Corporation, one of the world's largest sellers of database software and information management services. Like Microsoft, its success depends on continuing to improve its existing products while developing new products to keep pace with rapid changes in technology. Oracle's free cash flow for 2009 was $7.5 billion. This is impressive but significantly less than Microsoft's amazing ability to generate cash.

> DO IT!

Free Cash Flow

Chicago Corporation issued the following statement of cash flows for 2014.

Chicago Corporation Statement of Cash Flows—Indirect Method For the Year Ended December 31, 2014		
Cash flows from operating activities		
Net income		$ 19,000
Adjustments to reconcile net income to net cash provided by operating activities:		
Depreciation expense	$ 8,100	
Loss on disposal of plant assets	1,300	
Decrease in accounts receivable	6,900	
Increase in inventory	(4,000)	
Decrease in accounts payable	(2,000)	10,300
Net cash provided by operating activities		29,300
Cash flows from investing activities		
Sale of investments	1,100	
Purchase of equipment	(19,000)	
Net cash used by investing activities		(17,900)

Cash flows from financing activities		
Issuance of stock	10,000	
Payment on long-term note payable	(5,000)	
Payment for dividends	(9,000)	
Net cash used by financing activities		(4,000)
Net increase in cash		7,400
Cash at beginning of year		10,000
Cash at end of year		$ 17,400

(a) Compute free cash flow for Chicago Corporation. (b) Explain why free cash flow often provides better information than "Net cash provided by operating activities."

Solution

Action Plan

✔ Compute free cash flow as: Cash provided by operating activities − Capital expenditures − Cash dividends.

(a) Free cash flow = $29,300 − $19,000 − $9,000 = $1,300

(b) Cash provided by operating activities fails to take into account that a company must invest in new plant assets just to maintain the current level of operations. Companies must also maintain dividends at current levels to satisfy investors. The measurement of free cash flow provides additional insight regarding a company's cash-generating ability.

Related exercise material: **BE13-8, BE13-9, BE13-10, BE13-11, E13-7, E13-9, and** **DO IT!** **13-3.**

 The Navigator

> Comprehensive **DO IT! 1**

The income statement for the year ended December 31, 2014, for Kosinski Company contains the following condensed information.

Kosinski Company
Income Statement
For the Year Ended December 31, 2014

Sales revenue		$6,583,000
Operating expenses (excluding depreciation)	$4,920,000	
Depreciation expense	880,000	5,800,000
Income before income taxes		783,000
Income tax expense		353,000
Net income		$ 430,000

Included in operating expenses is a $24,000 loss resulting from the sale of machinery for $270,000 cash. Machinery was purchased at a cost of $750,000.

The following balances are reported on Kosinski's comparative balance sheets at December 31.

Kosinski Company
Comparative Balance Sheets (partial)

	2014	2013
Cash	$672,000	$130,000
Accounts receivable	775,000	610,000
Inventory	834,000	867,000
Accounts payable	521,000	501,000

Income tax expense of $353,000 represents the amount paid in 2014. Dividends declared and paid in 2014 totaled $200,000.

Instructions

Prepare the statement of cash flows using the indirect method.

Solution to Comprehensive DO IT! 1

Action Plan

✔ Determine net cash from operating activities. Operating activities generally relate to changes in current assets and current liabilities.

✔ Determine net cash from investing activities. Investing activities generally relate to changes in noncurrent assets.

✔ Determine net cash from financing activities. Financing activities generally relate to changes in long-term liabilities and stockholders' equity accounts.

Kosinski Company
Statement of Cash Flows—Indirect Method
For the Year Ended December 31, 2014

Cash flows from operating activities		
Net income		$ 430,000
Adjustments to reconcile net income to net cash provided by operating activities:		
Depreciation expense	$ 880,000	
Loss on disposal of plant assets	24,000	
Increase in accounts receivable	(165,000)	
Decrease in inventory	33,000	
Increase in accounts payable	20,000	792,000
Net cash provided by operating activities		1,222,000
Cash flows from investing activities		
Disposal of plant assets	270,000	
Purchase of machinery	(750,000)	
Net cash used by investing activities		(480,000)
Cash flows from financing activities		
Payment of cash dividends		(200,000)
Net increase in cash		542,000
Cash at beginning of period		130,000
Cash at end of period		$ 672,000

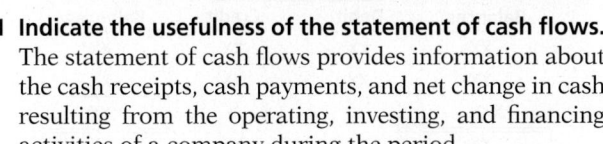 The Navigator

 The Navigator

SUMMARY OF LEARNING OBJECTIVES

1 **Indicate the usefulness of the statement of cash flows.** The statement of cash flows provides information about the cash receipts, cash payments, and net change in cash resulting from the operating, investing, and financing activities of a company during the period.

2 **Distinguish among operating, investing, and financing activities.** Operating activities include the cash effects of transactions that enter into the determination of net income. Investing activities involve cash flows resulting from changes in investments and long-term asset items. Financing activities involve cash flows resulting from changes in long-term liability and stockholders' equity items.

3 **Prepare a statement of cash flows using the indirect method.** The preparation of a statement of cash flows involves three major steps: (1) Determine net cash provided/used by operating activities by converting net income from an accrual basis to a cash basis. (2) Analyze changes in noncurrent asset and liability accounts and record as investing and financing activities, or disclose as noncash transactions. (3) Compare the net change in cash on the statement of cash flows with the change in the Cash account reported on the balance sheet to make sure the amounts agree.

4 **Analyze the statement of cash flows.** Free cash flow indicates the amount of cash a company generated during the current year that is available for the payment of additional dividends or for expansion.

GLOSSARY

Direct method A method that shows operating cash receipts and payments, making it more consistent with the objective of the statement of cash flows. (p. 650).

Financing activities Cash flow activities that include (a) obtaining cash from issuing debt and repaying the amounts borrowed and (b) obtaining cash from stockholders, repurchasing shares, and paying dividends. (p. 647).

Free cash flow Cash provided by operating activities adjusted for capital expenditures and dividends paid. (p. 662).

Indirect method A method of preparing a statement of cash flows in which net income is adjusted for items that do not affect cash, to determine net cash provided by operating activities. (p. 650).

Investing activities Cash flow activities that include (a) acquiring and disposing of investments and property, plant, and equipment and (b) lending money and collecting the loans. (p. 646).

Operating activities Cash flow activities that include the cash effects of transactions that create revenues and expenses and thus enter into the determination of net income. (p. 646).

Statement of cash flows A basic financial statement that provides information about the cash receipts, cash payments, and net change in cash during a period, resulting from operating, investing, and financing activities. (p. 646).

APPENDIX 13A USING A WORKSHEET TO PREPARE THE STATEMENT OF CASH FLOWS—INDIRECT METHOD

LEARNING OBJECTIVE 5

Explain how to use a worksheet to prepare the statement of cash flows using the indirect method.

When preparing a statement of cash flows, companies may need to make numerous adjustments of net income. In such cases, they often use **a worksheet to assemble and classify the data that will appear on the statement**. The worksheet is merely an aid in preparing the statement. Its use is optional. Illustration 13A-1 shows the skeleton format of the worksheet for preparation of the statement of cash flows.

Illustration 13A-1
Format of worksheet

XYZ Company.xls

XYZ Company
Worksheet
Statement of Cash Flows For the Year Ended . . .

Balance Sheet Accounts	End of Last Year Balances	Reconciling Items Debit	Reconciling Items Credit	End of Current Year Balances
Debit balance accounts	XX	XX	XX	XX
	XX	XX	XX	XX
Totals	XXX			XXX
Credit balance accounts	XX	XX	XX	XX
	XX	XX	XX	XX
Totals	XXX			XXX
Statement of Cash				
Flows Effects				
Operating activities				
Net income		XX		
Adjustments to net income		XX	XX	
Investing activities				
Receipts and payments		XX	XX	
Financing activities				
Receipts and payments		XX	XX	
Totals		XXX	XXX	
Increase (decrease) in cash		(XX)	XX	
Totals		XXX	XXX	

The following guidelines are important in preparing a worksheet.

1. In the balance sheet accounts section, **list accounts with debit balances separately from those with credit balances**. This means, for example, that Accumulated Depreciation appears under credit balances and not as a contra account under debit balances. Enter the beginning and ending balances of each account in the appropriate columns. Enter as reconciling items in the two middle columns the transactions that caused the change in the account balance during the year.

   After all reconciling items have been entered, each line pertaining to a balance sheet account should "foot across." That is, the beginning balance plus or minus the reconciling item(s) must equal the ending balance. When this agreement exists for all balance sheet accounts, all changes in account balances have been reconciled.

2. The bottom portion of the worksheet consists of the operating, investing, and financing activities sections. It provides the information necessary to prepare the formal statement of cash flows. **Enter inflows of cash as debits in the reconciling columns. Enter outflows of cash as credits in the reconciling columns.** Thus, in this section, the sale of equipment for cash at book value appears as a debit under investing activities. Similarly, the purchase of land for cash appears as a credit under investing activities.

3. **The reconciling items shown in the worksheet are not entered in any journal or posted to any account.** They do not represent either adjustments or corrections of the balance sheet accounts. They are used only to facilitate the preparation of the statement of cash flows.

Preparing the Worksheet

As in the case of worksheets illustrated in earlier chapters, preparing a worksheet involves a series of prescribed steps. The steps in this case are:

1. Enter in the balance sheet accounts section the balance sheet accounts and their beginning and ending balances.

2. Enter in the reconciling columns of the worksheet the data that explain the changes in the balance sheet accounts other than cash and their effects on the statement of cash flows.

3. Enter on the cash line and at the bottom of the worksheet the increase or decrease in cash. This entry should enable the totals of the reconciling columns to be in agreement.

   To illustrate the preparation of a worksheet, we will use the 2014 data for Computer Services Company. Your familiarity with these data (from the chapter) should help you understand the use of a worksheet. For ease of reference, the comparative balance sheets, income statement, and selected data for 2014 are presented in Illustration 13A-2 (page 668).

DETERMINING THE RECONCILING ITEMS

Companies can use one of several approaches to determine the reconciling items. For example, they can first complete the changes affecting net cash provided by operating activities, and then can determine the effects of financing and investing transactions. Or, they can analyze the balance sheet accounts in the order in which they are listed on the worksheet. We will follow this latter approach for Computer Services, except for cash. As indicated in Step 3, **cash is handled last**.

Illustration 13A-2
Comparative balance sheets, income statement, and additional information for Computer Services Company

---

Computer Services Company.xls

Home | Insert | Page Layout | Formulas | Data | Review | View

P18   fx

	A	B	C	D

Computer Services Company
Comparative Balance Sheets
December 31

Assets	2014	2013	Change in Account Balance Increase/Decrease	
Current assets				
Cash	$ 55,000	$ 33,000	$ 22,000	Increase
Accounts receivable	20,000	30,000	10,000	Decrease
Inventory	15,000	10,000	5,000	Increase
Prepaid expenses	5,000	1,000	4,000	Increase
Property, plant, and equipment				
Land	130,000	20,000	110,000	Increase
Buildings	160,000	40,000	120,000	Increase
Accumulated depreciation—buildings	(11,000)	(5,000)	6,000	Increase
Equipment	27,000	10,000	17,000	Increase
Accumulated depreciation—equipment	(3,000)	(1,000)	2,000	Increase
Total assets	$398,000	$138,000		
Liabilities and Stockholders' Equity				
Current liabilities				
Accounts payable	$ 28,000	$ 12,000	$ 16,000	Increase
Income taxes payable	6,000	8,000	2,000	Decrease
Long-term liabilities				
Bonds payable	130,000	20,000	110,000	Increase
Stockholders' equity				
Common stock	70,000	50,000	20,000	Increase
Retained earnings	164,000	48,000	116,000	Increase
Total liabilities and stockholders' equity	$398,000	$138,000		

Computer Services Company.xls

Home | Insert | Page Layout | Formulas | Data | Review | View

P18   fx

	A	B	C	D

Computer Services Company
Income Statement
For the Year Ended December 31, 2014

Sales revenue			$507,000
Cost of goods sold		$150,000	
Operating expenses (excluding depreciation)		111,000	
Depreciation expense		9,000	
Loss on disposal of plant assets		3,000	
Interest expense		42,000	315,000
Income before income tax			192,000
Income tax expense			47,000
Net income			$145,000

Additional information for 2014:
1. Depreciation expense was comprised of $6,000 for building and $3,000 for equipment.
2. The company sold equipment with a book value of $7,000 (cost $8,000, less accumulated depreciation $1,000) for $4,000 cash.
3. Issued $110,000 of long-term bonds in direct exchange for land.
4. A building costing $120,000 was purchased for cash. Equipment costing $25,000 was also purchased for cash.
5. Issued common stock for $20,000 cash.
6. The company declared and paid a $29,000 cash dividend.

ACCOUNTS RECEIVABLE The decrease of $10,000 in accounts receivable means that cash collections from sales revenue are higher than the sales revenue reported in the income statement. To convert net income to net cash provided by operating activities, we add the decrease of $10,000 to net income. The entry in the reconciling columns of the worksheet is:

(a)	Operating—Decrease in Accounts Receivable	10,000	
	Accounts Receivable		10,000

INVENTORY Computer Services Company's inventory balance increases $5,000 during the period. The Inventory account reflects the difference between the amount of inventory that the company purchased and the amount that it sold. For Computer Services, this means that the cost of merchandise purchased exceeds the cost of goods sold by $5,000. As a result, cost of goods sold does not reflect $5,000 of cash payments made for merchandise. We deduct this inventory increase of $5,000 during the period from net income to arrive at net cash provided by operating activities. The worksheet entry is:

(b)	Inventory	5,000	
	Operating—Increase in Inventory		5,000

PREPAID EXPENSES An increase of $4,000 in prepaid expenses means that expenses deducted in determining net income are less than expenses that were paid in cash. We deduct the increase of $4,000 from net income in determining net cash provided by operating activities. The worksheet entry is:

(c)	Prepaid Expenses	4,000	
	Operating—Increase in Prepaid Expenses		4,000

LAND The increase in land of $110,000 resulted from a purchase through the issuance of long-term bonds. The company should report this transaction as a significant noncash investing and financing activity. The worksheet entry is:

(d)	Land	110,000	
	Bonds Payable		110,000

> **Helpful Hint**
> These amounts are asterisked in the worksheet to indicate that they result from a significant noncash transaction.

BUILDINGS The cash purchase of a building for $120,000 is an investing activity cash outflow. The entry in the reconciling columns of the worksheet is:

(e)	Buildings	120,000	
	Investing—Purchase of Building		120,000

EQUIPMENT The increase in equipment of $17,000 resulted from a cash purchase of $25,000 and the sale of equipment costing $8,000. The book value of the equipment was $7,000, the cash proceeds were $4,000, and a loss of $3,000 was recorded. The worksheet entries are:

(f)	Equipment	25,000	
	Investing—Purchase of Equipment		25,000

(g)	Investing—Disposal of Plant Assets	4,000	
	Operating—Loss on Disposal of Plant Assets	3,000	
	Accumulated Depreciation—Equipment	1,000	
	Equipment		8,000

ACCOUNTS PAYABLE We must add the increase of $16,000 in accounts payable to net income to determine net cash provided by operating activities. The worksheet entry is:

(h)	Operating—Increase in Accounts Payable	16,000	
	Accounts Payable		16,000

INCOME TAXES PAYABLE When a company incurs income tax expense but has not yet paid its taxes, it records income taxes payable. A change in the Income Taxes Payable account reflects the difference between income tax expense incurred and income tax actually paid. Computer Services' Income Taxes Payable account decreases by $2,000. That means the $47,000 of income tax expense reported on the income statement was $2,000 less than the amount of taxes paid during the period of $49,000. To adjust net income to a cash basis, we must reduce net income by $2,000. The worksheet entry is:

(i)	Income Taxes Payable	2,000	
	Operating—Decrease in Income Taxes Payable		2,000

BONDS PAYABLE The increase of $110,000 in this account resulted from the issuance of bonds for land. This is a significant noncash investing and financing activity. Worksheet entry (d) above is the only entry necessary.

COMMON STOCK The balance sheet reports an increase in Common Stock of $20,000. The additional information section notes that this increase resulted from the issuance of new shares of stock. This is a cash inflow reported in the financing section. The worksheet entry is:

(j)	Financing—Issuance of Common Stock	20,000	
	Common Stock		20,000

ACCUMULATED DEPRECIATION—BUILDINGS, AND ACCUMULATED DEPRECIATION—EQUIPMENT Increases in these accounts of $6,000 and $3,000, respectively, resulted from depreciation expense. Depreciation expense is a **noncash charge that we must add to net income** to determine net cash provided by operating activities. The worksheet entries are:

(k)	Operating—Depreciation Expense	6,000	
	Accumulated Depreciation—Buildings		6,000
(l)	Operating—Depreciation Expense	3,000	
	Accumulated Depreciation—Equipment		3,000

RETAINED EARNINGS The $116,000 increase in retained earnings resulted from net income of $145,000 and the declaration and payment of a $29,000 cash dividend. Net income is included in net cash provided by operating activities, and the dividends are a financing activity cash outflow. The entries in the reconciling columns of the worksheet are:

(m)	Operating—Net Income	145,000	
	Retained Earnings		145,000
(n)	Retained Earnings	29,000	
	Financing—Payment of Dividends		29,000

DISPOSITION OF CHANGE IN CASH The firm's cash increased $22,000 in 2014. The final entry on the worksheet, therefore, is:

(o)	Cash	22,000	
	Increase in Cash		22,000

As shown in the worksheet, we enter the increase in cash in the reconciling credit column as a **balancing** amount. This entry should complete the reconciliation of the changes in the balance sheet accounts. Also, it should permit the totals of the reconciling columns to be in agreement. When all changes have been explained and the reconciling columns are in agreement, the reconciling columns are ruled to complete the worksheet. The completed worksheet for Computer Services Company is shown in Illustration 13A-3.

Illustration 13A-3
Completed worksheet—
indirect method

	Computer Services Company.xls				
Home Insert Page Layout Formulas Data Review View					
P18 *fx*					

	A	B	C	D	E
1	**Computer Services Company**				
2	Worksheet				
3	Statement of Cash Flows For the Year Ended December 31, 2014				
4					
5		**Balance**	**Reconciling Items**		**Balance**
6	**Balance Sheet Accounts**	**12/31/13**	**Debit**	**Credit**	**12/31/14**
7	Debits				
8	Cash	33,000	(o) 22,000		55,000
9	Accounts Receivable	30,000		(a) 10,000	20,000
10	Inventory	10,000	(b) 5,000		15,000
11	Prepaid Expenses	1,000	(c) 4,000		5,000
12	Land	20,000	(d) 110,000*		130,000
13	Buildings	40,000	(e) 120,000		160,000
14	Equipment	10,000	(f) 25,000	(g) 8,000	27,000
15	Total	144,000			412,000
16	Credits				
17	Accounts Payable	12,000		(h) 16,000	28,000
18	Income Taxes Payable	8,000	(i) 2,000		6,000
19	Bonds Payable	20,000		(d) 110,000*	130,000
20	Accumulated Depreciation—Buildings	5,000		(k) 6,000	11,000
21	Accumulated Depreciation—Equipment	1,000	(g) 1,000	(l) 3,000	3,000
22	Common Stock	50,000		(j) 20,000	70,000
23	Retained Earnings	48,000	(n) 29,000	(m) 145,000	164,000
24	Total	144,000			412,000
25					
26	**Statement of Cash Flows Effects**				
27	Operating activities				
28	Net income		(m) 145,000		
29	Decrease in accounts receivable		(a) 10,000		
30	Increase in inventory			(b) 5,000	
31	Increase in prepaid expenses			(c) 4,000	
32	Increase in accounts payable		(h) 16,000		
33	Decrease in income taxes payable			(i) 2,000	
34	Depreciation expense		(k) 6,000		
35			(l) 3,000		
36	Loss on disposal of plant assets		(g) 3,000		
37	Investing activities				
38	Purchase of building			(e) 120,000	
39	Purchase of equipment			(f) 25,000	
40	Disposal of plant assets		(g) 4,000		
41	Financing activities				
42	Issuance of common stock		(j) 20,000		
43	Payment of dividends			(n) 29,000	
44	Totals		525,000	503,000	
45	Increase in cash			(o) 22,000	
46	Totals		525,000	525,000	
47					
	* Significant noncash investing and financing activity.				

5 Explain how to use a worksheet to prepare the statement of cash flows using the indirect method. When there are numerous adjustments, a worksheet can be a helpful tool in preparing the statement of cash flows. Key guidelines for using a worksheet are: (1) List accounts with debit balances separately from those with credit balances. (2) In the reconciling columns in the bottom portion of the worksheet, show cash inflows as debits and cash outflows as credits. (3) Do not enter reconciling items in any journal or account, but use them only to help prepare the statement of cash flows.

The steps in preparing the worksheet are: (1) Enter beginning and ending balances of balance sheet accounts. (2) Enter debits and credits in reconciling columns. (3) Enter the increase or decrease in cash in two places as a balancing amount.

APPENDIX **13B** STATEMENT OF CASH FLOWS—DIRECT METHOD

LEARNING OBJECTIVE 6

Prepare a statement of cash flows using the direct method.

To explain and illustrate the direct method, we will use the transactions of Computer Services Company for 2014, to prepare a statement of cash flows. Illustration 13B-1 presents information related to 2014 for Computer Services Company.

Illustration 13B-1
Comparative balance sheets, income statement, and additional information for Computer Services Company

Computer Services Company
Comparative Balance Sheets
December 31

Assets	2014	2013	Change in Account Balance Increase/Decrease
Current assets			
Cash	$ 55,000	$ 33,000	$ 22,000 Increase
Accounts receivable	20,000	30,000	10,000 Decrease
Inventory	15,000	10,000	5,000 Increase
Prepaid expenses	5,000	1,000	4,000 Increase
Property, plant, and equipment			
Land	130,000	20,000	110,000 Increase
Buildings	160,000	40,000	120,000 Increase
Accumulated depreciation— buildings	(11,000)	(5,000)	6,000 Increase
Equipment	27,000	10,000	17,000 Increase
Accumulated depreciation— equipment	(3,000)	(1,000)	2,000 Increase
Total assets	$398,000	$138,000	

Liabilities and Stockholders' Equity			
Current liabilities			
Accounts payable	$ 28,000	$ 12,000	$ 16,000 Increase
Income taxes payable	6,000	8,000	2,000 Decrease
Long-term liabilities			
Bonds payable	130,000	20,000	110,000 Increase
Stockholders' equity			
Common stock	70,000	50,000	20,000 Increase
Retained earnings	164,000	48,000	116,000 Increase
Total liabilities and stockholders' equity	$398,000	$138,000	

Illustration 13B-1
(cont'd.)

Computer Services Company Income Statement For the Year Ended December 31, 2014		
Sales revenue		$507,000
Cost of goods sold	$150,000	
Operating expenses (excluding depreciation)	111,000	
Depreciation expense	9,000	
Loss on disposal of plant assets	3,000	
Interest expense	42,000	315,000
Income before income tax		192,000
Income tax expense		47,000
Net income		$145,000

Additional information for 2014:
1. Depreciation expense was comprised of $6,000 for building and $3,000 for equipment.
2. The company sold equipment with a book value of $7,000 (cost $8,000, less accumulated depreciation $1,000) for $4,000 cash.
3. Issued $110,000 of long-term bonds in direct exchange for land.
4. A building costing $120,000 was purchased for cash. Equipment costing $25,000 was also purchased for cash.
5. Issued common stock for $20,000 cash.
6. The company declared and paid a $29,000 cash dividend.

To prepare a statement of cash flows under the direct approach, we will apply the three steps outlined in Illustration 13-3 (page 651).

Step 1: Operating Activities

DETERMINE NET CASH PROVIDED/USED BY OPERATING ACTIVITIES BY CONVERTING NET INCOME FROM AN ACCRUAL BASIS TO A CASH BASIS
Under the **direct method**, companies compute net cash provided by operating activities by **adjusting each item in the income statement** from the accrual basis to the cash basis. To simplify and condense the operating activities section, companies **report only major classes of operating cash receipts and cash payments**. For these major classes, the difference between cash receipts and cash payments is the net cash provided by operating activities. These relationships are as shown in Illustration 13B-2 (page 674).

An efficient way to apply the direct method is to analyze the items reported in the income statement in the order in which they are listed. We then determine cash receipts and cash payments related to these revenues and expenses. The following pages present the adjustments required to prepare a statement of cash flows for Computer Services Company using the direct approach.

CASH RECEIPTS FROM CUSTOMERS The income statement for Computer Services Company reported revenues from customers of $507,000. How much of that was cash receipts? To answer that, companies need to consider the change in accounts receivable during the year. When accounts receivable increase during the year, revenues on an accrual basis are higher than cash receipts from customers. Operations led to revenues, but not all of these revenues resulted in cash receipts.

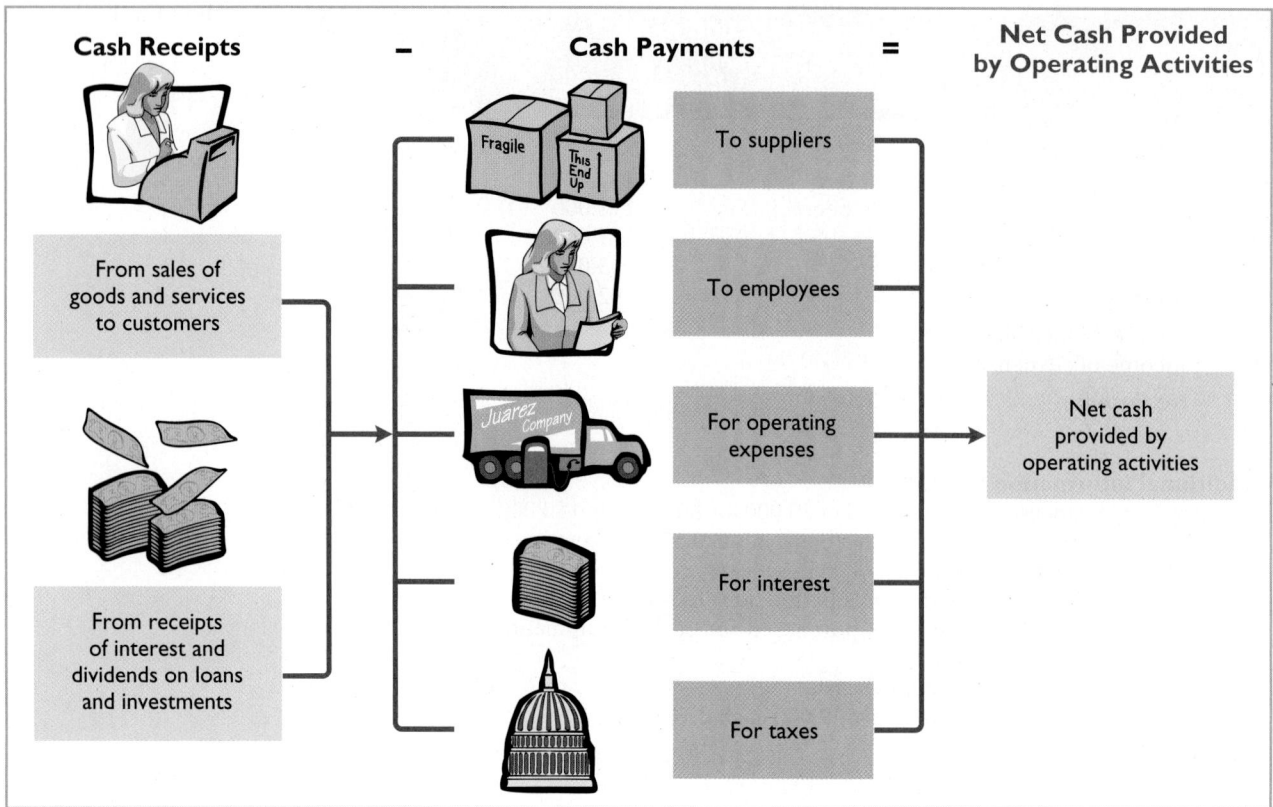

Illustration 13B-2
Major classes of cash receipts and payments

To determine the amount of cash receipts, the company deducts from sales revenues the increase in accounts receivable. On the other hand, there may be a decrease in accounts receivable. That would occur if cash receipts from customers exceeded sales revenues. In that case, the company adds to sales revenues the decrease in accounts receivable. For Computer Services Company, accounts receivable decreased $10,000. Thus, cash receipts from customers were $517,000, computed as shown in Illustration 13B-3.

Illustration 13B-3
Computation of cash receipts from customers

Revenues from sales	$ 507,000
Add: Decrease in accounts receivable	10,000
Cash receipts from customers	**$517,000**

Computer Services can also determine cash receipts from customers from an analysis of the Accounts Receivable account, as shown in Illustration 13B-4.

Illustration 13B-4
Analysis of accounts receivable

Helpful Hint
The T-account shows that revenue plus decrease in receivables equals cash receipts.

		Accounts Receivable			
1/1/14	Balance		30,000	**Receipts from customers**	**517,000**
	Revenues from sales		507,000		
12/31/14	Balance		20,000		

Illustration 13B-5 shows the relationships among cash receipts from customers, revenues from sales, and changes in accounts receivable.

Cash Receipts from Customers	=	Revenues from Sales	{	+ Decrease in Accounts Receivable
				or
				− Increase in Accounts Receivable

Illustration 13B-5
Formula to compute cash receipts from customers—direct method

CASH PAYMENTS TO SUPPLIERS Computer Services Company reported cost of goods sold of $150,000 on its income statement. How much of that was cash payments to suppliers? To answer that, it is first necessary to find purchases for the year. To find purchases, companies adjust cost of goods sold for the change in inventory. When inventory increases during the year, purchases for the year have exceeded cost of goods sold. As a result, to determine the amount of purchases, the company adds to cost of goods sold the increase in inventory.

In 2014, Computer Services Company's inventory increased $5,000. It computes purchases as follows.

Cost of goods sold	$ 150,000
Add: Increase in inventory	5,000
Purchases	**$155,000**

Illustration 13B-6
Computation of purchases

After computing purchases, a company can determine cash payments to suppliers. This is done by adjusting purchases for the change in accounts payable. When accounts payable increase during the year, purchases on an accrual basis are higher than they are on a cash basis. As a result, to determine cash payments to suppliers, a company deducts from purchases the increase in accounts payable. On the other hand, if cash payments to suppliers exceed purchases, there is a decrease in accounts payable. In that case, a company adds to purchases the decrease in accounts payable. For Computer Services Company, cash payments to suppliers were $139,000, computed as follows.

Purchases	$ 155,000
Deduct: Increase in accounts payable	16,000
Cash payments to suppliers	**$139,000**

Illustration 13B-7
Computation of cash payments to suppliers

Computer Services also can determine cash payments to suppliers from an analysis of the Accounts Payable account, as shown in Illustration 13B-8.

Accounts Payable

Payments to suppliers	139,000	1/1/14	Balance	12,000
			Purchases	155,000
		12/31/14	Balance	28,000

Illustration 13B-8
Analysis of accounts payable

Helpful Hint
The T-account shows that purchases less increase in accounts payable equals payments to suppliers.

Illustration 13B-9 (page 676) shows the relationships among cash payments to suppliers, cost of goods sold, changes in inventory, and changes in accounts payable.

Illustration 13B-9
Formula to compute cash payments to suppliers—direct method

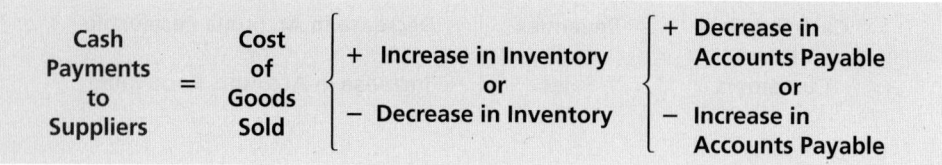

CASH PAYMENTS FOR OPERATING EXPENSES Computer Services reported on its income statement operating expenses of $111,000. How much of that amount was cash paid for operating expenses? To answer that, we need to adjust this amount for any changes in prepaid expenses and accrued expenses payable. For example, if prepaid expenses increased during the year, cash paid for operating expenses is higher than operating expenses reported on the income statement. To convert operating expenses to cash payments for operating expenses, a company adds the increase in prepaid expenses to operating expenses. On the other hand, if prepaid expenses decrease during the year, it deducts the decrease from operating expenses.

Companies must also adjust operating expenses for changes in accrued expenses payable. When accrued expenses payable increase during the year, operating expenses on an accrual basis are higher than they are in a cash basis. As a result, to determine cash payments for operating expenses, a company deducts from operating expenses an increase in accrued expenses payable. On the other hand, a company adds to operating expenses a decrease in accrued expenses payable because cash payments exceed operating expenses.

Computer Services Company's cash payments for operating expenses were $115,000, computed as follows.

Illustration 13B-10
Computation of cash payments for operating expenses

Operating expenses	$ 111,000
Add: Increase in prepaid expenses	4,000
Cash payments for operating expenses	**$115,000**

Illustration 13B-11 shows the relationships among cash payments for operating expenses, changes in prepaid expenses, and changes in accrued expenses payable.

Illustration 13B-11
Formula to compute cash payments for operating expenses—direct method

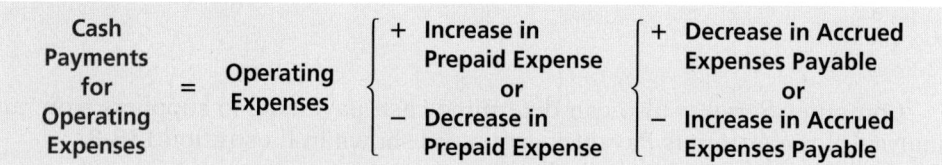

DEPRECIATION EXPENSE AND LOSS ON DISPOSAL OF PLANT ASSETS Computer Services' depreciation expense in 2014 was $9,000. Depreciation expense is not shown on a statement of cash flows under the direct method because it is a non-cash charge. If the amount for operating expenses includes depreciation expense, operating expenses must be reduced by the amount of depreciation to determine cash payments for operating expenses.

The loss on disposal of plant assets of $3,000 is also a noncash charge. The loss on disposal of plant assets reduces net income, but it does not reduce cash. Thus, the loss on disposal of plant assets is not shown on the statement of cash flows under the direct method.

Other charges to expense that do not require the use of cash, such as the amortization of intangible assets, depletion expense, and bad debt expense, are treated in the same manner as depreciation.

CASH PAYMENTS FOR INTEREST Computer Services reported on the income statement interest expense of $42,000. Since the balance sheet did not include an accrual for interest payable for 2013 or 2014, the amount reported as expense is the same as the amount of interest paid.

CASH PAYMENTS FOR INCOME TAXES Computer Services reported income tax expense of $47,000 on the income statement. Income taxes payable, however, decreased $2,000. This decrease means that income taxes paid were more than income taxes reported in the income statement. Cash payments for income taxes were, therefore, $49,000 as shown below.

Income tax expense	$ 47,000
Add: Decrease in income taxes payable	2,000
Cash payments for income taxes	**$49,000**

Illustration 13B-12
Computation of cash payments for income taxes

Illustration 13B-13 shows the relationships among cash payments for income taxes, income tax expense, and changes in income taxes payable.

Cash Payments for Income Taxes	=	Income Tax Expense	{ + Decrease in Income Taxes Payable
			or
			− Increase in Income Taxes Payable

Illustration 13B-13
Formula to compute cash payments for income taxes—direct method

The operating activities section of the statement of cash flows of Computer Services Company is shown in Illustration 13B-14.

Cash flows from operating activities		
Cash receipts from customers		$517,000
Less: Cash payments:		
To suppliers	$139,000	
For operating expenses	115,000	
For interest expense	42,000	
For income taxes	49,000	345,000
Net cash provided by operating activities		$172,000

Illustration 13B-14
Operating activities section of the statement of cash flows

When a company uses the direct method, it must also provide in a **separate schedule** (not shown here) the net cash flows from operating activities as computed under the indirect method.

Step 2: Investing and Financing Activities

ANALYZE CHANGES IN NONCURRENT ASSET AND LIABILITY ACCOUNTS AND RECORD AS INVESTING AND FINANCING ACTIVITIES, OR DISCLOSE AS NONCASH TRANSACTIONS

INCREASE IN LAND As indicated from the change in the Land account and the additional information, the company purchased land of $110,000 by directly exchanging bonds for land. The exchange of bonds payable for land has no effect on

Helpful Hint
The investing and financing activities are measured and reported the same under both the direct and indirect methods.

cash. But, it is a significant noncash investing and financing activity that merits disclosure in a separate schedule. (See Illustration 13B-16 on page 679.)

INCREASE IN BUILDINGS As the additional data indicate, Computer Services Company acquired an office building for $120,000 cash. This is a cash outflow reported in the investing section. (See Illustration 13B-16.)

INCREASE IN EQUIPMENT The Equipment account increased $17,000. The additional information explains that this was a net increase that resulted from two transactions: (1) a purchase of equipment of $25,000, and (2) the sale for $4,000 of equipment costing $8,000. These transactions are investing activities. The company should report each transaction separately. The statement in Illustration 13B-16 reports the purchase of equipment as an outflow of cash for $25,000. It reports the sale as an inflow of cash for $4,000. The T-account below shows the reasons for the change in this account during the year.

Illustration 13B-15
Analysis of equipment

Equipment				
1/1/14	Balance	10,000	Cost of equipment sold	8,000
	Purchase of equipment	**25,000**		
12/31/14	Balance	27,000		

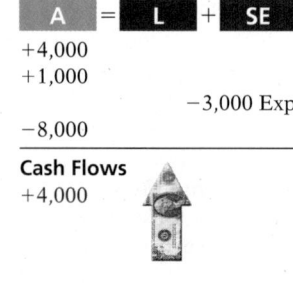

A = L + SE
+4,000
+1,000
−3,000 Exp
−8,000

Cash Flows
+4,000

The following entry shows the details of the equipment sale transaction.

Cash	4,000	
Accumulated Depreciation—Equipment	1,000	
Loss on Disposal of Plant Assets	3,000	
Equipment		8,000

INCREASE IN BONDS PAYABLE The Bonds Payable account increased $110,000. As indicated in the additional information, the company acquired land by directly exchanging bonds for land. Illustration 13B-16 reports this noncash transaction in a separate schedule at the bottom of the statement.

INCREASE IN COMMON STOCK The balance sheet reports an increase in Common Stock of $20,000. The additional information section notes that this increase resulted from the issuance of new shares of stock. This is a cash inflow reported in the financing section in Illustration 13B-16.

INCREASE IN RETAINED EARNINGS Retained earnings increased $116,000 during the year. This increase can be explained by two factors: (1) Net income of $145,000 increased retained earnings and (2) dividends of $29,000 decreased retained earnings. The company adjusts net income to net cash provided by operating activities in the operating activities section. **Payment** of the dividends (not the declaration) is a **cash outflow that the company reports as a financing activity in Illustration 13B-16**.

Helpful Hint
When companies issue stocks or bonds for cash, the actual proceeds will appear in the statement of cash flows as a financing inflow (rather than the par value of the stocks or face value of bonds).

STATEMENT OF CASH FLOWS—2014
Illustration 13B-16 shows the statement of cash flows for Computer Services Company.

Step 3: Net Change in Cash

COMPARE THE NET CHANGE IN CASH ON THE STATEMENT OF CASH FLOWS WITH THE CHANGE IN THE CASH ACCOUNT REPORTED ON THE BALANCE SHEET TO MAKE SURE THE AMOUNTS AGREE

Illustration 13B-16 indicates that the net change in cash during the period was an increase of $22,000. This agrees with the change in balances in the cash account reported on the balance sheets in Illustration 13B-1 (pages 672–673).

Illustration 13B-16
Statement of cash flows, 2014—direct method

Computer Services Company Statement of Cash Flows—Direct Method For the Year Ended December 31, 2014		
Cash flows from operating activities		
Cash receipts from customers		$ 517,000
Less: Cash payments:		
To suppliers	$ 139,000	
For operating expenses	115,000	
For income taxes	49,000	
For interest expense	42,000	345,000
Net cash provided by operating activities		172,000
Cash flows from investing activities		
Purchase of building	(120,000)	
Purchase of equipment	(25,000)	
Disposal of plant assets	4,000	
Net cash used by investing activities		(141,000)
Cash flows from financing activities		
Issuance of common stock	20,000	
Payment of cash dividends	(29,000)	
Net cash used by financing activities		(9,000)
Net increase in cash		22,000
Cash at beginning of period		33,000
Cash at end of period		$ 55,000
Noncash investing and financing activities		
Issuance of bonds payable to purchase land		$ 110,000

SUMMARY OF LEARNING OBJECTIVE FOR APPENDIX 13B   ✔ The Navigator

6 Prepare a statement of cash flows using the direct method. The preparation of the statement of cash flows involves three major steps: (1) Determine net cash provided/used by operating activities by converting net income from an accrual basis to a cash basis. (2) Analyze changes in noncurrent asset and liability accounts and record as investing and financing activities, or disclose as noncash transactions. (3) Compare the net change in cash on the statement of cash flows with the change in the cash account reported on the balance sheet to make sure the amounts agree. The direct method reports cash receipts less cash payments to arrive at net cash provided by operating activities.

GLOSSARY FOR APPENDIX 13B

Direct method A method of determining net cash provided by operating activities by adjusting each item in the income statement from the accrual basis to the cash basis. (p. 673).

> **Comprehensive DO IT! 2**

The income statement for Kosinski Company contains the following condensed information.

Kosinski Company
Income Statement
For the Year Ended December 31, 2014

Sales revenue		$6,583,000
Operating expenses, excluding depreciation	$4,920,000	
Depreciation expense	880,000	5,800,000
Income before income taxes		783,000
Income tax expense		353,000
Net income		$ 430,000

Included in operating expenses is a $24,000 loss resulting from the sale of machinery for $270,000 cash. Machinery was purchased at a cost of $750,000. The following balances are reported on Kosinski's comparative balance sheet at December 31.

Kosinski Company
Comparative Balance Sheets (partial)

	2014	2013
Cash	$672,000	$130,000
Accounts receivable	775,000	610,000
Inventory	834,000	867,000
Accounts payable	521,000	501,000

Income tax expense of $353,000 represents the amount paid in 2014. Dividends declared and paid in 2014 totaled $200,000.

Instructions
Prepare the statement of cash flows using the direct method.

Solution to Comprehensive DO IT! 2

Action Plan

✔ Determine net cash from operating activities. Each item in the income statement must be adjusted to the cash basis.

✔ Determine net cash from investing activities. Investing activities generally relate to changes in noncurrent assets.

✔ Determine net cash from financing activities. Financing activities generally relate to changes in long-term liabilities and stockholders' equity accounts.

Kosinski Company
Statement of Cash Flows—Direct Method
For the Year Ended December 31, 2014

Cash flows from operating activities		
Cash collections from customers		$6,418,000*
Cash payments:		
For operating expenses	$4,843,000**	
For income taxes	353,000	5,196,000
Net cash provided by operating activities		1,222,000
Cash flows from investing activities		
Disposal of plant assets	270,000	
Purchase of machinery	(750,000)	
Net cash used by investing activities		(480,000)
Cash flows from financing activities		
Payment of cash dividends	(200,000)	
Net cash used by financing activities		(200,000)
Net increase in cash		542,000
Cash at beginning of period		130,000
Cash at end of period		$ 672,000

Direct-Method Computations:

*Computation of cash collections from customers:

Sales revenue per the income statement	$6,583,000
Deduct: Increase in accounts receivable	(165,000)
Cash collections from customers	$6,418,000

**Computation of cash payments for operating expenses:

Operating expenses per the income statement	$4,920,000
Deduct: Loss on disposal of plant assets	(24,000)
Deduct: Decrease in inventories	(33,000)
Deduct: Increase in accounts payable	(20,000)
Cash payments for operating expenses	$4,843,000

✔ **The Navigator**

APPENDIX 13C STATEMENT OF CASH FLOWS—T-ACCOUNT APPROACH

Many people like to use T-accounts to provide structure to the preparation of a statement of cash flows. The use of T-accounts is based on the accounting equation. The basic equation is:

Assets = Liabilities + Equity

Now, let's rewrite the left-hand side as:

Cash + Noncash Assets = Liabilities + Equity

Next, rewrite the equation by subtracting Noncash Assets from each side to isolate Cash on the left-hand side:

Cash = Liabilities + Equity − Noncash Assets

Finally, if we insert the Δ symbol (which means "change in"), we have:

Δ Cash = Δ Liabilities + Δ Equity − Δ Noncash Assets

What this means is that the change in cash is equal to the change in all of the other balance sheet accounts. Another way to think about this is that if we analyze the changes in all of the noncash balance sheet accounts, we will explain the change in the Cash account. This, of course, is exactly what we are trying to do with the statement of cash flows.

To implement this approach, first prepare a large Cash T-account, with sections for operating, investing, and financing activities. Then, prepare smaller T-accounts for all of the other noncash balance sheet accounts. Insert the beginning and ending balances for each of these accounts. Once you have done this, then walk through the steps outlined on page 682. As you walk through the steps, enter debit and credit amounts into the affected accounts. When all of the changes in the T-accounts have been explained, you are done. To demonstrate, we will apply this approach to the example of Computer Services Company that is presented in the chapter. Each of the adjustments in Illustration 13C-1 is numbered so you can follow them through the T-accounts.

1. Post net income as a debit to the operating section of the Cash T-account and a credit to Retained Earnings. Make sure to label all adjustments to the Cash T-account. It also helps to number each adjustment so you can trace all of them if you make an error.

2. Post depreciation expense as a debit to the operating section of Cash and a credit to each of the appropriate accumulated depreciation accounts.

3. Post any gains or losses on the sale of property, plant, and equipment. To do this, it is best to first prepare the journal entry that was recorded at the time of the sale and then post each element of the journal entry. For example, for Computer Services the entry was:

Cash	4,000	
Accumulated Depreciation—Equipment	1,000	
Loss on Disposal of Plant Assets	3,000	
Equipment		8,000

The $4,000 cash entry is a source of cash in the investing section of the Cash account. Accumulated Depreciation—Equipment is debited for $1,000. The Loss on Disposal of Plant Assets is a debit to the operating section of the Cash T-account. Finally, Equipment is credited for $8,000.

Illustration 13C-1
T-account approach

Cash

Operating

(1) Net income	145,000	5,000	Inventory (5)	
(2) Depreciation expense	9,000	4,000	Prepaid expenses (6)	
(3) Loss on disposal of plant assets	3,000	2,000	Income taxes payable (8)	
(4) Accounts receivable	10,000			
(7) Accounts payable	16,000			
Net cash provided by operating activities	172,000			

Investing

(3) Disposal of plant assets	4,000	120,000	Purchased building (10)	
		25,000	Purchased equipment (11)	
		141,000	Net cash used by investing activities	

Financing

(12) Issued common stock	20,000	29,000	Dividend paid (13)	
		9,000	Net cash used by financing activities	
	22,000			

Accounts Receivable			Inventory			Prepaid Expenses			Land	
30,000			10,000			1,000			20,000	
	10,000 (4)	(5) 5,000			(6) 4,000			(9) 110,000		
20,000		15,000			5,000			130,000		

Buildings			Accumulated Depreciation—Buildings			Equipment			Accumulated Depreciation—Equipment	
40,000				5,000		10,000				1,000
(10) 120,000				6,000 (2)	(11) 25,000		8,000 (3)	(3) 1,000		3,000 (2)
160,000				11,000		27,000				3,000

Accounts Payable			Income Taxes Payable			Bonds Payable			Common Stock			Retained Earnings	
	12,000			8,000			20,000			50,000			48,000
	16,000 (7)	(8) 2,000					110,000 (9)			20,000 (12)			145,000 (1)
	28,000			6,000			130,000			70,000	(13) 29,000		
													164,000

4–8. Next, post each of the changes to the noncash current asset and current liability accounts. For example, to explain the $10,000 decline in Computer Services' Accounts Receivable, credit Accounts Receivable for $10,000 and debit the operating section of the Cash T-account for $10,000.

9. Analyze the changes in the noncurrent accounts. Land was purchased by issuing Bonds Payable. This requires a debit to Land for $110,000 and a credit to Bonds Payable for $110,000. Note that this is a significant noncash event that requires disclosure at the bottom of the statement of cash flows.

10. Buildings is debited for $120,000, and the investing section of the Cash T-account is credited for $120,000 as a use of cash from investing.

11. Equipment is debited for $25,000 and the investing section of the Cash T-account is credited for $25,000 as a use of cash from investing.

12. Common Stock is credited for $20,000 for the issuance of shares of stock, and the financing section of the Cash T-account is debited for $20,000.

13. Retained Earnings is debited to reflect the payment of the $29,000 dividend, and the financing section of the Cash T-account is credited to reflect the use of Cash.

At this point, all of the changes in the noncash accounts have been explained. All that remains is to subtotal each section of the Cash T-account and agree the total change in cash with the change shown on the balance sheet. Once this is done, the information in the Cash T-account can be used to prepare a statement of cash flows.

 Self-Test, Brief Exercises, Exercises, Problem Set A, and many more resources are available for practice in WileyPLUS.

Note: All Questions, Exercises, and Problems marked with an asterisk relate to material in the appendices to the chapter.

SELF-TEST QUESTIONS

Answers are on page 706.

(LO 1) **1.** Which of the following is *incorrect* about the statement of cash flows?
  (a) It is a fourth basic financial statement.
  (b) It provides information about cash receipts and cash payments of an entity during a period.
  (c) It reconciles the ending cash account balance to the balance per the bank statement.
  (d) It provides information about the operating, investing, and financing activities of the business.

(LO 1) **2.** Which of the following will *not* be reported in the statement of cash flows?
  (a) The net change in plant assets during the year.
  (b) Cash payments for plant assets purchased during the year.
  (c) Cash receipts from sales of plant assets during the year.
  (d) How acquisitions of plant assets during the year were financed.

(LO 2) **3.** The statement of cash flows classifies cash receipts and cash payments by these activities:
  (a) operating and nonoperating.
  (b) investing, financing, and operating.

  (c) financing, operating, and nonoperating.
  (d) investing, financing, and nonoperating.

(LO 2) **4.** Which is an example of a cash flow from an operating activity?
  (a) Payment of cash to lenders for interest.
  (b) Receipt of cash from the sale of capital stock.
  (c) Payment of cash dividends to the company's stockholders.
  (d) None of the above.

(LO 2) **5.** Which is an example of a cash flow from an investing activity?
  (a) Receipt of cash from the issuance of bonds payable.
  (b) Payment of cash to repurchase outstanding capital stock.
  (c) Receipt of cash from the sale of equipment.
  (d) Payment of cash to suppliers for inventory.

(LO 2) **6.** Cash dividends paid to stockholders are classified on the statement of cash flows as:
  (a) operating activities.
  (b) investing activities.
  (c) a combination of (a) and (b).
  (d) financing activities.

(LO 2) 7. Which is an example of a cash flow from a financing activity?
 (a) Receipt of cash from sale of land.
 (b) Issuance of debt for cash.
 (c) Purchase of equipment for cash.
 (d) None of the above.

(LO 2) 8. Which of the following is *incorrect* about the statement of cash flows?
 (a) The direct method may be used to report cash provided by operations.
 (b) The statement shows the cash provided (used) for three categories of activity.
 (c) The operating section is the last section of the statement.
 (d) The indirect method may be used to report cash provided by operations.

Questions 9 through 11 apply only to the indirect method.

(LO 3) 9. Net income is $132,000, accounts payable increased $10,000 during the year, inventory decreased $6,000 during the year, and accounts receivable increased $12,000 during the year. Under the indirect method, what is net cash provided by operating activities?
 (a) $102,000.   (c) $124,000.
 (b) $112,000.   (d) $136,000.

(LO 3) 10. Items that are added back to net income in determining cash provided by operating activities under the indirect method do *not* include:
 (a) depreciation expense.
 (b) an increase in inventory.
 (c) amortization expense.
 (d) loss on sale of equipment.

(LO 3) 11. The following data are available for Allen Clapp Corporation.

Net income	$200,000
Depreciation expense	40,000
Dividends paid	60,000
Gain on sale of land	10,000
Decrease in accounts receivable	20,000
Decrease in accounts payable	30,000

Net cash provided by operating activities is:
 (a) $160,000.   (c) $240,000.
 (b) $220,000.   (d) $280,000.

(LO 3) 12. The following data are available for Orange Peels Corporation.

Sale of land	$100,000
Sale of equipment	50,000
Issuance of common stock	70,000
Purchase of equipment	30,000
Payment of cash dividends	60,000

Net cash provided by investing activities is:
 (a) $120,000.   (c) $150,000.
 (b) $130,000.   (d) $190,000.

(LO 3) 13. The following data are available for Something Strange!

Increase in accounts payable	$ 40,000
Increase in bonds payable	100,000
Sale of investment	50,000
Issuance of common stock	60,000
Payment of cash dividends	30,000

Net cash provided by financing activities is:
 (a) $90,000.   (c) $160,000.
 (b) $130,000.   (d) $170,000.

(LO 4) 14. The statement of cash flows should *not* be used to evaluate an entity's ability to:
 (a) earn net income.
 (b) generate future cash flows.
 (c) pay dividends.
 (d) meet obligations.

(LO 4) 15. Free cash flow provides an indication of a company's ability to:
 (a) generate net income.
 (b) generate cash to pay dividends.
 (c) generate cash to invest in new capital expenditures.
 (d) Both (b) and (c).

(LO 5) *16. In a worksheet for the statement of cash flows, a decrease in accounts receivable is entered in the reconciling columns as a credit to Accounts Receivable and a debit in the:
 (a) investing activities section.
 (b) operating activities section.
 (c) financing activities section.
 (d) None of the above.

(LO 5) *17. In a worksheet for the statement of cash flows, a worksheet entry that includes a credit to accumulated depreciation will also include a:
 (a) credit in the operating section and a debit in another section.
 (b) debit in the operating section.
 (c) debit in the investing section.
 (d) debit in the financing section.

Questions 18 and 19 apply only to the direct method.

(LO 6) *18. The beginning balance in accounts receivable is $44,000, the ending balance is $42,000, and sales during the period are $129,000. What are cash receipts from customers?
 (a) $127,000.   (c) $131,000.
 (b) $129,000.   (d) $141,000.

(LO 6) *19. Which of the following items is reported on a statement of cash flows prepared by the direct method?
 (a) Loss on sale of building.
 (b) Increase in accounts receivable.
 (c) Depreciation expense.
 (d) Cash payments to suppliers.

Go to the book's companion website, www.wiley.com/college/weygandt, for additional Self-Test Questions.

✔ **The Navigator**

QUESTIONS

1. (a) What is a statement of cash flows?
   (b) Nick Johns maintains that the statement of cash flows is an optional financial statement. Do you agree? Explain.
2. What questions about cash are answered by the statement of cash flows?
3. Distinguish among the three types of activities reported in the statement of cash flows.
4. (a) What are the major sources (inflows) of cash in a statement of cash flows?
   (b) What are the major uses (outflows) of cash?
5. Why is it important to disclose certain noncash transactions? How should they be disclosed?
6. Wilma Flintstone and Barny Rublestone were discussing the format of the statement of cash flows of Saltwater Candy Co. At the bottom of Saltwater Candy's statement of cash flows was a separate section entitled "Noncash investing and financing activities." Give three examples of significant noncash transactions that would be reported in this section.
7. Why is it necessary to use comparative balance sheets, a current income statement, and certain transaction data in preparing a statement of cash flows?
8. Contrast the advantages and disadvantages of the direct and indirect methods of preparing the statement of cash flows. Are both methods acceptable? Which method is preferred by the FASB? Which method is more popular?
9. When the total cash inflows exceed the total cash outflows in the statement of cash flows, how and where is this excess identified?
10. Describe the indirect method for determining net cash provided (used) by operating activities.
11. Why is it necessary to convert accrual-based net income to cash-basis income when preparing a statement of cash flows?

12. The president of Ferneti Company is puzzled. During the last year, the company experienced a net loss of $800,000, yet its cash increased $300,000 during the same period of time. Explain to the president how this could occur.
13. Identify five items that are adjustments to convert net income to net cash provided by operating activities under the indirect method.
14. Why and how is depreciation expense reported in a statement prepared using the indirect method?
15. Why is the statement of cash flows useful?
16. During 2014, Singletree Company exchanged $1,700,000 of its common stock for land. Indicate how the transaction would be reported on a statement of cash flows, if at all.
17. ☁ PEPSICO In its 2010 statement of cash flows, what amount did PepsiCo report for net cash (a) provided by operating activities, (b) used for investing activities, and (c) used for financing activities?
*18. Why is it advantageous to use a worksheet when preparing a statement of cash flows? Is a worksheet required to prepare a statement of cash flows?
*19. Describe the direct method for determining net cash provided by operating activities.
*20. Give the formulas under the direct method for computing (a) cash receipts from customers and (b) cash payments to suppliers.
*21. Aloha Inc. reported sales of $2 million for 2014. Accounts receivable decreased $140,000 and accounts payable increased $300,000. Compute cash receipts from customers, assuming that the receivable and payable transactions related to operations.
*22. In the direct method, why is depreciation expense not reported in the cash flows from operating activities section?

BRIEF EXERCISES

BE13-1 Each of the items below must be considered in preparing a statement of cash flows for Alpha-Omega Co. for the year ended December 31, 2014. For each item, state how it should be shown in the statement of cash flows for 2014.
(a) Issued bonds for $150,000 cash.
(b) Purchased equipment for $200,000 cash.
(c) Sold land costing $50,000 for $50,000 cash.
(d) Declared and paid a $20,000 cash dividend.

Indicate statement presentation of selected transactions.
(LO 2)

BE13-2 Classify each item as an operating, investing, or financing activity. Assume all items involve cash unless there is information to the contrary.
(a) Purchase of equipment.   (d) Depreciation.
(b) Sale of building.   (e) Payment of dividends.
(c) Redemption of bonds.   (f) Issuance of capital stock.

Classify items by activities.
(LO 2)

*Identify financing activity
transactions.*

(LO 2)

BE13-3 The following T-account is a summary of the Cash account of Wiegman Company.

Cash (Summary Form)

Balance, Jan. 1	8,000		
Receipts from customers	364,000	Payments for goods	200,000
Dividends on stock investments	6,000	Payments for operating expenses	140,000
Proceeds from sale of equipment	36,000	Interest paid	10,000
Proceeds from issuance of		Taxes paid	8,000
bonds payable	500,000	Dividends paid	60,000
Balance, Dec. 31	496,000		

What amount of net cash provided (used) by financing activities should be reported in the statement of cash flows?

*Compute cash provided by
operating activities—indirect
method.* **(LO 3)**

BE13-4 Mokena, Inc. reported net income of $2.0 million in 2014. Depreciation for the year was $160,000, accounts receivable increased $350,000, and accounts payable increased $280,000. Compute net cash provided by operating activities using the indirect method.

*Compute cash provided by
operating activities—indirect
method.* **(LO 3)**

BE13-5 The net income for Lodi Co. for 2014 was $250,000. For 2014, depreciation on plant assets was $70,000, and the company incurred a gain on disposal of plant assets of $12,000. Compute net cash provided by operating activities under the indirect method.

*Compute net cash provided
by operating activities—
indirect method.*

(LO 3)

BE13-6 The comparative balance sheets for Tobemory Company show these changes in noncash current asset accounts: accounts receivable increase $80,000, prepaid expenses decrease $28,000, and inventories decrease $30,000. Compute net cash provided by operating activities using the indirect method assuming that net income is $250,000.

*Determine cash received from
sale of equipment.*

(LO 3)

BE13-7 The T-accounts for Equipment and the related Accumulated Depreciation—Equipment for Ada Company at the end of 2014 are shown here.

Equipment					**Accumulated Depreciation—Equipment**			
Beg. bal.	80,000	Disposals	22,000		Disposals	8,500	Beg. bal.	44,500
Acquisitions	41,600						Depr. exp.	12,000
End. bal.	99,600						End. bal.	48,000

In addition, Ada Company's income statement reported a loss on disposal of plant assets of $6,500. What amount was reported on the statement of cash flows as "cash flow from disposal of plant assets"?

Calculate free cash flow.

(LO 4)

BE13-8 In a recent year, Cypress Semiconductor Corporation reported cash provided by operating activities of $155,397,000, cash used in investing of $207,628,000, and cash used in financing of $33,372,000. In addition, cash spent for fixed assets during the period was $130,820,000. No dividends were paid. Calculate free cash flow.

Calculate free cash flow.

(LO 4)

BE13-9 Wruck Corporation reported cash provided by operating activities of $450,000, cash used by investing activities of $150,000, and cash provided by financing activities of $80,000. In addition, cash spent for capital assets during the period was $250,000. No dividends were paid. Calculate free cash flow.

Calculate free cash flow.

(LO 4)

BE13-10 In a recent quarter, Alliance Atlantis Communications Inc. reported cash provided by operating activities of $45,000,000 and revenues of $265,800,000. Cash spent on plant asset additions during the quarter was $1,400,000. Calculate free cash flow.

*Calculate and analyze free
cash flow.*

(LO 4)

BE13-11 The management of Russel Inc. is trying to decide whether it can increase its dividend. During the current year, it reported net income of $875,000. It had cash provided by operating activities of $643,000, paid cash dividends of $80,000, and had capital expenditures of $280,000. Compute the company's free cash flow, and discuss whether an increase in the dividend appears warranted. What other factors should be considered?

Indicate entries in worksheet.

(LO 5)

***BE13-12** During the year, prepaid expenses decreased $6,500, and accrued expenses increased $2,000. Indicate how the changes in prepaid expenses and accrued expenses payable should be entered in the reconciling columns of a worksheet. Assume that beginning balances were prepaid expenses $18,600 and accrued expenses payable $8,200.

*BE13-13 Columbia Sportswear Company had accounts receivable of $205,025,000 at the beginning of a recent year, and $267,653,000 at year-end. Sales revenues were $1,085,307,000 for the year. What is the amount of cash receipts from customers?

Compute receipts from customers—direct method.
(LO 6)

*BE13-14 Kinsey Corporation reported income taxes of $360,000,000 on its 2014 income statement, income taxes payable of $277,000,000 at December 31, 2013, and $525,000,000 at December 31, 2014. What amount of cash payments were made for income taxes during 2014?

Compute cash payments for income taxes—direct method.
(LO 6)

*BE13-15 Yaddof Corporation reports operating expenses of $70,000 excluding depreciation expense of $15,000 for 2014. During the year, prepaid expenses decreased $6,800 and accrued expenses payable increased $4,500. Compute the cash payments for operating expenses in 2014.

Compute cash payments for operating expenses—direct method.
(LO 6)

> DO IT! REVIEW

DO IT! 13-1 Piekarski Corporation had the following transactions.

1. Issued $200,000 of bonds payable.
2. Paid utilities expense.
3. Issued 500 shares of preferred stock for $45,000.
4. Sold land and a building for $250,000.
5. Lent $30,000 to Zarembski Corporation, receiving Zarembski's 1-year, 12% note.

Classify each of these transactions by type of cash flow activity (operating, investing, or financing).

Classify transactions by type of cash flow activity.
(LO 2)

DO IT! 13-2 Jojo Photography reported net income of $100,000 for 2014. Included in the income statement were depreciation expense of $4,000, amortization expense of $3,000, and a gain on disposal of plant assets of $3,900. Jojo's comparative balance sheets show the following balances.

Calculate net cash from operating activities.
(LO 3)

	12/31/13	12/31/14
Accounts receivable	$27,000	$21,000
Accounts payable	6,000	9,200

Calculate net cash provided by operating activities for Jojo Photography.

DO IT! 13-3 Zielinski Corporation issued the following statement of cash flows for 2014.

Compute and discuss free cash flow.
(LO 4)

Zielinski Corporation
Statement of Cash Flows—Indirect Method
For the Year Ended December 31, 2014

Cash flows from operating activities		
Net income		$ 59,000
Adjustments to reconcile net income to net cash provided by operating activities:		
Depreciation expense	$ 9,100	
Decrease in accounts receivable	8,500	
Loss on disposal of plant assets	3,300	
Increase in inventory	(5,000)	
Decrease in accounts payable	(2,500)	13,400
Net cash provided by operating activities		72,400
Cash flows from investing activities		
Sale of investments	3,100	
Purchase of equipment	(26,000)	
Net cash used by investing activities		(22,900)

Cash flows from financing activities
  Issuance of stock   20,000
  Payment on long-term note payable   (10,000)
  Payment for dividends   (18,000)
    Net cash used by financing activities   (8,000)
Net increase in cash   41,500
Cash at beginning of year   13,000
Cash at end of year $ 54,500

(a) Compute free cash flow for Zielinski Corporation. (b) Explain why free cash flow often provides better information than "Net cash provided by operating activities."

 **The Navigator**

EXERCISES

Classify transactions by type of activity.

(LO 2)

E13-1 Quarshee Corporation had these transactions during 2014.

(a) Issued $50,000 par value common stock for cash.
(b) Purchased a machine for $30,000, giving a long-term note in exchange.
(c) Issued $200,000 par value common stock upon conversion of bonds having a face value of $200,000.
(d) Declared and paid a cash dividend of $18,000.
(e) Sold a long-term investment with a cost of $15,000 for $15,000 cash.
(f) Collected $16,000 of accounts receivable.
(g) Paid $18,000 on accounts payable.

Instructions
Analyze the transactions and indicate whether each transaction resulted in a cash flow from operating activities, investing activities, financing activities, or noncash investing and financing activities.

Classify transactions by type of activity.

(LO 2)

E13-2 An analysis of comparative balance sheets, the current year's income statement, and the general ledger accounts of Solomon Corp. uncovered the following items. Assume all items involve cash unless there is information to the contrary.

(a) Payment of interest on notes payable.
(b) Exchange of land for patent.
(c) Sale of building at book value.
(d) Payment of dividends.
(e) Depreciation.
(f) Receipt of dividends on investment in stock.
(g) Receipt of interest on notes receivable.
(h) Issuance of capital stock.
(i) Amortization of patent.
(j) Issuance of bonds for land.
(k) Purchase of land.
(l) Conversion of bonds into common stock.
(m) Loss on sale of land.
(n) Retirement of bonds.

Instructions
Indicate how each item should be classified in the statement of cash flows using these four major classifications: operating activity (indirect method), investing activity, financing activity, and significant noncash investing and financing activity.

Prepare journal entry and determine effect on cash flows.

(LO 2)

E13-3 Tim Latimer Corporation had the following transactions.

1. Sold land (cost $12,000) for $10,000.
2. Issued common stock at par value for $22,000.
3. Recorded depreciation on buildings for $14,000.
4. Paid salaries of $7,000.
5. Issued 1,000 shares of $1 par value common stock for equipment worth $9,000.
6. Sold equipment (cost $10,000, accumulated depreciation $8,000) for $3,200.

Instructions
For each transaction above, (a) prepare the journal entry, and (b) indicate how it would affect the statement of cash flows under the direct method.

E13-4 Bracewell Company reported net income of $195,000 for 2014. Bracewell also reported depreciation expense of $40,000 and a gain of $5,000 on disposal of plant assets. The comparative balance sheet shows an increase in accounts receivable of $15,000 for the year, a $17,000 increase in accounts payable, and a $4,000 decrease in prepaid expenses.

Prepare the operating activities section—indirect method.

(LO 3)

Instructions
Prepare the operating activities section of the statement of cash flows for 2014. Use the indirect method.

E13-5 The current sections of Nasreen Inc.'s balance sheets at December 31, 2013 and 2014, are presented here. Nasreen's net income for 2014 was $153,000. Depreciation expense was $24,000.

Prepare the operating activities section—indirect method.

(LO 3)

	2014	2013
Current assets		
Cash	$105,000	$ 99,000
Accounts receivable	110,000	79,000
Inventory	158,000	172,000
Prepaid expenses	27,000	25,000
Total current assets	$400,000	$375,000
Current liabilities		
Accrued expenses payable	$ 15,000	$ 9,000
Accounts payable	85,000	95,000
Total current liabilities	$100,000	$104,000

Instructions
Prepare the net cash provided by operating activities section of the company's statement of cash flows for the year ended December 31, 2014, using the indirect method.

E13-6 The three accounts shown below appear in the general ledger of Chaudry Corp. during 2014.

Prepare partial statement of cash flows—indirect method.

(LO 3)

Equipment

Date		Debit	Credit	Balance
Jan. 1	Balance			160,000
July 31	Purchase of equipment	70,000		230,000
Sept. 2	Cost of equipment constructed	53,000		283,000
Nov. 10	Cost of equipment sold		49,000	234,000

Accumulated Depreciation—Equipment

Date		Debit	Credit	Balance
Jan. 1	Balance			71,000
Nov. 10	Accumulated depreciation on equipment sold	28,000		43,000
Dec. 31	Depreciation for year		23,000	66,000

Retained Earnings

Date		Debit	Credit	Balance
Jan. 1	Balance			105,000
Aug. 23	Dividends (cash)	17,000		88,000
Dec. 31	Net income		67,000	155,000

Instructions
From the postings in the accounts, indicate how the information is reported on a statement of cash flows using the indirect method. The loss on disposal of plant assets was $5,000. (*Hint:* Cost of equipment constructed is reported in the investing activities section as a decrease in cash of $53,000.)

Prepare statement of cash flows and compute free cash flow.

(LO 3, 4)

E13-7 Meera Corporation's comparative balance sheets are presented below.

Meera Corporation
Comparative Balance Sheets
December 31

	2014	2013
Cash	$ 14,700	$ 10,700
Accounts receivable	20,800	23,400
Land	20,000	26,000
Buildings	70,000	70,000
Accumulated depreciation—buildings	(15,000)	(10,000)
Total	$110,500	$120,100
Accounts payable	$ 12,370	$ 28,100
Common stock	75,000	72,000
Retained earnings	23,130	20,000
Total	$110,500	$120,100

Additional information:

1. Net income was $22,630. Dividends declared and paid were $19,500.
2. All other changes in noncurrent account balances had a direct effect on cash flows, except the change in accumulated depreciation. The land was sold for $5,000.

Instructions
(a) Prepare a statement of cash flows for 2014 using the indirect method.
(b) Compute free cash flow.

Prepare a statement of cash flows—indirect method.

(LO 3)

E13-8 Here are comparative balance sheets for Syal Company.

Syal Company
Comparative Balance Sheets
December 31

Assets	2014	2013
Cash	$ 73,000	$ 33,000
Accounts receivable	85,000	71,000
Inventory	170,000	187,000
Land	73,000	100,000
Equipment	260,000	200,000
Accumulated depreciation—equipment	(66,000)	(34,000)
Total	$595,000	$557,000

Liabilities and Stockholders' Equity		
Accounts payable	$ 35,000	$ 47,000
Bonds payable	150,000	200,000
Common stock ($1 par)	216,000	174,000
Retained earnings	194,000	136,000
Total	$595,000	$557,000

Additional information:

1. Net income for 2014 was $103,000.
2. Depreciation expense was $32,000.
3. Cash dividends of $45,000 were declared and paid.
4. Bonds payable amounting to $50,000 were redeemed for cash $50,000.
5. Common stock was issued for $42,000 cash.
6. No equipment was sold during 2014.
7. Land was sold for its book value of $27,000.

Instructions
Prepare a statement of cash flows for 2014 using the indirect method.

E13-9 Cassandra Corporation's comparative balance sheets are presented below.

Prepare statement of cash flows and compute free cash flow.

(LO 3, 4)

Cassandra Corporation
Comparative Balance Sheets
December 31

	2014	2013
Cash	$ 17,000	$ 17,700
Accounts receivable	25,200	22,300
Investments	20,000	16,000
Equipment	60,000	70,000
Accumulated depreciation—equipment	(14,000)	(10,000)
Total	$108,200	$116,000
Accounts payable	$ 14,600	$ 11,100
Bonds payable	10,000	30,000
Common stock	50,000	45,000
Retained earnings	33,600	29,900
Total	$108,200	$116,000

Additional information:

1. Net income was $18,300. Dividends declared and paid were $14,600.
2. Equipment which cost $10,000 and had accumulated depreciation of $1,800 was sold for $3,500.
3. All other changes in noncurrent account balances had a direct effect on cash flows, except the change in accumulated depreciation.

Instructions
(a) Prepare a statement of cash flows for 2014 using the indirect method.
(b) Compute free cash flow.

*E13-10 Comparative balance sheets for Erisa Magambo Company are presented below.

Prepare a worksheet.

(LO 5)

Erisa Magambo Company
Comparative Balance Sheets
December 31

Assets	2014	2013
Cash	$ 58,000	$ 22,000
Accounts receivable	85,000	76,000
Inventory	180,000	187,000
Land	75,000	100,000
Equipment	250,000	200,000
Accumulated depreciation—equipment	(66,000)	(42,000)
Total	$582,000	$543,000
Liabilities and Stockholders' Equity		
Accounts payable	$ 34,000	$ 45,000
Bonds payable	150,000	200,000
Common stock ($1 par)	214,000	164,000
Retained earnings	184,000	134,000
Total	$582,000	$543,000

Additional information:

1. Net income for 2014 was $120,000.
2. Cash dividends of $70,000 were declared and paid.
3. Bonds payable amounting to $50,000 were redeemed for cash $50,000.
4. Common stock was issued for $50,000 cash.
5. Depreciation expense was $24,000.
6. Sales for the year were $978,000.

Instructions
Prepare a worksheet for a statement of cash flows for 2014 using the indirect method. Enter the reconciling items directly on the worksheet, using letters to cross-reference each entry.

Compute cash provided by operating activities—direct method.

(LO 6)

*E13-11 Dumezweni Company completed its first year of operations on December 31, 2014. Its initial income statement showed that Dumezweni had revenues of $195,000 and operating expenses of $78,000. Accounts receivable and accounts payable at year-end were $60,000 and $25,000, respectively. Assume that accounts payable related to operating expenses. (Ignore income taxes.)

Instructions

Compute net cash provided by operating activities using the direct method.

Compute cash payments— direct method.

(LO 6)

*E13-12 A recent income statement for McDonald's Corporation shows cost of goods sold $4,527.8 million and operating expenses (including depreciation expense of $1,120 million) $10,517.6 million. The comparative balance sheet for the year shows that inventory increased $17.1 million, prepaid expenses increased $65.3 million, accounts payable (merchandise suppliers) increased $139.6 million, and accrued expenses payable increased $190.6 million.

Instructions

Using the direct method, compute (a) cash payments to suppliers and (b) cash payments for operating expenses.

Compute cash flow from operating activities—direct method.

(LO 6)

*E13-13 The 2014 accounting records of Liz Ten Transport reveal these transactions and events.

Payment of interest	$10,000	Collection of accounts receivable	$190,000
Cash sales	50,000	Payment of salaries and wages	57,000
Receipt of dividend		Depreciation expense	16,000
revenue	18,000	Proceeds from disposal of	
Payment of income taxes	16,000	plant assets	12,000
Net income	38,000	Purchase of equipment for cash	22,000
Payment of accounts payable		Loss on disposal of plant assets	3,000
for merchandise	115,000	Payment of dividends	14,000
Payment for land	74,000	Payment of operating expenses	28,000

Instructions

Prepare the cash flows from operating activities section using the direct method. (Not all of the items will be used.)

Calculate cash flows—direct method.

(LO 6)

*E13-14 The following information is taken from the 2014 general ledger of Okonedo Company.

Rent	Rent expense	$ 40,000
	Prepaid rent, January 1	5,600
	Prepaid rent, December 31	9,000
Salaries	Salaries and wages expense	$ 65,000
	Salaries and wages payable, January 1	10,000
	Salaries and wages payable, December 31	8,000
Sales	Sales revenue	$170,000
	Accounts receivable, January 1	19,000
	Accounts receivable, December 31	7,000

Instructions

In each case, compute the amount that should be reported in the operating activities section of the statement of cash flows under the direct method.

EXERCISES: SET B AND CHALLENGE EXERCISES

Visit the book's companion website, at **www.wiley.com/college/weygandt**, and choose the Student Companion site to access Exercise Set B and Challenge Exercises.

PROBLEMS: SET A

Distinguish among operating, investing, and financing activities. (LO 2)

P13-1A You are provided with the following transactions that took place during a recent fiscal year.

Transaction	Statement of Cash Flow Activity Affected	Cash Inflow, Outflow, or No Effect?
(a) Recorded depreciation expense on the plant assets.		
(b) Recorded and paid interest expense.		
(c) Recorded cash proceeds from a sale of plant assets.		
(d) Acquired land by issuing common stock.		
(e) Paid a cash dividend to preferred stockholders.		
(f) Paid a cash dividend to common stockholders.		
(g) Recorded cash sales.		
(h) Recorded sales on account.		
(i) Purchased inventory for cash.		
(j) Purchased inventory on account.		

Instructions

Complete the table indicating whether each item (1) affects operating (O) activities, investing (I) activities, financing (F) activities, or is a noncash (NC) transaction reported in a separate schedule; and (2) represents a cash inflow or cash outflow or has no cash flow effect. Assume use of the indirect approach.

P13-2A The following account balances relate to the stockholders' equity accounts of Chipo Corp. at year-end.

Determine cash flow effects of changes in equity accounts.

(LO 3)

	2014	2013
Common stock, 10,500 and 10,000 shares, respectively, for 2014 and 2013	$155,000	$130,000
Preferred stock, 5,000 shares	125,000	125,000
Retained earnings	300,000	250,000

A small stock dividend was declared and issued in 2014. The market value of the shares was $11,200. Cash dividends were $16,000 in both 2014 and 2013. The common stock has no par or stated value.

Instructions

(a) What was the amount of net income reported by Chipo Corp. in 2014?

(b) Determine the amounts of any cash inflows or outflows related to the common stock and dividend accounts in 2014.

(c) Indicate where each of the cash inflows or outflows identified in (b) would be classified on the statement of cash flows.

(a) Net income $77,200

P13-3A The income statement of Toby Zed Company is presented here.

Prepare the operating activities section—indirect method.

(LO 3)

Toby Zed Company
Income Statement
For the Year Ended November 30, 2014

Sales revenue		$7,500,000
Cost of goods sold		
Beginning inventory	$1,900,000	
Purchases	4,400,000	
Goods available for sale	6,300,000	
Ending inventory	1,400,000	
Total cost of goods sold		4,900,000
Gross profit		2,600,000
Operating expenses		1,150,000
Net income		$1,450,000

Additional information:

1. Accounts receivable increased $200,000 during the year, and inventory decreased $500,000.
2. Prepaid expenses increased $175,000 during the year.

3. Accounts payable to suppliers of merchandise decreased $340,000 during the year.
4. Accrued expenses payable decreased $105,000 during the year.
5. Operating expenses include depreciation expense of $85,000.

Instructions

Prepare the operating activities section of the statement of cash flows for the year ended November 30, 2014, for Toby Zed Company, using the indirect method.

Cash from operations $1,215,000

Prepare the operating activities section—direct method.

(LO 6)

Cash from oper. $1,215,000

Prepare the operating activities section—indirect method.

(LO 3)

***P13-4A** Data for Toby Zed Company are presented in P13-3A.

Instructions

Prepare the operating activities section of the statement of cash flows using the direct method.

P13-5A Rattigan Company's income statement contained the condensed information below.

Rattigan Company
Income Statement
For the Year Ended December 31, 2014

Service revenue		$970,000
Operating expenses, excluding depreciation	$624,000	
Depreciation expense	55,000	
Loss on disposal of plant assets	25,000	704,000
Income before income taxes		266,000
Income tax expense		40,000
Net income		$226,000

Rattigan's balance sheet contained the comparative data at December 31, shown below.

	2014	2013
Accounts receivable	$75,000	$60,000
Accounts payable	41,000	27,000
Income taxes payable	13,000	7,000

Accounts payable pertain to operating expenses.

Instructions

Prepare the operating activities section of the statement of cash flows using the indirect method.

Cash from operations $311,000

Prepare the operating activities section—direct method.

(LO 6)

Cash from oper. $311,000

***P13-6A** Data for Rattigan Company are presented in P13-5A.

Instructions

Prepare the operating activities section of the statement of cash flows using the direct method.

P13-7A Presented below and on the next page are the financial statements of Rajesh Company.

Prepare a statement of cash flows—indirect method, and compute free cash flow.

(LO 3, 4)

Rajesh Company
Comparative Balance Sheets
December 31

Assets	2014	2013
Cash	$ 37,000	$ 20,000
Accounts receivable	33,000	14,000
Inventory	30,000	20,000
Equipment	60,000	78,000
Accumulated depreciation—equipment	(29,000)	(24,000)
Total	$131,000	$108,000

Liabilities and Stockholders' Equity		
Accounts payable	$ 29,000	$ 15,000
Income taxes payable	7,000	8,000
Bonds payable	27,000	33,000
Common stock	18,000	14,000
Retained earnings	50,000	38,000
Total	$131,000	$108,000

Rajesh Company
Income Statement
For the Year Ended December 31, 2014

Sales revenue	$242,000
Cost of goods sold	175,000
Gross profit	67,000
Operating expenses	24,000
Income from operations	43,000
Interest expense	3,000
Income before income taxes	40,000
Income tax expense	8,000
Net income	$ 32,000

Additional data:

1. Depreciation expense is 13,300.
2. Dividends declared and paid were $20,000.
3. During the year, equipment was sold for $9,700 cash. This equipment cost $18,000 originally and had accumulated depreciation of $8,300 at the time of sale.

Instructions
(a) Prepare a statement of cash flows using the indirect method.
(b) Compute free cash flow.

(a) Cash from operations
    $29,300

*P13-8A Data for Rajesh Company are presented in P13-7A. Further analysis reveals the following.

1. Accounts payable pertain to merchandise suppliers.
2. All operating expenses except for depreciation were paid in cash.
3. All depreciation expense is in the operating expenses.
4. All sales and purchases are on account.

Prepare a statement of cash flows—direct method, and compute free cash flow.

(LO 4, 6)

Instructions
(a) Prepare a statement of cash flows for Rajesh Company using the direct method.
(b) Compute free cash flow.

(a) Cash from operations
    $29,300

P13-9A Condensed financial data of Sinjh Inc. follow.

Prepare a statement of cash flows—indirect method.

(LO 3)

Sinjh Inc.
Comparative Balance Sheets
December 31

Assets	2014	2013
Cash	$100,350	$ 48,400
Accounts receivable	92,800	33,000
Inventory	112,500	102,850
Prepaid expenses	29,300	26,000
Long-term investments	140,000	114,000
Plant assets	265,000	242,500
Accumulated depreciation	(47,000)	(52,000)
Total	$692,950	$514,750

Liabilities and Stockholders' Equity		
Accounts payable	$112,000	$ 67,300
Accrued expenses payable	16,500	17,000
Bonds payable	110,000	150,000
Common stock	220,000	175,000
Retained earnings	234,450	105,450
Total	$692,950	$514,750

Sinjh Inc.
Income Statement
For the Year Ended December 31, 2014

Sales revenue	$392,780	
Gain on disposal of plant assets	5,000	$397,780
Less:		
Cost of goods sold	135,460	
Operating expenses, excluding depreciation	12,410	
Depreciation expense	45,000	
Income tax expense	27,280	
Interest expense	4,730	224,880
Net income		$172,900

Additional information:

1. New plant assets costing $80,000 were purchased for cash during the year.
2. Old plant assets having an original cost of $57,500 and accumulated depreciation of $50,000 were sold for $12,500 cash.
3. Bonds payable matured and were paid off at face value for cash.
4. A cash dividend of $43,900 was declared and paid during the year.

Instructions

Cash from operations $184,350

Prepare a statement of cash flows using the indirect method.

Prepare a statement of cash flows—direct method.

(LO 6)

Cash from operations $184,350

*P13-10A Data for Sinjh Inc. are presented in P13-9A. Further analysis reveals that accounts payable pertain to merchandise creditors.

Instructions

Prepare a statement of cash flows for Sinjh Inc. using the direct method.

Prepare a statement of cash flows—indirect method.

(LO 3)

P13-11A The comparative balance sheets for Strackman Lux Company as of December 31 are presented below.

Strackman Lux Company
Comparative Balance Sheets
December 31

Assets	2014	2013
Cash	$ 59,520	$ 45,000
Accounts receivable	44,000	62,000
Inventory	154,550	142,000
Prepaid expenses	15,280	21,000
Land	145,000	130,000
Buildings	200,000	200,000
Accumulated depreciation—buildings	(60,000)	(40,000)
Equipment	228,000	155,000
Accumulated depreciation—equipment	(45,000)	(35,000)
Total	$741,350	$680,000

Liabilities and Stockholders' Equity	2014	2013
Accounts payable	$ 46,350	$ 40,000
Bonds payable	300,000	300,000
Common stock, $1 par	195,000	160,000
Retained earnings	200,000	180,000
Total	$741,350	$680,000

Additional information:

1. Operating expenses include depreciation expense of $40,000.
2. Land was sold for cash at book value of $20,000.

3. Cash dividends of $25,000 were paid.
4. Net income for 2014 was $45,000.
5. Equipment was purchased for $95,000 cash. In addition, equipment costing $22,000 with a book value of $12,000 was sold for $6,000 cash.
6. Issued 35,000 shares of $1 par value common stock in exchange for land with a fair value of $35,000.

Cash from operations $108,520

Instructions

Prepare a statement of cash flows for the year ended December 31, 2014, using the indirect method.

*P13-12A Condensed financial data of Jhutti Company appear below.

Prepare a worksheet—indirect method.

(LO 5)

Jhutti Company
Comparative Balance Sheets
December 31

Assets	2014	2013
Cash	$ 90,300	$ 47,250
Accounts receivable	80,900	57,000
Inventory	121,900	102,650
Investments	84,000	87,000
Equipment	250,000	205,000
Accumulated depreciation—equipment	(46,600)	(40,000)
	$580,500	$458,900

Liabilities and Stockholders' Equity		
Accounts payable	$ 53,400	$ 48,280
Accrued expenses payable	12,100	18,830
Bonds payable	100,000	70,000
Common stock	240,000	200,000
Retained earnings	175,000	121,790
	$580,500	$458,900

Jhutti Company
Income Statement
For the Year Ended December 31, 2014

Sales revenue	$297,500	
Gain on disposal of plant assets	8,550	$306,050
Less:		
Cost of goods sold	99,460	
Operating expenses (excluding depreciation expense)	14,670	
Depreciation expense	47,900	
Income tax expense	7,270	
Interest expense	2,940	172,240
Net income		$133,810

Additional information:

1. Equipment costing $92,000 was purchased for cash during the year.
2. Investments were sold at cost.
3. Equipment costing $47,000 was sold for $14,250, resulting in gain of $8,550.
4. A cash dividend of $80,600 was declared and paid during the year.

Instructions

Prepare a worksheet for the statement of cash flows using the indirect method. Enter the reconciling items directly in the worksheet columns, using letters to cross-reference each entry.

Reconciling items total
$580,910

Distinguish among operating, investing, and financing activities.

(LO 2)

P13-1B You are provided with the following transactions that took place during a recent fiscal year.

Transaction	Statement of Cash Flow Activity Affected	Cash Inflow, Outflow, or No Effect?
(a) Recorded depreciation expense on the plant assets.		
(b) Incurred a loss on disposal of plant assets.		
(c) Acquired a building by paying cash.		
(d) Made principal repayments on a mortgage.		
(e) Issued common stock.		
(f) Purchased shares of another company to be held as a long-term equity investment.		
(g) Paid cash dividends to common stockholders.		
(h) Sold inventory on credit. The company uses a perpetual inventory system.		
(i) Purchased inventory on credit.		
(j) Paid wages to employees.		

Instructions

Complete the table indicating whether each item (1) affects operating (O) activities, investing (I) activities, financing (F) activities, or is a noncash (NC) transaction reported in a separate schedule; and (2) represents a cash inflow or cash outflow or has no cash flow effect. Assume use of the indirect approach.

Determine cash flow effects of changes in plant asset accounts.

(LO 3)

P13-2B The following selected account balances relate to the plant asset accounts of Raji Inc. at year-end.

	2014	2013
Accumulated depreciation—buildings	$337,500	$300,000
Accumulated depreciation—equipment	145,000	93,000
Buildings	750,000	750,000
Depreciation expense	101,500	85,500
Equipment	300,000	250,000
Land	100,000	70,000
Loss on disposal of plant assets	7,000	0

Additional information:

1. Raji purchased $90,000 of equipment and $30,000 of land for cash in 2014.
2. Raji also sold equipment in 2014.
3. Depreciation expense in 2014 was $37,500 on building and $64,000 on equipment.

Instructions

(a) Cash proceeds $21,000

(a) Determine the amounts of any cash inflows or outflows related to the plant asset accounts in 2014.
(b) Indicate where each of the cash inflows or outflows identified in (a) would be classified on the statement of cash flows.

Prepare the operating activities section—indirect method.

(LO 3)

P13-3B The income statement of Asquith Company is presented on the next page.

Additional information:

1. Accounts receivable decreased $230,000 during the year, and inventory increased $120,000.
2. Prepaid expenses increased $125,000 during the year.

3. Accounts payable to merchandise suppliers increased $50,000 during the year.
4. Accrued expenses payable increased $155,000 during the year.

Asquith Company
Income Statement
For the Year Ended December 31, 2014

Service revenue		$5,250,000
Cost of goods sold		
Beginning inventory	$1,780,000	
Purchases	3,430,000	
Goods available for sale	5,210,000	
Ending inventory	1,900,000	
Total cost of goods sold		3,310,000
Gross profit		1,940,000
Operating expenses		
Depreciation expense	95,000	
Amortization expense	20,000	
Other expenses	945,000	1,060,000
Net income		$ 880,000

Instructions

Prepare the operating activities section of the statement of cash flows for the year ended December 31, 2014, for Asquith Company, using the indirect method.

Cash from operations $1,185,000

*P13-4B Data for Asquith Company are presented in P13-3B.

Prepare the operating activities section—direct method.

(LO 6)

Instructions

Prepare the operating activities section of the statement of cash flows using the direct method.

Cash from operations $1,185,000

P13-5B The income statement of Anne Droid Inc. reported the following condensed information.

Prepare the operating activities section—indirect method.

(LO 3)

Anne Droid Inc.
Income Statement
For the Year Ended December 31, 2014

Service revenue	$551,000
Operating expenses	400,000
Income from operations	151,000
Income tax expense	36,000
Net income	$115,000

Anne Droid's balance sheet contained these comparative data at December 31.

	2014	2013
Accounts receivable	$55,000	$70,000
Accounts payable	40,000	51,000
Income taxes payable	12,000	4,000

Anne Droid has no depreciable assets. Accounts payable pertain to operating expenses.

Instructions

Prepare the operating activities section of the statement of cash flows using the indirect method.

Cash from operations $127,000

*P13-6B Data for Anne Droid Inc. are presented in P13-5B.

Prepare the operating activities section—direct method.

(LO 6)

Instructions

Prepare the operating activities section of the statement of cash flows using the direct method.

Cash from operations $127,000

Prepare a statement of cash flows—indirect method, and compute free cash flow.

(LO 3, 4)

P13-7B Presented below are the financial statements of Rocastle Company.

Rocastle Company
Comparative Balance Sheets
December 31

Assets		2014		2013
Cash		$ 18,000		$ 33,000
Accounts receivable		25,000		14,000
Inventory		45,000		25,000
Equipment	$ 70,000		$ 78,000	
Less: Accumulated depreciation— equipment	(27,000)	43,000	(24,000)	54,000
Total		$131,000		$126,000

Liabilities and Stockholders' Equity		2014		2013
Accounts payable		$ 31,000		$ 43,000
Income taxes payable		24,000		20,000
Bonds payable		20,000		10,000
Common stock		25,000		25,000
Retained earnings		31,000		28,000
Total		$131,000		$126,000

Rocastle Company
Income Statement
For the Year Ended December 31, 2014

Sales revenue	$286,000
Cost of goods sold	204,000
Gross profit	82,000
Operating expenses	37,000
Income from operations	45,000
Interest expense	7,000
Income before income taxes	38,000
Income tax expense	10,000
Net income	$ 28,000

Additional data:

1. Depreciation expense was $6,000.
2. Dividends of $25,000 were declared and paid.
3. During the year, equipment was sold for $12,000 cash. This equipment cost $15,000 originally and had accumulated depreciation of $3,000 at the time of sale.
4. Additional equipment was purchased for $7,000 cash.

Instructions

(a) Cash from operations
    $(5,000)

(a) Prepare a statement of cash flows using the indirect method.
(b) Compute free cash flow.

Prepare a statement of cash flows—direct method, and compute free cash flow.

(LO 4, 6)

*P13-8B Data for Rocastle Company are presented in P13-7B. Further analysis reveals the following.

1. Accounts payable pertains to merchandise creditors.
2. All operating expenses except for depreciation are paid in cash.
3. All depreciation expense is in the operating expenses.
4. All sales and purchases are on account.

Instructions

(a) Cash from operations
    $(5,000)

(a) Prepare a statement of cash flows using the direct method.
(b) Compute free cash flow.

P13-9B Condensed financial data of Minnie Hooper Company are shown below.

Prepare a statement of cash flows—indirect method.

(LO 3)

Minnie Hooper Company
Comparative Balance Sheets
December 31

Assets	2014	2013
Cash	$ 93,600	$ 33,400
Accounts receivable	63,200	37,000
Inventory	124,500	102,650
Investments	79,500	107,000
Plant assets	318,000	205,000
Accumulated depreciation	(44,000)	(40,000)
Total	$634,800	$445,050

Liabilities and Stockholders' Equity		
Accounts payable	$ 56,600	$ 48,280
Accrued expenses payable	15,100	18,830
Bonds payable	140,000	70,000
Common stock	250,000	200,000
Retained earnings	173,100	107,940
Total	$634,800	$445,050

Minnie Hooper Company
Income Statement
For the Year Ended December 31, 2014

Sales revenue		$297,500
Less:		
Cost of goods sold	$99,460	
Operating expenses, excluding depreciation expense	19,670	
Depreciation expense	25,000	
Loss on disposal of plant assets	5,000	
Income tax expense	37,270	
Interest expense	2,940	189,340
Net income		$108,160

Additional information:

1. New plant assets costing $149,000 were purchased for cash during the year.
2. Investments were sold at cost.
3. Plant assets costing $36,000 were sold for $10,000, resulting in a loss of $5,000.
4. A cash dividend of $43,000 was declared and paid during the year.

Instructions
Prepare a statement of cash flows using the indirect method.

Cash from operations $94,700

*P13-10B Data for Minnie Hooper Company are presented in P13-9B. Further analysis reveals that accounts payable pertain to merchandise creditors.

Prepare a statement of cash flows—direct method.

(LO 6)

Instructions
Prepare a statement of cash flows for Minnie Hooper Company using the direct method.

Cash from operations $94,700

P13-11B Presented on the next page are the comparative balance sheets for Vernet Company at December 31.

Prepare a statement of cash flows—indirect method.

(LO 3)

Vernet Company
Comparative Balance Sheets
December 31

Assets	2014	2013
Cash	$ 41,460	$ 57,000
Accounts receivable	77,000	64,000
Inventory	170,000	140,000
Prepaid expenses	12,140	16,540
Land	140,000	150,000
Buildings	250,000	250,000
Accumulated depreciation—buildings	(70,000)	(50,000)
Equipment	215,000	175,000
Accumulated depreciation—equipment	(70,000)	(42,000)
Total	$765,600	$760,540

Liabilities and Stockholders' Equity		
Accounts payable	$ 58,000	$ 45,000
Bonds payable	265,000	265,000
Common stock, $1 par	275,000	250,000
Retained earnings	167,600	200,540
Total	$765,600	$760,540

Additional information:

1. Operating expenses include depreciation expense $57,000 and charges from prepaid expenses of $4,400.
2. Land was sold for cash at cost for $35,000
3. Cash dividends of $82,940 were paid.
4. Net income for 2014 was $50,000.
5. Equipment was purchased for $80,000 cash. In addition, equipment costing $40,000 with a book value of $31,000 was sold for $37,000 cash.
6. Issued 25,000 shares of $1 par value common stock in exchange for land with a fair value of $25,000.

Instructions

Cash from operations $75,400   Prepare a statement of cash flows for 2014 using the indirect method.

PROBLEMS: SET C

Visit the book's companion website, at **www.wiley.com/college/weygandt**, and choose the Student Companion site to access Problem Set C.

CONTINUING COOKIE CHRONICLE

(*Note:* This is a continuation of the Cookie Chronicle from Chapters 1–12.)

CCC13 Natalie has prepared the balance sheet and income statement of Cookie & Coffee Creations Inc. and would like you to prepare the statement of cash flows.

Go to the book's companion website, www.wiley.com/college/weygandt, to see the completion of this problem.

Broadening Your PERSPECTIVE

Financial Reporting and Analysis

Financial Reporting Problem: PepsiCo, Inc.

BYP13-1 Refer to the financial statements of PepsiCo Inc., presented in Appendix A, and answer the following questions.

(a) What was the amount of net cash provided by operating activities for the year ended December 25, 2010? For the year ended December 26, 2009?
(b) What was the amount of increase or decrease in cash and cash equivalents for the year ended December 25, 2010? For the year ended December 26, 2009?
(c) Which method of computing net cash provided by operating activities does PepsiCo use?
(d) From your analysis of the 2010 statement of cash flows, did the change in accounts and notes receivable require or provide cash? Did the change in inventories require or provide cash? Did the change in accounts payable and other current liabilities require or provide cash?
(e) What was the net outflow or inflow of cash from investing activities for the year ended December 25, 2010?
(f) What was the amount of interest paid in the year ended December 25, 2010? What was the amount of income taxes paid in the year ended December 25, 2010? (See Note 14.)

Comparative Analysis Problem: PepsiCo, Inc. vs. The Coca-Cola Company

BYP13-2 PepsiCo's financial statements are presented in Appendix A. Financial statements of The Coca-Cola Company are presented in Appendix B.

Instructions
(a) Based on the information contained in these financial statements, compute free cash flow for each company.
(b) What conclusions concerning the management of cash can be drawn from these data?

Real-World Focus

BYP13-3 Purpose: Learn about the SEC.

Address: **www.sec.gov/index.html,** or go to **www.wiley.com/college/weygandt**

From the SEC homepage, choose **About the SEC.**

Instructions
Answer the following questions.
(a) How many enforcement actions does the SEC take each year against securities law violators? What are typical infractions?
(b) After the Depression, Congress passed the Securities Acts of 1933 and 1934 to improve investor confidence in the markets. What two "common sense" notions are these laws based on?
(c) Who was the President of the United States at the time of the creation of the SEC? Who was the first SEC Chairperson?

BYP13-4 Purpose: Use the Internet to view SEC filings.

Address: **biz.yahoo.com/i/** or go to **www.wiley.com/college/weygandt**

Steps:
1. Type in a company name.
2. Choose **Profile.**
3. Choose **SEC Filings**. (This will take you to Yahoo-Edgar Online.)

Instructions
Answer the following questions.

(a) What company did you select?
(b) Which filing is the most recent? What is the date?
(c) What other recent SEC filings are available for your viewing?

Critical Thinking

Decision-Making Across the Organization

BYP13-5 Norman Roads and Sara Mesa are examining the following statement of cash flows for Del Carpio Company for the year ended January 31, 2014.

Del Carpio Company
Statement of Cash Flows
For the Year Ended January 31, 2014

Sources of cash	
From sales of merchandise	$350,000
From sale of capital stock	405,000
From sale of investment (purchased below)	85,000
From depreciation	75,000
From issuance of note for truck	25,000
From interest on investments	6,000
Total sources of cash	946,000
Uses of cash	
For purchase of fixtures and equipment	320,000
For merchandise purchased for resale	245,000
For operating expenses (including depreciation)	160,000
For purchase of investment	75,000
For purchase of truck by issuance of note	25,000
For purchase of treasury stock	15,000
For interest on note payable	5,000
Total uses of cash	845,000
Net increase in cash	$101,000

Norman claims that Del Carpio's statement of cash flows is an excellent portrayal of a superb first year with cash increasing $101,000. Sara replies that it was not a superb first year. Rather, she says, the year was an operating failure, the statement is presented incorrectly, and $101,000 is not the actual increase in cash. The cash balance at the beginning of the year was $140,000.

Instructions
With the class divided into groups, answer the following.

(a) Using the data provided, prepare a statement of cash flows in proper form using the indirect method. The only noncash items in the income statement are depreciation and the gain from the sale of the investment.
(b) With whom do you agree, Norman or Sara? Explain your position.

Communication Activity

BYP13-6 Bart Sampson, the owner-president of Computer Services Company, is unfamiliar with the statement of cash flows that you, as his accountant, prepared. He asks for further explanation.

Instructions
Write him a brief memo explaining the form and content of the statement of cash flows as shown in Illustration 13-13 (pages 659–660).

Ethics Case

BYP13-7 Babbit Corp. is a medium-sized wholesaler of automotive parts. It has 10 stockholders who have been paid a total of $1 million in cash dividends for 8 consecutive years. The board's policy requires that, for this dividend to be declared, net cash provided by operating activities as reported in Babbit's current year's statement of cash flows must exceed $1 million. President and CEO Milton Williams's job is secure so long as he produces annual operating cash flows to support the usual dividend.

At the end of the current year, controller Jerry Roberts presents president Milton Williams with some disappointing news: The net cash provided by operating activities is calculated by the indirect method to be only $970,000. The president says to Jerry, "We must get that amount above $1 million. Isn't there some way to increase operating cash flow by another $30,000?" Jerry answers, "These figures were prepared by my assistant. I'll go back to my office and see what I can do." The president replies, "I know you won't let me down, Jerry."

Upon close scrutiny of the statement of cash flows, Jerry concludes that he can get the operating cash flows above $1 million by reclassifying a $60,000, 2-year note payable listed in the financing activities section as "Proceeds from bank loan—$60,000." He will report the note instead as "Increase in payables—$60,000" and treat it as an adjustment of net income in the operating activities section. He returns to the president, saying, "You can tell the board to declare their usual dividend. Our net cash flow provided by operating activities is $1,030,000." "Good man, Jerry! I knew I could count on you," exults the president.

Instructions

(a) Who are the stakeholders in this situation?
(b) Was there anything unethical about the president's actions? Was there anything unethical about the controller's actions?
(c) Are the board members or anyone else likely to discover the misclassification?

All About You

BYP13-8 In this chapter, you learned that companies prepare a statement of cash flows in order to keep track of their sources and uses of cash and to help them plan for their future cash needs. Planning for your own short- and long-term cash needs is every bit as important as it is for a company.

Instructions

Read the article ("Financial Uh-Oh? No Problem") provided at **www.fool.com/personal-finance/saving/index.aspx**, and answer the following questions.

(a) Describe the three factors that determine how much money you should set aside for short-term needs.
(b) How many months of living expenses does the article suggest to set aside?
(c) Estimate how much you should set aside based upon your current situation. Are you closer to Cliff's scenario or to Prudence's?

FASB Codification Activity

BYP13-9 If your school has a subscription to the FASB Codification, go to *http://aaahq.org/ascLogin.cfm* to log in and prepare response to the following. Use the Master Glossary to determine the proper definitions.

(a) What are cash equivalents?
(b) What are financing activities?
(c) What are investing activities?
(d) What are operating activities?
(e) What is the primary objective for the statement of cash flows? Is working capital the basis for meeting this objective?
(f) Do companies need to disclose information about investing and financing activities that do not affect cash receipts or cash payments? If so, how should such information be disclosed?

Answers to Chapter Questions

Answers to Insight and Accounting Across the Organization Questions

p. 648 Net *What*? Q: In general, why do differences exist between net income and net cash provided by operating activities? **A:** The differences are explained by differences in the timing of the reporting of revenues and expenses under accrual accounting versus cash. Under accrual accounting, companies report revenues when earned, even if cash hasn't been received, and they report expenses when incurred, even if cash hasn't been paid.

p. 657 Cash Flow Isn't Always What It Seems Q: For what reasons might managers at WorldCom and at Dynegy take the actions noted above? **A:** Analysts increasingly use cash flow-based measures of income, such as cash flow provided by operations, in addition to net income. More investors now focus on cash flow from operations, and some compensation contracts now have bonuses tied to cash flow numbers. Thus, some managers have taken actions that artificially increase cash flow from operations.

Answers to Self-Test Questions

1. c **2.** a **3.** b **4.** a **5.** c **6.** d **7.** b **8.** c **9.** d ($132,000 + $10,000 + $6,000 − $12,000)
10. b **11.** b ($200,000 + $40,000 − $10,000 + $20,000 − $30,000) **12.** a ($100,000 + $50,000 − $30,000) **13.** b ($100,000 + $60,000 − $30,000) **14.** a **15.** d *16. b *17. b *18. c [$129,000 + ($44,000 − $42,000)] *19. d

A Look at IFRS

As in GAAP, the statement of cash flows is a required statement for IFRS. In addition, the content and presentation of an IFRS statement of cash flows is similar to the one used for GAAP. However, the disclosure requirements related to the statement of cash flows are more extensive under GAAP. *IAS 7* ("Cash Flow Statements") provides the overall IFRS requirements for cash flow information.

Key Points

- Companies preparing financial statements under IFRS must prepare a statement of cash flows as an integral part of the financial statements.

- Both IFRS and GAAP require that the statement of cash flows should have three major sections—operating, investing, and financing—along with changes in cash and cash equivalents.

- Similar to GAAP, the cash flow statement can be prepared using either the indirect or direct method under IFRS. In both U.S. and international settings, companies choose for the most part to use the indirect method for reporting net cash flows from operating activities.

- The definition of cash equivalents used in IFRS is similar to that used in GAAP. A major difference is that in certain situations, bank overdrafts are considered part of cash and cash equivalents under IFRS (which is not the case in GAAP). Under GAAP, bank overdrafts are classified as financing activities in the statement of cash flows and are reported as liabilities on the balance sheet.

- IFRS requires that noncash investing and financing activities be excluded from the statement of cash flows. Instead, these noncash activities should be reported elsewhere. This requirement is interpreted to mean that noncash investing and financing activities should be disclosed in the notes to the financial statements instead of in the financial statements. Under GAAP, companies may present this information on the face of the cash flow statement.

- One area where there can be substantial differences between IFRS and GAAP relates to the classification of interest, dividends, and taxes. The following table indicates the differences between the two approaches.

Item	IFRS	GAAP
Interest paid	Operating or financing	Operating
Interest received	Operating or investing	Operating
Dividends paid	Operating or financing	Financing
Dividends received	Operating or investing	Operating
Taxes paid	Operating—unless specific identification with financing or investing activity	Operating

- Under IFRS, some companies present the operating section in a single line item, with a full reconciliation provided in the notes to the financial statements. This presentation is not seen under GAAP.

- Similar to GAAP, under IFRS companies must disclose the amount of taxes and interest paid. Under GAAP, companies disclose this in the notes to the financial statements. Under IFRS, some companies disclose this information in the notes, but others provide individual line items on the face of the statement. In order to provide this information on the face of the statement, companies first add back the amount of interest expense and tax expense (similar to adding back depreciation expense) and then further down the statement they subtract the cash amount paid for interest and taxes. This treatment can be seen in the statement of cash flows provided for Zetar in Appendix C.

Looking to the Future

Presently, the FASB and the IASB are involved in a joint project on the presentation and organization of information in the financial statements. One interesting approach, revealed in a published proposal from that project, is that in the future the income statement and balance sheet would adopt headings similar to those of the statement of cash flows. That is, the income statement and balance sheet would be broken into operating, investing, and financing sections.

With respect to the cash flow statement specifically, the notion of *cash equivalents* will probably not be retained. That is, cash equivalents will not be combined with cash but instead will be reported as a form of highly liquid, low-risk investment. The definition of cash in the existing literature would be retained, and the statement of cash flows would present information on changes in cash only. In addition, the FASB favors presentation of operating cash flows using the direct method only. However, the majority of IASB members express a preference for not requiring use of the direct method of reporting operating cash flows. The two Boards will have to resolve their differences in this area in order to issue a converged standard for the statement of cash flows.

IFRS Practice

IFRS Self-Test Questions

1. Under IFRS, interest paid can be reported as:
   - (a) only a financing element.
   - (b) a financing element or an investing element.
   - (c) a financing element or an operating element.
   - (d) only an operating element.

2. IFRS requires that noncash items:
   - (a) be reported in the section to which they relate, that is, a noncash investing activity would be reported in the investing section.
   - (b) be disclosed in the notes to the financial statements.
   - (c) do not need to be reported.
   - (d) be treated in a fashion similar to cash equivalents.

3. In the future, it appears likely that:
   (a) the income statement and balance sheet will have headings of operating, investing, and financing, much like the statement of cash flows.
   (b) cash and cash equivalents will be combined in a single line item.
   (c) the IASB will not allow companies to use the direct approach to the statement of cash flows.
   (d) None of the above.

4. Under IFRS:
   (a) taxes are always treated as an operating item.
   (b) the income statement uses the headings operating, investing, and financing.
   (c) dividends received can be either an operating or investing item.
   (d) dividends paid can be either an operating or investing item.

5. Which of the following is *correct*?
   (a) Under IFRS, the statement of cash flows is optional.
   (b) IFRS requires use of the direct approach in preparing the statement of cash flows.
   (c) The majority of companies following GAAP and the majority following IFRS employ the indirect approach to the statement of cash flows.
   (d) Cash and cash equivalents are reported as separate line items under IFRS.

IFRS Exercises

IFRS13-1 Discuss the differences that exist in the treatment of bank overdrafts under GAAP and IFRS.

IFRS13-2 Describe the treatment of each of the following items under IFRS versus GAAP.
(a) Interest paid.
(b) Interest received.
(c) Dividends paid.
(d) Dividends received.

IFRS13-3 Explain how the treatment of cash equivalents will probably change in the future.

International Financial Reporting Problem: Zetar plc

IFRS13-4 The financial statements of Zetar plc are presented in Appendix C. The company's complete annual report, including the notes to its financial statements, is available at **www.zetarplc.com**.

Instructions

Use the company's annual report to answer the following questions.

(a) In which section (operating, investing, or financing) does Zetar report interest paid (finance cost)?

(b) Explain why the amount that Zetar reports for cash and cash equivalents in its statement of cash flows is negative.

(c) If Zetar reported under GAAP rather than IFRS, how would its treatment of bank overdrafts differ?

(d) Zetar's statement of cash flows reports negative "net movement in working capital" in 2010 of £179 (in thousands). According to the statement of cash flows, what were the components of this "net movement"?

Answers to IFRS Self-Test Questions

1. c   2. b   3. a   4. c   5. c

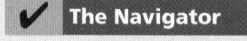
✔ **The Navigator**

✔ Remember to go back to The Navigator box on the chapter opening page and check off your completed work.

Chapter 14

Financial Statement Analysis

It Pays to Be Patient

A recent issue of *Forbes* magazine listed Warren Buffett as the richest person in the world. His estimated wealth was $62 billion, give or take a few million. How much is $62 billion? If you invested $62 billion in an investment earning just 4%, you could spend $6.8 million per day—every day—forever. How did Mr. Buffett amass this wealth? Through careful investing.

However, if you think you might want to follow Mr. Buffett's example and transform your humble nest-egg into a mountain of cash, be warned: His techniques have been widely circulated and emulated, but never practiced with the same degree of success.

Mr. Buffett epitomizes a "value investor." To this day, he applies the same basic techniques he learned in the 1950s from the great value investor Benjamin Graham. That means he spends his time looking for companies that have good long-term potential but are currently underpriced. He invests in companies that have low exposure to debt and that reinvest their earnings for future growth. He does not get caught up in fads or the latest trend. Instead, he looks for companies in industries with sound economics and ones that have high returns on stockholders' equity. He looks for steady earnings trends and high margins.

Mr. Buffett sat out on the dot-com mania in the 1990s. When other investors put lots of money into

The Navigator

- Scan Learning Objectives
- Read Feature Story
- Read Preview
- Read Text and answer **DO IT!** p. 716
  - p. 729 ▢ p. 734 ▢ p. 736
- Work Comprehensive **DO IT!** p. 737
- Review Summary of Learning Objectives
- Answer Self-Test Questions
- Complete Assignments
- Go to **WileyPLUS** for practice and tutorials
- Read A Look at IFRS p. 760

Learning Objectives

After studying this chapter, you should be able to:

1 Discuss the need for comparative analysis.

2 Identify the tools of financial statement analysis.

3 Explain and apply horizontal analysis.

4 Describe and apply vertical analysis.

5 Identify and compute ratios used in analyzing a firm's liquidity, profitability, and solvency.

6 Understand the concept of earning power, and how irregular items are presented.

7 Understand the concept of quality of earnings.

The Navigator

fledgling high-tech firms, Mr. Buffett did not bite. He simply did not find any dot-com companies that met his criteria. Of course, he didn't get to enjoy the stock price boom on the way up. On the other hand, he didn't have to ride the price back down to Earth either. Instead, when the dot-com bubble burst, and nearly everyone else was suffering from investment shock, he swooped in and scooped up deals on companies that he had been following for years.

So, how does Mr. Buffett spend his money? Basically, he doesn't! He still lives in the same house that he purchased in Omaha, Nebraska, in 1958 for $31,500. He still drives his own car (a Cadillac DTS). And in case you were thinking that his kids are riding the road to Easy Street, think again. Mr. Buffett has committed to giving virtually all of his money to charity before he dies.

So, given that neither you nor anyone else will be inheriting Mr. Buffett's riches, you should probably start honing your financial analysis skills. A good way for you to begin your career as a successful investor is to master the fundamentals of financial analysis discussed in this chapter.

 **The Navigator**

Preview of **Chapter 14**

We can learn an important lesson from Warren Buffett: Study companies carefully if you wish to invest. Do not get caught up in fads but instead find companies that are financially healthy. Using some of the basic decision tools presented in this book, you can perform a rudimentary analysis on any U.S. company and draw basic conclusions about its financial health. Although it would not be wise for you to bet your life savings on a company's stock relying solely on your current level of knowledge, we strongly encourage you to practice your new skills wherever possible. Only with practice will you improve your ability to interpret financial numbers.

Before unleashing you on the world of high finance, we will present a few more important concepts and techniques, as well as provide you with one more comprehensive review of corporate financial statements. We use all of the decision tools presented in this text to analyze a single company—J.C. Penney Company, one of the country's oldest and largest retail store chains.

The content and organization of Chapter 14 are as follows.

FINANCIAL STATEMENT ANALYSIS				
Basics of Financial Statement Analysis	**Horizontal and Vertical Analysis**	**Ratio Analysis**	**Earning Power and Irregular Items**	**Quality of Earnings**
• Need for comparative analysis • Tools of analysis	• Balance sheet • Income statement • Retained earnings statement	• Liquidity • Profitability • Solvency • Summary	• Discontinued operations • Extraordinary items • Changes in accounting principle • Comprehensive income	• Alternative accounting methods • Pro forma income • Improper recognition

✔ **The Navigator**

Basics of Financial Statement Analysis

Analyzing financial statements involves evaluating three characteristics: a company's liquidity, profitability, and solvency. A **short-term creditor**, such as a bank, is primarily interested in liquidity—the ability of the borrower to pay obligations when they come due. The liquidity of the borrower is extremely important in evaluating the safety of a loan. A **long-term creditor**, such as a bondholder, looks to profitability and solvency measures that indicate the company's ability to survive over a long period of time. Long-term creditors consider such measures as the amount of debt in the company's capital structure and its ability to meet interest payments. Similarly, **stockholders** look at the profitability and solvency of the company. They want to assess the likelihood of dividends and the growth potential of the stock.

Need for Comparative Analysis

LEARNING OBJECTIVE 1

Discuss the need for comparative analysis.

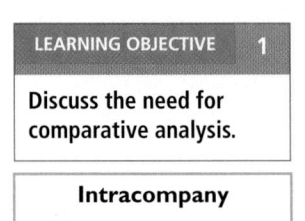

Intracompany

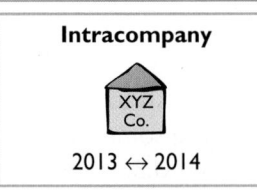

XYZ Co.

2013 ↔ 2014

Industry Averages

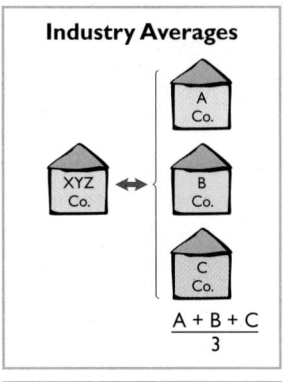

XYZ Co. ↔ A Co. / B Co. / C Co.

$\dfrac{A + B + C}{3}$

Intercompany

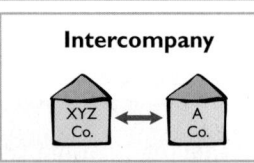

XYZ Co. ↔ A Co.

LEARNING OBJECTIVE 2

Identify the tools of financial statement analysis.

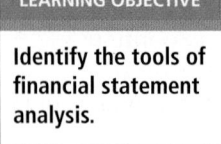

Every item reported in a financial statement has significance. When J.C. Penney Company, Inc. reports cash and cash equivalents of $3 billion on its balance sheet, we know the company had that amount of cash on the balance sheet date. But, we do not know whether the amount represents an increase over prior years, or whether it is adequate in relation to the company's need for cash. To obtain such information, we need to compare the amount of cash with other financial statement data.

Comparisons can be made on a number of different bases. Three are illustrated in this chapter.

1. **Intracompany basis.** Comparisons within a company are often useful to detect changes in financial relationships and significant trends. For example, a comparison of J.C. Penney's current year's cash amount with the prior year's cash amount shows either an increase or a decrease. Likewise, a comparison of J.C. Penney's year-end cash amount with the amount of its total assets at year-end shows the proportion of total assets in the form of cash.

2. **Industry averages.** Comparisons with industry averages provide information about a company's relative position within the industry. For example, financial statement readers can compare J.C. Penney's financial data with the averages for its industry compiled by financial rating organizations such as Dun & Bradstreet, Moody's, and Standard & Poor's, or with information provided on the Internet by organizations such as Yahoo! on its financial site.

3. **Intercompany basis.** Comparisons with other companies provide insight into a company's competitive position. For example, investors can compare J.C. Penney's total sales for the year with the total sales of its competitors in retail, such as Sears.

Tools of Analysis

We use various tools to evaluate the significance of financial statement data. Three commonly used tools are as follows.

- **Horizontal analysis** evaluates a series of financial statement data over a period of time.
- **Vertical analysis** evaluates financial statement data by expressing each item in a financial statement as a percentage of a base amount.
- **Ratio analysis** expresses the relationship among selected items of financial statement data.

Horizontal analysis is used primarily in intracompany comparisons. Two features in published financial statements and annual report information facilitate this type of comparison. First, each of the basic financial statements presents comparative financial data for a minimum of two years. Second, a summary of selected financial data is presented for a series of five to 10 years or more. *Vertical analysis* is used in both intra- and intercompany comparisons. *Ratio analysis* is used in all three types of comparisons. In the following sections, we explain and illustrate each of the three types of analysis.

Horizontal Analysis

Horizontal analysis, also called **trend analysis**, is a technique for evaluating a series of financial statement data over a period of time. Its purpose is to determine the increase or decrease that has taken place. This change may be expressed as either an amount or a percentage. For example, Illustration 14-1 shows recent net sales figures of J.C. Penney Company.

LEARNING OBJECTIVE 3

Explain and apply horizontal analysis.

J.C. Penney Company
Net Sales (In millions)

2009	2008	2007
$17,556	$18,486	$19,860

Illustration 14-1
J.C. Penney Company's net sales

If we assume that 2007 is the base year, we can measure all percentage increases or decreases from this base period amount as follows.

$$\text{Change Since Base Period} = \frac{\text{Current Year Amount} - \text{Base Year Amount}}{\text{Base Year Amount}}$$

Illustration 14-2
Formula for horizontal analysis of changes since base period

For example, we can determine that net sales for J.C. Penney decreased from 2007 to 2008 approximately 6.9% [($18,486 − $19,860) ÷ $19,860]. Similarly, we can determine that net sales decreased from 2007 to 2009 approximately 11.6% [($17,556 − $19,860) ÷ $19,860].

Alternatively, we can express current year sales as a percentage of the base period. We do this by dividing the current year amount by the base year amount, as shown below.

$$\text{Current Results in Relation to Base Period} = \frac{\text{Current Year Amount}}{\text{Base Year Amount}}$$

Illustration 14-3
Formula for horizontal analysis of current year in relation to base year

Illustration 14-4 presents this analysis for J.C. Penney for a three-year period using 2007 as the base period.

J.C. Penney Company
Net Sales (in millions)
in Relation to Base Period 2007

2009	2008	2007
$17,556	$18,486	$19,860
88.4%	93.1%	100%

Illustration 14-4
Horizontal analysis of J.C. Penney Company's net sales in relation to base period

Balance Sheet

To further illustrate horizontal analysis, we will use the financial statements of Quality Department Store Inc., a fictional retailer. Illustration 14-5 presents a horizontal analysis of its two-year condensed balance sheets, showing dollar and percentage changes.

Illustration 14-5
Horizontal analysis of balance sheets

Quality Department Store Inc. Condensed Balance Sheets December 31				
			Increase or (Decrease) during 2009	
	2009	**2008**	**Amount**	**Percent**
Assets				
Current assets	$1,020,000	$ 945,000	$ 75,000	7.9%
Plant assets (net)	800,000	632,500	167,500	26.5%
Intangible assets	15,000	17,500	(2,500)	(14.3%)
Total assets	$1,835,000	$1,595,000	$240,000	15.0%
Liabilities				
Current liabilities	$ 344,500	$ 303,000	$ 41,500	13.7%
Long-term liabilities	487,500	497,000	(9,500)	(1.9%)
Total liabilities	832,000	800,000	32,000	4.0%
Stockholders' Equity				
Common stock, $1 par	275,400	270,000	5,400	2.0%
Retained earnings	727,600	525,000	202,600	38.6%
Total stockholders' equity	1,003,000	795,000	208,000	26.2%
Total liabilities and stockholders' equity	$1,835,000	$1,595,000	$240,000	15.0%

The comparative balance sheets in Illustration 14-5 show that a number of significant changes have occurred in Quality Department Store's financial structure from 2008 to 2009:

- In the assets section, plant assets (net) increased $167,500, or 26.5%.

- In the liabilities section, current liabilities increased $41,500, or 13.7%.

- In the stockholders' equity section, retained earnings increased $202,600, or 38.6%.

These changes suggest that the company expanded its asset base during 2009 and **financed this expansion primarily by retaining income** rather than assuming additional long-term debt.

Income Statement

Illustration 14-6 presents a horizontal analysis of the two-year condensed income statements of Quality Department Store Inc. for the years 2009 and 2008. Horizontal analysis of the income statements shows the following changes:

- Net sales increased $260,000, or 14.2% ($260,000 ÷ $1,837,000).

- Cost of goods sold increased $141,000, or 12.4% ($141,000 ÷ $1,140,000).

- Total operating expenses increased $37,000, or 11.6% ($37,000 ÷ $320,000).

Overall, gross profit and net income were up substantially. Gross profit increased 17.1%, and net income, 26.5%. Quality's profit trend appears favorable.

Illustration 14-6
Horizontal analysis of income statements

Quality Department Store Inc. Condensed Income Statements For the Years Ended December 31				
			Increase or (Decrease) during 2009	
	2009	**2008**	**Amount**	**Percent**
Sales revenue	$2,195,000	$1,960,000	$235,000	12.0%
Sales returns and allowances	98,000	123,000	(25,000)	(20.3%)
Net sales	2,097,000	1,837,000	260,000	14.2%
Cost of goods sold	1,281,000	1,140,000	141,000	12.4%
Gross profit	816,000	697,000	119,000	17.1%
Selling expenses	253,000	211,500	41,500	19.6%
Administrative expenses	104,000	108,500	(4,500)	(4.1%)
Total operating expenses	357,000	320,000	37,000	11.6%
Income from operations	459,000	377,000	82,000	21.8%
Other revenues and gains				
Interest and dividends	9,000	11,000	(2,000)	(18.2%)
Other expenses and losses				
Interest expense	36,000	40,500	(4,500)	(11.1%)
Income before income taxes	432,000	347,500	84,500	24.3%
Income tax expense	168,200	139,000	29,200	21.0%
Net income	$ 263,800	$ 208,500	$ 55,300	26.5%

Helpful Hint
Note that though the amount column is additive (the total is $55,300), the percentage column is not additive (26.5% is not the column total). A separate percentage has been calculated for each item.

Retained Earnings Statement

Illustration 14-7 presents a horizontal analysis of Quality Department Store's comparative retained earnings statements. Analyzed horizontally, net income increased $55,300, or 26.5%, whereas dividends on the common stock increased only $1,200, or 2%. We saw in the horizontal analysis of the balance sheet that ending retained earnings increased 38.6%. As indicated earlier, the company retained a significant portion of net income to finance additional plant facilities.

Illustration 14-7
Horizontal analysis of retained earnings statements

Quality Department Store Inc. Retained Earnings Statements For the Years Ended December 31				
			Increase or (Decrease) during 2009	
	2009	**2008**	**Amount**	**Percent**
Retained earnings, Jan. 1	$525,000	$376,500	$148,500	39.4%
Add: Net income	263,800	208,500	55,300	26.5%
	788,800	585,000	203,800	
Deduct: Dividends	61,200	60,000	1,200	2.0%
Retained earnings, Dec. 31	$727,600	$525,000	$202,600	38.6%

Horizontal analysis of changes from period to period is relatively straightforward and is quite useful. But, complications can occur in making the computations. If an item has no value in a base year or preceding year but does have a value in the next year, we cannot compute a percentage change. Similarly, if a negative amount appears in the base or preceding period and a positive amount exists the following year (or vice versa), no percentage change can be computed.

> DO IT!

Horizontal Analysis

Summary financial information for Rosepatch Company is as follows.

	December 31, 2014	December 31, 2013
Current assets	$234,000	$180,000
Plant assets (net)	756,000	420,000
Total assets	$990,000	$600,000

Compute the amount and percentage changes in 2014 using horizontal analysis, assuming 2013 is the base year.

Solution

Action Plan

✔ Find the percentage change by dividing the amount of the increase by the 2013 amount (base year).

		Increase in 2014	
	Amount	Percent
Current assets	$ 54,000	30% [($234,000 − $180,000) ÷ $180,000]
Plant assets (net)	336,000	80% [($756,000 − $420,000) ÷ $420,000]
Total assets	$390,000	65% [($990,000 − $600,000) ÷ $600,000]

Related exercise material: **BE14-2, BE14-3, BE14-5, BE14-6, BE14-7, E14-1, E14-3, E14-4,** and **14-1.**

✔ **The Navigator**

Vertical Analysis

LEARNING OBJECTIVE 4

Describe and apply vertical analysis.

Vertical analysis, also called **common-size analysis**, is a technique that expresses each financial statement item as a percentage of a base amount. On a balance sheet we might say that current assets are 22% of total assets—*total assets* being the base amount. Or on an income statement, we might say that selling expenses are 16% of net sales—net sales being the base amount.

Balance Sheet

Illustration 14-8 presents the vertical analysis of Quality Department Store Inc.'s comparative balance sheets. The base for the asset items is **total assets**. The base for the liability and stockholders' equity items is **total liabilities and stockholders' equity**.

Vertical analysis shows the relative size of each category in the balance sheet. It also can show the **percentage change** in the individual asset, liability, and stockholders' equity items. For example, we can see that current assets decreased from 59.2% of total assets in 2008 to 55.6% in 2009 (even though the absolute dollar amount increased $75,000 in that time). Plant assets (net) have increased from 39.7% to 43.6% of total assets. Retained earnings have increased from 32.9% to 39.7% of total liabilities and stockholders' equity. These results reinforce the earlier observations that **Quality Department Store is choosing to finance its growth through retention of earnings rather than through issuing additional debt.**

Income Statement

Illustration 14-9 shows vertical analysis of Quality Department Store's income statements. Cost of goods sold as a percentage of net sales declined 1% (62.1% vs. 61.1%), and total operating expenses declined 0.4% (17.4% vs. 17.0%). As a result, it is not surprising to see net income as a percentage of net sales increase from 11.4% to 12.6%. Quality Department Store appears to be a profitable business that is becoming even more successful.

Illustration 14-8
Vertical analysis of balance
sheets

Quality Department Store Inc.
Condensed Balance Sheets
December 31

	2009		2008	
	Amount	Percent	Amount	Percent
Assets				
Current assets	$1,020,000	55.6%	$ 945,000	59.2%
Plant assets (net)	800,000	43.6%	632,500	39.7%
Intangible assets	15,000	0.8%	17,500	1.1%
Total assets	$1,835,000	100.0%	$1,595,000	100.0%
Liabilities				
Current liabilities	$ 344,500	18.8%	$ 303,000	19.0%
Long-term liabilities	487,500	26.5%	497,000	31.2%
Total liabilities	832,000	45.3%	800,000	50.2%
Stockholders' Equity				
Common stock, $1 par	275,400	15.0%	270,000	16.9%
Retained earnings	727,600	39.7%	525,000	32.9%
Total stockholders' equity	1,003,000	54.7%	795,000	49.8%
Total liabilities and stockholders' equity	$1,835,000	100.0%	$1,595,000	100.0%

Helpful Hint
The formula for calculating
these balance sheet
percentages is:
$$\frac{\text{Each item on B/S}}{\text{Total assets}} = \%$$

Quality Department Store Inc.
Condensed Income Statements
For the Years Ended December 31

Illustration 14-9
Vertical analysis of income
statements

	2009		2008	
	Amount	Percent	Amount	Percent
Sales revenue	$2,195,000	104.7%	$1,960,000	106.7%
Sales returns and allowances	98,000	4.7%	123,000	6.7%
Net sales	2,097,000	100.0%	1,837,000	100.0%
Cost of goods sold	1,281,000	61.1%	1,140,000	62.1%
Gross profit	816,000	38.9%	697,000	37.9%
Selling expenses	253,000	12.0%	211,500	11.5%
Administrative expenses	104,000	5.0%	108,500	5.9%
Total operating expenses	357,000	17.0%	320,000	17.4%
Income from operations	459,000	21.9%	377,000	20.5%
Other revenues and gains Interest and dividends	9,000	0.4%	11,000	0.6%
Other expenses and losses Interest expense	36,000	1.7%	40,500	2.2%
Income before income taxes	432,000	20.6%	347,500	18.9%
Income tax expense	168,200	8.0%	139,000	7.5%
Net income	$ 263,800	12.6%	$ 208,500	11.4%

Helpful Hint
The formula for calculating
these income statement
percentages is:
$$\frac{\text{Each item on I/S}}{\text{Net sales}} = \%$$

An associated benefit of vertical analysis is that it enables you to compare companies of different sizes. For example, Quality Department Store's main competitor is a J.C. Penney store in a nearby town. Using vertical analysis, we can compare the condensed income statements of Quality Department Store Inc.

(a small retail company) with J.C. Penney Company, Inc.[1] (a giant international retailer), as shown in Illustration 14-10.

Illustration 14-10
Intercompany income
statement comparison

	Condensed Income Statements (in thousands)			
	Quality Department Store Inc.		**J.C. Penney Company**	
	Dollars	**Percent**	**Dollars**	**Percent**
Net sales	$2,097	100.0%	$17,556,000	100.0%
Cost of goods sold	1,281	61.1%	10,646,000	60.6%
Gross profit	816	38.9%	6,910,000	39.4%
Selling and administrative expenses	357	17.0%	6,247,000	35.7%
Income from operations	459	21.9%	663,000	3.7%
Other expenses and revenues (including income taxes)	195	9.3%	412,000	2.3%
Net income	$ 264	12.6%	$ 251,000	1.4%

J.C. Penney's net sales are 8,372 times greater than the net sales of relatively tiny Quality Department Store. But vertical analysis eliminates this difference in size. The percentages show that Quality's and J.C. Penney's gross profit rates were comparable at 38.9% and 39.4%. However, the percentages related to income from operations were significantly different at 21.9% and 3.7%. This disparity can be attributed to Quality's selling and administrative expense percentage (17%) which is much lower than J.C. Penney's (35.7%). Although J.C. Penney earned net income more than 951 times larger than Quality's, J.C. Penney's net income as a **percentage of each sales dollar** (1.4%) is only 11% of Quality's (12.6%).

Ratio Analysis

LEARNING OBJECTIVE **5**

Identify and compute ratios used in analyzing a firm's liquidity, profitability, and solvency.

Ratio analysis expresses the relationship among selected items of financial statement data. A **ratio** expresses the mathematical relationship between one quantity and another. The relationship is expressed in terms of either a percentage, a rate, or a simple proportion. To illustrate, in 2010 Nike, Inc., had current assets of $10,959.2 million and current liabilities of $3,364.2 million. We can find the relationship between these two measures by dividing current assets by current liabilities. The alternative means of expression are:

Percentage: Current assets are 326% of current liabilities.
Rate: Current assets are 3.26 times current liabilities.
Proportion: The relationship of current assets to liabilities is 3.26:1.

To analyze the primary financial statements, we can use ratios to evaluate liquidity, profitability, and solvency. Illustration 14-11 describes these classifications.

Ratios can provide clues to underlying conditions that may not be apparent from individual financial statement components. However, a single ratio by itself is not very meaningful. Thus, in the discussion of ratios we will use the following types of comparisons.

1. **Intracompany comparisons** for two years for Quality Department Store.

2. **Industry average comparisons** based on median ratios for department stores.

3. **Intercompany comparisons** based on J.C. Penney Company as Quality Department Store's principal competitor.

---

[1]*2009 Annual Report*, J.C. Penney Company, Inc. (Dallas, Texas).

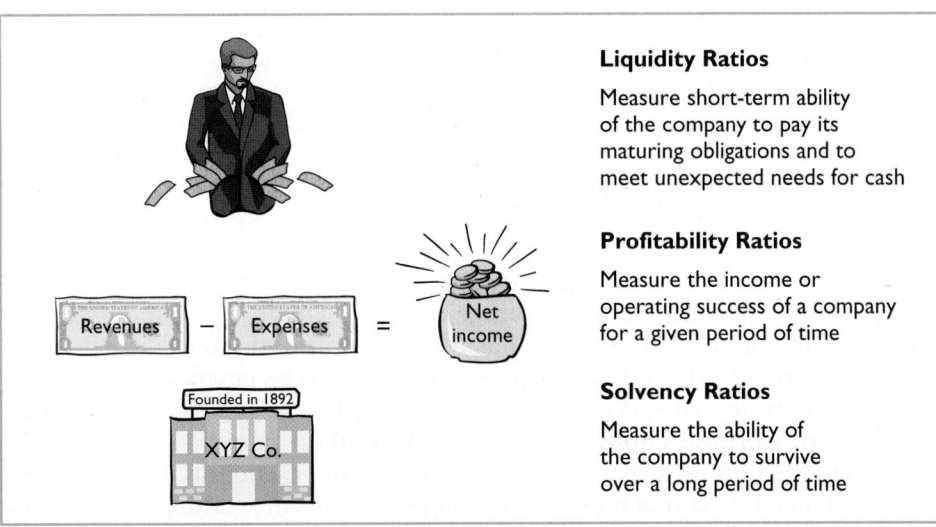

Illustration 14-11
Financial ratio classifications

Liquidity Ratios

Measure short-term ability of the company to pay its maturing obligations and to meet unexpected needs for cash

Profitability Ratios

Measure the income or operating success of a company for a given period of time

Solvency Ratios

Measure the ability of the company to survive over a long period of time

---

ANATOMY OF A FRAUD

Sometimes, relationships between numbers can be used by companies to detect fraud. The numeric relationships that can reveal fraud can be such things as financial ratios that appear abnormal, or statistical abnormalities in the numbers themselves. For example, the fact that WorldCom's line costs, as a percentage of either total expenses or revenues, differed very significantly from its competitors should have alerted people to the possibility of fraud. Or, consider the case of a bank manager, who cooperated with a group of his friends to defraud the bank's credit card department. The manager's friends would apply for credit cards and then run up balances of slightly less than $5,000. The bank had a policy of allowing bank personnel to write off balances of less than $5,000 without seeking supervisor approval. The fraud was detected by applying statistical analysis based on Benford's Law. Benford's Law states that in a random collection of numbers, the frequency of lower digits (e.g., 1, 2, or 3) should be much higher than higher digits (e.g., 7, 8, or 9). In this case, bank auditors analyzed the first two digits of amounts written off. There was a spike at 48 and 49, which was not consistent with what would be expected if the numbers were random.

Total take: Thousands of dollars

THE MISSING CONTROL
Independent internal verification. While it might be efficient to allow employees to write off accounts below a certain level, it is important that these write-offs be reviewed and verified periodically. Such a review would likely call attention to an employee with large amounts of write-offs, or in this case, write-offs that were frequently very close to the approval threshold.

Source: Mark J. Nigrini, "I've Got Your Number," *Journal of Accountancy Online* (May 1999).

Liquidity Ratios

Liquidity ratios measure the short-term ability of the company to pay its maturing obligations and to meet unexpected needs for cash. Short-term creditors such as bankers and suppliers are particularly interested in assessing liquidity. The ratios we can use to determine the company's short-term debt-paying ability are the current ratio, the acid-test ratio, accounts receivable turnover, and inventory turnover.

International Note

As more countries adopt international accounting standards, the ability of analysts to compare companies from different countries should improve. However, international standards are open to widely varying interpretations. In addition, some countries adopt international standards "with modifications." As a consequence, most cross-country comparisons are still not as transparent as within-country comparisons.

1. CURRENT RATIO

The **current ratio** is a widely used measure for evaluating a company's liquidity and short-term debt-paying ability. The ratio is computed by dividing current assets by current liabilities. Illustration 14-12 shows the 2009 and 2008 current ratios for Quality Department Store and comparative data.

What does the ratio actually mean? The 2009 ratio of 2.96:1 means that for every dollar of current liabilities, Quality has $2.96 of current assets. Quality's current ratio has decreased in the current year. But, compared to the industry average of 1.70:1, Quality appears to be reasonably liquid. J.C. Penney has a current ratio of 2.05:1, which indicates it has adequate current assets relative to its current liabilities.

The current ratio is sometimes referred to as the **working capital ratio; working capital** is current assets minus current liabilities. The current ratio is a more dependable indicator of liquidity than working capital. Two companies with the same amount of working capital may have significantly different current ratios.

Illustration 14-12
Current ratio

Helpful Hint
Can any company operate successfully without working capital? Yes, if it has very predictable cash flows and solid earnings. A number of companies (e.g., Whirlpool, American Standard, and Campbell's Soup) are pursuing this goal. The rationale: Less money tied up in working capital means more money to invest in the business.

$$\text{Current Ratio} = \frac{\text{Current Assets}}{\text{Current Liabilities}}$$

Quality Department Store

2009		**2008**	
$\dfrac{\$1,020,000}{\$344,500} = 2.96:1$		$\dfrac{\$945,000}{\$303,000} = 3.12:1$	
Industry average		J.C. Penney Company	
1.70:1		**2.05:1**	

The current ratio is only one measure of liquidity. It does not take into account the **composition** of the current assets. For example, a satisfactory current ratio does not disclose the fact that a portion of the current assets may be tied up in slow-moving inventory. A dollar of cash would be more readily available to pay the bills than a dollar of slow-moving inventory.

2. ACID-TEST RATIO

The **acid-test (quick) ratio** is a measure of a company's immediate short-term liquidity. We compute this ratio by dividing the sum of cash, short-term investments, and net receivables by current liabilities. Thus, it is an important complement to the current ratio. For example, assume that the current assets of Quality Department Store for 2009 and 2008 consist of the items shown in Illustration 14-13.

Illustration 14-13
Current assets of Quality Department Store

Quality Department Store Inc. Balance Sheet (partial)		
	2009	**2008**
Current assets		
Cash	$ 100,000	$155,000
Short-term investments	20,000	70,000
Receivables (net*)	230,000	180,000
Inventory	620,000	500,000
Prepaid expenses	50,000	40,000
Total current assets	$1,020,000	$ 945,000

*Allowance for doubtful accounts is $10,000 at the end of each year.

Cash, short-term investments, and receivables (net) are highly liquid compared to inventory and prepaid expenses. The inventory may not be readily saleable, and the prepaid expenses may not be transferable to others. Thus, the acid-test ratio measures **immediate** liquidity. The 2009 and 2008 acid-test ratios for Quality Department Store and comparative data are as follows.

Illustration 14-14
Acid-test ratio

$$\text{Acid-Test Ratio} = \frac{\text{Cash + Short-Term Investments + Receivables (Net)}}{\text{Current Liabilities}}$$

Quality Department Store	
2009	**2008**
$\dfrac{\$100{,}000 + \$20{,}000 + \$230{,}000}{\$344{,}500} = 1.02{:}1$	$\dfrac{\$155{,}000 + \$70{,}000 + \$180{,}000}{\$303{,}000} = 1.34{:}1$
Industry average	J.C. Penney Company
0.70:1	**1.05:1**

The ratio has declined in 2009. Is an acid-test ratio of 1.02:1 adequate? This depends on the industry and the economy. When compared with the industry average of 0.70:1 and J.C. Penney's of 1.05:1, Quality's acid-test ratio seems adequate.

INVESTOR INSIGHT

How to Manage the Current Ratio

The apparent simplicity of the current ratio can have real-world limitations because adding equal amounts to both the numerator and the denominator causes the ratio to decrease.

Assume, for example, that a company has $2,000,000 of current assets and $1,000,000 of current liabilities; its current ratio is 2:1. If it purchases $1,000,000 of inventory on account, it will have $3,000,000 of current assets and $2,000,000 of current liabilities; its current ratio decreases to 1.5:1. If, instead, the company pays off $500,000 of its current liabilities, it will have $1,500,000 of current assets and $500,000 of current liabilities; its current ratio increases to 3:1. Thus, any trend analysis should be done with care because the ratio is susceptible to quick changes and is easily influenced by management.

? How might management influence a company's current ratio? (See page 759.)

3. ACCOUNTS RECEIVABLE TURNOVER

We can measure liquidity by how quickly a company can convert certain assets to cash. How liquid, for example, are the receivables? The ratio used to assess the liquidity of the receivables is the **accounts receivable turnover**. It measures the number of times, on average, the company collects receivables during the period. We compute the accounts receivable turnover by dividing net credit sales (net sales less cash sales) by the average net accounts receivable. Unless seasonal factors are significant, average net accounts receivable can be computed from the beginning and ending balances of the net accounts receivable.[2]

Assume that all sales are credit sales. The balance of net accounts receivable at the beginning of 2008 is $200,000. Illustration 14-15 (page 722) shows the accounts

---

[2]If seasonal factors are significant, the average accounts receivable balance might be determined by using monthly amounts.

receivable turnover for Quality Department Store and comparative data. Quality's accounts receivable turnover improved in 2009. The turnover of 10.2 times is substantially lower than J.C. Penney's 37.2 times, and is also lower than the department store industry's average of 46.4 times.

Illustration 14-15
Accounts receivable turnover

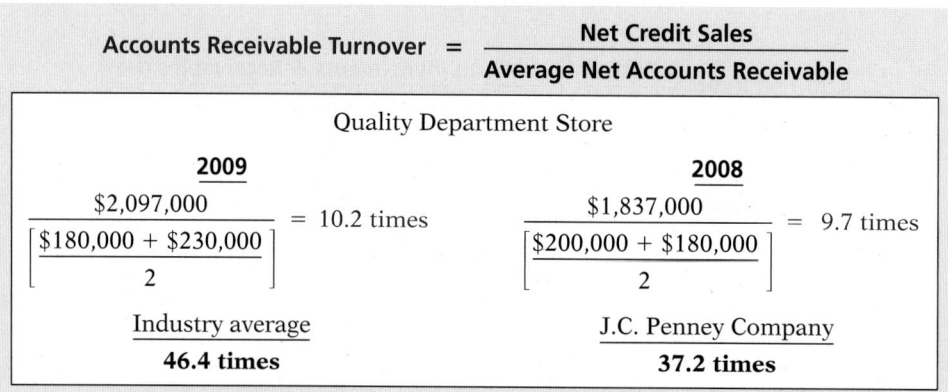

AVERAGE COLLECTION PERIOD A popular variant of the accounts receivable turnover ratio is to convert it to an **average collection period** in terms of days. To do so, we divide the accounts receivable turnover ratio into 365 days. For example, the accounts receivable turnover of 10.2 times divided into 365 days gives an average collection period of approximately 36 days. This means that receivables are collected on average every 36 days, or about every 5 weeks. Analysts frequently use the average collection period to assess the effectiveness of a company's credit and collection policies. The general rule is that the collection period should not greatly exceed the credit term period (the time allowed for payment).

4. INVENTORY TURNOVER

Inventory turnover measures the number of times, on average, the inventory is sold during the period. Its purpose is to measure the liquidity of the inventory. We compute the inventory turnover by dividing cost of goods sold by the average inventory. Unless seasonal factors are significant, we can use the beginning and ending inventory balances to compute average inventory.

Assuming that the inventory balance for Quality Department Store at the beginning of 2008 was $450,000, its inventory turnover and comparative data are as shown in Illustration 14-16. Quality's inventory turnover declined slightly in 2009. The turnover of 2.3 times is low compared with the industry average of 4.3 and J.C. Penney's 3.1. Generally, the faster the inventory turnover, the less cash a company has tied up in inventory and the less the chance of inventory obsolescence.

Illustration 14-16
Inventory turnover

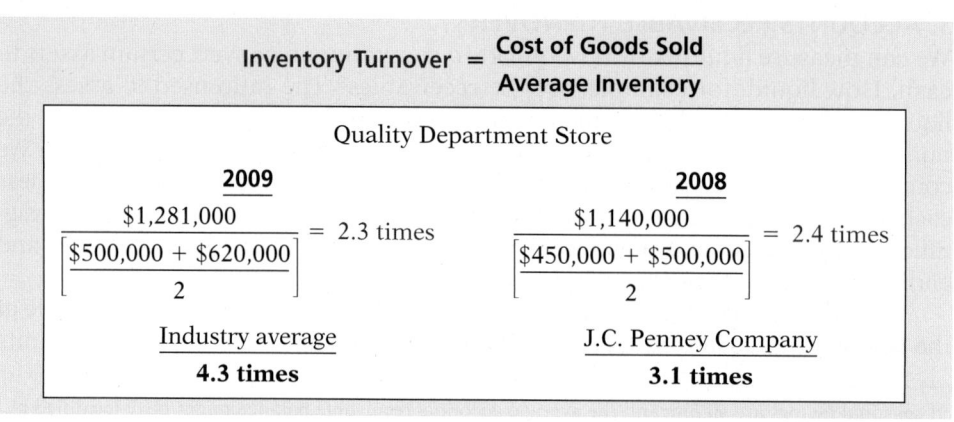

DAYS IN INVENTORY A variant of inventory turnover is the **days in inventory**. We calculate it by dividing the inventory turnover into 365. For example, Quality's 2009 inventory turnover of 2.3 times divided into 365 is approximately 159 days. An average selling time of 159 days is also high compared with the industry average of 84.9 days (365 ÷ 4.3) and J.C. Penney's 117.7 days (365 ÷ 3.1).

Inventory turnover ratios vary considerably among industries. For example, grocery store chains have a turnover of 17.1 times and an average selling period of 21 days. In contrast, jewelry stores have an average turnover of 0.80 times and an average selling period of 456 days.

Profitability Ratios

Profitability ratios measure the income or operating success of a company for a given period of time. Income, or the lack of it, affects the company's ability to obtain debt and equity financing. It also affects the company's liquidity position and the company's ability to grow. As a consequence, both creditors and investors are interested in evaluating earning power—profitability. Analysts frequently use profitability as the ultimate test of management's operating effectiveness.

5. PROFIT MARGIN

Profit margin is a measure of the percentage of each dollar of sales that results in net income. We can compute it by dividing net income by net sales. Illustration 14-17 shows Quality Department Store's profit margin and comparative data.

Alternative Terminology
Profit margin is also called the *rate of return on sales.*

Illustration 14-17
Profit margin

$$\text{Profit Margin} = \frac{\text{Net Income}}{\text{Net Sales}}$$

Quality Department Store

2009	2008
$\dfrac{\$263,800}{\$2,097,000} = 12.6\%$	$\dfrac{\$208,500}{\$1,837,000} = 11.4\%$
Industry average	J.C. Penney Company
8.0%	**1.4%**

Quality experienced an increase in its profit margin from 2008 to 2009. Its profit margin is unusually high in comparison with the industry average of 8% and J.C. Penney's 1.4%.

High-volume (high inventory turnover) businesses, such as grocery stores (Safeway or Kroger) and discount stores (Kmart or Wal-Mart), generally experience low profit margins. In contrast, low-volume businesses, such as jewelry stores (Tiffany & Co.) or airplane manufacturers (Boeing Co.), have high profit margins.

6. ASSET TURNOVER

Asset turnover measures how efficiently a company uses its assets to generate sales. It is determined by dividing net sales by average assets. The resulting number shows the dollars of sales produced by each dollar invested in assets. Unless seasonal factors are significant, we can use the beginning and ending balance of total assets to determine average total assets. Assuming that total assets at the beginning of 2008 were $1,446,000, the 2009 and 2008 asset turnover for Quality Department Store and comparative data are shown in Illustration 14-18 (page 724).

Illustration 14-18
Asset turnover

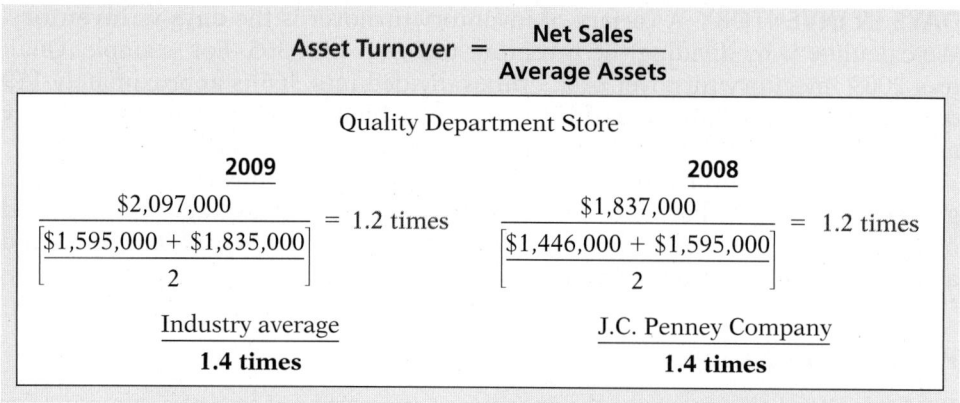

$$\text{Asset Turnover} = \frac{\text{Net Sales}}{\text{Average Assets}}$$

Quality Department Store

2009		2008	
$\dfrac{\$2,097,000}{\left[\dfrac{\$1,595,000 + \$1,835,000}{2}\right]} = 1.2 \text{ times}$		$\dfrac{\$1,837,000}{\left[\dfrac{\$1,446,000 + \$1,595,000}{2}\right]} = 1.2 \text{ times}$	
Industry average		J.C. Penney Company	
1.4 times		**1.4 times**	

Asset turnover shows that in 2009 Quality generated sales of approximately $1.20 for each dollar it had invested in assets. The ratio changed very little from 2008 to 2009. Quality's asset turnover is below both the industry average of 1.4 times and J.C. Penney's ratio of 1.4 times.

Asset turnover ratios vary considerably among industries. For example, a large utility company like Consolidated Edison (New York) has a ratio of 0.4 times, and the large grocery chain Kroger Stores has a ratio of 3.4 times.

7. RETURN ON ASSETS

An overall measure of profitability is **return on assets**. We compute this ratio by dividing net income by average assets. The 2009 and 2008 return on assets for Quality Department Store and comparative data are shown below.

Illustration 14-19
Return on assets

$$\text{Return on Assets} = \frac{\text{Net Income}}{\text{Average Assets}}$$

Quality Department Store

2009		2008	
$\dfrac{\$263,800}{\left[\dfrac{\$1,595,000 + \$1,835,000}{2}\right]} = 15.4\%$		$\dfrac{\$208,500}{\left[\dfrac{\$1,446,000 + \$1,595,000}{2}\right]} = 13.7\%$	
Industry average		J.C. Penney Company	
8.9%		**2.4%**	

Quality's return on assets improved from 2008 to 2009. Its return of 15.4% is very high compared with the department store industry average of 8.9% and J.C. Penney's 2.4%.

8. RETURN ON COMMON STOCKHOLDERS' EQUITY

Another widely used profitability ratio is **return on common stockholders' equity**. It measures profitability from the common stockholders' viewpoint. This ratio shows how many dollars of net income the company earned for each dollar invested by the owners. We compute it by dividing net income available to common stockholders by average common stockholders' equity. When a company has preferred stock, we must deduct **preferred dividend** requirements from net income to compute income available to common stockholders. Similarly, we deduct the par value of preferred stock (or call price, if applicable) from total stockholders' equity to determine the amount of common stockholders' equity used in this ratio. Assuming that common stockholders' equity at the beginning of 2008 was $667,000, Illustration 14-20 shows the 2009 and 2008 ratios for Quality Department Store and comparative data.

Illustration 14-20
Return on common
stockholders' equity

$$\text{Return on Common Stockholders' Equity} = \frac{\text{Net Income} - \text{Preferred Dividends}}{\text{Average Common Stockholders' Equity}}$$

Quality Department Store

2009	2008
$\dfrac{\$263,800 - \$0}{\left[\dfrac{\$795,000 + \$1,003,000}{2}\right]} = 29.3\%$	$\dfrac{\$208,500 - \$0}{\left[\dfrac{\$667,000 + \$795,000}{2}\right]} = 28.5\%$
Industry average	J.C. Penney Company
18.3%	**6.4%**

Quality's rate of return on common stockholders' equity is high at 29.3%, considering an industry average of 18.3% and a rate of 6.4% for J.C. Penney.

Note also that Quality's rate of return on stockholders' equity (29.3%) is substantially higher than its rate of return on assets (15.4%). The reason is that Quality has made effective use of **leverage**. **Leveraging** or **trading on the equity** at a gain means that the company has borrowed money at a lower rate of interest than it is able to earn by using the borrowed money. Leverage enables Quality Department Store to use money supplied by nonowners to increase the return to the owners. A comparison of the rate of return on total assets with the rate of interest paid for borrowed money indicates the profitability of trading on the equity. Quality Department Store earns more on its borrowed funds than it has to pay in the form of interest. Thus, the return to stockholders exceeds the return on the assets, due to benefits from the positive leveraging.

9. EARNINGS PER SHARE (EPS)

Earnings per share (EPS) is a measure of the net income earned on each share of common stock. It is computed by dividing net income available to common stockholders by the number of weighted-average common shares outstanding during the year. A measure of net income earned on a per share basis provides a useful perspective for determining profitability. Assuming that there is no change in the number of outstanding shares during 2008 and that the 2009 increase occurred midyear, Illustration 14-21 shows the net income per share for Quality Department Store for 2009 and 2008.

Illustration 14-21
Earnings per share

$$\text{Earnings per Share} = \frac{\text{Net Income} - \text{Preferred Dividends}}{\text{Weighted-Average Common Shares Outstanding}}$$

Quality Department Store

2009	2008
$\dfrac{\$263,800 - \$0}{\left[\dfrac{270,000 + 275,400}{2}\right]} = \$0.97$	$\dfrac{\$208,500 - \$0}{270,000} = \$0.77$

Note that no industry or J.C. Penney data are presented. Such comparisons are not meaningful because of the wide variations in the number of shares of outstanding stock among companies. The only meaningful EPS comparison is an intracompany trend comparison: Quality's earnings per share increased 20 cents per share in 2009. This represents a 26% increase over the 2008 earnings per share of 77 cents.

The terms "earnings per share" and "net income per share" refer to the amount of net income applicable to each share of **common stock**. Therefore, in computing EPS, if there are preferred dividends declared for the period, we must deduct them from net income to determine income available to the common stockholders.

10. PRICE-EARNINGS RATIO

The **price-earnings (P-E) ratio** is an oft-quoted measure of the ratio of the market price of each share of common stock to the earnings per share. The price-earnings (P-E) ratio reflects investors' assessments of a company's future earnings. We compute it by dividing the market price per share of the stock by earnings per share. Assuming that the market price of Quality Department Store Inc. stock is $8 in 2008 and $12 in 2009, the price-earnings ratio computation is as follows.

Illustration 14-22
Price-earnings ratio

$$\text{Price-Earnings Ratio} = \frac{\text{Market Price per Share of Stock}}{\text{Earnings per Share}}$$

Quality Department Store

2009	2008
$\frac{\$12.00}{\$0.97} = 12.4 \text{ times}$	$\frac{\$8.00}{\$0.77} = 10.4 \text{ times}$
Industry average	J.C. Penney Company
21.3 times	**17.2 times**

In 2009, each share of Quality's stock sold for 12.4 times the amount that the company earned on each share. Quality's price-earnings ratio is lower than the industry average of 21.3 times, and also lower than the ratio of 17.2 times for J.C. Penney. The average price-earnings ratio for the stocks that constitute the Standard and Poor's 500 Index (500 largest U.S. firms) in early 2009 was approximately 19.1 times.

11. PAYOUT RATIO

The **payout ratio** measures the percentage of earnings distributed in the form of cash dividends. We compute it by dividing cash dividends by net income. Companies that have high growth rates generally have low payout ratios because they reinvest most of their net income into the business. The 2009 and 2008 payout ratios for Quality Department Store are computed as shown in Illustration 14-23.

Illustration 14-23
Payout ratio

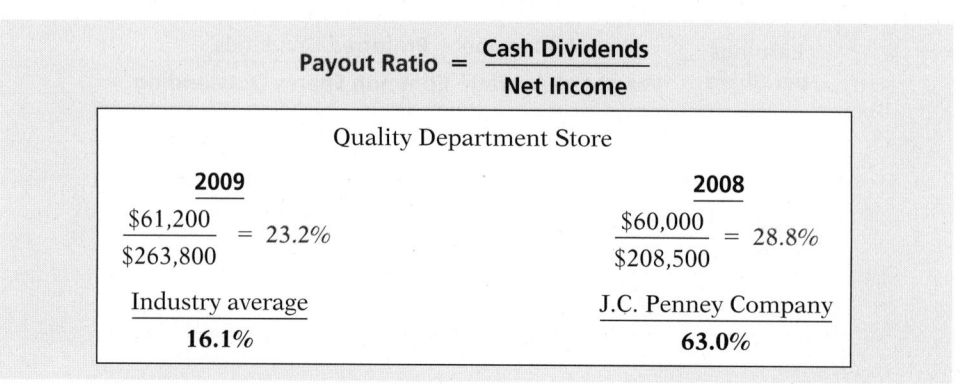

$$\text{Payout Ratio} = \frac{\text{Cash Dividends}}{\text{Net Income}}$$

Quality Department Store

2009	2008
$\frac{\$61,200}{\$263,800} = 23.2\%$	$\frac{\$60,000}{\$208,500} = 28.8\%$
Industry average	J.C. Penney Company
16.1%	**63.0%**

Quality's payout ratio is higher than the industry average payout ratio of 16.1%. J.C. Penney's ratio is very high because its net income in 2009 was quite low.

Solvency Ratios

Solvency ratios measure the ability of a company to survive over a long period of time. Long-term creditors and stockholders are particularly interested in a company's ability to pay interest as it comes due and to repay the face value of debt at maturity. Debt to total assets and times interest earned are two ratios that provide information about debt-paying ability.

12. DEBT TO TOTAL ASSETS RATIO

The **debt to total assets ratio** measures the percentage of the total assets that creditors provide. We compute it by dividing total debt (both current and long-term liabilities) by total assets. This ratio indicates the company's degree of leverage. It also provides some indication of the company's ability to withstand losses without impairing the interests of creditors. The higher the percentage of debt to total assets, the greater the risk that the company may be unable to meet its maturing obligations. The 2009 and 2008 ratios for Quality Department Store and comparative data are as follows.

Illustration 14-24
Debt to total assets ratio

$$\text{Debt to Total Assets Ratio} = \frac{\text{Total Debt}}{\text{Total Assets}}$$

Quality Department Store

2009	2008
$\dfrac{\$832,000}{\$1,835,000} = 45.3\%$	$\dfrac{\$800,000}{\$1,595,000} = 50.2\%$
Industry average	J.C. Penney Company
34.2%	**62.0%**

A ratio of 45.3% means that creditors have provided 45.3% of Quality Department Store's total assets. Quality's 45.3% is above the industry average of 34.2%. It is considerably below the high 62.0% ratio of J.C. Penney. The lower the ratio, the more equity "buffer" there is available to the creditors. Thus, from the creditors' point of view, a low ratio of debt to total assets is usually desirable.

The adequacy of this ratio is often judged in the light of the company's earnings. Generally, companies with relatively stable earnings (such as public utilities) have higher debt to total assets ratios than cyclical companies with widely fluctuating earnings (such as many high-tech companies).

13. TIMES INTEREST EARNED

Times interest earned provides an indication of the company's ability to meet interest payments as they come due. We compute it by dividing income before interest expense and income taxes by interest expense. Illustration 14-25 (page 728) shows the 2009 and 2008 ratios for Quality Department Store and comparative data. Note that times interest earned uses income before income taxes and interest expense. This represents the amount available to cover interest. For Quality Department Store, the 2009 amount of $468,000 is computed by taking the income before income taxes of $432,000 and adding back the $36,000 of interest expense.

Alternative Terminology
Times interest earned is also called *interest coverage*.

Illustration 14-25
Times interest earned

$$\text{Times Interest Earned} = \frac{\text{Income before Income Taxes and Interest Expense}}{\text{Interest Expense}}$$

Quality Department Store

2009	2008
$\dfrac{\$468,000}{\$36,000} = 13$ times	$\dfrac{\$388,000}{\$40,500} = 9.6$ times
Industry average	J.C. Penney Company
16.1 times	**2.9 times**

Quality's interest expense is well covered at 13 times, compared with the industry average of 16.1 times and J.C. Penney's 2.9 times.

Summary of Ratios

Illustration 14-26
Summary of liquidity, profitability, and solvency ratios

Illustration 14-26 summarizes the ratios discussed in this chapter. The summary includes the formula and purpose or use of each ratio.

Ratio	Formula	Purpose or Use
Liquidity Ratios		
1. Current ratio	$\dfrac{\text{Current assets}}{\text{Current liabilities}}$	Measures short-term debt-paying ability.
2. Acid-test (quick) ratio	$\dfrac{\text{Cash + Short-term investments + Receivables (net)}}{\text{Current liabilities}}$	Measures immediate short-term liquidity.
3. Accounts receivable turnover	$\dfrac{\text{Net credit sales}}{\text{Average net accounts receivable}}$	Measures liquidity of accounts receivable.
4. Inventory turnover	$\dfrac{\text{Cost of goods sold}}{\text{Average inventory}}$	Measures liquidity of inventory.
Profitability Ratios		
5. Profit margin	$\dfrac{\text{Net income}}{\text{Net sales}}$	Measures net income generated by each dollar of sales.
6. Asset turnover	$\dfrac{\text{Net sales}}{\text{Average assets}}$	Measures how efficiently assets are used to generate sales.
7. Return on assets	$\dfrac{\text{Net income}}{\text{Average assets}}$	Measures overall profitability of assets.
8. Return on common stockholders' equity	$\dfrac{\text{Net income} - \text{Preferred dividends}}{\text{Average common stockholders' equity}}$	Measures profitability of owners' investment.
9. Earnings per share (EPS)	$\dfrac{\text{Net income} - \text{Preferred dividends}}{\text{Weighted-average common shares outstanding}}$	Measures net income earned on each share of common stock.
10. Price-earnings (P-E) ratio	$\dfrac{\text{Market price per share of stock}}{\text{Earnings per share}}$	Measures the ratio of the market price per share to earnings per share.
11. Payout ratio	$\dfrac{\text{Cash dividends}}{\text{Net income}}$	Measures percentage of earnings distributed in the form of cash dividends.

Illustration 14-26

(cont'd.)

Ratio	Formula	Purpose or Use
Solvency Ratios		
12. Debt to total assets ratio	$\dfrac{\text{Total debt}}{\text{Total assets}}$	Measures the percentage of total assets provided by creditors.
13. Times interest earned	$\dfrac{\text{Income before income taxes and interest expense}}{\text{Interest expense}}$	Measures ability to meet interest payments as they come due.

> DO IT!

Ratio Analysis

The condensed financial statements of John Cully Company, for the years ended June 30, 2014 and 2013, are presented below.

John Cully Company
Balance Sheets
June 30

	(in thousands)	
Assets	**2014**	**2013**
Current assets		
Cash and cash equivalents	$ 553.3	$ 611.6
Accounts receivable (net)	776.6	664.9
Inventory	768.3	653.5
Prepaid expenses and other current assets	204.4	269.2
Total current assets	2,302.6	2,199.2
Property, plant, and equipment (net)	694.2	647.0
Investments	12.3	12.6
Intangibles and other assets	876.7	849.3
Total assets	$3,885.8	$3,708.1
Liabilities and Stockholders' Equity		
Current liabilities	$1,497.7	$1,322.0
Long-term liabilities	679.5	637.1
Stockholders' equity—common	1,708.6	1,749.0
Total liabilities and stockholders' equity	$3,885.8	$3,708.1

John Cully Company
Income Statements
For the Year Ended June 30

	(in thousands)	
	2014	**2013**
Sales revenue	$6,336.3	$5,790.4
Costs and expenses		
Cost of goods sold	1,617.4	1,476.3
Selling and administrative expenses	4,007.6	3,679.0
Interest expense	13.9	27.1
Total costs and expenses	5,638.9	5,182.4
Income before income taxes	697.4	608.0
Income tax expense	291.3	232.6
Net income	$ 406.1	$ 375.4

Compute the following ratios for 2014 and 2013.

(a) Current ratio.

(b) Inventory turnover. (Inventory on 6/30/12 was $599.0.)

(c) Profit margin ratio.

(d) Return on assets. (Assets on 6/30/12 were $3,349.9.)

(e) Return on common stockholders' equity. (Stockholders' equity on 6/30/12 was $1,795.9.)

(f) Debt to total assets ratio.

(g) Times interest earned.

Solution

Action Plan

✔ Remember that the current ratio includes all current assets. The acid-test ratio uses only cash, short-term investments, and net receivables.

✔ Use average balances for turnover ratios like inventory, receivables, and assets.

	2014	2013
(a) Current ratio:		
$2,302.6 ÷ $1,497.7 =	1.5:1	
$2,199.2 ÷ $1,322.0 =		1.7:1
(b) Inventory turnover:		
$1,617.4 ÷ [($768.3 + $653.5) ÷ 2] =	2.3 times	
$1,476.3 ÷ [($653.5 + $599.0) ÷ 2] =		2.4 times
(c) Profit margin:		
$406.1 ÷ $6,336.3 =	6.4%	
$375.4 ÷ $5,790.4 =		6.5%
(d) Return on assets:		
$406.1 ÷ [($3,885.8 + $3,708.1) ÷ 2] =	10.7%	
$375.4 ÷ [($3,708.1 + $3,349.9) ÷ 2] =		10.6%
(e) Return on common stockholders' equity:		
($406.1 − $0) ÷ [($1,708.6 + $1,749.0) ÷ 2] =	23.5%	
($375.4 − $0) ÷ [($1,749.0 + $1,795.9) ÷ 2] =		21.2%
(f) Debt to total assets ratio:		
($1,497.7 + $679.5) ÷ $3,885.8 =	56.0%	
($1,322.0 + $637.1) ÷ $3,708.1 =		52.8%
(g) Times interest earned:		
($406.1 + $291.3 + $13.9) ÷ $13.9 =	51.2 times	
($375.4 + $232.6 + $27.1) ÷ $27.1 =		23.4 times

Related exercise material: **BE14-9, BE14-10, BE14-12, BE14-13, E14-5, E14-7, E14-8, E14-9, E14-10, E14-11, and DO IT! 14-2.**

 The Navigator

Earning Power and Irregular Items

LEARNING OBJECTIVE 6

Understand the concept of earning power, and how irregular items are presented.

Users of financial statements are interested in the concept of earning power. **Earning power** means the normal level of income to be obtained in the future. Earning power differs from actual net income by the amount of irregular revenues, expenses, gains, and losses. Users are interested in earning power because it helps them derive an estimate of future earnings without the "noise" of irregular items.

For users of financial statements to determine earning power or regular income, the "irregular" items are separately identified on the income statement. Companies report two types of "irregular" items.

1. Discontinued operations.

2. Extraordinary items.

These "irregular" items are reported net of income taxes. That is, the income statement first reports income tax on the income before "irregular" items. Then the amount of tax for each of the listed "irregular" items is computed. The general concept is "let the tax follow income or loss."

Discontinued Operations

Discontinued operations refers to the disposal of a **significant component** of a business, such as the elimination of a major class of customers, or an entire activity. For example, to downsize its operations, General Dynamics Corp. sold its missile business to Hughes Aircraft Co. for $450 million. In its income statement, General Dynamics reported the sale in a separate section entitled "Discontinued operations."

Following the disposal of a significant component, the company should report on its income statement both income from continuing operations and income (or loss) from discontinued operations. **The income (loss) from discontinued operations consists of two parts: the income (loss) from operations** and **the gain (loss) on disposal of the segment**.

To illustrate, assume that during 2014 Acro Energy Inc. has income before income taxes of $800,000. During 2014, Acro discontinued and sold its unprofitable chemical division. The loss in 2014 from chemical operations (net of $60,000 taxes) was $140,000. The loss on disposal of the chemical division (net of $30,000 taxes) was $70,000. Assuming a 30% tax rate on income, Illustration 14-27 shows Acro's income statement presentation.

Illustration 14-27
Statement presentation of discontinued operations

Acro Energy Inc. Income Statement (partial) For the Year Ended December 31, 2014		
Income before income taxes		$800,000
Income tax expense		240,000
Income from continuing operations		560,000
Discontinued operations		
Loss from operations of chemical division, **net of $60,000 income tax saving**	$140,000	
Loss from disposal of chemical division, **net of $30,000 income tax saving**	70,000	210,000
Net income		$350,000

Helpful Hint
Observe the dual disclosures: (1) The results of operations of the discontinued division must be eliminated from the results of continuing operations. (2) The company must also report the disposal of the operation.

Note that the statement uses the caption "Income from continuing operations," and adds a new section "Discontinued operations." **The new section reports both the operating loss and the loss on disposal net of applicable income taxes.** This presentation clearly indicates the separate effects of continuing operations and discontinued operations on net income.

Extraordinary Items

Extraordinary items are events and transactions that meet two conditions: They are (1) **unusual in nature**, and (2) **infrequent in occurrence**. To be *unusual*, the item should be abnormal and only incidentally related to the company's customary activities. To be *infrequent*, the item should not be reasonably expected to recur in the foreseeable future.

A company must evaluate both criteria in terms of its operating environment. Thus, Weyerhaeuser Co. reported the $36 million in damages to its timberland caused by the volcanic eruption of Mount St. Helens as an extraordinary item. The eruption was both unusual and infrequent. In contrast, Florida Citrus Company does not report frost damage to its citrus crop as an extraordinary item, because frost damage is not infrequent. Illustration 14-28 shows the classification of extraordinary and ordinary items.

Illustration 14-28

Examples of extraordinary and ordinary items

Extraordinary Items

1. Effects of major natural casualties, if rare in the area.

2. Expropriation (takeover) of property by a foreign government.

3. Effects of a newly enacted law or regulation, such as a property condemnation action.

Ordinary Items

1. Effects of major natural casualties, not uncommon in the area.

2. Write-down of inventories or write-off of receivables.

3. Losses attributable to labor strikes.

4. Gains or losses from sales of property, plant, or equipment.

Companies report extraordinary items net of taxes in a separate section of the income statement, immediately below discontinued operations. To illustrate, assume that in 2014 a foreign government expropriated property held as an investment by Acro Energy Inc. If the loss is $70,000 before applicable income taxes of $21,000, the income statement will report a deduction of $49,000, as shown in Illustration 14-29. When there is an extraordinary item to report, the company adds the caption "Income before extraordinary item" immediately before the section for the extraordinary item. This presentation clearly indicates the effect of the extraordinary item on net income.

What if a transaction or event meets one (but not both) of the criteria for an extraordinary item? In that case, the company reports it under either "Other revenues and gains" or "Other expenses and losses" at its gross amount (not net of tax). This is true, for example, of gains (losses) resulting from the sale of property, plant, and equipment. It is quite common for companies to use the label "Non-recurring charges" for losses that do not meet the extraordinary item criteria.

Acro Energy Inc. Income Statement (partial) For the Year Ended December 31, 2014		
Income before income taxes		$800,000
Income tax expense		240,000
Income from continuing operations		560,000
Discontinued operations		
Loss from operations of chemical division, net of $60,000 income tax saving	$140,000	
Loss from disposal of chemical division, net of $30,000 income tax saving	70,000	210,000
Income before extraordinary item		350,000
Extraordinary item		
Expropriation of investment, net of $21,000 income tax saving		49,000
Net income		$301,000

Illustration 14-29
Statement presentation of extraordinary items

Helpful Hint
If there are no discontinued operations, the third line of the income statement would be labeled "Income before extraordinary item."

INVESTOR INSIGHT

What Does "Non-Recurring" Really Mean?

Many companies incur restructuring charges as they attempt to reduce costs. They often label these items in the income statement as "non-recurring" charges to suggest that they are isolated events which are unlikely to occur in future periods. The question for analysts is, are these costs really one-time, "non-recurring" events, or do they reflect problems that the company will be facing for many periods in the future? If they are one-time events, they can be largely ignored when trying to predict future earnings.

But some companies report "one-time" restructuring charges over and over again. For example, toothpaste and other consumer-goods giant Procter & Gamble Co. reported a restructuring charge in 12 consecutive quarters. Motorola had "special" charges in 14-consecutive quarters. On the other hand, other companies have a restructuring charge only once in a five- or ten-year period. There appears to be no substitute for careful analysis of the numbers that comprise net income.

 If a company takes a large restructuring charge, what is the effect on the company's current income statement versus future ones? (See page 760.)

Changes in Accounting Principle

For ease of comparison, users of financial statements expect companies to prepare such statements on a basis **consistent** with the preceding period. A **change in accounting principle** occurs when the principle used in the current year is different from the one used in the preceding year. Accounting rules permit a change when management can show that the new principle is preferable to the old principle. An example is a change in inventory costing methods (such as FIFO to average-cost).

Companies report most changes in accounting principle retroactively. That is, they report both the current period and previous periods using the new principle. As a result the same principle applies in all periods. This treatment improves the ability to compare results across years.

Ethics Note

Changes in accounting principle should result in financial statements that are more informative for statement users. They should *not* be used to artificially improve the reported performance or financial position of the corporation.

Comprehensive Income

The income statement reports most revenues, expenses, gains, and losses recognized during the period. However, over time, specific exceptions to this general practice have developed. Certain items now bypass income and are reported directly in stockholders' equity.

Companies do not include in income any unrealized gains and losses on non-trading securities. Instead, they report such gains and losses in the balance sheet as adjustments to stockholders' equity. Why are these gains and losses on non-trading securities excluded from net income? Because disclosing them separately (1) reduces the volatility of net income due to fluctuations in fair value, yet (2) informs the financial statement user of the gain or loss that would be incurred if the securities were sold at fair value.

Many analysts have expressed concern over the significant increase in the number of items that bypass the income statement. They feel that such reporting has reduced the usefulness of the income statement. To address this concern, in addition to reporting net income, a company must also report comprehensive income. **Comprehensive income** includes all changes in stockholders' equity during a period except those resulting from investments by stockholders and distributions to stockholders. A number of alternative formats for reporting comprehensive income are allowed. These formats are discussed in advanced accounting courses.

> DO IT!

Irregular Items

Action Plan

✔ Recall that a loss is extraordinary if it is both unusual and infrequent.

✔ Disclose the income tax effect of each component of income, beginning with income before any irregular items.

✔ Show discontinued operations before extraordinary items.

In its proposed 2014 income statement, AIR Corporation reports income before income taxes $400,000, extraordinary loss due to earthquake $100,000, income taxes $120,000 (not including irregular items), loss on operation of discontinued flower division $50,000, and loss on disposal of discontinued flower division $90,000. The income tax rate is 30%. Prepare a correct income statement, beginning with "Income before income taxes."

Solution

AIR Corporation
Income Statement (partial)
For the Year Ended December 31, 2014

Income before income taxes		$400,000
Income tax expense		120,000
Income from continuing operations		280,000
Discontinued operations		
Loss from operation of flower division, net of $15,000 tax saving	$35,000	
Loss on disposal of flower division, net of $27,000 tax saving	63,000	98,000
Income before extraordinary item		182,000
Extraordinary earthquake loss, net of $30,000 tax saving		70,000
Net income		$112,000

Related exercise material: **BE14-14, BE14-15, E14-12, E14-13, and DO IT! 14-3.**

 The Navigator

Quality of Earnings

In evaluating the financial performance of a company, the quality of a company's earnings is of extreme importance to analysts. A company that has a high **quality of earnings** provides full and transparent information that will not confuse or mislead users of the financial statements.

LEARNING OBJECTIVE   7

Understand the concept of quality of earnings.

The issue of quality of earnings has taken on increasing importance because recent accounting scandals suggest that some companies are spending too much time managing their income and not enough time managing their business. Here are some of the factors affecting quality of earnings.

Alternative Accounting Methods

Variations among companies in the application of generally accepted accounting principles may hamper comparability and reduce quality of earnings. For example, one company may use the FIFO method of inventory costing, while another company in the same industry may use LIFO. If inventory is a significant asset to both companies, it is unlikely that their current ratios are comparable. For example, if General Motors Corporation had used FIFO instead of LIFO for inventory valuation, its inventories in a recent year would have been 26% higher, which significantly affects the current ratio (and other ratios as well).

In addition to differences in inventory costing methods, differences also exist in reporting such items as depreciation, depletion, and amortization. Although these differences in accounting methods might be detectable from reading the notes to the financial statements, adjusting the financial data to compensate for the different methods is often difficult, if not impossible.

Pro Forma Income

Companies whose stock is publicly traded are required to present their income statement following generally accepted accounting principles (GAAP). In recent years, many companies have also reported a second measure of income, called pro forma income. **Pro forma income** usually excludes items that the company thinks are unusual or non-recurring. For example, at one time, Cisco Systems (a high-tech company) reported a quarterly net loss under GAAP of $2.7 billion. Cisco reported pro forma income for the same quarter as a profit of $230 million. This large difference in profits between GAAP income numbers and pro forma income is not unusual these days. For example, during one 9-month period the 100 largest firms on the Nasdaq stock exchange reported a total pro forma income of $19.1 billion, but a total loss as measured by GAAP of $82.3 billion—a difference of about $100 billion!

To compute pro forma income, companies generally can exclude any items they deem inappropriate for measuring their performance. Many analysts and investors are critical of the practice of using pro forma income because these numbers often make companies look better than they really are. As the financial press noted, pro forma numbers might be called EBS, which stands for "earnings before bad stuff." Companies, on the other hand, argue that pro forma numbers more clearly indicate sustainable income because they exclude unusual and non-recurring expenses. "Cisco's technique gives readers of financial statements a clear picture of Cisco's normal business activities," the company said in a statement issued in response to questions about its pro forma income accounting.

The SEC has provided guidance on how companies should present pro forma information. Stay tuned: Everyone seems to agree that pro forma numbers can be useful if they provide insights into determining a company's sustainable income. However, many companies have abused the flexibility that pro forma numbers allow and have used the measure as a way to put their companies in a good light.

Improper Recognition

Because some managers have felt pressure from Wall Street to continually increase earnings, they have manipulated the earnings numbers to meet these expectations. The most common abuse is the improper recognition of revenue. One practice that companies are using is **channel stuffing**: Offering deep discounts on their products to customers, companies encourage their customers to buy early (stuff the channel) rather than later. This lets the company report good earnings in the current period, but it often leads to a disaster in subsequent periods because customers have no need for additional goods. To illustrate, Bristol-Myers Squibb at one time indicated that it used sales incentives to encourage wholesalers to buy more drugs than needed to meet patients' demands. As a result, the company had to issue revised financial statements showing corrected revenues and income.

Another practice is the improper capitalization of operating expenses. The classic case is WorldCom. It capitalized over $7 billion dollars of operating expenses so that it would report positive net income. In other situations, companies fail to report all their liabilities. Enron had promised to make payments on certain contracts if financial difficulty developed, but these guarantees were not reported as liabilities. In addition, disclosure was so lacking in transparency that it was impossible to understand what was happening at the company.

> DO IT!

Quality of Earnings, Financial Statement Analysis

Match each of the following terms with the phrase that best describes it.

Comprehensive income   Vertical analysis
Quality of earnings   Pro forma income
Solvency ratio   Extraordinary item

1. _____ Measures the ability of the company to survive over a long period of time.
2. _____ Usually excludes items that a company thinks are unusual or non-recurring.
3. _____ Includes all changes in stockholders' equity during a period except those resulting from investments by stockholders and distributions to stockholders.
4. _____ Indicates the level of full and transparent information provided to users of the financial statements.
5. _____ Describes events and transactions that are unusual in nature and infrequent in occurrence.
6. _____ Expresses each item within a financial statement as a percentage of a base amount.

Solution

1. Solvency ratio: Measures the ability of the company to survive over a long period of time.
2. Pro forma income: Usually excludes items that a company thinks are unusual or non-recurring.
3. Comprehensive income: Includes all changes in stockholders' equity during a period except those resulting from investments by stockholders and distributions to stockholders.
4. Quality of earnings: Indicates the level of full and transparent information provided to users of the financial statements.
5. Extraordinary item: Describes events and transactions that are unusual in nature and infrequent in occurrence.
6. Vertical analysis: Expresses each item within a financial statement as a percentage of a base amount.

Action Plan

✔ Develop a sound understanding of basic methods used for financial reporting.

✔ Understand the use of fundamental analysis techniques.

Related exercise material: DO IT! **14-4.**

 The Navigator

> Comprehensive DO IT!

The events and transactions of Dever Corporation for the year ending December 31, 2014, resulted in the following data.

Cost of goods sold	$2,600,000
Net sales	4,400,000
Other expenses and losses	9,600
Other revenues and gains	5,600
Selling and administrative expenses	1,100,000
Income from operations of plastics division	70,000
Gain from disposal of plastics division	500,000
Loss from tornado disaster (extraordinary loss)	600,000

Analysis reveals that:

1. All items are before the applicable income tax rate of 30%.
2. The plastics division was sold on July 1.
3. All operating data for the plastics division have been segregated.

Instructions

Prepare an income statement for the year.

Solution to Comprehensive DO IT!

Action Plan

✔ Report material items not typical of continuing operations in separate sections, net of taxes.

✔ Associate income taxes with the item that affects the taxes.

✔ Apply the corporate tax rate to income before income taxes to determine tax expense.

✔ Recall that all data presented in determining income before income taxes are the same as for unincorporated companies.

Dever Corporation
Income Statement
For the Year Ended December 31, 2014

Net sales			$4,400,000
Cost of goods sold			2,600,000
Gross profit			1,800,000
Selling and administrative expenses			1,100,000
Income from operations			700,000
Other revenues and gains		$ 5,600	
Other expenses and losses		9,600	4,000
Income before income taxes			696,000
Income tax expense ($696,000 × 30%)			208,800
Income from continuing operations			487,200
Discontinued operations			
Income from operations of plastics division, net of			
$21,000 income taxes ($70,000 × 30%)		49,000	
Gain from disposal of plastics division, net of $150,000			
income taxes ($500,000 × 30%)		350,000	399,000
Income before extraordinary item			886,200
Extraordinary item			
Tornado loss, net of $180,000 income tax saving			
($600,000 × 30%)			420,000
Net income			$ 466,200

 The Navigator

SUMMARY OF LEARNING OBJECTIVES

1 Discuss the need for comparative analysis. There are three bases of comparison: (1) Intracompany, which compares an item or financial relationship with other data within a company. (2) Industry, which compares company data with industry averages. (3) Intercompany, which compares an item or financial relationship of a company with data of one or more competing companies.

2 Identify the tools of financial statement analysis. Financial statements can be analyzed horizontally, vertically, and with ratios.

3 Explain and apply horizontal analysis. Horizontal analysis is a technique for evaluating a series of data over a period of time to determine the increase or decrease that has taken place, expressed as either an amount or a percentage.

4 Describe and apply vertical analysis. Vertical analysis is a technique that expresses each item within a financial statement in terms of a percentage of a relevant total or a base amount.

5 Identify and compute ratios used in analyzing a firm's liquidity, profitability, and solvency. The formula and purpose of each ratio was presented in Illustration 14-26 (page 728).

6 Understand the concept of earning power, and how irregular items are presented. Earning power refers to a company's ability to sustain its profits from operations. "Irregular items"—discontinued operations and extraordinary items—are presented net of tax below income from continuing operations to highlight their unusual nature.

7 Understand the concept of quality of earnings. A high quality of earnings provides full and transparent information that will not confuse or mislead users of the financial statements. Issues related to quality of earnings are (1) alternative accounting methods, (2) pro forma income, and (3) improper recognition.

GLOSSARY

Accounts receivable turnover A measure of the liquidity of accounts receivable; computed by dividing net credit sales by average net accounts receivable. (p. 721).

Acid-test (quick) ratio A measure of a company's immediate short-term liquidity; computed by dividing the sum of cash, short-term investments, and net receivables by current liabilities. (p. 720).

Asset turnover A measure of how efficiently a company uses its assets to generate sales; computed by dividing net sales by average assets. (p. 723).

Change in accounting principle The use of a principle in the current year that is different from the one used in the preceding year. (p. 733).

Comprehensive income Includes all changes in stockholders' equity during a period except those resulting from investments by stockholders and distributions to stockholders. (p. 734).

Current ratio A measure used to evaluate a company's liquidity and short-term debt-paying ability; computed by dividing current assets by current liabilities. (p. 720).

Debt to total assets ratio Measures the percentage of total assets provided by creditors; computed by dividing total debt by total assets. (p. 727).

Discontinued operations The disposal of a significant segment of a business. (p. 731).

Earnings per share (EPS) The net income earned on each share of common stock; computed by dividing net income minus preferred dividends (if any) by the number of weighted-average common shares outstanding. (p. 725).

Extraordinary items Events and transactions that are unusual in nature and infrequent in occurrence. (p. 731).

Horizontal analysis A technique for evaluating a series of financial statement data over a period of time, to determine the increase (decrease) that has taken place, expressed as either an amount or a percentage. (p. 713).

Inventory turnover A measure of the liquidity of inventory; computed by dividing cost of goods sold by average inventory. (p. 722).

Leveraging See *Trading on the equity*. (p. 725).

Liquidity ratios Measures of the short-term ability of the company to pay its maturing obligations and to meet unexpected needs for cash. (p. 719).

Payout ratio Measures the percentage of earnings distributed in the form of cash dividends; computed by dividing cash dividends by net income. (p. 726).

Price-earnings (P-E) ratio Measures the ratio of the market price of each share of common stock to the earnings per share; computed by dividing the market price of the stock by earnings per share. (p. 726).

Profitability ratios Measures of the income or operating success of a company for a given period of time. (p. 723).

Profit margin Measures the percentage of each dollar of sales that results in net income; computed by dividing net income by net sales. (p. 723).

Pro forma income A measure of income that usually excludes items that a company thinks are unusual or non-recurring. (p. 735).

Quality of earnings Indicates the level of full and transparent information provided to users of the financial statements. (p. 735).

Ratio An expression of the mathematical relationship between one quantity and another. The relationship may be expressed either as a percentage, a rate, or a simple proportion. (p. 718).

Ratio analysis A technique for evaluating financial statements that expresses the relationship between selected financial statement data. (p. 718).

Return on assets An overall measure of profitability; computed by dividing net income by average assets. (p. 724).

Return on common stockholders' equity Measures the dollars of net income earned for each dollar invested by the owners; computed by dividing net income minus preferred dividends (if any) by average common stockholders' equity. (p. 724).

Solvency ratios Measures of the ability of the company to survive over a long period of time. (p. 727).

Times interest earned Measures a company's ability to meet interest payments as they come due; computed by dividing income before interest expense and income taxes by interest expense. (p. 727).

Trading on the equity Borrowing money at a lower rate of interest than can be earned by using the borrowed money. (p. 725).

Vertical analysis A technique for evaluating financial statement data that expresses each item within a financial statement as a percent of a base amount. (p. 716).

Self-Test, Brief Exercises, Exercises, Problem Set A, and many more resources are available for practice in WileyPLUS.

SELF-TEST QUESTIONS

Answers are on page 760.

(LO 1) **1.** Comparisons of data within a company are an example of the following comparative basis:
  (a) Industry averages.
  (b) Intracompany.
  (c) Intercompany.
  (d) Both (b) and (c).

(LO 3) **2.** In horizontal analysis, each item is expressed as a percentage of the:
  (a) net income amount.
  (b) stockholders' equity amount.
  (c) total assets amount.
  (d) base year amount.

(LO 4) **3.** In vertical analysis, the base amount for depreciation expense is generally:
  (a) net sales.
  (b) depreciation expense in a previous year.
  (c) gross profit.
  (d) fixed assets.

(LO 4) **4.** The following schedule is a display of what type of analysis?

	Amount	Percent
Current assets	$200,000	25%
Property, plant, and equipment	600,000	75%
Total assets	$800,000	

  (a) Horizontal analysis.   (c) Vertical analysis.
  (b) Differential analysis. (d) Ratio analysis.

(LO 3) **5.** Sammy Corporation reported net sales of $300,000, $330,000, and $360,000 in the years, 2012, 2013, and 2014, respectively. If 2012 is the base year, what is the trend percentage for 2014?

  (a) 77%.   (c) 120%.
  (b) 108%.   (d) 130%.

(LO 5) **6.** Which of the following measures is an evaluation of a firm's ability to pay current liabilities?
  (a) Acid-test ratio.   (c) Both (a) and (b).
  (b) Current ratio.   (d) None of the above.

(LO 5) **7.** A measure useful in evaluating the efficiency in managing inventories is:
  (a) inventory turnover.
  (b) average days to sell inventory.
  (c) Both (a) and (b).
  (d) None of the above.

Use the following financial statement information as of the end of each year to answer Self-Test Questions 8–12.

	2014	2013
Inventory	$ 54,000	$ 48,000
Current assets	81,000	106,000
Total assets	382,000	326,000
Current liabilities	27,000	36,000
Total liabilities	102,000	88,000
Preferred stock	40,000	40,000
Common stockholders' equity	240,000	198,000
Net sales	784,000	697,000
Cost of goods sold	306,000	277,000
Net income	134,000	90,000
Tax expense	22,000	18,000
Interest expense	12,000	12,000
Dividends paid to preferred stockholders	4,000	4,000
Dividends paid to common stockholders	15,000	10,000

(LO 5) **8.** Compute the days in inventory for 2014.
    (a) 64.4 days.   (c) 6 days.
    (b) 60.8 days.   (d) 24 days.

(LO 5) **9.** Compute the current ratio for 2014.
    (a) 1.26:1.   (c) .80:1.
    (b) 3.0:1.   (d) 3.75:1.

(LO 5) **10.** Compute the profit margin ratio for 2014.
    (a) 17.1%.   (c) 37.9%.
    (b) 18.1%.   (d) 5.9%.

(LO 5) **11.** Compute the return on common stockholders' equity for 2014.
    (a) 47.9%.   (c) 61.2%.
    (b) 51.7%.   (d) 59.4%.

(LO 5) **12.** Compute the times interest earned for 2014.
    (a) 11.2 times.   (c) 14.0 times.
    (b) 65.3 times.   (d) 13.0 times.

(LO 6) **13.** In reporting discontinued operations, the income statement should show in a special section:
    (a) gains and losses on the disposal of the discontinued segment.

(b) gains and losses from operations of the discontinued segment.
(c) Both (a) and (b).
(d) Neither (a) nor (b).

14. Scout Corporation has income before taxes of (LO 6) $400,000 and an extraordinary loss of $100,000. If the income tax rate is 25% on all items, the income statement should show income before extraordinary items and extraordinary items, respectively, of:
(a) $325,000 and $100,000.
(b) $325,000 and $75,000.
(c) $300,000 and $100,000
(d) $300,000 and $75,000.

15. Which situation below might indicate a company has (LO 7) a low quality of earnings?
(a) The same accounting principles are used each year.
(b) Revenue is recognized when earned.
(c) Maintenance costs are expensed as incurred.
(d) The company is continually reporting pro forma income numbers.

Go to the book's companion website, www.wiley.com/college/weygandt, for additional Self-Test Questions.

 **The Navigator**

QUESTIONS

1. (a) Kurt Gibson believes that the analysis of financial statements is directed at two characteristics of a company: liquidity and profitability. Is Kurt correct? Explain.
(b) Are short-term creditors, long-term creditors, and stockholders interested primarily in the same characteristics of a company? Explain.

2. (a) Distinguish among the following bases of comparison: (1) intracompany, (2) industry averages, and (3) intercompany.
(b) Give the principal value of using each of the three bases of comparison.

3. Two popular methods of financial statement analysis are horizontal analysis and vertical analysis. Explain the difference between these two methods.

4. (a) If Nimoy Company had net income of $350,000 in 2013 and it experienced a 22.4% increase in net income for 2014, what is its net income for 2014?
(b) If five cents of every dollar of Nimoy revenue is net income in 2013, what is the dollar amount of 2013 revenue?

5. What is a ratio? What are the different ways of expressing the relationship of two amounts? What information does a ratio provide?

6. Name the major ratios useful in assessing (a) liquidity and (b) solvency.

7. Maribel Ortiz is puzzled. Her company had a profit margin of 10% in 2014. She feels that this is an indication that the company is doing well. Gordon Liddy, her accountant, says that more information is needed to determine the firm's financial well-being. Who is correct? Why?

8. What do the following classes of ratios measure? (a) Liquidity ratios. (b) Profitability ratios. (c) Solvency ratios.

9. What is the difference between the current ratio and the acid-test ratio?

10. Monte Company, a retail store, has an accounts receivable turnover of 4.5 times. The industry average is 12.5 times. Does Monte have a collection problem with its accounts receivable?

11. Which ratios should be used to help answer the following questions?
(a) How efficient is a company in using its assets to produce sales?
(b) How near to sale is the inventory on hand?
(c) How many dollars of net income were earned for each dollar invested by the owners?
(d) How able is a company to meet interest charges as they fall due?

12. The price-earnings ratio of General Motors (automobile builder) was 8, and the price-earnings ratio of Microsoft (computer software) was 38. Which company did the stock market favor? Explain.

13. What is the formula for computing the payout ratio? Would you expect this ratio to be high or low for a growth company?

14. Holding all other factors constant, indicate whether each of the following changes generally signals good or bad news about a company.
    (a) Increase in profit margin.
    (b) Decrease in inventory turnover.
    (c) Increase in the current ratio.
    (d) Decrease in earnings per share.
    (e) Increase in price-earnings ratio.
    (f) Increase in debt to total assets ratio.
    (g) Decrease in times interest earned.

15. The return on assets for Miller Corporation is 7.6%. During the same year, Miller's return on common stockholders' equity is 12.8%. What is the explanation for the difference in the two rates?

16. Which two ratios do you think should be of greatest interest to:
    (a) A pension fund considering the purchase of 20-year bonds?
    (b) A bank contemplating a short-term loan?
    (c) A common stockholder?

17. Why must preferred stock dividends be subtracted from net income in computing earnings per share?

18. (a) What is meant by trading on the equity?
    (b) How would you determine the profitability of trading on the equity?

19. Tillman Inc. has net income of $160,000, weighted-average shares of common stock outstanding of 50,000, and preferred dividends for the period of $30,000. What is Tillman's earnings per share of common stock? Pat Tillman, the president of Tillman Inc., believes the computed EPS of the company is high. Comment.

20. Why is it important to report discontinued operations separately from income from continuing operations?

21. You are considering investing in Cherokee Transportation. The company reports 2014 earnings per share of $6.50 on income before extraordinary items and $4.75 on net income. Which EPS figure would you consider more relevant to your investment decision? Why?

22. MRT Inc. reported 2013 earnings per share of $3.20 and had no extraordinary items. In 2014, EPS on income before extraordinary items was $2.99, and EPS on net income was $3.49. Is this a favorable trend?

23. Indicate which of the following items would be reported as an extraordinary item in Muerte Corporation's income statement.
    (a) Loss from damages caused by volcano eruption.
    (b) Loss from sale of temporary investments.
    (c) Loss attributable to a labor strike.
    (d) Loss caused when manufacture of a product was prohibited by the Food and Drug Administration.
    (e) Loss from flood damage. (The nearby Black River floods every 2 to 3 years.)
    (f) Write-down of obsolete inventory.
    (g) Expropriation of a factory by a foreign government.

24. Identify and explain factors that affect quality of earnings.

25. **PEPSICO** Identify the specific sections in PepsiCo's 2010 annual report where horizontal and vertical analyses of financial data are presented.

BRIEF EXERCISES

Follow the rounding procedures used in the chapter.

BE14-1 You recently received a letter from your Uncle Liam. A portion of the letter is presented below.

You know that I have a significant amount of money I saved over the years. I am thinking about starting an investment program. I want to do the investing myself, based on my own research and analysis of financial statements. I know that you are studying accounting, so I have a couple of questions for you. I have heard that different users of financial statements are interested in different characteristics of companies. Is this true, and, if so, why? Also, some of my friends, who are already investing, have told me that comparisons involving a company's financial data can be made on a number of different bases. Can you explain these bases to me?

Discuss need for comparative analysis.

(LO 1)

Instructions

▱▱▱▱▱▷ Write a letter to your Uncle Liam which answers his questions.

*Identify and use tools of
financial statement analysis.*
(LO 2, 3, 4, 5)

BE14-2 Maria Fierro Corporation reported the following amounts in 2012, 2013, and 2014.

	2012	2013	2014
Current assets	$220,000	$230,000	$240,000
Current liabilities	$160,000	$170,000	$184,000
Total assets	$500,000	$600,000	$630,000

Instructions
(a) Identify and describe the three tools of financial statement analysis. (b) Perform each of the three types of analysis on Maria Fierro's current assets.

Prepare horizontal analysis.
(LO 3)

BE14-3 Using the following data from the comparative balance sheet of Dotte Company, illustrate horizontal analysis.

	December 31, 2014	December 31, 2013
Accounts receivable	$ 520,000	$ 350,000
Inventory	$ 840,000	$ 500,000
Total assets	$2,500,000	$3,000,000

Prepare vertical analysis.
(LO 4)

BE14-4 Using the same data presented above in BE14-3 for Dotte Company, illustrate vertical analysis.

*Calculate percentage of
change.*
(LO 3)

BE14-5 Net income was $550,000 in 2012, $475,000 in 2013, and $525,000 in 2014. What is the percentage of change from (a) 2012 to 2013 and (b) 2013 to 2014? Is the change an increase or a decrease?

Calculate net income.
(LO 3)

BE14-6 If Valdamorte Company had net income of $560,000 in 2014 and it experienced a 40% increase in net income over 2013, what was its 2013 net income?

*Calculate change in net
income.*
(LO 3)

BE14-7 Horizontal analysis (trend analysis) percentages for Kemplar Company's sales, cost of goods sold, and expenses are shown below.

Horizontal Analysis	2014	2013	2012
Sales	97.8	105.3	100.0
Cost of goods sold	103.0	96.0	100.0
Expenses	108.2	99.3	100.0

Did Kemplar's net income increase, decrease, or remain unchanged over the 3-year period?

*Calculate change in net
income.*
(LO 4)

BE14-8 Vertical analysis (common size) percentages for Dagman Company's sales, cost of goods sold, and expenses are shown below.

Vertical Analysis	2014	2013	2012
Sales	100.0	100.0	100.0
Cost of goods sold	59.2	62.4	64.5
Expenses	25.0	25.6	27.5

Did Dagman's net income as a percentage of sales increase, decrease, or remain unchanged over the 3-year period? Provide numerical support for your answer.

Calculate liquidity ratios.
(LO 5)

BE14-9 Selected condensed data taken from a recent balance sheet of Morino Inc. are as follows.

Morino Inc.
Balance Sheet (partial)

Cash	$ 8,113,000
Short-term investments	4,947,000
Accounts receivable	12,545,000
Inventory	14,814,000
Other current assets	6,271,000
Total current assets	$46,690,000
Total current liabilities	$40,600,000

What are the (a) working capital, (b) current ratio, and (c) acid-test ratio?

BE14-10 Huntsinger Corporation has net income of $12.76 million and net revenue of $88 million in 2014. Its assets are $14 million at the beginning of the year and $18 million at the end of the year. What are Huntsinger's (a) asset turnover and (b) profit margin?

Calculate profitability ratios.
(LO 5)

BE14-11 The following data are taken from the financial statements of Gladow Company.

Evaluate collection of accounts receivable.
(LO 5)

	2014	**2013**
Accounts receivable (net), end of year	$ 550,000	$ 520,000
Net sales on account	3,745,000	3,000,000
Terms for all sales are 1/10, n/60.		

(a) Compute for each year (1) the accounts receivable turnover and (2) the average collection period. At the end of 2012, accounts receivable (net) was $480,000.
(b) ▭▭▭▭▷ What conclusions about the management of accounts receivable can be drawn from these data?

BE14-12 The following data are from the income statements of Charles Company.

Evaluate management of inventory.
(LO 5)

	2014	**2013**
Sales	$6,420,000	$6,240,000
Beginning inventory	980,000	860,000
Purchases	4,440,000	4,720,000
Ending inventory	1,020,000	980,000

(a) Compute for each year (1) the inventory turnover and (2) the average days to sell the inventory.
(b) ▭▭▭▭▷ What conclusions concerning the management of the inventory can be drawn from these data?

BE14-13 Ming Company has stockholders' equity of $400,000 and net income of $68,000. It has a payout ratio of 20% and a rate of return on assets of 16%. How much did Ming pay in cash dividends, and what were its average assets?

Calculate amounts from profitability ratios.
(LO 5)

BE14-14 An inexperienced accountant for Reeves Corporation showed the following in the income statement: income before income taxes and extraordinary item $500,000, and extraordinary loss from flood (before taxes) $80,000. The extraordinary loss and taxable income are both subject to a 30% tax rate. Prepare a correct income statement.

Prepare income statement including extraordinary items.
(LO 6)

BE14-15 On June 30, Blevins Corporation discontinued its operations in Europe. During the year, the operating loss was $350,000 before taxes. On September 1, Blevins disposed of its European facilities at a pretax loss of $150,000. The applicable tax rate is 30%. Show the discontinued operations section of the income statement.

Prepare discontinued operations section of income statement.
(LO 6)

Prepare horizontal analysis.
(LO 3)

DO IT! 14-1 Summary financial information for Rapture Company is as follows.

	December 31, 2014	December 31, 2013
Current assets	$ 199,000	$225,000
Plant assets	821,000	750,000
Total assets	$1,020,000	$975,000

Compute the amount and percentage changes in 2014 using horizontal analysis, assuming 2013 is the base year.

Compute ratios.
(LO 5)

DO IT! 14-2 The condensed financial statements of Soule Company for the years 2013 and 2014 are presented below.

Soule Company
Balance Sheets
December 31

	2014	2013
Current assets		
Cash and cash equivalents	$ 330	$ 360
Accounts receivable (net)	470	433
Inventory	430	390
Prepaid expenses	120	160
Total current assets	1,350	1,343
Property, plant, and equipment	420	380
Investments	10	10
Intangibles and other assets	530	510
Total assets	$2,310	$2,243
Current liabilities	$ 900	$ 810
Long-term liabilities	390	393
Stockholders' equity—common	1,020	1,040
Total liabilities and stockholders' equity	$2,310	$2,243

Soule Company
Income Statements
For the Years Ended December 31

	2014	2013
Sales revenue	$4,000	$3,600
Costs and expenses		
Cost of goods sold	984	895
Selling and administrative expenses	2,400	2,330
Interest expense	10	20
Total costs and expenses	3,394	3,245
Income before income taxes	606	355
Income tax expense	242	142
Net income	$ 364	$ 213

Compute the following ratios for 2014 and 2013.
(a) Current ratio.
(b) Inventory turnover. (Inventory on 12/31/12 was $326.)
(c) Profit margin ratio.
(d) Return on assets. (Assets on 12/31/12 were $2,100.)

(e) Return on common stockholders' equity. (Stockholders' equity on 12/31/12 was $960.)
(f) Debt to total assets ratio.
(g) Times interest earned.

DO IT! 14-3 In its proposed 2014 income statement, Grinders Corporation reports income before income taxes $500,000, extraordinary loss due to earthquake $160,000, income taxes $175,000 (not including irregular items), loss on operation of discontinued music division $60,000, and gain on disposal of discontinued music division $40,000. The income tax rate is 35%. Prepare a correct income statement, beginning with income before income taxes.

Prepare income statement, including irregular items.

(LO 6)

DO IT! 14-4 Match each of the following terms with the phrase that best describes it.

Match terms relating to quality of earnings and financial statement analysis.

(LO 3, 5, 6, 7)

Quality of earnings   Pro forma income
Current ratio   Discontinued operations
Horizontal analysis   Comprehensive income

1. _____ A measure used to evaluate a company's liquidity.
2. _____ Usually excludes items that a company thinks are unusual or non-recurring.
3. _____ Indicates the level of full and transparent information provided to users of the financial statements.
4. _____ The disposal of a significant segment of a business.
5. _____ Determines increases or decreases in a series of financial statement data.
6. _____ Includes all changes in stockholders' equity during a period except those resulting from investments by stockholders and distributions to stockholders.

✔ **The Navigator**

EXERCISES

Follow the rounding procedures used in the chapter.

E14-1 Financial information for Gallup Inc. is presented below.

Prepare horizontal analysis.

(LO 3)

	December 31, 2014	**December 31, 2013**
Current assets	$128,000	$100,000
Plant assets (net)	396,000	330,000
Current liabilities	91,000	70,000
Long-term liabilities	138,700	95,000
Common stock, $1 par	159,000	115,000
Retained earnings	135,300	150,000

Instructions
Prepare a schedule showing a horizontal analysis for 2014 using 2013 as the base year.

E14-2 Operating data for Conard Corporation are presented below.

Prepare vertical analysis.

(LO 4)

	2014	**2013**
Net sales	$750,000	$600,000
Cost of goods sold	480,000	408,000
Selling expenses	105,000	84,000
Administrative expenses	75,000	54,000
Income tax expense	36,000	18,000
Net income	54,000	36,000

Instructions
Prepare a schedule showing a vertical analysis for 2014 and 2013.

Prepare horizontal and vertical analyses.

(LO 3, 4)

E14-3 The comparative condensed balance sheets of Garcia Corporation are presented below.

Garcia Corporation
Comparative Condensed Balance Sheets
December 31

	2014	2013
Assets		
Current assets	$ 76,000	$ 80,000
Property, plant, and equipment (net)	100,000	90,000
Intangibles	24,000	40,000
Total assets	$200,000	$210,000
Liabilities and stockholders' equity		
Current liabilities	$ 40,000	$ 48,000
Long-term liabilities	140,000	150,000
Stockholders' equity	20,000	12,000
Total liabilities and stockholders' equity	$200,000	$210,000

Instructions
(a) Prepare a horizontal analysis of the balance sheet data for Garcia Corporation using 2013 as a base.
(b) Prepare a vertical analysis of the balance sheet data for Garcia Corporation in columnar form for 2014.

Prepare horizontal and vertical analyses.

(LO 3, 4)

E14-4 The comparative condensed income statements of Hendi Corporation are shown below.

Hendi Corporation
Comparative Condensed Income Statements
For the Years Ended December 31

	2014	2013
Net sales	$600,000	$500,000
Cost of goods sold	468,000	400,000
Gross profit	132,000	100,000
Operating expenses	60,000	54,000
Net income	$ 72,000	$ 46,000

Instructions
(a) Prepare a horizontal analysis of the income statement data for Hendi Corporation using 2013 as a base. (Show the amounts of increase or decrease.)
(b) Prepare a vertical analysis of the income statement data for Hendi Corporation in columnar form for both years.

Compute liquidity ratios and compare results.

(LO 5)

E14-5 Nordstrom, Inc. operates department stores in numerous states. Selected financial statement data for the year ending January 30, 2010, are shown below.

Nordstrom, Inc.
Balance Sheet (partial)

(in millions)	End-of-Year	Beginning-of-Year
Cash and cash equivalents	$ 795	$ 72
Accounts receivable (net)	2,035	1,942
Merchandise inventory	898	900
Prepaid expenses	88	93
Other current assets	238	210
Total current assets	$4,054	$3,217
Total current liabilities	$2,014	$1,601

For the year, net sales were $8,258 and cost of goods sold was $5,328 (in millions).

Instructions
(a) Compute the four liquidity ratios at the end of the year.
(b) Using the data in the chapter, compare Nordstrom's liquidity with (1) that of J.C. Penney Company, and (2) the industry averages for department stores.

E14-6 Bennis Incorporated had the following transactions occur involving current assets and current liabilities during February 2014.

Perform current and acid-test ratio analysis.

(LO 5)

Feb.	3	Accounts receivable of $15,000 are collected.
	7	Equipment is purchased for $28,000 cash.
	11	Paid $3,000 for a 3-year insurance policy.
	14	Accounts payable of $12,000 are paid.
	18	Cash dividends of $5,000 are declared.

Additional information:

1. As of February 1, 2014, current assets were $140,000, and current liabilities were $50,000.
2. As of February 1, 2014, current assets included $10,000 of inventory and $5,000 of prepaid expenses.

Instructions
(a) Compute the current ratio as of the beginning of the month and after each transaction.
(b) Compute the acid-test ratio as of the beginning of the month and after each transaction.

E14-7 Willingham Company has the following comparative balance sheet data.

Compute selected ratios.

(LO 5)

Willingham Company
Balance Sheets
December 31

	2014	**2013**
Cash	$ 10,000	$ 30,000
Accounts receivable (net)	70,000	50,000
Inventory	60,000	50,000
Plant assets (net)	205,000	190,000
	$345,000	$320,000
Accounts payable	$ 50,000	$ 60,000
Mortgage payable (15%)	100,000	100,000
Common stock, $10 par	140,000	120,000
Retained earnings	55,000	40,000
	$345,000	$320,000

Additional information for 2014:

1. Net income was $25,000.
2. Sales on account were $410,000. Sales returns and allowances were $20,000.
3. Cost of goods sold was $187,000.

Instructions
Compute the following ratios at December 31, 2014.

(a) Current. (c) Accounts receivable turnover.
(b) Acid-test. (d) Inventory turnover.

E14-8 Selected comparative statement data for Molini Products Company are presented below. All balance sheet data are as of December 31.

Compute selected ratios.

(LO 5)

	2014	**2013**
Net sales	$700,000	$680,000
Cost of goods sold	480,000	400,000
Interest expense	7,000	5,000
Net income	42,000	34,000
Accounts receivable	120,000	100,000
Inventory	85,000	75,000
Total assets	580,000	540,000
Total common stockholders' equity	425,000	325,000

Instructions

Compute the following ratios for 2014.

(a) Profit margin.
(b) Asset turnover.
(c) Return on assets.
(d) Return on common stockholders' equity.

Compute selected ratios.

(LO 5)

E14-9 The income statement for Christiansen, Inc., appears below.

Christiansen, Inc.
Income Statement
For the Year Ended December 31, 2014

Net sales	$400,000
Cost of goods sold	235,000
Gross profit	165,000
Expenses (including $14,000 interest and $17,000 income taxes)	105,000
Net income	$ 60,000

Additional information:

1. The weighted-average common shares outstanding in 2014 were 30,000 shares.
2. The market price of Christiansen, Inc. stock was $10.80 in 2014.
3. Cash dividends of $21,000 were paid, $6,000 of which were to preferred stockholders.

Instructions

Compute the following ratios for 2014.

(a) Earnings per share.
(b) Price-earnings.
(c) Payout.
(d) Times interest earned.

Compute amounts from ratios.

(LO 5)

E14-10 Rees Corporation experienced a fire on December 31, 2014, in which its financial records were partially destroyed. It has been able to salvage some of the records and has ascertained the following balances.

	December 31, 2014	December 31, 2013
Cash	$ 30,000	$ 10,000
Accounts receivable (net)	73,000	126,000
Inventory	200,000	180,000
Accounts payable	50,000	90,000
Notes payable	30,000	60,000
Common stock, $100 par	400,000	400,000
Retained earnings	134,000	122,000

Additional information:

1. The inventory turnover is 3.4 times.
2. The return on common stockholders' equity is 25%. The company had no additional paid-in capital.
3. The accounts receivable turnover is 8.8 times.
4. The return on assets is 20%.
5. Total assets at December 31, 2013, were $650,000.

Instructions

Compute the following for Rees Corporation.

(a) Cost of goods sold for 2014.
(b) Net sales (credit) for 2014.
(c) Net income for 2014.
(d) Total assets at December 31, 2014.

E14-11 Yadier Corporation's comparative balance sheets are presented below.

Compute ratios.

(LO 5)

Yadier Corporation
Balance Sheets
December 31

	2014	2013
Cash	$ 4,300	$ 3,700
Accounts receivable	22,000	24,000
Inventory	10,000	7,000
Land	20,000	26,000
Buildings	70,000	70,000
Accumulated depreciation—buildings	(15,000)	(10,000)
Total	$111,300	$120,700
Accounts payable	$ 12,000	$ 31,100
Common stock	75,000	69,000
Retained earnings	24,300	20,600
Total	$111,300	$120,700

Yadier's 2014 income statement included net sales of $100,000, cost of goods sold of $60,350, and net income of $14,000.

Instructions

Compute the following ratios for 2014.

(a) Current ratio.
(b) Acid-test ratio.
(c) Accounts receivable turnover.
(d) Inventory turnover.
(e) Profit margin.
(f) Asset turnover.
(g) Return on assets.
(h) Return on common stockholders' equity.
(i) Debt to total assets ratio.

E14-12 For its fiscal year ending October 31, 2014, Douglas Corporation reports the following partial data shown below.

Prepare a correct income statement.

(LO 6)

Income before income taxes	$550,000
Income tax expense (30% × $410,000)	123,000
Income before extraordinary items	427,000
Extraordinary loss from flood	140,000
Net income	$287,000

The flood loss is considered an extraordinary item. The income tax rate is 30% on all items.

Instructions

(a) Prepare a correct income statement, beginning with income before income taxes.
(b) ▭▭▭▷ Explain in memo form why the income statement data are misleading.

E14-13 Maulder Corporation has income from continuing operations of $290,000 for the year ended December 31, 2014. It also has the following items (before considering income taxes).

Prepare income statement.

(LO 6)

1. An extraordinary loss of $70,000.
2. A gain of $35,000 on the discontinuance of a division.
3. A correction of an error in last year's financial statements that resulted in a $25,000 understatement of 2013 net income.

Assume all items are subject to income taxes at a 30% tax rate.

Instructions

(a) Prepare an income statement, beginning with income from continuing operations.
(b) Indicate the statement presentation of any item not included in (a) above.

EXERCISES: SET B AND CHALLENGE EXERCISES

Visit the book's companion website, at **www.wiley.com/college/weygandt**, and choose the Student Companion site to access Exercise Set B and Challenge Exercises.

PROBLEMS

Follow the rounding procedures used in the chapter.

Prepare vertical analysis and comment on profitability.

(LO 4, 5)

P14-1 Comparative statement data for Lionel Company and Barrymore Company, two competitors, appear below. All balance sheet data are as of December 31, 2014, and December 31, 2013.

	Lionel Company		Barrymore Company	
	2014	**2013**	**2014**	**2013**
Net sales	$1,549,035		$339,038	
Cost of goods sold	1,053,345		237,325	
Operating expenses	278,825		77,979	
Interest expense	7,745		2,034	
Income tax expense	61,960		8,476	
Current assets	401,584	$388,020	86,450	$ 82,581
Plant assets (net)	596,920	575,610	142,842	128,927
Current liabilities	65,015	75,507	19,618	14,654
Long-term liabilities	102,500	84,000	16,711	11,989
Common stock, $5 par	578,765	578,765	137,435	137,435
Retained earnings	252,224	225,358	55,528	47,430

Instructions

(a) Prepare a vertical analysis of the 2014 income statement data for Lionel Company and Barrymore Company in columnar form.

(b) ▭▭▭▭▭▭▷ Comment on the relative profitability of the companies by computing the return on assets and the return on common stockholders' equity ratios for both companies.

Compute ratios from balance sheet and income statement.

(LO 5)

P14-2 The comparative statements of Larker Tool Company are presented below.

Larker Tool Company
Income Statement
For the Years Ended December 31

	2014	**2013**
Net sales	$1,818,500	$1,750,500
Cost of goods sold	1,011,500	996,000
Gross profit	807,000	754,500
Selling and administrative expense	516,000	479,000
Income from operations	291,000	275,500
Other expenses and losses		
Interest expense	15,000	14,000
Income before income taxes	276,000	261,500
Income tax expense	84,000	77,000
Net income	$ 192,000	$ 184,500

Larker Tool Company
Balance Sheets
December 31

Assets	2014	2013
Current assets		
Cash	$ 60,100	$ 64,200
Short-term investments	69,000	50,000
Accounts receivable (net)	105,750	102,800
Inventory	110,950	115,500
Total current assets	345,800	332,500
Plant assets (net)	600,300	520,300
Total assets	$946,100	$852,800
Liabilities and Stockholders' Equity		
Current liabilities		
Accounts payable	$160,000	$145,400
Income taxes payable	43,500	42,000
Total current liabilities	203,500	187,400
Bonds payable	200,000	200,000
Total liabilities	403,500	387,400
Stockholders' equity		
Common stock ($5 par)	300,000	300,000
Retained earnings	242,600	165,400
Total stockholders' equity	542,600	465,400
Total liabilities and stockholders' equity	$946,100	$852,800

All sales were on account.

Instructions
Compute the following ratios for 2014. (Weighted-average common shares in 2014 were 60,000.)

(a) Earnings per share.
(b) Return on common stockholders' equity.
(c) Return on assets.
(d) Current.
(e) Acid-test.

(f) Accounts receivable turnover.
(g) Inventory turnover.
(h) Times interest earned.
(i) Asset turnover.
(j) Debt to total assets.

P14-3 Condensed balance sheet and income statement data for Clarence Corporation appear below and on page 752.

Perform ratio analysis, and evaluate financial position and operating results.

(LO 5)

Clarence Corporation
Balance Sheets
December 31

	2014	2013	2012
Cash	$ 25,000	$ 20,000	$ 18,000
Receivables (net)	50,000	45,000	48,000
Other current assets	90,000	95,000	64,000
Investments	75,000	70,000	45,000
Plant and equipment (net)	400,000	370,000	358,000
	$640,000	$600,000	$533,000
Current liabilities	$ 70,000	$ 75,000	$ 70,000
Long-term debt	80,000	85,000	50,000
Common stock, $10 par	345,000	315,000	300,000
Retained earnings	145,000	125,000	113,000
	$640,000	$600,000	$533,000

Clarence Corporation
Income Statement
For the Years Ended December 31

	2014	2013
Sales revenue	$740,000	$700,000
Less: Sales returns and allowances	40,000	60,000
Net sales	700,000	640,000
Cost of goods sold	420,000	400,000
Gross profit	280,000	240,000
Operating expenses (including income taxes)	238,000	208,000
Net income	$ 42,000	$ 32,000

Additional information:

1. The market price of Clarence's common stock was $4.00, $5.00, and $8.00 for 2012, 2013, and 2014, respectively.
2. All dividends were paid in cash.

Instructions
(a) Compute the following ratios for 2013 and 2014.
  (1) Profit margin.
  (2) Asset turnover.
  (3) Earnings per share. (Weighted-average common shares in 2014 were 32,000 and in 2013 were 31,000.)
  (4) Price-earnings.
  (5) Payout.
  (6) Debt to total assets.
(b) ▭▭▭▷ Based on the ratios calculated, discuss briefly the improvement or lack thereof in financial position and operating results from 2013 to 2014 of Clarence Corporation.

Compute ratios, and comment on overall liquidity and profitability.

(LO 5)

P14-4 Financial information for Ernie Bishop Company is presented below.

Ernie Bishop Company
Balance Sheets
December 31

Assets	2013	2012
Cash	$ 70,000	$ 65,000
Short-term investments	52,000	40,000
Receivables (net)	98,000	80,000
Inventory	125,000	135,000
Prepaid expenses	29,000	23,000
Land	130,000	130,000
Building and equipment (net)	168,000	175,000
	$672,000	$648,000

Liabilities and Stockholders' Equity		
Notes payable	$100,000	$100,000
Accounts payable	48,000	42,000
Accrued liabilities	44,000	40,000
Bonds payable, due 2016	150,000	150,000
Common stock, $10 par	200,000	200,000
Retained earnings	130,000	116,000
	$672,000	$648,000

Ernie Bishop Company
Income Statement
For the Years Ended December 31

	2013	2012
Net sales	$858,000	$798,000
Cost of goods sold	611,000	575,000
Gross profit	247,000	223,000
Operating expenses	204,500	181,000
Net income	$ 42,500	$ 42,000

Additional information:

1. Inventory at the beginning of 2012 was $118,000.
2. Total assets at the beginning of 2012 were $632,000.
3. No common stock transactions occurred during 2012 or 2013.
4. All sales were on account.
5. Receivables (net) at the beginning of 2012 were $88,000.

Instructions

(a) Indicate, by using ratios, the change in liquidity and profitability of Ernie Bishop Company from 2012 to 2013. (*Note:* Not all profitability ratios can be computed.)

(b) Given below are three independent situations and a ratio that may be affected. For each situation, compute the affected ratio (1) as of December 31, 2013, and (2) as of December 31, 2014, after giving effect to the situation. Net income for 2014 was $50,000. Total assets on December 31, 2014, were $700,000.

Situation	Ratio
(1) 18,000 shares of common stock were sold at par on July 1, 2014.	Return on common stockholders' equity
(2) All of the notes payable were paid in 2014. The only change in liabilities was that the notes payable were paid.	Debt to total assets
(3) Market price of common stock was $9 on December 31, 2013, and $12.50 on December 31, 2014.	Price-earnings ratio

P14-5 Selected financial data of Target and Wal-Mart Stores, Inc. for a recent year are presented here (in millions).

Compute selected ratios, and compare liquidity, profitability, and solvency for two companies.

(LO 5)

	Target Corporation	Wal-Mart Stores, Inc.
	Income Statement Data for Year	
Net sales	$67,390	$405,046
Cost of goods sold	45,725	304,657
Selling and administrative expenses	13,469	79,607
Interest expense	757	1,884
Other income (expense)	(2,944)	2,576
Income tax expense	1,575	7,139
Net income	$ 2,920	$ 14,335

	Balance Sheet Data (End of Year)	
Current assets	$17,213	$ 48,331
Noncurrent assets	26,492	122,375
Total assets	$43,705	$170,706
Current liabilities	$10,070	$ 55,561
Long-term debt	18,148	44,396
Total stockholders' equity	15,487	70,749
Total liabilities and stockholders' equity	$43,705	$170,706

	Target Corporation	Wal-Mart Stores, Inc.
	Beginning-of-Year Balances	
Total assets	$44,533	$163,429
Total stockholders' equity	15,347	65,285
Current liabilities	11,327	55,390
Total liabilities	29,186	98,144

	Other Data	
Average net accounts receivable	$ 6,560	$ 4,025
Average inventory	7,388	33,836
Net cash provided by operating activities	5,271	26,249

Instructions

(a) For each company, compute the following ratios.

(1) Current.	(7) Asset turnover.
(2) Accounts receivable turnover.	(8) Return on assets.
(3) Average collection period.	(9) Return on common stockholders' equity.
(4) Inventory turnover.	(10) Debt to total assets.
(5) Days in inventory.	(11) Times interest earned.
(6) Profit margin.	

(b) Compare the liquidity, profitability, and solvency of the two companies.

Compute numerous ratios.

(LO 5)

P14-6 The comparative statements of Beulah Company are presented below.

Beulah Company
Income Statement
For the Years Ended December 31

	2014	2013
Net sales (all on account)	$500,000	$420,000
Expenses		
Cost of goods sold	315,000	254,000
Selling and administrative	120,800	114,800
Interest expense	7,500	6,500
Income tax expense	20,000	15,000
Total expenses	463,300	390,300
Net income	$ 36,700	$ 29,700

Beulah Company
Balance Sheets
December 31

Assets	2014	2013
Current assets		
Cash	$ 21,000	$ 18,000
Short-term investments	18,000	15,000
Accounts receivable (net)	85,000	75,000
Inventory	80,000	60,000
Total current assets	204,000	168,000
Plant assets (net)	423,000	383,000
Total assets	$627,000	$551,000

Liabilities and Stockholders' Equity

Current liabilities		
Accounts payable	$122,000	$110,000
Income taxes payable	12,000	11,000
Total current liabilities	134,000	121,000
Long-term liabilities		
Bonds payable	120,000	80,000
Total liabilities	254,000	201,000
Stockholders' equity		
Common stock ($5 par)	150,000	150,000
Retained earnings	223,000	200,000
Total stockholders' equity	373,000	350,000
Total liabilities and stockholders' equity	$627,000	$551,000

Additional data:
The common stock recently sold at $19.50 per share.

Instructions
Compute the following ratios for 2014.

(a) Current.
(b) Acid-test.
(c) Accounts receivable turnover.
(d) Inventory turnover.
(e) Profit margin.
(f) Asset turnover.
(g) Return on assets.

(h) Return on common stockholders' equity.
(i) Earnings per share.
(j) Price-earnings.
(k) Payout.
(l) Debt to total assets.
(m) Times interest earned.

P14-7 Presented below is an incomplete income statement and an incomplete comparative balance sheet of Bondi Corporation.

Compute missing information given a set of ratios.

(LO 5)

Bondi Corporation
Income Statement
For the Year Ended December 31, 2014

Net sales	$10,500,000
Cost of goods sold	?
Gross profit	?
Operating expenses	1,500,000
Income from operations	?
Other expenses and losses	
Interest expense	?
Income before income taxes	?
Income tax expense	550,000
Net income	$?

Bondi Corporation
Balance Sheets
December 31

Assets	2014	2013
Current assets		
Cash	$ 480,000	$ 375,000
Accounts receivable (net)	?	950,000
Inventory	?	1,720,000
Total current assets	?	3,045,000
Plant assets (net)	4,620,000	4,455,000
Total assets	$?	$7,500,000

Assets	2014	2013
Liabilities and Stockholders' Equity		
Current liabilities	$?	$ 825,000
Long-term notes payable	?	3,300,000
Total liabilities	?	4,125,000
Common stock, $1 par	3,000,000	3,000,000
Retained earnings	400,000	375,000
Total stockholders' equity	3,400,000	3,375,000
Total liabilities and stockholders' equity	$?	$7,500,000

Additional information:

1. The accounts receivable turnover for 2014 is 10 times.
2. All sales are on account.
3. The profit margin for 2014 is 14.5%.
4. Return on assets is 20% for 2014.
5. The current ratio on December 31, 2014, is 3.0.
6. The inventory turnover for 2014 is 4.2 times.

Instructions

Compute the missing information given the ratios above. Show computations. (*Note:* Start with one ratio and derive as much information as possible from it before trying another ratio. List all missing amounts under the ratio used to find the information.)

Prepare income statement with discontinued operations and extraordinary loss.

(LO 6)

P14-8 Violet Bick Corporation owns a number of cruise ships and a chain of hotels. The hotels, which have not been profitable, were discontinued on September 1, 2014. The 2014 operating results for the company were as follows.

Operating revenues	$12,900,000
Operating expenses	8,700,000
Operating income	$ 4,200,000

Analysis discloses that these data include the operating results of the hotel chain, which were operating revenues $2,000,000 and operating expenses $2,500,000. The hotels were sold at a gain of $300,000 before taxes. This gain is not included in the operating results. During the year, Violet Bick suffered an extraordinary loss of $700,000 before taxes, which is not included in the operating results. In 2014, the company had other expenses and losses of $200,000, which are not included in the operating results. The corporation is in the 30% income tax bracket.

Instructions

Prepare a condensed income statement.

Prepare income statement with nontypical items.

(LO 6)

P14-9 The ledger of Gower Corporation at December 31, 2014, contains the following summary data.

Net sales	$1,600,000	Cost of goods sold	$1,100,000
Selling expenses	70,000	Administrative expenses	90,000
Other revenues and gains	22,000	Other expenses and losses	28,000

Your analysis reveals the following additional information that is not included in the above data.

1. The entire puzzles division was discontinued on August 31. The income from operations for this division before income taxes was $15,000. The puzzles division was sold at a loss of $80,000 before income taxes.
2. On May 15, company property was expropriated for an interstate highway. The settlement resulted in an extraordinary gain of $100,000 before income taxes.
3. The income tax rate on all items is 30%.

Instructions

Prepare an income statement for the year ended December 31, 2014. Use the format illustrated in the Comprehensive **DO IT!** (page 737).

PROBLEMS: SET B

Visit the book's companion website, at **www.wiley.com/college/weygandt**, and choose the Student Companion site to access Problem Set B.

CONTINUING COOKIE CHRONICLE

(*Note:* This is a continuation of the Cookie Chronicle from Chapters 1–13.)

CCC14 Natalie and Curtis have comparative balance sheets and income statements for Cookie & Coffee Creations Inc. They have been told that they can use these financial statements to prepare horizontal and vertical analyses, and to calculate financial ratios, to analyze how their business is doing and to make some decisions they have been considering.

Go to the book's companion website, www.wiley.com/college/weygandt, to see the completion of this problem.

Broadening Your **PERSPECTIVE**

Financial Reporting and Analysis

Financial Reporting Problem: PepsiCo, Inc.

BYP14-1 Your parents are considering investing in PepsiCo, Inc. common stock. They ask you, as an accounting expert, to make an analysis of the company for them. Fortunately, excerpts from a current annual report of PepsiCo are presented in Appendix A. Note that all dollar amounts are in millions.

Instructions
(Follow the approach in the chapter for rounding numbers.)
(a) Make a 5-year trend analysis, using 2006 as the base year, of (1) net sales and (2) net income. Comment on the significance of the trend results.
(b) Compute for 2010 and 2009 the (1) profit margin, (2) asset turnover, (3) return on assets, and (4) return on common stockholders' equity. How would you evaluate PepsiCo's profitability? Total assets at December 31, 2008, were $35,994 and total stockholders' equity at December 31, 2008, was $12,203.
(c) Compute for 2010 and 2009 the (1) debt to total assets and (2) times interest earned ratio. How would you evaluate PepsiCo's long-term solvency?
(d) What information outside the annual report may also be useful to your parents in making a decision about PepsiCo, Inc.?

Comparative Analysis Problem:
PepsiCo, Inc. vs. The Coca-Cola Company

BYP14-2 PepsiCo's financial statements are presented in Appendix A. Financial statements of The Coca-Cola Company are presented in Appendix B.

Instructions
(a) Based on the information contained in these financial statements, determine each of the following for each company.
   (1) The percentage increase (decrease) in (i) net sales and (ii) net income from 2009 to 2010.
   (2) The percentage increase in (i) total assets and (ii) total common stockholders' (shareholders') equity from 2009 to 2010.

(3) The basic earnings per share and price-earnings ratio for 2010. (For both PepsiCo and Coca-Cola, use the basic earnings per share.) Coca-Cola's common stock had a market price of $65.77 at the end of fiscal-year 2010, and PepsiCo's common stock had a market price of $65.69.

(b) What conclusions concerning the two companies can be drawn from these data?

Critical Thinking

Decision-Making Across the Organization

BYP14-3 As the CPA for Bonita Inc., you have been asked to develop some key ratios from the comparative financial statements. This information is to be used to convince creditors that the company is solvent and will continue as a going concern. The data requested and the computations developed from the financial statements follow.

	2014	2013
Current ratio	3.4 times	2.1 times
Acid-test ratio	.8 times	1.3 times
Asset turnover	2.6 times	2.2 times
Net income	Up 32%	Down 9%
Earnings per share	$3.30	$2.50

Instructions
With the class divided into groups, complete the following.

Bonita Inc. asks you to prepare a list of brief comments stating how each of these items supports the solvency and going-concern potential of the business. The company wishes to use these comments to support its presentation of data to its creditors. You are to prepare the comments as requested, giving the implications and the limitations of each item separately. Then prepare a collective inference that may be drawn from the individual items about Bonita's solvency and going-concern potential.

Real-World Focus

BYP14-4 The Management Discussion and Analysis section of an annual report addresses corporate performance for the year, and sometimes uses financial ratios to support its claims.

Address: **www.ibm.com/investor/tools/index.phtml** or go to **www.wiley.com/college/weygandt**

Steps
1. Choose **How to read annual reports** (in the Guides section).
2. Choose **Anatomy**.

Instructions
Using the information from the above site, answer the following questions.

(a) What are the optional elements that are often included in an annual report?
(b) What are the elements of an annual report that are required by the SEC?
(c) Describe the contents of the Management Discussion.
(d) Describe the contents of the Auditors' Report.
(e) Describe the contents of the Selected Financial Data.

Communication Activity

BYP14-5 Kyle Benson is the CEO of McCarty's Electronics. Benson is an expert engineer but a novice in accounting. He asks you to explain (1) the bases for comparison in analyzing McCarty's financial statements, and (2) the factors affecting quality of earnings.

Instructions
Write a letter to Kyle Benson that explains the bases for comparison and factors affecting quality of earnings.

Ethics Case

BYP14-6 Robert Turnbull, president of Turnbull Industries, wishes to issue a press release to bolster his company's image and maybe even its stock price, which has been gradually falling. As controller, you have been asked to provide a list of 20 financial ratios along with some other operating statistics relative to Turnbull Industries' first quarter financials and operations.

Two days after you provide the ratios and data requested, Perry Jarvis, the public relations director of Turnbull, asks you to prove the accuracy of the financial and operating data contained in the press release written by the president and edited by Perry. In the press release, the president highlights the sales increase of 25% over last year's first quarter and the positive change in the current ratio from 1.5:1 last year to 3:1 this year. He also emphasizes that production was up 50% over the prior year's first quarter.

You note that the press release contains only positive or improved ratios and none of the negative or deteriorated ratios. For instance, no mention is made that the debt to total assets ratio has increased from 35% to 55%, that inventories are up 89%, and that while the current ratio improved, the acid-test ratio fell from 1:1 to .5:1. Nor is there any mention that the reported profit for the quarter would have been a loss had not the estimated lives of Turnbull's plant and machinery been increased by 30%. Perry emphasized, "The prez wants this release by early this afternoon."

Instructions
(a) Who are the stakeholders in this situation?
(b) Is there anything unethical in president Turnbull's actions?
(c) Should you as controller remain silent? Does Perry have any responsibility?

All About You

BYP14-7 In this chapter, you learned how to use many tools for performing a financial analysis of a company. When making personal investments, however, it is most likely that you won't be buying stocks and bonds in individual companies. Instead, when most people want to invest in stock, they buy mutual funds. By investing in a mutual fund, you reduce your risk because the fund diversifies by buying the stock of a variety of different companies, bonds, and other investments, depending on the stated goals of the fund.

Before you invest in a fund, you will need to decide what type of fund you want. For example, do you want a fund that has the potential of high growth (but also high risk), or are you looking for lower risk and a steady stream of income? Do you want a fund that invests only in U.S. companies, or do you want one that invests globally? Many resources are available to help you with these types of decisions.

Instructions
Go to **http://web.archive.org/web/20050210200843/http://www.cnb1.com/invallocmdl.htm** and complete the investment allocation questionnaire. Add up your total points to determine the type of investment fund that would be appropriate for you.

FASB Codification Activity

BYP14-8 If your school has a subscription to the FASB Codification, go to *http://aaahq.org/ ascLogin.cfm* to log in and prepare responses to the following. Use the Master Glossary for determining the proper definitions.

(a) Discontinued operations.
(b) Extraordinary items.
(c) Comprehensive income.

Answers to Chapter Questions

Answers to Insight and Accounting Across the Organization Questions

p. 721 How to Manage the Current Ratio Q: How might management influence a company's current ratio? **A:** Management can affect the current ratio by speeding up or withholding payments on accounts payable just before the balance sheet date. Management can alter the cash balance by increasing or decreasing long-term assets or long-term debt, or by issuing or purchasing common stock.

p. 733 What Does "Non-Recurring" Really Mean? Q: If a company takes a large restructuring charge, what is the effect on the company's current income statement versus future ones? **A:** The current period's net income can be greatly diminished by a large restructuring charge. The net incomes in future periods can be enhanced because they are relieved of costs (e.g., depreciation and labor expenses) that would have been charged to them.

Answers to Self-Test Questions

1. b **2.** d **3.** a **4.** c **5.** c ($360,000 ÷ 300,000) **6.** c **7.** c **8.** b $306,000 ÷ [($54,000 + $48,000) ÷ 2] = 6; 365 ÷ 6 **9.** b ($81,000 ÷ $27,000) **10.** a $134,000 ÷ $784,000 **11.** d ($134,000 − $4,000) ÷ [($240,000 + $198,000) ÷ 2] **12.** c ($134,000 + $22,000 + $12,000) ÷ $12,000 **13.** c **14.** d ($400,000 − (25% × $400,000); $100,000 − (25% × $100,000) **15.** d

A Look at IFRS

The tools of financial analysis, covered in the first sections of this chapter, are the same throughout the world. Techniques such as vertical and horizontal analysis, for example, are tools used by analysts regardless of whether GAAP- or IFRS-related financial statements are being evaluated. In addition, the ratios provided in the textbook are the same ones that are used internationally.

The latter part of this chapter relates to the income statement and irregular items. As in GAAP, the income statement is a required statement under IFRS. In addition, the content and presentation of an IFRS income statement is similar to the one used for GAAP. *IAS 1* (revised), "Presentation of Financial Statements," provides general guidelines for the reporting of income statement information. In general, the differences in the presentation of financial statement information are relatively minor.

Key Points

- The tools of financial statement analysis covered in this chapter are universal and therefore no significant differences exist in the analysis methods used.

- The basic objectives of the income statement are the same under both GAAP and IFRS. As indicated in the textbook, a very important objective is to ensure that users of the income statement can evaluate the earning power of the company. Earning power is the normal level of income to be obtained in the future. Thus, both the IASB and the FASB are interested in distinguishing normal levels of income from irregular items in order to better predict a company's future profitability.

- The basic accounting for discontinued operations is the same under IFRS and GAAP.

- Under IFRS, there is no classification for extraordinary items. In other words, extraordinary item treatment is prohibited under IFRS. All revenue and expense items are considered ordinary in nature. Disclosure, however, is extensive for items that are considered material to the financial results. Examples are write-downs of inventory or plant assets, or gains and losses on the sale of plant assets.

- The accounting for changes in accounting principles and changes in accounting estimates are the same for both GAAP and IFRS.

- Both IFRS and GAAP follow the same approach in reporting comprehensive income. The statement of comprehensive income can be prepared under the one-statement approach or the two-statement approach.

    Under the one-statement approach, all components of revenue and expense are reported in the income statement. This combined statement of comprehensive income first computes net income or loss, which is then followed by components of other comprehensive income or loss items to arrive at comprehensive income. An example appears on the next page.

Walter Company
Statement of Comprehensive Income
For the Year Ended December 31, 2014

Sales revenue	$5,100,000
Cost of goods sold	3,800,000
Gross profit	1,300,000
Operating expenses	700,000
Net income	600,000
Other comprehensive income	
Unrealized gain on non-trading securities	75,000
Comprehensive income	$ 675,000

Under the two-statement approach, all the components of revenues and expenses are reported in a traditional income statement *except* for other comprehensive income or loss. In addition, a second statement (the statement of comprehensive income) is then prepared, starting with net income and followed by other comprehensive income or loss items to arrive at comprehensive income. An example of the two-statement approach, using the same data as that used above for Walter Company, appears below.

Walter Company
Income Statement
For the Year Ended December 31, 2014

Sales revenue	$5,100,000
Cost of goods sold	3,800,000
Gross profit	1,300,000
Operating expenses	700,000
Net income	$ 600,000

Walter Company
Statement of Comprehensive Income
For the Year Ended December 31, 2014

Net income	$600,000
Other comprehensive income	
Unrealized gain on non-trading securities	75,000
Comprehensive income	$675,000

- The issues related to quality of earnings are the same under both GAAP and IFRS. It is hoped that by adopting a more principles-based approach, as found in IFRS, many of the earnings' quality issues will disappear.

Looking to the Future

The FASB and the IASB are working on a project that would rework the structure of financial statements. Recently, the IASB decided to require a statement of comprehensive income, similar to what was required under GAAP. In addition, another part of this project addresses the issue of how to classify various items in the income statement. A main goal of this new approach is to provide information that better represents how businesses are run. In addition, the approach draws attention away from one number—net income.

IFRS Practice

IFRS Self-Test Questions

1. The basic tools of financial analysis are the same under both GAAP and IFRS *except* that:
   (a) horizontal analysis cannot be done because the format of the statements is sometimes different.
   (b) analysis is different because vertical analysis cannot be done under IFRS.
   (c) the current ratio cannot be computed because current liabilities are often reported before current assets in IFRS statements of position.
   (d) None of the above.

2. Under IFRS:
   (a) the reporting of discontinued items is different than GAAP.
   (b) the reporting of extraordinary items is prohibited.
   (c) the reporting of changes in accounting principles is different than under GAAP.
   (d) None of the above.

3. Presentation of comprehensive income must be reported under IFRS in:
   (a) the statement of stockholders' equity.
   (b) the income statement ending with net income.
   (c) the notes to the financial statements.
   (d) a statement of comprehensive income.

4. Parmalane reports the following information:

Sales revenue	$500,000
Cost of goods sold	200,000
Operating expense	40,000
Unrealized loss on non-trading securities	10,000

   Parmalane should report the following under the two-statement approach using IFRS:
   (a) net income of $260,000 and comprehensive income of $270,000.
   (b) net income of $270,000 and comprehensive income of $260,000.
   (c) other comprehensive income of $10,000 and comprehensive income of $270,000.
   (d) other comprehensive loss of $10,000 and comprehensive income of 250,000.

5. Assuming the same information as in Question 4, Parmalane should report the following using a one-statement approach under IFRS:
   (a) net income of $260,000 and comprehensive income of $270,000.
   (b) net income of $270,000 and comprehensive income of $260,000.
   (c) other comprehensive income of $10,000 and comprehensive income of $270,000.
   (d) other comprehensive loss of $10,000 and comprehensive income of $250,000.

IFRS Exercises

IFRS14-1 Chen Company reports the following information for the year ended December 31, 2014: sales revenue $1,000,000, cost of goods sold $700,000, operating expenses $200,000, and an unrealized gain on non-trading securities of $75,000. Prepare a statement of comprehensive income using the one-statement approach.

IFRS14-2 Assume the same information for Chen Company as in IFRS14-1. Prepare the income statement using the two-statement approach.

International Financial Reporting Problem: Zetar plc

IFRS14-3 The financial statements of Zetar plc are presented in Appendix C. The company's complete annual report, including the notes to its financial statements, is available at **www.zetarplc. com**.

Instructions

Use the company's annual report to answer the following questions.

(a) The company's 2009 income statement reports a loss on discontinued operations. What business did the company discontinue, and why did it choose to discontinue the business?

(b) For the year ended April 30, 2009, what amount did the company lose on the operation of the discontinued business, and what amount did it lose on disposal?

(c) What was the total recorded value of the net assets at the date of disposal, and what was the amount of costs incurred to dispose of the business?

Answers to IFRS Self-Test Questions

1. d   **2.** b   **3.** d   **4.** d   **5.** d

Chapter 15

Managerial Accounting

Feature Story

Just Add Water ... and Paddle

Mike Cichanowski grew up on the Mississippi River in Winona, Minnesota. At a young age, he learned to paddle a canoe so he could explore the river. Before long, Mike began crafting his own canoes from bent wood and fiberglass in his dad's garage. Then, when his canoe-making shop outgrew the garage, he moved it into an old warehouse. When that was going to be torn down, Mike came to a critical juncture in his life. He took out a bank loan and built his own small shop, giving birth to the company Wenonah Canoe.

Wenonah Canoe soon became known as a pioneer in developing techniques

to get the most out of new materials such as plastics, composites, and carbon fibers—maximizing strength while minimizing weight.

In the 1990s, as kayaking became popular, Mike made another critical decision when he acquired Current Designs, a premier Canadian kayak manufacturer. This venture allowed Wenonah to branch out with new product lines while providing Current Designs with much-needed capacity expansion as well as manufacturing expertise. Mike moved Current Designs' headquarters to Minnesota and made a big (and potentially risky) investment in a new production facility. Today, the company's 90 employees produce and sell about

---

Learning Objectives

After studying this chapter, you should be able to:

1 Explain the distinguishing features of managerial accounting.

2 Identify the three broad functions of management.

3 Define the three classes of manufacturing costs.

4 Distinguish between product and period costs.

5 Explain the difference between a merchandising and a manufacturing income statement.

6 Indicate how cost of goods manufactured is determined.

7 Explain the difference between a merchandising and a manufacturing balance sheet.

8 Identify trends in managerial accounting.

 The Navigator

12,000 canoes and kayaks per year, across the country and around the world.

Mike will tell you that business success is "a three-legged stool." The first leg is the knowledge and commitment to make a great product. Wenonah's canoes and Current Designs' kayaks are widely regarded as among the very best. The second leg is the ability to sell your product. Mike's company started off making great canoes, but it took a little longer to figure out how to sell them. The third leg is not something that most of you would immediately associate with entrepreneurial success. It is what goes on behind the scenes—accounting. Good accounting

Source: www.wenonah.com.

information is absolutely critical to the countless decisions, big and small, that ensure the survival and growth of the company.

Bottom line: No matter how good your product is, and no matter how many units you sell, if you don't have a firm grip on your numbers, you are up a creek without a paddle.

*Watch the **What Is Managerial Accounting?** video in WileyPLUS for an introduction to managerial accounting and the topics presented in this course.*

✔ **The Navigator**

Preview of Chapter 15

This chapter focuses on issues illustrated in the Feature Story about Current Designs and its parent company Wenonah Canoe. To succeed, the company needs to determine and control the costs of material, labor, and overhead, and understand the relationship between costs and profits. Managers often make decisions that determine their company's fate—and their own. Managers are evaluated on the results of their decisions. Managerial accounting provides tools for assisting management in making decisions and for evaluating the effectiveness of those decisions.

The content and organization of this chapter are as follows.

MANAGERIAL ACCOUNTING			
Managerial Accounting Basics	**Managerial Cost Concepts**	**Manufacturing Costs in Financial Statements**	**Managerial Accounting Today**
• Comparing managerial and financial accounting • Management functions • Organizational structure • Business ethics	• Manufacturing costs • Product vs. period costs	• Income statement • Cost of goods manufactured • Balance sheet • Cost concepts—A review • Product costing for service industries	• Focus on the value chain • Balanced scorecard • Corporate social responsibility

✔ **The Navigator**

Managerial Accounting Basics

Managerial accounting provides economic and financial information for managers and other internal users. The skills that you will learn in this course will be vital to your future success in business. You don't believe us? Let's look at some examples of some of the crucial activities of employees at Current Designs, and where those activities are addressed in this textbook.

In order to know whether it is making a profit, Current Designs needs accurate information about the cost of each kayak (Chapters 16, 17, and 18). And to stay profitable, Current Designs must adjust the number of kayaks it produces in light of changes in economic conditions and consumer tastes. It then needs to understand how changes in the number of kayaks it produces impact its production costs and profitability (Chapters 19 and 20). Further, Current Designs' managers must often consider alternative courses of action. For example, should the company accept a special order from a customer, produce a particular kayak component internally or outsource it, or continue or discontinue a particular product line (Chapter 21)? Finally, one of the most important, and most difficult, decisions is what price to charge for the kayaks (Chapter 22).

In order to plan for the future, Current Designs prepares budgets (Chapter 23), and it then compares its budgeted numbers with its actual results to evaluate performance and identify areas that need to change (Chapters 24 and 25). Finally, it sometimes needs to make substantial investment decisions, such as the building of a new plant or the purchase of new equipment (Chapter 26).

Someday, you are going to face decisions just like these. You may end up in sales, marketing, management, production, or finance. You may work for a company that provides medical care, produces software, or serves up mouth-watering meals. No matter what your position is, and no matter what your product, the skills you acquire in this class will increase your chances of business success. Put another way, in business you can either guess, or you can make an informed decision. As the CEO of Microsoft once noted: "If you're supposed to be making money in business and supposed to be satisfying customers and building market share, there are numbers that characterize those things. And if somebody can't speak to me quantitatively about it, then I'm nervous." This course gives you the skills you need to quantify information so you can make informed business decisions.

Comparing Managerial and Financial Accounting

LEARNING OBJECTIVE   1

Explain the distinguishing features of managerial accounting.

There are both similarities and differences between managerial and financial accounting. First, each field of accounting deals with the economic events of a business. For example, *determining* the unit cost of manufacturing a product is part of managerial accounting. *Reporting* the total cost of goods manufactured and sold is part of financial accounting. In addition, both managerial and financial accounting require that a company's economic events be quantified and communicated to interested parties. Illustration 15-1 summarizes the principal differences between financial accounting and managerial accounting.

Management Functions

LEARNING OBJECTIVE   2

Identify the three broad functions of management.

Managers' activities and responsibilities can be classified into three broad functions:

1. Planning.
2. Directing.
3. Controlling.

Feature	Financial Accounting	Managerial Accounting
Primary Users of Reports	External users: stockholders, creditors, and regulators.	Internal users: officers and managers.
Types and Frequency of Reports	Financial statements. Quarterly and annually.	Internal reports. As frequently as needed.
Purpose of Reports	General-purpose.	Special-purpose for specific decisions.
Content of Reports	Pertains to business as a whole. Highly aggregated (condensed). Limited to double-entry accounting and cost data. Generally accepted accounting principles.	Pertains to subunits of the business. Very detailed. Extends beyond double-entry accounting to any relevant data. Standard is relevance to decisions.
Verification Process	Audited by CPA.	No independent audits.

Illustration 15-1
Differences between financial and managerial accounting

In performing these functions, managers make decisions that have a significant impact on the organization.

Planning requires managers to look ahead and to establish objectives. These objectives are often diverse: maximizing short-term profits and market share, maintaining a commitment to environmental protection, and contributing to social programs. For example, Hewlett-Packard, in an attempt to gain a stronger foothold in the computer industry, has greatly reduced its prices to compete with Dell. A key objective of management is to **add value** to the business under its control. Value is usually measured by the trading price of the company's stock and by the potential selling price of the company.

Directing involves coordinating a company's diverse activities and human resources to produce a smooth-running operation. This function relates to implementing planned objectives and providing necessary incentives to motivate employees. For example, manufacturers such as Campbell Soup Company, General Motors, and Dell must coordinate purchasing, manufacturing, warehousing, and selling. Service corporations such as American Airlines, Federal Express, and AT&T must coordinate scheduling, sales, service, and acquisitions of equipment and supplies. Directing also involves selecting executives, appointing managers and supervisors, and hiring and training employees.

The third management function, **controlling**, is the process of keeping the company's activities on track. In controlling operations, managers determine whether planned goals are being met. When there are deviations from targeted objectives, managers must decide what changes are needed to get back on track. Scandals at companies like Enron, Lucent, and Xerox attest to the fact that companies must have adequate controls to ensure that the company develops and distributes accurate information.

How do managers achieve control? A smart manager in a very small operation can make personal observations, ask good questions, and know how to evaluate the answers. But using this approach in a larger organization would result in chaos. Imagine the president of Current Designs attempting to determine whether the company is meeting its planned objectives, without some record of what has happened and what is expected to occur. Thus, large businesses typically use a formal system of evaluation. These systems include such features as budgets, responsibility centers, and performance evaluation reports—all of which are features of managerial accounting.

Decision-making is not a separate management function. Rather, it is the outcome of the exercise of good judgment in planning, directing, and controlling.

MANAGEMENT INSIGHT

Even the Best Have to Get Better

Louis Vuitton is a French manufacturer of high-end handbags, wallets, and suitcases. Its reputation for quality and style allows it to charge extremely high prices–for example, $700 for a tote bag. But often in the past, when demand was hot, supply was nonexistent–shelves were empty, and would-be buyers left empty-handed.

Luxury-goods manufacturers used to consider stockouts to be a good thing, but recently Louis Vuitton changed its attitude. The company adopted "lean" processes used by car manufacturers and electronics companies to speed up production of "hot" products. Work is done by flexible teams, with jobs organized based on how long a task takes. By reducing wasted time and eliminating bottlenecks, what used to take 20 to 30 workers eight days to do now takes 6 to 12 workers one day. Also, production employees who used to specialize on a single task on a single product are now multiskilled. This allows them to quickly switch products to meet demand.

To make sure that the factory is making the right products, within a week of a product launch, Louis Vuitton stores around the world feed sales information to the headquarters in France, and production is adjusted accordingly. Finally, the new production processes have also improved quality. Returns of some products are down by two-thirds, which makes quite a difference to the bottom line when the products are pricey.

Source: Christina Passariello, "Louis Vuitton Tries Modern Methods on Factory Lines," *Wall Street Journal* (October 9, 2006).

 ? What are some of the steps that this company has taken in order to ensure that production meets demand? (See page 807.)

Organizational Structure

Most companies prepare **organization charts** to show the interrelationships of activities and the delegation of authority and responsibility within the company. Illustration 15-2 shows a typical organization chart.

Stockholders own the corporation, but they manage it indirectly through a **board of directors** they elect. The board formulates the operating policies for the company or organization. The board also selects officers, such as a president and one or more vice presidents, to execute policy and to perform daily management functions.

The **chief executive officer (CEO)** has overall responsibility for managing the business. As the organization chart on the next page shows, the CEO delegates responsibilities to other officers.

Responsibilities within the company are frequently classified as either line or staff positions. Employees with **line positions** are directly involved in the company's primary revenue-generating operating activities. Examples of line positions include the vice president of operations, vice president of marketing, plant managers, supervisors, and production personnel. Employees with **staff positions** are involved in activities that support the efforts of the line employees. In a company like General Electric or Facebook, employees in finance, legal, and human

Illustration 15-2
Corporation's organization
chart

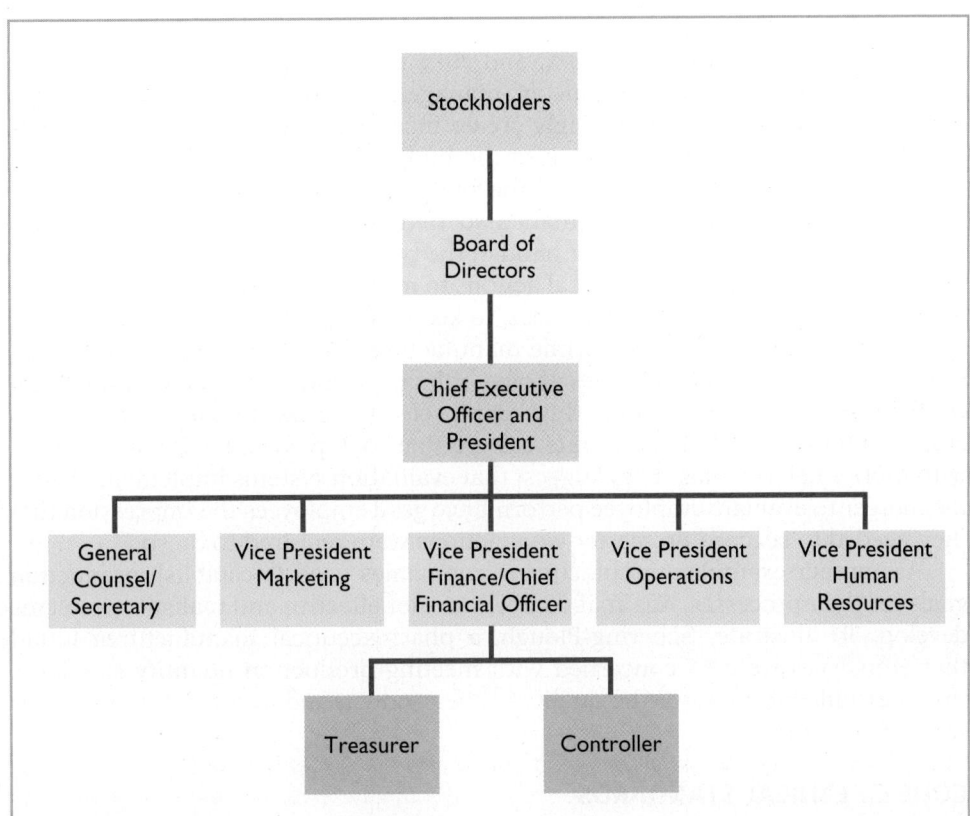

resources have staff positions. While activities of staff employees are vital to the company, these employees are nonetheless there to serve the line employees who engage in the company's primary operations.

The **chief financial officer (CFO)** is responsible for all of the accounting and finance issues the company faces. The CFO is supported by the **controller** and the **treasurer**. The controller's responsibilities include (1) maintaining the accounting records, (2) maintaining an adequate system of internal control, and (3) preparing financial statements, tax returns, and internal reports. The treasurer has custody of the corporation's funds and is responsible for maintaining the company's cash position.

Also serving the CFO is the internal audit staff. The staff's responsibilities include reviewing the reliability and integrity of financial information provided by the controller and treasurer. Staff members also ensure that internal control systems are functioning properly to safeguard corporate assets. In addition, they investigate compliance with policies and regulations, and in many companies they determine whether resources are being used in the most economical and efficient fashion.

The vice president of operations oversees employees with line positions. For example, the company might have multiple plant managers, each of whom would report to the vice president of operations. Each plant would also have department managers, such as fabricating, painting, and shipping, each of whom would report to the plant manager.

Business Ethics

All employees within an organization are expected to act ethically in their business activities. Given the importance of ethical behavior to corporations and their owners (stockholders), an increasing number of organizations provide codes of business ethics for their employees.

CREATING PROPER INCENTIVES

Companies like Amazon.com, IBM, and Nike use complex systems to monitor, control, and evaluate the actions of managers. Unfortunately, these systems and controls sometimes unwittingly create incentives for managers to take unethical actions. For example, because the budget is also used as an evaluation tool, some managers try to "game" the budgeting process by underestimating their division's predicted performance so that it will be easier to meet their performance targets. On the other hand, if the budget is set at unattainable levels, managers sometimes take unethical actions to meet the targets in order to receive higher compensation or, in some cases, to keep their jobs.

For example, at one time, airline manufacturer Boeing was plagued by a series of scandals including charges of over-billing, corporate espionage, and illegal conflicts of interest. Some long-time employees of Boeing blame the decline in ethics on a change in the corporate culture that took place after Boeing merged with McDonnell Douglas. They suggest that evaluation systems implemented after the merger to evaluate employee performance gave employees the impression that they needed to succeed no matter what actions were required to do so.

As another example, manufacturing companies need to establish production goals for their processes. Again, if controls are not effective and realistic, problems develop. To illustrate, Schering-Plough, a pharmaceutical manufacturer, found that employees were so concerned with meeting production quantity standards that they failed to monitor the quality of the product, and as a result the dosages were often wrong.

CODE OF ETHICAL STANDARDS

In response to corporate scandals, the U.S. Congress enacted the **Sarbanes-Oxley Act (SOX)** to help prevent lapses in internal control. One result of SOX was to clarify top management's responsibility for the company's financial statements. CEOs and CFOs must now certify that financial statements give a fair presentation of the company's operating results and its financial condition. In addition, top managers must certify that the company maintains an adequate system of internal controls to safeguard the company's assets and ensure accurate financial reports.

Another result of SOX is that companies now pay more attention to the composition of the board of directors. In particular, the audit committee of the board of directors must be comprised entirely of independent members (that is, non-employees) and must contain at least one financial expert. Finally, the law substantially increases the penalties for misconduct.

To provide guidance for managerial accountants, the Institute of Management Accountants (IMA) has developed a code of ethical standards, entitled *IMA Statement of Ethical Professional Practice*. Management accountants should not commit acts in violation of these standards. Nor should they condone such acts by others within their organizations. We include the IMA code of ethical standards in Appendix H. Throughout the textbook, we will address various ethical issues managers face.

> **DO IT!**

Managerial Accounting Concepts

Indicate whether the following statements are true or false.

1. Managerial accountants have a single role within an organization, collecting and reporting costs to management.

2. Financial accounting reports are general-purpose and intended for external users.

3. Managerial accounting reports are special-purpose and issued as frequently as needed.

4. Managers' activities and responsibilities can be classified into three broad functions: cost accounting, budgeting, and internal control.

5. As a result of the Sarbanes-Oxley Act, managerial accounting reports must now comply with generally accepted accounting principles (GAAP).

6. Top managers must certify that a company maintains an adequate system of internal controls.

Action Plan

✔ Understand that managerial accounting is a field of accounting that provides economic and financial information for managers and other internal users.

✔ Understand that financial accounting provides information for external users.

✔ Analyze which users require which different types of information.

Solution

1. False. Managerial accountants determine product costs. In addition, managerial accountants are now held responsible for evaluating how well the company is employing its resources. As a result, when the company makes critical strategic decisions, managerial accountants serve as team members alongside personnel from production, marketing, and engineering.

2. True.

3. True.

4. False. Managers' activities are classified into three broad functions: planning, directing, and controlling. Planning requires managers to look ahead to establish objectives. Directing involves coordinating a company's diverse activities and human resources to produce a smooth-running operation. Controlling keeps the company's activities on track.

5. False. SOX clarifies top management's responsibility for the company's financial statements. In addition, top managers must certify that the company maintains an adequate system of internal control to safeguard the company's assets and ensure accurate financial reports.

6. True.

Related exercise material: **BE15-1, BE15-2, BE15-3, E15-1, and** **DO IT!** **15-1.**

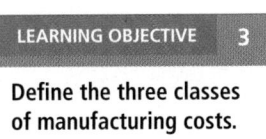
✔ **The Navigator**

Managerial Cost Concepts

In order for managers at a company like Current Designs to plan, direct, and control operations effectively, they need good information. One very important type of information is related to costs. Managers should ask questions such as the following.

1. What costs are involved in making a product or providing a service?

2. If we decrease production volume, will costs decrease?

3. What impact will automation have on total costs?

4. How can we best control costs?

To answer these questions, managers need reliable and relevant cost information. We now explain and illustrate the various cost categories that companies use.

Manufacturing Costs

Manufacturing consists of activities and processes that convert raw materials into finished goods. Contrast this type of operation with merchandising, which sells merchandise in the form in which it is purchased. Manufacturing costs are classified as direct materials, direct labor, and manufacturing overhead.

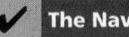
LEARNING OBJECTIVE   3

Define the three classes of manufacturing costs.

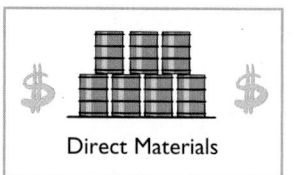

Direct Materials

DIRECT MATERIALS

To obtain the materials that will be converted into the finished product, the manufacturer purchases raw materials. **Raw materials** are the basic materials and parts used in the manufacturing process.

Raw materials that can be physically and directly associated with the finished product during the manufacturing process are **direct materials**. Examples include flour in the baking of bread, syrup in the bottling of soft drinks, and steel in the making of automobiles. A primary direct material of many Current Designs' kayaks is polyethylene powder. Some of its high-performance kayaks use Kevlar®.

Some raw materials cannot be easily associated with the finished product. These are called indirect materials. **Indirect materials** have one of two characteristics: (1) They do not physically become part of the finished product (such as lubricants used by Current Designs in its equipment and polishing compounds used for the finishing touches on kayaks). Or, (2) they are impractical to trace to the finished product because their physical association with the finished product is too small in terms of cost (such as cotter pins and lock washers). Companies account for indirect materials as part of **manufacturing overhead**.

Direct Labor

DIRECT LABOR

The work of factory employees that can be physically and directly associated with converting raw materials into finished goods is **direct labor**. Bottlers at Coca-Cola, bakers at Sara Lee, and equipment operators at Current Designs are employees whose activities are usually classified as direct labor. **Indirect labor** refers to the work of employees that has no physical association with the finished product, or for which it is impractical to trace costs to the goods produced. Examples include wages of factory maintenance people, factory time-keepers, and factory supervisors. Like indirect materials, companies classify indirect labor as **manufacturing overhead**.

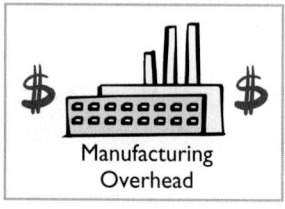

Manufacturing Overhead

MANUFACTURING OVERHEAD

Manufacturing overhead consists of costs that are indirectly associated with the manufacture of the finished product. Overhead costs also include manufacturing costs that cannot be classified as direct materials or direct labor. Manufacturing overhead includes indirect materials, indirect labor, depreciation on factory buildings and machines, and insurance, taxes, and maintenance on factory facilities.

Alternative Terminology
Some companies use terms such as *factory overhead*, *indirect manufacturing costs*, and *burden* instead of manufacturing overhead.

One study of manufactured goods found the following magnitudes of the three different product costs as a percentage of the total product cost: direct materials 54%, direct labor 13%, and manufacturing overhead 33%. Note that the direct labor component is the smallest. This component of product cost is dropping substantially because of automation. Companies are working hard to increase productivity by decreasing labor. In some companies, direct labor has become as little as 5% of the total cost.

Allocating direct materials and direct labor costs to specific products is fairly straightforward. Good recordkeeping can tell a company how much plastic it used in making each type of gear, or how many hours of factory labor it took to assemble a part. But allocating overhead costs to specific products presents problems. How much of the purchasing agent's salary is attributable to the hundreds of different products made in the same plant? What about the grease that keeps the machines humming, or the computers that make sure paychecks come out on time? Boiled down to its simplest form, the question becomes: Which products cause the incurrence of which costs? In subsequent chapters, we show various methods of allocating overhead to products.

MANAGEMENT INSIGHT

Why Manufacturing Matters for U.S. Workers

Prior to 2010, U.S. manufacturing employment fell at an average rate of 0.1% per year for 60 years. At the same time, U.S. factory output increased by an average rate of 3.4%. As manufacturers relied more heavily on automation, the number of people they needed declined. However, factory jobs are important because the average wage of a factory worker is $22, twice the average wage of employees in the service sector. Fortunately, manufacturing jobs in the United States increased by 1.2% in 2010, and they are forecast to continue to increase through at least 2015. Why? Because companies like Whirlpool, Caterpillar, and Dow are building huge new plants in the United States to replace old, inefficient U.S. facilities. For many products that are ultimately sold in the United States, it makes more sense to produce them domestically and save on the shipping costs. In addition, these efficient new plants, combined with an experienced workforce, will make it possible to compete with manufacturers in other countries, thereby increasing export potential.

Source: Bob Tita, "Whirlpool to Invest in Tennessee Plant," *Wall Street Journal Online* (September 1, 2010); and James R. Hagerty, "U.S. Factories Buck Decline," *Wall Street Journal Online* (January 19, 2011).

 In what ways does the shift to automated factories change the amount and composition of product costs? (See page 807.)

Product versus Period Costs

Each of the manufacturing cost components—direct materials, direct labor, and manufacturing overhead—are product costs. As the term suggests, **product costs** are costs that are a necessary and integral part of producing the finished product. Companies record product costs, when incurred, as inventory. These costs do not become expenses until the company sells the finished goods inventory. At that point, the company records the expense as cost of goods sold.

Period costs are costs that are matched with the revenue of a specific time period rather than included as part of the cost of a salable product. These are nonmanufacturing costs. Period costs include selling and administrative expenses. In order to determine net income, companies deduct these costs from revenues in the period in which they are incurred.

Illustration 15-3 summarizes these relationships and cost terms. Our main concern in this chapter is with product costs.

> **LEARNING OBJECTIVE   4**
>
> **Distinguish between product and period costs.**

Alternative Terminology
Product costs are also called *inventoriable costs.*

Illustration 15-3
Product versus period costs

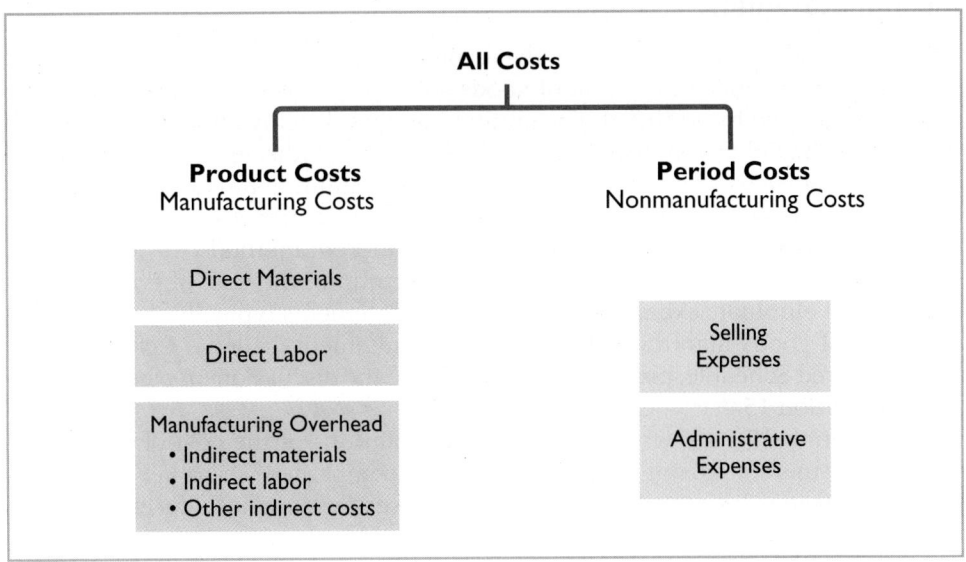

> DO IT!

Managerial Cost Concepts

Action Plan

✔ Classify as direct materials any raw materials that can be physically and directly associated with the finished product.

✔ Classify as direct labor the work of factory employees that can be physically and directly associated with the finished product.

✔ Classify as manufacturing overhead any costs that are indirectly associated with the finished product.

A bicycle company has these costs: tires, salaries of employees who put tires on the wheels, factory building depreciation, lubricants, spokes, salary of factory manager, handlebars, and salaries of factory maintenance employees. Classify each cost as direct materials, direct labor, or overhead.

Solution

Tires, spokes, and handlebars are direct materials. Salaries of employees who put tires on the wheels are direct labor. All of the other costs are manufacturing overhead.

Related exercise material: **BE15-4, BE15-5, BE15-6, BE15-7, E15-2, E15-3, E15-4, E15-5, E15-6, E15-7, and DO IT! 15-2.**

✔ **The Navigator**

Manufacturing Costs in Financial Statements

The financial statements of a manufacturer are very similar to those of a merchandiser. For example, you will find many of the same sections and same accounts in the financial statements of Procter & Gamble that you find in the financial statements of Dick's Sporting Goods. The principal differences between their financial statements occur in two places: the cost of goods sold section in the income statement and the current assets section in the balance sheet.

Income Statement

LEARNING OBJECTIVE 5

Explain the difference between a merchandising and a manufacturing income statement.

Under a periodic inventory system, the income statements of a merchandiser and a manufacturer differ in the cost of goods sold section. Merchandisers compute cost of goods sold by adding the beginning merchandise inventory to the **cost of goods purchased** and subtracting the ending merchandise inventory. Manufacturers compute cost of goods sold by adding the beginning finished goods inventory to the **cost of goods manufactured** and subtracting the ending finished goods inventory. Illustration 15-4 shows these different methods.

A number of accounts are involved in determining the cost of goods manufactured. To eliminate excessive detail, income statements typically show only the total cost of goods manufactured. A separate statement, called a Cost of Goods Manufactured Schedule, presents the details. (See the discussion on pages 775–776 and Illustration 15-7.)

Illustration 15-5 shows the different presentations of the cost of goods sold sections for merchandising and manufacturing companies. The other sections of an income statement are similar for merchandisers and manufacturers.

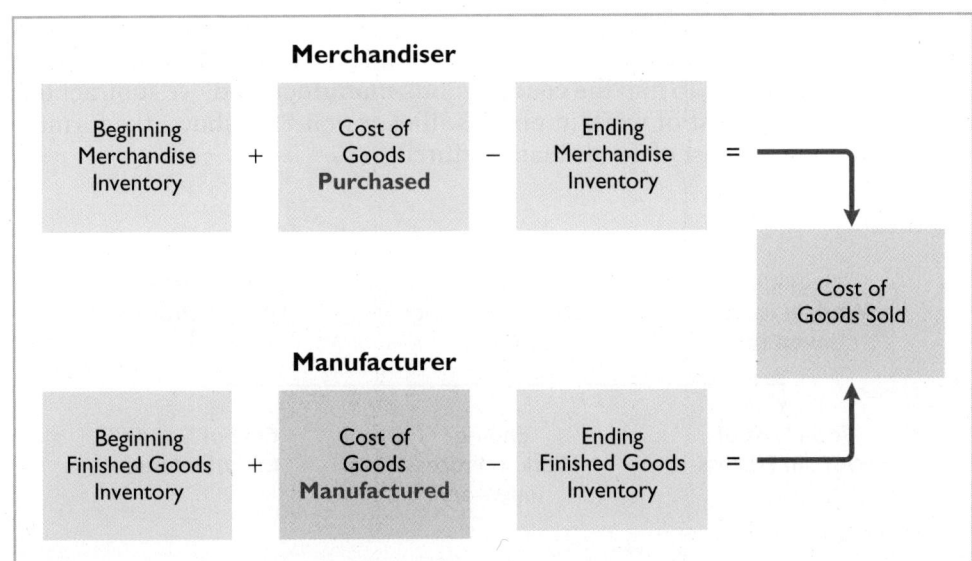

Illustration 15-4
Cost of goods sold components

Helpful Hint
We assume a periodic inventory system in this illustration.

Illustration 15-5
Cost of goods sold sections of merchandising and manufacturing income statements

Merchandising Company Income Statement (partial) For the Year Ended December 31, 2014		Manufacturing Company Income Statement (partial) For the Year Ended December 31, 2014	
Cost of goods sold		Cost of goods sold	
Merchandise inventory, Jan. 1	**$ 70,000**	**Finished goods inventory, Jan. 1**	**$ 90,000**
Cost of goods purchased	**650,000**	**Cost of goods manufactured**	
		(see Illustration 15-7)	**370,000**
Cost of goods available for sale	720,000	Cost of goods available for sale	460,000
Less: Merchandise inventory,		**Less: Finished goods inventory,**	
Dec. 31	400,000	Dec. 31	80,000
Cost of goods sold	$ 320,000	Cost of goods sold	$ 380,000

Cost of Goods Manufactured

An example may help show how companies determine the cost of goods manufactured. Assume that on January 1, Current Designs has a number of kayaks in various stages of production. In total, these partially completed units are called **beginning work in process inventory**. The costs the company assigns to beginning work in process inventory are based on the **manufacturing costs incurred in the prior period**.

Current Designs first incurs manufacturing costs in the current year to complete the work that was in process on January 1. It then incurs manufacturing costs for production of new orders. The sum of the direct materials costs, direct labor costs, and manufacturing overhead incurred in the current year is the **total manufacturing costs** for the current period.

We now have two cost amounts: (1) the cost of the beginning work in process and (2) the total manufacturing costs for the current period. The sum of these costs is the **total cost of work in process** for the year.

LEARNING OBJECTIVE   6

Indicate how cost of goods manufactured is determined.

At the end of the year, Current Designs may have some kayaks that are only partially completed. The costs of these units become the cost of the **ending work in process inventory**. To find the **cost of goods manufactured**, we subtract this cost from the total cost of work in process. Illustration 15-6 shows the formula for determining the cost of goods manufactured.

Illustration 15-6
Cost of goods manufactured formula

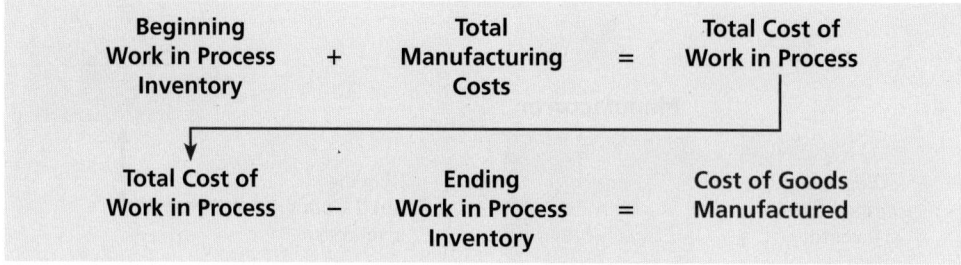

Cost of Goods Manufactured Schedule

The **cost of goods manufactured schedule** reports cost elements used in calculating cost of goods manufactured. Illustration 15-7 shows the schedule for Current Designs (using assumed data). The schedule presents detailed data for direct materials and for manufacturing overhead.

Review Illustration 15-6 and then examine the cost of goods manufactured schedule in Illustration 15-7. You should be able to distinguish between "Total manufacturing costs" and "Cost of goods manufactured." The difference is the effect of the change in work in process during the period.

Illustration 15-7
Cost of goods manufactured schedule

Current Designs		
Cost of Goods Manufactured Schedule		
For the Year Ended December 31, 2014		
Work in process, January 1		$ 18,400
Direct materials		
Raw materials inventory, January 1	$ 16,700	
Raw materials purchases	152,500	
Total raw materials available for use	169,200	
Less: Raw materials inventory, December 31	22,800	
Direct materials used		$146,400
Direct labor		175,600
Manufacturing overhead		
Indirect labor	14,300	
Factory repairs	12,600	
Factory utilities	10,100	
Factory depreciation	9,440	
Factory insurance	8,360	
Total manufacturing overhead		54,800
Total manufacturing costs		376,800
Total cost of work in process		395,200
Less: Work in process, December 31		25,200
Cost of goods manufactured		**$370,000**

> **DO IT!**

Cost of Goods Manufactured

Action Plan

✔ Start with beginning work in process as the first item in the cost of goods manufactured schedule.

✔ Sum direct materials used, direct labor, and manufacturing overhead to determine total manufacturing costs.

✔ Sum beginning work in process and total manufacturing costs to determine total cost of work in process.

✔ Cost of goods manufactured is the total cost of work in process less ending work in process.

The following information is available for Keystone Company.

	March 1	March 31
Raw materials inventory	$12,000	$10,000
Work in process inventory	2,500	4,000
Materials purchased in March	$ 90,000	
Direct labor in March	75,000	
Manufacturing overhead in March	220,000	

Prepare the cost of goods manufactured schedule for the month of March.

Solution

Keystone Company
Cost of Goods Manufactured Schedule
For the Month Ended March 31

Work in process, March 1			$ 2,500
Direct materials			
Raw materials, March 1	$ 12,000		
Raw material purchases	90,000		
Total raw materials available for use	102,000		
Less: Raw materials, March 31	10,000		
Direct materials used		$ 92,000	
Direct labor		75,000	
Manufacturing overhead		220,000	
Total manufacturing costs			387,000
Total cost of work in process			389,500
Less: Work in process, March 31			4,000
Cost of goods manufactured			$385,500

Related exercise material: **BE15-8, BE15-10, BE15-11, E15-8, E15-9, E15-10, E15-11, E15-12, E15-13, E15-14, E15-15, E15-16, E15-17, and DO IT! 15-3.**

✔ **The Navigator**

Balance Sheet

The balance sheet for a merchandising company shows just one category of inventory. In contrast, the balance sheet for a manufacturer may have three inventory accounts, as shown in Illustration 15-8.

LEARNING OBJECTIVE   7

Explain the difference between a merchandising and a manufacturing balance sheet.

Raw Materials Inventory

Shows the cost of raw materials on hand.

Work in Process Inventory

Shows the cost applicable to units that have been started into production but are only partially completed.

Finished Goods Inventory

Shows the cost of completed goods on hand.

Illustration 15-8
Inventory accounts for a manufacturer

Finished Goods Inventory is to a manufacturer what Merchandise Inventory is to a merchandiser. Each of these classifications represents the goods that the company has available for sale.

The current assets sections presented in Illustration 15-9 contrast the presentations of inventories for merchandising and manufacturing companies. Manufacturing companies generally list their inventories in the order of their liquidity—the order in which they are expected to be realized in cash. Thus, finished goods inventory comes first. The remainder of the balance sheet is similar for the two types of companies.

Illustration 15-9

Current assets sections of merchandising and manufacturing balance sheets

Merchandising Company Balance Sheet December 31, 2014			**Manufacturing Company** Balance Sheet December 31, 2014		
Current assets			Current assets		
Cash		$100,000	Cash		$180,000
Receivables (net)		210,000	Receivables (net)		210,000
Merchandise inventory		**400,000**	**Inventories**		
Prepaid expenses		22,000	Finished goods	$80,000	
Total current assets		$732,000	Work in process	25,200	
			Raw materials	22,800	128,000
			Prepaid expenses		18,000
			Total current assets		$536,000

Each step in the accounting cycle for a merchandiser applies to a manufacturer. For example, prior to preparing financial statements, manufacturers make adjusting entries. The adjusting entries are essentially the same as those of a merchandiser. The closing entries are also similar for manufacturers and merchandisers.

Cost Concepts—A Review

You have learned a number of cost concepts in this chapter. Because many of these concepts are new, we provide here an extended example for review. Suppose you started your own snowboard factory, Terrain Park Boards. Think that's impossible? Burton Snowboards was started by Jake Burton Carpenter, when he was only 23 years old. Jake initially experimented with 100 different prototype designs before settling on a final design. Then Jake, along with two relatives and a friend, started making 50 boards per day in Londonderry, Vermont. Unfortunately, while they made a lot of boards in their first year, they were only able to sell 300 of them. To get by during those early years, Jake taught tennis and tended bar to pay the bills.

Here are some of the costs that your snowboard factory would incur.

1. The materials cost of each snowboard (wood cores, fiberglass, resins, metal screw holes, metal edges, and ink) is $30.

2. The labor costs (for example, to trim and shape each board using jig saws and band saws) are $40.

3. Depreciation on the factory building and equipment (for example, presses, grinding machines, and lacquer machines) used to make the snowboards is $25,000 per year.

4. Property taxes on the factory building (where the snowboards are made) are $6,000 per year.

5. Advertising costs (mostly online and catalogue) are $60,000 per year.

6. Sales commissions related to snowboard sales are $20 per snowboard.

7. Salaries for factory maintenance employees are $45,000 per year.

8. The salary of the plant manager is $70,000.

9. The cost of shipping is $8 per snowboard.

Illustration 15-10 shows how Terrain Park Boards would assign these manufacturing and selling costs to the various categories.

Terrain Park Boards

| | Product Costs | | | |
Cost Item	Direct Materials	Direct Labor	Manufacturing Overhead	Period Costs
1. Material cost ($30 per board)	X			
2. Labor costs ($40 per board)		X		
3. Depreciation on factory equipment ($25,000 per year)			X	
4. Property taxes on factory building ($6,000 per year)			X	
5. Advertising costs ($60,000 per year)				X
6. Sales commissions ($20 per board)				X
7. Maintenance salaries (factory facilities) ($45,000 per year)			X	
8. Salary of plant manager ($70,000 per year)			X	
9. Cost of shipping boards ($8 per board)				X

Illustration 15-10
Assignment of costs to cost categories

Remember that total manufacturing costs are the sum of the **product costs**—direct materials, direct labor, and manufacturing overhead. If Terrain Park Boards produces 10,000 snowboards the first year, the total manufacturing costs would be $846,000 as shown in Illustration 15-11 (page 780).

Illustration 15-11
Computation of total
manufacturing costs

Cost Number and Item	Manufacturing Cost
1. Material cost ($30 × 10,000)	$300,000
2. Labor cost ($40 × 10,000)	400,000
3. Depreciation on factory equipment	25,000
4. Property taxes on factory building	6,000
7. Maintenance salaries (factory facilities)	45,000
8. Salary of plant manager	70,000
Total manufacturing costs	**$846,000**

Knowing the total manufacturing costs, Terrain Park Boards can compute the manufacturing cost per unit. Assuming 10,000 units, the cost to produce one snowboard is $84.60 ($846,000 ÷ 10,000 units).

In subsequent chapters, we will use extensively the cost concepts discussed in this chapter. So study Illustration 15-10 carefully. If you do not understand any of these classifications, go back and reread the appropriate section in this chapter.

Product Costing for Service Industries

Much of the U.S. economy has shifted toward an emphasis on services. Today, more than 50% of U.S. workers are employed by service companies. Airlines, marketing agencies, cable companies, and governmental agencies are just a few examples of service companies. How do service companies differ from manufacturing companies? One difference is that services are consumed immediately. For example, when a restaurant produces a meal, that meal is not put in inventory, but it is instead consumed immediately. An airline uses special equipment to provide its product, but again, the output of that equipment is consumed immediately by the customer in the form of a flight. And a marketing agency performs services for its clients that are immediately consumed by the customer in the form of a marketing plan. For a manufacturing company, like Boeing, it often has a long lead time before its airplane is used or consumed by the customer.

Ethics Note

Do telecommunications companies have an obligation to provide service to remote or low-user areas for a fee that may be less than the cost of the service?

This chapter's examples used manufacturing companies because accounting for the manufacturing environment requires the use of the broadest range of accounts. That is, the accounts used by service companies represent a subset of those used by manufacturers because service companies are not producing inventory. Neither the restaurant, the airline, or the marketing agency discussed above produces an inventoriable product. However, just like a manufacturer, each needs to keep track of the costs of its services in order to know whether it is generating a profit. A successful restaurateur needs to know the cost of each offering on the menu, an airline needs to know the cost of flight service to each destination, and a marketing agency needs to know the cost to develop a marketing plan. Thus, the techniques shown in this chapter, to accumulate manufacturing costs to determine manufacturing inventory, are equally useful for determining the costs of providing services.

For example, let's consider the costs that Hewlett-Packard (HP) might incur on a consulting engagement. A significant portion of its costs would be salaries of consulting personnel. It might also incur travel costs, materials, software costs, and depreciation charges on equipment used by the employees to provide the consulting service. In the same way that it needs to keep track of the cost of manufacturing its computers and printers, HP needs to know what its costs are on each consulting job. It could prepare a cost of services provided schedule similar to the cost of goods manufactured schedule in Illustration 15-7 (page 776). The structure would be essentially the same as the cost of goods manufactured schedule, but section headings would be reflective of the costs of the particular service organization.

Many of the examples we present in subsequent chapters will be based on service companies. To highlight the relevance of the techniques used in this course for service companies, we have placed a service company icon next to those items in the text and end-of-chapter materials that relate to nonmanufacturing companies.

SERVICE COMPANY INSIGHT

Low Fares but Decent Profits

During 2008, when other airlines were cutting flight service due to the recession, Allegiant Airlines increased capacity by 21%. Sounds crazy, doesn't it? But it must know something, because while the other airlines were losing money, it was generating profits. Consider also that its average one-way fare is only $83. So how does it make money? As a low-budget airline, it focuses on controlling costs. It purchases used planes for $4 million each rather than new planes for $40 million. It flies out of small towns, so wages are low and competition is nonexistent. It only flies a route if its 150-passenger planes are nearly full (it averages about 90% of capacity). If a route isn't filling up, it quits flying it as often or cancels it altogether. It adjusts its prices weekly. The bottom line is that it knows its costs to the penny. Knowing what your costs are might not be glamorous, but it sure beats losing money.

Source: Susan Carey, "For Allegiant, Getaways Mean Profits," *Wall Street Journal Online* (February 18, 2009).

? What are some of the line items that would appear in the cost of services provided schedule of an airline? (See page 807.)

Managerial Accounting Today

The business environment never stands still. Regulations are always changing, global competition continues to intensify, and technology is a source of constant upheaval. In this rapidly changing world, managerial accounting must continue to innovate in order to provide managers with the information they need.

LEARNING OBJECTIVE   8

Identify trends in managerial accounting.

Focus on the Value Chain

The **value chain** refers to all business processes associated with providing a product or service. Illustration 15-12 depicts the value chain for a manufacturer. Many of the most significant business innovations in recent years have resulted either directly, or indirectly, from a focus on the value chain. For example, so-called **lean manufacturing**, originally pioneered by Japanese automobile manufacturer Toyota but now widely practiced, reviews all business processes in an effort to increase productivity and eliminate waste, all while continually trying to improve quality.

Illustration 15-12
A manufacturer's value chain

| Research & development and product design | Acquisition of raw materials | Production | Sales and marketing | Delivery | Customer relations and subsequent services |

Just-in-time (JIT) inventory methods, which have significantly lowered inventory levels and costs for many companies, are one innovation that resulted from the focus on the value chain. Under the JIT inventory method, goods are manufactured or purchased just in time for sale. For example, Dell can deliver a computer within 48 hours of a customer's custom order. However, JIT also necessitates increased emphasis on product quality. Because JIT companies do not have excess inventory on hand, they cannot afford to stop production because of defects or machine breakdowns. If they have to stop production, deliveries will be delayed and customers will be unhappy. For example, a recent design flaw in an Intel computer chip was estimated to cost the company $1 billion in repairs and reduced revenue. As a consequence, many companies now focus on **total quality management (TQM)** to reduce defects in finished products, with the goal of zero defects. The TQM philosophy has been employed by some of the most successful businesses to improve all aspects of the value chain.

Another innovation, the **theory of constraints**, involves identification of "bottlenecks"—constraints within the value chain that limit a company's profitability. Once a major constraint has been identified and eliminated, the company moves on to fix the next most significant constraint. General Motors found that by eliminating bottlenecks, it improved its use of overtime labor while meeting customer demand. An application of the theory of constraints is presented in Chapter 20.

Technology has played a big role in the focus on the value chain and the implementation of lean manufacturing. For example, **enterprise resource planning (ERP) systems**, such as those provided by SAP, provide a comprehensive, centralized, integrated source of information to manage all major business processes—from purchasing, to manufacturing, to sales, to human resources. ERP systems have, in some large companies, replaced as many as 200 individual software packages. In addition, the focus on improving efficiency in the value chain has also resulted in adoption of automated manufacturing processes. Many companies now use computer-integrated manufacturing. These systems often reduce the reliance on manual labor by using robotic equipment. This increases overhead costs as a percentage of total product costs.

As overhead costs increased because of factory automation, the accuracy of overhead cost allocation to specific products became more important. Managerial accounting devised an approach, called **activity-based costing (ABC)**, which allocates overhead based on each product's use of particular activities in making the product. In addition to providing more accurate product costing, ABC also can contribute to increased efficiency in the value chain. For example, suppose one of a company's overhead pools is allocated based on the number of setups that each product requires. If a particular product's cost is high because it is allocated a lot of overhead due to a high number of setups, management will be motivated to try to reduce the number of setups and thus reduce its overhead allocation. ABC is discussed further in Chapter 18.

Balanced Scorecard

As companies implement various business practice innovations, managers sometimes focus too enthusiastically on the latest innovation, to the detriment of other areas of the business. For example, by focusing on total quality management, companies sometimes lose sight of cost/benefit considerations. Similarly, in focusing on reducing inventory levels through just-in-time inventory methods, companies sometimes lose sales due to inventory shortages. The **balanced scorecard** corrects for this limited perspective: This approach uses both financial and nonfinancial measures to evaluate all aspects of a company's operations in an integrated fashion. The performance measures are linked in a cause-and-effect fashion to ensure that they all tie to the company's overall objectives. For example, to increase return on assets, the company could try to increase sales. To increase sales, the company could try to increase customer satisfaction. To increase customer satisfaction, the company could try to reduce product defects. Finally, to reduce product defects, the company could increase employee training. The balanced scorecard, which is discussed further in Chapter 25, is now used by many companies, including Hilton Hotels, Wal-Mart Stores, Inc., and HP.

Corporate Social Responsibility

The balanced scorecard attempts to take a broader, more inclusive view of corporate profitability measures. Many companies, however, have begun to evaluate not just corporate profitability but also **corporate social responsibility**. In addition to profitability, corporate social responsibility considers a company's efforts to employ sustainable business practices with regard to its employees and the environment. This is sometimes referred to as the **triple bottom line** because it evaluates a company's performance with regard to **people, planet, and profit**. Make no mistake, these companies are still striving to maximize profits—in a competitive world, they won't survive long if they don't. In fact, you might recognize a few of the names on the Forbes.com list of the 100 most sustainable companies in the world. Ever hear of General Electric, adidas, Toyota, Coca-Cola, or Starbucks? These companies have learned that with a long-term, sustainable approach, they can maximize profits while also acting in the best interest of their employees, their communities, and the environment. At various points within this textbook, we will discuss situations where real companies use the very skills that you are learning to evaluate decisions from a sustainable perspective.

> DO IT!

Trends in Managerial Accounting

Match the descriptions that follow with the corresponding terms.

Descriptions:

1. _____ All activities associated with providing a product or service.

2. _____ A method of allocating overhead based on each product's use of activities in making the product.

3. _____ Systems implemented to reduce defects in finished products with the goal of achieving zero defects.

4. _____ A performance-measurement approach that uses both financial and nonfinancial measures, tied to company objectives, to evaluate a company's operations in an integrated fashion.

5. _____ Inventory system in which goods are manufactured or purchased just as they are needed for use.

Terms:

a. Activity-based costing

b. Balanced scorecard

c. Just-in-time (JIT) inventory

d. Total quality management (TQM)

e. Value chain

Action Plan

✔ Develop a forward-looking view, in order to advise and provide information to various members of the organization.

✔ Understand current business trends and issues.

Solution

1. e   2. a   3. d   4. b   5. c

Related exercise material: **E15-18 and DO IT! 15-4.**

 The Navigator

> **Comprehensive DO IT!**

Superior Company has the following cost and expense data for the year ending December 31, 2014.

Raw materials, 1/1/14	$ 30,000	Insurance, factory	$ 14,000
Raw materials, 12/31/14	20,000	Property taxes, factory building	6,000
Raw materials purchases	205,000	Sales revenue	1,500,000
Indirect materials	15,000	Delivery expenses	100,000
Work in process, 1/1/14	80,000	Sales commissions	150,000
Work in process, 12/31/14	50,000	Indirect labor	90,000
Finished goods, 1/1/14	110,000	Factory machinery rent	40,000
Finished goods, 12/31/14	120,000	Factory utilities	65,000
Direct labor	350,000	Depreciation, factory building	24,000
Factory manager's salary	35,000	Administrative expenses	300,000

Instructions

(a) Prepare a cost of goods manufactured schedule for Superior Company for 2014.

(b) Prepare an income statement for Superior Company for 2014.

(c) Assume that Superior Company's accounting records show the balances of the following current asset accounts: Cash $17,000, Accounts Receivable (net) $120,000, Prepaid Expenses $13,000, and Short-Term Investments $26,000. Prepare the current assets section of the balance sheet for Superior Company as of December 31, 2014.

Action Plan

✔ Start with beginning work in process as the first item in the cost of goods manufactured schedule.

✔ Sum direct materials used, direct labor, and total manufacturing overhead to determine total manufacturing costs.

✔ Sum beginning work in process and total manufacturing costs to determine total cost of work in process.

✔ Cost of goods manufactured is the total cost of work in process less ending work in process.

✔ In the cost of goods sold section of the income statement, show beginning and ending finished goods inventory and cost of goods manufactured.

✔ In the balance sheet, list manufacturing inventories in the order of their expected realization in cash, with finished goods first.

Solution to Comprehensive DO IT!

(a)
Superior Company
Cost of Goods Manufactured Schedule
For the Year Ended December 31, 2014

Work in process, 1/1			$ 80,000
Direct materials			
Raw materials inventory, 1/1	$ 30,000		
Raw materials purchases	205,000		
Total raw materials available for use	235,000		
Less: Raw materials inventory, 12/31	20,000		
Direct materials used		$215,000	
Direct labor		350,000	
Manufacturing overhead			
Indirect labor	90,000		
Factory utilities	65,000		
Factory machinery rent	40,000		
Factory manager's salary	35,000		
Depreciation, factory building	24,000		
Indirect materials	15,000		
Insurance, factory	14,000		
Property taxes, factory building	6,000		
Total manufacturing overhead		289,000	
Total manufacturing costs			854,000
Total cost of work in process			934,000
Less: Work in process, 12/31			50,000
Cost of goods manufactured			$ 884,000

(b)

Superior Company
Income Statement
For the Year Ended December 31, 2014

Sales revenue		$1,500,000
Cost of goods sold		
Finished goods inventory, January 1	$110,000	
Cost of goods manufactured	884,000	
Cost of goods available for sale	994,000	
Less: Finished goods inventory, December 31	120,000	
Cost of goods sold		874,000
Gross profit		626,000
Operating expenses		
Administrative expenses	300,000	
Sales commissions	150,000	
Delivery expenses	100,000	
Total operating expenses		550,000
Net income		$ 76,000

(c)

Superior Company
Balance Sheet (partial)
December 31, 2014

Current assets		
Cash		$ 17,000
Short-term investments		26,000
Accounts receivable (net)		120,000
Inventories		
Finished goods	$120,000	
Work in process	50,000	
Raw materials	20,000	190,000
Prepaid expenses		13,000
Total current assets		$366,000

The Navigator

SUMMARY OF LEARNING OBJECTIVES

The Navigator

1 Explain the distinguishing features of managerial accounting. The *primary users* of managerial accounting reports are internal users, who are officers, department heads, managers, and supervisors in the company. Managerial accounting issues internal reports as frequently as the need arises. The purpose of these reports is to provide special-purpose information for a particular user for a specific decision. The content of managerial accounting reports pertains to subunits of the business, may be very detailed, and may extend beyond the double-entry accounting system. The reporting standard is relevance to the decision being made. No independent audits are required in managerial accounting.

2 Identify the three broad functions of management. The three functions are planning, directing, and controlling. Planning requires management to look ahead and to establish objectives. Directing involves coordinating the diverse activities and human resources of a company to produce a smooth-running operation. Controlling is the process of keeping the activities on track.

3 Define the three classes of manufacturing costs. Manufacturing costs are typically classified as either (1) direct materials, (2) direct labor, or (3) manufacturing overhead. Raw materials that can be physically and directly associated with the finished product during the manufacturing process are called direct materials. The work of factory employees that can be physically and directly associated with converting raw materials into finished goods is considered direct labor. Manufacturing overhead consists of costs that are indirectly associated with the manufacture of the finished product.

4 Distinguish between product and period costs. Product costs are costs that are a necessary and integral part of producing the finished product. Product costs are also called inventoriable costs. Under the expense recognition principle, these costs do not become expenses until the company sells the finished goods inventory. Period costs are costs that are identified with a specific time period rather than with a salable product. These costs relate to nonmanufacturing costs and therefore are not inventoriable costs.

5 Explain the difference between a merchandising and a manufacturing income statement. The difference between a merchandising and a manufacturing income statement is in the cost of goods sold section. A manufacturing cost of goods sold section shows beginning and ending finished goods inventories and the cost of goods manufactured.

6 Indicate how cost of goods manufactured is determined. Companies add the cost of the beginning work in process to the total manufacturing costs for the current year to arrive at the total cost of work in process for the year. They then subtract the ending work in process from the total cost of work in process to arrive at the cost of goods manufactured.

7 Explain the difference between a merchandising and a manufacturing balance sheet. The difference between a merchandising and a manufacturing balance sheet is in the current assets section. The current assets section of a manufacturing company's balance sheet presents three inventory accounts: finished goods inventory, work in process inventory, and raw materials inventory.

8 Identify trends in managerial accounting. Managerial accounting has experienced many changes in recent years. Improved practices include a focus on managing the value chain through techniques such as just-in-time inventory, total quality management, activity-based costing, and theory of constraints. The balanced scorecard is now used by many companies in order to attain a more comprehensive view of the company's operations. Finally, companies are now evaluating their performance with regard to their corporate social responsibility.

GLOSSARY

Activity-based costing (ABC) A method of allocating overhead based on each product's use of activities in making the product. (p. 782).

Balanced scorecard A performance-measurement approach that uses both financial and nonfinancial measures, tied to company objectives, to evaluate a company's operations in an integrated fashion. (p. 782).

Board of directors The group of officials elected by the stockholders of a corporation to formulate operating policies, select officers, and otherwise manage the company. (p. 768).

Chief executive officer (CEO) Corporate officer who has overall responsibility for managing the business and delegates responsibilities to other corporate officers. (p. 768).

Chief financial officer (CFO) Corporate officer who is responsible for all of the accounting and finance issues of the company. (p. 769).

Controller Financial officer responsible for a company's accounting records, system of internal control, and preparation of financial statements, tax returns, and internal reports. (p. 769).

Corporate social responsibility The efforts of a company to employ sustainable business practices with regard to its employees and the environment. (p. 783).

Cost of goods manufactured Total cost of work in process less the cost of the ending work in process inventory. (p. 776).

Direct labor The work of factory employees that can be physically and directly associated with converting raw materials into finished goods. (p. 772).

Direct materials Raw materials that can be physically and directly associated with manufacturing the finished product. (p. 772).

Enterprise resource planning (ERP) system Software that provides a comprehensive, centralized, integrated source of information used to manage all major business processes. (p. 782).

Indirect labor Work of factory employees that has no physical association with the finished product, or for which it is impractical to trace the costs to the goods produced. (p. 772).

Indirect materials Raw materials that do not physically become part of the finished product or for which it is impractical to trace to the finished product because their physical association with the finished product is too small. (p. 772).

Just-in-time (JIT) inventory Inventory system in which goods are manufactured or purchased just in time for sale. (p. 782).

Line positions Jobs that are directly involved in a company's primary revenue-generating operating activities. (p. 768).

Managerial accounting A field of accounting that provides economic and financial information for managers and other internal users. (p. 766).

Manufacturing overhead Manufacturing costs that are indirectly associated with the manufacture of the finished product. (p. 772).

Period costs Costs that are matched with the revenue of a specific time period and charged to expense as incurred. (p. 773).

Product costs Costs that are a necessary and integral part of producing the finished product. (p. 773).

Sarbanes-Oxley Act (SOX) Law passed by Congress intended to reduce unethical corporate behavior. (p. 770).

Staff positions Jobs that support the efforts of line employees. (p. 768).

Theory of constraints A specific approach used to identify and manage constraints in order to achieve the company's goals. (p. 782).

Total cost of work in process Cost of the beginning work in process plus total manufacturing costs for the current period. (p. 775).

Total manufacturing costs The sum of direct materials, direct labor, and manufacturing overhead incurred in the current period. (p. 775).

Total quality management (TQM) Systems implemented to reduce defects in finished products with the goal of achieving zero defects. (p. 782).

Treasurer Financial officer responsible for custody of a company's funds and for maintaining its cash position. (p. 769).

Triple bottom line The evaluation of a company's social responsibility performance with regard to people, planet, and profit. (p. 783).

Value chain All activities that a business processes with providing a product or service. (p. 781).

 **Self-Test, Brief Exercises, Exercises, Problem Set A, and many more resources are available for practice in WileyPLUS.**

SELF-TEST QUESTIONS

Answers are at the end of the chapter.

(LO 1) **1.** Managerial accounting:
  (a) is governed by generally accepted accounting principles.
  (b) places emphasis on special-purpose information.
  (c) pertains to the entity as a whole and is highly aggregated.
  (d) is limited to cost data.

(LO 2) **2.** The management of an organization performs several broad functions. They are:
  (a) planning, directing, and selling.
  (b) planning, directing, and controlling.
  (c) planning, manufacturing, and controlling.
  (d) directing, manufacturing, and controlling.

(LO 2) **3.** After passage of the Sarbanes-Oxley Act:
  (a) reports prepared by managerial accountants must by audited by CPAs.
  (b) CEOs and CFOs must certify that financial statements give a fair presentation of the company's operating results.
  (c) the audit committee, rather than top management, is responsible for the company's financial statements.
  (d) reports prepared by managerial accountants must comply with generally accepted accounting principles (GAAP).

4. Direct materials are a: (LO 3)

	Product Cost	Manufacturing Overhead	Period Cost
(a)	Yes	Yes	No
(b)	Yes	No	No
(c)	Yes	Yes	Yes
(d)	No	No	No

5. Which of the following costs would a computer manufacturer include in manufacturing overhead?   (LO 3)
  (a) The cost of the disk drives.
  (b) The wages earned by computer assemblers.
  (c) The cost of the memory chips.
  (d) Depreciation on testing equipment.

6. Which of the following is *not* an element of manufacturing overhead?   (LO 3)
  (a) Sales manager's salary.
  (b) Plant manager's salary.
  (c) Factory repairman's wages.
  (d) Product inspector's salary.

7. Indirect labor is a: (LO 4)
  (a) nonmanufacturing cost.
  (b) raw material cost.
  (c) product cost.
  (d) period cost.

(LO 4) **8.** Which of the following costs are classified as a period cost?
  (a) Wages paid to a factory custodian.
  (b) Wages paid to a production department supervisor.
  (c) Wages paid to a cost accounting department supervisor.
  (d) Wages paid to an assembly worker.

(LO 5) **9.** For the year, Redder Company has cost of goods manufactured of $600,000, beginning finished goods inventory of $200,000, and ending finished goods inventory of $250,000. The cost of goods sold is:
  (a) $450,000.
  (b) $500,000.
  (c) $550,000.
  (d) $600,000.

(LO 5) **10.** Cost of goods available for sale is a step in the calculation of cost of goods sold of:
  (a) a merchandising company but not a manufacturing company.
  (b) a manufacturing company but not a merchandising company.
  (c) a merchandising company and a manufacturing company.
  (d) neither a manufacturing company nor a merchandising company.

(LO 6) **11.** A cost of goods manufactured schedule shows beginning and ending inventories for:
  (a) raw materials and work in process only.
  (b) work in process only.
  (c) raw materials only.
  (d) raw materials, work in process, and finished goods.

(LO 6) **12.** The formula to determine the cost of goods manufactured is:
  (a) Beginning raw materials inventory + Total manufacturing costs − Ending work in process inventory.

  (b) Beginning work in process inventory + Total manufacturing costs − Ending finished goods inventory.
  (c) Beginning finished good inventory + Total manufacturing costs − Ending finished goods inventory.
  (d) Beginning work in process inventory + Total manufacturing costs − Ending work in process inventory.

13. A manufacturer may report three inventories on its (LO 7) balance sheet: (1) raw materials, (2) work in process, and (3) finished goods. Indicate in what sequence these inventories generally appear on a balance sheet.
  (a) (1), (2), (3)
  (b) (2), (3), (1)
  (c) (3), (1), (2)
  (d) (3), (2), (1)

14. Which of the following managerial accounting tech- (LO 8) niques attempts to allocate manufacturing overhead in a more meaningful fashion?
  (a) Just-in-time inventory.
  (b) Total quality management.
  (c) Balanced scorecard.
  (d) Activity-based costing.

15. Corporate social responsibility refers to: (LO 8)
  (a) the practice by management of reviewing all business processes in an effort to increase productivity and eliminate waste.
  (b) an approach used to allocate overhead based on each product's use of activities.
  (c) the attempt by management to identify and eliminate constraints within the value chain.
  (d) efforts by companies to employ sustainable business practices with regard to employees and the environment.

Go to the book's companion website, www.wiley.com/college/weygandt, for additional Self-Test Questions.

 **The Navigator**

QUESTIONS

1. (a) "Managerial accounting is a field of accounting that provides economic information for all interested parties." Do you agree? Explain.
  (b) Joe Delong believes that managerial accounting serves only manufacturing firms. Is Joe correct? Explain.

2. Distinguish between managerial and financial accounting as to (a) primary users of reports, (b) types and frequency of reports, and (c) purpose of reports.

3. How do the content of reports and the verification of reports differ between managerial and financial accounting?

4. In what ways can the budgeting process create incentives for unethical behavior?

5. Linda Olsen is studying for the next accounting midterm examination. Summarize for Linda what she should know about management functions.

6. "Decision-making is management's most important function." Do you agree? Why or why not?

7. Explain the primary difference between line positions and staff positions, and give examples of each.

8. What new rules were enacted under the Sarbanes-Oxley Act to address unethical accounting practices?

9. Tony Andres is studying for his next accounting examination. Explain to Tony what he should know about the differences between the income statements for a manufacturing and for a merchandising company.

10. Jerry Lang is unclear as to the difference between the balance sheets of a merchandising company and a manufacturing company. Explain the difference to Jerry.

11. How are manufacturing costs classified?

12. Mel Finney claims that the distinction between direct and indirect materials is based entirely on physical association with the product. Is Mel correct? Why?

13. Tina Burke is confused about the differences between a product cost and a period cost. Explain the differences to Tina.

14. Identify the differences in the cost of goods sold section of an income statement between a merchandising company and a manufacturing company.

15. The determination of the cost of goods manufactured involves the following factors: (A) beginning work in process inventory, (B) total manufacturing costs, and (C) ending work in process inventory. Identify the meaning of x in the following formulas:
    (a) A + B = x
    (b) A + B − C = x

16. Sealy Company has beginning raw materials inventory $12,000, ending raw materials inventory $15,000, and raw materials purchases $170,000. What is the cost of direct materials used?

17. Tate Inc. has beginning work in process $26,000, direct materials used $240,000, direct labor $220,000, total manufacturing overhead $180,000, and ending work in process $32,000. What are the total manufacturing costs?

18. Using the data in Question 17, what are (a) the total cost of work in process and (b) the cost of goods manufactured?

19. In what order should manufacturing inventories be listed in a balance sheet?

20. How does the output of manufacturing operations differ from that of service operations?

21. Discuss whether the product costing techniques discussed in this chapter apply equally well to manufacturers and service companies.

22. What is the value chain? Describe, in sequence, the main components of a manufacturer's value chain.

23. What is an enterprise resource planning (ERP) system? What are its primary benefits?

24. Why is product quality important for companies that implement a just-in-time inventory system?

25. Explain what is meant by "balanced" in the balanced scorecard approach.

26. What is activity-based costing, and what are its potential benefits?

BRIEF EXERCISES

BE15-1 Complete the following comparison table between managerial and financial accounting.

Distinguish between managerial and financial accounting.

(LO 1)

	Financial Accounting	Managerial Accounting
Primary users of reports		
Types of reports		
Frequency of reports		
Purpose of reports		
Content of reports		
Verification process		

BE15-2 The Sarbanes-Oxley Act (SOX) has important implications for the financial community. Explain two implications of SOX.

Identify important regulatory changes.

(LO 2)

BE15-3 Listed below are the three functions of the management of an organization.
1. Planning   2. Directing   3. Controlling

Identify which of the following statements best describes each of the above functions.
(a) _____ requires management to look ahead and to establish objectives. A key objective of management is to add value to the business.
(b) _____ involves coordinating the diverse activities and human resources of a company to produce a smooth-running operation. This function relates to the implementation of planned objectives.
(c) _____ is the process of keeping the activities on track. Management must determine whether goals are being met and what changes are necessary when there are deviations.

Identify the three management functions.

(LO 2)

BE15-4 Determine whether each of the following costs should be classified as direct materials (DM), direct labor (DL), or manufacturing overhead (MO).
(a) _____ Frames and tires used in manufacturing bicycles.
(b) _____ Wages paid to production workers.
(c) _____ Insurance on factory equipment and machinery.
(d) _____ Depreciation on factory equipment.

Classify manufacturing costs.

(LO 3)

Classify manufacturing costs.

(LO 3)

BE15-5 Indicate whether each of the following costs of an automobile manufacturer would be classified as direct materials, direct labor, or manufacturing overhead.

(a) _____ Windshield.   (e) _____ Factory machinery lubricants.
(b) _____ Engine.   (f) _____ Tires.
(c) _____ Wages of assembly line worker.   (g) _____ Steering wheel.
(d) _____ Depreciation of factory machinery. (h) _____ Salary of painting supervisor.

Identify product and period costs.

(LO 4)

BE15-6 Identify whether each of the following costs should be classified as product costs or period costs.

(a) _____ Manufacturing overhead.   (d) _____ Advertising expenses.
(b) _____ Selling expenses.   (e) _____ Direct labor.
(c) _____ Administrative expenses. (f) _____ Direct material.

Classify manufacturing costs.

(LO 3)

BE15-7 Presented below are Dieker Company's monthly manufacturing cost data related to its personal computer products.

(a) Utilities for manufacturing equipment $116,000
(b) Raw material (CPU, chips, etc.) $ 85,000
(c) Depreciation on manufacturing building $880,000
(d) Wages for production workers $191,000

Enter each cost item in the following table, placing an "X" under the appropriate headings.

| | **Product Costs** | | |
	Direct Materials	Direct Labor	Factory Overhead
(a)			
(b)			
(c)			
(d)			

Compute total manufacturing costs and total cost of work in process.

(LO 6)

BE15-8 Francum Company has the following data: direct labor $209,000, direct materials used $180,000, total manufacturing overhead $208,000, and beginning work in process $25,000. Compute (a) total manufacturing costs and (b) total cost of work in process.

Prepare current assets section.

(LO 7)

BE15-9 In alphabetical order below are current asset items for Ruiz Company's balance sheet at December 31, 2014. Prepare the current assets section (including a complete heading).

Accounts receivable	$200,000
Cash	62,000
Finished goods	91,000
Prepaid expenses	38,000
Raw materials	73,000
Work in process	87,000

Determine missing amounts in computing total manufacturing costs.

(LO 6)

BE15-10 Presented below are incomplete manufacturing cost data. Determine the missing amounts for three different situations.

	Direct Materials Used	Direct Labor Used	Factory Overhead	Total Manufacturing Costs
(1)	$40,000	$61,000	$ 50,000	?
(2)	?	$75,000	$140,000	$296,000
(3)	$55,000	?	$111,000	$310,000

Determine missing amounts in computing cost of goods manufactured.

(LO 6)

BE15-11 Use the same data from BE15–10 above and the data below. Determine the missing amounts.

	Total Manufacturing Costs	Work in Process (1/1)	Work in Process (12/31)	Cost of Goods Manufactured
(1)	?	$120,000	$82,000	?
(2)	$296,000	?	$98,000	$321,000
(3)	$310,000	$463,000	?	$715,000

> DO IT! REVIEW

DO IT! 15-1 Indicate whether the following statements are true or false.

1. Managerial accountants explain and report manufacturing and nonmanufacturing costs, determine cost behaviors, and perform cost-volume-profit analysis, but are not involved in the budget process.
2. Financial accounting reports pertain to subunits of the business and are very detailed.
3. Managerial accounting reports must follow GAAP and are audited by CPAs.
4. Managers' activities and responsibilities can be classified into three broad functions: planning, directing, and controlling.
5. As a result of the Sarbanes-Oxley Act (SOX), top managers must certify that the company maintains an adequate system of internal control.
6. Management accountants follow a code of ethics developed by the Institute of Management Accountants.

Identify managerial accounting concepts.

(LO 1, 2)

DO IT! 15-2 A music company has these costs:

Advertising	Paper inserts for CD cases
Blank CDs	CD plastic cases
Depreciation of CD image burner	Salaries of sales representatives
	Salaries of factory maintenance employees
Salary of factory manager	Salaries of employees who burn music onto CDs
Factory supplies used	

Classify each cost as a period or a product cost. Within the product cost category, indicate if the cost is part of direct materials (DM), direct labor (DL), or manufacturing overhead (MO).

Identify managerial cost concepts.

(LO 3, 4)

DO IT! 15-3 The following information is available for Fishel Company.

	April 1	April 30
Raw materials inventory	$10,000	$14,000
Work in process inventory	5,000	3,500

Materials purchased in April	$ 98,000
Direct labor in April	80,000
Manufacturing overhead in April	180,000

Prepare the cost of goods manufactured schedule for the month of April.

Prepare cost of goods manufactured schedule.

(LO 6)

DO IT! 15-4 Match the descriptions that follow with the corresponding terms.
Descriptions:

1. _____ Inventory system in which goods are manufactured or purchased just as they are needed for sale.
2. _____ A method of allocating overhead based on each product's use of activities in making the product.
3. _____ Systems that are especially important to firms adopting just-in-time inventory methods.
4. _____ One part of the value chain for a manufacturing company.
5. _____ The U.S. economy is trending toward this.
6. _____ A performance-measurement approach that uses both financial and nonfinancial measures, tied to company objectives, to evaluate a company's operations in an integrated fashion.

Identify trends in managerial accounting.

(LO 8)

Terms:

(a) Activity-based costing
(b) Balanced scorecard
(c) Total quality management (TQM)
(d) Research and development, and product design
(e) Service industries
(f) Just-in-time (JIT) inventory

 The Navigator

EXERCISES

Identify distinguishing features of managerial accounting.

(LO 1)

E15-1 Richard Larkin has prepared the following list of statements about managerial accounting and financial accounting.

1. Financial accounting focuses on providing information to internal users.
2. Analyzing cost-volume-profit relationships is part of managerial accounting.
3. Preparation of budgets is part of financial accounting.
4. Managerial accounting applies only to merchandising and manufacturing companies.
5. Both managerial accounting and financial accounting deal with many of the same economic events.
6. Managerial accounting reports are prepared only quarterly and annually.
7. Financial accounting reports are general-purpose reports.
8. Managerial accounting reports pertain to subunits of the business.
9. Managerial accounting reports must comply with generally accepted accounting principles.
10. Although managerial accountants are expected to behave ethically, there is no code of ethical standards for managerial accountants.

Instructions
Identify each statement as true or false. If false, indicate how to correct the statement.

Classify costs into three classes of manufacturing costs.

(LO 3)

E15-2 Presented below is a list of costs and expenses usually incurred by Barnum Corporation, a manufacturer of furniture, in its factory.

1. Salaries for assembly line inspectors.
2. Insurance on factory machines.
3. Property taxes on the factory building.
4. Factory repairs.
5. Upholstery used in manufacturing furniture.
6. Wages paid to assembly line workers.
7. Factory machinery depreciation.
8. Glue, nails, paint, and other small parts used in production.
9. Factory supervisors' salaries.
10. Wood used in manufacturing furniture.

Instructions
Classify the above items into the following categories: (a) direct materials, (b) direct labor, and (c) manufacturing overhead.

Identify types of cost and explain their accounting.

(LO 3, 4)

E15-3 Ryan Corporation incurred the following costs while manufacturing its product.

Materials used in product	$100,000	Advertising expense	$45,000
Depreciation on plant	60,000	Property taxes on plant	14,000
Property taxes on store	7,500	Delivery expense	21,000
Labor costs of assembly-line workers	110,000	Sales commissions	35,000
Factory supplies used	13,000	Salaries paid to sales clerks	50,000

Instructions
(a) Identify each of the above costs as direct materials, direct labor, manufacturing overhead, or period costs.
(b) Explain the basic difference in accounting for product costs and period costs.

Determine the total amount of various types of costs.

(LO 3, 4)

E15-4 Knight Company reports the following costs and expenses in May.

Factory utilities	$ 15,500	Direct labor	$69,100
Depreciation on factory		Sales salaries	46,400
equipment	12,650	Property taxes on factory	
Depreciation on delivery trucks	3,800	building	2,500
Indirect factory labor	48,900	Repairs to office equipment	1,300
Indirect materials	80,800	Factory repairs	2,000
Direct materials used	137,600	Advertising	15,000
Factory manager's salary	8,000	Office supplies used	2,640

Instructions

From the information, determine the total amount of:

(a) Manufacturing overhead.

(b) Product costs.

(c) Period costs.

E15-5 Ikerd Company is a manufacturer of personal computers. Various costs and expenses associated with its operations are as follows.

1. Property taxes on the factory building.
2. Production superintendents' salaries.
3. Memory boards and chips used in assembling computers.
4. Depreciation on the factory equipment.
5. Salaries for assembly-line quality control inspectors.
6. Sales commissions paid to sell personal computers.
7. Electrical components used in assembling computers.
8. Wages of workers assembling personal computers.
9. Soldering materials used on factory assembly lines.
10. Salaries for the night security guards for the factory building.

The company intends to classify these costs and expenses into the following categories: (a) direct materials, (b) direct labor, (c) manufacturing overhead, and (d) period costs.

Classify various costs into different cost categories.

(LO 3, 4)

Instructions

List the items (1) through (10). For each item, indicate the cost category to which it belongs.

E15-6 The administrators of Crawford County's Memorial Hospital are interested in identifying the various costs and expenses that are incurred in producing a patient's X-ray. A list of such costs and expenses is presented below.

1. Salaries for the X-ray machine technicians.
2. Wages for the hospital janitorial personnel.
3. Film costs for the X-ray machines.
4. Property taxes on the hospital building.
5. Salary of the X-ray technicians' supervisor.
6. Electricity costs for the X-ray department.
7. Maintenance and repairs on the X-ray machines.
8. X-ray department supplies.
9. Depreciation on the X-ray department equipment.
10. Depreciation on the hospital building.

The administrators want these costs and expenses classified as: (a) direct materials, (b) direct labor, or (c) service overhead.

Classify various costs into different cost categories.

(LO 3)

Instructions

List the items (1) through (10). For each item, indicate the cost category to which the item belongs.

E15-7 Kwik Delivery Service reports the following costs and expenses in June 2014.

Classify various costs into different cost categories.

(LO 4)

Indirect materials	$ 5,400	Drivers' salaries	$16,000
Depreciation on delivery equipment	11,200	Advertising	3,600
Dispatcher's salary	5,000	Delivery equipment repairs	300
Property taxes on office building	870	Office supplies	650
CEO's salary	12,000	Office utilities	990
Gas and oil for delivery trucks	2,200	Repairs on office equipment	180

Instructions

Determine the total amount of (a) delivery service (product) costs and (b) period costs.

E15-8 Lopez Corporation incurred the following costs while manufacturing its product.

Compute cost of goods manufactured and sold.

(LO 5, 6)

Materials used in product	$120,000	Advertising expense	$45,000
Depreciation on plant	60,000	Property taxes on plant	14,000
Property taxes on store	7,500	Delivery expense	21,000
Labor costs of assembly-line		Sales commissions	35,000
workers	110,000	Salaries paid to sales	
Factory supplies used	23,000	clerks	50,000

Work in process inventory was $12,000 at January 1 and $15,500 at December 31. Finished goods inventory was $60,000 at January 1 and $45,600 at December 31.

Instructions
(a) Compute cost of goods manufactured.
(b) Compute cost of goods sold.

Determine missing amounts in cost of goods manufactured schedule.

(LO 6)

E15-9 An incomplete cost of goods manufactured schedule is presented below.

Molina Company
Cost of Goods Manufactured Schedule
For the Year Ended December 31, 2014

Work in process (1/1)			$210,000
Direct materials			
Raw materials inventory (1/1)	$?		
Add: Raw materials purchases	158,000		
Total raw materials available for use	?		
Less: Raw materials inventory (12/31)	22,500		
Direct materials used		$190,000	
Direct labor		?	
Manufacturing overhead			
Indirect labor	18,000		
Factory depreciation	36,000		
Factory utilities	68,000		
Total overhead		122,000	
Total manufacturing costs			?
Total cost of work in process			?
Less: Work in process (12/31)			81,000
Cost of goods manufactured			$530,000

Instructions
Complete the cost of goods manufactured schedule for Molina Company.

Determine the missing amount of different cost items.

(LO 6)

E15-10 Manufacturing cost data for Copa Company are presented below.

	Case A	Case B	Case C
Direct materials used	$ (a)	$68,400	$130,000
Direct labor	57,000	86,000	(g)
Manufacturing overhead	46,500	81,600	102,000
Total manufacturing costs	195,650	(d)	253,700
Work in process 1/1/14	(b)	16,500	(h)
Total cost of work in process	221,500	(e)	337,000
Work in process 12/31/14	(c)	11,000	70,000
Cost of goods manufactured	185,275	(f)	(i)

Instructions
Indicate the missing amount for each letter (a) through (i).

Determine the missing amount of different cost items, and prepare a condensed cost of goods manufactured schedule.

(LO 6)

E15-11 Incomplete manufacturing cost data for Colaw Company for 2014 are presented as follows for four different situations.

	Direct Materials Used	Direct Labor Used	Manufac- turing Overhead	Total Manufac- turing Costs	Work in Process 1/1	Work in Process 12/31	Cost of Goods Manufac- tured
(1)	$127,000	$140,000	$ 87,000	$ (a)	$33,000	$ (b)	$360,000
(2)	(c)	200,000	132,000	450,000	(d)	40,000	470,000
(3)	80,000	100,000	(e)	255,000	60,000	80,000	(f)
(4)	70,000	(g)	75,000	288,000	45,000	(h)	270,000

Instructions

(a) Indicate the missing amount for each letter.

(b) Prepare a condensed cost of goods manufactured schedule for situation (1) for the year ended December 31, 2014.

E15-12 Cepeda Corporation has the following cost records for June 2014.

Indirect factory labor	$ 4,500	Factory utilities	$ 400
Direct materials used	20,000	Depreciation, factory equipment	1,400
Work in process, 6/1/14	3,000	Direct labor	40,000
Work in process, 6/30/14	3,800	Maintenance, factory equipment	1,800
Finished goods, 6/1/14	5,000	Indirect materials	2,200
Finished goods, 6/30/14	7,500	Factory manager's salary	3,000

Prepare a cost of goods manufactured schedule and a partial income statement.

(LO 5, 6)

Instructions

(a) Prepare a cost of goods manufactured schedule for June 2014.

(b) Prepare an income statement through gross profit for June 2014 assuming sales revenue is $92,100.

E15-13 Joyce Tombert, the bookkeeper for Marks Consulting, a political consulting firm, has recently completed a managerial accounting course at her local college. One of the topics covered in the course was the cost of goods manufactured schedule. Joyce wondered if such a schedule could be prepared for her firm. She realized that, as a service-oriented company, it would have no work in process inventory to consider.

Classify various costs into different categories and prepare cost of services provided schedule.

(LO 4, 5, 6)

Listed below are the costs her firm incurred for the month ended August 31, 2014.

Supplies used on consulting contracts	$ 1,200
Supplies used in the administrative offices	1,500
Depreciation on equipment used for contract work	900
Depreciation used on administrative office equipment	1,050
Salaries of professionals working on contracts	15,600
Salaries of administrative office personnel	7,700
Janitorial services for professional offices	400
Janitorial services for administrative offices	500
Insurance on contract operations	800
Insurance on administrative operations	900
Utilities for contract operations	1,400
Utilities for administrative offices	1,300

Instructions

(a) Prepare a schedule of cost of contract services provided (similar to a cost of goods manufactured schedule) for the month.

(b) For those costs not included in (a), explain how they would be classified and reported in the financial statements.

E15-14 The following information is available for Aikman Company.

Prepare a cost of goods manufactured schedule and a partial income statement.

(LO 5, 6, 7)

	January 1, 2014	2014	December 31, 2014
Raw materials inventory	$21,000		$30,000
Work in process inventory	13,500		17,200
Finished goods inventory	27,000		21,000
Materials purchased		$150,000	
Direct labor		220,000	
Manufacturing overhead		180,000	
Sales revenue		910,000	

Instructions

(a) Compute cost of goods manufactured.

(b) Prepare an income statement through gross profit.

(c) Show the presentation of the ending inventories on the December 31, 2014, balance sheet.

(d) How would the income statement and balance sheet of a merchandising company be different from Aikman's financial statements?

Indicate in which schedule or financial statement(s) different cost items will appear.

(LO 5, 6, 7)

E15-15 Chambers Company produces blankets. From its accounting records, it prepares the following schedule and financial statements on a yearly basis.

(a) Cost of goods manufactured schedule.

(b) Income statement.

(c) Balance sheet.

The following items are found in its ledger and accompanying data.

1. Direct labor
2. Raw materials inventory, 1/1
3. Work in process inventory, 12/31
4. Finished goods inventory, 1/1
5. Indirect labor
6. Depreciation on factory machinery
7. Work in process, 1/1
8. Finished goods inventory, 12/31
9. Factory maintenance salaries
10. Cost of goods manufactured
11. Depreciation on delivery equipment
12. Cost of goods available for sale
13. Direct materials used
14. Heat and electricity for factory
15. Repairs to roof of factory building
16. Cost of raw materials purchases

Instructions

List the items (1)–(16). For each item, indicate by using the appropriate letter or letters, the schedule and/or financial statement(s) in which the item will appear.

Prepare a cost of goods manufactured schedule, and present the ending inventories on the balance sheet.

(LO 6, 7)

E15-16 An analysis of the accounts of Roberts Company reveals the following manufacturing cost data for the month ended June 30, 2014.

Inventories	Beginning	Ending
Raw materials	$9,000	$13,100
Work in process	5,000	7,000
Finished goods	9,000	8,000

Costs incurred: raw materials purchases $54,000, direct labor $47,000, manufacturing overhead $19,900. The specific overhead costs were: indirect labor $5,500, factory insurance $4,000, machinery depreciation $4,000, machinery repairs $1,800, factory utilities $3,100, miscellaneous factory costs $1,500. Assume that all raw materials used were direct materials.

Instructions

(a) Prepare the cost of goods manufactured schedule for the month ended June 30, 2014.

(b) Show the presentation of the ending inventories on the June 30, 2014, balance sheet.

Determine the amount of cost to appear in various accounts, and indicate in which financial statements these accounts would appear.

(LO 5, 6, 7)

E15-17 Buhler Motor Company manufactures automobiles. During September 2014, the company purchased 5,000 head lamps at a cost of $10 per lamp. Buhler withdrew 4,650 lamps from the warehouse during the month. Fifty of these lamps were used to replace the head lamps in autos used by traveling sales staff. The remaining 4,600 lamps were put in autos manufactured during the month.

Of the autos put into production during September 2014, 90% were completed and transferred to the company's storage lot. Of the cars completed during the month, 70% were sold by September 30.

Instructions

(a) Determine the cost of head lamps that would appear in each of the following accounts at September 30, 2014: Raw Materials, Work in Process, Finished Goods, Cost of Goods Sold, and Selling Expenses.

(b) ▓▓▓▭▭▭▷ Write a short memo to the chief accountant, indicating whether and where each of the accounts in (a) would appear on the income statement or on the balance sheet at September 30, 2014.

E15-18 The following is a list of terms related to managerial accounting practices.

Identify various managerial accounting practices.

(LO 8)

1. Activity-based costing.
2. Just-in-time inventory.
3. Balanced scorecard.
4. Value chain.

Instructions

Match each of the terms with the statement below that best describes the term.

(a) _____ A performance-measurement technique that attempts to consider and evaluate all aspects of performance using financial and nonfinancial measures in an integrated fashion.

(b) _____ The group of activities associated with providing a product or service.

(c) _____ An approach used to reduce the cost associated with handling and holding inventory by reducing the amount of inventory on hand.

(d) _____ A method used to allocate overhead to products based on each product's use of the activities that cause the incurrence of the overhead cost.

EXERCISES: SET B AND CHALLENGE EXERCISES

Visit the book's companion website, at **www.wiley.com/college/weygandt**, and choose the Student Companion site to access Exercise Set B and Challenge Exercises.

PROBLEMS: SET A

P15-1A Lott Company specializes in manufacturing a unique model of bicycle helmet. The model is well accepted by consumers, and the company has enough orders to keep the factory production at 10,000 helmets per month (80% of its full capacity). Lott's monthly manufacturing cost and other expense data are as follows.

Classify manufacturing costs into different categories and compute the unit cost.

(LO 3, 4)

Rent on factory equipment	$ 9,000
Insurance on factory building	1,500
Raw materials (plastics, polystyrene, etc.)	75,000
Utility costs for factory	900
Supplies for general office	300
Wages for assembly line workers	53,000
Depreciation on office equipment	800
Miscellaneous materials (glue, thread, etc.)	1,100
Factory manager's salary	5,700
Property taxes on factory building	400
Advertising for helmets	14,000
Sales commissions	10,000
Depreciation on factory building	1,500

Instructions

(a) Prepare an answer sheet with the following column headings.

(a) DM $75,000
    DL $53,000
    MO $20,100
    PC $25,100

	Product Costs			
Cost Item	Direct Materials	Direct Labor	Manufacturing Overhead	Period Costs

Enter each cost item on your answer sheet, placing the dollar amount under the appropriate headings. Total the dollar amounts in each of the columns.

(b) Compute the cost to produce one helmet.

P15-2A Bell Company, a manufacturer of audio systems, started its production in October 2014. For the preceding 3 years, Bell had been a retailer of audio systems. After a thorough survey of audio system markets, Bell decided to turn its retail store into an audio equipment factory.

Classify manufacturing costs into different categories and compute the unit cost.

(LO 3, 4)

Raw materials cost for an audio system will total $74 per unit. Workers on the production lines are on average paid $12 per hour. An audio system usually takes 5 hours to complete. In addition, the rent on the equipment used to assemble audio systems amounts to $4,900 per month. Indirect materials cost $5 per system. A supervisor was hired to oversee production; her monthly salary is $3,000.

Factory janitorial costs are $1,300 monthly. Advertising costs for the audio system will be $9,500 per month. The factory building depreciation expense is $7,800 per year. Property taxes on the factory building will be $9,000 per year.

Instructions

(a) Prepare an answer sheet with the following column headings.

| | Product Costs | | | |
Cost Item	Direct Materials	Direct Labor	Manufacturing Overhead	Period Costs

Assuming that Bell manufactures, on average, 1,500 audio systems per month, enter each cost item on your answer sheet, placing the dollar amount per month under the appropriate headings. Total the dollar amounts in each of the columns.
(b) Compute the cost to produce one audio system.

(a) DM $111,000
DL $ 90,000
MO $ 18,100
PC $ 9,500

Indicate the missing amount of different cost items, and prepare a condensed cost of goods manufactured schedule, an income statement, and a partial balance sheet.

(LO 5, 6, 7)

P15-3A Incomplete manufacturing costs, expenses, and selling data for two different cases are as follows.

| | Case | |
	1	2
Direct materials used	$ 9,600	$ (g)
Direct labor	5,000	8,000
Manufacturing overhead	8,000	4,000
Total manufacturing costs	(a)	16,000
Beginning work in process inventory	1,000	(h)
Ending work in process inventory	(b)	3,000
Sales revenue	24,500	(i)
Sales discounts	2,500	1,400
Cost of goods manufactured	17,000	22,000
Beginning finished goods inventory	(c)	3,300
Goods available for sale	20,000	(j)
Cost of goods sold	(d)	(k)
Ending finished goods inventory	3,400	2,500
Gross profit	(e)	7,000
Operating expenses	2,500	(l)
Net income	(f)	5,000

Instructions

(a) Indicate the missing amount for each letter.
(b) Prepare a condensed cost of goods manufactured schedule for Case 1.
(c) Prepare an income statement and the current assets section of the balance sheet for Case 1. Assume that in Case 1 the other items in the current assets section are as follows: Cash $4,000, Receivables (net) $15,000, Raw Materials $600, and Prepaid Expenses $400.

(b) Ending WIP $ 6,600
(c) Current assets $30,000

Prepare a cost of goods manufactured schedule, a partial income statement, and a partial balance sheet.

(LO 5, 6, 7)

P15-4A The following data were taken from the records of Clarkson Company for the fiscal year ended June 30, 2014.

Raw Materials		Factory Insurance	$ 4,600
Inventory 7/1/13	$ 48,000	Factory Machinery	
Raw Materials		Depreciation	16,000
Inventory 6/30/14	39,600	Factory Utilities	27,600
Finished Goods		Office Utilities Expense	8,650
Inventory 7/1/13	96,000	Sales Revenue	534,000
Finished Goods		Sales Discounts	4,200
Inventory 6/30/14	75,900	Plant Manager's Salary	58,000

Work in Process		Factory Property Taxes	$ 9,600
Inventory 7/1/13	$ 19,800	Factory Repairs	1,400
Work in Process		Raw Materials Purchases	96,400
Inventory 6/30/14	18,600	Cash	32,000
Direct Labor	139,250		
Indirect Labor	24,460		
Accounts Receivable	27,000		

Instructions

(a) Prepare a cost of goods manufactured schedule. (Assume all raw materials used were direct materials.)

(b) Prepare an income statement through gross profit.

(c) Prepare the current assets section of the balance sheet at June 30, 2014.

(a) CGM $386,910

(b) Gross profit $122,790

(c) Current assets $193,100

P15-5A Phillips Company is a manufacturer of computers. Its controller resigned in October 2014. An inexperienced assistant accountant has prepared the following income statement for the month of October 2014.

Prepare a cost of goods manufactured schedule and a correct income statement.

(LO 5, 6)

XLS

Phillips Company
Income Statement
For the Month Ended October 31, 2014

Sales revenue		$780,000
Less: Operating expenses		
Raw materials purchases	$264,000	
Direct labor cost	190,000	
Advertising expense	90,000	
Selling and administrative salaries	75,000	
Rent on factory facilities	60,000	
Depreciation on sales equipment	45,000	
Depreciation on factory equipment	31,000	
Indirect labor cost	28,000	
Utilities expense	12,000	
Insurance expense	8,000	803,000
Net loss		$ (23,000)

Prior to October 2014, the company had been profitable every month. The company's president is concerned about the accuracy of the income statement. As her friend, you have been asked to review the income statement and make necessary corrections. After examining other manufacturing cost data, you have acquired additional information as follows.

1. Inventory balances at the beginning and end of October were:

	October 1	October 31
Raw materials	$18,000	$29,000
Work in process	16,000	14,000
Finished goods	30,000	45,000

2. Only 75% of the utilities expense and 60% of the insurance expense apply to factory operations. The remaining amounts should be charged to selling and administrative activities.

Instructions

(a) Prepare a schedule of cost of goods manufactured for October 2014.

(b) Prepare a correct income statement for October 2014.

(a) CGM $577,800

(b) NI $ 1,000

P15-1B Agler Company specializes in manufacturing motorcycle helmets. The company has enough orders to keep the factory production at 1,000 motorcycle helmets per month. Agler's monthly manufacturing cost and other expense data are shown on the next page.

Classify manufacturing costs into different categories and compute the unit cost.

(LO 3, 4)

Maintenance costs on factory building	$ 1,500
Factory manager's salary	5,500
Advertising for helmets	8,000
Sales commissions	4,000
Depreciation on factory building	700
Rent on factory equipment	6,000
Insurance on factory building	3,000
Raw materials (plastic, polystyrene, etc.)	25,000
Utility costs for factory	800
Supplies for general office	200
Wages for assembly line workers	54,000
Depreciation on office equipment	500
Miscellaneous materials (glue, thread, etc.)	2,000

Instructions

(a) DM $25,000
DL $54,000
MO $19,500
PC $12,700

(a) Prepare an answer sheet with the following column headings.

	Product Costs			
Cost Item	**Direct Materials**	**Direct Labor**	**Manufacturing Overhead**	**Period Costs**

Enter each cost item on your answer sheet, placing the dollar amount under the appropriate headings. Total the dollar amounts in each of the columns.

(b) Compute the cost to produce one motorcycle helmet.

Classify manufacturing costs into different categories and compute the unit cost.

(LO 3, 4)

P15-2B Elliott Company, a manufacturer of tennis rackets, started production in November 2013. For the preceding 5 years, Elliott had been a retailer of sports equipment. After a thorough survey of tennis racket markets, Elliott decided to turn its retail store into a tennis racket factory.

Raw materials cost for a tennis racket will total $23 per racket. Workers on the production lines are paid on average $15 per hour. A racket usually takes 2 hours to complete. In addition, the rent on the equipment used to produce rackets amounts to $1,300 per month. Indirect materials cost $3 per racket. A supervisor was hired to oversee production; her monthly salary is $3,500.

Janitorial costs are $1,400 monthly. Advertising costs for the rackets will be $8,000 per month. The factory building depreciation expense is $8,400 per year. Property taxes on the factory building will be $9,600 per year.

Instructions

(a) DM $57,500
DL $75,000
MO $15,200
PC $ 8,000

(a) Prepare an answer sheet with the following column headings.

	Product Costs			
Cost Item	**Direct Materials**	**Direct Labor**	**Manufacturing Overhead**	**Period Costs**

Assuming that Elliott manufactures, on average, 2,500 tennis rackets per month, enter each cost item on your answer sheet, placing the dollar amount per month under the appropriate headings. Total the dollar amounts in each of the columns.

(b) Compute the cost to produce one racket.

Indicate the missing amount of different cost items, and prepare a condensed cost of goods manufactured schedule, an income statement, and a partial balance sheet.

(LO 5, 6, 7)

P15-3B Incomplete manufacturing costs, expenses, and selling data for two different cases are as follows.

	Case	
	A	**B**
Direct materials used	$ 6,300	$ (g)
Direct labor	3,000	4,000
Manufacturing overhead	6,000	5,000
Total manufacturing costs	(a)	16,000
Beginning work in process inventory	1,000	(h)
Ending work in process inventory	(b)	2,000
Sales revenue	22,500	(i)
Sales discounts	1,500	1,200
Cost of goods manufactured	15,800	20,000

	Case	
	A	B
Beginning finished goods inventory	$ (c)	$ 5,000
Goods available for sale	18,300	(j)
Cost of goods sold	(d)	(k)
Ending finished goods inventory	1,200	2,500
Gross profit	(e)	6,000
Operating expenses	2,700	(l)
Net income	(f)	2,200

Instructions
(a) Indicate the missing amount for each letter.
(b) Prepare a condensed cost of goods manufactured schedule for Case A.
(c) Prepare an income statement and the current assets section of the balance sheet for Case A. Assume that in Case A the other items in the current assets section are as follows: Cash $3,000, Receivables (net) $10,000, Raw Materials $700, and Prepaid Expenses $200.

(b) Beg. WIP $1,000
(c) Current assets $15,600

P15-4B The following data were taken from the records of Moxie Company for the year ended December 31, 2014.

Prepare a cost of goods manufactured schedule, a partial income statement, and a partial balance sheet.

(LO 5, 6, 7)

Raw Materials		Factory Insurance	$ 7,400
Inventory 1/1/14	$ 47,000	Factory Machinery	
Raw Materials		Depreciation	7,700
Inventory 12/31/14	44,200	Factory Utilities	12,900
Finished Goods		Office Utilities Expense	8,600
Inventory 1/1/14	85,000	Sales Revenue	465,000
Finished Goods		Sales Discounts	2,500
Inventory 12/31/14	57,800	Plant Manager's Salary	60,000
Work in Process		Factory Property Taxes	6,100
Inventory 1/1/14	9,500	Factory Repairs	800
Work in Process		Raw Materials Purchases	62,500
Inventory 12/31/14	8,000	Cash	18,000
Direct Labor	145,100		
Indirect Labor	18,100		
Accounts Receivable	27,000		

Instructions
(a) Prepare a cost of goods manufactured schedule. (Assume all raw materials used were direct materials.)
(b) Prepare an income statement through gross profit.
(c) Prepare the current assets section of the balance sheet at December 31.

(a) CGM $324,900

(b) Gross profit $110,400
(c) Current assets $155,000

P15-5B Ortiz Company is a manufacturer of toys. Its controller resigned in August 2014. An inexperienced assistant accountant has prepared the following income statement for the month of August 2014.

Prepare a cost of goods manufactured schedule and a correct income statement.

(LO 5, 6)

Ortiz Company
Income Statement
For the Month Ended August 31, 2014

Sales revenue		$675,000
Less: Operating expenses		
Raw materials purchases	$220,000	
Direct labor cost	160,000	
Advertising expense	75,000	
Selling and administrative salaries	70,000	
Rent on factory facilities	60,000	
Depreciation on sales equipment	50,000	
Depreciation on factory equipment	35,000	
Indirect labor cost	20,000	
Utilities expense	10,000	
Insurance expense	5,000	705,000
Net loss		$ (30,000)

Prior to August 2014, the company had been profitable every month. The company's president is concerned about the accuracy of the income statement. As her friend, you have been asked to review the income statement and make necessary corrections. After examining other manufacturing cost data, you have acquired additional information as follows.
1. Inventory balances at the beginning and end of August were:

	August 1	August 31
Raw materials	$19,500	$35,000
Work in process	25,000	21,000
Finished goods	40,000	52,000

2. Only 60% of the utilities expense and 70% of the insurance expense apply to factory operations; the remaining amounts should be charged to selling and administrative activities.

Instructions

(a) CGM $493,000
(b) NL $ (6,500)

(a) Prepare a cost of goods manufactured schedule for August 2014.
(b) Prepare a correct income statement for August 2014.

PROBLEMS: SET C

Visit the book's companion website, at **www.wiley.com/college/weygandt**, and choose the Student Companion site to access Problem Set C.

WATERWAYS CONTINUING PROBLEM

(*Note:* The Waterways Problem begins in Chapter 15 and continues in the remaining chapters. You can also find this problem at the book's Student Companion site.)

WCP15 Waterways Corporation is a private corporation formed for the purpose of providing the products and the services needed to irrigate farms, parks, commercial projects, and private lawns. It has a centrally located factory in a U.S. city that manufactures the products it markets to retail outlets across the nation. It also maintains a division that provides installation and warranty servicing in six metropolitan areas.

The mission of Waterways is to manufacture quality parts that can be used for effective irrigation projects that also conserve water. By that effort, the company hopes to satisfy its customers, provide rapid and responsible service, and serve the community and the employees who represent them in each community.

The company has been growing rapidly, so management is considering new ideas to help the company continue its growth and maintain the high quality of its products.

Waterways was founded by Will Winkman, who is the company president and chief executive officer (CEO). Working with him from the company's inception is Will's brother, Ben, whose sprinkler designs and ideas about the installation of proper systems have been a major basis of the company's success. Ben is the vice president who oversees all aspects of design and production in the company.

The factory itself is managed by Todd Senter who hires his line managers to supervise the factory employees. The factory makes all of the parts for the irrigation systems. The purchasing department is managed by Hector Hines.

The installation and training division is overseen by vice president Henry Writer, who supervises the managers of the six local installation operations. Each of these local managers hires his or her own local service people. These service employees are trained by the home office under Henry Writer's direction because of the uniqueness of the company's products.

There is a small human resources department under the direction of Sally Fenton, a vice president who handles the employee paperwork, though hiring is actually performed by the separate departments. Sam Totter is the vice president who heads the sales and marketing area; he oversees 10 well-trained salespeople.

The accounting and finance division of the company is run by Abe Headman, who is the chief financial officer (CFO) and a company vice president. He is a member of the Institute of Management Accountants and holds a certificate in management accounting.

He has a small staff of certified public accountants, including a controller and a treasurer, and a staff of accounting input operators who maintain the financial records.

A partial list of Waterways' accounts and their balances for the month of November follows.

Accounts Receivable	$ 275,000
Advertising Expenses	54,000
Cash	260,000
Depreciation—Factory Equipment	16,800
Depreciation—Office Equipment	2,400
Direct Labor	42,000
Factory Supplies Used	16,800
Factory Utilities	10,200
Finished Goods Inventory, November 30	68,800
Finished Goods Inventory, October 31	72,550
Indirect Labor	48,000
Office Supplies Expense	1,600
Other Administrative Expenses	72,000
Prepaid Expenses	41,250
Raw Materials Inventory, November 30	52,700
Raw Materials Inventory, October 31	38,000
Raw Materials Purchases	184,500
Rent—Factory Equipment	47,000
Repairs—Factory Equipment	4,500
Salaries	325,000
Sales Revenue	1,350,000
Sales Commissions	40,500
Work in Process Inventory, October 31	52,700
Work in Process Inventory, November 30	42,000

Instructions

(a) Based on the information given, construct an organizational chart of Waterways Corporation.

(b) A list of accounts and their values are given above. From this information, prepare a cost of goods manufactured schedule, an income statement, and a partial balance sheet for Waterways Corporation for the month of November.

Broadening Your PERSPECTIVE

Management Decision-Making

Chapters 15–26 contain an exercise based on Current Designs, the company that was featured at the beginning of this chapter. We are excited to present managerial accounting situations that are based on the operations of a real company. However, to protect the proprietary nature of this information, the amounts in these exercises are realistic but not necessarily the actual data that would be found in Current Designs' accounting records. We sincerely appreciate the cooperation of the people at Current Designs, particularly Mike Cichanowski, Jim Brown, Diane Buswell, and Jake Greseth, who made these exercises possible.

Decision-Making at Current Designs

BYP15-1 Mike Cichanowski founded Wenonah Canoe and later purchased Current Designs, a company that designs and manufactures kayaks. The kayak-manufacturing facility is located just a few minutes from the canoe company's headquarters in Winona, Minnesota.

Current Designs makes kayaks using two different processes. (See *www.cdkayak.com/craftsmanship/index.php* for the details of each method.) The rotational molding process uses high

temperature to melt polyethylene powder in a closed rotating metal mold to produce a complete kayak hull and deck in a single piece. These kayaks are less labor-intensive and less expensive for the company to produce and sell.

Its other kayaks use the vacuum-bagged composite lamination process (which we will refer to as the composite process). Layers of fiberglass or Kevlar® are carefully placed by hand in a mold and are bonded with resin. Then, a high-pressure vacuum is used to eliminate any excess resin that would otherwise add weight and reduce strength of the finished kayak. These kayaks require a great deal of skilled labor as each boat is individually finished. The exquisite finish of the vacuum-bagged composite kayaks gave rise to Current Designs' tag line, "A work of art, made for life."

Current Designs has the following managers:

Mike Cichanowski, CEO
Diane Buswell, Controller
Deb Welch, Purchasing Manager
Bill Johnson, Sales Manager
Dave Thill, Kayak Plant Manager
Rick Thrune, Production Manager for Composite Kayaks

Instructions

(a) What are the primary information needs of each manager?
(b) Name one special-purpose management accounting report that could be designed for each manager. Include the name of the report, the information it would contain, and how frequently it should be issued.
(c) When Diane Buswell, controller for Current Designs, reviewed the accounting records for a recent period, she noted the following items. Classify each item as a product cost or a period cost. If an item is a product cost, note if it is a direct materials, direct labor, or manufacturing overhead item.

Payee	Purpose	Product Costs			Period Costs
		Direct Materials	Direct Labor	Manufacturing Overhead	
Winona Agency	Property insurance for the manufacturing plant				
Bill Johnson (sales manager)	Payroll check—payment to sales manager				
Xcel Energy	Electricity for manufacturing plant				
Winona Printing	Price lists for salespeople				
Jim Kaiser (sales representative)	Sales commissions				
Dave Thill (plant manager)	Payroll check—payment to plant manager				
Dana Schultz (kayak assembler)	Payroll check—payment to kayak assembler				
Composite One	Bagging film used when kayaks are assembled; it is discarded after use				
Fastenal	Shop supplies—brooms, paper towels, etc.				
Ravago	Polyethylene powder which is the main ingredient for the rotational molded kayaks				
Winona County	Property taxes on manufacturing plant				
North American Composites	Kevlar® fabric for composite kayaks				
Waste Management	Trash disposal for the company office building				
None	Journal entry to record depreciation of manufacturing equipment				

Decision-Making Across the Organization

BYP15-2 Wendall Company specializes in producing fashion outfits. On July 31, 2014, a tornado touched down at its factory and general office. The inventories in the warehouse and the factory were completely destroyed as was the general office nearby. Next morning, through a careful search of the disaster site, however, Bill Francis, the company's controller, and Elizabeth Walton, the cost accountant, were able to recover a small part of manufacturing cost data for the current month.

"What a horrible experience," sighed Bill "And the worst part is that we may not have enough records to use in filing an insurance claim."

"It was terrible," replied Elizabeth. "However, I managed to recover some of the manufacturing cost data that I was working on yesterday afternoon. The data indicate that our direct labor cost in July totaled $250,000 and that we had purchased $365,000 of raw materials. Also, I recall that the amount of raw materials used for July was $350,000. But I'm not sure this information will help. The rest of our records are blown away."

"Well, not exactly," said Bill. "I was working on the year-to-date income statement when the tornado warning was announced. My recollection is that our sales in July were $1,240,000 and our gross profit ratio has been 40% of sales. Also, I can remember that our cost of goods available for sale was $770,000 for July."

"Maybe we can work something out from this information!" exclaimed Elizabeth. "My experience tells me that our manufacturing overhead is usually 60% of direct labor."

"Hey, look what I just found," cried Elizabeth. "It's a copy of this June's balance sheet, and it shows that our inventories as of June 30 are Finished goods $38,000, Work in process $25,000, and Raw materials $19,000."

"Super," yelled Bill. "Let's go work something out."

In order to file an insurance claim, Wendall Company must determine the amount of its inventories as of July 31, 2014, the date of the tornado touchdown.

Instructions

With the class divided into groups, determine the amount of cost in the Raw Materials, Work in Process, and Finished Goods inventory accounts as of the date of the tornado touchdown.

Managerial Analysis

BYP15-3 Tenrack is a fairly large manufacturing company located in the southern United States. The company manufactures tennis rackets, tennis balls, tennis clothing, and tennis shoes, all bearing the company's distinctive logo, a large green question mark on a white flocked tennis ball. The company's sales have been increasing over the past 10 years.

The tennis racket division has recently implemented several advanced manufacturing techniques. Robot arms hold the tennis rackets in place while glue dries, and machine vision systems check for defects. The engineering and design team uses computerized drafting and testing of new products. The following managers work in the tennis racket division:

Jason Dennis, Sales Manager (supervises all sales representatives)
Peggy Groneman, Technical Specialist (supervises computer programmers)
Dave Marley, Cost Accounting Manager (supervises cost accountants)
Kevin Carson, Production Supervisor (supervises all manufacturing employees)
Sally Renner, Engineer (supervises all new-product design teams)

Instructions

(a) What are the primary information needs of each manager?
(b) Which, if any, financial accounting report(s) is each likely to use?
(c) Name one special-purpose management accounting report that could be designed for each manager. Include the name of the report, the information it would contain, and how frequently it should be issued.

Real-World Focus

BYP15-4 Anchor Glass Container Corporation, the third largest manufacturer of glass containers in the United States, supplies beverage and food producers and consumer products manufacturers nationwide. Parent company Consumers Packaging Inc. (*Toronto Stock Exchange:* CGC) is a leading international designer and manufacturer of glass containers.

The management discussion on page 806 appeared in a recent annual report of Anchor Glass.

> ### Anchor Glass Container Corporation
> #### Management Discussion

Cost of Products Sold   Cost of products sold as a percentage of net sales was 89.3% in the current year compared to 87.6% in the prior year. The increase in cost of products sold as a percentage of net sales principally reflected the impact of operational problems during the second quarter of the current year at a major furnace at one of the Company's plants, higher downtime, and costs and expenses associated with an increased number of scheduled capital improvement projects, increases in labor, and certain other manufacturing costs (with no corresponding selling price increases in the current year). Reduced fixed costs from the closing of the Streator, Illinois, plant in June of the current year and productivity and efficiency gains partially offset these cost increases.

Instructions
What factors affect the costs of products sold at Anchor Glass Container Corporation?

BYP15-5 The Institute of Management Accountants (IMA) is an organization dedicated to excellence in the practice of management accounting and financial management.

Address: **www.imanet.org**, or go to **www.wiley.com/college/weygandt**

Instructions
At the IMA's home page, locate the answers to the following questions.
(a) How many members does the IMA have, and what are their job titles?
(b) What are some of the benefits of joining the IMA as a student?
(c) Use the chapter locator function to locate the IMA chapter nearest you, and find the name of the chapter president.

Critical Thinking

Communication Activity

BYP15-6 Refer to P15–5A (page 799) and add the following requirement.

Prepare a letter to the president of the company, Shelly Phillips, describing the changes you made. Explain clearly why net income is different after the changes. Keep the following points in mind as you compose your letter.

1. This is a letter to the president of a company, who is your friend. The style should be generally formal, but you may relax some requirements. For example, you may call the president by her first name.
2. Executives are very busy. Your letter should tell the president your main results first (for example, the amount of net income).
3. You should include brief explanations so that the president can understand the changes you made in the calculations.

Ethics Case

BYP15-7 Steve Morgan, controller for Newton Industries, was reviewing production cost reports for the year. One amount in these reports continued to bother him—advertising. During the year, the company had instituted an expensive advertising campaign to sell some of its slower-moving products. It was still too early to tell whether the advertising campaign was successful.

There had been much internal debate as how to report advertising cost. The vice president of finance argued that advertising costs should be reported as a cost of production, just like direct materials and direct labor. He therefore recommended that this cost be identified as manufacturing overhead and reported as part of inventory costs until sold. Others disagreed. Morgan believed that this cost should be reported as an expense of the current period, so as not to overstate net income. Others argued that it should be reported as prepaid advertising and reported as a current asset.

The president finally had to decide the issue. He argued that these costs should be reported as inventory. His arguments were practical ones. He noted that the company was experiencing financial difficulty and expensing this amount in the current period might jeopardize a planned bond offering. Also, by reporting the advertising costs as inventory rather than as prepaid advertising, less attention would be directed to it by the financial community.

Instructions
(a) Who are the stakeholders in this situation?
(b) What are the ethical issues involved in this situation?
(c) What would you do if you were Steve Morgan?

All About You

BYP15-8 The primary purpose of managerial accounting is to provide information useful for management decisions. Many of the managerial accounting techniques that you learn in this course will be useful for decisions you make in your everyday life.

Instructions
For each of the following managerial accounting techniques, read the definition provided and then provide an example of a personal situation that would benefit from use of this technique.
(a) Break-even point (page 961).
(b) Budget (page 1132).
(c) Balanced scorecard (page 1257).
(d) Capital budgeting (page 1291).

Considering Your Costs and Benefits

BYP15-9 As noted in this chapter, because of global competition, companies have become increasingly focused on reducing costs. To reduce costs and remain competitive, many companies are turning to outsourcing. Outsourcing means hiring an outside supplier to provide elements of a product or service rather than producing them internally.

Suppose you are the managing partner in a CPA firm with 30 full-time staff. Larger firms in your community have begun to outsource basic tax-return preparation work to India. Should you outsource your basic tax-return work to India as well? You estimate that you would have to lay off six staff members if you outsource the work. The basic arguments for and against are as follows.

YES: The wages paid to Indian accountants are very low relative to U.S. wages. You will not be able to compete unless you outsource.

NO: Tax-return data is highly sensitive. Many customers will be upset to learn that their data is being emailed around the world.

Instructions
Write a response indicating your position regarding this situation. Provide support for your view.

Answers to Chapter Questions

Answers to Insight and Accounting Across the Organization Questions

p. 768 Even the Best Have to Get Better Q: What are some of the steps that this company has taken in order to ensure that production meets demand? **A:** The company has organized flexible teams, with jobs arranged by the amount of time a task takes. Employees now are multiskilled, so they can switch between tasks and products. Also, the stores now provide sales data more quickly to the manufacturing facility, so that production levels can be changed more quickly in response to demand.
p. 773 Why Manufacturing Matters for U.S. Workers Q: In what ways does the shift to automated factories change the amount and composition of product costs? **A:** As factories become more automated, they become more efficient, increasing output and decreasing cost per unit. The composition of those costs also switches: Factory labor costs decline, and factory overhead costs (e.g., depreciation and maintenance on equipment) increase.
p. 781 Low Fares but Decent Profits Q: What are some of the line items that would appear in the cost of services provided schedule of an airline? **A:** Some of the line items that would appear in the cost of services provided schedule of an airline would be fuel, flight crew salaries, maintenance wages, depreciation on equipment, airport gate fees, and food-service costs.

Answers to Self-Test Questions

1. b **2.** b **3.** b **4.** b **5.** d **6.** a **7.** c **8.** c **9.** c ($200,000 + $600,000 − $250,000) **10.** c
11. a **12.** d **13.** d **14.** d **15.** d

✔ **Remember to go back to The Navigator box on the chapter opening page and check off your completed work.**

Chapter 16

Job Order Costing

Feature Story

She Succeeds Where Others Have Failed

The financial press is fond of highlighting the fact that, sporting stilettos and leather skirts, Lynn Tilton does not dress like your typical manufacturing executive. Much more important, however, is the fact that her business success is also far from typical. In fact, as the full or partial owner of 74 companies with revenues of more than $8 billion, Tilton is one of the wealthiest female entrepreneurs in the United States. Her company, Patriarch Partners, is sometimes referred to as the largest woman-owned business in America.

Her path to success is an inspiring tale of determination. Tilton started on Wall Street as a single mother, working 15-hour days as she put herself through business school. During years of employment at numerous financial institutions, she developed a knack for analyzing balance sheets and interpreting complex financial information. Eventually, Tilton started her own company, Patriarch Partners, and invested in the debt of a number of distressed companies. She quickly figured out that the only way she was going to make money on those investments was to take control of the companies and try to make them profitable. Thus, seemingly almost by accident, she became the CEO of dozens of failing manufacturing companies. Amazingly, she was able to make these companies profitable when others had given up on them.

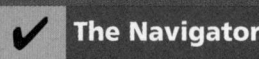

The Navigator

Learning Objectives

After studying this chapter, you should be able to:

1 Explain the characteristics and purposes of cost accounting.

2 Describe the flow of costs in a job order cost system.

3 Explain the nature and importance of a job cost sheet.

4 Indicate how the predetermined overhead rate is determined and used.

5 Prepare entries for jobs completed and sold.

6 Distinguish between under- and overapplied manufacturing overhead.

The Navigator

As a result of this initial success, Tilton made corporate turn-arounds the focus of her company. Once a business is acquired, she installs a new management team, improves productivity, and identifies new products for the company to produce. For example, she turned a failed paper mill into a producer of alternative fuels, and saved a helicopter company by identifying new customers. When others were fleeing the auto industry, she dove in and bought a number of auto-parts companies.

While she is a tough negotiator, Tilton also has the respect of her workers. Duane Ludgon, a union negotiator says, "Workers really take to Lynn. She's just human and honest with people. I don't say that about many CEOs." In fact,

Tilton is a crusader for U.S. manufacturing. She says, "The key to America's future is manufacturing. We simply have to become a country that can make things again."

Not all of her investments are immediate successes. Her investment in a fire-truck manufacturer, American LaFrance, was slow to turn a profit. But everyone involved figured it was only a matter of time before her persistent approach made this fire-truck maker another business that she saved before it went up in smoke.

*Watch the **Making a Hollywood Movie** video in WileyPLUS to learn more about job order costing in the real world.*

Source: Robert Frank, "Tilton Flaunts Her Style at Patriarch," *Wall Street Journal Online* (January 8, 2011).

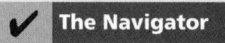

✔ **The Navigator**

Preview of **Chapter 16**

The Feature Story about Patriarch Partners describes the approach Lynn Tilton uses to turn around a failing company. Accurate costing is critical to this process. For example, in order to submit accurate bids on new jobs and to know whether it profited from past jobs, the company needs a good costing system. This chapter illustrates how these costs are assigned to specific jobs, such as the manufacture of individual fire trucks at one of Tilton's companies, American LaFrance. We begin the discussion in this chapter with an overview of the flow of costs in a job order cost accounting system. We then use a case study to explain and illustrate the documents, entries, and accounts in this type of cost accounting system.

The content and organization of Chapter 16 are as follows.

JOB ORDER COSTING

Cost Accounting Systems	Job Order Cost Flow	Reporting Job Cost Data
• Job order cost system • Process cost system	• Accumulating costs • Assigning costs to work in process • Assigning costs to finished goods • Assigning costs to cost of goods sold • Summary of job order cost flows • Job order costing for service companies • Advantages and disadvantages	• Cost of goods manufactured schedule • Income statement presentation • Under- or overapplied manufacturing overhead

✔ **The Navigator**

Cost Accounting Systems

LEARNING OBJECTIVE   1

Explain the characteristics and purposes of cost accounting.

Cost accounting involves measuring, recording, and reporting product costs. Companies determine both the total cost and the unit cost of each product. The accuracy of the product cost information is critical to the success of the company. Companies use this information to determine which products to produce, what price to charge, and the amounts to produce. Accurate product cost information is also vital for effective evaluation of employee performance.

A **cost accounting system** consists of accounts for the various manufacturing costs. These accounts are fully integrated into the general ledger of a company. An important feature of a cost accounting system is the use of **a perpetual inventory system**. Such a system **provides immediate, up-to-date information on the cost of a product**.

There are two basic types of cost accounting systems: (1) a job order cost system and (2) a process cost system. Although cost accounting systems differ widely from company to company, most involve one of these two traditional product costing systems.

Job Order Cost System

Under a **job order cost system**, the company assigns costs to each **job** or to each **batch** of goods. An example of a job is the manufacture of a mainframe computer by IBM, the production of a movie by Disney, or the making of a fire truck by American LaFrance. An example of a batch is the printing of 225 wedding invitations by a local print shop, or the printing of a weekly issue of *Fortune* magazine by a high-tech printer such as Quad Graphics.

An important feature of job order costing is that each job or batch has its own distinguishing characteristics. For example, each house is custom built, each consulting engagement by a CPA firm is unique, and each printing job is different. **The objective is to compute the cost per job**. At each point in manufacturing a product or providing a service, the company can identify the job and its associated costs. A job order cost system measures costs for each completed job, rather than for set time periods. Illustration 16-1 shows the recording of costs in a job order cost system.

Illustration 16-1
Job order cost system

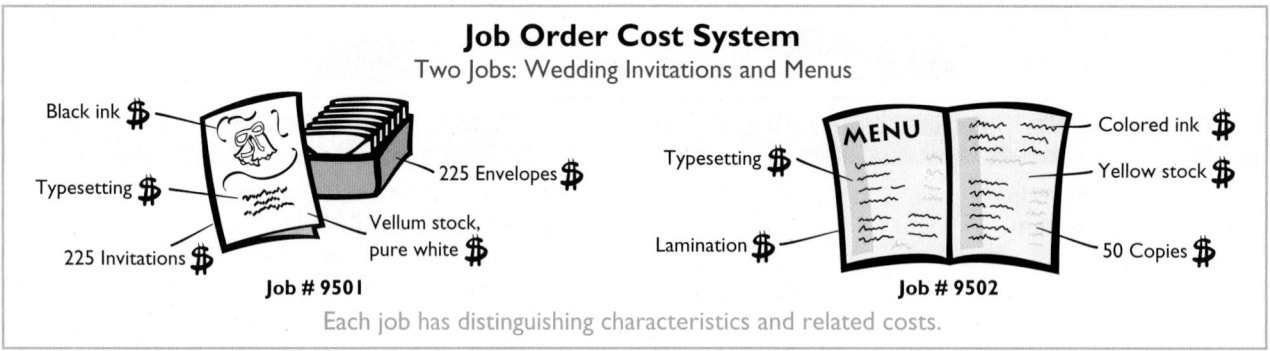

Job Order Cost System
Two Jobs: Wedding Invitations and Menus

Black ink $
Typesetting $
225 Invitations $
225 Envelopes $
Vellum stock, pure white $
Job # 9501

Typesetting $
Lamination $
MENU
Colored ink $
Yellow stock $
50 Copies $
Job # 9502

Each job has distinguishing characteristics and related costs.

Process Cost System

A company uses a **process cost system** when it manufactures a large volume of similar products. Production is continuous. Examples of a process cost system are the manufacture of cereal by Kellogg, the refining of petroleum by ExxonMobil, and the production of ice cream by Ben & Jerry's. Process costing accumulates product-related costs **for a period of time** (such as a week or a month) instead of assigning costs to specific products or job orders. In process costing, companies assign the costs to departments or processes for the specified period of time. Illustration 16-2 shows examples of the use of a process cost system. We will discuss the process cost system further in Chapter 17.

Illustration 16-2
Process cost system

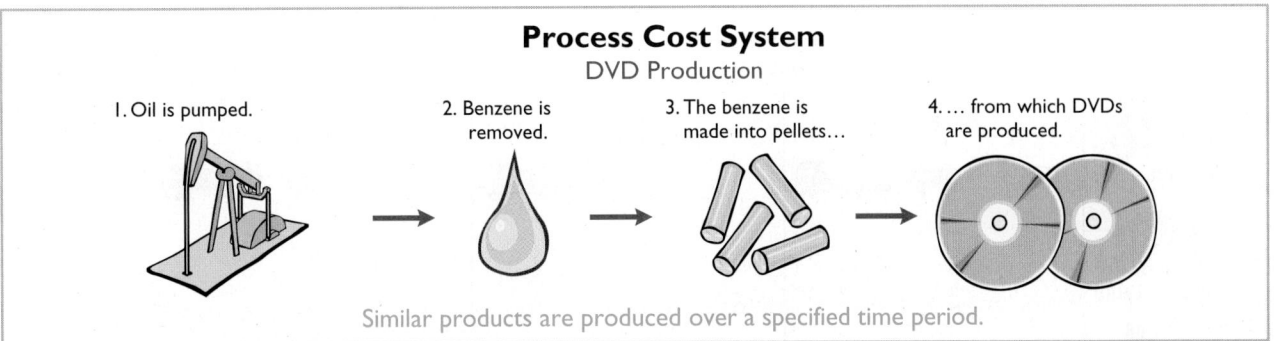

Process Cost System
DVD Production

1. Oil is pumped. 2. Benzene is removed. 3. The benzene is made into pellets... 4. ... from which DVDs are produced.

Similar products are produced over a specified time period.

Can a company use both types of cost systems? Yes. For example, General Motors uses process cost accounting for its standard model cars, such as Malibus and Corvettes, and job order cost accounting for a custom-made limousine for the President of the United States.

The objective of both cost accounting systems is to provide unit cost information for product pricing, cost control, inventory valuation, and financial statement presentation.

MANAGEMENT INSIGHT

Jobs Won, Money Lost

Many companies suffer from poor cost accounting. As a result, they sometimes make products they should not be selling at all, or they buy product components that they could more profitably make themselves. Also, inaccurate cost data leads companies to misallocate capital and frustrates efforts by plant managers to improve efficiency.

For example, consider the case of a diversified company in the business of rebuilding diesel locomotives. The managers thought they were making money, but a consulting firm found that the company had seriously underestimated costs. The company bailed out of the business, and not a moment too soon. Says the consultant who advised the company, "The more contracts it won, the more money it lost." Given that situation, a company cannot stay in business very long!

 What type of costs do you think the company had been underestimating? (See page 851.)

Job Order Cost Flow

The flow of costs (direct materials, direct labor, and manufacturing overhead) in job order cost accounting parallels the physical flow of the materials as they are converted into finished goods. As shown in Illustration 16-3 (page 812), companies first **accumulate** manufacturing costs in the form of raw materials, factory labor,

LEARNING OBJECTIVE   2

Describe the flow of costs in a job order cost system.

Illustration 16-3
Flow of costs in job order costing

or manufacturing overhead. They then **assign** manufacturing costs to the Work in Process Inventory account. When a job is completed, the company transfers the cost of the job to Finished Goods Inventory. Later when the goods are sold, the company transfers their cost to Cost of Goods Sold.

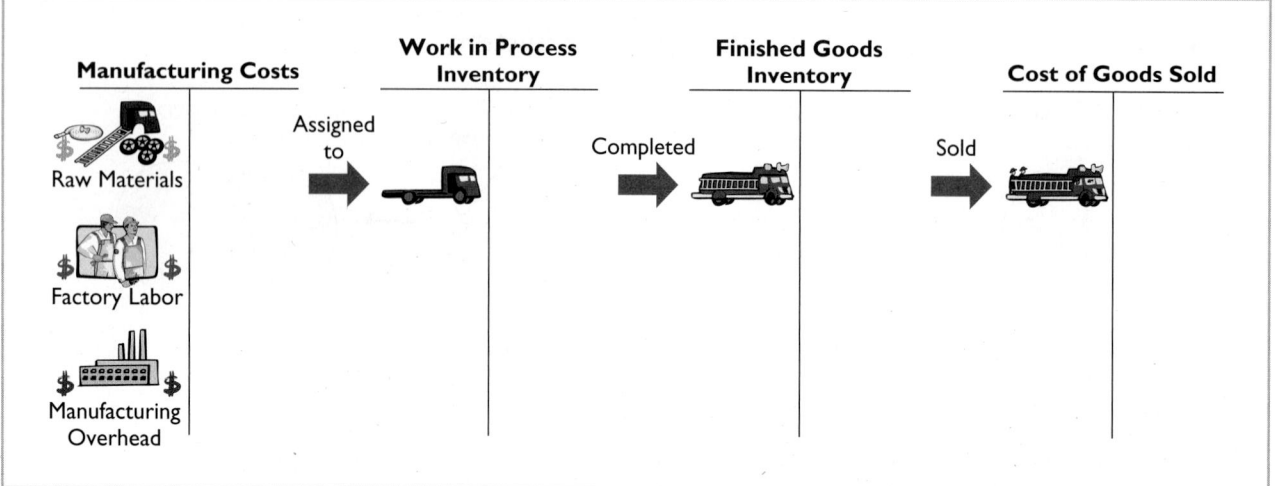

Illustration 16-3 provides a basic overview of the flow of costs in a manufacturing setting. A more detailed presentation of the flow of costs is summarized near the end of this chapter in Illustration 16-15. There are two major steps in the flow of costs: (1) *accumulating* the manufacturing costs incurred, and (2) *assigning* the accumulated costs to the work done. The following discussion shows that the company accumulates manufacturing costs incurred by debits to Raw Materials Inventory, Factory Labor, and Manufacturing Overhead. When the company incurs these costs, it does not attempt to associate the costs with specific jobs. The company makes additional entries to assign manufacturing costs incurred. In the remainder of this chapter, we will use a case study to explain how a job order cost system operates.

Accumulating Manufacturing Costs

To illustrate a job order cost system, we will use the January transactions of Wallace Company, which makes custom electronic sensors for corporate safety applications (such as fire and carbon monoxide) and security applications (such as theft and corporate espionage).

RAW MATERIALS COSTS

When Wallace receives the raw materials it has purchased, **it debits the cost of the materials to Raw Materials Inventory**. The company would debit this account for the invoice cost of the raw materials and freight costs chargeable to the purchaser. It would credit the account for purchase discounts taken and purchase returns and allowances. Wallace makes **no effort at this point to associate the cost of materials with specific jobs or orders**.

To illustrate, assume that Wallace purchases 2,000 lithium batteries (Stock No. AA2746) at $5 per unit ($10,000) and 800 electronic modules (Stock No. AA2850) at $40 per unit ($32,000) for a total cost of $42,000 ($10,000 + $32,000). The entry to record this purchase on January 4 is:

	(1)[1]			**Raw Materials Inventory**
Jan. 4	Raw Materials Inventory	42,000		42,000
	Accounts Payable		42,000	
	(Purchase of raw materials			
	on account)			

At this point, Raw Materials Inventory has a balance of $42,000, as shown in the T-account in the margin. As we will explain later in the chapter, the company subsequently assigns direct raw materials inventory to work in process and indirect raw materials inventory to manufacturing overhead.

FACTORY LABOR COSTS

Some of a company's employees are involved in the manufacturing process, while others are not. As discussed in Chapter 15, wages and salaries of nonmanufacturing employees are expensed as period costs (e.g., Salaries and Wages Expense). Costs related to manufacturing employees are accumulated in Factory Labor to ensure their treatment as product costs. Factory labor consists of three costs: (1) gross earnings of factory workers, (2) employer payroll taxes on these earnings, and (3) fringe benefits (such as sick pay, pensions, and vacation pay) incurred by the employer. **Companies debit labor costs to Factory Labor as they incur those costs**.

To illustrate, assume that Wallace incurs $32,000 of factory labor costs. Of that amount, $27,000 relates to wages payable and $5,000 relates to payroll taxes payable in February. The entry to record factory labor for the month is:

	(2)			**Factory Labor**
Jan. 31	Factory Labor	32,000		32,000
	Factory Wages Payable		27,000	
	Employer Payroll Taxes Payable		5,000	
	(To record factory labor costs)			

At this point, Factory Labor has a balance of $32,000, as shown in the T-account in the margin. The company subsequently assigns direct factory labor to work in process and indirect factory labor to manufacturing overhead.

MANUFACTURING OVERHEAD COSTS

A company has many types of overhead costs. If these overhead costs, such as property taxes, depreciation, insurance, and repairs, relate to overhead costs of a nonmanufacturing facility, such as an office building, then these costs are expensed as period costs (e.g., Property Tax Expense, Depreciation Expense, Insurance Expense, and Repairs Expense). If the costs relate to the manufacturing process, then they are accumulated in Manufacturing Overhead, to ensure their treatment as product costs.

Using assumed data, the summary entry for manufacturing overhead in Wallace Company is:

	(3)			**Manufacturing Overhead**
Jan. 31	Manufacturing Overhead	13,800		13,800
	Utilities Payable		4,800	
	Prepaid Insurance		2,000	
	Accounts Payable (for repairs)		2,600	
	Accumulated Depreciation		3,000	
	Property Taxes Payable		1,400	
	(To record overhead costs)			

---

[1]The numbers placed above the entries for Wallace Company are used for reference purposes in the summary provided in Illustration 16-15.

At this point, Manufacturing Overhead has a balance of $13,800, as shown in the T-account in the margin. The company subsequently assigns manufacturing overhead to work in process.

> DO IT!

Manufacturing Costs

Action Plan

✔ In accumulating manufacturing costs, debit at least one of three accounts: Raw Materials Inventory, Factory Labor, and Manufacturing Overhead.

✔ Manufacturing overhead costs may be recognized daily. Or manufacturing overhead may be recorded periodically through a summary entry.

During the current month, Ringling Company incurs the following manufacturing costs:

(a) Raw material purchases of $4,200 on account.

(b) Incurs factory labor of $18,000. Of that amount, $15,000 relates to wages payable and $3,000 relates to payroll taxes payable.

(c) Factory utilities of $2,200 are payable, prepaid factory insurance of $1,800 has expired, and depreciation on the factory building is $3,500.

Prepare journal entries for each type of manufacturing cost.

Solution

(a) Raw Materials Inventory	4,200	
Accounts Payable		4,200
(Purchases of raw materials on account)		
(b) Factory Labor	18,000	
Factory Wages Payable		15,000
Employer Payroll Taxes Payable		3,000
(To record factory labor costs)		
(c) Manufacturing Overhead	7,500	
Utilities Payable		2,200
Prepaid Insurance		1,800
Accumulated Depreciation		3,500
(To record overhead costs)		

Related exercise material: **BE16-1, BE16-2, E16-1, E16-7, E16-8, E16-11, and** **16-1.**

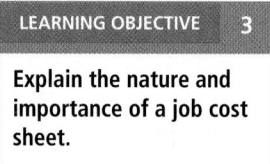

Assigning Manufacturing Costs to Work in Process

LEARNING OBJECTIVE   3

Explain the nature and importance of a job cost sheet.

Assigning manufacturing costs to work in process results in the following entries.

1. **Debits** made to Work in Process Inventory.

2. **Credits** made to Raw Materials Inventory, Factory Labor, and Manufacturing Overhead.

An essential accounting record in assigning costs to jobs is a **job cost sheet**, as shown in Illustration 16-4. A **job cost sheet** is a form used to record the costs chargeable to a specific job and to determine the total and unit costs of the completed job.

Companies keep a separate job cost sheet for each job. The job cost sheets constitute the subsidiary ledger for the Work in Process Inventory account. A **subsidiary ledger** consists of individual records for each individual item—in this case, each job. The Work in Process account is referred to as a **control account** because it summarizes the detailed data regarding specific jobs contained in the job cost sheets. **Each entry to Work in Process Inventory must be accompanied by a corresponding posting to one or more job cost sheets.**

Illustration 16-4
Job cost sheet

Job Cost Sheet

Job No. _____   Quantity _____
Item _____   Date Requested _____
For _____   Date Completed _____

Date	Direct Materials	Direct Labor	Manufacturing Overhead

Cost of completed job
  Direct materials $ _____
  Direct labor
  Manufacturing overhead _____
Total cost $ _____
Unit cost (total dollars ÷ quantity) $ _____

Helpful Hint
In today's electronic environment, companies typically maintain job cost sheets as computer files.

RAW MATERIALS COSTS

Companies assign raw materials costs to jobs when their materials storeroom issues the materials in response to requests. Requests for issuing raw materials are made on a prenumbered **materials requisition slip**. The materials issued may be used directly on a job, or they may be considered indirect materials. As Illustration 16-5 shows, the requisition should indicate the quantity and type of materials withdrawn and the account to be charged. The company will charge direct materials to Work in Process Inventory, and indirect materials to Manufacturing Overhead.

Helpful Hint
Approvals are an important part of a materials requisition slip because they help to establish individual accountability over inventory.

Illustration 16-5
Materials requisition slip

Wallace Company
Materials Requisition Slip

Deliver to: Assembly Department   Req. No. R247
Charge to: Work in Process—Job No. 101   Date: 1/6/14

Quantity	Description	Stock No.	Cost per Unit	Total
200	Lithium batteries	AA2746	$5.00	$1,000

Requested by _Bruce Howart_   Received by _Herb Crowley_
Approved by _Kap Shin_   Costed by _Heather Remmers_

Helpful Hint
Note the specific job to be charged.

Ethics Note
The internal control principle of documentation includes prenumbering to enhance accountability.

The company may use any of the inventory costing methods (FIFO, LIFO, or average-cost) in costing the requisitions **to the individual job cost sheets**.

Periodically, the company journalizes the requisitions. For example, if Wallace uses $24,000 of direct materials and $6,000 of indirect materials in January, the entry is:

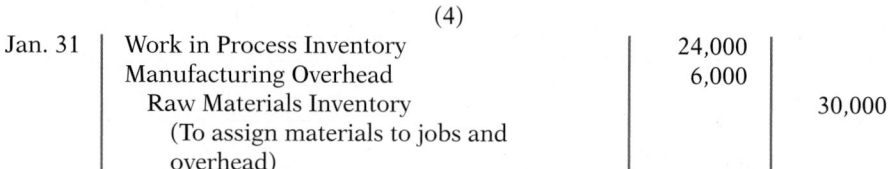

(4)

Jan. 31	Work in Process Inventory		24,000	
	Manufacturing Overhead		6,000	
	Raw Materials Inventory			30,000
	(To assign materials to jobs and			
	overhead)			

This entry reduces Raw Materials Inventory by $30,000, increases Work in Process Inventory by $24,000, and increases Manufacturing Overhead by $6,000, as shown below.

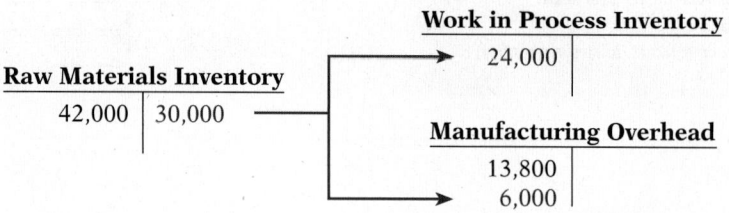

Illustration 16-6 shows the posting of requisition slip R247 to Job No. 101 and other assumed postings to the job cost sheets for materials. The requisition slips provide

Illustration 16-6
Job cost sheets–direct materials

Helpful Hint
Companies post to control accounts monthly, and post to job cost sheets daily.

Helpful Hint
Prove the $24,000 direct materials charge to Work in Process Inventory by totaling the charges by jobs:

101	$12,000
102	7,000
103	5,000
	$24,000

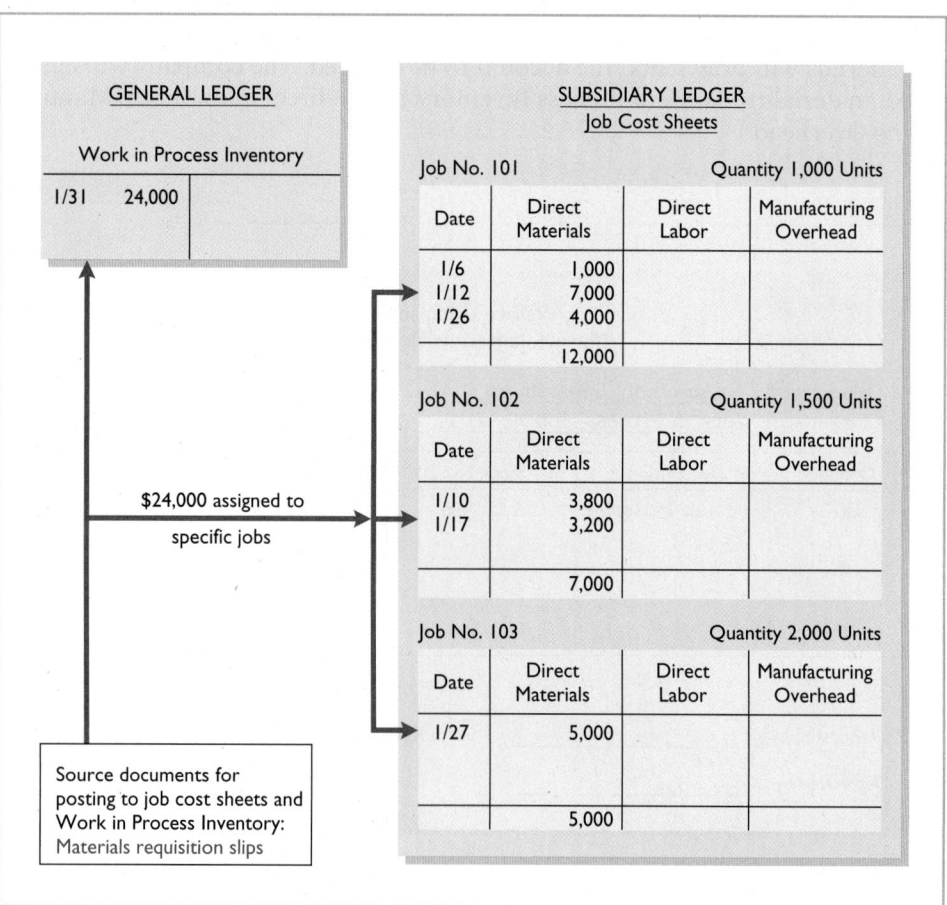

the basis for total direct materials costs of $12,000 for Job No. 101, $7,000 for Job No. 102, and $5,000 for Job No. 103. After the company has completed all postings, the sum of the direct materials columns of the job cost sheets (the subsidiary account amounts of $12,000, $7,000, and $5,000) should equal the direct materials debited to Work in Process Inventory (the control account amount of $24,000).

MANAGEMENT INSIGHT

The Cost of an iPhone? Just Tear One Apart

All companies need to know what it costs to make their own products—but a lot of companies would also like to know the cost of their competitors' products as well. That's where iSuppli steps in. For a price, iSuppli will tear apart sophisticated electronic devices to tell you what it would cost to replicate. In the case of smart-phones, which often have more than 1,000 tiny components, that is no small feat. As shown in the chart below, components of many smart-phones cost about $170. Assembly is only about another $6.50. The difference between what you pay and the "cost" is not all profit. Consider the additional nonproduction costs of research, design, marketing, patent fees, and selling costs.

Sum of the Parts
Cost of components[a], 2009

	Palm Pre	Apple iPhone[b]	Toshiba TG01	Motorola Droid
Integrated circuits	$ 83.96	$ 91.38	$ 68.39	$ 60.83
Display/ touchscreen	38.80	34.65	35.30	35.25
Mechanical[c]	19.63	17.80	21.88	20.23
Camera	7.50	9.35	12.80	14.25
Battery	4.25	5.07	4.71	4.25
Other	16.51	11.82	30.60	44.30
Total	**$170.65**	**$170.07**	**$173.68**	**$179.11**

[a] Latest data available
[b] 3GS 16GB
[c] Includes electromechanical
Source: iSuppli.

Source: "The Business of Dissecting Electronics: The Lowdown on Teardowns," *The Economist.com* (January 21, 2010).

 What type of costs are marketing and selling costs, and how are they treated for accounting purposes? (See page 851.)

FACTORY LABOR COSTS

Companies assign factory labor costs to jobs on the basis of time tickets prepared when the work is performed. The **time ticket** indicates the employee, the hours worked, the account and job to be charged, and the total labor cost. Many companies accumulate these data through the use of bar coding and scanning devices. When they start and end work, employees scan bar codes on their identification badges and bar codes associated with each job they work on. When direct labor is involved, the time ticket must indicate the job number, as shown in Illustration 16-7 (page 818). The employee's supervisor should approve all time tickets.

Illustration 16-7
Time ticket

Wallace Company
Time Ticket

Date: 1/6/14

Employee _____ John Nash _____   Employee No. 124
Charge to: _____ Work in Process _____   Job No. 101

Time			Hourly Rate	Total Cost
Start	Stop	Total Hours		
0800	1200	4	10.00	40.00

Approved by _Bob Kadler_   Costed by _M. Cher_

The time tickets are later sent to the payroll department, which applies the employee's hourly wage rate and computes the total labor cost. Finally, the company journalizes the time tickets. It debits the account Work in Process Inventory for direct labor and debits Manufacturing Overhead for indirect labor. For example, if the $32,000 total factory labor cost consists of $28,000 of direct labor and $4,000 of indirect labor, the entry is:

(5)

Jan. 31	Work in Process Inventory	28,000	
	Manufacturing Overhead	4,000	
	Factory Labor		32,000
	(To assign labor to jobs and		
	overhead)		

As a result of this entry, Factory Labor is reduced by $32,000 so it has a zero balance, and labor costs are assigned to the appropriate manufacturing accounts. The entry increases Work in Process Inventory by $28,000 and increases Manufacturing Overhead by $4,000, as shown below.

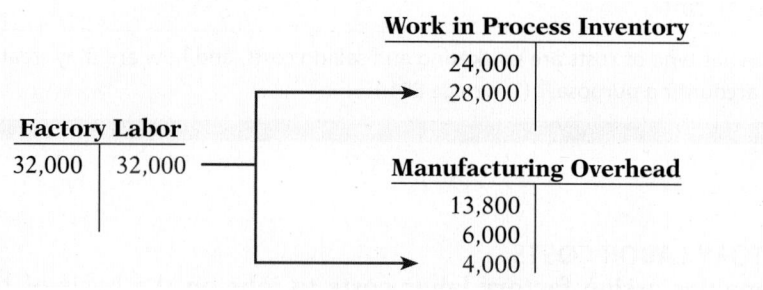

Let's assume that the labor costs chargeable to Wallace's three jobs are $15,000, $9,000, and $4,000. Illustration 16-8 shows the Work in Process Inventory and job cost sheets after posting. As in the case of direct materials, the postings to the direct labor columns of the job cost sheets should equal the posting of direct labor to Work in Process Inventory.

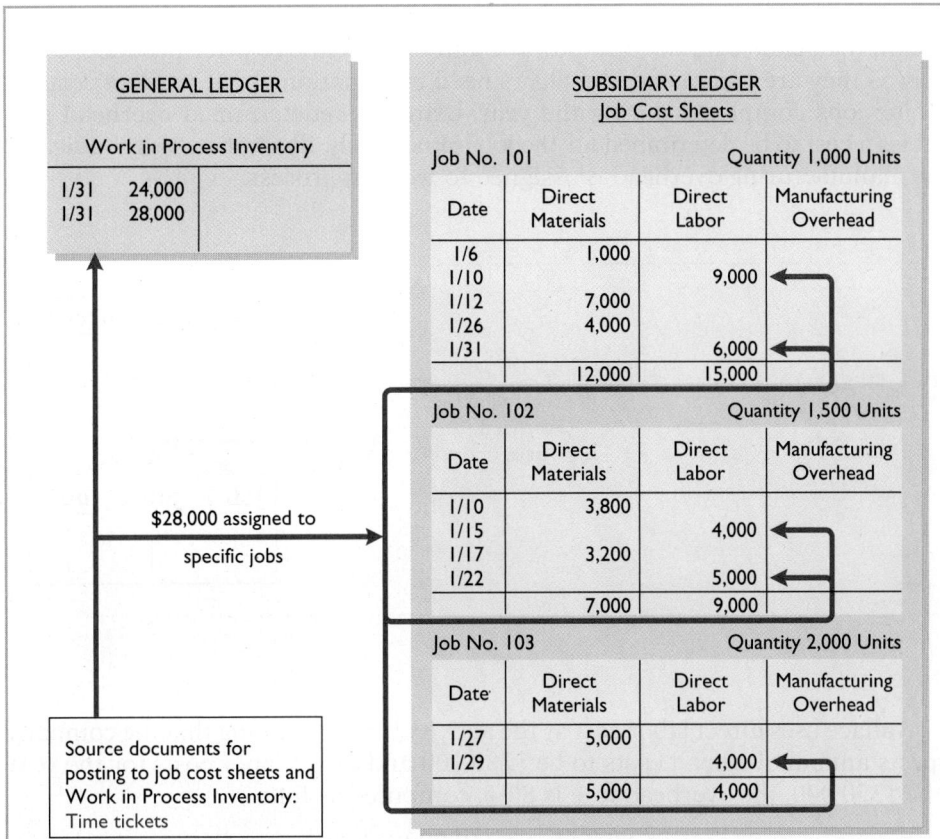

Illustration 16-8
Job cost sheets–direct labor

Helpful Hint
Prove the $28,000 direct labor charge to Work in Process Inventory by totaling the charges by jobs:

101	$15,000
102	9,000
103	4,000
	$28,000

Manufacturing Overhead Costs

Companies charge the actual costs of direct materials and direct labor to specific jobs. In contrast, manufacturing **overhead** relates to production operations **as a whole**. As a result, overhead costs cannot be assigned to specific jobs on the basis of actual costs incurred. Instead, companies assign manufacturing overhead to work in process and to specific jobs **on an estimated basis through the use of a predetermined overhead rate**.

The **predetermined overhead rate** is based on the relationship between estimated annual overhead costs and expected annual operating activity, expressed in terms of a common **activity base**. The company may state the activity in terms of direct labor costs, direct labor hours, machine hours, or any other measure that will provide an equitable basis for applying overhead costs to jobs. Companies establish the predetermined overhead rate at the beginning of the year. Small companies often use a single, company-wide predetermined overhead rate. Large companies often use rates that vary from department to department. The formula for a predetermined overhead rate is as follows.

LEARNING OBJECTIVE	4

Indicate how the predetermined overhead rate is determined and used.

$$\text{Estimated Annual Overhead Costs} \div \text{Expected Annual Operating Activity} = \text{Predetermined Overhead Rate}$$

Illustration 16-9
Formula for predetermined overhead rate

Overhead relates to production operations as a whole. To know what "the whole" is, the logical thing is to wait until the end of the year's operations. At that time, the company knows all of its costs for the period. As a practical matter, though, managers cannot wait until the end of the year. To price products effectively as they are completed, managers need information about product costs of specific jobs completed during the year. Using a predetermined overhead rate enables a cost to be determined for the job immediately. Illustration 16-10 indicates how manufacturing overhead is assigned to work in process.

Illustration 16-10
Using predetermined overhead rates

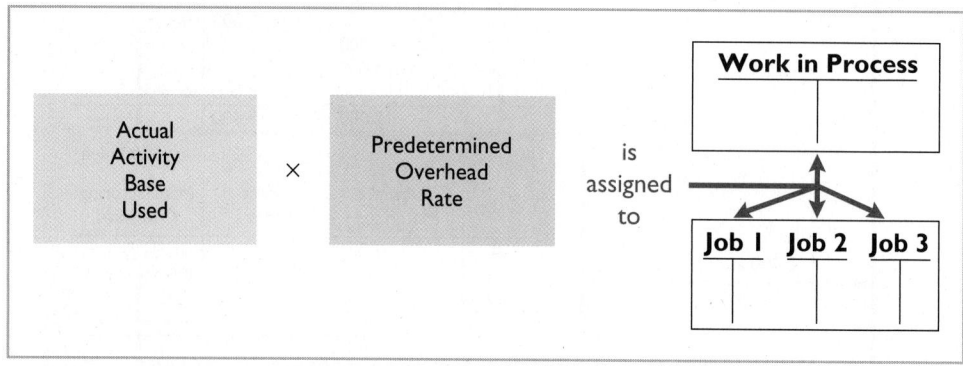

Wallace uses direct labor cost as the activity base. Assuming that the company expects annual overhead costs to be $280,000 and direct labor costs for the year to be $350,000, the overhead rate is 80%, computed as follows.

$$\$280,\!000 \div \$350,\!000 = 80\%$$

This means that for every dollar of direct labor, Wallace will assign 80 cents of manufacturing overhead to a job. The use of a predetermined overhead rate enables the company to determine the approximate total cost of each job **when it completes the job**.

Historically, companies used direct labor costs or direct labor hours as the activity base. The reason was the relatively high correlation between direct labor and manufacturing overhead. Today more companies are using **machine hours as the activity base, due to increased reliance on automation in manufacturing operations**. Or, as mentioned in Chapter 15 (and discussed more fully in Chapter 18), many companies now use activity-based costing to more accurately allocate overhead costs based on the activities that give rise to the costs.

A company may use more than one activity base. For example, if a job is manufactured in more than one factory department, each department may have its own overhead rate. In the Feature Story, American LaFrance might use two bases in assigning overhead to fire-truck jobs: direct materials dollars for indirect materials, and direct labor hours for such costs as insurance and supervisors' salaries.

Wallace Company applies manufacturing overhead to work in process when it assigns direct labor costs. It also applies manufacturing overhead to specific jobs at the same time. For January, Wallace applied overhead of $22,400 in response to its assignment of $28,000 of direct labor costs (direct labor cost of $28,000 × 80%). The following entry records this application.

(6)

Jan. 31	Work in Process Inventory	22,400	
	Manufacturing Overhead		22,400
	(To assign overhead to jobs)		

This entry reduces the balance in Manufacturing Overhead and increases Work in Process Inventory by $22,400, as shown on the next page.

Manufacturing Overhead		Work in Process Inventory	
13,800	22,400	24,000	
6,000		28,000	
4,000		22,400	

The overhead that Wallace applies to each job will be 80% of the direct labor cost of the job for the month. Illustration 16-11 shows the Work in Process Inventory account and the job cost sheets after posting. Note that the debit of $22,400 to Work in Process Inventory equals the sum of the overhead applied to jobs: Job 101 $12,000 + Job 102 $7,200 + Job 103 $3,200.

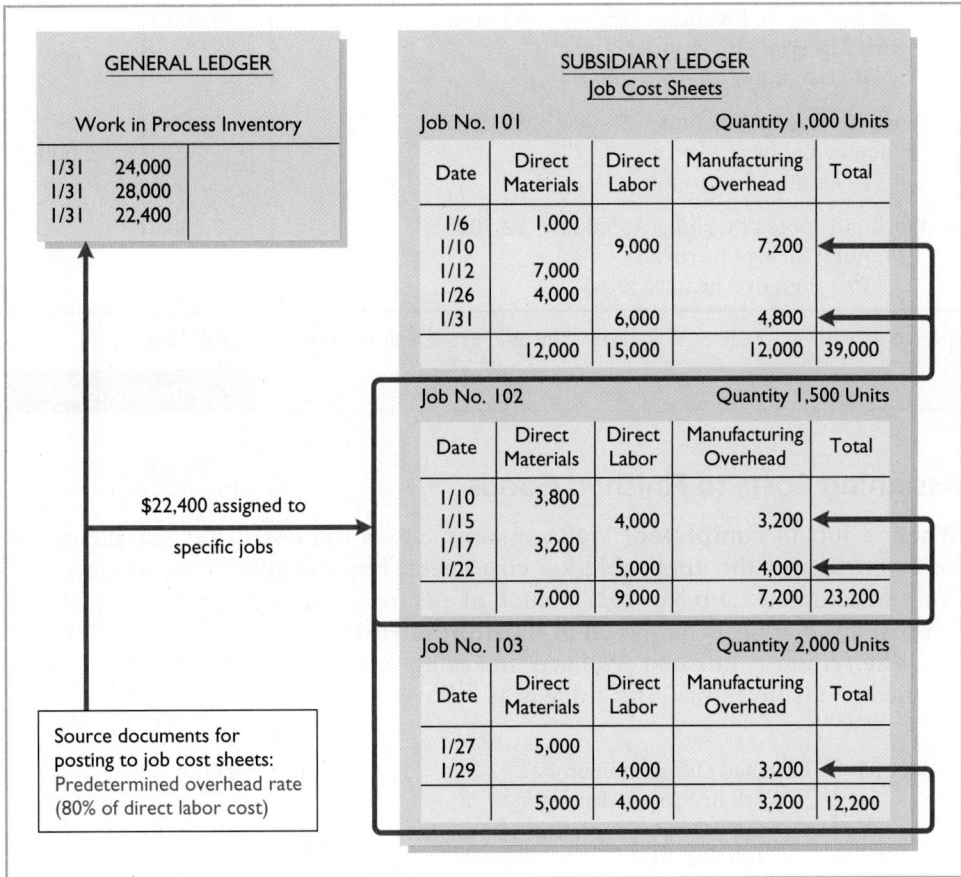

Illustration 16-11
Job cost sheets–manufacturing overhead applied

At the end of each month, the **balance in Work in Process Inventory should equal the sum of the costs shown on the job cost sheets of unfinished jobs**. Illustration 16-12 presents proof of the agreement of the control and subsidiary accounts in Wallace. (It assumes that all jobs are still in process.)

Work in Process Inventory				Job Cost Sheets	
Jan. 31	24,000			No. 101	$ 39,000
31	28,000			102	23,200
31	22,400			103	12,200
	74,400				**$74,400**

Illustration 16-12
Proof of job cost sheets to work in process inventory

> DO IT!

Work in Process

Danielle Company is working on two job orders. The job cost sheets show the following:

Direct materials—Job 120 $6,000; Job 121 $3,600
Direct labor—Job 120 $4,000; Job 121 $2,000
Manufacturing overhead—Job 120 $5,000; Job 121 $2,500

Prepare the three summary entries to record the assignment of costs to Work in Process from the data on the job cost sheets.

Action Plan

✔ Recognize that Work in Process Inventory is the control account for all unfinished job cost sheets.

✔ Debit Work in Process Inventory for the materials, labor, and overhead charged to the job cost sheets.

✔ Credit the accounts that were debited when the manufacturing costs were accumulated.

Solution

The three summary entries are:

Work in Process Inventory ($6,000 + $3,600)	9,600	
Raw Materials Inventory		9,600
(To assign materials to jobs)		
Work in Process Inventory ($4,000 + $2,000)	6,000	
Factory Labor		6,000
(To assign labor to jobs)		
Work in Process Inventory ($5,000 + $2,500)	7,500	
Manufacturing Overhead		7,500
(To assign overhead to jobs)		

Related exercise material: **BE16-3, BE16-4, BE16-7, E16-2, E16-7, E16-8, and** **DO IT!** **16-2.**

✔ **The Navigator**

Assigning Costs to Finished Goods

LEARNING OBJECTIVE 5

Prepare entries for jobs completed and sold.

When a job is completed, Wallace summarizes the costs and completes the lower portion of the applicable job cost sheet. For example, if we assume that Wallace completes Job No. 101, a batch of electronic sensors, on January 31, the job cost sheet appears as shown in Illustration 16-13.

When a job is finished, Wallace makes an entry to transfer its total cost to finished goods inventory. The entry is as follows.

(7)

Jan. 31	Finished Goods Inventory	39,000	
	Work in Process Inventory		39,000
	(To record completion of		
	Job No. 101)		

This entry increases Finished Goods Inventory and reduces Work in Process Inventory by $39,000, as shown in the T-accounts below.

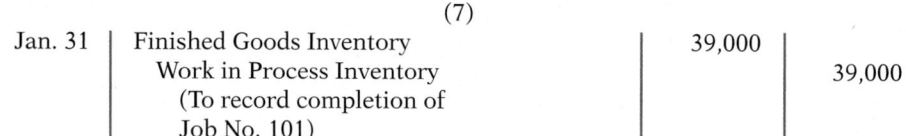

Work in Process Inventory		Finished Goods Inventory	
24,000	39,000 →	→ 39,000	
28,000			
22,400			

Finished Goods Inventory is a control account. It controls individual finished goods records in a finished goods subsidiary ledger. The company posts directly from completed job cost sheets to the receipts columns. Illustration 16-14 shows the finished goods inventory record for Job No. 101.

Illustration 16-13
Completed job cost sheet

Job Cost Sheet

Job No. _____ 101 _____   Quantity _____ 1,000 _____
Item _____ Electronic Sensors _____   Date Requested _____ February 5 _____
For _____ Tanner Company _____   Date Completed _____ January 31 _____

Date	Direct Materials	Direct Labor	Manufacturing Overhead
1/6	$ 1,000		
1/10		$ 9,000	$ 7,200
1/12	7,000		
1/26	4,000		
1/31		6,000	4,800
	$12,000	$15,000	$12,000

Cost of completed job
  Direct materials $ 12,000
  Direct labor   15,000
  Manufacturing overhead   12,000
  Total cost $ 39,000
  Unit cost ($39,000 ÷ 1,000) $ 39.00

Assigning Costs to Cost of Goods Sold

Companies recognize cost of goods sold when each sale occurs. To illustrate the entries a company makes when it sells a completed job, assume that on January 31 Wallace sells on account Job 101. The job cost $39,000, and it sold for $50,000. The entries to record the sale and recognize cost of goods sold are:

(8)

Jan. 31	Accounts Receivable	50,000	
	Sales Revenue		50,000
	(To record sale of Job No. 101)		
31	Cost of Goods Sold	39,000	
	Finished Goods Inventory		39,000
	(To record cost of Job No. 101)		

As Illustration 16-14 shows, Wallace records, in the issues section of the finished goods record, the units sold, the cost per unit, and the total cost of goods sold for each job sold.

Illustration 16-14
Finished goods record

Finished Goods.xls

Home | Insert | Page Layout | Formulas | Data | Review | View

P18   fx

	A	B	C	D	E	F	G	H	I	J
1	**Item: Electronic Sensors**								**Job No: 101**	
2										
3			Receipts			Issues			Balance	
4	Date	Units	Cost	Total	Units	Cost	Total	Units	Cost	Total
5	1/31	1,000	$39	$39,000				1,000	$39	$39,000
6	1/31				1,000	$39	$39,000			– 0 –
7										

Summary of Job Order Cost Flows

Illustration 16-15 shows a completed flowchart for a job order cost accounting system. All postings are keyed to entries 1–8 in the example presented in the previous pages for Wallace Company.

The cost flows in the diagram can be categorized as one of four types:

- **Accumulation.** The company first accumulates costs by (1) purchasing raw materials, (2) incurring labor costs, and (3) incurring manufacturing overhead costs.

- **Assignment to jobs.** Once the company has incurred manufacturing costs, it must assign them to specific jobs. For example, as it uses raw materials on specific jobs (4), it assigns them to work in process, or treats them as manufacturing overhead if the raw materials cannot be associated with a specific job. Similarly, it either assigns factory labor (5) to work in process, or treats it as manufacturing overhead if the factory labor cannot be associated with a specific job. Finally it assigns manufacturing overhead (6) to work in process using a *predetermined overhead rate*. This deserves emphasis: **Do not assign overhead using actual overhead costs, but instead use a predetermined rate.**

- **Completed jobs.** As jobs are completed (7), the company transfers the cost of the completed job out of work in process inventory into finished goods inventory.

- **When goods are sold.** As specific items are sold (8), the company transfers their cost out of finished goods inventory into cost of goods sold.

Illustration 16-15
Flow of costs in a job order cost system

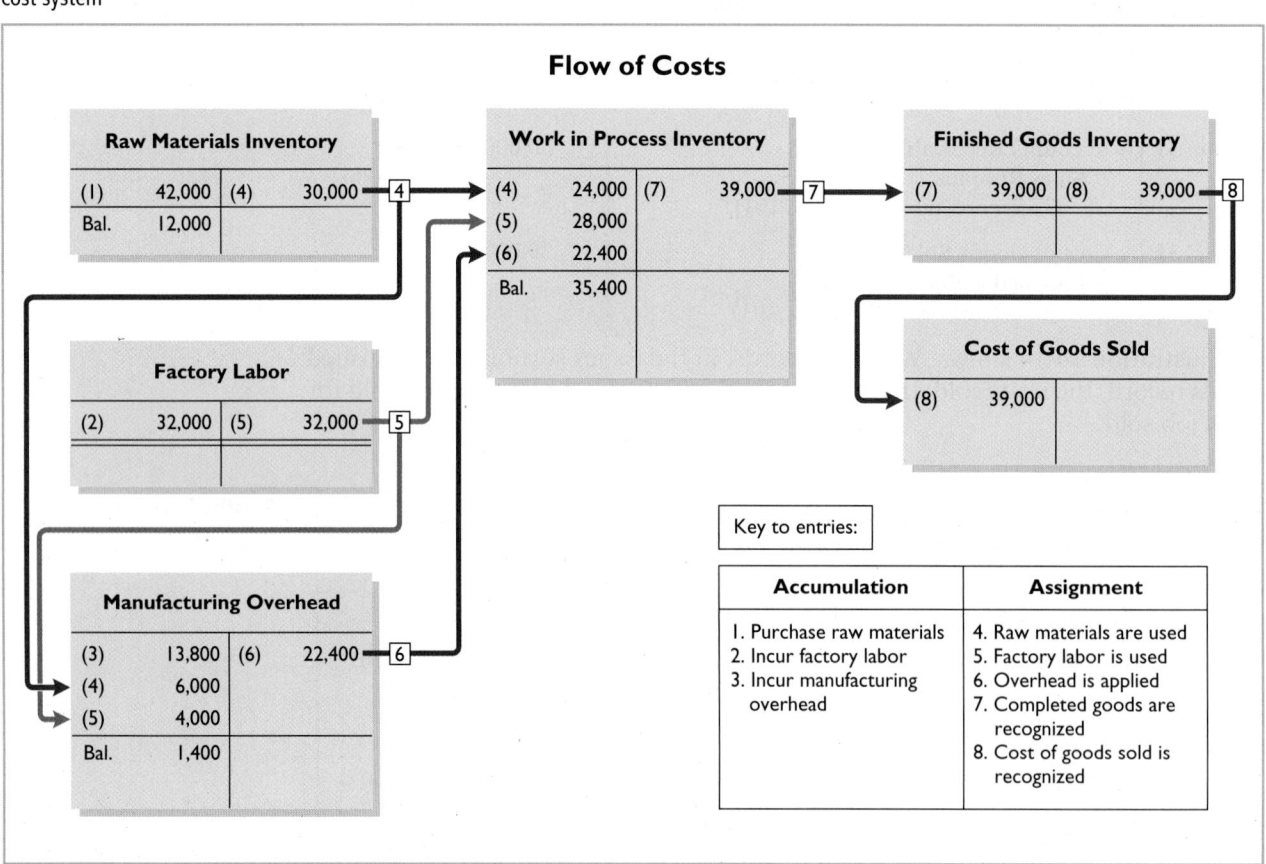

Illustration 16-16 summarizes the flow of documents in a job order cost system.

Illustration 16-16
Flow of documents in a job
order cost system

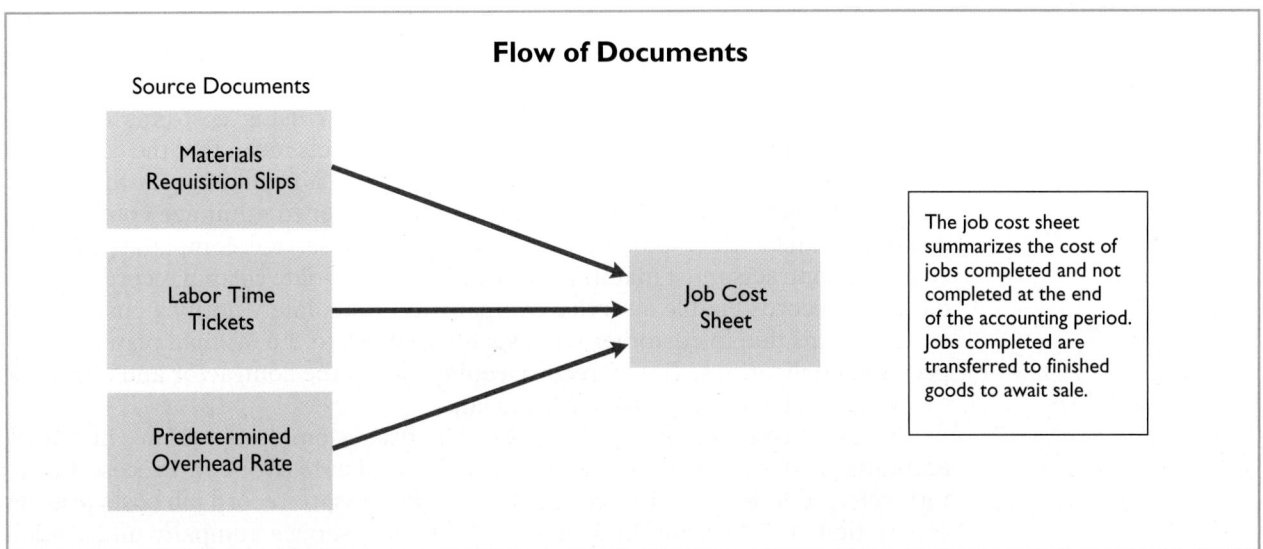

Flow of Documents

Source Documents

Materials
Requisition Slips

Labor Time
Tickets

Predetermined
Overhead Rate

Job Cost
Sheet

The job cost sheet
summarizes the cost of
jobs completed and not
completed at the end
of the accounting period.
Jobs completed are
transferred to finished
goods to await sale.

> DO IT!

Completion and Sale of Jobs

Action Plan

✔ Debit Finished Goods Inventory for the cost of completed jobs.

✔ Debit Cost of Goods Sold for the cost of jobs sold.

During the current month, Onyx Corporation completed Job 109 and Job 112. Job 109 cost $19,000 and Job 112 cost $27,000. Job 112 was sold on account for $42,000. Journalize the entries for the completion of the two jobs and the sale of Job 112.

Solution

Finished Goods Inventory	46,000	
Work in Process Inventory		46,000
(To record completion of Job 109,		
costing $19,000 and Job 112,		
costing $27,000)		
Accounts Receivable	42,000	
Sales Revenue		42,000
(To record sale of Job 112)		
Cost of Goods Sold	27,000	
Finished Goods Inventory		27,000
(To record cost of goods sold for Job 112)		

Related exercise material: **BE16-8, E16-2, E16-3, E16-4, E16-6, E16-7, E16-10, and DO IT! 16-3.**

 The Navigator

Job Order Costing for Service Companies

Our extended job order costing example focuses on a manufacturer so that you see the flow of costs through the inventory accounts. It is important to understand, however, that job order costing is also commonly used by service companies. While service companies do not have inventory, the techniques of job order costing are still quite useful in many service-industry environments. Consider, for example, the Mayo Clinic (health care), PriceWaterhouseCoopers (accounting), and Goldman Sachs (investment banking). These companies need to keep track of the cost of jobs performed for specific customers to evaluate the profitability of medical treatments, audits, or investment banking engagements.

Many service organizations bill their customers using cost-plus contracts (discussed more fully in Chapter 22). Cost-plus contracts mean that the customer's bill is the sum of the costs incurred on the job, plus a profit amount that is calculated as a percentage of the costs incurred. In order to minimize conflict with customers and reduce potential contract disputes, service companies that use cost-plus contracts must maintain accurate and up-to-date costing records. Up-to-date cost records enable a service company to immediately notify a customer of cost overruns due to customer requests for changes to the original plan or unexpected complications. Timely recordkeeping allows the contractor and customer to consider alternatives before it is too late.

A service company that uses a job order cost system does not have inventory accounts. It does, however, use an account similar to Work in Process Inventory, referred to here as Service Contracts in Process, to record job costs prior to completion. To illustrate the journal entries for a service company under a job order cost system, consider the following transactions for Frugal Interiors, an interior design company. The entry to record the assignment of $9,000 of supplies to projects ($7,000 direct and $2,000 indirect) is:

Service Contracts in Process	7,000	
Operating Overhead	2,000	
Supplies		9,000
(To assign supplies to projects)		

The entry to record the assignment of service salaries and wages of $100,000 ($84,000 direct and $16,000 indirect) is:

Service Contracts in Process	84,000	
Operating Overhead	16,000	
Service Salaries and Wages		100,000
(To assign personnel costs to projects)		

Frugal Interiors applies operating overhead at a rate of 50% of direct labor costs. The entry to record the application of overhead ($84,000 × 50%) based on the direct labor costs is:

Service Contracts in Process	42,000	
Operating Overhead		42,000
(To assign operating overhead to projects)		

Finally, upon completion, the job cost sheet of a design project for Sampson Corporation shows a total cost of $34,000. The entry to record completion of this project is:

Cost of Completed Service Contracts	34,000	
Service Contracts in Process		34,000
(To record completion of Sampson project)		

Job cost sheets for a service company keep track of materials, labor, and overhead used on a particular job similar to a manufacturer. A number of exercises at the end of this chapter apply job order costing to service companies.

SERVICE COMPANY INSIGHT

Sales Are Nice, but Service Revenue Pays the Bills

Jet engines are one of the many products made by the industrial operations division of General Electric (GE). At prices as high as $30 million per engine, you can bet that GE does its best to keep track of costs. It might surprise you that GE doesn't make much profit on the sale of each engine. So why does it bother making them? Service revenue–during one recent year, about 75% of the division's revenues came from servicing its own products. One estimate is that the $13 billion in aircraft engines sold during a recent three-year period will generate about $90 billion in service revenue over the 30-year life of the engines. Because of the high product costs, both the engines themselves and the subsequent service are most likely accounted for using job order costing. Accurate service cost records are important because GE needs to generate high profit margins on its service jobs to make up for the low margins on the original sale. It also needs good cost records for its service jobs in order to control its costs. Otherwise, a competitor, such as Pratt and Whitney, might submit lower bids for service contracts and take lucrative service jobs away from GE.

Source: Paul Glader, "GE's Focus on Services Faces Test," *Wall Street Journal Online* (March 3, 2009).

 ? Explain why GE would use job order costing to keep track of the cost of repairing a malfunctioning engine for a major airline. (See page 851.)

Advantages and Disadvantages of Job Order Costing

An advantage of job order costing is it is more precise in assignment of costs to projects than process costing. For example, assume that a construction company, Juan Company, builds 10 custom homes a year at a total cost of $2,000,000. One way to determine the cost of the homes is to divide the total construction cost incurred during the year by the number of homes produced during the year. For Juan Company, an average cost of $200,000 ($2,000,000 ÷ 10) is computed. If the homes are nearly identical, then this approach is adequate for purposes of determining profit per home. But if the homes vary in terms of size, style, and material types, using the average cost of $200,000 to determine profit per home is inappropriate. Instead, Juan Company should use a job order cost system to determine the specific cost incurred to build each home and the amount of profit made on each. Thus, job order costing provides more useful information for determining the profitability of particular projects and for estimating costs when preparing bids on future jobs.

One disadvantage of job order costing is that it requires a significant amount of data entry. For Juan Company, it is much easier to simply keep track of total costs incurred during the year than it is to keep track of the costs incurred on each job (home built). Recording this information is time-consuming, and if the data is not entered accurately, then the product costs are not accurate. In recent years, technological advances, such as bar-coding devices for both labor costs and materials, have increased the accuracy and reduced the effort needed to record costs on specific jobs. These innovations expand the opportunities to apply job order costing in a wider variety of business settings, thus improving management's ability to control costs and make better informed decisions.

A common problem of all costing systems is how to allocate overhead to the finished product. Overhead often represents more than 50% of a product's cost, and this cost is often difficult to allocate meaningfully to the product. How, for example, is the salary of a project manager allocated to the various homes, which may differ in size, style, and materials used, that she oversees? The accuracy of the job order cost system is largely dependent on the accuracy of the overhead allocation process. Even if the company does a good job of keeping track of the specific amounts of materials and labor used on each job, if the overhead costs are not allocated to individual jobs in a meaningful way, the product costing information is not useful. This issue will be addressed in more detail in Chapter 18.

Reporting Job Cost Data

LEARNING OBJECTIVE 6

Distinguish between under- and overapplied manufacturing overhead.

At the end of a period, companies prepare financial statements that present aggregate data on all jobs manufactured and sold. The cost of goods manufactured schedule in job order costing is the same as in Chapter 15 with one exception: **The schedule shows manufacturing overhead applied, rather than actual overhead costs. The company adds this amount to direct materials and direct labor to determine total manufacturing costs.**

Companies prepare the cost of goods manufactured schedule directly from the Work in Process Inventory account. Illustration 16-17 shows a condensed schedule for Wallace Company for January.

Helpful Hint
Companies usually prepare monthly financial statements for management use only.

Wallace Company		
Cost of Goods Manufactured Schedule		
For the Month Ending January 31, 2014		
Work in process, January 1		$ —0—
Direct materials used	$ 24,000	
Direct labor	28,000	
Manufacturing overhead applied	**22,400**	
Total manufacturing costs		74,400
Total cost of work in process		74,400
Less: Work in process, January 31		35,400
Cost of goods manufactured		$39,000

Illustration 16-17
Cost of goods manufactured schedule

Note that the cost of goods manufactured ($39,000) agrees with the amount transferred from Work in Process Inventory to Finished Goods Inventory in journal entry No. 7 in Illustration 16-15 (page 824).

The income statement and balance sheet are the same as those illustrated in Chapter 15. For example, Illustration 16-18 shows the partial income statement for Wallace for the month of January.

Illustration 16-18
Partial income statement

Wallace Company		
Income Statement (partial)		
For the Month Ending January 31, 2014		
Sales revenue		$50,000
Cost of goods sold		
Finished goods inventory, January 1	$ –0–	
Cost of goods manufactured (see Illustration 16-17)	**39,000**	
Cost of goods available for sale	39,000	
Less: Finished goods inventory, January 31	–0–	
Cost of goods sold		39,000
Gross profit		$11,000

Under- or Overapplied Manufacturing Overhead

When Manufacturing Overhead has a **debit balance**, overhead is said to be underapplied. **Underapplied overhead** means that the overhead assigned to work in process is less than the overhead incurred. Conversely, when manufacturing overhead has a **credit balance**, overhead is overapplied. **Overapplied overhead** means that the overhead assigned to work in process is greater than the overhead incurred. Illustration 16-19 shows these concepts.

Illustration 16-19
Under- and overapplied overhead

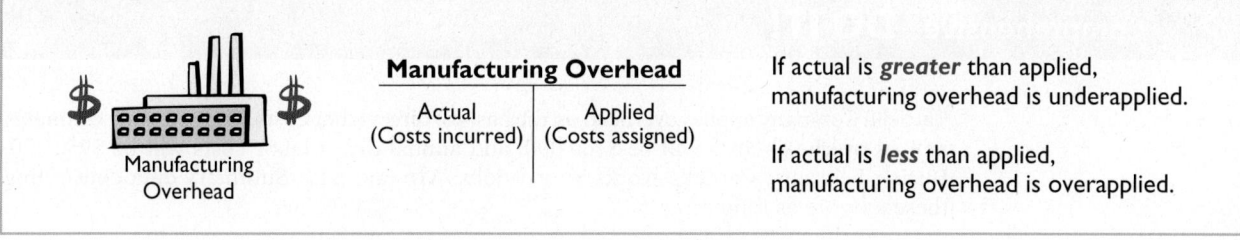

YEAR-END BALANCE

At the end of the year, all manufacturing overhead transactions are complete. There is no further opportunity for offsetting events to occur. At this point, Wallace eliminates any balance in Manufacturing Overhead by an adjusting entry. It considers under- or overapplied overhead to be an **adjustment to cost of goods sold**. Thus, Wallace **debits underapplied overhead to Cost of Goods Sold**. It **credits overapplied overhead to Cost of Goods Sold**.

To illustrate, assume that Wallace has a $2,500 credit balance in Manufacturing Overhead at December 31. The adjusting entry for the overapplied overhead is:

Dec. 31	Manufacturing Overhead	2,500	
	Cost of Goods Sold		2,500
	(To transfer overapplied overhead to cost of goods sold)		

After Wallace posts this entry, Manufacturing Overhead has a zero balance. In preparing an income statement for the year, Wallace reports cost of goods sold **after adjusting it** for either under- or overapplied overhead.

Conceptually, some argue, under- or overapplied overhead at the end of the year should be allocated among ending work in process, finished goods, and cost of goods sold. The discussion of this possible allocation approach is left to more advanced courses.

> DO IT!

Applied Manufacturing Overhead

Action Plan

✔ Calculate the amount of overhead applied by multiplying the predetermined overhead rate by actual activity.

✔ If actual manufacturing overhead is greater than applied, manufacturing overhead is underapplied.

✔ If actual manufacturing overhead is less than applied, manufacturing overhead is overapplied.

For Karr Company, the predetermined overhead rate is 140% of direct labor cost. During the month, Karr incurred $90,000 of factory labor costs, of which $80,000 is direct labor and $10,000 is indirect labor. Actual overhead incurred was $119,000.

Compute the amount of manufacturing overhead applied during the month. Determine the amount of under- or overapplied manufacturing overhead.

Solution

Manufacturing overhead applied = (140% × $80,000) = $112,000
Underapplied manufacturing overhead = ($119,000 − $112,000) = $7,000

Related exercise material: **BE16-10, E16-5, E16-12, E16-13, and DO IT! 16-4.**

✔ **The Navigator**

> Comprehensive DO IT!

Cardella Company applies overhead on the basis of direct labor costs. The company estimates annual overhead costs will be $760,000, and annual direct labor costs will be $950,000. During February, Cardella works on two jobs: A16 and B17. Summary data concerning these jobs are as follows.

Manufacturing Costs Incurred
Purchased $54,000 of raw materials on account.
Factory labor $76,000, plus $4,000 employer payroll taxes.
Manufacturing overhead exclusive of indirect materials and indirect labor $59,800.

Assignment of Costs

Direct materials:	Job A16 $27,000, Job B17 $21,000
Indirect materials:	$3,000
Direct labor:	Job A16 $52,000, Job B17 $26,000
Indirect labor:	$2,000

The company completed Job A16 and sold it on account for $150,000. Job B17 was only partially completed.

Instructions

(a) Compute the predetermined overhead rate.

(b) Journalize the February transactions in the sequence followed in the chapter.

(c) What was the amount of under- or overapplied manufacturing overhead?

Solution to Comprehensive DO IT!

(a) Estimated annual overhead costs	÷	Expected annual operating activity	=	Predetermined overhead rate
$760,000	÷	$950,000	=	80%

Action Plan

✔ Predetermined overhead rate = Estimated annual overhead cost ÷ Expected annual operating activity.

✔ In accumulating costs, debit three accounts: Raw Materials Inventory, Factory Labor, and Manufacturing Overhead.

✔ When Work in Process Inventory is debited, credit one of the three accounts listed above.

✔ Debit Finished Goods Inventory for the cost of completed jobs. Debit Cost of Goods Sold for the cost of jobs sold.

✔ Overhead is underapplied when Manufacturing Overhead has a debit balance.

(b)

1.

Feb. 28	Raw Materials Inventory		54,000	
	Accounts Payable			54,000
	(Purchase of raw materials on account)			

2.

28	Factory Labor		80,000	
	Factory Wages Payable			76,000
	Employer Payroll Taxes Payable			4,000
	(To record factory labor costs)			

3.

28	Manufacturing Overhead		59,800	
	Accounts Payable, Accumulated Depreciation, and Prepaid Insurance			59,800
	(To record overhead costs)			

4.

28	Work in Process Inventory		48,000	
	Manufacturing Overhead		3,000	
	Raw Materials Inventory			51,000
	(To assign raw materials to production)			

5.

28	Work in Process Inventory		78,000	
	Manufacturing Overhead		2,000	
	Factory Labor			80,000
	(To assign factory labor to production)			

6.

28	Work in Process Inventory		62,400	
	Manufacturing Overhead			62,400
	(To assign overhead to jobs— 80% × $78,000)			

7.

28	Finished Goods Inventory		120,600	
	Work in Process Inventory			120,600
	(To record completion of Job A16: direct materials $27,000, direct labor $52,000, and manufacturing overhead $41,600)			

8.

28	Accounts Receivable		150,000	
	Sales Revenue			150,000
	(To record sale of Job A16)			
28	Cost of Goods Sold		120,600	
	Finished Goods Inventory			120,600
	(To record cost of sale for Job A16)			

(c) Manufacturing Overhead has a debit balance of $2,400 as shown below.

Manufacturing Overhead

(3)	59,800	(6)	62,400
(4)	3,000		
(5)	2,000		
Bal.	2,400		

Thus, manufacturing overhead is underapplied for the month.

SUMMARY OF LEARNING OBJECTIVES

✔ The Navigator

1 Explain the characteristics and purposes of cost accounting. Cost accounting involves the procedures for measuring, recording, and reporting product costs. From the data accumulated, companies determine the total cost and the unit cost of each product. The two basic types of cost accounting systems are job order cost and process cost.

2 Describe the flow of costs in a job order cost system. In job order costing, companies first accumulate manufacturing costs in three accounts: Raw Materials Inventory, Factory Labor, and Manufacturing Overhead. They then assign the accumulated costs to Work in Process Inventory and eventually to Finished Goods Inventory and Cost of Goods Sold.

3 Explain the nature and importance of a job cost sheet. A job cost sheet is a form used to record the costs chargeable to a specific job and to determine the total and unit costs of the completed job. Job cost sheets constitute the subsidiary ledger for the Work in Process Inventory control account.

4 Indicate how the predetermined overhead rate is determined and used. The predetermined overhead rate is based on the relationship between estimated annual overhead costs and expected annual operating activity. This is expressed in terms of a common activity base, such as direct labor cost. Companies use this rate to assign overhead costs to work in process and to specific jobs.

5 Prepare entries for jobs completed and sold. When jobs are completed, companies debit the cost to Finished Goods Inventory and credit it to Work in Process Inventory. When a job is sold, the entries are (a) debit Cash or Accounts Receivable and credit Sales Revenue for the selling price; and (b) debit Cost of Goods Sold and credit Finished Goods Inventory for the cost of the goods.

6 Distinguish between under- and overapplied manufacturing overhead. Underapplied manufacturing overhead indicates that the overhead assigned to work in process is less than the overhead incurred. Overapplied overhead indicates that the overhead assigned to work in process is greater than the overhead incurred.

GLOSSARY

Cost accounting An area of accounting that involves measuring, recording, and reporting product costs. (p. 810).

Cost accounting system Manufacturing-cost accounts that are fully integrated into the general ledger of a company. (p. 810).

Job cost sheet A form used to record the costs chargeable to a specific job and to determine the total and unit costs of the completed job. (p. 814).

Job order cost system A cost accounting system in which costs are assigned to each job or batch. (p. 810).

Materials requisition slip A document authorizing the issuance of raw materials from the storeroom to production. (p. 815).

Overapplied overhead A situation in which overhead assigned to work in process is greater than the overhead incurred. (p. 829).

Predetermined overhead rate A rate based on the relationship between estimated annual overhead costs and expected annual operating activity, expressed in terms of a common activity base. (p. 819).

Process cost system A cost accounting system used when a company manufactures a large volume of similar products. (p. 810).

Time ticket A document that indicates the employee, the hours worked, the account and job to be charged, and the total labor cost. (p. 817).

Underapplied overhead A situation in which overhead assigned to work in process is less than the overhead incurred. (p. 829).

SELF-TEST QUESTIONS

Answers are at the end of the chapter.

(LO 1) **1.** Cost accounting involves the measuring, recording, and reporting of:
(a) product costs.
(b) future costs.
(c) manufacturing processes.
(d) managerial accounting decisions.

(LO 1) **2.** A company is more likely to use a job order cost system if:
(a) it manufactures a large volume of similar products.
(b) its production is continuous.
(c) it manufactures products with unique characteristics.
(d) it uses a periodic inventory system.

(LO 2) **3.** In accumulating raw materials costs, companies debit the cost of raw materials purchased in a perpetual system to:
(a) Raw Materials Purchases.
(b) Raw Materials Inventory.
(c) Purchases.
(d) Work in Process.

(LO 2) **4.** When incurred, factory labor costs are debited to:
(a) Work in Process.
(b) Factory Wages Expense.
(c) Factory Labor.
(d) Factory Wages Payable.

(LO 2) **5.** The flow of costs in job order costing:
(a) begins with work in process inventory and ends with finished goods inventory.
(b) begins as soon as a sale occurs.
(c) parallels the physical flow of materials as they are converted into finished goods.
(d) is necessary to prepare the cost of goods manufactured schedule.

(LO 3) **6.** Raw materials are assigned to a job when:
(a) the job is sold.
(b) the materials are purchased.
(c) the materials are received from the vendor.
(d) the materials are issued by the materials storeroom.

(LO 3) **7.** The source documents for assigning costs to job cost sheets are:
(a) invoices, time tickets, and the predetermined overhead rate.
(b) materials requisition slips, time tickets, and the actual overhead costs.
(c) materials requisition slips, payroll register, and the predetermined overhead rate.
(d) materials requisition slips, time tickets, and the predetermined overhead rate.

(LO 3) **8.** In recording the issuance of raw materials in a job order cost system, it would be *incorrect* to:

(a) debit Work in Process Inventory.
(b) debit Finished Goods Inventory.
(c) debit Manufacturing Overhead.
(d) credit Raw Materials Inventory.

(LO 3) **9.** The entry when direct factory labor is assigned to jobs is a debit to:
(a) Work in Process Inventory and a credit to Factory Labor.
(b) Manufacturing Overhead and a credit to Factory Labor.
(c) Factory Labor and a credit to Manufacturing Overhead.
(d) Factory Labor and a credit to Work in Process Inventory.

(LO 4) **10.** The formula for computing the predetermined manufacturing overhead rate is estimated annual overhead costs divided by an expected annual operating activity, expressed as:
(a) direct labor cost.   (c) machine hours.
(b) direct labor hours.   (d) Any of the above.

(LO 4) **11.** In Crawford Company, the predetermined overhead rate is 80% of direct labor cost. During the month, Crawford incurs $210,000 of factory labor costs, of which $180,000 is direct labor and $30,000 is indirect labor. Actual overhead incurred was $200,000. The amount of overhead debited to Work in Process Inventory should be:
(a) $200,000.   (c) $168,000.
(b) $144,000.   (d) $160,000.

(LO 5) **12.** Mynex Company completes Job No. 26 at a cost of $4,500 and later sells it for $7,000 cash. A *correct* entry is:
(a) debit Finished Goods Inventory $7,000 and credit Work in Process Inventory $7,000.
(b) debit Cost of Goods Sold $7,000 and credit Finished Goods Inventory $7,000.
(c) debit Finished Goods Inventory $4,500 and credit Work in Process Inventory $4,500.
(d) debit Accounts Receivable $7,000 and credit Sales Revenue $7,000.

(LO 5) **13.** At the end of an accounting period, a company using a job order cost system calculates the cost of goods manufactured:
(a) from the job cost sheet.
(b) from the Work in Process Inventory account.
(c) by adding direct materials used, direct labor incurred, and manufacturing overhead incurred.
(d) from the Cost of Goods Sold account.

(LO 5) **14.** Which of the following statements is *true*?
(a) Job order costing requires less data entry than process costing.
(b) Allocation of overhead is easier under job order costing than process costing.

(c) Job order costing provides more precise costing for custom jobs than process costing.

(d) The use of job order costing has declined because more companies have adopted automated accounting systems.

(LO 6) **15.** At end of the year, a company has a $1,200 debit balance in Manufacturing Overhead. The company:

(a) makes an adjusting entry by debiting Manufacturing Overhead Applied for $1,200 and crediting Manufacturing Overhead for $1,200.

(b) makes an adjusting entry by debiting Manufacturing Overhead Expense for $1,200 and crediting Manufacturing Overhead for $1,200.

(c) makes an adjusting entry by debiting Cost of Goods Sold for $1,200 and crediting Manufacturing Overhead for $1,200.

(d) makes no adjusting entry because differences between actual overhead and the amount applied are a normal part of job order costing and will average out over the next year.

16. Manufacturing overhead is underapplied if: (LO 6)

(a) actual overhead is less than applied.

(b) actual overhead is greater than applied.

(c) the predetermined rate equals the actual rate.

(d) actual overhead equals applied overhead.

Go to the book's companion website, www.wiley.com/college/weygandt, for additional Self-Test Questions.

 ✔ **The Navigator**

QUESTIONS

1. (a) Mary Barett is not sure about the difference between cost accounting and a cost accounting system. Explain the difference to Mary.

(b) What is an important feature of a cost accounting system?

2. (a) Distinguish between the two types of cost accounting systems.

(b) Can a company use both types of cost accounting systems?

3. What type of industry is likely to use a job order cost system? Give some examples.

4. What type of industry is likely to use a process cost system? Give some examples.

5. Your roommate asks your help in understanding the major steps in the flow of costs in a job order cost system. Identify the steps for your roommate.

6. There are three inventory control accounts in a job order system. Identify the control accounts and their subsidiary ledgers.

7. What source documents are used in accumulating direct labor costs?

8. "Entries to Manufacturing Overhead normally are only made daily." Do you agree? Explain.

9. Stan Kaiser is confused about the source documents used in assigning materials and labor costs.

Identify the documents and give the entry for each document.

10. What is the purpose of a job cost sheet?

11. Indicate the source documents that are used in charging costs to specific jobs.

12. Explain the purpose and use of a "materials requisition slip" as used in a job order cost system.

13. Sam Bowden believes actual manufacturing overhead should be charged to jobs. Do you agree? Why or why not?

14. What elements are involved in computing a predetermined overhead rate?

15. How can the agreement of Work in Process Inventory and job cost sheets be verified?

16. Jane Neff believes that the cost of goods manufactured schedule in job order cost accounting is the same as shown in Chapter 15. Is Jane correct? Explain.

17. Matt Litkee is confused about under- and overapplied manufacturing overhead. Define the terms for Matt, and indicate the balance in the manufacturing overhead account applicable to each term.

18. "At the end of the year, under- or overapplied overhead is closed to Income Summary." Is this correct? If not, indicate the customary treatment of this amount.

BRIEF EXERCISES

Prepare a flowchart of a job order cost accounting system, and identify transactions.

(LO 2)

BE16-1 Knox Company begins operations on January 1. Because all work is done to customer specifications, the company decides to use a job order cost system. Prepare a flowchart of a typical job order system with arrows showing the flow of costs. Identify the eight transactions.

BE16-2 During January, its first month of operations, Knox Company accumulated the following manufacturing costs: raw materials $4,000 on account, factory labor $6,000 of which $5,200 relates to factory wages payable and $800 relates to payroll taxes payable, and utilities payable $2,000. Prepare separate journal entries for each type of manufacturing cost.

Prepare entries in accumulating manufacturing costs.
(LO 2)

BE16-3 In January, Knox Company requisitions raw materials for production as follows: Job 1 $900, Job 2 $1,400, Job 3 $700, and general factory use $600. Prepare a summary journal entry to record raw materials used.

Prepare entry for the assignment of raw materials costs.
(LO 3)

BE16-4 Factory labor data for Knox Company is given in BE16-2. During January, time tickets show that the factory labor of $6,000 was used as follows: Job 1 $2,200, Job 2 $1,600, Job 3 $1,400, and general factory use $800. Prepare a summary journal entry to record factory labor used.

Prepare entry for the assignment of factory labor costs.
(LO 3)

BE16-5 Data pertaining to job cost sheets for Knox Company are given in BE16-3 and BE16-4. Prepare the job cost sheets for each of the three jobs. (*Note:* You may omit the column for Manufacturing Overhead.)

Prepare job cost sheets.
(LO 3)

BE16-6 Marquis Company estimates that annual manufacturing overhead costs will be $900,000. Estimated annual operating activity bases are direct labor cost $500,000, direct labor hours 50,000, and machine hours 100,000. Compute the predetermined overhead rate for each activity base.

Compute predetermined overhead rates.
(LO 4)

BE16-7 During the first quarter, Roland Company incurs the following direct labor costs: January $40,000, February $30,000, and March $50,000. For each month, prepare the entry to assign overhead to production using a predetermined rate of 80% of direct labor cost.

Assign manufacturing overhead to production.
(LO 4)

BE16-8 In March, Stinson Company completes Jobs 10 and 11. Job 10 cost $20,000 and Job 11 $30,000. On March 31, Job 10 is sold to the customer for $35,000 in cash. Journalize the entries for the completion of the two jobs and the sale of Job 10.

Prepare entries for completion and sale of completed jobs.
(LO 5)

BE16-9 Preprah Engineering Contractors incurred service salaries and wages of $32,000 ($24,000 direct and $8,000 indirect) on an engineering project. The company applies overhead at a rate of 25% of direct labor. Record the entries to assign service salaries and wages and to apply overhead.

Prepare entries for service salaries and wages and operating overhead.
(LO 5)

BE16-10 At December 31, balances in Manufacturing Overhead are Shimeca Company—debit $1,200, Garcia Company—credit $900. Prepare the adjusting entry for each company at December 31, assuming the adjustment is made to cost of goods sold.

Prepare adjusting entries for under- and overapplied overhead.
(LO 6)

> DO IT! REVIEW

DO IT! 16-1 During the current month, Tomlin Company incurs the following manufacturing costs.

(a) Purchased raw materials of $16,000 on account.
(b) Incurred factory labor of $40,000. Of that amount, $31,000 relates to wages payable and $9,000 relates to payroll taxes payable.
(c) Factory utilities of $3,100 are payable, prepaid factory property taxes of $2,400 have expired, and depreciation on the factory building is $9,500.

Prepare journal entries for each type of manufacturing cost. (Use a summary entry to record manufacturing overhead.)

Prepare journal entries for manufacturing costs.
(LO 2)

DO IT! 16-2 Milner Company is working on two job orders. The job cost sheets show the following.

Assign costs to work in process.
(LO 3, 4)

	Job 201	Job 202
Direct materials	$7,200	$9,000
Direct labor	4,000	8,000
Manufacturing overhead	5,200	9,800

Prepare the three summary entries to record the assignment of costs to Work in Process from the data on the job cost sheets.

DO IT! **16-3** During the current month, Reyes Corporation completed Job 310 and Job 312. Job 310 cost $60,000 and Job 312 cost $50,000. Job 312 was sold on account for $90,000. Journalize the entries for the completion of the two jobs and the sale of Job 312.

Prepare entries for completion and sale of jobs.

(LO 5)

DO IT! **16-4** For Eckstein Company, the predetermined overhead rate is 130% of direct labor cost. During the month, Eckstein incurred $100,000 of factory labor costs, of which $85,000 is direct labor and $15,000 is indirect labor. Actual overhead incurred was $115,000. Compute the amount of manufacturing overhead applied during the month. Determine the amount of under- or overapplied manufacturing overhead.

Apply manufacturing overhead and determine under- or overapplication.

(LO 6)

 **The Navigator**

EXERCISES

Prepare entries for factory labor.

(LO 2, 3)

E16-1 The gross earnings of the factory workers for Vargas Company during the month of January are $66,000. The employer's payroll taxes for the factory payroll are $8,000. The fringe benefits to be paid by the employer on this payroll are $6,000. Of the total accumulated cost of factory labor, 85% is related to direct labor and 15% is attributable to indirect labor.

Instructions

(a) Prepare the entry to record the factory labor costs for the month of January.
(b) Prepare the entry to assign factory labor to production.

Prepare journal entries for manufacturing costs.

(LO 2, 3, 4, 5)

E16-2 Stine Company uses a job order cost system. On May 1, the company has a balance in Work in Process Inventory of $3,500 and two jobs in process: Job No. 429 $2,000, and Job No. 430 $1,500. During May, a summary of source documents reveals the following.

Job Number	Materials Requisition Slips		Labor Time Tickets	
429	$2,500		$1,900	
430	3,500		3,000	
431	4,400	$10,400	7,600	$12,500
General use		800		1,200
		$11,200		$13,700

Stine Company applies manufacturing overhead to jobs at an overhead rate of 60% of direct labor cost. Job No. 429 is completed during the month.

Instructions

(a) Prepare summary journal entries to record (i) the requisition slips, (ii) the time tickets, (iii) the assignment of manufacturing overhead to jobs, and (iv) the completion of Job No. 429.
(b) Post the entries to Work in Process Inventory, and prove the agreement of the control account with the job cost sheets. (Use a T-account.)

E16-3 A job order cost sheet for Lowry Company is shown below.

Analyze a job cost sheet and prepare entries for manufacturing costs.

(LO 2, 3, 4, 5)

Job No. 92			For 2,000 Units
Date	Direct Materials	Direct Labor	Manufacturing Overhead
Beg. bal. Jan. 1	5,000	6,000	5,100
8	6,000		
12		8,000	6,400
25	2,000		
27		4,000	3,200
	13,000	18,000	14,700

Cost of completed job:	
Direct materials	$13,000
Direct labor	18,000
Manufacturing overhead	14,700
Total cost	$45,700
Unit cost ($45,700 ÷ 2,000)	$22.85

Instructions

(a) ▭▭▭▷ On the basis of the foregoing data, answer the following questions.
  (1) What was the balance in Work in Process Inventory on January 1 if this was the only unfinished job?
  (2) If manufacturing overhead is applied on the basis of direct labor cost, what overhead rate was used in each year?
(b) Prepare summary entries at January 31 to record the current year's transactions pertaining to Job No. 92.

E16-4 Manufacturing cost data for Orlando Company, which uses a job order cost system, are presented below.

Analyze costs of manufacturing and determine missing amounts.

(LO 2, 6)

	Case A	Case B	Case C
Direct materials used	$ (a)	$ 83,000	$ 63,150
Direct labor	50,000	140,000	(h)
Manufacturing overhead applied	42,500	(d)	(i)
Total manufacturing costs	145,650	(e)	213,000
Work in process 1/1/14	(b)	15,500	18,000
Total cost of work in process	201,500	(f)	(j)
Work in process 12/31/14	(c)	11,800	(k)
Cost of goods manufactured	192,300	(g)	222,000

Instructions

Indicate the missing amount for each letter. Assume that in all cases manufacturing overhead is applied on the basis of direct labor cost and the rate is the same.

E16-5 Duggan Company applies manufacturing overhead to jobs on the basis of machine hours used. Overhead costs are expected to total $325,000 for the year, and machine usage is estimated at 125,000 hours.
  For the year, $342,000 of overhead costs are incurred and 130,000 hours are used.

Compute the manufacturing overhead rate and under- or overapplied overhead.

(LO 4, 6)

Instructions

(a) Compute the manufacturing overhead rate for the year.
(b) What is the amount of under- or overapplied overhead at December 31?
(c) Prepare the adjusting entry to assign the under- or overapplied overhead for the year to cost of goods sold.

Analyze job cost sheet and prepare entry for completed job.

(LO 2, 3, 4, 5)

E16-6 A job cost sheet of Sandoval Company is given below.

		Job Cost Sheet		

JOB NO.   469   Quantity   2,500

ITEM   White Lion Cages   Date Requested   7/2

FOR   Todd Company   Date Completed   7/31

Date	Direct Materials	Direct Labor	Manufacturing Overhead
7/10	700		
12	900		
15		440	550
22		380	475
24	1,600		
27	1,500		
31		540	675

Cost of completed job:

  Direct materials   ———

  Direct labor   ———

    Manufacturing overhead   ———

Total cost   ═══

Unit cost   ═══

Instructions

(a) ▭▭▭▭▷ Answer the following questions.
   (1) What are the source documents for direct materials, direct labor, and manufacturing overhead costs assigned to this job?
   (2) What is the predetermined manufacturing overhead rate?
   (3) What are the total cost and the unit cost of the completed job? (Round unit cost to nearest cent.)

(b) Prepare the entry to record the completion of the job.

Prepare entries for manufacturing and nonmanufacturing costs.

(LO 2, 3, 4, 5)

E16-7 Torre Corporation incurred the following transactions.

1. Purchased raw materials on account $46,300.
2. Raw materials of $36,000 were requisitioned to the factory. An analysis of the materials requisition slips indicated that $6,800 was classified as indirect materials.
3. Factory labor costs incurred were $55,900, of which $51,000 pertained to factory wages payable and $4,900 pertained to employer payroll taxes payable.
4. Time tickets indicated that $50,000 was direct labor and $5,900 was indirect labor.
5. Manufacturing overhead costs incurred on account were $80,500.
6. Depreciation on the company's office building was $8,100.
7. Manufacturing overhead was applied at the rate of 150% of direct labor cost.
8. Goods costing $88,000 were completed and transferred to finished goods.
9. Finished goods costing $75,000 to manufacture were sold on account for $103,000.

Instructions

Journalize the transactions. (Omit explanations.)

Prepare entries for manufacturing and nonmanufacturing costs.

(LO 2, 3, 4, 5)

E16-8 Enos Printing Corp. uses a job order cost system. The following data summarize the operations related to the first quarter's production.

1. Materials purchased on account $192,000, and factory wages incurred $87,300.
2. Materials requisitioned and factory labor used by job:

Job Number	Materials	Factory Labor
A20	$ 35,240	$18,000
A21	42,920	22,000
A22	36,100	15,000
A23	39,270	25,000
General factory use	4,470	7,300
	$158,000	$87,300

3. Manufacturing overhead costs incurred on account $49,500.
4. Depreciation on factory equipment $14,550.
5. Depreciation on the company's office building was $14,300.
6. Manufacturing overhead rate is 90% of direct labor cost.
7. Jobs completed during the quarter: A20, A21, and A23.

Instructions

Prepare entries to record the operations summarized above. (Prepare a schedule showing the individual cost elements and total cost for each job in item 7.)

E16-9 At May 31, 2014, the accounts of Mantle Company show the following.

1. May 1 inventories—finished goods $12,600, work in process $14,700, and raw materials $8,200.
2. May 31 inventories—finished goods $9,500, work in process $17,900, and raw materials $7,100.
3. Debit postings to work in process were direct materials $62,400, direct labor $50,000, and manufacturing overhead applied $40,000.
4. Sales revenue totaled $210,000.

Prepare a cost of goods manufactured schedule and partial financial statements.

(LO 2, 5)

Instructions

(a) Prepare a condensed cost of goods manufactured schedule.
(b) Prepare an income statement for May through gross profit.
(c) Indicate the balance sheet presentation of the manufacturing inventories at May 31, 2014.

E16-10 Tierney Company begins operations on April 1. Information from job cost sheets shows the following.

Compute work in process and finished goods from job cost sheets.

(LO 3, 5)

	Manufacturing Costs Assigned			
Job Number	**April**	**May**	**June**	**Month Completed**
10	$5,200	$4,400		May
11	4,100	3,900	$2,000	June
12	1,200			April
13		4,700	4,500	June
14		5,900	3,600	Not complete

Job 12 was completed in April. Job 10 was completed in May. Jobs 11 and 13 were completed in June. Each job was sold for 25% above its cost in the month following completion.

Instructions

(a) What is the balance in Work in Process Inventory at the end of each month?
(b) What is the balance in Finished Goods Inventory at the end of each month?
(c) What is the gross profit for May, June, and July?

E16-11 Shown below are the job cost related accounts for the law firm of Jack, Bob, and Will and their manufacturing equivalents:

Prepare entries for costs of services provided.

(LO 2, 4, 5)

Law Firm Accounts	**Manufacturing Firm Accounts**
Supplies	Raw Materials
Salaries and Wages Payable	Factory Wages Payable
Operating Overhead	Manufacturing Overhead
Service Contracts in Process	Work in Process
Cost of Completed Service Contracts	Cost of Goods Sold

Cost data for the month of March follow.

1. Purchased supplies on account $1,500.
2. Issued supplies $1,200 (60% direct and 40% indirect).
3. Assigned labor costs based on time cards for the month which indicated labor costs of $60,000 (80% direct and 20% indirect).
4. Operating overhead costs incurred for cash totaled $40,000.
5. Operating overhead is applied at a rate of 90% of direct attorney cost.
6. Work completed totaled $75,000.

Instructions
(a) Journalize the transactions for March. (Omit explanations.)
(b) Determine the balance of the Service Contracts in Process account. (Use a T-account.)

Determine cost of jobs and ending balance in work in process and overhead accounts.

(LO 3, 4, 6)

E16-12 Don Lieberman and Associates, a CPA firm, uses job order costing to capture the costs of its audit jobs. There were no audit jobs in process at the beginning of November. Listed below are data concerning the three audit jobs conducted during November.

	Lynn	**Brian**	**Mike**
Direct materials	$600	$400	$200
Auditor labor costs	$5,400	$6,600	$3,375
Auditor hours	72	88	45

Overhead costs are applied to jobs on the basis of auditor hours, and the predetermined overhead rate is $50 per auditor hour. The Lynn job is the only incomplete job at the end of November. Actual overhead for the month was $11,000.

Instructions
(a) Determine the cost of each job.
(b) Indicate the balance of the Service Contracts in Process account at the end of November.
(c) Calculate the ending balance of the Operating Overhead account for November.

Determine predetermined overhead rate, apply overhead and determine whether balance under- or overapplied.

(LO 4, 6)

E16-13 Pure Decorating uses a job order cost system to collect the costs of its interior decorating business. Each client's consultation is treated as a separate job. Overhead is applied to each job based on the number of decorator hours incurred. Listed below are data for the current year.

Estimated overhead	$920,000
Actual overhead	$942,800
Estimated decorator hours	40,000
Actual decorator hours	40,500

The company uses Operating Overhead in place of Manufacturing Overhead.

Instructions
(a) Compute the predetermined overhead rate.
(b) Prepare the entry to apply the overhead for the year.
(c) Determine whether the overhead was under- or overapplied and by how much.

EXERCISES: SET B AND CHALLENGE EXERCISES

Visit the book's companion website, at **www.wiley.com/college/weygandt**, and choose the Student Companion site to access Exercise Set B and Challenge Exercises.

PROBLEMS: SET A

Prepare entries in a job order cost system and job cost sheets.

(LO 2, 3, 4, 5, 6)

P16-1A Degelman Company uses a job order cost system and applies overhead to production on the basis of direct labor costs. On January 1, 2014, Job No. 50 was the only job in process. The costs incurred prior to January 1 on this job were as follows: direct materials

$20,000, direct labor $12,000, and manufacturing overhead $16,000. As of January 1, Job No. 49 had been completed at a cost of $90,000 and was part of finished goods inventory. There was a $15,000 balance in the Raw Materials Inventory account.

During the month of January, Degelman Company began production on Jobs 51 and 52, and completed Jobs 50 and 51. Jobs 49 and 50 were also sold on account during the month for $122,000 and $158,000, respectively. The following additional events occurred during the month.

1. Purchased additional raw materials of $90,000 on account.
2. Incurred factory labor costs of $70,000. Of this amount $16,000 related to employer payroll taxes.
3. Incurred manufacturing overhead costs as follows: indirect materials $17,000; indirect labor $20,000; depreciation expense on equipment $19,000; and various other manufacturing overhead costs on account $16,000.
4. Assigned direct materials and direct labor to jobs as follows.

Job No.	Direct Materials	Direct Labor
50	$10,000	$ 5,000
51	39,000	25,000
52	30,000	20,000

Instructions

(a) Calculate the predetermined overhead rate for 2014, assuming Degelman Company estimates total manufacturing overhead costs of $980,000, direct labor costs of $700,000, and direct labor hours of 20,000 for the year.

(b) Open job cost sheets for Jobs 50, 51, and 52. Enter the January 1 balances on the job cost sheet for Job No. 50.

(c) Prepare the journal entries to record the purchase of raw materials, the factory labor costs incurred, and the manufacturing overhead costs incurred during the month of January.

(d) Prepare the journal entries to record the assignment of direct materials, direct labor, and manufacturing overhead costs to production. In assigning manufacturing overhead costs, use the overhead rate calculated in (a). Post all costs to the job cost sheets as necessary.

(e) Total the job cost sheets for any job(s) completed during the month. Prepare the journal entry (or entries) to record the completion of any job(s) during the month.

(f) Prepare the journal entry (or entries) to record the sale of any job(s) during the month.

(g) What is the balance in the Finished Goods Inventory account at the end of the month? What does this balance consist of?

(h) What is the amount of over- or underapplied overhead?

(e) Job 50, $70,000
Job 51, $99,000

P16-2A For the year ended December 31, 2014, the job cost sheets of Cinta Company contained the following data.

Prepare entries in a job order cost system and partial income statement.

(LO 2, 3, 4, 5, 6)

Job Number	Explanation	Direct Materials	Direct Labor	Manufacturing Overhead	Total Costs
7640	Balance 1/1	$25,000	$24,000	$28,800	$ 77,800
	Current year's costs	30,000	36,000	43,200	109,200
7641	Balance 1/1	11,000	18,000	21,600	50,600
	Current year's costs	43,000	48,000	57,600	148,600
7642	Current year's costs	58,000	55,000	66,000	179,000

Other data:

1. Raw materials inventory totaled $15,000 on January 1. During the year, $140,000 of raw materials were purchased on account.
2. Finished goods on January 1 consisted of Job No. 7638 for $87,000 and Job No. 7639 for $92,000.
3. Job No. 7640 and Job No. 7641 were completed during the year.
4. Job Nos. 7638, 7639, and 7641 were sold on account for $530,000.

5. Manufacturing overhead incurred on account totaled $120,000.
6. Other manufacturing overhead consisted of indirect materials $14,000, indirect labor $18,000, and depreciation on factory machinery $8,000.

Instructions

(a) $179,000; Job 7642:
$179,000

(a) Prove the agreement of Work in Process Inventory with job cost sheets pertaining to unfinished work. (*Hint:* Use a single T-account for Work in Process Inventory.) Calculate each of the following, then post each to the T-account: (1) beginning balance, (2) direct materials, (3) direct labor, (4) manufacturing overhead, and (5) completed jobs.

(b) Amount = $6,800

(b) Prepare the adjusting entry for manufacturing overhead, assuming the balance is allocated entirely to Cost of Goods Sold.

(c) $158,600

(c) Determine the gross profit to be reported for 2014.

Prepare entries in a job order cost system and cost of goods manufactured schedule.

(LO 2, 3, 4, 5)

P16-3A Stellar Inc. is a construction company specializing in custom patios. The patios are constructed of concrete, brick, fiberglass, and lumber, depending upon customer preference. On June 1, 2014, the general ledger for Stellar Inc. contains the following data.

Raw Materials Inventory	$4,200	Manufacturing Overhead Applied	$32,640
Work in Process Inventory	$5,540	Manufacturing Overhead Incurred	$31,650

Subsidiary data for Work in Process Inventory on June 1 are as follows.

Job Cost Sheets

	Customer Job		
Cost Element	**Gannon**	**Rosenthal**	**Linton**
Direct materials	$ 600	$ 800	$ 900
Direct labor	320	540	580
Manufacturing overhead	400	675	725
	$1,320	$2,015	$2,205

During June, raw materials purchased on account were $4,900, and all wages were paid. Additional overhead costs consisted of depreciation on equipment $700 and miscellaneous costs of $400 incurred on account.

A summary of materials requisition slips and time tickets for June shows the following.

Customer Job	**Materials Requisition Slips**	**Time Tickets**
Gannon	$ 800	$ 450
Koss	2,000	800
Rosenthal	500	360
Linton	1,300	1,200
Gannon	300	390
	4,900	3,200
General use	1,500	1,200
	$6,400	$4,400

Overhead was charged to jobs at the same rate of $1.25 per dollar of direct labor cost. The patios for customers Gannon, Rosenthal, and Linton were completed during June and sold for a total of $18,900. Each customer paid in full.

Instructions

(a) Journalize the June transactions: (i) for purchase of raw materials, factory labor costs incurred, and manufacturing overhead costs incurred; (ii) assignment of direct materials, labor, and overhead to production; and (iii) completion of jobs and sale of goods.

(b) Post the entries to Work in Process Inventory.

(d) Cost of goods
manufactured $13,840

(c) Reconcile the balance in Work in Process Inventory with the costs of unfinished jobs.

(d) Prepare a cost of goods manufactured schedule for June.

P16-4A Agassi Company uses a job order cost system in each of its three manufacturing departments. Manufacturing overhead is applied to jobs on the basis of direct labor cost in Department D, direct labor hours in Department E, and machine hours in Department K.

Compute predetermined overhead rates, apply overhead, and calculate under- or overapplied overhead.

(LO 4, 6)

In establishing the predetermined overhead rates for 2014, the following estimates were made for the year.

	Department		
	D	**E**	**K**
Manufacturing overhead	$1,200,000	$1,500,000	$900,000
Direct labor costs	$1,500,000	$1,250,000	$450,000
Direct labor hours	100,000	125,000	40,000
Machine hours	400,000	500,000	120,000

During January, the job cost sheets showed the following costs and production data.

	Department		
	D	**E**	**K**
Direct materials used	$140,000	$126,000	$78,000
Direct labor costs	$120,000	$110,000	$37,500
Manufacturing overhead incurred	$ 99,000	$124,000	$79,000
Direct labor hours	8,000	11,000	3,500
Machine hours	34,000	45,000	10,400

Instructions
(a) Compute the predetermined overhead rate for each department.
(b) Compute the total manufacturing costs assigned to jobs in January in each department.
(c) Compute the under- or overapplied overhead for each department at January 31.

(a) 80%, $12, $7.50
(b) $356,000, $368,000, $193,500
(c) $3,000, $(8,000), $1,000

P16-5A Rodman Corporation's fiscal year ends on November 30. The following accounts are found in its job order cost accounting system for the first month of the new fiscal year.

Analyze manufacturing accounts and determine missing amounts.

(LO 2, 3, 4, 5, 6)

Raw Materials Inventory

Dec. 1	Beginning balance	(a)	Dec. 31	Requisitions	16,850
31	Purchases	19,225			
Dec. 31	Ending balance	7,975			

Work in Process Inventory

Dec. 1	Beginning balance	(b)	Dec. 31	Jobs completed	(f)
31	Direct materials	(c)			
31	Direct labor	8,800			
31	Overhead	(d)			
Dec. 31	Ending balance	(e)			

Finished Goods Inventory

Dec. 1	Beginning balance	(g)	Dec. 31	Cost of goods sold	(i)
31	Completed jobs	(h)			
Dec. 31	Ending balance	(j)			

Factory Labor

Dec. 31	Factory wages	12,025	Dec. 31	Wages assigned	(k)

Manufacturing Overhead

Dec. 31	Indirect materials	1,900	Dec. 31	Overhead applied	(m)
31	Indirect labor	(l)			
31	Other overhead	1,245			

Other data:

1. On December 1, two jobs were in process: Job No. 154 and Job No. 155. These jobs had combined direct materials costs of $9,750 and direct labor costs of $15,000. Overhead was applied at a rate that was 75% of direct labor cost.

2. During December, Job Nos. 156, 157, and 158 were started. On December 31, Job No. 158 was unfinished. This job had charges for direct materials $3,800 and direct labor $4,800, plus manufacturing overhead. All jobs, except for Job No. 158, were completed in December.
3. On December 1, Job No. 153 was in the finished goods warehouse. It had a total cost of $5,000. On December 31, Job No. 157 was the only job finished that was not sold. It had a cost of $4,000.
4. Manufacturing overhead was $230 overapplied in December.

(c) $14,950
(f) $54,150
(i) $55,150

Instructions
List the letters (a) through (m) and indicate the amount pertaining to each letter.

PROBLEMS: SET B

Prepare entries in a job order cost system and job cost sheets.

(LO 2, 3, 4, 5, 6)

P16-1B Pedriani Company uses a job order cost system and applies overhead to production on the basis of direct labor hours. On January 1, 2014, Job No. 25 was the only job in process. The costs incurred prior to January 1 on this job were as follows: direct materials $10,000; direct labor $6,000; and manufacturing overhead $9,000. Job No. 23 had been completed at a cost of $42,000 and was part of finished goods inventory. There was a $5,000 balance in the Raw Materials Inventory account.

During the month of January, the company began production on Jobs 26 and 27, and completed Jobs 25 and 26. Jobs 23 and 25 were sold on account during the month for $63,000 and $74,000, respectively. The following additional events occurred during the month.

1. Purchased additional raw materials of $45,000 on account.
2. Incurred factory labor costs of $33,500. Of this amount, $7,500 related to employer payroll taxes.
3. Incurred manufacturing overhead costs as follows: indirect materials $10,000; indirect labor $9,500; depreciation expense on equipment $12,000; and various other manufacturing overhead costs on account $11,000.
4. Assigned direct materials and direct labor to jobs as follows.

Job No.	Direct Materials	Direct Labor
25	$ 5,000	$ 3,000
26	17,000	12,000
27	13,000	9,000

5. The company uses direct labor hours as the activity base to assign overhead. Direct labor hours incurred on each job were as follows: Job No. 25, 200; Job No. 26, 800; and Job No. 27, 600.

Instructions
(a) Calculate the predetermined overhead rate for the year 2014, assuming Pedriani Company estimates total manufacturing overhead costs of $440,000, direct labor costs of $300,000, and direct labor hours of 20,000 for the year.
(b) Open job cost sheets for Jobs 25, 26, and 27. Enter the January 1 balances on the job cost sheet for Job No. 25.
(c) Prepare the journal entries to record the purchase of raw materials, the factory labor costs incurred, and the manufacturing overhead costs incurred during the month of January.
(d) Prepare the journal entries to record the assignment of direct materials, direct labor, and manufacturing overhead costs to production. In assigning manufacturing overhead costs, use the overhead rate calculated in (a). Post all costs to the job cost sheets as necessary.

(e) Job 25, $37,400
Job 26, $46,600

(e) Total the job cost sheets for any job(s) completed during the month. Prepare the journal entry (or entries) to record the completion of any job(s) during the month.
(f) Prepare the journal entry (or entries) to record the sale of any job(s) during the month.
(g) What is the balance in the Work in Process Inventory account at the end of the month? What does this balance consist of?
(h) What is the amount of over- or underapplied overhead?

P16-2B For the year ended December 31, 2014, the job cost sheets of Dosey Company contained the following data.

Prepare entries in a job order cost system and partial income statement.

(LO 2, 3, 4, 5, 6)

Job Number	Explanation	Direct Materials	Direct Labor	Manufacturing Overhead	Total Costs
7650	Balance 1/1	$18,000	$20,000	$25,000	$ 63,000
	Current year's costs	32,000	36,000	45,000	113,000
7651	Balance 1/1	12,000	16,000	20,000	48,000
	Current year's costs	30,000	40,000	50,000	120,000
7652	Current year's costs	35,000	68,000	85,000	188,000

Other data:

1. Raw materials inventory totaled $20,000 on January 1. During the year, $100,000 of raw materials were purchased on account.
2. Finished goods on January 1 consisted of Job No. 7648 for $93,000 and Job No. 7649 for $62,000.
3. Job No. 7650 and Job No. 7651 were completed during the year.
4. Job Nos. 7648, 7649, and 7650 were sold on account for $490,000.
5. Manufacturing overhead incurred on account totaled $135,000.
6. Other manufacturing overhead consisted of indirect materials $12,000, indirect labor $16,000, and depreciation on factory machinery $19,500.

Instructions
(a) Prove the agreement of Work in Process Inventory with job cost sheets pertaining to unfinished work. (*Hint:* Use a single T-account for Work in Process Inventory.) Calculate each of the following, then post each to the T-account: (1) beginning balance, (2) direct materials, (3) direct labor, (4) manufacturing overhead, and (5) completed jobs.
(b) Prepare the adjusting entry for manufacturing overhead, assuming the balance is allocated entirely to cost of goods sold.
(c) Determine the gross profit to be reported for 2014.

(a) (1) $111,000
(4) $180,000
Unfinished job 7652,
$188,000
(b) Amount = $2,500

(c) $156,500

P16-3B Robert Perez is a contractor specializing in custom-built jacuzzis. On May 1, 2014, his ledger contains the following data.

Prepare entries in a job order cost system and cost of goods manufactured schedule.

(LO 2, 3, 4, 5)

Raw Materials Inventory	$30,000
Work in Process Inventory	12,200
Manufacturing Overhead	2,500 (dr.)

The Manufacturing Overhead account has debit totals of $12,500 and credit totals of $10,000. Subsidiary data for Work in Process Inventory on May 1 include:

Job Cost Sheets

Job by Customer	Direct Materials	Direct Labor	Manufacturing Overhead
Stiner	$2,500	$2,000	$1,400
Alton	2,000	1,200	840
Herman	900	800	560
	$5,400	$4,000	$2,800

During May, the following costs were incurred: raw materials purchased on account $4,000, labor paid $7,000, and manufacturing overhead paid $1,400.

A summary of materials requisition slips and time tickets for the month of May reveals the following.

Job by Customer	Materials Requisition Slips	Time Tickets
Stiner	$ 500	$ 400
Alton	600	1,000
Herman	2,300	1,300
Smith	1,900	2,300
	5,300	5,000
General use	1,500	2,000
	$6,800	$7,000

Overhead was charged to jobs on the basis of $0.70 per dollar of direct labor cost. The jacuzzis for customers Stiner, Alton, and Herman were completed during May. The three jacuzzis were sold for a total of $36,000.

Instructions
(a) Prepare journal entries for the May transactions: (i) for purchase of raw materials, factory labor costs incurred, and manufacturing overhead costs incurred; (ii) assignment of raw materials, labor, and overhead to production; and (iii) completion of jobs and sale of goods.
(b) Post the entries to Work in Process Inventory.
(c) Reconcile the balance in Work in Process Inventory with the costs of unfinished jobs.
(d) Prepare a cost of goods manufactured schedule for May.

(d) Cost of goods
    manufactured $20,190

Compute predetermined overhead rates, apply overhead, and calculate under- or overapplied overhead.

(LO 4, 6)

P16-4B Net Play Company uses a job order cost system in each of its three manufacturing departments. Manufacturing overhead is applied to jobs on the basis of direct labor cost in Department A, direct labor hours in Department B, and machine hours in Department C.

In establishing the predetermined overhead rates for 2014, the following estimates were made for the year.

	Department		
	A	**B**	**C**
Manufacturing overhead	$720,000	$640,000	$900,000
Direct labor cost	$600,000	$100,000	$600,000
Direct labor hours	50,000	40,000	40,000
Machine hours	100,000	120,000	150,000

During January, the job cost sheets showed the following costs and production data.

	Department		
	A	**B**	**C**
Direct materials used	$92,000	$86,000	$64,000
Direct labor cost	$48,000	$35,000	$50,400
Manufacturing overhead incurred	$60,000	$60,000	$72,100
Direct labor hours	4,000	3,500	4,200
Machine hours	8,000	10,500	12,600

(a) 120%, $16, $6
(b) $197,600, $177,000,
    $190,000
(c) $2,400 $4,000, $(3,500)

Instructions
(a) Compute the predetermined overhead rate for each department.
(b) Compute the total manufacturing costs assigned to jobs in January in each department.
(c) Compute the under- or overapplied overhead for each department at January 31.

Analyze manufacturing accounts and determine missing amounts.

(LO 2, 3, 4, 5, 6)

P16-5B Bell Company's fiscal year ends on June 30. The following accounts are found in its job order cost accounting system for the first month of the new fiscal year.

Raw Materials Inventory

July	1	Beginning balance	19,000	July 31	Requisitions	(a)
	31	Purchases	90,400			
July 31		Ending balance	(b)			

Work in Process Inventory

July	1	Beginning balance	(c)	July 31	Jobs completed	(f)
	31	Direct materials	80,000			
	31	Direct labor	(d)			
	31	Overhead	(e)			
July 31		Ending balance	(g)			

Finished Goods Inventory

July	1	Beginning balance	(h)	July 31	Cost of goods sold	(j)
	31	Completed jobs	(i)			
July 31		Ending balance	(k)			

Factory Labor				
July 31	Factory wages	(l)	July 31 Wages assigned	(m)

Manufacturing Overhead				
July 31	Indirect materials	8,900	July 31 Overhead applied	117,000
31	Indirect labor	16,000		
31	Other overhead	(n)		

Other data:

1. On July 1, two jobs were in process: Job No. 4085 and Job No. 4086, with costs of $19,000 and $8,200, respectively.
2. During July, Job Nos. 4087, 4088, and 4089 were started. On July 31, only Job No. 4089 was unfinished. This job had charges for direct materials $2,000 and direct labor $1,500, plus manufacturing overhead. Manufacturing overhead was applied at the rate of 130% of direct labor cost.
3. On July 1, Job No. 4084, costing $145,000, was in the finished goods warehouse. On July 31, Job No. 4088, costing $138,000, was in finished goods.
4. Overhead was $3,000 underapplied in July.

Instructions

List the letters (a) through (n) and indicate the amount pertaining to each letter. Show computations.

(d) $ 90,000
(f) $308,750
(l) $106,000

PROBLEMS: SET C

Visit the book's companion website, at **www.wiley.com/college/weygandt**, and choose the Student Companion site to access Problem Set C.

WATERWAYS CONTINUING PROBLEM

(*Note:* This is a continuation of the Waterways Problem from Chapter 15.)

WCP16 Waterways has two major public-park projects to provide with comprehensive irrigation in one of its service locations this month. Job J57 and Job K52 involve 15 acres of landscaped terrain which will require special-order sprinkler heads to meet the specifications of the project. This problem asks you to help Waterways use a job order cost system to account for production of these parts.

Go to the book's companion website, at **www.wiley.com/college/weygandt**, *to find the completion of this problem.*

Broadening Your PERSPECTIVE

Management Decision-Making

Decision-Making at Current Designs

BYP16-1 Huegel Hollow Resort has ordered 20 rotomolded kayaks from Current Designs. Each kayak will be formed in the rotomolded oven, cooled, and then the excess plastic trimmed away. Then, the hatches, seat, ropes, and bungees will be attached to the kayak.

Dave Thill, the kayak plant manager, knows that manufacturing each kayak requires 54 pounds of polyethylene powder and a finishing kit (rope, seat, hardware, etc.). The polyethylene powder used in these kayaks costs $1.50 per pound, and the finishing kits cost $170 each. Each kayak will use two kinds of labor: 2 hours of more-skilled type I labor from people who run the oven and trim the plastic, and 3 hours of less-skilled type II labor from people who attach the hatches and seat and other hardware. The type I employees are paid $15 per hour, and the type II employees are paid $12 per hour. For purposes of this problem, assume that overhead is allocated to all jobs at a rate of 150% of direct labor costs.

Instructions
Determine the total cost of the Huegel Hollow order and the cost of each individual kayak in the order. Identify costs as direct materials, direct labor, or manufacturing overhead.

Decision-Making Across the Organization

BYP16-2 Khan Products Company uses a job order cost system. For a number of months, there has been an ongoing rift between the sales department and the production department concerning a special-order product, TC-1. TC-1 is a seasonal product that is manufactured in batches of 1,000 units. TC-1 is sold at cost plus a markup of 40% of cost.

The sales department is unhappy because fluctuating unit production costs significantly affect selling prices. Sales personnel complain that this has caused excessive customer complaints and the loss of considerable orders for TC-1.

The production department maintains that each job order must be fully costed on the basis of the costs incurred during the period in which the goods are produced. Production personnel maintain that the only real solution to the problem is for the sales department to increase sales in the slack periods.

Andrea Parley, president of the company, asks you as the company accountant to collect quarterly data for the past year on TC-1. From the cost accounting system, you accumulate the following production quantity and cost data.

Costs	Quarter			
	1	2	3	4
Direct materials	$100,000	$220,000	$ 80,000	$200,000
Direct labor	60,000	132,000	48,000	120,000
Manufacturing overhead	105,000	153,000	97,000	125,000
Total	$265,000	$505,000	$225,000	$445,000
Production in batches	5	11	4	10
Unit cost (per batch)	$ 53,000	$ 45,909	$ 56,250	$ 44,500

Instructions
With the class divided into groups, answer the following questions.
(a) What manufacturing cost element is responsible for the fluctuating unit costs? Why?
(b) What is your recommended solution to the problem of fluctuating unit cost?
(c) Restate the quarterly data on the basis of your recommended solution.

Managerial Analysis

BYP16-3 In the course of routine checking of all journal entries prior to preparing year-end reports, Betty Eller discovered several strange entries. She recalled that the president's son Joe had come in to help out during an especially busy time and that he had recorded some journal entries. She was relieved that there were only a few of his entries, and even more relieved that he had included rather lengthy explanations. The entries Joe made were:

1.

Work in Process Inventory	25,000	
Cash		25,000

(This is for materials put into process. I don't find the record that we paid for these, so I'm crediting Cash because I know we'll have to pay for them sooner or later.)

2.

| Manufacturing Overhead | 12,000 | |
| Cash | | 12,000 |

(This is for bonuses paid to salespeople. I know they're part of overhead, and I can't find an account called "Non-Factory Overhead" or "Other Overhead" so I'm putting it in Manufacturing Overhead. I have the check stubs, so I know we paid these.)

3.

| Wages Expense | 120,000 | |
| Cash | | 120,000 |

(This is for the factory workers' wages. I have a note that payroll taxes are $18,000. I still think that's part of wages expense and that we'll have to pay it all in cash sooner or later, so I credited Cash for the wages and the taxes.)

4.

| Work in Process Inventory | 3,000 | |
| Raw Materials Inventory | | 3,000 |

(This is for the glue used in the factory. I know we used this to make the products, even though we didn't use very much on any one of the products. I got it out of inventory, so I credited an inventory account.)

Instructions

(a) How should Joe have recorded each of the four events?

(b) If the entry was not corrected, which financial statements (income statement or balance sheet) would be affected? What balances would be overstated or understated?

Real-World Focus

BYP 16-4 Founded in 1970, Parlex Corporation is a world leader in the design and manufacture of flexible interconnect products. Utilizing proprietary and patented technologies, Parlex produces custom flexible interconnects including flexible circuits, polymer thick film, laminated cables, and value-added assemblies for sophisticated electronics used in automotive, telecommunications, computer, diversified electronics, and aerospace applications. In addition to manufacturing sites in Methuen, Massachusetts; Salem, New Hampshire; Cranston, Rhode Island; San Jose, California; Shanghai, China; Isle of Wight, UK; and Empalme, Mexico, Parlex has logistic support centers and strategic alliances throughout North America, Asia, and Europe.

The following information was provided in the company's annual report.

Parlex Company
Notes to the Financial Statements

The Company's products are manufactured on a job order basis to customers' specifications. Customers submit requests for quotations on each job, and the Company prepares bids based on its own cost estimates. The Company attempts to reflect the impact of changing costs when establishing prices. However, during the past several years, the market conditions for flexible circuits and the resulting price sensitivity haven't always allowed this to transpire. Although still not satisfactory, the Company was able to reduce the cost of products sold as a percentage of sales to 85% this year versus 87% that was experienced in the two immediately preceding years. Management continues to focus on improving operational efficiency and further reducing costs.

Instructions

(a) Parlex management discusses the job order cost system employed by their company. What are several advantages of using the job order approach to costing?

(b) Contrast the products produced in a job order environment, like Parlex, to those produced when process cost systems are used.

BYP16-5 The Institute of Management Accountants sponsors a certification for management accountants, allowing them to obtain the title of Certified Management Accountant.

Address: **www.imanet.org**, or go to **www.wiley.com/college/weygandt**

Steps
1. Go to the site shown above.
2. Choose **CMA Certification**, and then, **Earning & Maintaining Your Credential**.

Instructions
(a) What is the experience qualification requirement?
(b) How many hours of continuing education are required, and what types of courses qualify?

Critical Thinking

Communication Activity

BYP16-6 You are the management accountant for Williams Company. Your company does custom carpentry work and uses a job order cost system. Williams sends detailed job cost sheets to its customers, along with an invoice. The job cost sheets show the date materials were used, the dollar cost of materials, and the hours and cost of labor. A predetermined overhead application rate is used, and the total overhead applied is also listed.

Nancy Kopay is a customer who recently had custom cabinets installed. Along with her check in payment for the work done, she included a letter. She thanked the company for including the detailed cost information but questioned why overhead was estimated. She stated that she would be interested in knowing exactly what costs were included in overhead, and she thought that other customers would, too.

Instructions
Prepare a letter to Ms. Kopay (address: 123 Cedar Lane, Altoona, KS 66651) and tell her why you did not send her information on exact costs of overhead included in her job. Respond to her suggestion that you provide this information.

Ethics Case

BYP16-7 LRF Printing provides printing services to many different corporate clients. Although LRF bids most jobs, some jobs, particularly new ones, are negotiated on a "cost-plus" basis. Cost-plus means that the buyer is willing to pay the actual cost plus a return (profit) on these costs to LRF.

Alice Reiley, controller for LRF, has recently returned from a meeting where LRF's president stated that he wanted her to find a way to charge more costs to any project that was on a cost-plus basis. The president noted that the company needed more profits to meet its stated goals this period. By charging more costs to the cost-plus projects and therefore fewer costs to the jobs that were bid, the company should be able to increase its profit for the current year.

Alice knew why the president wanted to take this action. Rumors were that he was looking for a new position and if the company reported strong profits, the president's opportunities would be enhanced. Alice also recognized that she could probably increase the cost of certain jobs by changing the basis used to allocate manufacturing overhead.

Instructions
(a) Who are the stakeholders in this situation?
(b) What are the ethical issues in this situation?
(c) What would you do if you were Alice Reiley?

All About You

BYP16-8 Many of you will work for a small business. Some of you will even own your own business. In order to operate a small business, you will need a good understanding of managerial accounting, as well as many other skills. Much information is available to assist people who are interested in starting a new business. A great place to start is the website provided by the Small Business Administration, which is an agency of the federal government whose purpose is to support small business.

Instructions

Go to **www.sba.gov** and in the Small Business Planner, Plan Your Business link, review the material under "Get Ready." Answer the following questions.

(a) What are some of the characteristics required of a small business owner?

(b) What are the top 10 reasons given for business failure?

Considering Your Costs and Benefits

BYP16-9 After graduating, you might decide to start a small business. As discussed in this chapter, owners of any business need to know how to calculate the cost of their products. In fact, many small businesses fail because they don't accurately calculate their product costs, so they don't know if they are making a profit or losing money—until it's too late.

Suppose that you decide to start a landscape business. You use an old pickup truck that you've fully paid for. You store the truck and other equipment in your parents' barn, and you store trees and shrubs on their land. Your parents will not charge you for the use of these facilities for the first two years, but beginning in the third year they will charge a reasonable rent. Your mother helps you by answering phone calls and providing customers with information. She doesn't charge you for this service, but she plans on doing it for only your first two years in business. In pricing your services, should you include charges for the truck, the barn, the land, and your mother's services when calculating your product cost? The basic arguments for and against are as follows.

YES: If you don't include charges for these costs, your costs are understated and your profitability is overstated.

NO: At this point, you are not actually incurring costs related to these activities; therefore, you shouldn't record charges.

Instructions

Write a response indicating your position regarding this situation. Provide support for your view.

Answers to Chapter Questions

Answers to Insight and Accounting Across the Organization Questions

p. 811 Jobs Won, Money Lost Q: What type of costs do you think the company had been underestimating? **A:** It is most likely that the company failed to estimate and track overhead. In a highly diversified company, overhead associated with the diesel locomotive jobs may have been "lost" in the total overhead pool for the entire company.

p. 817 The Cost of an iPhone? Just Tear One Apart Q: What type of costs are marketing and selling costs, and how are they treated for accounting purposes? **A:** Product costs include materials, labor, and overhead. Costs not related to production, such as marketing and selling costs, are period costs which are expensed in the period that they are incurred.

p. 827 Sales Are Nice, but Service Revenue Pays the Bills Q: Explain why GE would use job order costing to keep track of the cost of repairing a malfunctioning engine for a major airline. **A:** GE operates in a competitive environment. Other companies offer competing bids to win service contracts on GE's airplane engines. GE needs to know what it costs to repair engines, so that it can present competitive bids while still generating a reasonable profit.

Answers to Self-Test Questions

1. a **2.** c **3.** b **4.** c **5.** c **6.** d **7.** d **8.** b **9.** a **10.** d **11.** b ($180,000 × 80%) **12.** c **13.** b **14.** c **15.** c **16.** b

✔ Remember to go back to The Navigator box on the chapter opening page and check off your completed work.

Ben & Jerry's Tracks Its Mix-Ups

Ben & Jerry's Homemade, Inc., based in Waterbury, Vermont, started its first ice cream shop in a former gas station in 1978.

Making ice cream is a process—a movement of product from a mixing department to a prepping department to a pint department. The mixing department is where the ice cream is created. In the prep area, the production process adds extras such as cherries and dark chocolate to make plain ice cream into "Cherry Garcia," Ben & Jerry's most popular flavor, or fudge-covered waffle cone pieces

and a swirl of caramel for "Stephen Colbert's Americone Dream." The pint department is where the ice cream is actually put into containers. As the product is processed from one department to the next, the appropriate materials, labor, and overhead are added to determine its cost.

"The incoming ingredients from the shipping and receiving departments are stored in certain locations, either in a freezer or dry warehouse," says Beecher Eurich, staff accountant. "As ingredients get added, so do the costs associated with them." How much ice cream is produced? Running plants around the clock, the company produces 18 million gallons a year.

Learning Objectives

After studying this chapter, you should be able to:

1. Understand who uses process cost systems.

2. Explain the similarities and differences between job order cost and process cost systems.

3. Explain the flow of costs in a process cost system.

4. Make the journal entries to assign manufacturing costs in a process cost system.

5. Compute equivalent units.

6. Explain the four steps necessary to prepare a production cost report.

7. Prepare a production cost report.

 The Navigator

With the company's process cost system, Eurich can tell you how much a certain batch of ice cream costs to make—its materials, labor, and overhead in each of the production departments. She generates reports for the production department heads but makes sure not to overdo it. "You can get bogged down in numbers," says Eurich. "If you're generating a report that no one can use, then that's a waste of time."

It's more likely, though, that Ben & Jerry's production people want to know how efficient they are. Why? Many own stock in the company.

Watch the Jones Soda video in WileyPLUS to learn more about process costing in the real world.

Preview of Chapter 17

The cost accounting system used by companies such as Ben & Jerry's is **process cost accounting**. In contrast to job order cost accounting, which focuses on the individual job, process cost accounting focuses on the *processes* involved in mass-producing products that are identical or very similar in nature. The primary objective of this chapter is to explain and illustrate process costing.

The content and organization of this chapter are as follows.

PROCESS COSTING

Nature of Process Cost Systems	Equivalent Units	Production Cost Report
• Uses • Service companies • Similarities and differences • Process cost flow • Assigning manufacturing costs	• Weighted-average method • Refinements	• Physical units • Equivalent units of production • Unit production costs • Cost reconciliation schedule • Production cost report • Costing systems—Final comments

✔ **The Navigator**

The Nature of Process Cost Systems

Uses of Process Cost Systems

Companies use **process cost systems** to apply costs to similar products that are mass-produced in a continuous fashion. Ben & Jerry's uses a process cost system: Production of the ice cream, once it begins, continues until the ice cream emerges, and the processing is the same for the entire run—with precisely the same amount of materials, labor, and overhead. Each finished pint of ice cream is indistinguishable from another.

A company such as USX uses process costing in the manufacturing of steel. Kellogg and General Mills use process costing for cereal production; Exxon-Mobil uses process costing for its oil refining. Sherwin Williams uses process costing for its paint products. At a bottling company like Coca-Cola, the manufacturing process begins with the blending of ingredients. Next, automated machinery moves the bottles into position and fills them. The production process then caps, packages, and forwards the bottles to the finished goods warehouse. Illustration 17-1 shows this process.

Illustration 17-1
Manufacturing processes

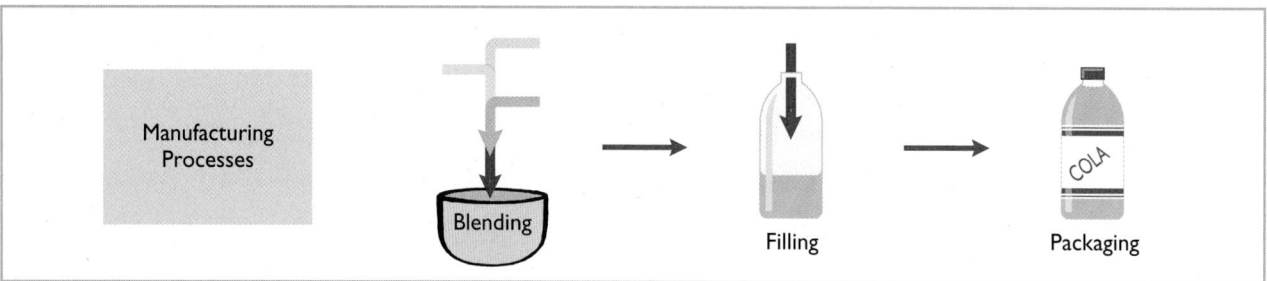

For Coca-Cola, as well as the other companies just mentioned, once production begins, it continues until the finished product emerges, and each unit of finished product is like every other unit.

In comparison, a job order cost system assigns costs to a *specific job*. Examples are the construction of a customized home, the making of a motion picture, or the manufacturing of a specialized machine. Illustration 17-2 provides examples of companies that primarily use either a process cost system or a job order cost system.

Illustration 17-2
Process cost and job order cost companies and products

Process Cost System		Job Order Cost System	
Company	**Product**	**Company**	**Product**
Coca-Cola, PepsiCo	Soft drinks	Young & Rubicam, J. Walter Thompson	Advertising
ExxonMobil, Royal Dutch Shell	Oil	Walt Disney, Warner Brothers	Motion pictures
Intel, Advanced Micro Devices	Computer chips	Center Ice Consultants, Ice Pro	Ice rinks
Dow Chemical, DuPont	Chemicals	Kaiser, Mayo Clinic	Patient health care

Process Costing for Service Companies

Frequently, when we think of service companies, we think of specific, nonroutine tasks, such as rebuilding an automobile engine, providing consulting services on a business acquisition, or working on a major lawsuit. However, many service companies specialize in performing repetitive, routine aspects of a particular business. For example, auto-care vendors such as Jiffy Lube focus on the routine aspects of car care. H&R Block focuses on the routine aspects of basic tax practice, and many large law firms focus on routine legal services, such as uncomplicated divorces. Service companies that provide specific, nonroutine services will probably benefit from using a job order cost system. Those that perform routine, repetitive services will probably be better off with a process cost system.

Similarities and Differences Between Job Order Cost and Process Cost Systems

In a job order cost system, companies assign costs to each job. In a process cost system, companies track costs through a series of connected manufacturing processes or departments, rather than by individual jobs. Thus, companies use process cost systems when they produce a large volume of uniform or relatively homogeneous products. Illustration 17-3 shows the basic flow of costs in these two systems.

The following analysis highlights the basic similarities and differences between these two systems.

LEARNING OBJECTIVE   2

Explain the similarities and differences between job order cost and process cost systems.

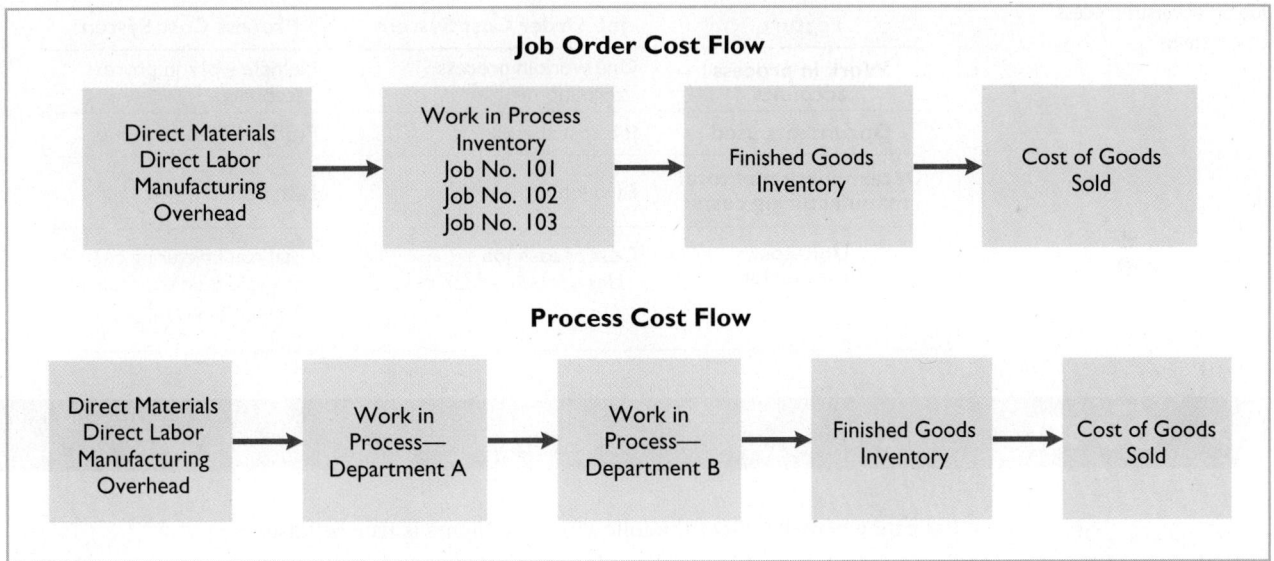

Illustration 17-3
Job order cost and process cost flow

SIMILARITIES

Job order cost and process cost systems are similar in three ways:

1. **The manufacturing cost elements.** Both costing systems track three manufacturing cost elements—direct materials, direct labor, and manufacturing overhead.

2. **The accumulation of the costs of materials, labor, and overhead.** Both costing systems debit raw materials to Raw Materials Inventory, factory labor to Factory Labor, and manufacturing overhead costs to Manufacturing Overhead.

3. **The flow of costs.** As noted above, both systems accumulate all manufacturing costs by debits to Raw Materials Inventory, Factory Labor, and Manufacturing

Overhead. Both systems then assign these costs to the same accounts—Work in Process, Finished Goods Inventory, and Cost of Goods Sold. **The methods of assigning costs, however, differ significantly.** These differences are explained and illustrated later in the chapter.

DIFFERENCES

The differences between a job order cost and a process cost system are as follows.

1. **The number of work in process accounts used.** A job order cost system uses only one work in process account. A process cost system uses multiple work in process accounts.

2. **Documents used to track costs.** A job order cost system charges costs to individual jobs and summarizes them in a job cost sheet. A process cost system summarizes costs in a production cost report for each department.

3. **The point at which costs are totaled.** A job order cost system totals costs when the job is completed. A process cost system totals costs at the end of a period of time.

4. **Unit cost computations.** In a job order cost system, the unit cost is the total cost per job divided by the units produced. In a process cost system, the unit cost is total manufacturing costs for the period divided by the units produced during the period.

Illustration 17-4 summarizes the major differences between a job order cost and a process cost system.

Illustration 17-4
Job order versus process cost systems

Feature	Job Order Cost System	Process Cost System
Work in process accounts	One work in process account	Multiple work in process accounts
Documents used	Job cost sheets	Production cost reports
Determination of total manufacturing costs	Each job	Each period
Unit-cost computations	Cost of each job ÷ Units produced for the job	Total manufacturing costs ÷ Equivalent units produced during the period

---

> DO IT!

Compare Job Order and Process Cost Systems

Action Plan

✔ Use job order costing in situations where unit costs are high, unit volume is low, and products are unique.

✔ Use process costing when there is a large volume of relatively homogeneous products.

Indicate whether each of the following statements is true or false.

1. A law firm is likely to use process costing for major lawsuits.

2. A manufacturer of paintballs is likely to use process costing.

3. Both job order and process costing determine product costs at the end of a period of time, rather than when a product is completed.

4. Process costing does not keep track of manufacturing overhead.

Solution

1. false. 2. true. 3. false. 4. false.

Related exercise material: **E17-1 and DO IT! 17-1.**

 **The Navigator**

Process Cost Flow

Illustration 17-5 shows the flow of costs in the process cost system for Tyler Company. Tyler Company manufactures roller blade and skateboard wheels that it sells to manufacturers and retail outlets. Manufacturing consists of two processes: machining and assembly. The Machining Department shapes, hones, and drills the raw materials. The Assembly Department assembles and packages the parts.

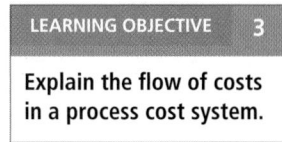

LEARNING OBJECTIVE   3

Explain the flow of costs in a process cost system.

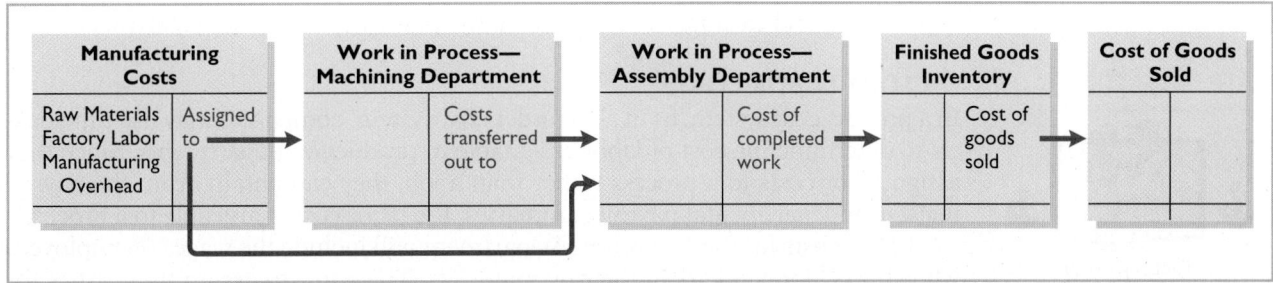

Illustration 17-5
Flow of costs in process cost system

As the flow of costs indicates, the company can add materials, labor, and manufacturing overhead in both the Machining and Assembly departments. When it finishes its work, the Machining Department transfers the partially completed units to the Assembly Department. The Assembly Department finishes the goods and then transfers them to the finished goods inventory. Upon sale, Tyler removes the goods from the finished goods inventory. Within each department, a similar set of activities is performed on each unit processed.

Assigning Manufacturing Costs—Journal Entries

As indicated, the accumulation of the costs of materials, labor, and manufacturing overhead is the same in a process cost system as in a job order cost system. That is, both systems follow these procedures:

- Companies debit all raw materials to Raw Materials Inventory at the time of purchase.
- They debit all factory labor to Factory Labor as the labor costs are incurred.
- They debit overhead costs to Manufacturing Overhead as these costs are incurred.

However, the assignment of the three manufacturing cost elements to Work in Process in a process cost system is different from a job order cost system. Here we'll look at how companies assign these manufacturing cost elements in a process cost system.

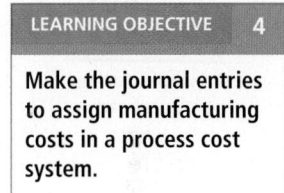

LEARNING OBJECTIVE   4

Make the journal entries to assign manufacturing costs in a process cost system.

MATERIALS COSTS

All raw materials issued for production are a materials cost to the producing department. A process cost system may use materials requisition slips, but **it generally requires fewer requisitions than in a job order cost system, because the materials are used for processes rather than for specific jobs** and therefore typically are for larger quantities.

At the beginning of the first process, a company usually adds most of the materials needed for production. However, other materials may be added at various points. For example, in the manufacture of Hershey candy bars, the chocolate and other ingredients are added at the beginning of the first process, and the wrappers and cartons are added at the end of the packaging process. Tyler Company adds materials at the beginning of each process. Tyler makes the following entry to record the materials used.

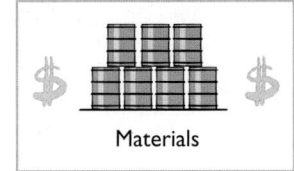
Materials

Work in Process—Machining	XXXX	
Work in Process—Assembly	XXXX	
Raw Materials Inventory		XXXX
(To record materials used)		

Ice cream maker Ben & Jerry's adds materials in three departments: milk and flavoring in the mixing department, extras such as cherries and dark chocolate in the prepping department, and cardboard containers in the pinting (packaging) department.

FACTORY LABOR COSTS

Factory Labor

In a process cost system, as in a job order cost system, companies may use time tickets to determine the cost of labor assignable to production departments. Since they assign labor costs to a process rather than a job, they can obtain, from the payroll register or departmental payroll summaries, the labor cost chargeable to a process.

Labor costs for the Machining Department will include the wages of employees who shape, hone, and drill the raw materials. The entry to assign these costs for Tyler Company is:

Work in Process—Machining	XXXX	
Work in Process—Assembly	XXXX	
Factory Labor		XXXX
(To assign factory labor to production)		

MANUFACTURING OVERHEAD COSTS

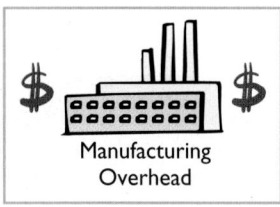

Manufacturing
Overhead

The objective in assigning overhead in a process cost system is to allocate the overhead costs to the production departments on an objective and equitable basis. That basis is the activity that "drives" or causes the costs. A primary driver of overhead costs in continuous manufacturing operations is **machine time used**, not direct labor. Thus, companies **widely use machine hours** in allocating manufacturing overhead costs using predetermined overhead rates. Tyler's entry to allocate overhead to the two processes is:

Work in Process—Machining	XXXX	
Work in Process—Assembly	XXXX	
Manufacturing Overhead		XXXX
(To assign overhead to production)		

MANAGEMENT INSIGHT

Choosing a Cost Driver

In one of its automated cost centers, Caterpillar feeds work into the cost center, where robotic machines process it and transfer the finished job to the next cost center without human intervention. One person tends all of the machines and spends more time maintaining machines than operating them. In such cases, overhead rates based on direct labor hours may be misleading. Surprisingly, some companies continue to assign manufacturing overhead on the basis of direct labor despite the fact that there is no cause-and-effect relationship between labor and overhead.

 What is the result if a company uses the wrong "cost driver" to assign manufacturing overhead? (See page 898.)

TRANSFER TO NEXT DEPARTMENT

At the end of the month, Tyler needs an entry to record the cost of the goods transferred out of the Machining Department. In this case, the transfer is to the Assembly Department, and Tyler makes the following entry.

Work in Process—Assembly	XXXXX	
Work in Process—Machining		XXXXX
(To record transfer of units to the Assembly		
Department)		

TRANSFER TO FINISHED GOODS

When the Assembly Department completes the units, it transfers them to the finished goods warehouse. The entry for this transfer is as follows.

Finished Goods Inventory	XXXXX	
Work in Process—Assembly		XXXXX
(To record transfer of units to finished goods)		

TRANSFER TO COST OF GOODS SOLD

When Tyler sells the finished goods, it records the cost of goods sold as follows.

Cost of Goods Sold	XXXXX	
Finished Goods Inventory		XXXXX
(To record cost of units sold)		

> DO IT!

Manufacturing Costs in Process Costing

Ruth Company manufactures ZEBO through two processes: blending and bottling. In June, raw materials used were Blending $18,000 and Bottling $4,000. Factory labor costs were Blending $12,000 and Bottling $5,000. Manufacturing overhead costs were Blending $6,000 and Bottling $2,500. The company transfers units completed at a cost of $19,000 in the Blending Department to the Bottling Department. The Bottling Department transfers units completed at a cost of $11,000 to Finished Goods. Journalize the assignment of these costs to the two processes and the transfer of units as appropriate.

Solution

Action Plan

✔ In process cost accounting, keep separate work in process accounts for each process.

✔ When the costs are assigned to production, debit the separate work in process accounts.

✔ Transfer cost of completed units to the next process or to Finished Goods.

The entries are:		
Work in Process—Blending	18,000	
Work in Process—Bottling	4,000	
Raw Materials Inventory		22,000
(To record materials used)		
Work in Process—Blending	12,000	
Work in Process—Bottling	5,000	
Factory Labor		17,000
(To assign factory labor to production)		
Work in Process—Blending	6,000	
Work in Process—Bottling	2,500	
Manufacturing Overhead		8,500
(To assign overhead to production)		

Work in Process—Bottling		19,000	
Work in Process—Blending			19,000
(To record transfer of units to the Bottling			
Department)			
Finished Goods Inventory		11,000	
Work in Process—Bottling			11,000
(To record transfer of units to finished goods)			

Related exercise material: **BE17-1, BE17-2, BE17-3, E17-2, E17-4,** and **DO IT!** **17-2.**

✔ **The Navigator**

Equivalent Units

LEARNING OBJECTIVE **5**

Compute equivalent units.

Suppose you have a work-study job in the office of your college's president, and she asks you to compute the cost of instruction per full-time equivalent student at your college. The college's vice president for finance provides the following information.

Illustration 17-6
Information for full-time student example

Costs:	
Total cost of instruction	$9,000,000
Student population:	
Full-time students	900
Part-time students	1,000

Part-time students take 60% of the classes of a full-time student during the year. To compute the number of full-time equivalent students per year, you would make the following computation.

Illustration 17-7
Full-time equivalent unit computation

Full-Time Students	+	Equivalent Units of Part-Time Students	=	Full-Time Equivalent Students
900	+	(60% × 1,000)	=	1,500

The cost of instruction per full-time equivalent student is therefore the total cost of instruction ($9,000,000) divided by the number of full-time equivalent students (1,500), which is $6,000 ($9,000,000 ÷ 1,500).

A process cost system uses the same idea, called equivalent units of production. **Equivalent units of production** measure the work done during the period, expressed in fully completed units. Companies use this measure to determine the cost per unit of completed product.

Weighted-Average Method

The formula to compute equivalent units of production is as follows.

Illustration 17-8
Equivalent units of production formula

Units Completed and Transferred Out	+	Equivalent Units of Ending Work in Process	=	Equivalent Units of Production

To better understand this concept of equivalent units, consider the following two separate examples.

> **Example 1.** In a specific period, the entire output of Sullivan Company's Blending Department consists of ending work in process of 4,000 units which are 60% complete as to materials, labor, and overhead. The equivalent units of production for the Blending Department are therefore 2,400 units (4,000 × 60%).
>
> **Example 2.** The output of Kori Company's Packaging Department during the period consists of 10,000 units completed and transferred out, and 5,000 units in ending work in process which are 70% completed. The equivalent units of production are therefore 13,500 [10,000 + (5,000 × 70%)].

This method of computing equivalent units is referred to as the **weighted-average method**. It considers the degree of completion (weighting) of the units completed and transferred out and the ending work in process.

Refinements on the Weighted-Average Method

Kellogg Company has produced Eggo® Waffles since 1970. Three departments produce these waffles: Mixing, Baking, and Freezing/Packaging. The Mixing Department combines dry ingredients, including flour, salt, and baking powder, with liquid ingredients, including eggs and vegetable oil, to make waffle batter. Illustration 17-9 provides information related to the Mixing Department at the end of June.

Mixing Department			
		Percentage Complete	
	Physical Units	**Materials**	**Conversion Costs**
Work in process, June 1	100,000	100%	70%
Started into production	800,000		
Total units	900,000		
Units transferred out	700,000		
Work in process, June 30	200,000	100%	60%
Total units	900,000		

Illustration 17-9
Information for Mixing Department

Illustration 17-9 indicates that the beginning work in process is 100% complete as to materials cost and 70% complete as to conversion costs. **Conversion costs are the sum of labor costs and overhead costs.** In other words, Kellogg adds both the dry and liquid ingredients (materials) at the beginning of the waffle-making process, and the conversion costs (labor and overhead) related to the mixing of these ingredients are incurred uniformly and are 70% complete. The ending work in process is 100% complete as to materials cost and 60% complete as to conversion costs.

We then use the Mixing Department information to determine equivalent units. **In computing equivalent units, the beginning work in process is not part of the equivalent-units-of-production formula.** The units transferred out to the Baking Department are fully complete as to both materials and conversion costs. The ending work in process is fully complete as to materials, but only 60% complete as to conversion costs. We therefore need to make **two equivalent unit computations**: one

Helpful Hint
When are separate unit cost computations needed for materials and conversion costs? Answer: Whenever the two types of costs do not occur in the process at the same time.

Ethics Note

An unethical manager might use incorrect completion percentages when determining equivalent units. This results in either raising or lowering costs. Since completion percentages are somewhat subjective, this form of income manipulation can be difficult to detect.

for materials, and the other for conversion costs. Illustration 17-10 shows these computations.

Illustration 17-10
Computation of equivalent units—Mixing Department

Mixing Department		
	Equivalent Units	
	Materials	**Conversion Costs**
Units transferred out	700,000	700,000
Work in process, June 30		
200,000 × 100%	200,000	
200,000 × 60%		120,000
Total equivalent units	900,000	820,000

We can refine the earlier formula used to compute equivalent units of production (Illustration 17-8, page 860) to show the computations for materials and for conversion costs, as follows.

Illustration 17-11
Refined equivalent units of production formula

Units Completed and Transferred Out— Materials	+	Equivalent Units of Ending Work in Process—Materials	=	Equivalent Units of Production— Materials
Units Completed and Transferred Out— Conversion Costs	+	Equivalent Units of Ending Work in Process—Conversion Costs	=	Equivalent Units of Production— Conversion Costs

 PEOPLE, PLANET, AND PROFIT INSIGHT

Haven't I Seen That Before?

For a variety of reasons, many companies, including Caterpillar, General Electric, and Eastman Kodak, are making a big push to remanufacture goods that have been thrown away. Items getting a second chance include cell phones, computers, home appliances, car parts, vacuum cleaners, and medical equipment. Businesses have figured out that profit margins on remanufactured goods are significantly higher than on new goods. As commodity prices such as copper and steel increase, reusing parts makes more sense. Also, as more local governments initiate laws requiring that electronics and appliances be recycled rather than thrown away, the cost of remanufacturing declines because the gathering of used goods becomes far more efficient. Besides benefitting the manufacturer, remanufacturing provides goods at a much lower price to consumers, reduces waste going to landfills, saves energy, reuses scarce resources, and reduces emissions. For example, it was estimated that a remanufactured car starter results in about 50% less carbon dioxide emissions than making a new one.

Source: James R. Hagerty and Paul Glader, "From Trash Heap to Store Shelf," *Wall Street Journal Online* (January 24, 2011).

 In what ways might the relative composition (materials, labor, and overhead) of a remanufactured product's cost differ from that of a newly made product? (See page 898.)

> DO IT!

Equivalent Units

The fabricating department has the following production and cost data for the current month.

Beginning Work in Process	Units Transferred Out	Ending Work in Process
–0–	15,000	10,000

Materials are entered at the beginning of the process. The ending work in process units are 30% complete as to conversion costs. Compute the equivalent units of production for (a) materials and (b) conversion costs.

Action Plan

✔ To measure the work done during the period, expressed in fully completed units, compute equivalent units of production.

✔ Use the appropriate formula: Units completed and transferred out + Equivalent units of ending work in process = Equivalent units of production.

Solution

(a) Since materials are entered at the beginning of the process, the equivalent units of ending work in process are 10,000. Thus, 15,000 units + 10,000 units = 25,000 equivalent units of production for materials.

(b) Since ending work in process is only 30% complete as to conversion costs, the equivalent units of ending work in process are 3,000 (30% × 10,000 units). Thus, 15,000 units + 3,000 units = 18,000 equivalent units of production for conversion costs.

Related exercise material: **BE17-5, BE17-10, E17-5, E17-6, E17-8, E17-9, E17-10, E17-11, E17-13, E17-14, E17-15, and DO IT! 17-3.**

✔ The Navigator

Production Cost Report

As mentioned earlier, companies prepare a production cost report for each department. A **production cost report** is the key document that management uses to understand the activities in a department; it shows the production quantity and cost data related to that department. For example, in producing Eggo® Waffles, Kellogg Company uses three production cost reports: Mixing, Baking, and Freezing/Packaging. Illustration 17-12 shows the flow of costs to make an Eggo® Waffle and the related production cost reports for each department.

LEARNING OBJECTIVE   6

Explain the four steps necessary to prepare a production cost report.

Illustration 17-12
Flow of costs in making Eggo® Waffles

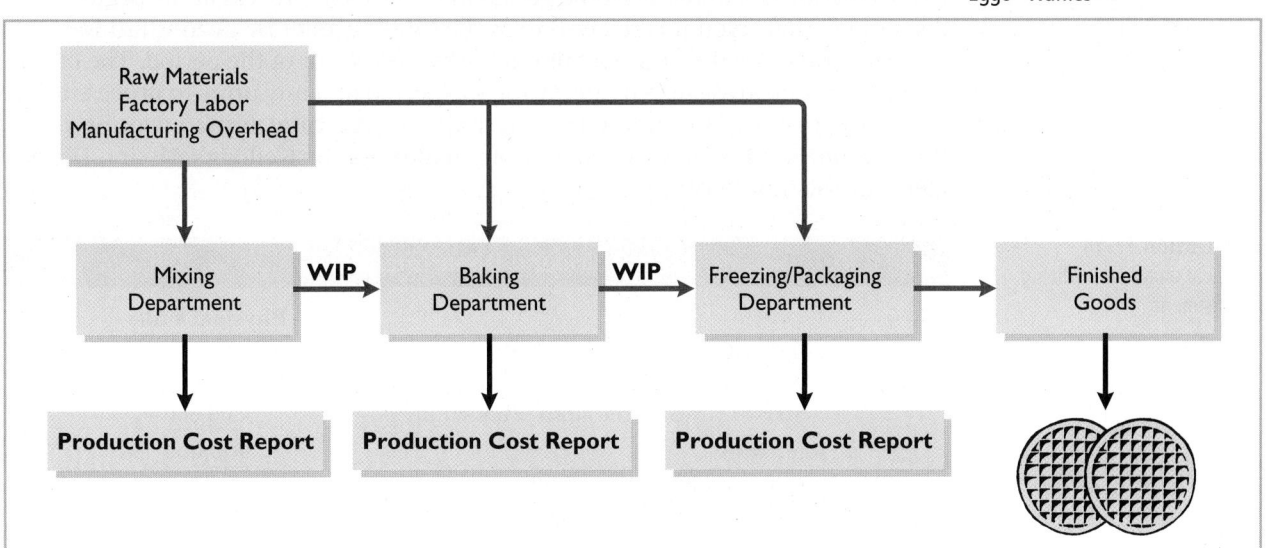

In order to complete a production cost report, the company must perform four steps, which, as a whole, make up the process cost system.

1. Compute the physical unit flow.
2. Compute the equivalent units of production.
3. Compute unit production costs.
4. Prepare a cost reconciliation schedule.

Illustration 17-13 shows assumed data for the Mixing Department at Kellogg Company for the month of June. We will use this information to complete a production cost report for the Mixing Department.

Illustration 17-13
Unit and cost data—Mixing Department

Mixing Department	
Units	
Work in process, June 1	100,000
Direct materials: 100% complete	
Conversion costs: 70% complete	
Units started into production during June	800,000
Units completed and transferred out to Baking Department	700,000
Work in process, June 30	200,000
Direct materials: 100% complete	
Conversion costs: 60% complete	
Costs	
Work in process, June 1	
Direct materials: 100% complete	$ 50,000
Conversion costs: 70% complete	35,000
Cost of work in process, June 1	$ 85,000
Costs incurred during production in June	
Direct materials	$400,000
Conversion costs	170,000
Costs incurred in June	$570,000

Compute the Physical Unit Flow (Step 1)

Physical units are the actual units to be accounted for during a period, irrespective of any work performed. To keep track of these units, add the units started (or transferred) into production during the period to the units in process at the beginning of the period. This amount is referred to as the **total units to be accounted for**.

The total units then are accounted for by the output of the period. The output consists of units transferred out during the period and any units in process at the end of the period. This amount is referred to as the **total units accounted for**. Illustration 17-14 shows the flow of physical units for Kellogg's Mixing Department for the month of June.

Illustration 17-14
Physical unit flow—Mixing Department

Mixing Department	
	Physical Units
Units to be accounted for	
Work in process, June 1	100,000
Started (transferred) into production	800,000
Total units	**900,000**
Units accounted for	
Completed and transferred out	700,000
Work in process, June 30	200,000
Total units	**900,000**

The records indicate that the Mixing Department must account for 900,000 units. Of this sum, 700,000 units were transferred to the Baking Department and 200,000 units were still in process.

Compute the Equivalent Units of Production (Step 2)

Once the physical flow of the units is established, Kellogg must measure the Mixing Department's productivity in terms of equivalent units of production. The Mixing Department adds materials at the beginning of the process, and it incurs conversion costs uniformly during the process. Thus, we need two computations of equivalent units: one for materials and one for conversion costs. The equivalent unit computation is as follows.

Helpful Hint
Materials are not always added at the beginning of the process. For example, materials are sometimes added uniformly during the process.

Illustration 17-15
Computation of equivalent units—Mixing Department

| | Equivalent Units | |
	Materials	Conversion Costs
Units transferred out	700,000	700,000
Work in process, June 30		
200,000 × 100%	200,000	
200,000 × 60%		120,000
Total equivalent units	900,000	820,000

Helpful Hint
Remember that we ignore the beginning work in process in this computation.

Compute Unit Production Costs (Step 3)

Armed with the knowledge of the equivalent units of production, we can now compute the unit production costs. **Unit production costs** are costs expressed in terms of equivalent units of production. When equivalent units of production are different for materials and conversion costs, we compute three unit costs: (1) materials, (2) conversion, and (3) total manufacturing.

The computation of total materials cost related to Eggo® Waffles is as follows.

Illustration 17-16
Total materials cost computation

Work in process, June 1	
Direct materials cost	$ 50,000
Costs added to production during June	
Direct materials cost	400,000
Total materials cost	$450,000

The computation of unit materials cost is as follows.

Illustration 17-17
Unit materials cost computation

Total Materials Cost	÷	Equivalent Units of Materials	=	Unit Materials Cost
$450,000	÷	900,000	=	$0.50

Illustration 17-18 shows the computation of total conversion costs.

Illustration 17-18
Total conversion costs computation

Work in process, June 1	
Conversion costs	$ 35,000
Costs added to production during June	
Conversion costs	170,000
Total conversion costs	$205,000

The computation of unit conversion cost is as follows.

Illustration 17-19
Unit conversion cost computation

Total Conversion Costs	÷	Equivalent Units of Conversion Costs	=	Unit Conversion Cost
$205,000	÷	820,000	=	$0.25

Total manufacturing cost per unit is therefore computed as shown in Illustration 17-20.

Illustration 17-20
Total manufacturing cost per unit

Unit Materials Cost	+	Unit Conversion Cost	=	Total Manufacturing Cost per Unit
$0.50	+	$0.25	=	$0.75

Prepare a Cost Reconciliation Schedule (Step 4)

We are now ready to determine the cost of goods transferred out of the Mixing Department to the Baking Department and the costs in ending work in process. Kellogg charged total costs of $655,000 to the Mixing Department in June, calculated as follows.

Illustration 17-21
Costs charged to Mixing Department

Costs to be accounted for	
Work in process, June 1	$ 85,000
Started into production	570,000
Total costs	**$655,000**

The company then prepares a cost reconciliation schedule to assign these costs to (a) units transferred out to the Baking Department and (b) ending work in process.

Illustration 17-22
Cost reconciliation schedule—Mixing Department

Mixing Department Cost Reconciliation Schedule		
Costs accounted for		
Transferred out (700,000 × $0.75)		$ 525,000
Work in process, June 30		
Materials (200,000 × $0.50)	$100,000	
Conversion costs (120,000 × $0.25)	30,000	130,000
Total costs		**$655,000**

Kellogg uses the total manufacturing cost per unit, $0.75, in costing the **units completed** and transferred to the Baking Department. In contrast, the unit cost of materials and the unit cost of conversion are needed in costing **units in process**. The **cost reconciliation schedule** shows that the total costs accounted for (Illustration 17-22) equal the total costs to be accounted for (Illustration 17-21).

Preparing the Production Cost Report

At this point, Kellogg is ready to prepare the production cost report for the Mixing Department. As indicated earlier, this report is an internal document for management that shows production quantity and cost data for a production department.

LEARNING OBJECTIVE 7

Prepare a production cost report.

There are four steps in preparing a production cost report:

1. Compute the physical unit flow.
2. Compute the equivalent units of production.
3. Compute unit production costs.
4. Prepare a cost reconciliation schedule.

Illustration 17-23 shows the production cost report for the Mixing Department. The report identifies the four steps.

Illustration 17-23
Production cost report

Mixing Department.xls				
Home Insert Page Layout Formulas Data Review View				
P18 fx				
A	B	C	D	E
	Mixing Department			
	Production Cost Report			
	For the Month Ended June 30, 2014			
		Equivalent Units		
	Physical Units	Materials	Conversion Costs	
6 **QUANTITIES**	Step 1	Step 2		
7 Units to be accounted for				
8 Work in process, June 1	100,000			
9 Started into production	800,000			
10 Total units	900,000			
11 Units accounted for				
12 Transferred out	700,000	700,000	700,000	
13 Work in process, June 30	200,000	200,000	120,000	(200,000 × 60%)
14 Total units	900,000	900,000	820,000	
15 **COSTS**				
16 Unit costs Step 3		Materials	Conversion Costs	Total
17 Total cost	(a)	$450,000	$205,000	$655,000
18 Equivalent units	(b)	900,000	820,000	
19 Unit costs [(a) ÷ (b)]		$0.50	$0.25	$0.75
20 Costs to be accounted for				
21 Work in process, June 1				$85,000
22 Started into production				570,000
23 Total costs				$655,000
24 **Cost Reconciliation Schedule** Step 4				
25 Costs accounted for				
26 Transferred out (700,000 × $0.75)				$525,000
27 Work in process, June 30				
28 Materials (200,000 × $0.50)			$100,000	
29 Conversion costs (120,000 × $0.25)			30,000	130,000
30 Total costs				$655,000
31				

Production cost reports provide a basis for evaluating the productivity of a department. In addition, managers can use the cost data to assess whether unit costs and total costs are reasonable. By comparing the quantity and cost data with predetermined goals, top management can also judge whether current performance is meeting planned objectives.

> DO IT!

Cost Reconciliation Schedule

In March, Rodayo Manufacturing had the following unit production costs: materials $6 and conversion costs $9. On March 1, it had zero work in process. During March, Rodayo transferred out 12,000 units. As of March 31, 800 units that were 25% complete as to conversion costs and 100% complete as to materials were in ending work in process. Assign the costs to the units transferred out and in process.

Solution

The assignment of costs is as follows.

Costs accounted for		
Transferred out (12,000 × $15)		$180,000
Work in process, March 31		
Materials (800 × $6)	$4,800	
Conversion costs (200ª × $9)	1,800	6,600
Total costs		$186,600

ª800 × 25%

Action Plan

✔ Assign the total manufacturing cost of $15 per unit to the 12,000 units transferred out.

✔ Assign the materials cost and conversion costs based on equivalent units of production to units in ending work in process.

Related exercise material: **BE17-4, BE17-6, BE17-7, BE17-8, BE17-9, BE17-10, E17-5, E17-6, E17-8, E17-9, E17-10, E17-11, E17-14, E17-15, and DO IT! 17-4.**

 The Navigator

Costing Systems—Final Comments

Companies often use a combination of a process cost and a job order cost system. Called **operations costing**, this hybrid system is similar to process costing in its assumption that standardized methods are used to manufacture the product. At the same time, the product may have some customized, individual features that require the use of a job order cost system.

Consider, for example, the automobile manufacturer Ford Motor Company. Each vehicle at a given plant goes through the same assembly line, but Ford uses different materials (such as seat coverings, paint, and tinted glass) for different vehicles. Similarly, Kellogg's Pop-Tarts® toaster pastries go through numerous standardized processes—mixing, filling, baking, frosting, and packaging. The pastry dough, though, comes in different flavors—plain, chocolate, and graham—and fillings include Smucker's® real fruit, chocolate fudge, vanilla creme, brown sugar cinnamon, and s'mores.

A cost-benefit trade-off occurs as a company decides which costing system to use. A job order cost system, for example, provides detailed information related to the cost of the product. Because each job has its own distinguishing characteristics, the system can provide an accurate cost per job. This information is useful in controlling costs and pricing products. However, the cost of implementing a job order cost system is often expensive because of the accounting costs involved.

On the other hand, for a company like Intel, which makes computer chips, is there a benefit in knowing whether the cost of the one-hundredth chip produced is different from the one-thousandth chip produced? Probably not. An average cost of the product will suffice for control and pricing purposes.

In summary, when deciding to use one of these systems, or a combination system, a company must weigh the costs of implementing the system against the benefits from the additional information provided.

> Comprehensive **DO IT!**

Karlene Industries produces plastic ice cube trays in two processes: heating and stamping. All materials are added at the beginning of the Heating Department process. Karlene uses the weighted-average method to compute equivalent units.

On November 1, the Heating Department had in process 1,000 trays that were 70% complete. During November, it started into production 12,000 trays. On November 30, 2014, 2,000 trays that were 60% complete were in process.

The following cost information for the Heating Department was also available.

Work in process, November 1:		Costs incurred in November:	
Materials	$ 640	Material	$3,000
Conversion costs	360	Labor	2,300
Cost of work in process, Nov. 1	$1,000	Overhead	4,050

Instructions

(a) Prepare a production cost report for the Heating Department for the month of November 2014, using the weighted-average method.

(b) Journalize the transfer of costs to the Stamping Department.

Solution to Comprehensive **DO IT!**

Action Plan

✔ Compute the physical unit flow—that is, the total units to be accounted for.

✔ Compute the equivalent units of production.

✔ Compute the unit production costs, expressed in terms of equivalent units of production.

✔ Prepare a cost reconciliation schedule, which shows that the total costs accounted for equal the total costs to be accounted for.

(a)

Karlene Industries
Heating Department
Production Cost Report
For the Month Ended November 30, 2014

	Physical Units	Equivalent Units	
		Materials	Conversion Costs
Quantities	Step 1	Step 2	
Units to be accounted for			
Work in process, November 1	1,000		
Started into production	12,000		
Total units	13,000		
Units accounted for			
Transferred out	11,000	11,000	11,000
Work in process, November 30	2,000	2,000	1,200
Total units	13,000	13,000	12,200

Costs

Unit costs Step 3		Materials	Conversion Costs	Total
Total cost	(a)	$ 3,640*	$ 6,710**	$10,350
Equivalent units	(b)	13,000	12,200	
Unit costs [(a) ÷ (b)]		$0.28	$0.55	$0.83

Costs to be accounted for	
Work in process, November 1	$ 1,000
Started into production	9,350
Total costs	$10,350

*$640 + $3,000
**$360 + $2,300 + $4,050

Cost Reconciliation Schedule Step 4

Costs accounted for		
Transferred out (11,000 × $0.83)		$ 9,130
Work in process, November 30		
Materials (2,000 × $0.28)	$560	
Conversion costs (1,200 × $0.55)	660	1,220
Total costs		$10,350

(b)	Work in Process—Stamping	9,130	
	Work in Process—Heating		9,130
	(To record transfer of units to the Stamping Department)		

SUMMARY OF LEARNING OBJECTIVES

1 Understand who uses process cost systems. Companies that mass-produce similar products in a continuous fashion use process cost systems. Once production begins, it continues until the finished product emerges. Each unit of finished product is indistinguishable from every other unit.

2 Explain the similarities and differences between job order cost and process cost systems. Job order cost systems are similar to process cost systems in three ways: (1) Both systems track the same cost elements—direct materials, direct labor, and manufacturing overhead. (2) Both accumulate costs in the same accounts—Raw Materials Inventory, Factory Labor, and Manufacturing Overhead. (3) Both assign accumulated costs to the same accounts—Work in Process, Finished Goods Inventory, and Cost of Goods Sold. However, the method of assigning costs differs significantly.

There are four main differences between the two cost systems: (1) A process cost system uses separate accounts for each department or manufacturing process, rather than only one work in process account used in a job order cost system. (2) A process cost system summarizes costs in a production cost report for each department. A job order cost system charges costs to individual jobs and summarizes them in a job cost sheet. (3) Costs are totaled at the end of a time period in

a process cost system, but at the completion of a job in a job order cost system. (4) A process cost system calculates unit cost as: Total manufacturing costs for the period ÷ Units produced during the period. A job order cost system calculates unit cost as: Total cost per job ÷ Units produced.

3 Explain the flow of costs in a process cost system. A process cost system assigns manufacturing costs for raw materials, labor, and overhead to work in process accounts for various departments or manufacturing processes. It transfers the costs of partially completed units from one department to another as those units move through the manufacturing process. The system transfers the costs of completed work to Finished Goods Inventory. Finally, when inventory is sold, the system transfers the costs to Cost of Goods Sold.

4 Make the journal entries to assign manufacturing costs in a process cost system. Entries to assign the costs of raw materials, labor, and overhead consist of a credit to Raw Materials Inventory, Factory Labor, and Manufacturing Overhead, and a debit to Work in Process for each department. Entries to record the cost of goods transferred to another department are a credit to Work in Process for the department whose work is finished and a debit to the department to which the goods are transferred. The entry to record units completed and transferred to the warehouse is a credit to Work in Process for the department whose work is finished and a debit to Finished Goods Inventory. The entry to record the sale of goods is a credit to Finished Goods Inventory and a debit to Cost of Goods Sold.

5 Compute equivalent units. Equivalent units of production measure work done during a period, expressed in fully completed units. Companies use this measure to determine the cost per unit of completed product. Equivalent units are the sum of units completed and transferred out plus equivalent units of ending work in process.

6 Explain the four steps necessary to prepare a production cost report. The four steps to complete a production

cost report are: (1) Compute the physical unit flow—that is, the total units to be accounted for. (2) Compute the equivalent units of production. (3) Compute the unit production costs, expressed in terms of equivalent units of production. (4) Prepare a cost reconciliation schedule, which shows that the total costs accounted for equal the total costs to be accounted for.

7 Prepare a production cost report. The production cost report contains both quantity and cost data for a production department. There are four sections in the report: (1) number of physical units, (2) equivalent units determination, (3) unit costs, and (4) cost reconciliation schedule.

APPENDIX 17A FIFO METHOD

In this chapter, we demonstrated the weighted-average method of computing equivalent units. Some companies use a different method, referred to as the **first-in, first-out (FIFO) method**, to compute equivalent units. The purpose of this appendix is to illustrate how companies use the FIFO method to prepare a production cost report.

LEARNING OBJECTIVE 8

Compute equivalent units using the FIFO method.

Equivalent Units Under FIFO

Under the FIFO method, companies compute equivalent units on a first-in, first-out basis. Some companies favor the FIFO method because the FIFO cost assumption usually corresponds to the actual physical flow of the goods. Under the FIFO method, companies therefore assume that the beginning work in process is completed before new work is started.

Using the FIFO method, equivalent units are the sum of the work performed to:

1. Finish the units of beginning work in process inventory.

2. Complete the units started into production during the period (referred to as the **units started and completed**).

3. Start, but only partially complete, the units in ending work in process inventory.

Normally, in a process cost system, some units will always be in process at both the beginning and end of the period.

ILLUSTRATION

Illustration 17A-1 shows the physical flow of units for the Assembly Department of Shutters Inc. In addition, it indicates the degree of completion of the work in process accounts in regard to conversion costs.

Assembly Department	Physical Units
Units to be accounted for	
Work in process, June 1 (40% complete)	500
Started (transferred) into production	8,000
Total units	8,500
Units accounted for	
Completed and transferred out	8,100
Work in process, June 30 (75% complete)	400
Total units	8,500

Illustration 17A-1
Physical unit flow—Assembly Department

In Illustration 17A-1, the units completed and transferred out (8,100) plus the units in ending work in process (400) equal the total units to be accounted for (8,500). Using FIFO, we then compute equivalent units as follows.

1. The 500 units of beginning work in process were 40% complete. Thus, 300 equivalent units (60% × 500 units) were required to complete the beginning inventory.

2. The units started and completed during the current month are the units transferred out minus the units in beginning work in process. For the Assembly Department, units started and completed are 7,600 (8,100 − 500).

3. The 400 units of ending work in process were 75% complete. Thus, equivalent units were 300 (75% × 400).

Equivalent units for the Assembly Department are 8,200, computed as follows.

Illustration 17A-2
Computation of equivalent units—FIFO method

Assembly Department			
Production Data	**Physical Units**	**Work Added This Period**	**Equivalent Units**
Work in process, June 1	500	60%	300
Started and completed	7,600	100%	7,600
Work in process, June 30	400	75%	300
Total	8,500		8,200

Comprehensive Example

To provide a complete illustration of the FIFO method, we will use the data for the Mixing Department at Kellogg Company for the month of June, as shown in Illustration 17A-3.

Illustration 17A-3
Unit and cost data—Mixing Department

Mixing Department	
Units	
Work in process, June 1	100,000
Direct materials: 100% complete	
Conversion costs: 70% complete	
Units started into production during June	800,000
Units completed and transferred out to Baking Department	700,000
Work in process, June 30	200,000
Direct materials: 100% complete	
Conversion costs: 60% complete	
Costs	
Work in process, June 1	
Direct materials: 100% complete	$ 50,000
Conversion costs: 70% complete	35,000
Cost of work in process, June 1	$ 85,000
Costs incurred during production in June	
Direct materials	$400,000
Conversion costs	170,000
Costs incurred in June	$570,000

COMPUTE THE PHYSICAL UNIT FLOW (STEP 1)

Illustration 17A-4 shows the physical flow of units for Kellogg for the month of June for the Mixing Department.

Illustration 17A-4
Physical unit flow—Mixing Department

Mixing Department	
	Physical Units
Units to be accounted for	
Work in process, June 1	100,000
Started (transferred) into production	800,000
Total units	900,000
Units accounted for	
Completed and transferred out	700,000
Work in process, June 30	200,000
Total units	900,000

Under the FIFO method, companies often expand the physical units schedule, as shown in Illustration 17A-5 to explain the transferred-out section. As a result, this section reports the beginning work in process and the units started and completed. These two items further explain the completed and transferred-out section.

Illustration 17A-5
Physical unit flow (FIFO)—
Mixing Department

Mixing Department	
	Physical Units
Units to be accounted for	
Work in process, June 1	100,000
Started (transferred) into production	800,000
Total units	900,000
Units accounted for	
Completed and transferred out	
Work in process, June 1	100,000
Started and completed	600,000
	700,000
Work in process, June 30	200,000
Total units	900,000

The records indicate that the Mixing Department must account for 900,000 units. Of this sum, 700,000 units were transferred to the Baking Department and 200,000 units were still in process.

COMPUTE EQUIVALENT UNITS OF PRODUCTION (STEP 2)

As with the method presented in the chapter, once they determine the physical flow of the units, companies need to determine equivalent units of production. The Mixing Department adds materials at the beginning of the process, and it incurs conversion costs uniformly during the process. Thus, Kellogg must make two computations of equivalent units: one for materials and one for conversion costs.

EQUIVALENT UNITS FOR MATERIALS Since Kellogg adds materials at the beginning of the process, no additional materials costs are required to complete the beginning work in process. In addition, 100% of the materials costs has been

Helpful Hint
Materials are not always added at the beginning of the process. For example, companies sometimes add materials uniformly during the process.

incurred on the ending work in process. Thus, the computation of equivalent units for materials is as follows.

Illustration 17A-6
Computation of equivalent
units—materials

		Mixing Department—Materials	
Production Data	**Physical Units**	**Materials Added This Period**	**Equivalent Units**
Work in process, June 1	100,000	–0–	–0–
Started and finished	600,000	100%	600,000
Work in process, June 30	200,000	100%	200,000
Total	900,000		800,000

EQUIVALENT UNITS FOR CONVERSION COSTS The 100,000 units of beginning work in process were 70% complete in terms of conversion costs. Thus, the Mixing Department required 30,000 equivalent units (30% × 100,000 units) of conversion costs to complete the beginning inventory. In addition, the 200,000 units of ending work in process were 60% complete in terms of conversion costs. Thus, the equivalent units for conversion costs is 750,000, computed as follows.

Illustration 17A-7
Computation of equivalent
units—conversion costs

		Mixing Department—Conversion Costs	
Production Data	**Physical Units**	**Work Added This Period**	**Equivalent Units**
Work in process, June 1	100,000	30%	30,000
Started and finished	600,000	100%	600,000
Work in process, June 30	200,000	60%	120,000
Total	900,000		750,000

COMPUTE UNIT PRODUCTION COSTS (STEP 3)

Armed with the knowledge of the equivalent units of production, Kellogg can now compute the unit production costs. Unit production costs are costs expressed in terms of equivalent units of production. When equivalent units of production are different for materials and conversion costs, companies compute three unit costs: (1) materials, (2) conversion, and (3) total manufacturing.

Under the FIFO method, the unit costs of production are based entirely on the production costs incurred during the month. Thus, the costs in the beginning work in process are not relevant, because they were incurred on work done in the preceding month. As Illustration 17A-3 (page 872) indicated, the costs incurred during production in June were:

Illustration 17A-8
Costs incurred during
production in June

Direct materials	$400,000
Conversion costs	170,000
Total costs	$570,000

Illustration 17A-9 shows the computation of unit materials cost, unit conversion costs, and total unit cost related to Eggo® Waffles.

(1)	Total Materials Cost	÷	Equivalent Units of Materials	=	Unit Materials Cost
	$400,000	÷	800,000	=	$0.50
(2)	Total Conversion Costs	÷	Equivalent Units of Conversion Costs	=	Unit Conversion Cost
	$170,000	÷	750,000	=	$0.227 (rounded)*
(3)	Unit Materials Cost	+	Unit Conversion Cost	=	Total Manufacturing Cost per Unit
	$0.50	+	$0.227	=	$0.727

For homework problems, round unit costs to three decimal places.

Illustration 17A-9
Unit cost formulas and computations—Mixing Department

As shown, the unit costs are $0.50 for materials, $0.227 for conversion costs, and $0.727 for total manufacturing costs.

PREPARE A COST RECONCILIATION SCHEDULE (STEP 4)

Kellogg is now ready to determine the cost of goods transferred out of the Mixing Department to the Baking Department and the costs in ending work in process. The total costs charged to the Mixing Department in June are $655,000, calculated as follows.

Illustration 17A-10
Costs charged to Mixing Department

Costs to be accounted for	
Work in process, June 1	$ 85,000
Started into production	570,000
Total costs	$655,000

Kellogg next prepares a cost reconciliation to assign these costs to (1) units transferred out to the Baking Department and (2) ending work in process. Under the FIFO method, the first goods to be completed during the period are the units in beginning work in process. Thus, the cost of the beginning work in process is always assigned to the goods transferred to the next department (or finished goods, if processing is complete). Under the FIFO method, ending work in process also will be assigned only the production costs incurred in the current period. Illustration 17A-11 shows a cost reconciliation schedule for the Mixing Department.

Illustration 17A-11
Cost reconciliation report

Mixing Department Cost Reconciliation Schedule		
Costs accounted for		
Transferred out		
Work in process, June 1		$ 85,000
Costs to complete beginning work in process		
Conversion costs (30,000 × $0.227)		6,810
Total costs		91,810
Units started and completed (600,000 × $0.727)		435,950*
Total costs transferred out		527,760
Work in process, June 30		
Materials (200,000 × $0.50)	$100,000	
Conversion costs (120,000 × $0.227)	27,240	127,240
Total costs		$655,000

*Any rounding errors should be adjusted in the "Units started and completed" calculation.

As you can see, the total costs accounted for ($655,000 from Illustration 17A-11) equal the total costs to be accounted for ($655,000 from Illustration 17A-10).

PREPARING THE PRODUCTION COST REPORT

At this point, Kellogg is ready to prepare the production cost report for the Mixing Department. This report is an internal document for management that shows production quantity and cost data for a production department.

As discussed on page 864, there are four steps in preparing a production cost report:

1. Compute the physical unit flow.
2. Compute the equivalent units of production.
3. Compute unit production costs.
4. Prepare a cost reconciliation schedule.

Illustration 17A-12 shows the production cost report for the Mixing Department, with the four steps identified in the report.

As indicated in the chapter, production cost reports provide a basis for evaluating the productivity of a department. In addition, managers can use the cost data to assess whether unit costs and total costs are reasonable. By comparing the quantity and cost data with predetermined goals, top management can also judge whether current performance is meeting planned objectives.

FIFO and Weighted-Average

The weighted-average method of computing equivalent units has **one major advantage**: It is simple to understand and apply. In cases where prices do not fluctuate significantly from period to period, the weighted-average method will be very similar to the FIFO method. In addition, companies that have been using just-in-time procedures effectively for inventory control purposes will have minimal inventory balances, and therefore differences between the weighted-average and the FIFO methods will not be material.

Conceptually, the FIFO method is superior to the weighted-average method because it measures **current performance** using only costs incurred in the current period. Managers are, therefore, not held responsible for costs from prior periods over which they may not have had control. In addition, the FIFO method **provides current cost information**, which the company can use to establish **more accurate pricing strategies** for goods manufactured and sold in the current period.

Helpful Hint
What are the two self-checks in the report? Answer: (1) Total physical units accounted for must equal the total units to be accounted for. (2) Total costs accounted for must equal the total costs to be accounted for.

		A	B	C	D	E	

Mixing Department.xls

Home Insert Page Layout Formulas Data Review View

P18

	A	B	C	D	E
1	**Mixing Department**				
2	**Production Cost Report**				
3	**For the Month Ended June 30, 2014**				
4			**Equivalent Units**		
5		Physical Units	Materials	Conversion Costs	
6	**QUANTITIES**	Step 1	Step 2		
7	Units to be accounted for				
8	Work in process (WIP), June 1	100,000			
9	Started into production	800,000			
10	Total units	900,000			
11	Units accounted for				
12	Completed and transferred out				
13	Work in process, June 1	100,000	0	30,000	
14	Started and completed	600,000	600,000	600,000	
15	Work in process, June 30	200,000	200,000	120,000	
16	Total units	900,000	800,000	750,000	
17	**COSTS**				
18	Unit costs Step 3		Materials	Conversion Costs	Total
19	Costs in June (excluding beginning WIP) (a)		$400,000	$170,000	$570,000
20	Equivalent units (b)		800,000	750,000	
21	Unit costs [(a) ÷ (b)]		$0.50	$0.227	$0.727
22	Costs to be accounted for				
23	Work in process, June 1				$85,000
24	Started into production				570,000
25	Total costs				$655,000
26	**Cost Reconciliation Schedule** Step 4				
27	Costs accounted for				
28	Transferred out				
29	Work in process, June 1				$85,000
30	Costs to complete beginning work in process				
31	Conversion costs (30,000 × $0.227)				6,810
32	Total costs				91,810
33	Units started and completed (600,000 × $0.727)*				435,950
34	Total costs transferred out				527,760
35	Work in process, June 30				
36	Materials (200,000 × $0.50)			$100,000	
37	Conversions costs (120,000 × $0.227)			27,240	127,240
38	Total costs				$655,000
39	*Any rounding errors should be adjusted in the "Units started and completed"				

Illustration 17A-12
Production cost report—
FIFO method

SUMMARY OF LEARNING OBJECTIVE FOR APPENDIX 17A

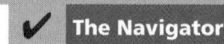 ✔ **The Navigator**

8 Compute equivalent units using the FIFO method. Equivalent units under the FIFO method are the sum of the work performed to: (1) Finish the units of beginning work in process inventory, if any; (2) complete the units started into production during the period; and (3) start, but only partially complete, the units in ending work in process inventory.

GLOSSARY

Conversion costs The sum of labor costs and overhead costs. (p. 861).

Cost reconciliation schedule A schedule that shows that the total costs accounted for equal the total costs to be accounted for. (p. 866).

Equivalent units of production A measure of the work done during the period, expressed in fully completed units. (p. 860).

Operations costing A combination of a process cost and a job order cost system, in which products are manufactured primarily by standardized methods, with some customization. (p. 868).

Physical units Actual units to be accounted for during a period, irrespective of any work performed. (p. 864).

Process cost system An accounting system used to apply costs to similar products that are mass-produced in a continuous fashion. (p. 854).

Production cost report An internal report for management that shows both production quantity and cost data for a production department. (p. 863).

Total units (costs) accounted for The sum of the units (costs) transferred out during the period plus the units (costs) in process at the end of the period. (p. 864).

Total units (costs) to be accounted for The sum of the units (costs) started (or transferred) into production during the period plus the units (costs) in process at the beginning of the period. (p. 864).

Unit production costs Costs expressed in terms of equivalent units of production. (p. 865).

Weighted-average method Method of computing equivalent units of production which considers the degree of completion (weighting) of the units completed and transferred out and the ending work in process. (p. 861).

 Self-Test, Brief Exercises, Exercises, Problem Set A, and many more resources are available for practice in WileyPLUS.

Note: All asterisked Questions, Exercises, and Problems relate to material in the appendix to the chapter.

SELF-TEST QUESTIONS

Answers are at the end of the chapter.

(LO 1) **1.** Which of the following items is *not* characteristic of a process cost system?
   (a) Once production begins, it continues until the finished product emerges.
   (b) The products produced are heterogeneous in nature.
   (c) The focus is on continually producing homogeneous products.
   (d) When the finished product emerges, all units have precisely the same amount of materials, labor, and overhead.

2. Indicate which of the following statements is *not* (LO 2) correct.
   (a) Both a job order and a process cost system track the same three manufacturing cost elements—direct materials, direct labor, and manufacturing overhead.
   (b) A job order cost system uses only one work in process account, whereas a process cost system uses multiple work in process accounts.
   (c) Manufacturing costs are accumulated the same way in a job order and in a process cost system.
   (d) Manufacturing costs are assigned the same way in a job order and in a process cost system.

(LO 3) **3.** In a process cost system, the flow of costs is:
  (a) work in process, cost of goods sold, finished goods.
  (b) finished goods, work in process, cost of goods sold.
  (c) finished goods, cost of goods sold, work in process.
  (d) work in process, finished goods, cost of goods sold.

(LO 4) **4.** In making journal entries to assign raw materials costs, a company using process costing:
  (a) debits Finished Goods Inventory.
  (b) often debits two or more work in process accounts.
  (c) generally credits two or more work in process accounts.
  (d) credits Finished Goods Inventory.

(LO 4) **5.** In a process cost system, manufacturing overhead:
  (a) is assigned to finished goods at the end of each accounting period.
  (b) is assigned to a work in process account for each job as the job is completed.
  (c) is assigned to a work in process account for each production department on the basis of a predetermined overhead rate.
  (d) is assigned to a work in process account for each production department as overhead costs are incurred.

(LO 5) **6.** Conversion costs are the sum of:
  (a) fixed and variable overhead costs.
  (b) labor costs and overhead costs.
  (c) direct material costs and overhead costs.
  (d) direct labor and indirect labor costs.

(LO 5) **7.** The Mixing Department's output during the period consists of 20,000 units completed and transferred out, and 5,000 units in ending work in process 60% complete as to materials and conversion costs. Beginning inventory is 1,000 units, 40% complete as to materials and conversion costs. The equivalent units of production are:
  (a) 22,600.
  (b) 23,000.
  (c) 24,000.
  (d) 25,000.

(LO 6) **8.** In RYZ Company, there are zero units in beginning work in process, 7,000 units started into production, and 500 units in ending work in process 20% completed. The physical units to be accounted for are:
  (a) 7,000.
  (b) 7,360.
  (c) 7,500.
  (d) 7,340.

(LO 6) **9.** Mora Company has 2,000 units in beginning work in process, 20% complete as to conversion costs, 23,000 units transferred out to finished goods, and 3,000 units in ending work in process $33\frac{1}{3}\%$ complete as to conversion costs.

The beginning and ending inventory is fully complete as to materials costs. Equivalent units for materials and conversion costs are, respectively:
  (a) 22,000, 24,000.
  (b) 24,000, 26,000.
  (c) 26,000, 24,000.
  (d) 26,000, 26,000.

(LO 6) **10.** Fortner Company has no beginning work in process; 9,000 units are transferred out and 3,000 units in ending work in process are one-third finished as to conversion costs and fully complete as to materials cost. If total materials cost is $60,000, the unit materials cost is:
  (a) $5.00.
  (b) $5.45 rounded.
  (c) $6.00.
  (d) No correct answer is given.

(LO 6) **11.** Largo Company has unit costs of $10 for materials and $30 for conversion costs. If there are 2,500 units in ending work in process, 40% complete as to conversion costs, and fully complete as to materials cost, the total cost assignable to the ending work in process inventory is:
  (a) $45,000.
  (b) $55,000.
  (c) $75,000.
  (d) $100,000.

(LO 7) **12.** A production cost report:
  (a) is an external report.
  (b) shows both the production quantity and cost data related to a department.
  (c) shows equivalent units of production but not physical units.
  (d) contains six sections.

(LO 7) **13.** In a production cost report, units to be accounted for are calculated as:
  (a) Units started into production + Units in ending work in process.
  (b) Units started into production − Units in beginning work in process.
  (c) Units transferred out + Units in beginning work in process.
  (d) Units started into production + Units in beginning work in process.

(LO 8) ***14.** Hollins Company uses the FIFO method to compute equivalent units. It has 2,000 units in beginning work in process, 20% complete as to conversion costs, 25,000 units started and completed, and 3,000 units in ending work in process, 30% complete as to conversion costs. All units are 100% complete as to materials. Equivalent units for materials and conversion costs are, respectively:
  (a) 28,000 and 26,600.
  (b) 28,000 and 27,500.
  (c) 27,000 and 26,200.
  (d) 27,000 and 29,600.

(LO 8) ***15.** KLM Company uses the FIFO method to compute equivalent units. It has no beginning work in process;

9,000 units are started and completed and 3,000 units in ending work in process are one-third completed. All material is added at the beginning of the process. If total materials cost is $60,000, the unit materials cost is:

(a) $5.00.
(b) $6.00.
(c) $6.67 (rounded).
(d) No correct answer given.

*16. Toney Company uses the FIFO method to compute  equivalent units. It has unit costs of $10 for materials and $30 for conversion costs. If there are 2,500 units in ending work in process, 100% complete as to materials and 40% complete as to conversion costs, the total cost assignable to the ending work in process inventory is:

(a) $45,000.   (c) $75,000.
(b) $55,000.   (d) $100,000.

Go to the book's companion website, www.wiley.com/college/weygandt, for additional Self-Test Questions.

✔ **The Navigator**

QUESTIONS

1. Identify which costing system—job order or process cost—the following companies would primarily use: (a) Quaker Oats, (b) Jif Peanut Butter, (c) Gulf Craft (luxury yachts), and (d) Warner Bros. Motion Pictures.
2. Contrast the primary focus of job order cost accounting and of process cost accounting.
3. What are the similarities between a job order and a process cost system?
4. Your roommate is confused about the features of process cost accounting. Identify and explain the distinctive features for your roommate.
5. Sam Bowyer believes there are no significant differences in the flow of costs between job order cost accounting and process cost accounting. Is Bowyer correct? Explain.
6. (a) What source documents are used in assigning (1) materials and (2) labor to production in a process cost system?
   (b) What criterion and basis are commonly used in allocating overhead to processes?
7. At Ely Company, overhead is assigned to production departments at the rate of $5 per machine hour. In July, machine hours were 3,000 in the Machining Department and 2,400 in the Assembly Department. Prepare the entry to assign overhead to production.
8. Mark Haley is uncertain about the steps used to prepare a production cost report. State the procedures that are required in the sequence in which they are performed.
9. John Harbeck is confused about computing physical units. Explain to John how physical units to be accounted for and physical units accounted for are determined.
10. What is meant by the term "equivalent units of production"?
11. How are equivalent units of production computed?
12. Coats Company had zero units of beginning work in process. During the period, 9,000 units were com-

pleted, and there were 600 units of ending work in process. What were the units started into production?
13. Sanchez Co. has zero units of beginning work in process. During the period, 12,000 units were completed, and there were 500 units of ending work in process one-fifth complete as to conversion cost and 100% complete as to materials cost. What were the equivalent units of production for (a) materials and (b) conversion costs?
14. Hindi Co. started 3,000 units during the period. Its beginning inventory is 500 units one-fourth complete as to conversion costs and 100% complete as to materials costs. Its ending inventory is 300 units one-fifth complete as to conversion costs and 100% complete as to materials costs. How many units were transferred out this period?
15. Clauss Company transfers out 14,000 units and has 2,000 units of ending work in process that are 25% complete. Materials are entered at the beginning of the process and there is no beginning work in process. Assuming unit materials costs of $3 and unit conversion costs of $5, what are the costs to be assigned to units (a) transferred out and (b) in ending work in process?
16. (a) Ann Quinn believes the production cost report is an external report for stockholders. Is Ann correct? Explain.
    (b) Identify the sections in a production cost report.
17. What purposes are served by a production cost report?
18. At Trent Company, there are 800 units of ending work in process that are 100% complete as to materials and 40% complete as to conversion costs. If the unit cost of materials is $3 and the total costs assigned to the 800 units is $6,000, what is the per unit conversion cost?
19. What is the difference between operations costing and a process cost system?
20. How does a company decide whether to use a job order or a process cost system?

*21. Soria Co. started and completed 2,000 units for the period. Its beginning inventory is 800 units 25% complete and its ending inventory is 400 units 20% complete. Soria uses the FIFO method to compute equivalent units. How many units were transferred out this period?

*22. Reyes Company transfers out 12,000 units and has 2,000 units of ending work in process that are 25% complete. Materials are entered at the beginning of the process and there is no beginning work in process. Reyes uses the FIFO method to compute equivalent units. Assuming unit materials costs of $3 and unit conversion costs of $7, what are the costs to be assigned to units (a) transferred out and (b) in ending work in process?

BRIEF EXERCISES

BE17-1 Weber Company purchases $45,000 of raw materials on account, and it incurs $60,000 of factory labor costs. Journalize the two transactions on March 31 assuming the labor costs are not paid until April.

Journalize entries for accumulating costs.

(LO 4)

BE17-2 Data for Weber Company are given in BE17-1. Supporting records show that (a) the Assembly Department used $24,000 of raw materials and $35,000 of the factory labor, and (b) the Finishing Department used the remainder. Journalize the assignment of the costs to the processing departments on March 31.

Journalize the assignment of materials and labor costs.

(LO 4)

BE17-3 Factory labor data for Weber Company are given in BE17-2. Manufacturing overhead is assigned to departments on the basis of 200% of labor costs. Journalize the assignment of overhead to the Assembly and Finishing Departments.

Journalize the assignment of overhead costs.

(LO 4)

BE17-4 Goode Company has the following production data for selected months.

Compute equivalent units of production.

(LO 5)

| | | | Ending Work in Process | |
Month	Beginning Work in Process	Units Transferred Out	Units	% Complete as to Conversion Cost
January	–0–	35,000	10,000	40%
March	–0–	40,000	8,000	75
July	–0–	45,000	16,000	25

Compute equivalent units of production for materials and conversion costs, assuming materials are entered at the beginning of the process.

BE17-5 In Lopez Company, total material costs are $36,000, and total conversion costs are $54,000. Equivalent units of production are materials 10,000 and conversion costs 12,000. Compute the unit costs for materials, conversion costs, and total manufacturing costs.

Compute unit costs of production.

(LO 6)

BE17-6 Trek Company has the following production data for April: units transferred out 40,000, and ending work in process 5,000 units that are 100% complete for materials and 40% complete for conversion costs. If unit materials cost is $4 and unit conversion cost is $7, determine the costs to be assigned to the units transferred out and the units in ending work in process.

Assign costs to units transferred out and in process.

(LO 6)

BE17-7 Production costs chargeable to the Finishing Department in June in Cascio Company are materials $16,000, labor $29,500, overhead $18,000. Equivalent units of production are materials 20,000 and conversion costs 19,000. Compute the unit costs for materials and conversion costs.

Compute unit costs.

(LO 6)

BE17-8 Data for Cascio Company are given in BE17-7. Production records indicate that 18,000 units were transferred out, and 2,000 units in ending work in process were 50% complete as to conversion cost and 100% complete as to materials. Prepare a cost reconciliation schedule.

Prepare cost reconciliation schedule.

(LO 6)

BE17-9 The Smelting Department of Mathews Company has the following production and cost data for November.

Compute equivalent units of production.

(LO 5)

Production: Beginning work in process 2,000 units that are 100% complete as to materials and 20% complete as to conversion costs; units transferred out 8,000 units; and ending work in process 7,000 units that are 100% complete as to materials and 40% complete as to conversion costs.

Compute the equivalent units of production for (a) materials and (b) conversion costs for the month of November.

Assign costs to units transferred out and in process.

(LO 8)

*BE17-10 Sanderson Company has the following production data for March: no beginning work in process, units started and completed 30,000, and ending work in process 5,000 units that are 100% complete for materials and 40% complete for conversion costs. Sanderson uses the FIFO method to compute equivalent units. If unit materials cost is $6 and unit conversion cost is $12, determine the costs to be assigned to the units transferred out and the units in ending work in process. The total costs to be assigned are $594,000.

Prepare a partial production cost report.

(LO 7, 8)

Compute unit costs.

(LO 8)

*BE17-11 Using the data in BE17-10, prepare the cost section of the production cost report for Sanderson Company.

*BE17-12 Production costs chargeable to the Finishing Department in May at Kim Company are materials $8,000, labor $20,000, overhead $18,000, and transferred-in costs $67,000. Equivalent units of production are materials 20,000 and conversion costs 19,000. Kim uses the FIFO method to compute equivalent units. Compute the unit costs for materials and conversion costs. Transferred-in costs are considered materials costs.

> DO IT! REVIEW

Compare job order and process cost systems.

(LO 1, 2)

DO IT! 17-1 Indicate whether each of the following statements is true or false.

1. Many hospitals use job order costing for small, routine medical procedures.
2. A manufacturer of computer flash drives would use a job order cost system.
3. A process cost system uses multiple work in process accounts.
4. A process cost system keeps track of costs on job cost sheets.

Assign and journalize manufacturing costs.

(LO 4)

DO IT! 17-2 Kopa Company manufactures CH-21 through two processes: Mixing and Packaging. In July, the following costs were incurred.

	Mixing	Packaging
Raw materials used	$10,000	$28,000
Factory labor costs	8,000	36,000
Manufacturing overhead costs	12,000	54,000

Units completed at a cost of $21,000 in the Mixing Department are transferred to the Packaging Department. Units completed at a cost of $106,000 in the Packaging Department are transferred to Finished Goods. Journalize the assignment of these costs to the two processes and the transfer of units as appropriate.

Compute equivalent units.

(LO 5)

DO IT! 17-3 The assembly department has the following production data for the current month.

Beginning Work in Process	Units Transferred Out	Ending Work in Process
–0–	20,000	12,000

Materials are entered at the beginning of the process. The ending work in process units are 70% complete as to conversion costs. Compute the equivalent units of production for (a) materials and (b) conversion costs.

Prepare cost reconciliation schedule.

(LO 6, 7)

DO IT! 17-4 In March, Kelly Company had the following unit production costs: materials $10 and conversion costs $8. On March 1, it had zero work in process. During March, Kelly transferred out 22,000 units. As of March 31, 4,000 units that were 40% complete as to conversion costs and 100% complete as to materials were in ending work in process.

(a) Compute the total units to be accounted for.
(b) Compute the equivalent units of production.
(c) Prepare a cost reconciliation schedule, including the costs of materials transferred out and the costs of materials in process.

EXERCISES

E17-1 Robert Mallory has prepared the following list of statements about process cost accounting.

1. Process cost systems are used to apply costs to similar products that are mass-produced in a continuous fashion.
2. A process cost system is used when each finished unit is indistinguishable from another.
3. Companies that produce soft drinks, motion pictures, and computer chips would all use process cost accounting.
4. In a process cost system, costs are tracked by individual jobs.
5. Job order costing and process costing track different manufacturing cost elements.
6. Both job order costing and process costing account for direct materials, direct labor, and manufacturing overhead.
7. Costs flow through the accounts in the same basic way for both job order costing and process costing.
8. In a process cost system, only one work in process account is used.
9. In a process cost system, costs are summarized in a job cost sheet.
10. In a process cost system, the unit cost is total manufacturing costs for the period divided by the equivalent units produced during the period.

Instructions
Identify each statement as true or false. If false, indicate how to correct the statement.

E17-2 Harrelson Company manufactures pizza sauce through two production departments: Cooking and Canning. In each process, materials and conversion costs are incurred evenly throughout the process. For the month of April, the work in process accounts show the following debits.

	Cooking	**Canning**
Beginning work in process	$ –0–	$ 4,000
Materials	21,000	9,000
Labor	8,500	7,000
Overhead	31,500	25,800
Costs transferred in		53,000

Instructions
Journalize the April transactions.

E17-3 The ledger of Custer Company has the following work in process account.

Work in Process—Painting					
5/1	Balance	3,590	5/31	Transferred out	?
5/31	Materials	5,160			
5/31	Labor	2,740			
5/31	Overhead	1,380			
5/31	Balance	?			

Production records show that there were 400 units in the beginning inventory, 30% complete, 1,400 units started, and 1,500 units transferred out. The beginning work in process had materials cost of $2,040 and conversion costs of $1,550. The units in ending inventory were 40% complete. Materials are entered at the beginning of the painting process.

Instructions
(a) How many units are in process at May 31?
(b) What is the unit materials cost for May?
(c) What is the unit conversion cost for May?
(d) What is the total cost of units transferred out in May?
(e) What is the cost of the May 31 inventory?

E17-4 Schrager Company has two production departments: Cutting and Assembly. July 1 inventories are Raw Materials $4,200, Work in Process—Cutting $2,900, Work in Process—

Assembly $10,600, and Finished Goods $31,000. During July, the following transactions occurred.

1. Purchased $62,500 of raw materials on account.
2. Incurred $60,000 of factory labor. (Credit Wages Payable.)
3. Incurred $70,000 of manufacturing overhead; $40,000 was paid and the remainder is unpaid.
4. Requisitioned materials for Cutting $15,700 and Assembly $8,900.
5. Used factory labor for Cutting $33,000 and Assembly $27,000.
6. Applied overhead at the rate of $18 per machine hour. Machine hours were Cutting 1,680 and Assembly 1,720.
7. Transferred goods costing $67,600 from the Cutting Department to the Assembly Department.
8. Transferred goods costing $134,900 from Assembly to Finished Goods.
9. Sold goods costing $150,000 for $200,000 on account.

Instructions
Journalize the transactions. (Omit explanations.)

Compute physical units and equivalent units of production.

(LO 5, 6)

E17-5 In Wayne Company, materials are entered at the beginning of each process. Work in process inventories, with the percentage of work done on conversion costs, and production data for its Sterilizing Department in selected months during 2014 are as follows.

	Beginning Work in Process		Units	Ending Work in Process	
Month	**Units**	**Conversion Cost%**	**Transferred Out**	**Units**	**Conversion Cost%**
January	–0–	—	9,000	2,000	60
March	–0–	—	12,000	3,000	30
May	–0–	—	16,000	7,000	80
July	–0–	—	10,000	1,500	40

Instructions
(a) Compute the physical units for January and May.
(b) Compute the equivalent units of production for (1) materials and (2) conversion costs for each month.

Determine equivalent units, unit costs, and assignment of costs.

(LO 5, 6)

E17-6 The Cutting Department of Cassel Company has the following production and cost data for July.

Production	Costs	
1. Transferred out 12,000 units.	Beginning work in process	$ –0–
2. Started 3,000 units that are 60%	Materials	45,000
complete as to conversion	Labor	16,200
costs and 100% complete as	Manufacturing overhead	18,300
to materials at July 31.		

Materials are entered at the beginning of the process. Conversion costs are incurred uniformly during the process.

Instructions
(a) Determine the equivalent units of production for (1) materials and (2) conversion costs.
(b) Compute unit costs and prepare a cost reconciliation schedule.

Prepare a production cost report.

(LO 5, 6, 7)

E17-7 The Sanding Department of Richards Furniture Company has the following production and manufacturing cost data for March 2014, the first month of operation.

Production: 9,000 units finished and transferred out; 3,000 units started that are 100% complete as to materials and 20% complete as to conversion costs.

Manufacturing costs: Materials $33,000; labor $24,000; overhead $36,000.

Instructions
Prepare a production cost report.

Determine equivalent units, unit costs, and assignment of costs.

(LO 5, 6)

E17-8 The Blending Department of Luongo Company has the following cost and production data for the month of April.

Costs:

Work in process, April 1
    Direct materials: 100% complete $100,000
    Conversion costs: 20% complete   70,000
      Cost of work in process, April 1 $170,000

Costs incurred during production in April
    Direct materials $ 800,000
    Conversion costs   365,000
      Costs incurred in April $1,165,000

Units transferred out totaled 17,000. Ending work in process was 1,000 units that are 100% complete as to materials and 40% complete as to conversion costs.

Instructions

(a) Compute the equivalent units of production for (1) materials and (2) conversion costs for the month of April.
(b) Compute the unit costs for the month.
(c) Determine the costs to be assigned to the units transferred out and in ending work in process.

E17-9 Kostrivas Company has gathered the following information.

Units in beginning work in process	–0–
Units started into production	40,000
Units in ending work in process	6,000
Percent complete in ending work in process:	
Conversion costs	40%
Materials	100%
Costs incurred:	
Direct materials	$72,000
Direct labor	$81,000
Overhead	$101,000

Determine equivalent units, unit costs, and assignment of costs.

(LO 5, 6)

Instructions

(a) Compute equivalent units of production for materials and for conversion costs.
(b) Determine the unit costs of production.
(c) Show the assignment of costs to units transferred out and in process.

E17-10 Overton Company has gathered the following information.

Units in beginning work in process	20,000
Units started into production	164,000
Units in ending work in process	24,000
Percent complete in ending work in process:	
Conversion costs	60%
Materials	100%
Costs incurred:	
Direct materials	$101,200
Direct labor	$164,800
Overhead	$184,000

Determine equivalent units, unit costs, and assignment of costs.

(LO 5, 6)

Instructions

(a) Compute equivalent units of production for materials and for conversion costs.
(b) Determine the unit costs of production.
(c) Show the assignment of costs to units transferred out and in process.

E17-11 The Polishing Department of Harbin Company has the following production and manufacturing cost data for September. Materials are entered at the beginning of the process.

Production: Beginning inventory 1,600 units that are 100% complete as to materials and 30% complete as to conversion costs; units started during the period are 38,400; ending inventory of 5,000 units 10% complete as to conversion costs.

Compute equivalent units, unit costs, and costs assigned.

(LO 5, 6)

Manufacturing costs: Beginning inventory costs, comprised of $20,000 of materials and $43,180 of conversion costs; materials costs added in Polishing during the month, $177,200; labor and overhead applied in Polishing during the month, $125,680 and $257,140, respectively.

Instructions

(a) Compute the equivalent units of production for materials and conversion costs for the month of September.
(b) Compute the unit costs for materials and conversion costs for the month.
(c) Determine the costs to be assigned to the units transferred out and in process.

Explain the production cost report.

(LO 7)

E17-12 David Skaros has recently been promoted to production manager, and so he has just started to receive various managerial reports. One of the reports he has received is the production cost report that you prepared. It showed that his department had 2,000 equivalent units in ending inventory. His department has had a history of not keeping enough inventory on hand to meet demand. He has come to you, very angry, and wants to know why you credited him with only 2,000 units when he knows he had at least twice that many on hand.

Instructions

 Explain to him why his production cost report showed only 2,000 equivalent units in ending inventory. Write an informal memo. Be kind and explain very clearly why he is mistaken.

Prepare a production cost report.

(LO 5, 6, 7)

E17-13 The Welding Department of Thorpe Company has the following production and manufacturing cost data for February 2014. All materials are added at the beginning of the process.

Manufacturing Costs			Production Data	
Beginning work in process			Beginning work in process	15,000 units
Materials	$18,000			1/10 complete
Conversion costs	14,175	$ 32,175	Units transferred out	49,000
Materials		180,000	Units started	45,000
Labor		52,380	Ending work in process	11,000 units
Overhead		61,445		1/5 complete

Instructions

Prepare a production cost report for the Welding Department for the month of February.

Compute physical units and equivalent units of production.

(LO 5, 6)

E17-14 Remington Shipping, Inc. is contemplating the use of process costing to track the costs of its operations. The operation consists of three segments (departments): receiving, shipping, and delivery. Containers are received at Remington's docks and sorted according to the ship they will be carried on. The containers are loaded onto a ship, which carries them to the appropriate port of destination. The containers are then off-loaded and delivered to the receiving company.

Remington Shipping wants to begin using process costing in the shipping department. Direct materials represent the fuel costs to run the ship, and "Containers in transit" represents work in process. Listed below is information about the shipping department's first month's activity.

Containers in transit, April 1	0
Containers loaded	1,200
Containers in transit, April 30	350, 40% of direct materials and 20% of conversion costs

Instructions

(a) Determine the physical flow of containers for the month.
(b) Calculate the equivalent units for direct materials and conversion costs.

Determine equivalent units, unit costs, and assignment of costs.

(LO 5, 6)

E17-15 Royale Mortgage Company uses a process cost system to accumulate costs in its loan application department. When an application is completed, it is forwarded to the loan department for final processing. The following processing and cost data pertain to September.

1. Applications in process on
   September 1, 100
2. Applications started in
   September, 900
3. Completed applications during
   September, 800
4. Applications still in process at
   September 30 were 100%
   complete as to materials (forms)
   and 60% complete as to conversion
   costs.

Beginning WIP:
Direct materials	$ 1,000
Conversion costs	3,960

September costs:
Direct materials	$ 4,500
Direct labor	12,000
Overhead	9,340

Materials are the forms used in the application process, and these costs are incurred at the beginning of the process. Conversion costs are incurred uniformly during the process.

Instructions
(a) Determine the equivalent units of service (production) for materials and conversion costs.
(b) Compute the unit costs and prepare a cost reconciliation schedule.

*E17-16 Using the data in E17-15, assume Royale Mortgage Company uses the FIFO method. Also assume that the applications in process on September 1 were 100% complete as to materials (forms) and 40% complete as to conversion costs.

Compute equivalent units, unit costs, and costs assigned.

(LO 6, 8)

Instructions
(a) Determine the equivalent units of service (production) for materials and conversion costs.
(b) Compute the unit costs and prepare a cost reconciliation schedule.

*E17-17 The Cutting Department of Keigi Company has the following production and cost data for August.

Determine equivalent units, unit costs, and assignment of costs.

(LO 6, 8)

Production	Costs	
1. Started and completed 8,000 units.	Beginning work in process	$ –0–
2. Started 2,000 units that are 40%	Materials	45,000
completed at August 31.	Labor	14,700
	Manufacturing overhead	16,100

Materials are entered at the beginning of the process. Conversion costs are incurred uniformly during the process. Keigi Company uses the FIFO method to compute equivalent units.

Instructions
(a) Determine the equivalent units of production for (1) materials and (2) conversion costs.
(b) Compute unit costs and show the assignment of manufacturing costs to units transferred out and in work in process.

*E17-18 The Smelting Department of Polzin Company has the following production and cost data for September.

Compute equivalent units, unit costs, and costs assigned.

(LO 6, 8)

Production: Beginning work in process 2,000 units that are 100% complete as to materials and 20% complete as to conversion costs; units started and finished 9,000 units; and ending work in process 1,000 units that are 100% complete as to materials and 40% complete as to conversion costs.

Manufacturing costs: Work in process, September 1, $15,200; materials added $60,000; labor and overhead $132,000.

Polzin uses the FIFO method to compute equivalent units.

Instructions
(a) Compute the equivalent units of production for (1) materials and (2) conversion costs for the month of September.
(b) Compute the unit costs for the month.
(c) Determine the costs to be assigned to the units transferred out and in process.

Answer questions on costs and production.

(LO 6, 8)

*E17-19 The ledger of Hannon Company has the following work in process account.

Work in Process—Painting

3/1	Balance	3,680	3/31	Transferred out	?
3/31	Materials	6,600			
3/31	Labor	2,500			
3/31	Overhead	1,150			
3/31	Balance	?			

Production records show that there were 800 units in the beginning inventory, 30% complete, 1,200 units started, and 1,500 units transferred out. The units in ending inventory were 40% complete. Materials are entered at the beginning of the painting process. Hannon uses the FIFO method to compute equivalent units.

Instructions
Answer the following questions.
(a) How many units are in process at March 31?
(b) What is the unit materials cost for March?
(c) What is the unit conversion cost for March?
(d) What is the total cost of units started in February and completed in March?
(e) What is the total cost of units started and finished in March?
(f) What is the cost of the March 31 inventory?

Prepare a production cost report for a second process.

(LO 8)

*E17-20 The Welding Department of Majestic Company has the following production and manufacturing cost data for February 2014. All materials are added at the beginning of the process. Majestic uses the FIFO method to compute equivalent units.

Manufacturing Costs		**Production Data**	
Beginning work in process	$ 32,175	Beginning work in process	15,000 units, 10% complete
Costs transferred in	135,000		
Materials	57,000	Units transferred out	54,000
Labor	35,100	Units transferred in	64,000
Overhead	68,400	Ending work in process	25,000, 20% complete

Instructions
Prepare a production cost report for the Welding Department for the month of February. Transferred-in costs are considered materials costs.

EXERCISES: SET B AND CHALLENGE EXERCISES

Visit the book's companion website, at **www.wiley.com/college/weygandt**, and choose the Student Companion site to access Exercise Set B and Challenge Exercises.

PROBLEMS: SET A

Journalize transactions.

(LO 3, 4)

P17-1A Conwell Company manufactures its product, Vitadrink, through two manufacturing processes: Mixing and Packaging. All materials are entered at the beginning of each process. On October 1, 2014, inventories consisted of Raw Materials $26,000, Work in Process—Mixing $0, Work in Process—Packaging $250,000, and Finished Goods $289,000. The beginning inventory for Packaging consisted of 10,000 units that were 50% complete as to conversion costs and fully complete as to materials. During October, 50,000 units were started into production in the Mixing Department and the following transactions were completed.

1. Purchased $300,000 of raw materials on account.
2. Issued raw materials for production: Mixing $210,000 and Packaging $45,000.

3. Incurred labor costs of $258,900.
4. Used factory labor: Mixing $182,500 and Packaging $76,400.
5. Incurred $810,000 of manufacturing overhead on account.
6. Applied manufacturing overhead on the basis of $24 per machine hour. Machine hours were 28,000 in Mixing and 6,000 in Packaging.
7. Transferred 45,000 units from Mixing to Packaging at a cost of $979,000.
8. Transferred 53,000 units from Packaging to Finished Goods at a cost of $1,315,000.
9. Sold goods costing $1,604,000 for $2,500,000 on account.

Instructions
Journalize the October transactions.

P17-2A Rosenthal Company manufactures bowling balls through two processes: Molding and Packaging. In the Molding Department, the urethane, rubber, plastics, and other materials are molded into bowling balls. In the Packaging Department, the balls are placed in cartons and sent to the finished goods warehouse. All materials are entered at the beginning of each process. Labor and manufacturing overhead are incurred uniformly throughout each process. Production and cost data for the Molding Department during June 2014 are presented below.

Complete four steps necessary to prepare a production cost report.

(LO 5, 6, 7)

Production Data	June
Beginning work in process units	–0–
Units started into production	22,000
Ending work in process units	2,000
Percent complete—ending inventory	40%

Cost Data	
Materials	$198,000
Labor	53,600
Overhead	112,800
Total	$364,400

Instructions
(a) Prepare a schedule showing physical units of production.
(b) Determine the equivalent units of production for materials and conversion costs.
(c) Compute the unit costs of production.
(d) Determine the costs to be assigned to the units transferred out and in process for June.
(e) Prepare a production cost report for the Molding Department for the month of June.

(c) Materials $9.00
    CC $8.00
(d) Transferred
    out $340,000
    WIP $ 24,400

P17-3A Seagren Industries Inc. manufactures in separate processes furniture for homes. In each process, materials are entered at the beginning, and conversion costs are incurred uniformly. Production and cost data for the first process in making two products in two different manufacturing plants are as follows.

Complete four steps necessary to prepare a production cost report.

(LO 5, 6, 7)

	Cutting Department	
	Plant 1	Plant 2
Production Data—July	T12-Tables	C10-Chairs
Work in process units, July 1	–0–	–0–
Units started into production	19,000	16,000
Work in process units, July 31	3,000	500
Work in process percent complete	60	80

Cost Data—July		
Work in process, July 1	$ –0–	$ –0–
Materials	380,000	288,000
Labor	234,200	110,000
Overhead	104,000	96,700
Total	$718,200	$494,700

(a) (3) T12:
    Materials $20
    CC $19
  (4) T12:
    Transferred
      out $624,000
      WIP $ 94,200

Assign costs and prepare production cost report.

(LO 5, 6, 7)

Instructions

(a) For each plant:
  (1) Compute the physical units of production.
  (2) Compute equivalent units of production for materials and for conversion costs.
  (3) Determine the unit costs of production.
  (4) Show the assignment of costs to units transferred out and in process.
(b) Prepare the production cost report for Plant 1 for July 2014.

P17-4A Rivera Company has several processing departments. Costs charged to the Assembly Department for November 2014 totaled $2,280,000 as follows.

Work in process, November 1		
Materials	$79,000	
Conversion costs	48,150	$ 127,150
Materials added		1,589,000
Labor		225,920
Overhead		337,930

Production records show that 35,000 units were in beginning work in process 30% complete as to conversion costs, 660,000 units were started into production, and 25,000 units were in ending work in process 40% complete as to conversion costs. Materials are entered at the beginning of each process.

Instructions

(b) Transferred
    out $2,211,000
    WIP $ 69,000

(a) Determine the equivalent units of production and the unit production costs for the Assembly Department.
(b) Determine the assignment of costs to goods transferred out and in process.
(c) Prepare a production cost report for the Assembly Department.

Determine equivalent units and unit costs and assign costs.

(LO 5, 6, 7)

P17-5A Morse Company manufactures basketballs. Materials are added at the beginning of the production process and conversion costs are incurred uniformly. Production and cost data for the month of July 2014 are as follows.

Production Data—Basketballs	Units	Percent Complete
Work in process units, July 1	500	60%
Units started into production	1,250	
Work in process units, July 31	600	40%

Cost Data—Basketballs		
Work in process, July 1		
Materials	$750	
Conversion costs	600	$1,350
Direct materials		2,400
Direct labor		1,580
Manufacturing overhead		1,295

Instructions

(a) (2) Materials $1.80
  (3) Transferred
      out $4,945
      WIP $1,680

(a) Calculate the following.
  (1) The equivalent units of production for materials and conversion costs.
  (2) The unit costs of production for materials and conversion costs.
  (3) The assignment of costs to units transferred out and in process at the end of the accounting period.
(b) Prepare a production cost report for the month of July for the basketballs.

Compute equivalent units and complete production cost report.

(LO 5, 7)

P17-6A Hamilton Processing Company uses a weighted-average process cost system and manufactures a single product—a premium rug shampoo and cleaner. The manufacturing activity for the month of October has just been completed. A partially completed production cost report for the month of October for the Mixing and Cooking Department is shown on the next page.

Instructions

(a) Materials $1.60
(b) Transferred
    out $282,000
    WIP $ 63,000

(a) Prepare a schedule that shows how the equivalent units were computed so that you can complete the "Quantities: Units accounted for" equivalent units section shown in the production cost report, and compute October unit costs.
(b) Complete the "Cost Reconciliation Schedule" part of the production cost report below.

Hamilton Processing Company
Mixing and Cooking Department
Production Cost Report
For the Month Ended October 31

		Equivalent Units	
Quantities	**Physical Units**	**Materials**	**Conversion Costs**
Units to be accounted for			
Work in process, October 1 (all materials, 70% conversion costs)	20,000		
Started into production	150,000		
Total units	170,000		
Units accounted for			
Transferred out	120,000	?	?
Work in process, October 31 (60% materials, 40% conversion costs)	50,000	?	?
Total units accounted for	170,000	?	?

Costs

Unit costs

	Materials	**Conversion Costs**	**Total**
Total cost	$240,000	$105,000	$345,000
Equivalent units	?	?	
Unit costs	$? +	$? =	$?

Costs to be accounted for		
Work in process, October 1		$ 30,000
Started into production		315,000
Total costs		$345,000

Cost Reconciliation Schedule

Costs accounted for		
Transferred out		$?
Work in process, October 31		
Materials	$?	
Conversion costs	?	?
Total costs		$?

P17-7A Rondeli Company manufactures bicycles and tricycles. For both products, materials are added at the beginning of the production process, and conversion costs are incurred uniformly. Rondeli Company uses the FIFO method to compute equivalent units. Production and cost data for the month of March are as follows.

Determine equivalent units and unit costs and assign costs for processes; prepare production cost report.

(LO 8)

Production Data—Bicycles	Units	Percent Complete
Work in process units, March 1	200	80%
Units started into production	1,250	
Work in process units, March 31	300	40%

Cost Data—Bicycles	Units	Percent Complete
Work in process, March 1	$19,280	
Direct materials	50,000	
Direct labor	25,500	
Manufacturing overhead	30,000	

Production Data—Tricycles	Units	Percent Complete
Work in process units, March 1	100	75%
Units started into production	800	
Work in process units, March 31	60	25%

Cost Data—Tricycles	
Work in process, March 1	$ 6,125
Direct materials	30,400
Direct labor	15,100
Manufacturing overhead	20,000

Instructions

(a) Bicycles:
(1) Materials   1,250
(2) Materials $40
(3) Transferred
      out $106,780
      WIP $ 18,000

(a) Calculate the following for both the bicycles and the tricycles.
    (1) The equivalent units of production for materials and conversion costs.
    (2) The unit costs of production for materials and conversion costs.
    (3) The assignment of costs to units transferred out and in process at the end of the accounting period.

(b) Prepare a production cost report for the month of March for the bicycles only.

PROBLEMS: SET B

Journalize transactions.

(LO 3, 4)

P17-1B Wilbury Company manufactures a nutrient, Everlife, through two manufacturing processes: Blending and Packaging. All materials are entered at the beginning of each process. On August 1, 2014, inventories consisted of Raw Materials $5,000, Work in Process—Blending $0, Work in Process—Packaging $3,945, and Finished Goods $7,500. The beginning inventory for Packaging consisted of 500 units, two-fifths complete as to conversion costs and fully complete as to materials. During August, 9,000 units were started into production in Blending, and the following transactions were completed.

1. Purchased $25,000 of raw materials on account.
2. Issued raw materials for production: Blending $18,930 and Packaging $9,140.
3. Incurred labor costs of $25,770.
4. Used factory labor: Blending $15,320 and Packaging $10,450.
5. Incurred $36,500 of manufacturing overhead on account.
6. Applied manufacturing overhead at the rate of $28 per machine hour. Machine hours were Blending 900 and Packaging 300.
7. Transferred 8,200 units from Blending to Packaging at a cost of $44,940.
8. Transferred 8,600 units from Packaging to Finished Goods at a cost of $67,490.
9. Sold goods costing $62,000 for $90,000 on account.

Instructions
Journalize the August transactions.

Complete four steps necessary to prepare a production cost report.

(LO 5, 6, 7)

P17-2B Steiner Corporation manufactures water skis through two processes: Molding and Packaging. In the Molding Department, fiberglass is heated and shaped into the form of a ski. In the Packaging Department, the skis are placed in cartons and sent to the finished goods warehouse. Materials are entered at the beginning of both processes. Labor and manufacturing overhead are incurred uniformly throughout each process. Production and cost data for the Molding Department for January 2014 are presented below.

Production Data	January
Beginning work in process units	–0–
Units started into production	50,000
Ending work in process units	2,500
Percent complete—ending inventory	40%

Cost Data	January
Materials	$510,000
Labor	92,500
Overhead	150,000
Total	$752,500

Instructions

(a) Compute the physical units of production.

(b) Determine the equivalent units of production for materials and conversion costs.

(c) Compute the unit costs of production.

(d) Determine the costs to be assigned to the units transferred out and in process.

(e) Prepare a production cost report for the Molding Department for the month of January.

(c) Materials $10.20
CC $5
(d) Transferred out $722,000
WIP $ 30,500

P17-3B Borman Corporation manufactures in separate processes refrigerators and freezers for homes. In each process, materials are entered at the beginning and conversion costs are incurred uniformly. Production and cost data for the first process in making two products in two different manufacturing plants are as follows.

Complete four steps necessary to prepare a production cost report.

(LO 5, 6, 7)

	Stamping Department	
	Plant A	**Plant B**
Production Data—June	**R12 Refrigerators**	**F24 Freezers**
Work in process units, June 1	–0–	–0–
Units started into production	20,000	20,000
Work in process units, June 30	4,000	2,500
Work in process percent complete	75	60

Cost Data—June		
Work in process, June 1	$ –0–	$ –0–
Materials	840,000	720,000
Labor	245,000	259,000
Overhead	420,000	292,000
Total	$1,505,000	$1,271,000

Instructions

(a) For each plant:

(1) Compute the physical units of production.

(2) Compute equivalent units of production for materials and for conversion costs.

(3) Determine the unit costs of production.

(4) Show the assignment of costs to units transferred out and in process.

(b) Prepare the production cost report for Plant A for June 2014.

(a) (3) R12:
Materials $42
CC $35
(4) R12:
Transferred
out $1,232,000
WIP $ 273,000

P17-4B Luxman Company has several processing departments. Costs charged to the Assembly Department for October 2014 totaled $1,298,400 as follows.

Assign costs and prepare production cost report.

(LO 5, 6, 7)

Work in process, October 1		
Materials	$29,000	
Conversion costs	16,500	$ 45,500
Materials added		1,006,000
Labor		138,900
Overhead		108,000

Production records show that 25,000 units were in beginning work in process 40% complete as to conversion cost, 435,000 units were started into production, and 35,000 units were in ending work in process 40% complete as to conversion costs. Materials are entered at the beginning of each process.

Instructions

(a) Determine the equivalent units of production and the unit production costs for the Assembly Department.

(b) Determine the assignment of costs to goods transferred out and in process.

(c) Prepare a production cost report for the Assembly Department.

(b) Transferred out $1,211,250
WIP $ 87,150

Determine equivalent units and unit costs and assign costs.

(LO 5, 6, 7)

P17-5B Swinn Company manufactures bicycles. Materials are added at the beginning of the production process, and conversion costs are incurred uniformly. Production and cost data for the month of May are as follows.

Production Data—Bicycles	Units	Percent Complete
Work in process units, May 1	500	80%
Units started in production	2,000	
Work in process units, May 31	800	40%

Cost Data—Bicycles		
Work in process, May 1 Materials	$15,000	
Conversion costs	18,000	$33,000
Direct materials		50,000
Direct labor		19,020
Manufacturing overhead		33,680

Instructions
(a) Calculate the following.
  (1) The equivalent units of production for materials and conversion.
  (2) The unit costs of production for materials and conversion costs.
  (3) The assignment of costs to units transferred out and in process at the end of the accounting period.
(b) Prepare a production cost report for the month of May for the bicycles.

(2) Materials $26
    CC $35
(3) Transferred
    out $103,700
    WIP $ 32,000

Compute equivalent units and complete production cost report.

(LO 5, 7)

P17-6B Venuchi Cleaner Company uses a weighted-average process cost system and manufactures a single product—an all-purpose liquid cleaner. The manufacturing activity for the month of March has just been completed. A partially completed production cost report for the month of March for the mixing and blending department is shown below.

Venuchi Cleaner Company
Mixing and Blending Department
Production Cost Report
For the Month Ended March 31

Quantities	Physical Units	Materials	Conversion Costs
Units to be accounted for			
Work in process, March 1	10,000		
Started into production	76,000		
Total units	86,000		
Units accounted for			
Transferred out	66,000	?	?
Work in process, March 31 (60% materials, 20% conversion costs)	20,000	?	?
Total units	86,000	?	?

Costs	Materials	Conversion Costs	Total
Unit costs			
Total cost	$156,000	$98,000	$254,000
Equivalent units	?	?	
Unit costs	$? +	$? =	$?
Costs to be accounted for			
Work in process, March 1			$ 8,700
Started into production			245,300
Total costs			$254,000

Cost Reconciliation Schedule	Materials	Conversion Costs	Total
Costs accounted for			
Transferred out			$?
Work in process, March 31			
Materials		?	
Conversion costs		$?	?
Total costs			$?

Instructions

(a) Prepare a schedule that shows how the equivalent units were computed so that you can complete the "Quantities: Units accounted for" equivalent units section shown in the production cost report above, and compute March unit costs.

(b) Complete the "Cost Reconciliation Schedule" part of the production cost report above.

(a) Materials $2.00

(b) Transferred out $224,400
    WIP $ 29,600

*P17-7B Holiday Company manufactures basketballs and soccer balls. For both products, materials are added at the beginning of the production process and conversion costs are incurred uniformly. Holiday uses the FIFO method to compute equivalent units. Production and cost data for the month of August are shown below.

Determine equivalent units and unit costs and assign costs for processes; prepare production cost report.

(LO 8)

Production Data—Basketballs	Units	Percent Complete	Production Data—Soccer Balls	Units	Percent Complete
Work in process units, August 1	500	60%	Work in process units, August 1	200	80%
Units started into production	2,000		Units started into production	2,000	
Work in process units, August 31	600	50%	Work in process units, August 31	150	70%

Cost Data—Basketballs		Cost Data—Soccer Balls	
Work in process, August 1	$1,125	Work in process, August 1	$ 450
Direct materials	1,600	Direct materials	2,800
Direct labor	1,280	Direct labor	1,000
Manufacturing overhead	1,000	Manufacturing overhead	1,394

Instructions

(a) Calculate the following for both the basketballs and the soccer balls.
  (1) The equivalent units of production for materials and conversion costs.
  (2) The unit costs of production for materials and conversion costs.
  (3) The assignment of costs to units transferred out and in process at the end of the accounting period.

(b) Prepare a production cost report for the month of August for the basketballs only.

(a) Basketballs:
(1) Materials   2,000
(2) Materials $.80
(3) Transferred out $4,165
    WIP $840

PROBLEMS: SET C

Visit the book's companion website, at **www.wiley.com/college/weygandt**, and choose the Student Companion site to access Problem Set C.

WATERWAYS CONTINUING PROBLEM

(*Note:* This is a continuation of the Waterways Problem from Chapters 15–16.)

WCP17 Because most of the parts for its irrigation systems are standard, Waterways handles the majority of its manufacturing as a process cost system. There are multiple process departments. Three of these departments are the Molding, Cutting, and Welding departments. All items eventually end up in the Packaging department which prepares items for sale in kits or individually. This problem asks you to help Waterways calculate equivalent units and prepare a production cost report.

*Go to the book's companion website, at **www.wiley.com/college/weygandt**, to see the completion of this problem.*

Broadening Your **PERSPECTIVE**

Management Decision-Making

Decision-Making at Current Designs

BYP17-1 Building a kayak using the composite method is a very labor-intensive process. In the fabrication department, the kayaks go through several steps as employees carefully place layers of Kevlar® in a mold and then use resin to fuse together the layers. The excess resin is removed with a vacuum process, and the upper shell and lower shell are removed from the molds and assembled. The seat, hatch, and other components are added in the finishing department.

At the beginning of April, Current Designs had 30 kayaks in process in the fabrication department. Rick Thrune, the production manager, estimated that about 80% of the material costs had been added to these boats, which were about 50% complete with respect to the conversion costs. The cost of this inventory had been calculated to be $8,400 in materials and $9,000 in conversion costs.

During April, 72 boats were started. At the end of the month, the 35 kayaks in the ending inventory had 20% of the materials and 40% of the conversion costs already added to them.

A review of the accounting records for April showed that materials with a cost of $17,500 had been requisitioned by this department and that the conversion costs for the month were $39,600.

Instructions
Complete a production cost report for April 2014 for the fabrication department using the weighted-average method.

Decision-Making Across the Organization

BYP17-2 Florida Beach Company manufactures suntan lotion, called Surtan, in 11-ounce plastic bottles. Surtan is sold in a competitive market. As a result, management is very cost-conscious. Surtan is manufactured through two processes: mixing and filling. Materials are entered at the beginning of each process, and labor and manufacturing overhead occur uniformly throughout each process. Unit costs are based on the cost per gallon of Surtan using the weighted-average costing approach.

On June 30, 2014, Mary Ritzman, the chief accountant for the past 20 years, opted to take early retirement. Her replacement, Joe Benili, had extensive accounting experience with motels in the area but only limited contact with manufacturing accounting. During July, Joe correctly accumulated the following production quantity and cost data for the Mixing Department.

Production quantities: Work in process, July 1, 8,000 gallons 75% complete; started into production 100,000 gallons; work in process, July 31, 5,000 gallons 20% complete. Materials are added at the beginning of the process.

Production costs: Beginning work in process $88,000, comprised of $21,000 of materials costs and $67,000 of conversion costs; incurred in July: materials $573,000, conversion costs $765,000.

Joe then prepared a production cost report on the basis of physical units started into production. His report showed a production cost of $14.26 per gallon of Surtan. The management of Florida Beach was surprised at the high unit cost. The president comes to you, as Mary's top assistant, to review Joe's report and prepare a correct report if necessary.

Instructions
With the class divided into groups, answer the following questions.
(a) Show how Joe arrived at the unit cost of $14.26 per gallon of Surtan.
(b) What error(s) did Joe make in preparing his production cost report?
(c) Prepare a correct production cost report for July.

Managerial Analysis

BYP17-3 Harris Furniture Company manufactures living room furniture through two departments: Framing and Upholstering. Materials are entered at the beginning of each process. For May, the following cost data are obtained from the two work in process accounts.

	Framing	Upholstering
Work in process, May 1	$ –0–	$?
Materials	450,000	?
Conversion costs	261,000	330,000
Costs transferred in	–0–	600,000
Costs transferred out	600,000	?
Work in process, May 31	111,000	?

Instructions

Answer the following questions.

(a) If 3,000 sofas were started into production on May 1 and 2,500 sofas were transferred to Upholstering, what was the unit cost of materials for May in the Framing Department?

(b) Using the data in (a) above, what was the per unit conversion cost of the sofas transferred to Upholstering?

(c) Continuing the assumptions in (a) above, what is the percentage of completion of the units in process at May 31 in the Framing Department?

Real-World Focus

BYP17-4 Paintball is now played around the world. The process of making paintballs is actually quite similar to the process used to make certain medical pills. In fact, paintballs were previously often made at the same factories that made pharmaceuticals.

Address: **http://video.google.com/videoplay?docid=6864066340713942400**, or go to **www.wiley.com/college/weygandt**

Instructions

View that video at the site listed above and then answer the following questions.

(a) Describe in sequence the primary steps used to manufacture paintballs.

(b) Explain the costs incurred by the company that would fall into each of the following categories: materials, labor, and overhead. Of these categories, which do you think would be the greatest cost in making paintballs?

(c) Discuss whether a paintball manufacturer would use job order costing or process costing.

Critical Thinking

Communication Activity

BYP17-5 Diane Barone was a good friend of yours in high school and is from your home town. While you chose to major in accounting when you both went away to college, she majored in marketing and management. You have recently been promoted to accounting manager for the Snack Foods Division of Melton Enterprises, and your friend was promoted to regional sales manager for the same division of Melton. Diane recently telephoned you. She explained that she was familiar with job cost sheets, which had been used by the Special Projects division where she had formerly worked. She was, however, very uncomfortable with the production cost reports prepared by your division. She emailed you a list of her particular questions:

1. Since Melton occasionally prepares snack foods for special orders in the Snack Foods Division, why don't we track costs of the orders separately?
2. What is an equivalent unit?
3. Why am I getting four production cost reports? Isn't there one Work in Process account?

Instructions

Prepare a memo to Diane. Answer her questions, and include any additional information you think would be helpful. You may write informally, but do use proper grammar and punctuation.

Ethics Case

BYP17-6 R. B. Dillman Company manufactures a high-tech component that passes through two production processing departments, Molding and Assembly. Department managers are partially compensated on the basis of units of products completed and transferred out relative to units of product put into production. This was intended as encouragement to be efficient and to minimize waste.

Jan Wooten is the department head in the Molding Department, and Tony Ferneti is her quality control inspector. During the month of June, Jan had three new employees who were not yet technically skilled. As a result, many of the units produced in June had minor molding defects. In order to maintain the department's normal high rate of completion, Jan told Tony to pass through inspection and on to the Assembly Department all units that had defects nondetectable to the human eye. "Company and industry tolerances on this product are too high anyway," says Jan. "Less than 2% of the units we produce are subjected in the market to the stress tolerance we've designed into them. The odds of those 2% being any of this month's units are even less. Anyway, we're saving the company money."

Instructions
(a) Who are the potential stakeholders involved in this situation?
(b) What alternatives does Tony have in this situation? What might the company do to prevent this situation from occurring?

Considering People, Planet, and Profit

BYP17-7 In a recent year, an oil refinery in Texas City, Texas, on the Houston Ship Channel exploded. The explosion killed 14 people and sent a plume of smoke hundreds of feet into the air. The blast started as a fire in the section of the plant that increased the octane of the gasoline that was produced at the refinery. The Houston Ship Channel is the main waterway that allows commerce to flow from the Gulf of Mexico into Houston.

The Texas Commission on Environmental Quality expressed concern about the release of nitrogen oxides, benzene, and other known carcinogens as a result of the blast. Neighbors of the plant complained that the plant had been emitting carcinogens for years and that the regulators had ignored their complaints about emissions and unsafe working conditions.

Instructions
Answer the following questions.
(a) Outline the costs that the company now faces as a result of the accident.
(b) How could the company have reduced the costs associated with the accident?

Answers to Chapter Questions

Answers to Insight and Accounting Across the Organization Questions

p. 858 Choosing a Cost Driver Q: What is the result if a company uses the wrong "cost driver" to assign manufacturing overhead? **A:** Incorrect assignment of manufacturing overhead will result in some products receiving too much overhead and others receiving too little.
p. 862 Haven't I Seen That Before? Q: In what ways might the relative composition (materials, labor, and overhead) of a remanufactured product's cost differ from that of a newly made product? **A:** We would expect that the materials costs would be substantially reduced since the bulk of the physical product is being reused. The labor component might increase, and the level of automation might decrease, since remanufacturing a product requires identification and replacement of malfunctioning components. This process might not be as easily automated as the production of a new product.

Answers to Self-Test Questions

1. b **2.** d **3.** d **4.** b **5.** c **6.** b **7.** b $[20,000 + (5,000 \times 60\%)]$ **8.** a $(7,000 + 0)$ **9.** c $(23,000 + 3,000), [23,000 + (3,000 \times 33\frac{1}{3}\%)]$ **10.** a $[\$60,000 \div (9,000 + 3,000)]$ **11.** b $[(\$10 \times 2,500) + (\$30 \times 2,500 \times 40\%)]$ **12.** b **13.** d ***14.** b $[25,000 + (3,000 \times 100\%)]; [(2,000 \times 80\%) + 25,000 + (3,000 \times 30\%)]$ ***15.** a $[\$60,000 \div (9,000 + 3,000)]$ ***16.** b $[(\$10 \times 2,500) + (\$30 \times 2,500 \times 40\%)]$

✔ **Remember to go back to The Navigator box on the chapter opening page and check off your completed work.**

Chapter 18

Activity-Based Costing

Precor Is on Your Side

Do you feel like the whole world is conspiring against your efforts to get in shape? Is it humanly possible to resist the constant barrage of advertisements and fast-food servers who pleasantly encourage us to "supersize" it? Lest we think that we have no allies in our battle against the bulge, consider Precor.

Ever since it made the first ergonomically sound rowing machine in 1980, Precor's sole mission has been to provide exercise equipment. It makes elliptical trainers, exercise bikes, rowing machines, treadmills, multistation strength systems, and many other forms of equipment designed to erase the cumulative effects of a fast-food nation. Its equipment is widely used in Hilton hotels, Gold's Gym franchises, and even in Madonna's Hard Candy fitness center in Moscow.

Building high-quality fitness equipment requires sizable investments by Precor in buildings and machinery. For example, Precor recently moved its facilities from Valencia, California, to Greensboro, North Carolina. In order to reduce costs and minimize environmental impact, the company installed low-flow water fixtures, high-efficiency heating and cooling systems, and state-of-the-art lighting in its $26 million, 230,000-square-foot facility. As a result of these efforts, Precor's new facility received a Leadership in Energy and Efficient Design (LEED) CI Gold Certification.

Learning Objectives

After studying this chapter, you should be able to:

1 Recognize the difference between traditional costing and activity-based costing.

2 Identify the steps in the development of an activity-based costing system.

3 Know how companies identify the activity cost pools used in activity-based costing.

4 Know how companies identify and use cost drivers in activity-based costing.

5 Understand the benefits and limitations of activity-based costing.

6 Differentiate between value-added and non–value-added activities.

7 Understand the value of using activity levels in activity-based costing.

8 Apply activity-based costing to service industries.

✔ The Navigator

Because of its huge investments in property, plant, and equipment, overhead costs represent a large percentage of the cost of Precor's exercise equipment. The combination of high overhead costs and a wide variety of products means that it is important that Precor allocates its overhead accurately to its various products. Without accurate cost information, Precor would not know whether its elliptical trainers and recumbent bicycles are making money, whether its AMT 100i adaptive motion trainer is priced high enough to cover its costs, or if its 240i Stretchtrainer is losing money. To increase the accuracy of its costs, Precor uses a method of overhead allocation

that focuses on identifying the types of activities that cause the company to incur costs. It then assigns more overhead to those products that rely most heavily on cost-incurring activities. By doing this, the allocation of overhead is less arbitrary than traditional overhead allocation methods. In short, before it can help us burn off the pounds, Precor needs to understand what drives its overhead costs.

Watch the Precor video in WileyPLUS to learn more about activity-based costing in the real world.

Source: www.precor.com.

✔ **The Navigator**

Preview of **Chapter 18**

As indicated in the Feature Story about Precor, the traditional costing systems described in earlier chapters are not the best answer for every company. Because Precor suspected that the traditional system was masking significant differences in its real cost structure, it sought a new method of assigning costs. Similar searches by other companies for ways to improve operations and gather more accurate data for decision-making have resulted in the development of powerful new management tools, including **activity-based costing (ABC)**. The primary objective of this chapter is to explain and illustrate this concept.

The content and organization of this chapter are as follows.

ACTIVITY-BASED COSTING

Traditional Costing and ABC	Example of ABC versus Traditional Costing	ABC: A Closer Look	ABC in Service Industries
• Traditional costing • Need for a new approach • Activity-based costing	• Identify activities and allocate to cost pools • Identify cost drivers • Compute overhead rates • Assign overhead costs to products • Compare unit costs	• Benefits • Limitations • When to use ABC • Value-added versus non–value-added activities • Classification of activity levels	• Traditional costing example • ABC example

✔ **The Navigator**

Traditional Costing and Activity-Based Costing

Traditional Costing Systems

It is probably impossible to determine the *exact* cost of a product or service. However, in order to achieve improved management decisions, companies strive to provide decision-makers with the most accurate cost estimates they can. The most accurate estimate of product cost occurs when the costs are traceable directly to the product produced or the service provided. Direct material and direct labor costs are the easiest to trace directly to the product through the use of material requisition forms and payroll time sheets. Overhead costs, on the other hand, are an indirect or common cost that generally cannot be easily or directly traced to individual products or services. Instead, companies use estimates to assign overhead costs to products and services.

Often the most difficult part of computing accurate unit costs is determining the proper amount of **overhead cost** to assign to each product, service, or job. In our coverage of job order costing in Chapter 16 and of process costing in Chapter 17, we used a single or plantwide overhead rate throughout the year for the entire factory operation. That rate was called the **predetermined overhead rate**. For job order costing, we assumed that **direct labor cost** was the relevant activity base for assigning all overhead costs to jobs. For process costing, we assumed that **machine hours** was the relevant activity base for assigning all overhead to the process or department.

The use of direct labor as the activity base made sense when overhead cost allocation systems were first developed. At that time, direct labor made up a large portion of total manufacturing cost. Therefore, it was widely accepted that there was a high correlation between direct labor and the incurrence of overhead cost. As a result, direct labor became the most popular basis for allocating overhead.

Even in today's increasingly automated environment, direct labor is sometimes the appropriate basis for assigning overhead cost to products. It is appropriate to use direct labor when (a) direct labor constitutes a significant part of total product cost, and (b) a high correlation exists between direct labor and changes in the amount of overhead costs. Illustration 18-1 displays a simplified (one-stage) traditional costing system relying on direct labor to assign overhead.

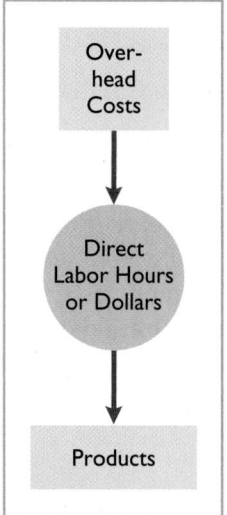

Illustration 18-1
Traditional one-stage costing system

The Need for a New Approach

In recent years, manufacturers and service providers have experienced tremendous change. Advances in computerized systems, technological innovation, global competition, and automation have changed the manufacturing environment drastically. As a result, the amount of direct labor used in many industries has greatly decreased, and total overhead costs resulting from depreciation on expensive equipment and machinery, utilities, repairs, and maintenance have significantly increased. When there is not a correlation between direct labor and overhead, it is inappropriate to use plantwide predetermined overhead rates based on direct labor. Companies that use overhead rates based on direct labor when this correlation does not exist experience significant product-cost distortions.

To avoid such distortions, many companies now use machine hours as the basis on which to allocate overhead in an automated manufacturing environment. But even machine hours may not suffice as the only plantwide basis for allocating all overhead. If the manufacturing process is complex, then only multiple allocation bases can result in more accurate product-cost computations. In such situations, managers need to consider an overhead cost allocation method that uses *multiple* bases. That method is **activity-based costing**.

Activity-Based Costing

Broadly, **activity-based costing (ABC)** is an approach for allocating overhead costs. More specifically, ABC allocates overhead to multiple activity cost pools, and it then assigns the activity cost pools to products and services by means of cost drivers. To understand this more clearly, we need to apply some new meanings to the rather common-sounding words that make up the definition: In activity-based costing, an **activity** is any event, action, transaction, or work sequence that incurs costs when producing a product or providing a service. An **activity cost pool** is the overhead cost attributed to a distinct type of activity (e.g., ordering materials or setting up machines). A **cost driver** is any factor or activity that has a direct cause-effect relationship with the resources consumed. The reasoning behind ABC cost allocation is simple: **Products consume activities, and activities consume resources**.

These definitions of terms will become clearer as we look more closely at how ABC works. ABC allocates overhead in a two-stage process. The first stage allocates overhead costs to activity cost pools. (Traditional costing systems, in contrast, allocate these costs to departments or to jobs.) Examples of overhead cost pools are ordering materials, setting up machines, assembling products, and inspecting products.

The second stage assigns the overhead allocated to the activity cost pools to products, using cost drivers. The cost drivers measure the number of individual activities undertaken or performed to produce products or provide services. Examples are number of purchase orders, number of setups, labor hours, and number of inspections. Illustration 18-2 shows examples of activities, and possible

Illustration 18-2
Activities and related cost drivers

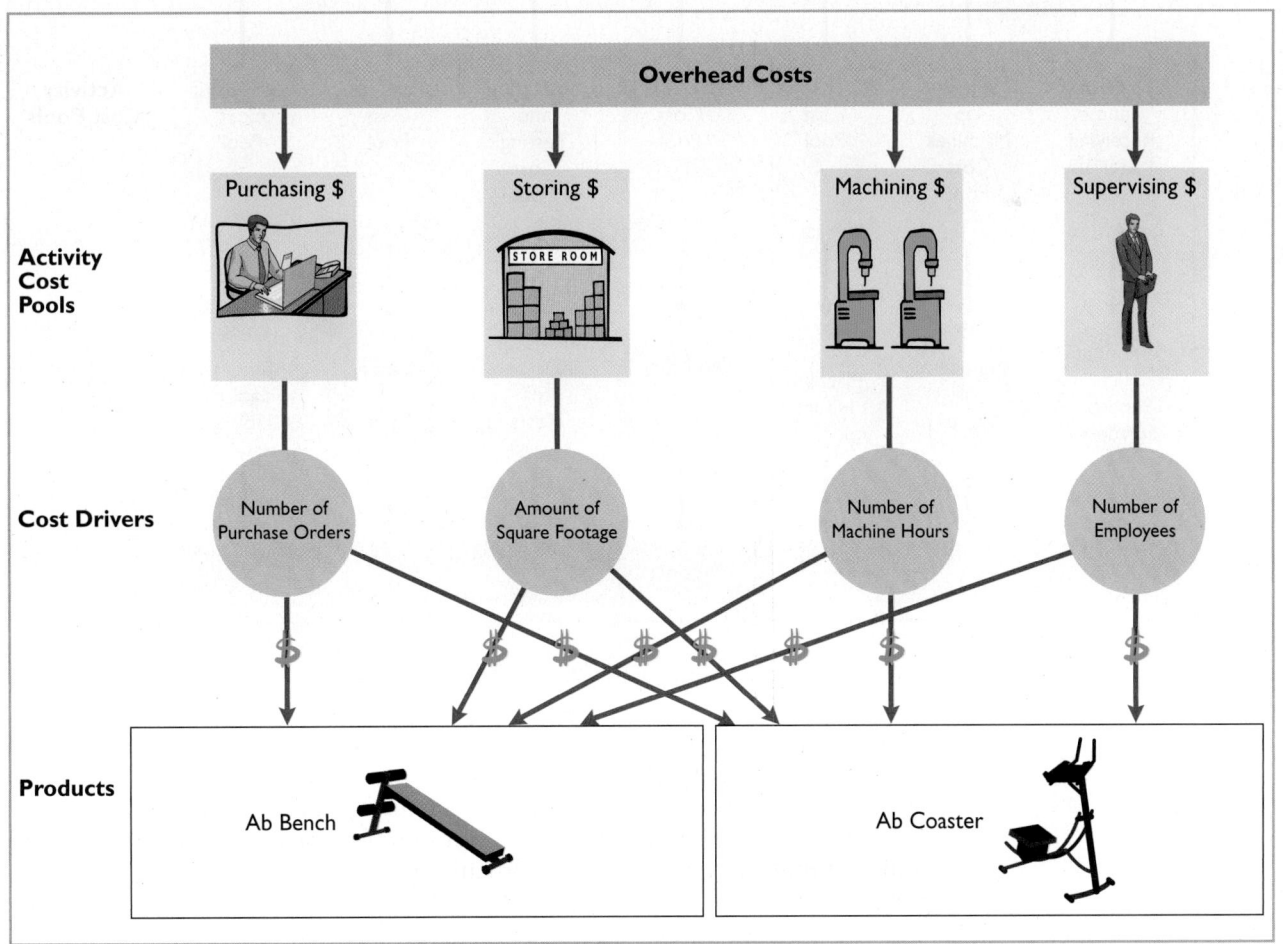

cost drivers to measure them, for a company that manufactures two types of abdominal exercise equipment—Ab Benches and Ab Coasters.

In the first step (as shown at the top of Illustration 18-2 on page 903), the company allocates overhead costs to activity cost pools. In this simplified example, the company has identified four activity cost pools: purchasing, storing, machining, and supervising. After the costs are allocated to the activity cost pools, the company uses cost drivers to determine the costs to assign to the individual products based on each product's use of each activity. For example, if Ab Benches require more activity by the purchasing department, as measured by the number of required purchase orders, then more of the overhead costs from the purchasing pool are allocated to the Ab Benches.

The more complex a product's manufacturing operation, the more activities and cost drivers it is likely to have. If there is little or no correlation between changes in the cost driver and consumption of the overhead cost, inaccurate product costs are inevitable.

Illustration 18-3 shows the design of a more complex activity-based costing system with seven activity cost pools for Lift Jack Company. Lift Jack Company manufactures two automotive jacks—an automobile scissors jack and a truck hydraulic jack.

Illustration 18-3
ABC system design—Lift
Jack Company

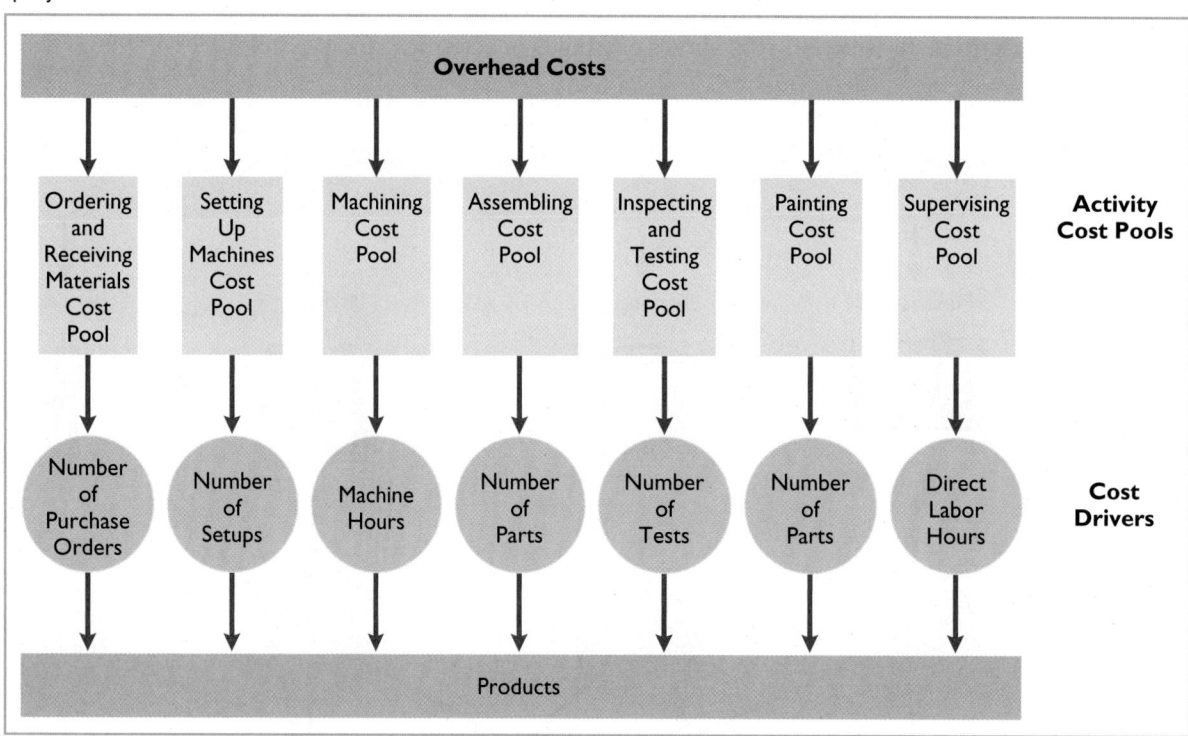

The Lift Jack Company illustration contains seven activity cost pools. In some companies, the number of activities can be substantial. For example, Clark-Hurth (a division of Clark Equipment Company), a manufacturer of axles and transmissions, identified over 170 activities. Compumotor (a division of Parker Hannifin) identified over 80 activities in just the procurement function of its Material Control Department.

> DO IT!

Costing Systems

Action Plan

✔ Understand that a traditional costing system allocates overhead on the basis of a single predetermined overhead rate.

✔ Understand that an ABC system allocates overhead to identified activity cost pools, and then assigns costs to products using related cost drivers that measure the resources consumed.

Indicate whether the following statements are true or false.

1. A traditional costing system allocates overhead by means of multiple overhead rates.

2. Activity-based costing allocates overhead costs in a two-stage process.

3. Direct material and direct labor costs are easier to trace to products than overhead.

4. As manufacturing processes have become more automated, more companies have chosen to allocate overhead on the basis of direct labor costs.

5. In activity-based costing, an activity is any event, action, transaction, or work sequence that incurs cost when producing a product.

Solution

1. false.   2. true.   3. true.   4. false.   5. true.

Related exercise material: **BE18-1, BE18-2, E18-1,** and **DO IT!** **18-1.**

✔ **The Navigator**

Example of ABC versus Traditional Costing

In this section, we present a simple case example that compares activity-based costing with traditional costing. It illustrates how ABC eliminates the distortion that can occur in traditional overhead cost allocation. As you study this example, you should understand that ABC does not *replace* an existing job order or process cost system. What ABC does is to segregate overhead into various cost pools in an effort to provide more accurate cost information. As a result, ABC supplements—rather than replaces—these cost systems.

LEARNING OBJECTIVE   2

Identify the steps in the development of an activity-based costing system.

Assume that Atlas Company produces two products—the Ab Bench and the Ab Coaster abdominal trainers. The Ab Bench is a high-volume item totaling 25,000 units annually. The Ab Coaster is a low-volume item totaling only 5,000 units per year. The direct materials cost per unit is $40 for the Ab Bench and $30 for the Ab Coaster. The direct labor cost is $12 per unit for each product. Each product requires one hour of direct labor for completion. Therefore, total annual direct labor hours are 30,000 (25,000 + 5,000). Expected annual manufacturing overhead costs are $900,000. Thus, the predetermined overhead rate under traditional costing, using direct labor hours, is $30 ($900,000 ÷ 30,000) per direct labor hour. Since both products require one direct labor hour per unit, both products are allocated overhead costs of **$30 per unit under traditional costing**.

Let's now calculate unit costs under ABC. Activity-based costing involves the following four steps.

1. **Identify and classify the activities** involved in the manufacture of specific products, and **allocate overhead to cost pools**.

2. **Identify the cost driver** that has a strong correlation to the costs accumulated in the cost pool.

3. **Compute the activity-based overhead rate** for each cost driver.

4. **Assign overhead costs to products**, using the overhead rates determined for each cost pool (cost per driver).

Identify and Classify Activities and Allocate Overhead to Cost Pools (Step 1)

LEARNING OBJECTIVE 3

Know how companies identify the activity cost pools used in activity-based costing.

Activity-based costing starts with an analysis of the activities performed to manufacture a product or provide a service. This analysis should identify all resource-consuming activities. It requires documenting every activity undertaken to accomplish a task. Atlas Company identified three activity cost pools: setting up machines, machining, and inspecting.

Next, the system assigns overhead costs directly to the appropriate activity cost pool. For example, all overhead costs directly associated with Atlas Company's machine setups (such as salaries, supplies, and depreciation) would be assigned to the machine setup cost pool. Illustration 18-4 shows the three cost pools, along with the estimated overhead allocated to each cost pool.

Illustration 18-4
Activity cost pools and estimated overhead

Activity Cost Pools	Estimated Overhead
Setting up machines	$300,000
Machining	500,000
Inspecting	100,000
Total	$ 900,000

Identify Cost Drivers (Step 2)

LEARNING OBJECTIVE 4

Know how companies identify and use cost drivers in activity-based costing.

After costs are allocated to the activity cost pools, the company must identify the cost drivers for each cost pool. The cost driver must accurately measure the actual consumption of the activity by the various products. To achieve accurate costing, a **high degree of correlation** must exist between the cost driver and the actual consumption of the overhead costs in the cost pool.

Illustration 18-5 shows the cost drivers identified by Atlas and their total expected use per activity cost pool.

Illustration 18-5
Cost drivers and their expected use

Activity Cost Pools	Cost Drivers	Expected Use of Cost Drivers per Activity
Setting up machines	Number of setups	**1,500** setups
Machining	Machine hours	**50,000** machine hours
Inspecting	Number of inspections	**2,000** inspections

Availability and ease of obtaining data relating to the cost driver is an important factor that must be considered in its selection.

Compute Activity-Based Overhead Rates (Step 3)

Next, the company computes an **activity-based overhead rate** per cost driver by dividing the estimated overhead per activity by the number of cost drivers expected to be used per activity. Illustration 18-6 shows the formula for this computation.

Illustration 18-6
Formula for computing activity-based overhead rate

$$\frac{\text{Estimated Overhead per Activity}}{\text{Expected Use of Cost Drivers per Activity}} = \frac{\text{Activity-Based}}{\text{Overhead Rate}}$$

Atlas Company computes its activity-based overhead rates by using the estimated overhead per activity cost pool, shown in Illustration 18-4, and the expected use of cost drivers per activity, shown in Illustration 18-5. These computations are presented in Illustration 18-7.

Activity Cost Pools	Estimated Overhead	÷	Expected Use of Cost Drivers per Activity	=	Activity-Based Overhead Rates
Setting up machines	$300,000		1,500 setups		$200 per setup
Machining	500,000		50,000 machine hours		$10 per machine hour
Inspecting	100,000		2,000 inspections		$50 per inspection
Total	$900,000				

Illustration 18-7
Computation of activity-based overhead rates

Assign Overhead Costs to Products (Step 4)

In assigning overhead costs, it is necessary to know the expected use of cost drivers **for each product**. Because of its low volume, the Ab Coaster requires more setups and inspections than the Ab Bench. Illustration 18-8 shows the expected use of cost drivers per product for each of Atlas's products.

Activity Cost Pools	Cost Drivers	Expected Use of Cost Drivers per Activity	Expected Use of Cost Drivers per Product	
			Ab Bench	Ab Coaster
Setting up machines	Number of setups	1,500 setups	500	1,000
Machining	Machine hours	50,000 machine hours	30,000	20,000
Inspecting	Number of inspections	2,000 inspections	500	1,500

Illustration 18-8
Expected use of cost drivers per product

To assign overhead costs to each product, Atlas multiplies the activity-based overhead rates per cost driver (Illustration 18-7) by the number of cost drivers expected to be used per product (Illustration 18-8). Illustration 18-9 shows the overhead cost assigned to each product.

Illustration 18-9
Assignment of activity cost pools to products

Atlas Company.xls

Home   Insert   Page Layout   Formulas   Data   Review   View

P18   fx

	A	B	C	D	E	F	G	H	I	J	K	L
1				Atlas Company								
2				Ab Bench						Ab Coaster		
3	Activity Cost Pools	Expected Use of Cost Drivers per Product	×	Activity-Based Overhead Rates	=	Cost Assigned		Expected Use of Cost Drivers per Product	×	Activity-Based Overhead Rates	=	Cost Assigned
4	Setting up machines	500		$200		$100,000		1,000		$200		$200,000
5	Machining	30,000		$10		300,000		20,000		$10		200,000
6	Inspecting	500		$50		25,000		1,500		$50		75,000
7	Total costs assigned [(a)]					$425,000						$475,000
8	Units produced [(b)]					25,000						5,000
9	Overhead cost per unit [(a)÷(b)]					$17						$95
10												
11												

Under ABC, the overhead cost per unit is $17 for the Ab Bench and $95 for the Ab Coaster. When compared to the $30 per unit overhead charge under traditional costing, ABC shifts costs from the high-volume product (Ab Bench) to the low-volume product (Ab Coaster). This shift occurs because low-volume products often require more special handling, such as machine setups and inspections. This is true for Atlas Company. Thus, the low-volume product frequently is responsible for more overhead costs per unit than is a high-volume product.[1] Assigning overhead using ABC will usually increase the cost per unit for low-volume products as compared to a traditional overhead allocation. Therefore, traditional cost drivers such as direct labor hours are usually not appropriate for assigning overhead costs to low-volume products.

Comparing Unit Costs

Illustration 18-10 shows the unit cost for each product under traditional costing.

Illustration 18-10
Computation of unit costs—traditional costing

	Products	
Manufacturing Costs	**Ab Bench**	**Ab Coaster**
Direct materials	$40	$30
Direct labor	12	12
Overhead	30*	30*
Total unit cost	**$82**	**$72**

*Predetermined overhead rate × Direct labor hours = $30 × 1 hr. = $30

A comparison of unit manufacturing costs under traditional costing and ABC shows the following significant differences.

Illustration 18-11
Comparison of unit product costs

	Ab Bench		**Ab Coaster**	
Manufacturing Costs	**Traditional Costing**	**ABC**	**Traditional Costing**	**ABC**
Direct materials	$40	$40	$30	$ 30
Direct labor	12	12	12	12
Overhead	30	17*	30	95*
Total cost per unit	**$82**	**$69**	**$72**	**$137**
		Overstated		Understated
		$13		$65

*Overhead per Illustration 18-9

The comparison shows that unit costs under traditional costing are significantly distorted. The cost of producing the Ab Bench is overstated by $13 per unit ($82 − $69), and the cost of producing the Ab Coaster is understated by $65 per unit ($137 − $72). These differences are attributable entirely to how Atlas Company assigns manufacturing overhead. A likely consequence of the differences in assigning overhead is that Atlas has been overpricing the Ab Bench and possibly losing market share to competitors. It also has been sacrificing profitability by underpricing the Ab Coaster.

Activity-based costing was pioneered in the United States: John Deere Company coined the term about 25 years ago. Numerous well-known U.S. companies,

---

[1]Robin Cooper and Robert S. Kaplan, "How Cost Accounting Distorts Product Costs," *Management Accounting* 69, No. 10 (April 1988), pp. 20–27.

including IBM, AT&T, Hewlett-Packard, Procter & Gamble, Tektronix, Hughes Aircraft, Caterpillar, and American Express, have adopted ABC. Its use outside the United States, however, is limited. The cost of implementation may discourage some foreign companies.

In Japan, activity-based costing is less widely used. Companies prefer volume measures such as direct labor hours to assign overhead cost to products. Japanese managers are convinced that reducing direct labor is essential to continuous cost reduction. Using direct labor as the basis for overhead allocation forces Japanese companies to watch direct labor more closely.

SERVICE COMPANY INSIGHT

Traveling Light

Have you flown on an airplane since baggage fees have been implemented? Did the fee make you so mad that you swore that the next time you flew, you would pack fewer clothes so you could use a carry-on bag instead? That is exactly how the airlines hoped that you would react. Baggage handling is extremely labor-intensive. All that tagging, sorting, loading on carts, loading in planes, unloading, and sorting again add up to about $9 per bag. They also have equipment costs: sorters, carts, conveyors, tractors, and storage facilities. That's about another $4 of equipment-related overhead per bag. Finally, there is additional fuel cost of a 40-pound item—about $2 in fuel for a 3-hour flight. These costs add up to $15 ($9 + $4 + $2). Since airlines have implemented their baggage fees, fewer customers are checking bags. Not only does this save the airlines money, it also increases the amount of space available for hauling cargo. An airline can charge at least $80 for hauling a small parcel for same-day delivery service.

Source: Scott McCartney, "What It Costs an Airline to Fly Your Luggage," *Wall Street Journal Online* (November 25, 2008).

? Why do airlines charge even higher rates for heavier bags, bags that are odd shapes (e.g., ski bags), and bags with hazardous materials in them? (see page 947.)

> DO IT!

Apply ABC

Casey Company has five activity cost pools and two products. It expects to produce 200,000 units of its automobile scissors jack and 80,000 units of its truck hydraulic jack. Having identified its activity cost pools and the cost drivers for each cost pool, Casey Company accumulated the following data relative to those activity cost pools and cost drivers.

Annual Overhead Data				Expected Use of Cost Drivers per Product	
Activity Cost Pools	Cost Drivers	Estimated Overhead	Expected Use of Cost Drivers per Activity	Scissors Jacks	Hydraulic Jacks
Ordering and receiving	Purchase orders	$ 200,000	2,500 orders	1,000	1,500
Machine setup	Setups	600,000	1,200 setups	500	700
Machining	Machine hours	2,000,000	800,000 hours	300,000	500,000
Assembling	Parts	1,800,000	3,000,000 parts	1,800,000	1,200,000
Inspecting and testing	Tests	700,000	35,000 tests	20,000	15,000
		$5,300,000			

Using the data on page 909, do the following.

(a) Prepare a schedule showing the computations of the activity-based overhead rates per cost driver.

(b) Prepare a schedule assigning each activity's overhead cost to the two products.

(c) Compute the overhead cost per unit for each product.

(d) Comment on the comparative overhead cost per unit.

Solution

Action Plan

✔ Determine the activity-based overhead rate by dividing the estimated overhead per activity by the expected use of cost drivers per activity.

✔ Assign the overhead of each activity cost pool to the individual products by multiplying the expected use of cost driver per product times the activity-based overhead rate.

✔ Determine overhead cost per unit by dividing the overhead assigned to each product by the number of units of that product.

(a) Computations of activity-based overhead rates per cost driver:

Activity Cost Pools	Estimated Overhead	÷	Expected Use of Cost Drivers per Activity	=	Activity-Based Overhead Rates
Ordering and receiving	$ 200,000		2,500 purchase orders		$80 per order
Machine setup	600,000		1,200 setups		$500 per setup
Machining	2,000,000		800,000 machine hours		$2.50 per machine hour
Assembling	1,800,000		3,000,000 parts		$0.60 per part
Inspecting and testing	700,000		35,000 tests		$20 per test
	$5,300,000				

(b) Assignment of each activity's overhead cost to products using ABC:

	Scissors Jacks				Hydraulic Jacks			
Activity Cost Pools	Expected Use of Cost Drivers per Product	×	Activity-Based Overhead Rates	= Cost Assigned	Expected Use of Cost Drivers per Product	×	Activity-Based Overhead Rates	= Cost Assigned
Ordering and receiving	1,000		$80	$ 80,000	1,500		$80	$ 120,000
Machine setup	500		$500	250,000	700		$500	350,000
Machining	300,000		$2.50	750,000	500,000		$2.50	1,250,000
Assembling	1,800,000		$0.60	1,080,000	1,200,000		$0.60	720,000
Inspecting and testing	20,000		$20	400,000	15,000		$20	300,000
Total assigned costs				$2,560,000				$2,740,000

(c) Computation of overhead cost per unit:

	Scissors Jack	Hydraulic Jack
Total costs assigned	$2,560,000	$2,740,000
Total units produced	200,000	80,000
Overhead cost per unit	$12.80	$34.25

(d) These data show that the total overhead assigned to 80,000 hydraulic jacks exceeds the overhead assigned to 200,000 scissors jacks. The overhead cost per hydraulic jack is $34.25, but it is only $12.80 per scissors jack.

Related exercise material: **BE18-5, BE18-6, BE18-7, E18-1, E18-2, E18-3, E18-4, E18-5, E18-6, E18-11,** and **DO IT!** **18-2.**

✔ The Navigator

Activity-Based Costing: A Closer Look

As the use of activity-based costing has grown, both its practical benefits and its limitations have become apparent.

LEARNING OBJECTIVE   **5**

Understand the benefits and limitations of activity-based costing.

Benefits of ABC

The primary benefit of ABC is **more accurate product costing**. Here's why:

1. **ABC leads to more cost pools** being used to assign overhead costs to products. Instead of one plantwide pool (or even departmental pools) and a single cost driver, companies use numerous activity cost pools with more relevant cost drivers. Costs are assigned more directly on the basis of the cost drivers used to produce each product.

2. **ABC leads to enhanced control over overhead costs.** Under ABC, companies can trace many overhead costs directly to activities—allowing some indirect costs to be identified as direct costs. Thus, managers have become more aware of their responsibility to control the activities that generate those costs.

3. **ABC leads to better management decisions.** More accurate product costing should contribute to setting selling prices that can help achieve desired product profitability levels. In addition, more accurate cost data could be helpful in deciding whether to make or buy a product part or component, and sometimes even whether to eliminate a product.

Activity-based costing does not change the amount of overhead costs. What it does do is allocate those overhead costs in a more accurate manner. Furthermore, if the scorekeeping is more realistic and more accurate, managers should be able to better understand cost behavior and overall profitability.

Limitations of ABC

Although ABC systems often provide better product cost data than traditional volume-based systems, there are limitations:

1. **ABC can be expensive to use.** The increased cost of identifying multiple activities and applying numerous cost drivers discourages many companies from using ABC. Activity-based costing systems are more complex than traditional costing systems—sometimes significantly more complex. So companies must ask, is the cost of implementation greater than the benefit of greater accuracy? Sometimes it may be. For some companies, there may be no need to consider ABC at all because their existing system is sufficient. If the costs of ABC outweigh the benefits, then the company should not implement ABC.

2. **Some arbitrary allocations continue.** Even though more overhead costs can be assigned directly to products through ABC's multiple activity cost pools, certain overhead costs remain to be allocated by means of some arbitrary volume-based cost driver such as labor or machine hours.

SERVICE COMPANY INSIGHT

Using ABC to Aid in Employee Evaluation

Although most publicized ABC applications are in manufacturing companies or large service firms, very small service businesses can apply it also. Mahany Welding Supply, a small family-run welding service business in Rochester, New York, used ABC to determine the cost of servicing customers and to identify feasible cost-reduction opportunities.

Application of ABC at Mahany Welding's operations provided information about the five employees who were involved in different activities of revenue generation—i.e., delivery of supplies (rural versus city), welding services, repairs, telephone sales, field or door-to-door sales, repeat business sales, and cold-call sales. Managers applied activity cost pools to the five revenue-producing employees using relevant cost drivers. ABC revealed annual net income (loss) by employee as follows.

Employee #1	$65,431	Employee #4	$(10,957)
Employee #2	$35,154	Employee #5	$(46,180)
Employee #3	$13,731		

This comparative information was an eye-opener to the owner of Mahany Welding—who was Employee #5!

Source: Michael Krupnicki and Thomas Tyson, "Using ABC to Determine the Cost of Servicing Customers," *Management Accounting* (December 31, 1997), pp. 40–46.

 What positive implications does application of ABC have for the employees of this company? (See page 948.)

When to Use ABC

How does a company know when to use ABC? The presence of one or more of the following factors would point to its possible use:

1. Product lines differ greatly in volume and manufacturing complexity.
2. Product lines are numerous and diverse, and they require differing degrees of support services.
3. Overhead costs constitute a significant portion of total costs.
4. The manufacturing process or the number of products has changed significantly—for example, from labor-intensive to capital-intensive due to automation.
5. Production or marketing managers are ignoring data provided by the existing system and are instead using "bootleg" costing data or other alternative data when pricing or making other product decisions.

The redesign and installation of a product costing system is a significant decision that requires considerable cost and a major effort to accomplish. Therefore, financial managers need to be very cautious and deliberate when initiating changes in costing systems. A key factor in implementing a successful ABC system is the support of top management.

Value-Added versus Non–Value-Added Activities

Some companies that have experienced the benefits of activity-based costing have applied it to a broader range of management activities. **Activity-based management (ABM)** extends the use of ABC from product costing to a comprehensive management tool that focuses on reducing costs and improving processes and decision-making. A refinement of activity-based costing used in ABM is the classification of activities as either value-added or non–value-added.

Value-added activities are those activities of **a company's operations** that increase the perceived worth of a product or service to customers. Examples for the manufacture of Precor exercise equipment include engineering design, machining, assembly, and painting. Examples of value-added activities in a service company include performing surgery at a hospital, providing legal research at a law firm, or delivering packages by a freight company.

Non–value-added activities are those activities that, if eliminated, would not hinder the company's operations or reduce the perceived worth of its product or service. These activities simply **add cost to, or increase the time spent on, a product or service without increasing its perceived value**. One example is inventory storage. If a company eliminated the need to store inventory (for example, through just-in-time inventory processes), it would not hinder its operations or reduce the worth of its product, but it would decrease its product costs. Other examples include moving materials, work in process, or finished goods from one location to another in the plant during the production process; waiting for manufacturing equipment to become available; inspecting goods; and fixing defective goods under warranty.

Companies often use **activity flowcharts** to help identify the ABC activities. Illustration 18-12 shows an activity flowchart. The top part of this flowchart identifies activities as value-added or non–value-added. The value-added activities are highlighted in red. Two rows in the lower part of the flowchart show the number of days spent on each activity. The first row shows the number of days spent on each activity under the current manufacturing process. The second row shows the number of days expected to be spent on each activity under management's proposed reengineered manufacturing process.

LEARNING OBJECTIVE   6

Differentiate between value-added and non–value-added activities.

Illustration 18-12
Flowchart showing value-added and non–value-added activities

				Heartland Company								
				Activity Flowchart								

Activities

NVA	NVA	NVA	NVA	VA		NVA	NVA	VA	NVA	NVA	NVA	VA
Receive and Inspect Materials	Move and Store Materials	Move Materials to Production and Wait	Set Up Machines	Machining: Drill	Lathe	Inspect	Move and Wait	Assembly	Inspect and Test	Move to Storage	Store Finished Goods	Package and Ship
Current Days 1	12	2.5	1.5	2	1	0.2	6	2	0.3	0.5	14	1

Total Current Average Time = 44 days →

| **Proposed Days** 1 | 4 | 1.5 | 1.5 | 2 | 1 | 0.2 | 2 | 2 | 0.3 | 0.5 | 10 | 1 |

← Total Proposed Average Time = 27 days →

Proposed reduction in non–value-added time = 17 days

VA = Value-added   NVA = Non–value-added

The proposed changes would reduce time spent on non–value-added activities by 17 days. This 17-day improvement would be due entirely to moving inventory more quickly through the non–value-added processes—that is, by reducing inventory time in moving, storage, and waiting. The appendix at the end of this chapter discusses a just-in-time inventory system, which some companies use to eliminate non–value-added activities related to inventory.

Not all activities labeled non–value-added are totally wasteful, nor can they be totally eliminated. For example, although inspection time is a non–value-added activity from a customer's perspective, few companies would eliminate their quality control functions. Similarly, moving and waiting time is non–value-added, but it would be impossible to completely eliminate. Nevertheless, when managers recognize the non–value-added characteristic of these activities, they are motivated to minimize them as much as possible. Attention to such matters is part of the growing practice of activity-based management, which helps managers concentrate on **continuous improvement** of operations and activities.

> **DO IT!**

Value-Added Activities

Action Plan

✔ Recognize that value-added activities increase the worth of a product or service to customers.

✔ Understand that non–value-added activities simply add cost to or increase the time spent on a product or service without increasing its market value.

Classify each of the following activities within a water-ski manufacturer as value-added (VA) or non–value-added (NVA).

1. Inspecting completed skis.
2. Storing raw materials.
3. Machine setups.
4. Installing bindings on skis.
5. Packaging skis for shipment.
6. Reworking defective skis.

Solution

| 1. NVA. | 2. NVA. | 3. NVA. | 4. VA. | 5. VA. | 6. NVA. |

Related exercise material: **BE18-8, BE18-9, E18-13, E18-14, E18-15, E18-16, and** DO IT! **18-3.**

✔ **The Navigator**

MANAGEMENT INSIGHT

What Does NASCAR Have to Do with Breakfast Cereal?

Often the best way to improve a process is to learn from observing a different process. Production-line technicians from giant food producer General Mills were flown to North Carolina to observe firsthand how race-car pit crews operate. In a NASCAR race, the value-added activity is driving toward the finish line; any time spent in the pit is non–value-added. Every split second saved in the pit increases the chances of winning. From what the General Mills' technicians learned at the car race, as well as other efforts, they were able to reduce setup time from 5 hours to just 20 minutes.

? What are the benefits of reducing setup time? (See page 948.)

Classification of Activity Levels

As mentioned earlier, traditional costing systems are volume-driven—driven by unit-based cost drivers such as direct labor or machine hours. Some activity costs are strictly variable and are caused by the production or acquisition of a single unit of product or the performance of a single unit of service. However, the recognition that other activity costs are not driven by unit-based cost drivers has led to the development of a classification of ABC activities consisting of four levels, as follows.

LEARNING OBJECTIVE   7

Understand the value of using activity levels in activity-based costing.

1. **Unit-level activities** are performed for each unit of production. For example, the assembly of cell phones is a unit-level activity because the amount of assembly the company performs increases with each additional cell phone assembled.

2. **Batch-level activities** are performed every time a company produces another batch of a product. For example, suppose that to start processing a new batch of ice cream, an ice cream producer needs to set up its machines. The amount of time spent setting up machines increases with the number of batches produced, not with the number of units produced.

3. **Product-level activities** are performed every time a company produces a new type of product. For example, before a pharmaceutical company can produce and sell a new type of medicine, it must undergo very substantial product tests to ensure the product is effective and safe. The amount of time spent on testing activities increases with the number of products the company produces.

4. **Facility-level activities** are required to support or sustain an entire production process. Consider, for example, a hospital. The hospital building must be insured and heated, and the property taxes must be paid, no matter how many patients the hospital treats. These costs do not vary as a function of the number of units, batches, or products.

Companies may achieve greater accuracy in overhead cost allocation by recognizing these four different levels of activities and, from them, developing specific activity cost pools and their related cost drivers. Illustration 18-13 (page 916) graphically displays this four-level activity hierarchy, along with the types of activities and examples of cost drivers for those activities at each level.

This classification provides managers a structured way of thinking about the relationships between activities and the resources they consume. In contrast, traditional volume-based costing recognizes only unit-level costs. **Failure to recognize this classification of activities is one of the reasons that volume-based cost allocation causes distortions in product costing.**

As indicated earlier, allocating all overhead costs by unit-based cost drivers can send false signals to managers: Dividing batch-, product-, or facility-level costs by the number of units produced gives the mistaken impression that these costs vary with the number of units. **The resources consumed by batch-, product-, and facility-level supporting activities do not vary at the unit level**, nor can managers control them at the unit level. The number of activities performed at the batch level goes up as the *number of batches* rises—not as the number of units within the batches changes. Similarly, the number of product-level activities performed depends on the *number of different products*—not on how many units or batches are produced. Furthermore, facility-sustaining activity costs are not dependent upon the number of products, batches, or units produced. Companies can control batch-, product-, and facility-level costs only by modifying batch-, product-, and facility-level activities.

Illustration 18-13
Hierarchy of activity levels

Four Levels	Types of Activities	Examples of Cost Drivers
Unit-Level Activities		
	<u>Machine-related</u> Drilling, cutting, milling, trimming, pressing	Machine hours
	<u>Labor-related</u> Assembling, painting, sanding, sewing	Direct labor hours or cost
Batch-Level Activities		
	Equipment setups	Number of setups or setup time
	Purchase ordering	Number of purchase orders
	Inspection	Number of inspections or inspection time
	Material handling	Number of material moves
Product-Level Activities		
	Product design	Number of product designs
	Engineering changes	Number of changes
Facility-Level Activities		
	Plant management salaries	Number of employees managed
	Plant depreciation	Square footage
	Property taxes	Square footage
	Utilities	Square footage

There. This baby should keep the building cool.

CUTTING EDGE APPAREL COMPANY

> **DO IT!**

Classify Activity Levels

Action Plan

✔ You should use: **unit-level** activities for each unit of product; **batch-level** activities for each batch of product; **product-level** activities for an entire product line; and **facility-level** activities for across the entire range of products.

Morgan Toy Company manufactures six primary product lines of toys in its Morganville plant. As a result of an activity analysis, the accounting department has identified eight activity cost pools. Each of the toy products is produced in large batches, with the whole plant devoted to one product at a time. Classify each of the following activities as either unit-level, batch-level, product-level, or facility-level: (a) engineering design, (b) machine setup, (c) toy design, (d) interviews of prospective employees, (e) inspections after each setup, (f) polishing parts, (g) assembling parts, (h) health and safety.

Solution

(a) product-level. (b) batch-level. (c) product-level. (d) facility-level. (e) batch-level. (f) unit-level. (g) unit-level. (h) facility-level.

Related exercise material: **BE18-10, BE18-11, BE18-12, E18-15, E18-16,** and **DO IT!** **18-4.**

 The Navigator

Activity-Based Costing in Service Industries

Although initially developed and implemented by manufacturers, activity-based costing has been widely adopted in service industries as well. ABC is used by airlines, railroads, hotels, hospitals, banks, insurance companies, telephone companies, and financial services firms. The overall objective of ABC in service firms is no different than it is in a manufacturing company. That objective is to identify the key activities that generate costs and to keep track of how many of those activities are performed for each service provided (by job, service, contract, or customer).

The general approach to identifying activities, activity cost pools, and cost drivers is the same for service companies and for manufacturers. Also, the labeling of activities as value-added and non–value-added, and the attempt to reduce or eliminate non–value-added activities as much as possible, is just as valid in service industries as in manufacturing operations. What sometimes makes implementation of activity-based costing difficult in service industries is that, compared to manufacturers, **a larger proportion of overhead costs are company-wide costs** that cannot be directly traced to specific services provided by the company.

To illustrate the application of activity-based costing to a service company, contrasted to traditional costing, we use a public accounting firm. This illustration is equally applicable to a law firm, consulting firm, architect, or any service firm that performs numerous services for a client as part of a job.

> **LEARNING OBJECTIVE 8**
>
> Apply activity-based costing to service industries.

Traditional Costing Example

Assume that the public accounting firm of Check and Doublecheck prepares the condensed annual budget shown in Illustration 18-14. The firm engages in a number of services, including audit, tax, and computer consulting.

Check and Doublecheck, CPAs		
Annual Budget		
Revenue		$4,000,000
Direct labor	$1,200,000	
Overhead (expected)	600,000	
Total costs		1,800,000
Operating income		$2,200,000

$$\frac{\text{Estimated overhead}}{\text{Direct labor cost}} = \text{Predetermined overhead rate}$$

$$\frac{\$600,000}{\$1,200,000} = 50\%$$

Illustration 18-14
Condensed annual budget of a service firm under traditional costing

Direct labor is the professional service performed. Under traditional costing, direct labor is the basis for overhead application to each job. As shown in Illustration 18-14, the predetermined overhead rate of 50% is calculated by dividing the total estimated overhead costs by the total direct labor cost. To determine the operating income earned on any job, Check and Doublecheck applies overhead at the rate of 50% of actual direct professional labor costs incurred. For example, assume that Check and Doublecheck records $140,000 of actual direct professional labor cost during its audit of Plano Molding Company, which was billed an audit fee of $260,000. Under traditional costing, using 50% as the rate for applying overhead to the job, Check and Doublecheck would compute applied overhead and operating income related to the Plano Molding Company audit, as shown in Illustration 18-15.

Illustration 18-15
Overhead applied under traditional costing system

Check and Doublecheck, CPAs		
Plano Molding Company Audit		
Revenue		$260,000
Less: Direct professional labor	$140,000	
Applied overhead (50% × $140,000)	70,000	210,000
Operating income		$ 50,000

This example, under traditional costing, uses only one direct cost item and one overhead application rate.

Activity-Based Costing Example

Illustration 18-16
Condensed annual budget of a service firm under activity-based costing

Under *activity-based costing,* Check and Doublecheck distributes its estimated annual overhead costs of $600,000 to three activity cost pools. The firm computes activity-based overhead rates per cost driver by dividing each activity overhead cost pool by the expected number of cost drivers used per activity. Illustration 18-16 shows an annual overhead budget using an ABC system.

Check and Doublecheck, CPAs					
Annual Overhead Budget					
Activity Cost Pools	**Cost Drivers**	**Estimated Overhead**	÷	**Expected Use of Cost Drivers per Activity**	=	**Activity-Based Overhead Rates**
Administration	Number of partner-hours	$335,000		3,350		$100 per partner-hour
Customer development	Revenue billed	160,000		$4,000,000		$0.04 per $1 of revenue
Recruiting and training	Direct professional hours	105,000		30,000		$3.50 per hour
		$600,000				

The assignment of the individual overhead activity rates to the actual number of activities used in the performance of the Plano Molding Company audit results in total overhead assigned of $57,200, as shown in Illustration 18-17.

Illustration 18-17
Assigning overhead in a service company

	Check and Doublecheck CPA.xls				
Home Insert Page Layout Formulas Data Review View					
P18	*fx*				
	A	**B**	**C**	**D**	**E**
1	Check and Doublecheck, CPAs				
2	Plano Molding Company Audit				
3				Activity-	
4			Actual Use of	Based Overhead	Cost
5	Activity Cost Pools	Cost Drivers	Drivers	Rates	Assigned
6	Administration	Number of partner-hours	335	$100.00	$33,500
7	Customer development	Revenue billed	$260,000	$0.04	10,400
8	Recruiting and training	Direct professional hours	3,800	$3.50	13,300
9					$57,200
10					

Under activity-based costing, Check and Doublecheck assigns overhead costs of $57,200 to the Plano Molding Company audit, as compared to $70,000 under traditional costing. Illustration 18-18 compares total costs and operating margins under the two costing systems.

Check and Doublecheck, CPAS Plano Molding Company Audit			
	Traditional Costing		**ABC**
Revenue		$260,000	$260,000
Expenses			
Direct professional labor	$140,000		$140,000
Applied overhead	70,000		57,200
Total expenses		210,000	197,200
Operating income		**$ 50,000**	**$ 62,800**
Profit margin		**19.2%**	**24.2%**

Illustration 18-18
Comparison of traditional costing with ABC in a service company

The comparison shows that the assignment of overhead costs under traditional costing is distorted. The total cost assigned to performing the audit of Plano Molding Company is greater under traditional costing by $12,800, and the profit margin is significantly lower. Traditional costing understates the profitability of the audit.

MANAGEMENT INSIGHT

ABC Evaluated

Surveys of companies often show ABC usage of approximately 50%. Yet, in recent years, articles about ABC have expressed mixed opinions regarding its usefulness. To evaluate ABC practices and user satisfaction with ABC, a survey was conducted of 348 companies worldwide. Some of the interesting findings included: ABC methods are widely used across the entire value chain, rather than being primarily used to allocate production-specific costs; only 25% of non-ABC companies think they are accurately tracing the costs of activities, while 70% of ABC companies think their company does this well; and respondents felt that ABC provides greater support for financial, operational, and strategic decisions. More than 87% of respondents said that their ideal costing system would include some form of ABC. Since this significantly exceeds the 50% of the respondents actually using it, ABC usage may well increase in the future.

Source: William Stratton, Denis Desroches, Raef Lawson, and Toby Hatch, "Activity-Based Costing: Is It Still Relevant?" *Management Accounting Quarterly* (Spring, 2009), pp. 31–39.

 What might explain why so many companies say that ideally they would use ABC, but they haven't adopted it yet? (See page 948.)

> Comprehensive DO IT!

Spreadwell Paint Company manufactures two high-quality base paints: an *oil-based* paint and a *latex* paint. Both are housepaints and are manufactured in neutral white color only. Spreadwell sells the white base paints to franchised retail paint and decorating stores where pigments are added to tint (color) the paint as the customer desires. The oil-based paint is made with organic solvents (petroleum products) such as mineral spirits or turpentine. The latex paint is made with water; synthetic resin particles are suspended in the water, and dry and harden when exposed to the air.

Spreadwell uses the same processing equipment to produce both paints in different production runs. Between batches, the vats and other processing equipment must be washed and cleaned.

After analyzing the company's entire operations, Spreadwell's accountants and production managers have identified activity cost pools and accumulated annual budgeted overhead costs by pool as follows.

Activity Cost Pools	Estimated Overhead
Purchasing	$ 240,000
Processing (weighing and mixing, grinding, thinning and drying, straining)	1,400,000
Packaging (quarts, gallons, and 5-gallons)	580,000
Testing	240,000
Storage and inventory control	180,000
Washing and cleaning equipment	560,000
Total annual budgeted overhead	$3,200,000

Following further analysis, activity cost drivers were identified and their expected use by product and activity were scheduled as follows.

Activity Cost Pools	Cost Drivers	Expected Cost Drivers per Activity	Expected Use of Drivers per Product Oil-Based	Latex
Purchasing	Purchase orders	1,500 orders	800	700
Processing	Gallons processed	1,000,000 gallons	400,000	600,000
Packaging	Containers filled	400,000 containers	180,000	220,000
Testing	Number of tests	4,000 tests	2,100	1,900
Storing	Avg. gals. on hand	18,000 gallons	10,400	7,600
Washing	Number of batches	800 batches	350	450

Spreadwell has budgeted 400,000 gallons of oil-based paint and 600,000 gallons of latex paint for processing during the year.

Instructions

(a) Prepare a schedule showing the computations of the activity-based overhead rates.

(b) Prepare a schedule assigning each activity's overhead cost pool to each product.

(c) Compute the overhead cost per unit for each product.

Solution to Comprehensive DO IT!

Action Plan

✔ Identify the major activities that pertain to the manufacture of specific products and allocate manufacturing overhead costs to activity cost pools.

✔ Identify the cost drivers that accurately measure each activity's contribution to the finished product.

(a) Computations of activity-based overhead rates:

Activity Cost Pools	Estimated Overhead	÷	Expected Use of Cost Drivers	=	Activity-Based Overhead Rates
Purchasing	$ 240,000		1,500 orders		$160 per order
Processing	1,400,000		1,000,000 gallons		$1.40 per gallon
Packaging	580,000		400,000 containers		$1.45 per container
Testing	240,000		4,000 tests		$60 per test
Storing	180,000		18,000 gallons		$10 per gallon
Washing	560,000		800 batches		$700 per batch
	$3,200,000				

Action Plan (contd.)

✔ Compute the activity-based overhead rates.

✔ Assign manufacturing overhead costs for each activity cost pool to products, using the activity-based overhead rates.

(b) Assignment of activity cost pools to products:

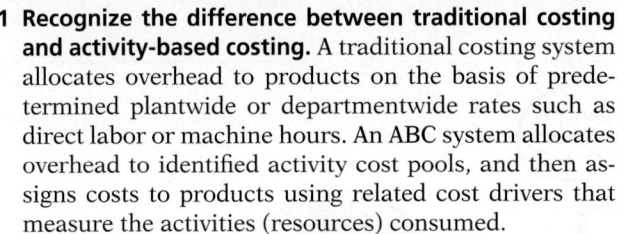

Activity Cost Pools	Oil-Based Paint			Latex Paint		
	Expected Use of Drivers	Overhead Rates	Cost Assigned	Expected Use of Drivers	Overhead Rates	Cost Assigned
Purchasing	800	$160	$ 128,000	700	$160	$ 112,000
Processing	400,000	$1.40	560,000	600,000	$1.40	840,000
Packaging	180,000	$1.45	261,000	220,000	$1.45	319,000
Testing	2,100	$60	126,000	1,900	$60	114,000
Storing	10,400	$10	104,000	7,600	$10	76,000
Washing	350	$700	245,000	450	$700	315,000
Total overhead assigned			$1,424,000			$1,776,000

(c) Computation of overhead cost assigned per unit:

	Oil-Based Paint	Latex Paint
Total overhead cost assigned	$1,424,000	$1,776,000
Total gallons produced	400,000	600,000
Overhead cost per gallon	$3.56	$2.96

✔ **The Navigator**

SUMMARY OF LEARNING OBJECTIVES

✔ **The Navigator**

1 Recognize the difference between traditional costing and activity-based costing. A traditional costing system allocates overhead to products on the basis of predetermined plantwide or departmentwide rates such as direct labor or machine hours. An ABC system allocates overhead to identified activity cost pools, and then assigns costs to products using related cost drivers that measure the activities (resources) consumed.

2 Identify the steps in the development of an activity-based costing system. The development of an activity-based costing system involves four steps: (1) Identify and classify the major activities involved in the manufacture of specific products, and allocate manufacturing overhead costs to the appropriate cost pools. (2) Identify the cost driver that has a strong correlation to the costs accumulated in the cost pool. (3) Compute the overhead rate per cost driver. (4) Assign manufacturing overhead costs for each cost pool to products or services using the overhead rates.

3 Know how companies identify the activity cost pools used in activity-based costing. To identify activity cost pools, a company must perform an analysis of each operation or process, documenting and timing every task, action, or transaction.

4 Know how companies identify and use cost drivers in activity-based costing. Cost drivers identified for assigning activity cost pools must (a) accurately measure the actual consumption of the activity by the various products and (b) have related data easily available.

5 Understand the benefits and limitations of activity-based costing. Features of ABC that make it a more accurate product costing system include: (1) the increased number of cost pools used to assign overhead, (2) the enhanced control over overhead costs, and (3) the better management decisions it makes possible. The limitations of ABC are: (1) the higher analysis and measurement costs that accompany multiple activity centers and cost drivers, and (2) the necessity still to allocate some costs arbitrarily.

6 Differentiate between value-added and non–value-added activities. Value-added activities are essential to operations of the business and often increase the worth of a product or service. Non–value-added are non-essential activities that simply add cost to or increase the time spent on a product or service without increasing its market value. Awareness of these classifications encourages managers to reduce or eliminate the time spent on non–value-added activities.

7 Understand the value of using activity levels in activity-based costing. Activities may be classified as unit-level, batch-level, product-level, and facility-level. Companies control overhead costs at unit-, batch-, product-, and facility-levels by modifying unit-, batch-, product-, and facility-level activities, respectively. Failure to recognize this classification of levels can result in distorted product costing.

8 Apply activity-based costing to service industries. The overall objective of using ABC in service industries is no different than for manufacturing industries—that is,

improved costing of services provided (by job, service, contract, or customer). The general approach to costing is the same: analyze operations, identify activities, accumulate overhead costs by activity cost pools, and identify and use cost drivers to assign the cost pools to the services.

APPENDIX 18A   JUST-IN-TIME PROCESSING

<table>
<tr><td>LEARNING OBJECTIVE   9</td></tr>
<tr><td>Explain just-in-time (JIT) processing.</td></tr>
</table>

Traditionally, continuous process manufacturing has been based on a **just-in-case** philosophy: Inventories of raw materials are maintained *just in case* some items are of poor quality or a key supplier is shut down by a strike. Similarly, subassembly parts are manufactured and stored *just in case* they are needed later in the manufacturing process. Finished goods are completed and stored *just in case* unexpected and rush customer orders are received. This philosophy often results in a "**push approach**," in which raw materials and subassembly parts are pushed through each process. Traditional processing often results in the buildup of extensive manufacturing inventories.

Primarily in response to foreign competition, many U.S. firms have switched to **just-in-time (JIT) processing**. JIT manufacturing is dedicated to having the right amount of materials, parts, or products just as they are needed. JIT first hit the United States in the early 1980s when automobile companies adopted it to compete with foreign automakers. Many companies, including Dell, Caterpillar, and Harley-Davidson, now successfully use JIT. Under JIT processing, companies receive raw materials **just in time** for use in production, they complete subassembly parts **just in time** for use in finished goods, and they complete finished goods **just in time** to be sold. Illustration 18A-1 shows the sequence of activities in just-in-time processing.

Illustration 18A-1
Just-in-time processing

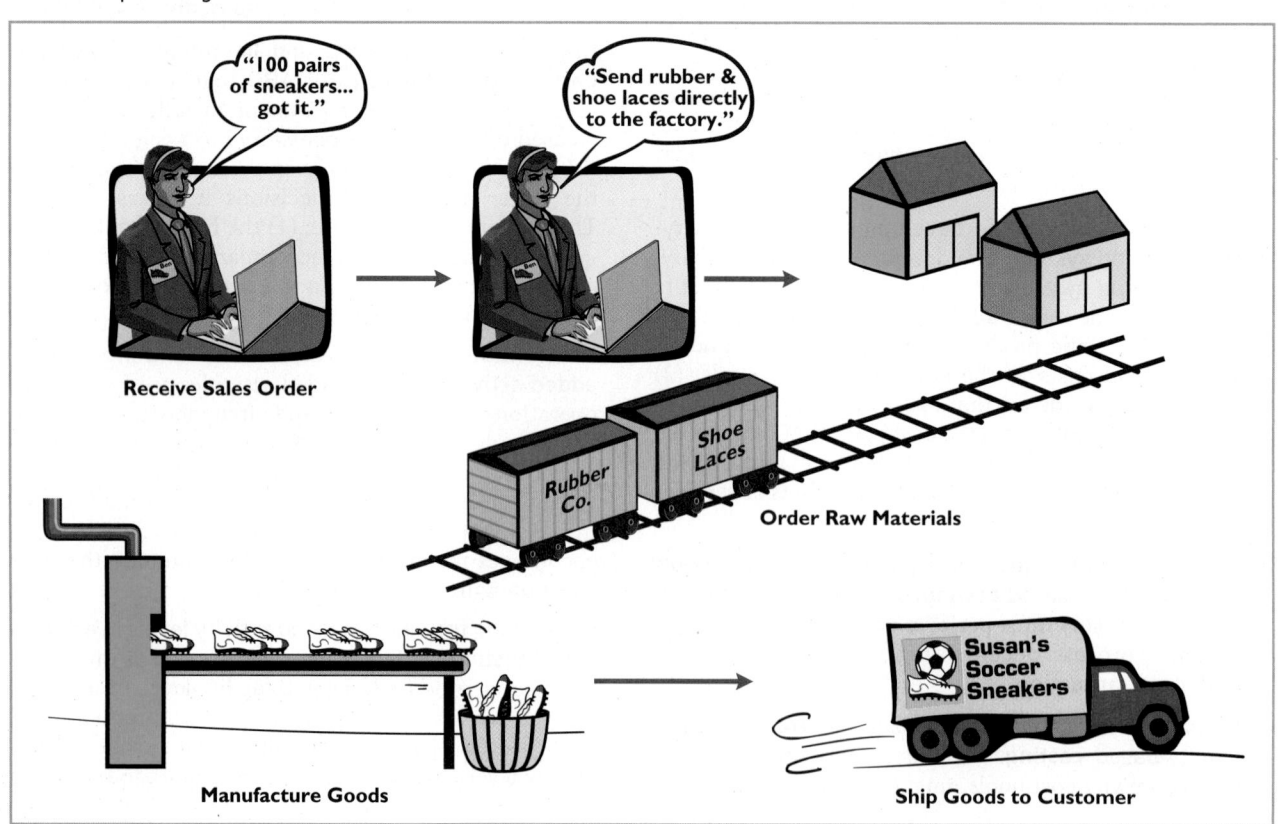

Objective of JIT Processing

A primary objective of JIT is to eliminate all manufacturing inventories. Inventories have an adverse effect on net income because they tie up funds and storage space that could be put to more productive uses. JIT strives to eliminate inventories by using a "**pull approach**" in manufacturing. This approach begins with the customer placing an order with the company, which starts the process of pulling the product through the manufacturing process. A computer at the final workstation sends a signal to the preceding workstation. This signal indicates the exact materials (parts and subassemblies) needed to complete the production of a specified product for a specified time period, such as an eight-hour shift. The next-preceding process, in turn, sends its signal to other processes back up the line. The goal is a smooth continuous flow in the manufacturing process, with no buildup of inventories at any point.

Elements of JIT Processing

There are three important elements in JIT processing:

1. **Dependable suppliers.** Suppliers must be willing to deliver on short notice exact quantities of raw materials according to precise quality specifications (even including multiple deliveries within the same day). Suppliers must also be willing to deliver the raw materials at specified workstations rather than at a central receiving department. This type of purchasing requires constant and direct communication. Such communication is facilitated by an online computer linkage between the company and its suppliers.

2. **A multiskilled work force.** Under JIT, machines are often strategically grouped into work cells or workstations. Much of the work is automated. As a result, one worker may operate and maintain several different types of machines.

3. **A total quality control system.** The company must establish total quality control throughout the manufacturing operations. Total quality control means **no defects**. Since the pull approach signals only required quantities, any defects at any workstation will shut down operations at subsequent workstations. Total quality control requires continuous monitoring by both line employees and supervisors at each workstation.

Helpful Hint
Buyer leverage is important in finding dependable suppliers. Companies like **GM** and **GE** have more success than smaller companies.

Helpful Hint
Without its emphasis on quality control, JIT would be impractical or even impossible. In JIT, quality is engineered into the production process.

Benefits of JIT Processing

The major benefits of implementing JIT processing are:

1. Significant reduction or elimination of manufacturing inventories.
2. Enhanced product quality.
3. Reduction or elimination of rework costs and inventory storage costs.
4. Production cost savings from the improved flow of goods through the processes.

The effects in many cases have been dramatic. For example, after using JIT for two years, a major division of Hewlett-Packard found that work in process inventories (in dollars) were down 82%, scrap/rework costs were down 30%, space utilization improved by 40%, and labor efficiency improved 50%. As indicated, JIT not only reduces inventory but also enables a manufacturer to produce a better product faster and with less waste.

One of the major accounting benefits of JIT is the elimination of separate raw materials and work in process inventory accounts. These accounts are replaced by **one account**, Raw and In-Process Inventory. All materials and conversion costs are charged to this account. The reduction (or elimination) of in-process inventories results in a simpler computation of equivalent units of production.

SUMMARY OF LEARNING OBJECTIVE FOR APPENDIX 18A

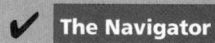 **The Navigator**

9 Explain just-in-time (JIT) processing. JIT is a processing system dedicated to having on hand the right materials and products just at the time they are needed, thereby reducing the amount of inventory and the time inventory is held. One of the principal accounting effects is that one account, Raw and In-Process Inventory, replaces both the raw materials and work-in-process inventory accounts.

GLOSSARY

Activity Any event, action, transaction, or work sequence that incurs cost when producing a product or providing a service. (p. 903).

Activity-based costing (ABC) An overhead cost-allocation system that allocates overhead to multiple activity cost pools and assigns the activity cost pools to products or services by means of cost drivers that represent the activities used. (p. 903).

Activity-based management (ABM) Extends ABC from product costing to a comprehensive management tool that focuses on reducing costs and improving processes and decision-making. (p. 913).

Activity cost pool The overhead cost attributed to a distinct type of activity or related activities. (p. 903).

Batch-level activities Activities performed for each batch of products rather than for each unit. (p. 915).

Cost driver Any factor or activity that has a direct cause–effect relationship with the resources consumed. In ABC, cost drivers are used to assign activity cost pools to products or services. (p. 903).

Facility-level activities Activities required to support or sustain an entire production process. (p. 915).

Just-in-time (JIT) processing A processing system dedicated to having the right amount of materials, parts, or products arrive as they are needed, thereby reducing the amount of inventory. (p. 922).

Non–value-added activity An activity that, if eliminated, would not hinder the company's operations or reduce the perceived worth of its product or service. (p. 913).

Product-level activities Activities performed in support of an entire product line, but not always performed every time a new unit or batch of products is produced. (p. 915).

Unit-level activities Activities performed for each unit of production. (p. 915).

Value-added activity An activity that increases the perceived worth of a product or service to a customer. (p. 913).

 **WILEY PLUS** Self-Test, Brief Exercises, Exercises, Problem Set A, and many more resources are available for practice in WileyPLUS.

Note: All asterisked Questions, Exercises, and Problems relate to material in the appendix to the chapter.

SELF-TEST QUESTIONS

Answers are at the end of the chapter.

(LO 1) **1.** Activity-based costing (ABC):
(a) can be used only in a process cost system.
(b) focuses on units of production.
(c) focuses on activities performed to produce a product.
(d) uses only a single basis of allocation.

2. Activity-based costing: (LO 1)
(a) is the initial phase of converting to a just-in-time operating environment.
(b) can be used only in a job order costing system.
(c) is a two-stage overhead cost allocation system that identifies activity cost pools and cost drivers.
(d) uses direct labor as its primary cost driver.

(LO 1, 4) **3.** Any activity that causes resources to be consumed is called a:
  (a) just-in-time activity.
  (b) facility-level activity.
  (c) cost driver.
  (d) non–value-added activity.

(LO 2) **4.** The first step in the development of an activity-based costing system is:
  (a) identify and classify activities and allocate overhead to cost pools.
  (b) assign overhead costs to products.
  (c) identify cost drivers.
  (d) compute overhead rates.

(LO 4) **5.** Which of the following would be the *best* cost driver for the assembling cost pool?
  (a) Number of product lines.
  (b) Number of parts.
  (c) Number of orders.
  (d) Amount of square footage.

(LO 4) **6.** The overhead rate for Machine Setups is $100 per setup. Products A and B have 80 and 60 setups, respectively. The overhead assigned to each product is:
  (a) Product A $8,000, Product B $8,000.
  (b) Product A $8,000, Product B $6,000.
  (c) Product A $6,000, Product B $6,000.
  (d) Product A $6,000, Product B $8,000.

(LO 4) **7.** Donna Crawford Co. has identified an activity cost pool to which it has allocated estimated overhead of $1,920,000. It has determined the expected use of cost drivers for that activity to be 160,000 inspections. Widgets require 40,000 inspections, Gadgets 30,000 inspections, and Targets 90,000 inspections. The overhead assigned to each product is:
  (a) Widgets $40,000, Gadgets $30,000, Targets $90,000.
  (b) Widgets $640,000, Gadgets $640,000, Targets $640,000.
  (c) Widgets $360,000, Gadgets $480,000, Targets $1,080,000.
  (d) Widgets $480,000, Gadgets $360,000, Targets $1,080,000.

(LO 5) **8.** A frequently cited limitation of activity-based costing is:
  (a) ABC results in more cost pools being used to assign overhead costs to products.

  (b) certain overhead costs remain to be allocated by means of some arbitrary volume-based cost driver such as labor or machine hours.
  (c) ABC leads to poorer management decisions.
  (d) ABC results in less control over overhead costs.

9. A company should consider using ABC if: (LO 5)
  (a) overhead costs constitute a small portion of total product costs.
  (b) it has only a few product lines that require similar degrees of support services.
  (c) direct labor constitutes a significant part of the total product cost and a high correlation exists between direct labor and changes in overhead costs.
  (d) its product lines differ greatly in volume and manufacturing complexity.

10. An activity that adds costs to the product but does (LO 6)
not increase its perceived market value is a:
  (a) value-added activity.
  (b) cost driver.
  (c) cost/benefit activity.
  (d) non–value-added activity.

11. The following activity is value-added: (LO 6)
  (a) Storage of raw materials.
  (b) Moving parts from machine to machine.
  (c) Shaping a piece of metal on a lathe.
  (d) All of the above.

12. A relevant facility-level cost driver for heating costs is: (LO 7)
  (a) machine hours.   (c) floor space.
  (b) direct material.   (d) direct labor cost.

*13. Under just-in-time processing: (LO 9)
  (a) raw materials are received just in time for use in production.
  (b) subassembly parts are completed just in time for use in assembling finished goods.
  (c) finished goods are completed just in time to be sold.
  (d) All of the above.

*14. The primary objective of just-in-time processing is to: (LO 9)
  (a) accumulate overhead in activity cost pools.
  (b) eliminate or reduce all manufacturing inventories.
  (c) identify relevant activity cost drivers.
  (d) identify value-added activities.

Go to the book's companion website, www.wiley.com/college/weygandt, for additional Self-Test Questions.

 ✔ **The Navigator**

QUESTIONS

1. Under what conditions is direct labor a valid basis for allocating overhead?

2. What has happened in recent industrial history to reduce the usefulness of direct labor as the primary basis for allocating overhead to products?

3. In an automated manufacturing environment, what basis of overhead allocation is frequently more relevant than direct labor hours?

4. What is generally true about overhead allocation to high-volume products versus low-volume products under a traditional costing system?

5. What are the principal differences between activity-based costing (ABC) and traditional product costing?

6. What is the formula for computing activity-based overhead rates?

7. What steps are involved in developing an activity-based costing system?
8. Explain the preparation and use of a value-added/non–value-added activity flowchart in an ABC system.
9. What is an activity cost pool?
10. What is a cost driver?
11. What makes a cost driver accurate and appropriate?
12. What is the formula for assigning activity cost pools to products?
13. What are the benefits of activity-based costing?
14. What are the limitations of activity-based costing?
15. Under what conditions is ABC generally the superior overhead costing system?

16. What refinement has been made to enhance the efficiency and effectiveness of ABC for use in managing costs?
17. Of what benefit is classifying activities as value-added and non–value-added?
18. In what ways is the application of ABC to service industries the same as its application to manufacturing companies?
19. What is the relevance of the classification of levels of activity to ABC?
*20. (a) Describe the philosophy and approach of just-in-time processing.
    (b) Identify the major elements of JIT processing.

BRIEF EXERCISES

Identify differences between costing systems.

(LO 1)

BE18-1 Warner Inc. sells a high-speed retrieval system for mining information. It provides the following information for the year.

	Budgeted	**Actual**
Overhead cost	$1,000,000	$950,000
Machine hours	50,000	45,000
Direct labor hours	100,000	92,000

Overhead is applied on the basis of direct labor hours. (a) Compute the predetermined overhead rate. (b) Determine the amount of overhead applied for the year. (c) Explain how an activity-based costing system might differ in terms of computing a predetermined overhead rate.

Identify differences between costing systems.

(LO 1)

BE18-2 Finney Inc. has conducted an analysis of overhead costs related to one of its product lines using a traditional costing system (volume-based) and an activity-based costing system. Here are its results.

	Traditional Costing	**ABC**
Sales revenue	$600,000	$600,000
Overhead costs:		
Product RX3	$ 34,000	$ 50,000
Product Y12	36,000	20,000
	$ 70,000	$ 70,000

Explain how a difference in the overhead costs between the two systems may have occurred.

Identify cost drivers.

(LO 4)

BE18-3 Storrer Co. identifies the following activities that pertain to manufacturing overhead: materials handling, machine setups, factory machine maintenance, factory supervision, and quality control. For each activity, identify an appropriate cost driver.

Identify cost drivers.

(LO 4)

BE18-4 Mason Company manufactures four products in a single production facility. The company uses activity-based costing. The following activities have been identified through the company's activity analysis: (a) inventory control, (b) machine setups, (c) employee training, (d) quality inspections, (e) material ordering, (f) drilling operations, and (g) building maintenance.

For each activity, name a cost driver that might be used to assign overhead costs to products.

Compute activity-based overhead rates.

(LO 4)

BE18-5 Mordica Company identifies three activities in its manufacturing process: machine setups, machining, and inspections. Estimated annual overhead cost for each activity is $150,000, $325,000, and $87,500, respectively. The cost driver for each activity and the expected annual usage are: number of setups 2,500, machine hours 25,000, and number of inspections 1,750. Compute the overhead rate for each activity.

BE18-6 Weisman, Inc. uses activity-based costing as the basis for information to set prices for its six lines of seasonal coats. Compute the activity-based overhead rates using the following budgeted data for each of the activity cost pools.

Compute activity-based overhead rates.

(LO 4)

Activity Cost Pools	Estimated Overhead	Expected Use of Cost Drivers per Activity
Designing	$ 450,000	10,000 designer hours
Sizing and cutting	4,000,000	160,000 machine hours
Stitching and trimming	1,440,000	80,000 labor hours
Wrapping and packing	336,000	32,000 finished units

BE18-7 Hollins, Inc., a manufacturer of computer chips, employs activity-based costing. The budgeted data for each of the activity cost pools is provided below for the year 2014.

Compute activity-based overhead rates.

(LO 4)

Activity Cost Pools	Estimated Overhead	Expected Use of Cost Drivers per Activity
Ordering and receiving	$ 90,000	12,000 orders
Etching	480,000	60,000 machine hours
Soldering	1,760,000	440,000 labor hours

For 2014, the company had 11,000 orders and used 50,000 machine hours, and labor hours totaled 500,000. What is the total overhead applied?

BE18-8 Rich Novelty Company identified the following activities in its production and support operations. Classify each of these activities as either value-added or non–value-added.

Classify activities as value- or non–value-added.

(LO 6)

(a) Machine setup.
(b) Design engineering.
(c) Storing inventory.
(d) Moving work in process.
(e) Inspecting and testing.
(f) Painting and packing.

BE18-9 Mendle and Kiner is an architectural firm that is contemplating the installation of activity-based costing. The following activities are performed daily by staff architects. Classify these activities as value-added or non–value-added: (a) designing and drafting, 2.5 hours; (b) staff meetings, 1 hour; (c) on-site supervision, 2 hours; (d) lunch, 1 hour; (e) consultation with client on specifications, 1.5 hours; (f) entertaining a prospective client for dinner, 2 hours.

Classify service company activities as value- or non–value-added.

(LO 6, 8)

BE18-10 Kwik Pix is a large digital processing center that serves 130 outlets in grocery stores, service stations, camera and photo shops, and drug stores in 16 nearby towns. Kwik Pix operates 24 hours a day, 6 days a week. Classify each of the following activity costs of Kwik Pix as either unit-level, batch-level, product-level, or facility-level.

Classify activities according to level.

(LO 7, 8)

(a) Color printing materials.
(b) Photocopy paper.
(c) Depreciation of machinery.
(d) Setups for enlargements.
(e) Supervisor's salary.
(f) Ordering materials.
(g) Pickup and delivery.
(h) Commission to dealers.
(i) Insurance on building.
(j) Loading developing machines.

BE18-11 Trammell, Inc. operates 20 injection molding machines in the production of tool boxes of four different sizes, named the Apprentice, the Handyman, the Journeyman, and the Professional. Classify each of the following costs as unit-level, batch-level, product-level, or facility-level.

Classify activities according to level.

(LO 7)

(a) First-shift supervisor's salary.
(b) Powdered raw plastic.
(c) Dies for casting plastic components.

(d) Depreciation on injection molding machines.
(e) Changing dies on machines.
(f) Moving components to assembly department.
(g) Engineering design.
(h) Employee health and medical insurance coverage.

Compute rates and activity levels.

(LO 4, 7)

BE18-12 Spin Cycle Company uses three activity pools to apply overhead to its products. Each activity has a cost driver used to allocate the overhead costs to the product. The activities and related overhead costs are as follows: product design $40,000; machining $300,000; and material handling $100,000. The cost drivers and expected use are as follows.

Activities	Cost Drivers	Expected Use of Cost Drivers per Activity
Product design	Number of product changes	10
Machining	Machine hours	150,000
Material handling	Number of setups	100

(a) Compute the predetermined overhead rate for each activity. (b) Classify each of these activities as unit-level, batch-level, product-level, or facility-level.

> DO IT! REVIEW

Identify characteristics of traditional and ABC costing systems.

(LO 1, 2)

DO IT! 18-1 Indicate whether the following statements are true or false.

(a) The reasoning behind ABC cost allocation is that products consume activities and activities consume resources.
(b) Activity-based costing is an approach for allocating direct labor to products.
(c) In today's increasingly automated environment, direct labor is never an appropriate basis for allocating costs to products.
(d) A cost driver is any factor or activity that has a direct cause-effect relationship with resources consumed.
(e) Activity-based costing segregates overhead into various cost pools in an effort to provide more accurate cost information.

Compute activity-based overhead rates and assign overhead using ABC.

(LO 4)

DO IT! 18-2 Flynn Industries has three activity cost pools and two products. It expects to produce 3,000 units of Product BC113 and 1,500 of Product AD908. Having identified its activity cost pools and the cost drivers for each pool, Flynn accumulated the following data relative to those activity cost pools and cost drivers.

	Annual Overhead Data			Expected Use of Cost Drivers per Product		
Activity Cost Pool	Cost Drivers	Estimated Overhead	Expected Use of Cost Drivers per Activity	Product BC113	Product AD908
Machine setup	Setups	$ 16,000	40	25	15
Machining	Machine hours	110,000	5,000	1,000	4,000
Packing	Orders	30,000	500	150	350

Using the above data, do the following:

(a) Prepare a schedule showing the computations of the activity-based overhead rates per cost driver.
(b) Prepare a schedule assigning each activity's overhead cost to the two products.
(c) Compute the overhead cost per unit for each product. (Round to nearest cent.)
(d) Comment on the comparative overhead cost per product.

Classify activities as value- or non–value-added.

(LO 6, 8)

DO IT! 18-3 Classify each of the following activities within a tax-preparation business as value-added (VA) or non–value-added (NVA).

(a) Advertising.
(b) Completing tax returns.

(c) Billing clients.
(d) Answering client questions.
(e) Accompanying clients to audit proceedings.

DO IT! **18-4** Adamson Company manufactures four lines of garden tools. As a result of an activity analysis, the accounting department has identified eight activity cost pools. Each of the product lines is produced in large batches, with the whole plant devoted to one product at a time. Classify each of the following activities or costs as either unit-level, batch level, product-level, or facility-level.

Classify activities according to level.

(LO 7)

(a) Machining parts.   (e) Assembling parts.
(b) Product design.   (f) Purchasing raw materials.
(c) Plant maintenance.   (g) Property taxes.
(d) Machine setup.   (h) Painting.

✔ **The Navigator**

EXERCISES

E18-1 Wilkins Inc. has two types of handbags: standard and custom. The controller has decided to use a plantwide overhead rate based on direct labor costs. The president has heard of activity-based costing and wants to see how the results would differ if this system were used. Two activity cost pools were developed: machining and machine setup. Presented below is information related to the company's operations.

Assign overhead using traditional costing and ABC.

(LO 1, 4)

	Standard	**Custom**
Direct labor costs	$50,000	$100,000
Machine hours	1,000	1,000
Setup hours	100	400

Total estimated overhead costs are $270,000. Overhead cost allocated to the machining activity cost pool is $170,000, and $100,000 is allocated to the machine setup activity cost pool.

Instructions
(a) Compute the overhead rate using the traditional (plantwide) approach.
(b) Compute the overhead rates using the activity-based costing approach.
(c) Determine the difference in allocation between the two approaches.

E18-2 Ayala Inc. has conducted the following analysis related to its product lines, using a traditional costing system (volume-based) and an activity-based costing system. Both the traditional and the activity-based costing systems include direct materials and direct labor costs.

Explain difference between traditional and activity-based costing.

(LO 1)

		Total Costs	
Products	**Sales Revenue**	**Traditional**	**ABC**
Product 540X	$180,000	$55,000	$50,000
Product 137Y	160,000	50,000	35,000
Product 249S	70,000	15,000	35,000

Instructions
(a) For each product line, compute operating income using the traditional costing system.
(b) For each product line, compute operating income using the activity-based costing system.
(c) Using the following formula, compute the percentage difference in operating income for each of the product lines of Ayala: [Operating Income (ABC) − Operating Income (traditional cost)] ÷ Operating Income (traditional cost). (Round the percentage to two decimals.)
(d) Provide a rationale as to why the costs for Product 540X are approximately the same using either the traditional or activity-based costing system.

*Assign overhead using
traditional costing and ABC.*

(LO 1, 4)

E18-3 American Fabrics has budgeted overhead costs of $990,000. It has allocated overhead on a plantwide basis to its two products (wool and cotton) using direct labor hours which are estimated to be 450,000 for the current year. The company has decided to experiment with activity-based costing and has created two activity cost pools and related activity cost drivers. These two cost pools are: cutting (cost driver is machine hours) and design (cost driver is number of setups). Overhead allocated to the cutting cost pool is $360,000 and $630,000 is allocated to the design cost pool. Additional information related to these pools is as follows.

	Wool	Cotton	Total
Machine hours	100,000	100,000	200,000
Number of setups	1,000	500	1,500

Instructions
(a) Determine the amount of overhead allocated to the wool product line and the cotton product line using activity-based costing.
(b) What amount of overhead would be allocated to the wool and cotton product lines using the traditional approach, assuming direct labor hours were incurred evenly between the wool and cotton? How does this compare with the amount allocated using ABC in part (a)?

*Assign overhead using
traditional costing and ABC.*

(LO 1, 4)

E18-4 Altex Inc. manufactures two products: car wheels and truck wheels. To determine the amount of overhead to assign to each product line, the controller, Robert Hermann, has developed the following information.

	Car	Truck
Estimated wheels produced	40,000	10,000
Direct labor hours per wheel	1	3

Total estimated overhead costs for the two product lines are $770,000.

Instructions
(a) Compute the overhead cost assigned to the car wheels and truck wheels, assuming that direct labor hours is used to allocate overhead costs.
(b) Hermann is not satisfied with the traditional method of allocating overhead because he believes that most of the overhead costs relate to the truck wheel product line because of its complexity. He therefore develops the following three activity cost pools and related cost drivers to better understand these costs.

Activity Cost Pools	Expected Use of Cost Drivers	Estimated Overhead Costs
Setting up machines	1,000 setups	$220,000
Assembling	70,000 labor hours	280,000
Inspection	1,200 inspections	270,000

Compute the activity-based overhead rates for these three cost pools.
(c) Compute the cost that is assigned to the car wheels and truck wheels product lines using an activity-based costing system, given the following information.

Expected Use of Cost Drivers per Product		
	Car	Truck
Number of setups	200	800
Direct labor hours	40,000	30,000
Number of inspections	100	1,100

(d) What do you believe Hermann should do?

*Assign overhead using
traditional costing and ABC.*

(LO 1, 4)

E18-5 Shady Lady sells window coverings (shades, blinds, and awnings) to both commercial and residential customers. The following information relates to its budgeted operations for the current year.

	Commercial		Residential	
Revenues		$300,000		$480,000
Direct material costs	$ 30,000		$ 50,000	
Direct labor costs	100,000		300,000	
Overhead costs	85,000	215,000	150,000	500,000
Operating income (loss)		$ 85,000		($ 20,000)

The controller, Peggy Kingman, is concerned about the residential product line. She cannot understand why this line is not more profitable given that the installations of window coverings are less complex for residential customers. In addition, the residential client base resides in close proximity to the company office, so travel costs are not as expensive on a per client visit for residential customers. As a result, she has decided to take a closer look at the overhead costs assigned to the two product lines to determine whether a more accurate product costing model can be developed. Here are the three activity cost pools and related information she developed:

Activity Cost Pools	Estimated Overhead	Cost Drivers
Scheduling and travel	$105,000	Hours of travel
Setup time	70,000	Number of setups
Supervision	60,000	Direct labor cost

Expected Use of Cost Drivers per Product		
	Commercial	Residential
Scheduling and travel	1,000	500
Setup time	450	250

Instructions

(a) Compute the activity-based overhead rates for each of the three cost pools, and determine the overhead cost assigned to each product line.

(b) Compute the operating income for each product line, using the activity-based overhead rates.

(c) What do you believe Peggy Kingman should do?

E18-6 Perdon Corporation manufactures safes—large mobile safes, and large walk-in stationary bank safes. As part of its annual budgeting process, Perdon is analyzing the profitability of its two products. Part of this analysis involves estimating the amount of overhead to be allocated to each product line. The information shown below relates to overhead.

Assign overhead using traditional costing and ABC.

(LO 1, 4)

	Mobile Safes	Walk-In Safes
Units planned for production	200	50
Material moves per product line	300	200
Purchase orders per product line	450	350
Direct labor hours per product line	800	1,700

Instructions

(a) The total estimated manufacturing overhead was $260,000. Under traditional costing (which assigns overhead on the basis of direct labor hours), what amount of manufacturing overhead costs are assigned to:

(1) One mobile safe?

(2) One walk-in safe?

(b) The total estimated manufacturing overhead of $260,000 was comprised of $160,000 for material handling costs and $100,000 for purchasing activity costs. Under activity-based costing (ABC):

(1) What amount of material handling costs are assigned to:

(a) One mobile safe?

(b) One walk-in safe?

(2) What amount of purchasing activity costs are assigned to:

(a) One mobile safe?

(b) One walk-in safe?

(c) Compare the amount of overhead allocated to one mobile safe and to one walk-in safe under the traditional costing approach versus under ABC.

E18-7 Quik Prints Company is a small printing and copying firm with three high-speed offset printing presses, five copiers (two color and three black-and-white), one collator, one cutting and folding machine, and one fax machine. To improve its pricing practices, owner-manager Terry Morton is installing activity-based accounting. Additionally, Terry employs five employees: two printers/designers, one receptionist/bookkeeper, one salesperson/copy-machine operator, and one janitor/delivery clerk. Terry can operate any of the machines and, in addition to managing the entire operation, he performs the training, designing, selling, and marketing functions.

Identify activity cost pools.

(LO 3)

Instructions

As Quik Prints' independent accountant who prepares tax forms and quarterly financial statements, you have been asked to identify the activities that would be used to accumulate overhead costs for assignment to jobs and customers. Using your knowledge of a small printing and copying firm (and some imagination), identify at least 12 activity cost pools as the start of an activity-based costing system for Quik Prints Company.

Identify activity cost pools and cost drivers.

(LO 3, 4)

E18-8 Santana Corporation manufactures snowmobiles in its Blue Mountain, Wisconsin, plant. The following costs are budgeted for the first quarter's operations.

Machine setup, indirect materials	$ 4,000
Inspections	16,000
Tests	4,000
Insurance, plant	110,000
Engineering design	140,000
Depreciation, machinery	520,000
Machine setup, indirect labor	20,000
Property taxes	29,000
Oil, heating	19,000
Electricity, plant lighting	21,000
Engineering prototypes	60,000
Depreciation, plant	210,000
Electricity, machinery	36,000
Machine maintenance wages	19,000

Instructions

Classify the above costs of Santana Corporation into activity cost pools using the following: engineering, machinery, machine setup, quality control, factory utilities, maintenance. Next, identify a cost driver that may be used to assign each cost pool to each line of snowmobiles.

Identify activity cost drivers.

(LO 4)

E18-9 Danny Baden's Verde Vineyards in Oakville, California, produces three varieties of wine: Merlot, Viognier, and Pinot Noir. His winemaster, Russel Hansen, has identified the following activities as cost pools for accumulating overhead and assigning it to products.

1. Culling and replanting. Dead or overcrowded vines are culled, and new vines are planted or relocated. (Separate vineyards by variety.)
2. Tying. The posts and wires are reset, and vines are tied to the wires for the dormant season.
3. Trimming. At the end of the harvest, the vines are cut and trimmed back in preparation for the next season.
4. Spraying. The vines are sprayed with chemicals for protection against insects and fungi.
5. Harvesting. The grapes are hand-picked, placed in carts, and transported to the crushers.
6. Stemming and crushing. Cartfuls of bunches of grapes of each variety are separately loaded into machines which remove stems and gently crush the grapes.
7. Pressing and filtering. The crushed grapes are transferred to presses which mechanically remove the juices and filter out bulk and impurities.
8. Fermentation. The grape juice, by variety, is fermented in either stainless-steel tanks or oak barrels.
9. Aging. The wines are aged in either stainless-steel tanks or oak barrels for one to three years depending on variety.
10. Bottling and corking. Bottles are machine-filled and corked.
11. Labeling and boxing. Each bottle is labeled, as is each nine-bottle case, with the name of the vintner, vintage, and variety.
12. Storing. Packaged and boxed bottles are stored awaiting shipment.
13. Shipping. The wine is shipped to distributors and private retailers.
14. Heating and air-conditioning of plant and offices.
15. Maintenance of buildings and equipment. Printing, repairs, replacements, and general maintenance are performed in the off-season.

Instructions

For each of Verde's 15 activity cost pools, identify a probable cost driver that might be used to assign overhead costs to its three wine varieties.

Identify activity cost drivers.

(LO 4)

E18-10 Wilmington, Inc. manufactures five models of kitchen appliances at its Mesa plant. The company is installing activity-based costing and has identified the following activities performed at its Mesa plant.

1. Designing new models.
2. Purchasing raw materials and parts.
3. Storing and managing inventory.
4. Receiving and inspecting raw materials and parts.
5. Interviewing and hiring new personnel.
6. Machine forming sheet steel into appliance parts.
7. Manually assembling parts into appliances.
8. Training all employees of the company.
9. Insuring all tangible fixed assets.
10. Supervising production.
11. Maintaining and repairing machinery and equipment.
12. Painting and packaging finished appliances.

Having analyzed its Mesa plant operations for purposes of installing activity-based costing, Wilmington, Inc. identified its activity cost centers. It now needs to identify relevant activity cost drivers in order to assign overhead costs to its products.

Instructions

Using the activities listed above, identify for each activity one or more cost drivers that might be used to assign overhead to Wilmington's five products.

E18-11 Major Instrument, Inc. manufactures two products: missile range instruments and space pressure gauges. During April, 50 range instruments and 300 pressure gauges were produced, and overhead costs of $94,500 were estimated. An analysis of estimated overhead costs reveals the following activities.

Compute overhead rates and assign overhead using ABC.

(LO 4, 5)

Activities	Cost Drivers	Total Cost
1. Materials handling	Number of requisitions	$40,000
2. Machine setups	Number of setups	27,500
3. Quality inspections	Number of inspections	27,000
		$94,500

The cost driver volume for each product was as follows.

Cost Drivers	Instruments	Gauges	Total
Number of requisitions	400	600	1,000
Number of setups	200	300	500
Number of inspections	200	400	600

Instructions

(a) Determine the overhead rate for each activity.
(b) Assign the manufacturing overhead costs for April to the two products using activity-based costing.
(c) ▭▭▭▷ Write a memorandum to the president of Major Instrument explaining the benefits of activity-based costing.

E18-12 Kragan Clothing Company manufactures its own designed and labeled sports attire and sells its products through catalog sales and retail outlets. While Kragan has for years used activity-based costing in its manufacturing activities, it has always used traditional costing in assigning its selling costs to its product lines. Selling costs have traditionally been assigned to Kragan's product lines at a rate of 70% of direct material costs. Its direct material costs for the month of March for Kragan's "high-intensity" line of attire are $400,000. The company has decided to extend activity-based costing to its selling costs. Data relating to the "high-intensity" line of products for the month of March are as follows.

Assign overhead using traditional costing and ABC.

(LO 1, 4, 6)

Activity Cost Pools	Cost Drivers	Overhead Rate	Number of Cost Drivers Used per Activity
Sales commissions	Dollar sales	$0.05 per dollar sales	$900,000
Advertising—TV/Radio	Minutes	$300 per minute	250
Advertising—Newspaper	Column inches	$10 per column inch	2,000
Catalogs	Catalogs mailed	$2.50 per catalog	60,000
Cost of catalog sales	Catalog orders	$1 per catalog order	9,000
Credit and collection	Dollar sales	$0.03 per dollar sales	$900,000

Instructions

(a) Compute the selling costs to be assigned to the "high-intensity" line of attire for the month of March (1) using the traditional product costing system (direct material cost is the cost driver), and (2) using activity-based costing.

(b) By what amount does the traditional product costing system undercost or overcost the "high-intensity" product line?

Assign overhead using traditional costing and ABC; classify activities as value- or non–value-added.

(LO 1, 4, 6)

E18-13 Healthy Products, Inc., uses a traditional product costing system to assign overhead costs uniformly to all products. To meet Food and Drug Administration requirements and to assure its customers of safe, sanitary, and nutritious food, Healthy engages in a high level of quality control. Healthy assigns its quality-control overhead costs to all products at a rate of 17% of direct labor costs. Its direct labor cost for the month of June for its low-calorie dessert line is $65,000. In response to repeated requests from its financial vice president, Healthy's management agrees to adopt activity-based costing. Data relating to the low-calorie dessert line for the month of June are as follows.

Activity Cost Pools	Cost Drivers	Overhead Rate	Number of Cost Drivers Used per Activity
Inspections of material received	Number of pounds	$0.80 per pound	6,000 pounds
In-process inspections	Number of servings	$0.33 per serving	10,000 servings
FDA certification	Customer orders	$12.00 per order	420 orders

Instructions

(a) Compute the quality-control overhead cost to be assigned to the low-calorie dessert product line for the month of June (1) using the traditional product costing system (direct labor cost is the cost driver), and (2) using activity-based costing.

(b) By what amount does the traditional product costing system undercost or overcost the low-calorie dessert line?

(c) Classify each of the activities as value-added or non–value-added.

Classify service company activities as value-added or non–value-added.

(LO 6)

E18-14 Lasso and Markowitz is a law firm that is initiating an activity-based costing system. Sam Lasso, the senior partner and strong supporter of ABC, has prepared the following list of activities performed by a typical attorney in a day at the firm.

Activities	Hours
Writing contracts and letters	1.5
Attending staff meetings	0.5
Taking depositions	1.0
Doing research	1.0
Traveling to/from court	1.0
Contemplating legal strategy	1.0
Eating lunch	1.0
Litigating a case in court	2.5
Entertaining a prospective client	1.5

Instructions

Classify each of the activities listed by Sam Lasso as value-added or non–value-added, and defend your classification. How much was value-added time and how much was non–value-added?

E18-15 Having itemized its costs for the first quarter of next year's budget, Santana Corporation desires to install an activity-based costing system. First, it identified the activity cost pools in which to accumulate factory overhead. Second, it identified the relevant cost drivers. (This was done in E18-8.)

Classify activities by level.
(LO 7)

Instructions
Using the activity cost pools identified in E18-8, classify each of those cost pools as either unit-level, batch-level, product-level, or facility-level.

E18-16 William Mendel & Sons, Inc. is a small manufacturing company in La Jolla that uses activity-based costing. Mendel & Sons accumulates overhead in the following activity cost pools.

Classify activities by level.
(LO 7)

1. Hiring personnel.
2. Managing parts inventory.
3. Purchasing.
4. Testing prototypes.
5. Designing products.
6. Setting up equipment.
7. Training employees.
8. Inspecting machined parts.
9. Machining.
10. Assembling.

Instructions
For each activity cost pool, indicate whether the activity cost pool would be unit-level, batch-level, product-level, or facility-level.

EXERCISES: SET B AND CHALLENGE EXERCISES

Visit the book's companion website, at **www.wiley.com/college/weygandt**, and choose the Student Companion site to access Exercise Set B and Challenge Exercises.

PROBLEMS: SET A

P18-1A FireOut, Inc. manufactures steel cylinders and nozzles for two models of fire extinguishers: (1) a home fire extinguisher and (2) a commercial fire extinguisher. The *home model* is a high-volume (54,000 units), half-gallon cylinder that holds 2 1/2 pounds of multi-purpose dry chemical at 480 PSI. The *commercial model* is a low-volume (10,200 units), two-gallon cylinder that holds 10 pounds of multi-purpose dry chemical at 390 PSI. Both products require 1.5 hours of direct labor for completion. Therefore, total annual direct labor hours are 96,300 or [1.5 hrs. × (54,000 + 10,200)]. Expected annual manufacturing overhead is $1,557,480. Thus, the predetermined overhead rate is $16.17 or ($1,557,480 ÷ 96,300) per direct labor hour. The direct materials cost per unit is $18.50 for the home model and $26.50 for the commercial model. The direct labor cost is $19 per unit for both the home and the commercial models.

The company's managers identified six activity cost pools and related cost drivers and accumulated overhead by cost pool as follows.

Assign overhead using traditional costing and ABC; compute unit costs; classify activities as value- or non–value-added.

(LO 1, 4, 6)

Activity Cost Pools	Cost Drivers	Estimated Overhead	Expected Use of Cost Drivers	Expected Use of Drivers by Product	
				Home	Commercial
Receiving	Pounds	$ 70,350	335,000	215,000	120,000
Forming	Machine hours	150,500	35,000	27,000	8,000
Assembling	Number of parts	412,300	217,000	165,000	52,000
Testing	Number of tests	51,000	25,500	15,500	10,000
Painting	Gallons	52,580	5,258	3,680	1,578
Packing and shipping	Pounds	820,750	335,000	215,000	120,000
		$1,557,480			

(a) Unit cost—H.M. $61.76

(c) Cost assigned—H.M. $1,069,300

(d) Cost/unit—H.M. $57.30

Assign overhead to products using ABC and evaluate decision.

(LO 4)

Instructions

(a) Under traditional product costing, compute the total unit cost of each product. Prepare a simple comparative schedule of the individual costs by product (similar to Illustration 18-10 on page 908).

(b) Under ABC, prepare a schedule showing the computations of the activity-based overhead rates (per cost driver).

(c) Prepare a schedule assigning each activity's overhead cost pool to each product based on the use of cost drivers. (Include a computation of overhead cost per unit, rounding to the nearest cent.)

(d) Compute the total cost per unit for each product under ABC.

(e) Classify each of the activities as a value-added activity or a non–value-added activity.

(f) Comment on (1) the comparative overhead cost per unit for the two products under ABC, and (2) the comparative total costs per unit under traditional costing and ABC.

P18-2A Schultz Electronics manufactures two large-screen television models: the Royale which sells for $1,600, and a new model, the Majestic, which sells for $1,300. The production cost computed per unit under traditional costing for each model in 2014 was as follows.

Traditional Costing	Royale	Majestic
Direct materials	$ 700	$420
Direct labor ($20 per hour)	120	100
Manufacturing overhead ($38 per DLH)	228	190
Total per unit cost	$1,048	$710

In 2014, Schultz manufactured 25,000 units of the Royale and 10,000 units of the Majestic. The overhead rate of $38 per direct labor hour was determined by dividing total expected manufacturing overhead of $7,600,000 by the total direct labor hours (200,000) for the two models.

Under traditional costing, the gross profit on the models was Royale $552 or ($1,600 − $1,048), and Majestic $590 or ($1,300 − $710). Because of this difference, management is considering phasing out the Royale model and increasing the production of the Majestic model.

Before finalizing its decision, management asks Schultz's controller to prepare an analysis using activity-based costing (ABC). The controller accumulates the following information about overhead for the year ended December 31, 2014.

Activities	Cost Drivers	Estimated Overhead	Expected Use of Cost Drivers	Activity-Based Overhead Rate
Purchasing	Number of orders	$1,200,000	40,000	$30/order
Machine setups	Number of setups	900,000	18,000	$50/setup
Machining	Machine hours	4,800,000	120,000	$40/hour
Quality control	Number of inspections	700,000	28,000	$25/inspection

The cost drivers used for each product were:

Cost Drivers	Royale	Majestic	Total
Purchase orders	17,000	23,000	40,000
Machine setups	5,000	13,000	18,000
Machine hours	75,000	45,000	120,000
Inspections	11,000	17,000	28,000

Instructions

(a) Assign the total 2014 manufacturing overhead costs to the two products using activity-based costing (ABC) and determine the overhead cost per unit.

(b) What was the cost per unit and gross profit of each model using ABC costing?

(c) ▐▍▍▍▍▶ Are management's future plans for the two models sound? Explain.

(a) Royale $4,035,000

(b) Cost/unit—Royale $981.40

P18-3A Thakin Stairs Co. designs and builds factory-made premium wooden stairways for homes. The manufactured stairway components (spindles, risers, hangers, hand rails) permit installation of stairways of varying lengths and widths. All are of white oak wood. Budgeted manufacturing overhead costs for the year 2014 are as follows.

Assign overhead costs using traditional costing and ABC; compare results.

(LO 1, 4)

Overhead Cost Pools	Amount
Purchasing	$ 69,000
Handling materials	82,000
Production (cutting, milling, finishing)	210,000
Setting up machines	95,000
Inspecting	90,000
Inventory control (raw materials and finished goods)	126,000
Utilities	180,000
Total budgeted overhead costs	$852,000

For the last 4 years, Thakin Stairs Co. has been charging overhead to products on the basis of machine hours. For the year 2014, 100,000 machine hours are budgeted.

Jeremy Nolan, owner-manager of Thakin Stairs Co., recently directed his accountant, Bill Seagren, to implement the activity-based costing system that he has repeatedly proposed. At Jeremy Nolan's request, Bill and the production foreman identify the following cost drivers and their usage for the previously budgeted overhead cost pools.

Activity Cost Pools	Cost Drivers	Expected Use of Cost Drivers
Purchasing	Number of orders	600
Handling materials	Number of moves	8,000
Production (cutting, milling, finishing)	Direct labor hours	100,000
Setting up machines	Number of setups	1,250
Inspecting	Number of inspections	6,000
Inventory control (raw materials and finished goods)	Number of components	168,000
Utilities	Square feet occupied	90,000

Steve Hannon, sales manager, has received an order for 250 stairways from Community Builders, Inc., a large housing development contractor. At Steve's request, Bill prepares cost estimates for producing components for 250 stairways so Steve can submit a contract price per stairway to Community Builders. He accumulates the following data for the production of 250 stairways.

Direct materials	$103,600
Direct labor	$112,000
Machine hours	14,500
Direct labor hours	5,000
Number of purchase orders	60
Number of material moves	800
Number of machine setups	100
Number of inspections	450
Number of components	16,000
Number of square feet occupied	8,000

(b) Cost/stairway $1,356.56

(c) Cost/stairway $1,134.20

Instructions
(a) Compute the predetermined overhead rate using traditional costing with machine hours as the basis.
(b) What is the manufacturing cost per stairway under traditional costing? (Round to the nearest cent.)
(c) What is the manufacturing cost per stairway under the proposed activity-based costing? (Round to the nearest cent. Prepare all of the necessary schedules.)
(d) ⬛▭▭▭▭▷ Which of the two costing systems is preferable in pricing decisions and why?

Assign overhead costs using traditional costing and ABC; compare results.

(LO 1, 4)

P18-4A Benton Corporation produces two grades of wine from grapes that it buys from California growers. It produces and sells roughly 3,000,000 liters per year of a low-cost, high-volume product called CoolDay. It sells this in 600,000 5-liter jugs. Benton also produces and sells roughly 300,000 liters per year of a low-volume, high-cost product called LiteMist. LiteMist is sold in 1-liter bottles. Based on recent data, the CoolDay product has not been as profitable as LiteMist. Management is considering dropping the inexpensive CoolDay line so it can focus more attention on the LiteMist product. The LiteMist product already demands considerably more attention than the CoolDay line.

Jack Eller, president and founder of Benton, is skeptical about this idea. He points out that for many decades the company produced only the CoolDay line and that it was always quite profitable. It wasn't until the company started producing the more complicated LiteMist wine that the profitability of CoolDay declined. Prior to the introduction of LiteMist, the company had simple equipment, simple growing and production procedures, and virtually no need for quality control. Because LiteMist is bottled in 1-liter bottles, it requires considerably more time and effort, both to bottle and to label and box than does CoolDay. The company must bottle and handle 5 times as many bottles of LiteMist to sell the same quantity as CoolDay. CoolDay requires 1 month of aging; LiteMist requires 1 year. CoolDay requires cleaning and inspection of equipment every 10,000 liters; LiteMist requires such maintenance every 600 liters.

Jack has asked the accounting department to prepare an analysis of the cost per liter using the traditional costing approach and using activity-based costing. The following information was collected.

	CoolDay	LiteMist
Direct materials per liter	$0.40	$1.20
Direct labor cost per liter	$0.50	$0.90
Direct labor hours per liter	0.05	0.09
Total direct labor hours	150,000	27,000

Activity Cost Pools	Cost Drivers	Estimated Overhead	Expected Use of Cost Drivers	Expected Use of Cost Drivers Per Product	
				CoolDay	LiteMist
Grape processing	Cart of grapes	$ 145,860	6,600	6,000	600
Aging	Total months	396,000	6,600,000	3,000,000	3,600,000
Bottling and corking	Number of bottles	270,000	900,000	600,000	300,000
Labeling and boxing	Number of bottles	189,000	900,000	600,000	300,000
Maintain and inspect equipment	Number of inspections	240,800	800	350	450
		$1,241,660			

Instructions
Answer each of the following questions. (Round all calculations to three decimal places.)

(a) Cost/liter—C.D. $1.251

(a) Under traditional product costing using direct labor hours, compute the total manufacturing cost per **liter** of both products.

(b) Under ABC, prepare a schedule showing the computation of the activity-based overhead rates (per cost driver).

(c) Prepare a schedule assigning each activity's overhead cost pool to each product, based on the use of cost drivers. Include a computation of overhead cost per liter.

(c) Cost/liter—C.D. $.241

(d) Compute the total manufacturing cost per liter for both products under ABC.

(e) ▭▭▭▷ Write a memo to Jack Eller discussing the implications of your analysis for the company's plans. In this memo, provide a brief description of ABC as well as an explanation of how the traditional approach can result in distortions.

P18-5A Polk and Stoneman is a public accounting firm that offers two primary services, auditing and tax-return preparation. A controversy has developed between the partners of the two service lines as to who is contributing the greater amount to the bottom line. The area of contention is the assignment of overhead. The tax partners argue for assigning overhead on the basis of 40% of direct labor dollars, while the audit partners argue for implementing activity-based costing. The partners agree to use next year's budgeted data for purposes of analysis and comparison. The following overhead data are collected to develop the comparison.

Assign overhead costs to services using traditional costing and ABC; compute overhead rates and unit costs; compare results.

(LO 1, 4, 6, 8)

Activity Cost Pools	Cost Drivers	Estimated Overhead	Expected Use of Cost Drivers	Expected Use of Cost Drivers Per Service	
				Audit	Tax
Employee training	Direct labor dollars	$216,000	$1,800,000	$1,050,000	$750,000
Typing and secretarial	Number of reports/ forms	76,200	2,500	800	1,700
Computing	Number of minutes	204,000	60,000	25,000	35,000
Facility rental	Number of employees	142,500	40	22	18
Travel	Per expense reports	81,300	Direct	56,000	25,300
		$720,000			

Instructions

(a) Using traditional product costing as proposed by the tax partners, compute the total overhead cost assigned to both services (audit and tax) of Polk and Stoneman.

(b) (1) Using activity-based costing, prepare a schedule showing the computations of the activity-based overhead rates (per cost driver).

(b) (2) Cost assigned—Tax $350,241

    (2) Prepare a schedule assigning each activity's overhead cost pool to each service based on the use of the cost drivers.

(c) ▭▭▭▷ Comment on the comparative overhead cost for the two services under both traditional costing and ABC.

(c) Difference—Audit $50,241

PROBLEMS: SET B

P18-1B VideoPlus, Inc. manufactures two types of DVD players, a deluxe model and a standard model. The deluxe model is a multi-format progressive-scan DVD player with networking capability, Dolby digital, and DTS decoder. The standard model's primary feature is progressive-scan. Annual production is 50,000 units for the deluxe and 20,000 units for the standard.

Assign overhead using traditional costing and ABC; compute unit costs; classify activities as value- or non–value-added.

(LO 1, 4, 6)

Both products require 2 hours of direct labor for completion. Therefore, total annual direct labor hours are 140,000 [2 hrs. × (20,000 + 50,000)]. Expected annual manufacturing overhead is $1,050,000. Thus, the predetermined overhead rate is $7.50 ($1,050,000 ÷ 140,000) per direct labor hour. The direct materials cost per unit is $42 for the deluxe model and $11 for the standard model. The direct labor cost is $18 per unit for both the deluxe and the standard models.

The company's managers identified six activity cost pools and related cost drivers and accumulated overhead by cost pool as follows.

Activity Cost Pool	Cost Driver	Estimated Overhead	Expected Use of Cost Drivers	Expected Use of Drivers by Product	
				Standard	Deluxe
Purchasing	Orders	$ 126,000	400	100	300
Receiving	Pounds	30,000	20,000	4,000	16,000
Assembling	Number of parts	444,000	74,000	20,000	54,000
Testing	Number of tests	115,000	23,000	10,000	13,000
Finishing	Units	140,000	70,000	20,000	50,000
Packing and shipping	Pounds	195,000	80,000	18,000	62,000
		$1,050,000			

Instructions

(a) Unit cost—Standard $44

(a) Under traditional product costing, compute the total unit cost of both products. Prepare a simple comparative schedule of the individual costs by product (similar to Illustration 18-10 on page 908).

(b) Under ABC, prepare a schedule showing the computations of the activity-based overhead rates (per cost driver).

(c) Cost assigned—Standard $291,375

(c) Prepare a schedule assigning each activity's overhead cost pool to each product based on the use of cost drivers. (Include a computation of overhead cost per unit, rounding to the nearest cent.)

(d) Cost/unit—Standard $43.57

(d) Compute the total cost per unit for each product under ABC.

(e) Classify each of the activities as a value-added activity or a non–value-added activity.

(f) Comment on (1) the comparative overhead cost per unit for the two products under ABC, and (2) the comparative total costs per unit under traditional costing and ABC.

Assign overhead to products using ABC and evaluate decision.

(LO 4)

P18-2B Kinnard Electronics manufactures two home theater systems: the Elite which sells for $1,400, and a new model, the Preferred, which sells for $1,100. The production cost computed per unit under traditional costing for each model in 2014 was as follows.

Traditional Costing	Elite	Preferred
Direct materials	$600	$320
Direct labor ($20 per hour)	100	80
Manufacturing overhead ($35 per DLH)	175	140
Total per unit cost	$875	$540

In 2014, Kinnard manufactured 20,000 units of the Elite and 10,000 units of the Preferred. The overhead rate of $35 per direct labor hour was determined by dividing total expected manufacturing overhead of $4,900,000 by the total direct labor hours (140,000) for the two models.

Under traditional costing, the gross profit on the models was Elite $525 ($1,400 − $875), and Preferred $560 ($1,100 − $540). Because of this difference, management is considering phasing out the Elite model and increasing the production of the Preferred model.

Before finalizing its decision, management asks Kinnard's controller to prepare an analysis using activity-based costing (ABC). The controller accumulates the following information about overhead for the year ended December 31, 2014.

Activity	Cost Driver	Estimated Overhead	Expected Use of Cost Drivers	Activity-Based Overhead Rate
Purchasing	Number of orders	$ 775,000	25,000	$31
Machine setups	Number of setups	580,000	20,000	29
Machining	Machine hours	3,100,000	100,000	31
Quality control	Number of inspections	445,000	5,000	89

The cost drivers used for each product were:

Cost Driver	Elite	Preferred	Total
Purchase orders	11,250	13,750	25,000
Machine setups	11,000	9,000	20,000
Machine hours	40,000	60,000	100,000
Inspections	2,750	2,250	5,000

Instructions
(a) Assign the total 2014 manufacturing overhead costs to the two products using activity-based costing (ABC) and determine the overhead cost per unit.
(b) What was the cost per unit and gross profit of each model using ABC costing?
(c) ▭▭▭▭▷ Are management's future plans for the two models sound? Explain.

(a) Elite $2,152,500

(b) Cost/unit—Elite $807.63

P18-3B Luxury Furniture designs and builds factory-made, premium, wood armoires for homes. All are of white oak. Its budgeted manufacturing overhead costs for the year 2014 are as follows.

Assign overhead costs using traditional costing and ABC; compare results.

(LO 1, 4)

Overhead Cost Pools	Amount
Purchasing	$ 45,000
Handling materials	50,000
Production (cutting, milling, finishing)	130,000
Setting up machines	85,000
Inspecting	60,000
Inventory control (raw materials and finished goods)	80,000
Utilities	100,000
Total budgeted overhead costs	$550,000

For the last 4 years, Luxury Furniture has been charging overhead to products on the basis of materials cost. For the year 2014, materials cost of $500,000 were budgeted.

Jim Brigham, owner-manager of Luxury Furniture, recently directed his accountant, Bob Borke, to implement the activity-based costing system that he has repeatedly proposed. At Jim Brigham's request, Bob and the production foreman identify the following cost drivers and their usage for the previously budgeted overhead cost pools.

Overhead Cost Pools	Activity Cost Drivers	Expected Use of Cost Drivers
Purchasing	Number of orders	500
Handling materials	Number of moves	5,000
Production (cutting, milling, finishing)	Direct labor hours	65,000
Setting up machines	Number of setups	1,000
Inspecting	Number of inspections	4,000
Inventory control (raw materials and finished goods)	Number of components	40,000
Utilities	Square feet occupied	50,000

Debbie Steiner, sales manager, has received an order for 12 luxury armoires from Thom's Interior Design. At Debbie's request, Bob prepares cost estimates for producing 12 armoires so Debbie can submit a contract price per armoire to Thom's. He accumulates the following data for the production of 12 armoires.

Direct materials	$5,200
Direct labor	$3,500
Direct labor hours	200
Number of purchase orders	3
Number of material moves	32
Number of machine setups	4
Number of inspections	20
Number of components	640
Number of square feet occupied	320

(b) Cost/armoire $1,201.67
(c) Cost/armoire $1,020.83

Assign overhead costs using traditional costing and ABC; compare results.

(LO 1, 4)

Instructions

(a) Compute the predetermined overhead rate using traditional costing with materials cost as the basis.

(b) What is the manufacturing cost per armoire under traditional costing?

(c) What is the manufacturing cost per armoire under the proposed activity-based costing? (Prepare all of the necessary schedules.)

(d) ▭▭▭▭▷ Which of the two costing systems is preferable in pricing decisions and why?

P18-4B Merando Corporation produces two grades of wine from grapes that it buys from California growers. It produces and sells roughly 600,000 gallon jugs per year of a low-cost, high-volume product called Valley Fresh. Merando also produces and sells roughly 200,000 gallons per year of a low-volume, high-cost product called Merando Valley. Merando Valley is sold in 1-liter bottles. Based on recent data, the Valley Fresh product has not been as profitable as Merando Valley. Management is considering dropping the inexpensive Valley Fresh line so it can focus more attention on the Merando Valley product. The Merando Valley product already demands considerably more attention than the Valley Fresh line.

Frankie Merando, president and founder of Merando, is skeptical about this idea. He points out that for many decades the company produced only the Valley Fresh line, and that it was always quite profitable. It wasn't until the company started producing the more complicated Merando Valley wine that the profitability of Valley Fresh declined. Prior to the introduction of Merando Valley, the company had simple equipment, simple growing and production procedures, and virtually no need for quality control. Because Merando Valley is bottled in 1-liter bottles, it requires considerably more time and effort, both to bottle and to label and box, than does Valley Fresh. The company must bottle and handle 4 times as many bottles of Merando Valley to sell the same quantity as Valley Fresh, since there are approximately 4 liters in a gallon. Valley Fresh requires 1 month of aging; Merando Valley requires 1 year. Valley Fresh requires cleaning and inspection of equipment every 2,500 gallons; Merando Valley requires such maintenance every 250 gallons.

Frankie has asked the accounting department to prepare an analysis of the cost per gallon using the traditional costing approach and using activity-based costing. The following information was collected.

	Valley Fresh	Merando Valley
Direct materials per gallon	$1.35	$3.60
Direct labor cost per gallon	$0.75	$1.50
Direct labor hours per gallon	0.05	0.10
Total direct labor hours	30,000	20,000

Activity Cost Pool	Cost Driver	Estimated Overhead	Expected Use of Cost Drivers	Expected Use of Cost Drivers per Product	
				Valley Fresh	Merando Valley
Grape processing	Cart of grapes	$ 146,000	8,000	6,000	2,000
Aging	Total months	420,000	3,000,000	600,000	2,400,000
Bottling and corking	Number of bottles	210,000	1,400,000	600,000	800,000
Labeling and boxing	Number of bottles	140,000	1,400,000	600,000	800,000
Maintain and inspect equipment	Number of inspections	234,000	1,040	240	800
		$1,150,000			

Instructions

Answer each of the following questions. (Round all calculations to three decimal places.)

(a) Cost/gallon—V.F. $3.25

(a) Under traditional product costing using direct labor hours, compute the total manufacturing cost per **gallon** of both products.

(b) Under ABC, prepare a schedule showing the computation of the activity-based overhead rates (per cost driver).

(c) Prepare a schedule assigning each activity's overhead cost pool to each product, based on the use of cost drivers. Include a computation of overhead cost per gallon.

(d) Compute the total manufacturing cost per gallon for both products under ABC.

(e) ▣▭▭▭▭▷ Write a memo to Frankie Merando discussing the implications of your analysis for the company's plans. In this memo, provide a brief description of ABC as well as an explanation of how the traditional approach can result in distortions.

(c) Cost/gallon—V.F. $0.663

P18-5B Smith and Jones is a law firm that serves both individuals and corporations. A controversy has developed between the partners of the two service lines as to who is contributing the greater amount to the bottom line. The area of contention is the assignment of overhead. The individual partners argue for assigning overhead on the basis of 30% of direct labor dollars, while the corporate partners argue for implementing activity-based costing. The partners agree to use next year's budgeted data for purposes of analysis and comparison. The following overhead data are collected to develop the comparison.

Assign overhead costs to services using traditional costing and ABC; compute overhead rates and unit costs; compare results.

(LO 1, 4, 6, 8)

Activity Cost Pool	Cost Driver	Estimated Overhead	Expected Use of Cost Drivers	Expected Use of Cost Drivers per Service	
				Corporate	Individual
Employee training	Direct labor dollars	$120,000	$1,600,000	$900,000	$700,000
Typing and secretarial	Number of reports/ forms	60,000	2,000	500	1,500
Computing	Number of minutes	130,000	40,000	17,000	23,000
Facility rental	Number of employees	100,000	25	14	11
Travel	Per expense reports	70,000	Direct	48,000	22,000
		$480,000			

Instructions

(a) Using traditional product costing, compute the total overhead cost assigned to both services (individual and corporate) of Smith and Jones.

(b) (1) Using activity-based costing, prepare a schedule showing the computations of the activity-based overhead rates (per cost driver).

(2) Prepare a schedule assigning each activity's overhead cost pool to each service based on the use of the cost drivers.

(c) ▣▭▭▭▭▷ Comment on the comparative overhead for the two service lines under both traditional costing and ABC.

(b) (2) Cost assigned— Individual $238,250

(c) Difference—Corporate $28,250

PROBLEMS: SET C

Visit the book's companion website, at **www.wiley.com/college/weygandt**, and choose the Student Companion site to access Problem Set C.

WATERWAYS CONTINUING PROBLEM

(*Note:* This is a continuation of the Waterways Problem from Chapters 15–17.)

WCP18 Waterways looked into ABC as a method of costing because of the variety of items it produces and the many different activities in which it is involved. This problem asks you to help Waterways use an activity-based costing system to account for its production activities.

Go to the book's companion website, at **www.wiley.com/college/weygandt**, *to find the completion of this problem.*

Broadening Your PERSPECTIVE

Management Decision-Making

Decision-Making at Current Designs

BYP18-1 As you learned in previous chapters, Current Designs has two main product lines—composite kayaks, which are handmade and very labor-intensive, and rotomolded kayaks, which require less labor but employ more expensive equipment. Current Designs' controller, Diane Buswell, is now evaluating several different methods of assigning overhead to these products. It is important to ensure that costs are appropriately assigned to the company's products. At the same time, the system that is used must not be so complex that its costs are greater than its benefits.

Diane has decided to use the following activities and costs to evaluate the methods of assigning overhead.

Activity	Cost
Designing new models	$121,100
Creating and testing prototypes	152,000
Creating molds for kayaks	188,500
Operating oven for the rotomolded kayaks	40,000
Operating the vacuum line for the composite kayaks	28,000
Supervising production employees	180,000
Curing time (the time that is needed for the chemical processes to finish before the next step in the production process; many of these costs are related to the space required in the building)	190,400
Total	$900,000

As Diane examines the data, she decides that the cost of operating the oven for the rotomolded kayaks and the cost of operating the vacuum line for the composite kayaks can be directly assigned to each of these product lines and do not need to be allocated with the other costs.

Instructions
For purposes of this analysis, assume that Current Designs uses $234,000 in direct labor costs to produce 1,000 composite kayaks and $286,000 in direct labor costs to produce 4,000 rotomolded kayaks each year.

(a) One method of allocating overhead would allocate the common costs to each product line by using an allocation basis such as the number of employees in working on each type of kayak or the amount of factory space used for the production of each type of kayak. Diane knows that about 50% of the area of the plant and 50% of the employees work on the composite kayaks, and the remaining space and other employees work on the rotomolded kayaks. Using this information, and remembering that the cost of operating the oven and vacuum line have been directly assigned, determine the total amount to be assigned to the composite kayak line and the rotomolded kayak line, and the amount to be assigned to each of the units in each line.

(b) Another method of allocating overhead is to use direct labor dollars as an allocation basis. Remembering that the costs of the oven and the vacuum line have been assigned directly to the product lines, allocate the remaining costs using direct labor dollars as the allocation basis. Then, determine the amount of overhead that should be assigned to each unit of each product line using this method.

(c) Activity-based costing requires a cost driver for each cost pool. Use the following information to assign the costs to the product lines using the activity-based costing approach.

Activity	Cost Driver	Driver Amount for Composite Kayaks	Driver Amount for Rotomolded Kayaks
Designing new models	Number of models	3	1
Creating and testing prototypes	Number of prototypes	6	2
Creating molds for kayaks	Number of molds	12	1
Supervising production employees	Number of employees	12	12
Curing time	Number of days of curing time	15,000	2,000

What amount of overhead should be assigned to each composite kayak using this method? What amount of overhead should be assigned to each rotomolded kayak using this method?

(d) Which of the three methods do you think Current Designs should use? Why?

Decision-Making Across the Organization

BYP18-2 East Valley Hospital is a primary medical care facility and trauma center that serves 11 small, rural midwestern communities within a 40-mile radius. The hospital offers all the medical/surgical services of a typical small hospital. It has a staff of 18 full-time doctors and 20 part-time visiting specialists. East Valley has a payroll of 150 employees consisting of technicians, nurses, therapists, managers, directors, administrators, dieticians, secretaries, data processors, and janitors.

Instructions
With the class divided into groups, discuss and answer the following.
(a) Using your (limited, moderate, or in-depth) knowledge of a hospital's operations, identify as many **activities** as you can that would serve as the basis for implementing an activity-based costing system.
(b) For each of the activities listed in (a), identify a **cost driver** that would serve as a valid measure of the resources consumed by the activity.

Managerial Analysis

BYP18-3 Ideal Manufacturing Company of Sycamore, Illinois, has supported a research and development (R&D) department that has for many years been the sole contributor to the company's new farm machinery products. The R&D activity is an overhead cost center that provides services only to in-house manufacturing departments (four different product lines), all of which produce agricultural/farm/ranch-related machinery products.

The department has never sold its services outside, but because of its long history of success, larger manufacturers of agricultural products have approached Ideal to hire its R&D department for special projects. Because the costs of operating the R&D department have been spiraling uncontrollably, Ideal's management is considering entertaining these outside approaches to absorb the increasing costs. But, (1) management doesn't have any cost basis for charging R&D services to outsiders, and (2) it needs to gain control of its R&D costs. Management decides to implement an activity-based costing system in order to determine the charges for both outsiders and the in-house users of the department's services.

R&D activities fall into four pools with the following annual costs.

Market analysis	$1,050,000
Product design	2,350,000
Product development	3,600,000
Prototype testing	1,400,000

Activity analysis determines that the appropriate cost drivers and their usage for the four activities are:

Activities	Cost Drivers	Total Estimated Drivers
Market analysis	Hours of analysis	15,000 hours
Product design	Number of designs	2,500 designs
Product development	Number of products	90 products
Prototype testing	Number of tests	500 tests

Instructions

(a) Compute the activity-based overhead rate for each activity cost pool.

(b) How much cost would be charged to an in-house manufacturing department that consumed 1,800 hours of market analysis time, was provided 280 designs relating to 10 products, and requested 92 engineering tests?

(c) How much cost would serve as the basis for pricing an R&D bid with an outside company on a contract that would consume 800 hours of analysis time, require 178 designs relating to 3 products, and result in 70 engineering tests?

(d) What is the benefit to Ideal Manufacturing of applying activity-based costing to its R&D activity for both in-house and outside charging purposes?

Real-World Focus

BYP18-4 An article in *Cost Management*, by Kocakulah, Bartlett, and Albin entitled "ABC for Calculating Mortgage Loan Servicing Expenses" (July/August 2009, p. 36), discusses a use of ABC in the financial services industry.

Instructions

Read the article and answer the following questions.

(a) What are some of the benefits of ABC that relate to the financial services industry?

(b) What are three things that the company's original costing method did not take into account?

(c) What were some of the cost drivers used by the company in the ABC approach?

BYP18-5 Activity-based costing methods are constantly being improved upon, and many websites discuss suggestions for improvement. The article in this activity outlines an alternative perspective on activity-based costing.

Address: **http://hbswk.hbs.edu/item/4587.html**, or go to **www.wiley.com/college/weygandt**

Instructions

Read the article provided at the site and answer the following questions.

(a) What concerns do the authors say are raised by "real-world use" of ABC? According to the authors, what benefits have companies enjoyed from the use of ABC?

(b) What method do the authors suggest for estimating practical capacity? How important is it to be precise in this estimate?

(c) Describe the steps that are taken after practical capacity has been estimated.

(d) What is one of the primary benefits obtained by management in the report entitled "ABC, the Time-Driven Way"? What is an example of how this worked for a real company?

Critical Thinking

Ethics Case

BYP18-6 Curtis Rich, the cost accountant for Hi-Power Mower Company, recently installed activity-based costing at Hi-Power's St. Louis lawn tractor (riding mower) plant where three models—the 8-horsepower Bladerunner, the 12-horsepower Quickcut, and the 18-horsepower Supercut—are manufactured. Curtis's new product costs for these three models show that the company's traditional costing system had been significantly undercosting the 18-horsepower Supercut. This was due primarily to the lower sales volume of the Supercut compared to the Bladerunner and the Quickcut.

Before completing his analysis and reporting these results to management, Curtis is approached by his friend Ed Gray, who is the production manager for the 18-horsepower Supercut model. Ed has heard from one of Curtis's staff about the new product costs and is upset and worried for his job because the new costs show the Supercut to be losing, rather than making, money.

At first, Ed condemns the new cost system, whereupon Curtis explains the practice of activity-based costing and why it is more accurate than the company's present system. Even more worried now, Ed begs Curtis, "Massage the figures just enough to save the line from being discontinued. You don't want me to lose my job, do you? Anyway, nobody will know."

Curtis holds firm but agrees to recompute all his calculations for accuracy before submitting his costs to management.

Instructions
(a) Who are the stakeholders in this situation?
(b) What, if any, are the ethical considerations in this situation?
(c) What are Curtis's ethical obligations to the company? To his friend?

All About You

BYP18-7 There are many resources available on the Web to assist people in time management. Some of these resources are designed specifically for college students.

Instructions
Go to **http://www.dartmouth.edu/~acskills/videos/video_tm.html** (or do an Internet search of Dartmouth's time-management video). Watch the video and then answer the following questions.
(a) What are the main tools of time management for students, and what is each used for?
(b) At what time of day are students most inclined to waste time? What time of day is the best for studying complex topics?
(c) How can employing time-management practices be a "liberating" experience?
(d) Why is goal-setting important? What are the characteristics of good goals, and what steps should you take to help you develop your goals?

Considering Your Costs and Benefits

BYP18-8 As discussed in the chapter, the principles underlying activity-based costing have evolved into the broader approach known as *activity-based management*. One of the common practices of activity-based management is to identify all business activities, classify each activity as either a value-added or a non–value-added activity, and then try to reduce or eliminate the time spent on non–value-added activities. Consider the implications of applying this same approach to your everyday life, at work and at school. How do you spend your time each day? How much of your day is spent on activities that help you accomplish your objectives, and how much of your day is spent on activities that do not add value?

Many "self-help" books and websites offer suggestions on how to improve your time management. Should you minimize the "non–value-added" hours in your life by adopting the methods suggested by these sources? The basic arguments for and against are as follows.

YES: There are a limited number of hours in a day. You should try to maximize your chances of achieving your goals by eliminating the time that you waste.
NO: Life is about more than working yourself to death. Being an efficiency expert doesn't guarantee that you will be happy. Schedules and daily planners are too constraining.

Instructions
Write a response indicating your position regarding this situation. Provide support for your view.

Answers to Chapter Questions

Answers to Insight and Accounting Across the Organization Questions

p. 909 Traveling Light Q: Why do airlines charge even higher rates for heavier bags, bags that are odd shapes (e.g., ski bags), and bags with hazardous materials in them? **A:** Each of these factors increases the costs to the airlines. Heavier baggage is more difficult to handle, thus increasing labor costs. It also uses up more fuel. Bags that are odd shapes complicate handling both for humans and machines. In addition, odd shapes take up more space in the cargo area. Finally, hazardous materials require special handling and storage procedures. All of these factors should be considered by an airline when it decides how much to charge for special baggage.

p. 912 Using ABC to Aid in Employee Evaluation Q: What positive implications does application of ABC have for the employees of this company? **A:** ABC will make these employees more aware of which activities cost the company more money. They will be motivated to reduce their use of these activities in order to improve their individual performance.

p. 914 What Does NASCAR Have to Do with Breakfast Cereal? Q: What are the benefits of reducing setup time? **A:** Setup time is a non–value-added activity. Customers are not willing to pay extra for more setup time. By reducing the time spent on setups, the company can reduce non–value-added costs. Also, by reducing setup time, the company can switch from producing one product to producing a different product more quickly. This enables it to respond to customers' demands more quickly, thus avoiding stockouts.

p. 919 ABC Evaluated Q: What might explain why so many companies say that ideally they would use ABC, but they haven't adopted it yet? **A:** As noted in the chapter, implementation of an ABC system can be very expensive. It may be difficult to justify an expenditure for a system that allocates overhead costs more accurately. The benefits of more accurate costing may not be as obvious as some of the other things a company might spend its money on, such as a machine that produces goods more efficiently.

Answers to Self-Test Questions

1. c **2.** c **3.** c **4.** a **5.** b **6.** b ($100 × 80), ($100 × 60) **7.** d [($1,920,000/160,000) × 40,000], [($1,920,000/160,000) × 30,000)], [($1,920,000/160,000) × 90,000)] **8.** b **9.** d **10.** d **11.** c **12.** c *13. d *14. b

Chapter 19

Cost-Volume-Profit

Feature Story

Don't Worry—Just Get Big

It wasn't that Jeff Bezos didn't have a good job. He was a vice president at a Wall Street firm. But, he quit his job, moved to Seattle, and started an online retailer, which he named Amazon.com. Like any good entrepreneur, Jeff strove to keep his initial investment small. Operations were run out of his garage. And, to avoid the need for a warehouse, he took orders for books and had them shipped from other distributors' warehouses. One board member recalls how excited the board was whenever an order came in from a customer in a state that Amazon had never serviced before.

By its fourth month, Amazon was selling 100 books a day. In its first full year, it had $15.7 million in sales. The next year, sales increased eightfold. Two years later, sales were $1.6 billion.

Although its sales growth was impressive, Amazon's ability to lose money was equally amazing. One analyst nicknamed it *Amazon.bomb*, while another, predicting its demise, called it *Amazon.toast*. Why was it losing money? The company used every available dollar to reinvest in itself. It built massive warehouses and bought increasingly sophisticated (and expensive) computer systems to improve its distribution system. This desire to grow as fast as possible was

Learning Objectives

After studying this chapter, you should be able to:

1 Distinguish between variable and fixed costs.

2 Explain the significance of the relevant range.

3 Explain the concept of mixed costs.

4 List the five components of cost-volume-profit analysis.

5 Indicate what contribution margin is and how it can be expressed.

6 Identify the three ways to determine the break-even point.

7 Give the formulas for determining sales required to earn target net income.

8 Define margin of safety, and give the formulas for computing it.

 The Navigator

captured in a T-shirt slogan at its company picnic, which read "Eat another hot dog, get big fast." This buying binge was increasing the company's fixed costs at a rate that exceeded its sales growth. Skeptics were predicting that Amazon would soon run out of cash. It didn't.

In the fourth quarter of 2010 (only 15 years after its world headquarters were located in a garage), Amazon reported quarterly revenues of $12.95 billion and quarterly income of $416 million. But, even as it announced record profits, its share price fell by 9%. Why? Because although the company was predicting that its sales revenue in the next quarter would increase by at least 28%, it predicted that its operating profit would fall by at least 2% and perhaps by as much as 34%.

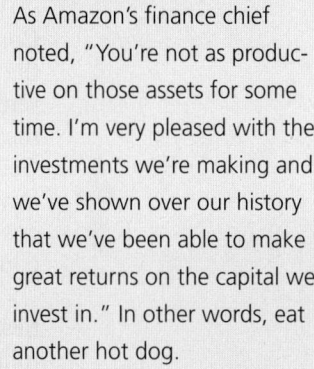

The company made no apologies. It explained that it was in the process of expanding from 39 distribution centers to 52. As Amazon's finance chief noted, "You're not as productive on those assets for some time. I'm very pleased with the investments we're making and we've shown over our history that we've been able to make great returns on the capital we invest in." In other words, eat another hot dog.

Watch the Southwest Airlines video in WileyPLUS to learn more about cost-volume-profit analysis in the real world.

Source: Christine Frey and John Cook, "How Amazon.com Survived, Thrived and Turned a Profit," *Seattle Post* (January 28, 2008); and Stu Woo, "Sticker Shock Over Amazon Growth," *Wall Street Journal Online* (January 28, 2011).

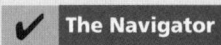

Preview of Chapter 19

As the Feature Story indicates, to manage any size business you must understand how costs respond to changes in sales volume and the effect of costs and revenues on profits. A prerequisite to understanding cost-volume-profit (CVP) relationships is knowledge of how costs behave. In this chapter, we first explain the considerations involved in cost behavior analysis. Then, we discuss and illustrate CVP analysis.

The content and organization of Chapter 19 are as follows.

COST-VOLUME-PROFIT

Cost Behavior Analysis	Cost-Volume-Profit Analysis
• Variable costs • Fixed costs • Relevant range • Mixed costs • Identifying variable and fixed costs	• Basic components • CVP income statement • Break-even analysis • Target net income • Margin of safety

✔ The Navigator

Cost Behavior Analysis

Cost behavior analysis is the study of how specific costs respond to changes in the level of business activity. As you might expect, some costs change, and others remain the same. For example, for an airline company such as Southwest or United, the longer the flight, the higher the fuel costs. On the other hand, Massachusetts General Hospital's costs to staff the emergency room on any given night are relatively constant regardless of the number of patients treated. A knowledge of cost behavior helps management plan operations and decide between alternative courses of action. Cost behavior analysis applies to all types of entities.

The starting point in cost behavior analysis is measuring the key business activities. Activity levels may be expressed in terms of sales dollars (in a retail company), miles driven (in a trucking company), room occupancy (in a hotel), or dance classes taught (by a dance studio). Many companies use more than one measurement base. A manufacturer, for example, may use direct labor hours or units of output for manufacturing costs, and sales revenue or units sold for selling expenses.

For an activity level to be useful in cost behavior analysis, changes in the level or volume of activity should be correlated with changes in costs. The activity level selected is referred to as the activity (or volume) index. The **activity index** identifies the activity that causes changes in the behavior of costs. With an appropriate activity index, companies can classify the behavior of costs in response to changes in activity levels into three categories: variable, fixed, or mixed.

Variable Costs

Variable costs are costs that vary **in total** directly and proportionately with changes in the activity level. If the level increases 10%, total variable costs will increase 10%. If the level of activity decreases by 25%, variable costs will decrease 25%. Examples of variable costs include direct materials and direct labor for a manufacturer; cost of goods sold, sales commissions, and freight-out for a merchandiser; and gasoline in airline and trucking companies. A variable cost may also be defined as a cost that **remains the same *per unit* at every level of activity**.

To illustrate the behavior of a variable cost, assume that Damon Company manufactures tablet computers that contain a $10 camera. The activity index is the number of tablet computers produced. As Damon manufactures each tablet, the total cost of cameras used increases by $10. As part (a) of Illustration 19-1

Illustration 19-1
Behavior of total and unit variable costs

Helpful Hint
True or false: Variable costs per unit change directly and proportionately with changes in activity.
Answer: False. Per unit costs remain constant at all levels of activity.

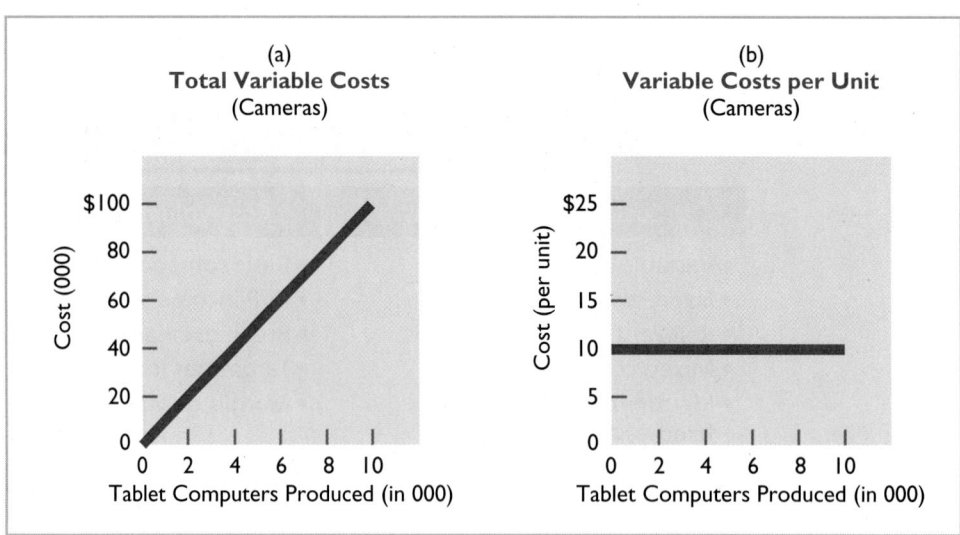

shows, total cost of the cameras will be $20,000 if Damon produces 2,000 tablets, and $100,000 when it produces 10,000 tablets. We also can see that a variable cost remains the same per unit as the level of activity changes. As part (b) of Illustration 19-1 shows, the unit cost of $10 for the cameras is the same whether Damon produces 2,000 or 10,000 tablets.

Companies that rely heavily on labor to manufacture a product, such as Nike or Reebok, or to provide a service, such as Hilton or Marriott, are likely to have many variable costs. In contrast, companies that use a high proportion of machinery and equipment in producing revenue, such as AT&T or Duke Energy Co., may have few variable costs.

Fixed Costs

Fixed costs are costs that **remain the same in total** regardless of changes in the activity level. Examples include property taxes, insurance, rent, supervisory salaries, and depreciation on buildings and equipment. Because total fixed costs remain constant as activity changes, it follows that **fixed costs *per unit* vary inversely with activity: As volume increases, unit cost declines, and vice versa**.

To illustrate the behavior of fixed costs, assume that Damon Company leases its productive facilities at a cost of $10,000 per month. Total fixed costs of the facilities will remain constant at every level of activity, as part (a) of Illustration 19-2 shows. But, **on a per unit basis, the cost of rent will decline as activity increases**, as part (b) of Illustration 19-2 shows. At 2,000 units, the unit cost per tablet computer is $5 ($10,000 ÷ 2,000). When Damon produces 10,000 tablets, the unit cost of the rent is only $1 per tablet ($10,000 ÷ 10,000).

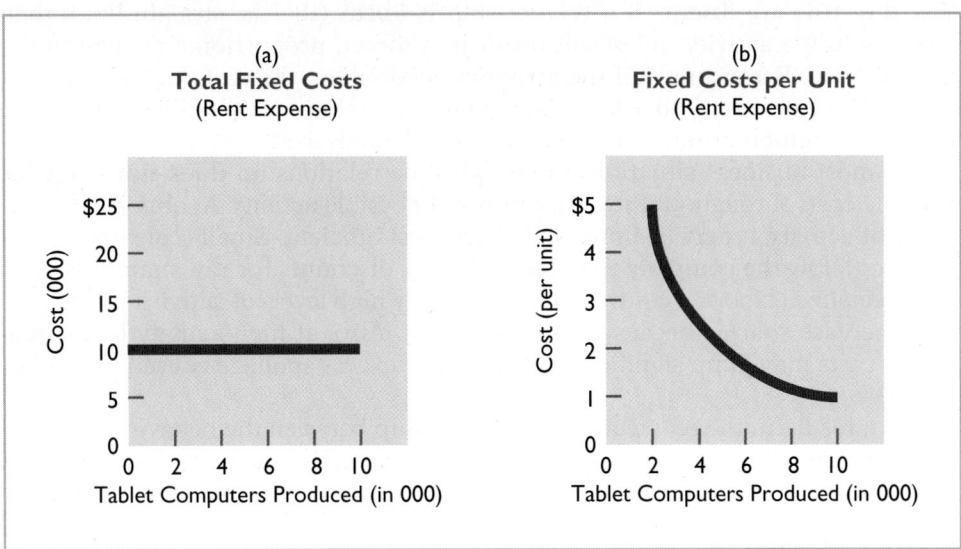

Illustration 19-2
Behavior of total and unit fixed costs

The trend for many manufacturers is to have more fixed costs and fewer variable costs. This trend is the result of increased use of automation and less use of employee labor. As a result, depreciation and lease charges (fixed costs) increase, whereas direct labor costs (variable costs) decrease.

PEOPLE, PLANET, AND PROFIT INSIGHT

Gardens in the Sky

Because of population increases, the United Nations' Food and Agriculture Organization estimates that food production will need to increase by 70% by 2050. Also, by 2050, roughly 70% of people will live in cities, which means more food needs to be hauled further to get it to the consumer. To address the lack of farmable land and reduce the cost of transporting produce, some have suggested building "vertical farming" skyscrapers in cities. This sounds great, but do the numbers work? Some variable costs would be reduced. For example, the use of pesticides, herbicides, fuel costs for shipping, and water would all drop. Soil erosion would be a non-issue since plants would be grown hydroponically (in a solution of water and minerals), and land requirements would be reduced because of vertical structures. But, other costs would be higher. First, there is the cost of the building. Also, any multistory building would require artificial lighting for plants on lower floors.

Until these cost challenges can be overcome, it appears that these skyscrapers will not break even. On the other hand, rooftop greenhouses on existing city structures already appear financially viable. For example, a 15,000 square-foot rooftop greenhouse in Brooklyn already produces roughly 30 tons of vegetables per year for local residents.

Source: "Vertical Farming: Does It Really Stack Up?" *The Economist* (December 9, 2010).

 What are some of the variable and fixed costs that are impacted by hydroponic farming? (See page 987.)

Relevant Range

LEARNING OBJECTIVE **2**

Explain the significance of the relevant range.

In Illustration 19-1 part (a) (page 952), a straight line is drawn throughout the entire range of the activity index for total variable costs. In essence, the assumption is that the costs are **linear**. If a relationship is linear (that is, straight-line), then changes in the activity index will result in a direct, proportional change in the variable cost. For example, if the activity level doubles, the cost doubles.

It is now necessary to ask: Is the straight-line relationship realistic? Does the linear assumption produce useful data for CVP analysis?

In most business situations, a straight-line relationship **does not exist** for variable costs throughout the entire range of possible activity. At abnormally low levels of activity, it may be impossible to be cost-efficient. Small-scale operations may not allow the company to obtain quantity discounts for raw materials or to use specialized labor. In contrast, at abnormally high levels of activity, labor costs may increase sharply because of overtime pay. Also, at high activity levels, materials costs may jump significantly because of excess spoilage caused by worker fatigue.

As a result, in the real world, the relationship between the behavior of a variable cost and changes in the activity level is often **curvilinear**, as shown in part (a) of Illustration 19-3. In the curved sections of the line, a change in the activity index will not result in a direct, proportional change in the variable cost. That is, a doubling of the activity index will not result in an exact doubling of the variable cost. The variable cost may more than double, or it may be less than double.

Total fixed costs also do not have a straight-line relationship over the entire range of activity. Some fixed costs will not change. But it is possible for management to change other fixed costs. For example, in some instances, salaried employees (fixed) are replaced with freelance workers (variable). Illustration 19-3, part (b), shows an example of the behavior of total fixed costs through all potential levels of activity.

Helpful Hint
Fixed costs that may be changeable include research, such as new product development, and management training programs.

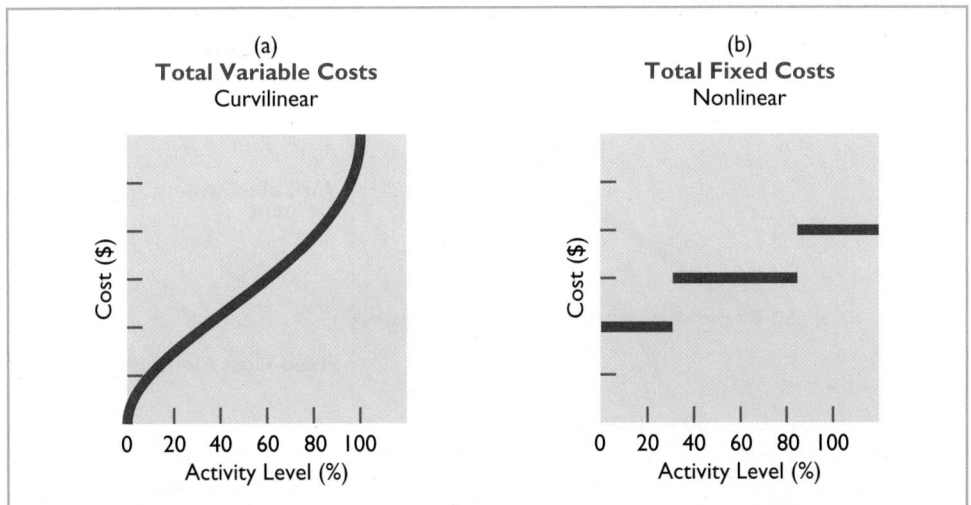

Illustration 19-3
Nonlinear behavior of variable and fixed costs

For most companies, operating at almost zero or at 100% capacity is the exception rather than the rule. Instead, companies often operate over a somewhat narrower range, such as 40–80% of capacity. The range over which a company expects to operate during a year is called the **relevant range** of the activity index. Within the relevant range, as both diagrams in Illustration 19-4 show, a straight-line relationship generally exists for both variable and fixed costs.

Alternative Terminology
The relevant range is also called the *normal* or *practical range*.

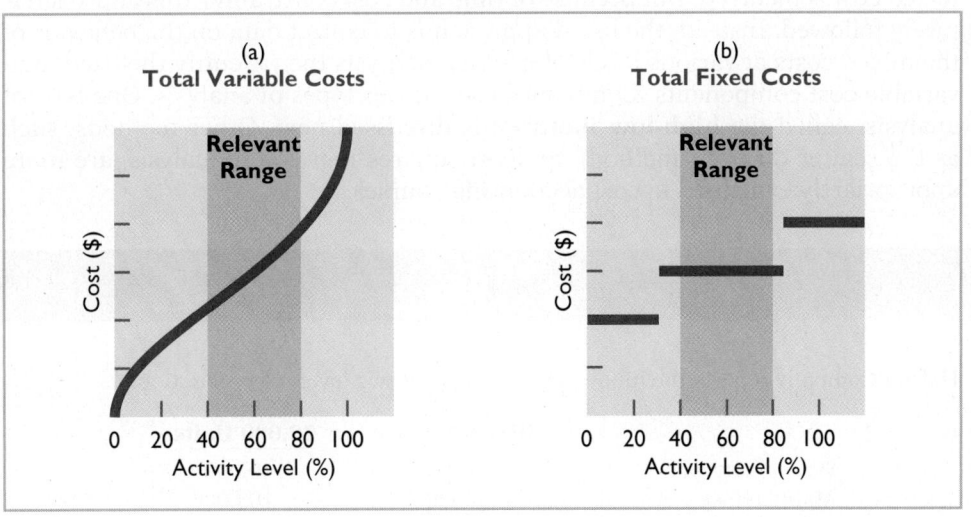

Illustration 19-4
Linear behavior within relevant range

As you can see, although the linear (straight-line) relationship may not be completely realistic, **the linear assumption produces useful data for CVP analysis as long as the level of activity remains within the relevant range**.

Mixed Costs

Mixed costs are costs that contain both a variable element and a fixed element. **Mixed costs, therefore, change in total but not proportionately with changes in the activity level.**

The rental of a U-Haul truck is a good example of a mixed cost. Assume that local rental terms for a 17-foot truck, including insurance, are $50 per day plus 50 cents per mile. When determining the cost of a one-day rental, the per day charge is a fixed cost (with respect to miles driven), whereas the mileage charge is a variable cost. The graphic presentation of the rental cost for a one-day rental is as follows.

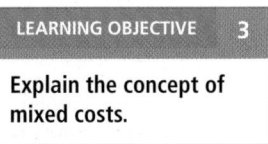

LEARNING OBJECTIVE 3

Explain the concept of mixed costs.

Illustration 19-5
Behavior of a mixed cost

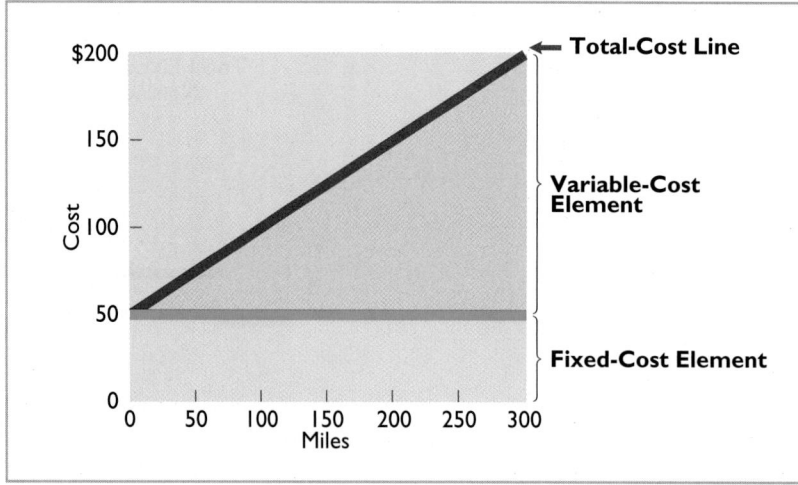

In this case, the fixed-cost element is the cost of having the service available. The variable-cost element is the cost of actually using the service. Another example of a mixed cost is utility costs (electric, telephone, and so on), where there is a flat service fee plus a usage charge.

For purposes of CVP analysis, **mixed costs must be classified into their fixed and variable elements**. How does management make the classification? One possibility is to determine the variable and fixed components each time a mixed cost is incurred. But because of time and cost constraints, this approach is rarely followed. Instead, the usual approach is to collect data on the behavior of the mixed costs at various levels of activity. Analysts then identify the fixed- and variable-cost components. Companies use various types of analysis. One type of analysis, called the **high-low method**, is discussed next. Other methods, such as the scatter diagram method and least squares regression analysis, are more appropriately explained in cost accounting courses.

> **DO IT!**

Types of Costs

Helena Company reports the following total costs at two levels of production.

	10,000 Units	20,000 Units
Direct materials	$20,000	$40,000
Maintenance	8,000	10,000
Direct labor	17,000	34,000
Indirect materials	1,000	2,000
Depreciation	4,000	4,000
Utilities	3,000	5,000
Rent	6,000	6,000

Action Plan

✔ Recall that a variable cost varies in total directly and proportionately with each change in activity level.

✔ Recall that a fixed cost remains the same in total with each change in activity level.

✔ Recall that a mixed cost changes in total but not proportionately with each change in activity level.

Classify each cost as variable, fixed, or mixed.

Solution

Direct materials, direct labor, and indirect materials are variable costs.
Depreciation and rent are fixed costs.
Maintenance and utilities are mixed costs.

Related exercise material: **BE19-1, BE19-2, E19-1, E19-2, E19-4, and** DO IT! **19-1.**

✔ **The Navigator**

HIGH-LOW METHOD

The **high-low method** uses the total costs incurred at the high and low levels of activity to classify mixed costs into fixed and variable components. The difference in costs between the high and low levels represents variable costs, since only the variable-cost element can change as activity levels change.

The steps in computing fixed and variable costs under this method are as follows.

1. Determine variable cost per unit from the following formula.

Change in Total Costs	÷	High minus Low Activity Level	=	Variable Cost per Unit

Illustration 19-6
Formula for variable cost per unit using high-low method

To illustrate, assume that Metro Transit Company has the following maintenance costs and mileage data for its fleet of buses over a 6-month period.

Illustration 19-7
Assumed maintenance costs and mileage data

Month	Miles Driven	Total Cost	Month	Miles Driven	Total Cost
January	20,000	$30,000	April	50,000	$63,000
February	40,000	48,000	May	30,000	42,000
March	35,000	49,000	June	43,000	61,000

The high and low levels of activity are 50,000 miles in April and 20,000 miles in January. The maintenance costs at these two levels are $63,000 and $30,000, respectively. The difference in maintenance costs is $33,000 ($63,000 − $30,000), and the difference in miles is 30,000 (50,000 − 20,000). Therefore, for Metro Transit, variable cost per unit is $1.10, computed as follows.

$$\$33,000 \div 30,000 = \$1.10$$

2. Determine the fixed costs by subtracting the total variable costs at either the high or the low activity level from the total cost at that activity level.

For Metro Transit, the computations are shown in Illustration 19-8.

Illustration 19-8
High-low method computation of fixed costs

	A	B	C	D
			\multicolumn{2}{c} METRO TRANSIT.xls	
	Home Insert Page Layout Formulas Data Review View			
	P18	fx		
1		Metro Transit		
2			Activity Level	
3			High	Low
4	Total cost		$63,000	$30,000
5	Less:	Variable costs		
6		50,000 × $1.10	55,000	
7		20,000 × $1.10		22,000
8	Total fixed costs		$ 8,000	$ 8,000
9				
10				

Maintenance costs are therefore $8,000 per month of fixed costs plus $1.10 per mile of variable costs. This is represented by the following formula:

$$\text{Maintenance costs} = \$8{,}000 + (\$1.10 \times \text{Miles driven})$$

For example, at 45,000 miles, estimated maintenance costs would be $8,000 fixed and $49,500 variable ($1.10 × 45,000) for a total of $57,500.

The graph in Illustration 19-9 plots the 6-month data for Metro Transit Company. The red line drawn in the graph connects the high and low data points, and therefore represents the equation that we just solved using the high-low method. The red, "high-low" line intersects the y-axis at $8,000 (the fixed-cost level), and it rises by $1.10 per unit (the variable cost per unit). Note that a completely different line would result if we chose any two of the other data points. That is, by choosing any two other data points, we would end up with a different estimate of fixed costs and a different variable cost per unit. Thus, from this scatter plot, we can see that while the high-low method is simple, the result is rather arbitrary. A better approach, which uses information from all the data points to estimate fixed and variable costs, is called *regression analysis*. A discussion of regression analysis is provided in a supplement on the book's companion website.

Illustration 19-9

Scatter plot for Metro Transit Company

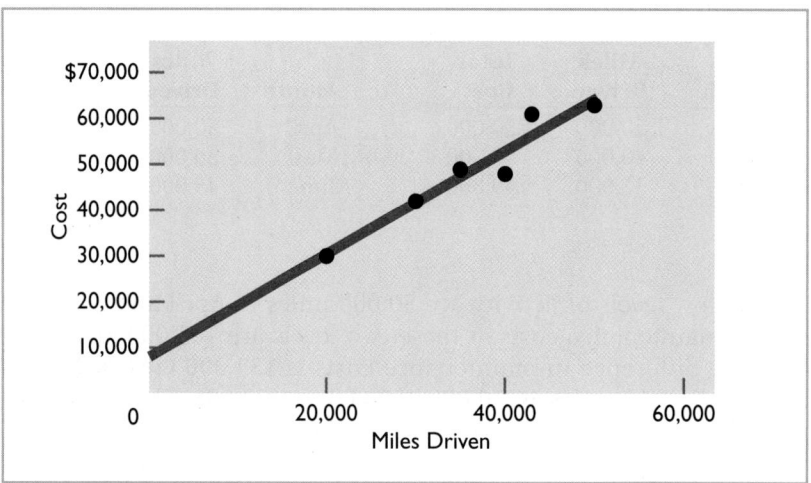

MANAGEMENT INSIGHT

Skilled Labor Is Truly Essential

The recession that started in 2008 had devastating implications for employment. But one surprise was that for some manufacturers, the number of jobs lost was actually lower than in previous recessions. One of the main explanations for this was that between 2000 and 2008, many factories adopted lean manufacturing practices. This meant that production relied less on large numbers of low-skilled workers, and more on machines and a few highly skilled workers. As a result of this approach, a single employee was supporting far more dollars in sales. Thus, it would require a larger decline in sales before an employee would need to be laid-off in order to continue to break even. Also, because the employees are highly skilled, employers are reluctant to lose them. Instead of lay-offs, many manufacturers have resorted to cutting employees hours.

Source: Timothy Aeppel and Justin Lahart, "Lean Factories Find It Hard to Cut Jobs Even in a Slump," *Wall Street Journal Online* (March 9, 2009).

 Would you characterize labor costs as being a fixed cost, a variable cost, or something else in this situation? (See page 987.)

Importance of Identifying Variable and Fixed Costs

Why is it important to segregate costs into variable and fixed elements? The answer may become apparent if we look at the following four business decisions.

1. If American Airlines is to make a profit when it reduces all domestic fares by 30%, what reduction in costs or increase in passengers will be required?
   Answer: To make a profit when it cuts domestic fares by 30%, American Airlines will have to increase the number of passengers or cut its variable costs for those flights. Its fixed costs will not change.

2. If Ford Motor Company meets workers' demands for higher wages, what increase in sales revenue will be needed to maintain current profit levels?
   Answer: Higher wages at Ford Motor Company will increase the variable costs of manufacturing automobiles. To maintain present profit levels, Ford will have to cut other variable costs or increase the price of its automobiles.

3. If United States Steel Corp.'s program to modernize plant facilities through significant equipment purchases reduces the work force by 50%, what will be the effect on the cost of producing one ton of steel?
   Answer: The modernizing of plant facilities at United States Steel Corp. changes the proportion of fixed and variable costs of producing one ton of steel. Fixed costs increase because of higher depreciation charges, whereas variable costs decrease due to the reduction in the number of steelworkers.

4. What happens if Kellogg's increases its advertising expenses but cannot increase prices because of competitive pressure?
   Answer: Sales volume must be increased to cover the increase in fixed advertising costs.

> **DO IT!**

High-Low Method   Byrnes Company accumulates the following data concerning a mixed cost, using units produced as the activity level.

	Units Produced	Total Cost
March	9,800	$14,740
April	8,500	13,250
May	7,000	11,100
June	7,600	12,000
July	8,100	12,460

Action Plan

✔ Determine the highest and lowest levels of activity.

✔ Compute variable cost per unit as: Change in total costs ÷ (High − low activity level) = Variable cost per unit.

✔ Compute fixed cost as: Total cost − (Variable cost per unit × Units produced) = Fixed cost.

(a) Compute the variable- and fixed-cost elements using the high-low method.
(b) Estimate the total cost if the company produces 6,000 units.

Solution

(a) Variable cost: ($14,740 − $11,100) ÷ (9,800 − 7,000) = $1.30 per unit
     Fixed cost: $14,740 − $12,740 ($1.30 × 9,800 units) = $2,000
          or $11,100 − $9,100 ($1.30 × 7,000) = $2,000
(b) Total cost to produce 6,000 units: $2,000 + $7,800 ($1.30 × 6,000) = $9,800

Related exercise material: **BE19-3, BE19-4, BE19-5, E19-3, E19-5, E19-6, and** **DO IT!** **19-2.**

 **The Navigator**

Cost-Volume-Profit Analysis

Cost-volume-profit (CVP) analysis is the study of the effects of changes in costs and volume on a company's profits. CVP analysis is important in profit planning. It also is a critical factor in such management decisions as setting selling prices, determining product mix, and maximizing use of production facilities.

LEARNING OBJECTIVE 4

List the five components of cost-volume-profit analysis.

Basic Components

CVP analysis considers the interrelationships among the components shown in Illustration 19-10.

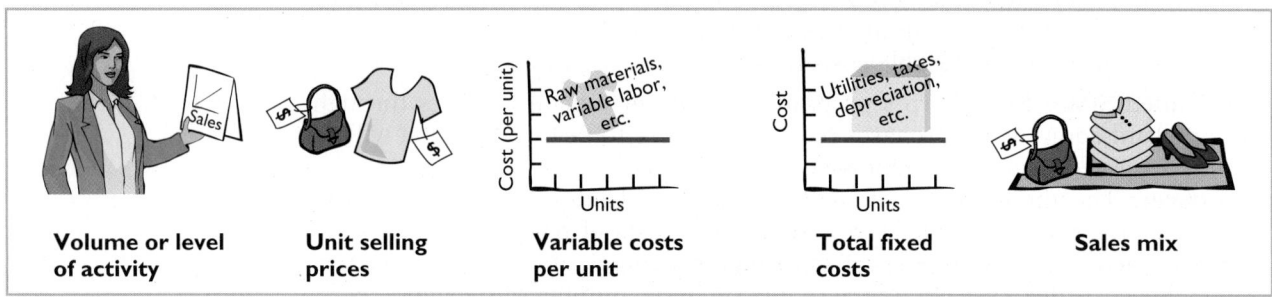

Volume or level of activity   **Unit selling prices**   **Variable costs per unit**   **Total fixed costs**   **Sales mix**

Illustration 19-10
Components of CVP analysis

The following assumptions underlie each CVP analysis.

1. The behavior of both costs and revenues is linear throughout the relevant range of the activity index.
2. Costs can be classified accurately as either variable or fixed.
3. Changes in activity are the only factors that affect costs.
4. All units produced are sold.
5. When more than one type of product is sold, the sales mix will remain constant. That is, the percentage that each product represents of total sales will stay the same. Sales mix complicates CVP analysis because different products will have different cost relationships. In this chapter, we assume a single product. (In Chapter 20, we relax this assumption.)

When these assumptions are not valid, the CVP analysis may be inaccurate.

CVP Income Statement

LEARNING OBJECTIVE 5

Indicate what contribution margin is and how it can be expressed.

Because CVP is so important for decision-making, management often wants this information reported in a **cost-volume-profit (CVP) income statement** format for internal use. The CVP income statement classifies costs as variable or fixed and computes a contribution margin. **Contribution margin (CM)** is the amount of revenue remaining after deducting variable costs. It is often stated both as a total amount and on a per unit basis.

We will use Vargo Video Company to illustrate a CVP income statement. Vargo Video produces a high-definition digital camcorder with 15× optical zoom and a wide-screen, high-resolution LCD monitor. Relevant data for the camcorders sold by this company in June 2014 are as follows.

Illustration 19-11
Assumed selling and cost data for Vargo Video

Unit selling price of camcorder	$500
Unit variable costs	$300
Total monthly fixed costs	$200,000
Units sold	1,600

The CVP income statement for Vargo Video therefore would be reported as follows.

Illustration 19-12
CVP income statement, with net income

Vargo Video Company
CVP Income Statement
For the Month Ended June 30, 2014

	Total
Sales (1,600 camcorders)	$ 800,000
Variable costs	480,000
Contribution margin	320,000
Fixed costs	200,000
Net income	$120,000

A traditional income statement and a CVP income statement both report the same net income of $120,000. However a traditional income statement does not classify costs as variable or fixed, and therefore it does not report a contribution margin. In addition, sometimes per unit amounts and percentage of sales amounts are shown on a CVP income statement to facilitate CVP analysis. *Homework assignments specify which columns to present.*

In the applications of CVP analysis that follow, we assume that the term "cost" includes all costs and expenses related to production and sale of the product. That is, cost includes manufacturing costs plus selling and administrative expenses.

CONTRIBUTION MARGIN PER UNIT

Illustration 19-14 shows Vargo Video's CVP income statement at the point where net income equals zero. It shows a contribution margin of $200,000, and a contribution margin per unit of $200 ($500 − $300). The formula for **contribution margin per unit** and the computation for Vargo Video are:

Illustration 19-13
Formula for contribution margin per unit

Unit Selling Price	−	Unit Variable Costs	=	Contribution Margin per Unit
$500	−	$300	=	$200

Contribution margin per unit indicates that for every camcorder sold, the selling price exceeds the variable costs by $200. Vargo generates $200 per unit sold to cover fixed costs and contribute to net income. Because Vargo Video has fixed costs of $200,000, it must sell 1,000 camcorders ($200,000 ÷ $200) to cover its fixed costs. At the point where total contribution margin exactly equals fixed costs, Vargo will report net income of zero. At this point, referred to as the **break-even point**, total costs (variable plus fixed) exactly equal total revenue.

Illustration 19-14
CVP income statement, with zero net income

Vargo Video Company
CVP Income Statement
For the Month Ended June 30, 2014

	Total	Per Unit
Sales (1,000 camcorders)	$ 500,000	$ 500
Variable costs	300,000	300
Contribution margin	200,000	$200
Fixed costs	200,000	
Net income	$ –0–	

It follows that for every camcorder sold above the break-even point of 1,000 units, **net income increases by the amount of the contribution margin per unit, $200.** For example, assume that Vargo sold one more camcorder, for a total of 1,001 camcorders sold. In this case, Vargo reports net income of $200, as shown in Illustration 19-15.

Illustration 19-15
CVP income statement, with net income and per unit data

Vargo Video Company
CVP Income Statement
For the Month Ended June 30, 2014

	Total	Per Unit
Sales (1,001 camcorders)	$500,500	$500
Variable costs	300,300	300
Contribution margin	200,200	$200
Fixed costs	200,000	
Net income	$ 200	

CONTRIBUTION MARGIN RATIO

Some managers prefer to use a contribution margin ratio in CVP analysis. The contribution margin ratio is the contribution margin expressed as a percentage of sales, as shown in Illustration 19-16.

Illustration 19-16
CVP income statement, with net income and percent of sales data

Vargo Video Company
CVP Income Statement
For the Month Ended June 30, 2014

	Total	Percent of Sales
Sales (1,001 camcorders)	$500,500	100%
Variable costs	300,300	60
Contribution margin	200,200	40%
Fixed costs	200,000	
Net income	$ 200	

Alternatively, the **contribution margin ratio** is the contribution margin per unit divided by the unit selling price. For Vargo Video, the ratio is as follows.

Illustration 19-17
Formula for contribution margin ratio

Contribution Margin per Unit	÷	Unit Selling Price	=	Contribution Margin Ratio
$200	÷	$500	=	40%

The contribution margin ratio of 40% means that Vargo generates 40 cents of contribution margin with each dollar of sales. That is, $0.40 of each sales dollar (40% × $1) is available to apply to fixed costs and to contribute to net income.

This expression of contribution margin is very helpful in determining the effect of changes in sales on net income. For example, if Vargo's sales increase $100,000, net income will increase $40,000 (40% × $100,000). Thus, by using the contribution margin ratio, managers can quickly determine increases in net income from any change in sales.

We can also see this effect through a CVP income statement. Assume that Vargo Video's current sales are $500,000 and it wants to know the effect of a $100,000 (200-unit) increase in sales. Vargo prepares a comparative CVP income statement analysis as follows.

Illustration 19-18
Comparative CVP income statements

	No Change			**With Change**		
	Total	**Per Unit**	**Percent of Sales**	**Total**	**Per Unit**	**Percent of Sales**
Sales	$500,000	$500	100%	$600,000	$500	100%
Variable costs	300,000	300	60	360,000	300	60
Contribution margin	**200,000**	**$200**	**40%**	**240,000**	**$200**	**40%**
Fixed costs	200,000			200,000		
Net income	**$ –0–**			**$ 40,000**		

Vargo Video Company
CVP Income Statements
For the Month Ended June 30, 2014

The $40,000 increase in net income can be calculated on either a contribution margin per unit basis (200 units × $200 per unit) or using the contribution margin ratio times the increase in sales dollars (40% × $100,000). Note that the contribution margin per unit and contribution margin as a percentage of sales remain unchanged by the increase in sales.

Study these CVP income statements carefully. The concepts presented in these statements are used extensively in this and later chapters.

Break-Even Analysis

A key relationship in CVP analysis is the level of activity at which total revenues equal total costs (both fixed and variable)—the **break-even point**. At this volume of sales, the company will realize no income but will suffer no loss. The process of finding the break-even point is called **break-even analysis**. Knowledge of the break-even point is useful to management when it decides whether to introduce new product lines, change sales prices on established products, or enter new market areas.

LEARNING OBJECTIVE 6

Identify the three ways to determine the break-even point.

The break-even point can be:

1. Computed from a mathematical equation.
2. Computed by using contribution margin.
3. Derived from a cost-volume-profit (CVP) graph.

The break-even point can be expressed either in **sales units** or **sales dollars**.

MATHEMATICAL EQUATION
The first line of Illustration 19-19 (page 964) shows a common equation used for CVP analysis. When net income is set to zero, this equation can be used to calculate the break-even point.

Illustration 19-19
Basic CVP equation

Required Sales	–	Variable Costs	–	Fixed Costs	=	Net Income
$500Q	–	$300Q	–	$200,000	=	$0

As shown in Illustration 19-14 (page 961), net income equals zero when the contribution margin (sales minus variable costs) is equal to fixed costs.

To reflect this, Illustration 19-20 rewrites the equation with contribution margin (sales minus variable costs) on the left side, and fixed costs and net income on the right. We can compute the break-even point **in units** by **using unit selling prices** and **unit variable costs**. The computation for Vargo Video is:

Illustration 19-20
Computation of break-even point in units

Required Sales	–	Variable Costs	–	Fixed Costs	=	Net Income
$500Q	–	$300Q	–	$200,000	=	$0
$500Q	–	$300Q	=	$200,000	+	$0

$$\$200Q = \$200,000$$

$$Q = \frac{\$200,000}{\$200} = \frac{\text{Fixed Costs}}{\text{Contribution Margin per Unit}}$$

$$Q = 1,000 \text{ units}$$

where

$$Q = \text{sales volume in units}$$
$$\$500 = \text{selling price}$$
$$\$300 = \text{variable costs per unit}$$
$$\$200,000 = \text{total fixed costs}$$

Thus, Vargo Video must sell 1,000 units to break even.

To find the amount of **sales dollars** required to break even, we multiply the units sold at the break-even point times the selling price per unit, as shown below.

$$1,000 \times \$500 = \$500,000 \text{ (break-even sales dollars)}$$

CONTRIBUTION MARGIN TECHNIQUE
Many managers employ the contribution margin to compute the break-even point.

CONTRIBUTION MARGIN IN UNITS The final step in Illustration 19-20 divides fixed costs by the contribution margin per unit (highlighted in red). Thus, rather than walk through all of the steps of the equation approach, we can simply employ this formula shown in Illustration 19-21.

Illustration 19-21
Formula for break-even point in units using contribution margin per unit

Fixed Costs	÷	Contribution Margin per Unit	=	Break-Even Point in Units
$200,000	÷	$200	=	1,000 units

Why does this formula work? The contribution margin per unit is the net amount by which each sale exceeds the variable costs per unit. Every sale generates this much money to pay off fixed costs. Consequently, if we divide fixed costs by the contribution margin per unit, we know how many units we need to sell to break even.

CONTRIBUTION MARGIN RATIO As we will see in the next chapter, when a company has numerous products, it is not practical to determine the contribution margin per unit for each product. In this case, using the contribution margin ratio is very useful for determining the break-even point in total dollars (rather than units). Recall that the contribution margin ratio is the amount of contribution margin that is generated from each dollar of sales. Therefore, to determine the sales dollars needed to cover fixed costs, we divide fixed costs by the contribution margin ratio, as shown in Illustration 19-22.

Fixed Costs	÷	Contribution Margin Ratio	=	Break-Even Point in Dollars
$200,000	÷	40%	=	$500,000

Illustration 19-22
Formula for break-even point in dollars using contribution margin ratio

To apply this formula to Vargo, consider that its 40% contribution margin ratio means that for every dollar sold, it generates 40 cents of contribution margin. The question is, how many dollars of sales does Vargo need in order to generate total contribution margin of $200,000 to pay off fixed costs? We divide the fixed costs of $200,000 by the 40 cents of contribution margin generated by each dollar of sales to arrive at $500,000 ($200,000 ÷ 40%). To prove this result, if we generate 40 cents of contribution margin for each dollar of sales, then the total contribution margin generated by $500,000 in sales is $200,000 ($500,000 × 40%).

SERVICE COMPANY INSIGHT

Charter Flights Offer a Good Deal

The Internet is wringing inefficiencies out of nearly every industry. While commercial aircraft spend roughly 4,000 hours a year in the air, chartered aircraft are flown only 500 hours annually. That means that they are sitting on the ground—not making any money—about 90% of the time. One company, FlightServe, saw a business opportunity in that fact. For about the same cost as a first-class ticket, FlightServe decided to match up executives with charter flights in small "private jets." The executive would get a more comfortable ride and could avoid the hassle of big airports. FlightServe noted that the average charter jet has eight seats. When all eight seats were full, the company would have an 80% profit margin. It would break even at an average of 3.3 full seats per flight.

Source: "Jet Set Go," *The Economist* (March 18, 2000), p. 68.

 How did FlightServe determine that it would break even with 3.3 seats full per flight? (See page 987.)

GRAPHIC PRESENTATION
An effective way to find the break-even point is to prepare a break-even graph. Because this graph also shows costs, volume, and profits, it is referred to as a **cost-volume-profit (CVP) graph**.

As the CVP graph in Illustration 19-23 shows, sales volume is recorded along the horizontal axis. This axis should extend to the maximum level of expected sales. Both total revenues (sales) and total costs (fixed plus variable) are recorded on the vertical axis.

Illustration 19-23
CVP graph

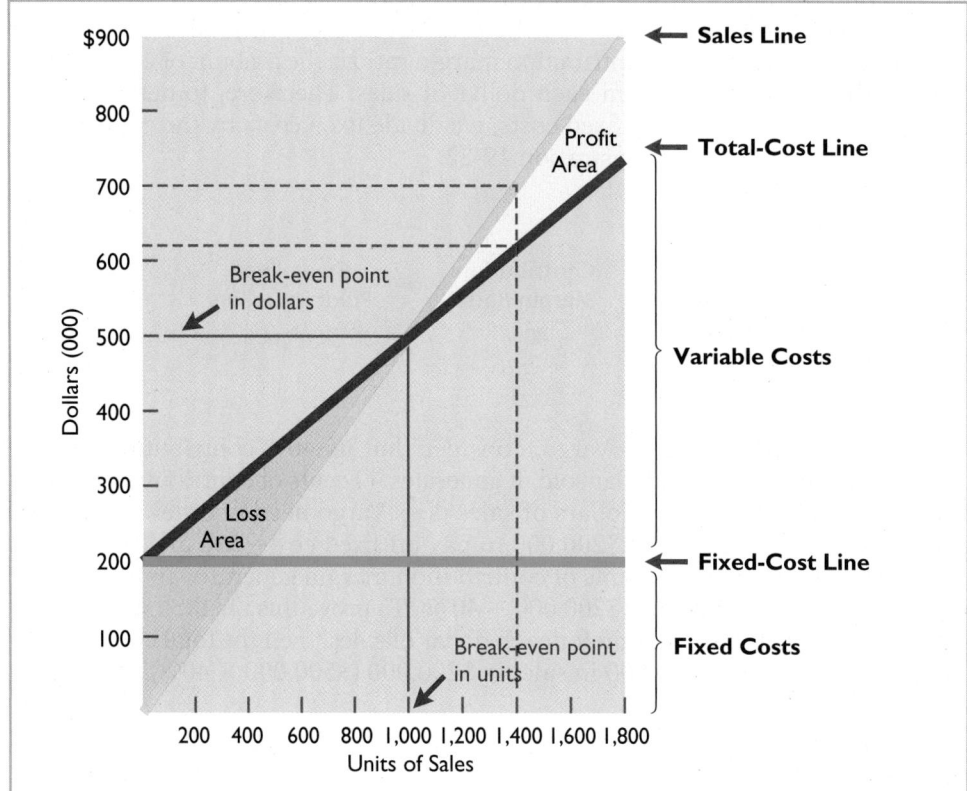

The construction of the graph, using the data for Vargo Video, is as follows.

1. Plot the sales line, starting at the zero activity level. For every camcorder sold, total revenue increases by $500. For example, at 200 units, sales are $100,000. At the upper level of activity (1,800 units), sales are $900,000. The revenue line is assumed to be linear through the full range of activity.

2. Plot the total fixed costs using a horizontal line. For the camcorders, this line is plotted at $200,000. The fixed costs are the same at every level of activity.

3. Plot the total-cost line. This starts at the fixed-cost line at zero activity. It increases by the variable costs at each level of activity. For each camcorder, variable costs are $300. Thus, at 200 units, total variable costs are $60,000, and the total cost is $260,000. At 1,800 units, total variable costs are $540,000, and total cost is $740,000. On the graph, the amount of the variable costs can be derived from the difference between the total-cost and fixed-cost lines at each level of activity.

4. Determine the break-even point from the intersection of the total-cost line and the sales line. The break-even point in dollars is found by drawing a horizontal line from the break-even point to the vertical axis. The break-even point in units is found by drawing a vertical line from the break-even point to the horizontal axis. For the camcorders, the break-even point is

$500,000 of sales, or 1,000 units. At this sales level, Vargo Video will cover costs but make no profit.

The CVP graph also shows both the net income and net loss areas. Thus, the amount of income or loss at each level of sales can be derived from the sales and total-cost lines.

A CVP graph is useful because the effects of a change in any element in the CVP analysis can be quickly seen. For example, a 10% increase in selling price will change the location of the sales line. Likewise, the effects on total costs of wage increases can be quickly observed.

> **DO IT!**

Break-Even Analysis

Action Plan

✔ Apply the formula: Sales = Variable costs + Fixed costs + Net income.

✔ Apply the formula: Fixed costs ÷ Contribution margin per unit = Break-even point in units.

Lombardi Company has a unit selling price of $400, variable costs per unit of $240, and fixed costs of $180,000. Compute the break-even point in units using (a) a mathematical equation and (b) contribution margin per unit.

Solution

(a) The equation is $400Q − $240Q − $180,000 = $0; ($400Q − $240Q) = $180,000. The break-even point in units is 1,125. (b) The contribution margin per unit is $160 ($400 − $240). The formula therefore is $180,000 ÷ $160, and the break-even point in units is 1,125.

Related exercise material: **BE19-6, BE19-7, BE19-8, BE19-9, E19-8, E19-9, E19-10, E19-11, E19-12, E19-13, and DO IT! 19-3.**

✔ **The Navigator**

Target Net Income

Rather than simply "breaking even," management usually sets an income objective often called **target net income**. It indicates the sales necessary to achieve a specified level of income. Companies determine the sales necessary to achieve target net income by using one of the three approaches discussed earlier.

MATHEMATICAL EQUATION

We know that at the break-even point no profit or loss results for the company. By adding an amount for target net income to the same basic equation, we obtain the following formula for determining required sales.

LEARNING OBJECTIVE **7**

Give the formulas for determining sales required to earn target net income.

Required Sales	−	Variable Costs	−	Fixed Costs	=	Target Net Income

Illustration 19-24
Formula for required sales to meet target net income

Recall that once the break-even point has been reached so that fixed costs are covered, each additional unit sold increases net income by the amount of the contribution margin per unit. We can rewrite the equation with contribution margin (sales minus variable costs) on the left-hand side, and fixed costs and net income on the right. Assuming that target net income is $120,000 for Vargo Video, the computation of required sales in units is as follows.

Illustration 19-25
Computation of required sales

Required Sales	–	Variable Costs	–	Fixed Costs	=	Target Net Income
$500Q	–	$300Q	–	$200,000	=	$120,000
$500Q	–	$300Q			=	$200,000 + $120,000

$$\$200Q = \$200,000 + \$120,000$$

$$Q = \frac{\$200,000 + \$120,000}{\$200} = \frac{\text{Fixed Costs} + \text{Net Target Income}}{\text{Contribution Margin per Unit}}$$

$$Q = 1,600$$

where
Q	=	sales volume
$500	=	selling price
$300	=	variable costs per unit
$200,000	=	total fixed costs
$120,000	=	target net income

Vargo must sell 1,600 units to achieve target net income of $120,000. The sales dollars required to achieve the target net income is found by multiplying the units sold by the unit selling price [(1,600 × $500) = $800,000].

CONTRIBUTION MARGIN TECHNIQUE

As in the case of break-even sales, we can compute in either units or dollars the sales required to meet target net income. The formula to compute required sales in units for Vargo Video using the contribution margin per unit can be seen in the final step of the equation approach in Illustration 19-25 (shown in red). We simply divide the sum of fixed costs and target net income by the contribution margin per unit. Illustration 19-26 shows this for Vargo.

Illustration 19-26
Formula for required sales in units using contribution margin per unit

$\left(\begin{array}{c}\text{Fixed Costs +}\\ \text{Target Net Income}\end{array}\right)$	÷	Contribution Margin per Unit	=	Required Sales in Units
($200,000 + $120,000)	÷	$200	=	1,600 units

To achieve its desired target net income of $120,000, Vargo must sell 1,600 camcorders.

The formula to compute the required sales in dollars for Vargo Video using the contribution margin ratio is shown below.

Illustration 19-27
Formula for required sales in dollars using contribution margin ratio

$\left(\begin{array}{c}\text{Fixed Costs +}\\ \text{Target Net Income}\end{array}\right)$	÷	Contribution Margin Ratio	=	Required Sales in Dollars
($200,000 + $120,000)	÷	40%	=	$800,000

To achieve its desired target net income of $120,000, Vargo must generate sales of $800,000.

GRAPHIC PRESENTATION

We also can use the CVP graph in Illustration 19-23 (on page 966) to find the sales required to meet target net income. In the profit area of the graph, the distance between the sales line and the total-cost line at any point equals net income. We can find required sales by analyzing the differences between the two lines until the desired net income is found.

For example, suppose Vargo Video sells 1,400 camcorders. Illustration 19-23 shows that a vertical line drawn at 1,400 units intersects the sales line at $700,000 and the total cost line at $620,000. The difference between the two amounts represents the net income (profit) of $80,000.

Margin of Safety

Margin of safety is the difference between actual or expected sales and sales at the break-even point. It measures the "cushion" that a particular level of sales provides. It tells us how far sales could fall before the company begins operating at a loss. The margin of safety is expressed in dollars or as a ratio.

The formula for stating the **margin of safety in dollars** is actual (or expected) sales minus break-even sales. Assuming that actual (expected) sales for Vargo Video are $750,000, the computation is:

LEARNING OBJECTIVE   **6**

Define margin of safety, and give the formulas for computing it.

Actual (Expected) Sales	−	Break-Even Sales	=	Margin of Safety in Dollars
$750,000	−	$500,000	=	$250,000

Illustration 19-28
Formula for margin of safety in dollars

Vargo's margin of safety is $250,000. Its sales could fall $250,000 before it operates at a loss.

The **margin of safety ratio** is the margin of safety in dollars divided by actual (or expected) sales. The formula and computation for determining the margin of safety ratio are:

Margin of Safety in Dollars	÷	Actual (Expected) Sales	=	Margin of Safety Ratio
$250,000	÷	$750,000	=	33%

Illustration 19-29
Formula for margin of safety ratio

This means that the company's sales could fall by 33% before it would be operating at a loss.

The higher the dollars or the percentage, the greater the margin of safety. Management continuously evaluates the adequacy of the margin of safety in terms of such factors as the vulnerability of the product to competitive pressures and to downturns in the economy.

SERVICE COMPANY INSIGHT

How a Rolling Stones' Tour Makes Money

Computation of break-even and margin of safety is important for service companies. Consider how the promoter for the Rolling Stones' tour used the break-even point and margin of safety. For example, one outdoor show should bring 70,000 individuals for a gross of $2.45 million. The promoter guarantees $1.2 million to the Rolling Stones. In addition, 20% of gross goes to the stadium in which the performance is staged. Add another $400,000 for other expenses such as ticket takers, parking attendants, advertising, and so on. The promoter also shares in sales of T-shirts and memorabilia for which the promoter will net over $7 million during the tour. From a successful Rolling Stones' tour, the promoter could make $35 million!

? What amount of sales dollars are required for the promoter to break even? (See page 987.)

> DO IT!

Break-Even, Margin of Safety, Target Net Income

Action Plan

✔ Apply the formula for the break-even point in dollars.

✔ Apply the formulas for the margin of safety in dollars and the margin of safety ratio.

✔ Apply the formula for the required sales in dollars.

Zootsuit Inc. makes travel bags that sell for $56 each. For the coming year, management expects fixed costs to total $320,000 and variable costs to be $42 per unit. Compute the following: (a) break-even point in dollars using the contribution margin (CM) ratio; (b) the margin of safety and margin of safety ratio assuming actual sales are $1,382,400; and (c) the sales dollars required to earn net income of $410,000.

Solution

(a) Contribution margin ratio = [($56 − $42) ÷ $56] = 25%
Break-even sales in dollars = $320,000 ÷ 25% = $1,280,000

(b) Margin of safety = $1,382,400 − $1,280,000 = $102,400
Margin of safety ratio = $102,400 ÷ $1,382,400 = 7.4%

(c) Required sales in dollars = ($320,000 + $410,000) ÷ 25% = $2,920,000

Related exercise material: **BE19-10, BE19-11, BE19-12, E19-14, E19-15, E19-16, and** DO IT! **19-4.**

✔ **The Navigator**

> Comprehensive DO IT!

Mabo Company makes calculators that sell for $20 each. For the coming year, management expects fixed costs to total $220,000 and variable costs to be $9 per unit.

Instructions

(a) Compute break-even point in units using the mathematical equation.

(b) Compute break-even point in dollars using the contribution margin (CM) ratio.

(c) Compute the margin of safety percentage assuming actual sales are $500,000.

(d) Compute the sales required in dollars to earn net income of $165,000.

Solution to Comprehensive

Action Plan

✔ Know the formulas.

✔ Recognize that variable costs change with sales volume; fixed costs do not.

✔ Avoid computational errors.

(a) Sales − Variable costs − Fixed costs = Net income
$$\$20Q − \$9Q − \$220,000 = \$0$$
$$\$11Q = \$220,000$$
$$Q = 20,000 \text{ units}$$

(b) Contribution margin per unit = Unit selling price − Unit variable costs
$$\$11 = \$20 − \$9$$
Contribution margin ratio = Contribution margin per unit ÷ Unit selling price
$$55\% = \$11 ÷ \$20$$
Break-even point in dollars = Fixed costs ÷ Contribution margin ratio
$$= \$220,000 ÷ 55\%$$
$$= \$400,000$$

(c) Margin of safety = $\dfrac{\text{Actual sales} − \text{Break-even sales}}{\text{Actual sales}}$

$$= \dfrac{\$500,000 − \$400,000}{\$500,000}$$

$$= 20\%$$

(d) Required sales − Variable costs − Fixed costs = Net income

$$\$20Q - \$9Q - \$220{,}000 = \$165{,}000$$
$$\$11Q = \$385{,}000$$
$$Q = 35{,}000 \text{ units}$$
$$35{,}000 \text{ units} \times \$20 = \$700{,}000 \text{ required sales}$$

 The Navigator

SUMMARY OF LEARNING OBJECTIVES

 **The Navigator**

1 **Distinguish between variable and fixed costs.** Variable costs are costs that vary in total directly and proportionately with changes in the activity index. Fixed costs are costs that remain the same in total regardless of changes in the activity index.

2 **Explain the significance of the relevant range.** The relevant range is the range of activity in which a company expects to operate during a year. It is important in CVP analysis because the behavior of costs is assumed to be linear throughout the relevant range.

3 **Explain the concept of mixed costs.** Mixed costs increase in total but not proportionately with changes in the activity level. For purposes of CVP analysis, mixed costs must be classified into their fixed and variable elements. One method that management may use to classify these costs is the high-low method.

4 **List the five components of cost-volume-profit analysis.** The five components of CVP analysis are (a) volume or level of activity, (b) unit selling prices, (c) variable costs per unit, (d) total fixed costs, and (e) sales mix.

5 **Indicate what contribution margin is and how it can be expressed.** Contribution margin is the amount of revenue remaining after deducting variable costs. It is

identified in a CVP income statement, which classifies costs as variable or fixed. It can be expressed as a total amount, as a per unit amount, or as a ratio.

6 **Identify the three ways to determine the break-even point.** The break-even point can be (a) computed from a mathematical equation, (b) computed by using a contribution margin technique, and (c) derived from a CVP graph.

7 **Give the formulas for determining sales required to earn target net income.** The general formula for required sales is: Required sales − Variable costs − Fixed costs = Target net income. Two other formulas are Required sales in units = (Fixed costs + Target net income) ÷ Contribution margin per unit, and Required sales in dollars = (Fixed costs + Target net income) ÷ Contribution margin ratio.

8 **Define margin of safety, and give the formulas for computing it.** Margin of safety is the difference between actual or expected sales and sales at the break-even point. The formulas for margin of safety are Actual (expected) sales − Break-even sales = Margin of safety in dollars; Margin of safety in dollars ÷ Actual (expected) sales = Margin of safety ratio.

GLOSSARY

Activity index The activity that causes changes in the behavior of costs. (p. 952).

Break-even point The level of activity at which total revenues equal total costs. (p. 961).

Contribution margin (CM) The amount of revenue remaining after deducting variable costs. (p. 960).

Contribution margin per unit The amount of revenue remaining per unit after deducting variable costs; calculated as unit selling price minus unit variable cost. (p. 961).

Contribution margin ratio The percentage of each dollar of sales that is available to apply to fixed costs and contribute to net income; calculated as contribution margin per unit divided by unit selling price. (p. 962).

Cost behavior analysis The study of how specific costs respond to changes in the level of business activity. (p. 952).

Cost-volume-profit (CVP) analysis The study of the effects of changes in costs and volume on a company's profits. (p. 960).

Cost-volume-profit (CVP) graph A graph showing the relationship between costs, volume, and profits. (p. 965).

Cost-volume-profit (CVP) income statement A statement for internal use that classifies costs as fixed or variable and reports contribution margin in the body of the statement. (p. 960).

Fixed costs Costs that remain the same in total regardless of changes in the activity level. (p. 953).

High-low method A mathematical method that uses the total costs incurred at the high and low levels of activity to classify mixed costs into fixed and variable components. (p. 957).

Margin of safety The difference between actual or expected sales and sales at the break-even point. (p. 969).

Mixed costs Costs that contain both a variable- and a fixed-cost element and change in total but not proportionately with changes in the activity level. (p. 955).

Relevant range The range of the activity index over which the company expects to operate during the year. (p. 955).

Target net income The income objective set by management. (p. 967).

Variable costs Costs that vary in total directly and proportionately with changes in the activity level. (p. 952).

 Self-Test, Brief Exercises, Exercises, Problem Set A, and many more resources are available for practice in WileyPLUS.

SELF-TEST QUESTIONS

Answers are at the end of the chapter.

(LO 1) **1.** Variable costs are costs that:
  (a) vary in total directly and proportionately with changes in the activity level.
  (b) remain the same per unit at every activity level.
  (c) Neither of the above.
  (d) Both (a) and (b) above.

(LO 2) **2.** The relevant range is:
  (a) the range of activity in which variable costs will be curvilinear.
  (b) the range of activity in which fixed costs will be curvilinear.
  (c) the range over which the company expects to operate during a year.
  (d) usually from zero to 100% of operating capacity.

(LO 3) **3.** Mixed costs consist of a:
  (a) variable-cost element and a fixed-cost element.
  (b) fixed-cost element and a controllable-cost element.
  (c) relevant-cost element and a controllable-cost element.
  (d) variable-cost element and a relevant-cost element.

(LO 3) **4.** Your phone service provider offers a plan that is classified as a mixed cost. The cost per month for 1,000 minutes is $50. If you use 2,000 minutes this month, your cost will be:
  (a) $50.   (c) more than $100.
  (b) $100.   (d) between $50 and $100.

(LO 3) **5.** Kendra Corporation's total utility costs during the past year were $1,200 during its highest month and $600 during its lowest month. These costs corresponded with 10,000 units of production during the high month and 2,000 units during the low month. What are the fixed and variable components of its utility costs using the high-low method?
  (a) $0.075 variable and $450 fixed.
  (b) $0.120 variable and $0 fixed.
  (c) $0.300 variable and $0 fixed.
  (d) $0.060 variable and $600 fixed.

6. Which of the following is *not* involved in CVP analysis? (LO 4)
  (a) Sales mix.
  (b) Unit selling prices.
  (c) Fixed costs per unit.
  (d) Volume or level of activity.

7. When comparing a traditional income statement to a (LO 5) CVP income statement:
  (a) net income will always be greater on the traditional statement.
  (b) net income will always be less on the traditional statement.
  (c) net income will always be identical on both.
  (d) net income will be greater or less depending on the sales volume.

8. Contribution margin: (LO 5)
  (a) is revenue remaining after deducting variable costs.
  (b) may be expressed as contribution margin per unit.
  (c) is selling price less cost of goods sold.
  (d) Both (a) and (b) above.

9. Cournot Company sells 100,000 wrenches for $12 (LO 5) a unit. Fixed costs are $300,000, and net income is $200,000. What should be reported as variable expenses in the CVP income statement?
  (a) $700,000.   (c) $500,000.
  (b) $900,000.   (d) $1,000,000.

10. Gossen Company is planning to sell 200,000 pliers for (LO 6) $4 per unit. The contribution margin ratio is 25%. If Gossen will break even at this level of sales, what are the fixed costs?
  (a) $100,000.   (c) $200,000.
  (b) $160,000.   (d) $300,000.

11. Brownstone Company's contribution margin ratio is (LO 6) 30%. If Brownstone's sales revenue is $100 greater than its break-even sales in dollars, its net income:
  (a) will be $100.
  (b) will be $70.
  (c) will be $30.
  (d) cannot be determined without knowing fixed costs.

(LO 7) **12.** The mathematical equation for computing required sales to obtain target net income is: Required sales =
(a) Variable costs + Target net income.
(b) Variable costs + Fixed costs + Target net income.
(c) Fixed costs + Target net income.
(d) No correct answer is given.

(LO 8) **13.** Margin of safety is computed as:
(a) Actual sales − Break-even sales.
(b) Contribution margin − Fixed costs.
(c) Break-even sales − Variable costs.
(d) Actual sales − Contribution margin.

14. Marshall Company had actual sales of $600,000 when (LO 8) break-even sales were $420,000. What is the margin of safety ratio?
(a) 25%. (c) 33⅓%.
(b) 30%. (d) 45%.

Go to the book's companion website, **www.wiley.com/college/weygandt**, for additional Self-Test Questions.

 **The Navigator**

QUESTIONS

1. (a) What is cost behavior analysis?
(b) Why is cost behavior analysis important to management?

2. (a) Scott Winter asks your help in understanding the term "activity index." Explain the meaning and importance of this term for Scott.
(b) State the two ways that variable costs may be defined.

3. Contrast the effects of changes in the activity level on total fixed costs and on unit fixed costs.

4. J. P. Alexander claims that the relevant range concept is important only for variable costs.
(a) Explain the relevant range concept.
(b) Do you agree with J. P.'s claim? Explain.

5. "The relevant range is indispensable in cost behavior analysis." Is this true? Why or why not?

6. Adam Antal is confused. He does not understand why rent on his apartment is a fixed cost and rent on a Hertz rental truck is a mixed cost. Explain the difference to Adam.

7. How should mixed costs be classified in CVP analysis? What approach is used to effect the appropriate classification?

8. At the high and low levels of activity during the month, direct labor hours are 90,000 and 40,000, respectively. The related costs are $165,000 and $100,000. What are the fixed and variable costs at any level of activity?

9. "Cost-volume-profit (CVP) analysis is based entirely on unit costs." Do you agree? Explain.

10. Faye Dunn defines contribution margin as the amount of profit available to cover operating expenses. Is there any truth in this definition? Discuss.

11. Marshall Company's GWhiz calculator sells for $40. Variable costs per unit are estimated to be $26. What are the contribution margin per unit and the contribution margin ratio?

12. "Break-even analysis is of limited use to management because a company cannot survive by just breaking even." Do you agree? Explain.

13. Total fixed costs are $26,000 for Daz Inc. It has a contribution margin per unit of $15, and a contribution margin ratio of 25%. Compute the break-even sales in dollars.

14. Peggy Turnbull asks your help in constructing a CVP graph. Explain to Peggy (a) how the break-even point is plotted, and (b) how the level of activity and dollar sales at the break-even point are determined.

15. Define the term "margin of safety." If Revere Company expects to sell 1,250 units of its product at $12 per unit, and break-even sales for the product are $13,200, what is the margin of safety ratio?

16. Huang Company's break-even sales are $500,000. Assuming fixed costs are $180,000, what sales volume is needed to achieve a target net income of $90,000?

17. The traditional income statement for Pace Company shows sales $900,000, cost of goods sold $600,000, and operating expenses $200,000. Assuming all costs and expenses are 70% variable and 30% fixed, prepare a CVP income statement through contribution margin.

BRIEF EXERCISES

BE19-1 Monthly production costs in Pesavento Company for two levels of production are as follows.

Classify costs as variable, fixed, or mixed.

(LO 1, 3)

Cost	2,000 Units	4,000 Units
Indirect labor	$10,000	$20,000
Supervisory salaries	5,000	5,000
Maintenance	4,000	7,000

Indicate which costs are variable, fixed, and mixed, and give the reason for each answer.

BE19-2 For Lodes Company, the relevant range of production is 40–80% of capacity. At 40% of capacity, a variable cost is $4,000 and a fixed cost is $6,000. Diagram the behavior of each cost within the relevant range assuming the behavior is linear.

BE19-3 For Hunt Company, a mixed cost is $15,000 plus $18 per direct labor hour. Diagram the behavior of the cost using increments of 500 hours up to 2,500 hours on the horizontal axis and increments of $15,000 up to $60,000 on the vertical axis.

BE19-4 Bruno Company accumulates the following data concerning a mixed cost, using miles as the activity level.

	Miles Driven	Total Cost		Miles Driven	Total Cost
January	8,000	$14,150	March	8,500	$15,000
February	7,500	13,500	April	8,200	14,490

Compute the variable- and fixed-cost elements using the high-low method.

BE19-5 Stiever Corp. has collected the following data concerning its maintenance costs for the past 6 months.

	Units Produced	Total Cost
July	18,000	$32,000
August	32,000	48,000
September	36,000	55,000
October	22,000	38,000
November	40,000	66,100
December	38,000	62,000

Compute the variable- and fixed-cost elements using the high-low method.

BE19-6 Determine the missing amounts.

	Unit Selling Price	Unit Variable Costs	Contribution Margin per Unit	Contribution Margin Ratio
1.	$640	$352	(a)	(b)
2.	$300	(c)	$93	(d)
3.	(e)	(f)	$325	25%

BE19-7 Radial Inc. had sales of $2,400,000 for the first quarter of 2014. In making the sales, the company incurred the costs and expenses shown below.

	Variable	Fixed
Cost of goods sold	$920,000	$440,000
Selling expenses	70,000	45,000
Administrative expenses	86,000	98,000

Prepare a CVP income statement for the quarter ended March 31, 2014.

BE19-8 Rice Company has a unit selling price of $520, variable costs per unit of $286, and fixed costs of $163,800. Compute the break-even point in units using (a) the mathematical equation and (b) contribution margin per unit.

BE19-9 Acorn Corp. had total variable costs of $180,000, total fixed costs of $170,000, and total revenues of $300,000. Compute the required sales in dollars to break even.

BE19-10 For Flynn Company, variable costs are 70% of sales, and fixed costs are $195,000. Management's net income goal is $75,000. Compute the required sales in dollars needed to achieve management's target net income of $75,000. (Use the contribution margin approach.)

BE19-11 For Stevens Company, actual sales are $1,000,000 and break-even sales are $840,000. Compute (a) the margin of safety in dollars and (b) the margin of safety ratio.

BE19-12 Deines Corporation has fixed costs of $480,000. It has a unit selling price of $6, unit variable costs of $4.40, and a target net income of $1,500,000. Compute the required sales in units to achieve its target net income.

> DO IT! REVIEW

Classify types of costs.
(LO 1, 3)

DO IT! 19-1 Helena Company reports the following total costs at two levels of production.

	5,000 Units	10,000 Units
Indirect labor	$ 3,000	$ 6,000
Property taxes	7,000	7,000
Direct labor	28,000	56,000
Direct materials	22,000	44,000
Depreciation	4,000	4,000
Utilities	5,000	7,000
Maintenance	9,000	11,000

Classify each cost as variable, fixed, or mixed.

Compute costs using high-low method and estimate total cost.
(LO 3)

DO IT! 19-2 Westerville Company accumulates the following data concerning a mixed cost, using units produced as the activity level.

	Units Produced	Total Cost
March	10,000	$18,000
April	9,000	16,650
May	10,500	18,580
June	8,800	16,200
July	9,500	17,100

(a) Compute the variable- and fixed-cost elements using the high-low method.
(b) Estimate the total cost if the company produces 9,200 units.

Compute break-even point in units.
(LO 6)

DO IT! 19-3 Larissa Company has a unit selling price of $250, variable costs per unit of $170, and fixed costs of $140,000. Compute the break-even point in units using (a) the mathematical equation and (b) contribution margin per unit.

Compute break-even point, margin of safety ratio, and sales for target net income.
(LO 6, 7, 8)

DO IT! 19-4 Presto Company makes radios that sell for $30 each. For the coming year, management expects fixed costs to total $220,000 and variable costs to be $18 per unit.

(a) Compute the break-even point in dollars using the contribution margin (CM) ratio.
(b) Compute the margin of safety ratio assuming actual sales are $800,000.
(c) Compute the sales dollars required to earn net income of $140,000.

✔ **The Navigator**

EXERCISES

E19-1 Turgro Company manufactures a single product. Annual production costs incurred in the manufacturing process are shown below for two levels of production.

Define and classify variable, fixed, and mixed costs.
(LO 1, 3)

Production in Units	Costs Incurred			
	5,000		10,000	
Production Costs	Total Cost	Cost/ Unit	Total Cost	Cost/ Unit
Direct materials	$8,000	$1.60	$16,000	$1.60
Direct labor	9,500	1.90	19,000	1.90
Utilities	2,000	0.40	3,500	0.35
Rent	4,000	0.80	4,000	0.40
Maintenance	800	0.16	1,100	0.11
Supervisory salaries	1,000	0.20	1,000	0.10

Instructions
(a) Define the terms variable costs, fixed costs, and mixed costs.
(b) Classify each cost above as either variable, fixed, or mixed.

Diagram cost behavior, determine relevant range, and classify costs.

(LO 1, 2)

E19-2 Shingle Enterprises is considering manufacturing a new product. It projects the cost of direct materials and rent for a range of output as shown below.

Output in Units	Rent Expense	Direct Materials
1,000	$ 5,000	$ 4,000
2,000	5,000	7,200
3,000	8,000	9,000
4,000	8,000	12,000
5,000	8,000	15,000
6,000	8,000	18,000
7,000	8,000	21,000
8,000	8,000	24,000
9,000	10,000	29,300
10,000	10,000	35,000
11,000	10,000	44,000

Instructions
(a) Diagram the behavior of each cost for output ranging from 1,000 to 11,000 units.
(b) Determine the relevant range of activity for this product.
(c) Calculate the variable costs per unit within the relevant range.
(d) Indicate the fixed cost within the relevant range.

Determine fixed and variable costs using the high-low method and prepare graph.

(LO 1, 3)

E19-3 The controller of Furgee Industries has collected the following monthly expense data for use in analyzing the cost behavior of maintenance costs.

Month	Total Maintenance Costs	Total Machine Hours
January	$2,500	300
February	3,000	350
March	3,600	500
April	4,500	690
May	3,200	400
June	4,900	700

Instructions
(a) Determine the fixed- and variable-cost components using the high-low method.
(b) Prepare a graph showing the behavior of maintenance costs, and identify the fixed- and variable-cost elements. Use 100-hour increments and $1,000 cost increments.

Classify variable, fixed, and mixed costs.

(LO 1, 3)

E19-4 Family Furniture Corporation incurred the following costs.

1. Wood used in the production of furniture.
2. Fuel used in delivery trucks.
3. Straight-line depreciation on factory building.
4. Screws used in the production of furniture.
5. Sales staff salaries.
6. Sales commissions.
7. Property taxes.
8. Insurance on buildings.
9. Hourly wages of furniture craftsmen.
10. Salaries of factory supervisors.
11. Utilities expense.
12. Telephone bill.

Instructions
Identify the costs above as variable, fixed, or mixed.

Determine fixed and variable costs using the high-low method and prepare graph.

(LO 1, 3)

E19-5 The controller of Dousmann Industries has collected the following monthly expense data for use in analyzing the cost behavior of maintenance costs.

Month	Total Maintenance Costs	Total Machine Hours
January	$2,750	3,500
February	3,000	4,000
March	3,600	6,000
April	4,500	7,900
May	3,200	5,000
June	5,000	8,000

Instructions
(a) Determine the fixed- and variable-cost components using the high-low method.
(b) Prepare a graph showing the behavior of maintenance costs, and identify the fixed- and variable-cost elements. Use 2,000-hour increments and $1,000 cost increments.

E19-6 PCB Corporation manufactures a single product. Monthly production costs incurred in the manufacturing process are shown below for the production of 3,000 units. The utilities and maintenance costs are mixed costs. The fixed portions of these costs are $300 and $200, respectively.

Determine fixed, variable, and mixed costs.

(LO 1, 3)

Production in Units	3,000
Production Costs	
Direct materials	$ 7,500
Direct labor	18,000
Utilities	2,100
Property taxes	1,000
Indirect labor	4,500
Supervisory salaries	1,900
Maintenance	1,100
Depreciation	2,400

Instructions
(a) Identify the above costs as variable, fixed, or mixed.
(b) Calculate the expected costs when production is 5,000 units.

E19-7 Jim Taylor wants Taylor Company to use CVP analysis to study the effects of changes in costs and volume on the company. Taylor has heard that certain assumptions must be valid in order for CVP analysis to be useful.

Explain assumptions underlying CVP analysis.

(LO 4)

Instructions
▭▭▭▶ Prepare a memo to Jim Taylor concerning the assumptions that underlie CVP analysis.

E19-8 All That Blooms provides environmentally friendly lawn services for homeowners. Its operating costs are as follows.

Compute break-even point in units and dollars.

(LO 5, 6)

Depreciation	$1,400 per month
Advertising	$200 per month
Insurance	$2,000 per month
Weed and feed materials	$12 per lawn
Direct labor	$10 per lawn
Fuel	$2 per lawn

All That Blooms charges $60 per treatment for the average single-family lawn.

Instructions
Determine the company's break-even point in (a) number of lawns serviced per month and (b) dollars.

E19-9 The Green Acres Inn is trying to determine its break-even point. The inn has 50 rooms that it rents at $60 a night. Operating costs are as follows.

Compute break-even point.

(LO 5, 6)

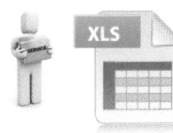

Salaries	$6,200 per month
Utilities	$1,100 per month
Depreciation	$1,000 per month
Maintenance	$100 per month
Maid service	$11 per room
Other costs	$28 per room

Instructions
Determine the inn's break-even point in (a) number of rented rooms per month and (b) dollars.

Compute contribution margin and break-even point.

(LO 5, 6)

E19-10 In the month of March, Style Salon services 560 clients at an average price of $120. During the month, fixed costs were $21,024 and variable costs were 60% of sales.

Instructions
(a) Determine the contribution margin in dollars, per unit, and as a ratio.
(b) Using the contribution margin technique, compute the break-even point in dollars and in units.

Compute break-even point.

(LO 5, 6)

E19-11 Kare Kars provides shuttle service between four hotels near a medical center and an international airport. Kare Kars uses two 10-passenger vans to offer 12 round trips per day. A recent month's activity in the form of a cost-volume-profit income statement is shown below.

Fare revenues (1,440 fares)		$36,000
Variable costs		
Fuel	$ 5,040	
Tolls and parking	3,100	
Maintenance	860	9,000
Contribution margin		27,000
Fixed costs		
Salaries	12,700	
Depreciation	1,300	
Insurance	1,000	15,000
Net income		$12,000

Instructions
(a) Calculate the break-even point in (1) dollars and (2) number of fares.
(b) Without calculations, determine the contribution margin at the break-even point.

Compute variable costs per unit, contribution margin ratio, and increase in fixed costs.

(LO 5, 6)

E19-12 In 2013, Manhoff Company had a break-even point of $350,000 based on a selling price of $5 per unit and fixed costs of $112,000. In 2014, the selling price and the variable costs per unit did not change, but the break-even point increased to $420,000.

Instructions
(a) Compute the variable costs per unit and the contribution margin ratio for 2013.
(b) Compute the increase in fixed costs for 2014.

Prepare CVP income statements.

(LO 5, 6)

E19-13 Cannes Company has the following information available for September 2014.

Unit selling price of video game consoles	$ 400
Unit variable costs	$ 275
Total fixed costs	$52,000
Units sold	600

Instructions
(a) Compute the contribution margin per unit.
(b) Prepare a CVP income statement that shows both total and per unit amounts.
(c) Compute Cannes' break-even point in units.
(d) Prepare a CVP income statement for the break-even point that shows both total and per unit amounts.

Compute various components to derive target net income under different assumptions.

(LO 6, 7)

E19-14 Naylor Company had $210,000 of net income in 2013 when the selling price per unit was $150, the variable costs per unit were $90, and the fixed costs were $570,000. Management expects per unit data and total fixed costs to remain the same in 2014. The president of Naylor Company is under pressure from stockholders to increase net income by $52,000 in 2014.

Instructions
(a) Compute the number of units sold in 2013.
(b) Compute the number of units that would have to be sold in 2014 to reach the stockholders' desired profit level.

(c) Assume that Naylor Company sells the same number of units in 2014 as it did in 2013. What would the selling price have to be in order to reach the stockholders' desired profit level?

E19-15 Cottonwood Company reports the following operating results for the month of August: sales $400,000 (units 5,000); variable costs $210,000; and fixed costs $90,000. Management is considering the following independent courses of action to increase net income.

Compute net income under different alternatives.

(LO 7)

1. Increase selling price by 10% with no change in total variable costs or units sold.
2. Reduce variable costs to 45% of sales.

Instructions
Compute the net income to be earned under each alternative. Which course of action will produce the highest net income?

E19-16 Glacial Company estimates that variable costs will be 62.5% of sales, and fixed costs will total $600,000. The selling price of the product is $4.

Prepare a CVP graph and compute break-even point and margin of safety.

(LO 6, 8)

Instructions
(a) Prepare a CVP graph, assuming maximum sales of $3,200,000. (*Note:* Use $400,000 increments for sales and costs and 100,000 increments for units.)
(b) Compute the break-even point in (1) units and (2) dollars.
(c) Compute the margin of safety in (1) dollars and (2) as a ratio, assuming actual sales are $2 million.

E19-17 Oak Bucket Co., a manufacturer of wood buckets, had the following data for 2013:

Determine contribution margin ratio, break-even point in dollars, and margin of safety.

(LO 5, 6, 7, 8)

Sales	2,600 units
Sales price	$40 per unit
Variable costs	$16 per unit
Fixed costs	$19,500

Instructions
(a) What is the contribution margin ratio?
(b) What is the break-even point in dollars?
(c) What is the margin of safety in dollars and as a ratio?
(d) If the company wishes to increase its total dollar contribution margin by 30% in 2014, by how much will it need to increase its sales if all other factors remain constant?

(CGA adapted)

EXERCISES: SET B AND CHALLENGE EXERCISES

Visit the book's companion website, at **www.wiley.com/college/weygandt**, and choose the Student Companion site to access Exercise Set B and Challenge Exercises.

PROBLEMS: SET A

P19-1A Telly Savalas owns the Bonita Barber Shop. He employs four barbers and pays each a base rate of $1,000 per month. One of the barbers serves as the manager and receives an extra $500 per month. In addition to the base rate, each barber also receives a commission of $4.50 per haircut.

Other costs are as follows.

Determine variable and fixed costs, compute break-even point, prepare a CVP graph, and determine net income.

(LO 1, 3, 5, 6)

Advertising	$200 per month
Rent	$1,100 per month
Barber supplies	$0.30 per haircut
Utilities	$175 per month plus $0.20 per haircut
Magazines	$25 per month

Telly currently charges $10 per haircut.

Instructions

(a) VC $5

(a) Determine the variable costs per haircut and the total monthly fixed costs.

(b) Compute the break-even point in units and dollars.

(c) Prepare a CVP graph, assuming a maximum of 1,800 haircuts in a month. Use increments of 300 haircuts on the horizontal axis and $3,000 on the vertical axis.

(d) Determine net income, assuming 1,700 haircuts are given in a month.

Prepare a CVP income statement, compute break-even point, contribution margin ratio, margin of safety ratio, and sales for target net income.

(LO 5, 6, 7, 8)

P19-2A Jorge Company bottles and distributes B-Lite, a diet soft drink. The beverage is sold for 50 cents per 16-ounce bottle to retailers, who charge customers 75 cents per bottle. For the year 2014, management estimates the following revenues and costs.

Sales	$1,800,000	Selling expenses—variable	$70,000
Direct materials	430,000	Selling expenses—fixed	65,000
Direct labor	360,000	Administrative expenses—	
Manufacturing overhead—		variable	20,000
variable	380,000	Administrative expenses—	
Manufacturing overhead—		fixed	60,000
fixed	280,000		

Instructions

(b) (1) 2,700,000 units
(c) CM ratio 30%

(a) Prepare a CVP income statement for 2014 based on management's estimates. (Show column for total amounts only.)

(b) Compute the break-even point in (1) units and (2) dollars.

(c) Compute the contribution margin ratio and the margin of safety ratio. (Round to nearest full percent.)

(d) Determine the sales dollars required to earn net income of $180,000.

Compute break-even point under alternative courses of action.

(LO 5, 6)

P19-3A Dousmann Corp.'s sales slumped badly in 2014. For the first time in its history, it operated at a loss. The company's income statement showed the following results from selling 500,000 units of product: sales $2,500,000; total costs and expenses $2,600,000; and net loss $100,000. Costs and expenses consisted of the amounts shown below.

	Total	Variable	Fixed
Cost of goods sold	$2,140,000	$1,540,000	$600,000
Selling expenses	250,000	92,000	158,000
Administrative expenses	210,000	68,000	142,000
	$2,600,000	$1,700,000	$900,000

Management is considering the following independent alternatives for 2015.

1. Increase unit selling price 20% with no change in costs, expenses, and sales volume.

2. Change the compensation of salespersons from fixed annual salaries totaling $150,000 to total salaries of $60,000 plus a 5% commission on sales.

Instructions

(b) Alternative 1 $2,093,023

(a) Compute the break-even point in dollars for 2014.

(b) Compute the break-even point in dollars under each of the alternative courses of action. (Round all ratios to nearest full percent.) Which course of action do you recommend?

Compute break-even point and margin of safety ratio, and prepare a CVP income statement before and after changes in business environment.

(LO 5, 6, 8)

P19-4A Mary Willis is the advertising manager for Bargain Shoe Store. She is currently working on a major promotional campaign. Her ideas include the installation of a new lighting system and increased display space that will add $24,000 in fixed costs to the $270,000 currently spent. In addition, Mary is proposing that a 5% price decrease ($40 to $38) will produce a 20% increase in sales volume (20,000 to 24,000). Variable costs will remain at $24 per pair of shoes. Management is impressed with Mary's ideas but concerned about the effects that these changes will have on the break-even point and the margin of safety.

Instructions

(b) Current margin of safety ratio 16%

(a) Compute the current break-even point in units, and compare it to the break-even point in units if Mary's ideas are used.

(b) Compute the margin of safety ratio for current operations and after Mary's changes are introduced. (Round to nearest full percent.)

(c) Prepare a CVP income statement for current operations and after Mary's changes are introduced. (Show column for total amounts only.) Would you make the changes suggested?

P19-5A Mozena Corporation has collected the following information after its first year of sales. Sales were $1,500,000 on 100,000 units; selling expenses $250,000 (40% variable and 60% fixed); direct materials $511,000; direct labor $290,000; administrative expenses $270,000 (20% variable and 80% fixed); manufacturing overhead $350,000 (70% variable and 30% fixed). Top management has asked you to do a CVP analysis so that it can make plans for the coming year. It has projected that unit sales will increase by 10% next year.

Compute contribution margin, fixed costs, break-even point, sales for target net income, and margin of safety ratio.

(LO 5, 6, 7, 8)

Instructions
(a) Compute (1) the contribution margin for the current year and the projected year, and (2) the fixed costs for the current year. (Assume that fixed costs will remain the same in the projected year.)
(b) Compute the break-even point in units and sales dollars for the current year.

(b) 157,000 units

(c) The company has a target net income of $200,000. What is the required sales in dollars for the company to meet its target?
(d) If the company meets its target net income number, by what percentage could its sales fall before it is operating at a loss? That is, what is its margin of safety ratio?

P19-6A Kaiser Industries carries no inventories. Its product is manufactured only when a customer's order is received. It is then shipped immediately after it is made. For its fiscal year ended October 31, 2014, Kaiser's break-even point was $1.3 million. On sales of $1.2 million, its income statement showed a gross profit of $180,000, direct materials cost of $400,000, and direct labor costs of $500,000. The contribution margin was $180,000, and variable manufacturing overhead was $50,000.

Determine contribution margin ratio, break-even point, and margin of safety.

(LO 1, 5, 7, 8)

Instructions
(a) Calculate the following:
(1) Variable selling and administrative expenses.
(2) Fixed manufacturing overhead.
(3) Fixed selling and administrative expenses.

(a) (2) $70,000

(b) Ignoring your answer to part (a), assume that fixed manufacturing overhead was $100,000 and the fixed selling and administrative expenses were $80,000. The marketing vice president feels that if the company increased its advertising, sales could be increased by 25%. What is the maximum increased advertising cost the company can incur and still report the same income as before the advertising expenditure?

(CGA adapted)

PROBLEMS: SET B

P19-1B The Sasoon Barber Shop employs four barbers. One barber, who also serves as the manager, is paid a salary of $3,000 per month. The other barbers are paid $1,500 per month. In addition, each barber is paid a commission of $3 per haircut. Other monthly costs are store rent $700 plus 60 cents per haircut, depreciation on equipment $400, barber supplies 40 cents per haircut, utilities $300, and advertising $100. The price of a haircut is $10.

Determine variable and fixed costs, compute break-even point, prepare a CVP graph, and determine net income.

(LO 1, 3, 5, 6)

Instructions
(a) Determine the variable costs per haircut and the total monthly fixed costs.
(b) Compute the break-even point in units and dollars.

(a) VC $4

(c) Prepare a CVP graph, assuming a maximum of 1,800 haircuts in a month. Use increments of 300 haircuts on the horizontal axis and $3,000 increments on the vertical axis.
(d) Determine the net income, assuming 1,800 haircuts are given in a month.

Prepare a CVP income statement, compute break-even point, contribution margin ratio, margin of safety ratio, and sales for target net income.

(LO 5, 6, 7, 8)

P19-2B All Frute Company bottles and distributes Frute Ade, a fruit drink. The beverage is sold for 50 cents per 16-ounce bottle to retailers, who charge customers 70 cents per bottle. For the year 2014, management estimates the following revenues and costs.

Sales	$2,500,000	Selling expenses—variable	$ 80,000
Direct materials	360,000	Selling expenses—fixed	250,000
Direct labor	450,000	Administrative expenses—	
Manufacturing overhead—		variable	40,000
variable	270,000	Administrative expenses—	
Manufacturing overhead—		fixed	150,000
fixed	380,000		

Instructions
(a) Prepare a CVP income statement for 2014 based on management's estimates. (Show column for total amounts only.)

(b) (1) 3,000,000 units
(c) CM ratio 52%

(b) Compute the break-even point in (1) units and (2) dollars.
(c) Compute the contribution margin ratio and the margin of safety ratio.
(d) Determine the sales dollars required to earn net income of $624,000.

Compute break-even point under alternative courses of action.

(LO 5, 6)

P19-3B Olgivie Company had a bad year in 2013. For the first time in its history, it operated at a loss. The company's income statement showed the following results from selling 60,000 units of product: sales $1,800,000; total costs and expenses $2,010,000; and net loss $210,000. Costs and expenses consisted of the amounts shown below.

	Total	Variable	Fixed
Cost of goods sold	$1,350,000	$ 930,000	$420,000
Selling expenses	480,000	125,000	355,000
Administrative expenses	180,000	115,000	65,000
	$2,010,000	$1,170,000	$840,000

Management is considering the following independent alternatives for 2014.

1. Increase unit selling price 25% with no change in costs, expenses, and sales volume.
2. Change the compensation of salespersons from fixed annual salaries totaling $200,000 to total salaries of $20,000 plus a 5% commission on net sales.
3. Purchase new high-tech factory machinery that will change the proportion between variable and fixed cost of goods sold to 50:50.

Instructions
(a) Compute the break-even point in dollars for 2013.

(b) Alternative 1, $1,750,000

(b) Compute the break-even point in dollars under each of the alternative courses of action. (Round all ratios to nearest full percent.) Which course of action do you recommend?

Compute break-even point and margin of safety ratio, and prepare a CVP income statement before and after changes in business environment.

(LO 5, 6, 8)

P19-4B Alma Ortiz is the advertising manager for CostLess Shoe Store. She is currently working on a major promotional campaign. Her ideas include the installation of a new lighting system and increased display space that will add $18,000 in fixed costs to the $216,000 currently spent. In addition, Alma is proposing that a 10% price decrease (from $30 to $27) will produce an increase in sales volume from 20,000 to 24,000 units. Variable costs will remain at $12 per pair of shoes. Management is impressed with Alma's ideas but concerned about the effects that these changes will have on the break-even point and the margin of safety.

Instructions
(a) Compute the current break-even point in units, and compare it to the break-even point in units if Alma's ideas are used.

(b) Current margin of safety ratio 40%

(b) Compute the margin of safety ratio for current operations and after Alma's changes are introduced. (Round to nearest full percent.)
(c) Prepare a CVP income statement for current operations and after Alma's changes are introduced. (Show column for total amounts only.) Would you make the changes suggested?

Compute break-even point and margin of safety ratio, and prepare a CVP income statement before and after changes in business environment.

(LO 5, 6, 7, 8)

P19-5B Isaac Corporation has collected the following information after its first year of sales. Sales were $1,800,000 on 100,000 units; selling expenses $400,000 (30% variable and 70% fixed); direct materials $456,000; direct labor $250,000; administrative expenses $484,000 (50% variable and 50% fixed); manufacturing overhead $480,000 (40% variable and 60% fixed). Top management has asked you to do a CVP analysis so that it can make plans for the coming year. It has projected that unit sales will increase by 20% next year.

Instructions

(a) Compute (1) the contribution margin for the current year and the projected year, and (2) the fixed costs for the current year. (Assume that fixed costs will remain the same in the projected year.)

(b) Compute the break-even point in units and sales dollars.

(c) The company has a target net income of $213,000. What is the required sales in dollars for the company to meet its target?

(d) If the company meets its target net income number, by what percentage could its sales fall before it is operating at a loss? That is, what is its margin of safety ratio?

(e) The company is considering a purchase of equipment that would reduce its direct labor costs by $100,000 and would change its manufacturing overhead costs to 10% variable and 90% fixed (assume total manufacturing overhead cost is $480,000, as above). It is also considering switching to a pure commission basis for its sales staff. This would change selling expenses to 80% variable and 20% fixed (assume total selling expense is $400,000, as above). Compute (1) the contribution margin and (2) the contribution margin ratio, and recompute (3) the break-even point in sales dollars. Comment on the effect each of management's proposed changes has on the break-even point.

(b) 150,000 units

P19-6B Mega Electronix carries no inventories. Its product is manufactured only when a customer's order is received. It is then shipped immediately after it is made. For its fiscal year ended October 31, 2014, Mega's break-even point was $2.4 million. On sales of $2 million, its income statement showed a gross profit of $400,000, direct materials cost of $600,000, and direct labor costs of $700,000. The contribution margin was $150,000, and variable manufacturing overhead was $200,000.

Determine contribution margin ratio, break-even point, and margin of safety.

(LO 1, 5, 7, 8)

Instructions

(a) Calculate the following:
1. Variable selling and administrative expenses.
2. Fixed manufacturing overhead.
3. Fixed selling and administrative expenses.

(a) 2. $100,000

(b) Ignoring your answer to part (a), assume that fixed manufacturing overhead was $100,000 and the fixed selling and administrative expenses were $80,000. The marketing vice president feels that if the company increased its advertising, sales could be increased by 15%. What is the maximum increased advertising cost the company can incur and still report the same income as before the advertising expenditure?

(CGA adapted)

PROBLEMS: SET C

Visit the book's companion website, at **www.wiley.com/college/weygandt**, and choose the Student Companion site to access Problem Set C.

WATERWAYS CONTINUING PROBLEM

(*Note:* This is a continuation of the Waterways Problem from Chapters 15–18.)

WCP19 The Vice President for Sales and Marketing at Waterways Corporation is planning for production needs to meet sales demand in the coming year. He is also trying to determine how the company's profits might be increased in the coming year. This problem asks you to use cost-volume-profit concepts to help Waterways understand contribution margins of some of its products and to decide whether to mass-produce certain products.

Go to the book's companion website, **www.wiley.com/college/weygandt**, *to find the remainder of this problem.*

Management Decision-Making

Decision-Making at Current Designs

BYP19-1 Bill Johnson, sales manager, and Diane Buswell, controller, at Current Designs are beginning to analyze the cost considerations for one of the composite models of the kayak division. They have provided the following production and operational costs necessary to produce one composite kayak.

Kevlar®	$250 per kayak
Resin and supplies	$100 per kayak
Finishing kit (seat, rudder, ropes, etc.)	$170 per kayak
Labor	$420 per kayak
Selling and administrative expenses—variable	$400 per kayak
Selling and administrative expenses—fixed	$119,700 per year
Manufacturing overhead—fixed	$240,000 per year

Bill and Diane have asked you to provide a cost-volume-profit analysis, to help them finalize the budget projections for the upcoming year. Bill has informed you that the selling price of the composite kayak will be $2,000.

Instructions
(a) Calculate variable costs per unit.
(b) Determine the contribution margin per unit.
(c) Using the contribution margin per unit, determine the break-even point in units for this product line.
(d) Assume that Current Designs plans to earn $270,600 on this product line. Using the contribution margin per unit, calculate the number of units that need to be sold to achieve this goal.
(e) Based on the most recent sales forecast, Current Designs plans to sell 1,000 units of this model. Using your results from part (c), calculate the margin of safety and the margin of safety ratio.

Decision-Making Across the Organization

BYP19-2 Creative Ideas Company has decided to introduce a new product. The new product can be manufactured by either a capital-intensive method or a labor-intensive method. The manufacturing method will not affect the quality of the product. The estimated manufacturing costs by the two methods are as follows.

	Capital- Intensive	Labor- Intensive
Direct materials	$5 per unit	$5.50 per unit
Direct labor	$6 per unit	$8.00 per unit
Variable overhead	$3 per unit	$4.50 per unit
Fixed manufacturing costs	$2,524,000	$1,550,000

Creative Ideas' market research department has recommended an introductory unit sales price of $32. The incremental selling expenses are estimated to be $502,000 annually plus $2 for each unit sold, regardless of manufacturing method.

Instructions
With the class divided into groups, answer the following.
(a) Calculate the estimated break-even point in annual unit sales of the new product if Creative Ideas Company uses the:
  (1) Capital-intensive manufacturing method.
  (2) Labor-intensive manufacturing method.
(b) Determine the annual unit sales volume at which Creative Ideas Company would be indifferent between the two manufacturing methods.
(c) Explain the circumstance under which Creative Ideas should employ each of the two manufacturing methods.

(CMA adapted)

Managerial Analysis

BYP19-3 The condensed income statement for the Peri and Paul partnership for 2014 is as follows.

Peri and Paul Company
Income Statement
For the Year Ended December 31, 2014

Sales (240,000 units)		$1,200,000
Cost of goods sold		800,000
Gross profit		400,000
Operating expenses		
Selling	$280,000	
Administrative	150,000	430,000
Net loss		($30,000)

A cost behavior analysis indicates that 75% of the cost of goods sold are variable, 42% of the selling expenses are variable, and 40% of the administrative expenses are variable.

Instructions

(Round to nearest unit, dollar, and percentage, where necessary. Use the CVP income statement format in computing profits.)

(a) Compute the break-even point in total sales dollars and in units for 2014.

(b) Peri has proposed a plan to get the partnership "out of the red" and improve its profitability. She feels that the quality of the product could be substantially improved by spending $0.25 more per unit on better raw materials. The selling price per unit could be increased to only $5.25 because of competitive pressures. Peri estimates that sales volume will increase by 25%. What effect would Peri's plan have on the profits and the break-even point in dollars of the partnership? (Round the contribution margin ratio to two decimal places.)

(c) Paul was a marketing major in college. He believes that sales volume can be increased only by intensive advertising and promotional campaigns. He therefore proposed the following plan as an alternative to Peri's: (1) Increase variable selling expenses to $0.59 per unit, (2) lower the selling price per unit by $0.25, and (3) increase fixed selling expenses by $40,000. Paul quoted an old marketing research report that said that sales volume would increase by 60% if these changes were made. What effect would Paul's plan have on the profits and the break-even point in dollars of the partnership?

(d) Which plan should be accepted? Explain your answer.

Real-World Focus

BYP19-4 The Coca-Cola Company hardly needs an introduction. A line taken from the cover of a recent annual report says it all: If you measured time in servings of Coca-Cola, "a billion Coca-Cola's ago was yesterday morning." On average, every U.S. citizen drinks 363 8-ounce servings of Coca-Cola products each year. Coca-Cola's primary line of business is the making and selling of syrup to bottlers. These bottlers then sell the finished bottles and cans of Coca-Cola to the consumer.

In the annual report of Coca-Cola, the information shown below was provided.

The Coca-Cola Company
Management Discussion

Our gross margin declined to 61 percent this year from 62 percent in the prior year, primarily due to costs for materials such as sweeteners and packaging.

The increases [in selling expenses] in the last two years were primarily due to higher marketing expenditures in support of our Company's volume growth.

We measure our sales volume in two ways: (1) gallon shipments of concentrates and syrups and (2) unit cases of finished product (bottles and cans of Coke sold by bottlers).

Instructions

Answer the following questions.

(a) Are sweeteners and packaging a variable cost or a fixed cost? What is the impact on the contribution margin of an increase in the per unit cost of sweeteners or packaging? What are the implications for profitability?

(b) In your opinion, are marketing expenditures a fixed cost, variable cost, or mixed cost to The Coca-Cola Company? Give justification for your answer.

(c) Which of the two measures cited for measuring volume represents the activity index as defined in this chapter? Why might Coca-Cola use two different measures?

BYP19-5 The May 21, 2010, edition of the *Wall Street Journal* includes an article by Jeffrey Trachtenberg entitled "E-Books Rewrite Bookselling."

Instructions

Read the article and answer the following questions.

(a) What aspect of Barnes and Noble's current structure puts it at risk if electronic books become a significant portion of book sales?

(b) What was Barnes and Noble's primary competitive advantage in a "paper book" world? How has this advantage been eliminated by e-books?

(c) What event do the authors say might eventually be viewed as the big turning point for e-books?

(d) What amount does Barnes and Noble earn on a $25 hardcover book? How much would it likely earn on an e-book version of the same title? What implications does this have for Barnes and Noble versus its competitors?

(e) What two mistakes does the author suggest that Barnes and Noble made that left it ill-prepared for an e-book environment?

Critical Thinking

Communication Activity

BYP19-6 Your roommate asks for your help on the following questions about CVP analysis formulas.

(a) How can the mathematical equation for break-even sales show both sales units and sales dollars?

(b) How do the formulas differ for contribution margin per unit and contribution margin ratio?

(c) How can contribution margin be used to determine break-even sales in units and in dollars?

Instructions

Write a memo to your roommate stating the relevant formulas and answering each question.

Ethics Case

BYP19-7 Scott Bestor is an accountant for Westfield Company. Early this year, Scott made a highly favorable projection of sales and profits over the next 3 years for Westfield's hot-selling computer PLEX. As a result of the projections Scott presented to senior management, the company decided to expand production in this area. This decision led to dislocations of some plant personnel who were reassigned to one of the company's newer plants in another state. However, no one was fired, and in fact the company expanded its work force slightly.

Unfortunately, Scott rechecked his computations on the projections a few months later and found that he had made an error that would have reduced his projections substantially. Luckily, sales of PLEX have exceeded projections so far, and management is satisfied with its decision. Scott, however, is not sure what to do. Should he confess his honest mistake and jeopardize his possible promotion? He suspects that no one will catch the error because sales of PLEX have exceeded his projections, and it appears that profits will materialize close to his projections.

Instructions

(a) Who are the stakeholders in this situation?

(b) Identify the ethical issues involved in this situation.

(c) What are the possible alternative actions for Scott? What would you do in Scott's position?

All About You

BYP19-8 Cost-volume-profit analysis can also be used in making personal financial decisions. For example, the purchase of a new car is one of your biggest personal expenditures. It is important that you carefully analyze your options.

Suppose that you are considering the purchase of a hybrid vehicle. Let's assume the following facts: The hybrid will initially cost an additional $4,500 above the cost of a traditional vehicle. The hybrid will get 40 miles per gallon of gas, and the traditional car will get 30 miles per gallon. Also, assume that the cost of gas is $3.60 per gallon.

Instructions
Using the facts above, answer the following questions.
(a) What is the variable gasoline cost of going one mile in the hybrid car? What is the variable cost of going one mile in the traditional car?
(b) Using the information in part (a), if "miles" is your unit of measure, what is the "contribution margin" of the hybrid vehicle relative to the traditional vehicle? That is, express the variable cost savings on a per-mile basis.
(c) How many miles would you have to drive in order to break even on your investment in the hybrid car?
(d) What other factors might you want to consider?

Answers to Chapter Questions

Answers to Insight and Accounting Across the Organization Questions

p. 954 Gardens in the Sky Q: What are some of the variable and fixed costs that are impacted by hydroponic farming? **A:** Compared to traditional methods, hydroponic farming would reduce the use of pesticides, herbicides, fuel, and water. Soil erosion would be eliminated, and land requirements would drop. But, fixed costs related to constructing greenhouses, suitable vertical planters, as well as investments in artificial lighting could be high.

p. 958 Skilled Labor Is Truly Essential Q: Would you characterize labor costs as being a fixed cost, a variable cost, or something else in this situation? **A:** Because these labor costs are essentially unchanged for most levels of production, they are primarily fixed. However, it could be described as being a "step function." If production gets too far outside the normal range, workers' hours will change. If production goes too low, hours are cut, and if it goes too high, overtime hours are needed.

p. 965 Charter Flights Offer a Good Deal Q: How did FlightServe determine that it would break even with 3.3 seats full per flight? **A:** FlightServe determined its break-even point with the following formula: Fixed costs ÷ Contribution margin per seat occupied = Break-even point in seats.

p. 969 How a Rolling Stones' Tour Makes Money Q: What amount of sales dollars are required for the promoter to break even?
A: Fixed costs = $1,200,000 + $400,000 = $1,600,000
   Contribution margin ratio = 80%
   Break-even sales = $1,600,000 ÷ .80 = $2,000,000

Answers to Self-Test Questions

1. d **2.** c **3.** a **4.** d **5.** a [($1,200 − $600) ÷ (10,000 − 2,000)] **6.** c **7.** c **8.** d
9. a [(100,000 × $12) − $300,000 − $200,000] **10.** c (200,000 × $4 × 25%) **11.** c ($100 × 30%)
12. b **13.** a **14.** b [($600,000 − $420,000) ÷ $600,000]

✔ Remember to go back to The Navigator box on the chapter opening page and check off your completed work.

Chapter 20

Cost-Volume-Profit Analysis: Additional Issues

Feature Story

Rapid Replay

Intel doesn't do things half-way. If you own a PC, then there is a roughly 85% chance that the microprocessor chip that runs your machine was made by Intel. In fact, for as long as most people can remember, Intel has had at least an 85% share of the market for PC computer chips. That doesn't mean, however, that life is easy for Intel. Its earnings swings, like every-thing else about the company, are major league. Consider these two *Wall Street Journal* headlines: "Intel's Net Plunges as Demand Dries Up" and then, only slightly more than a year later, "Intel Earnings Set High Bar."

If Intel is so dominant in the computer chip market, why does it experience such huge swings in its earnings? First, to produce computer chips, Intel must continually make huge investments in sophisticated equipment. Now, consider what you learned in the previous chapter. The higher a company's fixed costs, the more units it must sell to break even. In this chapter, you will learn that if a company has high fixed costs as a percentage of total costs, then its earnings will be very susceptible to economic swings.

Another way of saying this is that when the economy gets the sniffles,

Learning Objectives

After studying this chapter, you should be able to:

1 Describe the essential features of a cost-volume-profit income statement.

2 Apply basic CVP concepts.

3 Explain the term sales mix and its effects on break-even sales.

4 Determine sales mix when a company has limited resources.

5 Understand how operating leverage affects profitability.

 The Navigator

Intel gets the flu. A drop in Intel's sales results in a dispropor-tionately large drop in its profits. For example, during a recent quarter when Intel's sales fell 23%, its profits fell 90%. On the other hand, the minute the economy turns upward, Intel's profits do a sharp about-face. After the recent downturn, Intel's sales jumped 44%. While this was a nice bump in sales, consider what happened to its net income. Its net income increased by almost 10 times as much—nearly 400%.

Is there anything that Intel can do to tame this roller coaster ride? It can try to change its cost structure by reducing its

reliance on fixed costs. But to do this, it would have to rely more heavily on outside suppliers rather than producing its own chips. Intel is probably reluctant to make this change because it would lose some of its control over product quality.

Watch the Whole Foods video in WileyPLUS to learn more about the use of cost-volume-profit analysis in a changing business environment.

Source: Don Clark and Ben Worthen, "Intel's Net Plunges as Demand Dries Up," *Wall Street Journal Online* (January 16, 2009); and Don Clark, "Intel Earnings Set High Bar," *Wall Street Journal Online* (April 13, 2010).

✔ **The Navigator**

Preview of **Chapter 20**

As the Feature Story about Intel suggests, the relationship between a company's fixed and variable costs can have a huge impact on its profitability. In particular, the trend toward cost structures dominated by fixed costs has significantly increased the volatility of many companies' net income. The purpose of this chapter is to demonstrate additional uses of cost-volume-profit analysis in making sound business decisions.

The content and organization of this chapter are as follows.

COST-VOLUME-PROFIT ANALYSIS: ADDITIONAL ISSUES

Cost-Volume-Profit (CVP) Review	Sales Mix	Cost Structure and Operating Leverage
• Basic concepts • Basic computations • CVP and changes in the business environment	• Break-even sales in units • Break-even sales in dollars • Sales mix with limited resources	• Effect on contribution margin ratio • Effect on break-even point • Effect on margin of safety ratio • Operating leverage

✔ **The Navigator**

Cost-Volume-Profit (CVP) Review

As indicated in Chapter 19, cost-volume-profit (CVP) analysis is the study of the effects of changes in costs and volume on a company's profit. CVP analysis is important to profit planning. It is also a critical factor in determining product mix, maximizing use of production facilities, and setting selling prices.

Basic Concepts

LEARNING OBJECTIVE 1

Describe the essential features of a cost-volume-profit income statement.

Because CVP is so important for decision-making, management often wants this information reported in a CVP income statement format for internal use. The CVP income statement classifies costs as *variable* or *fixed* and computes a contribution margin. **Contribution margin** is the amount of revenue remaining after deducting variable costs. It is often stated both as a total amount and on a per unit basis.

Illustration 20-1 presents the CVP income statement for Vargo Video (which was shown in Illustration 19-12, on page 961). Note that Vargo's sales included 1,600 camcorders at $500 per unit.

Illustration 20-1
Basic CVP income statement

Vargo Video Company
CVP Income Statement
For the Month Ended June 30, 2014

	Total	Per Unit
Sales (1,600 camcorders)	$ 800,000	$ 500
Variable costs	480,000	300
Contribution margin	**320,000**	**$200**
Fixed costs	200,000	
Net income	**$120,000**	

Companies often prepare detailed CVP income statements. The CVP income statement in Illustration 20-2 uses the same base information as that presented in Illustration 20-1 but provides more detailed information (using assumed data) about the composition of expenses.

Illustration 20-2
Detailed CVP income statement

Vargo Video Company
CVP Income Statement
For the Month Ended June 30, 2014

		Total	Per Unit
Sales		$ 800,000	$ 500
Variable expenses			
Cost of goods sold	$400,000		
Selling expenses	60,000		
Administrative expenses	20,000		
Total variable expenses		480,000	300
Contribution margin		**320,000**	**$200**
Fixed expenses			
Cost of goods sold	120,000		
Selling expenses	40,000		
Administrative expenses	40,000		
Total fixed expenses		200,000	
Net income		**$120,000**	

Helpful Hint
The appendix to this chapter provides additional discussion of income statements used for decision-making.

In the applications of CVP analysis that follow, we assume that the term "cost" includes all costs and expenses related to production and sale of the product. That is, **cost includes manufacturing costs plus selling and administrative expenses.**

> ## > DO IT!

CVP Income Statement

Garner Inc. sold 20,000 units and recorded sales of $800,000 for the first quarter of 2014. In making the sales, the company incurred the following costs and expenses.

	Variable	Fixed
Cost of goods sold	$250,000	$110,000
Selling expenses	100,000	25,000
Administrative expenses	82,000	73,000

(a) Prepare a CVP income statement for the quarter ended March 31, 2014.

(b) Compute the contribution margin per unit.

(c) Compute the contribution margin ratio.

Solution

Action Plan

✔ Use the CVP income statement format.

✔ Use the formula for contribution margin per unit.

✔ Use the formula for the contribution margin ratio.

(a)

Garner Inc.
Income Statement
For the Quarter Ended March 31, 2014

Sales (20,000 units)		$800,000
Variable expenses		
Cost of goods sold	$250,000	
Selling expenses	100,000	
Administrative expenses	82,000	
Total variable expenses		432,000
Contribution margin		368,000
Fixed expenses		
Cost of goods sold	110,000	
Selling expenses	25,000	
Administrative expenses	73,000	
Total fixed expenses		208,000
Net income		$160,000

(b) Contribution margin per unit:
$368,000 ÷ 20,000 units = $18.40 per unit.

(c) Contribution margin ratio:
$368,000 ÷ $800,000 = 46% (or $18.40 ÷ $40 = 46%).

Related exercise material: **BE20-1, BE20-2, and DO IT! 20-1.**

✔ **The Navigator**

Basic Computations

Before we introduce additional issues of CVP analysis, let's review some of the basic concepts that you learned in Chapter 19, specifically break-even analysis, target net income, and margin of safety.

LEARNING OBJECTIVE   **2**

Apply basic CVP concepts.

BREAK-EVEN ANALYSIS

Vargo Video's CVP income statement (Illustration 20-2) shows that total contribution margin (sales minus variable expenses) is $320,000, and the company's contribution margin per unit is $200. Recall that contribution margin can also be expressed in the form of the **contribution margin ratio** (contribution margin divided by sales), which in the case of Vargo is 40% ($200 ÷ $500).

Illustration 20-3 demonstrates how to compute Vargo's break-even point in units (using contribution margin per unit).

Illustration 20-3
Break-even point in units

Fixed Costs	÷	Contribution Margin per Unit	=	Break-Even Point in Units
$200,000	÷	$200	=	1,000 units

Illustration 20-4 shows the computation for the break-even point in dollars (using contribution margin ratio).

Illustration 20-4
Break-even point in dollars

Fixed Costs	÷	Contribution Margin Ratio	=	Break-Even Point in Dollars
$200,000	÷	.40	=	$500,000

When a company is in its early stages of operation, its primary goal is to break even. Failure to break even will lead eventually to financial failure.

TARGET NET INCOME

Once a company achieves break-even, it then sets a sales goal that will generate a target net income. For example, assume that Vargo's management has a target net income of $250,000. Illustration 20-5 shows the required sales in units to achieve its target net income.

Illustration 20-5
Target net income in units

(Fixed Costs + Target Net Income)	÷	Contribution Margin per Unit	=	Required Sales in Units
($200,000 + $250,000)	÷	$200	=	2,250 units

Illustration 20-6 uses the contribution margin ratio to compute the required sales in dollars.

Illustration 20-6
Target net income in dollars

(Fixed Costs + Target Net Income)	÷	Contribution Margin Ratio	=	Required Sales in Dollars
($200,000 + $250,000)	÷	.40	=	$1,125,000

In order to achieve net income of $250,000, Vargo has to sell 2,250 camcorders, for a total price of $1,125,000.

MARGIN OF SAFETY

Another measure managers use to assess profitability is the margin of safety. The **margin of safety** tells us **how far sales can drop** before the company will be operating at a loss. Managers like to have a sense of how much cushion they have between their current situation and operating at a loss. This can be expressed in dollars or as a ratio. In Illustration 20-2, for example, Vargo reported sales of $800,000. At that sales level, its margin of safety in dollars and as a ratio are as follows.

Illustration 20-7
Margin of safety in dollars

Actual (Expected) Sales	–	Break-Even Sales	=	Margin of Safety in Dollars
$800,000	–	$500,000	=	$300,000

As shown in Illustration 20-8, Vargo's sales could drop by $300,000, or 37.5%, before the company would operate at a loss.

Illustration 20-8
Margin of safety ratio

Margin of Safety in Dollars	÷	Actual (Expected) Sales	=	Margin of Safety Ratio
$300,000	÷	$800,000	=	37.5%

CVP and Changes in the Business Environment

To better understand how CVP analysis works, let's look at three independent situations that might occur at Vargo Video. Each case uses the original camcorder sales and cost data, which were:

Illustration 20-9
Original camcorder sales
and cost data

Unit selling price	$500
Unit variable cost	$300
Total fixed costs	$200,000
Break-even sales	$500,000 or 1,000 units

CASE I

A competitor is offering a 10% discount on the selling price of its camcorders. Management must decide whether to offer a similar discount.

Question: What effect will a 10% discount on selling price have on the break-even point for camcorders?

Answer: A 10% discount on selling price reduces the selling price per unit to $450 [$500 − ($500 × 10%)]. Variable costs per unit remain unchanged at $300. Thus, the contribution margin per unit is $150. Assuming no change in fixed costs, break-even sales are 1,333 units, computed as follows.

Illustration 20-10
Computation of break-even
sales in units

Fixed Costs	÷	Contribution Margin per Unit	=	Break-Even Sales
$200,000	÷	$150	=	1,333 units (rounded)

For Vargo Video, this change requires monthly sales to increase by 333 units, or 33⅓%, in order to break even. In reaching a conclusion about offering a 10% discount to customers, management must determine how likely it is to achieve the increased sales. Also, management should estimate the possible loss of sales if the competitor's discount price is not matched.

CASE II

To meet the threat of foreign competition, management invests in new robotic equipment that will lower the amount of direct labor required to make camcorders. The company estimates that total fixed costs will increase 30% and that variable cost per unit will decrease 30%.

Question: What effect will the new equipment have on the sales volume required to break even?

Answer: Total fixed costs become $260,000 [$200,000 + (30% × $200,000)]. The variable cost per unit becomes $210 [$300 − (30% × $300)]. The new break-even point is approximately 897 units, computed as shown on the next page.

Illustration 20-11
Computation of break-even sales in units

Fixed Costs	÷	Contribution Margin per Unit	=	Break-Even Sales
$260,000	÷	($500 − $210)	=	897 units (rounded)

These changes appear to be advantageous for Vargo Video. The break-even point is reduced by approximately 10%, or 100 units.

CASE III

Vargo's principal supplier of raw materials has just announced a price increase. The higher cost is expected to increase the variable cost of camcorders by $25 per unit. Management decides to hold the line on the selling price of the camcorders. It plans a cost-cutting program that will save $17,500 in fixed costs per month. Vargo is currently realizing monthly net income of $80,000 on sales of 1,400 camcorders.

Question: What increase in units sold will be needed to maintain the same level of net income?

Answer: The variable cost per unit increases to $325 ($300 + $25). Fixed costs are reduced to $182,500 ($200,000 − $17,500). Because of the change in variable cost, the contribution margin per unit becomes $175 ($500 − $325). The required number of units sold to achieve the target net income is computed as follows.

Illustration 20-12
Computation of required sales

$\left(\begin{array}{c}\text{Fixed Costs + Target}\\\text{Net Income}\end{array}\right)$	÷	Contribution Margin per Unit	=	Required Sales in Units
($182,500 + $80,000)	÷	$175	=	1,500

To achieve the required sales, Vargo Video will have to sell 1,500 camcorders, an increase of 100 units. If this does not seem to be a reasonable expectation, management will either have to make further cost reductions or accept less net income if the selling price remains unchanged.

We hope that the concepts reviewed in this section are now familiar to you. We are now ready to examine additional ways that companies use CVP analysis to assess profitability and to help in making effective business decisions.

MANAGEMENT INSIGHT

Don't Just Look—Buy Something

When analyzing an Internet business, analysts closely watch the so-called "conversion rate." This rate is calculated by dividing the number of people who actually take action at an Internet site (buy something) by the total number of people who visit the site. Average conversion rates are from 3% to 5%. A rate below 2% is poor, while a rate above 10% is great.

Conversion rates have an obvious effect on the break-even point. Suppose you spend $10,000 on your site, and you attract 5,000 visitors. If you get a 2% conversion rate (100 purchases), your site costs $100 per purchase ($10,000 ÷ 100). A 4% conversion rate gets you down to a cost of $50 per transaction, and an 8% conversion rate gets you down to $25. Studies show that conversion rates increase if the site has an easy-to-use interface, fast-performing screens, a convenient ordering process, and advertising that is both clever and clear.

Source: J. William Gurley, "The One Internet Metric That Really Counts" *Fortune* (March 6, 2000), p. 392.

? Besides increasing their conversion rates, what steps can online merchants use to lower their break-even points? (See page 1040.)

> **DO IT!**

CVP Analysis

Krisanne Company reports the following operating results for the month of June.

Krisanne Company
CVP Income Statement
For the Month Ended June 30, 2014

	Total	Per Unit
Sales (5,000 units)	$300,000	$60
Variable costs	180,000	36
Contribution margin	120,000	$24
Fixed expenses	100,000	
Net income	$ 20,000	

To increase net income, management is considering reducing the selling price by 10%, with no changes to unit variable costs or fixed costs. Management is confident that this change will increase unit sales by 25%.

Using the contribution margin technique, compute the break-even point in units and dollars and margin of safety in dollars (a) assuming no changes to sales price or costs, and (b) assuming changes to sales price and volume as described above. (c) Comment on your findings.

Solution

Action Plan

✔ Apply the formula for the break-even point in units.

✔ Apply the formula for the break-even point in dollars.

✔ Apply the formula for the margin of safety in dollars.

(a) Assuming no changes to sales price or costs:
Break-even point in units = 4,167 units (rounded) ($100,000 ÷ $24).
Break-even point in sales dollars = $250,000 ($100,000 ÷ .40[a]).
Margin of safety in dollars = $50,000 ($300,000 − $250,000).
[a]$24 ÷ $60.

(b) Assuming changes to sales price and volume:
Break-even point in units = 5,556 units (rounded) ($100,000 ÷ $18[b]).
Break-even point in sales dollars = $300,000 ($100,000 ÷ ($18 ÷ $54)).
Margin of safety in dollars = $37,500 ($337,500[c] − $300,000).
[b]$60 − (.10 × $60) − 36 = $18.
[c]5,000 + (.25 × 5,000) = 6,250 units, 6,250 units × $54 = $337,500.

(c) The increase in the break-even point and the decrease in the margin of safety indicate that management should not implement the proposed change. The increase in sales volume will result in contribution margin of $112,500 (6,250 × $18), which is $7,500 less than the current amount.

Related exercise material: **BE20-3, BE20-4, BE20-5, BE20-6, E20-1, E20-2, E20-3, E20-4, E20-5, and DO IT! 20-2.**

✔ **The Navigator**

Sales Mix

To this point, our discussion of CVP analysis has assumed that a company sells only one product. However, most companies sell multiple products. When a company sells many products, it is important that management understand its sales mix.

Sales mix is the relative percentage in which a company sells its multiple products. For example, if 80% of Hewlett Packard's unit sales are printers and the other 20% are PCs, its sales mix is 80% printers to 20% PCs.

LEARNING OBJECTIVE   3

Explain the term sales mix and its effects on break-even sales.

Sales mix is important to managers because different products often have substantially different contribution margins. For example, Ford's SUVs and F150 pickup trucks have higher contribution margins compared to its economy cars. Similarly, first-class tickets sold by United Airlines provide substantially higher contribution margins than coach-class tickets. Intel's sales of computer chips for netbook computers have increased, but the contribution margin on these chips is lower than for notebook and desktop PCs.

Break-Even Sales in Units

Companies can compute break-even sales for a mix of two or more products by determining the **weighted-average unit contribution margin of all the products**. To illustrate, assume that Vargo Video sells not only camcorders but high-definition TVs as well. Vargo sells its two products in the following amounts: 1,500 camcorders and 500 TVs. The sales mix, expressed as a percentage of the 2,000 total units sold, is as follows.

Illustration 20-13
Sales mix as a function of units sold

Camcorders	TVs
1,500 units ÷ 2,000 units = 75%	500 units ÷ 2,000 units = 25%

That is, 75% of the 2,000 units sold are camcorders, and 25% of the 2,000 units sold are TVs.

Illustration 20-14 shows additional information related to Vargo Video. The unit contribution margin for camcorders is $200, and for TVs it is $500. Vargo's fixed costs total $275,000.

Illustration 20-14
Per unit data—sales mix

Unit Data	Camcorders	TVs
Selling price	$500	$1,000
Variable costs	300	500
Contribution margin	$200	$500
Sales mix—units	75%	25%
Fixed costs = $275,000		

To compute break-even for Vargo, we must determine the weighted-average unit contribution margin for the two products. We use the *weighted-average* contribution margin because Vargo sells three times as many camcorders as TVs. As a result, in determining an average unit contribution margin, three times as much weight should be placed on the contribution margin of the camcorders as on the TVs. Therefore, the camcorders must be counted three times for every TV sold. The weighted-average contribution margin for a sales mix of 75% camcorders and 25% TVs is $275, which is computed as follows.

Illustration 20-15
Weighted-average unit contribution margin

Camcorders				TVs			
(Unit Contribution Margin	×	Sales Mix Percentage)	+	(Unit Contribution Margin	×	Sales Mix Percentage)	=	Weighted-Average Unit Contribution Margin
($200	×	.75)	+	($500	×	.25)	=	$275

Similar to our calculation in the single-product setting, we can compute the break-even point in units by dividing the fixed costs by the weighted-average unit contribution margin. Then, we use the weighted-average unit contribution margin of $275 to compute the break-even point in unit sales. The computation of break-even sales in units for Vargo Video, assuming $275,000 of fixed costs, is as follows.

Fixed Costs	÷	Weighted-Average Unit Contribution Margin	=	Break-Even Point in Units
$275,000	÷	$275	=	1,000 units

Illustration 20-16
Break-even point in units

Illustration 20-16 shows the break-even point for Vargo Video is 1,000 units—camcorders and TVs combined. Management needs to know how many of these 1,000 units are camcorders and how many are TVs. Applying the sales mix percentages that we computed previously of 75% for camcorders and 25% for TVs, these 1,000 units would be comprised of 750 camcorders (.75 × 1,000 units) and 250 TVs (.25 × 1,000). This can be verified by the computations in Illustration 20-17, which shows that the total contribution margin is $275,000 when 1,000 units are sold, which equals the fixed costs of $275,000.

Product	Unit Sales	×	Unit Contribution Margin	=	Total Contribution Margin
Camcorders	750	×	$200	=	$ 150,000
TVs	250	×	500	=	125,000
	1,000				**$275,000**

Illustration 20-17
Break-even proof—sales units

Management should continually review the company's sales mix. At any level of units sold, **net income will be greater if higher contribution margin units are sold, rather than lower contribution margin units**. For Vargo Video, the TVs produce the higher contribution margin. Consequently, if Vargo sells 300 TVs and 700 camcorders, net income would be higher than in the current sales mix even though total units sold are the same.

An analysis of these relationships shows that a shift from low-margin sales to high-margin sales may increase net income even though there is a decline in total units sold. Likewise, a shift from high- to low-margin sales may result in a decrease in net income even though there is an increase in total units sold.

Break-Even Sales in Dollars

The calculation of the break-even point presented for Vargo Video in the previous section works well if a company has only a *small number* of products. In contrast, consider 3M, the maker of Post-it Notes, which has more than 30,000 products. In order to calculate the break-even point for 3M using a weighted-average unit contribution margin, we would need to calculate 30,000 different unit contribution margins. That is not realistic.

Therefore, for a company with many products, we calculate the break-even point in terms of sales dollars (rather than units sold), using sales information for divisions or product lines (rather than individual products). This requires that we compute sales mix as a percentage of total dollars sales (rather than units sold) and we compute the contribution margin ratio (rather than contribution margin per unit).

To illustrate, suppose that Kale Garden Supply Company has two divisions—Indoor Plants and Outdoor Plants. Each division has hundreds of different types of plants and plant-care products. Illustration 20-18 provides information necessary for determining the sales mix percentages for the two divisions of Kale Garden Supply.

Illustration 20-18
Cost-volume-profit data for
Kale Garden Supply

	Indoor Plant Division	Outdoor Plant Division	Total
Sales	$ 200,000	$ 800,000	$1,000,000
Variable costs	120,000	560,000	680,000
Contribution margin	$ 80,000	$ 240,000	$ 320,000
Sales mix percentage (Division sales ÷ Total sales)	$\frac{\$\,200{,}000}{\$1{,}000{,}000} = .20$	$\frac{\$\,800{,}000}{\$1{,}000{,}000} = .80$	

As shown in Illustration 20-19, the contribution margin ratio for the combined company is 32%, which is computed by dividing the total contribution margin by total sales.

Illustration 20-19
Contribution margin ratio for
each division

	Indoor Plant Division	Outdoor Plant Division	Total
Contribution margin ratio (Contribution margin ÷ Sales)	$\frac{\$\,80{,}000}{\$200{,}000} = .40$	$\frac{\$240{,}000}{\$800{,}000} = .30$	$\frac{\$\,320{,}000}{\$1{,}000{,}000} = .32$

It is useful to note that the contribution margin ratio of 32% is a weighted average of the individual contribution margin ratios of the two divisions (40% and 30%). To illustrate, in Illustration 20-20 we multiply each division's contribution margin ratio by its sales mix percentage, based on dollar sales, and then sum these amounts. As shown later, the calculation in Illustration 20-20 is useful because it enables us to determine how the break-even point changes when the sales mix changes.

Illustration 20-20
Calculation of weighted-
average contribution margin

Indoor Plant Division		Outdoor Plant Division		
$\left(\begin{array}{c}\text{Contribution}\\ \text{Margin Ratio}\end{array} \times \begin{array}{c}\text{Sales Mix}\\ \text{Percentage}\end{array}\right)$	+	$\left(\begin{array}{c}\text{Contribution}\\ \text{Margin Ratio}\end{array} \times \begin{array}{c}\text{Sales Mix}\\ \text{Percentage}\end{array}\right)$	=	Weighted-Average Contribution Margin Ratio
(.40 × .20)	+	(.30 × .80)	=	.32

Kale Garden Supply's break-even point in dollars is then computed by dividing its fixed costs of $300,000 by the weighted-average contribution margin ratio of 32%, as shown in Illustration 20-21.

Illustration 20-21
Calculation of break-even
point in dollars

Fixed Costs	÷	Weighted-Average Contribution Margin Ratio	=	Break-Even Point in Dollars
$300,000	÷	.32	=	$937,500

The break-even point is based on the sales mix of 20% to 80%. We can determine the amount of sales contributed by each division by multiplying the sales mix percentage of each division by the total sales figure. Of the company's total break-even sales of $937,500, a total of $187,500 (.20 × $937,500) will come from the Indoor Plant Division, and $750,000 (.80 × $937,500) will come from the Outdoor Plant Division.

What would be the impact on the break-even point if a higher percentage of Kale Garden Supply's sales were to come from the Indoor Plant Division? Because the Indoor Plant Division enjoys a higher contribution margin ratio, this change in the sales mix would result in a higher weighted-average contribution margin ratio, and consequently a lower break-even point in dollars. For example, if the sales mix changes to 50% for the Indoor Plant Division and 50% for the Outdoor Plant Division, the weighted-average contribution margin ratio would be 35% [(.40 × .50) + (.30 × .50)]. The new, lower, break-even point is $857,143 ($300,000 ÷ .35). The opposite would occur if a higher percentage of sales were expected from the Outdoor Plant Division. As you can see, the information provided using CVP analysis can help managers better understand the impact of sales mix on profitability.

SERVICE COMPANY INSIGHT

Healthy for You, and Great for the Bottom Line

Zoom Kitchen, a chain of four restaurants in the Chicago area, is known for serving sizable portions of meat and potatoes. But the company's management is quite pleased with the fact that during the past four years, salad sales have increased from 18% of its sales mix to 40%. Why are they pleased? Because the contribution margin on salads is much higher than on meat. The restaurant made a conscious effort to encourage people to buy more salads by offering an interesting assortment of salad ingredients including jicama, beets, marinated mushrooms, grilled tuna, and carved turkey. Management has to be very sensitive to contribution margin—it costs about $600,000 to open up a new Zoom Kitchen restaurant.

Source: Amy Zuber, "Salad Sales 'Zoom' at Meat-and-Potatoes Specialist," *Nation's Restaurant News* (November 12, 2001), p. 26.

 Why do you suppose restaurants are so eager to sell beverages and desserts? (See page 1040.)

> DO IT!

Sales Mix Break-Even

Manzeck Bicycles International produces and sells three different types of mountain bikes. Information regarding the three models is shown below.

	Pro	Intermediate	Standard	Total
Units sold	5,000	10,000	25,000	40,000
Selling price	$800	$500	$350	
Variable costs	$500	$300	$250	

The company's total fixed costs to produce the bicycles are $7,500,000.

(a) Determine the sales mix as a function of units sold for the three products.

(b) Determine the weighted-average unit contribution margin.

Action Plan

✔ The sales mix is the relative percentage of each product sold in units.

✔ The weighted-average unit contribution margin is the sum of the per unit contribution margins multiplied by the respective sales mix percentage.

✔ Determine the break-even point in units by dividing the fixed costs by the weighted-average unit contribution margin.

✔ Determine the number of units of each model to produce by multiplying the total break-even units by the respective sales mix percentage for each product.

(c) Determine the total number of units that the company must produce to break even.

(d) Determine the number of units of each model that the company must produce to break even.

Solution

(a) The sales mix percentages as a function of units sold are:

Pro	Intermediate	Standard
5,000/40,000 = 12.5%	10,000/40,000 = 25%	25,000/40,000 = 62.5%

(b) The weighted-average unit contribution margin is:

$$[.125 \times (\$800 - \$500)] + [.25 \times (\$500 - \$300)] + [.625 \times (\$350 - \$250)] = \$150$$

(c) The break-even point in units is:

$$\$7,500,000 \div \$150 = 50,000 \text{ units}$$

(d) The break-even units to produce for each product are:

Pro:	50,000 units × 12.5% =	6,250 units
Intermediate:	50,000 units × 25% =	12,500 units
Standard:	50,000 units × 62.5% =	31,250 units
		50,000 units

Related exercise material: **BE20-7, BE20-8, BE20-9, BE20-10, E20-6, E20-7, E20-8, E20-9, E20-10, and DO IT! 20-3.**

✔ **The Navigator**

Determining Sales Mix with Limited Resources

LEARNING OBJECTIVE 4

Determine sales mix when a company has limited resources.

In the previous discussion, we assumed a certain sales mix and then determined the break-even point given that sales mix. We now discuss how limited resources influence the sales-mix decision.

Everyone's resources are limited. The limited resource may be floor space in a retail department store, or raw materials, direct labor hours, or machine capacity in a manufacturing company. When a company has limited resources, management must decide which products to make and sell in order to maximize net income.

To illustrate, recall that Vargo manufactures camcorders and TVs. The limiting resource is machine capacity, which is 3,600 hours per month. Relevant data consist of the following.

Illustration 20-22
Contribution margin and machine hours

	Camcorders	TVs
Contribution margin per unit	$200	$500
Machine hours required per unit	.2	.625

Helpful Hint
CM alone is not enough to make this decision. The key factor is CM per unit of limited resource.

The TVs may appear to be more profitable since they have a higher contribution margin per unit ($500) than the camcorders ($200). However, the camcorders take fewer machine hours to produce than the TVs. Therefore, it is necessary to find the **contribution margin per unit of limited resource**—in this case, contribution margin per machine hour. This is obtained by dividing the contribution margin per unit of each product by the number of units of the limited resource required for each product, as shown in Illustration 20-23.

	Camcorders	TVs
Contribution margin per unit (a)	$200	$500
Machine hours required (b)	0.2	0.625
Contribution margin per unit of limited resource [(a) ÷ (b)]	$1,000	$800

Illustration 20-23
Contribution margin per unit
of limited resource

The computation shows that the camcorders have a higher contribution margin per unit of limited resource. This would suggest that, given sufficient demand for camcorders, Vargo should shift the sales mix to produce more camcorders or increase machine capacity.

As indicated in Illustration 20-23, the constraint for the production of the TVs is the larger number of machine hours needed to produce them. In addressing this problem, we have taken the limited number of machine hours as a given and have attempted to maximize the contribution margin given the constraint. One question that Vargo should ask, however, is whether this constraint can be reduced or eliminated. If Vargo is able to increase machine capacity from 3,600 hours to 4,200 hours, the additional 600 hours could be used to produce either the camcorders or TVs. The total contribution margin under each alternative is found by multiplying the machine hours by the contribution margin per unit of limited resource, as shown below.

	Camcorders	TVs
Machine hours (a)	600	600
Contribution margin per unit of limited resource (b)	$ 1,000	$ 800
Contribution margin [(a) × (b)]	$600,000	$480,000

From this analysis, we can see that to maximize net income, all of the increased capacity should be used to make and sell the camcorders.

Vargo's manufacturing constraint might be due to a bottleneck in production or to poorly trained machine operators. In addition to finding ways to solve those problems, the company should consider other possible solutions, such as outsourcing part of the production, acquiring additional new equipment (discussed in Chapter 26), or striving to eliminate any non–value-added activities (see Chapter 18). As discussed in Chapter 15, this approach to evaluating constraints is referred to as the theory of constraints. The **theory of constraints** is a specific approach used to identify and manage constraints in order to achieve the company's goals. According to this theory, a company must continually identify its constraints and find ways to reduce or eliminate them, where appropriate.

MANAGEMENT INSIGHT

Something Smells

When fragrance sales went flat, retailers turned up the heat on fragrance manufacturers. They reduced the amount of floor space devoted to fragrances, leaving fragrance manufacturers fighting each other for the smaller space. The retailer doesn't just choose the fragrance with the highest contribution margin. Instead, it chooses the fragrance with the highest contribution margin per square foot for a given period of time. In this game, a product with a lower contribution margin, but a higher turnover, could well be the winner.

? What is the limited resource for a retailer, and what implications does this have for sales mix? (See page 1040.)

> DO IT!

Sales Mix with Limited Resources

Carolina Corporation manufactures and sells three different types of high-quality sealed ball bearings. The bearings vary in terms of their quality specifications—primarily with respect to their smoothness and roundness. They are referred to as Fine, Extra-Fine, and Super-Fine bearings. Machine time is limited. More machine time is required to manufacture the Extra-Fine and Super-Fine bearings. Additional information is provided below.

	Product		
	Fine	**Extra-Fine**	**Super-Fine**
Selling price	$6.00	$10.00	$16.00
Variable costs and expenses	4.00	6.50	11.00
Contribution margin	$2.00	$ 3.50	$ 5.00
Machine hours required	0.02	0.04	0.08

(a) Ignoring the machine time constraint, what strategy would appear optimal?

(b) What is the contribution margin per unit of limited resource for each type of bearing?

(c) If additional machine time could be obtained, how should the additional capacity be used?

Solution

Action Plan

✔ Calculate the contribution margin per unit of limited resource for each product.

✔ Apply the formula for the contribution margin per unit of limited resource.

✔ To maximize net income, shift sales mix to the product with the highest contribution margin per unit of limited resource.

(a) The Super-Fine bearings have the highest contribution margin per unit. Thus, ignoring any manufacturing constraints, it would appear that the company should shift toward production of more Super-Fine units.

(b) The contribution margin per unit of limited resource (machine hours) is calculated as:

	Fine	**Extra-Fine**	**Super-Fine**
$\dfrac{\text{Contribution margin per unit}}{\text{Limited resource consumed per unit}}$	$\dfrac{\$2}{.02} = \$100$	$\dfrac{\$3.5}{.04} = \$87.50$	$\dfrac{\$5}{.08} = \$62.50$

(c) The Fine bearings have the highest contribution margin per unit of limited resource even though they have the lowest contribution margin per unit. Given the resource constraint, any additional capacity should be used to make Fine bearings.

Related exercise material: **BE20-11, E20-11, E20-12, E20-13, and** **20-4.**

✔ **The Navigator**

Cost Structure and Operating Leverage

LEARNING OBJECTIVE 5

Understand how operating leverage affects profitability.

Cost structure refers to the relative proportion of fixed versus variable costs that a company incurs. Cost structure can have a significant effect on profitability. For example, computer equipment manufacturer Cisco Systems has substantially reduced its fixed costs by choosing to outsource much of its production. By minimizing its fixed costs, Cisco is now less susceptible to economic swings. However, as the following discussion shows, its reduced reliance on fixed costs has also reduced its ability to experience the incredible profitability that it used to have during economic booms.

The choice of cost structure should be carefully considered. There are many ways that companies can influence their cost structure. For example, by acquiring sophisticated robotic equipment, many companies have reduced their use of manual labor. Similarly, some brokerage firms, such as E*Trade, have reduced their reliance on human brokers and have instead invested heavily in computers and online technology. In so doing, they have increased their reliance on fixed costs (through depreciation on the robotic equipment or computer equipment) and reduced their reliance on variable costs (the variable employee labor cost). Alternatively, some companies have reduced their fixed costs and increased their variable costs by outsourcing their production. Nike, for example, does very little manufacturing but instead outsources the manufacture of nearly all of its shoes. It has consequently converted many of its fixed costs into variable costs and therefore changed its cost structure.

Consider the following example of Vargo Video and one of its competitors, New Wave Company. Both make camcorders. Vargo Video uses a traditional, labor-intensive manufacturing process. New Wave Company has invested in a completely automated system. The factory employees are involved only in setting up, adjusting, and maintaining the machinery. Illustration 20-25 shows CVP income statements for each company.

	Vargo Video	New Wave Company
Sales	$800,000	$800,000
Variable costs	480,000	160,000
Contribution margin	320,000	640,000
Fixed costs	200,000	520,000
Net income	$120,000	$120,000

Illustration 20-25
CVP income statements for two companies

Both companies have the same sales and the same net income. However, because of the differences in their cost structures, they differ greatly in the risks and rewards related to increasing or decreasing sales. Let's evaluate the impact of cost structure on the profitability of the two companies.

Effect on Contribution Margin Ratio

First let's look at the contribution margin ratio. Illustration 20-26 shows the computation of the contribution margin ratio for each company.

	Contribution Margin	÷	Sales	=	Contribution Margin Ratio
Vargo Video	$320,000	÷	$800,000	=	.40
New Wave	$640,000	÷	$800,000	=	.80

Illustration 20-26
Contribution margin ratio for two companies

Because of its lower variable costs, New Wave has a contribution margin ratio of 80% versus only 40% for Vargo. That means that with every dollar of sales, New Wave generates 80 cents of contribution margin (and thus an 80-cent increase in net income), versus only 40 cents for Vargo. However, it also means that for every dollar that sales decline, New Wave loses 80 cents in net income, whereas Vargo will lose only 40 cents. New Wave's cost structure, which relies more heavily on fixed costs, makes it more sensitive to changes in sales revenue.

Effect on Break-Even Point

The difference in cost structure also affects the break-even point. The break-even point for each company is calculated in Illustration 20-27 (page 1004).

Illustration 20-27
Computation of break-even point for two companies

	Fixed Costs	÷	Contribution Margin Ratio	=	Break-Even Point in Dollars
Vargo Video	$200,000	÷	.40	=	$500,000
New Wave	$520,000	÷	.80	=	$650,000

New Wave needs to generate $150,000 ($650,000 − $500,000) more in sales than Vargo before it breaks even. This makes New Wave riskier than Vargo because a company cannot survive for very long unless it at least breaks even.

Effect on Margin of Safety Ratio

We can also evaluate the relative impact that changes in sales would have on the two companies by computing the margin of safety ratio. Illustration 20-28 shows the computation of the **margin of safety ratio** for the two companies.

Illustration 20-28
Computation of margin of safety ratio for two companies

	(Actual Sales	−	Break-Even Sales)	÷	Actual Sales	=	Margin of Safety Ratio
Vargo Video	($800,000	−	$500,000)	÷	$800,000	=	.38
New Wave	($800,000	−	$650,000)	÷	$800,000	=	.19

The difference in the margin of safety ratio also reflects the difference in risk between the two companies. Vargo could sustain a 38% decline in sales before it would be operating at a loss. New Wave could sustain only a 19% decline in sales before it would be "in the red."

Operating Leverage

Operating leverage refers to the extent to which a company's net income reacts to a given change in sales. Companies that have higher fixed costs relative to variable costs have higher operating leverage. When a company's sales revenue is increasing, high operating leverage is a good thing because it means that profits will increase rapidly. But when sales are declining, too much operating leverage can have devastating consequences.

DEGREE OF OPERATING LEVERAGE

How can we compare operating leverage between two companies? The **degree of operating leverage** provides a measure of a company's earnings volatility and can be used to compare companies. Degree of operating leverage is computed by dividing contribution margin by net income. This formula is presented in Illustration 20-29 and applied to our two manufacturers of camcorders.

Illustration 20-29
Computation of degree of operating leverage

	Contribution Margin	÷	Net Income	=	Degree of Operating Leverage
Vargo Video	$320,000	÷	$120,000	=	2.67
New Wave	$640,000	÷	$120,000	=	5.33

New Wave's earnings would go up (or down) by about two times (5.33 ÷ 2.67 = 1.99) as much as Vargo's with an equal increase (or decrease) in sales. For example, suppose both companies experience a 10% decrease in sales. Vargo's net income will decrease by 26.7% (2.67 × 10%), while New Wave's will decrease by 53.3% (5.33 × 10%). Thus, New Wave's higher operating leverage exposes it to greater earnings volatility risk.

You should be careful not to conclude from this analysis that a cost structure that relies on higher fixed costs, and consequently has higher operating leverage, is necessarily bad. Some have suggested that Internet radio company Pandora has limited potential for growth in its profitability because it has very little operating leverage. When its revenues grow, its variable costs (fees it pays for the right to use music) grow proportionally. When used carefully, operating leverage can add considerably to a company's profitability. For example, computer equipment manufacturer Komag enjoyed a 66% increase in net income when its sales increased by only 8%. As one commentator noted, "Komag's fourth quarter illustrates the company's significant operating leverage; a small increase in sales leads to a big profit rise." However, as our illustration demonstrates, increased reliance on fixed costs increases a company's risk.

SERVICE COMPANY INSIGHT

There Is Something About a Train

Warren Buffett, arguably the most successful investor in history, recently bought a new train set—for $44 billion. The sage from Omaha bought Burlington Northern Railroad for a price that exceeded its market value by 31%. At a time when the rest of the investing public was obsessed with technology companies like Facebook and Twitter, what could Buffett possibly see in a railroad? What he sees is a business whose costs are between 50–60% fixed. With such high fixed costs, railways have huge operating leverage. And because he bought the railroad at the bottom of a recession, when the economy turns around, Burlington could take off as well. Add to that the fact that railroad transport is very energy-efficient, and it has high barriers to entry. So, as energy prices increase, more people will turn to the rails, but there are a limited number of railways. Makes sense to me.

Source: Liam Denning, "Buffett's Unusual Train of Thought," *Wall Street Journal* (November 4, 2009).

 Why did Warren Buffett think that this was a good time to invest in railroad stocks?
(See page 1040.)

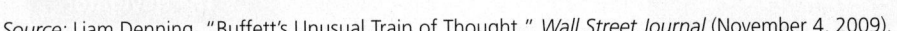

> Comprehensive **DO IT!**

Francis Corporation manufactures and sells three different types of water-sport wakeboards. The boards vary in terms of their quality specifications—primarily with respect to their smoothness and finish. They are referred to as Smooth, Extra-Smooth, and Super-Smooth boards. Machine time is limited. More machine time is required to manufacture the Extra-Smooth and Super-Smooth boards. Additional information is provided below.

	Product		
	Smooth	**Extra-Smooth**	**Super-Smooth**
Selling price	$60	$100	$160
Variable costs and expenses	50	75	130
Contribution margin	$10	$ 25	$ 30
Machine hours required	0.25	0.40	0.60
Total fixed costs: $234,000			

Instructions

Answer each of the following questions.

(a) Ignoring the machine time constraint, what strategy would appear optimal?

(b) What is the contribution margin per unit of limited resource for each type of board?

(c) If additional machine time could be obtained, how should the additional capacity be used?

Solution to Comprehensive DO IT!

Action Plan

✔ To determine how best to use a limited resource, calculate the contribution margin per unit of limited resource for each product type.

(a) The Super-Smooth boards have the highest contribution margin per unit. Thus, ignoring any manufacturing constraints, it would appear that the company should shift toward production of more Super-Smooth units.

(b) The contribution margin per unit of limited resource is calculated as:

	Smooth	Extra-Smooth	Super-Smooth
$\dfrac{\text{Contribution margin per unit}}{\text{Limited resource consumed per unit}}$	$\dfrac{\$10}{.25} = \$40$	$\dfrac{\$25}{.40} = \$62.50$	$\dfrac{\$30}{.60} = \$50$

(c) The Extra-Smooth boards have the highest contribution margin per unit of limited resource. Given the resource constraint, any additional capacity should be used to make Extra-Smooth boards.

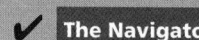 **The Navigator**

SUMMARY OF LEARNING OBJECTIVES

 The Navigator

1 **Describe the essential features of a cost-volume-profit income statement.** The CVP income statement classifies costs and expenses as variable or fixed and reports contribution margin in the body of the statement.

2 **Apply basic CVP concepts.** Contribution margin is the amount of revenue remaining after deducting variable costs. It can be expressed as a per unit amount or as a ratio. The break-even point in units is fixed costs divided by contribution margin per unit. The break-even point in dollars is fixed costs divided by the contribution margin ratio. These formulas can also be used to determine units or sales dollars needed to achieve target net income, simply by adding target net income to fixed costs before dividing by the contribution margin. Margin of safety indicates how much sales can decline before the company is operating at a loss. It can be expressed in dollar terms or as a percentage.

3 **Explain the term sales mix and its effects on break-even sales.** Sales mix is the relative proportion in which each product is sold when a company sells more than one product. For a company with a small number of products, break-even sales in units is determined by using the weighted-average unit contribution margin of

all the products. If the company sells many different products, then calculating the break-even point using unit information is not practical. Instead, in a company with many products, break-even sales in dollars is calculated using the weighted-average contribution margin ratio.

4 **Determine sales mix when a company has limited resources.** When a company has limited resources, it is necessary to find the contribution margin per unit of limited resource. This amount is then multiplied by the units of limited resource to determine which product maximizes net income.

5 **Understand how operating leverage affects profitability.** Operating leverage refers to the degree to which a company's net income reacts to a change in sales. Operating leverage is determined by a company's relative use of fixed versus variable costs. Companies with high fixed costs relative to variable costs have high operating leverage. A company with high operating leverage will experience a sharp increase (decrease) in net income with a given increase (decrease) in sales. The degree of operating leverage can be measured by dividing contribution margin by net income.

APPENDIX 20A ABSORPTION COSTING VERSUS VARIABLE COSTING

In earlier chapters, we classified both variable and fixed manufacturing costs as product costs. In job order costing, for example, a job is assigned the costs of direct materials, direct labor, and **both** variable and fixed manufacturing overhead. This costing approach is referred to as **full** or **absorption costing**. It is so named because all manufacturing costs are charged to, or absorbed by, the product. Absorption costing is the approach used for external reporting under generally accepted accounting principles.

An alternative approach is to use **variable costing**. Under variable costing, only direct materials, direct labor, and variable manufacturing overhead costs are considered product costs. Companies recognize fixed manufacturing overhead costs as period costs (expenses) when incurred. The difference between absorption costing and variable costing is shown graphically as follows.

> **LEARNING OBJECTIVE** **6**
>
> **Explain the difference between absorption costing and variable costing.**

Absorption Costing **Variable Costing**

Product Cost ←———— Fixed Manufacturing ————→ **Period Cost**
Overhead

Illustration 20A-1
Difference between absorption costing and variable costing

Under both absorption and variable costing, selling and administrative expenses are period costs.

Companies may not use variable costing for external financial reports because generally accepted accounting principles require that fixed manufacturing overhead be accounted for as a product cost.

Example Comparing Absorption Costing with Variable Costing

To illustrate absorption and variable costing, assume that Premium Products Corporation manufactures a polyurethane sealant, called Fix-It, for car windshields. Relevant data for Fix-It in January 2014, the first month of production, are as shown below.

Illustration 20A-2
Sealant sales and cost data for Premium Products Corporation

Selling price	$20 per unit.
Units	Produced 30,000; sold 20,000; beginning inventory zero.
Variable unit costs	Manufacturing $9 (direct materials $5, direct labor $3, and variable overhead $1).
	Selling and administrative expenses $2.
Fixed costs	Manufacturing overhead $120,000.
	Selling and administrative expenses $15,000.

The per unit manufacturing cost under each costing approach is computed in Illustration 20A-3 (page 1008).

Illustration 20A-3
Computation of per unit manufacturing cost

Type of Cost	Absorption Costing	Variable Costing
Direct materials	$ 5	$5
Direct labor	3	3
Variable manufacturing overhead	1	1
Fixed manufacturing overhead		
($120,000 ÷ 30,000 units produced)	4	0
Manufacturing cost per unit	**$13**	**$9**

The manufacturing cost per unit is $4 higher ($13 − $9) for absorption costing. This occurs because fixed manufacturing overhead costs are a product cost under absorption costing. Under variable costing, they are, instead, a period cost, and so they are expensed. Based on these data, each unit sold and each unit remaining in inventory is costed under absorption costing at $13 and under variable costing at $9.

ABSORPTION COSTING EXAMPLE

Illustration 20A-4 shows the income statement for Premium Products using absorption costing. It shows that cost of goods manufactured is $390,000, computed by multiplying the 30,000 units produced times the manufacturing cost per unit of $13 (see Illustration 20A-3). Cost of goods sold is $260,000, after subtracting ending inventory of $130,000. Under absorption costing, $40,000 of the fixed overhead (10,000 units × $4) is deferred to a future period as part of the cost of ending inventory.

Illustration 20A-4
Absorption costing income statement

Helpful Hint
The income statement format in Illustration 20A-4 is the same as that used under generally accepted accounting principles.

Premium Products Corporation		
Income Statement		
For the Month Ended January 31, 2014		
Absorption Costing		
Sales (20,000 units × $20)		$400,000
Cost of goods sold		
Inventory, January 1	$ –0–	
Cost of goods manufactured (30,000 units × $13)	390,000	
Cost of goods available for sale	390,000	
Inventory, January 31 (10,000 units × $13)	**130,000**	
Cost of goods sold (20,000 units × $13)		260,000
Gross profit		140,000
Variable selling and administrative expenses		
(20,000 × $2)	40,000	
Fixed selling and administrative expenses	15,000	55,000
Net income		**$ 85,000**

VARIABLE COSTING EXAMPLE

As Illustration 20A-5 shows, companies use the cost-volume-profit format in preparing a variable costing income statement. The variable manufacturing cost of $270,000 is computed by multiplying the 30,000 units produced times variable manufacturing cost of $9 per unit (see Illustration 20A-3). As in absorption costing, both variable and fixed selling and administrative expenses are treated as period costs.

Premium Products Corporation
Income Statement
For the Month Ended January 31, 2014
Variable Costing

Sales (20,000 units × $20)		$400,000
Variable cost of goods sold		
Inventory, January 1	$ –0–	
Variable cost of goods manufactured		
(30,000 units × $9)	270,000	
Variable cost of goods available for sale	270,000	
Inventory, January 31 (10,000 units × $9)	**90,000**	
Variable cost of goods sold	180,000	
Variable selling and administrative expenses		
(20,000 units × $2)	40,000	220,000
Contribution margin		180,000
Fixed manufacturing overhead	120,000	
Fixed selling and administrative expenses	15,000	135,000
Net income		**$ 45,000**

There is one primary difference between variable and absorption costing: Under variable costing, companies charge the fixed manufacturing overhead as an expense in the current period. Fixed manufacturing overhead costs of the current period, therefore, are not deferred to future periods through the ending inventory. As a result, absorption costing will show a **higher net income number** than variable costing **whenever units produced exceed units sold**. This difference can be seen in the income statements in Illustrations 20A-4 and 20A-5. There is a $40,000 difference in the ending inventories ($130,000 under absorption costing versus $90,000 under variable costing). Under absorption costing, $40,000 of the fixed overhead costs (10,000 units × $4) has been deferred to a future period as part of inventory. In contrast, under variable costing, all fixed manufacturing costs are expensed in the current period.

As shown, when units produced exceed units sold, income under absorption costing is *higher*. When units produced are less than units sold, income under absorption costing is *lower*. When units produced and sold are the same, net income will be *equal* under the two costing approaches. In this case, there is no increase in ending inventory. So fixed overhead costs of the current period are not deferred to future periods through the ending inventory.

An Extended Example

To further illustrate the concepts underlying absorption and variable costing, we will look at an extended example using Overbay Inc., a manufacturer of small airplane drones. We assume that production volume stays the same each year over the 3-year period, but the number of units sold varies each year.

2013 RESULTS

As indicated in Illustration 20A-6 (page 1010), the variable manufacturing cost per drone is $240,000, and the fixed manufacturing overhead cost per drone is $60,000 (assuming 10 drones). Total manufacturing cost per drone under absorption costing is therefore $300,000 ($240,000 + $60,000). Overbay also has variable selling and administrative expenses of $5,000 per drone. The fixed selling and administrative expenses are $80,000.

Illustration 20A-6
Information for Overbay Inc.

	2013	2014	2015
Volume information			
Drones in beginning inventory	0	0	2
Drones produced	10	10	10
Drones sold	10	8	12
Drones in ending inventory	0	2	0
Financial information			
Selling price per drone	$400,000		
Variable manufacturing cost per drone	$240,000		
Fixed manufacturing overhead for the year	$600,000		
Fixed manufacturing overhead per drone	$ 60,000 ($600,000 ÷ 10)		
Variable selling and administrative expenses per drone	$ 5,000		
Fixed selling and administrative expenses	$ 80,000		

An absorption costing income statement for 2013 for Overbay Inc. is shown in Illustration 20A-7.

Illustration 20A-7
Absorption costing income statement—2013

Overbay Inc.
Income Statement
For the Year Ended December 31, 2013
Absorption Costing

Sales (10 drones × $400,000)		$4,000,000
Cost of goods sold (10 drones × $300,000)		3,000,000
Gross profit		1,000,000
Variable selling and administrative expenses (10 drones × $5,000)	$50,000	
Fixed selling and administrative expenses	80,000	130,000
Net income		$ 870,000

Overbay reports net income of $870,000 under absorption costing.

Under a variable costing system, the income statement follows a cost-volume-profit (CVP) format. In this case, the manufacturing cost is comprised solely of the variable manufacturing costs of $240,000 per drone. The fixed manufacturing overhead costs of $600,000 for the year are expensed in 2013. As in absorption costing, the fixed and variable selling and administrative expenses are period costs expensed in 2013. A variable costing income statement for Overbay Inc. for 2013 is shown in Illustration 20A-8.

As shown in Illustration 20A-8, the variable costing net income of $870,000 is the same as the absorption costing net income computed in Illustration 20A-7. **When the numbers of units produced and sold are the same, net income is equal under the two costing approaches.** Because no increase in ending inventory occurs, no fixed manufacturing overhead costs incurred in 2013 are deferred to future periods using absorption costing.

Overbay Inc. Income Statement For the Year Ended December 31, 2013 Variable Costing		
Sales (10 drones × $400,000)		$4,000,000
Variable cost of goods sold		
(10 drones × $240,000)	$2,400,000	
Variable selling and administrative expenses		
(10 drones × $5,000)	50,000	2,450,000
Contribution margin		1,550,000
Fixed manufacturing overhead	600,000	
Fixed selling and administrative expenses	80,000	680,000
Net income		$ 870,000

2014 RESULTS

In 2014, Overbay produced 10 drones but sold only eight drones. As a result, there are two drones in ending inventory. The absorption costing income statement for 2014 is shown in Illustration 20A-9.

Overbay Inc. Income Statement For the Year Ended December 31, 2014 Absorption Costing		
Sales (8 drones × $400,000)		$3,200,000
Cost of goods sold (8 drones × $300,000)		2,400,000
Gross profit		800,000
Variable selling and administrative expenses		
(8 drones × $5,000)	$40,000	
Fixed selling and administrative expenses	80,000	120,000
Net income		$ 680,000

Under absorption costing, the ending inventory of two drones is $600,000 ($300,000 × 2). Each unit of ending inventory includes $60,000 of fixed manufacturing overhead. Therefore, fixed manufacturing overhead costs of $120,000 ($60,000 × 2 drones) are deferred until a future period.

The variable costing income statement for 2014 is shown in Illustration 20A-10.

Overbay Inc. Income Statement For the Year Ended December 31, 2014 Variable Costing		
Sales (8 drones × $400,000)		$3,200,000
Variable cost of goods sold		
(8 drones × $240,000)	$1,920,000	
Variable selling and administrative expenses		
(8 drones × $5,000)	40,000	1,960,000
Contribution margin		1,240,000
Fixed manufacturing overhead	600,000	
Fixed selling and administrative expenses	80,000	680,000
Net income		$ 560,000

As shown, when units produced (10) exceeds units sold (8), net income under absorption costing ($680,000) is higher than net income under variable costing ($560,000). The reason: The cost of the ending inventory is higher under absorption costing than under variable costing. In 2014, under absorption costing, fixed manufacturing overhead of $120,000 is deferred and carried to future periods as part of inventory. Under variable costing, the $120,000 is expensed in the current period and, therefore the difference in the two net income numbers is $120,000 ($680,000 − $560,000).

2015 RESULTS

In 2015, Overbay produced 10 drones and sold 12 (10 drones from the current year's production and 2 drones from the beginning inventory). As a result, there are no drones in ending inventory. The absorption costing income statement for 2015 is shown in Illustration 20A-11.

Illustration 20A-11
Absorption costing income statement—2015

Overbay Inc. Income Statement For the Year Ended December 31, 2015 Absorption Costing		
Sales (12 drones × $400,000)		$4,800,000
Cost of goods sold (12 drones × $300,000)		3,600,000
Gross profit		1,200,000
Variable selling and administrative expenses (12 drones × $5,000)	$60,000	
Fixed selling and administrative expenses	80,000	140,000
Net income		$1,060,000

Fixed manufacturing costs of $720,000 ($60,000 × 12 drones) are expensed as part of cost of goods sold in 2015. This $720,000 includes $120,000 of fixed manufacturing costs incurred during 2014 and included in beginning inventory, plus $600,000 of fixed manufacturing costs incurred during 2015. Given this result for the absorption costing statement, what would you now expect the result to be under variable costing? Let's take a look.

The variable costing income statement for 2015 is shown in Illustration 20A-12.

Illustration 20A-12
Variable costing income statement—2015

Overbay Inc. Income Statement For the Year Ended December 31, 2015 Variable Costing		
Sales (12 drones × $400,000)		$4,800,000
Variable cost of goods sold (12 drones × $240,000)	$2,880,000	
Variable selling and administrative expenses (12 drones × $5,000)	60,000	2,940,000
Contribution margin		1,860,000
Fixed manufacturing overhead	600,000	
Fixed selling and administrative expenses	80,000	680,000
Net income		$1,180,000

When Drones produced (10) are less than Drones sold (12), net income under absorption costing ($1,060,000) is less than net income under variable costing

($1,180,000). This difference of $120,000 ($1,180,000 − $1,060,000) results because $120,000 of fixed manufacturing overhead costs in beginning inventory are charged to 2015 under absorption costing. Under variable costing, there is no fixed manufacturing overhead cost in beginning inventory.

Illustration 20A-13 summarizes the results of the three years.

Illustration 20A-13
Comparison of net income under two costing approaches

	Net Income under Two Costing Approaches		
	2013 **Production = Sales**	**2014** **Production > Sales**	**2015** **Production < Sales**
Absorption costing	$870,000	$ 680,000	$1,060,000
Variable costing	870,000	560,000	1,180,000
Difference	$ –0–	$120,000	$(120,000)

This relationship between production and sales and its effect on net income under the two costing approaches is shown graphically in Illustration 20A-14.

Illustration 20A-14
Summary of income effects under absorption costing and variable costing

Decision-Making Concerns

LEARNING OBJECTIVE

Discuss the merits of absorption versus variable costing for management decision-making.

Generally accepted accounting principles require that absorption costing be used for the costing of inventory for external reporting purposes. Net income measured under GAAP (absorption costing) is often used internally to evaluate performance, justify cost reductions, or evaluate new projects. Some companies, however, have recognized that net income calculated using GAAP does not highlight differences between variable and fixed costs and may lead to poor business decisions. Consequently, these companies use variable costing for internal reporting purposes. The following discussion and example highlight a significant problem related to the use of absorption costing for decision-making purposes.

When production exceeds sales, absorption costing reports a higher net income than variable costing. The reason is that some fixed manufacturing costs are not expensed in the current period but are deferred to future periods as part of inventory. As a result, management may be tempted to overproduce in a given period in order to increase net income. Although net income will increase, this decision to overproduce may not be in the company's best interest.

Suppose, for example, a division manager's compensation is based upon the division's net income. In such a case, the manager may decide to meet the net income targets by increasing production. While this overproduction may increase the manager's compensation, the buildup of inventories in the long run will lead to additional costs to the company. Variable costing avoids this situation because net income under variable costing is unaffected by changes in production levels, as the following illustration shows.

Warren Lund, a division manager of Walker Enterprises, is under pressure to boost the performance of the Lighting Division in 2014. Unfortunately, recent profits have not met expectations. The expected sales for this year are 20,000 units. As he plans for the year, Warren has to decide whether to produce 20,000 or 30,000 units. The following facts are available for the division.

Illustration 20A-15
Facts for Lighting
Division—2014

Beginning inventory	0
Expected sales in units	20,000
Selling price per unit	$15
Variable manufacturing cost per unit	$6
Fixed manufacturing overhead cost (total)	$60,000
Fixed manufacturing overhead costs per unit	
Based on 20,000 units	$3 per unit ($60,000 ÷ 20,000 units)
Based on 30,000 units	$2 per unit ($60,000 ÷ 30,000 units)
Total manufacturing cost per unit	
Based on 20,000 units	$9 per unit ($6 variable + $3 fixed)
Based on 30,000 units	$8 per unit ($6 variable + $2 fixed)
Variable selling and administrative expenses per unit	$1
Fixed selling and administrative expenses	$15,000

Illustration 20A-16 presents the division's results based upon the two possible levels of output under absorption costing.

Illustration 20A-16
Absorption costing income
statement—2014

Lighting Division
Income Statement
For the Year Ended December 31, 2014
Absorption Costing

	20,000 Produced	30,000 Produced
Sales (20,000 units × $15)	$300,000	$ 300,000
Cost of goods sold	180,000*	160,000**
Gross profit	120,000	140,000
Variable selling and administrative expenses (20,000 units × $1)	20,000	20,000
Fixed selling and administrative expenses	15,000	15,000
Net income	$ 85,000	$105,000

*20,000 units × $9
**20,000 units × $8

If the Lighting Division produces 20,000 units, its net income under absorption costing is $85,000. If it produces 30,000 units, its net income is $105,000. By producing 30,000 units, the division has inventory of 10,000 units. This excess inventory causes net income to increase $20,000 because $20,000 of fixed costs

(10,000 units × $2) are not charged to the current year, but are deferred to future periods.

What do you think Warren Lund might do in this situation? Given his concern about the profit numbers of the Lighting Division, he may be tempted to increase production. Although this increased production will increase 2014 net income, it may be costly to the company in the long run.

Now let's evaluate the same situation under variable costing. A variable costing income statement is shown for production at both 20,000 and 30,000 units, using the information from Illustration 20A-15.

Lighting Division
Income Statement
For the Year Ended December 31, 2014
Variable Costing

	20,000 Produced	30,000 Produced
Sales (20,000 units × $15)	$300,000	$300,000
Variable cost of goods sold (20,000 units × $6)	120,000	120,000
Variable selling and administrative expenses (20,000 units × $1)	20,000	20,000
Contribution margin	160,000	160,000
Fixed manufacturing overhead	60,000	60,000
Fixed selling and administrative expenses	15,000	15,000
Net income	$ 85,000	$ 85,000

From this example, we see that under variable costing, net income is not affected by the number of units produced. Net income is $85,000 whether the division produces 20,000 or 30,000 units. Why? Because fixed manufacturing overhead is treated as a period expense. Unlike absorption costing, no fixed manufacturing overhead is deferred through inventory buildup. Therefore, under variable costing, production does not increase income; sales do. As a result, if the company uses variable costing, managers like Warren Lund cannot affect profitability by increasing production.

Potential Advantages of Variable Costing

Variable costing has a number of potential advantages relative to absorption costing:

1. Net income computed under variable costing is unaffected by changes in production levels. As a result, it is much easier to understand the impact of fixed and variable costs on the computation of net income when variable costing is used.

2. The use of variable costing is consistent with the cost-volume-profit material presented in Chapters 19 and 20.

3. Net income computed under variable costing is closely tied to changes in sales levels (not production levels), and therefore provides a more realistic assessment of the company's success or failure during a period.

4. The presentation of fixed and variable cost components on the face of the variable costing income statement makes it easier to identify these costs and understand their effect on the business. Under absorption costing, the allocation of fixed costs to inventory makes it difficult to evaluate the impact of fixed costs on the company's results.

Companies that use just-in-time processing techniques to minimize their inventories will not have significant differences between absorption and variable costing net income.

> DO IT!

Variable Costing

Franklin Company produces and sells tennis balls. The following costs are available for the year ended December 31, 2014. The company has no beginning inventory. In 2014, 8,000,000 units were produced, but only 7,500,000 units were sold. The unit selling price was $0.50 per ball. Costs and expenses were:

Variable costs per unit	
Direct materials	$0.10
Direct labor	0.05
Variable manufacturing overhead	0.08
Variable selling and administrative expenses	0.02
Annual fixed costs and expenses	
Manufacturing overhead	$500,000
Selling and administrative expenses	100,000

(a) Compute the manufacturing cost of one unit of product using variable costing.

(b) Prepare a 2014 income statement for Franklin Company using variable costing.

Solution

Action Plan

✔ Recall that under variable costing, only variable manufacturing costs are treated as manufacturing (product) costs.

✔ Subtract all fixed costs, both manufacturing overhead and selling and administrative expenses, as period costs.

(a) The cost of one unit of product under variable costing would be:

Direct materials	$0.10
Direct labor	0.05
Variable manufacturing overhead	0.08
	$0.23

(b) The variable costing income statement would be as follows.

Franklin Company
Income Statement
For the Year Ended December 31, 2014
Variable Costing

Sales (7,500,000 × $0.50)		$3,750,000
Variable cost of goods sold (7,500,000 × $0.23)	$1,725,000	
Variable selling and administrative expenses		
(7,500,000 × .02)	150,000	1,875,000
Contribution margin		1,875,000
Fixed manufacturing overhead	500,000	
Fixed selling and administrative expenses	100,000	600,000
Net income		$1,275,000

Related exercise material: **BE20-16, BE20-17, BE20-18, BE20-19, E20-17, E20-18, and E20-19.**

 The Navigator

SUMMARY OF LEARNING OBJECTIVES FOR APPENDIX 20A

6 **Explain the difference between absorption costing and variable costing.** Under absorption costing, fixed manufacturing costs are product costs. Under variable costing, fixed manufacturing costs are period costs.

7 **Discuss net income effects under absorption costing versus variable costing.** If production volume exceeds sales volume, net income under absorption costing will exceed net income under variable costing by the amount of fixed manufacturing costs included in ending inventory that results from units produced but not sold during the period. If production volume is less than sales volume, net income under absorption costing will be

less than under variable costing by the amount of fixed manufacturing costs included in the units sold during the period that were not produced during the period.

8 **Discuss the merits of absorption versus variable costing for management decision-making.** The use of variable costing is consistent with cost–volume–profit analysis. Net income under variable costing is unaffected by changes in production levels. Instead, it is closely tied to changes in sales. The presentation of fixed costs in the variable costing approach makes it easier to identify fixed costs and to evaluate their impact on the company's profitability.

GLOSSARY

Absorption costing A costing approach in which all manufacturing costs are charged to the product. (p. 1007).

Cost structure The relative proportion of fixed versus variable costs that a company incurs. (p. 1002).

Degree of operating leverage A measure of the extent to which a company's net income reacts to a change in sales. It is calculated by dividing contribution margin by net income. (p. 1004).

Operating leverage The extent to which a company's net income reacts to a change in sales. Operating leverage

is determined by a company's relative use of fixed versus variable costs. (p. 1004).

Sales mix The relative percentage in which a company sells its multiple products. (p. 995).

Theory of constraints A specific approach used to identify and manage constraints in order to achieve the company's goals. (p. 1001).

Variable costing A costing approach in which only variable manufacturing costs are product costs, and fixed manufacturing costs are period costs (expenses). (p. 1007).

Self-Test, Brief Exercises, Exercises, Problem Set A, and many more resources are available for practice in WileyPLUS.

Note: All asterisked Questions, Exercises, and Problems relate to material contained in the appendix to the chapter.

SELF-TEST QUESTIONS

Answers are at the end of the chapter.

(LO 1) **1.** Which one of the following is the format of a CVP income statement?
 (a) Sales − Variable costs = Fixed costs + Net income.
 (b) Sales − Fixed costs − Variable costs − Operating expenses = Net income.
 (c) Sales − Cost of goods sold − Operating expenses = Net income.
 (d) Sales − Variable costs − Fixed costs = Net income.

(LO 1, 2) **2.** Croc Catchers calculates its contribution margin to be less than zero. Which statement is *true*?
 (a) Its fixed costs are less than the variable costs per unit.

 (b) Its profits are greater than its total costs.
 (c) The company should sell more units.
 (d) Its selling price is less than its variable costs.

3. Which one of the following describes the break-even (LO 2) point?
 (a) It is the point where total sales equals total variable plus total fixed costs.
 (b) It is the point where the contribution margin equals zero.
 (c) It is the point where total variable costs equal total fixed costs.
 (d) It is the point where total sales equals total fixed costs.

(LO 1)   **4.** The following information is available for Chap Company.

Sales	$350,000
Cost of goods sold	$120,000
Total fixed expenses	$60,000
Total variable expenses	$100,000

Which amount would you find on Chap's CVP income statement?
(a) Contribution margin of $250,000.
(b) Contribution margin of $190,000.
(c) Gross profit of $230,000.
(d) Gross profit of $190,000.

(LO 2)   **5.** Gabriel Corporation has fixed costs of $180,000 and variable costs of $8.50 per unit. It has a target income of $268,000. How many units must it sell at $12 per unit to achieve its target net income?
(a) 51,429 units.   (c) 76,571 units.
(b) 128,000 units.   (d) 21,176 units.

(LO 2)   **6.** Mackey Corporation has fixed costs of $150,000 and variable costs of $9 per unit. If sales price per unit is $12, what is break-even sales in dollars?
(a) $200,000.   (c) $480,000.
(b) $450,000.   (d) $600,000.

(LO 3)   **7.** Sales mix is:
(a) important to sales managers but not to accountants.
(b) easier to analyze on absorption costing income statements.
(c) a measure of the relative percentage of a company's variable costs to its fixed costs.
(d) a measure of the relative percentage in which a company's products are sold.

(LO 3)   **8.** Net income will be:
(a) greater if more higher-contribution margin units are sold than lower-contribution margin units.
(b) greater if more lower-contribution margin units are sold than higher-contribution margin units.
(c) equal as long as total sales remain equal, regardless of which products are sold.
(d) unaffected by changes in the mix of products sold.

(LO 4)   **9.** If the contribution margin per unit is $15 and it takes 3.0 machine hours to produce the unit, the contribution margin per unit of limited resource is:
(a) $25.   (c) $4.
(b) $5.   (d) None of the above.

(LO 4)   **10.** MEM manufactures two products. Product X has a contribution margin of $26 and requires 4 hours of machine time. Product Y has a contribution margin of $14 and requires 2 hours of machine time. Assuming that machine time is limited to 3,000 hours, how should it allocate the machine time to maximize its income?

(a) Use 1,500 hours to produce X and 1,500 hours to produce Y.
(b) Use 2,250 hours to produce X and 750 hours to produce Y.
(c) Use 3,000 hours to produce only X.
(d) Use 3,000 hours to produce only Y.

11. When a company has a limited resource, it should   (LO 4)
apply additional capacity of that resource to providing more units of the product or service that has:
(a) the highest contribution margin.
(b) the highest selling price.
(c) the highest gross profit.
(d) the highest contribution margin per unit of that limited resource.

12. The degree of operating leverage: (LO 5)
(a) can be computed by dividing total contribution margin by net income.
(b) provides a measure of the company's earnings volatility.
(c) affects a company's break-even point.
(d) All of the above.

13. A high degree of operating leverage: (LO 5)
(a) indicates that a company has a larger percentage of variable costs relative to its fixed costs.
(b) is computed by dividing fixed costs by contribution margin.
(c) exposes a company to greater earnings volatility risk.
(d) exposes a company to less earnings volatility risk.

14. Stevens Company has a degree of operating leverage   (LO 5)
of 3.5 at a sales level of $1,200,000 and net income of $200,000. If Stevens' sales fall by 10%, Stevens can be expected to experience a:
(a) decrease in net income of $70,000.
(b) decrease in contribution margin of $7,000.
(c) decrease in operating leverage of 35%.
(d) decrease in net income of $175,000.

*15. Fixed manufacturing overhead costs are recognized as: (LO 6)
(a) period costs under absorption costing.
(b) product costs under absorption costs.
(c) product costs under variable costing.
(d) part of ending inventory costs under both absorption and variable costing.

*16. Net income computed under absorption costing   (LO 6)
will be:
(a) higher than net income under variable costing in all cases.
(b) equal to net income under variable costing in all cases.
(c) higher than net income under variable costing when units produced are greater than units sold.
(d) higher than net income under variable costing when units produced are less than units sold.

Go to the book's companion website, www.wiley.com/college/weygandt, for additional Self-Test Questions.

✔ **The Navigator**

QUESTIONS

1. What is meant by CVP analysis?
2. Provide three examples of management decisions that benefit from CVP analysis.
3. Distinguish between a traditional income statement and a CVP income statement.
4. Describe the features of a CVP income statement that make it more useful for management decision-making than the traditional income statement that is prepared for external users.
5. The traditional income statement for Wheat Company shows sales $900,000, cost of goods sold $500,000, and operating expenses $200,000. Assuming all costs and expenses are 75% variable and 25% fixed, prepare a CVP income statement through contribution margin.
6. If management chooses to reduce its selling price to match that of a competitor, how will the break-even point be affected?
7. What is meant by the term sales mix? How does sales mix affect the calculation of the break-even point?
8. Performance Company sells two types of performance tires. The lower-priced model is guaranteed for only 50,000 miles; the higher-priced model is guaranteed for 150,000 miles. The unit contribution margin on the higher-priced tire is twice as high as that of the lower-priced tire. If the sales mix shifts so that the company begins to sell more units of the lower-priced tire, explain how the company's break-even point in units will change.
9. What approach should be used to calculate the break-even point of a company that has many products?
10. How is the contribution margin per unit of limited resource computed?
11. What is the theory of constraints? Provide some examples of possible constraints for a manufacturer.

12. What is meant by "cost structure?" Explain how a company's cost structure affects its break-even point.
13. What is operating leverage? How does a company increase its operating leverage?
14. How does the replacement of manual labor with automated equipment affect a company's cost structure? What implications does this have for its operating leverage and break-even point?
15. What is a measure of operating leverage, and how is it calculated?
16. Pine Company has a degree of operating leverage of 8. Fir Company has a degree of operating leverage of 4. Interpret these measures.
*17. Distinguish between absorption costing and variable costing.
*18. (a) What is the major rationale for the use of variable costing?
    (b) Discuss why variable costing may not be used for financial reporting purposes.
*19. Doc Rowan Corporation sells one product, its waterproof hiking boot. It began operations in the current year and had an ending inventory of 8,500 units. The company sold 20,000 units throughout the year. Fixed manufacturing overhead is $5 per unit, and total manufacturing cost per unit is $20 (including fixed manufacturing overhead costs). What is the difference in net income between absorption and variable costing?
*20. If production equals sales, what, if any, is the difference between net income under absorption costing versus under variable costing?
*21. If production is greater than sales, how does absorption costing net income differ from variable costing net income?
*22. In the long run, will net income be higher or lower under variable costing compared to absorption costing?

BRIEF EXERCISES

BE20-1 Determine the missing amounts.

	Unit Selling Price	Unit Variable Costs	Contribution Margin per Unit	Contribution Margin Ratio
1.	$250	$180	(a)	(b)
2.	$500	(c)	$300	(d)
3.	(e)	(f)	$330	30%

Determine missing amounts for contribution margin.

(LO 1, 2)

BE20-2 Hamby Inc. has sales of $2,000,000 for the first quarter of 2014. In making the sales, the company incurred the following costs and expenses.

	Variable	Fixed
Cost of goods sold	$760,000	$600,000
Selling expenses	95,000	60,000
Administrative expenses	79,000	66,000

Prepare a CVP income statement for the quarter ended March 31, 2014.

Prepare CVP income statement.

(LO 1, 2)

BE20-3 Wesland Corp. had total variable costs of $175,000, total fixed costs of $120,000, and total revenues of $250,000. Compute the required sales in dollars to break even.

BE20-4 Dilts Company has a unit selling price of $400, variable costs per unit of $250, and fixed costs of $210,000. Compute the break-even point in units using (a) the mathematical equation and (b) contribution margin per unit.

BE20-5 For Ortega Company, variable costs are 60% of sales, and fixed costs are $210,000. Management's net income goal is $60,000. Compute the required sales needed to achieve management's target net income of $60,000. (Use the mathematical equation approach.)

BE20-6 For Kosko Company actual sales are $1,200,000 and break-even sales are $960,000. Compute (a) the margin of safety in dollars and (b) the margin of safety ratio.

BE20-7 Markowis Corporation sells three different models of mosquito "zapper." Model A12 sells for $50 and has variable costs of $40. Model B22 sells for $100 and has variable costs of $70. Model C124 sells for $400 and has variable costs of $300. The sales mix of the three models is: A12, 60%; B22, 15%; and C124, 25%. What is the weighted-average unit contribution margin?

BE20-8 Information for Markowis Corporation is given in BE20-7. If the company has fixed costs of $213,000, how many units of each model must the company sell in order to break even?

BE20-9 Peine Candle Supply makes candles. The sales mix (as a percentage of total dollar sales) of its three product lines is birthday candles 30%, standard tapered candles 50%, and large scented candles 20%. The contribution margin ratio of each candle type is shown below.

Candle Type	Contribution Margin Ratio
Birthday	20%
Standard tapered	20%
Large scented	45%

(a) What is the weighted-average contribution margin ratio?
(b) If the company's fixed costs are $440,000 per year, what is the dollar amount of each type of candle that must be sold to break even?

BE20-10 Faune Furniture Co. consists of two divisions, Bedroom Division and Dining Room Division. The results of operations for the most recent quarter are:

	Bedroom Division	Dining Room Division	Total
Sales	$500,000	$750,000	$1,250,000
Variable costs	225,000	450,000	675,000
Contribution margin	$275,000	$300,000	$ 575,000

(a) Determine the company's sales mix.
(b) Determine the company's weighted-average contribution margin ratio.

BE20-11 In Briggs Company, data concerning two products are contribution margin per unit—Product A $12, Product B $15; machine hours required for one unit—Product A 2, Product B 3. Compute the contribution margin per unit of limited resource for each product.

BE20-12 Sam's Shingle Corporation is considering the purchase of a new automated shingle-cutting machine. The new machine will reduce variable labor costs but will increase depreciation expense. Contribution margin is expected to increase from $200,000 to $240,000. Net income is expected to be the same at $40,000. Compute the degree of operating leverage before and after the purchase of the new equipment. Interpret your results.

BE20-13 Presented on the next page are variable costing income statements for Logan Company and Morgan Company. They are in the same industry, with the same net incomes, but different cost structures.

	Logan Co.	Morgan Co.
Sales	$200,000	$200,000
Variable costs	80,000	50,000
Contribution margin	120,000	150,000
Fixed costs	60,000	90,000
Net income	$ 60,000	$ 60,000

Compute the break-even point in dollars for each company and comment on your findings.

BE20-14 The degree of operating leverage for Montana Corp. and APK Co. are 1.6 and 5.4, respectively. Both have net incomes of $50,000. Determine their respective contribution margins.

Determine contribution margin from degree of operating leverage.

(LO 5)

BE20-15 Ger Corporation manufactures two products with the following characteristics.

Show allocation of limited resources.

(LO 4)

	Contribution Margin per Unit	Machine Hours Required for Production
Product 1	$42	.15 hours
Product 2	$35	.10 hours

If Ger's machine hours are limited to 2,000 per month, determine which product it should produce.

*BE20-16 The Rock Company produces basketballs. It incurred the following costs during the year.

Compute product costs under variable costing.

(LO 6)

Direct materials	$14,400
Direct labor	$25,600
Fixed manufacturing overhead	$12,000
Variable manufacturing overhead	$32,400
Selling costs	$21,000

What are the total product costs for the company under variable costing?

*BE20-17 Information concerning The Rock Company is provided in BE20-16. What are the total product costs for the company under absorption costing?

Compute product costs under absorption costing.

(LO 6)

*BE20-18 Burns Company incurred the following costs during the year: direct materials $20 per unit; direct labor $14 per unit; variable manufacturing overhead $15 per unit; variable selling and administrative costs $8 per unit; fixed manufacturing overhead $128,000; and fixed selling and administrative costs $10,000. Burns produced 8,000 units and sold 6,000 units. Determine the manufacturing cost per unit under (a) absorption costing and (b) variable costing.

Determine manufacturing cost per unit under absorption and variable costing.

(LO 6)

*BE20-19 ▭▭▭▷ Howser Company's fixed overhead costs are $4 per unit, and its variable overhead costs are $8 per unit. In the first month of operations, 50,000 units are produced, and 48,000 units are sold. Write a short memo to the chief financial officer explaining which costing approach will produce the higher income and what the difference will be.

Compute net income under absorption and variable costing.

(LO 7)

> DO IT! REVIEW

DO IT! 20-1 Amanda Inc. sold 10,000 units and recorded sales of $400,000 for the first month of 2014. In making the sales, the company incurred the following costs and expenses.

Prepare CVP income statement and compute contribution margin.

(LO 1)

	Variable	Fixed
Cost of goods sold	$184,000	$70,000
Selling expenses	40,000	30,000
Administrative expenses	16,000	50,000

(a) Prepare a CVP income statement for the month ended January 31, 2014.
(b) Compute the contribution margin per unit.
(c) Compute the contribution margin ratio.

Compute the break-even point and margin of safety under different alternatives.

(LO 2)

DO IT! **20-2** Queensland Company reports the following operating results for the month of April.

Queensland Company
CVP Income Statement
For the Month Ended April 30, 2014

	Total	Per Unit
Sales (9,000 units)	$450,000	$50
Variable costs	270,000	30
Contribution margin	180,000	$20
Fixed expenses	150,000	
Net income	$ 30,000	

Management is considering the following course of action to increase net income: Reduce the selling price by 4%, with no changes to unit variable costs or fixed costs. Management is confident that this change will increase unit sales by 20%.

Using the contribution margin technique, compute the break-even point in units and dollars and margin of safety in dollars:

(a) Assuming no changes to selling price or costs, and
(b) Assuming changes to sales price and volume as described above.

Comment on your findings.

Compute sales mix, weighted-average contribution margin, and break-even point.

(LO 3)

DO IT! **20-3** Snow Cap Springs produces and sells water filtration systems for homeowners. Information regarding its three models is shown below.

	Basic	Basic Plus	Premium	Total
Units sold	750	450	300	1,500
Selling price	$250	$400	$800	
Variable costs	$195	$288	$416	

The company's total fixed costs to produce the filtration systems are $165,480.

(a) Determine the sales mix as a function of units sold for the three products.
(b) Determine the weighted-average unit contribution margin.
(c) Determine the total number of units that the company must produce to break even.
(d) Determine the number of units of each model that the company must produce to break even.

Determine sales mix with limited resources.

(LO 4)

DO IT! **20-4** Eye Spy Corporation manufactures and sells three different types of binoculars. They are referred to as Good, Better, and Best binoculars. Grinding and polishing time is limited. More time is required to grind and polish the lenses used in the Better and Best binoculars. Additional information is provided below.

	Product		
	Good	Better	Best
Selling price	$90.00	$330.00	$900.00
Variable costs and expenses	50.00	180.00	480.00
Contribution margin	$40.00	$150.00	$420.00
Grinding and polishing time required	0.5 hrs	1.5 hrs	6 hrs

(a) Ignoring the time constraint, what strategy would appear to be optimal?
(b) What is the contribution margin per unit of limited resource for each type of binocular?
(c) If additional grinding and polishing time could be obtained, how should the additional capacity be used?

 ✔ **The Navigator**

EXERCISES

E20-1 The Bonita Inn is trying to determine its break-even point. The inn has 75 rooms that are rented at $60 a night. Operating costs are as follows.

Compute break-even point and margin of safety.

(LO 2)

Salaries	$8,800 per month
Utilities	2,400 per month
Depreciation	1,500 per month
Maintenance	800 per month
Maid service	8 per room
Other costs	37 per room

Instructions
(a) Determine the inn's break-even point in (1) number of rented rooms per month and (2) dollars.
(b) If the inn plans on renting an average of 50 rooms per day (assuming a 30-day month), what is (1) the monthly margin of safety in dollars and (2) the margin of safety ratio?

E20-2 In the month of June, Jose Hebert's Beauty Salon gave 4,000 haircuts, shampoos, and permanents at an average price of $30. During the month, fixed costs were $16,800 and variable costs were 75% of sales.

Compute contribution margin, break-even point, and margin of safety.

(LO 2)

Instructions
(a) Determine the contribution margin in dollars, per unit and as a ratio.
(b) Using the contribution margin technique, compute the break-even point in dollars and in units.
(c) Compute the margin of safety in dollars and as a ratio.

E20-3 Norton Company reports the following operating results for the month of August: sales $310,000 (units 5,000); variable costs $210,000; and fixed costs $75,000. Management is considering the following independent courses of action to increase net income.

Compute net income under different alternatives.

(LO 2)

1. Increase selling price by 10% with no change in total variable costs or sales volume.
2. Reduce variable costs to 58% of sales.
3. Reduce fixed costs by $20,000.

Instructions
Compute the net income to be earned under each alternative. Which course of action will produce the highest net income?

E20-4 Comfi Airways, Inc., a small two-plane passenger airline, has asked for your assistance in some basic analysis of its operations. Both planes seat 10 passengers each, and they fly commuters from Comfi's base airport to the major city in the state, Metropolis. Each month, 40 round-trip flights are made. Shown below is a recent month's activity in the form of a cost-volume-profit income statement.

Compute break-even point and prepare CVP income statement.

(LO 2)

Fare revenue (400 fares)		$48,000
Variable costs		
Fuel	$14,000	
Snacks and drinks	800	
Landing fees	2,000	
Supplies and forms	1,200	18,000
Contribution margin		30,000
Fixed costs		
Depreciation	3,000	
Salaries	15,000	
Advertising	500	
Airport hangar fees	1,750	20,250
Net income		$ 9,750

Instructions

(a) Calculate the break-even point in (1) dollars and (2) number of fares.

(b) Without calculations, determine the contribution margin at the break-even point.

(c) If fares were decreased by 10%, an additional 100 fares could be generated. However, total variable costs would increase by 20%. Should the fare decrease be adopted?

Prepare a CVP income statement before and after changes in business environment.

(LO 2)

E20-5 Hall Company had sales in 2014 of $1,560,000 on 60,000 units. Variable costs totaled $720,000, and fixed costs totaled $500,000.

A new raw material is available that will decrease the variable costs per unit by 25% (or $3.00). However, to process the new raw material, fixed operating costs will increase by $150,000. Management feels that one-half of the decline in the variable costs per unit should be passed on to customers in the form of a sales price reduction. The marketing department expects that this sales price reduction will result in a 5% increase in the number of units sold.

Instructions

Prepare a projected CVP income statement for 2014 (a) assuming the changes have not been made, and (b) assuming that changes are made as described.

Compute break-even point in units for a company with more than one product.

(LO 3)

E20-6 Yard Tools manufactures lawnmowers, weed-trimmers, and chainsaws. Its sales mix and contribution margin per unit are as follows.

	Sales Mix	Contribution Margin per Unit
Lawnmowers	20%	$30
Weed-trimmers	50%	$20
Chainsaws	30%	$40

Yard Tools has fixed costs of $4,200,000.

Instructions

Compute the number of units of each product that Yard Tools must sell in order to break even under this product mix.

Compute service line break-even point and target net income in dollars for a company with more than one service.

(LO 3)

E20-7 Qwik Repairs has over 200 auto-maintenance service outlets nationwide. It provides primarily two lines of service: oil changes and brake repair. Oil change–related services represent 70% of its sales and provide a contribution margin ratio of 20%. Brake repair represents 30% of its sales and provides a 60% contribution margin ratio. The company's fixed costs are $16,000,000 (that is, $80,000 per service outlet).

Instructions

(a) Calculate the dollar amount of each type of service that the company must provide in order to break even.

(b) The company has a desired net income of $60,000 per service outlet. What is the dollar amount of each type of service that must be provided by each service outlet to meet its target net income per outlet?

Compute break-even point in dollars for a company with more than one service.

(LO 3)

E20-8 Express Delivery is a rapidly growing delivery service. Last year, 80% of its revenue came from the delivery of mailing "pouches" and small, standardized delivery boxes (which provides a 20% contribution margin). The other 20% of its revenue came from delivering non-standardized boxes (which provides a 70% contribution margin). With the rapid growth of Internet retail sales, Express believes that there are great opportunities for growth in the delivery of non-standardized boxes. The company has fixed costs of $12,000,000.

Instructions

(a) What is the company's break-even point in total sales dollars? At the break-even point, how much of the company's sales are provided by each type of service?

(b) The company's management would like to hold its fixed costs constant but shift its sales mix so that 60% of its revenue comes from the delivery of non-standardized boxes and the remainder from pouches and small boxes. If this were to occur, what would be the company's break-even sales, and what amount of sales would be provided by each service type?

E20-9 Palmer Golf Accessories sells golf shoes, gloves, and a laser-guided range-finder that measures distance. Shown below are unit cost and sales data.

Compute break-even point in units for a company with multiple products.

(LO 3)

	Pairs of Shoes	Pairs of Gloves	Range-Finder
Unit sales price	$100	$30	$260
Unit variable costs	60	10	200
Unit contribution margin	$ 40	$20	$ 60
Sales mix	30%	60%	10%

Fixed costs are $630,000.

Instructions
(a) Compute the break-even point in units for the company.
(b) Determine the number of units to be sold at the break-even point for each product line.
(c) Verify that the mix of sales units determined in (b) will generate a zero net income.

E20-10 Personal Electronix sells iPads and iPods. The business is divided into two divisions along product lines. CVP income statements for a recent quarter's activity are presented below.

Determine break-even point in dollars for two divisions.

(LO 3)

	iPad Division	iPod Division	Total
Sales	$600,000	$400,000	$1,000,000
Variable costs	420,000	260,000	680,000
Contribution margin	$180,000	$140,000	320,000
Fixed costs			120,000
Net income			$ 200,000

Instructions
(a) Determine sales mix percentage and contribution margin ratio for each division.
(b) Calculate the company's weighted-average contribution margin ratio.
(c) Calculate the company's break-even point in dollars.
(d) Determine the sales level in dollars for each division at the break-even point.

E20-11 Spencer Company manufactures and sells three products. Relevant per unit data concerning each product are given below.

Compute contribution margin and determine the product to be manufactured.

(LO 4)

	Product		
	A	**B**	**C**
Selling price	$8	$12	$15
Variable costs and expenses	$3	$10	$12
Machine hours to produce	2	1	2

Instructions
(a) Compute the contribution margin per unit of the limited resource (machine hours) for each product.
(b) Assuming 1,500 additional machine hours are available, which product should be manufactured?
(c) Prepare an analysis showing the total contribution margin if the additional hours are (1) divided equally among the products, and (2) allocated entirely to the product identified in (b) above.

E20-12 Dalton Inc. produces and sells three products. Unit data concerning each product is shown below.

Compute contribution margin and determine the products to be manufactured.

(LO 4)

	Product		
	D	**E**	**F**
Selling price	$200	$300	$250
Direct labor costs	30	80	35
Other variable costs	95	80	145

The company has 2,000 hours of labor available to build inventory in anticipation of the company's peak season. Management is trying to decide which product should be produced. The direct labor hourly rate is $10.

Instructions
(a) Determine the number of direct labor hours per unit.
(b) Determine the contribution margin per direct labor hour.
(c) Determine which product should be produced and the total contribution margin for that product.

Compute contribution margin and determine the products to be manufactured.

(LO 4)

E20-13 Billings Company manufactures and sells two products. Relevant per unit data concerning each product follow.

	Product	
	Basic	**Deluxe**
Selling price	$40	$52
Variable costs	$20	$22
Machine hours	.5	.8

Instructions
(a) Compute the contribution margin per machine hour for each product.
(b) If 1,000 additional machine hours are available, which product should Billings manufacture?
(c) Prepare an analysis showing the total contribution margin if the additional hours are:
    (1) Divided equally between the products.
    (2) Allocated entirely to the product identified in part (b).

Compute degree of operating leverage and evaluate impact of alternative cost structures on net income.

(LO 5)

E20-14 The CVP income statements shown below are available for Armstrong Company and Contador Company.

	Armstrong Co.	**Contador Co.**
Sales	$500,000	$500,000
Variable costs	240,000	50,000
Contribution margin	260,000	450,000
Fixed costs	160,000	350,000
Net income	$100,000	$100,000

Instructions
(a) Compute the degree of operating leverage for each company and interpret your results.
(b) Assuming that sales revenue increases by 10%, prepare a variable costing income statement for each company.
(c) Discuss how the cost structure of these two companies affects their operating leverage and profitability.

Compute degree of operating leverage and evaluate impact of alternative cost structures on net income and margin of safety.

(LO 5)

E20-15 Arquitectos Interiores of Juarez, Mexico, is contemplating a major change in its cost structure. Currenty, all of its drafting work is performed by skilled draftsmen. Alfonso Jiminez, Arquitectos' owner, is considering replacing the draftsmen with a computerized drafting system. However, before making the change, Alfonso would like to know the consequences of the change, since the volume of business varies significantly from year to year. Shown below are CVP income statements for each alternative.

	Manual System	**Computerized System**
Sales	$1,500,000	$1,500,000
Variable costs	1,200,000	600,000
Contribution margin	300,000	900,000
Fixed costs	50,000	650,000
Net income	$ 250,000	$ 250,000

Instructions

(a) Determine the degree of operating leverage for each alternative.
(b) Which alternative would produce the higher net income if sales increased by $150,000?
(c) Using the margin of safety ratio, determine which alternative could sustain the greater decline in sales before operating at a loss.

E20-16 An investment banker is analyzing two companies that specialize in the production and sale of candied yams. Traditional Yams uses a labor-intensive approach, and Auto-Yams uses a mechanized system. CVP income statements for the two companies are shown below.

Compute degree of operating leverage and impact on net income of alternative cost structures.

(LO 5)

	Traditional Yams	Auto-Yams
Sales	$400,000	$400,000
Variable costs	320,000	160,000
Contribution margin	80,000	240,000
Fixed costs	30,000	190,000
Net income	$ 50,000	$ 50,000

The investment banker is interested in acquiring one of these companies. However, she is concerned about the impact that each company's cost structure might have on its profitability.

Instructions

(a) Calculate each company's degree of operating leverage. Determine which company's cost structure makes it more sensitive to changes in sales volume.
(b) Determine the effect on each company's net income if sales decrease by 15% and if sales increase by 10%. Do not prepare income statements.
(c) Which company should the investment banker acquire? Discuss.

*E20-17 Felde Company builds custom fishing lures for sporting goods stores. In its first year of operations, 2014, the company incurred the following costs.

Compute product cost and prepare an income statement under variable and absorption costing.

(LO 6)

Variable Costs per Unit

Direct materials	$7.50
Direct labor	$2.45
Variable manufacturing overhead	$5.80
Variable selling and administrative expenses	$3.90

Fixed Costs per Year

Fixed manufacturing overhead	$225,000
Fixed selling and administrative expenses	$240,100

Felde Company sells the fishing lures for $25. During 2014, the company sold 80,000 lures and produced 90,000 lures.

Instructions

(a) Assuming the company uses variable costing, calculate Felde's manufacturing cost per unit for 2014.
(b) Prepare a variable costing income statement for 2014.
(c) Assuming the company uses absorption costing, calculate Felde's manufacturing cost per unit for 2014.
(d) Prepare an absorption costing income statement for 2014.

*E20-18 Langdon Company produced 9,000 units during the past year, but only 8,200 of the units were sold. The following additional information is also available.

Determine ending inventory under variable costing and determine whether absorption or variable costing would result in higher net income.

(LO 6, 7)

Direct materials used	$79,000
Direct labor incurred	$30,000
Variable manufacturing overhead	$21,500
Fixed manufacturing overhead	$45,000
Fixed selling and administrative expenses	$70,000
Variable selling and administrative expenses	$10,000

There was no work in process inventory at the beginning of the year, nor did Langdon have any beginning finished goods inventory.

Instructions

(a) What would be Langdon Company's finished goods inventory cost on December 31 under variable costing?

(b) Which costing method, absorption or variable costing, would show a higher net income for the year? By what amount?

Compute manufacturing cost under absorption and variable costing and explain difference.

(LO 6)

*E20-19 Creative Crates Co. produces wooden crates used for shipping products by ocean liner. In 2014, Creative incurred the following costs.

Wood used in crate production	$54,000
Nails (considered insignificant and a variable expense)	$ 350
Direct labor	$38,000
Utilities for the plant:	
$1,500 each month,	
plus $0.40 for each kilowatt-hour used each month	
Rent expense for the plant for the year	$21,400

Assume Creative used an average 500 kilowatt-hours each month over the past year.

Instructions

(a) What is Creative's total manufacturing cost if it uses a variable costing approach?

(b) What is Creative's total manufacturing cost if it uses an absorption costing approach?

(c) What accounts for the difference in manufacturing costs between these two costing approaches?

EXERCISES: SET B AND CHALLENGE EXERCISES

Visit the book's companion website, at **www.wiley.com/college/weygandt**, and choose the Student Companion site to access Exercise Set B and Challenge Exercises.

PROBLEMS: SET A

Compute break-even point under alternative courses of action.

(LO 1, 2)

P20-1A Fredonia Inc. had a bad year in 2013. For the first time in its history, it operated at a loss. The company's income statement showed the following results from selling 80,000 units of product: net sales $2,000,000; total costs and expenses $1,740,000; and net loss $135,000. Costs and expenses consisted of the following.

	Total	Variable	Fixed
Cost of goods sold	$1,468,000	$ 950,000	$ 518,000
Selling expenses	517,000	92,000	425,000
Administrative expenses	150,000	58,000	92,000
	$2,135,000	$1,100,000	$1,035,000

Management is considering the following independent alternatives for 2014.

1. Increase unit selling price 25% with no change in costs and expenses.
2. Change the compensation of salespersons from fixed annual salaries totaling $200,000 to total salaries of $40,000 plus a 5% commission on net sales.
3. Purchase new high-tech factory machinery that will change the proportion between variable and fixed cost of goods sold to 50:50.

Instructions

(a) Compute the break-even point in dollars for 2014.

(b) (2) $2,187,500

(b) Compute the break-even point in dollars under each of the alternative courses of action. (Round to the nearest dollar.) Which course of action do you recommend?

P20-2A Lorge Corporation has collected the following information after its first year of sales. Sales were $1,500,000 on 100,000 units; selling expenses $250,000 (40% variable and 60% fixed); direct materials $511,000; direct labor $290,000; administrative expenses $270,000 (20% variable and 80% fixed); manufacturing overhead $350,000 (70% variable and 30% fixed). Top management has asked you to do a CVP analysis so that it can make plans for the coming year. It has projected that unit sales will increase by 10% next year.

Compute break-even point and margin of safety ratio, and prepare a CVP income statement before and after changes in business environment.

(LO 1, 2)

Instructions
(a) Compute (1) the contribution margin for the current year and the projected year, and (2) the fixed costs for the current year. (Assume that fixed costs will remain the same in the projected year.)
(b) Compute the break-even point in units and sales dollars for the first year.

(b) 157,000 units

(c) The company has a target net income of $200,000. What is the required sales in dollars for the company to meet its target?
(d) If the company meets its target net income number, by what percentage could its sales fall before it is operating at a loss? That is, what is its margin of safety ratio?
(e) The company is considering a purchase of equipment that would reduce its direct labor costs by $104,000 and would change its manufacturing overhead costs to 30% variable and 70% fixed (assume total manufacturing overhead cost is $350,000, as above). It is also considering switching to a pure commission basis for its sales staff. This would change selling expenses to 90% variable and 10% fixed (assume total selling expense is $250,000, as above). Compute (1) the contribution margin and (2) the contribution margin ratio, and recompute (3) the break-even point in sales dollars. Comment on the effect each of management's proposed changes has on the break-even point.

(e) (3) $1,735,714

P20-3A Tanek Industries manufactures and sells three different models of wet-dry shop vacuum cleaners. Although the shop vacs vary in terms of quality and features, all are good sellers. Tanek is currently operating at full capacity with limited machine time.
    Sales and production information relevant to each model follows.

Determine sales mix with limited resources.

(LO 4)

	Product		
	Economy	**Standard**	**Deluxe**
Selling price	$30	$50	$100
Variable costs and expenses	$14	$15	$46
Machine hours required	.5	.8	1.6

Instructions
(a) Ignoring the machine time constraint, which single product should Tanek Industries produce?
(b) What is the contribution margin per unit of limited resource for each product?
(c) If additional machine time could be obtained, how should the additional time be used?

(b) Economy $32

P20-4A The Hillside Inn is a restaurant in Flagstaff, Arizona. It specializes in southwestern style meals in a moderate price range. Phil Weld, the manager of Hillside, has determined that during the last 2 years the sales mix and contribution margin ratio of its offerings are as follows.

Determine break-even sales under alternative sales strategies and evaluate results.

(LO 3)

	Percent of Total Sales	**Contribution Margin Ratio**
Appetizers	15%	50%
Main entrees	50%	25%
Desserts	10%	50%
Beverages	25%	80%

Phil is considering a variety of options to try to improve the profitability of the restaurant. His goal is to generate a target net income of $117,000. The company has fixed costs of $1,053,000 per year.

Instructions
(a) Calculate the total restaurant sales and the sales of each product line that would be necessary to achieve the desired target net income.

(a) Total sales $2,600,000

(b) Total sales $3,375,000

(b) Phil believes the restaurant could greatly improve its profitability by reducing the complexity and selling price of its entrees to increase the number of clients that it serves. It would then more heavily market its appetizers and beverages. He is proposing to reduce the contribution margin ratio on the main entrees to 10% by dropping the average selling price. He envisions an expansion of the restaurant that would increase fixed costs by $585,000. At the same time, he is proposing to change the sales mix to the following.

	Percent of Total Sales	Contribution Margin Ratio
Appetizers	25%	50%
Main entrees	25%	10%
Desserts	10%	50%
Beverages	40%	80%

Compute the total restaurant sales, and the sales of each product line that would be necessary to achieve the desired target net income.

(c) Suppose that Phil reduces the selling price on entrees and increases fixed costs as proposed in part (b), but customers are not swayed by the marketing efforts and the sales mix remains what it was in part (a). Compute the total restaurant sales and the sales of each product line that would be necessary to achieve the desired target net income. Comment on the potential risks and benefits of this strategy.

Compute degree of operating leverage and evaluate impact of operating leverage on financial results.

(LO 5)

P20-5A The following CVP income statements are available for Viejo Company and Nuevo Company.

	Viejo Company	Nuevo Company
Sales	$500,000	$500,000
Variable costs	280,000	180,000
Contribution margin	220,000	320,000
Fixed costs	180,000	280,000
Net income	$ 40,000	$ 40,000

Instructions

(a) BE, Viejo $409,091
BE, Nuevo $437,500

(b) DOL, Viejo 5.5
DOL, Nuevo 8.0

(a) Compute the break-even point in dollars and the margin of safety ratio for each company.
(b) Compute the degree of operating leverage for each company and interpret your results.
(c) Assuming that sales revenue increases by 20%, prepare a CVP income statement for each company.
(d) Assuming that sales revenue decreases by 20%, prepare a CVP income statement for each company.
(e) ⬛▬▬▶ Discuss how the cost structure of these two companies affects their operating leverage and profitability.

Determine contribution margin, break-even point, target sales, and degree of operating leverage.

(LO 2, 5)

P20-6A Bonita Beauty Corporation manufactures cosmetic products that are sold through a network of sales agents. The agents are paid a commission of 18% of sales. The income statement for the year ending December 31, 2014, is as follows.

Bonita Beauty Corporation
Income Statement
For the Year Ended December 31, 2014

Sales		$75,000,000
Cost of goods sold		
Variable	$31,500,000	
Fixed	8,610,000	40,110,000
Gross margin		34,890,000
Selling and marketing expenses		
Commissions	13,500,000	
Fixed costs	10,260,000	23,760,000
Operating income		$11,130,000

The company is considering hiring its own sales staff to replace the network of agents. It will pay its salespeople a commission of 8% and incur additional fixed costs of $7.5 million.

Instructions

(a) Under the current policy of using a network of sales agents, calculate the Bonita Beauty Corporation's break-even point in sales dollars for the year 2014.

(b) Calculate the company's break-even point in sales dollars for the year 2014 if it hires its own sales force to replace the network of agents.

(c) Calculate the degree of operating leverage at sales of $75 million if (1) Bonita Beauty uses sales agents, and (2) Bonita Beauty employs its own sales staff. Describe the advantages and disadvantages of each alternative.

(d) Calculate the estimated sales volume in sales dollars that would generate an identical net income for the year ending December 31, 2014, regardless of whether Bonita Beauty Corporation employs its own sales staff and pays them an 8% commission or continues to use the independent network of agents.

(a) $47,175

(c) (2) 3.37

(CMA-Canada adapted)

***P20-7A** Gardner Company produces plastic that is used for injection-molding applications such as gears for small motors. In 2013, the first year of operations, Gardner produced 4,000 tons of plastic and sold 2,500 tons. In 2014, the production and sales results were exactly reversed. In each year, the selling price per ton was $2,000, variable manufacturing costs were 15% of the sales price of units produced, variable selling expenses were 10% of the selling price of units sold, fixed manufacturing costs were $2,000,000, and fixed administrative expenses were $500,000.

Prepare income statements under absorption costing and variable costing for a company with beginning inventory, and reconcile differences.

(LO 6, 7)

Instructions

(a) Prepare income statements for each year using variable costing. (Use the format from Illustration 20A-5.)

(b) Prepare income statements for each year using absorption costing. (Use the format from Illustration 20A-4.)

(c) Reconcile the differences each year in net income under the two costing approaches.

(d) ▭▭▭▷ Comment on the effects of production and sales on net income under the two costing approaches.

(a) 2014 $3,500,000

(b) 2014 $2,750,000

***P20-8A** Dilithium Batteries is a division of Enterprise Corporation. The division manufactures and sells a long-life battery used in a wide variety of applications. During the coming year, it expects to sell 60,000 units for $30 per unit. Nyota Uthura is the division manager. She is considering producing either 60,000 or 90,000 units during the period. Other information is presented in the schedule.

Prepare absorption and variable costing income statements and reconcile differences between absorption and variable costing income statements when sales level and production level change. Discuss relative usefulness of absorption costing versus variable costing.

(LO 6, 7, 8)

Division Information for 2014

Beginning inventory	0
Expected sales in units	60,000
Selling price per unit	$30
Variable manufacturing costs per unit	$12
Fixed manufacturing overhead costs (total)	$540,000
Fixed manufacturing overhead costs per unit:	
Based on 60,000 units	$9 per unit ($540,000 ÷ 60,000)
Based on 90,000 units	$6 per unit ($540,000 ÷ 90,000)
Manufacturing costs per unit:	
Based on 60,000 units	$21 per unit ($12 variable + $9 fixed)
Based on 90,000 units	$18 per unit ($12 variable + $6 fixed)
Variable selling and administrative expenses	$2
Fixed selling and administrative expenses (total)	$50,000

Instructions

(a) Prepare an absorption costing income statement, with one column showing the results if 60,000 units are produced and one column showing the results if 90,000 units are produced.

(b) Prepare a variable costing income statement, with one column showing the results if 60,000 units are produced and one column showing the results if 90,000 units are produced.

(a) 90,000 units: NI $550,000

(b) 90,000 units: NI $370,000

(c) Reconcile the difference in net incomes under the two approaches and explain what accounts for this difference.

(d) ▣▭▭▭▷ Discuss the relative usefulness of the variable costing income statements versus the absorption costing income statements for decision making and for evaluating the manager's performance.

PROBLEMS: SET B

Compute break-even point under alternative courses of action.

(LO 1, 2)

P20-1B McCure Corporation had a bad year in 2013, operating at a loss for the first time in its history. The company's income statement showed the following results from selling 200,000 units of product: net sales $2,400,000; total costs and expenses $2,472,000; and net loss $72,000. Costs and expenses consisted of the following.

	Total	Variable	Fixed
Cost of goods sold	$1,486,000	$1,070,000	$416,000
Selling expenses	681,000	356,000	325,000
Administrative expenses	305,000	110,000	195,000
	$2,472,000	$1,536,000	$936,000

Management is considering the following independent alternatives for 2014.

1. Increase unit selling price 25% with no change in costs and expenses.
2. Change the compensation of salespersons from fixed annual salaries totaling $170,000 to total salaries of $50,000 plus a 6% commission on net sales.
3. Purchase new high-tech factory machinery that will change the proportion between variable and fixed cost of goods sold to 40:60.

Instructions
(a) Compute the break-even point in dollars for 2014.

(b) (2) $2,720,000

(b) Compute the break-even point in dollars under each of the alternative courses of action. Which course of action do you recommend? Round to the nearest dollar.

Compute break-even point and margin of safety ratio, and prepare a CVP income statement before and after changes in business environment.

(LO 1, 2)

P20-2B Huber Corporation has collected the following information after its first year of sales. Sales were $1,000,000 on 40,000 units; selling expenses $200,000 (30% variable and 70% fixed); direct materials $327,000; direct labor $190,000; administrative expenses $250,000 (30% variable and 70% fixed); manufacturing overhead $240,000 (20% variable and 80% fixed). Top management has asked you to do a CVP analysis so that it can make plans for the coming year. It has projected that unit sales will increase by 20% next year.

Instructions
(a) Compute (1) the contribution margin for the current year and the projected year, and (2) the fixed costs for the current year. (Assume that fixed costs will remain the same in the projected year.)

(b) 67,600 units

(b) Compute the break-even point in units and sales dollars for the current year.
(c) The company has a target net income of $120,000. What is the required sales in dollars for the company to meet its target?
(d) If the company meets its target net income number, by what percentage could its sales fall before it is operating at a loss? That is, what is its margin of safety ratio?

(e) (3) $1,372,611

(e) The company is considering a purchase of equipment that would reduce its direct labor costs by $90,000 and would change its manufacturing overhead costs to 10% variable and 90% fixed (assume total manufacturing overhead cost is $240,000, as above). It is also considering switching to a pure commission basis for its sales staff. This would change selling expenses to 80% variable and 20% fixed (assume total selling expense is $200,000, as above). Compute (1) the contribution margin and (2) the contribution margin ratio, and (3) recompute the break-even point in sales dollars. Comment on the effect each of management's proposed changes has on the break-even point.

Determine sales mix with limited resources.

(LO 4)

P20-3B Keppel Corporation manufactures and sells three different models of exterior doors. Although the doors vary in terms of quality and features, all are good sellers. Keppel is currently operating at full capacity with limited machine time.

Sales and production information relevant to each model is shown below.

	Product		
	Economy	**Standard**	**Deluxe**
Selling price	$270	$450	$650
Variable costs and expenses	$144	$260	$430
Machine hours required	.6	.8	1.1

Instructions

(a) Ignoring the machine time constraint, which single product should Keppel produce?

(b) What is the contribution margin per unit of limited resource for each product?

(c) If additional machine time could be obtained, how should the additional time be used?

(b) Economy $210

P20-4B The Eatery is a restaurant in DeKalb, Illinois. It specializes in deluxe sandwiches in a moderate price range. Michael Raye, the manager of The Eatery, has determined that during the last 2 years the sales mix and contribution margin ratio of its offerings are as follows.

Determine break-even sales under alternative sales strategies and evaluate results.

(LO 3)

	Percent of Total Sales	Contribution Margin Ratio
Appetizers	15%	60%
Main entrees	60%	25%
Desserts	10%	40%
Beverages	15%	80%

Michael is considering a variety of options to try to improve the profitability of the restaurant. His goal is to generate a target net income of $176,000. The company has fixed costs of $352,000 per year.

Instructions

(a) Calculate the total restaurant sales and the sales of each product line that would be necessary to achieve the desired target net income.

(a) Total sales, $1,320,000

(b) Michael believes the restaurant could greatly improve its profitability by reducing the complexity and selling price of its entrees to increase the number of clients that it serves. It would then more heavily market its appetizers and beverages. He is proposing to reduce the contribution margin ratio on the main entrees to 10% by dropping the average selling price and increasing the contribution margin ratio on desserts to 50% by reducing costs. He envisions an expansion of the restaurant that would increase fixed costs by 50%. At the same time, he is proposing to change the sales mix to the following.

(b) Total sales, $1,600,000

	Percent of Total Sales	Contribution Margin Ratio
Appetizers	25%	60%
Main entrees	40%	10%
Desserts	10%	50%
Beverages	25%	80%

Compute the total restaurant sales, and the sales of each product line that would be necessary to achieve the desired target net income.

(c) Suppose that Michael reduces the selling price on entrees and increases fixed costs as proposed in part (b), but customers are not swayed by the marketing efforts and the sales mix remains what it was in part (a). Compute the total restaurant sales and the sales of each product line that would be necessary to achieve the desired target net income. Comment on the potential risks and benefits of this strategy.

(c) Total sales, $2,200,000

P20-5B The following variable costing income statements are available for Lyte Company and Darke Company.

Compute degree of operating leverage and evaluate impact of operating leverage on financial results.

(LO 5)

	Lyte Company	**Darke Company**
Sales	$1,000,000	$1,000,000
Variable costs	600,000	200,000
Contribution margin	400,000	800,000
Fixed costs	200,000	600,000
Net income	$ 200,000	$ 200,000

Instructions
(a) Compute the break-even point in dollars and the margin of safety ratio for each company.
(b) Compute the degree of operating leverage for each company and interpret your results.
(c) Assuming that sales revenue increases by 30%, prepare a variable costing income statement for each company.
(d) Assuming that sales revenue decreases by 30%, prepare a variable costing income statement for each company.
(e) ▭▭▭▭▷ Discuss how the cost structure of these two companies affects their operating leverage and profitability.

Determine contribution margin, break-even point, target sales, and degree of operating leverage.

(LO 2, 5)

P20-6B Peaches and Cream Corporation manufactures cosmetic products that are sold through a network of sales agents. The agents are paid a commission of 16.25% of sales. The income statement for the year ending December 31, 2014, is shown below.

Peaches and Cream Corporation
Income Statement
For the Year Ended December 31, 2014

Sales		$120,000,000
Cost of goods sold		
Variable	$58,500,000	
Fixed	11,000,000	69,500,000
Gross margin		50,500,000
Selling and marketing expenses		
Commissions	19,500,000	
Fixed costs	10,000,000	29,500,000
Operating income		$ 21,000,000

The company is considering hiring its own sales staff to replace the network of agents. It will pay its salespeople a commission of 10% and incur additional fixed costs of $12.0 million.

Instructions

(a) Under the current policy of using a network of sales agents, calculate the Peaches and Cream Corporation's break-even point in sales dollars for the year 2014.
(b) Calculate the company's break-even point in sales dollars for the year 2014 if it hires its own sales force to replace the network of agents.

(c) Calculate the degree of operating leverage at sales of $120 million if (1) Peaches and Cream uses sales agents, and (2) Peaches and Cream employs its own sales staff. Describe the advantages and disadvantages of each alternative.
(d) Calculate the estimated sales volume in sales dollars that would generate an identical net income for the year ending December 31, 2014, regardless of whether Peaches and Cream Corporation employs its own sales staff and pays them a 10% commission as well as incurring additional fixed costs of $12.0 million, or continues to use the independent network of agents.

(CMA Canada-adapted)

Prepare income statements under absorption costing and variable costing for a company with beginning inventory, and reconcile differences.

(LO 6, 7)

*P20-7B FAB produces fabrics that are used for clothing and other applications. In 2013, the first year of operations, FAB produced 500,000 yards of fabric and sold 400,000 yards. In 2014, the production and sales results were exactly reversed. In each year, selling price per yard was $2.50, variable manufacturing costs were 30% of the sales price of units produced, variable selling expenses were 10% of the selling price of units sold, fixed manufacturing costs were $400,000, and fixed administrative expenses were $100,000.

Instructions

(a) Prepare income statements for each year using variable costing. (Use the format from Illustration 20A-10.)

(b) Prepare income statements for each year using absorption costing. (Use the format from Illustration 20A-11.)
(c) Reconcile the differences each year in income from operations under the two costing approaches.
(d) ▭▭▭▭▷ Comment on the effects of production and sales on net income under the two costing approaches.

P20-8B Electricoil is a division of Meier Products Corporation. The division manufactures and sells an electric coil used in a wide variety of applications. During the coming year, it expects to sell 200,000 units for $9 per unit. Mark Barnes is the division manager. He is considering producing either 200,000 or 250,000 units during the period. Other information is presented in the schedule.

Prepare absorption and variable costing income statements and reconcile differences between absorption and variable costing income statements when sales level and production level change. Discuss relative usefulness of absorption costing versus variable costing.

(LO 6, 7, 8)

Division Information for 2014

Beginning inventory	0
Expected sales in units	200,000
Selling price per unit	$9
Variable manufacturing costs per unit	$3
Fixed manufacturing overhead costs (total)	$500,000

Fixed manufacturing overhead costs per unit:

Based on 200,000 units	$2.50 per unit ($50,000 ÷ 200,000)
Based on 250,000 units	$2.00 per unit ($500,000 ÷ 250,000)

Manufacturing costs per unit:

Based on 200,000 units	$5.50 per unit ($3 variable + $2.50 fixed)
Based on 250,000 units	$5.00 per unit ($3 variable + $2.00 fixed)
Variable selling and administrative expense	$0.40
Fixed selling and administrative expense (total)	$15,000

Instructions

(a) Prepare an absorption costing income statement, with one column showing the results if 200,000 units are produced and one column showing the results if 250,000 units are produced.

(b) Prepare a variable costing income statement, with one column showing the results if 200,000 units are produced and one column showing the results if 250,000 units are produced.

(c) Reconcile the difference in net incomes under the two approaches and explain what accounts for this difference.

(d) ▭▭▭▷ Discuss the relative usefulness of the variable costing income statements versus the absorption costing income statements for decision making and for evaluating the manager's performance.

(a) 250,000 produced
NI, $705,000

(b) 250,000 produced
NI, $605,000

PROBLEMS: SET C

Visit the book's companion website, at **www.wiley.com/college/weygandt**, and choose the Student Companion site to access Problem Set C.

WATERWAYS CONTINUING PROBLEM

(*Note:* This is a continuation of the Waterways Problem from Chapters 15–19.)

WCP20 This problem asks you to perform break-even analysis based on Waterways' sales mix and to make sales mix decisions related to Waterways' use of its productive facilities. An optional extension of the problem (related to the chapter appendix) also asks you to prepare a variable costing income statement and an absorption costing income statement.

*Go to the book's companion website, **www.wiley.com/college/weygandt**, to find the remainder of this problem.*

Management Decision-Making

Decision-Making at Current Designs

BYP20-1 Current Designs manufactures two different types of kayaks, rotomolded kayaks and composite kayaks. The following information is available for each product line.

	Rotomolded	**Composite**
Sales price/unit	$950	$2,000
Variable costs/unit	$570	$1,340

The company's fixed costs are $820,000. An analysis of the sales mix identifies that rotomolded kayaks make up 80% of the total units sold.

Instructions
(a) Determine the weighted-average unit contribution margin for Current Designs.
(b) Determine the break-even point in units for Current Designs and identify how many units of each type of kayak will be sold at the break-even point. (Round to the nearest whole number.)
(c) Assume that the sales mix changes, and rotomolded kayaks now make up 70% of total units sold. Calculate the total number of units that would need to be sold to earn a net income of $2,000,000 and identify how many units of each type of kayak will be sold at this level of income. (Round to the nearest whole number.)
(d) Assume that Current Designs will have sales of $3,000,000 with two-thirds of the sales dollars in rotomolded kayaks and one-third of the sales dollars in composite kayaks. Assuming $660,000 of fixed costs are allocated to the rotomolded kayaks and $160,000 to the composite kayaks, prepare a CVP income statement for each product line.
(e) Using the information in part (d), calculate the degree of operating leverage for each product line and interpret your findings. (Round to two decimal places.)

Decision-Making Across The Organization

BYP20-2 E-Z Seats manufactures swivel seats for customized vans. It currently manufactures 10,000 seats per year, which it sells for $500 per seat. It incurs variable costs of $200 per seat and fixed costs of $2,000,000. It is considering automating the upholstery process, which is now largely manual. It estimates that if it does so, its fixed costs will be $3,000,000, and its variable costs will decline to $100 per seat.

Instructions
With the class divided into groups, answer the following questions.
(a) Prepare a CVP income statement based on current activity.
(b) Compute contribution margin ratio, break-even point in dollars, margin of safety ratio, and degree of operating leverage based on current activity.
(c) Prepare a CVP income statement assuming that the company invests in the automated upholstery system.
(d) Compute contribution margin ratio, break-even point in dollars, margin of safety ratio, and degree of operating leverage assuming the new upholstery system is implemented.
(e) Discuss the implications of adopting the new system.

Managerial Analysis

BYP20-3 For nearly 20 years, Specialized Coatings has provided painting and galvanizing services for manufacturers in its region. Manufacturers of various metal products have relied on the quality and quick turnaround time provided by Specialized Coatings and its 20 skilled employees. During the last year, as a result of a sharp upturn in the economy, the company's sales have increased by 30%

relative to the previous year. The company has not been able to increase its capacity fast enough, so Specialized Coatings has had to turn work away because it cannot keep up with customer requests.

Top management is considering the purchase of a sophisticated robotic painting booth. The booth would represent a considerable move in the direction of automation versus manual labor. If Specialized Coatings purchases the booth, it would most likely lay off 15 of its skilled painters. To analyze the decision, the company compiled production information from the most recent year and then prepared a parallel compilation assuming that the company would purchase the new equipment and lay off the workers. Those data are shown below. As you can see, the company projects that during the last year it would have been far more profitable if it had used the automated approach.

	Current Approach	Automated Approach
Sales	$2,000,000	$2,000,000
Variable costs	1,500,000	1,000,000
Contribution margin	500,000	1,000,000
Fixed costs	380,000	800,000
Net income	$ 120,000	$ 200,000

Instructions
(a) Compute and interpret the contribution margin ratio under each approach.
(b) Compute the break-even point in sales dollars under each approach. Discuss the implications of your findings.
(c) Using the current level of sales, compute the margin of safety ratio under each approach and interpret your findings.
(d) Determine the degree of operating leverage for each approach at current sales levels. How much would the company's net income decline under each approach with a 10% decline in sales?
(e) At what level of sales would the company's net income be the same under either approach?
(f) Discuss the issues that the company must consider in making this decision.

Real-World Focus

BYP20-4 In a recent report, the Del Monte Foods Company reported three separate operating segments: consumer products (which includes a variety of canned foods including tuna, fruit, and vegetables); pet products (which includes pet food and snacks and veterinary products); and soup and infant-feeding products (which includes soup, broth, and infant feeding and pureed products).

In its annual report, Del Monte uses absorption costing. As a result, information regarding the relative composition of its fixed and variable costs is not available. We have assumed that $860.3 million of its total operating expenses of $1,920.3 million are fixed and have allocated the remaining variable costs across the three divisions. Sales data, along with assumed expense data, are provided below.

	(in millions)	
	Sales	Variable Costs
Consumer products	$1,031.8	$ 610
Pet products	837.3	350
Soup and infant-feeding products	302.0	100
	$2,171.1	$1,060

Instructions
(a) Compute each segment's contribution margin ratio and the sales mix.
(b) Using the information computed in part (a), compute the company's break-even point in dollars, and then determine the amount of sales that would be generated by each division at the break-even point.

BYP20-5 The external financial statements published by publicly traded companies are based on absorption cost accounting. As a consequence, it is very difficult to gain an understanding of the relative composition of the companies' fixed and variable costs. It is possible, however, to learn about a company's sales mix and the relative profitability of its various divisions. This exercise looks at the financial statements of FedEx Corporation.

Address: www.fedex.com/us/investorrelations, or go to **www.wiley.com/college/weygandt**

Steps
1. Go to the site above.
2. Under "Financial Documents," choose "Annual Reports."
3. Choose "2008 Annual Report."

Instructions
(a) Read page 25 of the report under the heading "Description of Business." What are the three primary product lines of the company? What does the company identify as the key factors affecting operating results?
(b) Page 36 of the report lists the operating expenses of FedEx Ground. Assuming that rentals, depreciation, and "other" are all fixed costs, prepare a variable costing income statement for 2008, and compute the division's contribution margin ratio and the break-even point in dollars.
(c) Page 73, Note 13 ("Business segment information") provides additional information regarding the relative profitability of the three business segments.
   (i) Calculate the sales mix for 2006 and 2008. (*Note:* Exclude "other" when you calculate total revenue.)
   (ii) The company does not provide the contribution margin for each division, but it does provide "operating margin" (operating income divided by revenues) on pages 34, 36, and 37. List these for each division for 2006 and 2008.
   (iii) Assuming that the "operating margin" (operating income divided by revenues) moves in parallel with each division's contribution margin, how has the shift in sales mix affected the company's profitability from 2006 to 2008?

BYP20-6 The June 8, 2009, edition of the *Wall Street Journal* has an article by JoAnn Lublin entitled "Smart Balance Keeps Tight Focus on Creativity."

Instructions
Read the article and answer the following questions.
(a) Describe Smart Balance's approach to employment and cost structure.
(b) What function does it keep "in-house"?
(c) Based on the discussion in this chapter, what are the advantages to Smart Balance's approach?
(d) Based on the discussion in this chapter, what are the disadvantages to Smart Balance's approach?

Critical Thinking

Communication Activity

BYP20-7 Easton Corporation makes two different boat anchors—a traditional fishing anchor and a high-end yacht anchor—using the same production machinery. The contribution margin of the yacht anchor is three times as high as that of the other product. The company is currently operating at full capacity and has been doing so for nearly two years. Bjorn Borg, the company's CEO, wants to cut back on production of the fishing anchor so that the company can make more yacht anchors. He says that this is a "no-brainer" because the contribution margin of the yacht anchor is so much higher.

Instructions
Write a short memo to Bjorn Borg describing the analysis that the company should do before it makes this decision and any other considerations that would affect the decision.

Ethics Case

*BYP20-8 Brett Stern was hired during January 2014 to manage the home products division of Hi-Tech Products. As part of his employment contract, he was told that he would get $5,000 of additional bonus for every 1% increase that the division's profits exceeded those of the previous year.

Soon after coming on board, Brett met with his plant managers and explained that he wanted the plants to be run at full capacity. Previously, the plant had employed just-in-time inventory practices and had consequently produced units only as they were needed. Brett stated that under previous management the company had missed out on too many sales opportunities because it didn't have enough inventory on hand. Because previous management had employed just-in-time inventory practices, when Brett came on board there was virtually no beginning inventory. The selling price and variable costs per unit remained the same from 2013 to 2014. Additional information is provided below.

	2013	2014
Net income	$ 300,000	$ 525,000
Units produced	25,000	30,000
Units sold	25,000	25,000
Fixed manufacturing overhead costs	$1,350,000	$1,350,000
Fixed manufacturing overhead costs per unit	$ 54	$ 45

Instructions
(a) Calculate Brett's bonus based upon the net income shown above.
(b) Recompute the 2013 and 2014 results using variable costing.
(c) Recompute Brett's 2014 bonus under variable costing.
(d) Were Brett's actions unethical? Do you think any actions need to be taken by the company?

All About You

BYP20-9 Many of you will some day own your own business. One rapidly growing opportunity is no-frills workout centers. Such centers attract customers who want to take advantage of state-of-the-art fitness equipment but do not need the other amenities of full-service health clubs. One way to own your own fitness business is to buy a franchise. Snap Fitness is a Minnesota-based business that offers franchise opportunities. For a very low monthly fee ($26, without an annual contract), customers can access a Snap Fitness center 24 hours a day.

The Snap Fitness website (*www.snapfitness.com*) indicates that start-up costs range from $60,000 to $184,000. This initial investment covers the following pre-opening costs: franchise fee, grand opening marketing, leasehold improvements, utility/rent deposits, and training.

Instructions
(a) Suppose that Snap Fitness estimates that each location incurs $4,000 per month in fixed operating expenses plus $1,460 to lease equipment. A recent newspaper article describing no-frills fitness centers indicated that a Snap Fitness site might require only 300 members to break even. Using the information provided above and your knowledge of CVP analysis, estimate the amount of variable costs. (When performing your analysis, assume that the only fixed costs are the estimated monthly operating expenses and the equipment lease.)
(b) Using the information from part (a), what would monthly sales in members and dollars have to be to achieve a target net income of $3,640 for the month?
(c) Provide five examples of variable costs for a fitness center.
(d) Go to a fitness-business website, such as Curves, Snap Fitness, or Anytime Fitness, and find information about purchasing a franchise. Summarize the franchise information needed to decide whether entering into a franchise agreement would be a good idea.

Considering People, Planet, and Profit

BYP20-10 Many politicians, scientists, economists, and businesspeople have become concerned about the potential implications of global warming. The largest source of the emissions thought to contribute to global warming is from coal-fired power plants. The cost of alternative energy has declined, but it is still higher than coal. In 1980, wind-power electricity cost 80 cents per kilowatt hour. Using today's highly efficient turbines with rotor diameters of up to 125 meters, the cost can be as low as 4 cents (about the same as coal), or as much as 20 cents in places with less wind.

Some people have recently suggested that conventional cost comparisons are not adequate because they do not take environmental costs into account. For example, while coal is a very cheap energy source, it is also a significant contributor of greenhouse gases. Should environmental costs be incorporated into decision formulas when planners evaluate new power plants? The basic arguments for and against are as follows.

YES: As long as environmental costs are ignored, renewable energy will appear to be too expensive relative to coal.

NO: If one country decides to incorporate environmental costs into its decision-making process but other countries do not, the country that does so will be at a competitive disadvantage because its products will cost more to produce.

Instructions

Write a response indicating your position regarding this situation. Provide support for your view.

Answers to Chapter Questions

Answers to Insight and Accounting Across the Organization Questions

p. 994 Don't Just Look—Buy Something Q: Besides increasing their conversion rates, what steps can online merchants use to lower their break-even points? **A:** In theory, one of the principal advantages of online retailers is that they can minimize their investment in "bricks and mortar" and thus minimize their fixed costs. Some online merchants never even handle the merchandise they sell. Instead, they simply provide a centralized location for customers to view merchandise and to place orders. The online retailer then forwards the order to the supplier, and the supplier ships it directly to the customer.

However, some online merchants who originally planned on employing this model have since found it necessary to build their own warehouses and distribution centers to ensure timely and dependable product delivery. This increases their fixed costs and consequently increases their break-even point.

p. 999 Healthy for You, and Great for the Bottom Line Q: Why do you suppose restaurants are so eager to sell beverages and desserts? **A:** There is a reason why servers at restaurants keep your beverage glass full, and why they wave the dessert tray in your face at the end of the meal. Both of these items traditionally have very high contribution margins and require very minimal investments in fixed costs. As a consequence, they are a great mechanism by which a company can hit its break-even point.

p. 1001 Something Smells Q: What is the limited resource for a retailer, and what implications does this have for sales mix? **A:** For retailers, the limited resource is not just shelf space, but shelf space per day. At first, you might think that a product that is small and has a high contribution margin would be the product of choice. But, you also have to factor in the amount of time that a product sits on the shelf.

For example, suppose Product A and B are the same size. Product A has twice the contribution margin as product B, but A sits on the shelf five times as long as product B. In this case, once time spent on the shelf is taken into account, B's superior turnover more than makes up for its lower contribution margin.

p. 1005 There Is Something About a Train Q: Why did Warren Buffett think that this was a good time to invest in railroad stocks? **A:** Railroads have extremely high fixed costs. Mr. Buffett bought Burlington Northern Railroad at the bottom of a recession. He is counting on the railroad's high operating leverage to provide large profits once the economy rebounds.

Answers to Self-Test Questions

1. d **2.** d **3.** a **4.** a ($350,000 − $100,000) **5.** b [($180,000 + $268,000) ÷ ($12 − $8.50)]
6. d [$150,000 ÷ ($3 ÷ $12)] **7.** d **8.** a **9.** b ($15 ÷ 3.0) **10.** d [($26 ÷ 4) < ($14 ÷ 2)] **11.** d
12. d **13.** c **14.** a ($200,000 × 3.5 × 10%) *****15.** b *****16.** c

Chapter 21

Incremental Analysis

Make It or Buy It?

When is a manufacturer not a manufacturer? When it outsources. An extension of the classic "make or buy" decision, outsourcing involves hiring other companies to make all or part of a product or to perform services. Who is outsourcing? Nike, General Motors, Sara Lee, and Hewlett-Packard, to name a few. Even a recent trade journal article for small cabinet-makers outlined the pros and cons of building cabinet doors and drawers internally, or outsourcing them to other shops.

Gibson Greetings, Inc., one of the country's largest sellers of greeting cards, has experienced both the pros and cons of outsourcing. In April one year, it announced it would outsource the manufacturing of all of its cards and gift wrap. Gibson's stock price shot up quickly because investors believed the strategy could save the company $10 million a year, primarily by reducing manufacturing costs. But later in the same year, Gibson got a taste of the negative side of outsourcing: When one of its suppliers was unable to meet its production schedule, about $20 million of Christmas cards went to stores a month later than scheduled.

Outsourcing is often a point of dispute in labor negotiations. Although many of the jobs lost to outsourcing go overseas, that is not always the case. In fact, a recent trend is to hire out work to vendors located close to the company. This reduces shipping costs and can improve coordination of efforts.

✔ The Navigator

☐ Scan Learning Objectives

☐ Read Feature Story

☐ Read Preview

☐ Read Text and answer **DO IT!** p. 1047
   ☐ p. 1049 ☐ p. 1054 ☐ p. 1057

☐ Work Comprehensive **DO IT!** p. 1059

☐ Review Summary of Learning Objectives

☐ Answer Self-Test Questions

☐ Complete Assignments

☐ Go to **WileyPLUS** for practice and tutorials

Learning Objectives

After studying this chapter, you should be able to:

1 Identify the steps in management's decision-making process.

2 Describe the concept of incremental analysis.

3 Identify the relevant costs in accepting an order at a special price.

4 Identify the relevant costs in a make-or-buy decision.

5 Identify the relevant costs in determining whether to sell or process materials further.

6 Identify the relevant costs to be considered in repairing, retaining, or replacing equipment.

7 Identify the relevant costs in deciding whether to eliminate an unprofitable segment or product.

 The Navigator

One company that has benefited from local outsourcing is Solectron Corporation in Silicon Valley. It makes things like cell phones, printers, and computers for high-tech companies in the region. To the surprise of many, it has kept thousands of people employed in California rather than watching those jobs go overseas. What is its secret? It produces high-quality products efficiently. Solectron has to be efficient because it operates on a very thin profit margin—that is, it makes a tiny amount of money on each part—but it makes millions and millions of parts. It has proved the logic of outsourcing as a management decision, both for the companies for which it makes parts and for its owners and employees.

Watch the Method video in WileyPLUS to learn more about incremental analysis in the real world.

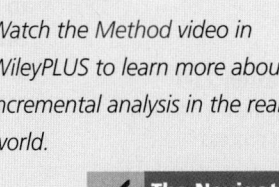
✔ **The Navigator**

Preview of **Chapter 21**

An important purpose of management accounting is to provide managers with relevant information for decision-making. Companies of all sorts must make product decisions. Philip Morris decided to cut prices to raise market share. Oral-B Laboratories opted to produce a new, higher-priced ($5) toothbrush. General Motors discontinued making the Buick Riviera and announced the closure of its Oldsmobile Division. Quaker Oats decided to sell off a line of beverages, at a price more than $1 billion less than it paid for that product line only a few years before. Ski manufacturers like Dynastar had to decide whether to use their limited resources to make snowboards instead of downhill skis.

This chapter explains management's decision-making process and a decision-making approach called incremental analysis. The use of incremental analysis is demonstrated in a variety of situations.

The content and organization of this chapter are as follows.

INCREMENTAL ANALYSIS

Management's Decision-Making Process	Types of Incremental Analysis	Other Considerations
• Incremental analysis • How incremental analysis works	• Accept an order at a special price • Make or buy • Sell or process further • Repair, retain, or replace equipment • Eliminate an unprofitable segment or product	• Qualitative factors • Incremental analysis and ABC

✔ **The Navigator**

Management's Decision-Making Process

Making decisions is an important management function. Management's decision-making process does not always follow a set pattern because decisions vary significantly in their scope, urgency, and importance. It is possible, though, to identify some steps that are frequently involved in the process. These steps are shown in Illustration 21-1 below.

Accounting's contribution to the decision-making process occurs primarily in Steps 2 and 4—evaluating possible courses of action, and reviewing results. In Step 2, for each possible course of action, relevant revenue and cost data are provided. These show the expected overall effect on net income. In Step 4, internal reports are prepared that review the actual impact of the decision.

Illustration 21-1
Management's decision-making process

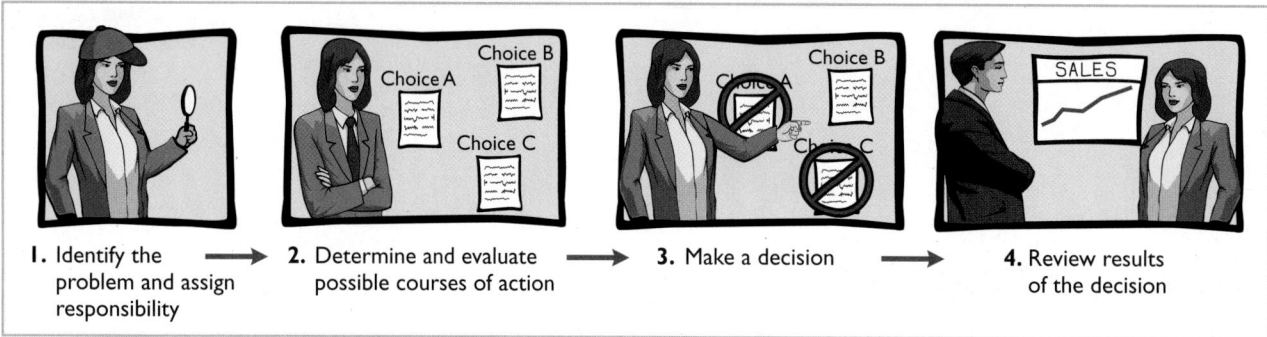

1. Identify the problem and assign responsibility ➔ 2. Determine and evaluate possible courses of action ➔ 3. Make a decision ➔ 4. Review results of the decision

In making business decisions, management ordinarily considers both financial and nonfinancial information. **Financial** information is related to revenues and costs and their effect on the company's overall profitability. **Nonfinancial** information relates to such factors as the effect of the decision on employee turnover, the environment, or the overall image of the company in the community. (These are considerations that we touched on in our Chapter 15 discussion of corporate social responsibility.) Although nonfinancial information can be as important as financial information, we will focus primarily on financial information that is relevant to the decision.

Incremental Analysis Approach

Decisions involve a choice among alternative courses of action. Suppose you face the personal financial decision of whether to purchase or lease a car. The financial data relate to the cost of leasing versus the cost of purchasing. For example, leasing would involve periodic lease payments; purchasing would require "up-front" payment of the purchase price. In other words, the financial data relevant to the decision are the data that would vary in the future among the possible alternatives. The process used to identify the financial data that change under alternative courses of action is called **incremental analysis**. In some cases, you will find that when you use incremental analysis, both costs **and** revenues will vary. In other cases, only costs **or** revenues will vary.

Just as your decision to buy or lease a car will affect your future financial situation, similar decisions, on a larger scale, will affect a company's future. Incremental analysis identifies the probable effects of those decisions on future earnings. Such analysis inevitably involves estimates and uncertainty. Gathering data for incremental analyses may involve market analysts, engineers, and accountants. In quantifying the data, the accountant is expected to produce the most reliable information available at the time the decision must be made.

Alternative Terminology
Incremental analysis is also called *differential analysis* because the analysis focuses on differences.

How Incremental Analysis Works

The basic approach in incremental analysis is illustrated in the following example.

Illustration 21-2
Basic approach in incremental analysis

		Incremental Analysis.xls		
	Home Insert Page Layout Formulas Data Review View			
	P18	fx		
	A	B	C	D
1		**Alternative A**	**Alternative B**	**Net Income Increase (Decrease)**
2	Revenues	$125,000	$110,000	$ (15,000)
3	Costs	100,000	80,000	20,000
4	Net income	$ 25,000	$ 30,000	$ 5,000
5				

This example compares alternative B with alternative A. The net income column shows the differences between the alternatives. In this case, incremental revenue will be $15,000 less under alternative B than under alternative A. But a $20,000 incremental cost saving will be realized.[1] Thus, alternative B will produce $5,000 more net income than alternative A.

In the following pages, you will encounter three important cost concepts used in incremental analysis, as defined and discussed in Illustration 21-3.

Illustration 21-3
Key cost concepts in incremental analysis

- **Relevant cost**   In incremental analysis, the only factors to be considered are those costs and revenues that differ across alternatives. Those factors are called **relevant costs**. Costs and revenues that do not differ across alternatives can be ignored when trying to choose between alternatives.

- **Opportunity cost**   Often in choosing one course of action, the company must give up the opportunity to benefit from some other course of action. For example, if a machine is used to make one type of product, the benefit of making another type of product with that machine is lost. This lost benefit is referred to as **opportunity cost**.

- **Sunk cost**   Costs that have already been incurred and will not be changed or avoided by any present or future decisions are referred to as **sunk costs**. For example, the amount you spent in the past to purchase or repair a machine should have no bearing on your decision whether to buy a new machine. **Sunk costs are not relevant costs.**

---

[1]Although income taxes are sometimes important in incremental analysis, they are ignored in the chapter for simplicity's sake.

Incremental analysis sometimes involves changes that at first glance might seem contrary to your intuition. For example, sometimes variable costs **do not change** under the alternative courses of action. Also, sometimes fixed costs **do change**. For example, direct labor, normally a variable cost, is not an incremental cost in deciding between two new factory machines if each asset requires the same amount of direct labor. In contrast, rent expense, normally a fixed cost, is an incremental cost in a decision whether to continue occupancy of a building or to purchase or lease a new building.

It is also important to understand that **the approaches to incremental analysis discussed in this chapter do not take into consideration the time value of money**. That is, amounts to be paid or received in future years are not discounted for the cost of interest. Time value of money is addressed in Chapter 26 and Appendix D.

SERVICE COMPANY INSIGHT

That Letter from AmEx Might Not Be a Bill

No doubt every one of you has received an invitation from a credit card company to open a new account—some of you have probably received three in one day. But how many of you have received an offer of $300 to close out your credit card account? American Express decided to offer some of its customers $300 if they would give back their credit card. You could receive the $300 even if you hadn't paid off your balance yet, as long as you agreed to give up your credit card.

Source: Aparajita Saha-Bubna and Lauren Pollock, "AmEx Offers Some Holders $300 to Pay and Leave," *Wall Street Journal Online* (February 23, 2009).

 What are the relevant costs that American Express would need to know in order to determine to whom to make this offer? (See page 1080.)

Types of Incremental Analysis

A number of different types of decisions involve incremental analysis. The more common types of decisions are whether to:

1. Accept an order at a special price.
2. Make or buy component parts or finished products.
3. Sell products or process them further.
4. Repair, retain, or replace equipment.
5. Eliminate an unprofitable business segment or product.

We will consider each of these types of decisions in the following pages.

Accept an Order at a Special Price

LEARNING OBJECTIVE **3**

Identify the relevant costs in accepting an order at a special price.

Sometimes a company may have an opportunity to obtain additional business if it is willing to make a major price concession to a specific customer. To illustrate, assume that Sunbelt Company produces 100,000 Smoothie blenders per month, which is 80% of plant capacity. Variable manufacturing costs are $8 per unit. Fixed manufacturing costs are $400,000, or $4 per unit. The Smoothie blenders are normally sold directly to retailers at $20 each. Sunbelt has an offer from Kensington Co. (a foreign wholesaler) to purchase an additional 2,000 blenders at

$11 per unit. Acceptance of the offer would not affect normal sales of the product, and the additional units can be manufactured without increasing plant capacity. What should management do?

If management makes its decision on the basis of the total cost per unit of $12 ($8 variable + $4 fixed), the order would be rejected because costs per unit ($12) would exceed revenues per unit ($11) by $1 per unit. However, since the units can be produced within existing plant capacity, the special order **will not increase fixed costs**. Let's identify the relevant data for the decision. First, the variable manufacturing costs will increase $16,000 ($8 × 2,000). Second, the expected revenue will increase $22,000 ($11 × 2,000). Thus, as shown in Illustration 21-4, Sunbelt will increase its net income by $6,000 by accepting this special order.

Helpful Hint
This is a good example of different costs for different purposes. In the long run all costs are relevant, but for this decision only costs that change are relevant.

	Incremental Analysis - Accepting an order at a special price.xls		
	Home Insert Page Layout Formulas Data Review View		
	P18 fx		
	A	B	C	D
1		**Reject Order**	**Accept Order**	**Net Income Increase (Decrease)**
2	Revenues	$0	$22,000	$ 22,000
3	Costs	0	16,000	(16,000)
4	Net income	$0	$ 6,000	$ 6,000
5				

Illustration 21-4
Incremental analysis— accepting an order at a special price

Two points should be emphasized: First, we assume that sales of the product in other markets **would not be affected by this special order**. If other sales were affected, then Sunbelt would have to consider the lost sales in making the decision. Second, if Sunbelt is operating **at full capacity**, it is likely that the special order would be rejected. Under such circumstances, the company would have to expand plant capacity. In that case, the special order would have to absorb these additional fixed manufacturing costs, as well as the variable manufacturing costs.

> **DO IT!**

Special Orders

Cobb Company incurs costs of $28 per unit ($18 variable and $10 fixed) to make a product that normally sells for $42. A foreign wholesaler offers to buy 5,000 units at $25 each. Cobb will incur additional shipping costs of $1 per unit. Compute the increase or decrease in net income Cobb will realize by accepting the special order, assuming Cobb has excess operating capacity. Should Cobb Company accept the special order?

Solution

Action Plan

✔ Identify all revenues that will change as a result of accepting the order.

✔ Identify all costs that will change as a result of accepting the order, and net this amount against the change in revenues.

	Reject	Accept	Net Income Increase (Decrease)
Revenues	$-0-	$125,000*	$125,000
Costs	-0-	95,000**	(95,000)
Net income	$-0-	$ 30,000	$ 30,000

*5,000 × $25
**(5,000 × $18) + (5,000 × $1)

The analysis indicates net income will increase by $30,000; therefore, Cobb Company should accept the special order.

Related exercise material: **BE21-3, E21-2, E21-3, E21-4, and** DO IT! **21-1.**

 ✔ **The Navigator**

Make or Buy

When a manufacturer assembles component parts in producing a finished product, management must decide whether to make or buy the components. The decision to buy parts or services is often referred to as outsourcing. For example, as discussed in the Feature Story, a company such as General Motors Corporation may either make or buy the batteries, tires, and radios used in its cars. Similarly, Hewlett-Packard Corporation may make or buy the electronic circuitry, cases, and printer heads for its printers. Boeing recently sold some of its commercial aircraft factories in an effort to cut production costs and focus instead on engineering and final assembly rather than manufacturing. The decision to make or buy components should be made on the basis of incremental analysis.

Baron Company makes motorcycles and scooters. It incurs the following annual costs in producing 25,000 ignition switches for scooters.

Illustration 21-5
Annual product cost data

Direct materials	$ 50,000
Direct labor	75,000
Variable manufacturing overhead	40,000
Fixed manufacturing overhead	60,000
Total manufacturing costs	$225,000
Total cost per unit ($225,000 ÷ 25,000)	**$9.00**

Instead of making its own switches, Baron Company might purchase the ignition switches from Ignition, Inc. at a price of $8 per unit. What should management do?

At first glance, it appears that management should purchase the ignition switches for $8 rather than make them at a cost of $9. However, a review of operations indicates that if the ignition switches are purchased from Ignition, Inc., *all* of Baron's variable costs but only $10,000 of its fixed manufacturing costs will be eliminated (avoided). Thus, $50,000 of the fixed manufacturing costs will remain if the ignition switches are purchased. The relevant costs for incremental analysis, therefore, are as shown below.

Illustration 21-6
Incremental analysis—make or buy

	Make	Buy	Net Income Increase (Decrease)
Direct materials	$ 50,000	$ 0	$ 50,000
Direct labor	75,000	0	75,000
Variable manufacturing costs	40,000	0	40,000
Fixed manufacturing costs	60,000	50,000	10,000
Purchase price (25,000 × $8)	0	200,000	(200,000)
Total annual cost	$225,000	$250,000	$ (25,000)

(Spreadsheet: Incremental Analysis - Make or buy.xls — cell P18)

This analysis indicates that Baron Company would incur $25,000 of additional costs by buying the ignition switches rather than making them. Therefore, Baron should continue to make the ignition switches even though the total manufacturing cost is $1 higher per unit than the purchase price. The primary cause of this result is that, even if the company purchases the ignition switches, it will still have fixed costs of $50,000 to absorb.

OPPORTUNITY COST

The foregoing make-or-buy analysis is complete only if it is assumed that the productive capacity used to make the ignition switches cannot be converted to another purpose. If there is an opportunity to use this productive capacity in some other manner, then this opportunity cost must be considered. As indicated earlier, **opportunity cost** is the potential benefit that may be obtained by following an alternative course of action.

To illustrate, assume that through buying the switches, Baron Company can use the released productive capacity to generate additional income of $38,000 from producing a different product. This lost income is an additional cost of continuing to make the switches in the make-or-buy decision. This opportunity cost is therefore added to the "Make" column for comparison. As shown in Illustration 21-7, it is now advantageous to buy the ignition switches. The company's income would increase by $13,000.

> ### Ethics Note
> In the make-or-buy decision, it is important for management to take into account the social impact of its choice. For instance, buying may be the most economically feasible solution, but such action could result in the closure of a manufacturing plant that employs many good workers.

Illustration 21-7
Incremental analysis—make or buy, with opportunity cost

Incremental Analysis - Make or buy with opportunity cost.xls

Home   Insert   Page Layout   Formulas   Data   Review   View

P18   fx

	A	B	C	D
1		**Make**	**Buy**	**Net Income Increase (Decrease)**
2	Total annual cost	$225,000	$250,000	$(25,000)
3	Opportunity cost	38,000	0	38,000
4	Total cost	$263,000	$250,000	$ 13,000
5				

The qualitative factors in this decision include the possible loss of jobs for employees who produce the ignition switches. In addition, management must assess how well the supplier will be able to satisfy the company's quality control standards at the quoted price per unit.

> DO IT!

Make or Buy

Juanita Company must decide whether to make or buy some of its components for the appliances it produces. The costs of producing 166,000 electrical cords for its appliances are as follows.

Direct materials	$90,000	Variable overhead	$32,000
Direct labor	$20,000	Fixed overhead	$24,000

Instead of making the electrical cords at an average cost per unit of $1.00 ($166,000 ÷ 166,000), the company has an opportunity to buy the cords at $0.90 per unit. If the company purchases the cords, all variable costs and one-fourth of the fixed costs will be eliminated.

(a) Prepare an incremental analysis showing whether the company should make or buy the electrical cords. (b) Will your answer be different if the released productive capacity will generate additional income of $5,000?

Solution

(a)

	Make	Buy	Net Income Increase (Decrease)
Direct materials	$ 90,000	$ –0–	$ 90,000
Direct labor	20,000	–0–	20,000
Variable manufacturing costs	32,000	–0–	32,000
Fixed manufacturing costs	24,000	18,000*	6,000
Purchase price	–0–	149,400**	(149,400)
Total cost	$166,000	$167,400	$ (1,400)

*.75 × $24,000
**$166,000 × .90

This analysis indicates that Juanita Company will incur $1,400 of additional costs if it buys the electrical cords rather than making them.

(b)

	Make	Buy	Net Income Increase (Decrease)
Total cost	$166,000	$167,400	$(1,400)
Opportunity cost	5,000	–0–	5,000
Total cost	$171,000	$167,400	$ 3,600

Yes, the answer is different: The analysis shows that net income will be increased by $3,600 if Juanita Company purchases the electrical cords rather than making them.

Related exercise material: **BE21-4, E21-5, E21-6, E21-7, E21-8, and** **21-2.**

✔ **The Navigator**

SERVICE COMPANY INSIGHT

Giving Away the Store?

In an earlier chapter, we discussed Amazon.com's incredible growth. However, some analysts have questioned whether some of the methods that Amazon uses to increase its sales make good business sense. For example, a few years ago, Amazon initiated a "Prime" free-shipping subscription program. For a $79 fee per year, Amazon's customers get free shipping on as many goods as they want to buy. At the time, CEO Jeff Bezos promised that the program would be costly in the short-term but benefit the company in the long-term. Six years later, it was true that Amazon's sales had grown considerably. It was also estimated that its Prime customers buy two to three times as much as non-Prime customers. But, its shipping costs rose from 2.8% of sales to 4% of sales, which is remarkably similar to the drop in its gross margin from 24% to 22.3%. Perhaps even less easy to justify is a proposal by Mr. Bezos to start providing a free Internet movie-streaming service to Amazon's Prime customers. Perhaps some incremental analysis is in order?

Source: Martin Peers, "Amazon's Prime Numbers," *Wall Street Journal Online* (February 3, 2011).

 ? What are the relevant revenues and costs that Amazon should consider relative to the decision whether to offer the Prime free-shipping subscription? (See page 1080.)

Sell or Process Further

Many manufacturers have the option of selling products at a given point in the production cycle or continuing to process with the expectation of selling them at a later point at a higher price. For example, a bicycle manufacturer such as Trek could sell its bicycles to retailers either unassembled or assembled. A furniture manufacturer such as Ethan Allen could sell its dining room sets to furniture stores either unfinished or finished. The sell-or-process-further decision should be made on the basis of incremental analysis. The basic decision rule is: **Process further as long as the incremental revenue from such processing exceeds the incremental processing costs.**

LEARNING OBJECTIVE   5

Identify the relevant costs in determining whether to sell or process materials further.

SINGLE-PRODUCT CASE

Assume, for example, that Woodmasters Inc. makes tables. It sells unfinished tables for $50. The cost to manufacture an unfinished table is $35, computed as follows.

Direct materials	$15
Direct labor	10
Variable manufacturing overhead	6
Fixed manufacturing overhead	4
Manufacturing cost per unit	**$35**

Illustration 21-8
Per unit cost of unfinished table

Woodmasters currently has unused productive capacity that is expected to continue indefinitely. Some of this capacity could be used to finish the tables and sell them at $60 per unit. For a finished table, direct materials will increase $2 and direct labor costs will increase $4. Variable manufacturing overhead costs will increase by $2.40 (60% of direct labor). No increase is anticipated in fixed manufacturing overhead.

    Should the company sell the unfinished tables, or should it process them further? The incremental analysis on a per unit basis is as follows.

Helpful Hint
Current net income is known. Net income from processing further is an estimate. In making its decision, management could add a "risk" factor for the estimate.

	Incremental Analysis - Sell or process further.xls		
	Home Insert Page Layout Formulas Data Review View		
P18	*fx*		
A	B	C	D
1	**Sell Unfinished**	**Process Further**	**Net Income Increase (Decrease)**
2 Sales price per unit	$50.00	$60.00	$10.00
3 Cost per unit			
4 Direct materials	15.00	17.00	(2.00)
5 Direct labor	10.00	14.00	(4.00)
6 Variable manufacturing overhead	6.00	8.40	(2.40)
7 Fixed manufacturing overhead	4.00	4.00	0.00
8 Total	35.00	43.40	(8.40)
9 Net income per unit	$ 15.00	$ 16.60	$ 1.60
10			

Illustration 21-9
Incremental analysis—sell or process further

It would be advantageous for Woodmasters to process the tables further. The incremental revenue of $10.00 from the additional processing is $1.60 higher than the incremental processing costs of $8.40.

MULTIPLE-PRODUCT CASE

Sell-or-process-further decisions are particularly applicable to production processes that produce multiple products simultaneously. In many industries, a number of end-products are produced from a single raw material and a common production process. These multiple end-products are commonly referred to as **joint products.** For example, in the meat-packing industry, Armour processes a cow or pig to produce meat, internal organs, hides, bones, and fat. In the petroleum industry, ExxonMobil refines crude oil to produce gasoline, lubricating oil, kerosene, paraffin, and ethylene.

Illustration 21-10 presents a joint product situation for Marais Creamery involving a decision **to sell or process further** cream and skim milk. Cream and skim milk are joint products that result from the processing of raw milk.

Illustration 21-10

Joint production process—
Creamery

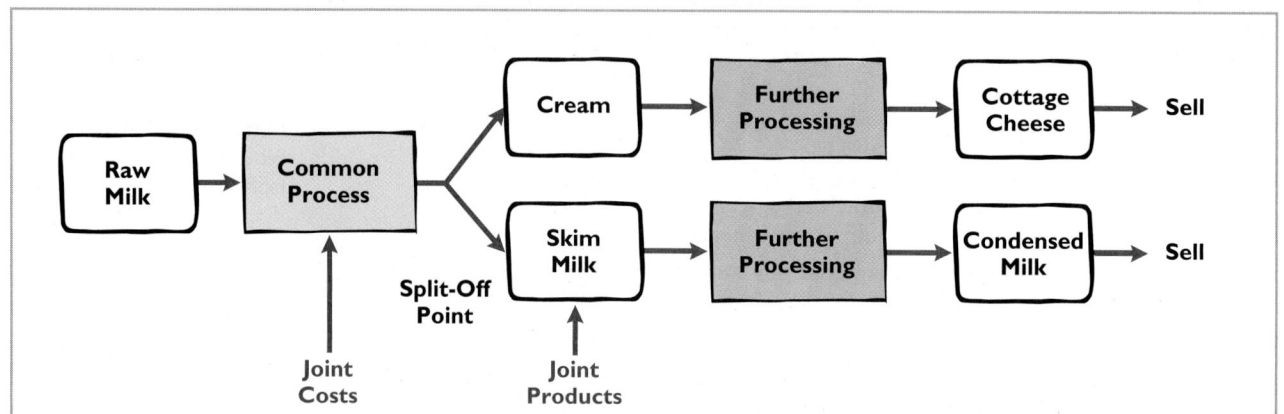

Marais incurs many costs prior to the manufacture of the cream and skim milk. All costs incurred prior to the point at which the two products are separately identifiable (the *split-off point*) are called **joint costs.** For purposes of determining the cost of each product, joint product costs must be allocated to the individual products. This is frequently done based on the relative sales value of the joint products. While this allocation is important for determination of product cost, **it is irrelevant for any sell-or-process-further decisions.** The reason is that these **joint product costs are sunk costs.** That is, they have already been incurred, and they cannot be changed or avoided by any subsequent decision.

Illustration 21-11 provides the daily cost and revenue data for Marais Creamery related to cream and cottage cheese.

Illustration 21-11

Cost and revenue data per day
for cream

Costs (per day)	
Joint cost allocated to cream	$ 9,000
Cost to process cream into cottage cheese	10,000

Revenues from Products (per day)	
Cream	$19,000
Cottage cheese	27,000

From this information, we can determine whether the company should simply sell the cream or process it further into cottage cheese. Illustration 21-12 shows the necessary analysis. Note that the joint cost that is allocated to the cream is not included in this decision. It is not relevant to the decision because it is a sunk cost. It has been incurred in the past and will remain the same no matter whether the cream is subsequently processed into cottage cheese or not.

◨ ೧ ▾ ᴖ ▾ ⋮	Incremental Analysis - Sell or process further - Cottage cheese.xls			
Home Insert Page Layout Formulas Data Review View				
P18	fx			
A	**B**	**C**	**D**	
1		**Sell**	**Process Further**	**Net Income Increase (Decrease)**
2	Sales per day	$19,000	$27,000	$ 8,000
3	Cost per day to process cream into cottage cheese	0	10,000	(10,000)
4		$19,000	$ 17,000	$ (2,000)
5				

Illustration 21-12

Analysis of whether to sell cream or process into cottage cheese

From this analysis, we can see that Marais should not process the cream further because it will sustain an incremental loss of $2,000.

Illustration 21-13 provides the daily cost and revenue data for the company related to skim milk and condensed milk.

Illustration 21-13

Cost and revenue data per day for skim milk

Costs (per day)	
Joint cost allocated to skim milk	$ 5,000
Cost to process skim milk into condensed milk	8,000
Revenues from Products (per day)	
Skim milk	$11,000
Condensed milk	26,000

Illustration 21-14 shows that Marais Company should process the skim milk into condensed milk, as it will increase net income by $7,000.

◨ ೧ ▾ ᴖ ▾ ⋮	Incremental Analysis - Sell or process further - Skim milk or process condensed milk.xls			
Home Insert Page Layout Formulas Data Review View				
P18	fx			
A	**B**	**C**	**D**	
1		**Sell**	**Process Further**	**Net Income Increase (Decrease)**
2	Sales per day	$11,000	$26,000	$15,000
3	Cost per day to process skim milk into condensed milk	0	8,000	(8,000)
4		$11,000	$ 18,000	$ 7,000
5				

Illustration 21-14

Analysis of whether to sell skim milk or process into condensed milk

Again, note that the $5,000 of joint cost allocated to the skim milk is irrelevant in deciding whether to sell or process further. Why? The joint cost remains the same, whether or not further processing is performed.

It is important to understand that these decisions need to be reevaluated as market conditions change. For example, if the price of skim milk increases relative to the price of condensed milk, it may become more profitable to sell the skim milk rather than process it into condensed milk. Consider also oil refineries. As market conditions change, they must constantly re-assess which products to produce from the oil they receive at their plants.

> **DO IT!**

Sell or Process Further

Easy Does It manufactures unpainted furniture for the do-it-yourself (DIY) market. It currently sells a child's rocking chair for $25. Production costs are $12 variable and $8 fixed. Easy Does It is considering painting the rocking chair and selling it for $35. Variable costs to paint each chair are expected to be $9, and fixed costs are expected to be $2.

Prepare an analysis showing whether Easy Does It should sell unpainted or painted chairs.

Solution

	Sell	Process Further	Net Income Increase (Decrease)
Revenues	$25	$35	$10
Variable costs	12	21	(9)
Fixed costs	8	10	(2)
Net income	$ 5	$ 4	$ (1)

The analysis indicates that the rocking chair should be sold unpainted because net income per chair will be $1 greater.

Related exercise material: **BE21-5, BE21-6, E21-9, E21-10, E21-11, E21-12, and DO IT! 21-3.**

✔ **The Navigator**

Repair, Retain, or Replace Equipment

Management often has to decide whether to continue using an asset, repair, or replace it. For example, Delta Airlines must decide whether to replace old jets with new, more fuel-efficient ones. To illustrate, assume that Jeffcoat Company has a factory machine that originally cost $110,000. It has a balance in Accumulated Depreciation of $70,000, so its book value is $40,000. It has a remaining useful life of four years. The company is considering replacing this machine with a new machine. A new machine is available that costs $120,000. It is expected to have zero salvage value at the end of its four-year useful life. If the new machine is acquired, variable manufacturing costs are expected to decrease from $160,000 to $125,000 annually, and the old unit could be sold for $5,000. The incremental analysis for the **four-year period** is as follows.

Illustration 21-15
Incremental analysis—retain or replace equipment

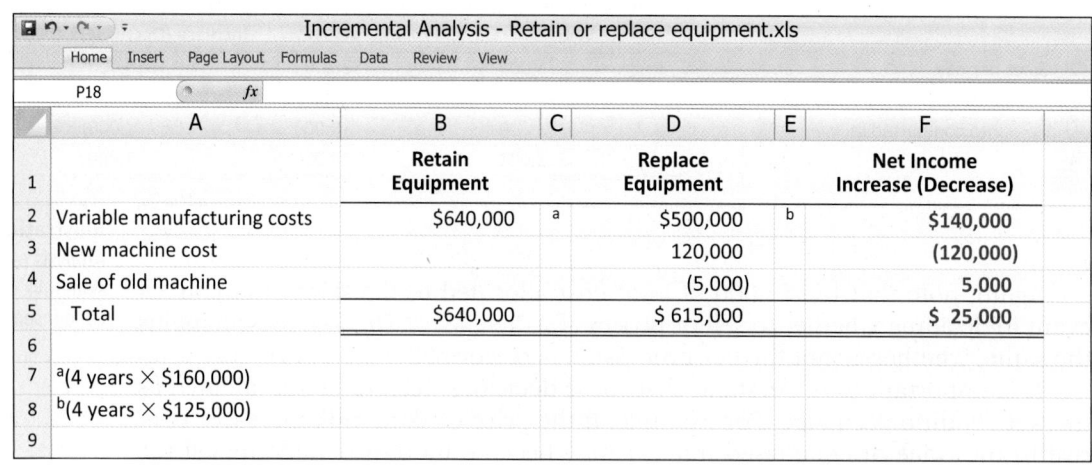

In this case, it would be to the company's advantage to replace the equipment. The lower variable manufacturing costs due to replacement more than offset the cost of the new equipment. Note that the $5,000 received from the sale of the old machine is relevant to the decision because it will only be received if the company chooses to replace its equipment. In general, any trade-in allowance or cash disposal value of existing assets is relevant to the decision to retain or replace equipment.

One other point should be mentioned regarding Jeffcoat's decision: **The book value of the old machine does not affect the decision.** Book value is a **sunk cost**, which is a cost that cannot be changed by any present or future decision. **Sunk costs are not relevant in incremental analysis.** In this example, if the asset is retained, book value will be depreciated over its remaining useful life. Or, if the new unit is acquired, book value will be recognized as a loss of the current period. Thus, the effect of book value on current and future earnings is the same regardless of the replacement decision.

Sometimes, decisions regarding whether to replace equipment are clouded by behavioral decision-making errors. For example, suppose a manager spent $90,000 repairing a machine two months ago. Now, suppose that the machine breaks down again today. The manager might be inclined to think that, because the company recently spent a large amount of money to repair the machine, the machine should now be repaired rather than replaced. However, the amount spent in the past to repair the machine is irrelevant to the current decision. It is a sunk cost.

Similarly, suppose a manager spent $5,000,000 to purchase a new machine. Six months later, a new machine comes on the market that is significantly more efficient than the one recently purchased. The manager might be inclined to think that he or she should not buy the new machine because of the recent purchase. In fact, the manager might fear that buying a different machine so quickly might call into question the merit of the previous decision. Again, the fact that the company recently bought a new machine is not relevant. Instead, the manager should use incremental analysis to determine whether the savings generated by the efficiencies of the new machine would justify its purchase.

Eliminate an Unprofitable Segment or Product

Management sometimes must decide whether to eliminate an unprofitable business segment or product. For example, in recent years, many airlines quit servicing certain cities or cut back on the number of flights. Goodyear quit producing several brands in the low-end tire market. Again, the key is to **focus on the relevant costs— the data that change under the alternative courses of action.** To illustrate, assume that Venus Company manufactures tennis racquets in three models: Pro, Master, and Champ. Pro and Master are profitable lines. Champ (highlighted in red in the table below) operates at a loss. Condensed income statement data are as follows.

LEARNING OBJECTIVE	7

Identify the relevant costs in deciding whether to eliminate an unprofitable segment or product.

Illustration 21-16
Segment income data

	Pro	Master	Champ	Total
Sales	$800,000	$300,000	$100,000	$1,200,000
Variable costs	520,000	210,000	90,000	820,000
Contribution margin	280,000	90,000	10,000	380,000
Fixed costs	80,000	50,000	30,000	160,000
Net income	$200,000	$ 40,000	$ (20,000)	$ 220,000

Helpful Hint
A decision to discontinue a segment based solely on the bottom line—net loss—is inappropriate.

You might think that total net income will increase by $20,000 to $240,000 if the unprofitable Champ line of racquets is eliminated. However, **net income may actually decrease if the Champ line is discontinued**. The reason is that the fixed costs allocated to the Champ racquets will have to be absorbed by the other products. To illustrate, assume that the $30,000 of fixed costs applicable to the unprofitable segment are allocated ⅔ to the Pro model and ⅓ to the Master model if the Champ model is eliminated. Fixed costs will increase to $100,000 ($80,000 + $20,000) in the Pro line and to $60,000 ($50,000 + $10,000) in the Master line. The revised income statement is shown in Illustration 21-17 (page 1056).

Illustration 21-17
Income data after eliminating
unprofitable product line

	Pro	Master	Total
Sales	$800,000	$300,000	$1,100,000
Variable costs	520,000	210,000	730,000
Contribution margin	280,000	90,000	370,000
Fixed costs	**100,000**	**60,000**	160,000
Net income	$180,000	$ 30,000	$ 210,000

Illustration 21-18
Incremental analysis—
eliminating unprofitable
segment with no reduction
in fixed costs

Total net income has decreased $10,000 ($220,000 − $210,000). This result is also obtained in the following incremental analysis of the Champ racquets.

Incremental Analysis - Eliminating an unprofitable segment.xls

Home   Insert   Page Layout   Formulas   Data   Review   View

P18   fx

	A	B	C	D
1		Continue	Eliminate	Net Income Increase (Decrease)
2	Sales	$100,000	$ 0	$(100,000)
3	Variable costs	90,000	0	90,000
4	Contribution margin	10,000	0	(10,000)
5	Fixed costs	30,000	30,000	0
6	Net income	$(20,000)	$(30,000)	$ (10,000)
7				

The loss in net income is attributable to the Champ line's contribution margin ($10,000) that will not be realized if the segment is discontinued.

Assume the same facts as above, except now assume that $22,000 of the fixed costs attributed to the Champ line can be eliminated if the line is discontinued. Illustration 21-19 presents the incremental analysis based on this revised assumption.

Incremental Analysis - Eliminating an unprofitable segment.xls

Home   Insert   Page Layout   Formulas   Data   Review   View

P18   fx

	A	B	C	D
1		Continue	Eliminate	Net Income Increase (Decrease)
2	Sales	$100,000	$ 0	$(100,000)
3	Variable costs	90,000	0	90,000
4	Contribution margin	10,000	0	(10,000)
5	Fixed costs	30,000	8,000	22,000
6	Net income	$(20,000)	$(8,000)	$ 12,000
7				

In this case, because the company is able to eliminate some of its fixed costs by eliminating the division, it can increase its net income by $12,000. **This occurs because the $22,000 savings that results from the eliminated fixed costs exceeds the $10,000 in lost contribution margin by $12,000 ($22,000 − $10,000).**

In deciding on the future status of an unprofitable segment, management should consider the effect of elimination on related product lines. It may be possible for continuing product lines to obtain some or all of the sales lost by the discontinued product line. In some businesses, services or products may be linked—for example, free checking accounts at a bank, or coffee at a donut shop. In addition, management should consider the effect of eliminating the product line on employees who may have to be discharged or retrained.

> DO IT!

Unprofitable Segments

Action Plan

✔ Identify the revenues that will change as a result of eliminating a product line.

✔ Identify all costs that will change as a result of eliminating a product line, and net the amount against the revenues.

Lambert, Inc. manufactures several types of accessories. For the year, the knit hats and scarves line had sales of $400,000, variable expenses of $310,000, and fixed expenses of $120,000. Therefore, the knit hats and scarves line had a net loss of $30,000. If Lambert eliminates the knit hats and scarves line, $20,000 of fixed costs will remain. Prepare an analysis showing whether the company should eliminate the knit hats and scarves line.

Solution

	Continue	Eliminate	Net Income Increase (Decrease)
Sales	$400,000	$ 0	$(400,000)
Variable costs	310,000	0	310,000
Contribution margin	90,000	0	(90,000)
Fixed costs	120,000	20,000	100,000
Net income	$(30,000)	$(20,000)	$ 10,000

The analysis indicates that Lambert should eliminate the knit hats and scarves line because net income will increase $10,000.

Related exercise material: **BE21-8, E21-15, E21-16, E21-17, and DO IT! 21-4.**

✔ **The Navigator**

MANAGEMENT INSIGHT

Time to Move to a New Neighborhood?

If you have ever moved, then you know how complicated and costly it can be. Now consider what it would be like for a manufacturing company with 260 employees and a 170,000-square-foot facility to move from southern California to Idaho. That is what Buck Knives did in order to save its company from financial ruin. Electricity rates in Idaho were half those in California, workers' compensation was one-third the cost, and factory wages were 20% lower. Combined, this would reduce manufacturing costs by $600,000 per year. Moving the factory would cost about $8.5 million, plus $4 million to move key employees. Offsetting these costs was the estimated $11 million selling price of the California property. Based on these estimates, the move would pay for itself in three years.

Ultimately, the company received only $7.5 million for its California property, only 58 of 75 key employees were willing to move, construction was delayed by a year which caused the new plant to increase in price by $1.5 million, and wages surged in Idaho due to low unemployment. Despite all of these complications, though, the company considers the move a great success.

Source: Chris Lydgate, "The Buck Stopped," *Inc. Magazine* (May 2006), pp. 87–95.

 What were some of the factors that complicated the company's decision to move? How should the company have incorporated such factors into its incremental analysis? (See page 1080.)

Other Considerations in Decision-Making

Qualitative Factors

In this chapter, we have focused primarily on the quantitative factors that affect a decision—those attributes that can be easily expressed in terms of numbers or dollars. However, many of the decisions involving incremental analysis have important qualitative features. Though not easily measured, they should not be ignored.

Consider, for example, the potential effects of the make-or-buy decision or of the decision to eliminate a line of business on existing employees and the community in which the plant is located. The cost savings that may be obtained from outsourcing or from eliminating a plant should be weighed against these qualitative attributes. One example would be the cost of lost morale that might result. Al "Chainsaw" Dunlap was a so-called "turnaround" artist who went into many companies, identified inefficiencies (using incremental analysis techniques), and tried to correct these problems to improve corporate profitability. Along the way, he laid off thousands of employees at numerous companies. As head of Sunbeam, it was Al Dunlap who lost his job because his Draconian approach failed to improve Sunbeam's profitability. It was widely reported that Sunbeam's employees openly rejoiced for days after his departure. Clearly, qualitative factors can matter.

Relationship of Incremental Analysis and Activity-Based Costing

In Chapter 18, we noted that many companies have shifted to activity-based costing to allocate overhead costs to products. The primary reason for using activity-based costing is that it results in a more accurate allocation of overhead. The concepts presented in this chapter are completely consistent with the use of activity-based costing. In fact, activity-based costing will result in better identification of relevant costs and, therefore, better incremental analysis.

MANAGEMENT INSIGHT

What Is the Real Cost of Packaging Options?

The existence of excess plant capacity is frequently the incentive for management to add new products. Adding one new product may not add much incremental cost. But continuing to add products will at some point create new constraints, perhaps requiring additional investments in people, equipment, and facilities.

The effects of product and product line proliferation are generally understood. But the effect on incremental overhead costs of changes *in servicing customers* is less understood. For example, if a company newly offers its customers the option of product delivery by case or by pallet, the new service may appear to be simple and low in cost. But, if the manufacturing process must be realigned to package in two different forms; if two sets of inventory records must be maintained; and if warehousing, handling, and shipping require two different arrangements or sets of equipment, the additional costs of this new option could be as high as a whole new product. If the customer service option were adopted for all products, the product line could effectively be doubled—but so might many overhead costs.

Source: Elizabeth Haas Edersheim and Joan Wilson, "Complexity at Consumer Goods Companies: Naming and Taming the Beast," *Journal of Cost Management* (Fall 1992), pp. 26–36.

 If your marketing director suggests that, in addition to selling your cereal in a standard-size box, you should sell a jumbo size and an individual size, what issues must you consider? (See page 1080.)

> Comprehensive **DO IT!**

Walston Company produces kitchen cabinets for homebuilders across the western United States. The cost of producing 5,000 cabinets is as follows.

Materials	$ 500,000
Labor	250,000
Variable overhead	100,000
Fixed overhead	400,000
Total	$1,250,000

Walston also incurs selling expenses of $20 per cabinet. Wellington Corp. has offered Walston $165 per cabinet for a special order of 1,000 cabinets. The cabinets would be sold to homebuilders in the eastern United States and thus would not conflict with Walston's current sales. Selling expenses per cabinet would be only $5 per cabinet. Walston has available capacity to do the work.

Instructions

(a) Prepare an incremental analysis for the special order.

(b) Should Walston accept the special order? Why or why not?

Solution to Comprehensive

Action Plan

✔ Determine the relevant cost per unit of the special order.

✔ Identify the relevant costs and revenues for the units to be produced.

✔ Compare the results related to accepting the special order versus rejecting the special order.

(a) Relevant costs per unit would be:

Materials	$500,000/5,000 = $100
Labor	250,000/5,000 = 50
Variable overhead	100,000/5,000 = 20
Selling expenses	5
Total relevant cost per unit	$175

	Reject Order	Accept Order	Net Income Increase (Decrease)
Revenues	$0	$165,000	$165,000
Costs	0	175,000	(175,000)
Net income	$0	$ (10,000)	$ (10,000)

(b) Walston should reject the offer. The incremental benefit of $165 per cabinet is less than the incremental cost of $175. By accepting the order, Walston's net income would actually decline by $10,000.

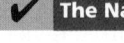 The Navigator

SUMMARY OF LEARNING OBJECTIVES

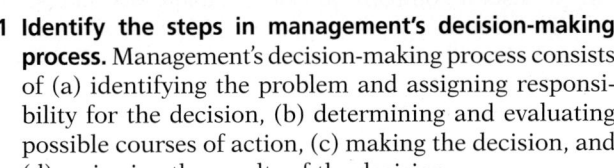 The Navigator

1 **Identify the steps in management's decision-making process.** Management's decision-making process consists of (a) identifying the problem and assigning responsibility for the decision, (b) determining and evaluating possible courses of action, (c) making the decision, and (d) reviewing the results of the decision.

2 **Describe the concept of incremental analysis.** Incremental analysis identifies financial data that change under alternative courses of action. These data are relevant to the decision because they will vary in the future among the possible alternatives.

3 **Identify the relevant costs in accepting an order at a special price.** The relevant costs are those that change if the order is accepted. The relevant information in accepting an order at a special price is the difference between the variable manufacturing costs to produce the special order and expected revenues. Any changes in fixed costs, opportunity cost, or other incremental costs or savings (such as additional shipping) should be considered.

4 **Identify the relevant costs in a make-or-buy decision.** In a make-or-buy decision, the relevant costs are (a) the variable manufacturing costs that will be saved as well

as changes to fixed manufacturing costs, (b) the purchase price, and (c) opportunity cost.

5 Identify the relevant costs in determining whether to sell or process materials further. The decision rule for whether to sell or process materials further is: Process further as long as the incremental revenue from processing exceeds the incremental processing costs.

6 Identify the relevant costs to be considered in repairing, retaining, or replacing equipment. The relevant costs to be considered in determining whether equipment

should be repaired, retained, or replaced are the effects on variable costs and the cost of the new equipment. Also, any disposal value of the existing asset must be considered.

7 Identify the relevant costs in deciding whether to eliminate an unprofitable segment or product. In deciding whether to eliminate an unprofitable segment or product, the relevant costs are the variable costs that drive the contribution margin, if any, produced by the segment or product. Disposition of the segment's or the product's fixed expenses and opportunity cost must also be considered.

GLOSSARY

Incremental analysis The process of identifying the financial data that change under alternative courses of action. (p. 1044).

Joint costs For joint products, all costs incurred prior to the point at which the two products are separately identifiable (known as the *split-off point*). (p. 1052).

Joint products Multiple end-products produced from a single raw material and a common production process. (p. 1052).

Opportunity cost The potential benefit that is lost when one course of action is chosen rather than an alternative course of action. (p. 1045).

Relevant costs Those costs and revenues that differ across alternatives. (p. 1045).

Sunk cost A cost that cannot be changed or avoided by any present or future decision. (p. 1045).

 Self-Test, Brief Exercises, Exercises, Problem Set A, and many more resources are available for practice in WileyPLUS.

SELF-TEST QUESTIONS

Answers are at the end of the chapter.

(LO 1) **1.** Three of the steps in management's decision-making process are (1) review results of decision, (2) determine and evaluate possible courses of action, and (3) make the decision. The steps are prepared in the following order:
  (a) (1), (2), (3).   (c) (2), (1), (3).
  (b) (3), (2), (1).   (d) (2), (3), (1).

(LO 2) **2.** Incremental analysis is the process of identifying the financial data that:
  (a) do not change under alternative courses of action.
  (b) change under alternative courses of action.
  (c) are mixed under alternative courses of action.
  (d) No correct answer is given.

(LO 1, 2) **3.** In making business decisions, management ordinarily considers:
  (a) quantitative factors but not qualitative factors.
  (b) financial information only.
  (c) both financial and nonfinancial information.
  (d) relevant costs, opportunity cost, and sunk costs.

(LO 2) **4.** A company is considering the following alternatives:

	Alternative A	Alternative B
Revenues	$50,000	$50,000
Variable costs	24,000	24,000
Fixed costs	12,000	15,000

Which of the following are relevant in choosing between these alternatives?
  (a) Revenues, variable costs, and fixed costs.
  (b) Variable costs and fixed costs.
  (c) Variable costs only.
  (d) Fixed costs only.

(LO 3) **5.** It costs a company $14 of variable costs and $6 of fixed costs to produce product Z200 that sells for $30. A foreign buyer offers to purchase 3,000 units at $18 each. If the special offer is accepted and produced with unused capacity, net income will:
  (a) decrease $6,000.   (c) increase $12,000.
  (b) increase $6,000.   (d) increase $9,000.

(LO 3) **6.** It costs a company $14 of variable costs and $6 of fixed costs to produce product Z200. Product Z200 sells for $30. A buyer offers to purchase 3,000 units at $18 each. The seller will incur special shipping costs of $5 per unit. If the special offer is accepted and produced with unused capacity, net income will:
  (a) increase $3,000.   (c) decrease $12,000.
  (b) increase $12,000.   (d) decrease $3,000.

(LO 3) **7.** Jobart Company is currently operating at full capacity. It is considering buying a part from an outside supplier rather than making it in-house. If Jobart purchases the part, it can use the released productive capacity

to generate additional income of $30,000 from producing a different product. When conducting incremental analysis in this make-or-buy decision, the company should:
(a) ignore the $30,000.
(b) add $30,000 to other costs in the "Make" column.
(c) add $30,000 to other costs in the "Buy" column.
(d) subtract $30,000 from the other costs in the "Make" column.

(LO 4) **8.** In a make-or-buy decision, relevant costs are:
(a) manufacturing costs that will be saved.
(b) the purchase price of the units.
(c) the opportunity cost.
(d) All of the above.

(LO 4) **9.** Derek is performing incremental analysis in a make-or-buy decision for Item X. If Derek buys Item X, he can use its released productive capacity to produce Item Z. Derek will sell Item Z for $12,000 and incur production costs of $8,000. Derek's incremental analysis should include an opportunity cost of:
(a) $12,000.   (c) $4,000.
(b) $8,000.   (d) $0.

(LO 5) **10.** The decision rule in a sell-or-process-further decision is: process further as long as the incremental revenue from processing exceeds:
(a) incremental processing costs.
(b) variable processing costs.
(c) fixed processing costs.
(d) No correct answer is given.

(LO 5) **11.** Walton, Inc. makes an unassembled product that it currently sells for $55. Production costs are $20. Walton is considering assembling the product and selling it for $68. The cost to assemble the product is estimated at $12. What decision should Walton make?
(a) Sell before assembly; net income per unit will be $12 greater.
(b) Sell before assembly; net income per unit will be $1 greater.
(c) Process further; net income per unit will be $13 greater.
(d) Process further; net income per unit will be $1 greater.

12. In a decision to retain or replace equipment, the book (LO 6) value of the old equipment is a (an):
(a) opportunity cost.   (c) incremental cost.
(b) sunk cost.   (d) marginal cost.

13. If an unprofitable segment is eliminated: (LO 7)
(a) net income will always increase.
(b) variable expenses of the eliminated segment will have to be absorbed by other segments.
(c) fixed expenses allocated to the eliminated segment will have to be absorbed by other segments.
(d) net income will always decrease.

14. A segment of Hazard Inc. has the following data. (LO 7)

Sales	$200,000
Variable expenses	140,000
Fixed expenses	100,000

If this segment is eliminated, what will be the effect on the remaining company? Assume that 50% of the fixed expenses will be eliminated and the rest will be allocated to the segments of the remaining company.
(a) $120,000 increase.   (c) $50,000 increase.
(b) $10,000 decrease.   (d) $10,000 increase.

Go to the book's companion website, www.wiley.com/college/weygandt, for additional Self-Test Questions.

 **The Navigator**

QUESTIONS

1. What steps are frequently involved in management's decision-making process?

2. Your roommate, Anna Polis, contends that accounting contributes to most of the steps in management's decision-making process. Is your roommate correct? Explain.

3. "Incremental analysis involves the accumulation of information concerning a single course of action." Do you agree? Why?

4. Sydney Greene asks for your help concerning the relevance of variable and fixed costs in incremental analysis. Help Sydney with her problem.

5. What data are relevant in deciding whether to accept an order at a special price?

6. Emil Corporation has an opportunity to buy parts at $9 each that currently cost $12 to make. What manufacturing costs are relevant to this make-or-buy decision?

7. Define the term "opportunity cost." How may this cost be relevant in a make-or-buy decision?

8. What is the decision rule in deciding whether to sell a product or process it further?

9. What are joint products? What accounting issue results from the production process that creates joint products?

10. How are allocated joint costs treated when making a sell-or-process-further decision?

11. Your roommate, Gale Dunham, is confused about sunk costs. Explain to your roommate the meaning of sunk costs and their relevance to a decision to retain or replace equipment.

12. Huang Inc. has one product line that is unprofitable. What circumstances may cause overall company net income to be lower if the unprofitable product line is eliminated?

Identify the steps in management's decision-making process.

(LO 1)

BE21-1 The steps in management's decision-making process are listed in random order below. Indicate the order in which the steps should be executed.

_____ Make a decision   _____ Review results of the decision

_____ Identify the problem and assign   _____ Determine and evaluate possible
responsibility   courses of action

Determine incremental changes.

(LO 2)

BE21-2 Bogart Company is considering two alternatives. Alternative A will have revenues of $160,000 and costs of $100,000. Alternative B will have revenues of $180,000 and costs of $125,000. Compare Alternative A to Alternative B showing incremental revenues, costs, and net income.

Determine whether to accept a special order.

(LO 3)

BE21-3 At Jaymes Company, it costs $30 per unit ($20 variable and $10 fixed) to make a product at full capacity that normally sells for $45. A foreign wholesaler offers to buy 3,000 units at $25 each. Jaymes will incur special shipping costs of $2 per unit. Assuming that Jaymes has excess operating capacity, indicate the net income (loss) Jaymes would realize by accepting the special order.

Determine whether to make or buy a part.

(LO 4)

BE21-4 Manson Industries incurs unit costs of $8 ($5 variable and $3 fixed) in making a subassembly part for its finished product. A supplier offers to make 10,000 of the assembly part at $6 per unit. If the offer is accepted, Manson will save all variable costs but no fixed costs. Prepare an analysis showing the total cost saving, if any, Manson will realize by buying the part.

Determine whether to sell or process further.

(LO 5)

BE21-5 Chudrick Inc. makes unfinished bookcases that it sells for $62. Production costs are $36 variable and $10 fixed. Because it has unused capacity, Chudrick is considering finishing the bookcases and selling them for $70. Variable finishing costs are expected to be $7 per unit with no increase in fixed costs. Prepare an analysis on a per unit basis showing whether Chudrick should sell unfinished or finished bookcases.

Determine whether to sell or process further, joint products.

(LO 5)

BE21-6 Each day, Adama Corporation processes 1 ton of a secret raw material into two resulting products, AB1 and XY1. When it processes 1 ton of the raw material, the company incurs joint processing costs of $60,000. It allocates $25,000 of these costs to AB1 and $35,000 of these costs to XY1. The resulting AB1 can be sold for $100,000. Alternatively, it can be processed further to make AB2 at an additional processing cost of $45,000, and sold for $150,000. Each day's batch of XY1 can be sold for $95,000. Alternatively, it can be processed further to create XY2, at an additional processing cost of $50,000, and sold for $130,000. Discuss what products Adama Corporation should make.

Determine whether to retain or replace equipment.

(LO 6)

BE21-7 Kobe Company has a factory machine with a book value of $90,000 and a remaining useful life of 5 years. It can be sold for $30,000. A new machine is available at a cost of $300,000. This machine will have a 5-year useful life with no salvage value. The new machine will lower annual variable manufacturing costs from $600,000 to $500,000. Prepare an analysis showing whether the old machine should be retained or replaced.

Determine whether to eliminate an unprofitable segment.

(LO 7)

BE21-8 Lisah, Inc., manufactures golf clubs in three models. For the year, the Big Bart line has a net loss of $10,000 from sales $200,000, variable costs $180,000, and fixed costs $30,000. If the Big Bart line is eliminated, $20,000 of fixed costs will remain. Prepare an analysis showing whether the Big Bart line should be eliminated.

> **DO IT! REVIEW**

Evaluate special order.

(LO 3)

DO IT! 21-1 Maize Company incurs a cost of $35 per unit, of which $20 is variable, to make a product that normally sells for $58. A foreign wholesaler offers to buy 6,000 units at $30 each. Maize will incur additional costs of $3 per unit to imprint a logo and to pay for shipping. Compute the increase or decrease in net income Maize will realize by accepting the special order, assuming Maize has sufficient excess operating capacity. Should Maize Company accept the special order?

DO IT! **21-2** Rubble Company must decide whether to make or buy some of its components. The costs of producing 60,000 switches for its generators are as follows.

Direct materials	$30,000	Variable overhead	$45,000
Direct labor	$42,000	Fixed overhead	$60,000

Instead of making the switches at an average cost of $2.95 ($177,000 ÷ 60,000), the company has an opportunity to buy the switches at $2.70 per unit. If the company purchases the switches, all the variable costs and one-fourth of the fixed costs will be eliminated.

(a) Prepare an incremental analysis showing whether the company should make or buy the switches. (b) Would your answer be different if the released productive capacity will generate additional income of $34,000?

Evaluate make-or-buy opportunity.

(LO 4)

DO IT! **21-3** Mesa Verde manufactures unpainted furniture for the do-it-yourself (DIY) market. It currently sells a table for $75. Production costs are $40 variable and $10 fixed. Mesa Verde is considering staining and sealing the table to sell it for $100. Variable costs to finish each table are expected to be $17, and fixed costs are expected to be $3.

Prepare an analysis showing whether Mesa Verde should sell unpainted or finished tables.

Sell or process further.

(LO 5)

DO IT! **21-4** Gator Corporation manufactures several types of accessories. For the year, the gloves and mittens line had sales of $500,000, variable expenses of $370,000, and fixed expenses of $150,000. Therefore, the gloves and mittens line had a net loss of $20,000. If Gator eliminates the line, $38,000 of fixed costs will remain.

Prepare an analysis showing whether the company should eliminate the gloves and mittens line.

Analyze whether to eliminate unprofitable segment.

(LO 7)

 The Navigator

EXERCISES

E21-1 Ortega has prepared the following list of statements about decision-making and incremental analysis.

1. The first step in management's decision-making process is, "Determine and evaluate possible courses of action."
2. The final step in management's decision-making process is to actually make the decision.
3. Accounting's contribution to management's decision-making process occurs primarily in evaluating possible courses of action and in reviewing the results.
4. In making business decisions, management ordinarily considers only financial information because it is objectively determined.
5. Decisions involve a choice among alternative courses of action.
6. The process used to identify the financial data that change under alternative courses of action is called incremental analysis.
7. Costs that are the same under all alternative courses of action sometimes affect the decision.
8. When using incremental analysis, some costs will always change under alternative courses of action, but revenues will not.
9. Variable costs will change under alternative courses of action, but fixed costs will not.

Analyze statements about decision-making and incremental analysis.

(LO 1, 2)

Instructions
Identify each statement as true or false. If false, indicate how to correct the statement.

E21-2 Gruden Company produces golf discs which it normally sells to retailers for $7 each. The cost of manufacturing 20,000 golf discs is:

Materials	$ 10,000
Labor	30,000
Variable overhead	20,000
Fixed overhead	40,000
Total	$100,000

Gruden also incurs 5% sales commission ($0.35) on each disc sold.

Use incremental analysis for special-order decision.

(LO 3)

McGee Corporation offers Gruden $4.80 per disc for 5,000 discs. McGee would sell the discs under its own brand name in foreign markets not yet served by Gruden. If Gruden accepts the offer, its fixed overhead will increase from $40,000 to $46,000 due to the purchase of a new imprinting machine. No sales commission will result from the special order.

Instructions
(a) Prepare an incremental analysis for the special order.
(b) Should Gruden accept the special order? Why or why not?
(c) What assumptions underlie the decision made in part (b)?

Use incremental analysis for special order.

(LO 3)

E21-3 Leno Company manufactures toasters. For the first 8 months of 2014, the company reported the following operating results while operating at 75% of plant capacity:

Sales (350,000 units)	$4,375,000
Cost of goods sold	2,600,000
Gross profit	1,775,000
Operating expenses	840,000
Net income	$ 935,000

Cost of goods sold was 70% variable and 30% fixed; operating expenses were 75% variable and 25% fixed.

In September, Leno Company receives a special order for 15,000 toasters at $7.60 each from Centro Company of Ciudad Juarez. Acceptance of the order would result in an additional $3,000 of shipping costs but no increase in fixed operating expenses.

Instructions
(a) Prepare an incremental analysis for the special order.
(b) ▭▭▭▭▷ Should Leno Company accept the special order? Why or why not?

Use incremental analysis for special order.

(LO 3)

E21-4 Klean Fiber Company is the creator of Y-Go, a technology that weaves silver into its fabrics to kill bacteria and odor on clothing while managing heat. Y-Go has become very popular as an undergarment for sports activities. Operating at capacity, the company can produce 1,000,000 undergarments of Y-Go a year. The per unit and the total costs for an individual garment when the company operates at full capacity are as follows.

	Per Undergarment	Total
Direct materials	$2.00	$2,000,000
Direct labor	0.75	750,000
Variable manufacturing overhead	1.00	1,000,000
Fixed manufacturing overhead	1.50	1,500,000
Variable selling expenses	0.25	250,000
Totals	$5.50	$5,500,000

The U.S. Army has approached Klean Fiber and expressed an interest in purchasing 250,000 Y-Go undergarments for soldiers in extremely warm climates. The Army would pay the unit cost for direct materials, direct labor, and variable manufacturing overhead costs. In addition, the Army has agreed to pay an additional $1 per undergarment to cover all other costs and provide a profit. Presently, Klean Fiber is operating at 70% capacity and does not have any other potential buyers for Y-Go. If Klean Fiber accepts the Army's offer, it will not incur any variable selling expenses related to this order.

Instructions
Using incremental analysis, determine whether Klean Fiber should accept the Army's offer.

Use incremental analysis for make-or-buy decision.

(LO 4)

E21-5 Schopp Inc. has been manufacturing its own shades for its table lamps. The company is currently operating at 100% of capacity, and variable manufacturing overhead is charged to production at the rate of 70% of direct labor cost. The direct materials and direct labor cost per unit to make the lamp shades are $4 and $5, respectively. Normal production is 30,000 table lamps per year.

A supplier offers to make the lamp shades at a price of $12.75 per unit. If Schopp Inc. accepts the supplier's offer, all variable manufacturing costs will be eliminated, but the $45,000 of fixed manufacturing overhead currently being charged to the lamp shades will have to be absorbed by other products.

Instructions

(a) Prepare the incremental analysis for the decision to make or buy the lamp shades.

(b) ▯▯▯▯▯▶ Should Schopp Inc. buy the lamp shades?

(c) ▯▯▯▯▯▶ Would your answer be different in (b) if the productive capacity released by not making the lamp shades could be used to produce income of $25,000?

E21-6 Jobs, Inc. has recently started the manufacture of Tri-Robo, a three-wheeled robot that can scan a home for fires and gas leaks and then transmit this information to a mobile phone. The cost structure to manufacture 20,000 Tri-Robos is as follows.

Use incremental analysis for make-or-buy decision.

(LO 4)

	Cost
Direct materials ($50 per robot)	$1,000,000
Direct labor ($40 per robot)	800,000
Variable overhead ($6 per robot)	120,000
Allocated fixed overhead ($30 per robot)	600,000
Total	$2,520,000

Jobs is approached by Tienh Inc., which offers to make Tri-Robo for $115 per unit or $2,300,000.

Instructions

(a) Using incremental analysis, determine whether Jobs should accept this offer under each of the following independent assumptions.

(1) Assume that $405,000 of the fixed overhead cost can be reduced (avoided).

(2) Assume that none of the fixed overhead can be reduced (avoided). However, if the robots are purchased from Tienh Inc., Jobs can use the released productive resources to generate additional income of $405,000.

(b) Describe the qualitative factors that might affect the decision to purchase the robots from an outside supplier.

E21-7 Gibbs Company purchases sails and produces sailboats. It currently produces 1,200 sailboats per year, operating at normal capacity, which is about 80% of full capacity. Gibbs purchases sails at $250 each, but the company is considering using the excess capacity to manufacture the sails instead. The manufacturing cost per sail would be $100 for direct materials, $80 for direct labor, and $100 for overhead. The $100 overhead is based on $78,000 of annual fixed overhead that is allocated using normal capacity.

Prepare incremental analysis for make-or-buy decision.

(LO 4)

The president of Gibbs has come to you for advice. "It would cost me $280 to make the sails," she says, "but only $250 to buy them. Should I continue buying them, or have I missed something?"

Instructions

(a) Prepare a per unit analysis of the differential costs. Briefly explain whether Gibbs should make or buy the sails.

(b) If Gibbs suddenly finds an opportunity to rent out the unused capacity of its factory for $77,000 per year, would your answer to part (a) change? Briefly explain.

(c) Identify three qualitative factors that should be considered by Gibbs in this make-or-buy decision.

(CGA adapted)

E21-8 Innova uses 1,000 units of the component IMC2 every month to manufacture one of its products. The unit costs incurred to manufacture the component are as follows.

Prepare incremental analysis concerning make-or-buy decision.

(LO 4)

Direct materials	$ 65.00
Direct labor	45.00
Overhead	126.50
Total	$236.50

Overhead costs include variable material handling costs of $6.50, which are applied to products on the basis of direct material costs. The remainder of the overhead costs are applied on the basis of direct labor dollars and consist of 60% variable costs and 40% fixed costs.

A vendor has offered to supply the IMC2 component at a price of $200 per unit.

Instructions

(a) Should Innova purchase the component from the outside vendor if Innova's capacity remains idle?

(b) Should Innova purchase the component from the outside vendor if it can use its facilities to manufacture another product? What information will Innova need to make an accurate decision? Show your calculations.

(c) What are the qualitative factors that Innova will have to consider when making this decision?

(CGA adapted)

Use incremental analysis for further processing of materials decision.

(LO 5)

E21-9 Rachel Rey recently opened her own basketweaving studio. She sells finished baskets in addition to the raw materials needed by customers to weave baskets of their own. Rachel has put together a variety of raw material kits, each including materials at various stages of completion. Unfortunately, owing to space limitations, Rachel is unable to carry all varieties of kits originally assembled and must choose between two basic packages.

The basic introductory kit includes undyed, uncut reeds (with dye included) for weaving one basket. This basic package costs Rachel $14 and sells for $30. The second kit, called Stage 2, includes cut reeds that have already been dyed. With this kit the customer need only soak the reeds and weave the basket. Rachel is able to produce the second kit by using the basic materials included in the first kit and adding one hour of her own time, which she values at $18 per hour. Because she is more efficient at cutting and dying reeds than her average customer, Rachel is able to make two kits of the dyed reeds, in one hour, from one kit of undyed reeds. The Stage 2 kit sells for $35.

Instructions

Determine whether Rachel's basketweaving shop should carry the basic introductory kit with undyed and uncut reeds or the Stage 2 kit with reeds already dyed and cut. Prepare an incremental analysis to support your answer.

Determine whether to sell or process further, joint products.

(LO 5)

E21-10 Stahl Inc. produces three separate products from a common process costing $100,000. Each of the products can be sold at the split-off point or can be processed further and then sold for a higher price. Shown below are cost and selling price data for a recent period.

	Sales Value at Split-Off Point	Cost to Process Further	Sales Value after Further Processing
Product 10	$60,000	$100,000	$190,000
Product 12	15,000	30,000	35,000
Product 14	55,000	150,000	215,000

Instructions

(a) Determine total net income if all products are sold at the split-off point.

(b) Determine total net income if all products are sold after further processing.

(c) Using incremental analysis, determine which products should be sold at the split-off point and which should be processed further.

(d) Determine total net income using the results from (c) and explain why the net income is different from that determined in (b).

Determine whether to sell or process further, joint products.

(LO 5)

E21-11 Chen Minerals processes materials extracted from mines. The most common raw material that it processes results in three joint products: Larco, Marco, and Narco. Each of these products can be sold as is, or each can be processed further and sold for a higher price. The company incurs joint costs of $180,000 to process one batch of the raw material that produces the three joint products. The following cost and sales information is available for one batch of each product.

	Sales Value at Split-Off Point	Allocated Joint Costs	Cost to Process Further	Sales Value of Processed Product
Larco	$200,000	$40,000	$110,000	$300,000
Marco	300,000	60,000	85,000	400,000
Narco	405,000	80,000	250,000	800,000

Instructions

Determine whether each of the three joint products should be sold as is, or processed further.

E21-12 A company manufactures three products using the same production process. The costs incurred up to the split-off point are $200,000. These costs are allocated to the products on the basis of their sales value at the split-off point. The number of units produced, the selling prices per unit of the three products at the split-off point and after further processing, and the additional processing costs are as follows.

Prepare incremental analysis for whether to sell or process materials further.

(LO 5)

Product	Number of Units Produced	Selling Price at Split-Off	Selling Price after Processing	Additional Processing Costs
D	4,000	$10.00	$15.00	$14,000
E	6,000	11.60	16.20	20,000
F	2,000	19.40	22.60	9,000

Instructions

(a) Which information is relevant to the decision on whether or not to process the products further? Explain why this information is relevant.

(b) Which product(s) should be processed further and which should be sold at the split-off point?

(c) Would your decision be different if the company was using the quantity of output to allocate joint costs? Explain.

(CGA adapted)

E21-13 On January 2, 2013, Benson Hospital purchased a $100,000 special radiology scanner from Picard Inc. The scanner had a useful life of 4 years and was estimated to have no disposal value at the end of its useful life. The straight-line method of depreciation is used on this scanner. Annual operating costs with this scanner are $105,000.

Use incremental analysis for retaining or replacing equipment decision.

(LO 6)

Approximately one year later, the hospital is approached by Dyno Technology salesperson, Meg Ryan, who indicated that purchasing the scanner in 2013 from Picard Inc. was a mistake. She points out that Dyno has a scanner that will save Benson Hospital $30,000 a year in operating expenses over its 3-year useful life. She notes that the new scanner will cost $110,000 and has the same capabilities as the scanner purchased last year. The hospital agrees that both scanners are of equal quality. The new scanner will have no disposal value. Ryan agrees to buy the old scanner from Benson Hospital for $40,000.

Instructions

(a) If Benson Hospital sells its old scanner on January 2, 2014, compute the gain or loss on the sale.

(b) Using incremental analysis, determine if Benson Hospital should purchase the new scanner on January 2, 2014.

(c) Explain why Benson Hospital might be reluctant to purchase the new scanner, regardless of the results indicated by the incremental analysis in (b).

E21-14 Johnson Enterprises uses a computer to handle its sales invoices. Lately, business has been so good that it takes an extra 3 hours per night, plus every third Saturday, to keep up with the volume of sales invoices. Management is considering updating its computer with a faster model that would eliminate all of the overtime processing.

Use incremental analysis for retaining or replacing equipment decision.

(LO 6)

	Current Machine	New Machine
Original purchase cost	$15,000	$25,000
Accumulated depreciation	$ 6,000	—
Estimated annual operating costs	$25,000	$20,000
Useful life	5 years	5 years

If sold now, the current machine would have a salvage value of $6,000. If operated for the remainder of its useful life, the current machine would have zero salvage value. The new machine is expected to have zero salvage value after 5 years.

Instructions

Should the current machine be replaced?

Use incremental analysis concerning elimination of division.

(LO 7)

E21-15 Judy Jean, a recent graduate of Rolling's accounting program, evaluated the operating performance of Artie Company's six divisions. Judy made the following presentation to Artie's board of directors and suggested the Huron Division be eliminated. "If the Huron Division is eliminated," she said, "our total profits would increase by $26,000."

	The Other Five Divisions	Huron Division	Total
Sales	$1,664,200	$100,000	$1,764,200
Cost of goods sold	978,520	76,000	1,054,520
Gross profit	685,680	24,000	709,680
Operating expenses	527,940	50,000	577,940
Net income	$ 157,740	$ (26,000)	$ 131,740

In the Huron Division, cost of goods sold is $61,000 variable and $15,000 fixed, and operating expenses are $26,000 variable and $24,000 fixed. None of the Huron Division's fixed costs will be eliminated if the division is discontinued.

Instructions

▭▭▭▷ Is Judy right about eliminating the Huron Division? Prepare a schedule to support your answer.

Use incremental analysis for elimination of a product line.

(LO 7)

E21-16 Cawley Company makes three models of tasers. Information on the three products is given below.

	Tingler	Shocker	Stunner
Sales	$300,000	$500,000	$200,000
Variable expenses	150,000	200,000	145,000
Contribution margin	150,000	300,000	55,000
Fixed expenses	120,000	230,000	95,000
Net income	$ 30,000	$ 70,000	$ (40,000)

Fixed expenses consist of $300,000 of common costs allocated to the three products based on relative sales, and additional fixed expenses of $30,000 (Tingler), $80,000 (Shocker), and $35,000 (Stunner). The common costs will be incurred regardless of how many models are produced. The other fixed expenses would be eliminated if a model is phased out.

James Watt, an executive with the company, feels the Stunner line should be discontinued to increase the company's net income.

Instructions

(a) Compute current net income for Cawley Company.
(b) Compute net income by product line and in total for Cawley Company if the company discontinues the Stunner product line. (*Hint:* Allocate the $300,000 common costs to the two remaining product lines based on their relative sales.)
(c) Should Cawley eliminate the Stunner product line? Why or why not?

Prepare incremental analysis concerning keeping or dropping a product to maximize operating income.

(LO 2, 7)

E21-17 Twyla Company operates a small factory in which it manufactures two products: C and D. Production and sales results for last year were as follows.

	C	D
Units sold	9,000	20,000
Selling price per unit	$95	$75
Variable cost per unit	50	40
Fixed cost per unit	22	22

For purposes of simplicity, the firm averages total fixed costs over the total number of units of C and D produced and sold.

The research department has developed a new product (E) as a replacement for product D. Market studies show that Twyla Company could sell 10,000 units of E next year at a price of $115; the variable cost per unit of E is $40. The introduction of product E will lead to a 10% increase in demand for product C and discontinuation of product D. If the company does not introduce the new product, it expects next year's results to be the same as last year's.

Instructions

Should Twyla Company introduce product E next year? Explain why or why not. Show calculations to support your decision.

(CMA-Canada adapted)

E21-18 The costs listed below relate to a variety of different decision situations.

Identify relevant costs for different decisions.

(LO 3, 4, 5, 6, 7)

Cost	Decision
1. Unavoidable fixed overhead	Eliminate an unprofitable segment
2. Direct labor	Make or buy
3. Original cost of old equipment	Equipment replacement
4. Joint production costs	Sell or process further
5. Opportunity cost	Accepting a special order
6. Segment manager's salary	Eliminate an unprofitable segment (manager will be terminated)
7. Cost of new equipment	Equipment replacement
8. Incremental production costs	Sell or process further
9. Direct materials	Equipment replacement (the amount of materials required does not change)
10. Rent expense	Purchase or lease a building

Instructions

For each cost listed above, indicate if it is relevant or not to the related decision. For those costs determined to be irrelevant, briefly explain why.

EXERCISES: SET B AND CHALLENGE EXERCISES

Visit the book's companion website, at **www.wiley.com/college/weygandt**, and choose the Student Companion site to access Exercise Set B and Challenge Exercises.

PROBLEMS: SET A

P21-1A ShurShot Sports Inc. manufactures basketballs for the National Basketball Association (NBA). For the first 6 months of 2014, the company reported the following operating results while operating at 80% of plant capacity and producing 120,000 units.

Use incremental analysis for special order and identify nonfinancial factors in the decision.

(LO 3)

	Amount
Sales	$4,800,000
Cost of goods sold	3,600,000
Selling and administrative expenses	405,000
Net income	$ 795,000

Fixed costs for the period were cost of goods sold $960,000, and selling and administrative expenses $225,000.

In July, normally a slack manufacturing month, ShurShot Sports receives a special order for 10,000 basketballs at $27 each from the Greek Basketball Association (GBA). Acceptance of the order would increase variable selling and administrative expenses $0.50 per unit because of shipping costs but would not increase fixed costs and expenses.

Instructions

(a) Prepare an incremental analysis for the special order.

(a) NI increase $30,000

(b) Should ShurShot Sports Inc. accept the special order? Explain your answer.

(c) What is the minimum selling price on the special order to produce net income of $4.00 per ball?

(d) ▭▭▭▭▷ What nonfinancial factors should management consider in making its decision?

P21-2A The management of Shatner Manufacturing Company is trying to decide whether to continue manufacturing a part or to buy it from an outside supplier. The part, called CISCO, is a component of the company's finished product.

The following information was collected from the accounting records and production data for the year ending December 31, 2014.

Use incremental analysis related to make or buy, consider opportunity cost, and identify nonfinancial factors.

(LO 4)

1. 8,000 units of CISCO were produced in the Machining Department.
2. Variable manufacturing costs applicable to the production of each CISCO unit were: direct materials $4.80, direct labor $4.30, indirect labor $0.43, utilities $0.40.
3. Fixed manufacturing costs applicable to the production of CISCO were:

Cost Item	Direct	Allocated
Depreciation	$2,100	$ 900
Property taxes	500	200
Insurance	900	600
	$3,500	$1,700

All variable manufacturing and direct fixed costs will be eliminated if CISCO is purchased. Allocated costs will have to be absorbed by other production departments.
4. The lowest quotation for 8,000 CISCO units from a supplier is $80,000.
5. If CISCO units are purchased, freight and inspection costs would be $0.35 per unit, and receiving costs totaling $1,300 per year would be incurred by the Machining Department.

Instructions

(a) Prepare an incremental analysis for CISCO. Your analysis should have columns for (1) Make CISCO, (2) Buy CISCO, and (3) Net Income Increase/(Decrease).
(b) Based on your analysis, what decision should management make?
(c) Would the decision be different if Shatner Company has the opportunity to produce $3,000 of net income with the facilities currently being used to manufacture CISCO? Show computations.
(d) ▯▭▭▭▶ What nonfinancial factors should management consider in making its decision?

(a) NI (decrease) $(1,160)

(c) NI increase $1,840

Determine if product should be sold or processed further.

(LO 5)

P21-3A Sutton Industrial Products Inc. (SIPI) is a diversified industrial-cleaner processing company. The company's Verde plant produces two products: a table cleaner and a floor cleaner from a common set of chemical inputs (CDG). Each week 900,000 ounces of chemical input are processed at a cost of $210,000 into 600,000 ounces of floor cleaner and 300,000 ounces of table cleaner. The floor cleaner has no market value until it is converted into a polish with the trade name FloorShine. The additional processing costs for this conversion amount to $240,000.

FloorShine sells at $20 per 30-ounce bottle. The table cleaner can be sold for $18 per 25-ounce bottle. However, the table cleaner can be converted into two other products by adding 300,000 ounces of another compound (TCP) to the 300,000 ounces of table cleaner. This joint process will yield 300,000 ounces each of table stain remover (TSR) and table polish (TP). The additional processing costs for this process amount to $100,000. Both table products can be sold for $14 per 25-ounce bottle.

The company decided not to process the table cleaner into TSR and TP based on the following analysis.

| | Table Cleaner | Process Further | | Total |
		Table Stain Remover (TSR)	Table Polish (TP)	
Production in ounces	300,000	300,000	300,000	
Revenue	$216,000	$168,000	$168,000	$336,000
Costs:				
CDG costs	70,000*	52,500	52,500	105,000**
TCP costs	0	50,000	50,000	100,000
Total costs	70,000	102,500	102,500	205,000
Weekly gross profit	$146,000	$ 65,500	$ 65,500	$131,000

*If table cleaner is not processed further, it is allocated 1/3 of the $210,000 of CDG cost, which is equal to 1/3 of the total physical output.

**If table cleaner is processed further, total physical output is 1,200,000 ounces. TSR and TP combined account for 50% of the total physical output and are each allocated 25% of the CDG cost.

Instructions
(a) Determine if management made the correct decision to not process the table cleaner further by doing the following.
  (1) Calculate the company's total weekly gross profit assuming the table cleaner is not processed further.
  (2) Calculate the company's total weekly gross profit assuming the table cleaner is processed further.
  (3) Compare the resulting net incomes and comment on management's decision.
(b) Using incremental analysis, determine if the table cleaner should be processed further.

(CMA adapted)

(2) Gross profit $186,000

P21-4A Last year (2013), Richter Condos installed a mechanized elevator for its tenants. The owner of the company, Ron Richter, recently returned from an industry equipment exhibition where he watched a computerized elevator demonstrated. He was impressed with the elevator's speed, comfort of ride, and cost efficiency. Upon returning from the exhibition, he asked his purchasing agent to collect price and operating cost data on the new elevator. In addition, he asked the company's accountant to provide him with cost data on the company's elevator. This information is presented below.

Compute gain or loss, and determine if equipment should be replaced.

(LO 6)

	Old Elevator	New Elevator
Purchase price	$120,000	$160,000
Estimated salvage value	0	0
Estimated useful life	5 years	4 years
Depreciation method	Straight-line	Straight-line
Annual operating costs other than depreciation:		
Variable	$ 35,000	$ 10,000
Fixed	23,000	8,500

Annual revenues are $240,000, and selling and administrative expenses are $29,000, regardless of which elevator is used. If the old elevator is replaced now, at the beginning of 2014, Richter Condos will be able to sell it for $25,000.

Instructions
(a) Determine any gain or loss if the old elevator is replaced.
(b) Prepare a 4-year summarized income statement for each of the following assumptions:
  (1) The old elevator is retained.
  (2) The old elevator is replaced.
(c) Using incremental analysis, determine if the old elevator should be replaced.
(d) ▭▭▭▷ Write a memo to Ron Richter explaining why any gain or loss should be ignored in the decision to replace the old elevator.

(b) (2) NI $539,000
(c) NI increase $23,000

P21-5A Gutierrez Company has four operating divisions. During the first quarter of 2014, the company reported aggregate income from operations of $213,000 and the following divisional results.

Prepare incremental analysis concerning elimination of divisions.

(LO 7)

	Division			
	I	II	III	IV
Sales	$250,000	$200,000	$500,000	$450,000
Cost of goods sold	200,000	192,000	300,000	250,000
Selling and administrative expenses	75,000	60,000	60,000	50,000
Income (loss) from operations	$ (25,000)	$ (52,000)	$140,000	$150,000

Analysis reveals the following percentages of variable costs in each division.

	I	II	III	IV
Cost of goods sold	75%	90%	80%	75%
Selling and administrative expenses	40	70	50	60

Discontinuance of any division would save 50% of the fixed costs and expenses for that division.

Top management is very concerned about the unprofitable divisions (I and II). Consensus is that one or both of the divisions should be discontinued.

(a) I $70,000

(c) Income III $133,800

Instructions

(a) Compute the contribution margin for Divisions I and II.

(b) Prepare an incremental analysis concerning the possible discontinuance of (1) Division I and (2) Division II. What course of action do you recommend for each division?

(c) Prepare a columnar condensed income statement for Gutierrez Company, assuming Division II is eliminated. (Use the CVP format.) Division II's unavoidable fixed costs are allocated equally to the continuing divisions.

(d) Reconcile the total income from operations ($213,000) with the total income from operations without Division II.

PROBLEMS: SET B

Use incremental analysis for special order and identify nonfinancial factors in decision.

(LO 3)

P21-1B Morello Inc. manufactures basketballs for the National Basketball Association (NBA). For the first 6 months of 2014, the company reported the following operating results while operating at 90% of plant capacity and producing 90,000 units.

	Amount	Per Unit
Sales	$4,500,000	$50
Cost of goods sold	3,060,000	34
Selling and administrative expenses	360,000	4
Net income	$1,080,000	$12

Fixed costs for the period were cost of goods sold $900,000, and selling and administrative expenses $180,000.

In July, normally a slack manufacturing month, Morello receives a special order for 10,000 basketballs at $30 each from the Chinese Basketball Association (CBA). Acceptance of the order would increase variable selling and administrative expenses $0.50 per unit because of shipping costs but would not increase fixed costs and expenses.

Instructions

(a) NI increase $35,000

(a) Prepare an incremental analysis for the special order.

(b) Should Morello Inc. accept the special order?

(c) What is the minimum selling price on the special order to produce net income of $5.50 per ball?

(d) ⬛⬛⬛⬛⬛➤ What nonfinancial factors should management consider in making its decision?

Use incremental analysis related to make or buy; consider opportunity cost and identify nonfinancial factors.

(LO 4)

P21-2B The management of Gill Corporation is trying to decide whether to continue manufacturing a part or to buy it from an outside supplier. The part, called FIZBE, is a component of the company's finished product.

The following information was collected from the accounting records and production data for the year ending December 31, 2014.

1. 5,000 units of FIZBE were produced in the Machining Department.

2. Variable manufacturing costs applicable to the production of each FIZBE unit were: direct materials $4.75, direct labor $4.60, indirect labor $0.45, utilities $0.35.

3. Fixed manufacturing costs applicable to the production of FIZBE were:

Cost Item	Direct	Allocated
Depreciation	$1,100	$ 900
Property taxes	500	200
Insurance	900	600
	$2,500	$1,700

All variable manufacturing and direct fixed costs will be eliminated if FIZBE is purchased. Allocated costs will have to be absorbed by other production departments.

4. The lowest quotation for 5,000 FIZBE units from a supplier is $56,000.

5. If FIZBE units are purchased, freight and inspection costs would be $0.30 per unit, and receiving costs totaling $500 per year would be incurred by the Machining Department.

Instructions

(a) Prepare an incremental analysis for FIZBE. Your analysis should have columns for (1) Make FIZBE, (2) Buy FIZBE, and (3) Net Income Increase/Decrease.

(b) Based on your analysis, what decision should management make?

(c) Would the decision be different if Gill Corporation has the opportunity to produce $6,000 of net income with the facilities currently being used to manufacture FIZBE? Show computations.

(d) ▐▐▐▬▬▬▶ What nonfinancial factors should management consider in making its decision?

(a) NI (decrease) ($4,750)

(c) NI increase $1,250

P21-3B Ohio Household Products Co. (OHPC) is a diversified household-cleaner processing company. The company's Mishawaka plant produces two products: an appliance cleaner and a general-purpose cleaner from a common set of chemical inputs (NPR). Each week 1,000,000 ounces of chemical input are processed at a cost of $200,000 into 750,000 ounces of appliance cleaner and 250,000 ounces of general-purpose cleaner. The appliance cleaner has no market value until it is converted into a polish with the trade name Shine Brite. The additional processing costs for this conversion amount to $300,000. Shine Brite sells at $15 per 25-ounce bottle. The general-purpose cleaner can be sold for $20 per 20-ounce bottle. However, the general-purpose cleaner can be converted into two other products by adding 250,000 ounces of another compound (PST) to the 250,000 ounces of general-purpose cleaner. This joint process will yield 250,000 ounces each of premium cleaner (PC) and premium stain remover (PSR). The additional processing costs for this process amount to $140,000. Both premium products can be sold for $16 per 20-ounce bottle.

Determine if product should be sold or processed further.
(LO 5)

The company decided not to process the general-purpose cleaner into PC and PSR based on the following analysis.

| | General-Purpose Cleaner | Process Further | | |
		Premium Cleaner (PC)	Premium Stain Remover (PSR)	Total
Production in ounces	250,000	250,000	250,000	
Revenue	$250,000	$200,000	$200,000	$400,000
Costs:				
NPR costs	50,000*	40,000	40,000	80,000**
PST costs	0	70,000	70,000	140,000
Total costs	50,000	110,000	110,000	220,000
Weekly gross profit	$200,000	$ 90,000	$ 90,000	$180,000

*If general-purpose cleaner is not processed further, it is allocated 1/4 of the $200,000 of NPR cost, which is equal to 1/4 of the total physical output.

**If general-purpose cleaner is processed further, total physical output is 1,250,000 ounces. PC and PSR combined account for 40% of the total output and are each allocated 20% of the NPR cost.

Instructions

(a) Determine if management made the correct decision to not process the general-purpose cleaner further by doing the following.
  (1) Calculate the company's total weekly gross profit assuming the general-purpose cleaner is not processed further.
  (2) Calculate the company's total weekly gross profit assuming the general-purpose cleaner is processed further.
  (3) Compare the resulting net incomes and comment on management's decision.

(b) Using incremental analysis, determine if the general-purpose cleaner should be processed further.

(a) (2) Gross profit $210,000

(CMA adapted)

P21-4B Last year (2013), Simmons Company installed new factory equipment. The owner of the company, Gene Simmons, recently returned from an industry equipment exhibition where he watched computerized equipment demonstrated. He was impressed with the equipment's speed and cost efficiency. Upon returning from the exhibition, he asked his purchasing

Compute gain or loss, and determine if equipment should be replaced.
(LO 6)

agent to collect price and operating cost data on the new equipment. In addition, he asked the company's accountant to provide him with cost data on the company's equipment. This information is presented below.

	Old Equipment	New Equipment
Purchase price	$210,000	$250,000
Estimated salvage value	0	0
Estimated useful life	5 years	4 years
Depreciation method	Straight-line	Straight-line
Annual operating costs other than depreciation:		
Variable	$50,000	$12,000
Fixed	30,000	5,000

Annual revenues are $360,000, and selling and administrative expenses are $45,000, regardless of which equipment is used. If the old equipment is replaced now, at the beginning of 2014, Simmons Company will be able to sell it for $58,000.

Instructions
(a) Determine any gain or loss if the old equipment is replaced.
(b) Prepare a 4-year summarized income statement for each of the following assumptions:
  (1) The old equipment is retained.
  (2) The old equipment is replaced.
(c) Using incremental analysis, determine if the old equipment should be replaced.
(d) ▭▭▭▶ Write a memo to Gene Simmons explaining why any gain or loss should be ignored in the decision to replace the old equipment.

(b) (2) NI $832,000

(c) NI increase $60,000

Prepare incremental analysis concerning elimination of divisions.

(LO 7)

P21-5B Panda Corporation has four operating divisions. During the first quarter of 2014, the company reported aggregate income from operations of $129,000 and the divisional results shown below.

	Division			
	I	**II**	**III**	**IV**
Sales	$510,000	$400,000	$310,000	$170,000
Cost of goods sold	300,000	250,000	270,000	156,000
Selling and administrative expenses	60,000	80,000	75,000	70,000
Income (loss) from operations	$150,000	$ 70,000	$ (35,000)	$ (56,000)

Analysis reveals the following percentages of variable costs in each division.

	I	**II**	**III**	**IV**
Cost of goods sold	70%	80%	70%	90%
Selling and administrative expenses	40	50	60	70

Discontinuance of any division would save 50% of the fixed costs and expenses for that division.

Top management is very concerned about the unprofitable divisions (III and IV). Consensus is that one or both of the divisions should be discontinued.

Instructions
(a) III $76,000
(a) Compute the contribution margin for Divisions III and IV.
(b) Prepare an incremental analysis concerning the possible discontinuance of (1) Division III and (2) Division IV. What course of action do you recommend for each division?
(c) II $63,900
(c) Prepare a columnar condensed income statement for Panda Corporation, assuming Division IV is eliminated. (Use the CVP format.) Division IV's unavoidable fixed costs are allocated equally to the continuing divisions.
(d) Reconcile the total income from operations ($129,000) with the total income from operations without Division IV.

PROBLEMS: SET C

Visit the book's companion website, at **www.wiley.com/college/weygandt**, and choose the Student Companion site to access Problem Set C.

WATERWAYS CONTINUING PROBLEM

(This is a continuation of the Waterways Problem from Chapters 15–20.)

WCP21 Waterways Corporation is considering various business opportunities. It wants to make the best use of its production facilities to maximize income. This problem asks you to help Waterways do incremental analysis on these various opportunities.

*Go to the book's companion website, **www.wiley.com/college/weygandt**, to find the remainder of this problem.*

Broadening Your **PERSPECTIVE**

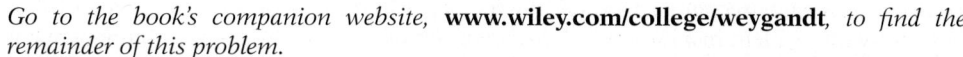

Management Decision-Making

Decision-Making at Current Designs

BYP21-1 Current Designs faces a number of important decisions that require incremental analysis. Consider each of the following situations independently.

Situation 1

Recently, Mike Cichanowski, owner and CEO of Current Designs, received a phone call from the president of a brewing company. He was calling to inquire about the possibility of Current Designs producing "floating coolers" for a promotion his company was planning. These coolers resemble a kayak but are about one-third the size. They are used to float food and beverages while paddling down the river on a weekend leisure trip. The company would be interested in purchasing 100 coolers for the upcoming summer. It is willing to pay $250 per cooler. The brewing company would pick up the coolers upon completion of the order.

Mike met with Diane Buswell, controller, to identify how much it would cost Current Designs to produce the coolers. After careful analysis, the following costs were identified.

Direct materials	$80/unit	Variable overhead	$20/unit
Direct labor	$60/unit	Fixed overhead	$1,000

Current Designs would be able to modify an existing mold to produce the coolers. The cost of these modifications would be approximately $2,000.

Instructions

(a) Prepare an incremental analysis to determine whether Current Designs should accept this special order to produce the coolers.

(b) Discuss additional factors that Mike and Diane should consider if Current Designs is currently operating at full capacity.

Situation 2

Current Designs is always working to identify ways to increase efficiency while becoming more environmentally conscious. During a recent brainstorming session, one employee suggested to Diane Buswell, controller, that the company should consider replacing the current rotomold oven as a way to realize savings from reduced energy consumption. The oven operates on natural gas, using 17,000 therms of natural gas for an entire year. A new, energy-efficient rotomold oven would operate on 15,000 therms of natural gas for an entire year. After seeking out price quotes from a few suppliers, Diane determined that it would cost approximately $250,000 to purchase a new, energy-efficient rotomold oven. She determines that the expected useful life of the new oven would be 10 years, and it would have no salvage value at the end of its useful life. Current Designs would be able to sell the current oven for $10,000.

Instructions

(a) Prepare an incremental analysis to determine if Current Designs should purchase the new roto-mold oven, assuming that the average price for natural gas over the next 10 years will be $0.65 per therm.

(b) Diane is concerned that natural gas prices might increase at a faster rate over the next 10 years. If the company projects that the average natural gas price of the next 10 years could be as high as $0.85 per therm, discuss how that might change your conclusion in (a).

Situation 3

One of Current Designs' competitive advantages is found in the ingenuity of its owner and CEO, Mike Cichanowski. His involvement in the design of kayak molds and production techniques has led to Current Designs being recognized as an industry leader in the design and production of kay-aks. This ingenuity was evident in an improved design of one of the most important components of a kayak, the seat. The "Revolution Seating System" is a one-of-a-kind, rotating axis seat that gives unmatched, full-contact, under-leg support. It is quickly adjustable with a lever-lock system that allows for a customizable seat position that maximizes comfort for the rider.

Having just designed the "Revolution Seating System," Current Designs must now decide whether to produce the seats internally or buy them from an outside supplier. The costs for Current Designs to produce the seats are as follows.

| Direct materials | $20/unit | Direct labor | $15/unit |
| Variable overhead | $12/unit | Fixed overhead | $20,000 |

Current Designs will need to produce 3,000 seats this year; 25% of the fixed overhead will be avoided if the seats are purchased from an outside vendor. After soliciting prices from outside suppliers, the company determined that it will cost $50 to purchase a seat from an outside vendor.

Instructions

(a) Prepare an incremental analysis showing whether Current Designs should make or buy the "Revolution Seating System."

(b) Would your answer in (a) change if the productive capacity released by not making the seats could be used to produce income of $20,000?

Decision-Making Across the Organization

BYP21-2 Aurora Company is considering the purchase of a new machine. The invoice price of the machine is $140,000, freight charges are estimated to be $4,000, and installation costs are expected to be $6,000. Salvage value of the new equipment is expected to be zero after a useful life of 5 years. Existing equipment could be retained and used for an additional 5 years if the new machine is not purchased. At that time, the salvage value of the equipment would be zero. If the new machine is purchased now, the existing machine would have to be scrapped. Aurora's accountant, Lisah Huang, has accumulated the following data regarding annual sales and expenses with and without the new machine.

1. Without the new machine, Aurora can sell 12,000 units of product annually at a per unit selling price of $100. If the new machine is purchased, the number of units produced and sold would increase by 10%, and the selling price would remain the same.

2. The new machine is faster than the old machine, and it is more efficient in its usage of materials. With the old machine the gross profit rate will be 25% of sales, whereas the rate will be 30% of sales with the new machine.

3. Annual selling expenses are $180,000 with the current equipment. Because the new equipment would produce a greater number of units to be sold, annual selling expenses are expected to increase by 10% if it is purchased.

4. Annual administrative expenses are expected to be $100,000 with the old machine, and $113,000 with the new machine.

5. The current book value of the existing machine is $36,000. Aurora uses straight-line depreciation.

Instructions

With the class divided into groups, prepare an incremental analysis for the 5 years showing whether Aurora should keep the existing machine or buy the new machine. (Ignore income tax effects.)

Managerial Analysis

BYP21-3 MiniTek manufactures private-label small electronic products, such as alarm clocks, calculators, kitchen timers, stopwatches, and automatic pencil sharpeners. Some of the products are sold as sets, and others are sold individually. Products are studied as to their sales potential, and then cost estimates are made. The Engineering Department develops production plans, and then production begins. The company has generally had very successful product introductions. Only two products introduced by the company have been discontinued.

One of the products currently sold is a multi-alarm clock. The clock has four alarms that can be programmed to sound at various times and for varying lengths of time. The company has experienced a great deal of difficulty in making the circuit boards for the clocks. The production process has never operated smoothly. The product is unprofitable at the present time, primarily because of warranty repairs and product recalls. Two models of the clocks were recalled, for example, because they sometimes caused an electric shock when the alarms were being shut off. The Engineering Department is attempting to revise the manufacturing process, but the revision will take another 6 months at least.

The clocks were very popular when they were introduced, and since they are private-label, the company has not suffered much from the recalls. Presently, the company has a very large order for several items from Kmart Stores. The order includes 5,000 of the multi-alarm clocks. When the company suggested that Kmart purchase the clocks from another manufacturer, Kmart threatened to rescind the entire order unless the clocks were included.

The company has therefore investigated the possibility of having another company make the clocks for them. The clocks were bid for the Kmart order based on an estimated $6.90 cost to manufacture:

Circuit board, 1 each @ $2.00	$2.00
Plastic case, 1 each @ $0.80	0.80
Alarms, 4 @ $0.15 each	0.60
Labor, 15 minutes @ $12/hour	3.00
Overhead, $2.00 per labor hour	0.50

MiniTek could purchase clocks to fill the Kmart order for $10 from Trans-Tech Asia, a Korean manufacturer with a very good quality record. Trans-Tech has offered to reduce the price to $7.50 after MiniTek has been a customer for 6 months, placing an order of at least 1,000 units per month. If MiniTek becomes a "preferred customer" by purchasing 15,000 units per year, the price would be reduced still further to $4.50.

Omega Products, a local manufacturer, has also offered to make clocks for MiniTek. They have offered to sell 5,000 clocks for $5 each. However, Omega Products has been in business for only 6 months. They have experienced significant turnover in their labor force, and the local press has reported that the owners may face tax evasion charges soon. The owner of Omega Products is an electronic engineer, however, and the quality of the clocks is likely to be good.

If MiniTek decides to purchase the clocks from either Trans-Tech or Omega, all the costs to manufacture could be avoided, except a total of $5,000 in overhead costs for machine depreciation. The machinery is fairly new, and has no alternate use.

Instructions

(a) What is the difference in profit under each of the alternatives if the clocks are to be sold for $14.50 each to Kmart?

(b) What are the most important nonfinancial factors that MiniTek should consider when making this decision?

(c) What do you think MiniTek should do in regard to the Kmart order? What should it do in regard to continuing to manufacture the multi-alarm clocks? Be prepared to defend your answer.

Real-World Focus

BYP21-4 Founded in 1983, Beverly Hills Fan Company is located in Woodland Hills, California. With 23 employees and sales of less than $10 million, the company is relatively small. Management feels that there is potential for growth in the upscale market for ceiling fans and lighting. They are particularly optimistic about growth in Mexican and Canadian markets.

Presented below is information from the president's letter in the company's annual report.

Beverly Hills Fan Company
President's Letter

An aggressive product development program was initiated during the past year resulting in new ceiling fan models planned for introduction this year. Award winning industrial designer Ron Rezek created several new fan models for the Beverly Hills Fan and L.A. Fan lines, including a new Showroom Collection, designed specifically for the architectural and designer markets. Each of these models has received critical acclaim, and order commitments for this year have been outstanding. Additionally, our Custom Color and special order fans continued to enjoy increasing popularity and sales gains as more and more customers desire fans that match their specific interior decors. Currently, Beverly Hills Fan Company offers a product line of over 100 models of contemporary, traditional, and transitional ceiling fans.

Instructions
(a) What points did the company management need to consider before deciding to offer the special-order fans to customers?
(b) How would incremental analysis be employed to assist in this decision?

BYP21-5 Outsourcing by both manufacturers and service companies is becoming increasingly common. There are now many firms that specialize in outsourcing consulting.

Address: **www.alsbridge.com**, or go to **www.wiley.com/college/weygandt**

Instructions
Go to the Web page of Alsbridge, Inc. at the address shown above, and answer the following questions.
(a) What are some of the types of outsourcing for which the company provides assistance?
(b) What is insourcing?
(c) What are some of the potential benefits of insourcing?

Critical Thinking

Communication Activity

BYP21-6 Hank Jewell is a production manager at a metal fabricating plant. Last night, he read an article about a new piece of equipment that would dramatically reduce his division's costs. Hank was very excited about the prospect, and the first thing he did this morning was to bring the article to his supervisor, Preston Thiese, the plant manager. The following conversation occurred:

Hank: Preston, I thought you would like to see this article on the new PDD1130; they've made some fantastic changes that could save us millions of dollars.

Preston: I appreciate your interest, Hank, but I actually have been aware of the new machine for two months. The problem is that we just bought a new machine last year. We spent $2 million on that machine, and it was supposed to last us 12 years. If we replace it now, we would have to write its book value off of the books for a huge loss. If I go to top management now and say that I want a new machine, they will fire me. I think we should use our existing machine for a couple of years, and then when it becomes obvious that we have to have a new machine, I will make the proposal.

Instructions
Hank just completed a course in managerial accounting, and he believes that Preston is making a big mistake. Write a memo from Hank to Preston explaining Preston's decision-making error.

Ethics Case

BYP21-7 Blake Romney became Chief Executive Officer of Peters Inc. two years ago. At the time, the company was reporting lagging profits, and Blake was brought in to "stir things up." The company has three divisions, electronics, fiber optics, and plumbing supplies. Blake has no interest in plumbing supplies, and one of the first things he did was to put pressure on his accountants to reallocate some of the company's fixed costs away from the other two divisions to the plumbing division. This had the effect of causing the plumbing division to report losses during the last two years; in the past it had always reported low, but acceptable, net income. Blake felt that this reallocation would shine a favorable light on him in front of the board of directors because it meant that the electronics and fiber optics divisions would look like they were improving. Given that these are "businesses of the future," he believed that the stock market would react favorably to these increases, while not penalizing the poor results of the plumbing division. Without this shift in the allocation of fixed costs, the profits of the electronics and fiber optics divisions would not have improved. But now the board of directors has suggested that the plumbing division be closed because it is reporting losses. This would mean that nearly 500 employees, many of whom have worked for Peters their whole lives, would lose their jobs.

Instructions
(a) If a division is reporting losses, does that necessarily mean that it should be closed?
(b) Was the reallocation of fixed costs across divisions unethical?
(c) What should Blake do?

All About You

BYP21-8 Managerial accounting techniques can be used in a wide variety of settings. As we have frequently pointed out, you can use them in many personal situations. They also can be useful in trying to find solutions for societal issues that appear to be hard to solve.

Instructions
Read the Fortune article, "The Toughest Customers: How Hardheaded Business Metrics Can Help the Hard-core Homeless," by Cait Murphy, available at *http://money.cnn.com/magazines/fortune/fortune_archive/2006/04/03/8373067/index.htm*. Answer the following questions.
(a) How does the article define "chronic" homelessness?
(b) In what ways does homelessness cost a city money? What are the estimated costs of a chronic homeless person to various cities?
(c) What are the steps suggested to address the problem?
(d) What is the estimated cost of implementing this program in New York? What results have been seen?
(e) In terms of incremental analysis, frame the relevant costs in this situation.

Considering Your Costs and Benefits

BYP21-9 School costs money. Is this an expenditure that you should have avoided? A year of tuition at a public four-year college costs about $8,655, and a year of tuition at a public two-year college costs about $1,359. If you did not go to college, you might avoid mountains of school-related debt. In fact, each year, about 600,000 students decide to drop out of school. Many of them never return. Suppose that you are working two jobs and going to college, and that you are not making ends meet. Your grades are suffering due to your lack of available study time. You feel depressed. Should you drop out of school?

> **YES:** You can always go back to school. If your grades are bad and you are depressed, what good is school doing you anyway?
> **NO:** Once you drop out, it is very hard to get enough momentum to go back. Dropping out will dramatically reduce your long-term opportunities. It is better to stay in school, even if you take only one class per semester. While you cannot go back and redo your initial decision, you can look at some facts to evaluate the wisdom of your decision.

Instructions
Write a response indicating your position regarding this situation. Provide support for your view.

Answers to Chapter Questions

Answers to Insight and Accounting Across the Organization Questions

p. 1046 That Letter from AmEx Might Not Be a Bill Q: What are the relevant costs that American Express would need to know in order to determine to whom to make this offer? **A:** Clearly, American Express would make this offer to those customers that are most likely to default on their bills. The most important relevant cost would be the "expected loss" that an at-risk customer posed. If a customer has a high probability of defaulting and if the expected loss exceeds the $300 cost, then American Express can probably save money by paying that customer to quit using its card so that the customer doesn't ring up an even bigger bill.

p. 1050 Giving Away the Store? Q: What are the relevant revenues and costs that Amazon should consider relative to the decision whether to offer the Prime free-shipping subscription? **A:** The relevant revenues to consider would be the estimated change in revenue that would result from offering free shipping and the $79 annual fee for a Prime subscription. The relevant costs would be the estimated additional shipping costs that the company would incur.

p. 1057 Time to Move to a New Neighborhood? Q: What were some of the factors that complicated the company's decision to move? How should the company have incorporated such factors into its incremental analysis? **A:** The company received only $7.5 million for its California property, only 58 of 75 key employees were willing to move, construction was delayed by a year which caused the new plant to increase in price by $1.5 million, and wages surged in Idaho due to low unemployment. In performing incremental analysis of the decision to move, a company should perform sensitivity analysis. This would include evaluating the impact on the decision if all costs were, for example, 10% higher than expected or if cost savings were 10% lower than expected.

p. 1058 What Is the Real Cost of Packaging Options? Q: If your marketing director suggests that, in addition to selling your cereal in a standard-size box, you should sell a jumbo size and an individual size, what issues must you consider? **A:** In evaluating this decision, you should identify the incremental revenues as well as incremental costs. The marketing manager is most likely focusing on the fact that by offering alternative packaging options, the company can market the product to a broader range of customers. However, alternative packaging options will also result in additional costs. It will increase the number of setups, require different types of storage and handling, and increase the need for additional storage space for the packages and the packaged products.

Answers to Self-Test Questions

1. d **2.** b **3.** c **4.** d **5.** c $(3,000 \times \$4)$ **6.** d $[\$18 - (\$14 + \$5)] \times 3,000$ **7.** b **8.** d **9.** c $(\$12,000 - \$8,000)$ **10.** a **11.** d $[(\$68 - \$55) - \$12]$ **12.** b **13.** c **14.** b $(.5 \times \$100,000) - (\$200,000 - \$140,000)$

✔ Remember to go back to The Navigator box on the chapter opening page and check off your completed work.

Chapter 22

Pricing

Feature Story

They've Got Your Size—and Color

Nick Swinmum was shopping for a pair of shoes. He found a store with the right style, but not the right color. The next store had the right color, but not the right size. After visiting numerous stores, he went home, figuring he would buy them on the Web. After all, it was 1999, so you could buy everything on the Web, right? Well, apparently not shoes. After an exhaustive search, Nick still came up shoeless.

Nick lived in San Francisco, where, in 1999, everybody with even half an idea started an Internet company and became a millionaire. Or so it seemed. So Nick started Zappos.com. The

company is dedicated to providing the best selection in shoes in terms of brands, styles, colors, size, and most importantly service.

To make sure that Zappos.com had a fighting chance of evolving from a half-baked idea to a thriving business, Nick brought in Tony Hsieh. At the age of 24, Tony had developed and recently sold a business to Microsoft for $265 million. Tony originally contributed to Zappos as an investor and advisor, but soon he took over as CEO. Tony then brought in Alfred Lin to manage the company's finances. Tony and Alfred had met when Tony was running a pizza business. (Alfred was Tony's best pizza customer, but his competencies apparently extended

Learning Objectives

After studying this chapter, you should be able to:

1 Compute a target cost when the market determines a product price.

2 Compute a target selling price using cost-plus pricing.

3 Use time-and-material pricing to determine the cost of services provided.

4 Determine a transfer price using the negotiated, cost-based, and market-based approaches.

5 Explain issues involved in transferring goods between divisions in different countries.

✔ The Navigator

beyond pizza consumption.) Together, Tony and Alfred have run Zappos based on 10 basic principles:

1. Deliver WOW through service.
2. Embrace and drive change.
3. Create fun and a little weirdness.
4. Be adventurous, creative, and open-minded.
5. Pursue growth and learning.
6. Build open and honest relationships with communication.
7. Build a positive team and family spirit.
8. Do more with less.
9. Be passionate and determined.
10. Be humble.

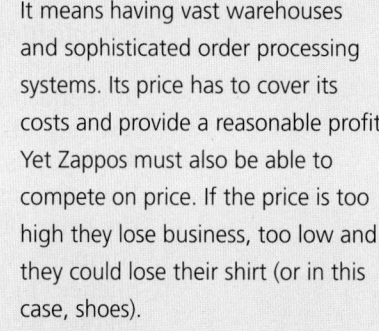

Are you looking for a pair of size 6 Giuseppe Zanotti heels for $1,295 or a pair of Keen size 17 sandals for $95? Zappos is

committed to having what you want and getting it to you as fast as possible. Providing this kind of service is not cheap. It means having vast warehouses and sophisticated order processing systems. Its price has to cover its costs and provide a reasonable profit. Yet Zappos must also be able to compete on price. If the price is too high they lose business, too low and they could lose their shirt (or in this case, shoes).

Watch the Zappos.com video in WileyPLUS to learn more about how the company sets prices.

Source: www.zappos.com.

Preview of **Chapter 22**

As the Feature Story about Zappos.com indicates, few management decisions are more important than setting prices. Intel, for example, must sell computer chips at a price that is high enough to cover its costs and ensure a reasonable profit. But if the price is too high, the chips will not sell. In this chapter, we examine two types of pricing situations. The first part of the chapter addresses pricing for goods sold or services provided to external parties. The second part of the chapter addresses pricing decisions managers face when they sell goods to other divisions within the company.

The content and organization of this chapter are as follows.

PRICING			
Pricing Goods for External Sales	**Pricing Services**	**Transfer Pricing for Internal Sales**	**Transfers Between Divisions in Different Countries**
• Target costing • Cost-plus pricing • Variable-cost pricing • Time-and-material pricing	• Calculating labor rate • Calculating material loading charge • Calculating job charges	• Negotiated transfer prices • Cost-based transfer prices • Market-based transfer prices • Effect of outsourcing on transfer pricing	• Tax considerations

✔ **The Navigator**

1083

Pricing Goods for External Sales

Establishing the price for any good or service is affected by many factors. Take the pharmaceutical industry as an example. Its approach to profitability has been to spend heavily on research and development in an effort to find and patent a few new drugs, price them high, and market them aggressively. However, the AIDS crisis in Africa placed the drug industry under considerable pressure to lower prices on drugs used to treat the disease. For example, Merck Co. lowered the price of its AIDS drug Crixivan to $600 per patient in these countries. This compares with the $6,016 it typically charged in the United States.[1] As a consequence, individuals in the United States questioned whether prices in the U.S. market were too high. The drug companies countered that to cover their substantial financial risks to develop these products, they need to set the prices high. Illustration 22-1 indicates the many factors that can affect pricing decisions.

Illustration 22-1
Pricing factors

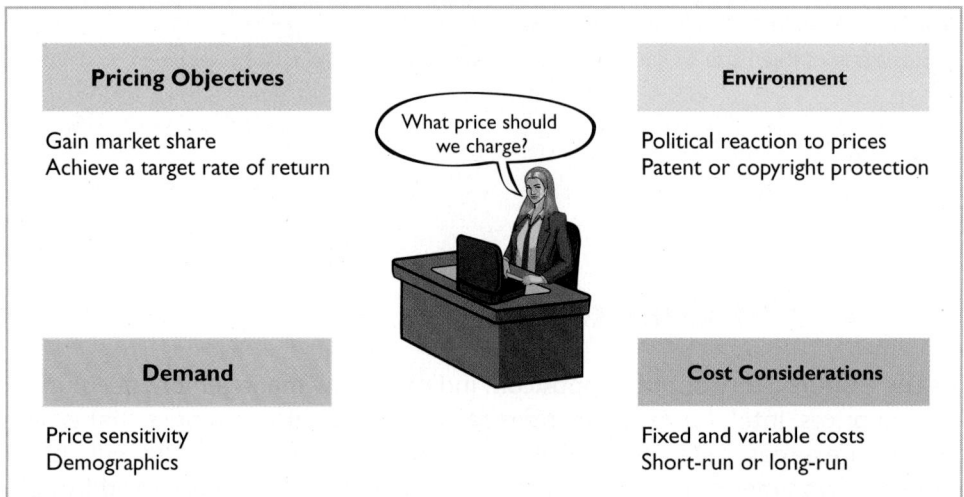

In the long run, a company must price its product to cover its costs and earn a reasonable profit. But to price its product appropriately, it must have a good understanding of market forces at work. In most cases, a company does not set the prices. Instead, the price is set by the competitive market (the laws of supply and demand). For example, a company such as ChevronTexaco or Exxon-Mobil cannot set the price of gasoline by itself. These companies are called **price takers** because the price of gasoline is set by market forces (the supply of oil and the demand by customers). This is the case for any product that is not easily differentiated from competing products, such as farm products (corn or wheat) or minerals (coal or sand).

In other situations, the company sets the prices. This would be the case where the product is specially made for a customer, as in a one-of-a-kind product such as a designer dress by Zoran or Armani. This also occurs when there are few or no other producers capable of manufacturing a similar item. An example would be a company that has a patent or copyright on a unique process, such as the case of computer chips by Intel. However, it is also the case when a company can effectively differentiate its product or service from others. Even in a competitive

---

[1]"AIDS Gaffes in Africa Come Back to Haunt Drug Industry at Home," *Wall Street Journal* (April 23, 2001), p. 1.

market like coffee, Starbucks has been able to differentiate its product and charge a premium for a cup of java.

MANAGEMENT INSIGHT

The Only Game in Town?

Pricing plays a critical role in corporate strategy. For example, almost 50% of tablet computer users say that they use them to read newspapers and magazines. And since Apple's iPad tablet computer at one time represented 75% of the tablets being sold, Apple felt like it had the newspaper and magazine publishers right where it wanted them. So it decided to charge the publishers a fee of 30% of subscription revenue for subscriptions sold at Apple's App Store. Publishers were outraged, but it didn't take long for somebody to come to their rescue. Within 1 day of Apple's announcement, Google announced that it would only charge a fee of about 10% of subscription revenue for users of its Android system. That might at least partially explain why *Sports Illustrated* provided an app to run on Android tablets before it provided one for iPads, even though at that time Android tablets only had a small share of the market.

Source: Martin Peers, "Apple Risks App-lash on iPad," *Wall Street Journal Online* (February 17, 2011).

 Do the substantially different prices that Apple and Google charge for a similar service reflect different costs incurred by each company, or is the price difference due to something else? (See page 1129.)

Target Costing

Automobile manufacturers like Ford or Toyota face a competitive market. The price of an automobile is affected greatly by the laws of supply and demand, so no company in this industry can affect the price to a significant degree. Therefore, to earn a profit, companies in the auto industry must focus on controlling costs. This requires setting a **target cost** that provides a desired profit. Illustration 22-2 shows the relationship and importance of a target cost to the price and desired profit.

> **LEARNING OBJECTIVE   1**
>
> Compute a target cost when the market determines a product price.

Market Price	−	Desired Profit	=	Target Cost

Illustration 22-2
Target cost as related to price and profit

If General Motors can produce its automobiles for the target cost (or less), it will meet its profit goal. If it cannot achieve its target cost, it will fail to produce the desired profit, which will disappoint its stockholders.

In a competitive market, a company chooses the segment of the market it wants to compete in—that is, its market niche. For example, it may choose between selling luxury goods or economy goods in order to focus its efforts on one segment or the other. Once the company has identified the segment of the market that it wants to compete in, it conducts market research. This determines the features its product should have, and what the market price is for a product with those features. Once the company has determined this price, it can determine its target cost by setting a desired profit. The difference between the market price and the desired profit is the target cost of the product (shown in Illustration 22-2). After the company determines the target cost, it assembles a team of employees with expertise in a variety of areas (production and operations, marketing, and finance). The team's task is to design and develop a product that can meet quality specifications while not exceeding the target cost. The target cost includes all product and period costs necessary to make and market the product or service.

MANAGEMENT INSIGHT

Wal-Mart Says the Price Is Too High

"And the price should be $19 per pair of jeans instead of $23," said the retailer Wal-Mart Stores Inc. to jean maker Levi Strauss. What happened to Levi Strauss is what happens to many manufacturers who deal with Wal-Mart. Wal-Mart often sets the price, and the manufacturer has to figure out how to make a profit, given that price. In Levi Strauss's case, it revamped its distribution and production to serve Wal-Mart and improve its overall record of timely deliveries. Producing a season of new jeans styles, from conception to store shelves, used to take Levi 12 to 15 months. Today, it takes just 10 months for Levi Strauss signature jeans; for regular Levi's, the time is down to 7 1/2 months. As the chief executive of Levi Strauss noted, "We had to change people and practice. It's been somewhat of a D-Day invasion approach."

Source: "In Bow to Retailers' New Clout, Levi Strauss Makes Alterations," *Wall Street Journal* (June 17, 2004), p A1.

? What are some issues that Levi Strauss should consider in deciding whether it should agree to meet Wal-Mart's target price? (See page 1129.)

> DO IT!

Target Costing

Fine Line Phones is considering introducing a fashion cover for its phones. Market research indicates that 200,000 units can be sold if the price is no more than $20. If Fine Line decides to produce the covers, it will need to invest $1,000,000 in new production equipment. Fine Line requires a minimum rate of return of 25% on all investments. Determine the target cost per unit for the cover.

Action Plan

✔ Recall that Market price − Desired profit = Target cost.

✔ The minimum rate of return is a company's desired profit.

Solution

The desired profit for this new product line is $250,000 ($1,000,000 × 25%).

Each cover must result in $1.25 of profit ($250,000/200,000 units).

Market price	−	Desired profit	=	Target cost per unit
$20	−	$1.25	=	$18.75 per unit

Related exercise material: **BE22-1, E22-1, E22-2, and** **22-1.**

✔ **The Navigator**

Cost-Plus Pricing

LEARNING OBJECTIVE 2

Compute a target selling price using cost-plus pricing.

As discussed, in a competitive product environment, the price of a product is set by the market. In order to achieve its desired profit, the company focuses on achieving a target cost. In a less competitive environment, companies have a greater ability to set the product price. Commonly, when a company sets a product price, it does so as a function of, or relative to, the cost of the product or service. This is referred to as **cost-plus pricing**. Under cost-plus pricing, a company first determines a cost base and then adds a **markup** to the cost base to determine the **target selling price**.

If the cost base includes all of the costs required to produce and sell the product, then the markup represents the desired profit. This can be seen in Illustration 22-3, where the markup represents the difference between the selling price and cost—the profit on the product.

Selling Price − Cost = Markup (Profit)

Illustration 22-3
Relation of markup to cost and selling price

The size of the markup (profit) depends on the return the company hopes to generate on the amount it has invested. In determining the optimal markup, the company must consider competitive and market conditions, political and legal issues, and other relevant factors. Once the company has determined its cost base and its desired markup, it can add the two together to determine the target selling price. The basic cost-plus pricing formula is expressed as follows.

Cost + Markup = Target Selling Price

Illustration 22-4
Cost-plus pricing formula

To illustrate, assume that Thinkmore Products, Inc. is in the process of setting a selling price on its new video camera pen. It is a functioning pen that will record up to 2 hours of audio and video. The per unit variable cost estimates for the video camera pen are as follows.

	Per Unit
Direct materials	$23
Direct labor	17
Variable manufacturing overhead	12
Variable selling and administrative expenses	8
Variable cost per unit	$60

Illustration 22-5
Variable cost per unit

To produce and sell its product, Thinkmore incurs fixed manufacturing overhead of $280,000 and fixed selling and administrative expenses of $240,000. To arrive at the cost per unit, we divide total fixed costs by the number of units the company expects to produce. Illustration 22-6 shows the computation of fixed cost per unit for Thinkmore, assuming the production of 10,000 units.

	Total Costs	÷	Budgeted Volume	=	Cost per Unit
Fixed manufacturing overhead	$280,000	÷	10,000	=	$28
Fixed selling and administrative expenses	240,000	÷	10,000	=	24
Fixed cost per unit					$52

Illustration 22-6
Fixed cost per unit, 10,000 units

Management is ultimately evaluated based on its ability to generate a high return on the company's investment. This is frequently expressed as a return on investment (ROI) percentage, calculated as income divided by the average amount invested in a product or service. A higher percentage reflects a greater success in generating profits from the investment in a product or service. Chapter 24 provides a more in-depth discussion of the use of ROI to evaluate the performance of investment center managers.

To achieve a desired return on investment percentage, a product's markup should be determined by calculating the desired return on investment (ROI) per unit. This is calculated by multiplying the desired ROI percentage times the amount invested to produce the product, and then dividing this by the number of units produced. Illustration 22-7 shows the computation used to determine a markup amount based on a desired ROI per unit for Thinkmore, assuming that the company desires a 20% ROI and that it has invested $1,000,000.

Illustration 22-7
Calculation of markup based on desired ROI per unit

$$\frac{\text{Desired ROI Percentage} \times \text{Amount Invested}}{\text{Units Produced}} = \text{Markup}$$

$$\frac{20\% \times \$1,000,000}{10,000 \text{ units}} = \$20$$

Thinkmore expects to receive income of $200,000 (20% × $1,000,000) on its $1,000,000 investment. On a per unit basis, the markup based on the desired ROI per unit is $20 ($200,000 ÷ 10,000 units). Given the per unit costs shown above, Illustration 22-8 computes the sales price to be $132.

Illustration 22-8
Computation of selling price, 10,000 units

	Per Unit
Variable cost	$ 60
Fixed cost	52
Total cost	112
Markup (desired ROI)	20
Selling price per unit	**$132**

In most cases, companies like Thinkmore use a percentage markup on cost to determine the selling price. The formula to compute the markup percentage to achieve a desired ROI of $20 per unit is as follows.

Illustration 22-9
Computation of markup percentage

$$\text{Markup (Desired ROI per Unit)} \div \text{Total Unit Cost} = \text{Markup Percentage}$$

$$\$20 \div \$112 = 17.86\%$$

Using a 17.86% markup on cost, Thinkmore Products would compute the target selling price as follows.

Illustration 22-10
Computation of selling price—markup approach

$$\text{Total Unit Cost} + (\text{Total Unit Cost} \times \text{Markup Percentage}) = \text{Target Selling Price per Unit}$$

$$\$112 + (\$112 \times 17.86\%) = \$132$$

Thinkmore should set the price for its video camera pen at $132 per unit.

LIMITATIONS OF COST-PLUS PRICING

The cost-plus pricing approach has a major advantage: It is simple to compute. However, the cost model does not give consideration to the demand side. That is, will customers pay the price Thinkmore computed for its video camera pen? In addition, sales volume plays a large role in determining per unit costs. The lower the sales volume, for example, the higher the price Thinkmore must charge to meet its desired ROI. To illustrate, if the budgeted sales volume was 8,000 instead of 10,000, Thinkmore's variable cost per unit would remain the same. However, the fixed cost per unit would change as follows.

	Total Costs	÷	Budgeted Volume	=	Cost per Unit
Fixed manufacturing overhead	$280,000	÷	8,000	=	$ 35
Fixed selling and administrative expenses	240,000	÷	8,000	=	30
Fixed cost per unit					$65

Illustration 22-11
Fixed cost per unit, 8,000 units

As indicated in Illustration 22-6, the fixed cost per unit for 10,000 units was $52. However, at a lower sales volume of 8,000 units, the fixed cost per unit increases to $65. Thinkmore's desired 20% ROI now results in a $25 ROI per unit [(20% × $1,000,000) ÷ 8,000]. Thinkmore computes the selling price at 8,000 units as follows.

	Per Unit
Variable cost	$ 60
Fixed cost	65
Total cost	125
Desired ROI	25
Selling price per unit	$150

Illustration 22-12
Computation of selling price, 8,000 units

As shown, the lower the budgeted volume, the higher the per unit price. The reason: Fixed costs and ROI are spread over fewer units, and therefore the fixed cost and ROI per unit increase. In this case, at 8,000 units, Thinkmore would have to mark up its total unit costs 20% to earn a desired ROI of $25 per unit, as shown below.

$$20\% = \frac{\$25 \text{ (desired ROI)}}{\$125 \text{ (total unit cost)}}$$

The target selling price would then be $150, as indicated earlier:

$$\$125 + (\$125 \times 20\%) = \$150$$

The opposite effect will occur if budgeted volume is higher (say, at 12,000 units) because fixed costs and ROI can be spread over more units. As a result, the cost-plus model of pricing will achieve its desired ROI only when Thinkmore sells the quantity it budgeted. If actual volume is much less than budgeted volume, Thinkmore may sustain losses unless it can raise its prices.

Variable-Cost Pricing

In determining the target price for Thinkmore's video camera pen, we calculated the cost base by including all costs incurred. This approach is referred to as **full-cost pricing**. Instead of using full costs to set prices, some companies simply add a markup to their variable costs (thus excluding fixed manufacturing and fixed selling and administrative costs). Using **variable-cost pricing** as the basis for setting prices avoids the problem of using uncertain cost information (as shown in Illustration 22-11) related to fixed-cost-per-unit computations. Variable-cost pricing also is helpful in pricing special orders or when excess capacity exists.

The major disadvantage of variable-cost pricing is that managers may set the price too low and consequently fail to cover their fixed costs. In the long run, failure to cover fixed costs will lead to losses. As a result, companies that use variable-cost pricing must adjust their markups to make sure that the price set will provide a fair return. The use of variable costs as the basis for setting prices is discussed in the appendix to this chapter.

MANAGEMENT INSIGHT

At Least It Was Simple

For nearly 90 years, Parker Hannifin used the same simple approach to price its industrial parts. It calculated the production cost, then added on a percentage of the cost (about 35%) to arrive at the price. It didn't matter if a product was a premium product or a standard product. And if Parker reduced its production costs, it then also cut the price for the product. The problem with this approach was that it made it difficult for the company to ever substantially increase its profit margins. So the company's CEO decided to break with tradition and implement strategic pricing schemes similar to those used by retailers. It determined that for about a third of its products, it had a competitive advantage that would allow it to charge a higher markup. For example, there might be limited competition for the product, or its product might be of higher quality, or it might have the ability to produce a product faster. The company determined that the price increases raised net income by $200 million—not bad considering that net income was $130 million before the price increases.

Source: Timothy Aeppel, "Changing the Formula: Seeking Perfect Prices, CEO Tears Up the Rules," *Wall Street Journal Online* (March 27, 2007).

? What kind of help might the sales staff need in implementing this new approach? (See page 1129.)

> DO IT!

Target Selling Price

Air Corporation produces air purifiers. The following per unit cost information is available: direct materials $16, direct labor $18, variable manufacturing overhead $11, variable selling and administrative expenses $6. Fixed selling and administrative expenses are $50,000, and fixed manufacturing overhead is $150,000. Using a 45% markup percentage on total per unit cost and assuming 10,000 units, compute the target selling price.

Action Plan

✔ Calculate the total cost per unit.

✔ Multiply the total cost per unit by the markup percentage, then add this amount to the total cost per unit to determine the target selling price.

Solution

Direct materials	$16
Direct labor	18
Variable manufacturing overhead	11
Variable selling and administrative expenses	6
Fixed selling and administrative expenses	5*
Fixed manufacturing overhead	15**
Total unit cost	$71

$$\begin{pmatrix}\text{Total}\\\text{unit cost}\end{pmatrix} + \left(\begin{pmatrix}\text{Total}\\\text{unit cost}\end{pmatrix} \times \begin{pmatrix}\text{Markup}\\\text{percentage}\end{pmatrix}\right) = \begin{pmatrix}\text{Target}\\\text{selling price}\end{pmatrix}$$

$$\$71 + (\$71 \times 45\%) = \$102.95$$

*$50,000 ÷ 10,000; **$150,000 ÷ 10,000

Related exercise material: **BE22-2, BE22-3, BE22-4, BE22-5, E22-3, E22-4, E22-5, E22-6, E22-7,** and DO IT! **22-2.**

✔ **The Navigator**

Pricing Services

Another variation on cost-plus pricing is **time-and-material pricing**. Under this approach, the company sets two pricing rates—one for the **labor** used on a job and another for the **material**. The labor rate includes direct labor time and other employee costs. The material charge is based on the cost of direct parts and materials used and a **material loading charge** for related overhead costs. Time-and-material pricing is widely used in service industries, especially professional firms such as public accounting, law, engineering, and consulting firms, as well as construction companies, repair shops, and printers.

To illustrate a time-and-material pricing situation, assume the following data for Lake Holiday Marina, a boat and motor repair shop.

 LEARNING OBJECTIVE   3

Use time-and-material pricing to determine the cost of services provided.

Illustration 22-13
Total annual budgeted time and material costs

Lake Holiday Marina Budgeted Costs for the Year 2014		
	Time Charges	**Material Loading Charges***
Mechanics' wages and benefits	$103,500	—
Parts manager's salary and benefits	—	$11,500
Office employee's salary and benefits	20,700	2,300
Other overhead (supplies, depreciation, property taxes, advertising, utilities)	26,800	14,400
Total budgeted costs	$151,000	$28,200

*The material loading charges exclude the invoice cost of the materials.

Using time-and-material pricing involves three steps: (1) calculate the per hour labor charge, (2) calculate the charge for obtaining and holding materials, and (3) calculate the charges for a particular job.

STEP 1: CALCULATE THE LABOR RATE.   The first step for time-and-material pricing is to determine a charge for labor time. The charge for labor time is expressed as a rate per hour of labor. This rate includes (1) the direct labor cost of the employee, including hourly rate or salary and fringe benefits; (2) selling, administrative, and similar overhead costs; and (3) an allowance for a desired profit or ROI per hour of employee time. In some industries, such as repair shops for autos and boats, the same hourly labor rate is charged regardless of which employee performs the work. In other industries, the rate that is charged is adjusted according to classification or level of the employee. A public accounting firm, for example, would charge different rates for the services of an assistant, senior, manager, or partner; a law firm would charge different rates for the work of a paralegal, associate, or partner.

Illustration 22-14 shows computation of the hourly charges for Lake Holiday Marina during 2014. The marina budgets 5,000 annual labor hours in 2014, and it desires a profit margin of $8 per hour of labor.

Illustration 22-14
Computation of hourly time-charge rate

	Lake Holiday Marina.xls					
	Home Insert Page Layout Formulas Data Review View					
	P18 *fx*					
	A	B	C	D	E	F
1	**Per Hour**	**Total Cost**	÷	**Total Hours**	=	**Per Hour Charge**
2	Hourly labor rate for repairs					
3	Mechanics' wages and benefits	$103,500	÷	5,000	=	$20.70
4	Overhead costs					
5	Office employee's salary and benefits	20,700	÷	5,000	=	4.14
6	Other overhead	26,800	÷	5,000	=	5.36
7	Total hourly cost	$151,000	÷	5,000	=	30.20
8	Profit margin					8.00
9	Rate charged per hour of labor					$38.20
10						

The marina multiplies this rate of $38.20 by the number of hours of labor used on any particular job to determine the labor charge for that job.

STEP 2: CALCULATE THE MATERIAL LOADING CHARGE.   The charge for materials typically includes the invoice price of any materials used on the job plus a material loading charge. The **material loading charge** covers the costs of purchasing, receiving, handling, and storing materials, plus any desired profit margin on the materials themselves. The material loading charge is expressed as a **percentage** of the total estimated costs of parts and materials for the year. To determine this percentage, the company does the following: (1) It estimates its total annual costs for purchasing, receiving, handling, and storing materials. (2) It divides this amount by the total estimated cost of parts and materials. (3) It adds a desired profit margin on the materials themselves.

Illustration 22-15 shows computation of the material loading charge used by Lake Holiday Marina during 2014. The marina estimates that the total invoice cost of parts and materials used in 2014 will be $120,000. The marina desires a 20% profit margin on the invoice cost of parts and materials.

	A	B	C	D	E	F
1		**Material Loading Charges**	÷	**Total Invoice Cost, Parts and Materials**	=	**Material Loading Percentage**
2	Overhead costs					
3	Parts manager's salary and benefits	$11,500				
4	Office employee's salary	2,300				
5		13,800	÷	$120,000	=	11.50%
6						
7	Other overhead	14,400	÷	120,000	=	12.00%
8		$28,200	÷	120,000	=	23.50%
9	Profit margin					20.00%
10	Material loading percentage					43.50%
11						

Illustration 22-15
Computation of material loading charge

The marina's material loading charge on any particular job is 43.50% multiplied by the cost of materials used on the job. For example, if the marina used $100 of parts, the additional material loading charge would be $43.50.

STEP 3: CALCULATE CHARGES FOR A PARTICULAR JOB. The charges for any particular job are the sum of (1) the labor charge, (2) the charge for the materials, and (3) the material loading charge. For example, suppose that Lake Holiday Marina prepares a price quotation to estimate the cost to refurbish a used 28-foot pontoon boat. Lake Holiday Marina estimates the job will require 50 hours of labor and $3,600 in parts and materials. Illustration 22-16 shows the marina's price quotation.

Illustration 22-16
Price quotation for time and material

Lake Holiday Marina		
Time-and-Material Price Quotation		
Job: Marianne Perino, repair of 28-foot pontoon boat		
Labor charges: 50 hours @ $38.20		$1,910
Material charges		
Cost of parts and materials	$3,600	
Material loading charge (43.5% × $3,600)	1,566	5,166
Total price of labor and material		$7,076

Included in the $7,076 price quotation for the boat repair are charges for labor costs, overhead costs, materials costs, materials handling and storage costs, and a profit margin on both labor and parts. Lake Holiday Marina used labor hours as a basis for computing the time rate. Other companies, such as machine shops, plastic molding shops, and printers, might use machine hours.

> **DO IT!**

Time-and-Material Pricing

Presented below are data for Harmon Electrical Repair Shop for next year.

Repair-technicians' wages	$130,000
Fringe benefits	30,000
Overhead	20,000

The desired profit margin per labor hour is $10. The material loading charge is 40% of invoice cost. Harmon estimates that 8,000 labor hours will be worked next year. If Harmon repairs a TV that takes 4 hours to repair and uses parts costing $50, compute the bill for this job.

Solution

Action Plan

✔ Calculate the labor charge.

✔ Calculate the material loading charge.

✔ Compute the bill for specific repair.

	Total Cost	÷	Total Hours	=	Per Hour Charge
Repair-technicians' wages	$130,000	÷	8,000	=	$16.25
Fringe benefits	30,000	÷	8,000	=	3.75
Overhead	20,000	÷	8,000	=	2.50
	$180,000	÷	8,000	=	22.50
Profit margin					10.00
Rate charged per hour of labor					$32.50

Job: Repair TV
Labor charges: 4 hours @ $32.50		$130
Material charges		
Cost of parts and materials	$50	
Material loading charge (40% × $50)	20	70
Total price of labor and material		$200

Related exercise material: **BE22-6, E22-8, E22-9, E22-10, and** DO IT! **22-3.**

✔ **The Navigator**

SERVICE COMPANY INSIGHT

It Ain't Like It Used to Be

For many decades, professionals in most service industries have used some form of hourly based price, regardless of the outcome. But the most recent recession appears to have brought an end to that practice. Many customers are now demanding that the bill be tied to actual performance, rather than to the amount of hours worked. For example, one communications company that used to charge about $15,000 or more per month as its "retainer fee" now instead charges based on achieving particular outcomes. Now, it might charge $10,000 if it obtains a desirable public speaking engagement for a company executive. Similarly, a digital marketing agency reduced its hourly fee from $135 to $80, but it gets a bonus if it achieves specified increases in the sales volume on a customer's website.

Source: Simona Covel, "Firms Try Alternative to Hourly Fees," *Wall Street Journal Online* (April 2, 2009).

 What implications does this have for a service company's need for managerial accounting? (See page 1129.)

Transfer Pricing for Internal Sales

In today's global economy, growth is often vital to survival. Some companies grow "vertically," meaning the company expands in the direction of either its suppliers or its customers. For example, a manufacturer of bicycles like Trek may acquire a bicycle component manufacturer or a chain of bicycle shops. A movie production company like Walt Disney or Time Warner may acquire a movie theater chain or a cable television company.

Divisions within vertically integrated companies normally transfer goods or services to other divisions within the same company, as well as make sales to customers outside the company. When goods are transferred between divisions of the same company, the price used to record the transaction is the **transfer price**. Illustration 22-17 shows transfers between divisions for Aerobic Bicycle Company. As shown, the Component Division sells goods to the company's Assembly Division, as well as to outside parties. Units sold to the Assembly Division are recorded at the transfer price.

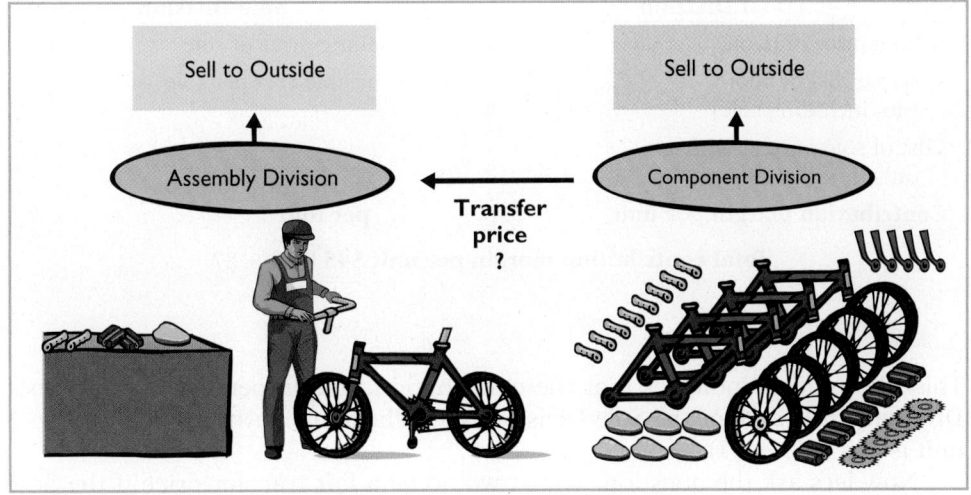

Illustration 22-17
Transfer pricing example

The primary objective of transfer pricing is the same as that of pricing a product to an outside party. The objective is to maximize the return to the company. An additional objective of transfer pricing is to measure divisional performance accurately. Setting a transfer price is complicated because of competing interests among divisions within the company. For example, in the case of the bicycle company shown in Illustration 22-17, setting the transfer price high will benefit the Component Division (the selling division), but will hurt the Assembly Division (the purchasing division).

There are three possible approaches for determining a transfer price:

1. Negotiated transfer prices.
2. Cost-based transfer prices.
3. Market-based transfer prices.

Conceptually, a negotiated transfer price should work best, but due to practical considerations, companies often use the other two methods.

Negotiated Transfer Prices

A **negotiated transfer price** is determined through agreement of division managers. To illustrate negotiated transfer pricing, we examine Alberta Company. Until recently, Alberta focused exclusively on making rubber soles for work boots and hiking boots. It sold these rubber soles to boot manufacturers. However, last year the company decided to take advantage of its strong reputation by expanding into the business of making hiking boots. As a consequence of this expansion, the company is now structured as two independent divisions, the Boot Division and the Sole Division. The company compensates the manager of each division based on achievement of profitability targets for that division.

The Boot Division manufactures leather uppers for hiking boots and attaches these uppers to rubber soles. During its first year, the Boot Division purchased its rubber soles from an *outside supplier* so as not to disrupt the operations of the Sole Division. However, top management now wants the Sole Division to provide at least some of the soles used by the Boot Division. Illustration 22-18 shows the computation of the contribution margin per unit for each division when the Boot Division purchases soles from an outside supplier.

Illustration 22-18
Computation of contribution margin for two divisions, when Boot Division purchases soles from an outside supplier

Boot Division		Sole Division	
Selling price of boots	$90	Selling price of sole	$18
Variable cost of boot (not including sole)	35	Variable cost per sole	11
Cost of sole purchased from outside supplier	17	**Contribution margin per unit**	**$ 7**
Contribution margin per unit	**$38**		

Total contribution margin per unit **$45** ($38 + $7)

This information indicates that the contribution margin per unit for the Boot Division is $38 and for the Sole Division is $7. The total contribution margin per unit is $45 ($38 + $7).

Now let's ask the question, "What would be a fair transfer price if the Sole Division sold 10,000 soles to the Boot Division?" The answer depends on how busy the Sole Division is—that is, whether it has excess capacity.

NO EXCESS CAPACITY

As indicated in Illustration 22-18, the Sole Division charges outside customers $18 and derives a contribution margin of $7 per sole. The Sole Division has **no excess capacity** and produces and sells 80,000 units (soles) to outside customers. Therefore, the Sole Division must receive from the Boot Division a payment that will at least cover its variable cost per sole **plus** its lost contribution margin per sole. (This lost contribution margin is often referred to as **opportunity cost**.) If the Sole Division cannot recover that amount—called the **minimum transfer price**—it should not sell its soles to the Boot Division. The minimum transfer price that would be acceptable to the Sole Division is $18, as shown below.

Illustration 22-19
Minimum transfer price—no excess capacity

Variable Cost	+	Opportunity Cost	=	Minimum Transfer Price
$11	+	$7	=	$18

From the perspective of the Boot Division (the buyer), the most it will pay is what the sole would cost from an outside supplier. In this case, therefore, the Boot Division would pay no more than $17. As shown in Illustration 22-20, an acceptable transfer price is not available in this situation.

Illustration 22-20
Transfer price negotiations—
no deal

EXCESS CAPACITY

What happens if the Sole Division **has excess capacity**? For example, assume the Sole Division can produce 80,000 soles but can sell only 70,000 soles in the open market. As a result, it has available capacity of 10,000 units. Because it has excess capacity, the Sole Division could provide 10,000 units to the Boot Division without losing its $7 contribution margin on these units. Therefore, the minimum price it would now accept is $11, as shown below.

Variable Cost	+	Opportunity Cost	=	Minimum Transfer Price
$11	+	$0	=	$11

Illustration 22-21
Minimum transfer price
formula—excess capacity

In this case, the Boot Division and the Sole Division should negotiate a transfer price within the range of $11 to $17, as shown in Illustration 22-22.

Illustration 22-22
Transfer pricing
negotiations—deal

Given excess capacity, Alberta Company will increase its overall net income if the Boot Division purchases the 10,000 soles internally. This is true as long as the Sole Division's variable cost is less than the outside price of $17. The Sole

Division will receive a positive contribution margin from any transfer price above its variable cost of $11. The Boot Division will benefit from any price below $17. At any transfer price above $17 the Boot Division will go to an outside supplier, a solution that would be undesirable to both divisions, as well as to the company as a whole.

VARIABLE COSTS

In the minimum transfer price formula, **variable cost is defined as the variable cost of units sold _internally_**. In some instances, the variable cost of units sold internally will differ from the variable cost of units sold externally. For example, companies often can avoid some variable selling expenses when units are sold internally. In this case, the variable cost of units sold internally will be lower than that of units sold externally.

Alternatively, the variable cost of units sold internally could be higher than normal if the internal division requests a special order that requires more expensive materials or additional labor. For example, assume that the Boot Division designs a new high-margin, heavy-duty boot. The sole for this boot will use denser rubber with an intricate lug design. Alberta Company is not aware of any supplier that currently makes such a sole, nor does it feel that any other supplier can meet its quality expectations. As a consequence, there is no available market price to use as the transfer price.

We can, however, employ the formula for the minimum transfer price to assist in arriving at a reasonable solution. After evaluating the special sole, the Sole Division determines that its variable cost would be $19 per sole. The Sole Division is at full capacity. The Sole Division's opportunity cost at full capacity is the $7 ($18 − $11) per sole that it earns producing the standard sole and selling it to an outside customer. Therefore, the minimum transfer price that the Sole Division would be willing to accept for the special-order sole would be:

Illustration 22-23
Minimum transfer price formula—special order

Variable Cost	+	Opportunity Cost	=	Minimum Transfer Price
$19	+	$7	=	$26

The transfer price of $26 provides the Sole Division with enough revenue to cover its increased variable cost and its opportunity cost (contribution margin on its standard sole).

SUMMARY OF NEGOTIATED TRANSFER PRICING

Under negotiated transfer pricing, the selling division establishes a minimum transfer price, and the purchasing division establishes a maximum transfer price. This system provides a sound basis for establishing a transfer price because both divisions are better off if the proper decision rules are used. However, companies often do not use negotiated transfer pricing because:

- Market price information is sometimes not easily obtainable.
- A lack of trust between the two negotiating divisions may lead to a breakdown in the negotiations.
- Negotiations often lead to different pricing strategies from division to division, which is cumbersome and sometimes costly to implement.

Many companies, therefore, often use simple systems based on cost or market information to develop transfer prices.

> **DO IT!**

Transfer Pricing

The clock division of Control Central Corporation manufactures clocks and then sells them to customers for $10 per unit. Its variable cost is $4 per unit, and its fixed cost per unit is $2.50. Management would like the clock division to transfer 8,000 of these clocks to another division within the company at a price of $5. The clock division could avoid $0.50 per clock of variable packaging costs by selling internally.

(a) Determine the minimum transfer price, assuming the clock division is not operating at full capacity. (b) Determine the minimum transfer price, assuming the clock division is operating at full capacity.

Solution

Action Plan

✔ Determine whether the company is at full capacity or not.

✔ Determine variable cost and opportunity cost.

✔ Apply minimum transfer price formula.

(a) If the clock division is not operating at full capacity, the opportunity cost for the clocks is $0. Since internal sales will eliminate $0.50 of packaging costs, the variable cost per clock is $3.50 ($4 − $0.50).

Minimum transfer price	=	Variable cost	+	Opportunity cost
$3.50	=	$3.50	+	$0

(b) If the clock division is already operating at full capacity, the opportunity cost for the clocks is $6 ($10 − $4). Since internal sales will eliminate $0.50 of packaging costs, the variable cost per clock is $3.50 ($4 − $0.50).

Minimum transfer price	=	Variable cost	+	Opportunity cost
$9.50	=	$3.50	+	$6

Related exercise material: **BE22-7, BE22-8, BE22-9, E22-11, E22-12, E22-13, E22-14, E22-15,** and **DO IT!** 22-4.

✔ **The Navigator**

Cost-Based Transfer Prices

An alternative to negotiated transfer pricing is cost-based pricing. A **cost-based transfer price** is based on the costs incurred by the division producing the goods or services. A cost-based transfer price can be based on variable costs alone, or on variable costs plus fixed costs. Also, in some cases the selling division may add a markup.

The cost-based approach sometimes results in improper transfer prices. Improper transfer prices can reduce company profits and provide unfair evaluations of division performance. To illustrate, assume that Alberta Company requires the division to use a transfer price based on the variable cost of the sole. With no excess capacity, the contribution margins per unit for the two divisions are:

Illustration 22-24
Cost-based transfer price—10,000 units

Boot Division		Sole Division	
Selling price of boots	$90	Selling price of sole	$11
Variable cost of boot (not including sole)	35	Variable cost per sole	11
Cost of sole purchased from sole division	11		
Contribution margin per unit	**$44**	**Contribution margin per unit**	**$ 0**

Total contribution margin per unit $44 ($44 + $0)

This cost-based transfer system is a bad deal for the Sole Division as it reports no profit on the transfer of 10,000 soles to the Boot Division. If the Sole Division could sell these soles to an outside customer, it would make $70,000 [10,000 × ($18 − $11)]. The Boot Division, on the other hand, is delighted: its contribution margin per unit increases from $38 to $44, or $6 per boot. Thus, this transfer price results in an unfair evaluation of these two divisions.

Further examination of this example reveals that this transfer price reduces the company's overall profits. The Sole Division lost a contribution margin per unit of $7 (Illustration 22-18, page 1096), and the Boot Division experiences only a $6 increase in its contribution margin per unit. Overall, Alberta Company loses $10,000 [10,000 boots × ($7 − $6)]. Illustration 22-25 illustrates this deficiency.

Illustration 22-25
Cost-based transfer price results—no excess capacity

The overall results change if the Sole Division **has excess capacity**. In this case, the Sole Division continues to report a zero profit on these 10,000 units but does not lose the $7 per unit of contribution margin (because it had excess capacity). The Boot Division gains $6. So overall, the company is better off by $60,000 (10,000 × $6). However, with a cost-based system, the Sole Division continues to report a zero profit on these 10,000 units.

We can see that a cost-based system does not reflect the division's true profitability. What's more, **it does not provide adequate incentive for the Sole Division to control costs**. The division's costs are simply passed on to the next division.

Notwithstanding these disadvantages, the cost system is simple to understand and easy to use because the information is already available in the accounting system. In addition, market information is sometimes not available, so the only alternative is some type of cost-based system. As a result, it is the most common method used by companies to establish transfer prices.

Market-Based Transfer Prices

The **market-based transfer price** is based on existing market prices of competing goods or services. A market-based system is often considered the best approach because it is objective and generally provides the proper economic incentives. For example, if the Sole Division can charge the market price, it is indifferent as to whether soles are sold to outside customers or internally to the Boot Division—it does not lose any contribution margin. Similarly, the Boot Division pays a price for the soles that is at or reasonably close to market.

When the Sole Division has no excess capacity, the market-based system works reasonably well. The Sole Division receives market price, and the Boot Division pays market price.

If the Sole Division has excess capacity, however, the market-based system can lead to actions that are not in the best interest of the company. The minimum transfer price that the Sole Division should receive is its variable cost plus opportunity cost. If the Sole Division has excess capacity, its opportunity cost is zero. However, under the market-based system, the Sole Division transfers the goods at the market price of $18, for a contribution margin per unit of $7 ($18 − $11). The Boot Division manager has to accept the $18 sole price. This price may not accurately reflect a fair cost of the sole, given that the Sole Division had excess capacity. As a result, the Boot Division may overprice its boots in the market if it uses the market price of the sole plus a markup in setting the price of the boot. This action can lead to losses for Alberta overall.

As indicated earlier, in many cases, there simply is not a well-defined market for the good or service being transferred. When this is the case, a reasonable market value cannot be developed, so companies often resort to a cost-based system.

Effect of Outsourcing on Transfer Pricing

An increasing number of companies rely on **outsourcing**. Outsourcing involves contracting with an external party to provide a good or service, rather than performing the work internally. Some companies have taken outsourcing to the extreme by outsourcing all of their production. Many of these so-called **virtual companies** have well-established brand names though they do not manufacture any of their own products. Companies use incremental analysis (Chapter 21) to determine whether outsourcing is profitable. When companies outsource, fewer components are transferred internally between divisions. This reduces the need for transfer prices.

Transfers Between Divisions in Different Countries

As more companies "globalize" their operations, an increasing number of inter-company transfers are between divisions that are located in different countries. One estimate suggests that 60% of trade between countries is simply transfers between company divisions. Differences in tax rates across countries can complicate the determination of the appropriate transfer price.

LEARNING OBJECTIVE	5

Explain issues involved in transferring goods between divisions in different countries.

Companies must pay income tax in the country where they generate the income. In order to maximize income and minimize income tax, many companies prefer to report more income in countries with low tax rates, and less income in countries with high tax rates. They accomplish this by adjusting the transfer prices they use on internal transfers between divisions located in different countries. They allocate more contribution margin to the division in the low-tax-rate country, and allocate less to the division in the high-tax-rate country.

To illustrate, suppose that Alberta's Boot Division is located in a country with a corporate tax rate of 10%, and the Sole Division is located in a country with a tax rate of 30%. Illustration 22-26 (page 1102) compares the after-tax contribution margin to the company using a transfer price of $18 versus a transfer price of $11.

Note that the *before-tax* total contribution margin to Alberta Company is $44 regardless of whether the transfer price is $18 or $11. However, the *after-tax* total contribution margin to Alberta Company is $38.20 using the $18 transfer price, and $39.60 using the $11 transfer price. The reason: When Alberta uses the $11 transfer price, more of the contribution margin is attributed to the division that is in the country with the lower tax rate, so it pays $1.40 less per shoe in taxes [($3.70 + $2.10) − $4.40].

As this analysis shows, Alberta Company would be better off using the $11 transfer price. However, this presents some concerns. First, the Sole Division

Illustration 22-26
After-tax contribution margin per unit under alternative transfer prices

At $18 Transfer Price

Boot Division		Sole Division	
Selling price of boots	$90.00	Selling price of sole	$18.00
Variable cost of boot (not including sole)	35.00	Variable cost per sole	11.00
Cost of sole purchased internally	18.00		
Before-tax contribution margin	37.00	Before-tax contribution margin	7.00
Tax at 10%	3.70	Tax at 30%	2.10
After-tax contribution margin	$33.30	After-tax contribution margin	$ 4.90

Before-tax total contribution margin per unit to company = $37 + $7 = **$44**
After-tax total contribution margin per unit to company = $33.30 + $4.90 = **$38.20**

At $11 Transfer Price

Boot Division		Sole Division	
Selling price of boots	$90.00	Selling price of sole	$11.00
Variable cost of boot (not including sole)	35.00	Variable cost per sole	11.00
Cost of sole purchased internally	11.00		
Before-tax contribution margin	44.00	Before-tax contribution margin	0.00
Tax at 10%	4.40	Tax at 30%	0.00
After-tax contribution margin	$39.60	After-tax contribution margin	$ 0.00

Before-tax total contribution margin per unit to company = $44 + $0 = **$44**
After-tax total contribution margin per unit to company = $39.60 + $0 = **$39.60**

manager won't be happy with an $11 transfer price. This price may lead to unfair evaluations of the Sole Division's manager. Second, the company must ask whether it is legal and ethical to use an $11 transfer price when the market price clearly is higher than that.

Additional consideration of international transfer pricing is presented in advanced accounting texts.

ETHICS INSIGHT

Transferring Profits and Reducing Taxes

International transfer pricing issues create a huge headache for the Internal Revenue Service. Some estimates suggest that the United States loses over $25 billion in underpaid taxes due to transfer price abuses. Occasionally, violators are caught. Toyota, for example, reportedly paid a $1 billion settlement. But enforcement is complicated and time-consuming, and many foreign firms are reluctant to give access to their records.

U.S. companies have also been accused of transfer pricing abuse. It has been noted that at one time, U.S. giant Westinghouse booked over 25% of its profit in the tiny island of Puerto Rico. At the time, the corporate tax rate there was zero. The rules require that the transfer price be based on the current market price that a nonrelated party would pay for the goods. But often this current market price is difficult to determine.

? What are the implications for other taxpayers if companies reduce their taxes by using improper transfer prices to shift profits to lower-tax countries? (See page 1129.)

Revco Electronics is a division of International Motors, an automobile manufacturer. Revco produces car radio/CD players. Revco sells its products to International Motors, as well as to other car manufacturers and electronics distributors. The following information is available regarding Revco's car radio/CD player.

Selling price of car radio/CD player to external customers	$49
Variable cost per unit	$28
Capacity	200,000 units

Instructions

Determine whether the goods should be transferred internally or purchased externally and what the appropriate transfer price should be under each of the following **independent** situations.

(a) Revco Electronics is operating at full capacity. There is a saving of $4 per unit for variable cost if the car radio is made for internal sale. International Motors can purchase a comparable car radio from an outside supplier for $47.

(b) Revco Electronics has sufficient existing capacity to meet the needs of International Motors. International Motors can purchase a comparable car radio from an outside supplier for $47.

(c) International Motors wants to purchase a special-order car radio/CD player with additional features. It needs 15,000 units. Revco Electronics has determined that the additional variable cost would be $12 per unit. Revco Electronics has no spare capacity. It will have to forgo sales of 15,000 units to external parties in order to provide this special order.

Solution to Comprehensive DO IT!

Action Plan

✔ Determine whether company is at full capacity or not.

✔ Find the minimum transfer price, using formulas.

✔ Compare maximum price the buyer would pay to the minimum price for the seller.

✔ Determine if a deal can be made.

(a) Revco Electronics' opportunity cost (its lost contribution margin) would be $21 ($49 − $28). Using the formula for minimum transfer price, we determine:

$$\begin{array}{ccccc} \text{Minimum transfer price} & = & \text{Variable cost} & + & \text{Opportunity cost} \\ \$45 & = & (\$28 - \$4) & + & \$21 \end{array}$$

Since this minimum transfer price is less than the $47 it would cost if International Motors purchases from an external party, internal transfer should take place. Revco Electronics and International Motors should negotiate a transfer price between $45 and $47.

(b) Since Revco Electronics has available capacity, its opportunity cost (its lost contribution margin) would be $0. Using the formula for minimum transfer price, we determine the following.

$$\begin{array}{ccccc} \text{Minimum transfer price} & = & \text{Variable cost} & + & \text{Opportunity cost} \\ \$28 & = & \$28 & + & \$0 \end{array}$$

Since International Motors can purchase the unit for $47 from an external party, the most it would be willing to pay would be $47. It is in the best interest of the company as a whole, as well as the two divisions, for a transfer to take place. The two divisions must reach a negotiated transfer price between $28 and $47 that recognizes the costs and benefits to each party and is acceptable to both.

(c) Revco Electronics' opportunity cost (its lost contribution margin per unit) would be $21 ($49 − $28). Its variable cost would be $40 ($28 + $12). Using the formula for minimum transfer price, we determine the following.

$$\begin{array}{ccccc} \text{Minimum transfer price} & = & \text{Variable cost} & + & \text{Opportunity cost} \\ \$61 & = & \$40 & + & \$21 \end{array}$$

Note that in this case Revco Electronics has no available capacity. Its management may decide that it does not want to provide this special order because to do so will require that it cut off the supply of the standard unit to some of its existing customers. This may anger those customers and result in the loss of customers.

✔ The Navigator

1 Compute a target cost when the market determines a product price. To compute a target cost, the company determines its target selling price. Once the target selling price is set, it determines its target cost by setting a desired profit. The difference between the target price and desired profit is the target cost of the product.

2 Compute a target selling price using cost-plus pricing. Cost-plus pricing involves establishing a cost base and adding to this cost base a markup to determine a target selling price. The cost-plus pricing formula is expressed as follows: Target selling price = Cost + (Markup percentage × Cost).

3 Use time-and-material pricing to determine the cost of services provided. Under time-and-material pricing, two pricing rates are set—one for the labor used on a job and another for the material. The labor rate includes direct labor time and other employee costs. The material charge is based on the cost of direct parts and materials used and a material loading charge for related overhead costs.

4 Determine a transfer price using the negotiated, cost-based, and market-based approaches. The negotiated price is determined through agreement of division managers. Under a cost-based approach, the transfer price may be based on variable cost alone or on variable costs plus fixed costs. Companies may add a markup to these numbers. The cost-based approach often leads to poor performance evaluations and purchasing decisions. The advantage of the cost-based system is its simplicity. A market-based transfer price is based on existing competing market prices and services. A market-based system is often considered the best approach because it is objective and generally provides the proper economic incentives.

5 Explain issues involved in transferring goods between divisions in different countries. Companies must pay income tax in the country where they generate the income. In order to maximize income and minimize income tax, many companies prefer to report more income in countries with low tax rates, and less income in countries with high tax rates. This is accomplished by adjusting the transfer prices they use on internal transfers between divisions located in different countries.

APPENDIX 22A   OTHER COST APPROACHES TO PRICING

LEARNING OBJECTIVE   6

Determine prices using absorption-cost pricing and variable-cost pricing.

In determining the target price for Thinkmore's video camera pen in the chapter, we calculated the cost base **by including all costs incurred**. This approach is referred to as **full-cost pricing**. Using total cost as the basis of the markup makes sense conceptually because, in the long run, the price must cover all costs and provide a reasonable profit. However, total cost is difficult to determine in practice. This is because period costs (selling and administrative expenses) are difficult to trace to a specific product. Activity-based costing can be used to overcome this difficulty to some extent.

In practice, companies sometimes use two other cost approaches: (1) absorption-cost pricing or (2) variable-cost pricing. Absorption-cost pricing is more popular than variable-cost pricing.[2] We illustrate both approaches because both have merit.

Absorption-Cost Pricing

Absorption-cost pricing is consistent with generally accepted accounting principles (GAAP). The reason: It includes both variable and fixed manufacturing costs as product costs. **It excludes from this cost base both variable and fixed**

---

[2]For a discussion of cost-plus pricing, see Eunsup Skim and Ephraim F. Sudit, "How Manufacturers Price Products," *Management Accounting* (February 1995), pp. 37–39; and V. Govindarajan and R.N. Anthony, "How Firms Use Cost Data in Pricing Decisions," *Management Accounting* (65, no. 1), pp. 30–36.

selling and administrative costs. Thus, companies must somehow provide for selling and administrative costs plus the target ROI, and they do this through the markup.

The **first step** in absorption-cost pricing is to compute the unit **manufacturing cost.** For Thinkmore Products, Inc., this amounts to $80 per unit at a volume of 10,000 units, as shown in Illustration 22A-1.

	Per Unit
Direct materials	$23
Direct labor	17
Variable manufacturing overhead	12
Fixed manufacturing overhead ($280,000 ÷ 10,000)	28
Total unit manufacturing cost (absorption cost)	$80

Illustration 22A-1
Computation of unit manufacturing cost

In addition, Thinkmore provides the following information regarding selling and administrative expenses per unit and desired ROI per unit.

Variable selling and administrative expenses	$ 8
Fixed selling and administrative expenses ($240,000 ÷ 10,000)	$24
Desired ROI per unit	$20

Illustration 22A-2
Other information

The **second step** in absorption-cost pricing is to compute the markup percentage using the formula in Illustration 22A-3. Note that when companies use manufacturing cost per unit as the cost base to compute the markup percentage, the **percentage must cover the desired ROI and also the selling and administrative expenses.**

Illustration 22A-3
Markup percentage—absorption-cost pricing

Desired ROI per Unit	+	Selling and Administrative Expenses per Unit	=	Markup Percentage	×	Manufacturing Cost per Unit
$20	+	$32	=	MP	×	$80

Solving we find:

$$MP = (\$20 + \$32) \div \$80 = 65\%$$

The **third** and final **step** is to set the target selling price. Using a markup percentage of 65% and absorption-cost pricing, Thinkmore computes the target selling price as shown in Illustration 22A-4.

Illustration 22A-4
Computation of target price—absorption-cost pricing

Manufacturing Cost per Unit	+	(Markup Percentage	×	Manufacturing Cost per Unit)	=	Target Selling Price
$80	+	(65%	×	$80)	=	$132

Using a target price of $132 will produce the desired 20% return on investment for Thinkmore Products on its video camera pen at a volume level of 10,000 units, as shown in Illustration 22A-5 (page 1106).

Thinkmore Products, Inc.		
Budgeted Absorption-Cost Income Statement		
Revenue (10,000 camera pens × $132)		$1,320,000
Cost of goods sold (10,000 camera pens × $80)		800,000
Gross profit		520,000
Selling and administrative expenses [10,000 camera pens × ($8 + $24)]		320,000
Net income		$ 200,000

Budgeted ROI

$$\frac{\text{Net income}}{\text{Invested assets}} = \frac{\$200,000}{\$1,000,000} = \textbf{20\%}$$

Markup Percentage

$$\frac{\text{Net income} + \text{Selling and administrative expenses}}{\text{Cost of goods sold}} = \frac{\$200,000 + \$320,000}{\$800,000} = \textbf{65\%}$$

Because of the fixed-cost element, if Thinkmore sells more than 10,000 units, the ROI will be greater than 20%. If it sells fewer than 10,000 units, the ROI will be less than 20%. The markup percentage is also verified by adding $200,000 (the net income) and $320,000 (selling and administrative expenses) and then dividing by $800,000 (the cost of goods sold or the cost base).

Most companies that use cost-plus pricing use either absorption cost or full cost as the basis. The reasons for this tendency are as follows.

1. Absorption-cost information is most readily provided by a company's cost accounting system. Because absorption-cost data already exist in general ledger accounts, it is cost-effective to use the data for pricing.

2. Basing the cost-plus formula on only variable costs could encourage managers to set too low a price to boost sales. There is the fear that if managers use only variable costs, they will substitute variable costs for full costs, which can lead to suicidal price cutting.

3. Absorption-cost or full-cost pricing provides the most defensible base for justifying prices to all interested parties—managers, customers, and government.

Variable-Cost Pricing

Under **variable-cost pricing**, the cost base consists of all of the **variable costs** associated with a product, including variable selling and administrative costs. **Because fixed costs are not included in the base, the markup must provide for all fixed costs (manufacturing, and selling and administrative) and the target ROI.** Variable-cost pricing is more useful for making short-run decisions because it considers variable-cost and fixed-cost behavior patterns separately.

The **first step** in variable-cost pricing is to compute the unit variable cost. For Thinkmore Products, Inc., this amounts to $60 per unit, as shown in Illustration 22A-6.

	Per Unit
Direct materials	$23
Direct labor	17
Variable manufacturing overhead	12
Variable selling and administrative expense	8
Total unit variable cost	$60

Illustration 22A-6
Computation of unit variable cost

The **second step** in variable-cost pricing is to compute the markup percentage. Illustration 22A-7 shows the formula for the markup percentage. For Thinkmore, fixed costs include fixed manufacturing overhead of $28 per unit ($280,000 ÷ 10,000) and fixed selling and administrative expenses of $24 per unit ($240,000 ÷ 10,000).

Desired ROI per Unit	+	Fixed Cost per Unit	=	Markup Percentage	×	Variable Cost per Unit
$20	+	($28 + $24)	=	MP	×	$60

Illustration 22A-7
Computation of markup percentage—variable-cost pricing

Solving, we find:

$$MP = \frac{\$20 + (\$28 + \$24)}{\$60} = 120\%$$

The **third step** is to set the target selling price. Using a markup percentage of 120% and the contribution approach, Thinkmore computes the selling price as shown in Illustration 22A-8.

Variable Cost per Unit	+	(Markup Percentage	×	Variable Cost per Unit)	=	Target Selling Price
$60	+	(120%	×	$60)	=	$132

Illustration 22A-8
Computation of target price—variable-cost pricing

Using a target price of $132 will produce the desired 20% return on investment for Thinkmore Products on its video camera pen at a volume level of 10,000 units, as shown in Illustration 22A-9.

Illustration 22A-9
Proof of 20% ROI—contribution approach

Thinkmore Products, Inc.
Budgeted Variable-Cost Income Statement

Revenue (10,000 camera pens × $132)		$1,320,000
Variable costs (10,000 camera pens × $60)		600,000
Contribution margin		720,000
Fixed manufacturing overhead (10,000 camera pens × $28)	$280,000	
Fixed selling and administrative expenses (10,000 camera pens × $24)	240,000	520,000
Net income		$ 200,000

Budgeted ROI

$$\frac{\text{Net income}}{\text{Invested assets}} = \frac{\$200,000}{\$1,000,000} = \mathbf{20\%}$$

Markup Percentage

$$\frac{\text{Net income} + \text{Fixed costs}}{\text{Variable costs}} = \frac{\$200,000 + \$520,000}{\$600,000} = \mathbf{120\%}$$

Under any of the three pricing approaches we have looked at (full-cost, absorption-cost, and variable-cost), the desired ROI will be attained only if the budgeted sales volume for the period is attained. None of these approaches guarantees a profit or a desired ROI. Achieving a desired ROI is the result of many factors, some of which are beyond the company's control, such as market conditions, political and legal issues, customers' tastes, and competitive actions.

Because absorption-cost pricing includes allocated fixed costs, it does not make clear how the company's costs will change as volume changes. To avoid blurring the effects of cost behavior on net income, some managers therefore prefer variable-cost pricing. The specific reasons for using variable-cost pricing, even though the basic accounting data are less accessible, are as follows.

1. Variable-cost pricing, being based on variable cost, is more consistent with cost-volume-profit analysis used by managers to measure the profit implications of changes in price and volume.

2. Variable-cost pricing provides the type of data managers need for pricing special orders. It shows the incremental cost of accepting one more order.

3. Variable-cost pricing avoids arbitrary allocation of common fixed costs (such as executive salaries) to individual product lines.

SUMMARY OF LEARNING OBJECTIVE FOR APPENDIX 22A

 **The Navigator**

6 Determine prices using absorption-cost pricing and variable-cost pricing. Absorption-cost pricing uses total manufacturing cost as the cost base and provides for selling and administrative costs plus the target ROI through the markup. The target selling price is computed as: Manufacturing cost per unit + (Markup percentage × Manufacturing cost per unit).

Variable-cost pricing uses all of the variable costs, including selling and administrative costs, as the cost base and provides for fixed costs and target ROI through the markup. The target selling price is computed as: Variable cost per unit + (Markup percentage × Variable cost per unit).

GLOSSARY

Absorption-cost pricing An approach to pricing that defines the cost base as the manufacturing cost; it excludes both variable and fixed selling and administrative costs. (p. 1104).

Cost-based transfer price A transfer price that uses as its foundation the costs incurred by the division producing the goods. (p. 1099).

Cost-plus pricing A process whereby a product's selling price is determined by adding a markup to a cost base. (p. 1086).

Full-cost pricing An approach to pricing that defines the cost base as all costs incurred. (p. 1090).

Market-based transfer price A transfer price that is based on existing market prices of competing products. (p. 1100).

Markup The amount added to a product's cost base to determine the product's selling price. (p. 1086).

Material loading charge A charge added to cover the cost of purchasing, receiving, handling, and storing materials, plus any desired profit margin on the materials themselves. (p. 1092).

Negotiated transfer price A transfer price that is determined by the agreement of the division managers. (p. 1096).

Outsourcing Contracting with an external party to provide a good or service, rather than performing the work internally. (p. 1101).

Target cost The cost that will provide the desired profit on a product when the seller does not have control over the product's price. (p. 1085).

Target selling price The selling price that will provide the desired profit on a product when the seller has the ability to determine the product's price. (p. 1086).

Time-and-material pricing An approach to cost-plus pricing in which the company uses two pricing rates, one for the labor used on a job and another for the material. (p. 1091).

Transfer price The price used to record the transfer of goods between two divisions of a company. (p. 1095).

Variable-cost pricing An approach to pricing that defines the cost base as all variable costs; it excludes both fixed manufacturing and fixed selling and administrative costs. (pp. 1090, 1106).

 **Self-Test, Brief Exercises, Exercises, Problem Set A, and many more resources are available for practice in WileyPLUS.**

Note: All asterisked Questions, Exercises, and Problems relate to material in the appendix to the chapter.

SELF-TEST QUESTIONS

Answers are at the end of the chapter.

(LO 1) **1.** Target cost related to price and profit means that:
  (a) cost and desired profit must be determined before selling price.
  (b) cost and selling price must be determined before desired profit.
  (c) price and desired profit must be determined before costs.
  (d) costs can be achieved only if the company is at full capacity.

(LO 1) **2.** Classic Toys has examined the market for toy train locomotives. It believes there is a market niche in which it can sell locomotives at $80 each. It estimates that it could sell 10,000 of these locomotives annually. Variable costs to make a locomotive are expected to be $25. Classic anticipates a profit of $15 per locomotive. The target cost for the locomotive is:
  (a) $80.   (c) $40.
  (b) $65.   (d) $25.

(LO 1, 2) **3.** In a competitive, common-product environment, a seller would most likely use:
  (a) time-and-material pricing.
  (b) variable costing.
  (c) target costing.
  (d) cost-plus pricing.

(LO 2) **4.** Cost-plus pricing means that:
  (a) Selling price = Variable cost + (Markup percentage + Variable cost).
  (b) Selling price = Cost + (Markup percentage × Cost).
  (c) Selling price = Manufacturing cost + (Markup percentage + Manufacturing cost).
  (d) Selling price = Fixed cost + (Markup percentage × Fixed cost).

(LO 2) **5.** Adler Company is considering developing a new product. The company has gathered the following information on this product.

Expected total unit cost	$25
Estimated investment for new product	$500,000
Desired ROI	10%
Expected number of units to be produced and sold	1,000

Given this information, the desired markup percentage and selling price are:
  (a) markup percentage 10%; selling price $55.
  (b) markup percentage 200%; selling price $75.
  (c) markup percentage 10%; selling price $50.
  (d) markup percentage 100%; selling price $55.

(LO 2) **6.** Mystique Co. provides the following information for the new product it recently introduced.

Total unit cost	$30
Desired ROI per unit	$10
Target selling price	$40

What would be Mystique Co.'s percentage markup on cost?
  (a) 125%.   (c) 33⅓%.
  (b) 75%.   (d) 25%.

(LO 3) **7.** Crescent Electrical Repair has decided to price its work on a time-and-material basis. It estimates the following costs for the year related to labor.

Technician wages and benefits	$100,000
Office employee's salary and benefits	$ 40,000
Other overhead	$ 80,000

Crescent desires a profit margin of $10 per labor hour and budgets 5,000 hours of repair time for the year. The office employee's salary, benefits, and other overhead costs should be divided evenly between time charges and material loading charges. Crescent labor charge per hour would be:
  (a) $42.   (c) $32.
  (b) $34.   (d) $30.

(LO 3) **8.** Time-and-material pricing would most likely be used by a:
  (a) garden-fertilizer producer.
  (b) lawn-mower manufacturer.
  (c) tree farm.
  (d) lawn-care provider.

(LO 4) **9.** The Plastics Division of Weston Company manufactures plastic molds and then sells them to customers for $70 per unit. Its variable cost is $30 per unit, and its fixed cost per unit is $10. Management would like the Plastics Division to transfer 10,000 of these molds to another division within the company at a price of $40. The Plastics Division is operating at full capacity. What is the minimum transfer price that the Plastics Division should accept?
  (a) $10.   (c) $40.
  (b) $30.   (d) $70.

(LO 4) **10.** Assume the same information as Question 9, except that the Plastics Division has available capacity of 10,000 units for plastic moldings. What is the minimum transfer price that the Plastics Division should accept?
  (a) $10.   (c) $40.
  (b) $30.   (d) $70.

(LO 4) **11.** The most common method used to establish transfer prices is the:
(a) negotiated transfer pricing approach.
(b) opportunity costing transfer pricing approach.
(c) cost-based transfer pricing approach.
(d) market-based transfer pricing approach.

(LO 4) **12.** When a company uses time-and-material pricing, the material loading charge is expressed as a percentage of:
(a) the total estimated labor costs for the year.
(b) the total estimated costs of parts and materials for the year.
(c) the total estimated overhead costs for the year.
(d) the total estimated costs of parts, materials, and labor for the year.

(LO 5) **13.** Global Industries transfers parts between divisions in two countries, Eastland and Westland. Eastland's tax rate is 8%, and Westland's tax rate is 16%. To minimize tax payments and maximize net income, Global should establish transfer prices that:
(a) allocate contribution margin equally between Eastland and Westland.
(b) allocate more contribution margin to Eastland.

(c) allocate more contribution margin to Westland.
(d) allocate half as much contribution margin to Eastland as it does to Westland.

*14. AST Electrical provides the following cost information (LO 6) related to its production of electronic circuit boards.

	Per Unit
Variable manufacturing cost	$40
Fixed manufacturing cost	$30
Variable selling and administrative expenses	$ 8
Fixed selling and administrative expenses	$12
Desired ROI per unit	$15

What is its markup percentage assuming that AST Electrical uses absorption-cost pricing?
(a) 16.67%.   (c) 54.28%.
(b) 50%.   (d) 118.75%.

*15. Assume the same information as question 14 and (LO 6) determine AST Electrical's markup percentage using variable-cost pricing.
(a) 16.67%.   (c) 54.28%.
(b) 50%.   (d) 118.75%.

Go to the book's companion website, www.wiley.com/college/weygandt, for additional Self-Test Questions.

 The Navigator

QUESTIONS

1. What are the two types of pricing environments for sales to external parties?

2. In what situation does a company place the greatest focus on its target cost? How is the target cost determined?

3. What is the basic formula to determine the target selling price in cost-plus pricing?

4. Benz Corporation produces a filter that has a per unit cost of $18. The company would like a 30% markup. Using cost-plus pricing, determine the per unit selling price.

5. What is the basic formula for the markup percentage?

6. What are some of the factors that affect a company's desired ROI?

7. Stanley Corporation manufactures an electronic switch for dishwashers. The cost base per unit, excluding selling and administrative expenses, is $60. The per unit cost of selling and administrative expenses is $15. The company's desired ROI per unit is $6. Calculate its markup percentage on total unit cost.

8. Sheen Co. manufactures a standard cabinet for a DVD player. The variable cost per unit is $16. The fixed cost per unit is $9. The desired ROI per unit is $6. Compute the markup percentage on total unit cost and the target selling price for the cabinet.

9. In what circumstances is time-and-material pricing most often used?

10. What is the material loading charge? How is it expressed?

11. What is a transfer price? Why is determining a fair transfer price important to division managers?

12. When setting a transfer price, what objective(s) should the company have in mind?

13. What are the three approaches for determining transfer prices?

14. Describe the cost-based approach to transfer pricing. What is the strength of this approach? What are the weaknesses of this approach?

15. What is the general formula for determining the minimum transfer price that the selling division should be willing to accept?

16. When determining the minimum transfer price, what is meant by the "opportunity cost"?

17. In what circumstances will a negotiated transfer price be used instead of a market-based price?

18. Explain how companies use transfer pricing between divisions located in different countries to reduce tax payments, and discuss the propriety of this approach.

*19. What costs are excluded from the cost base when absorption-cost pricing is used to determine the markup percentage?

*20. Marie Corporation manufactures a fiber optic connector. The variable cost per unit is $16. The fixed cost per unit is $9. The company's desired ROI per unit is $3. Compute the markup percentage using variable-cost pricing.

BRIEF EXERCISES

BE22-1 Voorhees Company manufactures computer hard drives. The market for hard drives is very competitive. The current market price for a computer hard drive is $45. Voorhees would like a profit of $15 per drive. How can Voorhees Company accomplish this objective?

Compute target cost.
(LO 1)

BE22-2 Mussatto Corporation produces snowboards. The following per unit cost information is available: direct materials $12; direct labor $8; variable manufacturing overhead $6; fixed manufacturing overhead $14; variable selling and administrative expenses $4; and fixed selling and administrative expenses $12. Using a 30% markup percentage on total per unit cost, compute the target selling price.

Use cost-plus pricing to determine selling price.
(LO 2)

BE22-3 Hannon Corporation produces high-performance rotors. It expects to produce 50,000 rotors in the coming year. It has invested $10,000,000 to produce rotors. The company has a required return on investment of 16%. What is its ROI per unit?

Compute ROI per unit.
(LO 2)

BE22-4 Morales Corporation produces microwave units. The following per unit cost information is available: direct materials $36; direct labor $24; variable manufacturing overhead $18; fixed manufacturing overhead $40; variable selling and administrative expenses $14; and fixed selling and administrative expenses $28. Its desired ROI per unit is $30. Compute its markup percentage using a total-cost approach.

Compute markup percentage.
(LO 2)

BE22-5 During the current year, Mast Corporation expects to produce 10,000 units and has budgeted the following: net income $300,000; variable costs $1,100,000; and fixed costs $100,000. It has invested assets of $1,500,000. The company's budgeted ROI was 24%. What was its budgeted markup percentage using a full-cost approach?

Compute ROI and markup percentage.
(LO 2)

BE22-6 Rooney Small Engine Repair charges $42 per hour of labor. It has a material loading percentage of 40%. On a recent job replacing the engine of a riding lawnmower, Rooney worked 10.5 hours and used parts with a cost of $700. Calculate Rooney's total bill.

Use time-and-material pricing to determine bill.
(LO 3)

BE22-7 The Heating Division of KLM International produces a heating element that it sells to its customers for $45 per unit. Its variable cost per unit is $20, and its fixed cost per unit is $10. Top management of KLM International would like the Heating Division to transfer 15,000 heating units to another division within the company at a price of $29. The Heating Division is operating at full capacity. What is the minimum transfer price that the Heating Division should accept?

Determine minimum transfer price.
(LO 4)

BE22-8 Use the data from BE22-7, but assume that the Heating Division has sufficient excess capacity to provide the 15,000 heating units to the other division. What is the minimum transfer price that the Heating Division should accept?

Determine minimum transfer price with excess capacity.
(LO 4)

BE22-9 Use the data from BE22-7, but assume that the units being requested are special high-performance units and that the division's variable cost would be $24 per unit (rather than $20). What is the minimum transfer price that the Heating Division should accept?

Determine minimum transfer price for special order.
(LO 4)

*BE22-10** Using the data in BE22-4, compute the markup percentage using absorption-cost pricing.

Compute markup percentage using absorption-cost pricing.
(LO 6)

*BE22-11** Using the data in BE22-4, compute the markup percentage using variable-cost pricing.

Compute markup percentage using variable-cost pricing.
(LO 6)

> ## DO IT! REVIEW

DO IT! 22-1 Krystal Water is considering introducing a water filtration device for its 20-ounce water bottles. Market research indicates that 1,000,000 units can be sold if the price is no more than $3. If Krystal Water decides to produce the filters, it will need to

Determine target cost.
(LO 1)

invest $2,000,000 in new production equipment. Krystal Water requires a minimum rate of return of 18% on all investments.

Determine the target cost per unit for the filter.

DO IT! **22-2** Gundy Corporation produces area rugs. The following per unit cost information is available: direct materials $18, direct labor $9, variable manufacturing overhead $5, fixed manufacturing overhead $6, variable selling and administrative expenses $3, and fixed selling and administrative expenses $7.

Using a 30% markup on total per unit cost, compute the target selling price.

DO IT! **22-3** Presented below are data for Kwik Appliance Repair Shop.

Repair-technicians' wages	$120,000
Fringe benefits	40,000
Overhead	50,000

The desired profit margin per hour is $20. The material loading charge is 60% of invoice cost. Kwik estimates that 5,000 labor hours will be worked next year. If Kwik repairs a dishwasher that takes 1.5 hours to repair and uses parts of $80, compute the bill for the job.

DO IT! **22-4** The fastener division of Southern Fasteners manufactures zippers and then sells them to customers for $8 per unit. Its variable cost is $3 per unit, and its fixed cost per unit is $1.50. Management would like the fastener division to transfer 12,000 of these zippers to another division within the company at a price of $3. The fastener division could avoid $0.20 per zipper of variable packaging costs by selling internally.

Determine the minimum transfer price (a) assuming the fastener division is not operating at full capacity, and (b) assuming the fastener division is operating at full capacity.

✔ **The Navigator**

EXERCISES

E22-1 Jarlsberg Cheese Company has developed a new cheese slicer called Slim Slicer. The company plans to sell this slicer through its catalog, which it issues monthly. Given market research, Jarlsberg believes that it can charge $20 for the Slim Slicer. Prototypes of the Slim Slicer, however, are costing $22. By using cheaper materials and gaining efficiencies in mass production, Jarlsberg believes it can reduce Slim Slicer's cost substantially. Jarlsberg wishes to earn a return of 30% of the selling price.

Instructions
(a) Compute the target cost for the Slim Slicer.
(b) When is target costing particularly helpful in deciding whether to produce a given product?

E22-2 Eckert Company is involved in producing and selling high-end golf equipment. The company has recently been involved in developing various types of laser guns to measure yardages on the golf course. One small laser gun, called LittleLaser, appears to have a very large potential market. Because of competition, Eckert does not believe that it can charge more than $90 for LittleLaser. At this price, Eckert believes it can sell 100,000 of these laser guns. Eckert will require an investment of $8,000,000 to manufacture, and the company wants an ROI of 20%.

Instructions
Determine the target cost for one LittleLaser.

E22-3 Hannon Company makes swimsuits and sells these suits directly to retailers. Although Hannon has a variety of suits, it does not make the All-Body suit used by highly skilled swimmers. The market research department believes that a strong market exists for this type of suit. The department indicates that the All-Body suit would sell for approximately $100. Given its experience, Hannon believes the All-Body suit would have the following manufacturing costs.

Direct materials	$ 25
Direct labor	30
Manufacturing overhead	45
Total costs	$100

Instructions

(a) Assume that Hannon uses cost-plus pricing, setting the selling price 20% above its costs. (1) What would be the price charged for the All-Body swimsuit? (2) Under what circumstances might Hannon consider manufacturing the All-Body swimsuit given this approach?

(b) Assume that Hannon uses target costing. What is the price that Hannon would charge the retailer for the All-Body swimsuit?

(c) What is the highest acceptable manufacturing cost Hannon would be willing to incur to produce the All-Body swimsuit, if it desired a profit of $20 per unit? (Assume target costing.)

E22-4 Kaspar Corporation makes a commercial-grade cooking griddle. The following information is available for Kaspar Corporation's anticipated annual volume of 30,000 units.

Use cost-plus pricing to determine selling price.

(LO 2)

	Per Unit	Total
Direct materials	$17	
Direct labor	$ 8	
Variable manufacturing overhead	$11	
Fixed manufacturing overhead		$300,000
Variable selling and administrative expenses	$ 4	
Fixed selling and administrative expenses		$150,000

The company uses a 40% markup percentage on total cost.

Instructions

(a) Compute the total cost per unit.

(b) Compute the target selling price.

E22-5 Paige Corporation makes a mechanical stuffed alligator that sings the Martian national anthem. The following information is available for Paige Corporation's anticipated annual volume of 500,000 units.

Use cost-plus pricing to determine various amounts.

(LO 2)

	Per Unit	Total
Direct materials	$ 7	
Direct labor	$ 9	
Variable manufacturing overhead	$15	
Fixed manufacturing overhead		$3,000,000
Variable selling and administrative expenses	$14	
Fixed selling and administrative expenses		$1,500,000

The company has a desired ROI of 25%. It has invested assets of $26,000,000.

Instructions

(a) Compute the total cost per unit.

(b) Compute the desired ROI per unit.

(c) Compute the markup percentage using total cost per unit.

(d) Compute the target selling price.

E22-6 Alma's Recording Studio rents studio time to musicians in 2-hour blocks. Each session includes the use of the studio facilities, a digital recording of the performance, and a professional music producer/mixer. Anticipated annual volume is 1,000 sessions. The company has invested $2,352,000 in the studio and expects a return on investment (ROI) of 20%. Budgeted costs for the coming year are as follows.

Use cost-plus pricing to determine various amounts.

(LO 2)

	Per Session	Total
Direct materials (tapes, CDs, etc)	$ 20	
Direct labor	$400	
Variable overhead	$ 50	
Fixed overhead		$950,000
Variable selling and administrative expenses	$ 40	
Fixed selling and administrative expenses		$500,000

Instructions
(a) Determine the total cost per session.
(b) Determine the desired ROI per session.
(c) Calculate the markup percentage on the total cost per session.
(d) Calculate the target price per session.

Use cost-plus pricing to determine various amounts.

(LO 2)

E22-7 Pargo Corporation produces industrial robots for high-precision manufacturing. The following information is given for Pargo Corporation.

	Per Unit	Total
Direct materials	$380	
Direct labor	$290	
Variable manufacturing overhead	$ 72	
Fixed manufacturing overhead		$1,800,000
Variable selling and administrative expenses	$ 55	
Fixed selling and administrative expenses		$ 324,000

The company has a desired ROI of 20%. It has invested assets of $51,000,000. It anticipates production of 3,000 units per year.

Instructions
(a) Compute the cost per unit of the fixed manufacturing overhead and the fixed selling and administrative expenses.
(b) Compute the desired ROI per unit. (Round to the nearest dollar.)
(c) Compute the target selling price.

Use time-and-material pricing to determine bill.

(LO 3)

E22-8 Second Chance Welding rebuilds spot welders for manufacturers. The following budgeted cost data for 2014 is available for Second Chance.

	Time Charges	Material Loading Charges
Technicians' wages and benefits	$228,000	—
Parts manager's salary and benefits	—	$42,500
Office employee's salary and benefits	38,000	9,000
Other overhead	15,200	24,000
Total budgeted costs	$281,200	$75,500

The company desires a $30 profit margin per hour of labor and a 20% profit margin on parts. It has budgeted for 7,600 hours of repair time in the coming year, and estimates that the total invoice cost of parts and materials in 2014 will be $400,000.

Instructions
(a) Compute the rate charged per hour of labor.
(b) Compute the material loading percentage. (Round to three decimal places.)
(c) Pace Corporation has requested an estimate to rebuild its spot welder. Second Chance estimates that it would require 40 hours of labor and $2,000 of parts. Compute the total estimated bill.

Use time-and-material pricing to determine bill.

(LO 3)

E22-9 Ignatenko's Custom Electronics (ICE) sells and installs complete security, computer, audio, and video systems for homes. On newly constructed homes it provides bids using time-and-material pricing. The following budgeted cost data are available.

	Time Charges	Material Loading Charges
Technicians' wages and benefits	$150,000	—
Parts manager's salary and benefits	—	$34,000
Office employee's salary and benefits	28,000	15,000
Other overhead	15,000	42,000
Total budgeted costs	$193,000	$91,000

The company has budgeted for 6,250 hours of technician time during the coming year. It desires a $38 profit margin per hour of labor and a 100% profit on parts. It estimates the total invoice cost of parts and materials in 2014 will be $700,000.

Instructions
(a) Compute the rate charged per hour of labor. (Round to two decimal places.)
(b) Compute the material loading percentage. (Round to two decimal places.)
(c) ICE has just received a request for a bid from Buil Builders on a $1,200,000 new home. The company estimates that it would require 80 hours of labor and $40,000 of parts. Compute the total estimated bill.

E22-10 Wasson's Classic Cars restores classic automobiles to showroom status. Budgeted data for the current year are:

Use time-and-material pricing to determine bill.

(LO 3)

	Time Charges	Material Loading Charges
Restorers' wages and fringe benefits	$270,000	
Purchasing agent's salary and fringe benefits		$ 67,500
Administrative salaries and fringe benefits	54,000	21,960
Other overhead costs	24,000	77,490
Total budgeted costs	$348,000	$166,950

The company anticipated that the restorers would work a total of 12,000 hours this year. Expected parts and materials were $1,260,000.

In late January, the company experienced a fire in its facilities that destroyed most of the accounting records. The accountant remembers that the hourly labor rate was $70.00 and that the material loading charge was 83.25%.

Instructions
(a) Determine the profit margin per hour on labor.
(b) Determine the profit margin on materials.
(c) Determine the total price of labor and materials on a job that was completed after the fire that required 150 hours of labor and $60,000 in parts and materials.

E22-11 Wellstone Company's Small Motor Division manufactures a number of small motors used in household and office appliances. The Household Division of Wellstone then assembles and packages such items as blenders and juicers. Both divisions are free to buy and sell any of their components internally or externally. The following costs relate to small motor LN233 on a per unit basis.

Determine minimum transfer price.

(LO 4)

Fixed cost per unit	$ 5
Variable cost per unit	$ 9
Selling price per unit	$30

Instructions
(a) Assuming that the Small Motor Division has excess capacity, compute the minimum acceptable price for the transfer of small motor LN233 to the Household Division.
(b) Assuming that the Small Motor Division does not have excess capacity, compute the minimum acceptable price for the transfer of the small motor to the Household Division.
(c) ▭▭▭▷ Explain why the level of capacity in the Small Motor Division has an effect on the transfer price.

Determine effect on income from transfer price.

(LO 4)

E22-12 The Cycle Division of Ayala Company has the following per unit data related to its most recent cycle called Roadbuster.

Selling price		$2,200
Variable cost of goods sold		
Body frame	$300	
Other variable costs	900	1,200
Contribution margin		$1,000

Presently, the Cycle Division buys its body frames from an outside supplier. However Ayala has another division, FrameBody, that makes body frames for other cycle companies. The Cycle Division believes that FrameBody's product is suitable for its new Roadbuster cycle. Presently, FrameBody sells its frames for $350 per frame. The variable cost for FrameBody is $270. The Cycle Division is willing to pay $280 to purchase the frames from FrameBody.

Instructions

(a) Assume that FrameBody has excess capacity and is able to meet all of the Cycle Division's needs. If the Cycle Division buys 1,000 frames from FrameBody, determine the following: (1) effect on the income of the Cycle Division; (2) effect on the income of FrameBody; and (3) effect on the income of Ayala.

(b) Assume that FrameBody does not have excess capacity and therefore would lose sales if the frames were sold to the Cycle Division. If the Cycle Division buys 1,000 frames from FrameBody, determine the following: (1) effect on the income of the Cycle Division; (2) effect on the income of FrameBody; and (3) effect on the income of Ayala.

Determine minimum transfer price.

(LO 4)

E22-13 Venetian Corporation manufactures car stereos. It is a division of Berna Motors, which manufactures vehicles. Venetian sells car stereos to Berna, as well as to other vehicle manufacturers and retail stores. The following information is available for Venetian's standard unit: variable cost per unit $35; fixed cost per unit $23; and selling price to outside customer $86. Berna currently purchases a standard unit from an outside supplier for $80. Because of quality concerns and to ensure a reliable supply, the top management of Berna has ordered Venetian to provide 200,000 units per year at a transfer price of $35 per unit. Venetian is already operating at full capacity. Venetian can avoid $4 per unit of variable selling costs by selling the unit internally.

Instructions

Answer each of the following questions.

(a) What is the minimum transfer price that Venetian should accept?

(b) What is the potential loss to the corporation as a whole resulting from this forced transfer?

(c) How should the company resolve this situation?

Compute minimum transfer price.

(LO 4)

E22-14 The Bathtub Division of Kirk Plumbing Corporation has recently approached the Faucet Division with a proposal. The Bathtub Division would like to make a special "ivory" tub with gold-plated fixtures for the company's 50-year anniversary. It would make only 5,000 of these units. It would like the Faucet Division to make the fixtures and provide them to the Bathtub Division at a transfer price of $160. If sold externally, the estimated variable cost per unit would be $140. However, by selling internally, the Faucet Division would save $6 per unit on variable selling expenses. The Faucet Division is currently operating at full capacity. Its standard unit sells for $50 per unit and has variable costs of $29.

Instructions

Compute the minimum transfer price that the Faucet Division should be willing to accept, and discuss whether it should accept this offer.

Determine minimum transfer price.

(LO 4)

E22-15 The Appraisal Department of Bonita Bank performs appraisals of business properties for loans being considered by the bank and appraisals for home buyers that are financing their purchase through some other financial institution. The department charges $162 per home appraisal, and its variable costs are $130 per appraisal.

Recently, Bonita Bank has opened its own Home-Loan Department and wants the Appraisal Department to perform 1,200 appraisals on all Bonita Bank–financed home loans. Bank management feels that the cost of these appraisals to the Home-Loan Department should be $150. The variable cost per appraisal to the Home-Loan Department would be $6 less than those performed for outside customers due to savings in administrative costs.

Instructions

(a) Determine the minimum transfer price, assuming the Appraisal Department has excess capacity.

(b) Determine the minimum transfer price, assuming the Appraisal Department has no excess capacity.

(c) Assuming the Appraisal Department has no excess capacity, should management force the department to charge the Home-Loan Department only $150? Discuss.

E22-16 Crede Inc. has two divisions. Division A makes and sells student desks. Division B manufactures and sells reading lamps.

Determine minimum transfer price under different situations.

(LO 4)

Each desk has a reading lamp as one of its components. Division A can purchase reading lamps at a cost of $10 from an outside vendor. Division A needs 10,000 lamps for the coming year.

Division B has the capacity to manufacture 50,000 lamps annually. Sales to outside customers are estimated at 40,000 lamps for the next year. Reading lamps are sold at $12 each. Variable costs are $7 per lamp and include $1 of variable sales costs that are not incurred if lamps are sold internally to Division A. The total amount of fixed costs for Division B is $80,000.

Instructions

Consider the following independent situations.

(a) What should be the minimum transfer price accepted by Division B for the 10,000 lamps and the maximum transfer price paid by Division A? Justify your answer.

(b) Suppose Division B could use the excess capacity to produce and sell externally 15,000 units of a new product at a price of $7 per unit. The variable cost for this new product is $5 per unit. What should be the minimum transfer price accepted by Division B for the 10,000 lamps and the maximum transfer price paid by Division A? Justify your answer.

(c) If Division A needs 15,000 lamps instead of 10,000 during the next year, what should be the minimum transfer price accepted by Division B and the maximum transfer price paid by Division A? Justify your answer.

(CGA adapted)

E22-17 The Pacific Company is a multidivisional company. Its managers have full responsibility for profits and complete autonomy to accept or reject transfers from other divisions. Division A produces a subassembly part for which there is a competitive market. Division B currently uses this subassembly for a final product that is sold outside at $2,400. Division A charges Division B market price for the part, which is $1,500 per unit. Variable costs are $1,050 and $1,200 for Divisions A and B, respectively.

Determine minimum transfer price under different situations.

(LO 4)

The manager of Division B feels that Division A should transfer the part at a lower price than market because at market, Division B is unable to make a profit.

Instructions

(a) Calculate Division B's contribution margin if transfers are made at the market price, and calculate the company's total contribution margin.

(b) Assume that Division A can sell all its production in the open market. Should Division A transfer the goods to Division B? If so, at what price?

(c) Assume that Division A can sell in the open market only 500 units at $1,500 per unit out of the 1,000 units that it can produce every month. Assume also that a 20% reduction in price is necessary to sell all 1,000 units each month. Should transfers be made? If so, how many units should the division transfer and at what price? To support your decision, submit a schedule that compares the contribution margins under three different alternatives.

(CMA-Canada adapted)

*E22-18 Information for Paige Corporation is given in E22-5.

Compute total cost per unit, ROI, and markup percentages using absorption-cost pricing and variable-cost pricing.

(LO 6)

Instructions

Using the information given in E22-5, answer the following.

(a) Compute the total cost per unit.

(b) Compute the desired ROI per unit.

(c) Using absorption-cost pricing, compute the markup percentage.

(d) Using variable-cost pricing, compute the markup percentage.

Compute markup percentage using absorption-cost pricing and variable-cost pricing.

(LO 6)

*E22-19 Rensing Corporation produces outdoor portable fireplace units. The following per unit cost information is available: direct materials $20; direct labor $25; variable manufacturing overhead $14; fixed manufacturing overhead $21; variable selling and administrative expenses $9; and fixed selling and administrative expenses $11. The company's ROI per unit is $20.

Instructions
Compute Rensing Corporation's markup percentage using (a) absorption-cost pricing and (b) variable-cost pricing.

Compute various amounts using absorption-cost pricing and variable-cost pricing.

(LO 6)

*E22-20 Information for Pargo Corporation is given in E22-7.

Instructions
Using the information given in E22-7, answer the following.
(a) Compute the cost per unit of the fixed manufacturing overhead and the fixed selling and administrative expenses.
(b) Compute the desired ROI per unit. (Round to the nearest dollar.)
(c) Compute the markup percentage and target selling price using absorption-cost pricing. (Round the markup percentage to three decimal places.)
(d) Compute the markup percentage and target selling price using variable-cost pricing. (Round the markup percentage to three decimal places.)

EXERCISES: SET B AND CHALLENGE EXERCISES

Visit the book's companion website, at **www.wiley.com/college/weygandt**, and choose the Student Companion site to access Exercise Set B and Challenge Exercises.

PROBLEMS: SET A

Use cost-plus pricing to determine various amounts.

(LO 2)

P22-1A Dewitt Corporation needs to set a target price for its newly designed product M14–M16. The following data relate to this new product.

	Per Unit	Total
Direct materials	$20	
Direct labor	$40	
Variable manufacturing overhead	$10	
Fixed manufacturing overhead		$1,440,000
Variable selling and administrative expenses	$ 5	
Fixed selling and administrative expenses		$ 960,000

These costs are based on a budgeted volume of 80,000 units produced and sold each year. Dewitt uses cost-plus pricing methods to set its target selling price. The markup percentage on total unit cost is 30%.

Instructions
(a) Compute the total variable cost per unit, total fixed cost per unit, and total cost per unit for M14–M16.
(b) Compute the desired ROI per unit for M14–M16.
(c) Compute the target selling price for M14–M16.
(d) Compute variable cost per unit, fixed cost per unit, and total cost per unit assuming that 60,000 M14–M16s are sold during the year.

(a) Variable cost per unit $75

Use cost-plus pricing to determine various amounts.

(LO 2)

P22-2A Lovell Computer Parts Inc. is in the process of setting a selling price on a new component it has just designed and developed. The following cost estimates for this new component have been provided by the accounting department for a budgeted volume of 50,000 units.

	Per Unit	Total
Direct materials	$50	
Direct labor	$26	
Variable manufacturing overhead	$20	
Fixed manufacturing overhead		$600,000
Variable selling and administrative expenses	$19	
Fixed selling and administrative expenses		$400,000

Lovell Computer Parts management requests that the total cost per unit be used in cost-plus pricing its products. On this particular product, management also directs that the target price be set to provide a 25% return on investment (ROI) on invested assets of $1,000,000.

Instructions
(Round all calculations to two decimal places.)
(a) Compute the markup percentage and target selling price that will allow Lovell Computer Parts to earn its desired ROI of 25% on this new component.
(b) Assuming that the volume is 40,000 units, compute the markup percentage and target selling price that will allow Lovell Computer Parts to earn its desired ROI of 25% on this new component.

(b) Target selling price $146.25

P22-3A Jose's Electronic Repair Shop has budgeted the following time and material for 2014.

Use time-and-material pricing to determine bill.

(LO 3)

Jose's Electronic Repair Shop
Budgeted Costs for the Year 2014

	Time Charges	Material Loading Charges
Shop employees' wages and benefits	$108,000	—
Parts manager's salary and benefits	—	$25,400
Office employee's salary and benefits	23,500	13,600
Overhead (supplies, depreciation, advertising, utilities)	26,000	16,000
Total budgeted costs	$157,500	$55,000

Jose's budgets 5,000 hours of repair time in 2014 and will bill a profit of $5 per labor hour along with a 30% profit markup on the invoice cost of parts. The estimated invoice cost for parts to be used is $100,000.

On January 5, 2014, Jose's is asked to submit a price estimate to fix a 72-inch flat-screen TV. Jose's estimates that this job will consume 5 hours of labor and $200 in parts.

Instructions
(a) Compute the labor rate for Jose's Electronic Repair Shop for the year 2014.
(b) Compute the material loading charge percentage for Jose's Electronic Repair Shop for the year 2014.
(c) Prepare a time-and-material price quotation for fixing the flat-screen TV.

(c) $1,655

P22-4A Word Wizard is a publishing company with a number of different book lines. Each line has contracts with a number of different authors. The company also owns a printing operation called Quick Press. The book lines and the printing operation each operate as a separate profit center. The printing operation earns revenue by printing books by authors under contract with the book lines owned by Word Wizard, as well as authors under contract with other companies. The printing operation bills out at $0.01 per page, and a typical book requires 500 pages of print. A manager from Business Books, one of the Word Wizard's book lines, has approached the manager of the printing operation offering to pay $0.007 per page for 1,500 copies of a 500-page book. The book line pays outside printers $0.009 per page. The printing operation's variable cost per page is $0.004.

Determine minimum transfer price with no excess capacity and with excess capacity.

(LO 4)

Instructions
Determine whether the printing should be done internally or externally, and the appropriate transfer price, under each of the following situations.

(a) Assume that the printing operation is booked solid for the next 2 years, and it would have to cancel an obligation with an outside customer in order to meet the needs of the internal division.

(b) Assume that the printing operation has available capacity.

(c)  The top management of Word Wizard believes that the printing operation should always do the printing for the company's authors. On a number of occasions, it has forced the printing operation to cancel jobs with outside customers in order to meet the needs of its own lines. Discuss the pros and cons of this approach.

(d) Loss to company ($750)

(d) Calculate the change in contribution margin to each division, and to the company as a whole, if top management forces the printing operation to accept the $0.007 per page transfer price when it has no available capacity.

Determine minimum transfer price with no excess capacity.

(LO 4)

P22-5A Watts Company makes various electronic products. The company is divided into a number of autonomous divisions that can either sell to internal units or sell externally. All divisions are located in buildings on the same piece of property. The Board Division has offered the Chip Division $20 per unit to supply it with chips for 30,000 boards. It has been purchasing these chips for $22 per unit from outside suppliers. The Chip Division receives $22.50 per unit for sales made to outside customers on this type of chip. The variable cost of chips sold externally by the Chip Division is $14.50. It estimates that it will save $4.50 per chip of selling expenses on units sold internally to the Board Division. The Chip Division has no excess capacity.

Instructions

(a) Calculate the minimum transfer price that the Chip Division should accept. Discuss whether it is in the Chip Division's best interest to accept the offer.

(b) Total loss to company
$120,000

(b) Suppose that the Chip Division decides to reject the offer. What are the financial implications for each division, and for the company as a whole, of this decision?

Determine minimum transfer price under different situations.

(LO 4)

P22-6A Comm Devices (CD) is a division of Worldwide Communications, Inc. CD produces pagers and other personal communication devices. These devices are sold to other Worldwide divisions, as well as to other communication companies. CD was recently approached by the manager of the Personal Communications Division regarding a request to make a special pager designed to receive signals from anywhere in the world. The Personal Communications Division has requested that CD produce 12,000 units of this special pager. The following facts are available regarding the Comm Devices Division.

Selling price of standard pager	$95
Variable cost of standard pager	$50
Additional variable cost of special pager	$30

Instructions

For each of the following independent situations, calculate the minimum transfer price, and discuss whether the internal transfer should take place or whether the Personal Communications Division should purchase the pager externally.

(a) The Personal Communications Division has offered to pay the CD Division $105 per pager. The CD Division has no available capacity. The CD Division would have to forego sales of 10,000 pagers to existing customers in order to meet the request of the Personal Communications Division.

(b) Minimum price $140

(b) The Personal Communications Division has offered to pay the CD Division $150 per pager. The CD Division has no available capacity. The CD Division would have to forego sales of 16,000 pagers to existing customers in order to meet the request of the Personal Communications Division.

(c) The Personal Communications Division has offered to pay the CD Division $100 per pager. The CD Division has available capacity.

Compute the target price using absorption-cost pricing and variable-cost pricing.

(LO 6)

XLS

*P22-7A Gonzalez Corporation needs to set a target price for its newly designed product EverReady. The following data relate to this new product.

	Per Unit	Total
Direct materials	$20	
Direct labor	$40	
Variable manufacturing overhead	$10	
Fixed manufacturing overhead		$1,200,000
Variable selling and administrative expenses	$ 5	
Fixed selling and administrative expenses		$1,120,000

The costs shown above are based on a budgeted volume of 80,000 units produced and sold each year. Gonzalez uses cost-plus pricing methods to set its target selling price. Because some managers prefer absorption-cost pricing and others prefer variable-cost pricing, the accounting department provides information under both approaches using a markup of 50% on absorption cost and a markup of 70% on variable cost.

Instructions

(a) Compute the target price for one unit of EverReady using absorption-cost pricing.

(b) Compute the target price for one unit of EverReady using variable-cost pricing.

(a) Markup $42.50
(b) Markup $52.50

P22-8A Anderson Windows Inc. is in the process of setting a target price on its newly designed tinted window. Cost data relating to the window at a budgeted volume of 4,000 units are as follows.

Compute various amounts using absorption-cost pricing and variable-cost pricing.

(LO 6)

	Per Unit	Total
Direct materials	$100	
Direct labor	$ 70	
Variable manufacturing overhead	$ 20	
Fixed manufacturing overhead		$120,000
Variable selling and administrative expenses	$ 10	
Fixed selling and administrative expenses		$102,000

Anderson Windows uses cost-plus pricing methods that are designed to provide the company with a 25% ROI on its tinted window line. A total of $1,016,000 in assets is committed to production of the new tinted window.

Instructions

(a) Compute the markup percentage under absorption-cost pricing that will allow Anderson Windows to realize its desired ROI.

(a) 45%

(b) Compute the target price of the window under absorption-cost pricing, and show proof that the desired ROI is realized.

(c) Compute the markup percentage under variable-cost pricing that will allow Anderson Windows to realize its desired ROI. (Round to three decimal places.)

(d) Compute the target price of the window under variable-cost pricing, and show proof that the desired ROI is realized.

(e) ▮▮▭▭▻ Since both absorption-cost pricing and variable-cost pricing produce the same target price and provide the same desired ROI, why do both methods exist? Isn't one method clearly superior to the other?

PROBLEMS: SET B

P22-1B Harrington Corporation needs to set a target price for its newly designed product R2–D2. The following data relate to this new product.

Use cost-plus pricing to determine various amounts.

(LO 2)

	Per Unit	Total
Direct materials	$ 8	
Direct labor	$14	
Variable manufacturing overhead	$ 7	
Fixed manufacturing overhead		$2,000,000
Variable selling and administrative expenses	$ 6	
Fixed selling and administrative expenses		$1,200,000

These costs are based on a budgeted volume of 100,000 units produced and sold each year. Harrington uses cost-plus pricing methods to set its target selling price. The markup on total unit cost is 30%.

Instructions

(a) Compute the total variable cost per unit, total fixed cost per unit, and total cost per unit for R2–D2.

(a) Variable cost per unit $35

(b) Compute the desired ROI per unit for R2–D2.

(c) Compute the target selling price for R2–D2.

(d) Compute variable cost per unit, fixed cost per unit, and total cost per unit assuming that 80,000 R2–D2s are sold during the year.

Use cost-plus pricing to determine various amounts.

(LO 2)

P22-2B Robo Parts Inc. is in the process of setting a selling price on a new robotics component it has just designed and developed. The following cost estimates for this new component have been provided by the accounting department for a budgeted volume of 100,000 units.

	Per Unit	Total
Direct materials	$30	
Direct labor	$20	
Variable manufacturing overhead	$17	
Fixed manufacturing overhead		$2,500,000
Variable selling and administrative expenses	$ 8	
Fixed selling and administrative expenses		$ 500,000

Robo's management requests that the total cost per unit be used in cost-plus pricing its products. On this particular product, management also directs that the target price be set to provide a 30% return on investment (ROI) on invested assets of $3,000,000.

Instructions

(Round all calculations to two decimal places.)

(a) Compute the markup percentage and target selling price that will allow Robo to earn its desired ROI of 30% on this new component.

(b) Target selling price $123.75

(b) Assuming that the volume is 80,000 units, compute the markup percentage and target selling price that will allow Robo to earn its desired ROI of 30% on this new component.

Use time-and-material pricing to determine bill.

(LO 3)

P22-3B Armstrong Bike Repair Shop has budgeted the following time and material for 2014.

Armstrong Bike Repair Shop
Budgeted Costs for the Year 2014

	Time Charges	Material Loading Charges
Shop employees' wages and benefits	$36,000	—
Parts supervisor's salary and benefits	—	$20,000
Office employee's salary and benefits	15,000	10,000
Overhead (supplies, depreciation, advertising, utilities)	19,000	15,000
Total budgeted costs	$70,000	$45,000

Armstrong budgets 2,500 hours of repair time in 2014 and will bill a profit of $5 per labor hour along with a 15% profit markup on the invoice cost of parts. The estimated invoice cost for parts to be used is $75,000.

On January 5, 2014, Armstrong is asked to submit a price estimate to fix a Superior Mountain bike. Armstrong estimates that this job will consume 4 hours of labor and $200 in parts.

Instructions

(a) Compute the labor rate for Armstrong Bike Repair Shop for the year 2014.

(b) Compute the material loading charge percentage for Armstrong Bike Repair Shop for the year 2014.

(c) $482.00

(c) Prepare a time-and-material price quotation for fixing the Superior Mountain bike.

Determine minimum transfer price with no excess capacity and with excess capacity.

(LO 4)

P22-4B Deitz is a publishing company with a number of different magazines and other publications. The company also owns a printing operation called Saira Press. The publications and the printing operation each operate as a separate profit center. The printing operation earns revenue by printing magazines and other publications owned by Deitz, as well as publications of other companies. The printing operation bills out at $0.025 per page. A manager from *Winner!*, one of Deitz's magazines, has approached the manager of the printing operation offering to pay $0.016 per page for 20,000 copies of a 64-page magazine. The magazine pays outside printers $0.018 per page. The printing operation's variable cost per page is $0.014.

Instructions

Determine whether the printing should be done internally or externally, and the appropriate transfer price, under each of the following situations.

(a) Assume that the printing operation is booked solid for the next two years, and it would have to cancel an obligation with an outside customer in order to meet the needs of the internal division.

(b) Assume that the printing operation has available capacity.

(c) ▯▭▭▭▷ The top management of Deitz believes that the printing operation should always do the printing for the company's magazines. On a number of occasions, it has forced the printing operation to cancel jobs with outside customers in order to meet the needs of its own publications. Discuss the pros and cons of this approach.

(d) Calculate the change in contribution margin to each division, and to the company as a whole, if top management forces the printing operation to accept the $0.016 per page transfer price when it has no available capacity.

(d) Loss to company $8,960

P22-5B Dolby Ukes makes various types of ukeleles. The company is divided into a number of autonomous divisions that can either sell to internal units or sell externally. All divisions are located in buildings on the same piece of property. The Alto Division has offered the Peg Division $0.26 per peg to supply it with 200,000 pegs. It has been purchasing these pegs for $0.28 per unit from outside suppliers. The Peg Division receives $0.30 per unit for sales made to outside customers on this type of peg. The variable cost of pegs sold externally by the Peg Division is $0.18. It estimates that it will save $0.04 per peg of selling expenses on units sold internally to the Alto Division. The Peg Division has no excess capacity.

Determine minimum transfer price with no excess capacity.
(LO 4)

Instructions

(a) Calculate the minimum transfer price that the Peg Division should accept. Discuss whether it is in the Peg Division's best interest to accept the offer.

(b) Suppose that the Peg Division decides to reject the offer. What are the financial implications for each division, and for the company as a whole, of this decision?

(b) Total loss to company $4,000

P22-6B Innovative Systems (IS) is a division of Global Electronics, Inc. IS produces videogame systems. These systems are sold to retailers. IS recently approached the manager of the Laptop Computer Division regarding a request to buy a special circuit board for a new advanced video game system. IS has requested that the laptop computer division produce 200,000 units of this special circuit board. The following facts are available regarding the Laptop (LT) Division.

Determine minimum transfer price under different situations.
(LO 4)

Selling price of standard circuit board	$54
Variable cost of standard circuit board	30
Additional variable cost of special circuit board	20

Instructions

For each of the following independent situations, calculate the minimum transfer price, and discuss whether the internal transfer should take place or whether IS should purchase the circuit board externally.

(a) IS has offered to pay the LT Division $62 per circuit board. The LT Division has no available capacity. The LT Division would have to forgo sales of 200,000 circuit boards to existing customers in order to meet the request of IS.

(b) IS has offered to pay the LT Division $90 per circuit board. The LT Division has no available capacity. The LT Division would have to forgo sales of 250,000 circuit boards to existing customers in order to meet the request of IS.

(b) Minimum price $80

(c) IS has offered to pay the LT Division $62 per circuit board. The LT Division has available capacity.

*P22-7B Zelmer Corporation needs to set a target price for its newly designed product QB-14. The following data relate to this new product.

Compute the target price using absorption-cost and variable-cost pricing.
(LO 6)

	Per Unit	Total
Direct materials	$50	
Direct labor	$30	
Variable manufacturing overhead	$13	
Fixed manufacturing overhead		$8,000,000
Variable selling and administrative expenses	$ 7	
Fixed selling and administrative expenses		$2,000,000

The costs above are based on a budgeted volume of 250,000 units produced and sold each year. Zelmer uses cost-plus pricing methods to set its target selling price. Because some managers prefer absorption-cost pricing and others prefer variable-cost pricing, the accounting department provides information under both approaches using a markup of 60% on unit manufacturing cost and a markup of 100% on variable cost.

(a) Markup $75
(b) Markup $100

Instructions
(a) Compute the target price for one unit of QB-14 using absorption-cost pricing.
(b) Compute the target price for one unit of QB-14 using variable-cost pricing.

Compute various amounts using absorption-cost pricing and variable-cost pricing.

(LO 6)

*P22-8B Georgia Gould Bikes Inc. is in the process of setting a target price on its newly designed mountain bike. Cost data relating to the bike at a budgeted volume of 20,000 units are as follows.

	Per Unit	Total
Direct materials	$200	
Direct labor	$100	
Variable manufacturing overhead	$ 30	
Fixed manufacturing overhead		$1,400,000
Variable selling and administrative expenses	$ 20	
Fixed selling and administrative expenses		$ 200,000

Georgia Gould Bikes uses cost-plus pricing methods that are designed to provide the company with a 25% ROI on its mountain bike line. A total of $20,000,000 in assets is committed to production of the new mountain bike.

(a) 70%

Instructions
(a) Compute the markup percentage under absorption-cost pricing that will allow Georgia Gould Bikes to realize its desired ROI.
(b) Compute the target price of the bike under absorption-cost pricing, and show proof that the desired ROI is realized.
(c) Compute the markup percentage under variable-cost pricing that will allow Georgia Gould Bikes to realize its desired ROI. (Round to three decimal places.)
(d) Compute the target price of the bike under variable-cost pricing, and show proof that the desired ROI is realized. (Round to nearest dollar.)
(e) Since both the absorption-cost pricing and variable-cost pricing produce the same target price and provide the same desired ROI, why do both methods exist? Isn't one method clearly superior to the other?

PROBLEMS: SET C

Visit the book's companion website, at **www.wiley.com/college/weygandt**, and choose the Student Companion site to access Problem Set C.

WATERWAYS CONTINUING PROBLEM

(This is a continuation of the Waterways Problem from Chapters 15–21.)

WCP22 Waterways Corporation competes in a market economy in which its products must be sold at market prices. Its emphasis is therefore on manufacturing its products at a cost that allows the company to earn its desired profit. This problem asks you to consider various pricing situations for Waterways' projects.

*Go to the book's companion website, **www.wiley.com/college/weygandt**, to find the remainder of this problem.*

Broadening Your PERSPECTIVE

Management Decision-Making

Decision-Making at Current Designs

BYP22-1 As a service to its customers, Current Designs repairs damaged kayaks. This is especially valuable to customers that have made a significant investment in the composite kayaks. To price the repair jobs, Current Designs uses time-and-material pricing with a desired profit margin of $20 per labor hour and a 50% materials loading charge.

Recently, Bill Johnson, Vice President of Sales and Marketing, received a phone call from a dealer in Brainerd, Minnesota. The dealer has a customer who recently damaged his composite kayak and would like an estimate of the cost to repair it. After the dealer emailed pictures of the damage, Bill reviewed the pictures with the repair technician and determined that the total materials charges for the repair would be $100. Bill estimates that the job will take 3 labor hours to complete. Following is the budgeted cost data for Current Designs:

Repair technician wages	$30,000
Fringe benefits	$10,000
Overhead	$10,000

Current Designs has allocated 2,000 hours of repair time for the upcoming year. The customer has agreed to transport the kayak to the Winona production facility for the repairs.

Instructions
Determine the price that Current Designs would charge to complete the repairs for the customer.

Decision-Making Across the Organization

BYP22-2 Lanier Manufacturing has multiple divisions that make a wide variety of products. Recently, the Bearing Division and the Wheel Division got into an argument over a transfer price. The Wheel Division needed bearings for garden tractor wheels. It normally buys its bearings from an outside supplier for $25 per set. The company's top management recently initiated a campaign to persuade the different divisions to buy their materials from within the company whenever possible. As a result, Hank Sherril, the purchasing manager for the Wheel Division, received a letter from the vice president of Purchasing, ordering him to contact the Bearing Division to discuss buying bearings from this division.

To comply with this request, Hank from the Wheel Division called Mary Plimpton of the Bearing Division, and asked the price for 15,000 bearings. Mary responded that the bearings normally sell for $36 per set. However, Mary noted that the Bearing Division would save $3 on marketing costs by selling internally, and would pass this cost savings on to the Wheel Division. She further commented that they were at full capacity, and therefore would not be able to provide any bearings presently. In the future, if they had available capacity, they would be happy to provide bearings.

Hank responded indignantly, "Thanks but no thanks." He said, "We can get all the bearings we need from Falk Manufacturing for $24 per set." Mary snorted back, "Falk makes junk. It costs us $22 per set just to make our bearings. Our bearings can withstand heat of 2,000 degrees centigrade, and are good to within .00001 centimeters. If you guys are happy buying junk, then go ahead and buy from Falk."

Two weeks later, Hank's boss from the central office stopped in to find out whether he had placed an order with the Bearing Division. Hank responded that he would sooner buy his bearings from his worst enemy than from the Bearing Division.

Instructions
With the class divided into groups, prepare answers to the following questions.

(a) Why might the company's top management want the divisions to start doing more business with one another?

(b) Under what conditions should a buying division be forced to buy from an internal supplier? Under what conditions should a selling division be forced to sell to an internal division rather than to an outside customer?

(c) The vice president of Purchasing thinks that this problem should be resolved by forcing the Bearing Division to sell to the Wheel Division at its cost of $22. Is this a good solution for the Wheel Division? Is this a good solution for the Bearing Division? Is this a good solution for the company?

(d) Provide at least two other possible solutions to this problem. Discuss the merits and drawbacks of each.

Managerial Analysis

BYP22-3 Construction on the Bonita Full-Service Car Wash is nearing completion. The owner is Dave Kear, a retired accounting professor. The car wash is strategically located on a busy street that separates an affluent suburban community from a middle-class community. It has two state-of-the-art stalls. Each stall can provide anything from a basic two-stage wash and rinse to a five-stage luxurious bath. It is all "touchless," that is, there are no brushes to potentially damage the car. Outside each stall, there is also a 400 horse-power vacuum. Dave likes to joke that these vacuums are so strong that they will pull the carpet right out of your car if you aren't careful.

Dave has some important decisions to make before he can open the car wash. First, he knows that there is one drive-through car wash only a 10-minute drive away. It is attached to a gas station; it charges $5 for a basic wash, and $4 if you also buy at least 8 gallons of gas. It is a "brush"-type wash with rotating brush heads. There is also a self-serve "stand outside your car and spray until you are soaked" car wash a 15-minute drive away from Dave's location. He went over and tried this out. He went through $3 in quarters to get the equivalent of a basic wash. He knows that both of these locations always have long lines, which is one reason why he decided to build a new car wash.

Dave is planning to offer three levels of wash service—Basic, Deluxe, and Premium. The Basic is all automated; it requires no direct intervention by employees. The Deluxe is all automated except that at the end an employee will wipe down the car and will put a window treatment on the windshield that reduces glare and allows rainwater to run off more quickly. The Premium level is a "pampered" service. This will include all the services of the Deluxe, plus a special wax after the machine wax, and an employee will vacuum the car, wipe down the entire interior, and wash the inside of the windows. To provide the Premium service, Dave will have to hire a couple of "car wash specialists" to do the additional pampering.

Dave has pulled together the following estimates, based on data he received from the local Chamber of Commerce and information from a trade association.

	Per Unit	Total
Direct materials per Basic wash	$0.30	
Direct materials per Deluxe wash	$0.80	
Direct materials per Premium wash	$1.10	
Direct labor per Basic wash	na	
Direct labor per Deluxe wash	$0.40	
Direct labor per Premium wash	$2.40	
Variable overhead per Basic wash	$0.10	
Variable overhead per Deluxe and Premium washes	$0.20	
Fixed overhead		$117,000
Variable selling and administrative expenses all washes	$0.10	
Fixed selling and administrative expenses		$130,500

The total estimated number of washes of any type is 45,000. Dave has invested assets of $393,750. He would like a return on investment (ROI) of 20%.

Instructions
Answer each of the following questions.

(a) Identify the issues that Dave must consider in deciding on the price of each level of service of his car wash. Also discuss what issues he should consider in deciding on what levels of service to provide.

(b) Dave estimates that of the total 45,000 washes, 20,000 will be Basic, 20,000 will be Deluxe, and 5,000 will be Premium. Calculate the selling price, using cost-plus pricing, that Dave should use for each type of wash to achieve his desired ROI of 20%.

(c) During the first year, instead of selling 45,000 washes, Dave sold 43,000 washes. He was quite accurate in his estimate of first-year sales, but he was way off on the types of washes that he sold. He sold 3,000 Basic, 31,000 Deluxe, and 9,000 Premium. His actual total fixed expenses were as he expected, and his variable cost per unit was as estimated. Calculate Dave's actual net income and his actual ROI. (Round to two decimal places.)

(d) Dave is using a traditional approach to allocate overhead. As a consequence, he is allocating overhead equally to all three types of washes, even though the Basic wash is considerably less complicated and uses very little of the technical capabilities of the machinery. What should Dave do to determine more accurate costs per unit? How will this affect his pricing and, consequently, his sales?

Real-World Focus

BYP22-4 Merck & Co., Inc. is a global, research-driven pharmaceutical company that discovers, develops, manufactures, and markets a broad range of human and animal health products. The following are excerpts from the financial review section of the company's annual report.

| **Merck & Co., Inc.** |
| Financial Review Section (partial) |

In the United States, the Company has been working with private and governmental employers to slow the increase of health care costs.

Outside of the United States, in difficult environments encumbered by government cost containment actions, the Company has worked with payers to help them allocate scarce resources to optimize health care outcomes, limiting potentially detrimental effects of government actions on sales growth.

Several products face expiration of product patents in the near term.

The Company, along with other pharmaceutical manufacturers, received a notice from the Federal Trade Commission (FTC) that it was conducting an investigation into pricing practices.

Instructions
Answer each of the following questions.

(a) In light of the above excerpts from Merck's annual report, discuss some unique pricing issues faced by companies that operate in the pharmaceutical industry.

(b) What are some reasons why the same company often sells identical drugs for dramatically different prices in different countries? How can the same drug used for both humans and animals cost significantly different prices?

(c) Suppose that Merck has just developed a revolutionary new drug. Discuss the steps it would go through in setting a price. Include a discussion of the information it would need to gather, and the issues it would need to consider.

BYP22-5 Shopping "robots" have become very popular on the Web. These are sites that will find the price of a specified product that is listed by retailers on the Web ("e-tailers"). This allows the customer to search for the lowest possible price.

Address: **www.dealtime.com** or go to **www.wiley.com/college/weygandt**

Steps
1. Go to the Web page of DealTime.
2. Under the heading "**Electronics**," click on **DVD players**.
3. Choose one of the models.

Instructions
(a) Write down the name of the retailer and the price of the two lowest-priced units and the two highest-priced units.

(b) As a consumer, what concerns might you have in clicking on the "buy" button?

(c) Why might a consumer want to purchase a unit from a retailer that isn't offering the lowest price?

(d) What implications does the existence of these sites have for retailers?

Critical Thinking

Communication Activity

BYP22-6 Jane Fleming recently graduated from college with a degree in landscape architecture. Her father runs a tree, shrub, and perennial-flower nursery, and her brother has a business delivering topsoil, mulch, and compost. Jane has decided that she would like to start a landscape business. She believes that she can generate a nice profit for herself, while providing an opportunity for both her brother's and father's businesses to grow.

One potential problem that Jane is concerned about is that her father and brother tend to charge the highest prices of any local suppliers for their products. She is hoping that she can demonstrate that it would be in her interest, as well as theirs, for them to sell to her at a discounted price.

Instructions

Write a memo to Jane explaining what information she must gather, and what issues she must consider in working out an arrangement with her father and brother. In your memo, discuss how this situation differs from a "standard" transfer pricing problem, but also how it has many of the characteristics of a transfer pricing problem.

Ethics Case

BYP22-7 Jumbo Airlines operates out of three main "hub" airports in the United States. Recently, Econo Airlines began operating a flight from Reno, Nevada, into Jumbo's Metropolis hub for $190. Jumbo Airlines offers a price of $425 for the same route. The management of Jumbo is not happy about Econo invading its turf. In fact, Jumbo has driven off nearly every other competing airline from its hub, so that today 90% of flights into and out of Metropolis are Jumbo Airline flights. Econo is able to offer a lower fare because its pilots are paid less, it uses older planes, and it has lower overhead costs. Econo has been in business for only 6 months, and it services only two other cities. It expects the Metropolis route to be its most profitable.

Jumbo estimates that it would have to charge $210 just to break even on this flight. It estimates that Econo can break even at a price of $160. Within one day of Econo's entry into the market, Jumbo dropped its price to $140, whereupon Econo matched its price. They both maintained this fare for a period of 9 months, until Econo went out of business. As soon as Econo went out of business, Jumbo raised its fare back to $425.

Instructions

Answer each of the following questions.

(a) Who are the stakeholders in this case?
(b) What are some of the reasons why Econo's break-even point is lower than that of Jumbo?
(c) What are the likely reasons why Jumbo was able to offer this price for this period of time, while Econo couldn't?
(d) What are some of the possible courses of action available to Econo in this situation?
(e) Do you think that this kind of pricing activity is ethical? What are the implications for the stakeholders in this situation?

Considering Your Costs and Benefits

BYP22-8 The January 2011 issue of *Strategic Finance* includes an article by J. Lockhart, A. Taylor, K. Thomas, B. Levetsovitis, and J. Wise entitled "When a Higher Price Pays Off."

Instructions

Read the article and answer the following questions.

(a) Explain what is meant by a "low-cost" supplier versus a "low-priced" supplier.
(b) Clarus Technologies' products are typically priced significantly higher than its competitors' products. How is it able to overcome the initial "sticker shock"?
(c) List the five categories of costs that the authors used to compare the Tornado to competing products. Give examples of specific types of costs in each category.
(d) The article discusses full-cost accounting as developed by the Environmental Protection Agency (EPA). What are the characteristics of this approach, and what implications does the approach used in this article have for corporate social responsibility?

Answers to Chapter Questions

Answers to Insight and Accounting Across the Organization Questions

p. 1085 The Only Game in Town? Q: Do the substantially different prices that Apple and Google charge for a similar service reflect different costs incurred by each company, or is the price difference due to something else? **A:** While it is possible that the companies incur different costs to provide this service, that would not explain this huge price difference. Instead, Apple apparently felt that its commanding lead in terms of the percentage of tablet computer users enabled it to charge a substantial premium for subscription services. On the other hand, Google's decision most likely reflects a strategic decision to try to grow its market share by providing a substantially lower price.

p. 1086 Wal-Mart Says the Price Is Too High Q: What are some issues that Levi Strauss should consider in deciding whether it should agree to meet Wal-Mart's target price? **A:** Levi may be tempted to reduce the quality of its product, or it may be forced to move more of its operations to low-wage suppliers. A big concern is that other retailers may complain that Levi is selling its jeans to Wal-Mart at a price that is lower than they receive. Also, customers may no longer be willing to pay for Levi's other models of higher-priced jeans that it sells in other stores because they can get the low-price jeans (those with the lower gross margin) at Wal-Mart. All of these are issues that a manufacturer must consider in deciding whether to be a supplier to Wal-Mart.

p. 1090 At Least It Was Simple Q: What kind of help might the sales staff need in implementing this new approach? **A:** Many customers might object to the price increases, and some might even threaten to buy a competing product. The company needed to provide the sales staff with justifications for the product. For example, salespeople needed evidence to demonstrate that the superior quality of the product justified the higher price.

p. 1094 It Ain't Like It Used to Be Q: What implications does this have for a service company's need for managerial accounting? **A:** When service companies billed by the hour, they were better able to ensure their profitability because labor hours is their primary cost. But when billing schemes become performance-based, the company cannot be assured that the bill will cover its hourly costs. As a consequence, companies will need to be far more accurate in their estimates of the likelihood of achieving desired outcomes, or their costs may well exceed their revenues.

p. 1102 Transferring Profits and Reducing Taxes Q: What are the implications for other taxpayers if companies reduce their taxes by using improper transfer prices to shift profits to lower-tax countries? **A:** If companies reduce their taxes by using improper transfer prices, then more of the tax burden will fall on law-abiding companies or on individual taxpayers. As countries such as Ireland, for example, have drawn increased foreign investment by non-Irish companies, many other European countries have complained that Ireland is using unfair tax incentives. Many countries are beginning to scrutinize the transfer pricing practices of multinational companies more closely in order to reduce cheating and increase tax revenues.

Answers to Self-Test Questions

1. c **2.** b ($80 − $15) **3.** c **4.** b **5.** b [(.10 × $500,000) ÷ 1,000]/$25; $25 + $50 **6.** c ($10 ÷ $30) **7.** a $10 + [$100,000 + .5(40,000) + .5(80,000)] ÷ 5,000 **8.** d **9.** d ($70 − $30) + $30 **10.** b **11.** c **12.** b **13.** b ***14.** b [$15 + ($8 + 12)] ÷ ($40 + $30) ***15.** d [$15 + ($30 + $12)] ÷ ($40 + $8)

✔ **Remember to go back to The Navigator box on the chapter opening page and check off your completed work.**

Chapter 23

Budgetary Planning

✔ The Navigator

☐ Scan Learning Objectives

☐ Read Feature Story

☐ Scan Preview

☐ Read Text and answer **DO IT!** p. 1136
☐ p. 1139 ☐ p. 1141 ☐ p. 1146
☐ p. 1151

☐ Work Comprehensive **DO IT!** **1** p. 1154
☐ **2** p. 1156

☐ Review Summary of Learning Objectives

☐ Answer Self-Test Questions

☐ Complete Assignments

☐ Go to **WileyPLUS** for practice and tutorials

Feature Story

Was This the Next Amazon.com? Not Quite

So you came up with a great idea for a product. You started a company, and you are selling stuff so fast that you can barely keep up. No problem, right? However, without proper planning and budgeting, your success could be short-lived. In some cases, failure is actually brought on by rapid, uncontrolled growth.

One such example was online discount bookseller, www.Positively-You.com. One of the website's co-founders, Lyle Bowline, had never run a business. However, his experience as an assistant director of an entrepreneurial center had provided him with knowledge about the do's and don'ts of small business. To minimize costs, he started the company small and simple. He invested $5,000 in computer equipment and ran the business out of his basement. In the early months, even though sales were only about $2,000 a month, the company actually made a profit because it kept its costs low (a feat few other dot-coms could boast of).

Things changed dramatically when the company received national publicity in the financial press. Suddenly, the company's sales increased to $50,000 a month—fully 25 times the previous level. The "simple" little business suddenly needed a business plan, a strategic plan, and a budget. It needed to rent office space and to hire employees.

Learning Objectives

After studying this chapter, you should be able to:

1 Indicate the benefits of budgeting.

2 State the essentials of effective budgeting.

3 Identify the budgets that comprise the master budget.

4 Describe the sources for preparing the budgeted income statement.

5 Explain the principal sections of a cash budget.

6 Indicate the applicability of budgeting in nonmanufacturing companies.

 The Navigator

Initially, members of a local book club donated time to help meet the sudden demand. Some put in so much time that eventually the company hired them. Quickly, the number of paid employees ballooned. The sudden growth necessitated detailed planning and budgeting. The need for a proper budget was accentuated by the fact that the company's gross profit was only 16 cents on each dollar of goods sold. This meant that after paying for its inventory, the company had only 16 cents of every dollar to cover its remaining operating costs.

Unfortunately, the company never got things under control. Within a few months, sales had plummeted to $12,000 per month. At this level of sales, the company could not meet the mountain of monthly expenses that it had accumulated in trying to grow. Ironically, the company's sudden success, and the turmoil it created, appears to have been what eventually caused the company to fail.

Watch the Babycakes video in WileyPLUS to learn more about budgetary planning in the real world.

✔ **The Navigator**

Preview of Chapter 23

As the Feature Story about Positively-You.com indicates, budgeting is critical to financial well-being. As a student, you budget your study time and your money. Families budget income and expenses. Governmental agencies budget revenues and expenditures. Businesses use budgets in planning and controlling their operations.

Our primary focus in this chapter is budgeting—specifically, how budgeting is used as a *planning tool* by management. Through budgeting, it should be possible for management to maintain enough cash to pay creditors, to have sufficient raw materials to meet production requirements, and to have adequate finished goods to meet expected sales.

The content and organization of Chapter 23 are as follows.

BUDGETARY PLANNING			
Budgeting Basics	**Preparing the Operating Budgets**	**Preparing the Financial Budgets**	**Budgeting in Non-manufacturing Companies**
• Budgeting and accounting • Benefits • Essentials of effective budgeting • Length of budget period • Budgeting process • Budgeting and human behavior • Budgeting and long-range planning • The master budget	• Sales • Production • Direct materials • Direct labor • Manufacturing overhead • Selling and administrative expense • Budgeted income statement	• Cash • Budgeted balance sheet	• Merchandisers • Service • Not-for-profit

✔ **The Navigator**

Budgeting Basics

One of management's major responsibilities is planning. As explained in Chapter 15, **planning** is the process of establishing company-wide objectives. A successful organization makes both long-term and short-term plans. These plans establish the objectives of the company and the proposed way of accomplishing them.

A **budget** is a formal written statement of management's plans for a specified future time period, expressed in financial terms. It represents the primary method of communicating agreed-upon objectives throughout the organization. Once adopted, a budget becomes an important basis for evaluating performance. It promotes efficiency and serves as a deterrent to waste and inefficiency. We consider the role of budgeting as a **control device** in Chapter 24.

Budgeting and Accounting

Accounting information makes major contributions to the budgeting process. From the accounting records, companies can obtain historical data on revenues, costs, and expenses. These data are helpful in formulating future budget goals.

Normally, accountants have the responsibility for presenting management's budgeting goals in financial terms. In this role, they translate management's plans and communicate the budget to employees throughout the company. They prepare periodic budget reports that provide the basis for measuring performance and comparing actual results with planned objectives. The budget itself, and the administration of the budget, however, are entirely management responsibilities.

The Benefits of Budgeting

The primary benefits of budgeting are:

1. It requires all levels of management to **plan ahead** and to formalize goals on a recurring basis.
2. It provides **definite objectives** for evaluating performance at each level of responsibility.
3. It creates an **early warning system** for potential problems so that management can make changes before things get out of hand.
4. It facilitates the **coordination of activities** within the business. It does this by correlating the goals of each segment with overall company objectives. Thus, the company can integrate production and sales promotion with expected sales.
5. It results in greater **management awareness** of the entity's overall operations and the impact on operations of external factors, such as economic trends.
6. It **motivates personnel** throughout the organization to meet planned objectives.

A budget is an aid to management; it is not a *substitute* for management. A budget cannot operate or enforce itself. Companies can realize the benefits of budgeting only when managers carefully administer budgets.

Essentials of Effective Budgeting

Effective budgeting depends on a **sound organizational structure**. In such a structure, authority and responsibility for all phases of operations are clearly defined. Budgets based on **research and analysis** are more likely to result in realistic goals that will contribute to the growth and profitability of a company. And, the effectiveness of a budget program is directly related to its **acceptance by all levels of management**.

Once adopted, the budget is an important tool for evaluating performance. Managers should systematically and periodically review variations between actual and expected results to determine their cause(s). However, individuals should not be held responsible for variations that are beyond their control.

Length of the Budget Period

The budget period is not necessarily one year in length. **A budget may be prepared for any period of time.** Various factors influence the length of the budget period. These factors include the type of budget, the nature of the organization, the need for periodic appraisal, and prevailing business conditions.

The budget period should be long enough to provide an attainable goal under normal business conditions. Ideally, the time period should minimize the impact of seasonal or cyclical fluctuations. On the other hand, the budget period should not be so long that reliable estimates are impossible.

The **most common budget period is one year**. The annual budget, in turn, is often supplemented by monthly and quarterly budgets. Many companies use **continuous 12-month budgets**. These budgets drop the month just ended and add a future month. One advantage of continuous budgeting is that it keeps management planning a full year ahead.

ACCOUNTING ACROSS THE ORGANIZATION

Businesses Often Feel Too Busy to Plan for the Future

A study by Willard & Shullman Group Ltd. found that fewer than 14% of businesses with less than 500 employees do an annual budget or have a written business plan. For many small businesses, the basic assumption is that, "As long as I sell as much as I can, and keep my employees paid, I'm doing OK." A few small business owners even say that they see no need for budgeting and planning. Most small business owners, though, say that they understand that budgeting and planning are critical for survival and growth. But given the long hours that they already work addressing day-to-day challenges, they also say that they are "just too busy to plan for the future."

 Describe a situation in which a business "sells as much as it can" but cannot "keep its employees paid." (See page 1178.)

The Budgeting Process

The development of the budget for the coming year generally starts several months before the end of the current year. The budgeting process usually begins with the collection of data from each organizational unit of the company. Past performance is often the starting point from which future budget goals are formulated.

The budget is developed within the framework of a **sales forecast**. This forecast shows potential sales for the industry and the company's expected share of such sales. Sales forecasting involves a consideration of various factors: (1) general economic conditions, (2) industry trends, (3) market research studies, (4) anticipated advertising and promotion, (5) previous market share, (6) changes in prices, and (7) technological developments. The input of sales personnel and top management is essential to the sales forecast.

In small companies like Positively-You.com, the budgeting process is often informal. In larger companies, a **budget committee** has responsibility for coordinating the preparation of the budget. The committee ordinarily includes the president, treasurer, chief accountant (controller), and management personnel from each of the major areas of the company, such as sales, production, and research. The budget committee serves as a review board where managers can defend their budget goals and requests. Differences are reviewed, modified if necessary, and reconciled. The budget is then put in its final form by the budget committee, approved, and distributed.

Budgeting and Human Behavior

A budget can have a significant impact on human behavior. If done well, it can inspire managers to higher levels of performance. However, if done poorly, budgets can discourage additional effort and pull down the morale of managers. Why do these diverse effects occur? The answer is found in how the budget is developed and administered.

In developing the budget, each level of management should be invited to participate. This "bottom-to-top" approach is referred to as **participative budgeting**. One advantage of participative budgeting is that lower-level managers have more detailed knowledge of their specific area and thus are able to provide more accurate budgetary estimates. Also, when lower-level managers participate in the budgeting process, they are more likely to perceive the resulting budget as fair. The overall goal is to reach agreement on a budget that the managers consider fair and achievable, but which also meets the corporate goals set by top management. When this goal is met, the budget will provide positive motivation for the managers. In contrast, if managers view the budget as unfair and unrealistic, they may feel discouraged and uncommitted to budget goals. The risk of having unrealistic budgets is generally greater when the budget is developed from top management down to lower management than vice versa. Illustration 23-1 graphically displays the flow of budget data from bottom to top under participative budgeting.

Illustration 23-1
Flow of budget data under participative budgeting

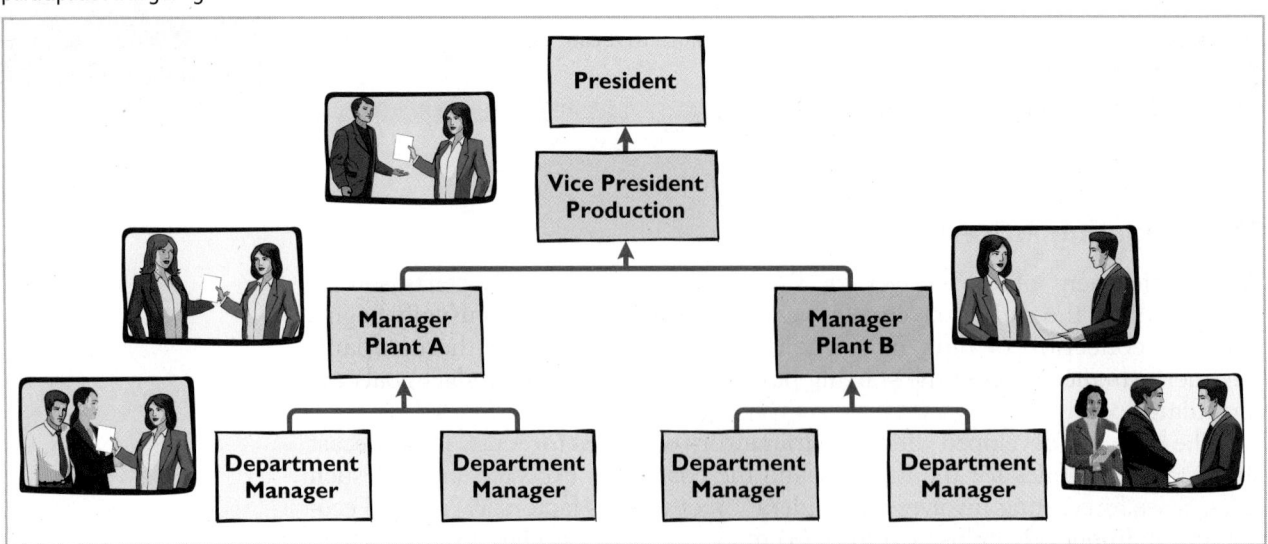

For example, at one time, in an effort to revive its plummeting stock, Time Warner's top management determined and publicly announced bold new financial goals for the coming year. Unfortunately, these goals were not reached. The next year, the company got a new CEO who said the company would now actually set reasonable goals that it could meet. The new budgets were developed with each operating unit setting what it felt were optimistic but attainable goals. In the words of one manager, using this approach created a sense of teamwork.

Participative budgeting does, however, have potential disadvantages. First, the "give and take" of participative budgeting is time-consuming (and thus more costly). Under a "top-down" approach, the budget is simply developed by top management and then dictated to lower-level managers. A second disadvantage is that participative budgeting can foster budgetary "gaming" through budgetary slack. **Budgetary slack** occurs when managers intentionally underestimate budgeted revenues or overestimate budgeted expenses in order to make it easier to achieve budgetary goals. To minimize budgetary slack, higher-level managers must carefully review and thoroughly question the budget projections provided to them by employees whom they supervise.

For the budget to be effective, top management must completely support the budget. The budget is an important basis for evaluating performance. It also can be used as a positive aid in achieving projected goals. The effect of an evaluation is positive when top management tempers criticism with advice and assistance. In contrast, a manager is likely to respond negatively if top management uses the budget exclusively to assess blame. A budget should not be used as a pressure device to force improved performance. In sum, a budget can be a manager's friend or a foe.

Ethics Note

Unrealistic budgets can lead to unethical employee behavior such as cutting corners on the job or distorting internal financial reports.

Budgeting and Long-Range Planning

Budgeting and long-range planning are not the same. One important difference is the **time period involved**. The maximum length of a budget is usually one year, and budgets are often prepared for shorter periods of time, such as a month or a quarter. In contrast, long-range planning usually encompasses a period of at least five years.

A second significant difference is in **emphasis**. Budgeting focuses on achieving specific short-term goals, such as meeting annual profit objectives. **Long-range planning**, on the other hand, identifies long-term goals, selects strategies to achieve those goals, and develops policies and plans to implement the strategies. In long-range planning, management also considers anticipated trends in the economic and political environment and how the company should cope with them.

The final difference between budgeting and long-range planning relates to the **amount of detail presented**. Budgets, as you will see in this chapter, can be very detailed. Long-range plans contain considerably less detail. The data in long-range plans are intended more for a review of progress toward long-term goals than as a basis of control for achieving specific results. The primary objective of long-range planning is to develop the best strategy to maximize the company's performance over an extended future period.

Helpful Hint

In comparing a budget with a long-range plan:
(1) Which has more detail?
(2) Which is done for a longer period of time?
(3) Which is more concerned with short-term goals?
Answers: (1) Budget.
(2) Long-range plan.
(3) Budget.

The Master Budget

The term "budget" is actually a shorthand term to describe a variety of budget documents. All of these documents are combined into a master budget. The **master budget** is a set of interrelated budgets that constitutes a plan of action for a specified time period.

The master budget contains two classes of budgets. **Operating budgets** are the individual budgets that result in the preparation of the budgeted income statement.

LEARNING OBJECTIVE   3

Identify the budgets that comprise the master budget.

These budgets establish goals for the company's sales and production personnel. In contrast, **financial budgets** focus primarily on the cash resources needed to fund expected operations and planned capital expenditures. Financial budgets include the capital expenditure budget, the cash budget, and the budgeted balance sheet.

Illustration 23-2 pictures the individual budgets included in a master budget, and the sequence in which they are prepared. The company first develops the operating budgets, beginning with the sales budget. Then, it prepares the financial budgets. We will explain and illustrate each budget shown in Illustration 23-2 except the capital expenditure budget. That budget is discussed under the topic of capital budgeting in Chapter 26.

Illustration 23-2

Components of the master budget

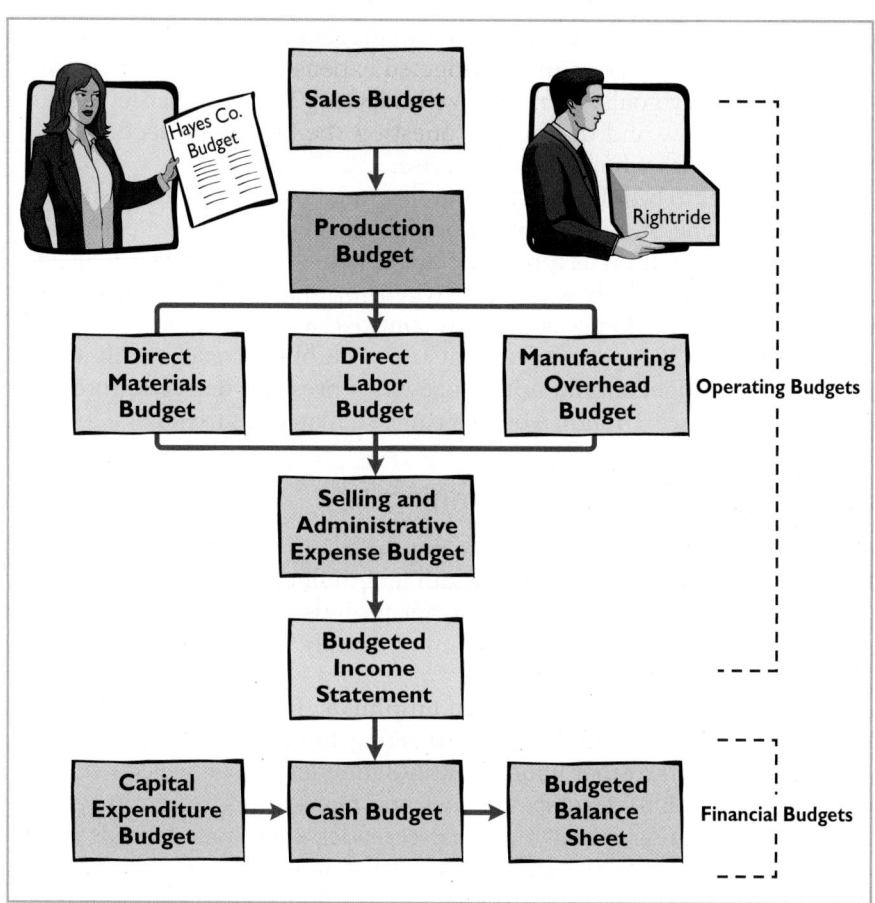

> DO IT!

Budget Terminology

Use this list of terms to complete the sentences that follow.

Long-range planning   Participative budgeting
Sales forecast   Operating budgets
Master budget   Financial budgets

1. A _____ shows potential sales for the industry and a company's expected share of such sales.

2. _____ are used as the basis for the preparation of the budgeted income statement.

3. The _____ is a set of interrelated budgets that constitutes a plan of action for a specified time period.

Action Plan

✔ Understand the budgeting process, including the importance of the sales forecast.

✔ Understand the difference between an operating budget and a financial budget.

✔ Differentiate budgeting from long-range planning.

✔ Realize that the master budget is a set of interrelated budgets.

4. _____ identifies long-term goals, selects strategies to achieve these goals, and develops policies and plans to implement the strategies.

5. Lower-level managers are more likely to perceive results as fair and achievable under a _____ approach.

6. _____ focus primarily on the cash resources needed to fund expected operations and planned capital expenditures.

Solution

1. Sales forecast.	4. Long-range planning.
2. Operating budgets.	5. Participative budgeting.
3. Master budget.	6. Financial budgets.

Related exercise material: **BE23-1, E23-1, and DO IT! 23-1.**

 The Navigator

Preparing the Operating Budgets

We use a case study of Hayes Company in preparing the operating budgets. Hayes manufactures and sells a single product, an ergonomically designed bike seat with multiple customizable adjustments, called the Rightride. The budgets are prepared by quarters for the year ending December 31, 2014. Hayes Company begins its annual budgeting process on September 1, 2013, and it completes the budget for 2014 by December 1, 2013.

Sales Budget

As shown in the master budget in Illustration 23-2, **the sales budget is prepared first**. Each of the other budgets depends on the sales budget. The **sales budget** is derived from the sales forecast. It represents management's best estimate of sales revenue for the budget period. An inaccurate sales budget may adversely affect net income. For example, an overly optimistic sales budget may result in excessive inventories that may have to be sold at reduced prices. In contrast, an unduly pessimistic sales budget may result in loss of sales revenue due to inventory shortages.

For example, at one time Amazon.com significantly underestimated demand for its e-book reader, the Kindle. As a consequence, it did not produce enough Kindles and was completely sold out well before the holiday shopping season. Not only did this represent a huge lost opportunity for Amazon.com, but it exposed it to potential competitors, who were eager to provide customers with alternatives to the Kindle.

Forecasting sales is challenging. For example, consider the forecasting challenges faced by major sports arenas, whose revenues depend on the success of the home team. Madison Square Garden's revenues from April to June were $193 million during a year when the Knicks made the NBA playoffs. But revenues were only $133.2 million a couple of years later when the team did not make the playoffs. Or, consider the challenges faced by Hollywood movie producers in predicting the complicated revenue stream produced by a new movie. Movie theater ticket sales represent only 20% of total revenue. The bulk of revenue comes from global sales, DVDs, video-on-demand, merchandising products, and videogames, all of which are difficult to forecast.

The sales budget is prepared by multiplying the expected unit sales volume for each product by its anticipated unit selling price. Hayes Company expects sales volume to be 3,000 units in the first quarter, with 500-unit increases in each succeeding quarter. Illustration 23-3 (page 1138) shows the sales budget for the year, by quarter, based on a sales price of $60 per unit.

Helpful Hint

For a retail or manufacturing company, what is the starting point in preparing the master budget, and why? Answer: The sales budget is the starting point for the master budget. It sets the level of activity for other functions such as production and purchasing.

Illustration 23-3
Sales budget

		Quarter				
		1	2	3	4	Year
6	Expected unit sales	3,000	3,500	4,000	4,500	15,000
7	Unit selling price	× $60	× $60	× $60	× $60	× $60
8	Total sales	$180,000	$210,000	$240,000	$270,000	$900,000

Hayes Company
Sales Budget
For the Year Ending December 31, 2014

Some companies classify the anticipated sales revenue as cash or credit sales and by geographical regions, territories, or salespersons.

SERVICE COMPANY INSIGHT

The Implications of Budgetary Optimism

Companies aren't the only ones that have to estimate revenues. Governments at all levels (e.g., local, state or federal) prepare annual budgets. Most are required to submit balanced budgets, that is, estimated revenues are supposed to cover anticipated expenditures. Unfortunately, estimating government revenues can be as difficult as, or even more difficult than, estimating company revenues. The accuracy of government estimates is most critical during economic downturns. If governments fail to anticipate lower revenues during the planning stage, they then often have to make much larger, more disruptive cuts than would have been originally necessary.

For example, during 2009, the median state government overestimated revenues by 10.2%, with four state governments missing by more than 25%. What makes estimation so difficult for these governments? Most states rely on income taxes, which fluctuate widely with economic gyrations. Some states rely on sales taxes, which are problematic because the laws regarding sales taxes haven't adjusted for the shift from manufacturing to service companies and from brick-and-mortar stores to online sales.

Source: Conor Dougherty, "States Fumble Revenue Forecasts," *Wall Street Journal Online* (March 2, 2011).

 Why is it important that government budgets accurately estimate future revenues during economic downturns? (See page 1178.)

Production Budget

The **production budget** shows the number of units of a product to produce to meet anticipated sales demand. Production requirements are determined from the following formula.[1]

Illustration 23-4
Production requirements formula

Budgeted Sales Units	+	Desired Ending Finished Goods Units	−	Beginning Finished Goods Units	=	Required Production Units

A realistic estimate of ending inventory is essential in scheduling production requirements. Excessive inventories in one quarter may lead to cutbacks in

---

[1]This formula ignores any work in process inventories, which are assumed to be nonexistent in Hayes Company.

production and employee layoffs in a subsequent quarter. On the other hand, inadequate inventories may result either in added costs for overtime work or in lost sales. Hayes Company believes it can meet future sales requirements by maintaining an ending inventory equal to 20% of the next quarter's budgeted sales volume. For example, the ending finished goods inventory for the first quarter is 700 units (20% × anticipated second-quarter sales of 3,500 units). Illustration 23-5 shows the production budget.

Units of Finished Goods Inventory	
Beg. Inv.	
Required Prod. Units	Sales
End. Inv.	

Hayes Company Production Budget.xls

Home   Insert   Page Layout   Formulas   Data   Review   View

P18   fx

Hayes Company
Production Budget
For the Year Ending December 31, 2014

	Quarter					
	1	2	3	4	Year	
Expected unit sales (Illustration 23-3)	3,000	3,500	4,000	4,500		
Add: Desired ending finished goods units[a]	700	800	900	1,000 [b]		
Total required units	3,700	4,300	4,900	5,500		
Less: Beginning finished goods units	600 [c]	700	800	900		
Required production units	3,100	3,600	4,100	4,600	15,400	

[a]20% of next quarter's sales
[b]Expected 2015 first-quarter sales, 5,000 units × 20%
[c]20% of estimated first-quarter 2014 sales units

Units of Finished Goods Inventory	
600	
3,100	3,000
700	

Illustration 23-5
Production budget

The production budget, in turn, provides the basis for the budgeted costs for each manufacturing cost element, as explained in the following pages.

> DO IT!

Production Budget

Becker Company estimates that 2014 unit sales will be 12,000 in quarter 1, 16,000 in quarter 2, and 20,000 in quarter 3, at a unit selling price of $30. Management desires to have ending finished goods inventory equal to 15% of the next quarter's expected unit sales. Prepare a production budget by quarter for the first six months of 2014.

Solution

Action Plan

✔ Begin with budgeted sales in units.

✔ Add desired ending finished goods inventory.

✔ Subtract beginning finished goods inventory.

Becker Company
Production Budget
For the Six Months Ending June 30, 2014

	Quarter		Six Months
	1	2	
Expected unit sales	12,000	16,000	
Add: Desired ending finished goods	2,400	3,000	
Total required units	14,400	19,000	
Less: Beginning finished goods inventory	1,800	2,400	
Required production units	12,600	16,600	29,200

Related exercise material: **BE23-3, E23-4, E23-6, and DO IT! 23-2.**

✔ The Navigator

Direct Materials Budget

The **direct materials budget** shows both the quantity and cost of direct materials to be purchased. The quantities of direct materials are derived from the following formula.

Illustration 23-6
Formula for direct materials quantities

Direct Materials Units Required for Production	+	Desired Ending Direct Materials Units	−	Beginning Direct Materials Units	=	Required Direct Materials Units to Be Purchased

Units of Direct Materials

Beg. Inv.	
Direct Materials to Prod.	Direct Materials Required for Prod.
End. Inv.	

After the company determines the number of units to purchase, it can compute the budgeted cost of direct materials to be purchased. It does so by multiplying the required units of direct materials by the anticipated cost per unit.

The desired ending inventory is again a key component in the budgeting process. For example, inadequate inventories could result in temporary shutdowns of production. Because of its close proximity to suppliers, Hayes Company maintains an ending inventory of raw materials equal to 10% of the next quarter's production requirements. The manufacture of each Rightride requires 2 pounds of raw materials, and the expected cost per pound is $4. Illustration 23-7 shows the direct materials budget. Assume that the desired ending direct materials amount is 1,020 pounds for the fourth quarter of 2014.

Illustration 23-7
Direct materials budget

Units of Direct Materials (1ˢᵗ Qtr.)

620	
6,300	6,200
720	

Hayes Company Direct Materials Budget.xls							

Home Insert Page Layout Formulas Data Review View

P18

	A	B C D E F G H I J K

	A	1	2	3	4	Year
1	**Hayes Company**					
2	**Direct Materials Budget**					
3	**For the Year Ending December 31, 2014**					
4		Quarter				
5		1	2	3	4	Year
6	Units to be produced (Illustration 23-5)	3,100	3,600	4,100	4,600	
7	Direct materials per unit	× 2	× 2	× 2	× 2	
8	Total pounds needed for production	6,200	7,200	8,200	9,200	
9	Add: Desired ending direct materials (pounds)ᵃ	720	820	920	1,020	
10	Total materials required	6,920	8,020	9,120	10,220	
11	Less: Beginning direct materials (pounds)	620 ᵇ	720	820	920	
12	Direct materials purchases	6,300	7,300	8,300	9,300	
13	Cost per pound	× $4	× $4	× $4	× $4	
14	Total cost of direct materials purchases	$25,200	$29,200	$33,200	$37,200	$124,800
15						
16	ᵃ10% of next quarter's production requirements					
17	ᵇ10% of estimated first-quarter pounds needed for production					
18						

MANAGEMENT INSIGHT

Betting That Prices Won't Fall

Sometimes things happen that cause managers to reevaluate their normal purchasing patterns. Consider, for example, the predicament that businesses faced when the price of many raw materials recently skyrocketed. Rubber, cotton, oil, corn, wheat, steel, copper, and spices—prices for seemingly everything were going straight up. Anticipating that prices might continue to go up, many managers decided to stockpile much larger quantities of raw materials to avoid paying even higher prices in the future. For example, after cotton prices rose 92%, one manager of a printed T-shirt manufacturer decided to stockpile a huge supply of plain T-shirts in anticipation of additional price increases. While he normally has about 30 boxes of T-shirts in inventory, he purchased 2,500 boxes.

Source: Liam Pleven and Matt Wirz, "Companies Stock Up as Commodities Prices Rise," *Wall Street Journal Online* (February 3, 2011).

? What are the potential downsides of stockpiling a huge amount of raw materials? (See page 1179.)

> DO IT!

Master Budget

Action Plan

✔ Know the form and content of the sales budget.

✔ Prepare the sales budget first, as the basis for the other budgets.

✔ Determine the units that must be produced to meet anticipated sales.

✔ Know how to compute the beginning and ending finished goods units.

✔ Determine the materials required to meet production needs.

✔ Know how to compute the beginning and ending direct materials units.

Soriano Company is preparing its master budget for 2014. Relevant data pertaining to its sales, production, and direct materials budgets are as follows.

Sales. Sales for the year are expected to total 1,200,000 units. Quarterly sales, as a percentage of total sales, are 20%, 25%, 30%, and 25%, respectively. The sales price is expected to be $50 per unit for the first three quarters and $55 per unit beginning in the fourth quarter. Sales in the first quarter of 2015 are expected to be 10% higher than the budgeted sales for the first quarter of 2014.

Production. Management desires to maintain the ending finished goods inventories at 25% of the next quarter's budgeted sales volume.

Direct materials. Each unit requires 3 pounds of raw materials at a cost of $5 per pound. Management desires to maintain raw materials inventories at 5% of the next quarter's production requirements. Assume the production requirements for the first quarter of 2015 are 810,000 pounds.

Prepare the sales, production, and direct materials budgets by quarters for 2014.

Solution

Soriano Company Sales Budget.xls

Home   Insert   Page Layout   Formulas   Data   Review   View

P18   *fx*

	A	B	C	D	E	F
1		**Soriano Company**				
2		**Sales Budget**				
3		**For the Year Ending December 31, 2014**				
4				Quarter		
5		1	2	3	4	Year
6	Expected unit sales	240,000	300,000	360,000	300,000	1,200,000
7	Unit selling price	× $50	× $50	× $50	× $55	—
8	Total sales	$12,000,000	$15,000,000	$18,000,000	$16,500,000	$61,500,000

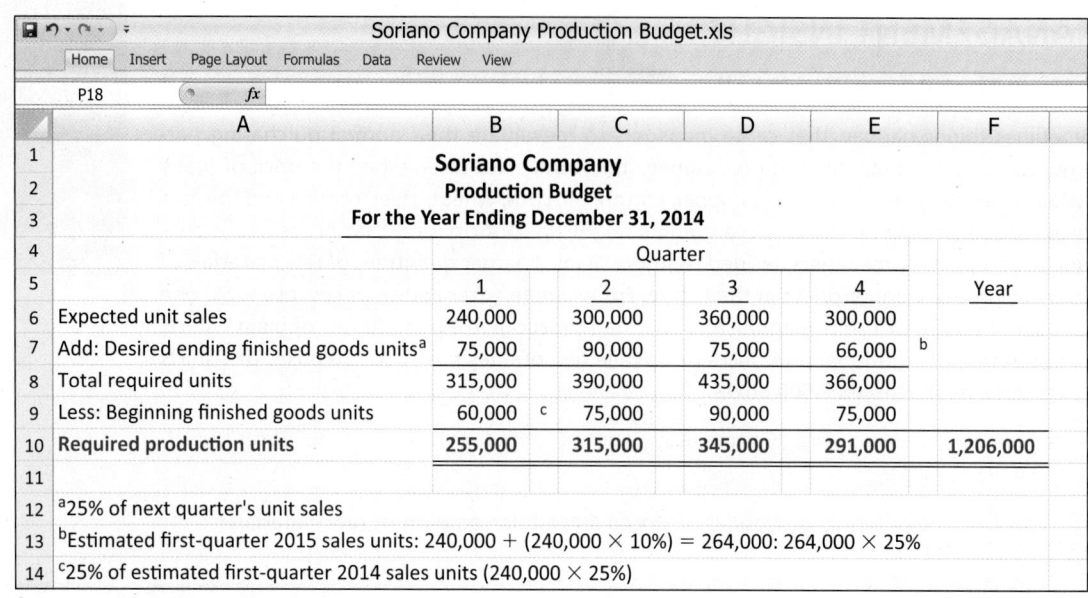

Soriano Company Production Budget.xls

Home   Insert   Page Layout   Formulas   Data   Review   View

P18   *fx*

Soriano Company
Production Budget
For the Year Ending December 31, 2014

	Quarter				Year
	1	2	3	4	
Expected unit sales	240,000	300,000	360,000	300,000	
Add: Desired ending finished goods units[a]	75,000	90,000	75,000	66,000 [b]	
Total required units	315,000	390,000	435,000	366,000	
Less: Beginning finished goods units	60,000 [c]	75,000	90,000	75,000	
Required production units	255,000	315,000	345,000	291,000	1,206,000

[a]25% of next quarter's unit sales
[b]Estimated first-quarter 2015 sales units: 240,000 + (240,000 × 10%) = 264,000: 264,000 × 25%
[c]25% of estimated first-quarter 2014 sales units (240,000 × 25%)

Soriano Company Direct Materials Budget.xls

Home   Insert   Page Layout   Formulas   Data   Review   View

P18   *fx*

Soriano Company
Direct Materials Budget
For the Year Ending December 31, 2014

	Quarter				Year
	1	2	3	4	
Units to be produced	255,000	315,000	345,000	291,000	
Direct materials per unit	× 3	× 3	× 3	× 3	
Total pounds needed for production	765,000	945,000	1,035,000	873,000	
Add: Desired ending direct materials (pounds)	47,250	51,750	43,650	40,500 [a]	
Total materials required	812,250	996,750	1,078,650	913,500	
Less: Beginning direct materials (pounds)	38,250 [b]	47,250	51,750	43,650	
Direct materials purchases	774,000	949,500	1,026,900	869,850	
Cost per pound	× $5	× $5	× $5	× $5	
Total cost of direct materials purchases	$3,870,000	$4,747,500	$5,134,500	$4,349,250	$18,101,250

[a]Estimated first-quarter 2015 production requirements: 810,000 × 5% = 40,500
[b]5% of estimated first-quarter pounds needed for production

Related exercise material: **BE23-2, BE23-3, BE23-4, E23-2, E23-3, E23-4, E23-5, E23-6, and DO IT! 23-3.**

✔ **The Navigator**

Direct Labor Budget

Like the direct materials budget, the **direct labor budget** contains the quantity (hours) and cost of direct labor necessary to meet production requirements. The total direct labor cost is derived from the following formula.

Illustration 23-8
Formula for direct labor cost

Units to Be Produced	×	Direct Labor Time per Unit	×	Direct Labor Cost per Hour	=	Total Direct Labor Cost

Direct labor hours are determined from the production budget. At Hayes Company, two hours of direct labor are required to produce each unit of finished goods. The anticipated hourly wage rate is $10. Illustration 23-9 shows these data.

Illustration 23-9
Direct labor budget

Hayes Company Direct Labor Budget.xls

Home | Insert | Page Layout | Formulas | Data | Review | View

P18

	A	B	C	D	E	F	G	H	I	J
1			Hayes Company							
2			Direct Labor Budget							
3			For the Year Ending December 31, 2014							
4					Quarter					
5			1		2		3		4	Year
6	Units to be produced (Illustration 23-5)		3,100		3,600		4,100		4,600	
7	Direct labor time (hours) per unit		× 2		× 2		× 2		× 2	
8	Total required direct labor hours		6,200		7,200		8,200		9,200	
9	Direct labor cost per hour		× $10		× $10		× $10		× $10	
10	Total direct labor cost		$62,000		$72,000		$82,000		$92,000	$308,000
11										

The direct labor budget is critical in maintaining a labor force that can meet the expected levels of production.

Manufacturing Overhead Budget

The **manufacturing overhead budget** shows the expected manufacturing overhead costs for the budget period. As Illustration 23-10 (page 1144) shows, **this budget distinguishes between variable and fixed overhead costs**. Hayes Company expects variable costs to fluctuate with production volume on the basis of the following rates per direct labor hour: indirect materials $1.00, indirect labor $1.40, utilities $0.40, and maintenance $0.20. Thus, for the 6,200 direct labor hours to produce 3,100 units, budgeted indirect materials are $6,200 (6,200 × $1), and budgeted indirect labor is $8,680 (6,200 × $1.40). Hayes also recognizes that some maintenance is fixed. The amounts reported for fixed costs are assumed for our example. The accuracy of budgeted overhead cost estimates can be greatly improved by employing activity-based costing.

Helpful Hint
An important assumption in Illustration 23-9 is that the company can add to and subtract from its work force as needed so that the $10 per hour labor cost applies to a wide range of possible production activity.

Illustration 23-10
Manufacturing overhead
budget

	Hayes Company Manufacturing Overhead Budget.xls					
	Home Insert Page Layout Formulas Data Review View					
	P18 *fx*					
	A	B	C	D	E	F
1	**Hayes Company**					
2	**Manufacturing Overhead Budget**					
3	**For the Year Ending December 31, 2014**					
4		Quarter				
5		1	2	3	4	Year
6	Variable costs					
7	Indirect materials ($1.00/hour)	$ 6,200	$ 7,200	$ 8,200	$ 9,200	$ 30,800
8	Indirect labor ($1.40/hour)	8,680	10,080	11,480	12,880	43,120
9	Utilities ($0.40/hour)	2,480	2,880	3,280	3,680	12,320
10	Maintenance ($0.20/hour)	1,240	1,440	1,640	1,840	6,160
11	Total variable costs	18,600	21,600	24,600	27,600	92,400
12	Fixed costs					
13	Supervisory salaries	20,000	20,000	20,000	20,000	80,000
14	Depreciation	3,800	3,800	3,800	3,800	15,200
15	Property taxes and insurance	9,000	9,000	9,000	9,000	36,000
16	Maintenance	5,700	5,700	5,700	5,700	22,800
17	Total fixed costs	38,500	38,500	38,500	38,500	154,000
18	Total manufacturing overhead	$57,100	$60,100	$63,100	$66,100	$246,400
19	Direct labor hours (Illustration 23-9)	6,200	7,200	8,200	9,200	30,800
20	Manufacturing overhead rate per direct labor hour ($246,400 ÷ 30,800)					$8
21						

At Hayes Company, overhead is applied to production on the basis of direct labor hours. Thus, as Illustration 23-10 shows, the budgeted annual rate is $8 per hour ($246,400 ÷ 30,800).

Selling and Administrative Expense Budget

Hayes Company combines its operating expenses into one budget, the **selling and administrative expense budget**. This budget projects anticipated selling and administrative expenses for the budget period. This budget (Illustration 23-11) also classifies expenses as either variable or fixed. In this case, the variable expense rates per unit of sales are sales commissions $3 and freight-out $1. Variable expenses per quarter are based on the unit sales from the sales budget (Illustration 23-3, page 1138). For example, Hayes expects sales in the first quarter to be 3,000 units. Thus, Sales Commissions Expense is $9,000 (3,000 × $3), and Freight-Out is $3,000 (3,000 × $1). Fixed expenses are based on assumed data.

LEARNING OBJECTIVE 4

Describe the sources for preparing the budgeted income statement.

Budgeted Income Statement

The **budgeted income statement** is the important end-product of the operating budgets. This budget indicates the expected profitability of operations for the budget period. The budgeted income statement provides the basis for evaluating company performance. Budgeted income statements often act as a call to action.

	A	B	C	D	E	F
	Hayes Company Manufacturing Selling and Administrative Expense Budget.xls					
	Home Insert Page Layout Formulas Data Review View					
	P18 fx					
1	**Hayes Company**					
2	**Selling and Administrative Expense Budget**					
3	**For the Year Ending December 31, 2014**					
4				Quarter		
5		1	2	3	4	Year
6	Budgeted sales in units (Illustration 23-3)	3,000	3,500	4,000	4,500	15,000
7	Variable expenses					
8	Sales commissions ($3 per unit)	$ 9,000	$10,500	$12,000	$13,500	$ 45,000
9	Freight-out ($1 per unit)	3,000	3,500	4,000	4,500	15,000
10	Total variable expenses	12,000	14,000	16,000	18,000	60,000
11	Fixed expenses					
12	Advertising	5,000	5,000	5,000	5,000	20,000
13	Sales salaries	15,000	15,000	15,000	15,000	60,000
14	Office salaries	7,500	7,500	7,500	7,500	30,000
15	Depreciation	1,000	1,000	1,000	1,000	4,000
16	Property taxes and insurance	1,500	1,500	1,500	1,500	6,000
17	Total fixed expenses	30,000	30,000	30,000	30,000	120,000
18	Total selling and administrative expenses	$42,000	$44,000	$46,000	$48,000	$180,000
19						

Illustration 23-11
Selling and administrative
expense budget

For example, a board member at XM Satellite Radio Holdings felt that budgeted costs were too high relative to budgeted revenues. When management refused to cut its marketing and programming costs, the board member resigned. He felt that without the cuts, the company risked financial crisis.

As you would expect, the budgeted income statement is prepared from the various operating budgets. For example, to find the cost of goods sold, Hayes Company must first determine the total unit cost of producing one Rightride, as follows.

Illustration 23-12
Computation of total unit cost

Cost of One Rightride

Cost Element	Illustration	Quantity	Unit Cost	Total
Direct materials	23-7	2 pounds	$ 4.00	$ 8.00
Direct labor	23-9	2 hours	$10.00	20.00
Manufacturing overhead	23-10	2 hours	$ 8.00	16.00
Total unit cost				**$44.00**

Hayes Company then determines cost of goods sold by multiplying the units sold by the unit cost. Its budgeted cost of goods sold is $660,000 (15,000 × $44). All data for the income statement come from the individual operating budgets except the following: (1) interest expense is expected to be $100, and (2) income taxes are estimated to be $12,000. Illustration 23-13 (page 1146) shows the budgeted income statement.

Illustration 23-13
Budgeted income statement

Hayes Company	
Budgeted Income Statement	
For the Year Ending December 31, 2014	
Sales (Illustration 23-3)	$900,000
Cost of goods sold (15,000 × $44)	660,000
Gross profit	240,000
Selling and administrative expenses (Illustration 23-11)	180,000
Income from operations	60,000
Interest expense	100
Income before income taxes	59,900
Income tax expense	12,000
Net income	$ 47,900

> ## DO IT!

Budgeted Income Statement

Soriano Company is preparing its budgeted income statement for 2014. Relevant data pertaining to its sales, production, and direct materials budgets can be found in the DO IT! exercise on page 1141.

In addition, Soriano budgets 0.5 hours of direct labor per unit, labor costs at $15 per hour, and manufacturing overhead at $25 per direct labor hour. Its budgeted selling and administrative expenses for 2014 are $12,000,000.

(a) Calculate the budgeted total unit cost. (b) Prepare the budgeted income statement for 2014.

Solution

Action Plan

✔ Recall that total unit cost consists of direct materials, direct labor, and manufacturing overhead.

✔ Recall that direct materials costs are included in the direct materials budget.

✔ Know the form and content of the income statement.

✔ Use the total unit sales information from the sales budget to compute annual sales and cost of goods sold.

(a)

Cost Element	**Quantity**	**Unit Cost**	**Total**
Direct materials	3.0 pounds	$ 5	$ 15.00
Direct labor	0.5 hours	$15	7.50
Manufacturing overhead	0.5 hours	$25	12.50
Total unit cost			**$35.00**

(b)

Soriano Company	
Budgeted Income Statement	
For the Year Ending December 31, 2014	
Sales (1,200,000 units from sales budget, page 1141)	$61,500,000
Cost of goods sold (1,200,000 × $35.00/unit)	42,000,000
Gross profit	19,500,000
Selling and administrative expenses	12,000,000
Net income	$ 7,500,000

Related exercise material: **BE23-8, E23-11, E23-13, and** DO IT! **23-4.**

✔ **The Navigator**

As shown in Illustration 23-2 (page 1136), the financial budgets consist of the capital expenditure budget, the cash budget, and the budgeted balance sheet. We will discuss the capital expenditure budget in Chapter 26. The other budgets are explained in the following sections.

Cash Budget

The **cash budget** shows anticipated cash flows. Because cash is so vital, this budget is often considered to be the most important financial budget.

The cash budget contains three sections (cash receipts, cash disbursements, and financing) and the beginning and ending cash balances, as shown in Illustration 23-14.

Any Company Cash Budget	
Beginning cash balance	$X,XXX
Add: Cash receipts (itemized)	X,XXX
Total available cash	X,XXX
Less: Cash disbursements (itemized)	X,XXX
Excess (deficiency) of available cash over cash disbursements	X,XXX
Financing	X,XXX
Ending cash balance	$X,XXX

> **LEARNING OBJECTIVE 5**
> Explain the principal sections of a cash budget.

Illustration 23-14
Basic form of a cash budget

Helpful Hint
Why is the cash budget prepared after the other budgets are prepared? Answer: Because the information generated by the other budgets dictates the expected inflows and outflows of cash.

The **cash receipts section** includes expected receipts from the company's principal source(s) of revenue. These are usually cash sales and collections from customers on credit sales. This section also shows anticipated receipts of interest and dividends, and proceeds from planned sales of investments, plant assets, and the company's capital stock.

The **cash disbursements section** shows expected cash payments. Such payments include direct materials, direct labor, manufacturing overhead, and selling and administrative expenses. This section also includes projected payments for income taxes, dividends, investments, and plant assets.

The **financing section** shows expected borrowings and the repayment of the borrowed funds plus interest. Companies need this section when there is a cash deficiency or when the cash balance is below management's minimum required balance.

Data in the cash budget are prepared in sequence. The ending cash balance of one period becomes the beginning cash balance for the next period. Companies obtain data for preparing the cash budget from other budgets and from information provided by management. In practice, cash budgets are often prepared for the year on a monthly basis.

To minimize detail, we will assume that Hayes Company prepares an annual cash budget by quarters. Its cash budget is based on the following assumptions.

1. The January 1, 2014, cash balance is expected to be $38,000. Hayes wishes to maintain a balance of at least $15,000.

2. Sales (Illustration 23-3, page 1138): 60% are collected in the quarter sold and 40% are collected in the following quarter. Accounts receivable of $60,000 at December 31, 2013, are expected to be collected in full in the first quarter of 2014.

3. Short-term investments are expected to be sold for $2,000 cash in the first quarter.

4. Direct materials (Illustration 23-7, page 1140): 50% are paid in the quarter purchased and 50% are paid in the following quarter. Accounts payable of $10,600 at December 31, 2013, are expected to be paid in full in the first quarter of 2014.

5. Direct labor (Illustration 23-9, page 1143): 100% is paid in the quarter incurred.

6. Manufacturing overhead (Illustration 23-10, page 1144) and selling and administrative expenses (Illustration 23-11, page 1145): All items except depreciation are paid in the quarter incurred.

7. Management plans to purchase a truck in the second quarter for $10,000 cash.

8. Hayes makes equal quarterly payments of its estimated annual income taxes.

9. Loans are repaid in the earliest quarter in which there is sufficient cash (that is, when the cash on hand exceeds the $15,000 minimum required balance).

In preparing the cash budget, it is useful to prepare schedules for collections from customers (assumption No. 2) and cash payments for direct materials (assumption No. 4). These schedules are shown in Illustrations 23-15 and 23-16.

Illustration 23-15
Collections from customers

			Hayes Company		
		Schedule of Expected Collections from Customers			
		Collections by Quarter			
	Sales[a]	**1**	**2**	**3**	**4**
Accounts receivable, 12/31/13		$ 60,000			
First quarter	$180,000	108,000[b]	$ 72,000[c]		
Second quarter	210,000		126,000	$ 84,000	
Third quarter	240,000			144,000	$ 96,000
Fourth quarter	270,000				162,000
Total collections		$168,000	$198,000	$228,000	$258,000

[a]Per Illustration 23-3; [b]$180,000 × .60; [c]$180,000 × .40

Illustration 23-16
Payments for direct materials

			Hayes Company		
		Schedule of Expected Payments for Direct Materials			
		Payments by Quarter			
	Purchases[a]	**1**	**2**	**3**	**4**
Accounts payable, 12/31/13		$10,600			
First quarter	$25,200	12,600[b]	$12,600[c]		
Second quarter	29,200		14,600	$14,600	
Third quarter	33,200			16,600	$16,600
Fourth quarter	37,200				18,600
Total payments		$23,200	$27,200	$31,200	$35,200

[a]Per Illustration 23-7; [b]$25,200 × .50; [c]$25,200 × .50

Illustration 23-17 shows the cash budget for Hayes Company. The budget indicates that Hayes will need $3,000 of financing in the second quarter to maintain a minimum cash balance of $15,000. Since there is an excess of available cash over disbursements of $22,500 at the end of the third quarter, the borrowing, plus $100 interest, is repaid in this quarter.

	Home	Insert	Page Layout	Formulas	Data	Review	View

	P18			fx						

	A	B	C	D	E	F	G	H	I	J
1			**Hayes Company**							
2			Cash Budget							
3			For the Year Ending December 31, 2014							
4							Quarter			
5		Assumption	1		2		3		4	
6	Beginning cash balance	1	$ 38,000		$ 25,500		$ 15,000		$ 19,400	
7	**Add: Receipts**									
8	Collections from customers	2	168,000		198,000		228,000		258,000	
9	Sale of securities	3	2,000		0		0		0	
10	Total receipts		170,000		198,000		228,000		258,000	
11	Total available cash		208,000		223,500		243,000		277,400	
12	**Less: Disbursements**									
13	Direct materials	4	23,200		27,200		31,200		35,200	
14	Direct labor	5	62,000		72,000		82,000		92,000	
15	Manufacturing overhead	6	53,300	a	56,300		59,300		62,300	
16	Selling and administrative expenses	6	41,000	b	43,000		45,000		47,000	
17	Purchase of truck	7	0		10,000		0		0	
18	Income tax expense	8	3,000		3,000		3,000		3,000	
19	Total disbursements		182,500		211,500		220,500		239,500	
20	Excess (deficiency) of available cash over cash disbursements		25,500		12,000		22,500		37,900	
21	**Financing**									
22	Add: Borrowings		0		**3,000**		0		0	
23	Less: Repayments including interest	9	0		0		**3,100**		0	
24	Ending cash balance		$ 25,500		$ 15,000		$ 19,400		$ 37,900	
25										
26	[a]$57,100 − $3,800 depreciation									
27	[b]$42,000 − $1,000 depreciation									

Illustration 23-17
Cash budget

SERVICE COMPANY INSIGHT

Without a Budget, Can the Games Begin?

Behind the grandeur of the Olympic Games lies a huge financial challenge—how to keep budgeted costs in line with revenues. For example, the 2006 Winter Olympics in Turin, Italy, narrowly avoided going into bankruptcy before the Games even started. In order for the event to remain solvent, organizers cancelled glitzy celebrations and shifted promotional responsibilities to an Italian state-run agency. Despite these efforts, after the Games were over, the Italian government created a lottery game to cover its financial losses.

As another example, organizers of the 2002 Winter Olympics in Salt Lake City cut budgeted costs by $200 million shortly before the events began. According to the chief operating and financial officer, the organizers went through every line item in the budget, sorting each one into "must have" versus "nice to have." As a result, the Salt Lake City Games produced a surplus of $100 million.

Source: Gabriel Kahn and Roger Thurow, "In Turin, Paying for Games Went Down to the Wire," *Wall Street Journal* (February 10, 2006).

? Why does it matter whether the Olympic Games exceed their budget? (See page 1179.)

A cash budget contributes to more effective cash management. It shows managers when additional financing is necessary well before the actual need arises. And, it indicates when excess cash is available for investments or other purposes.

Budgeted Balance Sheet

The **budgeted balance sheet** is a projection of financial position at the end of the budget period. This budget is developed from the budgeted balance sheet for the preceding year and the budgets for the current year. Pertinent data from the budgeted balance sheet at December 31, 2013, are as follows.

Buildings and equipment	$182,000	Common stock	$225,000
Accumulated depreciation	$ 28,800	Retained earnings	$ 46,480

Illustration 23-18 shows Hayes Company's budgeted balance sheet at December 31, 2014.

Illustration 23-18
Budgeted balance sheet

Hayes Company
Budgeted Balance Sheet
December 31, 2014

Assets

Cash		$ 37,900
Accounts receivable		108,000
Finished goods inventory		44,000
Raw materials inventory		4,080
Buildings and equipment	$192,000	
Less: Accumulated depreciation	48,000	144,000
Total assets		$337,980

Liabilities and Stockholders' Equity

Accounts payable	$ 18,600
Common stock	225,000
Retained earnings	94,380
Total liabilities and stockholders' equity	$337,980

The computations and sources of the amounts are explained below.

Cash: Ending cash balance $37,900, shown in the cash budget (Illustration 23-17, page 1149).

Accounts receivable: 40% of fourth-quarter sales $270,000, shown in the schedule of expected collections from customers (Illustration 23-15, page 1148).

Finished goods inventory: Desired ending inventory 1,000 units, shown in the production budget (Illustration 23-5, page 1139) times the total unit cost $44 (shown in Illustration 23-12, page 1145).

Raw materials inventory: Desired ending inventory 1,020 pounds, times the cost per pound $4, shown in the direct materials budget (Illustration 23-7, page 1140).

Buildings and equipment: December 31, 2013, balance $182,000, plus purchase of truck for $10,000 (Illustration 23-17, page 1149).

Accumulated depreciation: December 31, 2013, balance $28,800, plus $15,200 depreciation shown in manufacturing overhead budget (Illustration 23-10, page 1144) and $4,000 depreciation shown in selling and administrative expense budget (Illustration 23-11, page 1145).

Accounts payable: 50% of fourth-quarter purchases $37,200, shown in schedule of expected payments for direct materials (Illustration 23-16, page 1148).

Common stock: Unchanged from the beginning of the year.

Retained earnings: December 31, 2013, balance $46,480, plus net income $47,900, shown in budgeted income statement (Illustration 23-13, page 1146).

After budget data are entered into the computer, Hayes prepares the various budgets (sales, cash, etc.), as well as the budgeted financial statements. Using spreadsheets, management can also perform "what if" (sensitivity) analyses based on different hypothetical assumptions. For example, suppose that sales managers project that sales will be 10% higher in the coming quarter. What impact does this change have on the rest of the budgeting process and the financing needs of the business? The impact of the various assumptions on the budget is quickly determined by the spreadsheet. Armed with these analyses, managers make more informed decisions about the impact of various projects. They also anticipate future problems and business opportunities. As seen in this chapter, budgeting is an excellent use of electronic spreadsheets.

> DO IT!

Cash Budget

Martian Company management wants to maintain a minimum monthly cash balance of $15,000. At the beginning of March, the cash balance is $16,500, expected cash receipts for March are $210,000, and cash disbursements are expected to be $220,000. How much cash, if any, must be borrowed to maintain the desired minimum monthly balance?

Solution

Action Plan

✔ Write down the basic form of the cash budget, starting with the beginning cash balance, adding cash receipts for the period, deducting cash disbursements, and identifying the needed financing to achieve the desired minimum ending cash balance.

✔ Insert the data given into the outlined form of the cash budget.

Martian Company Cash Budget For the Month Ending March 31, 2014	
Beginning cash balance	$ 16,500
Add: Cash receipts for March	210,000
Total available cash	226,500
Less: Cash disbursements for March	220,000
Excess of available cash over cash disbursements	6,500
Financing	8,500
Ending cash balance	$ 15,000

To maintain the desired minimum cash balance of $15,000, Martian Company must borrow $8,500 of cash.

Related exercise material: **BE23-9, E23-13, E23-14, E23-15, E23-16, and** **23-5.**

✔ **The Navigator**

Budgeting in Nonmanufacturing Companies

LEARNING OBJECTIVE　6

Indicate the applicability of budgeting in nonmanufacturing companies.

Budgeting is not limited to manufacturers. Budgets are also used by merchandisers, service companies, and not-for-profit organizations.

Merchandisers

As in manufacturing operations, the sales budget for a merchandiser is both the starting point and the key factor in the development of the master budget. The major differences between the master budgets of a merchandiser and a manufacturer are these:

1. A merchandiser **uses a merchandise purchases budget instead of a production budget**.

2. A merchandiser **does not use the manufacturing budgets (direct materials, direct labor, and manufacturing overhead)**.

The **merchandise purchases budget** shows the estimated cost of goods to be purchased to meet expected sales. The formula for determining budgeted merchandise purchases is:

Illustration 23-19
Merchandise purchases formula

Budgeted Cost of Goods Sold	+	Desired Ending Merchandise Inventory	−	Beginning Merchandise Inventory	=	Required Merchandise Purchases

To illustrate, assume that the budget committee of Lima Company is preparing the merchandise purchases budget for July 2014. It estimates that budgeted sales will be $300,000 in July and $320,000 in August. Cost of goods sold is expected to be 70% of sales—that is, $210,000 in July (.70 × $300,000) and $224,000 in August (.70 × $320,000). The company's desired ending inventory is 30% of the following month's cost of goods sold. Required merchandise purchases for July are $214,200, computed as follows.

Illustration 23-20
Merchandise purchases budget

Lima Company	
Merchandise Purchases Budget	
For the Month Ending July 31, 2014	
Budgeted cost of goods sold ($300,000 × 70%)	$ 210,000
Add: Desired ending merchandise inventory ($224,000 × 30%)	67,200
Total	277,200
Less: Beginning merchandise inventory ($210,000 × 30%)	63,000
Required merchandise purchases for July	**$214,200**

When a merchandiser is departmentalized, it prepares separate budgets for each department. For example, a grocery store prepares sales budgets and purchases budgets for each of its major departments, such as meats, dairy, and produce. The store then combines these budgets into a master budget for the store. When a retailer has branch stores, it prepares separate master budgets for each store. Then, it incorporates these budgets into master budgets for the company as a whole.

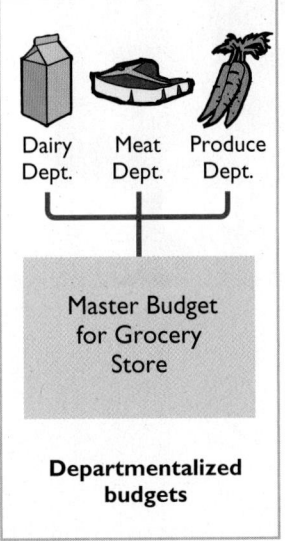

Dairy   Meat   Produce
Dept.   Dept.   Dept.

Master Budget
for Grocery
Store

**Departmentalized
budgets**

Service Companies

In a service company, such as a public accounting firm, a law office, or a medical practice, the critical factor in budgeting is **coordinating professional staff needs with anticipated services**. If a firm is overstaffed, several problems may result: Labor costs are disproportionately high. Profits are lower because of the additional salaries. Staff turnover sometimes increases because of lack of challenging work. In contrast, if a service company is understaffed, it may lose revenue because existing and prospective client needs for service cannot be met. Also, professional staff may seek other jobs because of excessive work loads.

Service companies can obtain budget data for service revenue from **expected output** or **expected input**. When output is used, it is necessary to determine the expected billings of clients for services provided. In a public accounting firm, for example, output is the sum of its billings in auditing, tax, and consulting services. When input data are used, each professional staff member projects his or her billable time. The firm then applies billing rates to billable time to produce expected service revenue.

Not-for-Profit Organizations

Budgeting is just as important for not-for-profit organizations as for profit-oriented businesses. The budget process, however, is different. In most cases, not-for-profit entities budget **on the basis of cash flows (expenditures and receipts), rather than on a revenue and expense basis**. Further, the starting point in the process is usually expenditures, not receipts. For the not-for-profit entity, management's task generally is to find the receipts needed to support the planned expenditures. The activity index is also likely to be significantly different. For example, in a not-for-profit entity, such as a university, budgeted faculty positions may be based on full-time equivalent students or credit hours expected to be taught in a department.

For some governmental units, voters approve the budget. In other cases, such as state governments and the federal government, legislative approval is required. After the budget is adopted, it must be followed. Overspending is often illegal. In governmental budgets, authorizations tend to be on a line-by-line basis. That is, the budget for a municipality may have a specified authorization for police and fire protection, garbage collection, street paving, and so on. The line-item authorization of governmental budgets significantly limits the amount of discretion management can exercise. The city manager often cannot use savings from one line item, such as street paving, to cover increased spending in another line item, such as snow removal.

SERVICE COMPANY INSIGHT

Budget Shortfalls as Far as the Eye Can See

All organizations need to stick to budgets. The Museum of Contemporary Art in Los Angeles learned this the hard way. Over a 10-year period, its endowment shrunk from $50 million to $6 million as its newly hired director strove to build the museum's reputation through spending. The director consistently ran budget deficits, which eventually threatened the museum's survival.

The most recent recession has created budgeting challenges for nearly all governmental agencies. Tax revenues dropped rapidly as earnings declined and unemployment skyrocketed. At the same time, sources of debt financing dried up. To meet a projected shortfall of nearly $50 billion, California proposed to cut the school year by five days, give state workers two unpaid days off per month, and raise the state's sales tax percentage. Even Princeton University, with the largest endowment per student of any U.S. university ($2 million per student), experienced a 25% drop in the value of its endowment when the financial markets plunged. Because the endowment supports 45% of the university's $1.25 billion budget, when the endowment fell the university had to make cuts. Many raises were capped at $2,000, administrative budgets were cut by 5%, and major construction projects were put on hold.

Source: Edward Wyatt and Jori Finkel, "Soaring in Art, Museum Trips Over Finances," *Wall Street Journal Online* (December 4, 2008); and Stu Woo, "California's Plans to Close Gap Become More Drastic," *Wall Street Journal Online* (January 8, 2009); and John Hechinger, "Princeton Cuts Budget as Endowment Slides," *Wall Street Journal Online* (January 9, 2009).

? Why would a university's budgeted scholarships probably fall when the stock market suffers a serious drop? (See page 1179.)

 > Comprehensive **DO IT! 1**

Barrett Company has completed all operating budgets other than the income statement for 2014. Selected data from these budgets follow.

Sales: $300,000
Purchases of raw materials: $145,000
Ending inventory of raw materials: $15,000
Direct labor: $40,000
Manufacturing overhead: $73,000, including $3,000 of depreciation expense
Selling and administrative expenses: $36,000 including depreciation expense of $1,000
Interest expense: $1,000
Principal payment on note: $2,000
Dividends declared: $2,000
Income tax rate: 30%

Other information:

Assume that the number of units produced equals the number sold.
Year-end accounts receivable: 4% of 2014 sales.
Year-end accounts payable: 50% of ending inventory of raw materials.

Interest, direct labor, manufacturing overhead, and selling and administrative expenses other than depreciation are paid as incurred.

Dividends declared and income taxes for 2014 will not be paid until 2015.

Barrett Company
Balance Sheet
December 31, 2013

Assets

Cash		$20,000
Raw materials inventory		10,000
Equipment	$40,000	
Less: Accumulated depreciation	4,000	36,000
Total assets		$66,000

Liabilities and Stockholders' Equity

Accounts payable	$ 5,000	
Notes payable	22,000	
Total liabilities		$27,000
Common stock	25,000	
Retained earnings	14,000	39,000
Total liabilities and stockholders' equity		$66,000

Instructions

(a) Calculate budgeted cost of goods sold.

(b) Prepare a budgeted income statement for the year ending December 31, 2014.

(c) Prepare a budgeted balance sheet as of December 31, 2014.

Solution to Comprehensive DO IT! 1

Action Plan

✔ Recall that beginning raw materials inventory plus purchases less ending raw materials inventory equals direct materials used.

✔ Prepare the budgeted income statement before the budgeted balance sheet.

✔ Use the standard form of a cash budget to determine cash on the budgeted balance sheet.

✔ Add budgeted depreciation expense to accumulated depreciation at the beginning of the year to determine accumulated depreciation on the budgeted balance sheet.

(a) Beginning raw materials + Purchases − Ending raw materials = Cost of direct materials used ($10,000 + $145,000 − $15,000 = $140,000)

Direct materials used + Direct labor + Manufacturing overhead = Cost of goods sold ($140,000 + $40,000 + $73,000 = $253,000)

(b)

Barrett Company
Budgeted Income Statement
For the Year Ending December 31, 2014

Sales		$300,000
Cost of goods sold		253,000
Gross profit		47,000
Selling and administrative expenses	$36,000	
Interest expense	1,000	37,000
Income before income tax expense		10,000
Income tax expense (30%)		3,000
Net income		$ 7,000

Action Plan (cont'd.)

✔ Add budgeted net income to retained earnings from the beginning of the year and subtract dividends declared to determine retained earnings on the budgeted balance sheet.

✔ Verify that total assets equal total liabilities and stockholders' equity on the budgeted balance sheet.

(c)

Barrett Company
Budgeted Balance Sheet
December 31, 2014

Assets

Cash[1]		$17,500
Accounts receivable (4% × $300,000)		12,000
Raw materials inventory		15,000
Equipment	$40,000	
Less: Accumulated depreciation	8,000	32,000
Total assets		$76,500

Liabilities and Stockholders' Equity

Accounts payable (50% × $15,000)	$ 7,500	
Income taxes payable	3,000	
Dividends payable	2,000	
Note payable	20,000	
Total liabilities		$32,500
Common stock	25,000	
Retained earnings[2]	19,000	44,000
Total liabilities and stockholders' equity		$76,500

[1]Beginning cash balance		$ 20,000
Add: Collections from customers		
(96% × $300,000 sales)		288,000
Total available cash		308,000
Less: Disbursements		
Direct materials ($5,000 + $145,000 − $7,500)	$142,500	
Direct labor	40,000	
Manufacturing overhead	70,000	
Selling and administrative expenses	35,000	
Total disbursements		287,500
Excess of available cash over cash disbursements		20,500
Financing		
Less: Repayment of principal and interest		3,000
Ending cash balance		$ 17,500

[2]Beginning retained earnings + Net income − Dividends declared = Ending retained earnings ($14,000 + $7,000 − $2,000 = $19,000)

 **The Navigator**

> Comprehensive DO IT! 2

Action Plan

✔ Know the form and content of the sales budget.

✔ Prepare the sales budget first as the basis for the other budgets.

Asheville Company is preparing its master budget for 2014. Relevant data pertaining to its sales and production budgets are as follows.

Sales. Sales for the year are expected to total 2,100,000 units. Quarterly sales, as a percentage of total sales, are 15%, 25%, 35%, and 25%, respectively. The sales price is expected to be $70 per unit for the first three quarters and $75 per unit beginning

Action Plan (cont'd.)

✔ Determine the units that must be produced to meet anticipated sales.

✔ Know how to compute the beginning and ending finished goods units.

in the fourth quarter. Sales in the first quarter of 2015 are expected to be 10% higher than the budgeted sales volume for the first quarter of 2014.

Production. Management desires to maintain ending finished goods inventories at 20% of the next quarter's budgeted sales volume.

Instructions

Prepare the sales budget and production budget by quarters for 2014.

Solution to Comprehensive DO IT! 2

Asheville Company
Sales Budget
For the Year Ending December 31, 2014

	Quarter				
	1	**2**	**3**	**4**	**Year**
Expected unit sales	315,000	525,000	735,000	525,000	2,100,000
Unit selling price	× $70	× $70	× $70	× $75	—
Total sales	$22,050,000	$36,750,000	$51,450,000	$39,375,000	$149,625,000

Asheville Company
Production Budget
For the Year Ending December 31, 2014

	Quarter				
	1	**2**	**3**	**4**	**Year**
Expected unit sales	315,000	525,000	735,000	525,000	
Add: Desired ending finished goods units	105,000	147,000	105,000	69,300[a]	
Total required units	420,000	672,000	840,000	594,300	
Less: Beginning finished goods units	63,000[b]	105,000	147,000	105,000	
Required production units	357,000	567,000	693,000	489,300	2,106,300

[a]Estimated first-quarter 2015 sales volume 315,000 + (315,000 × 10%) = 346,500; 346,500 × 20%

[b]20% of estimated first-quarter 2014 sales units (315,000 × 20%)

 The Navigator

 **The Navigator**

SUMMARY OF LEARNING OBJECTIVES

1 Indicate the benefits of budgeting. The primary advantages of budgeting are that it (a) requires management to plan ahead, (b) provides definite objectives for evaluating performance, (c) creates an early warning system for potential problems, (d) facilitates coordination of activities, (e) results in greater management awareness, and (f) motivates personnel to meet planned objectives.

2 State the essentials of effective budgeting. The essentials of effective budgeting are (a) sound organizational structure, (b) research and analysis, and (c) acceptance by all levels of management.

3 Identify the budgets that comprise the master budget. The master budget consists of the following budgets:

(a) sales, (b) production, (c) direct materials, (d) direct labor, (e) manufacturing overhead, (f) selling and administrative expense, (g) budgeted income statement, (h) capital expenditure budget, (i) cash budget, and (j) budgeted balance sheet.

4 Describe the sources for preparing the budgeted income statement. The budgeted income statement is prepared from (a) the sales budget; (b) the budgets for direct materials, direct labor, and manufacturing overhead; and (c) the selling and administrative expense budget.

5 Explain the principal sections of a cash budget. The cash budget has three sections (receipts, disbursements, and financing) and the beginning and ending cash balances.

6 Indicate the applicability of budgeting in nonmanufacturing companies. Budgeting may be used by merchandisers for development of a merchandise purchases budget. In service companies, budgeting is a critical factor in coordinating staff needs with anticipated services. In not-for-profit organizations, the starting point in budgeting is usually expenditures, not receipts.

GLOSSARY

Budget A formal written statement of management's plans for a specified future time period, expressed in financial terms. (p. 1132).

Budget committee A group responsible for coordinating the preparation of the budget. (p. 1134).

Budgetary slack The amount by which a manager intentionally underestimates budgeted revenues or overestimates budgeted expenses in order to make it easier to achieve budgetary goals. (p. 1135).

Budgeted balance sheet A projection of financial position at the end of the budget period. (p. 1150).

Budgeted income statement An estimate of the expected profitability of operations for the budget period. (p. 1144).

Cash budget A projection of anticipated cash flows. (p. 1147).

Direct labor budget A projection of the quantity and cost of direct labor necessary to meet production requirements. (p. 1143).

Direct materials budget An estimate of the quantity and cost of direct materials to be purchased. (p. 1140).

Financial budgets Individual budgets that focus primarily on the cash resources needed to fund expected operations and planned capital expenditures. (p. 1136).

Long-range planning A formalized process of identifying long-term goals, selecting strategies to achieve those goals, and developing policies and plans to implement the strategies. (p. 1135).

Manufacturing overhead budget An estimate of expected manufacturing overhead costs for the budget period. (p. 1143).

Master budget A set of interrelated budgets that constitutes a plan of action for a specific time period. (p. 1135).

Merchandise purchases budget The estimated cost of goods to be purchased by a merchandiser to meet expected sales. (p. 1152).

Operating budgets Individual budgets that result in a budgeted income statement. (p. 1135).

Participative budgeting A budgetary approach that starts with input from lower-level managers and works upward so that managers at all levels participate. (p. 1134).

Production budget A projection of the units that must be produced to meet anticipated sales. (p. 1138).

Sales budget An estimate of expected sales revenue for the budget period. (p. 1137).

Sales forecast The projection of potential sales for the industry and the company's expected share of such sales. (p. 1133).

Selling and administrative expense budget A projection of anticipated selling and administrative expenses for the budget period. (p. 1144).

 Self-Test, Brief Exercises, Exercises, Problem Set A, and many more resources are available for practice in WileyPLUS.

SELF-TEST QUESTIONS

Answers are at the end of the chapter.

(LO 1) **1.** Which of the following is *not* a benefit of budgeting?
  (a) Management can plan ahead.
  (b) An early warning system is provided for potential problems.
  (c) It enables disciplinary action to be taken at every level of responsibility.
  (d) The coordination of activities is facilitated.

2. A budget: (LO 1)
  (a) is the responsibility of management accountants.
  (b) is the primary method of communicating agreed-upon objectives throughout an organization.
  (c) ignores past performance because it represents management's plans for a future time period.
  (d) may promote efficiency but has no role in evaluating performance.

(LO 2) **3.** The essentials of effective budgeting do *not* include:
(a) top-down budgeting.
(b) management acceptance.
(c) research and analysis.
(d) sound organizational structure.

(LO 2) **4.** Compared to budgeting, long-range planning generally has the:
(a) same amount of detail.
(b) longer time period.
(c) same emphasis.
(d) same time period.

(LO 3) **5.** A sales budget is:
(a) derived from the production budget.
(b) management's best estimate of sales revenue for the year.
(c) not the starting point for the master budget.
(d) prepared only for credit sales.

(LO 3) **6.** The formula for the production budget is budgeted sales in units plus:
(a) desired ending merchandise inventory less beginning merchandise inventory.
(b) beginning finished goods units less desired ending finished goods units.
(c) desired ending direct materials units less beginning direct materials units.
(d) desired ending finished goods units less beginning finished goods units.

(LO 3) **7.** Direct materials inventories are kept in pounds in Byrd Company, and the total pounds of direct materials needed for production is 9,500. If the beginning inventory is 1,000 pounds and the desired ending inventory is 2,200 pounds, the total pounds to be purchased is:
(a) 9,400.   (c) 9,700.
(b) 9,500.   (d) 10,700.

(LO 3) **8.** The formula for computing the direct labor budget is to multiply the direct labor cost per hour by the:
(a) total required direct labor hours.
(b) physical units to be produced.
(c) equivalent units to be produced.
(d) No correct answer is given.

(LO 4) **9.** Each of the following budgets is used in preparing the budgeted income statement *except* the:
(a) sales budget.
(b) selling and administrative budget.
(c) capital expenditure budget.
(d) direct labor budget.

10. The budgeted income statement is: (LO 4)
(a) the end-product of the operating budgets.
(b) the end-product of the financial budgets.
(c) the starting point of the master budget.
(d) dependent on cash receipts and cash disbursements.

11. The budgeted balance sheet is: (LO 5)
(a) developed from the budgeted balance sheet for the preceding year and the budgets for the current year.
(b) the last operating budget prepared.
(c) used to prepare the cash budget.
(d) All of the above.

12. The format of a cash budget is: (LO 5)
(a) Beginning cash balance + Cash receipts + Cash from financing − Cash disbursements = Ending cash balance.
(b) Beginning cash balance + Cash receipts − Cash disbursements +/− Financing = Ending cash balance.
(c) Beginning cash balance + Net income − Cash dividends = Ending cash balance.
(d) Beginning cash balance + Cash revenues − Cash expenses = Ending cash balance.

13. Expected direct materials purchases in Read Com- (LO 5) pany are $70,000 in the first quarter and $90,000 in the second quarter. Forty percent of the purchases are paid in cash as incurred, and the balance is paid in the following quarter. The budgeted cash payments for purchases in the second quarter are:
(a) $96,000.   (c) $78,000.
(b) $90,000.   (d) $72,000.

14. The budget for a merchandiser differs from a budget (LO 6) for a manufacturer because:
(a) a merchandise purchases budget replaces the production budget.
(b) the manufacturing budgets are not applicable.
(c) None of the above.
(d) Both (a) and (b) above.

15. In most cases, not-for-profit entities: (LO 6)
(a) prepare budgets using the same steps as those used by profit-oriented businesses.
(b) know budgeted cash receipts at the beginning of a time period, so they budget only for expenditures.
(c) begin the budgeting process by budgeting expenditures rather than receipts.
(d) can ignore budgets because they are not expected to generate net income.

Go to the book's companion website, www.wiley.com/college/weygandt, for additional Self-Test Questions.

 ✔ **The Navigator**

QUESTIONS

1. (a) What is a budget?
(b) How does a budget contribute to good management?

2. Kate Cey and Joe Coulter are discussing the benefits of budgeting. They ask you to identify the

primary advantages of budgeting. Comply with their request.

3. Jane Gilligan asks your help in understanding the essentials of effective budgeting. Identify the essentials for Jane.

4. (a) "Accounting plays a relatively unimportant role in budgeting." Do you agree? Explain.
   (b) What responsibilities does management have in budgeting?

5. What criteria are helpful in determining the length of the budget period? What is the most common budget period?

6. Lori Wilkins maintains that the only difference between budgeting and long-range planning is time. Do you agree? Why or why not?

7. What is participative budgeting? What are its potential benefits? What are its potential disadvantages?

8. What is budgetary slack? What incentive do managers have to create budgetary slack?

9. Distinguish between a master budget and a sales forecast.

10. What budget is the starting point in preparing the master budget? What may result if this budget is inaccurate?

11. "The production budget shows both unit production data and unit cost data." Is this true? Explain.

12. Alou Company has 20,000 beginning finished goods units. Budgeted sales units are 160,000. If management desires 15,000 ending finished goods units, what are the required units of production?

13. In preparing the direct materials budget for Quan Company, management concludes that required purchases are 64,000 units. If 52,000 direct materials units are required in production and there are 9,000 units of beginning direct materials, what is the desired units of ending direct materials?

14. The production budget of Justus Company calls for 80,000 units to be produced. If it takes 45 minutes to make one unit and the direct labor rate is $16 per hour, what is the total budgeted direct labor cost?

15. Ortiz Company's manufacturing overhead budget shows total variable costs of $198,000 and total fixed costs of $162,000. Total production in units is expected to be 150,000. It takes 20 minutes to make one unit, and the direct labor rate is $15 per hour. Express the manufacturing overhead rate as (a) a percentage of direct labor cost, and (b) an amount per direct labor hour.

16. Everly Company's variable selling and administrative expenses are 12% of net sales. Fixed expenses are $50,000 per quarter. The sales budget shows expected sales of $200,000 and $240,000 in the first and second quarters, respectively. What are the total budgeted selling and administrative expenses for each quarter?

17. For Goody Company, the budgeted cost for one unit of product is direct materials $10, direct labor $20, and manufacturing overhead 80% of direct labor cost. If 25,000 units are expected to be sold at $65 each, what is the budgeted gross profit?

18. Indicate the supporting schedules used in preparing a budgeted income statement through gross profit for a manufacturer.

19. Identify the three sections of a cash budget. What balances are also shown in this budget?

20. Noterman Company has credit sales of $600,000 in January. Past experience suggests that 40% is collected in the month of sale, 50% in the month following the sale, and 10% in the second month following the sale. Compute the cash collections from January sales in January, February, and March.

21. What is the formula for determining required merchandise purchases for a merchandiser?

22. How may expected revenues in a service company be computed?

BRIEF EXERCISES

Prepare a diagram of a master budget.

(LO 3)

BE23-1 Chicksaw Company uses the following budgets: Balance Sheet, Capital Expenditure, Cash, Direct Labor, Direct Materials, Income Statement, Manufacturing Overhead, Production, Sales, and Selling and Administrative. Prepare a diagram of the interrelationships of the budgets in the master budget. Indicate whether each budget is an operating or a financial budget.

Prepare a sales budget.

(LO 3)

BE23-2 Palermo Company estimates that unit sales will be 10,000 in quarter 1; 12,000 in quarter 2; 15,000 in quarter 3; and 18,000 in quarter 4. Using a sales price of $70 per unit, prepare the sales budget by quarters for the year ending December 31, 2014.

Prepare a production budget for 2 quarters.

(LO 3)

BE23-3 Sales budget data for Palermo Company are given in BE23-2. Management desires to have an ending finished goods inventory equal to 25% of the next quarter's expected unit sales. Prepare a production budget by quarters for the first 6 months of 2014.

Prepare a direct materials budget for 1 month.

(LO 3)

BE23-4 Perine Company has 2,000 pounds of raw materials in its December 31, 2013, ending inventory. Required production for January and February of 2014 are 4,000 and 5,000 units, respectively. Two pounds of raw materials are needed for each unit, and the estimated cost per pound is $6. Management desires an ending inventory equal to 25% of next month's materials requirements. Prepare the direct materials budget for January.

Prepare a direct labor budget for 2 quarters.

(LO 3)

BE23-5 For Mize Company, units to be produced are 5,000 in quarter 1 and 6,000 in quarter 2. It takes 1.6 hours to make a finished unit, and the expected hourly wage rate is $15 per hour. Prepare a direct labor budget by quarters for the 6 months ending June 30, 2014.

BE23-6 For Roche Inc., variable manufacturing overhead costs are expected to be $20,000 in the first quarter of 2014, with $5,000 increments in each of the remaining three quarters. Fixed overhead costs are estimated to be $40,000 in each quarter. Prepare the manufacturing overhead budget by quarters and in total for the year.

Prepare a manufacturing overhead budget.

(LO 3)

BE23-7 Noble Company classifies its selling and administrative expense budget into variable and fixed components. Variable expenses are expected to be $22,000 in the first quarter, and $4,000 increments are expected in the remaining quarters of 2014. Fixed expenses are expected to be $40,000 in each quarter. Prepare the selling and administrative expense budget by quarters and in total for 2014.

Prepare a selling and administrative expense budget.

(LO 3)

BE23-8 North Company has completed all of its operating budgets. The sales budget for the year shows 50,000 units and total sales of $2,250,000. The total unit cost of making one unit of sales is $25. Selling and administrative expenses are expected to be $300,000. Income taxes are estimated to be $210,000. Prepare a budgeted income statement for the year ending December 31, 2014.

Prepare a budgeted income statement for the year.

(LO 4)

BE23-9 Bruno Industries expects credit sales for January, February, and March to be $200,000, $260,000, and $300,000, respectively. It is expected that 75% of the sales will be collected in the month of sale, and 25% will be collected in the following month. Compute cash collections from customers for each month.

Prepare data for a cash budget.

(LO 5)

BE23-10 Moore Wholesalers is preparing its merchandise purchases budget. Budgeted sales are $400,000 for April and $480,000 for May. Cost of goods sold is expected to be 65% of sales. The company's desired ending inventory is 20% of the following month's cost of goods sold. Compute the required purchases for April.

Determine required merchandise purchases for 1 month.

(LO 6)

> DO IT! REVIEW

Identify budget terminology.

(LO 2, 3)

DO IT! 23-1 Use this list of terms to complete the sentences that follow.

Long-range plans   Participative budgeting
Sales forecast   Operating budgets
Master budget   Financial budgets

1. _____ establish goals for the company's sales and production personnel.
2. The _____ is a set of interrelated budgets that constitutes a plan of action for a specified time period.
3. _____ reduces the risk of having unrealistic budgets.
4. _____ include the cash budget and the budgeted balance sheet.
5. The budget is formed within the framework of a _____.
6. _____ contain considerably less detail than budgets.

Production budget.

(LO 3)

DO IT! 23-2 Zeller Company estimates that 2014 unit sales will be 20,000 in quarter 1, 24,000 in quarter 2, and 29,000 in quarter 3, at a unit selling price of $20. Management desires to have ending finished goods inventory equal to 10% of the next quarter's expected unit sales. Prepare a production budget by quarter for the first 6 months of 2014.

Prepare sales, production, and direct materials budgets.

(LO 3)

DO IT! 23-3 Ash Creek Company is preparing its master budget for 2014. Relevant data pertaining to its sales, production, and direct materials budgets are as follows.

Sales. Sales for the year are expected to total 1,000,000 units. Quarterly sales are 20%, 20%, 30%, and 30%, respectively. The sales price is expected to be $40 per unit for the first three quarters and $45 per unit beginning in the fourth quarter. Sales in the first quarter of 2015 are expected to be 20% higher than the budgeted sales for the first quarter of 2014.

Production. Management desires to maintain the ending finished goods inventories at 25% of the next quarter's budgeted sales volume.

Direct materials. Each unit requires 2 pounds of raw materials at a cost of $12 per pound. Management desires to maintain raw materials inventories at 10% of the next quarter's production requirements. Assume the production requirements for first quarter of 2015 are 450,000 pounds.

Prepare the sales, production, and direct materials budgets by quarters for 2014.

Calculate budgeted total unit cost and prepare budgeted income statement.

(LO 4)

DO IT! **23-4** Ash Creek Company is preparing its budgeted income statement for 2014. Relevant data pertaining to its sales, production, and direct materials budgets can be found in **DO IT!** 23-3.

In addition, Ash Creek budgets 0.3 hours of direct labor per unit, labor costs at $15 per hour, and manufacturing overhead at $20 per direct labor hour. Its budgeted selling and administrative expenses for 2014 are $6,000,000.

(a) Calculate the budgeted total unit cost.
(b) Prepare the budgeted income statement for 2014.

Determine amount of financing needed.

(LO 5)

DO IT! **23-5** Batista Company management wants to maintain a minimum monthly cash balance of $20,000. At the beginning of April, the cash balance is $25,000, expected cash receipts for April are $245,000, and cash disbursements are expected to be $255,000. How much cash, if any, must be borrowed to maintain the desired minimum monthly balance?

✔ **The Navigator**

EXERCISES

Explain the concept of budgeting.

(LO 1, 2, 3)

E23-1 ◁▭▭▭▷ Adler Company has always done some planning for the future, but the company has never prepared a formal budget. Now that the company is growing larger, it is considering preparing a budget.

Instructions
Write a memo to Jim Dixon, the president of Adler Company, in which you define budgeting, identify the budgets that comprise the master budget, identify the primary benefits of budgeting, and discuss the essentials of effective budgeting.

Prepare a sales budget for 2 quarters.

(LO 3)

E23-2 Edington Electronics Inc. produces and sells two models of pocket calculators, XQ-103 and XQ-104. The calculators sell for $15 and $25, respectively. Because of the intense competition Edington faces, management budgets sales semiannually. Its projections for the first 2 quarters of 2014 are as follows.

	Unit Sales	
Product	**Quarter 1**	**Quarter 2**
XQ-103	20,000	22,000
XQ-104	12,000	15,000

No changes in selling prices are anticipated.

Instructions
Prepare a sales budget for the 2 quarters ending June 30, 2014. List the products and show for each quarter and for the 6 months, units, selling price, and total sales by product and in total.

E23-3 Garza and Neely, CPAs, are preparing their service revenue (sales) budget for the coming year (2014). The practice is divided into three departments: auditing, tax, and consulting. Billable hours for each department, by quarter, are provided below.

Prepare a sales budget for 4 quarters.

(LO 3, 6)

Department	Quarter 1	Quarter 2	Quarter 3	Quarter 4
Auditing	2,300	1,600	2,000	2,400
Tax	3,000	2,200	2,000	2,500
Consulting	1,500	1,500	1,500	1,500

Average hourly billing rates are auditing $80, tax $90, and consulting $100.

Instructions

Prepare the service revenue (sales) budget for 2014 by listing the departments and showing for each quarter and the year in total, billable hours, billable rate, and total revenue.

E23-4 Turney Company produces and sells automobile batteries, the heavy-duty HD-240. The 2014 sales forecast is as follows.

Prepare quarterly production budgets.

(LO 3)

Quarter	HD-240
1	5,000
2	7,000
3	8,000
4	10,000

The January 1, 2014, inventory of HD-240 is 2,000 units. Management desires an ending inventory each quarter equal to 40% of the next quarter's sales. Sales in the first quarter of 2015 are expected to be 25% higher than sales in the same quarter in 2014.

Instructions

Prepare quarterly production budgets for each quarter and in total for 2014.

E23-5 Dallas Industries has adopted the following production budget for the first 4 months of 2014.

Prepare a direct materials purchases budget.

(LO 3)

Month	Units	Month	Units
January	10,000	March	5,000
February	8,000	April	4,000

Each unit requires 2 pounds of raw materials costing $2 per pound. On December 31, 2013, the ending raw materials inventory was 4,000 pounds. Management wants to have a raw materials inventory at the end of the month equal to 20% of next month's production requirements.

Instructions

Prepare a direct materials purchases budget by month for the first quarter.

E23-6 On January 1, 2014, the Hardin Company budget committee has reached agreement on the following data for the 6 months ending June 30, 2014.

Prepare production and direct materials budgets by quarters for 6 months.

(LO 3)

Sales units: First quarter 5,000; second quarter 6,000; third quarter 7,000.

Ending raw materials inventory: 40% of the next quarter's production requirements.

Ending finished goods inventory: 25% of the next quarter's expected sales units.

Third-quarter production: 7,200 units.

The ending raw materials and finished goods inventories at December 31, 2013, follow the same percentage relationships to production and sales that occur in 2014. Three pounds of raw materials are required to make each unit of finished goods. Raw materials purchased are expected to cost $4 per pound.

Instructions

(a) Prepare a production budget by quarters for the 6-month period ended June 30, 2014.
(b) Prepare a direct materials budget by quarters for the 6-month period ended June 30, 2014.

*Prepare raw materials
purchase budget in dollars.*

(LO 3)

E23-7 Chandler Ltd. estimates sales for the second quarter of 2014 will be as follows.

Month	Units
April	2,550
May	2,475
June	2,390

The target ending inventory of finished products is as follows.

March 31	2,000
April 30	2,230
May 31	2,200
June 30	2,310

Two units of material are required for each unit of finished product. Production for July is estimated at 2,700 units to start building inventory for the fall sales period. Chandler's policy is to have an inventory of raw materials at the end of each month equal to 50% of the following month's production requirements.

Raw materials are expected to cost $4 per unit throughout the period.

Instructions

Calculate the May raw materials purchases in dollars.

(CGA adapted)

Prepare a direct labor budget.

(LO 3)

E23-8 Rodriguez, Inc., is preparing its direct labor budget for 2014 from the following production budget based on a calendar year.

Quarter	Units	Quarter	Units
1	20,000	3	35,000
2	25,000	4	30,000

Each unit requires 1.5 hours of direct labor.

Instructions

Prepare a direct labor budget for 2014. Wage rates are expected to be $16 for the first 2 quarters and $18 for quarters 3 and 4.

*Prepare production and direct
labor budgets.*

(LO 3)

E23-9 Donnegal Company makes and sells artistic frames for pictures. The controller is responsible for preparing the master budget and has accumulated the following information for 2014.

	January	February	March	April	May
Estimated unit sales	12,000	14,000	10,000	11,000	11,000
Sales price per unit	$50.00	$47.50	$47.50	$47.50	$47.50
Direct labor hours per unit	2.0	2.0	1.5	1.5	1.5
Wage per direct labor hour	$8.00	$8.00	$8.00	$9.00	$9.00

Donnegal has a labor contract that calls for a wage increase to $9.00 per hour on April 1. New labor-saving machinery has been installed and will be fully operational by March 1.

Donnegal expects to begin the year with 17,600 frames on hand and has a policy of carrying an end-of-month inventory of 100% of the following month's sales, plus 40% of the second following month's sales.

Instructions

Prepare a production budget and a direct labor budget for Donnegal Company by month and for the first quarter of the year. The direct labor budget should include direct labor hours.

(CMA-Canada adapted)

*Prepare a manufacturing
overhead budget for the year.*

(LO 3)

E23-10 Atlanta Company is preparing its manufacturing overhead budget for 2014. Relevant data consist of the following.

Units to be produced (by quarters): 10,000, 12,000, 14,000, 16,000.

Direct labor: time is 1.5 hours per unit.

Variable overhead costs per direct labor hour: indirect materials $0.80; indirect labor $1.20; and maintenance $0.50.

Fixed overhead costs per quarter: supervisory salaries $35,000; depreciation $15,000; and maintenance $12,000.

Instructions
Prepare the manufacturing overhead budget for the year, showing quarterly data.

E23-11 Duncan Company combines its operating expenses for budget purposes in a selling and administrative expense budget. For the first 6 months of 2014, the following data are available.

1. Sales: 20,000 units quarter 1; 22,000 units quarter 2.
2. Variable costs per dollar of sales: sales commissions 5%, delivery expense 2%, and advertising 4%.
3. Fixed costs per quarter: sales salaries $10,000, office salaries $8,000, depreciation $4,200, insurance $1,500, utilities $800, and repairs expense $500.
4. Unit selling price: $20.

Prepare a selling and administrative expense budget for 2 quarters.

(LO 3)

Instructions
Prepare a selling and administrative expense budget by quarters for the first 6 months of 2014.

E23-12 Fuqua Company's sales budget projects unit sales of part 198Z of 10,000 units in January, 12,000 units in February, and 13,000 units in March. Each unit of part 198Z requires 4 pounds of materials, which cost $2 per pound. Fuqua Company desires its ending raw materials inventory to equal 40% of the next month's production requirements, and its ending finished goods inventory to equal 20% of the next month's expected unit sales. These goals were met at December 31, 2013.

Prepare a production and a direct materials budget.

(LO 3)

Instructions
(a) Prepare a production budget for January and February 2014.
(b) Prepare a direct materials budget for January 2014.

E23-13 Dalby Company has accumulated the following budget data for the year 2014.

1. Sales: 30,000 units, unit selling price $85.
2. Cost of one unit of finished goods: direct materials 2 pounds at $5 per pound, direct labor 3 hours at $15 per hour, and manufacturing overhead $5 per direct labor hour.
3. Inventories (raw materials only): beginning, 10,000 pounds; ending, 15,000 pounds.
4. Selling and administrative expenses: $200,000.
5. Income taxes: 30% of income before income taxes.

Prepare a budgeted income statement for the year.

(LO 4)

Instructions
(a) Prepare a schedule showing the computation of cost of goods sold for 2014.
(b) Prepare a budgeted income statement for 2014.

E23-14 Danner Company expects to have a cash balance of $45,000 on January 1, 2014. Relevant monthly budget data for the first 2 months of 2014 are as follows.

Prepare a cash budget for 2 months.

(LO 5)

Collections from customers: January $85,000, February $150,000.

Payments for direct materials: January $50,000, February $75,000.

Direct labor: January $30,000, February $45,000. Wages are paid in the month they are incurred.

Manufacturing overhead: January $21,000, February $25,000. These costs include depreciation of $1,500 per month. All other overhead costs are paid as incurred.

Selling and administrative expenses: January $15,000, February $20,000. These costs are exclusive of depreciation. They are paid as incurred.

Sales of marketable securities in January are expected to realize $12,000 in cash. Danner Company has a line of credit at a local bank that enables it to borrow up to $25,000. The company wants to maintain a minimum monthly cash balance of $20,000.

Instructions
Prepare a cash budget for January and February.

E23-15 Aaron Corporation is projecting a cash balance of $30,000 in its December 31, 2013, balance sheet. Aaron's schedule of expected collections from customers for the first quarter of 2014 shows total collections of $180,000. The schedule of expected payments for direct materials for the first quarter of 2014 shows total payments of $41,000. Other

Prepare a cash budget.

(LO 5)

information gathered for the first quarter of 2014 is sale of equipment $3,000; direct labor $70,000, manufacturing overhead $35,000, selling and administrative expenses $45,000; and purchase of securities $14,000. Aaron wants to maintain a balance of at least $25,000 cash at the end of each quarter.

Instructions
Prepare a cash budget for the first quarter.

Prepare cash budget for a month.

(LO 5)

E23-16 The controller of Trenshaw Company wants to improve the company's control system by preparing a month-by-month cash budget. The following information is for the month ending July 31, 2014.

June 30, 2014, cash balance	$45,000
Dividends to be declared on July 15*	12,000
Cash expenditures to be paid in July for operating expenses	40,800
Amortization expense in July	4,500
Cash collections to be received in July	90,000
Merchandise purchases to be paid in cash in July	56,200
Equipment to be purchased for cash in July	20,000

*Dividends are payable 30 days after declaration to shareholders of record on the declaration date.

Trenshaw Company wants to keep a minimum cash balance of $25,000.

Instructions
(a) Prepare a cash budget for the month ended July 31, 2014, and indicate how much money, if any, Trenshaw Company will need to borrow to meet its minimum cash requirement.
(b) Explain how cash budgeting can reduce the cost of short-term borrowing.

(CGA adapted)

Prepare schedules of expected collections and payments.

(LO 5)

E23-17 LRF Company's budgeted sales and direct materials purchases are as follows.

	Budgeted Sales	Budgeted D.M. Purchases
January	$200,000	$30,000
February	220,000	36,000
March	270,000	40,000

LRF's sales are 30% cash and 70% credit. Credit sales are collected 10% in the month of sale, 50% in the month following sale, and 36% in the second month following sale; 4% are uncollectible. LRF's purchases are 50% cash and 50% on account. Purchases on account are paid 40% in the month of purchase, and 60% in the month following purchase.

Instructions
(a) Prepare a schedule of expected collections from customers for March.
(b) Prepare a schedule of expected payments for direct materials for March.

Prepare schedules for cash receipts and cash payments, and determine ending balances for balance sheet.

(LO 5, 6)

E23-18 Green Landscaping Inc. is preparing its budget for the first quarter of 2014. The next step in the budgeting process is to prepare a cash receipts schedule and a cash payments schedule. To that end the following information has been collected.

Clients usually pay 60% of their fee in the month that service is provided, 30% the month after, and 10% the second month after receiving service.

Actual service revenue for 2013 and expected service revenues for 2014 are November 2013, $80,000; December 2013, $90,000; January 2014, $100,000; February 2014, $120,000; March 2014, $140,000.

Purchases of landscaping supplies (direct materials) are paid 60% in the month of purchase and 40% the following month. Actual purchases for 2013 and expected purchases for 2014 are December 2013, $14,000; January 2014, $12,000; February 2014, $15,000; March 2014, $18,000.

Instructions
(a) Prepare the following schedules for each month in the first quarter of 2014 and for the quarter in total:
(1) Expected collections from clients.
(2) Expected payments for landscaping supplies.

(b) Determine the following balances at March 31, 2014:
  (1) Accounts receivable.
  (2) Accounts payable.

E23-19 Lager Dental Clinic is a medium-sized dental service specializing in family dental care. The clinic is currently preparing the master budget for the first 2 quarters of 2014. All that remains in this process is the cash budget. The following information has been collected from other portions of the master budget and elsewhere.

Prepare a cash budget for 2 quarters.

(LO 5, 6)

Beginning cash balance	$ 30,000
Required minimum cash balance	25,000
Payment of income taxes (2nd quarter)	4,000
Professional salaries:	
1st quarter	140,000
2nd quarter	140,000
Interest from investments (2nd quarter)	7,000
Overhead costs:	
1st quarter	75,000
2nd quarter	100,000
Selling and administrative costs, including	
$2,000 depreciation:	
1st quarter	50,000
2nd quarter	70,000
Purchase of equipment (2nd quarter)	50,000
Sale of equipment (1st quarter)	12,000
Collections from clients:	
1st quarter	230,000
2nd quarter	380,000
Interest payments (2nd quarter)	400

Instructions
Prepare a cash budget for each of the first two quarters of 2014.

E23-20 In May 2014, the budget committee of Grand Stores assembles the following data in preparation of budgeted merchandise purchases for the month of June.

Prepare a purchases budget and budgeted income statement for a merchandiser.

(LO 6)

1. Expected sales: June $500,000, July $600,000.
2. Cost of goods sold is expected to be 75% of sales.
3. Desired ending merchandise inventory is 30% of the following (next) month's cost of goods sold.
4. The beginning inventory at June 1 will be the desired amount.

Instructions
(a) Compute the budgeted merchandise purchases for June.
(b) Prepare the budgeted income statement for June through gross profit.

EXERCISES: SET B AND CHALLENGE EXERCISES

Visit the book's companion website, at **www.wiley.com/college/weygandt**, and choose the Student Companion site to access Exercise Set B and Challenge Exercises.

PROBLEMS: SET A

P23-1A Glendo Farm Supply Company manufactures and sells a pesticide called Snare. The following data are available for preparing budgets for Snare for the first 2 quarters of 2014.

Prepare budgeted income statement and supporting budgets.

(LO 3, 4)

1. Sales: quarter 1, 30,000 bags; quarter 2, 42,000 bags. Selling price is $60 per bag.
2. Direct materials: each bag of Snare requires 4 pounds of Gumm at a cost of $3.80 per pound and 6 pounds of Tarr at $1.50 per pound.

3. Desired inventory levels:

Type of Inventory	January 1	April 1	July 1
Snare (bags)	8,000	15,000	18,000
Gumm (pounds)	9,000	10,000	13,000
Tarr (pounds)	14,000	20,000	25,000

4. Direct labor: direct labor time is 15 minutes per bag at an hourly rate of $16 per hour.
5. Selling and administrative expenses are expected to be 15% of sales plus $175,000 per quarter.
6. Income taxes are expected to be 30% of income from operations.

Your assistant has prepared two budgets: (1) The manufacturing overhead budget shows expected costs to be 150% of direct labor cost. (2) The direct materials budget for Tarr shows the cost of Tarr purchases to be $297,000 in quarter 1 and $439,500 in quarter 2.

Instructions

Prepare the budgeted income statement for the first 6 months and all required operating budgets by quarters. (*Note:* Use variable and fixed in the selling and administrative expense budget.) Do not prepare the manufacturing overhead budget or the direct materials budget for Tarr.

Prepare sales, production, direct materials, direct labor, and income statement budgets.

(LO 3, 4)

P23-2A Deleon Inc. is preparing its annual budgets for the year ending December 31, 2014. Accounting assistants furnish the data shown below.

	Product JB 50	Product JB 60
Sales budget:		
Anticipated volume in units	400,000	200,000
Unit selling price	$20	$25
Production budget:		
Desired ending finished goods units	30,000	15,000
Beginning finished goods units	25,000	10,000
Direct materials budget:		
Direct materials per unit (pounds)	2	3
Desired ending direct materials pounds	30,000	10,000
Beginning direct materials pounds	40,000	15,000
Cost per pound	$3	$4
Direct labor budget:		
Direct labor time per unit	0.4	0.6
Direct labor rate per hour	$12	$12
Budgeted income statement:		
Total unit cost	$13	$20

An accounting assistant has prepared the detailed manufacturing overhead budget and the selling and administrative expense budget. The latter shows selling expenses of $560,000 for product JB 50 and $360,000 for product JB 60, and administrative expenses of $540,000 for product JB 50 and $340,000 for product JB 60. Income taxes are expected to be 30%.

Instructions

Prepare the following budgets for the year. Show data for each product. Quarterly budgets should not be prepared.

(a) Sales
(b) Production
(c) Direct materials

(d) Direct labor
(e) Income statement (*Note:* Income taxes are not allocated to the products.)

Prepare sales and production budgets and compute cost per unit under two plans.

(LO 3, 4)

P23-3A Marsh Industries had sales in 2013 of $6,400,000 and gross profit of $1,100,000. Management is considering two alternative budget plans to increase its gross profit in 2014.

Plan A would increase the selling price per unit from $8.00 to $8.40. Sales volume would decrease by 10% from its 2013 level. Plan B would decrease the selling price per unit by $0.50. The marketing department expects that the sales volume would increase by 100,000 units.

At the end of 2013, Marsh has 38,000 units of inventory on hand. If Plan A is accepted, the 2014 ending inventory should be equal to 5% of the 2014 sales. If Plan B is accepted, the ending inventory should be equal to 60,000 units. Each unit produced will cost $1.80 in direct labor, $1.30 in direct materials, and $1.20 in variable overhead. The fixed overhead for 2014 should be $1,895,000.

Instructions
(a) Prepare a sales budget for 2014 under each plan.
(b) Prepare a production budget for 2014 under each plan.
(c) Compute the production cost per unit under each plan. Why is the cost per unit different for each of the two plans? (Round to two decimals.)
(d) Which plan should be accepted? (*Hint:* Compute the gross profit under each plan.)

(c) Unit cost: Plan A $6.94
Plan B $6.36
(d) Gross profit:
Plan A $1,051,200
Plan B $1,026,000

P23-4A Colter Company prepares monthly cash budgets. Relevant data from operating budgets for 2014 are:

Prepare cash budget for 2 months.

(LO 5)

	January	February
Sales	$360,000	$400,000
Direct materials purchases	120,000	125,000
Direct labor	90,000	100,000
Manufacturing overhead	70,000	75,000
Selling and administrative expenses	79,000	85,000

All sales are on account. Collections are expected to be 50% in the month of sale, 30% in the first month following the sale, and 20% in the second month following the sale. Sixty percent (60%) of direct materials purchases are paid in cash in the month of purchase, and the balance due is paid in the month following the purchase. All other items above are paid in the month incurred except for selling and administrative expenses that include $1,000 of depreciation per month.

Other data:

1. Credit sales: November 2013, $250,000; December 2013, $320,000.
2. Purchases of direct materials: December 2013, $100,000.
3. Other receipts: January—collection of December 31, 2013, notes receivable $15,000; February—proceeds from sale of securities $6,000.
4. Other disbursements: February—payment of $6,000 cash dividend.

The company's cash balance on January 1, 2014, is expected to be $60,000. The company wants to maintain a minimum cash balance of $50,000.

(a) January: collections $326,000 payments $112,000
(b) Ending cash balance:
January $51,000
February $50,000

Instructions
(a) Prepare schedules for (1) expected collections from customers and (2) expected payments for direct materials purchases for January and February.
(b) Prepare a cash budget for January and February in columnar form.

P23-5A The budget committee of Litwin Company collects the following data for its San Miguel Store in preparing budgeted income statements for May and June 2014.

Prepare purchases and income statement budgets for a merchandiser.

(LO 6)

1. Sales for May are expected to be $800,000. Sales in June and July are expected to be 5% higher than the preceding month.
2. Cost of goods sold is expected to be 75% of sales.
3. Company policy is to maintain ending merchandise inventory at 15% of the following month's cost of goods sold.
4. Operating expenses are estimated to be:

Sales salaries	$30,000 per month
Advertising	6% of monthly sales
Delivery expense	3% of monthly sales
Sales commissions	5% of monthly sales
Rent expense	$5,000 per month
Depreciation	$800 per month
Utilities	$600 per month
Insurance	$500 per month

5. Income taxes are estimated to be 30% of income from operations.

Prepare budgeted income statement and balance sheet.

(LO 4, 5)

Instructions

(a) Prepare the merchandise purchases budget for each month in columnar form.
(b) Prepare budgeted income statements for each month in columnar form. Show in the statements the details of cost of goods sold.

P23-6A Krause Industries' balance sheet at December 31, 2013, is presented below.

Krause Industries
Balance Sheet
December 31, 2013

Assets

Current assets		
Cash		$ 7,500
Accounts receivable		82,500
Finished goods inventory (1,000 units)		15,000
Total current assets		105,000
Property, plant, and equipment		
Equipment	$40,000	
Less: Accumulated depreciation	10,000	30,000
Total assets		$135,000

Liabilities and Stockholders' Equity

Liabilities		
Notes payable		$ 25,000
Accounts payable		45,000
Total liabilities		70,000
Stockholders' equity		
Common stock	$40,000	
Retained earnings	25,000	
Total stockholders' equity		65,000
Total liabilities and stockholders' equity		$135,000

Additional information accumulated for the budgeting process is as follows. Budgeted data for the year 2014 include the following.

	4th Qtr. of 2014	Year 2014 Total
Sales budget (8,000 units at $32)	$76,800	$256,000
Direct materials used	17,000	62,500
Direct labor	12,500	50,900
Manufacturing overhead applied	10,000	48,600
Selling and administrative expenses	18,000	75,000

To meet sales requirements and to have 3,000 units of finished goods on hand at December 31, 2014, the production budget shows 9,000 required units of output. The total unit cost of production is expected to be $18. Krause Industries uses the first-in, first-out (FIFO) inventory costing method. Selling and administrative expenses include $4,000 for depreciation on equipment. Interest expense is expected to be $3,500 for the year. Income taxes are expected to be 40% of income before income taxes.

All sales and purchases are on account. It is expected that 60% of quarterly sales are collected in cash within the quarter and the remainder is collected in the following quarter. Direct materials purchased from suppliers are paid 50% in the quarter incurred and the remainder in the following quarter. Purchases in the fourth quarter were the same as the materials used. In 2014, the company expects to purchase additional equipment costing $9,000. It expects to pay $8,000 on notes payable plus all interest due and payable to December 31 (included in interest expense $3,500, above). Accounts payable at December 31, 2014, include amounts due suppliers (see above) plus other accounts payable of $6,500. In 2014, the company expects to declare and pay an $8,000 cash dividend. Unpaid income taxes at December 31 will be $5,000. The company's cash budget shows an expected cash balance of $6,980 at December 31, 2014.

Instructions

Prepare a budgeted income statement for 2014 and a budgeted balance sheet at December 31, 2014. In preparing the income statement, you will need to compute cost of goods manufactured (direct materials + direct labor + manufacturing overhead) and finished goods inventory (December 31, 2014).

Net income $32,700
Total assets $126,700

PROBLEMS: SET B

P23-1B Mercer Farm Supply Company manufactures and sells a fertilizer called Basic II. The following data are available for preparing budgets for Basic II for the first 2 quarters of 2014.

Prepare budgeted income statement and supporting budgets.

(LO 3, 4)

1. Sales: quarter 1, 40,000 bags; quarter 2, 50,000 bags. Selling price is $63 per bag.
2. Direct materials: each bag of Basic II requires 5 pounds of Crup at a cost of $3.80 per pound and 10 pounds of Dert at $1.50 per pound.
3. Desired inventory levels:

Type of Inventory	January 1	April 1	July 1
Basic II (bags)	10,000	15,000	20,000
Crup (pounds)	9,000	12,000	15,000
Dert (pounds)	15,000	20,000	25,000

4. Direct labor: direct labor time is 15 minutes per bag at an hourly rate of $12 per hour.
5. Selling and administrative expenses are expected to be 10% of sales plus $150,000 per quarter.
6. Income taxes are expected to be 30% of income from operations.

   Your assistant has prepared two budgets: (1) The manufacturing overhead budget shows expected costs to be 100% of direct labor cost. (2) The direct materials budget for Dert which shows the cost of Dert to be $682,500 in quarter 1 and $832,500 in quarter 2.

Instructions

Prepare the budgeted income statement for the first 6 months of 2014 and all required supporting budgets by quarters. (*Note:* Use variable and fixed in the selling and administrative expense budget.) Do not prepare the manufacturing overhead budget or the direct materials budget for Dert.

Net income $842,100
Cost per bag $40.00

P23-2B Urbina Inc. is preparing its annual budgets for the year ending December 31, 2014. Accounting assistants furnish the following data.

Prepare sales, production, direct materials, direct labor, and income statement budgets.

(LO 3, 4)

	Product LN 35	Product LN 40
Sales budget:		
Anticipated volume in units	400,000	240,000
Unit selling price	$25	$35
Production budget:		
Desired ending finished goods units	20,000	25,000
Beginning finished goods units	30,000	15,000
Direct materials budget:		
Direct materials per unit (pounds)	2	3
Desired ending direct materials pounds	50,000	10,000
Beginning direct materials pounds	40,000	20,000
Cost per pound	$2	$3
Direct labor budget:		
Direct labor time per unit	0.5	0.75
Direct labor rate per hour	$12	$12
Budgeted income statement:		
Total unit cost	$12	$22

An accounting assistant has prepared the detailed manufacturing overhead budget and the selling and administrative expense budget. The latter shows selling expenses of $750,000 for product LN 35 and $580,000 for product LN 40, and administrative expenses of $420,000 for product LN 35 and $380,000 for product LN 40. Income taxes are expected to be 30%.

(a) Total sales $18,400,000
(b) Required production units:
    LN 35, 390,000
(c) Total cost of direct materials purchases $3,800,000
(d) Total direct labor cost $4,590,000
(e) Net income $4,333,000

Instructions

Prepare the following budgets for the year. Show data for each product. You do not need to prepare quarterly budgets.

(a) Sales   (d) Direct labor
(b) Production   (e) Income statement (*Note:* Income taxes are
(c) Direct materials   not allocated to the products.)

Prepare sales and production budgets and compute cost per unit under two plans.

(LO 3, 4)

P23-3B Ogleby Industries has sales in 2013 of $5,600,000 (800,000 units) and gross profit of $1,344,000. Management is considering two alternative budget plans to increase its gross profit in 2014.

Plan A would increase the selling price per unit from $7.00 to $7.60. Sales volume would decrease by 5% from its 2013 level. Plan B would decrease the selling price per unit by 5%. The marketing department expects that the sales volume would increase by 150,000 units.

At the end of 2013, Ogleby has 70,000 units on hand. If Plan A is accepted, the 2014 ending inventory should be equal to 90,000 units. If Plan B is accepted, the ending inventory should be equal to 100,000 units. Each unit produced will cost $2.00 in direct materials, $1.50 in direct labor, and $0.50 in variable overhead. The fixed overhead for 2014 should be $980,000.

(c) Unit cost:
    Plan A $5.26
    Plan B $5.00
(d) Gross profit:
    Plan A $1,778,400
    Plan B $1,567,500

Instructions

(a) Prepare a sales budget for 2014 under (1) Plan A and (2) Plan B.
(b) Prepare a production budget for 2014 under (1) Plan A and (2) Plan B.
(c) Compute the cost per unit under (1) Plan A and (2) Plan B. Explain why the cost per unit is different for each of the two plans. (Round to two decimals.)
(d) Which plan should be accepted? (*Hint:* Compute the gross profit under each plan.)

Prepare cash budget for 2 months.

(LO 5)

P23-4B Derby Company prepares monthly cash budgets. Relevant data from operating budgets for 2014 are:

	January	February
Sales	$350,000	$400,000
Direct materials purchases	110,000	120,000
Direct labor	85,000	115,000
Manufacturing overhead	60,000	75,000
Selling and administrative expenses	75,000	80,000

All sales are on account. Collections are expected to be 60% in the month of sale, 25% in the first month following the sale, and 15% in the second month following the sale. Thirty percent (30%) of direct materials purchases are paid in cash in the month of purchase, and the balance due is paid in the month following the purchase. All other items above are paid in the month incurred. Depreciation has been excluded from manufacturing overhead and selling and administrative expenses.

Other data:

1. Credit sales: November 2013, $200,000; December 2013, $290,000.
2. Purchases of direct materials: December 2013, $90,000.
3. Other receipts: January—collection of December 31, 2013, interest receivable $3,000; February—proceeds from sale of securities $5,000.
4. Other disbursements: February—payment of $20,000 for land.

The company's cash balance on January 1, 2014, is expected to be $50,000. The company wants to maintain a minimum cash balance of $40,000.

(a) January:
    collections $312,500
    payments $96,000
(b) Ending cash balance:
    January $49,500
    February $40,000

Instructions

(a) Prepare schedules for (1) expected collections from customers and (2) expected payments for direct materials purchases.
(b) Prepare a cash budget for January and February in columnar form.

P23-5B The budget committee of Widner Company collects the following data for its West-wood Store in preparing budgeted income statements for July and August 2014.

1. Expected sales: July $400,000, August $450,000, September $500,000.
2. Cost of goods sold is expected to be 65% of sales.
3. Company policy is to maintain ending merchandise inventory at 15% of the following month's cost of goods sold.
4. Operating expenses are estimated to be:

Sales salaries	$50,000 per month
Advertising	5% of monthly sales
Delivery expense	2% of monthly sales
Sales commissions	4% of monthly sales
Rent expense	$3,000 per month
Depreciation	$700 per month
Utilities	$500 per month
Insurance	$300 per month

5. Income taxes are estimated to be 30% of income from operations.

Instructions
(a) Prepare the merchandise purchases budget for each month in columnar form.
(b) Prepare budgeted income statements for each month in columnar form. Show the details of cost of goods sold in the statements.

Prepare purchases and income statement budgets for a merchandiser.

(LO 6)

(a) Purchases: July $264,875
    August $297,375
(b) Net income: July $29,050
    August $37,450

PROBLEMS: SET C

Visit the book's companion website, at **www.wiley.com/college/weygandt**, and choose the Student Companion site to access Problem Set C.

WATERWAYS CONTINUING PROBLEM

(This is a continuation of the Waterways Problem from Chapters 15–22.)

WCP23 Waterways Corporation is preparing its budget for the coming year, 2014. The first step is to plan for the first quarter of that coming year. The company has gathered information from its managers in preparation of the budgeting process. This problem asks you to prepare the various budgets that comprise the master budget for 2014.

Go to the book's companion website, at **www.wiley.com/college/weygandt***, to see the completion of this problem.*

Broadening Your **PERSPECTIVE**

Management Decision-Making

Decision-Making at Current Designs

BYP23-1 Diane Buswell is preparing the 2013 budget for one of Current Designs' rotomolded kayaks. Extensive meetings with members of the sales department and executive team have resulted in the following unit sales projections for 2013.

Quarter 1	1,000 kayaks
Quarter 2	1,500 kayaks
Quarter 3	750 kayaks
Quarter 4	750 kayaks

Current Designs' policy is to have finished goods ending inventory in a quarter equal to 20% of the next quarter's anticipated sales. Preliminary sales projections for 2014 are 1,100 units for the first quarter and 1,500 units for the second quarter. Ending inventory of finished goods at December 31, 2012, will be 200 rotomolded kayaks.

Production of each kayak requires 54 pounds of polyethylene powder and a finishing kit (rope, seat, hardware, etc). Company policy is that the ending inventory of polyethylene powder should be 25% of the amount needed for production in the next quarter. Assume that the ending inventory of polyethylene powder on December 31, 2012, is 19,400 pounds. The finishing kits can be assembled as they are needed. As a result, Current Designs does not maintain a significant inventory of the finishing kits.

The polyethylene powder used in these kayaks costs $1.50 per pound, and the finishing kits cost $170 each. Production of a single kayak requires 2 hours of time by more experienced, type I employees and 3 hours of finishing time by type II employees. The type I employees are paid $15 per hour, and the type II employees are paid $12 per hour.

Selling and administrative expenses for this line are expected to be $45 per unit sold plus $7,500 per quarter. Manufacturing overhead is assigned at 150% of labor costs.

Instructions

Prepare the production budget, direct materials budget, direct labor budget, manufacturing overhead budget, and selling and administrative budget for this product line by quarter and in total for 2013.

Decision-Making Across the Organization

BYP23-2 Palmer Corporation operates on a calendar-year basis. It begins the annual budgeting process in late August when the president establishes targets for the total dollar sales and net income before taxes for the next year.

The sales target is given first to the marketing department. The marketing manager formulates a sales budget by product line in both units and dollars. From this budget, sales quotas by product line in units and dollars are established for each of the corporation's sales districts. The marketing manager also estimates the cost of the marketing activities required to support the target sales volume and prepares a tentative marketing expense budget.

The executive vice president uses the sales and profit targets, the sales budget by product line, and the tentative marketing expense budget to determine the dollar amounts that can be devoted to manufacturing and corporate office expense. The executive vice president prepares the budget for corporate expenses. She then forwards to the production department the product-line sales budget in units and the total dollar amount that can be devoted to manufacturing.

The production manager meets with the factory managers to develop a manufacturing plan that will produce the required units when needed within the cost constraints set by the executive vice president. The budgeting process usually comes to a halt at this point because the production department does not consider the financial resources allocated to be adequate.

When this standstill occurs, the vice president of finance, the executive vice president, the marketing manager, and the production manager meet together to determine the final budgets for each of the areas. This normally results in a modest increase in the total amount available for manufacturing costs and cuts in the marketing expense and corporate office expense budgets. The total sales and net income figures proposed by the president are seldom changed. Although the participants are seldom pleased with the compromise, these budgets are final. Each executive then develops a new detailed budget for the operations in his or her area.

None of the areas has achieved its budget in recent years. Sales often run below the target. When budgeted sales are not achieved, each area is expected to cut costs so that the president's profit target can be met. However, the profit target is seldom met because costs are not cut enough. In fact, costs often run above the original budget in all functional areas (marketing, production, and corporate office).

The president is disturbed that Palmer has not been able to meet the sales and profit targets. He hired a consultant with considerable experience with companies in Palmer's industry. The consultant reviewed the budgets for the past 4 years. He concluded that the product line sales budgets were reasonable and that the cost and expense budgets were adequate for the budgeted sales and production levels.

Instructions

With the class divided into groups, answer the following.

(a) Discuss how the budgeting process employed by Palmer Corporation contributes to the failure to achieve the president's sales and profit targets.

(b) Suggest how Palmer Corporation's budgeting process could be revised to correct the problems.

(c) Should the functional areas be expected to cut their costs when sales volume falls below budget? Explain your answer.

(CMA adapted)

Managerial Analysis

BYP23-3 Elliot & Hesse Inc. manufactures ergonomic devices for computer users. Some of its more popular products include glare screens (for computer monitors), keyboard stands with wrist rests, and carousels that allow easy access to discs. Over the past 5 years, it experienced rapid growth, with sales of all products increasing 20% to 50% each year.

Last year, some of the primary manufacturers of computers began introducing new products with some of the ergonomic designs, such as glare screens and wrist rests, already built in. As a result, sales of Elliot & Hesse's accessory devices have declined somewhat. The company believes that the disc carousels will probably continue to show growth, but that the other products will probably continue to decline. When the next year's budget was prepared, increases were built into research and development so that replacement products could be developed or the company could expand into some other product line. Some product lines being considered are general-purpose ergonomic devices including back supports, foot rests, and sloped writing pads.

The most recent results have shown that sales decreased more than was expected for the glare screens. As a result, the company may have a shortage of funds. Top management has therefore asked that all expenses be reduced 10% to compensate for these reduced sales. Summary budget information is as follows.

Direct materials	$240,000
Direct labor	110,000
Insurance	50,000
Depreciation	90,000
Machine repairs	30,000
Sales salaries	50,000
Office salaries	80,000
Factory salaries (indirect labor)	50,000
Total	$700,000

Instructions

Using the information above, answer the following questions.

(a) What are the implications of reducing each of the costs? For example, if the company reduces direct materials costs, it may have to do so by purchasing lower-quality materials. This may affect sales in the long run.

(b) Based on your analysis in (a), what do you think is the best way to obtain the $70,000 in cost savings requested? Be specific. Are there any costs that cannot or should not be reduced? Why?

Real-World Focus

BYP23-4 Network Computing Devices, Inc. was founded in 1988 in Mountain View, California. The company develops software products such as X-terminals, Z-mail, PC X-ware, and related hardware products. The following is a discussion by management in its annual report.

Network Computing Devices, Inc.
Management Discussion

The Company's operating results have varied significantly, particularly on a quarterly basis, as a result of a number of factors, including general economic conditions affecting industry demand for computer products, the timing and market acceptance of new product introductions by the Company and its competitors, the timing of significant orders from large customers, periodic changes in product pricing and discounting due to competitive factors, and the availability of key components, such as video monitors and electronic subassemblies, some of which require substantial order lead times. The Company's operating results may fluctuate in the future as a result of these and other factors, including the Company's success in developing and introducing new products, its product and customer mix, and the level of competition which it experiences. The Company operates with a small backlog. Sales and operating results, therefore, generally depend on the volume and timing of orders received, which are difficult to forecast. The Company has experienced slowness in orders from some customers during the first quarter of each calendar year due to budgeting cycles common in the computer industry. In addition, sales in Europe typically are adversely affected in the third calendar quarter as many European customers reduce their business activities during the month of August.

Due to the Company's rapid growth rate and the effect of new product introductions on quarterly revenues, these seasonal trends have not materially impacted the Company's results of operations to date. However, as the Company's product lines mature and its rate of revenue growth declines, these seasonal factors may become more evident. Additionally, the Company's international sales are denominated in U.S. dollars, and an increase or decrease in the value of the U.S. dollar relative to foreign currencies could make the Company's products less or more competitive in those markets.

Instructions
(a) Identify the factors that affect the budgeting process at Network Computing Devices, Inc.
(b) Explain the additional budgeting concerns created by the international operations of the company.

BYP23-5 Information regarding many approaches to budgeting can be found on the Web. The following activity investigates the merits of "zero-based" budgeting, as discussed by Michael LaFaive, Director of Financial Policy of the Mackinac Center for Public Policy.

Address: **www.mackinac.org/article.aspx?ID=5928**, or go to **www.wiley.com/college/weygandt**

Instructions
Read the article at the website and answer the following questions.

(a) How does zero-based budgeting differ from standard budgeting procedures?
(b) What are some potential advantages of zero-based budgeting?
(c) What are some potential disadvantages of zero-based budgeting?
(d) How often do departments in Oklahoma undergo zero-based budgeting?

Critical Thinking

Communication Activity

BYP23-6 In order to better serve their rural patients, Drs. Joe and Rick Parcells (brothers) began giving safety seminars. Especially popular were their "emergency-preparedness" talks given to farmers. Many people asked whether the "kit" of materials the doctors recommended for common farm emergencies was commercially available.

After checking with several suppliers, the doctors realized that no other company offered the supplies they recommended in their seminars, packaged in the way they described. Their wives, Megan and Sue, agreed to make a test package by ordering supplies from various medical supply companies and assembling them into a "kit" that could be sold at the seminars. When these kits proved a runaway success, the sisters-in-law decided to market them. At the advice of their accountant, they organized this venture as a separate company, called Life Protection Products (LPP), with Megan Parcells as CEO and Sue Parcells as Secretary-Treasurer.

LPP soon started receiving requests for the kits from all over the country, as word spread about their availability. Even without advertising, LPP was able to sell its full inventory every month. However, the company was becoming financially strained. Megan and Sue had about $100,000 in savings, and they invested about half that amount initially. They believed that this venture would allow them to make money. However, at the present time, only about $30,000 of the cash remains, and the company is constantly short of cash.

Megan has come to you for advice. She does not understand why the company is having cash flow problems. She and Sue have not even been withdrawing salaries. However, they have rented a local building and have hired two more full-time workers to help them cope with the increasing demand. They do not think they could handle the demand without this additional help.

Megan is also worried that the cash problems mean that the company may not be able to support itself. She has prepared the cash budget shown below. All seminar customers pay for their products in full at the time of purchase. In addition, several large companies have ordered the kits for use by employees who work in remote sites. They have requested credit terms and have been allowed to pay in the month following the sale. These large purchasers amount to about 25% of the sales at the present time. LPP purchases the materials for the kits about 2 months ahead of time. Megan and Sue are considering slowing the growth of the company by simply purchasing less materials, which will mean selling fewer kits.

The workers are paid weekly. Megan and Sue need about $15,000 cash on hand at the beginning of the month to pay for purchases of raw materials. Right now they have been using cash from their savings, but as noted, only $30,000 is left.

Instructions

Write a response to Megan Parcells. Explain why LPP is short of cash. Will this company be able to support itself? Explain your answer. Make any recommendations you deem appropriate.

Life Protection Products
Cash Budget
For the Quarter Ending June 30, 2014

	April	May	June
Cash balance, beginning	$15,000	$15,000	$15,000
Cash received			
From prior month sales	5,000	7,500	12,500
From current sales	15,000	22,500	37,500
Total cash on hand	35,000	45,000	65,000
Cash payments			
To employees	3,000	3,000	3,000
For products	25,000	35,000	45,000
Miscellaneous expenses	5,000	6,000	7,000
Postage	1,000	1,000	1,000
Total cash payments	34,000	45,000	56,000
Cash balance	$ 1,000	$ 0	$ 9,000
Borrow from savings	$14,000	$15,000	$ 1,000
Borrow from bank?	$ 0	$ 0	$ 5,000

Ethics Case

BYP23-7 You are an accountant in the budgetary, projections, and special projects department of Fernetti Conductor, Inc., a large manufacturing company. The president, Richard Brown, asks you on very short notice to prepare some sales and income projections covering the next 2 years of the company's much heralded new product lines. He wants these projections for a series of speeches he is making while on a 2-week trip to eight East Coast brokerage firms. The president hopes to bolster Fernetti's stock sales and price.

You work 23 hours in 2 days to compile the projections, hand-deliver them to the president, and are swiftly but graciously thanked as he departs. A week later, you find time to go over some of your computations and discover a miscalculation that makes the projections grossly overstated. You quickly inquire about the president's itinerary and learn that he has made half of his speeches and has half yet to make. You are in a quandary as to what to do.

Instructions
(a) What are the consequences of telling the president of your gross miscalculations?
(b) What are the consequences of not telling the president of your gross miscalculations?
(c) What are the ethical considerations to you and the president in this situation?

All About You

BYP23-8 In order to get your personal finances under control, you need to prepare a personal budget. Assume that you have compiled the following information regarding your expected cash flows for a typical month.

Rent payment	$ 500	Miscellaneous costs	$210
Interest income	50	Savings	50
Income tax withheld	300	Eating out	150
Electricity bill	85	Telephone and Internet costs	125
Groceries	100	Student loan payments	375
Wages earned	2,500	Entertainment costs	250
Insurance	100	Transportation costs	150

Instructions
Using the information above, prepare a personal budget. In preparing this budget, use the format found at *http://financialplan.about.com/cs/budgeting/l/blbudget.htm*. Just skip any unused line items.

Considering Your Costs and Benefits

BYP23-9 You might hear people say that they "need to learn to live within a budget." The funny thing is that most people who say this haven't actually prepared a personal budget, nor do they intend to. Instead, what they are referring to is a vaguely defined, poorly specified collection of rough ideas of how much they should spend on various aspects of their lives. However, you can't live within or even outside of something that doesn't exist. With that in mind, let's take a look at one aspect of personal-budget templates.

Many personal-budget worksheet templates that are provided for college students treat student loans as an income source. See, for example, the template provided at *http://financialplan. about.com/cs/budgeting/l/blmocolbud.htm*. Based on your knowledge of accounting, is this correct?

YES: Student loans provide a source of cash, which can be used to pay costs. As the saying goes, "It all spends the same." Therefore, student loans are income.
NO: Student loans must eventually be repaid; therefore, they are not income. As the name suggests, they are loans.

Instructions
Write a response indicating your position regarding this situation. Provide support for your view.

Answers to Chapter Questions

Answers to Insight and Accounting Across the Organization Questions

p. 1133 Businesses Often Feel Too Busy to Plan for the Future Q: Describe a situation in which a business "sells as much as it can" but cannot "keep its employees paid." **A:** If sales are made to customers on credit and collection is slow, the company may find that it does not have enough cash to pay employees or suppliers. Without these resources, the company will fail to survive.
p. 1138 The Implications of Budgetary Optimism Q: Why is it important that government budgets accurately estimate future revenues during economic downturns? **A:** Accuracy of government

revenue estimates is especially important during economic downturns because most governments must balance their budgets. If anticipated revenues in one period do not match expectations, then the shortfall must be made up in the next period. This can result in much steeper, more disruptive cuts than might have been necessary had the government anticipated the revenue decline more accurately and consequently started cutting expenditures sooner.

p. 1141 Betting That Prices Won't Fall Q: What are the potential downsides of stockpiling a huge amount of raw materials? **A:** If prices continue to go up, these managers will avoid paying higher prices until their inventory runs out. However, it is a risky strategy. First of all, prices fluctuate. If a price goes up by 90% in a year, it can also go down by 90%. If this happens, the managers will be stuck with overpriced raw materials. Second, if the economy slows down, it might take a lot longer to sell their inventory than they had planned. There are many costs associated with holding large quantities of inventory. The additional storage, insurance, and handling costs can be very expensive, and obsolescence can occur.

p. 1149 Without a Budget, Can the Games Begin? Q: Why does it matter whether the Olympic Games exceed their budget? **A:** If the Olympic Games exceed their budget, taxpayers of the sponsoring community and country will end up footing the bill. Depending on the size of the losses, and the resources of the community, this could produce a substantial burden. As a result, other communities might be reluctant to host the Olympics in the future.

p. 1154 Budget Shortfalls as Far as the Eye Can See Q: Why would a university's budgeted scholarships probably fall when the stock market suffers a serious drop? **A:** Scholarships typically cannot be paid out of the "principal" portion of donations made to scholarship endowment funds. Instead, scholarships are usually funded through earnings generated by endowment investments. Any excess earnings above current-year scholarship needs can be used for scholarships in subsequent years. But a serious drop in the value of endowment investments can wipe out previous earnings, in some cases completely eliminating funds available for scholarships.

Answers to Self-Test Questions

1. c   **2.** b   **3.** a   **4.** b   **5.** b   **6.** d   **7.** d $(9,500 + 2,200 - 1,000)$ **8.** a   **9.** c   **10.** a   **11.** a   **12.** b   **13.** c $[(\$70,000 \times 60\%) + (\$90,000 \times 40\%)]$ **14.** d   **15.** c

✔ Remember to go back to The Navigator box on the chapter opening page and check off your completed work.

Turning Trash Into Treasure

Vancouver teenager Brian Scudamore needed to raise money to pay his way through college. With $700 and a strong desire to do it on his own, he established a junk removal company. Fifteen years later, 1-800-GOT-JUNK? had 113 franchise partners across Canada and the United States, and projected revenues of more than $60 million.

"It was a high-school business project that was out of control," says Cameron Herold, vice president of operations.

While the exponential growth of 1-800-GOT-JUNK? may seem unwieldy (at one point it had five consecutive years of 100-percent compounded growth), it has in fact involved sound financial planning, budgeting, and cash management. The company only spends money it has; it has no outside investors or debt.

Managing this growth involves forecasting everything by creating a "painted picture" of what the company will look like in three years. The company knows its staffing plans, training requirements, and overhead and office space needs well in advance. "That filters back to our budgeting process," Mr. Herold says. "We'll sit down and say, 'If this is where we're going, what are all the components of that?' . . . Then we

Learning Objectives

After studying this chapter, you should be able to:

1　Describe the concept of budgetary control.

2　Evaluate the usefulness of static budget reports.

3　Explain the development of flexible budgets and the usefulness of flexible budget reports.

4　Describe the concept of responsibility accounting.

5　Indicate the features of responsibility reports for cost centers.

6　Identify the content of responsibility reports for profit centers.

7　Explain the basis and formula used in evaluating performance in investment centers.

✔ The Navigator

bring it back to zero and say, 'What's it going to cost us? Where does it fit into the budget?'"

Key to the company's growth management was the introduction of franchising. "We chose franchising because our franchise partners would actually finance our growth," Mr. Herold says. In addition to the initial franchise fee, franchisees pay the head office 8 percent of their sales, plus another 7 percent to run the centralized call center.

While the company has used franchising to manage growth, a frugal approach to

day-to-day costs has also been integral to its budgeting success. "We're always looking for ways to cut costs," Mr. Herold says. This includes establishing strategic relationships with the local coffee shop, doing regular cost analyses of office equipment and changing suppliers when needed, and buying office furniture in bulk from liquidators at 10 cents on the dollar. "All those little things start to really add up," he says.

Watch the Tribeca Grand video in WileyPLUS to learn more about budgeting in the real world.

 ✔ **The Navigator**

Preview of **Chapter 24**

In contrast to Chapter 23, we now consider how budgets are used by management to control operations. In the Feature Story on 1-800-GOT-JUNK?, we saw that management uses the budget to adapt to the business environment. This chapter focuses on two aspects of management control: (1) budgetary control and (2) responsibility accounting.

The content and organization of Chapter 24 are as follows.

BUDGETARY CONTROL AND RESPONSIBILITY ACCOUNTING

Budgetary Control	Static Budget Reports	Flexible Budgets	Responsibility Accounting	Types of Responsibility Centers
• Budget reports • Control activities • Reporting systems	• Examples • Uses and limitations	• Why flexible budgets? • Development • Case study • Reports	• Controllable vs. noncontrollable • Performance evaluation • Reporting system	• Cost centers • Profit centers • Investment centers

✔ **The Navigator**

Budgetary Control

One of management's functions is to control company operations. Control consists of the steps taken by management to see that planned objectives are met. We now ask: How do budgets contribute to control of operations?

The use of budgets in controlling operations is known as **budgetary control**. Such control takes place by means of **budget reports** that compare actual results with planned objectives. The use of budget reports is based on the belief that planned objectives lose much of their potential value without some monitoring of progress along the way. Just as your professors give midterm exams to evaluate your progress, top management requires periodic reports on the progress of department managers toward their planned objectives.

Budget reports provide management with feedback on operations. The feedback for a crucial objective, such as having enough cash on hand to pay bills, may be made daily. For other objectives, such as meeting budgeted annual sales and operating expenses, monthly budget reports may suffice. Budget reports are prepared as frequently as needed. From these reports, management analyzes any differences between actual and planned results and determines their causes. Management then takes corrective action, or it decides to modify future plans. Budgetary control involves the activities shown in Illustration 24-1.

Illustration 24-1
Budgetary control activities

Budgetary control works best when a company has a formalized reporting system. The system does the following:

1. Identifies the name of the budget report, such as the sales budget or the manufacturing overhead budget.
2. States the frequency of the report, such as weekly or monthly.
3. Specifies the purpose of the report.
4. Indicates the primary recipient(s) of the report.

Illustration 24-2 provides a partial budgetary control system for a manufacturing company. Note the frequency of the reports and their emphasis on control. For example, there is a daily report on scrap and a weekly report on labor.

Name of Report	Frequency	Purpose	Primary Recipient(s)
Sales	Weekly	Determine whether sales goals are met	Top management and sales manager
Labor	Weekly	Control direct and indirect labor costs	Vice president of production and production department managers
Scrap	Daily	Determine efficient use of materials	Production manager
Departmental overhead costs	Monthly	Control overhead costs	Department manager
Selling expenses	Monthly	Control selling expenses	Sales manager
Income statement	Monthly and quarterly	Determine whether income goals are met	Top management

Illustration 24-2
Budgetary control reporting system

Static Budget Reports

You learned in Chapter 23 that the master budget formalizes management's planned objectives for the coming year. When used in budgetary control, each budget included in the master budget is considered to be static. A **static budget** is a projection of budget data **at one level of activity**. These budgets do not consider data for different levels of activity. As a result, companies always compare actual results with budget data at the activity level that was used in developing the master budget.

> **LEARNING OBJECTIVE 2**
> Evaluate the usefulness of static budget reports.

Examples

To illustrate the role of a static budget in budgetary control, we will use selected data prepared for Hayes Company in Chapter 23. Budget and actual sales data for the Rightride product in the first and second quarters of 2014 are as follows.

Illustration 24-3
Budget and actual sales data

Sales	First Quarter	Second Quarter	Total
Budgeted	$180,000	$210,000	$390,000
Actual	179,000	199,500	378,500
Difference	$ 1,000	$ 10,500	$ 11,500

The sales budget report for Hayes Company's first quarter is shown below. The right-most column reports the difference between the budgeted and actual amounts.

Illustration 24-4
Sales budget report—first quarter

Hayes Company
Sales Budget Report
For the Quarter Ended March 31, 2014

Product Line	Budget	Actual	Difference Favorable F Unfavorable U
Rightride[a]	$180,000	$179,000	**$1,000 U**

[a]In practice, each product line would be included in the report.

Alternative Terminology
The difference between budget and actual is sometimes called a *budget variance*.

The report shows that sales are $1,000 under budget—an unfavorable result. This difference is less than 1% of budgeted sales ($1,000 ÷ $180,000 = .0056).

Top management's reaction to unfavorable differences is often influenced by the materiality (significance) of the difference. Since the difference of $1,000 is immaterial in this case, we assume that Hayes Company management takes no specific corrective action.

Illustration 24-5 shows the budget report for the second quarter. It contains one new feature: cumulative year-to-date information. This report indicates that sales for the second quarter are $10,500 below budget. This is 5% of budgeted sales ($10,500 ÷ $210,000). Top management may now conclude that the difference between budgeted and actual sales requires investigation.

Hayes Company
Sales Budget Report
For the Quarter Ended June 30, 2014

| | Second Quarter | | | Year-to-Date | | |
| | | | Difference | | | Difference |
Product Line	Budget	Actual	Favorable F Unfavorable U	Budget	Actual	Favorable F Unfavorable U
Rightride	$210,000	$199,500	**$10,500 U**	$390,000	$378,500	**$11,500 U**

Illustration 24-5
Sales budget report—second quarter

Management's analysis should start by asking the sales manager the cause(s) of the shortfall. Managers should consider the need for corrective action. For example, management may decide to spur sales by offering sales incentives to customers or by increasing the advertising of Rightrides. Or, if management concludes that a downturn in the economy is responsible for the lower sales, it may modify planned sales and profit goals for the remainder of the year.

Uses and Limitations

From these examples, you can see that a master sales budget is useful in evaluating the performance of a sales manager. It is now necessary to ask: Is the master budget appropriate for evaluating a manager's performance in controlling costs? Recall that in a static budget, data are not modified or adjusted, regardless of changes in activity. It follows, then, that a static budget is appropriate in evaluating a manager's effectiveness in controlling costs when:

1. The actual level of activity closely approximates the master budget activity level, and/or

2. The behavior of the costs in response to changes in activity is fixed.

A static budget report is, therefore, appropriate for **fixed manufacturing costs** and for **fixed selling and administrative expenses**. But, as you will see shortly, static budget reports may not be a proper basis for evaluating a manager's performance in controlling variable costs.

Static budgets report a single level of activity

Flexible Budgets

LEARNING OBJECTIVE 3

Explain the development of flexible budgets and the usefulness of flexible budget reports.

In contrast to a static budget, which is based on one level of activity, a **flexible budget** projects budget data for various levels of activity. In essence, **the flexible budget is a series of static budgets at different levels of activity**. The flexible budget recognizes that the budgetary process is more useful if it is adaptable to changed operating conditions.

Flexible budgets can be prepared for each of the types of budgets included in the master budget. For example, Marriott Hotels can budget revenues and net income on the basis of 60%, 80%, and 100% of room occupancy. Similarly, American Van Lines can budget its operating expenses on the basis of various levels of truck-miles driven. Duke Energy can budget revenue and net income on the basis of estimated billions of kwh (kilowatt hours) of residential, commercial, and industrial electricity generated. In the following pages, we will illustrate a flexible budget for manufacturing overhead.

Why Flexible Budgets?

Assume that you are the manager in charge of manufacturing overhead in the Assembly Department of Barton Robotics. In preparing the manufacturing overhead budget for 2014, you prepare the following static budget based on a production volume of 10,000 units of robotic controls.

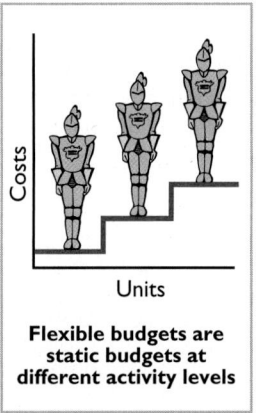

Flexible budgets are static budgets at different activity levels

Barton Robotics
Manufacturing Overhead Budget (Static)
Assembly Department
For the Year Ended December 31, 2014

Budgeted production in units (robotic controls)	10,000
Budgeted costs	
Indirect materials	$ 250,000
Indirect labor	260,000
Utilities	190,000
Depreciation	280,000
Property taxes	70,000
Supervision	50,000
	$1,100,000

Helpful Hint
The master budget described in Chapter 23 is based on a static budget.

Illustration 24-6
Static overhead budget

Fortunately for the company, the demand for robotic controls has increased, and Barton produces and sells 12,000 units during the year, rather than 10,000. You are elated: Increased sales means increased profitability, which should mean a bonus or a raise for you and the employees in your department. Unfortunately, a comparison of Assembly Department actual and budgeted costs has put you on the spot. The budget report is shown below.

Illustration 24-7
Overhead static budget report

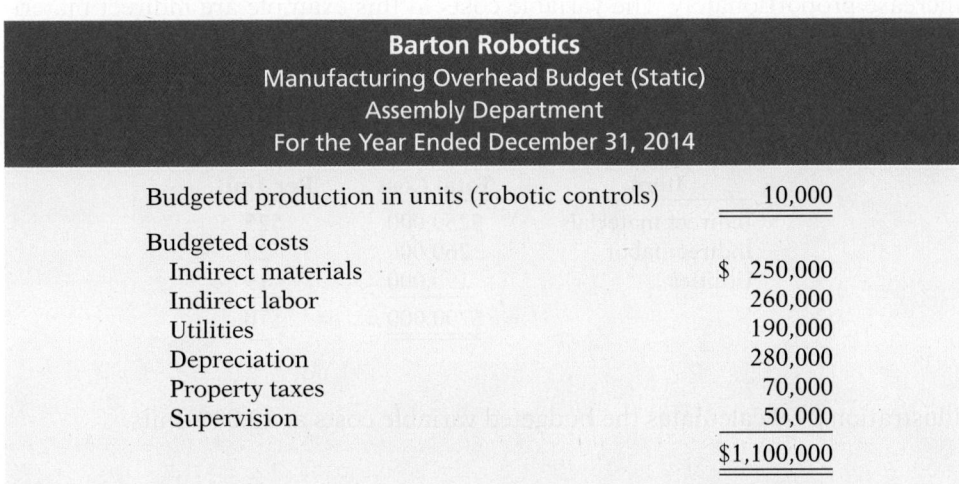

Barton Robotics.xls

	A	B	C	D	E
1			**Barton Robotics**		
2		**Manufacturing Overhead Static Budget Report**			
3		**For the Year Ended December 31, 2014**			
4				Difference	
5		Budget	Actual	Favorable - F Unfavorable - U	
6	Production in units	10,000	12,000		
7					
8	Costs				
9	Indirect materials	$ 250,000	$ 295,000	$ 45,000	U
10	Indirect labor	260,000	312,000	52,000	U
11	Utilities	190,000	225,000	35,000	U
12	Depreciation	280,000	280,000	0	
13	Property taxes	70,000	70,000	0	
14	Supervision	50,000	50,000	0	
15		$1,100,000	$1,232,000	$132,000	U
16					

Helpful Hint
A static budget is not useful for performance evaluation if a company has substantial variable costs.

This comparison uses budget data based on the original activity level (10,000 robotic controls). It indicates that the Assembly Department is significantly **over budget** for three of the six overhead costs. There is a total unfavorable difference of $132,000, which is 12% over budget ($132,000 ÷ $1,100,000). Your supervisor is very unhappy! Instead of sharing in the company's success, you may find yourself looking for another job. What went wrong?

When you calm down and carefully examine the manufacturing overhead budget, you identify the problem: The budget data are not relevant! At the time the budget was developed, the company anticipated that only 10,000 units would be produced, **not** 12,000. Comparing actual with budgeted variable costs is meaningless. As production increases, the budget allowances for variable costs should increase proportionately. The variable costs in this example are indirect materials, indirect labor, and utilities.

Analyzing the budget data for these costs at 10,000 units, you arrive at the following per unit results.

Illustration 24-8
Variable costs per unit

Item	Total Cost	Per Unit
Indirect materials	$250,000	$25
Indirect labor	260,000	26
Utilities	190,000	19
	$700,000	$70

Illustration 24-9 calculates the budgeted variable costs at 12,000 units.

Illustration 24-9
Budgeted variable costs, 12,000 units

Item	Computation	Total
Indirect materials	$25 × 12,000	$300,000
Indirect labor	26 × 12,000	312,000
Utilities	19 × 12,000	228,000
		$840,000

Because fixed costs do not change in total as activity changes, the budgeted amounts for these costs remain the same. Illustration 24-10 shows the budget report based on the flexible budget for **12,000 units** of production. (Compare this with Illustration 24-7.)

This report indicates that the Assembly Department's costs are *under budget*—a favorable difference. Instead of worrying about being fired, you may be in line for a bonus or a raise after all! As this analysis shows, the only appropriate comparison is between actual costs at 12,000 units of production and budgeted costs at 12,000 units. Flexible budget reports provide this comparison.

Developing the Flexible Budget

The flexible budget uses the master budget as its basis. To develop the flexible budget, management uses the following steps.

1. Identify the activity index and the relevant range of activity.
2. Identify the variable costs, and determine the budgeted variable cost per unit of activity for each cost.
3. Identify the fixed costs, and determine the budgeted amount for each cost.
4. Prepare the budget for selected increments of activity within the relevant range.

Illustration 24-10
Overhead flexible budget report

	Barton Robotics.xls			

Home   Insert   Page Layout   Formulas   Data   Review   View

P18   fx

	A	B	C	D	E
1			**Barton Robotics**		
2			**Manufacturing Overhead Flexible Budget Report**		
3			**For the Year Ended December 31, 2014**		
4				Difference	
				Favorable - F	
5		Budget	Actual	Unfavorable - U	
6	Production in units	12,000	12,000		
7					
8	Variable costs				
9	Indirect materials ($25)	$ 300,000	$ 295,000	$5,000	F
10	Indirect labor ($26)	312,000	312,000	0	
11	Utilities ($19)	228,000	225,000	3,000	F
12	Total variable costs	840,000	832,000	8,000	F
13					
14	Fixed costs				
15	Depreciation	280,000	280,000	0	
16	Property taxes	70,000	70,000	0	
17	Supervision	50,000	50,000	0	
18	Total fixed costs	400,000	400,000	0	
19	Total costs	$1,240,000	$1,232,000	$8,000	F
20					

The activity index chosen should significantly influence the costs being budgeted. For manufacturing overhead costs, for example, the activity index is usually the same as the index used in developing the predetermined overhead rate—that is, direct labor hours or machine hours. For selling and administrative expenses, the activity index usually is sales or net sales.

The choice of the increment of activity is largely a matter of judgment. For example, if the relevant range is 8,000 to 12,000 direct labor hours, increments of 1,000 hours may be selected. The flexible budget is then prepared for each increment within the relevant range.

SERVICE COMPANY INSIGHT

Just What the Doctor Ordered?

Nobody is immune from the effects of declining revenues—not even movie stars. When the number of viewers of the television show "House," a medical drama, declined by almost 20%, Fox Broadcasting said it wanted to cut the license fee that it paid to NBCUniversal by 20%. What would NBCUniversal do in response? It might cut the size of the show's cast, which would reduce the payroll costs associated with the show. Or, it could reduce the number of episodes that take advantage of the full cast. Alternatively, it might threaten to quit providing the show to Fox altogether and instead present the show on its own NBC-affiliated channels.

Source: Sam Schechner, "Media Business Shorts: NBCU, Fox Taking Scalpel to 'House'," *Wall Street Journal Online* (April 17, 2011).

? Explain how the use of flexible budgets might help to identify the best solution to this problem. (See page 1235.)

Flexible Budget—A Case Study

To illustrate the flexible budget, we use Fox Company. Fox's management uses a **flexible budget for monthly comparisons** of actual and budgeted manufacturing overhead costs of the Finishing Department. The master budget for the year ending December 31, 2014, shows expected **annual** operating capacity of 120,000 direct labor hours and the following overhead costs.

Illustration 24-11
Master budget data

Variable Costs		Fixed Costs	
Indirect materials	$180,000	Depreciation	$180,000
Indirect labor	240,000	Supervision	120,000
Utilities	60,000	Property taxes	60,000
Total	$480,000	Total	$360,000

The four steps for developing the flexible budget are applied as follows.

STEP 1. Identify the activity index and the relevant range of activity. The activity index is direct labor hours. The relevant range is 8,000–12,000 direct labor hours per **month.**

STEP 2. Identify the variable costs, and determine the budgeted variable cost per unit of activity for each cost. There are three variable costs. The variable cost per unit is found by dividing each total budgeted cost by the direct labor hours used in preparing the annual master budget (120,000 hours). For Fox Company, the computations are:

Illustration 24-12
Computation of variable cost per direct labor hour

Variable Costs	Computation	Variable Cost per Direct Labor Hour
Indirect materials	$180,000 ÷ 120,000	$1.50
Indirect labor	$240,000 ÷ 120,000	2.00
Utilities	$ 60,000 ÷ 120,000	0.50
Total		$4.00

STEP 3. Identify the fixed costs, and determine the budgeted amount for each cost. There are three fixed costs. Since Fox desires **monthly budget data,** it divides each annual budgeted cost by 12 to find the monthly amounts. For Fox Company, the monthly budgeted fixed costs are depreciation $15,000, supervision $10,000, and property taxes $5,000.

STEP 4. Prepare the budget for selected increments of activity within the relevant range. Management prepares the budget in increments of 1,000 direct labor hours.

Illustration 24-13 shows Fox's flexible budget.

Illustration 24-13
Monthly overhead flexible budget

Fox Company.xls

Home | Insert | Page Layout | Formulas | Data | Review | View

P18   fx

	A	B	C	D	E	F
1		**Fox Company**				
2		**Monthly Manufacturing Overhead Flexible Budget**				
3		**Finishing Department**				
4		**For Months During the Year 2014**				
5	Activity level					
6	Direct labor hours	8,000	9,000	10,000	11,000	12,000
7	Variable costs					
8	Indirect materials ($1.50)[a]	$12,000[b]	$13,500	$15,000	$16,500	$18,000
9	Indirect labor ($2.00)[a]	16,000[c]	18,000	20,000	22,000	24,000
10	Utilities ($0.50)[a]	4,000[d]	4,500	5,000	5,500	6,000
11	Total variable costs	32,000	36,000	40,000	44,000	48,000
12	Fixed costs					
13	Depreciation	15,000	15,000	15,000	15,000	15,000
14	Supervision	10,000	10,000	10,000	10,000	10,000
15	Property taxes	5,000	5,000	5,000	5,000	5,000
16	Total fixed costs	30,000	30,000	30,000	30,000	30,000
17	Total costs	$62,000	$66,000	$70,000	$74,000	$78,000
18						
19	[a]Cost per direct labor hour; [b]8,000 x $1.50; [c]8,000 x $2.00; [d]8,000 x $0.50					

Fox uses the formula below to determine total budgeted costs at any level of activity.

Illustration 24-14
Formula for total budgeted costs

$$\text{Fixed Costs} + \text{Variable Costs*} = \text{Total Budgeted Costs}$$

*Total variable cost per unit of activity × Activity level.

For Fox, fixed costs are $30,000, and total variable cost per direct labor hour is $4 ($1.50 + $2.00 + $0.50). At 9,000 direct labor hours, total budgeted costs are $66,000 [$30,000 + ($4 × 9,000)]. At 8,622 direct labor hours, total budgeted costs are $64,488 [$30,000 + ($4 × 8,622)].

Total budgeted costs can also be shown graphically, as in Illustration 24-15 (page 1190). In the graph, the horizontal axis represents the activity index, and costs are indicated on the vertical axis. The graph highlights two activity levels (10,000 and 12,000). As shown, total budgeted costs at these activity levels are $70,000 [$30,000 + ($4 × 10,000)] and $78,000 [$30,000 + ($4 × 12,000)], respectively.

Helpful Hint
Using the data given for Fox, what amount of total costs would be budgeted for 10,600 direct labor hours? Answer: $30,000 fixed + $42,400 variable (i.e., 10,600 × $4) = $72,400 total.

Illustration 24-15
Graphic flexible budget data highlighting 10,000 and 12,000 activity levels

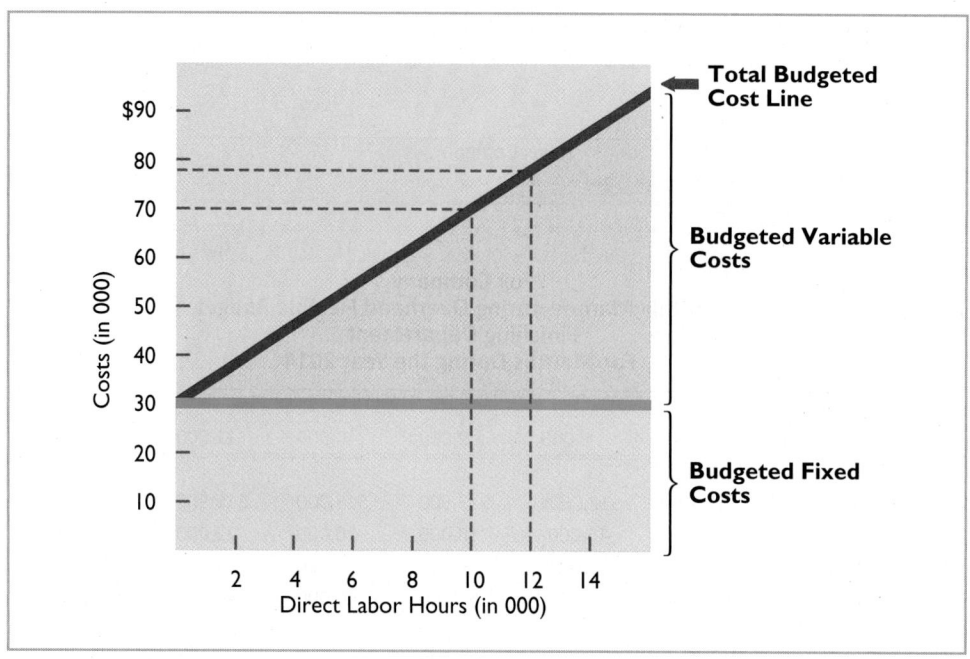

> **DO IT!**

Flexible Budgets

In Strassel Company's flexible budget graph, the fixed cost line and the total budgeted cost line intersect the vertical axis at $36,000. The total budgeted cost line is $186,000 at an activity level of 50,000 direct labor hours. Compute total budgeted costs at 30,000 direct labor hours.

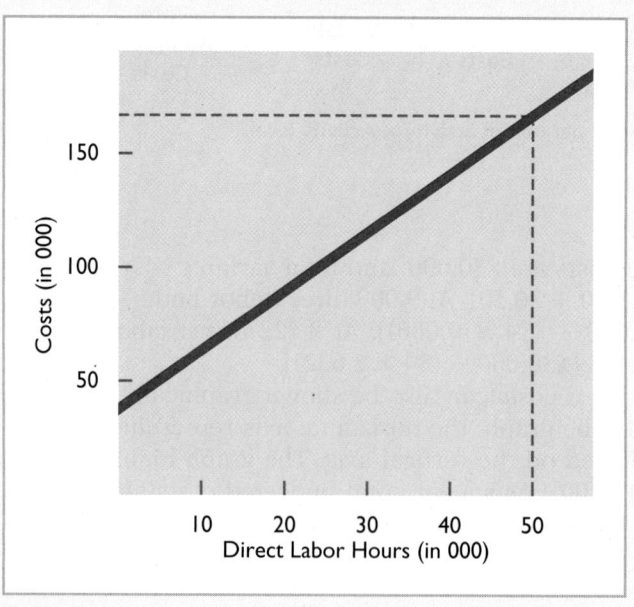

Action Plan

✔ Apply the formula:
Fixed costs + Variable
costs (Total variable
cost per unit × Activity
level) = Total budgeted
costs.

Solution

Using the graph, fixed costs are $36,000, and variable costs are $3 per direct labor hour [($186,000 − $36,000) ÷ 50,000]. Thus, at 30,000 direct labor hours, total budgeted costs are $126,000 [$36,000 + ($3 × 30,000)].

Related exercise material: **BE24-4, E24-3, E24-5, and** **24-1.**

✔ **The Navigator**

Flexible Budget Reports

Flexible budget reports are another type of internal report. The flexible budget report consists of two sections: (1) production data for a selected activity index, such as direct labor hours, and (2) cost data for variable and fixed costs. The report provides a basis for evaluating a manager's performance in two areas: production control and cost control. Flexible budget reports are widely used in production and service departments.

Illustration 24-16 shows a budget report for the Finishing Department of Fox Company for the month of January. In this month, 9,000 hours are worked. The budget data are therefore based on the flexible budget for 9,000 hours in Illustration 24-13 (page 1189). The actual cost data are assumed.

Illustration 24-16
Overhead flexible budget report

Fox Company.xls

	A	B	C	D	E
1		**Fox Company**			
2		**Manufacturing Overhead Flexible Budget Report**			
3		**Finishing Department**			
4		**For the Month Ended January 31, 2014**			
5				Difference	
6		Budget at	Actual costs at	Favorable - F	
7	Direct labor hours (DLH)	9,000 DLH	9,000 DLH	Unfavorable - U	
8					
9	Variable costs				
10	Indirect materials ($1.50)[a]	$13,500	$14,000	$ 500	U
11	Indirect labor ($2.00)[a]	18,000	17,000	1,000	F
12	Utilities ($0.50)[a]	4,500	4,600	100	U
13	Total variable costs	36,000	35,600	400	F
14					
15	Fixed costs				
16	Depreciation	15,000	15,000	0	
17	Supervision	10,000	10,000	0	
18	Property taxes	5,000	5,000	0	
19	Total fixed costs	30,000	30,000	0	
20	Total costs	$66,000	$65,600	$ 400	F
21					
22	[a]Cost per direct labor hour				

How appropriate is this report in evaluating the Finishing Department manager's performance in controlling overhead costs? The report clearly provides a reliable basis. Both actual and budget costs are based on the activity level worked during January. Since variable costs generally are incurred directly by the department, the difference between the budget allowance for those hours and the actual costs is the responsibility of the department manager.

In subsequent months, Fox Company will prepare other flexible budget reports. For each month, the budget data are based on the actual activity level attained. In February that level may be 11,000 direct labor hours, in July 10,000, and so on.

Note that this flexible budget is based on a single cost driver. A more accurate budget often can be developed using the activity-based costing concepts explained in Chapter 18.

SERVICE COMPANY INSIGHT

Budgets and the Exotic Newcastle Disease

Exotic Newcastle Disease, one of the most infectious bird diseases in the world, kills so swiftly that many victims die before any symptoms appear. When it broke out in Southern California, it could have spelled disaster for the San Diego Zoo. "We have one of the most valuable collections of birds in the world, if not *the* most valuable," says Paula Brock, CFO of the Zoological Society of San Diego, which operates the zoo.

Bird exhibits were closed to the public for several months (the disease, which is harmless to humans, can be carried on clothes and shoes). The tires of arriving delivery trucks were sanitized, as were the shoes of anyone visiting the zoo's nonpublic areas. Zookeeper uniforms had to be changed and cleaned daily. And ultimately, the zoo, with $150 million in revenues, spent almost half a million dollars on quarantine measures.

It worked: No birds got sick. Better yet, the damage to the rest of the zoo's budget was minimized by another protective measure: the monthly budget reforecast. "When we get a hit like this, we still have to find a way to make our bottom line," says Brock. Thanks to a new planning process Brock had introduced a year earlier, the zoo's scientists were able to raise the financial alarm as they redirected resources to ward off the disease. "Because we had timely awareness," she says, "we were able to make adjustments to weather the storm."

Budget reforecasting is nothing new. (The San Diego Zoo's annual static budget was behind the times before Brock took over as CFO.) But the reaction of the zoo's staff shows the benefits of Brock's immediate efforts to link strategy to the process. It's a move long touted by consultants as a key way to improve people's involvement in budgeting.

"To keep your company on a path, it has to have some kind of map," says Brock. "The budgeting-and-planning process is that map. I cannot imagine an organization feeling in control if it didn't have that sort of discipline."

Source: Tim Reason, "Budgeting in the Real World," *CFO Magazine* (July 12, 2005), *www.cfodirect.com/cfopublic.nsf/vContentPrint/649A82C8FF8AB06B85257037004* (accessed July 2005).

 What is the major benefit of tying a budget to the overall goals of the company? (See page 1236.)

> DO IT!

Flexible Budget Reports

Lawler Company expects to produce 40,000 units of product CV93 during the current year. Budgeted variable manufacturing costs per unit are direct materials $6, direct labor $15, and overhead $24. Annual budgeted fixed manufacturing overhead costs are $120,000 for depreciation and $60,000 for supervision.

In the current month, Lawler produced 5,000 units and incurred the following costs: direct materials $33,900, direct labor $74,200, variable overhead $120,500, depreciation $10,000, and supervision $5,000.

Prepare a flexible budget report. (*Note:* You do not have to prepare the heading.) Were costs controlled?

Solution

Action Plan

✔ Use budget for actual units produced.

✔ Classify each cost as variable or fixed.

✔ Determine monthly fixed costs by dividing annual amounts by 12.

✔ Determine the difference as favorable or unfavorable.

✔ Determine the difference in total variable costs, total fixed costs, and total costs.

Lawler Company.xls

Home   Insert   Page Layout   Formulas   Data   Review   View

P18   fx

	A	B	C	D	
1				Difference	
2		Budget at	Actual costs at	Favorable - F	
3	Units produced	5,000 units	5,000 units	Unfavorable - U	
4					
5	Variable costs				
6	Direct materials ($6)	$ 30,000	$ 33,900	$3,900	U
7	Direct labor ($15)	75,000	74,200	800	F
8	Overhead ($24)	120,000	120,500	500	U
9	Total variable costs	225,000	228,600	3,600	U
10					
11	Fixed costs				
12	Depreciation	10,000	10,000	0	
13	Supervision	5,000	5,000	0	
14	Total fixed costs	15,000	15,000	0	
15	Total costs	$240,000	$243,600	$3,600	U
16					
17					

The responsibility report indicates that actual direct labor was only about 1% different from the budget, and overhead was less than half a percent different. Both appear to have been well-controlled.

This was not the case for direct materials. Its 13% unfavorable difference should probably be investigated.

Actual fixed costs had no difference from budget and were well-controlled.

Related exercise material: **BE24-5, E24-4, E24-6, E24-7, E24-8, E24-10, and DO IT! 24-2.**

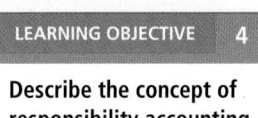 **The Navigator**

Responsibility Accounting

Like budgeting, responsibility accounting is an important part of management accounting. **Responsibility accounting** involves accumulating and reporting costs (and revenues, where relevant) on the basis of the manager who has the authority to make the day-to-day decisions about the items. Under responsibility accounting, a manager's performance is evaluated on matters directly under that manager's control. Responsibility accounting can be used at every level of management in which the following conditions exist.

 LEARNING OBJECTIVE   4

Describe the concept of responsibility accounting.

1. Costs and revenues can be directly associated with the specific level of management responsibility.

2. The costs and revenues can be controlled by employees at the level of responsibility with which they are associated.

3. Budget data can be developed for evaluating the manager's effectiveness in controlling the costs and revenues.

Illustration 24-17 depicts levels of responsibility for controlling costs.

Illustration 24-17
Responsibility for controllable costs at varying levels of management

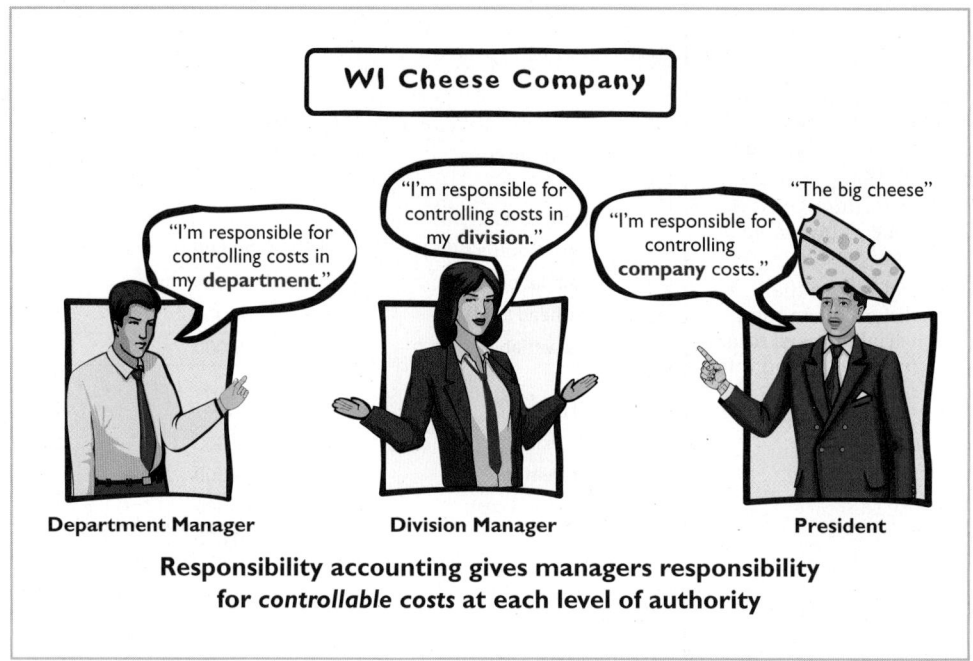

WI Cheese Company

"I'm responsible for controlling costs in my **department**."

"I'm responsible for controlling costs in my **division**."

"I'm responsible for controlling **company** costs."

"The big cheese"

Department Manager   Division Manager   President

Responsibility accounting gives managers responsibility for *controllable* costs at each level of authority

Helpful Hint
All companies use responsibility accounting. Without some form of responsibility accounting, there would be chaos in discharging management's control function.

Under responsibility accounting, any individual who controls a specified set of activities can be a responsibility center. Thus, responsibility accounting may extend from the lowest level of control to the top strata of management. Once responsibility is established, the company first measures and reports the effectiveness of the individual's performance for the specified activity. It then reports that measure upward throughout the organization.

Responsibility accounting is especially valuable in a decentralized company. **Decentralization** means that the control of operations is delegated to many managers throughout the organization. The term **segment** is sometimes used to identify an area of responsibility in decentralized operations. Under responsibility accounting, companies prepare segment reports periodically, such as monthly, quarterly, and annually, to evaluate managers' performance.

Responsibility accounting is an essential part of any effective system of budgetary control. The reporting of costs and revenues under responsibility accounting differs from budgeting in two respects:

1. A distinction is made between controllable and noncontrollable items.

2. Performance reports either emphasize or include only items controllable by the individual manager.

Responsibility accounting applies to both profit and not-for-profit entities. For-profit entities seek to maximize net income. Not-for-profit entities wish to provide services as efficiently as possible.

MANAGEMENT INSIGHT

Competition versus Collaboration

Many compensation and promotion programs encourage competition among employees for pay raises. To get ahead you have to perform better than your fellow employees. While this may encourage hard work, it does not foster collaboration, and it can lead to distrust and disloyalty. Such results have led some companies to believe that cooperation and collaboration are essential in order to succeed in today's environment. For example, division managers might increase collaboration (and reduce costs) by sharing design and marketing resources or by jointly negotiating with suppliers. In addition, companies can reduce the need to hire and lay off employees by sharing employees across divisions as human resource needs increase and decrease.

As a consequence, many companies now explicitly include measures of collaboration in their performance measures. For example, Procter & Gamble measures collaboration in employees' annual performance reviews. At Cisco Systems the assessment of an employee's teamwork can affect the annual bonus by as much as 20%.

Source: Carol Hymowitz, "Rewarding Competitors Over Collaboration No Longer Makes Sense," *Wall Street Journal* (February 13, 2006).

 How might managers of separate divisions be able to reduce division costs through collaboration? (See page 1236.)

Controllable versus Noncontrollable Revenues and Costs

All costs and revenues are controllable at some level of responsibility within a company. This truth underscores the adage by the CEO of any organization that "the buck stops here." Under responsibility accounting, the critical issue is **whether the cost or revenue is controllable at the level of responsibility with which it is associated**. A cost over which a manager has control is called a **controllable cost**. From this definition, it follows that:

1. All costs are controllable by top management because of the broad range of its authority.

2. Fewer costs are controllable as one moves down to each lower level of managerial responsibility because of the manager's decreasing authority.

In general, **costs incurred directly by a level of responsibility are controllable at that level**. In contrast, costs incurred indirectly and allocated to a responsibility level are **noncontrollable costs** at that level.

> **Helpful Hint**
> Are there more or fewer controllable costs as you move to higher levels of management?
> Answer: More.

> **Helpful Hint**
> The longer the time span, the more likely that the cost becomes controllable.

Principles of Performance Evaluation

Performance evaluation is at the center of responsibility accounting. It is a management function that compares actual results with budget goals. It involves both behavioral and reporting principles.

MANAGEMENT BY EXCEPTION

Management by exception means that top management's review of a budget report is focused either entirely or primarily on differences between actual results and planned objectives. This approach enables top management to focus on problem areas. For example, many companies now use online reporting systems for employees to file their travel and entertainment expense reports. In addition to cutting reporting time in half, the online system enables managers to quickly analyze variances from travel budgets. This cuts down on expense account "padding" such as spending too much on meals or falsifying documents for costs that were never actually incurred.

Management by exception does not mean that top management will investigate every difference. For this approach to be effective, there must be guidelines for identifying an exception. The usual criteria are materiality and controllability.

MATERIALITY Without quantitative guidelines, management would have to investigate every budget difference regardless of the amount. Materiality is usually expressed as a percentage difference from budget. For example, management may set the percentage difference at 5% for important items and 10% for other items. Managers will investigate all differences either over or under budget by the specified percentage. Costs over budget warrant investigation to determine why they were not controlled. Likewise, costs under budget merit investigation to determine whether costs critical to profitability are being curtailed. For example, if maintenance costs are budgeted at $80,000 but only $40,000 is spent, major unexpected breakdowns in productive facilities may occur in the future.

Alternatively, a company may specify a single percentage difference from budget for all items and supplement this guideline with a minimum dollar limit. For example, the exception criteria may be stated at 5% of budget or more than $10,000.

CONTROLLABILITY OF THE ITEM Exception guidelines are more restrictive for controllable items than for items the manager cannot control. In fact, there may be no guidelines for noncontrollable items. For example, a large unfavorable difference between actual and budgeted property tax expense may not be flagged for investigation because the only possible causes are an unexpected increase in the tax rate or in the assessed value of the property. An investigation into the difference would be useless: The manager cannot control either cause.

BEHAVIORAL PRINCIPLES

The human factor is critical in evaluating performance. Behavioral principles include the following.

1. **Managers of responsibility centers should have direct input into the process of establishing budget goals of their area of responsibility.** Without such input, managers may view the goals as unrealistic or arbitrarily set by top management. Such views adversely affect the managers' motivation to meet the targeted objectives.

2. **The evaluation of performance should be based entirely on matters that are controllable by the manager being evaluated.** Criticism of a manager on matters outside his or her control reduces the effectiveness of the evaluation process. It leads to negative reactions by a manager and to doubts about the fairness of the company's evaluation policies.

3. **Top management should support the evaluation process.** As explained earlier, the evaluation process begins at the lowest level of responsibility and extends upward to the highest level of management. Managers quickly lose faith in the process when top management ignores, overrules, or bypasses established procedures for evaluating a manager's performance.

4. **The evaluation process must allow managers to respond to their evaluations.** Evaluation is not a one-way street. Managers should have the opportunity to defend their performance. Evaluation without feedback is both impersonal and ineffective.

5. The evaluation should identify both good and poor performance. Praise for good performance is a powerful motivating factor for a manager. This is especially true when a manager's compensation includes rewards for meeting budget goals.

REPORTING PRINCIPLES

Performance evaluation under responsibility accounting should be based on certain reporting principles. These principles pertain primarily to the internal reports that provide the basis for evaluating performance. Performance reports should:

1. Contain only data that are controllable by the manager of the responsibility center.

2. Provide accurate and reliable budget data to measure performance.

3. Highlight significant differences between actual results and budget goals.

4. Be tailor-made for the intended evaluation.

5. Be prepared at reasonable time intervals.

In recent years, companies have come under increasing pressure from influential shareholder groups to do a better job of linking executive pay to corporate performance. For example, software maker Siebel Systems unveiled a new incentive plan after lengthy discussions with the California Public Employees' Retirement System. One unique feature of the plan is that managers' targets will be publicly disclosed at the beginning of each year for investors to evaluate.

MANAGEMENT INSIGHT

Flexible Manufacturing Requires Flexible Accounting

Flexible budgeting is useful because it enables managers to evaluate performance in light of changing conditions. But the ability to react quickly to changing conditions is even more important. Among automobile manufacturing facilities in the U.S., nobody's plants are more flexible than Honda. The manufacturing facilities of some auto companies can make slight alterations to the features of a vehicle in response to changes in demand for particular features. But for most plants, to switch from production of one type of vehicle to a completely different type of vehicle, when demand for types of vehicles shifts, typically takes months and costs hundreds of millions of dollars. But at the Honda plant, the switch takes minutes. For example, it takes about five minutes to install different hand-like parts on the robots so they can switch from making Civic compacts to the longer, taller CR-V crossover. This ability to adjust quickly to changing demand gave Honda a huge advantage when gas prices surged and demand for more fuel-efficient cars increased quickly.

Source: Kate Linebaugh, "Honda's Flexible Plants Provide Edge," *Wall Street Journal Online* (September 23, 2008).

 What implications do these improvements in production capabilities have for management accounting information and performance evaluation within the organization? (See page 1236.)

Responsibility Reporting System

A **responsibility reporting system** involves the preparation of a report for each level of responsibility in the company's organization chart. To illustrate such a system, we use the partial organization chart and production departments of Francis Chair Company in Illustration 24-18 (page 1198).

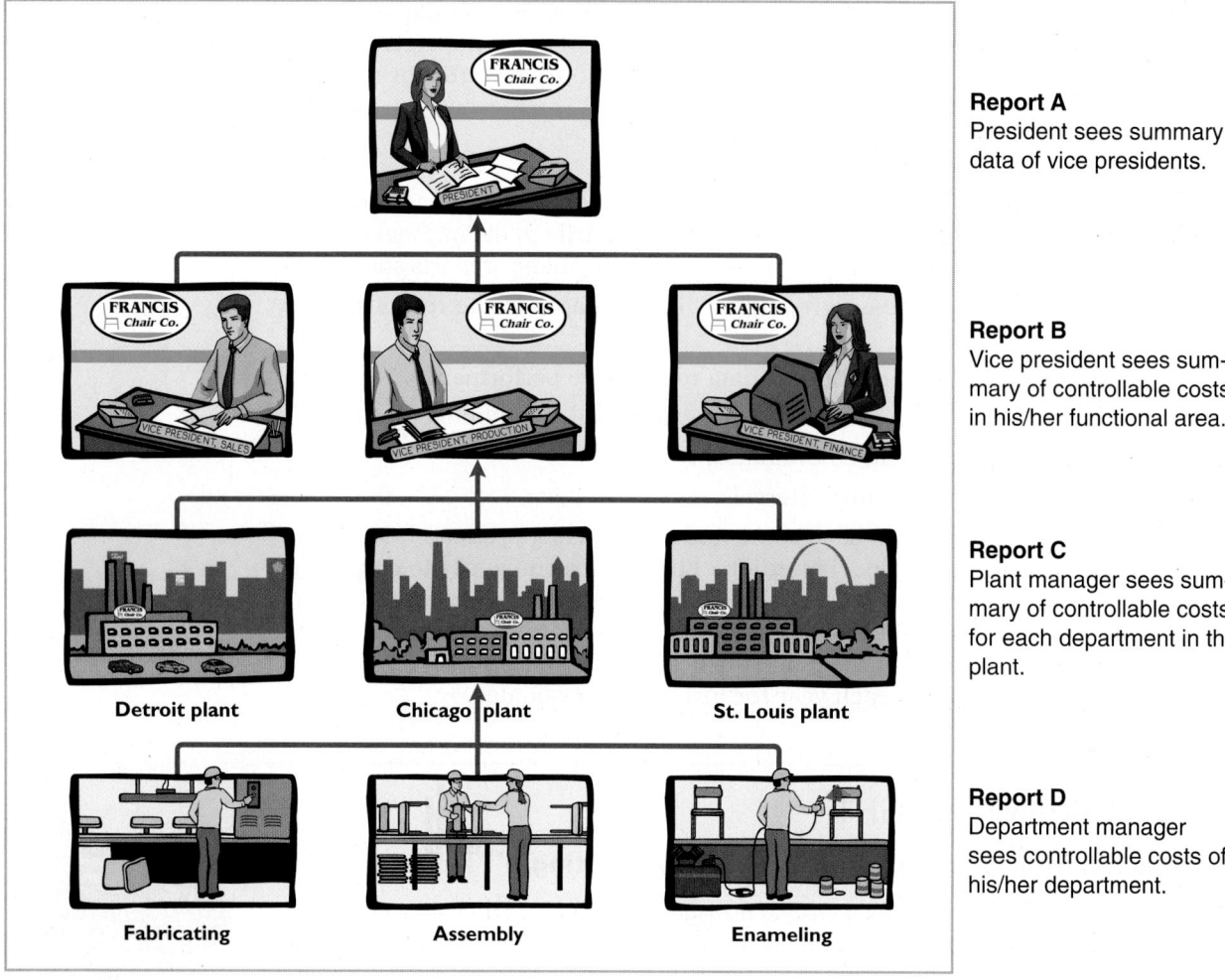

Report A
President sees summary data of vice presidents.

Report B
Vice president sees summary of controllable costs in his/her functional area.

Report C
Plant manager sees summary of controllable costs for each department in the plant.

Report D
Department manager sees controllable costs of his/her department.

Detroit plant   Chicago plant   St. Louis plant

Fabricating   Assembly   Enameling

Illustration 24-18
Partial organization chart

The responsibility reporting system begins with the lowest level of responsibility for controlling costs and moves upward to each higher level. Illustration 24-19 details the connections between levels.

A brief description of the four reports for Francis Chair Company is as follows.

1. **Report D** is typical of reports that go to department managers. Similar reports are prepared for the managers of the Fabricating, Assembly, and Enameling Departments.

2. **Report C** is an example of reports that are sent to plant managers. It shows the costs of the Chicago plant that are controllable at the second level of responsibility. In addition, Report C shows summary data for each department that is controlled by the plant manager. Similar reports are prepared for the Detroit and St. Louis plant managers.

3. **Report B** illustrates the reports at the third level of responsibility. It shows the controllable costs of the vice president of production and summary data on the three assembly plants for which this officer is responsible. Similar reports are prepared for the vice presidents of sales and finance.

4. **Report A** is typical of reports that go to the top level of responsibility—the president. It shows the controllable costs and expenses of this office and summary data on the vice presidents that are accountable to the president.

Illustration 24-19
Responsibility reporting system

Report A
President sees summary data of vice presidents.

Report A.xls

	A	B	C	D	E
1			**Report A**		
2					
3	To President			Month: January	
4	Controllable Costs:	Budget	Actual	Fav/Unfav	
5	President	$ 150,000	$ 151,500	$ 1,500	U
6	Vice Presidents:				
7	Sales	185,000	187,000	2,000	U
8	Production	1,179,000	1,186,300	7,300	U
9	Finance	100,000	101,000	1,000	U
10	Total	$1,614,000	$1,625,800	$11,800	U
11					

Report B
Vice president sees summary of controllable costs in his/her functional area.

Report B.xls

	A	B	C	D	E
1			**Report B**		
2					
3	To Vice President Production			Month: January	
4	Controllable Costs:	Budget	Actual	Fav/Unfav	
5	VP Production	$ 125,000	$ 126,000	$ 1,000	U
6	Assembly Plants:				
7	Detroit	420,000	418,000	2,000	F
8	Chicago	304,000	309,300	5,300	U
9	St. Louis	330,000	333,000	3,000	U
10	Total	$1,179,000	$1,186,300	$ 7,300	U
11					

Report C
Plant manager sees summary of controllable costs for each department in the plant.

Report C.xls

	A	B	C	D	E
1			**Report C**		
2					
3	To Plant Manager-Chicago			Month: January	
4	Controllable Costs:	Budget	Actual	Fav/Unfav	
5	Chicago Plant	$110,000	$113,000	$3,000	U
6	Departments:				
7	Fabricating	84,000	85,300	1,300	U
8	Enameling	62,000	64,000	2,000	U
9	Assembly	48,000	47,000	1,000	F
10	Total	$304,000	$309,300	$5,300	U
11					

Report D
Department manager sees controllable costs of his/her department.

Report D.xls

	A	B	C	D	E
1			**Report D**		
2					
3	To Fabricating Dept. Manager			Month: January	
4	Controllable Costs:	Budget	Actual	Fav/Unfav	
5	Direct Materials	$20,000	$20,500	$ 500	U
6	Direct Labor	40,000	41,000	1,000	U
7	Overhead	24,000	23,800	200	F
8	Total	$84,000	$85,300	$1,300	U
9					

A responsibility reporting system permits management by exception at each level of responsibility. And, each higher level of responsibility can obtain the detailed report for each lower level of responsibility. For example, the vice president of production in the Francis Chair Company may request the Chicago plant manager's report because this plant is $5,300 over budget.

This type of reporting system also permits comparative evaluations. In Illustration 24-19, the Chicago plant manager can easily rank the department managers' effectiveness in controlling manufacturing costs. Comparative rankings provide further incentive for a manager to control costs.

Types of Responsibility Centers

There are three basic types of responsibility centers: cost centers, profit centers, and investment centers. These classifications indicate the degree of responsibility the manager has for the performance of the center.

A **cost center** incurs costs (and expenses) but does not directly generate revenues. Managers of cost centers have the authority to incur costs. They are evaluated on their ability to control costs. **Cost centers are usually either production departments or service departments.** Production departments participate directly in making the product. Service departments provide only support services. In a Ford Motor Company automobile plant, the welding, painting, and assembling departments are production departments. Ford's maintenance, cafeteria, and human resources departments are service departments. All of them are cost centers.

A **profit center** incurs costs (and expenses) and also generates revenues. Managers of profit centers are judged on the profitability of their centers. Examples of profit centers include the individual departments of a retail store, such as clothing, furniture, and automotive products, and branch offices of banks.

Like a profit center, an **investment center** incurs costs (and expenses) and generates revenues. In addition, an investment center has control over decisions regarding the assets available for use. Investment center managers are evaluated on both the profitability of the center and the rate of return earned on the funds invested. Investment centers are often associated with subsidiary companies. Utility Duke Energy has operating divisions such as electric utility, energy trading, and natural gas. Investment center managers control or significantly influence investment decisions related to such matters as plant expansion and entry into new market areas. Illustration 24-20 depicts the three types of responsibility centers.

Helpful Hint
(1) Is the jewelry department of Macy's department store a profit center or a cost center?
(2) Is the props department of a movie studio a profit center or a cost center?
Answers: (1) Profit center.
(2) Cost center.

Illustration 24-20
Types of responsibility centers

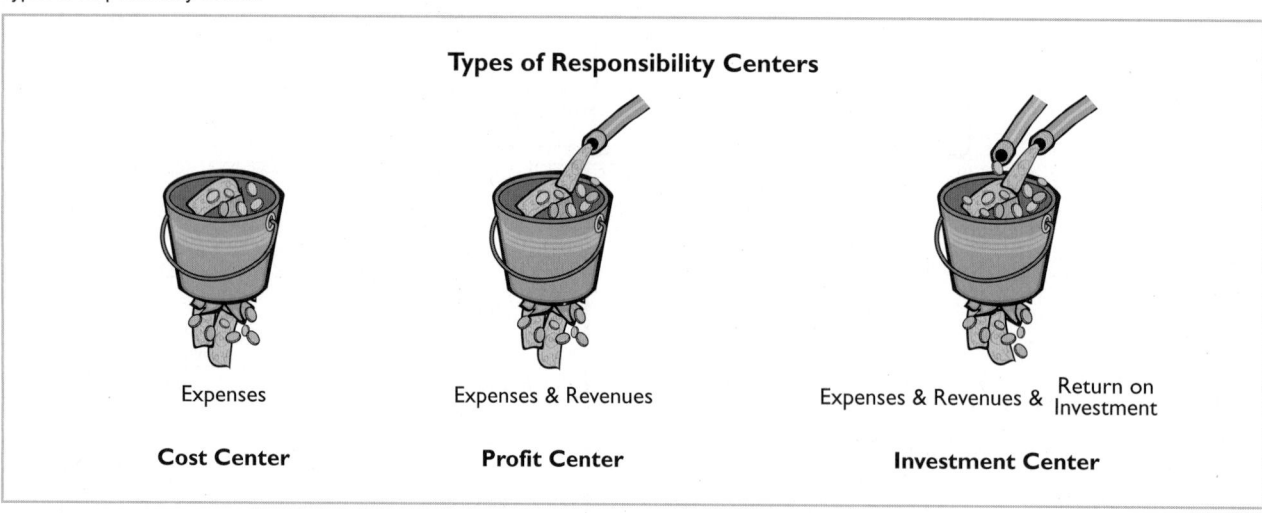

Types of Responsibility Centers

Expenses

Cost Center

Expenses & Revenues

Profit Center

Expenses & Revenues & Return on Investment

Investment Center

Responsibility Accounting for Cost Centers

The evaluation of a manager's performance for cost centers is based on his or her ability to meet budgeted goals for controllable costs. **Responsibility reports for cost centers compare actual controllable costs with flexible budget data.**

Illustration 24-21 shows a responsibility report. The report is adapted from the flexible budget report for Fox Company in Illustration 24-16 (page 1191). It assumes that the Finishing Department manager is able to control all manufacturing overhead costs except depreciation, property taxes, and his own monthly salary of $6,000. The remaining $4,000 ($10,000 − $6,000) of supervision costs are assumed to apply to other supervisory personnel within the Finishing Department, whose salaries are controllable by the manager.

LEARNING OBJECTIVE   5

Indicate the features of responsibility reports for cost centers.

	Fox Company.xls				
Home Insert Page Layout Formulas Data Review View					
P18		fx			
	A	B	C	D	E
1		**Fox Company**			
2		**Finishing Department**			
3		**Responsibility Report**			
4		**For the Month Ended January 31, 2014**			
5				Difference	
				Favorable - F	
6	Controllable Costs	Budget	Actual	Unfavorable - U	
7	Indirect materials	$13,500	$14,000	$ 500	U
8	Indirect labor	18,000	17,000	$1,000	F
9	Utilities	4,500	4,600	100	U
10	**Supervision**	4,000	4,000	0	
11		$40,000	$39,600	$ 400	F
12					

Illustration 24-21
Responsibility report for a cost center

The report in Illustration 24-21 includes **only controllable costs**, and no distinction is made between variable and fixed costs. The responsibility report continues the concept of management by exception. In this case, top management may request an explanation of the $1,000 favorable difference in indirect labor and/or the $500 unfavorable difference in indirect materials.

Responsibility Accounting for Profit Centers

To evaluate the performance of a profit center manager, upper management needs detailed information about both controllable revenues and controllable costs. The operating revenues earned by a profit center, such as sales, are controllable by the manager. All variable costs (and expenses) incurred by the center are also controllable by the manager because they vary with sales. However, to determine the controllability of fixed costs, it is necessary to distinguish between direct and indirect fixed costs.

LEARNING OBJECTIVE   6

Identify the content of responsibility reports for profit centers.

DIRECT AND INDIRECT FIXED COSTS

A profit center may have both direct and indirect fixed costs. **Direct fixed costs** relate specifically to one center and are incurred for the sole benefit of that center. Examples of such costs include the salaries established by the profit center manager for supervisory personnel and the cost of a timekeeping department for the center's employees. Since these fixed costs can be traced directly to a center, they are also called **traceable costs. Most direct fixed costs are controllable by the profit center manager.**

In contrast, **indirect fixed costs** pertain to a company's overall operating activities and are incurred for the benefit of more than one profit center. Management allocates indirect fixed costs to profit centers on some type of equitable basis. For example, property taxes on a building occupied by more than one center may be allocated on the basis of square feet of floor space used by each center. Or, the costs of a company's human resources department may be allocated to profit centers on the basis of the number of employees in each center. Because these fixed costs apply to more than one center, they are also called **common costs. Most indirect fixed costs are not controllable by the profit center manager.**

Helpful Hint
Recognize that we are emphasizing *financial* measures of performance. These days companies are also making an effort to stress *nonfinancial* performance measures such as product quality, labor productivity, market growth, materials' yield, manufacturing flexibility, and technological capability.

RESPONSIBILITY REPORT

The responsibility report for a profit center shows budgeted and actual **controllable revenues and costs.** The report is prepared using the cost-volume-profit income statement explained in Chapter 19. In the report:

1. Controllable fixed costs are deducted from contribution margin.

2. The excess of contribution margin over controllable fixed costs is identified as **controllable margin.**

3. Noncontrollable fixed costs are not reported.

Illustration 24-22 shows the responsibility report for the manager of the Marine Division, a profit center of Mantle Company. For the year, the Marine Division also had $60,000 of indirect fixed costs that were not controllable by the profit center manager.

Illustration 24-22
Responsibility report for profit center

		Budget	Actual	Difference Favorable - F Unfavorable - U	
7	Sales	$1,200,000	$1,150,000	$50,000	U
8	Variable costs				
9	Cost of goods sold	500,000	490,000	10,000	F
10	Selling and administrative	160,000	156,000	4,000	F
11	Total	660,000	646,000	14,000	F
12	Contribution margin	540,000	504,000	36,000	U
13	Controllable fixed costs				
14	Cost of goods sold	100,000	100,000	0	
15	Selling and administrative	80,000	80,000	0	
16	Total	180,000	180,000	0	
17	Controllable margin	$ 360,000	$ 324,000	$36,000	U

Mantle Company
Marine Division
Responsibility Report
For the Year Ended December 31, 2014

Controllable margin is considered to be the best measure of the manager's performance **in controlling revenues and costs**. The report in Illustration 24-22 shows that the manager's performance was below budgeted expectations by 10% ($36,000 ÷ $360,000). Top management would likely investigate the causes of this unfavorable result. Note that the report does not show the Marine Division's noncontrollable fixed costs of $60,000. These costs would be included in a report on the profitability of the profit center.

Management also may choose to see **monthly** responsibility reports for profit centers. In addition, responsibility reports may include cumulative year-to-date results.

> **DO IT!**

Profit Center Responsibility Report

Midwest Division operates as a profit center. It reports the following for the year:

	Budget	Actual
Sales	$1,500,000	$1,700,000
Variable costs	700,000	800,000
Controllable fixed costs	400,000	400,000
Noncontrollable fixed costs	200,000	200,000

Prepare a responsibility report for the Midwest Division for December 31, 2014.

Solution

Action Plan

✔ Deduct variable costs from sales to show contribution margin.

✔ Deduct controllable fixed costs from the contribution margin to show controllable margin.

✔ Do not report noncontrollable fixed costs.

Midwest Division
Responsibility Report
For the Year Ended December 31, 2014

	Budget	Actual	Difference Favorable F Unfavorable U
Sales	$1,500,000	$1,700,000	$200,000 F
Variable costs	700,000	800,000	100,000 U
Contribution margin	800,000	900,000	100,000 F
Controllable fixed costs	400,000	400,000	–0–
Controllable margin	$ 400,000	$ 500,000	$100,000 F

Related exercise material: **BE24-7, E24-15, and** DO IT! **24-3.**

 The Navigator

Responsibility Accounting for Investment Centers

As explained earlier, an investment center manager can control or significantly influence the investment funds available for use. Thus, the primary basis for evaluating the performance of a manager of an investment center is **return on investment (ROI)**. The return on investment is considered to be a useful performance measurement because it shows the **effectiveness of the manager in utilizing the assets at his or her disposal**.

LEARNING OBJECTIVE 7

Explain the basis and formula used in evaluating performance in investment centers.

RETURN ON INVESTMENT (ROI)

The formula for computing ROI for an investment center, together with assumed illustrative data, is shown in Illustration 24-23 (page 1204).

Both factors in the formula are controllable by the investment center manager. Operating assets consist of current assets and plant assets used in operations by the

Illustration 24-23
ROI formula

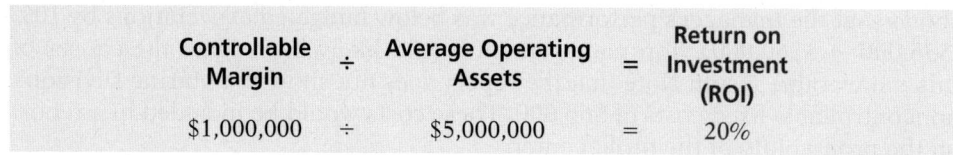

Controllable Margin	÷	Average Operating Assets	=	Return on Investment (ROI)
$1,000,000	÷	$5,000,000	=	20%

center and controlled by the manager. Nonoperating assets such as idle plant assets and land held for future use are excluded. Average operating assets are usually based on the cost or book value of the assets at the beginning and end of the year.

RESPONSIBILITY REPORT

The scope of the investment center manager's responsibility significantly affects the content of the performance report. Since an investment center is an independent entity for operating purposes, **all fixed costs are controllable by its manager**. For example, the manager is responsible for depreciation on investment center assets. Therefore, more fixed costs are identified as controllable in the performance report for an investment center manager than in a performance report for a profit center manager. The report also shows budgeted and actual ROI below controllable margin.

To illustrate this responsibility report, we will now assume that the Marine Division of Mantle Company is an investment center. It has budgeted and actual average operating assets of $2,000,000. The manager can control $60,000 of fixed costs that were not controllable when the division was a profit center. Illustration 24-24 shows the division's responsibility report.

Illustration 24-24
Responsibility report for investment center

	Mantle Company.xls			
Home Insert Page Layout Formulas Data Review View				
P18	fx			

	A	B	C	D	E
1		**Mantle Company**			
2		**Marine Division**			
3		**Responsibility Report**			
4		**For the Year Ended December 31, 2014**			
5				Difference	
6		Budget	Actual	Favorable - F Unfavorable - U	
7	Sales	$ 1,200,000	$ 1,150,000	$ 50,000	U
8	Variable costs				
9	Cost of goods sold	500,000	490,000	10,000	F
10	Selling and administrative	160,000	156,000	4,000	F
11	Total	660,000	646,000	14,000	F
12	Contribution margin	540,000	504,000	36,000	U
13	Controllable fixed costs				
14	Cost of goods sold	100,000	100,000	0	
15	Selling and administrative	80,000	80,000	0	
16	Other fixed costs	60,000	60,000	0	
17	Total	$ 240,000	$ 240,000	0	
18	Controllable margin	$ 300,000	$ 264,000	$ 36,000	U
19	Return on investment	15.0%	13.2%	1.8%	U
20		(a)	(b)	(c)	
21					
22		(a) $ 300,000 / $2,000,000	(b) $ 264,000 / $2,000,000	(c) $ 36,000 / $2,000,000	
23					

The report shows that the manager's performance based on ROI was below budget expectations by 1.8% (15.0% versus 13.2%). Top management would likely want an explanation of the reasons for this unfavorable result.

JUDGMENTAL FACTORS IN ROI

The return on investment approach includes two judgmental factors:

1. **Valuation of operating assets.** Operating assets may be valued at acquisition cost, book value, appraised value, or fair value. The first two bases are readily available from the accounting records.

2. **Margin (income) measure.** This measure may be controllable margin, income from operations, or net income.

   Each of the alternative values for operating assets can provide a reliable basis for evaluating a manager's performance as long as it is consistently applied between reporting periods. However, the use of income measures other than controllable margin will not result in a valid basis for evaluating the performance of an investment center manager.

IMPROVING ROI

The manager of an investment center can improve ROI by increasing controllable margin, and/or reducing average operating assets. To illustrate, we will use the following assumed data for the Laser Division of Berra Company.

Sales	$2,000,000
Variable costs	1,100,000
Contribution margin (45%)	900,000
Controllable fixed costs	300,000
Controllable margin (a)	$ 600,000
Average operating assets (b)	$5,000,000
Return on investment (a) ÷ (b)	12%

Illustration 24-25
Assumed data for Laser Division

INCREASING CONTROLLABLE MARGIN Controllable margin can be increased by increasing sales or by reducing variable and controllable fixed costs as follows.

1. **Increase sales 10%.** Sales will increase $200,000 ($2,000,000 × .10). Assuming no change in the contribution margin percentage of 45%, contribution margin will increase $90,000 ($200,000 × .45). Controllable margin will increase by the same amount because controllable fixed costs will not change. Thus, controllable margin becomes $690,000 ($600,000 + $90,000). The new ROI is 13.8%, computed as follows.

$$ ROI = \frac{\text{Controllable margin}}{\text{Average operating assets}} = \frac{\$690,000}{\$5,000,000} = \textbf{13.8\%} $$

Illustration 24-26
ROI computation—increase in sales

An increase in sales benefits both the investment center and the company if it results in new business. It would not benefit the company if the increase was achieved at the expense of other investment centers.

2. Decrease variable and fixed costs 10%. Total costs decrease $140,000 [($1,100,000 + $300,000) × .10]. This reduction results in a corresponding increase in controllable margin. Thus, controllable margin becomes $740,000 ($600,000 + $140,000). The new ROI is 14.8%, computed as follows.

Illustration 24-27
ROI computation—decrease in costs

$$\text{ROI} = \frac{\text{Controllable margin}}{\text{Average operating assets}} = \frac{\$740,000}{\$5,000,000} = \mathbf{14.8\%}$$

This course of action is clearly beneficial when the reduction in costs is the result of eliminating waste and inefficiency. But, a reduction in costs that results from cutting expenditures on vital activities, such as required maintenance and inspections, is not likely to be acceptable to top management.

REDUCING AVERAGE OPERATING ASSETS Assume that average operating assets are reduced 10% or $500,000 ($5,000,000 × .10). Average operating assets become $4,500,000 ($5,000,000 − $500,000). Since controllable margin remains unchanged at $600,000, the new ROI is 13.3%, computed as follows.

Illustration 24-28
ROI computation—decrease in operating assets

$$\text{ROI} = \frac{\text{Controllable margin}}{\text{Average operating assets}} = \frac{\$600,000}{\$4,500,000} = \mathbf{13.3\%}$$

Reductions in operating assets may or may not be prudent. It is beneficial to eliminate overinvestment in inventories and to dispose of excessive plant assets. However, it is unwise to reduce inventories below expected needs or to dispose of essential plant assets.

ACCOUNTING ACROSS THE ORGANIZATION

Does Hollywood Look at ROI?

If Hollywood were run like a real business, where things like return on investment mattered, there would be one unchallenged, sacred principle that studio chieftains would never violate: Make lots of G-rated movies.

No matter how you slice the movie business—by star vehicles, by budget levels, or by sequels or franchises—by far the best return on investment comes from the not-so-glamorous world of G-rated films. The problem is, these movies represent only 3% of the total films made in a typical year.

Take 2003: According to Motion Picture Association of America statistics, of the 940 movies released that year, only 29 were G-rated. Yet the highest-grossing movie of the year, *Finding Nemo*, was G-rated. . . . On the flip side are the R-rated films, which dominate the total releases and yet yield the worst return on investment. A whopping 646 R-rated films were released in 2003—69% of the total output—but only four of the top-20 grossing movies of the year were R-rated films.

This trend—G-rated movies are good for business but underproduced; R-rated movies are bad for business, and yet overdone—is something that has been driving economists batty for the past several years.

Source: David Grainger, "The Dysfunctional Family-Film Business," *Fortune* (January 10, 2005), pp. 20–21.

 What might be the reason that movie studios do not produce G-rated movies as much as R-rated ones? (See page 1236.)

> DO IT!

Performance Evaluation

The service division of Metro Industries reported the following results for 2014.

Sales	$400,000
Variable costs	320,000
Controllable fixed costs	40,800
Average operating assets	280,000

Management is considering the following independent courses of action in 2015 in order to maximize the return on investment for this division.

1. Reduce average operating assets by $80,000, with no change in controllable margin.
2. Increase sales $80,000, with no change in the contribution margin percentage.

(a) Compute the controllable margin and the return on investment for 2014.

(b) Compute the controllable margin and the expected return on investment for each proposed alternative.

Solution

Action Plan

✔ Recall key formulas: Sales − Variable costs = Contribution margin.

✔ Contribution margin ÷ Sales = Contribution margin percentage.

✔ Contribution margin − Controllable fixed costs = Controllable margin.

✔ Return on investment = Controllable margin ÷ Average operating assets.

(a) Return on investment for 2014

Sales	$400,000
Variable costs	320,000
Contribution margin	80,000
Controllable fixed costs	40,800
Controllable margin	$ 39,200

$$\text{Return on investment} \quad \frac{\$39,200}{\$280,000} = 14\%$$

(b) Expected return on investment for alternative 1:

$$\frac{\$39,200}{\$280,000 - \$80,000} = 19.6\%$$

Expected return on investment for alternative 2:

Sales ($400,000 + $80,000)	$480,000
Variable costs ($320,000/$400,000 × $480,000)	384,000
Contribution margin	96,000
Controllable fixed costs	40,800
Controllable margin	$ 55,200

$$\text{Return on investment} \quad \frac{\$55,200}{\$280,000} = 19.7\%$$

Related exercise material: **BE24-8, BE24-9, BE24-10, E24-16, E24-17, and** **24-4.**

✔ **The Navigator**

> Comprehensive **DO IT!**

Glenda Company uses a flexible budget for manufacturing overhead based on direct labor hours. For 2014, the master overhead budget for the Packaging Department based on 300,000 direct labor hours was as follows.

	Variable Costs		Fixed Costs	
Indirect labor		$360,000	Supervision	$ 60,000
Supplies and lubricants		150,000	Depreciation	24,000
Maintenance		210,000	Property taxes	18,000
Utilities		120,000	Insurance	12,000
		$840,000		$114,000

During July, 24,000 direct labor hours were worked. The company incurred the following variable costs in July: indirect labor $30,200, supplies and lubricants $11,600, maintenance $17,500, and utilities $9,200. Actual fixed overhead costs were the same as monthly budgeted fixed costs.

Instructions

Prepare a flexible budget report for the Packaging Department for July.

Solution to Comprehensive DO IT!

Action Plan

✔ Classify each cost as variable or fixed.

✔ Compute the budgeted cost per direct labor hour for all variable costs.

✔ Use budget data for actual direct labor hours worked.

✔ Determine the difference between budgeted and actual costs.

✔ Identify the difference as favorable or unfavorable.

✔ Determine the difference in total variable costs, total fixed costs, and total costs.

Glenda Company
Manufacturing Overhead Budget Report (Flexible)
Packaging Department
For the Month Ended July 31, 2014

Direct labor hours (DLH)	Budget 24,000 DLH	Actual Costs 24,000 DLH	Difference Favorable F Unfavorable U
Variable costs			
Indirect labor ($1.20[a])	$28,800	$30,200	$1,400 U
Supplies and lubricants ($0.50[a])	12,000	11,600	400 F
Maintenance ($0.70[a])	16,800	17,500	700 U
Utilities ($0.40[a])	9,600	9,200	400 F
Total variable	67,200	68,500	1,300 U
Fixed costs			
Supervision	$ 5,000[b]	$ 5,000	–0–
Depreciation	2,000[b]	2,000	–0–
Property taxes	1,500[b]	1,500	–0–
Insurance	1,000[b]	1,000	–0–
Total fixed	9,500	9,500	–0–
Total costs	$76,700	$78,000	$1,300 U

[a]($360,000 ÷ 300,000; $150,000 ÷ 300,000; $210,000 ÷ 300,000; $120,000 ÷ 300,000).
[b]Annual cost divided by 12.

 The Navigator

SUMMARY OF LEARNING OBJECTIVES  **The Navigator**

1 Describe the concept of budgetary control. Budgetary control consists of (a) preparing periodic budget reports that compare actual results with planned objectives, (b) analyzing the differences to determine their causes, (c) taking appropriate corrective action, and (d) modifying future plans, if necessary.

2 Evaluate the usefulness of static budget reports. Static budget reports are useful in evaluating the progress toward planned sales and profit goals. They are also appro-

priate in assessing a manager's effectiveness in controlling costs when (a) actual activity closely approximates the master budget activity level, and/or (b) the behavior of the costs in response to changes in activity is fixed.

3 Explain the development of flexible budgets and the usefulness of flexible budget reports. To develop the flexible budget it is necessary to: (a) Identify the activity index and the relevant range of activity. (b) Identify the variable costs, and determine the budgeted variable cost per unit of activity for each cost. (c) Identify the fixed costs, and determine the budgeted amount for each cost. (d) Prepare the budget for selected increments of activity within the relevant range. Flexible budget reports permit an evaluation of a manager's performance in controlling production and costs.

4 Describe the concept of responsibility accounting. Responsibility accounting involves accumulating and reporting revenues and costs on the basis of the individual manager who has the authority to make the day-to-day decisions about the items. The evaluation of a manager's performance is based on the matters directly under the manager's control. In responsibility accounting, it is necessary to distinguish between controllable and noncontrollable fixed costs and to identify three types of responsibility centers: cost, profit, and investment.

5 Indicate the features of responsibility reports for cost centers. Responsibility reports for cost centers compare actual costs with flexible budget data. The reports show only controllable costs, and no distinction is made between variable and fixed costs.

6 Identify the content of responsibility reports for profit centers. Responsibility reports show contribution margin, controllable fixed costs, and controllable margin for each profit center.

7 Explain the basis and formula used in evaluating performance in investment centers. The primary basis for evaluating performance in investment centers is return on investment (ROI). The formula for computing ROI for investment centers is: Controllable margin ÷ Average operating assets.

APPENDIX 24A   RESIDUAL INCOME—ANOTHER PERFORMANCE MEASUREMENT

Although most companies use ROI in evaluating their investment performance, ROI has a significant disadvantage. To illustrate, let's look at the Electronics Division of Pujols Company. It has an ROI of 20% computed as follows.

LEARNING OBJECTIVE   8

Explain the difference between ROI and residual income.

Controllable Margin	÷	Average Operating Assets	=	Return on Investment (ROI)
$1,000,000	÷	$5,000,000	=	20%

Illustration 24A-1
ROI formula

The Electronics Division is considering producing a new product, a GPS device (hereafter referred to as Tracker), for its boats. To produce Tracker, operating assets will have to increase $2,000,000. Tracker is expected to generate an additional $260,000 of controllable margin. Illustration 24A-2 shows how Tracker will effect ROI.

Illustration 24A-2
ROI comparison

	Without Tracker	Tracker	With Tracker
Controllable margin (a)	$1,000,000	$ 260,000	$1,260,000
Average operating assets (b)	$5,000,000	$2,000,000	$7,000,000
Return on investment [(a) ÷ (b)]	20%	13%	18%

The investment in Tracker reduces ROI from 20% to 18%.

Let's suppose that you are the manager of the Electronics Division and must make the decision to produce or not produce Tracker. If you were evaluated using ROI, you probably would not produce Tracker because your ROI would drop from 20% to 18%. The problem with this ROI analysis is that it ignores an important variable, the minimum rate of return on a company's operating assets. The **minimum rate of return** is the rate at which the Electronics Division can cover its costs and earn a profit. Assuming that the Electronics Division has a minimum rate of return of 10%, it should invest in Tracker because its ROI of 13% is greater than 10%.

Residual Income Compared to ROI

To evaluate performance using the minimum rate of return, companies use the residual income approach. **Residual income** is the income that remains after subtracting from the controllable margin the minimum rate of return on a company's average operating assets. The residual income for Tracker would be computed as follows.

Illustration 24A-3
Residual income formula

Controllable Margin	−	Minimum Rate of Return × Average Operating Assets	=	Residual Income
$260,000	−	10% × $2,000,000	=	$60,000

As shown, the residual income related to the Tracker investment is $60,000. Illustration 24A-4 indicates how residual income changes as the additional investment is made.

Illustration 24A-4
Residual income comparison

	Without Tracker	Tracker	With Tracker
Controllable margin (a)	$1,000,000	$260,000	$1,260,000
Average operating assets × 10% (b)	500,000	200,000	700,000
Residual income [(a) − (b)]	$ 500,000	$ 60,000	$ 560,000

This example illustrates how performance evaluation based on ROI can be misleading and can even cause managers to reject projects that would actually increase income for the company. As a result, many companies such as Coca-Cola, Briggs and Stratton, Eli Lilly, and Siemens AG use residual income (or a variant often referred to as economic value added) to evaluate investment alternatives and measure company performance.

Residual Income Weakness

It might appear from the above discussion that the goal of any company should be to maximize the total amount of residual income in each division. This goal, however, ignores the fact that one division might use substantially fewer assets to attain the same level of residual income as another division. For example, we know that to produce Tracker, the Electronics Division of Pujols Company used $2,000,000 of average operating assets to generate $260,000 of controllable margin. Now let's say a different division produced a product called SeaDog, which used $4,000,000 to generate $460,000 of controllable margin, as shown in Illustration 24A-5.

Illustration 24A-5
Comparison of two products

	Tracker	SeaDog
Controllable margin (a)	$260,000	$460,000
Average operating assets × 10% (b)	200,000	400,000
Residual income [(a) − (b)]	$ 60,000	$ 60,000

If the performance of these two investments were evaluated using residual income, they would be considered equal: Both products have the same total residual income. This ignores, however, the fact that SeaDog required **twice** as many operating assets to achieve the same level of residual income.

SUMMARY OF LEARNING OBJECTIVE FOR APPENDIX 24A

8 Explain the difference between ROI and residual income. ROI is controllable margin divided by average operating assets. Residual income is the income that remains after subtracting the minimum rate of return on a company's average operating assets. ROI sometimes provides misleading results because profitable investments are often rejected when the investment reduces ROI but increases overall profitability.

GLOSSARY

Budgetary control The use of budgets to control operations. (p. 1182).

Controllable cost A cost over which a manager has control. (p. 1195).

Controllable margin Contribution margin less controllable fixed costs. (p. 1202).

Cost center A responsibility center that incurs costs but does not directly generate revenues. (p. 1200).

Decentralization Control of operations is delegated to many managers throughout the organization. (p. 1194).

Direct fixed costs Costs that relate specifically to a responsibility center and are incurred for the sole benefit of the center. (p. 1201).

Flexible budget A projection of budget data for various levels of activity. (p. 1184).

Indirect fixed costs Costs that are incurred for the benefit of more than one profit center. (p. 1202).

Investment center A responsibility center that incurs costs, generates revenues, and has control over decisions regarding the assets available for use. (p. 1200).

Management by exception The review of budget reports by top management focused entirely or primarily on differences between actual results and planned objectives. (p. 1195).

Noncontrollable costs Costs incurred indirectly and allocated to a responsibility center that are not controllable at that level. (p. 1195).

Profit center A responsibility center that incurs costs and also generates revenues. (p. 1200).

Residual income The income that remains after subtracting from the controllable margin the minimum rate of return on a company's average operating assets. (p. 1210).

Responsibility accounting A part of management accounting that involves accumulating and reporting revenues and costs on the basis of the manager who has the authority to make the day-to-day decisions about the items. (p. 1193).

Responsibility reporting system The preparation of reports for each level of responsibility in the company's organization chart. (p. 1197).

Return on investment (ROI) A measure of management's effectiveness in utilizing assets at its disposal in an investment center. (p. 1203).

Segment An area of responsibility in decentralized operations. (p. 1194).

Static budget A projection of budget data at one level of activity. (p. 1183).

Self-Test, Brief Exercises, Exercises, Problem Set A, and many more resources are available for practice in WileyPLUS.

Note: All asterisked Questions, Exercises, and Problems relate to material in the appendix to the chapter.

SELF-TEST QUESTIONS

Answers are at the end of the chapter.

(LO 1) **1.** Budgetary control involves all but one of the following:
  (a) modifying future plans.
  (b) analyzing differences.
  (c) using static budgets.
  (d) determining differences between actual and planned results.

2. Budget reports are prepared: (LO 1)
  (a) daily.   (c) monthly.
  (b) weekly.   (d) All of the above.

3. A production manager in a manufacturing company   (LO 1) would most likely receive a:
  (a) sales report.
  (b) income statement.

(c) scrap report.

(d) shipping department overhead report.

(LO 2) **4.** A static budget is:

(a) a projection of budget data at several levels of activity within the relevant range of activity.

(b) a projection of budget data at a single level of activity.

(c) compared to a flexible budget in a budget report.

(d) never appropriate in evaluating a manager's effectiveness in controlling costs.

(LO 2) **5.** A static budget is useful in controlling costs when cost behavior is:

(a) mixed.   (c) variable.

(b) fixed.   (d) linear.

(LO 3) **6.** At zero direct labor hours in a flexible budget graph, the total budgeted cost line intersects the vertical axis at $30,000. At 10,000 direct labor hours, a horizontal line drawn from the total budgeted cost line intersects the vertical axis at $90,000. Fixed and variable costs may be expressed as:

(a) $30,000 fixed plus $6 per direct labor hour variable.

(b) $30,000 fixed plus $9 per direct labor hour variable.

(c) $60,000 fixed plus $3 per direct labor hour variable.

(d) $60,000 fixed plus $6 per direct labor hour variable.

(LO 3) **7.** At 9,000 direct labor hours, the flexible budget for indirect materials is $27,000. If $28,000 of indirect materials costs are incurred at 9,200 direct labor hours, the flexible budget report should show the following difference for indirect materials:

(a) $1,000 unfavorable.   (c) $400 favorable.

(b) $1,000 favorable.   (d) $400 unfavorable.

(LO 4) **8.** Under responsibility accounting, the evaluation of a manager's performance is based on matters that the manager:

(a) directly controls.

(b) directly and indirectly controls.

(c) indirectly controls.

(d) has shared responsibility for with another manager.

(LO 4) **9.** Responsibility centers include:

(a) cost centers.   (c) investment centers.

(b) profit centers.   (d) All of the above.

(LO 5) **10.** Responsibility reports for cost centers:

(a) distinguish between fixed and variable costs.

(b) use static budget data.

(c) include both controllable and noncontrollable costs.

(d) include only controllable costs.

(LO 5) **11.** The accounting department of a manufacturing company is an example of:

(a) a cost center.   (c) an investment center.

(b) a profit center.   (d) a contribution center.

(LO 6) **12.** To evaluate the performance of a profit center manager, upper management needs detailed information about:

(a) controllable costs.

(b) controllable revenues.

(c) controllable costs and revenues.

(d) controllable costs and revenues and average operating assets.

(LO 6) **13.** In a responsibility report for a profit center, controllable fixed costs are deducted from contribution margin to show:

(a) profit center margin.

(b) controllable margin.

(c) net income.

(d) income from operations.

(LO 7) **14.** In the formula for return on investment (ROI), the factors for controllable margin and operating assets are, respectively:

(a) controllable margin percentage and total operating assets.

(b) controllable margin dollars and average operating assets.

(c) controllable margin dollars and total assets.

(d) controllable margin percentage and average operating assets.

(LO 7) **15.** A manager of an investment center can improve ROI by:

(a) increasing average operating assets.

(b) reducing sales.

(c) increasing variable costs.

(d) reducing variable and/or controllable fixed costs.

Go to the book's companion website, www.wiley.com/college/weygandt, for additional Self-Test Questions.

 **The Navigator**

QUESTIONS

1. (a) What is budgetary control?

(b) Fred Barone is describing budgetary control. What steps should be included in Fred's description?

2. The following purposes are part of a budgetary reporting system: (a) Determine efficient use of materials. (b) Control overhead costs. (c) Determine whether income objectives are being met. For each purpose, indicate the name of the report, the frequency of the report, and the primary recipient(s) of the report.

3. How may a budget report for the second quarter differ from a budget report for the first quarter?

4. Ken Bay questions the usefulness of a master sales budget in evaluating sales performance. Is there justification for Ken's concern? Explain.

5. Under what circumstances may a static budget be an appropriate basis for evaluating a manager's effectiveness in controlling costs?

6. "A flexible budget is really a series of static budgets." Is this true? Why?

7. The static manufacturing overhead budget based on 40,000 direct labor hours shows budgeted indirect labor costs of $54,000. During March, the department incurs $64,000 of indirect labor while working 45,000 direct labor hours. Is this a favorable or unfavorable performance? Why?

8. A static overhead budget based on 40,000 direct labor hours shows Factory Insurance $6,500 as a fixed cost. At the 50,000 direct labor hours worked in March, factory insurance costs were $6,300. Is this a favorable or unfavorable performance? Why?

9. Megan Pedigo is confused about how a flexible budget is prepared. Identify the steps for Megan.

10. Cali Company has prepared a graph of flexible budget data. At zero direct labor hours, the total budgeted cost line intersects the vertical axis at $20,000. At 10,000 direct labor hours, the line drawn from the total budgeted cost line intersects the vertical axis at $85,000. How may the fixed and variable costs be expressed?

11. The flexible budget formula is fixed costs $50,000 plus variable costs of $4 per direct labor hour. What is the total budgeted cost at (a) 9,000 hours and (b) 12,345 hours?

12. What is management by exception? What criteria may be used in identifying exceptions?

13. What is responsibility accounting? Explain the purpose of responsibility accounting.

14. Eve Rooney is studying for an accounting examination. Describe for Eve what conditions are necessary for responsibility accounting to be used effectively.

15. Distinguish between controllable and noncontrollable costs.

16. How do responsibility reports differ from budget reports?

17. What is the relationship, if any, between a responsibility reporting system and a company's organization chart?

18. Distinguish among the three types of responsibility centers.

19. (a) What costs are included in a performance report for a cost center? (b) In the report, are variable and fixed costs identified?

20. How do direct fixed costs differ from indirect fixed costs? Are both types of fixed costs controllable?

21. Jane Nott is confused about controllable margin reported in an income statement for a profit center. How is this margin computed, and what is its primary purpose?

22. What is the primary basis for evaluating the performance of the manager of an investment center? Indicate the formula for this basis.

23. Explain the ways that ROI can be improved.

24. Indicate two behavioral principles that pertain to (a) the manager being evaluated and (b) top management.

*25. What is a major disadvantage of using ROI to evaluate investment and company performance?

*26. What is residual income, and what is one of its major weaknesses?

BRIEF EXERCISES

BE24-1 For the quarter ended March 31, 2014, Maris Company accumulates the following sales data for its product, Garden-Tools: $310,000 budget; $305,000 actual. Prepare a static budget report for the quarter.

Prepare static budget report.
(LO 2)

BE24-2 Data for Maris Company are given in BE24-1. In the second quarter, budgeted sales were $380,000, and actual sales were $384,000. Prepare a static budget report for the second quarter and for the year to date.

Prepare static budget report for 2 quarters.
(LO 2)

BE24-3 In Paige Company, direct labor is $20 per hour. The company expects to operate at 10,000 direct labor hours each month. In January 2014, direct labor totaling $204,000 is incurred in working 10,400 hours. Prepare (a) a static budget report and (b) a flexible budget report. Evaluate the usefulness of each report.

Show usefulness of flexible budgets in evaluating performance.
(LO 3)

BE24-4 Gundy Company expects to produce 1,200,000 units of Product XX in 2014. Monthly production is expected to range from 80,000 to 120,000 units. Budgeted variable manufacturing costs per unit are direct materials $5, direct labor $6, and overhead $8. Budgeted fixed manufacturing costs per unit for depreciation are $2 and for supervision are $1. Prepare a flexible manufacturing budget for the relevant range value using 20,000 unit increments.

Prepare a flexible budget for variable costs.
(LO 3)

BE24-5 Data for Gundy Company are given in BE24-4. In March 2014, the company incurs the following costs in producing 100,000 units: direct materials $525,000, direct labor $596,000, and variable overhead $805,000. Actual fixed costs were equal to budgeted fixed costs. Prepare a flexible budget report for March. Were costs controlled?

Prepare flexible budget report.
(LO 3)

BE24-6 In the Assembly Department of Hannon Company, budgeted and actual manufacturing overhead costs for the month of April 2014 were as follows.

Prepare a responsibility report for a cost center.
(LO 5)

	Budget	**Actual**
Indirect materials	$16,000	$14,300
Indirect labor	20,000	20,600
Utilities	10,000	10,850
Supervision	5,000	5,000

All costs are controllable by the department manager. Prepare a responsibility report for April for the cost center.

Prepare a responsibility report for a profit center.

(LO 6)

BE24-7 Elbert Company accumulates the following summary data for the year ending December 31, 2014, for its Water Division, which it operates as a profit center: sales—$2,000,000 budget, $2,080,000 actual; variable costs—$1,000,000 budget, $1,060,000 actual; and controllable fixed costs—$300,000 budget, $305,000 actual. Prepare a responsibility report for the Water Division.

Prepare a responsibility report for an investment center.

(LO 7)

BE24-8 For the year ending December 31, 2014, Cobb Company accumulates the following data for the Plastics Division which it operates as an investment center: contribution margin—$700,000 budget, $710,000 actual; controllable fixed costs—$300,000 budget, $302,000 actual. Average operating assets for the year were $2,000,000. Prepare a responsibility report for the Plastics Division beginning with contribution margin.

Compute return on investment using the ROI formula.

(LO 7)

BE24-9 For its three investment centers, Kaspar Company accumulates the following data:

	I	**II**	**III**
Sales	$2,000,000	$4,000,000	$ 4,000,000
Controllable margin	1,300,000	2,000,000	3,600,000
Average operating assets	5,000,000	8,000,000	12,000,000

Compute the return on investment (ROI) for each center.

Compute return on investment under changed conditions.

(LO 7)

BE24-10 Data for the investment centers for Kaspar Company are given in BE24-9. The centers expect the following changes in the next year: (I) increase sales 15%; (II) decrease costs $400,000; (III) decrease average operating assets $500,000. Compute the expected return on investment (ROI) for each center. Assume center I has a contribution margin percentage of 70%.

Compute ROI and residual income.

(LO 8)

*BE24-11 Voorhees, Inc. reports the following financial information.

Average operating assets	$3,000,000
Controllable margin	$ 660,000
Minimum rate of return	10%

Compute the return on investment and the residual income.

Compute ROI and residual income.

(LO 8)

*BE24-12 Presented below is information related to the Southern Division of Lumber, Inc.

Contribution margin	$1,200,000
Controllable margin	$ 800,000
Average operating assets	$4,000,000
Minimum rate of return	15%

Compute the Southern Division's return on investment and residual income.

> **DO IT!** REVIEW

Compute total budgeted costs in flexible budget.

(LO 3)

DO IT! 24-1 In Pargo Company's flexible budget graph, the fixed cost line and the total budgeted cost line intersect the vertical axis at $90,000. The total budgeted cost line is $330,000 at an activity level of 50,000 direct labor hours. Compute total budgeted costs at 65,000 direct labor hours.

DO IT! 24-2 Mussatto Company expects to produce 50,000 units of product IOA during the current year. Budgeted variable manufacturing costs per unit are direct materials $7, direct labor $13, and overhead $18. Annual budgeted fixed manufacturing overhead costs are $96,000 for depreciation and $45,600 for supervision.

Prepare and evaluate a flexible budget report.

(LO 3)

In the current month, Mussatto produced 6,000 units and incurred the following costs: direct materials $38,850, direct labor $76,440, variable overhead $116,640, depreciation $8,000, and supervision $4,000.

Prepare a flexible budget report. (*Note:* You do not need to prepare the heading.) Were costs controlled?

DO IT! 24-3 The Wellstone Division operates as a profit center. It reports the following for the year.

Prepare a responsibility report.

(LO 6)

	Budget	**Actual**
Sales	$2,000,000	$1,860,000
Variable costs	800,000	760,000
Controllable fixed costs	550,000	550,000
Noncontrollable fixed costs	250,000	250,000

Prepare a responsibility report for the Wellstone Division at December 31, 2014.

DO IT! 24-4 The service division of Raney Industries reported the following results for 2013.

Compute ROI and expected return on investments.

(LO 7)

Sales	$500,000
Variable costs	300,000
Controllable fixed costs	75,000
Average operating assets	625,000

Management is considering the following independent courses of action in 2014 in order to maximize the return on investment for this division.

1. Reduce average operating assets by $125,000, with no change in controllable margin.
2. Increase sales $100,000, with no change in the contribution margin percentage.

(a) Compute the controllable margin and the return on investment for 2013. (b) Compute the controllable margin and the expected return on investment for each proposed alternative.

 The Navigator

EXERCISES

E24-1 Mike Trusler has prepared the following list of statements about budgetary control.

Understand the concept of budgetary control.

(LO 1, 2, 3)

1. Budget reports compare actual results with planned objectives.
2. All budget reports are prepared on a weekly basis.
3. Management uses budget reports to analyze differences between actual and planned results and determine their causes.
4. As a result of analyzing budget reports, management may either take corrective action or modify future plans.
5. Budgetary control works best when a company has an informal reporting system.
6. The primary recipients of the sales report are the sales manager and the vice president of production.
7. The primary recipient of the scrap report is the production manager.
8. A static budget is a projection of budget data at one level of activity.
9. Top management's reaction to unfavorable differences is not influenced by the materiality of the difference.
10. A static budget is not appropriate in evaluating a manager's effectiveness in controlling costs unless the actual activity level approximates the static budget activity level or the behavior of the costs is fixed.

Instructions

Identify each statement as true or false. If false, indicate how to correct the statement.

E24-2 Crede Company budgeted selling expenses of $30,000 in January, $35,000 in February, and $40,000 in March. Actual selling expenses were $31,200 in January, $34,525 in February, and $46,000 in March.

Instructions
(a) Prepare a selling expense report that compares budgeted and actual amounts by month and for the year to date.
(b) What is the purpose of the report prepared in (a), and who would be the primary recipient?
(c) What would be the likely result of management's analysis of the report?

E24-3 Thome Company uses a flexible budget for manufacturing overhead based on direct labor hours. Variable manufacturing overhead costs per direct labor hour are as follows.

Indirect labor	$1.00
Indirect materials	0.60
Utilities	0.40

Fixed overhead costs per month are supervision $4,000, depreciation $1,200, and property taxes $800. The company believes it will normally operate in a range of 7,000–10,000 direct labor hours per month.

Instructions
Prepare a monthly manufacturing overhead flexible budget for 2014 for the expected range of activity, using increments of 1,000 direct labor hours.

E24-4 Using the information in E24-3, assume that in July 2014, Thome Company incurs the following manufacturing overhead costs.

Variable Costs		Fixed Costs	
Indirect labor	$8,800	Supervision	$4,000
Indirect materials	5,300	Depreciation	1,200
Utilities	3,200	Property taxes	800

Instructions
(a) Prepare a flexible budget performance report, assuming that the company worked 9,000 direct labor hours during the month.
(b) Prepare a flexible budget performance report, assuming that the company worked 8,500 direct labor hours during the month.
(c) ▭▭▭▭▷ Comment on your findings.

E24-5 DeWitt Company uses flexible budgets to control its selling expenses. Monthly sales are expected to range from $170,000 to $200,000. Variable costs and their percentage relationship to sales are sales commissions 6%, advertising 4%, traveling 3%, and delivery 2%. Fixed selling expenses will consist of sales salaries $35,000, depreciation on delivery equipment $7,000, and insurance on delivery equipment $1,000.

Instructions
Prepare a monthly flexible budget for each $10,000 increment of sales within the relevant range for the year ending December 31, 2014.

E24-6 The actual selling expenses incurred in March 2014 by DeWitt Company are as follows.

Variable Expenses		Fixed Expenses	
Sales commissions	$11,000	Sales salaries	$35,000
Advertising	6,900	Depreciation	7,000
Travel	5,100	Insurance	1,000
Delivery	3,450		

Instructions
(a) Prepare a flexible budget performance report for March using the budget data in E24-5, assuming that March sales were $170,000.
(b) Prepare a flexible budget performance report, assuming that March sales were $180,000.
(c) ▭▭▭▭▷ Comment on the importance of using flexible budgets in evaluating the performance of the sales manager.

E24-7 Kitchen Help Inc. (KHI) is a manufacturer of toaster ovens. To improve control over operations, the president of KHI wants to begin using a flexible budgeting system, rather than use only the current master budget. The following data are available for KHI's expected costs at production levels of 90,000, 100,000, and 110,000 units.

Prepare flexible budget report for cost center.

(LO 3)

Variable costs	
Manufacturing	$6 per unit
Administrative	$4 per unit
Selling	$2 per unit
Fixed costs	
Manufacturing	$160,000
Administrative	$ 80,000

Instructions

(a) Prepare a flexible budget for each of the possible production levels: 90,000, 100,000, and 110,000 units.

(b) If KHI sells the toaster ovens for $16 each, how many units will it have to sell to make a profit of $200,000 before taxes?

(CGA adapted)

E24-8 Rensing Groomers is in the dog-grooming business. Its operating costs are described by the following formulas:

Prepare flexible budget report; compare flexible and static budgets.

(LO 2, 3)

Grooming supplies (variable)	$y = \$0 + \$5x$
Direct labor (variable)	$y = \$0 + \$14x$
Overhead (mixed)	$y = \$10,000 + \$1x$

Milo, the owner, has determined that direct labor is the cost driver for all three categories of costs.

Instructions

(a) Prepare a flexible budget for activity levels of 550, 600, and 700 direct labor hours.

(b) ▨▨▨▨▷ Explain why the flexible budget is more informative than the static budget.

(c) Calculate the total cost per direct labor hour at each of the activity levels specified in part (a).

(d) The groomers at Rensing normally work a total of 650 direct labor hours during each month. Each grooming job normally takes a groomer 1.3 hours. Milo wants to earn a profit equal to 40% of the costs incurred. Determine what he should charge each pet owner for grooming.

(CGA adapted)

E24-9 Lowell Company's manufacturing overhead budget for the first quarter of 2014 contained the following data.

Prepare flexible budget and responsibility report for manufacturing overhead.

(LO 3, 5)

Variable Costs		Fixed Costs	
Indirect materials	$12,000	Supervisory salaries	$36,000
Indirect labor	10,000	Depreciation	7,000
Utilities	8,000	Property taxes and insurance	8,000
Maintenance	6,000	Maintenance	5,000

Actual variable costs were indirect materials $13,900, indirect labor $9,500, utilities $8,700, and maintenance $5,000. Actual fixed costs equaled budgeted costs except for property taxes and insurance, which were $8,400. The actual activity level equaled the budgeted level.

All costs are considered controllable by the production department manager except for depreciation, and property taxes and insurance.

Instructions

(a) Prepare a manufacturing overhead flexible budget report for the first quarter.

(b) Prepare a responsibility report for the first quarter.

E24-10 As sales manager, Joe Batista was given the following static budget report for selling expenses in the Clothing Department of Soria Company for the month of October.

Prepare flexible budget report, and answer question.

(LO 2, 3)

Soria Company
Clothing Department
Budget Report
For the Month Ended October 31, 2014

	Budget	Actual	Difference Favorable F Unfavorable U
Sales in units	8,000	10,000	2,000 F
Variable expenses			
Sales commissions	$ 2,400	$ 2,600	$ 200 U
Advertising expense	720	850	130 U
Travel expense	3,600	4,100	500 U
Free samples given out	1,600	1,400	200 F
Total variable	8,320	8,950	630 U
Fixed expenses			
Rent	1,500	1,500	–0–
Sales salaries	1,200	1,200	–0–
Office salaries	800	800	–0–
Depreciation—autos (sales staff)	500	500	–0–
Total fixed	4,000	4,000	–0–
Total expenses	$12,320	$12,950	$ 630 U

As a result of this budget report, Joe was called into the president's office and congratulated on his fine sales performance. He was reprimanded, however, for allowing his costs to get out of control. Joe knew something was wrong with the performance report that he had been given. However, he was not sure what to do, and comes to you for advice.

Instructions
(a) Prepare a budget report based on flexible budget data to help Joe.
(b) Should Joe have been reprimanded? Explain.

*Prepare and discuss a
responsibility report.*

(LO 3, 5)

E24-11 Kirkland Plumbing Company is a newly formed company specializing in plumbing services for home and business. The owner, Lenny Kirkland, had divided the company into two segments: Home Plumbing Services and Business Plumbing Services. Each segment is run by its own supervisor, while basic selling and administrative services are shared by both segments.

Lenny has asked you to help him create a performance reporting system that will allow him to measure each segment's performance in terms of its profitability. To that end, the following information has been collected on the Home Plumbing Services segment for the first quarter of 2014.

	Budget	Actual
Service revenue	$25,000	$26,000
Allocated portion of:		
Building depreciation	11,000	11,000
Advertising	5,000	4,200
Billing	3,500	3,000
Property taxes	1,200	1,000
Material and supplies	1,600	1,200
Supervisory salaries	9,000	9,500
Insurance	4,000	3,600
Wages	3,000	3,250
Gas and oil	2,800	3,400
Equipment depreciation	1,500	1,300

Instructions
(a) Prepare a responsibility report for the first quarter of 2014 for the Home Plumbing Services segment.
(b) ▭▭▭▷ Write a memo to Lenny Kirkland discussing the principles that should be used when preparing performance reports.

E24-12 Venetian Company has two production departments, Fabricating and Assembling. At a department managers' meeting, the controller uses flexible budget graphs to explain total budgeted costs. Separate graphs based on direct labor hours are used for each department. The graphs show the following.

State total budgeted cost formulas, and prepare flexible budget graph.

(LO 3)

1. At zero direct labor hours, the total budgeted cost line and the fixed cost line intersect the vertical axis at $50,000 in the Fabricating Department and $40,000 in the Assembling Department.
2. At normal capacity of 50,000 direct labor hours, the line drawn from the total budgeted cost line intersects the vertical axis at $150,000 in the Fabricating Department, and $120,000 in the Assembling Department.

Instructions
(a) State the total budgeted cost formula for each department.
(b) Compute the total budgeted cost for each department, assuming actual direct labor hours worked were 53,000 and 47,000, in the Fabricating and Assembling Departments, respectively.
(c) Prepare the flexible budget graph for the Fabricating Department, assuming the maximum direct labor hours in the relevant range is 100,000. Use increments of 10,000 direct labor hours on the horizontal axis and increments of $50,000 on the vertical axis.

E24-13 Fultz Company's organization chart includes the president; the vice president of production; three assembly plants—Dallas, Atlanta, and Tucson; and two departments within each plant—Machining and Finishing. Budget and actual manufacturing cost data for July 2014 are as follows.

Prepare reports in a responsibility reporting system.

(LO 4, 5)

Finishing Department—Dallas: direct materials $41,500 actual, $44,000 budget; direct labor $83,400 actual, $82,000 budget; manufacturing overhead $51,000 actual, $49,200 budget.

Machining Department—Dallas: total manufacturing costs $220,000 actual, $219,000 budget.

Atlanta Plant: total manufacturing costs $424,000 actual, $421,000 budget.

Tucson Plant: total manufacturing costs $494,200 actual, $496,500 budget.

The Dallas plant manager's office costs were $95,000 actual and $92,000 budget. The vice president of production's office costs were $132,000 actual and $130,000 budget. Office costs are not allocated to departments and plants.

Instructions
Using the format on page 1199, prepare the reports in a responsibility system for:

(a) The Finishing Department—Dallas.
(b) The plant manager—Dallas.
(c) The vice president of production.

E24-14 The Mixing Department manager of Malone Company is able to control all overhead costs except rent, property taxes, and salaries. Budgeted monthly overhead costs for the Mixing Department, in alphabetical order, are:

Prepare a responsibility report for a cost center.

(LO 5)

Indirect labor	$12,000	Property taxes	$ 1,000
Indirect materials	7,700	Rent	1,800
Lubricants	1,675	Salaries	10,000
Maintenance	3,500	Utilities	5,000

Actual costs incurred for January 2014 are indirect labor $12,250; indirect materials $10,200; lubricants $1,650; maintenance $3,500; property taxes $1,100; rent $1,800; salaries $10,000; and utilities $6,400.

Instructions
(a) Prepare a responsibility report for January 2014.
(b) What would be the likely result of management's analysis of the report?

E24-15 Deitz Inc. has three divisions which are operated as profit centers. Actual operating data for the divisions listed alphabetically are as follows.

Compute missing amounts in responsibility reports for three profit centers, and prepare a report.

(LO 6)

Operating Data	Women's Shoes	Men's Shoes	Children's Shoes
Contribution margin	$250,000	(3)	$180,000
Controllable fixed costs	100,000	(4)	(5)
Controllable margin	(1)	$ 90,000	95,000
Sales	600,000	450,000	(6)
Variable costs	(2)	320,000	250,000

Instructions

(a) Compute the missing amounts. Show computations.

(b) Prepare a responsibility report for the Women's Shoes Division assuming (1) the data are for the month ended June 30, 2014, and (2) all data equal budget except variable costs which are $10,000 over budget.

Prepare a responsibility report for a profit center, and compute ROI.

(LO 6, 7)

E24-16 The Sports Equipment Division of Harrington Company is operated as a profit center. Sales for the division were budgeted for 2014 at $900,000. The only variable costs budgeted for the division were cost of goods sold ($440,000) and selling and administrative ($60,000). Fixed costs were budgeted at $100,000 for cost of goods sold, $90,000 for selling and administrative, and $70,000 for noncontrollable fixed costs. Actual results for these items were:

Sales	$880,000
Cost of goods sold	
Variable	408,000
Fixed	105,000
Selling and administrative	
Variable	61,000
Fixed	66,000
Noncontrollable fixed	90,000

Instructions

(a) Prepare a responsibility report for the Sports Equipment Division for 2014.

(b) Assume the division is an investment center, and average operating assets were $1,000,000. The noncontrollable fixed costs are controllable at the investment center level. Compute ROI.

Compute ROI for current year and for possible future changes.

(LO 7)

E24-17 The West Division of Nieto Company reported the following data for the current year.

Sales	$3,000,000
Variable costs	1,980,000
Controllable fixed costs	600,000
Average operating assets	5,000,000

Top management is unhappy with the investment center's return on investment (ROI). It asks the manager of the West Division to submit plans to improve ROI in the next year. The manager believes it is feasible to consider the following independent courses of action.

1. Increase sales by $320,000 with no change in the contribution margin percentage.
2. Reduce variable costs by $150,000.
3. Reduce average operating assets by 4%.

Instructions

(a) Compute the return on investment (ROI) for the current year.

(b) Using the ROI formula, compute the ROI under each of the proposed courses of action. (Round to one decimal.)

Prepare a responsibility report for an investment center.

(LO 7)

E24-18 The Dinkle and Frizell Dental Clinic provides both preventive and orthodontic dental services. The two owners, Reese Dinkle and Anita Frizell, operate the clinic as two separate investment centers: Preventive Services and Orthodontic Services. Each of them is in charge of one of the centers: Reese for Preventive Services and Anita for Orthodontic Services. Each month, they prepare an income statement for the two centers to evaluate performance and make decisions about how to improve the operational efficiency and profitability of the clinic.

Recently, they have been concerned about the profitability of the Preventive Services operations. For several months, it has been reporting a loss. The responsibility report for the month of May 2014 is shown on page 1221.

	Actual	Difference from Budget
Service revenue	$40,000	$1,000 F
Variable costs		
Filling materials	5,000	100 U
Novocain	3,900	100 U
Supplies	1,900	350 F
Dental assistant wages	2,500	–0–
Utilities	500	110 U
Total variable costs	13,800	40 F
Fixed costs		
Allocated portion of receptionist's salary	3,000	200 U
Dentist salary	9,800	400 U
Equipment depreciation	6,000	–0–
Allocated portion of building depreciation	15,000	1,000 U
Total fixed costs	33,800	1,600 U
Operating income (loss)	$(7,600)	$ 560 U

In addition, the owners know that the investment in operating assets at the beginning of the month was $82,400, and it was $77,600 at the end of the month. They have asked for your assistance in evaluating their current performance reporting system.

Instructions
(a) Prepare a responsibility report for an investment center as illustrated in the chapter.
(b) ▭▬▬▷ Write a memo to the owners discussing the deficiencies of their current reporting system.

E24-19 The Pletcher Transportation Company uses a responsibility reporting system to measure the performance of its three investment centers: Planes, Taxis, and Limos. Segment performance is measured using a system of responsibility reports and return on investment calculations. The allocation of resources within the company and the segment managers' bonuses are based in part on the results shown in these reports.

Prepare missing amounts in responsibility reports for three investment centers.

(LO 7)

Recently, the company was the victim of a computer virus that deleted portions of the company's accounting records. This was discovered when the current period's responsibility reports were being prepared. The printout of the actual operating results appeared as follows.

	Planes	Taxis	Limos
Service revenue	$?	$500,000	$?
Variable costs	5,500,000	?	300,000
Contribution margin	?	250,000	480,000
Controllable fixed costs	1,500,000	?	?
Controllable margin	?	80,000	240,000
Average operating assets	25,000,000	?	1,500,000
Return on investment	13%	10%	?

Instructions
Determine the missing pieces of information above.

*E24-20 Presented below is selected information for three regional divisions of Medina Company.

Compare ROI and residual income.

(LO 8)

	Divisions		
	North	West	South
Contribution margin	$ 300,000	$ 500,000	$ 400,000
Controllable margin	$ 140,000	$ 360,000	$ 210,000
Average operating assets	$1,000,000	$2,000,000	$1,500,000
Minimum rate of return	13%	16%	10%

Instructions

(a) Compute the return on investment for each division.

(b) Compute the residual income for each division.

(c) Assume that each division has an investment opportunity that would provide a rate of return of 16%.

  (1) If ROI is used to measure performance, which division or divisions will probably make the additional investment?

  (2) If residual income is used to measure performance, which division or divisions will probably make the additional investment?

Fill in information related to ROI and residual income.

(LO 8)

*E24-21 Presented below is selected financial information for two divisions of Yono Brewing.

	Lager	Lite Lager
Contribution margin	$500,000	$ 300,000
Controllable margin	200,000	(c)
Average operating assets	(a)	$1,200,000
Minimum rate of return	(b)	13%
Return on investment	20%	(d)
Residual income	$100,000	$ 204,000

Instructions

Supply the missing information for the lettered items.

EXERCISES: SET B AND CHALLENGE EXERCISES

Visit the book's companion website, at **www.wiley.com/college/weygandt**, and choose the Student Companion site to access Exercise Set B and Challenge Exercises.

PROBLEMS: SET A

Prepare flexible budget and budget report for manufacturing overhead.

(LO 3)

P24-1A Cook Company estimates that 300,000 direct labor hours will be worked during the coming year, 2014, in the Packaging Department. On this basis, the budgeted manufacturing overhead cost data, shown below, are computed for the year.

Fixed Overhead Costs		**Variable Overhead Costs**	
Supervision	$ 96,000	Indirect labor	$126,000
Depreciation	72,000	Indirect materials	90,000
Insurance	30,000	Repairs	54,000
Rent	24,000	Utilities	72,000
Property taxes	18,000	Lubricants	18,000
	$240,000		$360,000

It is estimated that direct labor hours worked each month will range from 27,000 to 36,000 hours.

During October, 27,000 direct labor hours were worked and the following overhead costs were incurred.

Fixed overhead costs: supervision $8,000, depreciation $6,000, insurance $2,460, rent $2,000, and property taxes $1,500.

Variable overhead costs: indirect labor $12,432, indirect materials $7,680, repairs $4,800, utilities $6,840, and lubricants $1,920.

Instructions

(a) Total costs: DLH 27,000, $52,400; DLH 36,000, $63,200

(b) Total $1,232 U

(a) Prepare a monthly manufacturing overhead flexible budget for each increment of 3,000 direct labor hours over the relevant range for the year ending December 31, 2014.

(b) Prepare a flexible budget report for October.

(c) ▬▬▬▷ Comment on management's efficiency in controlling manufacturing overhead costs in October.

P24-2A Zelmer Company manufactures tablecloths. Sales have grown rapidly over the past 2 years. As a result, the president has installed a budgetary control system for 2014. The following data were used in developing the master manufacturing overhead budget for the Ironing Department, which is based on an activity index of direct labor hours.

Prepare flexible budget, budget report, and graph for manufacturing overhead.

(LO 3)

Variable Costs	Rate per Direct Labor Hour	Annual Fixed Costs	
Indirect labor	$0.40	Supervision	$48,000
Indirect materials	0.50	Depreciation	18,000
Factory utilities	0.30	Insurance	12,000
Factory repairs	0.20	Rent	30,000

The master overhead budget was prepared on the expectation that 480,000 direct labor hours will be worked during the year. In June, 41,000 direct labor hours were worked. At that level of activity, actual costs were as shown below.

Variable—per direct labor hour: indirect labor $0.44, indirect materials $0.48, factory utilities $0.32, and factory repairs $0.25.

Fixed: same as budgeted.

Instructions
(a) Prepare a monthly manufacturing overhead flexible budget for the year ending December 31, 2014, assuming production levels range from 35,000 to 50,000 direct labor hours. Use increments of 5,000 direct labor hours.
(b) Prepare a budget report for June comparing actual results with budget data based on the flexible budget.
(c) Were costs effectively controlled? Explain.
(d) State the formula for computing the total budgeted costs for the Ironing Department.
(e) Prepare the flexible budget graph, showing total budgeted costs at 35,000 and 45,000 direct labor hours. Use increments of 5,000 direct labor hours on the horizontal axis and increments of $10,000 on the vertical axis.

(a) Total costs: 35,000 DLH, $58,000; 50,000 DLH, $79,000

(b) Budget $66,400
Actual $70,090

P24-3A Hill Company uses budgets in controlling costs. The August 2014 budget report for the company's Assembling Department is as follows.

State total budgeted cost formula, and prepare flexible budget reports for 2 time periods.

(LO 2, 3)

Hill Company
Budget Report
Assembling Department
For the Month Ended August 31, 2014

Manufacturing Costs	Budget	Actual	Difference Favorable F Unfavorable U
Variable costs			
Direct materials	$ 48,000	$ 47,000	$1,000 F
Direct labor	54,000	51,200	2,800 F
Indirect materials	24,000	24,200	200 U
Indirect labor	18,000	17,500	500 F
Utilities	15,000	14,900	100 F
Maintenance	6,000	6,200	200 U
Total variable	165,000	161,000	4,000 F
Fixed costs			
Rent	12,000	12,000	–0–
Supervision	17,000	17,000	–0–
Depreciation	6,000	6,000	–0–
Total fixed	35,000	35,000	–0–
Total costs	$200,000	$196,000	$4,000 F

The monthly budget amounts in the report were based on an expected production of 60,000 units per month or 720,000 units per year. The Assembling Department manager is pleased with the report and expects a raise, or at least praise for a job well done. The company president, however, is unhappy with the results for August because only 58,000 units were produced.

(b) Budget $194,500

(c) Budget $211,000
Actual $212,100

Prepare responsibility report for a profit center.

(LO 6)

(a) Contribution margin
$85,000 F
Controllable margin
$80,000 F

Prepare responsibility report for an investment center, and compute ROI.

(LO 7)

(a) Controllable margin:
Budget $330;
Actual $350

Prepare reports for cost centers under responsibility accounting, and comment on performance of managers.

(LO 4)

Instructions

(a) State the total monthly budgeted cost formula.

(b) Prepare a budget report for August using flexible budget data. Why does this report provide a better basis for evaluating performance than the report based on static budget data?

(c) In September, 64,000 units were produced. Prepare the budget report using flexible budget data, assuming (1) each variable cost was 10% higher than its actual cost in August, and (2) fixed costs were the same in September as in August.

P24-4A Clarke Inc. operates the Patio Furniture Division as a profit center. Operating data for this division for the year ended December 31, 2014, are as shown below.

	Budget	Difference from Budget
Sales	$2,500,000	$50,000 F
Cost of goods sold		
Variable	1,300,000	41,000 F
Controllable fixed	200,000	3,000 U
Selling and administrative		
Variable	220,000	6,000 U
Controllable fixed	50,000	2,000 U
Noncontrollable fixed costs	70,000	4,000 U

In addition, Clarke incurs $180,000 of indirect fixed costs that were budgeted at $175,000. Twenty percent (20%) of these costs are allocated to the Patio Furniture Division.

Instructions

(a) Prepare a responsibility report for the Patio Furniture Division for the year.

(b) ▭▭▭▭▷ Comment on the manager's performance in controlling revenues and costs.

(c) Identify any costs excluded from the responsibility report and explain why they were excluded.

P24-5A Suppan Company manufactures a variety of tools and industrial equipment. The company operates through three divisions. Each division is an investment center. Operating data for the Home Division for the year ended December 31, 2014, and relevant budget data are as follows.

	Actual	Comparison with Budget
Sales	$1,400,000	$100,000 favorable
Variable cost of goods sold	675,000	55,000 unfavorable
Variable selling and administrative expenses	125,000	25,000 unfavorable
Controllable fixed cost of goods sold	170,000	On target
Controllable fixed selling and administrative expenses	80,000	On target

Average operating assets for the year for the Home Division were $2,000,000 which was also the budgeted amount.

Instructions

(a) Prepare a responsibility report (in thousands of dollars) for the Home Division.

(b) Evaluate the manager's performance. Which items will likely be investigated by top management?

(c) Compute the expected ROI in 2014 for the Home Division, assuming the following independent changes to actual data.

(1) Variable cost of goods sold is decreased by 5%.

(2) Average operating assets are decreased by 10%.

(3) Sales are increased by $200,000, and this increase is expected to increase contribution margin by $85,000.

P24-6A Durham Company uses a responsibility reporting system. It has divisions in Denver, Seattle, and San Diego. Each division has three production departments: Cutting, Shaping, and Finishing. The responsibility for each department rests with a manager who reports to the division production manager. Each division manager reports to the vice president of production. There are also vice presidents for marketing and finance. All vice presidents report to the president.

In January 2014, controllable actual and budget manufacturing overhead cost data for the departments and divisions were as shown below.

Manufacturing Overhead	Actual	Budget
Individual costs—Cutting Department—Seattle		
Indirect labor	$ 73,000	$ 70,000
Indirect materials	47,900	46,000
Maintenance	20,500	18,000
Utilities	20,100	17,000
Supervision	22,000	20,000
	$183,500	$171,000
Total costs		
Shaping Department—Seattle	$158,000	$148,000
Finishing Department—Seattle	210,000	205,000
Denver division	678,000	673,000
San Diego division	722,000	715,000

Additional overhead costs were incurred as follows: Seattle division production manager—actual costs $52,500, budget $51,000; vice president of production—actual costs $65,000, budget $64,000; president—actual costs $76,400, budget $74,200. These expenses are not allocated.

The vice presidents who report to the president, other than the vice president of production, had the following expenses.

Vice President	Actual	Budget
Marketing	$133,600	$130,000
Finance	109,000	104,000

Instructions

(a) Using the format on page 1199, prepare the following responsibility reports.
  (1) Manufacturing overhead—Cutting Department manager—Seattle division.
  (2) Manufacturing overhead—Seattle division manager.
  (3) Manufacturing overhead—vice president of production.
  (4) Manufacturing overhead and expenses—president.
(b) Comment on the comparative performances of:
  (1) Department managers in the Seattle division.
  (2) Division managers.
  (3) Vice presidents.

(a) (1) $12,500 U
(2) $29,000 U
(3) $42,000 U
(4) $52,800 U

*P24-7A Delby Industries has manufactured prefabricated houses for over 20 years. The houses are constructed in sections to be assembled on customers' lots. Delby expanded into the precut housing market when it acquired Jensen Company, one of its suppliers. In this market, various types of lumber are precut into the appropriate lengths, banded into packages, and shipped to customers' lots for assembly. Delby designated the Jensen Division as an investment center.

Compare ROI and residual income.

(LO 8)

Delby uses return on investment (ROI) as a performance measure with investment defined as average operating assets. Management bonuses are based in part on ROI. All investments are expected to earn a minimum rate of return of 18%. Jensen's ROI has ranged from 20.1% to 23.5% since it was acquired. Jensen had an investment opportunity in 2014 that had an estimated ROI of 19%. Jensen management decided against the investment because it believed the investment would decrease the division's overall ROI.

Selected financial information for Jensen are presented below. The division's average operating assets were $12,300,000 for the year 2014.

Jensen Division
Selected Financial Information
For the Year Ended December 31, 2014

Sales	$26,000,000
Contribution margin	9,100,000
Controllable margin	2,583,000

Instructions
(a) Calculate the following performance measures for 2014 for the Jensen Division.
  (1) Return on investment (ROI).
  (2) Residual income.
(b) ▭▭▭▷ Would the management of Jensen Division have been more likely to accept the investment opportunity it had in 2014 if residual income were used as a performance measure instead of ROI? Explain your answer.

(CMA adapted)

PROBLEMS: SET B

Prepare flexible budget and budget report for manufacturing overhead.

(LO 3)

P24-1B Speier Company estimates that 240,000 direct labor hours will be worked during 2014 in the Assembly Department. On this basis, the following budgeted manufacturing overhead data are computed.

Variable Overhead Costs		Fixed Overhead Costs	
Indirect labor	$ 72,000	Supervision	$ 75,600
Indirect materials	48,000	Depreciation	30,000
Repairs	36,000	Insurance	12,000
Utilities	24,000	Rent	9,600
Lubricants	12,000	Property taxes	6,000
	$192,000		$133,200

It is estimated that direct labor hours worked each month will range from 18,000 to 24,000 hours.
  During January, 20,000 direct labor hours were worked and the following overhead costs were incurred.

Variable Overhead Costs		Fixed Overhead Costs	
Indirect labor	$ 6,200	Supervision	$ 6,300
Indirect materials	3,600	Depreciation	2,500
Repairs	2,300	Insurance	1,000
Utilities	1,700	Rent	850
Lubricants	1,050	Property taxes	500
	$14,850		$11,150

Instructions
(a) Prepare a monthly flexible manufacturing overhead budget for each increment of 2,000 direct labor hours over the relevant range for the year ending December 31, 2014.
(b) Prepare a manufacturing overhead budget report for January.
(c) ▭▭▭▷ Comment on management's efficiency in controlling manufacturing overhead costs in January.

(a) Total costs: 18,000 DLH, $25,500; 24,000 DLH, $30,300
(b) Budget $27,100 Actual $26,000

Prepare flexible budget, budget report, and graph for manufacturing overhead.

(LO 3)

P24-2B Gonzalez Company produces one product, Olpe. Because of wide fluctuations in demand for Olpe, the Assembly Department experiences significant variations in monthly production levels.
  The annual master manufacturing overhead budget is based on 300,000 direct labor hours. In July, 27,500 labor hours were worked. The master manufacturing overhead budget for the year and the actual overhead costs incurred in July are as follows.

Overhead Costs	Master Budget (annual)	Actual in July
Variable		
Indirect labor	$300,000	$26,000
Indirect materials	150,000	11,350
Utilities	90,000	8,050
Maintenance	60,000	5,400
Fixed		
Supervision	144,000	12,000
Depreciation	96,000	8,000
Insurance and taxes	60,000	5,000
Total	$900,000	$75,800

Instructions

(a) Prepare a monthly flexible overhead budget for the year ending December 31, 2014, assuming monthly production levels range from 22,500 to 30,000 direct labor hours. Use increments of 2,500 direct labor hours.

(b) Prepare a budget report for the month of July 2014, comparing actual results with budget data based on the flexible budget.

(c) ▭▬▬▷ Were costs effectively controlled? Explain.

(d) State the formula for computing the total monthly budgeted costs in the Gonzalez Company.

(e) Prepare the flexible budget graph showing total budgeted costs at 25,000 and 27,500 direct labor hours. Use increments of 5,000 on the horizontal axis and increments of $10,000 on the vertical axis.

(a) Total costs: 22,500 DLH, $70,000; 30,000 DLH, $85,000

(b) Budget $80,000
Actual $75,800

P24-3B Hardesty Company uses budgets in controlling costs. The May 2014 budget report for the company's Packaging Department is as follows.

State total budgeted cost formula, and prepare flexible budget reports for 2 time periods.

(LO 2, 3)

Hardesty Company
Budget Report
Packaging Department
For the Month Ended May 31, 2014

Manufacturing Costs	Budget	Actual	Difference Favorable F Unfavorable U
Variable costs			
Direct materials	$ 40,000	$ 41,000	$1,000 U
Direct labor	45,000	47,300	2,300 U
Indirect materials	15,000	15,200	200 U
Indirect labor	12,500	13,000	500 U
Utilities	10,000	9,600	400 F
Maintenance	7,500	8,000	500 U
Total variable	130,000	134,100	4,100 U
Fixed costs			
Rent	10,000	10,000	–0–
Supervision	7,000	7,000	–0–
Depreciation	4,000	4,000	–0–
Total fixed	21,000	21,000	–0–
Total costs	$151,000	$155,100	$4,100 U

The monthly budget amounts in the report were based on an expected production of 50,000 units per month or 600,000 units per year.

The company president was displeased with the department manager's performance. The department manager, who thought he had done a good job, could not understand the unfavorable results. In May, 55,000 units were produced.

Instructions

(a) State the total budgeted cost formula.

(b) Prepare a budget report for May using flexible budget data. Why does this report provide a better basis for evaluating performance than the report based on static budget data?

(c) In June, 40,000 units were produced. Prepare the budget report using flexible budget data, assuming (1) each variable cost was 20% less in June than its actual cost in May, and (2) fixed costs were the same in the month of June as in May.

(b) Budget $164,000

(c) Budget $125,000
Actual $128,280

P24-4B Guzman Inc. operates the Home Appliance Division as a profit center. Operating data for this division for the year ended December 31, 2014, are shown on the next page.

Prepare responsibility report for a profit center.

(LO 6)

	Budget	Difference from Budget
Sales	$2,400,000	$90,000 U
Cost of goods sold		
Variable	1,200,000	58,000 U
Controllable fixed	200,000	8,000 F
Selling and administrative		
Variable	240,000	8,000 F
Controllable fixed	60,000	3,000 U
Noncontrollable fixed costs	50,000	2,000 U

In addition, Guzman incurs $150,000 of indirect fixed costs that were budgeted at $155,000. Twenty percent (20%) of these costs are allocated to the Home Appliance Division. None of these costs are controllable by the division manager.

Instructions

(a) Contribution margin
$140,000 U
Controllable margin
$135,000 U

(a) Prepare a responsibility report for the Home Appliance Division (a profit center) for the year.
(b) ▭▭▭▭▷ Comment on the manager's performance in controlling revenues and costs.
(c) Identify any costs excluded from the responsibility report and explain why they were excluded.

Prepare responsibility report for an investment center, and compute ROI.

(LO 7)

P24-5B Strauss Company manufactures a variety of garden and lawn equipment. The company operates through three divisions. Each division is an investment center. Operating data for the Lawnmower Division for the year ended December 31, 2014, and relevant budget data are as follows.

	Actual	Comparison with Budget
Sales	$2,900,000	$150,000 unfavorable
Variable cost of goods sold	1,400,000	100,000 unfavorable
Variable selling and administrative		
expenses	300,000	40,000 favorable
Controllable fixed cost of goods sold	270,000	On target
Controllable fixed selling and administrative		
expenses	140,000	On target

Average operating assets for the year for the Lawnmower Division were $5,000,000, which was also the budgeted amount.

Instructions

(a) Controllable margin:
Budget $1,000
Actual $790

(a) Prepare a responsibility report (in thousands of dollars) for the Lawnmower Division.
(b) Evaluate the manager's performance. Which items will likely be investigated by top management?
(c) Compute the expected ROI in 2014 for the Lawnmower Division, assuming the following independent changes.
  (1) Variable cost of goods sold is decreased by 20%.
  (2) Average operating assets are decreased by 24%.
  (3) Sales are increased by $700,000, and this increase is expected to increase contribution margin by $260,000.

Prepare reports for cost centers under responsibility accounting, and comment on performance of managers.

(LO 4)

P24-6B Gore Company uses a responsibility reporting system. It has divisions in San Francisco, Phoenix, and Tulsa. Each division has three production departments: Cutting, Shaping, and Finishing. The responsibility for each department rests with a manager who reports to the division production manager. Each division manager reports to the vice president of production. There are also vice presidents for marketing and finance. All vice presidents report to the president.

In January 2014, controllable actual and budget manufacturing overhead cost data for the departments and divisions were as shown on the next page.

Manufacturing Overhead	Actual	Budget
Individual costs—Cutting Department—Phoenix		
Indirect labor	$ 95,000	$ 90,000
Indirect materials	62,700	61,000
Maintenance	27,400	25,000
Utilities	25,200	20,000
Supervision	31,000	28,000
	$241,300	$224,000
Total costs		
Shaping Department—Phoenix	$190,000	$177,000
Finishing Department—Phoenix	250,000	245,000
San Francisco division	724,000	715,000
Tulsa division	760,000	750,000

Additional overhead costs were incurred as follows: Phoenix division production manager—actual costs $73,100, budget $70,000; vice president of production—actual costs $72,000, budget $70,000; president—actual costs $94,200, budget $91,300. These expenses are not allocated.

The vice presidents, who report to the president (other than the vice president of production), had the following expenses.

Vice President	Actual	Budget
Marketing	$167,200	$160,000
Finance	125,000	120,000

Instructions
(a) Using the format on page xxx, prepare the following responsibility reports.
  (1) Manufacturing overhead—Cutting Department manager—Phoenix division.
  (2) Manufacturing overhead—Phoenix division manager.
  (3) Manufacturing overhead—vice president of production.
  (4) Manufacturing overhead and expenses—president.
(b) Comment on the comparative performances of:
  (1) Department managers in the Phoenix division.
  (2) Division managers.
  (3) Vice presidents.

(a) (1) $17,300 U
(2) $38,400 U
(3) $59,400 U
(4) $74,500 U

*P24-7B Walton Industries has manufactured prefabricated garages for over 20 years. The garages are constructed in sections to be assembled on customers' lots. Walton expanded into the precut housing market when it acquired Washington Enterprises, one of its suppliers. In this market, various types of lumber are precut into the appropriate lengths, banded into packages, and shipped to customers' lots for assembly. Walton designated the Washington Division as an investment center.

Compare ROI and residual income.

(LO 8)

Walton uses return on investment (ROI) as a performance measure, with investment defined as average operating assets. Management bonuses are based in part on ROI. All investments are expected to earn a minimum rate of return of 15%. Washington's ROI has ranged from 19.9% to 23.3% since it was acquired. Washington had an investment opportunity in 2014 that had an estimated ROI of 18%. Washington's management decided against the investment because it believed the investment would decrease the division's overall ROI.

Selected financial information for Washington is presented below. The division's average operating assets were $7,500,000 for the year 2014.

Washington Division
Selected Financial Information
For the Year Ended December 31, 2014

Sales	$16,000,000
Contribution margin	5,600,000
Controllable margin	1,500,000

Instructions

(a) Calculate the following performance measures for 2014 for the Washington Division.
   (1) Return on investment (ROI).
   (2) Residual income.
(b)  Would the management of Washington have been more likely to accept the investment opportunity it had in 2014 if residual income were used as a performance measure instead of ROI? Explain your answer.

PROBLEMS: SET C

Visit the book's companion website, at **www.wiley.com/college/weygandt**, and choose the Student Companion site to access Problem Set C.

WATERWAYS CONTINUING PROBLEM

(*Note:* This is a continuation of the Waterways Problem from Chapters 15–23.)

WCP24 Waterways Corporation is continuing its budget preparations. This problem gives you static budget information as well as actual overhead costs, and asks you to calculate amounts related to budgetary control and responsibility accounting.

Go to the book's companion website, at **www.wiley.com/college/weygandt**, *to find the completion of this problem.*

Broadening Your **PERSPECTIVE**

Management Decision-Making

Decision-Making at Current Designs

BYP24-1 The Current Designs staff has prepared the annual manufacturing budget for the roto-molded line based on an estimated annual production of 4,000 kayaks during 2013. Each kayak will require 54 pounds of polyethylene powder and a finishing kit (rope, seat, hardware, etc.). The polyethylene powder used in these kayaks costs $1.50 per pound, and the finishing kits cost $170 each. Each kayak will use two kinds of labor—2 hours of type I labor from people who run the oven and trim the plastic, and 3 hours of work from type II workers who attach the hatches and seat and other hardware. The type I employees are paid $15 per hour, and the type II are paid $12 per hour. Manufacturing overhead is budgeted at $396,000 for 2013, broken down as follows.

Variable costs	
Indirect materials	$ 40,000
Manufacturing supplies	53,800
Maintenance and utilities	88,000
	181,800
Fixed costs	
Supervision	90,000
Insurance	14,400
Depreciation	109,800
	214,200
Total	$396,000

During the first quarter, ended March 31, 2013, 1,050 units were actually produced with the following costs.

Polyethylene powder	$ 87,000
Finishing kits	178,840
Type I labor	31,500
Type II labor	39,060
Indirect materials	10,500
Manufacturing supplies	14,150
Maintenance and utilities	26,000
Supervision	20,000
Insurance	3,600
Depreciation	27,450
Total	$438,100

Instructions
(a) Prepare the annual manufacturing budget for 2013, assuming that 4,000 kayaks will be produced.
(b) Prepare the flexible budget for manufacturing for the quarter ended March 31, 2013. Assume activity levels of 900, 1,000, and 1,050 units.
(c) Assuming the rotomolded line is treated as a profit center, prepare a flexible budget report for manufacturing for the quarter ended March 31, 2013, when 1,050 units were produced.

Decision-Making Across the Organization

BYP24-2 Green Pastures is a 400-acre farm on the outskirts of the Kentucky Bluegrass, specializing in the boarding of broodmares and their foals. A recent economic downturn in the thoroughbred industry has led to a decline in breeding activities, and it has made the boarding business extremely competitive. To meet the competition, Green Pastures planned in 2014 to entertain clients, advertise more extensively, and absorb expenses formerly paid by clients such as veterinary and blacksmith fees.

The budget report for 2014 is presented below. As shown, the static income statement budget for the year is based on an expected 21,900 boarding days at $25 per mare. The variable expenses per mare per day were budgeted: feed $5, veterinary fees $3, blacksmith fees $0.25, and supplies $0.55. All other budgeted expenses were either semifixed or fixed.

During the year, management decided not to replace a worker who quit in March, but it did issue a new advertising brochure and did more entertaining of clients.[1]

Green Pastures
Static Budget Income Statement
For the Year Ended December 31, 2014

	Actual	Master Budget	Difference
Number of mares	52	60	8 U
Number of boarding days	19,000	21,900	2,900 U
Sales	$380,000	$547,500	$167,500 U
Less: Variable expenses			
Feed	104,390	109,500	5,110 F
Veterinary fees	58,838	65,700	6,862 F
Blacksmith fees	4,984	5,475	491 F
Supplies	10,178	12,045	1,867 F
Total variable expenses	178,390	192,720	14,330 F
Contribution margin	201,610	354,780	153,170 U

---

[1]Data for this case are based on Hans Sprohge and John Talbott, "New Applications for Variance Analysis," *Journal of Accountancy* (AICPA, New York), April 1989, pp. 137–141.

	Actual	Master Budget	Difference
Less: Fixed expenses			
Depreciation	40,000	40,000	–0–
Insurance	11,000	11,000	–0–
Utilities	12,000	14,000	2,000 F
Repairs and maintenance	10,000	11,000	1,000 F
Labor	88,000	95,000	7,000 F
Advertisement	12,000	8,000	4,000 U
Entertainment	7,000	5,000	2,000 U
Total fixed expenses	180,000	184,000	4,000 F
Net income	$ 21,610	$170,780	$149,170 U

Instructions

With the class divided into groups, answer the following.

(a) Based on the static budget report:
   (1) What was the primary cause(s) of the loss in net income?
   (2) Did management do a good, average, or poor job of controlling expenses?
   (3) Were management's decisions to stay competitive sound?
(b) Prepare a flexible budget report for the year.
(c) Based on the flexible budget report, answer the three questions in part (a) above.
(d) What course of action do you recommend for the management of Green Pastures?

Managerial Analysis

BYP24-3 Lanier Company manufactures expensive watch cases sold as souvenirs. Three of its sales departments are Retail Sales, Wholesale Sales, and Outlet Sales. The Retail Sales Department is a profit center. The Wholesale Sales Department is a cost center. Its managers merely take orders from customers who purchase through the company's wholesale catalog. The Outlet Sales Department is an investment center because each manager is given full responsibility for an outlet store location. The manager can hire and discharge employees, purchase, maintain, and sell equipment, and in general is fairly independent of company control.

Mary Gammel is a manager in the Retail Sales Department. Stephen Flott manages the Wholesale Sales Department. Jose Gomez manages the Golden Gate Club outlet store in San Francisco. The following are the budget responsibility reports for each of the three departments.

	Budget		
	Retail Sales	**Wholesale Sales**	**Outlet Sales**
Sales	$ 750,000	$ 400,000	$200,000
Variable costs			
Cost of goods sold	150,000	100,000	25,000
Advertising	100,000	30,000	5,000
Sales salaries	75,000	15,000	3,000
Printing	10,000	20,000	5,000
Travel	20,000	30,000	2,000
Fixed costs			
Rent	50,000	30,000	10,000
Insurance	5,000	2,000	1,000
Depreciation	75,000	100,000	40,000
Investment in assets	1,000,000	1,200,000	800,000

	Actual Results		
	Retail Sales	Wholesale Sales	Outlet Sales
Sales	$ 750,000	$ 400,000	$200,000
Variable costs			
Cost of goods sold	192,000	122,000	26,500
Advertising	100,000	30,000	5,000
Sales salaries	75,000	15,000	3,000
Printing	10,000	20,000	5,000
Travel	14,000	21,000	1,500
Fixed costs			
Rent	40,000	50,000	12,300
Insurance	5,000	2,000	1,000
Depreciation	80,000	90,000	56,000
Investment in assets	1,000,000	1,200,000	800,000

Instructions

(a) Determine which of the items should be included in the responsibility report for each of the three managers.

(b) Compare the budgeted measures with the actual results. Decide which results should be called to the attention of each manager.

Real-World Focus

BYP24-4 Computer Associates International, Inc., the world's leading business software company, delivers the end-to-end infrastructure to enable e-business through innovative technology, services, and education. Computer Associates has 19,000 employees worldwide and recently had revenue of over $6 billion.

Presented below is information from the company's annual report.

Computer Associates International, Inc.
Management Discussion

The Company has experienced a pattern of business whereby revenue for its third and fourth fiscal quarters reflects an increase over first- and second-quarter revenue. The Company attributes this increase to clients' increased spending at the end of their calendar year budgetary periods and the culmination of its annual sales plan. Since the Company's costs do not increase proportionately with the third- and fourth-quarters' increase in revenue, the higher revenue in these quarters results in greater profit margins and income. Fourth-quarter profitability is traditionally affected by significant new hirings, training, and education expenditures for the succeeding year.

Instructions

(a) Why don't the company's costs increase proportionately as the revenues increase in the third and fourth quarters?

(b) What type of budgeting seems appropriate for the Computer Associates situation?

BYP24-5 There are many useful resources regarding budgeting available on websites. The following activity investigates the results of a comprehensive budgeting study.

Address: **http://www.accountingweb.com/whitepapers/centage_ioma.pdf**, or go to **www.wiley.com/college/weygandt**

Instructions

Go to the address above and then answer the following questions.

(a) What are cited as the two most common "pain points" of budgeting?

(b) What percentage of companies that participated in the survey said that they prepare annual budgets? Of those that prepare budgets, what percentage say that they start the budgeting process by first generating sales projections?

(c) What is the most common amount of time for the annual budgeting process?

(d) When evaluating variances from budgeted amounts, what was the most commonly defined range of acceptable tolerance levels?

(e) The study defines three types of consequences for varying from budgeted amounts. How does it describe "severe" consequences?

Critical Thinking

Communication Activity

BYP24-6 The manufacturing overhead budget for Fleming Company contains the following items.

Variable costs		Fixed costs	
Indirect materials	$22,000	Supervision	$17,000
Indirect labor	12,000	Inspection costs	1,000
Maintenance expense	10,000	Insurance expense	2,000
Manufacturing supplies	6,000	Depreciation	15,000
Total variable	$50,000	Total fixed	$35,000

The budget was based on an estimated 2,000 units being produced. During the past month, 1,500 units were produced, and the following costs incurred.

Variable costs		Fixed costs	
Indirect materials	$22,500	Supervision	$18,400
Indirect labor	13,500	Inspection costs	1,200
Maintenance expense	8,200	Insurance expense	2,200
Manufacturing supplies	5,000	Depreciation	14,700
Total variable	$49,200	Total fixed	$36,500

Instructions

(a) Determine which items would be controllable by Fred Bedner, the production manager.

(b) How much should have been spent during the month for the manufacture of the 1,500 units?

(c) Prepare a flexible manufacturing overhead budget report for Mr. Bedner.

(d) Prepare a responsibility report. Include only the costs that would have been controllable by Mr. Bedner. Assume that the supervision cost above includes Mr. Bedner's salary of $10,000, both at budget and actual. In an attached memo, describe clearly for Mr. Bedner the areas in which his performance needs to be improved.

Ethics Case

BYP24-7 American Products Corporation participates in a highly competitive industry. In order to meet this competition and achieve profit goals, the company has chosen the decentralized form of organization. Each manager of a decentralized investment center is measured on the basis of profit contribution, market penetration, and return on investment. Failure to meet the objectives established by corporate management for these measures has not been acceptable and usually has resulted in demotion or dismissal of an investment center manager.

An anonymous survey of managers in the company revealed that the managers feel the pressure to compromise their personal ethical standards to achieve the corporate objectives. For example, at certain plant locations there was pressure to reduce quality control to a level which could not assure that all unsafe products would be rejected. Also, sales personnel were encouraged to use questionable sales tactics to obtain orders, including gifts and other incentives to purchasing agents.

The chief executive officer is disturbed by the survey findings. In his opinion, such behavior cannot be condoned by the company. He concludes that the company should do something about this problem.

Instructions
(a) Who are the stakeholders (the affected parties) in this situation?
(b) Identify the ethical implications, conflicts, or dilemmas in the above described situation.
(c) What might the company do to reduce the pressures on managers and decrease the ethical conflicts?

(CMA adapted)

All About You

BYP24-8 It is one thing to prepare a personal budget; it is another thing to stick to it. Financial planners have suggested various mechanisms to provide support for enforcing personal budgets. One approach is called "envelope budgeting."

Instructions
Read the article provided at **http://en.wikipedia.org/wiki/Envelope_budgeting**, and answer the following questions.

(a) Summarize the process of envelope budgeting.
(b) Evaluate whether you think you would benefit from envelope budgeting. What do you think are its strengths and weaknesses relative to your situation?

Considering Your Costs and Benefits

BYP24-9 Preparing a personal budget is a great first step toward control over your personal finances. It is especially useful to prepare a budget when you face a big decision. For most people, the biggest decision they will ever make is whether to purchase a house. The percentage of people in the United States who own a home is high compared to many other countries. This is partially the result of U.S. government programs and incentives that encourage home ownership. For example, the interest on a home mortgage is tax-deductible.

Before purchasing a house, you should first consider whether buying it is the best choice for you. Suppose you just graduated from college and are moving to a new community. Should you immediately buy a new home?

> **YES:** If I purchase a home, I am making my housing cost more like a "fixed cost," thus minimizing increases in my future housing costs. Also, I benefit from the appreciation in my home's value. Although recent turbulence in the economy has caused home prices in many communities to decline, I know that over the long term, home prices have increased across the country.
>
> **NO:** I just moved to a new town, so I don't know the housing market. I am new to my job, so I don't know whether I will like it or my new community. Also, if my job does go well, it is likely that my income will increase in the next few years, so I will able to afford a better house if I wait. Therefore, the flexibility provided by renting is very valuable to me at this point in my life.

Instructions
Write a response indicating your position regarding this situation. Provide support for your view.

Answers to Chapter Questions

Answers to Insight and Accounting Across the Organization Questions

p. 1187 Just What the Doctor Ordered? Q: Explain how the use of flexible budgets might help to identify the best solution to this problem. **A:** A fixed budget assumes a particular level of activity. In the case of television shows, the number of viewers can impact revenues and costs. NBCUniversal could prepare alternative budgets at varying levels of activities and assume various cost structures depending on the number of cast members and other factors. Experimenting with different scenarios could help the network identify an approach that maintains an acceptable level of income as revenues decline.

p. 1192 Budgets and the Exotic Newcastle Disease Q: What is the major benefit of tying a budget to the overall goals of the company? **A:** People working on a budgeting process that is clearly guided and focused by strategic goals spend less time arguing about irrelevant details and more time focusing on the items that matter.

p. 1195 Competition versus Collaboration Q: How might managers of separate divisions be able to reduce division costs through collaboration? **A:** Division managers might reduce costs by sharing design and marketing resources or by jointly negotiating with suppliers. In addition, they can reduce the need to hire and lay off employees by sharing staff across divisions as human resource needs change.

p. 1197 Flexible Manufacturing Requires Flexible Accounting Q: What implications do these improvements in production capabilities have for management accounting information and performance evaluation within the organization? **A:** In order to maximize the potential of flexible manufacturing facilities, managers need to be supplied with information on a more frequent basis. In turn, the tools used to evaluate performance need to take into account what information management had at its disposal, and what decisions were made in response to this information.

p. 1206 Does Hollywood Look at ROI? Q: What might be the reason that movie studios do not produce G-rated movies as much as R-rated ones? **A:** Perhaps Hollywood believes that big-name stars or large budgets, both of which are typical of R-rated movies, sell movies. However, one study recently concluded, "We can't find evidence that stars help movies, and we can't find evidence that bigger budgets increase return on investment." Some film companies are going out of their way to achieve at least a PG rating.

Answers to Self-Test Questions

1. c **2.** d **3.** c **4.** b **5.** b **6.** a $(\$90,000 - \$30,000) \div 10,000$ **7.** d $\$28,000 - [9,200 \times (\$2,700 \div 9,000)]$ **8.** a **9.** d **10.** d **11.** a **12.** c **13.** b **14.** b **15.** d

✔ **Remember to go back to The Navigator box on the chapter opening page and check off your completed work.**

Chapter 25

Standard Costs and Balanced Scorecard

Feature Story

80,000 Different Caffeinated Combinations

When Howard Schultz purchased a small Seattle coffee-roasting business in 1987, he set out to create a new kind of company. He thought the company should sell coffee by the cup in its store, in addition to the bags of roasted beans it already sold. He also felt that the store shouldn't just sell coffee but also a pleasant atmosphere and experience. Schultz saw the store as a place where you could order a beverage, custom-made to your unique tastes, in an environment that would give you the sense that you had escaped, if only momentarily, from the chaos we call life. Finally, Schultz believed that the company would prosper if employees shared in its success.

In a little more than 20 years, Howard Schultz's company, Starbucks, grew from that one store to over 17,000 locations in 54 countries. That is an incredible rate of growth, and it didn't happen by accident. While Starbucks does everything it can to maximize the customer's experience, behind the scenes it needs to control costs. Consider the almost infinite options of beverage combinations and variations at Starbucks. The company must determine the most efficient way to make each beverage, it must communicate these methods in the form of standards to its employees, and it must then evaluate whether those standards are being met.

✔ The Navigator

Learning Objectives

After studying this chapter, you should be able to:

1. Distinguish between a standard and a budget.
2. Identify the advantages of standard costs.
3. Describe how companies set standards.
4. State the formulas for determining direct materials and direct labor variances.
5. State the formula for determining the total manufacturing overhead variance.
6. Discuss the reporting of variances.
7. Prepare an income statement for management under a standard costing system.
8. Describe the balanced scorecard approach to performance evaluation.

 The Navigator

Schultz's book, *Onward: How Starbucks Fought for Its Life Without Losing Its Soul*, describes a painful period in which Starbucks had to close 600 stores and lay off thousands of employees. However, when a prominent shareholder suggested that the company eliminate its employee health-care plan, as so many other companies had done, Schultz refused. The health-care plan represented one of the company's most tangible commitments to employee

well-being as well as to corporate social responsibility. Schultz feels strongly that providing health care to the company's employees is an essential part of the standard cost of a cup of Starbucks' coffee.

Watch the Starbucks video in WileyPLUS to learn more about how the company sets standards. Watch the Southwest Airlines video in WileyPLUS to learn more about the use of the balanced scorecard in the real world.

Preview of Chapter 25

Standards are a fact of life. You met the admission standards for the school you are attending. The vehicle that you drive had to meet certain governmental emissions standards. The hamburgers and salads that you eat in a restaurant have to meet certain health and nutritional standards before they can be sold. As described in our Feature Story, Starbucks has standards for the costs of its materials, labor, and overhead. The reason for standards in these cases is very simple: They help to ensure that overall product quality is high while keeping costs under control.

In this chapter, we continue the study of controlling costs. You will learn how to evaluate performance using standard costs and a balanced scorecard.

The content and organization of Chapter 25 are as follows.

STANDARD COSTS AND BALANCED SCORECARD

The Need for Standards	Setting Standard Costs	Analyzing and Reporting Variances from Standards	Balanced Scorecard
• Standards vs. budgets • Why standard costs?	• Ideal vs. normal • Case study	• Direct materials variances • Direct labor variances • Manufacturing overhead variances • Reporting variances • Statement presentation	• Financial perspective • Customer perspective • Internal process perspective • Learning and growth perspective

✔ The Navigator

The Need for Standards

Standards are common in business. Those imposed by government agencies are often called **regulations**. They include the Fair Labor Standards Act, the Equal Employment Opportunity Act, and a multitude of environmental standards. Standards established internally by a company may extend to personnel matters, such as employee absenteeism and ethical codes of conduct, quality control standards for products, and standard costs for goods and services. In managerial accounting, **standard costs** are predetermined unit costs, which companies use as measures of performance.

We will focus on manufacturing operations in this chapter. But you should also recognize that standard costs also apply to many types of service businesses as well. For example, a fast-food restaurant such as McDonald's knows the price it should pay for pickles, beef, buns, and other ingredients. It also knows how much time it should take an employee to flip hamburgers. If the company pays too much for pickles or if employees take too much time to prepare Big Macs, McDonald's notices the deviations and takes corrective action. Not-for-profit entities, such as universities, charitable organizations, and governmental agencies, also may use standard costs as measures of performance.

Distinguishing Between Standards and Budgets

> **LEARNING OBJECTIVE 1**
>
> **Distinguish between a standard and a budget.**

Both **standards** and **budgets** are predetermined costs, and both contribute to management planning and control. There is a difference, however, in the way the terms are expressed. A standard is a **unit** amount. A budget is a **total** amount. Thus, it is customary to state that the **standard cost** of direct labor for a unit of product is, say, $10. If the company produces 5,000 units of the product, the $50,000 of direct labor is the **budgeted** labor cost. A standard is the budgeted **cost per unit** of product. A standard is therefore concerned with each individual cost component that makes up the entire budget.

There are important accounting differences between budgets and standards. Except in the application of manufacturing overhead to jobs and processes, budget data are not journalized in cost accounting systems. In contrast, as we illustrate in the appendix to this chapter, standard costs may be incorporated into cost accounting systems. Also, a company may report its inventories at standard cost in its financial statements, but it would not report inventories at budgeted costs.

Why Standard Costs?

> **LEARNING OBJECTIVE 2**
>
> **Identify the advantages of standard costs.**

Standard costs offer a number of advantages to an organization, as shown in Illustration 25-1.

The organization will realize these advantages only when standard costs are carefully established and prudently used. Using standards solely as a way to place blame can have a negative effect on managers and employees. To minimize this effect, many companies offer wage incentives to those who meet the standards.

Setting Standard Costs

> **LEARNING OBJECTIVE 3**
>
> **Describe how companies set standards.**

The setting of standard costs to produce a unit of product is a difficult task. It requires input from all persons who have responsibility for costs and quantities. To determine the standard cost of direct materials, management consults purchasing agents, product managers, quality control engineers, and production supervisors. In setting the standard cost for direct labor, managers obtain pay

Advantages of Standard Costs

Facilitate management planning

Promote greater economy by making employees more "cost-conscious"

Useful in setting selling prices

Contribute to management control by providing basis for evaluation of cost control

Useful in highlighting variances in management by exception

Simplify costing of inventories and reduce clerical costs

Illustration 25-1
Advantages of standard costs

rate data from the payroll department. Industrial engineers generally determine the labor time requirements. The managerial accountant provides important input for the standard-setting process by accumulating historical cost data and by knowing how costs respond to changes in activity levels.

To be effective in controlling costs, standard costs need to be current at all times. Thus, standards are under continuous review. They should change whenever managers determine that the existing standard is not a good measure of performance. Circumstances that warrant revision of a standard include changed wage rates resulting from a new union contract, a change in product specifications, or the implementation of a new manufacturing method.

Ideal versus Normal Standards

Companies set standards at one of two levels: ideal or normal. **Ideal standards** represent optimum levels of performance under perfect operating conditions. **Normal standards** represent efficient levels of performance that are attainable under expected operating conditions.

Some managers believe ideal standards will stimulate workers to ever-increasing improvement. However, most managers believe that ideal standards lower the morale of the entire workforce because they are difficult, if not impossible, to meet. Very few companies use ideal standards.

Most companies that use standards set them at a normal level. Properly set, normal standards should be **rigorous but attainable**. Normal standards allow for rest periods, machine breakdowns, and other "normal" contingencies in the production process. In the remainder of this chapter, we will assume that standard costs are set at a normal level.

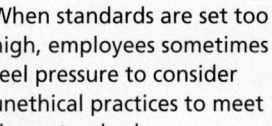

Ethics Note

When standards are set too high, employees sometimes feel pressure to consider unethical practices to meet these standards.

A Case Study

To establish the standard cost of producing a product, it is necessary to establish standards for each manufacturing cost element—direct materials, direct labor, and manufacturing overhead. The standard for each element is derived from the standard price to be paid and the standard quantity to be used.

To illustrate, we use an extended example. Xonic Beverage Company uses standard costs to measure performance at the production facility of its caffeinated energy drink, Xonic Tonic. Xonic produces one-gallon containers of concentrated syrup that it sells to coffee and smoothie shops, and other retail outlets. The syrup is mixed with ice water or ice "slush" before serving. The potency of the beverage varies depending on the amount of concentrated syrup used.

DIRECT MATERIALS

The **direct materials price standard** is the cost per unit of direct materials that should be incurred. This standard is based on the purchasing department's best estimate of the **cost of raw materials**. This cost is frequently based on current purchase prices. The price standard also includes an amount for related costs such as receiving, storing, and handling. The materials price standard per pound of material for Xonic Tonic is:

Illustration 25-2
Setting direct materials price standard

Item	Price
Purchase price, net of discounts	$ 2.70
Freight	0.20
Receiving and handling	0.10
Standard direct materials price per pound	**$3.00**

The **direct materials quantity standard** is the quantity of direct materials that should be used per unit of finished goods. This standard is expressed as a physical measure, such as pounds, barrels, or board feet. In setting the standard, management considers both the quality and quantity of materials required to manufacture the product. The standard includes allowances for unavoidable waste and normal spoilage. The standard quantity per unit for Xonic Tonic is as follows.

Item	Quantity (Pounds)
Required materials	3.5
Allowance for waste	0.4
Allowance for spoilage	0.1
Standard direct materials quantity per unit	**4.0**

Illustration 25-3
Setting direct materials quantity standard

The standard direct materials cost per unit is the standard direct materials price times the standard direct materials quantity. For Xonic, the standard direct materials cost per gallon of Xonic Tonic is $12.00 ($3 × 4 pounds).

DIRECT LABOR

The **direct labor price standard** is the rate per hour that should be incurred for direct labor. This standard is based on current wage rates, adjusted for anticipated changes such as cost of living adjustments (COLAs). The price standard also generally includes employer payroll taxes and fringe benefits, such as paid holidays and vacations. For Xonic, the direct labor price standard is as follows.

Alternative Terminology
The direct labor price standard is also called the *direct labor rate standard*.

Item	Price
Hourly wage rate	$ 12.50
COLA	0.25
Payroll taxes	0.75
Fringe benefits	1.50
Standard direct labor rate per hour	**$15.00**

Illustration 25-4
Setting direct labor price standard

The **direct labor quantity standard** is the time that should be required to make one unit of the product. This standard is especially critical in labor-intensive companies. Allowances should be made in this standard for rest periods, cleanup, machine setup, and machine downtime. For Xonic, the direct labor quantity standard is as follows.

Alternative Terminology
The direct labor quantity standard is also called the *direct labor efficiency standard.*

Illustration 25-5
Setting direct labor quantity standard

Item	Quantity (Hours)
Actual production time	1.5
Rest periods and cleanup	0.2
Setup and downtime	0.3
Standard direct labor hours per unit	**2.0**

The standard direct labor cost per unit is the standard direct labor rate times the standard direct labor hours. For Xonic, the standard direct labor cost per gallon is $30 ($15 × 2 hours).

MANUFACTURING OVERHEAD

For manufacturing overhead, companies use a **standard predetermined overhead rate** in setting the standard. This overhead rate is determined by dividing budgeted overhead costs by an expected standard activity index. For example, the index may be standard direct labor hours or standard machine hours.

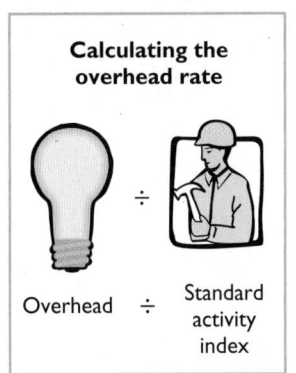

Calculating the overhead rate

Overhead ÷ Standard activity index

As discussed in Chapter 18, many companies employ activity-based costing (ABC) to allocate overhead costs. Because ABC uses multiple activity indices to allocate overhead costs, it results in a better correlation between activities and costs incurred than do other methods. As a result, the use of ABC can significantly improve the usefulness of standard costing for management decision-making.

Xonic uses standard direct labor hours as the activity index. The company expects to produce 13,200 gallons of Xonic Tonic during the year at normal capacity. **Normal capacity** is the average activity output that a company should experience over the long run. Since it takes two direct labor hours for each gallon, total standard direct labor hours are 26,400 (13,200 gallons × 2 hours).

At normal capacity of 26,400 direct labor hours, overhead costs are expected to be $132,000. Of that amount, $79,200 are variable and $52,800 are fixed. Illustration 25-6 shows computation of the standard predetermined overhead rates for Xonic.

Illustration 25-6
Computing predetermined overhead rates

Budgeted Overhead Costs	Amount	÷	Standard Direct Labor Hours	=	Overhead Rate per Direct Labor Hour
Variable	$ 79,200		26,400		$3.00
Fixed	52,800		26,400		2.00
Total	$132,000		26,400		$5.00

The standard manufacturing overhead rate per unit is the predetermined overhead rate times the activity index quantity standard. For Xonic, which uses direct labor hours as its activity index, the standard manufacturing overhead rate per gallon of Xonic Tonic is $10 ($5 × 2 hours).

TOTAL STANDARD COST PER UNIT

After a company has established the standard quantity and price per unit of product, it can determine the total standard cost. The total standard cost per unit is the sum of the standard costs of direct materials, direct labor, and manufacturing overhead. The total standard cost per gallon of Xonic Tonic is $52, as shown on the following standard cost card.

Illustration 25-7
Standard cost per gallon of Xonic Tonic

Product: Xonic Tonic		Unit Measure: Gallon		
Manufacturing Cost Elements	Standard Quantity ×	Standard Price =	Standard Cost	
Direct materials	4 pounds	$ 3.00	$12.00	
Direct labor	2 hours	$15.00	30.00	
Manufacturing overhead	2 hours	$ 5.00	10.00	
			$52.00	

The company prepares a standard cost card for each product. This card provides the basis for determining variances from standards.

MANAGEMENT INSIGHT

How Can We Make Susan's Chili Profitable?

Susan's Chili Factory manufactures and sells chili. The cost of manufacturing Susan's chili consists of the costs of raw materials, labor to convert the basic ingredients to chili, and overhead. Managers need to develop three standards for materials: (1) What should be the formula (mix) of ingredients for one gallon of chili? (2) What should be the normal wastage (or shrinkage) for the individual ingredients? (3) What should be the standard cost for the individual ingredients that go into the chili?

Susan's Chili Factory also illustrates how managers can use standard costs in controlling costs. Suppose that summer droughts have reduced crop yields. As a result, prices have doubled for beans, onions, and peppers. In this case, actual costs will be significantly higher than standard costs, which will cause management to evaluate the situation. Similarly, assume that poor maintenance caused the onion-dicing blades to become dull. As a result, usage of onions to make a gallon of chili tripled. Because this deviation is quickly highlighted through standard costs, managers can take corrective action promptly.

Source: Adapted from David R. Beran, "Cost Reduction Through Control Reporting," *Management Accounting* (April 1982), pp. 29–33.

? How might management use this raw materials cost information? (See page 1288.)

> DO IT!

Standard Costs

Action Plan

✔ Know that standard costs are predetermined unit costs.

✔ To establish the standard cost of producing a product, establish the standard for each manufacturing cost element—direct materials, direct labor, and manufacturing overhead.

✔ Compute the standard cost for each element from the standard price to be paid and the standard quantity to be used.

Ridette Inc. accumulated the following standard cost data concerning product Cty31.

Direct materials per unit: 1.5 pounds at $4 per pound
Direct labor per unit: 0.25 hours at $13 per hour.
Manufacturing overhead: predetermined rate is 120% of direct labor cost.

Compute the standard cost of one unit of product Cty31.

Solution

Manufacturing Cost Element	Standard Quantity	×	Standard Price	=	Standard Cost
Direct materials	1.5 pounds		$4.00		$ 6.00
Direct labor	0.25 hours		$13.00		3.25
Manufacturing overhead	120% of direct labor cost		$3.25		3.90
Total					$13.15

Related exercise material: **BE25-2, BE25-3, E25-1, E25-2, E25-3, and** **DO IT!** **25-1.**

 The Navigator

Analyzing and Reporting Variances from Standards

Alternative Terminology
In business, the term *variance* is also used to indicate differences between total budgeted and total actual costs.

One of the major management uses of standard costs is to identify variances from standards. **Variances** are the differences between total actual costs and total standard costs.

To illustrate, assume that in producing 1,000 gallons of Xonic Tonic in the month of June, Xonic incurred the following costs.

Illustration 25-8
Actual production costs

Direct materials	$13,020
Direct labor	31,080
Variable overhead	6,500
Fixed overhead	4,400
Total actual costs	$55,000

Companies determine total standard costs by multiplying the units produced by the standard cost per unit. The total standard cost of Xonic Tonic is $52,000 (1,000 gallons × $52). Thus, the total variance is $3,000, as shown below.

Illustration 25-9
Computation of total variance

Actual costs	$55,000
Less: Standard costs	52,000
Total variance	**$ 3,000**

Note that the variance is expressed in total dollars, and not on a per unit basis.

When actual costs exceed standard costs, the variance is **unfavorable**. The $3,000 variance in June for Xonic Tonic is unfavorable. An unfavorable variance has a negative connotation. It suggests that the company paid too much for one or more of the manufacturing cost elements or that it used the elements inefficiently.

If actual costs are less than standard costs, the variance is **favorable**. A favorable variance has a positive connotation. It suggests efficiencies in incurring manufacturing costs and in using direct materials, direct labor, and manufacturing overhead.

However, be careful: A favorable variance could be obtained by using inferior materials. In printing wedding invitations, for example, a favorable variance could result from using an inferior grade of paper. Or, a favorable variance might be achieved in installing tires on an automobile assembly line by tightening only half of the lug bolts. A variance is not favorable if the company has sacrificed quality control standards.

To interpret a variance, you must analyze its components. A variance can result from differences related to the cost of materials, labor, or overhead. Illustration 25-10 shows that the total variance is the sum of the materials, labor, and overhead variances.

Illustration 25-10
Components of total variance

Materials Variance + Labor Variance + Overhead Variance = Total Variance

In the following discussion, you will see that the materials variance and the labor variance are the sum of variances resulting from price differences and quantity differences. Illustration 25-11 shows a format for computing the price and quantity variances.

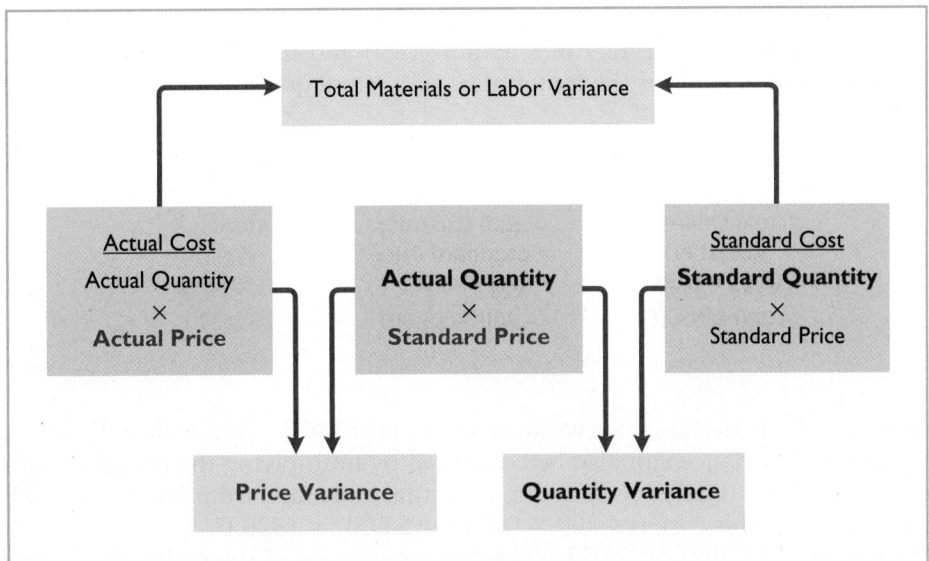

Illustration 25-11
Breakdown of materials or labor variance into price and quantity variances

Note that the left side of the matrix is actual cost (actual quantity times actual price). The right hand is standard cost (standard quantity times standard price). The only additional element you need in order to compute the price and quantity variances is the middle element, the actual quantity at the standard price.

Direct Materials Variances

Part of Xonic's total variance of $3,000 is due to a materials variance. In completing the order for 1,000 gallons of Xonic Tonic, the company used 4,200 pounds of direct materials. The direct materials were purchased at a price of $3.10 per unit. From Illustration 25-3, we know that Xonic's standards require it to use 4 pounds of materials per gallon produced, so it should have only used 4,000 (4 × 1,000) pounds of direct materials to produce 1,000 gallons. Illustration 25-2 shows that the standard cost of each pound of direct materials is $3 instead of the $3.10 actually paid. Illustration 25-12 shows that the **total materials variance** is computed as the difference between the amount paid (actual quantity times actual price) and the amount that should have been paid based on standards (standard quantity times standard price of materials).

LEARNING OBJECTIVE   **4**

State the formulas for determining direct materials and direct labor variances.

Actual Quantity × Actual Price (AQ) × (AP)		Standard Quantity × Standard Price (SQ) × (SP)		Total Materials Variance (TMV)
(4,200 × $3.10)	−	(4,000 × $3.00)	=	$1,020 U

Illustration 25-12
Formula for total materials variance

Thus, for Xonic, the total materials variance is $1,020 ($13,020 − $12,000) unfavorable.

The total materials variance could be caused by differences in the price paid for the materials or by differences in the amount of materials used. Illustration 25-13 shows that the total materials variance is the sum of the materials price variance and the materials quantity variance.

Materials Price Variance + Materials Quantity Variance = Total Materials Variance

Illustration 25-13
Components of total materials variance

The materials price variance results from a difference between the actual price and the standard price. Illustration 25-14 (page 1248) shows that the **materials**

price variance is computed as the difference between the actual amount paid (actual quantity of materials times actual price) and the standard amount that should have been paid for the materials used (actual quantity of materials times standard price).[1]

Illustration 25-14
Formula for materials price variance

Actual Quantity × Actual Price (AQ) × (AP)		Actual Quantity × Standard Price (AQ) × (SP)		Materials Price Variance (MPV)
(4,200 × $3.10)	−	(4,200 × $3.00)	=	$420 U

Helpful Hint
The alternative formula is:
$$\boxed{AQ} \times \boxed{AP - SP} = \boxed{MPV}$$

For Xonic, the materials price variance is $420 ($13,020 − $12,600) unfavorable.

The price variance can also be computed by multiplying the actual quantity purchased by the difference between the actual and standard price per unit. The computation in this case is 4,200 × ($3.10 − $3.00) = $420 U.

As seen in Illustration 25-13, the other component of the materials variance is the quantity variance. The quantity variance results from differences between the amount of material actually used and the amount that should have been used. As shown in Illustration 25-15, the **materials quantity variance** is computed as the difference between the standard cost of the actual quantity (actual quantity times standard price) and the standard cost of the amount that should have been used (standard quantity times standard price for materials).

Illustration 25-15
Formula for materials quantity variance

Actual Quantity × Standard Price (AQ) × (SP)		Standard Quantity × Standard Price (SQ) × (SP)		Materials Quantity Variance (MQV)
(4,200 × $3.00)	−	(4,000 × $3.00)	=	$600 U

Thus, for Xonic, the materials quantity variance is $600 ($12,600 − $12,000) unfavorable.

Helpful Hint
The alternative formula is:
$$\boxed{SP} \times \boxed{AQ - SQ} = \boxed{MQV}$$

The quantity variance can also be computed by applying the standard price to the difference between actual and standard quantities used. The computation in this example is $3.00 × (4,200 − 4,000) = $600 U.

The total materials variance of $1,020 U, therefore, consists of the following.

Illustration 25-16
Summary of materials variances

Materials price variance	$ 420 U
Materials quantity variance	600 U
Total materials variance	**$1,020 U**

Companies sometimes use a matrix to analyze a variance. **When the matrix is used, a company computes the amounts using the formulas for each cost element first and then computes the variances.** Illustration 25-17 shows the

---

[1]Assume that all materials purchased during the period are used in production and that no units remain in inventory at the end of the period.

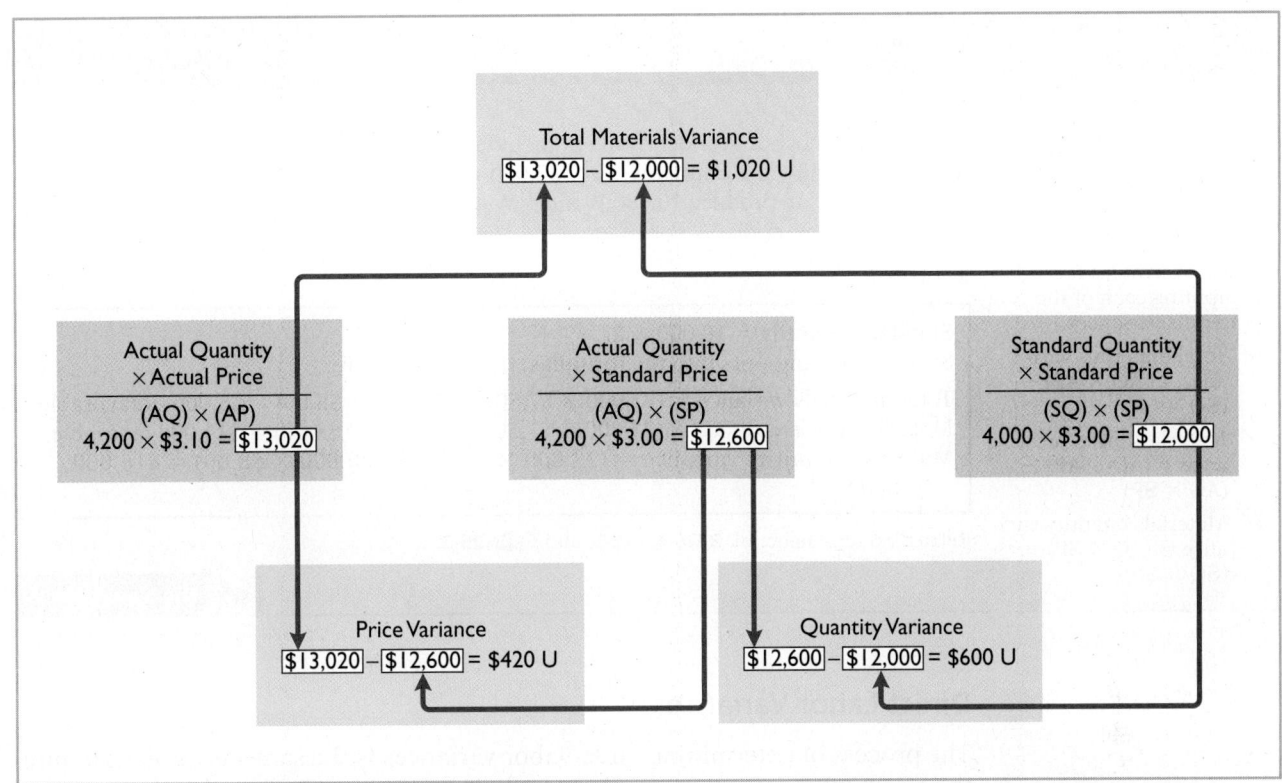

Illustration 25-17
Matrix for direct materials variances

completed matrix for the direct materials variance for Xonic. The matrix provides a convenient structure for determining each variance.

CAUSES OF MATERIALS VARIANCES

What are the causes of a variance? The causes may relate to both internal and external factors. The investigation of a **materials price variance usually begins in the purchasing department**. Many factors affect the price paid for raw materials. These include availability of quantity and cash discounts, the quality of the materials requested, and the delivery method used. To the extent that these factors are considered in setting the price standard, the purchasing department is responsible for any variances.

However, a variance may be beyond the control of the purchasing department. Sometimes, for example, prices may rise faster than expected. Moreover, actions by groups over which the company has no control, such as the OPEC nations' oil price increases, may cause an unfavorable variance. For example, during a recent year, Kraft Foods and Kellogg Company both experienced unfavorable materials price variances when the cost of dairy and wheat products jumped unexpectedly. There are also times when a production department may be responsible for the price variance. This may occur when a rush order forces the company to pay a higher price for the materials.

The starting point for determining the cause(s) of a significant **materials quantity variance is in the production department**. If the variances are due to inexperienced workers, faulty machinery, or carelessness, the production department is responsible. However, if the materials obtained by the purchasing department were of inferior quality, then the purchasing department is responsible.

> **DO IT!**

Direct Materials Variances

Action Plan

Use the formulas for computing each of the materials variances:

✔ Total materials variance = (AQ × AP) − (SQ × SP)

✔ Materials price variance = (AQ × AP) − (AQ × SP)

✔ Materials quantity variance = (AQ × SP) − (SQ × SP)

The standard cost of Wonder Walkers includes two units of direct materials at $8.00 per unit. During July, the company buys 22,000 units of direct materials at $7.50 and uses those materials to produce 10,000 Wonder Walkers. Compute the total, price, and quantity variances for materials.

Solution

Standard quantity = 10,000 × 2.
Substituting amounts into the formulas, the variances are:

Total materials variance = (22,000 × $7.50) − (20,000 × $8.00) = $5,000 unfavorable
Materials price variance = (22,000 × $7.50) − (22,000 × $8.00) = $11,000 favorable
Materials quantity variance = (22,000 × $8.00) − (20,000 × $8.00) = $16,000 unfavorable

Related exercise material: **BE25-4, E25-5, and** **DO IT!** **25-2.**

✔ **The Navigator**

Direct Labor Variances

The process of determining direct labor variances is the same as for determining the direct materials variances. In completing the Xonic Tonic order, the company incurred 2,100 direct labor hours at an average hourly rate of $14.80. The standard hours allowed for the units produced were 2,000 hours (1,000 gallons × 2 hours). The standard labor rate was $15 per hour.

The total labor variance is the difference between the amount actually paid for labor versus the amount that should have been paid. Illustration 25-18 shows that the **total labor variance** is computed as the difference between the amount actually paid for labor (actual hours times actual rate) and the amount that should have been paid (standard hours times standard rate for labor).

Illustration 25-18
Formula for total labor variance

Actual Hours × Actual Rate (AH) × (AR)		Standard Hours × Standard Rate (SH) × (SR)		Total Labor Variance (TLV)
(2,100 × $14.80)	−	(2,000 × $15.00)	=	$1,080 U

The total labor variance is $1,080 ($31,080 − $30,000) unfavorable.

The total labor variance is caused by differences in the labor rate or difference in labor hours. Illustration 25-19 shows that the total labor variance is the sum of the labor price variance and the labor quantity variance.

Illustration 25-19
Components of total labor variance

Labor Price Variance	+	Labor Quantity Variance	=	Total Labor Variance

The labor price variance results from the difference between the rate paid to workers versus the rate that was supposed to be paid. Illustration 25-20 shows that the **labor price variance** is computed as the difference between the actual amount paid (actual hours times actual rate) and the amount that should have been paid for the number of hours worked (actual hours times standard rate for labor).

Actual Hours × Actual Rate (AH) × (AR)		Actual Hours × Standard Rate (AH) × (SR)		Labor Price Variance (LPV)
(2,100 × $14.80)	−	(2,100 × $15.00)	=	$420 F

Illustration 25-20
Formula for labor price variance

For Xonic, the labor price variance is $420 ($31,080 − $31,500) favorable.

The labor price variance can also be computed by multiplying actual hours worked by the difference between the actual pay rate and the standard pay rate. The computation in this example is 2,100 × ($15.00 − $14.80) = $420 F.

The other component of the total labor variance is the labor quantity variance. The labor quantity variance results from the difference between the actual number of labor hours and the number of hours that should have been worked for the quantity produced. Illustration 25-21 shows that the **labor quantity variance** is computed as the difference between the amount that should have been paid for the hours worked (actual hours times standard rate) and the amount that should have been paid for the amount of hours that should have been worked (standard hours times standard rate for labor).

Helpful Hint
The alternative formula is:
$$AH \times (AR - SR) = LPV$$

Actual Hours × Standard Rate (AH) × (SR)		Standard Hours × Standard Rate (SH) × (SR)		Labor Quantity Variance (LQV)
(2,100 × $15.00)	−	(2,000 × $15.00)	=	$1,500 U

Illustration 25-21
Formula for labor quantity variance

Thus, for Xonic, the labor quantity variance is $1,500 ($31,500 − $30,000) unfavorable.

The same result can be obtained by multiplying the standard rate by the difference between actual hours worked and standard hours allowed. In this case, the computation is $15.00 × (2,100 − 2,000) = $1,500 U.

The total direct labor variance of $1,080 U, therefore, consists of:

Helpful Hint
The alternative formula is:
$$SR \times (AH - SH) = LQV$$

Labor price variance	$ 420 F
Labor quantity variance	1,500 U
Total direct labor variance	**$1,080 U**

Illustration 25-22
Summary of labor variances

These results can also be obtained from the matrix in Illustration 25-23 (page 1252).

"What caused labor price variances?"

Personnel decisions

CAUSES OF LABOR VARIANCES

Labor price variances usually result from two factors: (1) paying workers **different wages than expected**, and (2) **misallocation of workers**. In companies where pay rates are determined by union contracts, labor price variances should

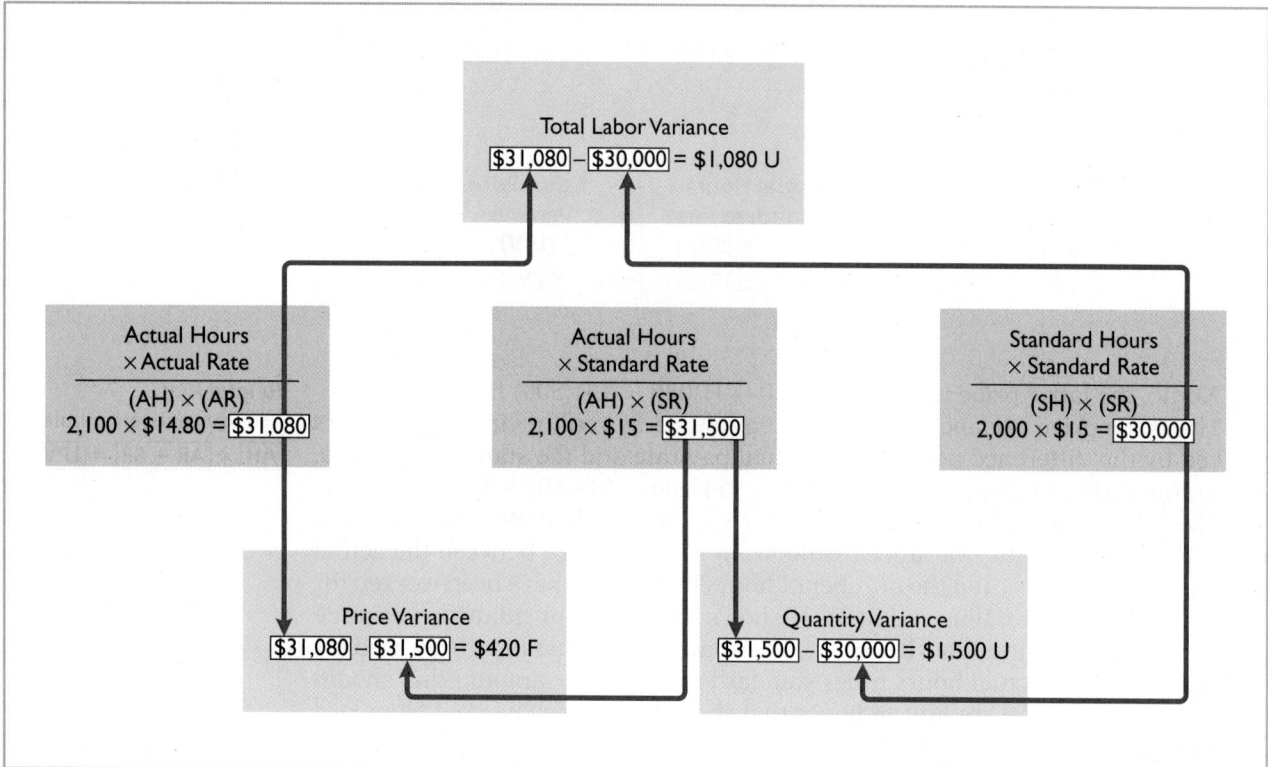

Illustration 25-23
Matrix for direct labor variances

"What caused labor quantity variances?"

Production Dept.

be infrequent. When workers are not unionized, there is a much higher likelihood of such variances. The responsibility for these variances rests with the manager who authorized the wage change.

Misallocation of the workforce refers to using skilled workers in place of unskilled workers and vice versa. The use of an inexperienced worker instead of an experienced one will result in a favorable price variance because of the lower pay rate of the unskilled worker. An unfavorable price variance would result if a skilled worker were substituted for an inexperienced one. The production department generally is responsible for labor price variances resulting from misallocation of the workforce.

Labor quantity variances relate to the **efficiency of workers**. The cause of a quantity variance generally can be traced to the production department. The causes of an unfavorable variance may be poor training, worker fatigue, faulty machinery, or carelessness. These causes are the responsibility of the **production department**. However, if the excess time is due to inferior materials, the responsibility falls outside the production department.

Manufacturing Overhead Variances

LEARNING OBJECTIVE 5

State the formula for determining the total manufacturing overhead variance.

The **total overhead variance** is the difference between the actual overhead costs and overhead costs applied based on standard hours allowed for the amount of goods produced. As indicated in Illustration 25-8 (page 1246), Xonic incurred overhead costs of $10,900 to produce 1,000 gallons of Xonic Tonic in June. The computation of the actual overhead is comprised of a variable and a fixed component. Illustration 25-24 shows this computation.

Variable overhead	$ 6,500
Fixed overhead	4,400
Total actual overhead	**$10,900**

Illustration 25-24
Actual overhead costs

To find the total overhead variance in a standard costing system, we determine the overhead costs applied based on standard hours allowed. **Standard hours allowed** are the hours that *should* have been worked for the units produced. Overhead costs for Xonic Tonic are applied based on direct labor hours. Because it takes two hours of direct labor to produce one gallon of Xonic Tonic, for the 1,000-gallon Xonic Tonic order, the standard hours allowed are 2,000 hours (1,000 gallons × 2 hours). We then apply the predetermined overhead rate to the 2,000 standard hours allowed.

Recall from Illustration 25-6 (page 1244) that the amount of budgeted overhead costs at normal capacity of $132,000 was divided by normal capacity of 26,400 direct labor hours, to arrive at a predetermined overhead rate of $5 ($132,000 ÷ 26,400). The predetermined rate of $5 is then multiplied by the 2,000 standard hours allowed, to determine the overhead costs applied.

Illustration 25-25 shows the formula for the total overhead variance and the calculation for Xonic for the month of June.

Actual Overhead	–	Overhead Applied*	=	Total Overhead Variance
$10,900	–	$10,000	=	$900 U
($6,500 + $4,400)		($5 × 2,000 hours)		

*Based on standard hours allowed.

Illustration 25-25
Formula for total overhead variance

Thus, for Xonic, the total overhead variance is $900 unfavorable.

The overhead variance is generally analyzed through a price and a quantity variance. (These computations are discussed in more detail in advanced courses.) The name usually given to the price variance is the **overhead controllable variance**; the quantity variance is referred to as the **overhead volume variance**. Appendix 25B discusses how the total overhead variance can be broken down into these two variances.

CAUSES OF MANUFACTURING OVERHEAD VARIANCES

One reason for an overhead variance relates to over- or underspending on overhead items. For example, overhead may include indirect labor for which a company paid wages higher than the standard labor price allowed. Or, the price of electricity to run the company's machines increased, and the company did not anticipate this additional cost. Companies should investigate any spending variances, to determine whether they will continue in the future. Generally, the responsibility for these variances rests with the production department.

The overhead variance can also result from the inefficient use of overhead. For example, because of poor maintenance, a number of the manufacturing

machines are experiencing breakdowns on a consistent basis, leading to reduced production. Or, the flow of materials through the production process is impeded because of a lack of skilled labor to perform the necessary production tasks, due to a lack of planning. In both of these cases, the production department is responsible for the cause of these variances. On the other hand, overhead can also be underutilized because of a lack of sales orders. When the cause is a lack of sales orders, the responsibility rests outside the production department. For example, at one point Chrysler experienced a very significant unfavorable overhead variance because plant capacity was maintained at excessively high levels, due to overly optimistic sales forecasts.

PEOPLE, PLANET, AND PROFIT INSIGHT

What's Brewing at Starbucks?

It is one thing for a company to say it is committed to corporate social responsibility. It is another thing for the company to actually spell out measurable goals. Recently, Starbucks published its 10th annual *Global Responsibility Report* in which it describes its goals, achievements, and even its shortcomings related to corporate social responsibility. For example, the company achieved its goal of getting more than 50% of its electricity from renewable sources. It then set its sights higher by setting a goal of 100% within five years. The company also has numerous goals related to purchasing coffee from sources that are certified as responsibly grown and ethically traded; providing funds for loans to coffee farmers; and partnerships with Conservation International to provide training to farmers on ecologically friendly growing. Further, the company reduced water consumption by more than 20% in a two-year period. Finally, it made a significant investment in programs to increase recycling of paper and plastic at its stores.

The report also candidly explains that the company did not meet its goal to cut energy consumption by 25%. It also fell far short of its goal of getting customers to reuse their cups. In those instances where it didn't achieve its goals, Starbucks set new goals and described steps it would take to achieve them. You can view the company's *Global Responsibility Report* at *www.starbucks.com/2010report*.

Source: "Starbucks Launches 10th Global Responsibility Report," *Business Wire* (April 18, 2011).

 What implications does Starbucks' commitment to corporate social responsibility have for the standard cost of a cup of coffee? (See page 1288.)

> DO IT!

Labor and Manufacturing Overhead Variances

The standard cost of Product YY includes 3 hours of direct labor at $12.00 per hour. The predetermined overhead rate is $20.00 per direct labor hour. During July, the company incurred 3,500 hours of direct labor at an average rate of $12.40 per hour and $71,300 of manufacturing overhead costs. It produced 1,200 units.

(a) Compute the total, price, and quantity variances for labor. (b) Compute the total overhead variance.

Action Plan

✔ Use the formulas for computing each of the variances:
Total labor variance = $(AH \times AR) - (SH \times SR)$
Labor price variance = $(AH \times AR) - (AH \times SR)$
Labor quantity variance = $(AH \times SR) - (SH \times SR)$
Total overhead variance = Actual overhead − Overhead applied*

*Based on standard hours allowed.

Solution

Substituting amounts into the formulas, the variances are:

Total labor variance = $(3,500 \times \$12.40) - (3,600 \times \$12.00) = \$200$ unfavorable

Labor price variance = $(3,500 \times \$12.40) - (3,500 \times \$12.00) = \$1,400$ unfavorable

Labor quantity variance = $(3,500 \times \$12.00) - (3,600 \times \$12.00) = \$1,200$ favorable

Total overhead variance = $\$71,300 - \$72,000^* = \$700$ favorable

*3,600 hours × \$20.00

Related exercise material: **BE25-5, BE25-6, E25-4, E25-6, E25-7, E25-8, E25-11, and** DO IT! **25-3.**

✔ **The Navigator**

Reporting Variances

All variances should be reported to appropriate levels of management as soon as possible. The sooner managers are informed, the sooner they can evaluate problems and take corrective action.

LEARNING OBJECTIVE 6

Discuss the reporting of variances.

The form, content, and frequency of variance reports vary considerably among companies. One approach is to prepare a weekly report for each department that has primary responsibility for cost control. Under this approach, materials price variances are reported to the purchasing department, and all other variances are reported to the production department that did the work. The following report for Xonic, with the materials for the Xonic Tonic order listed first, illustrates this approach.

Xonic Variance Report—Purchasing Department For Week Ended June 8, 2014					
Type of Materials	**Quantity Purchased**	**Actual Price**	**Standard Price**	**Price Variance**	**Explanation**
X100	4,200 lbs.	$3.10	$3.00	$ 420 U	Rush order
X142	1,200 units	2.75	2.80	60 F	Quantity discount
A85	600 doz.	5.20	5.10	60 U	Regular supplier on strike
Total price variance				**$420 U**	

Illustration 25-26
Materials price variance report

The explanation column is completed after consultation with the purchasing department manager.

Variance reports facilitate the principle of "management by exception" explained in Chapter 24. For example, the vice president of purchasing can use the report shown above to evaluate the effectiveness of the purchasing department manager. Or, the vice president of production can use production department variance reports to determine how well each production manager is controlling costs. In using variance reports, top management normally looks for **significant variances**. These may be judged on the basis of some quantitative measure, such as more than 10% of the standard or more than $1,000.

Statement Presentation of Variances

LEARNING OBJECTIVE   7

Prepare an income statement for management under a standard costing system.

In income statements **prepared for management** under a standard cost accounting system, **cost of goods sold is stated at standard cost and the variances are disclosed separately.** Unfavorable variances increase cost of goods sold, while favorable variances decrease cost of goods sold. Illustration 25-27 shows the presentation of variances in an income statement. This income statement is based on the production and sale of 1,000 units of Xonic Tonic at $70 per unit. It also assumes selling and administrative costs of $3,000. Observe that each variance is shown, as well as the total net variance. In this example, variations from standard costs reduced net income by $3,000.

Illustration 25-27
Variances in income statement for management

Xonic		
Income Statement		
For the Month Ended June 30, 2014		
Sales revenue		$70,000
Cost of goods sold (at standard)		52,000
Gross profit (at standard)		18,000
Variances		
Materials price	$ 420 U	
Materials quantity	600 U	
Labor price	420 F	
Labor quantity	1,500 U	
Overhead	900 U	
Total variance unfavorable		3,000
Gross profit (actual)		15,000
Selling and administrative expenses		3,000
Net income		$12,000

Standard costs may be used in financial statements prepared for stockholders and other external users. The costing of inventories at standard costs is in accordance with generally accepted accounting principles when there are no significant differences between actual costs and standard costs. Hewlett-Packard and Jostens, Inc., for example, report their inventories at standard costs. However, if there are significant differences between actual and standard costs, the financial statements must report inventories and cost of goods sold at actual costs.

It is also possible to show the variances in an income statement prepared in the variable costing (CVP) format. To do so, it is necessary to analyze the overhead variances into variable and fixed components. This type of analysis is explained in cost accounting textbooks.

Balanced Scorecard

LEARNING OBJECTIVE   8

Describe the balanced scorecard approach to performance evaluation.

Financial measures (measurement of dollars), such as variance analysis and return on investment (ROI), are useful tools for evaluating performance. However, many companies now supplement these financial measures with nonfinancial measures to better assess performance and anticipate future results. For example, airlines like Delta, American, and United use capacity utilization as an important measure to understand and predict future performance. Newspaper publishers such as the *New York Times* and the *Chicago Tribune* use circulation figures as another measure by which to assess performance. Penske Automotive

Group, the owner of 300 dealerships, rewards executives for meeting employee retention targets. Illustration 25-28 lists some key nonfinancial measures used in various industries.

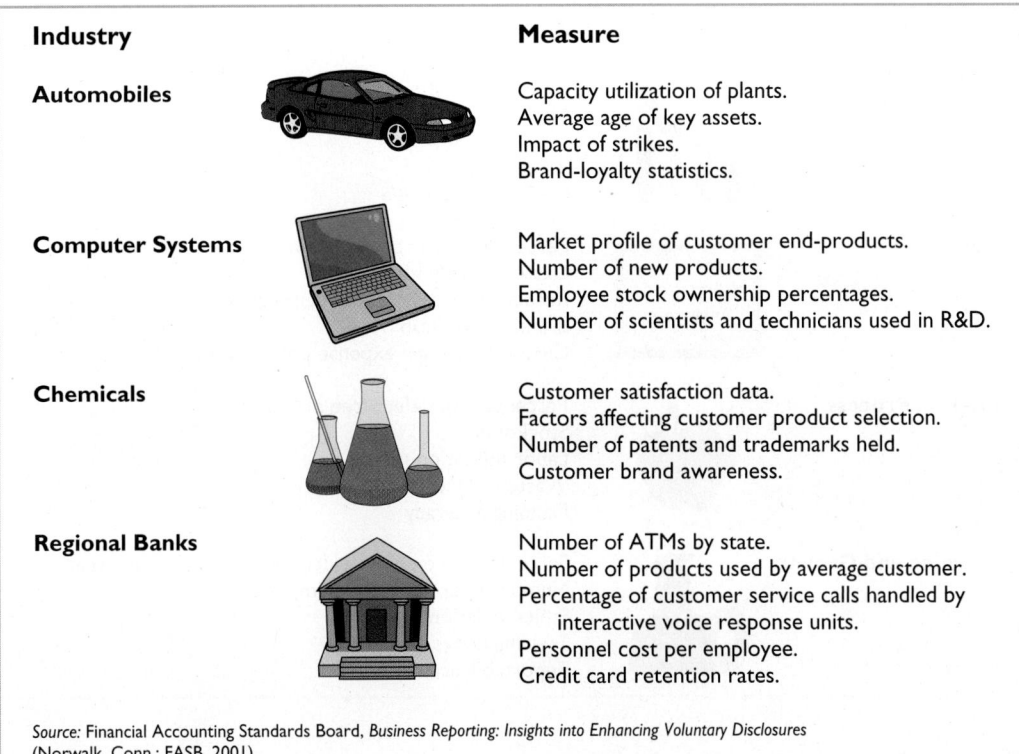

Industry	Measure
Automobiles	Capacity utilization of plants. Average age of key assets. Impact of strikes. Brand-loyalty statistics.
Computer Systems	Market profile of customer end-products. Number of new products. Employee stock ownership percentages. Number of scientists and technicians used in R&D.
Chemicals	Customer satisfaction data. Factors affecting customer product selection. Number of patents and trademarks held. Customer brand awareness.
Regional Banks	Number of ATMs by state. Number of products used by average customer. Percentage of customer service calls handled by interactive voice response units. Personnel cost per employee. Credit card retention rates.

Source: Financial Accounting Standards Board, *Business Reporting: Insights into Enhancing Voluntary Disclosures* (Norwalk, Conn.: FASB, 2001).

Illustration 25-28
Nonfinancial measures used in various industries

Most companies recognize that both financial and nonfinancial measures can provide useful insights into what is happening in the company. As a result, many companies now use a broad-based measurement approach, called the **balanced scorecard**, to evaluate performance. The **balanced scorecard** incorporates financial and nonfinancial measures in an integrated system that links performance measurement with a company's strategic goals. Nearly 50% of the largest companies in the United States, including Unilever, Chase, and Wal-Mart Stores Inc., are using the balanced scorecard approach.

The balanced scorecard evaluates company performance from a series of "perspectives." The four most commonly employed perspectives are as follows.

1. The **financial perspective** is the most traditional view of the company. It employs financial measures of performance used by most firms.

2. The **customer perspective** evaluates the company from the viewpoint of those people who buy its products or services. This view compares the company to competitors in terms of price, quality, product innovation, customer service, and other dimensions.

3. The **internal process perspective** evaluates the internal operating processes critical to success. All critical aspects of the value chain—including product development, production, delivery, and after-sale service—are evaluated to ensure that the company is operating effectively and efficiently.

4. The **learning and growth perspective** evaluates how well the company develops and retains its employees. This would include evaluation of such things as employee skills, employee satisfaction, training programs, and information dissemination.

Within each perspective, the balanced scorecard identifies objectives that contribute to attainment of strategic goals. Illustration 25-29 shows examples of objectives within each perspective.

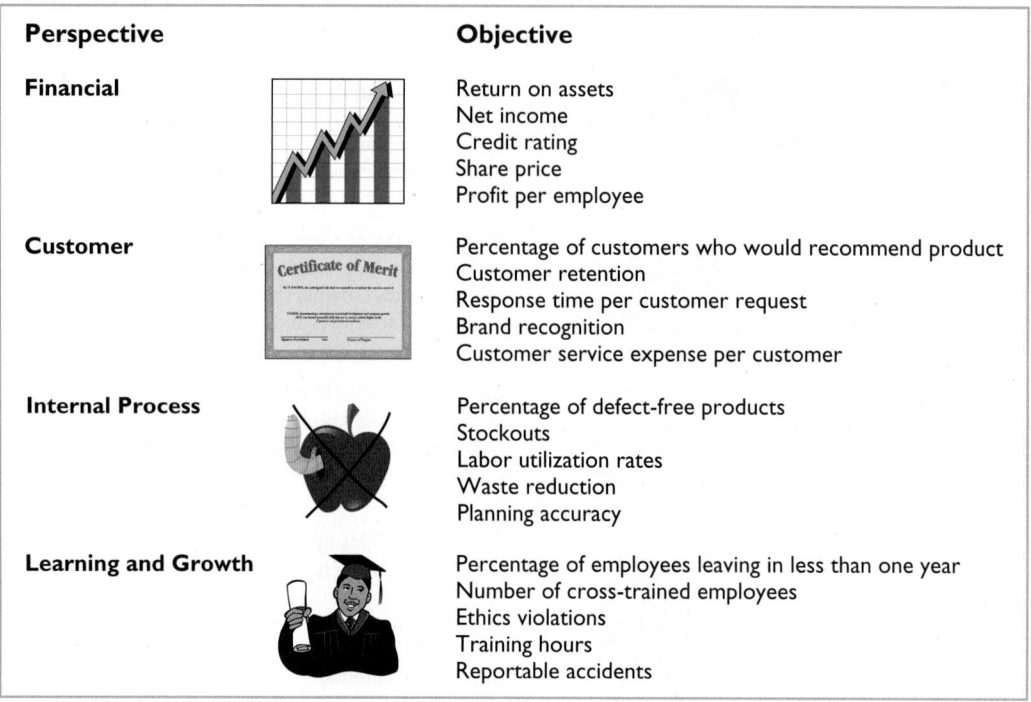

Perspective		Objective
Financial		Return on assets Net income Credit rating Share price Profit per employee
Customer		Percentage of customers who would recommend product Customer retention Response time per customer request Brand recognition Customer service expense per customer
Internal Process		Percentage of defect-free products Stockouts Labor utilization rates Waste reduction Planning accuracy
Learning and Growth		Percentage of employees leaving in less than one year Number of cross-trained employees Ethics violations Training hours Reportable accidents

Illustration 25-29
Examples of objectives within the four perspectives of balanced scorecard

The objectives are linked across perspectives in order to tie performance measurement to company goals. The financial-perspective objectives are normally set first, and then objectives are set in the other perspectives in order to accomplish the financial goals.

For example, within the financial perspective, a common goal is to increase profit per dollars invested as measured by ROI. In order to increase ROI, a customer-perspective objective might be to increase customer satisfaction as measured by the percentage of customers who would recommend the product to a friend. In order to increase customer satisfaction, an internal-process-perspective objective might be to increase product quality as measured by the percentage of defect-free units. Finally, in order to increase the percentage of defect-free units, the learning-and-growth-perspective objective might be to reduce factory employee turnover as measured by the percentage of employees leaving in under one year.

Illustration 25-30 illustrates this linkage across perspectives.

Illustration 25-30
Linked process across balanced scorecard perspectives

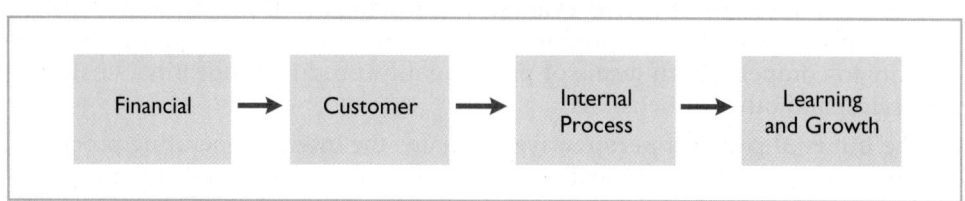

Through this linked process, the company can better understand how to achieve its goals and what measures to use to evaluate performance.

In summary, the balanced scorecard does the following:

1. Employs both **financial and nonfinancial measures**. (For example, ROI is a financial measure; employee turnover is a nonfinancial measure.)

2. **Creates linkages** so that high-level corporate goals can be communicated all the way down to the shop floor.

3. **Provides measurable objectives for nonfinancial measures** such as product quality, rather than vague statements such as "We would like to improve quality."

4. Integrates all of the company's goals into a single performance measurement system, so that **an inappropriate amount of weight will not be placed on any single goal**.

SERVICE COMPANY INSIGHT

It May Be Time to Fly United Again

Many of the benefits of a balanced scorecard approach are evident in the improved operations at United Airlines. At the time it filed for bankruptcy, United had a reputation for some of the worst service in the airline business. But when Glenn Tilton took over as United's chief executive officer, he recognized that things had to change.

He implemented an incentive program that allows all of United's 63,000 employees to earn a bonus of 2.5% or more of their wages if the company "exceeds its goals for on-time flight departures and for customer intent to fly United again." After instituting this program, the company's on-time departures were among the best, its customer complaints were reduced considerably, and the number of customers who said that they would fly United again was at its highest level ever.

Source: Susan Carey, "Friendlier Skies: In Bankruptcy, United Airlines Forges a Path to Better Service," *Wall Street Journal* (June 15, 2004).

? Which of the perspectives of a balanced scorecard were the focus of United's CEO? (See page 1288.)

> DO IT!

Balanced Scorecard

Action Plan

✔ The financial perspective employs traditional financial measures of performance.

✔ The customer perspective evaluates company performance as seen by the people who buy its products or services.

✔ The internal process perspective evaluates the internal operating processes critical to success.

✔ The learning and growth perspective evaluates how well the company develops and retains its employees.

Indicate which of the four perspectives in the balanced scorecard is most likely associated with the objectives that follow.

1. Percentage of repeat customers.
2. Number of suggestions for improvement from employees.
3. Contribution margin.
4. Brand recognition.
5. Number of cross-trained employees.
6. Amount of setup time.

Solution

1. Customer perspective.
2. Learning and growth perspective.
3. Financial perspective.
4. Customer perspective.
5. Learning and growth perspective.
6. Internal process perspective.

Related exercise material: **BE25-7, E25-17, and DO IT! 25-4.**

 The Navigator

> Comprehensive **DO IT!**

Manlow Company makes a cologne called Allure. The standard cost for one bottle of Allure is as follows.

Manufacturing Cost Elements	Quantity	×	Price	=	Cost
Direct materials	6 oz.	×	$ 0.90	=	$ 5.40
Direct labor	0.5 hrs.	×	$12.00	=	6.00
Manufacturing overhead	0.5 hrs.	×	$ 4.80	=	2.40
					$13.80

During the month, the following transactions occurred in manufacturing 10,000 bottles of Allure.

1. 58,000 ounces of materials were purchased at $1.00 per ounce.
2. All the materials purchased were used to produce the 10,000 bottles of Allure.
3. 4,900 direct labor hours were worked at a total labor cost of $56,350.
4. Variable manufacturing overhead incurred was $15,000 and fixed overhead incurred was $10,400.

The manufacturing overhead rate of $4.80 is based on a normal capacity of 5,200 direct labor hours. The total budget at this capacity is $10,400 fixed and $14,560 variable.

Instructions

(a) Compute the total variance and the variances for direct materials and direct labor elements.

(b) Compute the total variance for manufacturing overhead.

Solution to Comprehensive DO IT!

Action Plan

✔ Check to make sure the total variance and the sum of the individual variances are equal.

✔ Find the price variance first, then the quantity variance.

✔ Base budgeted overhead costs on flexible budget data.

✔ Base overhead applied on standard hours allowed.

✔ Ignore actual hours worked in computing overhead variances.

(a)

Total Variance

Actual costs incurred		
Direct materials	$ 58,000	
Direct labor	56,350	
Manufacturing overhead	25,400	
	139,750	
Standard cost (10,000 × $13.80)	138,000	
Total variance	$ 1,750 U	

Direct Materials Variances

Total = $58,000 (58,000 × $1.00) − $54,000 (60,000 × $0.90) = $4,000 U
Price = $58,000 (58,000 × $1.00) − $52,200 (58,000 × $0.90) = $5,800 U
Quantity = $52,200 (58,000 × $0.90) − $54,000 (60,000 × $0.90) = $1,800 F

Direct Labor Variances

Total = $56,350 (4,900 × $11.50) − $60,000 (5,000 × $12.00) = $3,650 F
Price = $56,350 (4,900 × $11.50) − $58,800 (4,900 × $12.00) = $2,450 F
Quantity = $58,800 (4,900 × $12.00) − $60,000 (5,000 × $12.00) = $1,200 F

(b)

Overhead Variance

Total = $25,400 ($15,000 + $10,400) − $24,000 (5,000 × $4.80) = $1,400 U

 The Navigator

SUMMARY OF LEARNING OBJECTIVES

✔ The Navigator

1 **Distinguish between a standard and a budget.** Both standards and budgets are predetermined costs. The primary difference is that a standard is a unit amount, whereas a budget is a total amount. A standard may be regarded as the budgeted cost per unit of product.

2 **Identify the advantages of standard costs.** Standard costs offer a number of advantages. They (a) facilitate management planning, (b) promote greater economy, (c) are useful in setting selling prices, (d) contribute to management control, (e) permit "management by exception," and (f) simplify the costing of inventories and reduce clerical costs.

3 **Describe how companies set standards.** The direct materials price standard should be based on the delivered cost of raw materials plus an allowance for receiving and handling. The direct materials quantity standard should establish the required quantity plus an allowance for waste and spoilage.

The direct labor price standard should be based on current wage rates and anticipated adjustments such as COLAs. It also generally includes payroll taxes and fringe benefits. Direct labor quantity standards should be based on required production time plus an allowance for rest periods, cleanup, machine setup, and machine downtime.

For manufacturing overhead, a standard pre determined overhead rate is used. It is based on an expected standard activity index such as standard direct labor hours or standard machine hours.

4 **State the formulas for determining direct materials and direct labor variances.** The formulas for the direct materials variances are:

$$\begin{pmatrix} \text{Actual quantity} \\ \times \text{ Actual price} \end{pmatrix} - \begin{pmatrix} \text{Standard quantity} \\ \times \text{ Standard price} \end{pmatrix} = \begin{matrix} \text{Total} \\ \text{materials} \\ \text{variance} \end{matrix}$$

$$\begin{pmatrix} \text{Actual quantity} \\ \times \text{ Actual price} \end{pmatrix} - \begin{pmatrix} \text{Actual quantity} \\ \times \text{ Standard price} \end{pmatrix} = \begin{matrix} \text{Materials} \\ \text{price} \\ \text{variance} \end{matrix}$$

$$\begin{pmatrix} \text{Actual quantity} \\ \times \text{ Standard price} \end{pmatrix} - \begin{pmatrix} \text{Standard quantity} \\ \times \text{ Standard price} \end{pmatrix} = \begin{matrix} \text{Materials} \\ \text{quantity} \\ \text{variance} \end{matrix}$$

The formulas for the direct labor variances are:

$$\begin{pmatrix} \text{Actual hours} \\ \times \text{ Actual rate} \end{pmatrix} - \begin{pmatrix} \text{Standard hours} \\ \times \text{ Standard rate} \end{pmatrix} = \begin{matrix} \text{Total} \\ \text{labor} \\ \text{variance} \end{matrix}$$

$$\begin{pmatrix} \text{Actual hours} \\ \times \text{ Actual rate} \end{pmatrix} - \begin{pmatrix} \text{Actual hours} \\ \times \text{ Standard rate} \end{pmatrix} = \begin{matrix} \text{Labor} \\ \text{price} \\ \text{variance} \end{matrix}$$

$$\begin{pmatrix} \text{Actual hours} \\ \times \text{ Standard rate} \end{pmatrix} - \begin{pmatrix} \text{Standard hours} \\ \times \text{ Standard rate} \end{pmatrix} = \begin{matrix} \text{Labor} \\ \text{quantity} \\ \text{variance} \end{matrix}$$

5 **State the formula for determining the total manufacturing overhead variance.** The formula for the total manufacturing overhead variance is:

$$\begin{pmatrix} \text{Actual} \\ \text{overhead} \end{pmatrix} - \begin{pmatrix} \text{Overhead} \\ \text{applied at} \\ \text{standard hours} \\ \text{allowed} \end{pmatrix} = \begin{matrix} \text{Total overhead} \\ \text{variance} \end{matrix}$$

6 **Discuss the reporting of variances.** Variances are reported to management in variance reports. The reports facilitate management by exception by highlighting significant differences.

7 **Prepare an income statement for management under a standard costing system.** Under a standard costing system, an income statement prepared for management will report cost of goods sold at standard cost and then disclose each variance separately.

8 **Describe the balanced scorecard approach to performance evaluation.** The balanced scorecard incorporates financial and nonfinancial measures in an integrated system that links performance measurement and a company's strategic goals. It employs four perspectives: financial, customer, internal process, and learning and growth. Objectives are set within each of these perspectives that link to objectives within the other perspectives.

APPENDIX 25A   STANDARD COST ACCOUNTING SYSTEM

A **standard cost accounting system** is a double-entry system of accounting. In this system, companies use standard costs in making entries, and they formally recognize variances in the accounts. Companies may use a standard cost system with either job order or process costing.

In this appendix, we will explain and illustrate a **standard cost, job order cost accounting system**. The system is based on two important assumptions:

LEARNING OBJECTIVE   9

Identify the features of a standard cost accounting system.

1. Variances from standards are recognized at the earliest opportunity.
2. The Work in Process account is maintained exclusively on the basis of standard costs.

In practice, there are many variations among standard cost systems. The system described here should prepare you for systems you see in the "real world."

Journal Entries

We will use the transactions of Xonic to illustrate the journal entries. Note as you study the entries that the major difference between the entries here and those for the job order cost accounting system in Chapter 16 is the **variance accounts**.

1. Purchase raw materials on account for $13,020 when the standard cost is $12,600.

Raw Materials Inventory	12,600	
Materials Price Variance	420	
Accounts Payable		13,020
(To record purchase of materials)		

Xonic debits the inventory account for actual quantities at standard cost. This enables the perpetual materials records to show actual quantities. Xonic debits the price variance, which is unfavorable, to Materials Price Variance.

2. Incur direct labor costs of $31,080 when the standard labor cost is $31,500.

Factory Labor	31,500	
Labor Price Variance		420
Factory Wages Payable		31,080
(To record direct labor costs)		

Like the raw materials inventory account, Xonic debits Factory Labor for actual hours worked at the standard hourly rate of pay. In this case, the labor variance is favorable. Thus, Xonic credits Labor Price Variance.

3. Incur actual manufacturing overhead costs of $10,900.

Manufacturing Overhead	10,900	
Accounts Payable/Cash/Acc. Depreciation		10,900
(To record overhead incurred)		

The controllable overhead variance (see Appendix 25B) is not recorded at this time. It depends on standard hours applied to work in process. This amount is not known at the time overhead is incurred.

4. Issue raw materials for production at a cost of $12,600 when the standard cost is $12,000.

Work in Process Inventory	12,000	
Materials Quantity Variance	600	
Raw Materials Inventory		12,600
(To record issuance of raw materials)		

Xonic debits Work in Process Inventory for standard materials quantities used at standard prices. It debits the variance account because the variance is unfavorable. The company credits Raw Materials Inventory for actual quantities at standard prices.

5. Assign factory labor to production at a cost of $31,500 when standard cost is $30,000.

Work in Process Inventory	30,000	
Labor Quantity Variance	1,500	
Factory Labor		31,500
(To assign factory labor to jobs)		

Xonic debits Work in Process Inventory for standard labor hours at standard rates. It debits the unfavorable variance to Labor Quantity Variance. The credit to Factory Labor produces a zero balance in this account.

6. Apply manufacturing overhead to production $10,000.

Work in Process Inventory	10,000	
Manufacturing Overhead		10,000
(To assign overhead to jobs)		

Xonic debits Work in Process Inventory for standard hours allowed multiplied by the standard overhead rate.

7. Transfer completed work to finished goods $52,000.

Finished Goods Inventory	52,000	
Work in Process Inventory		52,000
(To record transfer of completed work to		
finished goods)		

In this example, both inventory accounts are at standard cost.

8. Sell the 1,000 gallons of Xonic Tonic for $70,000.

Accounts Receivable	70,000	
Cost of Goods Sold	52,000	
Sales		70,000
Finished Goods Inventory		52,000
(To record sale of finished goods and the		
cost of goods sold)		

The company debits Cost of Goods Sold at standard cost. Gross profit, in turn, is the difference between sales and the standard cost of goods sold.

9. Recognize unfavorable total overhead variance:

Overhead Variance	900	
Manufacturing Overhead		900
(To recognize overhead variances)		

Prior to this entry, a debit balance of $900 existed in Manufacturing Overhead. This entry therefore produces a zero balance in the Manufacturing Overhead account. The information needed for this entry is often not available until the end of the accounting period.

Ledger Accounts

Illustration 25A-1 (page 1264) shows the cost accounts for Xonic after posting the entries. Note that five variance accounts are included in the ledger. The remaining accounts are the same as those illustrated for a job order cost system in Chapter 16, in which only actual costs were used.

Illustration 25A-1
Cost accounts with variances

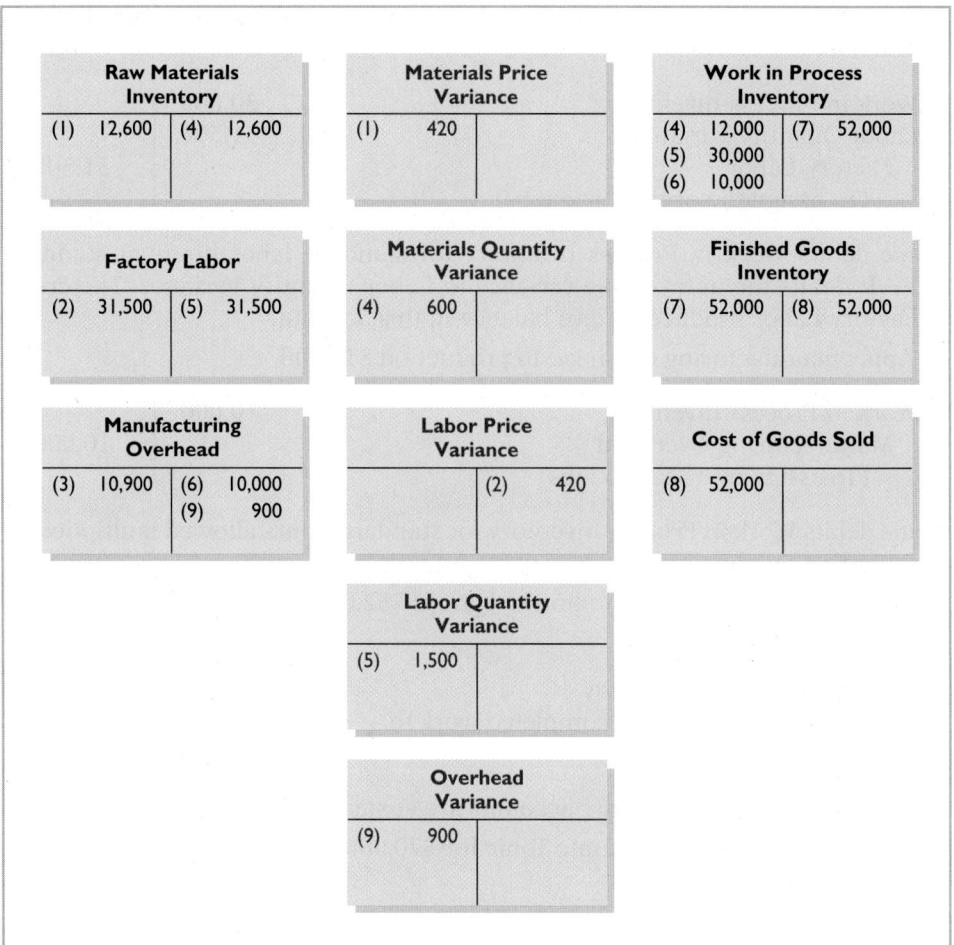

Helpful Hint
All debit balances in variance accounts indicate unfavorable variances; all credit balances indicate favorable variances.

SUMMARY OF LEARNING OBJECTIVE FOR APPENDIX 25A

✔ **The Navigator**

9 Identify the features of a standard cost accounting system. In a standard cost accounting system, companies journalize and post standard costs, and they maintain separate variance accounts in the ledger.

APPENDIX 25B A CLOSER LOOK AT OVERHEAD VARIANCES

LEARNING OBJECTIVE 10

Compute overhead controllable and volume variance.

As indicated in the chapter, the total overhead variance is generally analyzed through a price variance and a quantity variance. The name usually given to the price variance is the **overhead controllable variance**; the quantity variance is referred to as the **overhead volume variance**.

Overhead Controllable Variance

The **overhead controllable variance** shows whether overhead costs are effectively controlled. To compute this variance, the company compares actual overhead costs incurred with budgeted costs for the **standard hours allowed**. The budgeted costs are determined from a flexible manufacturing overhead budget. The concepts related to a flexible budget were discussed in Chapter 24.

For Xonic, the budget formula for manufacturing overhead is variable manufacturing overhead cost of $3 per hour of labor plus fixed manufacturing overhead costs of $4,400 ($52,800 ÷ 12, per Illustration 25-6 on page 1244). Illustration 25B-1 shows the monthly flexible budget for Xonic.

Illustration 25B-1
Flexible budget using standard direct labor hours

A	B	C	D	E
Xonic				
Flexible Manufacturing Overhead Monthly Budget				
Activity Index				
Standard direct labor hours	1,800	2,000	2,200	2,400
Costs				
Variable costs				
Indirect materials	$1,800	$ 2,000	$ 2,200	$ 2,400
Indirect labor	2,700	3,000	3,300	3,600
Utilities	900	1,000	1,100	1,200
Total variable costs	5,400	6,000	6,600	7,200
Fixed costs				
Supervision	3,000	3,000	3,000	3,000
Depreciation	1,400	1,400	1,400	1,400
Total fixed costs	4,400	4,400	4,400	4,400
Total costs	$9,800	$10,400	$11,000	$11,600

As shown, the budgeted costs for 2,000 standard hours are $10,400 ($6,000 variable and $4,400 fixed).

Illustration 25B-2 shows the formula for the overhead controllable variance and the calculation for Xonic at 1,000 units of output (2,000 standard labor hours).

Illustration 25B-2
Formula for overhead controllable variance

Actual Overhead	−	Overhead Budgeted*	=	Overhead Controllable Variance
$10,900	−	$10,400	=	$500 U
($6,500 + $4,400)		($6,000 + $4,400)		

*Based on standard hours allowed.

The overhead controllable variance for Xonic is $500 unfavorable.

Most controllable variances are associated with variable costs, which are controllable costs. Fixed costs are often known at the time the budget is prepared and are therefore not as likely to deviate from the budgeted amount. In Xonic's case, all of the overhead controllable variance is due to the difference between the actual variable overhead costs ($6,500) and the budgeted variable costs ($6,000).

Management can compare actual and budgeted overhead for each manufacturing overhead cost that contributes to the controllable variance. In addition, management can develop cost and quantity variances for each overhead cost, such as indirect materials and indirect labor.

Overhead Volume Variance

The **overhead volume variance** is the difference between normal capacity hours and standard hours allowed times the fixed overhead rate. The overhead volume variance relates to whether fixed costs were under- or overapplied during the year. For example, the overhead volume variance answers the question of whether Xonic effectively used its fixed costs. If Xonic produces less Xonic Tonic than normal capacity would allow, an unfavorable variance results. Conversely, if Xonic produces more Xonic Tonic than what is considered normal capacity, a favorable variance results.

The formula for computing the overhead volume variance is as follows.

Illustration 25B-3
Formula for overhead volume variance

Fixed Overhead Rate	×	(Normal Capacity Hours	−	Standard Hours Allowed)	=	Overhead Volume Variance

To illustrate the fixed overhead rate computation, recall that Xonic budgeted fixed overhead cost for the year of $52,800 (Illustration 25-6 on page 1244). At normal capacity, 26,400 standard direct labor hours are required. The fixed overhead rate is therefore $2 per hour ($52,800 ÷ 26,400 hours).

Xonic produced 1,000 units of Xonic Tonic in June. The standard hours allowed for the 1,000 gallons produced in June is 2,000 (1,000 gallons × 2 hours). For Xonic, normal capacity for June is 1,100, so standard direct labor hours for June at normal capacity is 2,200 (26,400 annual hours ÷ 12 months). The computation of the overhead volume variance in this case is as follows.

Illustration 25B-4
Computation of overhead volume variance for Xonic

Fixed Overhead Rate	×	(Normal Capacity Hours	−	Standard Hours Allowed)	=	Overhead Volume Variance
$2	×	(2,200	−	2,000)	=	$400 U

In Xonic's case, a $400 unfavorable volume variance results. The volume variance is unfavorable because Xonic produced only 1,000 gallons rather than the normal capacity of 1,100 gallons in the month of June. As a result, it underapplied fixed overhead for that period.

In computing the overhead variances, it is important to remember the following.

1. Standard hours allowed are used in each of the variances.
2. Budgeted costs for the controllable variance are derived from the flexible budget.
3. The controllable variance generally pertains to variable costs.
4. The volume variance pertains solely to fixed costs.

10 Compute overhead controllable and volume variance. The total overhead variance is generally analyzed through a price variance and a quantity variance. The name usually given to the price variance is the overhead controllable variance. The quantity variance is referred to as the overhead volume variance.

GLOSSARY

Balanced scorecard An approach that incorporates financial and nonfinancial measures in an integrated system that links performance measurement and a company's strategic goals. (p. 1257).

Customer perspective A viewpoint employed in the balanced scorecard to evaluate the company from the perspective of those people who buy and use its products or services. (p. 1257).

Direct labor price standard The rate per hour that should be incurred for direct labor. (p. 1243).

Direct labor quantity standard The time that should be required to make one unit of product. (p. 1243).

Direct materials price standard The cost per unit of direct materials that should be incurred. (p. 1242).

Direct materials quantity standard The quantity of direct materials that should be used per unit of finished goods. (p. 1242).

Financial perspective A viewpoint employed in the balanced scorecard to evaluate a company's performance using financial measures. (p. 1257).

Ideal standards Standards based on the optimum level of performance under perfect operating conditions. (p. 1241).

Internal process perspective A viewpoint employed in the balanced scorecard to evaluate the effectiveness and efficiency of a company's value chain, including product development, production, delivery, and after-sale service. (p. 1257).

Labor price variance The difference between the actual hours times the actual rate and the actual hours times the standard rate for labor. (p. 1250).

Labor quantity variance The difference between actual hours times the standard rate and standard hours times the standard rate for labor. (p. 1251).

Learning and growth perspective A viewpoint employed in the balanced scorecard to evaluate how well a company develops and retains its employees. (p. 1257).

Materials price variance The difference between the actual quantity times the actual price and the actual quantity times the standard price for materials. (p. 1247).

Materials quantity variance The difference between the actual quantity times the standard price and the standard quantity times the standard price for materials. (p. 1248).

Normal capacity The average activity output that a company should experience over the long run. (p. 1244).

Normal standards Standards based on an efficient level of performance that are attainable under expected operating conditions. (p. 1241).

Overhead controllable variance The difference between actual overhead incurred and overhead budgeted for the standard hours allowed. (p. 1264).

Overhead volume variance The difference between normal capacity hours and standard hours allowed times the fixed overhead rate. (p. 1266).

Standard cost accounting system A double-entry system of accounting in which standard costs are used in making entries, and variances are recognized in the accounts. (p. 1261).

Standard costs Predetermined unit costs which companies use as measures of performance. (p. 1240).

Standard hours allowed The hours that should have been worked for the units produced. (p. 1253).

Standard predetermined overhead rate An overhead rate determined by dividing budgeted overhead costs by an expected standard activity index. (p. 1243).

Total labor variance The difference between actual hours times the actual rate and standard hours times the standard rate for labor. (p. 1250).

Total materials variance The difference between the actual quantity times the actual price and the standard quantity times the standard price of materials. (p. 1247).

Total overhead variance The difference between actual overhead costs and overhead costs applied to work done, based on standard hours allowed. (p. 1252).

Variance The difference between total actual costs and total standard costs. (p. 1246).

Self-Test, Brief Exercises, Exercises, Problem Set A, and many more resources are available for practice in WileyPLUS.

Note: All asterisked Questions, Exercises, and Problems relate to material in the appendices to the chapter.

SELF-TEST QUESTIONS

Answers are at the end of the chapter.

(LO 1) **1.** Standards differ from budgets in that:
(a) budgets but not standards may be used in valuing inventories.
(b) budgets but not standards may be journalized and posted.
(c) budgets are a total amount and standards are a unit amount.
(d) only budgets contribute to management planning and control.

(LO 1) **2.** Standard costs:
(a) are imposed by governmental agencies.
(b) are predetermined unit costs which companies use as measures of performance.
(c) can be used by manufacturing companies but not by service or not-for-profit companies.
(d) All of the above.

(LO 2) **3.** The advantages of standard costs include all of the following *except*:
(a) management by exception may be used.
(b) management planning is facilitated.
(c) they may simplify the costing of inventories.
(d) management must use a static budget.

(LO 3) **4.** Normal standards:
(a) allow for rest periods, machine breakdowns, and setup time.
(b) represent levels of performance under perfect operating conditions.
(c) are rarely used because managers believe they lower workforce morale.
(d) are more likely than ideal standards to result in unethical practices.

(LO 3) **5.** The setting of standards is:
(a) a managerial accounting decision.
(b) a management decision.
(c) a worker decision.
(d) preferably set at the ideal level of performance.

(LO 4) **6.** Each of the following formulas is correct *except*:
(a) Labor price variance = (Actual hours × Actual rate) − (Actual hours × Standard rate).
(b) Total overhead variance = Actual overhead − Overhead applied.
(c) Materials price variance = (Actual quantity × Actual price) − (Standard quantity × Standard price).
(d) Labor quantity variance = (Actual hours × Standard rate) − (Standard hours × Standard rate).

(LO 4) **7.** In producing product AA, 6,300 pounds of direct materials were used at a cost of $1.10 per pound. The standard was 6,000 pounds at $1.00 per pound. The direct materials quantity variance is:
(a) $330 unfavorable.
(c) $600 unfavorable.
(b) $300 unfavorable.
(d) $630 unfavorable.

(LO 4) **8.** In producing product ZZ, 14,800 direct labor hours were used at a rate of $8.20 per hour. The standard was 15,000 hours at $8.00 per hour. Based on these data, the direct labor:
(a) quantity variance is $1,600 favorable.
(b) quantity variance is $1,600 unfavorable.
(c) price variance is $2,960 favorable.
(d) price variance is $2,960 unfavorable.

(LO 5) **9.** Which of the following is *correct* about the total overhead variance?
(a) Budgeted overhead and budgeted overhead applied are the same.
(b) Total actual overhead is composed of variable overhead, fixed overhead, and period costs.
(c) Standard hours actually worked are used in computing the variance.
(d) Standard hours allowed for the work done is the measure used in computing the variance.

(LO 5) **10.** The formula for computing the total overhead variance is:
(a) actual overhead less overhead applied.
(b) overhead budgeted less overhead applied.
(c) actual overhead less overhead budgeted.
(d) No correct answer is given.

(LO 6) **11.** Which of the following is *incorrect* about variance reports?
(a) They facilitate "management by exception."
(b) They should only be sent to the top level of management.
(c) They should be prepared as soon as possible.
(d) They may vary in form, content, and frequency among companies.

(LO 6) **12.** In using variance reports to evaluate cost control, management normally looks into:
(a) all variances.
(b) favorable variances only.
(c) unfavorable variances only.
(d) both favorable and unfavorable variances that exceed a predetermined quantitative measure such as a percentage or dollar amount.

(LO 7) **13.** Generally accepted accounting principles allow a company to:
  (a) report inventory at standard cost but cost of goods sold must be reported at actual cost.
  (b) report cost of goods sold at standard cost but inventory must be reported at actual cost.
  (c) report inventory and cost of goods sold at standard cost as long as there are no significant differences between actual and standard cost.
  (d) report inventory and cost of goods sold only at actual costs; standard costing is never permitted.

(LO 8) **14.** Which of the following would *not* be an objective used in the customer perspective of the balanced scorecard approach?
  (a) Percentage of customers who would recommend product to a friend.
  (b) Customer retention.
  (c) Brand recognition.
  (d) Earnings per share.

*15. Which of the following is *incorrect* about a standard cost accounting system?   (LO 9)
  (a) It is applicable to job order costing.
  (b) It is applicable to process costing.
  (c) It reports only favorable variances.
  (d) It keeps separate accounts for each variance.

*16. The formula to compute the overhead volume variance is: (LO 10)
  (a) Fixed overhead rate × (Standard hours − Actual hours).
  (b) Fixed overhead rate × (Normal capacity hours − Actual hours).
  (c) Fixed overhead rate × (Normal capacity hours − Standard hours allowed).
  (d) (Variable overhead rate + Fixed overhead rate) × (Normal capacity hours − Standard hours allowed).

Go to the book's companion website, www.wiley.com/college/weygandt, for additional Self-Test Questions.

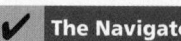 ✔ **The Navigator**

QUESTIONS

1. (a) "Standard costs are the expected total cost of completing a job." Is this correct? Explain.
  (b) "A standard imposed by a governmental agency is known as a regulation." Do you agree? Explain.

2. (a) Explain the similarities and differences between standards and budgets.
  (b) Contrast the accounting for standards and budgets.

3. Standard costs facilitate management planning. What are the other advantages of standard costs?

4. Contrast the roles of the management accountant and management in setting standard costs.

5. Distinguish between an ideal standard and a normal standard.

6. What factors should be considered in setting (a) the direct materials price standard and (b) the direct materials quantity standard?

7. "The objective in setting the direct labor quantity standard is to determine the aggregate time required to make one unit of product." Do you agree? What allowances should be made in setting this standard?

8. How is the predetermined overhead rate determined when standard costs are used?

9. What is the difference between a favorable cost variance and an unfavorable cost variance?

10. In each of the following formulas, supply the words that should be inserted for each number in parentheses.
  (a) (Actual quantity × (1)) − (Standard quantity × (2)) = Total materials variance
  (b) ((3) × Actual price) − (Actual quantity × (4)) = Materials price variance
  (c) (Actual quantity × (5)) − ((6) × Standard price) = Materials quantity variance

11. In the direct labor variance matrix, there are three factors: (1) Actual hours × Actual rate, (2) Actual hours × Standard rate, and (3) Standard hours × Standard rate. Using the numbers, indicate the formulas for each of the direct labor variances.

12. Mikan Company's standard predetermined overhead rate is $9 per direct labor hour. For the month of June, 26,000 actual hours were worked, and 27,000 standard hours were allowed. How much overhead was applied?

13. How often should variances be reported to management? What principle may be used with variance reports?

14. What circumstances may cause the purchasing department to be responsible for both an unfavorable materials price variance and an unfavorable materials quantity variance?

15. What are the four perspectives used in the balanced scorecard? Discuss the nature of each, and how the perspectives are linked.

16. Kerry James says that the balanced scorecard was created to replace financial measures as the primary mechanism for performance evaluation. He says that it uses only nonfinancial measures. Is this true?

17. What are some examples of nonfinancial measures used by companies to evaluate performance?

18. (a) How are variances reported in income statements prepared for management? (b) May standard costs be used in preparing financial statements for stockholders? Explain.

*19. (a) Explain the basic features of a standard cost accounting system. (b) What type of balance will exist in the variance account when (1) the materials price variance is unfavorable and (2) the labor quantity variance is favorable?

*20. If the $9 per hour overhead rate in Question 12 includes $5 variable, and actual overhead costs were $248,000, what is the overhead controllable variance for June? The normal capacity hours were 28,000. Is the variance favorable or unfavorable?

*21. What is the purpose of computing the overhead volume variance? What is the basic formula for this variance?

*22. Alma Ortiz does not understand why the overhead volume variance indicates that fixed overhead costs are under- or overapplied. Clarify this matter for Alma.

*23. John Hsu is attempting to outline the important points about overhead variances on a class examination. List four points that John should include in his outline.

BRIEF EXERCISES

Distinguish between a standard and a budget.
(LO 1)

BE25-1 Perez Company uses both standards and budgets. For the year, estimated production of Product X is 500,000 units. Total estimated cost for materials and labor are $1,300,000 and $1,700,000. Compute the estimates for (a) a standard cost and (b) a budgeted cost.

Set direct materials standard.
(LO 3)

BE25-2 Tang Company accumulates the following data concerning raw materials in making one gallon of finished product: (1) Price—net purchase price $2.30, freight-in $0.20, and receiving and handling $0.10. (2) Quantity—required materials 3.6 pounds, allowance for waste and spoilage 0.4 pounds. Compute the following.
(a) Standard direct materials price per gallon.
(b) Standard direct materials quantity per gallon.
(c) Total standard materials cost per gallon.

Set direct labor standard.
(LO 3)

BE25-3 Labor data for making one gallon of finished product in Tang Company are as follows: (1) Price—hourly wage rate $13.00, payroll taxes $0.80, and fringe benefits $1.20. (2) Quantity—actual production time 1.1 hours, rest periods and cleanup 0.25 hours, and setup and downtime 0.15 hours. Compute the following.
(a) Standard direct labor rate per hour.
(b) Standard direct labor hours per gallon.
(c) Standard labor cost per gallon.

Compute direct materials variances.
(LO 4)

BE25-4 Simba Company's standard materials cost per unit of output is $10 (2 pounds × $5). During July, the company purchases and uses 3,200 pounds of materials costing $16,192 in making 1,500 units of finished product. Compute the total, price, and quantity materials variances.

Compute direct labor variances.
(LO 4)

BE25-5 Hartley Company's standard labor cost per unit of output is $22 (2 hours × $11 per hour). During August, the company incurs 2,100 hours of direct labor at an hourly cost of $10.80 per hour in making 1,000 units of finished product. Compute the total, price, and quantity labor variances.

Compute total overhead variance.
(LO 5)

BE25-6 In October, Roby Company reports 21,000 actual direct labor hours, and it incurs $118,000 of manufacturing overhead costs. Standard hours allowed for the work done is 20,400 hours. The predetermined overhead rate is $6 per direct labor hour. Compute the total overhead variance.

Match balanced scorecard perspectives.
(LO 8)

BE25-7 The four perspectives in the balanced scorecard are (1) financial, (2) customer, (3) internal process, and (4) learning and growth. Match each of the following objectives with the perspective it is most likely associated with: (a) Plant capacity utilization. (b) Employee work days missed due to injury. (c) Return on assets. (d) Brand recognition.

Journalize materials variances.
(LO 9)

***BE25-8** Journalize the following transactions for Combs Company.
(a) Purchased 6,000 units of raw materials on account for $11,500. The standard cost was $12,000.
(b) Issued 5,600 units of raw materials for production. The standard units were 5,800.

Journalize labor variances.
(LO 9)

***BE25-9** Journalize the following transactions for Dewey, Inc.
(a) Incurred direct labor costs of $24,000 for 3,000 hours. The standard labor cost was $25,500.
(b) Assigned 3,000 direct labor hours costing $24,000 to production. Standard hours were 3,150.

*BE25-10 Some overhead data for Roby Company are given in BE25-6. In addition, the flexible manufacturing overhead budget shows that budgeted costs are $4 variable per direct labor hour and $50,000 fixed. Compute the overhead controllable variance.

Compute the overhead controllable variance.

(LO 10)

*BE25-11 Using the data in BE25-6 and BE25-10, compute the overhead volume variance. Normal capacity was 25,000 direct labor hours.

Compute overhead volume variance.

(LO 10)

> DO IT! REVIEW

DO IT! 25-1 Jacque Company accumulated the following standard cost data concerning product I-Tal.

Direct materials per unit: 2 pounds at $5 per pound
Direct labor per unit: 0.2 hours at $15 per hour
Manufacturing overhead: Predetermined rate is 125% of direct labor cost

Compute the standard cost of one unit of product I-Tal.

Compute standard cost.

(LO 3)

DO IT! 25-2 The standard cost of product 777 includes 2 units of direct materials at $6.00 per unit. During August, the company bought 29,000 units of materials at $6.30 and used those materials to produce 16,000 units. Compute the total, price, and quantity variances for materials.

Compute materials variance.

(LO 4)

DO IT! 25-3 The standard cost of product 5252 includes 1.9 hours of direct labor at $14.00 per hour. The predetermined overhead rate is $22.00 per direct labor hour. During July, the company incurred 4,100 hours of direct labor at an average rate of $14.30 per hour and $81,300 of manufacturing overhead costs. It produced 2,000 units.

(a) Compute the total, price, and quantity variances for labor. (b) Compute the total overhead variance.

Compute labor and manufacturing overhead variances.

(LO 4, 5)

DO IT! 25-4 Indicate which of the four perspectives in the balanced scorecard is most likely associated with the objectives that follow.

1. Ethics violations.
2. Credit rating.
3. Customer retention.
4. Stockouts.
5. Reportable accidents.
6. Brand recognition.

Match balance scorecard perspectives and their objectives.

(LO 8)

✔ **The Navigator**

EXERCISES

E25-1 Shannon Company is planning to produce 2,000 units of product in 2014. Each unit requires 3 pounds of materials at $5 per pound and a half-hour of labor at $15 per hour. The overhead rate is 70% of direct labor.

Compute budget and standard.

(LO 1, 2, 3)

Instructions
(a) Compute the budgeted amounts for 2014 for direct materials to be used, direct labor, and applied overhead.
(b) Compute the standard cost of one unit of product.
(c) What are the potential advantages to a corporation of using standard costs?

E25-2 Hank Itzek manufactures and sells homemade wine, and he wants to develop a standard cost per gallon. The following are required for production of a 50-gallon batch.

3,000 ounces of grape concentrate at $0.06 per ounce
54 pounds of granulated sugar at $0.30 per pound

Compute standard materials costs.

(LO 3)

60 lemons at $0.60 each
50 yeast tablets at $0.25 each
50 nutrient tablets at $0.20 each
2,600 ounces of water at $0.005 per ounce

Hank estimates that 4% of the grape concentrate is wasted, 10% of the sugar is lost, and 25% of the lemons cannot be used.

Instructions
Compute the standard cost of the ingredients for one gallon of wine. (Carry computations to two decimal places.)

Compute standard cost per unit.

(LO 3)

E25-3 Kimm Company has gathered the following information about its product.

Direct materials. Each unit of product contains 4.5 pounds of materials. The average waste and spoilage per unit produced under normal conditions is 0.5 pounds. Materials cost $5 per pound, but Kimm always takes the 2% cash discount all of its suppliers offer. Freight costs average $0.25 per pound.

Direct labor. Each unit requires 2 hours of labor. Setup, cleanup, and downtime average 0.3 hours per unit. The average hourly pay rate of Kimm's employees is $12. Payroll taxes and fringe benefits are an additional $3 per hour.

Manufacturing overhead. Overhead is applied at a rate of $7 per direct labor hour.

Instructions
Compute Kimm's total standard cost per unit.

Compute labor cost and labor quantity variance.

(LO 3, 4)

E25-4 Monte Services, Inc. is trying to establish the standard labor cost of a typical oil change. The following data have been collected from time and motion studies conducted over the past month.

Actual time spent on the oil change	1.0 hour
Hourly wage rate	$12
Payroll taxes	10% of wage rate
Setup and downtime	20% of actual labor time
Cleanup and rest periods	30% of actual labor time
Fringe benefits	25% of wage rate

Instructions
(a) Determine the standard direct labor hours per oil change.
(b) Determine the standard direct labor hourly rate.
(c) Determine the standard direct labor cost per oil change.
(d) If an oil change took 1.6 hours at the standard hourly rate, what was the direct labor quantity variance?

Compute materials price and quantity variances.

(LO 4)

E25-5 The standard cost of Product B manufactured by MIT Company includes three units of direct materials at $5.00 per unit. During June, 29,000 units of direct materials are purchased at a cost of $4.70 per unit, and 29,000 units of direct materials are used to produce 9,500 units of Product B.

Instructions
(a) Compute the total materials variance and the price and quantity variances.
(b) Repeat (a), assuming the purchase price is $5.15 and the quantity purchased and used is 28,000 units.

Compute labor price and quantity variances.

(LO 4)

E25-6 Lewis Company's standard labor cost of producing one unit of Product DD is 4 hours at the rate of $12.00 per hour. During August, 40,600 hours of labor are incurred at a cost of $12.15 per hour to produce 10,000 units of Product DD.

Instructions
(a) Compute the total labor variance.
(b) Compute the labor price and quantity variances.
(c) Repeat (b), assuming the standard is 4.1 hours of direct labor at $12.25 per hour.

Compute materials and labor variances.

(LO 4)

E25-7 Nona Inc., which produces a single product, has prepared the following standard cost sheet for one unit of the product.

Direct materials (8 pounds at $2.50 per pound)	$20
Direct labor (3 hours at $12.00 per hour)	$36

During the month of April, the company manufactures 235 units and incurs the following actual costs.

| Direct materials purchased and used (1,900 pounds) | $5,035 |
| Direct labor (700 hours) | $8,260 |

Instructions
Compute the total, price, and quantity variances for materials and labor.

E25-8 The following direct materials and direct labor data pertain to the operations of Laurel Company for the month of August.

Compute the materials and labor variances and list reasons for unfavorable variances.

(LO 4)

Costs		Quantities	
Actual labor rate	$13 per hour	Actual hours incurred and used	4,150 hours
Actual materials price	$128 per ton	Actual quantity of materials purchased and used	1,220 tons
Standard labor rate	$12.50 per hour	Standard hours used	4,300 hours
Standard materials price	$130 per ton	Standard quantity of materials used	1,200 tons

Instructions
(a) Compute the total, price, and quantity variances for materials and labor.
(b) ◼▭▭▭▭▷ Provide two possible explanations for each of the unfavorable variances calculated above, and suggest where responsibility for the unfavorable result might be placed.

E25-9 You have been given the following information about the production of Horatio Co., and are asked to provide the plant manager with information for a meeting with the vice president of operations.

Determine amounts from variance report.

(LO 4)

	Standard Cost Card
Direct materials (5 pounds at $4 per pound)	$20.00
Direct labor (0.8 hours at $10)	8.00
Variable overhead (0.8 hours at $3 per hour)	2.40
Fixed overhead (0.8 hours at $7 per hour)	5.60
	$36.00

The following is a variance report for the most recent period of operations.

		Variances	
Costs	Total Standard Cost	Price	Quantity
Direct materials	$405,000	$5,175 F	$9,000 U
Direct labor	180,000	3,840 U	6,000 U

Instructions
(a) How many units were produced during the period?
(b) How many pounds of raw materials were purchased and used during the period?
(c) What was the actual cost per pound of raw materials?
(d) How many actual direct labor hours were worked during the period?
(e) What was the actual rate paid per direct labor hour?

(CGA adapted)

E25-10 During March 2014, Toby Tool & Die Company worked on four jobs. A review of direct labor costs reveals the following summary data.

Prepare a variance report for direct labor.

(LO 4, 6)

Job Number	Actual Hours	Actual Costs	Standard Hours	Standard Costs	Total Variance
A257	221	$4,420	225	$4,500	$ 80 F
A258	450	9,450	430	8,600	850 U
A259	300	6,180	300	6,000	180 U
A260	116	2,088	110	2,200	112 F
Total variance					$838 U

Analysis reveals that Job A257 was a repeat job. Job A258 was a rush order that required overtime work at premium rates of pay. Job A259 required a more experienced replacement worker on one shift. Work on Job A260 was done for one day by a new trainee when a regular worker was absent.

Instructions

Prepare a report for the plant supervisor on direct labor cost variances for March. The report should have columns for (1) Job No., (2) Actual Hours, (3) Standard Hours, (4) Quantity Variance, (5) Actual Rate, (6) Standard Rate, (7) Price Variance, and (8) Explanation.

Compute overhead variance.

(LO 5)

E25-11 Manufacturing overhead data for the production of Product H by Smart Company are as follows.

Overhead incurred for 52,000 actual direct labor hours worked	$263,000
Overhead rate (variable $3; fixed $2) at normal capacity of 54,000 direct labor hours	$5
Standard hours allowed for work done	51,000

Instructions

Compute the total overhead variance.

Compute overhead variances.

(LO 5)

E25-12 Byrd Company produces one product, a putter called GO-Putter. Byrd uses a standard cost system and determines that it should take one hour of direct labor to produce one GO-Putter. The normal production capacity for this putter is 100,000 units per year. The total budgeted overhead at normal capacity is $850,000 comprised of $250,000 of variable costs and $600,000 of fixed costs. Byrd applies overhead on the basis of direct labor hours.

During the current year, Byrd produced 95,000 putters, worked 94,000 direct labor hours, and incurred variable overhead costs of $256,000 and fixed overhead costs of $600,000.

Instructions

(a) Compute the predetermined variable overhead rate and the predetermined fixed overhead rate.
(b) Compute the applied overhead for Byrd for the year.
(c) Compute the total overhead variance.

Compute variances for materials.

(LO 4)

E25-13 Wales Company purchased (at a cost of $10,800) and used 2,400 pounds of materials during May. Wales's standard cost of materials per unit produced is based on 2 pounds per unit at a cost $5 per pound. Production in May was 1,070 units.

Instructions

(a) Compute the total, price, and quantity variances for materials.
(b) Assume Wales also had an unfavorable labor quantity variance. What is a possible scenario that would provide one cause for the variances computed in (a) and the unfavorable labor quantity variance?

Prepare a variance report.

(LO 4, 6)

E25-14 Picard Landscaping plants grass seed as the basic landscaping for business campuses. During a recent month, the company worked on three projects (Remington, Chang, and Wyco). The company is interested in controlling the materials costs, namely the grass seed, for these plantings projects.

In order to provide management with useful cost control information, the company uses standard costs and prepares monthly variance reports. Analysis reveals that the purchasing agent mistakenly purchased poor-quality seed for the Remington project. The Chang project, however, received higher-than-standard-quality seed that was on sale. The Wyco project received standard-quality seed. However, the price had increased and a new employee was used to spread the seed.

Shown below are quantity and cost data for each project.

	Actual		Standard		Total
Project	**Quantity**	**Costs**	**Quantity**	**Costs**	**Variance**
Remington	500 lbs.	$1,200	460 lbs.	$1,150	$ 50 U
Chang	400	920	410	1,025	105 F
Wyco	550	1,430	480	1,200	230 U
Total variance					$175 U

Instructions

(a) Prepare a variance report for the purchasing department with the following columns: (1) Project, (2) Actual Pounds Purchased, (3) Actual Price, (4) Standard Price, (5) Price Variance, and (6) Explanation.

(b) Prepare a variance report for the production department with the following columns: (1) Project, (2) Actual Pounds, (3) Standard Pounds, (4) Standard Price, (5) Quantity Variance, and (6) Explanation.

E25-15 Burte Corporation prepared the following variance report.

Complete variance report.

(LO 6)

Burte Corporation
Variance Report—Purchasing Department
For the Week Ended January 9, 2014

Type of Materials	Quantity Purchased	Actual Price	Standard Price	Price Variance	Explanation
Rogue11	? lbs.	$5.20	$5.00	$5,000 ?	Price increase
Storm17	7,000 oz.	?	3.30	1,050 U	Rush order
Beast29	22,000 units	0.40	?	440 F	Bought larger quantity

Instructions

Fill in the appropriate amounts or letters for the question marks in the report.

E25-16 Fisk Company uses a standard cost accounting system. During January, the company reported the following manufacturing variances.

Prepare income statement for management.

(LO 7)

Materials price variance	$1,200 U	Labor quantity variance	$750 U
Materials quantity variance	800 F	Overhead variance	800 U
Labor price variance	550 U		

In addition, 8,000 units of product were sold at $8 per unit. Each unit sold had a standard cost of $5. Selling and administrative expenses were $8,000 for the month.

Instructions

Prepare an income statement for management for the month ended January 31, 2014.

E25-17 The following is a list of terms related to performance evaluation.

Identify performance evaluation terminology.

(LO 3, 8)

1. Balanced scorecard
2. Variance
3. Learning and growth perspective
4. Nonfinancial measures
5. Customer perspective
6. Internal process perspective
7. Ideal standards
8. Normal standards

Instructions

Match each of the following descriptions with one of the terms above.

(a) The difference between total actual costs and total standard costs.

(b) An efficient level of performance that is attainable under expected operating conditions.

(c) An approach that incorporates financial and nonfinancial measures in an integrated system that links performance measurement and a company's strategic goals.

(d) A viewpoint employed in the balanced scorecard to evaluate how well a company develops and retains its employees.

(e) An evaluation tool that is not based on dollars.

(f) A viewpoint employed in the balanced scorecard to evaluate the company from the perspective of those people who buy its products or services.

(g) An optimum level of performance under perfect operating conditions.

(h) A viewpoint employed in the balanced scorecard to evaluate the efficiency and effectiveness of the company's value chain.

*E25-18 Vista Company installed a standard cost system on January 1. Selected transactions for the month of January are as follows.

Journalize entries in a standard cost accounting system.

(LO 9)

1. Purchased 18,000 units of raw materials on account at a cost of $4.50 per unit. Standard cost was $4.40 per unit.

2. Issued 18,000 units of raw materials for jobs that required 17,500 standard units of raw materials.
3. Incurred 15,300 actual hours of direct labor at an actual rate of $5.00 per hour. The standard rate is $5.50 per hour. (Credit Factory Wages Payable.)
4. Performed 15,300 hours of direct labor on jobs when standard hours were 15,400.
5. Applied overhead to jobs at the rate of 100% of direct labor cost for standard hours allowed.

Instructions
Journalize the January transactions.

Answer questions concerning missing entries and balances.

(LO 4, 5, 9)

*E25-19 Stiller Company uses a standard cost accounting system. Some of the ledger accounts have been destroyed in a fire. The controller asks your help in reconstructing some missing entries and balances.

Instructions
Answer the following questions.

(a) Materials Price Variance shows a $2,000 unfavorable balance. Accounts Payable shows $128,000 of raw materials purchases. What was the amount debited to Raw Materials Inventory for raw materials purchased?
(b) Materials Quantity Variance shows a $3,000 favorable balance. Raw Materials Inventory shows a zero balance. What was the amount debited to Work in Process Inventory for direct materials used?
(c) Labor Price Variance shows a $1,500 favorable balance. Factory Labor shows a debit of $140,000 for wages incurred. What was the amount credited to Factory Wages Payable?
(d) Factory Labor shows a credit of $140,000 for direct labor used. Labor Quantity Variance shows a $900 favorable balance. What was the amount debited to Work in Process for direct labor used?
(e) Overhead applied to Work in Process totaled $165,000. If the total overhead variance was $1,200 favorable, what was the amount of overhead costs debited to Manufacturing Overhead?

Journalize entries for materials and labor variances.

(LO 9)

*E25-20 Data for Nona Inc. are given in E25-7.

Instructions
Journalize the entries to record the materials and labor variances.

Compute manufacturing overhead variances and interpret findings.

(LO 10)

*E25-21 The information shown below was taken from the annual manufacturing overhead cost budget of Samantha Company.

Variable manufacturing overhead costs	$34,650
Fixed manufacturing overhead costs	$19,800
Normal production level in labor hours	16,500
Normal production level in units	4,125
Standard labor hours per unit	4

During the year, 4,000 units were produced, 16,100 hours were worked, and the actual manufacturing overhead was $55,000. Actual fixed manufacturing overhead costs equaled budgeted fixed manufacturing overhead costs. Overhead is applied on the basis of direct labor hours.

Instructions
(a) Compute the total, fixed, and variable predetermined manufacturing overhead rates.
(b) Compute the total, controllable, and volume overhead variances.
(c) ▭▬▬▭▶ Briefly interpret the overhead controllable and volume variances computed in (b).

Compute overhead variances.

(LO 10)

*E25-22 The loan department of Calgary Bank uses standard costs to determine the overhead cost of processing loan applications. During the current month, a fire occurred, and the accounting records for the department were mostly destroyed. The following data were salvaged from the ashes.

Standard variable overhead rate per hour	$9
Standard hours per application	2
Standard hours allowed	2,000
Standard fixed overhead rate per hour	$6
Actual fixed overhead cost	$12,600
Variable overhead budget based on standard hours allowed	$18,000
Fixed overhead budget	$12,600
Overhead controllable variance	$ 1,200 U

Instructions
(a) Determine the following.
   (1) Total actual overhead cost.
   (2) Actual variable overhead cost.
   (3) Variable overhead costs applied.
   (4) Fixed overhead costs applied.
   (5) Overhead volume variance.
(b) Determine how many loans were processed.

*E25-23 Alona Company's overhead rate was based on estimates of $200,000 for overhead costs and 20,000 direct labor hours. Alona's standards allow 2 hours of direct labor per unit produced. Production in May was 900 units, and actual overhead incurred in May was $19,000. The overhead budgeted for 1,800 standard direct labor hours is $17,600 ($5,000 fixed and $12,600 variable).

Compute variances.

(LO 10)

Instructions
(a) Compute the total, controllable, and volume variances for overhead.
(b) What are possible causes of the variances computed in part (a)?

EXERCISES: SET B AND CHALLENGE EXERCISES

Visit the book's companion website, at **www.wiley.com/college/weygandt**, and choose the Student Companion site to access Exercise Set B and Challenge Exercises.

PROBLEMS: SET A

P25-1A Costello Corporation manufactures a single product. The standard cost per unit of product is shown below.

Compute variances.

(LO 4, 5)

Direct materials—1 pound plastic at $7.00 per pound	$ 7.00
Direct labor—1.6 hours at $12.00 per hour	19.20
Variable manufacturing overhead	12.00
Fixed manufacturing overhead	4.00
Total standard cost per unit	$42.20

The predetermined manufacturing overhead rate is $10 per direct labor hour ($16.00 ÷ 1.6). It was computed from a master manufacturing overhead budget based on normal production of 8,000 direct labor hours (5,000 units) for the month. The master budget showed total variable costs of $60,000 ($7.50 per hour) and total fixed overhead costs of $20,000 ($2.50 per hour). Actual costs for October in producing 4,900 units were as follows.

Direct materials (5,100 pounds)	$ 36,720
Direct labor (7,500 hours)	93,750
Variable overhead	59,700
Fixed overhead	21,000
Total manufacturing costs	$211,170

The purchasing department buys the quantities of raw materials that are expected to be used in production each month. Raw materials inventories, therefore, can be ignored.

Instructions
(a) Compute all of the materials and labor variances.
(b) Compute the total overhead variance.

(a) MPV $1,020 U

Compute variances, and prepare income statement.

(LO 4, 5, 7)

P25-2A Ayala Corporation accumulates the following data relative to jobs started and finished during the month of June 2014.

Costs and Production Data	Actual	Standard
Raw materials unit cost	$2.25	$2.10
Raw materials units used	10,600	10,000
Direct labor payroll	$120,960	$120,000
Direct labor hours worked	14,400	15,000
Manufacturing overhead incurred	$189,500	
Manufacturing overhead applied		$189,000
Machine hours expected to be used at normal capacity		42,500
Budgeted fixed overhead for June		$55,250
Variable overhead rate per machine hour		$3.00
Fixed overhead rate per machine hour		$1.30

Overhead is applied on the basis of standard machine hours. Three hours of machine time are required for each direct labor hour. The jobs were sold for $400,000. Selling and administrative expenses were $40,000. Assume that the amount of raw materials purchased equaled the amount used.

Instructions
(a) Compute all of the variances for (1) direct materials and (2) direct labor.
(b) Compute the total overhead variance.
(c) Prepare an income statement for management. (Ignore income taxes.)

(a) LQV $4,800 F

Compute and identify significant variances.

(LO 4, 5, 6)

P25-3A Hopkins Clothiers is a small company that manufactures tall-men's suits. The company has used a standard cost accounting system. In May 2014, 11,200 suits were produced. The following standard and actual cost data applied to the month of May when normal capacity was 14,000 direct labor hours. All materials purchased were used.

Cost Element	Standard (per unit)	Actual
Direct materials	8 yards at $4.40 per yard	$375,575 for 90,500 yards ($4.15 per yard)
Direct labor	1.2 hours at $13.40 per hour	$200,220 for 14,200 hours ($14.10 per hour)
Overhead	1.2 hours at $6.10 per hour (fixed $3.50; variable $2.60)	$49,000 fixed overhead $37,000 variable overhead

Overhead is applied on the basis of direct labor hours. At normal capacity, budgeted fixed overhead costs were $49,000, and budgeted variable overhead was $36,400.

Instructions
(a) Compute the total, price, and quantity variances for (1) materials and (2) labor.
(b) Compute the total overhead variance.
(c) ▭▭▭▭▷ Which of the materials and labor variances should be investigated if management considers a variance of more than 4% from standard to be significant?

(a) MPV $22,625 F

Answer questions about variances.

(LO 4, 5)

P25-4A Kansas Company uses a standard cost accounting system. In 2014, the company produced 28,000 units. Each unit took several pounds of direct materials and 1.6 standard hours of direct labor at a standard hourly rate of $12.00. Normal capacity was 50,000 direct labor hours. During the year, 117,000 pounds of raw materials were purchased at $0.92 per pound. All materials purchased were used during the year.

Instructions
(a) If the materials price variance was $3,510 favorable, what was the standard materials price per pound?
(b) If the materials quantity variance was $4,750 unfavorable, what was the standard materials quantity per unit?

(b) 4.0 pounds

(c) What were the standard hours allowed for the units produced?

(d) If the labor quantity variance was $7,200 unfavorable, what were the actual direct labor hours worked?

(e) If the labor price variance was $9,080 favorable, what was the actual rate per hour?

(f) If total budgeted manufacturing overhead was $360,000 at normal capacity, what was the predetermined overhead rate?

(f) $7.20 per DLH

(g) What was the standard cost per unit of product?

(h) How much overhead was applied to production during the year?

(i) Using one or more answers above, what were the total costs assigned to work in process?

P25-5A Pace Labs, Inc. provides mad cow disease testing for both state and federal governmental agricultural agencies. Because the company's customers are governmental agencies, prices are strictly regulated. Therefore, Pace Labs must constantly monitor and control its testing costs. Shown below are the standard costs for a typical test.

Compute variances, prepare an income statement, and explain unfavorable variances.

(LO 4, 5, 7)

Direct materials (2 test tubes @ $1.46 per tube)	$ 2.92
Direct labor (1 hour @ $24 per hour)	24.00
Variable overhead (1 hour @ $6 per hour)	6.00
Fixed overhead (1 hour @ $10 per hour)	10.00
Total standard cost per test	$42.92

The lab does not maintain an inventory of test tubes. Therefore, the tubes purchased each month are used that month. Actual activity for the month of November 2014, when 1,500 tests were conducted, resulted in the following.

Direct materials (3,050 test tubes)	$ 4,209
Direct labor (1,600 hours)	36,800
Variable overhead	7,400
Fixed overhead	15,000

Monthly budgeted fixed overhead is $14,000. Revenues for the month were $75,000, and selling and administrative expenses were $5,000.

Instructions

(a) Compute the price and quantity variances for direct materials and direct labor.

(b) Compute the total overhead variance.

(c) Prepare an income statement for management.

(d) Provide possible explanations for each unfavorable variance.

(a) LQV $2,400 U

*P25-6A Jorgensen Corporation uses standard costs with its job order cost accounting system. In January, an order (Job No. 12) for 1,900 units of Product B was received. The standard cost of one unit of Product B is as follows.

Journalize and post standard cost entries, and prepare income statement.

(LO 4, 5, 7, 9)

Direct materials	3 pounds at $1.00 per pound	$ 3.00
Direct labor	1 hour at $8.00 per hour	8.00
Overhead	2 hours (variable $4.00 per machine hour;	
	fixed $2.25 per machine hour)	12.50
Standard cost per unit		$23.50

Normal capacity for the month was 4,200 machine hours. During January, the following transactions applicable to Job No. 12 occurred.

1. Purchased 6,200 pounds of raw materials on account at $1.05 per pound.
2. Requisitioned 6,200 pounds of raw materials for Job No. 12.
3. Incurred 2,000 hours of direct labor at a rate of $7.80 per hour.
4. Worked 2,000 hours of direct labor on Job No. 12.
5. Incurred manufacturing overhead on account $25,000.
6. Applied overhead to Job No. 12 on basis of standard machine hours allowed.
7. Completed Job No. 12.
8. Billed customer for Job No. 12 at a selling price of $65,000.

Instructions

(a) Journalize the transactions.

(b) Post to the job order cost accounts.

(d) NI $15,890

(c) Prepare the entry to recognize the total overhead variance.
(d) Prepare the January 2014 income statement for management. Assume selling and administrative expenses were $2,000.

Compute overhead control-lable and volume variances.
(LO 10)

*P25-7A Using the information in P25-1A, compute the overhead controllable variance and the overhead volume variance.

Compute overhead control-lable and volume variances.
(LO 10)

*P25-8A Using the information in P25-2A, compute the overhead controllable variance and the overhead volume variance.

Compute overhead control-lable and volume variances.
(LO 10)

*P25-9A Using the information in P25-3A, compute the overhead controllable variance and the overhead volume variance.

Compute overhead controllable and volume variances.
(LO 10)

*P25-10A Using the information in P25-5A, compute the overhead controllable variance and the overhead volume variance.

PROBLEMS: SET B

Compute variances.
(LO 4, 5)

P25-1B Buil Corporation manufactures a single product. The standard cost per unit of product is as follows.

Direct materials—2 pounds of plastic at $6 per pound	$12
Direct labor—2 hours at $13 per hour	26
Variable manufacturing overhead	7
Fixed manufacturing overhead	5
Total standard cost per unit	$50

The master manufacturing overhead budget for the month based on normal productive capacity of 20,000 direct labor hours (10,000 units) shows total variable costs of $70,000 ($3.50 per labor hour) and total fixed costs of $50,000 ($2.50 per labor hour). Normal productive capacity is 20,000 direct labor hours. Overhead is applied on the basis of direct labor hours. Actual costs for November in producing 9,700 units were as follows.

Direct materials (20,000 pounds)	$119,000
Direct labor (19,600 hours)	256,760
Variable overhead	68,800
Fixed overhead	50,000
Total manufacturing costs	$494,560

The purchasing department normally buys the quantities of raw materials that are expected to be used in production each month. Raw materials inventories, therefore, can be ignored.

Instructions

(a) MPV $1,000 F

(a) Compute all of the materials and labor variances.
(b) Compute the total overhead variance.

Compute variances, and prepare income statement.
(LO 4, 5, 7)

P25-2B Huang Company uses a standard cost accounting system to account for the manufacture of exhaust fans. In July 2014, it accumulates the following data relative to 1,800 units started and finished.

Cost and Production Data	Actual	Standard
Raw materials		
Units purchased	21,000	
Units used	21,000	22,000
Unit cost	$3.70	$3.50
Direct labor		
Hours worked	3,450	3,600
Hourly rate	$11.50	$12.00
Manufacturing overhead		
Incurred	$94,800	
Applied		$100,800

Manufacturing overhead was applied on the basis of direct labor hours. Normal capacity for the month was 3,400 direct labor hours. At normal capacity, budgeted overhead costs were $16 per labor hour variable and $12 per labor hour fixed. Total budgeted fixed overhead costs were $40,800.

Jobs finished during the month were sold for $270,000. Selling and administrative expenses were $20,000.

Instructions

(a) Compute all of the variances for (1) direct materials and (2) direct labor.

(a) LQV $1,800 F

(b) Compute the total overhead variance.

(c) Prepare an income statement for management. (Ignore income taxes.)

P25-3B Zimmerman Clothiers manufactures women's business suits. The company uses a standard cost accounting system. In March 2014, 15,700 suits were made. The following standard and actual cost data applied to the month of March when normal capacity was 20,000 direct labor hours. All materials purchased were used in production.

Compute and identify significant variances.

(LO 4, 5, 6)

Cost Element	Standard (per unit)	Actual
Direct materials	5 yards at $6.75 per yard	$547,200 for 76,000 yards ($7.20 per yard)
Direct labor	1.0 hours at $11.45 per hour	$165,760 for 14,800 hours ($11.20 per hour)
Overhead	1.0 hours at $9.40 per hour (fixed $6.25; variable $3.15)	$120,000 fixed overhead $49,000 variable overhead

Overhead is applied on the basis of direct labor hours. At normal capacity, budgeted fixed overhead costs were $125,000, and budgeted variable overhead costs were $63,000.

Instructions

(a) Compute the total, price, and quantity variances for (1) materials and (2) labor.

(a) MPV $34,200 U

(b) Compute the total overhead variance.

(c) ◼▬▬▶ Which of the materials and labor variances should be investigated if management considers a variance of more than 5% from standard to be significant?

P25-4B Beta Company uses a standard cost accounting system. In 2014, 45,000 units were produced. Each unit took several pounds of direct materials and 2 standard hours of direct labor at a standard hourly rate of $12.00. Normal capacity was 86,000 direct labor hours. During the year, 200,000 pounds of raw materials were purchased at $1.00 per pound. All materials purchased were used during the year.

Answer questions about variances.

(LO 4, 5)

Instructions

(a) If the materials price variance was $10,000 unfavorable, what was the standard materials price per pound?

(b) If the materials quantity variance was $23,750 favorable, what was the standard materials quantity per unit?

(b) 5.0 pounds

(c) What were the standard hours allowed for the units produced?

(d) If the labor quantity variance was $10,080 unfavorable, what were the actual direct labor hours worked?

(e) If the labor price variance was $18,168 favorable, what was the actual rate per hour?

(f) If total budgeted manufacturing overhead was $713,800 at normal capacity, what was the predetermined overhead rate per direct labor hour?

(f) $8.30 per DLH

(g) What was the standard cost per unit of product?

(h) How much overhead was applied to production during the year?

(i) Using selected answers above, what were the total costs assigned to work in process?

P25-5B Bonita Labs performs steroid testing services to high schools, colleges, and universities. Because the company deals solely with educational institutions, the price of each test is strictly regulated. Therefore, the costs incurred must be carefully monitored and controlled. Shown below are the standard costs for a typical test.

Compute variances, prepare an income statement, and explain unfavorable variances.

(LO 4, 5, 7)

Direct materials (1 petri dish @ $1.80 per dish)	$ 1.80
Direct labor (0.5 hours @ $20.50 per hour)	10.25
Variable overhead (0.5 hours @ $8 per hour)	4.00
Fixed overhead (0.5 hours @ $5 per hour)	2.50
Total standard cost per test	$18.55

The lab does not maintain an inventory of petri dishes. Therefore, the dishes purchased each month are used that month. Actual activity for the month of May 2014, when 2,500 tests were conducted, resulted in the following.

Direct materials (2,530 dishes)	$ 5,060
Direct labor (1,240 hours)	26,040
Variable overhead	10,100
Fixed overhead	5,700

Monthly budgeted fixed overhead is $6,000. Revenues for the month were $55,000, and selling and administrative expenses were $2,000.

Instructions

(a) LQV $205 F

(a) Compute the price and quantity variances for direct materials and direct labor.
(b) Compute the total overhead variance.
(c) Prepare an income statement for management.
(d) Provide possible explanations for each unfavorable variance.

Journalize and post standard cost entries, and prepare income statement.

(LO 4, 5, 7, 9)

*P25-6B Frio Company uses standard costs with its job order cost accounting system. In January, an order (Job No. 84) was received for 5,500 units of Product D. The standard cost of 1 unit of Product D is as follows.

Direct materials—1.5 pounds at $4.00 per pound	$ 6.00
Direct labor—1 hour at $9.00 per hour	9.00
Overhead—1 hour (variable $7.40; fixed $8.00)	15.40
Standard cost per unit	$30.40

Overhead is applied on the basis of direct labor hours. Normal capacity for the month of January was 6,000 direct labor hours. During January, the following transactions applicable to Job No. 84 occurred.

1. Purchased 8,100 pounds of raw materials on account at $3.70 per pound.
2. Requisitioned 8,100 pounds of raw materials for production.
3. Incurred 5,200 hours of direct labor at $9.20 per hour.
4. Worked 5,200 hours of direct labor on Job No. 84.
5. Incurred $87,500 of manufacturing overhead on account.
6. Applied overhead to Job No. 84 on the basis of direct labor hours.
7. Transferred Job No. 84 to finished goods.
8. Billed customer for Job No. 84 at a selling price of $270,000.

Instructions

(a) Journalize the transactions.
(b) Post to the job order cost accounts.
(c) Prepare the entry to recognize the total overhead variance.

(d) NI $44,690

(d) Prepare the January 2014 income statement for management. Assume selling and administrative expenses were $60,000.

Compute overhead controllable and volume variances.

(LO 10)

*P25-7B Using the information in P25-1B, compute the overhead controllable variance and the overhead volume variance.

Compute overhead controllable and volume variances.

(LO 10)

*P25-8B Using the information in P25-2B, compute the overhead controllable variance and the overhead volume variance.

Compute overhead controllable and volume variances.

(LO 10)

*P25-9B Using the information in P25-3B, compute the overhead controllable variance and the overhead volume variance.

Compute overhead controllable and volume variances.

(LO 10)

*P25-10B Using the information in P25-5B, compute the overhead controllable variance and the overhead volume variance.

PROBLEMS: SET C

Visit the book's companion website, at **www.wiley.com/college/weygandt**, and choose the Student Companion site to access Problem Set C.

WATERWAYS CONTINUING PROBLEM

(This is a continuation of the Waterways Problem from Chapters 15–24.)

WCP25 Waterways Corporation uses very stringent standard costs in evaluating its manufacturing efficiency. These standards are not "ideal" at this point, but management is working toward that as a goal. This problem asks you to calculate and evaluate the company's variances.

Go to the book's companion website, at **www.wiley.com/college/weygandt**, *to find the completion of this problem.*

Broadening Your PERSPECTIVE

Management Decision-Making

Decision-Making at Current Designs

BYP25-1 The executive team at Current Designs has gathered to evaluate the company's operations for the last month. One of the topics on the agenda is the special order from Huegel Hollow, which was presented in BYP16-1. Recall that Current Designs had a special order to produce a batch of 20 kayaks for a client, and you were asked to determine the cost of the order and the cost per kayak.

Mike Cichanowski asked the others if the special order caused any particular problems in the production process. Dave Thill, the production manager, made the following comments: "Since we wanted to complete this order quickly and make a good first impression on this new customer, we had some of our most experienced type I workers run the rotomold oven and do the trimming. They were very efficient and were able to complete that part of the manufacturing process even more quickly than the regular crew. However, the finishing on these kayaks required a different technique than what we usually use, so our type II workers took a little longer than usual for that part of the process."

Deb Welch, who is in charge of the purchasing function, said, "We had to pay a little more for the polyethylene powder for this order because the customer wanted a color that we don't usually stock. We also ordered a little extra since we wanted to make sure that we had enough to allow us to calibrate the equipment. The calibration was a little tricky, and we used all of the powder that we had purchased. Since the number of kayaks in the order was fairly small, we were able to use some rope and other parts that were left over from last year's production in the finishing kits. We've seen a price increase for these components in the last year, so using the parts that we already had in inventory cut our costs for the finishing kits."

Instructions

(a) Based on the comments above, predict whether each of the following variances will be favorable or unfavorable. If you don't have enough information to make a prediction, use "NEI" to indicate "Not Enough Information."

    (1) Quantity variance for polyethylene powder.
    (2) Price variance for polyethylene powder.
    (3) Quantity variance for finishing kits.
    (4) Price variance for finishing kits.
    (5) Quantity variance for type I workers.
    (6) Price variance for type I workers.
    (7) Quantity variance for type II workers.
    (8) Price variance for type II workers.

(b) Diane Buswell examined some of the accounting records and reported that Current Designs purchased 1,200 pounds of pellets for this order at a total cost of $2,040. Twenty (20) finishing kits were assembled at a total cost of $3,240. The payroll records showed that the type I employees worked 38 hours on this project at a total cost of $570. The type II finishing employees worked 65 hours at a total cost of $796.25. A total of 20 kayaks were produced for this order.

The standards that had been developed for this model of kayak were used in BYP16-1 and are reproduced here. For each kayak:

54 pounds of polyethylene powder at $1.50 per pound

1 finishing kit (rope, seat, hardware, etc.) at $170

2 hours of type I labor from people who run the oven and trim the plastic at a standard wage rate of $15 per hour

3 hours of type II labor from people who attach the hatches and seat and other hardware at a standard wage rate of $12 per hour.

Calculate the eight variances that are listed in part (a) of this problem.

Decision-Making Across the Organization

BYP25-2 Milton Professionals, a management consulting firm, specializes in strategic planning for financial institutions. James Hahn and Sara Norton, partners in the firm, are assembling a new strategic planning model for use by clients. The model is designed for use on most personal computers and replaces a rather lengthy manual model currently marketed by the firm. To market the new model, James and Sara will need to provide clients with an estimate of the number of labor hours and computer time needed to operate the model. The model is currently being test-marketed at five small financial institutions. These financial institutions are listed below, along with the number of combined computer/labor hours used by each institution to run the model one time.

Financial Institutions	Computer/Labor Hours Required
Midland National	25
First State	45
Financial Federal	40
Pacific America	30
Lakeview National	30
Total	170
Average	34

Any company that purchases the new model will need to purchase user manuals for the system. User manuals will be sold to clients in cases of 20, at a cost of $320 per case. One manual must be used each time the model is run because each manual includes a nonreusable computer-accessed password for operating the system. Also required are specialized computer forms that are sold only by Milton. The specialized forms are sold in packages of 250, at a cost of $60 per package. One application of the model requires the use of 50 forms. This amount includes two forms that are generally wasted in each application due to printer alignment errors. The overall cost of the strategic planning model to clients is $12,000. Most clients will use the model four times annually.

Milton must provide its clients with estimates of ongoing costs incurred in operating the new planning model, and would like to do so in the form of standard costs.

Instructions
With the class divided into groups, answer the following.
(a) What factors should be considered in setting a standard for computer/labor hours?
(b) What alternatives for setting a standard for computer/labor hours might be used?
(c) What standard for computer/labor hours would you select? Justify your answer.
(d) Determine the standard materials cost associated with the user manuals and computer forms for each application of the strategic planning model.

Managerial Analysis

*BYP25-3 Ana Carillo and Associates is a medium-sized company located near a large metropolitan area in the Midwest. The company manufactures cabinets of mahogany, oak, and other fine woods for use in expensive homes, restaurants, and hotels. Although some of the work is custom, many of the cabinets are a standard size.

One such non-custom model is called Luxury Base Frame. Normal production is 1,000 units. Each unit has a direct labor hour standard of 5 hours. Overhead is applied to production based on standard direct labor hours. During the most recent month, only 900 units were produced; 4,500 direct labor hours were allowed for standard production, but only 4,000 hours were used. Standard and actual overhead costs were as follows.

	Standard (1,000 units)	Actual (900 units)
Indirect materials	$ 12,000	$ 12,300
Indirect labor	43,000	51,000
(Fixed) Manufacturing supervisors salaries	22,500	22,000
(Fixed) Manufacturing office employees salaries	13,000	12,500
(Fixed) Engineering costs	27,000	25,000
Computer costs	10,000	10,000
Electricity	2,500	2,500
(Fixed) Manufacturing building depreciation	8,000	8,000
(Fixed) Machinery depreciation	3,000	3,000
(Fixed) Trucks and forklift depreciation	1,500	1,500
Small tools	700	1,400
(Fixed) Insurance	500	500
(Fixed) Property taxes	300	300
Total	$144,000	$150,000

Instructions

(a) Determine the overhead application rate.
(b) Determine how much overhead was applied to production.
(c) Calculate the total overhead variance, controllable variance, and volume variance.
(d) Decide which overhead variances should be investigated.
(e) Discuss causes of the overhead variances. What can management do to improve its performance next month?

Real-World Focus

BYP25-4 Glassmaster Company is organized as two divisions and one subsidiary. One division focuses on the manufacture of filaments such as fishing line and sewing thread; the other division manufactures antennas and specialty fiberglass products. Its subsidiary manufactures flexible steel wire controls and molded control panels.

The annual report of Glassmaster provides the following information.

Glassmaster Company
Management Discussion

Gross profit margins for the year improved to 20.9% of sales compared to last year's 18.5%. All operations reported improved margins due in large part to improved operating efficiencies as a result of cost reduction measures implemented during the second and third quarters of the fiscal year and increased manufacturing throughout due to higher unit volume sales. Contributing to the improved margins was a favorable materials price variance due to competitive pricing by suppliers as a result of soft demand for petrochemical-based products. This favorable variance is temporary and will begin to reverse itself as stronger worldwide demand for commodity products improves in tandem with the economy. Partially offsetting these positive effects on profit margins were competitive pressures on sales prices of certain product lines. The company responded with pricing strategies designed to maintain and/or increase market share.

Instructions
(a) Is it apparent from the information whether Glassmaster utilizes standard costs?
(b) Do you think the price variance experienced should lead to changes in standard costs for the next fiscal year?

BYP25-5 The Balanced Scorecard Institute *(www.balancedscorecard.org)* is a great resource for information about implementing the balanced scorecard. One item of interest provided at its website is an example of a balanced scorecard for a regional airline.

Address: **http://www.balancedscorecard.org/portals/0/pdf/regional_airline.pdf**, or go to **www. wiley.com/college/weygandt**

Instructions
Go to the address above and answer the following questions.
(a) What are the objectives identified for the airline for each perspective?
(b) What measures are used for the objectives in the customer perspective?
(c) What initiatives are planned to achieve the objective in the learning perspective?

BYP25-6 The December 22, 2009, edition of the *Wall Street Journal* has an article by Kevin Kelliker entitled "In Risky Move, GM to Run Plants Around Clock."

Instructions
Read the article and answer the following questions.
(a) According to the article, what is the normal industry standard for plants to be considered operating at full capacity?
(b) What ideal standard is the company hoping to achieve?
(c) What reasons are given in the article for why most companies do not operate a third shift? How does GM propose to overcome these issues?
(d) What are some potential drawbacks of the midnight shift? What implications does this have for variances from standards?
(e) What potential sales/marketing disadvantage does the third shift create?

Critical Thinking

Communication Activity

BYP25-7 The setting of standards is critical to the effective use of standards in evaluating performance.

Instructions
Explain the following in a memo to your instructor.
(a) The comparative advantages and disadvantages of ideal versus normal standards.
(b) The factors that should be included in setting the price and quantity standards for direct materials, direct labor, and manufacturing overhead.

Ethics Case

BYP25-8 At Symond Company, production workers in the Painting Department are paid on the basis of productivity. The labor time standard for a unit of production is established through periodic time studies conducted by Douglas Management Consultants. In a time study, the actual time required to complete a specific task by a worker is observed. Allowances are then made for preparation time, rest periods, and cleanup time. Bill Carson is one of several veterans in the Painting Department.

Bill is informed by Douglas that he will be used in the time study for the painting of a new product. The findings will be the basis for establishing the labor time standard for the next 6 months. During the test, Bill deliberately slows his normal work pace in an effort to obtain a labor time standard that will be easy to meet. Because it is a new product, the Douglas representative who conducted the test is unaware that Bill did not give the test his best effort.

Instructions
(a) Who was benefited and who was harmed by Bill's actions?
(b) Was Bill ethical in the way he performed the time study test?
(c) What measure(s) might the company take to obtain valid data for setting the labor time standard?

All About You

BYP25-9 From the time you first entered school many years ago, instructors have been measuring and evaluating you by imposing standards. In addition, many of you will pursue professions that administer professional examinations to attain recognized certification. Recently, a federal commission presented proposals suggesting all public colleges and universities should require standardized tests to measure their students' learning.

Instructions
Read the article at **www.signonsandiego.com/uniontrib/20060811/news_1n11colleges.html**, and answer the following questions.
(a) What areas of concern did the panel's recommendations address?
(b) What are possible advantages of standard testing?
(c) What are possible disadvantages of standard testing?
(d) Would you be in favor of standardized tests?

Considering Your Costs and Benefits

BYP25-10 Do you think that standard costs are used only in making products like wheel bearings and hamburgers? Think again. Standards influence virtually every aspect of our lives. For example, the next time you call to schedule an appointment with your doctor, ask the receptionist how many minutes the appointment is scheduled for. Doctors are under increasing pressure to see more patients each day, which means the time spent with each patient is shorter. As insurance companies and employers push for reduced medical costs, every facet of medicine has been standardized and analyzed. Doctors, nurses, and other medical staff are evaluated in every part of their operations to ensure maximum efficiency. While keeping medical treatment affordable seems like a worthy goal, what are the potential implications for the quality of health care? Does a focus on the bottom line result in a reduction in the quality of health care?

A simmering debate has centered on a very basic question: To what extent should accountants, through financial measures, influence the type of medical care that you receive? Suppose that your local medical facility is in danger of closing because it has been losing money. Should the facility put in place incentives that provide bonuses to doctors if they meet certain standard-cost targets for the cost of treating specific ailments?

YES: If the facility is in danger of closing, then someone should take steps to change the medical practices to reduce costs. A closed medical facility is of no use to me, my family, or the community.

NO: I don't want an accountant deciding the right medical treatment for me. My family and I deserve the best medical care.

Instructions
Write a response indicating your position regarding this situation. Provide support for your view.

Answers to Chapter Questions

Answers to Insight and Accounting Across the Organization Questions

p. 1242 How Do Standards Help a Business? Q: How will the creation of such standards help a business or organization? **A:** A business or organization may use the data to compare its performance relative to others with regard to common practices such as processing a purchase order or filling a sales order. Armed with this information, an organization can determine which areas to focus on with improvement campaigns.

p. 1245 How Can We Make Susan's Chili Profitable? Q: How might management use this raw materials cost information? **A:** Management might decide to increase the price of its chili. Or, it might revise its recipes to use cheaper ingredients. Or, it might eliminate some products until ingredients are available at costs closer to standard. Regarding the waste due to dull blades, management should reconsider its maintenance policy, to balance the cost of maintenance versus the cost of wasted product.

p. 1254 What's Brewing at Starbucks? Q: What implications does Starbucks' commitment to corporate social responsibility have for the standard cost of a cup of coffee? **A:** Starbucks' *Global Responsibility Report* explicitly describes its goals related to corporate social responsibility. By including measurable objectives, it signals that it is committed to meeting these goals. As a consequence of setting measurable objectives, when the company determines the standard costs of its products, it needs to factor in the costs of these programs. For example, if renewable energy costs more per kilowatt, then the company must include this added cost in its determination of its products' costs.

p. 1259 It May Be Time to Fly United Again Q: Which of the perspectives of a balanced scorecard were the focus of United's CEO? **A:** Improving on-time flight departures is an objective within the internal process perspective. Customer intent to fly United again is an objective within the customer perspective.

Answers to Self-Test Questions

1. c **2.** b **3.** d **4.** a **5.** b **6.** c **7.** b [(6,300 × $1.00) − (6,000 × $1.00)] **8.** a [(14,800 × $8.00) − (15,000 × $8.00)] **9.** d **10.** a **11.** b **12.** d **13.** c **14.** d ***15.** c ***16.** c

Chapter 26

Planning for Capital Investments

Floating Hotels

Do you own a boat? Maybe it's a nice boat, but how many swimming pools, movie theaters, shopping malls, or restaurants does it have on board? If you are in the cruise-line business, like Holland America Line, you need all of these amenities and more just to stay afloat. Holland America Line is considered by many to be the leader of the premium luxury-liner segment.

Carnival Corporation, which owns Holland America Line and other cruise lines, is one of the largest vacation companies in the world. During one recent three-year period, Carnival spent more than $3 billion per year on capital expenditures. Those are big

numbers, but keep in mind that Carnival estimates that at any given time there are 270,000 people (200,000 customers and 70,000 crew) on one of its 100 ships somewhere in the world.

The cruise industry is a tricky business. When times are good, customers are looking for ways to splurge. But when times get tough, people are more inclined to take a trip in a minivan than a luxury yacht. So timing your investment properly is important. For example, during one stretch of solid global economic growth, many cruise lines decided to add capacity. The industry built 14 new ships at a total price of $4.7 billion. (That's an average price of about $330 million.) But, it takes

✔ **The Navigator**

☐ Scan Learning Objectives

☐ Read Feature Story

☐ Read Preview

☐ Read Text and answer **DO IT!** p. 1295
  ☐ p. 1299 ☐ p. 1307 ☐ p. 1309

☐ Work Comprehensive **DO IT!** p. 1310

☐ Review Summary of Learning Objectives

☐ Answer Self-Test Questions

☐ Complete Assignments

☐ Go to **WileyPLUS** for practice and tutorials

Learning Objectives

After studying this chapter, you should be able to:

1 Discuss capital budgeting evaluation, and explain inputs used in capital budgeting.

2 Describe the cash payback technique.

3 Explain the net present value method.

4 Identify the challenges presented by intangible benefits in capital budgeting.

5 Describe the profitability index.

6 Indicate the benefits of performing a post-audit.

7 Explain the internal rate of return method.

8 Describe the annual rate of return method.

 **The Navigator**

up to three years to build one of these giant vessels Unfortunately, by the time these ships were completed, the economy was in a nose-dive.

To maintain passenger numbers, cruise prices had to be cut by up to 40%. While the lower prices attracted lots of customers, that wasn't enough to offset

an overall decline in revenue of 10% in the middle of the recession. The industry had added capacity at just the wrong time.

Watch the Holland America Line video in WileyPLUS to learn more about capital budgeting in the real world.

✔ **The Navigator**

Preview of **Chapter 26**

Companies like Holland America Line must constantly determine how to invest their resources. Other examples: Dell announced plans to spend $1 billion on data centers for cloud computing. Exxon announced that two wells off the Brazilian coast, which it had spent hundreds of millions to drill, would produce no oil. Renault and Nissan spent over $5 billion during a nearly 20-year period to develop electric cars, such as the Leaf.

The process of making such capital expenditure decisions is referred to as **capital budgeting**. Capital budgeting involves choosing among various capital projects to find the one(s) that will maximize a company's return on its financial investment. The purpose of this chapter is to discuss the various techniques used to make effective capital budgeting decisions.

The content and organization of this chapter are as follows.

PLANNING FOR CAPITAL INVESTMENTS				
Capital Budgeting Evaluation Process	**Cash Payback**	**Net Present Value Method**	**Additional Considerations**	**Other Capital Budgeting Techniques**
• Cash flow information • Illustrative data	• Calculation • Evaluation	• Equal cash flows • Unequal cash flows • Choosing a discount rate • Simplifying assumptions • Comprehensive example	• Intangible benefits • Profitability index • Risk analysis • Post-audit of projects	• Internal rate of return method • Comparing discounted cash flow methods • Annual rate of return method

✔ **The Navigator**

The Capital Budgeting Evaluation Process

LEARNING OBJECTIVE   1

Discuss capital budgeting evaluation, and explain inputs used in capital budgeting.

Many companies follow a carefully prescribed process in capital budgeting. At least once a year, top management requests proposals for projects from each department. A capital budgeting committee screens the proposals and submits its findings to the officers of the company. The officers, in turn, select the projects they believe to be most worthy of funding. They submit this list of projects to the board of directors. Ultimately, the directors approve the capital expenditure budget for the year. Illustration 26-1 shows this process.

The involvement of top management and the board of directors in the process demonstrates the importance of capital budgeting decisions. These decisions often have a significant impact on a company's future profitability. In fact, poor capital budgeting decisions can cost a lot of money. Such decisions have even led to the bankruptcy of some companies.

1. Project proposals are requested from departments, plants, and authorized personnel.

2. Proposals are screened by a capital budget committee.

3. Officers determine which projects are worthy of funding.

4. Board of directors approves capital budget.

Illustration 26-1
Corporate capital budget authorization process

Cash Flow Information

In this chapter, we will look at several methods that help companies make effective capital budgeting decisions. Most of these methods employ **cash flow numbers**, rather than accrual accounting revenues and expenses. Remember from your financial accounting course that accrual accounting records *revenues* and *expenses*, rather than cash inflows and cash outflows. In fact, revenues and expenses measured during a period often differ significantly from their cash flow counterparts. Accrual accounting has advantages over cash accounting in many contexts. **For purposes of capital budgeting, though, estimated cash inflows and outflows are the preferred inputs.** Why? Because ultimately the value of all financial investments is determined by the value of cash flows received and paid.

Sometimes cash flow information is not available. In this case, companies can make adjustments to accrual accounting numbers to estimate cash flow. Often, they estimate net annual cash flow by adding back depreciation expense to net income. Depreciation expense is added back because it is an expense that does not require an outflow of cash. By adding back to net income the depreciation expense that was deducted in determining net income, companies approximate net annual cash flow. Suppose, for example, that Reno Company's net income of $13,000 includes a charge for depreciation expense of $26,000. Its estimated net annual cash flow would be $39,000 ($13,000 + $26,000).

Illustration 26-2 lists some typical cash outflows and inflows related to equipment purchase and replacement.

Illustration 26-2
Typical cash flows relating to
capital budgeting decisions

Cash Outflows

Initial investment
Repairs and maintenance
Increased operating costs
Overhaul of equipment

Cash Inflows

Sale of old equipment
Increased cash received from customers
Reduced cash outflows related to operating costs
Salvage value of equipment

These cash flows are the inputs that are considered relevant in capital budgeting decisions.

The capital budgeting decision, under any technique, depends in part on a variety of considerations:

- **The availability of funds:** Does the company have unlimited funds, or will it have to ration capital investments?

- **Relationships among proposed projects:** Are proposed projects independent of each other, or does the acceptance or rejection of one depend on the acceptance or rejection of another?

- **The company's basic decision-making approach:** Does the company want to produce an accept-reject decision or a ranking of desirability among possible projects?

- **The risk associated with a particular project:** How certain are the projected returns? The certainty of estimates varies with such issues as market considerations or the length of time before returns are expected.

Illustrative Data

For our initial discussion of quantitative capital budgeting techniques, we will use a continuing example, which will enable us to compare the results of the various techniques. Assume that Stewart Shipping Company is considering an investment of $130,000 in new equipment. The new equipment is expected to last 10 years. It will have a zero salvage value at the end of its useful life. The annual cash inflows are $200,000, and the annual cash outflows are $176,000. Illustration 26-3 summarizes these data.

Illustration 26-3
Investment information for
Stewart Shipping example

Initial investment	$130,000
Estimated useful life	10 years
Estimated salvage value	–0–
Estimated annual cash flows	
Cash inflows from customers	$200,000
Cash outflows for operating costs	176,000
Net annual cash flow	$ 24,000

In the following two sections, we will examine two popular techniques for evaluating capital investments: cash payback and the net present value method.

Cash Payback

LEARNING OBJECTIVE   2

Describe the cash payback technique.

The **cash payback technique** identifies the time period required to recover the cost of the capital investment from the net annual cash flow produced by the investment. Illustration 26-4 presents the formula for computing the cash payback period assuming equal annual cash flows.

Illustration 26-4
Cash payback formula

Cost of Capital Investment	÷	Net Annual Cash Flow	=	Cash Payback Period

Helpful Hint
Net annual cash flow can also be approximated by "Net cash provided by operating activities" from the statement of cash flows.

The cash payback period in the Stewart Shipping example is 5.42 years, computed as follows.

$$\$130,000 \div \$24,000 = 5.42 \text{ years}$$

The evaluation of the payback period is often related to the expected useful life of the asset. For example, assume that at Stewart Shipping a project is unacceptable if the payback period is longer than 60% of the asset's expected useful life. The 5.42-year payback period in this case is a bit over 50% of the project's expected useful life. Thus, the project is acceptable.

It follows that when the payback technique is used to decide among acceptable alternative projects, **the shorter the payback period, the more attractive the investment**. This is true for two reasons: First, the earlier the investment is recovered, the sooner the company can use the cash funds for other purposes. Second, the risk of loss from obsolescence and changed economic conditions is less in a shorter payback period.

The preceding computation of the cash payback period assumes **equal** net annual cash flows in each year of the investment's life. In many cases, this assumption is not valid. In the case of **uneven** net annual cash flows, the company determines the cash payback period when the cumulative net cash flows from the investment equal the cost of the investment.

To illustrate, assume that Chen Company proposes an investment in a new website that is estimated to cost $300,000. Illustration 26-5 shows the proposed investment cost, net annual cash flows, cumulative net cash flows, and the cash payback period.

Illustration 26-5
Computation of cash payback period—unequal cash flows

Year	Investment	Net Annual Cash Flow	Cumulative Net Cash Flow
0	$300,000		
1		$ 60,000	$ 60,000
2		90,000	150,000
3		90,000	240,000
4		120,000	360,000
5		100,000	460,000

Cash payback period = 3.5 years

As Illustration 26-5 shows, at the end of year 3, cumulative net cash flow of $240,000 is less than the investment cost of $300,000, but at the end of year 4 the cumulative cash inflow of $360,000 exceeds the investment cost. The cash flow needed in year 4 to equal the investment cost is $60,000 ($300,000 − $240,000). Assuming the cash inflow occurred evenly during year 4, we then divide this amount by the net annual cash flow in year 4 ($120,000) to determine the point during the year when the cash payback occurs. Thus, we get 0.50 ($60,000/$120,000), or half of the year, and the cash payback period is 3.5 years.

The cash payback technique may be useful as an initial screening tool. It may be the most critical factor in the capital budgeting decision for a company that desires a fast turnaround of its investment because of a weak cash position. It also is relatively easy to compute and understand.

However, cash payback should not ordinarily be the only basis for the capital budgeting decision because it **ignores the expected profitability of the project**. To illustrate, assume that Projects A and B have the same payback period, but Project A's useful life is double the useful life of Project B. Project A's earning power, therefore, is twice as long as Project B's. A further—and major—disadvantage of this technique is that it **ignores the time value of money**.

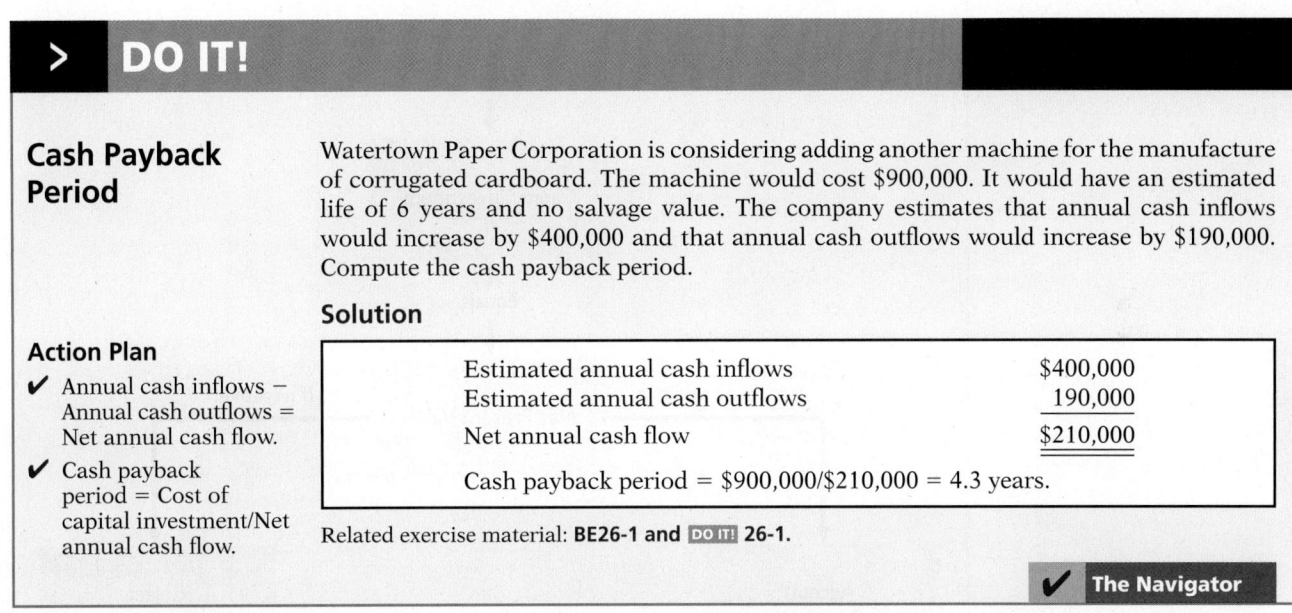

> **DO IT!**

Cash Payback Period

Watertown Paper Corporation is considering adding another machine for the manufacture of corrugated cardboard. The machine would cost $900,000. It would have an estimated life of 6 years and no salvage value. The company estimates that annual cash inflows would increase by $400,000 and that annual cash outflows would increase by $190,000. Compute the cash payback period.

Solution

Action Plan

✔ Annual cash inflows − Annual cash outflows = Net annual cash flow.

✔ Cash payback period = Cost of capital investment/Net annual cash flow.

Estimated annual cash inflows	$400,000
Estimated annual cash outflows	190,000
Net annual cash flow	$210,000

Cash payback period = $900,000/$210,000 = 4.3 years.

Related exercise material: **BE26-1 and DO IT! 26-1**.

✔ **The Navigator**

Net Present Value Method

Recognition of the time value of money can make a significant difference in the long-term impact of the capital budgeting decision. For example, cash flows that occur early in the life of an investment will be worth more than those that occur later—because of the time value of money. Therefore, it is useful to recognize the timing of cash flows when evaluating projects.

LEARNING OBJECTIVE 3

Explain the net present value method.

Capital budgeting techniques that take into account both the time value of money and the estimated net cash flow from an investment are called **discounted cash flow techniques**. They are generally recognized as the most informative and best conceptual approaches to making capital budgeting decisions. The expected net cash flow used in discounting cash flows consists of the annual net cash flows plus the estimated liquidation proceeds (salvage value) when the asset is sold for salvage at the end of its useful life.

The primary discounted cash flow technique is the **net present value method**. A second method, discussed later in the chapter, is the **internal rate of return**. At this point, before you read on, **we recommend that you examine Appendix D** to review time value of money concepts, upon which these methods are based.

The **net present value (NPV) method** involves discounting net cash flows to their present value and then comparing that present value with the capital outlay required by the investment. The difference between these two amounts is referred to as **net present value (NPV)**. Company management determines what interest rate to use in discounting the future net cash flows. This rate, often referred to as the **discount rate** or **required rate of return**, is discussed in a later section.

The NPV decision rule is this: **A proposal is acceptable when net present value is zero or positive**. At either of those values, the rate of return on the investment equals or exceeds the required rate of return. When net present value is negative, the project is unacceptable. Illustration 26-6 shows the net present value decision criteria.

Illustration 26-6
Net present value decision criteria

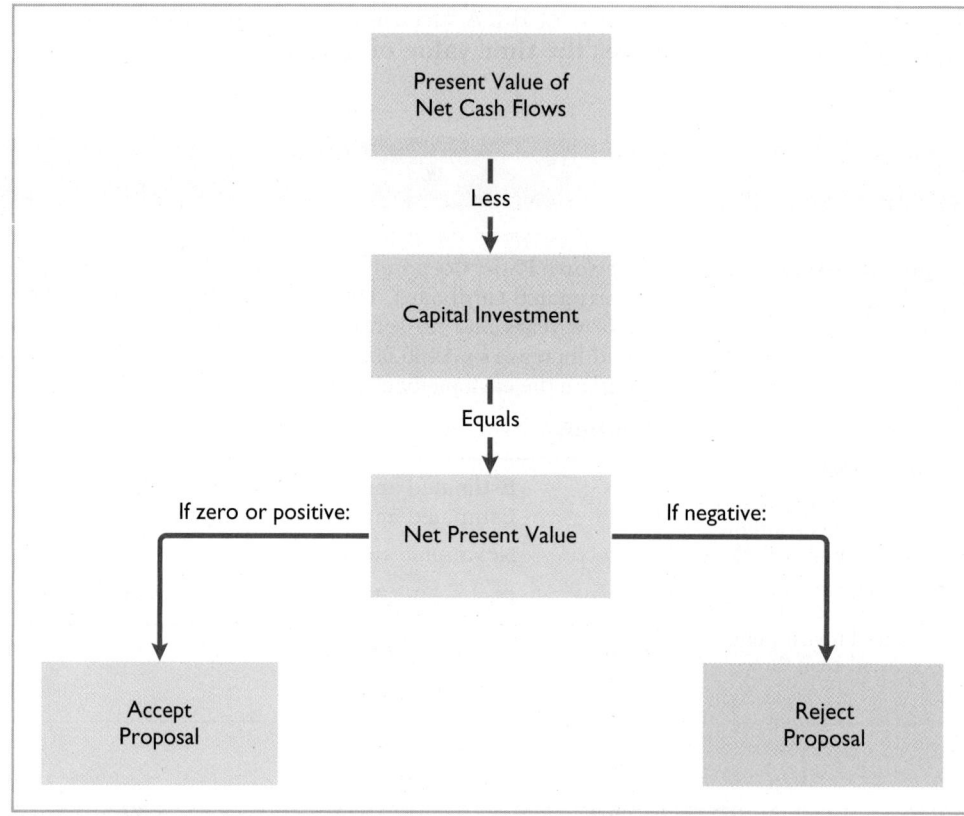

When making a selection among acceptable proposals, **the higher the positive net present value, the more attractive the investment**. The application of this method to two cases is described in the next two sections. In each case, we will assume that the investment has no salvage value at the end of its useful life.

Equal Annual Cash Flows

Helpful Hint
The ABC Co. expects equal cash flows over an asset's 5-year useful life. What discount factor should it use in determining present values if management wants (1) a 12% return or (2) a 15% return? Answer: Using Table 4, the factors are (1) 3.60478 and (2) 3.35216.

In our Stewart Shipping Company example, the company's net annual cash flows are $24,000. If we assume this amount **is uniform over the asset's useful life**, we can compute the present value of the net annual cash flows by using the present value of an annuity of 1 for 10 payments (from Table 4, Appendix D). Assuming a discount rate of 12%, the present value of net cash flows are as shown in Illustration 26-7 (rounded to the nearest dollar).

Illustration 26-7
Computation of present value of equal net annual cash flows

	Present Value at 12%
Discount factor for 10 payments	5.65022
Present value of net cash flows: $24,000 × 5.65022	**$135,605**

The analysis of the proposal by the net present value method is as follows.

	12%
Present value of net cash flows	$135,605
Capital investment	130,000
Net present value	**$ 5,605**

Illustration 26-8
Computation of net present value—equal net annual cash flows

The proposed capital expenditure is acceptable at a required rate of return of 12% because the net present value is positive.

Unequal Annual Cash Flows

When net annual cash flows are unequal, we cannot use annuity tables to calculate their present value. Instead, we use tables showing the **present value of a single future amount for each annual cash flow**.

To illustrate, assume that Stewart Shipping Company expects the same total net cash flows of $240,000 over the life of the investment. But because of a declining market demand for the new product over the life of the equipment, the net annual cash flows are higher in the early years and lower in the later years. The present value of the net annual cash flows is calculated as follows, using Table 3 in Appendix D.

Helpful Hint
Appendix D demonstrates the use of a financial calculator to solve time value of money problems.

Illustration 26-9
Computation of present value of unequal annual cash flows

Year	Assumed Net Annual Cash Flows	Discount Factor 12%	Present Value 12%
	(1)	(2)	(1) × (2)
1	$ 34,000	.89286	$ 30,357
2	30,000	.79719	23,916
3	27,000	.71178	19,218
4	25,000	.63552	15,888
5	24,000	.56743	13,618
6	22,000	.50663	11,146
7	21,000	.45235	9,499
8	20,000	.40388	8,078
9	19,000	.36061	6,852
10	18,000	.32197	5,795
	$240,000		$144,367

Therefore, the analysis of the proposal by the net present value method is as follows.

	12%
Present value of net cash flows	$144,367
Capital investment	130,000
Net present value	**$ 14,367**

Illustration 26-10
Computation of net present value—unequal annual cash flows

In this example, the present value of the net cash flows is greater than the $130,000 capital investment. Thus, the project is acceptable at a 12% required rate of return. The difference between the present values using the 12% rate under equal cash flows ($135,605) and unequal cash flows ($144,367) is due to the pattern of the flows. Since more money is received sooner under this particular uneven cash flow scenario, its present value is greater.

MANAGEMENT INSIGHT

Can You Hear Me—Better?

What's better than 3G wireless service? 4G. But the question for wireless service providers is whether customers will be willing to pay extra for that improvement. Verizon has already spent billions on the upgrade, but customer usage might be slow in coming. First, there aren't that many 4G-compatible devices, and coverage will be spotty. Also, most applications don't really need higher speeds. Verizon is hoping that its investment in 4G works out better than its $23 billion investment in its FIOS fiber-wired network for TV and ultrahigh-speed Internet. One analyst estimates that the present value of each FIOS customer is $800 less than the cost of the connection.

Source: Martin Peers, "Investors: Beware Verizon's Generation GAP," *Wall Street Journal Online* (January 26, 2010).

 Based on the potentially slow initial adoption of 4G by customers, how might the conclusions of a cash payback analysis of Verizon's 4G investment differ from a present value analysis? (See page 1327.)

Choosing a Discount Rate

Now that you understand how companies apply the net present value method, it is logical to ask a related question: How is a discount rate (required rate of return) determined in real capital budgeting decisions? In most instances, a company uses a required rate of return equal to its **cost of capital**—that is, the rate that it must pay to obtain funds from creditors and stockholders.

The cost of capital is a weighted average of the rates paid on borrowed funds as well as on funds provided by investors in the company's common stock and preferred stock. If management believes a project is riskier than the company's usual line of business, the discount rate should be increased. That is, the discount rate has two elements, a cost of capital element and a risk element. Often, companies assume the risk element is equal to zero.

Using an incorrect discount rate can lead to incorrect capital budgeting decisions. Consider again the Stewart Shipping example in Illustration 26-8, where we used a discount rate of 12%. Suppose that this rate does not take into account the fact that this project is riskier than most of the company's investments. A more appropriate discount rate, given the risk, might be 15%. Illustration 26-11 compares the net present values at the two rates. At the higher, more appropriate discount rate of 15%, the net present value is negative, and the company should reject the project (discount factors from Appendix D, Table 4).

Helpful Hint
Cost of capital is the rate that management expects to pay on all borrowed and equity funds. It does not relate to the cost of funding a *specific* project.

Illustration 26-11
Comparison of net present values at different discount rates

	Present Values at Different Discount Rates	
	12%	**15%**
Discount factor for 10 payments	5.65022	5.01877
Present value of net cash flows:		
$24,000 × 5.65022	$135,605	
$24,000 × 5.01877		$120,450
Capital investment	130,000	130,000
Positive (negative) net present value	$ 5,605	$ (9,550)

The discount rate is often referred to by alternative names, including the **required rate of return**, the **hurdle rate**, and the **cutoff rate**. Determination of the cost of capital varies somewhat depending on whether the entity is a for-profit or not-for-profit business. Calculation of the cost of capital is discussed more fully in advanced accounting and finance courses.

Simplifying Assumptions

In our examples of the net present value method, we have made a number of simplifying assumptions:

- **All cash flows come at the end of each year.** In reality, cash flows will come at uneven intervals throughout the year. However, it is far simpler to assume that all cash flows come at the end (or in some cases the beginning) of the year. In fact, this assumption is frequently made in practice.

- **All cash flows are immediately reinvested in another project that has a similar return.** In most capital budgeting situations, companies receive cash flows during each year of a project's life. In order to determine the return on the investment, some assumption must be made about how the cash flows are reinvested in the year that they are received. It is customary to assume that cash flows received are reinvested in some other project of similar return until the end of the project's life.

- **All cash flows can be predicted with certainty.** The outcomes of business investments are full of uncertainty, as the Holland America Line Feature Story shows. There is no way of knowing how popular a new product will be, how long a new machine will last, or what competitors' reactions might be to changes in a product. But, in order to make investment decisions, analysts must estimate future outcomes. In this chapter, we have assumed that future amounts are known with certainty.[1] In reality, little is known with certainty. More advanced capital budgeting techniques deal with uncertainty by considering the probability that various outcomes will occur.

> DO IT!

Net Present Value

Watertown Paper Corporation is considering adding another machine for the manufacture of corrugated cardboard. The machine would cost $900,000. It would have an estimated life of 6 years and no salvage value. The company estimates that annual cash inflows would increase by $400,000 and that annual cash outflows would increase by $190,000. Management has a required rate of return of 9%. Calculate the net present value on this project and discuss whether it should be accepted.

Action Plan

✔ Estimated annual cash inflows − Estimated annual cash outflows = Net annual cash flow.

✔ Use the NPV technique to calculate the difference between net cash flows and the initial investment.

✔ Accept the project if the net present value is positive.

Solution

Estimated annual cash inflows	$400,000
Estimated annual cash outflows	190,000
Net annual cash flow	$210,000

	Cash Flow	9% Discount Factor	Present Value
Present value of net annual cash flows	$210,000	4.48592[a]	$942,043
Capital investment			900,000
Net present value			$ 42,043

[a]Table 4, Appendix D, 9%, 6 years

Since the net present value is greater than zero, Watertown should accept the project.

Related exercise material: **BE26-2, BE26-3, E26-1, E26-2, E26-3, and DO IT! 26-2.**

 The Navigator

---

[1]One exception is a brief discussion of sensitivity analysis later in the chapter.

Comprehensive Example

Best Taste Foods is considering investing in new equipment to produce fat-free snack foods. Management believes that although demand for fat-free foods has leveled off, fat-free foods are here to stay. The following estimated costs, cost of capital, and cash flows were determined in consultation with the marketing, production, and finance departments.

Illustration 26-12

Investment information for Best Taste Foods example

Initial investment	$1,000,000
Cost of equipment overhaul in 5 years	$200,000
Salvage value of equipment in 10 years	$20,000
Cost of capital (discount rate)	15%
Estimated annual cash flows	
Cash inflows received from sales	$500,000
Cash outflows for cost of goods sold	$200,000
Maintenance costs	$30,000
Other direct operating costs	$40,000

Remember that we are using cash flows in our analysis, not accrual revenues and expenses. Thus, for example, the direct operating costs would not include depreciation expense, since depreciation expense does not use cash. Illustration 26-13 presents the computation of the net annual cash flows of this project.

Illustration 26-13

Computation of net annual cash flow

Cash inflows received from sales	$ 500,000
Cash outflows for cost of goods sold	(200,000)
Maintenance costs	(30,000)
Other direct operating costs	(40,000)
Net annual cash flow	**$230,000**

Illustration 26-14 shows computation of the net present value for this proposed investment (discount factors from Appendix D, Table 4).

Illustration 26-14

Computation of net present value for Best Taste Foods investment

Event	Time Period	Cash Flow	×	15% Discount Factor	=	Present Value
Equipment purchase	0	$1,000,000		1.00000		$(1,000,000)
Equipment overhaul	5	200,000		.49718		(99,436)
Net annual cash flow	1–10	230,000		5.01877		1,154,317
Salvage value	10	20,000		.24719		4,944
Net present value						**$ 59,825**

Because the net present value of the project is positive, Best Taste should accept the project.

Additional Considerations

Now that you understand how the net present value method works, we can add some "additional wrinkles." Specifically, these are the impact of intangible benefits, a way to compare mutually exclusive projects, refinements that take risk into account, and the need to conduct post-audits of investment projects.

Intangible Benefits

The NPV evaluation techniques employed thus far rely on tangible costs and benefits that can be relatively easily quantified. Some investment projects, especially high-tech projects, fail to make it through initial capital budget screens because only the project's tangible benefits are considered. *Intangible benefits* might include increased quality, improved safety, or enhanced employee loyalty. By ignoring intangible benefits, capital budgeting techniques might incorrectly eliminate projects that could be financially beneficial to the company.

LEARNING OBJECTIVE   **4**

Identify the challenges presented by intangible benefits in capital budgeting.

To avoid rejecting projects that actually should be accepted, analysts suggest two possible approaches:

1. Calculate net present value ignoring intangible benefits. Then, if the NPV is negative, ask whether the project offers any intangible benefits that are worth at least the amount of the negative NPV.

2. Project rough, conservative estimates of the value of the intangible benefits, and incorporate these values into the NPV calculation.

EXAMPLE

Assume that Berg Company is considering the purchase of a new mechanical robot to be used for soldering electrical connections. Illustration 26-15 shows the estimates related to this proposed purchase (discount factors from Appendix D, Table 4).

Initial investment	$200,000	
Annual cash inflows	$ 50,000	
Annual cash outflows	20,000	
Net annual cash flow	**$ 30,000**	
Estimated life of equipment	10 years	
Discount rate	12%	

	Cash Flows	×	12% Discount Factor	=	Present Value
Present value of net annual cash flows	$30,000	×	5.65022	=	$169,507
Initial investment					200,000
Net present value					**$(30,493)**

Illustration 26-15
Investment information for Berg Company example

Based on the negative net present value of $30,493, the proposed project is not acceptable. This calculation, however, ignores important information. First, the company's engineers believe that purchasing this machine will dramatically improve the quality of electrical connections in the company's products. As a result, future warranty costs will be reduced. Also, the company believes that this higher quality will translate into higher future sales. Finally, the new machine will be much safer than the previous one.

Berg can incorporate this new information into the capital budgeting decision in the two ways discussed earlier. First, management might simply ask whether the reduced warranty costs, increased sales, and improved safety benefits have an estimated total present value to the company of at least $30,493. If yes, then the project is acceptable.

Alternatively, analysts can estimate the annual cash flows of these benefits. In our initial calculation, we assumed each of these benefits to have a value of zero. It seems likely that their actual values are much higher than zero. Given the difficulty of estimating these benefits, however, conservative values should be assigned to them. If, after using conservative estimates, the net present value is positive, Berg should accept the project.

To illustrate, assume that Berg estimates that improved sales will increase cash inflows by $10,000 annually as a result of an increase in perceived quality. Berg also estimates that annual cost outflows would be reduced by $5,000 as a result of lower warranty claims, reduced injury claims, and missed work. Consideration of the intangible benefits results in the following revised NPV calculation (discount factors from Appendix D, Table 4).

Illustration 26-16
Revised investment information for Berg Company example, including intangible benefits

Initial investment	$200,000	
Annual cash inflows (revised)	$ 60,000	($50,000 + $10,000)
Annual cash outflows (revised)	15,000	($20,000 − $5,000)
Net annual cash flow	**$ 45,000**	
Estimated life of equipment	10 years	
Discount rate	12%	

	Cash Flows	×	12% Discount Factor	=	Present Value
Present value of net annual cash flows	$45,000	×	5.65022	=	$254,260
Initial investment					200,000
Net present value					**$ 54,260**

Using these conservative estimates of the value of the additional benefits, Berg should accept the project.

ETHICS INSIGHT

It Need Not Cost an Arm and a Leg

Most manufacturers say that employee safety matters above everything else. But how many back up this statement with investments that improve employee safety? Recently, a woodworking hobbyist, who also happens to be a patent attorney with a Ph.D. in physics, invented a mechanism that automatically shuts down a power saw when the saw blade comes in contact with human flesh. The blade stops so quickly that only minor injuries result.

Power saws injure 40,000 Americans each year, and 4,000 of those injuries are bad enough to require amputation. Therefore, one might think that power-saw companies would be lined up to incorporate this mechanism into their saws. But, in the words of one power-tool company, "Safety doesn't sell." Since existing saw manufacturers were unwilling to incorporate the device into their saws, eventually the inventor started his own company to build the devices and sell them directly to businesses that use power saws.

Source: Melba Newsome, "An Edgy New Idea," *Time: Inside Business* (May 2006), p. A16.

? In addition to the obvious humanitarian benefit of reducing serious injuries, how else might the manufacturer of this product convince potential customers of its worth? (See page 1327.)

Profitability Index for Mutually Exclusive Projects

In theory, companies should accept all projects with positive NPVs. However, companies rarely are able to adopt all positive-NPV proposals. First, proposals often are **mutually exclusive**. This means that if the company adopts one proposal, it would be impossible also to adopt the other proposal. For example, a company may be considering the purchase of a new packaging machine and is looking at various brands and models. It needs only one packaging machine. Once the company has determined which brand and model to purchase, the others will not be purchased—even though they also may have positive net present values.

Even in instances where projects are not mutually exclusive, managers often must choose between various positive-NPV projects because of **limited resources**. For example, the company might have ideas for two new lines of business, each of which has a projected positive NPV. However, both of these proposals require skilled personnel, and the company determines that it will not be able to find enough skilled personnel to staff both projects. Management will have to choose the project it thinks is a better option.

When choosing between alternative proposals, it is tempting simply to choose the project with the higher NPV. Consider the following example of two mutually exclusive projects. Each is assumed to have a 10-year life and a 12% discount rate (discount factors from Appendix D, Tables 3 and 4). Illustration 26-17 shows the estimates for each project and the computation of the present value of the net annual cash flows.

LEARNING OBJECTIVE 5

Describe the profitability index.

	Project A	Project B
Initial investment	$40,000	$ 90,000
Net annual cash inflow	10,000	19,000
Salvage value	5,000	10,000
Present value of net annual cash flows		
($10,000 × 5.65022) + ($5,000 × .32197)	58,112	
($19,000 × 5.65022) + ($10,000 × .32197)		110,574

Illustration 26-17
Investment information for mutually exclusive projects

Illustration 26-18 computes the net present values of Project A and Project B by subtracting the initial investment from the present value of the net annual cash flows.

	Project A	Project B
Present value of net annual cash flows	$ 58,112	$110,574
Initial investment	40,000	90,000
Net present value	$18,112	$ 20,574

Illustration 26-18
Net present value computation

Project B has the higher NPV, and so it would seem that the company should adopt B. Note, however, that Project B also requires more than twice the original investment of Project A. In choosing between the two projects, the company should also include in its calculations the amount of the original investment.

One relatively simple method of comparing alternative projects is the **profitability index**. This method takes into account both the size of the original investment and the discounted cash flows. The profitability index is calculated by dividing the present value of net cash flows that occur after the initial investment by the amount of the initial investment.

Present Value of Net Cash Flows	÷	Initial Investment	=	Profitability Index

Illustration 26-19
Formula for profitability index

The profitability index allows comparison of the relative desirability of projects that require differing initial investments. Note that any project with a positive NPV will have a profitability index above 1. The profitability index for each of the mutually exclusive projects is calculated below.

Illustration 26-20
Calculation of profitability index

| Profitability Index | $=$ | $\dfrac{\text{Present Value of Net Cash Flows}}{\text{Initial Investment}}$ |

Project A	Project B
$\dfrac{\$58,112}{\$40,000} = \mathbf{1.45}$	$\dfrac{\$110,574}{\$90,000} = \mathbf{1.23}$

In this case, the profitability index of Project A exceeds that of Project B. Thus, Project A is more desirable. Again, if these were not mutually exclusive projects and if resources were not limited, then the company should invest in both projects since both have positive NPVs. Additional considerations related to preference decisions are discussed in more advanced courses.

Risk Analysis

A simplifying assumption made by many financial analysts is that projected results are known with certainty. In reality, projected results are only estimates based upon the forecaster's belief as to the most probable outcome. One approach for dealing with such uncertainty is **sensitivity analysis**. Sensitivity analysis uses a number of outcome estimates to get a sense of the variability among potential returns. An example of sensitivity analysis was presented in Illustration 26-11 (page 1298), where we illustrated the impact on NPV of different discount rate assumptions. A higher-risk project would be evaluated using a higher discount rate.

Similarly, to take into account that more distant cash flows are often more uncertain, a higher discount rate can be used to discount more distant cash flows. Other techniques to address uncertainty are discussed in advanced courses.

MANAGEMENT INSIGHT

Wide-Screen Capacity

Building a new factory to produce 50- and even 60-inch TV screens can cost $4 billion. But for more than 10 years, manufacturers of these screens have continued to build new plants. By building so many plants, they have expanded productive capacity at a rate that has exceeded the demand for big-screen TVs. In fact, during one recent year, the supply of big-screen TVs was estimated to exceed demand by 12%, rising to 16% in the future. One state-of-the-art plant built by Sharp was estimated to be operating at only 50% of capacity. Experts say that the price of big-screen TVs will have to fall much further than they already have before demand may eventually catch up with productive capacity.

Source: James Simms, "Sharp's Payoff Delayed," *Wall Street Journal Online* (September 14, 2010).

 What implications does the excess capacity have for the cash payback and net present value calculations of these investments? (See page 1327.)

Post-Audit of Investment Projects

Any well-run organization should perform an evaluation, called a **post-audit**, of its investment projects after their completion. A post-audit is a thorough evaluation of how well a project's actual performance matches the original projections. An example of a post-audit is seen in a situation that occurred at Campbell Soup. The company made the original decision to invest in the Intelligent Quisine line based on management's best estimates of future cash flows. During the development phase of the project, Campbell hired an outside consulting firm to evaluate the project's potential for success. Because actual results during the initial years were far below the estimated results and because the future also did not look promising, the project was terminated.

LEARNING OBJECTIVE   6

Indicate the benefits of performing a post-audit.

Performing a post-audit is important for a variety of reasons. First, if managers know that the company will compare their estimates to actual results, they will be more likely to submit reasonable and accurate data when they make investment proposals. This clearly is better for the company than for managers to submit overly optimistic estimates in an effort to get pet projects approved. Second, as seen with Campbell Soup, a post-audit provides a formal mechanism by which the company can determine whether existing projects should be supported or terminated. Third, post-audits improve future investment proposals because, by evaluating past successes and failures, managers improve their estimation techniques.

A post-audit involves the same evaluation techniques used in making the original capital budgeting decision—for example, use of the NPV method. The difference is that, in the post-audit, analysts insert actual figures, where known, and they revise estimates of future amounts based on new information. The managers responsible for the estimates used in the original proposal must explain the reasons for any significant differences between their estimates and actual results.

Post-audits are not foolproof. In the case of Campbell Soup, some observers suggested that the company was too quick to abandon the project. Industry analysts suggested that with more time and more advertising expenditures, the company might have enjoyed success.

MANAGEMENT INSIGHT

Seeing the Big Picture

Inaccurate trend forecasting and market positioning are more detrimental to capital investment decisions than using the wrong discount rate. Ampex patented the VCR but failed to see its market potential. Westinghouse made the same mistake with the flat-screen video display. More often, companies adopt projects or businesses only to discontinue them in response to market changes. Texas Instruments announced it would stop manufacturing computer chips, after it had made substantial capital investments that enabled it to become one of the world's leading suppliers. The company dropped out of some 12 business lines in only a few years.

Source: World Research Advisory Inc. (London, August 1998), p. 4.

 How important is the choice of discount rate in making capital budgeting decisions? (See page 1327.)

Other Capital Budgeting Techniques

Some companies use capital budgeting techniques other than, or in addition to, the cash payback and net present value methods. In this section, we will briefly discuss these other approaches.

Internal Rate of Return Method

The **internal rate of return method** differs from the net present value method in that it finds the **interest yield of the potential investment**. The **internal rate of return (IRR)** is the interest rate that will cause the present value of the proposed capital expenditure to equal the present value of the expected net annual cash flows (that is, NPV equal to zero). Because it recognizes the time value of money, the internal rate of return method is (like the NPV method) a discounted cash flow technique.

How do we determine the internal rate of return? One way is to use a financial calculator (see Appendix D, Section Three) or computerized spreadsheet to solve for this rate. Or, we can use a trial-and-error procedure.

To illustrate, assume that Stewart Shipping Company is considering the purchase of a new front-end loader at a cost of $244,371. Net annual cash flows from this loader are estimated to be $100,000 a year for three years. To determine the internal rate of return on this front-end loader, the company finds the discount rate that results in a net present value of zero. As Illustration 26-21 shows, at a rate of return of 10%, Stewart Shipping has a positive net present value of $4,315. At a rate of return of 12%, it has a negative net present value of $4,188. At an 11% rate, the net present value is zero. Therefore, 11% is the internal rate of return for this investment (discount factors from Appendix D, Table 3).

Illustration 26-21
Estimation of internal rate of return

Year	Net Annual Cash Flows	Discount Factor 10%	Present Value 10%	Discount Factor 11%	Present Value 11%	Discount Factor 12%	Present Value 12%
1	$100,000	.90909	$ 90,909	.90090	$ 90,090	.89286	$ 89,286
2	$100,000	.82645	82,645	.81162	81,162	.79719	79,719
3	$100,000	.75132	75,132	.73119	73,119	.71178	71,178
			248,686		244,371		240,183
Less: Initial investment			244,371		244,371		244,371
Net present value			$ 4,315		$ –0–		$ (4,188)

An easier approach to solving for the internal rate of return can be used if the net annual cash flows are **equal**, as in the Stewart Shipping example. In this special case, we can find the internal rate of return using the following formula.

Illustration 26-22
Formula for internal rate of return—even cash flows

$$\text{Capital Investment} \div \text{Net Annual Cash Flows} = \text{Internal Rate of Return Factor}$$

Applying this formula to the Stewart Shipping example, we find:

$$\$244,371 \div \$100,000 = 2.44371$$

We then look up the factor 2.44371 in Table 4 of Appendix D in the three-payment row and find it under 11%. Row 3 is reproduced on the next page for your convenience.

(n) Payments	4%	5%	6%	7%	8%	9%	10%	11%	12%	15%
				Table 4 Present Value of an Annuity of 1						
3	2.77509	2.72325	2.67301	2.62432	2.57710	2.53130	2.48685	**2.44371**	2.40183	2.28323

Recognize that if the cash flows are **uneven**, then a trial-and-error approach or a financial calculator or computerized spreadsheet must be used.

Once managers know the internal rate of return, they compare it to the company's required rate of return (the discount rate). The IRR decision rule is as follows: **Accept the project when the internal rate of return is equal to or greater than the required rate of return. Reject the project when the internal rate of return is less than the required rate of return.** Illustration 26-23 shows these relationships. The internal rate of return method is widely used in practice, largely because most managers find the internal rate of return easy to interpret.

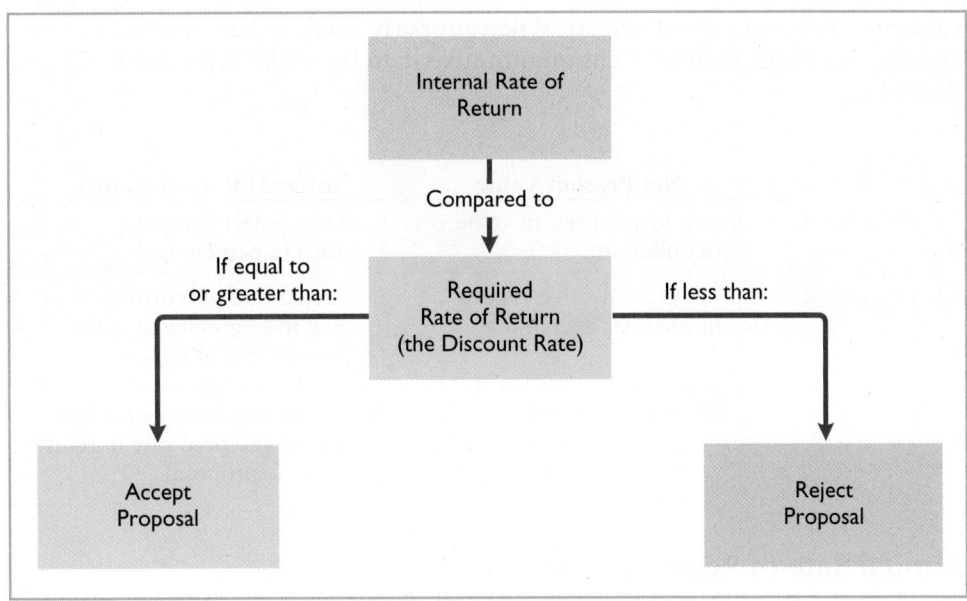

Illustration 26-23
Internal rate of return decision criteria

> **DO IT!**

Internal Rate of Return

Watertown Paper Corporation is considering adding another machine for the manufacture of corrugated cardboard. The machine would cost $900,000. It would have an estimated life of 6 years and no salvage value. The company estimates that annual cash inflows would increase by $400,000 and that annual cash outflows would increase by $190,000. Management has a required rate of return of 9%. Calculate the internal rate of return on this project and discuss whether it should be accepted.

Action Plan

✔ Estimated annual cash inflows − Estimated annual cash outflows = Net annual cash flow.

✔ Capital investment/Net annual cash flows = Internal rate of return factor.

✔ Look up the factor in the present value of an annuity table to find the internal rate of return.

✔ Accept the project if the internal rate of return is equal to or greater than the required rate of return.

Solution

Estimated annual cash inflows	$400,000
Estimated annual cash outflows	190,000
Net annual cash flow	$210,000

$900,000/210,000 = 4.285714. Using Table 4 of Appendix D and the factors that correspond with the six-payment row, 4.285714 is between the factors for 10% and 11%. Since the project has an internal rate that is greater than 10% and the required rate of return is only 9%, the project should be accepted.

Related exercise material: **BE26-7, BE26-8, E26-5, E26-6, E26-7, and** **DO IT!** **26-3.**

✔ **The Navigator**

Comparing Discounted Cash Flow Methods

Illustration 26-24 compares the two discounted cash flow methods—net present value and internal rate of return. When properly used, either method will provide management with relevant quantitative data for making capital budgeting decisions.

Illustration 26-24
Comparison of discounted cash flow methods

	Net Present Value	**Internal Rate of Return**
1. Objective	Compute net present value (a dollar amount).	Compute internal rate of return (a percentage).
2. Decision Rule	If net present value is zero or positive, accept the proposal. If net present value is negative, reject the proposal.	If internal rate of return is equal to or greater than the required rate of return, accept the proposal. If internal rate of return is less than the required rate of return, reject the proposal.

Annual Rate of Return Method

The final capital budgeting technique we will look at is the **annual rate of return method**. It is based directly on accrual accounting data rather than on cash flows. It indicates **the profitability of a capital expenditure** by dividing expected annual net income by the average investment. Illustration 26-25 shows the formula for computing annual rate of return.

Illustration 26-25
Annual rate of return formula

Expected Annual Net Income	÷	Average Investment	=	Annual Rate of Return

Assume that Reno Company is considering an investment of $130,000 in new equipment. The new equipment is expected to last five years and have zero salvage value at the end of its useful life. Reno uses the straight-line method of depreciation for accounting purposes. The expected annual revenues and costs of the new product that will be produced from the investment are:

Sales		$200,000
Less: Costs and expenses		
Manufacturing costs (exclusive of depreciation)	$132,000	
Depreciation expense ($130,000 ÷ 5)	26,000	
Selling and administrative expenses	22,000	180,000
Income before income taxes		20,000
Income tax expense		7,000
Net income		$ 13,000

Illustration 26-26
Estimated annual net income from Reno Company's capital expenditure

Reno's expected annual net income is $13,000. Average investment is derived from the formula shown below.

$$\frac{\text{Original Investment} + \text{Value at End of Useful Life}}{2} = \text{Average Investment}$$

Illustration 26-27
Formula for computing average investment

The value at the end of useful life is equal to the asset's salvage value, if any. For Reno, average investment is $65,000 [($130,000 + $0) ÷ 2]. The expected annual rate of return for Reno's investment in new equipment is therefore 20%, computed as follows.

$$\$13,000 \div \$65,000 = 20\%$$

Management then compares the annual rate of return with its **required rate of return** for investments of similar risk. The required rate of return is generally based on the company's cost of capital. The decision rule is: **A project is acceptable if its rate of return is greater than management's required rate of return. It is unacceptable when the reverse is true.** When companies use the rate of return technique in deciding among several acceptable projects, **the higher the rate of return for a given risk, the more attractive the investment**.

The principal advantages of this method are the simplicity of its calculation and management's familiarity with the accounting terms used in the computation. A major limitation of the annual rate of return method is that it does not consider the time value of money. For example, no consideration is given as to whether cash inflows will occur early or late in the life of the investment. As explained in Appendix D, recognition of the time value of money can make a significant difference between the future value and the discounted present value of an investment. A second disadvantage is that this method relies on accrual accounting numbers rather than expected cash flows.

Helpful Hint
A capital budgeting decision based on only one technique may be misleading. It is often wise to analyze an investment from a number of different perspectives.

> **DO IT!**

Annual Rate of Return

Watertown Paper Corporation is considering adding another machine for the manufacture of corrugated cardboard. The machine would cost $900,000. It would have an estimated life of 6 years and no salvage value. The company estimates that annual revenues would increase by $400,000 and that annual expenses excluding depreciation would increase by $190,000. It uses the straight-line method to compute depreciation expense. Management has a required rate of return of 9%. Compute the annual rate of return.

Solution

Action Plan

✔ Expected annual net income = Annual revenues − Annual expenses (including depreciation expense).

✔ Annual rate of return = Expected annual net income/ Average investment.

✔ Average investment = (Original investment + Value at end of useful life)/2.

Revenues		$400,000
Less:		
Expenses (excluding depreciation)	$190,000	
Depreciation ($900,000/6 years)	150,000	340,000
Annual net income		$ 60,000

Average investment = ($900,000 + 0)/2 = $450,000.
Annual rate of return = $60,000/$450,000 = 13.3%.

Since the annual rate of return (13.33%) is greater than Watertown's required rate of return (9%), the proposed project is acceptable.

Related exercise material: **BE26-9, E26-8, E26-9, E26-10, E26-11, and DO IT! 26-4.**

 The Navigator

> Comprehensive DO IT!

Cornfield Company is considering a long-term capital investment project in laser equipment. This will require an investment of $280,000, and it will have a useful life of 5 years. Annual net income is expected to be $16,000 a year. Depreciation is computed by the straight-line method with no salvage value. The company's cost of capital is 10%. (*Hint:* Assume cash flows can be computed by adding back depreciation expense.)

Instructions
(Round all computations to two decimal places.)
(a) Compute the cash payback period for the project. (Round to two decimals.)
(b) Compute the net present value for the project. (Round to nearest dollar.)
(c) Compute the annual rate of return for the project.
(d) Should the project be accepted? Why?

Solution to Comprehensive DO IT!

Action Plan

✔ Calculate the time it will take to pay back the investment: cost of the investment divided by net annual cash flows.

✔ When calculating NPV, remember that net annual cash flow equals annual net income plus annual depreciation expense.

✔ Be careful to use the correct discount factor in using the net present value method.

✔ Calculate the annual rate of return: expected annual net income divided by average investment.

(a) $280,000 ÷ $72,000 ($16,000 + $56,000) = 3.89 years

(b)

	Present Value at 10%
Discount factor for 5 payments	3.79079
Present value of net cash flows:	
$72,000 × 3.79079	$272,937
Capital investment	280,000
Negative net present value	$ (7,063)

(c) $16,000 ÷ $140,000 ($280,000 ÷ 2) = 11.4%
(d) The annual rate of return of 11.4% is good. However, the cash payback period is 78% of the project's useful life, and net present value is negative. The recommendation is to reject the project.

 The Navigator

SUMMARY OF LEARNING OBJECTIVES

✔ **The Navigator**

1 Discuss capital budgeting evaluation, and explain inputs used in capital budgeting. Management gathers project proposals from each department; a capital budget committee screens the proposals and recommends worthy projects. Company officers decide which projects to fund, and the board of directors approves the capital budget. In capital budgeting, estimated cash inflows and outflows, rather than accrual-accounting numbers, are the preferred inputs.

2 Describe the cash payback technique. The cash payback technique identifies the time period required to recover the cost of the investment. The formula when net annual cash flows are equal is: Cost of capital investment ÷ Estimated net annual cash flow = Cash payback period. The shorter the payback period, the more attractive the investment.

3 Explain the net present value method. The net present value method compares the present value of future cash inflows with the capital investment to determine net present value. The NPV decision rule is: Accept the project if net present value is zero or positive. Reject the project if net present value is negative.

4 Identify the challenges presented by intangible benefits in capital budgeting. Intangible benefits are difficult to quantify and thus are often ignored in capital budgeting decisions. This can result in incorrectly rejecting some projects. One method for considering intangible benefits is to calculate the NPV, ignoring intangible benefits. If the resulting NPV is below zero, evaluate whether the benefits are worth at least the amount of the negative net present value. Alternatively, intangible benefits can be incorporated into the NPV calculation, using conservative estimates of their value.

5 Describe the profitability index. The profitability index is a tool for comparing the relative merits of alternative capital investment opportunities. It is computed as: Present value of net cash flows ÷ Initial investment. The higher the index, the more desirable the project.

6 Indicate the benefits of performing a post-audit. A post-audit is an evaluation of a capital investment's actual performance. Post-audits create an incentive for managers to make accurate estimates. Post-audits also are useful for determining whether a company should continue, expand, or terminate a project. Finally, post-audits provide feedback that is useful for improving estimation techniques.

7 Explain the internal rate of return method. The objective of the internal rate of return method is to find the interest yield of the potential investment, which is expressed as a percentage rate. The IRR decision rule is: Accept the project when the internal rate of return is equal to or greater than the required rate of return. Reject the project when the internal rate of return is less than the required rate of return.

8 Describe the annual rate of return method. The annual rate of return uses accrual accounting data to indicate the profitability of a capital investment. It is calculated as: Expected annual net income ÷ Amount of the average investment. The higher the rate of return, the more attractive the investment.

GLOSSARY

Annual rate of return method The determination of the profitability of a capital expenditure, computed by dividing expected annual net income by the average investment. (p. 1308).

Capital budgeting The process of making capital expenditure decisions in business. (p. 1291).

Cash payback technique A capital budgeting technique that identifies the time period required to recover the cost of a capital investment from the net annual cash flow produced by the investment. (p. 1294).

Cost of capital The average rate of return that the firm must pay to obtain funds from creditors and stockholders. (p. 1298).

Discounted cash flow technique A capital budgeting technique that considers both the estimated net cash flows from the investment and the time value of money. (p. 1295).

Discount rate The interest rate used in discounting the future net cash flows to determine present value. (p. 1296).

Internal rate of return (IRR) The interest rate that will cause the present value of the proposed capital expenditure to equal the present value of the expected net annual cash flows. (p. 1306).

Internal rate of return (IRR) method A method used in capital budgeting that results in finding the interest yield of the potential investment. (p. 1306).

Net present value (NPV) The difference that results when the original capital outlay is subtracted from the discounted net cash flows. (p. 1296).

Net present value (NPV) method A method used in capital budgeting in which net cash flows are discounted to their present value and then compared to the capital outlay required by the investment. (p. 1295).

Post-audit A thorough evaluation of how well a project's actual performance matches the original projections. (p. 1305).

Profitability index A method of comparing alternative projects that takes into account both the size of the investment and its discounted future net cash flows. It is computed by dividing the present value of net future cash flows by the initial investment. (p. 1303).

Required rate of return The rate of return management expects on investments; also called the *discount rate or cost of capital*. (p. 1309).

 Self-Test, Brief Exercises, Exercises, Problem Set A, and many more resources are available for practice in WileyPLUS.

SELF-TEST QUESTIONS

Answers are at the end of the chapter.

(LO 1) **1.** Which of the following is *not* an example of a capital budgeting decision?
(a) Decision to build a new plant.
(b) Decision to renovate an existing facility.
(c) Decision to buy a piece of machinery.
(d) All of these are capital budgeting decisions.

(LO 1) **2.** What is the order of involvement of the following parties in the capital budgeting authorization process?
(a) Plant managers, officers, capital budget committee, board of directors.
(b) Board of directors, plant managers, officers, capital budget committee.
(c) Plant managers, capital budget committee, officers, board of directors.
(d) Officers, plant managers, capital budget committee, board of directors.

(LO 2) **3.** What is a weakness of the cash payback approach?
(a) It uses accrual-based accounting numbers.
(b) It ignores the time value of money.
(c) It ignores the useful life of alternative projects.
(d) Both (b) and (c) are true.

(LO 2) **4.** Siegel Industries is considering two capital budgeting projects. Project A requires an initial investment of $48,000. It is expected to produce net annual cash flows of $7,000. Project B requires an initial investment of $75,000 and is expected to produce net annual cash flows of $12,000. Using the cash payback technique to evaluate the two projects, Siegel should accept:
(a) Project A because it has a shorter cash payback period.
(b) Project B because it has a shorter cash payback period.
(c) Project A because it requires a smaller initial investment.
(d) Project B because it produces a larger net annual cash flow.

(LO 3) **5.** Which is a true statement regarding using a higher discount rate to calculate the net present value of a project?
(a) It will make it less likely that the project will be accepted.
(b) It will make it more likely that the project will be accepted.

(c) It is appropriate to use a higher rate if the project is perceived as being less risky than other projects being considered.
(d) It is appropriate to use a higher rate if the project will have a short useful life relative to other projects being considered.

6. A positive net present value means that the: (LO 3)
(a) project's rate of return is less than the cutoff rate.
(b) project's rate of return exceeds the required rate of return.
(c) project's rate of return equals the required rate of return.
(d) project is unacceptable.

7. Which of the following is *not* an alternative name for (LO 3) the discount rate?
(a) Hurdle rate.
(b) Required rate of return.
(c) Cutoff rate.
(d) All of these are alternative names for the discount rate.

8. If a project has intangible benefits whose value is (LO 4) hard to estimate, the best thing to do is:
(a) ignore these benefits, since any estimate of their value will most likely be wrong.
(b) include a conservative estimate of their value.
(c) ignore their value in your initial net present value calculation, but then estimate whether their potential value is worth at least the amount of the net present value deficiency.
(d) Either (b) or (c) is correct.

9. An example of an intangible benefit provided by a (LO 4) capital budgeting project is:
(a) the salvage value of the capital investment.
(b) a positive net present value.
(c) a decrease in customer complaints due to poor quality.
(d) an internal rate of return greater than zero.

10. The following information is available for a potential (LO 5) capital investment.

Initial investment	$80,000
Salvage value	10,000
Net annual cash flow	14,820
Net present value	18,112
Useful life	10 years

The potential investment's profitability index (rounded to two decimals) is:

(a) 5.40.   (c) 1.23.
(b) 1.19.   (d) 1.40.

(LO 6) **11.** A post-audit of an investment project should be performed:
(a) on all significant capital expenditure projects.
(b) on all projects that management feels might be financial failures.
(c) on randomly selected projects.
(d) only on projects that enjoy tremendous success.

(LO 7) **12.** A project should be accepted if its internal rate of return exceeds:
(a) zero.
(b) the rate of return on a government bond.
(c) the company's required rate of return.
(d) the rate the company pays on borrowed funds.

(LO 7) **13.** The following information is available for a potential capital investment.

Initial investment	$60,000
Net annual cash flow	15,400
Net present value	3,143
Useful life	5 years

The potential investment's internal rate of return is approximately:

(a) 5%.   (c) 4%.
(b) 10%.   (d) 9%.

14. Which of the following is *incorrect* about the annual (LO 8) rate of return technique?
(a) The calculation is simple.
(b) The accounting terms used are familiar to management.
(c) The timing of the cash inflows is not considered.
(d) The time value of money is considered.

15. The following information is available for a potential (LO 8) capital investment.

Initial investment	$120,000
Annual net income	15,000
Net annual cash flow	27,500
Salvage value	20,000
Useful life	8 years

The potential investment's annual rate of return is approximately:

(a) 21%.   (c) 30%.
(b) 15%.   (d) 39%.

Go to the book's companion website, www.wiley.com/college/weygandt, for additional Self-Test Questions.

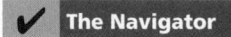 ✔ **The Navigator**

QUESTIONS

1. Describe the process a company may use in screening and approving the capital expenditure budget.

2. What are the advantages and disadvantages of the cash payback technique?

3. Tom Wells claims the formula for the cash payback technique is the same as the formula for the annual rate of return technique. Is Tom correct? What is the formula for the cash payback technique?

4. Two types of present value tables may be used with the discounted cash flow techniques. Identify the tables and the circumstance(s) when each table should be used.

5. What is the decision rule under the net present value method?

6. Discuss the factors that determine the appropriate discount rate to use when calculating the net present value.

7. What simplifying assumptions were made in the chapter regarding calculation of net present value?

8. What are some examples of potential intangible benefits of investment proposals? Why do these intangible benefits complicate the capital budgeting evaluation process? What might happen if intangible benefits are ignored in a capital budgeting decision?

9. What steps can be taken to incorporate intangible benefits into the capital budget evaluation process?

10. What advantages does the profitability index provide over direct comparison of net present value when comparing two projects?

11. What is a post-audit? What are the potential benefits of a post-audit?

12. Identify the steps required in using the internal rate of return method when the net annual cash flows are equal.

13. El Cajon Company uses the internal rate of return method. What is the decision rule for this method?

14. What are the strengths of the annual rate of return approach? What are its weaknesses?

15. Your classmate, Mike Dawson, is confused about the factors that are included in the annual rate of return technique. What is the formula for this technique?

16. Sveta Pace is trying to understand the term "cost of capital." Define the term and indicate its relevance to the decision rule under the internal rate of return technique.

BRIEF EXERCISES

Compute the cash payback period for a capital investment.
(LO 2)

BE26-1 Bella Company is considering purchasing new equipment for $450,000. It is expected that the equipment will produce net annual cash flows of $50,000 over its 10-year useful life. Annual depreciation will be $45,000. Compute the cash payback period.

Compute net present value of an investment.
(LO 3)

BE26-2 Hsung Company accumulates the following data concerning a proposed capital investment: cash cost $215,000, net annual cash flows $40,000, present value factor of cash inflows for 10 years 5.65 (rounded). Determine the net present value, and indicate whether the investment should be made.

Compute net present value of an investment.
(LO 3)

BE26-3 Magic Corporation, an amusement park, is considering a capital investment in a new exhibit. The exhibit would cost $136,000 and have an estimated useful life of 5 years. It will be sold for $65,000 at that time. (Amusement parks need to rotate exhibits to keep people interested.) It is expected to increase net annual cash flows by $25,000. The company's borrowing rate is 8%. Its cost of capital is 10%. Calculate the net present value of this project to the company.

Compute net present value of an investment and consider intangible benefits.
(LO 3, 4)

BE26-4 Caine Bottling Corporation is considering the purchase of a new bottling machine. The machine would cost $200,000 and has an estimated useful life of 8 years with zero salvage value. Management estimates that the new bottling machine will provide net annual cash flows of $34,000. Management also believes that the new bottling machine will save the company money because it is expected to be more reliable than other machines, and thus will reduce downtime. How much would the reduction in downtime have to be worth in order for the project to be acceptable? Assume a discount rate of 9%. (*Hint:* Calculate the net present value.)

Compute net present value and profitability index.
(LO 3, 5)

BE26-5 Beacon Company is considering two different, mutually exclusive capital expenditure proposals. Project A will cost $400,000, has an expected useful life of 10 years, a salvage value of zero, and is expected to increase net annual cash flows by $70,000. Project B will cost $280,000, has an expected useful life of 10 years, a salvage value of zero, and is expected to increase net annual cash flows by $50,000. A discount rate of 9% is appropriate for both projects. Compute the net present value and profitability index of each project. Which project should be accepted?

Perform a post-audit.
(LO 6)

BE26-6 Quillen Company is performing a post-audit of a project completed one year ago. The initial estimates were that the project would cost $250,000, would have a useful life of 9 years, zero salvage value, and would result in net annual cash flows of $46,000 per year. Now that the investment has been in operation for 1 year, revised figures indicate that it actually cost $260,000, will have a useful life of 11 years, and will produce net annual cash flows of $39,000 per year. Evaluate the success of the project. Assume a discount rate of 10%.

Calculate internal rate of return.
(LO 7)

BE26-7 Horowitz Company is evaluating the purchase of a rebuilt spot-welding machine to be used in the manufacture of a new product. The machine will cost $176,000, has an estimated useful life of 7 years, a salvage value of zero, and will increase net annual cash flows by $33,740. What is its approximate internal rate of return?

Calculate internal rate of return.
(LO 7)

BE26-8 Viera Corporation is considering investing in a new facility. The estimated cost of the facility is $2,045,000. It will be used for 12 years, then sold for $716,000. The facility will generate annual cash inflows of $400,000 and will need new annual cash outflows of $150,000. The company has a required rate of return of 7%. Calculate the internal rate of return on this project, and discuss whether the project should be accepted.

Compute annual rate of return.
(LO 8)

BE26-9 Mecha Oil Company is considering investing in a new oil well. It is expected that the oil well will increase annual revenues by $130,000 and will increase annual expenses by $70,000 including depreciation. The oil well will cost $470,000 and will have a $10,000 salvage value at the end of its 10-year useful life. Calculate the annual rate of return.

> DO IT! REVIEW

Compute the cash payback period for an investment.

(LO 2)

DO IT! 26-1 Wallowa Company is considering a long-term investment project called ZIP. ZIP will require an investment of $120,000. It will have a useful life of 4 years and no salvage value. Annual cash inflows would increase by $80,000, and annual cash outflows would increase by $40,000. Compute the cash payback period.

Calculate net present value of an investment.

(LO 3)

DO IT! 26-2 Wallowa Company is considering a long-term investment project called ZIP. ZIP will require an investment of $120,000. It will have a useful life of 4 years and no salvage value. Annual cash inflows would increase by $80,000, and annual cash outflows would increase by $40,000. The company's required rate of return is 12%. Calculate the net present value on this project and discuss whether it should be accepted.

Calculate internal rate of return.

(LO 7)

DO IT! 26-3 Wallowa Company is considering a long-term investment project called ZIP. ZIP will require an investment of $120,000. It will have a useful life of 4 years and no salvage value. Annual cash inflows would increase by $80,000, and annual cash outflows would increase by $40,000. The company's required rate of return is 12%. Calculate the internal rate of return on this project and discuss whether it should be accepted.

Calculate annual rate of return.

(LO 8)

DO IT! 26-4 Wallowa Company is considering a long-term investment project called ZIP. ZIP will require an investment of $120,000. It will have a useful life of 4 years and no salvage value. Annual revenues would increase by $80,000, and annual expenses (excluding depreciation) would increase by $40,000. Wallowa uses the straight-line method to compute depreciation expense. The company's required rate of return is 12%. Compute the annual rate of return.

 The Navigator

EXERCISES

E26-1 Palo Alto Corporation is considering purchasing a new delivery truck. The truck has many advantages over the company's current truck (not the least of which is that it runs). The new truck would cost $56,000. Because of the increased capacity, reduced maintenance costs, and increased fuel economy, the new truck is expected to generate cost savings of $7,500. At the end of 8 years the company will sell the truck for an estimated $27,000. Traditionally the company has used a rule of thumb that a proposal should not be accepted unless it has a payback period that is less than 50% of the asset's estimated useful life. Larry Newton, a new manager, has suggested that the company should not rely solely on the payback approach, but should also employ the net present value method when evaluating new projects. The company's cost of capital is 8%.

Compute cash payback and net present value.

(LO 2, 3)

Instructions
(a) Compute the cash payback period and net present value of the proposed investment.
(b) Does the project meet the company's cash payback criteria? Does it meet the net present value criteria for acceptance? Discuss your results.

E26-2 Doug's Custom Construction Company is considering three new projects, each requiring an equipment investment of $22,000. Each project will last for 3 years and produce the following net annual cash flows.

Compute cash payback period and net present value.

(LO 2, 3)

Year	AA	BB	CC
1	$ 7,000	$10,000	$13,000
2	9,000	10,000	12,000
3	12,000	10,000	11,000
Total	$28,000	$30,000	$36,000

The equipment's salvage value is zero, and Doug uses straight-line depreciation. Doug will not accept any project with a cash payback period over 2 years. Doug's required rate of return is 12%.

Instructions

(a) Compute each project's payback period, indicating the most desirable project and the least desirable project using this method. (Round to two decimals and assume in your computations that cash flows occur evenly throughout the year.)

(b) Compute the net present value of each project. Does your evaluation change? (Round to nearest dollar.)

Calculate net present value and apply decision rule.

(LO 3)

E26-3 Hiland Inc. manufactures snowsuits. Hiland is considering purchasing a new sewing machine at a cost of $2.45 million. Its existing machine was purchased five years ago at a price of $1.8 million; six months ago, Hiland spent $55,000 to keep it operational. The existing sewing machine can be sold today for $260,000. The new sewing machine would require a one-time, $85,000 training cost. Operating costs would decrease by the following amounts for years 1 to 7:

Year	1	$390,000
	2	400,000
	3	411,000
	4	426,000
	5	434,000
	6	435,000
	7	436,000

The new sewing machine would be depreciated according to the declining-balance method at a rate of 20%. The salvage value is expected to be $350,000. This new equipment would require maintenance costs of $100,000 at the end of the fifth year. The cost of capital is 9%.

Instructions

Use the net present value method to determine whether Hiland should purchase the new machine to replace the existing machine, and state the reason for your conclusion.

(CGA adapted)

Compute net present value and profitability index.

(LO 3, 5)

E26-4 BAK Corp. is considering purchasing one of two new diagnostic machines. Either machine would make it possible for the company to bid on jobs that it currently isn't equipped to do. Estimates regarding each machine are provided below.

	Machine A	Machine B
Original cost	$75,500	$180,000
Estimated life	8 years	8 years
Salvage value	–0–	–0–
Estimated annual cash inflows	$20,000	$40,000
Estimated annual cash outflows	$5,000	$10,000

Instructions

Calculate the net present value and profitability index of each machine. Assume a 9% discount rate. Which machine should be purchased?

Determine internal rate of return.

(LO 7)

E26-5 Eisler Corporation is involved in the business of injection molding of plastics. It is considering the purchase of a new computer-aided design and manufacturing machine for $430,000. The company believes that with this new machine it will improve productivity and increase quality, resulting in an increase in net annual cash flows of $101,000 for the next 6 years. Management requires a 10% rate of return on all new investments.

Instructions

Calculate the internal rate of return on this new machine. Should the investment be accepted?

Calculate cash payback period, internal rate of return, and apply decision rules.

(LO 2, 7)

E26-6 BSU Inc. wants to purchase a new machine for $29,300, excluding $1,500 of installation costs. The old machine was bought five years ago and had an expected economic life of 10 years without salvage value. This old machine now has a book value of $2,000, and BSU Inc. expects to sell it for that amount. The new machine would decrease operating costs by $7,000 each year of its economic life. The straight-line depreciation method would be used for the new machine, for a six-year period with no salvage value.

Instructions
(a) Determine the cash payback period.
(b) Determine the approximate internal rate of return.
(c) Assuming the company has a required rate of return of 10%, state your conclusion on whether the new machine should be purchased.

(CGA adapted)

E26-7 Ueker Company is considering three capital expenditure projects. Relevant data for the projects are as follows.

Determine internal rate of return.

(LO 7)

Project	Investment	Annual Income	Life of Project
22A	$240,000	$16,700	6 years
23A	270,000	20,600	9 years
24A	280,000	17,500	7 years

Annual income is constant over the life of the project. Each project is expected to have zero salvage value at the end of the project. Ueker Company uses the straight-line method of depreciation.

Instructions
(a) Determine the internal rate of return for each project. Round the internal rate of return factor to three decimals.
(b) If Ueker Company's required rate of return is 11%, which projects are acceptable?

E26-8 Pierre's Hair Salon is considering opening a new location in French Lick, California. The cost of building a new salon is $300,000. A new salon will normally generate annual revenues of $70,000, with annual expenses (including depreciation) of $41,500. At the end of 15 years the salon will have a salvage value of $80,000.

Calculate annual rate of return.

(LO 8)

Instructions
Calculate the annual rate of return on the project.

E26-9 Brady Service Center just purchased an automobile hoist for $35,000. The hoist has an 8-year life and an estimated salvage value of $3,000. Installation costs and freight charges were $3,300 and $700, respectively. Brady uses straight-line depreciation.

The new hoist will be used to replace mufflers and tires on automobiles. Brady estimates that the new hoist will enable his mechanics to replace five extra mufflers per week. Each muffler sells for $72 installed. The cost of a muffler is $36, and the labor cost to install a muffler is $12.

Compute cash payback period and annual rate of return.

(LO 2, 8)

Instructions
(a) Compute the cash payback period for the new hoist.
(b) Compute the annual rate of return for the new hoist. (Round to one decimal.)

E26-10 Vilas Company is considering a capital investment of $190,000 in additional productive facilities. The new machinery is expected to have a useful life of 5 years with no salvage value. Depreciation is by the straight-line method. During the life of the investment, annual net income and net annual cash flows are expected to be $12,000 and $50,000, respectively. Vilas has a 12% cost of capital rate, which is the required rate of return on the investment.

Compute annual rate of return, cash payback period, and net present value.

(LO 2, 3, 8)

Instructions
(Round to two decimals.)
(a) Compute (1) the cash payback period and (2) the annual rate of return on the proposed capital expenditure.
(b) Using the discounted cash flow technique, compute the net present value.

E26-11 BAP Corporation is reviewing an investment proposal. The initial cost and estimates of the book value of the investment at the end of each year, the net cash flows for each year, and the net income for each year are presented in the schedule on the next page. All cash flows are assumed to take place at the end of the year. The salvage value of the investment at the end of each year is equal to its book value. There would be no salvage value at the end of the investment's life.

Calculate payback, annual rate of return, and net present value.

(LO 2, 3, 8)

Investment Proposal

Year	Initial Cost and Book Value	Net Annual Cash Flows	Annual Net Income
0	$105,000		
1	70,000	$45,000	$10,000
2	42,000	40,000	12,000
3	21,000	35,000	14,000
4	7,000	30,000	16,000
5	0	25,000	18,000

BAP Corporation uses a 12% target rate of return for new investment proposals.

Instructions
(a) What is the cash payback period for this proposal?
(b) What is the annual rate of return for the investment?
(c) What is the net present value of the investment?

(CMA-Canada adapted)

EXERCISES: SET B AND CHALLENGE EXERCISES

Visit the book's companion website, at **www.wiley.com/college/weygandt**, and choose the Student Companion site to access Exercise Set B and Challenge Exercises.

PROBLEMS: SET A

Compute annual rate of return, cash payback, and net present value.

(LO 2, 3, 8)

P26-1A Henkel Company is considering three long-term capital investment proposals. Each investment has a useful life of 5 years. Relevant data on each project are as follows.

	Project Kilo	Project Lima	Project Oscar
Capital investment	$150,000	$165,000	$200,000
Annual net income:			
Year 1	14,000	18,000	27,000
2	14,000	17,000	23,000
3	14,000	16,000	21,000
4	14,000	12,000	13,000
5	14,000	9,000	12,000
Total	$ 70,000	$ 72,000	$ 96,000

Depreciation is computed by the straight-line method with no salvage value. The company's cost of capital is 15%. (Assume that cash flows occur evenly throughout the year.)

Instructions

(b) L $(4,016); O $2,163

(a) Compute the cash payback period for each project. (Round to two decimals.)
(b) Compute the net present value for each project. (Round to nearest dollar.)
(c) Compute the annual rate of return for each project. (Round to two decimals.) (*Hint:* Use average annual net income in your computation.)
(d) Rank the projects on each of the foregoing bases. Which project do you recommend?

Compute annual rate of return, cash payback, and net present value.

(LO 2, 3, 8)

P26-2A Lon Timur is an accounting major at a midwestern state university located approximately 60 miles from a major city. Many of the students attending the university are from the metropolitan area and visit their homes regularly on the weekends. Lon, an entrepreneur at heart, realizes that few good commuting alternatives are available for students doing weekend travel. He believes that a weekend commuting service could be organized and run profitably from several suburban and downtown shopping mall locations. Lon has gathered the following investment information.

1. Five used vans would cost a total of $75,000 to purchase and would have a 3-year useful life with negligible salvage value. Lon plans to use straight-line depreciation.
2. Ten drivers would have to be employed at a total payroll expense of $48,000.
3. Other annual out-of-pocket expenses associated with running the commuter service would include Gasoline $16,000, Maintenance $3,300, Repairs $4,000, Insurance $4,200, Advertising $2,500.
4. Lon has visited several financial institutions to discuss funding. The best interest rate he has been able to negotiate is 15%. Use this rate for cost of capital.
5. Lon expects each van to make ten round trips weekly and carry an average of six students each trip. The service is expected to operate 30 weeks each year, and each student will be charged $12.00 for a round-trip ticket.

Instructions

(a) Determine the annual (1) net income and (2) net annual cash flows for the commuter service.

(a) (1) $5,000

(b) Compute (1) the cash payback period and (2) the annual rate of return. (Round to two decimals.)

(b) (1) 2.5 years

(c) Compute the net present value of the commuter service. (Round to the nearest dollar.)
(d) ▭▭▭▶ What should Lon conclude from these computations?

P26-3A Goltra Clinic is considering investing in new heart-monitoring equipment. It has two options: Option A would have an initial lower cost but would require a significant expenditure for rebuilding after 4 years. Option B would require no rebuilding expenditure, but its maintenance costs would be higher. Since the Option B machine is of initial higher quality, it is expected to have a salvage value at the end of its useful life. The following estimates were made of the cash flows. The company's cost of capital is 8%.

Compute net present value, profitability index, and internal rate of return.

(LO 3, 5, 7)

	Option A	Option B
Initial cost	$160,000	$227,000
Annual cash inflows	$70,000	$80,000
Annual cash outflows	$30,000	$26,000
Cost to rebuild (end of year 4)	$50,000	$0
Salvage value	$0	$8,000
Estimated useful life	7 years	7 years

Instructions

(a) Compute the (1) net present value, (2) profitability index, and (3) internal rate of return for each option. (*Hint:* To solve for internal rate of return, experiment with alternative discount rates to arrive at a net present value of zero.)

(a) (1) NPV A $11,503
(3) IRR B 15%

(b) Which option should be accepted?

P26-4A Jane's Auto Care is considering the purchase of a new tow truck. The garage doesn't currently have a tow truck, and the $60,000 price tag for a new truck would represent a major expenditure. Jane Austen, owner of the garage, has compiled the estimates shown below in trying to determine whether the tow truck should be purchased.

Compute net present value considering intangible benefits.

(LO 3, 4)

Initial cost	$60,000
Estimated useful life	8 years
Net annual cash flows from towing	$8,000
Overhaul costs (end of year 4)	$6,000
Salvage value	$12,000

Jane's good friend, Rick Ryan, stopped by. He is trying to convince Jane that the tow truck will have other benefits that Jane hasn't even considered. First, he says, cars that need towing need to be fixed. Thus, when Jane tows them to her facility, her repair revenues will increase. Second, he notes that the tow truck could have a plow mounted on it, thus saving Jane the cost of plowing her parking lot. (Rick will give her a used plow blade for free if Jane will plow Rick's driveway.) Third, he notes that the truck will generate goodwill; people who are rescued by Jane's tow truck will feel grateful and might be more inclined to use her service station in the future or buy gas there. Fourth, the tow truck will have "Jane's Auto Care" on its doors, hood, and back tailgate—a form of free advertising wherever the tow truck goes. Rick estimates that, at a minimum, these benefits would be worth the following.

Additional annual net cash flows from repair work	$3,000
Annual savings from plowing	750
Additional annual net cash flows from customer "goodwill"	1,000
Additional annual net cash flows resulting from free advertising	750

The company's cost of capital is 9%.

Instructions

(a) NPV $(13,950)

(a) Calculate the net present value, ignoring the additional benefits described by Rick. Should the tow truck be purchased?

(b) NPV $16,491

(b) Calculate the net present value, incorporating the additional benefits suggested by Rick. Should the tow truck be purchased?

(c) Suppose Rick has been overly optimistic in his assessment of the value of the additional benefits. At a minimum, how much would the additional benefits have to be worth in order for the project to be accepted?

Compute net present value and internal rate of return with sensitivity analysis.

(LO 3, 7)

P26-5A Goldbloom Corp. is thinking about opening a soccer camp in southern California. To start the camp, Goldbloom would need to purchase land and build four soccer fields and a sleeping and dining facility to house 150 soccer players. Each year, the camp would be run for 8 sessions of 1 week each. The company would hire college soccer players as coaches. The camp attendees would be male and female soccer players ages 12–18. Property values in southern California have enjoyed a steady increase in value. It is expected that after using the facility for 20 years, Goldbloom can sell the property for more than it was originally purchased for. The following amounts have been estimated.

Cost of land	$300,000
Cost to build soccer fields, dorm and dining facility	$600,000
Annual cash inflows assuming 150 players and 8 weeks	$940,000
Annual cash outflows	$840,000
Estimated useful life	20 years
Salvage value	$1,500,000
Discount rate	8%

Instructions

(a) NPV $403,640

(a) Calculate the net present value of the project.

(b) To gauge the sensitivity of the project to these estimates, assume that if only 125 players attend each week, annual cash inflows will be $800,000 and annual cash outflows will be $750,000. What is the net present value using these alternative estimates? Discuss your findings.

(c) Assuming the original facts, what is the net present value if the project is actually riskier than first assumed and an 11% discount rate is more appropriate?

(d) IRR 12%

(d) Assume that during the first 5 years, the annual net cash flows each year were only $40,000. At the end of the fifth year, the company is running low on cash, so management decides to sell the property for $1,332,000. What was the actual internal rate of return on the project? Explain how this return was possible given that the camp did not appear to be successful.

PROBLEMS: SET B

Compute annual rate of return, cash payback, and net present value.

(LO 2, 3, 8)

P26-1B The Borders and Noble partnership is considering three long-term capital investment proposals. Each investment has a useful life of 5 years. Relevant data on each project are as follows.

	Project Mary	**Project Winnie**	**Project Sarah**
Capital investment	$140,000	$175,000	$190,000
Annual net income:			
Year 1	$10,000	$12,500	$19,000
2	10,000	12,000	16,000
3	10,000	11,000	14,000
4	10,000	8,000	9,000
5	10,000	6,000	8,000
Total	$50,000	$49,500	$66,000

Depreciation is computed by the straight-line method with no salvage value. The company's cost of capital is 12%. (Assume cash flows occur evenly throughout the year.)

Instructions
(a) Compute the cash payback period for each project. (Round to two decimals.)
(b) Compute the net present value for each project. (Round to nearest dollar.)
(c) Compute the annual rate of return for each project. (Round to two decimals.) (*Hint:* Use average annual net income in your computation.)
(d) Rank the projects on each of the foregoing bases. Which project do you recommend?

(b) M $(3,018); S $(3,075)

P26-2B Ben Paul is an accounting major at a western university located approximately 60 miles from a major city. Many of the students attending the university are from the metropolitan area and visit their homes regularly on the weekends. Ben, an entrepreneur at heart, realizes that few good commuting alternatives are available for students doing weekend travel. He believes that a weekend commuting service could be organized and run profitably from several suburban and downtown shopping mall locations. Ben has gathered the following investment information.

Compute annual rate of return, cash payback, and net present value.

(LO 2, 3, 8)

1. Five used vans would cost a total of $90,000 to purchase and would have a 3-year useful life with negligible salvage value. Ben plans to use straight-line depreciation.
2. Ten drivers would have to be employed at a total payroll expense of $43,000.
3. Other annual out-of-pocket expenses associated with running the commuter service would include Gasoline $26,000, Maintenance $4,000, Repairs $5,300, Insurance $4,500, Advertising $2,200.
4. Ben desires to earn a return of 15% on his investment.
5. Ben expects each van to make ten round trips weekly and carry an average of six students each trip. The service is expected to operate 32 weeks each year, and each student will be charged $15 for a round-trip ticket.

Instructions
(a) Determine the annual (1) net income and (2) net annual cash flows for the commuter service.
(b) Compute (1) the cash payback period and (2) the annual rate of return. (Round to two decimals.)
(c) Compute the net present value of the commuter service. (Round to the nearest dollar.)
(d) ▯▯▭▭➤ What should Ben conclude from these computations?

(a) (1) $29,000

(b) (1) 1.53 years

P26-3B Platteville Eye Clinic is considering investing in new optical-scanning equipment. It has two options: Option A would have an initial lower cost but would require a significant expenditure for rebuilding after 3 years. Option B would require no rebuilding expenditure, but its maintenance costs would be higher. Since the Option B machine is of initial higher quality, it is expected to have a salvage value at the end of its useful life. The following estimates were made of the cash flows. The company's cost of capital is 11%.

Compute net present value, profitability index, and internal rate of return.

(LO 3, 5, 7)

	Option A	**Option B**
Initial cost	$100,000	$160,000
Annual cash inflows	$56,000	$60,000
Annual cash outflows	$24,000	$24,000
Cost to rebuild (end of year 3)	$53,000	$0
Salvage value	$0	$24,000
Estimated useful life	6 years	6 years

Instructions

(a) Compute the (1) net present value, (2) profitability index, and (3) internal rate of return for each option. (*Hint:* To solve for internal rate of return, experiment with alternative discount rates to arrive at a net present value of zero.)

(b) Which option should be accepted?

Compute net present value considering intangible benefits.

(LO 3, 4)

P26-4B Isaac's Auto Repair is considering the purchase of a new tow truck. The garage doesn't currently have a tow truck, and the $65,000 price tag for a new truck would represent a major expenditure for the garage. Isaac Mayer, owner of the garage, has compiled the following estimates in trying to determine whether to purchase the truck.

Initial cost	$65,000
Estimated useful life	8 years
Net annual cash inflows from towing	$9,600
Overhaul costs (end of year 4)	$7,000
Salvage value	$16,000

Isaac's good friend, Brad Jolie, stopped by. He is trying to convince Isaac that the tow truck will have other benefits that Isaac hasn't even considered. First, he says, cars that need towing need to be fixed. Thus, when Isaac tows them to his facility his repair revenues will increase. Second, he notes that the tow truck could have a plow mounted on it, thus saving Isaac the cost of plowing his parking lot. (Brad will give him a used plow blade for free if Isaac will plow Brad's driveway.) Third, he notes that the truck will generate goodwill; that is, people who are rescued by Isaac and his tow truck will feel grateful and might be more inclined to use his service station in the future or buy gas there. Fourth, the tow truck will have "Isaac's Auto Repair" on its doors, hood, and back tailgate—a form of free advertising wherever the tow truck goes.

Brad estimates that, at a minimum, these benefits would be worth the following.

Additional annual net cash flows from repair work	$2,600
Annual savings from plowing	600
Additional annual net cash flows from customer "goodwill"	1,200
Additional annual net cash flows resulting from free advertising	500

The company's cost of capital is 10%.

Instructions

(a) Calculate the net present value, ignoring the additional benefits described by Brad. Should the tow truck be purchased?

(b) Calculate the net present value, incorporating the additional benefits suggested by Brad. Should the tow truck be purchased?

(c) Suppose Brad has been overly optimistic in his assessment of the value of the additional benefits. At a minimum, how much would the additional benefits have to be worth in order for the project to be accepted?

Compute net present value and internal rate of return with sensitivity analysis.

(LO 3, 7)

P26-5B Lewis Corp. is thinking about opening a basketball camp in Texas. In order to start the camp, the company would need to purchase land and build eight basketball courts and a dormitory-type sleeping and dining facility to house 110 basketball players. Each year, the camp would be run for 8 sessions of 1 week each. The company would hire college basketball players as coaches. The camp attendees would be male and female basketball players ages 12 to 18. Property values in Texas have enjoyed a steady increase in value. It is expected that after using the facility for 20 years, Lewis can sell the property for more than it was originally purchased for. The amounts shown below have been estimated.

Cost of land	$200,000
Cost to build dorm and dining facility	$350,000
Annual cash inflows assuming 110 players and 8 weeks	$700,000
Annual cash outflows	$570,000
Estimated useful life	20 years
Salvage value	$700,000
Discount rate	12%

Instructions

(a) Calculate the net present value of the project.

(b) To gauge the sensitivity of the project to these estimates, assume that if only 90 campers attend each week, annual cash inflows will be $570,000 and annual cash outflows will be $508,000. What is the net present value using these alternative estimates? Discuss your findings.

(c) Assuming the original facts, what is the net present value if the project is actually riskier than first assumed, and a 15% discount rate is more appropriate?

(d) Assume that during the first 5 years the annual net cash inflows each year were only $65,000. At the end of the fifth year, the company is running low on cash, so management decides to sell the property for $668,000. What was the actual internal rate of return on the project? Explain how this return was possible given that the camp did not appear to be successful.

(a) NPV $493,596

(d) IRR 15%

PROBLEMS: SET C

Visit the book's companion website, at **www.wiley.com/college/weygandt**, and choose the Student Companion site to access Problem Set C.

WATERWAYS CONTINUING PROBLEM

(This is a continuation of the Waterways Problem from Chapters 15–25.)

WCP26 Waterways Corporation puts much emphasis on cash flow when it plans for capital investments. The company chose its discount rate of 8% based on the rate of return it must pay its owners and creditors. Using that rate, Waterways then uses different methods to determine the best decisions for making capital outlays. Waterways is considering buying five new backhoes to replace the backhoes it now has. This problem asks you to evaluate that decision, using various capital budgeting techniques.

Go to the book's companion website, **www.wiley.com/college/weygandt**, *to find the remainder of this problem.*

Broadening Your PERSPECTIVE

Management Decision-Making

Decision-Making at Current Designs

BYP26-1 A company that manufactures recreational pedal boats has approached Mike Cichanowski to ask if he would be interested in using Current Designs' rotomold expertise and equipment to produce some of the pedal boat components. Mike is intrigued by the idea and thinks it would be an interesting way of complementing the present product line.

One of Mike's hesitations about the proposal is that the pedal boats are a different shape than the kayaks that Current Designs produces. As a result, the company would need to buy an additional rotomold oven in order to produce the pedal boat components. This project clearly involves risks, and

Mike wants to make sure that the returns justify the risks. In this case, since this is a new venture, Mike thinks that a 15% discount rate is appropriate to use to evaluate the project.

As an intern at Current Designs, Mike has asked you to prepare an initial evaluation of this proposal. To aid in your analysis, he has provided the following information and assumptions.

1. The new rotomold oven will have a cost of $256,000, a salvage value of $0, and an 8-year useful life. Straight-line depreciation will be used.
2. The projected revenues, costs, and results for each of the 8 years of this project are as follows.

Sales		$220,000
Less:		
Manufacturing costs	$140,000	
Depreciation	32,000	
Shipping and administrative costs	22,000	194,000
Income before income taxes		26,000
Income tax expense		10,800
Net income		$ 15,200

Instructions
(a) Compute the annual rate of return. (Round to two decimal places.)
(b) Compute the payback period. (Round to two decimal places.)
(c) Compute the NPV using a discount rate of 9%. (Round to nearest dollar.) Should the proposal be accepted using this discount rate?
(d) Compute the NPV using a discount rate of 15%. (Round to nearest dollar.) Should the proposal be accepted using this discount rate?

Decision-Making Across the Organization

BYP26-2 Luang Company is considering the purchase of a new machine. Its invoice price is $122,000, freight charges are estimated to be $3,000, and installation costs are expected to be $5,000. Salvage value of the new machine is expected to be zero after a useful life of 4 years. Existing equipment could be retained and used for an additional 4 years if the new machine is not purchased. At that time, the salvage value of the equipment would be zero. If the new machine is purchased now, the existing machine would be scrapped. Luang's accountant, Lisa Hsung, has accumulated the following data regarding annual sales and expenses with and without the new machine.

1. Without the new machine, Luang can sell 10,000 units of product annually at a per unit selling price of $100. If the new unit is purchased, the number of units produced and sold would increase by 25%, and the selling price would remain the same.
2. The new machine is faster than the old machine, and it is more efficient in its usage of materials. With the old machine the gross profit rate will be 28.5% of sales, whereas the rate will be 30% of sales with the new machine.
3. Annual selling expenses are $160,000 with the current equipment. Because the new equipment would produce a greater number of units to be sold, annual selling expenses are expected to increase by 10% if it is purchased.
4. Annual administrative expenses are expected to be $100,000 with the old machine, and $112,000 with the new machine.
5. The current book value of the existing machine is $40,000. Luang uses straight-line depreciation.
6. Luang's management has a required rate of return of 15% on its investment and a cash payback period of no more than 3 years.

Instructions
With the class divided into groups, answer the following. (Ignore income tax effects.)
(a) Calculate the annual rate of return for the new machine. (Round to two decimals.)
(b) Compute the cash payback period for the new machine. (Round to two decimals.)
(c) Compute the net present value of the new machine. (Round to the nearest dollar.)
(d) On the basis of the foregoing data, would you recommend that Luang buy the machine? Why?

Managerial Analysis

BYP26-3 Hawke Skateboards is considering building a new plant. Bob Skerritt, the company's marketing manager, is an enthusiastic supporter of the new plant. Lucy Liu, the company's chief financial officer, is not so sure that the plant is a good idea. Currently, the company purchases its skateboards from foreign manufacturers. The following figures were estimated regarding the construction of a new plant.

Cost of plant	$4,000,000	Estimated useful life	15 years
Annual cash inflows	4,000,000	Salvage value	$2,000,000
Annual cash outflows	3,540,000	Discount rate	11%

Bob Skerritt believes that these figures understate the true potential value of the plant. He suggests that by manufacturing its own skateboards the company will benefit from a "buy American" patriotism that he believes is common among skateboarders. He also notes that the firm has had numerous quality problems with the skateboards manufactured by its suppliers. He suggests that the inconsistent quality has resulted in lost sales, increased warranty claims, and some costly lawsuits. Overall, he believes sales will be $200,000 higher than projected above, and that the savings from lower warranty costs and legal costs will be $60,000 per year. He also believes that the project is not as risky as assumed above, and that a 9% discount rate is more reasonable.

Instructions
Answer each of the following.
(a) Compute the net present value of the project based on the original projections.
(b) Compute the net present value incorporating Bob's estimates of the value of the intangible benefits, but still using the 11% discount rate.
(c) Compute the net present value using the original estimates, but employing the 9% discount rate that Bob suggests is more appropriate.
(d) Comment on your findings.

Real-World Focus

BYP26-4 Tecumseh Products Company has its headquarters in Tecumseh, Michigan. It describes itself as "a global multinational corporation producing mechanical and electrical components essential to industries creating end-products for health, comfort, and convenience." The following was excerpted from the management discussion and analysis section of a recent annual report.

Tecumseh Products Company
Management Discussion and Analysis

The company has invested approximately $50 million in a scroll compressor manufacturing facility in Tecumseh, Michigan. After experiencing setbacks in developing a commercially acceptable scroll compressor, the Company is currently testing a new generation of scroll product. The Company is unable to predict when, or if, it will offer a scroll compressor for commercial sale, but it does anticipate that reaching volume production will require a significant additional investment. Given such additional investment and current market conditions, management is currently reviewing its options with respect to scroll product improvement, cost reductions, joint ventures and alternative new products.

Instructions
Discuss issues the company should consider and techniques the company should employ to determine whether to continue pursuing this project.

BYP26-5 Campbell Soup Company is an international provider of soup products. Management is very interested in continuing to grow the company in its core business, while "spinning off" those businesses that are not part of its core operation.

Address: **www.campbellsoups.com**, or go to **www.wiley.com/college/weygandt**

Steps
1. Go to the home page of Campbell Soup Company at the address shown above.
2. Choose the current annual report.

Instructions

Review the financial statements and management's discussion and analysis, and answer the following questions.

(a) What was the total amount of capital expenditures in the current year, and how does this amount compare with the previous year?

(b) What interest rate did the company pay on new borrowings in the current year?

(c) Assume that this year's capital expenditures are expected to increase cash flows by $42 million. What is the expected internal rate of return (IRR) for these capital expenditures? (Assume a 10-year period for the cash flows.)

Critical Thinking

Communication Activity

BYP26-6 Refer back to E26-9 to address the following.

Instructions

Prepare a memo to Maria Fierro, your supervisor. Show your calculations from E26-9, (a) and (b). In one or two paragraphs, discuss important nonfinancial considerations. Make any assumptions you believe to be necessary. Make a recommendation based on your analysis.

Ethics Case

BYP26-7 NuComp Company operates in a state where corporate taxes and workers' compensation insurance rates have recently doubled. NuComp's president has just assigned you the task of preparing an economic analysis and making a recommendation relative to moving the entire operation to Missouri. The president is slightly in favor of such a move because Missouri is his boyhood home and he also owns a fishing lodge there.

You have just completed building your dream house, moved in, and sodded the lawn. Your children are all doing well in school and sports and, along with your spouse, want no part of a move to Missouri. If the company does move, so will you because the town is a one-industry community and you and your spouse will have to move to have employment. Moving when everyone else does will cause you to take a big loss on the sale of your house. The same hardships will be suffered by your coworkers, and the town will be devastated.

In compiling the costs of moving versus not moving, you have latitude in the assumptions you make, the estimates you compute, and the discount rates and time periods you project. You are in a position to influence the decision singlehandedly.

Instructions

(a) Who are the stakeholders in this situation?

(b) What are the ethical issues in this situation?

(c) What would you do in this situation?

All About You

BYP26-8 Numerous articles have been written that identify early warning signs that you might be getting into trouble with your personal debt load. You can find many good articles on this topic on the Web.

Instructions

Find an article that identifies early warning signs of personal debt trouble. Write up a summary of the article and bring your summary and the article to class to share.

Considering Your Costs and Benefits

BYP26-9 The March 31, 2011, edition of the *Wall Street Journal* includes an article by Russell Gold entitled "Solar Gains Traction—Thanks to Subsidies."

Instructions
Read the article and answer the following questions.
(a) What was the total cost of the solar panels installed? What was the "out-of-pocket" cost to the couple?
(b) Using the total annual electricity bill of $5,000 mentioned in the story, what is the cash payback of the project using the total cost? What is the cash payback based on the "out-of-pocket" cost?
(c) Solar panel manufactures estimate that solar panels can last up to 40 years with only minor maintenance costs. Assuming no maintenance costs, a 6% rate of interest, a more conservative 20-year life, and zero salvage value, what is the net present value of the project based on the total cost? What is the net present value of the project based on the "out-of-pocket" cost?
(d) What was the wholesale price of panels per watt at the time the article was written? At what price per watt does the article say that subsidies no longer be needed? Does this price appear to be achievable?

Answers to Chapter Questions

Answers to Insight and Accounting Across the Organization Questions

p. 1298 Can You Hear Me—Better? Q: Based on the potentially slow initial adoption of 4G by customers, how might the conclusions of a cash payback analysis of Verizon's 4G investment differ from a present value analysis? **A:** If the initial adoption of 4G by customers is slow, then the amount of cash received in the early years will be low. This would lengthen the cash payback period, making it unlikely that the investment would get high marks with this test. However, the long-run potential of 4G is probably quite high as more people switch to smart phones and consequently increase their use of services that benefit from a high-speed connection. These later cash flows may well be large enough that they provide a positive net present value amount.

p. 1302 It Need Not Cost an Arm and a Leg Q: In addition to the obvious humanitarian benefit of reducing serious injuries, how else might the manufacturer of this product convince potential customers of its worth? **A:** Serious injuries cost employers huge sums, which can sometimes force small companies out of business. In addition to the obvious humanitarian benefit, the manufacturer can demonstrate that this device is a sound financial investment in terms of reduced healthcare and workers' compensation costs and fewer hours missed due to injury. Also, as the device gains wider acceptance, employers that do not have the device may ultimately be found negligent with regard to worker safety.

p. 1304 Wide-Screen Capacity Q: What implications does the excess capacity have for the cash payback and net present value calculations of these investments? **A:** Because the companies have excess capacity, they are not selling as many units as expected. Also, to increase sales, they are being forced to cut selling prices in order to sell units. Therefore, the revenues that they generate are lower than the amounts that would have been estimated when the plants were planned and built. This means that cash payback periods are longer and net present values are lower than desired levels.

p. 1305 Seeing the Big Picture Q: How important is the choice of discount rate in making capital budgeting decisions? **A:** The point of this discussion is that errors in implementation, as well as the accuracy of the estimated future benefits and costs as measured by cash inflows and outflows, are what matter the most when making capital expenditure decisions. While the choice of discount rates will result in incremental differences in present value calculations, "missing the big picture" has the potential to cause much bigger decision errors. Underestimating potential future cash inflows can result in missed opportunities. Underestimating future costs can result in failed investments.

Answers to Self-Test Questions

1. d **2.** c **3.** d **4.** b ($48,000 ÷ $7,000) > ($75,000 ÷ $12,000) **5.** a **6.** b **7.** d **8.** d **9.** c
10. c ($18,112 + $80,000) ÷ $80,000 **11.** a **12.** c **13.** d ($60,000 ÷ $15,400) = IRR factor **14.** d
15. a $15,000 ÷ [($120,000 + $20,000) ÷ 2]

✔ Remember to go back to The Navigator box on the chapter opening page and check off your completed work.

Appendix A

Specimen Financial Statements: PepsiCo, Inc.

The Annual Report

Once each year, a corporation communicates to its stockholders and other interested parties by issuing a complete set of audited financial statements. The **annual report**, as this communication is called, summarizes the financial results of the company's operations for the year and its plans for the future. Many annual reports are attractive, multicolored, glossy public relations pieces, containing pictures of corporate officers and directors as well as photos and descriptions of new products and new buildings. Yet, the basic function of every annual report is to report financial information, almost all of which is a product of the corporation's accounting system.

The content and organization of corporate annual reports have become fairly standardized. Excluding the public relations part of the report (pictures, products, etc.), the following are the traditional financial portions of the annual report:

- Financial Highlights
- Letter to the Stockholders
- Management's Discussion and Analysis
- Financial Statements
- Notes to the Financial Statements
- Management's Report on Internal Control
- Management Certification of Financial Statements
- Auditor's Report
- Supplementary Financial Information

In this appendix, we illustrate current financial reporting with a comprehensive set of corporate financial statements that are prepared in accordance with generally accepted accounting principles and audited by an international independent certified public accounting firm. We are grateful for permission to use the actual financial statements and other accompanying financial information from the annual report of a large, publicly held company, PepsiCo, Inc.

Financial Highlights

Companies usually present the financial highlights section inside the front cover of the annual report or on its first two pages. This section generally reports the total or per share amounts for five to ten financial items for the current year and one or more previous years. Financial items from the income statement and the balance sheet that typically are presented are sales, income from continuing operations, net income, net income per share, net cash provided by operating activities, dividends per common share, and the amount of capital expenditures. The financial highlights section from PepsiCo's Annual Report is shown on page A-2.

Financial Highlights

PepsiCo, Inc. and subsidiaries
(in millions except per share data; all per share amounts assume dilution)

	2010	2009	Chg(a)	Chg Constant Currency(a)(f)
Summary of Operations				
Total net revenue	$57,838	$43,232	34%	33%
Core division operating profit(b)	$10,626	$ 8,647	23%	23%
Core total operating profit(c)	$ 9,773	$ 7,856	24%	
Core net income attributable to PepsiCo(d)	$ 6,675	$ 5,846	14%	
Core earnings per share attributable to PepsiCo(d)	$ 4.13	$ 3.71	12%	12%
Other Data				
Management operating cash flow, excluding certain items(e)	$ 6,892	$ 5,583	23%	
Net cash provided by operating activities	$ 8,448	$ 6,796	24%	
Capital spending	$ 3,253	$ 2,128	53%	
Common share repurchases	$ 4,978	–	n/m	
Dividends paid	$ 2,978	$ 2,732	9%	
Long-term debt	$19,999	$ 7,400	170%	

Cumulative Total Shareholder Return

Return on PepsiCo stock investment (including dividends), the S&P 500 and the S&P Average of Industry Groups

PepsiCo, Inc.   S&P 500®   S&P® Average of Industry Groups***

***The S&P Average of Industry Groups is derived by weighting the returns of two applicable S&P Industry Groups (Non-Alcoholic Beverages and Food) by PepsiCo's sales in its beverages and foods businesses. The returns for PepsiCo, the S&P 500 and the S&P Average indices are calculated through December 31, 2010.

	Dec. 05	Dec. 06	Dec. 07	Dec. 08	Dec. 09	Dec. 10
PepsiCo Inc.	$100	$108	$134	$ 99	$113	$125
S&P 500®	$100	$116	$122	$ 77	$ 97	$112
S&P® Avg. of Industry Groups***	$100	$116	$129	$106	$128	$151

Mix of Net Revenue

Food 49%
Beverage 51%

Outside the U.S. 47%
U.S. 53%

Net Revenues

PepsiCo AMEA 12%
PepsiCo Europe 16%
PepsiCo Americas Beverages 35%
PepsiCo Americas Foods 37%

Division Operating Profit

PepsiCo AMEA 8%
PepsiCo Europe 10%
PepsiCo Americas Beverages 29%
PepsiCo Americas Foods 53%

(a) Percentage changes are based on unrounded amounts.

(b) Excludes corporate unallocated expenses and merger and integration charges in both years. In 2010, also excludes certain inventory fair value adjustments in connection with our bottling acquisitions and a one-time net charge related to the currency devaluation in Venezuela. In 2009, also excludes restructuring and impairment charges. See page 108 for a reconciliation to the most directly comparable financial measure in accordance with GAAP.

(c) Excludes merger and integration charges and the net mark-to-market impact of our commodity hedges in both years. In 2010, also excludes certain inventory fair value adjustments in connection with our bottling acquisitions, a one-time net charge related to the currency devaluation in Venezuela, an asset write-off charge for SAP software and a contribution to The PepsiCo Foundation, Inc. In 2009, also excludes restructuring and impairment charges. See page 108 for a reconciliation to the most directly comparable financial measure in accordance with GAAP.

(d) Excludes merger and integration charges and the net mark-to-market impact of our commodity hedges in both years. In 2010, also excludes a gain on previously held equity interests and certain inventory fair value adjustments in connection with our bottling acquisitions, a one-time net charge related to the currency devaluation in Venezuela, an asset write-off charge for SAP software, a contribution to The PepsiCo Foundation, Inc. and interest expense incurred in connection with our debt repurchase. In 2009, also excludes restructuring and impairment charges. See pages 64 and 108 for reconciliations to the most directly comparable financial measures in accordance with GAAP.

(e) Includes the impact of net capital spending, and excludes merger and integration payments and restructuring payments in both years. In 2010, also excludes discretionary pension and retiree medical payments, a contribution to The PepsiCo Foundation, Inc., interest paid related to our debt repurchase and capital expenditures related to the integration of our bottlers. In 2009, also excludes discretionary pension payments. See also "Our Liquidity and Capital Resources" in Management's Discussion and Analysis. See page 108 for a reconciliation to the most directly comparable financial measure in accordance with GAAP.

(f) Assumes constant currency exchange rates used for translation based on the rates in effect in 2009. See pages 64 and 108 for reconciliations to the most directly comparable financial measures in accordance with GAAP.

Letter to the Stockholders

Nearly every annual report contains a letter to the stockholders from the chairman of the board or the president, or both. This letter typically discusses the company's accomplishments during the past year and highlights significant events such as mergers and acquisitions, new products, operating achievements, business philosophy, changes in officers or directors, financing commitments, expansion plans, and future prospects. The letter to the stockholders is signed by Indra Nooyi, Chairman of the Board and Chief Executive Officer, of PepsiCo.

Only a short summary of the letter is provided below. The full letter can be accessed at the book's companion website at **www.wiley.com/college/weygandt**.

Dear Fellow Shareholders,

2010 was a good year for PepsiCo. I am delighted with the success we have achieved, and I am sure you are too.

Amid the continuing challenge of the most difficult global macroeconomic environment in decades, we delivered strong operating performance that puts us in the top tier in our industry while we generated significant operating cash flow.

• Net revenue grew 33 percent on a constant currency basis.[1]

• Core division operating profit rose 23 percent on a constant currency basis.[1]

• Core EPS grew 12 percent on a constant currency basis.[2]

• Management operating cash flow, excluding certain items, reached $6.9 billion, up 23 percent.[1]

• $8 billion was returned to our shareholders through share repurchases and dividends.

• We raised the annual dividend by 7 percent.

We can confidently say that PepsiCo continues to operate from a position of balance and strength. We are the second-largest food and beverage business in the world, and the largest food and beverage business in North America.

Indra Nooyi

Indra K. Nooyi
Chairman and
Chief Executive Officer

Management's Discussion and Analysis

The **management's discussion and analysis (MD&A)** section covers three financial aspects of a company: its results of operations, its ability to pay near-term obligations, and its ability to fund operations and expansion. Management must highlight favorable or unfavorable trends and identity significant events and uncertainties that affect these three factors. This discussion obviously involves a number of subjective estimates and opinions. In its MD&A section, PepsiCo breaks its discussion into three major headings: Our Business, Our Critical Accounting Policies, and Our Financial Results. You can access the full MD&A section at **www.wiley.com/college/weygandt**.

Financial Statements and Accompanying Notes

The standard set of financial statements consists of (1) a comparative income statement for three years, (2) a comparative statement of cash flows for three years, (3) a comparative balance sheet for two years, (4) a statement of stockholders' equity for three years, and (5) a set of accompanying notes that are considered an integral part of the financial statements. The auditor's report, unless stated otherwise, covers the financial statements and the accompanying notes. PepsiCo's financial statements and accompanying notes plus supplementary data and analyses follow.

Consolidated Statement of Income   PepsiCo, Inc. and Subsidiaries

(in millions except per share amounts)
Fiscal years ended December 25, 2010, December 26, 2009 and December 27, 2008

	2010	2009	2008
Net Revenue	$57,838	$43,232	$43,251
Cost of sales	26,575	20,099	20,351
Selling, general and administrative expenses	22,814	15,026	15,877
Amortization of intangible assets	117	63	64
Operating Profit	8,332	8,044	6,959
Bottling equity income	735	365	374
Interest expense	(903)	(397)	(329)
Interest income	68	67	41
Income before income taxes	8,232	8,079	7,045
Provision for income taxes	1,894	2,100	1,879
Net income	6,338	5,979	5,166
Less: Net income attributable to noncontrolling interests	18	33	24
Net Income Attributable to PepsiCo	$ 6,320	$ 5,946	$ 5,142
Net Income Attributable to PepsiCo per Common Share			
Basic	$ 3.97	$ 3.81	$ 3.26
Diluted	$ 3.91	$ 3.77	$ 3.21
Cash dividends declared per common share	$ 1.89	$ 1.775	$ 1.65

See accompanying notes to consolidated financial statements.

Consolidated Statement of Cash Flows

PepsiCo, Inc. and Subsidiaries

(in millions)
Fiscal years ended December 25, 2010, December 26, 2009 and December 27, 2008

	2010	2009	2008
Operating Activities			
Net income	$ 6,338	$ 5,979	$ 5,166
Depreciation and amortization	2,327	1,635	1,543
Stock-based compensation expense	299	227	238
Restructuring and impairment charges	–	36	543
Cash payments for restructuring charges	(31)	(196)	(180)
Merger and integration costs	808	50	–
Cash payments for merger and integration costs	(385)	(49)	–
Gain on previously held equity interests in PBG and PAS	(958)	–	–
Asset write-off	145	–	–
Non-cash foreign exchange loss related to Venezuela devaluation	120	–	–
Excess tax benefits from share-based payment arrangements	(107)	(42)	(107)
Pension and retiree medical plan contributions	(1,734)	(1,299)	(219)
Pension and retiree medical plan expenses	453	423	459
Bottling equity income, net of dividends	42	(235)	(202)
Deferred income taxes and other tax charges and credits	500	284	573
Change in accounts and notes receivable	(268)	188	(549)
Change in inventories	276	17	(345)
Change in prepaid expenses and other current assets	144	(127)	(68)
Change in accounts payable and other current liabilities	488	(133)	718
Change in income taxes payable	123	319	(180)
Other, net	(132)	(281)	(391)
Net Cash Provided by Operating Activities	8,448	6,796	6,999
Investing Activities			
Capital spending	(3,253)	(2,128)	(2,446)
Sales of property, plant and equipment	81	58	98
Acquisitions of PBG and PAS, net of cash and cash equivalents acquired	(2,833)	–	–
Acquisition of manufacturing and distribution rights from DPSG	(900)	–	–
Investment in WBD	(463)	–	–
Other acquisitions and investments in noncontrolled affiliates	(83)	(500)	(1,925)
Divestitures	12	99	6
Cash restricted for pending acquisitions	–	15	(40)
Cash proceeds from sale of PBG and PAS stock	–	–	358
Short-term investments, by original maturity			
More than three months — purchases	(12)	(29)	(156)
More than three months — maturities	29	71	62
Three months or less, net	(229)	13	1,376
Other investing, net	(17)	–	–
Net Cash Used for Investing Activities	(7,668)	(2,401)	(2,667)
Financing Activities			
Proceeds from issuances of long-term debt	$ 6,451	$ 1,057	$ 3,719
Payments of long-term debt	(59)	(226)	(649)
Debt repurchase	(500)	–	–
Short-term borrowings, by original maturity			
More than three months — proceeds	227	26	89
More than three months — payments	(96)	(81)	(269)
Three months or less, net	2,351	(963)	625
Cash dividends paid	(2,978)	(2,732)	(2,541)
Share repurchases — common	(4,978)	–	(4,720)
Share repurchases — preferred	(5)	(7)	(6)
Proceeds from exercises of stock options	1,038	413	620
Excess tax benefits from share-based payment arrangements	107	42	107
Acquisition of noncontrolling interest in Lebedyansky from PBG	(159)	–	–
Other financing	(13)	(26)	–
Net Cash Provided by/(Used for) Financing Activities	1,386	(2,497)	(3,025)
Effect of exchange rate changes on cash and cash equivalents	(166)	(19)	(153)
Net Increase in Cash and Cash Equivalents	2,000	1,879	1,154
Cash and Cash Equivalents, Beginning of Year	3,943	2,064	910
Cash and Cash Equivalents, End of Year	$ 5,943	$ 3,943	$ 2,064
Non-cash activity:			
Issuance of common stock and equity awards in connection with our acquisitions of PBG and PAS, as reflected in investing and financing activities	$ 4,451	–	–

See accompanying notes to consolidated financial statements.

Consolidated Balance Sheet

PepsiCo, Inc. and Subsidiaries

(in millions except per share amounts)
December 25, 2010 and December 26, 2009

	2010	2009
ASSETS		
Current Assets		
Cash and cash equivalents	$ 5,943	$ 3,943
Short-term investments	426	192
Accounts and notes receivable, net	6,323	4,624
Inventories	3,372	2,618
Prepaid expenses and other current assets	1,505	1,194
Total Current Assets	17,569	12,571
Property, Plant and Equipment, net	19,058	12,671
Amortizable Intangible Assets, net	2,025	841
Goodwill	14,661	6,534
Other nonamortizable intangible assets	11,783	1,782
Nonamortizable Intangible Assets	26,444	8,316
Investments in Noncontrolled Affiliates	1,368	4,484
Other Assets	1,689	965
Total Assets	$ 68,153	$ 39,848
LIABILITIES AND EQUITY		
Current Liabilities		
Short-term obligations	$ 4,898	$ 464
Accounts payable and other current liabilities	10,923	8,127
Income taxes payable	71	165
Total Current Liabilities	15,892	8,756
Long-Term Debt Obligations	19,999	7,400
Other Liabilities	6,729	5,591
Deferred Income Taxes	4,057	659
Total Liabilities	46,677	22,406
Commitments and Contingencies		
Preferred Stock, no par value	41	41
Repurchased Preferred Stock	(150)	(145)
PepsiCo Common Shareholders' Equity		
Common stock, par value 1⅔¢ per share (authorized 3,600 shares, issued 1,865 and 1,782 shares, respectively)	31	30
Capital in excess of par value	4,527	250
Retained earnings	37,090	33,805
Accumulated other comprehensive loss	(3,630)	(3,794)
Repurchased common stock, at cost (284 and 217 shares, respectively)	(16,745)	(13,383)
Total PepsiCo Common Shareholders' Equity	21,273	16,908
Noncontrolling interests	312	638
Total Equity	21,476	17,442
Total Liabilities and Equity	$ 68,153	$ 39,848

See accompanying notes to consolidated financial statements.

Consolidated Statement of Equity

PepsiCo, Inc. and Subsidiaries

(in millions)
Fiscal years ended December 25, 2010,
December 26, 2009 and December 27, 2008

	2010 Shares	2010 Amount	2009 Shares	2009 Amount	2008 Shares	2008 Amount
Preferred Stock	0.8	$ 41	0.8	$ 41	0.8	$ 41
Repurchased Preferred Stock						
Balance, beginning of year	(0.6)	(145)	(0.5)	(138)	(0.5)	(132)
Redemptions	(–)	(5)	(0.1)	(7)	(–)	(6)
Balance, end of year	(0.6)	(150)	(0.6)	(145)	(0.5)	(138)
Common Stock						
Balance, beginning of year	1,782	30	1,782	30	1,782	30
Shares issued in connection with our acquisitions of PBG and PAS	83	1	–	–	–	–
Balance, end of year	1,865	31	1,782	30	1,782	30
Capital in Excess of Par Value						
Balance, beginning of year		250		351		450
Stock-based compensation expense		299		227		238
Stock option exercises/RSUs converted[a]		(500)		(292)		(280)
Withholding tax on RSUs converted		(68)		(36)		(57)
Equity issued in connection with our acquisitions of PBG and PAS		4,451		–		–
Other		95		–		–
Balance, end of year		4,527		250		351
Retained Earnings						
Balance, beginning of year		33,805		30,638		28,184
Measurement date change		–		–		(89)
Adjusted balance, beginning of year		33,805		30,638		28,095
Net income attributable to PepsiCo		6,320		5,946		5,142
Cash dividends declared — common		(3,028)		(2,768)		(2,589)
Cash dividends declared — preferred		(1)		(2)		(2)
Cash dividends declared — RSUs		(12)		(9)		(8)
Other		6		–		–
Balance, end of year		37,090		33,805		30,638
Accumulated Other Comprehensive Loss						
Balance, beginning of year		(3,794)		(4,694)		(952)
Measurement date change		–		–		51
Adjusted balance, beginning of year		(3,794)		(4,694)		(901)
Currency translation adjustment		312		800		(2,484)
Cash flow hedges, net of tax:						
Net derivative (losses)/gains		(111)		(55)		16
Reclassification of net losses to net income		53		28		5
Pension and retiree medical, net of tax:						
Net pension and retiree medical (losses)/gains		(280)		21		(1,376)
Reclassification of net losses to net income		166		86		73
Unrealized gains/(losses) on securities, net of tax		23		20		(21)
Other		1		–		(6)
Balance, end of year		(3,630)		(3,794)		(4,694)
Repurchased Common Stock						
Balance, beginning of year	(217)	(13,383)	(229)	(14,122)	(177)	(10,387)
Share repurchases	(76)	(4,978)	–	–	(68)	(4,720)
Stock option exercises	24	1,487	11	649	15	883
Other	(15)	129	1	90	1	102
Balance, end of year	(284)	(16,745)	(217)	(13,383)	(229)	(14,122)
Total Common Shareholders' Equity		21,273		16,908		12,203
Noncontrolling Interests						
Balance, beginning of year		$ 638		$ 476		$ 62
Net income attributable to noncontrolling interests		18		33		24
(Distributions to)/contributions from noncontrolling interests, net		(332)		150		450
Currency translation adjustment		(13)		(12)		(48)
Other, net		1		(9)		(12)
Balance, end of year		312		638		476
Total Equity		$ 21,476		$ 17,442		$ 12,582
Comprehensive Income						
Net income		$ 6,338		$ 5,979		$ 5,166
Other Comprehensive Income/(Loss)						
Currency translation adjustment		299		788		(2,532)
Cash flow hedges, net of tax		(58)		(27)		21
Pension and retiree medical, net of tax:						
Net prior service credit/(cost)		22		(3)		55
Net (losses)/gains		(136)		110		(1,358)
Unrealized gains/(losses) on securities, net of tax		23		20		(21)
Other		1		–		(6)
		151		888		(3,841)
Comprehensive Income		6,489		6,867		1,325
Comprehensive (income)/loss attributable to noncontrolling interests		(5)		(21)		24
Comprehensive Income Attributable to PepsiCo		$ 6,484		$ 6,846		$ 1,349

(a) Includes total tax benefits of $75 million in 2010, $31 million in 2009 and $95 million in 2008.

See accompanying notes to consolidated financial statements.

Notes to Consolidated Financial Statements

Note 1 Basis of Presentation and Our Divisions

Basis of Presentation

Our financial statements include the consolidated accounts of PepsiCo, Inc. and the affiliates that we control. In addition, we include our share of the results of certain other affiliates based on our economic ownership interest. We do not control these other affiliates, as our ownership in these other affiliates is generally less than 50%. Intercompany balances and transactions are eliminated. Our fiscal year ends on the last Saturday of each December, resulting in an additional week of results every five or six years.

On February 26, 2010, we completed our acquisitions of The Pepsi Bottling Group, Inc. (PBG) and PepsiAmericas, Inc. (PAS). The results of the acquired companies in the U.S. and Canada are reflected in our consolidated results as of the acquisition date, and the international results of the acquired companies have been reported as of the beginning of our second quarter of 2010, consistent with our monthly international reporting calendar. The results of the acquired companies in the U.S., Canada and Mexico are reported within our PAB segment, and the results of the acquired companies in Europe, including Russia, are reported within our Europe segment. Prior to our acquisitions of PBG and PAS, we recorded our share of equity income or loss from the acquired companies in bottling equity income in our income statement. Our share of the net income of PBV is reflected in bottling equity income and our share of income or loss from other noncontrolled affiliates is reflected as a component of selling, general and administrative expenses. Additionally, in the first quarter of 2010, in connection with our acquisitions of PBG and PAS, we recorded a gain on our previously held equity interests of $958 million, comprising $735 million which is non-taxable and recorded in bottling equity income and $223 million related to the reversal of deferred tax liabilities associated with these previously held equity interests. See Notes 8 and 15 and for additional unaudited information on items affecting the comparability of our consolidated results, see "Items Affecting Comparability" in Management's Discussion and Analysis of Financial Condition and Results of Operations.

As of the beginning of our 2010 fiscal year, the results of our Venezuelan businesses are reported under hyperinflationary accounting. See "Our Business Risks" and "Items Affecting Comparability" in Management's Discussion and Analysis of Financial Condition and Results of Operations.

Raw materials, direct labor and plant overhead, as well as purchasing and receiving costs, costs directly related to production planning, inspection costs and raw material handling facilities, are included in cost of sales. The costs of moving, storing and delivering finished product are included in selling, general and administrative expenses.

The preparation of our consolidated financial statements in conformity with generally accepted accounting principles requires us to make estimates and assumptions that affect reported amounts of assets, liabilities, revenues, expenses and disclosure of contingent assets and liabilities. Estimates are used in determining, among other items, sales incentives accruals, tax reserves, stock-based compensation, pension and retiree medical accruals, useful lives for intangible assets, and future cash flows associated with impairment testing for perpetual brands, goodwill and other long-lived assets. We evaluate our estimates on an ongoing basis using our historical experience, as well as other factors we believe appropriate under the circumstances, such as current economic conditions, and adjust or revise our estimates as circumstances change. As future events and their effect cannot be determined with precision, actual results could differ significantly from these estimates.

While the majority of our results are reported on a weekly calendar basis, most of our international operations report on a monthly calendar basis. The following chart details our quarterly reporting schedule:

Quarter	U.S. and Canada	International
First Quarter	12 weeks	January, February
Second Quarter	12 weeks	March, April and May
Third Quarter	12 weeks	June, July and August
Fourth Quarter	16 weeks	September, October, November and December

See "Our Divisions" below and for additional unaudited information on items affecting the comparability of our consolidated results, see "Items Affecting Comparability" in Management's Discussion and Analysis of Financial Condition and Results of Operations.

Tabular dollars are in millions, except per share amounts. All per share amounts reflect common per share amounts, assume dilution unless noted, and are based on unrounded amounts. Certain reclassifications were made to prior years' amounts to conform to the 2010 presentation.

Our Divisions

We manufacture or use contract manufacturers, market and sell a variety of salty, convenient, sweet and grain-based snacks, carbonated and non-carbonated beverages, and foods in over 200 countries with our largest operations in North America (United States and Canada), Mexico, Russia and the United Kingdom. Division results are based on how our Chief Executive Officer assesses the performance of and allocates resources to our divisions. For additional unaudited information on our divisions, see "Our Operations" in Management's Discussion and Analysis of Financial Condition and Results of Operations. The accounting policies for the divisions are the same as those described in Note 2, except for the following allocation methodologies:

- stock-based compensation expense;
- pension and retiree medical expense; and
- derivatives.

Stock-Based Compensation Expense

Our divisions are held accountable for stock-based compensation expense and, therefore, this expense is allocated to our divisions as an incremental employee compensation cost. The allocation of stock-based compensation expense in 2010 was approximately 17% to FLNA, 2% to QFNA, 5% to LAF, 32% to PAB, 11% to Europe, 8% to AMEA and 25% to corporate unallocated expenses. We had similar allocations of stock-based compensation expense to our divisions in 2009 and 2008. The expense allocated to our divisions excludes any impact of changes in our assumptions during the year which reflect market conditions over which division management has no control. Therefore, any variances between allocated expense and our actual expense are recognized in corporate unallocated expenses.

Pension and Retiree Medical Expense

Pension and retiree medical service costs measured at a fixed discount rate, as well as amortization of costs related to certain pension plan amendments and gains and losses due to demographics, including salary experience, are reflected in division results for North American employees. Division results also include interest costs, measured at a fixed discount rate, for retiree medical plans. Interest costs for the pension plans, pension asset returns and the impact of pension funding, and gains and losses other than those due to demographics, are all reflected in corporate unallocated expenses. In addition, corporate unallocated expenses include the difference between the service costs measured at a fixed discount rate (included in division results as noted above) and the total service costs determined using the plans' discount rates as disclosed in Note 7.

Derivatives

We centrally manage commodity derivatives on behalf of our divisions. These commodity derivatives include energy, fruit and other raw materials. Certain of these commodity derivatives do not qualify for hedge accounting treatment and are marked to market with the resulting gains and losses recognized in corporate unallocated expenses. These gains and losses are subsequently reflected in division results when the divisions take delivery of the underlying commodity. Therefore, the divisions realize the economic effects of the derivative without experiencing any resulting mark-to-market volatility, which remains in corporate unallocated expenses. These derivatives hedge underlying commodity price risk and were not entered into for speculative purposes.

	2010	2009	2008	2010	2009	2008
		Net Revenue			Operating Profit[a]	
FLNA	$13,397	$13,224	$12,507	$3,549	$3,258	$2,959
QFNA	1,832	1,884	1,902	568	628	582
LAF	6,315	5,703	5,895	1,004	904	897
PAB[b]	20,401	10,116	10,937	2,776	2,172	2,026
Europe[b]	9,254	6,727	6,891	1,020	932	910
AMEA	6,639	5,578	5,119	742	716	592
Total division	57,838	43,232	43,251	9,659	8,610	7,966
Corporate Unallocated						
Net impact of mark-to-market on commodity hedges	–	–	–	91	274	(346)
Merger and integration costs	–	–	–	(191)	(49)	–
Restructuring and impairment charges	–	–	–	–	–	(10)
Venezuela currency devaluation	–	–	–	(129)	–	–
Asset write-off	–	–	–	(145)	–	–
Foundation contribution	–	–	–	(100)	–	–
Other	–	–	–	(853)	(791)	(651)
	$57,838	$43,232	$43,251	$8,332	$8,044	$6,959

(a) For information on the impact of restructuring, impairment and integration charges on our divisions, see Note 3.
(b) Changes in 2010 relate primarily to our acquisitions of PBG and PAS.

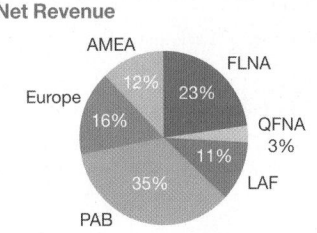

Net Revenue

AMEA 12%, FLNA 23%, QFNA 3%, LAF 11%, PAB 35%, Europe 16%

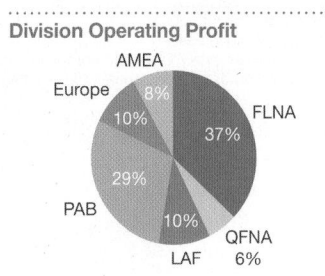

Division Operating Profit

AMEA 8%, Europe 10%, PAB 29%, LAF 10%, QFNA 6%, FLNA 37%

Corporate

Corporate includes costs of our corporate headquarters, centrally managed initiatives, such as our ongoing business transformation initiative and research and development projects, unallocated insurance and benefit programs, foreign exchange transaction gains and losses, certain commodity derivative gains and losses and certain other items.

Other Division Information

	2010	2009	2008	2010	2009	2008
	Total Assets			*Capital Spending*		
FLNA	$ 6,284	$ 6,337	$ 6,284	$ 526	$ 490	$ 553
QFNA	960	997	1,035	37	33	43
LAF	4,053	3,575	3,023	370	310	351
PAB(a)	31,622	7,670	7,673	973	182	344
Europe(a)	12,853	9,321	8,840	503	357	401
AMEA	5,748	4,937	3,756	624	585	479
Total division	61,520	32,837	30,611	3,033	1,957	2,171
Corporate(b)	6,394	3,933	2,729	220	171	275
Investments in bottling affiliates(a)	239	3,078	2,654	–	–	–
	$68,153	$39,848	$35,994	$3,253	$2,128	$2,446

(a) Changes in total assets in 2010 relate primarily to our acquisitions of PBG and PAS.
(b) Corporate assets consist principally of cash and cash equivalents, short-term investments, derivative instruments and property, plant and equipment.

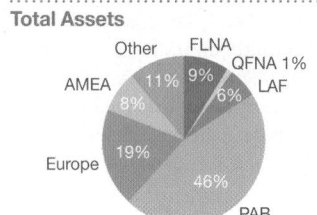

Total Assets

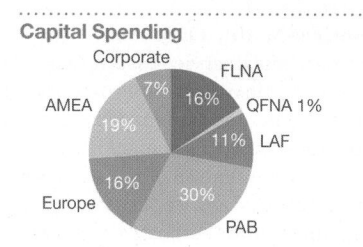

Capital Spending

	2010	2009	2008	2010	2009	2008
	Amortization of Intangible Assets			*Depreciation and Other Amortization*		
FLNA	$ 7	$ 7	$ 9	$ 462	$ 440	$ 441
QFNA	–	–	–	38	36	34
LAF	6	5	6	213	189	194
PAB(a)	56	18	16	749	345	334
Europe(a)	35	22	23	343	227	210
AMEA	13	11	10	306	248	213
Total division	117	63	64	2,111	1,485	1,426
Corporate	–	–	–	99	87	53
	$117	$63	$64	$2,210	$1,572	$1,479

(a) Increases in 2010 relate primarily to our acquisitions of PBG and PAS.

	2010	2009	2008	2010	2009	2008
	Net Revenue(b)			*Long-Lived Assets(c)*		
U.S.(a)	$30,618	$22,446	$22,525	$28,631	$12,496	$12,095
Mexico(a)	4,531	3,210	3,714	1,671	1,044	904
Canada(a)	3,081	1,996	2,107	3,133	688	556
Russia(a)	1,890	1,006	585	2,744	2,094	577
United Kingdom	1,888	1,826	2,099	1,019	1,358	1,509
All other countries	15,830	12,748	12,221	11,697	8,632	6,889
	$57,838	$43,232	$43,251	$48,895	$26,312	$22,530

(a) Increases in 2010 relate primarily to our acquisitions of PBG and PAS.
(b) Represents net revenue from businesses operating in these countries.
(c) Long-lived assets represent property, plant and equipment, nonamortizable intangible assets, amortizable intangible assets and investments in noncontrolled affiliates. These assets are reported in the country where they are primarily used.

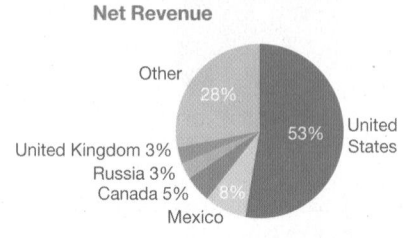

Net Revenue

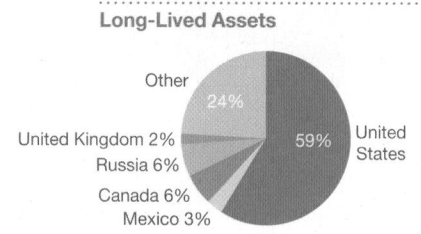

Long-Lived Assets

Note 2 Our Significant Accounting Policies

Revenue Recognition

We recognize revenue upon shipment or delivery to our customers based on written sales terms that do not allow for a right of return. However, our policy for DSD and certain chilled products is to remove and replace damaged and out-of-date products from store shelves to ensure that our consumers receive the product quality and freshness that they expect. Similarly, our policy for certain warehouse-distributed products is to replace damaged and out-of-date products. Based on our experience with this practice, we have reserved for anticipated damaged and out-of-date products. For additional unaudited information on our revenue recognition and related policies, including our policy on bad debts, see "Our Critical Accounting Policies" in Management's Discussion and Analysis of Financial Condition and Results of Operations. We are exposed to concentration of credit risk by our customers, including Wal-Mart. In 2010, Wal-Mart (including Sam's) represented approximately 12% of our total net revenue, including concentrate sales to our bottlers (including concentrate sales to PBG and PAS prior to the February 26, 2010 acquisition date) which are used in finished goods sold by them to Wal-Mart. We have not experienced credit issues with these customers.

Sales Incentives and Other Marketplace Spending

We offer sales incentives and discounts through various programs to our customers and consumers. Sales incentives and discounts are accounted for as a reduction of revenue and totaled $29.1 billion in 2010, $12.9 billion in 2009 and $12.5 billion in 2008. While most of these incentive arrangements have terms of no more than one year, certain arrangements, such as fountain pouring rights, may extend beyond one year. Costs incurred to obtain these arrangements are recognized over the shorter of the economic or contractual life, as a reduction of revenue, and the remaining balances of $296 million, as of both December 25, 2010 and December 26, 2009, are included in current assets and other assets on our balance sheet. For additional unaudited information on our sales incentives, see "Our Critical Accounting Policies" in Management's Discussion and Analysis of Financial Condition and Results of Operations.

Other marketplace spending, which includes the costs of advertising and other marketing activities, totaled $3.4 billion in 2010, $2.8 billion in 2009 and $2.9 billion in 2008 and is reported as selling, general and administrative expenses. Included in these amounts were advertising expenses of $1.9 billion in 2010 and $1.7 billion in both 2009 and 2008. Deferred advertising costs are not expensed until the year first used and consist of:
- media and personal service prepayments;
- promotional materials in inventory; and
- production costs of future media advertising.

Deferred advertising costs of $158 million and $143 million at year-end 2010 and 2009, respectively, are classified as prepaid expenses on our balance sheet.

Distribution Costs

Distribution costs, including the costs of shipping and handling activities, are reported as selling, general and administrative expenses. Shipping and handling expenses were $7.7 billion in 2010 and $5.6 billion in both 2009 and 2008.

Cash Equivalents

Cash equivalents are investments with original maturities of three months or less which we do not intend to rollover beyond three months.

Software Costs

We capitalize certain computer software and software development costs incurred in connection with developing or obtaining computer software for internal use when both the preliminary project stage is completed and it is probable that the software will be used as intended. Capitalized software costs include only (i) external direct costs of materials and services utilized in developing or obtaining computer software, (ii) compensation and related benefits for employees who are directly associated with the software project and (iii) interest costs incurred while developing internal-use computer software. Capitalized software costs are included in property, plant and equipment on our balance sheet and amortized on a straight-line basis when placed into service over the estimated useful lives of the software, which approximate five to ten years. Software amortization totaled $137 million in 2010, $119 million in 2009 and $58 million in 2008. Net capitalized software and development costs were $1.1 billion as of both December 25, 2010 and December 26, 2009.

Commitments and Contingencies

We are subject to various claims and contingencies related to lawsuits, certain taxes and environmental matters, as well as commitments under contractual and other commercial obligations. We recognize liabilities for contingencies and commitments when a loss is probable and estimable. For additional information on our commitments, see Note 9.

Research and Development

We engage in a variety of research and development activities. These activities principally involve the development of new products, improvement in the quality of existing products, improvement and modernization of production processes, and the development and implementation of new technologies to enhance the quality and value of both current and proposed product lines. Consumer research is excluded from research and development costs and included in other marketing costs. Research and development costs were $488 million in 2010, $414 million in 2009 and $388 million in 2008 and are reported within selling, general and administrative expenses.

Other Significant Accounting Policies

Our other significant accounting policies are disclosed as follows:

- *Property, Plant and Equipment and Intangible Assets* — Note 4, and for additional unaudited information on goodwill and other intangible assets, see "Our Critical Accounting Policies" in Management's Discussion and Analysis of Financial Condition and Results of Operations.
- *Income Taxes* — Note 5, and for additional unaudited information, see "Our Critical Accounting Policies" in Management's Discussion and Analysis of Financial Condition and Results of Operations.
- *Stock-Based Compensation* — Note 6.
- *Pension, Retiree Medical and Savings Plans* — Note 7, and for additional unaudited information, see "Our Critical Accounting Policies" in Management's Discussion and Analysis of Financial Condition and Results of Operations.
- *Financial Instruments* — Note 10, and for additional unaudited information, see "Our Business Risks" in Management's Discussion and Analysis of Financial Condition and Results of Operations.

Recent Accounting Pronouncements

In December 2007, the Financial Accounting Standards Board (FASB) amended its guidance on accounting for business combinations to improve, simplify and converge internationally the accounting for business combinations. The new accounting guidance continues the movement toward the greater use of fair value in financial reporting and increased transparency through expanded disclosures. We adopted the provisions of the new guidance as of the beginning of our 2009 fiscal year. The new accounting guidance changes how business acquisitions are accounted for and will impact financial statements both on the acquisition date and in subsequent periods. Additionally, under the new guidance, transaction costs are expensed rather than capitalized. Future adjustments made to valuation allowances on deferred taxes and acquired tax contingencies associated with acquisitions that closed prior to the beginning of our 2009 fiscal year apply the new provisions and will be evaluated based on the outcome of these matters.

In June 2009, the FASB amended its accounting guidance on the consolidation of variable interest entities (VIE). Among other things, the new guidance requires a qualitative rather than a quantitative assessment to determine the primary beneficiary of a VIE based on whether the entity (1) has the power to direct matters that most significantly impact the activities of the VIE and (2) has the obligation to absorb losses or the right to receive benefits of the VIE that could potentially be significant to the VIE. In addition, the amended guidance requires an ongoing reconsideration of the primary beneficiary. The provisions of this new guidance were effective as of the beginning of our 2010 fiscal year, and the adoption did not have a material impact on our financial statements.

In the second quarter of 2010, the Patient Protection and Affordable Care Act (PPACA) was signed into law. The PPACA changes the tax treatment related to an existing retiree drug subsidy (RDS) available to sponsors of retiree health benefit plans that provide a benefit that is at least actuarially equivalent to the benefits under Medicare Part D. As a result of the PPACA, RDS payments will effectively become taxable in tax years beginning in 2013, by requiring the amount of the subsidy received to be offset against our deduction for health care expenses. The provisions of the PPACA required us to record the effect of this tax law change beginning in our second quarter of 2010, and consequently we recorded a one-time related tax charge of $41 million in the second quarter of 2010. We continue to evaluate the longer-term impacts of this new legislation.

Note 3 Restructuring, Impairment and Integration Charges

In 2010, we incurred merger and integration charges of $799 million related to our acquisitions of PBG and PAS, as well as advisory fees in connection with our acquisition of WBD. $467 million of these charges were recorded in the PAB segment, $111 million recorded in the Europe segment, $191 million recorded in corporate unallocated expenses and $30 million recorded in interest expense. All of these charges, other than the interest expense portion, were recorded in selling, general and administrative expenses. The merger and integration charges related to our acquisitions of PBG and PAS are being incurred to help create a more fully integrated supply chain and go-to-market business model, to improve the effectiveness and efficiency of the distribution of our brands and to enhance our revenue growth. These charges also include closing costs, one-time financing costs and advisory fees related to our acquisitions of PBG and PAS. In addition, we recorded $9 million of merger-related charges, representing our share of the respective merger costs of PBG and PAS, in bottling equity income. Substantially all cash payments related to the above charges are expected to be paid by the end of 2011. In total, these charges had an after-tax impact of $648 million or $0.40 per share.

In 2009, we incurred $50 million of charges related to the merger of PBG and PAS, of which substantially all was paid in 2009. In 2009, we also incurred charges of $36 million ($29 million after-tax or $0.02 per share) in conjunction with our Productivity for Growth program that began in 2008. The program includes actions in all divisions of the business, including the closure of six plants that we believe will increase cost competitiveness across the supply chain, upgrade and streamline our product portfolio, and simplify the organization for more effective and timely decision-making. These charges were recorded in selling, general and administrative expenses. These initiatives were completed in the second quarter of 2009 and substantially all cash payments related to these charges were paid by the end of 2010.

In 2008, we incurred charges of $543 million ($408 million after-tax or $0.25 per share) in conjunction with our Productivity for Growth program. Approximately $455 million of the charge was recorded in selling, general and administrative expenses, with the remainder recorded in cost of sales.

A summary of our merger and integration activity in 2010 is as follows:

	Severance and Other Employee Costs[a]	Asset Impairment	Other Costs	Total
2010 merger and integration charges	$ 396	$ 132	$ 280	$ 808
Cash payments	(114)	–	(271)	(385)
Non-cash charges	(103)	(132)	16	(219)
Liability as of December 25, 2010	$ 179	$ –	$ 25	$ 204

(a) Primarily reflects termination costs for approximately 2,370 employees.

A summary of our restructuring and impairment charges in 2009 is as follows:

	Severance and Other Employee Costs[a]	Other Costs	Total
FLNA	$ –	$ 2	$ 2
QFNA	–	1	1
LAF	3	–	3
PAB	6	10	16
Europe	1	–	1
AMEA	7	6	13
	$17	$19	$36

(a) Primarily reflects termination costs for approximately 410 employees.

A summary of our restructuring and impairment charges in 2008 is as follows:

	Severance and Other Employee Costs	Asset Impairment	Other Costs	Total
FLNA	$ 48	$ 38	$ 22	$108
QFNA	14	3	14	31
LAF	30	8	2	40
PAB	68	92	129	289
Europe	39	6	5	50
AMEA	11	2	2	15
Corporate	2	–	8	10
	$212	$149	$182	$543

Severance and other employee costs primarily reflect termination costs for approximately 3,500 employees. Asset impairments relate to the closure of six plants and changes to our beverage product portfolio. Other costs include contract exit costs and third-party incremental costs associated with upgrading our product portfolio and our supply chain.

A summary of our Productivity for Growth program activity is as follows:

	Severance and Other Employee Costs	Asset Impairment	Other Costs	Total
2008 restructuring and impairment charges	$ 212	$ 149	$ 182	$ 543
Cash payments	(50)	–	(109)	(159)
Non-cash charge	(27)	(149)	(9)	(185)
Currency translation	(1)	–	–	(1)
Liability as of December 27, 2008	134	–	64	198
2009 restructuring and impairment charges	17	12	7	36
Cash payments	(128)	–	(68)	(196)
Currency translation	(14)	(12)	25	(1)
Liability as of December 26, 2009	9	–	28	37
Cash payments	(6)	–	(25)	(31)
Non-cash charge	(2)	–	(1)	(3)
Currency translation	–	–	(1)	(1)
Liability as of December 25, 2010	$ 1	$ –	$ 1	$ 2

Note 4 Property, Plant and Equipment and Intangible Assets

	Average Useful Life	2010	2009	2008
Property, plant and equipment, net				
Land and improvements	10–34 yrs.	$ 1,976	$ 1,208	
Buildings and improvements	15–44 yrs.	7,054	5,080	
Machinery and equipment, including fleet and software	5–15 yrs.	22,091	17,183	
Construction in progress		1,920	1,441	
		33,041	24,912	
Accumulated depreciation		(13,983)	(12,241)	
		$ 19,058	$ 12,671	
Depreciation expense		$ 2,124	$ 1,500	$1,422
Amortizable intangible assets, net				
Acquired franchise rights	56–60 yrs.	$ 949	$ –	
Reacquired franchise rights	1–14 yrs.	110	–	
Brands	5–40 yrs.	1,463	1,465	
Other identifiable intangibles	10–24 yrs.	747	505	
		3,269	1,970	
Accumulated amortization		(1,244)	(1,129)	
		$ 2,025	$ 841	
Amortization expense		$ 117	$ 63	$ 64

Property, plant and equipment is recorded at historical cost. Depreciation and amortization are recognized on a straight-line basis over an asset's estimated useful life. Land is not depreciated and construction in progress is not depreciated until ready for service. Amortization of intangible assets for each of the next five years, based on existing intangible assets as of December 25, 2010 and using average 2010 foreign exchange rates, is expected to be $121 million in 2011, $114 million in 2012, $106 million in 2013, $89 million in 2014 and $81 million in 2015.

Depreciable and amortizable assets are only evaluated for impairment upon a significant change in the operating or macro-economic environment. In these circumstances, if an evaluation of the undiscounted cash flows indicates impairment, the asset is written down to its estimated fair value, which is based on discounted future cash flows. Useful lives are periodically evaluated to determine whether events or circumstances have occurred which indicate the need for revision. For additional unaudited information on our policies for amortizable brands, see "Our Critical Accounting Policies" in Management's Discussion and Analysis of Financial Condition and Results of Operations.

Nonamortizable Intangible Assets

Perpetual brands and goodwill are assessed for impairment at least annually. If the carrying amount of a perpetual brand exceeds its fair value, as determined by its discounted cash flows, an impairment loss is recognized in an amount equal to that excess. No impairment charges resulted from these impairment evaluations. The change in the book value of nonamortizable intangible assets is as follows:

	Balance, Beginning 2009	Acquisitions	Translation and Other	Balance, End of 2009	Acquisitions	Translation and Other	Balance, End of 2010
FLNA							
Goodwill	$ 277	$ 6	$ 23	$ 306	$ —	$ 7	$ 313
Brands	–	26	4	30	–	1	31
	277	32	27	336	–	8	344
QFNA							
Goodwill	175	–	–	175	–	–	175
LAF							
Goodwill	424	17	38	479	–	18	497
Brands	127	1	8	136	–	7	143
	551	18	46	615	–	25	640
PAB[a]							
Goodwill	2,355	62	14	2,431	7,476	39	9,946
Reacquired franchise rights	–	–	–	–	7,229	54	7,283
Acquired franchise rights	–	–	–	–	660	905[b]	1,565
Brands	59	48	5	112	66	4	182
Other	–	–	–	–	10	–	10
	2,414	110	19	2,543	15,441	1,002	18,986
Europe[a]							
Goodwill	1,469	1,291	(136)	2,624	583	(168)	3,039
Reacquired franchise rights	–	–	–	–	810	(17)	793
Acquired franchise rights	–	–	–	–	232	(5)	227
Brands	844	572	(38)	1,378	88	(86)	1,380
	2,313	1,863	(174)	4,002	1,713	(276)	5,439
AMEA							
Goodwill	424	4	91	519	116	56	691
Brands	98	–	28	126	26	17	169
	522	4	119	645	142	73	860
Total goodwill	5,124	1,380	30	6,534	8,175	(48)	14,661
Total reacquired franchise rights	–	–	–	–	8,039	37	8,076
Total acquired franchise rights	–	–	–	–	892	900	1,792
Total brands	1,128	647	7	1,782	180	(57)	1,905
Total other	–	–	–	–	10	–	10
	$6,252	$2,027	$ 37	$8,316	$17,296	$ 832	$26,444

(a) Net increases in 2010 relate primarily to our acquisitions of PBG and PAS.
(b) Includes $900 million related to our upfront payment to DPSG to manufacture and distribute Dr Pepper and certain other DPSG products.

Note 5 Income Taxes

		2010	2009	2008
Income before income taxes				
U.S.		$4,008	$4,209	$3,274
Foreign		4,224	3,870	3,771
		$8,232	$8,079	$7,045
Provision for income taxes				
Current:	U.S. Federal	$ 932	$1,238	$ 815
	Foreign	728	473	732
	State	137	124	87
		1,797	1,835	1,634
Deferred:	U.S. Federal	78	223	313
	Foreign	18	21	(69)
	State	1	21	1
		97	265	245
		$1,894	$2,100	$1,879
Tax rate reconciliation				
U.S. Federal statutory tax rate		35.0%	35.0%	35.0%
State income tax, net of U.S. Federal tax benefit		1.1	1.2	0.8
Lower taxes on foreign results		(9.4)	(7.9)	(8.0)
Acquisitions of PBG and PAS		(3.1)	–	–
Other, net		(0.6)	(2.3)	(1.1)
Annual tax rate		23.0%	26.0%	26.7%
Deferred tax liabilities				
Investments in noncontrolled affiliates		$ 74	$1,120	
Debt guarantee of wholly owned subsidiary		828	–	
Property, plant and equipment		1,984	1,056	
Intangible assets other than nondeductible goodwill		3,726	417	
Other		647	68	
Gross deferred tax liabilities		7,259	2,661	
Deferred tax assets				
Net carryforwards		1,264	624	
Stock-based compensation		455	410	
Retiree medical benefits		579	508	
Other employee-related benefits		527	442	
Pension benefits		291	179	
Deductible state tax and interest benefits		320	256	
Long-term debt obligations acquired		291	–	
Other		904	560	
Gross deferred tax assets		4,631	2,979	
Valuation allowances		(875)	(586)	
Deferred tax assets, net		3,756	2,393	
Net deferred tax liabilities		$3,503	$ 268	

	2010	2009	2008
Deferred taxes included within:			
Assets:			
Prepaid expenses and other current assets	$ 554	$391	
Other assets	–	–	
Liabilities:			
Deferred income taxes	$4,057	$659	
Analysis of valuation allowances			
Balance, beginning of year	$ 586	$657	$695
Provision/(Benefit)	75	(78)	(5)
Other additions/(deductions)	214	7	(33)
Balance, end of year	$ 875	$586	$657

For additional unaudited information on our income tax policies, including our reserves for income taxes, see "Our Critical Accounting Policies" in Management's Discussion and Analysis of Financial Condition and Results of Operations.

Reserves

A number of years may elapse before a particular matter, for which we have established a reserve, is audited and finally resolved. The number of years with open tax audits varies depending on the tax jurisdiction. Our major taxing jurisdictions and the related open tax audits are as follows:

- U.S. — continue to dispute one matter related to tax years 1998 through 2002. During 2010, all but three issues were resolved for tax years 2003 through 2005. These three issues are currently under review by the IRS Appeals Division. Our U.S. tax returns for the years 2006 through 2007 are currently under audit;
- Mexico — audits have been substantially completed for all taxable years through 2005;
- United Kingdom — audits have been completed for all taxable years prior to 2008; and
- Canada — domestic audits have been substantially completed for all taxable years through 2007. International audits have been completed for all taxable years through 2003.

While it is often difficult to predict the final outcome or the timing of resolution of any particular tax matter, we believe that our reserves reflect the probable outcome of known tax contingencies. We adjust these reserves, as well as the related interest, in light of changing facts and circumstances. Settlement of any particular issue would usually require the use of cash. Favorable resolution would be recognized as a reduction to our annual tax rate in the year of resolution. For further unaudited information on the impact of the resolution of open tax issues, see "Other Consolidated Results."

As of December 25, 2010, the total gross amount of reserves for income taxes, reported in other liabilities, was $2,023 million. Any prospective adjustments to these reserves will be recorded as an increase or decrease to our provision for income taxes and would impact our effective tax rate. In addition, we accrue interest related to reserves for income taxes in our provision for income taxes and any associated penalties are recorded in selling, general and administrative expenses. The gross amount of interest accrued, reported in other liabilities, was $570 million as of December 25, 2010, of which $135 million was recognized in 2010. The gross amount of interest accrued was $461 million as of December 26, 2009, of which $30 million was recognized in 2009.

A rollforward of our reserves for all federal, state and foreign tax jurisdictions, is as follows:

	2010	2009
Balance, beginning of year	$1,731	$1,711
Additions for tax positions related to the current year	204	238
Additions for tax positions from prior years	517	79
Reductions for tax positions from prior years	(391)	(236)
Settlement payments	(30)	(64)
Statute of limitations expiration	(7)	(4)
Translation and other	(2)	7
Balance, end of year	$2,022(a)	$1,731

(a) Includes amounts related to our acquisitions of PBG and PAS.

Carryforwards and Allowances

Operating loss carryforwards totaling $9.1 billion at year-end 2010 are being carried forward in a number of foreign and state jurisdictions where we are permitted to use tax operating losses from prior periods to reduce future taxable income. These operating losses will expire as follows: $0.4 billion in 2011, $6.5 billion between 2012 and 2030 and $2.2 billion may be carried forward indefinitely. We establish valuation allowances for our deferred tax assets if, based on the available evidence, it is more likely than not that some portion or all of the deferred tax assets will not be realized.

Undistributed International Earnings

As of December 25, 2010, we had approximately $26.6 billion of undistributed international earnings. We intend to continue to reinvest earnings outside the U.S. for the foreseeable future and, therefore, have not recognized any U.S. tax expense on these earnings.

Note 6 Stock-Based Compensation

Our stock-based compensation program is designed to attract and retain employees while also aligning employees' interests with the interests of our shareholders. Stock options and restricted stock units (RSU) are granted to employees under the shareholder-approved 2007 Long-Term Incentive Plan (LTIP), the only stock-based plan under which we currently grant stock options and RSUs. Stock-based compensation expense was $352 million in 2010, $227 million in 2009 and $238 million in 2008. In 2010, $299 million was recorded as stock-based compensation expense and $53 million was included in merger and integration charges. $86 million of the $352 million recorded in 2010 was related to the unvested acquisition-related grants described below. Income tax benefits related to stock-based compensation expense and recognized in earnings were $89 million in 2010, $67 million in 2009 and $71 million in 2008. At year-end 2010, 154 million shares were available for future stock-based compensation grants.

In connection with our acquisition of PBG, we issued 13.4 million stock options and 2.7 million RSUs at weighted-average grant prices of $42.89 and $62.30, respectively, to replace previously held PBG equity awards. In connection with our acquisition of PAS, we issued 0.4 million stock options at a weighted-average grant price of $31.72 to replace previously held PAS equity awards. Our equity issuances included 8.3 million stock options and 0.6 million RSUs which were vested at the acquisition date and were included in the purchase price. The remaining 5.5 million stock options and 2.1 million RSUs issued are unvested and are being amortized over their remaining vesting period, up to three years.

As a result of our annual benefits review in 2010, the Company approved certain changes to our benefits programs to remain market competitive relative to other leading global companies. These changes included ending the Company's broad-based SharePower stock option program. Consequently, beginning in 2011, no new awards will be granted under the SharePower program. Outstanding SharePower awards from 2010 and earlier will continue to vest and be exercisable according to the terms and conditions of the program. See Note 7 for additional information regarding other related changes.

Method of Accounting and Our Assumptions

We account for our employee stock options under the fair value method of accounting using a Black-Scholes valuation model to measure stock option expense at the date of grant. All stock option grants have an exercise price equal to the fair market value of our common stock on the date of grant and generally have a 10-year term. We do not backdate, reprice or grant stock-based compensation awards retroactively. Repricing of awards would require shareholder approval under the LTIP.

The fair value of stock option grants is amortized to expense over the vesting period, generally three years. Executives who are awarded long-term incentives based on their performance are generally offered the choice of stock options or RSUs. Executives who elect RSUs receive one RSU for every four stock options that would have otherwise been granted. Senior officers do not have a choice and are granted 50% stock options and 50% performance-based RSUs. Vesting of RSU awards for senior officers is contingent upon the achievement of pre-established performance targets approved by the Compensation Committee of the Board of Directors. RSU expense is based on the fair value of PepsiCo stock on the date of grant and is amortized over the vesting period, generally three years. Each RSU is settled in a share of our stock after the vesting period.

Our weighted-average Black-Scholes fair value assumptions are as follows:

	2010	2009	2008
Expected life	5 yrs.	6 yrs.	6 yrs.
Risk-free interest rate	2.3%	2.8%	3.0%
Expected volatility	17%	17%	16%
Expected dividend yield	2.8%	3.0%	1.9%

The expected life is the period over which our employee groups are expected to hold their options. It is based on our historical experience with similar grants. The risk-free interest rate is based on the expected U.S. Treasury rate over the expected life. Volatility reflects movements in our stock price over the most recent historical period equivalent to the expected life. Dividend yield is estimated over the expected life based on our stated dividend policy and forecasts of net income, share repurchases and stock price.

A summary of our stock-based compensation activity for the year ended December 25, 2010 is presented below:

Our Stock Option Activity

	Options[a]	Average Price[b]	Average Life (years)[c]	Aggregate Intrinsic Value[d]
Outstanding at December 26, 2009	106,011	$51.68		
Granted	26,858	54.09		
Exercised	(23,940)	43.47		
Forfeited/expired	(2,726)	55.85		
Outstanding at December 25, 2010	106,203	$54.03	5.19	$1,281,596
Exercisable at December 25, 2010	67,304	$50.26	3.44	$1,040,510

(a) Options are in thousands and include options previously granted under PBG, PAS and Quaker plans. No additional options or shares may be granted under the PBG, PAS and Quaker plans.
(b) Weighted-average exercise price.
(c) Weighted-average contractual life remaining.
(d) In thousands.

Our RSU Activity

	RSUs[a]	Average Intrinsic Price[b]	Average Life (years)[c]	Aggregate Intrinsic Value[d]
Outstanding at December 26, 2009	6,092	$60.98		
Granted	8,326	65.01		
Converted	(3,183)	63.58		
Forfeited/expired	(573)	62.50		
Outstanding at December 25, 2010	10,662	$63.27	1.69	$700,397

(a) RSUs are in thousands and include RSUs previously granted under a PBG plan. No additional RSUs or shares may be granted under the PBG plan.
(b) Weighted-average intrinsic value at grant date.
(c) Weighted-average contractual life remaining.
(d) In thousands.

Other Stock-Based Compensation Data

	2010	2009	2008
Stock Options			
Weighted-average fair value of options granted	$ 13.93	$ 7.02	$ 11.24
Total intrinsic value of options exercised[a]	$502,354	$194,545	$410,152
RSUs			
Total number of RSUs granted[a]	8,326	2,653	2,135
Weighted-average intrinsic value of RSUs granted	$ 65.01	$ 53.22	$ 68.73
Total intrinsic value of RSUs converted[a]	$202,717	$124,193	$180,563

(a) In thousands.

As of December 25, 2010, there was $423 million of total unrecognized compensation cost related to nonvested share-based compensation grants. This unrecognized compensation is expected to be recognized over a weighted-average period of two years.

Note 7   Pension, Retiree Medical and Savings Plans

Our pension plans cover full-time employees in the U.S. and certain international employees. Benefits are determined based on either years of service or a combination of years of service and earnings. U.S. and Canada retirees are also eligible for medical and life insurance benefits (retiree medical) if they meet age and service requirements. Generally, our share of retiree medical costs is capped at specified dollar amounts, which vary based upon years of service, with retirees contributing the remainder of the costs.

Gains and losses resulting from actual experience differing from our assumptions, including the difference between the actual return on plan assets and the expected return on plan assets, and from changes in our assumptions are also determined at each measurement date. If this net accumulated gain or loss exceeds 10% of the greater of the market-related value of plan assets or plan liabilities, a portion of the net gain or loss is included in expense for the following year based upon the average remaining service period of active plan participants, which is approximately 11 years for pension expense and approximately eight years for retiree medical expense. The cost or benefit of plan changes that increase or decrease benefits for prior employee service (prior service cost/(credit)) is included in earnings on a straight-line basis over the average remaining service period of active plan participants.

In connection with our acquisitions of PBG and PAS, we assumed sponsorship of pension and retiree medical plans that provide benefits to U.S. and certain international employees. Subsequently, during the third quarter of 2010, we merged the pension plan assets of the legacy PBG and PAS U.S. pension plans with those of PepsiCo into one master trust.

During 2010, the Compensation Committee of PepsiCo's Board of Directors approved certain changes to the U.S. pension and retiree medical plans, effective January 1, 2011. Pension plan design changes include implementing a new employer contribution to the 401(k) savings plan for all future salaried new hires of the Company, as salaried new hires are no longer eligible to participate in the defined benefit pension plan, as well as implementing a new defined benefit pension formula for certain hourly new hires of the Company. Pension plan design changes also include implementing a new employer contribution to the 401(k) savings plan for certain legacy PBG and PAS salaried employees (as such employees are also not eligible to participate in the defined benefit pension plan), as well as implementing a new defined benefit pension formula for certain legacy PBG and PAS hourly employees. The retiree medical plan design change includes phasing out Company subsidies of retiree medical benefits.

As a result of these changes, we remeasured our pension and retiree medical expenses and liabilities in the third quarter of 2010, which resulted in a one-time pre-tax curtailment gain of $62 million included in retiree medical expense.

The provisions of both the PPACA and the Health Care and Education Reconciliation Act are reflected in our retiree medical expenses and liabilities and were not material to our financial statements.

Selected financial information for our pension and retiree medical plans is as follows:

	Pension				Retiree Medical	
	2010	2009	2010	2009	2010	2009
	U.S.		International			
Change in projected benefit liability						
Liability at beginning of year	$6,606	$ 6,217	$1,709	$1,270	$ 1,359	$ 1,370
Acquisitions	2,161	–	90	–	396	–
Service cost	299	238	81	54	54	44
Interest cost	506	373	106	82	93	82
Plan amendments	28	–	–	–	(132)	–
Participant contributions	–	–	3	10	–	–
Experience loss/(gain)	583	70	213	221	95	(63)
Benefit payments	(375)	(296)	(69)	(50)	(100)	(80)
Settlement/curtailment gain	(2)	–	(3)	(8)	–	–
Special termination benefits	45	–	3	–	3	–
Foreign currency adjustment	–	–	(18)	130	2	6
Other	–	4	27	–	–	–
Liability at end of year	$9,851	$ 6,606	$2,142	$1,709	$ 1,770	$ 1,359
Change in fair value of plan assets						
Fair value at beginning of year	$5,420	$ 3,974	$1,561	$1,165	$ 13	$ –
Acquisitions	1,633	–	52	–	–	–
Actual return on plan assets	943	697	164	159	7	2
Employer contributions/funding	1,249	1,041	215	167	270	91
Participant contributions	–	–	3	10	–	–
Benefit payments	(375)	(296)	(69)	(50)	(100)	(80)
Settlement	–	–	(2)	(8)	–	–
Foreign currency adjustment	–	–	(28)	118	–	–
Other	–	4	–	–	–	–
Fair value at end of year	$8,870	$ 5,420	$1,896	$1,561	$ 190	$ 13
Funded status	$ (981)	$(1,186)	$ (246)	$ (148)	$(1,580)	$(1,346)

	Pension				Retiree Medical	
	2010	2009	2010	2009	2010	2009
	U.S.		International			
Amounts recognized						
Other assets	$ 47	$ –	$ 66	$ 50	$ –	$ –
Other current liabilities	(54)	(36)	(10)	(1)	(145)	(105)
Other liabilities	(974)	(1,150)	(302)	(197)	(1,435)	(1,241)
Net amount recognized	$ (981)	$(1,186)	$ (246)	$ (148)	$(1,580)	$(1,346)
Amounts included in accumulated other comprehensive loss (pre-tax)						
Net loss	$2,726	$ 2,563	$ 767	$ 625	$ 270	$ 190
Prior service cost/(credit)	117	101	17	20	(150)	(102)
Total	$2,843	$ 2,664	$ 784	$ 645	$ 120	$ 88
Components of the increase/(decrease) in net loss						
Change in discount rate	$ 556	$ 47	$ 213	$ 97	$ 101	$ 11
Employee-related assumption changes	4	–	(4)	70	8	(38)
Liability-related experience different from assumptions	43	23	5	51	(22)	(36)
Actual asset return different from expected return	(300)	(235)	(41)	(54)	(6)	(2)
Amortization of losses	(119)	(111)	(24)	(9)	(9)	(11)
Other, including foreign currency adjustments	(21)	13	(7)	49	8	–
Total	$ 163	$ (263)	$ 142	$ 204	$ 80	$ (76)
Liability at end of year for service to date	$9,163	$ 5,784	$1,743	$1,414		

The components of benefit expense are as follows:

	Pension						Retiree Medical		
	2010	2009	2008	2010	2009	2008	2010	2009	2008
	U.S.			International					
Components of benefit expense									
Service cost	$ 299	$ 238	$ 244	$ 81	$ 54	$ 61	$ 54	$ 44	$ 45
Interest cost	506	373	371	106	82	88	93	82	82
Expected return on plan assets	(643)	(462)	(416)	(123)	(105)	(112)	(1)	–	–
Amortization of prior service cost/(credit)	12	12	19	2	2	3	(22)	(17)	(13)
Amortization of net loss	119	110	55	24	9	19	9	11	7
	293	271	273	90	42	59	133	120	121
Settlement/curtailment (gain)/loss	(2)	(13)	3	1	3	3	(62)	–	–
Special termination benefits	45	–	31	3	–	2	3	–	3
Total	$ 336	$ 258	$ 307	$ 94	$ 45	$ 64	$ 74	$120	$124

The estimated amounts to be amortized from accumulated other comprehensive loss into benefit expense in 2011 for our pension and retiree medical plans are as follows:

	Pension		Retiree Medical
	U.S.	International	
Net loss	$144	$39	$ 12
Prior service cost/(credit)	15	2	(28)
Total	$159	$41	$(16)

The following table provides the weighted-average assumptions used to determine projected benefit liability and benefit expense for our pension and retiree medical plans:

	Pension						Retiree Medical		
	2010	2009	2008	2010	2009	2008	2010	2009	2008
		U.S.			International				
Weighted-average assumptions									
Liability discount rate	5.7%	6.1%	6.2%	5.5%	5.9%	6.3%	5.2%	6.1%	6.2%
Expense discount rate	6.0%	6.2%	6.5%	6.0%	6.3%	5.6%	5.8%	6.2%	6.5%
Expected return on plan assets	7.8%	7.8%	7.8%	7.1%	7.1%	7.2%	7.8%		
Liability rate of salary increases	4.1%	4.4%	4.4%	4.1%	4.1%	4.1%			
Expense rate of salary increases	4.4%	4.4%	4.6%	4.1%	4.2%	3.9%			

The following table provides selected information about plans with liability for service to date and total benefit liability in excess of plan assets:

	Pension				Retiree Medical	
	2010	2009	2010	2009	2010	2009
		U.S.		International		
Selected information for plans with liability for service to date in excess of plan assets						
Liability for service to date	$ (525)	$(2,695)	$ (610)	$ (342)		
Fair value of plan assets	$　–	$ 2,220	$ 474	$ 309		
Selected information for plans with projected benefit liability in excess of plan assets						
Benefit liability	$(5,806)	$(6,603)	$(1,949)	$(1,566)	$(1,770)	$(1,359)
Fair value of plan assets	$ 4,778	$ 5,417	$ 1,638	$ 1,368	$ 190	$ 13

Of the total projected pension benefit liability at year-end 2010, $747 million relates to plans that we do not fund because the funding of such plans does not receive favorable tax treatment.

Future Benefit Payments and Funding

Our estimated future benefit payments are as follows:

	2011	2012	2013	2014	2015	2016–20
Pension	$480	$500	$520	$560	$595	$3,770
Retiree medical[a]	$155	$155	$160	$165	$170	$ 875

(a) Expected future benefit payments for our retiree medical plans do not reflect any estimated subsidies expected to be received under the 2003 Medicare Act. Subsidies are expected to be approximately $11 million for each of the years from 2011 through 2015 and approximately $90 million in total for 2016 through 2020.

These future benefits to beneficiaries include payments from both funded and unfunded pension plans.

In 2011, we expect to make pension contributions of approximately $160 million, with up to approximately $15 million expected to be discretionary. Our net cash payments for retiree medical are estimated to be approximately $145 million in 2011.

Plan Assets

Pension

Our pension plan investment strategy includes the use of actively managed securities and is reviewed annually based upon plan liabilities, an evaluation of market conditions, tolerance for risk and cash requirements for benefit payments. Our investment objective is to ensure that funds are available to meet the plans' benefit obligations when they become due. Our overall investment strategy is to prudently invest plan assets in a well-diversified portfolio of equity and high-quality debt securities to achieve our long-term

return expectations. Our investment policy also permits the use of derivative instruments which are primarily used to reduce risk. Our expected long-term rate of return on U.S. plan assets is 7.8%. Our target investment allocation is 40% for U.S. equity allocations, 20% for international equity allocations and 40% for fixed income allocations. Actual investment allocations may vary from our target investment allocations due to prevailing market conditions. We regularly review our actual investment allocations and periodically rebalance our investments to our target allocations. In an effort to enhance diversification, the pension plan divested its holdings of PepsiCo stock in the fourth quarter of 2010.

The expected return on pension plan assets is based on our pension plan investment strategy, our expectations for long-term rates of return by asset class, taking into account volatilities and correlation among asset classes, and our historical experience. We also review current levels of interest rates and inflation to assess the reasonableness of the long-term rates. We evaluate our expected return assumptions annually to ensure that they are reasonable. To calculate the expected return on pension plan assets, we use a market-related valuation method that recognizes investment gains or losses (the difference between the expected and actual return based on the market-related value of assets) for securities included in our equity strategies over a five-year period. This has the effect of reducing year-to-year volatility. For all other asset categories, the actual fair value is used for the market-related value of assets.

Retiree Medical

In 2010, we made nondiscretionary contributions of $100 million to fund the payment of U.S. retiree medical claims. During the fourth quarter of 2010, we made a discretionary contribution of $170 million to fund future U.S. retiree medical plan benefits. This contribution was invested consistent with the allocation of existing assets in the U.S. pension plan.

Fair Value

The guidance on fair value measurements defines fair value, establishes a framework for measuring fair value, and expands disclosures about fair value measurements. The fair value framework requires the categorization of assets and liabilities into three levels based upon the assumptions (inputs) used to price the assets. Level 1 provides the most reliable measure of fair value, whereas Level 3 generally requires significant management judgment.

Plan assets measured at fair value as of fiscal year-end 2010 and 2009 are categorized consistently by level in both years, and are as follows:

	2010*				2009
	Total	Level 1	Level 2	Level 3	Total
U.S. plan assets					
Equity securities:					
PepsiCo common stock[a]	$ –	$ –	$ –	$ –	$ 332
U.S. common stock[a]	304	304	–	–	229
U.S. commingled funds[b]	3,426	–	3,426	–	1,387
International common stock[a]	834	834	–	–	700
International commingled fund[c]	992	–	992	–	114
Preferred stock[d]	4	–	4	–	4
Fixed income securities:					
Government securities[d]	950	–	950	–	741
Corporate bonds[d]	2,374	–	2,374	–	1,214
Mortgage-backed securities[d]	20	–	20	–	201
Other:					
Contracts with insurance companies[f]	28	–	–	28	9
Cash and cash equivalents	81	81	–	–	457
Subtotal U.S. plan assets	9,013	$1,219	$7,766	$28	5,388
Dividends and interest receivable	47				32
Total U.S. plan assets	$9,060				$5,420
International plan assets					
Equity securities:					
U.S. commingled funds[b]	$ 193	$ –	$ 193	$ –	$ 180
International commingled funds[c]	779	–	779	–	661
Fixed income securities:					
Government securities[d]	184	–	184	–	139
Corporate bonds[d]	152	–	152	–	128
Fixed income commingled funds[e]	393	–	393	–	363
Other:					
Contracts with insurance companies[f]	28	–	–	28	29
Currency commingled funds[g]	42	–	42	–	44
Cash and cash equivalents	120	120	–	–	17
Subtotal international plan assets	1,891	$ 120	$1,743	$28	1,561
Dividends and interest receivable	5				–
Total international plan assets	$1,896				$1,561

(a) Based on quoted market prices in active markets.
(b) Based on the fair value of the investments owned by these funds that track various U.S. large, mid-cap and small company indices. Includes one large-cap fund that represents 32% and 25%, respectively, of total U.S. plan assets for 2010 and 2009.
(c) Based on the fair value of the investments owned by these funds that track various non-U.S. equity indices.
(d) Based on quoted bid prices for comparable securities in the marketplace and broker/dealer quotes that are not observable. Corporate bonds of U.S.-based companies represent 22% and 18%, respectively, of total U.S. plan assets for 2010 and 2009.
(e) Based on the fair value of the investments owned by these funds that track various government and corporate bond indices.
(f) Based on the fair value of the contracts as determined by the insurance companies using inputs that are not observable.
(g) Based on the fair value of the investments owned by these funds. Includes managed hedge funds that invest primarily in derivatives to reduce currency exposure.
 * 2010 amounts include $190 million of retiree medical plan assets that are restricted for purposes of providing health benefits for U.S. retirees and their beneficiaries.

Retiree Medical Cost Trend Rates

An average increase of 7% in the cost of covered retiree medical benefits is assumed for 2011. This average increase is then projected to decline gradually to 5% in 2020 and thereafter. These assumed health care cost trend rates have an impact on the retiree medical plan expense and liability. However, the cap on our share of retiree medical costs limits the impact. In addition, beginning January 1, 2011, the Company will start phasing out company subsidies of retiree medical benefits. A 1-percentage-point change in the assumed health care trend rate would have the following effects:

	1% Increase	1% Decrease
2010 service and interest cost components	$ 5	$ (4)
2010 benefit liability	$42	$(50)

Savings Plan

Our U.S. employees are eligible to participate in 401(k) savings plans, which are voluntary defined contribution plans. The plans are designed to help employees accumulate additional savings for retirement, and we make company matching contributions on a portion of eligible pay based on years of service. In 2010, in connection with our acquisitions of PBG and PAS, we also made company retirement contributions for certain employees on a portion of eligible pay based on years of service. In 2010 and 2009, our total contributions were $135 million and $72 million, respectively.

Beginning January 1, 2011, a new employer contribution to the 401(k) savings plan will become effective for certain eligible legacy PBG and PAS salaried employees as well as all future eligible salaried new hires of PepsiCo who are not eligible to participate in the defined benefit pension plan as a result of plan design changes approved during 2010.

For additional unaudited information on our pension and retiree medical plans and related accounting policies and assumptions, see "Our Critical Accounting Policies" in Management's Discussion and Analysis.

Note 8 Noncontrolled Bottling Affiliates

On February 26, 2010, we completed our acquisitions of PBG and PAS, at which time we gained control over their operations and began to consolidate their results. See Note 1. Prior to these acquisitions, PBG and PAS represented our most significant noncontrolled bottling affiliates. Sales to PBG in 2010 (prior to the acquisition date) represented less than 1% of our total net revenue in 2010, 6% of our total net revenue in 2009 and 7% of our total net revenue in 2008.

See Note 15 for additional information regarding our acquisitions of PBG and PAS.

The Pepsi Bottling Group

In addition to approximately 32% of PBG's outstanding common stock that we owned at year-end 2009, we owned 100% of PBG's class B common stock and approximately 7% of the equity of Bottling Group, LLC, PBG's principal operating subsidiary.

PBG's summarized financial information is as follows:

	2009	2008
Current assets	$ 3,412	
Noncurrent assets	10,158	
Total assets	$13,570	
Current liabilities	$ 1,965	
Noncurrent liabilities	7,896	
Total liabilities	$ 9,861	
Our investment	$ 1,775	
Net revenue	$13,219	$13,796
Gross profit	$ 5,840	$ 6,210
Operating income	$ 1,048	$ 649
Net income attributable to PBG	$ 612	$ 162

Our investment in PBG, which included the related goodwill, was $463 million higher than our ownership interest in their net assets less noncontrolling interests at year-end 2009.

During 2008, together with PBG, we jointly acquired Russia's leading branded juice company, Lebedyansky. See Note 14 for further information on this acquisition.

PepsiAmericas

At year-end 2009, we owned approximately 43% of the outstanding common stock of PAS.

PAS's summarized financial information is as follows:

	2009	2008
Current assets	$ 952	
Noncurrent assets	4,141	
Total assets	$5,093	
Current liabilities	$ 669	
Noncurrent liabilities	2,493	
Total liabilities	$3,162	
Our investment	$1,071	
Net revenue	$4,421	$4,937
Gross profit	$1,767	$1,982
Operating income	$ 381	$ 473
Net income attributable to PAS	$ 181	$ 226

Our investment in PAS, which included the related goodwill, was $322 million higher than our ownership interest in their net assets less noncontrolling interests at year-end 2009.

Related Party Transactions

Our significant related party transactions are with our non-controlled bottling affiliates, including PBG and PAS prior to our acquisitions on February 26, 2010. All such amounts are settled on terms consistent with other trade receivables and payables. The transactions primarily consist of (1) selling concentrate to these affiliates, which they use in the production of CSDs and non-carbonated beverages, (2) selling certain finished goods to these affiliates, (3) receiving royalties for the use of our trademarks for certain products and (4) paying these affiliates to act as our manufacturing and distribution agent for product associated with our national account fountain customers. Sales of concentrate and finished goods are reported net of bottler funding. For further unaudited information on these bottlers, see "Our Customers" in Management's Discussion and Analysis of Financial Condition and Results of Operations. These transactions with our bottling affiliates are reflected in our consolidated financial statements as follows:

	2010(a)	2009	2008
Net revenue	$993	$3,922	$4,049
Cost of sales	$116	$ 634	$ 660
Selling, general and administrative expenses	$ 6	$ 24	$ 30
Accounts and notes receivable	$ 27	$ 254	$ 248
Accounts payable and other liabilities	$ 42	$ 285	$ 198

(a) Includes transactions with PBG and PAS in 2010 prior to the date of acquisition. 2010 balance sheet information for PBG and PAS is not applicable as we consolidated their balance sheets at the date of acquisition.

We also coordinate, on an aggregate basis, the contract negotiations of sweeteners and other raw material requirements, including aluminum cans and plastic bottles and closures for certain of our independent bottlers. Once we have negotiated the contracts, the bottlers order and take delivery directly from the supplier and pay the suppliers directly. Consequently, these transactions are not reflected in our consolidated financial statements. As the contracting party, we could be liable to these suppliers in the event of any nonpayment by our bottlers, but we consider this exposure to be remote.

In addition, our joint ventures with Unilever (under the Lipton brand name) and Starbucks sell finished goods (ready-to-drink teas, coffees and water products) to our noncontrolled bottling affiliates. Consistent with accounting for equity method investments, our joint venture revenue is not included in our consolidated net revenue and therefore is not included in the above table.

In 2010, we repurchased $357 million (5.5 million shares) of PepsiCo stock from the Master Trust which holds assets of PepsiCo's U.S. qualified pension plans at market value. See Note 7.

Note 9 Debt Obligations and Commitments

	2010	2009
Short-term debt obligations		
Current maturities of long-term debt	$ 113	$ 102
Commercial paper (0.2%)	2,632	–
Notes due 2011 (4.4%)	1,513	–
Other borrowings (5.3% and 6.7%)	640	362
	$ 4,898	$ 464
Long-term debt obligations		
Notes due 2012 (3.1% and 1.9%)	$ 2,437	$1,079
Notes due 2013 (3.0% and 3.7%)	2,110	999
Notes due 2014 (5.3% and 4.0%)	2,888	1,026
Notes due 2015 (2.6%)	1,617	–
Notes due 2016–2040 (4.9% and 5.4%)	10,828	4,056
Zero coupon notes, due 2011–2012 (13.3%)	136	192
Other, due 2011–2019 (4.8% and 8.4%)	96	150
	20,112	7,502
Less: current maturities of long-term debt obligations	(113)	(102)
	$19,999	$7,400

The interest rates in the above table reflect weighted-average rates at year-end.

In the first quarter of 2010, we issued $1.25 billion of floating rate notes maturing in 2011 which bear interest at a rate equal to the three-month London Inter-Bank Offered Rate (LIBOR) plus 3 basis points, $1.0 billion of 3.10% senior notes maturing in 2015, $1.0 billion of 4.50% senior notes maturing in 2020 and $1.0 billion of 5.50% senior notes maturing in 2040. A portion of the net proceeds from the issuance of these notes was used to finance our acquisitions of PBG and PAS and the remainder was used for general corporate purposes.

On February 26, 2010, in connection with the transactions contemplated by the PBG merger agreement, Pepsi-Cola Metropolitan Bottling Company, Inc. (Metro) assumed the due and punctual payment of the principal of (and premium, if any) and interest on PBG's 7.00% senior notes due March 1, 2029 ($1 billion principal amount of which are outstanding). These notes are guaranteed by Bottling Group, LLC and PepsiCo.

On February 26, 2010, in connection with the transactions contemplated by the PAS merger agreement, Metro assumed the due and punctual payment of the principal of (and premium, if any) and interest on PAS's 7.625% notes due 2015 ($9 million principal amount of which are outstanding), 7.29% notes due 2026 ($100 million principal amount of which are outstanding), 7.44% notes due 2026 ($25 million principal amount of which are outstanding), 4.50% notes due 2013 ($150 million principal amount of which are outstanding), 5.625% notes due 2011 ($250 million principal amount of which are outstanding), 5.75% notes due 2012 ($300 million principal amount of which are outstanding), 4.375% notes due 2014 ($350 million principal amount of which are outstanding), 4.875% notes due 2015 ($300 million principal amount of which are outstanding), 5.00% notes due 2017 ($250 million principal amount of which are outstanding) and 5.50% notes due 2035 ($250 million principal amount of which are outstanding). These notes are guaranteed by PepsiCo.

On February 26, 2010, as a result of the transactions contemplated by the PBG merger agreement, Bottling Group, LLC became a wholly owned subsidiary of Metro. Bottling Group, LLC's 4.625% senior notes due 2012 ($1 billion principal amount of which are outstanding), 4.125% senior notes due 2015 ($250 million principal amount of which are outstanding), 5.00% senior notes due 2013 ($400 million principal amount of which are outstanding), 5.50% senior notes due 2016 ($800 million principal amount of which are outstanding), 6.95% senior notes due 2014 ($1.3 billion principal amount of which are outstanding) and 5.125% senior notes due 2019 ($750 million principal amount of which are outstanding) are guaranteed by PepsiCo.

As of December 25, 2010, the long-term debt acquired from our anchor bottlers (including debt previously issued by PBG, Bottling Group, LLC and PAS) in connection with our acquisitions of PBG and PAS has a total face value of approximately $7,484 million (fair value of $8,472 million) with a weighted-average stated interest rate of 5.7%. This acquired debt has a remaining weighted-average maturity of 6.6 years. See Note 15.

In the third quarter of 2010, we entered into a $2,575 million 364-day unsecured revolving credit agreement which expires in June 2011. We may request renewal of this facility for an additional 364-day period or convert any amounts outstanding into a term loan for a period of up to one year, which would mature no later than June 2012. This agreement replaced our $1,975 million 364-day unsecured revolving credit agreement and a $540 million amended PAS credit facility and is in addition to our existing $2,000 million unsecured revolving credit agreement and the $1,080 million amended PBG credit facility, both of which expire in 2012. Funds borrowed under these agreements may be used for general corporate purposes, including but not limited to repayment of our outstanding commercial paper, working capital, capital investments and/or acquisitions. Borrowings under the amended PBG credit facility are guaranteed by PepsiCo. Our lines of credit remain unused as of December 25, 2010.

In the fourth quarter of 2010, we paid $672 million in a cash tender offer to repurchase $500 million (aggregate principal amount) of our 7.90% senior unsecured notes maturing in 2018. As a result of this debt repurchase, we recorded a $178 million charge to interest expense, primarily representing the premium paid in the tender offer.

In the fourth quarter of 2010, we issued $500 million of 0.875% senior unsecured notes maturing in 2013, $1.0 billion of 3.125% senior unsecured notes maturing in 2020 and $750 million of 4.875% senior unsecured notes maturing in 2040. A portion of the net proceeds from the issuance of these notes was used to finance the debt repurchase and the remainder was used for general corporate purposes.

In addition, as of December 25, 2010, $657 million of our debt related to borrowings from various lines of credit that are maintained for our international divisions. These lines of credit are subject to normal banking terms and conditions and are fully committed at least to the extent of our borrowings.

Long-Term Contractual Commitments[a]

			Payments Due by Period		
	Total	2011	2012–2013	2014–2015	2016 and beyond
Long-term debt obligations[b]	$19,337	$ –	$4,569	$4,322	$10,446
Interest on debt obligations[c]	7,746	809	1,480	1,075	4,382
Operating leases	1,676	390	543	320	423
Purchasing commitments	2,433	765	1,159	481	28
Marketing commitments	824	294	268	151	111
	$32,016	$2,258	$8,019	$6,349	$15,390

(a) Reflects non-cancelable commitments as of December 25, 2010 based on year-end foreign exchange rates and excludes any reserves for uncertain tax positions as we are unable to reasonably predict the ultimate amount or timing of settlement.

(b) Excludes $662 million related to the fair value step-up of debt acquired in connection with our acquisitions of PBG and PAS, as well as $113 million related to current maturities of long-term debt.

(c) Interest payments on floating-rate debt are estimated using interest rates effective as of December 25, 2010.

Most long-term contractual commitments, except for our long-term debt obligations, are not recorded on our balance sheet. Non-cancelable operating leases primarily represent building leases. Non-cancelable purchasing commitments are primarily for packaging materials, oranges and orange juice. Non-cancelable marketing commitments are primarily for sports marketing. Bottler funding to independent bottlers is not reflected in our long-term contractual commitments as it is negotiated on an annual basis. Accrued liabilities for pension and retiree medical plans are not reflected in our long-term contractual commitments because they do not represent expected future cash outflows. See Note 7 for additional information regarding our pension and retiree medical obligations.

Off-Balance-Sheet Arrangements

It is not our business practice to enter into off-balance-sheet arrangements, other than in the normal course of business. See Note 8 regarding contracts related to certain of our bottlers.

See "Our Liquidity and Capital Resources" in Management's Discussion and Analysis of Financial Condition and Results of Operations for further unaudited information on our borrowings.

Note 10 Financial Instruments

We are exposed to market risks arising from adverse changes in:
- commodity prices, affecting the cost of our raw materials and energy,
- foreign exchange risks, and
- interest rates.

In the normal course of business, we manage these risks through a variety of strategies, including the use of derivatives. Certain derivatives are designated as either cash flow or fair value hedges and qualify for hedge accounting treatment, while others do not qualify and are marked to market through earnings. Cash flows from derivatives used to manage commodity, foreign exchange or interest risks are classified as operating activities. See "Our Business Risks" in Management's Discussion and Analysis of Financial Condition and Results of Operations for further unaudited information on our business risks.

For cash flow hedges, changes in fair value are deferred in accumulated other comprehensive loss within common shareholders' equity until the underlying hedged item is recognized in net income. For fair value hedges, changes in fair value are recognized immediately in earnings, consistent with the underlying hedged item. Hedging transactions are limited to an underlying exposure. As a result, any change in the value of our derivative instruments would be substantially offset by an opposite change in the value of the underlying hedged items. Hedging ineffectiveness and a net earnings impact occur when the change in the value of the hedge does not offset the change in the value of the underlying hedged item. Ineffectiveness of our hedges is not material. If the derivative instrument is terminated, we continue to defer the related gain or loss and then include it as a component of the cost of the underlying hedged item. Upon determination that the underlying hedged item will not be part of an actual transaction, we recognize the related gain or loss in net income immediately.

We also use derivatives that do not qualify for hedge accounting treatment. We account for such derivatives at market value with the resulting gains and losses reflected in our income statement. We do not use derivative instruments for trading or speculative purposes. We perform assessments of our counterparty credit risk regularly, including a review of credit ratings, credit default swap rates and potential nonperformance of the counterparty. Based on our most recent assessment of our counterparty credit risk, we consider this risk to be low. In addition, we enter into derivative contracts with a variety of financial institutions that we believe are creditworthy in order to reduce our concentration of credit risk and generally settle with these financial institutions on a net basis.

Commodity Prices

We are subject to commodity price risk because our ability to recover increased costs through higher pricing may be limited in the competitive environment in which we operate. This risk is managed through the use of fixed-price purchase orders, pricing agreements, geographic diversity and derivatives. We use derivatives, with terms of no more than three years, to economically hedge price fluctuations related to a portion of our anticipated commodity purchases, primarily for natural gas, diesel fuel and aluminum. For those derivatives that qualify for hedge accounting, any ineffectiveness is recorded immediately in corporate unallocated expenses. We classify both the earnings and cash flow impact from these derivatives consistent with the underlying hedged item. During the next 12 months, we expect to reclassify net gains of $12 million related to these hedges from accumulated other comprehensive loss into net income. Derivatives used to hedge commodity price risk that do not qualify for hedge accounting are marked to market each period and reflected in our income statement.

Our open commodity derivative contracts that qualify for hedge accounting had a face value of $590 million as of December 25, 2010 and $151 million as of December 26, 2009. These contracts resulted in net unrealized gains of $46 million as of December 25, 2010 and net unrealized losses of $29 million as of December 26, 2009.

Our open commodity derivative contracts that do not qualify for hedge accounting had a face value of $266 million as of December 25, 2010 and $231 million as of December 26, 2009. These contracts resulted in net gains of $26 million in 2010 and net losses of $57 million in 2009.

Foreign Exchange

Financial statements of foreign subsidiaries are translated into U.S. dollars using period-end exchange rates for assets and liabilities and weighted-average exchange rates for revenues and expenses. Adjustments resulting from translating net assets are reported as a separate component of accumulated other comprehensive loss within common shareholders' equity as currency translation adjustment.

Our operations outside of the U.S. generate over 45% of our net revenue, with Mexico, Canada, Russia and the United Kingdom comprising approximately 20% of our net revenue. As a result, we are exposed to foreign currency risks. We also enter into derivatives, primarily forward contracts with terms of no more than two years, to manage our exposure to foreign currency transaction risk. Exchange rate gains or losses related to foreign currency transactions are recognized as transaction gains or losses in our income statement as incurred.

Our foreign currency derivatives had a total face value of $1.7 billion as of December 25, 2010 and $1.2 billion as of December 26, 2009. The contracts that qualify for hedge accounting resulted in net unrealized losses of $15 million as of December 25, 2010 and $20 million as of December 26, 2009. During the next 12 months, we expect to reclassify net losses of $14 million related to these hedges from accumulated other comprehensive loss into net income. The contracts that do not qualify for hedge accounting resulted in net losses of $6 million in 2010 and a net gain of $1 million in 2009. All losses and gains were offset by changes in the underlying hedged items, resulting in no net material impact on earnings.

Interest Rates

We centrally manage our debt and investment portfolios considering investment opportunities and risks, tax consequences and overall financing strategies. We use various interest rate derivative instruments including, but not limited to, interest rate swaps, cross-currency interest rate swaps, Treasury locks and swap locks to manage our overall interest expense and foreign exchange risk. These instruments effectively change the interest rate and currency of specific debt issuances. Certain of our fixed rate indebtedness has been swapped to floating rates. The notional amount, interest payment and maturity date of the interest rate and cross-currency swaps match the principal, interest payment and maturity date of the related debt. Our Treasury locks and swap locks are entered into to protect against unfavorable interest rate changes relating to forecasted debt transactions.

The notional amounts of the interest rate derivative instruments outstanding as of December 25, 2010 and December 26, 2009 were $9.23 billion and $5.75 billion, respectively. For those interest rate derivative instruments that qualify for cash flow hedge accounting, any ineffectiveness is recorded immediately. We classify both the earnings and cash flow impact from these interest rate derivative instruments consistent with the underlying hedged item. During the next 12 months, we expect to reclassify net losses of $13 million related to these hedges from accumulated other comprehensive loss into net income.

As of December 25, 2010, approximately 43% of total debt (including indebtedness acquired in our acquisitions of PBG and PAS), after the impact of the related interest rate derivative instruments, was exposed to variable rates compared to 57% as of December 26, 2009.

Fair Value Measurements

The fair values of our financial assets and liabilities as of December 25, 2010 and December 26, 2009 are categorized as follows:

	2010		2009	
	Assets[a]	Liabilities[a]	Assets[a]	Liabilities[a]
Available-for-sale securities[b]	$ 636	$ –	$ 71	$ –
Short-term investments — index funds[c]	$ 167	$ –	$120	$ –
Deferred compensation[d]	$ –	$559	$ –	$461
Derivatives designated as hedging instruments:				
Forward exchange contracts[e]	$ 8	$ 23	$ 11	$ 31
Interest rate derivatives[f]	284	12	177	43
Commodity contracts — other[g]	70	2	8	5
Commodity contracts — futures[h]	1	23	–	32
	$ 363	$ 60	$196	$111
Derivatives not designated as hedging instruments:				
Forward exchange contracts[e]	$ 1	$ 7	$ 4	$ 2
Interest rate derivatives[f]	6	45	–	–
Commodity contracts — other[g]	28	1	7	60
Commodity contracts — futures[h]	–	1	–	3
Prepaid forward contracts[i]	48	–	46	–
	$ 83	$ 54	$ 57	$ 65
Total derivatives at fair value	$ 446	$114	$253	$176
Total	$1,249	$673	$444	$637

(a) Financial assets are classified on our balance sheet within other assets, with the exception of short-term investments. Financial liabilities are classified on our balance sheet within other current liabilities and other liabilities. Unless specifically indicated, all financial assets and liabilities are categorized as Level 2 assets or liabilities.
(b) Based on the price of common stock. Categorized as a Level 1 asset.
(c) Based on price changes in index funds used to manage a portion of market risk arising from our deferred compensation liability. Categorized as a Level 1 asset.
(d) Based on the fair value of investments corresponding to employees' investment elections. At December 25, 2010 and December 26, 2009, $170 million and $121 million, respectively, are categorized as Level 1 liabilities. The remaining balances are categorized as Level 2 liabilities.
(e) Based on observable market transactions of spot and forward rates.
(f) Based on LIBOR and recently reported transactions in the marketplace.
(g) Based on recently reported transactions in the marketplace, primarily swap arrangements.
(h) Based on average prices on futures exchanges. Categorized as a Level 1 asset or liability.
(i) Based primarily on the price of our common stock.

The effective portion of the pre-tax (gains)/losses on our derivative instruments are categorized in the tables below.

	Fair Value/Non-designated Hedges		Cash Flow Hedges			
	Losses/(Gains) Recognized in Income Statement[a]		Losses/(Gains) Recognized in Accumulated Other Comprehensive Loss		Losses/(Gains) Reclassified from Accumulated Other Comprehensive Loss into Income Statement[b]	
	2010	2009	2010	2009	2010	2009
Forward exchange contracts	$ 6	$ (29)	$ 26	$ 75	$40	$(64)
Interest rate derivatives	(104)	206	75	32	7	–
Prepaid forward contracts	(4)	(5)	–	–	–	–
Commodity contracts	(30)	(274)	(32)	(1)	28	90
Total	$(132)	$(102)	$ 69	$106	$75	$ 26

(a) Interest rate gains/losses are included in interest expense in our income statement. All other gains/losses are included in corporate unallocated expenses.
(b) Interest rate losses are included in interest expense in our income statement. All other gains/losses are included in cost of sales in our income statement.

The carrying amounts of our cash and cash equivalents and short-term investments approximate fair value due to the short-term maturity. Short-term investments consist principally of short-term time deposits and index funds used to manage a portion of market risk arising from our deferred compensation liability. The fair value of our debt obligations as of December 25, 2010 and December 26, 2009 was $25.9 billion and $8.6 billion, respectively, based upon prices of similar instruments in the marketplace.

The above table excludes guarantees. See Note 9 for additional information on our guarantees.

Note 11　Net Income Attributable to PepsiCo per Common Share

Basic net income attributable to PepsiCo per common share is net income available for PepsiCo common shareholders divided by the weighted average of common shares outstanding during the period. Diluted net income attributable to PepsiCo per common share is calculated using the weighted average of common shares outstanding adjusted to include the effect that would occur if in-the-money employee stock options were exercised and RSUs and preferred shares were converted into common shares. Options to purchase 24.4 million shares in 2010, 39.0 million shares in 2009 and 9.8 million shares in 2008 were not included in the calculation of diluted earnings per common share because these options were out-of-the-money. Out-of-the-money options had average exercise prices of $67.26 in 2010, $61.52 in 2009 and $67.59 in 2008.

The computations of basic and diluted net income attributable to PepsiCo per common share are as follows:

	2010		2009		2008	
	Income	Shares[a]	Income	Shares[a]	Income	Shares[a]
Net income attributable to PepsiCo	$6,320		$5,946		$5,142	
Preferred shares:						
Dividends	(1)		(1)		(2)	
Redemption premium	(5)		(5)		(6)	
Net income available for PepsiCo common shareholders	$6,314	1,590	$5,940	1,558	$5,134	1,573
Basic net income attributable to PepsiCo per common share	$ 3.97		$ 3.81		$ 3.26	
Net income available for PepsiCo common shareholders	$6,314	1,590	$5,940	1,558	$5,134	1,573
Dilutive securities:						
Stock options and RSUs	–	23	–	17	–	27
ESOP convertible preferred stock	6	1	6	2	8	2
Diluted	$6,320	1,614	$5,946	1,577	$5,142	1,602
Diluted net income attributable to PepsiCo per common share	$ 3.91		$ 3.77		$ 3.21	

(a) Weighted-average common shares outstanding (in millions).

Note 12　Preferred Stock

As of December 25, 2010 and December 26, 2009, there were 3 million shares of convertible preferred stock authorized. The preferred stock was issued for an ESOP established by Quaker and these shares are redeemable for common stock by the ESOP participants. The preferred stock accrues dividends at an annual rate of $5.46 per share. At year-end 2010 and 2009, there were 803,953 preferred shares issued and 227,653 and 243,553 shares outstanding, respectively. The outstanding preferred shares had a fair value of $74 million as of December 25, 2010 and $73 million as of December 26, 2009. Each share is convertible at the option of the holder into 4.9625 shares of common stock. The preferred shares may be called by us upon written notice at $78 per share plus accrued and unpaid dividends. Quaker made the final award to its ESOP plan in June 2001.

	2010		2009		2008	
	Shares[a]	Amount	Shares[a]	Amount	Shares[a]	Amount
Preferred stock	0.8	$ 41	0.8	$ 41	0.8	$ 41
Repurchased preferred stock						
Balance, beginning of year	0.6	$145	0.5	$138	0.5	$132
Redemptions	–	5	0.1	7	–	6
Balance, end of year	0.6	$150	0.6	$145	0.5	$138

(a) In millions.

Note 13 Accumulated Other Comprehensive Loss Attributable to PepsiCo

Comprehensive income is a measure of income which includes both net income and other comprehensive income or loss. Other comprehensive income or loss results from items deferred from recognition into our income statement. Accumulated other comprehensive loss is separately presented on our balance sheet as part of common shareholders' equity. Other comprehensive income/(loss) attributable to PepsiCo was $164 million in 2010, $900 million in 2009 and $(3,793) million in 2008. The accumulated balances for each component of other comprehensive loss attributable to PepsiCo were as follows:

	2010	2009	2008
Currency translation adjustment	$(1,159)	$(1,471)	$(2,271)
Cash flow hedges, net of tax(a)	(100)	(42)	(14)
Unamortized pension and retiree medical, net of tax(b)	(2,442)	(2,328)	(2,435)
Unrealized gain on securities, net of tax	70	47	28
Other	1	–	(2)
Accumulated other comprehensive loss attributable to PepsiCo	$(3,630)	$(3,794)	$(4,694)

(a) Includes $23 million after-tax gain in 2009 and $17 million after-tax loss in 2008 for our share of our equity investees' accumulated derivative activity.
(b) Net of taxes of $1,322 million in 2010, $1,211 million in 2009 and $1,288 million in 2008. Includes $51 million decrease to the opening balance of accumulated other comprehensive loss attributable to PepsiCo in 2008 due to a change in measurement date for our pension and retiree medical plans.

Note 14 Supplemental Financial Information

	2010	2009	2008
Accounts receivable			
Trade receivables	$5,514	$4,026	
Other receivables	953	688	
	6,467	4,714	
Allowance, beginning of year	90	70	$ 69
Net amounts charged to expense	12	40	21
Deductions(a)	(37)	(21)	(16)
Other(b)	79	1	(4)
Allowance, end of year	144	90	$ 70
Net receivables	$6,323	$4,624	
Inventories(c)			
Raw materials	$1,654	$1,274	
Work-in-process	128	165	
Finished goods	1,590	1,179	
	$3,372	$2,618	

(a) Includes accounts written off.
(b) Includes adjustments related to our acquisitions of PBG and PAS, currency translation effects and other adjustments.
(c) Inventories are valued at the lower of cost or market. Cost is determined using the average, first-in, first-out (FIFO) or last-in, first-out (LIFO) methods. Approximately 8% in 2010 and 10% in 2009 of the inventory cost was computed using the LIFO method. The differences between LIFO and FIFO methods of valuing these inventories were not material.

	2010	2009
Other assets		
Noncurrent notes and accounts receivable	$ 165	$ 118
Deferred marketplace spending	203	182
Unallocated purchase price for recent acquisitions	–	143
Pension plans	121	64
Other investments(a)	653	89
Other	547	369
	$ 1,689	$ 965
Accounts payable and other current liabilities		
Accounts payable	$ 3,865	$2,881
Accrued marketplace spending	1,841	1,656
Accrued compensation and benefits	1,779	1,291
Dividends payable	766	706
Other current liabilities	2,672	1,593
	$10,923	$8,127

(a) In 2010, includes our investment in WBD of $549 million. This investment is accounted for as an available-for-sale security with any unrealized gains or losses recorded in other comprehensive income.

	2010	2009	2008
Other supplemental information			
Rent expense	$ 526	$ 412	$ 357
Interest paid	$ 1,043	$ 456	$ 359
Income taxes paid, net of refunds	$ 1,495	$1,498	$ 1,477
Acquisitions(a)			
Fair value of assets acquired	$27,665	$ 851	$ 2,907
Cash paid, net of cash acquired	(3,044)	(466)	(1,925)
Equity issued	(4,451)	–	–
Previously held equity interests in PBG and PAS	(4,293)	–	–
Liabilities and noncontrolling interests assumed	$15,877	$ 385	$ 982

(a) In 2010, amounts primarily reflect our acquisitions of PBG and PAS. During 2008, together with PBG, we jointly acquired Lebedyansky, for a total purchase price of $1.8 billion.

Note 15 Acquisitions

PBG and PAS

On August 3, 2009, we entered into a Merger Agreement (the PBG Merger Agreement) with PBG and Metro pursuant to which PBG merged with and into Metro, with Metro continuing as the surviving corporation and a wholly owned subsidiary of PepsiCo. Also on August 3, 2009, we entered into a Merger Agreement (the PAS Merger Agreement and together with the PBG Merger Agreement, the Merger Agreements) with PAS and Metro pursuant to which PAS merged with and into Metro, with Metro continuing as the surviving corporation and a wholly owned subsidiary of PepsiCo. On February 26, 2010, we acquired PBG and PAS to create a more fully integrated supply chain and go-to-market business model, improving the effectiveness and efficiency of the distribution of our brands and enhancing our revenue growth. The total purchase price was approximately $12.6 billion, which included $8.3 billion of cash and equity and the fair value of our previously held equity interests in PBG and PAS of $4.3 billion.

Under the terms of the PBG Merger Agreement, each outstanding share of common stock of PBG not held by Metro, PepsiCo or a subsidiary of PepsiCo or held by PBG as treasury stock (each, a "PBG Share") was canceled and converted into the right to receive, at the holder's election, either 0.6432 shares of common stock of PepsiCo (the "PBG Per Share Stock Consideration") or $36.50 in cash, without interest (the "PBG Cash Election Price"), subject to proration provisions which provide that an aggregate 50% of such outstanding PBG Shares were converted into the right to receive common stock of PepsiCo and an aggregate 50% of such outstanding PBG Shares were converted into the right to receive cash and each PBG Share and share of Class B common stock of PBG held by Metro, PepsiCo or a subsidiary of PepsiCo was canceled or converted to the right to receive 0.6432 shares of common stock of PepsiCo. Under the terms of the PAS Merger Agreement, each outstanding share of common stock of PAS not held by Metro, PepsiCo or a subsidiary of PepsiCo or held by PAS as treasury stock (each, a "PAS Share") was canceled and converted into the right to receive, at the holder's election, either 0.5022 shares of common stock of PepsiCo (the "PAS Per Share Stock Consideration") or $28.50 in cash, without interest (the "PAS Cash Election Price"), subject to proration provisions which provide that an aggregate 50% of such outstanding PAS Shares were converted into the right to receive common stock of PepsiCo and an aggregate 50% of such outstanding PAS Shares were converted into the right to receive cash and each PAS Share held by Metro, PepsiCo or a subsidiary of PepsiCo was canceled or converted into the right to receive 0.5022 shares of common stock of PepsiCo.

Under the terms of the applicable Merger Agreement, each PBG or PAS stock option was converted into an adjusted PepsiCo stock option to acquire a number of shares of PepsiCo common stock, determined by multiplying the number of shares of PBG or PAS common stock subject to the PBG or PAS stock option by an exchange ratio (the "Closing Exchange Ratio") equal to the closing price of a share of PBG or PAS common stock on the business day immediately before the acquisition date divided by the closing price of a share of PepsiCo common stock on the business day immediately before the acquisition date. The exercise price per share of PepsiCo common stock subject to the adjusted PepsiCo stock option is equal to the per share exercise price of PBG or PAS stock option divided by the Closing Exchange Ratio.

Under the terms of the PBG Merger Agreement, each PBG restricted stock unit (RSU) was adjusted so that its holder is entitled to receive, upon settlement, a number of shares of PepsiCo common stock equal to the number of shares of PBG common stock subject to the PBG RSU multiplied by the PBG Per Share Stock Consideration. PBG performance-based RSUs were converted into PepsiCo RSUs based on 100% target achievement, and, following conversion, remain subject to continued service of the holder. Each PBG RSU held by a non-employee director was vested and canceled at the acquisition date, and, in exchange for cancellation of the PBG RSU, the holder received the PBG Per Share Stock Consideration for each share of PBG common stock subject to the PBG RSU.

Under the terms of the PAS Merger Agreement, each cash-settled PAS RSU was canceled in exchange for a cash payment equal to the closing price of a share of PAS common stock on the business day immediately before the closing of the PAS merger for each share of PAS common stock subject to each PAS RSU. Each PAS restricted share was converted into either the PAS Per Share Stock Consideration or the PAS Cash Election Price, at the election of the holder, with the same proration procedures applicable to PAS stockholders described above.

Pursuant to the terms of PBG's executive retention arrangements, PBG equity awards granted to certain executives prior to the PBG merger vest immediately upon a qualifying termination of the executive's employment except for certain PBG executives whose equity awards vested immediately at the effective time of the PBG merger pursuant to the terms of PepsiCo's executive retention agreements. Each PAS equity award granted prior to the PAS merger vested immediately at the effective time of the PAS merger pursuant to the original terms of the awards.

Prior to the acquisitions, we had equity investments in PBG and PAS. In addition to approximately 32% of PBG's outstanding common stock that we owned at year-end 2009, we owned 100% of PBG's class B common stock and approximately 7% of the equity of Bottling Group, LLC, PBG's principal operating subsidiary. At year-end 2009, we owned approximately 43% of the outstanding common stock of PAS.

The guidance on accounting for business combinations requires that an acquirer remeasure its previously held equity interest in an acquiree at its acquisition date fair value and recognize the resulting gain or loss in earnings. Thus, in connection with our acquisitions of PBG and PAS, the carrying amounts of our previously held equity interests in PBG and PAS were revalued to fair value at the acquisition date, resulting in a gain in the first quarter of 2010 of $958 million, comprising $735 million which is non-taxable and recorded in bottling equity income and $223 million related to the reversal of deferred tax liabilities associated with these previously held equity interests.

As discussed in Note 9, in January 2010, we issued $4.25 billion of fixed and floating rate notes. A portion of the net proceeds from the issuance of these notes was used to finance our acquisitions of PBG and PAS.

Our actual stock price on February 25, 2010 (the last trading day prior to the closing of the acquisitions) was used to determine the value of stock, stock options and RSUs issued as consideration in connection with our acquisitions of PBG and PAS and thus to calculate the actual purchase price.

The table below represents the computation of the purchase price excluding assumed debt and the fair value of our previously held equity interests in PBG and PAS as of the acquisition date:

	Total Number of Shares/ Awards Issued	Total Fair Value
Payment in cash, for the remaining (not owned by PepsiCo and its subsidiaries) outstanding shares of PBG and PAS common stock and equity awards vested at consummation of merger	–	$3,813
Payment to PBG and PAS of shares of PepsiCo common stock for the remaining (not owned by PepsiCo and its subsidiaries) outstanding shares of PBG and PAS common stock and equity awards vested at consummation of merger	67	4,175
Issuance of PepsiCo equity awards (vested and unvested) to replace existing PBG and PAS equity awards	16	276
Total purchase price	83	$8,264

The following table summarizes the fair value of identifiable assets acquired and liabilities assumed in the acquisitions of PBG and PAS and the resulting goodwill as of the acquisition date:

	Acquisition Date Fair Value
Inventory	$ 1,006
Property, plant and equipment	5,574
Amortizable intangible assets	1,298
Nonamortizable intangible assets, primarily reacquired franchise rights	9,036
Other current assets and current liabilities[a]	751
Other noncurrent assets	281
Debt obligations	(8,814)
Pension and retiree medical benefits	(962)
Other noncurrent liabilities	(744)
Deferred income taxes	(3,246)
Total identifiable net assets	4,180
Goodwill	8,059
Subtotal	12,239
Fair value of acquisition of noncontrolling interest	317
Total purchase price	$12,556

(a) Includes cash and cash equivalents, accounts receivable, prepaid expenses and other current assets, accounts payable and other current liabilities.

Goodwill is calculated as the excess of the purchase price paid over the net assets recognized. The goodwill recorded as part of the acquisitions of PBG and PAS primarily reflects the value of adding PBG and PAS to PepsiCo to create a more fully integrated supply chain and go-to-market business model, as well as any intangible assets that do not qualify for separate recognition. Goodwill is not amortizable nor deductible for tax purposes. Substantially all of the goodwill is recorded in our PAB segment.

In connection with our acquisitions of PBG and PAS, we reacquired certain franchise rights which had previously provided PBG and PAS with the exclusive and perpetual rights to manufacture and/or distribute beverages for sale in specified territories. Reacquired franchise rights totaling $8.0 billion were assigned a perpetual life and are, therefore, not amortizable. Amortizable acquired franchise rights of $0.9 billion have weighted-average estimated useful lives of 56 years. Other amortizable intangible assets, primarily customer relationships, have weighted-average estimated useful lives of 20 years.

Under the guidance on accounting for business combinations, merger and integration costs are not included as components of consideration transferred but are accounted for as expenses in the period in which the costs are incurred. See Note 3 for details on the expenses incurred during 2010.

The following table presents unaudited consolidated pro forma financial information as if the closing of our acquisitions of PBG and PAS had occurred on December 27, 2009 for purposes of the financial information presented for the year ended December 25, 2010; and as if the closing of our acquisitions of PBG and PAS had occurred on December 28, 2008 for purposes of the financial information presented for the year ended December 26, 2009.

	2010	2009
Net Revenue	$59,582	$57,471
Net Income Attributable to PepsiCo	$ 5,856	$ 6,752
Net Income Attributable to PepsiCo per Common Share – Diluted	$ 3.60	$ 4.09

The unaudited consolidated pro forma financial information was prepared in accordance with the acquisition method of accounting under existing standards, and the regulations of the U.S. Securities and Exchange Commission, and is not necessarily indicative of the results of operations that would have occurred if our acquisitions of PBG and PAS had been completed on the dates indicated, nor is it indicative of the future operating results of PepsiCo.

The historical unaudited consolidated financial information has been adjusted to give effect to pro forma events that are (1) directly attributable to the acquisitions, (2) factually supportable, and (3) expected to have a continuing impact on the combined results of PepsiCo, PBG and PAS.

The unaudited pro forma results have been adjusted with respect to certain aspects of our acquisitions of PBG and PAS to reflect:
- the consummation of the acquisitions;
- consolidation of PBG and PAS which are now owned 100% by PepsiCo and the corresponding gain resulting from the remeasurement of our previously held equity interests in PBG and PAS;
- the elimination of related party transactions between PepsiCo and PBG, and PepsiCo and PAS;
- changes in assets and liabilities to record their acquisition date fair values and changes in certain expenses resulting therefrom; and
- additional indebtedness, including, but not limited to, debt issuance costs and interest expense, incurred in connection with the acquisitions.

The unaudited pro forma results do not reflect future events that may occur after the acquisitions, including, but not limited to, the anticipated realization of ongoing savings from operating synergies in subsequent periods. They also do not give effect to certain one-time charges we expect to incur in connection with the acquisitions, including, but not limited to, charges that are expected to achieve ongoing cost savings and synergies.

WBD

On February 3, 2011, we announced that we had completed the previously announced acquisition of ordinary shares, American Depositary Shares and Global Depositary Shares of WBD, a company incorporated in the Russian Federation, which represent in the aggregate approximately 66% of WBD's outstanding ordinary shares, pursuant to the purchase agreement dated December 1, 2010 between PepsiCo and certain selling shareholders of WBD for approximately $3.8 billion. The acquisition increased PepsiCo's total ownership of WBD to approximately 77%.

PepsiCo expects to make an offer in Russia (Russian Offer) on or before March 11, 2011 to acquire all of the remaining ordinary shares, in accordance with the mandatory tender offer rules of the Russian Federation. The price to be paid in the Russian Offer will be 3,883.70 Russian rubles per ordinary share. This price is $132, which is the price per share PepsiCo paid to the selling shareholders pursuant to the purchase agreement, converted to Russian rubles at the Central Bank of Russia exchange rate established for February 3, 2011. Concurrently with the Russian Offer, we expect to make an offer (U.S. Offer) to all holders of American Depositary Shares at a price per American Depositary Share equal to 970.925 Russian rubles (which is one-fourth of 3,883.70 Russian rubles since each American Depositary Share represents one-fourth of an ordinary share), without interest and less any fees, conversion expenses and applicable taxes. This amount will be converted to U.S. dollars at the spot market rate on or about the date that PepsiCo pays for the American Depositary Shares tendered in the U.S. Offer.

Additional Information

In addition to the financial statements and accompanying notes, companies are required to provide a report on internal control over financial reporting and to have an auditor's report on the financial statements. In addition, PepsiCo has provided a report indicating that financial reporting is management's responsibility. Finally, PepsiCo also provides selected financial data it believes is useful. The two required reports are further explained below.

Management's Report on Internal Control over Financial Reporting

The Sarbanes-Oxley Act requires managers of publicly traded companies to establish and maintain systems of internal control over the company's financial reporting processes. In addition, management must express its responsibility for financial reporting, and it must provide certifications regarding the accuracy of the financial statements.

Auditor's Report

All publicly held corporations, as well as many other enterprises and organizations, engage the services of independent certified public accountants for the purpose of obtaining an objective, expert report on their financial statements. Based on a comprehensive examination of the company's accounting system, accounting records, and the financial statements, the outside CPA issues the auditor's report.

The standard auditor's report identifies who and what was audited and indicates the responsibilities of management and the auditor relative to the financial statements. It states that the audit was conducted in accordance with generally accepted auditing standards and discusses the nature and limitations of the audit. It then expresses an informed opinion as to (1) the fairness of the financial statements and (2) their conformity with generally accepted accounting principles. It also expresses an opinion regarding the effectiveness of the company's internal controls. All of this additional information for PepsiCo is provided on the following pages.

Management's Responsibility for Financial Reporting

To Our Shareholders:

At PepsiCo, our actions — the actions of all our associates — are governed by our Worldwide Code of Conduct. This Code is clearly aligned with our stated values — a commitment to sustained growth, through empowered people, operating with responsibility and building trust. Both the Code and our core values enable us to operate with integrity — both within the letter and the spirit of the law. Our Code of Conduct is reinforced consistently at all levels and in all countries. We have maintained strong governance policies and practices for many years.

The management of PepsiCo is responsible for the objectivity and integrity of our consolidated financial statements. The Audit Committee of the Board of Directors has engaged independent registered public accounting firm, KPMG LLP, to audit our consolidated financial statements, and they have expressed an unqualified opinion.

We are committed to providing timely, accurate and understandable information to investors. Our commitment encompasses the following:

Maintaining strong controls over financial reporting.
Our system of internal control is based on the control criteria framework of the Committee of Sponsoring Organizations of the Treadway Commission published in their report titled *Internal Control — Integrated Framework*. The system is designed to provide reasonable assurance that transactions are executed as authorized and accurately recorded; that assets are safeguarded; and that accounting records are sufficiently reliable to permit the preparation of financial statements that conform in all material respects with accounting principles generally accepted in the U.S. We maintain disclosure controls and procedures designed to ensure that information required to be disclosed in reports under the Securities Exchange Act of 1934 is recorded, processed, summarized and reported within the specified time periods. We monitor these internal controls through self-assessments and an ongoing program of internal audits. Our internal controls are reinforced through our Worldwide Code of Conduct, which sets forth our commitment to conduct business with integrity, and within both the letter and the spirit of the law.

Exerting rigorous oversight of the business.
We continuously review our business results and strategies. This encompasses financial discipline in our strategic and daily business decisions. Our Executive Committee is actively involved — from understanding strategies and alternatives to reviewing key initiatives and financial performance. The intent is to ensure we remain objective in our assessments, constructively challenge our approach to potential business opportunities and issues, and monitor results and controls.

Engaging strong and effective Corporate Governance from our Board of Directors.
We have an active, capable and diligent Board that meets the required standards for independence, and we welcome the Board's oversight as a representative of our shareholders. Our Audit Committee is comprised of independent directors with the financial literacy, knowledge and experience to provide appropriate oversight. We review our critical accounting policies, financial reporting and internal control matters with them and encourage their direct communication with KPMG LLP, with our General Auditor, and with our General Counsel. We also have a Compliance Department to coordinate our compliance policies and practices.

Providing investors with financial results that are complete, transparent and understandable.
The consolidated financial statements and financial information included in this report are the responsibility of management. This includes preparing the financial statements in accordance with accounting principles generally accepted in the U.S., which require estimates based on management's best judgment.

PepsiCo has a strong history of doing what's right.
We realize that great companies are built on trust, strong ethical standards and principles. Our financial results are delivered from that culture of accountability, and we take responsibility for the quality and accuracy of our financial reporting.

February 18, 2011

Peter A. Bridgman
Senior Vice President and Controller

Hugh F. Johnston
Chief Financial Officer

Indra K. Nooyi
Chairman of the Board of Directors and
Chief Executive Officer

Management's Report on Internal Control Over Financial Reporting

Our management is responsible for establishing and maintaining adequate internal control over financial reporting, as such term is defined in Rule 13a-15(f) of the Exchange Act. Under the supervision and with the participation of our management, including our Chief Executive Officer and Chief Financial Officer, we conducted an evaluation of the effectiveness of our internal control over financial reporting based upon the framework in *Internal Control — Integrated Framework* issued by the Committee of Sponsoring Organizations of the Treadway Commission. Based on that evaluation, our management concluded that our internal control over financial reporting is effective as of December 25, 2010.

KPMG LLP, an independent registered public accounting firm, has audited the consolidated financial statements included in this Annual Report on Form 10-K and, as part of their audit, has issued their report, included herein, on the effectiveness of our internal control over financial reporting.

During our fourth fiscal quarter of 2010, we continued migrating certain of our financial processing systems to an enterprise-wide systems solution. These systems implementations are part of our ongoing global business transformation initiative, and we plan to continue implementing such systems throughout other parts of our businesses over the course of the next few years. In connection with these implementations and resulting business process changes, we continue to enhance the design and documentation of our internal control processes to ensure suitable controls over our financial reporting.

Except as described above, there were no changes in our internal control over financial reporting during our fourth fiscal quarter of 2010 that have materially affected, or are reasonably likely to materially affect, our internal control over financial reporting.

February 18, 2011

Peter A. Bridgman
Senior Vice President and Controller

Hugh F. Johnston
Chief Financial Officer

Indra K. Nooyi
Chairman of the Board of Directors and
Chief Executive Officer

Report of Independent Registered
Public Accounting Firm

To the Board of Directors and Shareholders of
PepsiCo, Inc.:

We have audited the accompanying Consolidated Balance
Sheets of PepsiCo, Inc. and subsidiaries ("PepsiCo, Inc." or "the
Company") as of December 25, 2010 and December 26, 2009, and
the related Consolidated Statements of Income, Cash Flows and
Equity for each of the fiscal years in the three-year period ended
December 25, 2010. We also have audited PepsiCo, Inc.'s internal
control over financial reporting as of December 25, 2010, based on
criteria established in *Internal Control — Integrated Framework*
issued by the Committee of Sponsoring Organizations of the
Treadway Commission (COSO). PepsiCo, Inc.'s management
is responsible for these consolidated financial statements, for
maintaining effective internal control over financial reporting,
and for its assessment of the effectiveness of internal control over
financial reporting, included in the accompanying Management's
Report on Internal Control over Financial Reporting. Our responsibility is to express an opinion on these consolidated financial
statements and an opinion on the Company's internal control over
financial reporting based on our audits.

We conducted our audits in accordance with the standards of
the Public Company Accounting Oversight Board (United States).
Those standards require that we plan and perform the audits to
obtain reasonable assurance about whether the financial statements are free of material misstatement and whether effective
internal control over financial reporting was maintained in all
material respects. Our audits of the consolidated financial statements included examining, on a test basis, evidence supporting
the amounts and disclosures in the financial statements, assessing the accounting principles used and significant estimates made
by management, and evaluating the overall financial statement
presentation. Our audit of internal control over financial reporting included obtaining an understanding of internal control over
financial reporting, assessing the risk that a material weakness
exists, and testing and evaluating the design and operating effectiveness of internal control based on the assessed risk. Our audits
also included performing such other procedures as we considered
necessary in the circumstances. We believe that our audits provide
a reasonable basis for our opinions.

A company's internal control over financial reporting is a
process designed to provide reasonable assurance regarding the
reliability of financial reporting and the preparation of financial
statements for external purposes in accordance with generally
accepted accounting principles. A company's internal control
over financial reporting includes those policies and procedures
that (1) pertain to the maintenance of records that, in reasonable detail, accurately and fairly reflect the transactions and
dispositions of the assets of the company; (2) provide reasonable
assurance that transactions are recorded as necessary to permit
preparation of financial statements in accordance with generally
accepted accounting principles, and that receipts and expenditures of the company are being made only in accordance with
authorizations of management and directors of the company; and
(3) provide reasonable assurance regarding prevention or timely
detection of unauthorized acquisition, use, or disposition of the
company's assets that could have a material effect on the financial statements.

Because of its inherent limitations, internal control over financial reporting may not prevent or detect misstatements. Also,
projections of any evaluation of effectiveness to future periods
are subject to the risk that controls may become inadequate
because of changes in conditions, or that the degree of compliance with the policies or procedures may deteriorate.

In our opinion, the consolidated financial statements referred
to above present fairly, in all material respects, the financial position of PepsiCo, Inc. as of December 25, 2010 and December 26,
2009, and the results of its operations and its cash flows for each
of the fiscal years in the three-year period ended December 25,
2010, in conformity with U.S. generally accepted accounting
principles. Also in our opinion, PepsiCo, Inc. maintained, in
all material respects, effective internal control over financial
reporting as of December 25, 2010, based on criteria established
in *Internal Control — Integrated Framework* issued by COSO.

KPMG LLP

New York, New York
February 18, 2011

Selected Financial Data

Quarterly (in millions except per share amounts, unaudited)	2010				2009			
	First Quarter	Second Quarter	Third Quarter	Fourth Quarter	First Quarter	Second Quarter	Third Quarter	Fourth Quarter
Net revenue	$9,368	$14,801	$15,514	$18,155	$8,263	$10,592	$11,080	$13,297
Gross profit	$4,905	$ 8,056	$ 8,506	$ 9,796	$4,519	$ 5,711	$ 5,899	$ 7,004
Mark-to-market net impact[a]	$ (46)	$ 4	$ (16)	$ (33)	$ (62)	$ (100)	$ (29)	$ (83)
Merger and integration charges[b]	$ 321	$ 155	$ 69	$ 263	–	–	$ 9	$ 52
Gain on previously held equity interests[c]	$ (958)	–	–	–				
Inventory fair value adjustments[d]	$ 281	$ 76	$ 17	$ 24				
Venezuela currency devaluation[e]	$ 120	–	–	–				
Asset write-off[f]	$ 145	–	–	–				
Foundation contribution[g]	$ 100	–	–	–				
Debt repurchase[h]	–	–	–	$ 178				
Restructuring and impairment charges[i]					$ 25	$ 11	–	–
Net income attributable to PepsiCo	$1,430	$ 1,603	$ 1,922	$ 1,365	$1,135	$ 1,660	$ 1,717	$ 1,434
Net income attributable to PepsiCo per common share – basic	$ 0.90	$ 1.00	$ 1.21	$ 0.86	$ 0.73	$ 1.06	$ 1.10	$ 0.92
Net income attributable to PepsiCo per common share – diluted	$ 0.89	$ 0.98	$ 1.19	$ 0.85	$ 0.72	$ 1.06	$ 1.09	$ 0.90
Cash dividends declared per common share	$ 0.45	$ 0.48	$ 0.48	$ 0.48	$0.425	$ 0.45	$ 0.45	$ 0.45
Stock price per share[j]								
High	$66.98	$ 67.61	$ 66.83	$ 68.11	$56.93	$ 56.95	$ 59.64	$ 64.48
Low	$58.75	$ 61.04	$ 60.32	$ 63.43	$43.78	$ 47.50	$ 52.11	$ 57.33
Close	$66.56	$ 63.56	$ 65.57	$ 65.69	$50.02	$ 53.65	$ 57.54	$ 60.96

(a) In 2010, we recognized $91 million ($58 million after-tax or $0.04 per share) of mark-to-market net gains on commodity hedges in corporate unallocated expenses. In 2009, we recognized $274 million ($173 million after-tax or $0.11 per share) of mark-to-market net gains on commodity hedges in corporate unallocated expenses.

(b) In 2010, we incurred merger and integration charges of $799 million related to our acquisitions of PBG and PAS, as well as advisory fees in connection with our acquisition of WBD. In addition, we recorded $9 million of merger-related charges, representing our share of the respective merger costs of PBG and PAS. In total, these charges had an after-tax impact of $648 million or $0.40 per share. In 2009, we recognized $50 million of merger-related charges, as well as an additional $11 million of costs in bottling equity income representing our share of the respective merger costs of PBG and PAS. In total, these costs had an after-tax impact of $44 million or $0.03 per share. See Note 3.

(c) In 2010, in connection with our acquisitions of PBG and PAS, we recorded a gain on our previously held equity interests of $958 million ($0.60 per share), comprising $735 million which is non-taxable and recorded in bottling equity income and $223 million related to the reversal of deferred tax liabilities associated with these previously held equity interests. See Note 15.

(d) In 2010, we recorded $398 million ($333 million after-tax or $0.21 per share) of incremental costs related to fair value adjustments to the acquired inventory and other related hedging contracts included in PBG's and PAS's balance sheets at the acquisition date.

(e) In 2010, we recorded a one-time $120 million net charge ($120 million after-tax or $0.07 per share) related to our change to hyperinflationary accounting for our Venezuelan businesses and the related devaluation of the bolivar.

(f) In 2010, we recorded a $145 million charge ($92 million after-tax or $0.06 per share) related to a change in scope of one release in our ongoing migration to SAP software.

(g) In 2010, we made a $100 million ($64 million after-tax or $0.04 per share) contribution to The PepsiCo Foundation Inc., in order to fund charitable and social programs over the next several years.

(h) In 2010, we paid $672 million in a cash tender offer to repurchase $500 million (aggregate principal amount) of our 7.90% senior unsecured notes maturing in 2018. As a result of this debt repurchase, we recorded a $178 million charge to interest expense ($114 million after-tax or $0.07 per share), primarily representing the premium paid in the tender offer.

(i) Restructuring and impairment charges in 2009 were $36 million ($29 million after-tax or $0.02 per share). See Note 3.

(j) Represents the composite high and low sales price and quarterly closing prices for one share of PepsiCo common stock.

THE COCA-COLA COMPANY AND SUBSIDIARIES
CONSOLIDATED STATEMENTS OF INCOME

Year Ended December 31,	**2010**	2009	2008
(In millions except per share data)			
NET OPERATING REVENUES	**$35,119**	$30,990	$31,944
Cost of goods sold	**12,693**	11,088	11,374
GROSS PROFIT	**22,426**	19,902	20,570
Selling, general and administrative expenses	**13,158**	11,358	11,774
Other operating charges	**819**	313	350
OPERATING INCOME	**8,449**	8,231	8,446
Interest income	**317**	249	333
Interest expense	**733**	355	438
Equity income (loss)—net	**1,025**	781	(874)
Other income (loss)—net	**5,185**	40	39
INCOME BEFORE INCOME TAXES	**14,243**	8,946	7,506
Income taxes	**2,384**	2,040	1,632
CONSOLIDATED NET INCOME	**11,859**	6,906	5,874
Less: Net income attributable to noncontrolling interests	**50**	82	67
NET INCOME ATTRIBUTABLE TO SHAREOWNERS OF THE COCA-COLA COMPANY	**$11,809**	$ 6,824	$ 5,807
BASIC NET INCOME PER SHARE[1]	**$ 5.12**	$ 2.95	$ 2.51
DILUTED NET INCOME PER SHARE[1]	**$ 5.06**	$ 2.93	$ 2.49
AVERAGE SHARES OUTSTANDING	**2,308**	2,314	2,315
Effect of dilutive securities	**25**	15	21
AVERAGE SHARES OUTSTANDING ASSUMING DILUTION	**2,333**	2,329	2,336

[1]Basic net income per share and diluted net income per share are calculated based on net income attributable to shareowners of The Coca-Cola Company.

Refer to Notes to Consolidated Financial Statements.

The financial information herein is reprinted with permission from The Coca-Cola Company 2010 Annual Report. The accompanying Notes are an integral part of the consolidated financial statements. The complete financial statements are available through a link at the book's companion website.

THE COCA-COLA COMPANY AND SUBSIDIARIES
CONSOLIDATED BALANCE SHEETS

December 31,	2010	2009
(In millions except par value)		
ASSETS		
CURRENT ASSETS		
Cash and cash equivalents	$ 8,517	$ 7,021
Short-term investments	2,682	2,130
TOTAL CASH, CASH EQUIVALENTS AND SHORT-TERM INVESTMENTS	11,199	9,151
Marketable securities	138	62
Trade accounts receivable, less allowances of $48 and $55, respectively	4,430	3,758
Inventories	2,650	2,354
Prepaid expenses and other assets	3,162	2,226
TOTAL CURRENT ASSETS	21,579	17,551
EQUITY METHOD INVESTMENTS	6,954	6,217
OTHER INVESTMENTS, PRINCIPALLY BOTTLING COMPANIES	631	538
OTHER ASSETS	2,121	1,976
PROPERTY, PLANT AND EQUIPMENT—net	14,727	9,561
TRADEMARKS WITH INDEFINITE LIVES	6,356	6,183
BOTTLERS' FRANCHISE RIGHTS WITH INDEFINITE LIVES	7,511	1,953
GOODWILL	11,665	4,224
OTHER INTANGIBLE ASSETS	1,377	468
TOTAL ASSETS	$72,921	$48,671
LIABILITIES AND EQUITY		
CURRENT LIABILITIES		
Accounts payable and accrued expenses	$ 8,859	$ 6,657
Loans and notes payable	8,100	6,749
Current maturities of long-term debt	1,276	51
Accrued income taxes	273	264
TOTAL CURRENT LIABILITIES	18,508	13,721
LONG-TERM DEBT	14,041	5,059
OTHER LIABILITIES	4,794	2,965
DEFERRED INCOME TAXES	4,261	1,580
THE COCA-COLA COMPANY SHAREOWNERS' EQUITY		
Common stock, $0.25 par value; Authorized—5,600 shares;		
Issued—3,520 and 3,520 shares, respectively	880	880
Capital surplus	10,057	8,537
Reinvested earnings	49,278	41,537
Accumulated other comprehensive income (loss)	(1,450)	(757)
Treasury stock, at cost—1,228 and 1,217 shares, respectively	(27,762)	(25,398)
EQUITY ATTRIBUTABLE TO SHAREOWNERS OF THE COCA-COLA COMPANY	31,003	24,799
EQUITY ATTRIBUTABLE TO NONCONTROLLING INTERESTS	314	547
TOTAL EQUITY	31,317	25,346
TOTAL LIABILITIES AND EQUITY	$72,921	$48,671

Refer to Notes to Consolidated Financial Statements.

THE COCA-COLA COMPANY AND SUBSIDIARIES
CONSOLIDATED STATEMENTS OF CASH FLOWS

Year Ended December 31,	2010	2009	2008
(In millions)			
OPERATING ACTIVITIES			
Consolidated net income	$ 11,859	$ 6,906	$ 5,874
Depreciation and amortization	1,443	1,236	1,228
Stock-based compensation expense	380	241	266
Deferred income taxes	617	353	(360)
Equity (income) loss—net of dividends	(671)	(359)	1,128
Foreign currency adjustments	151	61	(42)
Significant (gains) losses on sales of assets—net	(645)	(43)	(130)
Other significant (gains) losses—net	(4,713)	—	—
Other operating charges	264	134	209
Other items	477	221	153
Net change in operating assets and liabilities	370	(564)	(755)
Net cash provided by operating activities	9,532	8,186	7,571
INVESTING ACTIVITIES			
Purchases of short-term investments	(4,579)	(2,130)	—
Proceeds from disposals of short-term investments	4,032	—	—
Acquisitions and investments	(2,511)	(300)	(759)
Purchases of other investments	(132)	(22)	(240)
Proceeds from disposals of bottling companies and other investments	972	240	479
Purchases of property, plant and equipment	(2,215)	(1,993)	(1,968)
Proceeds from disposals of property, plant and equipment	134	104	129
Other investing activities	(106)	(48)	(4)
Net cash provided by (used in) investing activities	(4,405)	(4,149)	(2,363)
FINANCING ACTIVITIES			
Issuances of debt	15,251	14,689	4,337
Payments of debt	(13,403)	(12,326)	(4,308)
Issuances of stock	1,666	664	595
Purchases of stock for treasury	(2,961)	(1,518)	(1,079)
Dividends	(4,068)	(3,800)	(3,521)
Other financing activities	50	(2)	(9)
Net cash provided by (used in) financing activities	(3,465)	(2,293)	(3,985)
EFFECT OF EXCHANGE RATE CHANGES ON CASH AND CASH EQUIVALENTS	(166)	576	(615)
CASH AND CASH EQUIVALENTS			
Net increase (decrease) during the year	1,496	2,320	608
Balance at beginning of year	7,021	4,701	4,093
Balance at end of year	$ 8,517	$ 7,021	$ 4,701

Refer to Notes to Consolidated Financial Statements.

THE COCA-COLA COMPANY AND SUBSIDIARIES
CONSOLIDATED STATEMENTS OF SHAREOWNERS' EQUITY

Year Ended December 31,	2010	2009	2008
(In millions except per share data)			
EQUITY ATTRIBUTABLE TO SHAREOWNERS OF THE COCA-COLA COMPANY			
NUMBER OF COMMON SHARES OUTSTANDING			
Balance at beginning of year	2,303	2,312	2,318
Purchases of treasury stock	(49)	(26)	(18)
Treasury stock issued to employees exercising stock options	38	17	12
Balance at end of year	2,292	2,303	2,312
COMMON STOCK	$ 880	$ 880	$ 880
CAPITAL SURPLUS			
Balance at beginning of year	8,537	7,966	7,378
Stock issued to employees related to stock compensation plans	855	339	324
Replacement share-based awards issued in connection with an acquisition	237	—	—
Tax benefit (charge) from employees' stock option and restricted stock plans	48	(6)	(1)
Stock-based compensation	380	238	265
Balance at end of year	10,057	8,537	7,966
REINVESTED EARNINGS			
Balance at beginning of year	41,537	38,513	36,235
Cumulative effect of the adoption of new accounting guidance for pension and other postretirement plans	—	—	(8)
Net income attributable to shareowners of The Coca-Cola Company	11,809	6,824	5,807
Dividends (per share—$1.76, $1.64, and $1.52 in 2010, 2009 and 2008, respectively)	(4,068)	(3,800)	(3,521)
Balance at end of year	49,278	41,537	38,513
ACCUMULATED OTHER COMPREHENSIVE INCOME (LOSS)			
Balance at beginning of year	(757)	(2,674)	626
Net foreign currency translation adjustment	(935)	1,824	(2,285)
Net gain (loss) on derivatives	(120)	34	1
Net change in unrealized gain on available-for-sale securities	102	(52)	(44)
Net change in pension liability	260	111	(972)
Net other comprehensive income (loss)	(693)	1,917	(3,300)
Balance at end of year	(1,450)	(757)	(2,674)
TREASURY STOCK			
Balance at beginning of year	(25,398)	(24,213)	(23,375)
Stock issued to employees related to stock compensation plans	824	333	243
Purchases of treasury stock	(3,188)	(1,518)	(1,081)
Balance at end of year	(27,762)	(25,398)	(24,213)
TOTAL EQUITY ATTRIBUTABLE TO SHAREOWNERS OF THE COCA-COLA COMPANY	$31,003	$24,799	$20,472
EQUITY ATTRIBUTABLE TO NONCONTROLLING INTERESTS			
Balance at beginning of year	$ 547	$ 390	$ 342
Net income attributable to noncontrolling interests	50	82	67
Net foreign currency translation adjustment	(12)	49	(25)
Dividends paid to noncontrolling interests	(32)	(14)	(20)
Contributions by noncontrolling interests	1	40	31
Increase due to business combinations	13	—	—
Deconsolidation of certain variable interest entities	(253)	—	(5)
TOTAL EQUITY ATTRIBUTABLE TO NONCONTROLLING INTERESTS	314	547	390
COMPREHENSIVE INCOME			
Consolidated net income	$11,859	$ 6,906	$ 5,874
Consolidated net other comprehensive income (loss)	(705)	1,966	(3,325)
CONSOLIDATED COMPREHENSIVE INCOME	$11,154	$ 8,872	$ 2,549

Refer to Notes to Consolidated Financial Statements.

CONSOLIDATED INCOME STATEMENT
FOR THE YEAR ENDED 30 APRIL 2010

	Note	2010 Adjusted* results £'000	2010 Adjusting items £'000	2010 Total £'000	2009 Adjusted results £'000	2009 Adjusting items £'000	2009 Total £'000
Continuing operations							
Revenue	3	131,922	—	131,922	118,602	—	118,602
Cost of sales		(105,112)	—	(105,112)	(93,857)	—	(93,857)
Gross profit		26,810	—	26,810	24,745	—	24,745
Distribution costs		(5,495)	—	(5,495)	(4,777)	—	(4,777)
Administrative expenses:							
– other administrative expenses		(14,003)	—	(14,003)	(13,917)	—	(13,917)
– one-off items	4	—	—	—	—	(1,508)	(1,508)
– amortisation of intangible assets	14	—	(299)	(299)	—	(456)	(456)
– share-based payments	9	—	(287)	(287)	—	116	116
Operating profit		7,312	(586)	6,726	6,051	(1,848)	4,203
Interest income	8	11	—	11	47	—	47
Finance costs	8	(968)	201	(767)	(1,556)	(680)	(2,236)
Profit from continuing operations before taxation		6,355	(385)	5,970	4,542	(2,528)	2,014
Tax on profit from continuing activities	10	(1,722)	20	(1,702)	(1,241)	—	(1,241)
Net result from continuing operations		4,633	(365)	4,268	3,301	(2,528)	773
Net result from discontinued operations	11	—	—	—	—	(5,836)	(5,836)
Net result for the period		4,633	(365)	4,268	3,301	(8,364)	(5,063)
Continuing basic earnings per share (p)	12			32.6			6.6
Continuing diluted earnings per share (p)	12			32.6			6.5
Basic earnings/(loss) per share (p)	12			32.6			(42.9)
Diluted earnings/(loss) per share (p)	12			32.6			(42.6)
Adjusted basic earnings per share (p)*	12	35.4			28.0		
Adjusted diluted earnings per share (p)*	12	35.4			27.8		

* Adjusted operating profit and adjusted earnings per share are from continuing activities before one-off items, amortisation of intangible assets, share-based payments and the fair value movement on financial instruments.

The accompanying notes and accounting policies form an integral part of the financial statements.

CONSOLIDATED STATEMENT OF COMPREHENSIVE INCOME
FOR THE YEAR ENDED 30 APRIL 2010

	2010 Total £'000	2009 Total £'000
Profit/(loss) for the year	4,268	(5,063)
Other comprehensive income:		
– currency translation differences	(917)	1,404
Other comprehensive income	(917)	1,404
Total comprehensive income for the year	3,351	(3,659)
Attributable to:		
– owners of the parent	3,351	(3,659)

CONSOLIDATED BALANCE SHEET
AT 30 APRIL 2010

	Note	2010 £'000	2009 £'000
Non-current assets			
Goodwill	13	30,342	30,821
Other intangible assets	14	309	623
Property, plant and equipment	15	14,886	15,283
Deferred tax asset	21	213	198
		45,750	46,925
Current assets			
Inventories	16	16,039	14,319
Trade and other receivables	17	19,062	19,190
Cash at bank	26	4,257	5,405
		39,358	38,914
Total assets		85,108	85,839
Current liabilities			
Trade and other payables	18	(25,176)	(23,763)
Performance related contingent consideration		—	(220)
Current tax liabilities		(524)	(252)
Obligations under finance leases	19	(90)	(214)
Derivative financial instruments	30	(406)	(607)
Borrowings and overdrafts	20	(12,885)	(15,712)
		(39,081)	(40,768)
Net current assets/(liabilities)		277	(1,854)
Non-current liabilities			
Performance related contingent consideration		(300)	(300)
Deferred tax liabilities	21	(1,605)	(1,575)
Obligations under finance leases	19	(77)	(167)
Borrowings and overdrafts	20	(2,290)	(4,676)
		(4,272)	(6,718)
Total liabilities		(43,353)	(47,486)
Net assets		41,755	38,353
Equity			
Share capital	22	1,324	1,324
Share premium account	23	28,266	28,252
Merger reserve		3,411	3,411
Equity reserve	24	2,089	2,719
Retained earnings	24	6,665	2,647
Total equity attributable to equity holders of the parent		41,755	38,353

The financial statements were approved by the Board for issue on 21 July 2010.

IAN BLACKBURN   **MARK STOTT**
CHIEF EXECUTIVE   **GROUP FINANCE DIRECTOR**
21 July 2010

CONSOLIDATED CASH FLOW STATEMENT
FOR THE YEAR ENDED 30 APRIL 2010

	Note	2010 £'000	2009 £'000
Cash flow from operating activities			
Profit from continuing operations before taxation		5,970	2,014
Finance costs		767	2,236
Interest income		(11)	(47)
Share-based payments		287	(116)
Depreciation	15	2,337	2,346
(Profit)/loss on sale of plant and equipment		(113)	22
Amortisation of intangible assets		299	457
One-off items		—	1,388
Net movement in working capital		(179)	(2,469)
(Increase) in inventories		(1,720)	(1,299)
Decrease/(increase) in receivables		128	(4,504)
Increase in payables		1,413	3,334
Cash flow from continuing operations		9,357	5,831
Cash flow from discontinued operations		—	(1,002)
Total cash flow from operations		9,357	4,829
Net interest paid	8	(957)	(1,510)
Tax paid		(1,415)	(782)
Cash generated from activities in continuing operations		6,985	3,539
Cash flow generated from operating activities in discontinued operations		—	(1,002)
Total cash flow from operating activities		6,985	2,537
Cash flow from investing activities			
Purchase of property, plant and equipment		(2,098)	(3,847)
Proceeds from sale of plant and equipment		259	42
Disposal of subsidiary	11	—	(220)
Total cash impact of acquisitions		(220)	(879)
Contingent consideration payment		(220)	(879)
Net borrowings assumed on acquisition		—	—
Net cash flow from investing activities		(2,059)	(4,904)
Cash flow from financing activities			
Net proceeds from issue of ordinary share capital		14	1,976
Purchase of own shares		(250)	(149)
Repayment of borrowings		(2,545)	(3,536)
Finance lease repayments		(214)	(457)
Net cash flow from financing activities		(2,995)	(2,166)
Net increase/(decrease) in cash and cash equivalents		1,931	(4,533)
Cash and cash equivalents at beginning of the year		(8,127)	(3,331)
Effect of foreign exchange rate movements		(412)	(263)
Cash and cash equivalents at end of the year		(6,608)	(8,127)
Cash and cash equivalents comprise:			
Cash at bank	26	4,257	5,405
Bank overdraft	26	(10,865)	(13,532)
		(6,608)	(8,127)

CONSOLIDATED STATEMENT OF CHANGES IN EQUITY
FOR THE YEAR ENDED 30 APRIL 2010

	Attributable to equity holders of the parent					
	Share capital £'000	Share premium account £'000	Merger reserve £'000	Equity reserve £'000	Retained earnings £'000	Total £'000
Balance at 1 May 2008	1,151	26,449	3,411	1,431	7,859	40,301
Loss for the year	—	—	—	—	(5,063)	(5,063)
Exchange gain on translation of foreign operation	—	—	—	1,404	—	1,404
Issue of new ordinary shares	173	1,803	—	—	—	1,976
Purchase of own shares	—	—	—	—	(149)	(149)
Prior year share-based payment reversal	—	—	—	(116)	—	(116)
Balance at 30 April 2009	1,324	28,252	3,411	2,719	2,647	38,353
Profit for the year	—	—	—	—	4,268	4,268
Exchange (loss) on translation of foreign operations	—	—	—	(917)	—	(917)
Issue of new ordinary shares	—	14	—	—	—	14
Purchase of own shares	—	—	—	—	(250)	(250)
Current year share-based payment charge	—	—	—	287	—	287
Balance at 30 April 2010	**1,324**	**28,266**	**3,411**	**2,089**	**6,665**	**41,755**

Appendix D

Time Value of Money

Learning Objectives

After studying this appendix, you should be able to:

1 Distinguish between simple and compound interest.

2 Solve for future value of a single amount.

3 Solve for future value of an annuity.

4 Identify the variables fundamental to solving present value problems.

5 Solve for present value of a single amount.

6 Solve for present value of an annuity.

7 Compute the present value of notes and bonds.

8 Compute the present values in capital budgeting situations.

9 Use a financial calculator to solve time value of money problems.

Would you rather receive $1,000 today or a year from now? You should prefer to receive the $1,000 today because you can invest the $1,000 and earn interest on it. As a result, you will have more than $1,000 a year from now. What this example illustrates is the concept of the **time value of money**. Everyone prefers to receive money today rather than in the future because of the interest factor.

Nature of Interest

Interest is payment for the use of another person's money. It is the difference between the amount borrowed or invested (called the **principal**) and the amount repaid or collected. The amount of interest to be paid or collected is usually stated as a rate over a specific period of time. The rate of interest is generally stated as an annual rate.

The amount of interest involved in any financing transaction is based on three elements:

1. Principal (p): The original amount borrowed or invested.

2. Interest Rate (i): An annual percentage of the principal.

3. Time (n): The number of years that the principal is borrowed or invested.

> **LEARNING OBJECTIVE 1**
>
> **Distinguish between simple and compound interest.**

Simple Interest

Simple interest is computed on the principal amount only. It is the return on the principal for one period. Simple interest is usually expressed as shown in Illustration D-1.

$$\text{Interest} = \underset{p}{\text{Principal}} \times \underset{i}{\text{Rate}} \times \underset{n}{\text{Time}}$$

For example, if you borrowed $5,000 for 2 years at a simple interest rate of 12% annually, you would pay $1,200 in total interest, computed as follows.

$$\begin{aligned}\text{Interest} &= p \times i \times n \\ &= \$5{,}000 \times .12 \times 2 \\ &= \$1{,}200\end{aligned}$$

Illustration D-1
Interest computation

Compound Interest

Compound interest is computed on principal **and** on any interest earned that has not been paid or withdrawn. It is the return on (or growth of) the principal for two or more time periods. Compounding computes interest not only on the principal but also on the interest earned to date on that principal, assuming the interest is left on deposit.

To illustrate the difference between simple and compound interest, assume that you deposit $1,000 in Bank Two, where it will earn simple interest of 9% per year, and you deposit another $1,000 in Citizens Bank, where it will earn compound interest of 9% per year compounded annually. Also assume that in both cases you will not withdraw any cash until three years from the date of deposit. Illustration D-2 shows the computation of interest to be received and the accumulated year-end balances.

Illustration D-2
Simple versus compound interest

Bank Two				**Citizens Bank**		
Simple Interest Calculation	Simple Interest	Accumulated Year-End Balance		Compound Interest Calculation	Compound Interest	Accumulated Year-End Balance
Year 1 $1,000.00 × 9%	$ 90.00	$1,090.00		Year 1 $1,000.00 × 9%	$ 90.00	$1,090.00
Year 2 $1,000.00 × 9%	90.00	$1,180.00		Year 2 $1,090.00 × 9%	98.10	$1,188.10
Year 3 $1,000.00 × 9%	90.00	$1,270.00		Year 3 $1,188.10 × 9%	106.93	$1,295.03
	$ 270.00				$ 295.03	

$25.03 Difference

Note in Illustration D-2 that simple interest uses the initial principal of $1,000 to compute the interest in all three years. Compound interest uses the accumulated balance (principal plus interest to date) at each year-end to compute interest in the succeeding year—which explains why your compound interest account is larger.

Obviously, if you had a choice between investing your money at simple interest or at compound interest, you would choose compound interest, all other things—especially risk—being equal. In the example, compounding provides $25.03 of additional interest income. For practical purposes, compounding assumes that unpaid interest earned becomes a part of the principal, and the accumulated balance at the end of each year becomes the new principal on which interest is earned during the next year.

Illustration D-2 indicates that you should invest your money at the bank that compounds interest. Most business situations use compound interest. Simple interest is generally applicable only to short-term situations of one year or less.

Future Value Concepts

LEARNING OBJECTIVE 2

Solve for future value of a single amount.

Future Value of a Single Amount

The **future value of a single amount** is the value at a future date of a given amount invested, assuming compound interest. For example, in Illustration D-2, $1,295.03 is the future value of the $1,000 investment earning 9% for three years. The $1,295.03 could be determined more easily by using the following formula.

$$FV = p \times (1 + i)^n$$

where:

FV = future value of a single amount
p = principal (or present value; the value today)
i = interest rate for one period
n = number of periods

The $1,295.03 is computed as follows.

$$
\begin{aligned}
FV &= \quad p \quad \times (1 + i)^n \\
&= \$1,000 \times (1 + .09)^3 \\
&= \$1,000 \times 1.29503 \\
&= \$1,295.03
\end{aligned}
$$

The 1.29503 is computed by multiplying (1.09 × 1.09 × 1.09). The amounts in this example can be depicted in the time diagram shown in Illustration D-4.

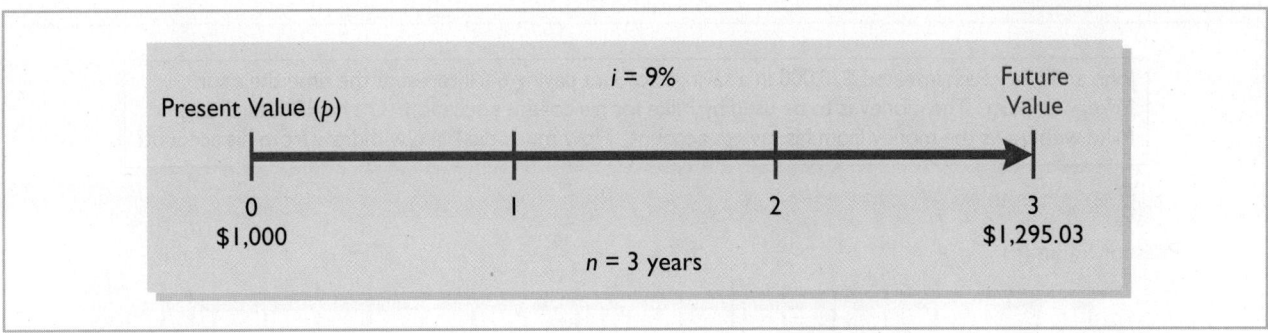

Another method used to compute the future value of a single amount involves a compound interest table. This table shows the future value of 1 for n periods. Table 1 on the next page is such a table.

In Table 1, n is the number of compounding periods, the percentages are the periodic interest rates, and the 5-digit decimal numbers in the respective columns are the future value of 1 factors. In using Table 1, you would multiply the principal amount by the future value factor for the specified number of periods and interest rate. For example, the future value factor for two periods at 9% is 1.18810. Multiplying this factor by $1,000 equals $1,188.10—which is the accumulated balance at the end of year 2 in the Citizens Bank example in Illustration D-2. The $1,295.03 accumulated balance at the end of the third year can be calculated from Table 1 by multiplying the future value factor for three periods (1.29503) by the $1,000.

The demonstration problem in Illustration D-5 (page D-4) shows how to use Table 1.

TABLE 1   Future Value of 1

(n) Periods	4%	5%	6%	7%	8%	9%	10%	11%	12%	15%
0	1.00000	1.00000	1.00000	1.00000	1.00000	1.00000	1.00000	1.00000	1.00000	1.00000
1	1.04000	1.05000	1.06000	1.07000	1.08000	1.09000	1.10000	1.11000	1.12000	1.15000
2	1.08160	1.10250	1.12360	1.14490	1.16640	1.18810	1.21000	1.23210	1.25440	1.32250
3	1.12486	1.15763	1.19102	1.22504	1.25971	1.29503	1.33100	1.36763	1.40493	1.52088
4	1.16986	1.21551	1.26248	1.31080	1.36049	1.41158	1.46410	1.51807	1.57352	1.74901
5	1.21665	1.27628	1.33823	1.40255	1.46933	1.53862	1.61051	1.68506	1.76234	2.01136
6	1.26532	1.34010	1.41852	1.50073	1.58687	1.67710	1.77156	1.87041	1.97382	2.31306
7	1.31593	1.40710	1.50363	1.60578	1.71382	1.82804	1.94872	2.07616	2.21068	2.66002
8	1.36857	1.47746	1.59385	1.71819	1.85093	1.99256	2.14359	2.30454	2.47596	3.05902
9	1.42331	1.55133	1.68948	1.83846	1.99900	2.17189	2.35795	2.55803	2.77308	3.51788
10	1.48024	1.62889	1.79085	1.96715	2.15892	2.36736	2.59374	2.83942	3.10585	4.04556
11	1.53945	1.71034	1.89830	2.10485	2.33164	2.58043	2.85312	3.15176	3.47855	4.65239
12	1.60103	1.79586	2.01220	2.25219	2.51817	2.81267	3.13843	3.49845	3.89598	5.35025
13	1.66507	1.88565	2.13293	2.40985	2.71962	3.06581	3.45227	3.88328	4.36349	6.15279
14	1.73168	1.97993	2.26090	2.57853	2.93719	3.34173	3.79750	4.31044	4.88711	7.07571
15	1.80094	2.07893	2.39656	2.75903	3.17217	3.64248	4.17725	4.78459	5.47357	8.13706
16	1.87298	2.18287	2.54035	2.95216	3.42594	3.97031	4.59497	5.31089	6.13039	9.35762
17	1.94790	2.29202	2.69277	3.15882	3.70002	4.32763	5.05447	5.89509	6.86604	10.76126
18	2.02582	2.40662	2.85434	3.37993	3.99602	4.71712	5.55992	6.54355	7.68997	12.37545
19	2.10685	2.52695	3.02560	3.61653	4.31570	5.14166	6.11591	7.26334	8.61276	14.23177
20	2.19112	2.65330	3.20714	3.86968	4.66096	5.60441	6.72750	8.06231	9.64629	16.36654

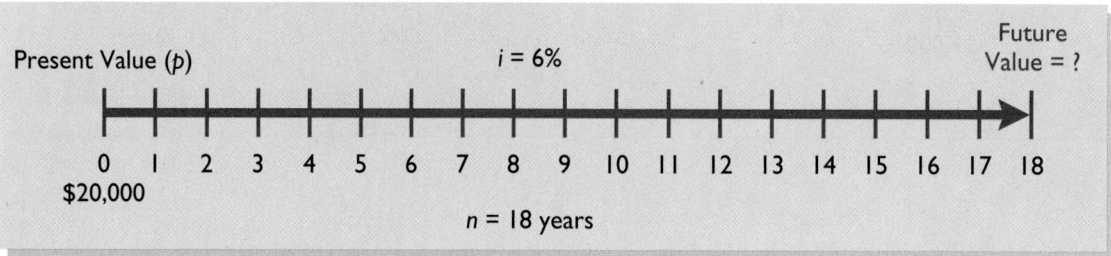

John and Mary Rich invested $20,000 in a savings account paying 6% interest at the time their son, Mike, was born. The money is to be used by Mike for his college education. On his 18th birthday, Mike withdraws the money from his savings account. How much did Mike withdraw from his account?

Present Value (p)   i = 6%   Future Value = ?

0 1 2 3 4 5 6 7 8 9 10 11 12 13 14 15 16 17 18
$20,000

n = 18 years

Answer: The future value factor from Table 1 is 2.85434 (18 periods at 6%). The future value of $20,000 earning 6% per year for 18 years is **$57,086.80** ($20,000 × 2.85434).

Illustration D-5
Demonstration problem—
Using Table 1 for *FV* of 1

LEARNING OBJECTIVE   3

Solve for future value of an annuity.

Future Value of an Annuity

The preceding discussion involved the accumulation of only a single principal sum. Individuals and businesses frequently encounter situations in which a **series** of equal dollar amounts are to be paid or received at evenly spaced time intervals (periodically), such as loans or lease (rental) contracts. A series of payments or receipts of equal dollar amounts is referred to as an **annuity**.

The **future value of an annuity** is the sum of all the payments (receipts) plus the accumulated compound interest on them. In computing the future value of an annuity, it is necessary to know (1) the interest rate, (2) the number of payments (receipts), and (3) the amount of the periodic payments (receipts).

To illustrate the computation of the future value of an annuity, assume that you invest $2,000 at the end of each year for three years at 5% interest compounded annually. This situation is depicted in the time diagram in Illustration D-6.

Illustration D-6
Time diagram for a three-year annuity

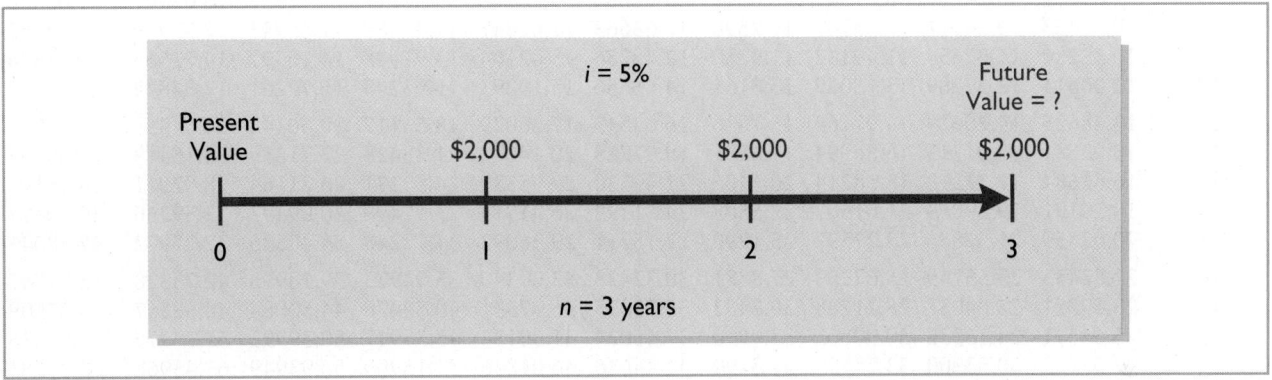

The $2,000 invested at the end of year 1 will earn interest for two years (years 2 and 3), and the $2,000 invested at the end of year 2 will earn interest for one year (year 3). However, the last $2,000 investment (made at the end of year 3) will not earn any interest. The future value of these periodic payments could be computed using the future value factors from Table 1, as shown in Illustration D-7.

Illustration D-7
Future value of periodic payment computation

Invested at End of Year	Number of Compounding Periods	Amount Invested	×	Future Value of 1 Factor at 5%	=	Future Value
1	2	$2,000	×	1.10250		$ 2,205
2	1	$2,000	×	1.05000		2,100
3	0	$2,000	×	1.00000		2,000
				3.15250		**$6,305**

The first $2,000 investment is multiplied by the future value factor for two periods (1.1025) because two years' interest will accumulate on it (in years 2 and 3). The second $2,000 investment will earn only one year's interest (in year 3) and therefore is multiplied by the future value factor for one year (1.0500). The final $2,000 investment is made at the end of the third year and will not earn any interest. Thus $n = 0$ and the future value factor is 1.00000. Consequently, the future value of the last $2,000 invested is only $2,000 since it does not accumulate any interest.

Calculating the future value of each individual cash flow is required when the periodic payments or receipts are not equal in each period. However, when the periodic payments (receipts) are **the same in each period**, the future value can be computed by using a future value of an annuity of 1 table. Table 2 (page D-6) is such a table.

TABLE 2 **Future Value of an Annuity of 1**

(n) Payments	4%	5%	6%	7%	8%	9%	10%	11%	12%	15%
1	1.00000	1.00000	1.00000	1.0000	1.00000	1.00000	1.00000	1.00000	1.00000	1.00000
2	2.04000	2.05000	2.06000	2.0700	2.08000	2.09000	2.10000	2.11000	2.12000	2.15000
3	3.12160	3.15250	3.18360	3.2149	3.24640	3.27810	3.31000	3.34210	3.37440	3.47250
4	4.24646	4.31013	4.37462	4.4399	4.50611	4.57313	4.64100	4.70973	4.77933	4.99338
5	5.41632	5.52563	5.63709	5.7507	5.86660	5.98471	6.10510	6.22780	6.35285	6.74238
6	6.63298	6.80191	6.97532	7.1533	7.33592	7.52334	7.71561	7.91286	8.11519	8.75374
7	7.89829	8.14201	8.39384	8.6540	8.92280	9.20044	9.48717	9.78327	10.08901	11.06680
8	9.21423	9.54911	9.89747	10.2598	10.63663	11.02847	11.43589	11.85943	12.29969	13.72682
9	10.58280	11.02656	11.49132	11.9780	12.48756	13.02104	13.57948	14.16397	14.77566	16.78584
10	12.00611	12.57789	13.18079	13.8164	14.48656	15.19293	15.93743	16.72201	17.54874	20.30372
11	13.48635	14.20679	14.97164	15.7836	16.64549	17.56029	18.53117	19.56143	20.65458	24.34928
12	15.02581	15.91713	16.86994	17.8885	18.97713	20.14072	21.38428	22.71319	24.13313	29.00167
13	16.62684	17.71298	18.88214	20.1406	21.49530	22.95339	24.52271	26.21164	28.02911	34.35192
14	18.29191	19.59863	21.01507	22.5505	24.21492	26.01919	27.97498	30.09492	32.39260	40.50471
15	20.02359	21.57856	23.27597	25.1290	27.15211	29.36092	31.77248	34.40536	37.27972	47.58041
16	21.82453	23.65749	25.67253	27.8881	30.32428	33.00340	35.94973	39.18995	42.75328	55.71747
17	23.69751	25.84037	28.21288	30.8402	33.75023	36.97351	40.54470	44.50084	48.88367	65.07509
18	25.64541	28.13238	30.90565	33.9990	37.45024	41.30134	45.59917	50.39593	55.74972	75.83636
19	27.67123	30.53900	33.75999	37.3790	41.44626	46.01846	51.15909	56.93949	63.43968	88.21181
20	29.77808	33.06595	36.78559	40.9955	45.76196	51.16012	57.27500	64.20283	72.05244	102.44358

Table 2 shows the future value of 1 to be received periodically for a given number of payments. It assumes that each payment is made at the **end** of each period. We can see from Table 2 that the future value of an annuity of 1 factor for three payments at 5% is 3.15250. The future value factor is the total of the three individual future value factors was shown in Illustration D-7. Multiplying this amount by the annual investment of $2,000 produces a future value of $6,305.

The demonstration problem in Illustration D-8 shows how to use Table 2.

Illustration D-8

Demonstration problem— Using Table 2 for *FV* of an annuity of 1

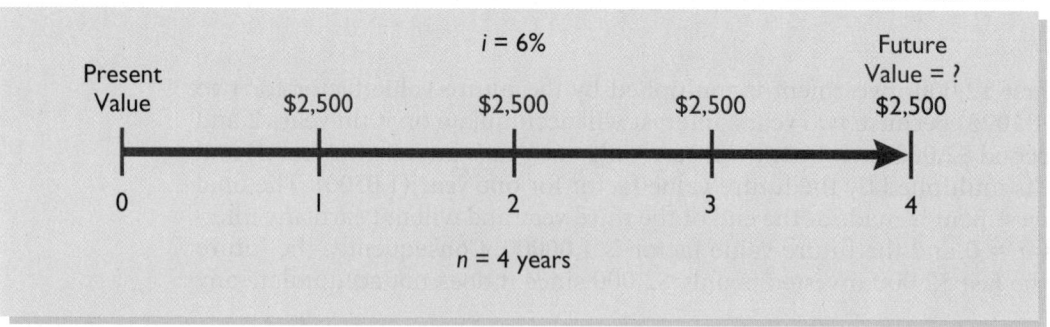

John and Char Lewis' daughter, Debra, has just started high school. They decide to start a college fund for her and will invest $2,500 in a savings account at the end of each year she is in high school (4 payments total). The account will earn 6% interest compounded annually. How much will be in the college fund at the time Debra graduates from high school?

Answer: The future value factor from Table 2 is 4.37462 (4 payments at 6%). The future value of $2,500 invested each year for 4 years at 6% interest is **$10,936.55** ($2,500 × 4.37462).

Present Value Concepts

Present Value Variables

The **present value** is the value now of a given amount to be paid or received in the future, assuming compound interest. The present value, like the future value, is based on three variables: (1) the dollar amount to be received (future amount), (2) the length of time until the amount is received (number of periods), and (3) the interest rate (the discount rate). The process of determining the present value is referred to as **discounting the future amount**.

Present value computations are used in measuring many items. For example, the present value of principal and interest payments is used to determine the market price of a bond. Determining the amount to be reported for notes payable and lease liabilities also involves present value computations. In addition, capital budgeting and other investment proposals are evaluated using present value computations. Finally, all rate of return and internal rate of return computations involve present value techniques.

Present Value of a Single Amount

To illustrate present value, assume that you want to invest a sum of money today that will provide $1,000 at the end of one year. What amount would you need to invest today to have $1,000 one year from now? If you want a 10% rate of return, the investment or present value is $909.09 ($1,000 ÷ 1.10). The formula for calculating present value is shown in Illustration D-9.

$$\text{Present Value} = \text{Future Value} \div (1 + i)^n$$

Illustration D-9
Formula for present value

The computation of $1,000 discounted at 10% for one year is as follows.

$$
\begin{aligned}
PV &= FV \div (1 + i)^n \\
&= \$1{,}000 \div (1 + .10)^1 \\
&= \$1{,}000 \div 1.10 \\
&= \$909.09
\end{aligned}
$$

The future amount ($1,000), the discount rate (10%), and the number of periods (1) are known. The variables in this situation can be depicted in the time diagram in Illustration D-10.

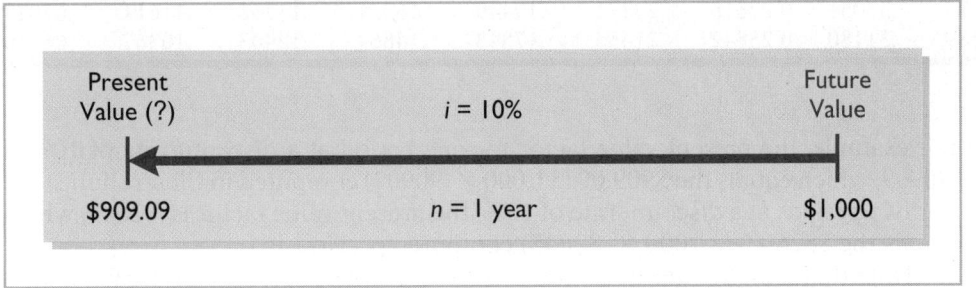

Illustration D-10
Finding present value if discounted for one period

If the single amount of $1,000 is to be received **in two years** and discounted at 10% [$PV = \$1{,}000 \div (1 + .10)^2$], its present value is $826.45 [($1,000 ÷ 1.21), depicted as shown in Illustration D-11 on the next page.

Illustration D-11
Finding present value if
discounted for two periods

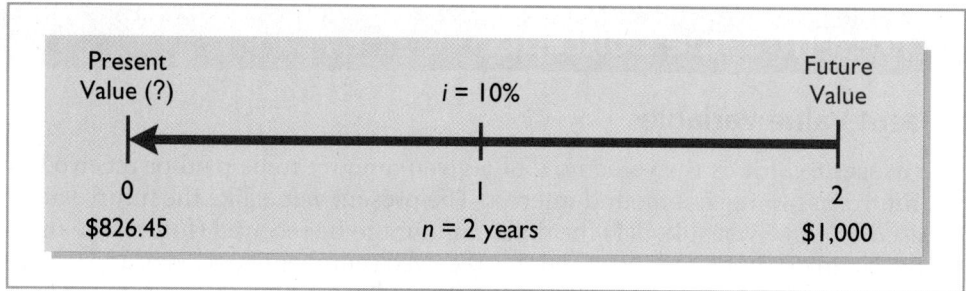

The present value of 1 may also be determined through tables that show the present value of 1 for *n* periods. In Table 3, below, *n* is the number of discounting periods involved. The percentages are the periodic interest rates or discount rates, and the 5-digit decimal numbers in the respective columns are the present value of 1 factors.

When using Table 3, the future value is multiplied by the present value factor specified at the intersection of the number of periods and the discount rate.

TABLE 3   Present Value of 1

(*n*) Periods	4%	5%	6%	7%	8%	9%	10%	11%	12%	15%
1	.96154	.95238	.94340	0.93458	.92593	.91743	.90909	.90090	.89286	.86957
2	.92456	.90703	.89000	0.87344	.85734	.84168	.82645	.81162	.79719	.75614
3	.88900	.86384	.83962	0.81630	.79383	.77218	.75132	.73119	.71178	.65752
4	.85480	.82270	.79209	0.76290	.73503	.70843	.68301	.65873	.63552	.57175
5	.82193	.78353	.74726	0.71299	.68058	.64993	.62092	.59345	.56743	.49718
6	.79031	.74622	.70496	0.66634	.63017	.59627	.56447	.53464	.50663	.43233
7	.75992	.71068	.66506	0.62275	.58349	.54703	.51316	.48166	.45235	.37594
8	.73069	.67684	.62741	0.58201	.54027	.50187	.46651	.43393	.40388	.32690
9	.70259	.64461	.59190	0.54393	.50025	.46043	.42410	.39092	.36061	.28426
10	.67556	.61391	.55839	0.50835	.46319	.42241	.38554	.35218	.32197	.24719
11	.64958	.58468	.52679	0.47509	.42888	.38753	.35049	.31728	.28748	.21494
12	.62460	.55684	.49697	0.44401	.39711	.35554	.31863	.28584	.25668	.18691
13	.60057	.53032	.46884	0.41496	.36770	.32618	.28966	.25751	.22917	.16253
14	.57748	.50507	.44230	0.38782	.34046	.29925	.26333	.23199	.20462	.14133
15	.55526	.48102	.41727	0.36245	.31524	.27454	.23939	.20900	.18270	.12289
16	.53391	.45811	.39365	0.33873	.29189	.25187	.21763	.18829	.16312	.10687
17	.51337	.43630	.37136	0.31657	.27027	.23107	.19785	.16963	.14564	.09293
18	.49363	.41552	.35034	0.29586	.25025	.21199	.17986	.15282	.13004	.08081
19	.47464	.39573	.33051	0.27615	.23171	.19449	.16351	.13768	.11611	.07027
20	.45639	.37689	.31180	0.25842	.21455	.17843	.14864	.12403	.10367	.06110

For example, the present value factor for one period at a discount rate of 10% is .90909, which equals the $909.09 ($1,000 × .90909) computed in Illustration D-10. For two periods at a discount rate of 10%, the present value factor is .82645, which equals the $826.45 ($1,000 × .82645) computed previously.

Note that a higher discount rate produces a smaller present value. For example, using a 15% discount rate, the present value of $1,000 due one year from now is $869.57, versus $909.09 at 10%. Also note that the further removed from the present the future value is, the smaller the present value. For example, using the same discount rate of 10%, the present value of $1,000 due in **five years** is $620.92. The present value of $1,000 due in **one year** is $909.09, a difference of $288.17.

The following two demonstration problems (Illustrations D-12 and D-13) illustrate how to use Table 3.

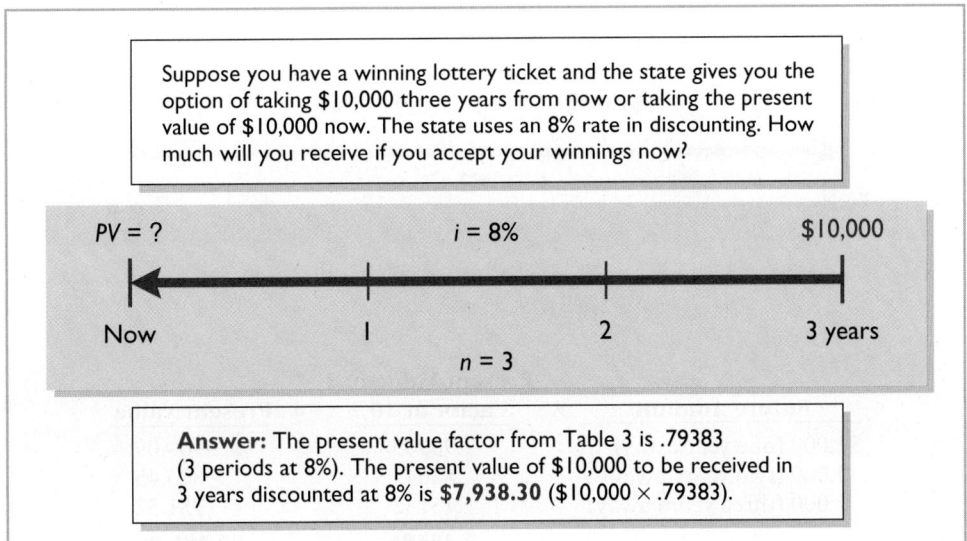

Illustration D-12
Demonstration problem—
Using Table 3 for *PV* of 1

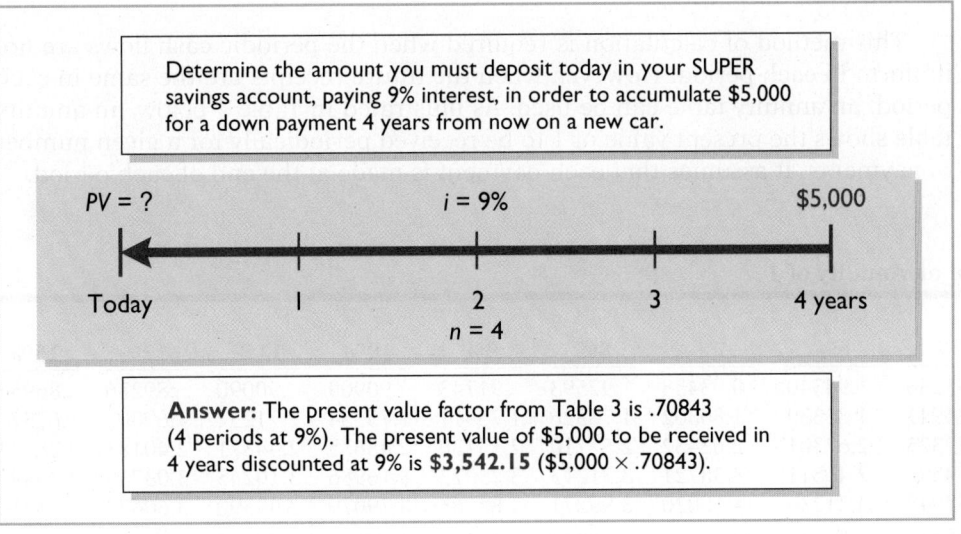

Illustration D-13
Demonstration problem—
Using Table 3 for *PV* of 1

Present Value of an Annuity

The preceding discussion involved the discounting of only a single future amount. Businesses and individuals frequently engage in transactions in which a series of equal dollar amounts are to be received or paid at evenly spaced time intervals (periodically). Examples of a series of periodic receipts or payments are loan agreements, installment sales, mortgage notes, lease (rental) contracts, and pension obligations. As discussed earlier, these periodic receipts or payments are **annuities**.

The **present value of an annuity** is the value now of a series of future receipts or payments, discounted assuming compound interest. In computing the present value of an annuity, it is necessary to know (1) the discount rate, (2) the number of payments (receipts), and (3) the amount of the periodic payments or receipts. To illustrate the computation of the present value of an annuity, assume that you

LEARNING OBJECTIVE   6

Solve for present value of an annuity.

will receive $1,000 cash annually for three years at a time when the discount rate is 10%. This situation is depicted in the time diagram in Illustration D-14. Illustration D-15 shows the computation of its present value in this situation.

Illustration D-14
Time diagram for a three-year annuity

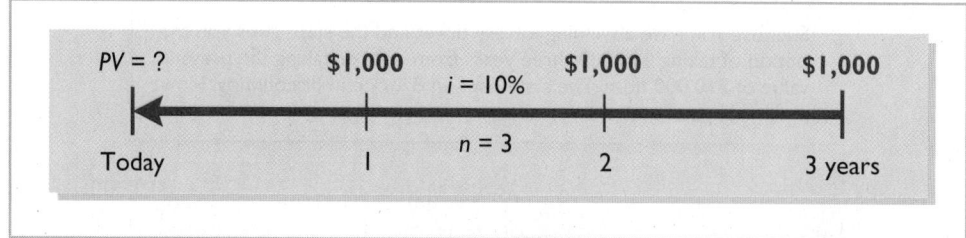

Illustration D-15
Present value of a series of future amounts computation

Future Amount	×	Present Value of 1 Factor at 10%	=	Present Value
$1,000 (one year away)		.90909		$ 909.09
1,000 (two years away)		.82645		826.45
1,000 (three years away)		.75132		751.32
		2.48686		**$2,486.86**

This method of calculation is required when the periodic cash flows are not uniform in each period. However, when the future receipts are the same in each period, an annuity table can be used. As illustrated in Table 4 below, an annuity table shows the present value of 1 to be received periodically for a given number of payments. It assumes that each payment is made at the end of each period.

TABLE 4   Present Value of an Annuity of 1

(n) Payments	4%	5%	6%	7%	8%	9%	10%	11%	12%	15%
1	.96154	.95238	.94340	0.93458	.92593	.91743	.90909	.90090	.89286	.86957
2	1.88609	1.85941	1.83339	1.80802	1.78326	1.75911	1.73554	1.71252	1.69005	1.62571
3	2.77509	2.72325	2.67301	2.62432	2.57710	2.53130	2.48685	2.44371	2.40183	2.28323
4	3.62990	3.54595	3.46511	3.38721	3.31213	3.23972	3.16986	3.10245	3.03735	2.85498
5	4.45182	4.32948	4.21236	4.10020	3.99271	3.88965	3.79079	3.69590	3.60478	3.35216
6	5.24214	5.07569	4.91732	4.76654	4.62288	4.48592	4.35526	4.23054	4.11141	3.78448
7	6.00205	5.78637	5.58238	5.38929	5.20637	5.03295	4.86842	4.71220	4.56376	4.16042
8	6.73274	6.46321	6.20979	5.97130	5.74664	5.53482	5.33493	5.14612	4.96764	4.48732
9	7.43533	7.10782	6.80169	6.51523	6.24689	5.99525	5.75902	5.53705	5.32825	4.77158
10	8.11090	7.72173	7.36009	7.02358	6.71008	6.41766	6.14457	5.88923	5.65022	5.01877
11	8.76048	8.30641	7.88687	7.49867	7.13896	6.80519	6.49506	6.20652	5.93770	5.23371
12	9.38507	8.86325	8.38384	7.94269	7.53608	7.16073	6.81369	6.49236	6.19437	5.42062
13	9.98565	9.39357	8.85268	8.35765	7.90378	7.48690	7.10336	6.74987	6.42355	5.58315
14	10.56312	9.89864	9.29498	8.74547	8.24424	7.78615	7.36669	6.98187	6.62817	5.72448
15	11.11839	10.37966	9.71225	9.10791	8.55948	8.06069	7.60608	7.19087	6.81086	5.84737
16	11.65230	10.83777	10.10590	9.44665	8.85137	8.31256	7.82371	7.37916	6.97399	5.95424
17	12.16567	11.27407	10.47726	9.76322	9.12164	8.54363	8.02155	7.54879	7.11963	6.04716
18	12.65930	11.68959	10.82760	10.05909	9.37189	8.75563	8.20141	7.70162	7.24967	6.12797
19	13.13394	12.08532	11.15812	10.33560	9.60360	8.95012	8.36492	7.83929	7.36578	6.19823
20	13.59033	12.46221	11.46992	10.59401	9.81815	9.12855	8.51356	7.96333	7.46944	6.25933

Table 4 shows that the present value of an annuity of 1 factor for three payments at 10% is 2.48685.[1] This present value factor is the total of the three individual present value factors, as shown in Illustration D-15. Applying this amount to the annual cash flow of $1,000 produces a present value of $2,486.85.

The following demonstration problem (Illustration D-16) illustrates how to use Table 4.

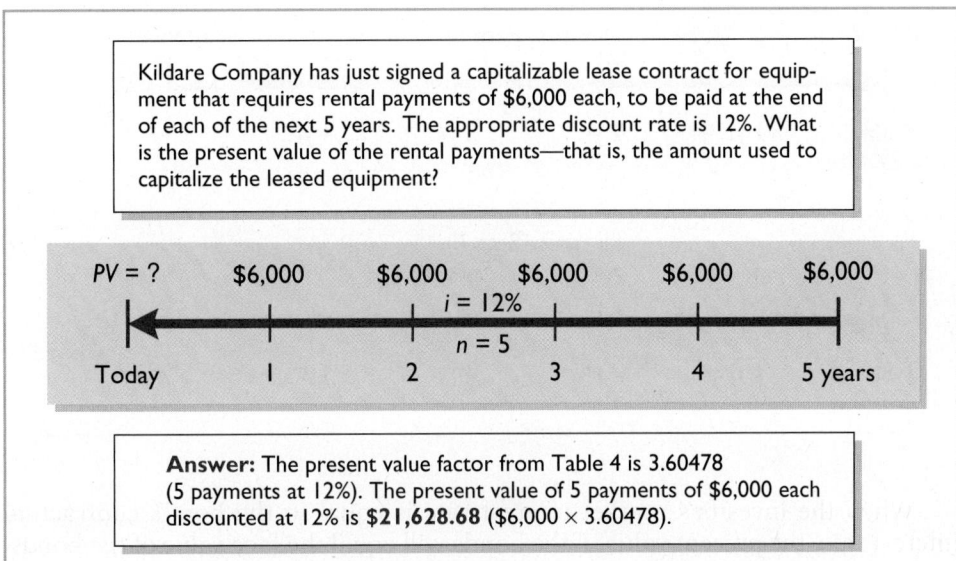

Kildare Company has just signed a capitalizable lease contract for equipment that requires rental payments of $6,000 each, to be paid at the end of each of the next 5 years. The appropriate discount rate is 12%. What is the present value of the rental payments—that is, the amount used to capitalize the leased equipment?

$PV = ?$ $6,000 $6,000 $6,000 $6,000 $6,000
$i = 12\%$
$n = 5$
Today   1   2   3   4   5 years

Answer: The present value factor from Table 4 is 3.60478 (5 payments at 12%). The present value of 5 payments of $6,000 each discounted at 12% is **$21,628.68** ($6,000 × 3.60478).

Illustration D-16
Demonstration problem—Using Table 4 for *PV* of an annuity of 1

Time Periods and Discounting

In the preceding calculations, the discounting was done on an annual basis using an annual interest rate. Discounting may also be done over shorter periods of time such as monthly, quarterly, or semiannually.

When the time frame is less than one year, it is necessary to convert the annual interest rate to the applicable time frame. Assume, for example, that the investor in Illustration D-14 received $500 **semiannually** for three years instead of $1,000 annually. In this case, the number of periods becomes six (3 × 2), the discount rate is 5% (10% ÷ 2), the present value factor from Table 4 is 5.07569 (6 periods at 5%), and the present value of the future cash flows is $2,537.85 (5.07569 × $500). This amount is slightly higher than the $2,486.86 computed in Illustration D-15 because interest is computed twice during the same year. That is, during the second half of the year, interest is earned on the first half-year's interest.

Computing the Present Value of a Long-Term Note or Bond

The present value (or market price) of a long-term note or bond is a function of three variables: (1) the payment amounts, (2) the length of time until the amounts are paid, and (3) the discount rate. Our illustration (on the next page) uses a five-year bond issue.

LEARNING OBJECTIVE   7

Compute the present value of notes and bonds.

---

[1]The difference of .00001 between 2.48686 and 2.48685 is due to rounding.

The first variable (dollars to be paid) is made up of two elements: (1) a series of interest payments (an annuity) and (2) the principal amount (a single sum). To compute the present value of the bond, both the interest payments and the principal amount must be discounted—two different computations. The time diagrams for a bond due in five years are shown in Illustration D-17.

Illustration D-17
Present value of a bond time diagram

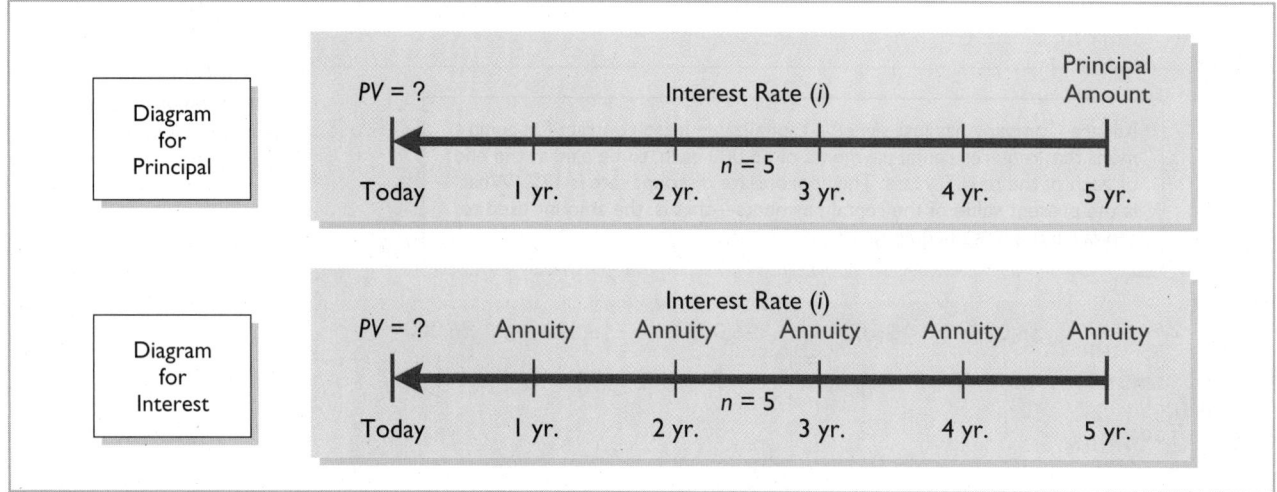

When the investor's market interest rate is equal to the bond's contractual interest rate, the present value of the bonds will equal the face value of the bonds. To illustrate, assume a bond issue of 10%, five-year bonds with a face value of $100,000 with interest payable **semiannually** on January 1 and July 1. If the discount rate is the same as the contractual rate, the bonds will sell at face value. In this case, the investor will receive (1) $100,000 at maturity and (2) a series of ten $5,000 interest payments [($100,000 × 10%) ÷ 2] over the term of the bonds. The length of time is expressed in terms of interest periods—in this case—10, and the discount rate per interest period, 5%. The following time diagram (Illustration D-18) depicts the variables involved in this discounting situation.

Illustration D-18
Time diagram for present value of a 10%, five-year bond paying interest semiannually

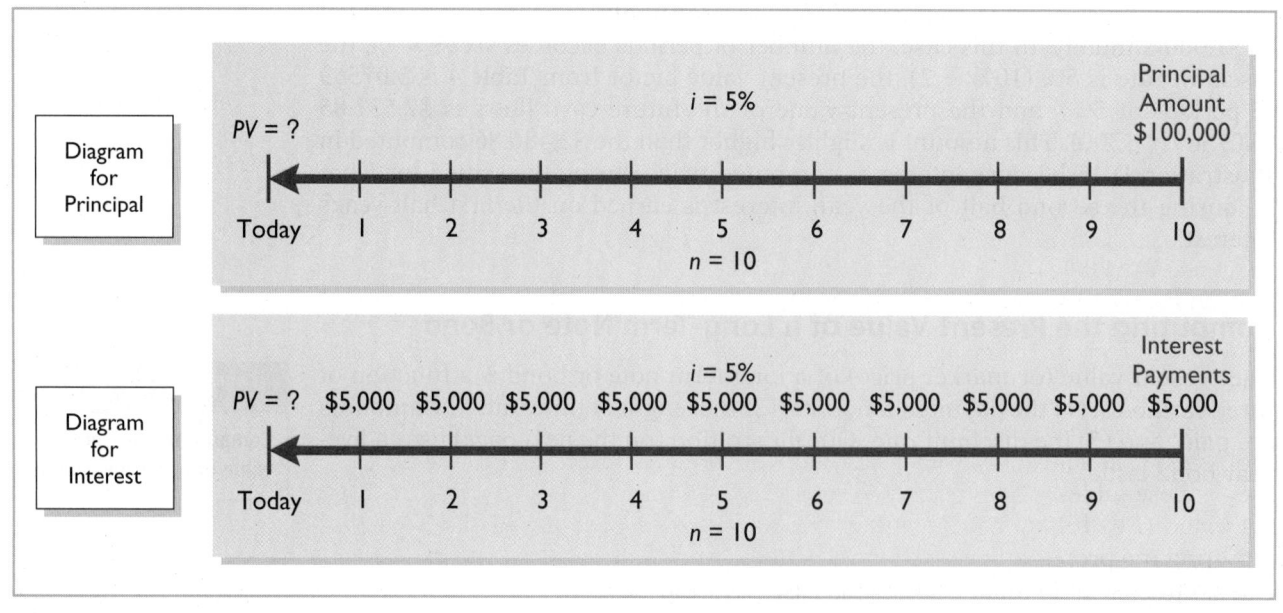

Illustration D-19 shows the computation of the present value of these bonds.

Illustration D-19
Present value of principal and interest—face value

10% Contractual Rate—10% Discount Rate

Present value of principal to be received at maturity	
$100,000 × *PV* of 1 due in 10 periods at 5%	
$100,000 × .61391 (Table 3)	$ 61,391
Present value of interest to be received periodically	
over the term of the bonds	
$5,000 × *PV* of 1 due periodically for 10 periods at 5%	
$5,000 × 7.72173 (Table 4)	38,609*
Present value of bonds	**$100,000**

_____

*Rounded

Now assume that the investor's required rate of return is 12%, not 10%. The future amounts are again $100,000 and $5,000, respectively, but now a discount rate of 6% (12% ÷ 2) must be used. The present value of the bonds is $92,639, as computed in Illustration D-20.

Illustration D-20
Present value of principal and interest—discount

10% Contractual Rate—12% Discount Rate

Present value of principal to be received at maturity	
$100,000 × .55839 (Table 3)	$ 55,839
Present value of interest to be received periodically	
over the term of the bonds	
$5,000 × 7.36009 (Table 4)	36,800
Present value of bonds	**$92,639**

Conversely, if the discount rate is 8% and the contractual rate is 10%, the present value of the bonds is $108,111, computed as shown in Illustration D-21.

Illustration D-21
Present value of principal and interest—premium

10% Contractual Rate—8% Discount Rate

Present value of principal to be received at maturity	
$100,000 × .67556 (Table 3)	$ 67,556
Present value of interest to be received periodically	
over the term of the bonds	
$5,000 × 8.11090 (Table 4)	40,555
Present value of bonds	**$108,111**

The above discussion relied on present value tables in solving present value problems. Calculators may also be used to compute present values without the use of these tables. Many calculators, especially financial calculators, have present value (*PV*) functions that allow you to calculate present values by merely inputting the proper amount, discount rate, periods, and pressing the PV key. We discuss the use of financial calculators in a later section.

Computing the Present Values in a Capital Budgeting Decision

Compute the present values in capital budgeting situations.

The decision to make long-term capital investments is best evaluated using discounting techniques that recognize the time value of money. To do this, many companies calculate the present value of the cash flows involved in a capital investment.

To illustrate, Nagel-Siebert Trucking Company, a cross-country freight carrier in Montgomery, Illinois, is considering adding another truck to its fleet because of a purchasing opportunity. Navistar Inc., Nagel-Siebert's primary supplier of overland rigs, is overstocked and offers to sell its biggest rig for $154,000 cash payable upon delivery. Nagel-Siebert knows that the rig will produce a net cash flow per year of $40,000 for five years (received at the end of each year), at which time it will be sold for an estimated salvage value of $35,000. Nagel-Siebert's discount rate in evaluating capital expenditures is 10%. Should Nagel-Siebert commit to the purchase of this rig?

The cash flows that must be discounted to present value by Nagel-Siebert are as follows.

Cash payable on delivery (today): $154,000.

Net cash flow from operating the rig: $40,000 for 5 years (at the end of each year).

Cash received from sale of rig at the end of 5 years: $35,000.

The time diagrams for the latter two cash flows are shown in Illustration D-22.

Illustration D-22
Time diagrams for Nagel-Siebert Trucking Company

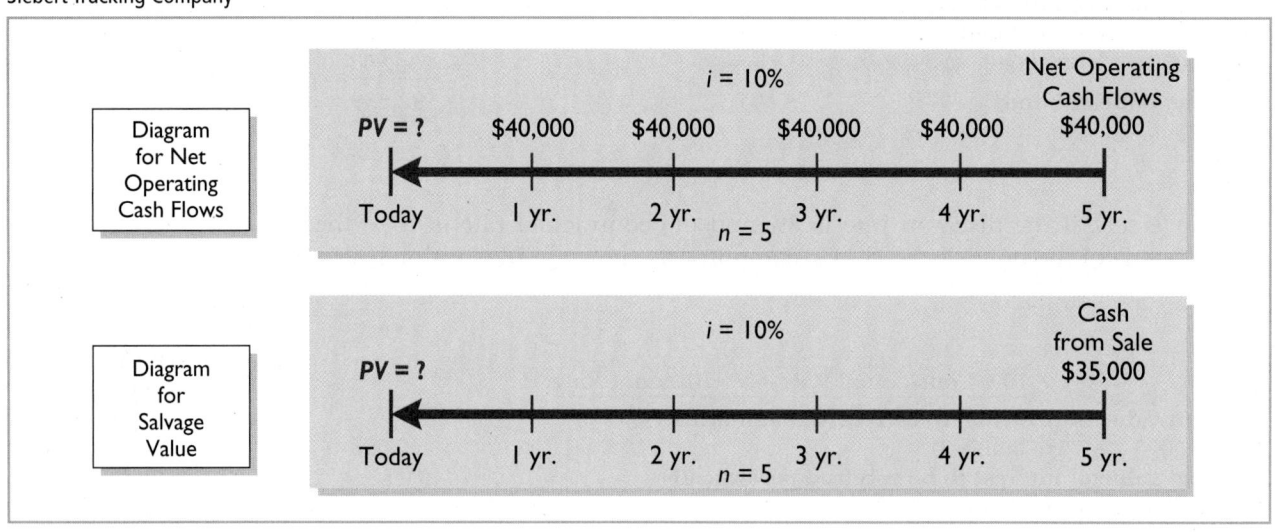

Notice from the diagrams that computing the present value of the net operating cash flows ($40,000 at the end of each year) is **discounting an annuity** (Table 4), while computing the present value of the $35,000 salvage value is **discounting a single sum** (Table 3). The computation of these present values is shown in Illustration D-23.

Present Values—10% Discount Rate

Present value of net operating cash flows received annually over 5 years:
  $40,000 × PV of 1 received annually for 5 years at 10%
  $40,000 × 3.79079 · $ 151,631.60
Present value of salvage value (cash) to be received in 5 years
  $35,000 × PV of 1 received in 5 years at 10%
  $35,000 × .62092 · 21,732.20
Present value of cash **inflows** · 173,363.80
Present value cash **outflows** (purchase price due today at 10%):
  $154,000 × PV of 1 due today
  $154,000 × 1.00000 · (154,000.00)
Net present value · **$ 19,363.80**

Because the present value of the cash receipts (inflows) of $173,363.80 ($151,631.60 + $21,732.20) exceeds the present value of the cash payments (outflows) of $154,000.00, the net present value of $19,363.80 is positive, and **the decision to invest should be accepted**.

Now assume that Nagle-Siebert uses a discount rate of 15%, not 10%, because it wants a greater return on it investments in capital assets. The cash receipts and cash payments by Nagel-Siebert are the same. The present values of these receipts and cash payments discounted at 15% are shown in Illustration D-24.

Present Values—15% Discount Rate

Present value of net operating cash flows received annually
over 5 years at 15%
  $40,000 × 3.35216 · $ 134,086.40
Present value of salvage value (cash) to be received in 5 years at 15%
  $35,000 × .49718 · 17,401.30
Present value of cash **inflows** · $ 151,487.70
Present value of cash **outflows** (purchase price due today at 15%):
  $154,000 × 1.00000 · (154,000.00)
Net present value · **$ (2,512.30)**

Because the present value of the cash payments (outflows) of $154,000 exceeds the present value of the cash receipts (inflows) of $151,487.70 ($134,086.40 + $17,401.30), the net present value of $2,512.30 is negative, and **the investment should be rejected**.

The above discussion relied on present value tables in solving present value problems. As we show in the next section, calculators may also be used to compute present values without the use of these tables. Some calculators, especially the "business" or financial calculators, have present value (PV) functions that allow you to calculate present values by merely identifying the proper amount, discount rate, periods, and pressing the PV key.

Using Financial Calculators

LEARNING OBJECTIVE   9

Use a financial calculator to solve time value of money problems.

Business professionals, once they have mastered the underlying concepts in sections 1 and 2, often use a financial calculator to solve time value of money problems. In many cases, they must use calculators if interest rates or time periods do not correspond with the information provided in the compound interest tables.

To use financial calculators, you enter the time value of money variables into the calculator. Illustration D-25 shows the five most common keys used to solve time value of money problems.[2]

Illustration D-25

Financial calculator keys

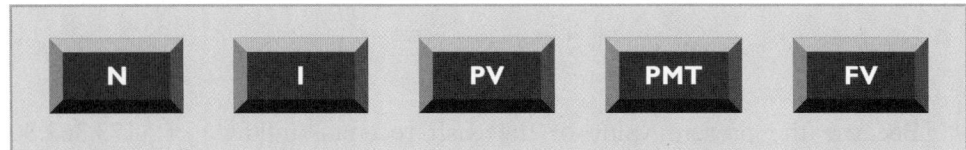

where:

N	=	number of periods
I	=	interest rate per period (some calculators use I/YR or i)
PV	=	present value (occurs at the beginning of the first period)
PMT	=	payment (all payments are equal, and none are skipped)
FV	=	future value (occurs at the end of the last period)

In solving time value of money problems in this appendix, you will generally be given three of four variables and will have to solve for the remaining variable. The fifth key (the key not used) is given a value of zero to ensure that this variable is not used in the computation.

Present Value of a Single Sum

To illustrate how to solve a present value problem using a financial calculator, assume that you want to know the present value of $84,253 to be received in five years, discounted at 11% compounded annually. Illustration D-26 depicts this problem.

Illustration D-26

Calculator solution for present value of a single sum

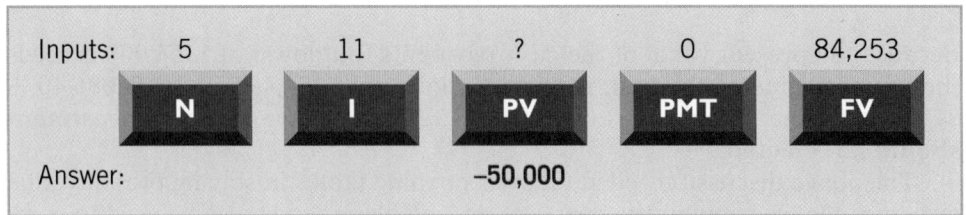

---

[2]On many calculators, these keys are actual buttons on the face of the calculator; on others, they appear on the display after the user accesses a present value menu.

Illustration D-26 shows you the information (inputs) to enter into the calculator: N = 5, I = 11, PMT = 0, and FV = 84,253. You then press PV for the answer: −$50,000. As indicated, the PMT key was given a value of zero because a series of payments did not occur in this problem.

PLUS AND MINUS

The use of plus and minus signs in time value of money problems with a financial calculator can be confusing. Most financial calculators are programmed so that the positive and negative cash flows in any problem offset each other. In the present value problem above, we identified the $84,253 future value initial investment as a positive (inflow); the answer −$50,000 was shown as a negative amount, reflecting a cash outflow. If the 84,253 were entered as a negative, then the final answer would have been reported as a positive 50,000.

Hopefully, the sign convention will not cause confusion. If you understand what is required in a problem, you should be able to interpret a positive or negative amount in determining the solution to a problem.

COMPOUNDING PERIODS

In the problem above, we assumed that compounding occurs once a year. Some financial calculators have a default setting, which assumes that compounding occurs 12 times a year. You must determine what default period has been programmed into your calculator and change it as necessary to arrive at the proper compounding period.

ROUNDING

Most financial calculators store and calculate using 12 decimal places. As a result, because compound interest tables generally have factors only up to five decimal places, a slight difference in the final answer can result. In most time value of money problems, the final answer will not include more than two decimal places.

Present Value of an Annuity

To illustrate how to solve a present value of an annuity problem using a financial calculator, assume that you are asked to determine the present value of rental receipts of $6,000 each to be received at the end of each of the next five years, when discounted at 12%, as pictured in Illustration D-27.

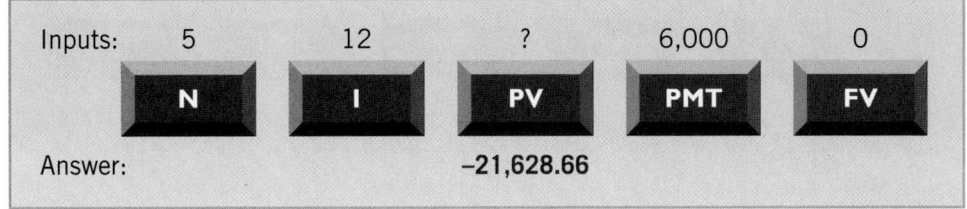

Illustration D-27
Calculator solution for present value of an annuity

In this case, you enter N = 5, I = 12, PMT = 6,000, FV = 0, and then press PV to arrive at the answer of −$21,628.66.

Useful Applications of the Financial Calculator

With a financial calculator, you can solve for any interest rate or for any number of periods in a time value of money problem. Here are some examples of these applications.

AUTO LOAN

Assume you are financing the purchase of a used car with a three-year loan. The loan has a 9.5% stated annual interest rate, compounded monthly. The price of the car is $6,000, and you want to determine the monthly payments, assuming that the payments start one month after the purchase. This problem is pictured in Illustration D-28.

Illustration D-28
Calculator solution for auto loan payments

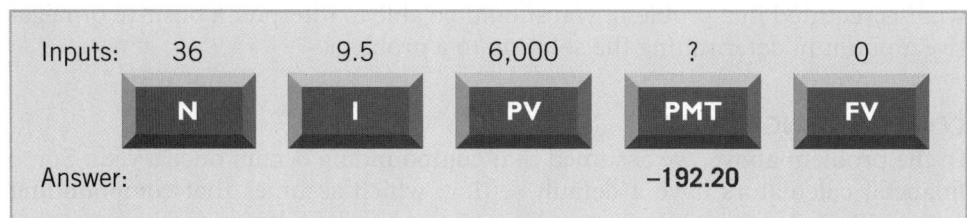

To solve this problem, you enter N = 36 (12 × 3), I = 9.5, PV = 6,000, FV = 0, and than press PMT. You will find that the monthly payments will be $192.20. Note that the payment key is usually programmed for 12 payments per year. Thus, you must change the default (compounding period) if the payments are other than monthly.

MORTGAGE LOAN AMOUNT

Let's say you evaluating financing options for a loan on a house. You decide that the maximum mortgage payment you can afford is $700 per month. The annual interest rate is 8.4%. If you get a mortgage that requires you to make monthly payments over a 15-year period, what is the maximum home loan you can afford? Illustration D-29 depicts this problem.

Illustration D-29
Calculator solution for mortgage amount

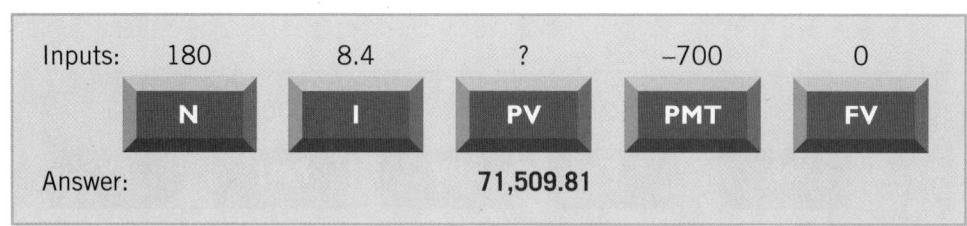

You enter N = 180 (12 × 15 years), I = 8.4, PMT = −700, FV = 0, and press PV. With the payments-per-year key set at 12, you find a present value of $71,509.81— the maximum home loan you can afford, given that you want to keep your mortgage payments at $700. Note that by changing any of the variables, you can quickly conduct "what-if" analyses for different situations.

SUMMARY OF LEARNING OBJECTIVES

✔ **The Navigator**

1 Distinguish between simple and compound interest. Simple interest is computed on the principal only, while compound interest is computed on the principal and any interest earned that has not been withdrawn.

2 Solve for future value of a single amount. Prepare a time diagram of the problem. Identify the principal amount, the number of compounding periods, and the interest rate. Using the future value of 1 table, multiply the principal amount by the future value factor specified at the intersection of the number of periods and the interest rate.

3 Solve for future value of an annuity. Prepare a time diagram of the problem. Identify the amount of the periodic payments (receipts), the number of payments (receipts), and the interest rate. Using the future value of an annuity of 1 table, multiply the amount of the payments by the future value factor specified at the intersection of the number of payments and the interest rate.

4 Identify the variables fundamental to solving present value problems. The following three variables are fundamental to solving present value problems: (1) the future amount, (2) the number of periods, and (3) the interest rate (the discount rate).

5 Solve for present value of a single amount. Prepare a time diagram of the problem. Identify the future amount, the number of discounting periods, and the discount (interest) rate. Using the present value of a single amount table, multiply the future amount by the present value factor specified at the intersection of the number of periods and the discount rate.

6 Solve for present value of an annuity. Prepare a time diagram of the problem. Identify the amount of future periodic receipts or payment (annuities), the number of payments (receipts), and the discount (interest) rate. Using the present value of an annuity of 1 table, multiply the amount of the annuity by the present value factor specified at the intersection of the number of payments and the interest rate.

7 Compute the present value of notes and bonds. Determine the present value of the principal amount: Multiply the principal amount (a single future amount) by the present value factor (from the present value of 1 table) intersecting at the number of periods (number of interest payments) and the discount rate. Determine the present value of the series of interest payments: Multiply the amount of the interest payment by the present value factor (from the present value of an annuity of 1 table) intersecting at the number of periods (number of interest payments) and the discount rate. Add the present value of the principal amount to the present value of the interest payments to arrive at the present value of the note or bond.

8 Compute the present values in capital budgeting situations. Compute the present values of all cash inflows and all cash outflows related to the capital budgeting proposal (an investment-type decision). If the **net** present value is positive, accept the proposal (make the investment). If the **net** present value is negative, reject the proposal (do not make the investment).

9 Use a financial calculator to solve time value of money problems. Financial calculators can be used to solve the same and additional problems as those solved with time value of money tables. Enter into the financial calculator the amounts for all of the known elements of a time value of money problem (periods, interest rate, payments, future or present value), and it solves for the unknown element. Particularly useful situations involve interest rates and compounding periods not presented in the tables.

GLOSSARY

Annuity A series of equal dollar amounts to be paid or received at evenly spaced time intervals (periodically). (p. D-4).

Compound interest The interest computed on the principal and any interest earned that has not been paid or withdrawn. (p. D-2).

Discounting the future amount(s) The process of determining present value. (p. D-7).

Future value of a single amount The value at a future date of a given amount invested, assuming compound interest. (p. D-2).

Future value of an annuity The sum of all the payments (receipts) plus the accumulated compound interest on them. (p. D-5).

Interest Payment for the use of another person's money. (p. D-1).

Present value The value now of a given amount to be paid or received in the future assuming compound interest. (p. D-7).

Present value of an annuity The value now of a series of future receipts or payments, discounted assuming compound interest. (p. D-9).

Principal The amount borrowed or invested. (p. D-1).

Simple interest The interest computed on the principal only. (p. D-1).

BRIEF EXERCISES

(Use tables to solve exercises BED-1 to BED-25.)

Compute the future value of a single amount.

(LO 2)

BED-1 Randy Owen invested $9,000 at 5% annual interest, and left the money invested without withdrawing any of the interest for 12 years. At the end of the 12 years, Randy withdrew the accumulated amount of money. (a) What amount did Randy withdraw, assuming the investment earns simple interest? (b) What amount did Randy withdraw, assuming the investment earns interest compounded annually?

Use future value tables.

(LO 2, 3)

BED-2 For each of the following cases, indicate (a) to what interest rate columns and (b) to what number of periods you would refer in looking up the future value factor.

(1) In Table 1 (future value of 1):

	Annual Rate	Number of Years Invested	Compounded
Case A	5%	3	Annually
Case B	12%	4	Semiannually

(2) In Table 2 (future value of an annuity of 1):

	Annual Rate	Number of Years Invested	Compounded
Case A	3%	8	Annually
Case B	8%	6	Semiannually

Compute the future value of a single amount.

(LO 2)

BED-3 Joyce Company signed a lease for an office building for a period of 12 years. Under the lease agreement, a security deposit of $8,400 is made. The deposit will be returned at the expiration of the lease with interest compounded at 4% per year. What amount will Joyce receive at the time the lease expires?

Compute the future value of an annuity.

(LO 3)

BED-4 Bates Company issued $1,000,000, 12-year bonds and agreed to make annual sinking fund deposits of $78,000. The deposits are made at the end of each year into an account paying 6% annual interest. What amount will be in the sinking fund at the end of 12 years?

Compute the future value of a single amount and of an annuity.

(LO 2, 3)

BED-5 Frank and Maureen Fantazzi invested $5,000 in a savings account paying 5% annual interest when their daughter, Angela, was born. They also deposited $1,000 on each of her birthdays until she was 18 (including her 18th birthday). How much was in the savings account on her 18th birthday (after the last deposit)?

Compute the future value of a single amount.

(LO 2)

BED-6 Hugh Curtin borrowed $35,000 on July 1, 2014. This amount plus accrued interest at 8% compounded annually is to be repaid on July 1, 2019. How much will Hugh have to repay on July 1, 2019?

Use present value tables.

(LO 5, 6)

BED-7 For each of the following cases, indicate (a) to what interest rate columns and (b) to what number of periods you would refer in looking up the discount rate.

(1) In Table 3 (present value of 1):

	Annual Rate	Number of Years Involved	Discounts per Year
Case A	12%	7	Annually
Case B	8%	11	Annually
Case C	6%	8	Semiannually

(2) In Table 4 (present value of an annuity of 1):

	Annual Rate	Number of Years Involved	Number of Payments Involved	Frequency of Payments
Case A	10%	20	20	Annually
Case B	10%	7	7	Annually
Case C	8%	5	10	Semiannually

BED-8 (a) What is the present value of $25,000 due 9 periods from now, discounted at 10%?

(b) What is the present value of $25,000 to be received at the end of each of 6 periods, discounted at 9%?

Determine present values.

(LO 5, 6)

BED-9 Chaffee Company is considering an investment that will return a lump sum of $750,000 six years from now. What amount should Chaffee Company pay for this investment to earn an 8% return?

Compute the present value of a single amount investment.

(LO 5)

BED-10 Lloyd Company earns 6% on an investment that will return $450,000 eight years from now. What is the amount Lloyd should invest now to earn this rate of return?

Compute the present value of a single amount investment.

(LO 5)

BED-11 Arthur Company is considering investing in an annuity contract that will return $46,000 annually at the end of each year for 15 years. What amount should Arthur Company pay for this investment if it earns an 8% return?

Compute the present value of an annuity investment.

(LO 6)

BED-12 Kaehler Enterprises earns 5% on an investment that pays back $80,000 at the end of each of the next 6 years. What is the amount Kaehler Enterprises invested to earn the 5% rate of return?

Compute the present value of an annual investment.

(LO 6)

BED-13 Hanna Railroad Co. is about to issue $300,000 of 10-year bonds paying an 11% interest rate, with interest payable semiannually. The discount rate for such securities is 10%. How much can Hanna expect to receive for the sale of these bonds?

Compute the present value of bonds.

(LO 5, 6, 7)

BED-14 Assume the same information as BED-13 except that the discount rate is 12% instead of 10%. In this case, how much can Hanna expect to receive from the sale of these bonds?

Compute the present value of bonds.

(LO 5, 6, 7)

BED-15 Tomas Taco Company receives a $65,000, 6-year note bearing interest of 4% (paid annually) from a customer at a time when the discount rate is 6%. What is the present value of the note received by Tomas?

Compute the present value of a note.

(LO 5, 6, 7)

BED-16 Gleason Enterprises issued 6%, 8-year, $2,500,000 par value bonds that pay interest semiannually on October 1 and April 1. The bonds are dated April 1, 2014, and are issued on that date. The discount rate of interest for such bonds on April 1, 2014, is 8%. What cash proceeds did Gleason receive from issuance of the bonds?

Compute the present value of bonds.

(LO 5, 6, 7)

BED-17 Mark Barton owns a garage and is contemplating purchasing a tire retreading machine for $18,000. After estimating costs and revenues, Mark projects a net cash flow from the retreading machine of $3,200 annually for 8 years. Mark hopes to earn a return of 9% on such investments. What is the present value of the retreading operation? Should Mark purchase the retreading machine?

Compute the present value of a machine for purposes of making a purchase decision.

(LO 6, 7)

BED-18 Frazier Company issues a 10%, 5-year mortgage note on January 1, 2014, to obtain financing for new equipment. Land is used as collateral for the note. The terms provide for semiannual installment payments of $48,850. What were the cash proceeds received from the issuance of the note?

Compute the present value of a note.

(LO 6)

BED-19 Leffler Company is considering purchasing equipment. The equipment will produce the following cash flows: Year 1, $40,000; Year 2, $45,000; and Year 3, $50,000. Leffler requires a minimum rate of return of 8%. What is the maximum price Leffler should pay for this equipment?

Compute the maximum price to pay for a machine.

(LO 6, 7)

BED-20 If Colleen Mooney invests $4,765.50 now and she will receive $12,000 at the end of 12 years, what annual rate of interest will Colleen earn on her investment? (*Hint:* Use Table 3.)

Compute the interest rate on a single amount.

(LO 5)

BED-21 Wayne Kurt has been offered the opportunity of investing $29,319 now. The investment will earn 11% per year and at the end of that time will return Wayne $75,000. How many years must Wayne wait to receive $75,000? (*Hint:* Use Table 3.)

Compute the number of periods of a single amount.

(LO 5)

Compute the interest rate on an annuity.

(LO 6)

BED-22 Joanne Quick made an investment of $10,271.38. From this investment, she will receive $1,200 annually for the next 15 years starting one year from now. What rate of interest will Joanne's investment be earning for her? (*Hint:* Use Table 4.)

Compute the number of payments of an annuity.

(LO 6)

BED-23 Patty Schleis invests $6,542.83 now for a series of $1,300 annual returns beginning one year from now. Patty will earn a return of 9% on the initial investment. How many annual payments of $1,300 will Patty receive? (*Hint:* Use Table 4.)

Compute the present value of a machine for purposes of making a purchase decision.

(LO 8)

BED-24 Barney Googal owns a garage and is contemplating purchasing a tire retreading machine for $12,820. After estimating costs and revenues, Barney projects a net cash inflow from the retreading machine of $2,700 annually for 7 years. Barney hopes to earn a return of 9% on such investments. What is the present value of the retreading operation? Should Barney Googal purchase the retreading machine?

Compute the maximum price to pay for a machine.

(LO 8)

BED-25 Ramos Company is considering purchasing equipment. The equipment will produce the following cash flows: Year 1, $20,000; Year 2, $30,000; Year 3, $40,000. Ramos requires a minimum rate of return of 11%. What is the maximum price Ramos should pay for this equipment?

Determine interest rate.

(LO 8)

BED-26 Carly Simon wishes to invest $18,000 on July 1, 2014, and have it accumulate to $50,000 by July 1, 2024. Use a financial calculator to determine at what exact annual rate of interest Carly must invest the $18,000.

Determine interest rate.

(LO 9)

BED-27 On July 17, 2014, James Taylor borrowed $60,000 from his grandfather to open a clothing store. Starting July 17, 2015, James has to make 10 equal annual payments of $8,860 each to repay the loan. Use a financial calculator to determine what interest rate James is paying.

Determine interest rate.

(LO 9)

BED-28 As the purchaser of a new house, Carrie Underwood has signed a mortgage note to pay the Nashville National Bank and Trust Co. $8,400 every 6 months for 20 years, at the end of which time she will own the house. At the date the mortgage is signed, the purchase price was $198,000 and Underwood made a down payment of $20,000. The first payment will be made 6 months after the date the mortgage is signed. Using a financial calculator, compute the exact rate of interest earned on the mortgage by the bank.

Various time value of money situations.

(LO 9)

BED-29 Using a financial calculator, solve for the unknowns in each of the following situations.

(a) On June 1, 2013, Holly Golightly purchases lakefront property from her neighbor, George Peppard, and agrees to pay the purchase price in seven payments of $16,000 each, the first payment to be payable June 1, 2014. (Assume that interest compounded at an annual rate of 6.9% is implicit in the payments.) What is the purchase price of the property?

(b) On January 1, 2013, Sammis Corporation purchased 200 of the $1,000 face value, 7% coupon, 10-year bonds of Malone Inc. The bonds mature on January 1, 2023, and pay interest annually beginning January 1, 2014. Sammis purchased the bonds to yield 8.65%. How much did Sammis pay for the bonds?

Various time value of money situations.

(LO 9)

BED-30 Using a financial calculator, provide a solution to each of the following situations.

(a) Lynn Anglin owes a debt of $42,000 from the purchase of her new sport utility vehicle. The debt bears annual interest of 7.8% compounded monthly. Lynn wishes to pay the debt and interest in equal monthly payments over 8 years, beginning one month hence. What equal monthly payments will pay off the debt and interest?

(b) On January 1, 2014, Roger Molony offers to buy Dave Feeney's used snowmobile for $8,000, payable in five equal annual installments, which are to include 7.25% interest on the unpaid balance and a portion of the principal. If the first payment is to be made on December 31, 2014, how much will each payment be?

Cases for Management Decision-Making

The complete cases are available for viewing or download at the book's companion website that accompanies this textbook, at *www.wiley.com/college/weygandt*. To solve these cases, it will be necessary to use the tools learned within the chapters.

Suggested Uses of Cases

Case	Overview
CASE 1 *Greetings Inc.:* *Job Order Costing*	This case is the first in a series of four cases that presents a business situation in which a traditional retailer decides to employ Internet technology to expand its sales opportunities. It requires the student to employ traditional job order costing techniques and then requests an evaluation of the resulting product costs. (Related to Chapter 16, Job Order Costing.)
CASE 2 *Greetings Inc.:* *Activity-Based* *Costing*	This case focuses on decision-making benefits of activity-based costing relative to the traditional approach. It also offers an opportunity to discuss the cost/benefit trade-off between simple ABC systems versus refined systems, and the potential benefit of using capacity rather than expected sales when allocating fixed overhead costs. (Related to Chapter 18, Activity-Based Costing.)
CASE 3 *Greetings Inc.:* *Transfer Pricing* *Issues*	This case illustrates the importance of proper transfer pricing for decision-making as well as performance evaluation. The student is required to evaluate profitability using two different transfer pricing approaches and comment on the terms of the proposed transfer pricing agreement. (Related to Chapter 22, Pricing.)
CASE 4 *Greetings Inc.:* *Capital Budgeting*	This case is set in an environment in which the company is searching for new opportunities for growth. It requires evaluation of a proposal based on initial estimates as well as sensitivity analysis. It also requires evaluation of the underlying assumptions used in the analysis. (Related to Chapter 26, Planning for Capital Investments.)
CASE 5 *Auburn Circular* *Club Pro Rodeo* *Roundup*	This comprehensive case is designed to be used as a capstone activity at the end of the course. It deals with a not-for-profit service company. The case involves many managerial accounting issues that would be common for a start-up business. (Related to Chapter 19, Cost-Volume-Profit; Chapter 21, Incremental Analysis; and Chapter 23, Budgetary Planning.)

CASE 6	This case focuses on setting up a new business. In planning
Sweats Galore	for this new business, the preparation of budgets is empha-
	sized. In addition, an understanding of cost-volume-profit
	relationships is required. (Related to Chapter 19, Cost-
	Volume-Profit, and Chapter 23, Budgetary Planning.)

CASE 7	This comprehensive case involves finding the cost for a given
Armstrong Helmet	product. In addition, it explores cost-volume-profit relation-
Company	ships. It requires the preparation of a set of budgets. (Related to
	Chapter 15, Managerial Accounting; Chapter 19, Cost-Volume-
	Profit; Chapter 23, Budgetary Planning; Chapter 24, Budgetary
	Control and Responsibility Accounting; Chapter 25, Standard
	Costs and Balanced Scorecard; and Chapter 26, Planning for
	Capital Investments.)

To access the full text of these cases, go to the book's companion website at **www.wiley.com/college/weygandt**.

Photo Credits

Chapter 1 Opener: Brand X/Jupiterimages/Getty Images, Inc. Page 6: iStockphoto. Page 8: Gemunu Amarasinghe/AP Photo. Page 10: Toru Hanai/©AP/Wide World Photos. Page 12: Josef Volavka/iStockphoto. Page 25: Marek Uliasz/iStockphoto. Page 44: iStockphoto.

Chapter 2 Opener: Gary W. Green/MCT/NewsCom. Page 58: Jonathan Daniel/Getty Images, Inc. Page 63: Sciencefaction/SuperStock. Page 75: Enviromatic/iStockphoto.

Chapter 3 Opener: James Lauritz/Digital Vision/Getty Images, Inc. Page 104: Dan Chippendale/iStockphoto. Page 112: Apcuk/iStockphoto. Page 116: Gunay Mutlu/iStockphoto. Page 118: Nathan Gleave/iStockphoto.

Chapter 4 Opener: Comstock/Getty Images, Inc. Page 174: Alex Slobodkin/iStockphoto. Page 179: Christian Lagereek/iStockphoto. Page 181: Lowell Sannes/iStockphoto. Page 182 (top): Gunay Mutlu/iStockphoto. Page 182 (bottom): Denis Vorobyev/iStockphoto. Page 183 (top): Nikki Ward/iStockphoto. Page 183 (center): Gehringj/iStockphoto. Page 184: Brentmelissa/iStockphoto. Page 185 (top): Jorge Salcedo/iStockphoto. Page 185 (bottom): Vladislav Gurfinkel/iStockphoto. Page 186: iStockphoto.

Chapter 5 Opener: Stone/Getty Images, Inc. Page 223: Ben Blankenburg/iStockphoto. Page 230: Maciej Noskowski/iStockphoto. Page 231: Helen Sessions/Alamy. Page 237: Heizfrosch/iStockphoto.

Chapter 6 Opener: Steve Dunning/Getty Images, Inc. Page 273: Alexey Dudoladov/iStockphoto. Page 274: Yin Yang/iStockphoto. Page 284: John A. Rizzo/Getty Images, Inc. Page 285: AP/Wide World Photos. Page 288: Fred Hall/iStockphoto. Page 289: Jaap Hart/iStockphoto.

Chapter 7 Opener: Lauren King/iStockphoto. Page 327: Dino Ablakovic/iStockphoto. Page 334: Tom Nulens/iStockphoto. Page 335: Catherine Yeulet/iStockphoto. Page 343: Chris Fernig/iStockphoto. Page 351: AFP Photo/Timothy A. Clary/NewsCom. Page 352: iStockphoto.

Chapter 8 Opener: Shutterstock. Page 390: Michael Braun/iStockphoto. Page 394: iStockphoto. Page 396: Andy Dean/iStockphoto.

Chapter 9 Opener: David Trood/Getty Images, Inc. Page 427: iStockphoto. Page 440: Christian Uhrig/iStockphoto. Page 443: iStockphoto. Page 445 (top): Natallia Yaumenenka/iStockphoto. Page 445 (bottom): Linda Steward/iStockphoto.

Chapter 10 Opener: Cary Westfall/iStockphoto. Page 479: Katie Nesling/iStockphoto. Page 482: iStockphoto. Page 487: iStockphoto. Page 497: Corbis/Stock Market.

Chapter 11 Opener: Scott Heavey/Getty Images. Page 541: Paul Sakuma/©AP/Wide World Photos. Page 544: Rick Bowmer/©AP/Wide World Photos. Page 547: Robert Churchill/iStockphoto. Page 552: Paul Vidler/Alamy. Page 559: Palto/iStockphoto. Page 563: Dietmar Klement/iStockphoto. Page 565: Stephen Strathdee/iStockphoto. Page 566: Editorial12/iStockphoto.

Chapter 12 Opener: Topham/The Image Works. Page 608: Jacob Wackerhausen/iStockphoto.

Chapter 13 Opener: Jason Stitt/iStockphoto. Page 648: Suzy Oliveira/iStockphoto. Page 657: Svetlana Tebenkova/iStockphoto. Page 662: PhotoDisc, Inc./Getty Images.

Chapter 14 Opener: Daniel Acker/Bloomberg/Getty Images, Inc. Page 713: Don Wilkie/iStockphoto. Page 721: SuperStock. Page 733: Kenneth C. Zirkel/iStockphoto.

Chapter 15 Opener: courtesy Current Designs. Page 768: Peter Kramer/Getty Images, Inc. Page 773: Brian Snyder/Reuters/Landov LLC. Page 781: David Joyner/iStockphoto. Page 802: Perry Kroll/iStockphoto.

Chapter 16 Opener: Mark Peterson/Redux Pictures. Page 811: iStockphoto. Page 817: iStockphoto. Page 827: Christian Lagereek/iStockphoto.

Chapter 17 Opener: Richard B. Levine/Alamy. Page 858: iStockphoto. Page 862: Michael Ventura/Alamy.

Chapter 18   Opener: mediaphotos/iStockphoto. Page 909: Oleksiy Maksymenko Photography/Alamy. Page 912: Jeffery Hochstrasser/iStockphoto. Page 914: Sam Greenwood/Getty Images, Inc. Page 919: CGinspiration/iStockphoto.

Chapter 19   Opener: Eric Gerrard/iStockphoto. Page 954: Jani Bryson/iStockphoto. Page 958: pidjoe/iStockphoto. Page 965: Digital Vision/Getty Images. Page 969: Yael/Retna.

Chapter 20   Opener: Paul Sakuma/©AP/Wide World Photos. Page 994: Warchi/iStockphoto. Page 999: dem10/iStockphoto. Page 1001: Liv Friis-Larsen/iStockphoto. Page 1005: Michele Wassell/Age Fotostock America, Inc.

Chapter 21   Opener: iStockphoto. Page 1046: Tina Spruce/iStockphoto. Page 1050: iStockphoto. Page 1057: Max Blain/iStockphoto. Page 1058: Mitch Kezar/Stone/Getty Images.

Chapter 22   Opener: Tomasz Kobiela/iStockphoto. Page 1085: Frank Gartner/iStockphoto. Page 1086: Paul Hart/iStockphoto. Page 1090: Wesley VanDinter/iStockphoto.

Page 1094: Don Bayley/iStockphoto. Page 1102: Rob Colvin/Getty Images.

Chapter 23   Opener: Vladimir Melnikov/iStockphoto. Page 1133: Thinkstock/Comstock/Getty Images, Inc. Page 1138: Marcela Barsse/iStockphoto. Page 1141: ranplett/iStockphoto. Page 1149: Wolfgang Rattya/Reuters/Corbis. Page 1154: ©AP/Wide World Photos.

Chapter 24   Opener: Marcus Clackson/iStockphoto. Page 1187: Fox Broadcasting Company/Album/Newscom. Page 1192: Eric Isselee/iStockphoto. Page 1195: Khuong Hoang/iStockphoto. Page 1197: Kyodo/©AP/Wide World Photos. Page 1206: Brentmelissa/iStockphoto.

Chapter 25   Opener: Bloomberg/Getty Images. Page 1242: SpotX/iStockphoto. Page 1245: Hywit Dimyadi/iStockphoto. Page 1254: Archer Colin/SIPA/NewsCom. Page 1259: PhotoDisc, Inc./Getty Images.

Chapter 26   Opener: Engel & Gielen/Photolibrary. Page 1298: Trevor Smith/iStockphoto. Page 1302: Carol Gering/iStockphoto. Page 1304: Matjaz Boncina/iStockphoto. Page 1305: Matjaz Boncina/iStockphoto.

Company Index

BASIC ACCOUNTING EQUATION (Chapter 2)

Basic Equation	Assets = Liabilities +				Stockholders' Equity								
Expanded Equation	Assets	=	Liabilities	+	Common Stock	+	Retained Earnings	−	Dividends	+	Revenues	−	Expenses
Debit/Credit Effects	Dr. Cr. + −		Dr. Cr. − +		Dr. Cr. − +		Dr. Cr. − +		Dr. Cr. + −		Dr. Cr. − +		Dr. Cr. + −

ADJUSTING ENTRIES (Chapter 3)

	Type	Adjusting Entry	
Deferrals	1. Prepaid expenses 2. Unearned revenues	Dr. Expenses Dr. Liabilities	Cr. Assets Cr. Revenues
Accruals	1. Accrued revenues 2. Accrued expenses	Dr. Assets Dr. Expenses	Cr. Revenues Cr. Liabilities

Note: Each adjusting entry will affect one or more income statement accounts and one or more balance sheet accounts.

Interest Computation

Interest = Face value of note × Annual interest rate × Time in terms of one year

CLOSING ENTRIES (Chapter 4)

Purpose: (1) Update the Retained Earnings account in the ledger by transferring net income (loss) and dividends to retained earnings. (2) Prepare the temporary accounts (revenue, expense, dividends) for the next period's postings by reducing their balances to zero.

Process

1. Debit each revenue account for its balance (assuming normal balances) and credit Income Summary for total revenues.
2. Debit Income Summary for total expenses and credit each expense account for its balance (assuming normal balances).

   STOP AND CHECK: Does the balance in your Income Summary account equal the net income (loss) reported in the income statement?

3. Debit (credit) Income Summary and credit (debit) Retained Earnings for the amount of net income (loss).
4. Debit Retained Earnings for the balance in the Dividends account and credit Dividends for the same amount.

   STOP AND CHECK: Does the balance in your Retained Earnings account equal the ending balance reported in the balance sheet and the retained earnings statement? Are all of your temporary account balances zero?

ACCOUNTING CYCLE (Chapter 4)

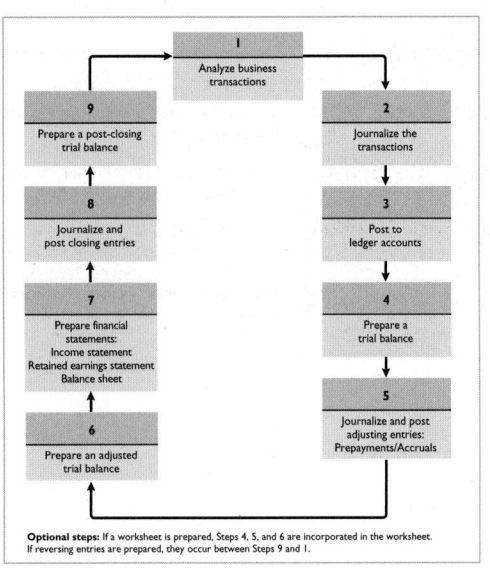

Optional steps: If a worksheet is prepared, Steps 4, 5, and 6 are incorporated in the worksheet. If reversing entries are prepared, they occur between Steps 9 and 1.

INVENTORY (Chapters 5 and 6)

Ownership

Freight Terms	Ownership of goods on public carrier resides with:	Who pays freight costs:
FOB shipping point	Buyer	Buyer
FOB destination	Seller	Seller

Perpetual vs. Periodic Journal Entries

Event	Perpetual	Periodic
Purchase of goods	Inventory Cash (A/P)	Purchases Cash (A/P)
Freight (shipping point)	Inventory Cash	Freight-In Cash
Return of goods	Cash (or A/P) Inventory	Cash (or A/P) Purchase Returns and Allowances
Sale of goods	Cash (or A/R) Sales Revenue Cost of Goods Sold Inventory	Cash (or A/R) Sales Revenue No entry
End of period	No entry	Closing or adjusting entry required

Cost Flow Methods

- Specific identification
- First-in, first-out (FIFO)
- Weighted-average
- Last-in, first-out (LIFO)

FRAUD, INTERNAL CONTROL, AND CASH (Chapter 7)

The Fraud Triangle	Principles of Internal Control Activities
Opportunity Financial △ Rationalization pressure	• Establishment of responsibility • Segregation of duties • Documentation procedures • Physical controls • Independent internal verification • Human resource controls

Bank Reconciliation

Bank	Books
Balance per bank statement Add: Deposits in transit	Balance per books Add: Unrecorded credit memoranda from bank statement
Deduct: Outstanding checks	Deduct: Unrecorded debit memoranda from bank statement
Adjusted cash balance	Adjusted cash balance

Note: 1. Errors should be offset (added or deducted) on the side that made the error.
2. Adjusting journal entries should only be made on the books.

STOP AND CHECK: Does the adjusted cash balance in the Cash account equal the reconciled balance?

RECEIVABLES (Chapter 8)

Methods to Account for Uncollectible Accounts

Direct write-off method	Record bad debt expense when the company determines a particular account to be uncollectible.
Allowance methods: Percentage-of-sales	At the end of each period, estimate the amount of credit sales uncollectible. Debit Bad Debt Expense and credit Allowance for Doubtful Accounts for this amount. As specific accounts become uncollectible, debit Allowance for Doubtful Accounts and credit Accounts Receivable.
Percentage-of-receivables	At the end of each period, estimate the amount of uncollectible receivables. Debit Bad Debt Expense and credit Allowance for Doubtful Accounts in an amount that results in a balance in the allowance account equal to the estimate of uncollectibles. As specific accounts become uncollectible, debit Allowance for Doubtful Accounts and credit Accounts Receivable.

Chapter Content

PLANT ASSETS (Chapter 9)

Presentation

Tangible Assets	Intangible Assets
Property, plant, and equipment	Intangible assets (patents, copyrights, trademarks, franchises, goodwill)
Natural resources	

Computation of Annual Depreciation Expense

Straight-line	$\dfrac{\text{Cost} - \text{Salvage value}}{\text{Useful life (in years)}}$
Units-of-activity	$\dfrac{\text{Depreciable cost}}{\text{Useful life (in units)}} \times \text{Units of activity during year}$
Declining-balance	Book value at beginning of year $\times$ Declining-balance rate* *Declining-balance rate $= 1 \div$ Useful life (in years)

Note: If depreciation is calculated for partial periods, the straight-line and declining-balance methods must be adjusted for the relevant proportion of the year. Multiply the annual depreciation expense by the number of months expired in the year divided by 12 months.

BONDS (Chapter 10)

Premium	Market interest rate < Contractual interest rate
Face value	Market interest rate = Contractual interest rate
Discount	Market interest rate > Contractual interest rate

Computation of Annual Bond Interest Expense

Interest expense = Interest paid (payable) + Amortization of discount
(OR − Amortization of premium)

Straight-line amortization	$\dfrac{\text{Bond discount (premium)}}{\text{Number of interest periods}}$	
Effective-interest amortization (preferred method)	Bond interest expense	Bond interest paid
	Carrying value of bonds at beginning of period × Effective-interest rate	Face amount of bonds × Contractual interest rate

STOCKHOLDERS' EQUITY (Chapter 11)

No-Par Value vs. Par Value Stock Journal Entries

No-Par Value	Par Value

Cash
    Common Stock
	Cash
	    Common Stock (par value)
	    Paid-in Capital in Excess of Par

Comparison of Dividend Effects

	Cash	Common Stock	Retained Earnings
Cash dividend	↓	No effect	↓
Stock dividend	No effect	↑	↓
Stock split	No effect	No effect	No effect

Debits and Credits to Retained Earnings

Retained Earnings	
Debits (Decreases)	Credits (Increases)
1. Net loss	1. Net income
2. Prior period adjustments for overstatement of net income	2. Prior period adjustments for understatement of net income
3. Cash dividends and stock dividends	
4. Some disposals of treasury stock	

INVESTMENTS (Chapter 12)

Comparison of Long-Term Bond Investment and Liability Journal Entries

Event	Investor	Investee

Purchase / issue of bonds	Debt Investments
	    Cash
		Cash
		    Bonds Payable

Interest receipt / payment	Cash
	    Interest Revenue
		Interest Expense
		    Cash

Comparison of Cost and Equity Methods of Accounting for Long-Term Stock Investments

Event	Cost	Equity

Acquisition	Stock Investments
	    Cash
		Stock Investments
		    Cash

Investee reports earnings	No entry	Stock Investments Revenue from Stock Investments

Investee pays dividends	Cash
	    Dividend Revenue
		Cash
		    Stock Investments

Trading and Non-Trading Securities

Trading	Report at fair value with changes reported in net income.
Non-trading	Report at fair value with changes reported in the stockholders' equity section.

STATEMENT OF CASH FLOWS (Chapter 13)

Cash flows from operating activities (**indirect method**)
Net income

Add:	Losses on disposals of assets	$ X
	Amortization and depreciation	X
	Decreases in noncash current assets	X
	Increases in current liabilities	X
Deduct:	Gains on disposals of assets	(X)
	Increases in noncash current assets	(X)
	Decreases in current liabilities	(X)
Net cash provided (used) by operating activities		$ X

Cash flows from operating activities (**direct method**)
Cash receipts
  (Examples: from sales of goods and services to customers, from receipts
  of interest and dividends on loans and investments) $ X
Cash payments
  (Examples: to suppliers, for operating expenses, for interest, for taxes)   (X)
Cash provided (used) by operating activities $ X

PRESENTATION OF NON-TYPICAL ITEMS (Chapter 14)

Prior period adjustments (Chapter 11)	Retained earnings statement (adjustment of beginning retained earnings)
Discontinued operations	Income statement (presented separately after "Income from continuing operations")
Extraordinary items	Income statement (presented separately after "Income before extraordinary items")
Changes in accounting principle	In most instances, use the new method in current period and restate previous years' results using new method. For changes in depreciation and amortization methods, use the new method in the current period but do not restate previous periods.

MANAGERIAL ACCOUNTING (Chapter 15)

Characteristics of Managerial Accounting

Primary users	Internal users
Reports	Internal reports issued as needed
Purpose	Special purpose for a particular user
Content	Pertains to subunits, may be detailed, use of relevant data
Verification	No independent audits

Types of Manufacturing Costs

Direct materials	Raw materials directly associated with finished product
Direct labor	Work of employees directly associated with turning raw materials into finished product
Manufacturing overhead	Costs indirectly associated with manufacture of finished product

JOB ORDER AND PROCESS COSTING (Chapters 16 and 17)

Types of Accounting Systems

Job order	Costs are assigned to each unit or each batch of goods
Process cost	Costs are applied to similar products that are mass-produced in a continuous fashion

Job Order and Process Cost Flow

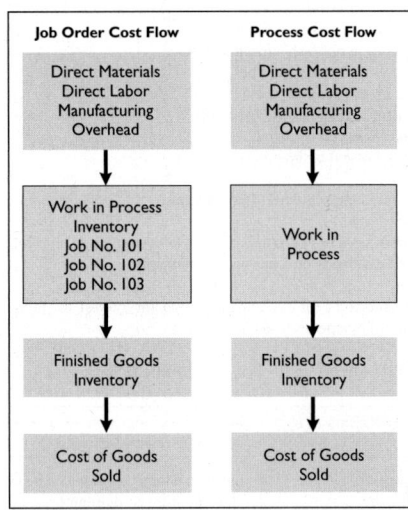

ACTIVITY-BASED COSTING (Chapter 18)

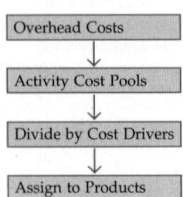

Activity-based costing involves the following four steps:
1. Identify and classify the major activities involved in the manufacture of specific products, and allocate the manufacturing overhead costs to the appropriate cost pools.
2. Identify the cost driver that has a strong correlation to the costs accumulated in the cost pool.
3. Compute the overhead rate for each cost driver.
4. Assign manufacturing overhead costs for each cost pool to products, using the overhead rates (cost per driver).

COST-VOLUME-PROFIT (Chapters 19 and 20)

Types of Costs

Variable costs	Vary in total directly and proportionately with changes in activity level
Fixed costs	Remain the same in total regardless of change in activity level
Mixed costs	Contain both a fixed and a variable element

CVP Income Statement Format

	Total	Per Unit
Sales	$xx	$xx
Variable costs	xx	xx
Contribution margin	xx	$xx
Fixed costs	xx	
Net income	$xx	

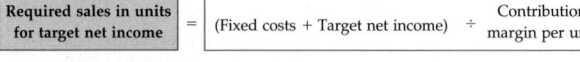

$$\text{Contribution margin per unit} = \text{Unit selling price} - \text{Unit variable costs}$$

$$\text{Break-even point in units} = \text{Fixed costs} \div \text{Unit contribution margin*}$$

$$\text{Break-even point in dollars} = \text{Fixed costs} \div \text{Contribution margin ratio*}$$

$$\text{Required sales in units for target net income} = (\text{Fixed costs} + \text{Target net income}) \div \text{Contribution margin per unit}$$

$$\text{Degree of operating leverage} = \text{Contribution margin} \div \text{Net income}$$

*For multiple products, use weighted-average.

INCREMENTAL ANALYSIS (Chapter 21)

1. Identify the relevant costs associated with each alternative. **Relevant costs** are those costs and revenues that differ across alternatives. Choose the alternative that maximizes net income.
2. **Opportunity costs** are those benefits that are given up when one alternative is chosen instead of another one. Opportunity costs are relevant costs.
3. **Sunk costs** have already been incurred and will not be changed or avoided by any future decision. Sunk costs are not relevant costs.

PRICING (Chapter 22)

External Pricing

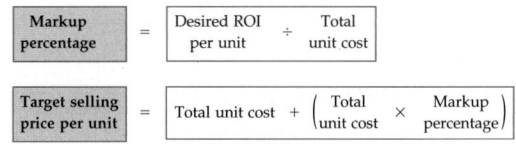

$$\text{Markup percentage} = \text{Desired ROI per unit} \div \text{Total unit cost}$$

$$\text{Target selling price per unit} = \text{Total unit cost} + \left(\text{Total unit cost} \times \text{Markup percentage}\right)$$

Transfer Pricing

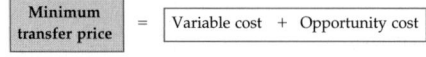

$$\text{Minimum transfer price} = \text{Variable cost} + \text{Opportunity cost}$$

BUDGETS (Chapter 23)

Components of the Master Budget

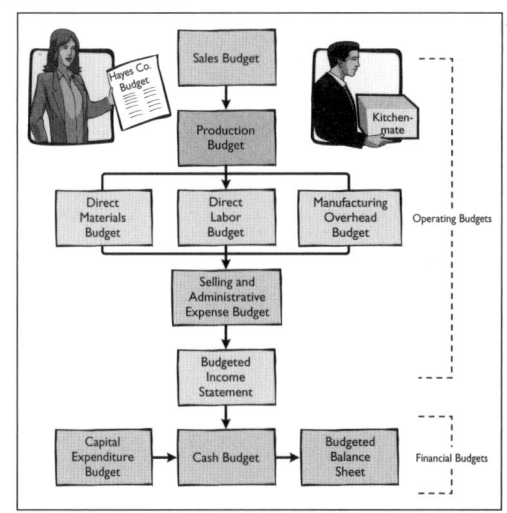

RESPONSIBILITY ACCOUNTING (Chapter 24)

Types of Responsibility Centers

Cost	Profit	Investment
Expenses only	Expenses and Revenues	Expenses and Revenues and ROI

Return on Investment

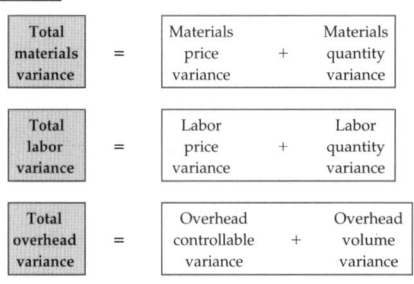

$$\text{Return on investment (ROI)} = \frac{\text{Investment center controllable margin}}{\text{Average investment center operating assets}}$$

STANDARD COSTS (Chapter 25)

Standard Cost Variances

$$\text{Total materials variance} = \text{Materials price variance} + \text{Materials quantity variance}$$

$$\text{Total labor variance} = \text{Labor price variance} + \text{Labor quantity variance}$$

$$\text{Total overhead variance} = \text{Overhead controllable variance} + \text{Overhead volume variance}$$

Balanced Scorecard

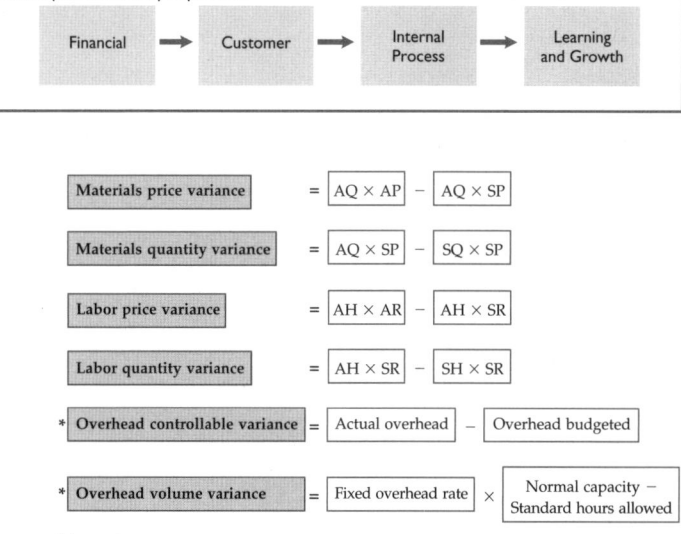

Linked process across perspectives:

Financial → Customer → Internal Process → Learning and Growth

Materials price variance	$= (AQ \times AP) - (AQ \times SP)$
Materials quantity variance	$= (AQ \times SP) - (SQ \times SP)$
Labor price variance	$= (AH \times AR) - (AH \times SR)$
Labor quantity variance	$= (AH \times SR) - (SH \times SR)$
* Overhead controllable variance	$= \text{Actual overhead} - \text{Overhead budgeted}$
* Overhead volume variance	$= \text{Fixed overhead rate} \times (\text{Normal capacity} - \text{Standard hours allowed})$

*Appendix coverage

CAPITAL BUDGETING (Chapter 26)

Annual Rate of Return

$$\text{Annual rate of return} = \text{Expected annual net income} \div \text{Average investment}$$

Cash Payback

$$\text{Cash payback period} = \text{Cost of capital investment} \div \text{Annual cash inflow}$$

Discounted Cash Flow Approaches

Net Present Value	Internal Rate of Return
Compute net present value (a dollar amount). If net present value is zero or positive, accept the proposal. If net present value is negative, reject the proposal.	Compute internal rate of return (a percentage). If internal rate of return is equal to or greater than the minimum required rate of return, accept the proposal. If internal rate of return is less than the minimum rate, reject the proposal.

RAPID REVIEW
Financial Statements

Order of Preparation

Statement Type	Date
1. Income statement	For the period ended
2. Retained earnings statement	For the period ended
3. Balance sheet	As of the end of the period
4. Statement of cash flows	For the period ended

Income Statement (perpetual inventory system)

Name of Company **Income Statement** **For the Period Ended**		
Sales revenues		
Sales revenue	$ X	
Less: Sales returns and allowances	X	
Sales discounts	X	
Net sales		$ X
Cost of goods sold		X
Gross profit		X
Operating expenses		
(Examples: salaries and wages, advertising, rent,		
depreciation, utilities, insurance)		X
Income from operations		X
Other revenues and gains		
(Examples: interest, gains)	X	
Other expenses and losses		
(Examples: interest, losses)	X	X
Income before income taxes		X
Income tax expense		X
Net income		$ X

Income Statement (periodic inventory system)

Name of Company **Income Statement** **For the Period Ended**			
Sales revenues			
Sales revenue		$ X	
Less: Sales returns and allowances		X	
Sales discounts		X	
Net sales			$ X
Cost of goods sold			
Beginning inventory		X	
Purchases	$ X		
Less: Purchase returns and allowances	X		
Net purchases	X		
Add: Freight-in	X		
Cost of goods purchased		X	
Cost of goods available for sale		X	
Less: Ending inventory		X	
Cost of goods sold			X
Gross profit			X
Operating expenses			
(Examples: salaries and wages, advertising, rent,			
depreciation, utilities, insurance)			X
Income from operations			X
Other revenues and gains			
(Examples: interest, gains)		X	
Other expenses and losses			
(Examples: interest, losses)		X	X
Income before income taxes			X
Income tax expense			X
Net income			$ X

Retained Earnings Statement

Name of Company **Retained Earnings Statement** **For the Period Ended**	
Retained earnings, beginning of period	$ X
Add: Net income (or deduct net loss)	X
	X
Deduct: Dividends	X
Retained earnings, end of period	$ X

STOP AND CHECK: Net income (loss) presented on the retained earnings statement must equal the net income (loss) presented on the income statement.

Balance Sheet

Name of Company **Balance Sheet** **As of the End of the Period**			
Assets			
Current assets			
(Examples: cash, short-term investments, accounts			
receivable, inventory, prepaid expenses)			$ X
Long-term investments			
(Examples: investments in bonds, investments in stocks)			X
Property, plant, and equipment			
Land		$ X	
Buildings and equipment	$ X		
Less: Accumulated depreciation	X	X	X
Intangible assets			X
Total assets			$ X
Liabilities and Stockholders' Equity			
Liabilities			
Current liabilities			
(Examples: notes payable, accounts payable, accruals,			
unearned revenues, current portion of notes payable)			$ X
Long-term liabilities			
(Examples: notes payable, bonds payable)			X
Total liabilities			X
Stockholders' equity			
Common stock			X
Retained earnings			X
Total liabilities and stockholders' equity			$ X

STOP AND CHECK: Total assets on the balance sheet must equal total liabilities and stockholders' equity, and ending retained earnings on the balance sheet must equal ending retained earnings on the retained earnings statement.

Statement of Cash Flows

Name of Company **Statement of Cash Flows** **For the Period Ended**	
Cash flows from operating activities	
(*Note:* May be prepared using the direct or indirect method)	
Cash provided (used) by operating activities	$ X
Cash flows from investing activities	
(Examples: purchase/sale of long-term assets)	
Cash provided (used) by investing activities	X
Cash flows from financing activities	
(Examples: issue/repayment of long-term liabilities,	
issue of stock, payment of dividends)	
Net cash provided (used) by financing activities	X
Net increase (decrease) in cash	X
Cash, beginning of the period	X
Cash, end of the period	$ X

STOP AND CHECK: Cash, end of the period, on the statement of cash flows must equal cash presented on the balance sheet.